75.00

T_{16}

30 00

D1481307

A Concordance to the Poems of
SIR PHILIP SIDNEY

THE CORNELL CONCORDANCES

S. M. Parrish, *General Editor*

Supervisory Committee

M. H. Abrams
Donald D. Eddy
Ephim Fogel
Alain Seznec

POEMS OF MATTHEW ARNOLD, *edited by S. M. Parrish*
POEMS OF W. B. YEATS, *edited by S. M. Parrish*
POEMS OF EMILY DICKINSON, *edited by S. P. Rosenbaum*
WRITINGS OF WILLIAM BLAKE, *edited by David V. Erdman*
BYRON'S *DON JUAN*, *edited by C. W. Hagelman, Jr., and R. J. Barnes*
THÉÂTRE ET POÉSIES DE JEAN RACINE, *edited by Byrant C. Freeman*
BEOWULF, *edited by J. B. Bessinger, Jr.*
PLAYS OF W. B. YEATS, *edited by Eric Domville*
POEMS OF JONATHAN SWIFT, *edited by Michael Shinagel*
PLAYS OF WILLIAM CONGREVE, *edited by David Mann*
POEMS OF SAMUEL JOHNSON, *edited by Helen Naugle*
FABLES AND TALES OF JEAN DE LA FONTAINE, *edited by J. Allen Tyler*
POEMS OF OSIP MANDELSTAM, *edited by Demetrius J. Koubourlis*
POEMS OF SIR PHILIP SIDNEY, *edited by Herbert S. Donow*

A Concordance to the Poems of
SIR PHILIP SIDNEY

Edited by

HERBERT S. DONOW

With Programming by

TREVOR J. SWANSON

Cornell University Press

ITHACA AND LONDON

First published 1975 by Cornell University Press.
Published in the United Kingdom by Cornell University Press Ltd., 2–4 Brook Street, London W1Y 1AA.

International Standard Book Number 0-8014-0805-9
Library of Congress Catalog Card Number 73-20816

Printed in the United States of America

For Michael and Jennifer

CONTENTS

Preface ix

Concordance to the Poems of Sir Philip Sidney 1

Appendix: Index Words in Order of Frequency 615

PREFACE

Sir Philip Sidney's importance to his contemporaries and to us cannot be measured by the bulk of his literary output (although he was remarkably prolific for his thirty-one years), nor by the degree of his modern popularity. His distinction lies in his having been better attuned to the literary temper of his time than any other single figure. A critic, poet, writer of prose romance, translator, and student of literary form, Sidney was an exemplar, possibly the best, of what sixteenth-century humanism could produce. His life and his writing attest to his faculty for assimilating the elements of his education, his reading, his travel, and his catholic acquaintanceship without depriving each of these influences of its discrete identity. In contrast to Shakespeare, whose relationship to his contemporaries and to his age is often ambiguous and rarely agreed upon, Sidney is emphatically a product of his time and his renaissance education. One has the feeling, if not the assurance, that Shakespeare could use a rhetorical figure without knowing its name or could imitate a form without knowing its source. This could hardly be said of Sidney, whose meticulous use of nearly every poetic meter known in his time would attest to the level of self-consciousness that he brought to his art. He might, indeed, be called the quintessence of the educated man as poet.

Without meaning to become rhapsodic about Sidney's merits, I make these observations principally to point out how appropriate a concordance of his poetry is. Sidney was, unlike Shakespeare, restrained in his use of imagery. But if he eschewed imaginative pyrotechnics, his verbal wit and classical elegance individualized him—a judgment, I hope, that this concordance will validate.

When the imperfections and crudities of machine-made concordances are rehearsed by reviewers, one observes a persistent tendency to lay the blame on the machine for its inelegancies and mindless mishandling of the text. The editor is similarly found culpable for not having added by hand or by an infinitely sophisticated program a thousand and one amenities to make the concordance more civilized and universally pleasing.

The fault, however, generally lies not with the machine nor even with the editor but with the medium by which the concordance is transmitted to the reader, that is, the printed page. If a scholar had at his disposal a computer of modest proportions, a terminal which gave him the capability of communicating quickly and easily with the computer, a good concordance program, and the necessary texts in machine-readable form stored in a nonsequential

mode,[1] he could have as good a concordance, one as suitable to his needs, as he could wish. If he wanted large quantities of the concordance, he could instruct the material to be printed at incredible rates of speed (20,000 to 40,000 lines per minute) on microfilm; or if he wanted to browse here and there, he could view the output on a video display screen. If dissatisfied with the amount of context he was receiving, he could demand expanded or contracted contexts. If he wanted to see only those lines that contained a certain word in the initial position of a line or sentence, say lines of poetry beginning with "what," or if he wanted to see how many lines began with present or past participles (for which he would require a reverse-spelling concordance feature), all of this could be immediately available. By exercising the various options of the true computer concordance, the user, not the editor or publisher, could determine the contents of the concordance each and every time he chose to use it.

The printed concordance has none of this flexibility, and no matter what form the editor designs for his concordance, it cannot prove as serviceable as what I have just described. Unfortunately, the printed concordance with all of its faults is for the present the only practical form of concordance. The machines and know-how for producing an interactive, dynamic concordance exist today, but there are at best only a dozen or so academic institutions with the facilities, as modest as they need be, that can provide the services necessary for the true computer concordance. My main purpose in making these remarks is to remind the concordance user, not to mention the maker, that his most frequent and justified objections are not so much to the manner in which the concordance was compiled and created as to the inflexible medium through which it is transmitted.

The remainder of this preface is an explanation of the choices that my medium has forced me to make. The decisions were ones with which I was not always happy, because the choices generally imposed unpleasant limitations. Apologies would, therefore, be fruitless, for were I to repent and choose again, I should fall, as inevitably, once more into error.

Variants

The text used for this concordance is *The Poems of Sir Philip Sidney*, edited by William A. Ringler, Jr. (Oxford, 1962). The copy text used, according to Ringler, was "the most readable sixteenth-century version." Professor Ringler explains that his general practice was "to list all departures from the copy text, but otherwise only variants occurring in two or more substantive texts" (lxvii). The bulk of the variants are the products of scribal or other error; for that reason most variants have been excluded from the text of the printed concordance. However, I have preserved all the variant readings included in Ringler's edition in a machine-readable transcription of the entire text of the poems as well as in an unabridged version of this concordance. Copies of these tapes can be made available to scholars on request.

---

[1] A bit of jargon which means that the data file can be entered at any point just as a book can be opened to any page. This type of processing is not possible with magnetic tape or punch cards, both of which must be paged sequentially.

The variants included in this text are those which, according to modern editors, have some authority. Most of the variant readings from the poems of the *Old Arcadia,* which I have included, are those which Jean Robertson preferred in her excellent modern-spelling edition of *The Countess of Pembroke's Arcadia.*[2] There are approximately twenty of these readings. In passing I should note that Robertson prefers the monosyllabic "ill" in many places where the disyllabic "evil" occurs in the Ringler text; however, I have not included "ill" among the variants in the concordance. Some variants from *Astrophil and Stella* and from the miscellaneous poems referred to as "Certain Sonnets" are also included in this concordance. In this connection, some modern editions, but principally the A. W. Pollard edition, *Sir Philip Sidney's Astrophel & Stella,*[3] have been consulted.

I have made no attempt to edit or correct the Ringler edition except in one instance—occurring in the third poem from the "First Book or Act" of the *Old Arcadia.* Ringler's lines read:

Like great god *Saturn* faire, and like faire *Venus* chaste;

As smooth as *Pan* as *Juno* milde, like goddess *Isis* faste. (5–6)

Ringler's preference for Isis over Iris was an emendation that seemed, at one time, called for in order to preserve the ironic character of the divine allusions. The emendation seemed further reinforced by the better rhyme in "chaste/faced" than in "chaste/fast," an observation which has also been made by Jean Robertson.[4] But Ringler has since withdrawn his own emendation, and I have restored Sidney's word, "Iris."

In another disputed reading, we have a line in sonnet 6 of *Astrophil and Stella* which Ringler prints as "Broadred with buls and swans. . . ." Most modern editors seem to prefer "Bordered with bulls and swans. . . ," but the word "brodred," according to the OED a form of "embroidered," makes more sense in the context than "bordered" and is therefore the reading preferred in this concordance: the entry appears here under its normalized form, "Brodered."

General Format and Contents

The format of the concordance is patterned after the more recent volumes in the Cornell Concordances. Since only a few of the poems are titled, all poems are identified by giving the source, corresponding to the main sections of Ringler's text. Following is a list of the titles of Ringler's sections with my own sometimes abbreviated titles opposite.

Ringler's Sections	*Concordance Titles*
Poems from the *Lady of May*	Lady of May
Poems from the *Old Arcadia*	
The First Book or Act	Arcadia I
The First Eclogues	Ist Eclogues
The Second Book or Act	Arcadia II

[2] Oxford, 1973.
[3] London, 1888.
[4] Page 424.

The Second Eclogues	2nd Eclogues
The Third Book or Act	Arcadia III
The Third Eclogues	3rd Eclogues
The Fourth Book or Act	Arcadia IV
The Fourth Eclogues	4th Eclogues
The Fifth Book or Act	Arcadia V
Certain Sonnets	Cert Sonnets
Astrophil and Stella	
(If one of the sonnets)	Astrophil
(If one of the songs)	A&S 1st Song, A&S 2nd Song, etc.
Other Poems	Other Poems
The *Psalms of David*	Psalms
Poems Possibly by Sidney	Possibly

The reference to the section is followed by an Arabic numeral corresponding to the poem number assigned in the Ringler text, except for the Psalms, which are followed by Roman numerals. Line numbers are also given, together with the pertinent page number in the Ringler edition. If a line is a variant, the line number is preceded by a V.

Except for the romanizing of italics, the lines are printed exactly as they appear in the Ringler text. That is, the text is in old spelling with the addition of apostrophes and quotation marks and the normalization of *i, j, u,* and *v.*[5] For the convenience of the user, however, the spelling of the index words has been normalized in accordance with modern American practice. This procedure was followed in order to prevent proliferation of entries and to obviate the need for cross-indexing, and yet to retain the text exactly as it appears in the edition upon which this concordance is based. As has often been noted, there is no generally accepted authority for an old-spelling version of Sidney's poetry. Retention of the old spelling for this text was not, therefore, motivated out of a sense of misguided purism, but to keep this concordance compatible with that text which it is indexing. In modernizing spelling for the index words, I have been somewhat conservative about altering words that might be construed as archaisms or special dialectal forms. Thus I have preserved the spelling of "ure" instead of changing it to "ore," "tyran" rather than "tyrant" (which has its own entry), and a number of others of similar character.

Index words are marked with an asterisk if they are homographs. The indication of homographs has no logical boundaries, and for this reason the system here incorporated is an incomplete one aimed only at noting the most obvious cases where the same spelling occurs for words with different etymologies or radically different meanings or functions.

Excluded Words

For reasons of economy and convenience, few "complete" concordances have been published. The general practice, which I have followed, is to delete common high-frequency words from the printed concordance. Although some words in this concordance were excluded according to category (for example,

---

[5] Ringler, lxvii.

articles, personal pronouns, and so on), the overriding consideration was frequency. Thus certain words belonging to an excludable category were retained if they were of relatively low frequency. The high-frequency words selected for exclusion belonged mainly to the following categories: (1) personal pronouns, (2) articles, (3) coordinating conjunctions, (4) auxiliary verbs—to be, to have, to do, and (5) prepositions. Words like "will" or "art," which occur as auxiliary verbs but also as "content words," are selectively included; in the following list of excluded words, such words are marked with a dagger symbol.

a	be	for	him	†may	on	that	thou	†will
am	but	from	his	me	or	the	thy	with
an	by	†hath	I	my	our	thee	to	would
and	†did	†have	in	nor	shall	their	was	you
are	†do	he	is	not	she	them	we	your
†art	†doth	her	it	of	should	they	were	

Appendix

The last section of the book contains a list of words in the Sidney poems in modern-spelling form, arranged in order of descending frequency. Words occurring only once are not listed.

Acknowledgments

I was extremely fortunate, thanks to the Graduate School and Department of English of Southern Illinois University, to have had financial support that enabled me to employ several able assistants in helping me prepare this concordance. Although I did much of my own programming, a major programming contribution was made by Trevor J. Swanson, a doctoral student in English whose background as a computer professional proved most valuable. Much of the coding of the text was done by Rosemary Elkins, one of my former students. Finally, Charles A. Lawler, another graduate student in English, was assiduous in troubleshooting and proofreading of the final text. To these people and to the Academic Computing staff in the Southern Illinois University Computer Center, I owe my deepest thanks.

I also owe a debt of gratitude to William A. Ringler, Jr., of the University of Chicago, for his conversation with me regarding this project when I was first beginning it, and to Ephim Fogel and Stephen M. Parrish of Cornell University for their kind and useful advice.

I am indebted to Oxford University Press for its kind permission to make use of the text of William A. Ringler, Jr., ed., *The Poems of Sir Philip Sidney*.

HERBERT S. DONOW

Carbondale, Illinois

A Concordance to the Poems of
SIR PHILIP SIDNEY

ABANDONED
    Abandond me, yet my decay. . . . . 308 Psalm XXVII   50
    Therfore, O Lord, abandond thus of all,. . . . . 333 Psalm XLI   33
ABANDONS
    Of mine eyes abandons me.. . . . . 328 Psalm XXXVIII   30
ABASE
    Yet now the roote of him abase you would.. . . . . 106 3rd Eclogues 67   99
    Abase her praise, saying she doth excell:. . . . . 183 Astrophil   37   8
ABASED
    That to thy advauncement their wisdomes have thee abased.. . 32 1st Eclogues 13 34
    That to my advauncement their wisdomes have me abased. . . . 32 1st Eclogues 13 36
ABASH
    You, though feares do abash, in you still possible hopes be: 32 1st Eclogues 13 23
ABASHED
    Nor be abasht, since such a guest you finde, ... 13 Arcadia I   4   3
    Nature abasht went back: fortune blusht: yet she replide
       thus:. . . . . 30 1st Eclogues 11 17
    Those names abasht me much, when those great names I hard: . 119 4th Eclogues 73 79
    Reason abasht retyred, ... 154 Cert Sonnets 25   7
ABED
    Now brought abed, hath brought nought foorth, but nought.. . 278 Psalm VII   39
    Abed on mischief museth he,. . . . . 323 Psalm XXXVI   11
ABHOR
    With much more: now what doo I finde, but Care to abhor me,. 124 4th Eclogues 74 81
ABHORRED
    For he hath not abhorrd nor yet disdain'd. . . . . 300 Psalm XXII   55
    Imputes not sins to be abhord, ... 314 Psalm XXXII   5
ABHORS
    But hates, abhorrs the wycked braines, ... 284 Psalm XI   18
ABIDE
    Yet patient must abide. . . . . 20 1st Eclogues 7 V960
    But so unheard, condemn'd, kept thence we do seeke to abide
      in,. . . . . 32 1st Eclogues 13 25
    R. Dare Passions then abide in Reason's light? . . . . 46 2nd Eclogues 27 17
    R. We with ourselves abide a daily strife. . . . . 46 2nd Eclogues 27 25
    Dev'lls? if in hell such dev'lls do abide, to the hells I do
      go. Go. . . . . 65 2nd Eclogues 31 50
    Nor ramper did abide; my braine was up blowne, ... 68 2nd Eclogues 33 15
    He made the simple wench his wrath abide.. . . . . 95 3rd Eclogues 64 30
    Shall prove that fiercenes can with a white dove abide?. . . 123 4th Eclogues 74 34
    The babe cries "nay, for that abide I waking". . . . . 139 Cert Sonnets 6   9
    As treasure house where her best gifts abyde.. . . . . 141 Cert Sonnets 8   8
    Can abide to keepe no measure, ... 221 A&S 9th Song   7
    By Thee preserv'd, in Thee they shall abide, ... 285 Psalm XII   23
    To them that trust in Thee a shield thou dost abide. . . . . 292 Psalm XVIII   56
    And long yea long abide I shall, ... 301 Psalm XXIII   25
    I do abide of wicked wight. . . . . 329 Psalm XXXIX   4
    So maist thou long abide . . . . 258 Other Poems   5 67
    Scarce each other can abide, ... 263 Other Poems   7 52
ABIDES
    In meane caves oft treasure abides, to an hostry a king
      comes. . . . . 36 1st Eclogues 13 153
    Where well couched abides a coffer of pearle,. . . . . 67 2nd Eclogues 33 10
    The God in whom abides . . . . 303 Psalm XXV   15
ABIDING
    Nor meek abiding of the patient wight. . . . . 281 Psalm IX   58
    "But may Love abiding bee. . . . . 262 Other Poems   7 25
ABILITY
    Good Lalus mine, I yeld to thy abilitie; . . . . 20 1st Eclogues 7 V974
    Then may I hope, my pipe may have abilitie,. . . . . 48 2nd Eclogues 28 26
    Yet Reason saith, Reason should have abilitie, ... 60 2nd Eclogues 30 131
ABJECT
    Their abject lips no breath but flattery move. . . . . 284 Psalm XII   5
ABJECTS
    Then abjects, while I was unwitting quite, ... 322 Psalm XXXV   39
ABLE
    Who shall be able me to fright?. . . . . 306 Psalm XXVII   3
    Drew dainty Nous, that she not able so . . . . 250 Other Poems   4 335
ABOLISH
    Joyn'd, by thy beauty adorn'd, be no meanes these greefes to
      abolish:. . . . . 34 1st Eclogues 13 99
ABOLISHED
    But what's this for a fault, for which such faieth be
      abolisht,. . . . . 124 4th Eclogues 74 69
ABOMINATION
    From much abomination. 295 Psalm XIX   60
ABOUND
    Let heere thy skill abound,. . . . . 260 Other Poems   6 15
ABOUNDED
    All Thy floods on me abounded, ... 335 Psalm XLII   33
ABOUT
    The circle is my (round about her) sight:. . . . . 17 1st Eclogues 7 103
    Fortune, Nature, Love, long have contended about me, ... 29 1st Eclogues 11   1
    Since no refuge doth serve from woundes we do carry about
      us . . . . 33 1st Eclogues 13 51
    But, woe is me, the yeare is gone about, ... 115 4th Eclogues 72 56
    With hugy darknes, which about his feet did wend.. . . . . . 291 Psalm XVIII 21
    About which hee dimme clouds like a Pavilion brings, ... 291 Psalm XVIII 24
    About that Vault he goeth, ... 294 Psalm XIX   26

```
ABOUT                          (CONTINUED)                    PAGE    TITLE           LINE
      With mowes and nodds they stand about me flocking. . . . . .   299 Psalm XXII        18
      Nay Basan mighty Bulls close me about. . . . . . . . . . . .   299 Psalm XXII        28
      For bawling doggs have compast me about,. . . . . . . . . .    299 Psalm XXII        39
      And with those hands about Thy Altar waite,. . . . . . . . .   305 Psalm XXVI        21
      About them pitch who him do feare, . . . . . . . . . . . . .   319 Psalm XXXIV       26
      About these never conquered walles to swarme,. . . . . . . .   346 Possibly      5   10
      While daunce about the may-pole is begun,. . . . . . . . . .   243 Other Poems   4   55
      How rosy moist'ned lipps about his beake . . . . . . . . . .   244 Other Poems   4   95
      I go about, but then is all my best. . . . . . . . . . . . .   254 Other Poems   4  470
      Still to be hers, about her aye to flie, . . . . . . . . . .   255 Other Poems   4  501
      As this same sprite about my fancies blinde, . . . . . . . .   255 Other Poems   4  502
ABOVE
      Such force hath Love above poore Nature's power. . . . . . .    19 1st Eclogues  7  161
      Dorus. Such force hath Love above poore Nature's power,. . .    19 1st Eclogues  7  162
      To those high powers, which idly sit above,. . . . . . . . .    58 2nd Eclogues 30   63
      But nowe successe hathe gott above annoyes,. . . . . . . . .    71 Arcadia III  36   17
      Thou art farre off, thy kingdome is above: . . . . . . . . .    72 Arcadia III  38    7
      But above all away vile jealousie. . . . . . . . . . . . . .    93 3rd Eclogues 63   82
      Nature above all things requireth this,. . . . . . . . . . .   105 3rd Eclogues 67   70
      The crowne above you both for ever I appoint". . . . . . . .   121 4th Eclogues 73  166
      Or art thou from above bid play this part, . . . . . . . . .   142 Cert Sonnets 10   11
      The wood, above doth soone consuming rest. . . . . . . . . .   150 Cert Sonnets 22   44
      Whose talents held young Ganimed above:. . . . . . . . . . .   171 Astrophil    13    4
      Do they above love to be lov'd, and yet. . . . . . . . . . .   180 Astrophil    31   12
      Curb'd in with feare, but with guilt bosse above . . . . . .   189 Astrophil    49    7
      Nor ought do care, though some above me sit, . . . . . . . .   198 Astrophil    64   11
      Then sent he from above, and took me from below, . . . . . .   291 Psalm XVIII       34
      Should be restor'd by him above. . . . . . . . . . . . . . .   308 Psalm XXVII       51
      Thy truth above the Clouds, most high, . . . . . . . . . . .   323 Psalm XXXVI       14
ABRIDGE
      As that hatefull death can abridge them of powre,. . . . . .    31 1st Eclogues 12   18
ABROAD
      Or all abroade if but a Cubb start out.. . . . . . . . . . .    27 1st Eclogues 10   30
      Her horned head abroad doth raunge:. . . . . . . . . . . . .    86 Arcadia III  62   12
      We care abroad, and they of home have care.. . . . . . . . .   106 3rd Eclogues 67  108
      Striving abroad a foraging to go,. . . . . . . . . . . . . .   192 Astrophil    55    6
      Then rise and come abroad, . . . . . . . . . . . . . . . . .   282 Psalm X           49
      Defend Thee still from all Thy foes abroad.. . . . . . . . .   295 Psalm XX           5
      No sooner my child eyes could look abroad, . . . . . . . . .   299 Psalm XXII        23
      And mercy spredd abroad. . . . . . . . . . . . . . . . . . .   304 Psalm XXV         40
      And who abroad . . . . . . . . . . . . . . . . . . . . . . .   317 Psalm XXXIII      29
      Abroad his stepps be wrongly sett. . . . . . . . . . . . . .   323 Psalm XXXVI       12
      So then be blest now, then, at home, abroad, . . . . . . . .   334 Psalm XLI         45
      I will sing abroad . . . . . . . . . . . . . . . . . . . . .   337 Psalm XLIII       29
      By neighbors prai'd she went abroad therby,. . . . . . . . .   247 Other Poems   4  207
      (He staying thus) was faine abroad to stray. . . . . . . . .   250 Other Poems   4  331
      One day he with his flock abroad did raunge: . . . . . . . .   253 Other Poems   4  438
ABSENCE
      Hate fully growne, Absence new sprongen out. . . . . . . . .   115 4th Eclogues 72   58
      O hideous absence, by thee am I thralled.. . . . . . . . . .   138 Cert Sonnets  5   13
      I deemd it best some absence for to prove, . . . . . . . . .   149 Cert Sonnets 21    3
      In absence blind, and wearied with that woe, . . . . . . . .   149 Cert Sonnets 21    9
      Whose presence, absence, absence presence is;. . . . . . . .   195 Astrophil    60   13
      Their rayes to me, who in her tedious absence lay. . . . . .   204 Astrophil    76    2
      Out traytour absence, darest thou counsell me, . . . . . . .   223 Astrophil    88    1
      Tush absence, while thy mistes eclipse that light, . . . . .   223 Astrophil    88    9
      Now that of absence the most irksome night,. . . . . . . . .   223 Astrophil    89    1
      With absence' Vaile, I live in Sorowe's night. . . . . . . .   224 Astrophil    91    4
      With no worse curse then absence makes me tast.. . . . . . .   235 Astrophil   105   14
      Whether absence have had force . . . . . . . . . . . . . . .   225 A&S 10th Song      4
      "Well in absence this will dy, . . . . . . . . . . . . . . .   234 A&S 11th Song     11
      Absence sure will helpe, if I. . . . . . . . . . . . . . . .   234 A&S 11th Song     13
      Meaning with absence to refresh the thought. . . . . . . . .   246 Other Poems   4  175
      Strephon, whose absence seem'd unto thee long, . . . . . . .   247 Other Poems   4  220
      Which absence wisht: love plai'd a victor's part:. . . . . .   248 Other Poems   4  223
      For then wise Klaius found no absence can. . . . . . . . . .   253 Other Poems   4  419
      Of Mira's beames eclipst by absence bad. . . . . . . . . . .   256 Other Poems   5   11
      "Absence is death, or worse, to them that love." . . . . . .   259 Other Poems   5   94
ABSENT
      Yet harvest brings. Doth she alas absent herselfe? . . . . .    49 2nd Eclogues 28   62
      That if she absent were but halfe a daye, . . . . . . . . .     94 3rd Eclogues 64   10
      He will absent himselfe, least he should move. . . . . . . .    95 3rd Eclogues 64   58
      Shewes love and pitie to my absent case. . . . . . . . . . .   195 Astrophil    60    8
      O absent presence Stella is not here;. . . . . . . . . . . .   235 Astrophil   106    1
      O lord, do not absent Thy self from me!. . . . . . . . . . .   322 Psalm XXXV        56
      Doth not thy selfe, when he long absent is,. . . . . . . . .   257 Other Poems   5   24
      Be absent farre from thee, . . . . . . . . . . . . . . . . .   258 Other Poems   5   64
      Absent alone canst thou then piping be?. . . . . . . . . . .   258 Other Poems   5   65
ABSENTED
      But now those living lights absented be, . . . . . . . . . .   116 4th Eclogues 72   85
      For see alas, who is from you absented.. . . . . . . . . . .   128 4th Eclogues 75  124
      Absented? nay I say for ever banished. . . . . . . . . . . .   128 4th Eclogues 75  125
      Absented quite from you, . . . . . . . . . . . . . . . . . .   257 Other Poems   5   38
ABSTRACTED
      Because I oft in darke abstracted guise, . . . . . . . . . .   178 Astrophil    27    1
ABUNDANCE
      Is chaunced to my life, that from such muddy abundance . . .    34 1st Eclogues 13   96
ABUSE
      Naught in himselfe ech other to abuse. . . . . . . . . . . .    21 1st Eclogues  8   24
```

```
ABUSE                     (CONTINUED)                    PAGE    TITLE          LINE
    Let not a puppet abuse thy sprite, Kings' Crownes do not
       helpe them. . . . . . . . . . . . . . . . . . . .    34  1st Eclogues 13    84
    Keepe thy sprite from abuse, here no abuse doth haunte. . . .  69  2nd Eclogues 34    27
    And can with foule abuse such beauties blot; . . . . . . . .  177  Astrophil    24    11
ABUSED
    The witts abusde with will no counsayle take. . . . . . . .   23  1st Eclogues  9    22
    To such an end as he might be abus'de. . . . . . . . . . .    95  3rd Eclogues 64    28
    And when they were well us'de to be abused, . . . . . . . .  102  3rd Eclogues 66   144
    Princes in subjects wrongd, must deeme themselves abused. . .  213  A&S 5th Song       30
ABUSETH
    Where her who should rule paine, false paine abuseth. . . . .  142  Cert Sonnets 11    14
ACCENTS
    And doo not onely marke the accents last, . . . . . . . . .  126  4th Eclogues 75    32
ACCEPT
    Before all flies the Waspe accept I would. . . . . . . . .   104  3rd Eclogues 67    18
ACCEPTATION
    Receive good acceptation!. . . . . . . . . . . . . . . . .   295  Psalm XIX          64
ACCESS
    Farre more happy be you, whose greatnes gets a free accesse,   33  1st Eclogues 13    54
ACCCMPT
    So small accompt of time the shepeheard feeles . . . . . .    28  1st Eclogues 10    49
ACCORD
    Just accord all musike makes; . . . . . . . . . . . . . . .  140  Cert Sonnets  7    14
    In thee just accord excelleth, . . . . . . . . . . . . . .   140  Cert Sonnets  7    15
    And song accord. . . . . . . . . . . . . . . . . . . . . .   307  Psalm XXVII        35
    O now accord . . . . . . . . . . . . . . . . . . . . . . .   316  Psalm XXXIII        8
ACCORDED
    To whom precedence shall of both accorded be. . . . . . . .   120  4th Eclogues 73   136
ACCORDING
    According to my Lord Love's owne behest: . . . . . . . . .   189  Astrophil    50     6
    According to his heavnly equity. . . . . . . . . . . . . .   278  Psalm VII          47
    According as he saw the pureness of my hand. . . . . . . .   292  Psalm XVIII        49
ACCOUNT
    What coye account she makes of estimation? . . . . . . . .    15  1st Eclogues  7    34
    God keeps account of good men's dayes, . . . . . . . . . .   325  Psalm XXXVII       45
    A heardman rich of much account was he, . . . . . . . . . .  245  Other Poems   4   117
ACCOUNTED
    Let all the Sea thy teares accounted be: . . . . . . . . .   125  4th Eclogues 75    20
    Among the wisest was accounted wise, . . . . . . . . . . .   243  Other Poems   4    34
    Who earnest found what they accounted play. . . . . . . . .  251  Other Poems   4   366
ACCOUNTING
    But fore-accounting oft makes builders misse, . . . . . . .  244  Other Poems   4    79
ACCURSED
    Long sham'd to be accurst in every place, . . . . . . . . .  141  Cert Sonnets  8     3
    Delight protests he is not for the accurst, . . . . . . . .  228  Astrophil    95     7
ACCUSE
    Some hurt accuse a third with horny head. . . . . . . . . .   21  1st Eclogues  8    12
    To lye, faine, gloze, to steale, pry, and accuse, . . . . .   21  1st Eclogues  8    23
    To lye, to steale, to pry, and to accuse, . . . . . . . . .   21  1st Eclogues  8  V 23
    Ne could my soule it selfe accuse of such a faulte, . . . .  117  4th Eclogues 73    19
ACCUSED
    As loving not, accus'd, in Love I die. . . . . . . . . . .    41  Arcadia II   20     2
    So I my self accus'd to God, . . . . . . . . . . . . . . .   315  Psalm XXXII        16
    While guilty thoughts accus'd his Reason weake) . . . . . .  255  Other Poems   4   532
ACHE
    My harte doth ake, my life faints, . . . . . . . . . . . .    66  2nd Eclogues 32    14
    Whose braines boile not in woes, nor brests with beatings
       ake, . . . . . . . . . . . . . . . . . . . . . . . . .   117  4th Eclogues 73    13
    To yeeld she found hir noble heart did ake: . . . . . . . .  245  Other Poems   4   125
ACHIEVE
    Then may I hope t'atchieve grace of a heavenly tiger. . . .  122  4th Eclogues 74    22
ACHING
    Thy cries, o Babie, set mine head on aking: . . . . . . . .  139  Cert Sonnets  6     2
ACKNOWLEDGE
    Know my words their faults acknowledge. . . . . . . . . . .  157  Cert Sonnets 27    36
    Their Course doth it acknowledg, . . . . . . . . . . . . .   293  Psalm XIX           6
    His faults know and acknowledg?. . . . . . . . . . . . . .   295  Psalm XIX          50
ACQUAINT
    Teach me what circle may acquaint her sprite, . . . . . . .    17  1st Eclogues  7   101
ACQUAINTANCE
    For neere acquaintance dooth diminish reverent feare. . . .  121  4th Eclogues 73   160
    Vouchsafe of all acquaintance this to tell, . . . . . . . .  181  Astrophil    32     9
    Angels to acquaintance bringeth. . . . . . . . . . . . . .   219  A&S 8th Song       40
ACQUAINTED
    Nor brooke oughte els but well acquainted woe. . . . . . .    74  Arcadia III  41     6
    Or as the silly birde in well acquainted nest. . . . . . .   117  4th Eclogues 73    23
    Sure, if that long with Love acquainted eyes . . . . . . .   180  Astrophil    31     5
    The courtly Nymphs, acquainted with the mone . . . . . . .   191  Astrophil    54     5
    Thou that by proofe acquainted art . . . . . . . . . . . .   289  Psalm XVII          7
ACQUAINTS
    Who seekes to knowe, acquaintes hym self with hell; . . . .    71  Arcadia III  36    16
ACROSS
    One said he brake acrosse; full well it so might be: . . . .  241  Other Poems   1     3
A-CRYING
    I saw that riches fall, and fell a crying; . . . . . . . .    17  1st Eclogues  7    88
ACT
    Mercury kill'd his false sire for this act, . . . . . . . .    21  1st Eclogues  8    17
    Shew forth his Acts, and this as Act most high, . . . . . .  280  Psalm IX           32
```

```
ACTION                                                          PAGE    TITLE           LINE
     In action aptly graced:. . . . . . . . . . . . . . . . .   216 A&S 6th Song         28
ACTIVE
     Such active minde but seldome passion sees.. . . . . . .    26 1st Eclogues  9     134
     The Lion, harte; the Ounce gave active might;. . . . . .   101 3rd Eclogues 66      80
ACTS
     That evry folk Thy wondrous Acts may see.. . . . . . . .   277 Psalm VII            21
     Shew forth his Acts, and this as Act most high,. . . . .   280 Psalm IX             32
ADD
     Doth add her force unto the sting of fortune:. . . . . .   109 Arcadia IV   70      10
ADDERS
     Our best defenses are to flie these adders.. . . . . . .    50 2nd Eclogues 28      89
ADDRESS
     Some that know how my spring I did addresse, . . . . . .   176 Astrophil    23       5
     And yet to breake more staves did me addresse: . . . . .   191 Astrophil    53       2
     But I my self will to Thy house addresse . . . . . . . .   275 Psalm V              17
ADDRESSED
     Whose trust is so addressed, . . . . . . . . . . . . . .   331 Psalm XL             16
ADDS
     Nay former blisse addes to present paine,. . . . . . . .   153 Cert Sonnets 24      13
ADHERENT
     Of carking agonies (to estates which still be adherent). . .    34 1st Eclogues 13  97
ADIEU
     Gives an adieu to the world, as to his onely delight:. . . .    123 4th Eclogues 74 26
     Then adieu, deere flocke adieu:. . . . . . . . . . . . .   222 A&S 9th Song         46
ADMIRE
     Since best wits thinke it wit thee to admire;. . . . . .   206 Astrophil    80       2
ADMIRED
     And Mira I admirde: her shape sank in my brest.. . . . .   119 4th Eclogues 73     100
     We have a fish, by strangers much admirde, . . . . . . .   150 Cert Sonnets 22      21
ADMIRES
     Only fond youth admires a rotten stocke. . . . . . . . .    25 1st Eclogues  9      89
ADMITTED
     Admitted late by your best-graced grace, . . . . . . . .   208 Astrophil    82      10
ADONIS'
     Adonis' end, Venus' nett,. . . . . . . . . . . . . . . .    66 2nd Eclogues 32      27
ADOPTIVE
     Gallein's adoptive sonnes, who by a beaten way . . . . .   232 Astrophil   102       9
ADORE
     And, fooles, adore in temple of our hart,. . . . . . . .   167 Astrophil     5       7
ADORING
     Heare then, but then with wonder heare; see but adoring see,   217 A&S 7th Song     13
ADORNED
     And vertue is gratefull with bewty and richnes adorned,. . .    33 1st Eclogues 13  57
     Joyn'd, by thy beauty adorn'd, be no meanes these greefes to
          abolish:. . . . . . . . . . . . . . . . . . . . . .    34 1st Eclogues 13      99
     By north or south still rich adorned live: . . . . . . .   256 Other Poems   5      16
ADULTERY
     Thou, with thy wife, adultry shalt commit. . . . . . . .    11 Arcadia I     1      10
ADUST
     Choler adust is joyed in woman-kinde.. . . . . . . . . .   147 Cert Sonnets 17      52
ADUSTED
     But so his humor I frame, in a mould of choller adusted, . .    29 1st Eclogues 11   9
ADVANCE
     Horsemen my skill in horsmanship advaunce; . . . . . . .   185 Astrophil    41       5
ADVANCEMENT
     That to thy advauncement their wisdomes have thee abased.. . .    32 1st Eclogues 13 34
     That to my advauncement their wisdomes have me abased. . . .    32 1st Eclogues 13   36
ADVERSITY
     As perjur'd cowards in adversity . . . . . . . . . . . .   248 Other Poems   4     239
ADVICE
     In those weake harts that his advice receave.. . . . . .    21 1st Eclogues  8      34
     Yet say againe thy advise for th' ev'lls that I told thee. I
          told thee.. . . . . . . . . . . . . . . . . . . . .    63 2nd Eclogues 31      18
     Dick. Good Will, I cannot take thy good advice, before . . .   344 Possibly      1   43
ADVISE
     I way them not, but still will thee advize . . . . . . .    25 1st Eclogues  9     109
AEOL'S
     To Strephon Aeole's land first breathing lent: . . . . .   242 Other Poems   4      26
     And faine those Aeols' youthes there would their stay. . . .   233 Astrophil   103   9
AESCULAPIUS
     Of any since God AEsculapius ceased. . . . . . . . . . .   128 4th Eclogues 75     116
AFFECTED
     Desire's best meane, harvest of hartes affected, . . . .   108 Arcadia IV   69       2
     Love more affected seemes. . . . . . . . . . . . . . . .   216 A&S 6th Song         31
AFFECTION
     (Although simply atyrde) your manly affection utter. . . .    32 1st Eclogues 13    16
     Farewell with thee, farewell all our affection.. . . . .   129 4th Eclogues 76       6
     For what place now is lefte for our affection. . . . . .   129 4th Eclogues 76       7
     For he our father was in all affection,. . . . . . . . .   129 4th Eclogues 76      14
     Shall we now finde a guide of such affection,. . . . . .   129 4th Eclogues 76      22
     For ever banish'd from well plac'd affection;. . . . . .   130 4th Eclogues 76      29
     Let hating of our selves be our affection, . . . . . . .   130 4th Eclogues 76      33
     Farewell direction, farewell all affection. . . . . . .   130 4th Eclogues 76      39
     That who indeed infelt affection beares, . . . . . . . .   195 Astrophil    61       5
     With time still th' affection groweth. . . . . . . . . .   234 A&S 11th Song        19
     Will not they stir new affection?" . . . . . . . . . . .   234 A&S 11th Song        22
AFFECTION'S
     We finde most sweete affection's snare,. . . . . . . . .    14 1st Eclogues  6       3
     Affection's charmes in my behalfe to prove.. . . . . . .    17 1st Eclogues  7     102
```

4

		PAGE	TITLE		LINE
AFFECTION'S	(CONTINUED)				
Hardned, and coulde, farr from affectione's snare.		344	Possibly	2	5
AFFECTIONS					
Such mindes with sweet affections for to fill, ...		92	3rd Eclogues	63	61
AFFECTS					
Yee Muses all which chaste affects allow, ...		91	3rd Eclogues	63	19
On those affectes which easily yeeld to sight, ...		135	Cert Sonnets	2	6
AFFIRM					
That in one speech two Negatives affirme..		196	Astrophil	63	14
AFFLICTED					
Th' afflicted cry.		280	Psalm IX		35
The' afflicted then shall eat, and be well pleased, ...		300	Psalm XXII		61
In sprite afflicted finds.		320	Psalm XXXIV		68
Judg of th' afflicted man;		332	Psalm XLI		2
AFFLICTION					
While that my soule, she, she lives in affliction;		61	2nd Eclogues	30	146
Unto the caitife wretch, whom long affliction holdeth, . . .		122	4th Eclogues	74	1
The aire in raine for my affliction weepeth:		136	Cert Sonnets	3	2
The seely wretch with foule affliction staind, ...		300	Psalm XXII		56
AFFLICTION'S					
Of huge despaire, and foule affliction's vallies, ...		111	4th Eclogues	71	17
AFFORD					
Thus to my sonne do I yeeld, such lookes her beames do aforde me.		36	1st Eclogues	13	133
To whether with best cause the Nymphes faire flowers affoord		52	2nd Eclogues	29	28
Which the deere tongue would afford, ...		218	A&S 8th Song		22
So in my mouth he did a song afford, ...		331	Psalm XL		11
That did his death, hir death afford..		241	Other Poems	3	6
AFFORDED					
O not but such love you say you could have afoorded, ...		124	4th Eclogues	74	63
He thought gray haires afforded subtletie.		248	Other Poems	4	256
AFFORDS					
To some a sweetest plaint, a sweetest stile affords, ...		168	Astrophil	6	9
Fiercly affords.		308	Psalm XXVII		59
AFIELD					
A-field they goe, where many lookers be, ...		247	Other Poems	4	217
AFLYING					
I now should Fall aflying?		283	Psalm XI		4
A-FORAGING					
Striving abroad a foraging to go, ...		192	Astrophil	55	6
AFRAID					
I will not be afraid		272	Psalm III		19
AFRIKE					
Of herbes or beastes, which Inde or Afrike hold.		166	Astrophil	3	8
AFTER					
That after death, to heav'n in woods' resound, ...		56	2nd Eclogues	29	133
For mischeefes greate, daye after day doth showe:		82	Arcadia III	56	13
Like to the Moone when after chaunge		86	Arcadia III	62	11
One word of woe another after traineth:		128	4th Eclogues	75	103
After parting ought forgot, ...		226	A&S 10th Song		8
Long I will not after tary, ...		226	A&S 10th Song		15
After my clearness, and my Equity.		277	Psalm VII		24
That after God he never sought, ...		281	Psalm X		14
Seek peace and follow after it, ...		320	Psalm XXXIV		54
Look after him, he shall be vannisht		325	Psalm XXXVII		27
To follow after lyes..		331	Psalm XL		20
After ever living thee;		334	Psalm XLII		6
For as Urania after Cosma ran, ...		249	Other Poems	4	281
And Strephon single, turned after him.		249	Other Poems	4	287
But after this to greater rage it broke, ...		253	Other Poems	4	429
AFTER-FOLKS					
The after-folkes shall wonder still at thee.		56	2nd Eclogues	29	131
AFTER-FOLLOWING					
Who oft fore-judge my after-following race, ...		178	Astrophil	26	13
AFTER-LIVERS					
Unto my selfe let after-livers know.		40	Arcadia II	18	10
AFTER-MEWING					
Deepe musing to himselfe, which after-mewing showes, ...		53	2nd Eclogues	29	35
AFTERWARDS					
Which being done he afterwards would kill.		102	3rd Eclogues	66	126
AGAIN					
And they againe resolve.		19	1st Eclogues	7	153
Goe graft againe, and seeke to graft them right, ...		26	1st Eclogues	9	129
Nico. Who doubts but Pas' fine pipe againe will bring. . . .		53	2nd Eclogues	29	51
Yet say againe thy advise for th' ev'lls that I told thee. I told thee..		63	2nd Eclogues	31	18
Tell yet againe me the names of these faire form'd to do ev'lls. Dev'lls.		65	2nd Eclogues	31	49
Till my frayle barke his haven agayn do fynde.		70	Arcadia III	35	8
But there againe the flesh doth rise		89	Arcadia III	62	101
So much more strong againe let fastest concorde make.. . . .		120	4th Eclogues	73	120
And getting youth againe, in youth doth flourish:		127	4th Eclogues	75	83
(With gall cut out) closde up againe by art, ...		150	Cert Sonnets	22	23
Cald it anew, and wooed sleepe againe:		184	Astrophil	38	13
Looke on againe, the faire text better trie:		199	Astrophil	67	7
That Anger" selfe I needs must kisse againe.		203	Astrophil	73	14
And safe again He rear'd mee		272	Psalm III		18
I say again that I have calld on Thee.		289	Psalm XVII		17
Therfore I say again this goodness he me sent.		292	Psalm XVIII		47

5

```
AGAIN                    (CONTINUED)                          PAGE    TITLE              LINE
    I say, and say again,. . . . . . . . . . . . . . . . . .   305  Psalm XXV             75
    Doth rise again, new joyes shall rise. . . . . . . . . .   311  Psalm XXX             18
    Have power again to raised be. . . . . . . . . . . . . .   324  Psalm XXXVI           36
    And never found again shal be. . . . . . . . . . . . . .   325  Psalm XXXVII          28
    As pin'd a face as mine I saw againe.. . . . . . . . . .   254  Other Poems     4    476
AGAINST
    Since all his force against himselfe he tries,. . . . . .   23  1st Eclogues    9     37
    Here Laelaps, here, in deed against the foen . . . . . .    27  1st Eclogues   10     13
    Nature against we do seeme to rebell, seeme fooles in a
      vaine sute... . . . . . . . . . . . . . . . . . . . . .   32  1st Eclogues   13     24
    Unto a silly caban, though weake, yet stronger against woes.  34  1st Eclogues  13     93
    That sorrowe's worke against my will I prove.. . . . . .    60  2nd Eclogues   30    127
    Boulon. Who still doth seeke against himselfe offences,. . .  62  2nd Eclogues  30    167
    Their ireful shotte against so weake a marke,. . . . . . .   73  Arcadia III    40      6
    And (though against his will) on him she leand,. . . . . .   95  3rd Eclogues   64     44
    Ah let us all against foule Nature crie: . . . . . . . . .  127  4th Eclogues   75     92
    Let us against our selves employ our might,. . . . . . . .  130  4th Eclogues   76     35
    Let folke orecharg'd with braine against me crie,. . . . .  198  Astrophil      64      4
    And yet against thy Prince thy force dost dayly prove: . .  214  A&S 5th Song          65
    While she doth against me prove. . . . . . . . . . . . . .  226  A&S 10th Song         35
    Tho against me shee persever,. . . . . . . . . . . . . . .  221  A&S 9th Song          19
    Against the lord of lords, the lord of every thing,. . . .  271  Psalm II               5
    That all against poore me. . . . . . . . . . . . . . . . .  272  Psalm III              5
    Which all against me gather: . . . . . . . . . . . . . . .  272  Psalm III             21
    Against such rage of foes: Awake for me. . . . . . . . . .  277  Psalm VII             17
    He against me doth throw, but down it shall. . . . . . . .  278  Psalm VII             43
    Against the Innocent,. . . . . . . . . . . . . . . . . . .  282  Psalm X               36
    Against all them, that against him do swell, . . . . . . .  285  Psalm XII             17
    On whom against my Foes my only safty stayes?. . . . . . .  291  Psalm XVIII            7
    Against their guilty faces.. . . . . . . . . . . . . . . .  298  Psalm XXI             48
    Then though against me armys were, . . . . . . . . . . . .  307  Psalm XXVII           13
    Against me witnesses unjust, . . . . . . . . . . . . . . .  308  Psalm XXVII           57
    Do throw their words against the most upright. . . . . . .  313  Psalm XXXI            51
    Is bent, but bent against those same . . . . . . . . . . .  320  Psalm XXXIV           58
    Speake thou for me against wrong speaking foes,. . . . . .  321  Psalm XXXV             1
    Thy force O Lord against their force oppose, . . . . . . .  321  Psalm XXXV             2
    Who did me wrong, against me witness beare . . . . . . . .  322  Psalm XXXV            25
    Against me swarm, ceaseless to raile at me.. . . . . . . .  322  Psalm XXXV            40
    Against them usd by wicked wretches, . . . . . . . . . . .  327  Psalm XXXVII         103
    Did kick against my state. . . . . . . . . . . . . . . . .  333  Psalm XLI             32
AGANIPPE
    I never dranke of Aganippe well, . . . . . . . . . . . . .  203  Astrophil      74      1
AGE
    O noble age who place their only blisse. . . . . . . . . .   24  1st Eclogues    9     69
    Histor. Thus may you see, howe youthe estemeth aige. . . .   26  1st Eclogues    9    138
    Till age it self do make it self esteemde.. . . . . . . . .  26  1st Eclogues    9    141
    (For age doth make him of a wolvish hew) . . . . . . . . .   27  1st Eclogues   10     17
    Youth will have will: Age must to age therefore. . . . . .   27  1st Eclogues   10     24
    To age thus doe they draw there youthfull pryme, . . . . .   28  1st Eclogues   10     52
    Let not old age disgrace my high desire, . . . . . . . . .   38  Arcadia II     15      1
    Old age is wise and full of constant truth:. . . . . . . .   39  Arcadia II     15      9
    Old age well stayed from raunging humor lives:. . . . . . .  39  Arcadia II     15     10
    Old age hath knowne what ever was in youth:. . . . . . . .   39  Arcadia II     15     11
    Old age orecome, the greater honour gives. . . . . . . . .   39  Arcadia II     15     12
    And to old age since you your selfe aspire,. . . . . . . .   39  Arcadia II     15     13
    Let not old age disgrace my high desire. . . . . . . . . .   39  Arcadia II     15     14
    His youth delight, his age the soule's oppression: . . . .   48  2nd Eclogues   28     39
    But unto Man, age ever death doth sende. . . . . . . . . .  127  4th Eclogues   75     84
    And age pull'd on with paines all freshness fretteth:. . .  276  Psalm VI              22
    Yea in no age thy blisse from them departs.. . . . . . . .  285  Psalm XII             24
    But He, staffe of my age, He staid my stumbling state. . .  291  Psalm XVIII           39
    From age to age life joyes doth fill.. . . . . . . . . . .  311  Psalm XXX             15
AGED
    No man doth wish his horse should aged bee.. . . . . . . .   24  1st Eclogues    9     86
    Olde aged oke cutt downe, of newe works serves to the
      building:. . . . . . . . . . . . . . . . . . . . . . . .   36  1st Eclogues   13    134
    The filthy snake her aged coate can mende, . . . . . . . .  127  4th Eclogues   75     82
    Geron strave hard, but aged were his feet, . . . . . . . .  248  Other Poems     4    254
    She mov'd hir lims, and drew the aged man, . . . . . . . .  249  Other Poems     4    283
AGE'S
    Preserve those beames, this age's onely lighte:. . . . . .   79  Arcadia III    51      2
    With age's force decay'd, yet once the heaven was his. . .  120  4th Eclogues   73    124
    Her face (this age's praise) the thiefe doth kisse.. . . .  141  Cert Sonnets    9     12
    Each way, as she, that age's praise, did bend. . . . . . .  251  Other Poems     4    376
AGES
    Throughout all ages last.. . . . . . . . . . . . . . . . .  317  Psalm XXXIII          39
AGHAST
    The courtlie shepheard much agast at this, . . . . . . . .   96  3rd Eclogues   64     67
    I that was first agast, when first I saw their showe:. . .  121  4th Eclogues   73    158
    Yea neighbors, more, my mates were so agast. . . . . . . .  313  Psalm XXXI            32
AGO
    A neighbor mine not long agoe there was, . . . . . . . . .   94  3rd Eclogues   64      1
AGONIES
    Infernall agonies unto a bewtye divine,. . . . . . . . . .   30  1st Eclogues   11     14
    Of carking agonies (to estates which still be adherent). . .  34  1st Eclogues  13     97
AGREE
    And witnesse am, how ill agree in one, . . . . . . . . . .   40  Arcadia II     19      5
    May witnesse beare, how ill agree in one,. . . . . . . . .   41  Arcadia II     19     11
    In whom all joyes so well agree, . . . . . . . . . . . . .  139  Cert Sonnets    7      2
```

		PAGE	TITLE		LINE
AGREE	(CONTINUED)				
Above line repeated at following locations		139	Cert Sonnets	7	12
. . . .		140	Cert Sonnets	7	22
. . . .		140	Cert Sonnets	7	32
If French can yet three parts in one agree;.		180	Astrophil	30	5
Where Nature doth with infinite agree?		182	Astrophil	35	4
And eke their pipes did well, as frends, agree..		242	Other Poems	4	32
Who would have hir in will and worde agree		245	Other Poems	4	115
AGREED					
At length to Love's decrees, I forc'd, agreed, ...		165	Astrophil	2	7
AGREES					
Woe, but seems to me joy, that agrees to my thought so. I					
thought so..		64	2nd Eclogues	31	38
AH					
Dorus. Such Kala is: but ah, my fancies raysed be.		15	1st Eclogues	7	37
But ah my Muse I would thou hadst facilitie, ...		19	1st Eclogues	7	176
Nico. Ah now I see, why thou art in thy selfe so blind:. . .		52	2nd Eclogues	29	5
Pas. Ah foole; so Courtiers do. But who did lively skippe, .		52	2nd Eclogues	29	11
Ah where was first that cruell cunning found,.		57	2nd Eclogues	30	11
But ah, alas! (In vayne) my minde, sight, thought, ...		84	Arcadia III	60	11
But ah the more I hate, the more I thinke.		85	Arcadia III	61	9
Ah woe is me, my woes renewe;.		90	Arcadia III	62	120
And out gan cry, "ah well away for shame,.		95	3rd Eclogues	64	45
But ah her flight hath my dead reliques spent.		115	4th Eclogues	72	80
Strephon. But ah her flight hath my dead reliques spent, . .		115	4th Eclogues	72	81
A living coarse I lay: but ah, my wakefull minde		117	4th Eclogues	73	31
Ah, that, that do I not conceive, though that to me leefe					
were		122	4th Eclogues	74	19
Ah, that, that do I not conceive; to the heaven when a mouse					
climes.		122	4th Eclogues	74	21
Ah let us all against foule Nature crie:		127	4th Eclogues	75	92
His death our death. But ah; my Muse hath swarved, ...		129	4th Eclogues	75	136
Where ys Ah that face, that a Sunne defaces?		138	Cert Sonnets	5	9
Ah saucy paine let not thy errour last,.		141	Cert Sonnets	8	13
Ah haire, how many dayes,.		158	Cert Sonnets	28	9
Ah haire are you not griev'd,.		158	Cert Sonnets	28	29
And ah what hope, that hope should once see day, ...		182	Astrophil	35	7
"But ah," Desire still cries, "give me some food."		201	Astrophil	71	14
My heart cries "ah", it burnes, mine eyes now dazled be: . .		205	Astrophil	76	11
Yet ah, my Mayd'n Muse doth blush to tell the best..		205	Astrophil	77	14
But ah poore Night, in love with Phoebus' light, ...		229	Astrophil	97	5
Ah bed, the field where joye's peace some do see,.		230	Astrophil	98	1
Ah, is it not enough, that I am thence,.		233	Astrophil	104	5
Ah what doth Phoebus' gold that wretch availe, ...		237	Astrophil	108	10
Oh sweet kisse, but ah she is waking,.		203	A&S 2nd Song		25
Ah, my sute granted is, I feele my breast doth swell:. . . .		213	A&S 5th Song		34
Being (ah) exild, disdayneth		233	A&S 11th Song		4
Then think I, Ah, what is this Man,.		278	Psalm VIII		13
Ah, now even for their sakes, that taste of Woe, ...		285	Psalm XII		13
Ah, when from syon shall the saver come, ...		287	Psalm XIV		22
Ah! from the sword yet save my vital sprite, ...		299	Psalm XXII		47
But, ah he strait his face did hide, ...		311	Psalm XXX		23
Ah! yet from me let Thy plagues be displac't,.		330	Psalm XXXIX		31
Ah, when comes my blessed being, ...		334	Psalm XLII		7
Ah my soul it self appaleth, ...		334	Psalm XLII		23
Dick. Ah Will, though I grudge not, I count it feeble glee .		343	Possibly	1	3
Was Klaius cald, (ah Klaius, wofull wight!).		242	Other Poems	4	23
But, ah! hir darts did farre more depely goe		251	Other Poems	4	352
AHA					
Aha! Sir, now we see you where we should..		322	Psalm XXXV		54
Aha! This is good game.		332	Psalm XL		60
AI					
O Hiacinthe let Ai be on thee still.		125	4th Eclogues	75	29
AID					
Great be Physitions' brags, but aid is beggerly, ...		128	4th Eclogues	75	112
Muses, I oft invoked your holy ayde, ...		192	Astrophil	55	1
From whence shall come to us such ayd?		274	Psalm IV		25
O be thou still the Orphan's aide.		283	Psalm X		77
Since all my ayd in Thee I got..		308	Psalm XXVII		44
To looke and run to him for aid, ...		319	Psalm XXXIV		18
He shall be their true strength and aid.		327	Psalm XXXVII		100
Above line repeated at following location.		327	Psalm XXXVII		101
By thy aid;.		329	Psalm XXXVIII		65
Who is still my present aid;		335	Psalm XLII		54
Sure aid present comfort..		337	Psalm XLIII		36
And cal'd, now wounded, purpose to his aide:		246	Other Poems	4	162
AIDING					
By aiding when fierce unicorns come neare me..		299	Psalm XXII		50
AIL					
But if he nought do desire, what can Heraclitus aile?. . . .		30	1st Eclogues	11	12
AILETH					
What ayleth thee, and if they knew thy minde		23	1st Eclogues	9	42
AILS					
My muse what ails this ardour.		65	2nd Eclogues	32	1
Above line repeated at following locations		66	2nd Eclogues	32	9
. . . .		66	2nd Eclogues	32	19
. . . .		66	2nd Eclogues	32	30
. . . .		67	2nd Eclogues	32	40
What ayles this heathenish rage? What do theis people meane.		271	Psalm II		1
What ayles Thy discomfort?		337	Psalm XLIII		33

		PAGE	TITLE		LINE

AIM
With idle paines, and missing ayme, do guesse. . . . . 176 Astrophil 23 4

AIMED
Nico. Well aimed by my hat: for as thou sangst last day; . . 52 2nd Eclogues 29 25

AIMS
Only thought aymes at the pleasure.. . . . . 226 A&S 10th Song 12

AIR
To aire of sighes, sighes to the harte's fire turne, ... 19 1st Eclogues 7 154
Earth, sea, ayre, fire, heav'n, hell, and gastly sprite. . . 23 1st Eclogues 9 40
Aire, we do still with sighes encrease; to the fire? we do
want none. . . . . 32 1st Eclogues 13 30
The sound to this strange aier no sooner goes, ... 42 Arcadia II 21 9
Since streame, aier, sand, mine eyes and eares conspire: . . 42 Arcadia II 21 17
Where drawing breath, I sucke the aire of woe: . . . . 73 Arcadia III 40 10
Man oft is plag'de with aire, is burnt with fire,. . . . . . 105 3rd Eclogues 67 67
This cheerefull aire with your obscured cheere,. . . . . . . 127 4th Eclogues 75 68
The aire in raine for my affliction weepeth: . . . . 136 Cert Sonnets 3 2
Aire let me draw no more thy breath in anguish;. . . . . . . 136 Cert Sonnets 3 14
Fire, aire, sea, earth, fame, time, place, shew your power.. 136 Cert Sonnets 3 20
My Foe came on, and beat the aire for me,. . . . . 191 Astrophil 53 13
With wings of Love in aire of wonder flie, ... 212 Astrophil 86 8
But when birds charme, and that sweete aire, which is. . . . 231 Astrophil 99 9
Smiling ayre allowes my reason, ... 219 A&S 8th Song 55
The Bird free Burgesse of the ayre, ... 279 Psalm VIII 29
Cloudes even of Waters dark, and thickest ayre compos'd; . . 291 Psalm XVIII 25
A salve, freshe ayre, and hyghe contented mynde. . . . . . . 345 Possibly 2 14
The aire hir swete race mov'd doth blow the fire.. . . . . . 249 Other Poems 4 300
Who nothing earthly, but of fire and aire, ... 250 Other Poems 4 338
Come she, and sweet the aire with open brest,. . . . . 254 Other Poems 4 466
So may your Make, this wholsome springtime aire, ... 257 Other Poems 5 42

AIRS
O how the pleasant aires of true love be . . . . 205 Astrophil 78 1

ALABASTER
Hath his front built of Alabaster pure;. . . . . 169 Astrophil 9 3

ALABLASTER
A spotlesse mine of Alablaster.. . . . . 88 Arcadia III 62 80
Like Alablaster faire and sleeke, ... 88 Arcadia III 62 81
Decke that poore place with Alablaster linde.. . . . . 150 Cert Sonnets 22 34
Of trueth, farre more then Alablaster pure,. . . . . 150 Cert Sonnets 22 39

ALARM
Allarme allarme, here will no yeelding be, ... 346 Possibly 5 1
That naught withstandes Desire, Allarme allarme. . . . . . . 346 Possibly 5 4
Allarme allarme, let not their beauties move . . . . 346 Possibly 5 5
No force, though force be used, Allarme allarme. . . . . . . 346 Possibly 5 8
Allarme allarme, companions nowe beginne, ... 346 Possibly 5 9
Much may that was not yet, Allarme allarme.. . . . . 346 Possibly 5 12
Allarme allarme, when once the fight is warme, ... 346 Possibly 5 13
Then shall you see them yelde, Allarme allarme.. . . . . . . 346 Possibly 5 14

ALAS
Geron. Alas what falls are falne unto thy minde? . . . . . . 23 1st Eclogues 9 32
Of yeeres (alas) since I good Mastix knewe.. . . . . 27 1st Eclogues 10 21
Thus, thus, alas! wofull in nature, unhappy by fortune,. . . 30 1st Eclogues 11 19
What meane is there, alas, we can hope our losse to recover? 32 1st Eclogues 13 27
But yet, alas! O but yet alas! our happs be but hard happs,. 32 1st Eclogues 13 37
Well may a Pastor plaine, but alas his plaints be not
esteem de. . . . . 32 1st Eclogues 13 39
For yet (weigh this alas!) great is not great to a greater.. 34 1st Eclogues 13 74
For both, alas, their strengthes together tie: . . . . 42 Arcadia II 22 4
My sonne alas from me for ever goes. . . . . 43 Arcadia II 24 6
Yet harvest brings. Doth she alas absent herselfe? . . . . . 49 2nd Eclogues 28 62
The neighbours all did crie, "alas what asse doth bray?" . . 52 2nd Eclogues 29 26
If thou (alas poore if) do winne, then winne thou this,. . . 53 2nd Eclogues 29 37
Nico. Alas how oft I looke on cherries ripe, ... 54 2nd Eclogues 29 75
Pas. Alas, when I in spring meet roses rathe,. . . . . 54 2nd Eclogues 29 78
Alas (said I) this babe dooth nurce my thought.. . . . . . . 55 2nd Eclogues 29 113
Plangus. Alas how long this pilgrimage doth last?. . . . . . 57 2nd Eclogues 30 5
Alas while we are wrapt in foggie mist . . . . 59 2nd Eclogues 30 68
Alas, if you a Phoenix new will have . . . . 60 2nd Eclogues 30 102
Therefore, alas, you use vile Vulcan's spight, ... 60 2nd Eclogues 30 107
Alas it is no glory. . . . . 65 2nd Eclogues 32 3
Alas it is no comfort. 65 2nd Eclogues 32 5
Alas it is no wisdome. 65 2nd Eclogues 32 7
"Alas" she saith "I am thine,. . . . . 67 2nd Eclogues 32 41
Seeing, Alas, so mightie powers bende. . . . . 73 Arcadia III 40 5
No smaller wound, alas! farr deeper have.. . . . . 77 Arcadia III 47 4
But ah, alas! (In vayne) my minde, sight, thought, ... 84 Arcadia III 60 11
"Alas", quoth she, "thus women's shame doth creepe". . . . . 96 3rd Eclogues 64 87
"Long have I love'd, (alas thou worthy arte) . . . . 97 3rd Eclogues 64 97
Long have I lov'd, (alas love craveth love). . . . . 97 3rd Eclogues 64 98
Long have I lov'd thy selfe, alas my harte . . . . 97 3rd Eclogues 64 99
Choosing alas! this our theatre publique,. . . . . 109 Arcadia IV 70 11
Strephon. Long since alas, my deadly Swannish musique. . . . 112 4th Eclogues 71 25
Thus, thus alas, I had my losse in chase.. . . . . 115 4th Eclogues 72 70
Klaius. Thus, thus alas, I had my losse in chase. . . . . . 115 4th Eclogues 72 71
Alas I doo; from which to finde release, ... 116 4th Eclogues 72 92
O faire, o onely faire, from thee, alas, ... 116 4th Eclogues 72 96
Unarmde (alas) unwarn'd to take a man asleepe? . . . . 122 4th Eclogues 73 186
O you (alas so I find) cause of his onely ruine. . . . . . . 122 4th Eclogues 74 4
But, but alas, like a man condemn'd doth crave to be heard
speake,. . . . . 122 4th Eclogues 74 23

```
ALAS                      (CONTINUED)                    PAGE    TITLE        LINE
  Alas, me thinkes, my weakned voice but spilleth,  . . . . . .  127  4th Eclogues 75   97
  Approach of death, alas thou helpest meagerly,  . . . . . . .  128  4th Eclogues 75  110
  Justice, justice is now (alas) oppressed:. . . . . . . . . .   128  4th Eclogues 75  118
  For see alas, who is from you absented.. . . . . . . . . .     128  4th Eclogues 75  124
  Whence, whence alas, shall we seeke our direction!  . . . . .  129  4th Eclogues 76   19
  Alas, all onely she no pitie taketh, . . . . . . . . . . . .   136  Cert Sonnets  3    9
  Alas, from all their helps I am exiled,. . . . . . . . . . .   137  Cert Sonnets  3   21
  Alas she hath no other cause of anguish. . . . . . . . . . .   137  Cert Sonnets  4   13
  If thus, alas: yet while those partes have wo, . . . . . . .   142  Cert Sonnets 10   13
  Alas sweet Brookes do in my teares augment:. . . . . . . .    147  Cert Sonnets 18   12
  For me alas I am full resolv'd . . . . . . . . . . . . . .     153  Cert Sonnets 24   19
  Those bands alas shall not be dissolv'd. . . . . . . . . . .   153  Cert Sonnets 24   20
  Joyned alas to your beames,. . . . . . . . . . . . . . . . .   154  Cert Sonnets 25    4
  As you, alas, my Sunne bends;. . . . . . . . . . . . . . . .   154  Cert Sonnets 25   26
  Wo to me, alas she weepeth!. . . . . . . . . . . . . . . . .   157  Cert Sonnets 27   25
  Alas how oft with teares,. . . . . . . . . . . . . . . . . .   158  Cert Sonnets 28   13
  Alas, I lie: rage hath this errour bred, . . . . . . . . . .   160  Cert Sonnets 30   31
  Vertue alas, now let me take some rest,. . . . . . . . . . .   166  Astrophil     4    1
  Alas have I not paine enough my friend,. . . . . . . . . . .   171  Astrophil    14    1
  O fooles, or over-wise, alas the race. . . . . . . . . . . .   176  Astrophil    23   12
  Alas, if from the height of Vertue's throne, . . . . . . . .   184  Astrophil    40    5
  Alas, what cause is there so overthwart, . . . . . . . . . .   186  Astrophil    44    7
  Alas, if Fancy drawne by imag'd things,. . . . . . . . . . .   187  Astrophil    45    9
  Alas poore wag, that now a scholler art. . . . . . . . . . .   188  Astrophil    46    9
  But now that I, alas, do want her sight, . . . . . . . . . .   193  Astrophil    56    9
  Alas, if you graunt only such delight. . . . . . . . . . . .   194  Astrophil    59   12
  Alas, if this the only mettall be. . . . . . . . . . . . . .   196  Astrophil    62   12
  Mine eyes, my light, my heart, my life, alas,. . . . . . . .   198  Astrophil    65    9
  Now banisht art, but yet alas how shall? . . . . . . . . . .   202  Astrophil    72   14
  Most sweet-faire, most faire-sweet, do not alas, . . . . . .   208  Astrophil    82    7
  Alas, whence came this change of lookes? If I. . . . . . . .   212  Astrophil    86    1
  Alas I found, that she with me did smart,. . . . . . . . . .   223  Astrophil    87    5
  But, but (alas) night's side the ods hath fur, . . . . . . .   229  Astrophil    96   12
  Even so (alas) a Lady Dian's peere,. . . . . . . . . . . . .   230  Astrophil    97    9
  So strangely (alas) thy works in me prevaile,. . . . . . . .   237  Astrophil   108   12
  Now will I alas refraine,. . . . . . . . . . . . . . . . . .   203  A&S 2nd Song      19
  Sweet alas, why strive you thus? . . . . . . . . . . . . . .   211  A&S 4th Song      43
  Alas, that I am forst such evill of thee to say, . . . . . .   215  A&S 5th Song      80
  You witch, you Divill, (alas) you still of me beloved,  . . .  215  A&S 5th Song      87
  "Why alas, and are you he? . . . . . . . . . . . . . . . . .   234  A&S 11th Song      6
  Wept they had, alas the while, . . . . . . . . . . . . . . .   218  A&S 8th Song      13
  "Graunt, o graunt, but speech alas,. . . . . . . . . . . . .   219  A&S 8th Song      45
  Yet alas before you go,. . . . . . . . . . . . . . . . . . .   221  A&S 9th Song      11
  Why alas doth she then sweare, . . . . . . . . . . . . . . .   222  A&S 9th Song      31
  But alas, if in your straying. . . . . . . . . . . . . . . .   222  A&S 9th Song      47
  Alas, how long, my God, wilt Thou delay me?. . . . . . . . .   276  Psalm VI          10
  For what, alas, have just men done?. . . . . . . . . . . . .   284  Psalm XI          11
  And now am brought, alas, brought by Thy power  . . . . . . .  299  Psalm XXII        37
  What serves alas the blood of me . . . . . . . . . . . . . .   311  Psalm XXX         26
  While thus, alas, they say:. . . . . . . . . . . . . . . . .   333  Psalm XLI         18
  She troubled was (alas that it mought be!) . . . . . . . . .   245  Other Poems   4  113
  "Alas! what weights are these that lode my heart!. . . . . .   253  Other Poems   4  441
  "Alas! a cloud hath overcast mine eies:. . . . . . . . . . .   255  Other Poems   4  505
  Alas! of ghostes I heare the gastly cries: . . . . . . . . .   255  Other Poems   4  507
  "I will, I will, alas! alas! I will: . . . . . . . . . . . .   255  Other Poems   4  513
ALBEIT
  Pas. My gray-hood is mine owne, all be it be but gray,  . . .  52  2nd Eclogues 29    7
ALBION
  That Albion clives in whitenes passe:. . . . . . . . . . . .   88  Arcadia III  62   91
  Of ships, by shipwrack cast on Albion coast, . . . . . . . .  151  Cert Sonnets 22   51
ALIVE
  But I in me am chang'd, I am alive and dead: . . . . . . . .   215  A&S 5th Song      76
ALL
  To one whose state is raised over all, . . . . . . . . . . .    3  Lady of May   1    1
  Are all my thoughts, in which I live or die: . . . . . . . .    3  Lady of May   2   10
  All this I give, let me possesse thy grace,. . . . . . . . .    4  Lady of May   2   22
  Judge you to whom all beautie's force is lent. . . . . . . .    4  Lady of May   2   31
  Judge you of Love, to whom all Love is bent. . . . . . . . .    4  Lady of May   2   32
  And ere that all these blowes thy head doo hit,. . . . . . .   11  Arcadia I     1    9
  All this one the this fatall yere shall hitte. . . . . . . .   11  Arcadia I     1 V807
  For (woe is me) my powers all I finde. . . . . . . . . . . .   11  Arcadia I     2    3
  Thus all my thoughts are slaves to one thought still:. . . .   12  Arcadia I     2   10
  Since what I see, thinke, know is all but you? . . . . . . .   12  Arcadia I     2   14
  And for a tast of all these gifts, she borowes Momus' grace.   12  Arcadia I     3    8
  My Kala's giftes: who with all good gifts filled is. . . . .   15  1st Eclogues  7   26
  How nice to touch? how all her speeches peized be? . . . . .   15  1st Eclogues  7   35
  Since vertues all, to make her title, pleased be.. . . . . .   15  1st Eclogues  7   39
  Love well thine owne: me thinkes, woolle's whitenes passeth
     all:. . . . . . . . . . . . . . . . . . . . . . . . . . .   16  1st Eclogues  7   53
  This winde he spent: but when my Kala glasseth all . . . . .   16  1st Eclogues  7   55
  Not rotten sheepe, but high crownes she surpasseth all.. . .   16  1st Eclogues  7   57
  Lay all your feare upon your fearefull lover:. . . . . . . .   17  1st Eclogues  7   91
  Whose sprite all sprites can spoile, raise, damne, or save:.   17  1st Eclogues  7  110
  Yet all my health I place in your good-will. . . . . . . . .   18  1st Eclogues  7  120
  The thought of which doth passe all worldly pelfe. . . . . .   18  1st Eclogues  7  130
  Nature made all, but me of dolours made: . . . . . . . . . .   18  1st Eclogues  7  143
  Or naked he, disguis'd in all untruth? . . . . . . . . . . .   21  1st Eclogues  8    8
  To narrow brests he comes all wrapt in gaine:. . . . . . . .   21  1st Eclogues  8   37
  To open eyes all beauties he doth raine; . . . . . . . . . .   22  1st Eclogues  8   39
```

ALL	(CONTINUED)	PAGE	TITLE		LINE
Of all those fooles that will have all they see.......		22	1st Eclogues	8	48
And all the starres conspired to my good,..........		23	1st Eclogues	9	27
Since all his force against himselfe he tries........		23	1st Eclogues	9	37
Where all my paines one looke of hers hath paid.......		26	1st Eclogues	9	137
Either a sleepe be all if nought assaile,..........		27	1st Eclogues	10	29
Or all abroade if but a Cubb start out.............		27	1st Eclogues	10	30
Doe speake high wordes, when all the coaste is cleare, ...		27	1st Eclogues	10	32
The third his lesson mist, till all do smarte........		27	1st Eclogues	10	45
A Cage (guilded perchaunce) is all his lott.........		28	1st Eclogues	10	69
Who once all birdes, in sweetly-singing past,........		28	1st Eclogues	10	74
Of all the birdes, but namely those were grieved,......		29	1st Eclogues	10	83
Then who makes us such judges over all?............		29	1st Eclogues	10	96
Fortune thus gan say; "misery and misfortune is all one, ...		29	1st Eclogues	11	3
"Tush, tush", said nature, "this is all but a trifle, a man's selfe......................		29	1st Eclogues	11	7
Where thou poore nature left'st all thy due glory, to fortune.....................		30	1st Eclogues	11	15
With the voyce of truth to recorde to all worldes, ...		31	1st Eclogues	12	19
All to a lesson he draws, norr hills nor caves can avoide him......................		31	1st Eclogues	13	7
Cleofila. Worthy shepeheard, by my song to my selfe all favor is happned,...................		31	1st Eclogues	13	8
Sacred Muse, who in one contaynes what nine do in all them..		31	1st Eclogues	13	10
Dorus. Unto the Gods with a thanckfull heart all thankes I do render,.....................		32	1st Eclogues	13	35
Her praise, whence to the world all praise had his only beginning:....................		33	1st Eclogues	13	69
Desteny keepes me aloofe. For if all thy estate to thy verture.....................		34	1st Eclogues	13	98
But perforce disgest, all bitter juices of horror......		35	1st Eclogues	13	105
And since in vaine I find were all my strife,........		38	Arcadia II	14	13
Which makes all eyes doo honour unto you..........		38	Arcadia II	15	8
That onely light doth all my life maintaine;........		39	Arcadia II	16	4
Since in sweete you all goods so richly raigne,.......		39	Arcadia II	16	5
My sheepehooke is wanne hope, which all upholdes:......		39	Arcadia II	17	5
My words in store, the marble all alone;..........		41	Arcadia II	19	8
O blessed sonne whence all this blessing goes........		43	Arcadia II	23	6
You beare no woll, and losse is all my gayne........		44	Arcadia II	24	14
Who hath sav'd all? it is even I................		44	Arcadia II	25	12
P. Because our weaknes weakeneth all your might.......		46	2nd Eclogues	27	22
All numbring artes her endlesse graces number not:.....		49	2nd Eclogues	28	59
Thus I commend to thee all our former love.........		51	2nd Eclogues	28	102
As thou doest thinke) should most of all disquiet me		51	2nd Eclogues	28	115
Among us all we should find out some thing of nought....		51	2nd Eclogues	29	2
Despairde in all this flocke to find a knave, but thee....		52	2nd Eclogues	29	4
The neighbours all did crie, "alas what asse doth bray?" ..		52	2nd Eclogues	29	26
Nico. O Faunes, O Fairies all, and do you see, ...		54	2nd Eclogues	29	63
And all but jests, save onely sorrowe's rage.........		57	2nd Eclogues	30	22
Where all good haps a perfect state maintaine?		58	2nd Eclogues	30	40
For all these certaine blowes the surest shield.......		58	2nd Eclogues	30	43
Hath all thy whirling course so small effect?........		58	2nd Eclogues	30	60
Serve all thy starrie eyes this shame to see?........		58	2nd Eclogues	30	61
Thus Death becomes a rivall to us all,...........		59	2nd Eclogues	30	89
That sweetens all the place; she is the guest........		59	2nd Eclogues	30	99
And shall (o me) all this in ashes rest?..........		60	2nd Eclogues	30	101
Which while it is, it is all Asia's light..........		60	2nd Eclogues	30	109
Let all for her, and unto her be bent............		60	2nd Eclogues	30	124
Where but a baiting place is all our portion........		61	2nd Eclogues	30	136
To that strange stroke which conquer'd all my senses,....		61	2nd Eclogues	30	165
So greate a passion all feele,...............		66	2nd Eclogues	32	16
Of all thy harmes: Lo here she,..............		67	2nd Eclogues	32	47
But all thy songe herein knitt:..............		67	2nd Eclogues	32	51
The life we leade is all love,...............		67	2nd Eclogues	32	52
The love we holde is all death,..............		67	2nd Eclogues	32	53
Her legges carriage is of all the sweet campe:		67	2nd Eclogues	33	11
Doth proclaime with a sound made all by men's mouths		68	2nd Eclogues	33	20
Commands all creatures, to yeeld obeysance		68	2nd Eclogues	33	22
Nought disturbs thy quiet, all to thy service yeeld, ...		69	2nd Eclogues	34	10
But feare forgott, and paynes all overpaste, ...		70	Arcadia III	36	5
Seeking the Sainct in whome all graces dwell,.......		71	Arcadia III	36	14
Since all the thinges which give mine eyes their light ...		73	Arcadia III	39	5
Where too much sight, makes all the bodie blinde,......		73	Arcadia III	40	11
Due sighes blowe out all sparkes of joyfull light, ...		74	Arcadia III	42	11
I plaine with cause, my woes are all myne owne........		75	Arcadia III	43	6
All is but this, this is our labour's hire,.........		75	Arcadia III	44	6
O toong in which, all honyed likoures bee, ...		76	Arcadia III	46	3
Of waiting thoughts all to her service ment?		78	Arcadia III	49	12
Where hers, whom worth makes highest over all,.......		78	Arcadia III	49	17
Yet all well knit to one faire end do passe:		78	Arcadia III	50	8
All what I am, still one, his owne, doe finde........		78	Arcadia III	50	10
All what you are still one, his owne to finde,.......		79	Arcadia III	50	11
O harbour all her partes in easefull plighte:.......		79	Arcadia III	51	7
Bend all thy light to see.................		80	Arcadia III	52	5
Fancie we feele, encludes all passion's mighte,......		82	Arcadia III	57	3
All thoughts so spronge, are from their dwelling driv'n, ..		83	Arcadia III	57	5
In whose each part all pens may dwell?...........		85	Arcadia III	62	2
Can liken them without all peere,.............		86	Arcadia III	62	19
But bow all knees, now of her knees,...........		89	Arcadia III	62	93
Whose motion makes all graces move..		89	Arcadia III	62	96

10

ALL	(CONTINUED)	PAGE	TITLE		LINE
Whose steppe on earth all beautie sets..		89	Arcadia III	62	108
To all her limmes a spetiall grace,.		90	Arcadia III	62	135
How all this is but a faire Inne		90	Arcadia III	62	139
In whose each part all pens may dwell.		90	Arcadia III	62	146
Yee Muses all which chaste affects allow,.		91	3rd Eclogues	63	19
That they all vice may kill:		91	3rd Eclogues	63	23
Do please all eyes, and spotlesse do endure.		91	3rd Eclogues	63	25
Where that all blisse may raigne,.		91	3rd Eclogues	63	26
All churlish wordes, shrewd answeres, crabbed lookes,. . . .		93	3rd Eclogues	63	64
All privatenes, selfe-seeking, inward spite, ...		93	3rd Eclogues	63	65
All waywardnes, which nothing kindly brookes,.		93	3rd Eclogues	63	66
All strife for toyes, and clayming master's right:		93	3rd Eclogues	63	67
All sturring husband's hate.		93	3rd Eclogues	63	69
All peacock pride, and fruites of peacock's pride.		93	3rd Eclogues	63	73
But above all away vile jealousie, ...		93	3rd Eclogues	63	82
He farre did passe the rest of Shepheards all.		94	3rd Eclogues	64	18
And so she was, and all with good intent,.		95	3rd Eclogues	64	25
And this was all, and this the husband read.		97	3rd Eclogues	64	109
Al filthy mouths that glory in their vice.		98	3rd Eclogues	65	12
When all this Earth, this damme or mould of ours,.		100	3rd Eclogues	66	44
Or that they all to chaunging did encline, ...		100	3rd Eclogues	66	59
Rulers will thinke all things made them to please, ...		100	3rd Eclogues	66	73
They all consented were to give him wings:.		101	3rd Eclogues	66	101
That from thenceforth to all eternitie,.		101	3rd Eclogues	66	104
Before all flies the Waspe accept I would.		104	3rd Eclogues	67	18
Nature above all things requireth this,.		105	3rd Eclogues	67	70
Which drawne-out line doth hold all humane blisse.		105	3rd Eclogues	67	72
And yet in all this time, betwixt us tway, ...		106	3rd Eclogues	67	91
Mothers and Nurses of all vaine annoy.		107	3rd Eclogues	67	117
Turning all nature's course to selfe displeasure..		108	Arcadia IV	69	8
Since sorow then concludeth all our fortune,.		110	Arcadia IV	70	37
With all our deathes shew we this damage publique.		110	Arcadia IV	70	38
So darkened am, that all my day is evening,.		111	4th Eclogues	71	22
Strephon. I wish to fire the trees of all these forrests;. .		112	4th Eclogues	71	49
Strephon. I Joye in griefe, and doo detest all joyes:. . . .		113	4th Eclogues	72	1
I turne my minde to all formes of annoyes,.		113	4th Eclogues	72	3
All what I am: if I my selfe will save,.		114	4th Eclogues	72	23
The diffrence is; all folkes those stormes forbeare: . . .		114	4th Eclogues	72	38
Are all in me: what helpe then can I trie?		114	4th Eclogues	72	43
I harowe it with Thoughts, which all conspire.		115	4th Eclogues	72	54
Therefore esteeming all good blessings toyes,.		116	4th Eclogues	72	99
I joy in griefe, and doo detest all joyes.		116	4th Eclogues	72	100
Strephon. I joye in griefe, and doo detest all joyes.. . . .		116	4th Eclogues	72	101
Free all my powers were from those captiving snares, . . .		117	4th Eclogues	73	17
What life it is, and how that all these lives doo gather,. .		118	4th Eclogues	73	47
Or canons thunder-like, all shot togither, lende).		118	4th Eclogues	73	54
All things that earst I sawe, as orient pearles exceed,. . .		119	4th Eclogues	73	83
Of all those Graces' giftes the heavens have ever lent.. . .		119	4th Eclogues	73	86
The bande of beauties all, the little world of Love. . . .		119	4th Eclogues	73	90
In whom of all my rules the perfect proofe I finde,. . . .		119	4th Eclogues	73	94
To all what I decreed, did thus my verdict saye.		121	4th Eclogues	73	162
First having all their giftes upon faire Mira spred. . . .		121	4th Eclogues	73	178
And found with deadly feare that all my sinewes shak'd.. . .		121	4th Eclogues	73	180
All my'offence was Love: with Love then must I be chastned,.		123	4th Eclogues	74	41
Farewell, long farewell, all my woe, all my delight. . . .		124	4th Eclogues	74	86
Let all the Sea thy teares accounted be:		125	4th Eclogues	75	20
Thy bowels with all killing mettals arme..		125	4th Eclogues	75	21
O Echo, all these woods with roaring fill, ...		126	4th Eclogues	75	31
But all, for all reach not my wailefull will:.		126	4th Eclogues	75	33
Till that it hath all woods and waters past.		126	4th Eclogues	75	36
In one true chest to rob all Vertue's treasure?.		126	4th Eclogues	75	47
Thus, thus the mindes, which over all doo clime, ...		127	4th Eclogues	75	88
Ah let us all against foule Nature crie:		127	4th Eclogues	75	92
I have my selfe, and all what life containeth, ...		128	4th Eclogues	75	101
They leave off al, and say, death comes too eagerlie.. . . .		128	4th Eclogues	75	114
While he did live, farre, farre was all disorder;.		128	4th Eclogues	75	130
Farewell with thee, farewell all our affection..		129	4th Eclogues	76	6
Now that the mine is lost of all our treasure,.		129	4th Eclogues	76	10
We Orphans lefte, void of all publique might?.		129	4th Eclogues	76	12
For he our father was in all affection,.		129	4th Eclogues	76	14
In our well-doing placing all his pleasure,.		129	4th Eclogues	76	15
Who for our sakes will thinke all travaile light,.		129	4th Eclogues	76	23
No, no, for ever gone is all our pleasure;		130	4th Eclogues	76	25
For ever wandring from all good direction;		130	4th Eclogues	76	26
Let teares for him therefore be all our treasure,.		130	4th Eclogues	76	31
Farewell direction, farewell all affection..		130	4th Eclogues	76	39
For all his strife can onlie bondage gaine..		135	Cert Sonnets	2	8
Dead palsie sicke of all my chiefest parts:.		136	Cert Sonnets	2	10
Alas, all onely she no pitie taketh, ...		136	Cert Sonnets	3	9
Alas, from all their helps I am exiled,.		137	Cert Sonnets	3	21
Wherein she suffring all her spirits' languish,.		137	Cert Sonnets	4	15
In whom all joyes so well agree, ...		139	Cert Sonnets	7	2
Above line repeated at following locations		139	Cert Sonnets	7	12
. . . .		140	Cert Sonnets	7	22
. . . .		140	Cert Sonnets	7	32
Just accord all musike makes;.		140	Cert Sonnets	7	14
Since then truth to all minds telleth, ...		140	Cert Sonnets	7	18
Or doth she thinke all paine the minde forbeares?.		142	Cert Sonnets	11	5
But for all this I can not her remove.		145	Cert Sonnets	17	4

11

ALL	(CONTINUED)	PAGE	TITLE		LINE
That all the earth my woes, sighes, teares may know, ...	146	Cert Sonnets	17	39
But that good part, wherein all comforts be, ...	148	Cert Sonnets	20	11
Myne eyes thence drawne, where lived all their light, ...	149	Cert Sonnets	21	5
From fancie's earth passing all numbers' bound, ...	149	Cert Sonnets	22	7
Passing all ghesse, whence into me should fly.	149	Cert Sonnets	22	8
But all the rest, which feare durst not applie, ...	151	Cert Sonnets	22	49
On whome all love, in whom no love is plaste, ...	151	Cert Sonnets	22	63
She is the cause that all the rest I am.	151	Cert Sonnets	22	70
Left me devoid of all life;	154	Cert Sonnets	25	11
Where by the death of all deaths, ...	154	Cert Sonnets	25	13
Lady the life of all love;	154	Cert Sonnets	25	20
All what I am, it is you.	155	Cert Sonnets	25	34
All the places, ...	155	Cert Sonnets	26	6
Where that heat of all heates springeth, ...	155	Cert Sonnets	26	7
End the way, where all men stay. No, no, no, no.	155	Cert Sonnets	26	22
Al my sense thy sweetnesse gained, ...	156	Cert Sonnets	27	1
And all my life I will confesse, ...	157	Cert Sonnets	27	39
All Love is dead, infected	159	Cert Sonnets	30	3
Band of all evils, cradle of causelesse care, ...	161	Cert Sonnets	31	3
In vaine thou kindlest all thy smokie fire;	161	Cert Sonnets	31	11
Draw in thy beames, and humble all thy might, ...	161	Cert Sonnets	32	5
To make my selfe beleeve, that all is well, ...	166	Astrophil	2	13
What Love and Beautie be, then all my deed	166	Astrophil	3	13
But thinke that all the Map of my state I display, ...	168	Astrophil	6	13
She even in blacke doth make all beauties flow?	168	Astrophil	7	11
To honor all their deaths, who for her bleed.	168	Astrophil	7	14
Crie, "Victorie, this faire day all is ours.".	171	Astrophil	12	11
That to win it, is all the skill and paine..	171	Astrophil	12	14
While Love on me doth all his quiver spend, ...	171	Astrophil	14	4
A loathing of all loose unchastitie, ...	172	Astrophil	14	13
Of all those goods, which heav'n to me hath lent:	173	Astrophil	18	4
For though she passe all things, yet what is all	174	Astrophil	19	9
Of all my thoughts hath neither stop nor start, ...	176	Astrophil	23	13
As sacred things, far from all daunger's show.	177	Astrophil	24	8
Bends all his powers, even unto Stella's grace.	178	Astrophil	27	14
Do easly yeeld, that all their coasts may be	179	Astrophil	29	3
Use all to helpe his other conquerings:.	179	Astrophil	29	8
Vouchsafe of all acquaintance this to tell, ...	181	Astrophil	32	9
In all sweete stratagems sweete Arte can show, ...	183	Astrophil	36	11
Rich in all beauties which man's eye can see:	183	Astrophil	37	6
To leave the scepter of all subject things, ...	183	Astrophil	38	4
Whose beames be joyes, whose joyes all vertues be, ...	185	Astrophil	42	2
From all the world, her heart is then his rome, ...	186	Astrophil	43	13
Of all the grave conceits your braine doth breed;	190	Astrophil	51	6
Her eyes, her lips, her all, saith Love do this, ...	190	Astrophil	52	3
Th' anatomy of all my woes I wrate, ...	194	Astrophil	58	10
Where all my good I do in Stella see, ...	194	Astrophil	60	2
That wholly hers, all selfnesse he forbeares, ...	195	Astrophil	61	7
Let all the earth with scorne recount my case, ...	198	Astrophil	64	7
And yet amid all feares a hope there is.	199	Astrophil	66	9
Will she take time, before all wracked be?	199	Astrophil	67	4
And all in vaine, for while thy breath most sweet, ...	200	Astrophil	68	9
My friend, that oft saw through all maskes my wo, ...	200	Astrophil	69	5
There shall he find all vices' overthrow, ...	201	Astrophil	71	5
Thy selfe, doest strive all minds that way to move, ...	201	Astrophil	71	10
But thou Desire, because thou wouldst have all, ...	202	Astrophil	72	13
Of all the kings that ever here did raigne, ...	204	Astrophil	75	1
Loathing all lies, doubting this Flatterie is:	207	Astrophil	80	11
Breathing all blisse and sweetning to the heart, ...	207	Astrophil	81	3
How faine would I paint thee to all men's eyes, ...	207	Astrophil	81	7
Nymph of the gard'n, where all beauties be:	207	Astrophil	82	1
With doing all, leave nothing done but paine.	210	Astrophil	85	8
Thou but of all the kingly Tribute take.	210	Astrophil	85	14
But if all faith, like spotlesse Ermine ly	212	Astrophil	86	5
Then those blest eyes, where all my hopes do dwell, ...	212	Astrophil	86	13
Stella whose eyes make all my tempests cleere, ...	222	Astrophil	87	3
If thou praise not, all other praise is shame.	224	Astrophil	90	4
Since all my words thy beauty doth endite, ...	224	Astrophil	90	13
Say all, and all well sayd, still say the same..	225	Astrophil	92	14
That all thy hurts in my hart's wracke I reede;	227	Astrophil	93	13
The field where all my thoughts to warre be traind, ...	230	Astrophil	98	2
All mirth farewell, let me in sorrow live.	231	Astrophil	100	14
All folkes prest at thy will thy paine to "swage, ...	232	Astrophil	101	11
Where rigrows exile lockes up all my sense?.	233	Astrophil	104	8
Of all the powers which life bestowes on me, ...	236	Astrophil	107	2
To you, to you, all song of praise is due, ...	196	A&S 1st Song		3
Above line repeated at following locations	197	A&S 1st Song		7
. . . .	197	A&S 1st Song		11
. . . .	197	A&S 1st Song		15
. . . .	197	A&S 1st Song		19
. . . .	197	A&S 1st Song		23
. . . .	197	A&S 1st Song		27
. . . .	197	A&S 1st Song		31
. . . .	197	A&S 1st Song		35
Only for you the heav'n forgate all measure.	197	A&S 1st Song		8
Who hath the feet, whose step all sweetnesse planteth, . . .	197	A&S 1st Song		13
Onely at you all envie hopelesse rueth..	197	A&S 1st Song		24
Night hath closd all in her cloke, ...	210	A&S 4th Song		7
Dumbe sleepe holdeth all the house:	211	A&S 4th Song		26

12

ALL	(CONTINUED)	PAGE	TITLE	LINE
Cursed be my destines all, ...		211	A&S 4th Song	51
I thought all words were lost, that were not spent of thee:.		212	A&S 5th Song	4
And all eares worse then deafe, that heard not out thy storie.		212	A&S 5th Song	6
And all I said so well, as no man it denied.		212	A&S 5th Song	12
But thou rich in all joyes, doest rob my joyes from me,. . .		214	A&S 5th Song	46
If Rule by force without all claime a Tyran showeth, ...		214	A&S 5th Song	57
That all these cruell words your praises shall be proved...		215	A&S 5th Song	90
Seaze on all to her belonging;		226	A&S 10th Song	21
Senses all asunder breakes;.		219	A&S 8th Song	38
Whose face all, all beauty passeth,.		219	A&S 8th Song	43
Gave repulse all grace excelling.		219	A&S 8th Song	68
All my blisse in thee I lay;		220	A&S 8th Song	90
For all love, all faith is meant thee, ...		220	A&S 8th Song	92
Leave a wretch, in whom all wo		221	A&S 9th Song	6
All her hate, death soone would seaze me,.		222	A&S 9th Song	44
So all things whereto that man doth bend,.		270	Psalm I	11
Wherof if but a sparke once kindled be, you all.		272	Psalm II	29
That all against poore me.		272	Psalm III	5
Which all against me gather:		272	Psalm III	21
Sinne from all rule in you depose, ...		273	Psalm IV	17
Thou hatest all whose works in evill are plac't.		275	Psalm V	13
For all I neede, that with such foes do byde..		275	Psalm V	24
So shall all they that trust in thee do bend,.		275	Psalm V	33
And age pull'd on with paines all freshness fretteth:. . . .		276	Psalm VI	22
In all whose workes vainess is ever raigning:.		276	Psalm VI	26
So shall all men with laudes inviron thee.		277	Psalm VII	19
And all my help from none but Thee is sent,.		277	Psalm VII	29
Which all from Thee their Essence took		278	Psalm VIII	10
Thou placest him upon all lands.		279	Psalm VIII	21
And so thou hast all things ordained		279	Psalm VIII	23
And all the beasts for ever breeding		279	Psalm VIII	27
With all my heart O lord I will prayse Thee, ...		279	Psalm IX	1
My speeches all Thy marvailes shall descry:.		279	Psalm IX	2
Thence he to all his judgments shall apply		280	Psalm IX	24
May only joy in all Thy saving wayes		280	Psalm IX	44
Therfore he doth defy all those.		282	Psalm X	21
He leasure wants to mark all this.		282	Psalm X	48
All wrong and mischeife lyes,.		283	Psalm X	58
To hearts that hate all lying.		284	Psalm XI	8
Of things vain, with vaine mates they bable all, ...		284	Psalm XII	4
Our tongues, say they, beyond them all shall go, ...		285	Psalm XII	10
Against all them, that against him do swell,.		285	Psalm XII	17
Which if it last, Woe to all simple Hearts.		285	Psalm XII	27
And so thereafter He, and all his Mates.		286	Psalm XIV	4
And, lo, he finds that all astraying went,.		286	Psalm XIV	10
All plung'd in stinking filth, not One well bent,.		286	Psalm XIV	11
All the hope of all my heart,.		287	Psalm XVI	2
This is all the best I prove,.		288	Psalm XVI	7
All the fulness of delight,.		289	Psalm XVI	41
When silent night might seeme all faults to hide,.		289	Psalm XVII	9
Thee will I love, O Lord, with all my heart's delight, . . .		290	Psalm XVIII	1
His heat to all he throweth.		294	Psalm XIX	28
All his commandments being		294	Psalm XIX	34
Most secret from all knowledg.		295	Psalm XIX	52
Defend Thee still from all Thy foes abroad..		295	Psalm XX	5
But let all our conceit.		296	Psalm XX	28
And why all this? Because Our King		297	Psalm XXI	25
But all their bad mischeivous skill.		298	Psalm XXI	43
Let God save him, in whom was all his lust..		299	Psalm XXII	20
On me all this, who do like water slide;		299	Psalm XXII	31
Who feare the lord all prayse and glory beare him;		300	Psalm XXII	53
And turn to God, and all the Nations be.		300	Psalm XXII	67
And that by right upon all Realmes he raigneth..		300	Psalm XXII	70
Thus shall all thy days be fede, ...		301	Psalm XXIII	22
There where the Lord of all.		301	Psalm XXIII	26
And all who in that Globe do dwell;.		302	Psalm XXIV	2
All pureness ever to embrace;.		302	Psalm XXIV	8
Outward, all outward goods		304	Psalm XXV	51
For I am poore, and left of all.		304	Psalm XXV	60
And pardon all my faults.		304	Psalm XXV	64
My hope is all in thee....		305	Psalm XXV	76
O Lord from all his troubles fell.		305	Psalm XXV	78
Of all my trustfull hope,.		305	Psalm XXVI	5
Since all my ayd in Thee I got...		308	Psalm XXVII	44
All my trust on him was sett;.		309	Psalm XXVIII	27
Ascribe all glory and all might.		309	Psalm XXIX	3
All, all my trust lord I have put in Thee, ...		312	Psalm XXXI	1
For all my hope fixt upon God doth ly.		312	Psalm XXXI	18
For troubles of all sides have me within..		312	Psalm XXXI	26
All my fierce Foes reproach on mee did cast;		313	Psalm XXXI	31
All to this point, how my poore life to take..		313	Psalm XXXI	39
Then love him ye all ye that feel his grace, ...		314	Psalm XXXI	64
All mercys shall be swarmed.		315	Psalm XXXII	39
God's goodness fills all lands,.		316	Psalm XXXIII	21
And all that Host.		316	Psalm XXXIII	23
Let all the earth feare God, ...		317	Psalm XXXIII	28
His Counsells all.		317	Psalm XXXIII	38
Throughout all ages last..		317	Psalm XXXIII	39

13

ALL	(CONTINUED)	PAGE	TITLE		LINE
Of all their hope.		318	Psalm XXXIII		71
From out his troubles all.		319	Psalm XXXIV		24
Whose trust is all on thee..		319	Psalm XXXIV		32
All trouble, all reproche.		320	Psalm XXXIV		64
His bones he keepeth all		320	Psalm XXXIV		73
God doth all soules redeeme.		321	Psalm XXXIV		77
His deeds, yea thoughtes all good forgett;		323	Psalm XXXVI		10
Guide Thee by him, lay all thy trusting.		324	Psalm XXXVII		11
Though all his plotts without misfortune		325	Psalm XXXVII		19
Then fly all ev'ill and goodness nourish,		326	Psalm XXXVII		67
He shall save them from all the fetches.		327	Psalm XXXVII		102
At these my words all cloath'd in teares;		330	Psalm XXXIX		38
Therfore, O Lord, abandond thus of all,		333	Psalm XLI		33
Whome Thou, O place of places all, dost place.		334	Psalm XLI		43
All Thy floods on me abounded,		335	Psalm XLII		33
Over me all thy waves went;		335	Psalm XLII		34
Judg of all, judg me		336	Psalm XLIII		1
Shaking off all sadnes,		336	Psalm XLIII		21
God of all my blisse,		336	Psalm XLIII		23
God of all my gladness.		336	Psalm XLIII		24
Shew that we do not grudge at all when others do rejoyce..		343	Possibly	1	2
Will. A tyme there is for all, my Mother often sayes,		343	Possibly	1	9
As all the rest, so now the stone.		241	Other Poems	3	7
As bragging that free of all passions' mone.		244	Other Poems	4	71
But fearing lest all white might seeme too good,		246	Other Poems	4	151
So as good thoughts of him in all arise,		247	Other Poems	4	198
With others' blott, till all do tast of shame.		248	Other Poems	4	232
From Nous and Cosma all their beauty tooke..		248	Other Poems	4	248
So laughing all, yet Pas to ease some dell,		249	Other Poems	4	263
And all to second barly-brake are bent:		249	Other Poems	4	266
But all this while another course he fet.		249	Other Poems	4	280
With whose fine stepps all loves and joyes conspire.		250	Other Poems	4	302
Though him to meete at all she sturred nought.		250	Other Poems	4	326
And past all hope his chapps to frustrate so.		251	Other Poems	4	344
More then, besides hir, all the earth could show..		252	Other Poems	4	408
Then those delights through all their sinews breed		252	Other Poems	4	411
First killing mirth, then banishing all rest,		253	Other Poems	4	431
Then sports grew paines, all talking tediouse,		253	Other Poems	4	433
All visions seeme, at every bush I start:		253	Other Poems	4	445
I go about, but then is all my best.		254	Other Poems	4	470
Of all the games that here ere now I met:		254	Other Poems	4	494
Leave sheepe, leave all, I will no piecing have.		255	Other Poems	4	512
Like Rogue, all ragged goe,		257	Other Poems	5	25
Say all, and I with them,		259	Other Poems	5	93
Cause all the mirth you can,		261	Other Poems	6	37
Of all men to thee retaining,		263	Other Poems	7	65
ALLAY					
What Nestor's counsell can my flames alay,		182	Astrophil	35	5
ALL-BEHOLDING					
Rather then have thy all-beholding eye		126	4th Eclogues	75	56
ALLEGE					
That since they still alledge, When they were yong:		24	1st Eclogues	9	79
ALLEGIANCE					
O deue allegiance, by thee am I called		138	Cert Sonnets	5	15
Peace Due alledgeance, Duty must bee broken,		138	Cert Sonnets	5	19
ALLEGORY'S					
You that with allegorie's curious frame,		178	Astrophil	28	1
ALLOTTED					
Then couples three be streight allotted there,		248	Other Poems	4	225
ALLOW					
And charge of her to Argus did allow..		21	1st Eclogues	8	16
He is a beast, that beaste's use will allowe		25	1st Eclogues	9	99
Yee Muses all which chaste affects allow,		91	3rd Eclogues	63	19
Each other still allow:		92	3rd Eclogues	63	50
Allow good company, but kepe from thence		98	3rd Eclogues	65	11
And are not forst fonde thraldome to allow..		106	3rd Eclogues	67	105
That you allow me them by so small rate?		225	Astrophil	92	2
ALLOWS					
Then Love allowes, our pleasures to enrich,		18	1st Eclogues	7	129
Smiling ayre allowes my reason,		219	A&S 8th Song		55
ALLSEEING					
Naught his allseing sight can miss,		284	Psalm XI		15
ALLURE					
Least it might thee allure home to thy selfe to returne, ..		122	4th Eclogues	74	8
ALMIGHTY					
This God then girded me in his Almighty pow'rs,		292	Psalm XVIII		59
Made worshipers before Almighty Thee..		300	Psalm XXII		68
ALMOST					
Dicus. Thy words well voic'd, well gra'ste had almost heaved me.		48	2nd Eclogues	28	31
ALMS					
May get no almes but scorne of beggerie.		188	Astrophil	47	8
ALOFT					
The one aloft doth holde the other hie..		42	Arcadia II	22	5
Can fancies want eies, or he fall that steppeth aloft? Oft..		64	2nd Eclogues	31	22
When worthlesse corke, aloft doth floting lye.		81	Arcadia III	54	14
ALONE					
That she, whose looke alone might make me blessed,		17	1st Eclogues	7	83
My words in store, the marble all alone;		41	Arcadia II	19	8

14

```
ALONE                       (CONTINUED)                     PAGE    TITLE          LINE
  Now is the time we may be here alone,. . . . . . . . . . . .  97 3rd Eclogues 64  105
  A better life it is to lye alone. . . . . . . . . . . . . .  105 3rd Eclogues 67   57
  Stella alone with face unarmed marcht, . . . . . . . . . .  176 Astrophil    22    9
  Seeme most alone in greatest companie, . . . . . . . . . .  178 Astrophil    27    2
  If Love learne not alone to love and see,. . . . . . . . .  187 Astrophil    46    7
  He cannot love: no, no, let him alone.". . . . . . . . . .  191 Astrophil    54    8
  Hoping that when they might find Stella alone, . . . . . .  193 Astrophil    57    5
  My crying plaints to him alone, . . . . . . . . . . . . .   273 Psalm IV          14
  My bed, while I with black night mourn alone,. . . . . . .  276 Psalm VI          19
  His being was in her alone:. . . . . . . . . . . . . . .    241 Other Poems   3    1
  And comming where he hop'd to be alone,. . . . . . . . . .  253 Other Poems   4  439
  I still do see, though I be still alone. . . . . . . . . .  254 Other Poems   4  462
  This morne alone to lonely walke did passe,. . . . . . . .  255 Other Poems   4  533
  Absent alone canst thou then piping be?. . . . . . . . . .  258 Other Poems   5   65
  The other left alone,. . . . . . . . . . . . . . . . . . .  258 Other Poems   5   88
  It belongs to such alone . . . . . . . . . . . . . . . . .  262 Other Poems   7   27
ALONELY
  Then hers, to whom my thoughts alonely thrall. . . . . . .   78 Arcadia III  49   15
ALONG
  Along whose ridge such bones are met,. . . . . . . . . . .   89 Arcadia III  62  111
  In Lillies' neast, where Love's selfe lies along. . . . .   208 Astrophil    83    8
ALOOF
  Desteny keepes me aloofe. For if all thy estate to thy
    verture. . . . . . . . . . . . . . . . . . . . . . . . .   34 1st Eclogues 13   98
ALPS
  Klaius. For she, with whom compar'd, the Alpes are vallies,.  113 4th Eclogues 71   67
ALREADY
  Did piping leade, the Sunne already sanke. . . . . . . . .   98 3rd Eclogues 66    3
  Ev'n then Despaire did Hope already kill:. . . . . . . . .  115 4th Eclogues 72   64
  Yet since my death-wound is already got, . . . . . . . . .  189 Astrophil    48   12
  On me the paines of death already gan to prey, . . . . . .  291 Psalm XVIII        8
  Like in a winding sheet, wretch I already lay, . . . . . .  291 Psalm XVIII       10
  All ready, ready to my snaring grave to go.. . . . . . . .  291 Psalm XVIII       11
  But what? This doth already well appeare . . . . . . . . .  333 Psalm XLI         37
ALSO
  Thou lord also th' Oppressed wilt defend . . . . . . . . .  280 Psalm IX          26
ALTAR
  Of my owne harte, where thoughts be the temple, sighte is an
    aultar. . . . . . . . . . . . . . . . . . . . . . . . . .  37 1st Eclogues 13  171
  And with those hands about Thy Altar waite,. . . . . . . .  305 Psalm XXVI        21
  Yearely decke thine Altar shall: . . . . . . . . . . . . .  264 Other Poems   7   70
ALTARS
  Let doltes in haste some altars faire erect. . . . . . . .   58 2nd Eclogues 30   62
  Those thousand altars faire now in the dust to lie?. . . .  119 4th Eclogues 73  112
  To God's Altars tho. . . . . . . . . . . . . . . . . . . .  336 Psalm XLIII       19
ALTERED
  Save what a worke, by thy selfe is wrought: and since I am
    altred . . . . . . . . . . . . . . . . . . . . . . . . .  36 1st Eclogues 13  151
  Think what a world is now, think who hath altred her hart. .  124 4th Eclogues 74   76
ALTERINGS
  Till these straunge altrings you did hap to trie, . . . . .  125 4th Eclogues 75   26
ALTHOUGH
  "Poore Pan" (he sayd) "although thou beaten be,. . . . . .    5 Lady of May   3   11
  Disdaine me not, although I be not faire.. . . . . . . . .   18 1st Eclogues  7  116
  (Although simply atyrde) your manly affection utter. . . .   32 1st Eclogues 13   16
  Not so; although my mettall were most mutable, . . . . . .   47 2nd Eclogues 28   10
  And saith, although I seeke my life to flie, . . . . . . .   58 2nd Eclogues 30   54
  But still, although we faile of perfect rightfulnes, . . .   61 2nd Eclogues 30  137
  And did the same, although with mickle feare.. . . . . . .   96 3rd Eclogues 64   64
  So that I see, although my sight empaire,. . . . . . . . .  115 4th Eclogues 72   59
  Although their fame (me seemd) from truth had greatly jard..  119 4th Eclogues 73   80
  Although we be divine, our grandsire Saturne is. . . . . .  120 4th Eclogues 73  123
  Up to the sunne, although the sunne my wings do frie:. . .  153 Cert Sonnets 24   25
  Although with cruell fire, . . . . . . . . . . . . . . . .  155 Cert Sonnets 26    2
  Above line repeated at following locations . . . . . . . .  155 Cert Sonnets 26   13
                                                             156 Cert Sonnets 26   24
  And then, thinke thus, although thy beautie be . . . . . .  185 Astrophil    40    9
  Although lesse gifts impe feathers oft on Fame,. . . . . .  204 Astrophil    75    4
  Yet perish shall (although his paine be sore). . . . . . .  281 Psalm IX          59
  Although some Worldly losse therby he may sustaine,. . . .  287 Psalm XV          10
  To spend for harms, although they touch you not: . . . . .  242 Other Poems   4   10
  Although they be of meaner parents gott: . . . . . . . . .  242 Other Poems   4   12
  Till she brake from their armes (although in deed. . . . .  252 Other Poems   4  413
ALWAY
  Unto my children alway good rest taking: . . . . . . . . .  139 Cert Sonnets  6    5
  Forced are to sing alway;. . . . . . . . . . . . . . . . .  140 Cert Sonnets  7   27
ALWAYS
  But always one my selfe with eagle eyde trueth to flie, . .  153 Cert Sonnets 24   24
  I ev'en I will always. . . . . . . . . . . . . . . . . . .  318 Psalm XXXIV        1
  Yet let them say, laud to God alwayes . . . . . . . . . .   323 Psalm XXXV        69
  And alwaies westward eying,. . . . . . . . . . . . . . . .  259 Other Poems   5  125
  From alwayes with you beeing.. . . . . . . . . . . . . . .  261 Other Poems   6   46
  "So shall I to thee alwayes, . . . . . . . . . . . . . . .  264 Other Poems   7   67
AMAIN
  Large roomes within, where droppes distill amaine: . . . .  150 Cert Sonnets 22   32
AMATED
  These mates to be amated.. . . . . . . . . . . . . . . . .  297 Psalm XXI         32
A-MAYING
  With mery maids a Maying they do go, . . . . . . . . . . .  243 Other Poems   4   50
```

	PAGE	TITLE		LINE
AMAZE				
Know, that small Love is quicke, and great Love doth amaze:.	209	A&S 3rd Song		16
AMAZED				
My fancy amazde, my thoughtes dull'd,.	66	2nd Eclogues	32	13
Her minde amaz'de can neither's helpe applie..	81	Arcadia III	54	4
Place standeth still amazed.	136	Cert Sonnets	3	7
They are amaz'd, but you with reason armed,.	209	A&S 3rd Song		17
That at me so amaz'd my fellowes jest:	254	Other Poems	4	468
AMBASSAGE				
Let it ambassage beare your grieves to showe..	125	4th Eclogues	75	V 12
AMBER				
This crowne of amber faire (an amber crowne she held). . . .	120	4th Eclogues	73	141
Some beautie's peece, as amber coloured hed,.	225	Astrophil	91	6
AMBITION				
But one worse fault, Ambition, I confesse, ...	178	Astrophil	27	11
AMBITION'S				
But harder Judges judge ambition's rage, ...	176	Astrophil	23	9
AMBITIOUS				
What, doth high place ambitious thoughts augment?.	208	Astrophil	83	9
Nor so ambitious am I, as to frame	224	Astrophil	90	5
Now the ambitiouse Larke with mirror cleare.	243	Other Poems	4	45
AMBROSIAN				
And then, a heav'nly child, gave her Ambrosian pap:.	213	A&S 5th Song		26
AMEND				
Geron. What can amend where physick is refusde?.	23	1st Eclogues	9	21
In vaine, mine Eyes, you labour to amende.	38	Arcadia II	14	1
Hurte not the face, which nothing can amende".	82	Arcadia III	55	15
AMENDING				
The very soul amending,.	294	Psalm XIX		30
AMENDMENT				
Thus plag'de how can I frame to my soare any hope of				
amendemente?	37	1st Eclogues	13	160
AMENDS				
Not that he hopes for amends of the desaster he feeles,. . .	122	4th Eclogues	74	24
AMETISTS				
With amatists they headed are.	90	Arcadia III	62	132
AMID				
Amid my sheepe, though I sawe nought to feare, ...	99	3rd Eclogues	66	15
And yet amid all feares a hope there is.	199	Astrophil	66	9
Me thinks amid my heart I heare.	323	Psalm XXXVI		1
Amid my flock with woe my voice I teare, ...	254	Other Poems	4	459
And yet I see her shine amid the cloud..	255	Other Poems	4	506
AMISS				
As of a friend that meant not much amisse:.	193	Astrophil	56	8
Me thought some staves he mist: if so, not much amisse:. . .	241	Other Poems	1	1
So to have done amisse, so to be shent..	244	Other Poems	4	104
AMONG				
Among his flocke so sweete a treasure keepe.	4	Lady of May	2	18
Among us all we should find out some thing of nought.. . . .	51	2nd Eclogues	29	2
Silly rewarde! yet among women hath she of vertu the most.				
Most.	64	2nd Eclogues	31	36
Am banisht now among the monstrous mountaines.	111	4th Eclogues	71	16
But if among yourselves some one tree growe, ...	125	4th Eclogues	75	10
Among the Gentiles then I, Lord, yeild thanks to Thee, . . .	293	Psalm XVIII		88
And from among the humane race	297	Psalm XXI		39
Among you, who is here	320	Psalm XXXIV		45
Among the wisest was accounted wise, ...	243	Other Poems	4	34
And thou, seke-sorow Klaius, them among:	247	Other Poems	4	218
Of Barly-brake among the six befell.	250	Other Poems	4	317
Among the rest that there did take delight	251	Other Poems	4	361
One among the rest electing.	262	Other Poems	7	17
Mixing mirth our Songs among, ...	263	Other Poems	7	46
Learning this among the rest,.	264	Other Poems	7	75
AMPHION'S				
With voice more fit to wed Amphion's lyre, ...	200	Astrophil	68	6
To cadence of the tunes, which Amphyon's lyre did yeeld, . .	208	A&S 3rd Song		4
AMPLE				
So ample eares as never good newes know:	206	Astrophil	78	13
ANATOMY				
My selfe unto th' Anatomy desirde, ...	150	Cert Sonnets	22	27
Th' anatomy of all my woes I wrate,.	194	Astrophil	58	10
ANCHOR				
Be thow, sweete glove, the Anker of my mynde, ...	70	Arcadia III	35	7
Her cable, Reason, breakes from anchor, Hope:.	114	4th Eclogues	72	46
And anchor fast my selfe on Vertue's shore..	196	Astrophil	62	11
ANCIENT				
The ancient oke well makes a fired blocke:	25	1st Eclogues	9	87
The auncient prayse to Arcad shepheards' skill?.	53	2nd Eclogues	29	52
ANEW				
Turned anew by your meanes,.	154	Cert Sonnets	25	24
Cald it anew, and wooed sleepe againe:	184	Astrophil	38	13
ANGEL				
A woman's mould, but like an Angell graste,.	151	Cert Sonnets	22	66
When my good Angell guides me to the place,.	194	Astrophil	60	1
Let Angel thine a scattring make them go..	321	Psalm XXXV		12
Let Angel thine persue them as they fly, ...	321	Psalm XXXV		13
ANGEL'S				
An Angell's mind; but in a woman caste:	151	Cert Sonnets	22	67
Driv'n else to graunt by Angel's sophistrie, ...	195	Astrophil	61	13
Thy fingers Cupid's shafts, thy voyce the Angel's lay: . . .	212	A&S 5th Song		11

ANGEL'S	(CONTINUED)	PAGE	TITLE		LINE
I say thou art a Devill, though clothd in Angel's shining: .		215	A&S 5th Song		81
For though in lesse than Angel's state		279	Psalm VIII		17
Who hid in Angel's shape my life would ende.		254	Other Poems	4	464

ANGELS
In whose sweete heav'n Angels of high thoughts swarme? . . .		142	Cert Sonnets 10		8
The very essence of their tunes, when Angels do rejoyce. . .		217	A&S 7th Song		18
Angels to acquaintance bringeth.		219	A&S 8th Song		40
His Angels Armys round		319	Psalm XXXIV		25

ANGER
Her love my life; her anger my Instruction;.		49	2nd Eclogues 28		71
Such anger bringing: as for me, my fancie.		50	2nd Eclogues 28		95
The fire to see my wrongs for anger burneth:		136	Cert Sonnets 3		1
Anger invests with such a lovely grace,.		203	Astrophil 73		13
That Anger' selfe I needs must kisse againe.		203	Astrophil 73		14
Love feares nothing else but anger..		203	A&S 2nd Song		20
Come no more, least I get anger."		234	A&S 11th Song		37
Nor in anger chastise me;.		327	Psalm XXXVIII		3
That Thy anger being spent,.		335	Psalm XLII		36

ANGLE
| For so did I, when with my angle, Will,. . . . . | | 115 | 4th Eclogues 72 | | 62 |
| Lamde with the angle, which it selfe did beare,. . . . . . . | | 115 | 4th Eclogues 72 | | 67 |

ANGLES
| Whose equall lynes their angles bowes, ... | | 86 | Arcadia III 62 | | 10 |

ANGRIER
| We oft are angrier, with the feeble flie . . . . | | 28 | 1st Eclogues 10 | | 64 |

ANGRY
Leaping at every flie, and angrie with a flea:		53	2nd Eclogues 29		44
Must I be onely the marke, shall prove that Vertue is					
angrie		123	4th Eclogues 74		33
Pas Cosma matcht, yet angry with his fault,.		250	Other Poems	4	318

ANGUISH
And hope therby to ease their inward horrible anguish, . . .		33	1st Eclogues 13		45
Then shall those thinges ease their inward horrible angwish.		33	1st Eclogues 13		46
Come from marble bowers, many times the gay harbor of					
anguish, ...		34	1st Eclogues 13		92
The sorry fruites of anguish,.		66	2nd Eclogues 32		33
Grant yet, grant yet a looke, to the last monument of his					
anguish, ...		122	4th Eclogues 74		3
Aire let me draw no more thy breath in anguish:.		136	Cert Sonnets 3		14
Alas she hath no other cause of anguish.		137	Cert Sonnets 4		13
With glad moning passed anguish, ...		227	A&S 10th Song		39
Let me, fed with hellish anguish,.		220	A&S 8th Song		79
With cruel anguish.		276	Psalm VI		8
In anguish?.		285	Psalm XIII		6

ANNOY
To be a player of thine owne annoy..		25	1st Eclogues 9		119
R. Who Passion doth ensue, lives in annoy.		46	2nd Eclogues 27		13
Mothers and Nurses of all vaine annoy.		107	3rd Eclogues 67		117
Frcm joy I part still living in annoy.		148	Cert Sonnets 20		14
Sonets be not bound prentise to annoy:		201	Astrophil 70		5
Or if such heavenly signes must prove annoy, ...		231	Astrophil 100		13
And in my joyes for thee my only annoy..		237	Astrophil 108		14
Faire triumpher of annoy,.		218	A&S 8th Song		30
Let not those foes that me annoy		303	Psalm XXV		5
On me, from me help this annoy..		311	Psalm XXX		32
But hunt with craft the quiet man's annoy;		322	Psalm XXXV		52
Will. Then Dick let us go hence lest wee great folkes annoy.		344	Possibly	1	45

ANNOYED
Philisides. O gods, how long this old foole hath annoi'd . .		24	1st Eclogues 9		66
When with the kawing crowes their musicke is annoide.. . . .		52	2nd Eclogues 29		18
From out Thy land by them anoy'd..		283	Psalm X		72

ANNOYS
Philisides. Who minds to please the minde drownd in annoyes.		22	1st Eclogues 9		6
No sword soe bytes as that evill toole annoyes..		29	1st Eclogues 10		90
That to the sacred Muse my anoyes somewhat be revealed,. . .		31	1st Eclogues 13		9
Woe to poore man: ech outward thing annoyes him.		62	2nd Eclogues 30		170
But nowe successe hathe gott above annoyes,.		71	Arcadia III 36		17
Jcyne with thy sonne, to ease my long annoys..		81	Arcadia III 53		13
I turne my minde to all formes of annoyes, ...		113	4th Eclogues 72		3
Which for reward spoile it with vaine annoyes		174	Astrophil 11		13
That once come there, the sobs of mine annoyes		187	Astrophil 44		13
For my annoyes have come before thyne eye, ...		312	Psalm XXXI		20

ANOINT
| For David his Anoynt, and his seed ever more.. . . . . | | 293 | Psalm XVIII | | 91 |
| With oyle Thou dost anoynt my head,. . . . . | | 301 | Psalm XXIII | | 19 |

ANOINTED
And his anoynted King?		271	Psalm II		6
That God from fall his own Anoynted stayes..		296	Psalm XX		22
Who his Anoynted helped have..		309	Psalm XXVIII		32

ANOTHER
My hart doth seeke another estimation.		19	1st Eclogues 7		175
Sucking one's ill, another to infect..		21	1st Eclogues 7		36
But if I had bene there, th'adst met another mate.		52	2nd Eclogues 29		22
Pas. Another sure as is a gander from a goose:		52	2nd Eclogues 29		23
One Echo to another Echo cast.		126	4th Eclogues 75		34
One word of woe another after traineth:.		128	4th Eclogues 75		103
Another humbler wit to shepheard's pipe retires, ...		167	Astrophil 6		7
Nor hope, nor wishe another course to frame, ...		198	Astrophil 64		12
Who faileth one, is false, though trusty to another.		214	A&S 5th Song		72

17

ANOTHER   (CONTINUED)   PAGE   TITLE   LINE
   Another man be stonge. . . . . 320 Psalm XXXIV   52
   Such was his minde, if you another take: . . . . 345 Possibly   4   11
   "Another time", quoth she, "become more wise". . . . . . . 249 Other Poems   4 275
   But all this while another course he fet.. . . . . 249 Other Poems   4 280
   The Ewe another loved, ... 259 Other Poems   5 122
ANOTHER'S
   I am no pick-purse of another's wit. . . . . 204 Astrophil   74   8
   With sight made dymme with dayly teares another's sport to
      see. . . . . 343 Possibly   1   4
   Canst thou, poore lamme, become another's lamme? . . . . . 258 Other Poems   5   76
ANSWER
   Pleasd to receave that name by rebounding answere of Echo, . 33 1st Eclogues 13   44
   When by the winde it maketh a noyse, I do thinke she doth
      answer.. . . . .   36 1st Eclogues 13 145
   To speake without an answere.. . . . .   65 2nd Eclogues 32   6
   Reason sighes but in end he thus doth answere. . . . . . .   68 2nd Eclogues 33   25
   And thinke not that thy answere answere is,. . . . .   97 3rd Eclogues 64 101
   Such thing cannot I seeke (Despaire hath giv'n me my answer. 122 4th Eclogues 74   11
   With a cruell answer stong.. . . . . 139 Cert Sonnets 7   7
   Her breath which makes a sower answer sweete,. . . . . . . 141 Cert Sonnets 9   6
   Rockes, woods, hilles, caves, dales, meads, brookes, answere
      me, ... 147 Cert Sonnets 18   13
   Doth answere well the paine: . . . . 152 Cert Sonnets 23   18
   I, cumbred with good maners, answer do,. . . . . 180 Astrophil   30   13
   Least, if answer Thou forbeare,. . . . . 308 Psalm XXVIII   3
   "O earth, once answere give, ... 256 Other Poems   5   14
   I aske, now answere me.. . . . . 256 Other Poems   5   20
ANSWERED
   She answer'd was with looke, and well performed behest:. . . 119 4th Eclogues 73   99
   In Truth of heart I answerd Thee,. . . . . 307 Psalm XXVII   40
ANSWERS
   All churlish wordes, shrewd answeres, crabbed lookes,. . . .   93 3rd Eclogues 63   64
   With dearth of words, or answers quite awrie,. . . . . . . 178 Astrophil   27   3
   "Foole," answers he, "no Indes such treasures hold,. . . . 181 Astrophil   32   12
ANT
   Ante, industrie; and Connie, skill to builde;. . . . . . . 101 3rd Eclogues 66   93
ANTAXIUS
   To wedd Antaxius their neighbour neare.. . . . . 245 Other Poems   4 116
ANY
   Philisides. Hath any man heard what this old man said? . . .   26 1st Eclogues 9 135
   Which shootes strongly with out any noyse and deadly without
      smarte. . . . .   35 1st Eclogues 13 122
   Thus plag'de how can I frame to my soare any hope of
      amendemente? . . . .   37 1st Eclogues 13 160
   Whence may I show to my minde any light of a possible
      escape . . . .   37 1st Eclogues 13 161
   Without her love, then any mind who fairer is. . . . . . .   51 2nd Eclogues 28 116
   From any joy, which might her griefe occasion. . . . . . .   51 2nd Eclogues 28 122
   As farre as any shepheards piping be:. . . . .   56 2nd Eclogues 29 127
   As farre as Love possesseth any head.. . . . .   56 2nd Eclogues 29 128
   Made uniforme to any state reposed.. . . . .   57 2nd Eclogues 30   31
   Plangus. If through mine eares pearce any consolacyons . . .   61 2nd Eclogues 30 143
   From any joy, know fortune's vile displacing her,. . . . .   61 2nd Eclogues 30 150
   Nor envie's snaky ey, finds any harbor here, ...   69 2nd Eclogues 34   18
   And you o trees (if any life there lies. . . . . 125 4th Eclogues 75   4
   And if that any counsell you to measure. . . . . 126 4th Eclogues 75   49
   Of any since God AEsculapius ceased. . . . . 128 4th Eclogues 75 116
   But so confusde, that neither any eye. . . . . 149 Cert Sonnets 22   2
   Such smart may pitie claime of any hart, ... 186 Astrophil   44   3
   By no pretence claime any maner place. . . . . 191 Astrophil   52   11
   Nor this, nor that, nor any such small cause,. . . . . . . 204 Astrophil   75   12
   That any laud to me thereof should grow, ... 224 Astrophil   90   10
   Thence, so farre thence, that scarcely any sparke. . . . . 233 Astrophil   104   7
   "If that any thought in me,. . . . . 220 A&S 8th Song   77
   I do any wish impart,. . . . . 220 A&S 8th Song   86
   While I am voyd of any helping pow'r. . . . . 277 Psalm VII   6
   Ever from deed of any such desart: . . . . 277 Psalm VII   8
   As for my tongue, while I have any dayes,. . . . . 323 Psalm XXXV   71
APACE
   But cald, she came apace; a pace wherein did move. . . . . 119 4th Eclogues 73   89
APAID
   How well apaid she was hir birde to finde: . . . . 244 Other Poems   4   92
APART
   And knowing, love, and loving, lay apart . . . . 177 Astrophil   24   7
APE
   Ape great thing gave, though he did mowing stand,. . . . . 101 3rd Eclogues 66   97
APES
   Or Pindare's Apes, flaunt they in phrases fine,. . . . . . 166 Astrophil   3   3
APOLLO
   Apollo great, whose beames the greater world do light, . . .   44 Arcadia II   26   1
   Apollo wakes, and bow hath sometime sparde.. . . . . 143 Cert Sonnets 12   15
   Then good Apollo do away thy bowe: . . . . 146 Cert Sonnets 17   36
APOLLO'S
   Pas. Who evermore will love Apollo's quill,. . . . .   53 2nd Eclogues 29   54
   Pas. O if I had Apollo's golden carre, ...   56 2nd Eclogues 29 120
   And now before we seeke by wise Apollo's skill . . . . . . 120 4th Eclogues 73 125
   Of God Apolloe's giving, ... 260 Other Poems   6   8
APPALL
   Whose mind is such, as wisest minds appall,. . . . .   3 Lady of May   1   3

APPALL   (CONTINUED)   PAGE   TITLE   LINE
  Evill happes do fill with hope, good happes appall . . . . .   143 Cert Sonnets 12   10
  Nay ev'n my soul fell troubles do appall; . . . .   276 Psalm VI   9
  And his own evill his own head shall appall. . . . .   278 Psalm VII   45
APPALLED
  They hop'd on Thee, and they were not appalled.. . . . . . .   298 Psalm XXII   14
APPALLETH
  Ah my soul it self appaleth, ...   334 Psalm XLII   23
APPARELLED
  Whose lyverie is such, as most I freeze apparelled most, . .   343 Possibly   1   21
APPEACH
  Of foule rebellion then I do appeach thee now; . . . . . .   214 A&S 5th Song   62
APPEAR
  Save when great need of them perforce apeare.. . . . .   27 1st Eclogues 10   36
  Nico. When Leuca dooth appeare, the Sunne for shame.. . . .   55 2nd Eclogues 29   93
  To Westerne wightes, what starres in East appeare? . . . .   80 Arcadia III 52   4
  In speedie helpe, thanke worthie frends appeare. . . . . .   81 Arcadia III 53   14
  When two Sunnes do appeare . . . .   81 Arcadia III 55   1
  Where azurde veines well mixt appeere. . . . .   87 Arcadia III 62   56
  For to my dimmed eyes beganne t'appeare. . . . .   103 3rd Eclogues 66 159
  As little hunting minde (God knowes) did there appeere.. . .   118 4th Eclogues 73   70
  Shall to the world appeare that faith and love be rewarded .   123 4th Eclogues 74   35
  And if, o Sunne, thou ever didst appeare, ...   127 4th Eclogues 75   70
  Who Stoick-like in clowdie hew appeare:. . . . .   147 Cert Sonnets 17   48
  Feare to offend, will worthie to appeare, ...   202 Astrophil   72   10
  But no scuse serves, she makes her wrath appeare . . . . .   203 Astrophil   73   9
  I saw that teares did in her eyes appeare; . . . .   223 Astrophil   87   6
  Stella, I say my Stella, should appeare. . . . .   235 Astrophil   106   4
  A witch I say thou art, though thou so faire appeare;. . . .   214 A&S 5th Song   74
  And turn their backs, and strait on backs appeare. . . . .   276 Psalm VI   31
  When as to him Our Prayers do appeare. . . . .   296 Psalm XX   35
  As life may good appeare?. . . . .   320 Psalm XXXIV   48
  From him whose force did in their spoiles appeare. . . . .   321 Psalm XXXV   24
  Noe feare of God doth once appeare . . . .   323 Psalm XXXVI   5
  But what? This doth already well appeare . . . .   333 Psalm XLI   37
  In whome no evill did raigne, nor good appeare,. . . . . .   245 Other Poems   4 118
APPEARED
  Where snugging well he well appear'd content . . . .   244 Other Poems   4 103
APPEARETH
  O God my God I cry while day appeareth;. . . . .   298 Psalm XXII   5
APPEARING
  Make me still feare, thy faire appearing showe.. . . . . . .   82 Arcadia III 56   14
  Cranes, order; Storkes, to be appearing holie; . . . . . .   101 3rd Eclogues 66   94
  Nor hidd from him his face's faire appearing;. . . . . . .   300 Psalm XXII   57
  Friends like to blacke Swannes appearing,. . . . .   263 Other Poems   7   53
APPEARS
  And herein most their folly vaine appeares . . . .   24 1st Eclogues 9   78
  Monstrous appeares, long trueth receaved late, ...   85 Arcadia III 61   6
  So that therein appeares some blood, ...   86 Arcadia III 62   29
  In such a case where it appeares that nature . . . .   109 Arcadia IV   70   9
  My spring appeares, o see what here doth grow. . . . . . .   200 Astrophil   69   8
  Benighted in cold wo, but now appeares my day, ...   204 Astrophil   76   3
APPLE
  Then keep me as the Apple of an Eye, ...   290 Psalm XVII   25
APPLE'S
  Or like the fresh Queene-apple's side, ...   86 Arcadia III 62   25
APPLES
  That from those eies where heav'nly apples bene, ...   253 Other Poems   4 450
APPLIES
  Towne-folkes my strength; a daintier judge applies . . . .   185 Astrophil   41   6
  Who his owne joy to his owne hurt applies, ...   206 Astrophil   78   7
  Behold they cry, but who to them his help applys?. . . . .   292 Psalm XVIII   74
APPLY
  Her minde amaz'de can neither's helpe applie.. . . . .   81 Arcadia III 54   4
  And Parot, ready tongue, that to applie. . . . .   101 3rd Eclogues 66   84
  Goe to, goe to, and Cupid now applie . . . .   106 3rd Eclogues 67 100
  Your dolefull tunes sweete Muses now applie. . . . .   125 4th Eclogues 75   3
  Above line repeated at following locations . . . .   125 4th Eclogues 75   15
    . . . .   125 4th Eclogues 75   30
    . . . .   126 4th Eclogues 75   48
    . . . .   126 4th Eclogues 75   60
    . . . .   127 4th Eclogues 75   78
    . . . .   127 4th Eclogues 75   96
    . . . .   128 4th Eclogues 75 117
  Cease Muse therfore: thy dart o Death applie;. . . . .   129 4th Eclogues 75 141
  But all the rest, which feare durst not applie,. . . . . . .   151 Cert Sonnets 22   49
  Since to himselfe he doth your gifts apply,. . . . .   186 Astrophil   43   3
  Thence he to all his judgments shall apply . . . .   280 Psalm IX   24
  Let him come down, and help to Thee apply. . . . .   295 Psalm XX   7
  To thy self those words apply. . . . .   309 Psalm XXVIII   9
APPOINT
  The crowne above you both for ever I appoint". . . . . . .   121 4th Eclogues 73 166
APPREHEND
  Where piercing witts do quickly apprehend, ...   245 Other Poems   4 142
APPREHENDING
  In weakened minds, quicke apprehending breed,. . . . . . .   199 Astrophil   66   3
APPROACH
  You doo approch to the fruite your onely desirs be to
    gather . . . .   33 1st Eclogues 13   63
  With sonne's approche your pasture fertill growes, ...   43 Arcadia II   23   2

19

  Well mett Echo, aproche: then tell me thy will too. I will
    too. . . . .   63 2nd Eclogues 31   4
  At whose approach the Sunne rase in the evening, ...   113 4th Eclogues 71   69
  But finding th'approch of death with an inly relenting,. . .   123 4th Eclogues 74   25
  Approach of death, alas thou helpest meagerly, ...   128 4th Eclogues 75 110
  Once to approch this hayer. . . . .   158 Cert Sonnets 28   8
  The night as tedious, wooes th'approch of day; . . . .   224 Astrophil   89   6
  The just when harms approach . . . .   320 Psalm XXXIV   61
APPROACHING
  Moste lothe to loose, the moste approching hope. . . . . . .   71 Arcadia III 37   6
  Approching warmes (not else) dead logges up sends, ...   150 Cert Sonnets 22   12
APPROVE
  For god doth know, and knowing doth approve. . . . .   271 Psalm I   19
APPROVES
  He righteousness approves. . . . .   316 Psalm XXXIII   19
APRIL
  The Nightingale, as soone as aprill bringeth . . . .   137 Cert Sonnets 4   1
APRIL'S
  Proudly bedeckt in Aprill's livory, ...   253 Other Poems   4 453
APT
  Was ever apt: but you my pastimes did despise. . . . .   121 4th Eclogues 73 149
  In nature apt to like when I did see . . . .   172 Astrophil   16   1
  Least joy, by Nature apt sprites to enlarge, ...   210 Astrophil   85   3
  But give apt servants their due place, let eyes. . . . . . .   210 Astrophil   85   9
  By love were made apt to consort with me. . . . .   229 Astrophil   95   11
  Never roome more apt for it; . . . .   219 A&S 8th Song   54
APTEST
  That aptest is to figure miserie, ...   125 4th Eclogues 75   11
APTLY
  In action aptly graced: . . . .   216 A&S 6th Song   28
ARABS
  Ev'en Deserts where the Arabs byde. . . . .   310 Psalm XXIX   21
ARBITER
  Be Arbiter of this, ...   216 A&S 6th Song   44
ARCADE
  The auncient prayse to Arcad shepheards' skill? . . . . . .   53 2nd Eclogues 29   52
ARCADIA
  If many Kalaes our Arcadia gave, ...   104 3rd Eclogues 67   22
ARCADIANS'
  Who long have gap't to get Arcadians' treasure. . . . . . .   129 4th Eclogues 76   21
ARCADIA'S
  Arcadia's gemme the noblest childe of nature. . . . .   109 Arcadia IV   70   18
  Farewell o Sunn, Arcadia's clearest light: . . . .   129 4th Eclogues 76   1
ARCHER
  That busie archer his sharpe arrowes tries? . . . .   180 Astrophil   31   4
ARCHES
  And arches be to heavenly lids, ...   86 Arcadia III 62   13
ARDOR
  My muse what ails this ardour. . . . .   65 2nd Eclogues 32   1
  Above line repeated at following locations . . . .   66 2nd Eclogues 32   9
    . . . .   66 2nd Eclogues 32   19
    . . . .   66 2nd Eclogues 32   30
    . . . .   67 2nd Eclogues 32   40
ARGALUS
  Argalus and Parthenia.   241 Other Poems   3   9
ARGUES
  But rotten bleeding argues evill complection . . . .   50 2nd Eclogues 28 V883
ARGUMENTS
  Hast thou found such and such like arguments? . . . .   199 Astrophil   67   10
ARGUS
  By Argus got on Io, then a cow: . . . .   21 1st Eclogues 8   14
  And charge of her to Argus did allow. . . . .   21 1st Eclogues 8   16
  (At Juno's suite who much did Argus love). . . . .   22 1st Eclogues 8   46
  Lest that Argus eyes perceive may." . . . .   235 A&S 11th Song   42
ARIGHT
  His cloven foote doth never treade aright. . . . .   21 1st Eclogues 8   30
  Give right sound to the eares, and enter aright to the
    judgement; . . . .   32 1st Eclogues 13   18
  That trusts in time, to finde the way aright . . . .   82 Arcadia III 56   3
  No man doth speake aright, who speakes in feare. . . . . . .   106 3rd Eclogues 67   84
  But who aright poore-minded be . . . .   283 Psalm X   61
ARIGHTLY
  And never hathe therof arightelye deemde . . . .   26 1st Eclogues 9 139
ARISE
  To them that would make speech of speech arise, ...   178 Astrophil   27   4
  Stella, whence doth this new assault arise, ...   182 Astrophil   36   1
  Infected by those vapours, which arise . . . .   205 Astrophil   78   2
  So darke with misty vapors, which arise. . . . .   228 Astrophil   94   2
  Arise, O lord, in wrath thy self upsett. . . . .   277 Psalm VII   16
  For then Urania homeward did arise, ...   246 Other Poems   4 167
  So as good thoughts of him in all arise, ...   247 Other Poems   4 198
ARISTOTLE'S
  I do not envie Aristotle's wit, ...   198 Astrophil   64   9
ARM
  I sawe her arme, where purest Lillies cleave. . . . .   55 2nd Eclogues 29 104
  First, second, last, did binde, enforce, and arme, ...   84 Arcadia III 60   3
  Her right arme naked was, discovered was her breast. . . . .   118 4th Eclogues 73   68
  Thy bowels with all killing mettals arme. . . . .   125 4th Eclogues 75   21
  Whom curst do blesse, whose weakenesse vertues arme, ...   142 Cert Sonnets 10   6

```
ARM                        (CONTINUED)                        PAGE  TITLE              LINE
     Breake Thou the wyked arm. . . . . . . . . . . . . . . .  283 Psalm X                   65
     So that Uran, whose arme old Geron bore, . . . . . . . .  250 Other Poems      4   309
     Tell me if greedy arme, . . . . . . . . . . . . . . . .   258 Other Poems      5    85
ARMED
     O Mars, for what doth serve thy armed axe? . . . . . . .   60 2nd Eclogues 30     110
     Her ribbes in white well armed be. . . . . . . . . . . .   88 Arcadia III  62      68
     Since naked sence can conquer reason armed: . . . . . . . 135 Cert Sonnets  1       6
     He would not arm'd with beautie, only raigne . . . . . . 135 Cert Sonnets  2       5
     Her soule, arm'd but with such a dainty rind, . . . . . . 193 Astrophil    57       7
     They are amaz'd, but you with reason armed, . . . . . . . 209 A&S 3rd Song         17
     In chariots arm'd, Others in chivalry; . . . . . . . . .  296 Psalm XX             27
     Your hearts with clearness armed. . . . . . . . . . . . . 316 Psalm XXXII          42
     Therefore Love arm'd in hir now takes the fielde, . . . . 245 Other Poems      4   145
ARMIES
     Whole armies of thy beauties entred in. . . . . . . . . . 182 Astrophil    36       4
     Who is This Glorious King? The lord of armyes guiding, . . 302 Psalm XXIV          23
     Then though against me armys were, . . . . . . . . . . .  307 Psalm XXVII          13
     His Angels Armys round . . . . . . . . . . . . . . . . .  319 Psalm XXXIV          25
ARMOR
     With armour of my hart, he cried "O vanitie, . . . . . .   16 1st Eclogues  7      62
     Her flesh his food, her skin his armour brave, . . . . .  179 Astrophil    29      12
     If I but stars upon mine armour beare, . . . . . . . . .  233 Astrophil   104      10
ARMORY
     Clos'd with their quivers in sleep's armory; . . . . . .  230 Astrophil    99       4
*ARMS
     Let him drinke this, whome long in armes to folde. . . .   83 Arcadia III  58       1
     And thence those armes derived are; . . . . . . . . . . .   89 Arcadia III  62     117
     Yet craving law of armes, whose rule doth teach, . . . .  135 Cert Sonnets  1      10
     But betweene those armes, never else do leave mee; . . .  138 Cert Sonnets  5      23
     Of those three gods, whose armes the fairest were: . . .  171 Astrophil    13       2
     Thinke Nature me a man of armes did make. . . . . . . . . 185 Astrophil    41      11
     Since in thine armes, if learnd fame truth hath spread, . . 198 Astrophil  65      13
     Let breath sucke up those sweetes, let armes embrace . . .  210 Astrophil  85      12
     With armes crost, yet testifying . . . . . . . . . . . .  218 A&S 8th Song         19
     Though oft himselfe my mate-in-armes he sware. . . . . .  228 Astrophil    95       8
     And hast Thy deadly armes in order brought . . . . . . .  278 Psalm VII            35
     Strengthning mine arms that they could break an Iron bow. . 292 Psalm XVIII        63
     For wycked arms shall breake asunder, . . . . . . . . . .  325 Psalm XXXVII         43
     The trees spred out their armes to shade hir face, . . .  245 Other Poems      4   109
     Now runnes, and takes hir in his clipping armes. . . . .  252 Other Poems      4   384
     Till she brake from their armes (although in deed. . . .  252 Other Poems      4   413
A-ROW
     In chastest plaies, till home they walke a rowe, . . . .  243 Other Poems      4    54
ARRAY
     Because in brave array heere marcheth she, . . . . . . .  223 Astrophil    88       3
ARRAYED
     Might winne some grace in your sweet skill arraid. . . .  192 Astrophil    55       4
     Still in mourning chear arayd. . . . . . . . . . . . . .  328 Psalm XXXVIII        18
ARROGANCE
     Nor causelesse duty, nor comber of arrogance, . . . . . .   69 2nd Eclogues 34      23
ARROW
     (Since no estates be so base, but love vouchsafeth his
          arrow . . . . . . . . . . . . . . . . . . . . . . .   33 1st Eclogues 13      50
     Thou bear'st the arrow, I the arrow head. . . . . . . . . 198 Astrophil    65      14
     For like a marke Thou shalt arow . . . . . . . . . . . .  298 Psalm XXI            45
     The Arrow being shot from far, doth give the smaller blowe. . 344 Possibly    1      42
ARROWS
     A naked god, young, blind, with arrowes two. . . . . . .   20 1st Eclogues  8       6
     But arrowes two, and tipt with gold or leade: . . . . . .   21 1st Eclogues  8      11
     Tuckt up even with the knees, with bowe and arrowes prest: . 118 4th Eclogues 73    67
     And in her eyes of arrowes infinit. . . . . . . . . . . .  173 Astrophil    17      11
     That busie archer his sharpe arrowes tries?. . . . . . .  180 Astrophil    31       4
     And ready art to let Thyne arrowes go. . . . . . . . . .  278 Psalm VII            36
     And set their arrows in a rowe . . . . . . . . . . . . .  284 Psalm XI              6
     Then out his arrowes fly, and streight they scatterd been, . 291 Psalm XVIII       29
ART
     That sport it is to see with howe great art . . . . . . .   27 1st Eclogues 10      41
     But when I first did fal, what brought most fall to my hart?
          Arte. . . . . . . . . . . . . . . . . . . . . . . .   64 2nd Eclogues 31      28
     Arte? what can be that art which thou dost meane by thy
          speche? Speche. . . . . . . . . . . . . . . . . . .   64 2nd Eclogues 31      29
     What be the fruites of speaking arte? what growes by the
          words? Words. . . . . . . . . . . . . . . . . . . .   64 2nd Eclogues 31      30
     And yet as hard, as brawne made hard by arte: . . . . . .   76 Arcadia III  46      16
     No lampe, whose light by Art is got, . . . . . . . . . .   86 Arcadia III  62      17
     Avoydes thy hurtfull arte, . . . . . . . . . . . . . . .   92 3rd Eclogues 63      59
     The other had with arte (more then our women knowe, . . .  118 4th Eclogues 73      71
     (With gall cut out) closde up againe by art, . . . . . .  150 Cert Sonnets 22      23
     Where with most ease and warmth he might employ his art: . . 168 Astrophil   8       7
     Love onely reading unto me this art. . . . . . . . . . .  179 Astrophil    28      14
     In all sweete stratagems sweete Arte can show, . . . . .  183 Astrophil    36      11
     Professe in deed I do not Cupid's art; . . . . . . . . .  192 Astrophil    54      10
     By linkes of Love, and only Nature's art: . . . . . . . .  207 Astrophil    81       6
     To whom nor art nor nature graunteth light, . . . . . . .  230 Astrophil    99       2
     To this great cause, which needs both use and art, . . .  236 Astrophil   107       8
     Klaius for skill of herbs and shepheard's art. . . . . .  243 Other Poems      4    33
     To whome arte of Love is knowne: . . . . . . . . . . . .  262 Other Poems      7    28
     What in art of Love is fitting. . . . . . . . . . . . . . 262 Other Poems      7    30
     "Nay, what neede the Arte to those, . . . . . . . . . . . 263 Other Poems      7    31
```

21

Text	PAGE	TITLE		LINE
All numbring artes her endlesse graces number not:	49	2nd Eclogues	28	59
AS				
Whose mind is such, as wisest minds appall,	3	Lady of May	1	3
As shallow brookes do yeeld the greatest sound,	4	Lady of May	2	14
Two thousand sheepe I have as white as milke,	4	Lady of May	2	19
Though not so white as is thy lovely face,	4	Lady of May	2	20
The pasture rich, the wooll as soft as silke,	4	Lady of May	2	21
Who at thy beer, as at a barre, shall plead.	11	Arcadia I	1	6
Whose vertues strange, and beuties such, as no man them may know?.	12	Arcadia I	3	2
As smooth as Pan, as Juno milde, like goddesse Iris faste.	12	Arcadia I	3	6
As for those parts unknowne, which hidden sure are best:	12	Arcadia I	3	13
For as the Moone the eie doth please,	13	Arcadia I	5	7
As without breath, no pipe doth move,	14	1st Eclogues	6	7
Milde as a Lambe, more daintie then a Conie is:	15	1st Eclogues	7	31
Such as you see, such still you shall me finde.	18	1st Eclogues	7	122
In flowrie fielde; and as the day begins	18	1st Eclogues	7	125
And pastimes make, as Nature things hath made.	18	1st Eclogues	7	127
As well may thincke with oyle to coole the fire:	22	1st Eclogues	9	8
Yet not of wemen Judging as he said,	24	1st Eclogues	9	64
(As his beard him, not he his beard did beare)	25	1st Eclogues	9	91
Seeke to espie her faultes as well as praise,	25	1st Eclogues	9	121
Be as thou art, but be with mine at one.	27	1st Eclogues	10	15
Because I red him, as I would my son.	27	1st Eclogues	10	23
As for the rest, howe shepeheardes spend their daies,	28	1st Eclogues	10	46
As fishe sure tryall hath of muddy slyme.	28	1st Eclogues	10	54
No sword soe bytes as that evill toole annoyes.	29	1st Eclogues	10	90
Gives happs or mishapps, ev'n as he ordreth his hearte.	29	1st Eclogues	11	8
As that hatefull death can abridge them of powre,	31	1st Eclogues	12	18
How to the woods love runnes as well as rydes to the Pallace	31	1st Eclogues	13	4
Ease I do feele (such ease as falls to one wholy diseased)	35	1st Eclogues	13	114
Pine is hye, hope is as hie, sharpe leav'd, sharpe yet be my hope's budds.	36	1st Eclogues	13	130
And shall sensive things be so sencelesse as to resist sence	36	1st Eclogues	13	138
Cleofila. Hardy shephearde, such as thy meritts, such may be her insight	37	1st Eclogues	13	155
Bownd and bownd by so noble bandes, as loth to be unbownd,	37	1st Eclogues	13	162
My head you seeke, as to your strongest forte:	38	Arcadia II	14	10
This marble chose, as of like temper knowne:	40	Arcadia II	19	2
As loving not, accus'd, in Love I die.	41	Arcadia II	20	2
Still seeking Love, love found as much I flie.	41	Arcadia II	20	4
Enjoye my joyes, as you dyd taste my payne,	43	Arcadia II	23	11
As for your doubts; her voice was it deceaved me,	48	2nd Eclogues	28	29
As thou wilt give our soules a deare refection,	49	2nd Eclogues	28	52
Such anger bringing: as for me, my fancie.	50	2nd Eclogues	28	95
As for thy wish to my enraged spitefulnesse,	51	2nd Eclogues	28	111
As thou doest thinke) should most of all disquiet me	51	2nd Eclogues	28	115
Not as the scrippe thou stalest, while Dorcas sleeping lay.	52	2nd Eclogues	29	8
Pas. Another sure as is a gander from a goose:	52	2nd Eclogues	29	23
Nico. Well aimed by my hat: for as thou sangst last day;	52	2nd Eclogues	29	25
Nico. As I of late, neer bushes usde my sive,	54	2nd Eclogues	29	81
As white as milke, and comming to the call,	54	2nd Eclogues	29	85
Pas. As in a glasse I held she once did looke,	55	2nd Eclogues	29	114
As farre as any shepheards piping be:	56	2nd Eclogues	29	127
As farre as Love possesseth any head.	56	2nd Eclogues	29	128
As I behynde a Busshe dyd sitt	57	2nd Eclogues	30	1
As in it selfe to nourish mortall strife.	57	2nd Eclogues	30	28
As let them come or go with even facilitie.	60	2nd Eclogues	30	133
As if by death she onely might be saved?	61	2nd Eclogues	30	160
In divers kinds; yet as he were not filled,	62	2nd Eclogues	30	171
Thou li'st false Echo, their minds as vertu be just. Just.	65	2nd Eclogues	31	46
As sweete as violetts, faire as a lilly is,	69	2nd Eclogues	34	32
Streight as Cedar, a voice staines the Cannary birds,	69	2nd Eclogues	34	33
As neere his home, when storme or shelf he feares;	71	Arcadia III	37	4
As happie shewes of corne when harvest sendes;	71	Arcadia III	37	10
Make her as much more base by loving me.	72	Arcadia III	38	17
Since, as I say, both minde and sences darke	73	Arcadia III	39	9
For as from me, on him his hurt did light,	76	Arcadia III	45	11
That she is myne, as I to her am true.	76	Arcadia III	46	6
Lips red and plum, as cherrie's ruddy side,	76	Arcadia III	46	8
That she be myne, as I to her am true.	76	Arcadia III	46	12
But thou white skinne, as white as cruddes well prest,	76	Arcadia III	46	13
So smooth as sleekestone-like, it smoothes each parte,	76	Arcadia III	46	14
And thou deare flesh, as soft as wooll new drest,	76	Arcadia III	46	15
And yet as hard, as brawne made hard by arte:	76	Arcadia III	46	16
Since that my thoughtes, as streight as streightnes thine,	77	Arcadia III	47	3
Such pearcing wordes as no thoughts els conceave:	78	Arcadia III	49	8
As thou drawest on, so let my blisse draw neere.	80	Arcadia III	53	10
Weare these my words as mourning weedes of woes,	81	Arcadia III	54	5
As Prince's losse or change:	81	Arcadia III	55	3
As oh! my selfe, whose woes are never lighte	82	Arcadia III	56	9
Save one as much as other cleere:	86	Arcadia III	62	20
With hanches smooth as looking glasse.	88	Arcadia III	62	92
As for the fingers of the hand,	90	Arcadia III	62	130
As I began, so must I ende.	90	Arcadia III	62	144
As for the Starres, those spheares conteene,	86	Arcadia III	62 V	15
Be fled as things most vaine,	93	3rd Eclogues	63	71

AS   (CONTINUED)   PAGE   TITLE   LINE

As in a sommer day a man might see: . . . .   94 3rd Eclogues 64   4
And as a courtier was with cheere receaved, ...   94 3rd Eclogues 64   20
To such an end as he might be abus'de. . . . .   95 3rd Eclogues 64   28
And as for me (sweete husband) I must beare". . . . .   96 3rd Eclogues 64   62
So may each thing, even as thou wishest lighte, ...   96 3rd Eclogues 64   94
As thou wilt deigne to reade, and gentlie reede, ...   96 3rd Eclogues 64   95
Then such be he, as she his worth may see, ...   98 3rd Eclogues 65   3
As farre from want, as farre from vaine expence, ...   98 3rd Eclogues 65   9
As I my little flocke on Ister banke . . . .   98 3rd Eclogues 66   1
As for the Nightingale, woodmusique's King, ...   99 3rd Eclogues 66   13
For faithfull hart, cleane hands, and mouth as true: . . .   99 3rd Eclogues 66   25
Was onely won'd with such as beastes begot: . . . .   100 3rd Eclogues 66   45
Unknowne as then were they that buylden towers: . . . . . .   100 3rd Eclogues 66   46
Might freely rome, or rest, as seemed them: . . . .   100 3rd Eclogues 66   48
(As even in beasts their dammes leave chaunging parts) . . . 100 3rd Eclogues 66   60
As if he meant his lordship common be. . . . .   102 3rd Eclogues 66 112
(As Tygers, leopards, beares, and Lions' seed) . . . . . .   102 3rd Eclogues 66 122
By those great beastes, as for the weaker's good, ...   102 3rd Eclogues 66 128
As horse and dogge, not great, but gentle blood: . . . . .   102 3rd Eclogues 66 131
As for the gentle birds, like case might rewe. . . . . . .   102 3rd Eclogues 66 139
As for to finde a pasture strowed with golde, ...   104 3rd Eclogues 67   14
With meager lookes, as if they still did smart; . . . . . .   104 3rd Eclogues 67   28
As you paint them: but well in you I finde, ...   106 3rd Eclogues 67   83
In lawlesse games, and love not as you should, ...   106 3rd Eclogues 67   95
As we to get are fram'd, so they to spare: . . . .   106 3rd Eclogues 67 106
As soon as Sunne begins to clime the mountaines: . . . . .   112 4th Eclogues 71   44
Then decke me as thine owne; thy helpe I borowe, ...   114 4th Eclogues 72   28
To death, as then disguisde in her faire face. . . . . . .   115 4th Eclogues 72   69
Till by such hap, as I must ever rewe, ...   115 4th Eclogues 72   74
My senses such release, as they which quiet live, ...   117 4th Eclogues 73   12
As tender conscience might with furious panges assaulte. . . 117 4th Eclogues 73   20
Or as the silly birde in well acquainted nest. . . . . . .   117 4th Eclogues 73   23
On Nature's sweet repast, as healthfull senses ledd. . . . . 117 4th Eclogues 73   40
(Or such a noise it was, as highest thunders sende, ...   118 4th Eclogues 73   53
The first with cloth's tuckt up as Nymphes in woods do
   range , ...   118 4th Eclogues 73   66
As little hunting minde (God knowes) did there appeere.. . . 118 4th Eclogues 73   70
As stuffe meant for the sale set out to glaring showe) . . . 118 4th Eclogues 73   72
As I thus musing stood, Diana cald to her. . . . .   119 4th Eclogues 73   81
Her waiting Nymphe, a Nymphe that did excell as farr . . . . 119 4th Eclogues 73   82
All things that earst I sawe, as orient pearles exceed, . . . 119 4th Eclogues 73   83
And so she was attirde, as one that did not prize. . . . . . 119 4th Eclogues 73   87
So as if I prevaile, you give your giftes to me: . . . . .   120 4th Eclogues 73 133
(She beckned unto me) as yet of spotlesse truth, ...   120 4th Eclogues 73 138
And be it as he saith". Venus was glad to heare. . . . . . . 120 4th Eclogues 73 143
As though she were the same, as when by Paris' doome . . . . 120 4th Eclogues 73 145
Gives an adieu to the world, as to his onely delight:. . . . 123 4th Eclogues 74   26
As th'offence was done, and goe beyond if he can.. . . . .   123 4th Eclogues 74   40
Ev'n as I am, so I should unto that haire be a thrall. . . . 123 4th Eclogues 74   54
As might learne Temp'rance voyde of a rage's events. . . . . 124 4th Eclogues 74   64
As for to lose thy gemme, our earthly Sainct, ...   125 4th Eclogues 75   18
Such cursed harmes as cannot be redressed. . . . .   126 4th Eclogues 75   63
From such as were to dye for him contented.. . . . .   128 4th Eclogues 75 126
As in his health we healthfull were preserved. . . . . . .   128 4th Eclogues 75 134
From such deepe plaint as should such woes descrie, ...   129 4th Eclogues 75 137
So high, as should make such a paine notorious: . . . . . .   129 4th Eclogues 75 140
As well he was in peace a safest treasure: . . . .   129 4th Eclogues 76   17
As nature's worke: why should we feare to dye? . . . . . .   131 Arcadia V   77   2
The Nightingale, as soone as aprill bringeth . . . .   137 Cert Sonnets 4   1
As to Swanne in last disease: . . . .   140 Cert Sonnets 7   37
As treasure house where her best gifts abyde.. . . . . . .   141 Cert Sonnets 8   8
(First sealing up my heart as pray of his) . . . .   141 Cert Sonnets 9   10
Hath not such paine as it makes others have: . . . .   142 Cert Sonnets 11   10
Hath yet such health, as it my life can save.. . . . . . .   142 Cert Sonnets 11   12
Fowle Winters as they come, away they shall. . . . .   143 Cert Sonnets 12   12
Like as the Dove which seeled up doth flie, ...   144 Cert Sonnets 15   1
As this poore beast who did his rest forsake, ...   145 Cert Sonnets 16   7
As in their moodes to take a lingring pawse? . . . .   146 Cert Sonnets 17   24
As for my mirth, how could I but be glad, ...   147 Cert Sonnets 17   41
Sweet Ladie, as for those whose sullen cheare, ...   147 Cert Sonnets 17   46
Even as the flye, which to the flame doth goe, ...   149 Cert Sonnets 21   11
Which as of inward glorie. . . . .   152 Cert Sonnets 23   29
And as you like my double lot, ...   153 Cert Sonnets 24   17
As you, alas, my Sunne bends; . . . .   154 Cert Sonnets 25   26
As her words had it bent? . . . .   158 Cert Sonnets 28   24
To see me as you see? . . . .   158 Cert Sonnets 28   32
Worth as nought worth rejected, ...   159 Cert Sonnets 30   5
I can speake what I feele, and feele as much as they, ... 168 Astrophil   6   12
For soone as they strake thee with Stella's rayes, ...   170 Astrophil   10   12
As do bewray a want of inward tuch: . . . .   172 Astrophil   15   10
As who by being poisond doth poison know.. . . . .   173 Astrophil   16   14
And yet my words, as them my pen doth frame, ...   174 Astrophil   19   7
As that sweete blacke which vailes the heav'nly eye: . . .   175 Astrophil   20   7
Hath this world ought so faire as Stella is? . . . .   175 Astrophil   21   14
As what their hands do hold, their heads do know, ...   177 Astrophil   24   6
As sacred things, far from all daunger's show: . . . . . .   177 Astrophil   24   8
Are Beauties there as proud as here they be? . . . .   180 Astrophil   31   11
A Poet eke, as humours fly or creepe, ...   181 Astrophil   32   4
Him as thy slave, and now long needy Fame. . . . .   182 Astrophil   35   10

And if these things, as being thine by right,. . . . . 184 Astrophil   39   12
As good to write as for to lie and grone. . . . .   184 Astrophil   40   1
As his maine force, choise sport, and easefull stay. . . . . 186 Astrophil   43   4
And yet as soone as they so formed be, ... 189 Astrophil   50   5
As of a friend that meant not much amisse: . . . . 193 Astrophil   56   8
But as he them more short or slacke doth raine,. . . . . . . 194 Astrophil   58   4
As my young Dove may in your precepts wise . . . . 196 Astrophil   63   3
As I may well recount, but none can prize: . . . . 198 Astrophil   65   4
Trebles sing high, as well as bases deepe: . . . . 201 Astrophil   70   6
Hath cheekes to smile, as well as eyes to weepe. . . . . . . 201 Astrophil   70   8
As fast thy Vertue bends that love to good:. . . . . 201 Astrophil   71   13
Edward named fourth, as first in praise I name,. . . . . . . 204 Astrophil   75   2
As consterd in true speech, the name of heav'n it beares,. . 205 Astrophil   77   11
So piercing pawes, as spoyle when they embrace,. . . . . . . 206 Astrophil   78   10
So nimble feet as stirre still, though on thornes: . . . . . 206 Astrophil   78   11
So ample eares as never good newes know: . . . . 206 Astrophil   78   13
As though that faire soft hand did you great wrong.. . . . . 208 Astrophil   83   4
(As his sole object of felicitie). . . . . 212 Astrophil   86   7
The night as tedious, wooes th'approch of day; . . . . 224 Astrophil   89   6
Nor so ambitious am I, as to frame . . . . 224 Astrophil   90   5
Some beautie's peece, as amber colourd hed,. . . . . 225 Astrophil   91   6
As of a caitife worthy so to die,. . . . . 228 Astrophil   94   10
By being placed in such a wretch as I. . . . . 228 Astrophil   94   14
But as you with my breast I oft have nurst,. . . . . 228 Astrophil   95   3
As can refresh the hell where my soule fries.. . . . . 231 Astrophil   100   8
Sweetnesse, that breathes and pants as oft as she: . . . . . 231 Astrophil   101   2
As thy lookes sturre, runs up and downe to make. . . . . . . 232 Astrophil   101   10
As grudging me my sorrowe's eloquence? . . . . 233 Astrophil   104   4
As what my hart still sees thou canst not spie?. . . . . . . 235 Astrophil   105   4
Sure they prevaile as much with me, as he. . . . . 236 Astrophil   106   12
Which pants as though it still should leape to thee: . . . . 236 Astrophil   107   6
And as a Queene, who from her presence sends . . . . 236 Astrophil   107   9
But soone as thought of thee breeds my delight,. . . . . . . 236 Astrophil   108   5
Through pores of sencelesse trees, as it could make them
    move:. . . . . 208 A&S 3rd Song   2
As his light was her eyes, her death his endlesse night: . . 209 A&S 3rd Song   10
And all I said so well, as no man it denied. . . . . 212 A&S 5th Song   12
As where thou soone mightst helpe, most faith dost most
    oppresse,. . . . . 213 A&S 5th Song   41
No witchcraft is so evill, as which man's mind destroyeth. . 215 A&S 5th Song   78
Time doth as the subject prove,. . . . . 234 A&S 11th Song   18
Beauty as farre excels.. . . . . 216 A&S 6th Song   27
As both in both are spent.. . . . . 216 A&S 6th Song   36
As no exceptions tutch.. . . . . 216 A&S 6th Song   42
As with sententious lips to set a title vaine on it: . . . . 217 A&S 7th Song   4
Who have so leaden eyes, as not to see sweet beautie's show, 217 A&S 7th Song   7
Or seeing, have so wodden wits, as not that worth to know; . 217 A&S 7th Song   8
Or knowing, have so muddy minds, as not to be in love; . . . 217 A&S 7th Song   9
Or loving, have so frothy thoughts, as easly thence to move: 217 A&S 7th Song   10
As not eares but hart did tuch:. . . . . 220 A&S 8th Song   70
As yet love she signified. . . . . 220 A&S 8th Song   72
Half so deere as you to me,. . . . . 220 A&S 8th Song   82
The straying stepps as wicked Counsel leads; . . . . 270 Psalm I   2
Farr as World's farthest end.. . . . . 271 Psalm II   20
With kindest care, as with a certain shield. . . . . 275 Psalm V   40
Shew forth his Acts, and this as Act most high,. . . . . . . 280 Psalm IX   32
These Canibals, who as if they were bread. . . . . 286 Psalm XIV   14
Then keep me as the Apple of an Eye, ... 290 Psalm XVII   25
As how to watch our overthrow, ... 290 Psalm XVII   32
Save me from them Thou usest as thy blade, ... 290 Psalm XVII   37
As he before his eyes did see my justice stand,. . . . . . . 292 Psalm XVIII   48
According as he saw the pureness of my hand. . . . . 292 Psalm XVIII   49
I bett those folks as small as dust, which wind doth rayse;. 293 Psalm XVIII   76
I bett them as the clay is bett in beaten wayes. . . . . . . 293 Psalm XVIII   77
As glad is he, as Giants be. . . . . 294 Psalm XIX   23
Nay soon as he but moved . . . . 297 Psalm XXI   6
He had as him behoved. 297 Psalm XXI   8
Thou as in fiery Ov'en shalt make. . . . . 297 Psalm XXI   31
As they so theirs, Him shall their ofspring serve, ... 300 Psalm XXII   75
Guide me as Thy Truth guides;. . . . . 303 Psalm XXV   13
To such as keep his Covenant. . . . . 304 Psalm XXV   41
As their deeds have purchas'd it,. . . . . 309 Psalm XXVIII   17
As deserves their wicked witt; . . . . 309 Psalm XXVIII   18
Fare they as their hands have far'd, ... 309 Psalm XXVIII   19
In clouds of teares, but soon as sun . . . . 311 Psalm XXX   17
As life may good appeare?. . . . . 320 Psalm XXXIV   48
That hunt so poore a prey as is my soule.. . . . . 321 Psalm XXXV   8
And as vile chaff away the wind doth blow, ... 321 Psalm XXXV   11
Let Angel thine persue them as they fly, ... 321 Psalm XXXV   13
Laying such things, as never in mee weare; . . . . 322 Psalm XXXV   26
As Brothers, or as Friends beloved much; . . . . 322 Psalm XXXV   34
But lo, soon as they did me staggering see,. . . . . 322 Psalm XXXV   37
And said to me wide mowing as they could,. . . . . 322 Psalm XXXV   53
As for my tongue, while I have any dayes,. . . . . 323 Psalm XXXV   71
I ev'en as such kind of wight, ... 328 Psalm XXXVIII   40
And as I mus'd such World to see,. . . . . 329 Psalm XXXIX   10
But baiting, as my Fathers came; . . . . 330 Psalm XXXIX   40
As now to say to me, ... 332 Psalm XL   59
As soon as out they go.. . . . . 333 Psalm XLI   24

AS   (CONTINUED)   PAGE   TITLE   LINE
As the chafed hart which brayeth . . . . 334 Psalm XLII   1
If this in them be true, as true in men think I. . . . . . . 343 Possibly   1   7
Whose lyverie is such, as most I freeze apparelled most, . . 343 Possibly   1   21
Dick. Bound as I neither power have, nor would have power to
      stir. . . . . 343 Possibly   1   24
As all the rest, so now the stone. . . . . 241 Other Poems   3   7
Who share in woe, weygh others have as much. . . . . 242 Other Poems   4   16
As Strephon's eare and heart to Klaius bent: . . . . 242 Other Poems   4   28
As if they would of owners' humour be, ... 242 Other Poems   4   31
And eke their pipes did well, as frends, agree.. . . . . . . 242 Other Poems   4   32
Yet not so wise, as of unstained harte:. . . . . 243 Other Poems   4   35
As bragging that free of all passions' mone. . . . . 244 Other Poems   4   71
As she a black-silke cap on him begunne. . . . . 244 Other Poems   4   85
Should price of hir, as in a market, make. . . . . 245 Other Poems   4   123
Whose boiling heat encreased as she wept:. . . . . 246 Other Poems   4   155
Which soone as it did batefull question frame, ... 247 Other Poems   4   189
So as good thoughts of him in all arise, ... 247 Other Poems   4   198
That they, aswell as they, Hell may supplie: . . . . 248 Other Poems   4   230
There may you see, soone as the middle two . . . . 248 Other Poems   4   233
As perjur'd cowards in adversity . . . . 248 Other Poems   4   239
For as Urania after Cosma ran, ... 249 Other Poems   4   281
But as his heate with running did augment, ... 249 Other Poems   4   297
But he drew hir as love his fancy drew,. . . . . 250 Other Poems   4   323
Though with soft leggs, did run as fast as he. . . . . 250 Other Poems   4   339
As Venus' bird the white, swift, lovely Dove . . . . 251 Other Poems   4   353
(Yet beauty still as fast as she did sturre) . . . . 251 Other Poems   4   358
He stood, but turn'd, as Girosol, to Sun:. . . . . 251 Other Poems   4   370
His soule did fly as she was seen to run.. . . . . 251 Other Poems   4   372
Each way, as she, that age's praise, did bend. . . . . 251 Other Poems   4   376
As heart-bound slaves: and happy then embrace. . . . . 252 Other Poems   4   391
As rubies lustre, when they rubbed be. . . . . 252 Other Poems   4   396
As on sweet flowrs when morning's drops we see.. . . . . . . 252 Other Poems   4   398
Began at least to be conceiv'd as woe. . . . . 252 Other Poems   4   418
I am as dull as winter-sterved sheep,. . . . . 253 Other Poems   4   442
Tir'de as a jade in overloden carte, ... 253 Other Poems   4   443
In river as I look'd my pining face, ... 254 Other Poems   4   475
As pin'd a face as mine I saw againe.. . . . . 254 Other Poems   4   476
As this same sprite about my fancies blinde, ... 255 Other Poems   4   502
As much more loving, as lesse combersome.. . . . . 255 Other Poems   4   504
With heart as carefull, as with carelesse grace, ... 255 Other Poems   4   522
As three most joyntly set, ... 260 Other Poems   6   21
And as the Turtle-Dove . . . . 261 Other Poems   6   49
As one for ever joyned bee.. . . . . 261 Other Poems   6   60
A-SCATTERING
Let Angel thine a scattring make them go.. . . . . 321 Psalm XXXV   12
ASCEND
Then let my Words, my Crys ascend, ... 290 Psalm XVII   19
ASCRIBE
Ascribe unto the lord of light,.. . . . . 309 Psalm XXIX   1
Ascribe all glory and all might. . . . . 309 Psalm XXIX   3
Ascribe due glory to his Name, ... 310 Psalm XXIX   4
ASH
Ashe makes speares which shieldes do resist, her force no
      repulse takes: . . . .   36 1st Eclogues 13   136
ASHAMED
And if for want of use thy minde ashamed is, ...   14 1st Eclogues 7   2
Within thy selfe, thou soone wilt be ashamed . . . .   25 1st Eclogues 9   118
"Art not asham'd to publish thy disease?".. . . . . 182 Astrophil   34   5
Forst by their Lord, who is asham'd to find. . . . . 231 Astrophil   99   13
ASHES
Which doth to ashes burne: . . . .   19 1st Eclogues 7   155
My Lyvelye joyes to dolefull ashes turne:. . . . .   42 Arcadia II   22   10
And shall (o me) all this in ashes rest? . . . .   60 2nd Eclogues 30   101
In ashes of despaire (though burnt) shall make thee live". . 121 4th Eclogues 73   174
Thy offrings so that they to ashes turn. . . . . 296 Psalm XX   15
Yet will not I greife, ashes, thralldom change . . . . 345 Possibly   2   9
ASIA'S
Which while it is, it is all Asia's light. . . . .   60 2nd Eclogues 30   109
ASIDE
Nor ever turns aside . . . . 331 Psalm XL   19
ASK
And aske the reason of that speciall grace,. . . . . 126 4th Eclogues 75   40
Aske, if in great men good men so do thronge,. . . . . 126 4th Eclogues 75   43
Ask I will give yt Thee, ... 271 Psalm II   18
Yea thou prevent'st e're ask he could, ... 297 Psalm XXI   9
He did but ask a life of Thee, ... 297 Psalm XXI   13
When foes ask with foule deriding, ... 335 Psalm XLII   47
I aske, now answere me.. . . . . 256 Other Poems   5   20
ASKED
When being askt, now that he did obtaine . . . .   4 Lady of May   3   3
The goodman starting, askt what did her move?. . . . .   95 3rd Eclogues 64   47
ASKING
Asking her how she tasted Courtier's lips, ...   95 3rd Eclogues 64   33
ASLEEP
Either a sleepe be all if nought assaile,. . . . .   27 1st Eclogues 10   29
Unarmde (alas) unwarn'd to take a man asleepe? . . . . 122 4th Eclogues 73   186
Too long, too long asleepe thou hast me brought, ... 161 Cert Sonnets 31   7
In sport I suckt, while she asleepe did lie, ... 203 Astrophil   73   6
Yet a sleepe, me thinkes they say, ... 211 A&S 4th Song   27

25

		PAGE	TITLE		LINE
ASPECT					
With proud aspect, disdaining greater hast..		249	Other Poems	4	293
ASPIRE					
Fondly blame that to which your selves aspire.		25	1st Eclogues	9	104
Olive paintes me the peace that I must aspire to by					
conquest		35	1st Eclogues	13	117
And to old age since you your selfe aspire,.		39	Arcadia II	15	13
Hid heere his hopes, by which he might aspire.		75	Arcadia III	44	3
My hopes which do but to mine owne aspire?		80	Arcadia III	53	4
Far from my thoughts was ought, whereto their minds aspire,.		117	4th Eclogues	73	15
In vaine thou madest me to vaine things aspire,.		161	Cert Sonnets	31	10
And thou my mind aspire to higher things:.		161	Cert Sonnets	32	2
Nor do aspire to Caesar's bleeding fame, ...		198	Astrophil	64	10
Chiefe good, whereto my hope doth only aspire, ...		200	Astrophil	68	3
Let no tongue aspire to tell,.		226	A&S 10th Song		10
ASPIRES					
I then, whose burd'ned brest but thus aspires.		242	Other Poems	4	5
ASPIRETH					
And wisdome to his wonted seate aspireth..		83	Arcadia III	57	12
ASS					
The neighbours all did crie, "alas what asse doth bray?" . .		52	2nd Eclogues	29	26
The asse did hurt when he did thinke to kisse.		62	2nd Eclogues	30	184
Asse, pacience; the Mole, a working thought;		101	3rd Eclogues	66	86
ASSAIl					
Either a sleepe be all if nought assaile,.		27	1st Eclogues	10	29
While our sonne shynes no clowdie greeves assaile.		43	Arcadia II	23	12
My sun is gon, Nowe clowdie greeves assayle.		44	Arcadia II	24	12
Such living beames should her black seate assaile, ...		82	Arcadia III	55	10
I Stella's eyes assayll, invade her eares;		195	Astrophil	61	3
ASSAILED					
Assailed..		286	Psalm XIII		16
ASSAULT					
As tender conscience might with furious panges assaulte. . .		117	4th Eclogues	73	20
Stella, whence doth this new assault arise,.		182	Astrophil	36	1
Before thassault beginne, O yeelde O yeelde.		345	Possibly	4	14
But so she must. And now the third assault		250	Other Poems	4	316
ASSAULTS					
Shield me from these assaults;		304	Psalm XXV		62
ASSAYED					
I Stella's eyes assaid, invade her eares;.		195	Astrophil	61 V	3
ASSEMBLED					
Who joy but they, when they assembled bee?		322	Psalm XXXV		38
ASSEMBLY					
Wher godly men do their assembly make.		270	Psalm I		18
ASSENT					
And worse of other more, till by assent.		29	1st Eclogues	10	82
You goodly pines, which still with brave assent.		77	Arcadia III	49	1
In Dales I see each way a hard assent:		147	Cert Sonnets	18	10
ASSIGNED					
Death wrapt in flesh, to living grave assign'd..		73	Arcadia III	40	14
That is their share assigned..		284	Psalm XI		20
ASSIST					
We thinke they hurt, when most they do assist.		59	2nd Eclogues	30	70
Assist us Saviour deare;		296	Psalm XX		33
ASS'S					
An Asse's shade ere now hath bred debate..		146	Cert Sonnets	17	20
ASSUAGE					
With such a will that nothing can asswage.		105	3rd Eclogues	67	51
ASSUMPTION					
O happie Gods, which by inward assumption.		15	1st Eclogues	7	40
ASSURE					
My sight in her faire limmes, I then assure my selfe,. . . .		16	1st Eclogues	7	56
ASSURED					
Let this assured holde our judgements ever take, ...		45	Arcadia II	26	15
Friendship true in hart assured, ...		263	Other Poems	7	35
ASTONISHED					
And hers on me, astonisht with that sight.		115	4th Eclogues	72	76
I, wretch, astonisht was, and thought the deathfull doome. .		118	4th Eclogues	73	61
ASTRAY					
Might of each side astray be brought,.		88	Arcadia III	62	72
Least yet I slip or go astray.		289	Psalm XVII		16
To play when that their loved dammes, are stoln or gone					
astray?.		343	Possibly	1	6
ASTRAYING					
And, lo, he finds that all astraying went, ...		286	Psalm XIV		10
ASTROLOGY					
Though dustie wits dare scorne Astrologie, ...		177	Astrophil	26	1
ASTROPHEL					
Astrophil with Stella sweete,.		218	A&S 8th Song		5
"Astrophil" sayd she, "my love		220	A&S 8th Song		73
Astrophil that so wel served,.		222	A&S 9th Song		27
ASUNDER					
The moone a sunder rent (O godes, o pardon me, ...		118	4th Eclogues	73	55
The Moone a sunder rent; whereat with sodaine fall		118	4th Eclogues	73	57
Love did set his lips asunder, ...		218	A&S 8th Song		27
Senses all asunder breakes;		219	A&S 8th Song		38
For wycked arms shall breake asunder,.		325	Psalm XXXVII		43
Let them be ne'r a sunder, ...		261	Other Poems	6	56
AT					
At length obtain the point of his desire, ...		4	Lady of May	3	2

AT   (CONTINUED)   PAGE   TITLE   LINE

Who at thy beer, as at a barre, shall plead. . . . .   11 Arcadia I   1   6
Who frownes at others' feastes, dooth better bide away.. . .   15 1st Eclogues   7   15
Lalus. Kala at length conclude my lingring lotte:. . . . . .   18 1st Eclogues   7 115
With Jove's disdaine at such a rival's seed, ...   21 1st Eclogues   8   20
Till now at length that Jove him office gives, ...   22 1st Eclogues   8   45
(At Juno's suite who much did Argus love). . . . .   22 1st Eclogues   8   46
Though woes now live, at length thy woes must dye. . . . . .   22 1st Eclogues   9   12
Be as thou art, but be with mine at one. . . . .   27 1st Eclogues   10   15
At blowe point, hotcocles, or els at keeles. . . . .   28 1st Eclogues   10   47
If the Swanne's sweet voice be not heard, but at death,. . .   30 1st Eclogues   12   14
Will at length perceave these flames by her beames to be
   kindled, ...   37 1st Eclogues   13 167
Burnt in my selfe, I muse at others' fire: . . . .   41 Arcadia II   20   5
R. Yet Passion, yeeld at length to Reason's stroke.. . . . .   47 2nd Eclogues   27   33
Leaping at every flie, and angrie with a flea: . . . .   53 2nd Eclogues   29   44
She ranne away, and threw at me a ball.. . . . .   54 2nd Eclogues   29   89
The after-folkes shall wonder still at thee. . . . .   56 2nd Eclogues   29 131
Pas. My father hath at home a prettie Jay, ...   56 2nd Eclogues   29 138
While that we do at his sweete scourge repine, ...   59 2nd Eclogues   30   75
Which at firste voly gave too open entry,. . . . .   68 2nd Eclogues   33   14
But at no change, so pinching care he takes, ...   71 Arcadia III   37   9
I like this place, wheare at the least the darke . . . . . .   73 Arcadia III   39   13
Looke further then, so shalt thou finde at least,. . . . . .   75 Arcadia III   44   9
Blushing at sight of Phoebus' pride. . . . .   86 Arcadia III   62   26
Grumbling at her when she his kindnes sought, ...   95 3rd Eclogues   64   32
The courtlie shepheard much agast at this, ...   96 3rd Eclogues   64   67
At which, whether the others did repine, ...   100 3rd Eclogues   66   57
Who at the first, wanting, or hiding pride,. . . . .   101 3rd Eclogues   66 107
At length for glutton taste he did them kill:. . . . .   103 3rd Eclogues   66 146
At last for sport their sillie lives did spill.. . . . . . .   103 3rd Eclogues   66 147
At whose approach the Sunne rase in the evening, ...   113 4th Eclogues   71   69
Our morning hymne this is, and song at evening.. . . . . . .   113 4th Eclogues   71   75
Till deadly sleepe at length possest my living coarse. . . .   117 4th Eclogues   73   30
Sweete thinke not I am at ease, ...   140 Cert Sonnets   7   34
Oft have I musde, but now at length I finde, ...   148 Cert Sonnets   20   1
Not at first sight, nor with a dribbed shot. . . . .   165 Astrophil   2   1
At length to Love's decrees, I forc'd, agreed, ...   165 Astrophil   2   7
Yet with repining at so partiall lot.. . . . .   165 Astrophil   2   8
At length he perch'd himself in Stella's joyfull face, . . .   168 Astrophil   8   8
Or at the most on some fine picture stayes,. . . . .   170 Astrophil   11   7
And sure at length stolne goods do come to light . . . . . .   172 Astrophil   15   11
You seeke to nurse at fullest breasts of Fame, ...   172 Astrophil   15   13
Looke at my hands for no such quintessence;. . . . .   179 Astrophil   28   11
That not my soule, which at thy foot did fall, ...   183 Astrophil   36   12
Of those fierce darts, dispaire at me doth throw:. . . . . .   184 Astrophil   39   6
Each soule doth at Love's feet his weapons lay,. . . . . . .   186 Astrophil   43   7
But you faire maides, at length this true shall find,. . . .   192 Astrophil   54   11
But this at last is her sweet breath'd defence:. . . . . . .   195 Astrophil   61   4
Heav'ns envy not at my high triumphing:. . . . .   196 Astrophil   63   10
My Muse may well grudge at my heav'nly joy,. . . . .   201 Astrophil   70   1
Teaching the meane, at once to take and give . . . .   206 Astrophil   79   9
Or of thy gifts at least shade out some part.. . . . .   207 Astrophil   81   8
I caught at one of them a hungrie bit; . . . .   208 Astrophil   82   11
That do not leave your least friend at the wurst,. . . . . .   228 Astrophil   95   2
For that at length yet doth invite some rest,. . . . .   229 Astrophil   96   13
Shewes her oft at the full her fairest face, ...   229 Astrophil   97   2
All folkes prest at thy will thy paine to 'swage,. . . . . .   232 Astrophil   101   11
Who womankind at once both deckes and stayneth?. . . . . . .   197 A&S 1st Song   10
Onely at you all envie hopelesse rueth.. . . . .   197 A&S 1st Song   24
More cause a like effect at leastwise bringeth:. . . . . . .   208 A&S 3rd Song   5
Only thought aymes at the pleasure.. . . . .   226 A&S 10th Song   12
At her lips my Nectar drinking.. . . . .   227 A&S 10th Song   48
Love at length leave undertaking." . . . .   234 A&S 11th Song   32
And they are faln, nay perisht at Thy sight: . . . .   279 Psalm IX   7
Maugre their force I will set him at rest. . . . .   285 Psalm XII   18
And at my fall they joy that, troublous, me. . . . .   286 Psalm XIII   15
The lookers now at me poore wretch be mocking, ...   299 Psalm XXII   17
At mother's breastes, thou didst good hope betake me.. . . .   299 Psalm XXII   22
Against me swarm, ceaseless to raile at me.. . . . .   322 Psalm XXXV   40
Chafe not at some man's great good fortune . . . .   325 Psalm XXXVII   18
For those badd folks at last shall perish, ...   325 Psalm XXXVII   23
At best is merely vanity.. . . . .   330 Psalm XXXIX   18
At these my words all cloath'd in teares;. . . . .   330 Psalm XXXIX   38
Thus bound I said, lo, lord I am at hand,. . . . .   331 Psalm XL   31
My Friend I say, who at my table sate, ...   333 Psalm XLI   31
So then be blest now, then, at home, abroad, ...   334 Psalm XLI   45
Shew that we do not grudge at all when others do rejoyce.. .   343 Possibly   1   2
When she with skirts tuckt very hy, with girles at stoolball
   playes. . . . .   343 Possibly   1   10
Will. Thou seest my eares do itch at it: good Dick thy sorow
   tell.. . . . .   343 Possibly   1   18
And now at keels they trie a harmles chaunce,. . . . .   243 Other Poems   4   47
When, if nede were, they could at quintain run:. . . . . . .   243 Other Poems   4   56
Moving, she seem'd at once to kisse, and speake. . . . . . .   244 Other Poems   4   96
At length in rowes of Kisse-cheeke teares they raine.. . . .   245 Other Poems   4 128
Klaius streight felt, and groned at the blowe: . . . .   246 Other Poems   4 161
At Barly brake hir swete swift foot to trie. . . . .   247 Other Poems   4 208
And still, beleve me, Strephon was at hand.. . . . .   247 Other Poems   4 216
At other end Uran did Strephon lend. . . . .   248 Other Poems   4 246

27

AT   (CONTINUED)   PAGE   TITLE   LINE
        His heels grow'n proud did seme at heav'n to shake.. . . . . .   248 Other Poems   4 261
        Though him to meete at all she sturred nought. . . . .   250 Other Poems   4 326
        Began at least to be conceiv'd as woe, ...   252 Other Poems   4 418
        All visions seeme, at every bush I start:. . . . .   253 Other Poems   4 445
        That at me so amaz'd my fellowes jest: . . . .   254 Other Poems   4 468
        The courteous mountaines, griev'd at my disgrace,. . . . . .   254 Other Poems   4 477
        Though thus, and worse, though now I am at last, ...   254 Other Poems   4 493
        (With blushing soule at sight of judgement's glasse, ...   255 Other Poems   4 531
        His pipe was at his foote, ...   256 Other Poems   5   4
        This said, at length he ended. . . . .   259 Other Poems   5 114
ATHIRST
        Like dropsy folke still drinke to be a thyrst. . . . .   247 Other Poems   4 204
ATLAS
        Whose Atlas is a smallest small, ...   89 Arcadia III   62 103
        Of Atlas tyr'd, your wisedome's heav'nly sway. . . . .   190 Astrophil   51   8
        That hand, which without touch holds more then Atlas might;.   205 Astrophil   77   5
ATROPOS
        When once one is for Atropos distrained. . . . .   128 4th Eclogues 75 111
ATTAIN
        What Foes I did persue my force did them attaine,. . . . . .   292 Psalm XVIII   68
        Attain unto their wished scope.. . . . .   325 Psalm XXXVII   20
ATTAINT
        And thou poore Earth, whom fortune doth attaint. . . . . . .   125 4th Eclogues 75   16
ATTEMPT
        Yet high is my attempt. O Muse historifie. . . . .   15 1st Eclogues   7   23
        Whose winke ech bold attempt forbids.. . . . .   86 Arcadia III   62   14
        Where plagu'd for rash attempt, gives up his ghost,. . . . .   151 Cert Sonnets 22   57
        Now will I attempt to know,. . . . .   202 A&S 2nd Song   11
ATTEMPTS
        No, though the heav'ns for high attempts have blamed me, . .   15 1st Eclogues   7   22
ATTEND
        Come shepheard's weedes, attend my woefull cryes:. . . . . .   13 Arcadia I   4   5
        Us to attend, in this most private time and place. . . . . .   119 4th Eclogues 73   96
        Mark the upright, the just attend, ...   327 Psalm XXXVII   93
        I attend,. . . . .   328 Psalm XXXVIII   44
        The pleasure of my God attend, ...   330 Psalm XL   2
ATTENDED
        It should be ought of God attended.. . . . .   279 Psalm VIII   16
ATTENDS
        Hold deere his work, with sighes eache change attendes,. . .   71 Arcadia III   37   8
        Till it have wrought what thy owne will attends. . . . . . .   236 Astrophil   107   11
ATTENTION
        Seen, and unknowne; heard, but without attention.. . . . . .   19 1st Eclogues   7 179
        His childhood woonder, prenticeship attention, ...   48 2nd Eclogues 28   38
ATTIRE
        Will spoile the earth of his most rich attire. . . . .   59 2nd Eclogues 30   88
        Was vertue cladde in constant love's attire. . . . .   77 Arcadia III   48   2
        Since in such phrase his faith he did attire.. . . . .   80 Arcadia III   53   8
        Goodnes for best attire in dust is dressed.. . . . .   128 4th Eclogues 75 120
ATTIRED
        (Although simply atyrde) your manly affection utter. . . . .   32 1st Eclogues 13   16
        And so she was attirde, as one that did not prize. . . . . .   119 4th Eclogues 73   87
ATTIRES
        Some one his song in Jove, and Jove's strange tales attires,   167 Astrophil   6   5
ATTIRING
        Ech tree in his best attiring, ...   219 A&S 8th Song   59
ATTRIBUTED
        My harmes to me, my blisse to her attributed.. . . . .   49 2nd Eclogues 28   69
AUDIENCE
        Yet to my plaint Thou hast not audience lent.. . . . .   298 Psalm XXII   8
AUDIT
        When into Reason's audite I do go: . . . .   173 Astrophil   18   2
AUGHT
        If ought I cease these hideous exclamations, ...   61 2nd Eclogues 30 145
        Nor ought I crave to feed life,. . . . .   67 2nd Eclogues 32   54
        Nor ought I seeke to shun death, ...   67 2nd Eclogues 32   55
        Ncr brooke oughte els but well acquainted woe. . . . .   74 Arcadia III   41   6
        Nor of my fortune ought, but mischieve crave.. . . . .   114 4th Eclogues 72   20
        Strephon. Nor of my fortune ought but mischiefe crave, . . .   114 4th Eclogues 72   21
        Far from my thoughts was ought, whereto their minds aspire,.   117 4th Eclogues 73   15
        Ne yet for what I see, your beauties merite ought. . . . . .   121 4th Eclogues 73 164
        Hath this world ought so faire as Stella is? . . . .   175 Astrophil   21   14
        Nor ought do care, though some above me sit, ...   198 Astrophil   64   11
        That ere by them ought undertaken be,. . . . .   236 Astrophil   107   3
        After parting ought forgot,. . . . .   226 A&S 10th Song   8
        If ought my hands of wyckednes do bear:. . . . .   277 Psalm VII   9
        It should be ought of God attended.. . . . .   279 Psalm VIII   16
        Not weighing ought how fleshly fancys run, ...   289 Psalm XVII   13
AUGHTS
        Long be thy woes for such newes, but how recks she my
                thoughts? Oughts. . . . .   64 2nd Eclogues 31   33
AUGMENT
        My dreeades augment the more in passion's mighte,. . . . . .   72 Arcadia III   37   17
        Alas sweet Brookes do in my teares augment:. . . . .   147 Cert Sonnets 18   12
        What, doth high place ambitious thoughts augment?. . . . . .   208 Astrophil   83   9
        Lightning on lightning he did for their wrack augment; . . .   291 Psalm XVIII   30
        But as his heate with running did augment, ...   249 Other Poems   4 297
        Hir race did not hir beautie's beames augment, ...   252 Other Poems   4 393

28

```
AUGUST                                               PAGE   TITLE        LINE
   It August was, he daynde not then to sing. . . . . . . . .  99  3rd Eclogues 66   14
AURORA
   Aurora now thou shewst thy blushing light. . . . . . . . .  82  Arcadia III  56    1
   Aurora like new out of bed,. . . . . . . . . . . . . . . .  86  Arcadia III  62   24
   She comes with light and warmth, which like Aurora prove . . 205 Astrophil    76    5
   But when Aurora leades out Phoebus' daunce,. . . . . . . . 230  Astrophil    98   12
AURORA'S
   Towardes Aurora's Court a Nymph doth dwell,. . . . . . . . 183  Astrophil    37    5
AUSTERE
   Austere she is, when he would honest playes; . . . . . . . 104  3rd Eclogues 67   34
AUTHOR
   Besides, lo here the auther. . . . . . . . . . . . . . . .  67  2nd Eclogues 32   46
   Because that thou, the author of our sight,. . . . . . . .  80  Arcadia III  52   14
   Nor Fortune of thy fortune author is:. . . . . . . . . . . 181  Astrophil    33    8
   If th' author of thy blisse, . . . . . . . . . . . . . . . 257  Other Poems   5   21
AUTHORITY
   And therefore by her Love's authority, . . . . . . . . . . 196  Astrophil    62    9
AUTHORIZED
   Then who will heare a well autoris'd lye,. . . . . . . . .  24  1st Eclogues  9   72
AVAIL
   What can justice availe, to a man that tells not his owne
      case?. . . . . . . . . . . . . . . . . . . . . . . . .  32  1st Eclogues 13   22
   What pardon can availe? or who employes him. . . . . . . .  62  2nd Eclogues 30  168
   "Nought can reason availe in heav'nly matters".. . . . . .  68  2nd Eclogues 33   26
   That no more thy beames availe thee. . . . . . . . . . . . 156  Cert Sonnets 27   20
   Ah what doth Phoebus' gold that wretch availe, . . . . . . 237  Astrophil   108   10
AVISE
   Avise themselves that they are vainely spent. . . . . . . . 174 Astrophil    19    8
AVOID
   All to a lesson he draws, norr hills nor caves can avoide
      him. . . . . . . . . . . . . . . . . . . . . . . . . .  31  1st Eclogues 13    7
   Nico. Couldst thou make Lalus flie? so nightingales avoide,.  52  2nd Eclogues 29  17
   Yet noblest Conquerours do wreckes avoid.. . . . . . . . . 185  Astrophil    40   11
   Which to avoyde, quenche, loose noughte booted stryfe. . . 344  Possibly      2    8
AVOIDETH
   Whose shade safety doth hold, danger avoideth her: . . . .  69  2nd Eclogues 34   34
AVOIDS
   Avoydes thy hurtfull arte, . . . . . . . . . . . . . . . .  92  3rd Eclogues 63   59
AVOW
   To that where thou thy Cupid maist avowe,. . . . . . . . . 106  3rd Eclogues 67  101
AWAKE
   O heav'n awake shewe forth thy stately face, . . . . . . .  91  3rd Eclogues 63   10
   Vertue awake, Beautie but beautie is,. . . . . . . . . . . 188  Astrophil    47    9
   Against such rage of foes: Awake for me. . . . . . . . . . 277  Psalm VII         17
AWAKED
   Sight doth bewitch, the fancie evill awaked. . . . . . . .  82  Arcadia III  57    2
AWAKES
   But most wretched I am, now love awakes my desire. . . . .  30  1st Eclogues 11   20
AWARD
   Unto the man, whom now such miseries you awarde? . . . . . 124  4th Eclogues 74   74
AWAY
   Shallow brookes murmure most, deep silent slide away;. . .  14  1st Eclogues  7   11
   Who frownes at others' feastes, dooth better bide away.. .  15  1st Eclogues  7   15
   Did smile on me, and then away she leaped. . . . . . . . .  17  1st Eclogues  7   84
   She ranne away, and threw at me a ball.. . . . . . . . . .  54  2nd Eclogues 29   89
   Histor. Thus dyd they saye and then awaye dyd wende; . . .  62  2nd Eclogues 30  185
   Nor time pratled away, cradle of ignorance,. . . . . . . .  69  2nd Eclogues 34   22
   Why doost thou haste away. . . . . . . . . . . . . . . . .  80  Arcadia III  52    1
   Away vayne Cares, by which fewe men do finde . . . . . . .  83  Arcadia III  59    3
   For ever hence awaye:. . . . . . . . . . . . . . . . . . .  93  3rd Eclogues 63   77
   But above all away vile jealousie, . . . . . . . . . . . .  93  3rd Eclogues 63   82
   Let other fowler spots away be blowne; . . . . . . . . . . 105  3rd Eclogues 67   55
   Fancie, her tackling, torne away doth flie:. . . . . . . . 114  4th Eclogues 72   47
   And with that cursed curse away to heaven they fled, . . . 121  4th Eclogues 73  177
   Time runnes away for sorow:. . . . . . . . . . . . . . . . 136  Cert Sonnets  3    6
   Fowle Winters as they come, away they shall. . . . . . . . 143  Cert Sonnets 12   12
   A Satyre once did runne away for dread,. . . . . . . . . . 145  Cert Sonnets 16    1
   Then good Apollo do away thy bowe: . . . . . . . . . . . . 146  Cert Sonnets 17   36
   He burnt unwares his wings, and cannot fly away. . . . . . 169  Astrophil     8   14
   Was held, in opend sense it flies away,. . . . . . . . . . 184  Astrophil    38   10
   From my deare Captainnesse to run away?. . . . . . . . . . 223  Astrophil    88    2
   Only true sighs, you do not go away, . . . . . . . . . . . 229  Astrophil    95   12
   Now will I away hence flee:. . . . . . . . . . . . . . . . 203  A&S 2nd Song      27
   And from lowts to run away.. . . . . . . . . . . . . . . . 235  A&S 11th Song     45
   Therewithall away she went,. . . . . . . . . . . . . . . . 221  A&S 8th Song     101
   And cast their yoakes away.. . . . . . . . . . . . . . . . 271  Psalm II           8
   Doth melt away though it be inmost seated. . . . . . . . . 299  Psalm XXII        34
   Confounded be, and passe away like smoake, . . . . . . . . 313  Psalm XXXI        47
   And as vile chaff away the wind doth blow, . . . . . . . . 321  Psalm XXXV        11
   Ev'en with the smoake shall wast away. . . . . . . . . . . 326  Psalm XXXVII      52
   Let them be curst away that would me wast; . . . . . . . . 332  Psalm XL          54
   She chirping ran, he peeping flew away,. . . . . . . . . . 244  Other Poems   4   87
   Klaius in deede would faine have puld a way. . . . . . . . 246  Other Poems   4  171
   Or like a lambe whose dam away is fet. . . . . . . . . . . 254  Other Poems   4  490
   Away ragg'd rams, care I what murraine kill? . . . . . . . 255  Other Poems   4  515
   And pine away with daily wasting woe?. . . . . . . . . . . 257  Other Poems   5   26
   Do fondly take away. . . . . . . . . . . . . . . . . . . . 258  Other Poems   5   86
AWE
   And aye more awe towards him for to plant, . . . . . . . . 101  3rd Eclogues 66  102
```

```
AWFUL                                                      PAGE   TITLE           LINE
     So children still reade you with awfull eyes,. . . . . . . . 196 Astrophil    63    2
     O tremble then with awfull will: . . . . . . . . . . . . . . 273 Psalm IV           16
     Nor glorious Fooles stand in Thy awfull sight. . . . . . . . 274 Psalm V            12
AWRY
     With dearth of words, or answers quite awrie,. . . . . . . . 178 Astrophil    27    3
     How farre they shoote awrie! the true cause is,. . . . . . . 185 Astrophil    41   12
AXE
     O Mars, for what doth serve thy armed axe? . . . . . . . . .  60 2nd Eclogues 30  110
*AYE
     Should breed to her, let me for aye dejected be. . . . . . .  51 2nd Eclogues 28  121
     Can then a cause be so light that forceth a man to go die?
         Aye. . . . . . . . . . . . . . . . . . . . . . . . . . .  64 2nd Eclogues 31   24
     Be hence aye put to flight,. . . . . . . . . . . . . . . . .  93 3rd Eclogues 63   68
     And aye more awe towards him for to plant, . . . . . . . . . 101 3rd Eclogues 66  102
     Whereby that being aye must be conserved.. . . . . . . . . . 106 3rd Eclogues 67   81
     But mankind is for aye to nought resolved. . . . . . . . . . 127 4th Eclogues 75   81
     Her legges (O legges) her ay well stepping feete.. . . . . . 141 Cert Sonnets  9    8
     Unto the flowre that ay turnes,. . . . . . . . . . . . . . . 154 Cert Sonnets 25   25
     (Exil'd for ay from those high treasures, which. . . . . . . 177 Astrophil    24   13
     So manie eyes ay seeking their owne woe, . . . . . . . . . . 206 Astrophil    78   12
     Which ay most faire, now more then most faire show,. . . . . 231 Astrophil   100    3
     With winking eyes aye bent . . . . . . . . . . . . . . . . . 282 Psalm X            35
     Who thus proceeds, for aye, in sacred Mount shall raign. . . 287 Psalm XV           13
     God's witness sure for aye doth dure . . . . . . . . . . . . 294 Psalm XIX          31
     Feed and lift them up for aye. . . . . . . . . . . . . . . . 309 Psalm XXVIII       35
     And this his rule for aye remains. . . . . . . . . . . . . . 310 Psalm XXIX         27
     And thou hast not for aye enclosed me. . . . . . . . . . . . 312 Psalm XXXI         22
     Badd folks shall fall, and fall for aye, . . . . . . . . . . 326 Psalm XXXVII       49
     Thou art my help for aye;. . . . . . . . . . . . . . . . . . 332 Psalm XL           67
     For aye before Thy face. . . . . . . . . . . . . . . . . . . 334 Psalm XLI          44
     Still to be hers, about her aye to flie, . . . . . . . . . . 255 Other Poems   4  501
AZURED
     Where azurde veines well mixt appeere. . . . . . . . . . . .  87 Arcadia III  62   56
BABBLE
     Of things vain, with vaine mates they bable all, . . . . . . 284 Psalm XII           4
BABE
     Alas (said I) this babe dooth nurce my thought.. . . . . . .  55 2nd Eclogues 29  113
     Of Venus' babe the wanton nests: . . . . . . . . . . . . . .  87 Arcadia III  62   54
     The Babe cries "way, thy love doth keepe me waking". . . . . 139 Cert Sonnets  6    3
     Lully, lully, my babe, hope cradle bringeth. . . . . . . . . 139 Cert Sonnets  6    4
     The babe cries "way, thy love doth keepe me waking". . . . . 139 Cert Sonnets  6    6
     The babe cries "nay, for that abide I waking". . . . . . . . 139 Cert Sonnets  6    9
     Yet but a babe, with milke of Sight he nurst:. . . . . . . . 247 Other Poems   4  202
BABERY
     With golden leaves, and painted babery,. . . . . . . . . . . 246 Other Poems   4  181
BABES
     Pan store of babes, vertue their thoughts well staid,. . . .  93 3rd Eclogues 63   93
     I thought those babes of some pinne's hurt did whine,. . . . 173 Astrophil    16    7
     While those poore babes their death in birth do find:. . . . 190 Astrophil    50   11
     Sweet babes must babies have, but shrewd gyrles must be
         beat n.. . . . . . . . . . . . . . . . . . . . . . . . . 213 A&S 5th Song       36
BABIES
     Stella, thou straight lookst babies in her eyes, . . . . . . 170 Astrophil    11   10
     Sweet babes must babies have, but shrewd gyrles must be
         beat n.. . . . . . . . . . . . . . . . . . . . . . . . . 213 A&S 5th Song       36
BABY
     She byd me spie her babie in the brooke, . . . . . . . . . .  55 2nd Eclogues 29  112
     Sleepe Babie mine, Desire, nurse Beautie singeth:. . . . . . 139 Cert Sonnets  6    1
     Thy cries, o Babie, set mine head on aking:. . . . . . . . . 139 Cert Sonnets  6    2
     Since babie mine, from me thy watching springeth,. . . . . . 139 Cert Sonnets  6    7
BABY'S
     Thy force hath flow'd from Babie's tongue. . . . . . . . . . 278 Psalm VIII          6
BACK
     Nature abasht went back: fortune blusht: yet she replide
         thus:. . . . . . . . . . . . . . . . . . . . . . . . . .  30 1st Eclogues 11   17
     But back unto her back, my Muse, . . . . . . . . . . . . . .  89 Arcadia III  62  109
     But when mine eyes backe to their heav'n did move, . . . . . 199 Astrophil    66   13
     Came to hir back, and so with double warde . . . . . . . . . 252 Other Poems   4  389
BACK-PARTS
     Strephon, whose eies on hir back-parts did play, . . . . . . 250 Other Poems   4  333
BACKS
     And turn their backs, and strait on backs appeare. . . . . . 276 Psalm VI           31
     The Cherubins their backs, the winds did yeild their wings,. 291 Psalm XVIII        22
BACK-TURNED
     With shafts shott out from their back-turned bow.. . . . . . 251 Other Poems   4  351
BACKWARDLY
     Though they do fly, yet backwardly do glowe. . . . . . . . . 249 Other Poems   4  292
BACKWARDNESS
     When Strephon, cursing his owne backwardnes, . . . . . . . . 252 Other Poems   4  388
*BAD
     The goodman bad his wife be serviceable. . . . . . . . . . .  94 3rd Eclogues 64   24
     She sigh'd and sayd, the bad guest sought her love.. . . . .  95 3rd Eclogues 64   48
     But this bad world, few golden fieldes doth bring, . . . . . 104 3rd Eclogues 67   19
     But let us pick our good from out much bad:. . . . . . . . . 105 3rd Eclogues 67   62
     While that blacke hue from me the bad guest hid: . . . . . . 175 Astrophil    20   11
     That mine owne writings like bad servants show . . . . . . . 175 Astrophil    21    3
     With such bad mixture of my night and day, . . . . . . . . . 224 Astrophil    89   12
     Curst be the page from whome the bad torch fell, . . . . . . 235 Astrophil   105   11
     That bad his friend, but then new maim'd, to be. . . . . . . 236 Astrophil   106   13
```

```
*BAD                        (CONTINUED)                   PAGE    TITLE            LINE
   Ne for bad mates in way of sinning waiteth . . . . . . . . . 270  Psalm I              3
   Of these bad folkes, more lifted up with pride . . . . . . . 285  Psalm XII           26
   Shall these bad wights devouer.. . . . . . . . . . . . . . . 297  Psalm XXI           36
   But all their bad mischeivous skill. . . . . . . . . . . . . 298  Psalm XXI           43
   And from the haunts of such bad folks did fly. . . . . . . . 305  Psalm XXVI          18
   He badd and it did stand.. . . . . . . . . . . . . . . . . . 317  Psalm XXXIII        33
   For those badd folks at last shall perish, . . . . . . . . . 325  Psalm XXXVII        23
   Than of bad folks the wealthy wonder,. . . . . . . . . . . . 325  Psalm XXXVII        42
   Badd folks shall fall, and fall for aye, . . . . . . . . . . 326  Psalm XXXVII        49
   Save me from bad wights. . . . . . . . . . . . . . . . . . . 336  Psalm XLIII          5
   And ti'de them fast to leade his triumph badd, . . . . . . . 245  Other Poems    4   131
   Of Mira's beames eclipst by absence bad. . . . . . . . . . . 256  Other Poems    5    11
   O fortune too too badd,. . . . . . . . . . . . . . . . . . . 259  Other Poems    5    98
BADGE
   Seekes to make ech thing badge of his sweet passion. . . . .  47  2nd Eclogues 28     6
   Since they do weare his badge, most firmely prove. . . . . . 190  Astrophil    52     4
   That his right badge is but worne in the hart: . . . . . . . 192  Astrophil    54    12
   The height of honor in the kindly badge of shame?. . . . . . 232  Astrophil   102     3
   For wearing Venus' badge, in every part of thee, . . . . . . 214  A&S 5th Song        70
BAGGAGE
   That bagged baggage of a miser's mudd, . . . . . . . . . . . 245  Other Poems    4   122
BAGGED
   That bagged baggage of a miser's mudd, . . . . . . . . . . . 245  Other Poems    4   122
BAGPIPE
   Nico would needes with Pas his bagpipe blowe.. . . . . . . .  54  2nd Eclogues 29    68
   Will. What? is thy Bagpipe broke, or are thy lambs miswent;. 343  Possibly      1    15
BAIT
   And try with bayt how fish will bite sometime. . . . . . . .  26  1st Eclogues  9   128
   A baite most fit, for hungrie minded guest.. . . . . . . . .  75  Arcadia III  44    10
   (Which oft to hope laies out a guilefull baite,. . . . . . .  82  Arcadia III  56     2
   On pensive soules (in steede of restfull baite). . . . . . .  82  Arcadia III  56     6
   (Tide to the stake of doubt) strange passions baite, . . . .  82  Arcadia III  56    10
BAITING
   Where but a baiting place is all our portion.. . . . . . . .  61  2nd Eclogues 30   136
   The baiting place of wit, the balme of woe,. . . . . . . . . 184  Astrophil    39     2
   But baiting, as my Fathers came; . . . . . . . . . . . . . . 330  Psalm XXXIX         40
BAKE
   Save me from foes who seek my bane to bake.. . . . . . . . . 313  Psalm XXXI          42
BALANCE
   She holdes the ballance of my contentation:. . . . . . . . .  51  2nd Eclogues 28   118
   That sorrowe's weight dothe balance up thies joyes.. . . . .  71  Arcadia III  36    18
   While he each thing in sense's ballance wayes, . . . . . . . 177  Astrophil    25     6
   That Ballance weigh'd what sword did late obtaine, . . . . . 204  Astrophil    75     8
   The ballance evnly stands; . . . . . . . . . . . . . . . . . 283  Psalm X             60
BALD
   His voice makes bald the forest wast;. . . . . . . . . . . . 310  Psalm XXIX          23
BALE
   But that it is my doome of bale or blisse. . . . . . . . . .  97  3rd Eclogues 64   102
   Who jointly sought my bale to frame; . . . . . . . . . . . . 332  Psalm XL            53
BALEFUL
   Now fancie's fits, now fortune's balefull stowers: . . . . . 103  3rd Eclogues 66   157
BALL
   She ranne away, and threw at me a ball.. . . . . . . . . . .  54  2nd Eclogues 29    89
BALLS
   Balles to the starres, and thralles to Fortune's raigne; . .  57  2nd Eclogues 30    17
BALM
   The baiting place of wit, the balme of woe,. . . . . . . . . 184  Astrophil    39     2
BAND
   Trew harte, whose trewthe dothe yeeld to trewest bande,. . .  70  Arcadia III  35    11
   Chief band I saye, which tyes my chiefest parte, . . . . . .  70  Arcadia III  35    12
   Thinges rightelie prizde, love is the bande of love. . . . .  83  Arcadia III  57    14
   Of my first love the fatall band.. . . . . . . . . . . . . .  90  Arcadia III  62   122
   The bande of beauties all, the little world of Love. . . . . 119  4th Eclogues 73    90
   Band of all evils, cradle of causelesse care,. . . . . . . . 161  Cert Sonnets 31     3
   W. What seale? D. My hart deepe graven. W. Who made the band
      so fast?. . . . . . . . . . . . . . . . . . . . . . . . . 343  Possibly      1    27
   Will. What keepeth safe thy band? D. Remembrance is the
      Chest. . . . . . . . . . . . . . . . . . . . . . . . . . 344  Possibly      1    29
   Which made hir yeeld to deck this shepheards' band,. . . . . 247  Other Poems    4   215
   In firmest band of Unitie. . . . . . . . . . . . . . . . . . 260  Other Poems    6    22
BANDS
   My eyes the bandes, my thoughts the fatall knot. . . . . . .  17  1st Eclogues  7   113
   Bownd and bownd by so noble bandes, as loth to be unbownd, .  37  1st Eclogues 13   162
   If noble be thy bandes, make them notorious: . . . . . . . .  47  2nd Eclogues 28    14
   Bandes, favour, faith, to breake, defile, and kill.. . . . .  84  Arcadia III  60     8
   Those bands alas shall not be dissolv'd. . . . . . . . . . . 153  Cert Sonnets 24    20
   But linkt in binding bands . . . . . . . . . . . . . . . . . 261  Other Poems    6    57
BANE
   Save me from foes who seek my bane to bake.. . . . . . . . . 313  Psalm XXXI          42
   That seek my bane, O make me understand. . . . . . . . . . . 321  Psalm XXXV           5
BANISH
   For she protests to banish thee her face,. . . . . . . . . . 187  Astrophil    46     5
   From comming neare those Cherries banish me: . . . . . . . . 208  Astrophil    82     8
   But her sight his cares did banish,. . . . . . . . . . . . . 218  A&S 8th Song        11
BANISHED
   Her minde, beames, state farre from thy weake wings
      banished . . . . . . . . . . . . . . . . . . . . . . . .  16  1st Eclogues  7    65
   Selfe-lost and wandring, banished that place we doe come
      from,. . . . . . . . . . . . . . . . . . . . . . . . . .  32  1st Eclogues 13    26
```

```
BANISHED                    (CONTINUED)                         PAGE    TITLE           LINE
   A Banisht man, long bard from his desire . . . . . . . . .     75  Arcadia III    44     1
   Am banisht now among the monstrous mountaines. . . . . . .    111  4th Eclogues   71    16
   Care that I sinke in griefe, Care that I live banished?. . .   124  4th Eclogues   74    82
   And banished doo I live, nor now will seeke a recov'rie, . .   124  4th Eclogues   74    83
   Absented? nay I say for ever banished. . . . . . . . . . . .   128  4th Eclogues   75   125
   For ever banish'd from well plac'd affection;. . . . . . . .   130  4th Eclogues   76    29
   Now banisht art, but yet alas how shall? . . . . . . . . . .   202  Astrophil      72    14
   The wicked by his own pride bannisht;. . . . . . . . . . . .   325  Psalm XXXVII         26
BANISHING
   First killing mirth, then banishing all rest,. . . . . . . .   253  Other Poems     4   431
BANK
   Nico. To river's banke, being a walking brought, . . . . . .    55  2nd Eclogues   29   111
   As I my little flocke on Ister banke . . . . . . . . . . . .    98  3rd Eclogues   66     1
   On sandie banke of late,. . . . . . . . . . . . . . . . . .    158  Cert Sonnets   28    33
BANKRCUT
   And by just counts my selfe a banckrout know . . . . . . .    173  Astrophil      18     3
BANKS
   Lift up their stately swelling bankes; . . . . . . . . . . .    88  Arcadia III    62    90
   Shunn lothed-loving bankes with conning crooke:. . . . . . .   257  Other Poems     5    29
BANNER
   Where sweet graces erect the stately banner. . . . . . . . .    67  2nd Eclogues   33     3
   How their blacke banner might be best displaid.. . . . . . .   192  Astrophil      55     8
BANNERS
   My forces razde, thy banners raisd within: . . . . . . . . .   183  Astrophil      36     6
   May joy and banners raise. . . . . . . . . . . . . . . . . .   296  Psalm XX             19
*BAR
   Who at thy beer, as at a barre, shall plead. . . . . . . . .    11  Arcadia I       1     6
   Hastened from us with barre of shadow darke, . . . . . . . .    80  Arcadia III    52    13
   Shall barr that wrong, and though it not prevaile. . . . . .    82  Arcadia III    55    13
   The barre to plead their right,. . . . . . . . . . . . . . .   215  A&S 6th Song         11
*BARE
   Who, where she went, bare in her forhead morning,. . . . . .   113  4th Eclogues   71    70
   While late bare earth, proud of new clothing springeth,. . .   137  Cert Sonnets    4     3
   But in Vert field Mars bare a golden speare, . . . . . . . .   171  Astrophil      13     5
   Her daintiest bare went free; the cause was this,. . . . . .   176  Astrophil      22    13
   Because their forefront bare sweet Stella's name.. . . . . .   190  Astrophil      50    14
   The World's foundations then lay bare because he shent . . .   291  Psalm XVIII          32
   Never the earth on his round shoulders bare. . . . . . . . .   247  Other Poems     4   209
BARED
   A widow turtle neere on bared root . . . . . . . . . . . . .   256  Other Poems     5     6
BARGAIN
   There never was a better bargaine driv'ne. . . . . . . . . .    75  Arcadia III    45     4
BARGE
   Beware full sailes drowne not thy tottring barge:. . . . . .   209  Astrophil      85     2
*BARK
   Till my frayle barke his haven agayn do fynde. . . . . . . .    70  Arcadia III    35     8
   And in this growing barke growe verses myne. . . . . . . . .    77  Arcadia III    47    12
   And gives her kidds no food, but willow's barke.". . . . . .   259  Other Poems     5   113
BARKING
   With neighing, blaying, braying, and barking,. . . . . . . .   100  3rd Eclogues   66    62
*BARKS
   With her faire hande, your tender barkes to cleave,. . . . .    78  Arcadia III    49     6
   In trees) now through your porous barkes receave . . . . . .   125  4th Eclogues   75     5
   He barks, my songs thine owne voyce oft doth prove:. . . . .   194  Astrophil      59     6
BARLEY-BREAK
   With daunces, carols, or with barlybreake: . . . . . . . . .    54  2nd Eclogues   29    70
   At Barly brake hir swete swift foot to trie. . . . . . . . .   247  Other Poems     4   208
   And all to second barly-brake are bent:. . . . . . . . . . .   249  Other Poems     4   266
   And he by law of Barly-brake must run. . . . . . . . . . . .   249  Other Poems     4   296
   Of Barly-brake among the six befell. . . . . . . . . . . . .   250  Other Poems     4   317
   And so that even the barly-brake did end.. . . . . . . . . .   252  Other Poems     4   416
BARRED
   Bard of my will, I have beyond desire: . . . . . . . . . . .    41  Arcadia II     20     7
   Barr'd from their chiefest object of delightfulnesse,. . . .    51  2nd Eclogues   28   109
   A Banish man, long bard from his desire  . . . . . . . . . .    75  Arcadia III    44     1
   Which barde desires, (barde by my selfe) imparte. . . . . .    77  Arcadia III    47    11
   Night bard from Sun, thou from thy owne sunne's light; . . .   229  Astrophil      96     4
   And by his care from them is barr'd. . . . . . . . . . . . .   320  Psalm XXXIV          63
BARREN
   Firr trees great and greene, fixt on a hye hill but a
      barrein,  . . . . . . . . . . . . . . . . . . . . . . . .    35  1st Eclogues   13   123
   On barren sweetes they feede, and feeding sterve:. . . . . .    39  Arcadia II     17     3
   My sonne is gon, your pasture barrein growes,. . . . . . . .    43  Arcadia II     24     2
BARS
   Sweet vertue's lawe barres not a causefull mone. . . . . . .    22  1st Eclogues    9    18
   Peace? what barrs me my tongue? who is it that comes me so
      ny? I. . . . . . . . . . . . . . . . . . . . . . . . . . .    62  2nd Eclogues   31     2
BASAN
   Nay Basan mighty Bulls close me about. . . . . . . . . . . .   299  Psalm XXII           28
BASE
   No stile is held for base, where Love well named is: . . . .    14  1st Eclogues    7     4
   (Since no estates be so base, but love vouchsafeth his
      arrow  . . . . . . . . . . . . . . . . . . . . . . . . . .    33  1st Eclogues   13    50
   Silence doth seeme the maske of base oppression. . . . . . .    47  2nd Eclogues   28    15
   Then base and sower is Love's most high vocation.. . . . . .    48  2nd Eclogues   28    24
   Make her as much more base by loving me. . . . . . . . . . .    72  Arcadia III    38    17
   My state more base, then are the basest vallies: . . . . . .   112  4th Eclogues   71    57
   Who under courtly pompes doo hatch a base desire.. . . . . .   117  4th Eclogues   73    16
   Rich fooles there be, whose base and filthy hart . . . . . .   176  Astrophil      24     1
```

```
BASE                            (CONTINUED)                 PAGE    TITLE          LINE
    From base desire on earthly cates to pray? . . . . . . . .  223 Astrophil    88    8
    So from base slip is stayed. . . . . . . . . . . . . . . .  297 Psalm XXI          28
    Nor kept with base dissemblers company;. . . . . . . . . .  305 Psalm XXVI         15
    Let me not be thrown down to so base shame . . . . . . . .  330 Psalm XXXIX        27
    In poore shepheard's base degree?. . . . . . . . . . . . .  262 Other Poems   7   26
BASER
    Yet yeeld your graunt, a baser hand may leave. . . . . . .   78 Arcadia III  49    9
BASEST
    The highest note comes oft from basest mind, . . . . . . .    4 Lady of May   2   13
    My state more base, then are the basest vallies: . . . . .  112 4th Eclogues 71   57
    That hast my mind, none of the basest, brought . . . . . .  184 Astrophil    40    3
BASHFUL
    So dare I, wretch, my bashfull feare subdue, . . . . . . .    3 Lady of May   1   11
    The honest Bridegroome, and the bashfull Bride,. . . . . .   91 3rd Eclogues 63   13
    Since bashfull dread seekes where he knowes me harmed: . . . 135 Cert Sonnets  1    2
BASILISK
    When first that crowned Basiliske I knewe, . . . . . . . .  115 4th Eclogues 72   72
BASSES
    Trebles sing high, as well as bases deepe: . . . . . . . .  201 Astrophil    70    6
BATE
    Thou setst a bate betweene my will and wit,. . . . . . . .  166 Astrophil     4    2
    Feare not to judge this bate,. . . . . . . . . . . . . . .  215 A&S 6th Song       5
BATEFUL
    Which soone as it did batefull question frame, . . . . . .  247 Other Poems   4  189
BATHE
    I leave mine eyes unwipte my cheekes to bathe. . . . . . .   54 2nd Eclogues 29   80
    Nico. She once starke nak'd did bathe a little tine; . . . .  55 2nd Eclogues 29  105
BATTERED
    Whereto long since, through my long battred eyes,. . . . .  182 Astrophil    36    3
BATTLE
    With him proud battell proved. . . . . . . . . . . . . . .  259 Other Poems   5  123
BATTLE'S
    Though battaile's brunt I needs must beare,. . . . . . . .  307 Psalm XXVII        15
    While battaile's brunt on me were laid . . . . . . . . . .  307 Psalm XXVII        16
BATTLES
    The lord whose strength makes battails fight . . . . . . .  302 Psalm XXIV         20
BAWLING
    For bawling doggs have compast me about, . . . . . . . . .  299 Psalm XXII         39
    Go bawling curre, thy hungry maw go fill,. . . . . . . . .  255 Other Poems   4  517
*BAY
    Which made a Bay, made Bay a holy tree:. . . . . . . . . .   54 2nd Eclogues 29   61
    Beaten with waves, no sooner kennes the baye . . . . . . .   70 Arcadia III  36    3
    While they did ward sun-beames with shady bay, . . . . . .  243 Other Poems   4   66
BEAK
    How rosy moist'ned lipps about his beake . . . . . . . . .  244 Other Poems   4   95
BEAMS
    With gentle beames not hurting sight:. . . . . . . . . . .   13 Arcadia I     5    8
    Her minde, beames, state farre from thy weake wings
        banished . . . . . . . . . . . . . . . . . . . . . . .   16 1st Eclogues  7   65
    My beautie's hewe your beames, my health your deeds; . . .   18 1st Eclogues  7  136
    Thus to my sonne do I yeeld, such lookes her beames do
        aforde me. . . . . . . . . . . . . . . . . . . . . . .   36 1st Eclogues 13  133
    Will at length perceave these flames by her beames to be
        kindled, . . . . . . . . . . . . . . . . . . . . . . .   37 1st Eclogues 13  167
    Apollo great, whose beames the greater world do light, . .   44 Arcadia II   26    1
    Her beames have wrought therin most suer impression: . . .   47 2nd Eclogues 28   11
    Dorus. If Sunnie beames shame heav'nly habitation; . . . .   48 2nd Eclogues 28   22
    Her staines are beames; vertue the fault she blamed is . .   49 2nd Eclogues 28   57
    Cosma's faire beames emblemish much his raies. . . . . . .   55 2nd Eclogues 29   98
    Those beames that set so many harts on fire? . . . . . . .   59 2nd Eclogues 30   84
    Such beames so like his owne, which might have might . . .   60 2nd Eclogues 30  105
    Thy beames I like, but her cleare rayes I love:. . . . . .   72 Arcadia III  38    9
    Howe is my Sunn, whose beames are shining bright,. . . . .   74 Arcadia III  42    1
    Preserve those beames, this age's onely lighte:. . . . . .   79 Arcadia III  51    2
    Is left a Sunne, whose beames thy place may use? . . . . .   80 Arcadia III  52    6
    Such living beames should her blacke seate assaile, . . . .   82 Arcadia III  55   10
    The great beames gone, the house on shoulders light: . . .  102 3rd Eclogues 66  136
    Blinded with beames, fell darkenes is my sight:. . . . . .  113 4th Eclogues 72    8
    Yet living still in her, while her beames lent . . . . . .  115 4th Eclogues 72   83
    "Nay thou (said both) shalt see such beames shine in her
        face . . . . . . . . . . . . . . . . . . . . . . . . .  121 4th Eclogues 73  175
    Within her beames wrapping his cruell staines. . . . . . .  141 Cert Sonnets  8   12
    Finding those beames, which I must ever love,. . . . . . .  149 Cert Sonnets 21    1
    Joyned alas to your beames, . . . . . . . . . . . . . . . .  154 Cert Sonnets 25    4
    So that I in her beames dying, . . . . . . . . . . . . . .  156 Cert Sonnets 26   31
    That no more thy beames availe thee. . . . . . . . . . . .  156 Cert Sonnets 27   20
    That of those beames in you do tarie:. . . . . . . . . . .  159 Cert Sonnets 29   11
    Draw in thy beames, and humble all thy might,. . . . . . .  161 Cert Sonnets 32    5
    Of force of heav'nly beames, infusing hellish paine: . . .  167 Astrophil     6    3
    In colour blacke, why wrapt she beames so bright?. . . . .  168 Astrophil     7    2
    Long since forc'd by thy beames, but stone nor tree. . . .  183 Astrophil    36   13
    Sent forth the beames, which made so faire my race . . . .  185 Astrophil    41   14
    Whose beames be joyes, whose joyes all vertues be, . . . .  185 Astrophil    42    2
    Can those blacke beames such burning markes engrave. . . .  188 Astrophil    47    2
    Meane while my heart confers with Stella's beames, . . . .  190 Astrophil    51   12
    Stella's eyes sent to me the beames of blisse, . . . . . .  199 Astrophil    66   11
    With such a rosie morne, whose beames most freshly gay . .  205 Astrophil    76    7
    Pray that my sunne go downe with meeker beames to bed. . .  205 Astrophil    76   14
    Those lookes, whose beames be joy, whose motion is delight,. 205 Astrophil    77    1
```

BEAMS	(CONTINUED)	PAGE	TITLE		LINE
When Sun is hid, can starres such beames display?.		223	Astrophil	88	6
Where memory sets foorth the beames of love.		223	Astrophil	88	11
Serves thy beames but to disclose, ...		210	A&S 4th Song		20
Fearing her beames, take with thee		226	A&S 10th Song		23
O let them see these heavenly beames, and in faire letters reede.		217	A&S 7th Song		11
Whose beames, where they once are darted,.		218	A&S 8th Song		35
In beams of beauty guilded..		294	Psalm XIX		20
There be no Rea'ms hidd from his beames, ...		294	Psalm XIX		27
My freedom, with show of hir beames, with virtue my content.		344	Possibly	1	38
The darte, the beames, the stringe so stronge I prove; . . .		344	Possibly	2	1
Making hir beames his bravery and might:		246	Other Poems	4	146
Most mad with beames which he thought Cosma sent,.		249	Other Poems	4	270
Hir race did not hir beautie's beames augment, ...		252	Other Poems	4	393
Of Mira's beames eclipst by absence bad.		256	Other Poems	5	11
BEAMY					
Did light those beamye stars which greater light did darke:.		116	4th Eclogues	73	3
They to the beamie Sunnes went,.		154	Cert Sonnets	25	12
Would she in beamie blacke, like painter wise, ...		168	Astrophil	7	3
Whose faire skin, beamy eyes, like morning sun on snow,. . .		169	Astrophil	8	9
That through my heart their beamie darts be gone,.		189	Astrophil	48	10
BEAN					
O breath more sweete, then is the growing beane, ...		76	Arcadia III	46	2
That last day seem'd, he could not chew a beane.		103	3rd Eclogues	67	6
*BEAR					
Who can despaire, whom hope doth beare?.		14	1st Eclogues	6	5
(As his beard him, not he his beard did beare)		25	1st Eclogues	9	91
What be the pangs they beare, and whence those pangs be derived, ...		33	1st Eclogues	13	43
Justely to graunt thy rewarde, such envie I beare to thy fortune.		37	1st Eclogues	13	156
What wooll my sheepe shall beare, whyle thus they live,. . .		39	Arcadia II	17	7
To onely thee my constant course I beare..		40	Arcadia II	18	16
May witnesse beare, how ill agree in one,.		41	Arcadia II	19	11
You beare no woll, and losse is all my gayne..		44	Arcadia II	24	14
For that construction thy owne wordes do beare..		49	2nd Eclogues	28	74
Her sence too weake to beare her spirit's mighte..		79	Arcadia III	51	4
To whome our prince did beare a great good will,.		94	3rd Eclogues	64	16
And as for me (sweete husband) I must beare"..		96	3rd Eclogues	64	62
Least that some markes of jealousie you beare.		97	3rd Eclogues	64	124
Then founde I which thing is a charge to beare		99	3rd Eclogues	66	17
The sheep, mild-seeming face; climing, the Beare;.		101	3rd Eclogues	66	90
We beare our double yoke with such consent,.		106	3rd Eclogues	67	92
Lamde with the angle, which it selfe did beare,.		115	4th Eclogues	72	67
Now bolder waxt, waxt prowde, that I such sway might beare:.		121	4th Eclogues	73	159
Let it embassage beare your grieves to showe..		125	4th Eclogues	75	12
Let pearls be wan with woe their damme doth beare:		125	4th Eclogues	75	23
Who others' woes and plaints can chastly beare:.		142	Cert Sonnets	10	7
Else what in face, then in my fancie beare?.		146	Cert Sonnets	17	10
My hand doth not beare witnesse with my hart,.		146	Cert Sonnets	17	26
Joves golden shield did Eagle sables beare,.		171	Astrophil	13	3
But find some Hercules to beare, in steed.		190	Astrophil	51	7
Of them, who in their lips Love's standerd beare;.		191	Astrophil	54	6
And then with patience bid me beare my fire.		193	Astrophil	56	14
I bare (with Envie) yet I bare your song,.		208	Astrophil	83	5
Now blessed you, beare onward blessed me		209	Astrophil	84	5
O happie Tems, that didst my Stella beare, ...		232	Astrophil	103	1
If I but stars upon mine armour beare, ...		233	Astrophil	104	10
Bare me in hand, that in this Orphane place, ...		235	Astrophil	106	3
Her faire necke a foule yoke bare, ...		218	A&S 8th Song		10
Seing me so long to beare.		222	A&S 9th Song		33
Which beare his people's name, ...		273	Psalm III		35
If ought my hands of wyckednes do bear:.		277	Psalm VII		9
To beare his sacred flight, in secret place then clos'd, . .		291	Psalm XVIII		23
Of him the Feare doth cleaness beare		294	Psalm XIX		37
Our Fathers still in thee their trust did beare, ...		298	Psalm XXII		11
Who feare the lord all prayse and glory beare him;		300	Psalm XXII		53
Though battaile's brunt I needs must beare,.		307	Psalm XXVII		15
Upon his mercy beare..		318	Psalm XXXIII		72
And watch and ward for such do beare		319	Psalm XXXIV		27
Most great and grievous paines doth beare, ...		320	Psalm XXXIV		70
Who did me wrong, against me witness beare		322	Psalm XXXV		25
And whose? ev'n is who when they sickness bare.		322	Psalm XXXV		29
That yet beare love unto my righteousness;		323	Psalm XXXV		68
Which should Thy lessons beare		331	Psalm XL		29
Well might he others beare, but leane to none)		244	Other Poems	4	72
Of village-Lord that whitsontide to beare:		244	Other Poems	4	76
To catch of them, and them to hell to beare, ...		248	Other Poems	4	229
He thrise reacht, thrise deceiv'd when hir to beare.		250	Other Poems	4	340
To beare the bondes which Time nor wit could breake, ...		255	Other Poems	4	530
BEARD					
Who once a white long beard, well handle does, ...		25	1st Eclogues	9	90
(As his beard him, not he his beard did beare)		25	1st Eclogues	9	91
Till with lickt beard, his eye of fire espie his foes. . . .		53	2nd Eclogues	29	36
BEAREST					
Thou bear'st the arrow, I the arrow head..		198	Astrophil	65	14
*BEARS					
What circle then in so rare force beares swaye?.		17	1st Eclogues	7	109
Which so much reason beares, ...		18	1st Eclogues	7	148

```
*BEARS                        (CONTINUED)          PAGE    TITLE           LINE
    Whiche beares the bytt a weaker force doth guide,. . . . . .   20 1st Eclogues   7 V959
    Yet beares he still his parents' stately gifts,. . . . . . .   21 1st Eclogues   8   25
    Passion beares high when puffing wit doth blowe,. . . . . .    25 1st Eclogues   9  114
    Neither he beares reverence to a Prince nor pittie to
        begger . . . . . . . . . . . . . . . . . . . . . . . . .   31 1st Eclogues  13    5
    What horrors breede, wheare wynd dominion beares,. . . . . .   71 Arcadia III   37    2
    Then that which beares the mylken name.. . . . . . . . . . .   87 Arcadia III   62   60
    No Elephant so perfect beares. . . . . . . . . . . . . .       86 Arcadia III   62 V 28
    (As Tygers, leopards, beares, and Lions' seed) . . . . . .   102 3rd Eclogues  66  122
    While each conceate an ouglie figure beares, . . . . . . .   131 Arcadia V     77    7
    And doth she know what mould her beautie beares? . . . . .   142 Cert Sonnets  11    2
    That who indeed infelt affection beares, . . . . . . . . .   195 Astrophil     61    5
    As consterd in true speech, the name of heav'n it beares,. . 205 Astrophil     77   11
    Yet growest more wretched then thy nature beares,. . . . . .  228 Astrophil     94   13
    "But the wrongs love beares, will make . . . . . . . . . .   234 A&S 11th Song      31
BEAS
    He treble beas for helpe, but none can get:. . . . . . . .   254 Other Poems    4  492
BEAST
    But take this beast, if beasts you feare to misse, . . . .     4 Lady of May    2   29
    For of his beasts the greatest beast he is.. . . . . . . .     4 Lady of May    2   30
    That I growe like the beaste,. . . . . . . . . . . . . . .    20 1st Eclogues   7 V958
    His damme a beast was pardon'd beastly fact. . . . . . . .    21 1st Eclogues   8   18
    Thus halfe a beast, ech beastly vice he plants,. . . . . .    21 1st Eclogues   8   33
    Like beast for sacrifice, where save the tong. . . . . . .    24 1st Eclogues   9   81
    He is a beast, that beaste's use will allowe . . . . . . .    25 1st Eclogues   9   99
    This man, this talking beast, this walking tree. . . . . .    58 2nd Eclogues  30   34
    To let that witolde beast consume in flames. . . . . . . .    60 2nd Eclogues  30  111
    Ech other beast likewise his present brings: . . . . . . .   101 3rd Eclogues  66   99
    No beast should freely speake, but onely he. . . . . . . .   101 3rd Eclogues  66  105
    As this poore beast who did his rest forsake,. . . . . . .   145 Cert Sonnets  16    7
    And now man's wrongs in me, poore beast, descrie.. . . . .   189 Astrophil     49    4
BEASTLY
    His damme a beast was pardon'd beastly fact. . . . . . . .    21 1st Eclogues   8   18
    Thus halfe a beast, ech beastly vice he plants,. . . . . .    21 1st Eclogues   8   33
    The beastes had sure some beastly pollicie:. . . . . . . .   100 3rd Eclogues  66   50
BEAST'S
    He is a beast, that beaste's use will allowe . . . . . . .    25 1st Eclogues   9   99
BEASTS
    But take this beast, if beasts you feare to misse, . . . .     4 Lady of May    2   29
    For of his beasts the greatest beast he is.. . . . . . . .     4 Lady of May    2   30
    In hunting fearefull beastes, do spend some dayes, . . . .    25 1st Eclogues   9  123
    Was onely won'd with such as beastes begot:. . . . . . . .   100 3rd Eclogues  66   45
    The beastes had sure some beastly pollicie:. . . . . . . .   100 3rd Eclogues  66   50
    This thinke I well, the beasts with courage clad . . . . .   100 3rd Eclogues  66   55
    (As even in beasts their dammes leave chaunging parts) . .   100 3rd Eclogues  66   60
    "O beasts, take heed what you of me desire.. . . . . . . .   100 3rd Eclogues  66   72
    Then gan he factions in the beastes to breed;. . . . . . .   102 3rd Eclogues  66  120
    Where helping weaker sort, the nobler beastes, . . . . . .   102 3rd Eclogues  66  121
    By those great beastes, as for the weaker's good,. . . . .   102 3rd Eclogues  66  128
    And you poore beastes, in patience bide your hell, . . . .   103 3rd Eclogues  66  153
    Long since my thoughts chase me like beasts in forrests, .   112 4th Eclogues  71   35
    Of herbes or beastes, which Inde or Afrike hold. . . . . .   166 Astrophil      3    8
    O birds, o beasts, looke Love, lo, Stella shineth. . . . .   209 A&S 3rd Song       12
    The birds, beasts, stones and trees feele this, and feeling
        love: . . . . . . . . . . . . . . . . . . . . . . . . .  209 A&S 3rd Song       13
    Nor beasts, nor birds do come unto this blessed gaze,. . .   209 A&S 3rd Song       15
    And all the beasts for ever breeding . . . . . . . . . . .   279 Psalm VIII         27
    Knowing full well that beasts they be. . . . . . . . . . .   315 Psalm XXXII        34
    Yea beasts made safe thy goodness try. . . . . . . . . . .   323 Psalm XXXVI        18
BEASTS'
    He did to beastes' best use his cunning frame; . . . . . .   101 3rd Eclogues  66  108
BEAT
    Then him we kisse, whom late before we beatt . . . . . . .    27 1st Eclogues  10   37
    The kindly way to beate us on to blisse. . . . . . . . . .    59 2nd Eclogues  30   76
    My Foe came on, and beat the aire for me,. . . . . . . . .   191 Astrophil     53   13
    Did beate their hands, which durst so neere to presse. . .   252 Other Poems    4  406
    Nor beat you for your play,. . . . . . . . . . . . . . . .   257 Other Poems    5   36
BEATEN
    "Poore Pan" (he sayd) "although thou beaten be,. . . . . .     5 Lady of May    3   11
    Beaten with waves, no sooner kennes the baye . . . . . . .    70 Arcadia III   36    3
    Sore beaten doth her mast of Comforte spende:. . . . . . .   114 4th Eclogues  72   45
    Now I, wit-beaten long by hardest Fate,. . . . . . . . . .   195 Astrophil     60    9
    Gallein's adoptive sonnes, who by a beaten way . . . . . .   232 Astrophil    102    9
    Sweet babes must babies have, but shrewd gyrles must be
        beat n. . . . . . . . . . . . . . . . . . . . . . . . .  213 A&S 5th Song       36
    I bett them as the clay is bett in beaten wayes. . . . . .   293 Psalm XVIII        77
BEATING
    Biting my trewand pen, beating my selfe for spite, . . . .   165 Astrophil      1   13
BEATINGS
    Whose braines boile not in woes, nor brests with beatings
        ake, . . . . . . . . . . . . . . . . . . . . . . . . .  117 4th Eclogues  73   13
BEAUTIES
    Whose vertues strange, and beuties such, as no man them may
        know?. . . . . . . . . . . . . . . . . . . . . . . . .   12 Arcadia I      3    2
    Doth beauties keep, which never Sunne can burne, . . . . .    18 1st Eclogues   7  118
    To open eyes all beauties he doth raine; . . . . . . . . .    22 1st Eclogues   8   39
    Vertue, richesse, beawties of mine shall great be reputed. .  34 1st Eclogues  13   81
    But still (me thought) with beauties from her fell,. . . .    55 2nd Eclogues  29  106
    Shall I that saw those brests, where beauties flow,. . . .    58 2nd Eclogues  30   47
```

BEAUTIES	(CONTINUED)	PAGE	TITLE		LINE
She heav'n on earth with beauties doth preserve.		72	Arcadia III	38	8
Like divers flowers, whose divers beauties serve		78	Arcadia III	50	1
Thy running course cannot such beawties marke:		80	Arcadia III	52	11
Let not these slumbring clowds thy beawties hide,.		91	3rd Eclogues	63	11
Whose beawties shin'de more then the blushing morning, . . .		113	4th Eclogues	71	62
Her giftes my study was, her beauties were my sporte:. . . .		117	4th Eclogues	73	41
The bande of beauties all, the little world of Love.		119	4th Eclogues	73	90
Ne yet for what I see, your beauties merite ought.		121	4th Eclogues	73	164
So deepe in seas of vertue beauties ly..		151	Cert Sonnets	22	58
But eyes these beauties see not, ...		152	Cert Sonnets	23	25
She even in blacke doth make all beauties flow?.		168	Astrophil	7	11
Beauties, which were of manie Carrets fine,.		172	Astrophil	16	2
Yet were the hid and meaner beauties parcht, ...		176	Astrophil	22	12
And can with foule abuse such beauties blot;		177	Astrophil	24	11
Are Beauties there as proud as here they be?		180	Astrophil	31	11
Whole armies of thy beauties entred in..		182	Astrophil	36	4
Rich in all beauties which man's eye can see:.		183	Astrophil	37	6
Beauties so farre from reach of words, that we		183	Astrophil	37	7
Nymph of the gard'n, where all beauties be:.		207	Astrophil	82	1
Beauties which do in excellencie passe		207	Astrophil	82	2
While wanton winds with beauties so devine		232	Astrophil	103	6
"What if you new beauties see, ...		234	A&S 11th Song		21
The perfect beauties be..		216	A&S 6th Song		23
And hidden beauties find, ...		217	A&S 6th Song		52
Allarme allarme, let not their beauties move		346	Possibly	5	5
The hidden beauties seem'd in waite to lye,.		250	Other Poems	4	303
BEAUTIFIER					
Sweetner of musicke, wisedome's beautifier:.		207	Astrophil	80	6
BEAUTIFIES					
While gracefull pitty beauty beautifies.		231	Astrophil	100	4
For beautie beautifies,.		216	A&S 6th Song		19
BEAUTIFUL					
That I within the ports most beautyfull.		280	Psalm IX		41
BEAUTIFY					
Which doth even beautie beautifie, ...		90	Arcadia III	62	137
BEAUTY					
Infernall agonies unto a bewtye divine,.		30	1st Eclogues	11	14
And vertue is gratefull with bewty and richnes adorned,. . .		33	1st Eclogues	13	57
First shall vertue be vice, and bewty be counted a blemishe,		33	1st Eclogues	13	67
Joyn'd, by thy beauty adorn'd, be no meanes these greefes to					
abolish:.		34	1st Eclogues	13	99
Beautie his Booke, his play lovers' dissention:.		48	2nd Eclogues	28	42
Thy Venus' child, whose beautie Venus lackes?.		60	2nd Eclogues	30	112
Whence can pride come there, since springs of beawty be					
thence? Thence..		65	2nd Eclogues	31	44
Of fortune's Diademes, by beauty mustred..		67	2nd Eclogues	33	5
Yet joyning formes one sight of beautie breede..		78	Arcadia III	50	4
Beautie hath force to catche the humane sight.		82	Arcadia III	57	1
Vertue, beawtie, and speach, did strike, wound, charme,. . .		84	Arcadia III	60	1
A whiter beautie you may see..		85	Arcadia III	62	6
Whose steppe on earth all beautie sets..		89	Arcadia III	62	108
Which doth even beautie beautifie, ...		90	Arcadia III	62	137
Or with her beawtie fit to make a pray,.		94	3rd Eclogues	64	8
In her let beautie both, and chastnesse fully raigne.. . . .		120	4th Eclogues	73	132
She had chiefe Goddesses in beautie overcome..		120	4th Eclogues	73	146
Her beautie kindle shall within thy foolish minde, ...		121	4th Eclogues	73	171
Can death beautie become? must I be such a monument?		123	4th Eclogues	74	32
If the Love hate you dyd, you should your beautie have					
hidden:.		123	4th Eclogues	74	47
He would not arm'd with beautie, only raigne		135	Cert Sonnets	2	5
Sleepe Babie mine, Desire, nurse Beautie singeth:.		139	Cert Sonnets	6	1
One of other beautie takes..		140	Cert Sonnets	7	17
A seate where beauty shines and vertue raignes,.		141	Cert Sonnets	8	10
And doth she know what mould her beautie beares?		142	Cert Sonnets	11	2
Or cruell (still) time did your beautie staine:.		148	Cert Sonnets	19	8
Beautie tied to vertue,.		154	Cert Sonnets	25	6
No man doubts, whom beautie killeth, ...		156	Cert Sonnets	26	27
Who hath such beautie seene.		158	Cert Sonnets	28	25
What Love and Beautie be, then all my deed		166	Astrophil	3	13
True, that true Beautie Vertue is indeed,.		167	Astrophil	5	9
Whereof this Beautie can be but a shade, ...		167	Astrophil	5	10
Vertue's great beautie in that face I prove, ...		177	Astrophil	25	13
Princesse of Beautie, for whose only sake.		179	Astrophil	28	6
And then, thinke thus, although thy beautie be		185	Astrophil	40	9
O eyes, which do the Spheares of beautie move, ...		185	Astrophil	42	1
Vertue awake, Beautie but beautie is,.		188	Astrophil	47	9
And therefore, though her beautie and her grace.		191	Astrophil	52	9
How Vertue may best lodg'd in beautie be,.		201	Astrophil	71	2
So while thy beautie drawes the heart to love, ...		201	Astrophil	71	12
That face, whose lecture shewes what perfect beautie is: . .		205	Astrophil	77	2
Since all my words thy beauty doth endite, ...		224	Astrophil	90	13
While gracefull pitty beauty beautifies.		231	Astrophil	100	4
Beauty is sicke, but sicke in so faire guise,.		231	Astrophil	101	5
Who long dead beautie with increase reneweth?.		197	A&S 1st Song		22
Whose force but yours the bolts of beautie thunders?		197	A&S 1st Song		30
Lowring beautie chastens me:		203	A&S 2nd Song		26
Your power in your beautie stands:		211	A&S 4th Song		46
Beauty, musicke, sweetnesse, love..		226	A&S 10th Song		34
Never doth thy beauty florish.		234	A&S 11th Song		29

BEAUTY (CONTINUED) PAGE TITLE LINE
This side doth beauty take,. . . . . 215 A&S 6th Song 7
For beautie beautifies,. . . . . 216 A&S 6th Song 19
Beauty as farre excels,. . . . . 216 A&S 6th Song 27
Beauty brings to the hall,. . . . . 216 A&S 6th Song 39
Whose face all, all beauty passeth,. . . . . 219 A&S 8th Song 43
Woe, lyke a moth, my face's beauty eates . . . . 276 Psalm VI 21
In beams of beauty guilded.. . . . . 294 Psalm XIX 20
On beauty His my eyes to stay. . . . . 307 Psalm XXVII 22
Thou moth like mak'st his beauty fading be;. . . . . 330 Psalm XXXIX 35
To seek Thy beauty past conceit; . . . . 332 Psalm XL 62
So brave a shott, deere fyre and bewtye strange. . . . . . 345 Possibly 2 11
From Nous and Cosma all their beauty tooke.. . . . . 248 Other Poems 4 248
Left Nous to coast the loved beauty ny.. . . . . 249 Other Poems 4 284
(Yet beauty still as fast as she did sturre) . . . . 251 Other Poems 4 358
BEAUTY'S
Judge you to whom all beautie's force is lent. . . . . . . 4 Lady of May 2 31
Measure my case, how by thy beautie's filling. . . . . . . 16 1st Eclogues 7 77
My beautie's hewe your beames, my health your deeds; . . . 18 1st Eclogues 7 136
(Whiche hyding didest preserve that beawtie's light, . . . 70 Arcadia III 35 2
(Of passions darke, made darke by beautie's light) . . . . 72 Arcadia III 39 2
With beautie's seale, and vertue faire disguis'de, ... 85 Arcadia III 61 2
A way more worthie beautie's fame, ... 87 Arcadia III 62 59
Thus hath each part his beautie's part,. . . . . 90 Arcadia III 62 133
Though rapt with beautie's hooke, I did impart . . . . . . 150 Cert Sonnets 22 26
That whereas blacke seemes Beautie's contrary, ... 168 Astrophil 7 10
Which Cupid's selfe from Beautie's myne did draw:. . . . . 169 Astrophil 9 13
Where Vertue is made strong by Beautie's might,. . . . . . 188 Astrophil 48 2
In Beautie's throne, see now who dares come neare. . . . . 203 Astrophil 73 10
Beautie's plague, Vertue's scourge, succour of lies: . . . 206 Astrophil 78 6
Where Beautie's blush in Honour's graine is dide.. . . . . 207 Astrophil 80 8
See Beautie's totall summe summ'd in her face: . . . . . . 210 Astrophil 85 10
Some beautie's peece, as amber colourd hed,. . . . . 225 Astrophil 91 6
O teares, no teares, but raine from beautie's skies, . . . 231 Astrophil 100 1
That in that palenesse beautie's white we see; . . . . . . 231 Astrophil 101 6
While beautie's reddest inke Venus for him doth sturre.. . 232 Astrophil 102 14
The proofe of Beautie's worth, th'enheritrix of fame,. . . 213 A&S 5th Song 20
Nor debard from beautie's treasure. . . . . 226 A&S 10th Song 9
To beautie's lovely light, ... 216 A&S 6th Song 32
Who have so leaden eyes, as not to see sweet beautie's show, 217 A&S 7th Song 7
Yeelde yeelde O yeelde, trust not on beautie's pride,. . . 345 Possibly 4 5
Each motion seeming shott from beautie's bow,. . . . . . . 244 Other Poems 4 106
Vertue's proofe, fortune's victor, beautie's place.. . . . 252 Other Poems 4 392
Hir race did not hir beautie's beames augment, ... 252 Other Poems 4 393
BEA-WAYMENTING
Still for thy Dam with bea-waymenting crie?. . . . . 258 Other Poems 5 78
BECAME
The wretch compell'd a runnagate became, ... 21 1st Eclogues 8 21
Philisides. If fortune's lappe became my dwelling place, . 23 1st Eclogues 9 26
Thus Man was made; thus Man their Lord became: . . . . . . 101 3rd Eclogues 66 106
BECAUSE
Because from him doth come her light:. . . . . 13 Arcadia I 5 10
In painted clothes, because they call it love. . . . . . . 23 1st Eclogues 9 48
Because thou hast thy fellow overgone, ... 27 1st Eclogues 10 11
Because I red him, as I would my son.. . . . . 27 1st Eclogues 10 23
P. Because our weaknes weakeneth all your might. . . . . . 46 2nd Eclogues 27 22
I cherish his, because in me it bides. . . . . 76 Arcadia III 45 8
Because that thou, the author of our sight,. . . . . 80 Arcadia III 52 14
Because themselves they cannot see.. . . . . 86 Arcadia III 62 22
Who yet was good, because she knewe none ill,. . . . . . . 94 3rd Eclogues 64 14
Because in wrestling and in pastorall. . . . . 94 3rd Eclogues 64 17
He still hop'd well, because I loved truth;. . . . . 99 3rd Eclogues 66 38
Because (though hurt) they never heard her grone.. . . . . 102 3rd Eclogues 66 119
For because my cheefe part singeth, ... 140 Cert Sonnets 7 35
She saith, because I make no wofull laies, ... 146 Cert Sonnets 17 27
Whose eyes seeme chaste, because they looke on ground: . . 147 Cert Sonnets 17 50
Cupid, because thou shin'st in Stella's eyes,. . . . . . . 170 Astrophil 12 1
Because that Mars, growne slacker in her love, ... 173 Astrophil 17 2
Or carelesse of the wealth because her owne: . . . . 176 Astrophil 22 11
Others, because the Prince my service tries, ... 176 Astrophil 23 7
Because I oft in darke abstracted guise, ... 178 Astrophil 27 1
And I, but for because my prospect lies. . . . . 179 Astrophil 29 13
Others, because of both sides I do take. . . . . 185 Astrophil 41 9
Because their forefront bare sweet Stella's name.. . . . . 190 Astrophil 50 14
Because I breathe not love to everie one,. . . . . 191 Astrophil 54 1
But thou Desire, because thou wouldst have all,. . . . . . 202 Astrophil 72 13
And yet my Starre, because a sugred kisse. . . . . 203 Astrophil 73 5
Because in brave array heere marcheth she, ... 223 Astrophil 88 3
But why? because of you they models be,. . . . . 225 Astrophil 91 10
Because my Foes to fly are now constraind. . . . . 279 Psalm IX 6
The World's foundations then lay bare because he shent . . 291 Psalm XVIII 32
By him because I did find in his eyes' sight grace,. . . . 292 Psalm XVIII 41
Because I walk'd his wayes, nor gainst him ev'ly went, . . 292 Psalm XVIII 44
And why all this? Because Our King . . . . 297 Psalm XXI 25
Because of those . . . . 308 Psalm XXVII 53
Because that word of his . . . . 316 Psalm XXXIII 16
Because on him their trust is laid.. . . . . 327 Psalm XXXVII 104
Why? because I virtue chose. . . . . 329 Psalm XXXVIII 60
That Foxes leave to steale, because they finde they dy
   therefore. . . . . 344 Possibly 1 44

```
BECAUSE                 (CONTINUED)                          PAGE    TITLE           LINE
     Strephon, poor youth, because he saw no smoke, . . . . . . .   253 Other Poems      4   427
BECK
     Rules with a becke, so tyrannizeth thee, . . . . . . . . . .   187 Astrophil       46    3
BECKONED
     (She beckned unto me) as yet of spotlesse truth, . . . . . .   120 4th Eclogues 73  138
BECLOUDED
     Painted in my beclowded stormie face:. . . . . . . . . . . .   187 Astrophil       45    2
BECOME
     Come shepheard's weedes, become your master's minde: . . . .    13 Arcadia I        4    1
     So faire a fielde would well become an owner. . . . . . . . .    17 1st Eclogues     7   99
     That I become a vision, . . . . . . . . . . . . . . . . . .     20 1st Eclogues     7 V963
     Let not thy tonge become a firy matche,. . . . . . . . . . .    29 1st Eclogues    10   89
     So become our tombes monuments of her praise;. . . . . . . .    30 1st Eclogues    12   10
     Come cave, become my grave, come death, and lende. . . . . .    73 Arcadia III     40    7
     Become the cause of my darke ouglie night? . . . . . . . . .    74 Arcadia III     42    2
     O time, become the chariot of my joyes:. . . . . . . . . . .    80 Arcadia III     53    9
     Can death beautie become? must I be such a monument? . . . .   123 4th Eclogues    74   32
     No doome should make one's heav'n become his hell. . . . . .   212 Astrophil       86   14
     Become the measure. . . . . . . . . . . . . . . . . . . . .    276 Psalm VI              4
     That Jacob freed by Thee may glad become . . . . . . . . . .   287 Psalm XIV            23
     But I like a man become, . . . . . . . . . . . . . . . . . .   328 Psalm XXXVIII        37
     "Another time", quoth she, "become more wise". . . . . . . .   249 Other Poems      4  275
     Doth daily haunt: but so, that mine become . . . . . . . . .   255 Other Poems      4  503
     Tell me, if your diverted springs become . . . . . . . . . .   257 Other Poems      5   37
     Canst thou, poore lamme, become another's lamme? . . . . . .   258 Other Poems      5   76
BECOMES
     So becomes our losse the triumph of her gayne; . . . . . . .    30 1st Eclogues    12   11
     Thus Death becomes a rivall to us all, . . . . . . . . . . .    59 2nd Eclogues    30   89
     Blacke incke becommes the state wherein I dye. . . . . . . .    81 Arcadia III     54    6
     Knowing that evill becommes a houshold strife, . . . . . . .    96 3rd Eclogues    64   70
     And well (me thinks) becomes this vaultie skie . . . . . . .   126 4th Eclogues    75   58
     Whose necke becomes such yoke of tyranny?. . . . . . . . . .   188 Astrophil       47    4
     Becomes a clog) will soone ease me of it.. . . . . . . . . .   194 Astrophil       59   14
     When bedd from rest becomes his seat of woe, . . . . . . . .   333 Psalm XLI             9
BECOMETH
     Becommeth us: in us fortune determines not.. . . . . . . . .   120 4th Eclogues    73  140
     And thinke how evill becommeth him to slide, . . . . . . . .   144 Cert Sonnets    32   11
     My feete are turn'd to rootes, my hart becommeth lead, . . .   215 A&S 5th Song         77
BECOMING
     Becomming every time and place,. . . . . . . . . . . . . . .    90 Arcadia III     62  136
BED
     Came to the bed, where wound for kisse he got, . . . . . . .     5 Lady of May      3    8
     Aurora like new out of bed,. . . . . . . . . . . . . . . . .    86 Arcadia III     62   24
     His death-bed peacock's follie,. . . . . . . . . . . . . . .   160 Cert Sonnets    30   13
     Take thou of me smooth pillowes, sweetest bed, . . . . . . .   184 Astrophil       39    9
     Pray that my sunne go downe with meeker beames to bed. . . .   205 Astrophil       76   14
     Ah bed, the field where joye's peace some do see, . . . . . .   230 Astrophil       98    1
     Stella is sicke, and in that sicke bed lies. . . . . . . . .   231 Astrophil      101    1
     These sweet flowers on fine bed too,. . . . . . . . . . . . .   210 A&S 4th Song         15
     Your faire mother is a bed,. . . . . . . . . . . . . . . . .   211 A&S 4th Song         37
     My moystned bed proofes of my sorrow showeth:. . . . . . . .   276 Psalm VI             18
     My bed, while I with black night mourn alone,. . . . . . . .   276 Psalm VI             19
     Let them in bedd of endless silence dy.. . . . . . . . . . .   313 Psalm XXXI           48
     When bedd from rest becomes his seat of woe, . . . . . . . .   333 Psalm XLI             9
     Or scatter on her bedd,. . . . . . . . . . . . . . . . . . .   257 Other Poems      5   49
BEDECKED
     Her twinkling eies bedeckt with pearle, her lips of Saphir
     blew:. . . . . . . . . . . . . . . . . . . . . . . . . . . .    12 Arcadia I        3   10
     Proudly bedeckt in Aprill's livory,. . . . . . . . . . . . .   253 Other Poems      4  453
BEDIM
     Let clouds bedimme my face, breake in mine eye, . . . . . . .   198 Astrophil       64    5
BEDS
     Through him the floods to their beds fell. . . . . . . . . .   302 Psalm XXIV            4
BEE
     Who though she be no Bee, yet full of honie is:. . . . . . .    15 1st Eclogues     7   29
BEEN
     But if I had bene there, th'adst met another mate. . . . . .    52 2nd Eclogues    29   22
     Pas. If each day hath bene holy for your sake, . . . . . . .    54 2nd Eclogues    29   72
     He chose themselves his guarders for to bene,. . . . . . . .   102 3rd Eclogues    66  129
     These fiftie winters maried have I beene;. . . . . . . . . .   106 3rd Eclogues    67   86
     Or where one's love so constant bene,. . . . . . . . . . . .   158 Cert Sonnets    28   27
     That I had bene more foolish or more wise. . . . . . . . . .   181 Astrophil       33   14
     Doubt there hath bene, when with his golden chaine . . . . .   193 Astrophil       58    1
     I had bene vext, if vext I had not beene.. . . . . . . . . .   223 Astrophil       87   14
     Envious wits what hath bene mine offence,. . . . . . . . . .   233 Astrophil      104    1
     If I have been unkynd for friendly part: . . . . . . . . . .   277 Psalm VII            10
     Then out his arrowes fly, and streight they scatterd been, . .  291 Psalm XVIII          29
     What had I been, except I had. . . . . . . . . . . . . . . .   308 Psalm XXVII          61
     I have been younge now old I am, . . . . . . . . . . . . . .   326 Psalm XXXVII         61
     Have been my ill feeding food, . . . . . . . . . . . . . . .   334 Psalm XLII           10
     That from those eies where heav'nly apples bene . . . . . . .   253 Other Poems      4  450
BEES
     Cherish the hives of wisely painfull Bees: . . . . . . . . .    26 1st Eclogues     9  132
BEFALL
     And first Lambe that shall befall, . . . . . . . . . . . . .   264 Other Poems      7   69
BEFELL
     Of Barly-brake among the six befell. . . . . . . . . . . . .   250 Other Poems      4  317
BEFORE
     The wood cries most, before it throughly kindled be, . . . .    14 1st Eclogues     7    8
```

	PAGE	TITLE		LINE
BEFORE (CONTINUED)				
Then him we kisse, whom late before we beatt	27	1st Eclogues	10	37
Three dayes before that he must sure depart, ...	96	3rd Eclogues	64	79
Before all flies the Waspe accept I would.	104	3rd Eclogues	67	18
How well last day before our Prince you could.	106	3rd Eclogues	67	97
Full dead before, I now to dust should fall, ...	116	4th Eclogues	72	86
And now before we seeke by wise Apollo's skill	120	4th Eclogues	73	125
Having before me Nature's treasure, ...	159	Cert Sonnets	29	6
Having no scarfe of clowds before his face, ...	176	Astrophil	22	3
Before she could prepare to be unkind, ...	193	Astrophil	57	6
Will she take time, before all wracked be?	199	Astrophil	67	4
What sighes stolne out, or kild before full borne?	199	Astrophil	67	9
That where before hart loved and eyes did see, ...	223	Astrophil	88	12
Yet alas before you go, ...	221	A&S 9th Song		11
But nake'd before thine eyes	283	Psalm X		57
As he before his eyes did see my justice stand, ...	292	Psalm XVIII		48
Made worshipers before Almighty Thee..	300	Psalm XXII		68
Before me Thou a table setst, ...	301	Psalm XXIII		16
Before my eyes did stand	305	Psalm XXVI		11
For my annoyes have come before thyne eye, ...	312	Psalm XXXI		20
Before his eyes that so doth stray..	323	Psalm XXXVI		6
Lord before Thee I do lay.	328	Psalm XXXVIII		25
For aye before Thy face.	334	Psalm XLI		44
Dick. Good Will, I cannot take thy good advice, before . . .	344	Possibly	1	43
Before thassault beginne, O yeelde O yeelde.	345	Possibly	4	14
And so must see great cause before they love..	245	Other Poems	4	144
Made them his owne before they had it wist..	246	Other Poems	4	159
He that before shund hir to shun such harmes, ...	252	Other Poems	4	383
BEG				
I beg no subject to use eloquence, ...	179	Astrophil	28	9
Whose wages makes me beg the more, who feeds me till I				
sterve, ...	343	Possibly	1	20
BEGAN				
As I began, so must I ende..	90	Arcadia III	62	144
For to my dimmed eyes beganne t'appeare.	103	3rd Eclogues	66	159
And wanting use of eyes their eyes began to close:	116	4th Eclogues	73	6
Thus both did come to me, and both began to tell	121	4th Eclogues	73	154
But when the rod began to play his part, ...	246	Other Poems	4	183
The play began: Pas durst not Cosma chace, ...	248	Other Poems	4	249
It ended, but the others' woe began, ...	252	Other Poems	4	417
Began at least to be conceiv'd as woe.	252	Other Poems	4	418
BEGGAR				
Neither he beares reverence to a Prince nor pittie to				
begger	31	1st Eclogues	13	5
BEGGARLY				
Great be Physitions' brags, but aid is beggerly, ...	128	4th Eclogues	75	112
BEGGARS'				
Such planted gifts enrich even beggers' sight:	3	Lady of May	1	10
BEGGARY				
May get no almes but scorne of beggerie.	188	Astrophil	47	8
Of Love, new-coind to helpe my beggery, ...	196	Astrophil	62	13
Free of proud feares, brave begg'ry, smiling strife. . . .	243	Other Poems	4	60
BEGGING				
Nor that his seed to begging came.	326	Psalm XXXVII		64
BEGIN				
Begin (and halfe the worke is done) to prove	23	1st Eclogues	9	50
Now by thy words I begin, most famous Lady, to gather. . .	34	1st Eclogues	13	94
Fore-felt Desire, begin to savour parte.	83	Arcadia III	59	11
Diana did begin. "What mov'd me to invite.	119	4th Eclogues	73	102
Let them be clearde, and now begin to see, ...	131	Arcadia V	77	11
Stella behold, and then begin to endite.	172	Astrophil	15	14
But wilt new warre upon thine owne begin?.	183	Astrophil	36	8
Doth Stella now begin with piteous eye, ...	199	Astrophil	67	2
Now child, a lesson new you shall begin to spell:	213	A&S 5th Song		35
Thus I begin. I sought	319	Psalm XXXIV		13
Lo I now to mourn begin.	329	Psalm XXXVIII		52
O heale my soul, let there Thy cure begin.	333	Psalm XLI		15
Before thassault beginne, O yeelde O yeelde.	345	Possibly	4	14
Allarme allarme, companions nowe beginne, ...	346	Possibly	5	9
Speeche without ende were better not begin.	259	Other Poems	5	104
BEGINNING				
Her praise, whence to the world all praise had his only				
beginning:	33	1st Eclogues	13	69
Both cause, effect, beginning, and the ende.	114	4th Eclogues	72	42
BEGINS				
In flowrie fielde; and as the day begins	18	1st Eclogues	7	125
Or when an Echo begins unmov'd to sing them a love song. . .	33	1st Eclogues	13	48
Pan is not dead, since Pas beginnes to sing.	53	2nd Eclogues	29	53
My sowle beginnes to take leave.	66	2nd Eclogues	32	15
As soon as Sunne begins to clime the mountaines:	112	4th Eclogues	71	44
This night while sleepe begins with heavy wings.	183	Astrophil	38	1
Only in you my song begins and endeth.	196	A&S 1st Song		4
Above line repeated at following location.	197	A&S 1st Song		36
BEGOT				
Was onely won'd with such as beastes begot:	100	3rd Eclogues	66	45
Of hopes begot by feare, of wot not what desires:	167	Astrophil	6	2
Thou art my son in deed, this day begott by me:	271	Psalm II		17
BEGUILED				
Fie death, thou art beguiled.	137	Cert Sonnets	3	23
With what pastime, time's journey she beguilde, ...	225	Astrophil	92	12

```
                                                                PAGE    TITLE          LINE
BEGUN
    Who have their lesson so long time begonne?. . . . . . . .    27  1st Eclogues 10   27
    In stede of Thought, true pleasure be begunne, . . . . . .    84  Arcadia III  59   15
    Then from his depth with force in her begunne, . . . . . .   150  Cert Sonnets 22   17
    But that in building they begunne. . . . . . . . . . . .     284  Psalm XI           9
    While daunce about the may-pole is begun, . . . . . . . .    243  Other Poems   4   55
    As she a black-silke cap on him begunne. . . . . . . . . .   244  Other Poems   4   85
BEHALF
    Affection's charmes in my behalfe to prove.. . . . . . . .    17  1st Eclogues  7  102
BEHELD
    To worthiest let him give, when both he hath beheld: . . . .  120  4th Eclogues 73  142
    Mine eyes (shall I say curst or blest) beheld. . . . . . .   173  Astrophil    16   10
BEHEST
    She answer'd was with looke, and well performed behest:. . .  119  4th Eclogues 73   99
    According to my Lord Love's owne behest: . . . . . . . . .   189  Astrophil    50    6
BEHIND
    And so behinde foule clowdes full oft faire starres do ly
        hidden". . . . . . . . . . . . . . . . . . . . . . . .    36  1st Eclogues 13  154
    As I behynde a Busshe dyd sitt . . . . . . . . . . . . . .    57  2nd Eclogues 30    1
    (For both togither spake, each loth to be behinde) . . . .   121  4th Eclogues 73  155
    Yet of that best thou leav'st the best behind. . . . . . .   170  Astrophil    11    4
    He saw behind a bush where Klaius sate:. . . . . . . . . .   255  Other Poems   4  527
BEHOLD
    O descende for a while, from this greate height to behold
        me . . . . . . . . . . . . . . . . . . . . . . . . . .    36  1st Eclogues 13  149
    But nought els do behold (else is nought worth the
        beholding . . . . . . . . . . . . . . . . . . . . . . .   36  1st Eclogues 13  150
    Where senses do behold th'order of heav'nly hoste, . . . .    68  2nd Eclogues 34    5
    And wise thoughts do behold what the creator is: . . . . .    68  2nd Eclogues 34    6
    And so refuse to behold of these strange wounds the
        recitall . . . . . . . . . . . . . . . . . . . . . . .   122  4th Eclogues 74    7
    Behold Love's mightie hand . . . . . . . . . . . . . . . .   158  Cert Sonnets 28   38
    Stella behold, and then begin to endite. . . . . . . . . .   172  Astrophil    15   14
    And so nor will, nor can, behold those skies . . . . . . .   177  Astrophil    25    7
    Those faire wonders to behold, . . . . . . . . . . . . . .   226  A&S 10th Song     17
    Behold the evill have bent their bow . . . . . . . . . . .   284  Psalm XI           5
    Behold me, lord, let to Thy hearing creep. . . . . . . . .   285  Psalm XIII         9
    Behold they cry, but who to them his help applys?. . . . .   292  Psalm XVIII       74
    Behold their broken shame! . . . . . . . . . . . . . . . .   296  Psalm XX          31
    Behold my Foes, what store they be,. . . . . . . . . . . .   304  Psalm XXV         65
    Behold (beholding well it doth deserve). . . . . . . . . .   244  Other Poems   4   82
BEHOLDETH
    When Moone and starrs my thoughtes beholdeth . . . . . . .   278  Psalm VIII        11
BEHOLDING
    But nought els do behold (else is nought worth the
        beholding . . . . . . . . . . . . . . . . . . . . . . .   36  1st Eclogues 13  150
    Rather then have thy all-beholding eye . . . . . . . . . .   126  4th Eclogues 75   56
    Behold (beholding well it doth deserve). . . . . . . . . .   244  Other Poems   4   82
BEHOLDS
    Beholds our mortall race;. . . . . . . . . . . . . . . . .   317  Psalm XXXIII      51
BEHOOVED
    He had as him behoved. . . . . . . . . . . . . . . . . . .   297  Psalm XXI          8
BEING
    When being askt, now that he did obtaine . . . . . . . . .     4  Lady of May   3    3
    That Goddesse mine, my blessed being sees".. . . . . . . .     4  Lady of May   3    6
    Which being nought seems somewhat to the eyen, . . . . . .    19  1st Eclogues  7  164
    Which hath in others' head his only being. . . . . . . . .    20  1st Eclogues  7 V964
    In being heard untill the hearer dye . . . . . . . . . . .    24  1st Eclogues  9   70
    Nico. To river's banke, being a walking brought,. . . . .    55  2nd Eclogues 29  111
    Which being pure and plaine, . . . . . . . . . . . . . . .    93  3rd Eclogues 63   62
    Which being done he afterwards would kill. . . . . . . . .   102  3rd Eclogues 66  126
    His very being he hath not deserved, . . . . . . . . . . .   105  3rd Eclogues 67   79
    Whereby that being aye must be conserved.. . . . . . . . .   106  3rd Eclogues 67   81
    No being now, but sorowe I can have: . . . . . . . . . . .   114  4th Eclogues 72   27
    In face and eyes unmatched being,. . . . . . . . . . . . .   159  Cert Sonnets 29    7
    As who by being poisond doth poison know.. . . . . . . . .   173  Astrophil    16   14
    And if these things, as being thine by right,. . . . . . .   184  Astrophil    39   12
    I lodg'd thee in my heart, and being blind . . . . . . . .   198  Astrophil    65    7
    By being placed in such a wretch as I. . . . . . . . . . .   228  Astrophil    94   14
    Being (ah) exild, disdayneth . . . . . . . . . . . . . . .   233  A&S 11th Song      4
    All his commandments being . . . . . . . . . . . . . . . .   294  Psalm XIX         34
    Thus much I said, this being said. . . . . . . . . . . . .   311  Psalm XXX         33
    This being thus, For what O Lord wait I? . . . . . . . . .   330  Psalm XXXIX       23
    E're I my earthly being leave. . . . . . . . . . . . . . .   330  Psalm XXXIX       42
    Ah, when comes my blessed being, . . . . . . . . . . . . .   334  Psalm XLII         7
    That Thy anger being spent,. . . . . . . . . . . . . . . .   335  Psalm XLII        36
    The Arrow being shot from far, doth give the smaller blowe..  344  Possibly      1   42
    His being was in her alone:. . . . . . . . . . . . . . . .   241  Other Poems   3    1
    And he not being, she was none.. . . . . . . . . . . . . .   241  Other Poems   3    2
    From alwayes with you beeing... . . . . . . . . . . . . .    261  Other Poems   6   46
BELIEF
    Thus my beleefe was staid, . . . . . . . . . . . . . . . .   158  Cert Sonnets 28   37
BELIEVE
    Happie be they which well beleeve, and never seeke the rest.   12  Arcadia I     3   14
    When that noble toppe doth nodd, I beleeve she salutes me; .  36  1st Eclogues 13  144
    Beleeve me man, there is no greater blisse,. . . . . . . .   103  3rd Eclogues 67    7
    Beleeve them not, for Phisicke true doth finde,. . . . . .   147  Cert Sonnets 17   51
    To make my selfe beleeve, that all is well,. . . . . . . .   166  Astrophil     2   13
    Now be still, yet still beleeve me,. . . . . . . . . . . .   220  A&S 8th Song      75
    And still, beleve me, Strephon was at hand.. . . . . . . .   247  Other Poems   4  216
```

```
                                                              PAGE    TITLE          LINE
BELIEVED
    How much more we do love, so the lesse our loves be
      beleeved . . . . . . . . . . . . . . . . . . . . . .    32  1st Eclogues 13    20
    My love should not be beleeved, . . . . . . . . . . . .  222  A&S 9th Song       39
    Beleiv'd God's goodnesse for to see, . . . . . . . . . . 308  Psalm XXVII        62
BELIEVES
    And now fully beleeves helpe to be quite perished; . . . 122  4th Eclogues 74     2
BELL
    So caught, him seem'd he caught of joyes the bell, . . . 250  Other Poems   4   311
BELLIES
    Whose bellyes so with daintys Thou dost fill . . . . . . 290  Psalm XVII         41
BELLOWS
    For bellowes serve to kindle more the fire.. . . . . . .  38  Arcadia II   14     8
BELLS
    Ring out your belles, let mourning shewes be spread, . . 159  Cert Sonnets 30     1
BELLY
    And belly nought is left, such sure is he, . . . . . . .  24  1st Eclogues  9    82
    The bellie there gladde sight doth fill, . . . . . . . .  88  Arcadia III  62    77
BELONG
    Doth teach, to learne the good what travailes do belong: .  45  Arcadia II   26     8
    And with more, by the lawes that to Revenge doo belong. . . 123  4th Eclogues 74    42
    Salvation doth belong. . . . . . . . . . . . . . . . . . 273  Psalm III          31
BELONGING
    Seaze on all to her belonging; . . . . . . . . . . . . . 226  A&S 10th Song      21
    On yond foule flocke belonging not to me." . . . . . . . 255  Other Poems   4   518
BELONGS
    It belongs to such alone . . . . . . . . . . . . . . . . 262  Other Poems   7    27
BELOVED
    Faire seeke not to be feard, most lovely beloved by thy
      servants, . . . . . . . . . . . . . . . . . . . . . . 143  Cert Sonnets 14     1
    You witch, you Divill, (alas) you still of me beloved, . . . 215  A&S 5th Song       87
    Toward Lamkins best beloved. . . . . . . . . . . . . . . 221  A&S 9th Song       25
    Deare beloved Holy One, . . . . . . . . . . . . . . . . 288  Psalm XVI          35
    As Brothers, or as Friends beloved much; . . . . . . . . 322  Psalm XXXV         34
    To joyne sweet friends beloved.. . . . . . . . . . . . . 260  Other Poems   6    16
    The number best beloved, . . . . . . . . . . . . . . . . 261  Other Poems   6    26
BELOW
    Then sent he from above, and took me from below, . . . . 291  Psalm XVIII        34
BEMIRED
    And me from pitt bemyred, . . . . . . . . . . . . . . . 331  Psalm XL            5
BEMCAN
    Lalus. This mayde, thus made for joyes, o Pan bemone her, . .  17  1st Eclogues  7    97
    We mone that lost, which had we did bemone. . . . . . . .  59  2nd Eclogues 30    82
    But yet the common Damme none did bemone; . . . . . . . . 102  3rd Eclogues 66   118
    For though I oft my selfe of them bemone, . . . . . . . . 189  Astrophil    48     9
BEMOANS
    My mind bemones his sense of inward smart; . . . . . . . 186  Astrophil    44     2
BENAMED
    And therefore he a courtier was benamed, . . . . . . . .  94  3rd Eclogues 64    19
BEND
    Who doth his soule to endlesse malice bend.. . . . . . .  22  1st Eclogues  9    10
    She oft her lookes, the starres her favour bend to thee: . .  51  2nd Eclogues 28    99
    Seeing, Alas, so mightie powers bende. . . . . . . . . .  73  Arcadia III  40     5
    Bend all thy light to see. . . . . . . . . . . . . . . .  80  Arcadia III  52     9
    Iron to seeke, which gainst it selfe should bend, . . . . 102  3rd Eclogues 66   116
    My ship, my selfe, whose course to love doth bende, . . . 114  4th Eclogues 72    44
    And from our burning breath the trees doo bende. . . . . 116  4th Eclogues 72   104
    And to revenge who doo bend, would in that kind be revenged, 123  4th Eclogues 74    39
    Bend your thoghts to the dear sweet words which then to me
      giv'n were: . . . . . . . . . . . . . . . . . . . . . 124  4th Eclogues 74    75
    Till that they doo unto our dolours bende: . . . . . . . 126  4th Eclogues 75    39
    And unto death bend still our thoughts' direction. . . . 130  4th Eclogues 76    34
    I see my course to lose my selfe doth bend: . . . . . . . 174  Astrophil    18    12
    "Scholler," saith Love, "bend hitherward your wit.". . . 174  Astrophil    19    14
    Soule's joy, bend not those morning starres from me, . . . 188  Astrophil    48     1
    So all things whereto that man doth bend, . . . . . . . . 270  Psalm I            11
    And will my waiting eyes to thee ward bend.. . . . . . . 274  Psalm V             8
    So shall all they that trust in thee do bend, . . . . . . 275  Psalm V            33
    Who dost Thy saving health to true men bend. . . . . . . 277  Psalm VII          30
    They that know Thee, on Thee their trust will bend, . . . 280  Psalm IX           28
    Thyne Ears voutchsafe to bend to me. . . . . . . . . . . 289  Psalm XVII          4
    He did himself to me ward bend, . . . . . . . . . . . . . 330  Psalm XL            3
    But fill their hearts with joy, who bend their wayes . . . 332  Psalm XL           61
    Whose mettall stiff he knew he could not bende . . . . . 245  Other Poems   4   138
    Each way, as she, that age's praise, did bend. . . . . . 251  Other Poems   4   376
BENDED
    Then rase, but rase on leggs with faintnes bended, . . . 259  Other Poems   5   116
BENDING
    And bending humbled eyes (o eyes the Sunne of sight) . . 119  4th Eclogues 73    91
BENDS
    But when my Sunne her shining twinnes there bends, . . . 150  Cert Sonnets 22    16
    As you, alas, my Sunne bends; . . . . . . . . . . . . . . 154  Cert Sonnets 25    26
    Bends all his powers, even unto Stella's grace.. . . . . 178  Astrophil    27    14
    As fast thy Vertue bends that love to good:. . . . . . . 201  Astrophil    71    13
    Whose fury bends to harme: . . . . . . . . . . . . . . . 283  Psalm X            66
    Who bends not wandring eyes. . . . . . . . . . . . . . . 331  Psalm XL           17
BENDST
    Therfore thou whetst Thy sword, and bend'st Thy bow, . . . 278  Psalm VII          34
BENIGHTED
    Benighted in cold wo, but now appeares my day, . . . . . 204  Astrophil    76     3
```

41

BENT		PAGE	TITLE		LINE
Judge you of Love, to whom all Love is bent.		4	Lady of May	2	32
Bent to such one, in whom, my selfe must say,.		17	1st Eclogues	7	107
When that we see our ofspring gaily bent,.		28	1st Eclogues	10	59
Hardly remains fyer hid, where skill is bent to the hiding,.		33	1st Eclogues	13	59
R. Whom Passion leades unto his death is bent.		46	2nd Eclogues	27	9
Let all for her, and unto her be bent.		60	2nd Eclogues	30	124
If that to sing thou arte bent		66	2nd Eclogues	32	20
Or if to love thou art bent, ...		66	2nd Eclogues	32	25
Oh! if such a one have bent to a lonely life		69	2nd Eclogues	34	39
Rysing from lowe, are to the highest bente;.		78	Arcadia III	49	16
But that her husband thought her service bent.		95	3rd Eclogues	64	27
With mortall disdaine, bent to unendly revenge?.		123	4th Eclogues	74	36
For I to teach the world complainte am bent.		127	4th Eclogues	75	66
You fairer still, and still more cruell bent,.		148	Cert Sonnets	19	15
As her words had it bent?.		158	Cert Sonnets	28	24
On Cupid's bow how are my heart-strings bent,.		174	Astrophil	19	1
Was not in fault, who bent thy dazling race.		235	Astrophil	105	3
But both to both so bent, ...		216	A&S 6th Song		35
And shalt root out the tongues to lying bent:.		275	Psalm V		14
Bent to revenge and ever hating.		278	Psalm VIII		8
With winking eyes aye bent		282	Psalm X		35
Behold the evill have bent their bow		284	Psalm XI		5
All plung'd in stinking filth, not One well bent,.		286	Psalm XIV		11
My cryes clim'd up and he bent down from sacred throne,. . .		291	Psalm XVIII		13
The Mountains proudly high, and their ffoundations bent. . .		291	Psalm XVIII		16
Sound and upright with him, tc wickednes not bent.		292	Psalm XVIII		46
The firmament, so strangely bent,.		293	Psalm XIX		3
Who be to vaineness bent,.		305	Psalm XXVI		14
O now be bent.		316	Psalm XXXIII		11
Is bent, but bent against those same		320	Psalm XXXIV		58
In summe, I shew'd, that I to them was bent.		322	Psalm XXXV		33
The ev'ill bent bowes, and swords they drew,.		325	Psalm XXXVII		37
As Strephon's eare and heart to Klaius bent:		242	Other Poems	4	28
And all to second barly-brake are bent:.		249	Other Poems	4	266
I thinke you thinke Strephon bent thitherward.		250	Other Poems	4	320
BENUMBED					
Her hand benumde with fortune's daylie blows,.		81	Arcadia III	54	3
BEQUEATHING					
Praying, prayers still bequeathing		335	Psalm XLII		39
BEREAVE					
For how would you the mistresse' thoughts bereave.		78	Arcadia III	49	11
Sea drownd in thee, of tedious life bereave me:.		136	Cert Sonnets	3	15
And seek of life for to bereave him;		326	Psalm XXXVII		82
BEREAVED					
Till of these thoughts thy sodaine ende bereaved me.		48	2nd Eclogues	28	33
Now set thy triumph in this world, bereaved.		127	4th Eclogues	75	73
For it was of use bereaved,.		139	Cert Sonnets	7	6
Is so of skill bereaved, ...		293	Psalm XIX		10
BEREFT					
Have of joyes bereft me?		336	Psalm XLIII		12
BESEECH					
Cackling, and chattring, that of Jove beseech.		100	3rd Eclogues	66	67
BESETST					
For thou Deare lord Thou me besetst,.		301	Psalm XXIII		13
BESETIETH					
My life besetteth.		276	Psalm VI		24
BESIDE					
His lambs were him beside, ...		256	Other Poems	5	5
BESIDES					
Besides, lo here the auther.		67	2nd Eclogues	32	46
Though you besides such graces earth hath lent,.		77	Arcadia III	49	3
For who is God, besides this Great Jehova Ours?.		292	Psalm XVIII		57
And so besides our God, who is indue'd with might?		292	Psalm XVIII		58
Besides this force, within hir eies he kept.		246	Other Poems	4	153
More then, besides hir, all the earth could show.		252	Other Poems	4	408
BESIEGING					
On my beseiging Enemyes;		307	Psalm XXVII		32
BESOUGHT					
But ever since that well is well besought, ...		55	2nd Eclogues	29	109
BEST					
As for those parts unknowne, which hidden sure are best: . .		12	Arcadia I	3	13
Of best things then what world can yeeld confection.		15	1st Eclogues	7	46
She is her selfe, of best things the collection.		15	1st Eclogues	7	48
Our best defenses are to flie these adders.		50	2nd Eclogues	28	89
To whether with best cause the Nymphes faire flowers					
affoord		52	2nd Eclogues	29	28
That profit may ensue to him that best can do.		53	2nd Eclogues	29	30
Dicus. Enough, enough: so ill hath done the best,.		56	2nd Eclogues	29	147
Then to an earnest Love what doth best victorie lend? Ende..		63	2nd Eclogues	31	15
Bitter griefe tastes me best, paine is my ease,.		74	Arcadia III	41	7
Seeke then and see, what man esteemeth best, ...		75	Arcadia III	44	5
The best things still must be forgotten.		88	Arcadia III	62	86
Languet, the shepheard best swift Ister knewe, ...		99	3rd Eclogues	66	23
He said, the Musique best thilke powers pleasd		99	3rd Eclogues	66	29
He did to beastes' best use his cunning frame;		101	3rd Eclogues	66	108
Desire's best meane, harvest of hartes affected, ...		108	Arcadia IV	69	2
Turning to desarts our best pastur'de mountaines..		113	4th Eclogues	71	72
When they by yeares' experience get best graces, ...		127	4th Eclogues	75	89
That she her child, I say, her best child killeth?		127	4th Eclogues	75	95

```
BEST                       (CONTINUED)                          PAGE    TITLE          LINE
   Goodnes for best attire in dust is dressed.. . . . . . . . .  128  4th Eclogues  75   120
   Which to our darkned mindes was best direction;. . . . . .    129  4th Eclogues  76     9
   As treasure house where her best gifts abyde.. . . . . . . .  141  Cert Sonnets   8     8
   Then might I thinke what thoughts were best to thinke:  . . .  148  Cert Sonnets  19     5
   I deemd it best some absence for to prove, . . . . . . . . .  149  Cert Sonnets  21     3
   Burn'd by the light he best liked, . . . . . . . . . . . . .  154  Cert Sonnets  25    16
   In object best to knit and strength our sight, . . . . . . .  168  Astrophil      7     6
   Which dare claime from those lights the name of best,. . . .  169  Astrophil      9    11
   That when the heav'n to thee his best displayes, . . . . . .  170  Astrophil     11     3
   Yet of that best thou leav'st the best behind. . . . . . . .  170  Astrophil     11     4
   My best wits still their owne disgrace invent: . . . . . . .  174  Astrophil     19     5
   And not in Nature for best fruits unfit: . . . . . . . . . .  174  Astrophil     19    13
   That makes me oft my best friends overpasse, . . . . . . . .  178  Astrophil     27    12
   To portrait that which in this world is best.. . . . . . . .  189  Astrophil     50     8
   How their blacke banner might be best displaid.. . . . . . .  192  Astrophil     55     8
   In well raisde notes, my pen the best it may . . . . . . . .  201  Astrophil     70    10
   Wise silence is best musicke unto blisse.. . . . . . . . . .  201  Astrophil     70    14
   How Vertue may best lodg'd in beautie be,. . . . . . . . . .  201  Astrophil     71     2
   In verse, and that my verse best wits doth please? . . . . .  204  Astrophil     74    11
   Makes me in my best thoughts and quietst judgement see,. . .  205  Astrophil     77    12
   Yet ah, my Mayd'n Muse doth blush to tell the best.. . . . .  205  Astrophil     77    14
   Best charge, and bravest retrait in Cupid's fight, . . . . .  206  Astrophil     79     5
   Since best wits thinke it wit thee to admire;. . . . . . . .  206  Astrophil     80     2
   That sickenesse brags it selfe best graced to be.. . . . . .  231  Astrophil    101     4
   Us in their best language woo: . . . . . . . . . . . . . . .  210  A&S 4th Song        16
   Ech tree in his best attiring, . . . . . . . . . . . . . . .  219  A&S 8th Song        59
   Toward Lamkins best beloved. . . . . . . . . . . . . . . . .  221  A&S 9th Song        25
   This is all the best I prove,. . . . . . . . . . . . . . . .  288  Psalm XVI            7
   And count this life their Portion best . . . . . . . . . . .  290  Psalm XVII          40
   He shall be by best teacher taught.. . . . . . . . . . . . .  304  Psalm XXV           48
   Indeed the very best . . . . . . . . . . . . . . . . . . . .  320  Psalm XXXIV         69
   At best is merely vanity.. . . . . . . . . . . . . . . . . .  330  Psalm XXXIX         18
   Lockt fast with knowing that she is, of worldly things the
      best.. . . . . . . . . . . . . . . . . . . . . . . . . .  344  Possibly       1    30
   Where failing is a shame, and breaking is his best.. . . . .  241  Other Poems    1     6
   For they seem'd made even of skie-mettall best,. . . . . . .  244  Other Poems    4   100
   So is in her the best of Nature spent, . . . . . . . . . . .  249  Other Poems    4   299
   For they were ever in the best degree, . . . . . . . . . . .  252  Other Poems    4   394
   I go about, but then is all my best. . . . . . . . . . . . .  254  Other Poems    4   470
   Fearing the worst, not knowing what were best, . . . . . . .  255  Other Poems    4   525
   The number best beloved, . . . . . . . . . . . . . . . . . .  261  Other Poems    6    26
   Can Love's duties best fulfill:. . . . . . . . . . . . . . .  263  Other Poems    7    38
   That the meane estate is best, . . . . . . . . . . . . . . .  264  Other Poems    7    76
BEST-GRACED
   Admitted late by your best-graced grace, . . . . . . . . . .  208  Astrophil     82    10
BESTOW
   Which if you will (o doo) bestow on me,. . . . . . . . . . .   18  1st Eclogues   7   121
BESTOWS
   Of all the powers which life bestowes on me, . . . . . . . .  236  Astrophil    107     2
   This small light the Moone bestowes, . . . . . . . . . . . .  210  A&S 4th Song        19
BET
   I bett those folks as small as dust, which wind doth rayse;.  293  Psalm XVIII         76
   I bett them as the clay is bett in beaten wayes. . . . . . .  293  Psalm XVIII         77
BETAKE
   At mother's breastes, thou didst good hope betake me.. . . .  299  Psalm XXII          22
BETAKEN
   Yet I the man that was betaken . . . . . . . . . . . . . . .  326  Psalm XXXVII        62
BETEARED
   But to the Cedar, Queene of woods, when I lifte my beteard
      eyes,. . . . . . . . . . . . . . . . . . . . . . . . . .   36  1st Eclogues  13   141
BETHINK
   Ewe doth make me be thinke what kind of bow the boy holdeth.   35  1st Eclogues  13   121
BETIDE
   With recklesness what may thy house betide,. . . . . . . . .   93  3rd Eclogues  63    75
   Histor. No doubt to whom so good chance did betide,. . . . .  104  3rd Eclogues  67    13
   So may thee still betide . . . . . . . . . . . . . . . . . .  257  Other Poems    5    54
BETIME
   So shall my voice clime to thyne eares betime: . . . . . . .  274  Psalm V              5
BETOKEN
   Some say it doth betoken wonders neare . . . . . . . . . . .   81  Arcadia III   55     2
BETRAY
   Of mine owne wordes, my owne good hap betray,. . . . . . . .  145  Cert Sonnets  16    10
   Thus to betray my hart's fort, . . . . . . . . . . . . . . .  154  Cert Sonnets  25    10
BETRAYED
   What, have I thus betrayed my libertie?. . . . . . . . . . .  188  Astrophil     47     1
BETTER
   And plaine speach oft then quaint phrase better framed is. .   14  1st Eclogues   7     6
   Who frownes at others' feastes, dooth better bide away.. . .   15  1st Eclogues   7    15
   Then let thy minde with better bookes be tamed,. . . . . . .   25  1st Eclogues   9   120
   What if Laelaps a better morsell fyndes. . . . . . . . . . .   26  1st Eclogues  10     7
   Then do I thinke in deed, that better it is to be private. .   35  1st Eclogues  13   102
   Better yet do I live, that though by my thoughts I be
      plunged. . . . . . . . . . . . . . . . . . . . . . . . .   35  1st Eclogues  13   107
   And if I better sing, let me thy Cosma kisse.. . . . . . . .   53  2nd Eclogues  29    38
   Dicus. Sing then my lads, but sing with better vaine then
      yet, . . . . . . . . . . . . . . . . . . . . . . . . . .   53  2nd Eclogues  29    49
   Nico his place farre better furnish will.. . . . . . . . . .   53  2nd Eclogues  29    56
   Make present ease receave the better taste.. . . . . . . . .   70  Arcadia III   36     6
   There never was a better bargaine driv'ne. . . . . . . . . .   75  Arcadia III   45     4
```

BETTER	(CONTINUED)	PAGE	TITLE		LINE
(Better despisde) bewondre gasing eye.		81	Arcadia III	54	12
They better live that in a gaile doo lie..		105	3rd Eclogues	67	54
A better life it is to lye alone..		105	3rd Eclogues	67	57
Who may this doubt discerne: for better, witt, then lot. . .		120	4th Eclogues	73	139
You better sure shall live, not evermore		142	Cert Sonnets	12	1
Better like I thy Satyre deerest Dyer, ...		145	Cert Sonnets	16	13
Better then one captiv'd perceiveth, ...		159	Cert Sonnets	29	16
For vertue hath this better lesson taught,.		161	Cert Sonnets	31	12
Of Stella's browes made him two better bowes,.		173	Astrophil	17	10
I, seeing better sights in sight's decay,.		184	Astrophil	38	12
That giv'st no better eare to my just cries:		198	Astrophil	65	2
Looke on againe, the faire text better trie:		199	Astrophil	67	7
Better place no wit can find,.		210	A&S 4th Song		13
Concord better fitteth us:		211	A&S 4th Song		44
Seeke a better place of feeding, ...		221	A&S 9th Song		2
Small goodes in good men better is		325	Psalm XXXVII		41
That in her doings better could compare.		247	Other Poems	4	211
Speeche without ende were better not begin..		259	Other Poems	5	104
Better filled with contenting, ...		264	Other Poems	7	77
BETTER-LOVED					
To make thee nor thy better-loved rue:		258	Other Poems	5	81
BETWEEN					
Was jumpe concorde betweene our wit and will:.		99	3rd Eclogues	66	30
But betweene those armes, never else do leave mee;		138	Cert Sonnets	5	23
Thou setst a bate betweene my will and wit,.		166	Astrophil	4	2
Phoebus was Judge betweene Jove, Mars, and Love, ...		171	Astrophil	13	1
Th'indifferent Judge betweene the high and low;.		184	Astrophil	39	4
A strife is growne betweene Vertue and Love, ...		190	Astrophil	52	1
Betweene the jawes of hellish Jealousie.		205	Astrophil	78	4
How tenderly hir tender hands betweene		244	Other Poems	4	93
BETWIXT					
Betwixt the good and shade of good divided,.		62	2nd Eclogues	30	179
Betwixt which two in me I have this fight, ...		74	Arcadia III	42	7
Betwixt these two a way doth lie,.		87	Arcadia III	62	58
And yet in all this time, betwixt us tway, ...		106	3rd Eclogues	67	91
Betwixt us two; how much that discord foule hath stain'd . .		119	4th Eclogues	73	106
Let us a perfect peace betwixt us two resolve:		120	4th Eclogues	73	127
Sigh they did, but now betwixt		218	A&S 8th Song		17
Betwixt them two the peeper tooke his nest,.		244	Other Poems	4	102
BEWAIL					
These cocklinges cockred we bewaile to late, ...		28	1st Eclogues	10	58
Bewaile the case, and in the cause delight?.		74	Arcadia III	42	4
Shepheards bewaile your uttermost confusion;		128	4th Eclogues	75	121
Use thy words but to bewaile thee,.		156	Cert Sonnets	27	19
BEWAILING					
And mournfully bewailing,.		137	Cert Sonnets	4	5
BEWARE					
Beware full sailes drowne not thy tottring barge:.		209	Astrophil	85	2
BEWITCH					
Sight doth bewitch, the fancie evill awaked.		82	Arcadia III	57	2
And most bewitch the wretched eye, ...		90	Arcadia III	62	138
BEWITCHED					
Sure I bewitched am, it is even that:.		253	Other Poems	4	447
And, but bewitch'd, who to his flock would mone?		254	Other Poems	4	460
"Nay each thing is bewitcht to know my case:		254	Other Poems	4	473
BEWONDER					
(Better despisde) bewondre gasing eye.		81	Arcadia III	54	12
BEWRAY					
As do bewray a want of inward tuch:.		172	Astrophil	15	10
Bewray it selfe in my long setled eyes,.		176	Astrophil	23	2
BEYOND					
Looke to thy selfe; reach not beyond humanitie:.		16	1st Eclogues	7	64
Bard of my will, I have beyond desire:		41	Arcadia II	20	7
Her eyes the force beyond my possibilitie.		48	2nd Eclogues	28	30
Slander wants a pretext, flattery gone beyond:		69	2nd Eclogues	34	38
You onely yours, too farr beyond desarte..		79	Arcadia III	50	22
Beyond our worlde, and ere I gatt my boothe.		98	3rd Eclogues	66	4
Beyond the heaven, far more beyond your witts.		99	3rd Eclogues	66	28
But yet o man, rage not beyond thy neede:.		103	3rd Eclogues	66	148
As th'offence was done, and goe beyond if he can..		123	4th Eclogues	74	40
Thee to thy wracke beyond thy limits straine..		210	Astrophil	85	4
Our tongues, say they, beyond them all shall go, ...		285	Psalm XII		10
BIAS					
And that the bias of hir bloud was wrought..		244	Other Poems	4	101
BID					
She byd me spie her babie in the brooke, ...		55	2nd Eclogues	29	112
Or art thou from above bid play this part, ...		142	Cert Sonnets	10	11
And then with patience bid me beare my fire.		193	Astrophil	56	14
BIDDEN					
Bid'n, perhaps he fetcheth thee a glove, ...		194	Astrophil	59	7
BIDE					
Who frownes at others' feastes, dooth better bide away.. . .		15	1st Eclogues	7	15
Joie's strangers seeme, I cannot bide their showe, ...		74	Arcadia III	41	5
Whose loves may ever bide, ...		91	3rd Eclogues	63	14
And you poore beastes, in patience bide your hell, ...		103	3rd Eclogues	66	153
He were a foole, if there he did not bide..		104	3rd Eclogues	67	15
More happie I, might I in bondage bide..		144	Cert Sonnets	15	14
The new Pernassus, where the Muses bide, ...		207	Astrophil	80	5
For all I neede, that with such foes do byde..		275	Psalm V		24

BIDE   (CONTINUED)   PAGE   TITLE   LINE

	PAGE	TITLE		LINE
O let their wickedness no longer bide.	277	Psalm VII		25
His lovely face on them doth bide.	284	Psalm XI		22
So shall I bide well purify'd.	295	Psalm XIX		59
My cleaving tongue close to my roofe doth bide..	299	Psalm XXII		36
Within the bounds of Innocence to byde,	305	Psalm XXVI		3
Ev'en Deserts where the Arabs byde...	310	Psalm XXIX		21
When I within the pitt do bide;	311	Psalm XXX		27
The good mouth will in Wisdom bide,.	326	Psalm XXXVII		77
Lord while that thy rage doth bide,.	327	Psalm XXXVIII		1
Happy, o happy! if they so might bide,	252	Other Poems	4	401

BIDED
| Whose stormelike course staid not till hard by me it bided.. | 118 | 4th Eclogues 73 | | 60 |

BIDES
| I cherish his, because in me it bides. | 76 | Arcadia III | 45 | 8 |

BIDEST
| O well thou doost that thou no longer bidest; | 126 | 4th Eclogues 75 | | 53 |

BIDETH
| But who doth feare, or bideth muet wilfully, | 48 | 2nd Eclogues 28 | | 17 |
| For my mind on my God bideth, | 335 | Psalm XLII | | 25 |

BIDING
In my lips to have his biding,	226	A&S 10th Song		27
Lift up your heads you Gates, and you doores ever biding,.	302	Psalm XXIV		17
Above line repeated at following location.	302	Psalm XXIV		21
Ev'n where Thou makest Thy honour's biding place..	306	Psalm XXVI		27
To songs and joyfull byding.	315	Psalm XXXII		27
Where hath now your God his biding?.	335	Psalm XLII		48

BIDS
Thy father bids thee save, and chides for spilling..	16	1st Eclogues 7		79
She bids him goe, and yet from jorney stayes...	104	3rd Eclogues 67		36
Bids you leave such minds to nourish."	234	A&S 11th Song		27

BIER
| Who at thy beer, as at a barre, shall plead. | 11 | Arcadia I | 1 | 6 |

BILLING
| But you must needs with those lips billing be? | 208 | Astrophil | 83 | 12 |

BIND
Rebell, Rebell, in golden fetters binde.	23	1st Eclogues 9		44
That he, to whome these sondrie giftes I binde,	78	Arcadia III 50		9
First, second, last, did binde, enforce, and arme,	84	Arcadia III 60		3
For by and by the horse faire bitts did binde:	102	3rd Eclogues 66		137
(Which made of heav'nly stuffe no mortal chaunge doth bynde)	117	4th Eclogues 73		32
That they by solemne oth their Deities would binde	121	4th Eclogues 73		156
Since loosing long, the faster still I bind:	135	Cert Sonnets 1		5
But now the starres with their strange course do binde	148	Cert Sonnets 20		5
Of sorrowe's droppes, till colder reason binde	150	Cert Sonnets 22		37
This heaven in it doth binde..	152	Cert Sonnets 23		24
The Oratour so farre men's harts doth bind,	193	Astrophil	58	2
Thou whom to me such my good turnes should bind,	198	Astrophil	65	3
Cupid's yoke to loose or bind:	210	A&S 4th Song		14
But on god's law his heart's delight doth bind,	270	Psalm I		5
With perjury doth falsly bind.	302	Psalm XXIV		12
Most to Thy lawdes will I my speeches bind..	322	Psalm XXXV		48
Did me pearce, burne, and bynde, long since and late,.	345	Possibly	2	12
In ivory cage she did the micher binde:.	244	Other Poems	4	94
In which by will, my will and wits I binde:.	255	Other Poems	4	500

BINDING
| But linkt in binding bands | 261 | Other Poems | 6 | 57 |

BINDS
| No time within his limites binds... | 326 | Psalm XXXVII | | 76 |

BIRD
Wherein the birde doth never sing but cry;	105	3rd Eclogues 67		50
Or as the silly birde in well acquainted nest.	117	4th Eclogues 73		23
A bird which gets more life then ship had lost..	151	Cert Sonnets 22		54
The Bird free Burgess of the ayre,	279	Psalm VIII		29
That like a byrd to some strong hill	283	Psalm XI		3
How well apaid she was hir birde to finde:	244	Other Poems	4	92
As Venus' bird the white, swift, lovely Dove	251	Other Poems	4	353

BIRDS
With twenty ginnes we will the small birds take,	18	1st Eclogues 7		126
In which do light small birds of thoughts orethrowne:.	18	1st Eclogues 7		141
Or catch the birds with pitfalls, or with lyme,	26	1st Eclogues 9		124
Who once all birdes, in sweetly-singing past,	28	1st Eclogues 10		74
Of all the birdes, but namely those were grieved,	29	1st Eclogues 10		83
Thus children doo the silly birds they finde,	41	Arcadia II	20	11
Pas. Nay like to nightingales the other birds give eare:	52	2nd Eclogues 29		19
Sweet birds kindly do graunt harmony unto thee,	69	2nd Eclogues 34		12
Streight as Cedar, a voice staines the Cannary birds,	69	2nd Eclogues 34		33
The birdes likewise with chirpes, and puing could,	100	3rd Eclogues 66		66
As for the gentle birds, like case might rewe.	102	3rd Eclogues 66		139
Worst fell to smallest birds, and meanest heard,	102	3rd Eclogues 66		141
Of reason, from whose light those night-birds flie;	201	Astrophil	71	7
But when birds charme, and that sweete aire, which is.	231	Astrophil	99	9
O birds, o beasts, looke Love, lo, Stella shineth.	209	A&S 3rd Song		12
The birds, beasts, stones and trees feele this, and feeling love:	209	A&S 3rd Song		13
Nor beasts, nor birds do come unto this blessed gaze,	209	A&S 3rd Song		15
Where birds wanton musicke made,	217	A&S 8th Song		2
These birds sing: "Now use the season.".	219	A&S 8th Song		56
Sometimes we see small birds from nests do pull.	245	Other Poems	4	136
Like to Junoe's birdes of pride,	263	Other Poems	7	51

BIRDS'
    The birds' eyes closde, closed their chirping notes. . . .   98 3rd Eclogues 66 12
BIRTH
    Latona's sonne, whose birth in paine and travaile long . . .   45 Arcadia II   26   7
    In this small course which birth drawes out to death,. . . . 144 Cert Sonnets 32 10
    Such coltish gyres, that to my birth I owe . . . . 175 Astrophil   21   6
    While those poore babes their death in birth do find:. . . . 190 Astrophil   50 11
    From nobler course, fit for my birth and mind: . . . . . . 196 Astrophil   62   8
BIRTHRIGHT
    Which unto it by birthright I do ow: . . . . 174 Astrophil   18   6
    To have for no cause birthright in the skie, ... 178 Astrophil   26   5
    Ye men of Pow'er even by birth-right,. . . . . 309 Psalm XXIX   2
*BIT
    Whiche beares the bytt a weaker force doth guide,. . . . .   20 1st Eclogues 7 V959
    My mouth too tender is for thy hard bit. . . . . 166 Astrophil   4   8
    How Ulster likes of that same golden bit,. . . . . 180 Astrophil   30   9
    Are humbled thoughts, which bit of Reverence move, ... 189 Astrophil   49   6
    I caught at one of them a hungrie bit; . . . . 208 Astrophil   82 11
BITE
    And try with bayt how fish will bite sometime. . . . . . .   26 1st Eclogues 9 128
    Geron. Downe, downe Melampus; what? your fellow bite?. . .   26 1st Eclogues 10   1
    I will but kisse, I never more will bite. . . . . 208 Astrophil   82 14
    Thou those men's teeth which byte, ... 273 Psalm III   28
BITES
    No sword soe bytes as that evill toole annoyes.. . . . . .   29 1st Eclogues 10 90
BITING
    Biting my trewand pen, beating my selfe for spite, ... 165 Astrophil   1 13
    Frome bitinge Usury who ever doth refrain, ... 287 Psalm XV   11
BITS
    For by and by the horse faire bitts did binde: . . . . . . 102 3rd Eclogues 66 137
BITTEN
    Train'd in the life which on short-bitten grasse . . . . . 242 Other Poems   4 19
BITTER
    But perforce disgest, all bitter juices of horror. . . . .   35 1st Eclogues 13 105
    Bitter griefe tastes me best, paine is my ease,. . . . . .   74 Arcadia III 41   7
    With inward cries putts up a bitter role . . . .   85 Arcadia III 61   3
    Cupid's lust gone, and gone is bitter strife,. . . . . . .   93 3rd Eclogues 63 94
    The bitter juice of forsaken woes, ... 153 Cert Sonnets 24 11
    Thus while th' effect most bitter was to me, ... 223 Astrophil   87 12
BLACK
    My words blacke inke, the marble kindly white; . . . . . .   41 Arcadia II   19   9
    Blacke incke becommes the state wherein I dye. . . . . . .   81 Arcadia III 54   6
    Such living beames should her black seate assaile, ...   82 Arcadia III 55 10
    For the blacke starres those Spheares containe,. . . . . .   86 Arcadia III 62 15
    Each thing with mantle black the night doth soothe;. . . .   98 3rd Eclogues 66   5
    The night growne old, her blacke head waxen gray,. . . . . 103 3rd Eclogues 66 160
    Lilly in mourning blacke thy whitenes die: . . . . 125 4th Eclogues 75 28
    For mourning night her blacke weedes may display.. . . . . 126 4th Eclogues 75 54
    In colour blacke, why wrapt she beames so bright?. . . . . 168 Astrophil   7   5
    Would she in beamie blacke, like painter wise, ... 168 Astrophil   7   3
    That whereas blacke seemes Beautie's contrary, ... 168 Astrophil   7 10
    She even in blacke doth make all beauties flow?. . . . . . 168 Astrophil   7 11
    As that sweete blacke which vailes the heav'nly eye: . . . 175 Astrophil   20   7
    While that blacke hue from me the bad guest hid: . . . . . 175 Astrophil   20 11
    But for to spangle the blacke weeds of night: . . . . . . 178 Astrophil   26   6
    Can those blacke beames such burning markes engrave. . . . 188 Astrophil   47   2
    How their blacke banner might be best displaid.. . . . . . 192 Astrophil   55   8
    Shall paint out joy, though but in blacke and white. . . . 201 Astrophil   70 11
    Or seeing jets, blacke, but in blacknesse bright.. . . . . 225 Astrophil   91   8
    What inke is blacke inough to paint my wo? . . . . 227 Astrophil   93   3
    Both sadly blacke, both blackly darkned be,. . . . . 229 Astrophil   96   3
    While the blacke horrors of the silent night, ... 230 Astrophil   98   9
    Paint woe's blacke face so lively to my sight, ... 230 Astrophil   98 10
    My bed, while I with black night mourn alone,. . . . . . . 276 Psalm VI   19
    Ev'n when night with his black wing. . . . . 288 Psalm XVI   21
    D. Wonder that by two so black eyes the glittering stars be
        past.. . . . . 343 Possibly   1 28
    Friends like to blacke Swannes appearing,. . . . . 263 Other Poems   7 53
BLACKEST
    I sought fit words to paint the blackest face of woe,. . . . 165 Astrophil   1   5
    And this I sweare by blackest brooke of hell,. . . . . . . 204 Astrophil   74   7
    That living thus in blackest winter night, ... 224 Astrophil   89 13
BLACKLY
    Both sadly blacke, both blackly darkned be,. . . . . 229 Astrophil   96   3
BLACKNESS
    Or seeing jets, blacke, but in blacknesse bright.. . . . . 225 Astrophil   91   8
BLACK-SILK
    As she a black-silke cap on him begunne. . . . . 244 Other Poems   4 85
BLADE
    But eye from blade, and eare from crie:. . . . .   44 Arcadia II   25 11
    Save me from them Thou usest as thy blade, ... 290 Psalm XVII   37
BLAME
    Fondly blame that to which your selves aspire. . . . . . .   25 1st Eclogues 9 104
    Whether he needes must goe for feare of blame. . . . . . .   96 3rd Eclogues 64 78
    The fault I blame her chastnesse is. . . . . 157 Cert Sonnets 27 32
    His sole exec'tour blame. . . . . 160 Cert Sonnets 30 16
    Your words my friend (right healthfull caustiks) blame . . . 175 Astrophil   21   1
    On servants' shame oft Maister's blame doth sit; . . . . . 236 Astrophil 107 12
    That speech falles now to blame, which did thy honour raise, 213 A&S 5th Song   17
    But throw them down, put them to endlesse blame, ... 323 Psalm XXXV   63

		PAGE	TITLE		LINE
BLAMED					
No, though the heav'ns for high attempts have blamed me, . .		15	1st Eclogues	7	22
Her staines are beames; vertue the fault she blamed is. . . .		49	2nd Eclogues	28	57
(For they have toongs to make a poore man blamed		94	3rd Eclogues	64	21
Nor blam'd for bloud, nor sham'd for sinfull deed.		209	Astrophil	84	11
With how sweet sawes she blam'd their sawcines:		252	Other Poems	4	404
BLAMELESS					
(But namelesse he, for blamelesse he shall be)		94	3rd Eclogues	64	2
BLAMETH					
You be the cause that I love: what Reason blameth a shadowe,		123	4th Eclogues	74	45
BLASPHEME					
Was I to blaspheme enraged, ...		157	Cert Sonnets	27	27
BLASPHEMIES					
Staine with your blasphemys? till when		273	Psalm IV		8
BLASPHEMOUS					
Dorus. If I had thought to heare blasphemous wordes, ...		50	2nd Eclogues	28	79
Blasphemous words the speaker vaine do prove.		59	2nd Eclogues	30	67
BLASPHEMY					
Horrible is this blasphemy unto the most holy. O lie.		65	2nd Eclogues	31	45
BLAST					
Hailestones of teares, of sighes a monstrous blast, ...		114	4th Eclogues	72	33
BLASTING					
With blasting breath O Lord, that in thy chiding went. . . .		291	Psalm XVIII		33
BLASTS					
Torne you should disperse unto the blasts of a winde.		123	4th Eclogues	74	52
BLAYING					
With neighing, blaying, braying, and barking, ...		100	3rd Eclogues	66	62
Tell her in your piteous blaying, ...		222	A&S 9th Song		49
BLAZE					
My words, in hope to blaze my stedfast minde, ...		40	Arcadia II	19	1
To blase my onely secretts?		65	2nd Eclogues	32	2
Above line repeated at following location.		66	2nd Eclogues	32	31
To blaze these last, and sware devoutly then, ...		171	Astrophil	13	13
Walking in bright Phoebus' blaze		262	Other Poems	7	1
BLAZED					
Fame is with wonder blazed:		136	Cert Sonnets	3	5
BLEA					
With sluttish song: I pray thee learne to blea, ...		56	2nd Eclogues	29	136
BLEARED					
Dick. What joy the joyfull sunne gives unto bleared eyes: . .		343	Possibly	1	13
BLEED					
Deadly wounds inward bleed, ech sleight sore mattereth. . . .		14	1st Eclogues	7	9
This mourning inck, in which my hart doth bleede.		96	3rd Eclogues	64	96
Thou art of blood; joy not to make things bleede:		103	3rd Eclogues	66	150
Love gave the wound, which while I breathe will bleed: . . .		165	Astrophil	2	2
To honor all their deaths, who for her bleed.		168	Astrophil	7	14
Whose curelesse wounds even now most freshly bleed:		189	Astrophil	48	11
I cry thy sighs; my deere, thy teares I bleede.		227	Astrophil	93	14
BLEEDING					
But rotten bleeding argues evill complection		50	2nd Eclogues	28	V883
Which through a bleeding heart his point did shove:		171	Astrophil	13	6
Nor do aspire to Caesar's bleeding fame, ...		198	Astrophil	64	10
And even while I do speake, my death wounds bleeding be: . .		214	A&S 5th Song		52
BLEMISH					
First shall vertue be vice, and bewty be counted a blemishe,		33	1st Eclogues	13	67
BLEMISHED					
You should have your face (since Love is ill) blemished. . .		123	4th Eclogues	74	56
BLESS					
For pilfring Lalus' lambe, with crouch to blesse thy head. .		52	2nd Eclogues	29	14
O much more then words: those words serv'd more to me					
blesse Lesse.		64	2nd Eclogues	31	31
Whom curst do blesse, whose weakenesse vertues arme, ...		142	Cert Sonnets	10	6
Stella whom o heavens do blesse, ...		221	A&S 9th Song		18
Thy work it is to blesse, thou blessest them;		275	Psalm V		37
Ever, lord, I will blesse Thee, ...		288	Psalm XVI		19
Blesse Thyne heritage I say, ...		309	Psalm XXVIII		34
Then since my tongue delights that name to blesse, ...		312	Psalm XXXI		8
Who loves with good his servants good to blesse.		323	Psalm XXXV		70
BLESSED					
That Goddesse mine, my blessed being sees".		4	Lady of May	3	6
That she, whose looke alone might make me blessed, ...		17	1st Eclogues	7	83
O blessed sonne whence all this blessing goes.		43	Arcadia II	23	6
By her who was (O blessed you) content, ...		78	Arcadia III	49	5
And so by you (O blessed you) hath sent, ...		78	Arcadia III	49	7
Which blessed still themselves doo kisse.		87	Arcadia III	62	38
Now blessed you, beare onward blessed me		209	Astrophil	84	5
Nor beasts, nor birds do come unto this blessed gaze, ...		209	A&S 3rd Song		15
When I blessed shall devower, ...		226	A&S 10th Song		32
But each in the other blessed.		218	A&S 8th Song		8
He blessed is, who neither loosely treads.		270	Psalm I		1
And on those blessed same, ...		273	Psalm III		34
On thy blessed making hand		289	Psalm XVI		43
Then live Jehova still, my rock still blessed be;		293	Psalm XVIII		83
That they in peace shall blessed live.		310	Psalm XXIX		29
Bless'ed is the man whose filthy stain		314	Psalm XXXII		1
Blessed in deed to whom the lord		314	Psalm XXXII		4
Lord he is in thrice blessed case.		319	Psalm XXXIV		31
Who weare his blessed livery, ...		321	Psalm XXXIV		78
Lo whom God blest he blessed liveth, ...		326	Psalm XXXVII		55
O he indeed is blessed, ...		331	Psalm XL		15

```
BLESSED                    (CONTINUED)                  PAGE    TITLE           LINE
     He blessed is, who with wise temper can. . . . . . . . . .  332  Psalm XLI          1
     Ah, when comes my blessed being, . . . . . . . . . . . . .  334  Psalm XLII         7
     Ther was (o seldome blessed word of was!). . . . . . . . .  242  Other Poems   4   17
     Till my eies had their curse from blessed eine.. . . . . .  254  Other Poems   4  496
     On thy then blessed face,. . . . . . . . . . . . . . . . .  256  Other Poems   5   18
     A happy blessed Trinitie;. . . . . . . . . . . . . . . . .  260  Other Poems   6   20
BLESSEST
     Thy work it is to blesse, thou blessest them;. . . . . . .  275  Psalm V           37
BLESSING
     Comfort into my soule. I do finde, I do find what a blessing 34  1st Eclogues 13   95
     O blessed sonne whence all this blessing goes. . . . . . .   43  Arcadia II   23    6
     His blessing he extendeth. . . . . . . . . . . . . . . . .  273  Psalm III         36
     With many liberall blessing; . . . . . . . . . . . . . . .  297  Psalm XXI         10
     A blessing from the lord, from God of his salvation. . . .  302  Psalm XXIV        13
     Lo, how his blessing budds . . . . . . . . . . . . . . . .  304  Psalm XXV         49
     And blessing such with length desires, . . . . . . . . . .  320  Psalm XXXIV       47
     The more his seed in blessing flourish;. . . . . . . . . .  326  Psalm XXXVII      66
     Shall dwell thereon, and this their blessing . . . . . . .  326  Psalm XXXVII      75
     World without end, let still his blessing flow;. . . . . .  334  Psalm XLI         47
BLESSINGS
     Therefore esteeming all good blessings toyes,. . . . . . .  116  4th Eclogues 72   99
     Such blessings shall not wycked wretches see . . . . . . .  270  Psalm I           13
     Like storehouse Thou of blessings mad'st,. . . . . . . . .  297  Psalm XXI         21
     With blessings of the ground,. . . . . . . . . . . . . . .  333  Psalm XLI          6
     Sc may thy blessings swarme. . . . . . . . . . . . . . . .  258  Other Poems   5   82
BLEST
     Great to thee my estate seemes, thy estate is blest by my
          judgement:. . . . . . . . . . . . . . . . . . . . . .   33  1st Eclogues 13   72
     And yet neither of us great or blest deemeth his owne selfe.  33  1st Eclogues 13   73
     Dorus. Blest be the name, wherewith my mistres named is: . .  49  Arcadia II   28   55
     Who thinke themselves well blest, if they renew. . . . . .  146  Cert Sonnets 17   33
     Mine eyes (shall I say curst or blest) beheld. . . . . . .  173  Astrophil    16   10
     That in no more but these I might be fully blest:. . . . .  205  Astrophil    77   13
     Then those blest eyes, where all my hopes do dwell,. . . .  212  Astrophil    86   13
     O they be rightly blest. . . . . . . . . . . . . . . . . .  272  Psalm II          32
     Whose life doth seeme most greatly blest . . . . . . . . .  290  Psalm XVII        39
     Lo whom God blest he blessed liveth, . . . . . . . . . . .  326  Psalm XXXVII      55
     So then be blest now, then, at home, abroad, . . . . . . .  334  Psalm XLI         45
     But most cryed, "O well broke": O foole full gaily blest:. .  241  Other Poems  1    5
BLIND
     A naked god, young, blind, with arrowes two. . . . . . . .   20  1st Eclogues  8    6
     A naked god, blinde young, with arrowes two. . . . . . . .   20  1st Eclogues  8 V  6
     If he be blind, how hitteth he so right? . . . . . . . . .   21  1st Eclogues  8    9
     Geron. If that thy face were hid, or I were blinde,. . . .   25  1st Eclogues  9   96
     But loe, my words defaste, my fancies blinde,. . . . . . .   40  Arcadia II   19    3
     This is thy worke, thou God for ever blinde: . . . . . . .   41  Arcadia II   20    9
     R. Passion is blinde, and treades an unknowne trace. . . .   46  2nd Eclogues 27   15
     Nico. Ah now I see, why thou art in thy selfe so blind:. . .  52  2nd Eclogues 29    5
     What needed so high sprites such mansions blind? . . . . .   57  2nd Eclogues 30   14
     But if he know not his harms what guides hath he whil'st he
          be blind? Blind. . . . . . . . . . . . . . . . . . . .   63  2nd Eclogues 31   20
     What blinde guides can he have that leanes to a fancy? A
          fancy. . . . . . . . . . . . . . . . . . . . . . . . .   63  2nd Eclogues 31   21
     Where too much sight, makes all the bodie blinde,. . . . .   73  Arcadia III  40   11
     What were it els, but to make each thing blinde? . . . . .   79  Arcadia III  50   13
     She studied cunning how the same to blinde.. . . . . . . .   95  3rd Eclogues 64   42
     Not spying faults, nor in plaine errors blinde,. . . . . .   98  3rd Eclogues 65    7
     Who onely sees the ill is worse then blind.. . . . . . . .  106  3rd Eclogues 67   85
     Blinde Cupid's workes with wonder testifie?. . . . . . . .  106  3rd Eclogues 67   98
     Did suffer drousie lids mine eyes then cleare to blinde; . .  117  4th Eclogues 73  26
     That thou full oft shalt wish thy judging eyes were blinde".  121  4th Eclogues 73 172
     Since force doth faint, and sight doth make me blind:. . . .  135  Cert Sonnets  1   4
     Till wounded, blind, and wearied Spirites, lose. . . . . .  144  Cert Sonnets 15   11
     I heare a crye of spirits faint and blinde,. . . . . . . .  148  Cert Sonnets 20    7
     In absence blind, and wearied with that woe, . . . . . . .  149  Cert Sonnets 21    9
     Thou blind man's marke, thou foole's selfe chosen snare, . .  161  Cert Sonnets 31   1
     But that rich foole, who by blind Fortune's lot. . . . . .  177  Astrophil    24    9
     Teaching blind eyes both how to smile and weepe, . . . . .  181  Astrophil    32    8
     A chamber deafe to noise, and blind to light:. . . . . . .  184  Astrophil    39   10
     That love she did, but loved a Love not blind, . . . . . .  196  Astrophil    62    6
     I lodg'd thee in my heart, and being blind . . . . . . . .  198  Astrophil    65    7
     She could not shew my blind braine waies of joy, . . . . .  230  Astrophil    97   13
     Is not he blind that doth not find . . . . . . . . . . . .  294  Psalm XIX         17
     As this same sprite about my fancies blinde, . . . . . . .  255  Other Poems   4  502
BLINDED
     Whome wit makes vaine, or blinded with his eyes, . . . . .   23  1st Eclogues  9   35
     O nature doting olde, o blinded nature,. . . . . . . . . .  109  Arcadia IV   70   19
     Blinded with beames, fell darkenes is my sight:. . . . . .  113  4th Eclogues 72    8
     For ever blinded of our clearest light;. . . . . . . . . .  130  4th Eclogues 76   27
     Blinded forthwith in darke dispaire did lye, . . . . . . .  149  Cert Sonnets 21    6
     A blinded Mowlle, or else a burned flye. . . . . . . . . .  149  Cert Sonnets 21   14
     Fed by thy worth, and blinded by thy sight?. . . . . . . .  200  Astrophil    68 V  8
     Let me home returne, stark blinded . . . . . . . . . . . .  220  A&S 8th Song      83
BLINDER
     Of those eyes, and blinder minded. . . . . . . . . . . . .  220  A&S 8th Song      84
BLIND-HITTING
     Blind-hitting boy, since she that thee and me. . . . . . .  187  Astrophil    46    2
BLINDS
     Then jarle: lo, lo, even these how envie blindes.. . . . .   26  1st Eclogues 10    9
```

```
BLISS                                                        PAGE    TITLE            LINE
  Whose cleerest eyes I blisse, and sweetest voyce,. . . . . .    5 Lady of May    3    15
  Thy yonger shall with Nature's blisse embrace. . . . . . .    11 Arcadia I      1     3
  Helples his plaint, who spoyles himselfe of blisse.. . . . .   13 Arcadia I      4    10
  O noble age who place their only blisse. . . . . . . . . .    24 1st Eclogues   9    69
  R. Repent indeed, but that shall be your blisse. . . . . .    47 2nd Eclogues  27    37
  My harmes to me, my blisse to her attributed.. . . . . . .    49 2nd Eclogues  28    69
  The kindly way to beate us on to blisse. . . . . . . . . .    59 2nd Eclogues  30    76
  Think so, for of my desired blisse it is only the course.
       Curse. . . . . . . . . . . . . . . . . . . . . . .     64 2nd Eclogues  31    39
  Sweete glove the wittnes of my secrett blisse. . . . . . .    70 Arcadia III   35     1
  For reason will, great sight of hoped blisse,. . . . . . .    71 Arcadia III   37    11
  Both equall hurt, in this change sought our blisse:. . . . .   76 Arcadia III   45    13
  As thou drawest on, so let my blisse draw neere. . . . . .    80 Arcadia III   53    10
  Of whose high praise, and praiseful blisse, . . . . . . . .    90 Arcadia III   62   141
  Where that all blisse may raigne,. . . . . . . . . . . . .    91 3rd Eclogues  63    26
  But that it is my doome of bale or blisse. . . . . . . . . .    97 3rd Eclogues  64   102
  Beleeve me man, there is no greater blisse,. . . . . . . .   103 3rd Eclogues  67     7
  Which drawne-out line doth hold all humane blisse. . . . .   105 3rd Eclogues  67    72
  On rocke, Despaire, the buriall of my blisse. . . . . . . .   114 4th Eclogues  72    50
  Klaius. On rocke, Despaire, the buriall of my blisse . . . .  115 4th Eclogues  72    51
  Then let us holde the blisse of peacefull minde, . . . . . .  131 Arcadia V     77    13
  Where former blisse present evils do staine, . . . . . . .   153 Cert Sonnets  24    12
  Nay former blisse addes to present paine,. . . . . . . . .   153 Cert Sonnets  24    13
  Of this high grace with blisse conjoyn'd . . . . . . . . .   159 Cert Sonnets  29     1
  And then would not, or could not see my blisse:. . . . . .   181 Astrophil     33     2
  Which make the patents of true worldly blisse, . . . . . .   183 Astrophil     37    13
  Those daintie dores unto the Court of blisse,. . . . . . .   187 Astrophil     44    11
  That vertuous soule, sure heire of heav'nly blisse:. . . . .  190 Astrophil     52     7
  When I might reade those letters faire of blisse,. . . . .   193 Astrophil     56     5
  Blist in my curse, and cursed in my blisse.. . . . . . . .   195 Astrophil     60    14
  Stella's eyes sent to me the beames of blisse, . . . . . .   199 Astrophil     66    11
  O blisse, fit for a nobler state then me:. . . . . . . . .   200 Astrophil     69     2
  This realme of blisse, while vertuous course I take, . . . .  200 Astrophil     69    13
  Wise silence is best musicke unto blisse.. . . . . . . . .   201 Astrophil     70    14
  Those words, which do sublime the quintessence of blisse:. .  205 Astrophil     77     8
  Breathing all blisse and sweetning to the heart, . . . . .   207 Astrophil     81     3
  Of highest wish, I wish you so much blisse,. . . . . . . .   209 Astrophil     84    13
  O fate, o fault, o curse, child of my blisse,. . . . . . .   227 Astrophil     93     1
  Cals each wight to salute the floure of blisse;. . . . . .   231 Astrophil     99    11
  This large offer of our blisse,. . . . . . . . . . . . . .   211 A&S 4th Song        32
  The mansion seat of blisse, and just excuse of Lovers; . . .  213 A&S 5th Song        21
  Which do breath a sugred blisse, . . . . . . . . . . . . .   226 A&S 10th Song       29
  Blisse, I will my blisse forebeare,. . . . . . . . . . . .   234 A&S 11th Song       38
  Writ each character of blisse, . . . . . . . . . . . . . .   219 A&S 8th Song        42
  All my blisse in thee I lay; . . . . . . . . . . . . . . .   220 A&S 8th Song        90
  Tho I blisse enherit never.. . . . . . . . . . . . . . . .   221 A&S 9th Song        20
  So I in peace, and peacefull blisse. . . . . . . . . . . .   274 Psalm IV            31
  This gotten blisse shall never part, . . . . . . . . . . .   282 Psalm X             24
  Yea in no age thy blisse from them departs.. . . . . . . .   285 Psalm XII           24
  And of my Child's part the blisse, . . . . . . . . . . . .   288 Psalm XVI           14
  This lord with strength my life doth blisse; . . . . . . .   306 Psalm XXVII          4
  That Realm in deed hath blisse . . . . . . . . . . . . . .   317 Psalm XXXIII        43
  They have and shall have blisse. . . . . . . . . . . . . .   319 Psalm XXXIV         36
  Who stay for God, in blisse shall stay.. . . . . . . . . .   325 Psalm XXXVII        24
  But God upholds the just in blisse.. . . . . . . . . . . .   325 Psalm XXXVII        44
  He shall me restore to blisse, . . . . . . . . . . . . . .   334 Psalm XLII          22
  God of all my blisse,. . . . . . . . . . . . . . . . . . .   336 Psalm XLIII         23
  They found, they felt, they had no lease of blisse.. . . . .  244 Other Poems    4    80
  If th' author of thy blisse, . . . . . . . . . . . . . . .   257 Other Poems    5    21
BLISSED
  My soule is bliste, sence joyde, and fortune raysed. . . . .  108 Arcadia IV    69    14
  Wealth breeding want, more blist, more wretched grow.. . . .  177 Astrophil     24     4
  Blist in my curse, and cursed in my blisse.. . . . . . . .   195 Astrophil     60    14
BLISSES
  Slay mee not, for stay doo not hyde thy blisses, . . . . .   138 Cert Sonnets   5    22
BLITHE
  Blith were the commons, cattell of the fielde, . . . . . .   102 3rd Eclogues  66   132
BLOCK
  The ancient oke well makes a fired blocke: . . . . . . . .    25 1st Eclogues   9    87
BLOCKISH
  For who grieves not hath but a blockish braine,. . . . . .    58 2nd Eclogues  30    36
BLOOD
  Is past with me, my bloud is waxen colde.. . . . . . . . .    25 1st Eclogues   9   107
  A blooddy helpe with blood to save:. . . . . . . . . . . .    44 Arcadia II    25     2
  R. We are too strong: but Reason seekes not blood. . . . .    47 2nd Eclogues  27    29
  With losse of purest blood themselves to teare,. . . . . .    58 2nd Eclogues  30    46
  So that therein appeares some blood, . . . . . . . . . . .    86 Arcadia III   62    29
  As horse and dogge, not great, but gentle blood: . . . . .   102 3rd Eclogues  66   131
  Thou art of blood; joy not to make things bleede:. . . . .   103 3rd Eclogues  66   150
  From wooden bones, and blood of pitch doth flie. . . . . .   151 Cert Sonnets  22    53
  Yet hiding royall bloud full oft in rurall vaine.. . . . .   167 Astrophil      6     8
  My bloud from them, who did excell in this,. . . . . . . .   185 Astrophil     41    10
  Nor blam'd for bloud, not sham'd for sinfull deed. . . . .   209 Astrophil     84    11
  That He enquiringe, doth require just blood, . . . . . . .   280 Psalm IX            33
  Their blood offrings I do shun,. . . . . . . . . . . . . .   288 Psalm XVI           11
  What serves alas the blood of me . . . . . . . . . . . . .   311 Psalm XXX           26
  And that the bias of hir bloud was wrought.. . . . . . . .   244 Other Poems    4   101
  In cheeks and lipps the Tyran threatens bloud. . . . . . .   246 Other Poems    4   152
```

49

```
                                                           PAGE    TITLE          LINE
BLOODSEEKER'S
    Nor my life's cause match with bloodseeker's case, . . . . .  306  Psalm XXVI        30
BLOODY
    A bloody helpe with blood to save:. . . . . . . . . . . .   44  Arcadia II    25    2
    The bloudy shaftes of Cupid's warre, . . . . . . . . . . .   90  Arcadia III   62  131
    That eyes weepe worse then hart in bloodie teares? . . . .  142  Cert Sonnets  11    7
    Till bloudie bullet get him wrongfull pray.. . . . . . . .  175  Astrophil     20    4
    Those scarlet judges, threatning bloudy paine? . . . . . .  203  Astrophil     73   11
    Though strongly hedg'd of bloudy Lyon's pawes, . . . . . .  204  Astrophil     75   10
BLOT
    And can with foule abuse such beauties blot; . . . . . . .  177  Astrophil     24   11
    No vertue merits praise, once toucht with blot of Treason. .  214  A&S 5th Song       66
    Nor my Rebellious blott, . . . . . . . . . . . . . . . . .  303  Psalm XXV          27
    With others' blott, till all do tast of shame. . . . . . .  248  Other Poems    4  232
BLOTS
    Blots to the stone, shame to my selfe I finde: . . . . . .   40  Arcadia II    19    4
    A Shop of shame, a Booke where blots be rife . . . . . . .   57  2nd Eclogues  30   26
BLOTTED
    Like some which seeke to salve their blotted name. . . . .  248  Other Poems    4  231
*BLOW
    For from without came to mine eyes the blowe, . . . . . . .   11  Arcadia I      2    5
    Passion beares high when puffing wit doth blowe, . . . . .   25  1st Eclogues   9  114
    At blowe point, hotcocles, or els at keeles. . . . . . . .   28  1st Eclogues  10   47
    The lovely blowe with rare reward, my prayer is. . . . . .   51  2nd Eclogues  28  112
    Nico would needes with Pas his bagpipe blowe. . . . . . . .   54  2nd Eclogues  29   68
    Due sighes blowe out all sparkes of joyfull light, . . . .   74  Arcadia III   42   11
    Ye helplesse Sighes, blowe out your breath to nought,. . .   83  Arcadia III   59    5
    Then gave he him the blow which never smarted. . . . . . .   97  3rd Eclogues  64  120
    For lost, lost is by blowe of cruell fortune . . . . . . .  109  Arcadia IV    70   17
    With sound of horne, which he him selfe did blow, . . . . .  145  Cert Sonnets  16    2
    But to my selfe my selfe did give the blow, . . . . . . . .  181  Astrophil     33    9
    Since Reason's selfe doth blow the cole in me? . . . . . .  182  Astrophil     35    6
    While each doth blow the fier of my hart; . . . . . . . . .  202  Astrophil     72    4
    Wing'd with whose breath, so pleasing Zephires blow, . . .  231  Astrophil    100    7
    Revenge, revenge, my Muse, Defiance' trumpet blow: . . . .  213  A&S 5th Song       32
    To give unawares a Mortall blow. . . . . . . . . . . . . .  284  Psalm XI           7
    And as vile chaff away the wind doth blow, . . . . . . . .  321  Psalm XXXV        11
    The Arrow being shot from far, doth give the smaller blowe..  344  Possibly       1   42
    Klaius streight felt, and groned at the blowe, . . . . . .  246  Other Poems    4  161
    That to hir breast he gave a noysome blowe.. . . . . . . .  249  Other Poems    4  272
    The aire hir swete race mov'd doth blow the fire. . . . . .  249  Other Poems    4  300
    He quickly knew what witchcraft gave the blow. . . . . . .  256  Other Poems    4  539
BLOWN
    But such we are with inward tempest blowne . . . . . . . .   59  2nd Eclogues  30   80
    Nor ramper did abide; my braine was up blowne, . . . . . .   68  2nd Eclogues  33   15
    Let other fowler spots away be blowne; . . . . . . . . . .  105  3rd Eclogues  67   55
    Ruine, the winde, hath blowne her from her scope: . . . . .  114  4th Eclogues  72   48
    When it blowne up with myne a fall of ruine takes) . . . .  118  4th Eclogues  73   52
*BLOWS
    And ere that all these blowes thy head doo hit, . . . . . .   11  Arcadia I      1    9
    Their first caught sence prefers to teacher's blowes. . . .   28  1st Eclogues  10   57
    What hope to quench, where each thing blowes the fire? . . .   42  Arcadia II    21   18
    When rotten Fame will tell their blowes. . . . . . . . . .   44  Arcadia II    25   10
    For all these certaine blowes the surest shield. . . . . .   58  2nd Eclogues  30   43
    Her hand benumde with fortune's daylie blows, . . . . . . .   81  Arcadia III   54    3
    Invention, Nature's child, fled step-dame Studie's blowes, .  165  Astrophil      1   10
    Till downe-right blowes did foyle thy cunning fence: . . .  170  Astrophil     10   11
    The friendly fray, where blowes both wound and heale, . . .  206  Astrophil     79   10
    For thou with cruel blowes, . . . . . . . . . . . . . . . .  273  Psalm III          25
BLUE
    Her twinkling eies bedeckt with pearle, her lips of Saphir
        blew: . . . . . . . . . . . . . . . . . . . . . . . .   12  Arcadia I      3   10
BLUNTED
    Thinke, my harde haps have blunted death's sharpe knife, . .  113  4th Eclogues  72   14
BLUSH
    Blush on for shame: that still with thee do light. . . . .   82  Arcadia III   56    5
    Till that her blush taught me my shame to see. . . . . . .  191  Astrophil     53   14
    They fled with blush, which guiltie seem'd of love.. . . .  199  Astrophil     66   14
    Yet ah, my Mayd'n Muse doth blush to tell the best. . . . .  205  Astrophil     77   14
    Where Beautie's blush in Honour's graine is dide.. . . . .  207  Astrophil     80    8
    I should blush when thou art named." . . . . . . . . . . .  220  A&S 8th Song      100
    Shall never blush for shame. . . . . . . . . . . . . . . .  319  Psalm XXXIV       20
    Let them have shame, yea blush for shame, . . . . . . . . .  332  Psalm XL          52
    And now faire evenings blush my shame to see. . . . . . . .  254  Other Poems    4  480
BLUSHED
    Nature abasht went back: fortune blusht: yet she replide
        thus:. . . . . . . . . . . . . . . . . . . . . . . . .   30  1st Eclogues  11   17
    She so discheveld, blusht; from window I . . . . . . . . .  233  Astrophil    103   12
BLUSHING
    Aurora now thou shewst thy blushing light. . . . . . . . .   82  Arcadia III   56    1
    Blushing at sight of Phoebus' pride. . . . . . . . . . . .   86  Arcadia III   62   26
    Whose beawties shin'de more then the blushing morning, . . .  113  4th Eclogues  71   62
    Where blushing red, that Love's selfe them doth love, . . .  186  Astrophil     43   10
    What blushing notes doest thou in margine see? . . . . . .  199  Astrophil     67    8
    But she forbids, with blushing words, she sayes, . . . . .  207  Astrophil     81    9
    Nor blushing Lillies, nor pearles' ruby-hidden row, . . . .  213  A&S 5th Song      38
    (With blushing soule at sight of judgement's glasse) . . .  255  Other Poems    4  531
BOAST
    Whilst that methought I justly made my bost. . . . . . . .  147  Cert Sonnets  17   42
    What now the Dutch in their full diets boast; . . . . . . .  180  Astrophil     30    6
```

```
                                                         PAGE   TITLE        LINE
BOAT
    The bote for joy could not to daunce forbeare, . . . . . . .  232 Astrophil   103    5
BOBBED
    Let him be bob'd that bobs will have.. . . . . . . . . . . .   44 Arcadia II   25    4
BOBS
    Let him be bob'd that bobs will have.. . . . . . . . . . . .   44 Arcadia II   25    4
BODIES
    One grave their bodies seaze:.. . . . . . . . . . . . . . .   92 3rd Eclogues 63   32
    Our bodies be in living power maintained,. . . . . . . . . .  128 4th Eclogues 75  107
    And know those Bodies high raigne on the low.. . . . . . . .  178 Astrophil    26   11
    And whose bodys placed be. . . . . . . . . . . . . . . . .   289 Psalm XVI         42
    Make but one Minde in Bodies three.. . . . . . . . . . . . .  260 Other Poems   6    6
    Above line repeated at following locations . . . . . . . . .  260 Other Poems   6   12
        . . . . . . . . . . . . . . . . . . . . . . . . . . . .  260 Other Poems   6   18
        . . . . . . . . . . . . . . . . . . . . . . . . . . . .  260 Other Poems   6   24
        . . . . . . . . . . . . . . . . . . . . . . . . . . . .  261 Other Poems   6   30
        . . . . . . . . . . . . . . . . . . . . . . . . . . . .  261 Other Poems   6   36
        . . . . . . . . . . . . . . . . . . . . . . . . . . . .  261 Other Poems   6   42
        . . . . . . . . . . . . . . . . . . . . . . . . . . . .  261 Other Poems   6   48
        . . . . . . . . . . . . . . . . . . . . . . . . . . . .  261 Other Poems   6   54
    So should our sever'd bodies three . . . . . . . . . . . . .  261 Other Poems   6   59
BODILY
    Whose faire bodily gifts are fram'd most lovely to each ey..   33 1st Eclogues 13   55
    If then a boddily evill in a boddily gloze be not hidden,. .   34 1st Eclogues 13   87
BODY
    While that one body shine. . . . . . . . . . . . . . . . . .   19 1st Eclogues  7  165
    With name engrav'd: so though thy bodie die, . . . . . . . .   56 2nd Eclogues 29  130
    With so strong lives, that bodie cannot rest . . . . . . . .   56 2nd Eclogues 29  145
    In ease, untill that bodie life forgoes. . . . . . . . . . .   56 2nd Eclogues 29  146
    This bodie is: this bodie so composed, . . . . . . . . . . .   57 2nd Eclogues 30   27
    The labourer, whome tyred boddie makes . . . . . . . . . . .   71 Arcadia III  37    7
    Where too much sight, makes all the bodie blinde,. . . . . .   73 Arcadia III  40   11
    Let no strange dreme make her fayre body starte. . . . . . .   79 Arcadia III  51    8
    And keepe it still within this body thrall:. . . . . . . . .  116 4th Eclogues 72   88
    That with a body't goes? since by a body it is.. . . . . . .  123 4th Eclogues 74   46
    That Vertue but that body graunt to us.. . . . . . . . . . .  191 Astrophil    52   14
    Then some good body tell me how I do,. . . . . . . . . . . .  195 Astrophil    60   12
    "Stella, in whose body is. . . . . . . . . . . . . . . . . .  219 A&S 8th Song      41
    Ev'en the body of Thyne Own, . . . . . . . . . . . . . . . .  288 Psalm XVI         34
    Nothing in my body sound:. . . . . . . . . . . . . . . . . .  328 Psalm XXXVIII     21
    The dainty dew on face and body went . . . . . . . . . . . .  252 Other Poems   4  397
BODY'S
    Enjoy her soule, in bodie's faire possession,. . . . . . . .   15 1st Eclogues  7   41
BOIL
    Whose braines boile not in woes, nor brests with beatings
        ake, . . . . . . . . . . . . . . . . . . . . . . . . . .  117 4th Eclogues 73   13
BOILING
    Right so my boiling hart, enflam'de with fire of a faire
        eye . . . . . . . . . . . . . . . . . . . . . . . . . .  123 4th Eclogues 74   27
    My boiling sprites did thither soone incline,. . . . . . . .  172 Astrophil    16    3
    Melts downe his lead into my boyling brest,. . . . . . . . .  236 Astrophil   108    2
    Whose boiling heat encreased as she wept:. . . . . . . . . .  246 Other Poems   4  155
    Did draw his boyling braine. . . . . . . . . . . . . . . . .  256 Other Poems   5    9
BOISTROUS
    That streight was done with many a boistrous threat, . . . .   97 3rd Eclogues 64  115
BOLD
    These bolde words she did heare, this fruite I reaped, . . .   17 1st Eclogues  7   82
    But this light choller that doth make you bolde, . . . . . .   25 1st Eclogues  9  105
    With bolde clamor unheard, unmarckt, what I seeke what I
        suffer:. . . . . . . . . . . . . . . . . . . . . . . . .   35 1st Eclogues 13  112
    Whose winke ech bold attempt forbids.. . . . . . . . . . . .   86 Arcadia III  62   14
    There unseen thou maist be bold, . . . . . . . . . . . . . .  226 A&S 10th Song     16
    For what lord rules our bold emboldned breast. . . . . . . .  285 Psalm XII         12
    Where bold and hurtles many plays he tries,. . . . . . . . .  247 Other Poems   4  194
BOLDENED
    He flies to her, and boldned with desire,. . . . . . . . . .  141 Cert Sonnets  9   11
BOLDER
    Now bolder waxt, waxt prowde, that I such sway might beare:.  121 4th Eclogues 73  159
BOLDLY
    And boldly say Thou wilt give eare to me,. . . . . . . . . .  289 Psalm XVII        18
    Will I boldly go . . . . . . . . . . . . . . . . . . . . . .  336 Psalm XLIII       20
BOLT
    And makes our home good sport with daucing bolt upright...    53 2nd Eclogues 29   46
    The highest hills the bolt of thunder cleeves: . . . . . . .  143 Cert Sonnets 12    9
    Now bolt and cudgill squirrels' leape do move. . . . . . . .  243 Other Poems   4   44
BOLTS
    Whose force but yours the bolts of beautie thunders? . . . .  197 A&S 1st Song      30
BONDAGE
    No thralles like them that inward bondage have.. . . . . . .   17 1st Eclogues  7  114
    Into my live's bondage, yet may disburden a passion. . . . .   35 1st Eclogues 13  108
    Flew up with freer wings of fleshly bondage free;. . . . . .  117 4th Eclogues 73   33
    Or those golden lockes, those lockes which lock me to
        bondage, . . . . . . . . . . . . . . . . . . . . . . . .  123 4th Eclogues 74   51
    For all his strife can onlie bondage gaine.. . . . . . . . .  135 Cert Sonnets  2    8
    O happie Dove if she no bondage tried: . . . . . . . . . . .  144 Cert Sonnets 15   13
    More happie I, might I in bondage bide.. . . . . . . . . . .  144 Cert Sonnets 15   14
BONDS
    Come let us break their bonds, say they, and fondly say: . .  271 Psalm II           7
    And in my woundes, my flames and bondes I fynde. . . . . . .  345 Possibly      2   13
    To beare the bondes which Time nor wit could breake, . . . .  255 Other Poems   4  530
```

		PAGE	TITLE	LINE
BONE				
More white then whitest bone of whall.		89	Arcadia III 62	104
BONES				
Along whose ridge such bones are met,		89	Arcadia III 62	111
From wooden bones, and bloud of pitch doth flie.		151	Cert Sonnets 22	53
Lord help, for ev'en my bones their marrow spend		276	Psalm VI	7
Whose loosed bones quite out of joint be wryde;		299	Psalm XXII	32
They look, they gaze, my boanes might be rehearsed;		299	Psalm XXII	42
And ev'en my bones consume where they be plac't.		312	Psalm XXXI	30
Or roar'd, my bones still wasted;		315	Psalm XXXII	9
His bones he keepeth all		320	Psalm XXXIV	73
I both in mind, and bones shall gladded be.		321	Psalm XXXV	20
Ev'en bones shall say O God, who is Thy peere,		321	Psalm XXXV	21
Nor my sins let my bones rest;		327	Psalm XXXVIII	9
Wcund and rent me to the bones,		335	Psalm XLII	46
BONNET				
Yet to a passenger will bonnet vaile..		27	1st Eclogues 10	33
BONNY				
That married had a trick and bonny lasse		94	3rd Eclogues 64	3
BOOK				
Beautie his Booke, his play lovers' dissention:		48	2nd Eclogues 28	42
A Shop of shame, a Booke where blots be rife		57	2nd Eclogues 30	26
Sings out her woes, a thorne her song-booke making:		137	Cert Sonnets 4	4
For like a child that some faire booke doth find,		170	Astrophil 11	5
So long (though he from booke myche to desire)		188	Astrophil 46	13
Far far too long to learne it without booke:		192	Astrophil 56	2
Who will in fairest booke of Nature know,		201	Astrophil 71	1
From so fair book proceeding,		294	Psalm XIX	14
BOOK'S				
For in Thy book's roll I am writt,		331	Psalm XL	32
BOOKS				
Then let thy minde with better bookes be tamed,		25	1st Eclogues 9	120
Thus both trees and each thing ells, be the bookes of a fancy.		36	1st Eclogues 13	140
So have I sene trim bookes in velvet dight		246	Other Poems 4	180
BOOT				
Sate wailing without boot.		256	Other Poems 5	7
BOOTED				
Which to avoyde, quenche, loose noughte booted stryfe.		344	Possibly 2	8
BOOTH				
Beyond our worlde, and ere I gatt my boothe.		98	3rd Eclogues 66	4
BOPEEP				
And in her breast bopeepe or couching lyes,		170	Astrophil 11	12
BORDER				
Far was homestrife, and far was foe from border.		128	4th Eclogues 75	132
But what? I say from earth's remotest border		300	Psalm XXII	65
BORDERED				
Bordred with buls and swans, powdred with golden raine:		167	Astrophil 6 V	6
BORE				
Then ever for my selfe since I was bore:		99	3rd Eclogues 66	19
So that Uran, whose arme old Geron bore,		250	Other Poems 4	309
BOREAS				
In sum, proud Boreas never ruled fleet		251	Other Poems 4	373
BORN				
With cries first borne, the pressage of his life,		57	2nd Eclogues 30	24
You that are borne to be the worlde's eye,		79	Arcadia III 50	12
Fame say I was not borne:		136	Cert Sonnets 3	17
O the fayre Nymphe borne to doo woemen honor,		138	Cert Sonnets 5	3
Above line repeated at following location.		138	Cert Sonnets 5	27
Is gone, and now like slave-borne Muscovite,		166	Astrophil 2	10
Love borne in Greece, of late fled from his native place,		168	Astrophil 8	1
In my free side? or am I borne a slave,		188	Astrophil 47	3
By Nature borne, I gave to thee mine eyes.		198	Astrophil 65	8
What sighes stolne out, or kild before full borne?		199	Astrophil 67	9
For thou doest lord my heart, who am not borne thy slave,		214	A&S 5th Song	58
Thou, sweetest subject, werte borne in the realme of Love,		214	A&S 5th Song	64
The later borne, yet too soone, Strephon hight..		242	Other Poems 4	24
By fortune meane, in Nature borne a Queene,		244	Other Poems 4	91
BORNE				
P. Not so, but fellowlike together borne..		46	2nd Eclogues 27	12
Bownded with no limitts, borne with a wing of hope		68	2nd Eclogues 34	8
Where roses gueuls are borne in silver field..		171	Astrophil 13	11
Good brother Philip, I have borne you long,		208	Astrophil 83	1
But He shall them deride who by the heavns is borne,		271	Psalm II	9
My strength my strongest rock, which my defence hast borne,		290	Psalm XVIII	2
Nay like young Calves in leapes are born,		310	Psalm XXIX	16
BORROW				
Talking time borrowe for to spitt their vennim		50	2nd Eclogues 28	V886
Condoling cause of friendship he will borrow..		62	2nd Eclogues 30	178
Then decke me as thine owne; thy helpe I borowe,		114	4th Eclogues 72	28
BORROWS				
And for a tast of all these gifts, she borowes Momus' grace.		12	Arcadia I 3	8
The Naughty borrowes paying not,		326	Psalm XXXVII	53
BOSOM				
Till spotlesse soule unto thy bosome flye,		40	Arcadia II 18	17
Receipt to me, within thy bosome darke..		73	Arcadia III 40	8
Yet while I languish, him that bosome clips,		194	Astrophil 59	9
Whom Death to his cold bosom drawes.		311	Psalm XXX	9
Nor envy in thy bosome nourish		324	Psalm XXXVII	3
With inbow'd bosome well for hir prepar'd,		252	Other Poems 4	387

BOSOM   (CONTINUED)   PAGE   TITLE   LINE
    Dresse bosome hers or hedd,. . . . .   257 Other Poems   5   48
BOSS
    Curb'd in with feare, but with guilt bosse above . . . . . .   189 Astrophil   49   7
BOTCHES
    A foul infection kills or bredeth botches. . . . .   50 2nd Eclogues   28 V884
BOTH
    Both they themselves unto such two shall wed,. . . . .   11 Arcadia I   1   5
    Both these conspird poore Reason's overthrowe; . . . .   11 Arcadia I   2   7
    Shine eyes on me, that both our lives be guarded;. . . . . .   17 1st Eclogues   7   92
    Which both the pallate, and the eyes delight.. . . . .   26 1st Eclogues   9   131
    Hope we doo both dye..   30 1st Eclogues   12   8
    Thus both trees and each thing ells, be the bookes of a
       fancy. . . . .   36 1st Eclogues   13   140
    Whom both nature seemes to debarr from meanes to be helped,.   37 1st Eclogues   13   158
    My sheepe are thoughts, which I both guide and serve:. . . .   39 Arcadia II   17   1
    Both still do worke, in neither finde I rest:. . . . .   42 Arcadia II   22   3
    For both, alas, their strengthes together tie: . . . .   42 Arcadia II   22   4
    R.p. Then let us both to heavenly rules give place,. . . . .   47 2nd Eclogues   27   41
    Thou then, that framste both words and voice most skilfully,   48 2nd Eclogues   28   19
    Which do envenome both the soule and senses. . . . .   50 2nd Eclogues   28   88
    My pipe and song made him both songe and pipe forsweare. . .   52 2nd Eclogues   29   20
    Let cat and dog fight which shall have both you. . . . . . .   56 2nd Eclogues   29   149
    Of rarest price, both heav'n and earth her bower.. . . . . .   59 2nd Eclogues   30   100
    Since, as I say, both minde and sences darke . . . .   73 Arcadia III   39   9
    Both equall hurt, in this change sought our blisse:. . . . .   76 Arcadia III   45   13
    So both are yours: I, bound with gaged harte:. . . . .   79 Arcadia III   50   21
    One streame both streames containe,. . . . .   92 3rd Eclogues   63   35
    A young girle's hart, to that were shame for both, ...   95 3rd Eclogues   64   59
    The goodman read on both sides the content,. . . . .   96 3rd Eclogues   64   88
    Thus shall you both reward a lover true, ...   97 3rd Eclogues   64   107
    That it both seene and felte may with you live". . . . . . .   101 3rd Eclogues   66   77
    Both cause, effect, beginning, and the ende. . . . .   114 4th Eclogues   72   42
    Both our estates, while each the other did deprave,. . . . .   119 4th Eclogues   73   107
    Our yeares doo it require: you see we both doo feele . . . .   120 4th Eclogues   73   121
    And let her have the giftes that should in both remaine: . .   120 4th Eclogues   73   131
    In her let beautie both, and chastnesse fully raigne.. . . .   120 4th Eclogues   73   132
    To whom precedence shall of both accorded be.. . . . .   120 4th Eclogues   73   136
    To worthiest let him give, when both he hath beheld: . . . .   120 4th Eclogues   73   142
    Thus both did come to me, and both began to tell . . . . . .   121 4th Eclogues   73   154
    (For both togither spake, each loth to be behinde) . . . . .   121 4th Eclogues   73   155
    "How ill both you can rule, well hath your discord taught: .   121 4th Eclogues   73   163
    The crowne above you both for ever I appoint". . . . .   121 4th Eclogues   73   166
    I would have spoken crie: but out they both did crie; . . .   121 4th Eclogues   73   167
    "Nay thou (said both) shalt see such beames shine in her
       face . . . .   121 4th Eclogues   73   175
    Both force to flie and knowledge where to fall.. . . . . . .   144 Cert Sonnets   15   12
    Yea worse then death, death parts both woe and joy,. . . . .   148 Cert Sonnets   20   13
    While remembrance doth both states containe. . . . .   153 Cert Sonnets   24   14
    Yet do we both live in you.. . . . .   154 Cert Sonnets   25   23
    That doth both shine and give us sight to see. . . . .   161 Cert Sonnets   32   8
    Both so and thus, she minding Love should be . . . .   168 Astrophil   7   12
    But thou wouldst needs fight both with love and sence, . . .   170 Astrophil   10   9
    But if (both for your love and skill) your name. . . . . . .   172 Astrophil   15   12
    That unto me, who fare like him that both. . . . .   174 Astrophil   19   10
    Teaching blind eyes both how to smile and weepe, ...   181 Astrophil   32   8
    That I respects for both our sakes must show:. . . . .   181 Astrophil   33   11
    Both by the judgement of the English eyes, ...   185 Astrophil   41   3
    Others, because of both sides I do take. . . . .   185 Astrophil   41   9
    Pardon mine eares, both I and they do pray,. . . . .   190 Astrophil   51   1
    So captives to his Saint both soule and sence, ...   195 Astrophil   61   6
    The friendly fray, where blowes both wound and heale,. . . .   206 Astrophil   79   10
    In hart both sight and love now coupled be:. . . . .   223 Astrophil   88   13
    Suffering the evils both of the day and night, ...   224 Astrophil   89   9
    Since kind or chance gives both one liverie, ...   229 Astrophil   96   2
    Both sadly blacke, both blackly darkned be,. . . . .   229 Astrophil   96   3
    Silence in both displaies his sullen might,. . . . .   229 Astrophil   96   5
    Slow heavinesse in both holds one degree,. . . . .   229 Astrophil   96   6
    In both a mazefull solitarinesse:. . . . .   229 Astrophil   96   9
    To this great cause, which needs both use and art, ...   236 Astrophil   107   8
    Who womankind at once both deckes and stayneth?. . . . . . .   197 A&S 1st Song   10
    Suffer not her to laugh, while both we suffer paine: . . . .   213 A&S 5th Song   29
    Both Rebell to the Sonne, and Vagrant from the mother; . . .   214 A&S 5th Song   69
    But both to both so bent,. . . . .   216 A&S 6th Song   35
    As both in both are spent. . . . .   216 A&S 6th Song   36
    Both in their objects such,. . . . .   216 A&S 6th Song   41
    To both sides partiall is:. . . . .   216 A&S 6th Song   46
    A lesson fit, both sight and skill, love and firme love to
       breede,. . . . .   217 A&S 7th Song   12
    Both within themselves oppressed,. . . . .   218 A&S 8th Song   7
    Be both wish and I defaced. . . . .   220 A&S 8th Song   88
    Both sheep and Oxen wholy hast,. . . . .   279 Psalm VIII   26
    Both ruines, ruiners, and ruin'd plott . . . .   280 Psalm IX   19
    Both mischief and iniquity. . . . .   282 Psalm X   30
    Wee both have power, and will our tales to tell, ...   285 Psalm XII   11
    Both light and force of seing. . . . .   294 Psalm XIX   36
    For so both day and night did stand. . . . .   315 Psalm XXXII   10
    For causeless they both pitt and net did sett, ...   321 Psalm XXXV   15
    I both in mind, and bones shall gladded be.. . . . .   321 Psalm XXXV   20
    Thou shalt have both good food and place.. . . . .   324 Psalm XXXVII   8

BOTH   (CONTINUED)   PAGE   TITLE   LINE
    To ev'ill, both they and theirs shall wrack. . . . . 326 Psalm XXXVII   72
    Still both their flocks flocking togither went,. . . . . . 242 Other Poems   4   30
    Both free of minde, both did clear-dealing love, ... 243 Other Poems   4   39
    And both had skill in verse their voice to move. . . . . . 243 Other Poems   4   40
    Till hard by them both he and she did stay. . . . .   244 Other Poems   4   88
    They of both ends the middle two doe flie, ... 248 Other Poems   4   226
    Emprison hir, who both them did possesse . . . . 252 Other Poems   4   390
    Each thing both sweet and sadd . . . . 256 Other Poems   5   8
BOTTOM
    Thus noble golde, downe to the bottome goes, ...   81 Arcadia III   54   13
    With motion of his rage did to the bottom shake. . . . . . 291 Psalm XVIII   17
BOUGHS
    But when in shade we meet of mirtle bowes, ...   18 1st Eclogues   7   128
BOUGHT
    Is Late remorse in follie dearely bought.. . . . .   49 2nd Eclogues   28   78
    Whose bought incav'd doth yeeld such sight,. . . . .   89 Arcadia III   62   97
    Desire, desire I have too dearely bought,. . . . . 161 Cert Sonnets   31   5
BOULON
    Boulon. How long wilt thou with monefull musicke staine. . . 58 2nd Eclogues   30   38
    Boulon. O man, take heed, how thou the Gods do move. . . . . 59 2nd Eclogues   30   65
    Boulon. Thy wailing words do much my spirits move, ... 60 2nd Eclogues   30   125
    Boulon. Who still doth seeke against himselfe offences,. . . 62 2nd Eclogues   30   167
*BOUND
    Bound but to you, no wealth but you I would: . . . .   4 Lady of May   2   28
    Bownd and bownd by so noble bandes, as loth to be unbownd, . 37 1st Eclogues   13   162
    Where it should be to selfe-destruction bound? . . . . . .   57 2nd Eclogues   30   13
    Wheare he was bounde, to make his marting place, ...   70 Arcadia III   36   4
    So both are yours: I, bound with gaged harte:. . . . . . .   79 Arcadia III   50   21
    And though my mones be not in musicke bound, ...   81 Arcadia III   54   7
    Those lampes of heav'nly fire to fixed motion bound, ... 118 4th Eclogues   73   43
    And having bound them fast by Styx, they should obaye. . . . 121 4th Eclogues   73   161
    Is neither freed, nor yet to service bound, ... 144 Cert Sonnets   15   2
    To stranger wanting my minde's waste soile is bound, ... 149 Cert Sonnets   22   5
    From fancie's earth passing all numbers' bound, ... 149 Cert Sonnets   22   7
    Sonets be not bound prentise to annoy: . . . . 201 Astrophil   70   5
    Thus bound I said, lo, lord I am at hand,. . . . . 331 Psalm XL   31
    Will. What? these are riddles sure, art thou then bound to
         her? . . . . 343 Possibly   1   23
    Dick. Bound as I neither power have, nor would have power to
         stir. . . . . 343 Possibly   1   24
    W. Who bound thee? D. Love my Lord. W. What witnesses
         therto . . . . 343 Possibly   1   25
    As heart-bound slaves: and happy then embrace. . . . . . . 252 Other Poems   4   391
    To fasten knotts, which fancy first had bound. . . . . . . 253 Other Poems   4   424
BOUNDED
    Bownded with no limitts, borne with a wing of hope . . . .   68 2nd Eclogues   34   8
BOUNDS
    Within what bounds can one his liking stay,. . . . . 182 Astrophil   35   3
    To be (in things past bounds of wit) fooles, if they be not
         fooles.. . . . . 217 A&S 7th Song   6
    Within the bounds of Innocence to byde,. . . . . 305 Psalm XXVI   3
BOUNTIFULNESS
    Bcuntifulnes hath made his last conclusion:. . . . . 128 4th Eclogues   75   119
BOUT
    But did entend next bout with her to meete,. . . . . 248 Other Poems   4   250
*BOW
    Hath strongest soule, when most his raynes do bowe.. . . .   25 1st Eclogues   9   101
    Ewe doth make me be thinke what kind of bow the boy holdeth. 35 1st Eclogues   13   121
    But bow all knees, now of her knees. . . . .   89 Arcadia III   62   93
    To this chaste love your sacred favours bow, ...   91 3rd Eclogues   63   21
    He leane to her, she unto him do bow:. . . . .   92 3rd Eclogues   63   49
    Sweete supple mindes which soone to wisdome bowe . . . . . 106 3rd Eclogues   67   103
    Tuckt up even with the knees, with bowe and arrowes prest: . 118 4th Eclogues   73   67
    Apollo wakes, and bow hath sometime sparde.. . . . . 143 Cert Sonnets   12   15
    Then good Apollo do away thy bowe: . . . . 146 Cert Sonnets   17   36
    Brake bow, brake shafts, while Cupid weeping sate: . . . . 173 Astrophil   17   8
    On Cupid's bow how are my heart-strings bent,. . . . . . . 174 Astrophil   19   1
    And makes me then bow downe my head, and say,. . . . . . . 237 Astrophil   108   9
    Lo you grow proud with this, for tyrans make folke bow:. . 214 A&S 5th Song   61
    Therfore thou whetst Thy sword, and bend'st Thy bow, . . . 278 Psalm VII   34
    Behold the evill have bent their bow . . . . 284 Psalm XI   5
    Strengthning mine arms that they could break an Iron bow.. 292 Psalm XVIII   63
    And ready make Thy vengefull bowe. . . . . 298 Psalm XXI   47
    Bow down thine eare to heare how much I need,. . . . . . . 312 Psalm XXXI   4
    Earthly I do bow and crooke, ... 328 Psalm XXXVIII   16
    Each motion seeming shott from beautie's bow,. . . . . . . 244 Other Poems   4   106
    With shafts shott out from their back-turned bow.. . . . . 251 Other Poems   4   351
BOWED
    No knee once bowed, forsooth, for them they say we serve.. . 120 4th Eclogues   73   114
    He bow'd the heav'ns, and from the bow'd heav'ns did discend 291 Psalm XVIII   20
    Come shepheard's boy, let now thy heart be bowd. . . . . . 255 Other Poems   4   510
BOWELS
    To teare the bowels, that good corne should send.. . . . . 102 3rd Eclogues   66   117
    Thy bowels with all killing mettals arme.. . . . . 125 4th Eclogues   75   21
BOWER
    Of rarest price, both heav'n and earth her bower.. . . . .   59 2nd Eclogues   30   100
BOWERS
    And yet they say he talkes in greate men's bowers? . . . .   28 1st Eclogues   10   68
    Come from marble bowers, many times the gay harbor of
         anguish, ...   34 1st Eclogues   13   92

```
BOWERS                         (CONTINUED)           PAGE    TITLE           LINE
    Which skill dooth make in Princes' bowers. . . . . . . . . .  87 Arcadia III  62   50
    The cattell wild, or tame, in nature's bowers. . . . . . .  100 3rd Eclogues 66   47
BOWLS
    Which to their eies the bowles of Venus brought, . . . . . . 244 Other Poems   4   99
BOWS
    Whose equall lynes their angles bowes, . . . . . . . . . . .  86 Arcadia III  62   10
    Of Stella's browes made him two better bowes, . . . . . . . 173 Astrophil    17   10
    The ev'ill bent bowes, and swords they drew, . . . . . . . . 325 Psalm XXXVII      37
    But lo their bowes, they shall be broken, . . . . . . . . . 325 Psalm XXXVII      39
BOY
    Ewe doth make me be thinke what kind of bow the boy holdeth.  35 1st Eclogues 13  121
    Though thousands old, a Boy entit'led still. . . . . . . . .  41 Arcadia II   20   10
    In that sweete seate the Boy doth sport: . . . . . . . . . .  88 Arcadia III  62   83
    Unto Cupid that boy shall a Pedante be found?. . . . . . . . 124 4th Eclogues 74   66
    Deceiv'd the quaking boy, who thought from so pure light, .  169 Astrophil     8   10
    The boy refusde for feare of Marse's hate, . . . . . . . . . 173 Astrophil    17    5
    See there that boy, that murthring boy I say, . . . . . . . 174 Astrophil    20    2
    Blind-hitting boy, since she that thee and me. . . . . . . . 187 Astrophil    46    2
    For when, nak'd boy, thou couldst no harbour find. . . . . . 198 Astrophil    65    5
    Griefe but Love's winter liverie is, the Boy . . . . . . . . 201 Astrophil    70    7
    Love still a boy, and oft a wanton is, . . . . . . . . . . . 203 Astrophil    73    1
    Or hers whom naked the Trojan boy did see. . . . . . . . . . 207 Astrophil    82    4
    Now will I with that boy prove . . . . . . . . . . . . . . . 202 A&S 2nd Song      7
    If Love might sweet'n so a boy of shepheard' brood, . . . . 209 A&S 3rd Song      7
    Strephon, fond boy, delighted did not knowe, . . . . . . . . 246 Other Poems   4  163
    Come shepheard's boy, let now thy heart be bowd. . . . . . . 255 Other Poems   4  510
BOYISH
    In truth, o Love, with what a boyish kind. . . . . . . . . . 170 Astrophil    11    1
    And full, poore foole, of boyish bravery, . . . . . . . . . 244 Other Poems   4   77
BOYS
    Like busie boyes, to winne their tutor's harte, . . . . . . .  27 1st Eclogues 10   43
    O sheepheards' boyes, eschue these tongues of venome, . . . .  50 2nd Eclogues 28   87
    Of seely boies please unacquainted sight: . . . . . . . . . 246 Other Poems   4  182
BRABBLING
    Wouldst brabling be with sence and love in me: . . . . . . . 169 Astrophil    10    2
BRAG
    I cannot brag of word, much lesse of deed, . . . . . . . . . 199 Astrophil    66    5
    Least my Foe bragg, that in my ruin hee. . . . . . . . . . . 286 Psalm XIII        13
    More than they now do bragg, when He shall take. . . . . . . 286 Psalm XIII        17
BRAGGING
    O bragging Foe, where is the endless wast. . . . . . . . . . 280 Psalm IX          16
    And sayeth in his bragging heart, . . . . . . . . . . . . . 282 Psalm X           23
    As bragging that free of all passions' mone. . . . . . . . . 244 Other Poems   4   71
BRAGS
    Great be Physitions' brags, but aid is beggerly, . . . . . . 128 4th Eclogues 75  112
    That sickenesse brags it selfe best graced to be. . . . . . 231 Astrophil   101    4
BRAIN
    Thy too much zeale, I feare thy braine hath spent. . . . . .  28 1st Eclogues 10   63
    That in your sight they fixed have my braine; . . . . . . . .  39 Arcadia II   16    2
    For who grieves not hath but a blockish braine, . . . . . . .  58 2nd Eclogues 30   36
    O braine, where thought of her hath onely place; . . . . . .  60 2nd Eclogues 30  118
    Nor ramper did abide; my braine was up blowne, . . . . . . .  68 2nd Eclogues 33   15
    Fell jealousie did so his braine oppresse, . . . . . . . . .  94 3rd Eclogues 64    9
    The wife thus having settled husband's braine, . . . . . . .  96 3rd Eclogues 64   73
    First be mine eyes pulde out, first be my braine perished; . 124 4th Eclogues 74   60
    And in my braine some sacred humour flowe: . . . . . . . . . 146 Cert Sonnets 17   38
    Some fresh and fruitfull showers upon my sunne-burn'd
        braine. . . . . . . . . . . . . . . . . . . . . . . . . 165 Astrophil     1    8
    Holds my young braine captiv'd in golden cage. . . . . . . . 176 Astrophil    23   11
    Of all the grave conceits your braine doth breed; . . . . . 190 Astrophil    51    6
    Prints his owne lively forme in rudest braine. . . . . . . . 194 Astrophil    58    8
    Let folke orecharg'd with braine against me crie, . . . . . 198 Astrophil    64    4
    Not for his faire outside, nor well lined braine, . . . . . 204 Astrophil    75    3
    Nor do like Lords, whose weake confused braine, . . . . . . 210 Astrophil    85    5
    Griefe find the words, for thou hast made my braine. . . . . 228 Astrophil    94    1
    She could not shew my blind braine waies of joy, . . . . . . 230 Astrophil    97   13
    And to that braine of hers your hidnest gifts infused, . . . 213 A&S 5th Song      27
    These doubting clouds ore-casting heav'nly braine, . . . . . 245 Other Poems   4  127
    Did draw his boyling braine. . . . . . . . . . . . . . . . . 256 Other Poems   5    9
BRAINS
    Whose braines boile not in woes, nor brests with beatings
        ake, . . . . . . . . . . . . . . . . . . . . . . . . . 117 4th Eclogues 73   13
    And Muses scorne with vulgar braines to dwell, . . . . . . . 203 Astrophil    74    3
    But hates, abhorrs the wycked braines, . . . . . . . . . . . 284 Psalm XI          18
BRAKE
    She seald it first, then she the sealing brake, . . . . . . .  96 3rd Eclogues 64   83
    But let us wiser be; and what foule discorde brake, . . . . 120 4th Eclogues 73  119
    Brake on faire cleeves of constant chastitie: . . . . . . . 151 Cert Sonnets 22   56
    Brake bow, brake shafts, while Cupid weeping sate: . . . . . 173 Astrophil    17    8
    The fire took fire and forcibly out brake, . . . . . . . . . 329 Psalm XXXIX       11
    One said he brake acrosse; full well it so might be: . . . . 241 Other Poems   1    3
    At Barly brake hir swete swift foot to trie. . . . . . . . . 247 Other Poems   4  208
    And all to second barly-brake are bent: . . . . . . . . . . 249 Other Poems   4  266
    And he by law of Barly-brake must run. . . . . . . . . . . . 249 Other Poems   4  296
    Of Barly-brake among the six befell. . . . . . . . . . . . . 250 Other Poems   4  317
    To runne, brake from his hands, and let him goe. . . . . . . 250 Other Poems   4  336
    Till she brake from their armes (although in deed. . . . . . 252 Other Poems   4  413
    And so that even the barly-brake did end.. . . . . . . . . . 252 Other Poems   4  416
```

```
BRANCHES                                                      PAGE     TITLE           LINE
    And let my breath upon your braunches cleave,. . . . . . . .   125 4th Eclogues 75     7
    Whose braunches faile not timely fruite to nourish,. . . . .  270 Psalm I              9
BRASS
    Such hartes of brasse, wise heads, and garments trim . . . .   24 1st Eclogues  9     75
BRAVE
    Shew how thou canst deserve so brave desire, . . . . . . . .    3 Lady of May   2      2
    What length of verse can serve brave Mopsa's good to show, .   12 Arcadia I     3      1
    And of their wounds make brave lame showes:. . . . . . . . .   44 Arcadia II   25      8
    But if thy rage some brave revenge will finde, . . . . . . .   72 Arcadia III  38     13
    You goodly pines, which still with brave assent. . . . . . .   77 Arcadia III  49      1
    In her brave calves, like christall skies. . . . . . . . . .   89 Arcadia III  62    102
    Least if no vaile those brave gleames did disguise,. . . . .  168 Astrophil     7      7
    Her flesh his food, her skin his armour brave, . . . . . . .  179 Astrophil    29     12
    Because in brave array heere marcheth she, . . . . . . . . .  223 Astrophil    88      3
    With such brave wounds, that they under my feet did ly. . . .  292 Psalm XVIII        70
    So brave a shott, deere fyre and bewtye strange. . . . . . .  345 Possibly      2     11
    Free of proud feares, smiling strife. . . . .  243 Other Poems   4     60
    Brave crest to him hir scorn-gold haire did yeeld, . . . . .  246 Other Poems   4    149
BRAVELY
    That bravely maskt, their fancies may be told: . . . . . . .  166 Astrophil     3      2
    Enter bravely every where, . . . . . . . . . . . . . . . . .  226 A&S 10th Song       20
    And bravely speake to them, with breath of wrathful fire,. .  271 Psalm II            11
BRAVERY
    Or if sheepe's cries can helpe the Sunne's owne braverie,. .   48 2nd Eclogues 28     25
    And full, poore foole, of boyish bravery,. . . . . . . . . .  244 Other Poems   4     77
    Making hir beames his bravery and might: . . . . . . . . . .  246 Other Poems   4    146
BRAVEST
    Whose face doth oft the bravest sort enchaunt, . . . . . . .    3 Lady of May   1      2
    Old wood inflam'de, doth yeeld the bravest fire, . . . . . .   38 Arcadia II   15      3
    Best charge, and bravest retrait in Cupid's fight, . . . . .  206 Astrophil    79      5
BRAWL
    Or for some brawle, which in that chamber hie, . . . . . . .  178 Astrophil    26      7
BRAWLINGS
    With tedious brawlings of her parents deare, . . . . . . . .  245 Other Poems   4    114
BRAWN
    And yet as hard, as brawne made hard by arte:. . . . . . . .   76 Arcadia III  46     16
BRAY
    The neighbours all did crie, "alas what asse doth bray?" . .   52 2nd Eclogues 29     26
BRAYETH
    As the chafed hart which brayeth . . . . . . . . . . . . . .  334 Psalm XLII           1
BRAYING
    With neighing, blaying, braying, and barking,. . . . . . . .  100 3rd Eclogues 66     62
BRAZEN
    Seas in our eyes, and brasen tongues by nature,. . . . . . .  109 Arcadia IV   70     26
    I list not dig so deepe for brasen fame. . . . . . . . . . .  179 Astrophil    28      4
BREACH
    Or stop a breach, that never Cannon sawe?. . . . . . . . . .   22 1st Eclogues  9     17
    In justice quit, of honour made no breach: . . . . . . . . .  135 Cert Sonnets  1     12
    Having got up a breach by fighting well, . . . . . . . . . .  171 Astrophil    12     10
BREAD
    These Canibals, who as if they were bread. . . . . . . . . .  286 Psalm XIV           14
BREAK
    Bandes, favour, faith, to breake, defile, and kill. . . . . .   84 Arcadia III  60      8
    With daunces, carols, or with barlybreake: . . . . . . . . .   54 2nd Eclogues 29     70
    Doth breake, now toong unto thy name doth move,. . . . . . .   97 3rd Eclogues 64    100
    Nor breake my word though reward come late,. . . . . . . . .  153 Cert Sonnets 24     21
    And yet to breake more staves did me addresse: . . . . . . .  191 Astrophil    53      2
    Let clouds bedimme my face, breake in mine eye,. . . . . . .  198 Astrophil    64      5
    Thanke-worthiest yet when you shall breake my hart.. . . . .  229 Astrophil    95     14
    Love it selfe did silence breake;. . . . . . . . . . . . . .  218 A&S 8th Song        26
    Come let us break their bonds, say they, and fondly say: . .  271 Psalm II             7
    With Iron scepter bruse thou shalt, and peece meale breake .  271 Psalm II            21
    Breake Thou the wyked arm. . . . . . . . . . . . . . . . . .  283 Psalm X             65
    Strengthning mine arms that they could break an Iron bow.. .  292 Psalm XVIII         63
    He doth heath'n counsell breake, . . . . . . . . . . . . . .  317 Psalm XXXIII        34
    For wycked arms shall breake asunder,. . . . . . . . . . . .  325 Psalm XXXVII        43
    To beare the bondes which Time nor wit could breake, . . . .  255 Other Poems   4    530
BREAKFAST
    Breakefast of Love, but lo, lo, where she is, . . . . . . . .  206 Astrophil    79     13
BREAKING
    Where failing is a shame, and breaking is his best.. . . . .  241 Other Poems   1      6
BREAKS
    Her cable, Reason, breakes from anchor, Hope:. . . . . . . .  114 4th Eclogues 72     46
    Which breakes the clowdes and opens forth the light, . . . .  161 Cert Sonnets 32      7
    Senses all asunder breakes;. . . . . . . . . . . . . . . . .  219 A&S 8th Song        38
BREAST
    My brest to swords, my soule to hell have solde. . . . . . .   50 2nd Eclogues 28     80
    His breast doth fill with earth of others' woe,. . . . . . .   50 2nd Eclogues 28     85
    To put it with my hand in Cosma's brest. . . . . . . . . . .   54 2nd Eclogues 29     86
    O brest in which two white sheepe swell in pride:. . . . . .   76 Arcadia III  46     10
    Into my breste, and loves renewed swimme.. . . . . . . . . .   85 Arcadia III  61     12
    To vertue, fortune, time and woman's brest.. . . . . . . . .   98 3rd Eclogues 65     14
    Her right arme naked was, discovered was her breast. . . . .  118 4th Eclogues 73     68
    And Mira I admirde: her shape sank in my brest.. . . . . . .  119 4th Eclogues 73    100
    O Philomela with thy brest oppressed . . . . . . . . . . . .  126 4th Eclogues 75     61
    What griefe her breast oppresseth, . . . . . . . . . . . . .  137 Cert Sonnets  4      7
    O teares of guilefull breast,. . . . . . . . . . . . . . . .  158 Cert Sonnets 28     14
    Thy scepter use in some old Catoe's brest; . . . . . . . . .  166 Astrophil     4      5
    And in her breast bopeepe or couching lyes,. . . . . . . . .  170 Astrophil    11     12
```

BREAST	(CONTINUED)	PAGE	TITLE		LINE
That in her breast thy pap well sugred lies, ...		170	Astrophil	12	5
Upon whose breast a fiercer Gripe doth tire.		171	Astrophil	14	2
So in my swelling breast that only I		178	Astrophil	27	7
My mouth doth water, and my breast doth swell, ...		183	Astrophil	37	1
Pitie thereof gate in her breast such place.		187	Astrophil	45	7
Cannot be staid within my panting breast, ...		189	Astrophil	50	2
With that faire breast making woe's darknesse cleare:. . . .		193	Astrophil	57	11
But as you with my breast I oft have nurst, ...		228	Astrophil	95	3
O honied sighs, which from that breast do rise, ...		231	Astrophil	100	5
Melts downe his lead into my boyling brest, ...		236	Astrophil	108	2
Which now my breast orecharg'd to Musicke lendeth?		196	A&S 1st Song		2
Above line repeated at following location.		197	A&S 1st Song		34
Who hath the breast, whose milke doth passions nourish, . . .		197	A&S 1st Song		17
Ah, my sute granted is, I feele my breast doth swell:. . . .		213	A&S 5th Song		34
From the stormes in my breast breeding, ...		221	A&S 9th Song		4
But they that sinne, in sinfull breast do cherish;		271	Psalm I		21
By power of whose only brest, ...		274	Psalm IV		34
For what lord rules our bold emboldned breast.		285	Psalm XII		12
I prayd with prayers which my breast did touch;		322	Psalm XXXV		32
I then, whose burd'ned brest but thus aspires.		242	Other Poems	4	5
The happy wretch she putt into hir breast, ...		244	Other Poems	4	98
Desire the more he suckt, more sought the brest, ...		247	Other Poems	4	203
That to hir breast he gave a noysome blowe..		249	Other Poems	4	272
Filling his eies with teares, with sighs his brest..		253	Other Poems	4	432
Come she, and sweet the aire with open brest,.		254	Other Poems	4	466
With shrinking legges, but with a swelling brest, ...		255	Other Poems	4	523
With hand and mouth, with lapp and brest keepe warme, ...		258	Other Poems	5	84
BREASTS					
With sleeves turnde up, loose haire, and brestes enlarged, . .		16	1st Eclogues	7	74
To narrow brests he comes all wrapt in gaine:.		21	1st Eclogues	8	37
Shall I that saw those brests, where beauties flow, ...		58	2nd Eclogues	30	47
Her loose haire be the shott, the brestes the pykes be, . . .		67	2nd Eclogues	33	7
To over pressed brestes, more greevous waight.		82	Arcadia III	56	8
The lovely clusters of her brests, ...		87	Arcadia III	62	53
Whose braines boile not in woes, nor brests with beatings ake, ...		117	4th Eclogues	73	13
Her milken breasts the nurse of child-like love, ...		141	Cert Sonnets	9	7
You seeke to nurse at fullest breasts of Fame, ...		172	Astrophil	15	13
Her breasts his tents, legs his triumphall carre:.		179	Astrophil	29	11
I said, thine eyes were starres, thy breasts the milk'n way,		212	A&S 5th Song		10
At mother's breastes, thou didst good hope betake me.. . . .		299	Psalm XXII		22
BREATH					
As without breath, no pipe doth move,.		14	1st Eclogues	6	7
With flamie breathe doo issue oft in sound:.		42	Arcadia II	21	8
With words so vile, which viler breath doth breed.		50	2nd Eclogues	28	82
Her words in syrup laid of sweetest breath, ...		58	2nd Eclogues	30	51
Wherein I burne, thy breath is		67	2nd Eclogues	32	44
Where drawing breath, I sucke the aire of woe:		73	Arcadia III	40	10
O breath more sweete, then is the growing beane:		76	Arcadia III	46	2
Ye helplesse Sighes, blowe out your breath to nought, ...		83	Arcadia III	59	5
Monkie, sweet breath; the Cow, her faire eyes brought; . . .		101	3rd Eclogues	66	88
Breath made of flames, wits knowing nought but damage, . . .		109	Arcadia IV	70	28
Whereto I yeeld, and seeke no other breath, ...		114	4th Eclogues	72	18
And from our burning breath the trees doo bende.		116	4th Eclogues	72	104
Did not a rosed breath, from lips more rosie proceeding, . .		124	4th Eclogues	74	79
And let my breath upon your braunches cleave, ...		125	4th Eclogues	75	7
My breath distinguish'd into wordes of woe, ...		125	4th Eclogues	75	8
Aire let me draw no more thy breath in anguish:.		136	Cert Sonnets	3	14
Her breath which makes a sower answer sweete, ...		141	Cert Sonnets	9	6
Lives to impart my wearie clay some breath..		148	Cert Sonnets	20	10
Who seeketh heav'n and comes of heav'nly breath.		144	Cert Sonnets	32	12
That her sweete breath makes oft thy flames to rise, ...		170	Astrophil	12	4
That when the breath of my complaints doth tuch.		187	Astrophil	44	10
Stella's sweete breath the same to me did reed..		194	Astrophil	58	11
And all in vaine, for while thy breath most sweet, ...		200	Astrophil	68	9
But with short breath, long lookes, staid feet and walking hed, ...		205	Astrophil	76	13
Let breath sucke up those sweetes, let armes embrace		210	Astrophil	85	12
Yet truth (if Caitif's breath mighte call thee) this		227	Astrophil	93	5
Wing'd with whose breath, so pleasing Zephires blow, ...		231	Astrophil	100	7
And bravely speake to them, with breath of wrathful fire,. .		271	Psalm II		11
Their abject lips no breath but flattery move.		284	Psalm XII		5
With blasting breath O Lord, that in thy chiding went. . . .		291	Psalm XVIII		33
By breath of his mouth stands.		316	Psalm XXXIII		24
Her breath, then short, seem'd loth from home to pas, ...		252	Other Poems	4	399
Tell, if that breath, which thee thy sounding gives, ...		258	Other Poems	5	63
BREATHE					
That private panges can not breath out in publique		109	Arcadia IV	70	32
And mother Earth, now clad in mourning weeds, did breath . .		117	4th Eclogues	73	9
Bubling out doth breathe signes of his hugie dolours:. . . .		123	4th Eclogues	74	28
Love gave the wound, which while I breathe will bleed: . . .		165	Astrophil	2	2
While teares powre out his inke, and sighs breathe out his words, ...		168	Astrophil	6	10
Breathe out the flames which burne within my heart,.		179	Astrophil	28	13
Because I breathe not love to everie one, ...		191	Astrophil	54	1
If Orpheus' voyce had force to breathe such musicke's love .		208	A&S 3rd Song		1
Which do breath a sugred blisse, ...		226	A&S 10th Song		29
BREATHED					
Nurse inwarde maladyes, which have not scope to be breath'd out, ...		35	1st Eclogues	13	104

```
BREATHED              (CONTINUED)                              PAGE    TITLE         LINE
   This sowre-breath'd mate tast of those sugred lips.. . . . . .  194  Astrophil   59   11
   But this at last is her sweet breath'd defence:. . . . . . .  195  Astrophil   61    4
   Which thus breath'd out with earthquake of his hart. . . . .  256  Other Poems  4  544
BREATHER
   Breather of life, and fastner of desire, . . . . . . . . . .  207  Astrophil   80    7
BREATHES
   Sweetnesse, that breathes and pants as oft as she: . . . . .  231  Astrophil  101    2
BREATHING
   Breathing all blisse and sweetning to the heart, . . . . . .  207  Astrophil   81    3
   Tc my God that give me breathing.. . . . . . . . . . . . . .  335  Psalm XLII       40
   To Strephon Aeole's land first breathing lent: . . . . . . .  242  Other Poems  4   26
BREATHLESS
   Till with long race deare she was breathles brought, . . . .  251  Other Poems  4  359
BRED
   Desiring, that no griefe in him he bread . . . . . . . . . .   97  3rd Eclogues 64  111
   But such they say we be: this praise our discord bred, . . .  120  4th Eclogues 73  117
   My burning tongue hath bred my mistresse paine, . . . . . .  141  Cert Sonnets  9    2
   An Asse's shade ere now hath bred debate.. . . . . . . . . .  146  Cert Sonnets 17   20
   Alas, I lie: rage hath this errour bred, . . . . . . . . . .  160  Cert Sonnets 30   31
BREED
   Constant and kind: my sheep your foode shall breed,. . . . .   18  1st Eclogues  7  123
   New plucked from the place where it did breed, . . . . . . .   19  1st Eclogues  7  159
   And learn'd what ill a miser state doth breed, . . . . . . .   21  1st Eclogues  8   22
   O only sonne that suche a fruite can breede. . . . . . . . .   43  Arcadia II   23    3
   O cruell sonne thy hate this harme dothe breede. . . . . . .   43  Arcadia II   24    3
   R. But yet our strife sure peace in end doth breede. . . . .   46  2nd Eclogues 27   27
   With words so vile, which viler breath doth breed. . . . . .   50  2nd Eclogues 28   82
   Should breed to her, let me for aye dejected be. . . . . . .   51  2nd Eclogues 28  121
   For what can breed more peevish incongruities, . . . . . . .   61  2nd Eclogues 30  140
   What horrors breede, wheare wynd dominion beares, . . . . .   71  Arcadia III  37    2
   The high conceits thy heav'nly wisedomes breed . . . . . . .   72  Arcadia III  38    2
   Yet joyning formes one sight of beautie breede. . . . . . .   78  Arcadia III  50    4
   Then gan he factions in the beastes to breed;. . . . . . . .  102  3rd Eclogues 66  120
   Where life is death, and death cannot breed peace. . . . . .  116  4th Eclogues 72   95
   Would often kill to breed more feeling paine, . . . . . . .  135  Cert Sonnets  2    4
   A simple soule should breed so mixed woes. . . . . . . . . .  149  Cert Sonnets 22   10
   Which elements with mortall mixture breed: . . . . . . . . .  167  Astrophil    5   11
   If that be sinne which in fixt hearts doth breed . . . . . .  172  Astrophil   14   12
   Nay, that may breed my fame, it is so rare:. . . . . . . . .  182  Astrophil   34    6
   Wrackes Triumphs be, which Love (high set) doth breed. . . .  186  Astrophil   42   14
   Though false, yet with free scope more grace doth breed. . .  187  Astrophil   45   10
   Of all the grave conceits your braine doth breed;. . . . . .  190  Astrophil   51    6
   Even those sad words even in sad me did breed. . . . . . . .  194  Astrophil   58   14
   In weakened minds, quicke apprehending breed, . . . . . . .  199  Astrophil   66    3
   A lesson fit, both sight and skill, love and firme love to
      breede,. . . . . . . . . . . . . . . . . . . . . . . . .  217  A&S 7th Song      12
   To breed my grievous trouble,. . . . . . . . . . . . . . . .  272  Psalm III         3
   They shall be sham'd and vext, that breed my crying, . . . .  276  Psalm VI         30
   Delight in God and he shall breed. . . . . . . . . . . . . .  324  Psalm XXXVII      9
   To long-perplexed minde breed long delight.. . . . . . . . .  245  Other Poems  4  112
   Then those delights through all their sinews breed . . . . .  252  Other Poems  4  411
   So may no fortune breed. . . . . . . . . . . . . . . . . . .  258  Other Poems  5   80
BREEDETH
   A foul infection kills or bredeth botches. . . . . . . . . .   50  2nd Eclogues 28 V884
   Glorie breedeth: . . . . . . . . . . . . . . . . . . . . . .  156  Cert Sonnets 26   30
BREEDING
   Wealth breeding want, more blist, more wretched grow.. . . .  177  Astrophil   24    4
   From the stormes in my breast breeding, . . . . . . . . . .  221  A&S 9th Song      4
   And all the beasts for ever breeding . . . . . . . . . . . .  279  Psalm VIII       27
   Breeding huge stormes with in his inward parte, . . . . . .  256  Other Poems  4  543
BREEDS
   Which breeds nought else but gloses of deceits.. . . . . . .   20  1st Eclogues  8    4
   Unkindnes breedes, unkindnes fostreth hate.. . . . . . . . .   85  Arcadia III  61    8
   These wonders England breedes, the last remaines, . . . . .  151  Cert Sonnets 22   61
   But soone as thought of thee breeds my delight, . . . . . .  236  Astrophil  108    5
BRETHREN
   To Brethren then I will declare Thy Fame, . . . . . . . . .  299  Psalm XXII       51
BREW
   And rid me from the wrongs which cruel Wits did brew; . . .  293  Psalm XVIII      87
BREWED
   Sins brew'd in youthfull glass, . . . . . . . . . . . . . .  303  Psalm XXV        26
BRIBES
   That hand whose strength should help of bribes is full.. . .  306  Psalm XXVI       33
BRICKLE
   While brickle houreglas runnes, guide thou our panting race:   45  Arcadia II   26   10
BRIDE
   The honest Bridegroome, and the bashfull Bride, . . . . . .   91  3rd Eclogues 63   13
   We go unto the Bryde, and use this daye. . . . . . . . . . .  107  3rd Eclogues 67  119
BRIDEGROOM
   The honest Bridegroome, and the bashfull Bride, . . . . . .   91  3rd Eclogues 63   13
   Who forth doth come like a bridegrome. . . . . . . . . . . .  294  Psalm XIX        21
BRIDLE
   Hath power that Sex with bridle to withhold? . . . . . . . .   24  1st Eclogues  9   58
   Whose mouths Thy self dost bridle, . . . . . . . . . . . . .  315  Psalm XXXII      33
BRIGHT
   Howe is my Sunn, whose beames are shining bright, . . . . .   74  Arcadia III  42    1
   Burneth bright in fairest light. No, no, no, no. . . . . . .  155  Cert Sonnets 26   11
   In colour blacke, why wrapt she beames so bright?. . . . . .  168  Astrophil    7    2
   Or seeing jets, blacke, but in blacknesse bright.. . . . . .  225  Astrophil   91    8
```

58

BRIGHT	(CONTINUED)	PAGE	TITLE		LINE
Setting Thy self in Throne, which shined bright.		279	Psalm IX		9
In comes the King of glory bright.		302	Psalm XXIV		18
Above line repeated at following location.		302	Psalm XXIV		22
Walking in bright Phoebus' blaze		262	Other Poems	7	1
BRIM					
And thowe Laelaps let not pride make thee brim		26	1st Eclogues	10	10
BRIMFUL					
With seede of woes my hart brimme-full is charged.		16	1st Eclogues	7	78
BRIMSTONE					
On them storms, brimstone, coales he raines,		284	Psalm XI		19
BRING					
Do not thy hart, to plaintfull custome bring,		22	1st Eclogues	9	3
Nico. Who doubts but Pas' fine pipe againe will bring.		53	2nd Eclogues	29	51
I would climbe up, and bring a prettie starre,		55	2nd Eclogues	29	118
Which little time did fitlie bring to passe.		96	3rd Eclogues	64	76
But this bad world, few golden fieldes doth bring,		104	3rd Eclogues	67	19
The heav'ns doo not good haps in handfuls bring,		105	3rd Eclogues	67	61
You that do Dictionarie's methode bring.		172	Astrophil	15	5
A prety case! I hoped her to bring		193	Astrophil	57	12
And bring to naught those watching pawes..		290	Psalm XVII		36
Lord what delight to him doth bring.		296	Psalm XXI		3
To Thy remembrance bring		303	Psalm XXV		21
BRINGETH					
The Nightingale, as soone as aprill bringeth		137	Cert Sonnets	4	1
Lully, lully, my babe, hope cradle bringeth.		139	Cert Sonnets	6	4
For no dumbnesse nor death bringeth.		140	Cert Sonnets	7	38
That it bringeth		155	Cert Sonnets	26	8
More cause a like effect at leastwise bringeth:		208	A&S 3rd Song		5
Angels to acquaintance bringeth.		219	A&S 8th Song		40
BRINGING					
Such anger bringing: as for me, my fancie.		50	2nd Eclogues	28	95
Bringing with her those starry Nimphs, whose chace		229	Astrophil	97	3
Holy daunce to God's house bringing.		334	Psalm XLII		16
Bringing me to thy		336	Psalm XLIII		16
BRINGS					
One brings the stuffe, the other stamps the coine,		20	1st Eclogues	8	3
Yet harvest brings. Doth she alas absent herselfe?		49	2nd Eclogues	28	62
Ech other beast likewise his present brings:		101	3rd Eclogues	66	99
She, whose lest word brings from the spheares their musique,		113	4th Eclogues	71	68
What ever fades, but fading pleasure brings.		161	Cert Sonnets	32	4
When trembling voice brings forth that I do Stella love.		168	Astrophil	6	14
My youth doth waste, my knowledge brings forth toyes,		174	Astrophil	18	9
So Stella's heart, finding what power Love brings,		179	Astrophil	29	5
The first that straight my fancie's error brings		183	Astrophil	38	5
Then servant's wracke, where new doubts honor brings;		187	Astrophil	45	11
Beauty brings to the hall,		216	A&S 6th Song		39
About which hee dimme clouds like a Pavilion brings,		291	Psalm XVIII		24
To crammed mawes a spratt new Stomake brings..		245	Other Poems	4	134
BRODERED					
Broadred with buls and swans, powdred with golden raine:		167	Astrophil	6	6
BROILS					
To twist those broyles, which hardly would untwine:		146	Cert Sonnets	17	22
BROKE					
That hardly usde, who ever prison broke,		135	Cert Sonnets	1	11
So that not one of them is broke;		320	Psalm XXXIV		74
Will. What? is thy Bagpipe broke, or are thy lambs miswent;		343	Possibly	1	15
But most cryed, "O well broke": O foole full gaily blest:		241	Other Poems	1	5
But after this to greater rage it broke,		253	Other Poems	4	429
BROKEN					
Brused with waves of Care, but broken is		114	4th Eclogues	72	49
Full womanlike complaines her will was brokne.		137	Cert Sonnets	4	16
Peace Due alledgeance, Duty must bee broken,		138	Cert Sonnets	5	19
Nor of that golden sea, whose waves in curles are brok'n:		213	A&S 5th Song		39
That therewith my song is broken...		221	A&S 8th Song		104
Hast in their malice broken.		273	Psalm III		30
Behold their broken shame!		296	Psalm XX		31
The highest Cedars broken see,		310	Psalm XXIX		14
Or like a broken pott in myer tredd.		313	Psalm XXXI		36
To humble broken minds		320	Psalm XXXIV		65
But lo their bowes, they shall be broken,		325	Psalm XXXVII		39
I am weake and broken sore,		328	Psalm XXXVIII		22
His oft sigh-broken dittie,		259	Other Poems	5	115
BROOD					
If Love might sweet'n so a boy of shepheard' brood,		209	A&S 3rd Song		7
*BROOK					
She byd me spie her babie in the brooke,		55	2nd Eclogues	29	112
Nor brooke oughte els but well acquainted woe.		74	Arcadia III	41	6
Like Whitest Snowe, in silver Brooke,		88	Arcadia III	62 V	69
Which in her face teach vertue, I could brooke		193	Astrophil	56	6
And this I sweare by blackest brooke of hell,		204	Astrophil	74	7
Seeking some refreshing brook,		334	Psalm XLII		2
"Tell me you wanton brooke,		257	Other Poems	5	27
"Earth, brooke, flowrs, pipe, lambe, Dove.		259	Other Poems	5	92
*BROOKS					
As shallow brookes do yeeld the greatest sound,		4	Lady of May		14
Shallow brookes murmure most, deep silent slide away;		14	1st Eclogues	7	11
Seeke skill of hearbes in hills, haunt brookes neere night,		26	1st Eclogues	9	127
And to the woods or brookes, who do make such dreery recitall		33	1st Eclogues	13	42

*BROOKS	(CONTINUED)	PAGE	TITLE		LINE
Over these brookes trusting to ease mine eyes, ...		41	Arcadia II	21	1
There fall those Saphir-coloured brookes, ...		90	Arcadia III	62	127
All waywardnes, which nothing kindly brookes, ...		93	3rd Eclogues	63	66
Alas sweet Brookes do in my teares augment:		147	Cert Sonnets	18	12
Rockes, woods, hilles, caves, dales, meads, brookes, answere me, ...		147	Cert Sonnets	18	13

BROTHER
Brother to woe, and father of complaint:		141	Cert Sonnets	10	3
Good brother Philip, I have borne you long, ...		208	Astrophil	83	1
Brother his brother, frend doth frend forsake, ...		248	Other Poems	4	236

BROTHER'S
| Like to my brother's raies, yet those I sende. . . . . | | 82 | Arcadia III | 55 | 14 |

BROTHERS
| As Brothers, or as Friends beloved much; . . . . | | 322 | Psalm XXXV | | 34 |

BROTHERS'
| Like loving brothers' case . . . . | | 215 | A&S 6th Song | | 15 |

BROUGHT
And weakest harts to constant temper brought..		22	1st Eclogues	9	15
Nico. To river's banke, being a walking brought, ...		55	2nd Eclogues	29	111
But when I first did fal, what brought most fall to my hart? Arte.		64	2nd Eclogues	31	28
Yet never rock, nor race, suche terror brought, ...		71	Arcadia III	37	3
Might of each side astray be brought, ...		88	Arcadia III	62	72
Monkie, sweet breath; the Cow, her faire eyes brought; . . .		101	3rd Eclogues	66	88
And unto death, quite drownde in Dolours, brought.		115	4th Eclogues	72	68
The mountaines great with childe I thought brought foorth a mouse.		118	4th Eclogues	73	76
What force brought them to so unlikely ground.		149	Cert Sonnets	22	4
Too long, too long asleepe thou hast me brought, ...		161	Cert Sonnets	31	7
Doth fall to stray, and my chiefe powres are brought		183	Astrophil	38	3
That hast my mind, none of the basest, brought		184	Astrophil	40	3
That brought me so high to fall:		211	A&S 4th Song		52
While favour fed my hope, delight with hope was brought, . .		212	A&S 5th Song		1
And hast Thy deadly armes in order brought		278	Psalm VII		35
Now brought abed, hath brought nought foorth, but nought.. .		278	Psalm VII		39
And now am brought, alas, brought by Thy power		299	Psalm XXII		37
That I from trust in Thee was brought.		303	Psalm XXV		18
He me, he only brought..		319	Psalm XXXIV		16
Which to their eies the bowles of Venus brought, ...		244	Other Poems	4	99
To which hir presence such a feaver brought.		246	Other Poems	4	176
Who victor seem'd, was to his ruine brought:		251	Other Poems	4	346
Till with long race deare she was breathles brought, ...		251	Other Poems	4	359

BROWS
With sweatie browes, sometyme with watrie eyes, ...		71	Arcadia III	36	8
That doth present those even browes, ...		86	Arcadia III	62	9
The little coine his sweating browes have got, ...		104	3rd Eclogues	67	41
Of Stella's browes made him two better bowes, ...		173	Astrophil	17	10

BRUERTONS
| The Bruertons have a Lake, which when the Sunne. . . . . . . | | 150 | Cert Sonnets | 22 | 11 |

BRUISE
| With Iron scepter bruse thou shalt, and peece meale breake . | | 271 | Psalm II | | 21 |

BRUISED
| For hungrie throte their flesh with teeth he brused: . . . . | | 102 | 3rd Eclogues | 66 | 145 |
| Brused with waves of Care, but broken is . . . . | | 114 | 4th Eclogues | 72 | 49 |

BRUNT
| Though battaile's brunt I needs must beare, ... | | 307 | Psalm XXVII | | 15 |
| While battaile's brunt on me were laid . . . . | | 307 | Psalm XXVII | | 16 |

BUBBLING
| Bubling out doth breathe signes of his hugie dolours:. . . . | | 123 | 4th Eclogues | 74 | 28 |
| That poison foule of bubling pride doth lie. . . . . | | 178 | Astrophil | 27 | 6 |

BUD
| Since wayling is a bud of causefull sorowe, ... | | 108 | Arcadia IV | 70 | 1 |
| Where greene leaves did newly bud. . . . . | | 262 | Other Poems | 7 | 4 |

BUDS
Pine is hye, hope is as hie, sharpe leav'd, sharpe yet be my hope's budds.		36	1st Eclogues	13	130
The lothsome buds growne on sorrowe's tree..		153	Cert Sonnets	24	5
Lo, how his blessing budds		304	Psalm XXV		49

BUILD
Plangus. Curst be good haps, and curst be they that build. .		58	2nd Eclogues	30	41
Burnt by the Sunne, she first must build her nest.		60	2nd Eclogues	30	103
Ante, industrie; and Connie, skill to builde;		101	3rd Eclogues	66	93
We last short while, and build long lasting places:.		127	4th Eclogues	75	91
If stones good measure daunc'd, the Theban walles to build,.		208	A&S 3rd Song		3
In God on whom you build		272	Psalm III		10
The just in Thee, on thee and justice build:		275	Psalm V		38
On my complaint build up their joy..		303	Psalm XXV		6
Did it for just Desire's true children builde, ...		345	Possibly	4	10

BUILDED
| The tabernacle builded, ... | | 294 | Psalm XIX | | 18 |

BUILDEN
| Unknowne as then were they that buylden towers:. . . . . . . | | 100 | 3rd Eclogues | 66 | 46 |

BUILDERS
| But fore-accounting oft makes builders misse, ... | | 244 | Other Poems | 4 | 79 |

BUILDING
| Olde aged oke cutt downe, of newe works serves to the building:. . . . . | | 36 | 1st Eclogues | 13 | 134 |
| But that in building they begunne. . . . . | | 284 | Psalm XI | | 9 |

```
                                                        PAGE    TITLE          LINE
BUILDS
  She builds her fame on higher seated praise: . . . . . . . .  207 Astrophil    81   10
BUILT
  Hath his front built of Alabaster pure;. . . . . . . . . . .  169 Astrophil     9    3
BULLET
  Till bloudie bullet get him wrongfull pray.. . . . . . . . .  175 Astrophil    20    4
BULL'S
  I am enclosed with young Bulls' madded route,. . . . . . . .  299 Psalm XXII        27
BULLS
  Broadred with buls and swans, powdred with golden raine: . .  167 Astrophil     6    6
  Nay Basan mighty Bulls close me about. . . . . . . . . . . .  299 Psalm XXII        28
BURDEN
  Unto the heav'ns? our wings be too short; th' earth thinks
    us a burden; . . . . . . . . . . . . . . . . . . . . . . .   32 1st Eclogues 13   29
  But in a palme when I marke, how he doth rise under a
    burden . . . . . . . . . . . . . . . . . . . . . . . . . .   36 1st Eclogues 13  127
  But forced are to burthen feeble nature. . . . . . . . . . .  110 Arcadia IV   70   34
  On silly me do not the burthen lay,. . . . . . . . . . . . .  190 Astrophil    51    5
  Or doth the tedious burd'n of long wo. . . . . . . . . . . .  199 Astrophil    66    2
BURDENED
  Thus shrewdly burdned then, how can my Muse escape?. . . . .   12 Arcadia I     3    3
  A burthned hart. "How can words ease, which are. . . . . . .  181 Astrophil    34    2
  I then, whose burd'ned brest but thus aspires. . . . . . . .  242 Other Poems   4    5
BURDENOUS
  And cast from me part of my burdnous cares:. . . . . . . . .   42 Arcadia II   21   14
BURGESS
  Strephon. I that was once free-burges of the forrests, . . .  111 4th Eclogues 71   13
  The Bird free Burgess of the ayre, . . . . . . . . . . . . .  279 Psalm VIII        29
BURIAL
  In water dround, in earth his buriall is;. . . . . . . . . .  105 3rd Eclogues 67   68
  On rocke, Despaire, the buriall of my blisse.. . . . . . . .  114 4th Eclogues 72   50
  Klaius. On rocke, Despaire, the buriall of my blisse . . . .  115 4th Eclogues 72   51
BURIED
  In tombe of lids then buried are mine eyes,. . . . . . . . .  231 Astrophil    99   12
BURN
  Doth beauties keep, which never Sunne can burne, . . . . . .   18 1st Eclogues  7  118
  I finde no shade, but where my Sunne doth burne: . . . . . .   18 1st Eclogues  7  144
  Which doth to ashes burne: . . . . . . . . . . . . . . . . .   19 1st Eclogues  7  155
  Save that dayly we may discerne what fire we do burne in.. .   33 1st Eclogues 13   53
  Sweete Juniper saith this, thoh I burne, yet I burne in a
    sweete fire. . . . . . . . . . . . . . . . . . . . . . . .   35 1st Eclogues 13  120
  These fires increase: in these I dayly burne:. . . . . . . .   42 Arcadia II   22    8
  Leave of my sheepe, my sighes burne up your filde, . . . . .   43 Arcadia II   24    7
  That quickly they would her burne, drowne, or smother, . . .   61 2nd Eclogues 30  159
  Wherein I burne, thy breath is . . . . . . . . . . . . . . .   67 2nd Eclogues 32   44
  Fire burne me quite, till sense of burning leave me: . . . .  136 Cert Sonnets  3   13
  Pleased with the light, that his small corse doth burne: . .  149 Cert Sonnets 21   12
  For if those flames burne my desire, . . . . . . . . . . . .  153 Cert Sonnets 24   26
  And find th'effect, for I do burne in love.. . . . . . . . .  177 Astrophil    25   14
  Breathe out the flames which burne within my heart,. . . . .  179 Astrophil    28   13
  If he do love, I burne, I burne in love: . . . . . . . . . .  194 Astrophil    59    2
  Coles of love that burne so clearely;. . . . . . . . . . . .  222 A&S 9th Song      34
  Let fyre for tryall burn,. . . . . . . . . . . . . . . . . .  296 Psalm XX          13
  Did me pearce, burne, and bynde, long since and late,. . . .  345 Possibly      2   12
  A fire, to burne the prisoners he gaines,. . . . . . . . . .  246 Other Poems   4  154
BURNED
  In vaine, my Hart, now you with sight are burnd, . . . . . .   38 Arcadia II   14    5
  A blinded Mowlle, or else a burned flye. . . . . . . . . . .  149 Cert Sonnets 21   14
  Burn'd by the light he best liked, . . . . . . . . . . . . .  154 Cert Sonnets 25   16
  The Sunne which others burn'd, did her but kisse.. . . . . .  176 Astrophil    22   14
BURNETH
  The fire to see my wrongs for anger burneth: . . . . . . . .  136 Cert Sonnets  3    1
  Burneth bright in fairest light. No, no, no, no. . . . . . .  155 Cert Sonnets 26   11
BURNING
  And from our burning breath the trees doo bende. . . . . . .  116 4th Eclogues 72  104
  Fire burne me quite, till sense of burning leave me: . . . .  136 Cert Sonnets  3   13
  My burning tongue hath bred my mistresse paine,. . . . . . .  141 Cert Sonnets  9   21
  Can those blacke beames such burning markes engrave. . . . .  188 Astrophil    47    2
  Flames issued from his mouth, and burning coales out went; .  291 Psalm XVIII       19
BURNISHED
  Her skin like burnisht gold, her hands like silver ure
    untryde. . . . . . . . . . . . . . . . . . . . . . . . . .   12 Arcadia I     3   12
BURNS
  My heart cries "ah", it burnes, mine eyes now dazled be: . .  205 Astrophil    76   11
  But my heart burnes, I cannot silent be. . . . . . . . . . .  207 Astrophil    81   11
BURNT
  Where eares be burnt, eyes dazled, harts opprest?. . . . . .    3 Lady of May   1    6
  Burnt in my selfe, I muse at others' fire: . . . . . . . . .   41 Arcadia II   20    5
  Burnt by the Sunne, she first must build her nest. . . . . .   60 2nd Eclogues 30  103
  Man oft is plag'de with aire, is burnt with fire,. . . . . .  105 3rd Eclogues 67   67
  In ashes of despaire (though burnt) shall make thee live". .  121 4th Eclogues 73  174
  Who burnt his lips to kisse faire shining fire.. . . . . . .  145 Cert Sonnets 16   14
  He burnt unwares his wings, and cannot fly away. . . . . . .  169 Astrophil     8   14
  Burnt offring nor sin offring, . . . . . . . . . . . . . . .  331 Psalm XL          26
  Burnt Caban, lost my cloke,. . . . . . . . . . . . . . . . .  259 Other Poems   5  101
BURR
  This mote from out his eye, this inward burre, . . . . . . .  246 Other Poems   4  172
BURST
  With that (yet kissed first) his pipe he burst.. . . . . . .  255 Other Poems   4  520
```

BUSH
                                        PAGE   TITLE   LINE

	PAGE	TITLE		LINE
BUSH				
As I behynde a Busshe dyd sitt	57	2nd Eclogues	30	1
Who like a theefe, hid in darke bush doth ly,.	175	Astrophil	20	3
All visions seeme, at every bush I start:.	253	Other Poems	4	445
He saw behind a bush where Klaius sate:.	255	Other Poems	4	527
BUSHES				
Nico. As I of late, neer bushes usde my sive,.	54	2nd Eclogues	29	81
BUSINESS				
For busines, where it pertaines him not, ...	28	1st Eclogues	10	65
BUSSING				
Bussing her oft, and in his hart full faine, ...	95	3rd Eclogues	64	51
BUSY				
Like busie boyes, to winne their tutor's harte,.	27	1st Eclogues	10	43
In curious circle, busie sight:.	88	Arcadia III	62	74
These questions busie wits to me do frame;	180	Astrophil	30	12
That busie archer his sharpe arrowes tries?.	180	Astrophil	31	4
Tired with the dusty toiles of busie day,.	224	Astrophil	89	7
Busy with oker did their shoulders marke,.	243	Other Poems	4	69
BUY				
Dearely the servants doo their wages buy,.	105	3rd Eclogues	67	52
They are but words therefore which men do buy, ...	128	4th Eclogues	75	115
BYWAY				
In secret by-way villages.	282	Psalm X		32
BYWORDS				
Lord, what bywords they speake, what spite they spit?. . . .	105	3rd Eclogues	67	48
CABIN				
Unto a silly caban, though weake, yet stronger against woes.	34	1st Eclogues	13	93
Yet for that night, my Caban dyd them kepe	62	2nd Eclogues	30	188
Burnt Caban, lost my cloke,.	259	Other Poems	5	101
CABINET				
So when thou saw'st in Nature's cabinet.	170	Astrophil	11	9
CABLE				
Her cable, Reason, breakes from anchor, Hope:.	114	4th Eclogues	72	46
CACKLING				
Cackling, and chattring, that of Jove beseech.	100	3rd Eclogues	66	67
CADENCE				
To cadence of the tunes, which Amphyon's lyre did yeeld, . .	208	A&S 3rd Song		4
CAESAR'S				
Nor do aspire to Caesar's bleeding fame, ...	198	Astrophil	64	10
CAGE				
A Cage (guilded perchaunce) is all his lott.	28	1st Eclogues	10	69
Turnd from themselves, infected with their cage, ...	57	2nd Eclogues	30	18
The house is made a very lothsome cage,.	105	3rd Eclogues	67	49
Holds my young braine captiv'd in golden cage.	176	Astrophil	23	11
In ivory cage she did the micher binde:.	244	Other Poems	4	94
CAITIFF				
Unto the caitife wretch, whom long affliction holdeth, . . .	122	4th Eclogues	74	1
What courage strange hath caught thy caitife hart, ...	142	Cert Sonnets	10	9
As of a caitife worthy so to die,.	228	Astrophil	94	10
In this caitife hart to be,.	221	A&S 9th Song		23
CAITIFF'S				
Yet truth (if Caitif's breath mighte call thee) this	227	Astrophil	93	5
CALL				
In painted clothes, because they call it love.	23	1st Eclogues	9	48
What I call wrong, I doo the same, and more:	41	Arcadia II	20	6
My plaintes call wolves, my plagues in you prevaile, ...	43	Arcadia II	24	8
As white as milke, and comming to the call,.	54	2nd Eclogues	29	85
Nay higher thoughtes (though thralled thoughtes) I call. . .	78	Arcadia III	49	13
Call me but yours, my title is most hye:	79	Arcadia III	50	17
(More swift then falcon's stoope to feeding Falconer's call)	118	4th Eclogues	73	58
To call such wit a franzie,.	161	Cert Sonnets	30	38
I call it praise to suffer Tyrannie;	166	Astrophil	2	11
It is most true, what we call Cupid's dart,.	167	Astrophil	5	5
Queene Vertue's court, which some call Stella's face,. . . .	169	Astrophil	9	1
Do they call Vertue there ungratefulnesse?	180	Astrophil	31	14
Love by sure proofe I may call thee unkind,.	198	Astrophil	65	1
In justice paines come not till faults do call;.	212	Astrophil	86	10
Yet truth (if Caitif's breath mighte call thee) this	227	Astrophil	93	5
Musicke doth witnesse call	216	A&S 6th Song		37
Heare me, O heare me when I call	273	Psalm IV		1
I call to Thee..	280	Psalm IX		40
Lord help, it is high time for me to call, ...	284	Psalm XII		1
Nor ever call on god, but they shall quake	286	Psalm XIV		16
Wee may well call his glory great.	297	Psalm XXI		17
For lo, this Wretch did call,.	319	Psalm XXXIV		21
And lo, his Call the skyes did clime;.	319	Psalm XXXIV		22
Other deeps of Woes doth call, ...	335	Psalm XLII		30
CALLED				
A good foole call'd with paine, perhapps may be, ...	28	1st Eclogues	10	71
Of fowles there called was a parliament.	29	1st Eclogues	10	84
Let me forget that Plangus I am called:.	61	2nd Eclogues	30	162
Waste it is calde, for it doth waste	87	Arcadia III	62	65
For to the courte her man was calld by name, ...	96	3rd Eclogues	64	77
But then I homeward call'd my lambkins deare:.	103	3rd Eclogues	66	158
And loth this time, calld life, nay thinke, that life. . . .	113	4th Eclogues	72	12
(Which life is cald) were mov'd their spirits to repose, . .	116	4th Eclogues	73	5
As I thus musing stood, Diana cald to her.	119	4th Eclogues	73	81
But cald, she came apace; a pace wherein did move.	119	4th Eclogues	73	89
O deue allegiance, by thee am I called	138	Cert Sonnets	5	15
The smoke of hell, the monster called paine, ...	140	Cert Sonnets	8	2

```
CALLED              (CONTINUED)                          PAGE   TITLE         LINE
    Cald it anew, and wooed sleepe againe: . . . . . . . . . . .  184 Astrophil    38   13
    With rage of Love, I cald my Love unkind;. . . . . . . . . .  195 Astrophil    62    2
    Ungratefull who is cald, the worst of evils is spok'n. . . .  213 A&S 5th Song      42
    I say again that I have calld on Thee. . . . . . . . . . . .  289 Psalm XVII        17
    They were set free when they upon Thee called, . . . . . . .  298 Psalm XXII        13
    But when he calld this lord did give him hearing.. . . . . .  300 Psalm XXII        58
    For I have call'd on Thee, let wicked folk . . . . . . . . .  313 Psalm XXXI        46
    A paire of frends, or rather one cal'd two,. . . . . . . . .  242 Other Poems   4   18
    Was Klaius cald, (ah Klaius, wofull wight!). . . . . . . . .  242 Other Poems   4   23
    And cal'd, now wounded, purpose to his aide: . . . . . . . .  246 Other Poems   4  162
    The two that in mid place, Hell called were, . . . . . . . .  248 Other Poems   4  227
CALLS
    Since she faire fierce to such a state me calls, . . . . . .   23 1st Eclogues  9   30
    Cals each wight to salute the floure of blisse;. . . . . . .  231 Astrophil    99   11
    Which night and day he calls to marking mind.. . . . . . . .  270 Psalm I            6
    O, hearken to my voice, which calls on Thee, . . . . . . . .  274 Psalm V            3
    When mery May first early calls the morne, . . . . . . . . .  243 Other Poems   4   49
CALMY
    But there I was, and there my calmie thoughts I fedd . . . .  117 4th Eclogues 73   39
*CALVES
    In her brave calves, like christall skies. . . . . . . . . .   89 Arcadia III  62  102
    Nay like young Calves in leapes are born,. . . . . . . . . .  310 Psalm XXIX        16
    His voice makes hindes their calves to cast, . . . . . . . .  310 Psalm XXIX        22
CAME
    Came to the bed, where wound for kisse he got, . . . . . . .    5 Lady of May   3    8
    My foule mishap came yet from fairest mind.. . . . . . . . .    5 Lady of May   3   18
    For from without came to mine eyes the blowe,. . . . . . . .   11 Arcadia I     2    5
    Thus Reason said: but she came, Reason vanished; . . . . . .   16 1st Eclogues  7   67
    For me to come, and so she did: I came,. . . . . . . . . . .   55 2nd Eclogues 29   91
    And thus she did. One day to him she came, . . . . . . . . .   95 3rd Eclogues 64   43
    There came a chariot faire by doves and sparrowes guided:. .  118 4th Eclogues 73   59
    But cald, she came apace; a pace wherein did move. . . . . .  119 4th Eclogues 73   89
    But words came halting forth, wanting Invention's stay,. . .  165 Astrophil     1    9
    My Foe came on, and beat the aire for me,. . . . . . . . . .  191 Astrophil    53   13
    Alas, whence came this change of lookes? If I. . . . . . . .  212 Astrophil    86    1
    He came, but came with smoake from out his nostrills sent, .  291 Psalm XVIII       18
    Nor that his seed to begging came. . . . . . . . . . . . . .  326 Psalm XXXVII      64
    But baiting, as my Fathers came; . . . . . . . . . . . . . .  330 Psalm XXXIX       40
    Cosma this while to Strephon safely came,. . . . . . . . . .  249 Other Poems   4  265
    While Geron olde came safe to Cosma true,. . . . . . . . . .  250 Other Poems   4  325
    Came to hir back, and so with double warde . . . . . . . . .  252 Other Poems   4  389
CAMP
    Her legges carriage is of all the sweet campe: . . . . . . .   67 2nd Eclogues 33   11
CAMPS
    Ready to store their campes of needfull things:. . . . . . .  179 Astrophil    29    4
CAN
    Who in one selfe these diverse gifts can plant;. . . . . . .    3 Lady of May   1    4
    Them can I take, but you I cannot hold:. . . . . . . . . . .    4 Lady of May   2   26
    He is not poore who can his freedome save, . . . . . . . . .    4 Lady of May   2   27
    And thus my thoughtes, can thinke but one thing still. . . .   12 Arcadia I     2 V810
    What length of verse can serve brave Mopsa's good to show, .   12 Arcadia I     3    1
    Thus shrewdly burdned then, how can my Muse escape?. . . . .   12 Arcadia I     3    3
    Who can despaire, whom hope doth teare?. . . . . . . . . . .   14 1st Eclogues  6    5
    And who can hope, who feeles despaire? . . . . . . . . . . .   14 1st Eclogues  6    6
    Of best things then what world can yeeld confection. . . . .   15 1st Eclogues  7   46
    Can I be poore, that her golde haire procure my selfe? . . .   16 1st Eclogues  7   58
    Of fayrer death how can I make election? . . . . . . . . . .   16 1st Eclogues  7   72
    And if enchantment can a harde hart move,. . . . . . . . . .   17 1st Eclogues  7  100
    Nothing can mend one point that in her lies. . . . . . . . .   17 1st Eclogues  7  108
    Whose sprite all sprites can spoile, raise, damne, or save:.   17 1st Eclogues  7  110
    Doth beauties keep, which never Sunne can burne, . . . . . .   18 1st Eclogues  7  118
    Then vertue try, if she can worke in thee. . . . . . . . . .   22 1st Eclogues  9   13
    Geron. What can amend where physick is refusde?. . . . . . .   23 1st Eclogues  9   21
    What counsell can prevaile, or light give light? . . . . . .   23 1st Eclogues  9   36
    There is no hate that can thee more oppresse.. . . . . . . .   23 1st Eclogues  9   49
    Who well can set a passion out to show:. . . . . . . . . . .   25 1st Eclogues  9  112
    But if he nought do desire, what can Heraclitus aile?. . . .   30 1st Eclogues 11   12
    If mine eyes can speake to doo harty errande,. . . . . . . .   30 1st Eclogues 12    1
    As that hatefull death can abridge them of powre,. . . . . .   31 1st Eclogues 12   18
    But if eyes can speake to doo harty errande, . . . . . . . .   31 1st Eclogues 12   25
    All to a lesson he draws, norr hills nor caves can avoide
        him. . . . . . . . . . . . . . . . . . . . . . . . . . .   31 1st Eclogues 13    7
    What can justice availe, to a man that tells not his owne
        case?. . . . . . . . . . . . . . . . . . . . . . . . . .   32 1st Eclogues 13   22
    What meane is there, alas, we can hope our losse to recover?   32 1st Eclogues 13   27
    Fire no liquor can coole: Neptune's seate would be dryd up
        there. . . . . . . . . . . . . . . . . . . . . . . . . .   32 1st Eclogues 13   32
    None can speake of a wound with skill, if he have not a
        wound felt.. . . . . . . . . . . . . . . . . . . . . . .   33 1st Eclogues 13   71
    Oh no, no, hardye shepeheard, worth can never enter a title,   34 1st Eclogues 13   82
    But to my selfe what wish can I make for a salve to my
        sorrowes,. . . . . . . . . . . . . . . . . . . . . . . .   37 1st Eclogues 13  157
    Thus plag'de how can I frame to my soare any hope of
        amendemente? . . . . . . . . . . . . . . . . . . . . . .   37 1st Eclogues 13  160
    That where you are no wished good can want;. . . . . . . . .   39 Arcadia II   16    6
    How can you him unworthy then decree,. . . . . . . . . . . .   39 Arcadia II   16    9
    O only sonne that suche a fruite can breede. . . . . . . . .   43 Arcadia II   23    3
    No woolves dare howle, no murrayne can prevaile, . . . . . .   43 Arcadia II   23    8
    Your woll is riche: no tonge can tell my gayne.. . . . . . .   43 Arcadia II   23   14
```

(So humble knowledge can throw downe the snakish sinne). . .   44 Arcadia II   26   6
R. Can Reason then a Tyraunt counted be? . . . .   46 2nd Eclogues   27   3
Or if sheepe's cries can helpe the Sunne's owne braverie,. .   48 2nd Eclogues   28   25
A quiet mind none but thy selfe can lend to thee,. . . . . .   51 2nd Eclogues   28 101
Her onely cure from surfet-woes can diet me: . . . .   51 2nd Eclogues   28 117
Her cleared lookes, nought els, in stormes can quiet me. . .   51 2nd Eclogues   28 119
That profit may ensue to him that best can do. . . . .   53 2nd Eclogues   29   30
For Pas well knowes what layes can Nico make. . . . .   54 2nd Eclogues   29   74
That hath foure eyes, and onely two can frame. . . . . . .   56 2nd Eclogues   29 143
In this weake worke, that it can never be. . . . .   57 2nd Eclogues   30   30
What glorie from our losse can he receave? . . . .   59 2nd Eclogues   30   73
For what can breed more peevish incongruities, ...   61 2nd Eclogues   30 140
Can I, that know her sacred parts, restrained be . . . . .   61 2nd Eclogues   30 149
Can I forget, when they in prison placing her, ...   61 2nd Eclogues   30 152
Can I forget, from how much mourning plainfulnes . . . . .   61 2nd Eclogues   30 155
Can I forget in how straunge phrase she craved . . . . . .   61 2nd Eclogues   30 158
Can thoughts still thinking so rest unappalled?. . . . . .   61 2nd Eclogues   30 166
What pardon can availe? or who employes him. . . . .   62 2nd Eclogues   30 168
To hurt himselfe, what shields can be defenses?. . . . . .   62 2nd Eclogues   30 169
O poisonous medecin! what worse to me can be then it? It.. .   63 2nd Eclogues   31   7
End? but I can never end, love will not give me the leave.
    Leave. . . . .   63 2nd Eclogues   31   16
How be the minds dispos'd that can not tast thy physick?
    Sick.. . . . .   63 2nd Eclogues   31   17
What blinde guides can he have that leanes to a fancy? A
    fancy. . . . .   63 2nd Eclogues   31   21
Can fancies want eies, or he fall that steppeth aloft? Oft..   64 2nd Eclogues   31   22
Can then a cause be so light that forceth a man to go die?
    Aye. . . . .   64 2nd Eclogues   31   24
Arte? what can be that art which thou dost meane by thy
    speche? Speche..   64 2nd Eclogues   31   29
Howe can they be unkind? speake for th'hast narroly pri'de"
    pride.. . . . .   65 2nd Eclogues   31   43
Whence can pride come there, since springs of beawty be
    thence? Thence.   65 2nd Eclogues   31   44
Wherin no eare can have joy, ...   66 2nd Eclogues   32   37
That only can redresse thee, ...   67 2nd Eclogues   32   48
"Nought can reason availe in heav'nly matters". . . . . . .   68 2nd Eclogues   33   26
Thus sweete paine, I do yeeld, what ere I can yeelde.. . . .   68 2nd Eclogues   33   29
Can taste no sweetes, the sower onely please:. . . . . . .   74 Arcadia III   41   2
Can holde, shew, tell, my paines without reliefe.. . . . .   75 Arcadia III   43   8
Deeper engrav'd, which salve nor time can save,. . . . . .   77 Arcadia III   47   5
You none can clayme but you your selfe by right,. . . . . .   79 Arcadia III   50   19
Her minde amaz'de can neither's helpe applie. . . . .   81 Arcadia III   54   4
With circkled course, which no wise stay can trye,. . . . .   81 Arcadia III   54   10
Hurte not the face, which nothing can amende". . . . . . .   82 Arcadia III   55   15
For no thing, time, nor place, can loose, quench, ease,. . .   84 Arcadia III   60   13
What medicin then, can such desease remove . . . .   85 Arcadia III   61   13
What toong can her perfections tell. . . . .   85 Arcadia III   62   1
Can liken them without all peere,. . . . .   86 Arcadia III   62   19
No talke untaught can finde the way. . . . .   86 Arcadia III   62   34
But who those ruddie lippes can misse? . . . .   87 Arcadia III   62   37
No tongue can her perfections tell,. . . . .   90 Arcadia III   62 145
(How can he love suspecting treacherie?. . . . .   93 3rd Eclogues   63   84
How can she love where love cannot win trust?) . . . . . .   93 3rd Eclogues   63   85
Ne can he faile, for prince hath for him sent: . . . . . .   97 3rd Eclogues   64 104
For sure, no jealousie can that prevent, ...   97 3rd Eclogues   64 125
For nothing can endure where order n'is. . . . .   100 3rd Eclogues   66   51
With such a will that nothing can asswage. . . . .   105 3rd Eclogues   67   51
So well she can command, and yet obay,. . . . .   106 3rd Eclogues   67   89
My fire is more, then can be made with forrests;. . . . .   112 4th Eclogues   71   56
No being now, but sorowe I can have: . . . .   114 4th Eclogues   72   27
The darkened heav'n my soule which nought can see; . . . .   114 4th Eclogues   72   35
Are all in me: what helpe then can I trie? . . . .   114 4th Eclogues   72   43
"How ill both you can rule, well hath your discord taught: .   121 4th Eclogues   73 163
Can those eyes, that of eyes drownd in most harty flowing
    teares,. . . . .   122 4th Eclogues   74   15
Can those eyes now yeeld to the kind conceit of a sorow,. .   122 4th Eclogues   74   17
Can death beautie become? must I be such a monument? . . .   123 4th Eclogues   74   32
Shall prove that fiercenes can with a white dove abide?. .   123 4th Eclogues   74   34
As th'offence was done, and goe beyond if he can.. . . . .   123 4th Eclogues   74   40
The filthy snake her gilded coate can mende, ...   127 4th Eclogues   75   82
The very trees with grafting we can cherish. . . . .   127 4th Eclogues   75   85
So that we can long time produce their time: . . . .   127 4th Eclogues   75   86
For how can Nature unto this reply?. . . . .   127 4th Eclogues   75   94
The stile of heavie hart can never flie. . . . .   129 4th Eclogues   75 139
Since shunning paine, I ease can never find: . . . .   135 Cert Sonnets   1   1
Since naked sence can conquer reason armed:. . . . .   135 Cert Sonnets   1   6
For all his strife can onlie bondage gaine.. . . . .   135 Cert Sonnets   2   8
And can crie helpe with nought but grones and starts:. . .   136 Cert Sonnets   2   12
Who others' woes and plaints can chastly beare:. . . . . .   142 Cert Sonnets   10   7
Hath yet such health, as it my life can save. . . . . . .   142 Cert Sonnets   11   12
Can count them just, nor reason reason trye,. . . . . . .   149 Cert Sonnets   22   3
For no faire signe can credit winne, ...   156 Cert Sonnets   27   15
Who love can temper thus,. . . . .   161 Cert Sonnets   30   39
Whereof this Beautie can be but a shade, ...   167 Astrophil   5   10
I can speake what I feele, and feele as much as they,. . . .   168 Astrophil   6   12
Looks over the world, and can find nothing such, ...   169 Astrophil   9   10
And which is worse, no good excuse can show, ...   174 Astrophil   18   7

CAN   (CONTINUED)   PAGE   TITLE   LINE
     What can be hoped my harvest time will be? . . . . 175 Astrophil   21   11
     And can with foule abuse such beauties blot; . . . . 177 Astrophil   24   11
     And so nor will, nor can, behold those skies . . . . 177 Astrophil   25   7
     And fooles can thinke those Lampes of purest light,. . . . . 177 Astrophil   26   2
     If French can yet three parts in one agree;. . . . . 180 Astrophil   30   5
     Can judge of Love, thou feel'st a Lover's case;. . . . . . . 180 Astrophil   31   6
     A burthned hart. "How can words ease, which are. . . . . . . 181 Astrophil   34   2
     Within what bounds can one his liking stay,. . . . . 182 Astrophil   35   3
     What Nestor's counsell can my flames alay, ... 182 Astrophil   35   5
     In all sweete stratagems sweete Arte can show, ... 183 Astrophil   36   11
     By sence's priviledge, can scape from thee.. . . . . 183 Astrophil   36   14
     Rich in all beauties which man's eye can see:. . . . . 183 Astrophil   37   6
     Where well he knowes, no man to him can come.. . . . . 186 Astrophil   43   14
     Till without fewell you can make hot fire. . . . . 188 Astrophil   46   14
     Can those blacke beames such burning markes engrave. . . . . 188 Astrophil   47   2
     I may, I must, I can, I will, I do . . . . 188 Astrophil   47   10
     What, dost thou thinke that I can ever take. . . . . 193 Astrophil   56   10
     That no pace else their guided steps can find, ... 194 Astrophil   58   3
     If he be faire, yet but a dog can be.. . . . . 194 Astrophil   59   4
     As I may well recount, but none can prize: . . . . 198 Astrophil   65   4
     One from the other scarcely can descrie, ... 202 Astrophil   72   3
     No wind, no shade can coole, what helpe then in my case, . . 205 Astrophil   76   12
     And no spurre can his resty race renew,. . . . . 207 Astrophil   80   12
     When Sun is hid, can starres such beames display?. . . . . . 223 Astrophil   88   6
     What sobs can give words grace my griefe to show?. . . . . . 227 Astrophil   93   2
     Can scarce discerne the shape of mine owne paine.. . . . . . 228 Astrophil   94   4
     As can refresh the hell where my soule fries.. . . . . 231 Astrophil   100   8
     Knowing worlds passe, ere she enough can find. . . . . 232 Astrophil   101   13
     Better place no wit can find,. . . . . 210 A&S 4th Song   13
     Feare not else, none can us spie:. . . . . 211 A&S 4th Song   22
     The same key op'n can, which can locke up a treasure.. . . . 213 A&S 5th Song   18
     You see what I can say; mend yet your froward mind,. . . . . 215 A&S 5th Song   88
     Can learne, how my selfe to sunder . . . . 234 A&S 11th Song   14
     Which can make me thus to leave you, ... 235 A&S 11th Song   44
     Which Musicke can in sky . . . . 217 A&S 6th Song   51
     Can tast comfort but of thee,. . . . . 220 A&S 8th Song   78
     Can abide to keepe no measure, ... 221 A&S 9th Song   7
     Then can in good eawes be moved. . . . . 221 A&S 9th Song   24
     Can of thy prayse the tongues entombed make. . . . . 276 Psalm VI   15
     Whom that Great God remember can?. . . . . 278 Psalm VIII   14
     Still plagues the poore the most he can: . . . . 281 Psalm X   6
     Naught his allseing sight can miss,. . . . . 284 Psalm XI   15
     So can I not be opprest, ... 288 Psalm XVI   27
     Who is the man that ever can . . . . 295 Psalm XIX   49
     Even he whose life no help of man can quicken. . . . . 300 Psalm XXII   74
     And so can never I . . . . 301 Psalm XXIII   2
     For nothing they can ever want . . . . 319 Psalm XXXIV   34
     What man Thy thoughts can count to Thee. . . . . 331 Psalm XL   22
     But they are more than can by me be told.. . . . . 331 Psalm XL   24
     He blessed is, who with wise temper can. . . . . 332 Psalm XLI   1
     Dick. Faith in my self and worth in her, which no proofe can
          undoo.. . . . . 343 Possibly   1   26
     For nothing can more tedious bee, then plaint, in time of
          joy. . . . . 344 Possibly   1   46
     Desire's great force, no forces can withhold:. . . . . 345 Possibly   4   3
     Such marble eares, no cunning wordes can charme, ... 346 Possibly   5   2
     The plenteous sweets, (can sweets so sharply grow?). . . . . 243 Other Poems   4   52
     But golde can guild a rotten piece of wood,. . . . . 245 Other Poems   4   124
     Nous cri'de, and chafd, but he no other can. . . . . 249 Other Poems   4   285
     For then wise Klaius found no absence can. . . . . 253 Other Poems   4   419
     Help him, who can no more hir sight foregoe. . . . . 253 Other Poems   4   420
     Yet thoughts do flie, though I can scarcely creep. . . . . . 253 Other Poems   4   444
     Drowsy am I, and yet can rarely slepe. . . . . 253 Other Poems   4   446
     Those eies, which nothing like themselves can see, ... 253 Other Poems   4   451
     And none invisible, but Spirites, can goe. . . . . 253 Other Poems   4   456
     Say then, can this but of enchantment come?. . . . . 254 Other Poems   4   472
     He treble beas for helpe, but none can get:. . . . . 254 Other Poems   4   492
     Are you not dried? Can you your self renew?. . . . . 257 Other Poems   5   39
     Cause all the mirth you can, ... 261 Other Poems   6   37
     Can Love's duties best fulfill:. . . . . 263 Other Poems   7   38
     Scarce each other can abide, ... 263 Other Poems   7   52
CANARY
     Streight as Cedar, a voice staines the Cannary birds,. . . .   69 2nd Eclogues 34   33
CANDLE
     Or to the Sun for wonders seeme small sparks of a candle:. .   34 1st Eclogues 13   79
CANDLELIGHT
     If this darke place yet shew like candle light,. . . . . . . 225 Astrophil   91   5
CANDLES
     Candles out, and curtaines spread: . . . . 211 A&S 4th Song   38
CANKER
     Get hence foule Griefe, the canker of the minde: . . . . . .   83 Arcadia III 59   1
CANNIBALS
     These Canibals, who as if they were bread. . . . . 286 Psalm XIV   14
CANNON
     Or stop a breach, that never Cannon sawe?. . . . .   22 1st Eclogues 9   17
CANNONS
     Her cannons be her eys, myne eys the walls be, ...   68 2nd Eclogues 33   13
     Or canons thunder-like, all shot togither, lende'. . . . . . 118 4th Eclogues 73   54

CANNOT

		PAGE	TITLE		LINE
Them can I take, but you I cannot hold:.		4	Lady of May	2	26
With outward joyes, which inly cannot sincke,.		22	1st Eclogues	9	7
R. Though we cannot orecome, our cause is just.		47	2nd Eclogues	27	31
With so strong lives, that bodie cannot rest		56	2nd Eclogues	29	145
But cannot make resolved darkenes lighte:.		73	Arcadia III	39	12
Joie's strangers seeme, I cannot bide their showe, ...		74	Arcadia III	41	5
An ende, an ende, my dulde penn cannot write,.		74	Arcadia III	42	13
I holde his deare, and myne he cannot misse:		75	Arcadia III	45	3
Comming from her, cannot but downewarde fall..		78	Arcadia III	49	18
Thy running course cannot such beawties marke:		80	Arcadia III	52	11
Because themselves they cannot see...		86	Arcadia III	62	22
How can she love where love cannot win trust?)		93	3rd Eclogues	63	85
That private panges can not breath out in publique		109	Arcadia IV	70	32
But I cannot; who then my selfe should flie, ...		114	4th Eclogues	72	39
Where life is death, and death cannot breed peace.		116	4th Eclogues	72	95
But like the feeble flower (whose stalke cannot sustaine . .		117	4th Eclogues	73	21
The rest I cannot tell, for therewithall I wak'd		121	4th Eclogues	73	179
Such thing cannot I seeke (Despaire hath giv'n me my answer.		122	4th Eclogues	74	11
Such thing cannot he hope, that knowes thy determinat					
hardnes;		122	4th Eclogues	74	13
Such cursed harmes as cannot be redressed.		126	4th Eclogues	75	63
Why should we feare that which we cannot flye?		131	Arcadia V	77	4
Since this we feele, greate losse we cannot finde.		131	Arcadia V	77	14
Cannot have to content me, ...		137	Cert Sonnets	4	18
But for all this I can not her remove.		145	Cert Sonnets	17	4
No, no, no, no, I cannot hate my foe,.		155	Cert Sonnets	26	1
Above line repeated at following locations		155	Cert Sonnets	26	12
. . . .		156	Cert Sonnets	26	23
Though in paine, cannot complaine. No, no, no, no.		156	Cert Sonnets	26	33
He burnt unwares his wings, and cannot fly away.		169	Astrophil	8	14
But cannot skill to pitie my disgrace, ...		187	Astrophil	45	3
Cannot be staid within my panting breast, ...		189	Astrophil	50	2
So that I cannot chuse but write my mind,.		190	Astrophil	50	9
And cannot chuse but put out what I write, ...		190	Astrophil	50	10
He cannot love: no, no, let him alone.".		191	Astrophil	54	8
So dull am, that I cannot looke into		195	Astrophil	60	10
I cannot brag of word, much lesse of deed, ...		199	Astrophil	66	5
But my heart burnes, I cannot silent be.		207	Astrophil	81	11
Cannot such grace your silly selfe content,.		208	Astrophil	83	11
Cannot heavn's food, once felt, keepe stomakes free. . . .		223	Astrophil	88	7
Which cannot be restor'd by time nor industrie:.		214	A&S 5th Song		47
Trust in that lord, that cannot ly,.		274	Psalm IV		23
He cannot them espy, ...		282	Psalm X		20
So prest with sins I cannot see my case.		332	Psalm XL		44
Will. Dick, since we cannot dance, come let a chearefull					
voyce, ...		343	Possibly	1	1
Dick. Good Will, I cannot take thy good advice, before . . .		344	Possibly	1	43

CANST

		PAGE	TITLE		LINE
Shew how thou canst deserve so brave desire, ...		3	Lady of May	2	2
If neither by that helpe, thou canst clime up to thy fancie,		34	1st Eclogues	13	100
To causefull wrath, which thou canst not resist.		59	2nd Eclogues	30	66
Of lothsome dayes, whose losse how canst thou mone, ...		59	2nd Eclogues	30	78
Thus cruell to my selfe how canst thou crave		77	Arcadia III	47	7
My Muse therefore, for onely thou canst tell,.		146	Cert Sonnets	17	11
Thou canst vouchsafe the influence of a thought.		184	Astrophil	40	6
Do thou then (for thou canst) do thou complaine,.		228	Astrophil	94	5
As what my hart still sees thou canst not spie?.		235	Astrophil	105	4
Absent alone canst thou then piping be?.		258	Other Poems	5	65
Canst thou, poore lamme, become another's lamme?		258	Other Poems	5	76

CAP

		PAGE	TITLE		LINE
As she a black-silke cap on him begunne.		244	Other Poems	4	85

CAPTAINESSE

		PAGE	TITLE		LINE
From my deare Captainnesse to run away?.		223	Astrophil	88	2

CAPTAINS

		PAGE	TITLE		LINE
Wise Counsellors, stout Captaines, puissant Kings, ...		245	Other Poems	4	130

CAPTIVE

		PAGE	TITLE		LINE
Thus are my eyes still Captive to one sight:		12	Arcadia I	2	9
Ty me haire your captive wholly, ...		157	Cert Sonnets	27	34

CAPTIVE-KILLING

		PAGE	TITLE		LINE
This done, but done with captive-killing grace,.		244	Other Poems	4	105

CAPTIVED

		PAGE	TITLE		LINE
Or howe do I, captiv'd in this darke plight, ...		74	Arcadia III	42	3
Better then one captiv'd perceiveth, ...		159	Cert Sonnets	29	16
Holds my young braine captiv'd in golden cage.		176	Astrophil	23	11

CAPTIVES

		PAGE	TITLE		LINE
So captives to his Saint both soule and sence, ...		195	Astrophil	61	6

CAPTIVING

		PAGE	TITLE		LINE
Free all my powers were from those captiving snares, . . .		117	4th Eclogues	73	17

CAR

		PAGE	TITLE		LINE
Pas. O if I had Apollo's golden carre, ...		56	2nd Eclogues	29	120
Her breasts his tents, legs his triumphall carre:.		179	Astrophil	29	11

CARATS

		PAGE	TITLE		LINE
Beauties, which were of manie Carrets fine,.		172	Astrophil	16	2

CARE

		PAGE	TITLE		LINE
Thy elder care shall from thy carefull face.		11	Arcadia I	1	1
That sweete, but sower despairefull care..		14	1st Eclogues	6	4
Dorus. Farre other care, o Muse, my sorrow tries,.		17	1st Eclogues	7	106
Let speciall care upon thy flock be staid, ...		26	1st Eclogues	9	133
But at no change, so pinching care he takes, ...		71	Arcadia III	37	9

```
CARE                     (CONTINUED)                    PAGE    TITLE         LINE
  Synce love with care, and hope with feare do fight.. . . . . .  72 Arcadia III    37   18
  Care upon care (in steede of doing right). . . . . . . . . .  82 Arcadia III    56    7
  Whose care is cause that they in number growe, . . . . . . .  92 3rd Eclogues 63   38
  Have much more care of them that them do keepe, . . . . . . .  92 3rd Eclogues 63   39
  And with some words which shewed little care, . . . . . . . .  97 3rd Eclogues 64  118
  Must goe for that, if for her lowres he care: . . . . . . . . 104 3rd Eclogues 67   42
  We care abroad, and they of home have care.. . . . . . . . . 106 3rd Eclogues 67  108
  O Night, the ease of care, the pledge of pleasure, . . . . . 108 Arcadia IV     69    1
  Brused with waves of Care, but broken is . . . . . . . . . . 114 4th Eclogues 72   49
  Say, that I well shuld finde in what a care I was had? . . . 124 4th Eclogues 74   80
  With much more: now what doo I finde, but Care to abhor me,. 124 4th Eclogues 74   81
  Care that I sinke in griefe, Care that I live banished?. . . 124 4th Eclogues 74   82
  Ne doo I care how rude be my invention, . . . . . . . . . . 128 4th Eclogues 75  104
  Band of all evils, cradle of causelesse care, . . . . . . . 161 Cert Sonnets 31    3
  Vertue of late, with vertuous care to ster . . . . . . . . . 177 Astrophil    25    9
  The glasses of thy dayly vexing care?" . . . . . . . . . . . 181 Astrophil    34    3
  Nor ought do care, though some above me sit, . . . . . . . . 198 Astrophil    64   11
  Labour to kill in me this killing care: . . . . . . . . . . 200 Astrophil    68   12
  Care shining in mine eyes, faith in my sprite, . . . . . . . 202 Astrophil    72   11
  O God, thinke you that satisfies my care?. . . . . . . . . . 225 Astrophil    92    8
  But wit confus'd with too much care did misse. . . . . . . . 227 Astrophil    93    8
  So gratefull now you waite upon my care. . . . . . . . . . . 228 Astrophil    95    4
  Nature with care sweates for her darling's sake, . . . . . . 232 Astrophil   101   12
  That with such poysonous care my lookes you marke, . . . . . 233 Astrophil   104    2
  Fit to heare and ease my care: . . . . . . . . . . . . . . . 210 A&S 4th Song        2
  Danger hence good care doth keepe, . . . . . . . . . . . . . 210 A&S 4th Song        9
  Him great harmes had taught much care, . . . . . . . . . . . 218 A&S 8th Song        9
  With kindest care, as with a certain shield. . . . . . . . . 275 Psalm V            40
  Though Father's Care, and Mother's love. . . . . . . . . . . 308 Psalm XXVII        49
  And by his care from them is barr'd. . . . . . . . . . . . . 320 Psalm XXXIV        63
  Will. What care takes shee for thee? D. Hir care is to
    prevent. . . . . . . . . . . . . . . . . . . . . . . . . . 344 Possibly      1   37
  A careles comelines with comely care, . . . . . . . . . . . 247 Other Poems   4  213
  And you my flock, care of my carefull sight, . . . . . . . . 254 Other Poems   4  483
  While I was I, and so had cause to care; . . . . . . . . . . 254 Other Poems   4  484
  Away ragg'd rams, care I what murraine kill? . . . . . . . . 255 Other Poems   4  515
CARED
  Still to his judgments lookt, still for his statutes car'd,. 292 Psalm XVIII        45
CAREFUL
  Thy elder care shall from thy carefull face. . . . . . . . .  11 Arcadia I      1    1
  (A musique sweet to one in carefull musing plaste) . . . . . 117 4th Eclogues 73    8
  How long shall I consult with carefull sprite. . . . . . . . 285 Psalm XIII          5
  And you my flock, care of my carefull sight, . . . . . . . . 254 Other Poems   4  483
  With heart as carefull, as with carelesse grace, . . . . . . 255 Other Poems   4  522
CAREFULNESS
  Fancie his foode, his clothing is of carefulnes; . . . . . .  48 2nd Eclogues 28   41
CARELESS
  Or carelesse of the wealth because her owne: . . . . . . . . 176 Astrophil    22   11
  A careles comelines with comely care, . . . . . . . . . . . 247 Other Poems   4  213
  With heart as carefull, as with carelesse grace, . . . . . . 255 Other Poems   4  522
CARELESSNESS
  From carelesnesse did in no maner grow, . . . . . . . . . . 227 Astrophil    93    7
CARE'S
  Ruine's relique, care's web, and sorrowe's foode: . . . . .  23 1st Eclogues  9   29
  With care's hard hand) to turne and tosse in thee. . . . . . 230 Astrophil    98    8
CARES
  My day newe cares; my ginnes my daily sight, . . . . . . . .  18 1st Eclogues  7  140
  And cast from me part of my burdnous cares: . . . . . . . . .  42 Arcadia II     21   14
  Away vayne Cares, by which fewe men do finde . . . . . . . .  83 Arcadia III    59    3
  Which heav'nly purest gifts defile in muddy cares. . . . . . 117 4th Eclogues 73   18
  Doth hide his head with cares but onely how to rest: . . . . 117 4th Eclogues 73   24
  Then void of neerer cares, the depth of things to find.. . . 118 4th Eclogues 73   50
  But her sight his cares did banish, . . . . . . . . . . . . 218 A&S 8th Song       11
  And that forgetfull sort, which never cares. . . . . . . . . 281 Psalm IX           54
  Heeding himselfe, cares not how fellow doe, . . . . . . . . 248 Other Poems   4  237
CARK
  And Klaius taking for his yonglings carke, . . . . . . . . . 243 Other Poems   4   67
CARKING
  Of carking agonies (to estates which still be adherent). . .  34 1st Eclogues 13   97
CAROLS
  With daunces, carols, or with barlybreake: . . . . . . . . .  54 2nd Eclogues 29   70
CARRIAGE
  Her legges carriage is of all the sweet campe: . . . . . . .  67 2nd Eclogues 33   11
CARRIED
  Each had his creast, Mars caried Venus' glove, . . . . . . . 171 Astrophil    13    7
CARRY
  Since no refuge doth serve from woundes we do carry about
    us . . . . . . . . . . . . . . . . . . . . . . . . . . . .  33 1st Eclogues 13   51
  Is it to carry newes . . . . . . . . . . . . . . . . . . . .  80 Arcadia III    52    3
  To me mine eyes the true shape carie.. . . . . . . . . . . . 159 Cert Sonnets 29   13
  Which in them my hopes do cary. . . . . . . . . . . . . . . 226 A&S 10th Song      18
CART
  Make home more paine then following of the cart. . . . . . . 104 3rd Eclogues 67   30
  Tir'de as a jade in overloden carte, . . . . . . . . . . . . 253 Other Poems   4  443
CARTHAGE
  Thinke Hanniball did laugh when Carthage lost. . . . . . . . 147 Cert Sonnets 17   45
CARVE
  An image is, which for our selves we carve; . . . . . . . . 167 Astrophil     5    6
```

```
CASE                                                          PAGE    TITLE          LINE
Measure my case, how by thy beautie's filling. . . . . . .    16    1st Eclogues  7    77
Still were I one, this still should be my case,. . . . . .    23    1st Eclogues  9    28
What can justice availe, to a man that tells not his owne
    case?. . . . . . . . . . . . . . . . . . . . . . . . .    32    1st Eclogues 13    22
But yet well I doo finde each man most wise in his owne
    case . . . . . . . . . . . . . . . . . . . . . . . . .    33    1st Eclogues 13    70
P. Reason hath eyes to see his owne ill case. . . . . . . .   46    2nd Eclogues 27    16
And in thy case do glasse mine owne debilitie: . . . . . .    60    2nd Eclogues 30   129
Bewaile the case, and in the cause delight?. . . . . . . .    74    Arcadia III  42     4
As for the gentle birds, like case might rewe. . . . . . .   102    3rd Eclogues 66   139
In such a case where it appeares that nature . . . . . . .   109    Arcadia IV   70     9
That thou shalt never dare seeke helpe of wretched case".. .  121    4th Eclogues 73   176
If then a man in most ill case may give you a farewell;. . .  124    4th Eclogues 74    85
Can judge of Love, thou feel'st a Lover's case;. . . . . .   180    Astrophil    31     6
Of Lovers never knowne, a grievous case, . . . . . . . . .   187    Astrophil    45     6
I curst thee oft, I pitie now thy case,. . . . . . . . . .   187    Astrophil    46     1
A prety case! I hoped her to bring . . . . . . . . . . . .   193    Astrophil    57    12
Shewes love and pitie to my absent case. . . . . . . . . .   195    Astrophil    60     8
Let all the earth with scorne recount my case, . . . . . .   198    Astrophil    64     7
No wind, no shade can coole, what helpe then in my case, . .  205    Astrophil    76    12
Stella now learnes (strange case) to weepe in thee.. . . .   231    Astrophil   101     8
Thou toldst mine eyes should helpe their famisht case? . . .  235    Astrophil   106     6
Like loving brothers' case . . . . . . . . . . . . . . . .   215    A&S 6th Song       15
Show that Thy eyes respect a faithfull case; . . . . . . .   289    Psalm XVII         6
What would they more? And I would not their case.. . . . .   290    Psalm XVII        45
His eyes unto my Case, his eares unto my moane.. . . . . .   291    Psalm XVIII       14
Lord judg me, and my case, . . . . . . . . . . . . . . . .   305    Psalm XXVI         1
Nor my life's cause match with blcodseeker's case, . . . .   306    Psalm XXVI        30
Who savest me from troblous case,. . . . . . . . . . . . .   315    Psalm XXXII       26
Lord he is in thrice blessed case. . . . . . . . . . . . .   319    Psalm XXXIV       31
So prest with sins I cannot see my case. . . . . . . . . .   332    Psalm XL          44
Of shepheards two the seely case to show,. . . . . . . . .   242    Other Poems   4    6
With nature pleas'd, content with present case,. . . . . .   243    Other Poems   4   59
"Nay each thing is bewitcht to know my case: . . . . . . .   254    Other Poems   4  473
Taking pitty on his case,. . . . . . . . . . . . . . . . .   264    Other Poems   7   74
CASED
An Angell's mind, but in a woman caste:. . . . . . . . . .   151    Cert Sonnets 22   67
CAST
On me to cast those eyes, where shine nobilitie. . . . . .    19    1st Eclogues  7   178
Which should most miseries, cast on a worme that I am. . . .   29    1st Eclogues 11     2
And cast from me part of my burdnous cares:. . . . . . . .    42    Arcadia II   21    14
Cast thy stepmother eyes upon our sorowe,. . . . . . . . .   109    Arcadia IV   70    23
Hath cast me, wretch, into eternall evening,. . . . . . . .  113    4th Eclogues 71    65
One Echo to another Echo cast. . . . . . . . . . . . . . .   126    4th Eclogues 75    34
And thence cast off, where his sweete hurt he found, . . . .  144    Cert Sonnets 15    6
Of ships, by shipwrack cast on Albion coast, . . . . . . .   151    Cert Sonnets 22   51
And cast their yoakes away.. . . . . . . . . . . . . . . .   271    Psalm II           8
Up then thou liftst the poore, and down the proud wilt cast;  292    Psalm XVIII       52
And do cast lots, who should my vesture take.. . . . . . .   299    Psalm XXII        44
His voice makes hindes their calves to cast, . . . . . . .   310    Psalm XXIX        22
All my fierce Foes reproach on mee did cast; . . . . . . .   313    Psalm XXXI        31
I said that I from out Thy sight was cast; . . . . . . . .   313    Psalm XXXI        62
They are cast down, and never shal . . . . . . . . . . . .   324    Psalm XXXVI       35
Cast down in such dole,. . . . . . . . . . . . . . . . . .   337    Psalm XLIII       32
He ran, but ran with eye ore shoulder cast,. . . . . . . .   249    Other Poems   4  289
CASTING
On him Thy Count'nance casting.. . . . . . . . . . . . . .   297    Psalm XXI         24
CASTS
Whose owne fault casts him downe, hardly high seat recovers.  213    A&S 5th Song      24
CAT
I have (and long shall have) a white great nimble cat, . . .   53    2nd Eclogues 29   31
Let cat and dog fight which shall have both you. . . . . .    56    2nd Eclogues 29  149
The Hare, her sleights; the Cat, his melancholie;. . . . .   101    3rd Eclogues 66   92
If he do praise the dog, she likes the cat.. . . . . . . .   104    3rd Eclogues 67   33
Late neere a crosse I met an ougly Cat.. . . . . . . . . .   253    Other Poems   4  448
*CATCH
Or catch the birds with pitfalls, or with lyme,. . . . . .    26    1st Eclogues  9  124
That huntinge faultes, our selves we did not catch.. . . .    29    1st Eclogues 10   93
A prettie curre it is; his name iwis is Catch, . . . . . .    53    2nd Eclogues 29   40
Beautie hath force to catche the humane sight. . . . . . .    82    Arcadia III  57     1
I sought to catch the fish Torpedo faire.. . . . . . . . .   115    4th Eclogues 72   63
Catch harmful fall . . . . . . . . . . . . . . . . . . . .   318    Psalm XXXIII      65
They catch, while he (foole!) to himself makes love: . . . .  243    Other Poems   4   46
To catch hir sparrow which from hir did swerve,. . . . . .   244    Other Poems   4   84
To catch of them, and them to hell to beare, . . . . . . .   248    Other Poems   4  229
But Nous that slipt from Pas, did catch the clowne.. . . .   248    Other Poems   4  262
That she would faine the catch of Strephon flie, . . . . .   252    Other Poems   4  380
CATCHER
And this hath got; the catcher now is caught,. . . . . . .   115    4th Eclogues 72   66
CATES
From base desire on earthly cates to pray? . . . . . . . .   223    Astrophil    88     8
CATO'S
Thy scepter use in some old Catoe's brest; . . . . . . . .   166    Astrophil     4     5
CATTLE
The cattell wild, or tame, in nature's bowers. . . . . . .   100    3rd Eclogues 66   47
Blith were the commons, cattell of the fielde, . . . . . .   102    3rd Eclogues 66  132
Then quickly did the meaner cattell finde, . . . . . . . .   102    3rd Eclogues 66  135
And God forbid, women such cattell were, . . . . . . . . .   106    3rd Eclogues 67   82
```

```
                                                            PAGE   TITLE           LINE
CAUGHT
  Their first caught sence prefers to teacher's blowes.. . . .    28 1st Eclogues 10   57
  If Love tooke thee by force, or caught thee guilefully.. . .    48 2nd Eclogues 28   21
  And this hath got; the catcher now is caught,. . . . . . . .   115 4th Eclogues 72   66
  What courage strange hath caught thy caitife hart, . . . . .   142 Cert Sonnets 10    9
  Right so my minde, caught by his guiding eye . . . . . . . .   144 Cert Sonnets 15    5
  Which caught, to cruell search yeelds his chiefe part: . . .   150 Cert Sonnets 22   22
  I caught at one of them a hungrie bit; . . . . . . . . . . .   208 Astrophil    82   11
  Have I caught my heav'nly jewell,. . . . . . . . . . . . . .   202 A&S 2nd Song        1
  Most surely caught... . . . . . . . . . . . . . . . . . . .    280 Psalm IX          50
  O let proud him be throughly caught. . . . . . . . . . . . .   281 Psalm X            7
  For they had caught me up, when I was weake in Woe;. . . . .   291 Psalm XVIII       38
  Fall in self pitt, be caught in their own nett.. . . . . . .   321 Psalm XXXV        18
  So caught, him seem'd he caught of joyes the bell, . . . . .   250 Other Poems   4  311
  Who would be caught, that she should go to hell: . . . . . .   250 Other Poems   4  315
  For he was olde, and easly would be cought:. . . . . . . . .   250 Other Poems   4  322
  She fled, and tooke: he folow'd, and was cought. . . . . . .   251 Other Poems   4  348
  And then the Phoenix feared to be cought.. . . . . . . . . .   251 Other Poems   4  360
  Have cought of thy deare damme,. . . . . . . . . . . . . . .   258 Other Poems   5   73
CAUSE
  Honor, the cause, desart is not regarded.. . . . . . . . . .    17 1st Eclogues  7   96
  True cause of evils, and cause of causelesse woe.. . . . . .    25 1st Eclogues  9  116
  But thanke the cause, thou seest, when he is dim.. . . . . .    27 1st Eclogues 10   12
  R. Though we cannot orecome, our cause is just.. . . . . . .    47 2nd Eclogues 27   31
  To whether with best cause the Nymphes faire flowers
    affoord  . . . . . . . . . . . . . . . . . . . . . . . . .    52 2nd Eclogues 29   28
  Since cause of griefe no cause from life removes.. . . . . .    58 2nd Eclogues 30   37
  Condoling cause of friendship he will borrow.. . . . . . . .    62 2nd Eclogues 30  178
  Can then a cause be so light that forceth a man to go die?
    Aye. . . . . . . . . . . . . . . . . . . . . . . . . . . .    64 2nd Eclogues 31   24
  Become the cause of my darke ouglie night?. . . . . . . . .     74 Arcadia III  42    2
  Bewaile the case, and in the cause delight?. . . . . . . . .    74 Arcadia III  42    4
  I plaine with cause, my woes are all myne owne.. . . . . . .    75 Arcadia III  43    6
  Teares, drowne your selves, for woe (your cause) is wasted,.   83 Arcadia III  59    6
  Whose care is cause that they in number growe, . . . . . . .    92 3rd Eclogues 63   38
  The evill of evils, just cause to be unjust, . . . . . . . .    93 3rd Eclogues 63   83
  Whose light is cause we have our lives neglected . . . . . .   108 Arcadia IV   69    7
  Both cause, effect, beginning, and the ende. . . . . . . . .   114 4th Eclogues 72   42
  O you (alas so I find) cause of his onely ruine. . . . . . .   122 4th Eclogues 74    4
  You be the cause that I love: what Reason blameth a shadowe,   123 4th Eclogues 74   45
  Should my too-much sight cause so true a Sunne to be lost? .   124 4th Eclogues 74   58
  Her helpe to this, this justest cause of plaint. . . . . . .   125 4th Eclogues 75   14
  O Phoebus with good cause thy face thou hidest,. . . . . . .   126 4th Eclogues 75   55
  That here is juster cause of plaintfull sadnesse:. . . . . .   137 Cert Sonnets  4   10
  Alas she hath no other cause of anguish. . . . . . . . . . .   137 Cert Sonnets  4   13
  Have more cause to lament me,. . . . . . . . . . . . . . . .   137 Cert Sonnets  4   19
  That here is juster cause of plaintfull sadnesse:. . . . . .   137 Cert Sonnets  4   22
  But this she thinks, our paine hye cause excuseth, . . . . .   142 Cert Sonnets 11   13
  Tell me the cause of this my causelesse woe, . . . . . . . .   146 Cert Sonnets 17   12
  If Greekes themselves were mov'd with so small cause . . . .   146 Cert Sonnets 17   21
  Some cause there is, which of strange cause doth rise: . . .   147 Cert Sonnets 18    2
  She is the cause that all the rest I am. . . . . . . . . . .   151 Cert Sonnets 22   70
  Is cause the looker dyes. . . . . . . . . . . . . . . . . .    152 Cert Sonnets 23    8
  They have no cause to be sorie,. . . . . . . . . . . . . . .   155 Cert Sonnets 26   20
  Pleasure might cause her reade, reading might make her know,   165 Astrophil     1    3
  Her daintiest bare went free; the cause was this,. . . . . .   176 Astrophil    22   13
  To have for no cause birthright in the skie, . . . . . . . .   178 Astrophil    26    5
  How farre they shoote awrie! the true cause is,. . . . . . .   185 Astrophil    41   12
  Alas, what cause is there so overthwart,. . . . . . . . . . .   186 Astrophil    44    7
  Not though thereof the cause her selfe she know: . . . . . .   187 Astrophil    45    4
  And do I see some cause a hope to feede. . . . . . . . . . .   199 Astrophil    66    1
  Guesse we the cause: "What, is it thus?" Fie no: . . . . . .   204 Astrophil    74   12
  Nor this, nor that, nor any such small cause,. . . . . . . .   204 Astrophil    75   12
  And nothing then the cause more sweet could be,. . . . . . .   223 Astrophil    87   13
  Thought with good cause thou likest so well the night, . . .   229 Astrophil    96    1
  To this great cause, which needs both use and art, . . . . .   236 Astrophil   107    8
  More cause a like effect at leastwise bringeth:. . . . . . .   208 A&S 3rd Song        5
  To countenance his cause:. . . . . . . . . . . . . . . . . .   216 A&S 6th Song       30
  For Thou my cause, my right Thou hast maintaind, . . . . . .   279 Psalm IX           8
  Commit their Cause, themselves, to Thee, . . . . . . . . . .   283 Psalm X           62
  In them no cause is growing. . . . . . . . . . . . . . . . .   284 Psalm XI          12
  Who sells not guiltlesse cause, for filthy love of gain: . .   287 Psalm XV          12
  Nor my life's cause match with bloodseeker's case, . . . . .   306 Psalm XXVI        30
  In Cryes to Thee I shewd my Cause. . . . . . . . . . . . . .   311 Psalm XXX          5
  Who make a cause to joy of my decay; . . . . . . . . . . . .   323 Psalm XXXV        64
  I know that man's foule sin doth cause Thy wrath.. . . . . .   330 Psalm XXXIX       33
  Since foes nor have, nor shall have cause to be. . . . . . .   333 Psalm XLI         39
  Of my Cause oppressed. . . . . . . . . . . . . . . . . . . .   336 Psalm XLIII        3
  D. Her heavenly looks, which more and more do give me cause
    to crave.. . . . . . . . . . . . . . . . . . . . . . . . .   344 Possibly      1   32
  So have I cause my selfe to plaine, but no cause to
    complayne. . . . . . . . . . . . . . . . . . . . . . . . .   344 Possibly      1   36
  And so must see great cause before they love.. . . . . . . .   245 Other Poems   4  144
  While I was I, and so had cause to care; . . . . . . . . . .   254 Other Poems   4  484
  Where by his words his self-like cause he knew.. . . . . . .   256 Other Poems   4  536
  Cause all the mirth you can,. . . . . . . . . . . . . . . . .   261 Other Poems   6   37
CAUSED
  No sound part (causd by Thy wrath) . . . . . . . . . . . . .   327 Psalm XXXVIII      7
CAUSEFUL
  Sweet vertue's lawe barres not a causefull mone. . . . . . .    22 1st Eclogues  9   18
```

                                    69

```
CAUSEFUL                    (CONTINUED)                          PAGE    TITLE           LINE
    To causefull wrath, which thou canst not resist. . . . . . .    59  2nd Eclogues 30    66
    Since wayling is a bud of causefull sorowe, . . . . . . . .    108  Arcadia IV   70     1
    The straunge resounde of these my causefull cries: . . . . .  125  4th Eclogues 75     6
    Yet waile thy selfe, and waile with causefull teares, . . . .  228  Astrophil    94    11
    The Lord on them with causfull Ire . . . . . . . . . . . . .   297  Psalm XXI          33
CAUSELESS
    True cause of evils, and cause of causelesse woe. . . . . .     25  1st Eclogues  9   116
    Nor causelesse duty, nor comber of arrogance, . . . . . . . .   69  2nd Eclogues 34    23
    Such causelesse feares when coward minds do take, . . . . . .  145  Cert Sonnets 16     5
    Tell me the cause of this my causelesse woe, . . . . . . . .   146  Cert Sonnets 17    12
    Band of all evils, cradle of causelesse care, . . . . . . . .  161  Cert Sonnets 31     3
    My causeless wrongs hast wroken. . . . . . . . . . . . . . .   273  Psalm III          27
    Who causeless now, yeelds me a hatefull heart, . . . . . . .   277  Psalm VII          12
    That causeless wrongs do frame. . . . . . . . . . . . . . . .  303  Psalm XXV          10
    For causeless they both pitt and net did sett, . . . . . . .   321  Psalm XXXV         15
    For causeles they did seek to make me dy. . . . . . . . . . .  321  Psalm XXXV         16
    Let them not fleere, who me would causless stroy, . . . . . .  322  Psalm XXXV         50
CAUSELESSLY
    Not toying kinde, nor causiesly unkinde, . . . . . . . . . .    98  3rd Eclogues 65     5
CAUSES
    What causes first made these torments on me to light? Light.   64  2nd Eclogues 31    23
    And in himselfe new doubting causes nurst. . . . . . . . . .    94  3rd Eclogues 64    12
    And know great causes, great effects procure: . . . . . . .   178  Astrophil    26    10
CAUSTICS
    Your words my friend (right healthfull caustiks) blame . . .  175  Astrophil    21     1
CAVE
    Come cave, become my grave, come death, and lende. . . . . .    73  Arcadia III  40     7
    This cave is darke, but it had never light. . . . . . . . . .   75  Arcadia III  43     1
    No cave, no wasting waxe, no wordes of griefe, . . . . . . .    75  Arcadia III  43     7
    But foole, foole that I am, those eyes would shine from a
        dark cave. . . . . . . . . . . . . . . . . . . . . . . .   123  4th Eclogues 74    49
    Peake hath a Cave, whose narrow entries finde. . . . . . . .   150  Cert Sonnets 22    31
    Mine eyes the streight, the roomie cave, my minde, . . . . .   150  Cert Sonnets 22    35
    Who then in Lion's cave did enter fyrst, . . . . . . . . . .   247  Other Poems   4   206
CAVES
    All to a lesson he draws, norr hills nor caves can avoide
        him. . . . . . . . . . . . . . . . . . . . . . . . . . .    31  1st Eclogues 13     7
    In meane caves oft treasure abides, to an hostry a king
        comes. . . . . . . . . . . . . . . . . . . . . . . . . .    36  1st Eclogues 13   153
    The caves were full, the mountaines voide of goates: . . . .    98  3rd Eclogues 66    11
    The restfull Caves now restlesse visions give, . . . . . . .   147  Cert Sonnets 18     9
    Rockes, woods, hilles, caves, dales, meads, brookes, answere
        me, . . . . . . . . . . . . . . . . . . . . . . . . . .   147  Cert Sonnets 18    13
CAWING
    When with the kawing crowes their musicke is annoide. . . . .   52  2nd Eclogues 29    18
CEASE
    I cease to strive, with double conquest foild: . . . . . . .    11  Arcadia I     2     2
    First the rivers shall ceasse to repay their fludds to the
        Occean: . . . . . . . . . . . . . . . . . . . . . . . .    33  1st Eclogues 13    65
    But ceasse worthy shepheard, nowe ceasse we to weery the
        hearers. . . . . . . . . . . . . . . . . . . . . . . . .    37  1st Eclogues 13   172
    If ought I cease these hideous exclamations, . . . . . . . .    61  2nd Eclogues 30   145
    But vaine it is to thinke those paines should cease, . . . .   116  4th Eclogues 72    94
    Cease Muse therfore: thy dart o Death applie; . . . . . . .   129  4th Eclogues 75   141
    O make in me those civill warres to cease; . . . . . . . . .   184  Astrophil    39     7
    Cease eager Muse, peace pen, for my sake stay, . . . . . . .   201  Astrophil    70    12
    Cease we to praise, now pray we for a kisse. . . . . . . . .   206  Astrophil    79    14
    And I, mad with delight, want wit to cease, . . . . . . . . .  207  Astrophil    81    13
    But cease mine eyes, your teares do witnesse well. . . . . .   235  Astrophil   105     9
    Cease in these effects to prove: . . . . . . . . . . . . . .   220  A&S 8th Song       74
    That hatefull never cease. . . . . . . . . . . . . . . . . .   272  Psalm III           2
CEASED
    Of any since God AEsculapius ceased. . . . . . . . . . . . .   128  4th Eclogues 75   116
CEASELESS
    Against me swarm, ceaseless to raile at me. . . . . . . . . .  322  Psalm XXXV         40
CEDAR
    Then by my high Cedar, rich Ruby, and only shining Sunne, .    34  1st Eclogues 13    80
    But to the Cedar, Queene of woods, when I lifte my beteard
        eyes, . . . . . . . . . . . . . . . . . . . . . . . . .    36  1st Eclogues 13   141
    Streight as Cedar, a voice staines the Cannary birds, . . . .   69  2nd Eclogues 34    33
CEDAR'S
    This noble Cedar's pretious roote: . . . . . . . . . . . . .    89  Arcadia III  62   106
CEDARS
    When Cedars to the ground be opprest by the weight of an
        emmott, . . . . . . . . . . . . . . . . . . . . . . . .    34  1st Eclogues 13    77
    In straightnes past the Cedars of the forrests, . . . . . . .  113  4th Eclogues 71    64
    The highest Cedars broken see, . . . . . . . . . . . . . . .   310  Psalm XXIX         14
    Ev'en Cedars, which on liban be, . . . . . . . . . . . . . .   310  Psalm XXIX         15
CELESTIAL
    Celestiall powers to wormes, Jove's children serve to claye.  120  4th Eclogues 73   116
CENTAURS
    The warres of ougly Centaurs, . . . . . . . . . . . . . . . .   66  2nd Eclogues 32    22
CENTER
    The earth with pitie dull the center keepeth: . . . . . . . .  136  Cert Sonnets  3     8
CERTAIN
    For all these certaine blowes the surest shield. . . . . . .    58  2nd Eclogues 30    43
    Come sleepe, o sleepe, the certaine knot of peace, . . . . .   184  Astrophil    39     1
    With kindest care, as with a certain shield. . . . . . . . .   275  Psalm V            40
```

	PAGE	TITLE		LINE
CERTAINLY				
But certainly so long we may be glad,.	105	3rd Eclogues 67		64
CHAFE				
With chafe enough, till she him pacified:.	97	3rd Eclogues 64		110
But she in chafe him from her lap did shove, ...	173	Astrophil 17		7
Chafe not at some man's great good fortune	325	Psalm XXXVII		18
CHAFED				
As the chafed hart which brayeth	334	Psalm XLII		1
Nous cri'de, and chafd, but he no other can.	249	Other Poems 4		285
CHAFF				
But lyke vyle chaffe with wind shal scattred be.	270	Psalm I		14
And as vile chaff away the wind doth blow, ...	321	Psalm XXXV		11
CHAIN				
Doubt there hath bene, when with his golden chaine	193	Astrophil 58		1
Link not me in self same chain	309	Psalm XXVIII		11
CHAINS				
Whose fyrie chaines, uppon his freedome seaze, ...	74	Arcadia III 41		4
CHAIR				
But God shall sit in his Eternal chaire.	280	Psalm IX		21
CHALLENGE				
I challenge thee by shew of her perfection,.	15	1st Eclogues 7		17
Dorus. Thy challenge great, but greater my protection: . . .	15	1st Eclogues 7		19
Thy title great, I justlie chalenge may, ...	80	Arcadia III 53		7
(Lest greedy eies to them might challenge lay)	243	Other Poems 4		68
CHAMBER				
Or for some brawle, which in that chamber hie, ...	178	Astrophil 26		7
A chamber deafe to noise, and blind to light:.	184	Astrophil 39		10
More oft then to a chamber melodie;.	209	Astrophil 84		4
And when your chamber you do close,.	273	Psalm IV		19
CHAMELEON				
Camaeleon, ease to chaunge; Ducke, ease to yelde;.	101	3rd Eclogues 66		95
CHANCE				
Whyle upon chaunce, his fruite of labour lyes;	71	Arcadia III 36		10
Which that no chaunce may staine,.	91	3rd Eclogues 63		8
Histor. No doubt to whom so good chance did betide,.	104	3rd Eclogues 67		13
I praisde her eyes whom never chance doth move,.	141	Cert Sonnets 9		5
Some luckie wits impute it but to chaunce;	185	Astrophil 41		8
Since kind or chance gives both one liverie;	229	Astrophil 96		2
And now at keels they trie a harmles chaunce,.	243	Other Poems 4		47
CHANCED				
Is chaunced to my life, that from such muddy abundance . . .	34	1st Eclogues 13		96
CHANGE				
Yeld outward shew, what inward change he tryes:.	13	Arcadia I 4		2
The starres thy state, fortune may change thy happe.	23	1st Eclogues 9		25
To such a force soone chaunge were nothing sutable..	47	2nd Eclogues 28		12
Thou soone may have some helpe, or change of passion.. . . .	50	2nd Eclogues 28		98
Thus for ech change my changelesse hart I fortifie..	51	2nd Eclogues 28		126
Where chaunge of thoughts one foole to other shewes, ...	57	2nd Eclogues 30		21
Hold deere his work, with sighes eache change attendes,. . .	71	Arcadia III 37		8
But at no change, so pinching care he takes,.	71	Arcadia III 37		9
Both equall hurt, in this change sought our blisse:.	76	Arcadia III 45		13
As Prince's losse or change:.	81	Arcadia III 55		3
Like to the Moone when after chaunge	86	Arcadia III 62		11
Camaeleon, ease to chaunge; Ducke, ease to yelde;.	101	3rd Eclogues 66		95
Friend without change, playfellow without strife, ...	103	3rd Eclogues 67		10
And with the chaunge of them my fancie please.	113	4th Eclogues 72		4
(Which made of heav'nly stuffe no mortal chaunge doth bynde)	117	4th Eclogues 73		32
With feare of change, the courage well preparde:	143	Cert Sonnets 12		11
In wonted walkes, since wonted fancies change, ...	147	Cert Sonnets 18		1
If either you would change your cruell hart, ...	148	Cert Sonnets 19		7
Then might I hope a change or ease of minde, ...	148	Cert Sonnets 19		11
Who hath ever felt the change of love, ...	153	Cert Sonnets 24		1
Nor change in change, though change change my state.	153	Cert Sonnets 24		23
Changed to a change, I change not.	154	Cert Sonnets 25		29
Where, "sooner die then change my state",.	158	Cert Sonnets 28		35
Alas, whence came this change of lookes? If I.	212	Astrophil 86		1
We change eyes, and hart for hart, ...	227	A&S 10th Song		40
Deere when you find change in me,.	234	A&S 11th Song		8
Let my chaunge to ruine be..	234	A&S 11th Song		10
Yet will not I greife, ashes, thralldom change	345	Possibly 2		9
On thoughts he feeds, his lookes their figure chaunge, . . .	253	Other Poems 4		434
Rewing change of wonted state.	262	Other Poems 7		9
CHANGED				
Me seemes I heare in these ill-changed forrests, ...	112	4th Eclogues 71		39
Is chang'd to stone, in hardnesse, cold, and weight,. . . .	150	Cert Sonnets 22		43
Changed to a change, I change not.	154	Cert Sonnets 25		29
Have chang'd desert, let mine owne conscience be	212	Astrophil 86		2
But I in me am chang'd, I am alive and dead:	215	A&S 5th Song		76
Be not yet those fancies changed?"	234	A&S 11th Song		7
CHANGELESS				
Thus for ech change my changelesse hart I fortifie..	51	2nd Eclogues 28		126
CHANGELINGS				
Of other's children changelings use to make, ...	178	Astrophil 28		2
CHANGES				
What changes here, o haire,.	157	Cert Sonnets 28		1
So oft in feasts with costly chaunges cladd.	245	Other Poems 4		133
CHANGETH				
Popler changeth his hew from a rising sunne to a setting:. .	36	1st Eclogues 13		132
In one that changeth so, ...	158	Cert Sonnets 28		26

71

CHANGING   PAGE   TITLE   LINE

	PAGE	TITLE		LINE
CHANGING				
Or that they all to chaunging did encline, ...	100	3rd Eclogues	66	59
(As even in beasts their dammes leave chaunging parts) . . .	100	3rd Eclogues	66	60
For never day such changing wrought.	303	Psalm XXV		17
CHANNELS				
The gulfs of waters then were through their Chanels seen,. .	291	Psalm XVIII		31
CHAOS				
Throwne on this earth the Chaos of confusions.	51	2nd Eclogues	28	110
CHAPS				
And past all hope his chapps to frustrate so..	251	Other Poems	4	344
CHARACTER				
Writ each character of blisse, ...	219	A&S 8th Song		42
*CHARGE				
And charge of her to Argus did allow..	21	1st Eclogues	8	16
Feede on my sheepe, my chardge my comforte feede,.	43	Arcadia II	23	1
Hath sav'd his charge? it is even I.	44	Arcadia II	25	6
Then founde I which thing is a charge to beare	99	3rd Eclogues	66	17
Best charge, and bravest retrait in Cupid's fight, ...	206	Astrophil	79	5
I lay then to thy charge unjustest Tyrannie, ...	214	A&S 5th Song		56
*CHARGED				
With seede of woes my hart brimme-full is charged.	16	1st Eclogues	7	78
With gaping mouthes, these folks on me have charged, ...	299	Psalm XXII		29
CHARICT				
O time, become the chariot of my joyes:.	80	Arcadia III	53	9
There came a chariot faire by doves and sparrowes guided:. .	118	4th Eclogues	73	59
Fould with this sight, while thou thy chariot guidest. . . .	126	4th Eclogues	75	57
Which, coupling Doves, guides Venus' chariot right..	206	Astrophil	79	4
CHARIOTS				
In chariots arm'd, Others in chivalry;.	296	Psalm XX		27
CHARITY				
No men are left, that charity do love, ...	284	Psalm XII		2
CHARM				
My charme should be, she haunt me day and night.	17	1st Eclogues	7	105
No charme holdes her, but well possesse she may;	17	1st Eclogues	7	111
Vertue, beawtie, and speach, did strike, wound, charme,. . .	84	Arcadia III	60	1
But when birds charme, and that sweete aire, which is. . . .	231	Astrophil	99	9
Who may with charme of conversation sweete,.	236	Astrophil	106	10
Such marble eares, no cunning wordes can charme, ...	346	Possibly	5	2
CHARMED				
So love encroches on your charmed reason,.	50	2nd Eclogues	28	93
Since will is won, and stopped eares are charmed:.	135	Cert Sonnets	1	3
Since sweet sleep her eyes hath charmed, ...	202	A&S 2nd Song		5
O eyes, o eares of men, how are you charmed!	209	A&S 3rd Song		18
CHARMETH				
But from thy heart, while my sire charmeth thee, ...	181	Astrophil	32	13
CHARMING				
Not needing charming skill,.	92	3rd Eclogues	63	60
CHARMS				
Affection's charmes in my behalfe to prove..	17	1st Eclogues	7	102
"For, but by charms, how fall these things on me,.	253	Other Poems	4	449
CHASE				
Where rockes do wayte, for theym the wyndes do chase,. . . .	70	Arcadia III	36	2
Long since my thoughts chase me like beasts in forrests, . .	112	4th Eclogues	71	35
Thus, thus alas, I had my losse in chase..	115	4th Eclogues	72	70
Klaius. Thus, thus alas, I had my losse in chase,.	115	4th Eclogues	72	71
Bringing with her those starry Nimphs, whose chace	229	Astrophil	97	3
Then let my Foe chase me, and chasing take:.	277	Psalm VII		13
In rage Thy servant do not chase..	308	Psalm XXVII		45
The play began: Pas durst not Cosma chace, ...	248	Other Poems	4	249
CHASED				
Strephon so chas'd did seme in milke to swimme..	249	Other Poems	4	288
Like Numid Lions by the hunters chas'd,.	249	Other Poems	4	291
CHASING				
Then let my Foe chase me, and chasing take:.	277	Psalm VII		13
CHASTE				
Like great god Saturn faire, and like faire Venus chaste:. .	12	Arcadia I	3	5
Yee Muses all which chaste affects allow,.	91	3rd Eclogues	63	19
To this chaste love your sacred favours bow, ...	91	3rd Eclogues	63	21
Who doth desire that chaste his wife should be,.	98	3rd Eclogues	65	1
To know my miseries, but chaste and cruell:.	136	Cert Sonnets	3	10
For Thereus' force on her chaste will prevailing,.	137	Cert Sonnets	4	8
Whose eyes seeme chaste, because they looke on ground: . . .	147	Cert Sonnets	17	50
A Ladie in despite of nature chaste, ...	151	Cert Sonnets	22	62
Now since her chast mind hates this love in me,.	195	Astrophil	61	9
CHASTELY				
Who others' woes and plaints can chastly beare:.	142	Cert Sonnets	10	7
CHASTEN				
Use something else to chast'n me withall,.	212	Astrophil	86	12
CHASTENED				
All my'offence was Love: with Love then must I be chastned,.	123	4th Eclogues	74	41
With chastned mind, I straight must shew that she.	195	Astrophil	61	10
Chastned but thus, and thus his lesson tought, ...	244	Other Poems	4	97
CHASTENESS				
Where simple love, which chastnesse doth imparte,.	92	3rd Eclogues	63	58
In her let beautie both, and chastnesse fully raigne.. . . .	120	4th Eclogues	73	132
"Nay then (Diana said) the chastnesse I will give.	121	4th Eclogues	73	173
The fault I blame her chastnesse is.	157	Cert Sonnets	27	32
Where Love is chastnesse, Paine doth learne delight . .	188	Astrophil	48	3
CHASTENING				
Of my faults and chastening.	288	Psalm XVI		24

```
                                                              PAGE    TITLE              LINE
CHASTENS
    Lowring beautie chastens me: . . . . . . . . . . . . . .   203  A&S 2nd Song           26
CHASTEST
    In chastest plaies, till home they walke a rowe, . . . . .  243  Other Poems      4     54
CHASTISE
    Nor in anger chastise me;. . . . . . . . . . . . . . . . .  327  Psalm XXXVIII           3
CHASTISED
    Fearing least he chastisde be, . . . . . . . . . . . . . .  139  Cert Sonnets     7      9
CHASTITY
    O Chastitie, the chiefe of heavenly lightes, . . . . . . .   40  Arcadia II      18     13
    Brake on faire cleeves of constant chastitie:. . . . . . .  151  Cert Sonnets    22     56
    Where Cupid is sworne page to Chastity?. . . . . . . . . .  182  Astrophil       35      8
    The schooles where Venus hath learn'd Chastitie. . . . . .  185  Astrophil       42      4
CHAT
    Either dull silence, or eternall chat; . . . . . . . . . .  104  3rd Eclogues    67     31
    And cruel words their swelling tongues do chatt, . . . . .  290  Psalm XVII             30
CHATTERETH
    Dorus. Nightingales seldome sing, the Pie still chattereth:.  14  1st Eclogues     7      7
CHATTERING
    Goe winne of him (for chattering) praise or shame: . . . .   56  2nd Eclogues    29    139
    Cackling, and chattring, that of Jove beseech. . . . . . .  100  3rd Eclogues    66     67
    Dumbe Swannes, not chatring Pies, do Lovers prove, . . . .  192  Astrophil       54     13
CHAUCER'S
    Some good old dumpe, that Chaucer's mistresse knew,. . . .  146  Cert Sonnets    17     34
CHECKS
    With what sharpe checkes I in my selfe am shent, . . . . .  173  Astrophil       18      1
CHEEK
    At length in rowes of Kisse-cheeke teares they raine.. . .  245  Other Poems      4    128
CHEEK'S
    In her cheeke's pit thou didst thy pitfould set, . . . . .  170  Astrophil       11     11
CHEEKS
    Her forhead jacinth like, her cheekes of opall hue,. . . .   12  Arcadia I        3      9
    I leave mine eyes unwipte my cheekes to bathe. . . . . . .   54  2nd Eclogues    29     80
    Her cheekes with kindly claret spred.. . . . . . . . . . .   86  Arcadia III     62     23
    Whose porches rich (which name of cheekes endure). . . . .  169  Astrophil        9      7
    Hath cheekes to smile, as well as eyes to weepe. . . . . .  201  Astrophil       70      8
    Milke hands, rose cheeks, or lips more sweet, more red,. .  225  Astrophil       91      7
    Where those red cheeks, which oft with faire encrease did
        frame. . . . . . . . . . . . . . . . . . . . . . . . .  232  Astrophil      102      2
    In cheeks and lipps the Tyran threatens bloud. . . . . . .  246  Other Poems      4    152
CHEER
    And as a courtier was with cheere receaved,. . . . . . . .   94  3rd Eclogues    64     20
    But heavy was her pace, and such a meagre cheere,. . . . .  118  4th Eclogues    73     69
    Such proffer made, which she well showd with smiling cheere. 120  4th Eclogues    73    144
    This cheerefull aire with your obscured cheere,. . . . . .  127  4th Eclogues    75     68
    Sweet Ladie, as for those whose sullen cheare, . . . . . .  147  Cert Sonnets    17     46
    Dian that faine would cheare her friend the Night, . . . .  229  Astrophil       97      1
    Would faine drive cloudes from out my heavy cheere.. . . .  230  Astrophil       97     11
    What saist thou now, where is that dainty cheere . . . . .  235  Astrophil      106      5
    God's doomes be right, and cheer the sprite, . . . . . . .  294  Psalm XIX              33
    Still in mourning chear arayd. . . . . . . . . . . . . . .  328  Psalm XXXVIII          18
    Their chearfull minds, till pois'ned was their cheare, . .  243  Other Poems      4     41
CHEERFUL
    The cheerefull notes these pleasant places yeeld,. . . . .   58  2nd Eclogues    30     39
    Nowe that myne eyes their cheerefull sunn dothe misse. . .   70  Arcadia III     35      5
    But with thy cheerefull presence helpe to grace. . . . . .   91  3rd Eclogues    63     12
    This cheerefull aire with your obscured cheere,. . . . . .  127  4th Eclogues    75     68
    Upon thy cheerefull face, joye's livery weare: . . . . . .  232  Astrophil      103      3
    For cherfull thankfulness, . . . . . . . . . . . . . . . .  316  Psalm XXXIII            3
    Will. Dick, since we cannot dance, come let a cheerefull
        voyce. . . . . . . . . . . . . . . . . . . . . . . . .  343  Possibly         1      1
    Their chearfull minds, till pois'ned was their cheare, . .  243  Other Poems      4     41
CHEERING
    For warbling notes from inward chearing flow.. . . . . . .  242  Other Poems      4      4
CHERISH
    Cherish the hives of wisely painfull Bees: . . . . . . . .   26  1st Eclogues     9    132
    I cherish his, because in me it bides. . . . . . . . . . .   76  Arcadia III     45      8
    We made for paine, our paines they made to cherish:. . . .  106  3rd Eclogues    67    107
    Sorow then cherish me, for I am sorowe:. . . . . . . . . .  114  4th Eclogues    72     26
    The very trees with grafting we can cherish, . . . . . . .  127  4th Eclogues    75     85
    And onely cherish doth with injurie. . . . . . . . . . . .  206  Astrophil       78      5
    Whose grace is such, that when it chides doth cherish? . .  197  A&S 1st Song           18
    But they that sinne, in sinfull breast do cherish; . . . .  271  Psalm I                21
    Doth cherish rightfulness. . . . . . . . . . . . . . . . .  316  Psalm XXXIII            6
    Least such things sin in Thy self cherish, . . . . . . . .  325  Psalm XXXVII           22
CHERISHED
    Now fled, then cherished? then so nie, now so remote?. . .  124  4th Eclogues    74     78
CHERRIES
    Nico. Alas how oft I looke on cherries ripe, . . . . . . .   54  2nd Eclogues    29     75
    Rubies, Cherries, and Roses new, . . . . . . . . . . . . .   87  Arcadia III     62     39
    From comming neare those Cherries banish me: . . . . . . .  208  Astrophil       82      8
    So may the cheries redd. . . . . . . . . . . . . . . . . .  258  Other Poems      5     56
CHERRY
    Sweet gard'n Nymph, which keepes the Cherrie tree, . . . .  208  Astrophil       82      5
    Her chery lipps, milke hands, and golden haire . . . . . .  254  Other Poems      4    461
CHERRY'S
    Lips red and plum, as cherrie's ruddy side,. . . . . . . .   76  Arcadia III     46      8
CHERUBINS
    The Cherubins their backs, the winds did yeild their wings,.  291  Psalm XVIII            22
```

```
                                                              PAGE    TITLE          LINE
CHEST
    In one true chest to rob all Vertue's treasure?. . . . . . 126  4th Eclogues 75   47
    Will. What keepeth safe thy band? D. Remembrance is the
        Chest. . . . . . . . . . . . . . . . . . . . . . .  344  Possibly      1    29
CHESTS
    Where famine ravine taught their hungrie chestes,. . . . . 102  3rd Eclogues 66  124
CHEW
    That last day seem'd, he could not chew a beane. . . . . . 103  3rd Eclogues 67    6
CHIDE
    Doth lowre, nay, chide; nay, threat for only this: . . . . 203  Astrophil    73    7
    Do not chide . . . . . . . . . . . . . . . . . . . . . . . 327  Psalm XXXVIII       2
    She chide you not for stay,. . . . . . . . . . . . . . . . 257  Other Poems   5   35
CHIDES
    Thy father bids thee save, and chides for spilling.. . . .  16  1st Eclogues  7   79
    Whose grace is such, that when it chides doth cherish? . . 197  A&S 1st Song      18
CHIDING
    With blasting breath O Lord, that in thy chiding went. . . 291  Psalm XVIII       33
CHIEF
    Her length the earth in Love's chiefe clothing dressed.. .  17  1st Eclogues  7   87
    Therein his name, there his chiefe triumph lyes. . . . . .  22  1st Eclogues  8   42
    In whose chiefe parte your worthes implanted be? . . . . .  39  Arcadia II   16   10
    O Chastitie, the chiefe of heavenly lightes, . . . . . . .  40  Arcadia II   18   13
    Doth force us there to set our chiefe delightfulnes, . . .  61  2nd Eclogues 30  135
    Chief band I saye, which tyes my chiefest parte, . . . . .  70  Arcadia III  35   12
    Loath, I must leave his chiefe resort. . . . . . . . . . .  88  Arcadia III  62   84
    Vertue (if not a God) yet God's chiefe parte,. . . . . . .  92  3rd Eclogues 63   46
    Favour to make my chiefe and onely hire. . . . . . . . . . 115  4th Eclogues 72   55
    She had chiefe Goddesses in beautie overcome.. . . . . . . 120  4th Eclogues 73  146
    For because my cheefe part singeth,. . . . . . . . . . . . 140  Cert Sonnets  7   35
    Which caught, to cruell search yeelds his chiefe part: . . 150  Cert Sonnets 22   22
    When Nature made her chiefe worke, Stella's eyes,. . . . . 168  Astrophil     7    1
    But shining forth of heate in his chiefe pride;. . . . . . 176  Astrophil    22    4
    To keepe themselves and their chief cities free, . . . . . 179  Astrophil    29    2
    Doth fall to stray, and my chiefe powres are brought . . . 183  Astrophil    38    3
    Chiefe good, whereto my hope doth only aspire, . . . . . . 200  Astrophil    68    3
    Highway since you my chiefe Pernassus be,. . . . . . . . . 209  Astrophil    84    1
    Now God forbid. A theefe, and of worst theeves the cheefe: . 213  A&S 5th Song      44
    He layes on this chiefe praise,. . . . . . . . . . . . . . 216  A&S 6th Song      47
    Chiefe praise on that he laies.. . . . . . . . . . . . . . 216  A&S 6th Song      48
    Whiche my chefe partte, doth passe throughe, parche, and
        tye . . . . . . . . . . . . . . . . . . . . . . . .  344  Possibly      2    2
    "But you my pipe, whilome my chief delight,. . . . . . . . 254  Other Poems   4  481
CHIEFEST
    Barr'd from their chiefest object of delightfulnesse,. . .  51  2nd Eclogues 28  109
    Chief band I saye, which tyes my chiefest parte, . . . . .  70  Arcadia III  35   12
    My cheefest parte, wherin do chieflye stand. . . . . . . .  70  Arcadia III  35   13
    Dead palsie sicke of all my chiefest parts:. . . . . . . . 136  Cert Sonnets  2   10
    That parting thus my chiefest part I part. . . . . . . . . 148  Cert Sonnets 20    8
    In love, his chiefest part.. . . . . . . . . . . . . . . . 152  Cert Sonnets 23   12
    Prepar'd by Nature's chiefest furniture, . . . . . . . . . 169  Astrophil     9    2
    Who keepes the key of Nature's chiefest treasure?. . . . . 197  A&S 1st Song       6
CHIEFLY
    My cheefest parte, wherin do chieflye stand. . . . . . . .  70  Arcadia III  35   13
    Then must I save, what in my chiefly raignes,. . . . . . . 114  4th Eclogues 72   24
CHILD
    The child feeles that; the man that feeling knowes,. . . .  57  2nd Eclogues 30   23
    Thy Venus' child, whose beautie Venus lackes?. . . . . . .  60  2nd Eclogues 30  112
    Arcadia's gemme the noblest childe of nature.. . . . . . . 109  Arcadia IV   70   18
    The mountaines great with childe I thought brought foorth a
        mouse. . . . . . . . . . . . . . . . . . . . . . . . 118  4th Eclogues 73   76
    That she her child, I say, her best child killeth? . . . . 127  4th Eclogues 75   95
    The child of curse, man's weaknesse foster-child,. . . . . 141  Cert Sonnets 10    2
    Invention, Nature's child, fled step-dame Studie's blowes, . 165  Astrophil     1   10
    Thus great with child to speake, and helplesse in my
        throwes . . . . . . . . . . . . . . . . . . . . . . 165  Astrophil     1   12
    For like a child that some faire booke doth find,. . . . . 170  Astrophil    11    5
    O fate, o fault, o curse, child of my blisse,. . . . . . . 227  Astrophil    93    1
    And then, a heav'nly child, gave her Ambrosian pap:. . . . 213  A&S 5th Song      26
    Now child, a lesson new you shall begin to spell:. . . . . 213  A&S 5th Song      35
    And great with child of mischeif travaild long,. . . . . . 278  Psalm VII         38
    No sooner my child eyes could look abroad, . . . . . . . . 299  Psalm XXII        23
    On Creon's child his poison sooner throw,. . . . . . . . . 252  Other Poems   4  410
CHILDHOOD
    His childhood woonder, prenticeship attention, . . . . . .  48  2nd Eclogues 28   38
CHILDISH
    Seeke we to tame these childish superfluities: . . . . . .  61  2nd Eclogues 30  138
    That childish stuffe which knowes not frendes from foes, .  81  Arcadia III  54   11
    With thousand pretie childish plaies,. . . . . . . . . . . 158  Cert Sonnets 28   11
CHILDLIKE
    The gartring place with child-like signe,. . . . . . . . .  89  Arcadia III  62   99
    Her milken breasts the nurse of child-like love, . . . . . 141  Cert Sonnets  9    7
CHILDREN
    This paterne good, unto our children goes, . . . . . . . .  28  1st Eclogues 10   55
    Thus children doo the silly birds they finde,. . . . . . .  41  Arcadia II   20   11
    Riches of children passe a Prince's throne;. . . . . . . . 106  3rd Eclogues 67  112
    Celestiall powers to wormes, Jove's children serve to claye. 120  4th Eclogues 73  116
    Unto my children alway good rest taking: . . . . . . . . . 139  Cert Sonnets  6    5
    Of other's children changelings use to make, . . . . . . . 178  Astrophil    28    2
    So children still reade you with awfull eyes,. . . . . . . 196  Astrophil    63    2
    Kils his owne children, teares, finding that they. . . . . 229  Astrophil    95   10
```

		PAGE	TITLE		LINE
CHILDREN	(CONTINUED)				
And children have to leave it to................		290	Psalm XVII		44
They shall to children's children make notorious		300	Psalm XXII		77
Come children, lend your eare.................		319	Psalm XXXIV		41
Did it for just Desire's true children builde,........		345	Possibly	4	10
But with dew dropps engendre children hy:..........		257	Other Poems	5	45
CHILDREN'S					
They shall to children's children make notorious		300	Psalm XXII		77
CHILD'S					
The Heathen for thy Child's right, and will thy realme extend		271	Psalm II		19
And of my Child's part the blisse,.............		288	Psalm XVI		14
CHILLING					
Since heart in chilling feare with yce is warmed:......		135	Cert Sonnets	1	7
Scortch not, but onely do darke chilling sprites remove. . .		205	Astrophil	76	8
CHIN					
Her nose, her chinne pure ivorie weares:..........		86	Arcadia III	62	27
CHIRPING					
The birds' eyes closde, closed their chirping notes.		98	3rd Eclogues	66	12
She chirping ran, he peeping flew away,...........		244	Other Poems	4	87
CHIRPS					
The birdes likewise with chirpes, and puing could,.....		100	3rd Eclogues	66	66
CHIVALRY					
In chariots arm'd, Others in chivalry;...........		296	Psalm XX		27
CHOICE					
I warne thee therefore (since thou maist have choice). . . .		29	1st Eclogues	10	88
For why should I, whom free choise slave doth make,.....		146	Cert Sonnets	17	9
Faire choice I have, either to live or dye		149	Cert Sonnets	21	13
As his maine force, choise sport, and easefull stay.		186	Astrophil	43	4
With choise delights and rarest company,..........		230	Astrophil	97	10
Say whether of the choice.................		215	A&S 6th Song		3
CHOICEST					
Prepar'd by Nature's choisest furniture,..........		169	Astrophil	9 V	2
Or reach the fruite of Nature's choisest tree,.......		169	Astrophil	10	4
With choisest flowers my speech to engarland so;.......		192	Astrophil	55	2
With choisest words, thy words with reasons rare,......		200	Astrophil	68	10
CHOKE					
But malice shall the wicked choake,.............		320	Psalm XXXIV		75
For creeping rimes, which often sighings choke........		242	Other Poems	4	8
CHOKED					
I waile for want, and yet am chokte with store........		41	Arcadia II	20	8
CHOLER					
But this light choller that doth make you bolde, ...		25	1st Eclogues	9	105
But so his humor I frame, in a mould of choller adusted, . .		29	1st Eclogues	11	9
In choller put, with whom he would not fight........		96	3rd Eclogues	64	66
Choler adust is joyed in woman-kinde............		147	Cert Sonnets	17	52
CHOOSE					
Old men themselves, doe love young wives to choose:.....		25	1st Eclogues	9	88
So that I cannot chuse but write my mind,.........		190	Astrophil	50	9
And cannot chuse but put out what I write,........		190	Astrophil	50	10
CHOOSING					
Choosing alas! this our theatre publique,.........		109	Arcadia IV	70	11
CHOSE					
This marble chose, as of like temper knowne:		40	Arcadia II	19	2
He chose themselves his guarders for to bene,.......		102	3rd Eclogues	66	129
When He chose me, a godly One:...............		273	Psalm IV		12
Whom this lord chose,...................		317	Psalm XXXIII		47
Why? because I virtue chose................		329	Psalm XXXVIII		60
CHOSEN					
(Espilus) Thus joyfully in chosen tunes rejoyce, ...		5	Lady of May	3	13
Live long, and long witnesse my chosen smarte,.......		77	Arcadia III	47	10
Thou blind man's marke, thou foole's selfe chosen snare, . .		161	Cert Sonnets	31	1
For he then chosen was the dignitie............		244	Other Poems	4	75
CHRISTIAN					
To fill his hornes this yeare on Christian coast;.....		179	Astrophil	30	2
CHUMPISH					
With chumpish lookes, hard words, and secret nips, ...		95	3rd Eclogues	64	31
CHURCH					
Till that good God make Church and Churchman starve.		167	Astrophil	5	8
But in his church his Fame is plac't............		310	Psalm XXIX		24
CHURCHES					
Is this thy fruite O strife? those thousand churches hie,. .		119	4th Eclogues	73	111
Churches or schooles are for thy seate more fit:		166	Astrophil	4	6
CHURCHMAN					
Till that good God make Church and Churchman starve.		167	Astrophil	5	8
CHURLISH					
All churlish wordes, shrewd answeres, crabbed lookes,. . . .		93	3rd Eclogues	63	64
CIMMERIAN					
First let Cimmerian darknes be my onel'habitaco'n:		124	4th Eclogues	74	59
CIRCLE					
Teach me what circle may acquaint her sprite,.......		17	1st Eclogues	7	101
The circle is my (round about her) sight:.........		17	1st Eclogues	7	103
What circle then in so rare force heares swaye?.......		17	1st Eclogues	7	109
But (like a point in midst of a circle) is still of a neernesse, ...		31	1st Eclogues	13	6
In curious circle, busie sight:..............		88	Arcadia III	62	74
CIRCLED					
With circkled course, which no wise stay can trye, ...		81	Arcadia III	54	10
CIRCUMSPECTLY					
Most circumspectly guarded,................		295	Psalm XIX		46

CITADEL   PAGE   TITLE   LINE
    O no, her heart is such a Cittadell, ...   171 Astrophil   12   12
CITED
    Consist, when they to highest doome are cited, ...   270 Psalm I   16
CITHERN
    They shall not last: with Citherne silent muse . . . . . .   143 Cert Sonnets 12   14
CITIES
    To keepe themselves and their chief cities free, ...   179 Astrophil   29   2
CIVIL
    O make in me those civill warres to cease; . . . .   184 Astrophil   39   7
CLAD
    Was vertue cladde in constant love's attire. . . . .   77 Arcadia III   48   2
    This thinke I well, the beasts with courage clad . . . . .   100 3rd Eclogues 66   55
    And mother Earth, now clad in mourning weeds, did breath . . 117 4th Eclogues 73   9
    But now, if ere my face with joy be clad: . . . .   147 Cert Sonnets 17   44
    So in joy my glory clad, ...   288 Psalm XVI   29
    In land with living creatures clad?. . . . .   308 Psalm XXVII   63
    The poore-clad truth of love's wrong-ordred lot. . . . . .   242 Other Poems   4   14
    So oft in feasts with costly chaunges cladd. . . . .   245 Other Poems   4   133
CLAIM
    You none can clayme but you your selfe by right, ...   79 Arcadia III   50   19
    Which dare claime from those lights the name of best,. . . . 169 Astrophil   9   11
    Such smart may pitie claime of any hart, ...   186 Astrophil   44   3
    By no pretence claime any maner place. . . . .   191 Astrophil   52   11
    If Rule by force without all claime a Tyran showeth, ... 214 A&S 5th Song   57
CLAIMED
    With sense possest, and claim'd by reason's right: . . . . .   74 Arcadia III   42   6
CLAIMING
    All strife for toyes, and clayming master's right: . . . . .   93 3rd Eclogues 63   67
CLAIMS
    However they putt in their claimes,. . . . .   315 Psalm XXXII   23
    Claymes but to gaine his due, O yeelde O yeelde. . . . . . . 345 Possibly   4   8
CLAMOR
    With bolde clamor unheard, unmarckt, what I seeke what I
        suffer:. . . . .   35 1st Eclogues 13   112
CLARET
    Her cheekes with kindly claret spred. . . . .   86 Arcadia III   62   23
CLAUSE
    Despaire most tragicall clause to a deadly request). . . . . 122 4th Eclogues 74   12
CLAW
    Fine eares, long taile he hath, with Lion's curbed clawe,. .   53 2nd Eclogues 29   33
CLAY
    Which streight the Earth yclothed in his claye:. . . . . . . 101 3rd Eclogues 66   79
    Celestiall powers to wormes, Jove's children serve to claye. 120 4th Eclogues 73   116
    Lives to impart my wearie clay some breath.. . . . .   148 Cert Sonnets 20   10
    I bett them as the clay is bett in beaten wayes. . . . . .   293 Psalm XVIII   77
    And what was I but wretched clay?. . . . .   311 Psalm XXX   24
CLAYEY
    If of this Clayey race he could espy . . . .   286 Psalm XIV   8
CLEAN
    There ofte steales out that round cleane foote . . . . . .   89 Arcadia III   62   105
    For faithfull hart, cleane hands, and mouth as true: . . . .   99 3rd Eclogues 66   25
    The lord with pardon doth make cleane, ...   314 Psalm XXXII   2
CLEANLY
    A clenly cloth thy moistnes for to wipe: . . . .   257 Other Poems   5   55
CLEANNESS
    Of him the Feare doth cleaness beare . . . .   294 Psalm XIX   37
CLEANSE
    O lord cleanse me from faults that be. . . . .   295 Psalm XIX   51
CLEAR
    From those cleere notes which freely may rejoyce.. . . . .   13 Arcadia I   4   8
    Doe speake high wordes, when all the coaste is cleare, . . .   27 1st Eclogues 10   32
    And in our little world dost cleare our inward sight,. . . .   44 Arcadia II   26   2
    Thy beames I like, but her cleare rayes I love:. . . . . .   72 Arcadia III   38   9
    Let voice of Sighes into cleare musike runne,. . . . . . .   84 Arcadia III   59   13
    Save one as much as other cleere:. . . . .   86 Arcadia III   62   20
    Like pomels round of Marble cleere:. . . . .   87 Arcadia III   62   55
    Did suffer drousie lids mine eyes then cleare to blinde; . . 117 4th Eclogues 73   26
    That her cleare voyce lifts thy fame to the skies. . . . .   171 Astrophil   12   8
    With that faire breast making woe's darknesse cleare:. . . . 193 Astrophil   57   11
    Stella whose eyes make all my tempests cleere, ...   222 Astrophil   87   3
    For in their mouth not One cleere word is spent, ...   275 Psalm V   25
    Up Thou dost light my light, and cleare my darkned eye.. . . 292 Psalm XVIII   53
    In darkness teach cleere knowledg. . . . .   293 Psalm XIX   8
    And will save whom his sight cleere. . . . .   320 Psalm XXXIV   67
    Now the ambitiouse Larke with mirror cleare. . . . .   243 Other Poems   4   45
CLEAR-DEALING
    Both free of minde, both did clear-dealing love, ...   243 Other Poems   4   39
CLEARED
    Her cleared lookes, nought els, in stormes can quiet me. . .   51 2nd Eclogues 28   119
    Let them be clearde, and now begin to see, ...   131 Arcadia V   77   11
CLEAREST
    Whose cleerest eyes I blisse, and sweetest voyce,. . . . .   5 Lady of May   3   15
    I darkned am, who once had clearest sight. . . . .   75 Arcadia III   43   4
    Farewell o Sunn, Arcadia's clearest light: . . . .   129 4th Eclogues 76   1
    For ever blinded of our clearest light;. . . . .   130 4th Eclogues 76   27
CLEARLY
    Coles of love that burne so clearely;. . . . .   222 A&S 9th Song   34
CLEARNESS
    The shining clearness of thy face: . . . .   274 Psalm IV   27

CLEARNESS   (CONTINUED)   PAGE   TITLE   LINE

After my clearness, and my Equity. . . . . 277 Psalm VII   24
Your hearts with clearness armed.. . . . . 316 Psalm XXXII   42
CLEARS
Clusters of clowdes, which no Sunne ever cleares.. . . . . . 41 Arcadia II   21   4
CLEAVE
I sawe her arme, where purest Lillies cleave.. . . . . 55 2nd Eclogues 29 104
With her faire hande, your tender barkes to cleave,. . . . . 78 Arcadia III   49   6
And let my breath upon your braunches cleave,. . . . . 125 4th Eclogues 75   7
I hated have those men whose thoughts do cleave. . . . . . . 312 Psalm XXXI   16
CLEAVED
No, though tongue to roofe be cleaved, ... 139 Cert Sonnets 7   8
CLEAVES
My tong to this my roofe cleaves,. . . . . 66 2nd Eclogues 32   12
The highest hills the bolt of thunder cleeves: . . . . 143 Cert Sonnets 12   9
CLEAVING
My cleaving tongue close to my roofe doth bide.. . . . . . . 299 Psalm XXII   36
CLEEVES
Brake on faire cleeves of constant chastitie:. . . . . 151 Cert Sonnets 22   56
CLEOFILA
Cleofila. Worthy shepeheard, by my song to my selfe all
  favor is happned,. . . . . 31 1st Eclogues 13   8
Cleofila. First shall fertill grounds not yeeld increase of
  a good seed: . . . . 33 1st Eclogues 13   64
Cleofila. Hardy shepearde, such as thy meritts, such may be
  her insight . . . . 37 1st Eclogues 13 155
CLERKLY
For clerkly reed, and hating what is naught, ... 99 3rd Eclogues 66   24
CLIENT
Your Client poore my selfe, shall Stella handle so?. . . . . 213 A&S 5th Song   31
CLIMB
If neither by that helpe, thou canst clime up to thy fancie, 34 1st Eclogues 13 100
O tongues right ladders made to clime dishonour, ... 50 2nd Eclogues 28   90
I would climbe up, and bring a prettie starre, ... 55 2nd Eclogues 29 118
Those passions which to youthfull head doo clime,. . . . . . 107 3rd Eclogues 67 116
As soon as Sunne begins to clime the mountaines: . . . . . . 112 4th Eclogues 71   44
Thus, thus the mindes, which over all doo clime, ... 127 4th Eclogues 75   88
I rather wisht thee clime the Muses' hill, ... 169 Astrophil   10   3
When my leaping hart will clime, ... 226 A&S 10th Song   26
So shall my voice clime to thyne eares betime: . . . . 274 Psalm V   5
Who shall climb to the hill which God's own hill is named, . 302 Psalm XXIV   5
And lo, his Call the skyes did clime;. . . . . 319 Psalm XXXIV   22
When most his troubles clime.. . . . . 332 Psalm XLI   4
"My song clime thou the winde. . . . . 259 Other Poems   5 105
CLIMBED
And hath with wailing strength clim'd highest mountaines:. . 112 4th Eclogues 71   27
My cryes clim'd up and he bent down from sacred throne,. . . 291 Psalm XVIII   13
That I Climb'd highest hill, he me warr points did show, . . 292 Psalm XVIII   62
CLIMB-FALL
Of clime-fall Court, the envy-hatching place:. . . . . 243 Other Poems   4   61
CLIMBING
The sheep, mild-seeming face; climing, the Beare;. . . . . . 101 3rd Eclogues 66   90
In clyming steepe, now hard refusall show: . . . . 147 Cert Sonnets 18   6
Scourge of it selfe, still climing slipprie place, ... 176 Astrophil   23   10
CLIMBS
Clymes even unto the starres, Nature is under it.. . . . . . 68 2nd Eclogues 34   9
Ah, that, that do I not conceive; to the heaven when a mouse
  climes. . . . . 122 4th Eclogues 74   21
CLIMBST
With how sad steps, o Moone, thou climb'st the skies,. . . . 180 Astrophil   31   1
CLIMES
But finding these North clymes do coldly him embrace,. . . . 168 Astrophil   8   5
CLINGS
And oft so clings to my pure Love, that I. . . . . 202 Astrophil   72   2
CLIPPED
His wings desire oft clipt with desperation: . . . . 48 2nd Eclogues 28   44
CLIPPING
Now runnes, and takes hir in his clipping armes. . . . . . . 252 Other Poems   4 384
*CLIPS
Not usde to frozen clips, he strave to find some part, . . . 168 Astrophil   8   6
Yet while I languish, him that bosome clips, ... 194 Astrophil   59   9
Clips streight my wings, streight wraps me in his night, . . 236 Astrophil   108   8
CLIVES
That Albion clives in whitenes passe:. . . . . 88 Arcadia III   62   91
CLOAK
With ouglie cloke the darke envious night: . . . . 82 Arcadia III   55   8
Night hath closd all in her cloke, ... 210 A&S 4th Song   7
Who, their spotted thoughts to cloak,. . . . . 309 Psalm XXVIII   13
Burnt Caban, lost my cloke,. . . . . 259 Other Poems   5 101
Nor with Love to cloake Disdaine,. . . . . 263 Other Poems   7   40
CLOD-LIKE
Now for a clod-like hare in fourm they peere,. . . . . 243 Other Poems   4   43
CLOG
Becomes a clog) will soone ease me of it.. . . . . 194 Astrophil   59   14
CLOSE
Come clowdie feares, close up my daseled sight,. . . . . . . 74 Arcadia III   42   9
Let one time (but long first) close up their daies,. . . . . 92 3rd Eclogues 63   31
So close unto my selfe my wrackes doo lie. . . . . 114 4th Eclogues 72   40
Strephon. So close unto my selfe my wrackes doo lie; . . . . 114 4th Eclogues 72   41
And wanting use of eyes their eyes began to close: . . . . . 116 4th Eclogues 73   6

CLOSE	(CONTINUED)	PAGE	TITLE		LINE
Of what thou seest: close up in secrete knot thy will"....		119	4th Eclogues	73	98
To my close heart, where while some firebrands he did lay, .		169	Astrophil	8	13
There himselfe with his shot he close doth lay........		175	Astrophil	20	8
Then be they close, and so none shall displease.......		182	Astrophil	34	8
And when your chamber you do close,..............		273	Psalm IV		19
Nay Basan mighty Bulls close me about.............		299	Psalm XXII		28
My cleaving tongue close to my roofe doth bide........		299	Psalm XXII		36
For then their hatefull heads close whispring be		333	Psalm XLI		25
CLOSED					
Yet deare soile, if a soule closed in a mansion........		69	2nd Eclogues	34	31
With rebell force, hath closde in dungeon darke.......		73	Arcadia III	39	3
The birds' eyes closde, closed their chirping notes.		98	3rd Eclogues	66	12
(With gall cut out) closde up againe by art, ...		150	Cert Sonnets	22	23
Yet live with thoughts closde up, till that she will		150	Cert Sonnets	22	29
I start, looke, hearke, but what in closde up sence.		184	Astrophil	38	9
Or if they do delight therein, yet are so closde with wit, .		217	A&S 7th Song	V	3
Clos'd with their quivers in sleep's armory;		230	Astrophil	99	4
Night hath closd all in her cloke, ...		210	A&S 4th Song		7
To beare his sacred flight, in secret place then clos'd, . .		291	Psalm XVIII		23
CLOSED-UP					
That never I with clos'd-up sense do lie,..........		181	Astrophil	32	6
CLOSELY					
Hide me, ev'n closely in his Tent;		307	Psalm XXVII		27
CLOSEST					
And while o sleepe thou closest up her sight,........		79	Arcadia III	51	5
CLOTH					
A clenly cloth thy moistnes for to wipe:		257	Other Poems	5	55
CLOTHE					
Of such heaven stuffe, to cloath so heavenly mynde..		232	Astrophil	101	14
Well may the Evening cloath the eyes		311	Psalm XXX		16
CLOTHED					
Cloth'd in the shape which soonest may deceave:.......		21	1st Eclogues	8	32
And when I meete these trees, in the earth's faire lyvery clothed,..........................		35	1st Eclogues	13	113
Cloth'd with fine tropes, with strongest reasons lin'd,....		194	Astrophil	58	6
How cloth'd, how waited on, sighd she or smilde, ...		225	Astrophil	92	10
I say thou art a Devill, though clothd in Angel's shining: .		215	A&S 5th Song		81
Let them be cloathd in most confounding shame, ...		323	Psalm XXXV		65
At these my words all cloath'd in teares;..........		330	Psalm XXXIX		38
CLOTHES					
In painted clothes, because they call it love........		23	1st Eclogues	9	48
In earthly clothes enclosde a heavenly sparke........		80	Arcadia III	52	10
The first with cloth's tuckt up as Nymphes in woods do range ,.........................		118	4th Eclogues	73	66
CLOTHING					
Her length the earth in Love's chiefe clothing dressed....		17	1st Eclogues	7	87
Fancie his foode, his clothing is of carefulnes;		48	2nd Eclogues	28	41
While late bare earth, proud of new clothing springeth,. . .		137	Cert Sonnets	4	3
CLOUD					
"Alas! a cloud hath overcast mine eies:...........		255	Other Poems	4	505
And yet I see him shine amid the cloud:...........		255	Other Poems	4	506
CLOUDS					
And so behinde foule clowdes full oft faire starres do ly hidden"..........................		36	1st Eclogues	13	154
Clusters of clowdes, which no Sunne ever cleares.......		41	Arcadia II	21	4
Let not these slumbring clowds thy beawties hide,......		91	3rd Eclogues	63	11
In cofer of dimme clowdes his silver groates,........		98	3rd Eclogues	66	9
Yee dimmy clowdes, which well employ your stayning		127	4th Eclogues	75	67
Which breakes the clowdes and opens forth the light, ...		161	Cert Sonnets	32	7
Having no scarfe of clowds before his face,.........		176	Astrophil	22	3
Let clouds bedimme my face, breake in mine eye,.......		198	Astrophil	64	5
Would faine drive cloudes from out my heavy cheere.....		230	Astrophil	97	11
See what clouds of reproch small darke thy honour's skie,..		213	A&S 5th Song		23
About which hee dimme clouds like a Pavilion brings, ...		291	Psalm XVIII		24
Cloudes even of Waters dark, and thickest ayre compos'd; ..		291	Psalm XVIII		25
In clouds of teares, but soon as sun		311	Psalm XXX		17
Thy truth above the Clouds, most high,............		323	Psalm XXXVI		14
These doubting clouds ore-casting heav'nly braine, ...		245	Other Poems	4	127
CLOUDY					
While our sonne shynes no clowdie greeves assaile......		43	Arcadia II	23	12
My sun is gon, Nowe clowdie greeves assayle.........		44	Arcadia II	24	12
Ofte scorching sonne, ofte clowdie darkenes feares,.....		71	Arcadia III	36	9
Come clowdie feares, close up my daseled sight,.......		74	Arcadia III	42	9
Klaius. Me seemes I see a filthie clowdie evening, ...		112	4th Eclogues	71	43
Who Stoick-like in clowdie hew appeare:...........		147	Cert Sonnets	17	48
Whose clowdie thoughts let fall an inward raine.		150	Cert Sonnets	22	36
CLOUTED					
In shine or storme must sett the clowted shoe:		242	Other Poems	4	20
CLOVEN					
A horned head, cloven foote, and thousand eyes,.......		21	1st Eclogues	8	26
His cloven foote doth never treade aright.		21	1st Eclogues	8	30
CLOWN					
But Nous that slipt from Pas, did catch the clowne.....		248	Other Poems	4	262
CLOYED					
Or if they do delight therein, yet are so cloyed with wit, .		217	A&S 7th Song		3
Let them with shame be cloyed;		332	Psalm XL		55
CLUSTERS					
Clusters of clowdes, which no Sunne ever cleares......		41	Arcadia II	21	4
The lovely clusters of her brests, ...		87	Arcadia III	62	53

		PAGE	TITLE		LINE
COACHMAN					
Curst be the Cochman which did drive so fast,.		235	Astrophil	105	13
COAL					
Since Reason's selfe doth blow the cole in me?		182	Astrophil	35	6
COALS					
Coles of love that burne so clearely;.		222	A&S 9th Song		34
On them storms, brimstone, coales he raines, ...		284	Psalm XI		19
Flames issued from his mouth, and burning coales out went;. .		291	Psalm XVIII		19
Then hayle, then firie coales, then thundred heavnly sire, .		291	Psalm XVIII		27
Then spake he his lowd voyce, then hailestones coales and					
fire.		291	Psalm XVIII		28
COALY					
Upon thy face let coaly Ravens swarme:		125	4th Eclogues 75		19
COAST					
Doe speake high wordes, when all the coaste is cleare, . . .		27	1st Eclogues 10		32
Of ships, by shipwrack cast on Albion coast, ...		151	Cert Sonnets 22		51
Upon that coast, am giv'n up for a slave..		179	Astrophil	29	14
To fill his hornes this yeare on Christian coast;.		179	Astrophil	30	2
His Word made heavnly Coast, ...		316	Psalm XXXIII		22
Left Nous to coast the loved beauty ny..		249	Other Poems	4	284
COASTS					
Do easly yeeld, that all their coasts may be		179	Astrophil	29	3
COAT					
A ruddie haire his cote, with fine long specled face:. . . .		53	2nd Eclogues 29		42
The filthy snake her aged coate can mende, ...		127	4th Eclogues 75		82
COCKERED					
These cocklinges cockred we bewaile to late, ...		28	1st Eclogues 10		58
COCKLINGS					
These cocklinges cockred we bewaile to late, ...		28	1st Eclogues 10		58
COFFER					
Where well couched abides a coffer of pearle,.		67	2nd Eclogues 33		10
In cofer of dimme clowdes his silver groates,.		98	3rd Eclogues 66		9
COIN					
One brings the stuffe, the other stamps the coine, ...		20	1st Eclogues 8		3
The little coine his sweating browes have got, ...		104	3rd Eclogues 67		41
COINED					
Since that in selfe same metall coin'd,.		159	Cert Sonnets 29		3
Of Love, new-coind to helpe my beggery,.		196	Astrophil	62	13
COLD					
For water cold did never promise fire:		3	Lady of May	2	4
Is past with me, my bloud is waxen colde..		25	1st Eclogues 9		107
Nay even cold Death enflamde with hot desire		59	2nd Eclogues 30		86
Which on cold winter's face doth grow.		85	Arcadia III	62	8
Till knit with cold, though there unknowne remaine,.		150	Cert Sonnets 22		33
Is chang'd to stone, in hardnesse, cold, and weight, ...		150	Cert Sonnets 22		43
But she most faire, most cold, made him thence take his					
flight		169	Astrophil	8	12
To warme with ill-made fire cold Moscovy;.		180	Astrophil	30	4
In thy cold stuffe a flegmatike delight?		193	Astrophil	56	11
Benighted in cold wo, but now appeares my day, ...		204	Astrophil	76	3
Nature's praise, Vertue's stall, Cupid's cold fire,.		206	Astrophil	80	3
Whom Death to his cold bosom drawes.		311	Psalm XXX		9
Hardned, and coulde, farr from affectione's snare.		344	Possibly	2	5
For ev'n in forge colde water fire maintaines.		246	Other Poems	4	156
COLDER					
Of sorrowe's droppes, till colder reason binde		150	Cert Sonnets 22		37
COLDLY					
But finding these North clymes do coldly him embrace,. . . .		168	Astrophil	8	5
COLLAR					
The dogge was in a coller taught his kinde..		102	3rd Eclogues 66		138
COLLECTION					
She is her selfe, of best things the collection.		15	1st Eclogues 7		48
COLOR					
For hope the colour due.		157	Cert Sonnets 28		4
In colour blacke, why wrapt she beames so bright?.		168	Astrophil	7	2
How doth the colour vade of those vermillion dies, ...		232	Astrophil	102	5
COLORED					
To decke the earth with his well-colourde weede, ...		78	Arcadia III	50	2
There fall those Saphir-coloured brookes,.		90	Arcadia III	62	127
With guilded leaves or colourd Velume playes,.		170	Astrophil	11	6
Some beautie's peece, as amber colourd hed,.		225	Astrophil	91	6
COLORS					
He proules ech place stil in new colours deckt,.		21	1st Eclogues 8		35
Lay not thy colours more to view,.		157	Cert Sonnets 27		23
Nor do not use set colours for to weare, ...		191	Astrophil	54	2
In false colours dressed..		336	Psalm XLIII		6
COLT					
But still when thou dost sing, me thinkes a colt is loose. .		52	2nd Eclogues 29		24
COLTISH					
Such coltish gyres, that to my birth I owe		175	Astrophil	21	6
COLUMBINE					
Cowslipp and Columbine,.		257	Other Poems	5	41
COMB					
Hony or Comb of hony..		294	Psalm XIX		44
COME					
Come Espilus, come now declare thy skill,.		3	Lady of May	2	1
Come shepheard's weedes, become your master's minde:		13	Arcadia I	4	1
Come shepheard's weedes, attend my woefull cryes:.		13	Arcadia I	4	5
Because from him doth come her light:.		13	Arcadia I	5	10
Lalus. Come Dorus, come, let songs thy sorowes signifie: . .		14	1st Eclogues 7		1

COME	(CONTINUED)	PAGE	TITLE		LINE
Heare plaints come forth from dungeon of my minde.		18	1st Eclogues	7	133
Come narr good Mastix, tis now full tway score		27	1st Eclogues	10	20
Come, come my currs, tis late I will goe in.		29	1st Eclogues	10	98
Selfe-lost and wandring, banished that place we doe come from,		32	1st Eclogues	13	26
Come from marble bowers, many times the gay harbor of anguish,		34	1st Eclogues	13	92
A voice may come, which troubled soule doth yeld:		40	Arcadia II	18	4
Reason. Thou Rebell vile, come, to thy master yelde.		46	2nd Eclogues	27	1
But when I did come neere with heate and hope,		54	2nd Eclogues	29	88
For me to come, and so she did: I came,		55	2nd Eclogues	29	91
Pas. When Cosma doth come forth, the Sun displaies		55	2nd Eclogues	29	96
I would come downe, and yeeld to her my place,		56	2nd Eclogues	29	121
As let them come or go with even facilitie..		60	2nd Eclogues	30	133
Whence can pride come there, since springs of beawty be thence? Thence.		65	2nd Eclogues	31	44
But harveste come, and corne in fertill store,		71	Arcadia III	36	11
Come cave, become my grave, come death, and lende.		73	Arcadia III	40	7
Come clowdie feares, close up my daseled sight,		74	Arcadia III	42	9
And if forsooth there come some new found ware,		104	3rd Eclogues	67	40
Long since I see my joyes come to their evening,		112	4th Eclogues	71	29
Of heaven, of earth, of hell, of time and place was come..		118	4th Eclogues	73	62
When I such guests did see come out of such a house,		118	4th Eclogues	73	75
"Venus come on": said she, "Diane you are obaide".		119	4th Eclogues	73	78
Thus both did come to me, and both began to tell		121	4th Eclogues	73	154
Then come, O come, then do I come, receyve (mee),		138	Cert Sonnets	5	21
The stately towers come downe with greater fall:		143	Cert Sonnets	12	8
Fowle Winters as they come, away they shall.		143	Cert Sonnets	12	12
Come learners then to me, the modell of mishappe,		153	Cert Sonnets	24	15
Nor breake my word though reward come late,		153	Cert Sonnets	24	21
To come from whence you be,		158	Cert Sonnets	28	30
And sure at length stolne goods do come to light		172	Astrophil	15	11
Come let me write, "And to what end?" To ease.		181	Astrophil	34	1
Come sleepe, o sleepe, the certaine knot of peace,		184	Astrophil	39	1
Where well he knowes, no man to him can come..		186	Astrophil	43	14
That once come there, the sobs of mine annoyes		187	Astrophil	44	13
Her come, and heare with patience my desire,		193	Astrophil	56	13
Come, come, and let me powre my selfe on thee;		200	Astrophil	69	6
Come then my Muse, shew thou height of delight		201	Astrophil	70	9
In Beautie's throne, see now who dares come neare.		203	Astrophil	73	10
In justice paines come not till faults do call;		212	Astrophil	86	10
Of comfort dare come to this dungeon darke,		233	Astrophil	104	7
Nor beasts, nor birds do come unto this blessed gaze,		209	A&S 3rd Song		15
Come no more, least I get anger.".		234	A&S 11th Song		37
Come let us breake their bonds, say they, and fondly say:		271	Psalm II		7
From whence shall come to us such ayd?		274	Psalm IV		25
Then rise and come abroad,		282	Psalm X		49
Ah, when from syon shall the saver come,		287	Psalm XIV		22
Who forth doth come like a bridegrome.		294	Psalm XIX		21
Let him come down, and help to Thee apply.		295	Psalm XX		7
By aiding when fierce unicorns come neare me..		299	Psalm XXII		50
You Isra'el's seed, you come of Jacob, feare him..		300	Psalm XXII		54
For my annoyes have come before thyne eye,		312	Psalm XXXI		20
Shall never dare come neare him.		315	Psalm XXXII		24
Come, Come, the way I will teach Thee,		315	Psalm XXXII		29
Woes, woes shall come to wicked folks;		315	Psalm XXXII		37
Come then and join with me,		319	Psalm XXXIV		9
Come children, lend your eare.		319	Psalm XXXIV		41
Will. Dick, since we cannot dance, come let a chearefull voyce.		343	Possibly	1	1
Come she, and sweet the aire with open brest,		254	Other Poems	4	466
Say then, can this but of enchantment come?.		254	Other Poems	4	472
Come shepheard's boy, let now thy heart be bowd.		255	Other Poems	4	510
To mother sea you come,		257	Other Poems	5	34
Since I am now come hether,		261	Other Poems	6	38
COMEDY					
And is even irkt that so sweet Comedie,		190	Astrophil	51	13
COMELINESS					
A careles comelines with comely care,		247	Other Poems	4	213
COMELY					
It is a comely part.		316	Psalm XXXIII		4
A careles comelines with comely care,		247	Other Poems	4	213
COMES					
The highest note comes oft from basest mind,		4	Lady of May	2	13
To narrow brests he comes all wrapt in gaine:		21	1st Eclogues	8	37
Oft comes reliefe when most we seeme in trappe..		23	1st Eclogues	9	24
Cyprus promiseth helpe, but a helpe where comes no recomforte..		35	1st Eclogues	13	119
In meane caves oft treasure abides, to an hostry a king comes.		36	1st Eclogues	13	153
Peace? what barrs me my tongue? who is it that comes me so ny? I.		62	2nd Eclogues	31	2
They leave off al, and say, death comes too eagerlie..		128	4th Eclogues	75	114
Who seeketh heav'n and comes of heav'nly breath.		144	Cert Sonnets	32	12
The doore by which sometimes comes forth her Grace,		169	Astrophil	9	5
Let her go. Soft, but here she comes. Go to,		188	Astrophil	47	12
She comes, and streight therewith her shining twins do move.		204	Astrophil	76	1
She comes with light and warmth, which like Aurora prove		205	Astrophil	76	5
Nay sorrow comes with such maine rage, that he		229	Astrophil	95	9

COMES	(CONTINUED)	PAGE	TITLE	LINE
In comes the King of glory bright.		302	Psalm XXIV	18
Above line repeated at following location.		302	Psalm XXIV	22
What comes therof? he shall not slide.		326	Psalm XXXVII	80
Ah, when comes my blessed being, ...		334	Psalm XLII	7

COMETH
| What, is not this enough? nay farre worse commeth here;. . . | | 214 | A&S 5th Song | 73 |

COMFITS
| Like comfits round in marchpane set. . . . . | | 89 | Arcadia III 62 | 112 |

COMFORT
Till this he tooke for comfort of his lot:		5	Lady of May 3	10
Whose strongest hope in your weake comfort lyes.		13	Arcadia I 4	4
Comfort into my soule. I do finde, I do find what a blessing		34	1st Eclogues 13	95
Feede on my sheepe, my chardge my comforte feede,.		43	Arcadia II 23	1
Alas it is no comfort, ...		65	2nd Eclogues 32	5
That opened furthe my seale of compforte is)		70	Arcadia III 35	3
You have my thankes, Let me your comforte have..		70	Arcadia III 35	16
Comfort, step thou in place of wonted sadnes..		83	Arcadia III 59	10
"My sweetest joy, the comfort of my sprite,.		96	3rd Eclogues 64	92
Me seemes I feele the comfort of the morning		112	4th Eclogues 71	41
Sore beaten doth her mast of Comforte spende:.		114	4th Eclogues 72	45
Of everie image, which may comfort show?		199	Astrophil 66	4
Or art thou else to comfort me forsworne?.		199	Astrophil 67	11
Of comfort dare come to this dungeon darke,.		233	Astrophil 104	7
Doth make me most to wish thy comfort neere.		235	Astrophil 106	8
Did for mutuall comfort meete, ...		218	A&S 8th Song	6
Can tast comfort but of thee,.		220	A&S 8th Song	78
That I, even I of heavnly comfort full,.		280	Psalm IX	43
And Israel full of Comfort?.		287	Psalm XIV	24
But be not farr O Lord, my strength, my comfort;		299	Psalm XXII	45
To comfort me.		301	Psalm XXIII	15
Whose faces on his comfort staid		319	Psalm XXXIV	19
Sure aid present comfort.		337	Psalm XLIII	36
That comfort in these sports you like, my mynde his comfort				
tryes.		343	Possibly 1	14
Such comfort, fervent love		261	Other Poems 6	51

COMFORTS
But that good part, wherein all comforts be, ...		148	Cert Sonnets 20	11
That conversation sweet, where such high comforts be,. . . .		205	Astrophil 77	10
In Thee my joyes and comforts ever be, ...		279	Psalm IX	3

COMING
As white as milke, and comming to the call,.		54	2nd Eclogues 29	85
To couple comming harmes with sorrowes past?		57	2nd Eclogues 30	7
Comming from her, cannot but downewarde fall..		78	Arcadia III 49	18
Of comming gladnes..		83	Arcadia III 59	12
And scarce discerne the dawne cf comming day,.		131	Arcadia V 77	10
From comming neare those Cherries banish me:		208	Astrophil 82	8
From coming to the well deserved end,.		277	Psalm VII	26
And comming where he hop'd to be alone,.		253	Other Poems 4	439

COMMAND
| So well she can command, and yet obay, ... | | 106 | 3rd Eclogues 67 | 89 |

COMMANDING
| This song she singes in most commaunding wise: . . . . | | 255 | Other Poems 4 | 509 |

COMMANDMENTS
| All his commandments being . . . . | | 294 | Psalm XIX | 34 |

COMMANDS
| Commands all creatures, to yeeld obeysance . . . . | | 68 | 2nd Eclogues 33 | 22 |

COMMEND
| Thus I commend to thee all our former love.. . . . . | | 51 | 2nd Eclogues 28 | 102 |
| Into Thy hands I do commend my sprite, ... | | 312 | Psalm XXXI | 13 |

COMMIT
| Thou, with thy wife, adultry shalt commit. . . . . | | 11 | Arcadia I 1 | 10 |
| Commit their Cause, themselves, to Thee, ... | | 283 | Psalm X | 62 |

COMMITTETH
| Who may and will not save, murder in truth committeth. . . . | | 214 | A&S 5th Song | 54 |

COMMON
In this rare subject from thy common right:.		79	Arcadia III 51	10
As if he meant his lordship common be.		102	3rd Eclogues 66	112
But yet the common Damme none did bemone;.		102	3rd Eclogues 66	118
The common sence, which might.		216	A&S 6th Song	43
Their Counsills are your Common jesting stock, ...		287	Psalm XIV	20

COMMONLY
| But commonly like currs we them entreate,. . . . . | | 27 | 1st Eclogues 10 | 35 |

COMMONS
| Blith were the commons, cattell of the fielde, ... | | 102 | 3rd Eclogues 66 | 132 |

COMMONWEALTH
| Thy common-wealth may rightly grieved be,. . . . . | | 105 | 3rd Eclogues 67 | 76 |

COMPACT
| For there with strange compact dooth lie . . . . | | 90 | Arcadia III 62 | 125 |

COMPANION
| Desire, though thou my old companion art,. . . . . | | 202 | Astrophil 72 | 1 |

COMPANIONS
| Allarme allarme, companions nowe beginne,. . . . . | | 346 | Possibly 5 | 9 |

COMPANY
Dorus. Lady, reservd by the heav'ns to do pastors' company				
honnor,.		31	1st Eclogues 13	1
In silence, from a man's owne selfe with company robbed. . .		35	1st Eclogues 13	106
For such company decks such solitarines.		69	2nd Eclogues 34	42
Allow good company, but kepe from thence		98	3rd Eclogues 65	11
Seeme most alone in greatest companie, ...		178	Astrophil 27	2

81

```
COMPANY                 (CONTINUED)                    PAGE    TITLE          LINE
    With choise delights and rarest company, . . . . . . . . . .  230 Astrophil    97   10
    Nor kept with base dissemblers company;. . . . . . . . . . .  305 Psalm XXVI        15
COMPARE
    That in her doings better could compare. . . . . . . . . .    247 Other Poems   4  211
COMPARED
    Such this smale greatnes, doth seeme compar'd to the
        greatest.. . . . . . . . . . . . . . . . . . . . . . .     34 1st Eclogues 13   76
    That Nico must with Pas compared be? . . . . . . . . . . .     54 2nd Eclogues 29   65
    Klaius. For she, with whom compar'd, the Alpes are vallies,.  113 4th Eclogues 71   67
    Compar'd to me, made me in lightnesse found: . . . . . . .    147 Cert Sonnets 17   47
    (O happy Dove that art compar'd to hir!) . . . . . . . . . .  251 Other Poems   4  354
COMPARISON
    To liken her? Decke yours with your comparison:. . . . . . .   15 1st Eclogues  7   47
COMPASSED
    For bawling doggs have compast me about, . . . . . . . . . .  299 Psalm XXII        39
    For endless woes me compast have,. . . . . . . . . . . . . .  332 Psalm XL          43
COMPASSION
    Which of us two deserveth most compassion. . . . . . . . . .   15 1st Eclogues  7   18
    In sicke-man's franzie rather takes compassion,. . . . . . .   50 2nd Eclogues 28   96
    Selfe-guiltie folke must prove to feele compassion.. . . . .   60 2nd Eclogues 30  130
COMPEILED
    The wretch compell'd a runnagate became, . . . . . . . . . .   21 1st Eclogues  8   21
    Thus much my heart compeld my mouth to say,. . . . . . . . .  207 Astrophil    80    9
COMPLAIN
    Loved I am, and yet complaine of Love: . . . . . . . . . . .   41 Arcadia II   20    1
    He little looking that she should complaine. . . . . . . . .   95 3rd Eclogues 64   49
    Thy father justly may of thee complaine, . . . . . . . . . .  105 3rd Eclogues 67   73
    By them who of his rude resort complaine,. . . . . . . . . .  141 Cert Sonnets  8    4
    With her due praise did of my state complaine, . . . . . . .  141 Cert Sonnets  9    4
    Though in paine, cannot complaine. No, no, no, no. . . . . .  156 Cert Sonnets 26   33
    Do thou then (for thou canst) do thou complaine, . . . . . .  228 Astrophil    94    5
    So have I cause my selfe to plaine, but no cause to
        complayne. . . . . . . . . . . . . . . . . . . . . . . .  344 Possibly      1   36
COMPLAINING
    Of my complaining. . . . . . . . . . . . . . . . . . . . . .  276 Psalm VI          28
COMPLAININGS
    Nay to the heav'ns your just complayninges sende,. . . . . .  126 4th Eclogues 75   37
COMPLAINS
    Full womanlike complaines her will was brokne. . . . . . . .  137 Cert Sonnets  4   16
COMPLAINT
    Farewell Complaint, the miser's only pleasure: . . . . . . .   83 Arcadia III  59    2
    For I to teach the world complainte am bent. . . . . . . . .  127 4th Eclogues 75   66
    Brother to woe, and father of complaint: . . . . . . . . . .  141 Cert Sonnets 10    3
    On my complaint build up their joy. . . . . . . . . . . . .   303 Psalm XXV          6
COMPLAINTS
    Of huge complaintes, that now it is despis'de. . . . . . . .   85 Arcadia III  61    4
    That when the breath of my complaints doth tuch. . . . . . .  187 Astrophil    44   10
COMPLETE
    His compleat harneis was hir purest white. . . . . . . . . .  246 Other Poems   4  150
COMPLEXION
    But rotten bleeding argues evill complection . . . . . . . .   50 2nd Eclogues 28 V883
COMPOSED
    This bodie is: this bodie so composed, . . . . . . . . . . .   57 2nd Eclogues 30   27
    A yelling voice, and heartes compos'd of sorow,. . . . . . .  109 Arcadia IV   70   27
    Cloudes even of Waters dark, and thickest ayre compos'd; . .  291 Psalm XVIII       25
CON
    "I con thee thanke" to whom thy dogges be deare, . . . . . .   27 1st Eclogues 10   34
CONCEAL
    My heart shall not conceale. . . . . . . . . . . . . . . . .  331 Psalm XL          39
CONCEIT
    Then each conceit that enters in by sight, . . . . . . . . .   23 1st Eclogues  9   38
    One wonder yet farre passeth my conceate:. . . . . . . . . .   42 Arcadia II   22   13
    Who for a selfe-conceipt will that forbeare, . . . . . . . .  105 3rd Eclogues 67   80
    Can those eyes now yeeld to the kind conceit of a sorow, . .  122 4th Eclogues 74   17
    While each conceate an ouglie figure beares, . . . . . . . .  131 Arcadia V    77    7
    But let all our conceit. . . . . . . . . . . . . . . . . . .  296 Psalm XX          28
    To seek Thy beauty past conceit; . . . . . . . . . . . . . .  332 Psalm XL          62
CONCEITS
    To high conceipts the song must needes be high,. . . . . . .    3 Lady of May   2    8
    To fill the world with strange but vaine conceits: . . . . .   20 1st Eclogues  8    2
    (Opprest with ruinouse conceites) by the helpe of an
        outcrye . . . . . . . . . . . . . . . . . . . . . . . .    35 1st Eclogues 13  109
    The high conceits thy heav'nly wisedomes breed . . . . . . .   72 Arcadia III  38    2
    To hie conceits whose fruits are oft but small,. . . . . . .  144 Cert Sonnets 15   10
    Of all the grave conceits your braine doth breed;. . . . . .  190 Astrophil    51    6
    But this straunge race more straunge conceits did yeeld: . .  251 Other Poems   4  345
CONCEIVE
    Such pearcing wordes as no thoughts els conceave:. . . . . .   78 Arcadia III  49    8
    Ah, that, that do I not conceive, though that to me leefe
        were. . . . . . . . . . . . . . . . . . . . . . . . . .   122 4th Eclogues 74   19
    Ah, that, that do I not conceive; to the heaven when a mouse
        climes. . . . . . . . . . . . . . . . . . . . . . . . .   122 4th Eclogues 74   21
    Even thus might I, for doubts which I conceave . . . . . . .  145 Cert Sonnets 16    9
    Did not conceive what fire he had within.. . . . . . . . . .  253 Other Poems   4  428
CONCEIVED
    And by thy pompe our losse will be conceaved.. . . . . . . .  127 4th Eclogues 75   75
    Which once said what I conceaved,. . . . . . . . . . . . . .  139 Cert Sonnets  7    5
    Lo he that first conceiv'd a wretched thought, . . . . . . .  278 Psalm VII         37
    They have heard and conceived. . . . . . . . . . . . . . . .  293 Psalm XIX         12
```

```
CONCEIVED          (CONTINUED)                        PAGE    TITLE        LINE
  Began at least to be conceiv'd as woe, . . . . . . . . . . .  252 Other Poems   4  418
CONCLUDE
  Lalus. Kala at length conclude my lingring lotte:. . . . . .   18 1st Eclogues  7  115
  And to conclude thy mistresse is a woman. . . . . . . . . . .   24 1st Eclogues  9   61
CONCLUDETH
  Since sorow then concludeth all our fortune, . . . . . . . .  110 Arcadia IV   70   37
CONCLUSION
  Bountifulnes hath made his last conclusion:. . . . . . . . .  128 4th Eclogues 75  119
CONCLUSIONS
  And grace, sicke too, such fine conclusions tries, . . . . .  231 Astrophil   101    3
CONCORD
  Was jumpe concorde betweene our wit and will:. . . . . . . .   99 3rd Eclogues 66   30
  So much more strong againe let fastest concorde make. . . . .  120 4th Eclogues 73  120
  Concord better fitteth us: . . . . . . . . . . . . . . . . .  211 A&S 4th Song      44
CONDEMNED
  But so unneard, condemn'd, kept thence we do seeke to abide
    in,. . . . . . . . . . . . . . . . . . . . . . . . . . . .   32 1st Eclogues 13   25
  But, but alas, like a man condemn'd doth crave to be heard
    speake,. . . . . . . . . . . . . . . . . . . . . . . . . .  122 4th Eclogues 74   23
  Nor let him be condemn'd by such. . . . . . . . . . . . . . .  327 Psalm XXXVII      84
  Geron with Uran were condemn'd to hell. . . . . . . . . . . .  249 Other Poems   4  264
CONDEMNING
  A still felt plague, to selfe condemning me: . . . . . . . .  212 Astrophil    86    3
CONDITION
  And others long to tell their loves' condition:. . . . . . .   19 1st Eclogues  7  171
  And others long to tell their loves' condicion. . . . . . . .   20 1st Eclogues  7 V971
CONDITIONLY
  And though she give but thus conditionly . . . . . . . . . .  200 Astrophil    69   12
CONDOLING
  Condoling cause of friendship he will borrow. . . . . . . . .   62 2nd Eclogues 30  178
CONDUIT-LIKE
  Which conduit-like with curious crookes, . . . . . . . . . .   90 Arcadia III  62  128
CONFECTION
  Of best things then what world can yeeld confection. . . . .   15 1st Eclogues  7   46
CONFERS
  Meane while my heart confers with Stella's beames, . . . . .  190 Astrophil    51   12
CONFESS
  And all my life I will confesse, . . . . . . . . . . . . . .  157 Cert Sonnets 27   39
  I do confesse, pardon a fault confest, . . . . . . . . . . .  166 Astrophil     4    7
  But one worse fault, Ambition, I confesse, . . . . . . . . .  178 Astrophil    27   11
  While with the people's shouts I must confesse,. . . . . . .  191 Astrophil    53    3
  They please I do confesse, they please mine eyes,. . . . . .  225 Astrophil    91    9
  Yet I confess in that tempestuous haste. . . . . . . . . . .  313 Psalm XXXI        61
  Till my self did my faults confess . . . . . . . . . . . . .  315 Psalm XXXII       13
  He might on knees confesse his faulty part,. . . . . . . . .  247 Other Poems   4  190
CONFESSED
  That there where thou confest thy mischiefe lyes . . . . . .   23 1st Eclogues  9   33
  I do confesse, pardon a fault confest, . . . . . . . . . . .  166 Astrophil     4    7
CONFESSION
  How oft with raine of teares skies make confession,. . . . .   15 1st Eclogues  7   43
  Dicus. The harte well set doth never shunne confession:. . .   47 2nd Eclogues 28   13
CONFIRM
  But Grammer's force with sweet successe confirme,. . . . . .  196 Astrophil    63   11
  Bee strong I say his strength confirm in you,. . . . . . . .  314 Psalm XXXI        67
CONFOUND
  Confound those folks, thrust them in shamefull hole. . . . .  321 Psalm XXXV         7
CONFOUNDED
  Let them confounded be . . . . . . . . . . . . . . . . . . .  303 Psalm XXV          9
  Never therfore let me confounded be, . . . . . . . . . . . .  312 Psalm XXXI         2
  Confounded be, and passe away like smoake, . . . . . . . . .  313 Psalm XXXI        47
CONFOUNDING
  Let them be cloathd in most confounding shame, . . . . . . .  323 Psalm XXXV        65
CONFUSE
  Stella's great powrs, that so confuse my mind. . . . . . . .  182 Astrophil    34   14
CONFUSED
  But so confusde, that neither any eye. . . . . . . . . . . .  149 Cert Sonnets 22    2
  Nor do like Lords, whose weake confused braine,. . . . . . .  210 Astrophil    85    5
  But wit confus'd with too much care did misse. . . . . . . .  227 Astrophil    93    8
CONFUSION
  Shepheards bewaile your uttermost confusion; . . . . . . . .  128 4th Eclogues 75  121
CONFUSIONS
  Throwne on this earth the Chaos of confusions. . . . . . . .   51 2nd Eclogues 28  110
CONGREGATION
  In congregation great I will prayse Thee,. . . . . . . . . .  300 Psalm XXII        59
  I to great congregation, . . . . . . . . . . . . . . . . . .  331 Psalm XL          35
CONGREGATIONS
  I will thank Thee, where congregations sitt, . . . . . . . .  322 Psalm XXXV        46
CONGRUITIES
  Let us some grammar learne of more congruities. . . . . . . .   61 2nd Eclogues 30  142
CONJOINED
  Of this high grace with blisse conjoyn'd . . . . . . . . . .  159 Cert Sonnets 29    1
CONNING
  Nor conning humorists' puddled opinions, . . . . . . . . . .   69 2nd Eclogues 34   20
  Shunn lothed-loving bankes with conning crooke:. . . . . . .  257 Other Poems   5   29
CONQUER
  To conquere, and his conquest how to ratifie,. . . . . . . .   49 2nd Eclogues 28   47
  Since naked sence can conquer reason armed:. . . . . . . . .  135 Cert Sonnets  1    6
  Who while they make Love conquer, conquer Love,. . . . . . .  185 Astrophil    42    3
```

CONQUERED
                                        PAGE   TITLE   LINE

	PAGE	TITLE		LINE
CONQUERED				
To that strange stroke which conquer'd all my senses,. . . .	61	2nd Eclogues	30	165
Place Sorrowe's triumph on my conquered harte:	114	4th Eclogues	72	17
A conquerd, yelden, ransackt heart to winne?	182	Astrophil	36	2
Of Conquerd states, wherby such fame you gott?	280	Psalm IX		17
About these never conquered walles to swarme,.	346	Possibly	5	10
Cupid the wagg, that lately conquer'd had.	245	Other Poems	4	129
CONQUERINGS				
Use all to helpe his other conquerings:.	179	Astrophil	29	8
CONQUERORS				
Yet noblest Conquerours do wreckes avoid..	185	Astrophil	40	11
CONQUEST				
I cease to strive, with double conquest foild:	11	Arcadia I	2	2
Olive paintes me the peace that I must aspire to by				
conquest	35	1st Eclogues	13	117
To conquere, and his conquest how to ratifie,.	49	2nd Eclogues	28	47
For so yet of a conquest speake thou may.	56	2nd Eclogues	29	140
Thus nature's Diamond, receave thy conquest, ...	68	2nd Eclogues	33	27
Till by degrees it had full conquest got..	165	Astrophil	2	4
Of conquest, do not these effects suffice, ...	183	Astrophil	36	7
The ruines of her conquest to espie:	199	Astrophil	67	3
Till of his life it did full conquest win, ...	253	Other Poems	4	430
CONQUEST'S				
By conquest's right in steade of searching kill.	150	Cert Sonnets	22	30
CONSCIENCE				
As tender conscience might with furious panges assaulte. . .	117	4th Eclogues	73	20
Failing themselves, with withered conscience dye..	151	Cert Sonnets	22	50
Have chang'd desert, let mine owne conscience be	212	Astrophil	86	2
CONSENT				
We beare our double yoke with such consent,.	106	3rd Eclogues	67	92
A silence sweet each where with one consent embraste	117	4th Eclogues	73	7
Indeed a perfect hewe, indeed a sweet consent.	119	4th Eclogues	73	85
Ere that I should consent to doo such excessive a dammage. .	124	4th Eclogues	74	61
And so let him consent	296	Psalm XX		16
CONSENTED				
They all consented were to give him wings:	101	3rd Eclogues	66	101
CONSERVED				
Whereby that being aye must be conserved..	106	3rd Eclogues	67	81
O plaints conserv'd in such a sugred phraise,.	231	Astrophil	100	9
CONSIDER				
Consider what I meditate in me:.	274	Psalm V		2
CONSIDERATION				
Where man's mind hath a freed consideration.	68	2nd Eclogues	34	3
CONSIST				
Consist, when they to highest doome are cited, ...	270	Psalm I		16
CONSOLATIONS				
Plangus. If through mine eares pearce any consolacyons . . .	61	2nd Eclogues	30	143
CONSORT				
Pleasingst consort, where each sence holds a part, ...	206	Astrophil	79	3
By love were made apt to consort with me..	229	Astrophil	95	11
Whose senses in so evill consort, their stepdame Nature				
laies, ...	217	A&S 7th Song		1
CONSORTED				
The world doth yeeld such ill consorted shows, ...	81	Arcadia III	54	9
CONSPIRE				
Since streame, aier, sand, mine eyes and eares conspire: . .	42	Arcadia II	21	17
Then since such pow'rs conspire unto our damage.	109	Arcadia IV	70	13
I harowe it with Thoughts, which all conspire.	115	4th Eclogues	72	54
With whose fine stepps all loves and joyes conspire.	250	Other Poems	4	302
CONSPIRED				
Both these conspird poore Reason's overthrowe;	11	Arcadia I	2	7
And all the starres conspired to my good,.	23	1st Eclogues	9	27
The heavens conspir'd, to make my vitall sparke.	73	Arcadia III	40	3
Thou then whom partiall heavens conspir'd in one to frame, .	213	A&S 5th Song		19
CONSTANCY				
But who seek God with constancy.	319	Psalm XXXIV		39
While long I did with patient constancy.	330	Psalm XL		1
CONSTANT				
Constant and kind: my sheep your foode shall breed,.	18	1st Eclogues	7	123
And weakest harts to constant temper brought..	22	1st Eclogues	9	15
And me perchaunce your constant temper lend.	23	1st Eclogues	9	20
Old age is wise and full of constant truth;.	39	Arcadia II	15	9
To onely thee my constant course I beare..	40	Arcadia II	18	16
A woman's hand with constant marble stone.	40	Arcadia II	19	6
Above line repeated at following location.	41	Arcadia II	19	12
Harde to be gott, but got constant, to be helde like				
steeles Eeles..	65	2nd Eclogues	31	42
Was vertue cladde in constant love's attire.	77	Arcadia III	48	2
Where open hartes do holde so constant place, ...	93	3rd Eclogues	63	88
And stay the starrs' inconstant constant race, ...	126	4th Eclogues	75	38
In humble mind a constant faith to prove,.	145	Cert Sonnets	17	3
The Rockes which were of constant mind the marke	147	Cert Sonnets	18	5
Their running fall into a constant vaine	150	Cert Sonnets	22	38
Brake on faire cleeves of constant chastitie:.	151	Cert Sonnets	22	56
Or where one's love so constant bene,.	158	Cert Sonnets	28	27
Is constant Love deem'd there but want of wit?	180	Astrophil	31	10
Of foes the spoile is evill, far worse of constant lovers. .	214	A&S 5th Song		48
CONSTERED				
As consterd in true speech, the name of heav'n it beares,. .	205	Astrophil	77	11

```
                                                          PAGE    TITLE          LINE
CONSTRAINED
    To steale some rest, but wretch I am constraind, . . . . . .   230 Astrophil     98    6
    Because my Foes to fly are now constraind. . . . . . . . . .   279 Psalm IX             6
CONSTRAINT
    Thou paine the onely guest of loath'd constraint, . . . . . .  141 Cert Sonnets  10    1
    How holdst thou her, whose eyes constraint doth feare, . . .   142 Cert Sonnets  10    5
CONSTRUCTION
    For that construction thy owne wordes do beare.. . . . . . .    49 2nd Eclogues  28   74
CONSULT
    How long shall I consult with carefull sprite. . . . . . . .   285 Psalm XIII           5
CONSUME
    To let that witolde beast consume in flames. . . . . . . . .    60 2nd Eclogues  30  111
    And ev'en my bones consume where they be plac't. . . . . . .   312 Psalm XXXI          30
CONSUMED
    They live in force, I quite consumed die.. . . . . . . . . .    42 Arcadia II    22   12
    Like fatt of lambs shall be consumed, . . . . . . . . . . . .  326 Psalm XXXVII        51
CONSUMES
    Fleshly vaile consumes; but a soule hath his life, . . . . .    31 1st Eclogues  12   22
CONSUMING
    The wood, above doth soone consuming rest. . . . . . . . . .   150 Cert Sonnets  22   44
    Thou dost put out, and quite consuming send. . . . . . . . .   280 Psalm IX           14
CONSUMPTION
    And keep it joynde, fearing your seate's consumption.. . . .    15 1st Eclogues   7   42
CONTAIN
    For the blacke starres those Spheares containe, . . . . . . .   86 Arcadia III   62   15
    One streame both streames containe, . . . . . . . . . . . . .   92 3rd Eclogues  63   35
    That sense feeles more then what doth sense containe?. . . .   142 Cert Sonnets  11    8
    While remembrance doth both states containe. . . . . . . . .   153 Cert Sonnets  24   14
    I see the house, my heart thy selfe containe, . . . . . . . .  209 Astrophil     85    1
CONTAINED
    O heavenly soule, in humaine shape conteind: . . . . . . . .    38 Arcadia II    15    2
    In morall rules let raging woes contained be?. . . . . . . .    61 2nd Eclogues  30  151
CONTAINETH
    I have my selfe, and all what life containeth, . . . . . . .   128 4th Eclogues  75  101
    Which Epitaph containeth, . . . . . . . . . . . . . . . . . .  160 Cert Sonnets  30   25
    The earth is God's, and what the Globe of earth containeth, . 302 Psalm XXIV           1
CONTAINS
    Sacred Muse, who in one contaynes what nine do in all them..   31 1st Eclogues  13   10
    And seeke to nourish that, which now contaynes . . . . . . .   114 4th Eclogues  72   22
    A heaven on earth, or earth that heaven containes: . . . . .   151 Cert Sonnets  22   68
CONTEMPLATE
    Where from who may contemplate Thee . . . . . . . . . . . . .  289 Psalm XVI           39
CONTEMPLATION
    Quite from my selfe to love Love's contemplation; . . . . . .   48 2nd Eclogues  28   32
    Contemplation here holdeth his only seate: . . . . . . . . .    68 2nd Eclogues  34    7
CONTEMPT
    Hate of the firste, contempt of later feate: . . . . . . . .    27 1st Eclogues  10   39
    Which must frame contempt to the fittest purchase of
        honnour . . . . . . . . . . . . . . . . . . . . . . . . .   32 1st Eclogues  13   38
    Till wrong, contempt, deceipt, did growe, steale, creepe,. .    84 Arcadia III   60    7
CONTEND
    Or reason foyld would not in vaine contend: . . . . . . . . .  147 Cert Sonnets  19    4
    But with your Rubarb words yow must contend. . . . . . . . .   171 Astrophil     14    5
CONTENDED
    Fortune, Nature, Love, long have contended about me, . . . .    29 1st Eclogues  11    1
CONTENDS
    That each, while each contends, . . . . . . . . . . . . . . .  216 A&S 6th Song        17
*CONTENT
    P. And let him die, so that he die content.. . . . . . . . .    46 2nd Eclogues  27   10
    But when to give some grace she doth content herselfe, . . .    49 2nd Eclogues  28   64
    Nico. Content: but I will lay a wager hereunto, . . . . . . .    53 2nd Eclogues  29   29
    By her who was (O blessed you) content, . . . . . . . . . . .   78 Arcadia III   49    5
    The goodman read on both sides the content, . . . . . . . . .   96 3rd Eclogues  64   88
    And geve a long desire sweet content. . . . . . . . . . . . .   97 3rd Eclogues  64  106
    Whereto two parties once be full content.. . . . . . . . . .    97 3rd Eclogues  64  126
    Cannot have to content me, . . . . . . . . . . . . . . . . .   137 Cert Sonnets   4   18
    Sleepe then a litle, pap content is making:. . . . . . . . .   139 Cert Sonnets   6    8
    And not content to be Perfection's heire . . . . . . . . . .   201 Astrophil     71    9
    I was content you should in favour creepe, . . . . . . . . .   208 Astrophil     83    2
    Cannot such grace your silly selfe content, . . . . . . . . .  208 Astrophil     83   11
    If thou love, my love content thee, . . . . . . . . . . . . .  220 A&S 8th Song        91
    My freedom, with show of hir beames, with virtue my content.  344 Possibly       1   38
    With nature pleas'd, content with present case, . . . . . . .  243 Other Poems    4   59
    Where snugging well he well appear'd content . . . . . . . .   244 Other Poems    4  103
CONTENTATION
    She holdes the ballance of my contentation: . . . . . . . . .   51 2nd Eclogues  28  118
CONTENTED
    From such as were to dye for him contented.. . . . . . . . .   128 4th Eclogues  75  126
    A salve, freshe ayre, and hyghe contented mynde. . . . . . .   345 Possibly       2   14
CONTENTING
    Better filled with contenting, . . . . . . . . . . . . . . .   264 Other Poems    7   77
CONTENTION
    O Elements, by whose (they say) contention, . . . . . . . . .  128 4th Eclogues  75  106
CONTENTION'S
    For vaine equalitie is but contention's field. . . . . . . .   120 4th Eclogues  73  130
CONTENTS
    Well, how so thou interpret the contents, . . . . . . . . . .  199 Astrophil     67   12
CONTINUALLY
    And in my mouth continualy . . . . . . . . . . . . . . . . .   318 Psalm XXXIV          3
```

		PAGE	TITLE		LINE

CONTRARY
With strong foes on land, on seas with contrary tempests . . 29 1st Eclogues 11   5
But wretched be the soules which, vaild in a contrary
    subject,. . . . . 32 1st Eclogues 13   19
Of windes quite contrarie in waves of will:. . . . . 59 2nd Eclogues 30   81
Still contrarie to what her husband sayes; . . . . 104 3rd Eclogues 67   32
That whereas blacke seemes Beautie's contrary, ... 168 Astrophil   7   10
CONTRIBUTED
Thus then (I say) my mischiefes have contributed . . . . . 49 2nd Eclogues 28   67
CONTRITE
That hearing it the hearts contrite, ... 318 Psalm XXXIV   7
CONVERSATION
Her eyes my eyesight is, her conversation. . . . . 15 1st Eclogues 7   32
That conversation sweet, where such high comforts be,. . . 205 Astrophil   77   10
Who may with charme of conversation sweete,. . . . . 236 Astrophil 106   10
In thought and conversation, ... 295 Psalm XIX   58
CONY
Milde as a Lambe, more daintie then a Conie is:. . . . . . 15 1st Eclogues 7   31
Ante, industrie; and Connie, skill to builde;. . . . . . . 101 3rd Eclogues 66   93
COOL
As well may thincke with oyle to coole the fire: . . . . . 22 1st Eclogues 9   8
Fire no liquor can coole: Neptune's seate would be dryd up
    there. . . . . 32 1st Eclogues 13   32
With sighes you seeke to coole your hotte desire:. . . . . 38 Arcadia II 14   6
Pas. She once, to coole her selfe, stood in a well,. . . . 55 2nd Eclogues 29 108
No wind, no shade can coole, what helpe then in my case, . 205 Astrophil   76   12
COPARTNER
Copartner of the riches of that sight: . . . . 188 Astrophil   48   6
COPYING
But Copying is, what in her Nature writes. . . . . 166 Astrophil   3   14
CORK
When worthlesse corke, aloft doth floting lye. . . . . . . 81 Arcadia III 54   14
CORMORANT'S
Cormoraunt's glutt, Kite's spoile, king fisher's waste,. . 28 1st Eclogues 10   78
CORN
Her father's corne (moving her faire limmes) measure.. . . 16 1st Eclogues 7   75
But harveste come, and corne in fertill store,. . . . . . 71 Arcadia III 36   11
As happie shewes of corne when harvest sendes; . . . . . . 71 Arcadia III 37   10
To teare the bowels, that good corne should send.. . . . . 102 3rd Eclogues 66 117
CORNERS
But they do faile, and in their mazed corners rew. . . . . 293 Psalm XVIII   82
CORRECTION
His life a law, his looke a full correction: . . . . 128 4th Eclogues 75 133
CORRUPT
Do works which earth corrupt and Heaven hates, ... 286 Psalm XIV   5
CORRUPTING
From a foule corrupting end. . . . . 288 Psalm XVI   36
CORSE
Till deadly sleepe at length possest my living coarse. . . 117 4th Eclogues 73   30
A living coarse I lay: but ah, my wakefull minde . . . . . 117 4th Eclogues 73   31
Pleased with the light, that his small corse doth burne: . 149 Cert Sonnets 21   12
CORYDONS
To worthy Coredens he gave me ore. . . . . 99 3rd Eclogues 66   40
COSMA
And if I better sing, let me thy Cosma kisse.. . . . . . . 53 2nd Eclogues 29   38
Pas. Cosma once said, she left the wicket ope, ... 55 2nd Eclogues 29   90
Pas. When Cosma doth come forth, the Sun displaies . . . . 55 2nd Eclogues 29   96
Pas. Thy name (O Cosma) shall with praise be spread, . . . 56 2nd Eclogues 29 126
Pas. So oft these woods have heard me "Cosma" crie,. . . . 56 2nd Eclogues 29 132
With Echoe's help, shall "Cosma, Cosma" flie.. . . . . . . 56 2nd Eclogues 29 134
With Cosma, for whose love Pas past in woe.. . . . . 248 Other Poems 4 243
Pas thought it hell, while he was Cosma fro. . . . . 248 Other Poems 4 245
From Nous and Cosma all their beauty tooke.. . . . . 248 Other Poems 4 248
The play began: Pas durst not Cosma chace, ... 248 Other Poems 4 249
Cosma this while to Strephon safely came,. . . . . 249 Other Poems 4 265
The two in hell did toward Cosma frame,. . . . . 249 Other Poems 4 267
Most mad with beames which he thought Cosma sent,. . . . . 249 Other Poems 4 270
With such mad haste he did to Cosma goe, ... 249 Other Poems 4 271
For as Urania after Cosma ran,. . . . . 249 Other Poems 4 281
Till Uran seing Pas to Cosma fly,. . . . . 249 Other Poems 4 286
Pas Cosma matcht, yet angry with his fault,. . . . . 250 Other Poems 4 318
While Geron olde came safe to Cosma true,. . . . . 250 Other Poems 4 325
COSMA'S
Didst snatch from Cosma's hand her greene ywroughten glove.. 52 2nd Eclogues 29   10
And thinke from Cosma's sweet red lips I live, ... 54 2nd Eclogues 29   79
To put it with my hand in Cosma's brest. . . . . 54 2nd Eclogues 29   86
Cosma's faire beames emblemish much his raies. . . . . . . 55 2nd Eclogues 29   98
From Cosma's eyes, which full in darkenes shine, ... 55 2nd Eclogues 29 103
COST
And strange things cost too deare for my poore sprites.. . 166 Astrophil   3   11
COSTLY
So oft in feasts with costly chaunges cladd. . . . . 245 Other Poems 4 133
COUCH
And turn his couch, where sick he couched late,. . . . . . 333 Psalm XLI   11
COUCHED
Where well couched abides a coffer of pearle,. . . . . . . 67 2nd Eclogues 33   10
And turn his couch, where sick he couched late,. . . . . . 333 Psalm XLI   11
COUCHES
And preciouse couches full oft are shak't with a feaver. . . 34 1st Eclogues 13   86

```
                                                           PAGE   TITLE          LINE
COUCHING
    And in her breast bopeepe or couching lyes,. . . . . . . .  170 Astrophil      11   12
COULD
    His wished weale, what more he could require:. . . . . . .    4 Lady of May     3    4
    Largesse his hands could never skill of sparefulnesse. . .   48 2nd Eclogues 28   45
    Nought could impart such heates to friendly mind.. . . . .   51 2nd Eclogues 28  105
    In perfect light, which could not me deceave,. . . . . . .   55 2nd Eclogues 29  100
    I sate me downe: for see to goe ne could,. . . . . . .       99 3rd Eclogues 66   20
    The birdes likewise with chirpes, and puing could, . . . .  100 3rd Eclogues 66   66
    That last day seem'd, he could not chew a beane. . . . . .  103 3rd Eclogues 67    6
    Who would not have a Phoenix if he could?. . . . . . . . .  104 3rd Eclogues 67   16
    How well last day before our Prince you could. . . . . . .  106 3rd Eclogues 67   97
    Ne could my soule it selfe accuse of such a faulte,. . . .  117 4th Eclogues 73   19
    Too much her peerles parts, nor yet could them despise.. . .  119 4th Eclogues 73   88
    O not but such love you say you could have afoorded, . . . .  124 4th Eclogues 74   63
    As for my mirth, how could I but be glad,. . . . . . . . .  147 Cert Sonnets 17   41
    If I could thinke how these my thoughts to leave,. . . . .  147 Cert Sonnets 19    1
    So Tyran he no fitter place could spie,. . . . . . . . . .  175 Astrophil      20    5
    But ere I could flie thence, it pierc'd my heart. . . . . .  175 Astrophil      20   14
    And then would not, or could not see my blisse:. . . . . .  181 Astrophil      33    2
    And yet could not by rising Morne foresee. . . . . . . . .  181 Astrophil      33   12
    Could hope by Cupid's helpe on you to pray;. . . . . . . .  186 Astrophil      43    2
    Which in her face teach vertue, I could brooke . . . . . .  193 Astrophil      56    6
    Before she could prepare to be unkind, . . . . . . . . . .  193 Astrophil      57    6
    Nor that he could young-wise, wise-valiant frame . . . . .  204 Astrophil      75    5
    And gain'd by Mars, could yet mad Mars so tame,. . . . . .  204 Astrophil      75    7
    And nothing then the cause more sweet could be,. . . . . .  223 Astrophil      87   13
    Ne if I would, could I just title make,. . . . . . . . . .  224 Astrophil      90    9
    She could not shew my blind braine waies of joy, . . . . .  230 Astrophil      97   13
    The bote for joy could not to daunce forbeare, . . . . . .  232 Astrophil     103    5
    Through pores of sencelesse trees, as it could make them
        move:. . . . . . . . . . . . . . . . . . . . . . . . .  208 A&S 3rd Song         2
    If Eagle fierce could so in Grecian Mayd delight,. . . . .  209 A&S 3rd Song         9
    But when their tongues could not speake, . . . . . . . . .  218 A&S 8th Song        25
    If of this Clayey race he could espy . . . . . . . . . . .  286 Psalm XIV            8
    Strengthning mine arms that they could break an Iron bow.. .  292 Psalm XVIII         63
    Yea thou prevent'st e're ask he could, . . . . . . . . . .  297 Psalm XXI            9
    No sooner my child eyes could look abroad, . . . . . . . .  299 Psalm XXII          23
    And said to me wide mowing as they could,. . . . . . . . .  322 Psalm XXXV          53
    When, if nede were, they could at quintain run:. . . . . .  243 Other Poems     4   56
    Whose mettall stiff he knew he could not bende . . . . . .  245 Other Poems     4  138
    But if they had, could shephookes this resist? . . . . . .  246 Other Poems     4  160
    Faine would, but could not fly from golden smart.. . . . .  246 Other Poems     4  184
    That in her doings better could compare. . . . . . . . . .  247 Other Poems     4  211
    Pas could not stay, but over him did rake, . . . . . . . .  248 Other Poems     4  259
    Till that he spied old Geron could no more,. . . . . . . .  250 Other Poems     4  307
    More then, besides hir, all the earth could show.. . . . .  252 Other Poems     4  408
    Going from them, from them she could not go) . . . . . . .  252 Other Poems     4  414
    To beare the bondes which Time nor wit could breake, . . .  255 Other Poems     4  530
COULDST
    Nico. Couldst thou make Lalus flie? so nightingales avoide,..   52 2nd Eclogues 29   17
    For when, nak'd boy, thou couldst no harbour find. . . . .  198 Astrophil      65    5
COUNSEL
    The witts abusde with will no counsayle take.. . . . . . .   23 1st Eclogues  9   22
    What counsell can prevaile, or light give light? . . . . .   23 1st Eclogues  9   36
    Say then Reason, I say what is thy counsell? . . . . . . .   67 2nd Eclogues 33    6
    Above line repeated at following locations . . . . . . . .   67 2nd Eclogues 33   12
        . . . . . . . . . . . . . . . . . . . . . . . . . . .   68 2nd Eclogues 33   18
        . . . . . . . . . . . . . . . . . . . . . . . . . . .   68 2nd Eclogues 33   24
    Foode without fulnes, counsaile without pride, . . . . . .  103 3rd Eclogues 67   11
    And if that any counsell you to measure. . . . . . . . . .  126 4th Eclogues 75   49
    Where she his counsell keepeth,. . . . . . . . . . . . . .  160 Cert Sonnets 30   35
    What Nestor's counsell can my flames alay, . . . . . . . .  182 Astrophil      35    5
    Out traytour absence, darest thou counsell me, . . . . . .  223 Astrophil      88    1
    The straying stepps as wicked Counsel leads; . . . . . . .  270 Psalm I              2
    And counsel jointly take,. . . . . . . . . . . . . . . . .  271 Psalm II             4
    Who dost ever counsell mee,. . . . . . . . . . . . . . . .  288 Psalm XVI           20
    He doth heath'n counsell breake, . . . . . . . . . . . . .  317 Psalm XXXIII        34
    But Dick my counsell marke: run from the place of wo:. . .  344 Possibly        1   41
COUNSELED
    Nous counseld Strephon Geron to pursue,. . . . . . . . . .  250 Other Poems     4  321
COUNSELLORS
    Wise Counsellors, stout Captaines, puissant Kings, . . . .  245 Other Poems     4  130
COUNSELS
    Somewhat thy lead'n counsels, which I tooke. . . . . . . .  193 Astrophil      56    7
    No more, my deare, no more these counsels trie,. . . . . .  198 Astrophil      64    1
    Their Counsills are your Common jesting stock, . . . . . .  287 Psalm XIV           20
    Feare was each where, while they their counsells led . . . .  313 Psalm XXXI          38
    His Counsells all. . . . . . . . . . . . . . . . . . . . .  317 Psalm XXXIII        38
COUNT
    My life my death do counte hers.. . . . . . . . . . . . .   67 2nd Eclogues 32   57
    Can count them just, nor reason reason trye, . . . . . . .  149 Cert Sonnets 22    3
    And joy therein, though Nations count it shame.. . . . . .  179 Astrophil      28    8
    Heare you this soule-invading voice, and count it but a
        voice?. . . . . . . . . . . . . . . . . . . . . . . .  217 A&S 7th Song        17
    And count this life their Portion best . . . . . . . . . .  290 Psalm XVII          40
    What man Thy thoughts can count to Thee. . . . . . . . . .  331 Psalm XL            22
    Dick. Ah Will, though I grudge not, I count it feeble glee .  343 Possibly        1    3
COUNTED
    First shall vertue be vice, and bewty be counted a blemishe,   33 1st Eclogues 13   67
```

COUNTED	(CONTINUED)	PAGE	TITLE		LINE
R. Can Reason then a Tyraunt counted be?		46	2nd Eclogues	27	3
The sinke of filth, be counted huswifery:.		93	3rd Eclogues	63	79
COUNTENANCE					
To countenance his cause:.		216	A&S 6th Song		30
On him Thy Count'nance casting..		297	Psalm XXI		24
COUNTERFEITING					
Poorely counterfeting thee..		234	A&S 11th Song		25
COUNTEST					
Thou countest Stella thine, like those whose powers.		171	Astrophil	12	9
COUNTING					
Counting but dust what in the way did lie.		235	Astrophil	105	8
COUNTRY					
And should in soule up to our countrey move:		167	Astrophil	5	13
COUNTS					
And by just counts my selfe a banckrout know		173	Astrophil	18	3
COUPLE					
To couple comming harmes with sorrowes past?		57	2nd Eclogues	30	7
Do coupled towards either couple make, ...		248	Other Poems	4	234
COUPLED					
O Himen long their coupled joyes maintaine..		91	3rd Eclogues	63	9
Above line repeated at following locations		91	3rd Eclogues	63	18
. . . .		91	3rd Eclogues	63	27
. . . .		92	3rd Eclogues	63	36
. . . .		92	3rd Eclogues	63	45
. . . .		92	3rd Eclogues	63	54
. . . .		93	3rd Eclogues	63	63
. . . .		93	3rd Eclogues	63	72
. . . .		93	3rd Eclogues	63	81
. . . .		93	3rd Eclogues	63	90
For Himen will their coupled joyes maintaine..		94	3rd Eclogues	63	99
In hart both sight and love now coupled be;.		223	Astrophil	88	13
Do coupled towards either couple make, ...		248	Other Poems	4	234
COUPLES					
Then couples three be streight allotted there, ...		248	Other Poems	4	225
COUPLING					
Which, coupling Doves, guides Venus' chariot right..		206	Astrophil	79	4
COURAGE					
This thinke I well, the beasts with courage clad		100	3rd Eclogues	66	55
What courage strange hath caught thy caitife hart, ...		142	Cert Sonnets	10	9
With feare of change, the courage well preparde:		143	Cert Sonnets	12	11
Yet let this thought thy Tygrish courage passe:.		198	Astrophil	65	11
My Courage should not be dismaid..		307	Psalm XXVII		14
Courage therefore, and let the stately see		346	Possibly	5	3
COURSE					
And if a meane were found, fortune th' whole course of it hinders.		37	1st Eclogues	13	159
To onely thee my constant course I beare.		40	Arcadia II	18	16
Hath all thy whirling course so small effect?.		58	2nd Eclogues	30	60
Think so, for of my desired blisse it is only the course. Curse.		64	2nd Eclogues	31	39
Thy running course cannot such beawties marke:		80	Arcadia III	52	11
With circkled course, which no wise stay can trye, ...		81	Arcadia III	54	10
While thy known course, observing nature's right, ...		82	Arcadia III	56	11
Now course doth leade me to her hand, ...		90	Arcadia III	62	121
Turning all nature's course to selfe displeasure..		108	Arcadia IV	69	8
My ship, my selfe, whose course to love doth bende, ...		114	4th Eclogues	72	44
So I in simple course, and unentangled minde		117	4th Eclogues	73	25
Whose stormelike course staid not till hard by me it bided..		118	4th Eclogues	73	60
The vehement course of this just lamentation:		127	4th Eclogues	75	98
But now the starres with their strange course do binde . . .		148	Cert Sonnets	30	5
In this small course which birth drawes out to death, . . .		144	Cert Sonnets	32	10
Or seeke heavn's course, or heavn's inside to see:		169	Astrophil	10	5
I see my course to lose my selfe doth bend:		174	Astrophil	18	12
My still kept course, while others sleepe, to mone..		184	Astrophil	40	4
Thence his desires he learnes, his live's course thence. . .		195	Astrophil	61	8
From nobler course, fit for my birth and mind:		196	Astrophil	62	8
Nor hope, nor wishe another course to frame, ...		198	Astrophil	64	12
This realme of blisse, while vertuous course I take, ...		200	Astrophil	69	13
Their Course doth it acknowledg, ...		293	Psalm XIX		6
But all this while another course he fet..		249	Other Poems	4	280
While deare Uran, whose course was Pas to meet, ...		250	Other Poems	4	330
COURT					
For to the courte her man was calld by name, ...		96	3rd Eclogues	64	77
"The jealous wretch must now to Courte be gone:.		97	3rd Eclogues	64	103
Releast from Court, where envie needes must be..		143	Cert Sonnets	12	6
Queene Vertue's court, which some call Stella's face, ...		169	Astrophil	9	1
If in the Scottishe Court be weltring yet;		180	Astrophil	30	11
Towardes Aurora's Court a Nymph doth dwell, ...		183	Astrophil	37	5
Those daintie dores unto the Court of blisse, ...		187	Astrophil	44	11
And God shall them in his own court reserve.		300	Psalm XXII		76
Of clime-fall Court, the envy-hatching place:.		243	Other Poems	4	61
That were in Court a well proportion'd hooke, ...		245	Other Poems	4	141
Now in servile Court remayning..		262	Other Poems	7	12
COURTEOUS					
Nor courteous ruin of proffered usury, ...		69	2nd Eclogues	34	21
Saving the glowe worme, which would curteous be.		98	3rd Eclogues	66	6
Their courteous visitings are courting lyes, ...		333	Psalm XLI		21
The courteous mountaines, griev'd at my disgrace, ...		254	Other Poems	4	477

COURTESY   PAGE   TITLE   LINE

		PAGE	TITLE		LINE
COURTESY					
And therefore pray him that of courtesie		95	3rd Eclogues	64	57
Mirth with respect, few words with curtesy,		247	Other Poems	4	212
COURTIER					
Not limited to a whispringe note, the Lament of a Courtier,		35	1st Eclogues	13	110
And therefore he a courtier was benamed,		94	3rd Eclogues	64	19
And as a courtier was with cheere received,		94	3rd Eclogues	64	20
And for this Courtier should well like his table,		94	3rd Eclogues	64	23
She told him that the courtier had it sent:		96	3rd Eclogues	64	86
But now the courtier gan to smell the feate,		97	3rd Eclogues	64	117
COURTIER'S					
Asking her how she tasted Courtier's lips,		95	3rd Eclogues	64	33
COURTIERS					
Pas. Ah foole; so Courtiers do. But who did lively skippe,		52	2nd Eclogues	29	11
COURTING					
Their courteous visitings are courting lyes,		333	Psalm XLI		21
COURTLY					
The courtlie shepheard much agast at this,		96	3rd Eclogues	64	67
Who under courtly pompes doo hatch a base desire		117	4th Eclogues	73	16
For me, while you discourse of courtly tides,		190	Astrophil	51	9
The courtly Nymphs, acquainted with the mone		191	Astrophil	54	5
Then this false, fine, Courtly pleasure.		263	Other Poems	7	48
COUTH					
(A little flocke; but well my pipe they couthe).		98	3rd Eclogues	66	2
COVENANT					
To such as keep his Covenant		304	Psalm XXV		41
To such he doth his Cov'nant show.		304	Psalm XXV		54
COVENANTS					
No kings be crown'd but they some covenants make.		200	Astrophil	69	14
COVER					
"Let not dead earth enjoy so deare a cover,		17	1st Eclogues	7	89
A stately tombe to cover him deceased.		126	4th Eclogues	75	59
COVERED					
You should those faire eyes have with a veile covered.		123	4th Eclogues	74	48
COVERING					
Gold is the covering of that stately place.		169	Astrophil	9	4
COW					
By Argus got on Io, then a cow:		21	1st Eclogues	8	14
Monkie, sweet breath; the Cow, her faire eyes brought;		101	3rd Eclogues	66	88
COWARD					
Yet like a coward fearing stranger's pride,		95	3rd Eclogues	64	29
O cowarde Cupid thus doost thou my honour keepe,		122	4th Eclogues	73	185
Such causelesse feares when coward minds do take,		145	Cert Sonnets	16	5
Faint coward joy no longer tarry dare,		228	Astrophil	95	5
COWARDS					
Cowards Love with losse rewardeth.		202	A&S 2nd Song		16
As perjur'd cowards in adversity		248	Other Poems	4	239
COWSLIP					
Cowslipp and Columbine,		257	Other Poems	5	41
COY					
What coye account she makes of estimation?		15	1st Eclogues	7	34
COYED					
A servant Sex, soone prowde if they be coi'de,		24	1st Eclogues	9	60
COZENING					
Cursing and cosening,		282	Psalm X		28
Those lying lipps from Cousening head remove,		284	Psalm XII		8
CRABBED					
All churlish wordes, shrewd answeres, crabbed lookes,		93	3rd Eclogues	63	64
CRADLE					
Though cradle witted, must not honnor loose.		25	1st Eclogues	9	92
Nor time pratled away, cradle of ignorance,		69	2nd Eclogues	34	22
Lully, lully, my babe, hope cradle bringeth.		139	Cert Sonnets	6	4
Band of all evils, cradle of causelesse care,		161	Cert Sonnets	31	3
CRAFT					
The Foxe gave crafte; the Dog gave flatterie;		101	3rd Eclogues	66	85
In craft of his own crafty thought!		281	Psalm X		8
Which they for me with privy craft have set,		312	Psalm XXXI		11
But hunt with craft the quiet man's annoy;		322	Psalm XXXV		52
CRAFTILY					
That craftily he forst them to do ill,		102	3rd Eclogues	66	125
While craftily you seem'd your cut to keepe,		208	Astrophil	83	3
CRAFTY					
Or trayne the fox that traines so crafty laies.		26	1st Eclogues	9	125
Lyke crafty wretch by time and travell tought,		141	Cert Sonnets	8	5
In craft of his own crafty thought!		281	Psalm X		8
CRAMMED					
To crammed mawes a spratt new Stomake brings.		245	Other Poems	4	134
CRAMMING					
With stroking hurt, and too much cramming kill.		41	Arcadia II	20	12
CRANES					
Cranes, order; Storkes, to be appearing holie;		101	3rd Eclogues	66	94
CRAPAL-STONE					
Her haire pure Crapal-stone; her mouth O heavenly wyde;		12	Arcadia I	3	11
CRAVE					
When pittie most I crave, I cruell prove:		41	Arcadia II	20	3
Yet thus much Love, O Love, I crave of thee:		41	Arcadia II	20	13
Nor ought I crave to feede life,		67	2nd Eclogues	32	54
Thus cruell to my selfe how canst thou crave		77	Arcadia III	47	7
Graunt to the thing which we for Lalus crave.		92	3rd Eclogues	63	30
Nor of my fortune ought, but mischieve crave.		114	4th Eclogues	72	20

```
CRAVE                         (CONTINUED)                      PAGE    TITLE          LINE
       Strephon. Nor of my fortune ought but mischiefe crave, . . .  114  4th Eclogues 72    21
       But, but alas, like a man condemn'd doth crave to be heard
          speake,. . . . . . . . . . . . . . . . . . . . . . . . .   122  4th Eclogues 74    23
       Who for long faith, tho dayly helpe I crave, . . . . . . . .  188  Astrophil    47     7
       His lips to crave, what he would crave . . . . . . . . . . .  297  Psalm XXI           7
       For ever crave, that dwell I may . . . . . . . . . . . . . .  307  Psalm XXVII        20
       O helpe o help me, this farr yet I crave,. . . . . . . . . .  330  Psalm XXXIX        25
       Didst like, much lesse didst crave;. . . . . . . . . . . . .  331  Psalm XL           27
       D. Her heavenly looks, which more and more do give me cause
          to crave. . . . . . . . . . . . . . . . . . . . . . . . .  344  Possibly      1    32
CRAVED
       Can I forget in how straunge phrase she craved . . . . . . .   61  2nd Eclogues 30   158
       I crav'd the thing which ever she denies:. . . . . . . . . .  196  Astrophil    63     6
CRAVETH
       Long have I lov'd, (alas love craveth love). . . . . . . . .   97  3rd Eclogues 64    98
CRAVING
       Yet craving law of armes, whose rule doth teach, . . . . . .  135  Cert Sonnets  1    10
       But I who dayly craving, . . . . . . . . . . . . . . . . . .  137  Cert Sonnets  4    17
CREAM
       Whose pants do make unspilling creame to flow, . . . . . . .  231  Astrophil   100     6
CREATION
       So are we from our high creation slided. . . . . . . . . . .   62  2nd Eclogues 30   181
CREATOR
       And wise thoughts do behold what the creator is: . . . . . .   68  2nd Eclogues 34     6
CREATURES
       What be the sweet creatures wher lowly demaunds be not
          heard  Hard. . . . . . . . . . . . . . . . . . . . . . .    65  2nd Eclogues 31    41
       Commands all creatures, to yeeld obeysance . . . . . . . . .   68  2nd Eclogues 33    22
       In land with living creatures clad?. . . . . . . . . . . . .  308  Psalm XXVII        63
       "Where how many Creatures be,. . . . . . . . . . . . . . . .  263  Other Poems   7    49
CREDIT
       And one man still, credit with her preserve. . . . . . . . .   98  3rd Eclogues 65     9
       For no faire signe can credit winne, . . . . . . . . . . . .  156  Cert Sonnets 27    15
CREEP
       Till wrong, contempt, deceipt, did growe, steale, creepe,. .   84  Arcadia III  60     7
       "Alas", quoth she, "thus women's shame doth creepe". . . . .   96  3rd Eclogues 64    87
       A Poet eke, as humours fly or creepe,. . . . . . . . . . . .  181  Astrophil    32     4
       If still I force her in sad rimes to creepe: . . . . . . . .  201  Astrophil    70     2
       I was content you should in favour creepe, . . . . . . . . .  208  Astrophil    83     2
       Behold me, lord, let to Thy hearing creep. . . . . . . . . .  285  Psalm XIII          9
       Thy servant keep, least in him creep . . . . . . . . . . . .  295  Psalm XIX          53
       Yet thoughts do flie, though I can scarcely creep. . . . . .  253  Other Poems   4   444
CREEPETH
       Foole in me, what follie creepeth, . . . . . . . . . . . . .  157  Cert Sonnets 27    26
CREEPING
       Creeping to ech with flattering of desire. . . . . . . . . .   22  1st Eclogues  8    40
       For creeping rimes, which often sighings choke. . . . . . . .  242  Other Poems   4     8
       A creeping serpentlike of mortall woe. . . . . . . . . . . .  252  Other Poems   4   412
CREON'S
       On Creon's child his poison sooner throw,. . . . . . . . . .  252  Other Poems   4   410
CREST
       Each had his creast, Mars caried Venus' glove, . . . . . . .  171  Astrophil    13     7
       Cupid then smiles, for on his crest there lies . . . . . . .  171  Astrophil    13     9
       Brave crest to him hir scorn-gold haire did yeeld, . . . . .  246  Other Poems   4   149
CREW
       But of such wives we finde a slender crew; . . . . . . . . .  104  3rd Eclogues 67    25
CRIED
       Lalus. How oft my dolefull Sire cried to me, "tarrie sonne".   16  1st Eclogues  7    49
       With armour of my hart, he cried "O vanitie," . . . . . . . .   16  1st Eclogues  7    62
       "O" cried I, "of so meane worke be discharged: . . . . . . .   16  1st Eclogues  7    76
       I cried, and was with open rayes rewarded: . . . . . . . . .   17  1st Eclogues  7    94
       With sight thereof cride out; o faire disgrace,. . . . . . .  233  Astrophil   103    13
       Nay unto Thee they cry'd, but thou heardst not their cryes..  293  Psalm XVIII        75
       Then thus to Thee I praying cry'd: . . . . . . . . . . . . .  311  Psalm XXX          25
       But most cryed, "O well broke": O foole full gaily blest:. .  241  Other Poems   1     5
       Nous cri'de, and chafd, but he no other can. . . . . . . . .  249  Other Poems   4   285
CRIER
       Hath made it selfe a crier of the morning, . . . . . . . . .  112  4th Eclogues 71    26
CRIES
       Come shepheard's weedes, attend my woefull cryes:. . . . . .   13  Arcadia I     4     5
       The wood cries most, before it throughly kindled be, . . . .   14  1st Eclogues  7     8
       Then cries to sencelesse things, which neither knowes. . . .   23  1st Eclogues  9    41
       Or if sheepe's cries can helpe the Sunne's owne braverie,. .   48  2nd Eclogues 28    25
       Whose cries are ladders made to climb dishonor,. . . . . . .   50  2nd Eclogues 28 V  90
       With cries to skies, and curses to the ground, . . . . . . .   57  2nd Eclogues 30     9
       With cries first borne, the pressage of his life,. . . . . .   57  2nd Eclogues 30    24
       The tunes be cryes, the words plaints, . . . . . . . . . . .   66  2nd Eclogues 32    35
       With inward cries putts up a bitter role . . . . . . . . . .   85  Arcadia III  61     3
       Of willing teares, torne heare, and cries of sorrow. . . . .  109  Arcadia IV   70    16
       And fill the vales with cries in steed of musique. . . . . .  111  4th Eclogues 71    24
       The dreadfull cries of murdred men in forrests.. . . . . . .  112  4th Eclogues 71    48
       Thunders of cries; lightnings my wilde lookes be,. . . . . .  114  4th Eclogues 72    34
       The straunge resounde of these my causefull cries: . . . . .  125  4th Eclogues 75     4
       Thy cries, o Babie, set mine head on aking:. . . . . . . . .  139  Cert Sonnets  6     2
       The Babe cries "way, thy love doth keepe me waking". . . . .  139  Cert Sonnets  6     3
       Above line repeated at following location. . . . . . . . . .  139  Cert Sonnets  6     6
       The babe cries "nay, for that abide I waking". . . . . . . .  139  Cert Sonnets  6     9
       Nor trumpets sound I heard, nor friendly cries;. . . . . . .  191  Astrophil    53    12
       That giv'st no better eare to my just cries: . . . . . . . .  198  Astrophil    65     2
```

CRIES   (CONTINUED)   PAGE   TITLE   LINE
    "But ah," Desire still cries, "give me some food." . . . . .   201 Astrophil   71   14
    My heart cries "ah", it burnes, mine eyes now dazled be: . .   205 Astrophil   76   11
    Then let my Words, my Crys ascend, ...   290 Psalm XVII   19
    This my Distresse to God with wailfull cryes I show, ...   291 Psalm XVIII   12
    My cryes clim'd up and he bent down from sacred throne, . . . 291 Psalm XVIII   13
    Nay unto Thee they cry'd, but thou heardst not their cryes..   293 Psalm XVIII   75
    But of the skyes the teaching cryes. . . . .   293 Psalm XIX   11
    So farr from hearing to my roaring cryes.. . . . .   298 Psalm XXII   4
    In Cryes to Thee I shewd my Cause. . . . .   311 Psalm XXX   5
    Heare lord my suits and cryes, stop not thyn eares . . . . .   330 Psalm XXXIX   37
    Alas! of ghostes I heare the gastly cries: . . . .   255 Other Poems   4   507
    Thy liribliring cries, ...   258 Other Poems   5   62
CRIME
    Must finish then by death's detested crime.. . . . .   127 4th Eclogues 75   90
CRIMSON
    Who hath the crimson weeds stolne from my morning skies? . .   232 Astrophil   102   4
CROCODILE
    Crocodile, teares, which might be falsely spilde:. . . . . .   101 3rd Eclogues 66   96
CROOK
    Earthly I do bow and crooke, ...   328 Psalm XXXVIII   16
    Shunn lothed-loving bankes with conning crooke:. . . . . . .   257 Other Poems   5   29
CROOKED
    Pure to the pure, Thou dealst with crooked crookedly;. . . .   292 Psalm XVIII   51
CROOKEDLY
    Pure to the pure, Thou dealst with crooked crookedly;. . . .   292 Psalm XVIII   51
CROOKS
    Which conduit-like with curious crookes, ...   90 Arcadia III 62   128
CROSS
    Still doo I crosse this wretch, what so he taketh in hand"..   29 1st Eclogues 11   6
    Late neere a crosse I met an ougly Cat.. . . . .   253 Other Poems   4   448
CROSSED
    With armes crost, yet testifying . . . .   218 A&S 8th Song   19
    For never was there man more crossely crost then he. . . . .   241 Other Poems   1   4
CROSSLY
    For never was there man more crossely crost then he. . . . .   241 Other Poems   1   4
CROUCH
    Nico. In deed the witch thy dam her crouch from shoulder
       spred, ...   52 2nd Eclogues 29   13
    For pilfring Lalus' lambe, with crouch to blesse thy head. .   52 2nd Eclogues 29   14
CROWN
    This crowne of amber faire (an amber crowne she held). . . .   120 4th Eclogues 73   141
    The crowne above you both for ever I appoint". . . . .   121 4th Eclogues 73   166
    Rich in those gifts which give th'eternall crowne; . . . . .   183 Astrophil   37   11
    To lose his Crowne, rather then faile his Love.. . . . . . .   204 Astrophil   75   14
    Onely by you Cupid his crowne maintaineth. . . . .   197 A&S 1st Song   12
    Say whether thou wilt crowne,. . . . .   217 A&S 6th Song   53
    Of glorious Croune, and crouning honour. . . . .   279 Psalm VIII   20
    Croune of his head with croune of Gold . . . .   297 Psalm XXI   11
    And reason, since the Croune to God pertaineth,. . . . . . .   300 Psalm XXII   69
    And crown'd the earth with his first touching crowne:. . . .   248 Other Poems   4   260
CROWNED
    Mirtle makes my request, my request is crown'd with a
       willowe. . . . .   35 1st Eclogues 13   118
    When first that crowned Basiliske I knewe, ...   115 4th Eclogues 72   72
    No kings be crown'd but they some covenants make.. . . . . .   200 Astrophil   69   14
    And crown'd the earth with his first touching crowne:. . . .   248 Other Poems   4   260
CROWNING
    Of glorious Croune, and crouning honour. . . . .   279 Psalm VIII   20
CROWNS
    Not rotten sheepe, but high crownes she surpasseth all... .   16 1st Eclogues 7   57
    Let not a puppet abuse thy sprite, Kings' Crownes do not
       helpe them . . . .   34 1st Eclogues 13   84
CROWS
    Let crowes picke out mine eyes, which saw too much:. . . . .   19 1st Eclogues 7   149
    Let crowes picke out mine eyes which too much sawe.. . . . .   19 1st Eclogues 7   V149
    When with the kawing crowes their musicke is annoide.. . . .   52 2nd Eclogues 29   18
    Phoenix but one, of Crowes we milllions have:. . . . .   104 3rd Eclogues 67   20
    O how for joy he leapes, o how he crowes,. . . . .   173 Astrophil   17   12
CRUDS
    But thou white skinne, as white as cruddes well prest, . . .   76 Arcadia III 46   13
CRUEL
    But straight they fledde, summond by cruell honor, ...   17 1st Eclogues 7   95
    From the cruell headache, nor shooes of golde doo the gowt
       heale, ...   34 1st Eclogues 13   85
    When pittie most I crave, I cruell prove:. . . . .   41 Arcadia II   20   3
    O cruell sonne thy hate this harme dothe breede. . . . . . .   43 Arcadia II   24   3
    Ah where was first that cruell cunning found,. . . . .   57 2nd Eclogues 30   11
    Plangus. And shall shee dye? shall cruell fier spill . . . .   59 2nd Eclogues 30   83
    Thus cruell to my selfe how canst thou crave . . . .   77 Arcadia III 47   7
    Where they would leave trophees of cruell damage,. . . . . .   109 Arcadia IV   70   12
    For lost, lost is by blowe of cruell fortune . . . .   109 Arcadia IV   70   17
    Dread not a whit (O goodly cruell) that pittie may enter . .   122 4th Eclogues 74   5
    To know my miseries, but chaste and cruell:. . . . .   136 Cert Sonnets 3   10
    With a cruell answer stong. . . . .   139 Cert Sonnets 7   7
    Within her beames wrapping his cruell staines. . . . .   141 Cert Sonnets 8   12
    And have I heard her say, "o cruell paine!". . . . .   142 Cert Sonnets 11   1
    If either you would change your cruell hart, ...   148 Cert Sonnets 19   7
    Or cruell (still) time did your beautie staine:. . . . . . .   148 Cert Sonnets 19   8
    You fairer still, and still more cruell bent,. . . . .   148 Cert Sonnets 19   15

CRUEL	(CONTINUED)	PAGE	TITLE	LINE
Which caught, to cruell search yeelds his chiefe part: . . .		150	Cert Sonnets 22	22
Although with cruell fire, ...		155	Cert Sonnets 26	2
Above line repeated at following locations		155	Cert Sonnets 26	13
		156	Cert Sonnets 26	24
Oft cruell fights well pictured forth do please.		181	Astrophil 34	4
Deare Killer, spare not thy sweet cruell shot:		189	Astrophil 48	13
But that which once may win thy cruell hart:		198	Astrophil 64	13
Stella, while now by honour's cruell might, ...		224	Astrophil 91	1
When she wakes, is too too cruell.		202	A&S 2nd Song	4
Which (I protest) proceed from only Cruell thee, ...		214	A&S 5th Song	53
That all these cruell words your praises shall be proved.. .		215	A&S 5th Song	90
For thou with cruel blowes, ...		273	Psalm III	25
With cruel anguish.		276	Psalm VI	8
And cruel Words their swelling tongues do chatt, ...		290	Psalm XVII	30
And rid me from the wrongs which cruel Witts did brew; . .		293	Psalm XVIII	87
Most cruel words..		308	Psalm XXVII	60
With cruel minds my very soul to teare..		322	Psalm XXXV	28
Save me distrest from lion's cruel kind.		322	Psalm XXXV	45
By most cruel sprites, ...		336	Psalm XLIII	4
Dick. Oh hence! o cruell word! which even doggs do hate: . .		344	Possibly 1	47
CRUELIY				
And cruely in many peices teare.		277	Psalm IX	5
Who hate, yea hate me cruely.		304	Psalm XXV	66
CRUELTY				
Eagle, high looke; Wolfe secrete crueltie:		101	3rd Eclogues 66	87
Only lov'd Tyrants, just in cruelty, ...		185	Astrophil 42	6
Which full of spight, of Pride and cruelty, ...		313	Psalm XXXI	50
CRY				
But eye from blade, and eare from crie:		44	Arcadia II 25	11
The neighbours all did crie, "alas what asse doth bray?" . .		52	2nd Eclogues 29	26
Pas. So oft these woods have heard me "Cosma" crie, ...		56	2nd Eclogues 29	132
Thy mistresse' song is now a sorrow's crie, ...		81	Arcadia III 54	2
And out gan cry, "ah well away for shame, ...		95	3rd Eclogues 64	45
Wherein the birde doth never sing but cry;		105	3rd Eclogues 67	50
I would have spoken out: but out they both did crie; . . .		121	4th Eclogues 73	167
Ah let us all against foule Nature crie:		127	4th Eclogues 75	92
And can crie helpe with nought but grones and starts: . . .		136	Cert Sonnets 2	11
I heare a crye of spirits faint and blinde, ...		148	Cert Sonnets 20	7
Let daintie wits crie on the Sisters nine, ...		166	Astrophil 3	1
Crie, "Victorie, this faire day all is ours."		171	Astrophil 12	11
But more I crie, lesse grace she doth impart, ...		186	Astrophil 44	6
But on her name incessantly to crie:		192	Astrophil 55	11
Let folke orecharg'd with braine against me crie, ...		198	Astrophil 64	4
I cry thy sighs; my deere, thy teares I bleede..		227	Astrophil 93	14
Th' afflicted cry.		280	Psalm IX	35
Behold they cry, but who to them his help applys?		292	Psalm XVIII	74
When Thou on it dost cry, ...		295	Psalm XX	4
O God my God I cry while day appeareth;		298	Psalm XXII	5
To the Lord my cry I send..		308	Psalm XXVIII	1
Therfore while that I may cry, ...		309	Psalm XXVIII	6
To the Lord that heares my cry..		309	Psalm XXVIII	25
This lord and he did heare my cry, ...		319	Psalm XXXIV	14
Do cry, their cry of him is heard, ...		320	Psalm XXXIV	62
And hearkned hcw, and why that I did cry, ...		331	Psalm XL	4
A lustles song for sooth thinks hee that hath more lust to				
cry.		343	Possibly 1	8
"Be you with me while I unheard do cry, ...		255	Other Poems 4	497
Still for thy Dam with bea-waymenting crie?.		258	Other Poems 5	78
CRYING				
Crying in me: eye hopes deceitefull prove.		83	Arcadia III 57	13
I saw that riches fall, and fell a crying;		17	1st Eclogues 7	88
My crying plaints to him alone, ...		273	Psalm IV	14
They shall be sham'd and vext, that breed my crying, . . .		276	Psalm VI	30
My crying:		285	Psalm XIII	10
But God Thy eare my crying never heareth..		298	Psalm XXII	6
CRYSTAL				
In her brave calves, like christall skies.		89	Arcadia III 62	102
Like Christall, underlayde with Redd, ...		86	Arcadia III 62 V	24
CUB				
Or all abroade if but a Cubb start out..		27	1st Eclogues 10	30
CUCKOC'S				
The Cockow's shame, the Goose's good intent, ...		28	1st Eclogues 10	80
CUDGEL				
Now bolt and cudgill squirrels' leape do move.		243	Other Poems 4	44
CULLED				
The oldest Rammes are culled from the flocke:		24	1st Eclogues 9	85
CUMBER				
The Sunne is hid; his kindly shadows cumber not.		49	2nd Eclogues 28 V	63
Nor causelesse duty, nor comber of arrogance, ...		69	2nd Eclogues 34	23
CUMBERED				
I, cumbred with good maners, answer do, ...		180	Astrophil 30	13
CUMBERS				
The Sunne is hid; his kindly shadowe combers not..		49	2nd Eclogues 28	63
CUMBERSOME				
As much more loving, as lesse combersome..		255	Other Poems 4	504
CUMBROUS				
The Waspe seemes gay, but is a combrous thing.		104	3rd Eclogues 67	21
He made my cumbrous way to me most plainly right..		292	Psalm XVIII	60

92

```
CUNNING
   Ah where was first that cruell cunning found,. . . . . . . .   57  2nd Eclogues 30    11
   Like cunning Painter shadowing white.. . . . . . . . . . . .   89  Arcadia III  62    98
   She studied cunning how the same to blinde.. . . . . . . . .   95  3rd Eclogues 64    42
   He did to beastes' best use his cunning frame; . . . . . . .  101  3rd Eclogues 66   108
   Her haire, which by the helpe of painter's cunning, shinde..  118  4th Eclogues 73    74
   Till downe-right blowes did foyle thy cunning fence: . . . .  170  Astrophil    10    11
   Of cunning fishers in most troubled streames,. . . . . . . .  190  Astrophil    51 V 10
   In Martiall sports I had my cunning tride, . . . . . . . . .  191  Astrophil    53     1
   Such marble eares, no cunning wordes can charme, . . . . . .  346  Possibly      5     2
CUNNINGEST
   Of cunningst fishers in most troubled streames,. . . . . . .  190  Astrophil    51    10
CUP
   No mortall man the cuppe of suretie drinkes. . . . . . . . .  105  3rd Eclogues 67    60
   Nectar of Mirth, since I Jove's cup do keepe.. . . . . . . .  201  Astrophil    70     4
   And so my cup dost fill. . . . . . . . . . . . . . . . . . .  301  Psalm XXIII         20
CUPID
   With Cupid she fore-sees, and goes god Vulcan's pace:. . . .   12  Arcadia I     3     7
   Thus Painters Cupid paint, thus Poets do,. . . . . . . . . .   20  1st Eclogues  8     5
   Millions of yeares this old drivell Cupid lives; . . . . . .   22  1st Eclogues  8    43
   But thou foule Cupid, syre to lawlesse lust, . . . . . . . .   92  3rd Eclogues 63    55
   Goe to, goe to, and Cupid now applie . . . . . . . . . . . .  106  3rd Eclogues 67   100
   To that where thou thy Cupid maist avowe,. . . . . . . . . .  106  3rd Eclogues 67   101
   O cowarde Cupid thus doost thou my honour keepe, . . . . . .  122  4th Eclogues 73   185
   Unto Cupid that boy shall a Pedante be found?. . . . . . . .  124  4th Eclogues 74    66
   Cupid, because thou shin'st in Stella's eyes,. . . . . . . .  170  Astrophil    12     1
   Cupid then smiles, for on his crest there lies . . . . . . .  171  Astrophil    13     9
   His mother deare Cupid offended late,. . . . . . . . . . . .  173  Astrophil    17     1
   Brake bow, brake shafts, while Cupid weeping sate: . . . . .  173  Astrophil    17     8
   Where Cupid is sworne page to Chastity?. . . . . . . . . . .  182  Astrophil    35     8
   When Cupid, having me his slave describe . . . . . . . . . .  191  Astrophil    53     5
   O Doctor Cupid, thou for me reply, . . . . . . . . . . . . .  195  Astrophil    61    12
   Onely by you Cupid his crowne maintaineth. . . . . . . . . .  197  A&S 1st Song        12
   Cupid the wagg, that lately conquer'd had. . . . . . . . . .  245  Other Poems   4   129
   Hir feet be Pursevants from Cupid sent,. . . . . . . . . . .  249  Other Poems   4   301
CUPID'S
   "Thou art no souldier fitte for Cupid's garrison.. . . . . .   16  1st Eclogues  7    51
   Thy toong hath made of Cupid's deepe incision. . . . . . . .   20  1st Eclogues  7 V969
   Justly entitled Cupid's hill.. . . . . . . . . . . . . . . .   88  Arcadia III  62    78
   The bloudy shaftes of Cupid's warre, . . . . . . . . . . . .   90  Arcadia III  62   131
   Where justest love doth vanquish Cupid's powers. . . . . . .   91  3rd Eclogues 63     3
   Cupid's lust gone, and gone is bitter strife,. . . . . . . .   93  3rd Eclogues 63    94
   Blinde Cupid's workes with wonder testifie?. . . . . . . . .  106  3rd Eclogues 67    98
   To starving minds such is God Cupid's dish.. . . . . . . . .  136  Cert Sonnets  2    14
   And so for one that felt god Cupid's dart, . . . . . . . . .  146  Cert Sonnets 17    29
   It is most true, what we call Cupid's dart,. . . . . . . . .  167  Astrophil     5     5
   Which Cupid's selfe from Beautie's myne did draw:. . . . . .  169  Astrophil     9    13
   On Cupid's bow how are my heart-strings bent,. . . . . . . .  174  Astrophil    19     1
   Could hope for Cupid's helpe on you to pray;. . . . . . . . .  186  Astrophil    43     2
   Professe in deed I do not Cupid's art; . . . . . . . . . . .  192  Astrophil    54    10
   Vertue's gold now must head my Cupid's dart. . . . . . . . .  202  Astrophil    72     8
   Best charge, and bravest retrait in Cupid's fight, . . . . .  206  Astrophil    79     5
   Nature's praise, Vertue's stall, Cupid's cold fire,. . . . .  206  Astrophil    80     3
   Cupid's yoke to loose or bind: . . . . . . . . . . . . . . .  210  A&S 4th Song        14
   Thy fingers Cupid's shafts, thy voyce the Angel's lay: . . .  212  A&S 5th Song        11
   Are the lights of Cupid's skies, . . . . . . . . . . . . . .  218  A&S 8th Song        34
CUR
   A prettie curre it is; his name iwis is Catch, . . . . . . .   53  2nd Eclogues 29    40
   And now their curr they teach to fetch and daunce. . . . . .  243  Other Poems   4    48
   Go bawling curre, thy hungry maw go fill,. . . . . . . . . .  255  Other Poems   4   517
CURBED
   Fine eares, long taile he hath, with Lion's curbed clawe,. .   53  2nd Eclogues 29    33
   Curb'd in with feare, but with guilt bosse above . . . . . .  189  Astrophil    49     7
CURE
   A hatefull cure with hate to heale:. . . . . . . . . . . . .   44  Arcadia II   25     1
   Her onely cure from surfet-woes can diet me: . . . . . . . .   51  2nd Eclogues 28   117
   To shew the wound without cure.. . . . . . . . . . . . . . .   65  2nd Eclogues 32     8
   O heale my soul, let there Thy cure begin. . . . . . . . . .  333  Psalm XLI          15
   And lookes so neere unto my cure that I must needes be lost.  343  Possibly      1    22
CURED
   How elder rul'd their flocks, and cur'd their smart, . . . .  243  Other Poems   4    37
CURELESS
   Whose curelesse wounds even now most freshly bleed:. . . . .  189  Astrophil    48    11
CURIOUS
   His eyes are curious search, but vailde with warefulnesse:.   48  2nd Eclogues 28    43
   In curious circle, busie sight:. . . . . . . . . . . . . . .   88  Arcadia III  62    74
   Which conduit-like with curious crookes, . . . . . . . . . .   90  Arcadia III  62   128
   The curious wits, seeing dull pensivenesse . . . . . . . . .  176  Astrophil    23     1
   You that with allegorie's curious frame, . . . . . . . . . .  178  Astrophil    28     1
   By Love's owne selfe, but with so curious drought, . . . . .  184  Astrophil    38     7
CURLED
   In curled knots man's thought to hold: . . . . . . . . . . .   85  Arcadia III  62     4
   A wanton woman's face, and with curld knots had twinde . . .  118  4th Eclogues 73    73
CURLS
   Nor of that golden sea, whose waves in curles are brok'n:. .  213  A&S 5th Song        39
CURRISH
   Sweete speaking oft a currish hart reclaimes.. . . . . . . .   60  2nd Eclogues 30   115
CURS
   But commonly like currs we them entreate,. . . . . . . . . .   27  1st Eclogues 10    35
   Come, come my currs, tis late I will goe in. . . . . . . . .   29  1st Eclogues 10    98
```

93

```
CURSE                                                         PAGE   TITLE          LINE
        Think so, for of my desired blisse it is only the course.
            Curse. . . . . . . . . . . . . . . . . . . . . . . .   64  2nd Eclogues 31   39
        I curse the fidling finders out of Musicke:. . . . . . . .  112  4th Eclogues 71   51
        Klaius. Curse to my selfe my prayer is, the morning: . . . .  112  4th Eclogues 71   55
        And with that cursed curse away to heaven they fled, . . . .  121  4th Eclogues 73  177
        The child of curse, man's weaknesse foster-child,. . . . . .  141  Cert Sonnets 10    2
        I yeeld and strive, I kisse and curse the paine: . . . . . .  148  Cert Sonnets 19   17
        Blist in my curse, and cursed in my blisse.. . . . . . . . .  195  Astrophil    60   14
        O fate, o fault, o curse, child of my blisse,. . . . . . . .  227  Astrophil    93    1
        With no worse curse then absence makes me tast.. . . . . . .  235  Astrophil   105   14
        Whom he doth curse to naught shall rott. . . . . . . . . . .  326  Psalm XXXVII      56
        Till my eies had their curse from blessed eine.. . . . . . .  254  Other Poems   4  496
CURSED
        Plangus. Curst be good haps, and curst be they that build. .   58  2nd Eclogues 30   41
        Curs'd be thy selfe for cursing that which leades me to
            joies. Toies.. . . . . . . . . . . . . . . . . . . . . .   65  2nd Eclogues 31   40
        The laborer, which cursed earthe up teares . . . . . . . . .   71  Arcadia III  36    7
        And with that cursed curse away to heaven they fled, . . . .  121  4th Eclogues 73  177
        Such cursed harmes as cannot be redressed. . . . . . . . . .  126  4th Eclogues 75   63
        Whom curst do blesse, whose weakenesse vertues arme, . . . .  142  Cert Sonnets 10    6
        Mine eyes (shall I say curst or blest) beheld. . . . . . . .  173  Astrophil    16   10
        I curst thee oft, I pitie now thy case,. . . . . . . . . . .  187  Astrophil    46    1
        Blist in my curse, and cursed in my blisse.. . . . . . . . .  195  Astrophil    60   14
        Curst be the page from whome the bad torch fell, . . . . . .  235  Astrophil   105   11
        Curst be the night which did your strife resist, . . . . . .  235  Astrophil   105   12
        Curst be the Cochman which did drive so fast,. . . . . . . .  235  Astrophil   105   13
        Cursed be my destines all, . . . . . . . . . . . . . . . . .  211  A&S 4th Song      51
        Let them be curst away that would me wast; . . . . . . . . .  332  Psalm XL          54
        With that his dogge he henc'd, his flocke he curst:. . . . .  255  Other Poems   4  519
        Whose foote doth set a heav'n on cursed thee,. . . . . . . .  256  Other Poems   5   19
CURSES
        With cries to skies, and curses to the ground, . . . . . . .   57  2nd Eclogues 30    9
CURSING
        Curs'd be thy selfe for cursing that which leades me to
            joies. Toies.. . . . . . . . . . . . . . . . . . . . . .   65  2nd Eclogues 31   40
        Cursing and cosening,. . . . . . . . . . . . . . . . . . . .  282  Psalm X           28
        When Strephon, cursing his owne backwardnes, . . . . . . . .  252  Other Poems   4  388
CURTAINS
        Phoebus drew wide the curtaines of the skies . . . . . . . .  171  Astrophil    13   12
        Candles out, and curtaines spread: . . . . . . . . . . . . .  211  A&S 4th Song      38
CURTESY
        Is sawcinesse reward of curtesie?. . . . . . . . . . . . . .  208  Astrophil    83   10
CUSTOM
        Do not thy hart, to plaintfull custome bring,. . . . . . . .   22  1st Eclogues  9    3
CUT
        Olde aged oke cutt downe, of newe works serves to the
            building:. . . . . . . . . . . . . . . . . . . . . . . .   36  1st Eclogues 13  134
        So my desires by my feare, cutt downe, be the frames of her
            honour.. . . . . . . . . . . . . . . . . . . . . . . . .   36  1st Eclogues 13  135
        My weedes, Desire, cut out in endlesse foldes. . . . . . . .   39  Arcadia II   17    6
        Like late mowne meades, late cut from joy I live.. . . . . .  147  Cert Sonnets 18   11
        (With gall cut out) closde up againe by art, . . . . . . . .  150  Cert Sonnets 22   23
        While craftily you seem'd your cut to keepe, . . . . . . . .  208  Astrophil    83    3
        They soone shall be cutt down like grasse. . . . . . . . . .  324  Psalm XXXVII       5
        And quite cutt off, with helpless end. . . . . . . . . . . .  327  Psalm XXXVII      96
CUTTED
        Or do you cutted Spartanes imitate?. . . . . . . . . . . . .  225  Astrophil    92    3
CUTTING
        Of them, poore soules: and cutting Reason's raines,. . . . .  246  Other Poems   4  158
CYPRUS
        Of Phoebus' violence in shade of stately Ciprus tree,. . . .   31  1st Eclogues 13   12
        Cyprus promiseth helpe, but a helpe where comes no
            recomforte.. . . . . . . . . . . . . . . . . . . . . . .   35  1st Eclogues 13  119
D
        W. Who bound thee? D. Love my Lord. W. What witnesses
            therto . . . . . . . . . . . . . . . . . . . . . . . . .  343  Possibly      1   25
        W. What seale? D. My hart deepe graven. W. Who made the band
            so fast?. . . . . . . . . . . . . . . . . . . . . . . . .  343  Possibly      1   27
        D. Wonder that by two so black eyes the glittering stars be
            past.. . . . . . . . . . . . . . . . . . . . . . . . . .  343  Possibly      1   28
        Will. What keepeth safe thy band? D. Remembrance is the
            Chest.. . . . . . . . . . . . . . . . . . . . . . . . . .  344  Possibly      1   29
        D. Her heavenly looks, which more and more do give me cause
            to crave.. . . . . . . . . . . . . . . . . . . . . . . .  344  Possibly      1   32
        D. Teares drink, sorowes meat, wherewith, not I, but in me
            my death lives.. . . . . . . . . . . . . . . . . . . . .  344  Possibly      1   34
        Will. What living get you then? D. Disdayne; but just
            disdayne.. . . . . . . . . . . . . . . . . . . . . . . .  344  Possibly      1   35
        Will. What care takes shee for thee? D. Hir care is to
            prevent.. . . . . . . . . . . . . . . . . . . . . . . . .  344  Possibly      1   37
        Welcome my two to me, E.D. F.G. P.S. . . . . . . . . . . . .  261  Other Poems   6   25
        "Only for my two loves' sake, Sir Ed. D. and M. F. G.. . . .  263  Other Poems   7   61
DAILY
        My day newe cares; my ginnes my daily sight, . . . . . . . .   18  1st Eclogues  7  140
        Save that dayly we may discerne what fire we do burne in.. .   33  1st Eclogues 13   53
        And for a sure sacrifice I do dayly oblation offer . . . . .   37  1st Eclogues 13  170
        These fires increase: in these I dayly burne:. . . . . . . .   42  Arcadia II   22    8
        R. We with ourselves abide a daily strife. . . . . . . . . .   46  2nd Eclogues 27   25
        No, no: Despaire my dayly lesson saith,. . . . . . . . . . .   58  2nd Eclogues 30   53
```

		PAGE	TITLE		LINE
DAILY	(CONTINUED)				
And in whose eyes my dayly doome I reede............		72	Arcadia III	38	5
For what is life to dayly dyinge minde,............		73	Arcadia III	40	9
So to my minde, while passions daylie growe,........		74	Arcadia III	41	3
Her hand benumbe with fortune's daylie blows,........		81	Arcadia III	54	3
Witnesse your wofull teares with daily rayning..........		127	4th Eclogues 75		69
But I who dayly craving,..................		137	Cert Sonnets	4	17
The glasses of thy dayly vexing care?"..........		181	Astrophil	34	3
Who for long faith, tho dayly helpe I crave,........		188	Astrophil	47	7
Most rude dispaire my daily unbidden guest,........		236	Astrophil	108	7
And yet against thy Prince tny force dost dayly prove: ...		214	A&S 5th Song		65
With their dayly questions throwing:		334	Psalm XLII		11
With sight made dymme with dayly teares another's sport to see..................................		343	Possibly	1	4
Doth daily haunt: but so, that mine become		255	Other Poems	4	503
And pine away with daily wasting woe?..............		257	Other Poems	5	26
DAINTIER					
Towne-folkes my strength; a daintier judge applies		185	Astrophil	41	6
DAINTIES					
Whose bellyes so with daintys Thou dost fill		290	Psalm XVII		41
DAINTIEST					
Frame daintiest lustre, mixt of shades and light?......		168	Astrophil	7	4
Her daintiest bare went free; the cause was this,......		176	Astrophil	22	13
DAINTY					
Milde as a Lambe, more daintie then a Conie is:.......		15	1st Eclogues	7	31
A daintie seale of virgin-waxe,...............		88	Arcadia III	62	75
Let daintie wits crie on the Sisters nine, ...		166	Astrophil	3	1
Those daintie dores unto the Court of blisse,........		187	Astrophil	44	11
Her soule, arm'd but with such a dainty rind,........		193	Astrophil	57	7
What saist thou now, where is that dainty cheere		235	Astrophil	106	5
To make a Lyzard dull to taste Love's daintie food:.....		209	A&S 3rd Song		8
Drew dainty Nous, that she not able so		250	Other Poems	4	335
He hopes, with dainty turns she doth him flee........		251	Other Poems	4	341
The dainty dew on face and body went		252	Other Poems	4	397
DALES					
In Dales I see each way a hard assent:		147	Cert Sonnets 18		10
Rockes, woods, hilles, caves, dales, meads, brookes, answere me,.............................		147	Cert Sonnets 18		13
DALLYINGS					
Thinke, thinke of those dalyings,..............		226	A&S 10th Song		37
DAM					
His damme a beast was pardon'd beastly fact........		21	1st Eclogues	8	18
Nico. In deed the witch thy dam her crouch from shoulder spred,.............................		52	2nd Eclogues 29		13
In him, the thoughts of Phaeton's damme to grave......		60	2nd Eclogues 30		106
When all this Earth, this damme or mould of ours,......		100	3rd Eclogues 66		44
But yet the common Damme none did bemone;.........		102	3rd Eclogues 66		118
Let pearls be wan with woe their damme doth beare:		125	4th Eclogues 75		23
Or like a lambe whose dam away is fet, ...		254	Other Poems	4	490
Have cought of thy deare damme,.............		258	Other Poems	5	73
Still for thy Dam with bea-waymenting crie?.		258	Other Poems	5	78
DAMAGE					
Since no evill fortune equalls publique damage:.......		108	Arcadia IV	70	3
Now Prince's losse hath made our damage publique,......		109	Arcadia IV	70	4
Where they would leave trophees of cruell damage,......		109	Arcadia IV	70	12
Then since such pow'rs conspire unto our damage.		109	Arcadia IV	70	13
How just how torne thy selfe! sought thine owne damage! ...		109	Arcadia IV	70	20
Breath made of flames, wits knowing nought but damage, ...		109	Arcadia IV	70	28
With secret sense of our eternall damage,.........		110	Arcadia IV	70	35
With all our deathes shew we this damage publique.		110	Arcadia IV	70	38
Ere that I should consent to doo such excessive a dammage. .		124	4th Eclogues 74		61
DAMES					
Will. God shield us from such Dames. If so our Downes be sped,................................		344	Possibly	1	39
DAMN					
Whose sprite all sprites can spoile, raise, damne, or save:.		17	1st Eclogues	7	110
DAMNING					
And damning their owne selves to Tantal's smart, ...		177	Astrophil	24	3
DAMOETAS					
Miso mine owne pigsnie, thou shalt heare news o' Damaetas. .		241	Other Poems	2	1
DAMS					
(As even in beasts their dammes leave chaunging parts) ...		100	3rd Eclogues 66		60
To play when that their loved dammes, are stoln or gone astray?................................		343	Possibly	1	6
DAN					
Fa la la leridan, dan dan dan deridan:		156	Cert Sonnets 27		5
Above line repeated at following locations		156	Cert Sonnets 27		13
....		157	Cert Sonnets 27		21
....		157	Cert Sonnets 27		29
....		157	Cert Sonnets 27		37
Dan dan dan deridan deridan dei:		156	Cert Sonnets 27		6
Above line repeated at following locations		156	Cert Sonnets 27		14
....		157	Cert Sonnets 27		22
....		157	Cert Sonnets 27		30
....		157	Cert Sonnets 27		38
DANCE					
When trees daunce to the pype, and swift streames stay by the musicke, ...		33	1st Eclogues 13		47
They should still daunce to please a gazer's sight.......		178	Astrophil	26	8
But when Aurora leades out Phoebus' daunce,.		230	Astrophil	98	12

```
DANCE                     (CONTINUED)                           PAGE    TITLE           LINE
      The bote for joy could not to daunce forbeare, . . . . . . .   232 Astrophil  103      5
      Lo I that waild, now daunce for joy. . . . . . . . . . . . .   311 Psalm XXX            34
      Holy daunce to God's house bringing. . . . . . . . . . . . .   334 Psalm XLII           16
      Will. Dick, since we cannot dance, come let a chearefull
          voyce. . . . . . . . . . . . . . . . . . . . . . . . . .   343 Possibly     1       1
      And now their curr they teach to fetch and daunce. . . . . .   243 Other Poems  4      48
      While daunce about the may-pole is begun,. . . . . . . . . .   243 Other Poems  4      55
      With one good dawnce, or letter finely pend, . . . . . . . .   245 Other Poems  4     140
DANCED
      If stones good measure daunc'd, the Theban walles to build,.   208 A&S 3rd Song         3
DANCES
      With daunces, carols, or with barlybreake: . . . . . . . . .    54 2nd Eclogues 29     70
DANCING
      And makes our home good sport with dauncing bolt upright...     53 2nd Eclogues 29     46
DANGER
      Thus be her giftes most sweet, thus more danger to be neere
          her, . . . . . . . . . . . . . . . . . . . . . . . . . .    36 1st Eclogues 13    126
      Nor danger to thy selfe if be not in thy selfe.. . . . . . .    69 2nd Eclogues 34     14
      Whose shade safety doth hold, danger avoideth her: . . . . .    69 2nd Eclogues 34     34
      But o foole, thinke of the danger, . . . . . . . . . . . . .   203 A&S 2nd Song        17
      Danger hence good care doth keepe, . . . . . . . . . . . . .   210 A&S 4th Song         9
      Nor danger ever see: . . . . . . . . . . . . . . . . . . . .   282 Psalm X             26
DANGER'S
      As sacred things, far from all daunger's show. . . . . . . .   177 Astrophil   24       8
      (Who Neptune's webb on daunger's distaff spun) . . . . . . .   251 Other Poems  4     374
DANGERS
      Sturres me to thinke what dangers lye in waite.. . . . . . .    82 Arcadia III 56      12
DARE
      How dare I, wretch, seeke there my woes to rest, . . . . . .     3 Lady of May  1       5
      So dare I, wretch, my bashfull feare subdue, . . . . . . . .     3 Lady of May  1      11
      Dorus. Lady your selfe, whom nether name I dare, . . . . . .    18 1st Eclogues 7     131
      No woolves dare howle, no murrayne can prevaile, . . . . . .    43 Arcadia II  23       8
      R. Dare Passions then abide in Reason's light? . . . . . . .    46 2nd Eclogues 27     17
      R. Weakenes you are, dare you with our strength fight? . . .    46 2nd Eclogues 27     21
      Ne dare once shew thy face,. . . . . . . . . . . . . . . . .    93 3rd Eclogues 63     87
      There never past foule word, I dare well say.. . . . . . . .   106 3rd Eclogues 67     93
      That thou shalt never dare seeke helpe of wretched case".. .   121 4th Eclogues 73    176
      Which dare claime from those lights the name of best,. . . .   169 Astrophil    9      11
      Though dustie wits dare scorne Astrologie, . . . . . . . . .   177 Astrophil   26       1
      For when he will see who dare him gainesay,. . . . . . . . .   186 Astrophil   43       5
      "What he?" say they of me, "now I dare sweare, . . . . . . .   191 Astrophil   54       7
      Of gentle force, so that mine eyes dare gladly play. . . . .   205 Astrophil   76       6
      Faint coward joy no longer tarry dare, . . . . . . . . . . .   228 Astrophil   95       5
      Of comfort dare come to this dungeon darke,. . . . . . . . .   233 Astrophil  104       7
      That dare themselves to him oppose,. . . . . . . . . . . . .   282 Psalm X             22
      Shall never dare come neare him. . . . . . . . . . . . . . .   315 Psalm XXXII          24
DARES
      In Beautie's throne, see now who dares come neare. . . . . .   203 Astrophil   73      10
DAREST
      Out traytour absence, darest thou counsell me, . . . . . . .   223 Astrophil   88       1
DARING
      O toonge, then dumbe, not daring tell my smart;. . . . . . .    60 2nd Eclogues 30    121
      Daring not to tell to mee, . . . . . . . . . . . . . . . . .   262 Other Poems  7      15
DARK
      Since that the stormy rage of passions darcke. . . . . . . .    72 Arcadia III 39       1
      (Of passions darke, made darke by beautie's light) . . . . .    72 Arcadia III 39       2
      With rebell force, hath closde in dungeon darke. . . . . . .    73 Arcadia III 39       3
      Do foster still, the fruite of fancies darke:. . . . . . . .    73 Arcadia III 39       6
      Do serve, to make my inward powers darke:. . . . . . . . . .    73 Arcadia III 39       8
      Since, as I say, both minde and sences darke . . . . . . . .    73 Arcadia III 39       9
      While that the light may shewe the horrors darke . . . . . .    73 Arcadia III 39      11
      I like this place, wheare at the least the darke . . . . . .    73 Arcadia III 39      13
      Receipt to me, within thy bosome darke.. . . . . . . . . . .    73 Arcadia III 40       8
      Become the cause of my darke ouglie night? . . . . . . . . .    74 Arcadia III 42       2
      Or howe do I, captiv'd in this darke plight, . . . . . . . .    74 Arcadia III 42       3
      This cave is darke, but it had never light.. . . . . . . . .    75 Arcadia III 43       1
      Hastened from us with barre of shadow darke, . . . . . . . .    80 Arcadia III 52      13
      With ouglie cloke the darke envious night: . . . . . . . . .    82 Arcadia III 55       8
      By taking her two Sunnes from these darke vallies. . . . . .   113 4th Eclogues 71     66
      Did light those beamye stars which greater light did darke:.   116 4th Eclogues 73      3
      But foole, foole that I am, those eyes would shine from a
          dark cave. . . . . . . . . . . . . . . . . . . . . . . .   123 4th Eclogues 74     49
      The shading woods seeme now my Sunne to darke, . . . . . . .   147 Cert Sonnets 18      7
      Blinded forthwith in darke dispaire did lye, . . . . . . . .   149 Cert Sonnets 21      6
      Who like a theefe, hid in darke bush doth ly,. . . . . . . .   175 Astrophil   20       3
      Because I oft in darke abstracted guise, . . . . . . . . . .   178 Astrophil   27       1
      Scortch not, but onely do darke chilling sprites remove.. .    205 Astrophil   76       8
      That presence, which doth give darke hearts a living light:.   205 Astrophil   77       3
      While no night is more darke then is my day, . . . . . . . .   224 Astrophil   89      10
      If this darke place yet shew like candle light,. . . . . . .   225 Astrophil   91       5
      So darke with misty vapors, which arise. . . . . . . . . . .   228 Astrophil   94       2
      Of comfort dare come to this dungeon darke,. . . . . . . . .   233 Astrophil  104       7
      Through that darke fornace to my hart opprest, . . . . . . .   236 Astrophil  108       3
      I thought each place was darke but where thy lights would
          be . . . . . . . . . . . . . . . . . . . . . . . . . . .   212 A&S 5th Song         5
      See what clouds of reproch small darke thy honour's skie,..   213 A&S 5th Song         23
      "Who is it that this darke night,. . . . . . . . . . . . . .   233 A&S 11th Song        1
      Cloudes even of Waters dark, and thickest ayre compos'd; . .   291 Psalm XVIII         25
      Of death's dark shade I will . . . . . . . . . . . . . . . .   301 Psalm XXIII         11
```

DARK   (CONTINUED)   PAGE   TITLE   LINE
  But let their flight be dark and slippery; . . . .   321 Psalm XXXV   14
  One day (o day, that shin'de to make them darke!). . . . . .   243 Other Poems   4   65
  She is the heardesse faire that shines in darke. . . . . . .   259 Other Poems   5   112
DARKEN
  If Leuca live, she darken will my fame. . . . .   55 2nd Eclogues   29   95
DARKENED
  I darkned am, who once had clearest sight. . . . .   75 Arcadia III   43   4
  So darkened am, that all my day is evening,. . . . .   111 4th Eclogues   71   22
  The darkened heav'n my soule which nought can see; . . . . .   114 4th Eclogues   72   35
  Which to our darkned mindes was best direction;. . . . . . .   129 4th Eclogues   76   9
  Both sadly blacke, both blackly darkned be,. . . . .   229 Astrophil   96   3
  Such light in sense, with such a darkned mind. . . . .   231 Astrophil   99   14
  Up Thou dost light my light, and cleare my darkned eye.. . .   292 Psalm XVIII   53
DARKEST
  Be thow my starre in this my darkest night,. . . . .   70 Arcadia III   35   4
  Till her eyes shine, I live in darkest night.. . . . .   79 Arcadia III   51   14
  With darkest shade doth overcome my day; . . . .   223 Astrophil   89   2
DARKNESS
  Whose lights do ever live, but in our darkenesse fade; . . .   44 Arcadia II   26   4
  From Cosma's eyes, which full in darkenes shine, ...   55 2nd Eclogues   29   103
  Ofte scorching sonne, ofte clowdie darkenes feares,. . . . .   71 Arcadia III   36   9
  But cannot make resolved darkenes lighte:. . . . .   73 Arcadia III   39   12
  Blinded with beames, fell darkenes is my sight:. . . . . . .   113 4th Eclogues   72   8
  With Sunne's depart: and now the darkenes of the night . . .   116 4th Eclogues   73   2
  First let Cimmerian darknes be my onel'habitaco'n: . . . . .   124 4th Eclogues   74   59
  With that faire breast making woe's darknesse cleare:. . . .   193 Astrophil   57   11
  Viewing the shape of darknesse and delight,. . . . .   230 Astrophil   99   6
  Sleepy darkness doth o're cast,. . . . .   288 Psalm XVI   22
  With hugy darknes, which about his feet did wend.. . . . . .   291 Psalm XVIII   21
  In darkness teach cleere knowledg. . . . .   293 Psalm XIX   8
  Now let those lightsomme sights we see thy darknes overcome.   343 Possibly   1   12
DARLING
  Under this, this her owne, her only dearling. . . . .   68 2nd Eclogues   33   23
DARLING'S
  Nature with care sweates for her darling's sake, ...   232 Astrophil   101   12
DART
  (Her sight where love did forge his fayrest darte) . . . . .   79 Arcadia III   51   6
  Be thou farre hence with thy empoyson'd darte, ...   92 3rd Eclogues   63   56
  Cease Muse therfore: thy dart o Death applie;. . . . .   129 4th Eclogues   75   141
  And so for one that felt god Cupid's dart, ...   146 Cert Sonnets   17   29
  Weakely did seeme to paint death's ougly dart. . . . .   148 Cert Sonnets   20   4
  "Her eyes were once his dart". . . . .   160 Cert Sonnets   30   26
  It is most true, what we call Cupid's dart,. . . . .   167 Astrophil   5   5
  Is no fit marke to pierce with his fine pointed dart:. . . .   168 Astrophil   8   3
  And then descried the glistring of his dart: . . . .   175 Astrophil   20   13
  Yet still on me, o eyes, dart downe your rayes:. . . . . . .   186 Astrophil   42   11
  Vertue's gold now must head my Cupid's dart. . . . .   202 Astrophil   72   8
  The darte, the beames, the stringe so stronge I prove; . . .   344 Possibly   2   1
DARTED
  Whose beames, where they once are darted,. . . . .   218 A&S 8th Song   35
DARTS
  Of those fierce darts, dispaire at me doth throw:. . . . . .   184 Astrophil   39   6
  That through my heart their beamie darts be gone,. . . . . .   189 Astrophil   48   10
  The two only darts of Love:. . . . .   202 A&S 2nd Song   6
  Her strong darts, but weake defences.. . . . .   226 A&S 10th Song   36
  Were now his darts leaving his wonted fight. . . . .   246 Other Poems   4   148
  But, ah! hir darts did farre more depely goe . . . .   251 Other Poems   4   352
DASHED
  And now my pen these lines had dashed quite, ...   190 Astrophil   50   12
DAUGHTER
  Of syon's Daughter may sing forth Thy prayse:. . . . .   280 Psalm IX   42
DAUNTED
  Farewell our might, farewell our daunted pleasure: . . . . .   130 4th Eclogues   76   38
DAVID
  For David his Anoynt, and his seed ever more.. . . . .   293 Psalm XVIII   91
DAWN
  And scarce discerne the dawne of comming day,. . . . .   131 Arcadia V   77   10
DAY
  My charme should be, she haunt me day and night. . . . . . .   17 1st Eclogues   7   105
  In flowrie fielde; and as the day begins . . . .   18 1st Eclogues   7   125
  My day newe cares; my ginnes my daily sight, ...   18 1st Eclogues   7   140
  Nico. Well aimed by my hat: for as thou sangst last day; . .   52 2nd Eclogues   29   25
  Pas. If each day hath bene holy for your sake, ...   54 2nd Eclogues   29   72
  One day layes up stuffe of griefe for the morrow:. . . . . .   62 2nd Eclogues   30   176
  O Titan faire the giver of the daie? . . . .   80 Arcadia III   52   2
  For mischeefes greate, daye after day doth showe:. . . . . .   82 Arcadia III   56   13
  As in a sommer day a man might see:. . . . .   94 3rd Eclogues   64   4
  That if he absent were but halfe a daye, ...   94 3rd Eclogues   64   10
  And thus she did. One day to him she came, ...   95 3rd Eclogues   64   43
  Sure shepherd's signe, that morne would soone fetch day. . .   103 3rd Eclogues   66   161
  That last day seem'd, he could not chew a beane. . . . . . .   103 3rd Eclogues   67   6
  How well last day before our Prince you could. . . . .   106 3rd Eclogues   67   97
  We go unto the Bryde, and use this daye. . . . .   107 3rd Eclogues   67   119
  So darkened am, that all my day is evening,. . . . .   111 4th Eclogues   71   22
  I doo detest night, evening, day, and morning. . . . .   112 4th Eclogues   71   54
  O light of Sunne, which is entit'led day,. . . . .   126 4th Eclogues   75   52
  And scarce discerne the dawne of comming day,. . . . .   131 Arcadia V   77   10
  Crie, "Victorie, this faire day all is ours.". . . . .   171 Astrophil   12   11
  I find how heav'nly day wretch I did misse.. . . . .   181 Astrophil   33   4

DAY   (CONTINUED)   PAGE   TITLE   LINE

Line	Page	Title		Line
How faire a day was neare, o punisht eyes,	181	Astrophil	33	13
And ah what hope, that hope should once see day,	182	Astrophil	35	7
Having this day my horse, my hand, my launce	185	Astrophil	41	1
Stolne to my heart, since last faire night, nay day,	199	Astrophil	66	10
Benighted in cold wo, but now appeares my day,	204	Astrophil	76	3
With darkest shade doth overcome my day;	223	Astrophil	89	2
Since Stella's eyes, wont to give me my day,	223	Astrophil	89	3
Each day seemes long, and longs for long-staid night,	224	Astrophil	89	5
The night as tedious, wooes th'approch of day;	224	Astrophil	89	6
Tired with the dusty toiles of busie day,	224	Astrophil	89	7
Suffering the evils both of the day and night,	224	Astrophil	89	9
While no night is more darke then is my day,	224	Astrophil	89	10
Nor no day hath lesse quiet then my night:	224	Astrophil	89	11
With such bad mixture of my night and day,	224	Astrophil	89	12
I feele the flames of hottest sommer day.	224	Astrophil	89	14
Whom iron doores do keepe from use of day?	237	Astrophil	108	11
Which night and day he calls to marking mind.	270	Psalm I		6
Thou art my son in deed, this day begott by me:	271	Psalm II		17
Yet each day art provoakt, thyne Ire to show,	277	Psalm VII		32
Day unto day doth it display,	293	Psalm XIX		5
Ev'n in the day when most Thy troubles be;	295	Psalm XX		2
O God my God I cry while day appeareth;	298	Psalm XXII		5
For never day such changing wrought.	303	Psalm XXV		17
For so both day and night did stand.	315	Psalm XXXII		10
Day and night my teares out flowing.	334	Psalm XLII		9
I by day thy love shall tast,	335	Psalm XLII		37
One day (o day, that shin'de to make them darke!)	243	Other Poems	4	65
To see the sportes of double-shining day,	251	Other Poems	4	362
The day seemes long, but night is odious	253	Other Poems	4	435
One day he with his flock abroad did raunge:	253	Other Poems	4	438
The day well fed, the night in faithfull folde:	258	Other Poems	5	68

DAY-NETS
| That from her lockes, thy day-nets, none scapes free, | 170 | Astrophil | 12 | 2 |

DAY'S
| Which troubles their daye's worke, and joyes of evening: | 112 | 4th Eclogues | 71 | 33 |

DAYS
Were in his dayes: which heard, one nothing heares,	24	1st Eclogues	9	76
In hunting fearefull beastes, do spend some dayes,	25	1st Eclogues	9	123
As for the rest, howe shepeheardes spend their daies,	28	1st Eclogues	10	46
Nico. If never I did faile your holy-dayes,	54	2nd Eclogues	29	69
Of lothsome dayes, whose losse how canst thou mone,	59	2nd Eclogues	30	78
Let one time (but long first) close up their daies,	92	3rd Eclogues	63	31
But fewe dayes past while she good maner us'de,	95	3rd Eclogues	64	26
Three dayes before that he must sure depart,	96	3rd Eclogues	64	79
She thinks I leade and live too merrie daies.	146	Cert Sonnets	17	30
Ah haire, how many dayes,	158	Cert Sonnets	28	9
Throughout my days.	280	Psalm IX		45
Thus thus shall all my days be fede,	301	Psalm XXIII		22
As for my tongue, while I have any dayes,	323	Psalm XXXV		71
God keeps account of good men's dayes,	325	Psalm XXXVII		45

DAZZLE
| They sun-like should more dazle then delight? | 168 | Astrophil | 7 | 8 |

DAZZLED
Where eares be burnt, eyes dazled, harts opprest?	3	Lady of May	1	6
But still our dazeled eyes their way do misse,	59	2nd Eclogues	30	74
Come clowdie feares, close up my daseled sight,	74	Arcadia III	42	9
My heart then quak'd, then dazled were mine eyes,	191	Astrophil	53	10
My heart cries "ah", it burnes, mine eyes now dazled be:	205	Astrophil	76	11

DAZZLETH
| Nor trifling title of vanity dazleth us, | 69 | 2nd Eclogues | 34 | 24 |

DAZZLING
| Whiche dazeling still, dothe still maynteine my sight; | 70 | Arcadia III | 35 | 6 |
| Was not in fault, who bent thy dazling race. | 235 | Astrophil | 105 | 6 |

DEAD
Why thee a living man they had made dead.	11	Arcadia I	1	7
"Let not dead earth enjoy so deare a cover,	17	1st Eclogues	7	89
Life showing, dead indeed:	19	1st Eclogues	7	160
Yet dying, and dead, doo we sing her honour;	30	1st Eclogues	12	9
Thy sainte is dead, or dead is thy devotion.	47	2nd Eclogues	28	3
Pan is not dead, since Pas beginnes to sing.	53	2nd Eclogues	29	53
She lay for dead, till I helpt with unlasing her?	61	2nd Eclogues	30	154
That, leaving me for dead, to her it went:	115	4th Eclogues	72	79
But ah her flight hath my dead reliques spent.	115	4th Eclogues	72	80
Strephon. But ah her flight hath my dead reliques spent,	115	4th Eclogues	72	81
Her flight from me, from me, though dead to me,	115	4th Eclogues	72	82
Full dead before, I now to dust should fall,	116	4th Eclogues	72	86
Vertue is dead, now set thy triumph here.	127	4th Eclogues	75	72
Dead palsie sicke of all my chiefest parts:	136	Cert Sonnets	2	10
Now dead, doth shew departure is a death.	148	Cert Sonnets	20	12
Approching warmes (not else) dead logges up sends,	150	Cert Sonnets	22	12
But when that failes, my dead hopes up to take,	150	Cert Sonnets	22	19
And I be dead who want sense,	154	Cert Sonnets	25	22
For love is dead:	159	Cert Sonnets	30	2
All Love is dead, infected	159	Cert Sonnets	30	3
That Love is dead?	160	Cert Sonnets	30	12
For love is dead:	160	Cert Sonnets	30	22
Love is not dead.	160	Cert Sonnets	30	32
Love is not dead, but sleepeth	160	Cert Sonnets	30	33
Dead glasse, doost thou thy object so imbrace,	235	Astrophil	105	3

DEAD   (CONTINUED)   PAGE   TITLE   LINE
    Who long dead beautie with increase reneweth?. . . . . . . 197 A&S 1st Song   22
    But I in me am chang'd, I am alive and dead: . . . . 215 A&S 5th Song   76
    Ev'n like a dead man dreamed out of mind,. . . . . 313 Psalm XXXI   35
DEADLY
    Deadly wounds inward bleed, ech sleight sore mattereth.. . . 14 1st Eclogues 7   9
    Which shootes strongly with out any noyse and deadly without
        smarte. . . . . 35 1st Eclogues 13 122
    In what state was I then, when I tooke this deadly disease?
        ease. . . . . 63 2nd Eclogues 31   8
    To think a soare so deadly . . . .   66 2nd Eclogues 32   17
    Wrong sturres remorsed greefe, griefe's deadly sore. . . .   85 Arcadia III 61   7
    Strephon. Long since alas, my deadly Swannish musique. . . . 112 4th Eclogues 71   25
    Till deadly sleepe at length possest my living coarse. . . 117 4th Eclogues 73   30
    And found with deadly feare that all my sinewes shak'd.. . . 121 4th Eclogues 73 180
    Despaire most tragicall clause to a deadly request). . . . 122 4th Eclogues 74   12
    Like foe, whose wits inclin'd to deadly spite, ... 135 Cert Sonnets 2   3
    When to my deadlie pleasure, ... 154 Cert Sonnets 25   1
    Morpheus, the lively sonne of deadly sleepe, ... 180 Astrophil   32   1
    And hast Thy deadly armes in order brought . . . . 278 Psalm VII   35
    For I know the deadly grave. . . . . 288 Psalm XVI   31
    In deadly dust declared be?. . . . . 311 Psalm XXX   30
DEADMAN
    This life-deadman in this old dungeon flong. . . . .   24 1st Eclogues 9   83
DEAF
    A chamber deafe to noise, and blind to light:. . . . . . . 184 Astrophil   39   10
    And all eares worse then deafe, that heard not out thy
        storie. . . . . 212 A&S 5th Song   6
    Deaf and dumbe,. . . . . 328 Psalm XXXVIII   38
DEAL
    A foolish thing with fooles to deale:. . . . .   44 Arcadia II   25   3
    Leave what thou likest not, deale not thou with it.. . . . 166 Astrophil   4   4
    Deale thou with powers of thoughts, leave love to will.. . . 169 Astrophil   10   8
DEALING
    Both free of minde, both did clear-dealing love, ... 243 Other Poems   4   39
DEALST
    Pure to the pure, Thou dealst with crooked crookedly;. . . . 292 Psalm XVIII   51
DEAR
    "Let not dead earth enjoy so deare a cover,. . . . .   17 1st Eclogues 7   89
    "I con thee thanke" to whom thy dogges be deare, ...   27 1st Eclogues 10   34
    That that deare Dyamond, where wisdome holdeth a sure seate, 37 1st Eclogues 13 165
    As thou wilt give our soules a deare refection,. . . . . .   49 2nd Eclogues 28   52
    Yet deare soile, if a soule closed in a mansion. . . . . .   69 2nd Eclogues 34   31
    Hold deere his work, with sighes eache change attendes,. . . 71 Arcadia III 37   8
    I holde his deare, and myne he cannot misse: . . . .   75 Arcadia III 45   3
    And thou deare flesh, as soft as wooll new drest,. . . . .   76 Arcadia III 46   15
    Thou art the father of occasion deare: . . . .   81 Arcadia III 53   12
    So may thy flockes encrease, thy deere hart glad,. . . . .   96 3rd Eclogues 64   93
    But then I homeward call'd my lambkins deare:. . . . . . . 103 3rd Eclogues 66 158
    Your presence (sister deare) first to my Moony spheare,. . . 119 4th Eclogues 73 103
    Diana deare; my minde to love and not to hate. . . . . . . 120 4th Eclogues 73 148
    Bend your thoghts to the dear sweet words which then to me
        giv'n were:. . . . . 124 4th Eclogues 74   75
    Who silence force to make their words more deare:. . . . . 147 Cert Sonnets 17   49
    That the deare She might take some pleasure of my paine: . 165 Astrophil   1   2
    That she (deare she) might take some pleasure of my paine: . 165 Astrophil   1 V 2
    And strange things cost too deare for my poore sprites.. . . 166 Astrophil   3   11
    Of living deaths, deare wounds, faire stormes and freesing
        fires: . . . . 167 Astrophil   6   4
    His mother deare Cupid offended late, ... 173 Astrophil   17   1
    O Stella deare, how much thy power hath wrought, ... 184 Astrophil   40   2
    Faire eyes, sweet lips, deare heart, that foolish I. . . . 186 Astrophil   43   1
    Then thinke my deare, that you in me do reed . . . . 187 Astrophil   45   12
    Yet Deare, let me this pardon get of you,. . . . . 188 Astrophil   46   12
    Deare Killer, spare not thy sweet cruell shot:. . . . . . . 189 Astrophil   48   13
    That Stella (o deare name) that Stella is. . . . . 190 Astrophil   52   6
    Deare, why make you more of a dog then me? . . . . 194 Astrophil   59   1
    Deare, love me not, that you may love me more. . . . . . . 196 Astrophil   62   14
    For Grammer sayes (o this deare Stella weighe,). . . . . . 196 Astrophil   63   12
    No more, my deare, no more these counsels trie,. . . . . . 198 Astrophil   64   1
    These things are left me by my only Deare; . . . . 202 Astrophil   72   12
    When for so soft a rod deare play he trie? . . . . 203 Astrophil   73   4
    Then since (deare life) you faine would have me peace, . . 207 Astrophil   81   12
    When I was forst from Stella ever deere, ... 222 Astrophil   87   1
    From my deare Captainnesse to run away?. . . . . 223 Astrophil   88   2
    Deere, therefore be not jealous over me, ... 225 Astrophil   91   12
    I cry thy sighs; my deere, thy teares I bleede.. . . . . . 227 Astrophil   93   14
    Yet sighs, deere sighs, indeede true friends you are,. . . 228 Astrophil   95   1
    "No, no, no, no, my Deare, let be.". . . . . 210 A&S 4th Song   6
    Above line repeated at following locations . . . . 210 A&S 4th Song   12
        . . . . 210 A&S 4th Song   18
        . . . . 211 A&S 4th Song   24
        . . . . 211 A&S 4th Song   30
        . . . . 211 A&S 4th Song   36
        . . . . 211 A&S 4th Song   42
        . . . . 211 A&S 4th Song   48
        . . . . 211 A&S 4th Song   54
    O deare life, when shall it be,. . . . . 225 A&S 10th Song   1
    Deere when you find change in me,. . . . . 234 A&S 11th Song   8
    Deere, do reason no such spite,. . . . . 234 A&S 11th Song   28

```
DEAR                      (CONTINUED)                    PAGE    TITLE          LINE
    Which the deere tongue would afford, . . . . . . . . . . . .  218  A&S 8th Song      22
    "Graunt, o deere, on knees I pray, . . . . . . . . . . . . .  219  A&S 8th Song      49
    Half so deere as you to me, . . . . . . . . . . . . . . . .   220  A&S 8th Song      82
    "Therefore, Deere, this no more move, . . . . . . . . . . .   220  A&S 8th Song      97
    Then adieu, deere flocke adieu: . . . . . . . . . . . . . .   222  A&S 9th Song      46
    My Deare God stay me.. . . . . . . . . . . . . . . . . . . .  276  Psalm VI          12
    Deare beloved Holy One, . . . . . . . . . . . . . . . . . .   288  Psalm XVI         35
    Assist us Saviour deare; . . . . . . . . . . . . . . . . . .  296  Psalm XX          33
    For thou Deare lord Thou me besetst, . . . . . . . . . . . .  301  Psalm XXIII       13
    But his deare favour where it lyes . . . . . . . . . . . . .  311  Psalm XXX         14
    In that deare lord with true delight, . . . . . . . . . . .   318  Psalm XXXIV        6
    Which wicked folks do hold so deare; . . . . . . . . . . . .  323  Psalm XXXVI        3
    Thy deare presence farr from me; . . . . . . . . . . . . . .  329  Psalm XXXVIII     63
    That I to Thee am deare, . . . . . . . . . . . . . . . . . .  333  Psalm XLI         38
    Sc brave a shott, deere fyre and bewtye strange. . . . . . .  345  Possibly      2   11
    But you, o you, that thinke not teares too deare . . . . . .  242  Other Poems   4    9
    With tedious brawlings of her parents deare, . . . . . . . .  245  Other Poems   4  114
    While deare Uran, whose course was Pas to meet, . . . . . .   250  Other Poems   4  330
    Till with long race deare she was breathles brought, . . . . 251  Other Poems   4  359
    And yet, deare soule, I know she hurteth none: . . . . . . . 254  Other Poems   4  458
    With in himselfe of hir deare selfe to speake, . . . . . . . 255  Other Poems   4  534
    Have cought of thy deare damme, . . . . . . . . . . . . . .   258  Other Poems   5   73
DEAREST
    With dearest tops of porphyrie.. . . . . . . . . . . . . . .   87  Arcadia III  62   57
    Better like I thy Satyre deerest Dyer, . . . . . . . . . . .  145  Cert Sonnets 16   13
DEARLY
    I set you ore the flock I dearly love, . . . . . . . . . . .   26  1st Eclogues 10    2
    Is Late remorse in follie dearely bought.. . . . . . . . . .   49  2nd Eclogues 28   78
    Dearely the servants doo their wages buy, . . . . . . . . .   105  3rd Eclogues 67   52
    Desire, desire I have too dearely bought, . . . . . . . . .   161  Cert Sonnets 31    5
    That she loveth me so dearely, . . . . . . . . . . . . . . .  222  A&S 9th Song      32
DEARTH
    With dearth of words, or answers quite awrie, . . . . . . .   178  Astrophil    27    3
    Nor want in dearth their want to ease. . . . . . . . . . . .  325  Psalm XXXVII      48
DEATH
    Seeke other thoughts thy life or death to find; . . . . . .     4  Lady of May   2   15
    Of fayrer death how can I make election? . . . . . . . . . .   16  1st Eclogues  7   72
    Nor helpe by life or death who living dyes.. . . . . . . . .   18  1st Eclogues  7  146
    With father's death, and mother's guiltie shame, . . . . . .   21  1st Eclogues  8   19
    And when that time is paste, death holdes his heeles.. . . .   28  1st Eclogues 10   51
    If the Swanne's sweet voice be not heard, but at death, . . .  30  1st Eclogues 12   14
    As that hatefull death can abridge them of powre, . . . . .    31  1st Eclogues 12   18
    To this strange death I vainely yeeld my life. . . . . . . .   38  Arcadia II   14   14
    Such life to leade, such death I vow to dye. . . . . . . . .   40  Arcadia II   18   18
    R. Whom Passion leades unto his death is bent. . . . . . . .   46  2nd Eclogues 27    9
    Paine willes me die, yet will of death I mortifie: . . . . .   51  2nd Eclogues 28  124
    That after death, to heav'n in woods' resound, . . . . . . .   56  2nd Eclogues 29  133
    Where death is feard, and life is held with paine. . . . . .   57  2nd Eclogues 30   19
    Plangus must live to see Eronae's death. . . . . . . . . . .   58  2nd Eclogues 30   55
    Hath she not force even death with love to kill? . . . . . .   59  2nd Eclogues 30   85
    Nay even cold Death enflamde with hot desire . . . . . . . .   59  2nd Eclogues 30   86
    Thus Death becomes a rivall to us all, . . . . . . . . . . .   59  2nd Eclogues 30   89
    O Vertue weake, shall death his triumph set. . . . . . . . .   59  2nd Eclogues 30   92
    Let Death first dye; be thou his worthy let. . . . . . . . .   59  2nd Eclogues 30   94
    As if by death she onely might be saved? . . . . . . . . . .   61  2nd Eclogues 30  160
    What medecin may I finde for a paine that draw's me to
        death  Death.. . . . . . . . . . . . . . . . . . . . . .   63  2nd Eclogues 31    6
    The life, the death of Hector, . . . . . . . . . . . . . . .   66  2nd Eclogues 32   23
    The love we holde is all death, . . . . . . . . . . . . . .    67  2nd Eclogues 32   53
    Nor ought I seeke to shun death, . . . . . . . . . . . . . .   67  2nd Eclogues 32   55
    My life my death do counte hers. . . . . . . . . . . . . . .   67  2nd Eclogues 32   57
    Come cave, become my grave, come death, and lende. . . . . .   73  Arcadia III  40    7
    Death wrapt in flesh, to living grave assign'd.. . . . . . .   73  Arcadia III  40   14
    Sicke to the death, still loving my disease. . . . . . . . .   74  Arcadia III  41    8
    Thou fearest death; thinke they are loth to die. . . . . . .  103  3rd Eclogues 66  151
    And thinking this, thinke Nature, Life, and Death. . . . . .  114  4th Eclogues 72   16
    And unto death, quite drownde in Dolours, brought. . . . . .  115  4th Eclogues 72   68
    To death, as then disguisde in her faire face. . . . . . . .  115  4th Eclogues 72   69
    That thus I must, while in this death I dwell, . . . . . . .  116  4th Eclogues 72   89
    Where life is death, and death cannot breed peace. . . . . .  116  4th Eclogues 72   95
    A dull desire to kisse the image of our death: . . . . . . .  117  4th Eclogues 73   10
    But finding th'approch of death with an inly relenting, . .   123  4th Eclogues 74   25
    Can death beautie become? must I be such a monument? . . . .  123  4th Eclogues 74   32
    Or with a fair hand's nailes (o hand which nailes me to this
        death). . . . . . . . . . . . . . . . . . . . . . . . .   123  4th Eclogues 74   55
    Since that to death is gone the shepheard hie, . . . . . . .  125  4th Eclogues 75    1
    But unto Man, age ever death doth sende. . . . . . . . . . .  127  4th Eclogues 75   84
    Since Death on Vertue's fort hath made invasion. . . . . . .  128  4th Eclogues 75  102
    Was this man's death the fruite of your dissention?. . . . .  128  4th Eclogues 75  108
    Approach of death, alas thou helpest meagerly, . . . . . . .  128  4th Eclogues 75  110
    They leave off al, and say, death comes too eagerlie.. . . .  128  4th Eclogues 75  114
    Death is our home, life is but a delusion. . . . . . . . . .  128  4th Eclogues 75  123
    His death our death. But ah; my Muse hath swarved, . . . . .  129  4th Eclogues 75  136
    Cease Muse therfore: thy dart o Death applie; . . . . . . .   129  4th Eclogues 75  141
    Now death hath swallow'd up our worldly pleasure, . . . . .   129  4th Eclogues 76   11
    And unto death bend still our thoughts' direction. . . . . .  130  4th Eclogues 76   34
    Since nature's workes be good, and death doth serve. . . . .  131  Arcadia V    77    1
    For hers am I, and death feares her displeasure. . . . . . .  137  Cert Sonnets  3   22
    Fie death, thou art beguiled, . . . . . . . . . . . . . . .   137  Cert Sonnets  3   23
```

DEATH   (CONTINUED)   PAGE   TITLE   LINE
    For no dumbnesse nor death bringeth. . . . .   140 Cert Sonnets 7   38
    To paint my living death, and endlesse smart:. . . . . . .   146 Cert Sonnets 17   28
    Now dead, doth shew departure is a death. . . . . 148 Cert Sonnets 20   12
    Yea worse then death, death parts both woe and joy,. . . . . 148 Cert Sonnets 20   13
    Which rotting on the rockes, their death do dye: . . . . . . 151 Cert Sonnets 22   52
    But of his death flies up a purest love, ... 151 Cert Sonnets 22   59
    Thus is his death rewarded,. . . . . 152 Cert Sonnets 23   15
    Since she lives in his death. . . . .   152 Cert Sonnets 23   16
    Where by the death of all deaths,. . . . . 154 Cert Sonnets 25   13
    Yet, yet, a life to their death, ... 154 Cert Sonnets 25   18
    Faire death feeleth, ... 156 Cert Sonnets 26   28
    And in whome faire death proceedeth, ... 156 Cert Sonnets 26   29
    In this small course which birth drawes out to death,. . . . 144 Cert Sonnets 32   10
    Flie, fly, my friends, I have my death wound; fly, ... 174 Astrophil   20   1
    Oppressing mortall sense, my death proceed,. . . . . 186 Astrophil   42   13
    While those poore babes their death in birth do find:. . . . 190 Astrophil   50   11
    The prettie death, while each in other live. . . . . 206 Astrophil   79   11
    His who till death lookt in a watrie glasse, ... 207 Astrophil   82   3
    Though harbengers of death lodge there his traine. . . . . . 228 Astrophil   94   8
    As his light was her eyes, her death his endlesse night: . . 209 A&S 3rd Song   10
    Scone with my death I will please thee. . . . .   211 A&S 4th Song   53
    And even while I do speake, my death wounds bleeding be: . .   214 A&S 5th Song   52
    Thy griefe more then death would grieve me. . . . .   220 A&S 8th Song   76
    All her hate, death soone would seaze me,. . . . . 222 A&S 9th Song   44
    For death doth kill the witness of thy glory;. . . . . 276 Psalm VI   14
    Thou lord that from Death' gates hast lifted me, ... 280 Psalm IX   39
    Who for my Death still me enclose. . . . . 290 Psalm XVII   28
    On me the paines of death already gan to prey, ... 291 Psalm XVIII   8
    Whom Death to his cold bosom drawes. . . . . 311 Psalm XXX   9
    Like one that should his Mother's death lament. . . . . . .   322 Psalm XXXV   36
    When, when will death o'retake this wretched wight . . . . . 333 Psalm XLI   19
    D. Teares drink, sorowes meat, wherewith, not I, but in me
       my death lives. . . . . 344 Possibly   1   34
    Wounded, inflam'de, knitt to the deathe I dye. . . . . 344 Possibly   2   4
    That did his death, hir death afford. . . . .   241 Other Poems   3   6
    Wayling till death, shun you not to be seene?. . . . . 258 Other Poems   5   91
    "Absence is death, or worse, to them that love." . . . . . . 259 Other Poems   5   94
    He envied such a death in sight of lover,. . . . . 259 Other Poems   5   124
DEATH-BED
    His death-bed peacock's follie,. . . . . 160 Cert Sonnets 30   13
DEATHFUL
    I, wretch, astonisht was, and thought the deathfull doome. . 118 4th Eclogues 73   61
DEATH'S
    Thinke, my harde haps have blunted death's sharpe knife, . . 113 4th Eclogues 72   14
    Must finish then by death's detested crime. . . . .   127 4th Eclogues 75   90
    This song from deathe's sorrow springeth:. . . . . 140 Cert Sonnets 7   36
    The scourge of life, and death's extreame disgrace,. . . . . 140 Cert Sonnets 8   1
    Weakely did seeme to paint death's ougly dart. . . . . 148 Cert Sonnets 20   4
    Of deathe's power, ... 155 Cert Sonnets 26   19
    Those lips, which make death's pay a meane price for a
       kisse . . . . 205 Astrophil   77   6
    Unto the dust of my death's running hower; . . . . 299 Psalm XXII   38
    Of death's dark shade I will . . . . 301 Psalm XXIII   11
DEATHS
    With all our deathes shew we this damage publique. . . . . . 110 Arcadia IV   70   38
    Where by the death of all deaths,. . . . . 154 Cert Sonnets 25   13
    Of living deaths, deare wounds, faire stormes and freesing
       fires: . . . . 167 Astrophil   6   4
    To honor all their deaths, who for her bleed. . . . .   168 Astrophil   7   14
DEATH-WOUND
    Yet since my death-wound is already got, ... 189 Astrophil   48   12
DEBAR
    Whom both nature seemes to debarr from meanes to be helped,.   37 1st Eclogues 13   158
DEBARRED
    Nor debard from beautie's treasure,. . . . . 226 A&S 10th Song   9
DEBATE
    Gainst neighbors good for womanish debate. . . . .   93 3rd Eclogues 63   70
    And smirkly thus gan say. "I never sought debate . . . . . . 120 4th Eclogues 73   147
    An Asse's shade ere now hath bred debate. . . . .   146 Cert Sonnets 17   20
DEBILITY
    And in thy case do glasse mine owne debilitie: . . . .   60 2nd Eclogues 30   129
DEBT
    No further debt on me is laid, ... 159 Cert Sonnets 29   2
DECAY
    In whose decay Vertue's faire shrine must fall. . . . . . .   59 2nd Eclogues 30   91
    I, seeing better sights in sight's decay,. . . . . 184 Astrophil   38   12
    Abandond me, yet my decay. . . . . 308 Psalm XXVII   50
    Who make a Cause to joy of my decay; . . . . 323 Psalm XXXV   64
    Yea thou shalt see the ev'ill decay. . . . . 327 Psalm XXXVII   88
DECAYED
    Since outward pleasures be but halting helpes to decayd
       soules). . . . .   33 1st Eclogues 13   52
    To sing my owne decaid state. . . . .   65 2nd Eclogues 32   4
    With age's force decay'd, yet once the heaven was his. . . . 120 4th Eclogues 73   124
    Nay even the race of good men are decay'd. . . . . 284 Psalm XII   3
DECAYING
    Her poore slave's unjust decaying. . . . . 222 A&S 9th Song   50
DECEASED
    A stately tombe to cover him deceased. . . . . 126 4th Eclogues 75   59

```
DECEASED              (CONTINUED)                          PAGE    TITLE           LINE
    You that poore Petrarch's long deceased woes, . . . . . . . .  172 Astrophil    15    7
DECEIT
    Till wrong, contempt, deceipt, did growe, steale, creepe,. .   84 Arcadia III  60    7
    His words deceit, iniquity . . . . . . . . . . . . . . . . .  323 Psalm XXXVI        9
    Speaking ev'ill, thinking deceit. . . . . . . . .            328 Psalm XXXVIII      36
DECEITFUL
    Crying in me: eye hopes deceitefull prove. . . . . . . . . .   83 Arcadia III  57   13
    Who with deceitfull tongue hath never usd to faine,. . . . .  287 Psalm XV           5
DECEITS
    Which breeds nought else but gloses of deceits. . . . . . . .  20 1st Eclogues  8    4
DECEIVE
    Cloth'd in the shape which soonest may deceave:. . . . . . .   21 1st Eclogues  8   32
    In perfect light, which could not me deceave, . . . . . . .   55 2nd Eclogues 29  100
    Of our selfe-love (so passions do deceave) . . . . . . . .    59 2nd Eclogues 30   69
    Who never doth deceive, and much lesse his deceaving . . . .  302 Psalm XXIV        11
    To Vanitys, which most trust most deceave, . . . . . . . .   312 Psalm XXXI        17
DECEIVED
    (Therion) When wanton Pan, deceiv'd with Lion's skin,. . . .    5 Lady of May   3    7
    As for your doubts; her voice was it deceaved me,. . . . . .   48 2nd Eclogues 28   29
    Deceiv'd the quaking boy, who thought from so pure light,. .  169 Astrophil     8   10
    He thrise reacht, thrise deceiv'd when hir to beare. . . . .  250 Other Poems   4  340
DECEIVING
    Who never doth deceive, and much lesse his deceaving . . . .  302 Psalm XXIV        11
DECIPHER
    But sometimes to the woods, sometimes to the heavens do
        decyphire, . . . . . . . . . . . . . . . . . . . . . .    35 1st Eclogues 13  111
DECK
    To liken her? Decke yours with your comparison:. . . . . . .   15 1st Eclogues  7   47
    But deck therewith my soule for your sake dying. . . . . . .   17 1st Eclogues  7   90
    Let others deck their pride with skarres. . . . . . . . . .    44 Arcadia II   25    7
    To decke the earth with his well-coloured weede, . . . . . .   78 Arcadia III  50    2
    Let mother earth now decke her selfe in flowers, . . . . . .   91 3rd Eclogues 63    1
    Then decke me as thine owne; thy helpe I borowe, . . . . . .  114 4th Eclogues 72   28
    Decke that poore place with Alablaster linde. . . . . . . .   150 Cert Sonnets 22   34
    Which made hir yeeld to deck this shepheards' band,. . . . .  247 Other Poems   4  215
    Yearely decke thine Altar shall: . . . . . . . . . . . . .    264 Other Poems   7   70
DECKED
    He proules ech place stil in new colours deckt,. . . . . . .   21 1st Eclogues  8   35
    Thou God, whose youth was deckt with spoyle of Python's
        skin . . . . . . . . . . . . . . . . . . . . . . . . .    44 Arcadia II   26    5
    The earth is deckt with flowers, the heav'ns displaid, . . .   93 3rd Eclogues 63   91
    With length laid downe she deckt the lonely place. . . . . .  244 Other Poems   4  107
    Deckt with pyde flowers sweetely smelling. . . . . . . . . .  262 Other Poems   7    6
DECKS
    To helpe her praise, who decks me in her slaverie. . . . . .   48 2nd Eclogues 28   27
    For such company decks such solitarines. . . . . . . . . . .   69 2nd Eclogues 34   42
    Who womankind at once both deckes and stayneth?. . . . . . .  197 A&S 1st Song      10
DECLARATION
    Which thought doth marre my piping declaration, . . . . . .    19 1st Eclogues  7  168
    O well thou saiest! a feeling declaration. . . . . . . . . .   20 1st Eclogues  7 V968
    Thou knowst made declaration, . . . . . . . . . . . . . . .   331 Psalm XL          36
DECLARE
    Come Espilus, come now declare thy skill, . . . . . . . . .     3 Lady of May   2    1
    While Plangus dyd a storie strainge declare. . . . . . . . .   62 2nd Eclogues 30  189
    That to the duke, he would his sinne declare, . . . . . . .    97 3rd Eclogues 64  116
    To Brethren then I will declare Thy Fame, . . . . . . . . .   299 Psalm XXII        51
DECLARED
    In deadly dust declared be?. . . . . . . . . . . . . . . . .  311 Psalm XXX         30
DECLINE
    If now the May of my yeares much decline, . . . . . . . . .   175 Astrophil    21   10
    Which would not let me, whom she loved, decline. . . . . . .  196 Astrophil    62    7
    Do good, from faults decline, . . . . . . . . . . . . . . .   320 Psalm XXXIV       53
DECREASE
    Which never may decrease . . . . . . . . . . . . . . . . . .   91 3rd Eclogues 63    5
DECREE
    How can you him unworthy then decree, . . . . . . . . . . .    39 Arcadia II   16    9
    And I will (sayeth His King) the lord's decree display,. . .  271 Psalm II          15
DECREED
    To all what I decreed, did thus my verdict saye. . . . . . .  121 4th Eclogues 73  162
    I loved, but straight did not what Love decreed: . . . . . .  165 Astrophil     2    6
DECREES
    At length to Love's decrees, I forc'd, agreed, . . . . . . .  165 Astrophil     2    7
DEED
    Here Laelaps, here, in deed against the foen . . . . . . . .   27 1st Eclogues 10   13
    What Love and Beautie be, then all my deed . . . . . . . . .  166 Astrophil     3   13
    Well staid with truth in word and faith of deed, . . . . . .  172 Astrophil    14   10
    I cannot brag of word, much lesse of deed, . . . . . . . . .  199 Astrophil    66    5
    Nor blam'd for bloud, nor sham'd for sinfull deed. . . . . .  209 Astrophil    84   11
    Ever from deed of any such desart: . . . . . . . . . . . . .  277 Psalm VII          8
    Nor neighbour hurts by deed, nor doth with slaunder stain. .  287 Psalm XV           6
DEEDS
    My beautie's hewe your beames, my health your deeds; . . . .   18 1st Eclogues  7  136
    If thou doo not repay his deeds for thee, . . . . . . . . .   105 3rd Eclogues 67   74
    A rightfull Prince by unright deeds a Tyran groweth. . . . .  214 A&S 5th Song      60
    Whose deeds of Righteous heart, whose hearty words be plain, 287 Psalm XV           4
    As their deeds have purchas'd it, . . . . . . . . . . . . .   309 Psalm XXVIII      17
    And to the proud in deeds pays home their own. . . . . . . .  314 Psalm XXXI        66
    And his deeds faithfull bee. . . . . . . . . . . . . . . . .  316 Psalm XXXIII      18
    So my good deeds they pay with this ev'ill share, . . . . .   322 Psalm XXXV        27
```

```
DEEDS                        (CONTINUED)        PAGE    TITLE               LINE
    His deeds, yea thoughtes all good forgett; . . . . . . . . .   323 Psalm XXXVI          10
    Though ill deeds well succeeding be. . . . . . . . . . . . .   324 Psalm XXXVII          4
    And sought with deeds Thy will to hitt;. . . . . . . . . . .   331 Psalm XL             33
DEEM
    Showes, guilty harte doth deeme his state opprobrious. . . .    48 2nd Eclogues 28      18
    We pittie deeme that which but weakenes is:. . . . . . . . .    62 2nd Eclogues 30     180
    Deeme it no gloire to swell in tyrannie. . . . . . . . . . .   103 3rd Eclogues 66     149
    Deeme that my Muse some fruit of knowledge plies:. . . . . .   176 Astrophil     23      6
    They deeme, and of their doome the rumour flies, . . . . . .   178 Astrophil     27      5
    Princes in subjects wrongd, must deeme themselves abused.. .   213 A&S 5th Song         30
    And deigne to deeme your neighbors' mischefe neare,. . . . .   242 Other Poems    4     11
DEEMED
    And never hathe therof arightelye deemde . . . . . . . . . .    26 1st Eclogues  9     139
    I deemd it best some absence for to prove, . . . . . . . . .   149 Cert Sonnets 21      3
    Now thy sweetnesse sowre is deemed,. . . . . . . . . . . . .   156 Cert Sonnets 27      9
    Is constant Love deem'd there but want of wit? . . . . . . .   180 Astrophil     31     10
DEEMETH
    And yet neither of us great or blest deemeth his owne selfe.   33 1st Eclogues 13      73
DEEMING
    Deeming strange evill in that he did not know. . . . . . . .   145 Cert Sonnets 16      4
DEEP
    Shallow brookes murmure most, deep silent slide away;. . . .    14 1st Eclogues  7     11
    Thy toong hath made of Cupid's deepe incision. . . . . . . .    20 1st Eclogues  7   V969
    Deepe musing to himselfe, which after-mewing showes, . . . .    53 2nd Eclogues 29     35
    Thus honour, liking, trust, much, farre, and deepe,. . . . .    84 Arcadia III  60      5
    Which now in night's deepe shade sheep heard of me.. . . . .    99 3rd Eclogues 66     42
    Envying shallow toyes with malice deepe. . . . . . . . . . .   104 3rd Eclogues 67     39
    I long doo plowe with plough of deepe Desire:. . . . . . . .   115 4th Eclogues 72     52
    From such deepe plaint as should such woes descrie,. . . . .   129 4th Eclogues 75    137
    From deepe vaine thought that I may not be true. . . . . . .   145 Cert Sonnets 17      5
    Deepe plunged in earth, deprived of skie.. . . . . . . . . .   149 Cert Sonnets 21      8
    Deepe in the earth, what hath in earth receipt . . . . . . .   150 Cert Sonnets 22     42
    So deepe in seas of vertue beauties ly.. . . . . . . . . . .   151 Cert Sonnets 22     58
    With plague of deepe disdaine: . . . . . . . . . . . . . . .   159 Cert Sonnets 30      4
    Dig deepe with learning's spade, now tell me this, . . . . .   175 Astrophil     21     13
    I list not dig so deepe for brasen fame. . . . . . . . . . .   179 Astrophil     28      4
    Trebles sing high, as well as bases deepe: . . . . . . . . .   201 Astrophil     70      6
    Which too deep in me is framed,. . . . . . . . . . . . . . .   220 A&S 8th Song         99
    Hasten to help me, in this deep discomfort.. . . . . . . . .   299 Psalm XXII           46
    One deep with noyse of his fall. . . . . . . . . . . . . . .   335 Psalm XLII           29
    W. What seale? D. My hart deepe graven. W. Who made the band
        so fast?. . . . . . . . . . . . . . . . . . . . . . . .   343 Possibly      1      27
DEEPER
    No smaller wound, alas! farr deeper have.. . . . . . . . . .    77 Arcadia III  47      4
    Deeper engrav'd, which salve nor time can save,. . . . . . .    77 Arcadia III  47      5
    Deeper still they drive the stake. . . . . . . . . . . . . .   234 A&S 11th Song        35
DEEPLY
    The more his matchlesse giftes do deepely sinck. . . . . . .    85 Arcadia III  61     11
    But, ah! hir darts did farre more depely goe . . . . . . . .   251 Other Poems    4    352
DEEPS
    Other deeps of Woes doth call, . . . . . . . . . . . . . . .   335 Psalm XLII           30
DEER
    Two thousand deere in wildest woods I have,. . . . . . . . .     4 Lady of May    2     25
DEFACE
    Which Passions kill, and Reason do deface. . . . . . . . . .    47 2nd Eclogues 27     42
    Nico. Nothing (O Leuca) shall thy fame deface, . . . . . . .    56 2nd Eclogues 29    123
DEFACED
    For he woulde sing, but others were defaste; . . . . . . . .    28 1st Eclogues 10     76
    But loe, my words defaste, my fancies blinde,. . . . . . . .    40 Arcadia II   19      3
    By what eclipse shall that Sonne be defaste? . . . . . . . .    59 2nd Eclogues 30     95
    She doth possesse, thy Image is defaste, . . . . . . . . . .    72 Arcadia III  38     12
    Our names are quite forgot, our temples are defac'd: . . . .   119 4th Eclogues 73    109
    O wretch, what do I say? should that faire face be defaced?.   124 4th Eclogues 74     57
    Be both wish and I defaced.. . . . . . . . . . . . . . . . .   220 A&S 8th Song         88
DEFACES
    We Nature's workes doo helpe, she us defaces.. . . . . . . .   127 4th Eclogues 75     93
    Where ys Ah that face, that a Sunne defaces? . . . . . . . .   138 Cert Sonnets  5      9
DEFAULT
    Nous sware it was no right; for his default. . . . . . . . .   250 Other Poems    4    314
DEFEND
    Them to defend, not with your selves to fight. . . . . . . .    26 1st Eclogues 10      3
    My wit doth strive those passions to defend, . . . . . . . .   174 Astrophil     18     10
    Thou lord also th' Oppressed wilt defend . . . . . . . . . .   280 Psalm IX             26
    For I know thou wilt defend. . . . . . . . . . . . . . . . .   288 Psalm XVI            33
    Defend Thee still from all Thy foes abroad.. . . . . . . . .   295 Psalm XX              5
DEFENDETH
    He is he that defendeth; . . . . . . . . . . . . . . . . . .   273 Psalm III            33
DEFENSE
    Rather to wrong then unto just defence,. . . . . . . . . . .    25 1st Eclogues  9     106
    Theere seeke defence where weakenesse is the force:. . . . .    49 2nd Eclogues 28     77
    But this at last is her sweet breath'd defence:. . . . . . .   195 Astrophil     61      4
    Where you may have some defence. . . . . . . . . . . . . . .   221 A&S 9th Song          3
    My strength my strongest rock, which my defence hast borne,.   290 Psalm XVIII           2
    Defence herein doth wrong, O yeelde O yeelde,. . . . . . . .   345 Possibly      4      12
DEFENSES
    Our best defenses are to flie these adders.. . . . . . . . .    50 2nd Eclogues 28     89
    To hurt himselfe, what shields can be defenses?. . . . . . .    62 2nd Eclogues 30    169
    Her strong darts, but weake defences.. . . . . . . . . . . .   226 A&S 10th Song        36
```

```
DEFIANCE                                                         PAGE    TITLE           LINE
  Revenge, revenge, my Muse, Defiance' trumpet blow: . . . . .   213  A&S 5th Song         32
DEFILE
  I sooner would, then thus my eares defile. . . . . . . . . .    50  2nd Eclogues 28      81
  Bandes, favour, faith, to breake, defile, and kill.. . . . .    84  Arcadia III  60       8
  Which heav'nly purest gifts defile in muddy cares. . . . . .   117  4th Eclogues 73      18
  Least inward evills do them defile,. . . . . . . . . . . . .   320  Psalm XXXIV          50
DEFILED
  I soner would, then have my eares defylde. . . . . . . . . .    50  2nd Eclogues 28 V    81
DEFINE
  That doost so well their miseries define?. . . . . . . . . .    59  2nd Eclogues 30      79
DEFINING
  Who tempt, and tempted plague, are Devils in true defining..   215  A&S 5th Song         84
DEFY
  Therfore he doth defy all those. . . . . . . . . . . . . . .   282  Psalm X              21
DEGREE
  Slow heavinesse in both holds one degree,. . . . . . . . . .   229  Astrophil    96       6
  A maid train'd up from high or low degree, . . . . . . . . .   247  Other Poems   4     210
  For they were ever in the best degree, . . . . . . . . . . .   252  Other Poems   4     394
  In poore shepheard's base degree?. . . . . . . . . . . . . .   262  Other Poems   7      26
DEGREES
  Till by degrees it had full conquest got.. . . . . . . . . .   165  Astrophil     2       4
DEI
  Dan dan dan deridan deridan dei: . . . . . . . . . . . . . .   156  Cert Sonnets 27       6
  Above line repeated at following locations . . . . . . . . .   156  Cert Sonnets 27      14
     . . . . . . . . . . . . . . . . . . . . . . . . . . . . .   157  Cert Sonnets 27      22
     . . . . . . . . . . . . . . . . . . . . . . . . . . . . .   157  Cert Sonnets 27      30
     . . . . . . . . . . . . . . . . . . . . . . . . . . . . .   157  Cert Sonnets 27      38
DEIGN
  As thou wilt deigne to reade, and gentlie reede, . . . . . .    96  3rd Eclogues 64      95
  Let that King deign to heare,. . . . . . . . . . . . . . . .   296  Psalm XX             34
  When Thou wilt deign to heare him. . . . . . . . . . . . . .   315  Psalm XXXII          21
  And deigne to deeme your neighbors' mischefe neare,. . . . .   242  Other Poems   4      11
DEIGNED
  It August was, he daynde not then to sing. . . . . . . . . .    99  3rd Eclogues 66      14
  If her lips daignd to sweeten my poore name. . . . . . . . .   225  Astrophil    92      13
DEIGNS
  That he deigns to express. . . . . . . . . . . . . . . . . .   303  Psalm XXV            33
DEITIES
  That they by solemne oth their Deities would binde . . . . .   121  4th Eclogues 73     156
DEITY
  That shrines in flesh so true a Deitie,. . . . . . . . . . .   167  Astrophil     4      13
DEJECTED
  Should breed to her, let me for aye dejected be. . . . . . .    51  2nd Eclogues 28     121
  Transforme themselves to lowe dejected vallies:. . . . . . .   112  4th Eclogues 71      38
DELAY
  O Stealing time the subject of delaie, . . . . . . . . . . .    80  Arcadia III  53       1
  (Delay, the racke of unrefrain'd desire) . . . . . . . . . .    80  Arcadia III  53       2
  Geron. In faith, good Histor, long is your delay,. . . . . .   103  3rd Eclogues 67       1
  Alas, how long, my God, wilt Thou delay me?. . . . . . . . .   276  Psalm VI             10
DELICIOUS
  To witnes, that he thinkes his thoughts delicious, . . . . .    47  2nd Eclogues 28       5
DELIGHT
  Your face hurts oft, but still it doth delight,. . . . . . .     3  Lady of May   1       8
  Which both the pallate, and the eyes delight.. . . . . . . .    26  1st Eclogues  9     131
  His youth delight, his age the soule's oppression: . . . . .    48  2nd Eclogues 28      39
  O sweet woods the delight of solitarines!. . . . . . . . . .    68  2nd Eclogues 34       1
  O sweete woods the delight of solitarines! . . . . . . . . .    69  2nd Eclogues 34      15
  Above line repeated at following location. . . . . . . . . .    69  2nd Eclogues 34      29
  Bewaile the case, and in the cause delight?. . . . . . . . .    74  Arcadia III  42       4
  But wilt thy selfe in such a seate delighte, . . . . . . . .    79  Arcadia III  51      11
  My harte, eyes, eares, with wonder, love, delight: . . . . .    84  Arcadia III  60       2
  Despise delight, am tyrde with thought of ease;. . . . . . .   113  4th Eclogues 72       2
  Gives an adieu to the world, as to his onely delight:. . . .   123  4th Eclogues 74      26
  Farewell, long farewell, all my woe, all my delight. . . . .   124  4th Eclogues 74      86
  They sun-like should more dazle then delight?. . . . . . . .   168  Astrophil     7       8
  No force, no fraud, robd thee of thy delight,. . . . . . . .   181  Astrophil    33       7
  Where Love is chastnesse, Paine doth learne delight, . . . .   188  Astrophil    48       3
  That in the Manage myselfe takes delight.. . . . . . . . . .   189  Astrophil    49      14
  In thy cold stuffe a flegmatike delight? . . . . . . . . . .   193  Astrophil    56      11
  Which wooed wo, most ravishing delight . . . . . . . . . . .   194  Astrophil    58      13
  Alas, if you graunt only such delight. . . . . . . . . . . .   194  Astrophil    59      12
  World of my wealth, and heav'n of my delight.. . . . . . . .   200  Astrophil    68       4
  What Oceans of delight in me do flow.. . . . . . . . . . . .   200  Astrophil    69       4
  Come then my Muse, shew thou height of delight . . . . . . .   201  Astrophil    70       9
  Service and Honor, wonder with delight,. . . . . . . . . . .   202  Astrophil    72       9
  Those lookes, whose beames be joy, whose motion is delight,.   205  Astrophil    77       1
  Neast of young joyes, schoolmaster of delight, . . . . . . .   206  Astrophil    79       8
  And I, mad with delight, want wit to cease, . . . . . . . . .  207  Astrophil    81      13
  And I do sweare even by the same delight,. . . . . . . . . .   208  Astrophil    82      13
  Delight protests he is not for the accurst,. . . . . . . . .   228  Astrophil    95       7
  Viewing the shape of darknesse and delight,. . . . . . . . .   230  Astrophil    99       6
  To write therein more fresh the story of delight,. . . . . .   232  Astrophil   102      13
  But soone as thought of thee breeds my delight,. . . . . . .   236  Astrophil   108       5
  If Eagle fierce could so in Grecian Mayd delight,. . . . . .   209  A&S 3rd Song          9
  While favour fed my hope, delight with hope was brought,. . .  212  A&S 5th Song          1
  Thought waited on delight, and speech did follow thought:. .   212  A&S 5th Song          2
  But now that hope is lost, unkindnesse kils delight, . . . .   212  A&S 5th Song         13
  Is only true delight. . . . . . . . . . . . . . . . . . . .    215  A&S 6th Song         12
  That ravishing delight in them most sweete tunes do not
     raise; . . . . . . . . . . . . . . . . . . . . . . . . .    217  A&S 7th Song          2
```

```
DELIGHT                    (CONTINUED)             PAGE   TITLE            LINE
    Or if they do delight therein, yet are so cloyed with wit, .   217  A&S 7th Song         3
    But on god's law his heart's delight doth bind,. . . . . . .   270  Psalm I              5
    Where I have found more heart's delight. . . . . . . . . . .   274  Psalm IV            28
    For Thou art that same God, far from delight . . . . . . . .   274  Psalm V              9
    All the fulness of delight,. . . . . . . . . . . . . . . . .   289  Psalm XVI           41
    Thee will I love, O Lord, with all my heart's delight, . . .   290  Psalm XVIII          1
    Lord what delight to him doth bring. . . . . . . . . . . . .   296  Psalm XXI            3
    And so shall in Our songs' delight,. . . . . . . . . . . . .   298  Psalm XXI           51
    In that deare lord with true delight,. . . . . . . . . . . .   318  Psalm XXXIV          6
    With scoffers false I was their feast's delight, . . . . . .   322  Psalm XXXV          41
    Delight in God and he shall breed. . . . . . . . . . . . . .   324  Psalm XXXVII         9
    And this delight to them is granted, . . . . . . . . . . . .   325  Psalm XXXVII        31
    To long-perplexed minde breed long delight.. . . . . . . . .   245  Other Poems    4   112
    Thinking it just more therein to delight . . . . . . . . . .   246  Other Poems    4   178
    Among the rest that there did take delight . . . . . . . . .   251  Other Poems    4   361
    "But you my pipe, whilome my chief delight,. . . . . . . . .   254  Other Poems    4   481
    Till straunge delight, delight to nothing ware;. . . . . . .   254  Other Poems    4   482
    Only two do me delight . . . . . . . . . . . . . . . . . . .   263  Other Poems    7    63
DELIGHTED
    Klaius. I that was once delighted every morning, . . . . . .   111  4th Eclogues 71     19
    For neither shall the men in sin delighted . . . . . . . . .   270  Psalm I             15
    Strephon, fond boy, delighted did not knowe, . . . . . . . .   246  Other Poems    4   163
DELIGETFUL
    In which delightfull paine,. . . . . . . . . . . . . . . . .    91  3rd Eclogues 63     17
DELIGHTFULNESS
    Barr'd from their chiefest object of delightfulnesse,. . . .    51  2nd Eclogues 28    109
    Doth force us there to set our chiefe delightfulnes, . . . .    61  2nd Eclogues 30    135
DELIGHTS
    That the delights of life shall be to him dolorouse". . . . .   29  1st Eclogues 11     10
    In thies delights the wandring thought . . . . . . . . . . .    88  Arcadia III 62      71
    Where bee those movinges, the Delights, the graces?. . . . .   138  Cert Sonnets  5     11
    With choise delights and rarest company, . . . . . . . . . .   230  Astrophil     97    10
    Thy delights my woes increase,. . . . . . . . . . . . . . .    227  A&S 10th Song       44
    Then since my tongue delights that name to blesse, . . . . .   312  Psalm XXXI           8
    Then those delights through all their sinews breed . . . . .   252  Other Poems    4   411
DELIVER
    Good Lord deliver us.. . . . . . . . . . . . . . . . . . . .   160  Cert Sonnets 30     10
    Above line repeated at following locations . . . . . . . . .   160  Cert Sonnets 30     20
    . . . . . . . . . . . . . . . . . . . . . . . . . . . . . .   160  Cert Sonnets 30     30
    . . . . . . . . . . . . . . . . . . . . . . . . . . . . . .   161  Cert Sonnets 30     40
    Deliver me in my endangerd way . . . . . . . . . . . . . . .   277  Psalm VII            3
    In fine deliver Israel,. . . . . . . . . . . . . . . . . . .   305  Psalm XXV           77
    Deliver me, Deliver me in speed, . . . . . . . . . . . . . .   312  Psalm XXXI           5
    That dost deliver me,. . . . . . . . . . . . . . . . . . . .   332  Psalm XL            69
    For God shall him deliver in the time. . . . . . . . . . . .   332  Psalm XLI            3
DELIVERANCE
    Than true deliverance gain.. . . . . . . . . . . . . . . . .   318  Psalm XXXIII        66
DELIVERED
    They trusted and by Thee deliverd were... . . . . . . . . .    298  Psalm XXII          12
DELL
    So laughing all, yet Pas to ease some dell,. . . . . . . . .   249  Other Poems    4   263
DELUSION
    Death is our home, life is but a delusion. . . . . . . . . .   128  4th Eclogues 75    123
DELUSIONS
    Which who doth misse his eyes are but delusions, . . . . . .    51  2nd Eclogues 28    108
DEMAND
    Of her I will demaund helpe".. . . . . . . . . . . . . . . .    67  2nd Eclogues 32     49
    He did demaunde what remedy to finde;. . . . . . . . . . . .    95  3rd Eclogues 64     52
    When I demaund of Phenix Stella's state, . . . . . . . . . .   225  Astrophil     92     6
DEMANDS
    What be the sweet creatures wher lowly demaunds be not
        heard  Hard. . . . . . . . . . . . . . . . . . . . . .     65  2nd Eclogues 31     41
DEMEAN
    Our owne demeane, and soone we wondre shall. . . . . . . . .    29  1st Eclogues 10     92
DEMUR
    Well Love, since this demurre our sute doth stay,. . . . . .   191  Astrophil     52    12
DEN
    Like lurking lion in his denn. . . . . . . . . . . . . . . .   282  Psalm X             37
    Now like his Whelp in den that lurking stayes. . . . . . . .   290  Psalm XVII          34
DENIED
    And all I said so well, as no man it denied. . . . . . . . .   212  A&S 5th Song        12
    While such wise she love denied, . . . . . . . . . . . . . .   220  A&S 8th Song        71
DENIES
    Lalus. But if my Kala this my suite denies,. . . . . . . . .    18  1st Eclogues  7    147
    I crav'd the thing which ever she denies:. . . . . . . . . .   196  Astrophil     63     6
    Which even to sence, sence of it selfe denies, . . . . . . .   228  Astrophil     94     7
DENIZENED
    With new-borne sighes and denisend wit do sing;. . . . . . .   172  Astrophil     15     8
DENY
    The weeping Myrrhe I thinke will not denie . . . . . . . . .   125  4th Eclogues 75     13
    Do Stella love. Fooles, who doth it deny?. . . . . . . . . .   233  Astrophil    104     14
    "Trust me while I thee deny, . . . . . . . . . . . . . . . .   220  A&S 8th Song        93
DENYING
    Not sturring thoughts, nor yet denying right, . . . . . . .     98  3rd Eclogues 65      6
    That I, without thy denying, . . . . . . . . . . . . . . . .   263  Other Poems    7    59
DEPART
    But yet o dreame, if thou wilt not departe . . . . . . . . .    79  Arcadia III 51       9
    Three dayes before that he must sure depart, . . . . . . . .    96  3rd Eclogues 64     79
    With Sunne's depart: and now the darkenes of the night . . .   116  4th Eclogues 73      2
```

```
DEPART                    (CONTINUED)                        PAGE    TITLE           LINE
     If from my soule this love would once depart,. . . . . . . .  148  Cert Sonnets 19    9
     Why those that die, men say they do depart:. . . . . . . . .  148  Cert Sonnets 20    2
     Depart, a word so gentle to my minde,. . . . . . . . . . . .  148  Cert Sonnets 20    3
     By iron lawes of duty to depart: . . . . . . . . . . . . . .  222  Astrophil    87    4
     That from Thy truth will not depart. . . . . . . . . . . .   305  Psalm XXVI        12
DEPARTED
     He stayd untill the goodman was departed,. . . . . . . . . .   97  3rd Eclogues 64  119
DEPARTS
     Yea in no age thy blisse from them departs.. . . . . . . . .  285  Psalm XII         24
DEPARTURE
     Now dead, doth shew departure is a death.. . . . . . . . . .  148  Cert Sonnets 20   12
DEPOSE
     Sinne from all rule in you depose, . . . . . . . . . . . . .  273  Psalm IV          17
DEPRAVE
     Both our estates, while each the other did deprave,. . . . .  119  4th Eclogues 73  107
DEPRIVED
     There was the swan of dignitie deprived, . . . . . . . . . .   29  1st Eclogues 10   85
     Now was our heav'nly vaulte deprived of the light. . . . . .  116  4th Eclogues 73    1
     Orphans in deede, depriv'd of father's might:. . . . . . . .  129  4th Eclogues 76   13
     Deepe plunged in earth, deprived of the skie.. . . . . . . .  149  Cert Sonnets 21    8
     Yet eyes deprived be not,. . . . . . . . . . . . . . . . . .  152  Cert Sonnets 23   27
     Let him, deprived of sweet but unfelt joyes, . . . . . . . .  177  Astrophil    24   12
DEPTH
     Then void of neerer cares, the depth of things to find.. . .  118  4th Eclogues 73   50
     From hidnest depth, which tribute when it ends,. . . . . . .  150  Cert Sonnets 22   13
     Then from his depth with force in her begunne, . . . . . . .  150  Cert Sonnets 22   17
     Ev'n from the Waters' depth my God preserved me so.. . . . .  291  Psalm XVIII       35
DEPTHS
     And depths in treasure his.. . . . . . . . . . . . . . . . .  316  Psalm XXXIII      27
     Thy judgments like the depths do ly, . . . . . . . . . . . .  323  Psalm XXXVI       16
DERIDAN
     Fa la la leridan, dan dan dan deridan: . . . . . . . . . . .  156  Cert Sonnets 27    5
     Above line repeated at following locations . . . . . . . . .  156  Cert Sonnets 27   13
            . . . . . . . . . . . . . . . . . . . . . . . . . . .  156  Cert Sonnets 27   21
            . . . . . . . . . . . . . . . . . . . . . . . . . . .  157  Cert Sonnets 27   29
            . . . . . . . . . . . . . . . . . . . . . . . . . . .  157  Cert Sonnets 27   37
     Dan dan dan deridan deridan dei: . . . . . . . . . . . . . .  156  Cert Sonnets 27    6
     Above line repeated at following locations . . . . . . . . .  156  Cert Sonnets 27   14
            . . . . . . . . . . . . . . . . . . . . . . . . . . .  157  Cert Sonnets 27   22
            . . . . . . . . . . . . . . . . . . . . . . . . . . .  157  Cert Sonnets 27   30
            . . . . . . . . . . . . . . . . . . . . . . . . . . .  157  Cert Sonnets 27   38
DERIDE
     But He shall them deride who by the heavns is borne, . . . .  271  Psalm II           9
DERIDING
     When foes ask with foule deriding, . . . . . . . . . . . . .  335  Psalm XLII        47
DERIVED
     What be the pangs they beare, and whence those pangs be
         derived,. . . . . . . . . . . . . . . . . . . . . . . . .   33  1st Eclogues 13   43
     And thence those armes derived are;. . . . . . . . . . . . .   89  Arcadia III  62  117
     That, from that sea deriv'd, teares' spring did flow.. . . .  187  Astrophil    45    8
DESCEND
     O descende for a while, from this greate height to behold
         me . . . . . . . . . . . . . . . . . . . . . . . . . . .   36  1st Eclogues 13  149
     But mercy, lord, let Mercy thyne descend . . . . . . . . . .  276  Psalm VI           5
     He bow'd the heav'ns, and from the bow'd heav'ns did discend  291  Psalm XVIII       20
     I be like them that descend. . . . . . . . . . . . . . . . .  308  Psalm XXVIII       4
DESCENDED
     No mortall gifts, no earthly fruites, now here descended be:  217  A&S 7th Song      14
     And what the race of him descended . . . . . . . . . . . . .  279  Psalm VIII        15
DESCENT
     Whose eeven descent makes equall falle,. . . . . . . . . . .   89  Arcadia III  62 V104
DESCRIED
     And then descried the glistring of his dart: . . . . . . . .  175  Astrophil    20   13
     When Cupid, having me his slave describe . . . . . . . . . .  191  Astrophil    53    5
DESCRIES
     Nor sence that grace descryes: . . . . . . . . . . . . . . .  152  Cert Sonnets 23   26
     But for that man with paine this truth descries, . . . . . .  177  Astrophil    25    5
     To me that feele the like, thy state descries. . . . . . . .  180  Astrophil    31    8
DESCRY
     From such deepe plaint as should such woes descrie,. . . . .  129  4th Eclogues 75  137
     But by thy worke my Stella I descrie,. . . . . . . . . . . .  181  Astrophil    32    7
     And now man's wrongs in me, poore beast, descrie.. . . . . .  189  Astrophil    49    4
     One from the other scarcely can descrie, . . . . . . . . . .  202  Astrophil    72    3
     My speeches all Thy marvailes shall descry:. . . . . . . . .  279  Psalm IX           2
*DESERT
     That see my good, and judgeth my desert: . . . . . . . . . .    5  Lady of May   3   16
     Honor, the cause, desart is not regarded.. . . . . . . . . .   17  1st Eclogues  7   96
     Joyning your sweete voice to the rurall muse of a deserte, .   31  1st Eclogues 13    2
     You onely yours, too farr beyond desarte.. . . . . . . . . .   79  Arcadia III  50   22
     Leasure to weigh what due deserte requireth. . . . . . . . .   83  Arcadia III  57   10
     Thou arte therefore of these our desart places . . . . . . .  108  Arcadia IV   69   12
     Long since my thoughts more desert be then forrests: . . . .  112  4th Eclogues 71   28
     Till due desert she find. . . . . . . . . . . . . . . . . . .  160  Cert Sonnets 30   36
     Have chang'd desert, let mine owne conscience be . . . . . .  212  Astrophil    86    2
     Ever from deed of any such desart: . . . . . . . . . . . . .  277  Psalm VII          8
DESERTS
     But sawe they would, and he to deserts went. . . . . . . . .  100  3rd Eclogues 66   70
     Disdaind with this, in deserts sought their restes;. . . . .  102  3rd Eclogues 66  123
     Turning to desarts our best pastur'de mountaines.. . . . . .  113  4th Eclogues 71   72
```

		PAGE	TITLE		LINE

DESERTS   (CONTINUED)

His voice have trembling deserts try'd,. . . . . 310 Psalm XXIX 20
Ev'en Deserts where the Arabs byde. . . . . 310 Psalm XXIX 21

DESERVE

Shew how thou canst deserve so brave desire, ... 3 Lady of May 2 2
First be he true, for truth doth truth deserve:. . . . . . . 98 3rd Eclogues 65 2
Behold (beholding well it doth deserve). . . . . 244 Other Poems 4 82

DESERVED

His very being he hath not deserved, ... 105 3rd Eclogues 67 79
Which he of us for ever hath deserved. . . . . 129 4th Eclogues 75 138
Where bee those wellcomes by no worthe deserved? . . . . . . 138 Cert Sonnets 5 10
Rich in the treasure of deserv'd renowne,. . . . . 183 Astrophil 37 9
From coming to the well deserved end,. . . . . 277 Psalm VII 26

DESERVES

Deserves the former place: . . . . 215 A&S 6th Song 4
As deserves their wicked witt; . . . . 309 Psalm XXVIII 18

DESERVEST

"Onley Juell, O only Juell, which cnly deservest . . . . . 36 1st Eclogues 13 147

DESERVETH

Which of us two deserveth most compassion. . . . . 15 1st Eclogues 7 18

DESIGN

What strange dessein hast thou my hopes to staie,. . . . . 80 Arcadia III 53 3

DESIRE

Shew how thou canst deserve so brave desire, ... 3 Lady of May 2 2
At length obtaind the point of his desire, ... 4 Lady of May 3 2
Creeping to ech with flattering of desire. . . . . 22 1st Eclogues 8 40
But for that Love's desire most rules the eyes,. . . . . . . 22 1st Eclogues 8 41
Or with desire to make such foe a frend, ... 22 1st Eclogues 9 9
But fondlings fonde, know not your owne desire . . . . . . 25 1st Eclogues 9 102
Love smiled, and thus said; "want joynd to desire is
    unhappy . . . . 30 1st Eclogues 11 11
But if he nought do desire, what can Heraclitus aile?. . . . 30 1st Eclogues 11 12
None but I, workes by desire: by desire have I kindled in
    his soule. 30 1st Eclogues 11 13
But most wretched I am, now love awakes my desire. . . . . 30 1st Eclogues 11 20
With sighes you seeke to coole your hotte desire:. . . . . 38 Arcadia II 14 6
Let not old age disgrace my high desire, ... 38 Arcadia II 15 1
Above line repeated at following location. . . . . 39 Arcadia II 15 14
My weedes, Desire, cut out in endlesse foldes. . . . . . . 39 Arcadia II 17 6
Bard of my will, I have beyond desire: . . . . 41 Arcadia II 20 7
His wings desire oft clipt with desperation: . . . . 48 2nd Eclogues 28 44
Nay even cold Death enflamde with hot desire . . . . 59 2nd Eclogues 30 86
Hath not Reason enough vehemence the desire to reprove?
    Prove. . . . . 63 2nd Eclogues 31 10
Winde, tempests, and stormes, yet in ende what gives she
    desire? Ire. . . . . 64 2nd Eclogues 31 35
Thus tossed in my shipp of huge desyre,. . . . . 71 Arcadia III 37 13
A Banisht man, long bard from his desire . . . . 75 Arcadia III 44 1
Sweete roote say thou, the roote of my desire. . . . . . . 77 Arcadia III 48 1
(Delay, the racke of unrefrain'd desire) . . . . 80 Arcadia III 53 2
To ease those paines, which on desire do waite). . . . . . 82 Arcadia III 56 4
Thou doest desire, and with free power to holde. . . . . . 83 Arcadia III 58 2
Fore-felt Desire, begin to savour parte. . . . . 83 Arcadia III 59 11
And that it had enflam'd a new desire, ... 95 3rd Eclogues 64 38
And geve a long desire a sweet content.. . . . . 97 3rd Eclogues 64 106
Who doth desire that chaste his wife should be,. . . . . . 98 3rd Eclogues 65 1
"C beasts, take heed what you of me desire.. . . . . 100 3rd Eclogues 66 72
And shall we not therefore their use desire? . . . . 105 3rd Eclogues 67 69
I long doo plowe with plough of deepe Desire:. . . . . . . 115 4th Eclogues 72 52
A dull desire to kisse the image of our death:. . . . . . . 117 4th Eclogues 73 10
Who under courtly pompes doo hatch a base desire. . . . . . 117 4th Eclogues 73 16
Sleepe Babie mine, Desire, nurse Beautie singeth:. . . . . 139 Cert Sonnets 6 1
He flies to her, and boldned with desire,. . . . . 141 Cert Sonnets 9 11
My ship, desire, with winde of lust long tost, ... 151 Cert Sonnets 22 55
For if those flames burne my desire, ... 153 Cert Sonnets 24 26
First throwne on my desire,. . . . . 155 Cert Sonnets 26 3
Above line repeated at following locations . . . . 155 Cert Sonnets 26 14
    . . . . 156 Cert Sonnets 26 25
Desire, desire I have too dearely bought,. . . . . 161 Cert Sonnets 31 5
Desiring nought but how to kill desire.. . . . . 161 Cert Sonnets 31 14
To grieve me worse, in saying that Desire. . . . . 171 Astrophil 14 6
Without desire to feed of further grace. . . . . 187 Astrophil 46 1
So long (though he from booke myche to desire) . . . . . . 188 Astrophil 46 13
My horse, he spurres with sharpe desire my hart: . . . . . 189 Astrophil 49 11
Her come, and heare with patience my desire, ... 193 Astrophil 56 13
Desire still on the stilts of feare doth go. . . . . 199 Astrophil 66 8
Light of my life, and life of my desire, ... 200 Astrophil 68 2
"But ah," Desire still cries, "give me some food." . . . . 201 Astrophil 71 14
Desire, though thou my old companion art,. . . . . 202 Astrophil 72 1
But thou Desire, because thou wouldst have all,. . . . . . 202 Astrophil 72 13
Breather of life, and fastner of desire, ... 207 Astrophil 80 7
For though full of desire, emptie of wit,. . . . . 208 Astrophil 82 9
From base desire on earthly cates to pray? . . . . 223 Astrophil 88 8
Stella loadstar of desier. . . . . 218 A&S 8th Song 32
Whille I that syghte, desyre, and vowe forbare,. . . . . . 344 Possibly 2 7
Then to Desier's desire, O yeelde O yeelde.. . . . . 345 Possibly 4 4
When strong Desire, which vertue's love doth guide,. . . . 345 Possibly 4 7
That naught withstandes Desire, Allarme allarme. . . . . . 346 Possibly 5 4
In some such one she lik'd not his desire, ... 245 Other Poems 4 119
But glad Desire, his late embosom'd guest, ... 247 Other Poems 4 201

		PAGE	TITLE		LINE
DESIRE	(CONTINUED)				
	Desire the more he suckt, more sought the brest, ...	247	Other Poems	4	203
	Much more his sight encreast his hote desire:.	249	Other Poems	4	298
DESIRED					
	Think so, for of my desired blisse it is only the course.				
	Curse.	64	2nd Eclogues 31		39
	The sweete pursute of my desired pray.	145	Cert Sonnets 16		12
	My selfe unto th' Anatomy desirde, ...	150	Cert Sonnets 22		27
DESIRE'S					
	But our Desire's tyrannicall extortion	60	2nd Eclogues 30		134
	Desire's best meane, harvest of hartes affected, ...	108	Arcadia IV	69	2
	Desire's great force, no forces can withhold:.	345	Possibly	4	3
	Then to Desier's desire, O yeelde O yeelde..	345	Possibly	4	4
	Did it for just Desire's true children builde, ...	345	Possibly	4	10
DESIRES					
	Whyle hote desyres do Raigne in fancie's rage.	26	1st Eclogues 9		140
	You doo approch to the fruite your onely desirs be to				
	gather	33	1st Eclogues 13		63
	So my desires by my feare, cutt downe, be the frames of her				
	honour..	36	1st Eclogues 13		135
	Which barde desires, (barde by my selfe) imparte..	77	Arcadia III	47	11
	Of hopes begot by feare, of wot not what desires:.	167	Astrophil	6	2
	Nobler desires, least else that friendly foe, ...	175	Astrophil	21	7
	Thence his desires he learnes, his live's course thence. . .	195	Astrophil	61	8
	Of just desires, on justice stayd, ...	274	Psalm IV		22
	And blessing such with length desires, ...	320	Psalm XXXIV		47
	A Shepheard's tale no height of stile desires.	242	Other Poems	4	1
	While those restles desires in great men rife.	243	Other Poems	4	62
DESIRING					
	Desiring, that no griefe in him he bread	97	3rd Eclogues 64		111
	Desiring nought but how to kill desire..	161	Cert Sonnets 31		14
DESOLATED					
	My desolated life from dogged might.	299	Psalm XXII		48
DESOLATION					
	Send unto desolation	297	Psalm XXI		38
DESPAIR					
	Who can despaire, whom hope doth beare?.	14	1st Eclogues	6	5
	And who can hope, who feeles despaire?	14	1st Eclogues	6	6
	Despaire my fielde; the flowers spirits' warrs:.	18	1st Eclogues	7	139
	Their hopes on haps, and do not make despaire.	58	2nd Eclogues 30		42
	No, no: Despaire my dayly lesson saith,.	58	2nd Eclogues 30		53
	Though in despaire, for love so forcethe me;	58	2nd Eclogues 30		57
	Tyre on, despaier, uppon my tyred sprite..	74	Arcadia III	42	12
	Of huge despaire, and foule affliction's vallies, ...	111	4th Eclogues 71		17
	On rocke, Despaire, the buriall of my blisse..	114	4th Eclogues 72		50
	Klaius. On rocke, Despaire, the buriall of my blisse	115	4th Eclogues 72		51
	Vaine is their paine, who labour in Despaire..	115	4th Eclogues 72		60
	Strephon. Vaine is their paine, who labour in Despaire.. . .	115	4th Eclogues 72		61
	Ev'n then Despaire did Hope already kill:.	115	4th Eclogues 72		64
	In ashes of despaire (though burnt) shall make thee live". .	121	4th Eclogues 73		174
	Such thing cannot I seeke (Despaire hath giv'n me my answer.	122	4th Eclogues 74		11
	Despaire most tragicall clause to a deadly request).	122	4th Eclogues 74		12
	Blinded forthwith in darke dispaire did lye, ...	149	Cert Sonnets 21		6
	Engulfed in despaire, slid downe from fortune's lappe: . . .	153	Cert Sonnets 24		16
	His paper, pale dispaire, and paine his pen doth move. . . .	168	Astrophil	6	11
	Of those fierce darts, dispaire at me doth throw:.	184	Astrophil	39	6
	While I dispaire by Sunne's sight to enjoy..	230	Astrophil	97	14
	Most rude dispaire my daily unbidden guest,.	236	Astrophil	108	7
DESPAIRED					
	Despairde in all this flocke to find a knave, but thee.. . .	52	2nd Eclogues 29		4
DESPAIRFUL					
	That sweete, but sower despairefull care..	14	1st Eclogues	6	4
DESPAIRING					
	And endlesly dispairing of his grace,.	229	Astrophil	97	6
DESPAIRS					
	Be those despaires, which have my hopes quite wast..	114	4th Eclogues 72		37
DESPAIRST					
	Thy gray-hood hides the thing, that thou despairst to find..	52	2nd Eclogues 29		6
DESPERATION					
	His wings desire oft clipt with desperation:	48	2nd Eclogues 28		44
DESPISE					
	And with despite despise the humble vallies:	112	4th Eclogues 71		53
	Despise delight, am tyrde with thought of ease;.	113	4th Eclogues 72		2
	Too much her peerles parts, nor yet could them despise.. . .	119	4th Eclogues 73		88
	Was ever apt: but you my pastimes did despise.	121	4th Eclogues 73		149
	Fawne on my self, and others to despise:	178	Astrophil	27	8
	Why should the evill, so evill despise	283	Psalm X		53
	So that the grave did not his words despise.	243	Other Poems	4	38
	She quick, and proud, and who did Pas despise, ...	249	Other Poems	4	273
	To heare, and not despise.	258	Other Poems	5	61
DESPISED					
	(Better despisde) bewondre gasing eye.	81	Arcadia III	54	12
	Of huge complaintes, that now it is despis'de.	85	Arcadia III	61	4
	Which though despisde, yet still doth truth endure..	150	Cert Sonnets 22		40
	Which ever hath Love's yoke despised:.	159	Cert Sonnets 29		15
	That it, despisde in true but naked shew,.	192	Astrophil	55	3
DESPITE					
	And with despite despise the humble vallies:	112	4th Eclogues 71		53
	And in despite of that displeasure's might,.	113	4th Eclogues 72		6
	A Ladie in despite of nature chaste, ...	151	Cert Sonnets 22		62

```
                                                       PAGE    TITLE          LINE
DESPOILS
    Sweete glove, the sweete despoyles of sweetest hand, . . . .    70 Arcadia III   35     9
DESTINES
    Cursed be my destines all, . . . . . . . . . . . . . . . .     211 A&S 4th Song          51
DESTINY
    Desteny keepes me aloofe. For if all thy estate to thy
        verture. . . . . . . . . . . . . . . . . . . . . . . . .    34 1st Eclogues 13    98
    What essence dest'nie hath; if fortune be or no; . . . . . .   118 4th Eclogues 73    45
DESTROY
    If once thou maist that fancie glosse destroy. . . . . . . .    25 1st Eclogues  9   117
    R. O foolish thing, which glory doeste destroye. . . . . . .    46 2nd Eclogues 27    19
    Marrie therefore; for marriage will destroy. . . . . . . . .   107 3rd Eclogues 67   115
DESTROYED
    O do not let thy Temple be destroyd. . . . . . . . . . . . .   185 Astrophil    40    14
    Who hast the heath'ny folk destroyd. . . . . . . . . . . . .   283 Psalm X                71
    That I e're I return'd destroyd them utterly . . . . . . . .   292 Psalm XVIII           69
    But strayers vile shall be destroyed . . . . . . . . . . . .   327 Psalm XXXVII          95
    Yea let them be destroyed. . . . . . . . . . . . . . . . . .   332 Psalm XL              56
DESTROYETH
    No witchcraft is so evill, as which man's mind destroyeth. .   215 A&S 5th Song          78
DESTROYING
    From my destroying Wicked Foes . . . . . . . . . . . . . . .   290 Psalm XVII            27
    Shall use destroying power,. . . . . . . . . . . . . . . . .   297 Psalm XXI             34
DESTROYS
    And loden so puls downe, puld downe destroyes. . . . . . . .    50 2nd Eclogues 28    86
    He heapes in inward griefe, that most destroyes him. . . . .    62 2nd Eclogues 30   172
    Each moment lost, part of my hap destroyes:. . . . . . . . .    80 Arcadia III   53    11
    Embrace that most, that most my soule destroyes. . . . . . .   113 4th Eclogues 72     7
DESTRUCTION
    Dicus. Thy safetie sure is wrapped in destruction: . . . . .    49 2nd Eclogues 28    73
    Where it should be to selfe-destruction bound? . . . . . . .    57 2nd Eclogues 30    13
    Let their sly witts unwares destruction get, . . . . . . . .   321 Psalm XXXV            17
DETERMINATE
    Such thing cannot he hope, that knowes thy determinat
        hardnes; . . . . . . . . . . . . . . . . . . . . . . . .   122 4th Eclogues 74    13
DETERMINES
    Becommeth us: in us fortune determines not.. . . . . . . . .   120 4th Eclogues 73   140
DETEST
    I doo detest night, evening, day, and morning. . . . . . . .   112 4th Eclogues 71    54
    Strephon. I Joye in griefe, and doo detest all joyes:. . . .   113 4th Eclogues 72     1
    I joy in griefe, and doo detest all joyes. . . . . . . . . .   116 4th Eclogues 72   100
    Strephon. I joye in griefe, and doo detest all joyes. . . .   116 4th Eclogues 72   101
    Thou though still tired, yet still doost it detest.. . . . .   229 Astrophil    96    14
    Nay I did even detest. . . . . . . . . . . . . . . . . . . .   305 Psalm XXVI            16
DETESTATION
    I know not I, but once in detestation. . . . . . . . . . . .   128 4th Eclogues 75   100
DETESTED
    Must finish then by death's detested crime.. . . . . . . . .   127 4th Eclogues 75    90
DEVIL
    Is it not evill that such a Devill wants hornes? . . . . . .   206 Astrophil    78    14
    I say thou art a Devill, though clothd in Angel's shining: .   215 A&S 5th Song          81
    You witch, you Divill, (alas) you still of me beloved, . . .   215 A&S 5th Song          87
DEVILS
    Tell yet againe me the names of these faire form'd to do
        ev'lls. Dev'lls. . . . . . . . . . . . . . . . . . . . .    65 2nd Eclogues 31    49
    Dev'lls? if in hell such dev'lls do abide, to the hells I do
        go. Go. . . . . . . . . . . . . . . . . . . . . . . . . .    65 2nd Eclogues 31    50
    Who tempt, and tempted plague, are Devils in true defining..   215 A&S 5th Song          84
DEVISE
    Or did she else that sober hue devise, . . . . . . . . . . .   168 Astrophil     7     5
DEVISED
    Seeme to proceede, so well it was devisde. . . . . . . . . .    96 3rd Eclogues 64    82
    These sports shepheards deviz'd such faults to show. . . . .   248 Other Poems   4   241
DEVOID
    Left me devoid of all life;. . . . . . . . . . . . . . . . .   154 Cert Sonnets 25    11
    Wholy devoy'd of Reason's rule,. . . . . . . . . . . . . . .   315 Psalm XXXII           32
    (His marke a Piller was devoid of stay,. . . . . . . . . . .   243 Other Poems   4    70
DEVOTION
    Thy sainte is dead, or dead is thy devotion. . . . . . . . .    47 2nd Eclogues 28     3
DEVOUR
    When I blessed shall devower,. . . . . . . . . . . . . . . .   226 A&S 10th Song         32
    Least lion like He do my soule devoure,. . . . . . . . . . .   277 Psalm VII              4
    God's people do devower, . . . . . . . . . . . . . . . . . .   286 Psalm XIV             15
    Shall these bad wights devouer.. . . . . . . . . . . . . . .   297 Psalm XXI             36
    My very flesh for to devoure,. . . . . . . . . . . . . . . .   307 Psalm XXVII           10
    Why should grief my heart devower, . . . . . . . . . . . . .   335 Psalm XLII            43
DEVOURS
    Fear'st not a face that oft whole harts devowres,. . . . . .   142 Cert Sonnets 10    10
DEVOUTLY
    To blaze these last, and sware devoutly then, . . . . . . .   171 Astrophil    13    13
DEW
    O Words which fall like sommer deaw on me, . . . . . . . . .    76 Arcadia III   46     1
    The dainty dew on face and body went . . . . . . . . . . . .   252 Other Poems   4   397
DEWDROPS
    But with dew dropps engendre children hy:. . . . . . . . . .   257 Other Poems   5    45
DEWED
    Her heav'nly-dewed tongue to garde.. . . . . . . . . . . . .    87 Arcadia III   62    44
DEWS
    Shall such morning deaws be an ease to the heate of a love's
        fire? . . . . . . . . . . . . . . . . . . . . . . . . . .    34 1st Eclogues 13    88
```

DIADEM
    More then Nestor's yeares, more then a King's diademe. . . . 122 4th Eclogues 74 20
DIADEMS
    Of fortune's Diademes, by beauty mustred.. . . . . 67 2nd Eclogues 33 5
DIAMOND
    That that deare Dyamond, where wisdome holdeth a sure seate, 37 1st Eclogues 13 165
    With Diamond in window-glasse she graved,. . . . . 61 2nd Eclogues 30 156
    Thus nature's Diamond, receave thy conquest, ... 68 2nd Eclogues 33 27
    Hard like a rich marbell: hard, but a faire Diamond. . . . 122 4th Eclogues 74 14
DIAMONDS
    Mock'st thou those Diamonds which only be matcht by the
        gods Ods. . . . . 65 2nd Eclogues 31 47
    Let golde now rust, let Diamonds waste in thee:. . . . . . . 125 4th Eclogues 75 22
DIAN
    "Venus come on": said she, "Diane you are obaide". . . . . . 119 4th Eclogues 73 78
    My Diane made me shew, ... 158 Cert Sonnets 28 10
    Dian that faine would cheare her friend the Night, ... 229 Astrophil 97 1
DIANA
    Who would have sworne his spowse diana was,. . . . . 96 3rd Eclogues 64 74
    As I thus musing stood, Diana cald to her. . . . . 119 4th Eclogues 73 81
    Diana did begin. "What mov'd me to invite. . . . . 119 4th Eclogues 73 102
    Diana deare; my minde to love and not to hate. . . . . 120 4th Eclogues 73 148
    "Nay then (Diana said) the chastnesse I will give. . . . . . 121 4th Eclogues 73 173
DIANA'S
    Unto Dianae's train thou runaway didst flee: . . . . 214 A&S 5th Song 71
DIAN'S
    Venus is taught with Dian's wings to flie: . . . . 202 Astrophil 72 6
    Even so (alas) a Lady Dian's peere, ... 230 Astrophil 97 9
DICK
    Will. Dick, since we cannot dance, come let a chearefull
        voyce. . . . . 343 Possibly 1 1
    Dick. Ah Will, though I grudge not, I count it feeble glee . 343 Possibly 1 3
    Dick. What joy the joyfull sunne gives unto bleared eyes:. . 343 Possibly 1 13
    Dick. I would it were but thus, for thus it were too well. . 343 Possibly 1 17
    Will. Thou seest my eares do itch at it: good Dick thy sorow
        tell. . . . . 343 Possibly 1 18
    Dick. Here then and learn to sigh: a mistress I doo serve, . 343 Possibly 1 19
    Dick. Bound as I neither power have, nor would have power to
        stir. . . . . 343 Possibly 1 24
    Dick. Faith in my self and worth in her, which no proofe can
        undoo. . . . . 343 Possibly 1 26
    But Dick my counsell marke: run from the place of wo:. . . . 344 Possibly 1 41
    Dick. Good Will, I cannot take thy good advice, before . . . 344 Possibly 1 43
    Will. Then Dick let us go hence lest wee great folkes annoy. 344 Possibly 1 45
    Dick. Oh hence! o cruell word! which even doggs do hate: . . 344 Possibly 1 47
DICTICNARY'S
    You that do Dictionarie's methode bring. . . . . 172 Astrophil 15 5
DICUS
    Dicus. Dorus, tell me, where is thy wonted motion. . . . . . 47 2nd Eclogues 28 1
    Dorus. But what doth make thee Dicus so suspicious . . . . . 47 2nd Eclogues 28 7
    Dicus. The harte well set doth never shunne confession:. . . 47 2nd Eclogues 28 13
    Dicus. Thy words well voic'd, well gra'ste had almost heaved
        me. . . . . 48 2nd Eclogues 28 31
    Dicus. But so thy sheepe may thy good wishes satisfie. . . . 49 2nd Eclogues 28 49
    Dicus. Thy safetie sure is wrapped in destruction: . . . . . 49 2nd Eclogues 28 73
    Dicus. Dorus you wander farre in great reproches;. . . . . . 50 2nd Eclogues 28 92
    Pas. But here is Dicus old; let him then speake the woord, . 52 2nd Eclogues 29 27
    Dicus. Sing then my lads, but sing with better vaine then
        yet, ... 53 2nd Eclogues 29 49
    Dicus. Enough, enough: so ill hath done the best,. . . . . . 56 2nd Eclogues 29 147
DICUS'
    This is my pawne; the price let Dicus' judgement show: . . . 53 2nd Eclogues 29 47
DID
    For me to come, and so she did: I came,. . . . . 55 2nd Eclogues 29 91
    And thus she did. One day to him she came, ... 95 3rd Eclogues 64 43
    And did the same, although with mickle feare.. . . . . 96 3rd Eclogues 64 64
    For feare he did, least he the young man might . . . . 96 3rd Eclogues 64 65
    How sheepheards did of yore, how now they thrive,. . . . . . 99 3rd Eclogues 66 34
    For so did I, when with my angle, Will, ... 115 4th Eclogues 72 62
    As though that faire soft hand did you great wrong.. . . . . 208 Astrophil 83 4
    One thing in deed I did and will . . . . 307 Psalm XXVII 19
    And did the tribute of their wondring sight. . . . . 251 Other Poems 4 363
DIDST
    Didst snatch from Cosma's hand her greene ywroughten glove.. 52 2nd Eclogues 29 10
    (Whiche hyding didest preserve that beawtie's light, ... 70 Arcadia III 35 2
    Earth thou didst seeke, and store of earth thou hast.. . . . 108 Arcadia IV 68 2
    Since thou from me (o me) o Sunne didst passe. . . . . 116 4th Eclogues 72 98
    And if, o Sunne, thou ever didst appeare,. . . . . 127 4th Eclogues 75 70
    In her cheekes pit thou didst thy pitfould set, ... 170 Astrophil 11 11
    O happie Tems, that didst my Stella beare, ... 232 Astrophil 103 1
    Unto Dianae's train thou runaway didst flee: . . . . 214 A&S 5th Song 71
    Unto my strengthned stepps Thou didst enlarge the way, . . . 292 Psalm XVIII 66
    My heeles and plants thou didst from stumbling slip
        sustaine, ... 292 Psalm XVIII 67
    And yet ev'en from the womb thy self did'st take me; . . . . 299 Psalm XXII 21
    At mother's breastes, thou didst good hope betake me.. . . . 299 Psalm XXII 22
    My soul, which Thou didst make,. . . . . 304 Psalm XXV 67
    Seek my Face, when Thou didst say, ... 307 Psalm XXVII 39
    Thou didst ungird my dolefull sack . . . . 311 Psalm XXX 35
    But Thou didst heare, when I to Thee did moane.. . . . . . . 313 Psalm XXXI 63

DIDST   (CONTINUED)   PAGE TITLE   LINE
 Didst like, much lesse didst crave;. . . . . 331 Psalm XL   27
 But thou didst peirce my eare,. . . . . 331 Psalm XL   28
DIE
 Are all my thoughts, in which I live or die: . . . . 3 Lady of May 2 10
 Though woes now live, at length thy woes must dye. . . . . . 22 1st Eclogues 9 12
 In being heard untill the hearer dye . . . . 24 1st Eclogues 9 70
 Loth to dye young, and then you must be olde,. . . . . 25 1st Eclogues 9 103
 Hope we doo both dye.. . . . . 30 1st Eclogues 12 8
 Such life to leade, such death I vow to dye. . . . . 40 Arcadia II 18 18
 As loving not, accus'd, in Love I die. . . . . 41 Arcadia II 20 2
 They live in force, I quite consumed die.. . . . . 42 Arcadia II 22 12
 First let them die, then passe the starres,. . . . . 44 Arcadia II 25 9
 P. And let him die, so that he die content. . . . . 46 2nd Eclogues 27 10
 Paine willes me die, yet will of death I mortifie: . . . . . 51 2nd Eclogues 28 124
 With name engrav'd: so though thy bodie die, ... 56 2nd Eclogues 29 130
 Plangus doth live, and shall Erona dye?. . . . . 58 2nd Eclogues 30 58
 Erona dye? O heaven (if heaven there be) . . . . 58 2nd Eclogues 30 59
 If she must dye, then hath she past the line . . . . 59 2nd Eclogues 30 77
 Plangus. And shall shee dye? shall cruell fier spill . . . . 59 2nd Eclogues 30 83
 Let Death first dye; be thou his worthy let. . . . . 59 2nd Eclogues 30 94
 "Erona dye, and end this ougly painefulnes"? . . . . 61 2nd Eclogues 30 157
 Can then a cause be so light that forceth a man to go die?
  Aye. . . . . 64 2nd Eclogues 31 24
 Yet tell what light thinge I had in me to draw me to die?
  Eye. . . . . 64 2nd Eclogues 31 25
 Blacke incke becommes the state wherein I dye. . . . . 81 Arcadia III 54 6
 Thou fearest death; thinke they are loth to die. . . . . . . 103 3rd Eclogues 66 151
 His nature feares to die who lives still wailing.. . . . . . 110 Arcadia IV 70 39
 Lilly in mourning blacke thy whitenes die: . . . . 125 4th Eclogues 75 28
 That he for want of elbowe roome must die? . . . . 126 4th Eclogues 75 44
 From such as were to dye for him contented.. . . . . 128 4th Eclogues 75 126
 As nature's worke: why should we feare to dye? . . . . 131 Arcadia V 77 2
 Hath neither leave to live, nor doome to dye,. . . . . 144 Cert Sonnets 15 7
 Why those that die, men say they do depart:. . . . . 148 Cert Sonnets 20 2
 Faire choice I have, either to live or dye . . . . 149 Cert Sonnets 21 13
 Failing themselves, with withered conscience dye:. . . . . . 151 Cert Sonnets 22 50
 Which rotting on the rockes, their death do dye: . . . . . . 151 Cert Sonnets 22 52
 Looke then and dye, the pleasure . . . . 152 Cert Sonnets 23 17
 Which die not in that weale. . . . . 152 Cert Sonnets 23 32
 Yet I shall die in Phoenix fire. . . . . 153 Cert Sonnets 24 27
 Thus do I dye to live thus,. . . . . 154 Cert Sonnets 25 28
 Where, "sooner die then change my state",. . . . . 158 Cert Sonnets 28 35
 Witnesse of life to them that living die:. . . . . 180 Astrophil 32 2
 Glad if for her he give them leave to die. . . . . 186 Astrophil 43 8
 O looke, o shine, o let me die and see.. . . . . 188 Astrophil 48 8
 As of a caitife worthy so to die,. . . . . 228 Astrophil 94 10
 Thinke no more but die in me,. . . . . 227 A&S 10th Song 46
 "Well in absence this will dy,. . . . . 234 A&S 11th Song 11
 Which he forgetteth not, nor letteth dy. . . . . 280 Psalm IX   34
 Let them in bedd of endless silence dy.. . . . . 313 Psalm XXXI   48
 For causeles they did seek to make me dy.. . . . . 321 Psalm XXXV   16
 That Foxes leave to steale, because they finde they dy
  therefore. . . . . 344 Possibly 1 44
 Wounded, inflam'de, knitt to the deathe I dye. . . . . 344 Possibly 2 4
 To downe proud hearts that would not willing dye.. . . . . . 250 Other Poems 4 304
 Whither it would, so it would let him dy,. . . . . 252 Other Poems 4 382
 While I in heart my will write ere I die.. . . . . 255 Other Poems 4 499
 So may you never dy, ... 257 Other Poems 5 46
 Or rather, till thou die,. . . . . 258 Other Poems 5 77
DIED
 Where Beautie's blush in Honour's graine is dide.. . . . . . 207 Astrophil 80 8
 With skinne in sorrow died,. . . . . 259 Other Poems 5 117
DIES
 Nor helpe by life or death who living dyes.. . . . . 18 1st Eclogues 7 146
 With long large eares where never rumour dyes. . . . . 21 1st Eclogues 8 28
 This waxe doth waste it selfe, yet painelesse dyes.. . . . . 75 Arcadia III 43 2
 Is cause the looker dyes.. . . . . 152 Cert Sonnets 23 8
 She never dies but lasteth . . . . 152 Cert Sonnets 23 9
 He ever dies that wasteth. . . . . 152 Cert Sonnets 23 11
 If thou know not for whome thy Master dies,. . . . . 259 Other Poems 5 110
DIET
 Her onely cure from surfet-woes can diet me: . . . . 51 2nd Eclogues 28 117
DIETH
 Where envie's snaky ey, winketh or els dyeth,. . . . . 69 2nd Eclogues 34 37
 Who makes a man live then glad when he dieth?. . . . . 197 A&S 1st Song 26
DIETS
 What now the Dutch in their full diets boast;. . . . . 180 Astrophil 30 6
DIFFERENCE
 The diffrence is; all folkes those stormes forbeare: . . . . 114 4th Eclogues 72 38
DIG
 Dig deepe with learning's spade, now tell me this, ... 175 Astrophil 21 13
 I list not dig so deepe for brasen fame. . . . . 179 Astrophil 28 4
DIGGED
 A pitt was digg'd, by this man vainly strong,. . . . . 278 Psalm VII   40
DIGHT
 Silent and sad in mourning weedes doth dight:. . . . . 229 Astrophil 97 8
 So have I sene trim bookes in velvet dight . . . . 246 Other Poems 4 180
DIGNIFY
 That verie shame with Love's high title dignifie.. . . . . . 14 1st Eclogues 7 3

DIGNITY   PAGE   TITLE   LINE
     There was the swan of dignitie deprived, ...   29 1st Eclogues 10   85
     For he then chosen was the dignitie. . . . .   244 Other Poems   4   75
DIGRESSION
     From heav'nly throne to her heav'n use digression? . . . . .   15 1st Eclogues 7   45
DIM
     But thanke the cause, thou seest, when he is dim.. . . . . .   27 1st Eclogues 10   12
     My eys be dym, my lyms shake,. . . . .   66 2nd Eclogues 32   10
     In cofer of dimme clowdes his silver groates,. . . . .   98 3rd Eclogues 66   9
     About which hee dimme clouds like a Pavilion brings, ... 291 Psalm XVIII   24
     With sight made dymme with dayly teares another's sport to
       see. . . . . 343 Possibly   1   4
     And thus, with eyes made dimme . . . .   256 Other Poems   5   12
DIMINISH
     For neere acquaintance dooth diminish reverent feare.. . . . 121 4th Eclogues 73 160
DIMMED
     P. And is not Reason dimde with Passion's might? . . . . . .   46 2nd Eclogues 27   18
     For to my dimmed eyes beganne t'appeare. . . . . 103 3rd Eclogues 66 159
     Our owly eyes, which dimm'd with passions bee, ... 131 Arcadia V   77   9
DIMMY
     Yee dimmy clowdes, which well employ your stayning . . . . . 127 4th Eclogues 75   67
DIRECT
     Direct me how to go, and guide me right, ... 312 Psalm XXXI   9
DIRECTED
     Where they by wisdome's Rules directed are,. . . . . 106 3rd Eclogues 67 104
     While their eyes by love directed, ... 218 A&S 8th Song   15
DIRECTION
     Thus she is framde: her eyes are my direction; . . . . . .   49 2nd Eclogues 28   70
     Of goodnes to receive lovely direction.. . . . .   68 2nd Eclogues 34   4
     Example more prevailing then direction, ...   128 4th Eclogues 75 131
     Wisdome farewell, the skillesse man's direction: . . . . . . 129 4th Eclogues 76   5
     Which to our darkned mindes was best direction;. . . . . . . 129 4th Eclogues 76   9
     In warr his wit and word was our direction.. . . . . 129 4th Eclogues 76   18
     Whence, whence alas, shall we seeke our direction! . . . . . 129 4th Eclogues 76   19
     For ever wandring from all good direction; . . . . 130 4th Eclogues 76   26
     And unto death bend still our thoughts' direction. . . . . . 130 4th Eclogues 76   34
     Farewell direction, farewell all affection.. . . . . 130 4th Eclogues 76   39
DIRECTS
     The man whom God directs doth stand. . . . . 326 Psalm XXXVII   57
DIRGE
     Let Dirge be sung, and Trentals rightly read, ...   160 Cert Sonnets 30   21
DISARMED
     Some play, while he is disarmed. . . . . 202 A&S 2nd Song   8
DISARMING
     Disarming humane mindes of native might: . . . . 131 Arcadia V   77   6
DISASTER
     Not that he hopes for amends of the desaster he feeles,. . . 122 4th Eclogues 74   24
DISASTERS
     These foule, most foule, disastres to me fell; . . . . 116 4th Eclogues 72   97
DISBURDEN
     Into my live's bondage, yet may disburden a passion. . . . .   35 1st Eclogues 13 108
DISCERN
     Save that dayly we may discerne what fire we do burne in.. .   33 1st Eclogues 13   53
     Who may this doubt discerne: for doubt, witt, then lot. . .   120 4th Eclogues 73 139
     And scarce discerne the dawne of comming day,. . . . . 131 Arcadia V   77   10
     Can scarce discerne the shape of mine owne paine. . . . . . . 228 Astrophil   94   4
DISCERNETH
     Not One, that God discerneth.. . . . . 286 Psalm XIV   12
DISCHARGE
     Now in this sande I would discharge my minde, ...   42 Arcadia II   21   13
     While everie office themselves will discharge, ... 210 Astrophil   85   7
DISCHARGED
     "O" cried I, "of so meane worke be discharged: . . . .   16 1st Eclogues 7   76
DISCLOSE
     By justice' worke they their owne faultes disclose:. . . . .   27 1st Eclogues 10   42
     Serves thy beames but to disclose, ... 210 A&S 4th Song   20
     Yourselves yet to yourselves disclose. . . . . 273 Psalm IV   20
     To whom we our love disclose?. . . . . 263 Other Poems   7   32
DISCLOSED
     She waited mistresse' will: who thus disclosd her spright. . 119 4th Eclogues 73   92
     But streight his shining eyes this misty masse disclos'd.. . 291 Psalm XVIII   26
DISCOMFIT
     Let not ev'ill hands discomfit me; . . . . 324 Psalm XXXVI   32
DISCOMFORT
     Hasten to help me, in this deep discomfort.. . . . . 299 Psalm XXII   46
     What ayles Thy discomfort? . . . . 337 Psalm XLIII   33
DISCONTENT
     Wither not you, languisht with discontent? . . . . 257 Other Poems   5   52
DISCONTENTATION
     Nay rather then my ease discontentation. . . . .   51 2nd Eclogues 28 120
DISCORD
     And such discord twixt greatest shepheards flowes, ...   27 1st Eclogues 10   40
     I know full well you know, what discord long hath raign'd. . 119 4th Eclogues 73 105
     Betwixt us two; how much that discord foule hath stain'd . . 119 4th Eclogues 73 106
     But such they say we be: this praise our discord bred, . . . 120 4th Eclogues 73 117
     But let us wiser be; and what foule discorde brake,. . . . . 120 4th Eclogues 73 119
     "How ill both you can rule, well hath your discord taught: . 121 4th Eclogues 73 163
DISCOURSE
     By wise discourse, sweete tunes, or Poet's fiction;. . . . .   61 2nd Eclogues 30 144
     For me, while you discourse of courtly tides, ...   190 Astrophil   51   9

112

```
DISCOVER                                                            PAGE    TITLE          LINE
    Yet for my sake discover us thy griefe.. . . . . . . . . . .    23  1st Eclogues  9    23
    And in them thy mind discover, . . . . . . . . . . . . . . .   225  A&S 10th Song      3
DISCOVERED
    Her right arme naked was, discovered was her breast. . . . .   118  4th Eclogues 73   68
DISDAIN
    Disdaine me not, although I be not faire.. . . . . . . . .      18  1st Eclogues  7   116
    With Jove's disdaine at such a rival's seed, . . . . . . . .    21  1st Eclogues  8    20
    Thus by thy worke, disdaine not that which is by thy selfe
        done.. . . . . . . . . . . . . . . . . . . . . . . . . .    36  1st Eclogues 13   152
    Do not disdaine, o streight up raised Pine,. . . . . . . . .    77  Arcadia III  47    1
    Well grounded, noble, due, spite, rage, disdaine,. . . . . .    84  Arcadia III  60   10
    With mortall disdaine, bent to unendly revenge?. . . . . . .   123  4th Eclogues 74   36
    When Love puft up with rage of hy disdaine,. . . . . . . . .   135  Cert Sonnets  2    1
    And stately hilles disdaine to looke so low. . . . . . . . .   147  Cert Sonnets 18    8
    With plague of deepe disdaine: . . . . . . . . . . . . . . .   159  Cert Sonnets 30    4
    So fortified with wit, stor'd with disdaine, . . . . . . . .   171  Astrophil    12   13
    Or sprite, disdaine of such disdaine to have?. . . . . . . .   188  Astrophil    47    6
    Of her just and high disdaine: . . . . . . . . . . . . . . .   203  A&S 2nd Song      18
    Since she disdaining me, doth you in me disdaine:. . . . . .   213  A&S 5th Song      28
    But doth God' self disdain.. . . . . . . . . . . . . . . . .   281  Psalm X           12
    Whose eyes a person vile do hold in vile disdain . . . . . .   287  Psalm XV           7
    Nay to name their names disdain. . . . . . . . . . . . . . .   288  Psalm XVI         12
    Will. What living get you then? D. Disdayne; but just
        disdayne.. . . . . . . . . . . . . . . . . . . . . . . .   344  Possibly      1   35
    To visite so low folkes did much disdaine, . . . . . . . . .   243  Other Poems   4   63
    Disdaine not you the greene, . . . . . . . . . . . . . . . .   258  Other Poems   5   90
    Nor with Love to cloake Disdaine,. . . . . . . . . . . . . .   263  Other Poems   7   40
DISDAINED
    Disdaind with this, in deserts sought their restes;. . . . .   102  3rd Eclogues 66  123
    For he hath not abhorrd nor yet disdain'd. . . . . . . . . .   300  Psalm XXII        55
DISDAINETH
    Being (ah) exild, disdayneth . . . . . . . . . . . . . . . .   233  A&S 11th Song      4
DISDAINFULNESS
    With swelling hart in spite and due disdainfulnes. . . . . .    61  2nd Eclogues 30  153
DISDAINING
    Since she disdaining me, doth you in me disdaine:. . . . . .   213  A&S 5th Song      28
    Gnashing their teeth full of disdeigning;. . . . . . . . . .   325  Psalm XXXVII      34
    With proud aspect, disdaining greater hast.. . . . . . . . .   249  Other Poems   4  293
DISDAINS
    He eft would kill a mouse, but he disdaines the fight, . . .    53  2nd Eclogues 29   45
    Thundred disdaines and lightnings of disgrace: . . . . . . .   195  Astrophil    60    4
DISDAINST
    Disdainst we see thee staind with other's light. . . . . . .    80  Arcadia III  52   15
DISEASE
    Swelling with sighes, made pale with minde's disease,. . . .    58  2nd Eclogues 30   48
    In what state was I then, when I tooke this deadly disease?
        ease. . . . . . . . . . . . . . . . . . . . . . . . . .     63  2nd Eclogues 31    8
    Sicke to the death, still loving my disease. . . . . . . . .    74  Arcadia III  41    8
    Mine owne, embraced, sought, knot, fire, desease.. . . . . .    84  Arcadia III  60   14
    What medicin then, can such desease remove . . . . . . . . .    85  Arcadia III  61   13
    As to Swanne in last disease:. . . . . . . . . . . . . . . .   140  Cert Sonnets  7   37
    Feeling my pulse, misse my disease.. . . . . . . . . . . . .   153  Cert Sonnets 24    9
    "Art not asham'd to publish thy disease?". . . . . . . . . .   182  Astrophil    34    5
DISEASED
    Ease I do feele (such ease as falls to one wholy diseased) .    35  1st Eclogues 13  114
DISGEST
    But perforce disgest, all bitter juices of horror. . . . . .    35  1st Eclogues 13  105
DISGRACE
    Let not old age disgrace my high desire, . . . . . . . . . .    38  Arcadia II   15    1
    Above line repeated at following location. . . . . . . . . .    39  Arcadia II   15   14
    But for to find thy words did her disgrace,. . . . . . . . .    51  2nd Eclogues 28  106
    No eare nor taile he hath, least they should him disgrace, .    53  2nd Eclogues 29   41
    The scourge of life, and death's extreame disgrace,. . . . .   140  Cert Sonnets  8    1
    My best wits still their owne disgrace invent: . . . . . . .   174  Astrophil    19    5
    But cannot skill to pitie my disgrace, . . . . . . . . . . .   187  Astrophil    45    3
    Thundred disdaines and lightnings of disgrace: . . . . . . .   195  Astrophil    60    4
    Let Fortune lay on me her worst disgrace,. . . . . . . . . .   198  Astrophil    64    3
    With sight thereof cride out; o faire disgrace. . . . . . . .  233  Astrophil   103   13
    But thou art gone, now that selfe felt disgrace. . . . . . .   235  Astrophil   106    7
    Did hold hir fast for feare of more disgrace,. . . . . . . .   249  Other Poems   4  278
    The courteous mountaines, griev'd at my disgrace,. . . . . .   254  Other Poems   4  477
DISGRACED
    What sacriledge hath such a saint disgrast?. . . . . . . . .    59  2nd Eclogues 30   97
    When I, disgraced wretch, not wretched then, did give. . . .   117  4th Eclogues 73   11
    Tell how ill thought disgrac'd my doing well:. . . . . . . .   146  Cert Sonnets 17   13
DISGRACEFUL
    Seeme to your eyes of a disgracefull hewe: . . . . . . . . .    38  Arcadia II   15    6
DISGUISE
    Least if no vaile those brave gleames did disguise,. . . . .   168  Astrophil     7    7
    They inward ev'ills disguise,. . . . . . . . . . . . . . . .   333  Psalm XLI         22
DISGUISED
    Or naked he, disguis'd in all untruth? . . . . . . . . . . .    21  1st Eclogues  8    8
    With beautie's seale, and vertue faire disguis'de, . . . . .    85  Arcadia III  61    2
    She written had (but in a hand disguisde). . . . . . . . . .    96  3rd Eclogues 64   80
    To death, as then disguisde in her faire face. . . . . . . .   115  4th Eclogues 72   69
    The other sees it but disguised. . . . . . . . . . . . . . .   159  Cert Sonnets 29   18
DISH
    When for a treene-dish stolne, thy father did thee whippe!.    52  2nd Eclogues 29   12
    To starving minds such is God Cupid's dish.. . . . . . . . .   136  Cert Sonnets  2   14
```

	PAGE	TITLE		LINE
DISHEVELED				
She so discheveld, blusht; from window I	233	Astrophil	103	12
DISHONOR				
O tongues right ladders made to clime dishonour, ...	50	2nd Eclogues 28		90
DISMAYED				
My Courage should not be dismaid.	307	Psalm XXVII		14
And in me so much dismaid?	334	Psalm XLII		18
Above line repeated at following location.	335	Psalm XLII		50
DISMISS				
Whom she imployes, dismisse from thee my wit, ...	236	Astrophil	107	10
DISORDER				
While he did live, farre, farre was all disorder;	128	4th Eclogues 75		130
DISPERSE				
Torne you should disperse unto the blasts of a winde.	123	4th Eclogues 74		52
DISPERSED				
Thus be my thoughts disperst, thus thinking nurseth a				
thinking, ...	36	1st Eclogues 13		139
DISPLACE				
From earth quite to displace.	320	Psalm XXXIV		60
DISPLACED				
Our offrings spoil'd, our priests from priesthood are				
displac'd.	119	4th Eclogues 73		110
Ah! yet from me let Thy plagues be displac't, ...	330	Psalm XXXIX		31
DISPLACING				
From any joy, know fortune's vile displacing her, ...	61	2nd Eclogues 30		150
DISPLAY				
For mourning night her blacke weedes may display.	126	4th Eclogues 75		54
But thinke that all the Map of my state I display, ...	168	Astrophil	6	13
When Sun is hid, can starres such beames display?.	223	Astrophil	88	6
First did with puffing kisse those lockes display:	233	Astrophil	103	11
For she knowes, if she display	222	A&S 9th Song		43
And I will (sayeth His King) the lord's decree display, . . .	271	Psalm II		15
Day unto day doth it display, ...	293	Psalm XIX		5
Heare lord when I my voice display, ...	307	Psalm XXVII		37
Ev'n thus it self it doth display, ...	323	Psalm XXXVI		4
For like the light he shall display.	325	Psalm XXXVII		13
My Foes' ev'ill words their hate of me display	333	Psalm XLI		17
DISPLAYED				
The earth is deckt with flowers, the heav'ns displaid, . . .	93	3rd Eclogues 63		91
How their blacke banner might be best displaid.	192	Astrophil	55	8
In falsehood wrapt, but in their pride display'd.	284	Psalm XII		9
In my song shall be display'd.	334	Psalm XLII		20
Above line repeated at following location.	335	Psalm XLII		52
DISPLAYING				
She lightning Love, displaying Venus' skies, ...	196	Astrophil	63	7
DISPLAYS				
Pas. When Cosma doth come forth, the Sun displaies	55	2nd Eclogues 29		96
That when the heav'n to thee his best displayes, ...	170	Astrophil	11	3
Which inward sunne to Heroicke minde displaies, ...	177	Astrophil	25	8
Silence in both displaies his sullen might, ...	229	Astrophil	96	5
DISPLEASE				
Relent those thoughts, which then did so displease?.	58	2nd Eclogues 30		52
I studie that which moste may me displease, ...	113	4th Eclogues 72		5
Shall gesse, and faile, what doth displease, ...	153	Cert Sonnets 24		8
Then be they close, and so none shall displease.	182	Astrophil	34	8
DISPLEASURE				
Turning all nature's course to selfe displeasure.	108	Arcadia IV	69	8
For hers am I, and death feares her displeasure.	137	Cert Sonnets 3		22
Unto whom mirth is displeasure, ...	221	A&S 9th Song		9
While Thou art in the heat of thy displeasure:	276	Psalm VI		2
DISPLEASURE'S				
And in despite of that displeasure's might, ...	113	4th Eclogues 72		6
DISPOSED				
So divers be the Elements disposed	57	2nd Eclogues 30		29
How be the minds dispos'd that can not tast thy physick?				
Sick.	63	2nd Eclogues 31		17
Icleped starres; each thing to rest disposed:	98	3rd Eclogues 66		10
DISPRAISE				
With sword of wit, giving wounds of dispraise, ...	170	Astrophil	10	10
DISPROVE				
But Vertue thus that title doth disprove, ...	190	Astrophil	52	5
DISPUTATION				
Experience doubts, and schooles holde disputation.	49	2nd Eclogues 28		48
DISQUIET				
As thou doest thinke) should most of all disquiet me	51	2nd Eclogues 28		115
DISSEMBLERS				
Nor kept with base dissemblers company;	305	Psalm XXVI		15
DISSENSION				
Beautie his Booke, his play lovers' dissention:	48	2nd Eclogues 28		42
Was this man's death the fruite of your dissention?.	128	4th Eclogues 75		108
DISSEVER				
A light which doth dissever, ...	152	Cert Sonnets 23		5
Dissever?.	285	Psalm XIII		4
DISSIMULATION				
What man grafts in a tree dissimulation?	69	2nd Eclogues 34		28
DISSOLVE				
So doth my life within it selfe dissolve.	19	1st Eclogues 7		156
Lalus. So doth my life within it selfe dissolve, ...	19	1st Eclogues 7		157
Which lest the ruinous want of government dissolve;	120	4th Eclogues 73		128

114

```
DISSOLVED                                              PAGE    TITLE        LINE
    With too much griefe me thinkes you are dissolved. . . . . .  127  4th Eclogues 75   77
    Those bands alas shall not be dissolv'd. . . . . . . . . . .  153  Cert Sonnets 24   20
DISTAFF
    (Who Neptune's webb on daunger's distaff spun) . . . . . . .  251  Other Poems   4  374
DISTILL
    And so to him and her your giftes distill, . . . . . . . . .   91  3rd Eclogues 63   22
    Large roomes within, where droppes distill amaine: . . . . .  150  Cert Sonnets 22   32
DISTINGUISHED
    My breath distinguish'd into wordes of woe, . . . . . . . . .  125  4th Eclogues 75    8
DISTRAINED
    When once one is for Atropos distrained. . . . . . . . . . .  128  4th Eclogues 75  111
DISTRESS
    This my Distresse to God with wailfull cryes I show, . . . .  291  Psalm XVIII        12
DISTRESSED
    Even for the sighs, true sighs of man distrest . . . . . . .  285  Psalm XII          15
    Save me distrest from lion's cruel kind. . . . . . . . . . .  322  Psalm XXXV         45
DISTRIBUTE
    And in those gifts that years distribute doe, . . . . . . . .  242  Other Poems   4   22
DISTRIBUTED
    O then it shines; then are the heav'ns distributed, . . . . .   49  2nd Eclogues 28   65
DISTURBS
    Nought disturbs thy quiet, all to thy service yeeld, . . . .   69  2nd Eclogues 34   10
DISUSE
    Disuse your selves from sweete Menalcas' voice: . . . . . . .   13  Arcadia I     4    6
DITCH
    Lookes to the skies, and in a ditch doth fall? . . . . . . .  174  Astrophil    19   11
DITTIES
    When in her necke you did Love ditties peepe; . . . . . . . .  208  Astrophil    83    6
DITTY
    Song's Ditty. . . . . . . . . . . . . . . . . . . . . . . . .  286  Psalm XIII         20
    His oft sigh-broken dittie, . . . . . . . . . . . . . . . . .  259  Other Poems   5  115
DIVERS
    Who in one selfe these diverse gifts can plant; . . . . . . .    3  Lady of May   1    4
    So divers be the Elements disposed . . . . . . . . . . . . .   57  2nd Eclogues 30   29
    In divers kinds; yet as he were not filled, . . . . . . . . .   62  2nd Eclogues 30  171
    Like divers flowers, whose divers beauties serve . . . . . .   78  Arcadia III  50    1
    Though each possesse a divers working kinde, . . . . . . . .   78  Arcadia III  50    7
    When they though divers do together meete: . . . . . . . . .   92  3rd Eclogues 63   34
DIVERTED
    Tell me, if your diverted springs become . . . . . . . . . .  257  Other Poems   5   37
DIVIDE
    His voice doth flashing flames divide, . . . . . . . . . . .  310  Psalm XXIX         19
    Of Mira's lipps divide . . . . . . . . . . . . . . . . . . .  258  Other Poems   5   57
DIVIDED
    When they shall such devided weakenesse prove? . . . . . . .   26  1st Eclogues 10    6
    Betwixt the good and shade of good divided, . . . . . . . . .   62  2nd Eclogues 30  179
DIVIDING
    Opening rubies, pearles deviding. . . . . . . . . . . . . . .  226  A&S 10th Song      30
DIVINE
    Infernall agonies unto a bewtye divine, . . . . . . . . . . .   30  1st Eclogues 11   14
    Your scepters here, if to your eares divine. . . . . . . . .   40  Arcadia II   18    3
    A greater good by her divine reflection; . . . . . . . . . .   49  2nd Eclogues 28   68
    Although we be divine, our grandsire Saturne is. . . . . . .  120  4th Eclogues 73  123
    While wanton winds with beauties so devine . . . . . . . . .  232  Astrophil   103    6
DIVISION
    O wretched state of man in selfe division! . . . . . . . . .   20  1st Eclogues  7 V966
    Above line repeated at following location. . . . . . . . . .   20  1st Eclogues  7 V967
DIVORCE
    Thy remembrance to divorce, . . . . . . . . . . . . . . . . .  225  A&S 10th Song       5
DO
    Thus Painters Cupid paint, thus Poets do, . . . . . . . . . .   20  1st Eclogues  8    5
    If mine eyes can speake to doo harty errande, . . . . . . . .   30  1st Eclogues 12    1
    But if eyes can speake to doo harty errande, . . . . . . . .   31  1st Eclogues 12   25
    Sacred Muse, who in one contaynes what nine do in all them. .   31  1st Eclogues 13   10
    What I call wrong, I doo the same, and more: . . . . . . . .   41  Arcadia II   20    6
    Pas. Ah foole; so Courtiers do. But who did lively skippe, .   52  2nd Eclogues 29   11
    That profit may ensue to him that best can do. . . . . . . .   53  2nd Eclogues 29   30
    That craftily he forst them to do ill, . . . . . . . . . . .  102  3rd Eclogues 66  125
    Or know your strengths, and then you shall do well. . . . . .  103  3rd Eclogues 66  154
    While that we doo what nature doth require, . . . . . . . . .  105  3rd Eclogues 67   65
    Ere that I should consent to doo such excessive a dammage. .  124  4th Eclogues 74   61
    O the fayre Nymphe borne to doo woemen honor, . . . . . . . .  138  Cert Sonnets  5    3
    Above line repeated at following location. . . . . . . . . .  138  Cert Sonnets  5   27
    Then good Apollo do away thy bowe: . . . . . . . . . . . . .  146  Cert Sonnets 17   36
    I will good tribute pay if thou do so. . . . . . . . . . . .  184  Astrophil    39    8
    I may, I must, I can, I will, I do . . . . . . . . . . . . .  188  Astrophil    47   10
    Her eyes, her lips, her all, saith Love do this, . . . . . .  190  Astrophil    52    3
    Then some good body tell me how I do, . . . . . . . . . . . .  195  Astrophil    60   12
    Threat'n what may be done, yet do more then you threat'n. . .  213  A&S 5th Song       33
    Which fall he made to do his neighbor wrong. . . . . . . . .  278  Psalm VII          42
    Of sanctuary do the same. . . . . . . . . . . . . . . . . . .  310  Psalm XXIX          6
    Who do ev'ill for good, to me. . . . . . . . . . . . . . . .  329  Psalm XXXVIII      58
    Remorse in you to doe this Fortresse harme, . . . . . . . . .  346  Possibly      5    6
    Heeding himselfe, cares not how fellow doe, . . . . . . . . .  248  Other Poems   4  237
    He did not there doe homage of his eies, . . . . . . . . . .  251  Other Poems   4  367
    "The sportes wherin I wonted to do well, . . . . . . . . . .  254  Other Poems   4  465
    Then so I faile, when most I would do well, . . . . . . . . .  254  Other Poems   4  467
DOCTOR
    O Doctor Cupid, thou for me reply, . . . . . . . . . . . . .  195  Astrophil    61   12
```

		PAGE	TITLE		LINE
DOES					
	Who once a white long beard, well handle does, ...	25	1st Eclogues	9	90
DOG					
	Let cat and dog fight which shall have both you.	56	2nd Eclogues	29	149
	The Foxe gave crafte; the Dog gave flatterie;	101	3rd Eclogues	66	85
	As horse and dogge, not great, but gentle blood:	102	3rd Eclogues	66	131
	The dogge was in a coller taught his kinde..	102	3rd Eclogues	66	138
	If he do praise the dog, she likes the cat..	104	3rd Eclogues	67	33
	Deare, why make you more of a dog then me?	194	Astrophil	59	1
	If he be faire, yet but a dog can be..	194	Astrophil	59	4
	If I saw my good dog grieved,.	222	A&S 9th Song		37
	Then in good Dog, faire field, or shading tree..	246	Other Poems	4	179
	And thou my dogg, whose truth and valiant might.	254	Other Poems	4	485
	With that his dogge he henc'd, his flocke he curst:.	255	Other Poems	4	519
DOGGED					
	My desolated life from dogged might.	299	Psalm XXII		48
	But hence, even hence, I must needes goe; such is my dogged				
	fate..	344	Possibly	1	48
DOGS					
	Foole that I am that with my dogges speake grewe..	27	1st Eclogues	10	19
	"I con thee thanke" to whom thy dogges be deare, ...	27	1st Eclogues	10	34
	For bawling doggs have compast me about, ...	299	Psalm XXII		39
	Yea worse than doggs, a naughty wicked rout.	299	Psalm XXII		40
	Dick. Oh hence! o cruell word! which even doggs do hate: . .	344	Possibly	1	47
DOING					
	Care upon care (in steede of doing right).	82	Arcadia III	56	7
	In our well-doing placing all his pleasure,.	129	4th Eclogues	76	15
	Tell how ill thought disgrac'd my doing well:.	146	Cert Sonnets	17	13
	With doing all, leave nothing done but paine..	210	Astrophil	85	8
	His righteousness, and this his doing glorious..	300	Psalm XXII		78
DOINGS					
	That in her doings better could compare.	247	Other Poems	4	211
DOLE					
	Cast down in such dole,.	337	Psalm XLIII		32
DOLEFUL					
	Lalus. How oft my dolefull Sire cried to me, "tarrie sonne".	16	1st Eclogues	7	49
	My Lyvelye joyes to dolefull ashes turne:.	42	Arcadia II	22	10
	Your dolefull tunes sweete Muses now applie.	125	4th Eclogues	75	3
	Above line repeated at following locations	125	4th Eclogues	75	15
	. . . .	125	4th Eclogues	75	30
	. . . .	126	4th Eclogues	75	48
	. . . .	126	4th Eclogues	75	60
	. . . .	127	4th Eclogues	75	78
	. . . .	127	4th Eclogues	75	96
	. . . .	128	4th Eclogues	75	117
	Your dolefull tunes, to them still playning say, ...	126	4th Eclogues	75	50
	Thou didst ungird my dolefull sack	311	Psalm XXX		35
DOLOR					
	And drawes the dolor on till wery evening.	111	4th Eclogues	71	6
DOLORCUS					
	That the delights of life shall be to him dolorouse".. . . .	29	1st Eclogues	11	10
DOLORS					
	Nature made all, but me of dolours made:	18	1st Eclogues	7	143
	And unto death, quite drownde in Dolours, brought.	115	4th Eclogues	72	68
	Bubling out doth breathe signes of his hugie dolours:. . . .	123	4th Eclogues	74	28
	Till that they doo unto our dolours bende:	126	4th Eclogues	75	39
DOLTISH					
	Wry words, and stam'ring, or els doltish dombe,.	254	Other Poems	4	471
DOLTS					
	Let doltes in haste some altars faire erect.	58	2nd Eclogues	30	62
DOMINION					
	What horrors breede, wheare wynd dominion beares,.	71	Arcadia III	37	2
	And fellow-like let his dominion slide;.	101	3rd Eclogues	66	110
	Thou under his Dominion plac't	279	Psalm VIII		25
DONE					
	Begin (and halfe the worke is done) to prove	23	1st Eclogues	9	50
	Mastix. What marvaile if in youth such faults be done, . . .	27	1st Eclogues	10	25
	Thus by thy worke, disdaine not that which is by thy selfe				
	done..	36	1st Eclogues	13	152
	Dicus. Enough, enough: so ill hath done the best,.	56	2nd Eclogues	29	147
	That streight was done with many a boistrous threat, . . .	97	3rd Eclogues	64	115
	This done, thou hast no more, but leave the rest	98	3rd Eclogues	65	13
	Which being done he afterwards would kill.	102	3rd Eclogues	66	126
	For murdre done, which never erst was seene, ...	102	3rd Eclogues	66	127
	"Fie, fie, what have we done? ungodly rebell fie..	121	4th Eclogues	73	168
	As th'offence was done, and goe beyond if he can..	123	4th Eclogues	74	40
	With doing all, leave nothing done but paine..	210	Astrophil	85	8
	Threat'n what may be done, yet do more then you threat'n.. .	213	A&S 5th Song		33
	With what she had done and spoken, ...	221	A&S 8th Song		103
	For what, alas, have just men done?.	284	Psalm XI		11
	To whom feare Thee? what thou hast done for those.	313	Psalm XXXI		53
	Than it was done;.	317	Psalm XXXIII		32
	For ere that either had his purpose done,.	244	Other Poems	4	81
	So to have done amisse, so to be shent..	244	Other Poems	4	104
	This done, but done with captive-killing grace,.	244	Other Poems	4	105
	This said, this done, he rase even tir'd with rest,.	255	Other Poems	4	521
DOOM					
	And in whose eyes my dayly doome I reede..	72	Arcadia III	38	5
	But that it is my doome of bale or blisse.	97	3rd Eclogues	64	102
	I, wretch, astonisht was, and thought the deathfull doome. .	118	4th Eclogues	73	61

```
DOOM                 (CONTINUED)                          PAGE   TITLE          LINE
    As though she were the same, as when by Paris' doome . . . .  120  4th Eclogues  73   145
    Hath neither leave to live, nor doome to dye, . . . . . . . .  144  Cert Sonnets  15    7
    By Phoebus' doome, with sugred sentence sayes, . . . . . . .  177  Astrophil     25    2
    They deeme, and of their doome the rumour flies, . . . . . .  178  Astrophil     27    5
    No doome should make one's heav'n become his hell. . . . . .  212  Astrophil     86   14
    Consist, when they to highest doome are cited, . . . . . . .  270  Psalm I            16
    To that high doome, which I by Thee must get. . . . . . . .  277  Psalm VII          18
DOOMS
    God's doomes be right, and cheer the sprite, . . . . . . . .  294  Psalm XIX          33
DOOR
    The doore by which sometimes comes forth her Grace, . . . . .  169  Astrophil      9    5
    Thou openest heavnly Doore . . . . . . . . . . . . . . . . .  283  Psalm X            73
DOORS
    Those daintie dores unto the Court of blisse, . . . . . . .  187  Astrophil     44   11
    Whom iron doores do keepe from use of day? . . . . . . . . .  237  Astrophil    108   11
    Lift up your heads you Gates, and you doores ever biding, . .  302  Psalm XXIV         17
    Lift up your heads you Gates, and you doores ever biding, . .  302  Psalm XXIV         21
DORCAS
    Not as the scrippe thou stalest, while Dorcas sleeping lay. .   52  2nd Eclogues  29    8
DORUS
    Lalus. Come Dorus, come, let songs thy sorowes signifie: . .   14  1st Eclogues   7    1
    Dorus. Nightingales seldome sing, the Pie still chattereth: .   14  1st Eclogues   7    7
    Dorus. Thy challenge great, but greater my protection: . . .   15  1st Eclogues   7   19
    Dorus. Such Kala is: but ah, my fancies raysed be. . . . . .   15  1st Eclogues   7   37
    Dorus. How oft, when reason saw love of her harnished. . . .   16  1st Eclogues   7   61
    Dorus. Once, o sweete once, I saw with dread oppressed . . .   17  1st Eclogues   7   85
    Dorus. Farre other care, o Muse, my sorrow tries, . . . . .   17  1st Eclogues   7  106
    Dorus. Lady your selfe, whom nether name I dare, . . . . . .   18  1st Eclogues   7  131
    Dorus. My earthy moulde doth melte in watrie teares, . . . .   19  1st Eclogues   7  152
    Dorus. Such force hath Love above poore Nature's power, . . .   19  1st Eclogues   7  162
    Dorus. Of singing take to thee the reputation. . . . . . . .   19  1st Eclogues   7  173
    Dorus. Lady, reservd by the heav'ns to do pastors' company
        honnor, . . . . . . . . . . . . . . . . . . . . . . . .   31  1st Eclogues  13    1
    Dorus. Unto the Gods with a thanckfull heart all thankes I
        do render, . . . . . . . . . . . . . . . . . . . . . .   32  1st Eclogues  13   35
    Dorus. O glittring miseries of man, if this be the fortune .   34  1st Eclogues  13   89
    Dicus. Dorus, tell me, where is thy wonted motion. . . . . .   47  2nd Eclogues  28    1
    Dorus. But what doth make thee Dicus so suspicious . . . . .   47  2nd Eclogues  28    7
    Dorus. If Sunnie beames shame heav'nly habitation; . . . . .   48  2nd Eclogues  28   22
    Dorus. Sight is his roote, in thought is his progression, . .   48  2nd Eclogues  28   37
    Dorus. Blest be the name, wherewith my mistres named is: . .   49  2nd Eclogues  28   55
    Dorus. If I had thought to heare blasphemous wordes, . . . .   50  2nd Eclogues  28   79
    Dicus. Dorus you wander farre in great reproches; . . . . .   50  2nd Eclogues  28   92
    Dorus. Well do I prove, errour lies oft in zeale, . . . . .   51  2nd Eclogues  28  103
DOST
    Thy wit dost use still still more harmes to finde. . . . . .   23  1st Eclogues   9   34
    And in our little world dost cleare our inward sight, . . . .   44  Arcadia II    26    2
    R. O foolish thing, which glory doeste destroye. . . . . . .   46  2nd Eclogues  27   19
    As thou doest thinke) should most of all disquiet me . . . .   51  2nd Eclogues  28  115
    But still when thou dost sing, me thinkes a colt is loose. .   52  2nd Eclogues  29   24
    That doost so well their miseries define? . . . . . . . . .   59  2nd Eclogues  30   79
    Arte? what can be that art which thou dost meane by thy
        speche? Speche . . . . . . . . . . . . . . . . . . . .   64  2nd Eclogues  31   29
    Why doost thou haste away. . . . . . . . . . . . . . . . . .   80  Arcadia III   52    1
    Or doost thou thinke that heare. . . . . . . . . . . . . . .   80  Arcadia III   52    5
    Thou doest desire, and with free power to holde. . . . . . .   83  Arcadia III   58    2
    O cowarde Cupid thus doost thou my honour keepe, . . . . . .  122  4th Eclogues  73  185
    O well thou doost that thou no longer bidest; . . . . . . .  126  4th Eclogues  75   53
    Thou doest proceed in thy most serious wayes: . . . . . . .  170  Astrophil     11    2
    Since thou in me so sure a power doest keepe, . . . . . . .  181  Astrophil     32    5
    Hart rent thy selfe, thou doest thy selfe but right, . . . .  181  Astrophil     33    5
    Honour is honour'd, that thou doest possesse . . . . . . . .  182  Astrophil     35    9
    What, dost thou thinke that I can ever take. . . . . . . . .  193  Astrophil     56   10
    Hope, art thou true, or doest thou flatter me? . . . . . . .  199  Astrophil     67    1
    What blushing notes doest thou in margine see? . . . . . . .  199  Astrophil     67    8
    Why doest thou spend the treasures of thy sprite, . . . . .  200  Astrophil     68    5
    Thy selfe, doest strive all minds that way to move, . . . .  201  Astrophil     71   10
    O kisse, which doest thy ruddie gemmes impart, . . . . . . .  207  Astrophil     81    1
    Thou though still tired, yet still doost it detest . . . . .  229  Astrophil     96   14
    Dead glasse, doost thou thy object so imbrace, . . . . . . .  235  Astrophil    105    3
    As where thou soone mightst helpe, most faith dost most
        oppresse, . . . . . . . . . . . . . . . . . . . . . . .  213  A&S 5th Song       41
    But thou rich in all joyes, doest rob my joyes from me, . . .  214  A&S 5th Song       46
    For thou doest lord my heart, who am not borne thy slave, . .  214  A&S 5th Song       58
    And yet against thy Prince thy force dost dayly prove: . . .  214  A&S 5th Song       65
    Thou righteous proofes to hearts, and reines dost send, . . .  277  Psalm VII          28
    Who dost Thy saving health to true men bend. . . . . . . . .  277  Psalm VII          30
    Thou dost put out, and quite consuming send. . . . . . . . .  280  Psalm IX           14
    Say, Thou dost not Thyn Own regard? . . . . . . . . . . . .  283  Psalm X            56
    Who dost ever counsell mee, . . . . . . . . . . . . . . . .  288  Psalm XVI          20
    Whose bellyes so with daintys Thou dost fill . . . . . . . .  290  Psalm XVII         41
    Up Thou dost light my light, and cleare my darkned eye . . .  292  Psalm XVIII        53
    To them that trust in Thee a shield thou dost abide. . . . .  292  Psalm XVIII        56
    Yea Thou dost make me serv'd by folks I never knew; . . . .  293  Psalm XVIII        79
    When Thou on it dost cry, . . . . . . . . . . . . . . . . .  295  Psalm XX            4
    But Thou art Holy and dost hold Thy dwelling . . . . . . . .  298  Psalm XXII          9
    With oyle Thou dost anoynt my head, . . . . . . . . . . . .  301  Psalm XXIII        19
    And so my cup dost fill. . . . . . . . . . . . . . . . . . .  301  Psalm XXIII        20
    The House where Thou dost dwell, . . . . . . . . . . . . . .  306  Psalm XXVI         26
```

DOST	(CONTINUED)	PAGE	TITLE	LINE
Whose mouths Thy self dost bridle, ...		315	Psalm XXXII	33
Who poore and weake from rich and strong dost free, ...		321	Psalm XXXV	22
That dost deliver me, ...		332	Psalm XL	69
But triumph well may I, whom Thou dost stay.		334	Psalm XLI	41
Whome Thou, O place of places all, dost place.		334	Psalm XLI	43

DOTH
| But how he doth by might, or by persuasion . . . . | | 49 | 2nd Eclogues 28 | 46 |

DOTING
| O nature doting olde, o blinded nature, ... | | 109 | Arcadia IV 70 | 19 |

DOUBLE
I cease to strive, with double conquest foild:		11	Arcadia I 2	2
Of pretious pearle the double rowe, ...		87	Arcadia III 62	42
We beare our double yoke with such consent, ...		106	3rd Eclogues 67	92
And as you like my double lot, ...		153	Cert Sonnets 24	17
A double key, which opens to the heart, ...		206	Astrophil 79	6
Sent from false heart, on double meaning stay'd.		284	Psalm XII	6
Hir hands which pierc'd the soule's seav'n-double shield, . .		246	Other Poems 4	147
Came to hir back, and so with double warde		252	Other Poems 4	389

DOUBLE-SHINING
| To see the sportes of double-shining day, ... | | 251 | Other Poems 4 | 362 |

DOUBLING
| Is this sweet doubling of our single life. . . . . | | 103 | 3rd Eclogues 67 | 12 |

DOUBT
Quickly secure, and easilie in doubt, ...		27	1st Eclogues 10	28
Neither doubt you a whit, time will your passion utter. . . .		33	1st Eclogues 13	58
Who others' vertue doubt, themselves are vicious.		47	2nd Eclogues 28	9
Doubte is his sleepe, he waketh in invention;		48	2nd Eclogues 28	40
(Tide to the stake of doubt) strange passions baite, ...		82	Arcadia III 56	10
"Thus shall you show that him you do not doubt, ...		96	3rd Eclogues 64	61
Histor. No doubt to whom so good chance did betide, ...		104	3rd Eclogues 67	13
Are we their servants growne? no doubt a noble staye:		120	4th Eclogues 73	115
Who may this doubt discerne: for better, witt, then lot. . .		120	4th Eclogues 73	139
Thus write I while I doubt to write, and wreake.		182	Astrophil 34	12
Doubt there hath bene, when with his golden chaine		193	Astrophil 58	1
Doubt you to whom my Muse these notes entendeth, ...		196	A&S 1st Song	1
Above line repeated at following location.		197	A&S 1st Song	33
While into none doubt of his love did sinke, ...		247	Other Poems 4	199

DOUBTING
And in himselfe new doubting causes nurst.		94	3rd Eclogues 64	12
Loathing all lies, doubting this Flatterie is:		207	Astrophil 80	11
These doubting clouds ore-casting heav'nly braine, ...		245	Other Poems 4	127

DOUBTS
As for your doubts; her voice was it deceaved me, ...		48	2nd Eclogues 28	29
Experience doubts, and schooles holde disputation.		49	2nd Eclogues 28	48
Nico. Who doubts but Pas' fine pipe againe will bring. . . .		53	2nd Eclogues 29	51
Even thus might I, for doubts which I conceave		145	Cert Sonnets 16	9
No man doubts, whom beautie killeth, ...		156	Cert Sonnets 26	27
Then servant's wracke, where new doubts honor brings;		187	Astrophil 45	11
That full of doubts, thou of perplexity:		229	Astrophil 96	7

DOVE
Shall prove that fiercenes can with a white dove abide? . . .		123	4th Eclogues 74	34
Like as the Dove which seeled up doth flie, ...		144	Cert Sonnets 15	1
O happie Dove if she no bondage tried:		144	Cert Sonnets 15	13
As my young Dove may in your precepts wise		196	Astrophil 63	3
In the faithfull Turtle dove.		234	A&S 11th Song	20
As Venus' bird the white, swift, lovely Dove		251	Other Poems 4	353
(O happy Dove that art compar'd to hir!)		251	Other Poems 4	354
"Earth, brooke, flowrs, pipe, lambe, Dove.		259	Other Poems 5	92
And as the Turtle-Dove		261	Other Poems 6	49

DOVELIKE
| When with Dovelike murmurings, ... | | 226 | A&S 10th Song | 38 |

DOVES
Her shoulders be like two white Doves, ...		89	Arcadia III 62	113
There came a chariot faire by doves and sparrowes guided: . .		118	4th Eclogues 73	59
Which, coupling Doves, guides Venus' chariot right.		206	Astrophil 79	4

DOWN
Olde houses are throne downe for new we see:		24	1st Eclogues 9	84
Geron. Downe, downe Melampus; what? your fellow bite?. . . .		26	1st Eclogues 10	1
Olde aged oke cutt downe, of newe works serves to the building:		36	1st Eclogues 13	134
So my desires by my feare, cutt downe, be the frames of her honour.		36	1st Eclogues 13	135
(So humble knowledge can throw downe the snakish sinne). . .		44	Arcadia II 26	6
But so our hartes keepe downe, with vice they be not stainde		45	Arcadia II 26	14
And loden so puls downe, puld downe destroyes.		50	2nd Eclogues 28	86
I would come downe, and yeeld to her my place, ...		56	2nd Eclogues 29	121
What myne hath erst throwne downe so faire a tower?.		59	2nd Eclogues 30	96
Thus noble golde, downe to the bottome goes, ...		81	Arcadia III 54	13
I sate me downe: for see to goe ne could, ...		99	3rd Eclogues 66	20
And lowest sinke not downe to jote of ill:		99	3rd Eclogues 66	32
And state throwen downe to over-troden vallies.		112	4th Eclogues 71	30
And laying downe my head, did nature's rule observe, ...		117	4th Eclogues 73	27
The stately towers come downe with greater fall:		143	Cert Sonnets 12	8
Engulfed in despaire, slid downe from fortune's lappe: . . .		153	Cert Sonnets 24	16
Then did on him who first stale downe the fire, ...		171	Astrophil 14	3
Yet still on me, o eyes, dart downe your rayes:		186	Astrophil 42	11
That heav'n of joyes throwes onely downe on me		195	Astrophil 60	3
Pray that my sunne go downe with meeker beames to bed. . . .		205	Astrophil 76	14

DOWN   (CONTINUED)   PAGE   TITLE   LINE
    As thy lockes sturre, runs up and downe to make. . . . . . .   232 Astrophil   101   10
    Melts downe his lead into my boyling brest,. . . . .   236 Astrophil   108   2
    And makes me then bow downe my head, and say,. . . . .   237 Astrophil   108   9
    Whose owne fault casts him downe, hardly high seat recovers.   213 A&S 5th Song   24
    I layd me down and slept,. . . . .   272 Psalm III   16
    Will lay me down, and take my rest:. . . . .   274 Psalm IV   32
    He against me doth throw, but down it shall. . . . .   278 Psalm VII   43
    Down in the pitt, which they themselves had wrought: . . . .   280 Psalm IX   47
    Even god himself sent down his peircing ey . . . .   286 Psalm XIV   7
    My cryes clim'd up and he bent down from sacred throne,. . .   291 Psalm XVIII   13
    Up then thou liftst the poore, and down the proud wilt cast;   292 Psalm XVIII   52
    Not I but thou throw'st down those, who 'gainst me do rise;.   292 Psalm XVIII   72
    Let him come down, and help to Thee apply. . . . .   295 Psalm XX   7
    That down they go. . . . .   307 Psalm XXVII   12
    Let them be thrown down by Thee; . . . .   309 Psalm XXVIII   22
    Bow down thine eare to heare how much I need,. . . . .   312 Psalm XXXI   4
    Thus I prest down with weight of pain. . . . .   315 Psalm XXXII   7
    I did pull down my self, fasting for such;. . . . .   322 Psalm XXXV   31
    But throw them down, put them to endlesse blame, ...   323 Psalm XXXV   63
    They are cast down, and never shal . . . .   324 Psalm XXXVI   35
    They soone shall be cutt down like grasse. . . . .   324 Psalm XXXVII   5
    Let me not be thrown down to so base shame . . . .   330 Psalm XXXIX   27
    Cast down in such dole,. . . . .   337 Psalm XLIII   32
    With length laid downe she deckt the lonely place. . . . . .   244 Other Poems   4 107
    The fox on knees and elbowes tombled downe:. . . . .   248 Other Poems   4 258
    To downe proud hearts that would not willing dye.. . . . . .   250 Other Poems   4 304
    They looked down to triumph over pride:. . . . .   252 Other Poems   4 403
    Up and downe perplexed went, ...   262 Other Poems   7   14
DOWNRIGHT
    Till downe-right blowes did foyle thy cunning fence: . . . .   170 Astrophil   10   11
DOWNS
    Will. God shield us from such Dames. If so our Downes be
        sped,. . . . .   344 Possibly   1   39
    So on the downs we see, neere Wilton faire,. . . . .   251 Other Poems   4 342
DOWNWARD
    And highest thoughts, downeward most headlong throw? . . . .   73 Arcadia III 40   12
    Comming from her, cannot but downewarde fall.. . . . .   78 Arcadia III 49   18
    A little downward to espie,. . . . .   87 Arcadia III 62   52
    His weighty top) his top doth downeward drooping leane:. . .   117 4th Eclogues 73   22
DRANK
    I never dranke of Aganippe well, ...   203 Astrophil   74   1
DRAW
    To age thus doe they draw there youthfull pryme, ...   28 1st Eclogues 10   52
    Yet tell what light thinge I had in me to draw me to die?
        Eye. . . . .   64 2nd Eclogues 31   25
    As thou drawest on, so let my blisse draw neere. . . . . . .   80 Arcadia III 53   10
    Aire let me draw no more thy breath in anguish:. . . . . . .   136 Cert Sonnets 3   14
    In too full winde draw in thy swelling sailes. . . . .   143 Cert Sonnets 12   18
    Draw in thy beames, and humble all thy might,. . . . .   161 Cert Sonnets 32   5
    Which Cupid's selfe from Beautie's myne did draw:. . . . . .   169 Astrophil   9   13
    Then lord from me draw not Thy tender grace, ...   332 Psalm XL   41
    Not knowing who did draw with him therin;. . . . .   253 Other Poems   4 426
    Did draw his boyling braine. . . . .   256 Other Poems   5   9
DRAWEST
    As thou drawest on, so let my blisse draw neere. . . . . . .   80 Arcadia III 53   10
DRAWETH
    When hee once drau'th his wily nett. . . . .   282 Psalm X   40
DRAWING
    Where drawing breath, I sucke the aire of woe: . . . .   73 Arcadia III 40   10
DRAWN
    Myne eyes thence drawne, where lived all their light,. . . .   149 Cert Sonnets 21   5
    Alas, if Fancy drawne by imag'd things,. . . . .   187 Astrophil   45   9
    And thought it heav'n so to be drawn to hell.. . . . .   250 Other Poems   4 312
    With love drawne on, so fast with pace unmeet. . . . .   250 Other Poems   4 334
DRAWN-OUT
    Which drawne-out line doth hold all humane blisse. . . . . .   105 3rd Eclogues 67   72
DRAWS
    Drawes up; and if, hope fayling, ende live's pleasure, . . .   16 1st Eclogues 7   71
    All to a lesson he draws, norr hills nor caves can avoide
        him. . . . .   31 1st Eclogues 13   7
    What medecin may I finde for a paine that draw's me to
        death Death.. . . . .   63 2nd Eclogues 31   6
    Each sight draws on a thought, thought mother of science,. .   69 2nd Eclogues 34   11
    Where love draws hate, and hate engendreth love? . . . . . .   85 Arcadia III 61   14
    And drawes the dolor on till wery evening. . . . .   111 4th Eclogues 71   6
    More loving eyes she draws, more hate thou hast. . . . . . .   141 Cert Sonnets 8   14
    In this small course which birth drawes out to death,. . . .   144 Cert Sonnets 32   10
    So while thy beautie drawes the heart to love, ...   201 Astrophil   71   12
    A friend each party drawes,. . . . .   216 A&S 6th Song   29
    Whom Death to his cold bosom drawes. . . . .   311 Psalm XXX   9
DREAD
    Dorus. Once, o sweete once, I saw with dread oppressed . . .   17 1st Eclogues 7   85
    Her whom I dread; so that with prostrate lying . . . .   17 1st Eclogues 7   86
    And (but they drad their Prince they ofte should want) . . .   101 3rd Eclogues 66 100
    Dread not a whit (O goodly cruell) that pittie may enter . .   122 4th Eclogues 74   5
    Since bashfull dread seekes where he knowes me harmed: . . .   135 Cert Sonnets 1   2
    A Satyre once did runne away for dread,. . . . .   145 Cert Sonnets 16   1
DREADED
    For for my sheepe I dreaded mickle more. . . . .   99 3rd Eclogues 66   18

		PAGE	TITLE		LINE
DREADETH					
Faine would be free, but dreadeth parents' ire..	245	Other Poems	4	120
DREADFUL					
The dreadfull cries of murdred men in forrests..	112	4th Eclogues	71	48
Yea and from dreadfull misery.	319	Psalm XXXIV		15
DREADS					
My dreeades augment the more in passion's mighte,.	72	Arcadia III	37	17
DREAM					
Let no strange dreme make her fayre body starte.	79	Arcadia III	51	8
But yet o dreame, if thou wilt not departe	79	Arcadia III	51	9
Was it a dreame? O dreame, how hast thou wrought in me,. . .	121	4th Eclogues	73	181
DREAMED					
Ev'n like a dead man dreamed out of mind,.	313	Psalm XXXI		35
DREAMING					
That I things erst unseene should first in dreaming see? . .	121	4th Eclogues	73	182
DREAMS					
Like those whom dreames make uglie monsters see, ...	136	Cert Sonnets	2	11
No sleeps, but dreams, no dreams, but visions straunge,. . .	253	Other Poems	4	436
DREARY					
And to the woods or brookes, who do make such dreery					
recitall	33	1st Eclogues	13	42
DREGS					
Fond fancie's scum, and dregs of scattred thought, ...	161	Cert Sonnets	31	2
DRESS					
Let not a glittring name thy fancie dresse	23	1st Eclogues	9	47
Dresse bosome hers or hedd,.	257	Other Poems	5	48
DRESSED					
Her length the earth in Love's chiefe clothing dressed.. . .	17	1st Eclogues	7	87
Nor yet, fancy so drest, do receive more plausible hearing:.	35	1st Eclogues	13	101
Pas. But long have I a sparrow gailie drest, ...	54	2nd Eclogues	29	84
And thou deare flesh, as soft as wooll new drest,.	76	Arcadia III	46	15
Goodnes for best attire in dust is dressed..	128	4th Eclogues	75	120
In false colours dressed..	336	Psalm XLIII		6
DRESSING					
Of purest Metal dressing..	297	Psalm XXI		12
DREW					
With his sweet skill my skillesse youth he drewe,.	99	3rd Eclogues	66	26
Phoebus drew wide the curtaines of the skies	171	Astrophil	13	12
The ev'ill bent bowes, and swords they drew,.	325	Psalm XXXVII		37
The heav'n-love lodestone drew thy iron hart..	248	Other Poems	4	224
She mov'd hir lims, and drew the aged man,.	249	Other Poems	4	283
But he drew hir as love his fancy drew,.	250	Other Poems	4	323
Drew dainty Nous, that she not able so	250	Other Poems	4	335
Till Strephon's plaining voice him nearer drew,.	256	Other Poems	4	535
DRIBBED					
Not at first sight, nor with a dribbed shot.	165	Astrophil	2	1
DRIED					
Fire no liquor can coole: Neptune's seate would be dryd up					
there.	32	1st Eclogues	13	32
Thus be our noblest parts dryed up with sorrow:.	62	2nd Eclogues	30	174
My moystning strength is like a potsherd dride,.	299	Psalm XXII		35
Are you not dried? Can you your self renew?.	257	Other Poems	5	39
DRINK					
Let him drinke this, whome long in armes to folde.	83	Arcadia III	58	1
With water drinke, herbes meate, and naked hide, ...	101	3rd Eclogues	66	109
And through those lips drinke Nectar from that toong;. . . .	208	Astrophil	83	13
"Love makes earth the water drink, ...	219	A&S 8th Song		61
And drink from out Thy pleasures' spring,.	324	Psalm XXXVI		23
D. Teares drink, sorowes meat, wherewith, not I, but in me					
my death lives.	344	Possibly	1	34
Like dropsy folke still drinke to be a thyrst.	247	Other Poems	4	204
DRINKING					
At her lips my Nectar drinking..	227	A&S 10th Song		48
DRINKS					
No mortall man the cuppe of suretie drinkes.	105	3rd Eclogues	67	60
DRIVE					
Would faine drive cloudes from out my heavy cheere.. . . .	230	Astrophil	97	11
Curst be the Cochman which did drive so fast,.	235	Astrophil	105	13
Deeper still they drive the stake.	234	A&S 11th Song		35
DRIVEL					
Millions of yeares this old drivell Cupid lives;	22	1st Eclogues	8	43
DRIVEN					
There never was a better bargaine driv'ne.	75	Arcadia III	45	4
All thoughts so spronge, are from their dwelling driv'n, . .	83	Arcadia III	57	11
Let not mine eyes be hel-driv'n from that light:	188	Astrophil	48	7
Driv'n else to graunt by Angel's sophistrie, ...	195	Astrophil	61	13
DROOPING					
His weighty top) his top doth downeward drooping leane:. . .	117	4th Eclogues	73	22
DROPPING					
And now the dropping trees do wepe for me, ...	254	Other Poems	4	479
DROPS					
Or like the drops of raine..	92	3rd Eclogues	63	44
Large roomes within, where droppes distill amaine:	150	Cert Sonnets	22	32
Of sorrowe's droppes, till colder reason binde:	150	Cert Sonnets	22	37
As on sweet flowrs when morning's drops we see..	252	Other Poems	4	398
DROPSY					
Like dropsy folke still drinke to be a thyrst.	247	Other Poems	4	204
DROUGHT					
By Love's owne selfe, but with so curious drought, ...	184	Astrophil	38	7

```
DROWN                                                  PAGE   TITLE              LINE
    That quickly they would her burne, drowne, or smother, . . .    61 2nd Eclogues 30   159
    Teares, drowne your selves, for woe (your cause) is wasted,.    83 Arcadia III 59     6
    Beware full sailes drowne not thy tottring barge:. . . . . .   209 Astrophil 85       2
    With eyes which threatned they would drowne his face,. . . .   255 Other Poems  4    524
DROWNED
    Philisides. Who minds to please the minde drownd in annoyes.    22 1st Eclogues  9    6
    In water dround, in earth his buriall is;. . . . . . . . . .   105 3rd Eclogues 67   68
    And unto death, quite drownde in Dolours, brought. . . . . .   115 4th Eclogues 72   68
    Can those eyes, that of eyes drownd in most harty flowing
        teares,. . . . . . . . . . . . . . . . . . . . . . . . .   122 4th Eclogues 74   15
    Sea drownd in thee, of tedious life bereave me:. . . . . . .   136 Cert Sonnets  3   15
    Long drowned hopes to watrie eyes it lends:. . . . . . . .     150 Cert Sonnets 22   18
DROWSY
    Did suffer drousie lids mine eyes then cleare to blinde; . .   117 4th Eclogues 73   26
    Drowsy am I, and yet can rarely slepe. . . . . . . . . . . .   253 Other Poems  4   446
DRUNK
    She oft hath drunke my teares, now hopes to enjoy. . . . . .   201 Astrophil    70    3
DRY
    But hoarse and drye, my pipes I nowe must spare. . . . . . .    62 2nd Eclogues 30   190
    When rooted moisture failes, or groweth drie,. . . . . . . .   128 4th Eclogues 75   113
DUCK
    Camaeleon, ease to chaunge; Ducke, ease to yelde;. . . . . .   101 3rd Eclogues 66   95
DUE
    Where thou poore nature left'st all thy due glory, to
        fortune. . . . . . . . . . . . . . . . . . . . . . . . .    30 1st Eclogues 11   15
    Thus not ending, endes the due praise of her praise; . . . .    31 1st Eclogues 12   21
    Of my due faith, which needs must be immutable?. . . . . . .    47 2nd Eclogues 28    8
    That since the having them to neither's due, . . . . . . . .    56 2nd Eclogues 29   148
    With swelling hart in spite and due disdainfulnes. . . . . .    61 2nd Eclogues 30   153
    Nor ey receaves due object,. . . . . . . . . . . . . . . . .    66 2nd Eclogues 32   38
    Due sighes blowe out all sparkes of joyfull light, . . . . .    74 Arcadia III  42   11
    Do you say still, this is her promise due, . . . . . . . . .    76 Arcadia III  46    5
    Joyne you with me, to seale this promise due,. . . . . . . .    76 Arcadia III  46   11
    Leasure to weigh what due deserte requireth. . . . . . . . .    83 Arcadia III  57   10
    Well grounded, noble, due, spite, rage, disdaine,. . . . . .    84 Arcadia III  60   10
    And soone forget the swincke due to their hire.. . . . . . .   100 3rd Eclogues 66   74
    They seldome ponder what to them is due. . . . . . . . . . .   104 3rd Eclogues 67   27
    O deue allegiance, by thee am I called . . . . . . . . . . .   138 Cert Sonnets  5   15
    Peace Due alledgeance, Duty must bee broken, . . . . . . . .   138 Cert Sonnets  5   19
    With her due praise did of my state complaine, . . . . . . .   141 Cert Sonnets  9    4
    I do protest and seeke with service due, . . . . . . . . . .   145 Cert Sonnets 17    2
    For hope the colour due. . . . . . . . . . . . . . . . . . .   157 Cert Sonnets 28    4
    Till due desert she find.. . . . . . . . . . . . . . . . . .   160 Cert Sonnets 30   36
    But give apt servants their due place, let eyes. . . . . . .   210 Astrophil    85    9
    To you, to you, all song of praise is due, . . . . . . . . .   196 A&S 1st Song        3
    Above line repeated at following locations . . . . . . . . .   197 A&S 1st Song        7
    . . . . . . . . . . . . . . . . . . . . . . . . . . . . . .    197 A&S 1st Song       11
    . . . . . . . . . . . . . . . . . . . . . . . . . . . . . .    197 A&S 1st Song       15
    . . . . . . . . . . . . . . . . . . . . . . . . . . . . . .    197 A&S 1st Song       19
    . . . . . . . . . . . . . . . . . . . . . . . . . . . . . .    197 A&S 1st Song       23
    . . . . . . . . . . . . . . . . . . . . . . . . . . . . . .    197 A&S 1st Song       27
    . . . . . . . . . . . . . . . . . . . . . . . . . . . . . .    197 A&S 1st Song       31
    . . . . . . . . . . . . . . . . . . . . . . . . . . . . . .    197 A&S 1st Song       35
    Give them their due unto their guiltiness, . . . . . . . . .   275 Psalm V            29
    Ne let thy rage, of my due punishment. . . . . . . . . . . .   276 Psalm VI            3
    Who is our Lord, with due remembrance wayte. . . . . . . . .   296 Psalm XX           30
    Unto due thoughts mankind his thoughts shall order,. . . . .   300 Psalm XXII         66
    Ascribe due glory to his Name, . . . . . . . . . . . . . . .   310 Psalm XXIX          4
    And did due pain forgive me. . . . . . . . . . . . . . . . .   315 Psalm XXXII        18
    Somewhat to speake of his due praise,. . . . . . . . . . . .   319 Psalm XXXIV        10
    Claymes but to gaine his due, O yeelde O yeelde. . . . . . .   345 Possibly      4     8
    So when to pay your due. . . . . . . . . . . . . . . . . . .   257 Other Poems   5    33
DUKE
    That to the duke, he would his sinne declare,. . . . . . . .    97 3rd Eclogues 64   116
DULL
    Either dull silence, or eternall chat; . . . . . . . . . . .   104 3rd Eclogues 67   31
    A dull desire to kisse the image of our death: . . . . . . .   117 4th Eclogues 73   10
    The earth with pitie dull the center keepeth:. . . . . . . .   136 Cert Sonnets  3    4
    The curious wits, seeing dull pensivenesse . . . . . . . . .   176 Astrophil    23    1
    So dull am, that I cannot looke into . . . . . . . . . . . .   195 Astrophil    60   10
    To make a Lyzard dull to taste Love's daintie food:. . . . .   209 A&S 3rd Song        8
    I am as dull as winter-sterved sheep. . . . . . . . . . . .    253 Other Poems   4   442
DULLED
    My fancy amazde, my thoughtes dull'd,. . . . . . . . . . . .    66 2nd Eclogues 32   13
    An ende, an ende, my dulde penn cannot write,. . . . . . . .    74 Arcadia III  42   13
DUMB
    O toonge, then dumbe, not daring tell my smart;. . . . . . .    60 2nd Eclogues 30   121
    Dumbe Swannes, not chatring Pies, do Lovers prove, . . . . .   192 Astrophil    54   13
    Now with slow words, now with dumbe eloquence. . . . . . . .   195 Astrophil    61    2
    Teaching dumbe lips a nobler exercise. . . . . . . . . . . .   207 Astrophil    81    4
    Dumbe sleepe holdeth all the house:. . . . . . . . . . . . .   211 A&S 4th Song       26
    And if dumbe things be so witty, . . . . . . . . . . . . . .   219 A&S 8th Song       63
    Let those lips be made dumbe which love to ly, . . . . . . .   313 Psalm XXXI         49
    Deaf and dumbe,. . . . . . . . . . . . . . . . . . . . . . .   328 Psalm XXXVIII      38
    Wry words, and stam'ring, or els doltish dombe,. . . . . . .   254 Other Poems   4   471
DUMBNESS
    For no dumbnesse nor death bringeth. . . . . . . . . . . . .   140 Cert Sonnets  7    38
DUMP
    Some good old dumpe, that Chaucer's mistresse knew,. . . . .   146 Cert Sonnets 17   34
```

```
                                                           PAGE    TITLE          LINE
DUNGEON
   Heare plaints come forth from dungeon of my minde. . . . . .   18  1st Eclogues   7  133
   This life-deadman in this old dungeon flong. . . . . . . .   24  1st Eclogues   9   83
   With rebell force, hath closde in dungeon darke. . . . . .   73  Arcadia III   39    3
   Of comfort dare come to this dungeon darke,. . . . . . . . .  233  Astrophil    104    7
   From dungeon he retired, . . . . . . . . . . . . . . . . .  331  Psalm XL             6
DURE
   God's witness sure for aye doth dure . . . . . . . . . . .  294  Psalm XIX           31
DURST
   But all the rest, which feare durst not applie,. . . . . .  151  Cert Sonnets 22   49
   But only for this worthy knight durst prove. . . . . . . .  204  Astrophil    75   13
   The play began: Pas durst not Cosma chace, . . . . . . . .  248  Other Poems   4  249
   Did beate their hands, which durst so neere to presse. . .  252  Other Poems   4  406
DUST
   Goe snake hide thee in dust, . . . . . . . . . . . . . . .   93  3rd Eclogues 63   86
   Full dead before, I now to dust should fall, . . . . . . .  116  4th Eclogues 72   86
   Those thousand altars faire now in the dust to lie?. . . .  119  4th Eclogues 73  112
   Goodnes for best attire in dust is dressed.. . . . . . . .  128  4th Eclogues 75  120
   Leave me o Love, which reachest but to dust, . . . . . . .  161  Cert Sonnets 32    1
   Counting but dust what in the way did lie. . . . . . . . .  235  Astrophil    105    8
   Then in the Dust let him my honour rake. . . . . . . . . .  277  Psalm VII           15
   Of earthly man, a lord of dust.. . . . . . . . . . . . . .  283  Psalm X             80
   I bett those folks as small as dust, which wind doth rayse;.  293  Psalm XVIII         76
   Unto the dust of my death's running hower; . . . . . . . .  299  Psalm XXII          38
   To him shall kneel who to the dust be stricken,. . . . . .  300  Psalm XXII          73
   Shall ever dust give thanks to Thee, . . . . . . . . . . .  311  Psalm XXX           28
   In deadly dust declared be?. . . . . . . . . . . . . . . .  311  Psalm XXX           30
DUSTY
   Our life is but a step in dustie way.. . . . . . . . . . .  131  Arcadia V    77   12
   Though dustie wits dare scorne Astrologie, . . . . . . . .  177  Astrophil    26    1
   Tired with the dusty toiles of busie day,. . . . . . . . .  224  Astrophil    89    7
   Who dwell in dusty place.. . . . . . . . . . . . . . . . .  317  Psalm XXXIII        54
DUTCH
   What now the Dutch in their full diets boast;. . . . . . .  180  Astrophil    30    6
DUTIES
   Can Love's duties best fulfill:. . . . . . . . . . . . . .  263  Other Poems   7   38
DUTY
   Nor causelesse duty, nor comber of arrogance,. . . . . . .   69  2nd Eclogues 34   23
   If he to them his dutie misconceaved). . . . . . . . . . .   94  3rd Eclogues 64   22
   Though full of scorne, would not his duty misse, . . . . .   96  3rd Eclogues 64   69
   Peace Due alledgeance, Duty must bee broken, . . . . . . .  138  Cert Sonnets  5   19
   Yf Duety kill mee. . . . . . . . . . . . . . . . . . . . .  138  Cert Sonnets  5   20
   My Muse and I must you of dutie greet. . . . . . . . . . .  209  Astrophil    84    7
   By iron lawes of duty to depart: . . . . . . . . . . . . .  222  Astrophil    87    4
DWELL
   And thinke ther she do dwell and heare what plaintes I do
      utter: . . . . . . . . . . . . . . . . . . . . . . . .   36  1st Eclogues 13  143
   Seeking the Sainct in whome all graces dwell,. . . . . . .   71  Arcadia III  36   14
   In whose each part all pens may dwell? . . . . . . . . . .   85  Arcadia III  62    2
   In whose each part all pens may dwell. . . . . . . . . . .   90  Arcadia III  62  146
   Dwell in my ruines, feede with sucking smarte, . . . . .·. .  113  4th Eclogues 72    9
   That thus I must, while in this death I dwell, . . . . . .  116  4th Eclogues 72   89
   (Unto thy selfe I do meane those graces dwell so within
      thee . . . . . . . . . . . . . . . . . . . . . . . . .  122  4th Eclogues 74    9
   To honor turnd, doth dwell in honor's nest,. . . . . . . .  151  Cert Sonnets 22   47
   Towardes Aurora's Court a Nymph doth dwell,. . . . . . . .  183  Astrophil    37    5
   And Muses scorne with vulgar braines to dwell, . . . . . .  203  Astrophil    74    3
   Then those blest eyes, where all my hopes do dwell,. . . .  212  Astrophil    86   13
   In what high joyes I shall dwell,. . . . . . . . . . . . .  226  A&S 10th Song      11
   I dwell, layd up in safest neast.. . . . . . . . . . . . .  274  Psalm IV            35
   No, nor with Thee the naughty Ones shall dwel, . . . . . .  274  Psalm V             11
   And all who in that Globe do dwell;. . . . . . . . . . . .  302  Psalm XXIV           2
   The House where Thou dost dwell, . . . . . . . . . . . . .  306  Psalm XXVI          26
   For ever crave, that dwell I may . . . . . . . . . . . . .  307  Psalm XXVII         20
   Who dwell in dusty place.. . . . . . . . . . . . . . . . .  317  Psalm XXXIII        54
   Shall dwell thereon, and this their blessing . . . . . . .  326  Psalm XXXVII        75
   To hell he goes, and Nous with him must dwell. . . . . . .  250  Other Poems   4  313
DWELLER
   O prayse the lord, this Syon dweller good, . . . . . . . .  280  Psalm IX            31
   Of world a dweller is. . . . . . . . . . . . . . . . . . .  317  Psalm XXXIII        30
DWELLERS
   Their dwellers rapt with sight of her perfection . . . . .   15  1st Eclogues  7   44
   That nature, soverayne of earthly dwellers,. . . . . . . .   68  2nd Eclogues 33   21
   Klaius. Long since the happie dwellers of these vallies, . .  112  4th Eclogues 71   31
DWELLETH
   Where each part in such peace dwelleth,. . . . . . . . . .  140  Cert Sonnets  7   16
   Ev'en where he dwelleth hee. . . . . . . . . . . . . . . .  317  Psalm XXXIII        52
   For God's high law in his heart dwelleth.. . . . . . . . .  326  Psalm XXXVII        79
DWELLING
   Philisides. If fortune's lappe became my dwelling place, . .   23  1st Eclogues  9   26
   All thoughts so spronge, are from their dwelling driv'n, . .   83  Arcadia III  57   11
   My worke her workes to know, her dwelling my resorte.. . . .  117  4th Eclogues 73   42
   That thou must want or food, or dwelling place.. . . . . .  187  Astrophil    46    4
   But Thou art Holy and dost hold Thy dwelling . . . . . . .  298  Psalm XXII           9
   Ev'n from Hermon's dwelling led, . . . . . . . . . . . . .  335  Psalm XLII          26
   And of grasse was plenty dwelling, . . . . . . . . . . . .  262  Other Poems   7    5
DWELLINGS
   Man was not man their dwellings in to hem. . . . . . . . .  100  3rd Eclogues 66   49
DWELLS
   The power I will invoke dwelles in her eyes: . . . . . . .   17  1st Eclogues  7  104
```

DWELLS	(CONTINUED)	PAGE	TITLE		LINE
Of fairer quest, which dwells within,.		90	Arcadia III	62	140
DYED					
In time that, richly di'de,.		258	Other Poems	5	70
DYER					
Better like I thy Satyre deerest Dyer, ...		145	Cert Sonnets	16	13
DYES					
How doth the colour vade of those vermillion dies, ...		232	Astrophil	102	5
DYING					
But deck therewith my soule for your sake dying.		17	1st Eclogues	7	90
Yet dying, and dead, doo we sing her honour;		30	1st Eclogues	12	9
For what is life to dayly dyinge minde,.		73	Arcadia III	40	9
Time haste my dying hower:		136	Cert Sonnets	3	18
A light which dying never, ...		152	Cert Sonnets	23	7
In never dying faith:.		152	Cert Sonnets	23	14
To my dying heart some pleasure, ...		155	Cert Sonnets	26	9
So that I in her beames dying, ...		156	Cert Sonnets	26	31
Restlesse rest, and living dying..		218	A&S 8th Song		20
In dying..		285	Psalm XIII		12
E					
Welcome my two to me, E.D. F.G. P.S.		261	Other Poems	6	25
EACH					
Ech eare suckes up the words a true love scattereth, ...		14	1st Eclogues	7	5
Deadly wounds inward bleed, ech sleight sore mattereth.. . .		14	1st Eclogues	7	9
Naught in himselfe ech other to abuse.		21	1st Eclogues	8	24
Thus halfe a beast, ech beastly vice he plants,.		21	1st Eclogues	8	33
He proules ech place stil in new colours deckt,.		21	1st Eclogues	8	35
Creeping to ech with flattering of desire.		22	1st Eclogues	8	40
Geron. Yet sure an end, to each thing time doth give,. . . .		22	1st Eclogues	9	11
Then each conceit that enters in by sight, ...		23	1st Eclogues	9	38
With such intemperance, that each way grows.		27	1st Eclogues	10	38
While, "Let us passe our time" each shepeheard saies.. . . .		28	1st Eclogues	10	48
Whose faire bodily gifts are fram'd most lovely to each ey..		33	1st Eclogues	13	55
But yet well I doo finde each man most wise in his owne					
case		33	1st Eclogues	13	70
Thus both trees and each thing ells, be the bookes of a					
fancy.		36	1st Eclogues	13	140
What hope to quench, where each thing blowes the fire? . . .		42	Arcadia II	21	18
Eache flower eache herbe dothe to your service yeeld,. . . .		43	Arcadia II	23	5
Seekes to make ech thing badge of his sweet passion.		47	2nd Eclogues	28	6
Thus for ech change my changelesse hart I fortifie..		51	2nd Eclogues	28	126
Pas. If each day hath bene holy for your sake, ...		54	2nd Eclogues	29	72
Woe to poore man: ech outward thing annoyes him.		62	2nd Eclogues	30	170
Skowts ech motion is, the hands the horsmen,.		67	2nd Eclogues	33	8
Each sight draws on a thought, thought mother of science,. .		69	2nd Eclogues	34	11
Hold deere his work, with sighes eache change attendes,. . .		71	Arcadia III	37	8
So smooth as sleekestone-like, it smoothes each parte, . . .		76	Arcadia III	46	14
Though each of them, his private forme preserve, ...		78	Arcadia III	50	3
Though each possesse a divers working kinde, ...		78	Arcadia III	50	7
What were it els, but to make each thing blinde?		79	Arcadia III	50	13
Each moment lost, part of my hap destroyes:.		80	Arcadia III	53	11
But nowe each where doth range		82	Arcadia III	55	7
In whose each part all pens may dwell?		85	Arcadia III	62	2
Whose winke ech bold attempt forbids.		86	Arcadia III	62	14
Might of each side astray be brought,.		88	Arcadia III	62	72
Thus hath each part his beautie's part,.		90	Arcadia III	62	133
In whose each part all pens may dwell.		90	Arcadia III	62	146
Each other still allow:.		92	3rd Eclogues	63	50
So may each thing, even as thou wishest lighte,.		96	3rd Eclogues	64	94
Each thing with mantle black the night doth soothe;.		98	3rd Eclogues	66	5
Icleped starres: each thing to rest disposed:.		98	3rd Eclogues	66	10
Ech other beast likewise his present brings:		101	3rd Eclogues	66	99
Revil'd for ech small fault, sometimes for none:		105	3rd Eclogues	67	53
Geron. Who for ech fickle feare from vertue shrinkes,. . . .		105	3rd Eclogues	67	58
Am growne a shrich-owle to my selfe each morning..		111	4th Eclogues	71	18
I give the Sunne a last farewell each evening;		112	4th Eclogues	71	50
I wish no evenings more to see, each evening;.		112	4th Eclogues	71	58
Now each thing which enjoy'd that firie quickning sparke . .		116	4th Eclogues	73	4
A silence sweet each where with one consent embraste		117	4th Eclogues	73	7
Both our estates, while each the other did deprave,.		119	4th Eclogues	73	107
(For both togither spake, each loth to be behinde)		121	4th Eclogues	73	155
While each conceate an ouglie figure beares, ...		131	Arcadia V	77	7
Where each part in such peace dwelleth,.		140	Cert Sonnets	7	16
For in each thing wherto mine eye doth range, ...		147	Cert Sonnets	18	3
In Dales I see each way a hard assent:		147	Cert Sonnets	18	10
Infected mindes infect each thing they see,.		147	Cert Sonnets	18	14
Or with strange similies enrich each line, ...		166	Astrophil	3	7
Playing and shining in each outward part:.		170	Astrophil	11	13
Each had his creast, Mars caried Venus' glove, ...		171	Astrophil	13	7
Yet each prepar'd, with fanne's wel-shading grace, ...		176	Astrophil	22	7
While he each thing in sense's ballance wayes, ...		177	Astrophil	25	6
Each soule doth at Love's feet his weapons lay,.		186	Astrophil	43	7
While each pretends that Stella must be his:		190	Astrophil	52	2
Nor give each speech a full point of a grone,.		191	Astrophil	54	4
Each sence of mine, each gift, each power of mind, ...		193	Astrophil	57	2
While each doth blow the fier of my hart;.		202	Astrophil	72	4
Pleasingst consort, where each sence holds a part, ...		206	Astrophil	79	3
The prettie death, while each in other live.		206	Astrophil	79	11
Not pointing to fit folkes each undercharge, ...		210	Astrophil	85	6
United powers make each the stronger prove..		223	Astrophil	88	14

```
EACH            (CONTINUED)                                  PAGE    TITLE        LINE
   Each day seemes long, and longs for long-staid night,.. . . .  224  Astrophil   89    5
   From heavenly standing hits each mortall wight.. . . . . . .   229  Astrophil   97    4
   That tedious leasure marks each wrinckled line:.. . . . . .    230  Astrophil   98   11
   When far spent night perswades each mortall eye,. . . . . .    230  Astrophil   99    1
   Cals each wight to salute the floure of blisse;. . . . . . .   231  Astrophil   99   11
   That to each word, nay sigh of mine you harke, . . . . . . .   233  Astrophil  104    3
   Sweet then, while each thing doth frame: . . . . . . . . . .   211  A&S 4th Song     34
   I thought each place was darke but where . . . . . . . . . .   212  A&S 5th Song      5
   Each to other do imparte,. . . . . . . . . . . . . . . . . .   227  A&S 10th Song    41
   That each, while each contends,. . . . . . . . . . . . . . .   216  A&S 6th Song     17
   A friend each party drawes,. . . . . . . . . . . . . . . . .   216  A&S 6th Song     29
   But each in the other blessed. . . . . . . . . . . . . . . .   218  A&S 8th Song      8
   Their eares hungry of each word. . . . . . . . . . . . . . .   218  A&S 8th Song     21
   Writ each character of blisse, . . . . . . . . . . . . . . .   219  A&S 8th Song     42
   Ech tree in his best attiring, . . . . . . . . . . . . . . .   219  A&S 8th Song     59
   Yet each day art provoakt, thyne Ire to show,. . . . . . . .   277  Psalm VII        32
   Thou seest each side the walking doth endure . . . . . . . .   285  Psalm XII        25
   Feare was each where, while they their counsells led . . . .   313  Psalm XXXI       38
   Who for my hurt each way their thoughts did roll.. . . . . .   321  Psalm XXXV       10
   Each motion seeming shott from beautie's bow,. . . . . . . .   244  Other Poems  4  106
   And each way luckles, yet in humble guise. . . . . . . . . .   249  Other Poems  4  277
   Each way, as she, that age's praise, did bend. . . . . . . .   251  Other Poems  4  376
   "Nay each thing is bewitcht to know my case: . . . . . . . .   254  Other Poems  4  473
   Each thing both sweet and sadd . . . . . . . . . . . . . . .   256  Other Poems  5    8
   Oft each other's friendship proving, . . . . . . . . . . . .   262  Other Poems  7   23
   Scarce each other can abide, . . . . . . . . . . . . . . . .   263  Other Poems  7   52
EAGER
   These be her words, but a woman's words to a love that is
      eager,. . . . . . . . . . . . . . . . . . . . . . . . . .   143  Cert Sonnets 13   3
   Cease eager Muse, peace pen, for my sake stay, . . . . . . .   201  Astrophil   70   12
EAGERLY
   They leave off al, and say, death comes too eagerlie.. . . .   128  4th Eclogues 75 114
EAGLE
   Eagle, high looke; Wolfe secrete crueltie: . . . . . . . . .   101  3rd Eclogues 66  87
   But alwayes one my selfe with eagle eyde trueth to flie, . .   153  Cert Sonnets 24  24
   Joves golden shield did Eagle sables beare,. . . . . . . . .   171  Astrophil   13    3
   If Eagle fierce could so in Grecian Mayd delight,. . . . . .   209  A&S 3rd Song      9
EAR
   Ech eare suckes up the words a true love scattereth, . . . .    14  1st Eclogues  7   5
   But eye from blade, and eare from crie:. . . . . . . . . . .    44  Arcadia II   25  11
   The hart, eye, eare here onely find his treasure doth: . . .    49  2nd Eclogues 28  58
   Pas. Nay like to nightingales the other birds give eare: . .    52  2nd Eclogues 29  19
   No eare nor taile he hath, least they should him disgrace, .    53  2nd Eclogues 29  41
   Wherin no eare can have joy, . . . . . . . . . . . . . . . .    66  2nd Eclogues 32  37
   The tippe is jewell of the eare. . . . . . . . . . . . . . .    87  Arcadia III  62  36
   And hither now, vouchsafe to take with willing eare. . . . .   119  4th Eclogues 73 104
   Then give a quiet eare unto my playning: . . . . . . . . . .   127  4th Eclogues 75  65
   Listen then Lordings with good eare to me,. . . . . . . . .    183  Astrophil   37    3
   So sweete sounds straight mine eare and heart do hit,. . . .   192  Astrophil   55   13
   That giv'st no better eare to my just cries: . . . . . . . .   198  Astrophil   65    2
   "Peace, I thinke that some give eare:. . . . . . . . . . . .   234  A&S 11th Song    36
   The eare, his truth to trie: . . . . . . . . . . . . . . . .   216  A&S 6th Song     38
   He will give good eare to my moane.. . . . . . . . . . . . .   273  Psalm IV         15
   Then eare to them enclin'd.. . . . . . . . . . . . . . . . .   283  Psalm X          76
   And boldly say Thou wilt give eare to me,. . . . . . . . . .   289  Psalm XVII       18
   But God Thy eare my crying never heareth.. . . . . . . . . .   298  Psalm XXII        6
   O my strength stop not Thine eare, . . . . . . . . . . . . .   308  Psalm XXVIII      2
   Bow down thine eare to heare how much I need,. . . . . . . .   312  Psalm XXXI        4
   Come children, lend your eare. . . . . . . . . . . . . . . .   319  Psalm XXXIV      41
   But thou didst peirce my eare,. . . . . . . . . . . . . . .    331  Psalm XL         28
   As Strephon's eare and heart to Klaius bent: . . . . . . . .   242  Other Poems  4   28
EARLIEST
   With earlyest entry of the Morning prime,. . . . . . . . . .   274  Psalm V           7
EARLY
   Ly but to sleepe, and in the earely prime. . . . . . . . . .    26  1st Eclogues  9 126
   Which to my woes gives still an early morning: . . . . . . .   111  4th Eclogues 71   5
   When mery May first early calls the morne, . . . . . . . . .   243  Other Poems  4   49
EARNEST
   Then to an earnest Love what doth best victorie lend? Ende..    63  2nd Eclogues 31  15
   Who earnest found what they accounted play.. . . . . . . . .   251  Other Poems  4  366
EARS
   Where eares be burnt, eyes dazled, harts opprest?. . . . . .     3  Lady of May   1   6
   And feede mine eares, mine eyes, my hart in you. . . . . . .     3  Lady of May   1  12
   With long large eares where never rumour dyes. . . . . . . .    21  1st Eclogues  8  28
   My wearied ears! O gods yet graunt me this,. . . . . . . . .    24  1st Eclogues  9  67
   Give right sound to the eares, and enter aright to the
      judgement; . . . . . . . . . . . . . . . . . . . . . . .     32  1st Eclogues 13  18
   Your scepters here, if to your eares divine. . . . . . . . .    40  Arcadia II   18    3
   Since streame, aier, sand, mine eyes and eares conspire: . .    42  Arcadia II   21   17
   Yeeld to our eares a sweet and sound relation, . . . . . . .    48  2nd Eclogues 28  20
   I sooner would, then thus my eares defile. . . . . . . . . .    50  2nd Eclogues 28  81
   Fine eares, long taile he hath, with Lion's curbed clawe,. .    53  2nd Eclogues 29  33
   Shall I, whose eares her mournefull words did seaze, . . . .    58  2nd Eclogues 30  50
   Plangus. If through mine eares pearce any consolacyons . . .    61  2nd Eclogues 30 143
   My harte, eyes, eares, with wonder, love, delight: . . . . .    84  Arcadia III  60    2
   No purer then the pretie eares.. . . . . . . . . . . . . . .    86  Arcadia III  62   28
   With old true tales he woont mine eares to fill, . . . . . .    99  3rd Eclogues 66  33
   Vouchsafe your silent eares to playning musique, . . . . . .   111  4th Eclogues 71   4
   Above line repeated at following location. . . . . . . . . .   111  4th Eclogues 71  11
```

EARS   (CONTINUED)   PAGE   TITLE   LINE
      And stoppe mine eares, lest I growe mad with Musicke.. . . .   112 4th Eclogues 71   60
      Since will is won, and stopped eares are charmed:. . . . . .   135 Cert Sonnets 1   3
      The earth, her eares: the stake is my request: . . . . . .   151 Cert Sonnets 22   45
      Pardon mine eares, both I and they do pray,. . . . .   190 Astrophil   51   1
      I Stella's eyes assayll, invade her eares; . . . .   195 Astrophil   61   3
      That voyce, which makes the soule plant himselfe in the
         eares: . . . .   205 Astrophil   77   9
      So ample eares as never good newes know: . . . .   206 Astrophil   78   13
      And that my Muse to some eares not unsweet,. . . . .   209 Astrophil   84   2
      Let eares heare speech, which wit to wonder ties,. . . . . .   210 Astrophil   85   11
      Or do you meane my tender eares to spare,. . . . .   225 Astrophil   92   4
      O eyes, o eares of men, how are you charmed! . . . . . .   209 A&S 3rd Song   18
      And all eares worse then deafe, that heard not out thy
         storie.. . . . .   212 A&S 5th Song   6
      Their eares hungry of each word. . . . .   218 A&S 8th Song   21
      As not eares but hart did tuch:. . . . .   220 A&S 8th Song   70
      So shall my voice clime to thyne eares betime: . . . . . .   274 Psalm V   5
      Thyne Ears voutchsafe to bend to me. . . . .   289 Psalm XVII   4
      His eyes unto my Case, his eares unto my moane.. . . . . .   291 Psalm XVIII   14
      My name their eares, their eares their hearts to me
         enchaine , ...   293 Psalm XVIII   80
      And eares to them encline. . . . .   320 Psalm XXXIV   56
      Heare lord my suits and cryes, stop not thyn eares . . . . .   330 Psalm XXXIX   37
      Will. Thou seest my eares do itch at it: good Dick thy sorow
         tell. . . . .   343 Possibly   1   18
      Such marble eares, no cunning wordes can charme, ...   346 Possibly   5   2
      You I invite with easie eares to heare . . . .   242 Other Poems   4   13
      So may her eares be ledd,. . . . .   258 Other Poems   5   59
      Her eares where Musique lives, ...   258 Other Poems   5   60
      Her ears the weights of wit. . . . .   259 Other Poems   5 109
EARTH
      Her length the earth in Love's chiefe clothing dressed.. . .   17 1st Eclogues 7   87
      "Let not dead earth enjoy so deare a cover,. . . . .   17 1st Eclogues 7   89
      Earth, sea, ayre, fire, heav'n, hell, and gastly sprite. . .   23 1st Eclogues 9   40
      Unto the heav'ns? our wings be too short; th' earth thinks
         us a burden; . . . .   32 1st Eclogues 13   29
      Which ever shines, though hid from earth by earthly shade, .   44 Arcadia II   26   3
      That nothing winnes the heaven, but what doth earth forsake.   45 Arcadia II   26   16
      His breast doth fill with earth of others' woe,. . . . . . .   50 2nd Eclogues 28   85
      Throwne on this earth the Chaos of confusions. . . . .   51 2nd Eclogues 28 110
      To frame of Earth a vessell of the minde,. . . . .   57 2nd Eclogues 30   12
      Will spoile the earth of his most rich attire. . . . .   59 2nd Eclogues 30   88
      Of rarest price, both heav'n and earth her bower.. . . . . .   59 2nd Eclogues 30 100
      Then let my life long time on earth maintained be, ...   61 2nd Eclogues 30 147
      The laborer, which cursed earthe up teares . . . .   71 Arcadia III 36   7
      She heav'n on earth with beauties doth preserve. . . . . . .   72 Arcadia III 38   8
      Though you besides such graces earth hath lent,. . . . . . .   77 Arcadia III 49   3
      To decke the earth with his well-colourde weede, ...   78 Arcadia III 50   2
      Whose steppe on earth all beautie sets.. . . . .   89 Arcadia III 62 108
      Let mother earth now decke her selfe in flowers, ...   91 3rd Eclogues 63   1
      The earth is deckt with flowers, the heav'ns displaid, . . .   93 3rd Eclogues 63   91
      When all this Earth, this damme or mould of ours, ...   100 3rd Eclogues 66   44
      Which streight the Earth yclothed in his claye:. . . . . . .   101 3rd Eclogues 66   79
      Then gan in guiltlesse earth full many a wound,. . . . . . .   102 3rd Eclogues 66 115
      In water dround, in earth his buriall is;. . . . .   105 3rd Eclogues 67   68
      Earth thou didst seeke, and store of earth thou hast.. . . .   108 Arcadia IV   68   2
      I would the earth, I would the heavens sell. . . . .   116 4th Eclogues 72   93
      And mother Earth, now clad in mourning weeds, did breath . .   117 4th Eclogues 73   9
      Whence our immortall soules to mortall earth doo flowe:. . .   118 4th Eclogues 73   46
      Of heaven, of earth, of hell, of time and place was come.. .   118 4th Eclogues 73   62
      Unto the earth, by the hurt of this her heavenly jewell. . .   124 4th Eclogues 74   62
      And thou poore Earth, whom fortune doth attaint. . . . . . .   125 4th Eclogues 75   16
      The earth with pitie dull the center keepeth:. . . . .   136 Cert Sonnets 3   4
      Earth take this earth, wherein my spirits languish. . . . .   136 Cert Sonnets 3   16
      Fire, aire, sea, earth, fame, time, place, shew your power..   136 Cert Sonnets 3   20
      While late bare earth, proud of new clothing springeth,. . .   137 Cert Sonnets 4   3
      Thine earth now springs, mine fadeth. . . . .   137 Cert Sonnets 4   11
      Thine earth now springs, mine fadeth:. . . . .   137 Cert Sonnets 4   23
      That heavie earth, not fierie sprites may plaine?. . . . . .   142 Cert Sonnets 11   6
      That all the earth my woes, sighes, teares may know, ...   146 Cert Sonnets 17   39
      Deepe plunged in earth, deprived of the skie.. . . . .   149 Cert Sonnets 21   8
      From fancie's earth passing all numbers' bound,. . . . . . .   149 Cert Sonnets 22   7
      Deepe in the earth, what hath in earth receipt. . . . . . .   150 Cert Sonnets 22   42
      The earth, her eares: the stake is my request: . . . .   151 Cert Sonnets 22   45
      A heaven on earth, or earth that heaven containes: . . . . .   151 Cert Sonnets 22   68
      True, that on earth we are but pilgrims made,. . . . .   167 Astrophil   5   12
      Let all the earth with scorne recount my case, ...   198 Astrophil   64   7
      Earth gave that Love, heav'n I trow Love refineth: . . . . .   209 A&S 3rd Song   11
      "Love makes earth the water drink, ...   219 A&S 8th Song   61
      Love to earth makes water sinke; . . . .   219 A&S 8th Song   62
      Do works which earth corrupt and Heaven hates, ...   286 Psalm XIV   5
      And so the Earth did fall to tremble, and to quake . . . . .   291 Psalm XVIII   15
      The earth is God's, and what the Globe of earth containeth,.   302 Psalm XXIV   1
      Let all the earth feare God, ...   317 Psalm XXXIII   28
      From earth quite to displace.. . . . .   320 Psalm XXXIV   60
      But meek men shall the earth possesse, ...   325 Psalm XXXVII   29
      And of the earth make Thee an owner, ...   327 Psalm XXXVII   87
      For I with Thee on earth a stranger am . . . .   330 Psalm XXXIX   39
      Never the earth on his round shoulders bare. . . . .   247 Other Poems   4 209

125

```
EARTH                (CONTINUED)                              PAGE  TITLE              LINE
    And crown'd the earth with his first touching crowne:. . . .  248  Other Poems    4   260
    More then, besides hir, all the earth could show.. . . . . .  252  Other Poems    4   408
    "O earth, once answere give, . . . . . . . . . . . . . . . .  256  Other Poems    5    14
    "Earth, brooke, flowrs, pipe, lambe, Dove. . . . . . . . . .  259  Other Poems    5    92
EARTHLY
    Which ever shines, though hid from earth by earthly shade, .   44  Arcadia II     26    3
    That nature, soverayne of earthly dwellers,. . . . . . . . .   68  2nd Eclogues   33   21
    In earthly clothes enclosde a heavenly sparke. . . . . . . .   80  Arcadia III    52   10
    In earthly fetters feele a lasting hell. . . . . . . . . . .  116  4th Eclogues   72   90
    Klaius. In earthly fetters feele a lasting hell. . . . . . .  116  4th Eclogues   72   91
    As for to lose thy gemme, our earthly Sainct,. . . . . . . .  125  4th Eclogues   75   18
    From base desire on earthly cates to pray? . . . . . . . . .  223  Astrophil      88    8
    No mortall gifts, no earthly fruites, now here descended be:  217  A&S 7th Song         14
    Why do these earthly kings and lords such meetings make, . .  271  Psalm II              3
    Thou planted hast this earthly mate. . . . . . . . . . . . .  279  Psalm VIII           18
    Of earthly man, a lord of dust.. . . . . . . . . . . . . . .  283  Psalm X              80
    When fire seven times hath spent his earthly parts.. . . . .  285  Psalm XII            21
    With heavnly strength Thy earthly strength to prop.. . . . .  295  Psalm XX             10
    Their fruit shalt Thou from earthly face . . . . . . . . . .  297  Psalm XXI            37
    Earthly I do bow and crooke, . . . . . . . . . . . . . . . .  328  Psalm XXXVIII        16
    E're I my earthly being leave. . . . . . . . . . . . . . . .  330  Psalm XXXIX          42
    Who nothing earthly, but of fire and aire, . . . . . . . . .  250  Other Poems    4   338
EARTHQUAKE
    Which thus breath'd out with earthquake of his hart. . . . .  256  Other Poems    4   544
EARTH'S
    And when I meete these trees, in the earth's faire lyvery
        clothed, . . . . . . . . . . . . . . . . . . . . . . . .   35  1st Eclogues   13  113
    But what? I say from earth's remotest border . . . . . . . .  300  Psalm XXII           65
    They that be made even fatt, with earth's fatt good, . . . .  300  Psalm XXII           71
EARTHY
    My earthy moulde doth melte in watrie teares.. . . . . . . .   19  1st Eclogues    7  151
    Dorus. My earthy moulde doth melte in watrie teares, . . . .   19  1st Eclogues    7  152
    The honest sports of earthy lodging prove; . . . . . . . . .  243  Other Poems    4    42
EASE
    But let us sing, sweet tunes do passions ease, . . . . . . .   22  1st Eclogues    9    4
    And hope therby to ease their inward horrible anguish, . . .   33  1st Eclogues   13   45
    Then shall those thinges ease their inward horrible angwish.   33  1st Eclogues   13   46
    Shall such morning deaws be an ease to the heate of a love's
        fire? . . . . . . . . . . . . . . . . . . . . . . . . .   34  1st Eclogues   13   88
    Ease I do feele (such ease as falls to one wholy diseased) .   35  1st Eclogues   13  114
    Over these brookes trusting to ease mine eyes, . . . . . . .   41  Arcadia II     21    1
    Nay rather then my ease discontentation. . . . . . . . . . .   51  2nd Eclogues   28  120
    In ease, untill that bodie life forgoes. . . . . . . . . . .   56  2nd Eclogues   29  146
    In what state was I then, when I tooke this deadly disease?
        ease. . . . . . . . . . . . . . . . . . . . . . . . . .   63  2nd Eclogues   31    8
    Make present ease receave the better taste.. . . . . . . . .   70  Arcadia III    36    6
    Bitter griefe tastes me best, paine is my ease,. . . . . . .   74  Arcadia III    41    7
    To her sweete sence, sweete sleepe, some ease imparte, . . .   79  Arcadia III    51    3
    Joyne with thy sonne, to ease my long annoys.. . . . . . . .   81  Arcadia III    53   13
    To ease those paines, which on desire do waite). . . . . . .   82  Arcadia III    56    4
    Had reason's weight for passion's ease rejected. . . . . . .   83  Arcadia III    57    8
    For no thing, time, nor place, can loose, quench, ease,. . .   84  Arcadia III    60   13
    Camaeleon, ease to chaunge; Ducke, ease to yelde;. . . . . .  101  3rd Eclogues   66   95
    O Night, the ease of care, the pledge of pleasure, . . . . .  108  Arcadia IV     69    1
    Despise delight, am tyrde with thought of ease;. . . . . . .  113  4th Eclogues   72    2
    Since shunning paine, I ease can never find: . . . . . . . .  135  Cert Sonnets    1    1
    Sweete thinke not I am at ease,. . . . . . . . . . . . . . .  140  Cert Sonnets    7   34
    Then might I hope a change or ease of minde, . . . . . . . .  148  Cert Sonnets   19   11
    If further place might further me to ease. . . . . . . . . .  149  Cert Sonnets   21    4
    Where with most ease and warmth he might employ his art: . .  168  Astrophil       8    7
    Come let me write, "And to what end?" To ease. . . . . . . .  181  Astrophil      34    1
    A burthned hart. "How can words ease, which are. . . . . . .  181  Astrophil      34    2
    Becomes a clog) will soone ease me of it.. . . . . . . . . .  194  Astrophil      59   14
    How falles it then, that with so smooth an ease. . . . . . .  204  Astrophil      74    9
    O ease your hand, treate not so hard your slave: . . . . . .  212  Astrophil      86    9
    Fit to heare and ease my care: . . . . . . . . . . . . . . .  210  A&S 4th Song          2
    And of hideous torments ease me. . . . . . . . . . . . . . .  222  A&S 9th Song         45
    When he his lust doth ease,. . . . . . . . . . . . . . . . .  281  Psalm X              10
    Nor want in dearth their want to ease. . . . . . . . . . . .  325  Psalm XXXVII         48
    For other's ease, their frutte, or free estate,. . . . . . .  345  Possibly        2   10
    So laughing all, yet Pas to ease some dell,. . . . . . . . .  249  Other Poems    4   263
EASED
    Sorrowes ill easde, where sorrowes painted be. . . . . . . .   41  Arcadia II     21    6
    Witnesse his wrong which by thy helpe is eased:. . . . . . .  108  Arcadia IV     69   11
    Only with paines my paines thus eased be,. . . . . . . . . .  227  Astrophil      93   12
    And his sweet grace streight easd the rod. . . . . . . . . .  315  Psalm XXXII          17
EASEFUL
    O harbour all her partes in easefull plighte:. . . . . . . .   79  Arcadia III    51    7
    As his maine force, choise sport, and easefull stay. . . . .  186  Astrophil      43    4
EASILY
    Thus halfe a man, with man he easly haunts,. . . . . . . . .   21  1st Eclogues    8   31
    Quickly secure, and easilie in doubt,. . . . . . . . . . . .   27  1st Eclogues   10   28
    On those affectes which easily yeeld to sight, . . . . . . .  135  Cert Sonnets    2    6
    Do easly yeeld, that all their coasts may be . . . . . . . .  179  Astrophil      29    3
    Or loving, have so frothy thoughts, as easly thence to move:  217  A&S 7th Song          3
    For he was olde, and easly would be cought:. . . . . . . . .  250  Other Poems    4   322
EAST
    To Westerne wightes, what starres in East appeare? . . . . .   80  Arcadia III    52    4
    But East and West were join'd by frendship's hest. . . . . .  242  Other Poems    4   27
```

```
                                                      PAGE    TITLE          LINE
EASY
    Shewes easie print in mettall fine................  89 Arcadia III   62  100
    You I invite with easie eares to heare............ 242 Other Poems    4   13
EAT
    The' afflicted then shall eat, and be well pleased,.....  300 Psalm XXII         61
EATS
    Woe, lyke a moth, my face's beauty eates .......... 276 Psalm VI           21
EBB
    The sea to ebbe for griefe his flowing turneth:....... 136 Cert Sonnets  3    3
    To so lowe ebbe that wonted were to flowe. ........ 146 Cert Sonnets 17   15
ECHO
    Or pleasant mirtell, may teach th'unfortunate Echo .....  31 1st Eclogues 13   13
    Pleasd to receave that name by rebounding answere of Echo, .  33 1st Eclogues 13   44
    Or when an Echo begins unmov'd to sing them a love song. .  33 1st Eclogues 13   48
    Oh! I do know what guest I have mett; it is Echo. 'T is
        Echo...........................................  63 2nd Eclogues 31    3
    Well mett Echo, aproche: then tell me thy will too. I will
        too............................................  63 2nd Eclogues 31    4
    Echo, what do I gett yelding my sprite to my grieves?
        Grieves........................................  63 2nd Eclogues 31    5
    Thou li'st false Echo, their minds as vertu be just. Just. .  65 2nd Eclogues 31   46
    Which oft hath Echo tir'd in secrete forrests........ 111 4th Eclogues 71   12
    O Echo, all these woods with roaring fill, ........ 126 4th Eclogues 75   31
    One Echo to another Echo cast. ................... 126 4th Eclogues 75   34
ECHO'S
    But that it dooth with Echoe's force rebound ........  42 Arcadia II   21   10
    With Echoe's help, shall "Cosma, Cosma" flie........  56 2nd Eclogues 29  134
ECLIPSE
    By what eclipse shall that Sonne be defaste? .........  59 2nd Eclogues 30   95
    Tush absence, while thy mistes eclipse that light, ..... 223 Astrophil    88    9
ECLIPSED
    Of Mira's beames eclipst by absence bad. .......... 256 Other Poems    5   11
ED
    "Only for my two loves' sake, Sir Ed. D. and M. F. G..... 263 Other Poems    7   61
EDWARD
    Edward named fourth, as first in praise I name,....... 204 Astrophil    75    2
EELS
    Harde to be gott, but got constant, to be helde like
        steeles  Eeles.................................  65 2nd Eclogues 31   42
EFFECT
    Hath all thy whirling course so small effect?.......  58 2nd Eclogues 30   60
    Both cause, effect, beginning, and the ende........ 114 4th Eclogues 72   42
    And still th'effect of thy perswasions prove:....... 167 Astrophil     4   11
    And find th'effect, for I do burne in love.......... 177 Astrophil    25   14
    Thus while th' effect most bitter was to me,........ 223 Astrophil    87   12
    More cause a like effect at leastwise bringeth:....... 208 A&S 3rd Song        5
    To raise in words what in effect is lowe:........... 242 Other Poems    4    2
EFFECTING
    These same words, or this effecting: ............. 262 Other Poems    7   18
EFFECTS
    Effects of lively heat, must needs in nature grow....... 169 Astrophil     8   11
    And know great causes, great effects procure:........ 178 Astrophil    26   10
    Of conquest, do not these effects suffice:......... 183 Astrophil    36    7
    Cease in these effects to prove: ................. 220 A&S 8th Song       74
EFFEMINATE
    Women man-wood, and men effeminate................  28 1st Eclogues 10   60
EFT
    He eft would kill a mouse, but he disdaines the fight, . . .  53 2nd Eclogues 29   45
EIGHT
    Thus did I sing, and pipe eight sullen houres. ....... 103 3rd Eclogues 66  155
EITHER
    Either a sleepe be all if nought assaile,..........  27 1st Eclogues 10   29
    A letter such which might from either part ........  96 3rd Eclogues 64   81
    Either dull silence, or eternall chat; ........... 104 3rd Eclogues 67   31
    If either you would change your cruell hart, ....... 148 Cert Sonnets 19    7
    Faire choice I have, either to live or dye ........ 149 Cert Sonnets 21   13
    Either to do like him, which open shone, .......... 176 Astrophil    22   10
    With either lip he doth the other kisse: .......... 186 Astrophil    43   11
    For ere that either had his purpose done,.......... 244 Other Poems    4   81
    Do coupled towards either couple make,............ 248 Other Poems    4  234
EKE
    Then let me eke forget one hand from other:.........  61 2nd Eclogues 30  161
    And eke revenge his wrong suspecting you"..........  97 3rd Eclogues 64  108
    Klaius. These forrests eke, made wretched by our musique,. . 113 4th Eclogues 71   74
    A Poet eke, as humours fly or creepe,............. 181 Astrophil    32    4
    By his seed eke possest. ...................... 304 Psalm XXV          52
    Heare to have mercy eke of me.................... 307 Psalm XXVII        38
    And eke their pipes did well, as frends, agree........ 242 Other Poems    4   32
ELBOW
    That he for want of elbowe roome must die? ........ 126 4th Eclogues 75   44
    But she on elbow lean'd, with sighs did show ....... 245 Other Poems    4  110
ELBOWS
    The fox on knees and elbowes tombled downe:......... 248 Other Poems    4  258
ELDER
    Thy elder care shall from thy carefull face. .........  11 Arcadia I     1    1
    How elder rul'd their flocks, and cur'd their smart, .... 243 Other Poems    4   37
ELECTING
    One among the rest electing. .................... 262 Other Poems    7   17
ELECTION
    Of fayrer death how can I make election? .......... 16 1st Eclogues  7   72
```

```
ELEMENTS                                               PAGE     TITLE           LINE
    So divers be the Elements disposed . . . . . . . . . . .    57  2nd Eclogues  30     29
    O Elements, by whose (they say) contention,. . . . . . . .  128  4th Eclogues  75    106
    Which elements with mortall mixture breed: . . . . . . . .  167  Astrophil      5     11
ELEPHANT
    No Elephant so perfect beares. . . . . . . . . . . . . . .   86  Arcadia III   62  V 28
    Elephant gave a perfect memorie: . . . . . . . . . . . . .  101  3rd Eclogues  66     83
ELM
    Elme embraste by a vine, embracing fancy reviveth. . . . .   36  1st Eclogues  13    131
    Like to the Elme and Vyne, . . . . . . . . . . . . . . . .   91  3rd Eclogues  63     15
ELMY
    Within the Elmy grange,. . . . . . . . . . . . . . . . . .  261  Other Poems    6     33
ELOQUENCE
    I beg no subject to use eloquence, . . . . . . . . . . . .  179  Astrophil     28      9
    Leaving me nought but wailing eloquence: . . . . . . . . .  184  Astrophil     38     11
    That I well find no eloquence like it. . . . . . . . . . .  192  Astrophil     55     14
    Now with slow words, now with dumbe eloquence. . . . . . .  195  Astrophil     61      2
    That eloquence it selfe envies your praise,. . . . . . . .  231  Astrophil    100     10
    As grudging me my sorrowe's eloquence? . . . . . . . . . .  233  Astrophil    104      4
ELSE
    Be none of us, or els maintaine our fashion: . . . . . . .   15  1st Eclogues   7     14
    Which breeds nought else but gloses of deceits. . . . . . .   20  1st Eclogues   8      4
    At blowe point, hotcocles, or els at keeles. . . . . . . .   28  1st Eclogues  10     47
    Thus both trees and each thing ells, be the bookes of a
      fancy. . . . . . . . . . . . . . . . . . . . . . . . . .   36  1st Eclogues  13    140
    But nought els do behold (else is nought worth the
      beholding . . . . . . . . . . . . . . . . . . . . . . .   36  1st Eclogues  13    150
    Let me be lov'd, or els not loved be.. . . . . . . . . . .   41  Arcadia II    20     14
    Her cleared lookes, nought els, in stormes can quiet me. . .   51  2nd Eclogues  28    119
    Or else who singeth worse, my skill will hardly hit. . . . .   53  2nd Eclogues  29     50
    Where envie's snaky ey, winketh or els dyeth,. . . . . . .   69  2nd Eclogues  34     37
    Ncr brooke oughte els but well acquainted woe. . . . . . .   74  Arcadia III   41      6
    Such pearcing wordes as no thoughts els conceave: . . . . .   78  Arcadia III   49      8
    What were it els, but to make each thing blinde? . . . . .   79  Arcadia III   50     13
    Puiling, and whimpring, or else scolding flat, . . . . . .  104  3rd Eclogues  67     29
    Or els; "Nay faith, mine is the lucklest lot,. . . . . . .  104  3rd Eclogues  67     43
    Thy house by thee must live, or els be gone: . . . . . . .  106  3rd Eclogues  67    110
    That which their mother hight, or els their silly seed.. . .  119  4th Eclogues  73     84
    But betweene those armes, never else do leave mee; . . . .  138  Cert Sonnets   5     23
    Else what in face, then in my fancie beare?. . . . . . . .  146  Cert Sonnets  17     10
    A blinded Mowlle, or else a burned flye. . . . . . . . . .  149  Cert Sonnets  21     14
    Approching warmes (not else) dead logges up sends, . . . .  150  Cert Sonnets  22     12
    Or else let them in statelier glorie shine,. . . . . . . .  166  Astrophil      3      5
    Or did she else that sober hue devise, . . . . . . . . . .  168  Astrophil      7      5
    Nobler desires, least else that friendly foe, . . . . . . .  175  Astrophil     21      7
    That no pace else their guided steps can find, . . . . . .  194  Astrophil     58      3
    Or else pronouncing grace, wherewith his mind. . . . . . .  194  Astrophil     58      7
    Driv'n else to graunt by Angel's sophistrie, . . . . . . .  195  Astrophil     61     13
    Or art thou else to comfort me forsworne?. . . . . . . . .  199  Astrophil     67     11
    Use something else to chast'n me withall,. . . . . . . . .  212  Astrophil     86     12
    Who else for whom Fame worthy trumpets wanteth?. . . . . .  197  A&S 1st Song          14
    Love feares nothing else but anger. . . . . . . . . . . . .  203  A&S 2nd Song          20
    Feare not else, none can us spie:. . . . . . . . . . . . .  211  A&S 4th Song          22
    Which to stones I els would show:. . . . . . . . . . . . .  221  A&S 9th Song          13
    And what thinges els of waters traceth . . . . . . . . . .  279  Psalm VIII            31
    Wry words, and stam'ring, or els doltish dombe,. . . . . .  254  Other Poems    4    471
ELSEWHERE
    Livelier then else-where, Stella's image see.. . . . . . .  184  Astrophil     39     14
EMBASSAGE
    Let it embassage beare your grieves to showe.. . . . . . .  125  4th Eclogues  75     12
EMBLEMISH
    Cosma's faire beames emblemish much his raies. . . . . . .   55  2nd Eclogues  29     98
EMBOLDENED
    For what lord rules our bold emboldned breast. . . . . . .  285  Psalm XII             12
EMBOSCMED
    But glad Desire, his late embosom'd guest, . . . . . . . .  247  Other Poems    4    201
EMBRACE
    Thy yonger shall with Nature's blisse embrace. . . . . . .   11  Arcadia I      1      3
    When struling rocks he would imbrace. . . . . . . . . . . .   88  Arcadia III   62     70
    Shall in this life embrace no worthy thing:. . . . . . . .  105  3rd Eclogues  67     59
    Embrace that most, that most my soule destroyes. . . . . .  113  4th Eclogues  72      7
    But finding these North clymes do coldly him embrace,. . . .  168  Astrophil      8      5
    That see my wracke, and yet embrace the same?. . . . . . .  174  Astrophil     19      2
    So piercing pawes, as spoyle when they embrace,. . . . . .  206  Astrophil     78     10
    Let breath sucke up those sweetes, let armes embrace . . . .  210  Astrophil     85     12
    Dead glasse, doost thou thy object so imbrace, . . . . . .  235  Astrophil    105      3
    All pureness ever to embrace;. . . . . . . . . . . . . . .  302  Psalm XXIV             8
    As heart-bound slaves: and happy then embrace. . . . . . .  252  Other Poems    4    391
EMBRACED
    Elme embraste by a vine, embracing fancy reviveth. . . . .   36  1st Eclogues  13    131
    Mine owne, embraced, sought, knot, fire, desease.. . . . .   84  Arcadia III   60     14
    Men's lives, untill it be imbraste. . . . . . . . . . . . .   87  Arcadia III   62     66
    A silence sweet each where with one consent embraste . . . .  117  4th Eclogues  73      7
    With you embraced lie, . . . . . . . . . . . . . . . . . .  257  Other Poems    5     43
EMBRACEMENTS
    And hopes with foule embracements her to get,. . . . . . .   59  2nd Eclogues  30     90
    With mutuall embracements them to twyne: . . . . . . . . .   91  3rd Eclogues  63     16
EMBRACES
    Fcr so faire a flame embraces. . . . . . . . . . . . . . .  155  Cert Sonnets  26      5
```

```
                                                         PAGE    TITLE          LINE
EMBRACETH
    The unworn paths, his rule embraceth. . . . . . . . . . . .   279  Psalm VIII      32
EMBRACING
    Elme embraste by a vine, embracing fancy reviveth. . . . . .    36  1st Eclogues 13  131
EMBREW
    Their swords shall their own hearts embrew. . . . . . . . .   325  Psalm XXXVII     40
EMMET
    When Cedars to the ground be opprest by the weight of an
        emmott, . . . . . . . . . . . . . . . . . . . . . . . .    34  1st Eclogues 13   77
EMPIRE
    Yee Nymphes which in the waters empire have, . . . . . . . .    92  3rd Eclogues 63   28
    Like Senators a harmeles empire had. . . . . . . . . . . .    100  3rd Eclogues 66   56
EMPLOY
    Employ thy might, that she my fires may taste. . . . . . . .    72  Arcadia III  38   15
    Yet Fancie would perforce employ his skill, . . . . . . . .   115  4th Eclogues 72   65
    Yee dimmy clowdes, which well employ your stayning . . . . .   127  4th Eclogues 75   67
    Let us against our selves employ our might, . . . . . . . .   130  4th Eclogues 76   35
    And now employ the remnant of my wit, . . . . . . . . . . .   166  Astrophil     2   12
    Where with most ease and warmth he might employ his art: . .  168  Astrophil     8    7
EMPLOYED
    Upon his pate, his pain employed thus. . . . . . . . . . . .   278  Psalm VII        44
EMPLOYS
    What pardon can availe? or who employes him. . . . . . . . .    62  2nd Eclogues 30  168
    Whom she imployes, dismisse from thee my wit, . . . . . . .   236  Astrophil   107   10
EMPOISONED
    Be thou farre hence with thy empoyson'd darte, . . . . . . .    92  3rd Eclogues 63   56
EMPTY
    For though full of desire, emptie of wit, . . . . . . . . .   208  Astrophil    82    9
    Sicke, thirsty, glad (though but of empty glasse:) . . . . .   233  Astrophil   104   11
ENAMELED
    Nature her selfe enameld it. . . . . . . . . . . . . . . . .    90  Arcadia III  62  124
    Morne's messenger, with rose enameld skies . . . . . . . . .   231  Astrophil    99   10
ENAMELING
    Enam'ling with pied flowers their thoughts of gold: . . . .   166  Astrophil     3    4
ENCAVED
    Whose bought incav'd doth yeeld such sight, . . . . . . . .    89  Arcadia III  62   97
ENCHAIN
    My name their eares, their eares their hearts to me
        enchaine , . . . . . . . . . . . . . . . . . . . . . . .   293  Psalm XVIII      80
ENCHAINED
    Thy faire haire my heart enchained, . . . . . . . . . . . .   156  Cert Sonnets 27    2
ENCHANT
    Whose face doth oft the bravest sort enchaunt, . . . . . . .     3  Lady of May   1    2
ENCHANTMENT
    And if enchantment can a harde hart move, . . . . . . . . .    17  1st Eclogues  7  100
    Say then, can this but of enchantment come?. . . . . . . . .   254  Other Poems   4  472
ENCLOSE
    My Lute within thy selfe thy tunes enclose, . . . . . . . .    81  Arcadia III  54    1
    Who for my Death still me enclose. . . . . . . . . . . . . .   290  Psalm XVII       28
ENCLOSED
    Yee living powres enclosed in stately shrine . . . . . . . .    40  Arcadia II   18    1
    In earthly clothes enclosde a heavenly sparke. . . . . . . .    80  Arcadia III  52   10
    The welkin had full niggardly enclosed . . . . . . . . . . .    98  3rd Eclogues 66    8
    I am enclosed with young Bulls' madded route, . . . . . . .   299  Psalm XXII       27
    And thou hast not for aye enclosed me. . . . . . . . . . . .   312  Psalm XXXI       22
ENCROACHES
    So love encroches on your charmed reason, . . . . . . . . .    50  2nd Eclogues 28   93
ENCROACHMENT
    By no encrochment wrongd, nor time forgot: . . . . . . . . .   209  Astrophil    84   10
END
    Drawes up; and if, hope fayling, ende live's pleasure, . . .    16  1st Eclogues  7   71
    Geron. Yet sure an end, to each thing time doth give, . . .    22  1st Eclogues  9   11
    Time shall in one my life and sorrowes end, . . . . . . . .    23  1st Eclogues  9   19
    R. But yet our strife sure peace in end doth breede. . . . .    46  2nd Eclogues 27   27
    Till of these thoughts thy sodaine ende bereaved me. . . . .    48  2nd Eclogues 28   33
    But it is season for to end our singing, . . . . . . . . . .    50  2nd Eclogues 28   94
    "Erona dye, and end this ougly painefulnes"? . . . . . . . .    61  2nd Eclogues 30  157
    Or rubbing hurt the sore, I here doo end.. . . . . . . . . .    62  2nd Eclogues 30  183
    Then to an earnest Love what doth best victorie lend? Ende..    63  2nd Eclogues 31   15
    End? but I can never end, love will not give me the leave.
        Leave. . . . . . . . . . . . . . . . . . . . . . . . . .    63  2nd Eclogues 31   16
    Winde, tempests, and stormes, yet in ende what gives she
        desire? Ire. . . . . . . . . . . . . . . . . . . . . . .    64  2nd Eclogues 31   35
    Adonis' end, Venus' nett. . . . . . . . . . . . . . . . . .    66  2nd Eclogues 32   27
    Reason sighes but in end he thus doth answere. . . . . . . .    68  2nd Eclogues 33   25
    A wreched wracke, a glasse of Ruine's ende. . . . . . . . .    73  Arcadia III  40    4
    An ende, an ende, my dulde penn cannot write, . . . . . . .    74  Arcadia III  42   13
    Yet all well knit to one faire end do passe: . . . . . . . .    78  Arcadia III  50    8
    Thought, thinke to ende, too long the frute of thought . . .    83  Arcadia III  59    7
    As I began, so must I ende. . . . . . . . . . . . . . . . .    90  Arcadia III  62  144
    To such an end as he might be abus'de. . . . . . . . . . . .    95  3rd Eclogues 64   28
    Both cause, effect, beginning, and the ende. . . . . . . . .   114  4th Eclogues 72   42
    But now an ende, (o Klaius) now an ende, . . . . . . . . . .   116  4th Eclogues 72  102
    An honour to the world, while Honour was their ende, . . . .   117  4th Eclogues 73   37
    Now that he finds to what end his life and love be reserved,  123  4th Eclogues 74   29
    Sounde of my griefes, and let it never ende, . . . . . . . .   126  4th Eclogues 75   35
    Within it selfe, and never taketh ende: . . . . . . . . . .   127  4th Eclogues 75   80
    Or thinking still my thoughts might have good end: . . . . .   147  Cert Sonnets 19    2
    End the way, where all men stay. No, no, no, no. . . . . . .   155  Cert Sonnets 26   22
    Thou web of will, whose end is never wrought; . . . . . . .   161  Cert Sonnets 31    4
```

END	(CONTINUED)		PAGE	TITLE		LINE
Of sinfull thoughts, which do in ruine end?.	. . . .		172	Astrophil	14	8
Come let me write, "And to what end?" To ease.	. . . . . .		181	Astrophil	34	1
Shall prosper still, with well succeeding end.	. . . . . .		270	Psalm I		12
Farr as World's farthest end..	. . . .		271	Psalm II		20
From coming to the well deserved end,.	. . . .		277	Psalm VII		26
To endless end..	. . . .		280	Psalm IX		15
From a foule corrupting end.	. . . .		288	Psalm XVI		36
To the pitt where flesh doth end..	. . . .		308	Psalm XXVIII		5
No end shall find.	. . . .		317	Psalm XXXIII		41
And Thy good state shall never end..	. . . .		326	Psalm XXXVII		68
His end shall be in peace enjoyed;	. . . .		327	Psalm XXXVII		94
And quite cutt off, with helpless end.	. . . .		327	Psalm XXXVII		96
For on Thee, lord, without end	. . . .		328	Psalm XXXVIII		43
World without end, let still his blessing flow;.	. . . . .		334	Psalm XLI		47
Geron, though olde yet gamesome, kept one ende .	. . . . .		248	Other Poems	4	242
At other end Uran did Strephon lend.	. . . .		248	Other Poems	4	246
The other end Geron with Uran garde.	. . . .		250	Other Poems	4	319
And so that even the barly-brake did end..	. . . .		252	Other Poems	4	416
Who hid in Angel's shape my life would ende.	. . . .		254	Other Poems	4	464
Speeche without ende were better not begin..	. . . .		259	Other Poems	5	104
ENDANGER						
Fearing (sweete) you to endanger,.	. . . .		234	A&S 11th Song		39
ENDANGERED						
Deliver me in my endangerd way	. . . .		277	Psalm VII		3
ENDED						
Who ended hath this fearefull strife:.	. . . .		13	Arcadia I	5	4
And never ended.	. . . .		84	Arcadia III	59	16
Till their harts had ended talking..	. . . .		218	A&S 8th Song		24
Shall fruitlesly be ended.	. . . .		298	Psalm XXI		44
It ended, but the others' woe began,	. . . .		252	Other Poems	4	417
This said, at length he ended.	. . . .		259	Other Poems	5	114
ENDETH						
Only in you my song begins and endeth.	. . . .		196	A&S 1st Song		4
Only in you my song begins and endeth.	. . . .		197	A&S 1st Song		36
ENDING						
Thus not ending, endes the due praise of her praise;	. . . .		31	1st Eclogues	12	21
ENDLESS						
Who doth his soule to endlesse malice bend..	. . . .		22	1st Eclogues	9	10
That men's harts be thy seate and endlesse fame be thy						
servant,	. . . .		36	1st Eclogues	13	148
My weedes, Desire, cut out in endlesse foldes.	. . . . .		39	Arcadia II	17	6
All numbring artes her endlesse graces number not:	. . . .		49	2nd Eclogues	28	59
Why should we spare our voice from endlesse wailing,	. . . .		109	Arcadia IV	70	7
To paint my living death, and endlesse smart:	. . . . . .		146	Cert Sonnets	17	28
As his light was her eyes, her death his endlesse night:	. .		209	A&S 3rd Song		10
Joylesse, hopelesse, endlesse languish..	. . . .		220	A&S 8th Song		80
For Thou the lord in endless hatred hast.	. . . .		275	Psalm V		15
To endless end..	. . . .		280	Psalm IX		15
O bragging Foe, where is the endless wast.	. . . .		280	Psalm IX		16
Shall in endless pleasures stand!	. . . .		289	Psalm XVI		44
Thy endless prayse: O God my King.	. . . .		311	Psalm XXX		38
Let them in bedd of endless silence dy..	. . . .		313	Psalm XXXI		48
Oh! of thy grace what endlesse pleasure flowes	. . . . . .		313	Psalm XXXI		52
But throw them down, put them to endlesse blame,	. . . . .		323	Psalm XXXV		63
For endless woes me compast have,.	. . . .		332	Psalm XL		43
ENDLESSLY						
And endlesly dispairing of his grace,.	. . . .		229	Astrophil	97	6
*ENDS						
Thus not ending, endes the due praise of her praise;	. . . .		31	1st Eclogues	12	21
From hidnest depth, which tribute when it ends,.	. . . . .		150	Cert Sonnets	22	13
His race is even from ends of heaven	. . . .		294	Psalm XIX		25
For quickly ends his wrathfull Will,	. . . .		311	Psalm XXX		13
They of both ends the middle two doe flie,	. . . .		248	Other Poems	4	226
ENDURE						
Do please all eyes, and spotlesse do endure.	. . . .		91	3rd Eclogues	63	25
For nothing can endure where order n'is.	. . . .		100	3rd Eclogues	66	51
Which though despisde, yet still doth truth endure..	. . .		150	Cert Sonnets	22	40
Whose porches rich (which name of cheekes endure).	. . . .		169	Astrophil	9	7
Thou seest each side the walking doth endure	. . . .		285	Psalm XII		25
It shall endure,	. . . .		301	Psalm XXIII		24
ENDURES						
And so endures for ever,	. . . .		294	Psalm XIX		38
ENEMIES						
No sooner said, but (lo) myne Enemyes sink	. . . .		280	Psalm IX		46
On my beseiging Enemyes;	. . . .		307	Psalm XXVII		32
Enemys be-	. . . .		329	Psalm XXXVIII		59
ENEMY						
And of some sent from that sweet enemie Fraunce;	. . . . .		185	Astrophil	41	4
ENEMY'S						
Whereby Thou stop'st Thyne Enemy's prating	. . . .		278	Psalm VIII		7
ENFORCE						
First, second, last, did binde, enforce, and arme,	. . . . .		84	Arcadia III	60	3
ENGAGE						
Truly not I, who did my thoughts engage,	. . . .		26	1st Eclogues	9	136
ENGAGED						
Where my soule I have engaged?	. . . .		157	Cert Sonnets	27	28
ENGARLAND						
With choisest flowers my speech to engarland so;	. . . . .		192	Astrophil	55	2

130

ENGENDER   PAGE   TITLE   LINE

ENGENDER			
In tender harts, small things engender hate:	146	Cert Sonnets 17	17
But with dew dropps engendre children hy:	257	Other Poems 5	45
ENGENDERETH			
Where love draws hate, and hate engendreth love?	85	Arcadia III 61	14
ENGLAND			
These wonders England breedes, the last remaines,	151	Cert Sonnets 22	61
ENGLISH			
Both by the judgement of the English eyes,	185	Astrophil 41	3
Yet gentle English theeves do rob, but will not slay;	214	A&S 5th Song	49
Thou English murdring theefe, wilt have harts for thy pray:	214	A&S 5th Song	50
ENGRAINED			
Which Nature' selfe did make, and selfe engraind the same?	232	Astrophil 102	6
ENGRAVE			
Can those blacke beames such burning markes engrave.	188	Astrophil 47	2
ENGRAVED			
With name engrav'd: so though thy bodie die,	56	2nd Eclogues 29	130
Deeper engrav'd, which salve nor time can save,	77	Arcadia III 47	5
Part of my paine me seemes engraved lyes..	147	Cert Sonnets 18	4
ENGRAVEN			
Upon the heavns engrav'n the story..	278	Psalm VIII	4
ENGULFED			
Engulfed in despaire, slid downe from fortune's lappe:	153	Cert Sonnets 24	16
ENJOY			
Enjoy her soule, in bodie's faire possession,	15	1st Eclogues 7	41
"Let not dead earth enjoy so deare a cover,	17	1st Eclogues 7	89
Enjoye my joyes, as you dyd taste my payne,	43	Arcadia II 23	11
Her to enjoy, where joy it selfe is thrall,	59	2nd Eclogues 30	87
What do lovers seeke for, long seeking for to enjoy? Joy..	63	2nd Eclogues 31	13
What be the joyes for which to enjoy they went to the paines Paines..	63	2nd Eclogues 31	14
It is, so faire a Vertue to enjoy.	200	Astrophil 68	14
She oft hath drunke my teares, now hopes to enjoy.	201	Astrophil 70	3
While I dispaire by Sunne's sight to enjoy..	230	Astrophil 97	14
My joy shall be pure to enjoy thy face,	290	Psalm XVII	46
And madest me gladsom weeds enjoy,	311	Psalm XXX	36
Joy be to you, who do enjoy.	316	Psalm XXXII	41
Our hearts sure shall enjoy.	318	Psalm XXXIII	79
ENJOYED			
Now each thing which enjoy'd that firie quickning sparke	116	4th Eclogues 73	4
His end shall be in peace enjoyed;	327	Psalm XXXVII	94
ENJOYETH			
For I protest, my sight never thy face enjoyeth,	215	A&S 5th Song	75
ENJOYS			
The richest gemme of Love and life enjoyes,	177	Astrophil 24	10
ENLARGE			
Least joy, by Nature apt sprites to enlarge,	210	Astrophil 85	3
Unto my strengthned stepps Thou didst enlarge the way,	292	Psalm XVIII	66
ENLARGED			
With sleeves turnde up, loose haire, and brestes enlarged,	16	1st Eclogues 7	74
Like lions fierce, with roaring jawes enlarged..	299	Psalm XXII	30
But hast enlargd my feet from mortall ginn..	312	Psalm XXXI	24
ENMITY			
Within the hand of hatefull enmitie,	312	Psalm XXXI	23
ENNOBLE			
No, no: no wordes ennoble selfe-nobilitie.	48	2nd Eclogues 28	28
ENNOBLING			
Ennobling new found Tropes with problemes old:	166	Astrophil 3	6
ENOUGH			
Nature worketh enough with a small help for the revealing.	33	1st Eclogues 13	61
With monefull melodies, for enough our greefes be revealed,	37	1st Eclogues 13	173
Dicus. Enough, enough: so ill hath done the best,	56	2nd Eclogues 29	147
Hath not Reason enough vehemence the desire to reprove? Prove.	63	2nd Eclogues 31	10
Faire trees' shade is enough fortification,	69	2nd Eclogues 34	13
With chafe enough, till she him pacified:	97	3rd Eclogues 64	110
Enough to make a fertill minde lie waste..	114	4th Eclogues 72	30
Klaius. Enough to make a fertill minde lie waste	114	4th Eclogues 72	31
Alas have I not paine enough my friend,	171	Astrophil 14	1
What inke is blacke inough to paint my wo?	227	Astrophil 93	3
Knowing worlds passe, ere she enough can find.	232	Astrophil 101	13
Ah, is it not enough, that I am thence,	233	Astrophil 104	5
What, is not this enough? nay farre worse commeth here;	214	A&S 5th Song	73
ENRAGED			
As for thy wish to my enraged spitefulnesse,	51	2nd Eclogues 28	111
Was I to blaspheme enraged,	157	Cert Sonnets 27	27
ENRICH			
Such planted gifts enrich even beggers' sight:	3	Lady of May 1	10
Then Love allowes, our pleasures to enrich,	18	1st Eclogues 7	129
Or with strange similies enrich each line,	166	Astrophil 3	7
ENSUE			
R. Who Passion doth ensue, lives in annoy.	46	2nd Eclogues 27	13
That profit may ensue to him that best can do.	53	2nd Eclogues 29	30
Take heed therefore, how you ensue that trade,	97	3rd Eclogues 64	123
Lalus' example I would soone ensue,	104	3rd Eclogues 67	23
What ever may ensue, o let me be	188	Astrophil 48	5
ENTER			
To wo and shame the wretch did enter in,	5	Lady of May 3	9
Give right sound to the eares, and enter aright to the judgement;	32	1st Eclogues 13	18

ENTER	(CONTINUED)	PAGE	TITLE		LINE
Oh no, no, hardye shepeheard, worth can never enter a title,		34	1st Eclogues	13	82
Dread not a whit (O goodly cruell) that pittie may enter . .		122	4th Eclogues	74	5
Enter bravely every where, ...		226	A&S 10th Song		20
Who then in Lion's cave did enter fyrst, ...		247	Other Poems	4	206
ENTERED					
When once this entred was, in woman's hart, ...		95	3rd Eclogues	64	37
Whole armies of thy beauties entred in.		182	Astrophil	36	4
ENTERS					
Then each conceit that enters in by sight, ...		23	1st Eclogues	9	38
Into the faire looker on, pastime, not passion, enters.. . .		32	1st Eclogues	13	41
ENTERTAIN					
Studying inventions fine, her wits to entertaine:		165	Astrophil	1	6
Some Lovers speake when they their Muses entertaine, ...		167	Astrophil	6	1
But doth with honour great the Godly entertaine;		287	Psalm XV		8
Neighbors friendly entertain		309	Psalm XXVIII		14
ENTERTAINMENT					
To them that do such entertainment need, ...		190	Astrophil	51	3
ENTICE					
(The one doth force, the latter doth entise)		98	3rd Eclogues	65	10
ENTICING					
Nightingale, voice, entising songes to saye.		101	3rd Eclogues	66	82
ENTITLED					
Though thousands old, a Boy entit'led still.		41	Arcadia II	20	10
Justly entitled Cupid's hill.		88	Arcadia III	62	78
O lovelie starre, entitled of the morning, ...		111	4th Eclogues	71	9
O light of Sunne, which is entit'led day, ...		126	4th Eclogues	75	52
ENTOMBED					
Can of thy prayse the tongues entombed make.		276	Psalm VI		15
ENTREAT					
But commonly like currs we them entreate, ...		27	1st Eclogues	10	35
ENTRIES					
Peake hath a Cave, whose narrow entries finde.		150	Cert Sonnets	22	31
ENTRY					
Which at firste voly gave too open entry, ...		68	2nd Eclogues	33	14
With earlyest entry of the Morning prime, ...		274	Psalm V		7
ENVENOM					
Which do envenome both the soule and senses.		50	2nd Eclogues	28	88
ENVIED					
He envied such a death in sight of lover, ...		259	Other Poems	5	124
More envied Phoebus for his westerne flyinge		259	Other Poems	5	126
ENVIES					
That eloquence it selfe envies your praise, ...		231	Astrophil	100	10
ENVIOUS					
With ouglie cloke the darke envious night:		82	Arcadia III	55	8
Envious wits what hath bene mine offence, ...		233	Astrophil	104	1
Ev'en when foe's envious ey.		301	Psalm XXIII		17
ENVIRON					
So shall all men with laudes inviron thee.		277	Psalm VII		19
With rageing jaws environ me		307	Psalm XXVII		9
ENVY					
Then jarle: lo, lo, even these how envie blindes..		26	1st Eclogues	10	9
Justely to graunt thy rewarde, such envie I beare to thy					
fortune.		37	1st Eclogues	13	156
O Venus (if her praise no envy frames, ...		60	2nd Eclogues	30	113
(For envie harbreth most in feeblest hartes)		100	3rd Eclogues	66	58
With envie I doo hate the loftie mountaines;		112	4th Eclogues	71	52
And so no helpe gainst envy of those powers?		142	Cert Sonnets	10	12
Release from Court, where envie needes must be..		143	Cert Sonnets	12	6
Heav'ns envy not at my high triumphing:		196	Astrophil	63	10
I do not envie Aristotle's wit, ...		198	Astrophil	64	9
Envie, put out thine eyes, least thou do see		200	Astrophil	69	3
I bare (with Envie) yet I bare your song, ...		208	Astrophil	83	5
And that you know, I envy you no lot		209	Astrophil	84	12
Onely at you all envie hopelesse rueth...		197	A&S 1st Song		24
Nor envy in thy boscme nourish		324	Psalm XXXVII		3
ENVY-HATCHING					
Of clime-fall Court, the envy-hatching place:		243	Other Poems	4	61
ENVYING					
Envying shallow toyes with malice deepe.		104	3rd Eclogues	67	39
ENVY'S					
Nor envie's snaky ey, finds any harbor here, ...		69	2nd Eclogues	34	18
Where envie's snaky ey, winketh or els dyeth, ...		69	2nd Eclogues	34	37
ENWRAPT					
Or that by words enwrapt in guile.		320	Psalm XXXIV		51
EPEIRUS					
Epeirus high, was honest Klaius' nest, ...		242	Other Poems	4	25
EPISTLE					
Into thy hart by the sight of this Epistle I send:		122	4th Eclogues	74	6
EPITAPH					
Which Epitaph containeth, ...		160	Cert Sonnets	30	25
Graved in mine Epitaph a Poet's name:		224	Astrophil	90	8
EQUAL					
Wyth two strange fires of equall heate possest, ...		42	Arcadia II	22	1
Both equall hurt, in this change sought our blisse:		76	Arcadia III	45	13
What be her giftes, that make her equall thee, ...		80	Arcadia III	52	8
Whose equall lynes their angles bowes, ...		86	Arcadia III	62	10
Whose eeven descent makes equall falle, ...		89	Arcadia III	62	V104
EQUALITY					
For vaine equalitie is but contention's field.		120	4th Eclogues	73	130

132

```
                                                        PAGE    TITLE           LINE
EQUALS
    Since no evill fortune equalls publique damage:. . . . . . .  108  Arcadia IV     70    3
EQUITY
    O God, God of my Equity, . . . . . . . . . . . . . . . . .  273  Psalm IV             2
    After my clearness, and my Equity. . . . . . . . . . . . .  277  Psalm VII           24
    According to his heavnly equity. . . . . . . . . . . . . .  278  Psalm VII           47
    My lord my God ev'en to my equity. . . . . . . . . . . . .  322  Psalm XXXV          58
ERE
    And ere that all these blowes thy head doo hit,. . . . . . .   11  Arcadia I       1    9
    Yet thou art mickle warse then ere was I,. . . . . . . . . .   28  1st Eclogues   10   62
    I pray thee what hath ere the Parret gott, . . . . . . . . .   28  1st Eclogues   10   67
    Ere that I leave with song of praise her praise to
        solemnize . . . . . . . . . . . . . . . . . . . .   33  1st Eclogues   13   68
    My minde ere now led foorth by reason's light: . . . . . . .   73  Arcadia III    39    4
    Beyond our worlde, and ere I gatt my boothe. . . . . . . . .   98  3rd Eclogues   66    4
    Ere that I should consent to doo such excessive a dammage. .  124  4th Eclogues   74   61
    An Asse's shade ere now hath bred debate.. . . . . . . . . .  146  Cert Sonnets   17   20
    But now, if ere my face with joy be clad:. . . . . . . . . .  147  Cert Sonnets   17   44
    What words so ere she speakes perswades for thee,. . . . . .  171  Astrophil      12    7
    But ere I could flie thence, it pierc'd my heart.. . . . . .  175  Astrophil      20   14
    Knowing worlds passe, ere she enough can find. . . . . . . .  232  Astrophil     101   13
    That ere by them ought undertaken be,. . . . . . . . . . . .  236  Astrophil     107    3
    Long stay ere he graunt the same:. . . . . . . . . . . . . .  211  A&S 4th Song        33
    That I e're I return'd destroyd them utterly . . . . . . . .  292  Psalm XVIII         69
    Yea thou prevent'st e're ask he could, . . . . . . . . . . .  297  Psalm XXI            9
    E're I my earthly being leave. . . . . . . . . . . . . . . .  330  Psalm XXXIX         42
    For ere that either had his purpose done,. . . . . . . . . .  244  Other Poems     4   81
    Till one faire eav'n an howr ere Sun did rest, . . . . . . .  247  Other Poems     4  205
    Of all the games that here ere now I met:. . . . . . . . . .  254  Other Poems     4  494
    While I in heart my will write ere I die.. . . . . . . . . .  255  Other Poems     4  499
ERECT
    Let doltes in haste some altars faire erect. . . . . . . . .   58  2nd Eclogues   30   62
    Where sweet graces erect the stately banner. . . . . . . . .   67  2nd Eclogues   33    3
ERECTED
    The seate of peace, the throne which is erected. . . . . . .  108  Arcadia IV     69    3
ERECTION
    Her peereles height my minde to high erection. . . . . . . .   16  1st Eclogues    7   70
ERMELIN
    Passing the hate-spott Ermelin.. . . . . . . . . . . . . . .   89  Arcadia III    62  116
ERMINE
    But if all faith, like spotlesse Ermine ly . . . . . . . . .  212  Astrophil      86    5
    The Ermion, whitest skinne, spotted with nought; . . . . . .  101  3rd Eclogues   66   89
ERONA
    Plangus doth live, and shall Erona dye?. . . . . . . . . . .   58  2nd Eclogues   30   58
    Erona dye? O heaven (if heaven there be) . . . . . . . . . .   58  2nd Eclogues   30   59
    "Erona dye, and end this ougly painefulnes"? . . . . . . . .   61  2nd Eclogues   30  157
ERONA'S
    Shall I that saw Eronae's shining haire. . . . . . . . . . .   58  2nd Eclogues   30   44
    Plangus must live to see Eronae's death. . . . . . . . . . .   58  2nd Eclogues   30   55
ERR
    First thinke they erre, that thinke them gayly wise, . . . .   25  1st Eclogues    9  111
    Ods? what an ods is there since them to the heav'ns I
        prefer Erre.. . . . . . . . . . . . . . . . . . . .   65  2nd Eclogues   31   48
ERRAND
    If mine eyes can speake to doo harty errande,. . . . . . . .   30  1st Eclogues   12    1
    But if eyes can speake to doo harty errande, . . . . . . . .   31  1st Eclogues   12   25
ERROR
    Dorus. Well do I prove, errour lies oft in zeale,. . . . . .   51  2nd Eclogues   28  103
    Yet is it seale, though errour, of true hart.. . . . . . . .   51  2nd Eclogues   28  104
    Ah saucy paine let not thy errour last,. . . . . . . . . . .  141  Cert Sonnets    8   13
    Alas, I lie: rage hath this errour bred, . . . . . . . . . .  160  Cert Sonnets   30   31
    The first that straight my fancie's error brings . . . . . .  183  Astrophil      38    5
    Of straying wayes, when valiant errour guides: . . . . . . .  190  Astrophil      51   11
    I am resolv'd thy errour to maintaine, . . . . . . . . . . .  199  Astrophil      67   13
ERRORS
    Not spying faults, nor in plaine errors blinde,. . . . . . .   98  3rd Eclogues   65    7
    Thinke that I thinke state errours to redresse.. . . . . . .  176  Astrophil      23    8
ERST
    That erst I knewe, and with most plainefull muse;. . . . . .   24  1st Eclogues    9   63
    Then thow earst knew? rather take part with him. . . . . . .   26  1st Eclogues   10    8
    Then earste I knewe: But first dyd playne. . . . . . . . . .   57  2nd Eclogues   30    3
    What myne hath erst throwne downe so faire a tower?. . . . .   59  2nd Eclogues   30   96
    Not seeing earst such token in the wife, . . . . . . . . . .   96  3rd Eclogues   64   68
    For murdre done, which never erst was seene, . . . . . . . .  102  3rd Eclogues   66  127
    All things that earst I sawe, as orient pearles exceed,. . .  119  4th Eclogues   73   83
    That I things erst unseene should first in dreaming see? . .  121  4th Eclogues   73  182
ESCAPE
    Thus shrewdly burdned then, how can my Muse escape?. . . . .   12  Arcadia I       3    3
    Whence may I show to my minde any light of a possible
        escape . . . . . . . . . . . . . . . . . . . . .   37  1st Eclogues   13  161
ESCAPES
    And thus her heart escapes, but thus her eyes. . . . . . . .  179  Astrophil      29    9
ESCHEW
    O sheepheards' boyes, eschue these tongues of venome,. . . .   50  2nd Eclogues   28   87
ESCHEWING
    The Stagge did give the harme eschewing feare. . . . . . . .  101  3rd Eclogues   66   91
ESPIED
    Lalus. Once my well-waiting eyes espied my treasure, . . . .   16  1st Eclogues    7   73
    He rase, and streight espied . . . . . . . . . . . . . . . .  259  Other Poems     5  120
```

ESPILUS
    Come Espilus, come now declare thy skill,. . . . .   3 Lady of May   2   1
    (Espilus) Silvanus long in love, and long in vaine,. . . . .   4 Lady of May   3   1
    (Espilus) Thus joyfully in chosen tunes rejoyce, ...   5 Lady of May   3   13
ESPY
    Seeke to espie her faultes as well as praise,. . . . .   25 1st Eclogues   9 121
    Till with lickt beard, his eye of fire espie his foes. . . .   53 2nd Eclogues 29   36
    A little downward to espie,. . . . .   87 Arcadia III 62   52
    That yet the ground hereof he might espie. . . . .   96 3rd Eclogues 64   72
    Did Wisedome this our wretched time espie. . . . . 126 4th Eclogues 75   46
    The ruines of her conquest to espie: . . . . 199 Astrophil   67   3
    He cannot them espy,. . . . . 282 Psalm X   20
    If of this Clayey race he could espy . . . . 286 Psalm XIV   8
    Doth it espy.. . . . . 301 Psalm XXIII   18
ESSENCE
    What essence dest'nie hath; if fortune be or no; . . . . . . 118 4th Eclogues 73   45
    The very essence of their tunes, when Angels do rejoyce. . . 217 A&S 7th Song   18
    Which all from Thee their Essence took . . . . 278 Psalm VIII   10
    Since they Eternal Essence have. . . . . 303 Psalm XXV   24
ESTABLISH
    Holde thou my hart, establish thou my sprights:. . . . . . .   40 Arcadia II   18   15
ESTABLISHMENT
    And he shall your establishment renew. . . . . 314 Psalm XXXI   69
ESTATE
    Great to thee my estate seemes, thy estate is blest by my
       judgement: . . . .   33 1st Eclogues 13   72
    Desteny keepes me aloofe. For if all thy estate to thy
       verture. . . . .   34 1st Eclogues 13   98
    For that I finde in them parte of my estate represented. . .   35 1st Eclogues 13 115
    In hard estate with stowt shew valor use,. . . . . 143 Cert Sonnets 12   16
    For other's ease, their frutte, or free estate,. . . . . . . 345 Possibly   2   10
    That the meane estate is best, ... 264 Other Poems   7   76
ESTATES
    (Since no estates be so base, but love vouchsafeth his
       arrow . . . .   33 1st Eclogues 13   50
    Of carking agonies (to estates which still be adherent). . .   34 1st Eclogues 13   97
    Both our estates, while each the other did deprave,. . . . . 119 4th Eclogues 73 107
ESTEEM
    Who him their trust esteeme. . . . . 321 Psalm XXXIV   80
ESTEEMED
    Till aige it self do make it self esteemde.. . . . .   26 1st Eclogues   9 141
    Well may a Pastor plaine, but alas his plaints be not
       esteem de. . . . .   32 1st Eclogues 13   39
    I that was once esteem'd for pleasant musique. . . . . 111 4th Eclogues 71   15
    Thy haire not worth a haire esteemed:. . . . . 156 Cert Sonnets 27   10
ESTEEMETH
    Histor. Thus may you see, howe youthe estemeth aige. . . . .   26 1st Eclogues   9 138
    Seeke then and see, what man esteemeth best, ...   75 Arcadia III 44   5
ESTEEMING
    Therefore esteeming all good blessings toyes,. . . . . 116 4th Eclogues 72   99
ESTEEMS
    And wonder more esteemes . . . . 216 A&S 6th Song   33
ESTIMATION
    What coye account she makes of estimation? . . . .   15 1st Eclogues   7   34
    My hart doth seeke another estimation. . . . .   19 1st Eclogues   7 175
    For who doth holde his love in estimation, ...   47 2nd Eclogues 28   4
    In so high estimation. 297 Psalm XXI   20
ESTRANGED
    Though from me you be estranged, ... 234 A&S 11th Song   9
ETERNAL
    Either dull silence, or eternall chat; . . . . 104 3rd Eclogues 67   31
    With secret sense of our eternall damage,. . . . . 110 Arcadia IV   70   35
    Hath cast me, wretch, into eternall evening, ... 113 4th Eclogues 71   65
    But that eternall paines my soule have hent, ... 116 4th Eclogues 72   87
    Eternall Love maintaine thy life in me.. . . . . 144 Cert Sonnets 32   14
    Rich in those gifts which give th'eternall crowne; . . . . . 183 Astrophil   37   11
    But God shall sit in his Eternal chaire. . . . . 280 Psalm IX   21
    Since they Eternal Essence have. . . . . 303 Psalm XXV   24
ETERNITY
    That from thenceforth to all eternitie, ... 101 3rd Eclogues 66 104
    Whose numbers, wayes, greatnesse, eternitie, ... 178 Astrophil   26   3
    Lo! ev'en unto Eternity. . . . . 297 Psalm XXI   15
EUROPE
    Recount the rape of Europe,. . . . .   66 2nd Eclogues 32   26
*EVEN
    Such planted gifts enrich even beggers' sight: . . . .   3 Lady of May   1   10
    Then jarle: lo, lo, even these how envie blindes.. . . . . .   26 1st Eclogues 10   9
    Thou heardst even now a yong man snebb me sore,. . . . . . .   27 1st Eclogues 10   22
    But even for that shall suffer mightie Lovers. . . . .   28 1st Eclogues 10   72
    Even turtle toutcht he with hypocrisie.. . . . .   28 1st Eclogues 10   81
    Gives happs or mishapps, ev'n as he ordreth his hearte.. . .   29 1st Eclogues 11   8
    "And ev'n in that love, shall I reserve him a spite".. . . .   30 1st Eclogues 11   18
    (Mine eyes even great in labour with their teares) . . . . .   41 Arcadia II   21   2
    Hath sav'd his charge? it is even I. . . . .   44 Arcadia II   25   6
    Who hath sav'd all? it is even I.. . . . .   44 Arcadia II   25   12
    Nico. Peace, peace good Pas, thou weeriest even the ground .   56 2nd Eclogues 29 135
    (Even like a toppe which nought but whipping moves). . . . .   58 2nd Eclogues 30   33
    Hath she not force even death with love to kill? . . . . . .   59 2nd Eclogues 30   85
    Nay even cold Death enflamde with hot desire . . . .   59 2nd Eclogues 30   86
    As let them come or go with even facilitie.. . . . .   60 2nd Eclogues 30 133

```
*EVEN                    (CONTINUED)                PAGE    TITLE          LINE
  Clymes even unto the starres, Nature is under it. . . . . .   68  2nd Eclogues 34    9
  That doth present those even browes, . . . . . . . . . . .    86  Arcadia III  62    9
  The matchlesse paire, even praise doth staine. . . . . . .    86  Arcadia III  62   16
  Which doth even beautie beautifie, . . . . . . . . . . . .    90  Arcadia III  62  137
  Whose eeven descent makes equall falle, . . . . . . . . .     89  Arcadia III  62 V104
  So may each thing, even as thou wishest lighte, . . . . . .   96  3rd Eclogues 64   94
  Till forste to parte, with harte and eyes even sore, . . . .  99  3rd Eclogues 66   39
  (As even in beasts their dammes leave chaunging parts) . . . 100  3rd Eclogues 66   60
  Ev'n then Despaire did Hope already kill: . . . . . . . . .  115  4th Eclogues 72   64
  For even the hearbes our hatefull musique stroyes, . . . .   116  4th Eclogues 72  103
  Tuckt up even with the knees, with bowe and arrowes prest:   118  4th Eclogues 73   67
  Ev'n as I am, so I should unto that haire be a thrall. . . . 123  4th Eclogues 74   54
  Even thus might I, for doubts which I conceave . . . . . . . 145  Cert Sonnets 16    9
  If othes might serve, even by the Stygian lake, . . . . . .  146  Cert Sonnets 17    6
  Even as the flye, which to the flame doth goe, . . . . . .   149  Cert Sonnets 21   11
  Now even that footstep of lost libertie. . . . . . . . . .   166  Astrophil     2    9
  How then? even thus: in Stella's face I reed, . . . . . . .  166  Astrophil     3   12
  She even in blacke doth make all beauties flow?. . . . . .   168  Astrophil     7   11
  Doth plunge my wel-form'd soule even in the mire . . . . .   172  Astrophil    14    7
  I now have learn'd Love right, and learn'd even so, . . . .  173  Astrophil    16   13
  Unable quite to pay even Nature's rent, . . . . . . . . . .  174  Astrophil    18    5
  Bends all his powers, even unto Stella's grace.. . . . . .   178  Astrophil    27   14
  What, may it be that even in heav'nly place. . . . . . . .   180  Astrophil    31    3
  Then ev'n of fellowship, o Moone, tell me. . . . . . . . .   180  Astrophil    31    9
  Doth even grow rich, naming my stella's name.. . . . . . .   182  Astrophil    35   11
  Whose curelesse wounds even now most freshly bleed:. . . .   189  Astrophil    48   11
  And is even irkt that so sweet Comedie, . . . . . . . . . .  190  Astrophil    51   13
  Youth, lucke, and praise, even fild my veines with pride...  191  Astrophil    53    4
  Even those sad words even in sad me did breed. . . . . . .   194  Astrophil    58   14
  But I unbid, fetch even my soule to thee.. . . . . . . . .   194  Astrophil    59    8
  Late tyr'd with wo, even ready for to pine . . . . . . . .   195  Astrophil    62    1
  Which even of sweetnesse sweetest sweetner art: . . . . .    206  Astrophil    79    2
  O kisse, which soules, even soules together ties . . . . .   207  Astrophil    81    5
  And I do sweare even by the same delight, . . . . . . . . .  208  Astrophil    82   13
  Through me, wretch me, even Stella vexed is. . . . . . . .   227  Astrophil    93    4
  Which even to sence, sence of it selfe denies, . . . . . .   228  Astrophil    94    7
  Even so (alas) a Lady Dian's peere, . . . . . . . . . . . .  230  Astrophil    97    9
  And even while I do speake, my death wounds bleeding be: . . 214  A&S 5th Song        52
  And thy words of refuse, do powre even hell on mee: . . . .  215  A&S 5th Song        83
  Even multitudes be they. . . . . . . . . . . . . . . . . .   272  Psalm III            7
  Lord help, for ev'en my bones their marrow spend . . . . .   276  Psalm VI             7
  Nay ev'n my soul fell troubles do appall; . . . . . . . . .  276  Psalm VI             9
  Yet hast Thou made even him an owner . . . . . . . . . . .   279  Psalm VIII          19
  That even his feet have on them raigned. . . . . . . . . .   279  Psalm VIII          24
  Yea even my songs thy name shall magnify, . . . . . . . . .  279  Psalm IX             4
  That I, even I of heavnly comfort full, . . . . . . . . . .  280  Psalm IX            43
  Nay even the race of good men are decay'd. . . . . . . . .   284  Psalm XII            3
  Ah, now even for their sakes, that taste of Woe, . . . . .   285  Psalm XII           13
  Even for the sighs, true sighs of man distrest . . . . . .   285  Psalm XII           15
  Even god himself sent down his peircing ey . . . . . . . .   286  Psalm XIV            7
  Even he, that leads of life an uncorrupted traine, . . . .   287  Psalm XV             3
  Ev'n when night with his black wing. . . . . . . . . . . .   288  Psalm XVI           21
  Ev'en the body of Thyne Own, . . . . . . . . . . . . . . .   288  Psalm XVI           34
  Cloudes even of Waters dark, and thickest ayre compos'd; . . 291  Psalm XVIII         25
  Ev'n from the Waters' depth my God preserved me so.. . . .   291  Psalm XVIII         35
  Ev'en Feare makes strangers shew much love though much
      untrue. . . . . . . . . . . . . . . . . . . . . . . .    293  Psalm XVIII         81
  His race is even from ends of heaven . . . . . . . . . . .   294  Psalm XIX           25
  Ev'n in the day when most Thy troubles be; . . . . . . . .   295  Psalm XX             2
  Lo! ev'en unto Eternity. . . . . . . . . . . . . . . . . .   297  Psalm XXI           15
  And yet ev'en from the womb thy self did'st take me; . . .   299  Psalm XXII          21
  They that be made even fatt, with earth's fatt good, . . .   300  Psalm XXII          71
  Even he whose life no help of man can quicken. . . . . . .   300  Psalm XXII          74
  Ev'en when foe's envious ey. . . . . . . . . . . . . . . .   301  Psalm XXIII         17
  Even He the King of glory hight. . . . . . . . . . . . . .   302  Psalm XXIV          24
  Ev'n for Thy mercy's sake, O Lord. . . . . . . . . . . . .   303  Psalm XXV           30
  Ev'en spotless verity. . . . . . . . . . . . . . . . . . .   304  Psalm XXV           39
  Nay I did even detest. . . . . . . . . . . . . . . . . . .   305  Psalm XXVI          16
  Ev'n where Thou makest Thy honour's biding place.. . . . .   306  Psalm XXVI          27
  Even truth that for me sayes. . . . . . . . . . . . . . . .  306  Psalm XXVI          37
  When wicked folk, even they that be. . . . . . . . . . . .   307  Psalm XXVII          7
  Hide me, ev'n closely in his Tent; . . . . . . . . . . . .   307  Psalm XXVII         27
  Ev'n such I say, whose lying tongue. . . . . . . . . . . .   308  Psalm XXVII         58
  Ev'en so be their guerdon shar'd. . . . . . . . . . . . . .  309  Psalm XXVIII        20
  Ye men of Pow'er even by birth-right, . . . . . . . . . . .  309  Psalm XXIX           2
  Ev'en Cedars, which on liban be, . . . . . . . . . . . . .   310  Psalm XXIX          15
  Ev'en Deserts where the Arabs byde.. . . . . . . . . . . .   310  Psalm XXIX          21
  And ev'en my bones consume where they be plac't. . . . . .   312  Psalm XXXI          30
  Ev'n like a dead man dreamed out of mind, . . . . . . . . .  313  Psalm XXXI          35
  That trust in Thee, ev'n in most open sight! . . . . . . .   313  Psalm XXXI          54
  Ev'en people that, ev'en those . . . . . . . . . . . . . .   317  Psalm XXXIII        46
  Ev'en where he dwelleth hee. . . . . . . . . . . . . . . .   317  Psalm XXXIII        52
  Ev'en from the grave . . . . . . . . . . . . . . . . . . .   318  Psalm XXXIII        74
  I ev'en I will always. . . . . . . . . . . . . . . . . . .   318  Psalm XXXIV          1
  Ev'en bones shall say O God, who is Thy peere, . . . . . .   321  Psalm XXXV          21
  And whose? ev'n his who when they sickness bare. . . . . .   322  Psalm XXXV          29
  Ev'en gnashing teeth, to witness more their spight.. . . .   322  Psalm XXXV          42
  Even where I do most store of people find; . . . . . . . .   322  Psalm XXXV          47
  My lord my God ev'en to my equity. . . . . . . . . . . . .   322  Psalm XXXV          58
```

```
*EVEN                    (CONTINUED)                        PAGE    TITLE           LINE
     Judg lord, judg God, ev'en in Thy justice great, . . . . . .  322 Psalm XXXV        59
     Ev'n thus it self it doth display. . . . . . . . . . . . .    323 Psalm XXXVI        4
     Ev'en with the smoake shall wast away. . . . . . . . . . .    326 Psalm XXXVII      52
     Ev'en the light. . . . . . . . . . . . . . . . . . . . . .    328 Psalm XXXVIII     29
     I ev'en as such kind of wight, . . . . . . . . . . . . . .    328 Psalm XXXVIII     40
     I silence kept ev'n in the good. . . . . . . . . . . . . .    329 Psalm XXXIX        6
     Ev'en heapes of wicked thoughts which streight they show . .  333 Psalm XLI         23
     Ev'n from Hermon's dwelling led, . . . . . . . . . . . . .    335 Psalm XLII        26
     Dick. Oh hence! o cruell word! which even doggs do hate: . .  344 Possibly       1  47
     But hence, even hence, I must needes goe; such is my dogged
        fate. . . . . . . . . . . . . . . . . . . . . . . . . .    344 Possibly       1  48
     For they seem'd made even of skie-mettall best, . . . . . .   244 Other Poems    4 100
     For ev'n in forge colde water fire maintaines. . . . . . .    246 Other Poems    4 156
     Nay ev'n unto hir home he oft would go, . . . . . . . . . .   247 Other Poems    4 193
     Till one faire eav'n an howr ere Sun did rest, . . . . . .    247 Other Poems    4 205
     His eye, that ev'n did marke hir troden grasse, . . . . . .   251 Other Poems    4 379
     And so that even the barly-brake did end. . . . . . . . . .   252 Other Poems    4 416
     Sure I bewitched am, it is even that: . . . . . . . . . . .   253 Other Poems    4 447
     This said, this done, he rase even tir'd with rest, . . . .   255 Other Poems    4 521
EVENING
     And drawes the dolor on till wery evening. . . . . . . . .    111 4th Eclogues  71   6
     Klaius. O Mercurie, foregoer to the evening, . . . . . . .    111 4th Eclogues  71   7
     Where shade from Sunne, and sporte I sought in evening, . . . 111 4th Eclogues  71  14
     So darkened am, that all my day is evening, . . . . . . . .   111 4th Eclogues  71  22
     Long since I see my joyes come to their evening, . . . . .    112 4th Eclogues  71  29
     Which troubles their daye's worke, and joyes of evening: . .  112 4th Eclogues  71  33
     Turnde to the mortall serene of an evening. . . . . . . . .   112 4th Eclogues  71  42
     Klaius. Me seemes I see a filthie clowdie evening, . . . .    112 4th Eclogues  71  43
     I give the Sunne a last farewell each evening; . . . . . .    112 4th Eclogues  71  50
     I doo detest night, evening, day, and morning. . . . . . .    112 4th Eclogues  71  54
     I wish no evenings more to see, each evening; . . . . . . .   112 4th Eclogues  71  58
     Hath cast me, wretch, into eternall evening, . . . . . . .    113 4th Eclogues  71  65
     At whose approach the Sunne rase in the evening, . . . . .    113 4th Eclogues  71  69
     Our morning hymne this is, and song at evening. . . . . . .   113 4th Eclogues  71  75
     Well may the Evening cloath the eyes . . . . . . . . . . .    311 Psalm XXX         16
EVENINGS
     I wish no evenings more to see, each evening; . . . . . . .   112 4th Eclogues  71  58
     And now faire evenings blush my shame to see. . . . . . . .   254 Other Poems    4 480
EVENLY
     The ballance evnly stands; . . . . . . . . . . . . . . . .    283 Psalm X           60
EVENT
     O be it so, graunte such an event, O Gods, that event give. . 37 1st Eclogues  13 169
     And for th'event we never ought be sad. . . . . . . . . . .   105 3rd Eclogues  67  66
EVENTS
     As might learne Temp'rance voyde of a rage's events. . . . .  124 4th Eclogues  74  64
EVER
     No lovely praise was ever got with killing". . . . . . . .    16 1st Eclogues   7  81
     Is he a God, that ever flies the light? . . . . . . . . . .    21 1st Eclogues   8   7
     Philisides. Who ever taught a skillesse man to teach, . . .    22 1st Eclogues   9  16
     Clusters of clowdes, which no Sunne ever cleares. . . . . .    41 Arcadia II    21   4
     Which ever shines, though hid from earth by earthly shade, .   44 Arcadia II    26   3
     Whose lights do ever live, but in our darkenesse fade; . . .   44 Arcadia II    26   4
     Let this assured holde our judgements ever take, . . . . .     45 Arcadia II    26  15
     P. No Reason yet had ever skill tc show it. . . . . . . . .     47 2nd Eclogues  27  40
     Nico. And are you there old Pas? in troth I ever thought, . .   51 2nd Eclogues  29   1
     But ever since that well is well besought, . . . . . . . .      55 2nd Eclogues  29 109
     Whose loves may ever bide, . . . . . . . . . . . . . . . .      91 3rd Eclogues  63  14
     For ever hence awaye: . . . . . . . . . . . . . . . . . . .     93 3rd Eclogues  63  77
     Never hard hand, nor ever raines too light, . . . . . . . .     98 3rd Eclogues  65   8
     Then ever for my selfe since I was bore: . . . . . . . . .      99 3rd Eclogues  66  19
     She warre doth ever with his kinsfolke keepe, . . . . . . .    104 3rd Eclogues  67  37
     That ever fell to honest woman yet: . . . . . . . . . . . .    104 3rd Eclogues  67  44
     Till by such hap, as I must ever rewe, . . . . . . . . . .     115 4th Eclogues  72  74
     Of all those Graces' giftes the heavens have ever lent. . . .  119 4th Eclogues  73  86
     Was ever apt: but you my pastimes did despise. . . . . . .     121 4th Eclogues  73 149
     And if, o Sunne, thou ever didst appeare, . . . . . . . . .    127 4th Eclogues  75  70
     Time ever old, and yonge is still revolved . . . . . . . .     127 4th Eclogues  75  79
     But unto Man, age ever death doth sende. . . . . . . . . .     127 4th Eclogues  75  84
     That hardly usde, who ever prison broke, . . . . . . . . .     135 Cert Sonnets   1  11
     Where bee nowe those eyes ever Inly persers? . . . . . . .     138 Cert Sonnets   5   6
     Finding those beames, which I must ever love, . . . . . . .    149 Cert Sonnets  21   1
     He ever dies that wasteth. . . . . . . . . . . . . . . . .     152 Cert Sonnets  23  11
     Who hath ever felt the change of love, . . . . . . . . . .     153 Cert Sonnets  24   1
     Placed ever there, gave him this mourning weed, . . . . . .    168 Astrophil      7  13
     Keepe still my Zenith, ever shine on me. . . . . . . . . .     186 Astrophil     42   8
     What, dost thou thinke that I can ever hide: . . . . . . .     193 Astrophil     56  10
     I crav'd the thing which ever she denies: . . . . . . . . .    196 Astrophil     63   6
     Nor ever did in shade of Tempe sit: . . . . . . . . . . . .    203 Astrophil     74   2
     Of all the kings that ever here did raigne, . . . . . . . .    204 Astrophil     75   1
     When I was forst from Stella ever deere, . . . . . . . . .     222 Astrophil     87   1
     Fiercest but yet fairest ever; . . . . . . . . . . . . . .     221 A&S 9th Song      17
     They ever shall send thee their praysing voyce, . . . . . .    275 Psalm V           35
     Since ever thou to them wilt succour send. . . . . . . . .     275 Psalm V           36
     In all whose workes vainess is ever raigning: . . . . . . .    276 Psalm VI          26
     Ever from deed of any such desart: . . . . . . . . . . . .     277 Psalm VII          8
     Bent to revenge and ever hating. . . . . . . . . . . . . .     278 Psalm VIII         8
     In Thee my joyes and comforts ever be, . . . . . . . . . .     279 Psalm IX           3
     For Thou lord found by them wilt ever be . . . . . . . . .     280 Psalm IX          29
     Nor danger ever see: . . . . . . . . . . . . . . . . . . .     282 Psalm X           26
```

EVER   (CONTINUED)   PAGE   TITLE   LINE
    Ever and ever to be King,. . . . .   283 Psalm X   70
    Least we should ever feare the lust. . . . .   283 Psalm X   79
    These are God's words, God's words are ever pure,. . . . .   285 Psalm XII   19
    What? ever?. . . . .   285 Psalm XIII   2
    Nor ever call on god, but they shall quake . . . .   286 Psalm XIV   16
    Ever, lord, I will blesse Thee,. . . . .   288 Psalm XVI   19
    Who dost ever counsell mee,. . . . .   288 Psalm XVI   20
    My never peirced shield, my ever saving horn,. . . . . . .   290 Psalm XVIII   4
    Who is the man that ever can . . . .   295 Psalm XIX   49
    Where Israel Thy lawdes is ever telling; . . . .   298 Psalm XXII   10
    You shall the life that ever liveth find.. . . . .   300 Psalm XXII   64
    All pureness ever to embrace;. . . . .   302 Psalm XXIV   8
    Lift up your heads you Gates, and you doores ever biding,. . 302 Psalm XXIV   17
    Above line repeated at following location. . . . .   302 Psalm XXIV   21
    Unto whose ever hating lust. . . . .   308 Psalm XXVII   55
    And in his ever glorious frame . . . .   310 Psalm XXIX   5
    And ever, ever glorious. . . . .   310 Psalm XXIX   12
    Shall ever dust give thanks to Thee, ...   311 Psalm XXX   28
    But ever, ever shall . . . .   317 Psalm XXXIII   37
    For nothing they can ever want . . . .   319 Psalm XXXIV   34
    This lord is ever ever neare,. . . . .   320 Psalm XXXIV   66
    Nor ever turns aside . . . .   331 Psalm XL   19
    Who ever Lambkins saw (yet lambkins love to play). . . . .   343 Possibly   1   5
    For where he most would hit, he ever yet did misse.. . . .   241 Other Poems   1   2
    For they were ever in the best degree, ...   252 Other Poems   4 394
    So in you ever new . . . .   257 Other Poems   5 30
EVERLASTING
    This man for everlasting;. . . . .   297 Psalm XXI   22
EVER-LIVING
    After ever living thee;. . . . .   334 Psalm XLII   6
EVERMORE
    Pas. Who evermore will love Apollo's quill,. . . . .   53 2nd Eclogues 29   54
    You better sure shall live, not evermore . . . .   142 Cert Sonnets 12   1
    For David his Anoynt, and his seed ever more.. . . . . . .   293 Psalm XVIII   91
    Prayse, Prayse this lord then evermore . . . .   311 Psalm XXX   10
EVER-PLEASING
    With their ever-pleasing sight,. . . . .   263 Other Poems   7 64
EVER-TURNING
    The ever-turning spheares, the never-moving ground;. . . .   118 4th Eclogues 73   44
EVERY
    Leaping at every flie, and angrie with a flea: . . . . . .   53 2nd Eclogues 29   44
    Becomming every time and place,. . . . .   90 Arcadia III 62   136
    Klaius. I that was once delighted every morning, ...   111 4th Eclogues 71   19
    Long sham'd to be accurst in every place, ... 141 Cert Sonnets 8   3
    You that do search for everie purling spring,. . . . . . .   172 Astrophil   15   1
    And everie floure, not sweet perhaps, which growes . . . .   172 Astrophil   15   3
    Who though most rich in these and everie part, ...   183 Astrophil   37   12
    Of everie image, which may comfort show? . . . .   199 Astrophil   66   4
    While everie office themselves will discharge, ...   210 Astrophil   85   7
    For wearing Venus' badge, in every part of thee, ...   214 A&S 5th Song   70
    Every other vulgar light.. . . . .   233 A&S 11th Song   5
    That evry folk Thy wondrous Acts may see.. . . . .   277 Psalm VII   21
    Therfore shall evry godly One. . . . .   315 Psalm XXXII   19
    All visions seeme, at every bush I start:. . . . .   253 Other Poems   4 445
EVERYBODY'S
    For evry body's reading. . . . .   294 Psalm XIX   16
EVERYONE
    Because I breathe not love to everie one,. . . . .   191 Astrophil   54   1
EVERYTHING
    Against the lord of lords, the lord of every thing,. . . .   271 Psalm II   5
EVERYWHERE
    Enter bravely every where, ...   226 A&S 10th Song   20
EVIL
    No sword soe bytes as that evill toole annoyes.. . . . . .   29 1st Eclogues 10   90
    If then a boddily evill in a boddily gloze be not hidden,. . 34 1st Eclogues 10   87
    But rotten bleeding argues evill complection . . . .   50 2nd Eclogues 28 V883
    Doth th'infected wretch, of his ev'll th'extremity know? No. 63 2nd Eclogues 31   19
    Sight doth bewitch, the fancie evill awaked. . . . .   82 Arcadia III 57   2
    The evill of evils, just cause to be unjust, ...   93 3rd Eclogues 63   83
    Knowing that evill becommes a houshold strife, ...   96 3rd Eclogues 64   70
    Since sorow is the follower of evill fortune,. . . . . . .   108 Arcadia IV   70   2
    Since no evill fortune equalls publique damage:. . . . . .   108 Arcadia IV   70   3
    What? was I then worthie such good, now worthie so muche
        evill?. . . . .   124 4th Eclogues 74   77
    Which were not evill, well vew'd in reason's light.. . . .   131 Arcadia V   77   8
    His ugly evill in other's good to hide,. . . . .   141 Cert Sonnets 8   6
    Evill happes do fill with hope, good happes appall . . . .   143 Cert Sonnets 12   10
    Nor held in evill, nor suffered to be sound, ...   144 Cert Sonnets 15   8
    Deeming strange evill in that he did not know. . . . . . .   145 Cert Sonnets 16   4
    And thinke how evill becommeth him to slide, ...   144 Cert Sonnets 32   11
    Is it not evill that such a Devill wants hornes? . . . . .   206 Astrophil   78   14
    Of foes the spoile is evill, far worse of constant lovers. . 214 A&S 5th Song   48
    No witchcraft is so evill, as which man's mind destroyeth. . 215 A&S 5th Song   78
    Alas, that I am forst such evill of thee to say, ...   215 A&S 5th Song   80
    Whose senses in so evill consort, their stepdame Nature
        laies, ... 217 A&S 7th Song   1
    Thou hatest all whose works in evill are plac't. . . . . .   275 Psalm V   13
    Get hence you ev'ill, who in my ev'ill rejoyce,. . . . . .   276 Psalm VI   25
    And his own evill his own head shall appall. . . . .   278 Psalm VII   45

EVIL (CONTINUED)   PAGE   TITLE   LINE
   Why should the evill, so evill despise . . . .   283 Psalm X   53
   Behold the evill have bent their bow . . . .   284 Psalm XI   5
   That Thee so ev'ill have hated;. . . . .   297 Psalm XXI   30
   And was from evill by Thee upborn, ...   311 Psalm XXX   6
   So my good deeds they pay with this ev'ill share, ...   322 Psalm XXXV   27
   Till his known ev'ill do hatred get. . . . .   323 Psalm XXXVI   8
   Let not ev'ill hands discomfit me; . . . .   324 Psalm XXXVI   32
   Who do ev'ill works: lo I doe see. . . . .   324 Psalm XXXVI   34
   Ev'ill men work ill to utmost right, ...   325 Psalm XXXVII   33
   The ev'ill bent bowes, and swords they drew, ...   325 Psalm XXXVII   37
   Then fly all ev'ill and goodnesse nourish,. . . . .   326 Psalm XXXVII   67
   To ev'ill, both they and theirs shall wrack. . . . .   326 Psalm XXXVII   72
   Yea thou shalt see the ev'ill decay. . . . .   327 Psalm XXXVII   88
   Speaking ev'ill, thinking deceit.. . . . .   328 Psalm XXXVIII   36
   Who do ev'ill for good, to me. . . . .   329 Psalm XXXVIII   58
   My Foes' ev'ill words their hate of me display . . . .   333 Psalm XLI   17
   In whome no evill did raigne, nor good appeare, ...   245 Other Poems   4 118
   Till finding still his evill encreasing thus, ...   253 Other Poems   4 437
EVILLY
   Because I walk'd his wayes, nor gainst him ev'ly went, . . .   292 Psalm XVIII   44
EVILS
   True cause of evils, and cause of causelesse woe. . . . . .   25 1st Eclogues   9 116
   Yet say againe thy advise for th' ev'lls that I told thee. I
     told thee.. . . . .   63 2nd Eclogues 31   18
   Tell yet againe me the names of these faire form'd to do
     ev'lls. Dev'lls. . . . .   65 2nd Eclogues 31   49
   The evill of evils, just cause to be unjust, ...   93 3rd Eclogues 63   83
   To see my night of evils, which hath no morow. . . . . 136 Cert Sonnets   3   8
   Though present times and past with evils be snarde, ... 143 Cert Sonnets 12   13
   Where former blisse present evils do staine, ... 153 Cert Sonnets 24   12
   Band of all evils, cradle of causelesse care, ... 161 Cert Sonnets 31   3
   Suffering the evils both of the day and night, ... 224 Astrophil   89   9
   Ungratefull who is cald, the worst of evils is spok'n. . . . 213 A&S 5th Song   42
   Least inward evills do them defile, ... 320 Psalm XXXIV   50
   They inward ev'ills disguise. . . . . 333 Psalm XLI   22
EWE
   The Ewe another loved, ... 259 Other Poems   5 122
EWES
   Then can in good eawes be moved. . . . . 221 A&S 9th Song   24
   Made wolves (not inward wolves) my ewes to spare; . . . . . 254 Other Poems   4 486
EXALT
   He will exalt thee unto honour . . . . 327 Psalm XXXVII   86
EXALTED
   O lord Thou hast exalted me. . . . . 310 Psalm XXX   1
EXAMPLE
   Let swanne's example siker serve for thee, ...   28 1st Eclogues 10   73
   Lalus' example I would soone ensue, ... 104 3rd Eclogues 67   23
   Example more prevailing then direction, ... 128 4th Eclogues 75 131
EXCEED
   All things that earst I sawe, as orient pearles exceed, . . . 119 4th Eclogues 73   83
EXCEL
   The Indian odours doth excell. . . . .   87 Arcadia III   62   64
   Her waiting Nymphe, a Nymphe that did excell as farr . . . . 119 4th Eclogues 73   82
   Abase her praise, saying she doth excell: . . . . 183 Astrophil   37   8
   My bloud from them, who did excell in this, ... 185 Astrophil   41   10
EXCELLENCY
   Beauties which do in excellencie passe . . . . 207 Astrophil   82   2
EXCELLENT
   O Lord how excellent a thing . . . . 324 Psalm XXXVI   19
EXCELLENTLY
   When tis excellently sory. . . . . 221 A&S 9th Song   15
EXCELLETH
   In thee just accord excelleth, ... 140 Cert Sonnets   7   15
EXCELLING
   Gave repulse all grace excelling.. . . . . 219 A&S 8th Song   68
EXCELS
   Beauty as farre excels, ... 216 A&S 6th Song   27
EXCEPT
   What had I been, except I had. . . . . 308 Psalm XXVII   61
EXCEPTIONS
   As no exceptions tutch.. . . . . 216 A&S 6th Song   42
EXCESSIVE
   Ere that I should consent to doo such excessive a dammage. . 124 4th Eclogues 74   61
EXCHANGE
   By just exchange, one for the other giv'ne.. . . . .   75 Arcadia III   45   2
EXCLAIMING
   Have praide me leave my strange exclaiming musique, ... 112 4th Eclogues 71   32
EXCLAMATIONS
   If ought I cease these hideous exclamations, ...   61 2nd Eclogues 30 145
EXCUSE
   And which is worse, no good excuse can show, ... 174 Astrophil   18   7
   The mansion seat of blisse, and just excuse of Lovers; . . . 213 A&S 5th Song   21
EXCUSETH
   But this she thinks, our paine hye cause excuseth, ... 142 Cert Sonnets 11   13
EXECUTOR
   His sole exec'tour blame.. . . . . 160 Cert Sonnets 30   16
EXERCISE
   Teaching dumbe lips a nobler exercise. . . . . 207 Astrophil   81   4

```
                                                             PAGE    TITLE           LINE
EXILE
    Where rigrows exile lockes up all my sense?. . . . . . . .  233  Astrophil    104    8
EXILED
    Alas, from all their helps I am exiled,. . . . . . . . . .  137  Cert Sonnets   3   21
    Thou paine, thou hated paine, from heav'n exilde,. . . . .  141  Cert Sonnets  10    4
    (Exil'd for ay from those high treasures, which. . . . . .  177  Astrophil     24   13
    Being (ah) exild, disdayneth . . . . . . . . . . . . . . .  233  A&S 11th Song       4
EXPECTATION
    Great expectation, weare a traine of shame.. . . . . . . .  175  Astrophil     21    8
EXPENSE
    As farre from want, as farre from vaine expence, . . . . .   98  3rd Eclogues  65    9
EXPERIENCE
    Experience doubts, and schooles holde disputation. . . . .   49  2nd Eclogues  28   48
    When they by yeares' experience get best graces, . . . . .  127  4th Eclogues  75   89
EXPIRED
    A stranger fish, my selfe not yet expirde, . . . . . . . .  150  Cert Sonnets  22   25
EXPOSE
    And will not him unto the will expose. . . . . . . . . . .  333  Psalm XLI           7
EXPRESS
    Wit learnes in thee perfection to expresse,. . . . . . . .  182  Astrophil     35   12
    Thy teares expresse night's native moisture right. . . . .  229  Astrophil     96    8
    That he deigns to express. . . . . . . . . . . . . . . . .  303  Psalm XXV          33
    That I may still expresse. . . . . . . . . . . . . . . . .  305  Psalm XXVI         22
EXPRESSED
    Till that in words thy figure be exprest.. . . . . . . . .  189  Astrophil     50    4
EXPRESSETH
    Her throate in tunes expresseth. . . . . . . . . . . . . .  137  Cert Sonnets   4    6
EXTEND
    The Heathen for thy Child's right, and will thy realme
       extend . . . . . . . . . . . . . . . . . . . . . . . .  271  Psalm II           19
    O then extend Thy loving heart . . . . . . . . . . . . . .  324  Psalm XXXVI        27
EXTENDETH
    His blessing he extendeth. . . . . . . . . . . . . . . . .  273  Psalm III          36
EXTOLLING
    Extolling ravenous gain: . . . . . . . . . . . . . . . . .  281  Psalm X            11
EXTORTION
    But our Desire's tyrannicall extortion . . . . . . . . . .   60  2nd Eclogues  30  134
EXTREME
    The scourge of life, and death's extreame disgrace,. . . .  140  Cert Sonnets   8    1
EXTREMITY
    Doth th'infected wretch, of his ev'll th'extremity know? No.  63  2nd Eclogues  31   19
EYE
    For as the Moone the eie doth please,. . . . . . . . . . .   13  Arcadia I      5    7
    Whose faire bodily gifts are fram'd most lovely to each ey..  33  1st Eclogues  13   55
    Love wakes the jealous eye least thence it moves:. . . . .   42  Arcadia II    22    6
    The jealous eye, the more it lookes, it loves. . . . . . .   42  Arcadia II    22    7
    But eye from blade, and eare from crie:. . . . . . . . . .   44  Arcadia II    25   11
    The hart, eye, eare here onely find his treasure doth: . .   49  2nd Eclogues  28   58
    A man to feare a woman's moodie eye, . . . . . . . . . . .   49  2nd Eclogues  28   75
    Till with lickt beard, his eye of fire espie his foes. . .   53  2nd Eclogues  29   36
    Yet tell what light thinge I had in me to draw me to die?
       Eye. . . . . . . . . . . . . . . . . . . . . . . . . .   64  2nd Eclogues  31   25
    Nor ey receaves due object,. . . . . . . . . . . . . . . .   66  2nd Eclogues  32   38
    Nor envie's snaky ey, finds any harbor here, . . . . . . .   69  2nd Eclogues  34   18
    Where envie's snaky ey, winketh or els dyeth,. . . . . . .   69  2nd Eclogues  34   37
    You that are borne to be the worlde's eye, . . . . . . . .   79  Arcadia III   50   12
    (Better despisde) bewondre gasing eye. . . . . . . . . . .   81  Arcadia III   51   12
    Crying in me: eye hopes deceitefull prove. . . . . . . . .   83  Arcadia III   57   13
    So good a say invites the eye, . . . . . . . . . . . . . .   87  Arcadia III   62   51
    And most bewitch the wretched eye, . . . . . . . . . . . .   90  Arcadia III   62  138
    But (for his jealous eye she well did finde) . . . . . . .   95  3rd Eclogues  64   41
    Right so my boiling hart, enflam'de with fire of a faire
       eye . . . . . . . . . . . . . . . . . . . . . . . . . .  123  4th Eclogues  74   27
    Rather then have thy all-beholding eye . . . . . . . . . .  126  4th Eclogues  75   56
    In shape, which by man's eye might be perceived; . . . . .  127  4th Eclogues  75   71
    Right so my minde, caught by his guiding eye . . . . . . .  144  Cert Sonnets  15    5
    For in each thing wherto mine eye doth range,. . . . . . .  147  Cert Sonnets  18    3
    But so confusde, that neither any eye. . . . . . . . . . .  149  Cert Sonnets  22    2
    As that sweete blacke which vailes the heav'nly eye: . . .  175  Astrophil     20    7
    Rich in all beauties which man's eye can see:. . . . . . .  183  Astrophil     37    6
    Unkind, I love you not: O me, that eye . . . . . . . . . .  188  Astrophil     47   13
    Of Hope, which makes it seeme faire to the eye.. . . . . .  189  Astrophil     49    8
    Let clouds bedimme my face, breake in mine eye,. . . . . .  198  Astrophil     64    5
    Doth Stella now begin with piteous eye,. . . . . . . . . .  199  Astrophil     67    2
    School'd onely by his mother's tender eye: . . . . . . . .  203  Astrophil     73    2
    Let wo gripe on my heart, shame loade mine eye.. . . . . .  212  Astrophil     86    4
    When far spent night perswades each mortall eye, . . . . .  230  Astrophil     99    1
    The judgement of the eye,. . . . . . . . . . . . . . . . .  216  A&S 6th Song       40
    Even god himself sent down his peircing ey . . . . . . . .  286  Psalm XIV           7
    Then keep me as the Apple of an Eye, . . . . . . . . . . .  290  Psalm XVII         25
    Up Thou dost light my light, and cleare my darkned eye.. .  292  Psalm XVIII        53
    Ev'en when foe's envious ey. . . . . . . . . . . . . . . .  301  Psalm XXIII        17
    To Thy Works they give no ey.. . . . . . . . . . . . . . .  309  Psalm XXVIII       21
    For my annoyes have come before thyne eye, . . . . . . . .  312  Psalm XXXI         20
    My eye, my Gutts, yea my soul grief doth wast, . . . . . .  312  Psalm XXXI         27
    Full well his ey . . . . . . . . . . . . . . . . . . . . .  317  Psalm XXXIII       50
    I wait on Thee with hopefull ey. . . . . . . . . . . . . .  330  Psalm XXXIX        24
    This mote from out his eye, this inward burre, . . . . . .  246  Other Poems    4  172
    Must strive with waiting foot, and watching eye. . . . . .  248  Other Poems    4  228
    He ran, but ran with eye ore shoulder cast,. . . . . . . .  249  Other Poems    4  289
```

```
EYE                        (CONTINUED)                    PAGE    TITLE           LINE
  And surely taught by his love-open eye,. . . . . . . . . . .  251 Other Poems    4   378
  His eye, that ev'n did marke hir trodden grasse, . . . . . .  251 Other Poems    4   379
  In flowry fielde a gladder eye to please:. . . . . . . . . .  256 Other Poems    5    3
  Do turne from thee his eye,. . . . . . . . . . . . . . . . .  257 Other Poems    5   23
EYED
  But alwayes one my selfe with eagle eyde trueth to flie, . .  153 Cert Sonnets 24   24
EYE-JUDGMENT
  Eye-judgement of the eye,. . . . . . . . . . . . . . . . . .  216 A&S 6th Song    V 40
EYELIDS
  His eyelidds peyse our going. . . . . . . . . . . . . . . . .  284 Psalm XI           16
EYEN
  Which being nought seems somewhat to the eyen, . . . . . . .   19 1st Eclogues   7  164
  Giv'ne to my harte, by my fore wounded eyne: . . . . . . .    77 Arcadia III   47    6
  There be no eyn but reade the line . . . . . . . . . . . . .  294 Psalm XIX         13
  A span? nay nothing in Thyn eyne.. . . . . . . . . . . . . .  330 Psalm XXXIX       16
  Till my eies had their curse from blessed eine.. . . . . . .  254 Other Poems    4  496
EYES
  Where eares be burnt, eyes dazled, harts opprest?. . . . . .    3 Lady of May    1    6
  And feede mine eares, mine eyes, my hart in you. . . . . . .    3 Lady of May    1   12
  Whose cleerest eyes I blisse, and sweetest voyce,. . . . . .    5 Lady of May    3   15
  For from without came to mine eyes the blowe,. . . . . . . .   11 Arcadia I      2    5
  Thus are my eyes still Captive to one sight: . . . . . . . .   12 Arcadia I      2    9
  And thus my eyes, are plaste still in one sight. . . . . . .   12 Arcadia I      2 V809
  Her twinkling eies bedeckt with pearle, her lips of Saphir
    blew:. . . . . . . . . . . . . . . . . . . . . . . . . . .   12 Arcadia I      3   10
  Her eyes my eyesight is, her conversation. . . . . . . . . .   15 1st Eclogues   7   32
  Want I white wooll, whose eyes her white skinne garnished? .   16 1st Eclogues   7   59
  Her eyes so maistering me, that such objection . . . . . . .   16 1st Eclogues   7   68
  Lalus. Once my well-waiting eyes espied my treasure, . . . .   16 1st Eclogues   7   73
  Shine eyes on me, that both our lives be guarded;. . . . . .   17 1st Eclogues   7   92
  The power I will invoke dwelles in her eyes: . . . . . . . .   17 1st Eclogues   7  104
  My eyes the bandes, my thoughts the fatall knot. . . . . . .   17 1st Eclogues   7  113
  Let crowes picke out mine eyes, which saw too much:. . . . .   19 1st Eclogues   7  149
  Let crowes picke out mine eyes which too much sawe.. . . . .   19 1st Eclogues   7 V149
  On me to cast those eyes, where shine nobilitie. . . . . . .   19 1st Eclogues   7  178
  A horned head, cloven foote, and thousand eyes,. . . . . . .   21 1st Eclogues   8   26
  To open eyes all beauties he doth raine; . . . . . . . . . .   22 1st Eclogues   8   39
  But for that Love's desire most rules the eyes,. . . . . . .   22 1st Eclogues   8   41
  Whome wit makes vaine, or blinded with his eyes, . . . . . .   23 1st Eclogues   9   35
  Such sight have they that see with goggling eyes.. . . . . .   25 1st Eclogues   9  113
  And let thine eyes to other sports be framed.. . . . . . . .   25 1st Eclogues   9  122
  Which both the pallate, and the eyes delight.. . . . . . . .   26 1st Eclogues   9  131
  Lett our unpartiall eyes a litle watche. . . . . . . . . . .   29 1st Eclogues  10   91
  If mine eyes can speake to doo harty errande,. . . . . . . .   30 1st Eclogues  12    1
  But if eyes faile then, when I most doo need them, . . . . .   30 1st Eclogues  12    5
  But if eyes can speake to doo harty errande, . . . . . . . .   31 1st Eclogues  12   25
  But to the Cedar, Queene of woods, when I lifte my beteard
    eyes,. . . . . . . . . . . . . . . . . . . . . . . . . . .   36 1st Eclogues  13  141
  In vaine, mine Eyes, you labour to amende.. . . . . . . . . .   38 Arcadia II    14    1
  Since there mine eyes have played so false a parte,. . . . .   38 Arcadia II    14   11
  Seeme to your eyes of a disgracefull hewe: . . . . . . . . .   38 Arcadia II    15    6
  Which makes all eyes doo honour unto you.. . . . . . . . . .   38 Arcadia II    15    8
  Since so mine eyes are subject to your sight,. . . . . . . .   39 Arcadia II    16    1
  Over these brookes trusting to ease mine eyes, . . . . . . .   41 Arcadia II    21    1
  (Mine eyes even great in labour with their teares) . . . . .   41 Arcadia II    21    2
  In watry glasse my watrie eyes I see:. . . . . . . . . . . .   41 Arcadia II    21    5
  Since streame, aier, sand, mine eyes and eares conspire: . .   42 Arcadia II    21   17
  P. Reason hath eyes to see his owne ill case.. . . . . . . .   46 2nd Eclogues  27   16
  Her eyes the force beyond my possibilitie. . . . . . . . . .   48 2nd Eclogues  28   30
  His eyes are curious search, but vailde with warefulnesse: .   48 2nd Eclogues  28   43
  So she thy love, her eyes thy eyes may gratifie, . . . . . .   49 2nd Eclogues  28   51
  Thus she is framde: her eyes are my direction; . . . . . . .   49 2nd Eclogues  28   70
  Which who doth misse his eyes are but delusions, . . . . . .   51 2nd Eclogues  28  108
  And wanting her, my weeping eyes I wipe. . . . . . . . . . .   54 2nd Eclogues  29   77
  I leave mine eyes unwipte my cheekes to bathe. . . . . . . .   54 2nd Eclogues  29   80
  From Cosma's eyes, which full in darkenes shine, . . . . . .   55 2nd Eclogues  29  103
  I said, my hands well paide her for mine eyes, . . . . . . .   55 2nd Eclogues  29  115
  That hath foure eyes, and onely two can frame. . . . . . . .   56 2nd Eclogues  29  143
  And saw those eyes (those Sonnes) such shoures to shew,. . .   58 2nd Eclogues  30   49
  Serve all thy starrie eyes this shame to see?. . . . . . . .   58 2nd Eclogues  30   61
  But still our dazeled eyes their way do misse, . . . . . . .   59 2nd Eclogues  30   74
  O eyes of mine, where once she saw her face, . . . . . . . .   60 2nd Eclogues  30  116
  Can fancies want eies, or he fall that steppeth aloft? Oft..   64 2nd Eclogues  31   22
  Eysight made me to yeelde, but what first pierst to myne
    eies? Eies.. . . . . . . . . . . . . . . . . . . . . . . .   64 2nd Eclogues  31   26
  My eys be dym, my lyms shake,. . . . . . . . . . . . . . . .   66 2nd Eclogues  32   10
  Her cannons be her eys, myne eys the walls be, . . . . . . .   68 2nd Eclogues  33   13
  Her stepps, gladd we receave, gladd we receave her eys.. . .   69 2nd Eclogues  34   40
  Nowe that myne eyes their cheerefull sunn dothe misse. . . .   70 Arcadia III   35    5
  With sweatie browes, sometyme with watrie eyes,. . . . . . .   71 Arcadia III   36    8
  And in whose eyes my dayly doome I reede.. . . . . . . . . .   72 Arcadia III   38    5
  Since all the thinges which give mine eyes their light . . .   73 Arcadia III   39    5
  Eyes faire and great, like faire great oxe's eyes, . . . . .   76 Arcadia III   46    9
  Till her eyes shine, I live in darkest night.. . . . . . . .   79 Arcadia III   51   14
  Eyes, let your Teares with gazing now be mended, . . . . . .   84 Arcadia III   59   14
  My harte, eyes, eares, with wonder, love, delight: . . . . .   84 Arcadia III   60    2
  Your eyes may tread a Lover's maze.. . . . . . . . . . . . .   86 Arcadia III   62   32
  Do please all eyes, and spotlesse do endure. . . . . . . . .   91 3rd Eclogues  63   25
  With weeping eyes (her eyes she taught to weepe) . . . . . .   96 3rd Eclogues  64   85
```

EYES   (CONTINUED)   PAGE   TITLE   LINE

The birds' eyes closde, closed their chirping notes. . . . .   98 3rd Eclogues 66   12
Till forste to parte, with harte and eyes even sore, ...   99 3rd Eclogues 66   39
Monkie, sweet breath; the Cow, her faire eyes brought; . . .   101 3rd Eclogues 66   88
For to my dimmed eyes beganne t'appeare. . . . .   103 3rd Eclogues 66   159
Cast thy stepmother eyes upon our sorowe, ...   109 Arcadia IV   70   23
Seas in our eyes, and brasen tongues by nature, ...   109 Arcadia IV   70   26
Mine eyes did light upon her shining hewe, ...   115 4th Eclogues 72   75
Such vitall sparke, that her mine eyes might see. . . . . .   115 4th Eclogues 72   84
And wanting use of eyes their eyes began to close: . . . . .   116 4th Eclogues 73   6
Did suffer drousie lids mine eyes then cleare to blinde; . .   117 4th Eclogues 73   26
That forced with grief reveales what greeved eyes dyd see) .   118 4th Eclogues 73   56
And bending humbled eyes (o eyes the Sunne of sight) . . . .   119 4th Eclogues 73   91
But thus with irefull eyes, and face that shooke with spite.   119 4th Eclogues 73   101
That thou full oft shalt wish thy judging eyes were blinde".   121 4th Eclogues 73   172
Can those eyes, that of eyes drownd in most harty flowing
    teares, ...   122 4th Eclogues 74   15
Can those eyes now yeeld to the kind conceit of a sorow, . .   122 4th Eclogues 74   17
You should those faire eyes have with a veile covered. . . .   123 4th Eclogues 74   48
But foole, foole that I am, those eyes would shine from a
    dark cave. . . . .   123 4th Eclogues 74   49
First be mine eyes pulde out, first be my braine perished; .   124 4th Eclogues 74   60
And putting out our eyes seeke we our light. . . . .   130 4th Eclogues 76   36
Our owly eyes, which dimm'd with passions bee, ...   131 Arcadia V   77   9
Yet still her eyes give to my flames their fuell. . . . . .   136 Cert Sonnets 3   12
Where bee nowe those eyes ever Inly persers? . . . .   138 Cert Sonnets 5   5
More loving eyes she draws, more hate thou hast. . . . . . .   141 Cert Sonnets 8   14
I praisde her eyes whom never chance doth move, ...   141 Cert Sonnets 9   5
How holdst thou her, whose eyes constraint doth feare, . . .   142 Cert Sonnets 10   5
That weepe worse then hart in bloodie teares? . . . .   142 Cert Sonnets 11   7
Whose eyes seeme chaste, because they looke on ground: . . .   147 Cert Sonnets 17   50
Myne eyes thence drawne, where lived all their light, . . .   149 Cert Sonnets 21   5
Long drowned hopes to watrie eyes it lends: . . . .   150 Cert Sonnets 22   18
Mine eyes the streight, the roomie cave, my minde, ...   150 Cert Sonnets 22   35
Let here his eyes be raised. . . . .   151 Cert Sonnets 23   3
And yet unite the eyes, ...   152 Cert Sonnets 23   6
But eyes these beauties see not, ...   152 Cert Sonnets 23   25
Yet eyes deprived be not, ...   152 Cert Sonnets 23   27
From sight of her faire eyes: . . . .   152 Cert Sonnets 23   28
Let here his eyes be raysed. . . . .   152 Cert Sonnets 23   35
Ladie mine eyes remained, ...   154 Cert Sonnets 25   3
That trust those killing eyes, I would, ...   158 Cert Sonnets 28   19
In face and eyes unmatched being, ...   159 Cert Sonnets 29   7
What in your face mine eyes do measure. . . . .   159 Cert Sonnets 29   9
To me mine eyes the true shape carie. . . . .   159 Cert Sonnets 29   13
"Her eyes were once his dart". . . . .   160 Cert Sonnets 30   26
It is most true, that eyes are form'd to serve . . . . . .   167 Astrophil   5   1
When Nature made her chiefe worke, Stella's eyes, ...   168 Astrophil   7   1
Whose faire skin, beamy eyes, like morning sun on snow, . .   169 Astrophil   8   9
Stella, thou straight lookst babies in her eyes, ...   170 Astrophil   11   10
Cupid, because thou shin'st in Stella's eyes, ...   170 Astrophil   12   1
Mine eyes (shall I say curst or blest) beheld. . . . .   173 Astrophil   16   10
And in her eyes of arrowes infinit. . . . .   173 Astrophil   17   11
Bewray it selfe in my long setled eyes, ...   176 Astrophil   23   2
But only Stella's eyes and Stella's hart. . . . .   176 Astrophil   23   14
That Vertue, if it once met with our eyes, ...   177 Astrophil   25   3
To mortall eyes might sweetly shine in her. . . . .   177 Astrophil   25   11
And thus her heart escapes, but thus her eyes. . . . .   179 Astrophil   29   9
Sure, if that long with Love acquainted eyes . . . .   180 Astrophil   31   5
Teaching blind eyes both how to smile and weepe, ...   181 Astrophil   32   8
How faire a day was neare, o punish'd eyes, ...   181 Astrophil   33   13
Whereto long since, through my long battred eyes, ...   182 Astrophil   36   3
To hatch mine eyes, and that unbitted thought. . . . .   183 Astrophil   38   2
Both by the judgement of the English eyes, ...   185 Astrophil   41   3
O eyes, which do the Spheares of beautie move, ...   185 Astrophil   42   1
O eyes, where humble lookes most glorious prove, ...   185 Astrophil   42   5
Yet still on me, o eyes, dart downe your rayes: . . . . . .   186 Astrophil   42   11
Faire eyes, sweet lips, deare heart, that foolish I. . . . .   186 Astrophil   43   1
Then with those eyes he lookes, lo by and by . . . .   186 Astrophil   43   6
Let not mine eyes be hel-driv'n from that light: . . . . . .   188 Astrophil   48   7
With sad eyes I their weake proportion see, ...   189 Astrophil   50   7
Her eyes, her lips, her all, saith Love do this, ...   190 Astrophil   52   3
My heart then quak'd, then dazled were mine eyes, ...   191 Astrophil   53   10
I Stella's eyes assayll, invade her eares: . . . .   195 Astrophil   61   3
She in whose eyes Love, though unfelt, doth shine, ...   196 Astrophil   62   3
So children still reade you with awfull eyes, ...   196 Astrophil   63   2
For late with heart most high, with eyes most low, ...   196 Astrophil   63   5
By Nature borne, I gave to thee mine eyes. . . . .   198 Astrophil   65   8
Mine eyes, my light, my heart, my life, alas, ...   198 Astrophil   65   9
Stella's eyes sent to me the beames of blisse, ...   199 Astrophil   66   11
But when mine eyes backe to their heav'n did move, ...   199 Astrophil   66   13
Envie, put out thine eyes, least thou do see . . . .   200 Astrophil   69   3
Hath cheekes to smile, as well as eyes to weepe. . . . . . .   201 Astrophil   70   8
That inward sunne in thine eyes shineth so. . . . .   201 Astrophil   71   8
Care shining in mine eyes, faith in my sprite, ...   202 Astrophil   72   11
Of gentle force, so that mine eyes dare gladly play. . . . .   205 Astrophil   76   6
My heart cries "ah", it burnes, mine eyes now dazled be: . .   205 Astrophil   76   11
So manie eyes ay seeking their owne woe, ...   206 Astrophil   78   12
How faine would I paint thee to all men's eyes, ...   207 Astrophil   81   7
But give apt servants their due place, let eyes. . . . . . .   210 Astrophil   85   9

141

EYES   (CONTINUED)   PAGE   TITLE   LINE
        Then those blest eyes, where all my hopes do dwell,. . . . .   212 Astrophil 86   13
        Stella whose eyes make all my tempests cleere, ...   222 Astrophil 87   3
        I saw that teares did in her eyes appeare; . . . .   223 Astrophil 87   6
        That where before hart loved and eyes did see, ...   223 Astrophil 88   12
        Since Stella's eyes, wont to give me my day, ...   223 Astrophil 89   3
        Thine eyes my pride, thy lips my history:. . . . .   224 Astrophil 90   3
        They please I do confesse, they please mine eyes, ...   225 Astrophil 91   9
        From out thy heavy mould, that inbent eyes . . . .   228 Astrophil 94   3
        Mine eyes then only winke, for spite perchance, ...   230 Astrophil 98   13
        In tombe of lids then buried are mine eyes, ...   231 Astrophil 99   12
        And joy, which is inseperate from those eyes, ...   231 Astrophil 101   7
        Where be those Roses gone, which sweetned so our eyes? . . .   232 Astrophil 102   1
        But cease mine eyes, your teares do witnesse well. . . . . .   235 Astrophil 105   9
        Thou toldst mine eyes should helpe their famisht case? . . .   235 Astrophil 106   6
        Who hath the eyes which marrie state with pleasure, ...   197 A&S 1st Song   5
        Since sweet sleep her eyes hath charmed, ...   202 A&S 2nd Song   5
        As his light was her eyes, her death his endlesse night: . .   209 A&S 3rd Song   10
        O eyes, o eares of men, how are you charmed! . . . .   209 A&S 3rd Song   18
        I said, thine eyes were starres, thy breasts the milk'n way,   212 A&S 5th Song   10
        That mine eyes thine eyes may see? . . . .   225 A&S 10th Song   2
        We change eyes, and hart for hart, ...   227 A&S 10th Song   40
        Lest that Argus eyes perceive you.". . . . .   235 A&S 11th Song   42
        Who have so leaden eyes, as not to see sweet beautie's show,   217 A&S 7th Song   7
        Of which the two life-giving lights are figured in her eyes: 217 A&S 7th Song   16
        While their eyes by love directed, ...   218 A&S 8th Song   15
        "Stella, in whose shining eyes, ...   218 A&S 8th Song   33
        "If those eyes you praised, be . . . .   220 A&S 8th Song   81
        Of those eyes, and blinder minded. . . . .   220 A&S 8th Song   84
        And showers from mine eyes proceeding. . . . .   221 A&S 9th Song   5
        And will my waiting eyes to thee ward bend.. . . . .   274 Psalm V   8
        With winking eyes aye bent . . . .   282 Psalm X   35
        The power of Thy through-seing eyes? . . . .   283 Psalm X   54
        But nake'd before thine eyes . . . .   283 Psalm X   57
        Nay give me eyes, and light, least that I sleep. . . . . . .   285 Psalm XIII   11
        Whose eyes a person vile do hold in vile disdain . . . . . .   287 Psalm XV   7
        My eyes still my God regard. . . . .   288 Psalm XVI   25
        Show that Thy eyes respect a faithfull case; . . . .   289 Psalm XVII   6
        Their eyes do swim, their face doth shine in fatt, ...   290 Psalm XVII   29
        His eyes unto my Case, his eares unto my moane.. . . . . . .   291 Psalm XVIII   14
        But streight his shining eyes this misty masse disclos'd. . .   291 Psalm XVIII   26
        As he before his eyes did see my justice stand, ...   292 Psalm XVIII   48
        So purely wise it gives the eyes . . . .   294 Psalm XIX   35
        So farr from seing myne unhealthfull eyes, ...   298 Psalm XXII   3
        No sooner my child eyes could look abroad, ...   299 Psalm XXII   23
        Where then should my eyes be . . . .   304 Psalm XXV   55
        Before my eyes did stand . . . .   305 Psalm XXVI   11
        On beauty His my eyes to stay. . . . .   307 Psalm XXVII   22
        Well may the Evening cloath the eyes . . . .   311 Psalm XXX   16
        For God's own eyes on good men sit . . . .   320 Psalm XXXIV   55
        Before his eyes that so doth stray. . . . .   323 Psalm XXXVI   6
        For those same eyes his flatterers be. . . . .   323 Psalm XXXVI   7
        Of mine eyes abandons me.. . . . .   328 Psalm XXXVIII   30
        Who bends not wandring eyes. . . . .   331 Psalm XL   17
        Dick. What joy the joyfull sunne gives unto bleared eyes:. .   343 Possibly   1   13
        D. Wonder that by two so black eyes the glittering stars be
            past.. . . . .   343 Possibly   1   28
        Strephon was yonge, yet markt with humble eies . . . .   243 Other Poems 4   36
        (Lest greedy eies to them might challenge lay) . . . .   243 Other Poems 4   68
        Which to their eies the bowles of Venus brought, ...   244 Other Poems 4   99
        Besides this force, within hir eies he kept. . . . .   246 Other Poems 4   153
        Leaving in paine their wel-fed hungry eies.. . . . .   246 Other Poems 4   168
        For simple goodnes shined in his eyes. . . . .   247 Other Poems 4   196
        Strephon, whose eies on hir back-parts did play, ...   250 Other Poems 4   333
        He did not there doe homage of his eies, ...   251 Other Poems 4   367
        But on his eies his heart did sacrifise. . . . .   251 Other Poems 4   368
        To see hir eies, with how true humblenes . . . .   252 Other Poems 4   402
        Filling his eies with teares, with sighs his brest.. . . . .   253 Other Poems 4   432
        That from those eies where heav'nly apples bene, ...   253 Other Poems 4   450
        Those eies, which nothing like themselves can see, ...   253 Other Poems 4   451
        Till my eies had their curse from blessed eine.. . . . . . .   254 Other Poems 4   496
        "Alas! a cloud hath overcast mine eies:. . . . .   255 Other Poems 4   505
        With eyes which threatned they would drowne his face,. . . .   255 Other Poems 4   524
        And thus, with eyes made dimme . . . .   256 Other Poems 5   12
        Then want one hower those eyes which my joyes keepe. . . . .   259 Other Poems 5   102
EYES'
        Or mine eyes' language she doo hap to judge of, ...   30 1st Eclogues 12   2
        So that eyes' message be of her received, ...   30 1st Eclogues 12   3
        Or if eyes' language be not unto her knowne, ...   30 1st Eclogues 12   6
        So that eyes' message doo returne rejected, ...   30 1st Eclogues 12   7
        Or mine eyes' language she doo hap to judge of, ...   31 1st Eclogues 12 26
        So that eyes' message be of her received, ...   31 1st Eclogues 12 27
        Eies' hurters, eies hurt, but what from them to me fall's?
            Fall's.. . . . .   64 2nd Eclogues 31 27
        By him because I did find in his eyes' sight grace, ...   292 Psalm XVIII   41
        Guide Thee by my eyes' guiding. . . . .   315 Psalm XXXII   30
EYESIGHT
        Her eyes my eyesight is, her conversation. . . . .   15 1st Eclogues 7 32
        Eysight made me to yeelde, but what first pierst to myne
            eies? Eies.. . . . .   64 2nd Eclogues 31 26

```
                                                            PAGE   TITLE          LINE
EYES-SPEECH
    Her eye's-speech is translated thus by thee: . . . . . . . .  199 Astrophil    67    5
EYING
    And alwaies westward eying,. . . . . . . . . . . . . . . . .  259 Other Poems   5  125
F
    Welcome my two to me, E.D. F.G. P.S. . . . . . . . . . . . .  261 Other Poems   6   25
    "Only for my two loves' sake, Sir Ed. D. and M. F. G.. . . .  263 Other Poems   7   61
FA
    Fa la la leridan, dan dan dan deridan: . . . . . . . . . . .  156 Cert Sonnets 27    5
    Fa la la leridan dan dan dan deridan,. . . . . . . . . . . .  156 Cert Sonnets 27   13
    Fa la la leridan dan dan dan deridan,. . . . . . . . . . . .  157 Cert Sonnets 27   21
    Fa la la leridan, dan dan dan deridan: . . . . . . . . . . .  157 Cert Sonnets 27   29
    Fa la la leridan, dan dan dan deridan: . . . . . . . . . . .  157 Cert Sonnets 27   37
FABLE
    Yet hearing late a fable, which did show . . . . . . . . . .  187 Astrophil    45    5
    That Name of God a fable is. . . . . . . . . . . . . . . . .  281 Psalm X            16
FACE
    Whose face doth oft the bravest sort enchant, . . . . . . .    3 Lady of May   1    2
    Your face hurts oft, but still it doth delight,. . . . . . .    3 Lady of May   1    8
    Though not so white as is thy lovely face, . . . . . . . . .    4 Lady of May   2   20
    Thy elder care shall from thy carefull face. . . . . . . . .   11 Arcadia I     1    1
    Lalus. If thou wilt not be seene, thy face goe hide away,. .   15 1st Eclogues  7   13
    Geron. If that thy face were hid, or I were blinde,. . . . .   25 1st Eclogues  9   96
    Ne let white haires, which on my face doo grow,. . . . . . .   38 Arcadia II   15    5
    I layde my face; my face wherein there lyes. . . . . . . . .   41 Arcadia II   21    3
    Whose onely face the little heaven is, . . . . . . . . . . .   51 2nd Eclogues 28  107
    A ruddie haire his cote, with fine long specled face:. . . .   53 2nd Eclogues 29   42
    Or while that shepheards love a lovely face. . . . . . . . .   56 2nd Eclogues 29  125
    O eyes of mine, where once she saw her face, . . . . . . . .   60 2nd Eclogues 30  116
    Her face which was more lively in my hart; . . . . . . . . .   60 2nd Eclogues 30  117
    Hurte not the face, which nothing can amende". . . . . . . .   82 Arcadia III  55   15
    Doth him, his face, his words, leave, shunne, refraine,. . .   84 Arcadia III  60   12
    Which on cold winter's face doth grow. . . . . . . . . . . .   85 Arcadia III  62    8
    More white then Neptune's fomie face,. . . . . . . . . . . .   88 Arcadia III  62   69
    Her Horned face in Heaven dothe Range, . . . . . . . . . . .   86 Arcadia III  62 V 12
    O heav'n awake shewe forth thy stately face, . . . . . . . .   91 3rd Eclogues 63   10
    Ne dare once shew thy face,. . . . . . . . . . . . . . . . .   93 3rd Eclogues 63   87
    The sheep, mild-seeming face; climing, the Beare;. . . . . .  101 3rd Eclogues 66   90
    To death, as then disguisde in her faire face. . . . . . . .  115 4th Eclogues 72   69
    A wanton woman's face, and with curld knots had twinde . . .  118 4th Eclogues 73   73
    But thus with irefull eyes, and face that shooke with spite.  119 4th Eclogues 73  101
    "Nay thou (said both) shalt see such beames shine in her
        face . . . . . . . . . . . . . . . . . . . . . . . . . .  121 4th Eclogues 73  175
    You should have your face (since Love is ill) blemished. . .  123 4th Eclogues 74   56
    O wretch, what do I say? should that faire face be defaced?.  124 4th Eclogues 74   57
    Upon thy face let coaly Ravens swarme: . . . . . . . . . . .  125 4th Eclogues 75   19
    O Phoebus with good cause thy face thou hidest,. . . . . . .  126 4th Eclogues 75   55
    Where ys Ah that face, that a Sunne defaces? . . . . . . . .  138 Cert Sonnets  5    9
    In thy face I plainly see, . . . . . . . . . . . . . . . . .  140 Cert Sonnets  7   29
    Late harbors in her face whom nature wrought,. . . . . . . .  141 Cert Sonnets  8    7
    Her face (this age's praise) the thiefe doth kisse.. . . . .  141 Cert Sonnets  9   12
    Fear'st not a face that oft whole harts devowres,. . . . . .  142 Cert Sonnets 10   10
    No, no, she is too wise, she knowes her face . . . . . . . .  142 Cert Sonnets 11    9
    Else what in face, then in my fancie beare?. . . . . . . . .  146 Cert Sonnets 17   10
    But now, if ere my face with joy be clad:. . . . . . . . . .  147 Cert Sonnets 17   44
    May paint my face without seeing mee,. . . . . . . . . . . .  153 Cert Sonnets 24    3
    In face and eyes unmatched being,. . . . . . . . . . . . . .  159 Cert Sonnets 29    7
    What in your face mine eyes do measure.. . . . . . . . . . .  159 Cert Sonnets 29    9
    I sought fit words to paint the blackest face of woe,. . . .  165 Astrophil     1    5
    How then? even thus: in Stella's face I reed,. . . . . . . .  166 Astrophil     3   12
    At length he perch'd himself in Stella's joyfull face, . . .  168 Astrophil     8    8
    Queene Vertue's court, which some call Stella's face, . . . .  169 Astrophil     9    1
    Stella's faire haire, her face he makes his shield,. . . . .  171 Astrophil    13   10
    Having no scarfe of clowds before his face, . . . . . . . . .  176 Astrophil    22    3
    Stella alone with face unarmed marcht, . . . . . . . . . . .  176 Astrophil    22    9
    Vertue's great beautie in that face I prove, . . . . . . . .  177 Astrophil    25   13
    By only those two starres in Stella's face.. . . . . . . . .  178 Astrophil    26   14
    How silently, and with how wanne a face, . . . . . . . . . .  180 Astrophil    31    2
    Stella lookt on, and from her heavenly face. . . . . . . . .  185 Astrophil    41   13
    Stella oft sees the verie face of wo . . . . . . . . . . . .  187 Astrophil    45    1
    Painted in my beclowded stormie face:. . . . . . . . . . . .  187 Astrophil    45    2
    For she protests to banish thee her face,. . . . . . . . . .  187 Astrophil    46    5
    Her face? O Love, a Rogue thou then shouldst be, . . . . . .  187 Astrophil    46    6
    Which in her face teach vertue, I could brooke . . . . . . .  193 Astrophil    56    6
    To feele my griefes, and she with face and voice . . . . . .  193 Astrophil    57   13
    O voice, o face, maugre my speeche's might,. . . . . . . . .  194 Astrophil    58   12
    Let clouds bedimme my face, breake in mine eye,. . . . . . .  198 Astrophil    64    5
    O heav'nly foole, thy most kisse-worthie face, . . . . . . .  203 Astrophil    73   12
    That face, whose lecture shewes what perfect beautie is: . .  205 Astrophil    77    2
    See Beautie's totall summe summ'd in her face: . . . . . . .  210 Astrophil    85   10
    Shewes her oft at the full her fairest face, . . . . . . . .  229 Astrophil    97    2
    Paint woe's blacke face so lively to my sight, . . . . . . .  230 Astrophil    98   10
    Upon thy cheerefull face, joye's livery weare: . . . . . . .  232 Astrophil   103    3
    Onely unto the heav'n of Stella's face,. . . . . . . . . . .  235 Astrophil   105    7
    False flattering hope, that with so faire a face,. . . . . .  235 Astrophil   106    2
    For I protest, my sight never thy face enjoyeth, . . . . . .  215 A&S 5th Song       75
    For thy face tempts my soule to leave the heav'n for thee, .  215 A&S 5th Song       82
    O you that see this face, . . . . . . . . . . . . . . . . . .  215 A&S 6th Song        2
    Thus doth the voice and face,. . . . . . . . . . . . . . . .  215 A&S 6th Song       13
    And in this faultlesse face, . . . . . . . . . . . . . . . .  216 A&S 6th Song       22
```

FACE   (CONTINUED)   PAGE   TITLE   LINE
   See, do you see this face? a face? nay image of the skies, . 217 A&S 7th Song   15
   Whose face all, all beauty passeth,. . . . . 219 A&S 8th Song   43
   The shining clearness of thy face: . . . . 274 Psalm IV   27
   His lovely face on them doth bide. . . . . 284 Psalm XI   22
   How long wilt Thou Thy hidden face from me . . . . 285 Psalm XIII   3
   O let my sentence passe from Thyne own face; . . . . 289 Psalm XVII   5
   Their eyes do swim, their face doth shine in fatt, ... 290 Psalm XVII   29
   My joy shall be pure to enjoy thy face,. . . . . 290 Psalm XVII   46
   There by his Grace for sun's fair face . . . . 294 Psalm XIX   19
   Their fruit shalt Thou from earthly face . . . . 297 Psalm XXI   37
   Who search of God's face never leave. . . . . 302 Psalm XXIV   16
   Seek ye my Face, when Thou didst say,. . . . . 307 Psalm XXVII   39
   Seek Thy face still. . . . . 308 Psalm XXVII   42
   Hide not therfore from me that face, ... 308 Psalm XXVII   43
   But, ah he strait his face did hide, ... 311 Psalm XXX   23
   Thy Face to shine upon Thy servant make, ... 313 Psalm XXXI   43
   So his high heavnly face . . . . 320 Psalm XXXIV   57
   For aye before Thy face. . . . . 334 Psalm XLI   44
   Of Thy face to have a seing? . . . . 334 Psalm XLII   8
   The trees spred out their armes to shade hir face, ... 245 Other Poems   4   109
   Up with hir fist, and tooke him on the face, ... 249 Other Poems   4   274
   The dainty dew on face and body went . . . . 252 Other Poems   4   397
   In river as I look'd my pining face, ... 254 Other Poems   4   475
   As pin'd a face as mine I saw againe.. . . . . 254 Other Poems   4   476
   With eyes which threatned they would drowne his face,. . . . 255 Other Poems   4   524
   On thy then blessed face,. . . . . 256 Other Poems   5   18
   Mira may looke her face,. . . . . 257 Other Poems   5   31
   With face the plot cf pittie,. . . . . 259 Other Poems   5   118
FACE'S
   Woe, lyke a moth, my face's beauty eates . . . . 276 Psalm VI   21
   Shall feel in Thy face's sight . . . . 289 Psalm XVI   40
   Nor hidd from him his face's faire appearing;. . . . . 300 Psalm XXII   57
FACES
   These stately starrs in their now shining faces, ... 108 Arcadia IV   69   9
   Against their guilty faces.. . . . . 298 Psalm XXI   48
   Whose faces on his comfort staid . . . . 319 Psalm XXXIV   19
FACILITY
   But ah my Muse I would thou hadst facilitie, ...   19 1st Eclogues 7   176
   As let them come or go with even facilitie.. . . . .   60 2nd Eclogues 30   133
FACT
   His damme a beast was pardon'd beastly fact. . . . .   21 1st Eclogues 8   18
FACTICNS
   Then gan he factions in the beastes to breed;. . . . . 102 3rd Eclogues 66   120
FADE
   Whose lights do ever live, but in our darkenesse fade; . . .   44 Arcadia II   26   4
FADES
   What ever fades, but fading pleasure brings. . . . . 161 Cert Sonnets 32   4
FADETH
   Thine earth now springs, mine fadeth,. . . . . 137 Cert Sonnets 4   11
   Above line repeated at following location. . . . . 137 Cert Sonnets 4   23
FADING
   What ever fades, but fading pleasure brings. . . . . 161 Cert Sonnets 32   4
   Thou moth like mak'st his beauty fading be;. . . . . 330 Psalm XXXIX   35
FAIL
   Now my hoarse voice doth faile this occupation,. . . . . . .   19 1st Eclogues 7   170
   But now hoarse voyce, doth faile this occupation,. . . . . .   20 1st Eclogues 7 V970
   But if eyes faile then, when I most doo need them, ...   30 1st Eclogues 12   5
   Nico. If never I did faile your holy-dayes, ...   54 2nd Eclogues 29   69
   But still, although we faile of perfect rightfulnes, ...   61 2nd Eclogues 30   137
   Ne can he faile, for prince hath for him sent: . . . .   97 3rd Eclogues 64   104
   Shall gesse, and faile, what doth displease, ... 153 Cert Sonnets 24   8
   Nor faile my faith in my failing fate, ... 153 Cert Sonnets 24   22
   If that the substance faile within.. . . . . 156 Cert Sonnets 27   16
   And if these rules did faile, proofe makes me sure,. . . . . 178 Astrophil   26   12
   To lose his Crowne, rather then faile his Love,. . . . . . . 204 Astrophil   75   14
   Whose braunches faile not timely fruite to nourish,. . . . . 270 Psalm I   9
   Ncr withered leafe shall make yt faile to flourish.. . . . . 270 Psalm I   10
   But they do faile, and in their mazed corners rew. . . . . . 293 Psalm XVIII   82
   Then so I faile, when most I would do well,. . . . . 254 Other Poems   4   467
FAILED
   Pas. This is not he that failed her to gaine,. . . . .   54 2nd Eclogues 29   60
FAILETH
   Who faileth one, is false, though trusty to another. . . . . 214 A&S 5th Song   72
FAILING
   Drawes up; and if, hope fayling, ende live's pleasure, . . .   16 1st Eclogues 7   71
   For nature hathe that never fayling scoope,. . . . .   71 Arcadia III 37   5
   Failing themselves, with withered conscience dye.. . . . . . 151 Cert Sonnets 22   50
   Nor faile my faith in my failing fate, ... 153 Cert Sonnets 24   22
   Where failing is a shame, and breaking is his best.. . . . . 241 Other Poems   1   6
   And streight for failing, grav'd it in his heart:. . . . . . 247 Other Poems   4   186
FAILS
   When rooted moisture failes, or groweth drie, ... 128 4th Eclogues 75   113
   But when that failes, my dead hopes up to take,. . . . . . . 150 Cert Sonnets 22   19
   Failes me fearing on to passe, ... 219 A&S 8th Song   46
   Failes me, with ugly feares. . . . . 332 Psalm XL   50
FAILST
   But failst thou not in phrase so heav'nly hie? . . . . 199 Astrophil   67   6
FAIN
   Bussing her oft, and in his hart full faine, ...   95 3rd Eclogues 64   51

```
FAIN             (CONTINUED)                         PAGE    TITLE          LINE
   And now I faine would reape, I reape but this, . . . . . .  115  4th Eclogues 72   57
   It makes them flie that which they faine would have: . . . .  145  Cert Sonnets 16    6
   Loving in truth, and faine in verse my love to show, . . . .  165  Astrophil     1    1
   Sweet kisse, thy sweets I faine would sweetly endite,. . . .  206  Astrophil    79    1
   How faine would I paint thee to all men's eyes,. . . . . . .  207  Astrophil    81    7
   Then since (deare life) you faine would have me peace, . . .  207  Astrophil    81   12
   Dian that faine would cheare her friend the Night, . . . . .  229  Astrophil    97    1
   Would faine drive cloudes from out my heavy cheere. . . . .  230  Astrophil    97   11
   And faine those Aeols' youthes there would their stay. . . .  233  Astrophil   103    9
   There his hands in their speech, faine . . . . . . . . . . .  219  A&S 8th Song      65
   I fain of them would speaking be; . . . . . . . . . . . . .  331  Psalm XL          23
   Faine would be free, but dreadeth parents' ire.. . . . . . .  245  Other Poems   4  120
   But lickrous, Poison'd, faine to her would goe,. . . . . . .  246  Other Poems   4  165
   Klaius in deede would faine have puld a way. . . . . . . . .  246  Other Poems   4  171
   Faine would, but could not fly from golden smart.. . . . . .  246  Other Poems   4  184
   (He staying thus) was faine abroad to stray. . . . . . . . .  250  Other Poems   4  331
   That she would faine the catch of Strephon flie, . . . . . .  252  Other Poems   4  380
FAINT
   Though (yoked so) my minde with sicknes fainte,. . . . . . .   83  Arcadia III  57    7
   Since force doth faint, and sight doth make me blind:. . . .  135  Cert Sonnets  1    4
   I heare a crye of spirits faint and blinde,. . . . . . . . .  148  Cert Sonnets 20    7
   Faint coward joy no longer tarry dare, . . . . . . . . . . .  228  Astrophil    95    5
   And therfore finding force now faint to be,. . . . . . . . .  248  Other Poems   4  255
FAINTING
   My humble hands, my fainting feet they peirced;. . . . . . .  299  Psalm XXII        41
FAINTLY
   Whereto mine inward thoughts did faintly yeeld;. . . . . . .   11  Arcadia I     2    6
FAINTNESS
   Then rase, but rase on leggs with faintnes bended, . . . . .  259  Other Poems   5  116
FAINTS
   My harte doth ake, my life faints, . . . . . . . . . . . . .   66  2nd Eclogues 32   14
FAIR
   Like great god Saturn faire, and like faire Venus chaste:. .   12  Arcadia I     3    5
   Enjoy her soule, in bodie's faire possession,. . . . . . . .   15  1st Eclogues  7   41
   My sight in her faire limmes, I then assure my selfe,. . . .   16  1st Eclogues  7   56
   Her father's corne (moving her faire limmes) measure.. . . .   16  1st Eclogues  7   75
   So faire a fielde would well become an owner.. . . . . . . .   17  1st Eclogues  7   99
   Disdaine me not, although I be not faire.. . . . . . . . . .   18  1st Eclogues  7  116
   Since she faire fierce to such a state me calls, . . . . . .   23  1st Eclogues  9   30
   Into the faire looker on, pastime, not passion, enters.. . .   32  1st Eclogues 13   41
   Whose faire bodily gifts are fram'd most lovely to each ey..   33  1st Eclogues 13   55
   And when I meete these trees, in the earth's faire lyvery
      clothed, . . . . . . . . . . . . . . . . . . . . . . . .   35  1st Eclogues 13  113
   And so behinde foule clowdes full oft faire starres do ly
      hidden". . . . . . . . . . . . . . . . . . . . . . . . .   36  1st Eclogues 13  154
   Their pasture is faire hilles of fruitlesse Love:. . . . . .   39  Arcadia II   17    2
   Feede on my sheepe, your fayer sweete feeding flowes, . . .   43  Arcadia II   23    4
   To whether with best cause the Nymphes faire flowers
      affoord  . . . . . . . . . . . . . . . . . . . . . . . .   52  2nd Eclogues 29   28
   Cosma's faire beames emblemish much his raies. . . . . . . .   55  2nd Eclogues 29   98
   Let doltes in haste some altars faire erect. . . . . . . . .   58  2nd Eclogues 30   62
   In whose decay Vertue's faire shrine must fall.. . . . . . .   59  2nd Eclogues 30   91
   What myne hath erst throwne downe so faire a tower?.. . . .   59  2nd Eclogues 30   96
   Faire Rocks, goodly rivers, sweet woods, when shall I see
      peace... . . . . . . . . . . . . . . . . . . . . . . . .   62  2nd Eclogues 31    1
   Tell yet againe me the names of these faire form'd to do
      ev'lls. Dev'lls. . . . . . . . . . . . . . . . . . . . .   65  2nd Eclogues 31   49
   Faire trees' shade is enough fortification,. . . . . . . . .   69  2nd Eclogues 34   13
   As sweete as violetts, faire as a lilly is,. . . . . . . . .   69  2nd Eclogues 34   32
   Fayre hand, the fayrest pledge of fayrer harte,. . . . . . .   70  Arcadia III  35   10
   Eyes faire and great, like faire great oxe's eyes, . . . . .   76  Arcadia III  46    9
   Yet still, faire tree, lifte up thy stately line, . . . . .   77  Arcadia III  47    9
   With her faire hande, your tender barkes to cleave,. . . . .   78  Arcadia III  49    6
   Yet all well knit to one faire end do passe: . . . . . . . .   78  Arcadia III  50    8
   Locke up, faire liddes, the treasures of my harte: . . . . .   79  Arcadia III  51    1
   Let no strange dreme make her fayre body starte. . . . . . .   79  Arcadia III  51    8
   O Titan faire the giver of the daie? . . . . . . . . . . . .   80  Arcadia III  52    2
   "No" saies faire moone, "my lighte . . . . . . . . . . . . .   82  Arcadia III  55   12
   Make me still feare, thy faire appearing showe.. . . . . . .   82  Arcadia III  56   14
   With beautie's seale, and vertue faire disguis'de, . . . . .   85  Arcadia III  61    2
   Faire under these doth stately growe,. . . . . . . . . . . .   87  Arcadia III  62   46
   Like Alablaster faire and sleeke,. . . . . . . . . . . . . .   88  Arcadia III  62   81
   How all this is but a faire Inne . . . . . . . . . . . . . .   90  Arcadia III  62  139
   And Arches bee to those fayre Lyddes . . . . . . . . . . . .   86  Arcadia III  62 V 13
   Ffayre, thorow fayre strykes of heedefull Looke. . . . . . .   88  Arcadia III  62 V 70
   But like the turtells faire. . . . . . . . . . . . . . . . .   91  3rd Eclogues 63    6
   Monkie, sweet breath; the Cow, her faire eyes brought; . . .  101  3rd Eclogues 66   88
   For by and by the horse faire bitts did binde, . . . . . . .  102  3rd Eclogues 66  137
   I sought to catch the fish Torpedo faire.. . . . . . . . . .  115  4th Eclogues 72   63
   To death, as then disguisde in her faire face. . . . . . . .  115  4th Eclogues 72   69
   O faire, o onely faire, from thee, alas, . . . . . . . . . .  116  4th Eclogues 72   96
   There came a chariot faire by doves and sparrowes guided:. .  118  4th Eclogues 73   59
   Those thousand altars faire now in the dust to lie?. . . . .  119  4th Eclogues 73  112
   This crowne of amber faire (an amber crowne she held). . . .  120  4th Eclogues 73  141
   First having all their giftes upon faire Mira spred. . . . .  121  4th Eclogues 73  178
   Hard like a rich marbell: hard, but a faire Diamond. . . . .  122  4th Eclogues 74   14
   Right so my boiling hart, enflam'de with fire of a faire
      eye  . . . . . . . . . . . . . . . . . . . . . . . . . .  123  4th Eclogues 74   27
   O faire, O fairest, are such the triumphs to thy fairnesse?.  123  4th Eclogues 74   31
```

	PAGE	TITLE	LINE
You should those faire eyes have with a veile covered. . . .	123	4th Eclogues 74	48
Or with a fair hand's nailes (o hand which nailes me to this			
death).	123	4th Eclogues 74	55
O wretch, what do I say? should that faire face be defaced?.	124	4th Eclogues 74	57
O Philomela faire, o take some gladnesse,.	137	Cert Sonnets 4	9
Above line repeated at following location.	137	Cert Sonnets 4	21
O the fayre Nymphe borne to doo woemen honor,.	138	Cert Sonnets 5	3
Above line repeated at following location.	138	Cert Sonnets 5	27
O Faire, o sweet, when I do looke on thee, ...	139	Cert Sonnets 7	1
Above line repeated at following locations	139	Cert Sonnets 7	11
. . . .	140	Cert Sonnets 7	21
. . . .	140	Cert Sonnets 7	31
To see what faire sight there raigneth,.	140	Cert Sonnets 7	26
Faire seeke not to be feard, most lovely beloved by thy			
servants,.	143	Cert Sonnets 14	1
Who burnt his lips to kisse faire shining fire..	145	Cert Sonnets 16	14
Should Ladies faire be tyed to such hard lawes,.	146	Cert Sonnets 17	23
Faire choice I have, either to live or dye	149	Cert Sonnets 21	13
Their master is faire warn'd his will to make.	150	Cert Sonnets 22	20
Brake on faire cleeves of constant chastitie:.	151	Cert Sonnets 22	56
From sight of her faire eyes:.	152	Cert Sonnets 23	28
For so faire a flame embraces.	155	Cert Sonnets 26	5
Faire death feeleth, ...	156	Cert Sonnets 26	28
And in whome faire death proceedeth, ...	156	Cert Sonnets 26	29
Thy faire haire my heart enchained,.	156	Cert Sonnets 27	2
For no faire signe can credit winne.	156	Cert Sonnets 27	15
And Faith faire scorne doth gaine.	159	Cert Sonnets 30	6
Of living deaths, deare wounds, faire stormes and freesing			
fires:	167	Astrophil 6	4
Whose faire skin, beamy eyes, like morning sun on snow,. . .	169	Astrophil 8	9
But she most faire, most cold, made him thence take his			
flight	169	Astrophil 8	12
For like a child that some faire booke doth find,.	170	Astrophil 11	5
Crie, "Victorie, this faire day all is ours.".	171	Astrophil 12	11
Stella's faire haire, her face he makes his shield,.	171	Astrophil 13	10
Nor so faire levell in so secret stay, ...	175	Astrophil 20	6
Hath this world ought so faire as Stella is?	175	Astrophil 21	14
Progressing then from faire twinnes' gold'n place:	175	Astrophil 22	2
When some faire Ladies, by hard promise tied,.	176	Astrophil 22	5
How faire a day was neare, o punisht eyes,.	181	Astrophil 33	13
Sent forth the beames, which made so faire my race..	185	Astrophil 41	14
Faire eyes, sweet lips, deare heart, that foolish I.	186	Astrophil 43	1
Of Hope, which makes it seeme faire to the eye..	189	Astrophil 49	8
Not this faire outside, which our hearts doth move..	190	Astrophil 52	8
But you faire maides, at length this true shall find,. . . .	192	Astrophil 54	11
When I might reade those letters faire of blisse,.	193	Astrophil 56	5
With that faire breast making woe's darknesse cleare:. . . .	193	Astrophil 57	11
If he be faire, yet but a dog can be.	194	Astrophil 59	4
Stolne to my heart, since last faire night, nay day, ...	199	Astrophil 66	10
Looke on againe, the faire text better trie:	199	Astrophil 67	7
It is, so faire a Vertue to enjoy.	200	Astrophil 68	14
Stella, those faire lines, which true goodnesse show.. . . .	201	Astrophil 71	4
Who marke in thee their what is in thee most faire..	201	Astrophil 71	11
Not for his faire outside, nor well lined braine,.	204	Astrophil 75	3
Most sweet-faire, most faire-sweet, do not alas, ...	208	Astrophil 82	7
As though that faire soft hand did you great wrong..	208	Astrophil 83	4
Be you still faire, honourd by publike heed, ...	209	Astrophil 84	9
And that faire you my Sunne, thus overspred..	224	Astrophil 91	3
Which ay most faire, now more then most faire show,.	231	Astrophil 100	3
Beauty is sicke, but sicke in so faire guise,.	231	Astrophil 101	5
Where those red cheeks, which oft with faire encrease did			
frame.	232	Astrophil 102	2
While those faire planets on thy streames did shine.. . . .	232	Astrophil 103	4
With sight thereof cride out; o faire disgrace,.	233	Astrophil 103	13
False flattering hope, that with so faire a face,.	235	Astrophil 106	2
But heere I do store of faire Ladies meete,.	236	Astrophil 106	9
Teaching sleepe most faire to be?.	202	A&S 2nd Song	2
Your faire mother is a bed,.	211	A&S 4th Song	37
I said, thou wert most faire, and so indeed thou art:. . . .	212	A&S 5th Song	7
The name of murdrer now on thy faire forehead sitteth: . . .	214	A&S 5th Song	51
A witch I say thou art, though thou so faire appeare;. . . .	214	A&S 5th Song	74
Those faire wonders to behold, ...	226	A&S 10th Song	17
O let them see these heavenly beames, and in faire letters			
reede.	217	A&S 7th Song	11
Her faire necke a foule yoke bare, ...	218	A&S 8th Song	10
Faire triumpher of annoy,.	218	A&S 8th Song	30
Have not I fair partage gott?.	288	Psalm XVI	18
From so fair book proceeding,.	294	Psalm XIX	14
There by his Grace for sun's fair face	294	Psalm XIX	19
Nor hidd from him his face's faire appearing;.	300	Psalm XXII	57
Fayrenesse though fayer, is but a feeble shielde,.	345	Possibly 4	6
Then in good Dog, faire field, or shading tree..	246	Other Poems 4	179
Till one faire eav'n an howr ere Sun did rest,.	247	Other Poems 4	205
Faire Nous with Pas the lott to hell did sende:.	248	Other Poems 4	244
So on the downs we see, neere Wilton faire,.	251	Other Poems 4	342
To Nature's heir, the faire Urania, pay, ...	251	Other Poems 4	364
Of faire Urania, fairer then a greene,.	253	Other Poems 4	452
And now faire evenings blush my shame to see..	254	Other Poems 4	480
And make you faire with shadow of her hue:	257	Other Poems 5	32

```
FAIR              (CONTINUED)                           PAGE   TITLE          LINE
  "Tell me you flowers faire,. . . . . . . . . . . . .  257  Other Poems  5    40
  She is the heardesse faire that shines in darke. . . . .  259  Other Poems  5   112
FAIRER
  Of fayrer death how can I make election?. . . . . . . .   16  1st Eclogues  7   72
  Without her love, then any mind who fairer is. . . . . .   51  2nd Eclogues 28  116
  Fayre hand, the fayrest pledge of fayrer harte,. . . . .   70  Arcadia III  35   10
  Of fairer guest, which dwells within,. . . . . . . . . .   90  Arcadia III  62  140
  You fairer still, and still more cruell bent,. . . . . .  148  Cert Sonnets 19   15
  And saw this fairest maid of fairer minde, . . . . . . .  244  Other Poems  4    90
  Of faire Urania, fairer then a greene, . . . . . . . . .  253  Other Poems  4   452
FAIREST
  My foule mishap came yet from fairest mind.. . . . . . .    5  Lady of May  3    18
  Fayre hand, the fayrest pledge of fayrer harte,. . . . .   70  Arcadia III  35   10
  (Her sight where love did forge his fayrest darte) . . .   79  Arcadia III  51    6
  Me thought, nay sure I was, I was in fairest wood. . . .  117  4th Eclogues 73   35
  O faire, O fairest, are such the triumphs to thy fairnesse?.  123  4th Eclogues 74   31
  Burneth bright in fairest light. No, no, no, no. . . . .  155  Cert Sonnets 26   11
  Of those three gods, whose armes the fairest were: . . .  171  Astrophil    13    2
  Who will in fairest booke of Nature know,. . . . . . . .  201  Astrophil    71    1
  Shewes her oft at the full her fairest face, . . . . . .  229  Astrophil    97    2
  Fiercest but yet fairest ever; . . . . . . . . . . . . .  221  A&S 9th Song      17
  And saw this fairest maid of fairer minde, . . . . . . .  244  Other Poems  4    90
FAIRIES
  Nico. O Faunes, O Fairies all, and do you see, . . . . .   54  2nd Eclogues 29   63
FAIRNESS
  Nor stormes doo turne: fairenes serves oft to wealth.. . . .   18  1st Eclogues  7  119
  O faire, O fairest, are such the triumphs to thy fairnesse?.  123  4th Eclogues 74   31
  Where fairnesse yeelds to wisdome's shortest raines. . . . .  151· Cert Sonnets 22   64
  Who hath the lips, where wit in fairnesse raigneth,. . . . .  197  A&S 1st Song       9
  Fayrenesse though fayer, is but a feeble shielde,. . . . . .  345  Possibly     4     6
FAIR-SWEET
  Most sweet-faire, most faire-sweet, do not alas, . . . . . .  208  Astrophil    82    7
FAITH
  R. By nature you to Reason faith have sworne.. . . . . . . .   46  2nd Eclogues 27   11
  Of my due faith, which needs must be immutable?. . . . . .   47  2nd Eclogues 28    8
  Since in such phrase his faith he did attire.. . . . . . .   80  Arcadia III  53    8
  Bandes, favour, faith, to breake, defile, and kill.. . . .   84  Arcadia III  60    8
  Geron. In faith, good Histor, long is your delay,. . . . .  103  3rd Eclogues 67    1
  Or els; "Nay faith, mine is the lucklest lot,. . . . . . .  104  3rd Eclogues 67   43
  Shall to the world appeare that faith and love be rewarded .  123  4th Eclogues 74   35
  But what's this for a fault, for which such faieth be
        abolisht,. . . . . . . . . . . . . . . . . . . . . .  124  4th Eclogues 74   69
  Such faith, so stainles, inviolate, violent?. . . . . . .  124  4th Eclogues 74   70
  In humble mind a constant faith to prove,. . . . . . . . .  145  Cert Sonnets 17    3
  In never dying faith:. . . . . . . . . . . . . . . . . . .  152  Cert Sonnets 23   14
  Nor faile my faith in my failing fate, . . . . . . . . . .  153  Cert Sonnets 24   22
  Till that I sware my faith so stood, . . . . . . . . . . .  158  Cert Sonnets 28   23
  And Faith faire scorne doth gaine. . . . . . . . . . . . .  159  Cert Sonnets 30    6
  Reason, in faith thou art well serv'd, that still. . . . .  169  Astrophil    10    1
  Well staid with truth in word and faith of deed, . . . . .  172  Astrophil    14   10
  Who for long faith, tho dayly helpe I crave, . . . . . . .  188  Astrophil    47    7
  For Stella hath with words where faith doth shine, . . . .  200  Astrophil    69    9
  Care shining in mine eyes, faith in my sprite, . . . . . .  202  Astrophil    72   11
  But if all faith, like spotlesse Ermine ly . . . . . . . .  212  Astrophil    86    5
  Is faith so weake? Or is such force in thee? . . . . . . .  223  Astrophil    88    5
  As where thou soone mightst helpe, most faith dost most
        oppresse,. . . . . . . . . . . . . . . . . . . . . .  213  A&S 5th Song      41
  For all love, all faith is meant thee, . . . . . . . . . .  220  A&S 8th Song      92
  Dick. Faith in my self and worth in her, which no proofe can
        undoo.. . . . . . . . . . . . . . . . . . . . . . .  343  Possibly     1    26
FAITHFUL
  For faithfull hart, cleane hands, and mouth as true: . . . .   99  3rd Eclogues 66   25
  Love moves thy paine, and like a faithfull page, . . . . .  232  Astrophil   101    9
  In the faithfull Turtle dove.. . . . . . . . . . . . . . .  234  A&S 11th Song     20
  Show that Thy eyes respect a faithfull case; . . . . . . .  289  Psalm XVII         6
  That Thou by Faithfull Men wilt stand. . . . . . . . . . .  290  Psalm XVII        23
  For this Our lord preserves the faith full race. . . . . .  314  Psalm XXXI        65
  And his deeds faithfull bee. . . . . . . . . . . . . . . .  316  Psalm XXXIII      18
  Who faithfull feares in him do plant;. . . . . . . . . . .  319  Psalm XXXIV       35
  The day well fed, the night in faithfull folde:. . . . . .  258  Other Poems  5    68
FAITHFULLY
  Who word to neighbour given doth faithfully maintain . . . .  287  Psalm XV           9
FALCON
  When falcon they, and gossehauke saw in mewe.. . . . . . .  102  3rd Eclogues 66  140
  Finding the gripe of Falcon fierce not furr: . . . . . . .  251  Other Poems  4   356
  (More swift then falcon's stoope to feeding Falconer's call)  118  4th Eclogues 73   58
FALCON'S
  The Falcon's fercenes, Sparrow's letchery, . . . . . . . .   28  1st Eclogues 10   79
  (More swift then falcon's stoope to feeding Falconer's call)  118  4th Eclogues 73   58
FALL
  I saw that riches fall, and fell a crying; . . . . . . . .   17  1st Eclogues  7   88
  My pastimes none: time passeth on my fall: . . . . . . . .   18  1st Eclogues  7  142
  Into our mindes let us a little fall: . . . . . . . . . . .   29  1st Eclogues 10   94
  In whose decay Vertue's faire shrine must fall.. . . . . .   59  2nd Eclogues 30   91
  Can fancies want eies, or he fall that steppeth aloft? Oft..   64  2nd Eclogues 31   22
  But when I first did fal, what brought most fall to my hart?
        Arte. . . . . . . . . . . . . . . . . . . . . . . .   64  2nd Eclogues 31   28
  Go sing the fall of old Thebes,. . . . . . . . . . . . . .   66  2nd Eclogues 32   21
```

                                   147

FALL   (CONTINUED)   PAGE   TITLE   LINE

   O Words which fall like sommer deaw on me, ...   76 Arcadia III 46   1
   Comming from her, cannot but downewarde fall. . . . .   78 Arcadia III 49   18
   There fall those Saphir-coloured brookes, ...   90 Arcadia III 62   127
   Whose eeven descent makes equall falle, ...   89 Arcadia III 62 V104
   Full dead before, I now to dust should fall, ...   116 4th Eclogues 72   86
   When it blowne up with myne a fall of ruine takes) . . . . .   118 4th Eclogues 73   52
   The Moone a sunder rent; whereat with sodaine fall . . . . .   118 4th Eclogues 73   57
   My fall her glorie maketh, ...   136 Cert Sonnets 3   11
   The stately towers come downe with greater fall: . . . . . .   143 Cert Sonnets 12   8
   Till want of force do force her fall to ground; . . . .   144 Cert Sonnets 15   4
   Both force to flie and knowledge where to fall. . . . .   144 Cert Sonnets 15   12
   And see you not that I fall now to ryme? . . . .   146 Cert Sonnets 17   40
   Whose clowdie thoughts let fall an inward raine. . . . . . .   150 Cert Sonnets 22   36
   Their running fall into a constant vaine . . . .   150 Cert Sonnets 22   38
   Thus do I fall to rise thus, ...   154 Cert Sonnets 25   27
   Lookes to the skies, and in a ditch doth fall? . . . .   174 Astrophil   19   11
   That not my soule, which at thy foot did fall, ...   183 Astrophil   36   12
   Doth fall to stray, and my chiefe powres are brought . . . .   183 Astrophil   38   3
   Makes me fall from her sight, then sweetly she . . . .   195 Astrophil   60   6
   That brought me so high to fall: . . . .   211 A&S 4th Song   52
   Turne Thee, sweet lord, and from this Ougly fall . . . . . .   276 Psalm VI   11
   But in the pitt he ruind first did fall, ...   278 Psalm VII   41
   Which fall he made to do his neighbor wrong. . . . .   278 Psalm VII   42
   I now should Fall aflying? . . . .   283 Psalm XI   4
   With ground plot's fall shall be undone: . . . .   284 Psalm XI   10
   But Thou (O lord) give them a thorough fall, ...   284 Psalm XII   7
   And at my fall they joy that, troublous, me. . . . .   286 Psalm XIII   15
   And so the Earth did fall to tremble, and to quake . . . . .   291 Psalm XVIII   15
   That God from fall his own Anoynted stayes. . . . .   296 Psalm XX   22
   Wee stand upright, while they their fall did frame. . . . . .   296 Psalm XX   32
   O look, O help, let mercy fall, ...   304 Psalm XXV   59
   Catch harmful fall . . . .   318 Psalm XXXIII   65
   Who hate the good shall fall. . . . .   320 Psalm XXXIV   76
   Fall in self pitt, be caught in their own nett. . . . .   321 Psalm XXXV   18
   Lo there I now foresee their fall. . . . .   324 Psalm XXXVI   33
   Badd folks shall fall, and fall for aye, ...   326 Psalm XXXVII   49
   Though he do fall no wracke he proveth, ...   326 Psalm XXXVII   59
   Whom my fall doth make rejoyce. . . . .   328 Psalm XXXVIII   48
   On me let mercy fall, ...   333 Psalm XLI   34
   One deep with noyse of his fall. . . . .   335 Psalm XLII   29
   Of clime-fall Court, the envy-hatching place: . . . .   243 Other Poems   4   61
   Pas mad with fall, and madder with the shame, ...   249 Other Poems   4   269
   "For, but by charms, how fall these things on me, ...   253 Other Poems   4   449
FALLEN
   Thy stars be fal'n, plowed is thy flintie ground: . . . . . .   4 Lady of May   2   16
   Geron. Alas what falls are falne unto thy minde? . . . . . .   23 1st Eclogues 9   32
   And they are faln, nay perisht at Thy sight: . . . .   279 Psalm IX   7
FALLETH
   In such longing thoughts it falleth. . . . .   334 Psalm XLII   24
FALLS
   Geron. Alas what falls are falne unto thy minde? . . . . . .   23 1st Eclogues 9   32
   Ease I do feele (such ease as falls to one wholy diseased) .   35 1st Eclogues 13   114
   Eies' hurters, eies hurt, but what from them to me fall's?
         Fall's. . . . .   64 2nd Eclogues 31   27
   Our studies fixt upon the falles of fortune. . . . .   109 Arcadia IV   70   30
   Fals to shrewd turnes, and I was in his way. . . . .   173 Astrophil   17   14
   How falles it then, that with so smooth an ease. . . . . . .   204 Astrophil   74   9
   That speech falles now to blame, which did thy honour raise,   213 A&S 5th Song   17
FALSE
   False in my selfe, thus have I lost the field. . . . .   11 Arcadia I   2   8
   No, nothing so; an old false knave he is, ...   21 1st Eclogues 8   13
   Mercury kill'd his false sire for this act, ...   21 1st Eclogues 8   17
   That soone the world of his false tong be void. . . . .   24 1st Eclogues 9   68
   Since there mine eyes have played so false a parte, ...   38 Arcadia II   14   11
   Thou li'st false Echo, their minds as vertu be just. Just. .   65 2nd Eclogues 31   46
   Where her who should rule paine, false paine abuseth. . . . .   142 Cert Sonnets 11   14
   Though false, yet with free scope more grace doth breed. . .   187 Astrophil   45   10
   False flattering hope, that with so faire a face, ...   235 Astrophil   106   2
   Who faileth one, is false, though trusty to another. . . . .   214 A&S 5th Song   72
   Sent from false heart, on double meaning stay'd. . . . . . .   284 Psalm XII   6
   With scoffers false I was their feast's delight, ...   322 Psalm XXXV   41
   In false colours dressed. . . . .   336 Psalm XLIII   6
   They false and fearfull do their hands undoe, ...   248 Other Poems   4   235
   Then this false, fine, Courtly pleasure. . . . .   263 Other Poems   7   48
FALSE-SEEMING
   His will false-seeming holie . . . .   160 Cert Sonnets 30   15
   In falsehood wrapt, but in their pride display'd. . . . . . .   284 Psalm XII   9
   Whose spirit falshood flyeth. . . . .   314 Psalm XXXII   6
FALSELY
   Crocodile, teares, which might be falsely spilde: . . . . . .   101 3rd Eclogues 66   96
   With perjury doth falsly bind. . . . .   302 Psalm XXIV   12
FALSE-SEEMING
   His will false-seeming holie . . . .   160 Cert Sonnets 30   15
FALTERING
   Nor mas'de head thinke, nor faltring tonge recite. . . . . .   74 Arcadia III 42   14
FAME
   That men's harts be thy seate and endlesse fame be thy
         servant, ...   36 1st Eclogues 13   148
   When rotten Fame will tell their blowes. . . . .   44 Arcadia II   25   10

```
FAME                        (CONTINUED)                   PAGE    TITLE          LINE
    If Leuca live, she darken will my fame.. . . . . . . . . .   55 2nd Eclogues 29   95
    Nico. Nothing (O Leuca) shall thy fame deface, . . . . . .   56 2nd Eclogues 29  123
    Ne pleasure here, ne fame gott. . . . . . . . . . . . . .    66 2nd Eclogues 32   39
    And now fame the herald of her true honour,. . . . . . . .   68 2nd Eclogues 33   19
    A way more worthie beautie's fame, . . . . . . . . . . . .   87 Arcadia III  62   59
    The inke immortall fame dooth lende: . . . . . . . . . . .   90 Arcadia III  62  143
    Although their fame (me seemd) from truth had greatly jard.. 119 4th Eclogues 73   80
    Fame is with wonder blazed:. . . . . . . . . . . . . . . .  136 Cert Sonnets  3    5
    Fame say I was not borne:. . . . . . . . . . . . . . . . .  136 Cert Sonnets  3   17
    Fire, aire, sea, earth, fame, time, place, shew your power.. 136 Cert Sonnets  3   20
    That her cleare voyce lifts thy fame to the skies. . . . .  171 Astrophil    12    8
    You seeke to nurse at fullest breasts of Fame, . . . . . .  172 Astrophil    15   13
    I list not dig so deepe for brasen fame. . . . . . . . . .  179 Astrophil    28    4
    Nay, that may breed my fame, it is so rare:. . . . . . . .  182 Astrophil    34    6
    Him as thy slave, and now long needy Fame. . . . . . . . .  182 Astrophil    35   10
    Nor do aspire to Caesar's bleeding fame, . . . . . . . . .  198 Astrophil    64   10
    Since in thine armes, if learnd fame truth hath spread,. . .198 Astrophil    65   13
    Although lesse gifts impe feathers oft on Fame,. . . . . .  204 Astrophil    75    4
    She builds her fame on higher seated praise: . . . . . . .  207 Astrophil    81   10
    Stella thinke not that I by verse seeke fame, . . . . . . . 224 Astrophil    90    1
    Who else for whom Fame worthy trumpets wanteth?. . . . . .  197 A&S 1st Song      14
    The proofe of Beautie's worth, th'enheritrix of fame,. . . .213 A&S 5th Song      20
    But valiant Rebels oft in fooles' mouthes purchase fame:. . 214 A&S 5th Song      67
    Of Conquerd states, wherby such fame you gott? . . . . . .  280 Psalm IX          17
    The heavnly Frame sets forth the Fame. . . . . . . . . . .  293 Psalm XIX          1
    To Brethren then I will declare Thy Fame,. . . . . . . . .  299 Psalm XXII        51
    But in his church his Fame is plac't.. . . . . . . . . . .  310 Psalm XXIX        24
FAMINE
    Where famine ravine taught their hungrie chestes,. . . . .  102 3rd Eclogues 66  124
FAMINE'S
    And keep from Famin's paine. . . . . . . . . . . . . . . .  318 Psalm XXXIII      75
FAMISHED
    Seemde but to spoyle the foode of thoughts long famished.. . 16 1st Eclogues  7   69
    Thou toldst mine eyes should helpe their famisht case? . . .235 Astrophil   106    6
FAMOUS
    Now by thy words I begin, most famous Lady, to gather. . . . 34 1st Eclogues 13   94
    So may thy songe be famous;. . . . . . . . . . . . . . . .   66 2nd Eclogues 32   24
FANCIES
    Dorus. Such Kala is: but ah, my fancies raysed be. . . . .   15 1st Eclogues  7   37
    An olde man heare, who would thy fancies raise.. . . . . .   22 1st Eclogues  9    5
    But loe, my words defaste, my fancies blinde,. . . . . . .   40 Arcadia II   19    3
    Can fancies want eies, or he fall that steppeth aloft? Oft.. 64 2nd Eclogues 31   22
    Do foster still, the fruite of fancies darke:. . . . . . .   73 Arcadia III  39    6
    They first their use forgot, then fancies lost their force;. 117 4th Eclogues 73   29
    But with his wings of fancies up he goes,. . . . . . . . .  144 Cert Sonnets 15    9
    In wonted walkes, since wonted fancies change, . . . . . .  147 Cert Sonnets 18    1
    But who hath fancies pleased,. . . . . . . . . . . . . . .  152 Cert Sonnets 23   33
    And write the state how my fancies bee,. . . . . . . . . .  153 Cert Sonnets 24    4
    That bravely maskt, their fancies may be told: . . . . . .  166 Astrophil     3    2
    Be not yet those fancies changed?". . . . . . . . . . . . . 234 A&S 11th Song      7
    But rather much he fancys this . . . . . . . . . . . . . .  281 Psalm X           15
    Not weighing ought how fleshly fancys run, . . . . . . . .  289 Psalm XVII        13
    This shall men's fancys frame. . . . . . . . . . . . . . .  319 Psalm XXXIV       17
    His fancies still did hir in half-way meet,. . . . . . . .  251 Other Poems   4  371
    As this same sprite about my fancies blinde, . . . . . . .  255 Other Poems   4  502
FANCY
    Let not a glittring name thy fancie dresse . . . . . . . .   23 1st Eclogues  9   47
    If once thou maist that fancie glosse destroy. . . . . . .   25 1st Eclogues  9  117
    If neither by that helpe, thou canst clime up to thy fancie, 34 1st Eclogues 13  100
    Nor yet, fancy so drest, do receive more plausible hearing:. 35 1st Eclogues 13  101
    Elme embraste by a vine, embracing fancy reviveth. . . . .   36 1st Eclogues 13  131
    Thus both trees and each thing ells, be the bookes of a
        fancy. . . . . . . . . . . . . . . . . . . . . . . . .   36 1st Eclogues 13  140
    No fancy mine, nor others' wronge suspect. . . . . . . . .   40 Arcadia II   18   11
    Fancie his foode, his clothing is of carefulnes; . . . . .   48 2nd Eclogues 28   41
    Such anger bringing: as for me, my fancie. . . . . . . . .   50 2nd Eclogues 28   95
    What blinde guides can he have that leanes to a fancy? A
        fancy. . . . . . . . . . . . . . . . . . . . . . . . .   63 2nd Eclogues 31   21
    My fancy amazde, my thoughtes dull'd,. . . . . . . . . . .   66 2nd Eclogues 32   13
    Sight doth bewitch, the fancie evill awaked. . . . . . . .   82 Arcadia III  57    2
    Fancie we feele, encludes all passion's mighte,. . . . . .   82 Arcadia III  57    3
    And though thereby my fancie was infected, . . . . . . . .   83 Arcadia III  57    6
    My tongue doth tell what fancie sees. . . . . . . . . . . .  89 Arcadia III  62   94
    And with the chaunge of them my fancie please. . . . . . .  113 4th Eclogues 72    4
    Fancie, her tackling, torne away doth flie:. . . . . . . .  114 4th Eclogues 72   47
    Yet Fancie would perforce employ his skill,. . . . . . . .  115 4th Eclogues 72   65
    Else what in face, then in my fancie beare?. . . . . . . .  146 Cert Sonnets 17   10
    Who hath his fancie pleased, . . . . . . . . . . . . . . .  151 Cert Sonnets 23    1
    From so ungratefull fancie,. . . . . . . . . . . . . . . .  160 Cert Sonnets 30    7
    Above line repeated at following locations . . . . . . . .  160 Cert Sonnets 30   17
         . . . . . . . . . . . . . . . . . . . . . . . . . . .  160 Cert Sonnets 30   27
    Therefore from so vile fancie, . . . . . . . . . . . . . .  161 Cert Sonnets 30   37
    Alas, if Fancy drawne by imag'd things,. . . . . . . . . .  187 Astrophil    45    9
    The Wand is Will, thou Fancie Saddle art,. . . . . . . . .  189 Astrophil    49    9
    The foolish man by flesh and fancy led . . . . . . . . . .  286 Psalm XIV          1
    But he drew hir as love his fancy drew,. . . . . . . . . .  250 Other Poems   4  323
    To fasten knotts, which fancy first had bound. . . . . . .  253 Other Poems   4  424
FANCY'S
    And lives in fancye's seing. . . . . . . . . . . . . . . .   20 1st Eclogues  7 V965
```

FANCY'S   (CONTINUED)   PAGE   TITLE   LINE

Whyle hote desyres do Raigne in fancie's rage. . . . . . . 26 1st Eclogues   9   140
Now fancie's fits, now fortune's balefull stowers: . . . . 103 3rd Eclogues 66   157
From fancie's earth passing all numbers' bound,. . . . . . 149 Cert Sonnets 22   7
Fond fancie's scum, and dregs of scattred thought, ... 161 Cert Sonnets 31   2
The first that straight my fancie's error brings . . . . . 183 Astrophil   38   5
FAN'S
Yet each prepar'd, with fanne's wel-shading grace, ... 176 Astrophil   22   7
FAR
Her minde, beames, state farre from thy weake wings
   banished . . . .   16 1st Eclogues   7   65
Dorus. Farre other care, o Muse, my sorrow tries,. . . . . 17 1st Eclogues   7   106
Farre more happy be you, whose greatnes gets a free accesse, 33 1st Eclogues 13   54
One wonder yet farre passeth my conceate:. . . . . 42 Arcadia II   22   13
Dicus. Dorus you wander farre in great reproches;. . . . . 50 2nd Eclogues 28   92
Nico his place farre better furnish will. . . . . 53 2nd Eclogues 29   56
That (shining now) she then might shine more farre.. . . . 56 2nd Eclogues 29   122
As farre as any shepheards piping be:. . . . . 56 2nd Eclogues 29   127
As farre as Love possesseth any head.. . . . . 56 2nd Eclogues 29   128
Thou art farre off, thy kingdome is above: . . . . 72 Arcadia III   38   7
No smaller wound, alas! farr deeper have.. . . . . 77 Arcadia III   47   4
You onely yours, too farr beyond desarte.. . . . . 79 Arcadia III   50   22
Thus honour, liking, trust, much, farre, and deepe,. . . . 84 Arcadia III   60   5
Be thou farre hence with thy empoyson'd darte, ... 92 3rd Eclogues 63   56
And farre unfit to hold so good a roome. . . . . 94 3rd Eclogues 64   6
He farre did passe the rest of Shepheards all. . . . . . . 94 3rd Eclogues 64   18
As farre from want, as farre from vaine expence, ... 98 3rd Eclogues 65   9
Beyond the heaven, far more beyond your witts. . . . . . . 99 3rd Eclogues 66   28
Far from my thoughts was ought, whereto their minds aspire,. 117 4th Eclogues 73   15
Her waiting Nymphe, a Nymphe that did excell as farr . . . 119 4th Eclogues 73   82
While he did live, farre, farre was all disorder;. . . . . 128 4th Eclogues 75   130
Far was homestrife, and far was foe from border. . . . . . 128 4th Eclogues 75   132
Of trueth, farre more then Alablaster pure,. . . . . 150 Cert Sonnets 22   39
As sacred things, far from all daunger's show. . . . . . . 177 Astrophil   24   8
Beauties so farre from reach of words, that we . . . . . . 183 Astrophil   37   7
Since then thou hast so farre subdued me,. . . . . 185 Astrophil   40   12
How farre they shoote awrie! the true cause is,. . . . . . 185 Astrophil   41   12
Far far too long to learne it without booke: . . . . 192 Astrophil   56   2
The Oratour so farre men's harts doth bind,. . . . . 193 Astrophil   58   2
Without how farre this praise is short of you, ... 207 Astrophil   80   13
Whose fruit doth farre th' Esperian tast surpasse: . . . . 208 Astrophil   82   6
When far spent night perswades each mortall eye, ... 230 Astrophil   99   1
Thence, so farre thence, that scarcely any sparke. . . . . 233 Astrophil   104   6
Of foes the spoile is evill, far worse of constant lovers. . 214 A&S 5th Song   48
What, is not this enough? nay farre worse commeth here;. . . 214 A&S 5th Song   73
Yet witches may repent, thou art far worse then they,. . . 215 A&S 5th Song   79
Beauty as farre excels,. . . . . 216 A&S 6th Song   27
Farr as World's farthest end.. . . . . 271 Psalm II   20
For Thou art that same God, far from delight . . . . 274 Psalm V   9
Why standest Thou so farr,. . . . . 281 Psalm X   1
His farr off sight now hoodwinkt is, ... 282 Psalm X   47
So farr from seing myne unhealthfull eyes, ... 298 Psalm XXII   3
So farr from hearing to my roaring cryes.. . . . . 298 Psalm XXII   4
O be not farr, since pain so nearly presseth,. . . . . . . 299 Psalm XXII   25
But be not farr O Lord, my strength, my comfort;. . . . . . 299 Psalm XXII   45
Farr farr more sure, than walls most firmly fast.. . . . . 313 Psalm XXXI   60
Farr off wend; . . . . 328 Psalm XXXVIII   32
Thy deare presence farr from me; . . . . 329 Psalm XXXVIII   63
O helpe o help me, this farr yet I crave,. . . . . 330 Psalm XXXIX   25
The Arrow being shot from far, doth give the smaller blowe.. 344 Possibly   1   42
Hardned, and coulde, farr from affectione's snare. . . . . 344 Possibly   2   5
But, ah! hir darts did farre more depely goe . . . . 251 Other Poems   4   352
Be absent farre from thee, ... 258 Other Poems   5   64
FARE
That unto me, who fare like him that both. . . . . 174 Astrophil   19   10
Fare they as their hands have far'd, ... 309 Psalm XXVIII   19
FARED
Fare they as their hands have far'd, ... 309 Psalm XXVIII   19
FARES
And see therein how well the writer fares. . . . . 42 Arcadia II   21   16
FAREWELL
But farewell nowe, thy fault is no great sinne,. . . . . . 29 1st Eclogues 10   97
Phaebus farewell, a sweeter Saint I serve, ... 72 Arcadia III   38   1
Phaebus farewell, a sweeter Saint I serve. . . . . 72 Arcadia III   38   6
Farewell Complaint, the miser's only pleasure: . . . . . . 83 Arcadia III   59   2
I give the Sunne a last farewell each evening; . . . . . . 112 4th Eclogues 71   50
If then a man in most ill case may give you a farewell;. . 124 4th Eclogues 74   85
Farewell, long farewell, all my woe, all my delight. . . . 124 4th Eclogues 74   86
And farewell Prince, whom goodnesse hath made glorious.. . 129 4th Eclogues 75   142
Farewell o Sunn, Arcadia's clearest light: . . . . 129 4th Eclogues 76   1
Farewell o pearl, the poore man's plenteous treasure:. . . 129 4th Eclogues 76   2
Farewell o golden staffe, the weake man's might: . . . . . 129 4th Eclogues 76   3
Farewell o Joy, the wofull's onely pleasure: . . . . 129 4th Eclogues 76   4
Wisdome farewell, the skillesse man's direction: . . . . . 129 4th Eclogues 76   5
Farewell with thee, farewell all our affection.. . . . . . 129 4th Eclogues 76   6
Farewell our light, farewell our spoiled treasure: . . . . 130 4th Eclogues 76   37
Farewell our might, farewell our daunted pleasure: . . . . 130 4th Eclogues 76   38
Farewell direction, farewell all affection.. . . . . 130 4th Eclogues 76   39
Then farewell world, thy uttermost I see,. . . . . 144 Cert Sonnets 32   13
All mirth farewell, let me in sorrow live. . . . . 231 Astrophil   100   14

	PAGE	TITLE		LINE

FARE-WELLING
And fare-welling the flocke did homeward wend, ... 252 Other Poems 4 415
FAR-FET
You take wrong waies, those far-fet helpes be such,. . . . . 172 Astrophil 15 9
FARTHEST
Farr as World's farthest end.. . . . . 271 Psalm II   20
FASHICN
Be none of us, or els maintaine our fashion: . . . . 15 1st Eclogues 7 14
Goe on therefore, and tell us, by what fashion . . . . 48 2nd Eclogues 28 34
They uttred are in such a feeling fashion, ... 60 2nd Eclogues 30 126
FAST
As smooth as Pan, as Juno milde, like goddesse Iris faste. . 12 Arcadia I   3 6
Who hold this fast no greater wealth require.. . . . . 75 Arcadia III 44 8
And having bound them fast by Styx, they should obaye. . . . 121 4th Eclogues 73 161
O take fast hold, let that light be thy guide, ... 162 Cert Sonnets 32 9
Girt fast by memorie, and while I spurre . . . . 189 Astrophil 49 10
He sits me fast, how ever I do sturre: . . . . 189 Astrophil 49 12
And anchor fast my selfe on Vertue's shore. . . . . 196 Astrophil 62 11
As fast thy Vertue bends that love to good:. . . . . 201 Astrophil 71 13
Curst be the Cochman which did drive so fast,. . . . . 235 Astrophil 105 13
Farr farr more sure, than walls most firmly fast.. . . . . . 313 Psalm XXXI   60
W. What seale? D. My hart deepe graven. W. Who made the band
    so fast?.. . . . . 343 Possibly 1 27
Lockt fast with knowing that she is, of worldly things the
    best.. . . . . 344 Possibly 1 30
And ti'de them fast to leade his triumph badd, ... 245 Other Poems 4 131
With whome to joyne fast ran Urania sweet:. . . . . 248 Other Poems 4 252
Did hold hir fast for feare of more disgrace,. . . . . 249 Other Poems 4 278
Thus, fast he fled from her he follow'd sore,. . . . . 250 Other Poems 4 305
With love drawne on, so fast with eager pace. . . . . 250 Other Poems 4 334
Though with soft leggs, did run as fast as he. . . . . 250 Other Poems 4 339
(Yet beauty still as fast as she did sturre) . . . . 251 Other Poems 4 358
FASTEN
To fasten knotts, which fancy first had bound. . . . . 253 Other Poems 4 424
FASTENER
Breather of life, and fastner of desire, ... 207 Astrophil 80 7
FASTER
Since loosing long, the faster still I bind: . . . . 135 Cert Sonnets 1 5
FASTEST
So much more strong againe let fastest concorde make.. . . . 120 4th Eclogues 73 120
Who hath the haire which, loosest, fastest tieth,. . . . . . 197 A&S 1st Song   25
FASTING
I did pull down my self, fasting for such; . . . . 322 Psalm XXXV   31
FAST-MEANING
The seed Fast-meaning is, no truth to misse: . . . . 115 4th Eclogues 72 53
FAT
Their eyes do swim, their face doth shine in fatt, ... 290 Psalm XVII   29
They that be made even fatt, with earth's fatt good, ... 300 Psalm XXII   71
Like fatt of lambs shall be consumed,. . . . . 326 Psalm XXXVII   51
FATAL
All this one the this fatall yere shall hitte. . . . . 11 Arcadia I   1 V807
My eyes the bandes, my thoughts the fatall knot. . . . . . . 17 1st Eclogues 7 113
Of my first love the fatall band.. . . . . 90 Arcadia III 62 122
FATE
Nor faile my faith in my failing fate, ... 153 Cert Sonnets 24 22
Now I, wit-beaten long by hardest Fate,. . . . . 195 Astrophil 60 9
O fate, o fault, o curse, child of my blisse, ... 227 Astrophil 93 1
But hence, even hence, I must needes goe; such is my dogged
    fate.. . . . . 344 Possibly 1 48
FATHER
Thy father bids thee save, and chides for spilling.. . . . . 16 1st Eclogues 7 79
When for a treene-dish stolne, thy father did thee whippe! . 52 2nd Eclogues 29 12
Pas. My father hath at home a prettie Jay, ... 56 2nd Eclogues 29 138
Thou art the father of occasion deare: . . . . 81 Arcadia III 53 12
Pan, father Pan, the god of silly sheepe,. . . . . 92 3rd Eclogues 63 37
Thy father justly may of thee complaine, ... 105 3rd Eclogues 67 73
With outward maker's force, or like an inward father.. . . . 118 4th Eclogues 73 48
For he our father was in all affection. . . . . 129 4th Eclogues 76 14
Brother to woe, and father of complaint: . . . . 141 Cert Sonnets 10 3
Wherewith my father once made it halfe tame; . . . . 180 Astrophil 30 10
Help me my God and Father. . . . . 272 Psalm III   24
And Father of the Fatherlesse. . . . . 283 Psalm X   64
FATHERLESS
And Father of the Fatherlesse. . . . . 283 Psalm X   64
FATHER'S
Her father's corne (moving her faire limmes) measure.. . . . 16 1st Eclogues 7 75
With father's death, and mother's guiltie shame, ... 21 1st Eclogues 8 19
Which touch the father's hart with secret joy, ... 106 3rd Eclogues 67 113
Orphans in deede, depriv'd of father's might:. . . . . 129 4th Eclogues 76 13
For father's heritage, ... 215 A&S 6th Song   16
Though Father's Care, and Mother's love. . . . . 308 Psalm XXVII   49
FATHERS
O men, whose Fathers were but men, ... 273 Psalm IV   6
Our Fathers still in thee their trust did beare, ... 298 Psalm XXII   11
But baiting, as my Fathers came; . . . . 330 Psalm XXXIX   40
FATNESS
Who shall in Thy house fatness find. . . . . 324 Psalm XXXVI   22
FAULT
But farewell nowe, thy fault is no great sinne,. . . . . . . 29 1st Eclogues 10 97
With flowing teares your fault of hasty sight: . . . . 38 Arcadia II 14 2

151

```
FAULT               (CONTINUED)                        PAGE   TITLE           LINE
    Her staines are beames; vertue the fault she blamed is.. . .    49 2nd Eclogues 28   57
    That with his fault he might her goodnes know. . . . . . .      97 3rd Eclogues 64  114
    Revil'd for ech small fault, sometimes for none: . . . . . .   105 3rd Eclogues 67   53
    Ne could my soule it selfe accuse of such a faulte,. . . . .   117 4th Eclogues 73   19
    If that love be a fault, more fault in you to be lovely: . .   123 4th Eclogues 74   43
    But what's this for a fault, for which such faieth be
        abolisht,. . . . . . . . . . . . . . . . . . . . . . .     124 4th Eclogues 74   69
    The fault I blame her chastnesse is. . . . . . . . . . . . .   157 Cert Sonnets 27   32
    I do confesse, pardon a fault confest, . . . . . . . . . . .   166 Astrophil     4    7
    But one worse fault, Ambition, I confesse, . . . . . . . . .   178 Astrophil    27   11
    Pardon that fault, once more graunt me the place,. . . . . .   208 Astrophil    82   12
    O fate, o fault, o curse, child of my blisse,. . . . . . . .   227 Astrophil    93    1
    Their judgements hackney on, the fault on sicknesse lay, . .   232 Astrophil   102   10
    Was not in fault, who bent thy dazling race. . . . . . . . .   235 Astrophil   105    6
    Whose owne fault casts him downe, hardly high seat recovers.   213 A&S 5th Song      24
    But murder, private fault, seems but a toy to thee,. . . . .   214 A&S 5th Song      55
    But no fault there is in praying. . . . . . . . . . . . . . .  219 A&S 8th Song      48
    Whose fault well hidden lyeth. . . . . . . . . . . . . . . .   314 Psalm XXXII        3
    Pas Cosma matcht, yet angry with his fault,. . . . . . . . .   250 Other Poems   4  318
FAULTLESS
    For faultlesse length, and stainelesse hewe, . . . . . . . .    90 Arcadia III  62  119
    And in this faultlesse face, . . . . . . . . . . . . . . . .   216 A&S 6th Song      22
FAULTS
    Seeke to espie her faultes as well as praise,. . . . . . . .    25 1st Eclogues  9  121
    Mastix. What marvaile if in youth such faults be done, . . .    27 1st Eclogues 10   25
    By justice' worke they their owne faultes disclose:. . . . .    27 1st Eclogues 10   42
    That huntinge faultes, our selves we did not catch.. . . . .    29 1st Eclogues 10   93
    Not spying faults, nor in plaine errors blinde,. . . . . . .    98 3rd Eclogues 65    7
    And yet finde no such faults in womankind. . . . . . . . . .   106 3rd Eclogues 67   87
    Know my words their faults acknowledge.. . . . . . . . . . .   157 Cert Sonnets 27   36
    In justice paines come not till faults do call;. . . . . . .   212 Astrophil    86   10
    I thinke now of thy faults, who late thought of thy praise,.  213 A&S 5th Song      16
    Of my faults and chastening. . . . . . . . . . . . . . . . .   288 Psalm XVI         24
    When silent night might seeme all faults to hide,. . . . . .   289 Psalm XVII         9
    His faults know and acknowledg?. . . . . . . . . . . . . . .   295 Psalm XIX         50
    O lord cleanse me from faults that be. . . . . . . . . . . .   295 Psalm XIX         51
    And pardon all my faults.. . . . . . . . . . . . . . . . . .   304 Psalm XXV         64
    Till my self did my faults confess . . . . . . . . . . . . .   315 Psalm XXXII       13
    Do good, from faults decline,. . . . . . . . . . . . . . . .   320 Psalm XXXIV       53
    For my faults are highly spred . . . . . . . . . . . . . . .   327 Psalm XXXVIII     10
    Foul faults sore pains do reach me,. . . . . . . . . . . . .   332 Psalm XL          46
    These sports shepheards deviz'd such faults to show. . . . .   248 Other Poems   4  241
FAULTY
    Well: but faultie I was: Reason to my Passion yeelded, . . .   124 4th Eclogues 74   67
    If I then faultie be,. . . . . . . . . . . . . . . . . . . .   158 Cert Sonnets 28   18
    He might on knees confesse his faulty part,. . . . . . . . .   247 Other Poems   4  190
FAUNS
    Nico. O Faunes, O Fairies all, and do you see, . . . . . . .    54 2nd Eclogues 29   63
FAVOR
    Cleofila. Worthy shepeheard, by my song to my selfe all
        favor is happned,. . . . . . . . . . . . . . . . . . . .    31 1st Eclogues 13    8
    She oft her lookes, the starres her favour bend to thee: . .    51 2nd Eclogues 28   99
    Bandes, favour, faith, to breake, defile, and kill.. . . . .    84 Arcadia III  60    8
    Favour to make my chiefe and onely hire. . . . . . . . . . .   115 4th Eclogues 72   55
    Shall I not once object, that you, you graunted a favour . .   124 4th Eclogues 74   73
    An humble pride, a skorne that favour staines: . . . . . . .   151 Cert Sonnets 22   65
    I was content you should in favour creepe, . . . . . . . . .   208 Astrophil    83    2
    While favour fed my hope, delight with hope was brought, . .   212 A&S 5th Song       1
    But his deare favour where it lyes . . . . . . . . . . . . .   311 Psalm XXX         14
FAVORS
    To this chaste love your sacred favours bow, . . . . . . . .    91 3rd Eclogues 63   21
FAWN
    Fawne on my self, and others to despise: . . . . . . . . . .   178 Astrophil    27    8
FEAR
    So dare I, wretch, my bashfull feare subdue, . . . . . . . .     3 Lady of May   1   11
    But take this beast, if beasts you feare to misse, . . . . .     4 Lady of May   2   29
    Lay all your feare upon your fearefull lover:. . . . . . . .    17 1st Eclogues  7   91
    With vertue fraught and full of holy feare!. . . . . . . . .    25 1st Eclogues  9   95
    From former feare, they had of your good mindes, . . . . . .    26 1st Eclogues 10    5
    Thy too much zeale, I feare thy braine hath spent. . . . . .    28 1st Eclogues 10   63
    So my desires by my feare, cutt downe, be the frames of her
        honour.. . . . . . . . . . . . . . . . . . . . . . . . .    36 1st Eclogues 13  135
    But who doth feare, or bideth muet wilfully, . . . . . . . .    48 2nd Eclogues 28   17
    A man to feare a woman's moodie eye, . . . . . . . . . . . .    49 2nd Eclogues 28   75
    But feare forgott, and paynes all overpaste, . . . . . . . .    70 Arcadia III  36    5
    Make great the losse, so grete the feare to misse. . . . . .    71 Arcadia III  37   12
    Synce love with care, and hope with feare do fight.. . . . .    72 Arcadia III  37   18
    Thy force I feare, her force I still do prove. . . . . . . .    72 Arcadia III  38   10
    Make me still feare, thy faire appearing showe.. . . . . . .    82 Arcadia III  56   14
    And did the same, although with mickle feare.. . . . . . . .    96 3rd Eclogues 64   64
    For feare he did, least he the young man might . . . . . . .    96 3rd Eclogues 64   65
    Whether he needes must goe for feare of blame. . . . . . . .    96 3rd Eclogues 64   78
    The pandare of the thing, he most did feare, . . . . . . . .    97 3rd Eclogues 64  122
    Amid my sheepe, though I sawe nought to feare, . . . . . . .    99 3rd Eclogues 66   15
    The Stagge did give the harme eschewing feare. . . . . . . .   101 3rd Eclogues 66   91
    Gainst those of might, of whom in feare they stood,. . . . .   102 3rd Eclogues 66  130
    Geron. Who for ech fickle feare from vertue shrinkes,. . . .   105 3rd Eclogues 67   58
    No man doth speake aright, who speakes in feare. . . . . . .   106 3rd Eclogues 67   84
    For neere acquaintance dooth diminish reverent feare.. . . .   121 4th Eclogues 73  160
```

```
FEAR                         (CONTINUED)              PAGE    TITLE          LINE
    And found with deadly feare that all my sinewes shak'd....  121  4th Eclogues 73  180
    When that we feare our hatefull neighbours' might, .....    129  4th Eclogues 76   20
    As nature's worke: why should we feare to dye? .......     131  Arcadia V    77    2
    Since feare is vaine, but when it may preserve,.......     131  Arcadia V    77    3
    Why should we feare that which we cannot flye? ......      131  Arcadia V    77    4
    Feare is more paine, then is the paine it feares,......    131  Arcadia V    77    5
    Since heart in chilling feare with yce is warmed:......    135  Cert Sonnets  1    7
    How holdst thou her, whose eyes constraint doth feare, ... 142  Cert Sonnets 10    5
    With feare of change, the courage well preparde: ......    143  Cert Sonnets 12   11
    For true it is, that they feare many whom many feare.. ... 143  Cert Sonnets 14    2
    And thus might I for feare of may be, leave. ........     145  Cert Sonnets 16   11
    Which Poets say, the gods them selves do feare,.......    146  Cert Sonnets 17    7
    But all the rest, which feare durst not applie,.......    151  Cert Sonnets 22   49
    Though hope were mixt with feare,...............          158  Cert Sonnets 28    6
    Of hopes begot by feare, of wot not what desires:......   167  Astrophil     6    2
    The boy refusde for feare of Marse's hate, .........     173  Astrophil    17    5
    Curb'd in with feare, but with guilt bosse above .....    189  Astrophil    49    7
    Desire still on the stilts of feare doth go. ........     199  Astrophil    66    8
    Feare to offend, will worthie to appeare,..........      202  Astrophil    72   10
    Feare not else, none can us spie:..............          211  A&S 4th Song       22
    Feare not to judge this bate,................           215  A&S 6th Song        5
    Serve God, serve him with feare: Rejoyce in him but so,... 271  Psalm II          25
    And in thy feare knees of my heart will fold ........    275  Psalm V           19
    Least we should ever feare the lust. ............        283  Psalm X           79
    Ev'en Feare makes strangers shew much love though much
        untrue....................                         293  Psalm XVIII       81
    Of him the Feare doth cleaness beare ............        294  Psalm XIX         37
    Who feare the lord all prayse and glory beare him;.....   300  Psalm XXII        53
    You Isra'el's seed, you come of Jacob, feare him......    300  Psalm XXII        54
    Who feare Thee shall my vowes performed see. ........    300  Psalm XXII        60
    No whit feare ill. .....................                  301  Psalm XXIII       12
    Oh, is there one with his Feare fraught? ..........      304  Psalm XXV         47
    Feare might of men?.....................                  307  Psalm XXVII        6
    Feare was each where, while they their counsells led ....  313  Psalm XXXI        38
    To whom feare Thee? what thou hast done for those. .....  313  Psalm XXXI        53
    Let all the earth feare God, ................           317  Psalm XXXIII      28
    Who him do truly feare,....................              318  Psalm XXXIII      69
    About them pitch who him do feare,.............          319  Psalm XXXIV       26
    Feare God ye saints of his,..................            319  Psalm XXXIV       33
    How this Our lord to feare..................             320  Psalm XXXIV       44
    Noe feare of God doth once appeare ............         323  Psalm XXXVI        5
    To feare with trust, and trust with feare the Lord.. ...  331  Psalm XL          14
    With triumph's shews would shew he nought did feare. ...  244  Other Poems   4   78
    With sight of feare from frends to fremb'd do flie......   248  Other Poems   4  240
    Did hold hir fast for feare of more disgrace,.......      249  Other Poems   4  278
    For Pas, whether it were for feare, or love, ........     250  Other Poems   4  327
    "When I see her, my sinewes shake for feare,........      253  Other Poems   4  457
FEARED
    Where death is feard, and life is held with paine. .....   57  2nd Eclogues 30   19
    While thus he fear'd the silly innocent, .........       94  3rd Eclogues 64   13
    In that which he so fear'd that she should meet. ......    95  3rd Eclogues 64   36
    Of that, whereto he heard she was enclinde,........       95  3rd Eclogues 64   50
    Yet (for I nothing sawe) I feared sore:..........         99  3rd Eclogues 66   16
    Faire seeke not to be feard, most lovely beloved by thy
        servants,....................                        143  Cert Sonnets 14    1
    Fearing and feared thus from himselfe he fled, ......    145  Cert Sonnets 16    3
    To strive she fear'd how it with vertue stoode.......    245  Other Poems   4  126
    And then the Phoenix feared to be cought..........       251  Other Poems   4  360
FEAREST
    Thou fearest death; thinke they are loth to die. ......   103  3rd Eclogues 66  151
    Fear'st not a face that oft whole harts devowres,......   142  Cert Sonnets 10   10
FEARFUL
    Who ended hath this fearefull strife:...........          13  Arcadia I     5    4
    Lay all your feare upon your fearefull lover:.......      17  1st Eclogues  7   91
    In hunting fearefull beastes, do spend some dayes, ....   25  1st Eclogues  9  123
    The fearefull Hinde the Leopard did kisse: ........      100  3rd Eclogues 66   53
    Your fearfull words why do you spill ...........         283  Psalm XI           2
    They false and fearfull do their hands undoe,.......     248  Other Poems   4  235
FEARING
    And keep it joynde, fearing your seate's consumption.. ...  15  1st Eclogues  7   42
    Yet like a coward fearing stranger's pride,........       95  3rd Eclogues 64   29
    Fearing least he chastisde be, ...............           139  Cert Sonnets  7    9
    Fearing and feared thus from himselfe he fled, ......    145  Cert Sonnets 16    3
    Readie of wit and fearing nought but shame:........      172  Astrophil    14   11
    Fearing her beames, take with thee ............         226  A&S 10th Song      23
    Fearing (sweete) you to endanger,.............          234  A&S 11th Song      39
    Failes me fearing on to passe, ...............           219  A&S 8th Song       46
    But fearing lest all white might seeme too good, .....   246  Other Poems   4  151
    Fearing the worst, not knowing what were best, ......    255  Other Poems   4  525
FEARS
    You, though feares do abash, in you still possible hopes be:  32  1st Eclogues 13   23
    Ofte scorching sonne, ofte clowdie darkenes feares,....   71  Arcadia III  36    9
    As neere his home, when storme or shelf he feares; ....   71  Arcadia III  37    4
    Come clowdie feares, close up my daseled sight,......    74  Arcadia III  42    9
    His nature feares to die who lives still wailing.. .....  110  Arcadia IV   70   39
    Feare is more paine, then is the paine it feares,.....    131  Arcadia V    77    5
    For hers am I, and death feares her displeasure. .....   137  Cert Sonnets  3   22
    Feares she to feele, and feeles not others' feares?. ...  142  Cert Sonnets 11    4
    Such causelesse feares when coward minds do take,.....   145  Cert Sonnets 16    5
```

```
FEARS                    (CONTINUED)                          PAGE    TITLE              LINE
        She seemed full of jealous feares, . . . . . . . . . . . . .  158 Cert Sonnets 28    15
        And yet amid all feares a hope there is. . . . . . . . . . .  199 Astrophil    66     9
        Love feares nothing else but anger.. . . . . . . . . . . . .  203 A&S 2nd Song        20
        Who faithfull feares in him do plant;. . . . . . . . . . . .  319 Psalm XXXIV         35
        Failes me, with ugly feares. . . . . . . . . . . . . . . . .  332 Psalm XL            50
        Free of proud feares, brave begg'ry, smiling strife. . . . .  243 Other Poems  4     60
FEAST'S
        With scoffers false I was their feast's delight, . . . . . .  322 Psalm XXXV          41
FEASTS
        Who frownes at others' feastes, dooth better bide away.. . .   15 1st Eclogues  7     15
        So oft in feasts with costly chaunges cladd. . . . . . . . .  245 Other Poems  4    133
FEAT
        Hate of the firste, contempt of later feate: . . . . . . . .   27 1st Eclogues 10     39
        But now the courtier gan to smell the feate, . . . . . . . .   97 3rd Eclogues 64    117
FEATHERS
        Where Leda's swanne his feathers mewes, . . . . . . . . . . .   89 Arcadia III  62    110
        Yet first but wooll, or fethers off he teard: . . . . . . . .  102 3rd Eclogues 66    143
        Although lesse gifts impe feathers oft on Fame, . . . . . . .  204 Astrophil    75     4
        See now those feathers pluckt, wherewith thou flewst most
           high: . . . . . . . . . . . . . . . . . . . . . . . . . .  213 A&S 5th Song        22
FEATS
        The while a swarm of foes with vexing feates . . . . . . . .  276 Psalm VI            23
FED
        But there I was, and there my calmie thoughts I fedd . . . .  117 4th Eclogues 73     39
        While we for mutuall spight a striving passion fed.. . . . .  120 4th Eclogues 73    118
        Fed by thy worth, and kindled by thy sight?. . . . . . . . .  200 Astrophil    68      8
        While favour fed my hope, delight with hope was brought, . .  212 A&S 5th Song         1
        Let me, fed with hellish anguish, . . . . . . . . . . . . . .  220 A&S 8th Song        79
        His guiltie heart with this fond thought hath fed, . . . . .  286 Psalm XIV            2
        Thus thus shall all my days be fede, . . . . . . . . . . . .  301 Psalm XXIII         22
        The shepheards will grow leane I trow, their sheep will ill
           be fed.. . . . . . . . . . . . . . . . . . . . . . . . .  344 Possibly     1     40
        Leaving in paine their wel-fed hungry eies.. . . . . . . . .  246 Other Poems  4    168
        The day well fed, the night in faithfull folde: . . . . . .  258 Other Poems  5     68
FEE
        So that I live to pay a mortall fee, . . . . . . . . . . . .  136 Cert Sonnets  2      9
FEEBLE
        Would scorne in man (their king) such feeble shows.. . . . .   23 1st Eclogues  9     43
        We oft are angrier, with the feeble flie . . . . . . . . . .   28 1st Eclogues 10     64
        P. O Passion, passe on feeble Reason's spoiles.. . . . . . .   46 2nd Eclogues 27     24
        But forced are to burthen feeble nature. . . . . . . . . . .  110 Arcadia IV   70     34
        But like the feeble flower (whose stalke cannot sustaine . .  117 4th Eclogues 73     21
        Dick. Ah Will, though I grudge not, I count it feeble glee .  343 Possibly     1      3
        Fayrenesse though fayer, is but a feeble shielde, . . . . . .  345 Possibly     4      6
FEEBLEST
        (For envie harbreth most in feeblest hartes) . . . . . . . .  100 3rd Eclogues 66     58
FEED
        And feede mine eares, mine eyes, my hart in you. . . . . . .    3 Lady of May   1     12
        On barren sweetes they feede, and feeding sterve: . . . . .   39 Arcadia II   17      3
        They feede on me, and with my wings do flie: . . . . . . . .   42 Arcadia II   22      9
        Feede on my sheepe, my chardge my comforte feede, . . . . .   43 Arcadia II   23      1
        Feede on my sheepe, your fayer sweete feeding flowes, . . .   43 Arcadia II   23      4
        Feede on my sheepe, possesse your fruitefull fyeld, . . . .   43 Arcadia II   23      7
        Feede on my sheepe, sorrow hathe stricken sayle, . . . . . .   43 Arcadia II   23     10
        Feede on my sheepe, your Native joyes mayntayne, . . . . . .   43 Arcadia II   23     13
        Leave of my sheepe: it is no tyme to feede, . . . . . . . .   43 Arcadia II   24      1
        Nor ought I crave to feede life, . . . . . . . . . . . . . .   67 2nd Eclogues 32     54
        Right so my thoughts, whereon my hart I feede: . . . . . . .   78 Arcadia III  50      5
        And sorow feede, feeding our soules with sorow.. . . . . . .  110 Arcadia IV   70     36
        Dwell in my ruines, feede with sucking smarte, . . . . . . .  113 4th Eclogues 72      9
        Without desire to feed of further grace. . . . . . . . . . .  187 Astrophil    46      8
        And do I see some cause a hope to feede, . . . . . . . . . .  199 Astrophil    66      1
        Shall feed and laud the giver of their food. . . . . . . . .  300 Psalm XXII          72
        Feed and lift them up for aye. . . . . . . . . . . . . . . .  309 Psalm XXVIII        35
        That Mira may thee feede . . . . . . . . . . . . . . . . . .  258 Other Poems  5     83
FEEDING
        On barren sweetes they feede, and feeding sterve: . . . . .   39 Arcadia II   17      3
        Feede on my sheepe, your fayer sweete feeding flowes, . . .   43 Arcadia II   23      4
        And sorow feede, feeding our soules with sorow.. . . . . . .  110 Arcadia IV   70     36
        (More swift then falcon's stoope to feeding Falconer's call)  118 4th Eclogues 73     58
        Seeke a better place of feeding, . . . . . . . . . . . . . .  221 A&S 9th Song         2
        Which in the fertile fields be feeding, . . . . . . . . . .  279 Psalm VIII          28
        Have been my ill feeding food, . . . . . . . . . . . . . . .  334 Psalm XLII          10
FEEDS
        Whose wages makes me beg the more, who feeds me till I
           sterve,. . . . . . . . . . . . . . . . . . . . . . . . .  343 Possibly     1     20
        On thoughts he feeds, his lookes their figure chaunge, . . .  253 Other Poems  4    434
FEEL
        And doth not feele, that life is nought but time . . . . . .   28 1st Eclogues 10     50
        Ease I do feele (such ease as falls to one wholy diseased) .   35 1st Eclogues 13    114
        But more I plaine, I feele my woes the more. . . . . . . . .   57 2nd Eclogues 30     10
        Selfe-guiltie folke must prove to feele compassion.. . . . .   60 2nd Eclogues 30    130
        So greate a passion all feele, . . . . . . . . . . . . . . .   66 2nd Eclogues 32     16
        These wordes are full of woes, yet feele they none.. . . . .   75 Arcadia III  43      3
        And seeing feele in me . . . . . . . . . . . . . . . . . . .   81 Arcadia III  55      5
        Fancie we feele, encludes all passion's mighte, . . . . . .   82 Arcadia III  57      3
        Me seemes I feele the comfort of the morning . . . . . . . .  112 4th Eclogues 71     41
        Me seemes I feele a noysome sent, the morning. . . . . . . .  112 4th Eclogues 71     45
        In earthly fetters feele a lasting hell. . . . . . . . . . .  116 4th Eclogues 72     90
```

154

```
FEEL            (CONTINUED)                     PAGE    TITLE          LINE
    Klaius. In earthly fetters feele a lasting hell. . . . . . .  116  4th Eclogues 72    91
    Our yeares doo it require: you see we both doo feele . . . .  120  4th Eclogues 73   121
    Since this we feele, greate losse we cannot finde. . . . . .  131  Arcadia V      77    14
    Feares she to feele, and feeles not others' feares?. . . . . 142  Cert Sonnets 11     4
    I can speake what I feele, and feele as much as they,. . . .  168  Astrophil       6    12
    When most I glorie, then I feele most shame: . . . . . . . .  174  Astrophil      19     3
    To me that feele the like, thy state descries. . . . . . . . 180  Astrophil      31     8
    Or want I sense to feele my miserie? . . . . . . . . . . . .  188  Astrophil      47     5
    To feele my griefes, and she with face and voice . . . . . . 193  Astrophil      57    13
    I feele the flames of hottest sommer day.. . . . . . . . . . 224  Astrophil      89    14
    The birds, beasts, stones and trees feele this, and feeling
        love: . . . . . . . . . . . . . . . . . . . . . . . . .  209  A&S 3rd Song         13
    Ah, my sute granted is, I feele my breast doth swell:. . . . 213  A&S 5th Song         34
    Shall feel in Thy face's sight . . . . . . . . . . . . . . .  289  Psalm XVI            40
    Then love him ye all ye that feel his grace, . . . . . . . .  314  Psalm XXXI           64
    To feele the panting heart, which through hir syde . . . . . 252  Other Poems     4   405
    To see, to feele, to heare, to tast, to know . . . . . . . . 252  Other Poems     4   407
FEELETH
    Faire death feeleth, . . . . . . . . . . . . . . . . . . . . 156  Cert Sonnets 26     28
FEELING
    O well thou saiest! a feeling declaration. . . . . . . . . .  20  1st Eclogues    7  V968
    The child feeles that; the man that feeling knowes,. . . . .  57  2nd Eclogues 30     23
    They uttred are in such a feeling fashion, . . . . . . . . .  60  2nd Eclogues 30    126
    To have a feeling tast of him that sitts . . . . . . . . . .  99  3rd Eclogues 66     27
    Proofe speakes too much to us that feeling triall have.. . . 119  4th Eclogues 73    108
    Would often kill to breed more feeling paine,. . . . . . . . 135  Cert Sonnets  2      4
    Feeling my pulse, misse my disease.. . . . . . . . . . . . . 153  Cert Sonnets 24      9
    While with a feeling skill I paint my hell.. . . . . . . . . 166  Astrophil       2    14
    But feeling proofe makes me say they mistake it furre: . . . 232  Astrophil     102    11
    The birds, beasts, stones and trees feele this, and feeling
        love: . . . . . . . . . . . . . . . . . . . . . . . . .  209  A&S 3rd Song         13
FEELS
    And who can hope, who feeles despaire? . . . . . . . . . . .  14  1st Eclogues    6     6
    So small accompt of time the shepeheard feeles . . . . . . .  28  1st Eclogues   10    49
    The child feeles that; the man that feeling knowes,. . . . .  57  2nd Eclogues 30     23
    Not that he hopes for amends of the desaster he feeles,. . . 122  4th Eclogues 74     24
    Feares she to feele, and feeles not others' feares?. . . . . 142  Cert Sonnets 11      4
    That sense feeles more then what doth sense containe?. . . . 142  Cert Sonnets 11      8
FEELST
    Can judge of Love, thou feel'st a Lover's case;. . . . . . . 180  Astrophil      31     6
FEET
    Her legges (O legges) her ay well stepping feete.. . . . . . 141  Cert Sonnets  9      8
    And others' feete still seem'd but strangers in my way.. . . 165  Astrophil       1    11
    Each soule doth at Love's feet his weapons lay,. . . . . . . 186  Astrophil      43     7
    Thy reasons firmly set on Vertue's feet, . . . . . . . . . . 200  Astrophil      68    11
    But with short breath, long lookes, staid feet and walking
        hed, . . . . . . . . . . . . . . . . . . . . . . . . .  205  Astrophil      76    13
    So nimble feet as stirre still, though on thornes: . . . . . 206  Astrophil      78    11
    Tempers her words to trampling horses feet,. . . . . . . . . 209  Astrophil      84     3
    Hundreds of yeares you Stella's feet may kisse.. . . . . . . 209  Astrophil      84    14
    Who hath the feet, whose step all sweetnesse planteth, . . . 197  A&S 1st Song         13
    My feete are turn'd to rootes, my hart becommeth lead, . . . 215  A&S 5th Song         77
    That even his feet have on them raigned. . . . . . . . . . . 279  Psalm VIII           24
    In race of life their Feet to guide. . . . . . . . . . . . . 284  Psalm XI             23
    With hugy darknes, which about his feet did wend.. . . . . . 291  Psalm XVIII          21
    With such brave wounds, that they under my feet did ly.. . . 292  Psalm XVIII          70
    My humble hands, my fainting feet they peirced;. . . . . . . 299  Psalm XXII           41
    He guides my feet. . . . . . . . . . . . . . . . . . . . . . 301  Psalm XXIII           6
    My feet from tangling net. . . . . . . . . . . . . . . . . . 304  Psalm XXV            58
    But hast enlargd my feet from mortall ginn.. . . . . . . . . 312  Psalm XXXI           24
    Let not proud feet make me their thrall, . . . . . . . . . . 324  Psalm XXXVI          31
    Setting my feet upon . . . . . . . . . . . . . . . . . . . . 331  Psalm XL              8
    Geron strave hard, but aged were his feet, . . . . . . . . . 248  Other Poems     4   254
    Hir feet be Pursevants from Cupid sent,. . . . . . . . . . . 249  Other Poems     4   301
    With larger round, to shun the folowing feet.. . . . . . . . 250  Other Poems     4   332
    With gazing looks, short sighs, unsettled feet,. . . . . . . 251  Other Poems     4   369
FEIGN
    To lye, faine, gloze, to steale, pry, and accuse, . . . . . . 21  1st Eclogues    8    23
    P. Who be too weake, do feigne they be too good. . . . . . .  47  2nd Eclogues 27     30
    Mournes she in truth, and thinks that others faine?. . . . . 142  Cert Sonnets 11      3
    Who with deceitfull tongue hath never usd to faine,. . . . . 287  Psalm XV              5
    And since my lipps feign not with Thee,. . . . . . . . . . . 289  Psalm XVII            3
    Since they know not how to faine,. . . . . . . . . . . . . . 263  Other Poems     7    39
FEIGNING
    Faining love, somewhat to please me: . . . . . . . . . . . . 222  A&S 9th Song         42
FELICITY
    (As his sole object of felicitie). . . . . . . . . . . . . . 212  Astrophil      86     7
*FELL
    I saw that riches fall, and fell a crying; . . . . . . . . .  17  1st Eclogues    7    88
    But still (me thought) with beauties from her fell,. . . . .  55  2nd Eclogues 29    106
    Fell jealousie did so his braine oppresse, . . . . . . . . .  94  3rd Eclogues 64      9
    Worst fell to smallest birds, and meanest heard, . . . . . . 102  3rd Eclogues 66    141
    That ever fell to honest woman yet:. . . . . . . . . . . . . 104  3rd Eclogues 67     44
    Blinded with beames, fell darkenes is my sight:. . . . . . . 113  4th Eclogues 72      8
    These foule, most foule, disastres to me fell; . . . . . . . 116  4th Eclogues 72     97
    Tell how my joyes and hopes thus fowly fell. . . . . . . . . 146  Cert Sonnets 17     14
    Curst be the page from whome the bad torch fell, . . . . . . 235  Astrophil     105    11
    Nay ev'n my soul fell troubles do appall;. . . . . . . . . . 276  Psalm VI              9
    Through him the floods to their beds fell. . . . . . . . . . 302  Psalm XXIV            4
```

155

```
*FELL                    (CONTINUED)                     PAGE    TITLE          LINE
    O Lord from all his troubles fell. . . . . . . . . . . . .  305 Psalm XXV         78
FELLOW
    Geron. Downe, downe Melampus; what? your fellow bite?. . .   26 1st Eclogues 10    1
    Because thou hast thy fellow overgone, . . . . . . . . . .   27 1st Eclogues 10   11
    Heeding himselfe, cares not how fellow doe,. . . . . . . .  248 Other Poems   4  237
FELLOW-LIKE
    P. Not so, but fellowlike together borne. . . . . . . . .    46 2nd Eclogues 27   12
    And fellow-like let his dominion slide;. . . . . . . . . .  101 3rd Eclogues 66  110
FELLOWS
    That at me so amaz'd my fellowes jest: . . . . . . . . . .  254 Other Poems   4  468
FELLOWSHIP
    Then ev'n of fellowship, o Moone, tell me. . . . . . . . .  180 Astrophil     31    9
    Now from thy fellowship I needs must part, . . . . . . . .  202 Astrophil     72    5
FELT
    None can speake of a wound with skill, if he have not a
        wound felt. . . . . . . . . . . . . . . . . . . . . .    33 1st Eclogues 13   71
    Fore-felt Desire, begin to savour parte. . . . . . . . . .   83 Arcadia III  59   11
    That it both seene and felte may with you live". . . . . .  101 3rd Eclogues 66   77
    To well felte griefe, plainte is the onely pleasure. . . .  126 4th Eclogues 75   51
    And so for one that felt god Cupid's dart, . . . . . . . .  146 Cert Sonnets 17   29
    Who hath ever felt the change of love, . . . . . . . . . .  153 Cert Sonnets 24    1
    But who by hearesay speakes, and hath not fully felt . . .  153 Cert Sonnets 24    6
    A still felt plague, to selfe condemning me: . . . . . . .  212 Astrophil     86    3
    Cannot heavn's food, once felt, keepe stomakes free. . . .  223 Astrophil     88    7
    But thou art gone, now that selfe felt disgrace. . . . . .  235 Astrophil    106    7
    They found, they felt, they had no lease of blisse.. . . .  244 Other Poems   4   80
    Klaius streight felt, and groned at the blowe, . . . . . .  246 Other Poems   4  161
FEMALE
    Palmes do rejoyce to be joynd by the match of a male to a
        female,. . . . . . . . . . . . . . . . . . . . . . . .   36 1st Eclogues 13  137
    Then man to yeeld to female lamentations?. . . . . . . . .   61 2nd Eclogues 30  141
    From such a femall franzie . . . . . . . . . . . . . . . .  160 Cert Sonnets 30    8
    Above line repeated at following location. . . . . . . . .  160 Cert Sonnets 30   18
    From such femall franzie,. . . . . . . . . . . . . . . . .  160 Cert Sonnets 30   28
FENCE
    Till downe-right blowes did foyle thy cunning fence: . . .  170 Astrophil     10   11
FENCED
    The second sweetly-fenced warde, . . . . . . . . . . . . .   87 Arcadia III  62   43
FERTILE
    Cleofila. First shall fertill grounds not yeeld increase of
        a good seed: . . . . . . . . . . . . . . . . . . . . .   33 1st Eclogues 13   64
    With sonne's approche your pasture fertill growes, . . . .   43 Arcadia II   23    2
    But harveste come, and corne in fertill store, . . . . . .   71 Arcadia III  36   11
    Enough to make a fertill minde lie waste . . . . . . . . .  114 4th Eclogues 72   30
    Klaius. Enough to make a fertill minde lie waste . . . . .  114 4th Eclogues 72   31
    Which in the fertile fields be feeding,. . . . . . . . . .  279 Psalm VIII        28
FERVENT
    Such comfort, fervent love . . . . . . . . . . . . . . . .  261 Other Poems   6   51
FESTERED
    And will pitty the wound festred so strangely within me. .   37 1st Eclogues 13  168
FET
    You take wrong waies, those far-fet helpes be such,. . . .  172 Astrophil     15    9
    But all this while another course he fet.. . . . . . . . .  249 Other Poems   4  280
    Or like a lambe whose dam away is fet, . . . . . . . . . .  254 Other Poems   4  490
FETCH
    It shews they fetch their wit from youthfull yeares. . . .   24 1st Eclogues  9   80
    Sure shepherd's signe, that morne would soone fetch day. .  103 3rd Eclogues 66  161
    But I unbid, fetch even my soule to thee.. . . . . . . . .  194 Astrophil     59    8
    And now their curr they teach to fetch and daunce. . . . .  243 Other Poems   4   48
FETCHES
    He shall save them from all the fetches. . . . . . . . . .  327 Psalm XXXVII     102
FETCHETH
    Bid'n, perhaps he fetcheth thee a glove, . . . . . . . . .  194 Astrophil     59    7
FETTERS
    Rebell, Rebell, in golden fetters binde. . . . . . . . . .   23 1st Eclogues  9   44
    In earthly fetters feele a lasting hell. . . . . . . . . .  116 4th Eclogues 72   90
    Klaius. In earthly fetters feele a lasting hell. . . . . .  116 4th Eclogues 72   91
    Fetters tyed, do waite the hower . . . . . . . . . . . . .  155 Cert Sonnets 26   18
FEVER
    And precious couches full oft are shak't with a feaver. . .   34 1st Eclogues 13   86
    To which hir presence such a feaver brought. . . . . . . .  246 Other Poems   4  176
FEW
    Away vayne Cares, by which fewe men do finde . . . . . . .   83 Arcadia III  59    3
    But fewe dayes past while she good maner us'de,. . . . . .   95 3rd Eclogues 64   26
    But this bad world, few golden fieldes doth bring, . . . .  104 3rd Eclogues 67   19
    Mirth with respect, few words with curtesy,. . . . . . . .  247 Other Poems   4  212
FICKLE
    A fickle Sex, and trew in trust to no man, . . . . . . . .   24 1st Eclogues  9   59
    Geron. Who for ech fickle feare from vertue shrinkes,. . .  105 3rd Eclogues 67   58
FICTION
    By wise discourse, sweete tunes, or Poet's fiction;. . . .   61 2nd Eclogues 30  144
FIDDLING
    I curse the fidling finders out of Musicke:. . . . . . . .  112 4th Eclogues 71   51
FIE
    Geron. Fy man, fy man, what wordes hath thy tonge lent?. .   28 1st Eclogues 10   61
    "Fie, fie, what have we done? ungodly rebell fie.. . . . .  121 4th Eclogues 73  168
    Fie death, thou art beguiled,. . . . . . . . . . . . . . .  137 Cert Sonnets  3   23
    Fy, schoole of Patience, Fy, your lesson is. . . . . . . .  192 Astrophil     56    1
    Guesse we the cause: "What, is it thus?" Fie no: . . . . .  204 Astrophil     74   12
```

		PAGE	TITLE		LINE
FIELD					
More high then stars, more firme then flintie field.	. . . .	3	Lady of May	2	9
False in my selfe, thus have I lost the field.	. . . .	11	Arcadia I	2	8
A Lillie field, with plowe of Rose which tilled is..	. . . . .	15	1st Eclogues	7	30
So faire a fielde would well become an owner.	. . . .	17	1st Eclogues	7	99
In flowrie fielde; and as the day begins	. . . .	18	1st Eclogues	7	125
Despaire my fielde; the flowers spirits' warrs:.	. . . . . .	18	1st Eclogues	7	139
Feede on my sheepe, possesse your fruitefull fyeld,.	. . . .	43	Arcadia II	23	7
Leave of my sheepe, my sighes burne up your filde,	. . . . .	43	Arcadia II	24	7
Passion. No, Tyrant; no: mine, mine shall be the fielde.	. .	46	2nd Eclogues	27	2
This leades unto the joyous field,	. . . .	87	Arcadia III	62	61
Blith were the commons, cattell of the fielde,	. . . .	102	3rd Eclogues	66	132
For vaine equalitie is but contention's field.	. . . .	120	4th Eclogues	73	130
A field there is where, if a stake be prest.	. . . .	150	Cert Sonnets	22	41
But in Vert field Mars bare a golden speare,	. . . .	171	Astrophil	13	5
Where roses gueuls are borne in silver field..	. . . .	171	Astrophil	13	11
Ah bed, the field where joye's peace some do see,.	. . . . .	230	Astrophil	98	1
The field where all my thoughts to warre be traind,.	. . . .	230	Astrophil	98	2
Which seated is, in spotlesse honor's fielde,.	. . . .	345	Possibly	4	2
Therefore Love arm'd in hir now takes the fielde,.	. . . . .	245	Other Poems	4	145
Then in good Dog, faire field, or shading tree..	. . . . . .	246	Other Poems	4	179
Who seem'd orethrown was mistresse of the field:	. . . . . .	251	Other Poems	4	347
In flowry fielde a gladder eye to please:.	. . . .	256	Other Poems	5	3
Voyde of me in field to bee,	. . . .	262	Other Poems	7	20
FIELDS					
But this bad world, few golden fieldes doth bring,	. . . . .	104	3rd Eclogues	67	19
Which in the fertile fields be feeding,.	. . . .	279	Psalm VIII		28
FIEND					
Now make me thinke that there is not a fende,.	. . . .	254	Other Poems	4	463
FIERCE					
Since she faire fierce to such a state me calls,	. . . . . .	23	1st Eclogues	9	30
Of those fierce darts, dispaire at me doth throw:.	. . . . .	184	Astrophil	39	6
The ground of this fierce Love and lovely hate:.	. . . . . .	195	Astrophil	60	11
If Eagle fierce could so in Grecian Mayd delight,.	. . . . .	209	A&S 3rd Song		9
Like lions fierce, with roaring jawes enlarged..	. . . . . .	299	Psalm XXII		30
By aiding when fierce unicorns come neare me..	. . . .	299	Psalm XXII		50
All my fierce Foes reproach on mee did cast;	. . . .	313	Psalm XXXI		31
Thus proud and fierce unto the hearts he stept .	. . . . . .	246	Other Poems	4	157
Finding the gripe of Falcon fierce not furr:	. . . .	251	Other Poems	4	356
FIERCELY					
Fiercly affords.	. . . .	308	Psalm XXVII		59
FIERCENESS					
The Falcon's fercenes, Sparrow's letchery,	. . . .	28	1st Eclogues	10	79
Shall prove that fiercenes can with a white dove abide?.	. .	123	4th Eclogues	74	34
FIERCER					
Upon whose breast a fiercer Gripe doth tire.	. . . .	171	Astrophil	14	2
FIERCEST					
Stella fiercest shepherdesse,.	. . . .	221	A&S 9th Song		16
Fiercest but yet fairest ever;	. . . .	221	A&S 9th Song		17
FIERY					
Let not thy tonge become a firy matche,.	. . . .	29	1st Eclogues	10	89
But o happy be you, which safe from fyry reflection.	. . . .	31	1st Eclogues	13	11
Whose fyrie chaines, upon his freedome seaze,	. . . .	74	Arcadia III	41	4
Now each thing which enjoy'd that firie quickning sparke	. .	116	4th Eclogues	73	4
That heavie earth, not fierie sprites may plaine?.	. . . . .	142	Cert Sonnets	11	6
Then hayle, then firie coales, then thundred heavnly sire, .		291	Psalm XVIII		27
Thou as in fiery Ov'en shalt make.	. . . .	297	Psalm XXI		31
FIFTY					
These fiftie winters maried have I beene;.	. . . .	106	3rd Eclogues	67	86
FIG					
Figge that yeeldes most pleasante frute, his shaddow is					
hurtefull,	. . . .	35	1st Eclogues	13	125
FIGHT					
Them to defend, not with your selves to fight.	. . . .	26	1st Eclogues	10	3
R. Weakenes you are, dare you with our strength fight?	. . .	46	2nd Eclogues	27	21
He eft would kill a mouse, but he disdaines the fight,	. . .	53	2nd Eclogues	29	45
Let cat and dog fight which shall have both you.	. . . . . .	56	2nd Eclogues	29	149
Synce love with care, and hope with feare do fight..	. . . .	72	Arcadia III	37	18
Betwixt which two in me I have this fight,	. . . .	74	Arcadia III	43	7
In choller put, with whom he would not fight..	. . . .	96	3rd Eclogues	64	66
But thou wouldst needs fight both with love and sence,	. . .	170	Astrophil	10	9
One hand forgott to rule, th'other to fight.	. . . .	191	Astrophil	53	11
Best charge, and bravest retrait in Cupid's fight,	. . . . .	206	Astrophil	79	5
The lord whose strength makes battails fight..	. . . .	302	Psalm XXIV		20
Allarme allarme, when once the fight is warme,	. . . .	346	Possibly	5	13
Were now his darts leaving their wonted fight.	. . . .	246	Other Poems	4	148
FIGHTING					
Having got up a breach by fighting well,	. . . .	171	Astrophil	12	10
For why, my fighting strength by Thy strength strengthned					
was.	. . . .	292	Psalm XVIII		71
FIGHTS					
Oft cruell fights well pictured forth do please.	. . . . . .	181	Astrophil	34	4
Wo, having made with many fights his owne.	. . . .	193	Astrophil	57	1
FIGURE					
That aptest is to figure miserie,.	. . . .	125	4th Eclogues	75	11
While each conceate an ouglie figure beares,	. . . .	131	Arcadia V	77	7
Till that in words thy figure be exprest..	. . . .	189	Astrophil	50	4
On thoughts he feeds, his lookes their figure chaunge,	. . .	253	Other Poems	4	434
FIGURED					
Of which the two life-giving lights are figured in her eyes:		217	A&S 7th Song		16

FILL
                                                    PAGE   TITLE   LINE

	PAGE	TITLE		LINE
To fill the world with strange but vaine conceits:	20	1st Eclogues	8	2
His breast doth fill with earth of others' woe,	50	2nd Eclogues	28	85
Like players plast to fill a filthy stage,	57	2nd Eclogues	30	20
The bellie there gladde sight doth fill,	88	Arcadia III	62	77
Such mindes with sweet affections for to fill,	92	3rd Eclogues	63	61
With old true tales he woont mine eares to fill,	99	3rd Eclogues	66	33
By thy impe's losse to fill the world with wailing..	109	Arcadia IV	70	22
While that my voice doth fill these wofull vallies,	111	4th Eclogues	71	10
And fill the vales with cries in steed of musique.	111	4th Eclogues	71	24
O Echo, all these woods with roaring fill,	126	4th Eclogues	75	31
Evill happes do fill with hope, good happes appall	143	Cert Sonnets	12	10
To fill his hornes this yeare on Christian coast;	179	Astrophil	30	2
Whose bellyes so with daintys Thou dost fill	290	Psalm XVII		41
And so my cup dost fill.	301	Psalm XXIII		20
From age to age life joyes doth fill..	311	Psalm XXX		15
Thy mercy shall fill me with jollity,	312	Psalm XXXI		19
May learn their joyes to fill.	318	Psalm XXXIV		8
But fill their hearts with joy, who bend their wayes	332	Psalm XL		61
Go bawling curre, thy hungry maw go fill,	255	Other Poems	4	517
Be prest our reedes to fill,	260	Other Poems	6	9

FILLED
My Kala's giftes: who with all good gifts filled is.	15	1st Eclogues	7	26
Since so my harte is filled with that light,	39	Arcadia II	16	3
In divers kinds; yet as he were not filled,	62	2nd Eclogues	30	171
Youth, lucke, and praise, even fild my veines with pride..	191	Astrophil	53	4
So shall I with joy be filld,	309	Psalm XXVIII		29
Better filled with contenting,	264	Other Poems	7	77

FILLETH
Me thinkes, my sound no place with sorrow filleth.	127	4th Eclogues	75	99

FILLING
Measure my case, how by thy beautie's filling.	16	1st Eclogues	7	77
Filling his eies with teares, with sighs his brest..	253	Other Poems	4	432

FILLS
Of grain and wine fills stoaring place..	274	Psalm IV		30
God's goodness fills all lands,	316	Psalm XXXIII		21
Lord, how the heav'ns thy mercy fills,	323	Psalm XXXVI		13

FILTH
The sinke of filth, be counted huswifery:	93	3rd Eclogues	63	79
From filth of foreworne house, and quiet lives,	143	Cert Sonnets	12	5
All plung'd in stinking filth, not One well bent,	286	Psalm XIV		11

FILTHY
Like players plast to fill a filthy stage,	57	2nd Eclogues	30	20
Al filthy mouths that glory in their vice.	98	3rd Eclogues	65	12
In graunting such a scope to filthy fortune.	109	Arcadia IV	70	21
Klaius. Me seemes I see a filthie clowdie evening,	112	4th Eclogues	71	43
The filthy snake her aged coate can mende,	127	4th Eclogues	75	82
Rich fooles there be, whose base and filthy hart	176	Astrophil	24	1
Who sells not guiltlesse cause, for filthy love of gain:	287	Psalm XV		12
Bless'ed is the man whose filthy stain	314	Psalm XXXII		1
Of my filthy folly lai'd;	328	Psalm XXXVIII		15

FIND
Seeke other thoughts thy life or death to find;	4	Lady of May	2	15
(Therion) Thus wofully I in wo this salve do find,	5	Lady of May	3	17
For (woe is me) my powers all I finde.	11	Arcadia I	2	3
Nor be abasht, since such a guest you finde,	13	Arcadia I	4	3
We finde most sweete affection's snare,	14	1st Eclogues	6	3
Such as you see, such still you shall me finde..	18	1st Eclogues	7	122
I finde no shade, but where my Sunne doth burne:	18	1st Eclogues	7	144
Thy wit dost use still still more harmes to finde.	23	1st Eclogues	9	34
Such wandring reasons in thy speech I finde.	25	1st Eclogues	9	98
And we shall find more spottes then Leopard's skinne,	29	1st Eclogues	10	95
Here you fully do finde this strange operation of love,	31	1st Eclogues	13	3
But yet well I doo finde each man most wise in his owne case	33	1st Eclogues	13	70
Comfort into my soule. I do finde, I do find what a blessing	34	1st Eclogues	13	95
For that I finde in them parte of my estate represented...	35	1st Eclogues	13	115
And since in vaine I find were all my strife,	38	Arcadia II	14	13
Blots to the stone, shame to my selfe I finde:	40	Arcadia II	19	4
Thus children doo the silly birds they finde,	41	Arcadia II	20	11
But in the sandes my paynes foretolde I finde,	42	Arcadia II	21	15
Both still do worke, in neither finde I rest:	42	Arcadia II	22	3
The hart, eye, eare here onely find his treasure doth:	49	2nd Eclogues	28	58
But for to find thy words did her disgrace,	51	2nd Eclogues	28	106
Among us all we should find out some thing of nought..	51	2nd Eclogues	29	2
Despairde in all this flocke to find a knave, but thee..	52	2nd Eclogues	29	4
Thy gray-hood hides the thing, that thou despairst to find..	52	2nd Eclogues	29	6
What medecin may I finde for a paine that draw's me to death Death..	63	2nd Eclogues	31	6
Till my frayle barke his haven agayn do fynde.	70	Arcadia III	35	8
What stormes founde me, what tormentes I dyd fynde,	71	Arcadia III	36	15
But if thy rage some brave revenge will finde,	72	Arcadia III	38	13
Thus then my forme, and thus my state I finde,	73	Arcadia III	40	13
Of this wee live, in this wee finde our rest,	75	Arcadia III	44	7
Looke further then, so shalt thou finde at least,	75	Arcadia III	44	9
All what I am, still one, his owne, doe finde.	78	Arcadia III	50	10
All what you are still one, his owne to finde,	79	Arcadia III	50	11
That trusts in time, to finde the way aright	82	Arcadia III	56	3
Away vayne Cares, by which fewe men do finde	83	Arcadia III	59	3
No talke untaught can finde the way.	86	Arcadia III	62	34

FIND	(CONTINUED)	PAGE	TITLE		LINE
Whose gentle rayes suche Luster fynde, ...		89	Arcadia III	62	V115
But (for his jealous eye she well did finde)		95	3rd Eclogues	64	41
He did demaunde what remedy to finde;.		95	3rd Eclogues	64	52
And tell him that you finde I doo him love,.		95	3rd Eclogues	64	56
Then quickly did the meaner cattell finde, ...		102	3rd Eclogues	66	135
As for to finde a pasture strowed with golde,.		104	3rd Eclogues	67	14
But of such wives we finde a slender crew;		104	3rd Eclogues	67	25
As you paint them: but well in you I finde,.		106	3rd Eclogues	67	83
And yet finde no such faults in womankind.		106	3rd Eclogues	67	87
And thou shalt finde, in women vertues lie.		106	3rd Eclogues	67	102
Alas I doo; from which to finde release, ...		116	4th Eclogues	72	92
Then void of neerer cares, the depth of things to find.. . .		118	4th Eclogues	73	50
In whom of all my rules the perfect proofe I finde,.		119	4th Eclogues	73	94
O you (alas so I find) cause of his onely ruine.		122	4th Eclogues	74	4
Say, that I well shuld finde in what a care I was had? . . .		124	4th Eclogues	74	80
With much more: now what doo I finde, but Care to abhor me,.		124	4th Eclogues	74	81
Shall we now finde a guide of such affection,.		129	4th Eclogues	76	22
Since this we feele, greate losse we cannot finde.		131	Arcadia V	77	14
Since shunning paine, I ease can never find:		135	Cert Sonnets	1	1
Beleeve them not, for Phisicke true doth finde,.		147	Cert Sonnets	17	51
By your good helpe, or in my selfe to finde.		148	Cert Sonnets	19	12
Oft have I musde, but now at length I finde, ...		148	Cert Sonnets	20	1
Peake hath a Cave, whose narrow entries finde.		150	Cert Sonnets	22	31
Finde to what harme they hastned,.		154	Cert Sonnets	25	14
Till due desert she find..		160	Cert Sonnets	30	36
Not usde to frozen clips, he strave to find some part, . . .		168	Astrophil	8	6
Looks over the world, and can find nothing such, ...		169	Astrophil	9	10
For like a child that some faire booke doth find,.		170	Astrophil	11	5
And find th'effect, for I do burne in love..		177	Astrophil	25	14
I find how heav'nly day wretch I did misse..		181	Astrophil	33	4
My harmes on Ink's poore losse, perhaps some find.		182	Astrophil	34	13
And yet she heares, yet I no pitty find;		186	Astrophil	44	5
I much do guesse, yet find no truth save this, ...		187	Astrophil	44	9
And yet she heares, and yet no pitie I find;		186	Astrophil	44	V 5
While those poore babes their death in birth do find:. . . .		190	Astrophil	50	11
But find some Hercules to beare, in steed.		190	Astrophil	51	7
But you faire maides, at length this true shall find,. . . .		192	Astrophil	54	11
That I well find no eloquence like it.		192	Astrophil	55	14
Growne now his slaves, he forst them out to find		193	Astrophil	57	3
Hoping that when they might find Stella alone, ...		193	Astrophil	57	5
That no pace else their guided steps can find, ...		194	Astrophil	58	3
Sweet said that I true love in her should find..		196	Astrophil	62	4
For when, nak'd boy, thou couldst no harbour find.		198	Astrophil	65	5
There shall he find all vices' overthrow,.		201	Astrophil	71	5
Griefe find the words, for thou hast made my braine.		228	Astrophil	94	1
Forst by their Lord, who is asham'd to find.		231	Astrophil	99	13
Knowing worlds passe, ere she enough can find.		232	Astrophil	101	13
Better place no wit can find,.		210	A&S 4th Song		13
And such skill in my Muse you reconcil'd shall find, ...		215	A&S 5th Song		89
O if my self find not,.		226	A&S 10th Song		7
Deere when you find change in me,.		234	A&S 11th Song		8
And hidden beauties find,.		217	A&S 6th Song		52
That knowledg you may find..		271	Psalm II		24
By him because I did find in his eyes' sight grace,.		292	Psalm XVIII		41
Is not he blind that doth not find		294	Psalm XIX		17
You shall the life that ever liveth find..		300	Psalm XXII		64
Now I, now I my self forgotten find, ...		313	Psalm XXXI		34
No end shall find.		317	Psalm XXXIII		41
Even where I do most store of people find;		322	Psalm XXXV		47
Who shall in Thy house fatness find.		324	Psalm XXXVI		22
That Foxes leave to steale, because they finde they dy therefore.		344	Possibly	1	44
And in my woundes, my flames and bondes I fynde.		345	Possibly	2	13
How well apaid she was hir birde to finde:		244	Other Poems	4	92
That on his wings the leavell thou maist finde		259	Other Poems	5	107

FINDERS
| I curse the fidling finders out of Musicke:. . . . . | | 112 | 4th Eclogues | 71 | 51 |

FINDING
But finding th'approch of death with an inly relenting,. . .		123	4th Eclogues	74	25
Finding those beames, which I must ever love,.		149	Cert Sonnets	21	1
Finding that but wordes their love proved.		156	Cert Sonnets	27	12
But finding these North clymes do coldly him embrace,. . . .		168	Astrophil	8	5
But finding not those restlesse flames in me,.		173	Astrophil	16	5
So Stella's heart, finding what power Love brings,.		179	Astrophil	29	5
Kils his owne children, teares, finding that they.		229	Astrophil	95	10
And therfore finding force now faint to be,.		248	Other Poems	4	255
Finding the gripe of Falcon fierce not furr:		251	Other Poems	4	356
Till finding still his evill encreasing thus,.		253	Other Poems	4	437

FINDS
What if Laelaps a better morsell fyndes.		26	1st Eclogues	10	7
Nor envie's snaky ey, finds any harbor here, ...		69	2nd Eclogues	34	18
Now that he finds to what end his life and love be reserved,		123	4th Eclogues	74	29
And, lo, he finds that all astraying went, ...		286	Psalm XIV		10
In sprite afflicted finds.		320	Psalm XXXIV		68

FINE
With large encrease, and wooll of fine perfection, ...		49	2nd Eclogues	28	50
Fine eares, long taile he hath, with Lion's curbed clawe,. .		53	2nd Eclogues	29	33
A ruddie haire his cote, with fine long specled face:. . . .		53	2nd Eclogues	29	42
Nico. Who doubts but Pas' fine pipe againe will bring. . . .		53	2nd Eclogues	29	51

FINE	(CONTINUED)	PAGE	TITLE		LINE
She did the water wash, and make more fine..		55	2nd Eclogues	29	107
Her haire fine threeds of finest gould		85	Arcadia III	62	3
Shewes easie print in mettall fine..		89	Arcadia III	62	100
In fine he made her gesse, there was some sweet.		95	3rd Eclogues	64	35
In fine, since strife of thought but marres the mind,. . . .		135	Cert Sonnets	1	8
I would it not, their mettall is too fine, ...		146	Cert Sonnets	17	25
Studying inventions fine, her wits to entertaine:.		165	Astrophil	1	6
Or Pindare's Apes, flaunt they in phrases fine,.		166	Astrophil	3	3
Is no fit marke to pierce with his fine pointed dart:. . . .		168	Astrophil	8	3
Or at the most on some fine picture stayes,.		170	Astrophil	11	7
Beauties, which were of manie Carrets fine,.		172	Astrophil	16	2
Cloth'd with fine tropes, with strongest reasons lin'd,. . .		194	Astrophil	58	6
And grace, sicke too, such fine conclusions tries, ...		231	Astrophil	101	3
These sweet flowers on fine bed too, ...		210	A&S 4th Song		15
Thinke now no more to heare of warme fine odourd snow, . . .		213	A&S 5th Song		37
In fine deliver Israel,.		305	Psalm XXV		77
And in fine my soul be raysed, ...		335	Psalm XLII		55
With whose fine stepps all loves and joyes conspire.		250	Other Poems	4	302
Then this false, fine, Courtly pleasure.		263	Other Poems	7	48

FINELY
| With one good dawnce, or letter finely pend, ... | | 245 | Other Poems | 4 | 140 |

FINEST
| Griefe is the stone which finest judgement proves: . . . . . | | 58 | 2nd Eclogues | 30 | 35 |
| Her haire fine threeds of finest gould . . . . | | 85 | Arcadia III | 62 | 3 |

FINGER
| She with her finger writ:. . . . . | | 158 | Cert Sonnets | 28 | 36 |

FINGERS
| As for the fingers of the hand,. . . . . | | 90 | Arcadia III | 62 | 130 |
| Thy fingers Cupid's shafts, thy voyce the Angel's lay: . . . | | 212 | A&S 5th Song | | 11 |

FINISH
| Must finish then by death's detested crime.. . . . . | | 127 | 4th Eclogues | 75 | 90 |

FIR
| Firr trees great and greene, fixt on a hye hill but a barrein, ... | | 35 | 1st Eclogues | 13 | 123 |

FIRE
For water cold did never promise fire:		3	Lady of May	2	4
To aire of sighes, sighes to the harte's fire turne, ...		19	1st Eclogues	7	154
To swelling harts he shines in honour's fire:.		21	1st Eclogues	8	38
As well may thincke with oyle to coole the fire:		22	1st Eclogues	9	8
Earth, sea, ayre, fire, heav'n, hell, and gastly sprite. . .		23	1st Eclogues	9	40
For proofe of man, who sprong of heav'nly fire		25	1st Eclogues	9	100
Aire, we do still with sighes encrease; to the fire? we do want none.		32	1st Eclogues	13	30
Fire no liquor can coole: Neptune's seate would be dryd up there.		32	1st Eclogues	13	32
Save that dayly we may discerne what fire we do burne in.. .		33	1st Eclogues	13	53
Hardly remains fyer hid, where skill is bent to the hiding,.		33	1st Eclogues	13	59
Shall such morning deaws be an ease to the heate of a love's fire?		34	1st Eclogues	13	88
Sweete Juniper saith this, thoh I burne, yet I burne in a sweete fire.		35	1st Eclogues	13	120
For bellowes serve to kindle more the fire..		38	Arcadia II	14	8
Old wood inflam'de, doth yeeld the bravest fire, ...		38	Arcadia II	15	3
Burnt in my selfe, I muse at others' fire:		41	Arcadia II	20	5
What hope to quench, where each thing blowes the fire? . . .		42	Arcadia II	21	18
Till with lickt beard, his eye of fire espie his foes.. . .		53	2nd Eclogues	29	36
Plangus. And shall shee dye? shall cruell fier spill		59	2nd Eclogues	30	83
Those beames that set so many harts on fire?		59	2nd Eclogues	30	84
My greedy soule, with gripe of inward fire:.		80	Arcadia III	53	6
Mine owne, embraced, sought, knot, fire, desease..		84	Arcadia III	60	14
Fuell to seeke and not to quench the fire:		95	3rd Eclogues	64	40
But since you will, part of my heav'nly fire		100	3rd Eclogues	66	75
Man oft is plag'de with aire, is burnt with fire,.		105	3rd Eclogues	67	67
Strephon. I wish to fire the trees of all these forrests;. .		112	4th Eclogues	71	49
My fire is more, then can be made with forrests;		112	4th Eclogues	71	56
Those lampes of heav'nly fire to fixed motion bound, ...		118	4th Eclogues	73	43
"Yet thou shalt not go free (quoth Venus) such a fire. . . .		121	4th Eclogues	73	170
Right so my boiling hart, enflam'de with fire of a faire eye		123	4th Eclogues	74	27
The fire to see my wrongs for anger burneth:		136	Cert Sonnets	3	1
Fire burne me quite, till sense of burning leave me:		136	Cert Sonnets	3	13
Fire, aire, sea, earth, fame, time, place, shew your power..		136	Cert Sonnets	3	20
Paine heard her praise, and full of inward fire, ...		141	Cert Sonnets	9	9
Who burnt his lips to kisse faire shining fire..		145	Cert Sonnets	16	14
Yet I shall die in Phoenix fire.		153	Cert Sonnets	24	27
When with a fire he first met.		154	Cert Sonnets	25	17
Although with cruell fire, ...		155	Cert Sonnets	26	2
Above line repeated at following locations		155	Cert Sonnets	26	13
. . . .		156	Cert Sonnets	26	24
In vaine thou kindlest all thy smokie fire;.		161	Cert Sonnets	31	11
Then did on him who first stale downe the fire, ...		171	Astrophil	14	3
To warme with ill-made fire cold Moscovy;.		180	Astrophil	30	4
Till without fewell you can make hot fire.		188	Astrophil	46	14
And then with patience bid me beare my fire.		193	Astrophil	56	14
Seeking to quench in me the noble fire, ...		200	Astrophil	68	7
While each doth blow the fier of my hart;.		202	Astrophil	72	4
Nature's praise, Vertue's stall, Cupid's cold fire, ...		206	Astrophil	80	3
Stella starre of heavenly fier,.		218	A&S 8th Song		31
And bravely speake to them, with breath of wrathful fire,. .		271	Psalm II		11

```
FIRE                    (CONTINUED)                        PAGE    TITLE           LINE
    When fire seven times hath spent his earthly parts.. . . . .  285 Psalm XII          21
    Then spake he his lowd voyce, then hailestones coales and
        fire.. . . . . . . . . . . . . . . . . . . . . . . . . .  291 Psalm XVIII        28
    Let fyre for tryall burn,. . . . . . . . . . . . . . . . . .  296 Psalm XX           13
    Yea fire from himself sent,. . . . . . . . . . . . . . . . .  296 Psalm XX           14
    And flames of never quenched fire. . . . . . . . . . . . . .  297 Psalm XXI          35
    The fire took fire and forcibly out brake,. . . . . . . . .  329 Psalm XXXIX        11
    So brave a shott, deere fyre and bewtye strange. . . . . . .  345 Possibly        2  11
    A fire, to burne the prisoners he gaines,. . . . . . . . . .  246 Other Poems     4 154
    For ev'n in forge colde water fire maintaines. . . . . . . .  246 Other Poems     4 156
    The aire hir swete race mov'd doth blow the fire.. . . . . .  249 Other Poems     4 300
    Who nothing earthly, but of fire and aire, . . . . . . . . .  250 Other Poems     4 338
    Did not conceive what fire he had within.. . . . . . . . . .  253 Other Poems     4 428
FIREBRANDS
    To my close heart, where while some firebrands he did lay, .  169 Astrophil       8  13
FIRED
    The ancient oke well makes a fired blocke: . . . . . . . . .   25 1st Eclogues    9  87
FIRE'S
    When sorrow (using mine own fier's might). . . . . . . . . .  236 Astrophil     108   1
FIRES
    Wyth two strange fires of equall heate possest,. . . . . . .   42 Arcadia II     22   1
    These fires increase: in these I dayly burne:. . . . . . . .   42 Arcadia II     22   8
    The fuell small: how be the fires so great?. . . . . . . . .   42 Arcadia II     22  14
    Employ thy might, that she my fires may taste. . . . . . . .   72 Arcadia III    38  15
    What kind of fires they be in which those spirits melt,. . .  153 Cert Sonnets   24   7
    Of living deaths, deare wounds, faire stormes and freesing
        fires: . . . . . . . . . . . . . . . . . . . . . . . . .  167 Astrophil       6   4
FIRM
    More high then stars, more firme then flintie field. . . . .    3 Lady of May     2   9
    In a ground of so firme making,. . . . . . . . . . . . . . .  234 A&S 11th Song     34
    A lesson fit, both sight and skill, love and firme love to
        breede,. . . . . . . . . . . . . . . . . . . . . . . . .  217 A&S 7th Song      12
    Firm on his way, his way God loveth, . . . . . . . . . . . .  326 Psalm XXXVII      58
FIRMAMENT
    The firmament, so strangely bent,. . . . . . . . . . . . . .  293 Psalm XIX          3
FIRMEST
    In firmest band of Unitie. . . . . . . . . . . . . . . . . .  260 Other Poems     6  22
FIRMLY
    Since they do weare his badge, most firmely prove. . . . . .  190 Astrophil      52   4
    Thy reasons firmly set on Vertue's feet, . . . . . . . . . .  200 Astrophil      68  11
    Farr farr more sure, than walls most firmly fast.. . . . . .  313 Psalm XXXI         60
FIRST
    When first he spied my love? how oft he said to me,. . . . .   16 1st Eclogues    7  50
    First thinke they erre, that thinke them gayly wise, . . . .   25 1st Eclogues    9 111
    Hate of the firste, contempt of later feate: . . . . . . . .   27 1st Eclogues   10  39
    Their first caught sence prefers to teacher's blowes.. . . .   28 1st Eclogues   10  57
    Cleofila. First shall fertill grounds not yeeld increase of
        a good seed: . . . . . . . . . . . . . . . . . . . . . .   33 1st Eclogues   13  64
    First the rivers shall ceasse to repay their fludds to the
        Occean: . . . . . . . . . . . . . . . . . . . . . . . . .  33 1st Eclogues   13  65
    First may a trusty Greyhounde transforme himselfe to a
        Tigre . . . . . . . . . . . . . . . . . . . . . . . . . .  33 1st Eclogues   13  66
    First shall vertue be vice, and bewty be counted a blemishe,   33 1st Eclogues   13  67
    First let them die, then passe the starres,. . . . . . . . .   44 Arcadia II     25   9
    Raging in woes first pastors tought to plaine? . . . . . . .   53 2nd Eclogues   29  58
    Then earste I knewe: But first dyd playne. . . . . . . . . .   57 2nd Eclogues   30   3
    Ah where was first that cruell cunning found,. . . . . . . .   57 2nd Eclogues   30  11
    With cries first borne, the pressage of his life,. . . . . .   57 2nd Eclogues   30  24
    Let Death first dye; be thou his worthy let. . . . . . . . .   59 2nd Eclogues   30  94
    Burnt by the Sunne, she first must build her nest. . . . . .   60 2nd Eclogues   30 103
    What causes first made these torments on me to light? Light.   64 2nd Eclogues   31  23
    Eysight made me to yeelde, but what first pierst to myne
        eies? Eies.. . . . . . . . . . . . . . . . . . . . . . .   64 2nd Eclogues   31  26
    But when I first did fal, what brought most fall to my hart?
        Arte. . . . . . . . . . . . . . . . . . . . . . . . . . .  64 2nd Eclogues   31  28
    Which at firste voly gave too open entry,. . . . . . . . . .   68 2nd Eclogues   33  14
    First fower but say, next fowr their saying seale, . . . . .   76 Arcadia III    46  17
    My thoughtes then hers, who first your ryne did rente, . . .   78 Arcadia III    49  14
    First, second, last, did binde, enforce, and arme, . . . . .   84 Arcadia III    60   3
    Of my first love the fatall band.. . . . . . . . . . . . . .   90 Arcadia III    62 122
    Let one time (but long first) close up their daies,. . . . .   92 3rd Eclogues   63  31
    She seald it first, then she the sealing brake,. . . . . . .   96 3rd Eclogues   64  83
    First be he true, for truth doth truth deserve:. . . . . . .   98 3rd Eclogues   65   2
    Who at the first, wanting, or hiding pride,. . . . . . . . .  101 3rd Eclogues   66 107
    Yet first but wooll, or fethers off he teard:. . . . . . . .  102 3rd Eclogues   66 143
    When first that crowned Basiliske I knewe, . . . . . . . . .  115 4th Eclogues   72  72
    They first their use forgot, then fancies lost their force;.  117 4th Eclogues   73  29
    The first with cloth's tuckt up as Nymphes in woods do
        range ,. . . . . . . . . . . . . . . . . . . . . . . . .  118 4th Eclogues   73  66
    But walking forth, the first thus to the second saide, . . .  118 4th Eclogues   73  77
    Your presence (sister deare) first to my Moony spheare,. . .  119 4th Eclogues   73 103
    I that was first agast, when first I saw their showe:. . . .  121 4th Eclogues   73 158
    First having all their giftes upon faire Mira spred. . . . .  121 4th Eclogues   73 178
    That I things erst unseene should first in dreaming see? . .  121 4th Eclogues   73 182
    First let Cimmerian darknes be my onel'habitaco'n: . . . . .  124 4th Eclogues   74  59
    First be mine eyes pulde out, first be my braine perished;.  124 4th Eclogues   74  60
    (First sealing up my heart as pray of his) . . . . . . . . .  141 Cert Sonnets    9  10
    When with a fire he first met. . . . . . . . . . . . . . . .  154 Cert Sonnets   25  17
    First throwne on my desire,. . . . . . . . . . . . . . . . .  155 Cert Sonnets   26   3

                                   161
```

```
FIRST                 (CONTINUED)                      PAGE   TITLE           LINE
     Above line repeated at following locations . . . . . . . . .  155 Cert Sonnets 26    14
     . . . . . . . . . . . . . . . . . . . . . . . . . . . . . .  156 Cert Sonnets 26    25
Not at first sight, nor with a dribbed shot. . . . . . . . .       165 Astrophil     2     1
The first, thus matcht, were scarcely Gentlemen. . . . . . .       171 Astrophil    13    14
Then did on him who first stale downe the fire,. . . . . . .       171 Astrophil    14     3
To keepe the pace of their first loving state. . . . . . . .       173 Astrophil    17     4
The first that straight my fancie's error brings . . . . . .       183 Astrophil    38     5
Edward named fourth, as first in praise I name,. . . . . . .       204 Astrophil    75     2
Poore hope's first wealth, ostage of promist weale,. . . . .       206 Astrophil    79    12
Seeing hope yeeld when this wo strake him furst: . . . . . .       228 Astrophil    95     6
First did with puffing kisse those lockes display: . . . . .       233 Astrophil   103    11
They first resort unto that soveraigne part; . . . . . . . .       236 Astrophil   107     4
Who will read must first learne spelling.. . . . . . . . . .       203 A&S 2nd Song       24
Write, but first let me endite:. . . . . . . . . . . . . . .       211 A&S 4th Song       40
Write, but let me first endite:. . . . . . . . . . . . . . .       211 A&S 4th Song    V  40
Lo he that first conceiv'd a wretched thought, . . . . . . .       278 Psalm VII          37
But in the pitt he ruind first did fall, . . . . . . . . . .       278 Psalm VII          41
Thou first prepare'dst their mind. . . . . . . . . . . . . .       283 Psalm X            75
Yeelde yeelde O yeelde, who first this Port did make,. . . .       345 Possibly      4     9
To Strephon Aeole's land first breathing lent: . . . . . . .       242 Other Poems   4    26
When mery May first early calls the morne, . . . . . . . . .       243 Other Poems   4    49
Who then in Lion's cave did enter fyrst, . . . . . . . . . .       247 Other Poems   4   206
And crown'd the earth with his first touching crowne:. . . .       248 Other Poems   4   260
To fasten knotts, which fancy first had bound. . . . . . . .       253 Other Poems   4   424
First killing mirth, then banishing all rest,. . . . . . . .       253 Other Poems   4   431
With that (yet kissed first) his pipe he burst.. . . . . . .       255 Other Poems   4   520
And first Lambe that shall befall, . . . . . . . . . . . . .       264 Other Poems   7    69
FISH
And try with bayt how fish will bite sometime. . . . . . . .        26 1st Eclogues  9   128
As fishe sure tryall hath of muddy slyme.. . . . . . . . . .        28 1st Eclogues 10    54
I sought to catch the fish Torpedo faire.. . . . . . . . . .       115 4th Eclogues 72    63
We have a fish, by strangers much admirde, . . . . . . . . .       150 Cert Sonnets 22    21
A stranger fish, my selfe not yet expirde, . . . . . . . . .       150 Cert Sonnets 22    25
The Fish of Sea the Native heire,. . . . . . . . . . . . . .       279 Psalm VIII         30
FISHERS
Of cunningst fishers in most troubled streames,. . . . . . .       190 Astrophil    51    10
FIST
Up with hir fist, and tooke him on the face, . . . . . . . .       249 Other Poems   4   274
*FIT
"Thou art no souldier fitte for Cupid's garrison.. . . . . .        16 1st Eclogues  7    51
A baite most fit, for hungrie minded guest.. . . . . . . . .        75 Arcadia III  44    10
But now the fitt is past: and time hath giv'ne . . . . . . .        83 Arcadia III  57     9
A hill most fitte for such a master, . . . . . . . . . . . .        88 Arcadia III  62    79
Those thighes, for Ovid's song more fitte; . . . . . . . . .        88 Arcadia III  62    88
Or with her beawtie fit to make a pray,. . . . . . . . . . .        94 3rd Eclogues 64     8
They fit for heavenly places,. . . . . . . . . . . . . . . .       152 Cert Sonnets 23    23
I sought fit words to paint the blackest face of woe,. . . .       165 Astrophil     1     5
Churches or schooles are for thy seate more fit: . . . . . .       166 Astrophil     4     6
Is no fit marke to pierce with his fine pointed dart:. . . .       168 Astrophil     8     3
The thorowest words, fit for woe's selfe to grone, . . . . .       193 Astrophil    57     4
Frcm nobler course, fit for my birth and mind: . . . . . . .       196 Astrophil    62     8
With voice more fit to wed Amphion's lyre, . . . . . . . . .       200 Astrophil    68     6
O blisse, fit for a nobler state then me:. . . . . . . . . .       200 Astrophil    69     2
Not pointing to fit folkes each undercharge, . . . . . . . .       210 Astrophil    85     6
Fit to heare and ease my care: . . . . . . . . . . . . . . .       210 A&S 4th Song        2
Fit oratours to make . . . . . . . . . . . . . . . . . . . .       215 A&S 6th Song        9
A lesson fit, both sight and skill, love and firme love to
     breede,. . . . . . . . . . . . . . . . . . . . . . . .        217 A&S 7th Song       12
"Never season was more fit,. . . . . . . . . . . . . . . . .       219 A&S 8th Song       53
In time most fitt for Thee . . . . . . . . . . . . . . . . .       281 Psalm X             3
In fitt time make to Thee his moane, . . . . . . . . . . . .       315 Psalm XXXII        20
FITLY
Which little time did fitlie bring to passe. . . . . . . . .        96 3rd Eclogues 64    76
FITS
Now fancie's fits, now fortune's balefull stowers: . . . . .       103 3rd Eclogues 66   157
How ill fits you this greene to weare, . . . . . . . . . . .       157 Cert Sonnets 28     3
What fitts me now but teares, and sighings sadd? . . . . . .       259 Other Poems   5    97
FITTER
Pas. Kisse her? now mayst thou kisse. I have a fitter match;        53 2nd Eclogues 29    39
Sc Tyran he no fitter place could spie,. . . . . . . . . . .       175 Astrophil    20     5
FITTEST
Which must frame contempt to the fittest purchase of
     honnour  . . . . . . . . . . . . . . . . . . . . . . .         32 1st Eclogues 13    38
FITTETH
Concord better fitteth us: . . . . . . . . . . . . . . . . .       211 A&S 4th Song       44
FITTING
What in art of Love is fitting.. . . . . . . . . . . . . . .       262 Other Poems   7    30
FIX
Fix We our mind, . . . . . . . . . . . . . . . . . . . . . .       318 Psalm XXXIII       77
FIXED
Firr trees great and greene, fixt on a hye hill but a
     barrein,. . . . . . . . . . . . . . . . . . . . . . . .        35 1st Eclogues 13   123
Yet be my hopes thus plast, here fixed lives my recomforte,.        37 1st Eclogues 13   164
That in your sight they fixed have my braine;. . . . . . . .        39 Arcadia II   16     2
Our studies fixt upon the falles of fortune. . . . . . . . .       109 Arcadia IV   70    30
Those lampes of heav'nly fire to fixed motion bound, . . . .       118 4th Eclogues 73    43
If that be sinne which in fixt hearts doth breed . . . . . .       172 Astrophil    14    12
For all my hope fixt upon God doth ly. . . . . . . . . . . .       312 Psalm XXXI         18
```

```
                                                        PAGE    TITLE          LINE
FLAME
   Even as the flye, which to the flame doth goe, . . . . . . .  149 Cert Sonnets 21    11
   For so faire a flame embraces. . . . . . . . . . . . . . .   155 Cert Sonnets 26     5
FLAMES
   But in a minde that would his flames should not be
     repressed  . . . . . . . . . . . . . . . . . . . . . . .    33 1st Eclogues 13    60
   Will at length perceave these flames by her beames to be
     kindled, . . . . . . . . . . . . . . . . . . . . . . .      37 1st Eclogues 13   167
   Their flames mount up, my powers prostrate lie:. . . . . . .  42 Arcadia II    22    11
   To let that witolde beast consume in flames. . . . . . . .    60 2nd Eclogues 30   111
   Breath made of flames, wits knowing nought but damage, . . . 109 Arcadia IV    70    28
   Yet still her eyes give to my flames their fuell.. . . . . . 136 Cert Sonnets  3    12
   For if those flames burne my desire, . . . . . . . . . . .   153 Cert Sonnets 24    26
   That her sweete breath makes oft thy flames to rise, . . . . 170 Astrophil    12     4
   But finding not those restlesse flames in me,. . . . . . .   173 Astrophil    16     5
   Strange flames of Love it in our soules would raise; . . . . 177 Astrophil    25     4
   Breathe out the flames which burne within my heart,. . . . . 179 Astrophil    28    13
   What Nestor's counsell can my flames alay, . . . . . . . .   182 Astrophil    35     5
   I feele the flames of hottest sommer day.. . . . . . . . . . 224 Astrophil    89    14
   Flames issued from his mouth, and burning coales out went; . 291 Psalm XVIII        19
   And flames of never quenched fire. . . . . . . . . . . . .   297 Psalm XXI          35
   Whose heart with these huge flames, like wax o're heated,. . 299 Psalm XXII         33
   His voice doth flashing flames divide, . . . . . . . . . .   310 Psalm XXIX         19
   And in my woundes, my flames and bondes I fynde. . . . . . . 345 Possibly      2    13
FLAMY
   With flamie breathe doo issue oft in sound:. . . . . . . .    42 Arcadia II    21     8
   Her flamie glistring lights increase with time and place;. . 205 Astrophil    76    10
FLANKED
   Which flanked with two sugred flankes, . . . . . . . . . .    88 Arcadia III   62    89
FLANKS
   Which flanked with two sugred flankes, . . . . . . . . . .    88 Arcadia III   62    89
FLASHING
   His voice doth flashing flames divide, . . . . . . . . . .   310 Psalm XXIX         19
FLAT
   Puiling, and whimpring, or else scolding flat, . . . . . .   104 3rd Eclogues 67    29
FLATTER
   Hope, art thou true, or doest thou flatter me? . . . . . .   199 Astrophil    67     1
   When we doe but flatter men: . . . . . . . . . . . . . . .   263 Other Poems   7    34
FLATTERER
   Only of you the flatterer never lieth. . . . . . . . . . .   197 A&S 1st Song       28
FLATTERERS
   For those same eyes his flatterers be. . . . . . . . . . .   323 Psalm XXXVI         7
FLATTERERS'
   Nor flatterers' venomous insinuations, . . . . . . . . . .    69 2nd Eclogues 34    19
FLATTERING
   Creeping to ech with flattering of desire. . . . . . . . .    22 1st Eclogues  8    40
   False flattering hope, that with so faire a face,. . . . . . 235 Astrophil   106     2
   Wherto their tongue is flattring Instrument. . . . . . . .   275 Psalm V            28
FLATTERY
   The peacocke's pride, the pye's pild flatterye,. . . . . .    28 1st Eclogues 10    77
   Slander wants a pretext, flattery gone beyond: . . . . . .    69 2nd Eclogues 34    38
   The Foxe gave crafte; the Dog gave flatterie:. . . . . . .   101 3rd Eclogues 66    85
   Where truth it selfe must speake like flatterie? . . . . .   182 Astrophil    35     2
   Loathing all lies, doubting this Flatterie is: . . . . . .   207 Astrophil    80    11
   Their abject lips no breath but flattery move. . . . . . .   284 Psalm XII           5
FLAUNT
   Or Pindare's Apes, flaunt they in phrases fine,. . . . . .   166 Astrophil     3     3
FLEA
   Leaping at every flie, and angrie with a flea: . . . . . .    53 2nd Eclogues 29    44
FLED
   But straight they fledde, summond by cruell honor, . . . .    17 1st Eclogues  7    95
   Be fled as things most vaine,. . . . . . . . . . . . . . .    93 3rd Eclogues 63    71
   And with that cursed curse away to heaven they fled, . . . . 121 4th Eclogues 73   177
   Now fled, then cherished? then so nie, now so remote?. . . . 124 4th Eclogues 74    78
   Fearing and feared thus from himselfe he fled, . . . . . .   145 Cert Sonnets 16     3
   Invention, Nature's child, fled step-dame Studie's blowes, . 165 Astrophil     1    10
   Love borne in Greece, of late fled from his native place,. . 168 Astrophil     8     1
   They fled with blush, which guiltie seem'd of love.. . . . . 199 Astrophil    66    14
   That in the streets from sight of me they fled.. . . . . . . 313 Psalm XXXI         33
   Thus, fast he fled from her he follow'd sore,. . . . . . .   250 Other Poems   4   305
   She fled, and tooke: he folow'd, and was cought. . . . . .   251 Other Poems   4   348
FLEE
   Trying high seas, nor while Sea rage you flee, . . . . . .   142 Cert Sonnets 12     2
   Now will I away hence flee:. . . . . . . . . . . . . . . .   203 A&S 2nd Song       27
   Unto Dianae's train thou runaway didst flee: . . . . . . .   214 A&S 5th Song       71
   That they to Thee in troublous tyme may flee:. . . . . . .   280 Psalm IX           27
   He hopes, with dainty turns she doth him flee. . . . . . .   251 Other Poems   4   341
FLEER
   Let them not fleere, who me would causless stroy,. . . . .   322 Psalm XXXV         50
FLEET
   In sum, proud Boreas never ruled fleet . . . . . . . . . .   251 Other Poems   4   373
FLESH
   Or wrapt in flesh what do they here obtaine, . . . . . . .    57 2nd Eclogues 30    15
   Death wrapt in flesh, to living grave assign'd.. . . . . .    73 Arcadia III   40    14
   And thou deare flesh, as soft as wooll new drest,. . . . .    76 Arcadia III   46    15
   But there againe the flesh doth rise . . . . . . . . . . .    89 Arcadia III   62   101
   For hungrie throte their flesh with teeth he brused: . . . . 102 3rd Eclogues 66   145
   That shrines in flesh so true a Deitie,. . . . . . . . . .   167 Astrophil     4    13
   Her flesh his food, her skin his armour brave, . . . . . .   179 Astrophil    29    12
   The foolish man by flesh and fancy led . . . . . . . . . .   286 Psalm XIV           1
```

FLESH	(CONTINUED)	PAGE	TITLE	LINE
Yea my flesh in hope shall rest.		288	Psalm XVI	30
My very flesh for to devoure,.		307	Psalm XXVII	10
To the pitt where flesh doth end..		308	Psalm XXVIII	5
My flesh hath, ...		327	Psalm XXXVIII	8

FLESHLY

Fleshly vaile consumes; but a soule hath his life, ...		31	1st Eclogues 12	22
Flew up with freer wings of fleshly bondage free;.		117	4th Eclogues 73	33
Not weighing ought how fleshly fancys run, ...		289	Psalm XVII	13

FLEW

Flew up with freer wings of fleshly bondage free;.		117	4th Eclogues 73	33
See now those feathers pluckt, wherewith thou flew most high		213	A&S 5th Song	V 22
She chirping ran, he peeping flew away,.		244	Other Poems 4	87

FLEWST

See now those feathers pluckt, wherewith thou flewst most high:.		213	A&S 5th Song	22

FLICKERING

And hopes the flickring winde with net to holde, ...		24	1st Eclogues 9	54

FLIES

Is he a God, that ever flies the light?.		21	1st Eclogues 8	7
Before all flies the Waspe accept I would.		104	3rd Eclogues 67	18
He flies to her, and boldned with desire,.		141	Cert Sonnets 9	11
But of his death flies up a purest love, ...		151	Cert Sonnets 22	59
They deeme, and of their doome the rumour flies, ...		178	Astrophil 27	5
Was held, in opend sense it flies away,.		184	Astrophil 38	10
My Orphan sence flies to the inward sight, ...		223	Astrophil 88	10

FLIETH

Whose spirit falshood flyeth..		314	Psalm XXXII	6

FLIGHT

Wher who so wynns, I put my selfe to flight.		74	Arcadia III 42	8
Be hence aye put to flight,.		93	3rd Eclogues 63	68
But ah her flight hath my dead reliques spent.		115	4th Eclogues 72	80
Strephon. But ah her flight hath my dead reliques spent, . .		115	4th Eclogues 72	81
Her flight from me, from me, though dead to me,.		115	4th Eclogues 72	82
But she most faire, most cold, made him thence take his flight		169	Astrophil 8	12
To beare his sacred flight, in secret place then clos'd, . .		291	Psalm XVIII	23
But let their flight be dark and slippery;		321	Psalm XXXV	14

FLINTY

More high then stars, more firme then flintie field.		3	Lady of May 2	9
Thy stars be fal'n, plowed is thy flintie ground:.		4	Lady of May 2	16

FLOATING

When worthlesse corke, aloft doth floting lye.		81	Arcadia III 54	14

FLOCK

Among his flocke so sweete a treasure keepe.		4	Lady of May 2	18
The oldest Rammes are culled from the flocke:.		24	1st Eclogues 9	85
Let speciall care upon thy flock be staid, ...		26	1st Eclogues 9	133
I set you ore the flock I dearly love, ...		26	1st Eclogues 10	2
Despairde in all this flocke to find a knave, but thee.. . .		52	2nd Eclogues 29	4
As I my little flocke on Ister banke		98	3rd Eclogues 66	1
(A little flocke; but well my pipe they couthe).		98	3rd Eclogues 66	2
Spoiling their flock, or while twixt them they strive. . . .		99	3rd Eclogues 66	35
Go my flocke, go get you hence,.		221	A&S 9th Song	1
Merry flocke, such one forgo,.		221	A&S 9th Song	8
Then adieu, deere flocke adieu:.		222	A&S 9th Song	46
And fare-welling the flocke did homeward wend, ...		252	Other Poems 4	415
One day he with his flock abroad did raunge:		253	Other Poems 4	438
Amid my flock with woe my voice I teare, ...		254	Other Poems 4	459
And, but bewitch'd, who to his flock would mone?		254	Other Poems 4	460
And you my flock, care of my carefull sight, ...		254	Other Poems 4	483
On yond foule flocke belonging not to me."		255	Other Poems 4	518
With that his dogge he henc'd, his flocke he curst:.		255	Other Poems 4	519

FLOCKING

With mowes and nodds they stand about me flocking.		299	Psalm XXII	18
Still both their flocks flocking togither went,.		242	Other Poems 4	30

FLOCKS

So may thy flockes encrease, thy deere hart glad,.		96	3rd Eclogues 64	93
Still both their flocks flocking togither went,.		242	Other Poems 4	30
How elder rul'd their flocks, and cur'd their smart, ...		243	Other Poems 4	37
Give leave your flockes to range, ...		261	Other Poems 6	31
Your flockes will not be straying.		261	Other Poems 6	34

FLOODS

First the rivers shall ceasse to repay their fludds to the Occean:.		33	1st Eclogues 13	65
The floods of wickedness on me did horrors throw,.		291	Psalm XVIII	9
Through him the floods to their beds fell.		302	Psalm XXIV	4
Of furious floods he holds the reines, ...		310	Psalm XXIX	26
Sure, sure the Floods of straying streames		315	Psalm XXXII	22
All Thy floods on me abounded, ...		335	Psalm XLII	33

FLOUREDELUCE

Nor that he made the Flouredeluce so fraid,.		204	Astrophil 75	9

FLOURISH

Wherein do only flowrish		66	2nd Eclogues 32	32
O Histor, seeke within thy selfe to flourish:.		106	3rd Eclogues 67	109
And getting youth againe, in youth doth flourish:.		127	4th Eclogues 75	83
Onelie through you the tree of life doth flourish.		197	A&S 1st Song	20
Never doth thy beauty florish.		234	A&S 11th Song	29
Nor withered leafe shall make yt faile to flourish..		270	Psalm I	10
That they in riches flourish do.		290	Psalm XVII	43

				PAGE	TITLE		LINE
FLOURISH	(CONTINUED)						
That wicked men do seeme to flourish,.				324	Psalm XXXVII		2
The more his seed in blessing flourish;.				326	Psalm XXXVII		66
FLOW							
Shall I that saw those brests, where beauties flow,. . . .				58	2nd Eclogues	30	47
Like those sicke folkes, in whome strange humors flowe,. . .				74	Arcadia III	41	1
Whence never word in vaine did flowe..				87	Arcadia III	62	45
Since from these good the others' good doth flowe, ...				92	3rd Eclogues	63	40
Whence our immortall soules to mortall earth doo flowe:. . .				118	4th Eclogues	73	46
Tc so lowe ebbe that wonted were to flowe.				146	Cert Sonnets	17	15
And in my braine some sacred humour flowe:				146	Cert Sonnets	17	38
Oft turning others' leaves, to see if thence would flow. . .				165	Astrophil	1	7
She even in blacke doth make all beauties flow?.				168	Astrophil	7	11
Lies hatching still the goods wherein they flow:.				176	Astrophil	24	2
That, from that sea deriv'd, teares' spring did flow.. . . .				187	Astrophil	45	8
What Oceans of delight in me do flow..				200	Astrophil	69	4
My thoughts I speake, and what I speake doth flow.				204	Astrophil	74	10
For nothing from my wit or will doth flow,.				224	Astrophil	90	12
Whose pants do make unspilling creame to flow,.				231	Astrophil	100	6
World without end, let still his blessing flow;.				334	Psalm XLI		47
For warbling notes from inward chearing flow.				242	Other Poems	4	4
FLOWED							
Thy force hath flow'd from Babie's tongue.				278	Psalm VIII		6
FLOWER							
That I am like a flower.				19	1st Eclogues	7	158
Eache flower eache herbe dothe to your service yeeld,. . . .				43	Arcadia II	23	5
The world the garden is, she is the flower.				59	2nd Eclogues	30	98
Nowe that some flower of fruict, my paynes do prove, ...				72	Arcadia III	37	16
But like the feeble flower (whose stalke cannot sustaine . .				117	4th Eclogues	73	21
Unto the flowre that ay turnes,.				154	Cert Sonnets	25	25
And everie floure, not sweet perhaps, which growes				172	Astrophil	15	3
Cals each wight to salute the floure of blisse;.				231	Astrophil	99	11
And wither like green herb or flower;.				324	Psalm XXXVII		6
FLOWERS							
Despaire my fielde; the flowers spirits' warrs:.				18	1st Eclogues	7	139
Your sweetest flowers, your herbes, no service yeeld,. . . .				43	Arcadia II	24	5
To whether with best cause the Nymphes faire flowers							
affoord				52	2nd Eclogues	29	28
Like divers flowers, whose divers beauties serve				78	Arcadia III	50	1
Let mother earth now decke her selfe in flowers, ...				91	3rd Eclogues	63	1
The earth is deckt with flowers, the heav'ns displaid, . . .				93	3rd Eclogues	63	91
When I doo smell the flowers of these vallies:				112	4th Eclogues	71	46
And you, o flowers, which sometimes Princes were,.				125	4th Eclogues	75	25
Enam'ling with pied flowers their thoughts of gold:. . . .				166	Astrophil	3	4
With choisest flowers my speech to engarland so;				192	Astrophil	55	2
These sweet flowers on fine bed too, ...				210	A&S 4th Song		15
New perfumed with flowers fresh growing, ...				217	A&S 8th Song		4
While in pride flowers be preserved, ...				222	A&S 9th Song		29
As on sweet flowrs when morning's drops we see..				252	Other Poems	4	398
"Tell me you flowers faire,.				257	Other Poems	5	40
"Earth, brooke, flowrs, pipe, lambe, Dove.				259	Other Poems	5	92
Deckt with pyde flowers sweetely smelling.				262	Other Poems	7	6
FLOWERY							
In flowrie fielde; and as the day begins				18	1st Eclogues	7	125
In flowry fielde a gladder eye to please:.				256	Other Poems	5	3
FLOWETH							
With my teares floweth..				276	Psalm VI		20
FLOWING							
With flowing teares your fault of hasty sight:				38	Arcadia II	14	2
Can those eyes, that of eyes drownd in most harty flowing							
teares,.				122	4th Eclogues	74	15
The sea to ebbe for griefe his flowing turneth:.				136	Cert Sonnets	3	5
His safety from Thee flowing!.				296	Psalm XXI		4
Day and night my teares out flowing.				334	Psalm XLII		9
FLOWS							
And such discord twixt greatest shepheards flowes, ...				27	1st Eclogues	10	40
Feede on my sheepe, your fayer sweete feeding flowes,. . . .				43	Arcadia II	23	4
Which from the ribs of old Parnassus flowes,.				172	Astrophil	15	2
Oh! of thy grace what endlesse pleasure flowes				313	Psalm XXXI		52
FLUENTLY							
So may your tongue still fluently proceed, ...				190	Astrophil	51	2
FLUNG							
This life-deadman in this old dungeon flong.				24	1st Eclogues	9	83
FLUTTERS							
And my yong soule flutters to thee his nest, ...				236	Astrophil	108	6
*FLY							
What swarmes of vertues did in his youth flye.				24	1st Eclogues	9	74
We oft are angrier, with the feeble flie				28	1st Eclogues	10	64
Till spotlesse soule unto the present flye, ...				40	Arcadia II	18	17
Still seeking Love, love found as much I flie.				41	Arcadia II	20	4
They feede on me, and with my wings do flie:				42	Arcadia II	22	9
Our best defenses are to flie these adders..				50	2nd Eclogues	28	89
Nico. Couldst thou make Lalus flie? so nightingales avoide,.				52	2nd Eclogues	29	17
Leaping at every flie, and angrie with a flea:				53	2nd Eclogues	29	44
With Echoe's help, shall "Cosma, Cosma" flie:.				56	2nd Eclogues	29	134
And saith, although I seeke my life to flie, ...				58	2nd Eclogues	30	54
And to the sunne with waxen winges to flie?.				79	Arcadia III	50	14
But I cannot; who then my selfe should flie, ...				114	4th Eclogues	72	39
Fancie, her tackling, torne away doth flie:.				114	4th Eclogues	72	47
The stile of heavie hart can never flie.				129	4th Eclogues	75	139

165

```
*FLY                    (CONTINUED)                          PAGE   TITLE           LINE
  Why should we feare that which we cannot flye? . . . . . . .  131 Arcadia V     77    4
  Like as the Dove which seeled up doth flie,. . . . . . . . .  144 Cert Sonnets 15    1
  Both force to flie and knowledge where to fall.. . . . . . .  144 Cert Sonnets 15   12
  It makes them flie that which they faine would have: . . . .  145 Cert Sonnets 16    6
  Even as the flye, which to the flame doth goe, . . . . . . .  149 Cert Sonnets 21   11
  A blinded Mowlle, or else a burned flye. . . . . . . . . . .  149 Cert Sonnets 21   14
  Passing all ghesse, whence into me should fly. . . . . . . .  149 Cert Sonnets 22    8
  From wooden bones, and bloud of pitch doth flie. . . . . . .  151 Cert Sonnets 22   53
  But alwayes one my selfe with eagle eyde trueth to flie, . .  153 Cert Sonnets 24   24
  He burnt unwares his wings, and cannot fly away. . . . . . .  169 Astrophil     8    14
  Flie, fly, my friends, I have my death wound; fly, . . . . .  174 Astrophil    20     1
  But ere I could flie thence, it pierc'd my heart.. . . . . .  175 Astrophil    20    14
  A Poet eke, as humours fly or creepe,. . . . . . . . . . . .  181 Astrophil    32     4
  Willd me these tempests of vaine love to flie, . . . . . . .  196 Astrophil    62    10
  But do not will me from my Love to flie. . . . . . . . . . .  198 Astrophil    64     8
  Of reason, from whose light those night-birds flie;. . . . .  201 Astrophil    71     7
  Venus is taught with Dian's wings to flie: . . . . . . . . .  202 Astrophil    72     6
  With wings of Love in aire of wonder flie, . . . . . . . . .  212 Astrophil    86     8
  Have made, but forst by Nature still to flie, . . . . . . . . 233 Astrophil   103    10
  Because my Foes to fly are now constraind. . . . . . . . . .  279 Psalm IX           6
  Then out his arrowes fly, and streight they scatterd been, .  291 Psalm XVIII       29
  I hosts by thee orecome, by Thee ore walls I fly;. . . . . .  292 Psalm XVIII       54
  And from the haunts of such bad folks did fly. . . . . . . .  305 Psalm XXVI        18
  Which from suing voice do fly. . . . . . . . . . . . . . . .  309 Psalm XXVIII      10
  Let Angel thine persue them as they fly, . . . . . . . . . .  321 Psalm XXXV        13
  Then fly all ev'ill and goodness nourish,. . . . . . . . . .  326 Psalm XXXVII      67
  Faine would, but could not fly from golden smart.. . . . . .  246 Other Poems   4  184
  They of both ends the middle two doe flie, . . . . . . . . .  248 Other Poems   4  226
  With sight of feare from frends to fremb'd do flie. . . . . . 248 Other Poems   4  240
  Till Uran seing Pas to Cosma fly,. . . . . . . . . . . . . .  249 Other Poems   4  286
  Though they do fly, yet backwardly do glowe. . . . . . . . .  249 Other Poems   4  292
  His soule did fly as she was seen to run.. . . . . . . . . .  251 Other Poems   4  372
  That she would faine the catch of Strephon flie, . . . . . .  252 Other Poems   4  380
  Yet thoughts do flie, though I can scarcely creep. . . . . .  253 Other Poems   4  444
  Still to be hers, about her aye to flie, . . . . . . . . . .  255 Other Poems   4  501
FLYING
  The flying sprites which trees by rootes up teare. . . . . .  114 4th Eclogues 72   36
  And pleasd with our soft peace, staid here his flying race.. 168 Astrophil     8     4
  Their shamefull flying. . . . . . . . . . . . . . . . . . .  276 Psalm VI          32
  More envied Phoebus for his westerne flyinge . . . . . . . .  259 Other Poems   5  126
FOAMY
  More white then Neptune's fomie face,. . . . . . . . . . . .   88 Arcadia III  62   69
FOE
  Or with desire to make such foe a frend, . . . . . . . . . .   22 1st Eclogues  9    9
  A king upon a mouse, a strong foe to a rat,. . . . . . . . .   53 2nd Eclogues 29   32
  Far was homestrife, and far was foe from border. . . . . . .  128 4th Eclogues 75  132
  Like foe, whose wits inclin'd to deadly spite, . . . . . . .  135 Cert Sonnets  2    3
  No, no, no, no, I cannot hate my foe,. . . . . . . . . . . .  155 Cert Sonnets 26    1
  Above line repeated at following locations . . . . . . . . .  155 Cert Sonnets 26   12
    . . . . . . . . . . . . . . . . . . . . . . . . . . . . .  156 Cert Sonnets 26   23
  Nobler desires, least else that friendly foe, . . . . . . .  175 Astrophil    21     7
  My Foe came on, and beat the aire for me,. . . . . . . . . .  191 Astrophil    53    13
  Then let my Foe chase me, and chasing take:. . . . . . . . .  277 Psalm VII         13
  O bragging Foe, where is the endless wast. . . . . . . . . .  280 Psalm IX          16
  Least my Foe bragg, that in my ruin hee. . . . . . . . . . .  286 Psalm XIII        13
  So did he save me from my mighty furious foe,. . . . . . . .  291 Psalm XVIII       36
  While the Foe oppresseth me? . . . . . . . . . . . . . . . .  335 Psalm XLII        44
FOEN
  Here Laelaps, here, in deed against the foen . . . . . . . .   27 1st Eclogues 10   13
  Tho when they saw their foen of greatnes kilde.. . . . . . .  102 3rd Eclogues 66  133
FOE'S
  From that foe's wounds their tender skinnes to hide. . . . .  176 Astrophil    22     8
  Ev'en when foe's envious ey. . . . . . . . . . . . . . . . .  301 Psalm XXIII       17
FOES
  With strong foes on land, on seas with contrary tempests . .   29 1st Eclogues 11    5
  That to your strength your foes have sure resorte. . . . . .   38 Arcadia II   14   12
  Till with lickt beard, his eye of fire espie his foes. . . .   53 2nd Eclogues 29   36
  That childish stuffe which knowes not frendes from foes, . .   81 Arcadia III  54   11
  Of foes the spoile is evill, far worse of constant lovers. .  214 A&S 5th Song      48
  On jaw-bones of my foes,. . . . . . . . . . . . . . . . . .  273 Psalm III         26
  For all I neede, that with such foes do byde.. . . . . . . .  275 Psalm V           24
  The while a swarm of foes with vexing feates . . . . . . . .  276 Psalm VI          23
  Against such rage of foes: Awake for me. . . . . . . . . . .  277 Psalm VII         17
  Because my Foes to fly are now constraind. . . . . . . . . .  279 Psalm IX           6
  From my destroying Wicked Foes . . . . . . . . . . . . . . .  290 Psalm XVII        27
  On whom against my Foes my only safty stayes?. . . . . . . .  291 Psalm XVIII        7
  What Foes I did persue my force did them attaine,. . . . . .  292 Psalm XVIII       68
  Who freed me from my foes, from rebells guarded me,. . . . .  293 Psalm XVIII       86
  Defend Thee still from all Thy foes abroad.. . . . . . . . .  295 Psalm XX           5
  Thy hand thy foes shall overtake,. . . . . . . . . . . . . .  297 Psalm XXI         29
  Let not those foes that me annoy . . . . . . . . . . . . . .  303 Psalm XXV          5
  Behold my foes, what store they be,. . . . . . . . . . . . .  304 Psalm XXV         65
  My foes, to utmost of their pow'r. . . . . . . . . . . . . .  307 Psalm XXVII        8
  That be my Foes, . . . . . . . . . . . . . . . . . . . . . .  308 Psalm XXVII       54
  All my fierce Foes reproach on mee did cast; . . . . . . . .  313 Psalm XXXI        31
  Save me from foes who seek my bane to bake.. . . . . . . . .  313 Psalm XXXI        42
  Speake thou for me against wrong speaking foes,. . . . . . .  321 Psalm XXXV         1
  Then, then let not my foes unjustly joy; . . . . . . . . . .  322 Psalm XXXV        49
  Many mighty wrongfull foes,. . . . . . . . . . . . . . . . .  329 Psalm XXXVIII     57
```

		PAGE	TITLE	LINE

FOES   (CONTINUED)
  Of them that be his foes.................... 333 Psalm XLI   8
  Since foes nor have, nor shall have cause to be. ...... 333 Psalm XLI   39
  When foes ask with foule deriding,............. 335 Psalm XLII   47
  While prevayling foes..................... 336 Psalm XLIII   11
FOES'
  Hcw long shall I with foes' triumphant might .... 285 Psalm XIII   7
  And sav'd me from foes' laughing scorn;........... 310 Psalm XXX   2
  My Foes' ev'ill words their hate of me display .... 333 Psalm XLI   17
FOGGY
  Alas while we are wrapt in foggie mist .... 59 2nd Eclogues 30   68
FOIL
  Till downe-right blowes did foyle thy cunning fence: .... 170 Astrophil   10   11
  To sett, for foile of his milke-white to serve.. .... 244 Other Poems   4   86
FOILED
  I cease to strive, with double conquest foild: .... 11 Arcadia I   2   2
  Or reason foyld would not in vaine contend:. .... 147 Cert Sonnets 19   4
FOLD
  Let him drinke this, whome long in armes to folde. ..... 83 Arcadia III 58   1
  And in thy feare knees of my heart will fold .... 275 Psalm V   19
  The day well fed, the night in faithfull folde:. ...... 258 Other Poems   5   69
FOLDS
  My weedes, Desire, cut out in endlesse foldes. .... 39 Arcadia II   17   6
FOLK
  Selfe-guiltie folke must prove to feele compassion.. .... 60 2nd Eclogues 30 130
  Let folke orecharg'd with braine against me crie,...... 198 Astrophil   64   4
  Lo you grow proud with this, for tyrans make folke bow:. .. 214 A&S 5th Song   61
  That evry folk Thy wondrous Acts may see.. .... 277 Psalm VII   21
  Who hast the heath'ny folk destroyd. .... 283 Psalm X   71
  When wicked folk, even they that be. .... 307 Psalm XXVII   7
  With the wicked working folk .... 309 Psalm XXVIII   12
  For I have call'd on Thee, let wicked folk .... 313 Psalm XXXI   46
  Like dropsy folke still drinke to be a thyrst........ 247 Other Poems   4 204
FOLKS
  The after-folkes shall wonder still at thee. .... 56 2nd Eclogues 29 131
  Like those sicke folkes, in whome strange humors flowe,. .. 74 Arcadia III 41   1
  The diffrence is; all folkes those stormes forbeare: .... 114 4th Eclogues 72   38
  Not pointing to fit folkes each undercharge,........ 210 Astrophil   85   6
  All folkes prest at thy will thy paine to 'swage,...... 232 Astrophil   101   11
  Yong folkes, take time while you may:. .... 211 A&S 4th Song   28
  Indeed full many folkes have said, ... 274 Psalm IV   24
  And wyked folkes from thee to wrack do wend. .... 279 Psalm IX   12
  Of these bad folkes, more lifted up with pride ...... 285 Psalm XII   26
  O madness of these folks, thus loosely led,. .... 286 Psalm XIV   13
  I bett those folks as small as dust, which wind doth rayse:. 293 Psalm XVIII   76
  Yea Thou dost make me serv'd by folks I never knew;. .... 293 Psalm XVIII   79
  With gaping mouthes, these folks on me have charged, ... 299 Psalm XXII   29
  And from the haunts of such bad folks did fly........ 305 Psalm XXVI   18
  Woes, woes shall come to wicked folks; .... 315 Psalm XXXII   37
  Confound those folks, thrust them in shamefull hole. .... 321 Psalm XXXV   7
  Which wicked folks do hold so deare; .... 323 Psalm XXXVI   3
  For those badd folks at last shall perish, ... 325 Psalm XXXVII   23
  Than of bad folks the wealthy wonder,.. .... 325 Psalm XXXVII   42
  Badd folks shall fall, and fall for aye, ... 326 Psalm XXXVII   49
  Will. Then Dick let us go hence lest wee great folkes annoy. 344 Possibly   1   45
  To visite so low folkes did much disdaine, ... 243 Other Poems   4   63
FOLLOW
  Tread in my steppes, or follow not.. .... 153 Cert Sonnets 24   18
  Thought waited on delight, and speech did follow thought:. . 212 A&S 5th Song   2
  Seek peace and follow after it,................ 320 Psalm XXXIV   54
  To follow after lyes.. .... 331 Psalm XL   20
  And part must folowe where whole man doth goe. ...... 253 Other Poems   4 422
FOLLOWED
  Thus, fast he fled from her he follow'd sore,....... 250 Other Poems   4 305
  She fled, and tooke: he folow'd, and was cought. ..... 251 Other Poems   4 348
FOLLOWER
  Since sorow is the follower of evill fortune,....... 108 Arcadia IV   70   2
FOLLOWING
  Make home more paine then following of the cart. ..... 104 3rd Eclogues 67   30
  Who oft fore-judge my after-following race,......... 178 Astrophil   26   13
  Leave following that, which it is gaine to misse...... 188 Astrophil   47   11
  With larger round, to shun the folowing feet........ 250 Other Poems   4 332
FOLLY
  And herein most their folly vaine appeares .... 24 1st Eclogues 9   78
  Is Late remorse in follie dearely bought.. .... 49 2nd Eclogues 28   78
  Foole in me, what follie creepeth, ... 157 Cert Sonnets 27   26
  Sweetnesse sweetly pardon folly, ... 157 Cert Sonnets 27   33
  His death-bed peacock's follie,.. .... 160 Cert Sonnets 30   13
  He knowes not) grow in only follie rich. .... 177 Astrophil   24   14
  Of my filthy folly lai'd;. .... 328 Psalm XXXVIII   15
  From the paths of folly,. .... 336 Psalm XLIII   15
FOND
  Only fond youth admires a rotten stocke. .... 25 1st Eclogues 9   89
  But fondlings fonde, know not your owne desire ...... 25 1st Eclogues 9 102
  And are not forst fonde thraldome to allow.. .... 106 3rd Eclogues 67 105
  Fond fancie's scum, and dregs of scattred thought, ... 161 Cert Sonnets 31   2
  "But will not wise men thinke thy words fond ware?". ... 182 Astrophil   34   7
  His guiltie heart with this fond thought hath fed, ... 286 Psalm XIV   2
  Full of successe, fond I did say .... 311 Psalm XXX   20
  Strephon, fond boy, delighted did not knowe, ... 246 Other Poems   4 163

167

```
                                                               PAGE    TITLE           LINE
FONDLINGS
     But fondlings fonde, know not your owne desire . . . . . .   25  1st Eclogues   9  102
FONDLY
     Fondly blame that to which your selves aspire. . . . . . . .  25  1st Eclogues   9  104
     Come let us break their bonds, say they, and fondly say: . . 271  Psalm II          7
     Do fondly take away. . . . . . . . . . . . . . . . . . . . . 258  Other Poems    5   86
FOOD
     Seemde but to spoyle the foode of thoughts long famished.. .  16  1st Eclogues   7   69
     Constant and kind: my sheep your foode shall breed,. . . . .  18  1st Eclogues   7  123
     My foode is teares; my tunes waymenting yeeld: . . . . . . .  18  1st Eclogues   7  138
     Ruine's relique, care's web, and sorrowe's foode: . . . . .   23  1st Eclogues   9   29
     Fancie his foode, his clothing is of carefulnes; . . . . . .  48  2nd Eclogues  28   41
     Foode without fulnes, counsaile without pride, . . . . . . . 103  3rd Eclogues  67   11
     O My thoughts' sweete foode, my my onely owner, . . . . . .  138  Cert Sonnets   5    1
     Above line repeated at following location. . . . . . . . .   138  Cert Sonnets   5   25
     Her flesh his food, her skin his armour brave, . . . . . . . 179  Astrophil     29   12
     That thou must want or food, or dwelling place.. . . . . . . 187  Astrophil     46    4
     "Eut ah," Desire still cries, "give me some food." . . . . . 201  Astrophil     71   14
     Stella food of my thoughts, hart of my hart, . . . . . . . . 222  Astrophil     87    2
     Cannot heavn's food, once felt, keepe stomakes free. . . . . 223  Astrophil     88    7
     To make a Lyzard dull to taste Love's daintie food:. . . . . 209  A&S 3rd Song        8
     Shall feed and laud the giver of their food. . . . . . . . . 300  Psalm XXII         72
     The lions oft lack food, . . . . . . . . . . . . . . . . . . 319  Psalm XXXIV        37
     Thou shalt have both good food and place.. . . . . . . . . . 324  Psalm XXXVII        8
     Have been my ill feeding food, . . . . . . . . . . . . . . . 334  Psalm XLII         10
     W. If wages make you want, what food is that she gives?. . . 344  Possibly       1   33
     And taught his shepe hir shepe in food to thwart.. . . . . . 247  Other Poems    4  188
     And gives her kidds no food, but willow's barke.". . . . . . 259  Other Poems    5  113
FOOL
     Philisides. O gods, how long this old foole hath annoi'd . .  24  1st Eclogues   9   66
     Foole that I am that with my dogges speake grewe.. . . . . .  27  1st Eclogues  10   19
     A good foole call'd with paine, perhapps may be, . . . . . .  28  1st Eclogues  10   71
     Pas. Ah foole; so Courtiers do. But who did lively skippe, .  52  2nd Eclogues  29   11
     Where chaunge of thoughts one foole to other shewes, . . . .  57  2nd Eclogues  30   21
     He were a foole, if there he did not bide. . . . . . . . . . 104  3rd Eclogues  67   15
     But foole, foole that I am, those eyes would shine from a
          dark cave. . . . . . . . . . . . . . . . . . . . . . . 123  4th Eclogues  74   49
     But foole, foole that I am, tho I had but a hair of her head
          found,. . . . . . . . . . . . . . . . . . . . . . . . 123  4th Eclogues  74   53
     Foole in me, what follie creepeth, . . . . . . . . . . . . . 157  Cert Sonnets  27   26
     "Foole," said my Muse to me, "looke in thy heart and write." 165  Astrophil      1   14
     But, foole, seekst not to get intc her hart. . . . . . . . . 170  Astrophil     11   14
     But that rich foole, who by blind Fortune's lot. . . . . . . 177  Astrophil     24    9
     "Foole," answers he, "no Indes such treasures hold,. . . . . 181  Astrophil     32   12
     "What now sir foole," said he, "I would no lesse,. . . . . . 191  Astrophil     53    7
     O heav'nly foole, thy most kisse-worthie face, . . . . . . . 203  Astrophil     73   12
     Nay, more foole I, oft suffered you to sleepe. . . . . . . . 208  Astrophil     83    7
     But o foole, thinke of the danger, . . . . . . . . . . . . . 203  A&S 2nd Song       17
     Foole, more foole, for no more takinc. . . . . . . . . . . . 203  A&S 2nd Song       28
     But most cryed, "O well broke": O foole full gaily blest:. . 241  Other Poems    1    5
     They catch, while he (foole!) to himself makes love: . . . . 243  Other Poems    4   46
     And full, poore foole, of boyish bravery,. . . . . . . . . . 244  Other Poems    4   77
FOOLISH
     How thou from foolish love maist purge thy sense.. . . . . .  25  1st Eclogues   9  110
     A foolish thing with fooles to deale:. . . . . . . . . . . .  44  Arcadia II    25    3
     R. O foolish thing, which glory doeste destroye. . . . . . .  46  2nd Eclogues  27   19
     P. O glorious title of a foolish toye. . . . . . . . . . . .  46  2nd Eclogues  27   20
     Our foolish lustes in honest rules to stay.. . . . . . . . . 103  3rd Eclogues  67    3
     Her beautie kindle shall within thy foolish minde, . . . . . 121  4th Eclogues  73  171
     That I had bene more foolish or more wise. . . . . . . . . . 181  Astrophil     33   14
     Peace, foolish wit, with wit my wit is mard. . . . . . . . . 182  Astrophil     34   11
     Faire eyes, sweet lips, deare heart, that foolish I. . . . . 186  Astrophil     43    1
     The foolish man by flesh and fancy led . . . . . . . . . . . 286  Psalm XIV          1
FOOL'S
     Thou blind man's marke, thou foole's selfe chosen snare, . . 161  Cert Sonnets  31    1
FOOLS
     Of all those fooles that will have all they see. . . . . . .  22  1st Eclogues   8   48
     Nature against we do seeme to rebell, seeme fooles in a
          vaine sute.. . . . . . . . . . . . . . . . . . . . . .  32  1st Eclogues  13   24
     A foolish thing with fooles to deale:. . . . . . . . . . . .  44  Arcadia II    25    3
     And, fooles, adore in temple of our hart,. . . . . . . . . . 167  Astrophil      5    7
     O fooles, or over-wise, alas the race. . . . . . . . . . . . 176  Astrophil     23   12
     Rich fooles there be, whose base and filthy hart . . . . . . 176  Astrophil     24    1
     Yet to those fooles heav'n such wit doth impart, . . . . . . 177  Astrophil     24    5
     And fooles can thinke those Lampes of purest light,. . . . . 177  Astrophil     26    2
     Do Stella love. Fooles, who doth it deny?. . . . . . . . . . 233  Astrophil    104   14
     O let not fooles in me thy workes reprove, . . . . . . . . . 236  Astrophil    107   13
     No, the more fooles it do shake, . . . . . . . . . . . . . . 234  A&S 11th Song      33
     To be (in things past bounds of wit) fooles, if they be not
          fooles. . . . . . . . . . . . . . . . . . . . . . . . 217  A&S 7th Song        6
     Nor glorious Fooles stand in Thy awfull sight. . . . . . . . 274  Psalm V            12
     That fooles of me may make their game. . . . . . . . . . . . 330  Psalm XXXIX        28
FOOLS'
     But valiant Rebels oft in fooles' mouthes purchase fame: . . 214  A&S 5th Song       67
FOOT
     A horned head, cloven foote, and thousand eyes,. . . . . . .  21  1st Eclogues   8   26
     His cloven foote doth never treade aright. . . . . . . . . .  21  1st Eclogues   8   30
     There ofte steales out that round cleane foote . . . . . . .  89  Arcadia III   62  105
     A three foote stoole in Greece, made Trumpets sound, . . . . 146  Cert Sonnets  17   19
     That not my soule, which at thy foot did fall, . . . . . . . 183  Astrophil     36   12
```

```
FOOT                      (CONTINUED)                      PAGE    TITLE            LINE
    Then let his foot uppon my neck be set:. . . . . . . . . . .  277  Psalm VII           14
    Is their own foot, ledd by their own ill thought,. . . . . .  280  Psalm IX            49
    To match with light foot staggs he made my foot so light . .  292  Psalm XVIII         61
    My foot on justice stayes,. . . . . . . . . . . . . . . . . .  306  Psalm XXVI          38
    At Barly brake hir swete swift foot to trie. . . . . . . . .  247  Other Poems    4    208
    Must strive with waiting foot, and watching eye. . . . . . .  248  Other Poems    4    228
    His pipe was at his foote,. . . . . . . . . . . . . . . . . .  256  Other Poems    5     4
    Whose foote doth set a heav'n on cursed thee,. . . . . . . .  256  Other Poems    5    19
FOOTSTEP
    Now even that footstep of lost libertie. . . . . . . . . . .  166  Astrophil      2     9
FOOTSTEPS
    Whose footsteps I with kisses oft did trace, . . . . . . . .  115  4th Eclogues 72    73
FORAGING
    Striving abroad a foraging to go,. . . . . . . . . . . . . .  192  Astrophil     55     6
FORBARE
    Whille I that syghte, desyre, and vowe forbare,. . . . . . .  344  Possibly       2     7
FOREBEAR
    Who for a selfe-conceipt will that forbeare, . . . . . . . .  105  3rd Eclogues 67    80
    The diffrence is; all folkes those stormes forbeare: . . . .  114  4th Eclogues 72    38
    The bote for joy could not to daunce forbeare, . . . . . . .  232  Astrophil    103     5
    Me to hate? But I forbeare,. . . . . . . . . . . . . . . . .  211  A&S 4th Song        50
    Thought see thou no place forbeare,. . . . . . . . . . . . .  226  A&S 10th Song       19
    O lord, my God, if I did not forbeare. . . . . . . . . . . .  277  Psalm VII            7
    Least, if answer Thou forbeare,. . . . . . . . . . . . . . .  308  Psalm XXVIII         3
FORBEARS
    Or doth she thinke all paine the minde forbeares?. . . . . .  142  Cert Sonnets 11     5
    That wholly hers, all selfnesse he forbeares,. . . . . . . .  195  Astrophil     61     7
    Or if thy love of plaint yet mine forbeares, . . . . . . . .  228  Astrophil     94     9
FORBID
    And God forbid, women such cattell were, . . . . . . . . . .  106  3rd Eclogues 67    82
    Now God forbid. A theefe, and of worst theeves the cheefe: .  213  A&S 5th Song        44
FORBIDS
    Whose winke ech bold attempt forbids.. . . . . . . . . . . .   86  Arcadia III   62    14
    But she forbids, with blushing words, she sayes, . . . . . .  207  Astrophil     81     9
FORCE
    Judge you to whom all beautie's force is lent. . . . . . . .    4  Lady of May    2    31
    With outward force and inward treason spoild.. . . . . . . .   11  Arcadia I      2     4
    What circle then in so rare force beares swaye?. . . . . . .   17  1st Eclogues   7   109
    Such force hath Love above poore Nature's power. . . . . . .   19  1st Eclogues   7   161
    Dorus. Such force hath Love above poore Nature's power,. . .   19  1st Eclogues   7   162
    Whiche beares the bytt a weaker force doth guide,. . . . . .   20  1st Eclogues   7  V959
    Since all his force against himselfe he tries. . . . . . . .   23  1st Eclogues   9    37
    Ashe makes speares which shieldes do resist, her force no
      repulse takes: . . . . . . . . . . . . . . . . . . . . . .   36  1st Eclogues  13   136
    Whose force had such force so to transforme, nay to reforme
      me, . . . . . . . . . . . . . . . . . . . . . . . . . . .    37  1st Eclogues  13   166
    But that it dooth with Echoe's force rebound . . . . . . . .   42  Arcadia II    21    10
    They live in force, I quite consumed die.. . . . . . . . . .   42  Arcadia II    22    12
    To such a force soone chaunge were nothing sutable.. . . . .   47  2nd Eclogues  28    12
    If Love tooke thee by force, or caught thee guilefully.. . .   48  2nd Eclogues  28    21
    Her eyes the force beyond my possibilitie. . . . . . . . . .   48  2nd Eclogues  28    30
    Theere seeke defence where weakenesse is the force:. . . . .   49  2nd Eclogues  28    77
    Hath she not force even death with love to kill? . . . . . .   59  2nd Eclogues  30    85
    Doth force us there to set our chiefe delightfulnes, . . . .   61  2nd Eclogues  30   135
    Thy force I feare, her force I still do prove. . . . . . . .   72  Arcadia III   38    10
    With rebell force, hath closde in dungeon darke. . . . . . .   73  Arcadia III   39     3
    No no, such force with my small force to trye. . . . . . . .   79  Arcadia III   50    15
    Beautie hath force to catche the humane sight. . . . . . . .   82  Arcadia III   57     1
    (The one doth force, the latter doth entise) . . . . . . . .   98  3rd Eclogues  65    10
    Doth add her force unto the sting of fortune:. . . . . . . .  109  Arcadia IV    70    10
    They first their use forgot, then fancies lost their force;.  117  4th Eclogues  73    29
    With outward maker's force, or like an inward father,. . . .  118  4th Eclogues  73    48
    With age's force decay'd, yet once the heaven was his. . . .  120  4th Eclogues  73   124
    Since force doth faint, and sight doth make me blind:. . . .  135  Cert Sonnets   1     4
    For Thereus' force on her chaste will prevailing.. . . . . .  137  Cert Sonnets   4     8
    Till want of force do force her fall to ground;. . . . . . .  144  Cert Sonnets  15     4
    Both force to flie and knowledge where to fall.. . . . . . .  144  Cert Sonnets  15    12
    Who silence force to make their words more deare:. . . . . .  147  Cert Sonnets  17    49
    What force brought them to so unlikely ground. . . . . . . .  149  Cert Sonnets  22     4
    Then from his depth with force in her begunne, . . . . . . .  150  Cert Sonnets  22    17
    Of force of heav'nly beames, infusing hellish paine: . . . .  167  Astrophil      6     3
    No force, no fraud, robd thee of thy delight,. . . . . . . .  181  Astrophil     33     7
    As his maine force, choise sport, and easefull stay. . . . .  186  Astrophil     43     4
    But Grammer's force with sweet successe confirme,. . . . . .  196  Astrophil     63    11
    If still I force her in sad rimes to creepe: . . . . . . . .  201  Astrophil     70     2
    Not by rude force, but sweetest soveraigntie . . . . . . . .  201  Astrophil     71     6
    Of gentle force, so that mine eyes dare gladly play. . . . .  205  Astrophil     76     6
    Is faith so weake? Or is such force in thee? . . . . . . . .  223  Astrophil     88     5
    That hue, whose force my hart still unto thraldome ties? . .  232  Astrophil    102     8
    Whose force but yours the bolts of beautie thunders? . . . .  197  A&S 1st Song        30
    If Orpheus' voyce had force to breathe such musicke's love .  208  A&S 3rd Song         1
    Leave to Mars the force of hands,. . . . . . . . . . . . . .  211  A&S 4th Song        45
    If Rule by force without all claime a Tyran showeth, . . . .  214  A&S 5th Song        57
    And yet against thy Prince thy force dost dayly prove: . . .  214  A&S 5th Song        65
    Whether absence have had force . . . . . . . . . . . . . . .  225  A&S 10th Song        4
    Thy force hath flow'd from Babie's tongue. . . . . . . . . .  278  Psalm VIII           6
    Maugre their force I will set him at rest. . . . . . . . . .  285  Psalm XII           18
    What Foes I did persue my force did them attaine,. . . . . .  292  Psalm XVIII         68
    Both light and force of seing. . . . . . . . . . . . . . . .  294  Psalm XIX           36
```

FORCE	(CONTINUED)	PAGE	TITLE		LINE
And yet his force.		317	Psalm XXXIII		62
Thy force O Lord against their force oppose, ...		321	Psalm XXXV		2
From him whose force did in their spoiles appeare.		321	Psalm XXXV		24
Desire's great force, no forces can withhold:.		345	Possibly	4	3
No force, though force be used, Allarme allarme.		346	Possibly	5	8
Besides this force, within hir eies he kept.		246	Other Poems	4	153
And therfore finding force now faint to be,.		248	Other Poems	4	255
Urania name, whose force he knew so well,.		256	Other Poems	4	538
FORCED					
But forste with raige, his raige on theym upbrayde..		24	1st Eclogues	9	65
He forst her thinke that which she never thought..		95	3rd Eclogues	64	34
Till forste to parte, with harte and eyes even sore, ...		99	3rd Eclogues	66	39
That craftily he forst them to do ill, ...		102	3rd Eclogues	66	125
And are not forst fonde thraldome to allow..		106	3rd Eclogues	67	105
But forced are to burthen feeble nature.		110	Arcadia IV	70	34
That forced with grief reveales what greeved eyes dyd see) .		118	4th Eclogues	73	56
Forced are to sing alway;.		140	Cert Sonnets	7	27
At length to Love's decrees, I forc'd, agreed, ...		165	Astrophil	2	7
Forc'd by a tedious proofe, that Turkish hardned hart, . . .		168	Astrophil	8	2
Long since forc'd by thy beames, but stone nor tree.		183	Astrophil	36	13
Growne now his slaves, he forst them out to find		193	Astrophil	57	3
When I was forst from Stella ever deere, ...		222	Astrophil	87	1
Forst by their Lord, who is asham'd to find.		231	Astrophil	99	13
Have made, but forst by Nature still to flie,.		233	Astrophil	103	10
Alas, that I am forst such evill of thee to say, ...		215	A&S 5th Song		80
FORCES					
My forces razde, thy banners raisd within:		183	Astrophil	36	6
Desire's great force, no forces can withhold:.		345	Possibly	4	3
FORCETH					
Though in despaire, for love so forcethe me;		58	2nd Eclogues	30	57
Can then a cause be so light that forceth a man to go die?					
Aye.		64	2nd Eclogues	31	24
FORCIBLY					
The fire took fire and forcibly out brake, ...		329	Psalm XXXIX		11
FORE					
Giv'ne to my harte, by my fore wounded eyne:		77	Arcadia III	47	6
FORE-ACCOUNTING					
But fore-accounting oft makes builders misse,.		244	Other Poems	4	79
FOREBEAR					
Blisse, I will my blisse forebeare,.		234	A&S 11th Song		38
FORE-FELT					
Fore-felt Desire, begin to savour parte.		83	Arcadia III	59	11
FOREFRONT					
Because their forefront bare sweet Stella's name..		190	Astrophil	50	14
FOREGO					
Help him, who can no more hir sight foregoe.		253	Other Poems	4	420
FOREHEAD					
Her forhead jacinth like, her cheekes of opall hue,.		12	Arcadia I	3	9
But that her fore-head sayes in me		85	Arcadia III	62	5
Who, where she went, bare in her forhead morning,.		113	4th Eclogues	71	70
The name of murdrer now on thy faire forehead sitteth: . . .		214	A&S 5th Song		51
FOREIGN					
In thy owne seate a forraine state shall sit..		11	Arcadia I	1	8
And in thy throne, a forayne state shall sitte		11	Arcadia I	1	V806
FOREJUDGE					
Who oft fore-judge my after-following race,.		178	Astrophil	26	13
FOREMOST					
Where thou art not formost placed, ...		220	A&S 8th Song		87
FORESEE					
And yet could not by rising Morne foresee.		181	Astrophil	33	12
And forsee their wretched paine.		288	Psalm XVI		9
Lo there I now foresee their fall.		324	Psalm XXXVI		33
FORESEES					
With Cupid she fore-sees, and goes god Vulcan's pace:. . . .		12	Arcadia I	3	7
FORESIGHT					
What foresight tels; our thoughts upon thy knowledge staye..		45	Arcadia II	26	12
FORESIGHTFUL					
Give us foresightfull mindes: give us minds to obaye		45	Arcadia II	26	11
FOREST					
His voice makes bald the forest wast;.		310	Psalm XXIX		23
FORESTS					
Ye Satyrs joyde with free and quiet forrests,.		111	4th Eclogues	71	3
Which oft hath Echo tir'd in secrete forrests.		111	4th Eclogues	71	12
Strephon. I that was once free-burges of the forrests, . . .		111	4th Eclogues	71	13
Hunting the wilde inhabiters of forrests,.		111	4th Eclogues	71	20
Long since my thoughts more desert be then forrests:		112	4th Eclogues	71	28
Long since my thoughts chase me like beasts in forrests, . .		112	4th Eclogues	71	35
Me seemes I heare in these ill-changed forrests, ...		112	4th Eclogues	71	39
The dreadfull cries of murdred men in forrests..		112	4th Eclogues	71	48
Strephon. I wish to fire the trees of all these forrests;..		112	4th Eclogues	71	49
My fire is more, then can be made with forrests;		112	4th Eclogues	71	56
In straightnes past the Cedars of the forrests,.		113	4th Eclogues	71	64
Is gone, is gone from these our spoyled forrests,.		113	4th Eclogues	71	71
Klaius. These forrests eke, made wretched by our musique,..		113	4th Eclogues	71	74
FORETOLD					
But in the sandes my paynes foretolde I finde, ...		42	Arcadia II	21	15
FOREVER					
This is thy worke, thou God for ever blinde:		41	Arcadia II	20	9
My sonne alas from me for ever goes.		43	Arcadia II	24	6

FOREVER   (CONTINUED)   PAGE   TITLE   LINE
    Where whitenes dooth for ever sitte: . . . .   90 Arcadia III   62   123
    The crowne above you both for ever I appoint". . . . . . .   121 4th Eclogues   73   166
    Absented? nay I say for ever banished. . . . .   128 4th Eclogues   75   125
    Which he of us for ever hath deserved. . . . .   129 4th Eclogues   75   138
    No, no, for ever gone is all our pleasure; . . . .   130 4th Eclogues   76   25
    For ever wandring from all good direction; . . . .   130 4th Eclogues   76   26
    For ever blinded of our clearest light;. . . . .   130 4th Eclogues   76   27
    For ever lamed of our suerest might; . . . .   130 4th Eclogues   76   28
    For ever banish'd from well plac'd affection;. . . . .   130 4th Eclogues   76   29
    For ever robbed of our royall treasure.. . . . .   130 4th Eclogues   76   30
    And all the beasts for ever breeding . . . .   279 Psalm VIII   27
    And so endures for ever, ...   294 Psalm XIX   38
    For ever crave, that dwell I may . . . .   307 Psalm XXVII   20
    I will thee thanks for ever sing... . . . .   311 Psalm XXX   39
    Their heritage shall last for ever, ...   325 Psalm XXXVII   46
    As one for ever joyned bee.. . . . .   261 Other Poems   6   60
FOREVERMORE
    For ever more. . . . .   281 Psalm IX   60
FOREVER-WHIRLING
    The weakning worke of Time's for ever-whirling wheele. . . .   120 4th Eclogues   73   122
FORGAT
    Only for you the heav'n forgate all measure. . . . .   197 A&S 1st Song   8
FORGE
    (Her sight where love did forge his fayrest darte) . . . . .   79 Arcadia III   51   6
    For ev'n in forge colde water fire maintaines. . . . .   246 Other Poems   4   156
FORGET
    Can I forget, when they in prison placing her, ...   61 2nd Eclogues   30   152
    Can I forget, from how much mourning plainfulnes . . . . . .   61 2nd Eclogues   30   155
    Can I forget in how straunge phrase she craved . . . .   61 2nd Eclogues   30   158
    Then let me eke forget one hand from other:. . . . .   61 2nd Eclogues   30   161
    Let me forget that Plangus I am called:. . . . .   61 2nd Eclogues   30   162
    Let me forget I am sonne to my mother, ...   61 2nd Eclogues   30   163
    My thoughts forget: my thoughts, which never swerve. . . . .   72 Arcadia III   38   3
    And soone forget the swincke due to their hire.. . . . . . .   100 3rd Eclogues   66   74
    His deeds, yea thoughtes all good forgett; . . . .   323 Psalm XXXVI   10
FORGETFUL
    And that forgetfull sort, which never cares. . . . .   281 Psalm IX   54
FORGETS
    My life forgets to nourish languisht sprites;. . . . .   186 Astrophil   42   10
FORGETTETH
    Which he forgetteth not, nor letteth dy. . . . .   280 Psalm IX   34
FORGIVE
    Tho worlds quite me, shall I my selfe forgive? . . . .   227 Astrophil   93   11
    And did due pain forgive me. . . . .   315 Psalm XXXII   18
FORGO
    Merry flocke, such one forgo, ...   221 A&S 9th Song   8
    Let it suffise that he himselfe forgoe.. . . . .   254 Other Poems   4   488
FORGOER
    Klaius. O Mercurie, foregoer to the evening, ...   111 4th Eclogues   71   7
FORGOES
    In ease, untill that bodie life forgoes. . . . .   56 2nd Eclogues   29   146
FORGOT
    But feare forgott, and paynes all overpaste, ...   70 Arcadia III   36   5
    They first their use forgot, then fancies lost their force;.   117 4th Eclogues   73   29
    Our names are quite forgot, our temples are defac'd: . . . .   119 4th Eclogues   73   109
    One hand forgott to rule, th'other to fight. . . . .   191 Astrophil   53   11
    By no encrochment wrongd, nor time forgot: . . . .   209 Astrophil   84   10
    After parting ought forgot, ...   226 A&S 10th Song   8
    Be quite forgott.. . . . .   280 Psalm IX   20
    Why am I forgott by Thee?. . . . .   335 Psalm XLII   42
FORGOTTEN
    The best things still must be forgotten. . . . .   88 Arcadia III   62   86
    God sleeps, or hath forgotten quite, ...   282 Psalm X   46
    How long, O lord, shall I forgotten be?. . . . .   285 Psalm XIII   1
    Now I, now I my self forgotten find, ...   313 Psalm XXXI   34
FORLORN
    My refuge, refuge then, when moste I am forlorn; . . . . . .   291 Psalm XVIII   5
FORM
    Then do I shape to my selfe that forme which raigns so with
        in me, ...   36 1st Eclogues   13   142
    Thus then my forme, and thus my state I finde, ...   73 Arcadia III   40   13
    Though each of them, his private forme preserve, ...   78 Arcadia III   50   3
    Keeping that forme, though void of wonted heate: . . . . . .   151 Cert Sonnets   22   48
    Though he the lively forme receiveth:. . . . .   159 Cert Sonnets   29   17
    Prints his owne lively forme in rudest braine. . . . .   194 Astrophil   58   8
    Now for a clod-like hare in fourm they peere, ...   243 Other Poems   4   43
FORMED
    Tell yet againe me the names of these faire form'd to do
        ev'lls. Dev'lls. . . . .   65 2nd Eclogues   31   49
    It is most true, that eyes are form'd to serve . . . .   167 Astrophil   5   1
    Doth plunge my wel-form'd soule even in the mire . . . . . .   172 Astrophil   14   7
    And yet as soone as they so formed be, ...   189 Astrophil   50   5
FORMER
    From former feare, they had of your good mindes, ...   26 1st Eclogues   10   5
    Thus I commend to thee all our former love.. . . . .   51 2nd Eclogues   28   102
    Where former blisse present evils do staine, ...   153 Cert Sonnets   24   12
    Nay former blisse addes to present paine, ...   153 Cert Sonnets   24   13
    Deserves the former place: . . . .   215 A&S 6th Song   4

```
FORMS                                                     PAGE    TITLE           LINE
     Yet joyning formes one sight of beautie breede.. . . . . . .   78  Arcadia III  50    4
     I turne my minde to all formes of annoyes, . . . . . . . . .  113  4th Eclogues 72    3
FORSAKE
     That nothing winnes the heaven, but what doth earth forsake.   45  Arcadia II   26   16
     P. Who Passion doth forsake, lives void of joy.. . . . . . .   46  2nd Eclogues 27   14
     As this poore beast who did his rest forsake,. . . . . . . .  145  Cert Sonnets 16    7
     I never did my vowed word forsake: . . . . . . . . . . . . .  146  Cert Sonnets 17    8
     Forsake not me, O leave me not,. . . . . . . . . . . . . . .  308  Psalm XXVII       46
     God, loving right, doth not forsake. . . . . . . . . . . . .  326  Psalm XXXVII      69
     Dc not, Lord, then me forsake, . . . . . . . . . . . . . . .  329  Psalm XXXVIII     61
     Brother his brother, frend doth frend forsake, . . . . . . .  248  Other Poems   4  236
FORSAKEN
     The bitter juice of forsaken woes, . . . . . . . . . . . . .  153  Cert Sonnets 24   11
     My God my God why hast Thou me forsaken? . . . . . . . . . .  298  Psalm XXII         1
     To justice never saw forsaken, . . . . . . . . . . . . . . .  326  Psalm XXXVII      63
FORSOCTH
     Is made, forsooth, a Jurate of his woes, . . . . . . . . . .   23  1st Eclogues  9   39
     And if forsooth there come some new found ware,. . . . . . .  104  3rd Eclogues 67   40
     No knee once bowed, forsooth, for them they say we serve..    120  4th Eclogues 73  114
     While too much wit (forsooth) so troubled me,. . . . . . . .  181  Astrophil    33   10
     You say forsooth, you left her well of late. . . . . . . . .  225  Astrophil    92    7
     To be forsooth upright,. . . . . . . . . . . . . . . . . . .  216  A&S 6th Song      45
     Is that love? forsooth I trow, . . . . . . . . . . . . . . .  222  A&S 9th Song      36
     A lustles song for sooth thinks hee that hath more lust to
         cry. . . . . . . . . . . . . . . . . . . . . . . . . . .  343  Possibly      1    8
FORSWEAR
     My pipe and song made him both songe and pipe forsweare. . .   52  2nd Eclogues 29   20
FORSWCRN
     Or art thou else to comfort me forsworne?. . . . . . . . . .  199  Astrophil    67   11
FORT
     My head you seeke, as to your strongest forte: . . . . . . .   38  Arcadia II   14   10
     Since Death on Vertue's fort hath made invasion. . . . . . .  128  4th Eclogues 75  102
     Thus to betray my hart's fort, . . . . . . . . . . . . . . .  154  Cert Sonnets 25   10
     Now will I invade the fort;. . . . . . . . . . . . . . . . .  202  A&S 2nd Song      15
     Yeelde yeelde, O yeelde, you that this Forte do holde, . . .  345  Possibly      4    1
     Yeelde yeelde O yeelde, who first this Fort did make,. . . .  345  Possibly      4    9
FORTH
     Heare plaints come forth from dungeon of my minde. . . . . .   18  1st Eclogues  7  133
     Pas. When Cosma doth come forth, the Sun displaies . . . . .   55  2nd Eclogues 29   96
     That opened furthe my seale of comfforte is) . . . . . . . .   70  Arcadia III  35    3
     My minde ere now led foorth by reason's light: . . . . . . .   73  Arcadia III  39    4
     O heav'n awake shewe forth thy stately face, . . . . . . . .   91  3rd Eclogues 63   10
     But streight there issued forth two Ladies (Ladies sure..    118  4th Eclogues 73   63
     The mountaines great with childe I thought brought foorth a
         mouse. . . . . . . . . . . . . . . . . . . . . . . . . .  118  4th Eclogues 73   76
     But walking forth, the first thus to the second saide, . . .  118  4th Eclogues 73   77
     Which breakes the clowdes and opens forth the light, . . . .  161  Cert Sonnets 32    7
     But words came halting forth, wanting Invention's stay,. . .  165  Astrophil     1    9
     When trembling voice brings forth that I do Stella love. . .  168  Astrophil     6   14
     The doore by which sometimes comes forth her Grace,. . . . .  169  Astrophil     9    5
     My youth doth waste, my knowledge brings forth toyes,. . . .  174  Astrophil    18    9
     But shining forth of heate in his chiefe pride;. . . . . . .  176  Astrophil    22    4
     Oft cruell fights well pictured forth do please. . . . . . .  181  Astrophil    34    4
     Sent forth the beames, which made so faire my race.. . . . .  185  Astrophil    41   14
     My words I know do well set forth my mind, . . . . . . . . .  186  Astrophil    44    1
     But they do swell and struggle forth of me,. . . . . . . . .  189  Astrophil    50    3
     Who hard by made a window send forth light. . . . . . . . .  191  Astrophil    53    9
     Where memory sets foorth the beames of love. . . . . . . . .  223  Astrophil    88   11
     Now brought abed, hath brought nought foorth, but nought..   278  Psalm VII         39
     Shew forth his Acts, and this as Act most high,. . . . . . .  280  Psalm IX          32
     Of syon's Daughter may sing forth Thy prayse:. . . . . . . .  280  Psalm IX          42
     The heavnly Frame sets forth the Fame. . . . . . . . . . . .  293  Psalm XIX          1
     Who forth doth come like a bridegrome. . . . . . . . . . . .  294  Psalm XIX         21
     But yet a setting foorth it some way lent: . . . . . . . . .  252  Other Poems   4  395
FORTHWITH
     Blinded forthwith in darke dispaire did lye, . . . . . . . .  149  Cert Sonnets 21    6
FORTIFICATION
     Faire trees' shade is enough fortification,. . . . . . . . .   69  2nd Eclogues 34   13
FORTIFIED
     Sc fortified with wit, stor'd with disdaine, . . . . . . . .  171  Astrophil    12   13
FORTIFY
     Thus for ech change my changelesse hart I fortifie.. . . . .   51  2nd Eclogues 28  126
FORTRESS
     Be my strong rock, be Thou my forteress. . . . . . . . . . .  312  Psalm XXXI         6
     Indeed Thou art my rock, my Forteress; . . . . . . . . . . .  312  Psalm XXXI         7
     Remorse in you to doe this Fortresse harme,. . . . . . . . .  346  Possibly      5    6
FORTUNE
     The starres thy state, fortune may change thy happe. . . . .   23  1st Eclogues  9   25
     Whose wit the starres, whose fortune fortune thralls. . . .   23  1st Eclogues  9   31
     Fortune, Nature, Love, long have contended about me, . . . .   29  1st Eclogues 11    1
     Fortune thus gan say; "misery and misfortune is all one, . .   29  1st Eclogues 11    3
     And of misfortune, fortune hath only the gift. . . . . . . .   29  1st Eclogues 11    4
     Where thou poore nature left'st all thy due glory, to
         fortune. . . . . . . . . . . . . . . . . . . . . . . . .   30  1st Eclogues 11   15
     Her vertue is soveraine, fortune a vassal of hers".. . . . .   30  1st Eclogues 11   16
     Nature abasht went back: fortune blusht: yet she replide
         thus:. . . . . . . . . . . . . . . . . . . . . . . . . .   30  1st Eclogues 11   17
     Thus, thus, alas! wofull in nature, unhappy by fortune,. . .   30  1st Eclogues 11   19
     Dorus. O glittring miseries of man, if this be the fortune .   34  1st Eclogues 13   89
```

FORTUNE	(CONTINUED)	PAGE	TITLE		LINE
Of those fortune lulls, so small rest rests in a kingdome. .		34	1st Eclogues	13	90
Justely to graunt thy rewarde, such envie I beare to thy fortune.		37	1st Eclogues	13	156
And if a meane were found, fortune th' whole course of it hinders.		37	1st Eclogues	13	159
Fortune store, Nature health, Love grant perswasion.		51	2nd Eclogues	28	100
To vertue, fortune, time and woman's brest.		98	3rd Eclogues	65	14
My soule is bliste, sence joyde, and fortune raysed.		108	Arcadia IV	69	14
Since sorow is the follower of evill fortune, ...		108	Arcadia IV	70	2
Since no evill fortune equalls publique damage:		108	Arcadia IV	70	3
Doth add her force unto the sting of fortune:		109	Arcadia IV	70	10
For lost, lost is by blowe of cruell fortune		109	Arcadia IV	70	17
In graunting such a scope to filthy fortune, ...		109	Arcadia IV	70	21
Our studies fixt upon the falles of fortune.		109	Arcadia IV	70	30
No, no, our mischiefe growes in this vile fortune, ...		109	Arcadia IV	70	31
Since sorow then concludeth all our fortune, ...		110	Arcadia IV	70	37
Nor of my fortune ought, but mischieve crave.		114	4th Eclogues	72	20
Strephon. Nor of my fortune ought but mischiefe crave, . . .		114	4th Eclogues	72	21
What essence dest'nie hath; if fortune be or no;		118	4th Eclogues	73	45
Becommeth us: in us fortune determines not..		120	4th Eclogues	73	140
And thou poore Earth, whom fortune doth attaint.		125	4th Eclogues	75	16
Nor Fortune of thy fortune author is:		181	Astrophil	33	8
Let Fortune lay on me her worst disgrace, ...		198	Astrophil	64	11
Fortune wheeles still with me in one sort slow, ...		199	Astrophil	66	6
How is thy grace by my strange fortune staind!		230	Astrophil	98	3
Chafe not at some man's great good fortune		325	Psalm XXXVII		18
By fortune meane, in Nature borne a Queene, ...		244	Other Poems	4	91
So may no fortune breed.		258	Other Poems	5	80
O fortune too too badd, ...		259	Other Poems	5	98
FORTUNE'S					
Philisides. If fortune's lappe became my dwelling place, . .		23	1st Eclogues	9	26
Balles to the starres, and thralles to Fortune's raigne; . .		57	2nd Eclogues	30	17
From any joy, know fortune's vile displacing her, ...		61	2nd Eclogues	30	150
Of fortune's Diademes, by beauty mustred..		67	2nd Eclogues	33	5
Her hand benumde with fortune's daylie blows, ...		81	Arcadia III	54	3
Now fancie's fits, now fortune's balefull stowers:		103	3rd Eclogues	66	157
Engulfed in despaire, slid downe from fortune's lappe: . . .		153	Cert Sonnets	24	16
But that rich foole, who by blind Fortune's lot.		177	Astrophil	24	9
But when the ruggedst step of Fortune's race		195	Astrophil	60	5
O unjustest fortune's sway, ...		235	A&S 11th Song		43
Vertue's proofe, fortune's victor, beautie's place..		252	Other Poems	4	392
FORWORN					
From filth of foreworne house, and quiet lives, ...		143	Cert Sonnets	12	5
FOSTER					
Do foster still, the fruite of fancies darke:		73	Arcadia III	39	6
FOSTER-CHILD					
The child of curse, man's weaknesse foster-child, ...		141	Cert Sonnets	10	2
FOSTERETH					
Unkindnes breedes, unkindnes fostreth hate..		85	Arcadia III	61	8
FOUL					
My foule mishap came yet from fairest mind..		5	Lady of May	3	18
And so behinde foule clowdes full oft faire starres do ly hidden".		36	1st Eclogues	13	154
A foul infection kills or bredeth botches.		50	2nd Eclogues	28	V884
And hopes with foule embracements her to get, ...		59	2nd Eclogues	30	90
Get hence foule Griefe, the canker of the minde:		83	Arcadia III	59	1
But thou foule Cupid, syre to lawlesse lust, ...		92	3rd Eclogues	63	55
But he himselfe a foule unhansome groome, ...		94	3rd Eclogues	64	5
There never past foule word, I dare well say..		106	3rd Eclogues	67	93
Of huge despaire, and foule affliction's vallies, ...		111	4th Eclogues	71	17
These foule, most foule, disastres to me fell;		116	4th Eclogues	72	97
Betwixt us two; how much that discord foule hath stain'd . .		119	4th Eclogues	73	106
But let us wiser be; and what foule discorde brake, ...		120	4th Eclogues	73	119
Ah let us all against foule Nature crie:		127	4th Eclogues	75	92
Fowle Winters as they come, away they shall.		143	Cert Sonnets	12	12
And can with foule abuse such beauties blot;		177	Astrophil	24	11
That poison foule of bubling pride doth lie.		178	Astrophil	27	6
Witnesse with me, that my foule stumbling so, ...		227	Astrophil	93	6
Of foule rebellion then I do appeach thee now;		214	A&S 5th Song		62
Her faire necke a foule yoke bare, ...		218	A&S 8th Song		10
In that, which of fowle wickedness doth smel:		274	Psalm V		10
Their soules fowl sinns for inmost lyning have:		275	Psalm V		26
From a foule corrupting end.		288	Psalm XVI		36
The seely wretch with foule affliction staind, ...		300	Psalm XXII		56
Whose foule weights have me opprest.		327	Psalm XXXVIII		12
I know that man's foule sin doth cause Thy wrath..		330	Psalm XXXIX		33
Foul faults sore pains do reach me, ...		332	Psalm XL		46
When foes ask with foule deriding, ...		335	Psalm XLII		47
On yond foule flocke belonging not to me."		255	Other Poems	4	518
FOULED					
Fould with this sight, while thou thy chariot guidest. . . .		126	4th Eclogues	75	57
FOULER					
Let other fowler spots away be blowne;		105	3rd Eclogues	67	55
FOULLY					
Tell how my joyes and hopes thus fowly fell.		146	Cert Sonnets	17	14
FOUND					
I never found long love such wealth hath paide to me". . . .		16	1st Eclogues	7	54
And if a meane were found, fortune th' whole course of it hinders.		37	1st Eclogues	13	159

173

FOUND   (CONTINUED)   PAGE   TITLE   LINE

    Still seeking Love, love found as much I flie. . . . .   41 Arcadia II   20   4
    O heards take heed; for I a woolfe have found; . . . .   50 2nd Eclogues   28   83
    But in the place found nothing but a rope. . . . .   55 2nd Eclogues   29   92
    Ah where was first that cruell cunning found, ...   57 2nd Eclogues   30   11
    What stormes founde me, what tormentes I dyd fynde, ...   71 Arcadia III   36   15
    Thus in thy selfe, least strings are loudest founde, ...   81 Arcadia III   54   15
    Then founde I which thing is a charge to beare . . . . . .   99 3rd Eclogues   66   17
    But when his seate so rooted he had found, ...   102 3rd Eclogues   66   113
    And if forsooth there come some new found ware, ...   104 3rd Eclogues   67   40
    And found with deadly feare that all my sinewes shak'd. . . .   121 4th Eclogues   73   180
    But foole, foole that I am, tho I had but a hair of her head
       found, ...   123 4th Eclogues   74   53
    Unto Cupid that boy shall a Pedante be found?. . . . .   124 4th Eclogues   74   66
    And tnence cast off, where his sweete hurt he found, ...   144 Cert Sonnets   15   6
    O this it is, the knotted straw is found . . . .   146 Cert Sonnets   17   16
    Compar'd to me, made me in lightnesse found: . . . .   147 Cert Sonnets   17   47
    Neere Wilton sweete, huge heapes of stones are found, ...   149 Cert Sonnets   22   1
    Without the picture be found true. . . . .   157 Cert Sonnets   27   24
    Ennobling new found Tropes with problemes old: . . . .   166 Astrophil   3   6
    Hast thou found such and such like arguments?. . . . .   199 Astrophil   67   10
    Or gemmes, or frutes of new-found Paradise, ...   207 Astrophil   81   2
    Alas I found, that she with me did smart, ...   223 Astrophil   87   5
    Where I have found more heart's delight. . . . .   274 Psalm IV   28
    For Thou lord found by them wilt ever be . . . .   280 Psalm IX   29
    Say then, Is not my lot found. . . . .   288 Psalm XVI   16
    And then by Thee was guiltless found . . . .   289 Psalm XVII   11
    His voice is on the Waters found, ...   310 Psalm XXIX   7
    And never found again shal be. . . . .   325 Psalm XXXVII   28
    Though I did seek, I never found. . . . .   327 Psalm XXXVII   92
    In my heart such grief is found. . . . .   328 Psalm XXXVIII   24
    They found, they felt, they had no lease of blisse. . . . . .   244 Other Poems   4   80
    To yeeld she found hir noble heart did ake: . . . .   245 Other Poems   4   125
    Who earnest found what they accounted play. . . . .   251 Other Poems   4   366
    For then wise Klaius found no absence can. . . . .   253 Other Poems   4   419
    He found man's vertue is but part of man, ...   253 Other Poems   4   421
    He found that Reason's self now reasons found. . . . .   253 Other Poems   4   423
FOUNDATIONS
    The Mountains proudly high, and their ffoundations bent. . .   291 Psalm XVIII   16
    The World's foundations then lay bare because he shent . . .   291 Psalm XVIII   32
FOUR
    That hath foure legs, and with two onely goes, ...   56 2nd Eclogues   29   142
    That hath foure eyes, and onely two can frame. . . . . . .   56 2nd Eclogues   29   143
    First fower but say, next fowr their saying seale, ...   76 Arcadia III   46   17
FOURTH
    Edward named fourth, as first in praise I name, ...   204 Astrophil   75   2
FOWLS
    Of fowles there called was a parliament. . . . .   29 1st Eclogues   10   84
FOX
    Or trayne the fox that traines so crafty laies. . . . . . .   26 1st Eclogues   9   125
    The Foxe gave crafte; the Dog gave flatterie; . . . .   101 3rd Eclogues   66   85
    The fox on knees and elbowes tombled downe: . . . .   248 Other Poems   4   258
FOXES
    That Foxes leave to steale, because they finde they dy
       therefore. . . . .   344 Possibly   1   44
FRAID
    Nor that he made the Flouredeluce so fraid, ...   204 Astrophil   75   9
FRAIL
    Till my frayle barke his haven agayn do fynde. . . . . . .   70 Arcadia III   35   8
FRAME
    But so his humor I frame, in a mould of choller adusted, . .   29 1st Eclogues   11   9
    Which must frame contempt to the fittest purchase of
       honnour . . . .   32 1st Eclogues   13   38
    Thus plag'de how can I frame to my soare any hope of
       amendemente? . . . .   37 1st Eclogues   13   160
    That hath foure eyes, and onely two can frame. . . . .   56 2nd Eclogues   29   143
    To frame of Earth a vessell of the minde, ...   57 2nd Eclogues   30   12
    He did to beastes' best use his cunning frame; . . . .   101 3rd Eclogues   66   108
    Now thus this wonder to my selfe I frame, ...   151 Cert Sonnets   22   69
    Frame daintiest lustre, mixt of shades and light?. . . . . .   168 Astrophil   7   4
    If that be sinne which doth the maners frame, ...   172 Astrophil   14   9
    And yet my words, as them my pen doth frame, ...   174 Astrophil   19   7
    You that with allegorie's curious frame, ...   178 Astrophil   28   1
    These questions busie wits to me do frame; . . . .   180 Astrophil   30   12
    Nor hope, nor wishe another course to frame, ...   198 Astrophil   64   12
    Nor that he could young-wise, wise-valiant frame . . . . . .   204 Astrophil   75   5
    Ncr so ambitious am I, as to frame . . . .   224 Astrophil   90   5
    Where those red cheeks, which oft with faire encrease did
       frame. . . . .   232 Astrophil   102   2
    Sweet then, while each thing doth frame: . . . .   211 A&S 4th Song   34
    Thou then whom partiall heavens conspir'd in one to frame, .   213 A&S 5th Song   19
    The heavnly Frame sets forth the Fame. . . . .   293 Psalm XIX   1
    And who doth frame to keep the same. . . . .   295 Psalm XIX   47
    Wee stand upright, while they their fall did frame. . . . .   296 Psalm XX   32
    That causeless wrongs do frame. . . . .   303 Psalm XXV   10
    And in his ever glorious frame . . . .   310 Psalm XXIX   5
    Since he their hearts doth frame, ...   317 Psalm XXXIII   55
    This shall men's fancys frame. . . . .   319 Psalm XXXIV   17
    That lift themselves my ruin for to frame. . . . .   323 Psalm XXXV   66
    Who jointly sought my bale to frame; . . . .   332 Psalm XL   53

```
FRAME                        (CONTINUED)                   PAGE    TITLE           LINE
   Which soone as it did batefull question frame, . . . . . . .  247 Other Poems      4   189
   The two in hell did toward Cosma frame,. . . . . . . . . . .  249 Other Poems      4   267
FRAMED
   And plaine speach oft then quaint phrase better framed is. .   14 1st Eclogues     7     6
   Her praise, whose praise to learne your skill hath framed
   me . . . . . . . . . . . . . . . . . . . . . . . . . . . . .   15 1st Eclogues     7    24
   And let thine eyes to other sports be framed. . . . . . . .    25 1st Eclogues     9   122
   Whose faire bodily gifts are fram'd most lovely to each ey..   33 1st Eclogues    13    55
   By telling how she was, how now she framed is. . . . . . .     49 2nd Eclogues    28    53
   Thus she is framde: her eyes are my direction; . . . . . . .   49 2nd Eclogues    28    70
   As we to get are fram'd, so they to spare: . . . . . . . . .  106 3rd Eclogues    67   106
   How hast thou framde the paine wherewith I am opprest? . . .  121 4th Eclogues    73   184
   Which too deep in me is framed,. . . . . . . . . . . . . . .  220 A&S 8th Song          99
   He that hath hurtless hands, whose inward heart is framed. .  302 Psalm XXIV             7
FRAMES
   So my desires by my feare, cutt downe, be the frames of her
   honour.. . . . . . . . . . . . . . . . . . . . . . . . . . .   36 1st Eclogues    13   135
   O Venus (if her praise no envy frames, . . . . . . . . . . .   60 2nd Eclogues    30   113
FRAMEST
   Thou then, that framste both words and voice most skilfully,   48 2nd Eclogues    28    19
FRANCE
   And of some sent from that sweet enemie Fraunce; . . . . . .  185 Astrophil        41     4
FRANKLY
   Giving frankly niggard No: . . . . . . . . . . . . . . . . .  202 A&S 2nd Song          10
FRAUD
   No force, no fraud, robd thee of thy delight,. . . . . . . .  181 Astrophil        33     7
FRAUDULENT
   The murdrous man, and so the fraudulent. . . . . . . . . . .  275 Psalm V               16
FRAUGHT
   With vertue fraught and full of holy feare!. . . . . . . . .   25 1st Eclogues     9    95
   But of thy soule, so fraught with such ungratefulnesse,. . .  213 A&S 5th Song          40
   Oh, is there one with his Feare fraught? . . . . . . . . . .  304 Psalm XXV             47
FRAY
   The friendly fray, where blowes both wound and heale,. . . .  206 Astrophil        79    10
FREE
   Farre more happy be you, whose greatnes gets a free accesse,   33 1st Eclogues    13    54
   P. If Reason will, that Passions be not free.. . . . . . . .   46 2nd Eclogues    27     4
   Thou doest desire, and with free power to holde. . . . . . .   83 Arcadia III      58     2
   Ye Satyrs joyde with free and quiet forrests,. . . . . . . .  111 4th Eclogues    71     3
   Free all my powers were from those captiving snares, . . . .  117 4th Eclogues    73    17
   Flew up with freer wings of fleshly bondage free;. . . . . .  117 4th Eclogues    73    33
   "Yet thou shalt not go free (quoth Venus) such a fire. . . .  121 4th Eclogues    73   170
   The golden meane who loves, lives safely free. . . . . . . .  143 Cert Sonnets    12     4
   For why should I, whom free choise slave doth make,. . . . .  146 Cert Sonnets    17     9
   That from her lockes, thy day-nets, none scapes free,. . . .  170 Astrophil        12     2
   Her daintiest bare went free; the cause was this,. . . . . .  176 Astrophil        22    13
   To keepe themselves and their chief cities free, . . . . . .  179 Astrophil        29     2
   Though false, yet with free scope more grace doth breed. . .  187 Astrophil        45    10
   In my free side? or am I borne a slave,. . . . . . . . . . .  188 Astrophil        47     3
   Cannot heavn's food, once felt, keepe stomakes free. . . . .  223 Astrophil        88     7
   So neere, in so good time, so free a place?. . . . . . . . .  235 Astrophil       105     2
   Sleeping, grants a free resort:. . . . . . . . . . . . . . .  202 A&S 2nd Song          14
   Thou sett'st me free, when I was thrall, . . . . . . . . . .  273 Psalm IV               3
   The Bird free Burgess of the ayre, . . . . . . . . . . . . .  279 Psalm VIII            29
   They were set free when they upon Thee called, . . . . . . .  298 Psalm XXII            13
   Who doth, and will set free. . . . . . . . . . . . . . . . .  304 Psalm XXV             57
   Who poore and weake from rich and strong dost free,. . . . .  321 Psalm XXXV            22
   For other's ease, their frutte, or free estate,. . . . . . .  345 Possibly         2    10
   Both free of minde, both did clear-dealing love, . . . . . .  243 Other Poems      4    39
   Free of proud feares, brave begg'ry, smiling strife. . . . .  243 Other Poems      4    60
   As bragging that free of all passions' mone. . . . . . . . .  244 Other Poems      4    71
   Faine would be free, but dreadeth parents' ire.. . . . . . .  245 Other Poems      4   120
FREE-BURGESS
   Strephon. I that was once free-burges of the forrests, . . .  111 4th Eclogues    71    13
FREED
   Where man's mind hath a freed consideration. . . . . . . . .   68 2nd Eclogues    34     3
   Is neither freed, nor yet to service bound,. . . . . . . . .  144 Cert Sonnets    15     2
   That Jacob freed by Thee may glad become . . . . . . . . . .  287 Psalm XIV             23
   Thus freed from mutin men, thou makest me to raign,. . . . .  293 Psalm XVIII           78
   Who freed me from my foes, from rebells guarded me,. . . . .  293 Psalm XVIII           86
   And God freed him, in his worst time . . . . . . . . . . . .  319 Psalm XXXIV           23
FREEDOM
   He is not poore who can his freedome save, . . . . . . . . .    4 Lady of May      2    27
   What man is he that hath his freedome solde? . . . . . . . .   24 1st Eclogues     9    56
   Whose fyrie chaines, upon his freedome seaze, . . . . . . .    74 Arcadia III      41     4
   This much, yet more, when I by him this freedom gate,. . . .  292 Psalm XVIII           40
   My freedom, with show of hir beames, with virtue my content.  344 Possibly         1    38
FREEDOM'S
   From her, in whome is sowne their freedome's seede,. . . . .   72 Arcadia III      38     4
   Nay if I wrought not for his Freedome's sake . . . . . . . .  277 Psalm VII             11
FREEDOMS
   To that sweet yoke, where lasting freedomes be:. . . . . . .  161 Cert Sonnets    32     6
FREELY
   From those cleere notes which freely may rejoyce.. . . . . .   13 Arcadia I        4     8
   Might freely rome, or rest, as seemed them:. . . . . . . . .  100 3rd Eclogues    66    48
   No beast should freely speake, but onely he. . . . . . . . .  101 3rd Eclogues    66   105
   To speak with her, while freely speak we maye. . . . . . . .  107 3rd Eclogues    67   120
   Thus freely saith he in his sprite:. . . . . . . . . . . . .  282 Psalm X               45
   The good is kind and freely giveth;. . . . . . . . . . . . .  326 Psalm XXXVII          54
```

FREER
 Flew up with freer wings of fleshly bondage free;. . . . . . 117 4th Eclogues 73 33
FREEZE
 Whose lyverie is such, as most I freeze apparelled most, . . 343 Possibly 1 21
FREEZING
 Of living deaths, deare wounds, faire stormes and freesing
  fires: . . . . 167 Astrophil 6 4
FREMD
 And makes them fremb'd, who frendes by nature are, ... 104 3rd Eclogues 67 38
 With sight of feare from frends to fremb'd do flie. . . . . . 248 Other Poems 4 240
FRENCH
 If French can yet three parts in one agree;. . . . . 180 Astrophil 30 5
FRENZY
 In sicke-man's franzie rather takes compassion,. . . . . . . 50 2nd Eclogues 28 96
 From such a femall franzie . . . . 160 Cert Sonnets 30 8
 Above line repeated at following location. . . . . 160 Cert Sonnets 30 18
 From such femall franzie,. . . . . 160 Cert Sonnets 30 28
 To call such wit a franzie,. . . . . 161 Cert Sonnets 30 38
FREQUENT
 I did not them frequent. . . . . 305 Psalm XXVI 13
FRESH
 Or like the fresh Queene-apple's side, ... 86 Arcadia III 62 25
 Some fresh and fruitfull showers upon my sunne-burn'd
  braine . . . . 165 Astrophil 1 8
 To write therein more fresh the story of delight,. . . . . . 232 Astrophil 102 13
 New perfumed with flowers fresh growing, ... 217 A&S 8th Song 4
 Like laurell fresh himself out spreading.. . . . . 327 Psalm XXXVII 90
 A salve, freshe ayre, and hyghe contented mynde. . . . . . . 345 Possibly 2 14
FRESHLY
 Whose curelesse wounds even now most freshly bleed:. . . . . 189 Astrophil 48 11
 With such a rosie morne, whose beames most freshly gay . . . 205 Astrophil 76 7
 He shall be lyke a freshly planted tree, ... 270 Psalm I 7
FRESHNESS
 And age pull'd on with paines all freshness fretteth:. . . . 276 Psalm VI 22
FRET
 Frett not Thy self, if thou do see . . . . 324 Psalm XXXVII 1
 Fume not, rage not, frett not I say, ... 325 Psalm XXXVII 21
FRETTETH
 And age pull'd on with paines all freshness fretteth:. . . . 276 Psalm VI 22
FRIEND
 New friend of mine; I yeeld to thy habilitie:. . . . . 19 1st Eclogues 7 174
 Or with desire to make such foe a frend, ... 22 1st Eclogues 9 9
 Friend without change, playfellow without strife,. . . . . . 103 3rd Eclogues 67 10
 Alas have I not paine enough my friend,. . . . . 171 Astrophil 14 1
 Your words my friend (right healthfull caustiks) blame . . . 175 Astrophil 21 1
 As of a friend that meant not much amisse: . . . . 193 Astrophil 56 8
 My friend, that oft saw through all maskes my wo,. . . . . . 200 Astrophil 69 5
 That do not leave your least friend at the wurst,. . . . . . 228 Astrophil 95 2
 Dian that faine would cheare her friend the Night, ... 229 Astrophil 97 1
 That bad his friend, but then new maim'd, to be. . . . . . . 236 Astrophil 106 13
 A friend each party drawes,. . . . . 216 A&S 6th Song 29
 From my plague, kynn, neighbour, Friend, ... 328 Psalm XXXVIII 31
 O yea, my Friend to whom I did impart. . . . . 333 Psalm XLI 29
 My Friend I say, who at my table sate, ... 333 Psalm XLI 31
 In dede thou said'st it was thy frend to see,. . . . . 247 Other Poems 4 219
 Brother his brother, frend doth frend forsake. . . . . 248 Other Poems 4 236
 His well knowne friend, but yet his unknowne mate, ... 255 Other Poems 4 528
FRIENDLY
 Nought could impart such heates to friendly mind.. . . . . . 51 2nd Eclogues 28 105
 Nobler desires, least else that friendly foe, ... 175 Astrophil 21 7
 Nor trumpets sound I heard, nor friendly cries;. . . . . . . 191 Astrophil 53 12
 The friendly fray, where blowes both wound and heale,. . . . 206 Astrophil 79 10
 If I have been unkynd for friendly part: . . . . 277 Psalm VII 10
 Neighbors friendly entertain . . . . 309 Psalm XXVIII 14
FRIENDS
 In speedie helpe, thanke worthie frends appeare. . . . . . . 81 Arcadia III 53 14
 That childish stuffe which knowes not frendes from foes, . . 81 Arcadia III 54 11
 And makes them fremb'd, who frendes by nature are, ... 104 3rd Eclogues 67 38
 Flie, fly, my friends, I have my death wound; fly, ... 174 Astrophil 20 1
 That makes me oft my best friends overpasse, ... 178 Astrophil 27 12
 Yet sighs, deere sighs, indeede true friends you are,. . . . 228 Astrophil 95 1
 As Brothers, or as Friends beloved much; . . . . 322 Psalm XXXV 34
 A paire of frends, or rather one cal'd two,. . . . . 242 Other Poems 4 18
 And eke their pipes did well, as frends, agree.. . . . . . . 242 Other Poems 4 32
 With sight of feare from frends to fremb'd do flie.. . . . . 248 Other Poems 4 240
 To joyne sweet friends beloved.. . . . . 260 Other Poems 6 16
 Lovingly like friends did keepe, ... 262 Other Poems 7 22
 Friends like to blacke Swannes appearing,. . . . . 263 Other Poems 7 53
FRIENDSHIP
 Condoling cause of friendship he will borrow.. . . . . 62 2nd Eclogues 30 178
 In friendship unremoved. . . . . 261 Other Poems 6 28
 Oft each other's friendship proving, ... 262 Other Poems 7 23
 Friendship true in hart assured, ... 263 Other Poems 7 35
FRIENDSHIP'S
 But East and West were join'd by frendship's hest. . . . . . 242 Other Poems 4 27
FRIES
 No place to turne; without, within it fryes: . . . . 18 1st Eclogues 7 145
 As can refresh the hell where my soule fries.. . . . . 231 Astrophil 100 8
FRIGHT
 My mangled mind huge horrors still doe fright, ... 74 Arcadia III 42 5

FRIGHT   (CONTINUED)   PAGE   TITLE   LINE
    With terrors great, O Lord, do thou them fright: . . . . . . 281 Psalm IX   63
    Who shall be able me to fright?. . . . .   306 Psalm XXVII   3
FRISK
    Thou seest, how friske, and jolly now he is, ...   103 3rd Eclogues 67   5
FRO
    Pas thought it hell, while he was Cosma fro. . . . .   248 Other Poems   4   245
FRONT
    Hath his front built of Alabaster pure;. . . . .   169 Astrophil   9   3
FRONTIERS
    Doth willing graunt, that in the frontiers he. . . . . . .   179 Astrophil   29   7
FROTHY
    Or loving, have so frothy thoughts, as easly thence to move: 217 A&S 7th Song   10
FROWARD
    You see what I can say; mend yet your froward mind,. . . . . 215 A&S 5th Song   88
FROWNS
    Who frownes at others' feastes, dooth better bide away.. . .   15 1st Eclogues 7   15
FROZEN
    Not usde to frozen clips, he strave to find some part, . . . 168 Astrophil   8   6
FRUIT
    These bolde words she did heare, this fruite I reaped, . . .   17 1st Eclogues 7   82
    You doo approch to the fruite your onely desirs be to
        gather . . . .   33 1st Eclogues 13   63
    Figge that yeeldes most pleasant frute, his shaddow is
        hurtefull, ...   35 1st Eclogues 13   125
    O only sonne that suche a fruite can breede. . . . .   43 Arcadia II   23   3
    Whyle upon chaunce, his fruite of labour lyes;. . . . . . .   71 Arcadia III 36   10
    Nowe that some flower of fruict, my paynes do prove, ...   72 Arcadia III 37   16
    Do foster still, the fruite of fancies darke:. . . . . . .   73 Arcadia III 39   6
    Thought, thinke to ende, too long the frute of thought . . .   83 Arcadia III 59   7
    Is this thy fruite O strife? those thousand churches hie,. . 119 4th Eclogues 73   111
    Was this man's death the fruite of your dissention?. . . . . 128 4th Eclogues 75   108
    Or reach the fruite of Nature's choisest tree, ... 169 Astrophil   10   4
    But never heeds the fruit of writer's mind:. . . . .   170 Astrophil   11   8
    Deeme that my Muse some fruit of knowledge plies:. . . . . . 176 Astrophil   23   6
    Whose fruit doth farre th' Esperian tast surpasse:. . . . .   208 Astrophil   82   6
    Whose braunches faile not timely fruite to nourish,. . . . . 270 Psalm I   9
    Their fruit shalt Thou from earthly face . . . . 297 Psalm XXI   37
    And knowes not who the fruit shall reap. . . . . 330 Psalm XXXIX   22
    For other's ease, their frutte, or free estate,. . . . . . . 345 Possibly   2   10
FRUITFUL
    Those pleasant plants, those sweete and frutefull trees, . .   26 1st Eclogues 9   130
    Feede on my sheepe, possesse your fruitefull fyeld,. . . . .   43 Arcadia II   23   7
    Some fresh and fruitfull showers upon my sunne-burn'd
        braine . . . . 165 Astrophil   1   8
FRUITLESS
    Lyke to my noble thoughtes, still new, well plac'd, to me
        fruteles. . . . . 35 1st Eclogues 13   124
    Their pasture is faire hilles of fruitlesse Love:. . . . . .   39 Arcadia II   17   2
FRUITLESSLY
    Shall fruitlesly be ended. . . . . 298 Psalm XXI   44
FRUITS
    Let so our fruites grow up, that nature be maintainde: . . .   45 Arcadia II   26   13
    What be the fruites of speaking arte? what growes by the
        words? Words.. . . . .   64 2nd Eclogues 31   30
    The sorry fruites of anguish,. . . . .   66 2nd Eclogues 32   33
    All peacock pride, and fruites of peacock's pride. . . . . .   93 3rd Eclogues 63   73
    To hie conceits whose fruits are oft but small,. . . . . . . 144 Cert Sonnets 15   10
    With fruits of happie sight, ... 151 Cert Sonnets 23   2
    Above line repeated at following location. . . . . 152 Cert Sonnets 23   34
    And not in Nature for best fruits unfit: . . . . 174 Astrophil   19   13
    Or gemmes, or frutes of new-found Paradise,. . . . . 207 Astrophil   81   2
    No mortall gifts, no earthly fruites, now here descended be: 217 A&S 7th Song   14
FRUSTRATE
    And past all hope his chapps to frustrate so.. . . . . 251 Other Poems   4   344
FRY
    Up to the sunne, although the sunne my wings do frie:. . . . 153 Cert Sonnets 24   25
FUEL
    The fuell small: how be the fires so great?. . . . .   42 Arcadia II   22   14
    Fuell to seeke and not to quench the fire: . . . .   95 3rd Eclogues 64   40
    Yet still her eyes give to my flames their fuell.. . . . . . 136 Cert Sonnets 3   12
    Till without fewell you can make hot fire. . . . . 188 Astrophil   46   14
FULFILL
    Can Love's duties best fulfill:. . . . . 263 Other Poems   7   38
FULFILLS
    Thy grace with safety man fulfills,. . . . . 323 Psalm XXXVI   17
FULL
    Who though she be no Bee, yet full of honie is:. . . . . . .   15 1st Eclogues 7   29
    Such weight it hath which once is full possest,. . . . . . .   20 1st Eclogues 7   V961
    Above line repeated at following location. . . . .   20 1st Eclogues 7   V962
    With vertue fraught and full of holy feare!. . . . .   25 1st Eclogues 9   95
    Thy words, though full of malapert offence,. . . . .   25 1st Eclogues 9   108
    Come narr good Mastix, tis now full tway score . . . .   27 1st Eclogues 10   20
    And preciouse couches full oft are shak't with a feaver.. .   34 1st Eclogues 13   86
    And so behinde foule clowdes full oft faire starres do ly
        hidden". . . . .   36 1st Eclogues 13   154
    Old age is wise and full of constant truth;. . . . .   39 Arcadia II   15   9
    My words full weake, the marble full of might; . . . .   41 Arcadia II   19   7
    From Cosma's eyes, which full in darkenes shine, ...   55 2nd Eclogues 29   103
    These wordes are full of woes, yet feele they none.. . . . .   75 Arcadia III 43   3

```
FULL              (CONTINUED)                           PAGE   TITLE           LINE
    Who full of guiltie spite, . . . . . . . . . . . . . . . . .  82 Arcadia III  55    9
    Bussing her oft, and in his hart full faine, . . . . . . . .  95 3rd Eclogues 64   51
    Though full of scorne, would not his duty misse, . . . . . .  96 3rd Eclogues 64   69
    Whereto two parties once be full content.. . . . . . . . . .  97 3rd Eclogues 64  126
    The welkin had full niggardly enclosed . . . . . . . . . . .  98 3rd Eclogues 66    8
    The caves were full, the mountaines voide of goates: . . . .  98 3rd Eclogues 66   11
    Full glad they were and tooke the naked sprite,. . . . . . . 101 3rd Eclogues 66   78
    Then gan in guiltlesse earth full many a wound,. . . . . . . 102 3rd Eclogues 66  115
    Who now his owne, full like his owne he used.. . . . . . . . 102 3rd Eclogues 66  142
    Full dead before, I now to dust should fall, . . . . . . . . 116 4th Eclogues 72   86
    I know full well you know, what discord long hath raign'd. . 119 4th Eclogues 73  105
    That thou full oft shalt wish thy judging eyes were blinde". 121 4th Eclogues 73  172
    His life a law, his looke a full correction: . . . . . . . . 128 4th Eclogues 75  133
    Full womanlike complaines her will was brokne. . . . . . . . 137 Cert Sonnets  4   16
    Paine heard her praise, and full of inward fire, . . . . . . 141 Cert Sonnets  9    9
    In too full winde draw in thy swelling sailes. . . . . . . . 143 Cert Sonnets 12   18
    For me alas I am full resolv'd . . . . . . . . . . . . . . . 153 Cert Sonnets 24   19
    She seemed full of jealous feares, . . . . . . . . . . . . . 158 Cert Sonnets 28   15
    Till by degrees it had full conquest got.. . . . . . . . . . 165 Astrophil     2    4
    Yet hiding royall bloud full oft in rurall vaine.. . . . . . 167 Astrophil     6    8
    That those lips swell, so full of thee they bee, . . . . . . 170 Astrophil    12    3
    And, Love, I thought that I was full of thee:. . . . . . . . 172 Astrophil    16    4
    What now the Dutch in their full diets boast;. . . . . . . . 180 Astrophil    30    6
    Nor give each speech a full point of a grone,. . . . . . . . 191 Astrophil    54    4
    What sighes stolne out, or kild before full borne? . . . . . 199 Astrophil    67    9
    For though full of desire, emptie of wit,. . . . . . . . . . 208 Astrophil    82    9
    Beware full sailes drowne not thy tottring barge:. . . . . . 209 Astrophil    85    2
    That full of doubts, thou of perplexity; . . . . . . . . . . 229 Astrophil    96    7
    Shewes her oft at the full her fairest face, . . . . . . . . 229 Astrophil    97    2
    Indeed full many folkes have said, . . . . . . . . . . . . . 274 Psalm IV          24
    That I, even I of heavnly comfort full,. . . . . . . . . . . 280 Psalm IX          43
    And Israel full of Comfort?. . . . . . . . . . . . . . . . . 287 Psalm XIV         24
    Full Wylily intended;. . . . . . . . . . . . . . . . . . . . 298 Psalm XXI         42
    That hand whose strength should help of bribes is full.. . . 306 Psalm XXVI        33
    Full of successe, fond I did say . . . . . . . . . . . . . . 311 Psalm XXX         20
    Which full of spight, of Pride and cruelty,. . . . . . . . . 313 Psalm XXXI        50
    Knowing full well that beasts they be. . . . . . . . . . . . 315 Psalm XXXII       34
    Full well his ey . . . . . . . . . . . . . . . . . . . . . . 317 Psalm XXXIII      50
    But make such glad, and full of joyfulness,. . . . . . . . . 323 Psalm XXXV        67
    Gnashing their teeth full of disdeigning;. . . . . . . . . . 325 Psalm XXXVII      34
    I have the Wicked seen full sound, . . . . . . . . . . . . . 327 Psalm XXXVII      89
    One said he brake acrosse; full well it so might be: . . . . 241 Other Poems   1    3
    But most cryed, "O well broke": O foole full gaily blest:. . 241 Other Poems   1    5
    And full, poore foole, of boyish bravery,. . . . . . . . . . 244 Other Poems   4   77
    So Lords with sport of Stagg and Hearon full . . . . . . . . 245 Other Poems   4  135
    He met hir full, but full of warefulnes, . . . . . . . . . . 252 Other Poems   4  386
    Till of his life it did full conquest win, . . . . . . . . . 253 Other Poems   4  430
FULLEST
    You seeke to nurse at fullest breasts of Fame, . . . . . . . 172 Astrophil    15   13
FULLNESS
    Foode without fulnes, counsaile without pride, . . . . . . . 103 3rd Eclogues 67   11
    Stella, the fulnesse of my thoughts of thee. . . . . . . . . 189 Astrophil    50    1
    All the fulness of delight,. . . . . . . . . . . . . . . . . 289 Psalm XVI         41
    The fulness of thy own heart's lusting;. . . . . . . . . . . 324 Psalm XXXVII      10
FULLY
    Here you fully do finde this strange operation of love,. . .  31 1st Eclogues 13    3
    Hate fully growne, Absence new sprongen out. . . . . . . . . 115 4th Eclogues 72   58
    In her let beautie both, and chastnesse fully raigne.. . . . 120 4th Eclogues 73  132
    And now fully beleeves helpe to be quite perished; . . . . . 122 4th Eclogues 74    2
    Or if thy mourning notes be fully spent, . . . . . . . . . . 127 4th Eclogues 75   64
    But who by hearesay speakes, and hath not fully felt . . . . 153 Cert Sonnets 24    6
    That in no more but these I might be fully blest:. . . . . . 205 Astrophil    77   13
    So my heart is fully glad, . . . . . . . . . . . . . . . . . 288 Psalm XVI         28
    Shall fully be rewarded. . . . . . . . . . . . . . . . . . . 295 Psalm XIX         48
FUME
    Fume not, rage not, frett not I say, . . . . . . . . . . . . 325 Psalm XXXVII      21
FUMES
    Whence those same fumes of melancholy rise,. . . . . . . . . 176 Astrophil    23    3
FUR
    But, but (alas) night's side the ods hath fur, . . . . . . . 229 Astrophil    96   12
    But feeling proofe makes me say they mistake it furre: . . . 232 Astrophil   102   11
    The lesson which but late he learn'd too furre:. . . . . . . 246 Other Poems   4  174
    Finding the gripe of Falcon fierce not furr: . . . . . . . . 251 Other Poems   4  356
FURIES
    Harke plaintfull ghostes, infernall furies harke . . . . . .  73 Arcadia III  40    1
FURIOUS
    The furious inward griefes with hellish wailing: . . . . . . 109 Arcadia IV   70   33
    As tender conscience might with furious panges assaulte. . . 117 4th Eclogues 73   20
    On horsebacke met him in his furious race, . . . . . . . . . 176 Astrophil    22    6
    So did he save me from my mighty furious foe,. . . . . . . . 291 Psalm XVIII       36
    Of furious floods he holds the reines, . . . . . . . . . . . 310 Psalm XXIX        26
FURNACE
    Since sighes (into mine inward fornace turnd). . . . . . . .  38 Arcadia II   14    7
    Through that darke fornace to my hart opprest, . . . . . . . 236 Astrophil   108    3
FURNISH
    Nico his place farre better furnish will.. . . . . . . . . .  53 2nd Eclogues 29   56
FURNITURE
    Prepar'd by Nature's chiefest furniture, . . . . . . . . . . 169 Astrophil     9    2
```

```
FURTHER                                                    PAGE    TITLE          LINE
     Looke further then, so shalt thou finde at least,. . . . . . .  75 Arcadia III    44    9
     Watched when she a furder pont might gaine,. . . . . . . . .   96 3rd Eclogues 64   75
     If further place might further me to ease. . . . . . . . . .  149 Cert Sonnets 21    4
     No further debt on me is laid, . . . . . . . . . . . . . . .  159 Cert Sonnets 29    2
     Without desire to feed of further grace. . . . . . . . . . .  187 Astrophil      46    8
FURY
     But that they stopt his furie from the same, . . . . . . . .  190 Astrophil      50   13
     Some do I heare of Poets' furie tell,. . . . . . . . . . . .  204 Astrophil      74    5
     Whose fury bends to harme: . . . . . . . . . . . . . . . . .  283 Psalm X             66
G
     Welcome my two to me, E.D. F.G. P.S. . . . . . . . . . . . .  261 Other Poems     6   25
     "Only for my two loves' sake, Sir Ed. D. and M. F. G.. . . .  263 Other Poems     7   61
GAGE
     But you must pay, the gage of promist weale. . . . . . . . .   76 Arcadia III    46   18
GAGED
     So both are yours: I, bound with gaged harte:. . . . . . . .   79 Arcadia III    50   21
GAILY
     First thinke they erre, that thinke them gayly wise, . . . .   25 1st Eclogues    9  111
     When that we see our ofspring gaily bent,. . . . . . . . . .   28 1st Eclogues   10   59
     Pas. But long have I a sparrow gailie drest, . . . . . . . .   54 2nd Eclogues   29   84
     But most cryed, "O well broke": O foole full gaily blest:. .  241 Other Poems     1    5
GAIN
     To narrow brests he comes all wrapt in gaine:. . . . . . . .   21 1st Eclogues    8   37
     So becomes our losse the triumph of her gayne; . . . . . . .   30 1st Eclogues   12   11
     Your woll is riche: no tonge can tell my gayne.. . . . . . .   43 Arcadia II     23   14
     You beare no woll, and losse is all my gayne.. . . . . . . .   44 Arcadia II     24   14
     Pas. This is not he that failed her to gaine,. . . . . . . .   54 2nd Eclogues   29   60
     Then then what do I gaine, since unto hir will I do winde?
          Winde. . . . . . . . . . . . . . . . . . . . . . . . . .   64 2nd Eclogues   31   34
     The marchante man, whome gayne dothe teache the Sea. . . . .   70 Arcadia III    36    1
     Watched when she a furder point might gaine, . . . . . . . .   96 3rd Eclogues   64   75
     In granting unto him a grandsire's gaine.. . . . . . . . . .  105 3rd Eclogues   67   75
     For all his strife can onlie bondage gaine.. . . . . . . . .  135 Cert Sonnets    2    8
     But hopes to gaine some helpe by mounting hie, . . . . . . .  144 Cert Sonnets   15    3
     Who may immortall gaine. . . . . . . . . . . . . . . . . . .  152 Cert Sonnets   23   20
     And Faith faire scorne doth gaine. . . . . . . . . . . . . .  159 Cert Sonnets   30    6
     Leave following that, which it is gaine to misse.. . . . . .  188 Astrophil      47   11
     Whether with words this soveraignty he gaine,. . . . . . . .  194 Astrophil      58    5
     His Sire's revenge, joyn'd with a kingdome's gaine:. . . . .  204 Astrophil      75    6
     Extolling ravenous gain: . . . . . . . . . . . . . . . . . .  281 Psalm X             11
     Who sells not guiltlesse cause, for filthy love of gain: . .  287 Psalm XV            12
     Let my uprightness gaine . . . . . . . . . . . . . . . . . .  305 Psalm XXV           73
     Than true deliverance gain.. . . . . . . . . . . . . . . . .  318 Psalm XXXIII        66
     Claymes but to gaine his due, O yeelde O yeelde. . . . . . .  345 Possibly        4    8
GAINED
     Al my sense thy sweetnesse gained, . . . . . . . . . . . . .  156 Cert Sonnets   27    1
     And gain'd by Mars, could yet mad Mars so tame,. . . . . . .  204 Astrophil      75    7
GAINS
     A fire, to burne the prisoners he gaines,. . . . . . . . . .  246 Other Poems     4  154
GAINSAY
     For when he will see who dare him gainesay,. . . . . . . . .  186 Astrophil      43    5
     And now, proud Rebell gan for to gainsay . . . . . . . . . .  246 Other Poems     4  173
GAINST
     Gainst neighbors good for womanish debate. . . . . . . . . .   93 3rd Eclogues   63   70
     Iron to seeke, which gainst it selfe should bend,. . . . . .  102 3rd Eclogues   66  116
     Gainst those of might, of whom in feare they stood,. . . . .  102 3rd Eclogues   66  130
     And so no helpe gainst envy of those powers? . . . . . . . .  142 Cert Sonnets   10   12
     Because I walk'd his wayes, nor gainst him ev'ly went, . . .  292 Psalm XVIII         44
     Not I but thou throw'st down those, who 'gainst me do rise;.  292 Psalm XVIII         72
     Where 'gainst Thee lay my sin. . . . . . . . . . . . . . . .  333 Psalm XLI           16
GALL
     (With gall cut out) closde up againe by art, . . . . . . . .  150 Cert Sonnets   22   23
     In steade of gall, leaving to her my hart: . . . . . . . . .  150 Cert Sonnets   22   28
GALLED
     (Spurd with love's spur, though gald and shortly raind . . .  230 Astrophil      98    7
GALLEIN'S
     Gallein's adoptive sonnes, who by a beaten way . . . . . . .  232 Astrophil     102    9
GAME
     Nay shame of men, the people's scorning game.. . . . . . . .  299 Psalm XXII          16
     That fooles of me may make their game. . . . . . . . . . . .  330 Psalm XXXIX         28
     Aha! This is good game.. . . . . . . . . . . . . . . . . . .  332 Psalm XL            60
     While nought but game, the selfe-hurt wanton ment. . . . . .  247 Other Poems     4  192
GAMES
     In lawlesse games, and love not as you should, . . . . . . .  106 3rd Eclogues   67   95
     Of all the games that here ere now I met:. . . . . . . . . .  254 Other Poems     4  494
GAMESOME
     And gamesome then, when he thinkes on his sheepe;. . . . . .  104 3rd Eclogues   67   35
     Geron, though olde yet gamesome, kept one ende . . . . . . .  248 Other Poems     4  242
GAN
     Fortune thus gan say; "misery and misfortune is all one, . .   29 1st Eclogues   11    3
     And out gan cry, "ah well away for shame,. . . . . . . . . .   95 3rd Eclogues   64   45
     But now the courtier gan to smell the feate, . . . . . . . .   97 3rd Eclogues   64  117
     Then gan in guiltlesse earth full many a wound,. . . . . . .  102 3rd Eclogues   66  115
     Then gan he factions in the beastes to breed;. . . . . . . .  102 3rd Eclogues   66  120
     And smirkly thus gan say. "I never sought debate . . . . . .  120 4th Eclogues   73  147
     On me the paines of death already gan to prey, . . . . . . .  291 Psalm XVIII          8
     And now, proud Rebell gan for to gainsay . . . . . . . . . .  246 Other Poems     4  173
GANDER
     Pas. Another sure as is a gander from a goose: . . . . . . .   52 2nd Eclogues   29   23
```

	PAGE	TITLE		LINE
GANIMED				
Whose talents held young Ganimed above:	171	Astrophil	13	4
GAPE				
Since Nico doth to sing so widely gape?	53	2nd Eclogues	29	55
GAPED				
Who long have gap't to get Arcadians' treasure.	129	4th Eclogues	76	21
GAPING				
From out that noysome gulfe, which gaping lies	205	Astrophil	78	3
Now like a lion gaping to make preyes, ...	290	Psalm XVII		33
Up lord prevent those gaping jawes	290	Psalm XVII		35
With gaping mouthes, these folks on me have charged, ...	299	Psalm XXII		29
GARDEN				
The world the garden is, she is the flower	59	2nd Eclogues	30	98
Nymph of the gard'n, where all beauties be:	207	Astrophil	82	1
Sweet gard'n Nymph, which keepes the Cherrie tree, ...	208	Astrophil	82	5
GARLAND				
A rosie garland, and a wearie hed:	184	Astrophil	39	11
A garland made on temples for to weare, ...	244	Other Poems	4	74
GARMENTS				
Such hartes of brasse, wise heads, and garments trim	24	1st Eclogues	9	75
GARNISHED				
Want I white wooll, whose eyes her white skinne garnished? .	16	1st Eclogues	7	59
Private with welth, publike with quiet garnished.	128	4th Eclogues	75	129
GARRISON				
"Thou art no souldier fitte for Cupid's garrison.	16	1st Eclogues	7	51
GARTERING				
The gartring place with child-like signe, ...	89	Arcadia III	62	99
GAT				
Beyond our worlde, and ere I gatt my boothe.	98	3rd Eclogues	66	4
Pitie thereof gate in her breast such place.	187	Astrophil	45	7
This much, yet more, when I by him this freedom gate, ...	292	Psalm XVIII		40
GATES				
Thou lord that from Death' gates hast lifted me, ...	280	Psalm IX		39
Lift up your heads you Gates, and you doores ever biding, . .	302	Psalm XXIV		17
Above line repeated at following location.	302	Psalm XXIV		21
GATHER				
You doo approch to the fruite your onely desirs be to				
gather	33	1st Eclogues	13	63
Now by thy words I begin, most famous Lady, to gather. . . .	34	1st Eclogues	13	94
What life it is, and how that all these lives doo gather, . .	118	4th Eclogues	73	47
Which all against me gather:	272	Psalm III		21
GAVE				
Which at firste voly gave too open entry, ...	68	2nd Eclogues	33	14
Then gave he him the blow which never smarted.	97	3rd Eclogues	64	120
To worthy Coredens he gave me ore.	99	3rd Eclogues	66	40
The Lion, harte; the Ounce gave active might;	101	3rd Eclogues	66	80
Elephant gave a perfect memorie:	101	3rd Eclogues	66	83
The Foxe gave crafte; the Dog gave flatterie;	101	3rd Eclogues	66	85
Ape great thing gave, though he did mowing stand, ...	101	3rd Eclogues	66	97
If many Kalaes our Arcadia gave, ...	104	3rd Eclogues	67	22
O paine I now recant the praise I gave, ...	141	Cert Sonnets	9	13
Love gave the wound, which while I breathe will bleed: . . .	165	Astrophil	2	2
Placed ever there, gave him this mourning weed, ...	168	Astrophil	7	13
By Nature borne, I gave to thee mine eyes.	198	Astrophil	65	8
Earth gave that Love, heav'n I trow Love refineth:	209	A&S 3rd Song		11
And then, a heav'nly child, gave her Ambrosian pap:	213	A&S 5th Song		26
Gave repulse all grace excelling.	219	A&S 8th Song		68
That to hir breast he gave a noysome blowe.	249	Other Poems	4	272
A shot unheard gave me a wound unseene?.	253	Other Poems	4	454
He quickly knew what witchcraft gave the blow.	256	Other Poems	4	539
GAVEST				
Thou gavest me saving shield, Thy right hand was my stay; . .	292	Psalm XVIII		64
Thou gavest me their necks, on them Thou mad'est me passe. .	292	Psalm XVIII		73
Thou him a long life gavest;	297	Psalm XXI		14
GAY				
Come from marble bowers, many times the gay harbor of				
anguish, ...	34	1st Eclogues	13	92
Gay haire more gaie then straw when harvest lyes, ...	76	Arcadia III	46	7
Longing to be with losse of substance gay.	93	3rd Eclogues	63	74
The Waspe seemes gay, but is a cumbrous thing.	104	3rd Eclogues	67	21
With such a rosie morne, whose beames most freshly gay . . .	205	Astrophil	76	7
GAZE				
In whose Incirclets if you gaze, ...	86	Arcadia III	62	31
Nor beasts, nor birds do come unto this blessed gaze, ...	209	A&S 3rd Song		15
They look, they gaze, my boanes might be rehearsed;	299	Psalm XXII		42
GAZER'S				
They should still daunce to please a gazer's sight.	178	Astrophil	26	8
GAZING				
Some gazing still, some winking wilye shiftes, ...	21	1st Eclogues	8	27
(Better despisde) bewondre gasing eye.	81	Arcadia III	54	12
Eyes, let your Teares with gazing now be mended, ...	84	Arcadia III	59	14
With gazing looks, short sighs, unsettled feet, ...	251	Other Poems	4	369
GEM				
Arcadia's gemme the noblest childe of nature.	109	Arcadia IV	70	18
As for to lose thy gemme, our earthly Sainct, ...	125	4th Eclogues	75	18
The richest gemme of Love and life enjoyes, ...	177	Astrophil	24	10
And so to take the gemme Urania sought.	250	Other Poems	4	324
GEMS				
The knottes of joy, the gemmes of love, ...	89	Arcadia III	62	95
O kisse, which doest those ruddie gemmes impart, ...	207	Astrophil	81	1

GEMS   (CONTINUED)   PAGE   TITLE   LINE
     Or gemmes, or frutes of new-found Paradise,. . . . . 207 Astrophil 81   2
GENERATION
     Root out their generation. . . . .   297 Psalm XXI   40
     Jacob this is Thy seed, God seeking generation,. . . . . . 302 Psalm XXIV   15
GENTILES
     The Gentiles Thou rebuked sorely hast, ... 279 Psalm IX   11
     Up lord, and judg the Gentyls in Thy right . . . . 281 Psalm IX   61
     Among the Gentiles then I, Lord, yeild thanks to Thee, . . 293 Psalm XVIII   88
GENTLE
     With gentle beames not hurting sight:. . . . .   13 Arcadia I   5   8
     But well you know, the gentle Sunne would save . . . . . .   60 2nd Eclogues 30 104
     Whose gentle rayes suche Luster fynde, ...   89 Arcadia III 62 V115
     As horse and dogge, not great, but gentle blood: . . . . . 102 3rd Eclogues 66 131
     As for the gentle birds, like case might rewe. . . . . . . 102 3rd Eclogues 66 139
     Depart, a word so gentle to my minde,. . . . . 148 Cert Sonnets 20   3
     Of gentle force, so that mine eyes dare gladly play. . . . 205 Astrophil   76   6
     Yet gentle English theeves do rob, but will not slay;. . . 214 A&S 5th Song   49
     These gentle Lawyers wage, ... 215 A&S 6th Song   14
GENTLEMEN
     The first, thus matcht, were scarcely Gentlemen. . . . . . 171 Astrophil   13 14
GENTLY
     As thou wilt deigne to reade, and gentlie reede, ...   96 3rd Eclogues 64 95
     The lord my suite did heare, and gently heare, ... 276 Psalm VI   29
     Which Holland sweet now gently sendeth in, ... 259 Other Poems   5 106
GERON
     Geron. Up, up Philisides, let sorrowes goe,. . . . .   22 1st Eclogues 9   1
     Geron. Yet sure an end, to each thing time doth give,. . .   22 1st Eclogues 9 11
     Geron. What can amend where physick is refusde?. . . . . .   23 1st Eclogues 9 21
     Geron. Alas what falls are falne unto thy minde? . . . . .   23 1st Eclogues 9 32
     Geron. If that thy face were hid, or I were blinde, . . .   25 1st Eclogues 9 96
     Geron. Downe, downe Melampus; what? your fellow bite?. . .   26 1st Eclogues 10   1
     Geron. Fy man, fy man, what wordes hath thy tonge lent?. . . 28 1st Eclogues 10 61
     Geron. In faith, good Histor, long is your delay,. . . . . 103 3rd Eclogues 67   1
     Geron. Who for ech fickle feare from vertue shrinkes,. . . 105 3rd Eclogues 67 58
     Geron, though olde yet gamesome, kept one ende . . . . . . 248 Other Poems   4 242
     So he with Nous to Geron turn'd their race,. . . . . 248 Other Poems   4 251
     Geron strave hard, but aged were his feet, ... 248 Other Poems   4 254
     Geron with Uran were condemn'd to hell.. . . . . 249 Other Poems   4 264
     Till that he spied old Geron could no more,. . . . . 250 Other Poems   4 307
     So that Uran, whose arme old Geron bore, ... 250 Other Poems   4 309
     The other end Geron with Uran garde. . . . . 250 Other Poems   4 319
     Nous counseld Strephon Geron to pursue,. . . . . 250 Other Poems   4 321
     While Geron olde came safe to Cosma true,. . . . . 250 Other Poems   4 325
GET
     Till I get her, shall I to sheep enure my selfe? . . . . .   16 1st Eclogues 7 60
     Say then what vantage do we get, by the trade of a Pastor? . 33 1st Eclogues 13 49
     And may I not (say I then) gett up though griefs be so
         weightie?. . . . .   36 1st Eclogues 13 128
     And hopes with foule embracements her to get,. . . . . . .   59 2nd Eclogues 30 90
     In thy high minde) get her thy husband's grace. . . . . .   60 2nd Eclogues 30 114
     Echo, what do I gett yelding my sprite to my grieves?
         Grieves. . . . .   63 2nd Eclogues 31   5
     Get hence foule Griefe, the canker of the minde: . . . . .   83 Arcadia III 59   1
     How they might get that guest, from them to wend,. . . . .   95 3rd Eclogues 64 53
     As we to get are fram'd, so they to spare: . . . . 106 3rd Eclogues 67 106
     When they by yeares' experience get best graces, ... 127 4th Eclogues 75 89
     Who long have gap't to get Arcadians' treasure.. . . . . . 129 4th Eclogues 76 21
     But, foole, seekst not to get into her hart. . . . . 170 Astrophil   11 14
     Till bloudie bullet get him wrongfull pray.. . . . . 175 Astrophil   20   4
     Yet Deare, let me this pardon get of you,. . . . . 188 Astrophil   46 12
     May get no almes but scorne of beggerie. . . . . 188 Astrophil   47   8
     Rather then by more truth to get more paine. . . . . 199 Astrophil   67 14
     Come no more, least I get anger.". . . . . 234 A&S 11th Song   37
     Go my flocke, go get you hence,. . . . . 221 A&S 9th Song   1
     Get hence you ev'ill, who in my ev'ill rejoyce,. . . . . . 276 Psalm VI   25
     To that high doome, which I by Thee must get.. . . . . . . 277 Psalm VII   18
     Whom to their losse he still doth get. . . . . 282 Psalm X   39
     I will get up saith God, and my help show. . . . . 285 Psalm XII   16
     And, so I did safety gett, ... 309 Psalm XXVIII   28
     Let their sly witts unwares destruction get, ... 321 Psalm XXXV   17
     But rise, but wake that I may judgment gett. . . . . 322 Psalm XXXV   57
     Till his known ev'ill do hatred get. . . . . 323 Psalm XXXVI   8
     Will. What living get you then? D. Disdayne; but just
         disdayne.. . . . . 344 Possibly   1 35
     He treble beas for helpe, but none can get:. . . . . 254 Other Poems   4 492
GETS
     Farre more happy be you, whose greatnes gets a free accesse, 33 1st Eclogues 13 54
     In thy owne proofe he gets so straunge possession, ...   48 2nd Eclogues 28 35
     A bird which gets more life then ship had lost.. . . . . . 151 Cert Sonnets 22 54
GETTING
     And getting youth againe, in youth doth flourish:. . . . . 127 4th Eclogues 75 83
GHASTLINESS
     In thee or sprites or spirited gastlinesse:. . . . . 229 Astrophil   96 11
GHASTLY
     Earth, sea, ayre, fire, heav'n, hell, and gastly sprite. . . 23 1st Eclogues 9 40
     In night of sprites the gastly powers stur,. . . . . 229 Astrophil   96 10
     Alas! of ghostes I heare the gastly cries: . . . . 255 Other Poems   4 507
GHOST
     Where plagu'd for rash attempt, gives up his ghost,. . . . 151 Cert Sonnets 22 57

GHOSTS
Harke plaintfull ghostes, infernall furies harke . . . . . . 73 Arcadia III 40 1
Alas! of ghostes I heare the gastly cries: . . . . 255 Other Poems 4 507
GIANTS
As glad is he, as Giants be. . . . . 294 Psalm XIX 23
GIFT
And of misfortune, fortune hath only the gift. . . . . 29 1st Eclogues 11 4
The giver giv'n from gifte shall never parte. . . . . 77 Arcadia III 47 14
Each sence of mine, each gift, each power of mind, ... 193 Astrophil 57 2
GIFTS
Who in one selfe these diverse gifts can plant; . . . . 3 Lady of May 1 4
Such planted gifts enrich even beggers' sight; . . . . 3 Lady of May 1 10
And for a tast of all these gifts, she borowes Momus' grace. 12 Arcadia I 3 8
My Kala's giftes: who with all good gifts filled is. . . . . 15 1st Eclogues 7 26
Yet beares he still his parents' stately gifts, ... 21 1st Eclogues 8 25
whose faire bodily gifts are fram'd most lovely to each ey.. 33 1st Eclogues 13 55
Thus be her giftes most sweet, thus more danger to be neere
  her, ... 36 1st Eclogues 13 126
Time, place, life, wit scarcely her rare gifts measure doth. 49 2nd Eclogues 28 60
That he, to whome these sondrie giftes I binde, ... 78 Arcadia III 50 9
What be her giftes, that make her equall thee, ... 80 Arcadia III 52 8
The more his matchlesse giftes do deeply sinck. . . . . 85 Arcadia III 61 11
And so to him and her your giftes distill, ... 91 3rd Eclogues 63 22
Muses graunt guiftes, Nymphes long and joyned life . . . . . 93 3rd Eclogues 63 92
Which heav'nly purest gifts defile in muddy cares. . . . . . 117 4th Eclogues 73 18
Her giftes my study was, her beauties were my sporte: . . . 117 4th Eclogues 73 41
Of all those Graces' giftes the heavens have ever lent. . . 119 4th Eclogues 73 86
And let her have the giftes that should in both remaine: . . 120 4th Eclogues 73 131
So as if I prevaile, you give your giftes to me: . . . . . . 120 4th Eclogues 73 133
First having all their giftes upon faire Mira spred. . . . . 121 4th Eclogues 73 178
As treasure house where her best gifts abyde. . . . . 141 Cert Sonnets 8 8
Rich in those gifts which give th'eternall crowne; . . . . . 183 Astrophil 37 11
Since to himselfe he doth your gifts apply, ... 186 Astrophil 43 3
Although lesse gifts impe feathers oft on Fame, ... 204 Astrophil 75 4
Or of tny gifts at least shade out some part. . . . . 207 Astrophil 81 8
And to that braine of hers your hidnest gifts infused, . . . 213 A&S 5th Song 27
Nc mortall gifts, no earthly fruites, now here descended be: 217 A&S 7th Song 14
And in those gifts that years distribute doe, ... 242 Other Poems 4 22
Is by nature's giftes procured.. . . . . 263 Other Poems 7 36
GILD
But golde can guild a rotten piece of wood, ... 245 Other Poems 4 124
GILDED
A Cage (guilded perchaunce) is all his lott. . . . . 28 1st Eclogues 10 69
With guilded leaves or colourd Velume playes, ... 170 Astrophil 11 6
In beams of beauty guilded.. . . . . 294 Psalm XIX 20
GILT
Curb'd in with feare, but with guilt bosse above . . . . . . 189 Astrophil 49 7
GIN
But hast enlargd my feet from mortall ginn.. . . . . 312 Psalm XXXI 24
GINS
With twenty ginnes we will the small birds take, ... 18 1st Eclogues 7 126
My day newe cares; my ginnes my daily sight, ... 18 1st Eclogues 7 140
GIRDED
This God then girded me in his Almighty pow'rs, ... 292 Psalm XVIII 59
GIRL'S
A young girle's hart, to that were shame for both, ... 95 3rd Eclogues 64 59
GIRLS
Sweet babes must babies have, but shrewd gyrles must be
  beat n.. . . . . 213 A&S 5th Song 36
When she with skirts tuckt very hy, with girles at stoolball
  playes. . . . . 343 Possibly 1 10
GIROSOL
He stood, but turn'd, as Girosol, to Sun:. . . . . 251 Other Poems 4 370
GIRT
Girt fast by memorie, and while I spurre . . . . 189 Astrophil 49 10
GIVE
Greater is she who must the judgement give.. . . . . 3 Lady of May 2 6
All this I give, let me possesse thy grace, ... 4 Lady of May 2 22
Geron. Yet sure an end, to each thing time doth give . . . . 22 1st Eclogues 9 11
What counsell can prevaile, or light give light? . . . . . . 23 1st Eclogues 9 36
Give right sound to the eares, and enter aright to the
  judgement; . . . . 32 1st Eclogues 13 18
Give therefore to the Muse great praise in whose very
  likenes. . . . . 33 1st Eclogues 13 62
O be it so, graunte such an event, O Gods, that event give.. 37 1st Eclogues 13 169
In you it is, you must the judgement give. . . . . 39 Arcadia II 17 8
Give us foresightfull mindes: give us minds to obaye . . . . 45 Arcadia II 26 11
R.p. Then let us both to heavenly rules give place, ... 47 2nd Eclogues 27 41
As thou wilt give our soules a deare refection, ... 49 2nd Eclogues 28 52
But when to give some grace she doth content herselfe, . . . 49 2nd Eclogues 28 64
Pas. Nay like to nightingales the other birds give eare: . . 52 2nd Eclogues 29 19
That will I take, and to my Leuca give.. . . . . 54 2nd Eclogues 29 83
End? but I can never end, love will not give me the leave.
  Leave. . . . . 63 2nd Eclogues 31 16
What great name may I give to so heav'nly a woman? A
  woe-man . . . . 64 2nd Eclogues 31 37
Since all the thinges which give mine eyes their light . . . 73 Arcadia III 39 5
And geve a long desire a sweet content.. . . . . 97 3rd Eclogues 64 106
I will you lende; the rest your selves must give, ... 101 3rd Eclogues 66 76
The Stagge did give the harme eschewing feare. . . . . 101 3rd Eclogues 66 91

GIVE   (CONTINUED)   PAGE   TITLE   LINE

	PAGE	TITLE		LINE
They all consented were to give him wings:	101	3rd Eclogues	66	101
I give the Sunne a last farewell each evening;	112	4th Eclogues	71	50
When I, disgraced wretch, not wretched then, did give.	117	4th Eclogues	73	11
So as if I prevaile, you give your giftes to me:	120	4th Eclogues	73	133
To worthiest let him give, when both he hath beheld:	120	4th Eclogues	73	142
"Nay then (Diana said) the chastnesse I will give.	121	4th Eclogues	73	173
If then a man in most ill case may give you a farewell;	124	4th Eclogues	74	85
Then give a quiet eare unto my playning:	127	4th Eclogues	75	65
Yet still her eyes give to my flames their fuell..	136	Cert Sonnets	3	12
Give me my kisses.	138	Cert Sonnets	5	24
The restfull Caves now restlesse visions give,	147	Cert Sonnets	18	9
For if my place give me great pleasure,	159	Cert Sonnets	29	5
That doth both shine and give us sight to see.	161	Cert Sonnets	32	8
But to my selfe my selfe did give the blow,	181	Astrophil	33	9
Rich in those gifts which give th'eternall crowne;	183	Astrophil	37	11
Glad if for her he give them leave to die.	186	Astrophil	43	8
Doth make my heart give to my tongue the lie.	188	Astrophil	47	14
Nor give each speech a full point of a grone,	191	Astrophil	54	4
O give my passions leave to run their race:	198	Astrophil	64	2
And though she give but thus conditionly	200	Astrophil	69	12
I give you here my hand for truth of this,	201	Astrophil	70	13
"But ah," Desire still cries, "give me some food."	201	Astrophil	71	14
That presence, which doth give darke hearts a living light:	205	Astrophil	77	3
Teaching the meane, at once to take and give	206	Astrophil	79	9
But give apt servants their due place, let eyes.	210	Astrophil	85	9
Since Stella's eyes, wont to give me my day,	223	Astrophil	89	3
What sobs can give words grace my griefe to show?.	227	Astrophil	93	2
And do I then my selfe this vaine scuse give?	227	Astrophil	93	9
While sobd out words a perfect Musike give..	231	Astrophil	100	11
Sweete, for a while give respite to my hart,	236	Astrophil	107	5
And on my thoughts give thy Lieftenancy.	236	Astrophil	107	7
"Peace, I thinke that some give eare:	234	A&S 11th Song		36
Ask I will give yt Thee,	271	Psalm II		18
He will give good eare to my moane.	273	Psalm IV		15
Give them their due unto their guiltiness,	275	Psalm V		29
Then lord, my lord, give sentence on my side	277	Psalm VII		23
I will give thanks unto the lord of Us	278	Psalm VII		46
Which He prepar'd, to give his judgments high:	280	Psalm IX		22
To give unawares a Mortall blow.	284	Psalm XI		7
But Thou (O lord) give them a thorough fall,	284	Psalm XII		7
Nay give me eyes, and light, least that I sleep.	285	Psalm XIII		11
And boldly say Thou wilt give eare to me,	289	Psalm XVII		18
But when he calld this lord did give him hearing..	300	Psalm XXII		58
Oh, give me not, for there are sproong	308	Psalm XXVII		56
Spare not them, give them reward	309	Psalm XXVIII		16
To Thy Works they give no ey..	309	Psalm XXVIII		21
But let me give prayses high	309	Psalm XXVIII		24
God to his people strength shall give,	310	Psalm XXIX		28
Shall ever dust give thanks to Thee,	311	Psalm XXX		28
Wherto my heart did give me;	315	Psalm XXXII		15
Give hearty thanks to him on high,	318	Psalm XXXIV		2
Lord unto my time's just measure give,	329	Psalm XXXIX		13
To my God that give me breathing.	335	Psalm XLII		40
D. Her heavenly looks, which more and more do give me cause to crave.	344	Possibly	1	32
The Arrow being shot from far, doth give the smaller blowe..	344	Possibly	1	42
"O earth, once answere give,	256	Other Poems	5	14
Give leave your flockes to range,	261	Other Poems	6	31

GIVEN

	PAGE	TITLE		LINE
By just exchange, one for the other giv'ne..	75	Arcadia III	45	2
Giv'ne to my harte, by my fore wounded eyne:	77	Arcadia III	47	6
My harte my worde, my worde hath giv'ne my harte.	77	Arcadia III	47	13
The giver giv'n from gifte shall never parte.	77	Arcadia III	47	14
But now the fitt is past: and time hath show'd	83	Arcadia III	57	9
Such thing cannot I seeke (Despaire hath giv'n me my answer.	122	4th Eclogues	74	11
Bend your thoghts to the dear sweet words which then to me giv'n were:	124	4th Eclogues	74	75
Upon that coast, am giv'n up for a slave..	179	Astrophil	29	14
Of her high heart giv'n me the monarchie:	200	Astrophil	69	10
Who word to neighbour given doth faithfully maintain	287	Psalm XV		9
Thou hast given what his heart would have,	297	Psalm XXI		5
Than I was giv'en to Thee, Thou wert my God.	299	Psalm XXII		24

GIVER

	PAGE	TITLE		LINE
The giver giv'n from gifte shall never parte..	77	Arcadia III	47	14
O Titan faire the giver of the daie?	80	Arcadia III	52	2
Shall feed and laud the giver of their food.	300	Psalm XXII		72

GIVES

	PAGE	TITLE		LINE
Thus reason to his Servantes gyves his right	12	Arcadia I	2	V811
Till now at length that Jove him office gives,	22	1st Eclogues	8	45
Gives happs or mishapps, ev'n as he ordreth his hearte..	29	1st Eclogues	11	8
Old age orecome, the greater honour gives.	39	Arcadia II	15	12
Winde, tempests, and stormes, yet in ende what gives she desire? Ire.	64	2nd Eclogues	31	35
Which to my woes gives still an early morning:	111	4th Eclogues	71	5
Gives an adieu to the world, as to his onely delight:	123	4th Eclogues	74	26
Where plagu'd for rash attempt, gives up his ghost,	151	Cert Sonnets	22	57
The glasse to you but gives a shade,	159	Cert Sonnets	29	12
Since kind or chance gives both one liverie,	229	Astrophil	96	2
So purely wise it gives the eyes	294	Psalm XIX		35

```
GIVES              (CONTINUED)                        PAGE    TITLE              LINE
    He lends, he gives, more he doth spend . . . . . . . . . . .  326  Psalm XXXVII          65
    Dick. What joy the joyfull sunne gives unto bleared eyes:. .  343  Possibly        1     13
    W. If wages make you want, what food is that she gives?. . .  344  Possibly        1     33
    But God gives them instinct the man to shun, . . . . . . . .  249  Other Poems     4    295
    Tell, if that breath, which thee thy sounding gives, . . . .  258  Other Poems     5     63
    And gives her kidds no food, but willow's barke.". . . . . .  259  Other Poems     5    113
GIVEST
    That giv'st no better eare to my just cries: . . . . . . . .  198  Astrophil      65      2
GIVETH
    The good is kind and freely giveth;. . . . . . . . . . . . .  326  Psalm XXXVII          54
    Giveth me my might,. . . . . . . . . . . . . . . . . . . . .  336  Psalm XLIII            8
    Of you, to my hart giveth. . . . . . . . . . . . . . . . . .  261  Other Poems     6     52
GIVING
    With sword of wit, giving wounds of dispraise, . . . . . . .  170  Astrophil      10     10
    Giving frankly niggard No: . . . . . . . . . . . . . . . . .  202  A&S 2nd Song          10
    Of which the two life-giving lights are figured in her eyes:  217  A&S 7th Song          16
    Giving his reason pasport for to passe,. . . . . . . . . . .  252  Other Poems     4    381
    And giving to his sight a wandring race, . . . . . . . . . .  255  Other Poems     4    526
    Of God Apolloe's giving, . . . . . . . . . . . . . . . . . .  260  Other Poems     6      8
GLAD
    More gladde to me, then to a miser monie is. . . . . . . . .   15  1st Eclogues    7     33
    Her stepps, gladd we receave, gladd we receave her eys.. . .   69  2nd Eclogues   34     40
    The bellie there gladde sight doth fill, . . . . . . . . . .   88  Arcadia III    62     77
    Glad was the man when he had heard her out,. . . . . . . . .   96  3rd Eclogues   64     63
    So may thy flockes encrease, thy deere hart glad,. . . . . .   96  3rd Eclogues   64     93
    Full glad they were and tooke the naked sprite, . . . . . . .  101  3rd Eclogues   66     78
    But certainly so long we may be glad,. . . . . . . . . . . .  105  3rd Eclogues   67     64
    And be it as he saith". Venus was glad to heare. . . . . . .  120  4th Eclogues   73    143
    As for my mirth, how could I but be glad,. . . . . . . . . .  147  Cert Sonnets   17     41
    Glad if for her he give them leave to die. . . . . . . . . .  186  Astrophil      43      8
    Sicke, thirsty, glad (though but of empty glasse:) . . . . .  233  Astrophil     104     11
    Who makes a man live then glad when he dieth?. . . . . . . .  197  A&S 1st Song          26
    With glad moning passed anguish, . . . . . . . . . . . . . .  227  A&S 10th Song         39
    Sighs of woes were glad sighs mixt,. . . . . . . . . . . . .  218  A&S 8th Song          18
    That Jacob freed by Thee may glad become . . . . . . . . . .  287  Psalm XIV             23
    So my heart is fully glad, . . . . . . . . . . . . . . . . .  288  Psalm XVI             28
    As glad is he, as Giants be. . . . . . . . . . . . . . . . .  294  Psalm XIX             23
    Be glad you good, in God have joy, . . . . . . . . . . . . .  316  Psalm XXXII           40
    But make such glad, and full of joyfulness,. . . . . . . . .  323  Psalm XXXV            67
    Glad on me,. . . . . . . . . . . . . . . . . . . . . . . . .  328  Psalm XXXVIII         47
    Who may be glad, be glad you be not such:. . . . . . . . . .  242  Other Poems     4     15
    But glad Desire, his late embosom'd guest, . . . . . . . . .  247  Other Poems     4    201
GLADDED
    I both in mind, and bones shall gladded be.. . . . . . . . .  321  Psalm XXXV            20
GLADDER
    In flowry fielde a gladder eye to please:. . . . . . . . . .  256  Other Poems     5      3
GLADLY
    Who of his tongue the lickowr gladly powrs,. . . . . . . . .   28  1st Eclogues   10     70
    P. We gladly use the sweetnes of our life. . . . . . . . . .   46  2nd Eclogues   27     26
    Then might I wisely swimme or gladly sinke.. . . . . . . . .  148  Cert Sonnets   19      6
    Gladly my senses yeelded.. . . . . . . . . . . . . . . . . .  154  Cert Sonnets   25      8
    Gladly my senses yeelding, . . . . . . . . . . . . . . . . .  154  Cert Sonnets   25      9
    Of gentle force, so that mine eyes dare gladly play. . . . .  205  Astrophil      76      6
    Still gladly say, Unto our God bee prayse. . . . . . . . . .  332  Psalm XL              64
GLADNESS
    Of comming gladnes.. . . . . . . . . . . . . . . . . . . . .   83  Arcadia III    59     12
    O Philomela faire, o take some gladnesse,. . . . . . . . . .  137  Cert Sonnets    4      9
    Above line repeated at following location. . . . . . . . . .  137  Cert Sonnets    4     21
    God of all my gladness.. . . . . . . . . . . . . . . . . . .  336  Psalm XLIII           24
GLADS
    More in his owne he toyld he gladdes the more. . . . . . . .   71  Arcadia III    36     12
GLADSCME
    And madest me gladscm weeds enjoy, . . . . . . . . . . . . .  311  Psalm XXX             36
GLADST
    Unspeakably his heart Thou glad'st,. . . . . . . . . . . . .  297  Psalm XXI             23
GLARING
    As stuffe meant for the sale set out to glaring showe) . . .  118  4th Eclogues   73     72
GLASS
    In watry glasse my watrie eyes I see:. . . . . . . . . . . .   41  Arcadia II     21      5
    Pas. As in a glasse I held she once did looke, . . . . . . .   55  2nd Eclogues   29    114
    And in thy case do glasse mine owne debilitie: . . . . . . .   60  2nd Eclogues   30    129
    With Diamond in window-glasse she graved,. . . . . . . . . .   61  2nd Eclogues   30    156
    A wreched wracke, a glasse of Ruine's ende.. . . . . . . . .   73  Arcadia III    40      4
    Right so my inwarde partes, and outward glasse,. . . . . . .   78  Arcadia III    50      6
    With hanches smooth as looking glasse. . . . . . . . . . . .   88  Arcadia III    62     92
    The glasse to you but gives a shade, . . . . . . . . . . . .  159  Cert Sonnets   29     12
    Which lookes too oft in his unflattring glasse:. . . . . . .  178  Astrophil      27     10
    His who till death lookt in a watrie glasse, . . . . . . . .  207  Astrophil      82      3
    Sicke, thirsty, glad (though but of empty glasse:) . . . . .  233  Astrophil     104     11
    Dead glasse, doost thou thy object so imbrace, . . . . . . .  235  Astrophil     105      3
    Sins brew'd in youthfull glass,. . . . . . . . . . . . . . .  303  Psalm XXV             26
    (With blushing soule at sight of judgement's glasse, . . . .  255  Other Poems     4    531
GLASSES
    The glasses of thy dayly vexing care?" . . . . . . . . . . .  181  Astrophil      34      3
GLASSETH
    This winde he spent: but when my Kala glasseth all . . . . .   16  1st Eclogues    7     55
GLEAMING
    Two gleaming Sunnes of splendour like I see, . . . . . . . .   81  Arcadia III    55      4
```

	PAGE	TITLE		LINE
GLEAMS				
Least if no vaile those brave gleames did disguise,.	168	Astrophil	7	7
GLEE				
Dick. Ah Will, though I grudge not, I count it feeble glee .	343	Possibly	1	3
GLISTERING				
And then descried the glistring of his dart:	175	Astrophil	20	13
Her flamie glistring lights increase with time and place;. .	205	Astrophil	76	10
Models such be wood-globes of glistring skies.	225	Astrophil	91	11
GLITTERING				
Let not a glittring name thy fancie dresse	23	1st Eclogues	9	47
Dorus. O glittring miseries of man, if this be the fortune .	34	1st Eclogues	13	89
Which though of glittring golde, shall heere take rust . . .	92	3rd Eclogues	63	57
Or glittering golden mony?	294	Psalm XIX		42
D. Wonder that by two so black eyes the glittering stars be				
past.	343	Possibly	1	28
GLOBE				
The globe of weale, lips Love's indentures make:	210	Astrophil	85	13
The earth is God's, and what the Globe of earth containeth,.	302	Psalm XXIV		1
And all who in that Globe do dwell;.	302	Psalm XXIV		2
GLOBES				
Models such be wood-globes of glistring skies.	225	Astrophil	91	11
GLORIES				
Who glories in his love, doth make Love glorious:.	47	2nd Eclogues	28	16
GLORIFY				
Lalus. Muse hold your peace: but thou, my God Pan, glorify .	15	1st Eclogues	7	25
GLORICUS				
P. O glorious title of a foolish toye.	46	2nd Eclogues	27	20
Who glories in his love, doth make Love glorious:.	47	2nd Eclogues	28	16
But glorious name of wretched humaine-kind?.	57	2nd Eclogues	30	16
And farewell Prince, whom goodnesse hath made glorious.. . .	129	4th Eclogues	75	142
O eyes, where humble lookes most glorious prove, ...	185	Astrophil	42	5
Nor glorious Fooles stand in Thy awfull sight.	274	Psalm V		12
Of glorious Croune, and crouning honour.	279	Psalm VIII		20
His righteousness, and this his doing glorious..	300	Psalm XXII		78
Who is this glorious King in might and power riding?	302	Psalm XXIV		19
Who is This Glorious King? The lord of armyes guiding, . . .	302	Psalm XXIV		23
And in his ever glorious frame	310	Psalm XXIX		5
And ever, ever glorious.	310	Psalm XXIX		12
GLORY				
Where thou poore nature left'st all thy due glory, to				
fortune.	30	1st Eclogues	11	15
Hers be the glory.	30	1st Eclogues	12	12
R. O foolish thing, which glory doeste destroye.	46	2nd Eclogues	27	19
What glorie from our losse can he receave?	59	2nd Eclogues	30	73
Alas it is no glory.	65	2nd Eclogues	32	3
Al filthy mouths that glory in their vice.	98	3rd Eclogues	65	12
Deeme it no gloire to swell in tyrannie.	103	3rd Eclogues	66	149
My fall her glorie maketh, ...	136	Cert Sonnets	3	11
O my vayne worde gon, Ruyn of my glory..	138	Cert Sonnets	5	14
Which as of inward glorie.	152	Cert Sonnets	23	29
Who with glorie.	155	Cert Sonnets	26	21
Glorie breedeth:	156	Cert Sonnets	26	30
Glory trying,.	156	Cert Sonnets	26	32
Nc more in thy sweetnesse glorie, ...	156	Cert Sonnets	27	17
Or else let them in statelier glorie shine,.	166	Astrophil	3	5
When most I glorie, then I feele most shame:	174	Astrophil	19	3
Then grew my tongue and pen records unto thy glory:.	212	A&S 5th Song		3
Scrrow onely then hath glory,.	221	A&S 9th Song		14
In thee my glory raigneth.	272	Psalm III		12
For death doth kill the Witness of thy glory;.	276	Psalm VI		14
That hast of thine unmatched glory	278	Psalm VIII		3
So in joy my glory clad, ...	288	Psalm XVI		29
Wee may well call his glory great.	297	Psalm XXI		17
Who feare the lord all prayse and glory beare him;	300	Psalm XXII		53
In comes the King of glory bright.	302	Psalm XXIV		18
Above line repeated at following location.	302	Psalm XXIV		22
Even He the King of glory hight.	302	Psalm XXIV		24
Ascribe all glory and all might.	309	Psalm XXIX		3
Ascribe due glory to his Name, ...	310	Psalm XXIX		4
My soul shall glory still.	318	Psalm XXXIV		5
Like to the glory of noone day..	325	Psalm XXXVII		16
Wait on God, for yet his glory	334	Psalm XLII		19
Above line repeated at following location.	335	Psalm XLII		51
GLOSS				
To lye, faine, gloze, to steale, pry, and accuse,.	21	1st Eclogues	8	23
If once thou maist that fancie glosse destroy.	25	1st Eclogues	9	117
GLOSSES				
Which breeds nought else but gloses of deceits..	20	1st Eclogues	8	4
GLOVE				
Didst snatch from Cosma's hand her greene ywroughten glove..	52	2nd Eclogues	29	10
Sweete glove the wittnes of my secrett blisse.	70	Arcadia III	35	1
Be thow, sweete glove, the Anker of my mynde,.	70	Arcadia III	35	7
Sweete glove, the sweete despoyles of sweetest hand, ...	70	Arcadia III	35	9
Each had his creast, Mars caried Venus' glove, ...	171	Astrophil	13	7
Bid'n, perhaps he fetcheth thee a glove, ...	194	Astrophil	59	7
GLOW				
Though they do fly, yet backwardly do glowe.	249	Other Poems	4	292
GLOWWORM				
Saving the glowe worme, which would curteous be.	98	3rd Eclogues	66	6

GLOZE
    If then a boddily evill in a boddily gloze be not hidden,. .   34 1st Eclogues 13   87
GLUT
    Cormoraunt's glutt, Kite's spoile, king fisher's waste,. . .   28 1st Eclogues 10   78
GLUTTED
    Glutted with them now plaies with meanest things. . . . . . 245 Other Poems 4 132
GLUTTON
    At length for glutton taste he did them kill:. . . . . . . 103 3rd Eclogues 66 146
GNASHING
    Ev'en gnashing teeth, to witness more their spight. . . . . 322 Psalm XXXV   42
    Gnashing their teeth full of disdeigning;. . . . . 325 Psalm XXXVII   34
GO
    Lalus. If thou wilt not be seene, thy face goe hide away,. .   15 1st Eclogues 7   13
    Geron. Up, up Philisides, let sorrowes goe,. . . . .   22 1st Eclogues 9   1
    (And pacience hath) let him goe learne of him. . . . .   24 1st Eclogues 9   73
    Goe graft againe, and seeke to graft them right,. . . . . .   26 1st Eclogues 9 129
    Come, come my currs, tis late I will goe in. . . . .   29 1st Eclogues 10   98
    Goe on therefore, and tell us, by what fashion . . . .   48 2nd Eclogues 28   34
    Goe winne of him (for chattering) praise or shame: . . . . .   56 2nd Eclogues 29 139
    As let them come or go with even facilitie. . . . .   60 2nd Eclogues 30 133
    Can then a cause be so light that forceth a man to go die?
      Aye. . . . .   64 2nd Eclogues 31   24
    Dev'lls? if in hell such dev'lls do abide, to the hells I do
      go. Go. . . . .   65 2nd Eclogues 31   50
    Go sing the fall of old Thebes,. . . . .   66 2nd Eclogues 32   21
    Goe snake hide thee in dust, ...   93 3rd Eclogues 63   86
    "Husband", quoth she, "go to him by and by,. . . . .   95 3rd Eclogues 64   55
    Did goe his way, but sojourn'd neere thereby,. . . . .   96 3rd Eclogues 64   71
    Whether he needes must goe for feare of blame. . . . .   96 3rd Eclogues 64   78
    I sate me downe: for see to goe ne could,. . . . .   99 3rd Eclogues 66   20
    She bids him goe, and yet from jorney stayes.. . . . . 104 3rd Eclogues 67   36
    Must goe for that, if for her lowres he care:. . . . . 104 3rd Eclogues 67   42
    Goe to, goe to, and Cupid now applie . . . . 106 3rd Eclogues 67 100
    We go unto the Bryde, and use this daye. . . . . 107 3rd Eclogues 67 119
    "Yet thou shalt not go free (quoth Venus) such a fire. . . . 121 4th Eclogues 73 170
    As th'offence was done, and goe beyond if he can.. . . . . . 123 4th Eclogues 74   40
    Even as the flye, which to the flame doth goe, ... 149 Cert Sonnets 21   11
    When into Reason's audite I do go: . . . . 173 Astrophil   18   2
    Let her go. Soft, but here she comes. Go to, ... 188 Astrophil   47   12
    Striving abroad a foraging to go,. . . . . 192 Astrophil   55   6
    Desire still on the stilts of feare doth go. . . . . 199 Astrophil   66   8
    Pray that my sunne go downe with meeker beames to bed. . . . 205 Astrophil   76   14
    Only true sighs, you do not go away, ... 229 Astrophil   95   12
    Go my flocke, go get you hence,. . . . . 221 A&S 9th Song   1
    Yet alas before you go,. . . . . 221 A&S 9th Song   11
    The way they go shal be their way to perish. . . . . 271 Psalm I   22
    That joy with trembling go. . . . . 271 Psalm II   26
    And ready art to let Thyne arrowes go. . . . . 278 Psalm VII   36
    Our tongues, say they, beyond them all shall go, ... 285 Psalm XII   10
    Least yet I slip or go astray. . . . . 289 Psalm XVII   16
    All ready, ready to my snaring grave to go.. . . . . 291 Psalm XVIII 11
    Teach me, thus vext, what path to go. . . . . 303 Psalm XXV   12
    That down they go. . . . . 307 Psalm XXVII   12
    Direct me how to go, and guide me right, ... 312 Psalm XXXI   9
    Let Angel thine a scattring make them go.. . . . . 321 Psalm XXXV   12
    Sure I do but halting go,. . . . . 329 Psalm XXXVIII 49
    As soon as out they go. 333 Psalm XLI   24
    How in troops I wont to go, ... 334 Psalm XLII   14
    Will I boldly go . . . . 336 Psalm XLIII   20
    Will. Then Dick let us go hence lest wee great folkes annoy. 344 Possibly   1   45
    But hence, even hence, I must needes goe; such is my dogged
      fate.. . . . . 344 Possibly   1   48
    With mery maids a Maying they do go, ... 243 Other Poems 4   50
    But lickrous, Poison'd, faine to her would goe,. . . . . . . 246 Other Poems 4 165
    Nay ev'n unto hir home he oft would go,. . . . . 247 Other Poems 4 193
    A-field they goe, where many lookers be, ... 247 Other Poems 4 217
    With such mad haste he did to Cosma goe, ... 249 Other Poems 4 271
    More marking hir, then how himselfe did goe, ... 249 Other Poems 4 290
    Who would be caught, that she should go to hell: . . . . . . 250 Other Poems 4 315
    To runne, brake from his hands, and let him goe. . . . . . . 250 Other Poems 4 336
    A hast'ned Hare from greedy Grayhound goe, ... 251 Other Poems 4 343
    But, ah! hir darts did farre more depely goe . . . . 251 Other Poems 4 352
    Going from them, from them she could not go) . . . . 252 Other Poems 4 414
    And part must folowe where whole man doth goe. . . . . 253 Other Poems 4 422
    And none invisible, but Spirites, can goe. . . . . 253 Other Poems 4 456
    I go about, but then is all my best. . . . . 254 Other Poems 4 470
    Go you not from your master in his woe:. . . . . 254 Other Poems 4 487
    Go bawling curre, thy hungry maw go fill,. . . . . 255 Other Poems 4 517
    Like Rogue, all ragged goe,. . . . . 257 Other Poems 5   25
GOATHERD
    Strephon. Yee Gote-heard Gods, that love the grassie
      mountaines,. . . . . 111 4th Eclogues 71   1
GOATS
    The caves were full, the mountaines voide of goates: . . . .   98 3rd Eclogues 66   11
GOD
    Like great god Saturn faire, and like faire Venus chaste:. .   12 Arcadia I   3   5
    With Cupid she fore-sees, and goes god Vulcan's pace:. . . .   12 Arcadia I   3   7
    Now thanked be the great God Pan,. . . . .   13 Arcadia I   5   1
    Lalus. Muse hold your peace: but thou, my God Pan, glorify .   15 1st Eclogues 7   25
    A naked god, young, blind, with arrowes two. . . . .   20 1st Eclogues 8   6

GOD   (CONTINUED)   PAGE   TITLE   LINE
Is he a God, that ever flies the light?. . . . .   21 1st Eclogues 8   7
This is thy worke, thou God for ever blinde: . . . .   41 Arcadia II   20   9
Thou God, whose youth was deckt with spoyle of Python's
   skin . . . .   44 Arcadia II   26   5
Pan, father Pan, the god of silly sheepe, ...   92 3rd Eclogues 63   37
Vertue (if not a God) yet God's chiefe parte, ...   92 3rd Eclogues 63   46
No wife but I hath such a man, God wot". . . . .   104 3rd Eclogues 67   45
And God forbid, women such cattell were, ...   106 3rd Eclogues 67   82
As little hunting minde (God knowes) did there appeere.. . 118 4th Eclogues 73   70
Of any since God AEsculapius ceased. . . . .   128 4th Eclogues 75   116
To starving minds such is God Cupid's dish.. . . . . . .   136 Cert Sonnets   2   14
And so for one that felt god Cupid's dart, ...   146 Cert Sonnets 17   29
Till that good God make Church and Churchman starve. . . . 167 Astrophil   5   8
But (God wot) wot not what they meane by it: . . . . . .   204 Astrophil   74   6
O God, thinke you that satisfies my care?. . . . .   225 Astrophil   92   8
Now God forbid. A theefe, and of worst theeves the cheefe: . 213 A&S 5th Song   44
For god doth know, and knowing doth approve. . . . . . .   271 Psalm I   19
Serve God, serve him with feare: Rejoyce in him but so,. . . 271 Psalm II   25
In God on whom you build . . . .   272 Psalm III   10
Help me my God and Father. . . . .   272 Psalm III   24
O God, God of my Equity, ...   273 Psalm IV   2
Yet know this too, that God did take . . . .   273 Psalm IV   11
My King, my God for I to thee will pray. . . . .   274 Psalm V   4
For Thou art that same God, far from delight . . . . . .   274 Psalm V   9
Alas, how long, my God, wilt Thou delay me?. . . . . . .   276 Psalm VI   10
My Deare God stay me.. . . . .   276 Psalm VI   12
For god hath heard the weeping sobbing voice . . . . . .   276 Psalm VI   27
O Lord my God, Thou art my trustfull stay. . . . .   277 Psalm VII   1
O lord, my God, if I did not forbeare. . . . .   277 Psalm VII   7
Whom that Great God remember can?. . . . .   278 Psalm VIII   14
It should be ought of God attended.. . . . .   279 Psalm VIII   16
But God shall sit in his Eternal chaire. . . . .   280 Psalm IX   21
What God prepares.   281 Psalm IX   55
O God our only starr, ...   281 Psalm X   2
But doth God' self disdain.. . . . .   281 Psalm X   12
That after God he never sought,. . . . .   281 Psalm X   14
That Name of God a fable is. . . . .   281 Psalm X   16
God sleeps, or hath forgotten quite, ...   282 Psalm X   46
O lord Our only God, ...   282 Psalm X   50
God in his Holy Temple is, ...   284 Psalm XI   13
Who be to God enclined.. . . . .   284 Psalm XI   24
I will get up saith God, and my help show. . . . .   285 Psalm XII   16
There is no God that raigneth. . . . .   286 Psalm XIV   3
Even god himself sent down his peircing ey . . . .   286 Psalm XIV   7
Not One, that God discerneth.. . . . .   286 Psalm XIV   12
Nor ever call on god, but they shall quake . . . .   286 Psalm XIV   16
But God is Their recomfort.. . . . .   287 Psalm XIV   21
That to God my God I say . . . .   287 Psalm XVI   4
God my only portion is . . . .   288 Psalm XVI   13
My eyes still my God regard. . . . .   288 Psalm XVI   25
My God, and helping God, my might and trustfull might, . . . 290 Psalm XVIII   3
This my Distresse to God with wailfull cryes I show, . .   291 Psalm XVIII   12
Ev'n from the Waters' depth my God preserved me so.. . . . 291 Psalm XVIII   35
For who is God, besides this Great Jehova Ours?. . . . .   292 Psalm XVIII   57
And so besides our God, who is indue'd with might? . . . . 292 Psalm XVIII   58
This God then girded me in his Almighty pow'rs,. . . . . . 292 Psalm XVIII   59
Let God the lord heare Thee, ...   295 Psalm XX   1
Let name of Jacob's God, ...   295 Psalm XX   3
Up to Our God, when Thy suites granted be. . . . .   296 Psalm XX   20
That God from fall his own Anoynted stayes.. . . . . . .   296 Psalm XX   22
My God my God why hast Thou me forsaken? . . . .   298 Psalm XXII   1
O God my God I cry while day appeareth;. . . . .   298 Psalm XXII   5
But God Thy eare my crying never heareth.. . . . .   298 Psalm XXII   6
O God the night is privy to my plaint, ...   298 Psalm XXII   7
Let God help him (say they) whom he did trust; . . . . .   299 Psalm XXII   19
Let God save him, in whom was all his lust.. . . . . . .   299 Psalm XXII   20
Than I was giv'en to Thee, Thou wert my God. . . . . . .   299 Psalm XXII   24
And God shall be by those his seekers praysed. . . . . .   300 Psalm XXII   62
And turn to God, and all the Nations be. . . . .   300 Psalm XXII   67
And reason, since the Croune to God pertaineth,. . . . .   300 Psalm XXII   69
And God shall them in his own court reserve. . . . . . .   300 Psalm XXII   76
A blessing from the lord, from God of his salvation. . . . 302 Psalm XXIV   13
Jacob this is Thy seed, God seeking generation,. . . . . . 302 Psalm XXIV   15
My God in Thee I trust,. . . . .   302 Psalm XXV   3
The God in whom abides . . . .   303 Psalm XXV   15
The Paths of my great God? . . . .   304 Psalm XXV   38
The strong God my salvation is.. . . . .   306 Psalm XXVII   2
O God of my. . . . .   308 Psalm XXVII   47
Hope, Trust in God, bee strong, and he . . . .   308 Psalm XXVII   64
That God is my strength my shield; . . . .   309 Psalm XXVIII   26
God on them his strength doth lay. . . . .   309 Psalm XXVIII   31
God to his people strength shall give, ...   310 Psalm XXIX   28
For then my Hill Good God did stay;. . . . .   311 Psalm XXX   22
Thy endless prayse: O God my King. . . . .   311 Psalm XXX   38
O lord that art the God of verity. . . . .   312 Psalm XXXI   15
For all my hope fixt upon God doth ly. . . . .   312 Psalm XXXI   18
Thou art my God, my time on thee doth stay;. . . . . . .   313 Psalm XXXI   41
So I my self accus'd to God, ...   315 Psalm XXXII   16
But who on God his trust invokes,. . . . .   315 Psalm XXXII   38

GOD	(CONTINUED)	PAGE	TITLE		LINE
Be glad you good, in God have joy,		316	Psalm XXXII		40
Rejoice in God, O ye		316	Psalm XXXIII		1
Let all the earth feare God,		317	Psalm XXXIII		28
Whose God he is,		317	Psalm XXXIII		44
And God freed him, in his worst time		319	Psalm XXXIV		23
Feare God ye saints of his,		319	Psalm XXXIV		33
But who seek God with constancy.		319	Psalm XXXIV		39
But God shall him to safety reare.		320	Psalm XXXIV		71
God doth all soules redeeme.		321	Psalm XXXIV		77
Ev'en bones shall say O God, who is Thy peere,		321	Psalm XXXV		21
My lord my God ev'en to my equity.		322	Psalm XXXV		58
Judg lord, judg God, ev'en in Thy justice great,		322	Psalm XXXV		59
Yet let them say, laud be to God alwayes		323	Psalm XXXV		69
Noe feare of God doth once appeare		323	Psalm XXXVI		5
Delight in God and he shall breed.		324	Psalm XXXVII		9
Who stay for God, in blisse shall stay.		325	Psalm XXXVII		24
But God shall scorn their moody meaning,		325	Psalm XXXVII		35
But God upholds the just in blisse.		325	Psalm XXXVII		44
God keeps account of good men's dayes,		325	Psalm XXXVII		45
Who to make warr with God praesumed;		326	Psalm XXXVII		50
Lo whom God blest he blessed liveth,		326	Psalm XXXVII		55
The man whom God directs doth stand.		326	Psalm XXXVII		57
Firm on his way, his way God loveth,		326	Psalm XXXVII		58
God, loving right, doth not forsake.		326	Psalm XXXVII		69
But in their hand God will not leave him,		327	Psalm XXXVII		83
Wait thou on God and keep his way,		327	Psalm XXXVII		85
My God Thou wilt heare my voice;		328	Psalm XXXVIII		45
The pleasure of my God attend,		330	Psalm XL		2
New song unto our God of prayse,		331	Psalm XL		12
My God Thy wondrous works how manifold,		331	Psalm XL		21
Still gladly say, Unto our God bee prayse.		332	Psalm XL		64
Yet God on me is thinking,		332	Psalm XL		66
My God, O make no stay.		332	Psalm XL		70
For God shall him deliver in the time.		332	Psalm XLI		3
In God his strength shall grow,		333	Psalm XLI		10
Of Israel the God.		334	Psalm XLI		46
Thirsting on my God to look.		334	Psalm XLII		4
Where is now Thy God so good?		334	Psalm XLII		12
Wait on God, for yet his glory		334	Psalm XLII		19
For my mind on my God bideth,		335	Psalm XLII		25
While my God with wasting wonders.		335	Psalm XLII		31
To my God that give me breathing.		335	Psalm XLII		40
Where hath now your God his biding?		335	Psalm XLII		48
Wait on God, for yet his glory		335	Psalm XLII		51
God is my God, by me praysed.		335	Psalm XLII		56
For my God Thy sight		336	Psalm XLIII		7
To that God that is.		336	Psalm XLIII		22
God of all my blisse,		336	Psalm XLIII		23
God of all my gladness.		336	Psalm XLIII		24
Then God, yea my God,		337	Psalm XLIII		28
Wait on God, for still		337	Psalm XLIII		34
Thank my God I will,		337	Psalm XLIII		35
Will. God shield us from such Dames. If so our Downes be sped,		344	Possibly	1	39
But God gives them instinct the man to shun,		249	Other Poems	4	295
Let Pan our good God see,		260	Other Poems	6	3
Of God Apolloe's giving,		260	Other Poems	6	8
Once to Shepheard's God retayning,		262	Other Poems	7	11
May make treaty to god Pan).		263	Other Poems	7	58
GODDESSE					
That Goddesse mine, my blessed being sees".		4	Lady of May	3	6
As smooth as Pan, as Juno milde, like goddesse Iris faste.		12	Arcadia I	3	6
To worke my Goddesse so by thy invention,		19	1st Eclogues	7	177
In these woods to resounde the renowmed name of a goddesse.		31	1st Eclogues	13	14
But onely that my goddesse		67	2nd Eclogues	32	56
Reason looke to thy selfe, I serve a goddesse.		68	2nd Eclogues	33	30
GODDESSES					
She had chiefe Goddesses in beautie overcome.		120	4th Eclogues	73	146
GODLESS					
Venom'd with godless spight,		273	Psalm III		29
When Godless men be snar'd in their own snares:		281	Psalm IX		52
GODLINESS					
Where highest notes to godlines are raisd,		99	3rd Eclogues	66	31
GODLY					
Wher godly men do their assembly make.		270	Psalm I		18
When He chose me, a godly One:		273	Psalm IV		12
But doth with honour great the Godly entertaine;		287	Psalm XV		8
Good and godly men I love.		288	Psalm XVI		8
Therfore shall evry godly One.		315	Psalm XXXII		19
Still, still the godly shall be stay'd		327	Psalm XXXVII		97
GOD'S					
Vertue (if not a God) yet God's chiefe parte,		92	3rd Eclogues	63	46
With me those paines for God's sake do not take:		179	Astrophil	28	3
But on god's law his heart's delight doth bind,		270	Psalm I		5
These are God's words, God's words are ever pure,		285	Psalm XII		19
God's people do devower,		286	Psalm XIV		15
God's witness sure for aye doth dure		294	Psalm XIX		31
God's doomes be right, and cheer the sprite,		294	Psalm XIX		33
Upon God's holy name,		296	Psalm XX		29

188

GOD'S   (CONTINUED)   PAGE   TITLE   LINE
The earth is God's, and what the Globe of earth containeth,. 302 Psalm XXIV   1
Who shall climb to the hill which God's own hill is named, . 302 Psalm XXIV   5
Who search of God's face never leave. . . . .   302 Psalm XXIV   16
Beleiv'd God's goodness for to see,. . . . .   308 Psalm XXVII   62
God's goodness fills all lands,. . . . .   316 Psalm XXXIII   21
For God's own eyes on good men sit . . . .   320 Psalm XXXIV   55
For God's high law in his heart dwelleth. . . . .   326 Psalm XXXVII   79
By God's most sure, and sweet salvation; . . . .   327 Psalm XXXVII   98
Holy daunce to God's house bringing. . . . .   334 Psalm XLII   16
To God's Altars tho.   336 Psalm XLIII   19
GODS
The gods must help, and pretious things must serve to shew
    her shape. . . . .   12 Arcadia I   3   4
O happie Gods, which by inward assumption. . . . .   15 1st Eclogues   7   40
Philisides. O gods, how long this old foole hath annoi'd . .   24 1st Eclogues   9   66
My wearied ears! O gods yet graunt me this,. . . . .   24 1st Eclogues   9   67
Happy shepheard, with thanks to the Gods, still thinke to be
    thankfull,. . . . .   32 1st Eclogues 13   33
Dorus. Unto the Gods with a thanckfull heart all thankes I
    do render, ...   32 1st Eclogues 13   35
O be it so, graunte such an event, O Gods, that event give..   37 1st Eclogues 13 169
Of growing trees, yee rurall Gods that wield . . . .   40 Arcadia II   18   2
This vowe receave, this vowe o Gods maintaine; . . . . . .   40 Arcadia II   18   5
Boulon. O man, take heed, how thou the Gods do move. . . . .   59 2nd Eclogues 30   65
Mock'st thou those Diamonds which only be matcht by the
    gods Ods. . . . .   65 2nd Eclogues 31   47
Strephon. Yee Gote-heard Gods, that love the grassie
    mountaines,. . . . .   111 4th Eclogues 71   1
The moone a sunder rent (O godes, o pardon me, ...   118 4th Eclogues 73   55
Which Poets say, the gods them selves do feare,. . . . . .   146 Cert Sonnets 17   7
Of those three gods, whose armes the fairest were: . . . .   171 Astrophil   13   2
Who to other Gods do run,. . . . .   288 Psalm XVI   10
GOES
With Cupid she fore-sees, and goes god Vulcan's pace:. . . .   12 Arcadia I   3   7
This paterne good, unto our children goes, ...   28 1st Eclogues 10   55
The sound to this strange aier no sooner goes, ...   42 Arcadia II   21   9
O blessed sonne whence all this blessing goes. . . . . . .   43 Arcadia II   23   6
My sonne alas from me for ever goes. . . . .   43 Arcadia II   24   6
That hath foure legs, and with two onely goes, ...   56 2nd Eclogues 29 142
Thus noble golde, downe to the bottome goes, ...   81 Arcadia III   54   13
That with a body't goes? since by a body it is.. . . . . .   123 4th Eclogues 74   46
But with his wings of fancies up he goes,. . . . .   144 Cert Sonnets 15   9
To trap poor soules he goes! . . . .   282 Psalm X   44
To hell he goes, and Nous with him must dwell. . . . . . .   250 Other Poems   4 313
GOETH
About that Vault he goeth, ...   294 Psalm XIX   26
GOGGLING
Such sight have they that see with goggling eyes. . . . . .   25 1st Eclogues   9 113
GOING
His eyelidds peyse our going. . . . .   284 Psalm XI   16
Going from them, from them she could not go) . . . .   252 Other Poems   4 414
GOLD
Her skin like burnisht gold, her hands like silver ure
    untryde. . . . .   12 Arcadia I   3   12
Can I be poore, that her golde haire procure my selfe? . . .   16 1st Eclogues   7   58
But arrowes two, and tipt with gold or leade:. . . . . . .   21 1st Eclogues   8   11
From the cruell headache, nor shoces of golde doo the gowt
    heale,. . . . .   34 1st Eclogues 13   85
Thus noble golde, downe to the bottome goes, ...   81 Arcadia III   54   13
Her haire fine threeds of finest gould . . . .   85 Arcadia III   62   3
Which though of glittring golde, shall heere take rust . . .   92 3rd Eclogues 63   57
As for to finde a pasture strowed with golde,. . . . . . .   104 3rd Eclogues 67   14
Let golde now rust, let Diamonds waste in thee:. . . . . .   125 4th Eclogues 75   22
Tell me o haire of gold, ...   158 Cert Sonnets 28   17
Enam'ling with pied flowers their thoughts of gold:. . . . . 166 Astrophil   3   4
Gold is the covering of that stately place.. . . . .   169 Astrophil   9   4
Whence hast thou Ivorie, Rubies, pearle and gold,. . . . .   181 Astrophil   32   10
Vertue's gold now must head my Cupid's dart. . . . .   202 Astrophil   72   8
Ah what doth Phoebus' gold that wretch availe, ...   237 Astrophil   108   10
Then what man would so soon seek gold . . . .   294 Psalm XIX   41
Croune of his head with croune of Gold . . . .   297 Psalm XXI   11
But golde can guild a rotten piece of wood,. . . . .   245 Other Poems   4 124
Brave crest to him hir scorn-gold haire did yeeld, ...   246 Other Poems   4 149
"Tell me my lamb of gold,. . . . .   258 Other Poems   5   66
GOLDEN
Rebell, Rebell, in golden fetters binde. . . . .   23 1st Eclogues   9   44
Pas. O if I had Apollo's golden carre, ...   56 2nd Eclogues 29 120
Nor golden manacles, stand for a paradise, ...   69 2nd Eclogues 34   25
But this bad world, few golden fieldes doth bring, ...   104 3rd Eclogues 67   19
Be victor still of Phoebus' golden treasure: . . . .   108 Arcadia IV   69   5
Or those golden lockes, those lockes which lock me to
    bondage, ...   123 4th Eclogues 74   51
Farewell o golden staffe, the weake man's might: . . . . .   129 4th Eclogues 76   3
The golden meane who loves, lives safely free. . . . . . .   143 Cert Sonnets 12   4
Broadred with buls and swans, powdred with golden raine: . . 167 Astrophil   6   6
Joves golden shield did Eagle sables beare,. . . . .   171 Astrophil   13   3
But in Vert field Mars bare a golden speare. . . . .   171 Astrophil   13   5
Sure you say well, your wisdome's golden mine. . . . . . .   175 Astrophil   21   12
Progressing then from faire twinnes' gold'n place: . . . .   175 Astrophil   22   2

GOLDEN   (CONTINUED)   PAGE   TITLE   LINE
    Holds my young braine captiv'd in golden cage. . . . .   176 Astrophil   23   11
    How Ulster likes of that same golden bit,. . . . .   180 Astrophil   30   9
    A conquerd, golden, ransackt heart to winne? . . . .   182 Astrophil   36 V   2
    Doubt there hath bene, when with his golden chaine . . . . .   193 Astrophil   58   1
    Ravisht, staid not, till in her golden haire . . . .   232 Astrophil   103   7
    Nor of that golden sea, whose waves in curles are brok'n:. .   213 A&S 5th Song   39
    Or glittering golden mony? . . . .   294 Psalm XIX   42
    With golden leaves, and painted babery,. . . . .   246 Other Poems   4 181
    Faine would, but could not fly from golden smart.. . . . . .   246 Other Poems   4 184
    But never did Medea's golden weed. . . . .   252 Other Poems   4 409
    Her chery lipps, milke hands, and golden haire . . . .   254 Other Poems   4 461
GONE
    My sonne is gon, your pasture barrein growes,. . . . .   43 Arcadia II   24   2
    My sun is gon, from stormes what shall us sheelde? . . . . .   43 Arcadia II   24   9
    My sun is gon, Nowe clowdie greeves assayle. . . . .   44 Arcadia II   24   12
    Oft prove I: but what salve, when Reason seeks to be gone?
        One. . . . .   63 2nd Eclogues 31   11
    Slander wants a pretext, flattery gone beyond: . . . .   69 2nd Eclogues 34   38
    Cupid's lust gone, and gone is bitter strife,. . . . .   93 3rd Eclogues 63   94
    "The jealous wretch must now to Courte be gone:. . . . . . .   97 3rd Eclogues 64   103
    The great beames gone, the house on shoulders light: . . . .   102 3rd Eclogues 66   136
    Thy house by thee must live, or els be gone: . . . .   106 3rd Eclogues 67   110
    Is gone, is gone from these our spoyled forrests,. . . . . .   113 4th Eclogues 71   71
    But, woe is me, the yeare is gone about, ...   115 4th Eclogues 72   56
    Since that to death is gone the shepheard hie, ...   125 4th Eclogues 75   1
    No, no, for ever gone is all our pleasure; . . . .   130 4th Eclogues 76   25
    O my vayne worde gon, Ruyn of my glory. . . . .   138 Cert Sonnets 5   14
    Is gone, and now like slave-borne Muscovite, ...   166 Astrophil   2   10
    That through my heart their beamie darts be gone,. . . . . .   189 Astrophil   48   10
    Gone is the winter of my miserie,. . . . .   200 Astrophil   69   7
    Where be those Roses gone, which sweetned so our eyes? . . .   232 Astrophil   102   1
    But thou art gone, now that selfe felt disgrace. . . . . . .   235 Astrophil   106   7
    "Well, be gone, be gone I say, ...   235 A&S 11th Song   41
    Do pine, my strength with pain is wholy gon, ...   312 Psalm XXXI   29
    Lo, he was gon, print of his treading, ...   327 Psalm XXXVII   91
    My heart pants, gon is my might; . . . .   328 Psalm XXXVIII   28
    To play when that their loved dammes, are stoln or gone
        astray?. . . . .   343 Possibly   1   6
GOOD
    That see my good, and judgeth my desert: . . . .   5 Lady of May   3   16
    What length of verse can serve brave Mopsa's good to show, .   12 Arcadia I   3   1
    Hardly they heard, which by good hunters singled be. . . . .   14 1st Eclogues 7   10
    My Kala's giftes: who with all good gifts filled is. . . . .   15 1st Eclogues 7   26
    Good Lalus mine, I yeld to thy abilitie; . . . .   20 1st Eclogues 7 V974
    And all the starres conspired to my good, ...   23 1st Eclogues 9   27
    From former feare, they had of your good mindes, ...   26 1st Eclogues 10   5
    Of my good sheepe, thou never trews time tooke:. . . . . . .   27 1st Eclogues 10   14
    Come narr good Mastix, tis now full tway score . . . .   27 1st Eclogues 10   20
    Of yeeres (alas) since I good Mastix knewe.. . . . .   27 1st Eclogues 10   21
    This paterne good, unto our children goes, ...   28 1st Eclogues 10   55
    A good foole call'd with paine, perhapps may be, ...   28 1st Eclogues 10   71
    The Cockow's shame, the Goose's good intent, ...   28 1st Eclogues 10   80
    Cleofila. First shall fertill grounds not yeeld increase of
        a good seed: . . . .   33 1st Eclogues 13   64
    That where you are no wished good can want;. . . . .   39 Arcadia II   16   6
    Doth teach, to learne the good what travailes do belong: . .   45 Arcadia II   26   8
    P. Who be too weake, do feigne they be too good. . . . . . .   47 2nd Eclogues 27   30
    Dicus. But so thy sheepe may thy good wishes satisfie. . . .   49 2nd Eclogues 28   49
    A greater good by her divine reflection; . . . .   49 2nd Eclogues 28   68
    And makes our home good sport with dauncing bolt upright.. .   53 2nd Eclogues 29   46
    Nico. Peace, peace good Pas, thou weeriest even the ground .   56 2nd Eclogues 29   135
    For good thou mayst yet proove in sheepish sound.. . . . . .   56 2nd Eclogues 29   137
    Where all good haps a perfect state maintaine? . . . .   58 2nd Eclogues 30   40
    Plangus. Curst be good haps, and curst be they that build. .   58 2nd Eclogues 30   41
    And whose good happ, doth leave him unprovided, ...   62 2nd Eclogues 30   177
    Betwixt the good and shade of good divided,. . . . .   62 2nd Eclogues 30   179
    So good a say invites the eye, ...   87 Arcadia III 62   51
    To see her ofspring seeke a good increase, ...   91 3rd Eclogues 63   2
    Since from these good the others' good doth flowe, ...   92 3rd Eclogues 63   40
    Gainst neighbors good for womanish debate. . . . .   93 3rd Eclogues 63   70
    And farre unfit to hold so good a roome. . . . .   94 3rd Eclogues 64   6
    Who yet was good, because she knewe none ill,. . . . .   94 3rd Eclogues 64   14
    To whome our prince did beare a great good will, ...   94 3rd Eclogues 64   16
    And so she was, and all with good intent, ...   95 3rd Eclogues 64   25
    But fewe dayes past while she good maner us'de,. . . . . . .   95 3rd Eclogues 64   26
    Allow good company, but kepe from thence . . . .   98 3rd Eclogues 65   11
    His good strong staffe my slippry yeares upbore: . . . . . .   99 3rd Eclogues 66   37
    The Horse, good shape; the Sparrow, lust to playe; . . . . .   101 3rd Eclogues 66   81
    To teare the bowels, that good corne should send. . . . . .   102 3rd Eclogues 66   117
    By those great beastes, as for the weaker's good,. . . . . .   102 3rd Eclogues 66   128
    Geron. In faith, good Histor, long is your delay,. . . . . .   103 3rd Eclogues 67   1
    Histor. No doubt to whom so good chance did betide,. . . . .   104 3rd Eclogues 67   13
    The heav'ns doo not good haps in handfuls bring, ...   105 3rd Eclogues 67   61
    But let us pick our good from out much bad:. . . . .   105 3rd Eclogues 67   62
    Therefore esteeming all good blessings toyes, ...   116 4th Eclogues 72   99
    What? was I then worthie such good, now worthie so muche
        evill? . . . .   124 4th Eclogues 74   77
    Aske, if in great men good men so do thronge,. . . . .   126 4th Eclogues 75   43
    O Phoebus with good cause thy face thou hidest,. . . . . . .   126 4th Eclogues 75   55

GOOD   (CONTINUED)   PAGE   TITLE   LINE

	PAGE	TITLE		LINE
Of what was good, where now no good doth lie;	127	4th Eclogues	75	74
For ever wandring from all good direction;	130	4th Eclogues	76	26
Since nature's workes be good, and death doth serve.	131	Arcadia V	77	1
Unto my children alway good rest taking:	139	Cert Sonnets	6	5
His ugly evill in other's good to hide, ...	141	Cert Sonnets	8	6
Evill happes do fill with hope, good happes appall	143	Cert Sonnets	12	10
Of mine owne wordes, my owne good hap betray, ...	145	Cert Sonnets	16	10
Some good old dumpe, that Chaucer's mistresse knew, ...	146	Cert Sonnets	17	34
Then good Apollo do away thy bowe:	146	Cert Sonnets	17	36
Or thinking still my thoughts might have good end:	147	Cert Sonnets	19	2
By your good helpe, or in my selfe to finde.	148	Cert Sonnets	19	12
But that good part, wherein all comforts be, ...	148	Cert Sonnets	20	11
For messenger of inward good.	156	Cert Sonnets	27	8
Good Lord deliver us.	160	Cert Sonnets	30	10
Above line repeated at following locations	160	Cert Sonnets	30	20
. . . .	160	Cert Sonnets	30	30
. . . .	161	Cert Sonnets	30	40
Till that good God make Church and Churchman starve.	167	Astrophil	5	8
By reason good, good reason her to love.	170	Astrophil	10	14
And which is worse, no good excuse can show, ...	174	Astrophil	18	7
How Holland hearts, now so good townes be lost, ...	180	Astrophil	30	7
I, cumbred with good maners, answer do, ...	180	Astrophil	30	13
Listen then Lordings with good eare to me, ...	183	Astrophil	37	3
I will good tribute pay if thou do so.	184	Astrophil	39	8
As good to write as for to lie and grone.	184	Astrophil	40	1
His praise to sleight, which from good use doth rise;	185	Astrophil	41	7
No Patience, if thou wilt my good, then make	193	Astrophil	56	12
When my good Angell guides me to the place, ...	194	Astrophil	60	1
Where all my good I do in Stella see, ...	194	Astrophil	60	2
Then some good body tell me how I do, ...	195	Astrophil	60	12
Thou whom to me such my good turnes should bind, ...	198	Astrophil	65	3
Chiefe good, whereto my hope doth only aspire, ...	200	Astrophil	68	3
As fast thy Vertue bends that love to good:	201	Astrophil	71	13
So ample eares as never good newes know:	206	Astrophil	78	13
Good brother Philip, I have borne you long, ...	208	Astrophil	83	1
Be your words made (good Sir) of Indian ware, ...	225	Astrophil	92	1
Thought with good cause thou likest so well the night, . . .	229	Astrophil	96	1
So neere, in so good time, so free a place?.	235	Astrophil	105	2
If stones good measure daunc'd, the Theban walles to build,.	208	A&S 3rd Song		3
Danger hence good care doth keepe, ...	210	A&S 4th Song		9
Then can in good eawes be moved.	221	A&S 9th Song		24
If I saw my good dog grieved, ...	222	A&S 9th Song		37
He will give good eare to my moane.	273	Psalm IV		15
O prayse the lord, this Syon dweller good, ...	280	Psalm IX		31
Nay even the race of good men are decay'd.	284	Psalm XII		3
Then Thou (O lord) shalt keep the Good stil sure.	285	Psalm XII		22
Not One that good remaineth.	286	Psalm XIV		6
Good and godly men I love.	288	Psalm XVI		8
Meeke to the Meek Thou art, The good thy goodnesse taste; . .	292	Psalm XVIII		50
Receive good acceptation!.	295	Psalm XIX		64
That in good part he did Thy Offrings take;	296	Psalm XX		12
At mother's breastes, thou didst good hope betake me.	299	Psalm XXII		22
They that be made even fatt, with earth's fatt good, ...	300	Psalm XXII		71
For then my Hill Good God did stay;	311	Psalm XXX		22
Be glad you good, in God have joy, ...	316	Psalm XXXII		40
Shall need nought that is good.	319	Psalm XXXIV		40
As life may good appeare?.	320	Psalm XXXIV		48
Do good, from faults decline, ...	320	Psalm XXXIV		53
For God's own eyes on good men sit	320	Psalm XXXIV		55
Who hate the good shall fall.	320	Psalm XXXIV		76
So my good deeds they pay with this ev'ill share, ...	322	Psalm XXXV		27
Who loves with good his servants good to blesse.	323	Psalm XXXV		70
His deeds, yea thoughtes all good forgett;	323	Psalm XXXVI		10
Thou shalt have both good food and place.	324	Psalm XXXVII		8
Chafe not at some man's great good fortune	325	Psalm XXXVII		18
To have their hate on good soules wroken;	325	Psalm XXXVII		38
Small goodes in good men better is	325	Psalm XXXVII		41
God keeps account of good men's dayes, ...	325	Psalm XXXVII		45
The good is kind and freely giveth;	326	Psalm XXXVII		54
And Thy good state shall never end.	326	Psalm XXXVII		68
The good mouth will in Wisdom bide, ...	326	Psalm XXXVII		77
Who do ev'ill for good, to me.	329	Psalm XXXVIII		58
I silence kept ev'n in the good.	329	Psalm XXXIX		6
Aha! This is good game.	332	Psalm XL		60
Where is now Thy God so good?.	334	Psalm XLII		12
Will. Thou seest my eares do itch at it: good Dick thy sorow				
tell.	343	Possibly	1	18
Dick. Good Will, I cannot take thy good advice, before . . .	344	Possibly	1	43
In whome no evill did raigne, nor good appeare, ...	245	Other Poems	4	118
With one good dawnce, or letter finely pend, ...	245	Other Poems	4	140
But fearing lest all white might seeme too good, ...	246	Other Poems	4	151
Then in good Dog, faire field, or shading tree.	246	Other Poems	4	179
So as good thoughts of him in all arise, ...	247	Other Poems	4	198
Let Pan our good God see, ...	260	Other Poems	6	3
GOODLY				
Since in my hands selfe goodly sight she tooke.	55	2nd Eclogues	29	116
Faire Rocks, goodly rivers, sweet woods, when shall I see				
peace? Peace. . .	62	2nd Eclogues	31	1
You goodly pines, which still with brave assent.	77	Arcadia III	49	1

GOODLY   (CONTINUED)   PAGE   TITLE   LINE
    Dread not a whit (O goodly cruell) that pittie may enter . . 122 4th Eclogues 74   5
    In a goodly pleasant ground? . . . . 288 Psalm XVI   17
GOODMAN
    The goodman bad his wife be serviceable. . . . .   94 3rd Eclogues 64   24
    The goodman starting, askt what did her move?. . . . .   95 3rd Eclogues 64   47
    The goodman read on both sides the content,. . . . .   96 3rd Eclogues 64   88
    He stayd untill the goodman was departed,. . . . .   97 3rd Eclogues 64 119
GOODNESS
    Of goodnes to receive lovely direction.. . . . .   68 2nd Eclogues 34   4
    Such goodnes that in her simplicitie triumphs: . . . .   69 2nd Eclogues 34   36
    Goodnes the penne, heaven paper is,. . . . .   90 Arcadia III 62 142
    That with his fault he might her goodnes know. . . . .   97 3rd Eclogues 64 114
    Goodnes for best attire in dust is dressed.. . . . . 128 4th Eclogues 75 120
    And farewell Prince, whom goodnesse hath made glorious.. . . 129 4th Eclogues 75 142
    Stella, those faire lines, which true goodnesse show.. . . . 201 Astrophil   71   4
    Therfore I say again this goodness he me sent. . . . . 292 Psalm XVIII   47
    Meeke to the Meek Thou art, The good thy goodness taste; . . 292 Psalm XVIII   50
    Beleiv'd God's goodness for to see,. . . . . 308 Psalm XXVII   62
    God's goodness fills all lands,. . . . . 316 Psalm XXXIII   21
    Yea beasts made safe thy goodness try. . . . . 323 Psalm XXXVI   18
    Then fly all ev'ill and goodness nourish,. . . . . 326 Psalm XXXVII   67
    For simple goodnes shined in his eyes. . . . . 247 Other Poems   4 196
GOODS
    Since in sweete you all goods so richly raigne,. . . . . . .   39 Arcadia II   16   5
    And sure at length stolne goods do come to light . . . . . . 172 Astrophil   15   11
    Of all those goods, which heav'n to me hath lent:. . . . . . 173 Astrophil   18   4
    Lies hatching still the goods wherein they flow: . . . . . . 176 Astrophil   24   2
    Theeves steal for need, and steale but goods, which paine
        recovers,. . . . . 214 A&S 5th Song   45
    Outward, all outward goods . . . . 304 Psalm XXV   51
    Small goodes in good men better is . . . . 325 Psalm XXXVII   41
GOOD-WILL
    Yet all my health I place in your good-will. . . . .   18 1st Eclogues 7 120
GOOSE
    Pas. Another sure as is a gander from a goose: . . . .   52 2nd Eclogues 29   23
GOOSE'S
    The Cockow's shame, the Goose's good intent, ...   28 1st Eclogues 10   80
GOSHAWK
    When falcon they, and gossehauke saw in mewe.. . . . . 102 3rd Eclogues 66 140
*GOT
    Came to the bed, where wound for kisse he got, ...   5 Lady of May   3   8
    No lovely praise was ever got with killing". . . . .   16 1st Eclogues 7   81
    Of singing thou hast got the reputation. . . . .   20 1st Eclogues 7 V972
    Above line repeated at following location. . . . .   20 1st Eclogues 7 V973
    By Argus got on Io, then a cow:. . . . .   21 1st Eclogues 8   14
    I pray thee what hath ere the Parret gott, ...   28 1st Eclogues 10   67
    Harde to be gott, but got constant, to be helde like
        steeles Eeles.. . . . .   65 2nd Eclogues 31   42
    Ne pleasure here, ne fame gott.. . . . .   66 2nd Eclogues 32   39
    But nowe successe hathe gott above annoyes,. . . . .   71 Arcadia III 36   17
    No lampe, whose light by Art is got, ...   86 Arcadia III 62   17
    The little coine his sweating browes have got, ... 104 3rd Eclogues 67   41
    And this hath got; the catcher now is caught,. . . . . 115 4th Eclogues 72   66
    Till by degrees it had full conquest got.. . . . . 165 Astrophil   2   4
    Having got up a breach by fighting well,. . . . . 171 Astrophil   12   10
    And straight therewith, like wags new got to play, ... 173 Astrophil   17   13
    Yet since my death-wound is already got,. . . . . 189 Astrophil   48   12
    Of Conquerd states, wherby such fame you gott? . . . . 280 Psalm IX   17
    Have not I fair partage gott?. . . . . 288 Psalm XVI   18
    Since all my ayd in Thee I got.. . . . . 308 Psalm XXVII   44
    Although they be of meaner parents gott: . . . . 242 Other Poems   4 112
    But light-legd Pas had gott the middle space.. . . . . 248 Other Poems   4 253
    I got to a shady wood, ... 262 Other Poems   7   3
GOTTEN
    For such an use the world hath gotten, ...   88 Arcadia III 62   85
    This gotten blisse shall never part, ... 282 Psalm X   24
GOUT
    From the cruell headache, nor shooes of golde doo the gowt
        heale,. . . . .   34 1st Eclogues 13   85
GOVERN
    R. But Reason will, that Reason governe most.. . . . .   46 2nd Eclogues 27   5
GOVERNMENT
    Which lest the ruinous want of government dissolve;. . . . . 120 4th Eclogues 73 128
GOWNS
    Then some grene gowns are by the lasses worne. . . . . 243 Other Poems   4   53
GRACE
    All this I give, let me possesse thy grace,. . . . .   4 Lady of May   2   22
    And for a tast of all these gifts, she borowes Momus' grace.   12 Arcadia I   3   8
    But when to give some grace she doth content herselfe, . . .   49 2nd Eclogues 28   64
    In thy high minde) get her thy husband's grace.. . . . . . .   60 2nd Eclogues 30 114
    Of some late grace a greater grace receave,. . . . .   77 Arcadia III 49   4
    His workes, showes, suites, with wit, grace, and vow's
        might . . . .   84 Arcadia III 60   4
    To all her limmes a spetiall grace,. . . . .   90 Arcadia III 62 135
    But with thy cheerefull presence helpe to grace. . . . . . .   91 3rd Eclogues 63   12
    To onely thee thou seest we graunt this speciall grace . . . 119 4th Eclogues 73   95
    Then may I hope t'atchieve grace of a heavenly tiger.. . . . 122 4th Eclogues 74   22
    And aske the reason of that speciall grace,. . . . . 126 4th Eclogues 75   40
    That who so that grace obtaineth,. . . . . 140 Cert Sonnets 7   25

GRACE   (CONTINUED)   PAGE   TITLE   LINE
  Nor sence that grace descryes: . . . . 152 Cert Sonnets 23   26
  Of this high grace with blisse conjoyn'd . . . . 159 Cert Sonnets 29   1
  Knowledge might pitie winne, and pitie grace obtaine,. . . . 165 Astrophil   1   4
  The doore by which sometimes comes forth her Grace,. . . . . 169 Astrophil   9   5
  That her Grace gracious makes thy wrongs, that she . . . . . 170 Astrophil   12   6
  But straight I saw motions of lightning grace, ... 175 Astrophil   20   12
  Yet each prepar'd, with fanne's wel-shading grace, ... 176 Astrophil   22   7
  Bends all his powers, even unto Stella's grace.. . . . . . . 178 Astrophil   27   14
  I reade it in thy lookes, thy languisht grace. . . . . 180 Astrophil   31   7
  Move not thy heavy grace, thou shalt in me,. . . . . 184 Astrophil   39   13
  Upon a wretch, that long thy grace hath sought;. . . . . . . 185 Astrophil   40   7
  But more I crie, lesse grace she doth impart;. . . . . 186 Astrophil   44   6
  Though false, yet with free scope more grace doth breed. . . 187 Astrophil   45   10
  Without desire to feed of further grace. . . . . 187 Astrophil   46   8
  A kind of grace it is to slay with speed.. . . . . 189 Astrophil   48   14
  And therefore, though her beautie and her grace. . . . . . . 191 Astrophil   52   9
  Might winne some grace in your sweet skill arraid. . . . . . 192 Astrophil   55   4
  Might winne some grace in your sweet grace arraid. . . . . . 192 Astrophil   55 V 4
  Or else pronouncing grace, wherewith his mind. . . . . 194 Astrophil   58   7
  Anger invests with such a lovely grace,. . . . . 203 Astrophil   73   13
  That grace, which Venus weepes that she her selfe doth
    misse . . . . 205 Astrophil   77   4
  Who since he hath, by Nature's speciall grace, ... 206 Astrophil   78   9
  Admitted late by your best-graced grace, ... 208 Astrophil   82   10
  Cannot such grace your silly selfe content,. . . . . 208 Astrophil   83   11
  What sobs can give words grace my griefe to show?. . . . . . 227 Astrophil   93   2
  And endlesly dispairing of his grace,. . . . . 229 Astrophil   97   6
  How is thy grace by my strange fortune staind! . . . . 230 Astrophil   98   3
  And grace, sicke too, such fine conclusions tries, ... 231 Astrophil   101   3
  Whose grace is such, that when it chides doth cherish? . . . 197 A&S 1st Song   18
  With heavenly hew and grace, ... 216 A&S 6th Song   20
  Shall a heavenly grace want pitty?". . . . . 219 A&S 8th Song   64
  Gave repulse all grace excelling,. . . . . 219 A&S 8th Song   68
  By him because I did find in his eyes' sight grace,. . . . . 292 Psalm XVIII   41
  There by his Grace for sun's fair face . . . . 294 Psalm XIX   19
  Of grace and righteousness . . . . 303 Psalm XXV   31
  Oh! of thy grace what endlesse pleasure flowes . . . . 313 Psalm XXXI   52
  Then love him all ye that feel his grace,. . . . . 314 Psalm XXXI   64
  And his sweet grace streight easd the rod. . . . . 315 Psalm XXXII   17
  How sweet how gracious is his grace. . . . . 319 Psalm XXXIV   30
  Thy grace with safety man fulfills,. . . . . 323 Psalm XXXVI   17
  Then lord from me draw not Thy tender grace, ... 332 Psalm XL   41
  This done, but done with captive-killing grace,. . . . . . . 244 Other Poems   4 105
  Thus Pas did kisse hir hand with little grace. . . . . 249 Other Poems   4 276
  Laid hold on him with most lay-holding grace. . . . . 250 Other Poems   4 310
  With heart as carefull, as with carelesse grace, ... 255 Other Poems   4 522
  So may thy stately grace . . . . 256 Other Poems   5   15
GRACED
  Dicus. Thy words well voic'd, well gra'ste had almost heaved
    me. . . . .   48 2nd Eclogues 28   31
  A woman's mould, but like an Angell graste,. . . . . 151 Cert Sonnets 22   66
  Admitted late by your best-graced grace, ... 208 Astrophil   82   10
  That sickenesse brags it selfe best graced to be.. . . . . . 231 Astrophil   101   4
  In action aptly graced:. . . . . 216 A&S 6th Song   28
GRACEFUL
  While gracefull pitty beauty beautifies. . . . . 231 Astrophil   100   4
GRACEFULLY
  He ravished with sight how gracefully. . . . . 249 Other Poems   4 282
GRACES
  All numbring artes her endlesse graces number not: . . . . .   49 2nd Eclogues 28   59
  Where sweet graces erect the stately banner. . . . .   67 2nd Eclogues 33   3
  Seeking the Sainct in whome all graces dwell,. . . . .   71 Arcadia III 36   14
  Though you besides such graces earth hath lent,. . . . . . .   77 Arcadia III 49   3
  The neck, in which strange graces lurke. . . . .   87 Arcadia III 62   48
  Whose motion makes all graces move.. . . . .   89 Arcadia III 62   96
  But how the Graces doo impart. . . . .   90 Arcadia III 62 134
  (Unto thy selfe I do meane those graces dwell so within
    thee . . . . 122 4th Eclogues 74   9
  When they by yeares' experience get best graces, ... 127 4th Eclogues 75   89
  Where bee those movinges, the Delights, the graces?. . . . . 138 Cert Sonnets 5   11
  Immortall be her graces, ... 152 Cert Sonnets 23   21
  Whence words, not words, but heav'nly graces slide.. . . . . 206 Astrophil   80   4
  With passe-port of thy graces manifold:. . . . . 275 Psalm V   18
  Still therfore of Thy Graces shall be my . . . . 286 Psalm XIII   19
GRACES'
  Of all those Graces' giftes the heavens have ever lent.. . . 119 4th Eclogues 73   86
GRACIOUS
  That her Grace gracious makes thy wrongs, that she . . . . . 170 Astrophil   12   6
  Is strong though he be gracious, ... 310 Psalm XXIX   11
  Who was to me more than most gracious, ... 313 Psalm XXXI   59
  How sweet how gracious is his grace. . . . . 319 Psalm XXXIV   30
GRACIOUSNESS
  Thy Truth, health, gratiousness. . . . . 331 Psalm XL   40
GRAFT
  Goe graft againe, and seeke to graft them right, ...   26 1st Eclogues 9 129
GRAFTING
  The very trees with grafting we can cherish, ... 127 4th Eclogues 75   85
GRAFTS
  What man grafts in a tree dissimulation? . . . .   69 2nd Eclogues 34   28

193

```
                                                           PAGE    TITLE          LINE
GRAIN
    Where Beautie's blush in Honour's graine is dide.. . . . . .  207 Astrophil    80    8
    Of grain and wine fills stoaring place.. . . . . . . . . . .  274 Psalm IV          30
GRAMMAR
    Let us some grammar learne of more congruities.. . . . . . .   61 2nd Eclogues 30  142
    O Grammer rules, o now your vertues show;. . . . . . . . . .  196 Astrophil    63    1
    For Grammer sayes (o this deare Stella weighe,). . . . . . .  196 Astrophil    63   12
    For Grammer sayes (to Grammer who sayes nay) . . . . . . . .  196 Astrophil    63   13
GRAMMAR'S
    But Grammer's force with sweet successe confirme,. . . . . .  196 Astrophil    63   11
GRANDAME
    Till that his grandame Nature pittying it, . . . . . . . . .  173 Astrophil    17    9
GRANDSIRE
    Although we be divine, our grandsire Saturne is. . . . . . .  120 4th Eclogues 73  123
GRANDSIRE'S
    In granting unto him a grandsire's gaine.. . . . . . . . . .  105 3rd Eclogues 67   75
GRANGE
    Within the Elmy grange,. . . . . . . . . . . . . . . . . . .  261 Other Poems   6   33
GRANT
    My wearied ears! O gods yet graunt me this,. . . . . . . . .   24 1st Eclogues  9   67
    Justely to graunt thy rewarde, such envie I beare to thy
        fortune. . . . . . . . . . . . . . . . . . . . . . . . .   37 1st Eclogues 13  156
    O be it so, graunte such an event, O Gods, that event give..   37 1st Eclogues 13  169
    Fortune store, Nature health, Love grant perswasion. . . . .   51 2nd Eclogues 28  100
    Sweet birds kindly do graunt harmony unto thee,. . . . . . .   69 2nd Eclogues 34   12
    Yet yeeld your graunt, a baser hand may leave. . . . . . . .   78 Arcadia III  49    9
    Graunt to the thing which we for Lalus crave.. . . . . . . .   92 3rd Eclogues 63   30
    Muses graunt guiftes, Nymphes long and joyned life . . . . .   93 3rd Eclogues 63   92
    To their owne worke this priviledge they graunt, . . . . . .  101 3rd Eclogues 66  103
    To onely thee thou seest we graunt this speciall grace . . .  119 4th Eclogues 73   95
    Grant yet, grant yet a looke, to the last monument of his
        anguish, . . . . . . . . . . . . . . . . . . . . . . . .  122 4th Eclogues 74    3
    Doth willing graunt, that in the frontiers he. . . . . . . .  179 Astrophil    29    7
    That Vertue but that body graunt to us.. . . . . . . . . . .  191 Astrophil    52   14
    Alas, if you graunt only such delight. . . . . . . . . . . .  194 Astrophil    59   12
    Driv'n else to graunt by Angel's sophistrie, . . . . . . . .  195 Astrophil    61   13
    Her graunt to me, by her owne vertue know. . . . . . . . . .  196 Astrophil    63    4
    Pardon that fault, once more graunt me the place,. . . . . .  208 Astrophil    82   12
    Let honor selfe to thee graunt highest place.. . . . . . . .  233 Astrophil   103   14
    Long stay ere he graunt the same:. . . . . . . . . . . . . .  211 A&S 4th Song      33
    "Graunt, o graunt, but speech alas,. . . . . . . . . . . . .  219 A&S 8th Song      45
    Graunt, o me, what am I saying?. . . . . . . . . . . . . . .  219 A&S 8th Song      47
    "Graunt, o deere, on knees I pray, . . . . . . . . . . . . .  219 A&S 8th Song      49
    And so with hidden treasures grant their Will, . . . . . . .  290 Psalm XVII        42
    To grant Thy Will and perfect Thy entent,. . . . . . . . . .  296 Psalm XX          17
    Graunt pleasure to our meeting:. . . . . . . . . . . . . . .  260 Other Poems   6    2
    Grant, I say (if seely man . . . . . . . . . . . . . . . . .  263 Other Poems   7   57
    Grant me with those two remaining. . . . . . . . . . . . . .  263 Other Poems   7   66
GRANTED
    Shall I not once object, that you, you graunted a favour . .  124 4th Eclogues 74   73
    Ah, my sute granted is, I feele my breast doth swell:. . . .  213 A&S 5th Song      34
    Up to Our God, when Thy suites granted be. . . . . . . . . .  296 Psalm XX          20
    And this delight to them is granted, . . . . . . . . . . . .  325 Psalm XXXVII      31
GRANTETH
    To whom nor art nor nature graunteth light,. . . . . . . . .  230 Astrophil    99    2
    Onely to you her Scepter Venus granteth. . . . . . . . . . .  197 A&S 1st Song      16
GRANTING
    In granting unto him a grandsire's gaine.. . . . . . . . . .  105 3rd Eclogues 67   75
    In graunting such a scope to filthy fortune, . . . . . . . .  109 Arcadia IV   70   21
GRANTS
    Sleeping, grants a free resort:. . . . . . . . . . . . . . .  202 A&S 2nd Song      14
GRASS
    If three-leav'd grasse seeme to the sheepe unsavorie,. . . .   48 2nd Eclogues 28   23
    They soone shall be cutt down like grasse. . . . . . . . . .  324 Psalm XXXVII       5
    Train'd in the life which on short-bitten grasse . . . . . .  242 Other Poems   4   19
    Proud grew the grasse that under hir did growe,. . . . . . .  244 Other Poems   4  108
    No grasse, no trees, nor yet hir sparrow might . . . . . . .  245 Other Poems   4  111
    His eye, that ev'n did marke hir troden grasse,. . . . . . .  251 Other Poems   4  379
    And of grasse was plenty dwelling, . . . . . . . . . . . . .  262 Other Poems   7    5
GRASSY
    Strephon. Yee Gote-heard Gods, that love the grassie
        mountaines. . . . . . . . . . . . . . . . . . . . . . .  111 4th Eclogues 71    1
GRATEFUL
    And vertue is gratefull with bewty and richnes adorned,. . .   33 1st Eclogues 13   57
    Whereas if I a gratefull gardien have, . . . . . . . . . . .  135 Cert Sonnets  1   13
    So gratefull now you waite upon my care. . . . . . . . . . .  228 Astrophil    95    4
    Thinke of that most gratefull time,. . . . . . . . . . . . .  226 A&S 10th Song     25
    Gratefull meaning show thee, . . . . . . . . . . . . . . . .  337 Psalm XLIII       27
    How gratefull is our greeting. . . . . . . . . . . . . . . .  260 Other Poems   6    4
GRATEFULNESS
    Gratefulnes, sweetnes, holy love, hartie regard) . . . . . .  122 4th Eclogues 74   10
GRATIFY
    So she thy love, her eyes thy eyes may gratifie, . . . . . .   49 2nd Eclogues 28   51
*GRAVE
    In him, the thoughts of Phaeton's damme to grave.. . . . . .   60 2nd Eclogues 30  106
    Come cave, become my grave, come death, and lende. . . . . .   73 Arcadia III  40    7
    Death wrapt in flesh, to living grave assign'd.. . . . . . .   73 Arcadia III  40   14
    That wounding thee, my thoughtes in thee I grave:. . . . . .   77 Arcadia III  47    2
    One grave their bodies seaze:. . . . . . . . . . . . . . . .   92 3rd Eclogues 63   32
    But from the sent of some infectious grave:. . . . . . . . .  114 4th Eclogues 72   19
```

```
*GRAVE                    (CONTINUED)                          PAGE     TITLE          LINE
   Place see my grave uptorne:. . . . . . . . . . . . . . . .   136 Cert Sonnets  3    19
   Of all the grave conceits your braine doth breed;. . . . .   190 Astrophil    51     6
   Their throat, it is an Open swallowing grave,. . . . . . .   275 Psalm V            27
   For I know the deadly grave. . . . . . . . . . . . . . . .   288 Psalm XVI          31
   All ready, ready to my snaring grave to go. . . . . . . . .  291 Psalm XVIII        11
   Let those things Thy remembrance grave,. . . . . . . . . .   303 Psalm XXV          23
   Ev'en from the grave . . . . . . . . . . . . . . . . . . .   318 Psalm XXXIII       74
   So that the grave did not his words despise. . . . . . . .   243 Other Poems   4    38
GRAVED
   With Diamond in window-glasse she graved,. . . . . . . . . .  61 2nd Eclogues 30   156
   Graved in mine Epitaph a Poet's name:. . . . . . . . . . .   224 Astrophil    90     8
   And streight for failing, grav'd it in his heart:. . . . .   247 Other Poems   4   186
GRAVEN
   W. What seale? D. My hart deepe graven. W. Who made the band
      so fast?. . . . . . . . . . . . . . . . . . . . . . . .   343 Possibly      1    27
GRAVE'S
   Yea from the grave's most hungry jawes;. . . . . . . . . .   311 Psalm XXX           7
GRAY
   Pas. My gray-hood is mine owne, all be it be but gray, . .    52 2nd Eclogues 29     7
   The night growne old, her blacke head waxen gray,. . . . .   103 3rd Eclogues 66   160
   He thought gray haires afforded subtletie. . . . . . . . .   248 Other Poems   4   256
GRAY-HOOD
   Thy gray-hood hides the thing, that thou despairst to find..  52 2nd Eclogues 29     6
   Pas. My gray-hood is mine owne, all be it be but gray, . .    52 2nd Eclogues 29     7
GREAT
   Your state is great, your greatnesse is our shield,. . . . .   3 Lady of May   1     7
   Great sure is she, on whom our hopes do live,. . . . . . . .   3 Lady of May   2     5
   Let not wild woods so great a treasure have. . . . . . . . .   3 Lady of May   2    12
   Like great god Saturn faire, and like faire Venus chaste:. .  12 Arcadia I     3     5
   Now thanked be the great God Pan,. . . . . . . . . . . . . .  13 Arcadia I     5     1
   Dorus. Thy challenge great, but greater my protection: . . .  15 1st Eclogues  7    19
   Save when great need of them perforce apeare. . . . . . . .   27 1st Eclogues 10    36
   That sport it is to see with howe greate art . . . . . . .    27 1st Eclogues 10    41
   And yet they say he talkes in greate men's bowers? . . . .    28 1st Eclogues 10    68
   But farewell nowe, thy fault is no great sinne,. . . . . .    29 1st Eclogues 10    97
   Give therefore to the Muse great praise in whose very
      likenes. . . . . . . . . . . . . . . . . . . . . . . .     33 1st Eclogues 13    62
   Great to thee my estate seemes, thy estate is blest by my
      judgement: . . . . . . . . . . . . . . . . . . . . . .     33 1st Eclogues 13    72
   And yet neither of us great or blest deemeth his owne selfe.  33 1st Eclogues 13    73
   For yet (weigh this alas!) great is not great to a greater..  34 1st Eclogues 13    74
   Vertue, richesse, beawties of mine shall great be reputed. .  34 1st Eclogues 13    81
   Firr trees great and greene, fixt on a hye hill but a
      barrein, . . . . . . . . . . . . . . . . . . . . . . .     35 1st Eclogues 13   123
   O descende for a while, from this greate height to behold
      me . . . . . . . . . . . . . . . . . . . . . . . . . .     36 1st Eclogues 13   149
   (Mine eyes even great in labour with their teares) . . . .    41 Arcadia II   21     2
   The fuell small: how be the fires so great?. . . . . . . .    42 Arcadia II   22    14
   Apollo great, whose beames the greater world do light, . .    44 Arcadia II   26     1
   Dicus. Dorus you wander farre in great reproches;. . . . .    50 2nd Eclogues 28    92
   I have (and long shall have) a white great nimble cat, . .    53 2nd Eclogues 29    31
   What great name may I give to so heav'nly a woman? A
      woe-man. . . . . . . . . . . . . . . . . . . . . . . .     64 2nd Eclogues 31    37
   So greate a passion all feele, . . . . . . . . . . . . . .    66 2nd Eclogues 32    16
   For reason will, great sight of hoped blisse,. . . . . . .    71 Arcadia III  37    11
   Make great the losse, so grete the feare to misse. . . . .    71 Arcadia III  37    12
   Eyes faire and great, like faire great oxe's eyes, . . . .    76 Arcadia III  46     9
   Thy title great, I justlie chalenge may,. . . . . . . . . .   80 Arcadia III  53     7
   For mischeefes greate, daye after day doth showe:. . . . .    82 Arcadia III  56    13
   To whome our prince did beare a great good will, . . . . .    94 3rd Eclogues 64    16
   Ape great thing gave, though he did mowing stand,. . . . .   101 3rd Eclogues 66    97
   By those great beastes, as for the weaker's good,. . . . .   102 3rd Eclogues 66   128
   As horse and dogge, not great, but gentle blood: . . . . .   102 3rd Eclogues 66   131
   The great beames gone, the house on shoulders light: . . .   102 3rd Eclogues 66   136
   The mountaines great with childe I thought brought foorth a
      mouse. . . . . . . . . . . . . . . . . . . . . . . . .    118 4th Eclogues 73    76
   Those names abasht me much, when those great names I hard: .  119 4th Eclogues 73    79
   Aske, if in great men good men so do thronge,. . . . . . .   126 4th Eclogues 75    43
   Great be Physitions' brags, but aid is beggerly,. . . . . .  128 4th Eclogues 75   112
   Since this we feele, greate losse we cannot finde. . . . .   131 Arcadia V    77    14
   He hopes for some small praise since she hath great, . . .   141 Cert Sonnets  8    11
   For if my place give me great pleasure,. . . . . . . . . .   159 Cert Sonnets 29     5
   Thus great with child to speake, and helplesse in my
      throwes . . . . . . . . . . . . . . . . . . . . . . .    165 Astrophil     1    12
   Great expectation, weare a traine of shame.. . . . . . . .   175 Astrophil    21     8
   For since mad March great promise made of me,. . . . . . .   175 Astrophil    21     9
   Vertue's great beautie in that face I prove,. . . . . . . .  177 Astrophil    25    13
   And know great causes, great effects procure:. . . . . . .   178 Astrophil    26    10
   Stella's great powrs, that so confuse my mind. . . . . . .   182 Astrophil    34    14
   If so great services may scorned be: . . . . . . . . . . .   198 Astrophil    65    10
   As though that faire soft hand did you great wrong.. . . .   208 Astrophil    83     4
   To this great cause, which needs both use and art,. . . . .  236 Astrophil   107     8
   Know, that small Love is quicke, and great Love doth amaze:.  209 A&S 3rd Song       16
   Him great names had taught much care,. . . . . . . . . . .   218 A&S 8th Song        9
   And great with child of mischeif travaild long,. . . . . .   278 Psalm VII          38
   Whom that Great God remember can?. . . . . . . . . . . . .   278 Psalm VIII         14
   With terrors great, O Lord, do thou them fright: . . . . .   281 Psalm IX           63
   Great Pity.. . . . . . . . . . . . . . . . . . . . . . . .   286 Psalm XIII         18
   But doth with honour great the Godly entertaine; . . . . .   287 Psalm XV            8
```

GREAT   (CONTINUED)   PAGE   TITLE   LINE
    For who is God, besides this Great Jehova Ours?. . . . . . .   292 Psalm XVIII   57
    Their Words be set in letters great. . . . .   294 Psalm XIX   15
    Wee may well call his glory great. . . . .   297 Psalm XXI   17
    In congregation great I will prayse Thee,. . . . .   300 Psalm XXII   59
    The Paths of my great God? . . . .   304 Psalm XXV   38
    Though it be great in me. . . . .   304 Psalm XXV   46
    The works perform'd by Thee most wondrous great. . . . . . .   305 Psalm XXVI   24
    For when great griefes to me be ment,. . . . .   307 Psalm XXVII   25
    I understand what rayling great men spred; . . . .   313 Psalm XXXI   37
    O let thy mercy great.   318 Psalm XXXIII   82
    Most great and grievous paines doth beare, ...   320 Psalm XXXIV   70
    Judg lord, judg God, ev'en in Thy justice great, ...   322 Psalm XXXV   59
    Chafe not at some man's great good fortune . . . .   325 Psalm XXXVII   18
    In great show,. . . . .   329 Psalm XXXVIII   56
    To great men's peacock pride,. . . . .   331 Psalm XL   18
    I to great congregation,. . . . .   331 Psalm XL   35
    What great thanks I ow thee. . . . .   337 Psalm XLIII   30
    Will. Then Dick let us go hence lest wee great folkes annoy.   344 Possibly   1   45
    Desire's great force, no forces can withhold:. . . . .   345 Possibly   4   3
    While those restles desires in great men rife. . . . .   243 Other Poems   4   62
    And so must see great cause before they love. . . . .   245 Other Poems   4 144
GREATER
    Greater is she who must the judgement give.. . . . .   3 Lady of May   2   6
    Dorus. Thy challenge great, but greater my protection: . . .   15 1st Eclogues   7   19
    For yet (weigh this alas!) great is not great to a greater..   34 1st Eclogues 13   74
    Old age orecome, the greater honour gives. . . . .   39 Arcadia II   15   12
    Apollo great, whose beames the greater world do light, . . .   44 Arcadia II   26   1
    A greater good by her divine reflection: . . . .   49 2nd Eclogues 28   68
    What greater ills have now the heavens in store, ...   57 2nd Eclogues 30   6
    Who hold this fast no greater wealth require. . . . .   75 Arcadia III   44   8
    Of some late grace a greater grace receave,. . . . .   77 Arcadia III   49   4
    Beleeve me man, there is no greater blisse,. . . . .   103 3rd Eclogues 67   7
    Did light those beamye stars which greater light did darke:.   116 4th Eclogues 73   3
    The stately towers come downe with greater fall: . . . . . .   143 Cert Sonnets 12   8
    To greater woes by presence I returne, ...   149 Cert Sonnets 21   10
    I see and yet no greater sorow take, ...   174 Astrophil   18   13
    With proud aspect, disdaining greater hast.. . . . .   249 Other Poems   4 293
    With greater powr, then she did make them wend . . . .   251 Other Poems   4 375
    But after this to greater rage it broke, ...   253 Other Poems   4 429
    Greater was that shepheard's treasure, ...   263 Other Poems   7   47
GREATEST
    As shallow brookes do yeeld the greatest sound,. . . . . . .   4 Lady of May   2   14
    For of his beasts the greatest beast he is.. . . . .   4 Lady of May   2   30
    Yet hath sir Sunne the greatest praise,. . . . .   13 Arcadia I   5   9
    And such discord twixt greatest shepheards flowes, ...   27 1st Eclogues 10   40
    Such this smale greatnes, doth seeme compar'd to the
        greatest.. . . . .   34 1st Eclogues 13   76
    And vertue do in greatest need neglect.. . . . .   58 2nd Eclogues 30   64
    Seeme most alone in greatest companie, ...   178 Astrophil   27   2
    In time of greatest tribulation. . . . .   327 Psalm XXXVII   99
    What do we seeke? the greatest state I see . . . .   330 Psalm XXXIX   17
GREATLY
    Although their fame (me seemd) from truth had greatly jard..   119 4th Eclogues 73   80
    Whose life doth seeme most greatly blest . . . .   290 Psalm XVII   39
GREATNESS
    Your state is great, your greatnesse is our shield,. . . . .   3 Lady of May   1   7
    Farre more happy be you, whose greatnes gets a free accesse,   33 1st Eclogues 13   54
    Such this smale greatnes, doth seeme compar'd to the
        greatest.. . . . .   34 1st Eclogues 13   76
    Tho when they saw their foen of greatnes kilde.. . . . . . .   102 3rd Eclogues 66 133
    Whose numbers, wayes, greatnesse, eternitie, ...   178 Astrophil   26   3
GRECIAN
    If Eagle fierce could so in Grecian Mayd delight,. . . . . .   209 A&S 3rd Song   9
GREECE
    A three foote stoole in Greece, made Trumpets sound, ...   146 Cert Sonnets 17   19
    Love borne in Greece, of late fled from his native place,. .   168 Astrophil   8   1
GREEDY
    My greedy soule, with gripe of inward fire:. . . . .   80 Arcadia III   53   6
    With my greedy licorous sences,. . . . .   226 A&S 10th Song   33
    (Lest greedy eies to them might challenge lay) . . . .   243 Other Poems   4   68
    A hast'ned Hare from greedy Grayhound goe, ...   251 Other Poems   4 343
    Tell me if greedy arme,. . . . .   258 Other Poems   5   85
GREEKS
    If Greekes themselves were mov'd with so small cause . . . .   146 Cert Sonnets 17   21
GREEN
    Firr trees great and greene, fixt on a hye hill but a
        barrein, ...   35 1st Eclogues 13 123
    Didst snatch from Cosma's hand her greene ywroughten glove..   52 2nd Eclogues 29   10
    How ill fits you this greene to weare, ...   157 Cert Sonnets 28   3
    He rests me in green pasture his.. . . . .   301 Psalm XXIII   4
    And wither like green herb or flower;. . . . .   324 Psalm XXXVII   6
    Then some grene gowns are by the lasses worne. . . . .   243 Other Poems   4   53
    Of faire Urania, fairer then a greene, ...   253 Other Poems   4 452
    Disdaine not you the greene, ...   258 Other Poems   5   90
    Where greene leaves did newly bud. . . . .   262 Other Poems   7   4
GREET
    My Muse and I must you of dutie greet. . . . .   209 Astrophil   84   7
GREETING
    How gratefull is our greeting. . . . .   260 Other Poems   6   4

	PAGE	TITLE	LINE
*GREW			
Foole that I am that with my dogges speake grewe........	27	1st Eclogues 10	19
So in his sicknesse grew our sure infection.........	128	4th Eclogues 75	135
Then to my selfe, not though Jove grew a suter of hers....	143	Cert Sonnets 13	2
Then grew my tongue and pen records unto thy glory:.....	212	A&S 5th Song	3
Proud grew the grasse that under hir did growe,.......	244	Other Poems 4	108
Then sports grew paines, all talking tediouse,.......	253	Other Poems 4	433
GREYHOUND			
First may a trusty Greyhounde transforme himselfe to a			
Tigre................................	33	1st Eclogues 13	66
A hast'ned Hare from greedy Grayhound goe,.........	251	Other Poems 4	343
GRIEF			
Yet for my sake discover us thy griefe...........	23	1st Eclogues 9	23
P. But so we shall with griefe learne to repent.......	47	2nd Eclogues 27	36
From any joy, which might her griefe occasion........	51	2nd Eclogues 28	122
Griefe onely makes his wretched state to see	58	2nd Eclogues 30	32
Griefe is the stone which finest judgement proves:......	58	2nd Eclogues 30	35
Since cause of griefe no cause from life removes.......	58	2nd Eclogues 30	37
He heapes in inward griefe, that most destroyes him.....	62	2nd Eclogues 30	172
One day layes up stuffe of griefe for the morrow:.....	62	2nd Eclogues 30	176
Bitter griefe tastes me best, paine is my ease,......	74	Arcadia III 41	7
No cave, no wasting waxe, no wordes of griefe,.......	75	Arcadia III 43	7
Get hence foule Griefe, the canker of the minde:.....	83	Arcadia III 59	1
Then greefe, unkindnes, proofe, tooke, kindled, tought,...	84	Arcadia III 60	9
Wrong sturres remorsed greefe, griefe's deadly sore.....	85	Arcadia III 61	7
Desiring, that no griefe in him he bread	97	3rd Eclogues 64	111
And inward griefe seale up with outward wailing.......	109	Arcadia IV 70	6
Strephon. I Joye in griefe, and doo detest all joyes:....	113	4th Eclogues 72	1
I joy in griefe, and doo detest all joyes...........	116	4th Eclogues 72	100
Strephon. I joye in griefe, and doo detest all joyes.....	116	4th Eclogues 72	101
That forced with grief reveales what greeved eyes dyd see) .	118	4th Eclogues 73	56
Care that I sinke in griefe, Care that I live banished?...	124	4th Eclogues 74	82
To well felte griefe, plainte is the onely pleasure.....	126	4th Eclogues 75	51
By shame and griefe, helpe, helpe me to lament	126	4th Eclogues 75	62
With too much griefe me thinkes you are dissolved......	127	4th Eclogues 75	77
The sea to ebbe for griefe his flowing turneth:......	136	Cert Sonnets 3	3
What griefe her breast oppresseth,..............	137	Cert Sonnets 4	7
Griefe but Love's winter liverie is, the Boy	201	Astrophil 70	7
What sobs can give words grace my griefe to show?......	227	Astrophil 93	2
Griefe find the words, for thou hast made my braine.....	228	Astrophil 94	1
Thy griefe more then death would grieve me..	220	A&S 8th Song	76
My eye, my Gutts, yea my soul grief doth wast,.......	312	Psalm XXXI	27
In my heart such grief is found................	328	Psalm XXXVIII	24
Why should grief my heart devower,.............	335	Psalm XLII	43
Yet will not I greife, ashes, thralldom change	345	Possibly 2	9
They joi'd one joy, one griefe they griev'd,	241	Other Poems 3	3
GRIEF'S			
Wrong sturres remorsed greefe, griefe's deadly sore.....	85	Arcadia III 61	7
GRIEFS			
Joyn'd, by thy beauty adorn'd, be no meanes these greefes to			
abolish:...........................	34	1st Eclogues 13	99
And may I not (say I then) gett up though griefs be so			
weightie?...........................	36	1st Eclogues 13	128
With monefull melodies, for enough our greefes be revealed,.	37	1st Eclogues 13	173
Thus outward helps my inward griefes maintaine........	42	Arcadia II 21	12
While our sonne shynes no clowdie greeves assaile.....	43	Arcadia II 23	12
My sun is gon, Nowe clowdie greeves assayle........	44	Arcadia II 24	12
Echo, what do I gett yelding my sprite to my grieves?			
Grieves...............................	63	2nd Eclogues 31	5
Of written greefes, yet be the silent ground........	81	Arcadia III 54	8
The furious inward griefes with hellish wailing:.....	109	Arcadia IV 70	33
Let it embassage beare your grieves to showe........	125	4th Eclogues 75	12
Sounde of my griefes, and let it never ende,.......	126	4th Eclogues 75	35
To feele my griefes, and she with face and voice	193	Astrophil 57	13
For when great griefes to me be ment,............	307	Psalm XXVII	25
GRIEVE			
To grieve me worse, in saying that Desire..........	171	Astrophil 14	6
Thy griefe more then death would grieve me..	220	A&S 8th Song	76
Vain shades and vain, in vain to grieve...........	330	Psalm XXXIX	20
"My old mates I grieve to see,................	262	Other Poems 7	19
GRIEVED			
Of all the birdes, but namely those were grieved,......	29	1st Eclogues 10	83
Thy common-wealth may rightly grieved be,..........	105	3rd Eclogues 67	76
That forced with grief reveales what greeved eyes dyd see) .	118	4th Eclogues 73	56
Ah haire are you not griev'd,..................	158	Cert Sonnets 28	29
If I saw my good dog grieved,................	222	A&S 9th Song	37
They joi'd one joy, one griefe they griev'd,	241	Other Poems 3	3
The courteous mountaines, griev'd at my disgrace,.....	254	Other Poems 4	477
GRIEVES			
For who grieves not hath but a blockish braine,.......	58	2nd Eclogues 30	36
The wynde most oft the hugest Pine-tree greeves:......	143	Cert Sonnets 12	7
GRIEVOUS			
To over pressed brestes, more greevous waight........	82	Arcadia III 56	8
Of Lovers never knowne, a grievous case, ...	187	Astrophil 45	6
To breed my grievous trouble,.................	272	Psalm III	3
Most great and grievous paines doth beare, ...	320	Psalm XXXIV	70
*GRIPE			
My greedy soule, with gripe of inward fire:.........	80	Arcadia III 53	6
Upon whose breast a fiercer Gripe doth tire.........	171	Astrophil 14	2
Let wo gripe on my heart, shame loade mine eye.......	212	Astrophil 86	4

197

```
*GRIPE                     (CONTINUED)                        PAGE    TITLE          LINE
    Finding the gripe of Falcon fierce not furr: . . . . . . . .  251 Other Poems    4   356
GROAN
    Because (though hurt) they never heard her grone. . . . . . . 102 3rd Eclogues  66   119
    As good to write as for to lie and grone. . . . . . . . . . . 184 Astrophil     40    1
    Nor give each speech a full point of a grone, . . . . . . . . 191 Astrophil     54    4
    The thorowest words, fit for woe's selfe to grone, . . . . .  193 Astrophil     57    4
    Lo, I am tir'd, while still I sigh and groane: . . . . . . .  276 Psalm VI           17
GROANED
    Klaius streight felt, and groned at the blowe, . . . . . . .  246 Other Poems    4   161
GROANS
    And can crie helpe with nought but grones and starts: . . . . 136 Cert Sonnets   2    12
GROATS
    In cofer of dimme clowdes his silver groates, . . . . . . .   98 3rd Eclogues  66    9
GROCM
    But he himselfe a foule unhansome groome, . . . . . . . . .   94 3rd Eclogues  64    5
GROUND
    Thy stars be fal'n, plowed is thy flintie ground: . . . . .    4 Lady of May    2    16
    When Cedars to the ground be opprest by the weight of an
        emmott, . . . . . . . . . . . . . . . . . . . . . . . .   34 1st Eclogues  13    77
    Then kneling to the ground, oft thus do I speake to that
        Image: . . . . . . . . . . . . . . . . . . . . . . . .   36 1st Eclogues  13   146
    Nico. Peace, peace good Pas, thou weeriest even the ground .  56 2nd Eclogues  29   135
    With cries to skies, and curses to the ground, . . . . . . .  57 2nd Eclogues  30    9
    Of written greefes, yet be the silent ground. . . . . . . .   81 Arcadia III   54    8
    That yet the ground hereof he might espie. . . . . . . . . .  96 3rd Eclogues  64   72
    The ever-turning spheares, the never-moving ground; . . . . . 118 4th Eclogues  73   44
    Till want of force do force her fall to ground; . . . . . . . 144 Cert Sonnets  15    4
    A horse's worth laid wast the Troyan ground: . . . . . . . .  146 Cert Sonnets  17   18
    Whose eyes seeme chaste, because they looke on ground: . . .  147 Cert Sonnets  17   50
    What force brought them to so unlikely ground. . . . . . . .  149 Cert Sonnets  22    4
    The ground of this fierce Love and lovely hate: . . . . . . . 195 Astrophil     60   11
    In a ground of so firme making, . . . . . . . . . . . . . .   234 A&S 11th Song      34
    (Knees on ground he then did stay) . . . . . . . . . . . . .  219 A&S 8th Song       50
    With ground plot's fall shall be undone: . . . . . . . . . .  284 Psalm XI           10
    In a goodly pleasant ground? . . . . . . . . . . . . . . . .  288 Psalm XVI          17
    With blessings of the ground, . . . . . . . . . . . . . . .   333 Psalm XLI           6
    For since warre is the ground of vertue's love, . . . . . . . 346 Possibly       5    7
GROUNDED
    Well grounded, noble, due, spite, rage, disdaine, . . . . .   84 Arcadia III   60   10
    Yet thus still my hope is grounded, . . . . . . . . . . . . . 335 Psalm XLII         35
GROUNDS
    Cleofila. First shall fertill grounds not yeeld increase of
        a good seed: . . . . . . . . . . . . . . . . . . . . .   33 1st Eclogues  13    64
    From the grounds where Jordan slideth. . . . . . . . . . . .  335 Psalm XLII         27
GROVE
    In a grove most rich of shade, . . . . . . . . . . . . . . .  217 A&S 8th Song        1
GROW
    That I growe like a shade, . . . . . . . . . . . . . . . . .   19 1st Eclogues   7   163
    That I growe like the beaste, . . . . . . . . . . . . . . .    20 1st Eclogues   7  V958
    Ne let white haires, which on my face doo grow, . . . . . .   38 Arcadia II    15    5
    Let so our fruites grow up, that nature be maintainde: . . .  45 Arcadia II    26   13
    So to my minde, while passions daylie growe, . . . . . . . .  74 Arcadia III   41    3
    And in this growing barke growe verses myne. . . . . . . . .  77 Arcadia III   47   12
    Till wrong, contempt, deceit, did growe, steale, creepe, . .  84 Arcadia III   60    7
    Which on cold winter's face doth grow. . . . . . . . . . . .  85 Arcadia III   62    8
    Faire under these doth stately growe, . . . . . . . . . . .   87 Arcadia III   62   46
    Whose care is cause that they in number growe, . . . . . . .  92 3rd Eclogues  63   38
    Her strength from him, his praise from her do growe. . . . .  92 3rd Eclogues  63   52
    And stoppe mine eares, lest I growe mad with Musicke. . . .   112 4th Eclogues  71   60
    But if among yourselves some one tree growe, . . . . . . . .  125 4th Eclogues  75   10
    Grow rich in that which never taketh rust: . . . . . . . . .  161 Cert Sonnets  32    3
    Phrases and Problemes from my reach do grow, . . . . . . . .  166 Astrophil      3   10
    Effects of lively heat, must needs in nature grow. . . . . .  169 Astrophil      8   11
    Wealth breeding want, more blist, more wretched grow. . . .   177 Astrophil     24    4
    He knowes not) grow in only follie rich. . . . . . . . . . .  177 Astrophil     24   14
    Doth even grow rich, naming my stella's name. . . . . . . .   182 Astrophil     35   11
    My spring appeares, o see what here doth grow. . . . . . . .  200 Astrophil     69    8
    That any laud to me thereof should grow, . . . . . . . . . .  224 Astrophil     90   10
    From carelesnesse did in no maner grow, . . . . . . . . . .   227 Astrophil     93    7
    Making those Lillies and those Roses grow, . . . . . . . . .  231 Astrophil    100    2
    Make in my heavy mould new thoughts to grow: . . . . . . . .  236 Astrophil    106   11
    Lo you grow proud with this, for tyrans make folke bow: . .   214 A&S 5th Song       61
    But the while they live and grow . . . . . . . . . . . . . .  329 Psalm XXXVIII      55
    In God his strength shall grow, . . . . . . . . . . . . . .   333 Psalm XLI          15
    The shepheards will grow leane I trow, their sheep will ill
        be fed. . . . . . . . . . . . . . . . . . . . . . . . .  344 Possibly       1    40
    The plenteous sweets, (can sweets so sharply grow?). . . . .  243 Other Poems    4    52
    Proud grew the grasse that under hir did growe, . . . . . . . 244 Other Poems    4   108
    So grow thy wooll of note, . . . . . . . . . . . . . . . . .  258 Other Poems    5    69
GROWEST
    Yet growest more wretched then thy nature beares, . . . . .   228 Astrophil     94   13
GROWETH
    When rooted moisture failes, or groweth drie, . . . . . . .   128 4th Eclogues  75   113
    But lo, while I do speake, it groweth noone with me, . . . .  205 Astrophil     76    9
    A rightfull Prince by unright deeds a Tyran groweth. . . . .  214 A&S 5th Song       60
    With time still th' affection groweth. . . . . . . . . . . .  234 A&S 11th Song      19
GROWING
    Of growing trees, yee rurall Gods that wield . . . . . . . .  40 Arcadia II    18    2
    O breath more sweete, then is the growing beane, . . . . . .  76 Arcadia III   46    2
```

GROWING   (CONTINUED)   PAGE   TITLE   LINE
    And in this growing barke growe verses myne. . . . .   77 Arcadia III   47   12
    New perfumed with flowers fresh growing, ... 217 A&S 8th Song   4
    In them no cause is growing. . . . .   284 Psalm XI   12
    Lord from Thy strength is growing; . . . .   296 Psalm XXI   2
GROWN
    The night growne old, her blacke head waxen gray, ...   103 3rd Eclogues 66   160
    Am growne a shrich-owle to my selfe each morning. . . . . .   111 4th Eclogues 71   18
    Hate fully growne, Absence new sprongen out. . . . .   115 4th Eclogues 72   58
    Are we their servants growne? no doubt a noble staye: . . .   120 4th Eclogues 73   115
    The lothsome buds growne on sorrowe's tree. . . . .   153 Cert Sonnets 24   5
    Because that Mars, growne slacker in her love, ...   173 Astrophil   17   2
    A strife is growne betweene Vertue and Love, ...   190 Astrophil   52   1
    Growne now his slaves, he forst them out to find . . . . .   193 Astrophil   57   3
    In this old world, growne now so too too wise: . . . . . .   198 Astrophil   65   6
    His heels grow'n proud did seme at heav'n to shake. . . . .   248 Other Poems   4   261
GROWS
    With such intemperance, that each way grows. . . . .   27 1st Eclogues 10   38
    With sonne's approche your pasture fertill growes, ...   43 Arcadia II   23   2
    My sonne is gon, your pasture barrein growes, ...   43 Arcadia II   24   2
    Pas. Tell this (and Phoebus be) what monster growes. . . . .   56 2nd Eclogues 29   144
    What be the fruites of speaking arte? what growes by the
        words? Words. . . . .   64 2nd Eclogues 31   30
    No, no, our mischiefe growes in this vile fortune, ...   109 Arcadia IV   70   31
    So mazde a masse, or if in me it growes, ...   149 Cert Sonnets 22   9
    And everie floure, not sweet perhaps, which growes . . . .   172 Astrophil   15   3
    And Humblenesse growes one with Majestie. . . . .   188 Astrophil   48   4
GROWTH
    O let me prop my mind, yet in his growth . . . .   174 Astrophil   19   12
GRUDGE
    My Muse may well grudge at my heav'nly joy, ...   201 Astrophil   70   1
    Shew that we do not grudge at all when others do rejoyce. . . 343 Possibly   1   2
    Dick. Ah Will, though I grudge not, I count it feeble glee . 343 Possibly   1   3
GRUDGING
    As grudging me my sorrowe's eloquence? . . . .   233 Astrophil   104   4
GRUMBLING
    Grumbling at her when she his kindnes sought, ...   95 3rd Eclogues 64   32
GUARD
    Her heav'nly-dewed tongue to garde. . . . .   87 Arcadia III 62   44
    And he my right hand doth guard, ...   288 Psalm XVI   26
    Self-gard with mildnes, Sport with Majesty: . . . .   247 Other Poems   4   214
    The other end Geron with Uran garde. . . . .   250 Other Poems   4   319
    For with pretence from Strephon hir to garde, ...   252 Other Poems   4   385
GUARDED
    Shine eyes on me, that both our lives be guarded; . . . . .   17 1st Eclogues 7   92
    Thus is her life still guarded, ...   152 Cert Sonnets 23   13
    But if thou wouldst garded be, ...   226 A&S 10th Song   22
    Who freed me from my foes, from rebells guarded me, ...   293 Psalm XVIII   86
    Most circumspectly guarded, ...   295 Psalm XIX   46
GUARDERS
    He chose themselves his guarders for to bene, ...   102 3rd Eclogues 66   129
GUARDETH
    See the hand which waking gardeth, ...   202 A&S 2nd Song   13
GUARDIAN
    Whereas if I a gratefull gardien have, ...   135 Cert Sonnets 1   13
GUERDON
    Ev'en so be their guerdon shar'd. . . . .   309 Psalm XXVIII   20
    For guerdon of their shame, ...   332 Psalm XL   57
GUESS
    In fine he made her gesse, there was some sweet. . . . . .   95 3rd Eclogues 64   35
    Passing all ghesse, whence into me should fly. . . . . . .   149 Cert Sonnets 22   8
    Shall gesse, and faile, what doth displease, ...   153 Cert Sonnets 24   8
    With idle paines, and missing ayme, do guesse. . . . . . .   176 Astrophil   23   4
    I much do guesse, yet find no truth save this, ...   187 Astrophil   44   9
    Guesse we the cause: "What, is it thus?" Fie no: . . . . .   204 Astrophil   74   12
GUESSED
    He gest the worst (you wot what is the worst). . . . . . .   94 3rd Eclogues 64   11
GUEST
    Nor be abasht, since such a guest you finde, ...   13 Arcadia I   4   3
    That sweetens all the place; she is the guest. . . . . . .   59 2nd Eclogues 30   99
    Oh! I do know what guest I have mett; it is Echo. 'T is
        Echo . . . .   63 2nd Eclogues 31   3
    A baite most fit, for hungrie minded guest. . . . .   75 Arcadia III 44   10
    Of fairer guest, which dwells within, ...   90 Arcadia III 62   140
    She sigh'd and sayd, the bad guest sought her love. . . . .   95 3rd Eclogues 64   48
    How they might get that guest, from them to wend, ...   95 3rd Eclogues 64   53
    Thou paine the onely guest of loath'd constraint, ...   141 Cert Sonnets 10   1
    The windowes now through which this heav'nly guest . . . .   169 Astrophil   9   9
    While that blacke hue from me the bad guest hid: . . . . .   175 Astrophil   20   11
    But him her host that unkind guest had slaine. . . . . . .   184 Astrophil   38   14
    Most rude dispaire my daily unbidden guest, ...   236 Astrophil   108   7
    But glad Desire, his late embosom'd guest, ...   247 Other Poems   4   201
GUESTS
    When I such guests did see come out of such a house, ... 118 4th Eclogues 73   75
GUIDE
    Whiche beares the bytt a weaker force doth guide, ...   20 1st Eclogues 7 V959
    My sheepe are thoughts, which I both guide and serve: . . .   39 Arcadia II   17   1
    While brickle houreglas runnes, guide thou our panting race: 45 Arcadia II   26   10
    Shall we now finde a guide of such affection, ...   129 4th Eclogues 76   22
    O take fast hold, let that light be thy guide, ...   162 Cert Sonnets 32   9

GUIDE (CONTINUED)   PAGE   TITLE   LINE

Nor in hid wayes to guide Philosophie: . . . .   179 Astrophil   28   10
Guide me, O in thy justice be my guide:. . . . .   275 Psalm V   22
But still be Thou to just men justest guide. . . . .   277 Psalm VII   27
In race of life their Feet to guide. . . . .   284 Psalm XI   23
And pray that still Thou guide my way. . . . .   289 Psalm XVII   15
Guide me as Thy Truth guides;. . . . .   303 Psalm XXV   13
Direct me how to go, and guide me right, ...   312 Psalm XXXI   9
Guide Thee by my eyes' guiding. . . . .   315 Psalm XXXII   30
Guide Thee by him, lay all thy trusting. . . . .   324 Psalm XXXVII   11
Let them guide me right. . . . .   336 Psalm XLIII   14
When strong Desire, which vertue's love doth guide, ... 345 Possibly   4   7
GUIDED
There came a chariot faire by doves and sparrowes guided:. .   118 4th Eclogues 73   59
Guided so well, that I obtain'd the prize, ...   185 Astrophil   41   2
That no pace else their guided steps can find, ...   194 Astrophil   58   3
For rage now rules the reynes, which guided were by
   Pleasure . . . .   213 A&S 5th Song   15
My stepps shall guided be, ...   306 Psalm XXVI   35
GUIDES
But if he know not his harms what guides hath he whil'st he
   be blind? Blind. . . . .   63 2nd Eclogues 31   20
What blinde guides can he have that leanes to a fancy? A
   fancy. . . . .   63 2nd Eclogues 31   21
My hart in him, his thoughtes and senses guides: . . . . . .   76 Arcadia III 45   6
Of straying wayes, when valiant errour guides: . . . .   190 Astrophil   51   11
When my good Angell guides me to the place, ...   194 Astrophil   60   1
Which, coupling Doves, guides Venus' chariot right.. . . . .   206 Astrophil   79   4
He guides my feet. . . . .   301 Psalm XXIII   6
Guide me as Thy Truth guides;. . . . .   303 Psalm XXV   13
GUIDEST
Fould with this sight, while thou thy chariot guidest. . . .   126 4th Eclogues 75   57
GUIDING
Right so my minde, caught by his guiding eye . . . .   144 Cert Sonnets 15   5
Like to the Mowlle with want of guiding sight, ...   149 Cert Sonnets 21   7
Who is This Glorious King? The lord of armyes guiding, . . .   302 Psalm XXIV   23
Guide Thee by my eyes' guiding. . . . .   315 Psalm XXXII   30
GUILE
Or that by words enwrapt in guile. . . . .   320 Psalm XXXIV   51
GUILEFUL
(Which oft to hope laies out a guilefull baite, ...   82 Arcadia III 56   2
O teares of guilefull breast, ...   158 Cert Sonnets 28   14
GUILEFULLY
If Love tooke thee by force, or caught thee guilefully.. . .   48 2nd Eclogues 28   21
GUILTINESS
Give them their due unto their guiltiness, ...   275 Psalm V   29
GUILTLESS
Then gan in guiltlesse earth full many a wound, ...   102 3rd Eclogues 66 115
A plaint of guiltlesse hurt doth pierce the skie. . . . . .   103 3rd Eclogues 66 152
That you, guiltlesse thereof, your Nectar mist:. . . . . . .   235 Astrophil   105   10
And which is worse, makes me most guiltlesse torments have,.   214 A&S 5th Song   59
Who sells not guiltlesse cause, for filthy love of gain: . .   287 Psalm XV   12
And then by Thee was guiltless found . . . .   289 Psalm XVII   11
GUILTY
With father's death, and mother's guiltie shame, ...   21 1st Eclogues 8   19
Showes, guilty harte doth deeme his state opprobrious. . . .   48 2nd Eclogues 28   18
Selfe-guiltie folke must prove to feele compassion.. . . . .   60 2nd Eclogues 30 130
Who full of guiltie spite, ...   82 Arcadia III 55   9
They fled with blush, which guiltie seem'd of love.. . . . .   199 Astrophil   66   14
His guiltie heart with this fond thought hath fed, ...   286 Psalm XIV   2
Against their murdering guilty faces.. . . . .   298 Psalm XXI   48
What guilty wickedness doth say, ...   323 Psalm XXXVI   2
While guilty thoughts accus'd his Reason weake). . . . . . .   255 Other Poems   4 532
GUISE
Because I oft in darke abstracted guise, ...   178 Astrophil   27   1
Beauty is sicke, but sicke in so faire guise, ...   231 Astrophil   101   5
And each way luckles, yet in humble guise. . . . .   249 Other Poems   4 277
GULES
Where roses gueuls are borne in silver field.. . . . .   171 Astrophil   13   11
GULF
From out that noysome gulfe, which gaping lies . . . .   205 Astrophil   78   3
GULFS
The gulfs of waters then were through their Chanels seen,. .   291 Psalm XVIII   31
GUTS
My eye, my Gutts, yea my soul grief doth wast, ...   312 Psalm XXXI   27
GYRES
Such coltish gyres, that to my birth I owe . . . .   175 Astrophil   21   6
HABILITY
New friend of mine; I yeeld to thy habilitie:. . . . .   19 1st Eclogues 7 174
HABITATION
Dorus. If Sunnie beames shame heav'nly habitation; . . . . .   48 2nd Eclogues 28   22
First let Cimmerian darknes be my onel'habitaco'n: . . . . .   124 4th Eclogues 74   59
HACKNEY
Their judgements hackney on, the fault on sicknesse lay, . .   232 Astrophil   102   10
HAD
Why thee a living man they had made dead.. . . . .   11 Arcadia I   1   7
Frcm former feare, they had of your good mindes, ...   26 1st Eclogues 10   5
Her praise, whence to the world all praise had his only
   beginning: . . . .   33 1st Eclogues 13   69
Whose force had such force so to transforme, nay to reforme
   me, ...   37 1st Eclogues 13 166

```
HAD                          (CONTINUED)                    PAGE     TITLE           LINE
    P. No Reason yet had ever skill to show it.. . . . . . . . .  47  2nd Eclogues 27   40
    Dicus. Thy words well voic'd, well gra'ste had almost heaved
       me. . . . . . . . . . . . . . . . . . . . . . . . . . . .  48  2nd Eclogues 28   31
    Dorus. If I had thought to heare blasphemous wordes, . . . .  50  2nd Eclogues 28   79
    But if I had bene there, th'adst met another mate. . . . . .  52  2nd Eclogues 29   22
    Nico. O if I had a ladder for the skies, . . . . . . . . . .  55  2nd Eclogues 29  117
    Pas. O if I had Apollo's golden carre, . . . . . . . . . . .  56  2nd Eclogues 29  120
    We mone that lost, which had we did bemone.. . . . . . . . .  59  2nd Eclogues 30   82
    And what manner a mind which had to that humor a vaine?
       Vaine. . . . . . . . . . . . . . . . . . . . . . . . . .  63  2nd Eclogues 31    9
    Yet tell what light thinge I had in me to draw me to die?
       Eye. . . . . . . . . . . . . . . . . . . . . . . . . . .  64  2nd Eclogues 31   25
    This cave is darke, but it had never light.. . . . . . . . .  75  Arcadia III  43    1
    I darkned am, who once had clearest sight. . . . . . . . . .  75  Arcadia III  43    4
    Had reason's weight for passion's ease rejected. . . . . . .  83  Arcadia III  57    8
    That married had a trick and bonny lasse . . . . . . . . . .  94  3rd Eclogues 64    3
    And that it had enflam'd a new desire, . . . . . . . . . . .  95  3rd Eclogues 64   38
    Glad was the man when he had heard her out,. . . . . . . . .  96  3rd Eclogues 64   63
    She written had (but in a hand disguisde). . . . . . . . . .  96  3rd Eclogues 64   80
    She told him that the courtier had it sent:. . . . . . . . .  96  3rd Eclogues 64   86
    It title had, unto my only love, . . . . . . . . . . . . . .  96  3rd Eclogues 64   89
    The pistle selfe, such kinde of wordes it had, . . . . . . .  96  3rd Eclogues 64   91
    Now that he had her words so truely tried: . . . . . . . . .  97  3rd Eclogues 64  112
    The welkin had full niggardly enclosed . . . . . . . . . . .  98  3rd Eclogues 66    8
    The songe I sange old Languet had me taught, . . . . . . . .  99  3rd Eclogues 66   22
    The beastes had sure some beastly pollicie:. . . . . . . . . 100  3rd Eclogues 66   50
    Like Senators a harmeles empire had. . . . . . . . . . . . . 100  3rd Eclogues 66   56
    But when his seate so rooted he had found, . . . . . . . . . 102  3rd Eclogues 66  113
    The humming Waspe, if it had not a stinge, . . . . . . . . . 104  3rd Eclogues 67   17
    O that we had, to make our woes more publique, . . . . . . . 109  Arcadia IV   70   25
    Thus, thus alas, I had my losse in chase.. . . . . . . . . . 115  4th Eclogues 72   70
    Klaius. Thus, thus alas, I had my losse in chase, . . . . . . 115  4th Eclogues 72   71
    The other had with arte (more then our women knowe,. . . . . 118  4th Eclogues 73   71
    A wanton woman's face, and with curld knots had twinde . . . 118  4th Eclogues 73   73
    Although their fame (me seemd) from truth had greatly jard.. 119  4th Eclogues 73   80
    She had chiefe Goddesses in beautie overcome.. . . . . . . . 120  4th Eclogues 73  146
    (Teares and teares of a man) had no returne to remorse;. . . 122  4th Eclogues 74   16
    Love never had me opprest, but that I saw to be lov'd. . . . 123  4th Eclogues 74   44
    But foole, foole that I am, tho I had but a hair of her head
       found,. . . . . . . . . . . . . . . . . . . . . . . . . . 123  4th Eclogues 74   53
    What sweete joyes I had once, and what a place I did hold? . 124  4th Eclogues 74   72
    Say, that I well shuld finde in what a care I was had? . . . 124  4th Eclogues 74   80
    Unto no body my woman saith she had rather a wife be,. . . . 143  Cert Sonnets 13    1
    That onely I the onely Mistresse had:. . . . . . . . . . . . 147  Cert Sonnets 17   43
    A bird which gets more life then ship had lost.. . . . . . . 151  Cert Sonnets 22   54
    As her words had it bent?. . . . . . . . . . . . . . . . . . 158  Cert Sonnets 28   24
    Till by degrees it had full conquest got:. . . . . . . . . . 165  Astrophil          2    4
    Each had his creast, Mars caried Venus' glove, . . . . . . . 171  Astrophil        13    7
    That I had bene more foolish or more wise. . . . . . . . . . 181  Astrophil        33   14
    But him her host that unkind guest had slaine. . . . . . . . 184  Astrophil        38   14
    And now my pen these lines had dashed quite, . . . . . . . . 190  Astrophil        50   12
    In Martiall sports I had my cunning tride, . . . . . . . . . 191  Astrophil        53    1
    I had bene vext, if vext I had not beene.. . . . . . . . . . 223  Astrophil        87   14
    If Orpheus' voyce had force to breathe such musicke's love . 208  A&S 3rd Song       1
    I said, my soule was thine (o that I then had lyed). . . . . 212  A&S 5th Song       9
    Whether absence have had force . . . . . . . . . . . . . . . 225  A&S 10th Song      4
    Him great harmes had taught much care, . . . . . . . . . . . 218  A&S 8th Song       9
    Wept they had, alas the while, . . . . . . . . . . . . . . . 218  A&S 8th Song      13
    Till their harts had ended talking.. . . . . . . . . . . . . 218  A&S 8th Song      24
    With what she had done and spoken, . . . . . . . . . . . . . 221  A&S 8th Song     103
    Down in the pitt, which they themselves had wrought: . . . . 280  Psalm IX          47
    For they had caught me up, when I was weake in Woe;. . . . . 291  Psalm XVIII       38
    He had as him behoved. . . . . . . . . . . . . . . . . . . . 297  Psalm XXI          8
    What had I been, except I had. . . . . . . . . . . . . . . . 308  Psalm XXVII       61
    And both had skill in verse their voice to move. . . . . . . 243  Other Poems    4  40
    They found, they felt, they had no lease of blisse.. . . . . 244  Other Poems    4  80
    For ere that either had his purpose done,. . . . . . . . . . 244  Other Poems    4  81
    Cupid the wagg, that lately conquer'd had. . . . . . . . . . 245  Other Poems    4 129
    Made them his owne before they had it wist.. . . . . . . . . 246  Other Poems    4 159
    But if they had, could shephookes this resist? . . . . . . . 246  Other Poems    4 160
    If him new-learned manners had not stai'd. . . . . . . . . . 246  Other Poems    4 166
    But light-legd Pas had gott the middle space.. . . . . . . . 248  Other Poems    4 253
    To fasten knotts, which fancy first had bound. . . . . . . . 253  Other Poems    4 424
    Did not conceive what fire he had within.. . . . . . . . . . 253  Other Poems    4 428
    While I was I, and so had cause to care; . . . . . . . . . . 254  Other Poems    4 484
    Till my eies had their curse from blessed eine.. . . . . . . 254  Other Poems    4 496
HADST
    But ah my Muse I would thou hadst facilitie, . . . . . . . .  19  1st Eclogues  7  176
    But if I had bene there, th'adst met another mate. . . . . .  52  2nd Eclogues 29   22
    Thad'st killed with a stroke,. . . . . . . . . . . . . . . . 259  Other Poems    5 100
HAIL
    Then hayle, then firie coales, then thundred heavnly sire, . 291  Psalm XVIII       27
HAILSTONES
    Hailstones of teares, of sighes a monstrous blast,. . . . . 114  4th Eclogues 72   33
    Then spake he his lowd voyce, then hailestones coales and
       fire.. . . . . . . . . . . . . . . . . . . . . . . . . . 291  Psalm XVIII       28
HAIR
    Her haire pure Crapal-stone; her mouth O heavenly wyde;. . .  12  Arcadia I      3  11
    Can I be poore, that her golde haire procure my selfe? . . .  16  1st Eclogues  7  58
```

HAIR	(CONTINUED)	PAGE	TITLE		LINE
With sleeves turnde up, loose haire, and brestes enlarged, .		16	1st Eclogues	7	74
Oh when will men leave off to judge by haire,.		25	1st Eclogues	9	93
A ruddie haire his cote, with fine long specled face:. . . .		53	2nd Eclogues	29	42
Shall I that saw Eronae's shining haire.		58	2nd Eclogues	30	44
Her loose haire be the shott, the brestes the pykes be,. . .		67	2nd Eclogues	33	7
Gay haire more gaie then straw when harvest lyes,.		76	Arcadia III	46	7
Her haire fine threeds of finest gould		85	Arcadia III	62	3
Of willing teares, torne heare, and cries of sorrow.		109	Arcadia IV	70	16
Her haire, which by the helpe of painter's cunning, shinde..		118	4th Eclogues	73	74
But foole, foole that I am, tho I had but a hair of her head					
found,.		123	4th Eclogues	74	53
Ev'n as I am, so I should unto that haire be a thrall. . . .		123	4th Eclogues	74	54
Thy faire haire my heart enchained,.		156	Cert Sonnets	27	2
Thy haire not worth a haire esteemed:.		156	Cert Sonnets	27	10
For thy knitting haire be sorie:		156	Cert Sonnets	27	18
Ty me haire your captive wholly, ...		157	Cert Sonnets	27	34
What changes here, o haire,.		157	Cert Sonnets	28	1
Once to approch this hayer.		158	Cert Sonnets	28	8
Ah haire, how many dayes,.		158	Cert Sonnets	28	9
Tell me o haire of gold, ...		158	Cert Sonnets	28	17
Ah haire are you not griev'd,.		158	Cert Sonnets	28	29
Stella's faire haire, her face he makes his shield,.		171	Astrophil	13	10
Nor nourish speciall lockes of vowed haire,.		191	Astrophil	54	3
Ravisht, staid not, till in her golden haire		232	Astrophil	103	7
Who hath the haire which, loosest, fastest tieth,.		197	A&S 1st Song		25
Brave crest to him hir scorn-gold haire did yeeld,.		246	Other Poems	4	149
Her chery lipps, milke hands, and golden haire		254	Other Poems	4	461
Their snowy haire teare off in melting paine.		254	Other Poems	4	478
HAIRS					
Ne let white haires, which on my face doo grow,.		38	Arcadia II	15	5
More than my head hath haires;		332	Psalm XL		47
He thought gray haires afforded subtletie.		248	Other Poems	4	256
HALF					
Thus halfe a man, with man he easly haunts,.		21	1st Eclogues	8	31
Thus halfe a beast, ech beastly vice he plants,.		21	1st Eclogues	8	33
Begin (and halfe the worke is done) to prove		23	1st Eclogues	9	50
That if he absent were but halfe a daye, ...		94	3rd Eclogues	64	10
Which who so wants, halfe of himselfe doth misse.		103	3rd Eclogues	67	9
Wherewith my father once made it halfe tame;		180	Astrophil	30	10
Half so deere as you to me,.		220	A&S 8th Song		82
HALFWAY					
His fancies still did hir in half-way meet,.		251	Other Poems	4	371
HALL					
Beauty brings to the hall, ...		216	A&S 6th Song		39
Doth hold his hall.		301	Psalm XXIII		27
HALTING					
Since outward pleasures be but halting helpes to decayd					
soules)		33	1st Eclogues	13	52
But words came halting forth, wanting Invention's stay,. . .		165	Astrophil	1	9
Sure I do but halting go,.		329	Psalm XXXVIII		49
HAND					
Who hath his hopes laid up in woman's hand..		24	1st Eclogues	9	55
Still doo I crosse this wretch, what so he taketh in hand"..		29	1st Eclogues	11	6
A woman's hand with constant marble stone.		40	Arcadia II	19	6
Above line repeated at following location.		41	Arcadia II	19	12
Didst snatch from Cosma's hand her greene ywroughten glove..		52	2nd Eclogues	29	10
To put it with my hand in Cosma's brest.		54	2nd Eclogues	29	86
O hand, which toucht her hand when we did part;.		60	2nd Eclogues	30	119
O lippes, that kist that hand with my teares sprent;		60	2nd Eclogues	30	120
Then let me eke forget one hand from other:.		61	2nd Eclogues	30	161
Sweete glove, the sweete despoyles of sweetest hand, ...		70	Arcadia III	35	9
Fayre hand, the fayrest pledge of fayrer harte,.		70	Arcadia III	35	10
With her faire hande, your tender barkes to cleave,.		78	Arcadia III	49	6
Yet yeeld yur graunt, a baser hand may leave.		78	Arcadia III	49	9
Her hand benumde with fortune's daylie blows,.		81	Arcadia III	54	3
Now course doth leade me to her hand,.		90	Arcadia III	62	121
As for the fingers of the hand,.		90	Arcadia III	62	130
She written had (but in a hand disguisde).		96	3rd Eclogues	64	80
Never hard hand, nor ever raines too light..		98	3rd Eclogues	65	9
The instrument of instruments, the hand.		101	3rd Eclogues	66	98
Or with a fair hand's nailes (o hand which nailes me to this					
death).		123	4th Eclogues	74	55
Out of our sight in turne of hand is vanished.		128	4th Eclogues	75	127
But Thereus' love, on her by strong hand wrokne,.		137	Cert Sonnets	4	14
My hand doth not beare witnesse with my hart,.		146	Cert Sonnets	17	26
Behold Love's mightie hand		158	Cert Sonnets	28	38
Having this day my horse, my hand, my launce		185	Astrophil	41	1
And now hath made me to his hand so right, ...		189	Astrophil	49	13
One hand forgott to rule, th'other to fight.		191	Astrophil	53	11
I give you here my hand for truth of this, ...		201	Astrophil	70	13
That hand, which without touch holds more then Atlas might;.		205	Astrophil	77	5
As though that faire soft hand did you great wrong... . . .		208	Astrophil	83	4
O ease your hand, treate not so hard your slave:		212	Astrophil	86	9
And love doth hold my hand, and makes me write..		224	Astrophil	90	14
With care's hard hand) to turne and tosse in thee,.		230	Astrophil	98	8
Bare me in hand, that in this Orphane place, ...		235	Astrophil	106	3
Who hath the hand which without stroke subdueth, ...		197	A&S 1st Song		21
See the hand which waking gardeth, ...		202	A&S 2nd Song		13
And let not man have upper hand of Thee, ...		281	Psalm IX		62

202

```
HAND                    (CONTINUED)                      PAGE    TITLE          LINE
    Lift up Thy heavnly hand . . . . . . . . . . . . . .  282  Psalm X           51
    And he my right hand doth guard, . . . . . . . . . .  288  Psalm XVI         26
    On thy blessed making hand . . . . . . . . . . . . .  289  Psalm XVI         43
    And save them from rebellious hand.. . . . . . . . .  290  Psalm XVII        24
    According as he saw the pureness of my hand. . . . . .  292  Psalm XVIII      49
    Thou gavest me saving shield, Thy right hand was my stay;. .  292  Psalm XVIII  64
    Yea heares with powers and helps of helpfull hand. . . . .  296  Psalm XX     25
    Thy hand thy foes shall overtake,. . . . . . . . . . .  297  Psalm XXI        29
    For so Thy loving hand . . . . . . . . . . . . . . . .  305  Psalm XXVI       10
    That hand whose strength should help of bribes is full.. . .  306  Psalm XXVI  33
    Within the hand of hatefull enmitie, . . . . . . . . .  312  Psalm XXXI       23
    On wretched mee thy heavy hand, . . . . . . . . . . .  315  Psalm XXXII       11
    The might of people's hand.. . . . . . . . . . . . . .  317  Psalm XXXIII     36
    In sprite that I shall have Thy helping hand.. . . . . .  321  Psalm XXXV       6
    He is upheld by heavnly hand.. . . . . . . . . . . . .  326  Psalm XXXVII     60
    But in their hand God will not leave him,. . . . . . .  327  Psalm XXXVII     83
    Thus bound I said, lo, lord I am at hand,. . . . . . .  331  Psalm XL         31
    The hand was one, one was the sword. . . . . . . . . .  241  Other Poems   3   5
    And still, beleve me, Strephon was at hand.. . . . . .  247  Other Poems   4  216
    Her happy-making hand, of whome one looke. . . . . . .  248  Other Poems   4  247
    Thus Pas did kisse hir hand with little grace, . . . .  249  Other Poems   4  276
    But pulld by Mira's hande, . . . . . . . . . . . . . .  257  Other Poems   5   47
    With hand and mouth, with lapp and brest keepe warme,. . . .  258  Other Poems   5   84
HANDFULS
    The heav'ns doo not good haps in handfuls bring, . . . . .  105  3rd Eclogues 67  61
HANDLE
    Who once a white long beard, well handle does, . . . . . .   25  1st Eclogues  9  90
    The handle of this plesant worke,. . . . . . . . . . .   87  Arcadia III  62  47
    Your Client poore my selfe, shall Stella handle so?. . . . .  213  A&S 5th Song  31
    Whose hands do handle nought,. . . . . . . . . . . . .  306  Psalm XXVI       31
HAND-REACHED
    And so when Pas hand-reached him to take,. . . . . . . . .  248  Other Poems   4  257
HAND'S
    Or with a fair hand's nailes (o hand which nailes me to this
        death). . . . . . . . . . . . . . . . . . . . . .  123  4th Eclogues 74  55
HANDS
    Her skin like burnisht gold, her hands like silver ure
        untryde. . . . . . . . . . . . . . . . . . . . . .   12  Arcadia I     3  12
    Largesse his hands could never skill of sparefulnesse. . . .   48  2nd Eclogues 28  45
    I said, my hands well paide her for mine eyes, . . . . . .   55  2nd Eclogues 29  115
    Since in my hands selfe goodly sight she tooke.. . . . . .   55  2nd Eclogues 29  116
    Torne with her hands, and those same hands of snow . . . .   58  2nd Eclogues 30  45
    Skowts each motion is, the hands the horsmen,. . . . . .   67  2nd Eclogues 33   8
    For faithfull hart, cleane hands, and mouth as true: . . . .   99  3rd Eclogues 66  25
    You have the same in my hands, seeing. . . . . . . . . .  159  Cert Sonnets 29   8
    As what their hands do hold, their heads do know,. . . . .  177  Astrophil    24   6
    Looke at my hands for no such quintessence;. . . . . . .  179  Astrophil    28  11
    Milke hands, rose cheeks, or lips more sweet, more red,. . .  225  Astrophil    91   7
    Leave to Mars the force of hands,. . . . . . . . . . . .  211  A&S 4th Song     45
    There his hands in their speech, faine . . . . . . . . .  219  A&S 8th Song     65
    But her hands his hands repelling, . . . . . . . . . . .  219  A&S 8th Song     67
    If ought my hands of wyckednes do bear:. . . . . . . . .  277  Psalm VII         9
    To rule the Works of Thyne own hands . . . . . . . . . .  279  Psalm VIII       22
    For of them in Thy hands . . . . . . . . . . . . . . .  283  Psalm X          59
    My justice, my just hands thus did the lord reward,. . . . .  292  Psalm XVIII   43
    My humble hands, my fainting feet they peirced;. . . . . .  299  Psalm XXII       41
    He that hath hurtless hands, whose inward heart is framed. .  302  Psalm XXIV        7
    My hands shall washed be,. . . . . . . . . . . . . . . .  305  Psalm XXVI       20
    And with those hands about Thy Altar waite,. . . . . . .  305  Psalm XXVI       21
    Whose hands do handle nought,. . . . . . . . . . . . . .  306  Psalm XXVI       31
    While I that way hold my hands . . . . . . . . . . . . .  309  Psalm XXVIII      7
    Fare they as their hands have far'd, . . . . . . . . . .  309  Psalm XXVIII     19
    Into Thy hands I do commend my sprite, . . . . . . . . .  312  Psalm XXXI       13
    Their help from mighty hands.. . . . . . . . . . . . . .  317  Psalm XXXIII     60
    Let not ev'ill hands discomfit me; . . . . . . . . . . .  324  Psalm XXXVI      32
    Still Thy hands upon me be.. . . . . . . . . . . . . . .  327  Psalm XXXVIII     6
    How tenderly hir tender hands betweene . . . . . . . . .  244  Other Poems   4  93
    Hir hands which pierc'd the soule's seav'n-double shield,. .  246  Other Poems   4  147
    They false and fearfull do their hands undoe,. . . . . .  248  Other Poems   4  235
    To runne, brake from his hands, and let him goe. . . . .  250  Other Poems   4  336
    Did beate their hands, which durst so neere to presse. . . .  252  Other Poems   4  406
    Her chery lipps, milke hands, and golden haire . . . . .  254  Other Poems   4  461
    Joyne hearts and hands, so let it be,. . . . . . . . . .  260  Other Poems   6   5
    Above line repeated at following locations . . . . . . .  260  Other Poems   6  11
       . . . . . . . . . . . . . . . . . . . . . . . . . .  260  Other Poems   6  17
       . . . . . . . . . . . . . . . . . . . . . . . . . .  260  Other Poems   6  23
       . . . . . . . . . . . . . . . . . . . . . . . . . .  261  Other Poems   6  29
       . . . . . . . . . . . . . . . . . . . . . . . . . .  261  Other Poems   6  35
       . . . . . . . . . . . . . . . . . . . . . . . . . .  261  Other Poems   6  41
       . . . . . . . . . . . . . . . . . . . . . . . . . .  261  Other Poems   6  47
       . . . . . . . . . . . . . . . . . . . . . . . . . .  261  Other Poems   6  53
    Now joyned be our hands, . . . . . . . . . . . . . . . .  261  Other Poems   6  55
HANDWORKING
    Shewes his handworking wonders.. . . . . . . . . . . . .  293  Psalm XIX         4
HANDY
    For with thy handy stroakes I wast.. . . . . . . . . . .  330  Psalm XXXIX      32
HANGMAN
    In this our world a hang-man for to be,. . . . . . . . .   22  1st Eclogues  8  47
```

```
                                                           PAGE    TITLE         LINE
HANNIBAL
    Thinke Hanniball did laugh when Carthage lost. . . . . . .  147  Cert Sonnets 17   45
HAP
    The starres thy state, fortune may change thy happe. . . . .   23  1st Eclogues  9   25
    Or mine eyes' language she doo hap to judge of,. . . . . . .   30  1st Eclogues 12    2
    Above line repeated at following location. . . . . . . . . .   31  1st Eclogues 12   26
    And whose good happ, doth leave him unprovided,. . . . . . .   62  2nd Eclogues 30  177
    Each moment lost, part of my hap destroyes:. . . . . . . . .   80  Arcadia III  53   11
    Till by such hap, as I must ever rewe, . . . . . . . . . . .  115  4th Eclogues 72   74
    Till these straunge altrings you did hap to trie,. . . . . .  125  4th Eclogues 75   26
    Of mine owne wordes, my owne good hap betray,. . . . . . . .  145  Cert Sonnets 16   10
    So to raise my hap more hie;                                   211  A&S  4th Song      21
    Least by my tongue I hap to stray; . . . . . . . . . . . . .  329  Psalm XXXIX        2
HAPLESS
    I tolde you Klaius was the haples wight. . . . . . . . . . .  251  Other Poems   4  365
HAPPENED
    Cleofila. Worthy shepeheard, by my song to my selfe all
        favor is happned,. . . . . . . . . . . . . . . . . . . .   31  1st Eclogues 13    8
HAPPY
    Happie be they which well beleeve, and never seeke the rest.   12  Arcadia I     3   14
    O happie Gods, which by inward assumption. . . . . . . . . .   15  1st Eclogues  7   40
    But o happy be you, which safe from fyry reflection. . . . .   31  1st Eclogues 13   11
    Happy be you that may to the saint, your onely Idea, . . . .   32  1st Eclogues 13   15
    Happy be those mishapps which, justly proportion holding,. .   32  1st Eclogues 13   17
    Happy shepheard, with thanks to the Gods, still thinke to be
        thankfull,. . . . . . . . . . . . . . . . . . . . . . .   32  1st Eclogues 13   33
    Farre more happy be you, whose greatnes gets a free accesse,   33  1st Eclogues 13   54
    With so sweete plagues my happie harmes infected be: . . . .   51  2nd Eclogues 28  123
    As happie shewes of corne when harvest sendes; . . . . . . .   71  Arcadia III  37   10
    Happy man, happy wife. . . . . . . . . . . . . . . . . . . .   94  3rd Eclogues 63   95
    Klaius. Long since the happie dwellers of these vallies, . .  112  4th Eclogues 71   31
    O happie Dove if she no bondage tried: . . . . . . . . . . .  144  Cert Sonnets 15   13
    More happie I, might I in bondage bide.. . . . . . . . . . .  144  Cert Sonnets 15   14
    With fruits of happie sight, . . . . . . . . . . . . . . . .  151  Cert Sonnets 23    2
    Above line repeated at following location. . . . . . . . . .  152  Cert Sonnets 23   34
    O happie Tems, that didst my Stella beare, . . . . . . . . .  232  Astrophil   103    1
    But if I by a happy window passe,. . . . . . . . . . . . . .  233  Astrophil   104    9
    But so of happy other side . . . . . . . . . . . . . . . . .  284  Psalm XI          21
    The happy wretch she putt into hir breast, . . . . . . . . .  244  Other Poems   4   98
    (O happy Dove that art compar'd to hir!) . . . . . . . . . .  251  Other Poems   4  354
    As heart-bound slaves: and happy then embrace. . . . . . . .  252  Other Poems   4  391
    Happy, o happy! if they so might bide, . . . . . . . . . . .  252  Other Poems   4  401
    Their sugred selves to kisse thy happy hedd: . . . . . . . .  258  Other Poems   5   58
    A happy blessed Trinitie;. . . . . . . . . . . . . . . . . .  260  Other Poems   6   20
HAPPY-MAKING
    Her happy-making hand, of whome one looke. . . . . . . . . .  248  Other Poems   4  247
HAPS
    Gives happs or mishapps, ev'n as he ordreth his hearte.. . .   29  1st Eclogues 11    8
    But yet, alas! O but yet alas! our happs be but hard happs,.   32  1st Eclogues 13   37
    Where all good haps a perfect state maintaine? . . . . . . .   58  2nd Eclogues 30   40
    Plangus. Curst be good haps, and curst be they that build. .   58  2nd Eclogues 30   41
    Their hopes on haps, and do not make despaire. . . . . . . .   58  2nd Eclogues 30   42
    The heav'ns doo not good haps in handfuls bring, . . . . . .  105  3rd Eclogues 67   61
    Thinke, my harde haps have blunted death's sharpe knife, . .  113  4th Eclogues 72   14
    Evill happes do fill with hope, good happes appall . . . . .  143  Cert Sonnets 12   14
HARBINGERS
    Though harbengers of death lodge there his traine. . . . . .  228  Astrophil    94    8
HARBOR
    Come from marble bowers, many times the gay harbor of
        anguish, . . . . . . . . . . . . . . . . . . . . . . . .   34  1st Eclogues 13   92
    Nor envie's snaky ey, finds any harbor here, . . . . . . . .   69  2nd Eclogues 34   18
    O harbour all her partes in easefull plighte:. . . . . . . .   79  Arcadia III  51    7
    For when, nak'd boy, thou couldst no harbour find. . . . . .  198  Astrophil    65    5
    But my soule shall harbour there.. . . . . . . . . . . . . .  234  A&S 11th Song     40
HARBORED
    Pressing too much upon ill harbourd shore. . . . . . . . . .  142  Cert Sonnets 12    3
    Under his tongue do harbour'd ly . . . . . . . . . . . . . .  282  Psalm X           29
HARBORETH
    (For envie harbreth most in feeblest hartes) . . . . . . . .  100  3rd Eclogues 66   58
HARBORS
    Late harbors in her face whom nature wrought,. . . . . . . .  141  Cert Sonnets  8    7
HARD
    And if enchantment can a harde hart move,. . . . . . . . . .   17  1st Eclogues  7  100
    But yet, alas! O but yet alas! our happs be but hard happs,.   32  1st Eclogues 13   37
    My purest minde; whose temper hard doth showe. . . . . . . .   40  Arcadia II   18    8
    What be the sweet creatures wher lowly demaunds be not
        heard Hard. . . . . . . . . . . . . . . . . . . . . . .   65  2nd Eclogues 31   41
    Harde to be gott, but got constant, to be helde like
        steeles Eeles.. . . . . . . . . . . . . . . . . . . . .   65  2nd Eclogues 31   42
    And yet as hard, as brawne made hard by arte:. . . . . . . .   76  Arcadia III  46   16
    With chumpish lookes, hard words, and secret nips, . . . . .   95  3rd Eclogues 64   31
    Never hard hand, nor ever raines too light.. . . . . . . . .   98  3rd Eclogues 65   10
    Thinke, my harde haps have blunted death's sharpe knife, . .  113  4th Eclogues 72   14
    Whose stormelike course staid not till hard by me it bided..  118  4th Eclogues 73   60
    Hard like a rich marbell: hard, but a faire Diamond. . . . .  122  4th Eclogues 74   14
    In hard estate with stowt shew valor use,. . . . . . . . . .  143  Cert Sonnets 12   16
    Should Ladies faire be tyed to such hard lawes,. . . . . . .  146  Cert Sonnets 17   23
    In clyming steepe, now hard refusall show: . . . . . . . . .  147  Cert Sonnets 18    6
    In Dales I see each way a hard assent: . . . . . . . . . . .  147  Cert Sonnets 18   10
    My mouth too tender is for thy hard bit. . . . . . . . . . .  166  Astrophil     4    8
```

HARD   (CONTINUED)   PAGE   TITLE   LINE

	PAGE	TITLE		LINE
HARD (CONTINUED)				
When some faire Ladies, by hard promise tied,	176	Astrophil	22	5
"What idler thing, then speake and not be hard?"	182	Astrophil	34	9
Who hard by made a window send forth light..	191	Astrophil	53	9
O ease your hand, treate not so hard your slave:	212	Astrophil	86	9
With care's hard hand) to turne and tosse in thee.	230	Astrophil	98	8
And why should he in heart so hard	283	Psalm X		55
Till hard by them both he and she did stay..	244	Other Poems	4	88
Geron strave hard, but aged were his feet,	248	Other Poems	4	254
HARDENED				
Forc'd by a tedious proofe, that Turkish hardned hart,	168	Astrophil	8	2
Hardned, and coulde, farr from affectione's snare.	344	Possibly	2	5
HARDER				
But harder Judges judge ambition's rage,	176	Astrophil	23	9
What harder thing then smart, and not to speake?	182	Astrophil	34	10
HARDEST				
Now I, wit-beaten long by hardest Fate,	195	Astrophil	60	9
HARDLY				
Hardly they heard, which by good hunters singled be.	14	1st Eclogues	7	10
Hardly remains fyer hid, where skill is bent to the hiding,.	33	1st Eclogues	13	59
Or else who singeth worse, my skill will hardly hit.	53	2nd Eclogues	29	50
That hardly usde, who ever prison broke,	135	Cert Sonnets	1	11
To twist those broyles, which hardly would untwine:	146	Cert Sonnets	17	22
Whose owne fault casts him downe, hardly high seat recovers.	213	A&S 5th Song		24
HARDNESS				
Such thing cannot he hope, that knowes thy determinat hardnes;	122	4th Eclogues	74	13
Is chang'd to stone, in hardnesse, cold, and weight,	150	Cert Sonnets	22	43
HARDY				
Oh no, no, hardye shepeheard, worth can never enter a title,	34	1st Eclogues	13	82
Cleofila, Hardy shephearde, such as thy meritts, such may be her insight	37	1st Eclogues	13	155
HARE				
The Hare, her sleights; the Cat, his melancholie;	101	3rd Eclogues	66	92
Now for a clod-like hare in fourm they peere,	243	Other Poems	4	43
A hast'ned Hare from greedy Grayhound goe,	251	Other Poems	4	343
HARK				
Harke plaintfull ghostes, infernall furies harke	73	Arcadia III	40	1
I start, looke, hearke, but what in closde up sence.	184	Astrophil	38	9
That to each word, nay sigh of mine you harke,	233	Astrophil	104	3
My suite is just, just lord to my suite hark;	289	Psalm XVII		1
HARM				
O cruell sonne thy hate this harme dothe breede.	43	Arcadia II	24	3
To harme us wormes should that high Justice leave.	59	2nd Eclogues	30	71
The Stagge did give the harme eschewing feare.	101	3rd Eclogues	66	91
In Nature's name to suffer such a harme,	125	4th Eclogues	75	17
Finde to what harme they hastned,	154	Cert Sonnets	25	14
A monster, other's harme, selfe-miserie,	206	Astrophil	78	5
Whose fury bends to harme:	283	Psalm X		66
Remorse in you to doe this Fortresse harme,	346	Possibly	5	6
HARMED				
Since bashfull dread seekes where he knowes me harmed:	135	Cert Sonnets	1	2
I have (live I and know this) harmed thee,	227	Astrophil	93	10
HARMFUL				
Catch harmful fall	318	Psalm XXXIII		65
HARMING				
Hides their inward will of harming..	263	Other Poems	7	42
HARMLESS				
Like Senators a harmeles empire had.	100	3rd Eclogues	66	56
And now at keels they trie a harmles chaunce,	243	Other Poems	4	47
HARMONIES				
The heavenly harmonies;	216	A&S 6th Song		21
HARMONY				
Sweet birds kindly do graunt harmony unto thee,	69	2nd Eclogues	34	12
That in thee lives harmonie,	140	Cert Sonnets	7	19
Of his mazde powers keepes perfit harmony:	230	Astrophil	99	8
A perfect harmony.	216	A&S 6th Song		24
HARMS				
Thy wit dost use still still more harmes to finde.	23	1st Eclogues	9	34
My harmes to me, my blisse to her attributed..	49	2nd Eclogues	28	69
With so sweete plagues my happie harmes infected be:	51	2nd Eclogues	28	123
To couple coming harmes with sorrowes past?	57	2nd Eclogues	30	7
But if he know not his harms what guides hath he whil'st he be blind? Blind.	63	2nd Eclogues	31	20
Of all thy harmes: Lo here she,	67	2nd Eclogues	32	47
To have his harmes with wisdome's helpe redrest.	75	Arcadia III	44	4
Such cursed harmes as cannot be redressed.	126	4th Eclogues	75	63
My harmes on Ink's poore losse, perhaps some find.	182	Astrophil	34	13
Him great harmes had taught much care,	218	A&S 8th Song		9
The just when harms approach	320	Psalm XXXIV		61
To spend for harms, although they touch you not:	242	Other Poems	4	10
He that before shund hir to shun such harmes,	252	Other Poems	4	383
HARNESS				
Of vertue's regiment, shining in harnesse.	67	2nd Eclogues	33	4
His compleat harneis was hir purest white.	246	Other Poems	4	150
HARNESSED				
Dorus. How oft, when reason saw love of her harnished.	16	1st Eclogues	7	61
HARP				
Take harp and sing in this our versing time:	146	Cert Sonnets	17	37
O prayse with harp the lord,	316	Psalm XXXIII		7

HARP	(CONTINUED)	PAGE	TITLE		LINE
Sweete Orpheus' Harpe, whose sound		260	Other Poems	6	13

HARROW

I harowe it with Thoughts, which all conspire.	115	4th Eclogues	72	54

HARSH

Silly shepheard's poore pype, when his harsh sound testifis our woes,.	32	1st Eclogues	13	40

HART

The Lion, harte; the Ounce gave active might;.	101	3rd Eclogues	66	80
As the chafed hart which brayeth	334	Psalm XLII		1

HARVEST

Yet harvest brings. Doth she alas absent herselfe?	49	2nd Eclogues	28	62
But harveste come, and corne in fertill store, ...	71	Arcadia III	36	11
As happie shewes of corne when harvest sendes;	71	Arcadia III	37	10
Gay haire more gaie then straw when harvest lyes,.	76	Arcadia III	46	7
Desire's best meane, harvest of hartes affected, ...	108	Arcadia IV	69	2
What can be hoped my harvest time will be?	175	Astrophil	21	11
Than they whose stoare in harvest space.	274	Psalm IV		29

HAST

But if thou hast a Love, in that Love's passion, ...	15	1st Eclogues	7	16
Sing then, and see (for now thou hast inflamed me)	15	1st Eclogues	7	20
Of singing thou hast got the reputation.	20	1st Eclogues	7	V972
Above line repeated at following location.	20	1st Eclogues	7	V972
Because thou hast thy fellow overgone, ...	27	1st Eclogues	10	11
Howe can they be unkind? speake for th'hast narroly pri'de. pride..	65	2nd Eclogues	31	43
What strange dessein hast thou my hopes to staie,.	80	Arcadia III	53	3
Of yonglings, which thy selfe with love hast rearde, ...	92	3rd Eclogues	63	43
This done, thou hast no more, but leave the rest	98	3rd Eclogues	65	13
Earth thou didst seeke, and store of earth thou hast.. . . .	108	Arcadia IV	68	2
How hast thou torne thy selfe! sought thine owne damage! . .	109	Arcadia IV	70	20
Since thou my riches arte, and that thou haste	114	4th Eclogues	72	29
Was it a dreame? O dreame, how hast thou wrought in me,. . .	121	4th Eclogues	73	181
How hast thou framde the paine wherewith I am opprest? . . .	121	4th Eclogues	73	184
More loving eyes she draws, more hate thou hast.	141	Cert Sonnets	8	14
Too long, too long asleepe thou hast me brought, ...	161	Cert Sonnets	31	7
But yet in vaine thou hast my ruine sought,.	161	Cert Sonnets	31	9
Whence hast thou Ivorie, Rubies, pearle and gold,.	181	Astrophil	32	10
That hast my mind, none of the basest, brought	184	Astrophil	40	3
Since then thou hast so farre subdued me,.	185	Astrophil	40	12
Hast thou found such and such like arguments?.	199	Astrophil	67	10
Griefe find the words, for thou hast made my braine.	228	Astrophil	94	1
My causeless wrongs hast wroken.	273	Psalm III		27
Hast in their malice broken.	273	Psalm III		30
For Thou the lord in endless hatred hast	275	Psalm V		15
And hast Thy deadly armes in order brought	278	Psalm VII		35
That hast of thine unmatched glory	278	Psalm VIII		3
Thou planted hast this earthly mate.	279	Psalm VIII		18
Yet hast Thou made even him an owner	279	Psalm VIII		19
And so thou hast all things ordained	279	Psalm VIII		23
Both sheep and Oxen wholy hast,.	279	Psalm VIII		26
For Thou my cause, my right Thou hast maintaind, ...	279	Psalm IX		8
The Gentiles Thou rebuked sorely hast, ...	279	Psalm IX		11
Thou lord that from Death' gates hast lifted me, ...	280	Psalm IX		39
Who hast the heath'ny folk destroyd.	283	Psalm X		71
My strength my strongest rock, which my defence hast borne,.	290	Psalm XVIII		2
Thou hast given what his heart would have,.	297	Psalm XXI		5
Thou, Thou it is that hast him set	297	Psalm XXI		19
My God my God why hast Thou me forsaken?	298	Psalm XXII		1
Yet to my plaint Thou hast not audience lent..	298	Psalm XXII		8
O lord Thou hast exalted me.	310	Psalm XXX		1
For it is Thou, that hast restord my light,.	312	Psalm XXXI		14
Thou well hast known what plung my soul was in	312	Psalm XXXI		21
And thou hast not for aye enclosed me.	312	Psalm XXXI		22
But hast enlargd my feet from mortall ginn..	312	Psalm XXXI		24
To whom feare Thee? what thou hast done for those.	313	Psalm XXXI		53
Thou hast hid them: yet leaving them thy light,.	313	Psalm XXXI		56
This thou hast seen, and wilt thou silent be?.	322	Psalm XXXV		55
Why then hast thou left me?.	336	Psalm XLIII		9
When thou hast mynd to weepe, seeke out som smoky room:. . .	343	Possibly	1	11

HASTE

Let doltes in haste some altars faire erect.	58	2nd Eclogues	30	62
Why doost thou haste away.	80	Arcadia III	52	1
Time haste my dying hower:	136	Cert Sonnets	3	18
Yet I confess in that tempestuous haste.	313	Psalm XXXI		61
Hast O Lord, that I be stayd	329	Psalm XXXVIII		64
Vouchsafe me help O Lord, and help with hast;.	332	Psalm XL		51
With such mad haste he did to Cosma goe, ...	249	Other Poems	4	271
With proud aspect, disdaining greater hast..	249	Other Poems	4	293
(Stolne from her yoong by theeves' unchoosing hast).	254	Other Poems	4	491

HASTEN

Hasten to help me, in this deep discomfort..	299	Psalm XXII		46

HASTENED

Hastened from us with barre of shadow darke, ...	80	Arcadia III	52	13
Finde to what harme they hastned,.	154	Cert Sonnets	25	14
A hast'ned Hare from greedy Grayhound goe, ...	251	Other Poems	4	343

HASTILY

So hastily that which they would repent:	100	3rd Eclogues	66	69

HASTY

With flowing teares your fault of hasty sight:	38	Arcadia II	14	2

```
HASTY                    (CONTINUED)                  PAGE    TITLE         LINE
    Passion unto my rage, Rage to a hasty revenge. . . . . . .   124  4th Eclogues 74   68
HAT
    Nico. Well aimed by my hat: for as thou sangst last day; . .   52  2nd Eclogues 29   25
HATCH
    Who under courtly pompes doo hatch a base desire.. . . . . .   117  4th Eclogues 73   16
    To hatch mine eyes, and that unbitted thought. . . . . . . .   183  Astrophil    38    2
HATCHING
    Lies hatching still the goods wherein they flow: . . . . . .   176  Astrophil    24    2
    Of clime-fall Court, the envy-hatching place:. . . . . . . .   243  Other Poems   4   61
HATE
    If shee still hate love's lawe,. . . . . . . . . . . . . .    19  1st Eclogues  7  V150
    There is no hate that can thee more oppresse.. . . . . . .    23  1st Eclogues  9   49
    Hate of the firste, contempt of later feate: . . . . . . .    27  1st Eclogues 10   39
    For what they see their parents love or hate . . . . . . .    28  1st Eclogues 10   56
    O cruell sonne thy hate this harme dothe breede. . . . . .    43  Arcadia II   24    3
    A hatefull cure with hate to heale:. . . . . . . . . . . .    44  Arcadia II   25    1
    Nico. I thinke it well: such voice would make one musicke
        hate:. . . . . . . . . . . . . . . . . . . . . . . .    52  2nd Eclogues 29   21
    Unkindnes breedes, unkindnes fostreth hate.. . . . . . . .    85  Arcadia III  61    8
    But ah the more I hate, the more I thinke. . . . . . . . .    85  Arcadia III  61    9
    Whome I doe hate, the more I thinke on him,. . . . . . . .    85  Arcadia III  61   10
    Where love draws hate, and hate engendreth love? . . . . .    85  Arcadia III  61   14
    All sturring husband's hate. . . . . . . . . . . . . . . .    93  3rd Eclogues 63   69
    Long since I hate the night, more hate the morning:. . . .   112  4th Eclogues 71   34
    With envie I doo hate the loftie mountaines; . . . . . . .   112  4th Eclogues 71   52
    Shamed I hate my selfe in sight of mountaines, . . . . . .   112  4th Eclogues 71   59
    Hate fully growne, Absence new sprongen out. . . . . . . .   115  4th Eclogues 72   58
    Diana deare; my minde to love and not to hate. . . . . . .   120  4th Eclogues 73  148
    If the Love hate you dyd, you should your beautie have
        hidden:. . . . . . . . . . . . . . . . . . . . . . .   123  4th Eclogues 74   47
    More loving eyes she draws, more hate thou hast. . . . . .   141  Cert Sonnets  8   14
    In tender harts, small things engender hate: . . . . . . .   146  Cert Sonnets 17   17
    No, no, no, no, I cannot hate my foe,. . . . . . . . . . .   155  Cert Sonnets 26    1
    Above line repeated at following locations . . . . . . . .   155  Cert Sonnets 26   12
        . . . . . . . . . . . . . . . . . . . . . . . . . . .   156  Cert Sonnets 26   23
    The boy refusde for feare of Marse's hate, . . . . . . . .   173  Astrophil    17    5
    The ground of this fierce Love and lovely hate:. . . . . .   195  Astrophil    60   11
    Me to hate? But I forbeare,. . . . . . . . . . . . . . . .   211  A&S 4th Song       50
    For it is void of hate.. . . . . . . . . . . . . . . . . .   215  A&S 6th Song        6
    All her hate, death soone would seaze me,. . . . . . . . .   222  A&S 9th Song       44
    To hearts that hate all lying. . . . . . . . . . . . . . .   284  Psalm XI            8
    So did he save me from their then prevailing hate, . . . .   291  Psalm XVIII        37
    Who hate, yea hate me cruely.. . . . . . . . . . . . . . .   304  Psalm XXV          66
    Who hate the good shall fall.. . . . . . . . . . . . . . .   320  Psalm XXXIV        76
    To have their hate on good soules wroken;. . . . . . . . .   325  Psalm XXXVII       38
    My Foes' ev'ill words their hate of me display . . . . . .   333  Psalm XLI          17
    Dick. Oh hence! o cruell word! which even doggs do hate: . .   344  Possibly      1   47
HATED
    Thou paine, thou hated paine, from heav'n exilde,. . . . .   141  Cert Sonnets 10    4
    That Thee so ev'ill have hated;. . . . . . . . . . . . . .   297  Psalm XXI          30
    I hated have those men whose thoughts do cleave. . . . . .   312  Psalm XXXI         16
HATEFUL
    As that hatefull death can abridge them of powre,. . . . .    31  1st Eclogues 12   18
    A hatefull cure with hate to heale:. . . . . . . . . . . .    44  Arcadia II   25    1
    Unto my woes the hatefull heavens do sende,. . . . . . . .    73  Arcadia III  40    2
    Which is the hatefull web of Sorowe's paines.. . . . . . .   114  4th Eclogues 72   25
    For even the hearbes our hatefull musique stroyes, . . . .   116  4th Eclogues 72  103
    When that we feare our hatefull neighbours' might, . . . .   129  4th Eclogues 76   20
    That hatefull never cease. . . . . . . . . . . . . . . . .   272  Psalm III           2
    Who causeless now, yeelds me a hatefull heart, . . . . . .   277  Psalm VII          12
    By them whose minds on hatefull thoughts do stay:. . . . .   280  Psalm IX           38
    Within the hand of hatefull enmitie, . . . . . . . . . . .   312  Psalm XXXI         23
    For then their hatefull heads close whispring be . . . . .   333  Psalm XLI          25
HATES
    Now since her chast mind hates this love in me,. . . . . .   195  Astrophil    61    9
    Shall quickly me from what she hates remove. . . . . . . .   195  Astrophil    61   11
    No, she hates me, wellaway,. . . . . . . . . . . . . . . .   222  A&S 9th Song       41
    But hates, abhorrs the wycked braines, . . . . . . . . . .   284  Psalm XI           18
    Do works which earth corrupt and Heaven hates, . . . . . .   286  Psalm XIV           5
HATE-SPOT
    Passing the hate-spott Ermelin.. . . . . . . . . . . . . .    89  Arcadia III  62  116
HATEST
    Thou hatest all whose works in evill are plac't. . . . . .   275  Psalm V            13
HATETH
    An uncouth love, which Nature hateth most. . . . . . . . .    11  Arcadia I     1    4
HATH
    To one that hath no wealth, and wants his wit. . . . . . .     4  Lady of May   2   24
    Yet hath sir Sunne the greatest praise,. . . . . . . . . .    13  Arcadia I     5    9
    Such force hath Love above poore Nature's power. . . . . .    19  1st Eclogues  7  161
    Dorus. Such force hath Love above poore Nature's power,. . .    19  1st Eclogues  7  162
    Such weight it hath which once is full possest.. . . . . .    20  1st Eclogues  7  V961
    Above line repeated at following location. . . . . . . . .    20  1st Eclogues  7  V962
    Which hath in others' head his only being. . . . . . . . .    20  1st Eclogues  7  V964
    Hath power that Sex with bridle to withhold? . . . . . . .    24  1st Eclogues  9   58
    Hath strongest soule, when most his raynes do bowe.. . . .    25  1st Eclogues  9  101
    As fishe sure tryall hath of muddy slyme.. . . . . . . . .    28  1st Eclogues 10   54
    And of misfortune, fortune hath only the gift. . . . . . .    29  1st Eclogues 11    4
    Fleshly vaile consumes; but a soule hath his life, . . . .    31  1st Eclogues 12   22
    Old age hath knowne what ever was in youth:. . . . . . . .    39  Arcadia II   15   11
```

HATH   (CONTINUED)   PAGE   TITLE   LINE
    P. Will hath his will, when Reason's will doth misse.. . . .   46 2nd Eclogues 27   8
    P. Reason hath eyes to see his owne ill case.. . . . .   46 2nd Eclogues 27   16
    Who judge that honour, which hath scope to slander.. . . . .   50 2nd Eclogues 28   91
    Fine eares, long taile he hath, with Lion's curbed clawe,. .   53 2nd Eclogues 29   33
    No eare nor taile he hath, least they should him disgrace, .   53 2nd Eclogues 29   41
    Me thinkes I see the lippes my Leuca hath, ...   54 2nd Eclogues 29   76
    Pas. My father hath at home a prettie Jay, ...   56 2nd Eclogues 29 138
    That hath foure legs, and with two onely goes, ...   56 2nd Eclogues 29 142
    That hath foure eyes, and onely two can frame. . . . .   56 2nd Eclogues 29 143
    For who grieves not hath but a blockish braine,. . . . . . .   58 2nd Eclogues 30   36
    Hath all thy whirling course so small effect?. . . . .   58 2nd Eclogues 30   60
    Hath she not force even death with love to kill? . . . . . .   59 2nd Eclogues 30   85
    O braine, where thought of her hath only place; . . . . . .   60 2nd Eclogues 30 118
    Hath not Reason enough vehemence the desire to reprove?
        Prove. . . . .   63 2nd Eclogues 31   10
    But if he know not his harms what guides hath he whil'st he
        be blind? Blind. . . . .   63 2nd Eclogues 31   20
    Silly rewarde! yet among women hath she of vertu the most.
        Most.. . . . .   64 2nd Eclogues 31   36
    Where man's mind hath a freed consideration. . . . .   68 2nd Eclogues 34   3
    For nature hathe that never fayling scoope,. . . . .   71 Arcadia III 37   5
    My true love hath my hart, and I have his, ...   75 Arcadia III 45   1
    Above line repeated at following location. . . . .   76 Arcadia III 45   14
    Beautie hath force to catche the humane sight. . . . .   82 Arcadia III 57   1
    Thus hath each part his beautie's part,. . . . .   90 Arcadia III 62 133
    No wife but I hath such a man, God wot". . . . . 104 Arcadia III 67   45
    Who hath our sight with too much sight infected, ... 108 Arcadia IV   69   6
    What essence dest'nie hath; if fortune be or no; . . . . . . 118 4th Eclogues 73   45
    To see my night of evils, which hath no morow. . . . . 136 Cert Sonnets 3   8
    Alas she hath no other cause of anguish. . . . . 137 Cert Sonnets 4   13
    He hopes for some small praise since she hath great, ... 141 Cert Sonnets 8   11
    Hath not such paine as it makes others have: . . . . 142 Cert Sonnets 11   10
    Hath yet such health, as it my life can save.. . . . . 142 Cert Sonnets 11   12
    Hath neither leave to live, nor doome to dye,. . . . . 144 Cert Sonnets 15   7
    Peake hath a Cave, whose narrow entries finde. . . . . 150 Cert Sonnets 22   31
    Hath this world ought so faire as Stella is? . . . . 175 Astrophil   21   14
    Of all my thoughts hath neither stop nor start,. . . . . . . 176 Astrophil   23   13
    Hath no misfortune, but that Rich she is.. . . . . 183 Astrophil   37   14
    Hath cheekes to smile, as well as eyes to weepe. . . . . . . 201 Astrophil   70   8
    Who since he hath, by Nature's speciall grace, ... 206 Astrophil   78   9
    Nor no day hath lesse quiet then my night: . . . . 224 Astrophil   89   11
    But, but (alas) night's side the ods hath fur, ... 229 Astrophil   96   12
    Her selfe (to shew no other joy hath place). . . . . 229 Astrophil   97   7
    Who hath the eyes which marrie state with pleasure,. . . . . 197 A&S 1st Song   5
    Who hath the lips, where wit in fairnesse raigneth,. . . . . 197 A&S 1st Song   9
    Who hath the feet, whose step all sweetnesse planteth, . . . 197 A&S 1st Song   13
    Who hath the breast, whose milke doth passions nourish,. . . 197 A&S 1st Song   17
    Who hath the hand which without stroke subdueth, ... 197 A&S 1st Song   21
    Who hath the haire which, loosest, fastest tieth,. . . . . . 197 A&S 1st Song   25
    Who hath the voyce, which soule from sences sunders, ... 197 A&S 1st Song   29
    Sorrow onely then hath glory,. . . . . 221 A&S 9th Song   14
    With loving homage kisse that only son he hath,. . . . . . . 272 Psalm II   27
    He that hath hurtlesse hands, whose inward heart is framed. 302 Psalm XXIV   7
    The lord such plenty hath, ... 303 Psalm XXV   32
    That Realm in deed hath blisse . . . . 317 Psalm XXXIII   43
    My flesh hath, ... 327 Psalm XXXVIII   8
    For when his sin Thy scourging hath, ... 330 Psalm XXXIX   34
    More than my head hath haires; . . . . 332 Psalm XL   47
    Where hath now your God his biding?. . . . . 335 Psalm XLII   48
    A lustles song for sooth thinks hee that hath more lust to
        cry. . . . . 343 Possibly   1   8
HATING
    For clerkly reed, and hating what is naught, ...   99 3rd Eclogues 66   24
    Let hating of our selves be our affection, ... 130 4th Eclogues 76   33
    Bent to revenge and ever hating. . . . . 278 Psalm VIII   8
    Unto whose ever hating lust. . . . . 308 Psalm XXVII   55
HATRED
    For Thou the lord in endless hatred hast . . . . 275 Psalm V   15
    Till his known ev'ill do hatred get. . . . . 323 Psalm XXXVI   8
HAUNCHES
    With hanches smooth as looking glasse. . . . .   88 Arcadia III 62   92
HAUNT
    My charme should be, she haunt me day and night. . . . . . .   17 1st Eclogues 7 105
    Seeke skill of hearbes in hills, haunt brookes neere night,.   26 1st Eclogues 9 127
    Keepe thy sprite from abuse, here no abuse doth haunte.. . .   69 2nd Eclogues 34   27
    Yee Nimphes which haunt the springs in pleasant vallies, . . 111 4th Eclogues 71   2
    He knew hir haunt, and haunted in the same,. . . . . 247 Other Poems   4 187
    Doth daily haunt: but so, that mine become . . . . 255 Other Poems   4 503
HAUNTED
    He knew hir haunt, and haunted in the same,. . . . . 247 Other Poems   4 187
HAUNTS
    Thus halfe a man, with man he easly haunts,. . . . .   21 1st Eclogues 8   31
    And from the haunts of such bad folks did fly. . . . . 305 Psalm XXVI   18
HAVE
    Let not wild woods so great a treasure have. . . . .   3 Lady of May   2   12
    Two thousand sheepe I have as white as milke,. . . . .   4 Lady of May   2   19
    Two thousand deere in wildest woods I have,. . . . .   4 Lady of May   2   25
    So if my man must praises have,. . . . .   13 Arcadia I   5   5
    Above line repeated at following location. . . . .   13 Arcadia I   5   11

HAVE   (CONTINUED)   PAGE   TITLE   LINE
No thralles like them that inward bondage have.. . . . . . .   17 1st Eclogues 7 114
I have no shewes of wealth: my wealth is you,. . . . .   18 1st Eclogues 7 135
Of all those fooles that will have all they see. . . . . . .   22 1st Eclogues 8   48
And thinke them olde, that have the oldest minde,. . . . . .   25 1st Eclogues 9   94
Such sight have they that see with goggling eyes.. . . . . .   25 1st Eclogues 9 113
Youth will have will: Age must to age therefore. . . . . . .   27 1st Eclogues 10   24
Who have their lesson so long time begonne?. . . . .   27 1st Eclogues 10   27
And statute made he never shoulde have voice,. . . . .   29 1st Eclogues 10   86
I warne thee therefore (since thou maist have choice). . . .   29 1st Eclogues 10   88
Vertue you have, of vertue you have left proufes to the
  whole world, ...   33 1st Eclogues 13   56
Nurse inwarde maladyes, which have not scope to be breath'd
  out, ...   35 1st Eclogues 13 104
That to your strength your foes have sure resorte. . . . . .   38 Arcadia II   14   12
Bard of my will, I have beyond desire: . . . .   41 Arcadia II   20   7
Let him be bob'd that bobs will have. . . . .   44 Arcadia II   25   4
P. We now have peace, your peace we doo not neede. . . . . .   46 2nd Eclogues 27   28
R. The joyes you have shall be made permanent. . . . .   47 2nd Eclogues 27   35
Then may I hope, my pipe may have abilitie,. . . . .   48 2nd Eclogues 28   26
Thou soone may have some helpe, or change of passion.. . . .   50 2nd Eclogues 28   98
I have (and long shall have) a white great nimble cat, . . .   53 2nd Eclogues 29   31
Pas. Kisse her? now mayst thou kisse. I have a fitter match;   53 2nd Eclogues 29   39
Pas. But long have I a sparrow gailie drest, ...   54 2nd Eclogues 29   84
Let cat and dog fight which shall have both you. . . . . . .   56 2nd Eclogues 29 149
What greater ills have now the heavens in store, ...   57 2nd Eclogues 30   6
Where witt but serves, to have true tast of woes.. . . . . .   57 2nd Eclogues 30   25
Alas, if you a Phoenix new will have . . . .   60 2nd Eclogues 30 102
Such beames so like his owne, which might have might . . . .   60 2nd Eclogues 30 105
Yet Reason saith, Reason should have abilitie, ...   60 2nd Eclogues 30 131
What blinde guides can he have that leanes to a fancy? A
  fancy. . . . .   63 2nd Eclogues 31   21
Wherin no eare can have joy, ...   66 2nd Eclogues 32   37
You have my thankes, Let me your comforte have.. . . . . . .   70 Arcadia III 35   16
Betwixt which two in me I have this fight, ...   74 Arcadia III 42   7
To have his harmes with wisdome's helpe redrest. . . . . . .   75 Arcadia III 44   4
My true love hath my hart, and I have his, ...   75 Arcadia III 45   1
Above line repeated at following location. . . . .   76 Arcadia III 45   14
No smaller wound, alas! farr deeper have. . . . .   77 Arcadia III 47   4
That Limittes have in smallest smalle, ...   89 Arcadia III 62 V103
Yee Nymphes which in the waters empire have, ...   92 3rd Eclogues 63   28
Have much more care of them that them do keepe,. . . . . . .   92 3rd Eclogues 63   39
(For they have toongs to make a poore man blamed . . . . . .   94 3rd Eclogues 64   21
To have a feeling tast of him that sitts . . . .   99 3rd Eclogues 66   27
Roring, and howling for to have a King.. . . . . 100 3rd Eclogues 66   63
Who would not have a Phoenix if he could?. . . . . 104 3rd Eclogues 67   16
Phoenix but one, of Crowes we milllions have:. . . . . 104 3rd Eclogues 67   20
I have a wife worthie to be a Queene,. . . . . 106 3rd Eclogues 67   88
We care abroad, and they of home have care.. . . . . 106 3rd Eclogues 67 108
No being now, but sorowe I can have: . . . . 114 4th Eclogues 72   27
Proofe speakes too much to us that feeling triall have.. . . 119 4th Eclogues 73 108
And let her have the giftes that should in both remaine: . . 120 4th Eclogues 73 131
That they, which have no lives, should live so long, ... 126 4th Eclogues 75   41
Rather then have thy all-beholding eye . . . . 126 4th Eclogues 75   56
I have my selfe, and all what life containeth, ... 128 4th Eclogues 75 101
Whereas if I a gratefull gardien have, ... 135 Cert Sonnets 1   13
Longing to have, having no wit to wish,. . . . . 136 Cert Sonnets 2   13
Cannot have to content me, ... 137 Cert Sonnets 4   18
Have more cause to lament me, ... 137 Cert Sonnets 4   19
And sweare she is not worthy thee to have. . . . . 141 Cert Sonnets 9   14
If thus, alas! yet while those partes have wo, ... 142 Cert Sonnets 10   13
Hath not such paine as it makes others have: . . . . 142 Cert Sonnets 11   10
It makes them flie that which they faine would have: . . . . 145 Cert Sonnets 16   6
Or thinking still my thoughts might have good end: . . . . . 147 Cert Sonnets 19   2
Faire choice I have, either to live or dye . . . . 149 Cert Sonnets 21   13
The Bruertons have a Lake, which when the Sunne. . . . . . . 150 Cert Sonnets 22   11
We have a fish, by strangers much admirde, ... 150 Cert Sonnets 22   21
They have no cause to be sorie,. . . . . 155 Cert Sonnets 26   20
No other shepheard should have scope,. . . . . 158 Cert Sonnets 28   7
You have the same in my hands, seeing. . . . . 159 Cert Sonnets 29   8
Alas have I not paine enough my friend,. . . . . 171 Astrophil   14   1
Flie, fly, my friends, I have my death wound; fly, ... 174 Astrophil   20   1
To have for no cause birthright in the skie, ... 178 Astrophil   26   5
Or sprite, disdaine of such disdaine to have?. . . . . 188 Astrophil   47   6
So may you still have somewhat new to say. . . . . 190 Astrophil   51   4
Let Vertue have that Stella's selfe; yet thus, ... 191 Astrophil   52   13
But thou Desire, because thou wouldst have all,. . . . . . . 202 Astrophil   72   13
Then since (deare life) you faine would have me peace, . . . 207 Astrophil   81   12
Or if I needs (sweet Judge) must torments have,. . . . . . . 212 Astrophil   86   11
Thanke may you have for such a thankfull part, ... 229 Astrophil   95   13
That wormes should have their Sun, and I want mine.. . . . . 230 Astrophil   98   14
Sweet babes must babies have, but shrewd gyrles must be
  beat n. . . . . 213 A&S 5th Song   36
Thou English murdring theefe, wilt have harts for thy pray:. 214 A&S 5th Song   50
And which is worse, makes me most guiltlesse torments have,. 214 A&S 5th Song   59
In my lips to have his biding, ... 226 A&S 10th Song   27
Who have so leaden eyes, as not to see sweet beautie's show, 217 A&S 7th Song   7
Or seeing, have so wodden wits, as not that worth to know;   217 A&S 7th Song   8
Or knowing, have so muddy minds, as not to be in love; . . . 217 A&S 7th Song   9
Or loving, have so frothy thoughts, as easly thence to move: 217 A&S 7th Song   10

209

HAVE	(CONTINUED)	PAGE	TITLE		LINE
Where you may have some defence.		221	A&S 9th Song		3
Have mercy therfore still on me, ...		273	Psalm IV		4
Their soules fowl sinns for inmost lyning have:		275	Psalm V		26
Have mercie, mercie lord I once did say, ...		280	Psalm IX		36
And let not man have upper hand of Thee, ...		281	Psalm IX		62
Wee both have power, and will our tales to tell, ...		285	Psalm XII		11
On my soul no power shall have:		288	Psalm XVI		32
And children have to leave it to.		290	Psalm XVII		44
Let them not have me for their slave		295	Psalm XIX		55
Thou hast given what his heart would have, ...		297	Psalm XXI		5
Since they Eternal Essence have.		303	Psalm XXV		24
Heare to have mercy eke of me.		307	Psalm XXVII		38
For troubles of all sides have me within..		312	Psalm XXXI		26
Be glad you good, in God have joy, ...		316	Psalm XXXII		40
Nor strong men have.		317	Psalm XXXIII		59
We have no plea but trust.		318	Psalm XXXIII		84
They have and shall have blisse.		319	Psalm XXXIV		36
In sprite that I shall have Thy helping hand.		321	Psalm XXXV		6
As for my tongue, while I have any dayes, ...		323	Psalm XXXV		71
Have power again to raised be.		324	Psalm XXXVI		36
Thou shalt have both good food and place..		324	Psalm XXXVII		8
They shall have peace in plenteousness..		325	Psalm XXXVII		32
To have their hate on good soules wroken;		325	Psalm XXXVII		38
Shall have the land in their possessing.		326	Psalm XXXVII		74
Shew me how long I have to live.		329	Psalm XXXIX		14
Let them have shame, yea blush for shame, ...		332	Psalm XL		52
Have mercy lord on me, ...		333	Psalm XLI		14
And rayse me up that I may once have might		333	Psalm XLI		35
Since foes nor have, nor shall have cause to be.		333	Psalm XLI		39
Of Thy face to have a seing?		334	Psalm XLII		8
Dick. Bound as I neither power have, nor would have power to stir.		343	Possibly	1	24
Will. Thou late of wages playn'dst: what wages mayst thou have?.		344	Possibly	1	31
So have I cause my selfe to plaine, but no cause to complayne.		344	Possibly	1	36
Who share in woe, weygh others have as much.		242	Other Poems	4	16
Who would have hir in will and worde agree		245	Other Poems	4	115
Leave sheepe, leave all, I will no piecing have.		255	Other Poems	4	512
Wilt thou have more? more have, if more I be.		255	Other Poems	4	514
HAVEN					
Till my frayle barke his haven agayn do fynde.		70	Arcadia III	35	8
Nowe that I spye the haven my thoughtes requyre, ...		72	Arcadia III	37	15
HAVING					
That since the having them to neither's due, ...		56	2nd Eclogues	29	148
The wife thus having settled husband's braine, ...		96	3rd Eclogues	64	73
And having plaste my thoughts, my thoughts thus placed me. .		117	4th Eclogues	73	34
And having bound them fast by Styx, they should obaye. . . .		121	4th Eclogues	73	161
First having all their giftes upon faire Mira spred. . . .		121	4th Eclogues	73	178
Longing to have, having no wit to wish..		136	Cert Sonnets	2	13
Since wanting is more woe then too much having..		137	Cert Sonnets	4	20
Having before me Nature's treasure, ...		159	Cert Sonnets	29	6
Having got up a breach by fighting well, ...		171	Astrophil	12	10
Having no scarfe of clowds before his face, ...		176	Astrophil	22	3
Having this day my horse, my hand, my launce		185	Astrophil	41	1
When Cupid, having me his slave describe		191	Astrophil	53	5
Wo, having made with many fights his owne.		193	Astrophil	57	1
HEAD					
And ere that all these blowes thy head doo hit, ...		11	Arcadia I	1	9
Which hath in others' head his only being.		20	1st Eclogues	7	V964
Some hurt accuse a third with horny head..		21	1st Eclogues	8	12
A horned head, cloven foote, and thousand eyes, ...		21	1st Eclogues	8	26
His horned head doth soeme the heaven to spight:		21	1st Eclogues	8	29
My head you seeke, as to your strongest forte:		38	Arcadia II	14	10
For pilfring Lalus' lambe, with crouch to blesse thy head. .		52	2nd Eclogues	29	14
As farre as Love possesseth any head..		56	2nd Eclogues	29	128
Nor mas'de head thinke, nor faltring tonge recite.		74	Arcadia III	42	14
Her horned head abroad doth raunge:		86	Arcadia III	62	12
That still he be her head, she be his harte, ...		92	3rd Eclogues	63	48
The night growne old, her blacke head waxen gray, ...		103	3rd Eclogues	66	160
Those passions which to youthfull head doo clime, ...		107	3rd Eclogues	67	116
Doth hide his head with cares but onely how to rest: . . .		117	4th Eclogues	73	24
And laying downe my head, did nature's rule observe, ...		117	4th Eclogues	73	27
But foole, foole that I am, tho I had but a hair of her head found, ...		123	4th Eclogues	74	53
Thy cries, o Babie, set mine head on aking:		139	Cert Sonnets	6	2
To shew her skin, lips, teeth and head so well?.		181	Astrophil	32	11
A rosie garland, and a wearie hed:		184	Astrophil	39	11
Thou bear'st the arrow, I the arrow head..		198	Astrophil	65	14
Vertue's gold now must head my Cupid's dart.		202	Astrophil	72	8
But with short breath, long lookes, staid feet and walking hed, ...		205	Astrophil	76	13
Some beautie's peece, as amber colour hed, ...		225	Astrophil	91	6
And makes me then bow downe my head, and say, ...		237	Astrophil	108	9
The lord lifts up my head, ...		272	Psalm III		13
And his own evill his own head shall appall.		278	Psalm VII		45
Those lying lipps from Cousening head remove, ...		284	Psalm XII		8
Croune of his head with croune of Gold		297	Psalm XXI		11
With oyle Thou dost anoynt my head, ...		301	Psalm XXIII		19

HEAD   (CONTINUED)   PAGE   TITLE   LINE
     Now, Now shall He lift up my head. . . . .   307 Psalm XXVII   31
     On my head,. . . . .   327 Psalm XXXVIII   11
     More than my head hath haires; . . . .   332 Psalm XL   47
     And from Mizzar's hilly head.. . . . .   335 Psalm XLII   28
     Dresse bosome hers or hedd,. . . . .   257 Other Poems   5   48
     Their sugred selves to kisse thy happy hedd: . . . .   258 Other Poems   5   58
HEADACHE
     From the cruell headache, nor shooes of golde doo the gowt
        heale, ...   34 1st Eclogues 13   85
HEADED
     With amatists they headed are. . . . .   90 Arcadia III 62   132
HEADLONG
     And highest thoughts, downeward most headlong throw? . . . .   73 Arcadia III 40   12
HEADS
     Such hartes of brasse, wise heads, and garments trim . . . .   24 1st Eclogues 9   75
     In nature's pride your heads to heav'nwarde heave, ...   77 Arcadia III 49   2
     As what their hands do hold, their heads do know,. . . . . .   177 Astrophil   24   6
     Lift up your heads you Gates, and you doores ever biding,. .   302 Psalm XXIV   17
     Above line repeated at following location. . . . .   302 Psalm XXIV   21
     For then their hatefull heads close whispring be . . . . . .   333 Psalm XLI   25
HEAL
     From the cruell headache, nor shooes of golde doo the gowt
        heale, ...   34 1st Eclogues 13   85
     A hatefull cure with hate to heale:. . . . .   44 Arcadia II   25   1
     The friendly fray, where blowes both wound and heale,. . . .   206 Astrophil   79   10
     O heale my soul, let there Thy cure begin. . . . .   333 Psalm XLI   15
HEALTH
     Thy health too meane a match for my infection. . . . .   15 1st Eclogues 7   21
     Yet all my health I place in your good-will. . . . .   18 1st Eclogues 7   120
     My beautie's hewe your beames, my health your deeds; . . . .   18 1st Eclogues 7   136
     Fortune store, Nature health, Love grant perswasion. . . . .   51 2nd Eclogues 28   100
     As in his health we healthfull were preserved, ...   128 4th Eclogues 75   134
     Hath yet such health, as it my life can save.. . . . .   142 Cert Sonnets 11   12
     Who dost Thy saving health to true men bend. . . . .   277 Psalm VII   30
     Thy Truth, health, gratiousness. . . . .   331 Psalm XL   40
HEALTHFUL
     On Nature's sweet repast, as healthfull senses ledd. . . . .   117 4th Eclogues 73   40
     As in his health we healthfull were preserved, ...   128 4th Eclogues 75   134
     Your words my friend (right healthfull caustiks) blame . . .   175 Astrophil   21   1
HEAP
     A heape of sweetes she is, where nothing spilled is; . . . .   15 1st Eclogues 7   28
     Look but on this: man still doth riches heape. . . . .   330 Psalm XXXIX   21
HEAPED
     Save then my soule, spill not my thoughts well heaped, . . .   16 1st Eclogues 7   80
     With heaped weights of their own sins oppresse . . . .   275 Psalm V   31
HEAPS
     He heapes in inward griefe, that most destroyes him. . . . .   62 2nd Eclogues 30   172
     Neere Wilton sweete, huge heapes of stones are found,. . . .   149 Cert Sonnets 22   1
     In heapes he layes,. . . . .   316 Psalm XXXIII   26
     Ev'en heapes of wicked thoughts which streight they show . .   333 Psalm XLI   23
HEAR
     These bolde words she did heare, this fruite I reaped, . . .   17 1st Eclogues 7   82
     Heare plaints come forth from dungeon of my minde. . . . . .   18 1st Eclogues 7   133
     Then who will heare a well autoris'd lye,. . . . .   24 1st Eclogues 9   72
     And thinke ther she do dwell and heare what plaintes I do
        utter: . . . .   36 1st Eclogues 13   143
     And make me heare the plaints I would refraine:. . . . . . .   42 Arcadia II   21   11
     Dorus. If I had thought to heare blasphemous wordes, ...   50 2nd Eclogues 28   79
     Do you not heare his voice, and see his shape? . . . .   53 2nd Eclogues 29   59
     To sheepe, whom love, not knowledge, made to heare,. . . . .   103 3rd Eclogues 66   156
     Me seemes I heare in these ill-changed forrests, ...   112 4th Eclogues 71   39
     Me seemes I heare, when I doo heare sweete musique,. . . . .   112 4th Eclogues 71   47
     And be it as he saith". Venus was glad to heare. . . . . . .   120 4th Eclogues 73   143
     This you heare is not my tongue, ...   139 Cert Sonnets 7   4
     I heare a crye of spirits faint and blinde,. . . . .   148 Cert Sonnets 20   7
     Weepe neighbours, weepe, do you not heare it said, ...   160 Cert Sonnets 30   11
     Her come, and heare with patience my desire, ...   193 Astrophil   56   13
     She heard my plaints, and did not only heare,. . . . .   193 Astrophil   57   9
     Some do I heare of Poets' furie tell,. . . . .   204 Astrophil   74   5
     Let eares heare speech, which wit to wonder ties,. . . . . .   210 Astrophil   85   11
     And her sad words my sadded sence did heare. . . . .   223 Astrophil   87   8
     If you heare that they seeme my hart to move,. . . . .   225 Astrophil   91   13
     Fit to heare and ease my care: . . . .   210 A&S 4th Song   2
     Thinke now no more to heare of warme fine odourd snow, . . .   213 A&S 5th Song   37
     O You that heare this voice, ...   215 A&S 6th Song   1
     O let them heare these sacred tunes, and learne in wonder's
        schooles,. . . . .   217 A&S 7th Song   5
     Heare then, but then with wonder heare; see but adoring see,   217 A&S 7th Song   13
     Heare you this soule-invading voice, and count it but a
        voice? . . . .   217 A&S 7th Song   17
     Heare your wofull maister's story, ...   221 A&S 9th Song   12
     Heare me, O heare me when I call . . . .   273 Psalm IV   1
     The lord my suite did heare, and gently heare, ...   276 Psalm VI   29
     Let God the lord heare Thee, ...   295 Psalm XX   1
     Let that King deign to heare, ...   296 Psalm XX   34
     From lion's mouth O help, and shew to heare me . . . .   299 Psalm XXII   49
     Heare lord when I my voice display,. . . . .   307 Psalm XXVII   37
     Heare to have mercy eke of me. . . . .   307 Psalm XXVII   38
     Lord heare, let mercy thine be stay'd. . . . .   311 Psalm XXX   31

HEAR   (CONTINUED)   PAGE   TITLE   LINE
    Bow down thine eare to heare how much I need,. . . . . . .   312 Psalm XXXI   4
    But Thou didst heare, when I to Thee did moane.. . . . . .   313 Psalm XXXI   63
    When Thou wilt deign to heare him. . . . .   315 Psalm XXXII   21
    This lord and he did heare my cry, ...   319 Psalm XXXIV   14
    Me thinks amid my heart I heare. . . . .   323 Psalm XXXVI   1
    My God Thou wilt heare my voice; . . . .   328 Psalm XXXVIII   45
    For I sayd, heare, least they be . . . .   328 Psalm XXXVIII   46
    Heare lord my suits and cryes, stop not thyn eares . . . .   330 Psalm XXXIX   37
    Dick. Here then and learn to sigh: a mistress I doo serve, . 343 Possibly   1   19
    Miso mine owne pigsnie, thou shalt heare news o' Damaetas.   241 Other Poems   2   1
    You I invite with easie eares to heare . . . .   242 Other Poems   4   13
    To see, to feele, to heare, to tast, to know . . . .   252 Other Poems   4   407
    Alas! of ghostes I heare the gastly cries: . . . .   255 Other Poems   4   507
    Yet there, me seemes, I heare her singing loud.. . . . . .   255 Other Poems   4   508
    To heare, and not despise. . . . .   258 Other Poems   5   61
HEARD
    Seen, and unknowne; heard, but without attention.. . . . .   19 1st Eclogues   7   179
    In being heard untill the hearer dye . . . .   24 1st Eclogues   9   70
    Were in his dayes: which heard, one nothing heares,. . . .   24 1st Eclogues   9   76
    Philisides. Hath any man heard what this old man said? . . . 26 1st Eclogues   9   135
    If the Swanne's sweet voice be not heard, but at death,. . . 30 1st Eclogues 12   14
    While shepheards' tunes be heard, or rimes be read,. . . .   56 2nd Eclogues 29   124
    Pas. So oft these woods have heard me "Cosma" crie,. . . .   56 2nd Eclogues 29   132
    I silent herd more wordes of witt. . . . .   57 2nd Eclogues 30   2
    What be the sweet creatures wher lowly demaunds be not
       heard Hard. . . . .   65 2nd Eclogues 31   41
    Glad was the man when he had heard her out,. . . . .   96 3rd Eclogues 64   63
    Which now in night's deepe shade sheep heard of me.. . . .   99 3rd Eclogues 66   42
    Because (though hurt) they never heard her grone,. . . . .   102 3rd Eclogues 66   119
    Those names abasht me much, when those great names I hard: 119 4th Eclogues 73   79
    But, but alas, like a man condemn'd doth crave to be heard
       speake,. . . . . 122 4th Eclogues 74   23
    Paine heard her praise, and full of inward fire, ...   141 Cert Sonnets   9   9
    And have I heard her say, "o cruell paine!". . . . .   142 Cert Sonnets 11   1
    Nor trumpets sound I heard, nor friendly cries;. . . . . .   191 Astrophil   53   12
    She heard my plaints, and did not only heare,. . . . . . .   193 Astrophil   57   9
    Least once should not be heard, twise said, No, No.. . . .   196 Astrophil   63   8
    That you heard was but a Mouse,. . . . .   211 A&S 4th Song   25
    And all eares worse then deafe, that heard not out thy
       storie.. . . . . 212 A&S 5th Song   6
    From Holy hill he heard me.. . . . .   272 Psalm III   15
    For god hath heard the weeping sobbing voice . . . .   276 Psalm VI   27
    They have heard and conceived. . . . .   293 Psalm XIX   12
    Do cry, their cry of him is heard, ...   320 Psalm XXXIV   62
    So have I heard to pierce pursuing shield. . . . .   251 Other Poems   4   349
HEARDST
    Thou heardst even now a yong man snebb me sore,. . . . . .   27 1st Eclogues 10   22
    Nay unto Thee they cry'd, but thou heardst not their cryes.. 293 Psalm XVIII   75
HEARER
    In being heard untill the hearer dye . . . .   24 1st Eclogues   9   70
HEARERS
    But ceasse worthy shepheard, nowe ceasse we to weery the
       hearers. . . . .   37 1st Eclogues 13   172
HEARETH
    But God Thy eare my crying never heareth.. . . . .   298 Psalm XXII   6
HEARING
    Nor yet, fancy so drest, do receive more plausible hearing:. 35 1st Eclogues 13   101
    Yet hearing late a fable, which did show . . . .   187 Astrophil   45   5
    O stones, o trees, learne hearing, Stella singeth. . . . .   208 A&S 3rd Song   6
    Behold me, lord, let to Thy hearing creep. . . . .   285 Psalm XIII   9
    So farr remov'd from my roaring cryes.. . . . . 298 Psalm XXII   4
    But when he calld this lord did give him hearing.. . . . .   300 Psalm XXII   58
    That hearing it the hearts contrite, ...   318 Psalm XXXIV   7
    Little hearing, speaking lesse;. . . . .   328 Psalm XXXVIII   39
    For hearing him so oft with wordes of woe. . . . .   256 Other Poems   4   537
    Sooner these than those in hearing.. . . . .   263 Other Poems   7   54
HEARKEN
    And hearken how I pray to Thee. . . . . 273 Psalm IV   5
    O, hearken to my voice, which calls on Thee, ...   274 Psalm V   3
HEARKENED
    And hearkned how, and why that I did cry,. . . . .   331 Psalm XL   4
HEARS
    Were in his dayes: which heard, one nothing heares,. . . .   24 1st Eclogues   9   76
    And yet she heares, yet I no pitty find; . . . .   186 Astrophil   44   5
    I know that He heares Thee,. . . . .   296 Psalm XX   24
    Yea heares with powers and helps of helpfull hand. . . . .   296 Psalm XX   25
    To the Lord that heares my cry.. . . . .   309 Psalm XXVIII   25
HEARSAY
    But who by hearesay speakes, and hath not fully felt . . .   153 Cert Sonnets 24   6
    With hear-say, pictures, or a window looke,. . . . .   245 Other Poems   4   139
HEART
    And feede mine eares, mine eyes, my hart in you. . . . . .   3 Lady of May   1   12
    That such a one is witnesse of my hart,. . . . .   5 Lady of May   3   14
    With armour of my hart, he cried "O vanitie, ...   16 1st Eclogues   7   62
    With seede of woes my hart brimme-full is charged. . . . .   16 1st Eclogues   7   78
    And if enchantment can a harde hart move,. . . . .   17 1st Eclogues   7   100
    My hart doth seeke another estimation. . . . .   19 1st Eclogues   7   175
    Do not thy hart, to plaintfull custome bring,. . . . . . .   22 1st Eclogues   9   3
    Like busie boyes, to winne their tutor's harte,. . . . . .   27 1st Eclogues 10   43

212

HEART   (CONTINUED)   PAGE   TITLE   LINE
   Gives happs or mishapps, ev'n as he ordreth his hearte.. . .   29 1st Eclogues 11   8
Dorus. Unto the Gods with a thanckfull heart all thankes I
   do render, ...   32 1st Eclogues 13   35
Of my owne harte, where thoughts be the temple, sighte is an
   aultar. . . . .   37 1st Eclogues 13   171
Since to my hart her shape you so did sende; . . . .   38 Arcadia II   14   3
In vaine, my Hart, now you with sight are burnd, ...   38 Arcadia II   14   5
Reason, I vaine (now you have lost my hart). . . . .   38 Arcadia II   14   9
Since so my harte is filled with that light, ...   39 Arcadia II   16   3
My tempred hart; by thee my promise sent . . . .   40 Arcadia II   18   9
Holde thou my hart, establish thou my sprights:. . . . . . .   40 Arcadia II   18   15
Dicus. The harte well set doth never shunne confession:. . .   47 2nd Eclogues 28   13
Showes, guilty harte doth deeme his state opprobrious. . . .   48 2nd Eclogues 28   18
The hart, eye, eare here onely find his treasure doth: . . .   49 2nd Eclogues 28   58
Yet is it seale, though errour, of true hart. . . . .   51 2nd Eclogues 28   104
Thus for ech change my changelesse hart I fortifie.. . . . .   51 2nd Eclogues 28   126
Sweete speaking oft a currish hart reclaimes. . . . .   60 2nd Eclogues 30   115
Her face which was more lively in my hart; . . . .   60 2nd Eclogues 30   117
With swelling hart in spite and due disdainfulnes. . . . . .   61 2nd Eclogues 30   153
But when I first did fal, what brought most fall to my hart?
   Arte. . . . .   64 2nd Eclogues 31   28
My harte doth ake, my life faints, ...   66 2nd Eclogues 32   14
Thy heated harte my seat is. . . . .   67 2nd Eclogues 32   43
Fayre hand, the fayrest pledge of fayrer harte,. . . . . . .   70 Arcadia III 35   10
Trew harte, whose trewthe dothe yeeld to trewest bande,. . .   70 Arcadia III 35   11
I waste my harte, which still newe torment tryes.. . . . . .   75 Arcadia III 43   5
My true love hath my hart, and I have his, ...   75 Arcadia III 45   1
His hart in me, keepes me and him in one,. . . . .   76 Arcadia III 45   5
My hart in him, his thoughtes and senses guides: . . . . . .   76 Arcadia III 45   6
He loves my hart, for once it was his owne:. . . . .   76 Arcadia III 45   7
His hart his wound receaved from my sight: . . . .   76 Arcadia III 45   9
My hart was wounded, with his wounded hart,. . . . .   76 Arcadia III 45   10
My true love hath my hart and I have his.. . . . .   76 Arcadia III 45   14
Giv'ne to my harte, by my fore wounded eyne: . . . .   77 Arcadia III 47   6
My harte my worde, my worde hath giv'ne my harte.. . . . . .   77 Arcadia III 47   13
Right so my thoughts, whereon my hart I feede: . . . .   78 Arcadia III 50   5
So both are yours: I, bound with gaged harte:. . . . .   79 Arcadia III 50   21
Locke up, faire liddes, the treasures of my harte: . . . . .   79 Arcadia III 51   1
Of Prince's harte quite lost the ruine strange.. . . . . . .   81 Arcadia III 55   6
But thou, sure Hope, tickle my leaping heart.. . . . .   83 Arcadia III 59   9
My harte, eyes, eares, with wonder, love, delight: . . . . .   84 Arcadia III 60   2
That still he be her head, she be his harte, ...   92 3rd Eclogues 63   48
When once this entred was, in woman's hart,. . . . .   95 3rd Eclogues 64   37
Bussing her oft, and in his hart full faine, ...   95 3rd Eclogues 64   51
A young girle's hart, to that were shame for both, ...   95 3rd Eclogues 64   59
Whereto you knowe, his honest harte were loath.. . . . . . .   95 3rd Eclogues 64   60
So may thy flockes encrease, thy deere hart glad,. . . . . .   96 3rd Eclogues 64   93
This mourning inck, in which my hart doth bleede.. . . . . .   96 3rd Eclogues 64   96
Long have I lov'd thy selfe, alas my harte . . . .   97 3rd Eclogues 64   99
For faithfull hart, cleane hands, and mouth as true: . . . .   99 3rd Eclogues 66   25
Till forste to parte, with harte and eyes even sore, ...   99 3rd Eclogues 66   39
Shrewdnes so stirres, pride so puffes up their hart, ...   104 3rd Eclogues 67   26
Which touch the father's hart with secret joy, ...   106 3rd Eclogues 67   113
Place Sorrowe's triumph on my conquered harte: . . . .   114 4th Eclogues 72   17
Since then my harte did loose his wonted place,. . . . . . .   115 4th Eclogues 72   77
Into thy hart by the sight of this Epistle I send: . . . . .   122 4th Eclogues 74   6
Right so my boiling hart, enflam'de with fire of a faire
   eye . . . .   123 4th Eclogues 74   27
Think what a world is now, think who hath altred her hart. .   124 4th Eclogues 74   76
The stile of heavie hart can never flie. . . . .   129 4th Eclogues 75   139
Since heart in chilling feare with yce is warmed:. . . . . .   135 Cert Sonnets 1   7
Thy thorne without, my thorne my heart invadeth. . . . . . .   137 Cert Sonnets 4   12
Above line repeated at following location. . . . .   137 Cert Sonnets 4   24
Heart and soule do sing in me. . . . .   139 Cert Sonnets 7   3
Above line repeated at following locations . . . .   139 Cert Sonnets 7   10
   . . . .   139 Cert Sonnets 7   13
   . . . .   140 Cert Sonnets 7   20
   . . . .   140 Cert Sonnets 7   23
   . . . .   140 Cert Sonnets 7   30
   . . . .   140 Cert Sonnets 7   33
   . . . .   140 Cert Sonnets 7   40
For oft in paine to paine my painefull heart . . . .   141 Cert Sonnets 9   3
(First sealing up my heart as pray of his) . . . .   141 Cert Sonnets 9   10
What courage strange hath caught thy caitife hart, ...   142 Cert Sonnets 10   9
That eyes weepe worse then hart in bloodie teares? . . . . .   142 Cert Sonnets 11   7
My hand doth not beare witnesse with my hart,. . . . .   146 Cert Sonnets 17   26
If either you would change your cruell hart, ...   148 Cert Sonnets 19   7
Me one to leave, with whome I leave my hart. . . . .   148 Cert Sonnets 20   6
In steade of gall, leaving to her my hart: . . . .   150 Cert Sonnets 22   28
In life of lover's hart, ...   152 Cert Sonnets 23   10
To my dying heart some pleasure, ...   155 Cert Sonnets 26   9
Thy faire haire my heart enchained,. . . . .   156 Cert Sonnets 27   2
My mistresse' Marble hart, ...   160 Cert Sonnets 30   24
"Foole," said my Muse to me, "looke in thy heart and write."   165 Astrophil   1   14
I sweare, my heart such one shall shew to thee,. . . . . . .   167 Astrophil   4   12
And, fooles, adore in temple of our hart,. . . . .   167 Astrophil   5   7
Forc'd by a tedious proofe, that Turkish hardned hart, . . .   168 Astrophil   8   2
To my close heart, where while some firebrands he did lay, .   169 Astrophil   8   13
But, foole, seekst not to get into her hart. . . . .   170 Astrophil   11   14

```
HEART                        (CONTINUED)                    PAGE   TITLE          LINE
   O no, her heart is such a Cittadell, . . . . . . . . . . . .   171  Astrophil    12    12
   Which through a bleeding heart his point did shove:. . . . .   171  Astrophil    13     6
   But ere I could flie thence, it pierc'd my heart. . . . . .   175  Astrophil    20    14
   But only Stella's eyes and Stella's hart. . . . . . . . . .   176  Astrophil    23    14
   Rich fooles there be, whose base and filthy hart . . . . . .   176  Astrophil    24     1
   Breathe out the flames which burne within my heart, . . . .   179  Astrophil    28    13
   So Stella's heart, finding what power Love brings, . . . . .   179  Astrophil    29     5
   And thus her heart escapes, but thus her eyes. . . . . . . .   179  Astrophil    29     9
   But from thy heart, while my sire charmeth thee, . . . . . .   181  Astrophil    32    13
   Hart rent thy selfe, thou doest thy selfe but right, . . . .   181  Astrophil    33     5
   A burthned hart. "How can words ease, which are. . . . . . .   181  Astrophil    34     2
   A conquest, yelden, ransackt heart to winne? . . . . . . . .   182  Astrophil    36     2
   Rich in the riches of a royall hart, . . . . . . . . . . . .   183  Astrophil    37    10
   That in my heart I offer still to thee, . . . . . . . . . .   185  Astrophil    40    13
   Faire eyes, sweet lips, deare heart, that foolish I. . . . .   186  Astrophil    43     1
   From all the world, her heart is then his rome, . . . . . .   186  Astrophil    43    13
   Such smart may pitie claime of any hart, . . . . . . . . . .   186  Astrophil    44     3
   Her heart, sweete heart, is of no Tygre's kind:. . . . . . .   186  Astrophil    44     4
   Doth make my heart give to my tongue the lie. . . . . . . .   188  Astrophil    47    14
   That through my heart their beamie darts be gone, . . . . .   189  Astrophil    48    10
   My horse, he spurres with sharpe desire my hart: . . . . . .   189  Astrophil    49    11
   Meane while my heart confers with Stella's beames, . . . . .   190  Astrophil    51    12
   My heart then quak'd, then dazled were mine eyes, . . . . .   191  Astrophil    53    10
   That his right badge is but worne in the hart: . . . . . . .   192  Astrophil    54    12
   So sweete sounds straight mine eare and heart do hit, . . .   192  Astrophil    55    13
   For late with heart most high, with eyes most low, . . . . .   196  Astrophil    63     5
   But that which once may win thy cruell hart: . . . . . . . .   198  Astrophil    64    13
   I lodg'd thee in my heart, and being blind . . . . . . . . .   198  Astrophil    65     7
   Mine eyes, my light, my heart, my life, alas, . . . . . . .   198  Astrophil    65     9
   Stolne to my heart, since last faire night, nay day, . . . .   199  Astrophil    66    10
   Of her high heart giv'n me the monarchie:. . . . . . . . . .   200  Astrophil    69    10
   So while thy beautie drawes the heart to love, . . . . . . .   201  Astrophil    71    12
   While each doth blow the fier of my hart; . . . . . . . . .   202  Astrophil    72     4
   My heart cries "ah", it burnes, mine eyes now dazled be: . .   205  Astrophil    76    11
   A double key, which opens to the heart, . . . . . . . . . .   206  Astrophil    79     6
   Thus much my heart compeld my mouth to say, . . . . . . . .   207  Astrophil    80     9
   But now spite of my heart my mouth will stay, . . . . . . .   207  Astrophil    80    10
   Breathing all blisse and sweetning to the heart, . . . . . .   207  Astrophil    81     3
   But my heart burnes, I cannot silent be. . . . . . . . . . .   207  Astrophil    81    11
   To her, where I my heart safeliest shall meet. . . . . . . .   209  Astrophil    84     6
   I see the house, my heart thy selfe containe, . . . . . . .   209  Astrophil    85     1
   Let wo gripe on my heart, shame loade mine eye. . . . . . .   212  Astrophil    86     4
   Stella food of my thoughts, hart of my hart, . . . . . . . .   222  Astrophil    87     2
   That where before hart loved and eyes did see, . . . . . . .   223  Astrophil    88    12
   In hart both sight and love now coupled be;. . . . . . . . .   223  Astrophil    88    13
   If you heare that they seeme my hart to move, . . . . . . .   225  Astrophil    91    13
   Thanke-worthiest yet when you shall breake my hart. . . . .   229  Astrophil    95    14
   That hue, whose force my hart still unto thraldome ties? . .   232  Astrophil   102     8
   As what my hart still sees thou canst not spie?. . . . . . .   235  Astrophil   105     4
   Sweete, for a while give respite to my hart, . . . . . . . .   236  Astrophil   107     5
   Through that darke fornace to my hart opprest, . . . . . . .   236  Astrophil   108     3
   I said, thou wert most sweet, sweet poison to my heart:. . .   212  A&S 5th Song        8
   For thou doest lord my heart, who am not borne thy slave, . .  214  A&S 5th Song       58
   My feete are turn'd to rootes, my hart becommeth lead, . . .   215  A&S 5th Song       77
   When my leaping hart will clime, . . . . . . . . . . . . . .   226  A&S 10th Song      26
   We change eyes, and hart for hart, . . . . . . . . . . . . .   227  A&S 10th Song      40
   From what in my hart doth ly. . . . . . . . . . . . . . . .   234  A&S 11th Song      15
   As not eares but hart did tuch:. . . . . . . . . . . . . . .   220  A&S 8th Song       70
   "If to secret of my hart, . . . . . . . . . . . . . . . . .   220  A&S 8th Song       85
   In this caitife hart to be, . . . . . . . . . . . . . . . .   221  A&S 9th Song       23
   And in thy feare knees of my heart will fold . . . . . . . .   275  Psalm V            19
   Who causeless now, yeelds me a hatefull heart, . . . . . . .   277  Psalm VII          12
   With all my heart O lord I will prayse Thee, . . . . . . . .   279  Psalm IX            1
   And sayeth in his bragging heart, . . . . . . . . . . . . .   282  Psalm X            23
   And why should he in heart so hard . . . . . . . . . . . . .   283  Psalm X            55
   Sent from false heart, on double meaning stay'd. . . . . . .   284  Psalm XII           6
   His guiltie heart with this fond thought hath fed, . . . . .   286  Psalm XIV           2
   Whose deeds of Righteous heart, whose hearty words be plain, .  287  Psalm XV            4
   All the hope of all my heart, . . . . . . . . . . . . . . .   287  Psalm XVI           2
   So my heart is fully glad, . . . . . . . . . . . . . . . . .   288  Psalm XVI          28
   With Inward secrets of my heart. . . . . . . . . . . . . . .   289  Psalm XVII          8
   Thou hast given what his heart would have, . . . . . . . . .   297  Psalm XXI           5
   Unspeakably his heart Thou glad'st, . . . . . . . . . . . .   297  Psalm XXI          23
   Whose heart with these huge flames, like wax o're heated, . .  299  Psalm XXII         33
   He that hath hurtless hands, whose inward heart is framed. . .  302  Psalm XXIV          7
   Of whom the trust lives in my heart. . . . . . . . . . . . .   304  Psalm XXV          72
   Yea sound my reines, and inmost of my heart; . . . . . . . .   305  Psalm XXVI          9
   In Truth of heart I answerd Thee, . . . . . . . . . . . . .   307  Psalm XXVII        40
   Unto Thy heart . . . . . . . . . . . . . . . . . . . . . . .   308  Psalm XXVII        65
   For when my heart with woes was torn, . . . . . . . . . . .   311  Psalm XXX           4
   Wherto my heart did give me; . . . . . . . . . . . . . . . .   315  Psalm XXXII        15
   In them whose heart. . . . . . . . . . . . . . . . . . . . .   316  Psalm XXXIII        5
   Me thinks amid my heart I heare. . . . . . . . . . . . . . .   323  Psalm XXXVI         1
   O then extend Thy loving heart . . . . . . . . . . . . . . .   324  Psalm XXXVI        27
   For God's high law in his heart dwelleth. . . . . . . . . .   326  Psalm XXXVII       79
   In my heart such grief is found. . . . . . . . . . . . . . .   328  Psalm XXXVIII      24
   My heart pants, gon is my might; . . . . . . . . . . . . . .   328  Psalm XXXVIII      28
   The more me thought my heart was hott in me; . . . . . . . .   329  Psalm XXXIX         9
   Yea lord Thy law within my heart doth stand; . . . . . . . .   331  Psalm XL           34
```

```
HEART            (CONTINUED)                          PAGE   TITLE            LINE
   My heart shall not conceale. . . . . . . . . . . . . . . . .   331 Psalm XL            39
   My life-maintaining heart, . . . . . . . . . . . . . . . . .   332 Psalm XL            49
   The secrets of my heart, . . . . . . . . . . . . . . . . . .   333 Psalm XLI           30
   My heart melts remembring so,. . . . . . . . . . . . . . . .   334 Psalm XLII          13
   Why should grief my heart devower, . . . . . . . . . . . . .   335 Psalm XLII          43
   W. What seale? D. My hart deepe graven. W. Who made the band
      so fast?. . . . . . . . . . . . . . . . . . . . . . . . .   343 Possibly      1     27
   As Strephon's eare and heart to Klaius bent: . . . . . . . .   242 Other Poems   4     28
   Yet not so wise, as of unstained harte:. . . . . . . . . . .   243 Other Poems   4     35
   To yeeld she found hir noble heart did ake:. . . . . . . . .   245 Other Poems   4    125
   And streight for failing, grav'd it in his heart:. . . . . .   247 Other Poems   4    186
   The heav'n-love lodestone drew thy iron hart . . . . . . . .   248 Other Poems   4    224
   But on his eies his heart did sacrifise. . . . . . . . . . .   251 Other Poems   4    368
   To feele the panting heart, which through hir syde . . . . .   252 Other Poems   4    405
   "Alas! what weights are these that lode my heart!. . . . . .   253 Other Poems   4    441
   While I in heart my will write ere I die.. . . . . . . . . .   255 Other Poems   4    499
   Come shepheard's boy, let now thy heart be bowd. . . . . . .   255 Other Poems   4    510
   With heart as carefull, as with carelesse grace, . . . . . .   255 Other Poems   4    522
   Which thus breath'd out with earthquake of his hart. . . . .   256 Other Poems   4    544
   Within my heart you be . . . . . . . . . . . . . . . . . . .   261 Other Poems   6     27
   Of you, to my hart giveth. . . . . . . . . . . . . . . . . .   261 Other Poems   6     52
   Friendship true in hart assured, . . . . . . . . . . . . . .   263 Other Poems   7     35
HEART-BOUND
   As heart-bound slaves: and happy then embrace. . . . . . . .   252 Other Poems   4    391
HEARTBROKEN
   Hart-broken so, that molehilles seeme high mountaines, . . .   111 4th Eclogues 71     23
HEART'S
   To aire of sighes, sighes to the harte's fire turne, . . . .    19 1st Eclogues  7    154
   Thus to betray my hart's fort, . . . . . . . . . . . . . . .   154 Cert Sonnets 25     10
   That all thy hurts in my hart's wracke I reede;. . . . . . .   227 Astrophil     93     13
   But on god's law his heart's delight doth bind,. . . . . . .   270 Psalm I              5
   Where I have found more heart's delight. . . . . . . . . . .   274 Psalm IV            28
   Thee will I love, O Lord, with all my heart's delight, . . .   290 Psalm XVIII          1
   And my heart's meditation, . . . . . . . . . . . . . . . . .   295 Psalm XIX           62
   The fulness of thy own heart's lusting;. . . . . . . . . . .   324 Psalm XXXVII        10
HEARTS
   Where eares be burnt, eyes dazled, harts opprest?. . . . . .     3 Lady of May   1      6
   In those weake harts that his advice receave.. . . . . . . .    21 1st Eclogues  8     34
   To swelling harts he shines in honour's fire:. . . . . . . .    21 1st Eclogues  8     38
   And weakest harts to constant temper brought.. . . . . . . .    22 1st Eclogues  9     15
   Such hartes of brasse, wise heads, and garments trim . . . .    24 1st Eclogues  9     75
   That men's harts be thy seate and endlesse fame be thy
      servant. . . . . . . . . . . . . . . . . . . . . . . . .    36 1st Eclogues 13    148
   But so our hartes keepe downe, with vice they be not
      stainde . . . . . . . . . . . . . . . . . . . . . . . .    45 Arcadia II   26     14
   Those beames that set so many harts on fire? . . . . . . . .    59 2nd Eclogues 30     84
   Where open hartes do holde so constant place,. . . . . . . .    93 3rd Eclogues 63     88
   (For envie harbreth most in feeblest hartes) . . . . . . . .   100 3rd Eclogues 66     58
   Desire's best meane, harvest of hartes affected, . . . . . .   108 Arcadia IV   69      2
   Who justly make our hearts the seates of sorow?. . . . . . .   109 Arcadia IV   70      8
   A yelling voice, and heartes compos'd of sorow,. . . . . . .   109 Arcadia IV   70     27
   Fear'st not a face that oft whole harts devowres,. . . . . .   142 Cert Sonnets 10     10
   In tender harts, small things engender hate: . . . . . . . .   146 Cert Sonnets 17     17
   Whose hearts are set on measuring a verse: . . . . . . . . .   146 Cert Sonnets 17     32
   If that be sinne which in fixt hearts doth breed . . . . . .   172 Astrophil    14     12
   How Holland hearts, now so good townes be lost,. . . . . . .   180 Astrophil    30      7
   Not this faire outside, which our hearts doth move.. . . . .   190 Astrophil    52      8
   The Oratour so farre men's harts doth bind,. . . . . . . . .   193 Astrophil    58      2
   That presence, which doth give darke hearts a living light:.   205 Astrophil    77      3
   Thou English murdring theefe, wilt have harts for thy pray:.   214 A&S 5th Song        50
   Till their harts had ended talking.. . . . . . . . . . . . .   218 A&S 8th Song        24
   Talk with your hearts, and yet be still. . . . . . . . . . .   273 Psalm IV            18
   Thou righteous proofes to hearts, and reines dost send,. . .   277 Psalm VII           28
   To hearts that hate all lying. . . . . . . . . . . . . . . .   284 Psalm XI             8
   Which if it last, Woe to all simple Hearts.. . . . . . . . .   285 Psalm XII           27
   And yet their high hearts look so low. . . . . . . . . . . .   290 Psalm XVII          31
   My name their eares, their eares their hearts to me
      enchaine, . . . . . . . . . . . . . . . . . . . . . . . .   293 Psalm XVIII         80
   When in hearts they malice meane.. . . . . . . . . . . . . .   309 Psalm XXVIII        15
   Your hearts with clearness armed.. . . . . . . . . . . . . .   316 Psalm XXXII         42
   Since he their hearts doth frame,. . . . . . . . . . . . . .   317 Psalm XXXIII        55
   Our hearts sure shall enjoy. . . . . . . . . . . . . . . . .   318 Psalm XXXIII        79
   That hearing it the hearts contrite, . . . . . . . . . . . .   318 Psalm XXXIV          7
   Let them not, Lord, within their hearts thus say:. . . . . .   323 Psalm XXXV          61
   Their swords shall their own hearts embrew.. . . . . . . . .   325 Psalm XXXVII        40
   Which many seeing hearts shall rayse . . . . . . . . . . . .   331 Psalm XL            13
   But fill their hearts with joy, who bend their wayes . . . .   332 Psalm XL            61
   Thus proud and fierce unto the hearts he stept . . . . . . .   246 Other Poems   4    157
   To downe proud hearts that would not willing dye.. . . . . .   250 Other Poems   4    304
   Joyne hearts and hands, so let it be,. . . . . . . . . . . .   260 Other Poems   6      5
   Above line repeated at following locations . . . . . . . . .   260 Other Poems   6     11
      . . . . . . . . . . . . . . . . . . . . . . . . . . . . .   260 Other Poems   6     17
      . . . . . . . . . . . . . . . . . . . . . . . . . . . . .   260 Other Poems   6     23
      . . . . . . . . . . . . . . . . . . . . . . . . . . . . .   261 Other Poems   6     29
      . . . . . . . . . . . . . . . . . . . . . . . . . . . . .   261 Other Poems   6     35
      . . . . . . . . . . . . . . . . . . . . . . . . . . . . .   261 Other Poems   6     41
      . . . . . . . . . . . . . . . . . . . . . . . . . . . . .   261 Other Poems   6     47
      . . . . . . . . . . . . . . . . . . . . . . . . . . . . .   261 Other Poems   6     53
```

215

```
HEART-STRINGS                                                    PAGE    TITLE            LINE
    On Cupid's bow how are my heart-strings bent,. . . . . . . . 174  Astrophil    19     1
HEARTY
    If mine eyes can speake to doo harty errande,. . . . . . . .  30  1st Eclogues 12     1
    But if eyes can speake to doo harty errande, . . . . . . . .  31  1st Eclogues 12    25
    Gratefulnes, sweetnes, holy love, hartie regard) . . . . . . 122  4th Eclogues 74    10
    Can those eyes, that of eyes drownd in most harty flowing
        teares,. . . . . . . . . . . . . . . . . . . . . . . . . 122  4th Eclogues 74    15
    Whose deeds of Righteous heart, whose hearty words be plain, 287  Psalm XV            4
    Give hearty thanks to him on high, . . . . . . . . . . . . . 318  Psalm XXXIV         2
HEAT
    And yet his outward heate our teares would quench, but an
        inward . . . . . . . . . . . . . . . . . . . . . . . . .  32  1st Eclogues 13    31
    Shall such morning deaws be an ease to the heate of a love's
        fire? . . . . . . . . . . . . . . . . . . . . . . . . .   34  1st Eclogues 13    88
    Wyth two strange fires of equall heate possest,. . . . . . .  42  Arcadia II   22     1
    But when I did come neere with heate and hope, . . . . . . .  54  2nd Eclogues 29    88
    Keeping that forme, though void of wonted heate: . . . . . . 151  Cert Sonnets 22    48
    Where that heat of all heates springeth, . . . . . . . . . . 155  Cert Sonnets 26     7
    Effects of lively heat, must needs in nature grow. . . . . . 169  Astrophil     8    11
    But shining forth of heate in his chiefe pride;. . . . . . . 176  Astrophil    22     4
    While Thou art in the heat of thy displeasure: . . . . . . . 276  Psalm VI            2
    His heat to all he throweth. . . . . . . . . . . . . . . . . 294  Psalm XIX          28
    That of the stroke, the heat, and knott of love, . . . . . . 344  Possibly      2     3
    Whose boiling heat encreased as she wept:. . . . . . . . . . 246  Other Poems   4   155
    But as his heate with running did augment, . . . . . . . . . 249  Other Poems   4   297
    Where with heate oppreste I was, . . . . . . . . . . . . . . 262  Other Poems   7     2
HEATED
    Thy heated harte my seat is. . . . . . . . . . . . . . . . .  67  2nd Eclogues 32    43
HEATHEN
    The Heathen for thy Child's right, and will thy realme
        extend . . . . . . . . . . . . . . . . . . . . . . . . . 271  Psalm II           19
    That by sharp proofes, the heathen themselves may see. . . . 281  Psalm IX           64
    He doth heath'n counsell breake, . . . . . . . . . . . . . . 317  Psalm XXXIII       34
HEATHENISH
    What ayles this heathenish rage? What do theis people meane. 271  Psalm II            1
HEATHENY
    Who hast the heath'ny folk destroyd. . . . . . . . . . . . . 283  Psalm X            71
HEATS
    Nought could impart such heates to friendly mind. . . . . . .  51  2nd Eclogues 28   105
    Where that heat of all heates springeth, . . . . . . . . . . 155  Cert Sonnets 26     7
HEAVE
    In nature's pride your heads to heav'nwarde heave, . . . . .  77  Arcadia III  49     2
HEAVED
    Dicus. Thy words well voic'd, well gra'ste had almost heaved
        me. . . . . . . . . . . . . . . . . . . . . . . . . . . .  48  2nd Eclogues 28   31
HEAVEN
    From heav'nly throne to her heav'n use digression? . . . . .  15  1st Eclogues  7    45
    His horned head doth seeme the heaven to spight: . . . . . .  21  1st Eclogues  8    29
    Earth, sea, ayre, fire, heav'n, hell, and gastly sprite. . .  23  1st Eclogues  9    40
    That nothing winnes the heaven, but what doth earth forsake.  45  Arcadia II   26    16
    Whose onely face the little heaven is, . . . . . . . . . . .  51  2nd Eclogues 28   107
    That after death, to heav'n in woods' resound, . . . . . . .  56  2nd Eclogues 29   133
    Erona dye? O heaven (if heaven there be) . . . . . . . . . .  58  2nd Eclogues 30    59
    Of rarest price, both heav'n and earth her bower. . . . . . .  59  2nd Eclogues 30   100
    Those secrett joyes, which heaven to me emparte, . . . . . .  70  Arcadia III  35    14
    She heav'n on earth with beauties doth preserve. . . . . . .  72  Arcadia III  38     8
    Godnes the penne, heaven paper is,. . . . . . . . . . . . . .  90  Arcadia III  62   142
    Her Horned face in Heaven dothe Range, . . . . . . . . . . .  86  Arcadia III  62 V 12
    O heav'n awake shewe forth thy stately face, . . . . . . . .  91  3rd Eclogues 63    10
    Beyond the heaven, far more beyond your witts. . . . . . . .  99  3rd Eclogues 66    28
    The darkened heav'n my soule which nought can see; . . . . . 114  4th Eclogues 72    35
    Of heaven, of earth, of hell, of time and place was come.. . 118  4th Eclogues 73    62
    With age's force decay'd, yet once the heaven was his. . . . 120  4th Eclogues 73   124
    And with that cursed curse away to heaven they fled, . . . . 121  4th Eclogues 73   177
    Ah, that, that do I not conceive; to the heaven when a mouse
        climes. . . . . . . . . . . . . . . . . . . . . . . . . 122  4th Eclogues 74    21
    They that heav'n have knowne, do say . . . . . . . . . . . . 140  Cert Sonnets  7    24
    So then since that heaven remaineth, . . . . . . . . . . . . 140  Cert Sonnets  7    28
    Thou paine, thou hated paine, from heav'n exilde,. . . . . . 141  Cert Sonnets 10     4
    In whose sweete heav'n Angels of high thoughts swarme? . . . 142  Cert Sonnets 10     8
    A heaven on earth, or earth that heaven containes: . . . . . 151  Cert Sonnets 22    68
    This heaven in it doth binde.. . . . . . . . . . . . . . . . 152  Cert Sonnets 23    24
    So that thee like heaven I loved.. . . . . . . . . . . . . . 156  Cert Sonnets 27     4
    Who seeketh heav'n and comes of heav'nly breath. . . . . . . 144  Cert Sonnets 32    12
    That when the heav'n to thee his best displayes, . . . . . . 170  Astrophil    11     3
    Of all those goods, which heav'n to me hath lent:. . . . . . 173  Astrophil    18     4
    In highest way of heav'n the Sunne did ride, . . . . . . . . 175  Astrophil    22     1
    Yet to those fooles heav'n such wit doth impart, . . . . . . 177  Astrophil    24     5
    That heav'n of joyes throwes onely downe on me . . . . . . . 195  Astrophil    60     3
    But when mine eyes backe to their heav'n did move, . . . . . 199  Astrophil    66    13
    World of my wealth, and heav'n of my delight.. . . . . . . . 200  Astrophil    68     4
    As consterd in true speech, the name of heav'n it beares,. . 205  Astrophil    77    11
    No doome should make one's heav'n become his hell. . . . . . 212  Astrophil    86    14
    Of such heaven stuffe, to cloath so heavenly mynde.. . . . . 232  Astrophil   101    14
    Onely unto the heav'n of Stella's face,. . . . . . . . . . . 235  Astrophil   105    17
    Only for you the heav'n forgate all measure. . . . . . . . . 197  A&S 1st Song        8
    Earth gave that Love, heav'n I trow Love refineth: . . . . . 209  A&S 3rd Song       11
    For thy face tempts my soule to leave the heav'n for thee, . 215  A&S 5th Song       82
    The throne of Heav'n is only His:. . . . . . . . . . . . . . 284  Psalm XI           14
```

```
HEAVEN                       (CONTINUED)                        PAGE     TITLE            LINE
   Do works which earth corrupt and Heaven hates, . . . . . . .  286 Psalm XIV              5
   His race is even from ends of heaven . . . . . . . . . . . .  294 Psalm XIX             25
   In heaven his trust hath layed;. . . . . . . . . . . . . . .  297 Psalm XXI             26
   His heels grow'n proud did seme at heav'n to shake.. . . . .  248 Other Poems     4    261
   And thought it heav'n so to be drawn to hell.. . . . . . . .  250 Other Poems     4    312
   Whose foote doth set a heav'n on cursed thee, . . . . . . .   256 Other Poems     5     19
HEAVEN-LOVE
   The heav'n-love lodestone drew thy iron hart.. . . . . . . .  248 Other Poems     4    224
HEAVENLY
   Her haire pure Crapal-stone; her mouth O heavenly wyde;. . .   12 Arcadia I        3     11
   From heav'nly throne to her heav'n use digression? . . . . .   15 1st Eclogues     7     45
   For proofe of man, who sprong of heav'nly fire . . . . . . .   25 1st Eclogues     9    100
   O heavenly soule, in humaine shape conteind: . . . . . . . .   38 Arcadia II      15      2
   O Chastitie, the chiefe of heavenly lightes, . . . . . . . .   40 Arcadia II      18     13
   R.p. Then let us both to heavenly rules give place,. . . . .   47 2nd Eclogues    27     41
   Dorus. If Sunnie beames shame heav'nly habitation; . . . . .   48 2nd Eclogues    28     22
   What great name may I give to so heav'nly a woman? A
      woe-man . . . . . . . . . . . . . . . . . . . . . . . . .   64 2nd Eclogues    31     37
   "Nought can reason availe in heav'nly matters".. . . . . . .   68 2nd Eclogues    33     26
   Where senses do behold th'order of heav'nly hoste, . . . . .   68 2nd Eclogues    34      5
   The high conceits thy heav'nly wisedomes breed . . . . . . .   72 Arcadia III     38      2
   In earthly clothes enclosde a heavenly sparke. . . . . . . .   80 Arcadia III     52     10
   And arches be to heavenly lids, . . . . . . . . . . . . . .    86 Arcadia III     62     13
   But since you will, part of my heav'nly fire . . . . . . . .  100 3rd Eclogues    66     75
   O heavenlie huntresse of the savage mountaines,. . . . . . .  111 4th Eclogues    71      8
   Now was our heav'nly vaulte deprived of the light. . . . . .  116 4th Eclogues    73      1
   Which heav'nly purest gifts defile in muddy cares. . . . . .  117 4th Eclogues    73     18
   (Which made of heav'nly stuffe no mortal chaunge doth bynde)  117 4th Eclogues    73     32
   Those lampes of heav'nly fire to fixed motion bound, . . . .  118 4th Eclogues    73     43
   Then may I hope t'atchieve grace of a heavenly tiger.. . . .  122 4th Eclogues    74     22
   Unto the earth, by the hurt of this her heavenly jewell. . .  124 4th Eclogues    74     62
   O my heavens for taste by thie heavenly pleasure,. . . . . .  138 Cert Sonnets     5      2
   Above line repeated at following location. . . . . . . . . .  138 Cert Sonnets     5     26
   They fit for heavenly places,. . . . . . . . . . . . . . . .  152 Cert Sonnets    23     23
   With violence of heav'nly. . . . . . . . . . . . . . . . . .  154 Cert Sonnets    25      5
   Words, o words of heavenlie knowledge, . . . . . . . . . . .  157 Cert Sonnets    27     35
   Who seeketh heav'n and comes of heav'nly breath. . . . . . .  144 Cert Sonnets    32     12
   The inward light: and that the heavenly part . . . . . . . .  167 Astrophil        5      2
   Of force of heav'nly beames, infusing hellish paine: . . . .  167 Astrophil        6      3
   The windowes now through which this heav'nly guest . . . . .  169 Astrophil        9      9
   As that sweete blacke which vailes the heav'nly eye: . . . .  175 Astrophil       20      7
   What, may it be that even in heav'nly place. . . . . . . . .  180 Astrophil       31      3
   I find how heav'nly day wretch I did misse.. . . . . . . . .  181 Astrophil       33      4
   Stella lookt on, and from her heavenly face. . . . . . . . .  185 Astrophil       41     13
   The heav'nly nature of that place is such, . . . . . . . . .  187 Astrophil       44     12
   Of Atlas tyr'd, your wisedome's heav'nly sway. . . . . . . .  190 Astrophil       51      8
   That vertuous soule, sure heire of heav'nly blisse:. . . . .  190 Astrophil       52      7
   But failst thou not in phrase so heav'nly hie? . . . . . . .  199 Astrophil       67      6
   My Muse may well grudge at my heav'nly joy,. . . . . . . . .  201 Astrophil       70      1
   O heav'nly foole, thy most kisse-worthie face, . . . . . . .  203 Astrophil       73     12
   Whence words, not words, but heav'nly graces slide.. . . . .  206 Astrophil       80      4
   From heavenly standing hits each mortall wight.. . . . . . .  229 Astrophil       97      4
   Or if such heavenly signes must prove annoy, . . . . . . . .  231 Astrophil      100     13
   Of such heaven stuffe, to cloath so heavenly mynde.. . . . .  232 Astrophil      101     14
   Have I caught my heav'nly jewell, . . . . . . . . . . . . .   202 A&S 2nd Song            1
   And then, a heav'nly child, gave her Ambrosian pap:. . . . .  213 A&S 5th Song           26
   With heavenly hew and grace, . . . . . . . . . . . . . . . .  216 A&S 6th Song           20
   The heavenly harmonies;. . . . . . . . . . . . . . . . . . .  216 A&S 6th Song           21
   O let them see these heavenly beames, and in faire letters
      reede. . . . . . . . . . . . . . . . . . . . . . . . . .   217 A&S 7th Song           11
   Stella starre of heavenly fier,. . . . . . . . . . . . . . .  218 A&S 8th Song           31
   Shall a heavenly grace want pitty?". . . . . . . . . . . . .  219 A&S 8th Song           64
   Heavenly Stella meete with you,. . . . . . . . . . . . . . .  222 A&S 9th Song           48
   A heavn'ly story?. . . . . . . . . . . . . . . . . . . . . .  276 Psalm VI              16
   According to his heavnly equity. . . . . . . . . . . . . . .  278 Psalm VII             47
   That I, even I of heavnly comfort full,. . . . . . . . . . .  280 Psalm IX              43
   Shall not be scrap'd from out of heavnly scoar:. . . . . . .  281 Psalm IX              57
   Lift up Thy heavnly hand . . . . . . . . . . . . . . . . . .  282 Psalm X               51
   Thou openest heavnly Doore . . . . . . . . . . . . . . . . .  283 Psalm X               73
   Then hayle, then firie coales, then thundred heavnly sire, .  291 Psalm XVIII           27
   The heavnly Frame sets forth the Fame. . . . . . . . . . . .  293 Psalm XIX              1
   With heavnly strength Thy earthly strength to prop.. . . . .  295 Psalm XX              10
   From heavnly holy land . . . . . . . . . . . . . . . . . . .  296 Psalm XX              23
   His Word made heavnly Coast, . . . . . . . . . . . . . . . .  316 Psalm XXXIII          22
   So his high heavnly face . . . . . . . . . . . . . . . . . .  320 Psalm XXXIV           57
   Do well and trust on heavnly power,. . . . . . . . . . . . .  324 Psalm XXXVII           7
   He is upheld by heavnly hand.. . . . . . . . . . . . . . . .  326 Psalm XXXVII          60
   His tongue of heavnly judgments telleth, . . . . . . . . . .  326 Psalm XXXVII          78
   D. Her heavenly looks, which more and more do give me cause
      to crave.. . . . . . . . . . . . . . . . . . . . . . . .   344 Possibly         1     32
   These doubting clouds ore-casting heav'nly braine, . . . . .  245 Other Poems      4    127
   That from those eies where heav'nly apples bene, . . . . . .  253 Other Poems      4    450
HEAVENLY-DEWED
   Her heav'nly-dewed tongue to garde.. . . . . . . . . . . . .   87 Arcadia III     62     44
HEAVEN'S
   Or seeke heavn's course, or heavn's inside to see: . . . . .  169 Astrophil       10      5
   Cannot heavn's food, once felt, keepe stomakes free. . . . .  223 Astrophil       88      7
HEAVENS
   No, though the heav'ns for high attempts have blamed me, . .   15 1st Eclogues     7     22
```

217

HEAVENS	(CONTINUED)	PAGE	TITLE	LINE
Dorus. Lady, reservd by the heav'ns to do pastors' company honnor,		31	1st Eclogues 13	1
Unto the heav'ns? our wings be too short; th' earth thinks us a burden;		32	1st Eclogues 13	29
But sometimes to the woods, sometimes to the heavens do decyphire,		35	1st Eclogues 13	111
O then it shines; then are the heav'ns distributed,		49	2nd Eclogues 28	65
What greater ills have now the heavens in store,		57	2nd Eclogues 30	6
Ods? what an ods is there since them to the heav'ns I prefer Erre..		65	2nd Eclogues 31	48
Unto my woes the hatefull heavens do sende,		73	Arcadia III 40	2
The heavens conspir'd, to make my vitall sparke.		73	Arcadia III 40	3
The earth is deckt with flowers, the heav'ns displaid,		93	3rd Eclogues 63	91
The heav'ns doo not good haps in handfuls bring,		105	3rd Eclogues 67	61
I would the earth, I would the heavens sell.		116	4th Eclogues 72	93
Of all those Graces' giftes the heavens have ever lent..		119	4th Eclogues 73	86
Nay to the heav'ns your just complayninges sende,		126	4th Eclogues 75	37
O my heavens for taste by thie heavenly pleasure,		138	Cert Sonnets 5	2
Above line repeated at following location.		138	Cert Sonnets 5	26
Heav'ns envy not at my high triumphing:		196	Astrophil 63	10
Thou then whom partiall heavens conspir'd in one to frame,		213	A&S 5th Song	19
Stella whom o heavens do blesse,		221	A&S 9th Song	18
But He shall them deride who by the heavns is borne,		271	Psalm II	9
Upon the heavns engrav'n the story..		278	Psalm VIII	4
When I upon the Heav'ns do look.		278	Psalm VIII	9
He bow'd the heav'ns, and from the bow'd heav'ns did discend		291	Psalm XVIII	20
Lord, how the heav'ns thy mercy fills,		323	Psalm XXXVI	13
HEAVENWARD				
In nature's pride your heads to heav'nwarde heave,		77	Arcadia III 49	2
HEAVINESS				
Slow heavinesse in both holds one degree,		229	Astrophil 96	6
My life with heavyness, my yeares with moane		312	Psalm XXXI	28
HEAVY				
But heavy was her pace, and such a meagre cheere,		118	4th Eclogues 73	69
The stile of heavie hart can never flie.		129	4th Eclogues 75	139
That heavie earth, not fierie sprites may plaine?		142	Cert Sonnets 11	6
This night while sleepe begins with heavy wings.		183	Astrophil 38	1
Move not thy heavy grace, thou shalt in me,		184	Astrophil 39	13
From out thy heavy mould, that inbent eyes		228	Astrophil 94	3
Would faine drive cloudes from out my heavy cheere..		230	Astrophil 97	11
Make in my heavy mould new thoughts to grow:		236	Astrophil 106	11
On wretched mee thy heavy hand,		315	Psalm XXXII	11
HECTOR				
The life, the death of Hector,		66	2nd Eclogues 32	23
HEDGED				
Though strongly hedg'd of bloudy Lyon's pawes,		204	Astrophil 75	10
HEED				
But still take heede least thou thy selfe submit		4	Lady of May 2	23
O heards take heed; for I a woolfe have found;		50	2nd Eclogues 28	83
Boulon. O man, take heed, how thou the Gods do move.		59	2nd Eclogues 30	65
Take heed therefore, how you ensue that trade,		97	3rd Eclogues 64	123
"O beasts, take heed what you of me desire..		100	3rd Eclogues 66	72
Be you still faire, honourd by publike heed,		209	Astrophil 84	9
HEEDFUL				
Ffayre, thorow fayre strykes of heedefull Looke.		88	Arcadia III 62 V	70
HEEDING				
Heeding himselfe, cares not how fellow doe,		248	Other Poems 4	237
HEEDS				
But never heeds the fruit of writer's mind:		170	Astrophil 11	8
HEELS				
And when that time is paste, death holdes his heeles..		28	1st Eclogues 10	51
My heeles and plants thou didst from stumbling slip sustaine ,		292	Psalm XVIII	67
His heels grow'n proud did seme at heav'n to shake..		248	Other Poems 4	261
HEIGHT				
Her peereles height my minde to high erection.		16	1st Eclogues 7	70
O descende for a while, from this greate height to behold me		36	1st Eclogues 13	149
Alas, if from the height of Vertue's throne,		184	Astrophil 40	5
Come then my Muse, shew thou height of delight		201	Astrophil 70	9
The height of honor in the kindly badge of shame?		232	Astrophil 102	3
Yea noble hight of Rocky Hill.		307	Psalm XXVII	28
A Shepheard's tale no height of stile desires.		242	Other Poems 4	1
HEIR				
Who is an heire of many hundred sheep.		18	1st Eclogues 7	117
That vertuous soule, sure heire of heav'nly blisse:		190	Astrophil 52	7
And not content to be Perfection's heire		201	Astrophil 71	9
The Fish of Sea the Native heire,		279	Psalm VIII	30
To Nature's heir, the faire Urania, pay,		251	Other Poems 4	364
HELD				
No stile is held for base, where Love well named is:		14	1st Eclogues 7	4
Which is helde in love, love it is, that hath joynde		31	1st Eclogues 12	23
Pas. As in a glasse I held she once did looke,		55	2nd Eclogues 29	114
Where death is feard, and life is held with paine.		57	2nd Eclogues 30	19
Harde to be gott, but got constant, to be helde like steeles Eeles..		65	2nd Eclogues 31	42
Held, pearst, possest, my judgement, sence, and will,		84	Arcadia III 60	6
This crowne of amber faire (an amber crowne she held).		120	4th Eclogues 73	141
Nor held in evill, nor suffered to be sound,		144	Cert Sonnets 15	8

HELD   (CONTINUED)   PAGE   TITLE   LINE
  Whose talents held young Ganimed above:. . . . . 171 Astrophil   13   4
  Was held, in opend sense it flies away,. . . . .   184 Astrophil   38   10
  I held for sure that I should never slyde. . . . .   305 Psalm XXVI   6
HELEN
  No lovely Paris made thy Hellen his: . . . .   181 Astrophil   33   6
HELL
  Earth, sea, ayre, fire, heav'n, hell, and gastly sprite. . . 23 1st Eclogues   9   40
  My brest to swords, my soule to hell have solde. . . . . .   50 2nd Eclogues 28   80
  Dev'lls? if in hell such dev'lls do abide, to the hells I do
    go. Go. . . . .   65 2nd Eclogues 31   50
  Who seekes to knowe, acquaintes hym self with hell;. . . . . 71 Arcadia III   36   16
  And you poore beastes, in patience bide your hell, ... 103 3rd Eclogues 66 153
  In earthly fetters feele a lasting hell. . . . .   116 4th Eclogues 72   90
  Klaius. In earthly fetters feele a lasting hell. . . . . .   116 4th Eclogues 72   91
  Of heaven, of earth, of hell, of time and place was come.. . 118 4th Eclogues 73   62
  The smoke of hell, the monster called paine, ...   140 Cert Sonnets   8   2
  While with a feeling skill I paint my hell.. . . . .   166 Astrophil   2   14
  And this I sweare by blackest brooke of hell,. . . . . . .   204 Astrophil   74   7
  No doome should make one's heav'n become his hell. . . . .   212 Astrophil   86   14
  As can refresh the hell where my soule fries.. . . . . . .   231 Astrophil   100   8
  And thy words of refuse, do powre even hell on mee:. . . .   215 A&S 5th Song   83
  The two that in mid place, Hell called were,. . . . . . .   248 Other Poems   4 227
  To catch of them, and them to hell to beare, ...   248 Other Poems   4 229
  That they, aswell as they, Hell may supplie: . . . .   248 Other Poems   4 230
  Faire Nous with Pas the lott to hell did sende:. . . . . .   248 Other Poems   4 244
  Pas thought it hell, while he was Cosma fro. . . . .   248 Other Poems   4 245
  Geron with Uran were condemn'd to hell.. . . . .   249 Other Poems   4 264
  The two in hell did toward Cosma frame,. . . . .   249 Other Poems   4 267
  And thought it heav'n so to be drawn to hell.. . . . . . .   250 Other Poems   4 312
  To hell he goes, and Nous with him must dwell. . . . . . .   250 Other Poems   4 313
  Who would be caught, that she should go to hell: . . . . .   250 Other Poems   4 315
  Which made his Strephon think himself in hell.. . . . . .   256 Other Poems   4 540
HELL-DRIVEN
  Let not mine eyes be hel-driv'n from that light: . . . . .   188 Astrophil   48   7
HELLISH
  The furious inward griefes with hellish wailing: . . . . .   109 Arcadia IV   70   33
  Of force of heav'nly beames, infusing hellish paine: . . .   167 Astrophil   6   3
  Betweene the jawes of hellish Jealousie. . . . .   205 Astrophil   78   4
  Let me, fed with hellish anguish,. . . . .   220 A&S 8th Song   79
  When Wycked soules be turn'd to hellish paine, ...   281 Psalm IX   53
HELLS
  Dev'lls? if in hell such dev'lls do abide, to the hells I do
    go. Go. . . . .   65 2nd Eclogues 31   50
HELM
  Jove on his helme the thunderbolt did reare. . . . .   171 Astrophil   13   8
HELP
  The gods must help, and pretious things must serve to shew
    her shape. . . . .   12 Arcadia I   3   4
  Thy pipe, o Pan, shall helpe, though I sing sorilie. . . .   15 1st Eclogues   7   27
  Nor helpe by life or death who living dyes.. . . . .   18 1st Eclogues   7 146
  Nature worketh enough with a small help for the revealing. . 33 1st Eclogues 13   61
  Let not a puppet abuse thy sprite, Kings' Crownes do not
    helpe them . . . .   34 1st Eclogues 13   84
  If neither by that helpe, thou canst clime up to thy fancie. 34 1st Eclogues 13 100
  (Opprest with ruinouse conceites) by the helpe of an
    outcrye. . . . .   35 1st Eclogues 13 109
  Cyprus promiseth helpe, but a helpe where comes no
    recomforte.. . . . .   35 1st Eclogues 13 119
  A blooddy helpe with blood to save:. . . . .   44 Arcadia II   25   2
  R. O sacred Reason, helpe our vertuous toiles. . . . . . .   46 2nd Eclogues 27   23
  Or if sheepe's cries can helpe the Sunne's owne braverie,. . 48 2nd Eclogues 28   25
  To helpe her praise, who decks me in her slaverie. . . . .   48 2nd Eclogues 28   27
  To helpe, or hurt in thee her owne infection.. . . . . . .   49 2nd Eclogues 28   54
  Thou soone may have some helpe, or change of passion.. . .   50 2nd Eclogues 28   98
  Unto my pipe, O Nimphes, nowe helpe my pipe, ...   54 2nd Eclogues 29   73
  With Echoe's help, shall "Cosma, Cosma" flie.. . . . . . .   56 2nd Eclogues 29 134
  Plangus must live some helpe for her to trie . . . .   58 2nd Eclogues 30   56
  Of her I will demaund helpe".. . . . .   67 2nd Eclogues 32   49
  Thus weakned by my selfe, no helpe remaineth.. . . . . . .   68 2nd Eclogues 33   17
  To have his harmes with wisdome's helpe redrest. . . . . .   75 Arcadia III   44   4
  In speedie helpe, thanke worthie frends appeare. . . . . .   81 Arcadia III   53   14
  Her minde amaz'de can neither's helpe applie.. . . . . . .   81 Arcadia III   54   4
  But with thy cheerefull presence helpe to grace. . . . . .   91 3rd Eclogues 63   12
  If you helpe not our wedlocke will be staind". . . . . . .   95 3rd Eclogues 64   46
  Witnesse his wrong which by thy helpe is eased:. . . . . .   108 Arcadia IV   69   11
  Then decke me as thine owne: thy helpe I borowe, ...   114 4th Eclogues 72   28
  Are all in me: what helpe then can I trie? . . . .   114 4th Eclogues 72   43
  Her haire, which by the helpe of painter's cunning, shinde.. 118 4th Eclogues 73   74
  That thou shalt never dare seeke helpe of wretched case".. . 121 4th Eclogues 73 176
  And now fully beleeves helpe to be quite perished; . . . .   122 4th Eclogues 74   2
  Her helpe to this, this justest cause of plaint. . . . . .   125 4th Eclogues 75   14
  By shame and griefe, helpe, helpe me to lament . . . . . .   126 4th Eclogues 75   62
  We Nature's workes doo helpe, she us defaces.. . . . . . .   127 4th Eclogues 75   93
  And can crie helpe with nought but grones and starts:. . .   136 Cert Sonnets   2   12
  And so no helpe gainst envy of those powers? . . . .   142 Cert Sonnets 10   12
  But hopes to gaine some helpe by mounting hie, ...   144 Cert Sonnets 15   3
  By your good helpe, or in my selfe to finde. . . . .   148 Cert Sonnets 19   12
  Use all to helpe his other conquerings:. . . . .   179 Astrophil   29   8
  Could hope by Cupid's helpe on you to pray;. . . . .   186 Astrophil   43   2

HELP   (CONTINUED)   PAGE   TITLE   LINE

Who for long faith, tho dayly helpe I crave, ... 188 Astrophil   47   7
But now I meane no more your helpe to trie,. . . . . 192 Astrophil   55   9
Of Love, new-coind to helpe my beggery,. . . . . 196 Astrophil   62   13
No wind, no shade can coole, what helpe then in my case, . . 205 Astrophil   76   12
Thou toldst mine eyes should helpe their famisht case? . . . 235 Astrophil   106   6
As where thou soone mightst helpe, most faith dost most
    oppresse,. . . . . 213 A&S 5th Song   41
Absence sure will helpe, if I. . . . . 234 A&S 11th Song   13
And a helpe for him did know,. . . . . 222 A&S 9th Song   38
No help for you remaineth. . . . . 272 Psalm III   9
Help me my God and Father. . . . . 272 Psalm III   24
Lord help, for ev'en my bones their marrow spend . . . . . . 276 Psalm VI   7
And all my help from none but Thee is sent,. . . . . 277 Psalm VII   29
To help who vexed me.   281 Psalm X   4
Lord help, it is high time for me to call, ... 284 Psalm XII   1
I will get up saith God, and my help show. . . . . 285 Psalm XII   16
Behold they cry, but who to them his help applys?. . . . . . 292 Psalm XVIII   74
Let him come down, and help to Thee apply. . . . . 295 Psalm XX   7
Let God help him (say they) whom he did trust; . . . . 299 Psalm XXII   19
Hasten to help me, in this deep discomfort.. . . . . 299 Psalm XXII   46
From lion's mouth O help, and shew to heare me . . . . 299 Psalm XXII   49
Even he whose life no help of man can quicken. . . . . 300 Psalm XXII   74
O look, O help, let mercy fall,. . . . . 304 Psalm XXV   59
That hand whose strength should help of bribes is full.. . . 306 Psalm XXVI   33
On me, from me help this annoy.. . . . . 311 Psalm XXX   32
Their help from mighty hands.. . . . . 317 Psalm XXXIII   60
O helpe o help me, this farr yet I crave,. . . . . 330 Psalm XXXIX   25
Vouchsafe me help O Lord, and help with hast;. . . . . 332 Psalm XL   51
Thou art my help for aye;. . . . . 332 Psalm XL   67
Nede not the stately Muses' helpe invoke . . . . 242 Other Poems   4   7
But of a straunger mutuall help doth take: . . . . 248 Other Poems   4   238
Help him, who can no more hir sight foregoe. . . . . 253 Other Poems   4   420
He treble beas for helpe, but none can get:. . . . . 254 Other Poems   4   492
HELPED
Whom both nature seemes to debarr from meanes to be helped,.   37 1st Eclogues 13   158
She lay for dead, till I helpt with unlasing her?. . . . . .   61 2nd Eclogues 30   154
Are hurt, not helpt, with piercing of the light: . . . . . .   73 Arcadia III 39   10
(Which may be know'n, but never help't with wailing) . . . . 109 Arcadia IV   70   14
Who his Anoynted helped have.. . . . . 309 Psalm XXVIII   32
HELPEST
Approach of death, alas thou helpest meagerly, ... 128 4th Eclogues 75   110
Who helpest those, whose ruin was so neere,. . . . . 321 Psalm XXXV   23
HELPETH
But Man which helpeth them, helplesse must perish. . . . . . 127 4th Eclogues 75   87
HELPFUL
Yea heares with powers and helps of helpfull hand. . . . . . 296 Psalm XX   25
HELPING
Where helping weaker sort, the nobler beastes, ... 102 3rd Eclogues 66   121
While I am voyd of any helping pow'r.. . . . . 277 Psalm VII   6
My God, and helping God, my might and trustfull might, . . . 290 Psalm XVIII   3
In sprite that I shall have Thy helping hand.. . . . . 321 Psalm XXXV   6
HELPLESS
Helples his plaint, who spoyles himselfe of blisse.. . . . .   13 Arcadia I   4   10
Ye helplesse Sighes, blowe out your breath to nought,. . . .   83 Arcadia III 59   5
But Man which helpeth them, helplesse must perish. . . . . . 127 4th Eclogues 75   87
Thus great with child to speake, and helplesse in my
    throwes . . . . 165 Astrophil   1   12
And yet leave me helplesse meerely?. . . . . 222 A&S 9th Song   35
And quite cutt off, with helpless end. . . . . 327 Psalm XXXVII   96
HELPS
Since outward pleasures be but halting helpes to decayd
    soules). . . . .   33 1st Eclogues 13   52
Thus outward helps my inward griefes maintaine.. . . . . . .   42 Arcadia II   21   12
Alas, from all their helps I am exiled,. . . . . 137 Cert Sonnets 3   21
You take wrong waies, those far-fet helpes be such,. . . . . 172 Astrophil   15   9
Yea heares with powers and helps of helpfull hand. . . . . . 296 Psalm XX   25
HEM
Man was not man their dwellings in to hem. . . . . 100 3rd Eclogues 66   49
Thy work it is such men safe in to hemm. . . . . 275 Psalm V   39
Whome hills from her do hemme, ... 259 Other Poems   5   96
HEMISPHERE
Leaving my Hemisphere, leave me in night,. . . . . 223 Astrophil   89   4
HENCE
Get hence foule Griefe, the canker of the minde: . . . . . .   83 Arcadia III 59   1
Be thou farre hence with thy empoyson'd darte, ...   92 3rd Eclogues 63   56
Be hence aye put to flight,. . . . .   93 3rd Eclogues 63   68
For ever hence awaye:.   93 3rd Eclogues 63   77
Now will I away hence flee:. . . . . 203 A&S 2nd Song   27
Danger hence good care doth keepe, ... 210 A&S 4th Song   9
Go my flocke, go get you hence,. . . . . 221 A&S 9th Song   1
Get hence you ev'ill, who in my ev'ill rejoyce,. . . . . . . 276 Psalm VI   25
Will. Then Dick let us go hence lest wee great folkes annoy. 344 Possibly   1   45
Dick. Oh hence! o cruell word! which even doggs do hate: . . 344 Possibly   1   47
But hence, even hence, I must needes goe; such is my dogged
    fate.. . . . . 344 Possibly   1   48
HENCED
With that his dogge he henc'd, his flocke he curst:. . . . . 255 Other Poems   4   519
HENCEFORTH
Thy selfe henceforth the light doo never see.. . . . . 125 4th Eclogues 75   24

	PAGE	TITLE		LINE
HENT				
But that eternall paines my soule have hent, ...	116	4th Eclogues	72	87
HERACLITUS				
But if he nought do desire, what can Heraclitus aile?. . . .	30	1st Eclogues	11	12
HERALD				
And now fame the herald of her true honour, ...	68	2nd Eclogues	33	19
HERALDS				
Serve him with shot, her lips his heralds arre:	179	Astrophil	29	10
HERB				
Eache flower eache herbe dothe to your service yeeld, ...	43	Arcadia II	23	5
And wither like green herb or flower;	324	Psalm XXXVII		6
HERBS				
Seeke skill of hearbes in hills, haunt brookes neere night, .	26	1st Eclogues	9	127
Your sweetest flowers, your herbes, no service yeeld, ...	43	Arcadia II	24	5
With water drinke, herbes meate, and naked hide, ...	101	3rd Eclogues	66	109
For even the hearbes our hatefull musique stroyes, ...	116	4th Eclogues	72	103
Of herbes or beastes, which Inde or Afrike hold.	166	Astrophil	3	8
Klaius for skill of herbs and shepheard's art.	243	Other Poems	4	33
HERCULES				
It is no shame, since Hercules was he".	5	Lady of May	3	12
But find some Hercules to beare, in steed.	190	Astrophil	51	7
HERD				
Hardly they heard, which by good hunters singled be.	14	1st Eclogues	7	10
In number like the hearde.	92	3rd Eclogues	63	42
Worst fell to smallest birds, and meanest heard, ...	102	3rd Eclogues	66	141
HERDESS				
She is the heardesse faire that shines in darke.	259	Other Poems	5	112
HERDMAN				
A heardman rich of much account was he, ...	245	Other Poems	4	117
HERDS				
O heards take heed; for I a woolfe have found;	50	2nd Eclogues	28	83
HERE				
An olde man heare, who would thy fancies raise.	22	1st Eclogues	9	5
Here Laelaps, here, in deed against the foen	27	1st Eclogues	10	13
Here you fully do finde this strange operation of love, . . .	31	1st Eclogues	13	3
Yet be my hopes thus plast, here fixed lives my recomforte, .	37	1st Eclogues	13	164
Your scepters here, if to your eares divine.	40	Arcadia II	18	3
The hart, eye, eare here onely find his treasure doth: . . .	49	2nd Eclogues	28	58
Pas. And I am here the same, so mote I thrive and thee, . . .	52	2nd Eclogues	29	3
Pas. But here is Dicus old; let him then speake the woord, .	52	2nd Eclogues	29	27
Or wrapt in flesh what do they here obtaine, ...	57	2nd Eclogues	30	15
Or rubbing hurt the sore, I here doo end.	62	2nd Eclogues	30	183
Ne pleasure here, ne fame gott.	66	2nd Eclogues	32	39
Besides, lo here the auther.	67	2nd Eclogues	32	46
Of all thy harmes: Lo here she, ...	67	2nd Eclogues	32	47
Reason, tell me thy mind, if here be reason.	67	2nd Eclogues	33	1
Contemplation here holdeth his only seate:	68	2nd Eclogues	34	7
Here no treason is hidd, vailed in innocence, ...	69	2nd Eclogues	34	17
Nor envie's snaky ey, finds any harbor here, ...	69	2nd Eclogues	34	18
Here wrong's name is unheard: slander a monster is.	69	2nd Eclogues	34	26
Keepe thy sprite from abuse, here no abuse doth haunte. . . .	69	2nd Eclogues	34	27
Hid heere his hopes, by which he might aspire.	75	Arcadia III	44	3
Or doost thou thinke that heare.	80	Arcadia III	52	5
Which though of glittring golde, shall heere take rust . . .	92	3rd Eclogues	63	57
Now is the time we may be here alone, ...	97	3rd Eclogues	64	105
Vertue is dead, now set thy triumph here.	127	4th Eclogues	75	72
That here is juster cause of plaintfull sadnesse:	137	Cert Sonnets	4	10
Above line repeated at following location.	137	Cert Sonnets	4	22
Let here his eyes be raised.	151	Cert Sonnets	23	3
Above line repeated at following location.	152	Cert Sonnets	23	35
What changes here, o haire, ...	157	Cert Sonnets	28	1
And pleasd with our soft peace, staid here his flying race. .	168	Astrophil	8	4
Are Beauties there as proud as here they be?	180	Astrophil	31	11
Let her go. Soft, but here she comes. Go to, ...	188	Astrophil	47	12
Looke here, I say." I look'd, and Stella spide, ...	191	Astrophil	53	8
My spring appeares, o see what here doth grow.	200	Astrophil	69	8
I give you here my hand for truth of this, ...	201	Astrophil	70	13
Of all the kings that ever here did raigne, ...	204	Astrophil	75	1
Because in brave array heere marcheth she, ...	223	Astrophil	88	3
O absent presence Stella is not here;	235	Astrophil	106	1
But heere I do store of faire Ladies meete, ...	236	Astrophil	106	9
Onely joy, now here you are, ...	210	A&S 4th Song		1
What, is not this enough? nay farre worse commeth here; . . .	214	A&S 5th Song		73
No mortall gifts, no earthly fruites, now here descended be:	217	A&S 7th Song		14
Among you, who is here	320	Psalm XXXIV		45
Allarme allarme, here will no yeelding be, ...	346	Possibly	5	1
Of all the games that here ere now I met:	254	Other Poems	4	494
Let heere thy skill abound, ...	260	Other Poems	6	15
HEREBY				
For that (so that you like) hereby doth lie a youth.	120	4th Eclogues	73	137
HEREIN				
And herein most their folly vaine appeares	24	1st Eclogues	9	78
But all thy songe herein knitt:	67	2nd Eclogues	32	51
Defence herein doth wrong, O yeelde O yeelde, ...	345	Possibly	4	12
HEREOF				
That yet the ground hereof he might espie.	96	3rd Eclogues	64	72
HEREUNTO				
Nico. Content: but I will lay a wager hereunto, ...	53	2nd Eclogues	29	29
HERITAGE				
For father's heritage, ...	215	A&S 6th Song		16

HERITAGE   (CONTINUED)   PAGE   TITLE   LINE
    Blesse Thyne heritage I say, ... 309 Psalm XXVIII   34
    His heritage to make.. . . . . 317 Psalm XXXIII   48
    Their heritage shall last for ever,. . . . . 325 Psalm XXXVII   46
HERMON'S
    Ev'n from Hermon's dwelling led, ... 335 Psalm XLII   26
HEROIC
    Which inward sunne to Heroicke minde displaies,. . . . . . 177 Astrophil   25   8
HERCN
    So Lords with sport of Stagg and Hearon full . . . . 245 Other Poems   4   135
HERS
    Where all my paines one looke of hers hath paid. . . . . . 26 1st Eclogues 9   137
    Her vertue is soveraine, fortune a vassal of hers".. . . . 30 1st Eclogues 11   16
    Hers be the glory. . . . . 30 1st Eclogues 12   12
    My life my death do counte hers. . . . . 67 2nd Eclogues 32   57
    My thoughtes then hers, who first your ryne did rente, . . 78 Arcadia III 49   14
    Then hers, to whom my thoughts alonely thrall. . . . . . . 78 Arcadia III 49   15
    Where hers, whom worth makes highest over all, ... 78 Arcadia III 49   17
    And hers on me, astonisht with that sight. . . . . 115 4th Eclogues 72   76
    For hers am I, and death feares her displeasure. . . . . . 137 Cert Sonnets 3   22
    Though I be hers, she makes of me no treasure. . . . . . . 137 Cert Sonnets 3   24
    Then to my selfe, not though Jove grew a suter of hers.. . 143 Cert Sonnets 13   2
    That wholly hers, all selfnesse he forbeares,. . . . . . . 195 Astrophil   61   7
    Or hers whom naked the Trojan boy did see. . . . . 207 Astrophil   82   4
    And to that braine of hers your hidnest gifts infused, . . 213 A&S 5th Song   27
    Still to be hers, about her aye to flie, ... 255 Other Poems   4   501
    Dresse bosome hers or hedd,. . . . . 257 Other Poems   5   48
HERSELF
    She is her selfe, of best things the collection. . . . . . 15 1st Eclogues 7   48
    Yet harvest brings. Doth she alas absent herselfe? . . . . 49 2nd Eclogues 28   62
    But when to give some grace she doth content herselfe, . . 49 2nd Eclogues 28   64
    And Venus seemes, to make up her, she spent herselfe.. . . 49 2nd Eclogues 28   66
    Pas. She once, to coole her selfe, stood in a well,. . . . 55 2nd Eclogues 29   108
    Nature her selfe enameld it. . . . . 90 Arcadia III 62   124
    Let mother earth now decke her selfe in flowers, ... 91 3rd Eclogues 63   1
    Love of her selfe, takes Stella's shape, that she. . . . . 177 Astrophil   25   10
    Not though thereof the cause her selfe she know: . . . . . 187 Astrophil   45   4
    That grace, which Venus weepes that she her selfe doth
       misse . . . . 205 Astrophil   77   4
    Her selfe (to shew no other joy hath place). . . . . 229 Astrophil   97   7
HESPERIAN
    Whose fruit doth farre th' Esperian tast surpasse: . . . . 208 Astrophil   82   6
HEST
    But East and West were join'd by frendship's hest. . . . . 242 Other Poems   4   27
HID
    Geron. If that thy face were hid, or I were blinde,. . . . 25 1st Eclogues 9   96
    Hardly remains fyer hid, where skill is bent to the hiding,. 33 1st Eclogues 13   59
    Which ever shines, though hid from earth by earthly shade, . 44 Arcadia II   26   3
    The Sunne is hid; his kindly shadowe combers not.. . . . . 49 2nd Eclogues 28   63
    Here no treason is hidd, vailed in innocence,. . . . . . . 69 2nd Eclogues 34   17
    Hid heere his hopes, by which he might aspire. . . . . . . 75 Arcadia III 44   3
    Who like a theefe, hid in darke bush doth ly,. . . . . . . 175 Astrophil   20   3
    While that blacke hue from me the bad guest hid: . . . . . 175 Astrophil   20   11
    Yet were the hid and meaner beauties parcht, ... 176 Astrophil   22   12
    Nor in hid wayes to guide Philosophie: . . . . 179 Astrophil   28   10
    When Sun is hid, can starres such beames display?. . . . . 223 Astrophil   88   6
    Your morall notes straight my hid meaning teare. . . . . . 233 Astrophil   104   12
    There be no Rea'ms hidd from his beames, ... 294 Psalm XIX   27
    Nor hidd from him his face's faire appearing;. . . . . . . 300 Psalm XXII   57
    Thou hast hid them: yet leaving them thy light,. . . . . . 313 Psalm XXXI   56
    My sighs are not hid from thee;. . . . . 328 Psalm XXXVIII   27
    Who hid in Angel's shape my life would ende. . . . . 254 Other Poems   4   464
HIDDEN
    As for those parts unknowne, which hidden sure are best: . . 12 Arcadia I   3   13
    If then a boddily evill in a boddily gloze be not hidden,. . 34 1st Eclogues 13   87
    And so behinde foule clowdes full oft faire starres do ly
       hidden". . . . . 36 1st Eclogues 13   154
    If the Love hate you dyd, you should your beautie have
       hidden:. . . . . 123 4th Eclogues 74   47
    Nor blushing Lillies, nor pearles' ruby-hidden row,. . . . 213 A&S 5th Song   38
    And hidden beauties find,. . . . . 217 A&S 6th Song   52
    And in that nett, which they well hidden think,. . . . . . 280 Psalm IX   48
    How long wilt Thou Thy hidden face from me . . . . 285 Psalm XIII   3
    In Thy wings' shade then let me hidden ly. . . . . 290 Psalm XVII   26
    And so with hidden treasures grant their Will, ... 290 Psalm XVII   42
    Whose fault well hidden lyeth. . . . . 314 Psalm XXXII   3
    The hidden beauties seem'd in waite to lye,. . . . . 250 Other Poems   4   303
HIDDENEST
    From hidnest depth, which tribute when it ends,. . . . . . 150 Cert Sonnets 22   13
    And to that braine of hers your hidnest gifts infused, . . 213 A&S 5th Song   27
HIDE
    Lalus. If thou wilt not be seene, thy face goe hide away,. . 15 1st Eclogues 7   13
    Dooth hide himselfe: for to himselfe he sayes, ... 55 2nd Eclogues 29   94
    Let not these slumbring clowds thy beawties hide,. . . . . 91 3rd Eclogues 63   11
    Goe snake hide thee in dust, ... 93 3rd Eclogues 63   86
    With water drinke, herbes meate, and naked hide, ... 101 3rd Eclogues 66   109
    Doth hide his head with cares but onely how to rest: . . . 117 4th Eclogues 73   24
    Slay mee not, for stay doo not hyde thy blisses, ... 138 Cert Sonnets 5   22
    His ugly evill in other's good to hide,. . . . . 141 Cert Sonnets 8   6
    From that foe's wounds their tender skinnes to hide. . . . 176 Astrophil   22   8

HIDE   (CONTINUED)   PAGE   TITLE   LINE
    When silent night might seeme all faults to hide,. . . . . . 289 Psalm XVII   9
    Hide me, ev'n closely in his Tent; . . . . 307 Psalm XXVII   27
    Hide not therfore from me that face, ... 308 Psalm XXVII   43
    But, ah he strait his face did hide, ... 311 Psalm XXX   23
HIDEOUS
    If ought I cease these hideous exclamations, ...   61 2nd Eclogues 30   145
    O hideous absence, by thee am I thralled.. . . . . 138 Cert Sonnets 5   13
    And of hideous torments ease me. . . . . 222 A&S 9th Song   45
HIDES
    Thy gray-hood hides the thing, that thou despairst to find..   52 2nd Eclogues 29   6
    Hides their inward will of harming.. . . . . 263 Other Poems 7   42
HIDEST
    O Phoebus with good cause thy face thou hidest,. . . . . . . 126 4th Eclogues 75   55
HIDING
    Hardly remains fyer hid, where skill is bent to the hiding,.   33 1st Eclogues 13   59
    (Whiche hyding didest preserve that beawtie's light, ...   70 Arcadia III 35   2
    Who at the first, wanting, or hiding pride,. . . . . 101 3rd Eclogues 66   107
    Yet hiding royall bloud full oft in rurall vaine.. . . . . . 167 Astrophil 6   8
HIGH
    To high conceipts the song must needes be high,. . . . . . .   3 Lady of May 2   8
    More high then stars, more firme then flintie field. . . . .   3 Lady of May 2   9
    That verie shame with Love's high title dignifie.. . . . . .   14 1st Eclogues 7   3
    No, though the heav'ns for high attempts have blamed me, . .   15 1st Eclogues 7   22
    Yet high is my attempt. O Muse historifie. . . . .   15 1st Eclogues 7   23
    In one, whose name to name were high presumption,. . . . . .   15 1st Eclogues 7   38
    Not rotten sheepe, but high crownes she surpasseth all.. . .   16 1st Eclogues 7   57
    Her peereles height my minde to high erection. . . . .   16 1st Eclogues 7   70
    Passion beares high when puffing wit doth blowe, ...   25 1st Eclogues 9   114
    Doe speake high wordes, when all the coaste is cleare, . . .   27 1st Eclogues 10   32
    Then by my high Cedar, rich Ruby, and only shining Sunne,. .   34 1st Eclogues 13   80
    Firr trees great and greene, fixt on a hye hill but a
      barrein, ...   35 1st Eclogues 13   123
    Pine is hye, hope is as hie, sharpe leav'd, sharpe yet be my
      hope's budds. . . . .   36 1st Eclogues 13   130
    Let not old age disgrace my high desire, ...   38 Arcadia II 15   1
    Above line repeated at following location. . . . .   39 Arcadia II 15   14
    The one aloft doth holde the other hie.. . . . .   42 Arcadia II 22   5
    But who by meanes of wisdome hie . . . .   44 Arcadia II 25   5
    Then base and sower is Love's most high vocation.. . . . . .   48 2nd Eclogues 28   24
    What needed so high sprites such mansions blind? . . . . . .   57 2nd Eclogues 30   14
    To those high powers, which idly sit above,. . . . .   58 2nd Eclogues 30   63
    To harme us wormes should that high Justice leave. . . . . .   59 2nd Eclogues 30   71
    In thy high minde) get her thy husband's grace.. . . . . . .   60 2nd Eclogues 30   114
    So are we from our high creation slided. . . . .   62 2nd Eclogues 30   181
    Hye tyme for me, for scattered were my sheepe. . . . .   62 2nd Eclogues 30   186
    The high conceits thy heav'nly wisedomes breed . . . .   72 Arcadia III 38   2
    Call me but yours, my title is most hye: . . . .   79 Arcadia III 50   17
    Of whose high praise, and praisefull blisse, ...   90 Arcadia III 62   141
    Eagle, high looke; Wolfe secrete crueltie: . . . . 101 3rd Eclogues 66   87
    Hart-broken so, that molehilles seeme high mountaines, . . . 111 4th Eclogues 71   23
    Strephon. Me seemes I see the high and stately mountaines, . 112 4th Eclogues 71   37
    Is this thy fruite O strife? those thousand churches hie,. . 119 4th Eclogues 73   111
    Shall such high Plannets tend to the losse of a worme? . . . 123 4th Eclogues 74   38
    Since that to death is gone the shepheard hie, ... 125 4th Eclogues 75   1
    So high, as should make such a paine notorious:. . . . . . . 129 4th Eclogues 75   140
    When Love puft up with rage of hy disdaine,. . . . . 135 Cert Sonnets 2   1
    But vertue sets so high, that reason's light,. . . . . 135 Cert Sonnets 2   7
    In whose sweete heav'n Angels of high thoughts swarme? . . . 142 Cert Sonnets 10   8
    But this she thinks, our paine hye cause excuseth, ... 142 Cert Sonnets 11   13
    Trying high seas, nor while Sea rage you flee, ... 142 Cert Sonnets 12   2
    But hopes to gaine some helpe by mounting hie, ... 144 Cert Sonnets 15   3
    To hie conceits whose fruits are oft but small,. . . . . . . 144 Cert Sonnets 15   10
    Of this high grace with blisse conjoyn'd . . . . 159 Cert Sonnets 29   1
    (Exil'd for ay from those high treasures, which. . . . . . . 177 Astrophil 24   13
    Or for some brawle, which in that chamber hie, ... 178 Astrophil 26   7
    And know those Bodies high raigne on the low.. . . . . 178 Astrophil 26   11
    Th'indifferent Judge betweene the high and low;. . . . . . . 184 Astrophil 39   4
    Wrackes Triumphs be, which Love (high set) doth breed. . . . 186 Astrophil 42   14
    For late with heart most high, with eyes most low, ... 196 Astrophil 63   5
    Heav'ns envy not at my high triumphing:. . . . . 196 Astrophil 63   10
    But failst thou not in phrase so heav'nly hie? . . . . 199 Astrophil 67   6
    O joy, too high for my low stile to show:. . . . . 200 Astrophil 69   1
    Of her high heart giv'n me the monarchie:. . . . . 200 Astrophil 69   10
    Trebles sing high, as well as bases deepe: . . . . 201 Astrophil 70   6
    That conversation sweet, where such high comforts be,. . . . 205 Astrophil 77   10
    What, doth high place ambitious thoughts augment?. . . . . . 208 Astrophil 83   9
    Of her just and high disdaine: . . . . 203 A&S 2nd Song   18
    So to raise my hap more hie; . . . . 211 A&S 4th Song   21
    That brought me so high to fall: . . . . 211 A&S 4th Song   52
    See now those feathers pluckt, wherewith thou flewst most
      high:. . . . . 213 A&S 5th Song   22
    Whose owne fault casts him downe, hardly high seat recovers. 213 A&S 5th Song   24
    In what high joyes I shall dwell,. . . . . 226 A&S 10th Song   11
    Then reason, Princesse hy, ... 217 A&S 6th Song   49
    Till when will ye my honour high . . . . 273 Psalm IV   7
    To that high doome, which I by Thee must get.. . . . . 277 Psalm VII   18
    Therfore, O lord, lift up Thy throne on high . . . . 277 Psalm VII   20
    And will to highest Name yeild prayses high. . . . . 278 Psalm VII   48
    O Lord most high.. . . . . 279 Psalm IX   5

HIGH	(CONTINUED)	PAGE	TITLE		LINE
Which He prepar'd, to give his judgments high:		280	Psalm IX		22
Shew forth his Acts, and this as Act most high,.		280	Psalm IX		32
Thy judgments are too high		282	Psalm X		19
Lord help, it is high time for me to call,		284	Psalm XII		1
And yet their high hearts look so low.		290	Psalm XVII		31
The Mountains proudly high, and their ffoundations bent.		291	Psalm XVIII		16
From sanctuary high.		295	Psalm XX		6
In so high estimation.		297	Psalm XXI		20
Thy Honour high be raised.		298	Psalm XXI		50
Prove me O Lord most high,		305	Psalm XXVI		7
In house of High Jehova still,		307	Psalm XXVII		21
Salvation high..		308	Psalm XXVII		48
But let me give prayses high		309	Psalm XXVIII		24
By voice of high Jehova we		310	Psalm XXIX		13
Let me not tast of shame, O lord most high,		313	Psalm XXXI		45
Give hearty thanks to him on high,		318	Psalm XXXIV		2
So his high heavnly face		320	Psalm XXXIV		57
Thy truth above the Clouds, most high,		323	Psalm XXXVI		14
For God's high law in his heart dwelleth..		326	Psalm XXXVII		79
Tabernacle high.		336	Psalm XLIII		17
When she with skirts tuckt very hy, with girles at stoolball					
playes.		343	Possibly	1	10
A salve, freshe ayre, and hyghe contented mynde.		345	Possibly	2	14
Epeirus high, was honest Klaius' nest,		242	Other Poems	4	25
A maid train'd up from high or low degree,		247	Other Poems	4	210
Phoebus, that shepheard high,.		257	Other Poems	5	22
But with dew dropps engendre children hy:		257	Other Poems	5	45

HIGHER
Tune up my voice, a higher note I yeeld,		3	Lady of May	2	7
Nay higher thoughtes (though thralled thoughtes) I call.		78	Arcadia III	49	13
So that you may on hyer slippers stay.		93	3rd Eclogues	63	76
Who should my mind to higher things prepare.		161	Cert Sonnets	31	8
And thou my mind aspire to higher things:		161	Cert Sonnets	32	2
She builds her fame on higher seated praise:		207	Astrophil	81	10

HIGHEST
The highest note comes oft from basest mind,		4	Lady of May	2	13
And highest thoughts, downeward most headlong throw?		73	Arcadia III	40	12
Rysing from lowe, are to the highest bente;		78	Arcadia III	49	16
Where hers, whom worth makes highest over all,		78	Arcadia III	49	17
And lowest stops doo yeeld the hyest sounde.		81	Arcadia III	54	16
Where highest notes to godlines are raisd,		99	3rd Eclogues	66	31
And hath with wailing strength clim'd highest mountaines:		112	4th Eclogues	71	27
(Or such a noise it was, as highest thunders sende,		118	4th Eclogues	73	53
The highest hills the bolt of thunder cleeves:		143	Cert Sonnets	12	9
In highest way of heav'n the Sunne did ride,		175	Astrophil	22	1
Unseene, unheard, while thought to highest place		178	Astrophil	27	13
Of highest wish, I wish you so much blisse,		209	Astrophil	84	13
Let honor selfe to thee graunt highest place...		233	Astrophil	103	14
Consist, when they to highest doome are cited,		270	Psalm I		16
And will to highest Name yeild prayses high.		278	Psalm VII		48
That I Climb'd highest hill, he me warr points did show,		292	Psalm XVIII		62
He only leanes on highest Thing,		297	Psalm XXI		27
The highest Cedars broken see,		310	Psalm XXIX		14

HIGHLY
| For such a thought most highlie prized, | | 159 | Cert Sonnets | 29 | 14 |
| For my faults are highly spred | | 327 | Psalm XXXVIII | | 10 |

HIGHT
That which their mother hight, or els their silly seed..		119	4th Eclogues	73	84
Even He the King of glory hight.		302	Psalm XXIV		24
The later borne, yet too soone, Strephon hight..		242	Other Poems	4	24

HIGHWAY
| Highway since you my chiefe Pernassus be, | | 209 | Astrophil | 84 | 1 |

HILL
Firr trees great and greene, fixt on a hye hill but a					
barrein,		35	1st Eclogues	13	123
Justly entitled Cupid's hill.		88	Arcadia III	62	78
A hill most fitte for such a master,		88	Arcadia III	62	79
I rather wisht thee clime the Muses' hill,		169	Astrophil	10	3
My Holy Hill Syon.		271	Psalm II		14
From Holy hill he heard me..		272	Psalm III		15
That like a byrd to some strong hill		283	Psalm XI		3
Lord, of Thy Holy Hill who shall the rest obtayne?		287	Psalm XV		2
That I Climb'd highest hill, he me warr points did show,		292	Psalm XVIII		62
Who shall climb to the hill which God's own hill is named,		302	Psalm XXIV		5
Yea noble hight of Rocky Hill.		307	Psalm XXVII		28
For then my Hill Good God did stay;		311	Psalm XXX		22
In thy hill most holy.		336	Psalm XLIII		18

HILLOCK
| What judge you doth a hillocke shew, by the lofty Olympus? | | 34 | 1st Eclogues | 13 | 75 |
| Thus on a hillock set, he made his mone. | | 253 | Other Poems | 4 | 440 |

HILLS
Seeke skill of hearbes in hills, haunt brookes neere night,.		26	1st Eclogues	9	127
All to a lesson he draws, norr hills nor caves can avoide					
him.		31	1st Eclogues	13	7
Their pasture is faire hilles of fruitlesse Love:		39	Arcadia II	17	2
The highest hills the bolt of thunder cleeves:		143	Cert Sonnets	12	9
And stately hilles disdaine to looke so low.		147	Cert Sonnets	18	8
Rockes, woods, hilles, caves, dales, meads, brookes, answere					
me,		147	Cert Sonnets	18	13

HILLS   (CONTINUED)   PAGE   TITLE   LINE
      Of passyon's hilles reaching to reason's skie, ...   149 Cert Sonnets 22   6
      Thy Righteousness like hugest hills, ...   323 Psalm XXXVI   15
      Whome hills from her do hemme, ...   259 Other Poems   5 96
HILLY
      And from Mizzar's hilly head.. . . . .   335 Psalm XLII   28
HIMSELF
      Helples his plaint, who spoyles himselfe of blisse.. . . . .   13 Arcadia I   4 10
      Naught in himselfe ech other to abuse. . . . .   21 1st Eclogues   8 24
      Since all his force against himselfe he tries.. . . . .   23 1st Eclogues   9 37
      First may a trusty Greyhounde transforme himselfe to a
         Tigre .. . .   33 1st Eclogues 13 66
      What marvaile tho a Prince transforme himselfe to a Pastor?.   34 1st Eclogues 13 91
      Deepe musing to himselfe, which after-mewing showes, ...   53 2nd Eclogues 29 35
      He never musing standes, but with himselfe will play . . . .   53 2nd Eclogues 29 43
      Dooth hide himselfe: for to himselfe he sayes, ...   55 2nd Eclogues 29 94
      His nature? nay, himselfe? for so it is. . . . .   59 2nd Eclogues 30 72
      Boulon. Who still doth seeke against himselfe offences,. . .   62 2nd Eclogues 30 167
      To hurt himselfe, what shields can be defenses?. . . . . . .   62 2nd Eclogues 30 169
      Who seekes to knowe, acquaintes hym self with hell;. . . . .   71 Arcadia III   36 16
      But he himselfe a foule unhansome groome,. . . . .   94 3rd Eclogues 64   5
      And in himselfe new doubting causes nurst. . . . .   94 3rd Eclogues 64 12
      He will absent himselfe, least he should move. . . . .   95 3rd Eclogues 64 58
      Which who so wants, halfe of himselfe doth misse.. . . . . .   103 3rd Eclogues 67   9
      With sound of horne, which he him selfe did blow,. . . . . .   145 Cert Sonnets 16   2
      Fearing and feared thus from himselfe he fled, ...   145 Cert Sonnets 16   3
      Thinking not why, but how himselfe to save.. . . . .   145 Cert Sonnets 16   8
      At length he perch'd himself in Stella's joyfull face, . . .   168 Astrophil   8   8
      There himselfe with his shot he close doth lay.. . . . . . .   175 Astrophil   20   8
      Since to himselfe he doth your gifts apply,. . . . .   186 Astrophil   43   3
      That voyce, which makes the soule plant himselfe in the
         eares: . . . . 205 Astrophil   77   9
      Though oft himselfe my mate-in-armes he sware. . . . .   228 Astrophil   95   8
      Himselfe onely winter-sterved. . . . .   222 A&S 9th Song   30
      Nor yet himself with idle scorners seateth:. . . . .   270 Psalm I   4
      For he himself doth prayse,. . . . .   281 Psalm X   9
      Even god himself sent down his peircing ey . . . .   286 Psalm XIV   7
      Yea fire from himself sent,. . . . .   296 Psalm XX   14
      Like laurell fresh himself out spreading.. . . . .   327 Psalm XXXVII   90
      He did himself to me ward bend,. . . . .   330 Psalm XL   3
      They catch, while he (foole!) to himself makes love: . . . .   243 Other Poems   4 46
      And yeeld himselfe unto hir punishment,. . . . .   247 Other Poems   4 191
      For not himselfe to be in love did thinke. . . . .   247 Other Poems   4 200
      Heeding himselfe, cares not how fellow doe,. . . . .   248 Other Poems   4 237
      More marking hir, then how himselfe did goe, ...   249 Other Poems   4 290
      Mov'd not himselfe, nor suffred hir to move. . . . .   250 Other Poems   4 328
      Let it suffise that he himselfe forgoe.. . . . .   254 Other Poems   4 488
      With in himselfe of hir deare selfe to speake, ...   255 Other Poems   4 534
      Which made his Strephon think himselfe in hell.. . . . . . .   256 Other Poems   4 540
HIND
      The fearefull Hinde the Leopard did kisse: . . . .   100 3rd Eclogues 66 53
HINDERED
      By such unsuted speech should hindred be.. . . . .   190 Astrophil   51 14
HINDERS
      And if a meane were found, fortune th' whole course of it
         hinders. . . . .   37 1st Eclogues 13 159
HINDS
      His voice makes hindes their calves to cast, ...   310 Psalm XXIX   22
HIRE
      All is but this, this is our labour's hire,. . . . .   75 Arcadia III   44   6
      And soone forget the swincke due to their hire.. . . . . . .   100 3rd Eclogues 66 74
      Who hath his hire, hath well his labour plast: . . . .   108 Arcadia IV   68   1
      Favour to make my chiefe and onely hire. . . . .   115 4th Eclogues 72 55
      Within my selfe to seeke my onelie hire: . . . .   161 Cert Sonnets 31 13
HISS
      Uttring a serpent's minde with serpent's hisse.. . . . . . .   24 1st Eclogues   9 71
      Hurtles was Tyger's pawe and Serpent's hisse.. . . . .   100 3rd Eclogues 66 54
HISTOR
      Histor. Those woordes dyd once the Loveliest shepard use . .   24 1st Eclogues   9 62
      Histor. Thus may you see, howe youthe estemeth aige. . . . .   26 1st Eclogues   9 138
      Histor. Thus dyd they saye and then awaye dyd wende; . . . .   62 2nd Eclogues 30 185
      Geron. In faith, good Histor, long is your delay,. . . . . .   103 3rd Eclogues 67   1
      Histor. No doubt to whom so good chance did betide,. . . . .   104 3rd Eclogues 67 13
      O Histor, seeke within thy selfe to flourish:. . . . .   106 3rd Eclogues 67 109
      And then who shall the name of Histor nourish? . . . .   106 3rd Eclogues 67 111
      Histor. Perchaunce I will, but nowe me thinkes it tyme . . .   107 3rd Eclogues 67 118
HISTORIFY
      Yet high is my attempt. O Muse historifie. . . . .   15 1st Eclogues   7 23
HISTORY
      A Prophet oft, and oft an historie,. . . . .   181 Astrophil   32   3
      Thine eyes my pride, thy lips my history:. . . . .   224 Astrophil   90   3
HIT
      And ere that all these blowes thy head doo hit,. . . . . . .   11 Arcadia I   1   9
      All this one the this fatall yere shall hitte. . . . .   11 Arcadia I   1 V807
      Or else who singeth worse, my skill will hardly hit. . . . .   53 2nd Eclogues 29 50
      So sweete sounds straight mine eare and heart do hit,. . . .   192 Astrophil   55 13
      Oh! on my soul let not these tumults hitt. . . . .   322 Psalm XXXV   44
      And sought with deeds Thy will to hitt;. . . . .   331 Psalm XL   33
      For where he most would hit, he ever yet did misse.. . . . .   241 Other Poems   1   2
      To hit, but Kissing hit, ...   259 Other Poems   5 108

                                     225

		PAGE	TITLE		LINE
HITHER					
And hither now, vouchsafe to take with willing eare.		119	4th Eclogues	73	104
Since I am now come hether,		261	Other Poems	6	38
HITHERWARD					
"Scholler," saith Love, "bend hitherward your wit.".		174	Astrophil	19	14
HITS					
From heavenly standing hits each mortall wight..		229	Astrophil	97	4
HITTETH					
If he be blind, how hitteth he so right?		21	1st Eclogues	8	9
HITTING					
Blind-hitting boy, since she that thee and me.		187	Astrophil	46	2
HIVES					
Cherish the hives of wisely painfull Bees:		26	1st Eclogues	9	132
HOARSE					
Now my hoarse voice doth faile this occupation,		19	1st Eclogues	7	170
But now hoarse voyce, doth faile this occupation,		20	1st Eclogues	7	V970
Long since my voice is hoarce, and throte is sore,		57	2nd Eclogues	30	8
But hoarse and drye, my pipes I nowe must spare.		62	2nd Eclogues	30	190
My voice is hoarse, my throte scorcht,		66	2nd Eclogues	32	11
HOISED					
Leave of my sheepe, sorrowe hathe hoysed sayle,		44	Arcadia II	24	10
HOLD					
Them can I take, but you I cannot hold:		4	Lady of May	2	26
Lalus. Muse hold your peace: but thou, my God Pan, glorify .		15	1st Eclogues	7	25
And hopes the flickring winde with net to holde,		24	1st Eclogues	9	54
If the sencelesse spheares doo yet hold a musique,		30	1st Eclogues	12	13
Holde thou my hart, establish thou my sprights:		40	Arcadia II	18	15
The one aloft doth holde the other hie..		42	Arcadia II	22	5
Let this assured holde our judgements ever take,		45	Arcadia II	26	15
For who doth holde his love in estimation,		47	2nd Eclogues	28	4
Experience doubts, and schooles holde disputation.		49	2nd Eclogues	28	48
To hold these worldly things in such proportion,		60	2nd Eclogues	30	132
The love we holde is all death,		67	2nd Eclogues	32	53
Whose shade safety doth hold, danger avoideth her:		69	2nd Eclogues	34	34
Hold deere his work, with sighes eache change attendes,.		71	Arcadia III	37	8
Can holde, shew, tell, my paines without reliefe.		75	Arcadia III	43	8
Who hold this fast no greater wealth require..		75	Arcadia III	44	8
I holde his deare, and myne he cannot misse:		75	Arcadia III	45	3
Holde me most yours, then my longe suite is signde..		79	Arcadia III	50	18
Thou doest desire, and with free power to holde.		83	Arcadia III	58	2
In curled knots man's thought to hold:		85	Arcadia III	62	4
Where open hartes do holde so constant place,		93	3rd Eclogues	63	88
And farre unfit to hold so good a roome.		94	3rd Eclogues	64	6
Which drawne-out line doth hold all humane blisse.		105	3rd Eclogues	67	72
What sweete joyes I had once, and what a place I did hold? .		124	4th Eclogues	74	72
Then let us holde the blisse of peacefull minde,		131	Arcadia V	77	13
O take fast hold, let that light be thy guide,		162	Cert Sonnets	32	9
Of herbes or beastes, which Inde or Afrike hold.		166	Astrophil	3	8
As what their hands do hold, their heads do know,		177	Astrophil	24	6
"Foole," answers he, "no Indes such treasures hold,		181	Astrophil	32	12
And love doth hold my hand, and makes me write.		224	Astrophil	90	14
Whose eyes a person vile do hold in vile disdain		287	Psalm XV		7
But Thou art Holy and dost hold Thy dwelling		298	Psalm XXII		9
Doth hold his hall..		301	Psalm XXIII		27
My trust still hold.		307	Psalm XXVII		18
While I that way hold my hands		309	Psalm XXVIII		7
Which wicked folks do hold so deare;		323	Psalm XXXVI		3
But still the more that I did hold my peace,		329	Psalm XXXIX		7
Yeelde yeelde, O yeelde, you that this Forte do holde,		345	Possibly	4	1
Did hold hir fast for feare of more disgrace,		249	Other Poems	4	278
Laid hold on him with most lay-holding grace..		250	Other Poems	4	310
HOLDETH					
Ewe doth make me be thinke what kind of bow the boy holdeth.		35	1st Eclogues	13	121
That that deare Dyamond, where wisdome holdeth a sure seate,		37	1st Eclogues	13	165
Contemplation here holdeth his only seate:		68	2nd Eclogues	34	7
Unto the caitife wretch, whom long affliction holdeth,		122	4th Eclogues	74	1
Dumbe sleepe holdeth all the house:		211	A&S 4th Song		26
Whose life no life but of Thee holdeth,		278	Psalm VIII		12
HOLDING					
Happy be those mishapps which, justly proportion holding,.		32	1st Eclogues	13	17
Laid hold on him with most lay-holding grace..		250	Other Poems	4	310
HOLDS					
No charme holdes her, but well possesse she may;		17	1st Eclogues	7	111
And when that time is paste, death holdes his heeles..		28	1st Eclogues	10	51
She holdes the ballance of my contentation:		51	2nd Eclogues	28	118
Holds my young braine captiv'd in golden cage.		176	Astrophil	23	11
That hand, which without touch holds more then Atlas might;		205	Astrophil	77	5
Pleasingst consort, where each sence holds a part,		206	Astrophil	79	3
Slow heavinesse in both holds one degree,		229	Astrophil	96	6
Of furious floods he holds the reines,		310	Psalm XXIX		26
HOLDST					
How holdst thou her, whose eyes constraint doth feare,		142	Cert Sonnets	10	5
HOLE					
Confound those folks, thrust them in shamefull hole.		321	Psalm XXXV		7
HOLINESS					
Towards the Temple of Thy Holyness..		275	Psalm V		20
With thanks his Holyness therfore;		311	Psalm XXX		12
HOLLAND					
How Holland hearts, now so good townes be lost,		180	Astrophil	30	7
Which Holland sweet now gently sendeth in,		259	Other Poems	5	106

226

```
                                                         PAGE    TITLE           LINE
HOLY
   With vertue fraught and full of holy feare!. . . . . . . .   25  1st Eclogues  9    95
   Which made a Bay, made Bay a holy tree:. . . . . . . . . . .  54  2nd Eclogues 29    61
   Pas. If each day hath bene holy for your sake, . . . . . .   54  2nd Eclogues 29    72
   Horrible is this blasphemy unto the most holy. O lie.. . .   65  2nd Eclogues 31    45
   Cranes, order; Storkes, to be appearing holie; . . . . . .  101  3rd Eclogues 66    94
   From holy marriage, sweete and surest meane. . . . . . . .  103  3rd Eclogues 67     2
   Gratefulnes, sweetnes, holy love, hartie regard) . . . . .  122  4th Eclogues 74    10
   His will false-seeming holie . . . . . . . . . . . . . . .  160  Cert Sonnets 30    15
   Muses, I oft invoked your holy ayde, . . . . . . . . . . .  192  Astrophil    55     1
   My Holy Hill Syon. . . . . . . . . . . . . . . . . . . . .  271  Psalm II            14
   From Holy hill he heard me.. . . . . . . . . . . . . . . .  272  Psalm III           15
   God in his Holy Temple is, . . . . . . . . . . . . . . . .  284  Psalm XI            13
   Lord, of Thy Holy Hill who shall the rest obtayne? . . . .  287  Psalm XV             2
   Deare beloved Holy One,. . . . . . . . . . . . . . . . . .  288  Psalm XVI           35
   From Syon's holy top;. . . . . . . . . . . . . . . . . . .  295  Psalm XX             8
   From heavnly holy land . . . . . . . . . . . . . . . . . .  296  Psalm XX            23
   Upon God's holy name,. . . . . . . . . . . . . . . . . . .  296  Psalm XX            29
   But Thou art Holy and dost hold Thy dwelling . . . . . . .  298  Psalm XXII           9
   Who shall stand in his Holy place? . . . . . . . . . . . .  302  Psalm XXIV           6
   His Holy ones; they are preserved. . . . . . . . . . . . .  326  Psalm XXXVII        70
   Holy daunce to God's house bringing. . . . . . . . . . . .  334  Psalm XLII          16
   In thy hill most holy. . . . . . . . . . . . . . . . . . .  336  Psalm XLIII         18
HOLY-DAYS
   Nico. If never I did faile your holy-dayes,. . . . . . . .   54  2nd Eclogues 29    69
HOMAGE
   With loving homage kisse that only son he hath,. . . . . .  272  Psalm II            27
   He did not there doe homage of his eies, . . . . . . . . .  251  Other Poems   4   367
HOME
   And makes our home good sport with dauncing bolt upright.. .  53  2nd Eclogues 29    46
   Pas. My father hath at home a prettie Jay, . . . . . . . .   56  2nd Eclogues 29   138
   As neere his home, when storme or shelf he feares; . . . .   71  Arcadia III  37     4
   Make home more paine then following of the cart. . . . . .  104  3rd Eclogues 67    30
   We care abroad, and they of home have care.. . . . . . . .  106  3rd Eclogues 67   108
   With nature's praise are wont in safest home to take.. . .  117  4th Eclogues 73    14
   Least it might thee allure home to thy selfe to returne, . .  122  4th Eclogues 74     8
   Death is our home, life is but a delusion. . . . . . . . .  128  4th Eclogues 75   123
   Let me home returne, stark blinded . . . . . . . . . . . .  220  A&S 8th Song        83
   And to the proud in deeds pays home their own. . . . . . .  314  Psalm XXXI          66
   In quiet home they shall be planted, . . . . . . . . . . .  325  Psalm XXXVII        30
   So then be blest now, then, at home, abroad, . . . . . . .  334  Psalm XLI           45
   In chastest plaies, till home they walke a rowe, . . . . .  243  Other Poems   4    54
   Nay ev'n unto hir home he oft would go,. . . . . . . . . .  247  Other Poems   4   193
   Her breath, then short, seem'd loth from home to pas,. . . .  252  Other Poems   4   399
HOMESTRIFE
   Far was homestrife, and far was foe from border. . . . . .  128  4th Eclogues 75   132
HOMEWARD
   But then I homeward call'd my lambkins deare:. . . . . . .  103  3rd Eclogues 66   158
   For then Urania homeward did arise,. . . . . . . . . . . .  246  Other Poems   4   167
   And fare-welling the flocke did homeward wend, . . . . . .  252  Other Poems   4   415
HONEST
   The honest Bridegroome, and the bashfull Bride,. . . . . .   91  3rd Eclogues 63    13
   Whereto you knowe, his honest harte were loath.. . . . . .   95  3rd Eclogues 64    60
   Our foolish lustes in honest rules to stay.. . . . . . . .  103  3rd Eclogues 67     3
   Austere she is, when he would honest playes; . . . . . . .  104  3rd Eclogues 67    34
   That ever fell to honest woman yet:. . . . . . . . . . . .  104  3rd Eclogues 67    44
   Epeirus high, was honest Klaius' nest, . . . . . . . . . .  242  Other Poems   4    25
   The honest sports of earthy lodging prove; . . . . . . . .  243  Other Poems   4    42
HONEY
   Who though she be no Bee, yet full of honie is:. . . . . .   15  1st Eclogues  7    29
   Hony or Comb of hony.. . . . . . . . . . . . . . . . . . .  294  Psalm XIX           44
HONEYED
   O toong in which, all honyed likoures bee, . . . . . . . .   76  Arcadia III  46     3
   O honied sighs, which from that breast do rise,. . . . . .  231  Astrophil   100     5
HONOR
   But straight they fledde, summond by cruell honor, . . . .   17  1st Eclogues  7    95
   Honor, the cause, desart is not regarded.. . . . . . . . .   17  1st Eclogues  7    96
   Though cradle witted, must not honnor loose. . . . . . . .   25  1st Eclogues  9    92
   Yet dying, and dead, doo we sing her honour; . . . . . . .   30  1st Eclogues 12     9
   Dorus. Lady, reservd by the heav'ns to do pastors' company
      honnor,. . . . . . . . . . . . . . . . . . . . . . . .   31  1st Eclogues 13     1
   Which must frame contempt to the fittest purchase of
      honnour . . . . . . . . . . . . . . . . . . . . . . . .   32  1st Eclogues 13    38
   So my desires by my feare, cutt downe, be the frames of her
      honour.. . . . . . . . . . . . . . . . . . . . . . . .   36  1st Eclogues 13   135
   Which makes all eyes doo honour unto you.. . . . . . . . .   38  Arcadia II   15     8
   Old age orecome, the greater honour gives. . . . . . . . .   39  Arcadia II   15    12
   Who judge that honour, which hath scope to slander.. . . .   50  2nd Eclogues 28    91
   And now fame the herald of her true honour,. . . . . . . .   68  2nd Eclogues 33    19
   Thus honour, liking, trust, much, farre, and deepe,. . . .   84  Arcadia III  60     5
   An honour to the world, while Honour was their ende, . . .  117  4th Eclogues 73    37
   O cowarde Cupid thus doost thou my honour keepe, . . . . .  122  4th Eclogues 73   185
   In justice quit, of honour made no breach: . . . . . . . .  135  Cert Sonnets  1    12
   O the fayre Nymphe borne to doo woemen honor, . . . . . . .  138  Cert Sonnets  5     3
   Above line repeated at following location. . . . . . . . .  138  Cert Sonnets  5    27
   To honor turnd, doth dwell in honor's nest,. . . . . . . .  151  Cert Sonnets 22    47
   To honor all their deaths, who for her bleed.. . . . . . .  168  Astrophil     7    14
   Honour is honour'd, that thou doest possesse . . . . . . .  182  Astrophil    35     9
   Then servant's wracke, where new doubts honor brings;. . . .  187  Astrophil    45    11
   Service and Honor, wonder with delight,. . . . . . . . . .  202  Astrophil    72     9
```

HONOR	(CONTINUED)	PAGE	TITLE		LINE
The height of honor in the kindly badge of shame?.		232	Astrophil	102	3
Let honor selfe to thee graunt highest place..		233	Astrophil	103	14
That speech falles now to blame, which did thy honour raise,		213	A&S 5th Song		17
Tyran honour doth thus use thee, ...		220	A&S 8th Song		95
Till when will ye my honour high		273	Psalm IV		7
Then in the Dust let him my honour rake.		277	Psalm VII		15
From sucklings hath Thy honour sproong,.		278	Psalm VIII		5
Of glorious Croune, and crouning honour.		279	Psalm VIII		20
But doth with honour great the Godly entertaine;		287	Psalm XV		8
Thy Honour high be raised.		298	Psalm XXI		50
He will exalt thee unto honour		327	Psalm XXXVII		86

HONORED

Honour is honour'd, that thou doest possesse		182	Astrophil	35	9
Be you still faire, honourd by publike heed, ...		209	Astrophil	84	9
His Name may honourd be.		319	Psalm XXXIV		12

HONOR'S

To swelling harts he shines in honour's fire:.		21	1st Eclogues	8	38
To honor turnd, doth dwell in honor's nest,.		151	Cert Sonnets	22	47
Where Beautie's blush in Honour's graine is dide..		207	Astrophil	80	8
Stella, while now by honour's cruell might,.		224	Astrophil	91	1
See what clouds of reproch small darke thy honour's skie,. .		213	A&S 5th Song		23
Ev'n where Thou makest Thy honour's biding place.		306	Psalm XXVI		27
Which seated is, in spotlesse honor's fielde,.		345	Possibly	4	2

HOOD

| Thy gray-hood hides the thing, that thou despairst to find.. | | 52 | 2nd Eclogues | 29 | 6 |
| Pas. My gray-hood is mine owne, all be it be but gray, . . . | | 52 | 2nd Eclogues | 29 | 7 |

HOODWINKED

| His farr off sight now hoodwinkt is, ... | | 282 | Psalm X | | 47 |

HOOK

Though rapt with beautie's hooke, I did impart		150	Cert Sonnets	22	26
He oft layeth out his hook,.		282	Psalm X		42
That were in Court a well proportion'd hooke,.		245	Other Poems	4	141

HOPE

Whose strongest hope in your weake comfort lyes.		13	Arcadia I	4	4
Who can despaire, whom hope doth beare?.		14	1st Eclogues	6	5
And who can hope, who feeles despaire?		14	1st Eclogues	6	6
Drawes up; and if, hope fayling, ende live's pleasure, . . .		16	1st Eclogues	7	71
Hope we do live yet.		30	1st Eclogues	12	4
Above line repeated at following location.		31	1st Eclogues	12	28
Hope we doo both dye..		30	1st Eclogues	12	8
What meane is there, alas, we can hope our losse to recover?		32	1st Eclogues	13	27
What place is there left, we may hope our woes to recomfort?		32	1st Eclogues	13	28
And hope therby to ease their inward horrible anguish, . . .		33	1st Eclogues	13	45
Pine is a maste to a shippe, to my shippe shall hope for a maste serve?		36	1st Eclogues	13	129
Pine is hye, hope is as hie, sharpe leav'd, sharpe yet be my hope's budds.		36	1st Eclogues	13	130
Thus plag'de how can I frame to my soare any hope of amendemente?		37	1st Eclogues	13	160
My sheepehooke is wanne hope, which all upholdes:.		39	Arcadia II	17	5
My words, in hope to blaze my stedfast minde,.		40	Arcadia II	19	1
What hope to quench, where each thing blowes the fire? . . .		42	Arcadia II	21	18
Then may I hope, my pipe may have abilitie,.		48	2nd Eclogues	28	26
But when I did come neere with heate and hope,.		54	2nd Eclogues	29	88
Bownded with no limitts, borne with a wing of hope		68	2nd Eclogues	34	8
Moste lothe to loose, the moste approching hope..		71	Arcadia III	37	6
Synce love with care, and hope with feare do fight..		72	Arcadia III	37	18
(Which oft to loose laies out a guilefull baite,.		82	Arcadia III	56	2
But thou, sure Hope, tickle my leaping heart..		83	Arcadia III	59	9
Her cable, Reason, breakes from anchor, Hope:.		114	4th Eclogues	72	46
Ev'n then Despaire did Hope already kill:.		115	4th Eclogues	72	64
Such thing cannot he hope, that knowes thy determinat hardnes;		122	4th Eclogues	74	13
Then may I hope t'atchieve grace of a heavenly tiger.. . . .		122	4th Eclogues	74	22
Lully, lully, my babe, hope cradle bringeth.		139	Cert Sonnets	6	4
Evill happes do fill with hope, good happes appall		143	Cert Sonnets	12	10
Then might I hope a change or ease of minde		148	Cert Sonnets	19	11
For hope the colour due.		157	Cert Sonnets	28	4
Indeed I well did hope,.		158	Cert Sonnets	28	5
Though hope were mixt with feare,.		158	Cert Sonnets	28	6
And ah what hope, that hope should once see day, ...		182	Astrophil	35	7
Could hope by Cupid's helpe on you to pray;.		186	Astrophil	43	2
Of Hope, which makes it seeme faire to the eye..		189	Astrophil	49	8
To witlesse things, then Love I hope (since wit..		194	Astrophil	59	13
Nor new, nor wishe another course to frame, ...		198	Astrophil	64	12
And do I see some cause a hope to feede		199	Astrophil	66	1
And yet amid all feares a hope there is.		199	Astrophil	66	9
Hope, art thou true, or doest thou flatter me?		199	Astrophil	67	1
Chiefe good, whereto my hope doth only aspire, ...		200	Astrophil	68	3
Who seeke, who hope, who love, who live but thee;.		224	Astrophil	90	2
Seeing hope yeeld when this wo strake him furst:		228	Astrophil	95	6
False flattering hope, that with so faire a face,.		235	Astrophil	106	2
While favour fed my hope, delight with hope was brought,. .		212	A&S 5th Song		1
But now that hope is lost, unkindnesse kils delight, ...		212	A&S 5th Song		13
All the hope of all my heart,.		287	Psalm XVI		2
Yea my flesh in hope shall rest.		288	Psalm XVI		30
At mother's breastes, thou didst good hope betake me.. . . .		299	Psalm XXII		22
Sure, sure who hope in Thee.		303	Psalm XXV		7
My hope is all in thee..		305	Psalm XXV		76

HOPE   (CONTINUED)   PAGE   TITLE   LINE
    Of all my trustfull hope,. . . . .   305 Psalm XXVI   5
    Hope, Trust in God, bee strong, and he . . . . 308 Psalm XXVII   64
    For all my hope fixt upon God doth ly. . . . . 312 Psalm XXXI   18
    Of all their hope. . . . .   318 Psalm XXXIII   71
    Who hope on his Name just. . . . .   318 Psalm XXXIII   81
    Wait on the lord with patient hope,. . . . .   325 Psalm XXXVII   17
    Yet thus still my hope is grounded,. . . . .   335 Psalm XLII   35
    And past all hope his chapps to frustrate so. . . . . .   251 Other Poems   4   344
HOPED
    For reason will, great sight of hoped blisse,. . . . . .   71 Arcadia III   37   11
    He still hop'd well, because I loved truth;. . . . . . .   99 3rd Eclogues   66   38
    What can be hoped my harvest time will be? . . . . 175 Astrophil   21   11
    A prety case! I hoped her to bring . . . . 193 Astrophil   57   12
    They hop'd on Thee, and they were not appalled.. . . . . 298 Psalm XXII   14
    He single thus, hop'd soone with hir to be,. . . . . . . 250 Other Poems   4   337
    And comming where he hop'd to be alone,. . . . . 253 Other Poems   4   439
HOPEFUL
    I wait on Thee with hopefull ey. . . . . 330 Psalm XXXIX   24
HOPELESS
    Onely at you all envie hopelesse rueth.. . . . . 197 A&S 1st Song   24
    Joylesse, hopelesse, endlesse languish.. . . . . 220 A&S 8th Song   80
HOPE'S
    Pine is hye, hope is as hie, sharpe leav'd, sharpe yet be my
        hope's budds. . . . . 36 1st Eclogues   13   130
    Poore hope's first wealth, ostage of promist weale,. . . 206 Astrophil   79   12
HOPES
    Great sure is she, on whom our hopes do live,. . . . . .   3 Lady of May   2   5
    And hopes the flickring winde with net to holde, ...   24 1st Eclogues   9   54
    Who hath his hopes laid up in woman's hand.. . . . . . .   24 1st Eclogues   9   55
    You, though feares do abash, in you still possible hopes be: 32 1st Eclogues 13   23
    Yet be my hopes thus plast, here fixed lives my recomforte,. 37 1st Eclogues 13   164
    Their hopes on haps, and do not make despaire. . . . . .   58 2nd Eclogues   30   42
    And hopes with foule embracements her to get,. . . . . .   59 2nd Eclogues   30   90
    Hid heere his hopes, by which he might aspire. . . . . .   75 Arcadia III   44   3
    What strange dessein hast thou my hopes to staie,. . . .   80 Arcadia III   53   3
    My hopes which do but to mine owne aspire? . . . .   80 Arcadia III   53   4
    Crying in me: eye hopes deceitefull prove. . . . .   83 Arcadia III   57   13
    Be those despaires, which have my hopes quite wast.. . . 114 4th Eclogues   72   37
    Not that he hopes for amends of the desaster he feeles,. . . 122 4th Eclogues 74   24
    He hopes for some small praise since she hath great, . . 141 Cert Sonnets   8   11
    But hopes to gaine some helpe by mounting hie, ... 144 Cert Sonnets   15   3
    Tell how my joyes and hopes thus fowly fell. . . . . . . 146 Cert Sonnets   17   14
    Long drowned hopes to watrie eyes it lends:. . . . . . . 150 Cert Sonnets   22   18
    But when that failes, my dead hopes up to take,. . . . . 150 Cert Sonnets   22   19
    Of hopes begot by feare, of wot not what desires:. . . . 167 Astrophil   6   2
    She oft hath drunke my teares, now hopes to enjoy. . . . 201 Astrophil   70   3
    Then those blest eyes, where all my hopes do dwell,. . . 212 Astrophil   86   13
    Which in them my hopes do cary.. . . . . 226 A&S 10th Song   18
    He hopes, with dainty turns she doth him flee. . . . . . 251 Other Poems   4   341
HOPING
    Hoping that when they might find Stella alone, ... 193 Astrophil   57   5
HORN
    With sound of horne, which he him selfe did blow,. . . . 145 Cert Sonnets   16   2
    My never peirced shield, my ever saving horn,. . . . . . 290 Psalm XVIII   4
HORNED
    A horned head, cloven foote, and thousand eyes,. . . . .   21 1st Eclogues   8   26
    His horned head doth seeme the heaven to spight: . . . .   21 1st Eclogues   8   29
    Her horned head abroad doth raunge:. . . . .   86 Arcadia III   62   12
HORNS
    To fill his hornes this yeare on Christian coast;. . . . 179 Astrophil   30   2
    Is it not evill that such a Devill wants hornes? . . . . 206 Astrophil   78   14
HORNY
    Some hurt accuse a third with horny head.. . . . .   21 1st Eclogues   8   12
HORRIBLE
    And hope therby to ease their inward horrible anguish, . . .   33 1st Eclogues 13   45
    Then shall those thinges ease their inward horrible angwish.   33 1st Eclogues 13   46
    Horrible is this blasphemy unto the most holy. O lie. . .   65 2nd Eclogues   31   45
HORROR
    But perforce disgest, all bitter juices of horror. . . .   35 1st Eclogues   13   105
HORRORS
    What horrors breede, wheare wynd dominion beares,. . . .   71 Arcadia III   37   2
    While that the light may shewe the horrors darke . . . .   73 Arcadia III   39   11
    My mangled mind huge horrors still doe fright, ...   74 Arcadia III   42   5
    Languisht with horrors of the silent night,. . . . . . . 224 Astrophil   89   8
    While the blacke horrors of the silent night,. . . . . . 230 Astrophil   98   9
    The floods of wickedness on me did horrors throw,. . . . 291 Psalm XVIII   9
    Where I in horrors lay,. . . . . 331 Psalm XL   7
HORSE
    No man doth wish his horse should aged bee.. . . . . . .   24 1st Eclogues   9   86
    The Horse, good shape; the Sparrow, lust to playe; . . . 101 3rd Eclogues   66   81
    As horse and dogge, not great, but gentle blood: . . . . 102 3rd Eclogues   66   131
    For by and by the horse faire bitts did binde: . . . . . 102 3rd Eclogues   66   137
    Having this day my horse, my hand, my launce . . . . . . 185 Astrophil   41   1
    I on my horse, and Love on me doth trie. . . . . 189 Astrophil   49   1
    A horsman to my horse, a horse to Love;. . . . . 189 Astrophil   49   3
    My horse, he spurres with sharpe desire my hart: . . . . 189 Astrophil   49   11
    Oh be not like a horse or mule,. . . . . 315 Psalm XXXII   31
    Of quick strength is an horse, ... 317 Psalm XXXIII   61

HORSEBACK
    On horsebacke met him in his furious race, ... 176 Astrophil 22   6
HORSEMAN
    A horsman to my horse, a horse to Love;. . . . . 189 Astrophil 49   3
HORSEMANSHIP
    Horsemen my skill in horsmanship advaunce; . . . . 185 Astrophil 41   5
HORSEMANSHIPS
    Our horsmanships, while by strange worke I prove . . . . . . 189 Astrophil 49   2
HORSEMEN
    Skowts each motion is, the hands the horsmen, ... 67 2nd Eclogues 33   8
    Horsemen my skill in horsmanship advaunce; . . . . 185 Astrophil 41   5
HORSE'S
    A horse's worth laid wast the Troyan ground: . . . . 146 Cert Sonnets 17 18
HORSES'
    Tempers her words to trampling horses feet,. . . . . 209 Astrophil 84   3
*HOST
    Where senses do behold th'order of heav'nly hoste, ... 68 2nd Eclogues 34   5
    How Poles' right king meanes, without leave of hoast, ... 180 Astrophil 30   3
    But him her host that unkind guest had slaine. . . . . 184 Astrophil 38 14
    And all that Host. . . . . 316 Psalm XXXIII   23
HOSTAGE
    Poore hope's first wealth, ostage of promist weale, ... 206 Astrophil 79 12
HOSTRY
    In meane caves oft treasure abides, to an hostry a king
      comes. . . . . 36 1st Eclogues 13 153
HOSTS
    I hosts by thee orecome, by Thee ore walls I fly;. . . . . . 292 Psalm XVIII   54
    Hosts do the King not save, ... 317 Psalm XXXIII   58
HOT
    Whyle hote desyres do Raigne in fancie's rage. . . . . 26 1st Eclogues 9 140
    With sighes you seeke to coole your hotte desire:. . . . . . 38 Arcadia II 14   6
    Is she in rage? so is the Sunne in sommer hot, ... 49 2nd Eclogues 28 61
    Nay even cold Death enflamde with hot desire . . . . 59 2nd Eclogues 30 86
    My voice, too hott to keepe in.. . . . . 67 2nd Eclogues 32 45
    Till without fewell you can make hot fire. . . . . 188 Astrophil 46 14
    My life hott torments tasted.. . . . . 315 Psalm XXXII   12
    In my reines hot torment raignes, ... 328 Psalm XXXVIII   19
    The more me thought my heart was hott in me; . . . . 329 Psalm XXXIX   9
    Much more his sight encreast his hote desire:. . . . . 249 Other Poems 4 298
HOTCOCKLES
    At blowe point, hotcocles, or els at keeles. . . . . 28 1st Eclogues 10 47
HOTTEST
    I feele the flames of hottest sommer day.. . . . . 224 Astrophil 89 14
HOUR
    Time haste my dying hower: . . . . 136 Cert Sonnets 3 18
    Fetters tyed, do waite the hower . . . . 155 Cert Sonnets 26 18
    Unto the dust of my death's running hower; . . . . 299 Psalm XXII   38
    Till one faire eav'n an howr ere Sun did rest, ... 247 Other Poems 4 205
    Then want one hower those eyes which my joyes keepe. . . . . 259 Other Poems 5 102
HOURGLASS
    While brickle houreglas runnes, guide thou our panting race: 45 Arcadia II 26 10
HOURS
    Thus did I sing, and pipe eight sullen houres. . . . . 103 3rd Eclogues 66 155
HOUSE
    With recklesness what may thy house betide, ... 93 3rd Eclogues 63 75
    Unto his house a jollie shepheard went, ... 94 3rd Eclogues 64 15
    The great beames gone, the house on shoulders light: . . . . 102 3rd Eclogues 66 136
    The house is made a very lothsome cage, ... 105 3rd Eclogues 67 49
    In ruling of a house so well shee's seene. . . . . 106 3rd Eclogues 67 90
    Thy house by thee must live, or els be gone: . . . . 106 3rd Eclogues 67 110
    When I such guests did see come out of such a house, ... 118 4th Eclogues 73 75
    As treasure house where her best gifts abyde.. . . . . 141 Cert Sonnets 8   8
    From filth of foreworne house, and quiet lives, ... 143 Cert Sonnets 12   5
    I see the house, my heart thy selfe containe, ... 209 Astrophil 85   1
    Dumbe sleepe holdeth all the house:. . . . . 211 A&S 4th Song   26
    But I my self will to Thy house addresse . . . . 275 Psalm V   17
    The House where Thou dost dwell, ... 306 Psalm XXVI   26
    In house of High Jehova still, ... 307 Psalm XXVII   21
    Who shall in Thy house fatness find. . . . . 324 Psalm XXXVI   22
    Holy daunce to God's house bringing. . . . . 334 Psalm XLII   16
HOUSEHOLD
    Knowing that evill becommes a houshold strife, ... 96 3rd Eclogues 64 70
HOUSES
    Olde houses are throne downe for new we see: . . . . 24 1st Eclogues 9 84
HOW
    How dare I, wretch, seeke there my woes to rest, ... 3 Lady of May 1   5
    Shew how thou canst deserve so brave desire, ... 3 Lady of May 2   2
    Thus shrewdly burdned then, how can my Muse escape?. . . . . 12 Arcadia I 3   3
    How nice to touch? how all her speeches peized be? . . . . . 15 1st Eclogues 7 35
    How oft with raine of teares skies make confession, ... 15 1st Eclogues 7 43
    Lalus. How oft my dolefull Sire cried to me, "tarrie sonne". 16 1st Eclogues 7 49
    When first he spied my love? how oft he said to me, ... 16 1st Eclogues 7 50
    Dorus. How oft, when reason saw love of her harnished. . . . 16 1st Eclogues 7 61
    Of fayrer death how can I make election? . . . . 16 1st Eclogues 7 72
    Measure my case, how by thy beautie's filling. . . . . 16 1st Eclogues 7 77
    Thinking how it hath mard my shepheard's trade.. . . . . . . 19 1st Eclogues 7 169
    If he be blind, how hitteth he so right? . . . . 21 1st Eclogues 8   9
    How is he young, that tam'de old Phoebus' youth? . . . . . . 21 1st Eclogues 8 10
    Philisides. O gods, how long this old foole hath annoi'd . . 24 1st Eclogues 9 66
    How thou from foolish love maist purge thy sense.. . . . . . 25 1st Eclogues 9 110

And try with bayt how fish will bite sometime. . . . . . .   26 1st Eclogues 9 128
Histor. Thus may you see, howe youthe estemeth aige. . . . .   26 1st Eclogues 9 138
Then jarle: lo, lo, even these how envie blindes. . . . . .   26 1st Eclogues 10   9
That sport it is to see with howe greate art . . . .   27 1st Eclogues 10   41
As for the rest, howe shepeheardes spend their daies, ...   28 1st Eclogues 10   46
How to the woods love runnes as well as rydes to the
  Pallace . . . .   31 1st Eclogues 13   4
How much more we do love, so the lesse our loves be
  beleeved . . . .   32 1st Eclogues 13   20
Lawrell shews what I seeke, by the Mirre is show'd how I
  seeke it, ...   35 1st Eclogues 13 116
But in a palme when I marke, how he doth rise under a
  burden . . . .   36 1st Eclogues 13 127
Thus plag'de how can I frame to my soare any hope of
  amendemente? . . . .   37 1st Eclogues 13 160
How can you him unworthy then decree, ...   39 Arcadia II   16   9
And witnesse am, how ill agree in one, ...   40 Arcadia II   19   5
May witnesse beare, how ill agree in one, ...   41 Arcadia II   19   11
And see therein how well the writer fares. . . . .   42 Arcadia II   21   16
The fuell small: how be the fires so great?. . . . .   42 Arcadia II   22   14
P. How know we that, since present joyes we misse? . . . . .   47 2nd Eclogues 27   38
And how possest he strengthens his invasion? . . . .   48 2nd Eclogues 28   36
But how he doth by might, or by persuasion . . . .   49 2nd Eclogues 28   46
To conquere, and his conquest how to ratifie, ...   49 2nd Eclogues 28   47
By telling how she was, how now she framed is. . . . .   49 2nd Eclogues 28   53
Let Pas now know, how Nico maketh layes. . . . .   54 2nd Eclogues 29   71
Nico. Alas how oft I looke on cherries ripe, ...   54 2nd Eclogues 29   75
Plangus. Alas how long this pilgrimage doth last?. . . . . .   57 2nd Eclogues 30   5
Boulon. How long wilt thou with monefull musicke staine. . .   58 2nd Eclogues 30   38
Boulon. O man, take heed, how thou the Gods do move. . . . .   59 2nd Eclogues 30   65
Of lothsome dayes, whose losse how canst thou mone, ...   59 2nd Eclogues 30   78
Can I forget, from how much mourning plainfulnes . . . . . .   61 2nd Eclogues 30 155
Can I forget in how straunge phrase she craved . . . .   61 2nd Eclogues 30 158
How be the minds dispos'd that can not tast thy physick?
  Sick . . . .   63 2nd Eclogues 31   17
Long be thy woes for such newes, but how recks she my
  thoughts? Oughts . . . .   64 2nd Eclogues 31   33
Howe can they be unkind? speake for th'hast narroly pri'de.
  pride . . . .   65 2nd Eclogues 31   43
O how much I do like your solitarines! . . . .   68 2nd Eclogues 34   2
Above line repeated at following location. . . . .   69 2nd Eclogues 34   16
O how well I do like your solitarines! . . . .   69 2nd Eclogues 34   30
And how much more her worth surmounteth thee, ...   72 Arcadia III 38   16
Howe is my Sunn, whose beames are shining bright, ...   74 Arcadia III 42   1
Or howe do I, captiv'd in this darke plight, ...   74 Arcadia III 42   3
Thus cruell to my selfe how canst thou crave . . . .   77 Arcadia III 47   7
For how would you the mistresse' thoughts bereave. . . . . .   78 Arcadia III 49   11
But how the Graces doo impart. . . . .   90 Arcadia III 62 134
How all this is but a faire Inne . . . .   90 Arcadia III 62 139
(How can he love suspecting treacherie?. . . . .   93 3rd Eclogues 63   84
How can she love where love cannot win trust?) . . . .   93 3rd Eclogues 63   85
Asking her how she tasted Courtier's lips, ...   95 3rd Eclogues 64   33
She studied cunning how the same to blinde . . . .   95 3rd Eclogues 64   42
How they might get that guest, from them to wend, ...   95 3rd Eclogues 64   53
Take heed therefore, how you ensue that trade, ...   97 3rd Eclogues 64 123
How sheepheards did of yore, how now they thrive, ...   99 3rd Eclogues 66   34
That they now skilld not, how from him to wend; . . . . 102 3rd Eclogues 66 114
Thou seest, how friske, and jolly now he is, ... 103 3rd Eclogues 67   5
How well last day before our Prince you could. . . . . 106 3rd Eclogues 67   97
How hast thou torne thy selfe! sought thine owne damage! . . 109 Arcadia IV   70   20
Doth hide his head with cares but onely how to rest: . . . . 117 4th Eclogues 73   24
What life it is, and how that all these lives doo gather, . . 118 4th Eclogues 73   47
Betwixt us two; how much that discord foule hath stain'd . . 119 4th Eclogues 73 106
"How ill both you can rule, well hath your discord taught: . 121 4th Eclogues 73 163
Was it a dreame? O dreame, how hast thou wrought in me, . . . 121 4th Eclogues 73 181
How hast thou framde the paine wherewith I am opprest? . . . 121 4th Eclogues 73 184
For how can Nature unto this reply?. . . . . 127 4th Eclogues 75   94
Ne doo I care how rude be my invention, ... 128 4th Eclogues 75 104
Still studying how to us to be a light.. . . . . 129 4th Eclogues 76   16
Howe bee wee swerved?. 138 Cert Sonnets 5   12
How holdst thou her, whose eyes constraint doth feare, . . . 142 Cert Sonnets 10   5
Thinking not why, but how himselfe to save. . . . . 145 Cert Sonnets 16   8
Tell how ill thought disgrac'd my doing well: . . . . 146 Cert Sonnets 17   13
Tell how my joyes and hopes thus fowly fell. . . . . 146 Cert Sonnets 17   14
As for my mirth, how could I but be glad, ... 147 Cert Sonnets 17   41
If I could thinke how these my thoughts to leave, ... 147 Cert Sonnets 19   1
Of which, how much may pierce to that sweete seate, ... 151 Cert Sonnets 22   46
And write the state how my fancies bee, ... 153 Cert Sonnets 24   4
How ill fits you this greene to weare, ... 157 Cert Sonnets 28   3
Ah haire, how many dayes, ... 158 Cert Sonnets 28   9
Alas how oft with teares, ... 158 Cert Sonnets 28   13
Seeing how once you saw I liv'd, ... 158 Cert Sonnets 28   31
Desiring nought but how to kill desire. . . . . 161 Cert Sonnets 31   14
And thinke how evill becommeth him to slide, ... 144 Cert Sonnets 32   11
How then? even thus: in Stella's face I reed, ... 166 Astrophil   3   12
O how for joy he leapes, o how he crowes, ... 173 Astrophil   17   12
On Cupid's bow how are my heart-strings bent, ... 174 Astrophil   19   1
Some that know how my spring I did addresse, ... 176 Astrophil   23   5
How Poles' right king meanes, without leave of hoast, ... 180 Astrophil   30   3

How Holland hearts, now so good townes be lost,. . . . . . . 180 Astrophil 30 7
How Ulster likes of that same golden bit,. . . . . 180 Astrophil 30 9
But know not how, for still I thinke of you. . . . . 180 Astrophil 30 14
With how sad steps, o Moone, thou climb'st the skies,. . . . 180 Astrophil 31 1
How silently, and with how wanne a face, ... 180 Astrophil 31 2
Teaching blind eyes both how to smile and weepe, ... 181 Astrophil 32 8
I find how heav'nly day wretch I did misse.. . . . . 181 Astrophil 33 4
How faire a day was neare, o punisht eyes, ... 181 Astrophil 33 13
A burthned hart. "How can words ease, which are. . . . . . . 181 Astrophil 34 2
O Stella deare, how much thy power hath wrought, ... 184 Astrophil 40 2
Weigh then how I by thee am overthrowne: . . . . 185 Astrophil 40 8
How farre they shoote awrie! the true cause is,. . . . . . . 185 Astrophil 41 12
How their blacke banner might be best displaid.. . . . . . . 192 Astrophil 55 8
Then some good body tell me how I do,. . . . . 195 Astrophil 60 12
How Vertue may best lodg'd in beautie be,. . . . . 201 Astrophil 71 3
Now banisht art, but yet alas how shall? . . . . 202 Astrophil 72 14
How falles it then, that with so smooth an ease. . . . . . . 204 Astrophil 74 9
"Or so?" Much lesse: "How then?" Sure thus it is:. . . . . . 204 Astrophil 74 13
O how the pleasant aires of true love be . . . . 205 Astrophil 78 1
Without how farre this praise is short of you,. . . . . 207 Astrophil 80 13
How faine would I paint thee to all men's eyes,. . . . . . . 207 Astrophil 81 7
How cloth'd, how waited on, sighd she or smilde, ... 225 Astrophil 92 10
Whereof, with whom, how often did she talke, ... 225 Astrophil 92 11
How is thy grace by my strange fortune staind! . . . . 230 Astrophil 98 3
How thy lee shores by my sighes stormed be!. . . . . 230 Astrophil 98 4
How doth the colour vade of those vermillion dies, ... 232 Astrophil 102 5
O eyes, o eares of men, how are you charmed! . . . . 209 A&S 3rd Song 18
Can learne, how my selfe to sunder . . . . 234 A&S 11th Song 14
See how it the leaves doth kisse,. . . . . 219 A&S 8th Song 58
Lord how do they encrease. . . . . 272 Psalm III 1
How many Ones there be . . . . 272 Psalm III 4
And hearken how I pray to Thee.. . . . . 273 Psalm IV 5
Alas, how long, my God, wilt Thou delay me?. . . . . 276 Psalm VI 10
How through the World thy Name doth shine: . . . . 278 Psalm VIII 2
Above line repeated at following location. . . . . 279 Psalm VIII 34
O with how simple look . . . . 282 Psalm X 41
And with how humble showes . . . . 282 Psalm X 43
How long, O lord, shall I forgotten be?. . . . . 285 Psalm XIII 1
How long wilt Thou Thy hidden face from me . . . . 285 Psalm XIII 3
How long shall I consult with carefull sprite. . . . . 285 Psalm XIII 5
How long shall I with foes' triumphant might . . . . 285 Psalm XIII 7
Not weighing ought how fleshly fancys run, ... 289 Psalm XVII 13
As how to watch our overthrow, ... 290 Psalm XVII 32
O law of his How perfect 'tis. . . . . 294 Psalm XIX 29
And teach the humble how to tread. . . . . 303 Psalm XXV 36
Lo, how his blessing budds . . . . 304 Psalm XXV 49
See how I am opprest . . . . 304 Psalm XXV 63
Bow down thine eare to heare how much I need,. . . . . 312 Psalm XXXI 4
Direct me how to go, and guide me right, ... 312 Psalm XXXI 9
All to this point, how my poore life to take.. . . . . 313 Psalm XXXI 39
How sweet how gracious is his grace. . . . . 319 Psalm XXXIV 30
How this Our lord to feare.. . . . . 320 Psalm XXXIV 44
Lord, how the heav'ns thy mercy fills, ... 323 Psalm XXXVI 13
O Lord how excellent a thing . . . . 324 Psalm XXXVI 19
Shew me how long I have to live. . . . . 329 Psalm XXXIX 14
And hearkned how, and why that I did cry,. . . . . 331 Psalm XL 4
My God Thy wondrous works how manifold,. . . . . 331 Psalm XL 21
How in troops I wont to go,. . . . . 334 Psalm XLII 14
How elder rul'd their flocks, and cur'd their smart, ... 243 Other Poems 4 37
How well apaid she was hir birde to finde: . . . . 244 Other Poems 4 92
How tenderly hir tender hands betweene . . . . 244 Other Poems 4 93
How rosy moist'ned lipps about his beake . . . . 244 Other Poems 4 95
To strive she fear'd how it with vertue stoode.. . . . . . . 245 Other Poems 4 126
Heeding himselfe, cares not how fellow doe,. . . . . 248 Other Poems 4 237
He ravished with sight how gracefully. . . . . 249 Other Poems 4 282
More marking hir, then how himselfe did goe, ... 249 Other Poems 4 290
To see hir eies, with how true humblenes . . . . 252 Other Poems 4 402
With how sweet sawes she blam'd their sawcines:. . . . . . . 252 Other Poems 4 404
"For, but by charms, how fall these things on me,. . . . . . 253 Other Poems 4 449
How gratefull is our greeting. . . . . 260 Other Poems 6 4
Since they know not how to faine,. . . . . 263 Other Poems 7 39
"Where how many Creatures be,. . . . . 263 Other Poems 7 49
HOWEVER
He sits me fast, how ever I do sturre: . . . . 189 Astrophil 49 12
However they putt in their claimes,. . . . . 315 Psalm XXXII 23
HOWL
No woolves dare howle, no murrayne can prevaile, ... 43 Arcadia II 23 8
HOWLING
Roring, and howling for to have a King.. . . . . 100 3rd Eclogues 66 63
HOWSO
Well, how so thou interpret the contents,. . . . . 199 Astrophil 67 12
HUE
What marvaile then I take a woman's hew, ... 12 Arcadia I 2 13
Her forhead jacinth like, her cheekes of opall hue,. . . . . 12 Arcadia I 3 9
My beautie's hewe your beames, my health your deeds; . . . . 18 1st Eclogues 7 136
(For age doth make him of a wolvish hew) . . . . 27 1st Eclogues 10 17
Popler changeth his hew from a rising sunne to a setting:. . 36 1st Eclogues 13 132
Seeme to your eyes of a disgracefull hewe: . . . . 38 Arcadia II 15 6
In worth, in taste, in perfitte hewe:. . . . . 87 Arcadia III 62 40

HUE	(CONTINUED)	PAGE	TITLE		LINE
	Fcr faultlesse length, and stainelesse hewe, ...	90	Arcadia III	62	119
	Mine eyes did light upon her shining hewe, ...	115	4th Eclogues	72	75
	Indeed a perfect hewe, indeed a sweet consent.	119	4th Eclogues	73	85
	Who Stoick-like in clowdie hew appeare:.	147	Cert Sonnets	17	48
	Or did she else that sober hue devise, ...	168	Astrophil	7	5
	While that blacke hue from me the bad guest hid:	175	Astrophil	20	11
	That skin, whose passe-praise hue scorns this poore terme of white:.	205	Astrophil	77	7
	Takes in that sad hue, which with th'inward night.	230	Astrophil	99	7
	That hue, whose force my hart still unto thraldome ties? . .	232	Astrophil	102	8
	With heavenly hew and grace, ...	216	A&S 6th Song		20
	And make you faire with shadow of her hue:	257	Other Poems	5	32
HUGE					
	Thus tossed in my shipp of huge desyre,.	71	Arcadia III	37	13
	My mangled mind huge horrors still doe fright,.	74	Arcadia III	42	5
	Of huge complaintes, that now it is despis'de.	85	Arcadia III	61	4
	Of huge despaire, and foule affliction's vallies,.	111	4th Eclogues	71	17
	Is that huge storme, which powres it selfe on me:.	114	4th Eclogues	72	32
	Neere Wilton sweete, huge heapes of stones are found,. . . .	149	Cert Sonnets	22	1
	Whose heart with these huge flames, like wax o're heated,. .	299	Psalm XXII		33
	Breeding huge stormes with in his inward parte,.	256	Other Poems	4	543
HUGEST					
	When lo with hugest noise (such noise a tower makes.	118	4th Eclogues	73	51
	The wynde most oft the hugest Pine-tree greeves:	143	Cert Sonnets	12	7
	Thy Righteousness like hugest hills, ...	323	Psalm XXXVI		15
HUGEY					
	Bubling out doth breathe signes of his hugie dolours:. . . .	123	4th Eclogues	74	28
	With hugy darknes, which about his feet did wend..	291	Psalm XVIII		21
HUMAN					
	Are then humane mindes priviledg'd so meanly,.	31	1st Eclogues	12	17
	O heavenly soule, in humaine shape conteind:	38	Arcadia II	15	2
	Beautie hath force to catche the humane sight.	82	Arcadia III	57	1
	Which drawne-out line doth hold all humane blisse.	105	3rd Eclogues	67	72
	Of humane life to be the quiet measure,.	108	Arcadia IV	69	4
	Disarming humane mindes of native might:.	131	Arcadia V	77	6
	And from among the humane race	297	Psalm XXI		39
HUMANITY					
	Looke to thy selfe; reach not beyond humanitie:.	16	1st Eclogues	7	64
HUMANKIND					
	But glorious name of wretched humaine-kind?.	57	2nd Eclogues	30	16
HUMBLE					
	(So humble knowledge can throw downe the snakish sinne). . .	44	Arcadia II	26	6
	And with despite despise the humble vallies:	112	4th Eclogues	71	53
	In humble mind a constant faith to prove,.	145	Cert Sonnets	17	3
	An humble pride, a skorne that favour staines:	151	Cert Sonnets	22	65
	Draw in thy beames, and humble all thy might,.	161	Cert Sonnets	32	5
	O eyes, where humble lookes most glorious prove, ...	185	Astrophil	42	5
	Sweet, it was saucie Love, not humble I.	203	Astrophil	73	8
	And with how humble showes	282	Psalm X		43
	My humble hands, my fainting feet they peirced;.	299	Psalm XXII		41
	And teach the humble how to tread.	303	Psalm XXV		36
	To humble broken minds	320	Psalm XXXIV		65
	Strephon was yonge, yet markt with humble eies	243	Other Poems	4	36
	And each way luckles, yet in humble guise.	249	Other Poems	4	277
HUMBLED					
	And bending humbled eyes (o eyes the Sunne of sight)	119	4th Eclogues	73	91
	Are humbled thoughts, which bit of Reverence move, ...	189	Astrophil	49	6
HUMBLENESS					
	And Humblenesse growes one with Majestie..	188	Astrophil	48	4
	To see hir eies, with how true humblenes	252	Other Poems	4	402
HUMBLER					
	Another humbler wit to shepheard's pipe retires, ...	167	Astrophil	6	7
HUMBLY					
	Still still for them I humbly mourning went.	322	Psalm XXXV		35
HUMMING					
	The humming Waspe, if it had not a stinge, ...	104	3rd Eclogues	67	17
HUMOR					
	But so his humor I frame, in a mould of choller adusted, . .	29	1st Eclogues	11	9
	Old age well stayed from raunging humor lives:	39	Arcadia II	15	10
	And what manner a mind which had to that humor a vaine? Vaine..	63	2nd Eclogues	31	9
	And in my braine some sacred humour flowe:	146	Cert Sonnets	17	38
	As if they would of owners' humour be, ...	242	Other Poems	4	31
HUMORISTS'					
	Nor conning humorists' puddled opinions, ...	69	2nd Eclogues	34	20
HUMORS					
	Like those sicke folkes, in whome strange humors flowe,. . .	74	Arcadia III	41	1
	A Poet eke, as humours fly or creepe,.	181	Astrophil	32	4
HUNDRED					
	Who is an heire of many hundred sheep.	18	1st Eclogues	7	117
HUNDREDS					
	Hundreds of yeares you Stella's feet may kisse..	209	Astrophil	84	14
HUNGRY					
	A baite most fit, for hungrie minded guest..	75	Arcadia III	44	10
	Where famine ravine taught their hungrie chestes,.	102	3rd Eclogues	66	124
	For hungrie throte their flesh with teeth he brused:	102	3rd Eclogues	66	145
	I caught at one of them a hungrie bit;	208	Astrophil	82	11
	Their eares hungry of each word.	218	A&S 8th Song		21
	Yea from the grave's most hungry jawes;.	311	Psalm XXX		7

233

		PAGE	TITLE		LINE
HUNGRY	(CONTINUED)				
Leaving in paine their wel-fed hungry eies..		246	Other Poems	4	168
Go bawling curre, thy hungry maw go fill,.		255	Other Poems	4	517
HUNT					
And only hunt, where lyes do ly?		273	Psalm IV		10
That hunt so poore a prey as is my soule..		321	Psalm XXXV		8
But hunt with craft the quiet man's annoy;		322	Psalm XXXV		52
Who hunt me, ...		328	Psalm XXXVIII		35
HUNTERS					
Hardly they heard, which by good hunters singled be.		14	1st Eclogues	7	10
Like Numid Lions by the hunters chas'd,.		249	Other Poems	4	291
HUNTING					
In hunting fearefull beastes, do spend some dayes, ...		25	1st Eclogues	9	123
That huntinge faultes, our selves we did not catch..		29	1st Eclogues	10	93
Who hunting round the strongest for to kill, ...		50	2nd Eclogues	28	84
Hunting the wilde inhabiters of forrests,.		111	4th Eclogues	71	20
As little hunting minde (God knowes) did there appeere.. . .		118	4th Eclogues	73	70
HUNTRESS					
O heavenlie huntresse of the savage mountaines,.		111	4th Eclogues	71	8
HURT					
Some hurt accuse a third with horny head..		21	1st Eclogues	8	12
With stroking hurt, and too much cramming kill..		41	Arcadia II	20	12
To helpe, or hurt in thee her owne infection..		49	2nd Eclogues	28	54
We thinke they hurt, when most they do assist.		59	2nd Eclogues	30	70
To hurt himselfe, what shields can be defenses?.		62	2nd Eclogues	30	169
Or rubbing hurt the sore, I here doo end..		62	2nd Eclogues	30	183
The asse did hurt when he did thinke to kisse..		62	2nd Eclogues	30	184
Eies' hurters, eies hurt, but what from them to me fall's?					
Fall's.		64	2nd Eclogues	31	27
And thinke not she doth hurt our solitaries,.		69	2nd Eclogues	34	41
Are hurt, not helpt, with piercing of the light:		73	Arcadia III	39	10
For as from me, on him his hurt did light, ...		76	Arcadia III	45	11
So still me thought in me his hurt did smart:.		76	Arcadia III	45	12
Both equall hurt, in this change sought our blisse:.		76	Arcadia III	45	13
My inward hurte should spare thy outward rine?		77	Arcadia III	47	8
Hurte not the face, which nothing can amende".		82	Arcadia III	55	15
Because (though hurt) they never heard her grone..		102	3rd Eclogues	66	119
A plaint of guiltlesse hurt doth pierce the skie..		103	3rd Eclogues	66	152
Unto the earth, by the hurt of this her heavenly jewell. . .		124	4th Eclogues	74	62
And thence cast off, where his sweete hurt he found, ...		144	Cert Sonnets	15	6
To marre my minde, and with my hurt to please, ...		149	Cert Sonnets	21	2
I thought those babes of some pinne's hurt did whine,. . . .		173	Astrophil	16	7
Who his owne joy to his owne hurt applies, ...		206	Astrophil	78	7
Who for my hurt each way their thoughts did roll..		321	Psalm XXXV		10
While nought but game, the selfe-hurt wanton ment.		247	Other Poems	4	192
He was invisible that hurt me so,.		253	Other Poems	4	455
HURTERS					
Eies' hurters, eies hurt, but what from them to me fall's?					
Fall's..		64	2nd Eclogues	31	27
HURTETH					
And yet, deare soule, I know she hurteth none:		254	Other Poems	4	458
HURTFUL					
Figge that yeeldes most pleasant frute, his shaddow is					
hurtefull, ...		35	1st Eclogues	13	125
Avoydes thy hurtfull arte, ...		92	3rd Eclogues	63	59
With hurtfull thoughts to me..		333	Psalm XLI		26
HURTING					
With gentle beames not hurting sight:.		13	Arcadia I	5	8
HURTLESS					
Hurtles was Tyger's pawe and Serpent's hisse..		100	3rd Eclogues	66	54
To slay the hurtless One,.		282	Psalm X		34
He that hath hurtlesse hands, whose inward heart is framed. .		302	Psalm XXIV		7
Where bold and hurtles many plays he tries,.		247	Other Poems	4	194
HURTS					
Your face hurts oft, but still it doth delight,.		3	Lady of May	1	8
And Love, which lover hurts is inhumanitie".		16	1st Eclogues	7	66
That all thy hurts in my hart's wracke I reede;.		227	Astrophil	93	13
Nor neighbour hurts by deed, nor doth with slaunder stain. .		287	Psalm XV		6
HUSBAND					
But that her husband thought her service bent.		95	3rd Eclogues	64	27
"Husband", quoth she, "go to him by and by,.		95	3rd Eclogues	64	55
And as for me (sweete husband) I must beare".		96	3rd Eclogues	64	62
And to her jealous husband did it take..		96	3rd Eclogues	64	84
And this was all, and this the husband read..		97	3rd Eclogues	64	109
Still contrarie to what her husband sayes;		104	3rd Eclogues	67	32
Tell me, if husband springtime leave your lande, ...		257	Other Poems	5	50
HUSBAND'S					
In thy high minde) get her thy husband's grace..		60	2nd Eclogues	30	114
All sturring husband's hate.		93	3rd Eclogues	63	69
The wife thus having settled husband's braine, ...		96	3rd Eclogues	64	73
HUSH					
But I do hush, Why do I say thus much, ...		330	Psalm XXXIX		29
HUSWIFERY					
The sinke of filth, be counted huswifery:.		93	3rd Eclogues	63	79
HYACINTH					
O Hiacinthe let Ai be on thee still.		125	4th Eclogues	75	29
HYMEN					
O Himen long their coupled joyes maintaine..		91	3rd Eclogues	63	9
Above line repeated at following locations		91	3rd Eclogues	63	18
. . . .		91	3rd Eclogues	63	27

HYMEN   (CONTINUED)   PAGE   TITLE   LINE

```
HYMEN                      (CONTINUED)                PAGE    TITLE          LINE
    . . . . . . . . . . . . . . . . . . . . . . . .   92  3rd Eclogues 63   36
    . . . . . . . . . . . . . . . . . . . . . . . .   92  3rd Eclogues 63   45
    . . . . . . . . . . . . . . . . . . . . . . . .   92  3rd Eclogues 63   54
    . . . . . . . . . . . . . . . . . . . . . . . .   93  3rd Eclogues 63   63
    . . . . . . . . . . . . . . . . . . . . . . . .   93  3rd Eclogues 63   72
    . . . . . . . . . . . . . . . . . . . . . . . .   93  3rd Eclogues 63   81
    . . . . . . . . . . . . . . . . . . . . . . . .   93  3rd Eclogues 63   90
    For Himen will their coupled joyes maintaine...  94  3rd Eclogues 63   99
HYMN
    Our morning hymne this is, and song at evening.. 113  4th Eclogues 71   75
HYMNS
    Ye Hymnes and singing skill. . . . . . . . . . . 260  Other Poems   6    7
HYPOCRISY
    Even turtle toutcht he with hypocrisie.. . . . .  28  1st Eclogues 10   81
ICE
    Since heart in chilling feare with yce is warmed: 135 Cert Sonnets  1    7
IDEA
    Happy be you that may to the saint, your onely Idea,  32  1st Eclogues 13  15
IDLE
    With idle paines, and missing ayme, do guesse. . 176  Astrophil    23    4
    Nor yet himself with idle scorners seateth:. . . 270  Psalm I            4
    If Thou remainedst Idle. . . . . . . . . . . . . 315  Psalm XXXII       36
IDLER
    "What idler thing, then speake and not be hard?" 182  Astrophil    34    9
IDLY
    To those high powers, which idly sit above,. . .  58  2nd Eclogues 30   63
    Where bee now those wordes never Idelly wasted,. 138  Cert Sonnets  5    7
    But that my wealth I have most idly spent. . . . 174  Astrophil    18    8
    So they three did togither idly stay,. . . . . . 250  Other Poems   4  329
IF
    Warme well thy wits, if thou wilt win her will,.   3  Lady of May   2    3
    But take this beast, if beasts you feare to misse,  4  Lady of May   2   29
    So if my man must praises have,. . . . . . . . .  13  Arcadia I     5    5
    Above line repeated at following location. . . .  13  Arcadia I     5   11
    And if for want of use thy minde ashamed is, . .  14  1st Eclogues  7    2
    Lalus. If thou wilt not be seene, thy face goe hide away,.  15  1st Eclogues 7  13
    But if thou hast a Love, in that Love's passion,   15  1st Eclogues  7   16
    Drawes up; and if, hope fayling, ende live's pleasure, . . .  16  1st Eclogues  7   71
    And if enchantment can a harde hart move,. . . .  17  1st Eclogues  7  100
    Which if you will (o doo) bestow on me,. . . . .  18  1st Eclogues  7  121
    Lalus. But if my Kala this my suite denies,. . .  18  1st Eclogues  7  147
    If still her minde be such,. . . . . . . . . . .  19  1st Eclogues  7  150
    If shee still hate love's lawe,. . . . . . . . .  19  1st Eclogues  7 V150
    If he be blind, how hitteth he so right? . . . .  21  1st Eclogues  8    9
    Then vertue try, if she can worke in thee. . . .  22  1st Eclogues  9   13
    Philisides. If fortune's lappe became my dwelling place, . .  23  1st Eclogues  9   26
    What ayleth thee, and if they knew thy minde . .  23  1st Eclogues  9   42
    A servant Sex, soone prowde if they be coi'de, .  24  1st Eclogues  9   60
    If from his words the falshood he do skim. . . .  24  1st Eclogues  9   77
    Geron. If that thy face were hid, or I were blinde,.  25  1st Eclogues 9  96
    But is indeed a toy, if not a toy,. . . . . . . .  25  1st Eclogues  9  115
    If once thou maist that fancie glosse destroy. .  25  1st Eclogues  9  117
    What if Laelaps a better morsell fyndes. . . . .  26  1st Eclogues 10    7
    Mastix. What marvaile if in youth such faults be done, . . .  27  1st Eclogues 10   25
    Either a sleepe be all if nought assaile,. . . .  27  1st Eclogues 10   29
    Or all abroade if but a Cubb start out.. . . . .  27  1st Eclogues 10   30
    But if he nought do desire, what can Heraclitus aile?. . . .  30  1st Eclogues 11   12
    If mine eyes can speake to doo harty errande,. .  30  1st Eclogues 12    1
    But if eyes faile then, when I most doo need them,  30  1st Eclogues 12    5
    Or if eyes' language be not unto her knowne, . .  30  1st Eclogues 12    6
    If the sencelesse spheares doo yet hold a musique,  30  1st Eclogues 12   13
    If the Swanne's sweet voice be not heard, but at death,. . .  30  1st Eclogues 12   14
    If the mute timber when it hath the life lost, .  30  1st Eclogues 12   15
    But if eyes can speake to doo harty errande, . .  31  1st Eclogues 12   25
    None can speake of a wound with skill, if he have not a
        wound felt.. . . . . . . . . . . . . . . . .  33  1st Eclogues 13   71
    If then a boddily evill in a boddily gloze be not hidden,..  34  1st Eclogues 13   87
    Dorus. O glittring miseries of man, if this be the fortune .  34  1st Eclogues 13   89
    Desteny keepes me aloofe. For if all thy estate to thy
        verture. . . . . . . . . . . . . . . . . . .  34  1st Eclogues 13   98
    If neither by that helpe, thou canst clime up to thy fancie,  34  1st Eclogues 13  100
    And if a meane were found, fortune th' whole course of it
        hinders. . . . . . . . . . . . . . . . . . .  37  1st Eclogues 13  159
    If by the parties ment our meanings rightly be marked, . . .  37  1st Eclogues 13  174
    Your scepters here, if to your eares divine. . .  40  Arcadia II   18    3
    P. If Reason will, that Passions be not free.. .  46  2nd Eclogues 27    4
    If noble be thy bandes, make them notorious: . .  47  2nd Eclogues 28   14
    If Love tooke thee by force, or caught thee guilefully...  48  2nd Eclogues 28   21
    Dorus. If Sunnie beames shame heav'nly habitation; . . . . .  48  2nd Eclogues 28   22
    If three-leav'd grasse seeme to the sheepe unsavorie,. . . .  48  2nd Eclogues 28   23
    Or if sheepe's cries can helpe the Sunne's owne braverie,..  48  2nd Eclogues 28   25
    Dorus. If I had thought to heare blasphemous wordes, . . . .  50  2nd Eclogues 28   79
    But if I had bene there, th'adst met another mate. . . . . .  52  2nd Eclogues 29   22
    If thou (alas poore if) do winne, then winne thou this,. . .  53  2nd Eclogues 29   37
    And if I better sing, let me thy Cosma kisse.. .  53  2nd Eclogues 29   38
    Nico. If never I did faile your holy-dayes,. . .  54  2nd Eclogues 29   69
    Pas. If each day hath bene holy for your sake, .  54  2nd Eclogues 29   72
    If Leuca live, she darken will my fame.. . . . .  55  2nd Eclogues 29   95
    Nico. O if I had a ladder for the skies, . . . .  55  2nd Eclogues 29  117
```

	PAGE	TITLE	LINE
Pas. O if I had Apollo's golden carre, ...	56	2nd Eclogues 29	120
Erona dye? O heaven (if heaven there be)	58	2nd Eclogues 30	59
If she must dye, then hath she past the line	59	2nd Eclogues 30	77
Alas, if you a Phoenix new will have	60	2nd Eclogues 30	102
O Venus (if her praise no envy frames, ...	60	2nd Eclogues 30	113
Plangus. If through mine eares pearce any consolacyons . . .	61	2nd Eclogues 30	143
If ought I cease these hideous exclamations, ...	61	2nd Eclogues 30	145
As if by death she onely might be saved?	61	2nd Eclogues 30	160
But if my memory thus must be thralled	61	2nd Eclogues 30	164
But if he know not his harms what guides hath he whil'st he be blind? Blind.	63	2nd Eclogues 31	20
Dev'lls? if in hell such dev'lls do abide, to the hells I do go. Go.	65	2nd Eclogues 31	50
If that to sing thou arte bent	66	2nd Eclogues 32	17
Or if to love thou art bent, ...	66	2nd Eclogues 32	25
Reason, tell me thy mind, if here be reason.	67	2nd Eclogues 33	1
Nor danger to thy selfe if be not in thy selfe..	69	2nd Eclogues 34	14
Yet deare soile, if a soule closed in a mansion.	69	2nd Eclogues 34	31
Oh! if such a one have bent to a lonely life	69	2nd Eclogues 34	39
But if thy rage some brave revenge will finde, ...	72	Arcadia III 38	13
But yet o dreame, if thou wilt not departe	79	Arcadia III 51	9
In whose Incirclets if you gaze, ...	86	Arcadia III 62	31
Vertue (if not a God) yet God's chiefe parte, ...	92	3rd Eclogues 63	46
That if he absent were but halfe a daye, ...	94	3rd Eclogues 64	10
If he to them his dutie misconceaved).	94	3rd Eclogues 64	22
If you helpe not our wedlocke will be staind".	95	3rd Eclogues 64	46
Subscription was, yours most, if you will prove.	96	3rd Eclogues 64	90
As if he meant his lordship common be.	102	3rd Eclogues 66	112
He were a foole, if there he did not bide.	104	3rd Eclogues 67	15
Who would not have a Phoenix if he could?.	104	3rd Eclogues 67	16
The humming Waspe, if it had not a stinge, ...	104	3rd Eclogues 67	17
If many Kalaes our Arcadia gave, ...	104	3rd Eclogues 67	22
With meager lookes, as if they still did smart;.	104	3rd Eclogues 67	28
If he do praise the dog, she likes the cat,.	104	3rd Eclogues 67	33
And if forsooth there come some new found ware, ...	104	3rd Eclogues 67	40
Must goe for that, if for her lowres he care:.	104	3rd Eclogues 67	42
If thou doo not repay his deeds for thee,.	105	3rd Eclogues 67	74
If thus thou murther thy posteritie.	105	3rd Eclogues 67	78
All what I am: if I my selfe will save,.	114	4th Eclogues 72	23
What essence dest'nie hath; if fortune be or no;	118	4th Eclogues 73	45
So as if I prevaile, you give your giftes to me:	120	4th Eclogues 73	133
If you, on you I lay what in my office be.	120	4th Eclogues 73	134
As th'offence was done, and goe beyond if he can..	123	4th Eclogues 74	40
If that love be a fault, more fault in you to be lovely: . .	123	4th Eclogues 74	43
If the Love hate you dyd, you should your beautie have hidden:.	123	4th Eclogues 74	47
If then a man in most ill case may give you a farewell;. . .	124	4th Eclogues 74	85
And you o trees (if any life there lies.	125	4th Eclogues 75	4
But if among yourselves some one tree growe, ...	125	4th Eclogues 75	10
Aske, if in great men good men so do thronge, ...	126	4th Eclogues 75	43
Or if that they be skante, if this be wronge?.	126	4th Eclogues 75	45
And if that any counsell you to measure.	126	4th Eclogues 75	49
Or if thy mourning notes be fully spent, ...	127	4th Eclogues 75	64
And if, o Sunne, thou ever didst appeare,.	127	4th Eclogues 75	70
Whereas if I a gratefull gardien have, ...	135	Cert Sonnets 1	13
Yf Duety kill mee.	138	Cert Sonnets 5	20
If thus, alas: yet while those partes have wo, ...	142	Cert Sonnets 10	13
O happie Dove if she no bondage tried:	144	Cert Sonnets 15	13
If othes might serve, even by the Stygian lake, ...	146	Cert Sonnets 17	6
If Greekes themselves were mov'd with so small cause	146	Cert Sonnets 17	21
Who thinke themselves well blest, if they renew.	146	Cert Sonnets 17	33
But now, if ere my face with joy be clad:.	147	Cert Sonnets 17	44
If I could thinke how these my thoughts to leave,.	147	Cert Sonnets 19	1
If rebell sence would reason's law receave;.	147	Cert Sonnets 19	3
If either you would change your cruell hart, ...	148	Cert Sonnets 19	7
If from my soule this love would once depart, ...	148	Cert Sonnets 19	9
If further place might further me to ease.	149	Cert Sonnets 21	4
So mazde a masse, or if in me it growes, ...	149	Cert Sonnets 22	9
A field there is where, if a stake be prest.	150	Cert Sonnets 22	41
For if those flames burne my desire, ...	153	Cert Sonnets 24	26
If that the substance faile within..	156	Cert Sonnets 27	16
If I ware you or no, ...	158	Cert Sonnets 28	12
If I then faultie be, ...	158	Cert Sonnets 28	18
For if my place give me great pleasure, ...	159	Cert Sonnets 29	5
Oft turning others' leaves, to see if thence would flow. . .	165	Astrophil 1	7
If vaine love have my simple scule opprest, ...	166	Astrophil 4	3
But if that needs thou wilt usurping be, ...	167	Astrophil 4	9
Least if no vaile those brave gleames did disguise, ...	168	Astrophil 7	7
If that be sinne which doth the maners frame, ...	172	Astrophil 14	9
If that be sinne which in fixt hearts doth breed	172	Astrophil 14	12
But if (both for your love and skill) your name.	172	Astrophil 15	12
Who threatned stripes, if he his wrath did prove:	173	Astrophil 17	6
That Plato I read for nought, but if he tame	175	Astrophil 21	5
If now the May of my yeares much decline, ...	175	Astrophil 21	10
That Vertue, if it once met with our eyes, ...	177	Astrophil 25	3
And if these rules did faile, proofe makes me sure, ...	178	Astrophil 26	12
If French can yet three parts in one agree;	180	Astrophil 30	5
If in the Scottishe Court be weltring yet;	180	Astrophil 30	11
Sure, if that long with Love acquainted eyes	180	Astrophil 31	5

```
IF       (CONTINUED)                                   PAGE    TITLE          LINE
     I will good tribute pay if thou do so. . . . . . . . . . .  184 Astrophil    39    8
     And if these things, as being thine by right,. . . . . . . .  184 Astrophil    39   12
     Alas, if from the height of Vertue's throne, . . . . . . . .  184 Astrophil    40    5
     And if from Majestie of sacred lights, . . . . . . . . . . .  186 Astrophil    42   12
     Glad if for her he give them leave to die. . . . . . . . . .  186 Astrophil    43    8
     Alas, if Fancy drawne by imag'd things,. . . . . . . . . . .  187 Astrophil    45    9
     If Love learne not alone to love and see,. . . . . . . . . .  187 Astrophil    46    7
     No Patience, if thou wilt my good, then make . . . . . . . .  193 Astrophil    56   12
     If he do love, I burne, I burne in love: . . . . . . . . . .  194 Astrophil    59    2
     If he waite well, I never thence would move: . . . . . . . .  194 Astrophil    59    3
     If he be faire, yet but a dog can be.. . . . . . . . . . . .  194 Astrophil    59    4
     Alas, if you graunt only such delight. . . . . . . . . . . .  194 Astrophil    59   12
     Alas, if this the only mettall be. . . . . . . . . . . . . .  196 Astrophil    62   12
     If so great services may scorned be: . . . . . . . . . . . .  198 Astrophil    65   10
     Since in thine armes, if learnd fame truth hath spread,. . .  198 Astrophil    65   13
     If still I force her in sad rimes to creepe: . . . . . . . .  201 Astrophil    70    2
     What wonder then if he his lesson misse, . . . . . . . . . .  203 Astrophil    73    3
     Alas, whence came this change of lookes? If I. . . . . . . .  212 Astrophil    86    1
     But if all faith, like spotlesse Ermine ly . . . . . . . . .  212 Astrophil    86    5
     Or if I needs (sweet Judge) must torments have,. . . . . . .  212 Astrophil    86   11
     I had bene vext, if vext I had not beene.. . . . . . . . . .  223 Astrophil    87   14
     If thou praise not, all other praise is shame. . . . . . . .  224 Astrophil    90    4
     Ne if I would, could I just title make,. . . . . . . . . . .  224 Astrophil    90    9
     If this darke place yet shew like candle light,. . . . . . .  225 Astrophil    91    5
     If you heare that they seeme my hart to move,. . . . . . . .  225 Astrophil    91   13
     If her lips daignd to sweeten my poore name. . . . . . . . .  225 Astrophil    92   13
     Yet truth (if Caitif's breath mighte call thee) this . . . .  227 Astrophil    93    5
     Or if thy love of plaint yet mine forbeares, . . . . . . . .  228 Astrophil    94    9
     Or if such heavenly signes must prove annoy, . . . . . . . .  231 Astrophil   100   13
     But if I by a happy window passe,. . . . . . . . . . . . . .  233 Astrophil   104    9
     If I but stars upon mine armour beare, . . . . . . . . . . .  233 Astrophil   104   10
     If Orpheus' voyce had force to breathe such musicke's love .  208 A&S 3rd Song       1
     If stones good measure daunc'd, the Theban walles to build,.  208 A&S 3rd Song       3
     If Love might sweet'n so a boy of shepheard' brood,. . . . .  209 A&S 3rd Song       7
     If Eagle fierce could so in Grecian Mayd delight,. . . . . .  209 A&S 3rd Song       9
     And if the trees, nor stones stirre not the same to prove, .  209 A&S 3rd Song      14
     Niggard Time threats, if we misse. . . . . . . . . . . . . .  211 A&S 4th Song      31
     If Rule by force without all claime a Tyran showeth, . . . .  214 A&S 5th Song      57
     O if my self find not, . . . . . . . . . . . . . . . . . . .  226 A&S 10th Song      7
     But if thou wouldst garded be, . . . . . . . . . . . . . . .  226 A&S 10th Song     22
     Absence sure will helpe, if I. . . . . . . . . . . . . . . .  234 A&S 11th Song     13
     "What if you new beauties see, . . . . . . . . . . . . . . .  234 A&S 11th Song     21
     Or if they do delight therein, yet are so cloyed with wit, .  217 A&S 7th Song       3
     To be (in things past bounds of wit) fooles, if they be not
          fooles.. . . . . . . . . . . . . . . . . . . . . . . .  217 A&S 7th Song       6
     And if dumbe things be so witty, . . . . . . . . . . . . . .  219 A&S 8th Song      63
     "If that any thought in me,. . . . . . . . . . . . . . . . .  220 A&S 8th Song      77
     "If those eyes you praised, be . . . . . . . . . . . . . . .  220 A&S 8th Song      81
     "If to secret of my hart,. . . . . . . . . . . . . . . . . .  220 A&S 8th Song      85
     "If more may be sayd, I say, . . . . . . . . . . . . . . . .  220 A&S 8th Song      89
     If thou love, my love content thee,. . . . . . . . . . . . .  220 A&S 8th Song      91
     If I saw my good dog grieved,. . . . . . . . . . . . . . . .  222 A&S 9th Song      37
     For she knowes, if she display . . . . . . . . . . . . . . .  222 A&S 9th Song      43
     But alas, if in your straying. . . . . . . . . . . . . . . .  222 A&S 9th Song      47
     Wherof if but a sparke once kindled be, you all. . . . . . .  272 Psalm II          29
     O lord, my God, if I did not forbeare. . . . . . . . . . . .  277 Psalm VII          7
     If ought my hands of wyckednes do bear:. . . . . . . . . . .  277 Psalm VII          9
     If I have been unkynd for friendly part: . . . . . . . . . .  277 Psalm VII         10
     Nay if I wrought not for his Freedome's sake . . . . . . . .  277 Psalm VII         11
     Which if it last, Woe to all simple Hearts.. . . . . . . . .  285 Psalm XII         27
     If of this Clayey race he could espy . . . . . . . . . . . .  286 Psalm XIV          8
     These Canibals, who as if they were bread. . . . . . . . . .  286 Psalm XIV         14
     Least, if answer Thou forbeare,. . . . . . . . . . . . . . .  308 Psalm XXVIII       3
     If Thou remainedst Idle. . . . . . . . . . . . . . . . . . .  315 Psalm XXXII       36
     Frett not Thy self, if thou do see . . . . . . . . . . . . .  324 Psalm XXXVII       1
     If this in them be true, as true in men think I. . . . . . .  343 Possibly     1    7
     W. If wages make you want, what food is that she gives?. . .  344 Possibly     1   33
     Will. God shield us from such Dames. If so our Downes be
          sped,. . . . . . . . . . . . . . . . . . . . . . . . .  344 Possibly     1   39
     Such was his minde, if you another take: . . . . . . . . . .  345 Possibly     4   11
     Me thought some staves he mist: if so, not much amisse:. . .  241 Other Poems  1    1
     As if they would of owners' humour be, . . . . . . . . . . .  242 Other Poems  4   31
     When, if nede were, they could at quintain run:. . . . . . .  243 Other Poems  4   56
     But if they had, could shephookes this resist? . . . . . . .  246 Other Poems  4  160
     If him new-learned manners had not stai'd. . . . . . . . . .  246 Other Poems  4  166
     Happy, o happy! if they so might bide, . .. . . . . . . . .  252 Other Poems  4  401
     Wilt thou have more? more have, if more I be.. . . . . . . .  255 Other Poems  4  514
     If th' author of thy blisse. . . . . . . . . . . . . . . . .  257 Other Poems  5   21
     Tell me, if your diverted springs become . . . . . . . . . .  257 Other Poems  5   37
     Tell me, if husband springtime leave your lande, . . . . . .  257 Other Poems  5   50
     Tell, if that breath, which thee thy sounding gives, . . . .  258 Other Poems  5   63
     Tell me, if wolves the throte. . . . . . . . . . . . . . . .  258 Other Poems  5   72
     Tell me if greedy arme,. . . . . . . . . . . . . . . . . . .  258 Other Poems  5   85
     If thou know not for whome thy Master dies,. . . . . . . . .  259 Other Poems  5  110
     "Therefore Pan, if thou mayst be . . . . . . . . . . . . . .  263 Other Poems  7   55
     Grant, I say (if seely man . . . . . . . . . . . . . . . . .  263 Other Poems  7   57
     If it please thee be reflected,. . . . . . . . . . . . . . .  264 Other Poems  7   71
IGNORANCE
     Nor time pratled away, cradle of ignorance,. . . . . . . . .   69 2nd Eclogues 34   22
```

ILL

	PAGE	TITLE		LINE
And learn'd what ill a miser state doth breed, ...	21	1st Eclogues	8	22
Sucking one's ill, another to infect.	21	1st Eclogues	8	36
And witnesse am, how ill agree in one, ...	40	Arcadia II	19	5
May witnesse beare, how ill agree in one,.	41	Arcadia II	19	11
Sorrowes ill easde, where sorrowes painted be.	41	Arcadia II	21	6
P. Reason hath eyes to see his owne ill case.	46	2nd Eclogues	27	16
Dicus. Enough, enough: so ill hath done the best, ...	56	2nd Eclogues	29	147
The world doth yeeld such ill consorted shows, ...	81	Arcadia III	54	9
Who yet was good, because she knewe none ill,.	94	3rd Eclogues	64	14
And lowest sinke not downe to jote of ill:	99	3rd Eclogues	66	32
That craftily he forst them to do ill, ...	102	3rd Eclogues	66	125
Who onely sees the ill is worse then blind.	106	3rd Eclogues	67	85
"How ill both you can rule, well hath your discord taught: .	121	4th Eclogues	73	163
You should have your face (since Love is ill) blemished. . .	123	4th Eclogues	74	56
If then a man in most ill case may give you a farewell;. . .	124	4th Eclogues	74	85
Pressing too much upon ill harbour shore.	142	Cert Sonnets	12	3
Tell how ill thought disgrac'd my doing well:.	146	Cert Sonnets	17	13
How ill fits you this greene to weare, ...	157	Cert Sonnets	28	3
Is their own foot, ledd by their own ill thought,.	280	Psalm IX		49
From Ill word, and ill meaning sound.	289	Psalm XVII		12
No whit feare ill.	301	Psalm XXIII		12
Though ill deeds well succeeding be.	324	Psalm XXXVII		4
Ev'ill men work ill to utmost right, ...	325	Psalm XXXVII		33
Have been my ill feeding food, ...	334	Psalm XLII		10
The shepheards will grow leane I trow, their sheep will ill be fed.	344	Possibly	1	40

ILL-CHANGED

Me seemes I heare in these ill-changed forrests, ...	112	4th Eclogues	71	39

ILL-MADE

To warme with ill-made fire cold Moscovy;.	180	Astrophil	30	4

ILLS

What greater ills have now the heavens in store, ...	57	2nd Eclogues	30	6
And me from these ills take.	304	Psalm XXV		69

IMAGE

Then kneling to the ground, oft thus do I speake to that Image:	36	1st Eclogues	13	146
Since so your living image lives in me,.	39	Arcadia II	16	7
She doth possesse, thy Image is defaste, ...	72	Arcadia III	38	12
A dull desire to kisse the image of our death:	117	4th Eclogues	73	10
An image is, which for our selves we carve;.	167	Astrophil	5	6
Sweet Stella's image I do steale to mee".	181	Astrophil	32	14
Unto my mind, is Stella's image, wrought	183	Astrophil	38	7
Livelier then else-where, Stella's image see.	184	Astrophil	39	14
Of everie image, which may comfort show?	199	Astrophil	66	4
From the image of thy lover?	225	A&S 10th Song		6
(Image like of Saints' perfection)	234	A&S 11th Song		24
See, do you see this face? a face? nay image of the skies, .	217	A&S 7th Song		15
Which when he did in perfect image show, ...	256	Other Poems	4	541

IMAGED

Alas, if Fancy drawne by imag'd things,.	187	Astrophil	45	9

IMITATE

Or do you cutted Spartanes imitate?.	225	Astrophil	92	3

IMMORTAL

Which makes us most immortall shape to weare,.	40	Arcadia II	18	14
The inke immortall fame dooth lende:	90	Arcadia III	62	143
Which must by this immortall be preserved, ...	105	3rd Eclogues	67	77
Whence our immortall soules to mortall earth doo flowe:. . .	118	4th Eclogues	73	46
Who may immortall gaine.	152	Cert Sonnets	23	20
Immortall be her graces, ...	152	Cert Sonnets	23	21
Immortall is her minde:.	152	Cert Sonnets	23	22
Since our lives be not immortall,.	155	Cert Sonnets	26	16

IMMUTABLE

Of my due faith, which needs must be immutable?.	47	2nd Eclogues	28	8

IMP

Although lesse gifts impe feathers oft on Fame,.	204	Astrophil	75	4

IMPAIR

So that I see, although my sight empaire,.	115	4th Eclogues	72	59

IMPAIRER

The quiet mind (whereof my selfe empairer is,.	51	2nd Eclogues	28	114

IMPART

Nought could impart such heates to friendly mind.	51	2nd Eclogues	28	105
Those secrett joyes, which heaven to me emparte, ...	70	Arcadia III	35	14
Which barde desires, (barde by my selfe) imparte.	77	Arcadia III	47	11
To her sweete sence, sweete sleepe, some ease imparte, . . .	79	Arcadia III	51	3
But how the Graces doo impart.	90	Arcadia III	62	134
Where simple love, which chastnesse doth imparte,.	92	3rd Eclogues	63	58
Nature to me for torment did emparte;.	113	4th Eclogues	72	13
Lives to impart my wearie clay some breath.	148	Cert Sonnets	20	10
Though rapt with beautie's hooke, I did impart	150	Cert Sonnets	22	26
Yet to those fooles heav'n such wit doth impart, ...	177	Astrophil	24	5
But more I crie, lesse grace she doth impart, ...	186	Astrophil	44	6
Most rich, when most his riches it impart:	206	Astrophil	79	7
O kisse, which doest those ruddie gemmes impart, ...	207	Astrophil	81	1
Each to other do imparte, ...	227	A&S 10th Song		41
I do any wish impart,.	220	A&S 8th Song		86
Shall joy impart.	308	Psalm XXVII		66
O then Thy righteousness impart.	324	Psalm XXXVI		29
O yea, my Friend to whom I did impart.	333	Psalm XLI		29

		PAGE	TITLE	LINE

IMPARTED
Love therewith is streight imparted. . . . . 218 A&S 8th Song 36
IMPARTS
The multitude to Jove a suite empartes,. . . . . 100 3rd Eclogues 66 61
IMPLANTED
In whose chiefe parte your worthes implanted be? . . . . . . 39 Arcadia II 16 10
IMPRESSION
Her beames have wrought therin most suer impression: . . . . 47 2nd Eclogues 28 11
Where nothing but impression lackes. . . . . 88 Arcadia III 62 76
IMPRINTED
The love which is imprinted in my soule. . . . . 85 Arcadia III 61 1
IMPRISON
Emprison hir, who both them did possesse . . . . 252 Other Poems 4 390
IMPRISONED
My thoughts imprisonde in my secreat woes, ... 42 Arcadia II 21 7
IMP'S
By thy impe's losse to fill the world with wailing. . . . . . 109 Arcadia IV 70 22
IMPUTE
Some luckie wits impute it but to chaunce; . . . . 185 Astrophil 41 8
IMPUTES
Imputes not sins to be abhord, ... 314 Psalm XXXII 5
INBENT
From out thy heavy mould, that inbent eyes . . . . 228 Astrophil 94 3
INBOWED
With inbow'd bosome well for hir prepar'd, ... 252 Other Poems 4 387
INCESSANTLY
But on her name incessantly to crie: . . . . 192 Astrophil 55 11
INCIRCLETS
In whose Incirclets if you gaze, ... 86 Arcadia III 62 31
INCISION
Thy toong hath made of Cupid's deepe incision. . . . . 20 1st Eclogues 7 V969
INCLINE
Or that they all to chaunging did encline, ... 100 3rd Eclogues 66 59
My boiling sprites did thither soone incline,. . . . . 172 Astrophil 16 3
And eares to them encline. . . . . 320 Psalm XXXIV 56
INCLINED
Of that, whereto he feard she was enclinde,. . . . . 95 3rd Eclogues 64 50
Like foe, whose wits inclin'd to deadly spite, ... 135 Cert Sonnets 2 3
Then eare to them enclin'd.. . . . . 283 Psalm X 76
Who be to God enclined.. . . . . 284 Psalm XI 24
INCLUDES
Fancie we feele, encludes all passion's mighte, ... 82 Arcadia III 57 3
INCONGRUITIES
For what can breed more peevish incongruities, ... 61 2nd Eclogues 30 140
INCONSTANT
And stay the starrs' inconstant constant race, ... 126 4th Eclogues 75 38
INCREASE
Who yelds to woe, doth but encrease his smart. . . . . 22 1st Eclogues 9 2
Aire, we do still with sighes encrease; to the fire? we do
    want none. . . . . 32 1st Eclogues 13 30
Cleofila. First shall fertill grounds not yeeld increase of
    a good seed: . . . . 33 1st Eclogues 13 64
These fires increase: in these I dayly burne:. . . . . 42 Arcadia II 22 8
With large encrease, and wooll of fine perfection, ... 49 2nd Eclogues 28 50
To see her ofspring seeke a good increase, ... 91 3rd Eclogues 63 2
So may thy flockes encrease, thy deere hart glad,. . . . . . 96 3rd Eclogues 64 93
Her flamie glistring lights increase with time and place;. . 205 Astrophil 76 10
Where those red cheeks, which oft with faire encrease did
    frame. . . . . 232 Astrophil 102 2
Who long dead beautie with increase reneweth?. . . . . 197 A&S 1st Song 22
Thy delights my woes increase, ... 227 A&S 10th Song 44
Lord how do they encrease. . . . . 272 Psalm III 1
The more my sorrow did encrease, ... 329 Psalm XXXIX 8
INCREASED
My woes are still encreast;. . . . . 304 Psalm XXV 61
Whose boiling heat encreased as she wept:. . . . . 246 Other Poems 4 155
Much more his sight encreast his hote desire:. . . . . 249 Other Poems 4 298
INCREASING
Me in encreasing still, Thy kindness did maintaine;. . . . . 292 Psalm XVIII 65
Till finding still his evill encreasing thus,. . . . . 253 Other Poems 4 437
INDE
Of herbes or beastes, which Inde or Afrike hold. . . . . . . 166 Astrophil 3 8
INDEED
Life showing, dead indeed: . . . . 19 1st Eclogues 7 160
But is indeed a toy, if not a toy, ... 25 1st Eclogues 9 115
Then do I thinke in deed, that better it is to be private. . 35 1st Eclogues 13 102
R. Repent indeed, but that shall be your blisse. . . . . . . 47 2nd Eclogues 27 37
Nico. In deed the witch thy dam her crouch from shoulder
    spred, ... 52 2nd Eclogues 29 13
Whiter indeed; more white then snow, ... 85 Arcadia III 62 7
Indeed a perfect hewe, indeed a sweet consent. . . . . 119 4th Eclogues 73 85
Orphans in deede, depriv'd of father's might:. . . . . 129 4th Eclogues 76 13
Indeed I well did hope,. . . . . 158 Cert Sonnets 28 5
True, that true Beautie Vertue is indeed,. . . . . 167 Astrophil 5 9
Be Love's indeed, in Stella's selfe he may . . . . 191 Astrophil 52 10
Professe in deed I do not Cupid's art; . . . . 192 Astrophil 54 10
They love indeed, who quake to say they love:. . . . . 192 Astrophil 54 14
That who indeed infelt affection beares, ... 195 Astrophil 61 5
Yet sighs, deere sighs, indeede true friends you are,. . . . 228 Astrophil 95 1
I said, thou wert most faire, and so indeed thou art:. . . . 212 A&S 5th Song 7

INDEED	(CONTINUED)	PAGE	TITLE		LINE
Thou art my son in deed, this day begott by me:.		271	Psalm II		17
Indeed full many folkes have said, ...		274	Psalm IV		24
Indeed the poore opprest by you, you mock, ...		287	Psalm XIV		19
Indeed O you, you that be such of mind, ...		300	Psalm XXII		63
One thing in deed I did and will		307	Psalm XXVII		19
Indeed Thou art my rock, my Forteress;		312	Psalm XXXI		7
Blessed in deed to whom the lord		314	Psalm XXXII		4
That Realm in deed hath blisse		317	Psalm XXXIII		43
Indeed the very best		320	Psalm XXXIV		69
O he indeed is blessed, ...		331	Psalm XL		15
My soul thirsts indeed in me		334	Psalm XLII		5
While thus they liv'd, (this was indede a life).		243	Other Poems	4	58
Klaius in deede would faine have puld a way.		246	Other Poems	4	171
In dede thou said'st it was thy frend to see, ...		247	Other Poems	4	219
Till she brake from their armes (although in deed.		252	Other Poems	4	413
INDENTURES					
The globe of weale, lips Love's indentures make:		210	Astrophil	85	13
INDES					
"Foole," answers he, "no Indes such treasures hold, ...		181	Astrophil	32	12
INDIAN					
The Indian odours doth excell.		87	Arcadia III	62	64
Be your words made (good Sir) of Indian ware, ...		225	Astrophil	92	1
INDIFFERENT					
Th'indifferent Judge betweene the high and low;.		184	Astrophil	39	4
INDITE					
Stella behold, and then begin to endite.		172	Astrophil	15	14
Sweet kisse, thy sweets I faine would sweetly endite, ...		206	Astrophil	79	1
Since all my words thy beauty doth endite, ...		224	Astrophil	90	13
Write, but first let me endite:.		211	A&S 4th Song		40
Write, but let me first endite:.		211	A&S 4th Song		V 40
INDUED					
And so besides our God, who is indue'd with might?		292	Psalm XVIII		58
INDUSTRY					
Ante, industrie; and Connie, skill to builde;.		101	3rd Eclogues	66	93
Which cannot be restor'd by time nor industrie:.		214	A&S 5th Song		47
INFECT					
Sucking one's ill, another to infect.		21	1st Eclogues	8	36
Infected mindes infect each thing they see..		147	Cert Sonnets	18	14
INFECTED					
With so sweete plagues my happie harmes infected be:		51	2nd Eclogues	28	123
Turnd from themselves, infected with their cage, ...		57	2nd Eclogues	30	18
Doth th'infected wretch, of his ev'll th'extremity know? No.		63	2nd Eclogues	31	19
And though thereby my fancie was infected, ...		83	Arcadia III	57	6
Who hath our sight with too much sight infected, ...		108	Arcadia IV	69	6
Infected so with her sweet poyson's might, ...		115	4th Eclogues	72	78
Infected mindes infect each thing they see..		147	Cert Sonnets	18	14
All Love is dead, infected		159	Cert Sonnets	30	3
Infected by those vapours, which arise		205	Astrophil	78	2
INFECTION					
Thy health too meane a match for my infection.		15	1st Eclogues	7	21
To helpe, or hurt in thee her owne infection..		49	2nd Eclogues	28	54
A foul infection kills or bredeth botches..		50	2nd Eclogues	28	V884
So in his sicknesse grew our sure infection.		128	4th Eclogues	75	135
INFECTIOUS					
But from the sent of some infectious grave:.		114	4th Eclogues	72	19
INFELT					
That who indeed infelt affection beares, ...		195	Astrophil	61	5
INFERNAL					
Infernall agonies unto a bewtye divine, ...		30	1st Eclogues	11	14
Harke plaintfull ghostes, infernall furies harke		73	Arcadia III	40	1
Till now, wrapt in a most infernall night, ...		181	Astrophil	33	3
INFINITE					
And in her eyes of arrowes infinit..		173	Astrophil	17	11
Where Nature doth with infinite agree?		182	Astrophil	35	4
INFIRMITY					
What skill servethe a soare of a wrong infirmity judged? . .		32	1st Eclogues	13	21
Therfore I said in most infirmity, ...		333	Psalm XLI		13
INFLAME					
Least you enflame his wrath.		272	Psalm II		28
INFLAMED					
Sing then, and see (for now thou hast inflamed me)		15	1st Eclogues	7	20
Old wood inflam'de, doth yeeld the bravest fire, ...		38	Arcadia II	15	3
Nay even cold Death enflamde with hot desire		59	2nd Eclogues	30	86
And that it had enflam'd a new desire, ...		95	3rd Eclogues	64	38
Right so my boiling hart, enflam'de with fire of a faire eye		123	4th Eclogues	74	27
Wounded, inflam'de, knitt to the deathe I dye.		344	Possibly	2	4
INFLUENCE					
Thou canst vouchsafe the influence of a thought.		184	Astrophil	40	6
INFUSED					
And to that braine of hers your hidnest gifts infused, . . .		213	A&S 5th Song		27
INFUSING					
Of force of heav'nly beames, infusing hellish paine:		167	Astrophil	6	3
INHABIT					
Inhabit shall his prayse..		318	Psalm XXXIV		4
INHABITERS					
Hunting the wilde inhabiters of forrests, ...		111	4th Eclogues	71	20
INHERIT					
Tho I blisse enherit never..		221	A&S 9th Song		20

240

```
INHERITRIX                                                  PAGE    TITLE          LINE
   The proofe of Beautie's worth, th'enheritrix of fame,. . . .  213 A&S 5th Song     20
INHUMANITY
   And Love, which lover hurts is inhumanitie". . . . . . . . .   16 1st Eclogues  7   66
INIQUITIES
   Telling mine iniquityes. . . . . . . . . . . . . . . . . .    329 Psalm XXXVIII     54
INIQUITY
   Both mischief and iniquity.. . . . . . . . . . . . . . . . .  282 Psalm X          30
   Let my iniquity. . . . . . . . . . . . . . . . . . . . . . .  304 Psalm XXV        44
   His words deceit, iniquity . . . . . . . . . . . . . . . . .  323 Psalm XXXVI       9
INJURY
   And onely cherish doth with injurie. . . . . . . . . . . .    206 Astrophil    78   8
INK
   My words blacke inke, the marble kindly white; . . . . . .     41 Arcadia II   19   9
   Blacke incke becommes the state wherein I dye. . . . . . .     81 Arcadia III  54   6
   The inke immortall fame dooth lende: . . . . . . . . . . .     90 Arcadia III  62 143
   This mourning inck, in which my hart doth bleede. . . . . .    96 3rd Eclogues 64  96
   Which inke onely relates, but ne laments, ne replies?. . .    122 4th Eclogues 74  18
   While teares powre out his inke, and sighs breathe out his
      words: . . . . . . . . . . . . . . . . . . . . . . . . .   168 Astrophil     6  10
   My verie inke turnes straight to Stella's name;. . . . . .    174 Astrophil    19   6
   What inke is blacke inough to paint my wo? . . . . . . . .    227 Astrophil    93   3
   While beautie's reddest inke Venus for him doth sturre.. . .  232 Astrophil   102  14
INK'S
   My harmes on Ink's poore losse, perhaps some find. . . . .    182 Astrophil    34  13
INLY
   With outward joyes, which inly cannot sincke,. . . . . . .     22 1st Eclogues  9   7
   But finding th'approch of death with an inly relenting,. . .  123 4th Eclogues 74  25
   Where bee nowe those eyes ever Inly persers? . . . . . . .    138 Cert Sonnets  5   6
INMOST
   Their soules fowl sinns for inmost lyning have:. . . . . .    275 Psalm V          26
   Doth melt away though it be inmost seated. . . . . . . . .    299 Psalm XXII       34
   Yea sound my reines, and inmost of my heart; . . . . . . .    305 Psalm XXVI        9
INN
   How all this is but a faire Inne . . . . . . . . . . . . .     90 Arcadia III  62 139
INNOCENCE
   Here no treason is hidd, vailed in innocence,. . . . . . .     69 2nd Eclogues 34  17
   Within the bounds of Innocence to byde,. . . . . . . . . .    305 Psalm XXVI        3
   In th' Innocence of Me . . . . . . . . . . . . . . . . . .    305 Psalm XXVI       19
INNOCENT
   While thus he fear'd the silly innocent, . . . . . . . . .     94 3rd Eclogues 64  13
   Against the Innocent,. . . . . . . . . . . . . . . . . . .    282 Psalm X          36
INQUIRING
   That He enquiringe, doth require just blood, . . . . . . .    280 Psalm IX         33
INSEPARATE
   And joy, which is inseperate from those eyes,. . . . . . .    231 Astrophil   101   7
INSIDE
   Or seeke heavn's course, or heavn's inside to see: . . . .    169 Astrophil    10   5
INSIGHT
   Cleofila. Hardy shephearde, such as thy meritts, such may be
      her insight . . . . . . . . . . . . . . . . . . . . . .     37 1st Eclogues 13 155
   Then was I by thy searching insight try'd, . . . . . . . .    289 Psalm XVII       10
INSINUATIONS
   Nor flatterers' venomous insinuations, . . . . . . . . . .     69 2nd Eclogues 34  19
INSPIRED
   My lips are sweet, inspired with Stella's kisse. . . . . .    204 Astrophil    74  14
INSPIRING
   Untill by your inspiring I might know, . . . . . . . . . .    192 Astrophil    55   7
   Sense of love to love inspiring. . . . . . . . . . . . . .    219 A&S 8th Song     60
INSTEAD
   On pensive soules (in steede of restfull baite). . . . . .     82 Arcadia III  56   6
   Care upon care (in steede of doing right). . . . . . . . .     82 Arcadia III  56   7
   In stede of Thought, true pleasure be begunne, . . . . . .     84 Arcadia III  59  15
   And fill the vales with cries in steed of musique. . . . .    111 4th Eclogues 71  24
   In steade of gall, leaving to her my hart: . . . . . . . .    150 Cert Sonnets 22  28
   By conquest's right in steade of searching kill. . . . . .    150 Cert Sonnets 22  30
   But find some Hercules to beare, in steed. . . . . . . . .    190 Astrophil    51   7
INSTINCT
   But God gives them instinct the man to shun, . . . . . . .    249 Other Poems   4 295
INSTRUCTED
   But who so will instructed be. . . . . . . . . . . . . . .    315 Psalm XXXII      28
   Then did he slack his love-enstructed pace.. . . . . . . .    250 Other Poems   4 308
INSTRUCTION
   Her love my life; her anger my Instruction;. . . . . . . .     49 2nd Eclogues 28  71
INSTRUMENT
   The instrument of instruments, the hand. . . . . . . . . .    101 3rd Eclogues 66  98
   Wherto their tongue is flattring Instrument. . . . . . . .    275 Psalm V          28
   Let ten-stringd instrument . . . . . . . . . . . . . . . .    316 Psalm XXXIII     10
INSTRUMENTS
   The instrument of instruments, the hand. . . . . . . . . .    101 3rd Eclogues 66  98
INTEGRITY
   But in integrity . . . . . . . . . . . . . . . . . . . . .    306 Psalm XXVI       34
INTEMPERANCE
   With such intemperance, that each way grows. . . . . . . .     27 1st Eclogues 10  38
INTEND
   But did entend next bout with her to meete,. . . . . . . .    248 Other Poems   4 250
INTENDED
   Full Wylily intended;. . . . . . . . . . . . . . . . . . .    298 Psalm XXI        42
INTENDETH
   Doubt you to whom my Muse these notes entendeth, . . . . .    196 A&S 1st Song      1
```

INTENDETH   (CONTINUED)   PAGE   TITLE   LINE
    Doubt you to whom my Muse these notes intendeth, ...   197 A&S 1st Song   33
INTENT
    The Cockow's shame, the Goose's good intent, ...   28 1st Eclogues 10   80
    And so she was, and all with good intent, ...   95 3rd Eclogues 64   25
    To grant Thy Will and perfect Thy entent, ... 296 Psalm XX   17
INTEPRET
    Well, how so thou interpret the contents, ... 199 Astrophil   67   12
INTERCHANGEABLY
    Enterchangeably reflected. . . . . 218 A&S 8th Song   16
INTERLACE
    Marble mixt red and white do enterlace. . . . . 169 Astrophil   9   8
INTERPRET
    Well, how so thou interpret the contents, ... 199 Astrophil   67   12
INTO
    Into our mindes let us a little fall, ...   29 1st Eclogues 10   94
    Into the faire looker on, pastime, not passion, enters. . . .   32 1st Eclogues 13   41
    Comfort into my soule. I do finde, I do find what a blessing   34 1st Eclogues 13   95
    Into my live's bondage, yet may disburden a passion. . . . .   35 1st Eclogues 13   108
    Since sighes (into mine inward fornace turnd) . . . .   38 Arcadia II   14   7
    Let voice of Sighes into cleare musike runne, ...   84 Arcadia III   59   13
    Into my breste, and loves renewed swimme. . . . .   85 Arcadia III   61   12
    Man was not man their dwellings in to hem. . . . .   100 3rd Eclogues 66   49
    Hath cast me, wretch, into eternall evening, ...   113 4th Eclogues 71   65
    Into thy hart by the sight of this Epistle I send: . . . . .   122 4th Eclogues 74   6
    My breath distinguish'd into wordes of woe, ... 125 4th Eclogues 75   8
    Passing all ghesse, whence into me should fly. . . . .   149 Cert Sonnets 22   8
    Their running fall into a constant vaine . . . .   150 Cert Sonnets 22   38
    But, foole, seekst not to get into her hart. . . . .   170 Astrophil   11   14
    Neare therabout, into your Poesie wring; . . . .   172 Astrophil   15   4
    Into your rimes, running in ratling rowes: . . . .   172 Astrophil   15   6
    When into Reason's audite I do go: . . . .   173 Astrophil   18   2
    So dull am, that I cannot looke into . . . .   195 Astrophil   60   10
    Melts downe his lead into my boyling brest, ... 236 Astrophil   108   2
    The just into his power. . . . .   286 Psalm XIV   18
    And look into. . . . .   307 Psalm XXVII   23
    Into Thy hands I do commend my sprite, ...   312 Psalm XXXI   13
    The happy wretch she putt into hir breast, ...   244 Other Poems   4   98
    While into none doubt of his love did sinke, ...   247 Other Poems   4 199
INURE
    Till I get her, shall I to sheep enure my selfe? . . . . . .   16 1st Eclogues 7   60
INVADE
    I Stella's eyes assayll, invade her eares; . . . .   195 Astrophil   61   3
    Now will I invade the fort; . . . . 202 A&S 2nd Song   15
INVADETH
    Thy thorne without, my thorne my heart invadeth. . . . . . .   137 Cert Sonnets 4   12
    Above line repeated at following location. . . . .   137 Cert Sonnets 4   24
INVADING
    Heare you this soule-invading voice, and count it but a
        voice? . . . .   217 A&S 7th Song   17
INVASION
    And how possest he strengthens his invasion? . . . .   48 2nd Eclogues 28   36
    Since Death on Vertue's fort hath made invasion. . . . . . .   128 4th Eclogues 75   102
INVENT
    My best wits still their owne disgrace invent: . . . .   174 Astrophil   19   5
INVENTION
    To worke my Goddesse so by thy invention, ...   19 1st Eclogues 7   177
    Doubte is his sleepe, he waketh in invention; . . . .   48 2nd Eclogues 28   40
    Ne doo I care how rude be my invention, ... 128 4th Eclogues 75   104
    Invention, Nature's child, fled step-dame Studie's blowes, .   165 Astrophil   1   10
INVENTION'S
    But words came halting forth, wanting Invention's stay, . . . 165 Astrophil   1   9
INVENTIONS
    Studying inventions fine, her wits to entertaine: . . . . . . 165 Astrophil   1   6
INVESTS
    Anger invests with such a lovely grace, ... 203 Astrophil   73   13
INVIOLATE
    Such faith, so staineles, inviolate, violent? . . . . 124 4th Eclogues 74   70
INVISIBLE
    He was invisible that hurt me so, ... 253 Other Poems   4 455
    And none invisible, but Spirites, can goe. . . . .   253 Other Poems   4 456
INVITE
    Diana did begin. "What mov'd me to invite. . . . .   119 4th Eclogues 73   102
    Promising wonders, wonder to invite, ...   178 Astrophil   26   4
    For that at length yet doth invite some rest, ... 229 Astrophil   96   13
    Do invite a stealing kisse: . . . . 203 A&S 2nd Song   22
    You I invite with easie eares to heare . . . .   242 Other Poems   4   13
INVITES
    So good a say invites the eye, ...   87 Arcadia III   62   51
INVITEST
    With sweete soft shades thou oft invitest me . . . .   230 Astrophil   98   5
INVOKE
    The power I will invoke dwelles in her eyes: . . . .   17 1st Eclogues 7   104
    Whom then shall I invoke but Thee most worthy prayse, ... 291 Psalm XVIII   6
    Nede not the stately Muses' helpe invoke . . . .   242 Other Poems   4   7
INVOKED
    Muses, I oft invoked your holy ayde, ...   192 Astrophil   55   1
INVOKES
    But who on God his trust invokes, ... 315 Psalm XXXII   38

INWARD

		PAGE	TITLE		LINE
With outward force and inward treason spoild..		11	Arcadia I	2	4
Whereto mine inward thoughts did faintly yeeld;.		11	Arcadia I	2	6
Yeld outward shew, what inward change he tryes:.		13	Arcadia I	4	2
Deadly wounds inward bleed, ech sleight sore mattereth.. . . .		14	1st Eclogues	7	9
O happie Gods, which by inward assumption.		15	1st Eclogues	7	40
No thralles like them that inward bondage have..		17	1st Eclogues	7	114
And yet his outward heate our teares would quench, but an inward		32	1st Eclogues	13	31
And hope therby to ease their inward horrible anguish, . . .		33	1st Eclogues	13	45
Then shall those thinges ease their inward horrible angwish. .		33	1st Eclogues	13	46
Nurse inwarde maladyes, which have not scope to be breath'd out, ...		35	1st Eclogues	13	104
Since sighes (into mine inward fornace turnd).		38	Arcadia II	14	7
Thus outward helps my inward griefes maintaine..		42	Arcadia II	21	12
And in our little world dost cleare our inward sight,. . . .		44	Arcadia II	26	2
But such we are with inward tempest blowne		59	2nd Eclogues	30	80
He heapes in inward griefe, that most destroyes him.		62	2nd Eclogues	30	172
So that the windowes of my inward light.		73	Arcadia III	39	7
Do serve, to make my inward powers darke:.		73	Arcadia III	39	8
By inward letts, of them his state possest,.		75	Arcadia III	44	2
My inward hurte should spare thy outward rine?		77	Arcadia III	47	8
Right so my inwarde partes, and outward glasse,.		78	Arcadia III	50	6
My greedy soule, with gripe of inward fire:.		80	Arcadia III	53	6
With inward cries putts up a bitter role		85	Arcadia III	61	3
All privatenes, selfe-seeking, inward spite, ...		93	3rd Eclogues	63	65
And inward griefe seale up with outward wailing.		109	Arcadia IV	70	6
The furious inward griefes with hellish wailing:		109	Arcadia IV	70	33
With outward maker's force, or like an inward father.. . .		118	4th Eclogues	73	48
Paine heard her praise, and full of inward fire, ...		141	Cert Sonnets	9	9
Whose clowdie thoughts let fall an inward raine.		150	Cert Sonnets	22	36
Which as of inward glorie.		152	Cert Sonnets	23	29
For messenger of inward good..		156	Cert Sonnets	27	8
The inward light: and that the heavenly part		167	Astrophil	5	2
As do bewray a want of inward tuch:.		172	Astrophil	15	10
Which inward sunne to Heroicke minde displaies,.		177	Astrophil	25	8
My mind bemones his sense of inward smart;		186	Astrophil	44	2
That inward sunne in thine eyes shineth so..		201	Astrophil	71	8
My Orphan sence flies to the inward sight, ...		223	Astrophil	88	10
Takes in that sad hue, which with th'inward night.		230	Astrophil	99	7
In my inward reynes I taste.		288	Psalm XVI		23
With Inward secrets of my heart.		289	Psalm XVII		8
He that hath hurtless hands, whose inward heart is framed. .		302	Psalm XXIV		7
I lift my in ward sight;		302	Psalm XXV		2
Inward, an inward rest,.		304	Psalm XXV		50
Least inward evills do them defile,.		320	Psalm XXXIV		50
With inward wo, an outward sack cloth ware..		322	Psalm XXXV		30
They inward ev'ills disguise,.		333	Psalm XLI		22
For warbling notes from inward chearing flow..		242	Other Poems	4	4
This mote from out his eye, this inward burre.		246	Other Poems	4	172
Made wolves (not inward wolves) my ewes to spare;.		254	Other Poems	4	486
Breeding huge stormes with in his inward parte,.		256	Other Poems	4	543
Hides their inward will of harming..		263	Other Poems	7	42

IO

| By Argus got on Io, then a cow:. . . . . | | 21 | 1st Eclogues | 8 | 14 |
| Sing then my Muse, my Io Pean sing, ... | | 196 | Astrophil | 63 | 9 |

IRE

Winde, tempests, and stormes, yet in ende what gives she desire? Ire.		64	2nd Eclogues	31	35
And vex them in his ire.		271	Psalm II		12
Yet each day art provoakt, thyne Ire to show,.		277	Psalm VII		32
The Lord on them with causfull Ire		297	Psalm XXI		33
Faine would be free, but dreadeth parents' ire..		245	Other Poems	4	120

IREFUL

| Their ireful shotte against so weake a marke,. . . . . . | | 73 | Arcadia III | 40 | 6 |
| But thus with irefull eyes, and face that shooke with spite. | | 119 | 4th Eclogues | 73 | 101 |

IRIS

| As smooth as Pan, as Juno milde, like goddesse Iris faste. . | | 12 | Arcadia I | 3 | 6 |

IRKED

| And is even irkt that so sweet Comedie,. . . . . | | 190 | Astrophil | 51 | 13 |

IRKS

| For though life irkes, in life my loves protected be.. . . . | | 51 | 2nd Eclogues | 28 | 125 |

IRKSOME

| Now that of absence the most irksome night,. . . . . . . | | 223 | Astrophil | 89 | 1 |

IRON

Iron to seeke, which gainst it selfe should bend,.		102	3rd Eclogues	66	116
By iron lawes of duty to depart:		222	Astrophil	87	4
Whom iron doores do keepe from use of day?		237	Astrophil	108	11
With Iron scepter bruse thou shalt, and peece meale breake .		271	Psalm II		21
Strengthning mine arms that they could break an Iron bow.. .		292	Psalm XVIII		63
The heav'n-love lodestone drew thy iron hart..		248	Other Poems	4	224

ISIS

| As smooth as Pan, as Juno milde, like goddesse Isis faste. . | | 12 | Arcadia I | 3 | 6 |

ISLANDS

| Sweete Ilands make in that sweete land.. . . . . | | 90 | Arcadia III | 62 | 129 |

ISRAEL

And Israel full of Comfort?.		287	Psalm XIV		24
Where Israel Thy lawdes is ever telling;		298	Psalm XXII		10
In fine deliver Israel,.		305	Psalm XXV		77
Of Israel the God.		334	Psalm XLI		46

```
                                                     PAGE    TITLE          LINE
ISRAEL'S
     You Isra'el's seed, you come of Jacob, feare him.. . . . . .  300 Psalm XXII         54
ISSUE
     With flamie breathe doo issue oft in sound:. . . . . . . . .   42 Arcadia II    21     8
     And make their issue showe . . . . . . . . . . . . . . . . .   92 3rd Eclogues 63    41
ISSUED
     But streight there issued forth two Ladies (Ladies sure. . .  118 4th Eclogues 73    63
     Flames issued from his mouth, and burning coales out went; .  291 Psalm XVIII        19
ISTER
     As I my little flocke on Ister banke . . . . . . . . . . . .   98 3rd Eclogues 66     1
     Languet, the shepheard best swift Ister knewe, . . . . . . .   99 3rd Eclogues 66    23
ITCH
     My tongue doth itch, my thoughts in labour be: . . . . . . .  183 Astrophil     37     2
     Will. Thou seest my eares do itch at it: good Dick thy sorow
       tell. . . . . . . . . . . . . . . . . . . . . . . . . . .  343 Possibly       1    18
ITSELF
     So doth my life within it selfe dissolve.. . . . . . . . . .   19 1st Eclogues   7   156
     Lalus. So doth my life within it selfe dissolve, . . . . . .   19 1st Eclogues   7   157
     Till aige it self do make it self esteemde.. . . . . . . . .   26 1st Eclogues   9   141
     As in it selfe to nourish mortall strife.. . . . . . . . . .   57 2nd Eclogues 30    28
     Her to enjoy, where joy it selfe is thrall,. . . . . . . . .   59 2nd Eclogues 30    87
     This waxe doth waste it selfe, yet painelesse dyes.. . . . .   75 Arcadia III   43     7
     Iron to seeke, which gainst it selfe should bend,. . . . . .  102 3rd Eclogues 66   116
     Hath made it selfe a crier of the morning, . . . . . . . . .  112 4th Eclogues 71    26
     Is that huge storme, which powres it selfe on me:. . . . . .  114 4th Eclogues 72    32
     Lamde with the angle, which it selfe did beare,. . . . . . .  115 4th Eclogues 72    67
     Ne could my soule it selfe accuse of such a faulte,. . . . .  117 4th Eclogues 73    19
     Within it selfe, and never taketh ende:. . . . . . . . . . .  127 4th Eclogues 75    80
     Bewray it selfe in my long setled eyes,. . . . . . . . . . .  176 Astrophil     23     2
     Scourge of it selfe, still climing slipprie place, . . . . .  176 Astrophil     23    10
     To keepe it selfe in life and liberty, . . . . . . . . . . .  179 Astrophil     29     6
     Where truth it selfe must speake like flatterie? . . . . . .  182 Astrophil     35     2
     That Noblenesse it selfe makes thus unkind?. . . . . . . . .  186 Astrophil     44     8
     Which even to sence, sence of it selfe denies, . . . . . . .  228 Astrophil     94     7
     But wo is me, though joy it selfe were she,. . . . . . . . .  230 Astrophil     97    12
     That eloquence it selfe envies your praise,. . . . . . . . .  231 Astrophil    100    10
     That sickenesse brags it selfe best graced to be.. . . . . .  231 Astrophil    101     4
     Jealousie it selfe doth sleepe:. . . . . . . . . . . . . . .  210 A&S 4th Song        10
     It selfe to the other lends. . . . . . . . . . . . . . . . .  216 A&S 6th Song        18
     Love it selfe did silence breake;. . . . . . . . . . . . . .  218 A&S 8th Song        26
     Ev'n thus it self it doth display, . . . . . . . . . . . . .  323 Psalm XXXVI          4
     Ah my soul it self appaleth, . . . . . . . . . . . . . . . .  334 Psalm XLII          23
     Tc make it selfe to my least looke a slave:. . . . . . . . .  255 Other Poems    4   511
IVORY
     Her nose, her chinne pure ivorie weares: . . . . . . . . . .   86 Arcadia III   62    27
     Warme snow, moyst pearle, softe ivorie.. . . . . . . . . . .   90 Arcadia III   62   126
     Whence hast thou Ivorie, Rubies, pearle and gold,. . . . . .  181 Astrophil     32    10
     In ivory cage she did the micher binde:. . . . . . . . . . .  244 Other Poems    4    94
IWIS
     A prettie curre it is; his name iwis is Catch, . . . . . . .   53 2nd Eclogues 29    40
JACINTH
     Her forhead jacinth like, her cheekes of opall hue,. . . . .   12 Arcadia I      3     9
JACOB
     That Jacob freed by Thee may glad become . . . . . . . . . .  287 Psalm XIV          23
     You Isra'el's seed, you come of Jacob, feare him.. . . . . .  300 Psalm XXII         54
     Jacob this is Thy seed, God seeking generation,. . . . . . .  302 Psalm XXIV         15
JACOB'S
     Let name of Jacob's God, . . . . . . . . . . . . . . . . . .  295 Psalm XX            3
JADE
     Tir'de as a jade in overloden carte, . . . . . . . . . . . .  253 Other Poems    4   443
JAIL
     They better live that in a gaile doo lie.. . . . . . . . . .  105 3rd Eclogues 67    54
JAILER
     Jaylor I am to my selfe, prison and prisoner to myne owne
       selfe. . . . . . . . . . . . . . . . . . . . . . . . . .   37 1st Eclogues 13   163
JARL
     Then jarle: lo, lo, even these how envie blindes.. . . . . .   26 1st Eclogues 10     9
JARRED
     Although their fame (me seemd) from truth had greatly jard..  119 4th Eclogues 73    80
JAWBONES
     On jaw-bones of my foes, . . . . . . . . . . . . . . . . . .  273 Psalm III          26
JAWS
     Betweene the jawes of hellish Jealousie. . . . . . . . . . .  205 Astrophil     78     4
     Up lord prevent those gaping jawes . . . . . . . . . . . . .  290 Psalm XVII         35
     Like lions fierce, with roaring jawes enlarged.. . . . . . .  299 Psalm XXII         30
     With rageing jaws environ me . . . . . . . . . . . . . . . .  307 Psalm XXVII         9
     Yea from the grave's most hungry jawes;. . . . . . . . . . .  311 Psalm XXX           7
JAY
     Pas. My father hath at home a prettie Jay, . . . . . . . . .   56 2nd Eclogues 29   138
JEALOUS
     Love wakes the jealous eye least thence it moves:. . . . . .   42 Arcadia II    22     6
     The jealous eye, the more it lookes, it loves. . . . . . . .   42 Arcadia II    22     7
     But (for his jealous eye she well did finde) . . . . . . . .   95 3rd Eclogues 64    41
     And to her jealous husband did it take.. . . . . . . . . . .   96 3rd Eclogues 64    84
     "The jealous wretch must now to Courte be gone:. . . . . . .   97 3rd Eclogues 64   103
     Thus may you see, the jealous wretch was made. . . . . . . .   97 3rd Eclogues 64   121
     She seemed full of jealous feares, . . . . . . . . . . . . .  158 Cert Sonnets 28    15
     Deere, therefore be not jealous over me, . . . . . . . . . .  225 Astrophil     91    12
JEALOUSY
     The one of Love, the other Jealousie,. . . . . . . . . . . .   42 Arcadia II    22     2
```

JEALOUSY	(CONTINUED)	PAGE	TITLE		LINE
But above all away vile jealousie,		93	3rd Eclogues	63	82
And jealousie is slaine:		94	3rd Eclogues	63	98
Fell jealousie did so his braine oppresse,		94	3rd Eclogues	64	9
Least that some markes of jealousie you beare.		97	3rd Eclogues	64	124
For sure, no jealousie can that prevent,		97	3rd Eclogues	64	125
Betweene the jawes of hellish Jealousie.		205	Astrophil	78	4
Jealousie it selfe doth sleepe:		210	A&S 4th Song		10

JEHOVA
Since I do trust Jehova still,		283	Psalm XI		1
For who is God, besides this Great Jehova Ours?		292	Psalm XVIII		57
Then live Jehova still, my rock still blessed be;		293	Psalm XVIII		83
In house of High Jehova still,		307	Psalm XXVII		21
By voice of high Jehova we		310	Psalm XXIX		13

JEHOVA'S
| But lo Jehova's sight. | | 318 | Psalm XXXIII | | 67 |

JEST
| Whereat I did but jeast. | | 158 | Cert Sonnets | 28 | 16 |
| That at me so amaz'd my fellowes jest: | | 254 | Other Poems | 4 | 468 |

JESTING
| Their Counsills are your Common jesting stock, | | 287 | Psalm XIV | | 20 |

JESTS
| And all but jests, save onely sorrowe's rage. | | 57 | 2nd Eclogues | 30 | 22 |

JETS
| Or seeing jets, blacke, but in blacknesse bright. | | 225 | Astrophil | 91 | 8 |

JEWEL
"Onley Juell, O only Juell, which only deservest		36	1st Eclogues	13	147
The tippe no jewell needes to weare:		87	Arcadia III	62	35
The tippe is jewell of the eare.		87	Arcadia III	62	36
Unto the earth, by the hurt of this her heavenly jewell.		124	4th Eclogues	74	62
Have I caught my heav'nly jewell,		202	A&S 2nd Song		1

JOIN
Poore Painters oft with silly Poets joyne,		20	1st Eclogues	8	1
Joyne you with me, to seale this promise due,		76	Arcadia III	46	11
Joyne with thy sonne, to ease my long annoys.		81	Arcadia III	53	13
Come then and join with me,		319	Psalm XXXIV		9
With whome to joyne fast ran Urania sweet:		248	Other Poems	4	252
Joyne Mates in mirth to me,		260	Other Poems	6	1
Joyne hearts and hands, so let it be,		260	Other Poems	6	5
Above line repeated at following locations		260	Other Poems	6	11
		260	Other Poems	6	17
		260	Other Poems	6	23
		261	Other Poems	6	29
		261	Other Poems	6	35
		261	Other Poems	6	41
		261	Other Poems	6	47
		261	Other Poems	6	53
To joyne sweet friends beloved.		260	Other Poems	6	16

JOINED
And keep it joynde, fearing your seate's consumption.		15	1st Eclogues	7	42
Love smiled, and thus said; "Want joynd to desire is unhappy		30	1st Eclogues	11	11
Which is helde in love, love it is, that hath joynde		31	1st Eclogues	12	23
Joyn'd, by thy beauty adorn'd, be no meanes these greefes to abolish:		34	1st Eclogues	13	99
Palmes do rejoyce to be joynd by the match of a male to a female,		36	1st Eclogues	13	137
Muses graunt guiftes, Nymphes long and joyned life		93	3rd Eclogues	63	92
Joyned alas to your beames,		154	Cert Sonnets	25	4
His Sire's revenge, joyn'd with a kingdome's gaine:		204	Astrophil	75	6
But East and West were join'd by frendship's hest.		242	Other Poems	4	27
Now joyned be our hands,		261	Other Poems	6	55
As one for ever joyned bee.		261	Other Poems	6	60

JOINING
| Joyning your sweete voice to the rurall muse of a deserte, | | 31 | 1st Eclogues | 13 | 2 |
| Yet joyning formes one sight of beautie breede. | | 78 | Arcadia III | 50 | 4 |

JOINT
| Whose loosed bones quite out of joint be wryde; | | 299 | Psalm XXII | | 32 |

JOINTLY
And counsel jointly take,		271	Psalm II		4
Who jointly sought my bale to frame;		332	Psalm XL		53
As three most joyntly set,		260	Other Poems	6	21

JOLLITY
| Thy mercy shall fill me with jollity, | | 312 | Psalm XXXI | | 19 |
| Strephon did leape with joy and jolitie, | | 246 | Other Poems | 4 | 177 |

JOLLY
| Unto his house a jollie shepeheard went, | | 94 | 3rd Eclogues | 64 | 15 |
| Thou seest, how friske, and jolly now he is, | | 103 | 3rd Eclogues | 67 | 5 |

JORDAN
| From the grounds where Jordan slideth. | | 335 | Psalm XLII | | 27 |

JOT
| And lowest sinke not downe to jote of ill: | | 99 | 3rd Eclogues | 66 | 32 |

JOURNEY
| She bids him goe, and yet from jorney stayes. | | 104 | 3rd Eclogues | 67 | 36 |
| With what pastime, time's journey she beguilde, | | 225 | Astrophil | 92 | 12 |

JOVE
What time for her Juno her Jove did misse,		21	1st Eclogues	8	15
Till now at length that Jove him office gives,		22	1st Eclogues	8	45
The multitude to Jove a suite empartes,		100	3rd Eclogues	66	61
Cackling, and chattring, that of Jove beseech.		100	3rd Eclogues	66	67

JOVE   (CONTINUED)   PAGE   TITLE   LINE
   Jove wisely said (for wisedome wisely sayes) . . . .   100 3rd Eclogues 66   71
   Then to my selfe, not though Jove grew a suter of hers.. . .   143 Cert Sonnets 13   2
   Some one his song in Jove, and Jove's strange tales attires,   167 Astrophil   6   5
   Phoebus was Judge betweene Jove, Mars, and Love, ...   171 Astrophil   13   1
   Jove on his helme the thunderbolt did reare. . . . .   171 Astrophil   13   8
JOVE'S
   With Jove's disdaine at such a rival's seed, ...   21 1st Eclogues 8   20
   Celestiall powers to wormes, Jove's children serve to claye.   120 4th Eclogues 73   116
   Some one his song in Jove, and Jove's strange tales attires,   167 Astrophil   6   5
   Joves golden shield did Eagle sables beare,. . . . .   171 Astrophil   13   3
   Nectar of Mirth, since I Jove's cup do keepe.. . . . .   201 Astrophil   70   4
JOY
   "Nothing", sayd he, "for most I joy in this, ...   4 Lady of May   3   5
   P. Who Passion doth forsake, lives void of joy.. . . . . . .   46 2nd Eclogues 27   14
   From any joy, which might her griefe occasion. . . . .   51 2nd Eclogues 28   122
   Her to enjoy, where joy it selfe is thrall,. . . . .   59 2nd Eclogues 30   87
   From any joy, know fortune's vile displacing her,. . . . . .   61 2nd Eclogues 30   150
   What do lovers seeke for, long seeking for to enjoy? Joy.. .   63 2nd Eclogues 31   13
   Woe, but seems to me joy, that agrees to my thought so. I
     thought so.. . . . .   64 2nd Eclogues 31   38
   Wherin no eare can have joy, ...   66 2nd Eclogues 32   37
   The knottes of joy, the gemmes of love,. . . . .   89 Arcadia III 62   95
   "My sweetest joy, the comfort of my sprite,. . . . .   96 3rd Eclogues 64   92
   Thou art of blood; joy not to make things bleede:. . . . . .   103 3rd Eclogues 66   150
   Then is the quiet joy of loving wife;. . . . .   103 3rd Eclogues 67   8
   Which touch the father's hart with secret joy, ...   106 3rd Eclogues 67   113
   Strephon. I Joye in griefe, and doo detest all joyes:. . . .   113 4th Eclogues 72   9
   I joy in griefe, and doo detest all joyes. . . . .   116 4th Eclogues 72   100
   Strephon. I joye in griefe, and doo detest all joyes.. . . .   116 4th Eclogues 72   101
   Farewell o Joy, the wofull's onely pleasure. . . . .   129 4th Eclogues 76   4
   But now, if ere my face with joy be clad:. . . . .   147 Cert Sonnets 17   44
   Like late mowne meades, late cut from joy I live. . . . . .   147 Cert Sonnets 18   11
   Yea worse then death, death parts both woe and joy,. . . . .   148 Cert Sonnets 20   13
   From joy I part still living in annoy. . . . .   148 Cert Sonnets 20   14
   O how for joy he leapes, o how he crowes,. . . . .   173 Astrophil   17   12
   And joy therein, though Nations count it shame.. . . . . . .   179 Astrophil   24   8
   Soule's joy, bend not those morning starres from me, ...   188 Astrophil   48   1
   O thinke I then, what paradise of joy. . . . .   200 Astrophil   68   13
   O joy, too high for my low stile to show:. . . . .   200 Astrophil   69   1
   My Muse may well grudge at my heav'nly joy,. . . . .   201 Astrophil   70   1
   Shall paint out joy, though but in blacke and white. . . . .   201 Astrophil   70   11
   The onely light of joy, the onely warmth of Love. . . . . .   204 Astrophil   76   4
   Those lookes, whose beames be joy, whose motion is delight,.   205 Astrophil   77   1
   Who his owne joy to his owne hurt applies, ...   206 Astrophil   78   7
   Least joy, by Nature apt sprites to enlarge, ...   210 Astrophil   85   3
   Yet swam in joy, such love in her was seene. . . . .   223 Astrophil   87   11
   Faint coward joy no longer tarry dare, ...   228 Astrophil   95   5
   Her selfe (to shew no other joy hath place). . . . .   229 Astrophil   97   7
   But wo is me, though joy it selfe were she,. . . . .   230 Astrophil   97   12
   She could not shew my blind braine waies of joy, ...   230 Astrophil   97   13
   Such teares, sighs, plaints, no sorrow is, but joy:. . . . .   231 Astrophil   100   12
   And joy, which is inseperate from those eyes,. . . . .   231 Astrophil   101   7
   The bote for joy could not to daunce forbeare, ...   232 Astrophil   103   5
   There shines a joy from thee my only light;. . . . .   236 Astrophil   108   4
   That in my woes for thee thou art my joy,. . . . .   237 Astrophil   108   13
   Onely joy, now here you are,. . . . .   210 A&S 4th Song   1
   Joying till joy makes us languish. . . . .   227 A&S 10th Song   42
   "Stella soveraigne of my joy,. . . . .   218 A&S 8th Song   29
   That joy with trembling go. . . . .   271 Psalm II   26
   May only joy in all Thy saving wayes . . . .   280 Psalm IX   44
   And at my fall they joy that, troublous, me. . . . .   286 Psalm XIII   15
   No, No I trust on thee, and joy in Thy . . . .   286 Psalm XIII   17
   So in joy my glory clad, ...   288 Psalm XVI   29
   My joy shall be pure to enjoy thy face,. . . . .   290 Psalm XVII   46
   May joy and banners raise. . . . .   296 Psalm XX   19
   New joy, new joy unto Our King,. . . . .   296 Psalm XXI   1
   On my complaint build up their joy.. . . . .   303 Psalm XXV   6
   Offrings of joy in Temple His, ...   307 Psalm XXVII   34
   Shall joy impart.. . . . .   308 Psalm XXVII   66
   So shall I with joy be filld,. . . . .   309 Psalm XXVIII   29
   Lo I that waild, now daunce for joy. . . . .   311 Psalm XXX   34
   Be glad you good, in God have joy, ...   316 Psalm XXXII   40
   Joy be to you, who do enjoy. . . . .   316 Psalm XXXII   41
   In him much joy, ...   318 Psalm XXXIII   80
   Then shall I joy in thee, then sav'd by Thee . . . .   321 Psalm XXXV   19
   Who joy but they, when they assembled bee? . . . .   322 Psalm XXXV   38
   Then, then let not my foes unjustly joy; . . . .   322 Psalm XXXV   49
   Let not their joy upon my woes be sett.. . . . .   322 Psalm XXXV   60
   Who make a Cause to joy of my decay; . . . .   323 Psalm XXXV   64
   But fill their hearts with joy, who bend their wayes . . . .   332 Psalm XL   61
   Dick. What joy the joyfull sunne gives unto bleared eyes:. .   343 Possibly   1   13
   For nothing can more tedious bee, then plaint, in time of
     joy. . . . .   344 Possibly   1   46
   They joi'd one joy, one griefe they griev'd, ...   241 Other Poems   3   3
   Strephon did leape with joy and jolitie, ...   246 Other Poems   4   177
   Who never joy, but when. . . . .   261 Other Poems   6   39
   So joy I, in you seeing; . . . .   261 Other Poems   6   44
JOYED
   My soule is bliste, sence joyde, and fortune raysed. . . . .   108 Arcadia IV   69   14

		PAGE	TITLE		LINE
JOYED	(CONTINUED)				
Ye Satyrs joyde with free and quiet forrests,.		111	4th Eclogues	71	3
Choler adust is joyed in woman-kinde.		147	Cert Sonnets	17	52
I joyed, but straight thus watred was my wine, ...		196	Astrophil	62	5
They joi'd one joy, one griefe they griev'd, ...		241	Other Poems	3	3
JOYFUL					
Due sighes blowe out all sparkes of joyfull light, ...		74	Arcadia III	42	11
At length he perch'd himself in Stella's joyfull face, . . .		168	Astrophil	8	8
To songs and joyfull byding.		315	Psalm XXXII		27
Dick. What joy the joyfull sunne gives unto bleared eyes:. .		343	Possibly	1	13
JOYFULLY					
(Espilus) Thus joyfully in chosen tunes rejoyce, ...		5	Lady of May	3	13
JOYFULNESS					
But make such glad, and full of joyfulness,.		323	Psalm XXXV		67
JOYING					
Joying till joy makes us languish.		227	A&S 10th Song		42
JOYLESS					
Joylesse, hopelesse, endlesse languish..		220	A&S 8th Song		80
JOYOUS					
This leades unto the joyous field, ...		87	Arcadia III	62	61
JOY'S					
Joie's strangers seeme, I cannot bide their showe, ...		74	Arcadia III	41	5
Ah bed, the field where joye's peace some do see,.		230	Astrophil	98	1
Upon thy cheerefull face, joye's livery weare:		232	Astrophil	103	3
JOYS					
Lalus. This mayde, thus made for joyes, o Pan bemone her,. .		17	1st Eclogues	7	97
With outward joyes, which inly cannot sincke,.		22	1st Eclogues	9	7
My Lyvelye joyes to dolefull ashes turne:.		42	Arcadia II	22	10
Enjoye my joyes, as you dyd taste my payne,.		43	Arcadia II	23	11
Feede on my sheepe, your Native joyes mayntayne, ...		43	Arcadia II	23	13
R. The joyes you have shall be made permanent.		47	2nd Eclogues	27	35
P. How know we that, since present joyes we misse?		47	2nd Eclogues	27	38
What be the joyes for which to enjoy they went to the					
paines Paines..		63	2nd Eclogues	31	14
Curs'd be thy selfe for cursing that which leades me to					
joies. Toies..		65	2nd Eclogues	31	40
Those secrett joyes, which heaven to me emparte, ...		70	Arcadia III	35	14
That sorrowe's weight dothe balance up thies joyes..		71	Arcadia III	36	18
O time, become the chariot of my joyes:..		80	Arcadia III	53	9
O Himen long their coupled joyes maintaine..		91	3rd Eclogues	63	9
Above line repeated at following locations		91	3rd Eclogues	63	18
		91	3rd Eclogues	63	27
. . . .		92	3rd Eclogues	63	36
. . . .		92	3rd Eclogues	63	45
. . . .		92	3rd Eclogues	63	54
. . . .		93	3rd Eclogues	63	63
. . . .		93	3rd Eclogues	63	72
. . . .		93	3rd Eclogues	63	81
. . . .		93	3rd Eclogues	63	90
For Himen will their coupled joyes maintaine..		94	3rd Eclogues	63	99
Long since I see my joyes come to their evening, ...		112	4th Eclogues	71	29
Which troubles their daye's worke, and joyes of evening: . .		112	4th Eclogues	71	33
Strephon. I Joye in griefe, and doo detest all joyes:. . . .		113	4th Eclogues	72	1
I joy in griefe, and doo detest all joyes.		116	4th Eclogues	72	100
Strephon. I joye in griefe, and doo detest all joyes.. . . .		116	4th Eclogues	72	101
What sweete joyes I had once, and what a place I did hold? .		124	4th Eclogues	74	72
Where bee nowe those Joyes, that I lately tasted?.		138	Cert Sonnets	5	5
In whom all joyes so well agree, ...		139	Cert Sonnets	7	2
Above line repeated at following locations		139	Cert Sonnets	7	12
		140	Cert Sonnets	7	22
. . . .		140	Cert Sonnets	7	32
Tell how my joyes and hopes thus fowly fell.		146	Cert Sonnets	17	14
Let him, deprived of sweet but unfelt joyes, ...		177	Astrophil	24	12
Whose beames be joyes, whose joyes all vertues be, ...		185	Astrophil	42	2
Are metamorphosd straight to tunes of joyes.		187	Astrophil	44	14
That heav'n of joyes throwes onely downe on me		195	Astrophil	60	3
Neast of young joyes, schoolmaster of delight, ...		206	Astrophil	79	8
And in my joyes for thee my only annoy..		237	Astrophil	108	14
But thou rich in all joyes, doest rob my joyes from me,. . .		214	A&S 5th Song		46
In what high joyes I shall dwell,.		226	A&S 10th Song		11
In Thee my joyes and comforts ever be, ...		279	Psalm IX		3
From age to age life joyes doth fill..		311	Psalm XXX		15
Doth rise again, new joyes shall rise.		311	Psalm XXX		18
May learn their joyes to fill.		318	Psalm XXXIV		8
Have of joyes bereft me?		336	Psalm XLIII		12
With whose fine stepps all loves and joyes conspire.		250	Other Poems	4	302
So caught, him seem'd he caught of joyes the bell, ...		250	Other Poems	4	311
Then want one hower those eyes which my joyes keepe.		259	Other Poems	5	102
JUDGE					
Judge you to whom all beautie's force is lent.		4	Lady of May	2	31
Judge you of Love, to whom all Love is bent.		4	Lady of May	2	32
Oh when will men leave off to judge by haire,.		25	1st Eclogues	9	93
Or mine eyes' language she doo hap to judge of,.		30	1st Eclogues	12	2
Above line repeated at following location.		31	1st Eclogues	12	26
What judge you doth a hillocke shew, by the lofty Olympus? .		34	1st Eclogues	13	75
Who judge that honour, which hath scope to slander..		50	2nd Eclogues	28	91
Pas. My voice the lambe did winne, Menalcas was our judge: .		52	2nd Eclogues	29	15
And let him be our judge: the lad doth please me well".. . .		121	4th Eclogues	73	153
Phoebus was Judge betweene Jove, Mars, and Love, ...		171	Astrophil	13	1
But harder Judges judge ambition's rage, ...		176	Astrophil	23	9

JUDGE (CONTINUED)   PAGE   TITLE   LINE

	PAGE	TITLE		LINE
Can judge of Love, thou feel'st a Lover's case;	180	Astrophil	31	6
Th'indifferent Judge betweene the high and low;	184	Astrophil	39	4
Towne-folkes my strength; a daintier judge applies	185	Astrophil	41	6
Now judge by this: in piercing phrases late, ...	194	Astrophil	58	9
Or if I needs (sweet Judge) must torments have, ...	212	Astrophil	86	11
Feare not to judge this bate, ...	215	A&S 6th Song		5
Up lord, and judg the Gentyls in Thy right	281	Psalm IX		61
Lord judg me, and my case, ...	305	Psalm XXVI		1
Judg lord, judg God, ev'en in Thy justice great, ...	322	Psalm XXXV		59
Judg of th' afflicted man;	332	Psalm XLI		2
Judg of all, judg me	336	Psalm XLIII		1

JUDGED

What skill servethe a soare of a wrong infirmity judged? . .	32	1st Eclogues	13	21

JUDGES

Then who makes us such judges over all?.	29	1st Eclogues	10	96
But harder Judges judge ambition's rage, ...	176	Astrophil	23	9
Those scarlet judges, threatning bloudy paine?	203	Astrophil	73	11

JUDGETH

That see my good, and judgeth my desert:	5	Lady of May	3	16

JUDGING

Yet not of wemen Judging as he said, ...	24	1st Eclogues	9	64
That thou full oft shalt wish thy judging eyes were blinde".	121	4th Eclogues	73	172
By my love judging what Love's paine might be.	173	Astrophil	16	8
Of judging right.	279	Psalm IX		10

JUDGMENT

Greater is she who must the judgement give..	3	Lady of May	2	6
Give right sound to the eares, and enter aright to the judgement;	32	1st Eclogues	13	18
Great to thee my estate seemes, thy estate is blest by my judgement:	33	1st Eclogues	13	72
In you it is, you must the judgement give.	39	Arcadia II	17	8
This is my pawne; the price let Dicus' judgement show: . . .	53	2nd Eclogues	29	47
Griefe is the stone which finest judgement proves:	58	2nd Eclogues	30	35
Held, pearst, possest, my judgement, sence, and will, ...	84	Arcadia III	60	6
Both by the judgement of the English eyes, ...	185	Astrophil	41	3
Makes me in my best thoughts and quietst judgement see, . . .	205	Astrophil	77	12
The judgement of the eye, ...	216	A&S 6th Song		40
Eye-judgement of the eye, ...	216	A&S 6th Song	V	40
Thou, lord, the people shalt in judgment try:	277	Psalm VII		22
For then the lord in judgment shewes to raigne	281	Psalm IX		51
The meek he doth in judgment lead, ...	303	Psalm XXV		35
And judgment loves, ...	316	Psalm XXXIII		20
But rise, but wake that I may judgment gett.	322	Psalm XXXV		57
And of Thy Judgement make a muster	325	Psalm XXXVII		15

JUDGMENT'S

(With blushing soule at sight of judgement's glasse, ...	255	Other Poems	4	531

JUDGMENTS

Let this assured holde our judgements ever take, ...	45	Arcadia II	26	15
Their judgements hackney on, the fault on sicknesse lay, . .	232	Astrophil	102	10
The strongest judgements weake:	215	A&S 6th Song		10
Which He prepar'd, to give his judgments high:	280	Psalm IX		22
Thence he to all his judgments shall apply	280	Psalm IX		24
Thy judgments are too high	282	Psalm X		19
Still to his judgments lookt, still for his statutes car'd, .	292	Psalm XVIII		45
His judgments be self verity, ...	294	Psalm XIX		39
Thy judgments like the depths do ly, ...	323	Psalm XXXVI		16
His tongue of heavnly judgments telleth, ...	326	Psalm XXXVII		78

JUICE

The bitter juice of forsaken woes, ...	153	Cert Sonnets	24	11

JUICES

But perforce disgest, all bitter juices of horror.	35	1st Eclogues	13	105

JUMP

Was jumpe concorde betweene our wit and will:	99	3rd Eclogues	66	30

JUNIPER

Sweete Juniper saith this, thoh I burne, yet I burne in a sweete fire.	35	1st Eclogues	13	120

JUNO

As smooth as Pan, as Juno milde, like goddesse Iris faste. .	12	Arcadia I	3	6
What time for her Juno her Jove did misse, ...	21	1st Eclogues	8	15

JUNO'S

(At Juno's suite who much did Argus love).	22	1st Eclogues	8	46
Like to Junoe's birdes of pride, ...	263	Other Poems	7	51

JURAT

Is made, forsooth, a Jurate of his woes, ...	23	1st Eclogues	9	39

JUST

Rather to wrong then unto just defence, ...	25	1st Eclogues	9	106
Or when a rich rubie's just price be the worth of a walnut, .	34	1st Eclogues	13	78
R. Though we cannot orecome, our cause is just.	47	2nd Eclogues	27	31
Thou li'st false Echo, their minds as vertu be just. Just. .	65	2nd Eclogues	31	46
By just exchange, one for the other giv'ne..	75	Arcadia III	45	2
The evill of evils, just cause to be unjust, ...	93	3rd Eclogues	63	83
Nay to the heav'ns your just complayninges sende, ...	126	4th Eclogues	75	37
The vehement course of this just lamentation:	127	4th Eclogues	75	98
Just accord all musike makes;	140	Cert Sonnets	7	14
In thee just accord excelleth, ...	140	Cert Sonnets	7	15
Can count them just, nor reason reason trye, ...	149	Cert Sonnets	22	3
And by just counts my selfe a banckrout know	173	Astrophil	18	3
Only lov'd Tyrants, just in cruelty, ...	185	Astrophil	42	6
That giv'st no better eare to my just cries:	198	Astrophil	65	2

```
JUST                       (CONTINUED)                    PAGE   TITLE           LINE
   Ne if I would, could I just title make,. . . . . . . . . . .  224 Astrophil    90    9
   Of her just and high disdaine: . . . . . . . . . . . . . . .  203 A&S 2nd Song       18
   The mansion seat of blisse, and just excuse of Lovers; . . .  213 A&S 5th Song       21
   The trade of them, that just proceeding love;. . . . . . . .  271 Psalm I            20
   Of just desires, on justice stayd, . . . . . . . . . . . . .  274 Psalm IV           22
   The just in Thee, on thee and justice build: . . . . . . . .  275 Psalm V            38
   But still be Thou to just men justest guide. . . . . . . . .  277 Psalm VII          27
   That He enquiringe, doth require just blood, . . . . . . . .  280 Psalm IX           33
   For what, alas, have just men done?. . . . . . . . . . . . .  284 Psalm XI           11
   The lord doth search the just man's reines,. . . . . . . . .  284 Psalm XI           17
   The just into his power. . . . . . . . . . . . . . . . . . .  286 Psalm XIV          18
   My suite is just, just lord to my suite hark;. . . . . . . .  289 Psalm XVII          1
   My justice, my just hands thus did the lord reward,. . . . .  292 Psalm XVIII        43
   To thee, O Lord most just, . . . . . . . . . . . . . . . . .  302 Psalm XXV           1
   Who hope on his Name just. . . . . . . . . . . . . . . . . .  318 Psalm XXXIII       81
   The just when harms approach . . . . . . . . . . . . . . . .  320 Psalm XXXIV        61
   But God upholds the just in blisse.. . . . . . . . . . . . .  325 Psalm XXXVII       44
   Mark the upright, the just attend, . . . . . . . . . . . . .  327 Psalm XXXVII       93
   Lord unto me my time's just measure give,. . . . . . . . . .  329 Psalm XXXIX        13
   Will. What living get you then? D. Disdayne; but just
      disdayne.. . . . . . . . . . . . . . . . . . . . . . . . .  344 Possibly      1    35
   Did it for just Desire's true children builde, . . . . . . .  345 Possibly      4    10
   Thinking it just more therein to delight . . . . . . . . . .  246 Other Poems   4   178
JUSTER
   That here is juster cause of plaintfull sadnesse:. . . . . .  137 Cert Sonnets  4    10
   Above line repeated at following location. . . . . . . . . .  137 Cert Sonnets  4    22
JUSTEST
   Where justest love doth vanquish Cupid's powers. . . . . . .   91 3rd Eclogues 63    3
   Her helpe to this, this justest cause of plaint. . . . . . .  125 4th Eclogues 75   14
   But still be Thou to just men justest guide. . . . . . . . .  277 Psalm VII          27
JUSTICE
   By justice' worke they their owne faultes disclose:. . . . .   27 1st Eclogues 10   42
   What can justice availe, to a man that tells not his owne
      case?. . . . . . . . . . . . . . . . . . . . . . . . . . .   32 1st Eclogues 13   22
   To harme us wormes should that high Justice leave. . . . . .   59 2nd Eclogues 30   71
   Justice, justice is now (alas) oppressed:. . . . . . . . . .  128 4th Eclogues 75  118
   In justice quit, of honour made no breach: . . . . . . . . .  135 Cert Sonnets  1   12
   In justice paines come not till faults do call;. . . . . . .  212 Astrophil    86   10
   Of just desires, on justice stayd, . . . . . . . . . . . . .  274 Psalm IV           22
   Guide me, O in thy justice be my guide:. . . . . . . . . . .  275 Psalm V            22
   The just in Thee, on thee and justice build: . . . . . . . .  275 Psalm V            38
   Thither the World for justice shall repaire, . . . . . . . .  280 Psalm IX           23
   My justice, my just hands thus did the lord reward,. . . . .  292 Psalm XVIII        43
   As he before his eyes did see my justice stand,. . . . . . .  292 Psalm XVIII        48
   My foot on justice stayes, . . . . . . . . . . . . . . . . .  306 Psalm XXVI         38
   His justice seat the World sustains, . . . . . . . . . . . .  310 Psalm XXIX         25
   Judg lord, judg God, ev'en in Thy justice great, . . . . . .  322 Psalm XXXV         59
   Thy justice witness shall and speake Thy prayse. . . . . . .  323 Psalm XXXV         72
   Thy justice in most shining luster,. . . . . . . . . . . . .  325 Psalm XXXVII       14
   To justice never saw forsaken, . . . . . . . . . . . . . . .  326 Psalm XXXVII       63
JUSTLY
   Happy be those mishapps which, justly proportion holding,. .   32 1st Eclogues 13   17
   Where proofes justly do teach, thus matcht, such worth to be
      nought worth. . . . . . . . . . . . . . . . . . . . . . .   34 1st Eclogues 13   83
   Justely to graunt thy rewarde, such envie I beare to thy
      fortune. . . . . . . . . . . . . . . . . . . . . . . . . .   37 1st Eclogues 13  156
   Thy title great, I justlie chalenge may, . . . . . . . . . .   80 Arcadia III  53    7
   Justly entitled Cupid's hill.. . . . . . . . . . . . . . . .   88 Arcadia III  62   78
   Thy father justly may of thee complaine, . . . . . . . . . .  105 3rd Eclogues 67   73
   Who justly make our hearts the seates of sorow?. . . . . . .  109 Arcadia IV   70    8
   Whilst that methought I justly made my bost. . . . . . . . .  147 Cert Sonnets 17   42
   That tombes the two, is justly one.. . . . . . . . . . . . .  241 Other Poems   3    8
KALA
   Dorus. Such Kala is: but ah, my fancies raysed be. . . . . .   15 1st Eclogues  7   37
   This winde he spent: but when my Kala glasseth all . . . .    16 1st Eclogues  7   55
   Lalus. Kala at length conclude my lingring lotte:. . . . . .   18 1st Eclogues  7  115
   Lalus. But if my Kala this my suite denies,. . . . . . . . .   18 1st Eclogues  7  147
KALA'S
   My Kala's giftes: who with all good gifts filled is. . . . .   15 1st Eclogues  7   26
KALAS
   If many Kalaes our Arcadia gave, . . . . . . . . . . . . . .  104 3rd Eclogues 67   22
KEELS
   At blowe point, hotcocles, or els at keeles. . . . . . . . .   28 1st Eclogues 10   47
   And now at keels they trie a harmles chaunce,. . . . . . . .  243 Other Poems   4    47
KEEP
   Among his flocke so sweete a treasure keepe. . . . . . . . .    4 Lady of May   2   18
   Thanked be I that keepe a man, . . . . . . . . . . . . . . .   13 Arcadia I     5    3
   What then must I that keepe the knave? . . . . . . . . . . .   13 Arcadia I     5    6
   Above line repeated at following location. . . . . . . . . .   13 Arcadia I     5   12
   And keep it joynde, fearing your seate's consumption.. . . .   15 1st Eclogues  7   42
   My suite, keepe this, that my long toyle hath laide to me: .   16 1st Eclogues  7   52
   Till I get her, shall I to keepe enure my selfe? . . . . . .   16 1st Eclogues  7  V 60
   Doth beauties keep, which never Sunne can burne, . . . . . .   18 1st Eclogues  7  118
   But so our hartes keepe downe, with vice they be not
      stainde . . . . . . . . . . . . . . . . . . . . . . . . .   45 Arcadia II   26   14
   Yet for that night, my Caban dyd them kepe . . . . . . . . .   62 2nd Eclogues 30  188
   My voice, too hott to keepe in. . . . . . . . . . . . . . . .   67 2nd Eclogues 32   45
   Keepe thy sprite from abuse, here no abuse doth haunte.. . .   69 2nd Eclogues 34   27
   May keepe my thoughtes, from thought of wonted light.. . . .   73 Arcadia III  39   14
```

```
KEEP                    (CONTINUED)                      PAGE    TITLE           LINE
    Have much more care of them that them do keepe,. . . . . . . .  92  3rd Eclogues 63   39
    Allow good company, but kepe from thence . . . . . . . . . .  98  3rd Eclogues 65   11
    She warre doth ever with his kinsfolke keepe, . . . . . . . . 104  3rd Eclogues 67   37
    And keepe it still within this body thrall:. . . . . . . . .  116  4th Eclogues 72   88
    O cowarde Cupid thus doost thou my honour keepe, . . . . . .  122  4th Eclogues 73  185
    And make his paine to keepe us safe his pleasure?. . . . . .  129  4th Eclogues 76   24
    The Babe cries "way, thy love doth keepe me waking". . . . .  139  Cert Sonnets  6    3
    The babe cries "way, thy love doth keepe me waking". . . . .  139  Cert Sonnets  6    6
    To keepe the pace of their first loving state. . . . . . . .  173  Astrophil    17    4
    To keepe themselves and their chief cities free, . . . . . .  179  Astrophil    29    2
    To keepe it selfe in life and liberty, . . . . . . . . . . .  179  Astrophil    29    6
    Since thou in me so sure a power doest keepe,. . . . . . . .  181  Astrophil    32    5
    Keepe still my Zenith, ever shine on me. . . . . . . . . . .  186  Astrophil    42    8
    Nectar of Mirth, since I Jove's cup do keepe.. . . . . . . .  201  Astrophil    70    4
    While craftily you seem'd your cut to keepe, . . . . . . . .  208  Astrophil    83    3
    Cannot heavn's food, once felt, keepe stomakes free. . . . .  223  Astrophil    88    7
    Whom iron doores do keepe from use of day? . . . . . . . . .  237  Astrophil   108   11
    Danger hence good care doth keepe, . . . . . . . . . . . . .  210  A&S 4th Song       9
    Can abide to keepe no measure, . . . . . . . . . . . . . . .  221  A&S 9th Song       7
    Then Thou (O lord) shalt keep the Good stil sure.. . . . . .  285  Psalm XII         22
    Then keep me as the Apple of an Eye, . . . . . . . . . . . .  290  Psalm XVII        25
    And who doth frame to keep the same. . . . . . . . . . . . .  295  Psalm XIX         47
    Thy servant keep, least in him creep . . . . . . . . . . . .  295  Psalm XIX         53
    To such as keep his Covenant . . . . . . . . . . . . . . . .  304  Psalm XXV         41
    And keep from Famin's paine. . . . . . . . . . . . . . . . .  318  Psalm XXXIII      75
    To keep them safe and sound. . . . . . . . . . . . . . . . .  319  Psalm XXXIV       28
    Keep well thy lipps and tongue . . . . . . . . . . . . . . .  320  Psalm XXXIV       49
    Wait thou on God and keep his way, . . . . . . . . . . . . .  327  Psalm XXXVII      85
    The Lord will keep his life yet safe and sound . . . . . . .  333  Psalm XLI          5
    While most with hir he lesse did kepe with thee. . . . . . .  247  Other Poems   4  221
    With hand and mouth, with lapp and brest keepe warme,. . . .  258  Other Poems   5   84
    Then want one hower those eyes which my joyes keepe. . . . .  259  Other Poems   5  102
    Lovingly like friends did keepe, . . . . . . . . . . . . . .  262  Other Poems   7   22
KEEPETH
    The earth with pitie dull the center keepeth:. . . . . . . .  136  Cert Sonnets  3    4
    Where she his counsell keepeth,. . . . . . . . . . . . . . .  160  Cert Sonnets 30   35
    His bones he keepeth all . . . . . . . . . . . . . . . . . .  320  Psalm XXXIV       73
    Will. What keepeth safe thy band? D. Remembrance is the
       Chest. . . . . . . . . . . . . . . . . . . . . . . . . .  344  Possibly      1   29
KEEPING
    But keeping holesome meane,. . . . . . . . . . . . . . . . .  93  3rd Eclogues 63   80
    Keeping that forme, though void of wonted heate: . . . . . .  151  Cert Sonnets 22   48
KEEPS
    Desteny keepes me aloofe. For if all thy estate to thy
       verture. . . . . . . . . . . . . . . . . . . . . . . . .   34  1st Eclogues 13   98
    His hart in me, keepes me and him in one,. . . . . . . . . .   76  Arcadia III  45    5
    Sweet gard'n Nymph, which keepes the Cherrie tree, . . . . .  208  Astrophil    82    5
    Of his mazde powers keepes perfit harmony: . . . . . . . . .  230  Astrophil    99    8
    Who keepes the key of Nature's chiefest treasure?. . . . . .  197  A&S 1st Song       6
    He nobly saves his King, and kindness keeps in store,. . . .  293  Psalm XVIII       90
    God keeps account of good men's dayes, . . . . . . . . . . .  325  Psalm XXXVII      45
KENS
    Beaten with waves, no sooner kennes the baye . . . . . . . .   70  Arcadia III  36    3
KEPT
    But so unheard, condemn'd, kept thence we do seeke to abide
       in,. . . . . . . . . . . . . . . . . . . . . . . . . . .   32  1st Eclogues 13   25
    My still kept course, while others sleepe, to mone.. . . . .  184  Astrophil    40    4
    For he me safely kept. . . . . . . . . . . . . . . . . . . .  272  Psalm III         17
    Nor kept with base dissemblers company;. . . . . . . . . . .  305  Psalm XXVI        15
    I silence kept ev'n in the good. . . . . . . . . . . . . . .  329  Psalm XXXIX        6
    Well for to see they kept themselves unsene, . . . . . . . .  244  Other Poems   4   89
    Besides this force, within hir eies he kept. . . . . . . . .  246  Other Poems   4  153
    Geron, though olde yet gamesome, kept one ende . . . . . . .  248  Other Poems   4  242
KEY
    A double key, which opens to the heart,. . . . . . . . . . .  206  Astrophil    79    6
    Who keepes the key of Nature's chiefest treasure?. . . . . .  197  A&S 1st Song       6
    The same key op'n can, which can locke up a treasure.. . . .  213  A&S 5th Song      18
KICK
    Did kick against my state. . . . . . . . . . . . . . . . . .  333  Psalm XLI         32
KIDS
    And gives her kidds no food, but willow's barke.". . . . . .  259  Other Poems   5  113
KILL
    With stroking hurt, and too much cramming kill.. . . . . . .   41  Arcadia II   20   12
    Which Passions kill, and Reason do deface. . . . . . . . . .   47  2nd Eclogues 27   42
    Who hunting round the strongest for to kill, . . . . . . . .   50  2nd Eclogues 28   84
    He eft would kill a mouse, but he disdaines the fight, . . .   53  2nd Eclogues 29   45
    Hath she not force even death with love to kill? . . . . . .   59  2nd Eclogues 30   85
    Bandes, favour, faith, to breake, defile, and kill.. . . . .   84  Arcadia III  60    8
    That they all vice may kill: . . . . . . . . . . . . . . . .   91  3rd Eclogues 63   23
    Which being done he afterwards would kill. . . . . . . . . .  102  3rd Eclogues 66  126
    At length for glutton taste he did them kill:. . . . . . . .  103  3rd Eclogues 66  146
    Ev'n then Despaire did Hope already kill:. . . . . . . . . .  115  4th Eclogues 72   64
    Would often kill to breed more feeling paine,. . . . . . . .  135  Cert Sonnets  2    4
    Yf Duety kill mee. . . . . . . . . . . . . . . . . . . . . .  138  Cert Sonnets  5   20
    By conquest's right in steade of searching kill. . . . . . .  150  Cert Sonnets 22   30
    Desiring nought but how to kill desire.. . . . . . . . . . .  161  Cert Sonnets 31   14
    Labour to kill in me this killing care:. . . . . . . . . . .  200  Astrophil    68   12
    For death doth kill the Witness of thy glory;. . . . . . . .  276  Psalm VI          14
    Away ragg'd rams, care I what murraine kill? . . . . . . . .  255  Other Poems   4  515
```

	PAGE	TITLE		LINE
KILLED				
Mercury kill'd his false sire for this act,.	21	1st Eclogues	8	17
Tho when they saw their foen of greatnes kilde..	102	3rd Eclogues	66	133
What sighes stolne out, or kild before full borne?	199	Astrophil	67	9
Thad'st killed with a stroke,.	259	Other Poems	5	100
KILLER				
Deare Killer, spare not thy sweet cruell shot:	189	Astrophil	48	13
KILLETH				
That she her child, I say, her best child killeth?	127	4th Eclogues	75	95
No man doubts, whom beautie killeth, ...	156	Cert Sonnets	26	27
KILLING				
No lovely praise was ever got with killing".	16	1st Eclogues	7	81
Thy bowels with all killing mettals arme..	125	4th Eclogues	75	21
That trust those killing eyes, I would,.	158	Cert Sonnets	28	19
Labour to kill in me this killing care:.	200	Astrophil	68	12
This done, but done with captive-killing grace,.	244	Other Poems	4	105
First killing mirth, then banishing all rest,.	253	Other Poems	4	431
KILLS				
A foul infection kills or bredeth botches.	50	2nd Eclogues	28	V884
Kils his owne children, teares, finding that they.	229	Astrophil	95	10
But now that hope is lost, unkindnesse kils delight, ...	212	A&S 5th Song		13
KIN				
That I perhaps am somewhat kinne to thee;.	198	Astrophil	65	12
From my plague, kynn, neighbour, Friend, ...	328	Psalm XXXVIII		31
*KIND				
Constant and kind: my sheep your foode shall breed,.	18	1st Eclogues	7	123
The noblest kinde rejects not others' woes..	18	1st Eclogues	7	134
Those rebell thoughts which are thy slaves by kinde.	23	1st Eclogues	9	46
Ewe doth make me be thinke what kind of bow the boy holdeth.	35	1st Eclogues	13	121
Though each possesse a divers working kinde, ...	78	Arcadia III	50	7
The pistle selfe, such kinde of wordes it had, ...	96	3rd Eclogues	64	91
Nct toying kinde, nor causlesly unkinde, ...	98	3rd Eclogues	65	5
The dogge was in a coller taught his kinde..	102	3rd Eclogues	66	138
That we our kind doo labour to maintaine;.	105	3rd Eclogues	67	71
Can those eyes now yeeld to the kind conceit of a sorow, . .	122	4th Eclogues	74	17
And to revenge who doo bend, would in that kind be revenged,	123	4th Eclogues	74	39
What kind of fires they be in which those spirits melt,. . .	153	Cert Sonnets	24	7
In truth, o Love, with what a boyish kind.	170	Astrophil	11	1
Her heart, sweete heart, is of no Tygre's kind:.	186	Astrophil	44	4
A kind of grace it is to slay with speed,.	189	Astrophil	48	14
Since kind or chance gives both one liverie, ...	229	Astrophil	96	2
Then on that lord most kind.	318	Psalm XXXIII		76
Save me distrest from lion's cruel kind.	322	Psalm XXXV		45
The good is kind and freely giveth;.	326	Psalm XXXVII		54
I ev'en as such kind of wight, ...	328	Psalm XXXVIII		40
KINDER				
Now kindnesse profred is, none kinder is that I:	121	4th Eclogues	73	151
KINDEST				
With kindest care, as with a certain shield.	275	Psalm V		40
KINDLE				
For bellowes serve to kindle more the fire..	38	Arcadia II	14	8
Her beautie kindle shall within thy foolish minde, ...	121	4th Eclogues	73	171
KINDLED				
The wood cries most, before it throughly kindled be, ...	14	1st Eclogues	7	8
None but I, workes by desire: by desire have I kindled in				
his soule.	30	1st Eclogues	11	13
Will at length perceave these flames by her beames to be				
kindled, ...	37	1st Eclogues	13	167
Then greefe, unkindnes, proofe, tooke, kindled, tought,. . .	84	Arcadia III	60	9
Fed by thy worth, and kindled by thy sight?.	200	Astrophil	68	8
Wherof if but a sparke once kindled be, you all.	272	Psalm II		29
KINDLEST				
In vaine thou kindlest all thy smokie fire;.	161	Cert Sonnets	31	11
KINDLY				
No musike kindly without love.	14	1st Eclogues	6	8
My words blacke inke, the marble kindly white;.	41	Arcadia II	19	9
The Sunne is hid; his kindly shadowe combers not..	49	2nd Eclogues	28	63
The kindly way to beate us on to blisse.	59	2nd Eclogues	30	76
Sweet birds kindly do graunt harmony unto thee,.	69	2nd Eclogues	34	12
Her cheekes with kindly claret spred..	86	Arcadia III	62	23
All waywardnes, which nothing kindly brookes,.	93	3rd Eclogues	63	66
The height of honor in the kindly badge of shame?.	232	Astrophil	102	3
Kindly, sweete soule, she did unkindnes take,.	245	Other Poems	4	121
KINDNESS				
Grumbling at her when she his kindnes sought,.	95	3rd Eclogues	64	32
Now kindnesse profred is, none kinder is that I:	121	4th Eclogues	73	151
Shew then O Lord Thy wondrous kindness show,.	290	Psalm XVII		21
Me in encreasing still, Thy kindness did maintaine;.	292	Psalm XVIII		65
He nobly saves his King, and kindness keeps in store,. . . .	293	Psalm XVIII		90
Thy kindnes, lovingnes;.	303	Psalm XXV		22
But in Thy kindness me record, ...	303	Psalm XXV		29
KINDS				
In divers kinds; yet as he were not filled,.	62	2nd Eclogues	30	171
KING				
Would scorne in man (their king) such feeble shows..	23	1st Eclogues	9	43
In meane caves oft treasure abides, to an hostry a king				
comes.	36	1st Eclogues	13	153
A king upon a mouse, a strong foe to a rat,.	53	2nd Eclogues	29	32
As for the Nightingale, woodmusique's King, ...	99	3rd Eclogues	66	13
Roring, and howling for to have a King..	100	3rd Eclogues	66	63

251

KING	(CONTINUED)	PAGE	TITLE		LINE
A King, in language theirs they said they would:		100	3rd Eclogues	66	64
That still our little world may know his king.		105	3rd Eclogues	67	63
Ought to be king, from whose rules who do swerve, ...		167	Astrophil	5	3
How Poles' right king meanes, without leave of hoast, . . .		180	Astrophil	30	3
And his anoynted King?		271	Psalm II		6
And say (O kings) yet have I set my King upon.		271	Psalm II		13
And I will (sayeth His King) the lord's decree display, . .		271	Psalm II		15
My King, my God for I to thee will pray.		274	Psalm V		4
Ever and ever to be King, ...		283	Psalm X		70
He nobly saves his King, and kindness keeps in store, . . .		293	Psalm XVIII		90
Let that King deign to heare, ...		296	Psalm XX		34
New joy, new joy unto Our King, ...		296	Psalm XXI		1
And why all this? Because Our King		297	Psalm XXI		25
In comes the King of glory bright.		302	Psalm XXIV		18
Who is this glorious King in might and power riding?		302	Psalm XXIV		19
In comes the King of glory bright.		302	Psalm XXIV		22
Who is This Glorious King? The lord of armyes guiding, . . .		302	Psalm XXIV		23
Even He the King of glory hight.		302	Psalm XXIV		24
Remember, only King, ...		303	Psalm XXV		19
Thy endless prayse: O God my King.		311	Psalm XXX		38
Hosts do the King not save, ...		317	Psalm XXXIII		58
KINGDOM					
Of those fortune lulls, so small rest rests in a kingdome. .		34	1st Eclogues	13	90
Thou art farre off, thy kingdome is above:		72	Arcadia III	38	7
KINGDOM'S					
His Sire's revenge, joyn'd with a kingdome's gaine:		204	Astrophil	75	6
KINGFISHER'S					
Cormoraunt's glutt, Kite's spoile, king fisher's waste, . . .		28	1st Eclogues	10	78
KINGLY					
Thou but of all the kingly Tribute take.		210	Astrophil	85	14
KING'S					
More then Nestor's yeares, more then a king's diademe. . . .		122	4th Eclogues	74	20
KINGS					
Like some weake Lords, neighbord by mighty kings, ...		179	Astrophil	29	1
No kings be crown'd but they some covenants make.		200	Astrophil	69	14
Of all the kings that ever here did raigne, ...		204	Astrophil	75	1
Why do these earthly kings and lords such meetings make, . .		271	Psalm II		3
And say (O kings) yet have I set my King upon.		271	Psalm II		13
Therfore (O Kings), be wise, O Rulers rule your mind, . . .		271	Psalm II		23
Wise Counsellors, stout Captaines, puissant Kings, ...		245	Other Poems	4	130
KINGS'					
Let not a puppet abuse thy sprite, Kings' Crownes do not					
helpe them		34	1st Eclogues	13	84
KINSFOLK					
She warre doth ever with his kinsfolke keepe, ...		104	3rd Eclogues	67	37
KISS					
Came to the bed, where wound for kisse he got, ...		5	Lady of May	3	8
Then him we kisse, whom late before we beatt		27	1st Eclogues	10	37
And if I better sing, let me thy Cosma kisse.		53	2nd Eclogues	29	38
Pas. Kisse her? now mayst thou kisse. I have a fitter match;		53	2nd Eclogues	29	39
What ere you see, thinke, touch, kisse, speake, or love, . .		60	2nd Eclogues	30	123
The asse did hurt when he did thinke to kisse.		62	2nd Eclogues	30	184
The sleepy kisse the moone stale:		66	2nd Eclogues	32	28
Kisse her from me, and say unto her spirite, ...		79	Arcadia III	51	13
Which blessed still themselves doo kisse		87	Arcadia III	62	38
The fearefull Hinde the Leopard did kisse:		100	3rd Eclogues	66	53
A dull desire to kisse the image of our death:		117	4th Eclogues	73	10
Her face (this age's praise) the thiefe doth kisse		141	Cert Sonnets	9	12
Who burnt his lips to kisse faire shining fire.		145	Cert Sonnets	16	14
I yeeld and strive, I kisse and curse the paine:		148	Cert Sonnets	19	17
The Sunne which others burn'd, did her but kisse.		176	Astrophil	22	14
With either lip he doth the other kisse:		186	Astrophil	43	11
And yet my Starre, because a sugred kisse.		203	Astrophil	73	5
That Anger' selfe I needs must kisse againe.		203	Astrophil	73	14
My lips are sweet, inspired with Stella's kisse.		204	Astrophil	74	14
Those lips, which make death's pay a meane price for a					
kisse		205	Astrophil	77	6
Sweet kisse, thy sweets I faine would sweetly endite, . . .		206	Astrophil	79	1
Cease we to praise, now pray we for a kisse.		206	Astrophil	79	14
Sweet lip, you teach my mouth with one sweet kisse.		207	Astrophil	80	14
O kisse, which doest those ruddie gemmes impart, ...		207	Astrophil	81	1
O kisse, which soules, even soules together ties		207	Astrophil	81	5
I will but kisse, I never more will bite.		208	Astrophil	82	14
Hundreds of yeares you Stella's feet may kisse.		209	Astrophil	84	14
First did with puffing kisse those lockes display:		233	Astrophil	103	11
Do invite a stealing kisse:		203	A&S 2nd Song		22
Oh sweet kisse, but ah she is waking, ...		203	A&S 2nd Song		25
There those roses for to kisse, ...		226	A&S 10th Song		28
See how it the leaves doth kisse, ...		219	A&S 8th Song		58
With loving homage kisse that only son he hath, ...		272	Psalm II		27
Moving, she seem'd at once to kisse, and speake.		244	Other Poems	4	96
Thus Pas did kisse hir hand with little grace, ...		249	Other Poems	4	276
Their sugred selves to kisse thy happy hedd:		258	Other Poems	5	58
KISS-CHEEK					
At length in rowes of Kisse-cheeke teares they raine. . . .		245	Other Poems	4	128
KISSED					
O lippes, that kist that hand with my teares sprent;		60	2nd Eclogues	30	120
With that (yet kissed first) his pipe he burst.		255	Other Poems	4	520

```
                                                      PAGE    TITLE          LINE
KISSES
    Whose footsteps I with kisses oft did trace, . . . . . . . .  115  4th Eclogues 72   73
    Give me my kisses. . . . . . . . . . . . . . . . . . . . . .  138  Cert Sonnets  5   24
KISSING
    Stop you my mouth with still still kissing me. . . . . . . .  207  Astrophil    81   14
    To hit, but Kissing hit, . . . . . . . . . . . . . . . . . .  259  Other Poems   5  108
KISS-WORTHY
    O heav'nly foole, thy most kisse-worthie face, . . . . . . .  203  Astrophil    73   12
KITE'S
    Cormoraunt's glutt, Kite's spoile, king fisher's waste,. . .   28  1st Eclogues 10   78
KLAIUS
    Klaius. O Mercurie, foregoer to the evening, . . . . . . . .  111  4th Eclogues 71    7
    Klaius. I that was once delighted every morning, . . . . . .  111  4th Eclogues 71   19
    Klaius. Long since the happie dwellers of these vallies, . .  112  4th Eclogues 71   31
    Klaius. Me seemes I see a filthie clowdie evening, . . . . .  112  4th Eclogues 71   43
    Klaius. Curse to my selfe my prayer is, the morning: . . . .  112  4th Eclogues 71   55
    Klaius. For she, with whom compar'd, the Alpes are vallies,.  113  4th Eclogues 71   67
    Klaius. These forrests eke, made wretched by our musique,. .  113  4th Eclogues 71   74
    Klaius. I think from me, not from my woes to parte,. . . . .  113  4th Eclogues 72   11
    Klaius. Enough to make a fertill minde lie waste . . . . . .  114  4th Eclogues 72   31
    Klaius. On rocke, Despaire, the buriall of my blisse . . . .  115  4th Eclogues 72   51
    Klaius. Thus, thus alas, I had my losse in chase,. . . . . .  115  4th Eclogues 72   71
    Klaius. In earthly fetters feele a lasting hell. . . . . . .  116  4th Eclogues 72   91
    But now an ende, (o Klaius) now an ende, . . . . . . . . . .  116  4th Eclogues 72  102
    Was Klaius cald, (ah Klaius, wofull wight!). . . . . . . . .  242  Other Poems   4   23
    As Strephon's eare and heart to Klaius bent: . . . . . . . .  242  Other Poems   4   28
    Klaius for skill of herbs and shepheard's art. . . . . . . .  243  Other Poems   4   33
    And Klaius taking for his yonglings carke, . . . . . . . . .  243  Other Poems   4   67
    Klaius streight felt, and groned at the blowe, . . . . . . .  246  Other Poems   4  161
    Klaius in deede would faine have puld a way. . . . . . . . .  246  Other Poems   4  171
    And thou, seke-sorow Klaius, them among: . . . . . . . . . .  247  Other Poems   4  218
    I tolde you Klaius was the haples wight. . . . . . . . . . .  251  Other Poems   4  365
    For then wise Klaius found no absence can. . . . . . . . . .  253  Other Poems   4  419
    He saw behind a bush where Klaius sate:. . . . . . . . . . .  255  Other Poems   4  527
    Klaius the wretch, who lately yelden was . . . . . . . . . .  255  Other Poems   4  529
KLAIUS'
    Epeirus high, was honest Klaius' nest, . . . . . . . . . . .  242  Other Poems   4   25
    So Klaius' soule did in his Strephon rest. . . . . . . . . .  242  Other Poems   4   29
KNAVE
    What then must I that keepe the knave? . . . . . . . . . . .   13  Arcadia I     5    6
    Above line repeated at following location. . . . . . . . . .   13  Arcadia I     5   12
    No, nothing so; an old false knave he is,. . . . . . . . . .   21  1st Eclogues  8   13
    Despairde in all this flocke to find a knave, but thee.. . .   52  2nd Eclogues 29    4
KNEE
    No knee once bowed, forsooth, for them they say we serve.. .  120  4th Eclogues 73  114
KNEEL
    To him shall kneel who to the dust be stricken,. . . . . . .  300  Psalm XXII        73
KNEELEDST
    Reason thou kneel'dst, and offeredst straight to prove . . .  170  Astrophil    10   13
KNEELING
    Then kneling to the ground, oft thus do I speake to that
        Image: . . . . . . . . . . . . . . . . . . . . . . . . .   36  1st Eclogues 13  146
KNEES
    But bow all knees, now of her knees. . . . . . . . . . . . .   89  Arcadia III  62   93
    Tuckt up even with the knees, with bowe and arrowes prest: .  118  4th Eclogues 73   67
    "Graunt, o deere, on knees I pray, . . . . . . . . . . . . .  219  A&S 8th Song      49
    (Knees on ground he then did stay) . . . . . . . . . . . . .  219  A&S 8th Song      50
    And in thy feare knees of my heart will fold . . . . . . . .  275  Psalm V           19
    He might on knees confesse his faulty part,. . . . . . . . .  247  Other Poems   4  190
    The fox on knees and elbowes tombled downe:. . . . . . . . .  248  Other Poems   4  258
KNEW
    What ayleth thee, and if they knew thy minde . . . . . . . .   23  1st Eclogues  9   42
    That erst I knewe, and with most plainefull muse;. . . . . .   24  1st Eclogues  9   63
    Then thow earst knew? rather take part with him. . . . . . .   26  1st Eclogues 10    8
    Of yeeres (alas) since I good Mastix knewe . . . . . . . . .   27  1st Eclogues 10   21
    Then earste I knewe: But first dyd playne. . . . . . . . . .   57  2nd Eclogues 30    3
    Who yet was good, because she knewe none ill,. . . . . . . .   94  3rd Eclogues 64   14
    Languet, the shepheard best swift Ister knewe, . . . . . . .   99  3rd Eclogues 66   23
    When first that crowned Basiliske I knewe, . . . . . . . . .  115  4th Eclogues 72   72
    Some good old dumpe, that Chaucer's mistresse knew, . . . .  146  Cert Sonnets 17   34
    Yea Thou dost make me serv'd by folks I never knew;. . . . .  293  Psalm XVIII       79
    Whose mettall stiff he knew he could not bende . . . . . . .  245  Other Poems   4  138
    He knew hir haunt, and haunted in the same,. . . . . . . . .  247  Other Poems   4  187
    Where by his words his self-like cause he knew.. . . . . . .  256  Other Poems   4  536
    Urania name, whose force he knew so well,. . . . . . . . . .  256  Other Poems   4  538
    He quickly knew what witchcraft gave the blow. . . . . . . .  256  Other Poems   4  539
KNIFE
    Thinke, my harde haps have blunted death's sharpe knife, . .  113  4th Eclogues 72   14
KNIGHT
    But only for this worthy knight durst prove. . . . . . . . .  204  Astrophil    75   13
KNIT
    But all thy songe herein knitt:. . . . . . . . . . . . . . .   67  2nd Eclogues 32   51
    Yet all well knit to one faire end do passe: . . . . . . . .   78  Arcadia III  50    8
    Till knit with cold, though there unknowne remaine,. . . . .  150  Cert Sonnets 22   33
    In object best to knit and strength our sight, . . . . . . .  168  Astrophil     7    6
    Wounded, inflam'de, knitt to the deathe I dye. . . . . . . .  344  Possibly      2    4
KNITTING
    For thy knitting haire be sorie: . . . . . . . . . . . . . .  156  Cert Sonnets 27   18
KNOT
    My eyes the bandes, my thoughts the fatall knot. . . . . . .   17  1st Eclogues  7  113
```

KNOT   (CONTINUED)   PAGE   TITLE   LINE
      Mine owne, embraced, sought, knot, fire, desease.. . . . . .   84 Arcadia III 60   14
      Be thou the knot of this their open vowe,. . . . .   92 3rd Eclogues 63   47
      Of what thou seest: close up in secrete knot thy will". . . . 119 4th Eclogues 73   98
      Come sleepe, o sleepe, the certaine knot of peace, ...   184 Astrophil   39   1
      That of the stroke, the heat, and knott of love, ...   344 Possibly   2   3
KNOTS
      In curled knots man's thought to hold: . . . .   85 Arcadia III 62   4
      The knottes of joy, the gemmes of love, ...   89 Arcadia III 62   95
      A wanton woman's face, and with curld knots had twinde . . .   118 4th Eclogues 73   73
      To fasten knotts, which fancy first had bound. . . . .   253 Other Poems   4   424
KNOTTED
      O this it is, the knotted straw is found . . . .   146 Cert Sonnets 17   16
KNOW
      Since what I see, thinke, know is all but you? . . . .   12 Arcadia I   2   14
      Whose vertues strange, and beuties such, as no man them may
            know?. . . . .   12 Arcadia I   3   2
      Is he a manlike man, that doth not know man. . . . .   24 1st Eclogues 9   57
      I yet should know a young man speaketh now,. . . . .   25 1st Eclogues 9   97
      But fondlings fonde, know not your owne desire . . . .   25 1st Eclogues 9   102
      Unto my selfe let after-livers know. . . . .   40 Arcadia II   18   10
      P. How know we that, since present joyes we misse? . . . . .   47 2nd Eclogues 27   38
      R. You know it not: of Reason therefore know it. . . . . . .   47 2nd Eclogues 27   39
      Such oddes I willing lay; for him and you I know.. . . . . .   53 2nd Eclogues 29   48
      Pas. O Nymphes, I tell you newes, for Pas you knowe: . . . .   54 2nd Eclogues 29   66
      Let Pas now know, how Nico maketh layes. . . . .   54 2nd Eclogues 29   71
      His utmost light: for well his witte doth know,. . . . . . .   55 2nd Eclogues 29   97
      But well you know, the gentle Sunne would save . . . .   60 2nd Eclogues 30   104
      Can I, that know her sacred parts, restrained be . . . . . .   61 2nd Eclogues 30   149
      From any joy, know fortune's vile displacing her,. . . . . .   61 2nd Eclogues 30   150
      Oh! I do know what guest I have mett; it is Echo. 'T is
            Echo . . . .   63 2nd Eclogues 31   3
      Doth th'infected wretch, of his ev'll th'extremity know? No.   63 2nd Eclogues 31   19
      But if he know not his harms what guides hath he whil'st he
            be blind? Blind..   63 2nd Eclogues 31   20
      Who seekes to knowe, acquaintes hym self with hell;. . . . .   71 Arcadia III 36   16
      Whereto you knowe, his honest harte were loath.. . . . . . .   95 3rd Eclogues 64   60
      That with his fault he might her goodnes know. . . . .   97 3rd Eclogues 64   114
      Or know your strengths, and then you shall do weil.. . . . .   103 3rd Eclogues 66   154
      That still our little world may know his king. . . . .   105 3rd Eclogues 67   63
      My worke her workes to know, her dwelling my resorte.. . . .   117 4th Eclogues 73   42
      The other had with arte (more then our women knowe,. . . . .   118 4th Eclogues 73   71
      I know full well you know, what discord long hath raign'd. .   119 4th Eclogues 73   105
      To stand unto my will: their will they made me know. . . . .   121 4th Eclogues 73   157
      I know not I, but once in detestation. . . . .   128 4th Eclogues 75   100
      To know my miseries, but chaste and cruell:. . . . .   136 Cert Sonnets 3   10
      And doth she know what mould her beautie beares? . . . . . .   142 Cert Sonnets 11   2
      Deeming strange evill in that he did not know. . . . .   145 Cert Sonnets 16   4
      That all the earth my woes, sighes, teares may know, ...   146 Cert Sonnets 17   39
      Know my words their faults acknowledge.. . . . .   157 Cert Sonnets 27   36
      Pleasure might cause her reade, reading might make her know,   165 Astrophil   1   3
      For me in sooth, no Muse but one I know:. . . . .   166 Astrophil   3   9
      As who by being poisond doth poison know.. . . . .   173 Astrophil   16   14
      And by just counts my selfe a banckrout know . . . .   173 Astrophil   18   3
      Some that know how my spring I did addresse, ...   176 Astrophil   23   5
      As what their hands do hold, their heads do know,. . . . . .   177 Astrophil   24   6
      For me, I do Nature unidle know, ...   178 Astrophil   26   9
      And know great causes, great effects procure:. . . . .   178 Astrophil   26   10
      And know those Bodies high raigne on the low.. . . . .   178 Astrophil   26   11
      But know that I in pure simplicitie, ...   179 Astrophil   28   12
      But know not how, for still I thinke of you. . . . .   180 Astrophil   30   14
      My words I know do well set forth my mind, ...   186 Astrophil   44   1
      Not though thereof the cause her selfe she know: . . . . . .   187 Astrophil   45   4
      And thinke so still, so Stella know my mind, ...   192 Astrophil   54   9
      Untill by your inspiring I might know, ...   192 Astrophil   55   7
      Her graunt to me, by her owne vertue know. . . . .   196 Astrophil   63   4
      Who will in fairest booke of Nature know,. . . . .   201 Astrophil   71   1
      So ample eares as never good newes know: . . . .   206 Astrophil   78   13
      And that you know, I envy you no lot . . . .   209 Astrophil   84   12
      I would know whether she did sit or walke, ...   225 Astrophil   92   9
      I have (live I and know this) harmed thee, ...   227 Astrophil   93   10
      I would know by what right this palenesse overcame . . . . .   232 Astrophil   102   7
      Now will I attempt to know, ...   202 A&S 2nd Song   11
      Know, that small Love is quicke, and great Love doth amaze:.   209 A&S 3rd Song   16
      Or seeing, have so wodden wits, as not that worth to know; .   217 A&S 7th Song   8
      And a helpe for him did know,. . . . .   222 A&S 9th Song   38
      For god doth know, and knowing doth approve. . . . .   271 Psalm I   19
      Yet know this too, that God did take . . . .   273 Psalm IV   11
      They that know Thee, on Thee their trust will bend,. . . . .   280 Psalm IX   28
      For I know the deadly grave. . . . .   288 Psalm XVI   31
      For I know thou wilt defend. . . . .   288 Psalm XVI   33
      Make us in mervailes of Thy mercy know . . . .   290 Psalm XVII   22
      His faults know and acknowledg?. . . . .   295 Psalm XIX   50
      I know that He heares Thee, ...   296 Psalm XX   24
      For such he makes his secret know, ...   304 Psalm XXV   53
      To them them know Thee and Thy might, ...   324 Psalm XXXVI   28
      I know that man's foule sin doth cause Thy wrath.. . . . . .   330 Psalm XXXIX   33
      Strephon, fond boy, delighted did not knowe, ...   246 Other Poems   4   163
      To see, to feele, to heare, to tast, to know . . . .   252 Other Poems   4   407
      And yet, deare soule, I know she hurteth none: . . . .   254 Other Poems   4   458

```
KNOW                       (CONTINUED)            PAGE    TITLE           LINE
    "Nay each thing is bewitcht to know my case: . . . . . . . .  254 Other Poems    4   473
    If thou know not for whome thy Master dies,. . . . . . . . .  259 Other Poems    5   110
    Since they know not how to faine,. . . . . . . . . . . . . .  263 Other Poems    7    39
KNOWETH
    Time doth worke what no man knoweth.". . . . . . . . . . . .  234 A&S 11th Song      17
KNOWING
    Knowing no more, then what poore tryall showes,. . . . . . .   28 1st Eclogues 10    53
    Knowing that evill becommes a houshold strife, . . . . . . .   96 3rd Eclogues 64    70
    Breath made of flames, wits knowing nought but damage, . . .  109 Arcadia IV   28    28
    And knowing, love, and loving, lay apart . . . . . . . . . .  177 Astrophil    24     7
    Knowing worlds passe, ere she enough can find. . . . . . . .  232 Astrophil   101    13
    Or knowing, have so muddy minds, as not to be in love; . . .  217 A&S 7th Song       9
    For god doth know, and knowing doth approve. . . . . . . . .  271 Psalm I            19
    Knowing full well that beasts they be. . . . . . . . . . . .  315 Psalm XXXII        34
    Lockt fast with knowing that she is, of worldly things the
      best. . . . . . . . . . . . . . . . . . . . . . . . . . . .  344 Possibly     1    30
    Not knowing who did draw with him therin;. . . . . . . . . .  253 Other Poems    4   426
    Fearing the worst, not knowing what were best, . . . . . . .  255 Other Poems    4   525
KNOWLEDGE
    (So humble knowledge can throw downe the snakish sinne). . .   44 Arcadia II   26     6
    What foresight tels; our thoughts upon thy knowledge staye..   45 Arcadia II   26    12
    To sheepe, whom love, not knowledge, made to heare,. . . . .  103 3rd Eclogues 66   156
    Both force to flie and knowledge where to fall. . . . . . .   144 Cert Sonnets 15    12
    Words, o words of heavenlie knowledge, . . . . . . . . . . .  157 Cert Sonnets 27    35
    Knowledge might pitie winne, and pitie grace obtaine,. . . .  165 Astrophil     1     4
    My youth doth waste, my knowledge brings forth toyes,. . . .  174 Astrophil    18     9
    Deeme that my Muse some fruit of knowledge plies:. . . . . .  176 Astrophil    23     6
    That knowledg you may find.. . . . . . . . . . . . . . . . .  271 Psalm II           24
    In darkness teach cleere knowledg. . . . . . . . . . . . . .  293 Psalm XIX           8
    Most secret from all knowledg. . . . . . . . . . . . . . . .  295 Psalm XIX          52
    Now in mee knowledg sayes. . . . . . . . . . . . . . . . . .  296 Psalm XX           21
KNOWN
    Or if eyes' language be not unto her knowne, . . . . . . . .   30 1st Eclogues 12     6
    Old age hath knowne what ever was in youth:. . . . . . . . .   39 Arcadia II   15    11
    This marble chose, as of like temper knowne: . . . . . . . .   40 Arcadia II   19     2
    Oh when shall I be knowne, wher most to be knowne I do
      longe Long. . . . . . . . . . . . . . . . . . . . . . . . .   64 2nd Eclogues 31    32
    While thy known course, observing nature's right,. . . . . .   82 Arcadia III  56    11
    (Which may be know'n, but never help't with wailing) . . . .  109 Arcadia IV   70    14
    They that heav'n have knowne, do say . . . . . . . . . . . .  140 Cert Sonnets  7    24
    And knowne those pangs that the losers prove,. . . . . . . .  153 Cert Sonnets 24     2
    But knowne worth did in mine of time proceed,. . . . . . . .  165 Astrophil     2     3
    Of Lovers never knowne, a grievous case, . . . . . . . . . .  187 Astrophil    45     6
    And make Thy wayes to me more plainly known, . . . . . . . .  275 Psalm V            23
    Thou well hast known what plung my soul was in . . . . . . .  312 Psalm XXXI         21
    Till his known ev'ill do hatred get. . . . . . . . . . . . .  323 Psalm XXXVI         8
    His well knowne friend, but yet his unknowne mate, . . . . .  255 Other Poems    4   528
    To whome arte of Love is knowne: . . . . . . . . . . . . . .  262 Other Poems    7    28
KNOWS
    Then cries to sencelesse things, which neither knowes. . . .   23 1st Eclogues  9    41
    For Pas well knowes what layes can Nico make. . . . . . . .    54 2nd Eclogues 29    74
    The child feeles that; the man that feeling knowes,. . . . .   57 2nd Eclogues 30    23
    That childish stuffe which knowes not frendes from foes, . .   81 Arcadia III  54    11
    As little hunting minde (God knowes) did there appeere. . .   118 4th Eclogues 73    70
    Such thing cannot he hope, that knowes thy determinat
      hardnes; . . . . . . . . . . . . . . . . . . . . . . . . .  122 4th Eclogues 74    13
    Since bashfull dread seekes where he knowes me harmed: . . .  135 Cert Sonnets  1     2
    No, no, she is too wise, she knowes her face . . . . . . . .  142 Cert Sonnets 11     9
    She knowes the sicknesse of that perfect place. . . . . . .   142 Cert Sonnets 11    11
    He knowes not) grow in only follie rich. . . . . . . . . . .  177 Astrophil    24    14
    Where well he knowes, no man to him can come. . . . . . . .   186 Astrophil    43    14
    For she knowes, if she display . . . . . . . . . . . . . . .  222 A&S 9th Song       43
    He knowes the same,. . . . . . . . . . . . . . . . . . . . .  317 Psalm XXXIII       56
    And knowes not who the fruit shall reap. . . . . . . . . . .  330 Psalm XXXIX        22
KNOWST
    Thou knowst made declaration,. . . . . . . . . . . . . . . .  331 Psalm XL           36
LA
    Fa la la leridan, dan dan dan deridan: . . . . . . . . . . .  156 Cert Sonnets 27     5
    Above line repeated at following locations . . . . . . . . .  156 Cert Sonnets 27    13
    . . . . . . . . . . . . . . . . . . . . . . . . . . . . . .  157 Cert Sonnets 27    21
    . . . . . . . . . . . . . . . . . . . . . . . . . . . . . .  157 Cert Sonnets 27    29
    . . . . . . . . . . . . . . . . . . . . . . . . . . . . . .  157 Cert Sonnets 27    37
LABOR
    In vaine, mine Eyes, you labour to amende. . . . . . . . . .   38 Arcadia II   14     1
    (Mine eyes even great in labour with their teares) . . . . .   41 Arcadia II   21     2
    Whyle upon chaunce, his fruite of labour lyes; . . . . . . .   71 Arcadia III  36    10
    That we our kind doo labour to maintaine; . . . . . . . . .   105 3rd Eclogues 67    71
    Who hath his hire, hath well his labour plast. . . . . . . .  108 Arcadia IV   68     1
    Vaine is their paine, who labour in Despaire. . . . . . . .   115 4th Eclogues 72    60
    Strephon. Vaine is their paine, who labour in Despaire. . .   115 4th Eclogues 72    61
    My tongue doth itch, my thoughts in labour be: . . . . . . .  183 Astrophil    37     2
    Let me no steps but of lost labour trace,. . . . . . . . . .  198 Astrophil    64     6
    Labour to kill in me this killing care:. . . . . . . . . . .  200 Astrophil    68    12
LABORER
    The laborer, which cursed earthe up teares . . . . . . . . .   71 Arcadia III  36     7
    The labourer, whome tyred boddie makes . . . . . . . . . . .   71 Arcadia III  37     7
LABOR'S
    All is but this, this is our labour's hire,. . . . . . . . .   75 Arcadia III  44     6
```

LACK
    I sweare by her I love and lacke, that I . . . . 235 Astrophil 105 5
    Therfore my tongue shall never lack. . . . . 311 Psalm XXX 37
    The lions oft lack food, ... 319 Psalm XXXIV 37
LACKS
    Thy Venus' child, whose beautie Venus lackes? . . . . 60 2nd Eclogues 30 112
    Where nothing but impression lackes. . . . . 88 Arcadia III 62 76
LAD
    And let him be our judge: the lad doth please me well". . . . 121 4th Eclogues 73 153
    The ladd Philisides. . . . . 256 Other Poems 5 1
    So I unlucky lad . . . . 259 Other Poems 5 95
LADDER
    Nico. O if I had a ladder for the skies, ... 55 2nd Eclogues 29 117
LADDERS
    O tongues right ladders made to clime dishonour, ... 50 2nd Eclogues 28 90
WHOSE CRIES ARE LADD
LADIES
    But streight there issued forth two Ladies (Ladies sure. . . 118 4th Eclogues 73 63
    Should Ladies faire be tyed to such hard lawes, ... 146 Cert Sonnets 17 23
    When some faire Ladies, by hard promise tied, ... 176 Astrophil 22 5
    But heere I do store of faire Ladies meete, ... 236 Astrophil 106 9
LADIES'
    Straunge were the Ladies' weedes; yet more unfit then
        strange. . . . . 118 4th Eclogues 73 65
LADS
    Dicus. Sing then my lads, but sing with better vaine then
        yet, ... 53 2nd Eclogues 29 49
LADY
    Dorus. Lady your selfe, whom nether name I dare, ... 18 1st Eclogues 7 131
    Dorus. Lady, reservd by the heav'ns to do pastors' company
        honnor, ... 31 1st Eclogues 13 1
    Now by thy words I begin, most famous Lady, to gather. . . . 34 1st Eclogues 13 94
    Lady my Treasure. . . . . 138 Cert Sonnets 5 4
    Above line repeated at following location. . . . . 138 Cert Sonnets 5 28
    Sweet Ladie, as for those whose sullen cheare, ... 147 Cert Sonnets 17 46
    A Ladie in despite of nature chaste, ... 151 Cert Sonnets 22 62
    Ladie mine eyes remained, ... : . . 154 Cert Sonnets 25 3
    Lady have you reserved, ... 154 Cert Sonnets 25 19
    Lady the life of all love; . . . . 154 Cert Sonnets 25 20
    Sweet Ladie you remaine well paid. . . . . 159 Cert Sonnets 29 4
    Even so (alas) a Lady Dian's peere, ... 230 Astrophil 97 9
    You Rebell run away, to Lord and Lady untrue, ... 215 A&S 5th Song 86
LAELAPS
    What if Laelaps a better morsell fyndes. . . . . 26 1st Eclogues 10 7
    And thowe Laelaps let not pride make thee brim . . . . 26 1st Eclogues 10 10
    Here Laelaps, here, in deed against the foen . . . . 27 1st Eclogues 10 13
LAID
    My sonne, keepe this, that my long toyle hath laide to me: . 16 1st Eclogues 7 52
    Who hath his hopes laid up in woman's hand. . . . . 24 1st Eclogues 9 55
    I layde my face; my face wherein there lyes. . . . . 41 Arcadia II 21 3
    Nico. Thy monument is layd in many a tree, ... 56 2nd Eclogues 29 129
    Her words in syrup laid of sweetest breath, ... 58 2nd Eclogues 30 51
    And make me wish my selfe layd under mountaines, ... 112 4th Eclogues 71 36
    A horse's worth laid wast the Troyan ground: . . . . 146 Cert Sonnets 17 18
    No further debt on me is laid, ... 159 Cert Sonnets 29 2
    I layd me down and slept, ... 272 Psalm III 16
    Though legions round be layd, ... 272 Psalm III 20
    I dwell, layd up in safest neast. . . . . 274 Psalm IV 35
    In heaven his trust hath layed; . . . . . : . . . . 297 Psalm XXI 26
    While battaile's brunt on me were laid . . . . 307 Psalm XXVII 16
    Or shall Thy Truth on mankind layd . . . . 311 Psalm XXX 29
    Because on him their trust is laid. . . . . 327 Psalm XXXVII 104
    Of my filthy folly lai'd; . . . . 328 Psalm XXXVIII 15
    With length laid downe she deckt the lonely place. . . . . . 244 Other Poems 4 107
    Laid hold on him with most lay-holding grace. . . . . 250 Other Poems 4 310
LAIN
    For proof, oft lain in wait he is. . . . . 282 Psalm X 31
LAKE
    If othes might serve, even by the Stygian lake, ... 146 Cert Sonnets 17 6
    The Bruertons have a Lake, which when the Sunne. . . . . . . 150 Cert Sonnets 22 11
    My lake is sense, whose still streames never runne, ... 150 Cert Sonnets 22 15
LALUS
    Lalus. Come Dorus, come, let songs thy sorowes signifie: . . 14 1st Eclogues 7 1
    Lalus. If thou wilt not be seene, thy face goe hide away, . . 15 1st Eclogues 7 13
    Lalus. Muse hold your peace: but thou, my God Pan, glorify . 15 1st Eclogues 7 25
    Lalus. How oft my dolefull Sire cried to me, "tarrie sonne". 16 1st Eclogues 7 49
    Lalus. Once my well-waiting eyes espied my treasure, ... 16 1st Eclogues 7 73
    Lalus. This mayde, thus made for joyes, o Pan bemone her, . . 17 1st Eclogues 7 97
    Lalus. Kala at length conclude my lingring lotte: . . . . . . 18 1st Eclogues 7 115
    Lalus. But if my Kala this my suite denies, ... 18 1st Eclogues 7 147
    Lalus. So doth my life within it selfe dissolve, ... 19 1st Eclogues 7 157
    Lalus. Oh he is mard that is for others made. . . . . 19 1st Eclogues 7 167
    Good Lalus mine, I yeld to thy abilitie; . . . . 20 1st Eclogues 7 V974
    Nico. Couldst thou make Lalus flie? so nightingales avoide, . 52 2nd Eclogues 29 17
    And have to Lalus shewd your secret skill, ... 91 3rd Eclogues 63 20
    Graunt to the thing which we for Lalus crave. . . . . 92 3rd Eclogues 63 30
LALUS'
    For pilfring Lalus' lambe, with crouch to blesse thy head. . 52 2nd Eclogues 29 14
    Since Lalus' musick oft doth yeeld you praise, ... 92 3rd Eclogues 63 29
    I pray thee doo to Lalus' sample leane: . . . . 103 3rd Eclogues 67 4

	(CONTINUED)	PAGE	TITLE		LINE
LALUS'					
Lalus' example I would soone ensue,.	104	3rd Eclogues	67	23
LAMB					
Milde as a Lambe, more daintie then a Conie is:.	15	1st Eclogues	7	31
For pilfring Lalus' lambe, with crouch to blesse thy head. .	52	2nd Eclogues	29	14
Pas. My voice the lambe did winne, Menalcas was our judge:. .	52	2nd Eclogues	29	15
For once the Lion by the Lambe did lie;.	100	3rd Eclogues	66	52
Or like a lambe whose dam away is fet, ...	254	Other Poems	4	490
"Tell me my lamb of gold,.	258	Other Poems	5	66
Canst thou, poore lamme, become another's lamme?	258	Other Poems	5	76
"Earth, brooke, flowrs, pipe, lambe, Dove.	259	Other Poems	5	92
And first Lambe that shall befall, ...	264	Other Poems	7	69
LAMBKINS					
But then I homeward call'd my lambkins deare:.	103	3rd Eclogues	66	158
Toward Lamkins best beloved.	221	A&S 9th Song		25
Who ever Lambkins saw (yet lambkins love to play).	343	Possibly	1	5
LAMBS					
Like fatt of lambs shall be consumed,.	326	Psalm XXXVII		51
Will. What? is thy Bagpipe broke, or are thy lambs miswent;.	343	Possibly	1	15
His lambs were him beside, ...	256	Other Poems	5	5
LAME					
And of their wounds make brave lame showes:.	44	Arcadia II	25	8
My wits, quicke in vaine thoughts, in vertue lame:	175	Astrophil	21	4
LAMED					
Lamde with the angle, which it selfe did beare,.	115	4th Eclogues	72	67
For ever lamed of our suerest might;	130	4th Eclogues	76	28
LAMENT					
Not limited to a whispringe note, the Lament of a Courtier,.	35	1st Eclogues	13	110
By shame and griefe, helpe, helpe me to lament	126	4th Eclogues	75	62
Have more cause to lament me,.	137	Cert Sonnets	4	19
Like one that should his Mother's death lament..	322	Psalm XXXV		36
LAMENTATION					
To make these woods resounde thy lamentation?.	47	2nd Eclogues	28	2
The vehement course of this just lamentation:.	127	4th Eclogues	75	98
LAMENTATIONS					
Then man to yeeld to female lamentations?.	61	2nd Eclogues	30	141
LAMENTING					
On lamenting wholy set:.	262	Other Poems	7	8
LAMENTS					
Which inke onely relates, but ne laments, ne replies?. . . .	122	4th Eclogues	74	18
LAMP					
Nc lampe, whose light by Art is got, ...	86	Arcadia III	62	17
Now that of purest lampe is queint the light,.	129	4th Eclogues	76	8
LAMPS					
Those lampes of heav'nly fire to fixed motion bound, ...	118	4th Eclogues	73	43
And fooles can thinke those Lampes of purest light,.	177	Astrophil	26	2
LANCE					
Having this day my horse, my hand, my launce	185	Astrophil	41	1
Yea take Thy lance and stop the way of those	321	Psalm XXXV		4
LAND					
With strong foes on land, on seas with contrary tempests . .	29	1st Eclogues	11	5
Sweete Ilands make in that sweete land..	90	Arcadia III	62	129
Of samothea lande; a lande, which whilom stood	117	4th Eclogues	73	36
From out Thy land by them anoy'd..	283	Psalm X		72
From heavnly holy land	296	Psalm XX		23
For by his power the land upon the Ocean raigneth, ...	302	Psalm XXIV		3
In land with living creatures clad?.	308	Psalm XXVII		63
Shall have the land in their possessing, ...	326	Psalm XXXVII		74
To Strephon Aeole's land first breathing lent:	242	Other Poems	4	26
Tell me, if husband springtime leave your lande, ...	257	Other Poems	5	50
LANDS					
Thou placest him upon all lands.	279	Psalm VIII		21
Gcd's goodness fills all lands,.	316	Psalm XXXIII		21
LANGUAGE					
Or mine eyes' language she doo hap to judge of,.	30	1st Eclogues	12	2
Or if eyes' language be not unto her knowne, ...	30	1st Eclogues	12	6
Or mine eyes' language she doo hap to judge of,.	31	1st Eclogues	12	26
A King, in language theirs they said they would:	100	3rd Eclogues	66	64
(For then their language was a perfect speech)	100	3rd Eclogues	66	65
Us in their best language woo:	210	A&S 4th Song		16
Would have made tongue's language plaine;.	219	A&S 8th Song		66
There is no speech, no language which.	293	Psalm XIX		9
LANGUET					
The songe I sange old Languet had me taught, ...	99	3rd Eclogues	66	22
Languet, the shepheard best swift Ister knewe, ...	99	3rd Eclogues	66	23
LANGUISH					
Earth take this earth, wherein my spirits languish..	136	Cert Sonnets	3	16
Wherein she suffring all her spirits' languish,.	137	Cert Sonnets	4	15
Yet while I languish, him that bosome clips, ...	194	Astrophil	59	9
Joying till joy makes us languish.	227	A&S 10th Song		42
Joylesse, hopelesse, endlesse languish..	220	A&S 8th Song		80
For I am weake, and in my weakness languish;	276	Psalm VI		6
Thus languish?	285	Psalm XIII		8
LANGUISHED					
I reade it in thy lookes, thy languisht grace, ...	180	Astrophil	31	7
My life forgets to nourish languisht sprites;.	186	Astrophil	42	10
Languisht with horrors of the silent night,.	224	Astrophil	89	8
Wither not you, languisht with discontent?	257	Other Poems	5	52
LAP					
Philisides. If fortune's lappe became my dwelling place, . .	23	1st Eclogues	9	26

```
LAP                    (CONTINUED)                          PAGE    TITLE          LINE
   Engulfed in despaire, slid downe from fortune's lappe: . . .   153  Cert Sonnets 24   16
   But she in chafe him from her lap did shove, . . . . . . . .   173  Astrophil    17    7
   That lap doth lap, nay lets, in spite of spite, . . . . . . .  194  Astrophil    59   10
   And o my Muse, though oft you luld her in your lap, . . . . .  213  A&S 5th Song      25
   With hand and mouth, with lapp and brest keepe warme, . . . . 258  Other Poems   5   84
LARGE
   With long large eares where never rumour dyes. . . . . . . .   21   1st Eclogues  8   28
   With large encrease, and wooll of fine perfection, . . . . .   49   2nd Eclogues 28   50
   Large roomes within, where droppes distill amaine: . . . . .  150   Cert Sonnets 22   32
   And thinke I should not your large precepts misse? . . . . .  192   Astrophil    56    4
   This large offer of our blisse, . . . . . . . . . . . . . . . 211   A&S 4th Song      32
LARGELY
   He lifted me unto a largly noble place.. . . . . . . . . . .  292   Psalm XVIII       42
LARGER
   With larger round, to shun the folowing feet. . . . . . . .   250   Other Poems   4  332
LARGESS
   Largesse his hands could never skill of sparefulnesse. . . .   48   2nd Eclogues 28   45
LARK
   Now the ambitiouse Larke with mirror cleare. . . . . . . . .  243   Other Poems   4   45
LASS
   That married had a trick and bonny lasse . . . . . . . . . .   94   3rd Eclogues 64    3
LASSES
   Then some grene gowns are by the lasses worne. . . . . . . .  243   Other Poems   4   53
*LAST
   Nico. Well aimed by my hat: for as thou sangst last day; . .   52   2nd Eclogues 29   25
   Plangus. Alas how long this pilgrimage doth last?. . . . . .   57   2nd Eclogues 30    5
   To wretched me, the last worst malediction.. . . . . . . . .   61   2nd Eclogues 30  148
   The song thereof a last will, . . . . . . . . . . . . . . . .  66   2nd Eclogues 32   34
   First, second, last, did binde, enforce, and arme, . . . . .   84   Arcadia III  60    3
   At last for sport their sillie lives did spill.. . . . . . .  103   3rd Eclogues 66  147
   That last day seem'd, he could not chew a beane. . . . . . .  103   3rd Eclogues 67    6
   How well last day before our Prince you could. . . . . . . .  106   3rd Eclogues 67   97
   I give the Sunne a last farewell each evening; . . . . . . .  112   4th Eclogues 71   50
   Grant yet, grant yet a looke, to the last monument of his
      anguish, . . . . . . . . . . . . . . . . . . . . . . . . . 122   4th Eclogues 74    3
   And doo not onely marke the accents last, . . . . . . . . . . 126   4th Eclogues 75   32
   We last short while, and build long lasting places: . . . .  127   4th Eclogues 75   91
   Bountifulnes hath made his last conclusion: . . . . . . . .  128   4th Eclogues 75  119
   As to Swanne in last disease: . . . . . . . . . . . . . . . . 140   Cert Sonnets  7   37
   Ah saucy paine let not thy errour last, . . . . . . . . . . . 141   Cert Sonnets  8   13
   They shall not last: with Citherne silent muse . . . . . . .  143   Cert Sonnets 12   14
   Sore signe it is, the Lord's last thred is spun. . . . . . .  150   Cert Sonnets 22   14
   These wonders England breedes, the last remaines, . . . . . . 151   Cert Sonnets 22   61
   To blaze these last, and sware devoutly then, . . . . . . . . 171   Astrophil    13   13
   But this at last is her sweet breath'd defence: . . . . . . . 195   Astrophil    61    4
   Stolne to my heart, since last faire night, nay day, . . . .  199   Astrophil    66   10
   And their Renoune, which seemed so lyke to last, . . . . . .  280   Psalm IX          13
   What? Doth their Memory no longer last?. . . . . . . . . . .  280   Psalm IX          18
   Which if it last, Woe to all simple Hearts.. . . . . . . . .  285   Psalm XII         27
   Throughout all ages last.. . . . . . . . . . . . . . . . . .  317   Psalm XXXIII      39
   For those badd folks at last shall perish, . . . . . . . . .  325   Psalm XXXVII      23
   Their heritage shall last for ever, . . . . . . . . . . . . . 325   Psalm XXXVII      46
   I by night shall singing last, . . . . . . . . . . . . . . .  335   Psalm XLII        38
   Though thus, and worse, though now I am at last, . . . . . .  254   Other Poems   4  493
LASTETH
   She never dies but lasteth . . . . . . . . . . . . . . . . .  152   Cert Sonnets 23    9
LASTING
   In earthly fetters feele a lasting hell. . . . . . . . . . .  116   4th Eclogues 72   90
   Klaius. In earthly fetters feele a lasting hell. . . . . . .  116   4th Eclogues 72   91
   We last short while, and build long lasting places: . . . .  127   4th Eclogues 75   91
   To that sweet yoke, where lasting freedomes be: . . . . . .  161   Cert Sonnets 32    6
LASTLY
   Lastly what so she be, that's my protection. . . . . . . . .   49   2nd Eclogues 28   72
LATE
   Then him we kisse, whom late before we beatt . . . . . . . .   27   1st Eclogues 10   37
   These cocklinges cockred we bewaile to late, . . . . . . . .   28   1st Eclogues 10   58
   Come, come my currs, tis late I will goe in. . . . . . . . .   29   1st Eclogues 10   98
   Is Late remorse in follie dearely bought.. . . . . . . . . .   49   2nd Eclogues 28   78
   Nico. As I of late, neer bushes usde my sive, . . . . . . . .  54   2nd Eclogues 29   81
   Of some late grace a greater grace receave, . . . . . . . . .  77   Arcadia III  49    4
   Monstrous appeares, long trueth received late, . . . . . . .   85   Arcadia III  61    6
   But with much studie learne late to repent.. . . . . . . . .  106   3rd Eclogues 67   96
   While late bare earth, proud of new clothing springeth,. . .  137   Cert Sonnets  4    3
   Late harbors in her face whom nature wrought, . . . . . . . . 141   Cert Sonnets  8    7
   Like late mowne meades, late cut from joy I live.. . . . . .  147   Cert Sonnets 18   11
   Nor breake my word though reward come late, . . . . . . . . . 153   Cert Sonnets 24   21
   On sandie banke of late, . . . . . . . . . . . . . . . . . .  158   Cert Sonnets 28   33
   Love borne in Greece, of late fled from his native place,. .  168   Astrophil     8    1
   His mother deare Cupid offended late, . . . . . . . . . . . . 173   Astrophil    17    1
   Vertue of late, with vertuous care to ster . . . . . . . . .  177   Astrophil    25    9
   Yet hearing late a fable, which did show . . . . . . . . . .  187   Astrophil    45    5
   Now judge by this: in piercing phrases late, . . . . . . . .  194   Astrophil    58    9
   Late tyr'd with wo, even ready for to pine . . . . . . . . .  195   Astrophil    62    1
   For late with heart most high, with eyes most low, . . . . .  196   Astrophil    63    5
   That Ballance weigh'd what sword did late obtaine, . . . . .  204   Astrophil    75    8
   Admitted late by your best-graced grace, . . . . . . . . . .  208   Astrophil    82   10
   You say forsooth, you left her well of late. . . . . . . . .  225   Astrophil    92    7
   I think now of thy faults, who late thought of thy praise,.  213   A&S 5th Song      16
   And turn his couch, where sick he couched late, . . . . . .  333   Psalm XLI         11
```

```
LATE                    (CONTINUED)                          PAGE    TITLE              LINE
     Will. Thou late of wages playn'dst: what wages mayst thou
          have?. . . . . . . . . . . . . . . . . . . . . . . .   344  Possibly        1    31
     Did me pearce, burne, and bynde, long since and late,. . . .  345  Possibly        2    12
     The lesson which but late he learn'd too furre:. . . . . . .  246  Other Poems     4   174
     But glad Desire, his late embosom'd guest, . . . . . . . . .  247  Other Poems     4   201
     Late neere a crosse I met an ougly Cat.. . . . . . . . . . .  253  Other Poems     4   448
     Whence he was transformed late,. . . . . . . . . . . . . . .  262  Other Poems     7    10
LATELY
     Where bee nowe those Joyes, that I lately tasted?. . . . . .  138  Cert Sonnets    5     5
     Cupid the wagg, that lately conquer'd had. . . . . . . . . .  245  Other Poems     4   129
     Klaius the wretch, who lately yelden was . . . . . . . . . .  255  Other Poems     4   529
     And lately thence untwine: . . . . . . . . . . . . . . . . .  257  Other Poems     5    44
LATER
     Hate of the firste, contempt of later feate: . . . . . . . .   27  1st Eclogues   10    39
     The later borne, yet too soone, Strephon hight.. . . . . . .  242  Other Poems     4    24
LATONA'S
     Latona's sonne, whose birth in paine and travaile long . . .   45  Arcadia II     26     7
LATTER
     (The one doth force, the latter doth entise) . . . . . . . .   98  3rd Eclogues   65    10
LAUD
     That any laud to me thereof should grow, . . . . . . . . . .  224  Astrophil      90    10
     Shall feed and laud the giver of their food. . . . . . . . .  300  Psalm XXII           72
     Yet let them say, laud be to God alwayes . . . . . . . . . .  323  Psalm XXXV           69
LAUDS
     So shall all men with laudes inviron thee. . . . . . . . . .  277  Psalm VII            19
     Where Israel Thy lawdes is ever telling; . . . . . . . . . .  298  Psalm XXII           10
     So my songs his lauds shall yeeld. . . . . . . . . . . . . .  309  Psalm XXVIII         30
     Most to Thy lawdes will I my speeches bind.. . . . . . . . .  322  Psalm XXXV           48
LAUGH
     Thinke Hanniball did laugh when Carthage lost. . . . . . . .  147  Cert Sonnets   17    45
     Suffer not her to laugh, while both we suffer paine: . . . .  213  A&S 5th Song         29
     He shall laugh them to scorn,. . . . . . . . . . . . . . . .  271  Psalm II             10
     There did he make hir laugh in spite of woe, . . . . . . . .  247  Other Poems     4   197
LAUGHING
     And sav'd me from foes' laughing scorn;. . . . . . . . . . .  310  Psalm XXX             2
     So laughing all, yet Pas to ease some dell,. . . . . . . . .  249  Other Poems     4   263
LAUREL
     Lawrell shews what I seeke, by the Mirre is show'd how I
          seeke it,. . . . . . . . . . . . . . . . . . . . . . .   35  1st Eclogues   13   116
     A nest for my yong praise in Lawrell tree: . . . . . . . . .  224  Astrophil      90     6
     Like laurell fresh himself out spreading.. . . . . . . . . .  327  Psalm XXXVII         90
     Strephon with leavy twiggs of Laurell tree . . . . . . . . .  244  Other Poems     4    73
LAW
     If shee still hate love's lawe,. . . . . . . . . . . . . . .   19  1st Eclogues    7  V150
     Sweet vertue's lawe barres not a causefull mone. . . . . . .   22  1st Eclogues    9    18
     Since so she will, whose will is to me more then a lawe. . .  124  4th Eclogues   74    84
     His life a law, his looke a full correction: . . . . . . . .  128  4th Eclogues   75   133
     Yet craving law of armes, whose rule doth teach, . . . . . .  135  Cert Sonnets    1    10
     If rebell sence would reason's law receave;. . . . . . . . .  147  Cert Sonnets   19     3
     Rebell by Nature's law, Rebell by law of reason, . . . . . .  214  A&S 5th Song         63
     But on god's law his heart's delight doth bind,. . . . . . .  270  Psalm I               5
     O law of his How perfect 'tis. . . . . . . . . . . . . . . .  294  Psalm XIX            29
     For God's high law in his heart dwelleth.. . . . . . . . . .  326  Psalm XXXVII         79
     Yea lord Thy law within my heart doth stand; . . . . . . . .  331  Psalm XL             34
     And he by law of Barly-brake must run. . . . . . . . . . . .  249  Other Poems     4   296
LAWLESS
     But thou foule Cupid, syre to lawlesse lust, . . . . . . . .   92  3rd Eclogues   63    55
     In lawlesse games, and love not as you should, . . . . . . .  106  3rd Eclogues   67    95
LAWN
     Lyke thynnest Lawne with Tynsell lynde,. . . . . . . . . . .   89  Arcadia III    62  V116
LAWS
     Make me, o vertuous Shame, thy lawes neglect.. . . . . . . .   40  Arcadia II     18    12
     And with more, by the lawes that to Revenge doo belong.. . .  123  4th Eclogues   74    42
     Should Ladies faire be tyed to such hard lawes,. . . . . . .  146  Cert Sonnets   17    23
     By iron lawes of duty to depart: . . . . . . . . . . . . . .  222  Astrophil      87     4
LAWYERS
     These gentle Lawyers wage, . . . . . . . . . . . . . . . . .  215  A&S 6th Song         14
*LAY
     Lay all your feare upon your fearefull lover:. . . . . . . .   17  1st Eclogues    7    91
     Not as the scrippe thou stalest, while Dorcas sleeping lay..   52  2nd Eclogues   29     8
     Nico. Content: but I will lay a wager hereunto,. . . . . . .   53  2nd Eclogues   29    29
     Such odds I willing lay; for him and you I know.. . . . . . .   53  2nd Eclogues   29    48
     She lay for dead, till I helpt with unlasing her?. . . . . .   61  2nd Eclogues   30   154
     A living coarse I lay: but ah, my wakefull minde . . . . . .  117  4th Eclogues   73    31
     If you, on you I lay what in my office be. . . . . . . . . .  120  4th Eclogues   73   134
     Lay not thy colours more to view,. . . . . . . . . . . . . .  157  Cert Sonnets   27    23
     To my close heart, where while some firebrands he did lay, .  169  Astrophil       8    13
     There himselfe with his shot he close doth lay.. . . . . . .  175  Astrophil      20     8
     And knowing, love, and loving, lay apart . . . . . . . . . .  177  Astrophil      24     7
     Each soule doth at Love's feet his weapons lay,. . . . . . .  186  Astrophil      43     7
     On silly me do not the burthen lay,. . . . . . . . . . . . .  190  Astrophil      51     5
     Let Fortune lay on me her worst disgrace,. . . . . . . . . .  198  Astrophil      64     3
     Their rayes to me, who in her tedious absence lay. . . . . .  204  Astrophil      76     2
     To lay his then marke wanting shafts of sight, . . . . . . .  230  Astrophil      99     3
     Their judgements hackney on, the fault on sicknesse lay, . .  232  Astrophil     102    10
     Thy fingers Cupid's shafts, thy voyce the Angel's lay: . . .  212  A&S 5th Song         11
     I lay then to thy charge unjustest Tyrannie, . . . . . . . .  214  A&S 5th Song         56
     All my blisse in thee I lay; . . . . . . . . . . . . . . . .  220  A&S 8th Song         90
     Will lay me down, and take my rest:. . . . . . . . . . . . .  274  Psalm IV             32
```

```
*LAY                    (CONTINUED)                      PAGE    TITLE            LINE
     Like in a winding sheet, wretch I already lay, . . . . . . .  291 Psalm XVIII        10
     The World's foundations then lay bare because he shent . . .  291 Psalm XVIII        32
     God on them his strength doth lay. . . . . . . . . . . . . :.  309 Psalm XXVIII      31
     Guide Thee by him, lay all thy trusting. . . . . . . . : . .  324 Psalm XXXVII       11
     Lord before Thee I do lay. . . . . . . . . . . . . . . . . .  328 Psalm XXXVIII      25
     They lay snares they nimble be.. . . . . . . . . . . . . . .  328 Psalm XXXVIII      34
     Where I in horrors lay,. . . . . . . . . . . . . . . . . . .  331 Psalm XL            7
     Where 'gainst Thee lay my sin. . . . . . . . . . . . . . . .  333 Psalm XLI          16
     (lest greedy eies to them might challenge lay) . . . . . . .  243 Other Poems    4   68
     Lay by a river's side, . . . . . . . . . . . . . . . . . . .  256 Other Poems    5    2
LAYETH
     He oft layeth out his hook,. . . . . . . . . . . . . . . . .  282 Psalm X            42
LAY-HCLDING
     Laid hold on him with most lay-holding grace. . . . . . . .  250 Other Poems    4  310
LAYING
     And laying downe my head, did nature's rule observe, . . . .  117 4th Eclogues 73    27
     Laying such things, as never in mee weare; . . . . . . . . .  322 Psalm XXXV         26
LAYMAN
     Poore Layman I, for sacred rites unfit.. . . . . . . . . . .  203 Astrophil     74    4
*LAYS
     Or trayne the fox that traines so crafty laies.. . . . . . .   26 1st Eclogues  9  125
     Let Pas now know, how Nico maketh layes. . . . . . . . . . .   54 2nd Eclogues 29   71
     For Pas well knowes what layes can Nico make.. . . . . . . .   54 2nd Eclogues 29   74
     One day layes up stuffe of griefe for the morrow:. . . . . .   62 2nd Eclogues 30  176
     (Which oft to hope laies out a guilefull baite,. . . . . . .   82 Arcadia III  56    2
     She saith, because I make no wofull laies, . . . . . . . . .  146 Cert Sonnets 17   27
     He layes on this chiefe praise,. . . . . . . . . . . . . . .  216 A&S 6th Song      47
     Chiefe praise on that he laies.. . . . . . . . . . . . . . .  216 A&S 6th Song      48
     Whose senses in so evill consort, their stepdame Nature
       laies, . . . . . . . . . . . . . . . . . . . . . . . . . .  217 A&S 7th Song       1
     In heapes he layes,. . . . . . . . . . . . . . . . . . . . .  316 Psalm XXXIII      26
*LEAD
     But arrowes two, and tipt with gold or leade:. . . . . . . .   21 1st Eclogues  8   11
     Such life to leade, such death I vow to dye. . . . . . . . .   40 Arcadia II   18   18
     The life we leade is all love, . . . . . . . . . . . . . . .   67 2nd Eclogues 32   52
     Now course doth leade me to her hand,. . . . . . . . . . . .   90 Arcadia III  62  121
     Did piping leade, the Sunne already sanke. . . . . . . . . .   98 3rd Eclogues 66    3
     She thinks I leade and live too merrie daies.. . . . . . . .  146 Cert Sonnets 17   30
     Melts downe his lead into my boyling brest,. . . . . . . . .  236 Astrophil   108    2
     My feete are turn'd to rootes, my hart becommeth lead, . . .  215 A&S 5th Song      77
     Which to life true life doth lead: . . . . . . . . . . . . .  288 Psalm XVI         38
     The meek he doth in judgment lead, . . . . . . . . . . . . .  303 Psalm XXV         35
     Teach lord, lord lead me Thy right way,. . . . . . . . . . .  308 Psalm XXVII       52
     And ti'de them fast to leade his triumph badd, . . . . . . .  245 Other Poems    4  131
LEADED
     Which leaded are with silver skinne, . . . . . . . . . . . .   89 Arcadia III  62  115
LEADEN
     Somewhat thy lead'n counsels, which I tooke. . . . . . . . .  193 Astrophil    56    7
     Who have so leaden eyes, as not to see sweet beautie's show,  217 A&S 7th Song       7
LEADING
     Leading them his prayses singing,. . . . . . . . . . . . . .  334 Psalm XLII        15
LEADS
     R. Whom Passion leades unto his death is bent. . . . . . . .   46 2nd Eclogues 27    9
     Curs'd be thy selfe for cursing that which leades me to
       joies. Toies.. . . . . . . . . . . . . . . . . . . . . . .   65 2nd Eclogues 31   40
     This leades unto the joyous field, . . . . . . . . . . . . .   87 Arcadia III  62   61
     But when Aurora leades out Phoebus' daunce,. . . . . . . . .  230 Astrophil    98   12
     The straying stepps as wicked Counsel leads; . . . . . . . .  270 Psalm I            2
     Even he, that leads of life an uncorrupted traine, . . . . .  287 Psalm XV           3
     He me revives, leads me the way. . . . . . . . . . . . . . .  301 Psalm XXIII        7
LEAF
     Nor withered leafe shall make yt faile to flourish.. . . . .  270 Psalm I           10
*LEAN
     He leane to her, she unto him do bow:. . . . . . . . . . . .   92 3rd Eclogues 63   49
     I pray thee doo to Lalus' sample leane:. . . . . . . . . . .  103 3rd Eclogues 67    4
     His weighty top) his top doth downeward drooping leane:. . .  117 4th Eclogues 73   22
     The shepheards will grow leane I trow, their sheep will ill
       be fed.. . . . . . . . . . . . . . . . . . . . . . . . . .  344 Possibly      1   40
     Well might he others beare, but leane to none) . . . . . . .  244 Other Poems    4   72
LEANED
     And (though against his will) on him she leand,. . . . . . .   95 3rd Eclogues 64   44
     But she on elbow lean'd, with sighs did show . . . . . . . .  245 Other Poems    4  110
LEANS
     What blinde guides can he have that leanes to a fancy? A
       fancy. . . . . . . . . . . . . . . . . . . . . . . . . . .   63 2nd Eclogues 31   21
     He only leanes on highest Thing, . . . . . . . . . . . . . .  297 Psalm XXI         27
LEAP
     Which pants as though it still should leape to thee: . . . .  236 Astrophil   107    6
     Now bolt and cudgill squirrels' leape do move. . . . . . . .  243 Other Poems    4   44
     Strephon did leape with joy and jolitie, . . . . . . . . . .  246 Other Poems    4  177
LEAPED
     Did smile on me, and then away she leaped. . . . . . . . . .   17 1st Eclogues  7   84
LEAPING
     Leaping at every flie, and angrie with a flea: . . . . . . .   53 2nd Eclogues 29   44
     But thou, sure Hope, tickle my leaping heart.. . . . . . . .   83 Arcadia III  59    9
     When my leaping hart will clime, . . . . . . . . . . . . . .  226 A&S 10th Song     26
LEAPS
     O how for joy he leapes, o how he crowes,. . . . . . . . . .  173 Astrophil    17   12
     Nay like young Calves in leapes are born,. . . . . . . . . .  310 Psalm XXIX        16
```

LEARN   PAGE   TITLE   LINE

	PAGE	TITLE		LINE
Her praise, whose praise to learne your skill hath framed me	15	1st Eclogues	7	24
(And pacience hath) let him goe learne of him.	24	1st Eclogues	9	73
Doth teach, to learne the good what travailes do belong: . .	45	Arcadia II	26	8
P. But so we shall with griefe learne to repent.	47	2nd Eclogues	27	36
With sluttish song: I pray thee learne to blea,.	56	2nd Eclogues	29	136
Let us some grammar learne of more congruities..	61	2nd Eclogues	30	142
But with much studie learne late to repent..	106	3rd Eclogues	67	96
The Nightingales doo learne of Owles their musique:.	112	4th Eclogues	71	40
As might learne Temp'rance voyde of a rage's events.	124	4th Eclogues	74	64
If Love learne not alone to love and see,.	187	Astrophil	46	7
Where Love is chastnesse, Paine doth learne delight, ...	188	Astrophil	48	3
Far far too long to learne it without booke:	192	Astrophil	56	2
Let him but learne of Love to reade in thee, ...	201	Astrophil	71	3
Who will read must first learne spelling..	203	A&S 2nd Song		24
O stones, o trees, learne hearing, Stella singeth.	208	A&S 3rd Song		6
Can learne, how my selfe to sunder	234	A&S 11th Song		14
O let them heare these sacred tunes, and learne in wonder's schooles,.	217	A&S 7th Song		5
For this same man will not learn to repent,.	278	Psalm VII		33
May learn their joyes to fill.	318	Psalm XXXIV		8
Dick. Here then and learn to sigh: a mistress I doo serve, .	343	Possibly	1	19
LEARNED
And learn'd what ill a miser state doth breed, ...	21	1st Eclogues	8	22
O sweet simplicitie: from whence should Love be so learned?.	124	4th Eclogues	74	65
I now have learn'd Love right, and learn'd even so,.	173	Astrophil	16	13
The schooles where Venus hath learn'd Chastitie.	185	Astrophil	42	4
Since in thine armes, if learnd fame truth hath spread,. . .	198	Astrophil	65	13
If him new-learned manners had not stai'd.	246	Other Poems	4	166
The lesson which but late he learn'd too furre:.	246	Other Poems	4	174
He quickly learn'd Urania was her name,.	247	Other Poems	4	185
LEARNERS
Come learners then to me, the modell of mishappe,.	153	Cert Sonnets	24	15
LEARNETH
One that his Wisdom learneth..	286	Psalm XIV		9
LEARNING
Like the wiser sorte, whose learning,.	263	Other Poems	7	41
Learning this among the rest,.	264	Other Poems	7	75
LEARNING'S
Dig deepe with learning's spade, now tell me this, ...	175	Astrophil	21	13
LEARNS
Wit learnes in thee perfection to expresse,.	182	Astrophil	35	12
Thence his desires he learnes, his live's course thence. . .	195	Astrophil	61	8
Stella now learnes (strange case) to weepe in thee..	231	Astrophil	101	8
LEASE
They found, they felt, they had no lease of blisse..	244	Other Poems	4	80
LEAST
I like this place, wheare at the least the darke	73	Arcadia III	39	13
Looke further then, so shalt thou finde at least,.	75	Arcadia III	44	9
Thus in thy selfe, least strings are loudest founde, ...	81	Arcadia III	54	15
She, whose lest word brings from the spheares their musique,	113	4th Eclogues	71	68
Or of thy gifts at least shade out some part..	207	Astrophil	81	8
That do not leave your least friend at the wurst,.	228	Astrophil	95	2
Began at least to be conceiv'd as woe, ...	252	Other Poems	4	418
To make it selfe to my least looke a slave:.	255	Other Poems	4	511
LEASTWISE
More cause a like effect at leastwise bringeth:.	208	A&S 3rd Song		5
LEAVE
Oh when will men leave off to judge by haire,.	25	1st Eclogues	9	93
Ere that I leave with song of praise her praise to solemnize	33	1st Eclogues	13	68
Leave of my sheepe: it is no tyme to feede,.	43	Arcadia II	24	1
Leave of my sheepe, my shower of teeres oreflowes, ...	43	Arcadia II	24	4
Leave of my sheepe, my sighes burne up your filde, ...	43	Arcadia II	24	7
Leave of my sheepe, sorrowe hathe hoysed sayle,.	44	Arcadia II	24	10
Leave off my sheep my mourninge to maintayne,.	44	Arcadia II	24	13
I leave mine eyes unwipte my cheekes to bathe.	54	2nd Eclogues	29	80
To harme us wormes should that high Justice leave.	59	2nd Eclogues	30	71
And whose good happ, doth leave him unprovided,.	62	2nd Eclogues	30	177
End? but I can never end, love will not give me the leave. Leave.	63	2nd Eclogues	31	16
My sowle beginnes to take leave.	66	2nd Eclogues	32	15
Yet yeeld your graunt, a baser hand may leave.	78	Arcadia III	49	9
Doth him, his face, his words, leave, shunne, refraine, . .	84	Arcadia III	60	12
Loath, I must leave his chiefe resort.	88	Arcadia III	62	84
This done, thou hast no more, but leave the rest	98	3rd Eclogues	65	13
(As even in beasts their dammes leave chaunging parts) . . .	100	3rd Eclogues	66	60
Where they would leave trophees of cruell damage,.	109	Arcadia IV	70	12
Yet let us leave a monument in publique.	109	Arcadia IV	70	15
Have praide me leave my strange exclaiming musique,.	112	4th Eclogues	71	32
That so I may signes of my sorrowe leave..	125	4th Eclogues	75	9
They leave off al, and say, death comes too eagerlie.. . . .	128	4th Eclogues	75	114
Fire burne me quite, till sense of burning leave mee:	136	Cert Sonnets	3	13
But betweene those armes, never else do leave mee;	138	Cert Sonnets	5	23
Hath neither leave to live, nor doome to dye, ...	144	Cert Sonnets	15	7
And thus might I for feare of may be, leave.	145	Cert Sonnets	16	11
If I could thinke how these my thoughts to leave,.	147	Cert Sonnets	19	1
Me one to leave, with whome I leave my hart.	148	Cert Sonnets	20	6
Leave me o Love, which reachest but to dust, ...	161	Cert Sonnets	32	1

LEAVE	(CONTINUED)	PAGE	TITLE		LINE
Leave what thou likest not, deale not thou with it... . . .		166	Astrophil	4	4
Leave sense, and those which sense's objects be.		169	Astrophil	10	7
Deale thou with powers of thoughts, leave love to will.. . .		169	Astrophil	10	8
How Poles' right king meanes, without leave of hoast,. . . .		180	Astrophil	30	3
To leave the scepter of all subject things,.		183	Astrophil	38	4
Glad if for her he give them leave to die.		186	Astrophil	43	8
Leave following that, which it is gaine to misse...		188	Astrophil	47	11
That I love not, without I leave to love..		195	Astrophil	61	14
O give my passions leave to run their race:.		198	Astrophil	64	2
Leave that sir Phip, least off your necke be wroong.		208	Astrophil	83	14
With doing all, leave nothing done but paine...		210	Astrophil	85	8
Leaving my Hemisphere, leave me in night,.		223	Astrophil	89	4
That do not leave your least friend at the wurst,.		228	Astrophil	95	2
Leave to Mars the force of hands,.		211	A&S 4th Song		45
For thy face tempts my soule to leave the heav'n for thee, .		215	A&S 5th Song		82
Leave to see, and leave to wonder.".		234	A&S 11th Song		12
Bids you leave such minds to nourish."		234	A&S 11th Song		27
Love at length leave undertaking."		234	A&S 11th Song		32
Which can make me thus to leave you,.		235	A&S 11th Song		44
Least, though I leave not thy love,.		220	A&S 8th Song		98
Leave a wretch, in whom all wo		221	A&S 9th Song		6
And yet leave me helplesse meerely?.		222	A&S 9th Song		35
And children have to leave it to...		290	Psalm XVII		44
Who search of God's face never leave..		302	Psalm XXIV		16
Forsake not me, O leave me not,.		308	Psalm XXVII		46
But in their hand God will not leave him,.		327	Psalm XXXVII		83
E're I my earthly being leave.		330	Psalm XXXIX		42
That Foxes leave to steale, because they finde they dy therefore.		344	Possibly	1	44
Leave sheepe, leave all, I will no piecing have.		255	Other Poems	4	512
Tell me, if husband springtime leave your lande, ...		257	Other Poems	5	50
Give leave your flockes to range,.		261	Other Poems	6	31
LEAVED					
Pine is hye, hope is as hie, sharpe leav'd, sharpe yet be my hope's budds.		36	1st Eclogues	13	130
If three-leav'd grasse seeme to the sheepe unsavorie,. . . .		48	2nd Eclogues	28	23
*LEAVES					
Oft turning others' leaves, to see if thence would flow. . .		165	Astrophil	1	7
With guilded leaves or colourd Velume playes,.		170	Astrophil	11	6
See how it the leaves doth kisse,.		219	A&S 8th Song		58
With golden leaves, and painted babery,.		246	Other Poems	4	181
Where greene leaves did newly bud.		262	Other Poems	7	4
LEAVEST					
Yet of that best thou leav'st the best behind.		170	Astrophil	11	4
LEAVING					
Leave Leaving not my mourninge to maintayne, ...		44	Arcadia II	24 V	13
That, leaving me for dead, to her it went:		115	4th Eclogues	72	79
In steade of gall, leaving to her my hart:		150	Cert Sonnets	22	28
Leaving me nought but wailing eloquence:		184	Astrophil	38	11
Leaving my Hemisphere, leave me in night,.		223	Astrophil	89	4
Leaving him so passion rent, ...		221	A&S 8th Song		102
Leaving him to passion rent, ...		221	A&S 8th Song		V102
Who shunning vanity and works of vaineness leaving,.		302	Psalm XXIV		9
Thou hast hid them: yet leaving them thy light,.		313	Psalm XXXI		56
Were now his darts leaving his wonted fight.		246	Other Poems	4	148
Leaving in paine their wel-fed hungry eies..		246	Other Poems	4	168
LEAVY					
Strephon with leavy twiggs of Laurell tree		244	Other Poems	4	73
LECHERY					
The Falcon's fercenes, Sparrow's letchery, ...		28	1st Eclogues	10	79
LECTURE					
That face, whose lecture shewes what perfect beautie is: . .		205	Astrophil	77	2
LED					
My minde ere now led foorth by reason's light:		73	Arcadia III	39	4
On Nature's sweet repast, as healthfull senses ledd.		117	4th Eclogues	73	40
Is their own foot, ledd by their own ill thought,.		280	Psalm IX		49
The foolish man by flesh and fancy led		286	Psalm XIV		1
O madness of these folks, thus loosely led,.		286	Psalm XIV		13
Led by Thy Word the Rav'ner's stepps I shun, ...		289	Psalm XVII		14
But led by wicked thought.		306	Psalm XXVI		32
Feare was each where, while they their counsells led		313	Psalm XXXI		38
Ev'n from Hermon's dwelling led, ...		335	Psalm XLII		26
So may her eares be ledd,.		258	Other Poems	5	59
LEDA'S					
Where Leda's swanne his feathers mewes,.		89	Arcadia III	62	110
LEE					
How thy lee shores by my sighes stormed be!.		230	Astrophil	98	4
LEFT					
And belly nought is left, such sure is he, ...		24	1st Eclogues	9	82
What place is there left, we may hope our woes to recomfort?		32	1st Eclogues	13	28
Vertue you have, of vertue you have left proufes to the whole world, ...		33	1st Eclogues	13	56
Pas. Cosma once said, she left the wicket ope, ...		55	2nd Eclogues	29	90
Is left a Sunne, whose beames thy place may use?		80	Arcadia III	52	6
For what place now is lefte for our affection.		129	4th Eclogues	76	7
We Orphans lefte, void of all publique might?.		129	4th Eclogues	76	12
Left me devoid of all life;.		154	Cert Sonnets	25	11
The litle reason that is left in me, ...		167	Astrophil	4	10
These things are left me by my only Deare;		202	Astrophil	72	12

LEFT	(CONTINUED)	PAGE	TITLE		LINE
You say forsooth, you left her well of late.		225	Astrophil	92	7
No men are left, that charity do love, ...		284	Psalm XII		2
For I am poore, and left of all.		304	Psalm XXV		60
Why then hast thou left me?.		336	Psalm XLIII		9
Left Nous to coast the loved beauty ny.		249	Other Poems	4	284
The other left alone, ...		258	Other Poems	5	88
So I left him in that place, ...		264	Other Poems	7	73

LEFTST
| Where thou poore nature left'st all thy due glory, to fortune. . . . . | | 30 | 1st Eclogues | 11 | 15 |

LEG
| Her naked legge, more white then whitest snowe.. . . . . . | | 55 | 2nd Eclogues | 29 | 101 |

LEGGED
| But light-legd Pas had gott the middle space.. . . . . . . | | 248 | Other Poems | 4 | 253 |

LEGIONS
| Though legions round be layd, ... | | 272 | Psalm III | | 20 |

LEGS
That hath foure legs, and with two onely goes, ...		56	2nd Eclogues	29	142
Her legges carriage is of all the sweet campe:		67	2nd Eclogues	33	11
Her legges (O legges) her ay well stepping feete.		141	Cert Sonnets	9	8
Her breasts his tents, legs his triumphall carre:.		179	Astrophil	29	11
Though with soft leggs, did run as fast as he.		250	Other Poems	4	339
With shrinking legges, but with a swelling brest, ...		255	Other Poems	4	523
Then rase, but rase on leggs with faintnes bended, ...		259	Other Poems	5	116

LEISURE
Leasure to weigh what due deserte requireth.		83	Arcadia III	57	10
That tedious leasure marks each wrinckled line:.		230	Astrophil	98	11
He leasure wants to mark all this.		282	Psalm X		48

LEND
And me perchaunce your constant temper lend.		23	1st Eclogues	9	20
A quiet mind none but thy selfe can lend to thee, ...		51	2nd Eclogues	28	101
Then to an earnest Love what doth best victorie lend? Ende..		63	2nd Eclogues	31	15
Come cave, become my grave, come death, and lende.		73	Arcadia III	40	7
The inke immortall fame dooth lende:		90	Arcadia III	62	143
I will you lende; the rest your selves must give, ...		101	3rd Eclogues	66	76
Or canons thunder-like, all shot togither, lende)		118	4th Eclogues	73	54
Come children, lend your eare.		319	Psalm XXXIV		41
At other end Uran did Strephon lend.		248	Other Poems	4	246

LENDETH
| Which now my breast orecharg'd to Musicke lendeth? . . . . | | 196 | A&S 1st Song | | 2 |
| Above line repeated at following location. . . . . | | 197 | A&S 1st Song | | 34 |

LENDING
| To simplest Wisdom lending.. . . . . | | 294 | Psalm XIX | | 32 |

LENDS
Long drowned hopes to watrie eyes it lends:.		150	Cert Sonnets	22	18
It selfe to the other lends.		216	A&S 6th Song		18
He lends, he gives, more he doth spend		326	Psalm XXXVII		65

LENGTH
At length obtaind the point of his desire, ...		4	Lady of May	3	2
What length of verse can serve brave Mopsa's good to show, .		12	Arcadia I	3	1
Her length the earth in Love's chiefe clothing dressed.. . .		17	1st Eclogues	7	87
Lalus. Kala at length conclude my lingring lotte:.		18	1st Eclogues	7	115
Till now at length that Jove him office gives, ...		22	1st Eclogues	8	45
Though woes now live, at length thy woes must dye.		22	1st Eclogues	9	12
Will at length perceave these flames by her beames to be kindled, ...		37	1st Eclogues	13	167
R. Yet Passion, yeeld at length to Reason's stroke..		47	2nd Eclogues	27	33
For faultlesse length, and stainelesse hewe, ...		90	Arcadia III	62	119
At length for glutton taste he did them kill:.		103	3rd Eclogues	66	146
Till deadly sleepe at length possest my living coarse. . . .		117	4th Eclogues	73	30
Oft have I musde, but now at length I finde, ...		148	Cert Sonnets	20	1
At length to Love's decrees, I forc'd, agreed, ...		165	Astrophil	2	7
At length he perch'd himself in Stella's joyfull face, . . .		168	Astrophil	8	8
And sure at length stolne goods do come to light		172	Astrophil	15	11
But you faire maides, at length this true shall find, . . .		192	Astrophil	54	11
For that at length yet doth invite some rest, ...		229	Astrophil	96	13
Love at length leave undertaking."		234	A&S 11th Song		32
That life and length of life requires, ...		320	Psalm XXXIV		46
And blessing such with length desires, ...		320	Psalm XXXIV		47
Lo Thou a span's length madest my living line;		330	Psalm XXXIX		15
With length laid downe she deckt the lonely place..		244	Other Poems	4	107
At length in rowes of Kisse-cheeke teares they raine.. . . .		245	Other Poems	4	128
This said, at length he ended.		259	Other Poems	5	114

LENGTHEN
| Still shunning Nous to lengthen pleasing race, ... | | 250 | Other Poems | 4 | 306 |

LENT
Judge you to whom all beautie's force is lent.		4	Lady of May	2	31
Geron. Fy man, fy man, what wordes hath thy tonge lent?. . .		28	1st Eclogues	10	61
Though you besides such graces earth hath lent, ...		77	Arcadia III	49	3
Yet living still in her, while her beames lent		115	4th Eclogues	72	83
Of all those Graces' giftes the heavens have ever lent.. . .		119	4th Eclogues	73	86
Of all those goods, which heav'n to me hath lent:		173	Astrophil	18	4
Yet to my plaint Thou hast not audience lent..		298	Psalm XXII		8
To Strephon Aeole's land first breathing lent		242	Other Poems	4	26
But yet a setting foorth it some way lent:		252	Other Poems	4	395

LEOPARD
| The fearefull Hinde the Leopard did kisse: . . . . | | 100 | 3rd Eclogues | 66 | 53 |

LEOPARD'S
| And we shall find more spottes then Leopard's skinne.. . . . | | 29 | 1st Eclogues | 10 | 95 |

LEOPARDS   PAGE   TITLE   LINE

(As Tygers, leopards, beares, and Lions' seed) . . . . 102 3rd Eclogues 66 122
LERIDAN
Fa la la leridan, dan dan dan deridan: . . . . 156 Cert Sonnets 27   5
Above line repeated at following locations . . . . 156 Cert Sonnets 27 13
. . . . 157 Cert Sonnets 27 21
. . . . 157 Cert Sonnets 27 29
. . . . 157 Cert Sonnets 27 37
LESS
How much more we do love, so the lesse our loves be
  beleeved . . . . 32 1st Eclogues 13 20
O much more then words: those words serv'd more to me
  blesse Lesse. 64 2nd Eclogues 31 31
Which seeming lesse, yet nobler life doth move.. . . . . . . 151 Cert Sonnets 22 60
The lesse I love, I live the lesse.. . . . . 157 Cert Sonnets 27 40
But more I crie, lesse grace she doth impart,. . . . . 186 Astrophil   44   6
"What now sir foole," said he, "I would no lesse,. . . . . . 191 Astrophil   53   7
I cannot brag of word, much lesse of deed, ... 199 Astrophil   66   5
My wealth no more, and no whit lesse my need,. . . . . 199 Astrophil   66   7
"Or so?" Much lesse: "How then?" Sure thus it is:. . . . . . 204 Astrophil   74 13
Although lesse gifts impe feathers oft on Fame,. . . . . . . 204 Astrophil   75   4
Nor no day hath lesse quiet then my night: . . . . 224 Astrophil   89 11
For though in lesse than Angel's state . . . . 279 Psalm VIII   17
Who never doth deceive, and much lesse his deceaving . . . . 302 Psalm XXIV   11
Little hearing, speaking lesse;. . . . . 328 Psalm XXXVIII   39
Didst like, much lesse didst crave;. . . . . 331 Psalm XL   27
While most with hir he lesse did kepe with thee. . . . . . . 247 Other Poems   4 221
As much more loving, as lesse combersome.. . . . . 255 Other Poems   4 504
LESSON
Who have their lesson so long time begonne?. . . . . 27 1st Eclogues 10 27
The third his lesson mist, till all do smarte. . . . . 27 1st Eclogues 10 45
All to a lesson he draws, norr hills nor caves can avoide
  him. . . . . 31 1st Eclogues 13   7
No, no: Despaire my dayly lesson saith,. . . . . 58 2nd Eclogues 30 53
For vertue hath this better lesson taught, ... 161 Cert Sonnets 31 12
In her sight I a lesson new have speld,. . . . . 173 Astrophil   16 12
Fy, schoole of Patience, Fy, your lesson is. . . . . 192 Astrophil   56   1
What wonder then if he his lesson misse, ... 203 Astrophil   73   3
Now child, a lesson new you shall begin to spell:. . . . . . 213 A&S 5th Song   35
A lesson fit, both sight and skill, love and firme love to
  breede,. . . . . 217 A&S 7th Song   12
Chastned but thus, and thus his lesson tought, ... 244 Other Poems   4 97
The lesson which but late he learn'd too furre:. . . . . . . 246 Other Poems   4 174
LESSONS
To such a schoole-mistresse, whose lessons new . . . . 188 Astrophil   46 10
Which should Thy lessons beare . . . . 331 Psalm XL   29
LEST
But still take heede least thou thy selfe submit . . . . . . 4 Lady of May   2 23
Love wakes the jealous eye least thence it moves:. . . . . . 42 Arcadia II   22   6
No eare nor taile he hath, least they should him disgrace, . 53 2nd Eclogues 29 41
But Plangus, lest I may your sicknesse misse . . . . 62 2nd Eclogues 30 182
He will absent himselfe, least he should move. . . . . 95 3rd Eclogues 64 58
For feare he did, least he the young man might . . . . 96 3rd Eclogues 64 65
Least that some markes of jealousie you beare. . . . . 97 3rd Eclogues 64 124
And sange unto my sheepe lest stray they should. . . . . . . 99 3rd Eclogues 66 21
And stoppe mine eares, lest I growe mad with Musicke.. . . . 112 4th Eclogues 71 60
Which lest the ruinous want of government dissolve;. . . . . 120 4th Eclogues 73 128
Least it might thee allure home to thy selfe to returne, . . 122 4th Eclogues 74   8
Fearing least he chastisde be, ... 139 Cert Sonnets 7   9
Least if no vaile those brave gleames did disguise,. . . . . 168 Astrophil   7   7
Nobler desires, least else that friendly foe,. . . . . 175 Astrophil   21   7
Least once should not be heard, twise said, No, No.. . . . . 196 Astrophil   63   8
Envie, put out thine eyes, least thou do see . . . . 200 Astrophil   69   3
Leave that sir Phip, least off your necke be wroong. . . . . 208 Astrophil   83 14
Least joy, by Nature apt sprites to enlarge, ... 210 Astrophil   85   3
Come no more, least I get anger.". . . . . 234 A&S 11th Song   37
Lest that Argus eyes perceive you.". . . . . 235 A&S 11th Song   42
Least, though I leave not thy love,. . . . . 220 A&S 8th Song   98
Least you enflame his wrath. . . . . 272 Psalm II   28
Least lion like He do my soule devoure,. . . . . 277 Psalm VII   4
Least we should ever feare the lust. . . . . 283 Psalm X   79
Nay give me eyes, and light, least that I sleep. . . . . . . 285 Psalm XIII   11
Least my Foe bragg, that in my ruin hee. . . . . 286 Psalm XIII   13
Least yet I slip or go astray. . . . . 289 Psalm XVII   16
Thy servant keep, least in him creep . . . . 295 Psalm XIX   53
Least I rebuke sustain;. . . . . 304 Psalm XXV   70
Least, if answer Thou forbeare,. . . . . 308 Psalm XXVIII   3
Least inward evills do them defile,. . . . . 320 Psalm XXXIV   50
Least such things sin in Thy self cherish, ... 325 Psalm XXXVII 22
For I sayd, heare, least they be . . . . 328 Psalm XXXVIII 46
Least by my tongue I hap to stray; . . . . 329 Psalm XXXIX   2
Will. Then Dick let us go hence lest wee great folkes annoy. 344 Possibly   1 45
(Lest greedy eies to them might challenge lay) . . . . 243 Other Poems   4 68
But fearing lest all white might seeme too good, ... 246 Other Poems   4 151
LET
Let not wild woods so great a treasure have. . . . . 3 Lady of May   2 12
Sweete soule let not a wretch that serveth sheepe, ... 4 Lady of May   2 17
All this I give, let me possesse thy grace,. . . . . 4 Lady of May   2 22
Lalus. Come Dorus, come, let songs thy sorowes signifie: . . 14 1st Eclogues 7   1
"Let not dead earth enjoy so deare a cover,. . . . . 17 1st Eclogues 7 89

LET	(CONTINUED)	PAGE	TITLE		LINE
Let crowes picke out mine eyes, which saw too much:.		19	1st Eclogues	7	149
Let crowes picke out mine eyes which too much sawe..		19	1st Eclogues	7	V149
Geron. Up, up Philisides, let sorrowes goe,.		22	1st Eclogues	9	1
But let us sing, sweet tunes do passions ease, ...		22	1st Eclogues	9	4
Let not a glittring name thy fancie dresse		23	1st Eclogues	9	47
(And pacience hath) let him goe learne of him.		24	1st Eclogues	9	73
Then let thy minde with better bookes be tamed,.		25	1st Eclogues	9	120
And let thine eyes to other sports be framed..		25	1st Eclogues	9	122
Let speciall care upon thy flock be staid,.		26	1st Eclogues	9	133
And thowe Laelaps let not pride make thee brim		26	1st Eclogues	10	10
While, "Let us passe our time" each shepeheard saies.. . . .		28	1st Eclogues	10	48
Let swanne's example siker serve for thee, ...		28	1st Eclogues	10	73
Let not thy tonge become a firy matche,.		29	1st Eclogues	10	89
Lett our unpartiall eyes a litle waste.		29	1st Eclogues	10	91
Into our mindes let us a little fall,.		29	1st Eclogues	10	94
Let not a puppet abuse thy sprite, Kings' Crownes do not helpe them		34	1st Eclogues	13	84
Let not old age disgrace my high desire, ...		38	Arcadia II	15	1
Ne let white haires, which on my face doo grow,.		38	Arcadia II	15	5
Let not old age disgrace my high desire.		39	Arcadia II	15	14
Unto my selfe let after-livers know.		40	Arcadia II	18	10
Let me be lov'd, or els not loved be..		41	Arcadia II	20	14
Let him be bob'd that bobs will have..		44	Arcadia II	25	4
Let others deck their pride with skarres..		44	Arcadia II	25	7
First let them die, then passe the starres,.		44	Arcadia II	25	9
Let so our fruites grow up, that nature be maintainde: . . .		45	Arcadia II	26	13
Let this assured holde our judgements ever take, ...		45	Arcadia II	26	15
P. And let him die, so that he die content..		46	2nd Eclogues	27	10
P. Let us orecome, and let us be unjust..		47	2nd Eclogues	27	34
R.p. Then let us both to heavenly rules give place,.		47	2nd Eclogues	27	41
Should breed to her, let me for aye dejected be..		51	2nd Eclogues	28	121
Pas. But here is Dicus old; let him then speake the woord, .		52	2nd Eclogues	29	27
And if I better sing, let me thy Cosma kisse..		53	2nd Eclogues	29	38
This is my pawne; the price let Dicus' judgement show: . . .		53	2nd Eclogues	29	47
Let Pas now know, how Nico maketh layes.		54	2nd Eclogues	29	71
Let cat and dog fight which shall have both you.		56	2nd Eclogues	29	149
Let doltes in haste some altars faire erect..		58	2nd Eclogues	30	62
Let Death first dye; be thou his worthy let.		59	2nd Eclogues	30	94
To let that witolde beast consume in flames.		60	2nd Eclogues	30	111
Let all for her, and unto her be bent.		60	2nd Eclogues	30	124
As let them come or go with even facilitie..		60	2nd Eclogues	30	133
Let us not winke though void of purest sightfulnes..		61	2nd Eclogues	30	139
Let us some grammar learne of more congruities..		61	2nd Eclogues	30	142
Then let my life long time on earth maintained be, ...		61	2nd Eclogues	30	147
In morall rules let raging woes contained be?.		61	2nd Eclogues	30	151
Then let me eke forget one hand from other:.		61	2nd Eclogues	30	161
Let me forget that Plangus I am called:.		61	2nd Eclogues	30	162
Let me forget I am sonne to my mother, ...		61	2nd Eclogues	30	163
You have my thankes, Let me your comforte have..		70	Arcadia III	35	16
Let no strange dreme make her fayre body starte.		79	Arcadia III	51	8
As thou drawest on, so let my blisse draw neere.		80	Arcadia III	53	10
Let him drinke this, whome long in armes to folde.		83	Arcadia III	58	1
Let voice of Sighes into cleare musike runne,.		84	Arcadia III	59	13
Eyes, let your Teares with gazing now be mended,.		84	Arcadia III	59	14
Let mother earth now decke her selfe in flowers, ...		91	3rd Eclogues	63	1
Let not these slumbering clowds thy beawties hide,.		91	3rd Eclogues	63	14
Let one time (but long first) close up their daies,.		92	3rd Eclogues	63	31
Yet let not sluttery,.		93	3rd Eclogues	63	78
And fellow-like let his dominion slide;.		101	3rd Eclogues	66	110
But who doo let their tongues shew well their rage,.		105	3rd Eclogues	67	47
Let other fowler spots away be blowne;		105	3rd Eclogues	67	55
But let us pick our good from out much bad:.		105	3rd Eclogues	67	62
Yet let us leave a monument in publique.		109	Arcadia IV	70	15
But let us wiser be; and what foule discorde brake,.		120	4th Eclogues	73	119
So much more strong againe let fastest concorde make.. . . .		120	4th Eclogues	73	120
Let us a perfect peace betwixt us two resolve:		120	4th Eclogues	73	127
Let one the Princesse be, to her the other yeeld:.		120	4th Eclogues	73	129
And let her have the giftes that should in both remaine: . .		120	4th Eclogues	73	131
In her let beautie both, and chastnesse fully raigne:. . . .		120	4th Eclogues	73	132
To worthiest let him give, when both he hath beheld:		120	4th Eclogues	73	142
And let him be our judge: the lad doth please me well".. . .		121	4th Eclogues	73	153
First let Cimmerian darknes be my onel'habitaco'n:		124	4th Eclogues	74	59
And let my breath upon your braunches cleave,.		125	4th Eclogues	75	7
Let it embassage beare your grieves to showe..		125	4th Eclogues	75	12
Upon thy face let coaly Ravens swarme:		125	4th Eclogues	75	19
Let all the Sea thy teares accounted be:		125	4th Eclogues	75	20
Let golde now rust, let Diamonds waste in thee:.		125	4th Eclogues	75	22
Let pearls be wan with woe their damme doth beare:		125	4th Eclogues	75	23
O Hiacinthe let Ai be on thee still.		125	4th Eclogues	75	29
Sounde of my griefes, and let it never ende, ...		126	4th Eclogues	75	35
Ah let us all against foule Nature crie:		127	4th Eclogues	75	92
Let teares for him therefore be all our treasure,.		130	4th Eclogues	76	31
Let hating of our selves be our affection, ...		130	4th Eclogues	76	33
Let us against our selves employ our might,.		130	4th Eclogues	76	35
Let them be clearde, and now begin to see, ...		131	Arcadia V	77	11
Then let us holde the blisse of peacefull minde, ...		131	Arcadia V	77	13
Aire let me draw no more thy breath in anguish:.		136	Cert Sonnets	3	14
Ah saucy paine let not thy errour last,.		141	Cert Sonnets	8	13
Whose clowdie thoughts let fall an inward raine.		150	Cert Sonnets	22	36

265

Let here his eyes be raised. . . . .   151 Cert Sonnets 23   3
Let here his eyes be raysed. . . . .   152 Cert Sonnets 23   35
Ring out your belles, let mourning shewes be spread, ... 159 Cert Sonnets 30   1
Let Dirge be sung, and Trentals rightly read, ... 160 Cert Sonnets 30   21
O take fast hold, let that light be thy guide, ...   162 Cert Sonnets 32   9
Let daintie wits crie on the Sisters nine, ... 166 Astrophil   3   1
Or else let them in statelier glorie shine, ... 166 Astrophil   3   5
Vertue alas, now let me take some rest, ... 166 Astrophil   4   1
Then Love is sinne, and let me sinfull be. . . . .   172 Astrophil   14   14
O let me prop my mind, yet in his growth . . . .   174 Astrophil   19   12
Let him, deprived of sweet but unfelt joyes, ...   177 Astrophil   24   12
Come let me write, "And to what end?" To ease. . . . . . .   181 Astrophil   34   1
O do not let thy Temple be destroyd. . . . .   185 Astrophil   40   14
Yet Deare, let me this pardon get of you, ... 188 Astrophil   46   12
Let her go. Soft, but here she comes. Go to, ...   188 Astrophil   47   12
What ever may ensue, o let me be . . . .   188 Astrophil   48   5
Let not mine eyes be hel-driv'n from that light: . . . . .   188 Astrophil   48   7
O looke, o shine, o let me die and see. . . . . 188 Astrophil   48   8
Let Vertue have that Stella's selfe; yet thus, ...   191 Astrophil   52   13
He cannot love: no, no, let him alone.". . . . .   191 Astrophil   54   8
For let me but name her whom I do love, ... 192 Astrophil   55   12
Which would not let me, whom she loved, decline. . . . . .   196 Astrophil   62   7
Let Fortune lay on me her worst disgrace, ... 198 Astrophil   64   3
Let folke orecharg'd with braine against me crie, ... 198 Astrophil   64   4
Let clouds bedimme my face, breake in mine eye, ... 198 Astrophil   64   5
Let me no steps but of lost labour trace. . . . . 198 Astrophil   64   6
Let all the earth with scorne recount my case, ...   198 Astrophil   64   7
Yet let this thought thy Tygrish courage passe: . . . . . . 198 Astrophil   65   11
Come, come, and let me powre my selfe on thee; . . . . . .   200 Astrophil   69   6
Let him but learne of Love to reade in thee, ...   201 Astrophil   71   3
But give apt servants their due place, let eyes. . . . . .   210 Astrophil   85   9
Let eares heare speech, which wit to wonder ties, ... 210 Astrophil   85   11
Let breath sucke up those sweetes, let armes embrace . . . . 210 Astrophil   85   12
Have chang'd desert, let mine owne conscience be . . . . .   212 Astrophil   86   2
Let wo gripe on my heart, shame loade mine eye. . . . . . . 212 Astrophil   86   4
All mirth farewell, let me in sorrow live. . . . .   231 Astrophil   100   14
Let honor selfe to thee graunt highest place. . . . . 233 Astrophil   103   14
O let not fooles in me thy workes reprove, ...   236 Astrophil   107   13
Let my whispering voyce obtaine, ...   210 A&S 4th Song   3
"No, no, no, no, my Deare, let be.". . . . .   210 A&S 4th Song   6
Above line repeated at following locations . . . .   210 A&S 4th Song   12
                                        . . . . 210 A&S 4th Song   18
                                        . . . . 211 A&S 4th Song   24
                                        . . . . 211 A&S 4th Song   30
                                        . . . . 211 A&S 4th Song   36
                                        . . . . 211 A&S 4th Song   42
                                        . . . . 211 A&S 4th Song   48
                                        . . . . 211 A&S 4th Song   54
Write, but first let me endite: . . . . 211 A&S 4th Song   40
Let no tongue aspire to tell, ... 226 A&S 10th Song   10
Let my chaunge to ruine be. . . . . 234 A&S 11th Song   10
O let them heare these sacred tunes, and learne in wonder's
    schooles, ... 217 A&S 7th Song   5
O let them see these heavenly beames, and in faire letters
    reede. . . . . 217 A&S 7th Song   11
Let me, fed with hellish anguish, ... 220 A&S 8th Song   79
Let me home returne, stark blinded . . . .   220 A&S 8th Song   83
Come let us break their bonds, say they, and fondly say: . . 271 Psalm II   7
Let their vile thoughts the thinkers' ruin be. . . . . . .   275 Psalm V   30
Lord, let not me a worme by thee be shent, ...   276 Psalm VI   1
Ne let thy rage, of my due punishment. . . . .   276 Psalm VI   3
But mercy, lord, let Mercy thyne descend . . . .   276 Psalm VI   5
Then let my Foe chase me, and chasing take: . . . . 277 Psalm VII   13
Then let his foot uppon my neck be set: . . . . 277 Psalm VII   14
Then in the Dust let him my honour rake. . . . .   277 Psalm VII   15
O let their wickedness no longer bide. . . . .   277 Psalm VII   25
And ready art to let Thyne arrowes go. . . . .   278 Psalm VII   36
And let not man have upper hand of Thee, ...   281 Psalm IX   62
O let proud him be throughly caught. . . . .   281 Psalm X   7
Behold me, lord, let to Thy hearing creep. . . . .   285 Psalm XIII   9
O let my sentence passe from Thyne own face; . . . .   289 Psalm XVII   5
Then let my Words, my Crys ascend, ...   290 Psalm XVII   19
In Thy wings' shade then let me hidden ly. . . . .   290 Psalm XVII   26
Let him be lifted up, that hath preserved me! . . . . 293 Psalm XVIII   84
Let them not have me for their slave . . . .   295 Psalm XIX   55
So let words sprung from my weake tongue, ... 295 Psalm XIX   61
Let God the lord heare Thee, ...   295 Psalm XX   1
Let name of Jacob's God, ...   295 Psalm XX   3
Let him come down, and help to Thee apply. . . . .   295 Psalm XX   7
Thence let him undertake . . . .   295 Psalm XX   9
Let him notorious make . . . .   296 Psalm XX   11
Let fyre for tryall burn, ... 296 Psalm XX   13
And so let him consent . . . .   296 Psalm XX   16
Let trust of some men be . . . .   296 Psalm XX   26
But let all our conceit. . . . .   296 Psalm XX   28
Let that King deign to heare, ... 296 Psalm XX   34
Let God help him (say they) whom he did trust; . . . . . .   299 Psalm XXII   19
Let God save him, in whom was all his lust. . . . . 299 Psalm XXII   20
Let me not ruin quite; . . . .   302 Psalm XXV   4

```
LET               (CONTINUED)                        PAGE   TITLE            LINE
     Let not those foes that me annoy . . . . . . . . . . . . . .   303  Psalm XXV            5
     Let them confounded be. . . . . . . . . . . . . . . . . . .   303  Psalm XXV            9
     Let those things Thy remembrance grave,. . . . . . . . . . .   303  Psalm XXV           23
     Let my iniquity. . . . . . . . . . . . . . . . . . . . . . .   304  Psalm XXV           44
     O look, O help, let mercy fall,. . . . . . . . . . . . . . .   304  Psalm XXV           59
     Let my uprightness gaine . . . . . . . . . . . . . . . . . .   305  Psalm XXV           73
     Let them be thrown down by Thee; . . . . . . . . . . . . . .   309  Psalm XXVIII        22
     Let them not restored be;. . . . . . . . . . . . . . . . . .   309  Psalm XXVIII        23
     But let me give prayses high . . . . . . . . . . . . . . . .   309  Psalm XXVIII        24
     Lord heare, let mercy thine be stay'd. . . . . . . . . . . .   311  Psalm XXX           31
     Never therfore let me confounded be, . . . . . . . . . . . .   312  Psalm XXXI           2
     O Lord, of Thee let me still mercy winn, . . . . . . . . . .   312  Psalm XXXI          25
     Let me not tast of shame, O lord most high,. . . . . . . . .   313  Psalm XXXI          45
     For I have call'd on Thee, let wicked folk . . . . . . . . .   313  Psalm XXXI          46
     Let them in bedd of endless silence dy. . . . . . . . . . . .   313  Psalm XXXI          48
     Let those lips be made dumbe which love to ly, . . . . . . .   313  Psalm XXXI          49
     Let ten-stringd instrument . . . . . . . . . . . . . . . . .   316  Psalm XXXIII        10
     Let all the earth feare God, . . . . . . . . . . . . . . . .   317  Psalm XXXIII        28
     O let thy mercy great. . . . . . . . . . . . . . . . . . . .   318  Psalm XXXIII        82
     Let Angel thine a scattring make them go. . . . . . . . . . .   321  Psalm XXXV          12
     Let Angel thine persue them as they fly, . . . . . . . . . .   321  Psalm XXXV          13
     But let their flight be dark and slippery; . . . . . . . . .   321  Psalm XXXV          14
     Let their sly witts unwares destruction get, . . . . . . . .   321  Psalm XXXV          17
     Oh! on my soul let not these tumults hitt. . . . . . . . . .   322  Psalm XXXV          44
     Then, then let not my foes unjustly joy; . . . . . . . . . .   322  Psalm XXXV          49
     Let them not fleere, who me would causless stroy,. . . . . .   322  Psalm XXXV          50
     Let not their joy upon my woes be sett.. . . . . . . . . . .   322  Psalm XXXV          60
     Let them not, Lord, within their hearts thus say:. . . . . .   323  Psalm XXXV          61
     Let them be cloathd in most confounding shame, . . . . . . .   323  Psalm XXXV          65
     Yet let them say, laud be to God alwayes . . . . . . . . . .   323  Psalm XXXV          69
     Let not proud feet make me their thrall, . . . . . . . . . .   324  Psalm XXXVI         31
     Let not ev'ill hands discomfit me; . . . . . . . . . . . . .   324  Psalm XXXVI         32
     Nor let him be condemn'd by such.. . . . . . . . . . . . . .   327  Psalm XXXVII        84
     Nor my sins let my bones rest; . . . . . . . . . . . . . . .   327  Psalm XXXVIII        9
     Let me not be thrown down to so base shame . . . . . . . . .   330  Psalm XXXIX         27
     Ah! yet from me let Thy plagues be displac't,. . . . . . . .   330  Psalm XXXIX         31
     Let them have shame, yea blush for shame,. . . . . . . . . .   332  Psalm XL            52
     Let them be curst away that would me wast; . . . . . . . . .   332  Psalm XL            54
     Let them with shame be cloyed; . . . . . . . . . . . . . . .   332  Psalm XL            55
     Yea let them be destroyed. . . . . . . . . . . . . . . . . .   332  Psalm XL            56
     Let them that love Thy saving seat . . . . . . . . . . . . .   332  Psalm XL            63
     O heale my soul, let there Thy cure begin. . . . . . . . . .   333  Psalm XLI           15
     On me let mercy fall,. . . . . . . . . . . . . . . . . . . .   333  Psalm XLI           34
     World without end, let still his blessing flow;. . . . . . .   334  Psalm XLI           47
     Let them guide me right. . . . . . . . . . . . . . . . . . .   336  Psalm XLIII         14
     Will. Dick, since we cannot dance, come let a chearefull
       voyce. . . . . . . . . . . . . . . . . . . . . . . . . . .   343  Possibly     1       1
     Now let those lightsomme sights we see thy darknes overcome.   343  Possibly     1      12
     Will. Then Dick let us go hence lest wee great folkes annoy.   344  Possibly     1      45
     Courage therefore, and let the stately see . . . . . . . . .   346  Possibly     5       3
     Allarme allarme, let not their beauties move . . . . . . . .   346  Possibly     5       5
     To runne, brake from his hands, and let him goe. . . . . . .   250  Other Poems  4     336
     Whither it would, so it would let him dy,. . . . . . . . . .   252  Other Poems  4     382
     Let it suffise that he himselfe forgot.. . . . . . . . . . .   254  Other Poems  4     488
     Ccme shepheard's boy, let now thy heart be bowd. . . . . . .   255  Other Poems  4     510
     Let Pan our good God see,. . . . . . . . . . . . . . . . . .   260  Other Poems  6       3
     Jcyne hearts and hands, so let it be,. . . . . . . . . . . .   260  Other Poems  6       5
     Above line repeated at following locations . . . . . . . . .   260  Other Poems  6      11
         . . . . . . . . . . . . . . . . . . . . . . . . . . . .   260  Other Poems  6      17
         . . . . . . . . . . . . . . . . . . . . . . . . . . . .   260  Other Poems  6      23
         . . . . . . . . . . . . . . . . . . . . . . . . . . . .   261  Other Poems  6      29
         . . . . . . . . . . . . . . . . . . . . . . . . . . . .   261  Other Poems  6      35
         . . . . . . . . . . . . . . . . . . . . . . . . . . . .   261  Other Poems  6      41
         . . . . . . . . . . . . . . . . . . . . . . . . . . . .   261  Other Poems  6      47
         . . . . . . . . . . . . . . . . . . . . . . . . . . . .   261  Other Poems  6      53
     Let heere thy skill abound,. . . . . . . . . . . . . . . . .   260  Other Poems  6      15
     Let us the while be playing, . . . . . . . . . . . . . . . .   261  Other Poems  6      32
     Let nothing mee remove . . . . . . . . . . . . . . . . . . .   261  Other Poems  6      45
     Let them be ne'r a sunder, . . . . . . . . . . . . . . . . .   261  Other Poems  6      56
*LETS
     By inward letts, of them his state possest,. . . . . . . . .    75  Arcadia III 44       2
     That lap doth lap, nay lets, in spite of spite,. . . . . . .   194  Astrophil   59      10
LETTER
     A letter such which might from either part . . . . . . . . .    96  3rd Eclogues 64     81
     But that he would, to him the letter show. . . . . . . . . .    97  3rd Eclogues 64    113
     With one good dawnce, or letter finely pend, . . . . . . . .   245  Other Poems  4     140
LETTERS
     When I might reade those letters faire of blisse,. . . . . .   193  Astrophil   56       5
     She thinkes you do letters write:. . . . . . . . . . . . . .   211  A&S 4th Song        39
     O let them see these heavenly beames, and in faire letters
       reede. . . . . . . . . . . . . . . . . . . . . . . . . . .   217  A&S 7th Song        11
     Their Words be set in letters great. . . . . . . . . . . . .   294  Psalm XIX           15
LETTETH
     Which he forgetteth not, nor letteth dy. . . . . . . . . . .   280  Psalm IX            34
LEUCA
     Me thinkes I see the lippes my Leuca hath, . . . . . . . . .    54  2nd Eclogues 29     76
     That will I take, and to my Leuca give.. . . . . . . . . . .    54  2nd Eclogues 29     83
     Nico. I oft doo sue, and Leuca saith, I shall, . . . . . . .    54  2nd Eclogues 29     87
     Nico. When Leuca dooth appeare, the Sunne for shame. . . . .    55  2nd Eclogues 29     93
```

LEUCA   (CONTINUED)   PAGE   TITLE   LINE
  If Leuca live, she darken will my fame.. . . . .   55 2nd Eclogues 29   95
  Nico. Leuca to me did yester-morning showe . . . .   55 2nd Eclogues 29   99
  Nico. Nothing (O Leuca) shall thy fame deface, ...   56 2nd Eclogues 29   123
LEVEL
  Nor so faire levell in so secret stay, ...   175 Astrophil   20   6
  That on his wings the leavell thou maist finde . . . . . .   259 Other Poems   5   107
LEVELED
  While thus they ran a low, but leaveld race, ...   243 Other Poems   4   57
LEWIS
  That wittie Lewis to him a tribute paid. . . . .   204 Astrophil   75   11
LIBAN
  Ev'en Cedars, which on liban be, ...   310 Psalm XXIX   15
LIBAN'S
  And Liban' self with Nature's skorn, ...   310 Psalm XXIX   17
LIBERAL
  With many liberall blessing; . . . .   297 Psalm XXI   10
LIBERTY
  Now even that footstep of lost libertie. . . . .   166 Astrophil   2   9
  To keepe it selfe in life and liberty, ...   179 Astrophil   29   6
  What, have I thus betrayed my libertie?. . . . .   188 Astrophil   47   1
LICKED
  Till with lickt beard, his eye of fire espie his foes. . . .   53 2nd Eclogues 29   36
LICKEROUS
  With my greedy licorous sences, ...   226 A&S 10th Song   33
  But lickrous, Poison'd, faine to her would goe, ...   246 Other Poems   4   165
LIDS
  Locke up, faire liddes, the treasures of my harte: . . . . .   79 Arcadia III 51   1
  And arches be to heavenly lids, ...   86 Arcadia III 62   13
  Did suffer drousie lids mine eyes then cleare to blinde; . .   117 4th Eclogues 73   26
  In tombe of lids then buried are mine eyes, ...   231 Astrophil   99   12
*LIE
  To lye, faine, gloze, to steale, pry, and accuse, ...   21 1st Eclogues 8   23
  To lye, to steale, to pry, and to accuse, ...   21 1st Eclogues 8   V 23
  Then who will heare a well autoris'd lye, ...   24 1st Eclogues 9   72
  Ly but to sleepe, and in the earely prime. . . . .   26 1st Eclogues 9   126
  Then with the poisnous todes that quiet lie. . . . .   28 1st Eclogues 10   66
  And so behinde foule clowdes full oft faire starres do ly
    hidden". . . . .   36 1st Eclogues 13   154
  Their flames mount up, my powers prostrate lie: . . . . . .   42 Arcadia II   22   11
  Or Reason lie a slave to servile Sense, ...   49 2nd Eclogues 28   76
  Upon thy spoiles, which never should lye waste?. . . . . .   59 2nd Eclogues 30   93
  Horrible is this blasphemy unto the most holy. O lie.. . . .   65 2nd Eclogues 31   45
  When worthlesse corke, aloft doth floting lye. . . . . . .   81 Arcadia III 54   14
  Sturres me to thinke what dangers lye in waite.. . . . . .   82 Arcadia III 56   12
  Betwixt these two a way doth lie, ...   87 Arcadia III 62   58
  For there with strange compact dooth lie . . . .   90 Arcadia III 62   125
  For once the Lion by the Lambe did lie; . . . .   100 3rd Eclogues 66   52
  They better live that in a gaile doo lie.. . . . .   105 3rd Eclogues 67   54
  A better life it is to lye alone. . . . .   105 3rd Eclogues 67   57
  And thou shalt finde, in women vertues lie.. . . . .   106 3rd Eclogues 67   102
  Enough to make a fertill minde lie waste. . . . .   114 4th Eclogues 72   30
  Klaius. Enough to make a fertill minde lie waste . . . . .   114 4th Eclogues 72   31
  So close unto my selfe my wrackes doo lie. . . . .   114 4th Eclogues 72   40
  Strephon. So close unto my selfe my wrackes doo lie; . . . .   114 4th Eclogues 72   41
  Those thousand altars faire now in the dust to lie?. . . . .   119 4th Eclogues 73   112
  For that (so that you like) hereby doth lie a youth. . . . .   120 4th Eclogues 73   137
  Of what was good, where now no good doth lie; . . . .   127 4th Eclogues 75   74
  Blinded forthwith in darke dispaire did lye, ...   149 Cert Sonnets 21   6
  So deepe in seas of vertue beauties ly.. . . . .   151 Cert Sonnets 22   58
  Alas, I lie: rage hath this errour bred, ... · . . .   160 Cert Sonnets 30   31
  Who like a theefe, hid in darke bush doth ly, ...   175 Astrophil   20   3
  That poison foule of bubling pride doth lie. . . . .   178 Astrophil   27   6
  That never I with clos'd-up sense do lie, ...   181 Astrophil   32   6
  As good to write as for to lie and grone. . . . .   184 Astrophil   40   1
  Doth make my heart give to my tongue the lie.. . . . . . .   188 Astrophil   47   14
  I must no more in thy sweet passions lie; . . . .   202 Astrophil   72   7
  In sport I suckt, while she asleepe did lie, ...   203 Astrophil   73   6
  But if all faith, like spotlesse Ermine ly . . . .   212 Astrophil   86   5
  That though in wretchednesse thy life doth lie, ...   228 Astrophil   94   12
  With windowes ope then most my mind doth lie, ...   230 Astrophil   99   5
  Counting but dust what in the way did lie. . . . .   235 Astrophil   105   5
  From what in my hart doth ly.. . . . .   234 A&S 11th Song   15
  And only hunt, where lyes do ly? . . . .   273 Psalm IV   10
  Trust in that lord, that cannot ly, ...   274 Psalm IV   23
  Under his tongue do harbour'd ly . . . .   282 Psalm X   29
  In Thy wings' shade then let me hidden ly. . . . .   290 Psalm XVII   26
  With such brave wounds, that they under my feet did ly.. . .   292 Psalm XVIII   70
  For all my hope fixt upon God doth ly. . . . .   312 Psalm XXXI   18
  Let those lips be made dumbe which love to ly, ...   313 Psalm XXXI   49
  Thy judgments like the depths do ly, ...   323 Psalm XXXVI   16
  The hidden beauties seem'd in waite to lye, ...   250 Other Poems   4   303
  With you embraced lie, ...   257 Other Poems   5   43
LIED
  I said, my soule was thine (o that I then had lyed). . . . .   212 A&S 5th Song   9
LIEF
  Ah, that, that do I not conceive, though that to me leefe
    were . . . .   122 4th Eclogues 74   19
*LIES
  Whose strongest hope in your weake comfort lyes. . . . . . .   13 Arcadia I   4   4

*LIES   (CONTINUED)   PAGE   TITLE   LINE

	PAGE	TITLE		LINE
Nothing can mend one point that in her lies.	17	1st Eclogues	7	108
Therein his name, there his chiefe triumph lyes.	22	1st Eclogues	8	42
That there where thou confest thy mischiefe lyes	23	1st Eclogues	9	33
I layde my face; my face wherein there lyes.	41	Arcadia II	21	3
Dorus. Well do I prove, errour lies oft in zeale,.	51	2nd Eclogues	28	103
To weare upon her neck, that open lies.	55	2nd Eclogues	29	119
Whyle upon chaunce, his fruite of labour lyes;	71	Arcadia III	36	10
Gay haire more gaie then straw when harvest lyes,.	76	Arcadia III	46	7
And you o trees (if any life there lies.	125	4th Eclogues	75	4
Part of my paine me seemes engraved lyes..	147	Cert Sonnets	18	4
And in her breast bopeepe or couching lyes,.	170	Astrophil	11	12
That in her breast thy pap well sugred lies, ...	170	Astrophil	12	5
Cupid then smiles, for on his crest there lies	171	Astrophil	13	9
Lies hatching still the goodes wherein they flow:	176	Astrophil	24	2
And I, but for because my prospect lies.	179	Astrophil	29	13
And there long since, Love thy Lieutenant lies,.	183	Astrophil	36	5
From out that noysome gulfe, which gaping lies	205	Astrophil	78	3
Beautie's plague, Vertue's scourge, succour of lies:	206	Astrophil	78	6
Loathing all lies, doubting this Flatterie is:	207	Astrophil	80	11
In Lillies' neast, where Love's selfe lies along..	208	Astrophil	83	8
Stella is sicke, and in that sicke bed lies.	231	Astrophil	101	1
And only hunt, where lyes do ly?	273	Psalm IV		10
All wrong and mischeife lyes,..	283	Psalm X		58
But his deare favour where it lyes	311	Psalm XXX		14
To follow after lyes..	331	Psalm XL		20
Their courteous visitings are courting lyes, ...	333	Psalm XLI		21
Now is hee wrackt say they, lo, there he lyes.	333	Psalm XLI		27
LIEST				
Thou li'st false Echo, their minds as vertu be just. Just. .	65	2nd Eclogues	31	46
*LIETH				
Only of you the flatterer never lieth.	197	A&S 1st Song		28
Whose fault well hidden lyeth.	314	Psalm XXXII		3
LIEUTENANCY				
And on my thoughts give thy Lieftenancy.	236	Astrophil	107	7
LIEUTENANT				
And there long since, Love thy Lieutenant lies,.	183	Astrophil	36	5
LIFE				
Seeke other thoughts thy life or death to find;.	4	Lady of May	2	15
That thus preserves my loved life:	13	Arcadia I	5	2
Nor helpe by life or death who living dyes..	18	1st Eclogues	7	146
So doth my life within it selfe dissolve..	19	1st Eclogues	7	156
Lalus. So doth my life within it selfe dissolve, ...	19	1st Eclogues	7	157
Life showing, dead indeed:	19	1st Eclogues	7	160
Time shall in one my life and sorrowes end,.	23	1st Eclogues	9	19
And doth not feele, that life is nought but time	28	1st Eclogues	10	50
That the delights of life shall be to him dolorouse". . . .	29	1st Eclogues	11	10
If the mute timber when it hath the life lost, ...	30	1st Eclogues	12	15
Fleshly vaile consumes; but a soule hath his life, ...	31	1st Eclogues	12	22
Life to this our soule..	31	1st Eclogues	12	24
Is chaunced to my life, that from such muddy abundance . . .	34	1st Eclogues	13	96
To this strange death I vainely yeeld my life.	38	Arcadia II	14	14
That onely light doth all my life maintaine;	39	Arcadia II	16	4
My virgin life no spotted thought shall staine..	40	Arcadia II	18	6
Such life to leade, such death I vow to dye.	40	Arcadia II	18	18
In travaile of our life (a short but tedious space).	45	Arcadia II	26	9
P. We gladly use the sweetnes of our life.	46	2nd Eclogues	27	26
Time, place, life, wit scarcely her rare gifts measure doth.	49	2nd Eclogues	28	60
Her love my life; her anger my Instruction;.	49	2nd Eclogues	28	71
For though life irkes, in life my loves protected be.. . . .	51	2nd Eclogues	28	125
In ease, untill that bodie life forgoes.	56	2nd Eclogues	29	146
Where death is feard, and life is held with paine.	57	2nd Eclogues	30	19
With cries first borne, the pressage of his life,.	57	2nd Eclogues	30	24
Since cause of griefe no cause from life removes.	58	2nd Eclogues	30	37
And saith, although I seeke my life to flie, ...	58	2nd Eclogues	30	54
Then let my life long time on earth maintained be, ...	61	2nd Eclogues	30	147
My harte doth ake, my life faints,.	66	2nd Eclogues	32	14
The life, the death of Hector, ...	66	2nd Eclogues	32	23
The life we leade is all love, ...	67	2nd Eclogues	32	52
Nor ought I crave to feede life, ...	67	2nd Eclogues	32	54
My life my death do counte hers.	67	2nd Eclogues	32	57
Oh! if such a one have bent to a lonely life	69	2nd Eclogues	34	39
For what is life to dayly dyinge minde,.	73	Arcadia III	40	9
Muses graunt guiftes, Nymphes long and joyned life	93	3rd Eclogues	63	92
Is this sweet doubling of our single life.	103	3rd Eclogues	67	12
A better life it is to lye alone..	105	3rd Eclogues	67	57
Shall in this life embrace no worthy thing:.	105	3rd Eclogues	67	59
Of humane life to be the quiet measure,.	108	Arcadia IV	69	4
And loth this time, calld life, nay thinke, that life. . . .	113	4th Eclogues	72	12
And thinking this, thinke Nature, Life, and Death.	114	4th Eclogues	72	16
Where life is death, and death cannot breed peace.	116	4th Eclogues	72	95
(Which life is cald) were mov'd their spirits to repose, . .	116	4th Eclogues	73	5
What life it is, and how that all these lives doo gather,. .	118	4th Eclogues	73	47
Now that he finds to what end his life and love be reserved,	123	4th Eclogues	74	29
And you o trees (if any life there lies.	125	4th Eclogues	75	4
I have my selfe, and all what life containeth, ...	128	4th Eclogues	75	101
Death is our home, life is but a delusion.	128	4th Eclogues	75	123
His life a law, his looke a full correction:	128	4th Eclogues	75	133
Our life is but a step in dustie way..	131	Arcadia V	77	12
Sea drownd in thee, of tedious life bereave me:.	136	Cert Sonnets	3	15

LIFE   (CONTINUED)   PAGE   TITLE   LINE

	PAGE	TITLE	LINE
The scourge of life, and death's extreame disgrace,	140	Cert Sonnets 8	1
Hath yet such health, as it my life can save.	142	Cert Sonnets 11	12
Part of my life, the loathed part to me,	148	Cert Sonnets 20	9
Yet lives untill his life be new requirde.	150	Cert Sonnets 22	24
A bird which gets more life then ship had lost.	151	Cert Sonnets 22	54
Which seeming lesse, yet nobler life doth move.	151	Cert Sonnets 22	60
In life of lover's hart,	152	Cert Sonnets 23	10
Thus is her life still guarded,	152	Cert Sonnets 23	13
Left me devoid of all life;	154	Cert Sonnets 25	11
Yet, yet, a life to their death,	154	Cert Sonnets 25	18
Lady the life of all love;	154	Cert Sonnets 25	20
And all my life I will confesse,	157	Cert Sonnets 27	39
Eternall Love maintaine thy life in me.	144	Cert Sonnets 32	14
The richest gemme of Love and life enjoyes,	177	Astrophil 24	10
To keepe it selfe in life and liberty,	179	Astrophil 29	6
Witnesse of life to them that living die:	180	Astrophil 32	2
For of my life I must a riddle tell.	183	Astrophil 37	4
My life forgets to nourish languisht sprites;	186	Astrophil 42	10
Mine eyes, my light, my heart, my life, alas,	198	Astrophil 65	9
Light of my life, and life of my desire,	200	Astrophil 68	2
Breather of life, and fastner of desire,	207	Astrophil 80	7
Then since (deare life) you faine would have me peace,	207	Astrophil 81	12
I am from you, light of my life, mis-led,	224	Astrophil 91	2
That though in wretchednesse thy life doth lie,	228	Astrophil 94	12
Of all the powers which life bestowes on me,	236	Astrophil 107	2
Onelie through you the tree of life doth flourish.	197	A&S 1st Song	20
O deare life, when shall it be,	225	A&S 10th Song	1
My life melts with too much thinking;	227	A&S 10th Song	45
My life besetteth.	276	Psalm VI	24
Whose life no life but of Thee holdeth,	278	Psalm VIII	12
In race of life their Feet to guide.	284	Psalm XI	23
Even he, that leads of life an uncorrupted traine,	287	Psalm XV	3
Which to life true life doth lead:	288	Psalm XVI	38
Whose life doth seeme most greatly blest	290	Psalm XVII	39
And count this life their Portion best	290	Psalm XVII	40
He did but ask a life of Thee,	297	Psalm XXI	13
Thou him a long life gavest;	297	Psalm XXI	14
The life of him Thou savest.	297	Psalm XXI	16
My desolated life from dogged might.	299	Psalm XXII	48
You shall the life that ever liveth find.	300	Psalm XXII	64
Even he whose life no help of man can quicken.	300	Psalm XXII	74
This lord with strength my life doth blisse;	306	Psalm XXVII	4
From age to age life joyes doth fill.	311	Psalm XXX	15
My life with heavyness, my yeares with moane	312	Psalm XXXI	28
All to this point, how my poore life to take.	313	Psalm XXXI	39
My life hott torments tasted.	315	Psalm XXXII	12
That life and length of life requires,	320	Psalm XXXIV	46
As life may good appeare?.	320	Psalm XXXIV	48
For why the Well of life Thou art.	324	Psalm XXXVI	25
And seek of life for to bereave him;	326	Psalm XXXVII	82
But who for my life do waite,	328	Psalm XXXVIII	33
The Lord will keep his life yet safe and sound	333	Psalm XLI	5
Was once my mynde, my temper, and my lyfe,	344	Possibly 2	6
One love they lov'd, one life they liv'd.	241	Other Poems 3	4
Train'd in the life which on short-bitten grasse	242	Other Poems 4	19
While thus they liv'd, (this was indede a life).	243	Other Poems 4	58
Till of his life it did full conquest win,	253	Other Poems 4	430
Who hid in Angel's shape my life would ende.	254	Other Poems 4	464

LIFE-DEADMAN
This life-deadman in this old dungeon flong.	24	1st Eclogues 9	83

LIFE-GIVING
Of which the two life-giving lights are figured in her eyes:	217	A&S 7th Song	16

LIFE-MAINTAINING
My life-maintaining heart,	332	Psalm XL	49

LIFE'S
Into my live's bondage, yet may disburden a passion.	35	1st Eclogues 13	108
Thence his desires he learnes, his live's course thence.	195	Astrophil 61	8
Nor my life's cause match with bloodseeker's case,	306	Psalm XXVI	30

LIFT
But to the Cedar, Queene of woods, when I lifte my beteard eyes,	36	1st Eclogues 13	141
Yet still, faire tree, lifte up thy stately line,	77	Arcadia III 47	9
Lift up their stately swelling bankes;	88	Arcadia III 62	90
But, lord, lift Thou upon our sight.	274	Psalm IV	26
Therfore, O lord, lift up Thy throne on high	277	Psalm VII	20
Lift up Thy heavnly hand	282	Psalm X	51
Lift up your heads you Gates, and you doores ever biding,	302	Psalm XXIV	17
Lift up your heads you Gates, and you doores ever biding,	302	Psalm XXIV	21
I lift my inward sight;	302	Psalm XXV	2
Now, Now shall He lift up my head.	307	Psalm XXVII	31
Feed and lift them up for aye.	309	Psalm XXVIII	35
That lift themselves my ruin for to frame.	323	Psalm XXXV	66

LIFTED
Which oft he lifteth up, and stayes his lifted pawe,	53	2nd Eclogues 29	34
Thou lord that from Death' gates hast lifted me,	280	Psalm IX	39
Of these bad folkes, more lifted up with pride	285	Psalm XII	26
He lifted me unto a largly noble place.	292	Psalm XVIII	42
Let him be lifted up, that hath preserved me!	293	Psalm XVIII	84

```
                                                          PAGE   TITLE          LINE
LIFTETH
  Which oft he lifteth up, and stayes his lifted pawe, . . . .    53 2nd Eclogues 29   34
LIFTS
  That her cleare voyce lifts thy fame to the skies. . . . . .   171 Astrophil    12    8
  The lord lifts up my head, . . . . . . . . . . . . . . . .     272 Psalm III         13
LIFTST
  Up then thou liftst the poore, and down the proud wilt cast;  292 Psalm XVIII       52
*LIGHT
  Because from him doth come her light:. . . . . . . . . . .      13 Arcadia I     5   10
  In which do light small birds of thoughts orethrowne:. . . .    18 1st Eclogues  7  141
  Is he a God, that ever flies the light?. . . . . . . . . . .    21 1st Eclogues  8    7
  What counsell can prevaile, or light give light? . . . . . .    23 1st Eclogues  9   36
  But this light choller that doth make you bolde, . . . . . .    25 1st Eclogues  9  105
  Whence may I show to my minde any light of a possible
     escape . . . . . . . . . . . . . . . . . . . . . . . .      37 1st Eclogues 13  161
  That her I see, though you did lose your light.. . . . . . .    38 Arcadia II   14    4
  Since so my harte is filled with that light, . . . . . . .      39 Arcadia II   16    3
  That onely light doth all my life maintaine; . . . . . . .      39 Arcadia II   16    4
  Apollo great, whose beames the greater world do light, . . .    44 Arcadia II   26    1
  R. Dare Passions then abide in Reason's light? . . . . . . .    46 2nd Eclogues 27   17
  His utmost light: for well his witte doth know,. . . . . . .    55 2nd Eclogues 29   97
  In perfect light, which could not me deceave,. . . . . . . .    55 2nd Eclogues 29  100
  Pas. But yesternight by light I did receave. . . . . . . . .    55 2nd Eclogues 29  102
  Which while it is, it is all Asia's light. . . . . . . . . .    60 2nd Eclogues 30  109
  What causes first made these torments on me to light? Light.
  Can then a cause be so light that forceth a man to go die?
     Aye. . . . . . . . . . . . . . . . . . . . . . . . . .      64 2nd Eclogues 31   23
  Yet tell what light thinge I had in me to draw me to die?
     Eye. . . . . . . . . . . . . . . . . . . . . . . . . .      64 2nd Eclogues 31   24
  (Whiche hyding didest preserve that beawtie's light, . . . .    64 2nd Eclogues 31   25
  (Of passions darke, made darke by beautie's light) . . . . .    70 Arcadia III  35    2
  My minde ere now led foorth by reason's light: . . . . . .      72 Arcadia III  39    2
  Since all the thinges which give mine eyes their light . . .    73 Arcadia III  39    4
  So that the windowes of my inward light. . . . . . . . . .      73 Arcadia III  39    5
  Are hurt, not helpt, with piercing of the light: . . . . .      73 Arcadia III  39    7
  While that the light may shewe the horrors darke . . . . .      73 Arcadia III  39   10
  But cannot make resolved darkenes lighte:. . . . . . . . .      73 Arcadia III  39   11
  May keepe my thoughtes, from thought of wonted light.. . . .    73 Arcadia III  39   12
  Due sighes blowe out all sparkes of joyfull light, . . . .      73 Arcadia III  39   14
  This cave is darke, but it had never light.. . . . . . . .      74 Arcadia III  42   11
  For as from me, on him his hurt did light, . . . . . . . .      75 Arcadia III  43    1
  Preserve those beames, this age's onely lighte:. . . . . .      76 Arcadia III  45   11
  Bend all thy light to see. . . . . . . . . . . . . . . . .      79 Arcadia III  51    2
  Disdainst we see thee staind with other's light. . . . . .      80 Arcadia III  52    9
  "No" saies faire moone, "my lighte . . . . . . . . . . . .      80 Arcadia III  52   15
  Aurora now thou shewst thy blushing light. . . . . . . . .      82 Arcadia III  55   12
  Blush on for shame: that still with thee do light. . . . .      82 Arcadia III  56    1
  As oh! my selfe, whose woes are never lighte . . . . . . .      82 Arcadia III  56    5
  No lampe, whose light by Art is got, . . . . . . . . . . .      82 Arcadia III  56    9
  So may each thing, even as thou wishest lighte,. . . . . .      86 Arcadia III  62   17
  Never hard hand, nor ever raines too light.. . . . . . . .      96 3rd Eclogues 64   94
  Of that small light oft watching shepheards see. . . . . .      98 3rd Eclogues 65    8
  The great beames gone, the house on shoulders light: . . . .    98 3rd Eclogues 66    7
  Whose light is cause we have our lives neglected . . . . . .   102 3rd Eclogues 66  136
  Mine eyes did light upon her shining hewe, . . . . . . . .     108 Arcadia IV   69    7
  Now was our heav'nly vaulte deprived of the light. . . . .     115 4th Eclogues 72   75
  Did light those beamye stars which greater light did darke:.   116 4th Eclogues 73    1
  Thy selfe henceforth the light doo never see,. . . . . . .     116 4th Eclogues 73    3
  O light of Sunne, which is entit'led day,. . . . . . . . .     125 4th Eclogues 75   24
  Farewell o Sunn, Arcadia's clearest light: . . . . . . . .     126 4th Eclogues 75   52
  Now that of purest lampe is queint the light,. . . . . . .     129 4th Eclogues 76    1
  Still studying how to us to be a light.. . . . . . . . . .     129 4th Eclogues 76    8
  Who for our sakes will thinke all travaile light, . . . . .    129 4th Eclogues 76   16
  For ever blinded of our clearest light;. . . . . . . . . .     129 4th Eclogues 76   23
  And putting out our eyes seeke we our light. . . . . . . .     130 4th Eclogues 76   27
  Farewell our light, farewell our spoiled treasure: . . . .     130 4th Eclogues 76   36
  Which were not evill, well vew'd in reason's light.. . . .     130 4th Eclogues 76   37
  But vertue sets so high, that reason's light, . . . . . . .    131 Arcadia V    77    8
  Myne eyes thence drawne, where lived all their light,. . .     135 Cert Sonnets  2    7
  Pleased with the light, that his small corse doth burne: . .   149 Cert Sonnets 21    5
  On nature's sweetest light . . . . . . . . . . . . . . . .     149 Cert Sonnets 21   12
  A light which doth dissever, . . . . . . . . . . . . . . .     151 Cert Sonnets 23    4
  A light which dying never, . . . . . . . . . . . . . . . .     152 Cert Sonnets 23    5
  On nature's sweetest light.. . . . . . . . . . . . . . . .     152 Cert Sonnets 23    7
  Burn'd by the light he best liked, . . . . . . . . . . . .     152 Cert Sonnets 23   36
  Burneth bright in fairest light. No, no, no, no. . . . . .     154 Cert Sonnets 25   16
  Which breakes the clowdes and opens forth the light, . . . .   155 Cert Sonnets 26   11
  O take fast hold, let that light be thy guide, . . . . . .     161 Cert Sonnets 32    7
  The inward light: and that the heavenly part . . . . . . .     162 Cert Sonnets 32    9
  Frame daintiest lustre, mixt of shades and light?. . . . .     167 Astrophil     5    2
  Deceiv'd the quaking boy, who thought from so pure light,.     168 Astrophil     7    4
  And sure at length stolne goods do come to light . . . . .     169 Astrophil     8   10
  And fooles can thinke those Lampes of purest light, . . . .    172 Astrophil    15   11
  A chamber deafe to noise, and blind to light:. . . . . . .     177 Astrophil    26    2
  Let not mine eyes be hel-driv'n from that light: . . . . .     184 Astrophil    39   10
  Who hard by made a window send forth light.. . . . . . . .     188 Astrophil    48    7
  Mine eyes, my light, my heart, my life, alas,. . . . . . .     191 Astrophil    53    9
  Stella, the onely Planet of my light,. . . . . . . . . . .     198 Astrophil    65    9
  Light of my life, and life of my desire, . . . . . . . . .     200 Astrophil    68    1
  Of reason, from whose light those night-birds flie;. . . .     200 Astrophil    68    2
                                                                 201 Astrophil    71    7
```

```
*LIGHT                    (CONTINUED)                    PAGE  TITLE         LINE
    The onely light of joy, the onely warmth of Love.. . . . . .  204 Astrophil    76    4
    She comes with light and warmth, which like Aurora prove . .  205 Astrophil    76    5
    That presence, which doth give darke hearts a living light:.  205 Astrophil    77    3
    Tush absence, while thy mistes eclipse that light, . . . . .  223 Astrophil    88    9
    I am from you, light of my life, mis-led,. . . . . . . . . .  224 Astrophil    91    2
    Night bard from Sun, thou from thy owne sunne's light; . . .  229 Astrophil    96    4
    But ah poore Night, in love with Phoebus' light, . . . . . .  229 Astrophil    97    5
    To whom nor art nor nature graunteth light,. . . . . . . . .  230 Astrophil    99    2
    Such light in sense, with such a darkned mind. . . . . . . .  231 Astrophil    99   14
    There shines a joy from thee my only light:. . . . . . . . .  236 Astrophil   108    4
    As his light was her eyes, her death his endlesse night: . .  209 A&S 3rd Song      10
    This small light the Moone bestowes, . . . . . . . . . . . .  210 A&S 4th Song      19
    Every other vulgar light.. . . . . . . . . . . . . . . . . .  233 A&S 11th Song      5
    "But thy reason's purest light, . . . . . . . . . . . . . .   234 A&S 11th Song     26
    To beautie's lovely light, . . . . . . . . . . . . . . . . .  216 A&S 6th Song      32
    Nay give me eyes, and light, least that I sleep. . . . . . .  285 Psalm XIII        11
    Up Thou dost light my light, and cleare my darkned eye.. . .  292 Psalm XVIII       53
    To match with light foot staggs he made my foot so light . .  292 Psalm XVIII       61
    Both light and force of seing. . . . . . . . . . . . . . . .  294 Psalm XIX         36
    The shining Lord he is my light, . . . . . . . . . . . . . .  306 Psalm XXVII        1
    Ascribe unto the lord of light,. . . . . . . . . . . . . . .  309 Psalm XXIX         1
    For it is Thou, that hast restord my light,. . . . . . . . .  312 Psalm XXXI        14
    Thou hast hid them: yet leaving them thy light,. . . . . . .  313 Psalm XXXI        56
    On them doth light . . . . . . . . . . . . . . . . . . . . .  318 Psalm XXXIII      68
    And in thy light shall We see light. . . . . . . . . . . . .  324 Psalm XXXVI       26
    For like the light he shall display. . . . . . . . . . . . .  325 Psalm XXXVII      13
    Ev'en the light. . . . . . . . . . . . . . . . . . . . . . .  328 Psalm XXXVIII     29
    Send Thy truth and light,. . . . . . . . . . . . . . . . . .  336 Psalm XLIII       13
LIGHT-LEGGED
    But light-legd Pas had gott the middle space.. . . . . . . .  248 Other Poems    4  253
LIGHTNESS
    Compar'd to me, made me in lightnesse found: . . . . . . . .  147 Cert Sonnets  17   47
LIGHTNING
    But straight I saw motions of lightning grace, . . . . . . .  175 Astrophil    20   12
    She lightning Love, displaying Venus' skies, . . . . . . . .  196 Astrophil    63    7
    Lightning on lightning he did for their wrack augment; . . .  291 Psalm XVIII       30
LIGHTNINGS
    Thunders of cries; lightnings my wilde lookes be,. . . . . .  114 4th Eclogues 72   34
    Thundred disdaines and lightnings of disgrace: . . . . . . .  195 Astrophil    60    4
LIGHTS
    O Chastitie, the chiefe of heavenly lightes, . . . . . . . .   40 Arcadia II   18   13
    Whose lights do ever live, but in our darkenesse fade; . . .   44 Arcadia II   26    4
    But now those living lights absented be, . . . . . . . . . .  116 4th Eclogues 72   85
    Which dare claime from those lights the name of best,. . . .  169 Astrophil     9   11
    And if from Majestie of sacred lights, . . . . . . . . . . .  186 Astrophil    42   12
    Her flamie glistring lights increase with time and place;. .  205 Astrophil    76   10
    I thought each place was darke but where thy lights would
      be . . . . . . . . . . . . . . . . . . . . . . . . . . . .  212 A&S 5th Song       5
    Of which the two life-giving lights are figured in her eyes:  217 A&S 7th Song      16
    Are the lights of Cupid's skies, . . . . . . . . . . . . . .  218 A&S 8th Song      34
LIGHTSOME
    Now let those lightsomme sights we see thy darknes overcome.  343 Possibly      1   12
*LIKE
    Like great god Saturn faire, and like faire Venus chaste:. .   12 Arcadia I     3    5
    As smooth as Pan, as Juno milde, like goddesse IRis faste. .   12 Arcadia I     3    6
    Her forhead jacinth like, her cheekes of opall hue,. . . . .   12 Arcadia I     3    9
    Her skin like burnisht gold, her hands like silver ure
      untryde. . . . . . . . . . . . . . . . . . . . . . . . . .   12 Arcadia I     3   12
    No thralles like them that inward bondage have.. . . . . . .   17 1st Eclogues  7  114
    That I am like a flower. . . . . . . . . . . . . . . . . . .   19 1st Eclogues  7  158
    That I growe like a shade, . . . . . . . . . . . . . . . . .   19 1st Eclogues  7  163
    That I growe like the beaste,. . . . . . . . . . . . . . . .   20 1st Eclogues  7 V958
    Like beast for sacrifice, where save the tong. . . . . . . .   24 1st Eclogues  9   81
    For though Melampus like a wolfe doo looke,. . . . . . . . .   27 1st Eclogues 10   16
    We shepeheards are like them that under saile. . . . . . . .   27 1st Eclogues 10   31
    But commonly like currs we them entreate,. . . . . . . . . .   27 1st Eclogues 10   35
    Like busie boyes, to winne their tutor's harte,. . . . . . .   27 1st Eclogues 10   43
    But (like a point in midst of a circle) is still of a
      neernesse, . . . . . . . . . . . . . . . . . . . . . . . .   31 1st Eclogues 13    6
    Lyke to my noble thoughtes, still new, well plac'd, to me
      fruteles.. . . . . . . . . . . . . . . . . . . . . . . . .   35 1st Eclogues 13  124
    This marble chose, as of like temper knowne: . . . . . . . .   40 Arcadia II   19    2
    P. Not so, but fellowlike together borne.. . . . . . . . . .   46 2nd Eclogues 27   12
    Men tongd like lotches sucking others sorrowe. . . . . . . .   50 2nd Eclogues 28 V885
    Pas. Nay like to nightingales the other birds give eare: . .   52 2nd Eclogues 29   19
    Like players plast to fill a filthy stage, . . . . . . . . .   57 2nd Eclogues 30   20
    (Even like a toppe which nought but whipping moves). . . . .   58 2nd Eclogues 30   33
    Such beames so like his owne, which might have might . . . .   60 2nd Eclogues 30  105
    Harde to be gott, but got constant, to be helde like
      steeles Eeles.. . . . . . . . . . . . . . . . . . . . . .    65 2nd Eclogues 31   42
    O how much I do like your solitarines! . . . . . . . . . . .   68 2nd Eclogues 34    2
    Above line repeated at following location. . . . . . . . . .   69 2nd Eclogues 34   16
    O how well I do like your solitarines! . . . . . . . . . . .   69 2nd Eclogues 34   30
    Thy beames I like, but her cleare rayes I love:. . . . . . .   72 Arcadia III  38    9
    I like this place, wheare at the least the darke . . . . . .   73 Arcadia III  39   13
    Like those sicke folkes, in whome strange humors flowe,. . .   74 Arcadia III  41    1
    O Words which fall like sommer deaw on me, . . . . . . . . .   76 Arcadia III  46    1
    Eyes faire and great, like faire great oxe's eyes, . . . . .   76 Arcadia III  46    9
    So smooth as sleekestone-like, it smoothes each parte, . . .   76 Arcadia III  46   14
```

*LIKE	(CONTINUED)	PAGE	TITLE		LINE
Like divers flowers, whose divers beauties serve		78	Arcadia III	50	1
Two gleaming Sunnes of splendour like I see, ...		81	Arcadia III	55	4
Like to my brother's raies, yet those I sende.		82	Arcadia III	55	14
Like to the Moone when after chaunge		86	Arcadia III	62	11
Aurora like new out of bed,.		86	Arcadia III	62	24
Or like the fresh Queene-apple's side, ...		86	Arcadia III	62	25
Like wine and milke that mingled stood...		86	Arcadia III	62	30
Like pomels round of Marble cleere:.		87	Arcadia III	62	55
Like Alablaster faire and sleeke,.		88	Arcadia III	62	81
But soft and supple satten like.		88	Arcadia III	62	82
Like cunning Painter shadowing white.		89	Arcadia III	62	98
In her brave calves, like christall skies.		89	Arcadia III	62	102
Like comfits round in marchpane set.		89	Arcadia III	62	112
Her shoulders be like two white Doves, ...		89	Arcadia III	62	113
Which conduit-like with curious crookes, ...		90	Arcadia III	62	128
Like Whitest Snowe, in silver Brooke,.		88	Arcadia III	62 V	69
Lyke thynnest Lawne with Tynsell lynde,.		89	Arcadia III	62 V	116
But like the turtells faire.		91	3rd Eclogues	63	6
Like to the Elme and Vyne, ...		91	3rd Eclogues	63	15
And like to lillies pure		91	3rd Eclogues	63	24
And like two rivers sweete,.		92	3rd Eclogues	63	33
In number like the hearde.		92	3rd Eclogues	63	42
Or like the drops of raine..		92	3rd Eclogues	63	44
Like Oke and Mistletoe...		92	3rd Eclogues	63	51
And for this Courtier should well like his table,.		94	3rd Eclogues	64	23
Yet like a coward fearing stranger's pride,.		95	3rd Eclogues	64	29
Like Senators a harmeles empire had.		100	3rd Eclogues	66	56
And fellow-like let his dominion slide:.		101	3rd Eclogues	66	110
As for the gentle birds, like case might rewe.		102	3rd Eclogues	66	139
Who now his owne, full like his owne he used..		102	3rd Eclogues	66	142
Long since my thoughts chase me like beasts in forrests, . .		112	4th Eclogues	71	35
But like the feeble flower (whose stalke cannot sustaine . .		117	4th Eclogues	73	21
With outward maker's force, or like an inward father.. . . .		118	4th Eclogues	73	48
Or canons thunder-like, all shot togither, lende)		118	4th Eclogues	73	54
For that (so that you like) hereby doth lie a youth.		120	4th Eclogues	73	137
Hard like a rich marbell: hard, but a faire Diamond.		122	4th Eclogues	74	14
But, but alas, like a man condemn'd doth crave to be heard					
speake,.		122	4th Eclogues	74	23
Like foe, whose wits inclin'd to deadly spite, ...		135	Cert Sonnets	2	3
Like those whom dreames make uglie monsters see, ...		136	Cert Sonnets	2	11
Lyke crafty wretch by time and travell tought, ...		141	Cert Sonnets	8	5
Like as the Dove which seeled up doth flie, ...		144	Cert Sonnets	15	1
Better like I thy Satyre deerest Dyer, ...		145	Cert Sonnets	16	13
Who Stoick-like in clowdie hew appeare:.		147	Cert Sonnets	17	48
Like late mowne meades, late cut from joy I live..		147	Cert Sonnets	18	11
Like to the Mowlle with want of guiding sight, ...		149	Cert Sonnets	21	7
A woman's mould, but like an Angell graste,.		151	Cert Sonnets	22	66
And as you like my double lot, ...		153	Cert Sonnets	24	17
Like to the silly Sylvan,.		154	Cert Sonnets	25	15
So that thee like heaven I loved..		156	Cert Sonnets	27	4
Is gone, and now like slave-borne Muscovite, ...		166	Astrophil	2	10
Would she in beamie blacke, like painter wise, ...		168	Astrophil	7	3
They sun-like should more dazle then delight?.		168	Astrophil	7	8
Whose faire skin, beamy eyes, like morning sun on snow,. . .		169	Astrophil	8	9
For like a child that some faire booke doth find,.		170	Astrophil	11	5
Thou countest Stella thine, like those whose powers.		171	Astrophil	12	9
In nature apt to like when I did see		172	Astrophil	16	1
And straight therewith, like wags new got to play, ...		173	Astrophil	17	13
That unto me, who fare like him that both.		174	Astrophil	19	10
Who like a theefe, hid in darke bush doth ly,.		175	Astrophil	20	3
That mine owne writings like bad servants show		175	Astrophil	21	3
Either to do like him, which open shone, ...		176	Astrophil	22	10
Like some weake Lords, neighbord by mighty kings,.		179	Astrophil	29	1
To me that feele the like, thy state descries.		180	Astrophil	31	8
Where truth it selfe must speake like flatterie?		182	Astrophil	35	2
That I well find no eloquence like it.		192	Astrophil	55	14
Hast thou found such and such like arguments?.		199	Astrophil	67	10
She comes with light and warmth, which like Aurora prove . .		205	Astrophil	76	5
Nor do like Lords, whose weake confused braine,.		210	Astrophil	85	5
But if all faith, like spotlesse Ermine ly		212	Astrophil	86	5
If this darke place yet shew like candle light,.		225	Astrophil	91	5
Love moves thy paine, and like a faithfull page, ...		232	Astrophil	101	9
More cause a like effect at leastwise bringeth:.		208	A&S 3rd Song		5
(Image like of Saints' perfection)		234	A&S 11th Song		24
Like loving brothers' case		215	A&S 6th Song		15
He shall be lyke a freshly planted tree, ...		270	Psalm I		7
But lyke vyle chaffe with wind shal scattred be.		270	Psalm I		14
These men like potshards weake..		271	Psalm II		22
Woe, lyke a moth, my face's beauty eates		276	Psalm VI		21
Least lion like He do my soule devoure,.		277	Psalm VII		4
And their Renoune, which seemed so lyke to last, ...		280	Psalm IX		13
Like lurking lion in his denn.		282	Psalm X		37
That like a byrd to some strong hill		283	Psalm XI		3
Now like a lion gaping to make preyes, ...		290	Psalm XVII		33
Now like his Whelp in den that lurking stayes.		290	Psalm XVII		34
Like in a winding sheet, wretch I already lay, ...		291	Psalm XVIII		10
About which hee dimme clouds like a Pavilion brings, ...		291	Psalm XVIII		24
Who forth doth come like a bridegrome.		294	Psalm XIX		21
Like storehouse Thou of blessings mad'st,.		297	Psalm XXI		21

273

*LIKE	(CONTINUED)	PAGE	TITLE	LINE
For like a marke Thou shalt arow		298	Psalm XXI	45
Like lions fierce, with roaring jawes enlarged..		299	Psalm XXII	30
On me all this, who do like water slide;		299	Psalm XXII	31
Whose heart with these huge flames, like wax o're heated,. .		299	Psalm XXII	33
My moystning strength is like a potsherd dride,.		299	Psalm XXII	35
I be like them that descend.		308	Psalm XXVIII	4
Nay like young Calves in leapes are boin,.		310	Psalm XXIX	16
And shirion like young Unicorn..		310	Psalm XXIX	18
Ev'n like a dead man dreamed out of mind,.		313	Psalm XXXI	35
Or like a broken pott in myer tredd.		313	Psalm XXXI	36
Confounded be, and passe away like smoake, ...		313	Psalm XXXI	47
Oh be not like a horse or mule,.		315	Psalm XXXII	31
Like one that should his Mother's death lament..		322	Psalm XXXV	36
Thy Righteousness like hugest hills, ...		323	Psalm XXXVI	15
Thy judgments like the depths do ly, ...		323	Psalm XXXVI	16
They soone shall be cutt down like grasse.		324	Psalm XXXVII	5
And wither like green herb or flower;.		324	Psalm XXXVII	6
For like the light he shall display.		325	Psalm XXXVII	13
Like to the glory of noone day..		325	Psalm XXXVII	16
Like fatt of lambs shall be consumed,.		326	Psalm XXXVII	51
Like laurell fresh himself out spreading..		327	Psalm XXXVII	90
But I like a man become, ...		328	Psalm XXXVIII	37
Thou moth like mak'st his beauty fading be;.		330	Psalm XXXIX	35
Didst like, much lesse dost crave;.		331	Psalm XL	27
That comfort in these sports you like, my mynde his comfort tryes.		343	Possibly 1	14
Now for a clod-like hare in fourm they peere,.		243	Other Poems 4	43
Like dropsy folke still drinke to be a thyrst.		247	Other Poems 4	204
Like some which seeke to salve their blotted name.		248	Other Poems 4	231
Like Numid Lions by the hunters chas'd,.		249	Other Poems 4	291
A creeping serpentlike of mortall woe..		252	Other Poems 4	412
Those eies, which nothing like themselves can see,.		253	Other Poems 4	451
"For though like waxe, this magique makes me waste,.		254	Other Poems 4	489
Or like a lambe whose dam away is fet,.		254	Other Poems 4	490
Where by his words his self-like cause he knew..		256	Other Poems 4	536
Like Rogue, all ragged goe,.		257	Other Poems 5	25
Like Lovers do their Love, ...		261	Other Poems 6	43
Lovingly like friends did keepe, ...		262	Other Poems 7	22
Like the wiser sorte, whose learning,.		263	Other Poems 7	41
Like to Junoe's birdes of pride, ...		263	Other Poems 7	51
Friends like to blacke Swannes appearing,.		263	Other Poems 7	53
LIKED				
He liked me, but pitied lustfull youth:.		99	3rd Eclogues 66	36
Burn'd by the light he best liked, ...		154	Cert Sonnets 25	16
I saw and liked, I liked but loved not,.		165	Astrophil 2	5
In some such one she lik'd not his desire, ...		245	Other Poems 4	119
LIKEN				
To liken her? Decke yours with your comparison:.		15	1st Eclogues 7	47
Can liken them without all peere,.		86	Arcadia III 62	19
LIKENESS				
Give therefore to the Muse great praise in whose very likenes.		33	1st Eclogues 13	62
I shall see Thee in likeness Thine..		290	Psalm XVII	48
LIKES				
If he do praise the dog, she likes the cat..		104	3rd Eclogues 67	33
How Ulster likes of that same golden bit,.		180	Astrophil 30	9
LIKEST				
Leave what thou likest not, deale not thou with it..		166	Astrophil 4	4
Thought with good cause thou likest so well the night, . . .		229	Astrophil 96	1
LIKEWISE				
The birdes likewise with chirpes, and puing could, ...		100	3rd Eclogues 66	66
Ech other beast likewise his present brings:		101	3rd Eclogues 66	99
LIKING				
Thus honour, liking, trust, much, farre, and deepe,.		84	Arcadia III 60	5
Within what bounds can one his liking stay,.		182	Astrophil 35	3
Strength of liking, rage of longing,.		226	A&S 10th Song	24
Her parents liking well it should be so, ...		247	Other Poems 4	195
LILIES				
I sawe her arme, where purest Lillies cleave..		55	2nd Eclogues 29	104
Which onely still doth Lillies yeeld:.		87	Arcadia III 62	62
But Lillies such whose native smell.		87	Arcadia III 62	63
And like to lillies pure		91	3rd Eclogues 63	24
Making those Lillies and those Roses grow, ...		231	Astrophil 100	2
Nor blushing Lillies, nor pearles' ruby-hidden row,.		213	A&S 5th Song	38
LILIES'				
In Lillies' neast, where Love's selfe lies along..		208	Astrophil 83	8
LILY				
A Lillie field, with plowe of Rose which tilled is..		15	1st Eclogues 7	30
As sweete as violetts, faire as a lilly is,.		69	2nd Eclogues 34	32
Lilly in mourning blacke thy whitenes die:		125	4th Eclogues 75	28
LIMBS				
My sight in her faire limmes, I then assure my selfe,. . . .		16	1st Eclogues 7	56
Her father's corne (moving her faire limmes) measure.. . . .		16	1st Eclogues 7	75
My eys be dym, my lyms shake,.		66	2nd Eclogues 32	10
To all her limmes a spetiall grace,.		90	Arcadia III 62	135
She mov'd hir lims, and drew the aged man, ...		249	Other Poems 4	283
LIME				
Or catch the birds with pitfalls, or with lyme,.		26	1st Eclogues 9	124
With traitor lime the one, ...		258	Other Poems 5	87

LIMITED | PAGE | TITLE | LINE
Not limited to a whispringe note, the Lament of a Courtier,. | 35 | 1st Eclogues 13 | 110
LIMITLESS
With limitlesse renowne. . . . . | 217 | A&S 6th Song | 54
LIMITS
Bownded with no limitts, borne with a wing of hope . . . . . | 68 | 2nd Eclogues 34 | 8
That Limittes have in smallest smalle, ... | 89 | Arcadia III 62 | V103
Thee to thy wracke beyond thy limits straine. . . . . | 210 | Astrophil 85 | 4
No time within his limites binds.. . . . . | 326 | Psalm XXXVII | 76
LINE
If she must dye, then hath she past the line . . . . | 59 | 2nd Eclogues 30 | 77
Yet still, faire tree, lifte up thy stately line, ... | 77 | Arcadia III 47 | 9
Which drawne-out line doth hold all humane blisse. . . . . | 105 | 3rd Eclogues 67 | 72
And while their line of yeares they did in vertue spende.. | 117 | 4th Eclogues 73 | 38
Or with strange similies enrich each line, ... | 166 | Astrophil 3 | 7
That tedious leasure marks each wrinckled line:. . . . . . | 230 | Astrophil 98 | 11
I saw thy selfe with many a smiling line . . . . | 232 | Astrophil 103 | 2
O lord that rul'st Our mortall lyne. . . . . | 278 | Psalm VIII | 1
O lord that rulest Our mortall lyne, ... | 279 | Psalm VIII | 33
There be no eyn but reade the line . . . . | 294 | Psalm XIX | 13
Lo Thou a span's length madest my living line; . . . . . . | 330 | Psalm XXXIX | 15
LINED
Lyke thynnest Lawne with Tynsell lynde, ... | 89 | Arcadia III 62 | V116
Decke that poore place with Alablaster linde. . . . . | 150 | Cert Sonnets 22 | 34
Cloth'd with fine tropes, with strongest reasons lin'd, . . | 194 | Astrophil 58 | 6
Not for his faire outside, nor well lined braine, ... | 204 | Astrophil 75 | 3
LINES
Whose equall lynes their angles bowes, ... | 86 | Arcadia III 62 | 10
And now my pen these lines had dashed quite, ... | 190 | Astrophil 50 | 12
Stella, those faire lines, which true goodnesse show.. . . | 201 | Astrophil 71 | 4
LINGERING
Lalus. Kala at length conclude my lingring lotte:. . . . . | 18 | 1st Eclogues 7 | 115
As in their moodes to take a lingring pawse? . . . . | 146 | Cert Sonnets 17 | 24
LINING
Their soules fowl sinns for inmost lyning have:. . . . . . | 275 | Psalm V | 26
LINK
Link not me in self same chain . . . . | 309 | Psalm XXVIII | 11
LINKED
But linkt in binding bands . . . . | 261 | Other Poems 6 | 57
LINKS
By linkes of Love, and only Nature's art:. . . . . | 207 | Astrophil 81 | 6
LION
For once the Lion by the Lambe did lie;. . . . . | 100 | 3rd Eclogues 66 | 52
The Lion, harte; the Ounce gave active might;. . . . . . . | 101 | 3rd Eclogues 66 | 80
But while I thus with this yong Lyon plaid;. . . . . | 173 | Astrophil 16 | 9
Like lurking lion in his denn. . . . . | 282 | Psalm X | 37
Now like a lion gaping to make preyes, ... | 290 | Psalm XVII | 33
LION-LIKE
Least lion like He do my soule devoure, ... | 277 | Psalm VII | 4
LION'S
(Therion) When wanton Pan, deceiv'd with Lion's skin, . . . | 5 | Lady of May 3 | 7
Fine eares, long taile he hath, with Lion's curbed clawe,. | 53 | 2nd Eclogues 29 | 33
Though strongly hedg'd of bloudy Lyon's pawes, ... | 204 | Astrophil 75 | 10
From lion's mouth O help, and shew to heare me . . . . . . | 299 | Psalm XXII | 49
Save me distrest from lion's cruel kind. . . . . | 322 | Psalm XXXV | 45
Who then in Lion's cave did enter fyrst, ... | 247 | Other Poems 4 | 206
LIONS
Like lions fierce, with roaring jawes enlarged.. . . . . . | 299 | Psalm XXII | 30
The lions oft lack food, ... | 319 | Psalm XXXIV | 37
Like Numid Lions by the hunters chas'd, ... | 249 | Other Poems 4 | 291
LIONS'
(As Tygers, leopards, beares, and Lions' seed) . . . . . . | 102 | 3rd Eclogues 66 | 122
LIP
With either lip he doth the other kisse: . . . . | 186 | Astrophil 43 | 11
Sweet swelling lip, well maist thou swell in pride,. . . . | 206 | Astrophil 80 | 1
Sweet lip, you teach my mouth with one sweet kisse.. . . . | 207 | Astrophil 80 | 14
LIPS
Her twinkling eies bedeckt with pearle, her lips of Saphir
blew:. . . . . | 12 | Arcadia I 3 | 10
Me thinkes I see the lippes my Leuca hath, ... | 54 | 2nd Eclogues 29 | 76
And thinke from Cosma's sweet red lips I live, ... | 54 | 2nd Eclogues 29 | 79
O lippes, that kist that hand with my teares sprent; . . . | 60 | 2nd Eclogues 30 | 120
Her lipps are the riches the warres to maintaine, ... | 67 | 2nd Eclogues 33 | 9
Lips red and plum, as cherrie's ruddy side,. . . . . | 76 | Arcadia III 46 | 8
But who those ruddie lippes can misse? . . . . | 87 | Arcadia III 62 | 37
Asking her how she tasted Courtier's lips, ... | 95 | 3rd Eclogues 64 | 33
Did not a rosed breath, from lips more rosie proceeding, . | 124 | 4th Eclogues 74 | 79
Who burnt his lips to kisse faire shining fire.. . . . . . | 145 | Cert Sonnets 16 | 14
That those lips swell, so full of thee they bee, ... | 170 | Astrophil 12 | 3
Serve him with shot, her lips his heralds arre:. . . . . . | 179 | Astrophil 29 | 10
To shew her skin, lips, teeth and head so well? . . . . . | 181 | Astrophil 32 | 11
Faire eyes, sweet lips, deare heart, that foolish I. . . . | 186 | Astrophil 43 | 1
When he will play, then in her lips he is, ... | 186 | Astrophil 43 | 9
Her eyes, her lips, her all, saith Love do this, ... | 190 | Astrophil 52 | 3
Of them, who in their lips Love's standerd beare;. . . . . | 191 | Astrophil 54 | 6
This sowre-breath'd mate tast of those sugred lips.. . . . | 194 | Astrophil 59 | 11
My lips are sweet, inspired with Stella's kisse. . . . . . | 204 | Astrophil 74 | 14
Those lips, which make death's pay a meane price for a
kisse . . . . | 205 | Astrophil 77 | 6
Teaching dumbe lips a nobler exercise. . . . . | 207 | Astrophil 81 | 4

LIPS   (CONTINUED)   PAGE   TITLE   LINE
    But you must needs with those lips billing be? . . . .   208 Astrophil   83   12
    And through those lips drinke Nectar from that toong;. . . .   208 Astrophil   83   13
    The globe of weale, lips Love's indentures make: . . . . . .   210 Astrophil   85   13
    I saw that sighes her sweetest lips did part,. . . . .   223 Astrophil   87   7
    Thine eyes my pride, thy lips my history:. . . . .   224 Astrophil   90   3
    Milke hands, rose cheeks, or lips more sweet, more red,. . .   225 Astrophil   91   7
    If her lips daignd to sweeten my poore name. . . . .   225 Astrophil   92   13
    Who hath the lips, where wit in fairnesse raigneth,. . . . .   197 A&S 1st Song   9
    Yet those lips so sweetly swelling,. . . . .   203 A&S 2nd Song   21
    In my lips to have his biding, ...   226 A&S 10th Song   27
    At her lips my Nectar drinking.. . . . .   227 A&S 10th Song   48
    As with sententious lips to set a title vaine on it: . . . .   217 A&S 7th Song   4
    Love did set his lips asunder, ...   218 A&S 8th Song   27
    Their abject lips no breath but flattery move. . . . .   284 Psalm XII   5
    Those lying lipps from Cousening head remove,. . . . .   284 Psalm XII   8
    And since my lipps feign not with Thee,. . . . .   289 Psalm XVII   3
    His lips to crave, what he would crave . . . .   297 Psalm XXI   7
    Let those lips be made dumbe which love to ly, ...   313 Psalm XXXI   49
    Keep well thy lipps and tongue . . . .   320 Psalm XXXIV   49
    My lipps shall still reveale,. . . . .   331 Psalm XL   38
    How rosy moist'ned lipps about his beake . . . .   244 Other Poems   4 95
    In cheeks and lipps the Tyran threatens bloud. . . . .   246 Other Poems   4 152
    Her chery lipps, milke hands, and golden haire . . . .   254 Other Poems   4 461
    Of Mira's lipps divide . . . .   258 Other Poems   5   57
LIQUOR
    Who of his tongue the lickowr gladly powrs,. . . . .   28 1st Eclogues 10   70
LIQOURS
    O toong in which, all honyed likoures bee, ...   76 Arcadia III 46   3
LIQUOR
    Fire no liquor can coole: Neptune's seate would be bryd up
        there. . . . .   32 1st Eclogues 13   32
LICKEROUS
    With Lycoras stalkes of Porphiry,. . . . .   87 Arcadia III 62 V 57
LIRIBLIRING
    Thy liribliring cries, ...   258 Other Poems   5   62
LIST
    I list not dig so deepe for brasen fame. . . . .   179 Astrophil   28   4
LISTEN
    Listen then Lordings with good eare to me, ...   183 Astrophil   37   3
    Made to listen unto me,. . . . .   263 Other Poems   7   56
LITTLE
    Lett our unpartiall eyes a litle watche. . . . .   29 1st Eclogues 10   91
    Into our mindes let us a little fall,. . . . .   29 1st Eclogues 10   94
    And in our little world dost cleare our inward sight,. . . .   44 Arcadia II   26   2
    Whose onely face the little heaven is, ...   51 2nd Eclogues 28 107
    Nico. She once starke nak'd did bathe a little tine; . . . .   55 2nd Eclogues 29 105
    A little downward to espie,. . . . .   87 Arcadia III 62   52
    He little looking that she should complaine. . . . .   95 3rd Eclogues 64   49
    Which little time did fitlie bring to passe. . . . .   96 3rd Eclogues 64   76
    And with some words which shewed little care,. . . . .   97 3rd Eclogues 64 118
    As I my little flocke on Ister banke . . . .   98 3rd Eclogues 66   1
    (A little flocke; but well my pipe they couthe). . . . . . .   98 3rd Eclogues 66   2
    The little coine his sweating browes have got, ...   104 3rd Eclogues 67   41
    That still our little world may know his king. . . . .   105 3rd Eclogues 67   63
    As little hunting minde (God knowes) did there appeere.. . .   118 4th Eclogues 73   70
    The bande of beauties all, the little world of Love. . . . .   119 4th Eclogues 73   90
    Sleepe then a litle, pap content is making:. . . . .   139 Cert Sonnets 6   8
    The litle reason that is left in me, ...   167 Astrophil   4   10
    Litle he is, so litle worth is he; . . . .   194 Astrophil   59   5
    Little hearing, speaking lesse;. . . . .   328 Psalm XXXVIII   39
    Thus Pas did kisse hir hand with little grace, ...   249 Other Poems   4 276
LIVE
    Great sure is she, on whom our hopes do live,. . . . .   3 Lady of May   2   5
    Are all my thoughts, in which I live or die: . . . .   3 Lady of May   2   10
    Though woes now live, at length thy woes must dye. . . . . .   22 1st Eclogues 9   12
    Hope we do live yet. . . . .   30 1st Eclogues 12   4
    Above line repeated at following location. . . . .   31 1st Eclogues 12   28
    Better yet do I live, that though by my thoughts I be
        plunged. . . . .   35 1st Eclogues 13 107
    What wooll my sheepe shall beare, whyle thus they live,. . .   39 Arcadia II   17   7
    They live in force, I quite consumed die.. . . . .   42 Arcadia II   22   12
    Whose lights do ever live, but in our darkenesse fade; . . .   44 Arcadia II   26   4
    And thinke from Cosma's sweet red lips I live, ...   54 2nd Eclogues 29   79
    If Leuca live, she darken will my fame.. . . . .   55 2nd Eclogues 29   95
    Plangus must live to see Eronae's death. . . . .   58 2nd Eclogues 30   55
    Plangus must live some helpe for her to trie . . . .   58 2nd Eclogues 30   56
    Plangus doth live, and shall Erona dye?. . . . .   58 2nd Eclogues 30   58
    Of this we live, in this wee finde our rest, ...   75 Arcadia III 44   7
    Live long, and long witnesse my chosen smarte, ...   77 Arcadia III 47   10
    Till her eyes shine, I live in darkest night.. . . . .   79 Arcadia III 51   14
    Live one in two, a well united paire,. . . . .   91 3rd Eclogues 63   7
    That it both seene and felte may with you live". . . . . . .   101 3rd Eclogues 66   77
    They better live that in a gaile doo lie: . . . .   105 3rd Eclogues 67   54
    Thy house by thee must live, or els be gone: . . . .   106 3rd Eclogues 67 110
    My senses such release, as they which quiet live,. . . . . .   117 4th Eclogues 73   12
    In ashes of despaire (though burnt) shall make thee live".   121 4th Eclogues 73 174
    And that he thence must part where to live onely I lyved.. .   123 4th Eclogues 74   30
    Care that I sinke in griefe, Care that I live banished?. . .   124 4th Eclogues 74   82
    And banished doo I live, nor now will seeke a recov'rie, . .   124 4th Eclogues 74   83

```
LIVE                    (CONTINUED)                      PAGE   TITLE           LINE
    That they, which have no lives, should live so long, . . . .   126 4th Eclogues 75   41
    While he did live, farre, farre was all disorder;. . . . . .   128 4th Eclogues 75  130
    So that I live to pay a mortall fee, . . . . . . . . . . . .   136 Cert Sonnets  2    9
    You better sure shall live, not evermore . . . . . . . . . .   142 Cert Sonnets 12    1
    Hatn neither leave to live, nor doome to dye,. . . . . . .     144 Cert Sonnets 15    7
    She thinks I leade and live too merrie daies. . . . . . . .    146 Cert Sonnets 17   30
    Like late mowne meades, late cut from joy I live.. . . . .     147 Cert Sonnets 18   11
    Faire choice I have, either to live or dye . . . . . . . .     149 Cert Sonnets 21   13
    Yet live with thoughts closde up, till that she will . . . .   150 Cert Sonnets 22   29
    So may they live still sorie . . . . . . . . . . . . . . .     152 Cert Sonnets 23   31
    Yet do we both live in you.. . . . . . . . . . . . . . . . .   154 Cert Sonnets 25   23
    Thus do I dye to live thus,. . . . . . . . . . . . . . . .     154 Cert Sonnets 25   28
    The lesse I love, I live the lesse.. . . . . . . . . . . .     157 Cert Sonnets 27   40
    The prettie death, while each in other live. . . . . . . .     206 Astrophil    79   11
    Who seeke, who hope, who love, who live but thee;. . . . . .   224 Astrophil    90    2
    With absence' Vaile, I live in Sorowe's night. . . . . . .     224 Astrophil    91    4
    I have (live I and know this) harmed thee,. . . . . . . .      227 Astrophil    93   10
    All mirth farewell, let me in sorrow live. . . . . . . . .     231 Astrophil   100   14
    Who makes a man live then glad when he dieth?. . . . . . .     197 A&S 1st Song      26
    Yet thought and speech do live, though metamorphosd quite: .   212 A&S 5th Song      14
    Then live Jehova still, my rock still blessed be;. . . . . .   293 Psalm XVIII       83
    That they in peace shall blessed live. . . . . . . . . . .     310 Psalm XXIX        29
    But the while they live and grow . . . . . . . . . . . . .     329 Psalm XXXVIII     55
    Shew me how long I have to live. . . . . . . . . . . . . .     329 Psalm XXXIX       14
    They are but shades not true things where we live, . . . . .   330 Psalm XXXIX       19
    By north or south still rich adorned live: . . . . . . . .     256 Other Poems   5   16
LIVED
    Since when I thinke he hath in silence lived. . . . . . .       29 1st Eclogues 10   87
    And that he thence must part where to live onely I lyved.. .   123 4th Eclogues 74   30
    Myne eyes thence drawne, where lived all their light,. . . .   149 Cert Sonnets 21    5
    Seeing how once you saw I liv'd, . . . . . . . . . . . . .     158 Cert Sonnets 28   31
    One love they lov'd, one life they liv'd.. . . . . . . . .     241 Other Poems   3    4
    While thus they liv'd, (this was indede a life). . . . . .     243 Other Poems   4   58
LIVELIER
    Livelier then else-where, Stella's image see. . . . . . . .    184 Astrophil    39   14
LIVELY
    My Lyvelye joyes to dolefull ashes turne:. . . . . . . . .      42 Arcadia II   22   10
    Pas. Ah foole; so Courtiers do. But who did lively skippe, .    52 2nd Eclogues 29   11
    Her face which was more lively in my hart; . . . . . . . .      60 2nd Eclogues 30  117
    When to my livelie torment,. . . . . . . . . . . . . . . .     154 Cert Sonnets 25    2
    Though he the lively forme receiveth:. . . . . . . . . . .     159 Cert Sonnets 29   17
    Effects of lively heat, must needs in nature grow. . . . .     169 Astrophil     8   11
    Morpheus, the lively sonne of deadly sleepe, . . . . . . .     180 Astrophil    32    1
    Prints his owne lively forme in rudest braine. . . . . . .     194 Astrophil    58    8
    Paint woe's blacke face so lively to my sight, . . . . . .     230 Astrophil    98   10
LIVERS
    Unto my selfe let after-livers know. . . . . . . . . . . .      40 Arcadia II   18   10
LIVERY
    My minde for weeds your vertue's liverie weares. . . . . .      18 1st Eclogues  7  137
    And when I meete these trees, in the earth's faire lyvery
        clothed, . . . . . . . . . . . . . . . . . . . . . . .      35 1st Eclogues 13  113
    In Marse's liverie, prauncing in the presse: . . . . . . .     191 Astrophil    53    6
    Griefe but Love's winter liverie is, the Boy . . . . . . .     201 Astrophil    70    7
    Since kind or chance gives both one liverie, . . . . . . .     229 Astrophil    96    2
    Upon thy cheerefull face, joye's livery weare: . . . . . .     232 Astrophil   103    3
    Who weare his blessed livery;. . . . . . . . . . . . . . .     321 Psalm XXXIV       78
    Whose lyverie is such, as most I freeze apparelled most, .     343 Possibly      1   21
    Proudly bedeckt in Aprill's livory,. . . . . . . . . . . .     253 Other Poems   4  453
LIVE'S
    Drawes up; and if, hope fayling, ende live's pleasure, . . .    16 1st Eclogues  7   71
LIVES
    Shine eyes on me, that both our lives be guarded;. . . . .      17 1st Eclogues  7   92
    And lives in fancye's seing. . . . . . . . . . . . . . . .      20 1st Eclogues  7 V965
    Millions of yeares this old drivell Cupid lives; . . . . .      22 1st Eclogues  8   43
    Yet be my hopes thus plast, here fixed lives my recomforte,.    37 1st Eclogues 13  164
    Old age well stayed from raunging humor lives: . . . . . .      39 Arcadia II   15   10
    Since so your living image lives in me,. . . . . . . . . .      39 Arcadia II   16    7
    R. Who Passion doth ensue, lives in annoy. . . . . . . . .      46 2nd Eclogues 27   13
    P. Who Passion doth forsake, lives void of joy.. . . . . .      46 2nd Eclogues 27   14
    With so strong lives, that bodie cannot rest . . . . . . .      56 2nd Eclogues 29  145
    While that my soule, she, she lives in affliction; . . . .      61 2nd Eclogues 30  146
    Such wisedome, that in her lives speculation:. . . . . . .      69 2nd Eclogues 34   35
    Men's lives, untill it be imbraste.. . . . . . . . . . . .      87 Arcadia III  62   66
    At last for sport their sillie lives did spill.. . . . . .     103 3rd Eclogues 66  147
    Whose light is cause we have our lives neglected . . . . .     108 Arcadia IV   69    7
    His nature feares to die who lives still wailing.. . . . .     110 Arcadia IV   70   39
    What life it is, and how that all these lives doo gather,. .   118 4th Eclogues 73   47
    That they, which have no lives, should live so long, . . . .   126 4th Eclogues 75   41
    That in thee lives harmonie, . . . . . . . . . . . . . . .     140 Cert Sonnets  7   19
    The golden meane who loves, lives safely free. . . . . . .     143 Cert Sonnets 12    4
    From filth of foreworne house, and quiet lives,. . . . . .     143 Cert Sonnets 12    5
    Lives to impart my wearie clay some breath.. . . . . . . .     148 Cert Sonnets 20   10
    Yet lives untill his life be new requirde. . . . . . . . .     150 Cert Sonnets 22   24
    Since she lives in his death. . . . . . . . . . . . . . . .    152 Cert Sonnets 23   16
    Since our lives be not immortall,. . . . . . . . . . . . .     155 Cert Sonnets 26   16
    Of whom the trust lives in my heart. . . . . . . . . . . .     304 Psalm XXV         72
    D. Teares drink, sorrowes meat, wherewith, not I, but in me
        my deathlives. . . . . . . . . . . . . . . . . . . . .     344 Possibly      1   34
    Her eares where Musique lives, . . . . . . . . . . . . . .     258 Other Poems   5   60
```

277

LIVETH
    You shall the life that ever liveth find............. 300 Psalm XXII   64
    Lo whom God blest he blessed liveth, ... 326 Psalm XXXVII   55
    To mate with whom he liveth, ... 261 Other Poems 6   50
LIVING
    Why thee a living man they had made dead............ 11 Arcadia I   1   7
    Nor helpe by life or death who living dyes.......... 18 1st Eclogues 7 146
    Since so your living image lives in me............ 39 Arcadia II   16   7
    Yee living powres enclosed in stately shrine .... 40 Arcadia II   18   1
    Death wrapt in flesh, to living grave assign'd........ 73 Arcadia III 40 14
    Such living beames should her black seate assaile, ... 82 Arcadia III 55 10
    Yet living still in her, while her beames lent .... 115 4th Eclogues 72 83
    But now those living lights absented be, ... 116 4th Eclogues 72 85
    Till deadly sleepe at length possest my living coarse. ... 117 4th Eclogues 73 30
    A living coarse I lay: but ah, my wakefull minde ...... 117 4th Eclogues 73 31
    Our bodies be in living power maintained,.......... 128 4th Eclogues 75 107
    To paint my living death, and endlesse smart:........ 146 Cert Sonnets 17 28
    From joy I part still living in annoy............. 148 Cert Sonnets 20 14
    Of living deaths, deare wounds, faire stormes and freesing
       fires: .... 167 Astrophil   6   4
    Witnesse of life to them that living die:.......... 180 Astrophil   32   2
    That presence, which doth give darke hearts a living light:. 205 Astrophil   77   3
    That living thus in blackest winter night, ... 224 Astrophil   89 13
    Restlesse rest, and living dying..?............. 218 A&S 8th Song   20
    In land with living creatures clad? .... 308 Psalm XXVII   63
    Lo Thou a span's length madest my living line; .... 330 Psalm XXXIX   15
    After ever living thee:.................... 334 Psalm XLII   6
    Will. What living get you then? D. Disdayne; but just
       disdayne........................... 344 Possibly   1   35
    With sound of musicke living............... 260 Other Poems 6   10
LIZARD
    To make a Lyzard dull to taste Love's daintie food:..... 209 A&S 3rd Song   8
LO
    Then jarle: lo, lo, even these how envie blindes....... 26 1st Eclogues 10   9
    But loe, my words defaste, my fancies blinde,........ 40 Arcadia II   19   3
    Besides, lo here the auther. .... 67 2nd Eclogues 32 46
    Of all thy harmes: Lo here she,............... 67 2nd Eclogues 32 47
    When lo with hugest noise (such noise a tower makes...... 118 4th Eclogues 73 51
    Then with those eyes he lookes, lo by and by .... 186 Astrophil   43   6
    But lo, while I do speake, it groweth noone with me, ... 205 Astrophil   76   9
    Breakefast of Love, but lo, lo, where she is,........ 206 Astrophil   79 13
    O birds, o beasts, looke Love, lo, Stella shineth...... 209 A&S 3rd Song   12
    Lo you grow proud with this, for tyrans make folke bow:.. 214 A&S 5th Song   61
    Lo, I am tir'd, while still I sigh and groane:....... 276 Psalm VI   17
    Lo he that first conceiv'd a wretched thought, ... 278 Psalm VII   37
    No sooner said, but (lo) myne Enemyes sink .... 280 Psalm IX   46
    For lo with pride the wicked man .... 281 Psalm X   5
    And, lo, he finds that all astraying went,.......... 286 Psalm XIV   10
    Lo! ev'en unto Eternity..................... 297 Psalm XXI   15
    Lo, how his blessing budds .... 304 Psalm XXV   49
    Lo I that waild, now daunce for joy............. 311 Psalm XXX   34
    But lo Jehova's sight..................... 318 Psalm XXXIII   67
    For lo, this Wretch did call,................ 319 Psalm XXXIV   21
    And lo, his Call the skyes did clime;........... 319 Psalm XXXIV   22
    But lo, soon as they did me staggering see,......... 322 Psalm XXXV   37
    Lo there I now foresee their fall.............. 324 Psalm XXXVI   33
    Who do ev'ill works: lo I doe see.............. 324 Psalm XXXVI   34
    But lo their bowes, they shall be broken,.......... 325 Psalm XXXVII 39
    Lo whom God blest he blessed liveth, ... 326 Psalm XXXVII 55
    Lo, he was gon, print of his treading,........... 327 Psalm XXXVII 91
    Lo I now to mourn begin.................... 329 Psalm XXXVIII 52
    Lo Thou a span's length madest my living line; .... 330 Psalm XXXIX   15
    Thus bound I said, lo, lord I am at hand,.......... 331 Psalm XL   31
    Now is hee wrackt say they, lo, there he lyes........ 333 Psalm XLI   27
    Then lo, then I will .... 337 Psalm XLIII   25
LOAD
    Let wo gripe on my heart, shame loade mine eye....... 212 Astrophil   86   4
    "Alas! what weights are these that lode my heart!...... 253 Other Poems 4 441
LOADEN
    And loden so puls downe, puld downe destroyes........ 50 2nd Eclogues 28 86
    Ponder the paines, which on me loaden be .... 280 Psalm IX   37
LOADSTONE
    The heav'n-love lodestone drew thy iron hart......... 248 Other Poems 4 224
LOATH
    Loth to dye young, and then you must be olde,........ 25 1st Eclogues 9 103
    Bownd and bownd by so noble bandes, as loth to be unbownd, . 37 1st Eclogues 13 162
    Moste lothe to loose, the moste approching hope....... 71 Arcadia III 37   6
    Loath, I must leave his chiefe resort............ 88 Arcadia III 62 84
    Whereto you knowe, his honest harte were loath........ 95 3rd Eclogues 64 60
    Thou fearest death; thinke they are loth to die. ...... 103 3rd Eclogues 66 151
    (For both togither spake, each loth to be behinde) ..... 121 4th Eclogues 73 155
    Her breath, then short, seem'd loth from home to pas,.... 252 Other Poems 4 399
LOATHE
    And loth this time, calld life, nay thinke, that life. ... 113 4th Eclogues 72 12
LOATHED
    I yeeld, o Love, unto thy loathed yoke,.......... 135 Cert Sonnets 1   9
    Thou paine the onely guest of loath'd constraint,...... 141 Cert Sonnets 10 1
    Part of my life, the loathed part to me, ... 148 Cert Sonnets 20 9
LOATHED-LOVING
    Shunn lothed-loving bankes with conning crooke:....... 257 Other Poems 5 29

```
                                                        PAGE    TITLE          LINE
LOATHING
   A loathing of all loose unchastitie, . . . . . . . . . . . .  172 Astrophil   14   13
   Loathing all lies, doubting this Flatterie is: . . . . . . .  207 Astrophil   80   11
LOATHSOME
   Of lothsome dayes, whose losse how canst thou mone,. . . . .   59 2nd Eclogues 30  78
   Nor yet shall yeeld to loathsome sluttishnes,. . . . . . . .   94 3rd Eclogues 63  97
   The house is made a very lothsome cage,. . . . . . . . . . .  105 3rd Eclogues 67  49
   The lothsome buds growne on sorrowe's tree.. . . . . . . . .  153 Cert Sonnets 24   5
LOCK
   Locke up, faire liddes, the treasures of my harte: . . . . .   79 Arcadia III 51    1
   Or those golden lockes, those lockes which lock me to
      bondage, . . . . . . . . . . . . . . . . . . . . . . . .  123 4th Eclogues 74  51
   Red Porphir is, which locke of pearle makes sure:. . . . . .  169 Astrophil    9    6
   The same key op'n can, which can locke up a treasure.. . . .  213 A&S 5th Song     18
LOCKED
   Lcckt fast with knowing that she is, of worldly things the
      best.. . . . . . . . . . . . . . . . . . . . . . . . . .  344 Possibly     1   30
*LOCKS
   Or those golden lockes, those lockes which lock me to
      bondage, . . . . . . . . . . . . . . . . . . . . . . . .  123 4th Eclogues 74  51
   That from her lockes, thy day-nets, none scapes free,. . . .  170 Astrophil   12    2
   Ncr nourish speciall lockes of vowed haire,. . . . . . . . .  191 Astrophil   54    3
   First did with puffing kisse those lockes display: . . . . .  233 Astrophil  103   11
   Where rigrows exile lockes up all my sense?. . . . . . . . .  233 Astrophil  104    8
LODESTAR
   Stella loadstar of desier. . . . . . . . . . . . . . . . . .  218 A&S 8th Song     32
LODGE
   Though harbengers of death lodge there his traine. . . . . .  228 Astrophil   94    8
LODGED
   I lodg'd thee in my heart, and being blind . . . . . . . . .  198 Astrophil   65    7
   How Vertue may best lodg'd in beautie be,. . . . . . . . . .  201 Astrophil   71    2
LODGING
   The honest sports of earthy lcdging prove; . . . . . . . . .  243 Other Poems  4   42
LOFTLY
   Musicke more loftly swels. . . . . . . . . . . . . . . . . .  216 A&S 6th Song     25
LOFTY
   What judge you doth a hillocke shew, by the lofty Olympus? .   34 1st Eclogues 13  75
   With envie I doo hate the loftie mountaines; . . . . . . . .  112 4th Eclogues 71  52
LOGS
   Approching warmes (not else) dead logges up sends, . . . . .  150 Cert Sonnets 22  12
LONELY
   Oh! if such a one have bent to a lonely life . . . . . . . .   69 2nd Eclogues 34  39
   With length laid downe she deckt the lonely place. . . . . .  244 Other Poems  4  107
   This morne alone to lonely walke did passe,. . . . . . . . .  255 Other Poems  4  533
*LONG
   (Espilus) Silvanus long in love, and long in vaine,. . . . .    4 Lady of May  3    1
   My sonne, keepe this, that my long toyle hath laide to me:.   16 1st Eclogues  7  52
   I never found long love such wealth hath paide to me". . . .   16 1st Eclogues  7  54
   Seemde but to spoyle the foode of thoughts long famished..    16 1st Eclogues  7  69
   And others long to tell their loves' condition:. . . . . . .   19 1st Eclogues  7 171
   And others long to tell their loves' condicion. . . . . . .   20 1st Eclogues  7 V971
   With long large eares where never rumour dyes. . . . . . . .   21 1st Eclogues  8  28
   Philisides. O gods, how long this old foole hath annoi'd . .   24 1st Eclogues  9  66
   Who once a white long beard, well handle does, . . . . . . .   25 1st Eclogues  9  90
   Who have their lesson so long time begonne?. . . . . . . . .   27 1st Eclogues 10  27
   Fortune, Nature, Love, long have contended about me, . . . .   29 1st Eclogues 11   1
   Latona's sonne, whose birth in paine and travaile long . . .   45 Arcadia II  26    7
   I have (and long shall have) a white great nimble cat, . . .   53 2nd Eclogues 29  31
   Fine eares, long taile he hath, with Lion's curbed clawe,. .   53 2nd Eclogues 29  33
   A ruddie haire his cote, with fine long specled face:. . . .   53 2nd Eclogues 29  42
   Pas. But long have I a sparrow gailie drest, . . . . . . . .   54 2nd Eclogues 29  84
   Plangus. Alas how long this pilgrimage doth last?. . . . . .   57 2nd Eclogues 30   5
   Long since my voice is hoarce, and throte is sore, . . . . .   57 2nd Eclogues 30   8
   Boulon. How long wilt thou with monefull musicke staine. . .   58 2nd Eclogues 30  38
   Then let my life long time on earth maintained be, . . . . .   61 2nd Eclogues 30 147
   What do lovers seeke for, long seeking for to enjoy? Joy.. .   63 2nd Eclogues 31  13
   Oh when shall I be knowne, wher most to be knowne I do
      longe Long. . . . . . . . . . . . . . . . . . . . . . .   64 2nd Eclogues 31  32
   Long be thy woes for such newes, but how recks she my
      thoughts? Oughts.. . . . . . . . . . . . . . . . . . . .   64 2nd Eclogues 31  33
   A Banisht man, long bard from his desire . . . . . . . . . .   75 Arcadia III 44    1
   Live long, and long witnesse my chosen smarte, . . . . . . .   77 Arcadia III 47   10
   Holde me most yours, then my longe suite is signde.. . . . .   79 Arcadia III 50   18
   Jcyne with thy sonne, to ease my long annoys.. . . . . . . .   81 Arcadia III 53   13
   Let him drinke this, whome long in armes to folde. . . . . .   83 Arcadia III 58    1
   Thought, thinke to ende, too long the frute of thought . . .   83 Arcadia III 59    7
   Monstrous appeares, long trueth received late, . . . . . . .   85 Arcadia III 61    6
   O Himen long their coupled joyes maintaine.. . . . . . . . .   91 3rd Eclogues 63   9
   Above line repeated at following locations . . . . . . . . .   91 3rd Eclogues 63  18
   . . . . . . . . . . . . . . . . . . . . . . . . . . . . . .   91 3rd Eclogues 63  27
   . . . . . . . . . . . . . . . . . . . . . . . . . . . . . .   92 3rd Eclogues 63  45
   . . . . . . . . . . . . . . . . . . . . . . . . . . . . . .   92 3rd Eclogues 63  54
   . . . . . . . . . . . . . . . . . . . . . . . . . . . . . .   93 3rd Eclogues 63  63
   . . . . . . . . . . . . . . . . . . . . . . . . . . . . . .   93 3rd Eclogues 63  72
   . . . . . . . . . . . . . . . . . . . . . . . . . . . . . .   93 3rd Eclogues 63  81
   . . . . . . . . . . . . . . . . . . . . . . . . . . . . . .   93 3rd Eclogues 63  90
   Let one time (but long first) close up their daies,. . . . .   92 3rd Eclogues 63  31
   Muses graunt guiftes, Nymphes long and joyned life . . . . .   93 3rd Eclogues 63  92
   A neighbor mine not long agoe there was, . . . . . . . . . .   94 3rd Eclogues 64   1
   "Long have I love'd, (alas thou worthy arte) . . . . . . . .   97 3rd Eclogues 64  97
```

```
*LONG              (CONTINUED)                           PAGE    TITLE          LINE
    Long have I lov'd, (alas love craveth love). . . . . . . . .  97  3rd Eclogues  64   98
    Long have I lov'd thy selfe, alas my harte . . . . . . . . .  97  3rd Eclogues  64   99
    And geve a long desire a sweet content. . . . . . . . . . .   97  3rd Eclogues  64  106
    Geron. In faith, good Histor, long is your delay,. . . . . . 103  3rd Eclogues  67    1
    But certainly so long we may be glad,. . . . . . . . . . . . 105  3rd Eclogues  67   64
    Strephon. Long since alas, my deadly Swannish musique. . . . 112  4th Eclogues  71   25
    Long since my thoughts more desert be then forrests: . . . . 112  4th Eclogues  71   28
    Long since I see my joyes come to their evening, . . . . . . 112  4th Eclogues  71   29
    Klaius. Long since the happie dwellers of these vallies, . . 112  4th Eclogues  71   31
    Long since I hate the night, more hate the morning:. . . . . 112  4th Eclogues  71   34
    Long since my thoughts chase me like beasts in forrests, . . 112  4th Eclogues  71   35
    I long doo plowe with plough of deepe Desire:. . . . . . . . 115  4th Eclogues  72   52
    I know full well you know, what discord long hath raign'd. . 119  4th Eclogues  73  105
    Unto the caitife wretch, whom long affliction holdeth, . . . 122  4th Eclogues  74    1
    Farewell, long farewell, all my woe, all my delight. . . . . 124  4th Eclogues  74   86
    That they, which have no lives, should live so long, . . . . 126  4th Eclogues  75   41
    So that we can long time produce their time: . . . . . . . . 127  4th Eclogues  75   86
    We last short while, and build long lasting places:. . . . . 127  4th Eclogues  75   91
    Who long have gap't to get Arcadians' treasure.. . . . . . . 129  4th Eclogues  76   21
    Since loosing long, the faster still I bind:. . . . . . . . . 135  Cert Sonnets   1    5
    Long sham'd to be accurst in every place,. . . . . . . . . . 141  Cert Sonnets   8    3
    Long drowned hopes to watrie eyes it lends:. . . . . . . . . 150  Cert Sonnets  22   18
    My ship, desire, with winde of lust long tost, . . . . . . . 151  Cert Sonnets  22   55
    Too long, too long asleepe thou hast me brought, . . . . . . 161  Cert Sonnets  31    7
    You that poore Petrarch's long deceased woes,. . . . . . . . 172  Astrophil     15    7
    Bewray it selfe in my long setled eyes,. . . . . . . . . . . 176  Astrophil     23    2
    Sure, if that long with Love acquainted eyes . . . . . . . . 180  Astrophil     31    5
    Him as thy slave, and now long needy Fame. . . . . . . . . . 182  Astrophil     35   10
    Whereto long since, through my long battred eyes,. . . . . . 182  Astrophil     36    3
    And there long since, Love thy Lieutenant lies,. . . . . . . 183  Astrophil     36    5
    Long since forc'd by thy beames, but stone nor tree. . . . . 183  Astrophil     36   13
    Upon a wretch, that long thy grace hath sought;. . . . . . . 185  Astrophil     40    7
    So long (though he from booke myche to desire) . . . . . . . 188  Astrophil     46   13
    Who for long faith, the dayly helpe I crave, . . . . . . . . 188  Astrophil     47    7
    Far far too long to learne it without booke: . . . . . . . . 192  Astrophil     56    2
    Now I, wit-beaten long by hardest Fate,. . . . . . . . . . . 195  Astrophil     60    9
    Or doth the tedious burd'n of long wo. . . . . . . . . . . . 199  Astrophil     66    2
    But with short breath, long lookes, staid feet and walking
      hed, . . . . . . . . . . . . . . . . . . . . . . . . . . . 205  Astrophil     76   13
    Good brother Philip, I have borne you long,. . . . . . . . . 208  Astrophil     83    1
    Each day seemes long, and longs for long-staid night,. . . . 224  Astrophil     89    5
    Who long dead beautie with increase reneweth?. . . . . . . . 197  A&S 1st Song        22
    Long stay ere he graunt the same:. . . . . . . . . . . . . . 211  A&S 4th Song        33
    Long I will not after tary,. . . . . . . . . . . . . . . . . 226  A&S 10th Song       15
    Seing me so long to beare. . . . . . . . . . . . . . . . . . 222  A&S 9th Song        33
    Alas, how long, my God, wilt Thou delay me?. . . . . . . . . 276  Psalm VI            10
    And great with child of mischeif travaild long,. . . . . . . 278  Psalm VII           38
    How long, O lord, shall I forgotten be?. . . . . . . . . . . 285  Psalm XIII           1
    How long wilt Thou Thy hidden face from me . . . . . . . . . 285  Psalm XIII           3
    How long shall I consult with carefull sprite. . . . . . . . 285  Psalm XIII           5
    How long shall I with foes' triumphant might . . . . . . . . 285  Psalm XIII           7
    Thou him a long life gavest;. . . . . . . . . . . . . . . . . 297  Psalm XXI           14
    And long yea long abide I shall, . . . . . . . . . . . . . . 301  Psalm XXIII         25
    Shew me how long I have to live. . . . . . . . . . . . . . . 329  Psalm XXXIX         14
    While long I did with patient constancy. . . . . . . . . . . 330  Psalm XL             1
    Did me pearce, burne, and bynde, long since and late,. . . . 345  Possibly       2    12
    To long-perplexed minde breed long delight.. . . . . . . . . 245  Other Poems    4   112
    Strephon, whose absence seem'd unto thee long, . . . . . . . 247  Other Poems    4   220
    Till with long race deare she was breathles brought, . . . . 251  Other Poems    4   359
    The day seemes long, but night is odious . . . . . . . . . . 253  Other Poems    4   435
    So Mira long may be. . . . . . . . . . . . . . . . . . . . . 256  Other Poems    5    17
    Doth not thy selfe, when he long absent is,. . . . . . . . . 257  Other Poems    5    24
    So maist thou long abide . . . . . . . . . . . . . . . . . . 258  Other Poems    5    67
LONGER
    O well thou doost that thou no longer bidest;. . . . . . . . 126  4th Eclogues  75   53
    Faint coward joy no longer tarry dare, . . . . . . . . . . . 228  Astrophil     95    5
    O let their wickedness no longer bide. . . . . . . . . . . . 277  Psalm VII           25
    What? Doth their Memory no longer last?. . . . . . . . . . . 280  Psalm IX            18
LONGING
    Longing to be with losse of substance gay. . . . . . . . . .  93  3rd Eclogues  63   74
    Longing to have, having no wit to wish,. . . . . . . . . . . 136  Cert Sonnets   2   13
    Strength of liking, rage of longing. . . . . . . . . . . . . 226  A&S 10th Song       24
    In such longing thoughts it falleth. . . . . . . . . . . . . 334  Psalm XLII          24
LONG-PERPLEXED
    To long-perplexed minde breed long delight.. . . . . . . . . 245  Other Poems    4   112
LONGS
    Each day seemes long, and longs for long-staid night,. . . . 224  Astrophil     89    5
LONG-STAYED
    Each day seemes long, and longs for long-staid night,. . . . 224  Astrophil     89    5
LOOK
    Looke to thy selfe; reach not beyond humanitie:. . . . . . .  16  1st Eclogues   7   64
    That she, whose looke alone might make me blessed, . . . . .  17  1st Eclogues   7   83
    Where all my paines one looke of hers hath paid. . . . . . .  26  1st Eclogues   9  137
    For though Melampus like a wolfe doo looke,. . . . . . . . .  27  1st Eclogues  10   16
    Nico. Alas how oft I looke on cherries ripe, . . . . . . . .  54  2nd Eclogues  29   75
    Pas. As in a glasse I held she once did looke, . . . . . . .  55  2nd Eclogues  29  114
    Reason looke to thy selfe, I serve a goddesse. . . . . . . .  68  2nd Eclogues  33   30
    Looke further then, so shalt thou finde at least,. . . . . .  75  Arcadia III   44    9
    Ffayre, thorow fayre strykes of heedefull Looke. . . . . . .  88  Arcadia III   62 V 70
```

LOOK   (CONTINUED)   PAGE   TITLE   LINE
   Eagle, high looke; wolfe secrete crueltie: . . . .   101 3rd Eclogues 66   87
   She answer'd was with looke, and well performed behest: . . .   119 4th Eclogues 73   99
   Grant yet, grant yet a looke, to the last monument of his
       anguish, ...   122 4th Eclogues 74   3
   His life a law, his looke a full correction: . . . .   128 4th Eclogues 75 133
   O Faire, o sweet, when I do locke on thee, ...   139 Cert Sonnets 7   1
   Above line repeated at following locations . . . .   139 Cert Sonnets 7   11
   . . . .   140 Cert Sonnets 7   21
   . . . .   140 Cert Sonnets 7   31
   Whose eyes seeme chaste, because they looke on ground: . . .   147 Cert Sonnets 17   50
   And stately hilles disdaine to looke so low. . . . .   147 Cert Sonnets 18   8
   Looke then and dye, the pleasure . . . .   152 Cert Sonnets 23   17
   "Foole," said my Muse to me, "looke in thy heart and write."   165 Astrophil   1   14
   Looke at my hands for no such quintessence;. . . . .   179 Astrophil   28   11
   I start, looke, hearke, but what in closde up sence. . . . .   184 Astrophil   38   9
   O looke, o shine, o let me die and see. . . . .   188 Astrophil   48   8
   Looke here, I say." I look'd, and Stella spide,. . . . . . .   191 Astrophil   53   8
   What, a whole weeke without one peece of looke, ...   192 Astrophil   56   3
   Sc dull am, that I cannot looke into . . . .   195 Astrophil   60   10
   Looke on againe, the faire text better trie: . . . .   199 Astrophil   67   7
   O birds, o beasts, looke Love, lo, Stella shineth. . . . . .   209 A&S 3rd Song   12
   When I upon the Heav'ns do look. . . . .   278 Psalm VIII   9
   O with how simple look . . . .   282 Psalm X   41
   And yet their high hearts look so low. . . . .   290 Psalm XVII   31
   No sooner my child eyes could look abroad, ...   299 Psalm XXII   23
   They look, they gaze, my boanes might be rehearsed;. . . . .   299 Psalm XXII   42
   O look, O help, let mercy fall,. . . . .   304 Psalm XXV   59
   And look into. . . . .   307 Psalm XXVII   23
   Tc looke and run to him for aid, ...   319 Psalm XXXIV   18
   Look after him, he shall be vannisht . . . .   325 Psalm XXXVII   27
   With a look. . . . .   328 Psalm XXXVIII   17
   Look but on this: man still doth riches heape. . . . .   330 Psalm XXXIX   21
   Thirsting on my God to look. . . . .   334 Psalm XLII   4
   When but with one look of his. . . . .   334 Psalm XLII   21
   More prayse to us we never looke to winne, ...   346 Possibly   5   11
   With hear-say, pictures, or a window looke,. . . . .   245 Other Poems   4 139
   Her happy-making hand, of whome one looke. . . . .   248 Other Poems   4 247
   Tc make it selfe to my least looke a slave:. . . . .   255 Other Poems   4 511
   Mira may looke her face, ...   257 Other Poems   5   31
LOOKED
   Stella lookt on, and from her heavenly face. . . . .   185 Astrophil   41   13
   Looke here, I say." I look'd, and Stella spide,. . . . . . .   191 Astrophil   53   8
   Looking on me, while I lookt other way:. . . . .   199 Astrophil   66   12
   His who till death lookt in a watrie glasse, ...   207 Astrophil   82   3
   Still to his judgments lookt, still for his statutes car'd,.   292 Psalm XVIII   45
   They looked down to triumph over pride:. . . . .   252 Other Poems   4 403
   In river as I look'd my pining face, ...   254 Other Poems   4 475
LOOKER
   Into the faire looker on, pastime, not passion, enters.. . .   32 1st Eclogues 13   41
   Is cause the looker dyes.. . . . .   152 Cert Sonnets 23   8
LOOKERS
   The lookers now at me poore wretch be mocking, ...   299 Psalm XXII   17
   A-field they goe, where many lookers be, ...   247 Other Poems   4 217
LOOKING
   With hanches smooth as looking glasse. . . . .   88 Arcadia III 62   92
   He little looking that she should complaine. . . . .   95 3rd Eclogues 64   49
   Looking on me, while I lookt other way:. . . . .   199 Astrophil   66   12
LOOKS
   Thus to my sonne do I yeeld, such lookes her beames do
       aforde me. . . . .   36 1st Eclogues 13 133
   The jealous eye, the more it lookes, it loves. . . . .   42 Arcadia II   22   7
   She oft her lookes, the starres her favour bend to thee: . .   51 2nd Eclogues 28   99
   Her cleared lookes, nought els, in stormes can quiet me. . .   51 2nd Eclogues 28 119
   All churlish wordes, shrewd answeres, crabbed lookes,. . . .   93 3rd Eclogues 63   64
   With chumpish lookes, hard words, and secret nips, ...   95 3rd Eclogues 64   31
   With meager lookes, as if they still did smart;. . . . . . .   104 3rd Eclogues 67   28
   Thunders of cries; lightnings my wilde lookes be,. . . . . .   114 4th Eclogues 72   34
   Looks over the world, and can find nothing such, ...   169 Astrophil   9   10
   Lookes to the skies, and in a ditch doth fall? . . . .   174 Astrophil   19   11
   Which lookes too oft in his unflattring glasse:. . . . . . .   178 Astrophil   27   10
   I reade it in thy lookes, thy languisht grace, ...   180 Astrophil   31   7
   O eyes, where humble lookes most glorious prove, ...   185 Astrophil   42   5
   Then with those eyes he lookes, lo by and by , ...   186 Astrophil   43   6
   But with short breath, long lookes, staid feet and walking
       hed, ...   205 Astrophil   76   13
   Those lookes, whose beames be joy, whose motion is delight,.   205 Astrophil   77   1
   Alas, whence came this change of lookes? If I. . . . .   212 Astrophil   86   1
   As thy lookes sturre, runs up and downe to make. . . . . . .   232 Astrophil   101   10
   That with such poysonous care my lookes you marke, ...   233 Astrophil   104   2
   The lord looks from the sky, ...   317 Psalm XXXIII   49
   And lookes so neere unto my cure that I must needes be lost.   343 Possibly   1   22
   D. Her heavenly looks, which more and more do give me cause
       to crave. . . . .   344 Possibly   1   32
   With gazing looks, short sighs, unsettled feet,. . . . . . .   251 Other Poems   4 369
   On thoughts he feeds, his lookes their figure chaunge, . . .   253 Other Poems   4 434
LOOKST
   Stella, thou straight lookst babies in her eyes, ...   170 Astrophil   11   10
LOOSE
   With sleeves turnde up, loose haire, and brestes enlarged, .   16 1st Eclogues 7   74

281

		PAGE	TITLE		LINE
LOOSE	(CONTINUED)				
But still when thou dost sing, me thinkes a colt is loose..		52	2nd Eclogues	29	24
Her loose haire be the shott, the brestes the pykes be,...		67	2nd Eclogues	33	7
For no thing, time, nor place, can loose, quench, ease,...		84	Arcadia III	60	13
A loathing of all loose unchastitie,............		172	Astrophil	14	13
I see my course to loose my selfe doth bend:........		174	Astrophil	18 V	12
Cupid's yoke to loose or bind:..............		210	A&S 4th Song		14
Which to avoyde, quenche, loose noughte booted stryfe....		344	Possibly	2	8
LOOSED					
Whose loosed bones quite out of joint be wryde;......		299	Psalm XXII		32
LOOSELY					
He blessed is, who neither loosely treads.........		270	Psalm I		1
O madness of these folks, thus loosely led,........		286	Psalm XIV		13
LOOSEST					
Who hath the haire which, loosest, fastest tieth,.....		197	A&S 1st Song		25
LOOSING					
Since loosing long, the faster still I bind:.......		135	Cert Sonnets	1	5
LORD					
Thus Man was made; thus Man their Lord became:......		101	3rd Eclogues	66	106
Lord, what bywords they speake, what spite they spit?....		105	3rd Eclogues	67	48
Thou art my Lord, and I thy vowed slave..........		135	Cert Sonnets	1	14
Good Lord deliver us....................		160	Cert Sonnets	30	10
Above line repeated at following locations.........		160	Cert Sonnets	30	20
....		160	Cert Sonnets	30	30
....		161	Cert Sonnets	30	40
According to my Lord Love's owne behest:..........		189	Astrophil	50	6
Forst by their Lord, who is asham'd to find........		231	Astrophil	99	13
For thou doest lord my heart, who am not borne thy slave,..		214	A&S 5th Song		58
You Rebell run away, to Lord and Lady untrue,.......		215	A&S 5th Song		86
Against the lord of lords, the lord of every thing,.....		271	Psalm II		5
Lord how do they encrease.................		272	Psalm III		1
Yet lord thou art my shield,...............		272	Psalm III		11
The lord lifts up my head,...............		272	Psalm III		13
Up lord now time it is:..................		272	Psalm III		23
Unto the lord most strong:...............		273	Psalm III		32
Trust in that lord, that cannot ly,...........		274	Psalm IV		23
But, lord, lift Thou upon our sight...........		274	Psalm IV		26
For it is thou lord, Thou it is,.............		274	Psalm IV		33
Ponder the words, O lord, that I do say,.........		274	Psalm V		1
For Thou the lord in endless hatred hast.........		275	Psalm V		15
Thou lord, Thou lord, the saver of Thyne Owne.......		275	Psalm V		21
Lord, let not me a worme by thee be shent,........		276	Psalm VI		1
But mercy, lord, let Mercy thyne descend.........		276	Psalm VI		5
Lord help, for ev'en my bones their marrow spend.....		276	Psalm VI		7
Turne Thee, sweet lord, and from this Ougly fall.....		276	Psalm VI		11
Mercy, O Mercy lord, for Mercy's sake,..........		276	Psalm VI		13
The lord my suite did heare, and gently heare,......		276	Psalm VI		29
O Lord my God, Thou art my trustfull stay........		277	Psalm VII		1
O lord, my God, if I did not forbeare..........		277	Psalm VII		7
Arise, O lord, in wrath thy self upsett.........		277	Psalm VII		16
Therfore, O lord, lift up Thy throne on high.......		277	Psalm VII		20
Thou, lord, the people shalt in judgment try:......		277	Psalm VII		22
Then lord, my lord, give sentence on my side.......		277	Psalm VII		23
I will give thanks unto the lord of Us.........		278	Psalm VII		46
O lord that rul'st Our mortall lyne............		278	Psalm VIII		1
Above line repeated at following location.........		279	Psalm VIII		33
With all my heart O lord I will prayse Thee,.......		279	Psalm IX		1
O Lord most high....................		279	Psalm IX		5
Thou lord also th' Oppressed wilt defend.........		280	Psalm IX		26
For Thou lord found by them wilt ever be.........		280	Psalm IX		29
O prayse the lord, this Syon dweller good,........		280	Psalm IX		31
Have mercie, mercie lord I once did say,.........		280	Psalm IX		36
Thou lord that from Death' gates hast lifted me,.....		280	Psalm IX		39
For then the lord in judgment shewes to raigne.....		281	Psalm IX		51
Up lord, and judg the Gentyls in Thy right........		281	Psalm IX		61
With terrors great, O Lord, do thou them fright:.....		281	Psalm IX		63
O lord Our only God,..................		282	Psalm X		50
So lord we shall Thy Title sing.............		283	Psalm X		69
Of earthly man, a lord of dust..............		283	Psalm X		80
The lord doth search the just man's reines,.......		284	Psalm XI		17
Lord help, it is high time for me to call,........		284	Psalm XII		1
But Thou (O lord) give them a thorough fall,.......		284	Psalm XII		7
For what lord rules our bold emboldned breast.......		285	Psalm XII		12
Then Thou (O lord) shalt keep the Good stil sure.....		285	Psalm XII		22
How long, O lord, shall I forgotten be?.........		285	Psalm XIII		1
Behold me, lord, let to Thy hearing creep.........		285	Psalm XIII		9
In Tabernacle Thyne, O lord, who shall remayne?.....		287	Psalm XV		1
Lord, of Thy Holy Hill who shall the rest obtayne?....		287	Psalm XV		2
Save me lord, for why Thou art.............		287	Psalm XVI		1
Thou my lord, Thou art my stay,.............		287	Psalm XVI		5
Ever, lord, I will blesse Thee,.............		288	Psalm XVI		19
My suite is just, just lord to my suite hark;......		289	Psalm XVII		1
I plain sweet Lord, my plaint for pitty mark;......		289	Psalm XVII		2
Shew then O Lord Thy wondrous kindness show,.......		290	Psalm XVII		21
Up lord prevent those gaping jawes...........		290	Psalm XVII		35
Thee will I love, O Lord, with all my heart's delight...		290	Psalm XVIII		1
With blasting breath O Lord, that in thy chiding went..		291	Psalm XVIII		33
My justice, my just hands thus did the lord reward,....		292	Psalm XVIII		43
Among the Gentiles then I, Lord, yeild thanks to Thee,...		293	Psalm XVIII		88
O lord cleanse me from faults that be...........		295	Psalm XIX		51

282

LORD	(CONTINUED)	PAGE	TITLE	LINE
My saving might, lord in Thy sight, ...		295	Psalm XIX	63
Let God the lord heare Thee, ...		295	Psalm XX	1
Who is our Lord, with due remembrance wayte.		296	Psalm XX	30
Lord from Thy strength is growing;		296	Psalm XXI	2
Lord what delight to him doth bring.		296	Psalm XXI	3
The Lord on them with causfull Ire		297	Psalm XXI	33
Lord in Thy strength, lord in Thy might, ...		298	Psalm XXI	49
But be not farr O Lord, my strength, my comfort;		299	Psalm XXII	45
Who feare the lord all prayse and glory beare him;		300	Psalm XXII	53
But when he calld this lord did give him hearing..		300	Psalm XXII	58
The lord the lord my shepheard is, ...		301	Psalm XXIII	1
For thou Deare lord Thou me besetst, ...		301	Psalm XXIII	13
There where the Lord of all.		301	Psalm XXIII	26
A blessing from the lord, from God of his salvation.		302	Psalm XXIV	13
The lord whose strength makes battails fight.		302	Psalm XXIV	20
Who is This Glorious King? The lord of armyes guiding, . . .		302	Psalm XXIV	23
To thee, O Lord most just, ...		302	Psalm XXV	1
Yea Lord to me Thy wayes do show;		303	Psalm XXV	11
But Lord remember not.		303	Psalm XXV	25
Ev'n for Thy mercy's sake, O Lord.		303	Psalm XXV	30
The lord such plenty hath, ...		303	Psalm XXV	32
O Lord for Thy name's sake		304	Psalm XXV	43
But still on this Lord set?.		304	Psalm XXV	56
Now made, O Lord maintain, ...		304	Psalm XXV	68
For Thou the Lord, Thou only art, ...		304	Psalm XXV	71
O Lord from all his troubles fell.		305	Psalm XXV	78
Lord judg me, and my case, ...		305	Psalm XXVI	1
Prove me O Lord most high, ...		305	Psalm XXVI	7
Lord I have loved well		306	Psalm XXVI	25
Sweet lord, write not my soul.		306	Psalm XXVI	28
Then me redeem Lord then be mercifull.		306	Psalm XXVI	36
The shining Lord he is my light, ...		306	Psalm XXVII	1
This lord with strength my life doth blisse;		306	Psalm XXVII	4
To prayse the lord..		307	Psalm XXVII	36
Heare lord when I my voice display, ...		307	Psalm XXVII	37
O Lord I will.		308	Psalm XXVII	41
Teach lord, lord lead me Thy right way, ...		308	Psalm XXVII	52
To thee Lord my cry I send..		308	Psalm XXVIII	1
Tc the Lord that heares my cry..		309	Psalm XXVIII	25
Lord then still Thy people save, ...		309	Psalm XXVIII	33
Ascribe unto the lord of light, ...		309	Psalm XXIX	1
The Voice of that lord ruling us		310	Psalm XXIX	10
O lord Thou hast exalted me.		310	Psalm XXX	1
Prayse, Prayse this lord then evermore		311	Psalm XXX	10
Lord heare, let mercy thine be stay'd.		311	Psalm XXX	31
All, all my trust lord I have put in Thee, ...		312	Psalm XXXI	1
O lord that art the God of verity.		312	Psalm XXXI	15
O Lord, of Thee let me still mercy winn, ...		312	Psalm XXXI	25
But I did trust in Thee, lord, I did say		313	Psalm XXXI	40
Let me not tast of shame, O lord most high, ...		313	Psalm XXXI	45
Then prayse, then prayse I do the lord of us, ...		313	Psalm XXXI	58
For this Our lord preserves the faith full race.		314	Psalm XXXI	65
The lord with pardon doth make cleane, ...		314	Psalm XXXII	2
Blessed in deed to whom the lord		314	Psalm XXXII	4
O prayse with harp the lord, ...		316	Psalm XXXIII	7
Who him for their lord take;		317	Psalm XXXIII	45
Whom this lord chose, ...		317	Psalm XXXIII	47
The lord looks from the sky, ...		317	Psalm XXXIII	49
Then on that lord most kind.		318	Psalm XXXIII	76
In that deare lord with true delight, ...		318	Psalm XXXIV	6
This lord and he did heare my cry, ...		319	Psalm XXXIV	14
Lord he is in thrice blessed case.		319	Psalm XXXIV	31
How this Our lord to feare..		320	Psalm XXXIV	44
This lord is ever ever neare, ...		320	Psalm XXXIV	66
Thy force O Lord against their force oppose, ...		321	Psalm XXXV	2
Lord wilt thou see, and wilt Thou suffer it?		322	Psalm XXXV	43
O lord, do not absent Thy self from me!		322	Psalm XXXV	56
My lord my God ev'en to my equity.		322	Psalm XXXV	58
Judg lord, judg God, ev'en in Thy justice great, ...		322	Psalm XXXV	59
Let them not, Lord, within their hearts thus say:		323	Psalm XXXV	61
Lord, how the heav'ns thy mercy fills, ...		323	Psalm XXXVI	13
O Lord how excellent a thing		324	Psalm XXXVI	19
Wait on the lord with patient hope, ...		325	Psalm XXXVII	17
Lord while that thy rage doth bide, ...		327	Psalm XXXVIII	1
Lord before Thee I do lay.		328	Psalm XXXVIII	25
For on Thee, lord, without end		328	Psalm XXXVIII	43
Dc not, Lord, then me forsake, ...		329	Psalm XXXVIII	61
Hast O Lord, that I be stayd		329	Psalm XXXVIII	64
Lord unto me my time's just measure give, ...		329	Psalm XXXIX	13
This being thus, For what O Lord wait I?		330	Psalm XXXIX	23
Heare lord my suits and cryes, stop not thyn eares		330	Psalm XXXIX	37
To feare with trust, and trust with feare the Lord..		331	Psalm XL	14
Thus bound I said, lo, lord I am at hand, ...		331	Psalm XL	31
Yea lord Thy law within my heart doth stand;		331	Psalm XL	34
Then lord from me draw not Thy tender grace, ...		332	Psalm XL	41
Vouchsafe me help O Lord, and help with hast;		332	Psalm XL	51
The Lord will keep his life yet safe and sound		333	Psalm XLI	5
Have mercy lord on me, ...		333	Psalm XLI	14
Therfore, O Lord, abandond thus of all, ...		333	Psalm XLI	33

		PAGE	TITLE		LINE
LORD	(CONTINUED)				
I will say: O lord my tower, ...		335	Psalm XLII		41
W. Who bound thee? D. Love my Lord. W. What witnesses					
therto		343	Possibly	1	25
Of village-Lord that whitsontide to beare:		244	Other Poems	4	76
LORDINGS					
Listen then Lordings with good eare to me, ...		183	Astrophil	37	3
LORD'S					
Sore signe it is, the Lord's last thred is spun.		150	Cert Sonnets	22	14
And I will (sayeth His King) the lord's decree display,. . .		271	Psalm II		15
LORDS					
Like some weake Lords, neighbord by mighty kings,.		179	Astrophil	29	1
Ncr do like Lords, whose weake confused braine,.		210	Astrophil	85	5
Why do these earthly kings and lords such meetings make, . .		271	Psalm II		3
Against the lord of lords, the lord of every thing,.		271	Psalm II		5
So Lords with sport of Stagg and Hearon full		245	Other Poems	4	135
LORDSHIP					
As if he meant his lordship common be.		102	3rd Eclogues	66	112
LOSE					
Though cradle witted, must not honnor loose.		25	1st Eclogues	9	92
That her I see, though you did lose your light..		38	Arcadia II	14	4
Moste lothe to loose, the moste approching hope.		71	Arcadia III	37	6
Since then my harte did loose his wonted place,.		115	4th Eclogues	72	77
As for to lose thy gemme, our earthly Sainct,.		125	4th Eclogues	75	18
And vertuous soules so soone should lose their place?. . . .		126	4th Eclogues	75	42
Till wounded, blind, and wearied Spirites, lose.		144	Cert Sonnets	15	11
I see my course to lose my selfe doth bend:.		174	Astrophil	18	12
Then that I lose no more for Stella's sake..		174	Astrophil	18	14
To lose his Crowne, rather then faile his Love..		204	Astrophil	75	14
LOSERS					
And knowne those pangs that the losers prove,.		153	Cert Sonnets	24	2
LOSS					
So becomes our losse the triumph of her gayne;		30	1st Eclogues	12	11
What meane is there, alas, we can hope our losse to recover?		32	1st Eclogues	13	27
You beare no woll, and losse is all my gayne..		44	Arcadia II	24	14
With losse of purest blood themselves to teare,.		58	2nd Eclogues	30	46
What glorie from our losse can he receave?		59	2nd Eclogues	30	73
Of lothsome dayes, whose losse how canst thou mone,.		59	2nd Eclogues	30	78
Make great the losse, so grete the feare to misse.		71	Arcadia III	37	12
As Prince's losse or change:		81	Arcadia III	55	3
Longing to be with losse of substance gay.		93	3rd Eclogues	63	74
Now Prince's losse hath made our damage publique,.		109	Arcadia IV	70	4
By thy impe's losse to fill the world with wailing..		109	Arcadia IV	70	22
Publique our losse: so, see, thy shame is publique..		109	Arcadia IV	70	24
Thus, thus alas, I had my losse in chase..		115	4th Eclogues	72	70
Klaius. Thus, thus alas, I had my losse in chase,.		115	4th Eclogues	72	71
Shall such high Plannets tend to the losse of a worme? . . .		123	4th Eclogues	74	38
Of Prince's losse your selves for tokens reare..		125	4th Eclogues	75	27
And by thy pompe our losse will be conceaved..		127	4th Eclogues	75	75
Since this we feele, greate losse we cannot finde.		131	Arcadia V	77	14
Small losse of mortall treasure, ...		152	Cert Sonnets	23	19
My harmes on Ink's poore losse, perhaps some find.		182	Astrophil	34	13
Cowards Love with losse rewardeth.		202	A&S 2nd Song		16
Whcm to their losse he still doth get.		282	Psalm X		39
Although some Worldly losse therby he may sustaine,.		287	Psalm XV		10
LOSSES					
While I do score my losses on the winde, ...		255	Other Poems	4	498
LOST					
By princely meane be stolne, and yet not lost.		11	Arcadia I	1	2
False in my selfe, thus have I lost the field.		11	Arcadia I	2	8
If the mute timber when it hath the life lost, ...		30	1st Eclogues	12	15
Selfe-lost and wandring, banished that place we doe come					
from, ...		32	1st Eclogues	13	26
Reason, I vaine (now you have lost my hart).		38	Arcadia II	14	9
We mone that lost, which had we did bemone.		59	2nd Eclogues	30	82
Each moment lost, part of my hap destroyes:.		80	Arcadia III	53	11
Of Prince's harte quite lost the ruine strange..		81	Arcadia III	55	6
For lost, lost is by blowe of cruell fortune		109	Arcadia IV	70	17
They first their use forgot, then fancies lost their force;.		117	4th Eclogues	73	29
Should my too-much sight cause so true a Sunne to be lost? .		124	4th Eclogues	74	58
Now that the mine is lost of all our treasure, ...		129	4th Eclogues	76	10
Thinke Hanniball did laugh when Carthage lost.		147	Cert Sonnets	17	45
A bird which gets more life then ship had lost..		151	Cert Sonnets	22	54
Now even that footstep of lost libertie.		166	Astrophil	2	9
How Holland hearts, now so good townes be lost,.		180	Astrophil	30	7
Let me no steps but of lost labour trace,.		198	Astrophil	64	6
I thought all words were lost, that were not spent of thee:.		212	A&S 5th Song		4
But now that hope is lost, unkindnesse kils delight, ...		212	A&S 5th Song		13
Thy wallet or thy Tarbox lost, or thy new rayment rent?. . .		343	Possibly	1	16
And lookes so neere unto my cure that I must needes be lost.		343	Possibly	1	22
Burnt Caban, lost my cloke,.		259	Other Poems	5	101
*LOT					
Till this he tooke for comfort of his lot:		5	Lady of May	3	10
Lalus. Kala at length conclude my lingring lotte:.		18	1st Eclogues	7	115
A Cage (guilded perchaunce) is all his lott.		28	1st Eclogues	10	69
I waile their lotte, but will not other prove.		39	Arcadia II	17	4
Or els; "Nay faith, mine is the lucklest lot,.		104	3rd Eclogues	67	43
Who may this doubt discerne: for better, witt, then lot. . .		120	4th Eclogues	73	139
And as you like my double lot, ...		153	Cert Sonnets	24	17
Yet with repining at so partiall lot..		165	Astrophil	2	8

```
*LOT                     (CONTINUED)              PAGE    TITLE         LINE
  But that rich foole, who by blind Fortune's lot. . . . . . .   177  Astrophil   24     9
  And that you know, I envy you no lot . . . . . . . . . . . .   209  Astrophil   84    12
  He then shall maintayn my lott.. . . . . . . . . . . . . .   288  Psalm XVI          15
  Say then, Is not my lot found. . . . . . . . . . . . . . . .   288  Psalm XVI          16
  The poore-clad truth of love's wrong-ordred lot. . . . . . .   242  Other Poems  4    14
  Faire Nous with Pas the lott to hell did sende: . . . . . .   248  Other Poems  4   244
LOTCHES
  Men tongd like lotches sucking others sorrowe. . . . . . . .    50  2nd Eclogues 28  V885
LOTS
  And do cast lots, who should my vesture take.. . . . . . . .   299  Psalm XXII         44
LOUD
  Then spake he his lowd voyce, then hailestones coales and
      fire.. . . . . . . . . . . . . . . . . . . . . . . . . .   291  Psalm XVIII        28
  Sing lowd and merrily,. . . . . . . . . . . . . . . . . . .   316  Psalm XXXIII       15
  Yet there, me seemes, I heare her singing loud.. . . . . . .   255  Other Poems  4   508
LOUDEST
  Thus in thy selfe, least strings are loudest founde, . . . .    81  Arcadia III  54    15
LOUTS
  And from lowts to run away.. . . . . . . . . . . . . . . . .   235  A&S 11th Song      45
LOVE
  Judge you of Love, to whom all Love is bent. . . . . . . . .     4  Lady of May   2    32
  (Espilus) Silvanus long in love, and long in vaine,. . . . .     4  Lady of May   3     1
  An uncouth love, which Nature hateth most. . . . . . . . . .    11  Arcadia I     1     4
  We love, and have our loves rewarded.. . . . . . . . . . . .    14  1st Eclogues  6     1
  We love, and are no whit regarded. . . . . . . . . . . . . .    14  1st Eclogues  6     2
  No musike kindly without love. . . . . . . . . . . . . . . .    14  1st Eclogues  6     8
  No stile is held for base, where Love well named is: . . . .    14  1st Eclogues  7     4
  Ech eare suckes up the words a true love scattereth, . . . .    14  1st Eclogues  7     5
  Nor true love loves those loves with others mingled be.. . .    14  1st Eclogues  7    12
  But if thou hast a Love, in that Love's passion, . . . . . .    15  1st Eclogues  7    16
  When first he spied my love? how oft he said to me,. . . . .    16  1st Eclogues  7    50
  Love well thine owne: me thinkes, woolle's whitenes passeth
      all: . . . . . . . . . . . . . . . . . . . . . . . . . .    16  1st Eclogues  7    53
  I never found long love such wealth hath paide to me". . . .    16  1st Eclogues  7    54
  Dorus. How oft, when reason saw love of her harnished. . . .    16  1st Eclogues  7    61
  And Love, which lover hurts is inhumanitie". . . . . . . . .    16  1st Eclogues  7    66
  That without love she spends her yeares of love: . . . . . .    17  1st Eclogues  7    98
  Then Love allowes, our pleasures to enrich,. . . . . . . . .    18  1st Eclogues  7   129
  Such force hath Love above poore Nature's power. . . . . . .    19  1st Eclogues  7   161
  Dorus. Such force hath Love above poore Nature's power,. . .    19  1st Eclogues  7   162
  But for that Love is worst, which rules the eyes,. . . . . .    22  1st Eclogues  8  V 41
  (At Juno's suite who much did Argus love). . . . . . . . . .    22  1st Eclogues  8    46
  This tyran Love; or rather do suppresse. . . . . . . . . . .    23  1st Eclogues  9    45
  In painted clothes, because they call it love. . . . . . . .    23  1st Eclogues  9    48
  Old men themselves, doe love young wives to choose:. . . . .    25  1st Eclogues  9    88
  How thou from foolish love maist purge thy sense.. . . . . .    25  1st Eclogues  9   110
  I set you ore the flock I dearly love, . . . . . . . . . . .    26  1st Eclogues 10     2
  For what they see their parents love or hate . . . . . . . .    28  1st Eclogues 10    56
  Fortune, Nature, Love, long have contended about me, . . . .    29  1st Eclogues 11     1
  Love smiled, and thus said; "Want joynd to desire is
      unhappy . . . . . . . . . . . . . . . . . . . . . . . .    30  1st Eclogues 11    11
  "And ev'n in that love, shall I reserve him a spite".. . . .    30  1st Eclogues 11    18
  But most wretched I am, now love awakes my desire. . . . . .    30  1st Eclogues 11    20
  Which is helde in love, love it is, that hath joynde . . . .    31  1st Eclogues 12    23
  Here you fully do finde this strange operation of love,. . .    31  1st Eclogues 13     3
  How to the woods love runnes as well as rydes to the
      Pallace . . . . . . . . . . . . . . . . . . . . . . . .    31  1st Eclogues 13     4
  How much more we do love, so the lesse our loves be
      beleeved . . . . . . . . . . . . . . . . . . . . . . . .    32  1st Eclogues 13    20
  Or when an Echo begins unmov'd to sing them a love song. . .    33  1st Eclogues 13    48
  (Since no estates be so base, but love vouchsafeth his
      arrow . . . . . . . . . . . . . . . . . . . . . . . . .    33  1st Eclogues 13    50
  That in my selfe your selfe true love doth plant;. . . . . .    39  Arcadia II   16     8
  Their pasture is faire hilles of fruitlesse Love:. . . . . .    39  Arcadia II   17     2
  Loved I am, and yet complaine of Love: . . . . . . . . . . .    41  Arcadia II   20     1
  As loving not, accus'd, in Love I die. . . . . . . . . . . .    41  Arcadia II   20     2
  Still seeking Love, love found as much I flie. . . . . . . .    41  Arcadia II   20     4
  Yet thus much Love, O Love, I crave of thee: . . . . . . . .    41  Arcadia II   20    13
  The one of Love, the other Jealousie,. . . . . . . . . . . .    42  Arcadia II   22     2
  Love wakes the jealous eye least thence it moves:. . . . . .    42  Arcadia II   22     6
  For who doth holde his love in estimation, . . . . . . . . .    47  2nd Eclogues 28     4
  Who glories in his love, doth make Love glorious:. . . . . .    47  2nd Eclogues 28    16
  If Love tooke thee by force, or caught thee guilefully.. . .    48  2nd Eclogues 28    21
  Quite from my selfe to love Love's contemplation;. . . . . .    48  2nd Eclogues 28    32
  So she thy love, her eyes thy eyes may gratifie. . . . . . .    49  2nd Eclogues 28    51
  Her love my life; her anger my Instruction;. . . . . . . . .    49  2nd Eclogues 28    71
  So love encroches on your charmed reason,. . . . . . . . . .    50  2nd Eclogues 28    93
  Fortune store, Nature health, Love grant perswasion. . . . .    51  2nd Eclogues 28   100
  Thus I commend to thee all our former love.. . . . . . . . .    51  2nd Eclogues 28   102
  Thou mayest love her that I may see thy sightfulnesse. . . .    51  2nd Eclogues 28   113
  Without her love, then any mind who fairer is. . . . . . . .    51  2nd Eclogues 28   116
  Nico. Mine was the scrippe: but thou, that seeming raged
      with love,. . . . . . . . . . . . . . . . . . . . . . .    52  2nd Eclogues 29     9
  Pas. Who evermore will love Apollo's quill,. . . . . . . . .    53  2nd Eclogues 29    54
  Or while that shepheards love a lovely face. . . . . . . . .    56  2nd Eclogues 29   125
  As farre as Love possesseth any head.. . . . . . . . . . . .    56  2nd Eclogues 29   128
  Though in despaire, for love so forcethe me; . . . . . . . .    58  2nd Eclogues 30    57
  Of our selfe-love (so passions do deceave) . . . . . . . . .    59  2nd Eclogues 30    69
  Hath she not force even death with love to kill? . . . . . .    59  2nd Eclogues 30    85
```

```
LOVE                     (CONTINUED)                    PAGE   TITLE          LINE
    O soule, whose love in her is onely spent, . . . . . . . . .  60  2nd Eclogues 30  122
    What ere you see, thinke, touch, kisse, speake, or love, . .  60  2nd Eclogues 30  123
    Oh! what is it? what is it that may be a salve to my Love?
        Love. .  . . . . . . . . . . . . . . . . . . . . . . . .  63  2nd Eclogues 31   12
    Then to an earnest Love what doth best victorie lend? Ende..  63  2nd Eclogues 31   15
    End? but I can never end, love will not give me the leave.
        Leave. . . . . . . . . . . . . . . . . . . . . . . . . .  63  2nd Eclogues 31   16
    Or if to love thou art bent, . . . . . . . . . . . . . . . .  66  2nd Eclogues 32   25
    The life we leade is all love, . . . . . . . . . . . . . . .  67  2nd Eclogues 32   52
    The love we holde is all death, . . . . . . . . . . . . . .   67  2nd Eclogues 32   53
    Thus toyled in my work of raging love, . . . . . . . . . . .  71  Arcadia III  37   14
    Synce love with care, and hope with feare do fight.. . . . .  72  Arcadia III  37   18
    Thy beames I like, but her cleare rayes I love:. . . . . . .  72  Arcadia III  38    9
    My true love hath my hart, and I have his, . . . . . . . . .  75  Arcadia III  45    1
    Above line repeated at following location. . . . . . . . . .  76  Arcadia III  45   14
    (Her sight where love did forge his fayrest darte) . . . . .  79  Arcadia III  51    6
    Thinges rightelie prizde, love is the bande of love. . . . .  83  Arcadia III  57   14
    My harte, eyes, eares, with wonder, love, delight: . . . . .  84  Arcadia III  60    2
    The love which is imprinted in my soule. . . . . . . . . . .  85  Arcadia III  61    1
    Thus thus the more I love, the wronge the more . . . . . . .  85  Arcadia III  61    5
    Where love draws hate, and hate engendreth love? . . . . . .  85  Arcadia III  61   14
    The knottes of joy, the gemmes of love, . . . . . . . . . . . 89  Arcadia III  62   95
    Of my first love the fatall band.. . . . . . . . . . . . . .  90  Arcadia III  62  122
    Where justest love doth vanquish Cupid's powers. . . . . . .  91  3rd Eclogues 63    3
    To this chaste love your sacred favours bow, . . . . . . . .  91  3rd Eclogues 63   21
    Of yonglings, which thy selfe with love hast rearde, . . . .  92  3rd Eclogues 63   43
    Where simple love, which chastnesse doth imparte,. . . . . .  92  3rd Eclogues 63   58
    (How can he love suspecting treacherie?. . . . . . . . . . .  93  3rd Eclogues 63   84
    How can she love where love cannot win trust?) . . . . . . .  93  3rd Eclogues 63   85
    She sigh'd and sayd, the bad guest sought her love.. . . . .  95  3rd Eclogues 64   48
    And tell him that you finde I doo him love,. . . . . . . . .  95  3rd Eclogues 64   56
    It title had, unto my only love, . . . . . . . . . . . . . .  96  3rd Eclogues 64   89
    Long have I lov'd, (alas love craveth love). . . . . . . . .  97  3rd Eclogues 64   98
    To sheepe, whom love, not knowledge, made to heare,. . . . . 103  3rd Eclogues 66  156
    In lawlesse games, and love not as you should, . . . . . . . 106  3rd Eclogues 67   95
    Strephon. Yee Gote-heard Gods, that love the grassie
        mountaines,. . . . . . . . . . . . . . . . . . . . . . . 111  4th Eclogues 71    1
    My ship, my selfe, whose course to love doth bende,. . . . . 114  4th Eclogues 72   44
    The bande of beauties all, the little world of Love. . . . . 119  4th Eclogues 73   90
    Diana deare; my minde to love and not to hate. . . . . . . . 120  4th Eclogues 73  148
    Gratefulnes, sweetnes, holy love, hartie regard) . . . . . . 122  4th Eclogues 74   10
    Now that he finds to wnat end his life and love be reserved, 123  4th Eclogues 74   29
    Shall to the world appeare that faith and love be rewarded . 123  4th Eclogues 74   35
    All my'offence was Love: with Love then must I be chastned,. 123  4th Eclogues 74   41
    If that love be a fault, more fault in you to be lovely: . . 123  4th Eclogues 74   43
    Love never had me opprest, but that I saw to be lov'd. . . . 123  4th Eclogues 74   44
    You be the cause that I love: what Reason blameth a shadowe, 123  4th Eclogues 74   45
    If the Love hate you dyd, you should your beautie have
        hidden:. . . . . . . . . . . . . . . . . . . . . . . . . 123  4th Eclogues 74   47
    You should have your face (since Love is ill) blemished. . . 123  4th Eclogues 74   56
    O not but such love you say you could have afoorded, . . . . 124  4th Eclogues 74   63
    O sweet simplicitie: from whence should Love be so learned?. 124  4th Eclogues 74   65
    I yeeld, o Love, unto thy loathed yoke,. . . . . . . . . . . 135  Cert Sonnets  1    9
    When Love puft up with rage of hy disdaine,. . . . . . . . . 135  Cert Sonnets  2    1
    But Thereus' love, on her by strong hand wrokne, . . . . . . 137  Cert Sonnets  4   14
    The Babe cries "way, thy love doth keepe me waking". . . . . 139  Cert Sonnets  6    3
    The babe cries "way, thy love doth keepe me waking". . . . . 139  Cert Sonnets  6    6
    Her milken breasts the nurse of child-like love, . . . . . . 141  Cert Sonnets  9    7
    These be her words, but a woman's words to a love that is
        eager, . . . . . . . . . . . . . . . . . . . . . . . . . 143  Cert Sonnets 13    3
    My mistresse lowers and saith I do not love: . . . . . . . . 145  Cert Sonnets 17    1
    If from my soule this love would once depart, . . . . . . .  148  Cert Sonnets 19    9
    Or for my love some love I might obtaine,. . . . . . . . . . 148  Cert Sonnets 19   10
    I loving still a love that loveth none,. . . . . . . . . . . 148  Cert Sonnets 19   16
    Finding those beames, which I must ever love,. . . . . . . . 149  Cert Sonnets 21    1
    But of his death flies up a purest love, . . . . . . . . . . 151  Cert Sonnets 22   59
    On whome all love, in whom no love is plaste,. . . . . . . . 151  Cert Sonnets 22   63
    In love, his chiefest part.. . . . . . . . . . . . . . . . . 152  Cert Sonnets 23   12
    Who hath ever felt the change of love, . . . . . . . . . . . 153  Cert Sonnets 24    1
    Lady the life of all love; . . . . . . . . . . . . . . . . . 154  Cert Sonnets 25   20
    The lesse I love, I live the lesse.. . . . . . . . . . . . . 157  Cert Sonnets 27   40
    Or where one's love so constant bene,. . . . . . . . . . . . 158  Cert Sonnets 28   27
    For love is dead:. . . . . . . . . . . . . . . . . . . . . . 159  Cert Sonnets 30    2
    All Love is dead, infected . . . . . . . . . . . . . . . . . 159  Cert Sonnets 30    3
    That Love is dead? . . . . . . . . . . . . . . . . . . . . . 160  Cert Sonnets 30   12
    For love is dead:. . . . . . . . . . . . . . . . . . . . . . 160  Cert Sonnets 30   22
    Love is not dead.. . . . . . . . . . . . . . . . . . . . . . 160  Cert Sonnets 30   32
    Love is not dead, but sleepeth . . . . . . . . . . . . . . . 160  Cert Sonnets 30   33
    Who love can temper thus,. . . . . . . . . . . . . . . . . . 161  Cert Sonnets 30   39
    Leave me o Love, which reachest but to dust, . . . . . . . . 161  Cert Sonnets 32    1
    Eternall Love maintaine thy life in me.. . . . . . . . . . . 144  Cert Sonnets 32   14
    Loving in truth, and faine in verse my love to show, . . . . 165  Astrophil     1    1
    Love gave the wound, which while I breathe will bleed: . . . 165  Astrophil     2    2
    I loved, but straight did not what Love decreed: . . . . . . 165  Astrophil     2    6
    What Love and Beautie be, then all my deed . . . . . . . . . 166  Astrophil     3   13
    If vaine love have my simple soule opprest,. . . . . . . . . 166  Astrophil     4    3
    That Vertue, thou thy selfe shalt be in love.. . . . . . . . 167  Astrophil     4   14
    True, and yet true that I must Stella love.. . . . . . . . . 167  Astrophil     5   14
    When trembling voice brings forth that I do Stella love. . . 168  Astrophil     6   14
```

286

LOVE	(CONTINUED)	PAGE	TITLE		LINE
Both so and thus, she minding Love should be		168	Astrophil	7	12
Love borne in Greece, of late fled from his native place,. . .		168	Astrophil	8	1
Wouldst brabling be with sence and love in me:		169	Astrophil	10	2
Deale thou with powers of thoughts, leave love to will.. . . .		169	Astrophil	10	8
But thou wouldst needs fight both with love and sence, . . .		170	Astrophil	10	9
By reason good, good reason her to love.		170	Astrophil	10	14
In truth, o Love, with what a boyish kind.		170	Astrophil	11	1
Phoebus was Judge betweene Jove, Mars, and Love, ...		171	Astrophil	13	1
While Love on me doth all his quiver spend,.		171	Astrophil	14	4
Then Love is sinne, and let me sinfull be.		172	Astrophil	14	14
But if (both for your love and skill) your name.		172	Astrophil	15	12
And, Love, I thought that I was full of thee:.		172	Astrophil	16	4
By my love judging what Love's paine might be.		173	Astrophil	16	8
I now have learn'd Love right, and learn'd even so,.		173	Astrophil	16	13
Because that Mars, growne slacker in her love, ...		173	Astrophil	17	2
"Scholler," saith Love, "bend hitherward your wit.".		174	Astrophil	19	14
My young mind marde, whom Love doth windlas so,.		175	Astrophil	21	2
And knowing, love, and loving, lay apart		177	Astrophil	24	7
The richest gemme of Love and life enjoyes,.		177	Astrophil	24	10
Strange flames of Love it in our soules would raise;		177	Astrophil	25	4
Love of her selfe, takes Stella's shape, that she.		177	Astrophil	25	10
And find th'effect, for I do burne in love..		177	Astrophil	25	14
The raines of Love I love, though never slake, ...		179	Astrophil	28	7
Love onely reading unto me this art.		179	Astrophil	28	14
So Stella's heart, finding what power Love brings, ...		179	Astrophil	29	5
Sure, if that long with Love acquainted eyes		180	Astrophil	31	5
Can judge of Love, thou feel'st a Lover's case;.		180	Astrophil	31	6
Is constant Love deem'd there but want of wit?		180	Astrophil	31	10
Do they above love to be lov'd, and yet.		180	Astrophil	31	12
Those Lovers scorne whom that Love doth possesse?.		180	Astrophil	31	13
And there long since, Love thy Lieutenant lies,.		183	Astrophil	36	5
Who while they make Love conquer, conquer Love,.		185	Astrophil	42	3
Wrackes Triumphs be, which Love (high set) doth breed. . . .		186	Astrophil	42	14
Where blushing red, that Love's selfe them doth love,. . . .		186	Astrophil	43	10
Her face? O Love, a Rogue thou then shouldst be, ...		187	Astrophil	46	6
If Love learne not alone to love and see,.		187	Astrophil	46	7
Unkind, I love you not: O me, that eye		188	Astrophil	47	13
Where Love is chastnesse, Paine doth learne delight, ...		188	Astrophil	48	3
I on my horse, and Love on me doth trie.		189	Astrophil	49	1
A horsman to my horse, a horse to Love;.		189	Astrophil	49	3
A strife is growne betweene Vertue and Love, ...		190	Astrophil	52	1
Her eyes, her lips, her all, saith Love do this,.		190	Astrophil	52	3
Well Love, since this demurre our sute doth stay,.		191	Astrophil	52	12
Because I breathe not love to everie one,.		191	Astrophil	54	1
He cannot love: no, no, let him alone.".		191	Astrophil	54	8
They love indeed, who quake to say they love..		192	Astrophil	54	14
For let me but name her whom I do love,.		192	Astrophil	55	12
If he do love, I burne, I burne in love:		194	Astrophil	59	2
To witlesse things, then Love I hope (since wit.		194	Astrophil	59	13
Shewes love and pitie to my absent case.		195	Astrophil	60	8
The ground of this fierce Love and lovely hate:.		195	Astrophil	60	11
Now since her chast mind hates this love in me,.		195	Astrophil	61	9
That I love not, without I leave to love..		195	Astrophil	61	14
With rage of Love, I cald my Love unkind;.		195	Astrophil	62	2
She in whose eyes Love, though unfelt, doth shine, ...		196	Astrophil	62	3
Sweet said that I true love in her should find..		196	Astrophil	62	4
That love she did, but loved a Love not blind, ...		196	Astrophil	62	6
Willd me these tempests of vaine love to flie, ...		196	Astrophil	62	10
Of Love, new-coind to helpe my beggery,.		196	Astrophil	62	13
Deare, love me not, that you may love me more..		196	Astrophil	62	14
She lightning Love, displaying Venus' skies, ...		196	Astrophil	63	7
But do not will me from my Love to flie.		198	Astrophil	64	8
Love by sure proofe I may call thee unkind,.		198	Astrophil	65	1
They fled with blush, which guiltie seem'd of love..		199	Astrophil	66	14
Let him but learne of Love to reade in thee, ...		201	Astrophil	71	3
So while thy beautie drawes the heart to love, ...		201	Astrophil	71	12
As fast thy Vertue bends that love to good:.		201	Astrophil	71	13
And oft so clings to my pure love, that I.		202	Astrophil	72	2
Love still a boy, and oft a wanton is,.		203	Astrophil	73	1
Sweet, it was saucie Love, not humble I..		203	Astrophil	73	8
To lose his Crowne, rather then faile his Love..		204	Astrophil	75	14
The onely light of joy, the onely warmth of Love..		204	Astrophil	76	4
O how the pleasant aires of true love be		205	Astrophil	78	1
Breakefast of Love, but lo, lo, where she is,.		206	Astrophil	79	13
By linkes of Love, and only Nature's art:.		207	Astrophil	81	6
When in her necke you did Love ditties peepe;.		208	Astrophil	83	6
With wings of Love in aire of wonder flie, ...		212	Astrophil	86	8
Yet swam in joy, such love in her was seene.		223	Astrophil	87	11
Where memory sets foorth the beames of love.		223	Astrophil	88	11
In hart both sight and love now coupled be;.		223	Astrophil	88	13
Who seeke, who hope, who love, who live but thee;.		224	Astrophil	90	2
And love doth hold my hand, and makes me write..		224	Astrophil	90	14
Not them, o no, but you in them I love..		225	Astrophil	91	14
Or if thy love of plaint yet mine forbeares, ...		228	Astrophil	94	9
By love were made apt to consort with me..		229	Astrophil	95	11
But ah poore Night, in love with Phoebus' light, ...		229	Astrophil	97	5
Love moves thy paine, and like a faithfull page, ...		232	Astrophil	101	9
It is but love, which makes his paper perfit white		232	Astrophil	102	12
Do Stella love. Pooles, who doth it deny?.		233	Astrophil	104	14

```
LOVE                      (CONTINUED)                         PAGE    TITLE        LINE
      I sweare by her I love and lacke, that I . . . . . . . . . .  235 Astrophil  105    5
      And scorning say, "See what it is to love.". . . . . . . .   236 Astrophil  107   14
      The two only darts of Love:. . . . . . . . . . . . . . . .   202 A&S 2nd Song       6
      Cowards Love with losse rewardeth. . . . . . . . . . . . .   202 A&S 2nd Song      16
      Love feares nothing else but anger. . . . . . . . . . . . .  203 A&S 2nd Song      20
      If Orpheus' voyce had force to breathe such musicke's love . 208 A&S 3rd Song       1
      If Love might sweet'n so a boy of shepheard' brood,. . . . . 209 A&S 3rd Song       7
      Earth gave that Love, heav'n I trow Love refineth: . . . . . 209 A&S 3rd Song      11
      O birds, o beasts, looke Love, lo, Stella shineth. . . . . . 209 A&S 3rd Song      12
      The birds, beasts, stones and trees feele this, and feeling
          love: . . . . . . . . . . . . . . . . . . . . . . . . . 209 A&S 3rd Song      13
      Know, that small Love is quicke, and great Love doth amaze:. 209 A&S 3rd Song      16
      Thou, sweetest subject, werte borne in the realme of Love, . 214 A&S 5th Song      64
      Beauty, musicke, sweetnesse, love. . . . . . . . . . . . . . 226 A&S 10th Song     34
      "But the wrongs love beares, will make . . . . . . . . . . . 234 A&S 11th Song     31
      Love at length leave undertaking." . . . . . . . . . . . . . 234 A&S 11th Song     32
      Love more affected seemes. . . . . . . . . . . . . . . . . . 216 A&S 6th Song      31
      Or knowing, have so muddy minds, as not to be in love; . . . 217 A&S 7th Song       9
      A lesson fit, both sight and skill, love and firme love to
          breede,. . . . . . . . . . . . . . . . . . . . . . . .  217 A&S 7th Song      12
      While their eyes by love directed, . . . . . . . . . . . . . 218 A&S 8th Song      15
      Love it selfe did silence breake;. . . . . . . . . . . . . . 218 A&S 8th Song      26
      Love did set his lips asunder, . . . . . . . . . . . . . . . 218 A&S 8th Song      27
      Thus to speake in love and wonder: . . . . . . . . . . . . . 218 A&S 8th Song      28
      Love therewith is streight imparted. . . . . . . . . . . . . 218 A&S 8th Song      36
      That not I, but since I love you,. . . . . . . . . . . . . . 219 A&S 8th Song      51
      Sense of love to love inspiring. . . . . . . . . . . . . . . 219 A&S 8th Song      60
      "Love makes earth the water drink, . . . . . . . . . . . . . 219 A&S 8th Song      61
      Love to earth makes water sinke; . . . . . . . . . . . . . . 219 A&S 8th Song      62
      While such wise she love denied, . . . . . . . . . . . . . . 220 A&S 8th Song      71
      As yet love she signified. . . . . . . . . . . . . . . . . . 220 A&S 8th Song      72
      "Astrophil" sayd she, "my love . . . . . . . . . . . . . . . 220 A&S 8th Song      73
      If thou love, my love content thee,. . . . . . . . . . . . . 220 A&S 8th Song      91
      For all love, all faith is meant thee, . . . . . . . . . . . 220 A&S 8th Song      92
      Least, though I leave not thy love,. . . . . . . . . . . . . 220 A&S 8th Song      98
      Stella who more love hath proved,. . . . . . . . . . . . . . 221 A&S 9th Song      22
      Coles of love that burne so clearely;. . . . . . . . . . . . 222 A&S 9th Song      34
      Is that love? forsooth I trow, . . . . . . . . . . . . . . . 222 A&S 9th Song      36
      My love should not be beleeved,. . . . . . . . . . . . . . . 222 A&S 9th Song      39
      Faining love, somewhat to please me: . . . . . . . . . . . . 222 A&S 9th Song      42
      The trade of them, that just proceeding love;. . . . . . . . 271 Psalm I          20
      And love the sweet sound of thy name, rejoyce. . . . . . . . 275 Psalm V          34
      On them he sets his love:. . . . . . . . . . . . . . . . . . 282 Psalm X          18
      No men are left, that charity do love, . . . . . . . . . . . 284 Psalm XII         2
      Who sells not guiltlesse cause, for filthy love of gain: . . 287 Psalm XV         12
      Good and godly men I love. . . . . . . . . . . . . . . . . . 288 Psalm XVI         8
      Thee will I love, O Lord, with all my heart's delight, . . . 290 Psalm XVIII       1
      Ev'en Feare makes strangers shew much love though much
          untrue.. . . . . . . . . . . . . . . . . . . . . . . .  293 Psalm XVIII      81
      Though Father's Care, and Mother's love. . . . . . . . . . . 308 Psalm XXVII      49
      Let those lips be made dumbe which love to ly, . . . . . . . 313 Psalm XXXI       49
      Then love him ye all ye that feel his grace, . . . . . . . . 314 Psalm XXXI       64
      That yet beare love unto my righteousness; . . . . . . . . . 323 Psalm XXXV       68
      Let them that love Thy saving seat . . . . . . . . . . . . . 332 Psalm XL         63
      I by day thy love shall tast,. . . . . . . . . . . . . . . . 335 Psalm XLII       37
      Who ever Lambkins saw (yet lambkins love to play). . . . . . 343 Possibly     1     5
      W. Who bound thee? D. Love my Lord. W. What witnesses
          therto . . . . . . . . . . . . . . . . . . . . . . . .  343 Possibly     1    25
      That of the stroke, the heat, and knott of love, . . . . . . 344 Possibly     2     3
      When strong Desire, which vertue's love doth guide,. . . . . 345 Possibly     4     7
      For since warre is the ground of vertue's love,. . . . . . . 346 Possibly     5     7
      One love they lov'd, one life they liv'd.. . . . . . . . . . 241 Other Poems  3     4
      Both free of minde, both did clear-dealing love, . . . . . . 243 Other Poems  4    39
      They catch, while he (foole!) to himself makes love: . . . . 243 Other Poems  4    46
      And so must see great cause before they love.. . . . . . . . 245 Other Poems  4   144
      Therefore Love arm'd in hir now takes the fielde,. . . . . . 245 Other Poems  4   145
      That it was Love that shin'de in shining maid: . . . . . . . 246 Other Poems  4   164
      While into none doubt of his love did sinke, . . . . . . . . 247 Other Poems  4   199
      For not himselfe to be in love did thinke. . . . . . . . . . 247 Other Poems  4   200
      Which absence wisht: love plai'd a victor's part:. . . . . . 248 Other Poems  4   223
      The heav'n-love lodestone drew thy iron hart. . . . . . . .  248 Other Poems  4   224
      With Cosma, for whose love Pas past in woe.. . . . . . . . . 248 Other Poems  4   243
      What rage in them, that love in him did show.. . . . . . . . 249 Other Poems  4   294
      But he drew hir as love his fancy drew,. . . . . . . . . . . 250 Other Poems  4   323
      For Pas, whether it were for feare, or love, . . . . . . . . 250 Other Poems  4   327
      With love drawne on, so fast with pace unmeet. . . . . . . . 250 Other Poems  4   334
      "Absence is death, or worse, to them that love." . . . . . . 259 Other Poems  5    94
      Like Lovers do their Love, . . . . . . . . . . . . . . . . . 261 Other Poems  6    43
      Such comfort, fervent love . . . . . . . . . . . . . . . . . 261 Other Poems  6    51
      "But may Love abiding bee. . . . . . . . . . . . . . . . . . 262 Other Poems  7    25
      To whome arte of Love is knowne: . . . . . . . . . . . . . . 262 Other Poems  7    28
      What in art of Love is fitting.. . . . . . . . . . . . . . . 262 Other Poems  7    30
      To whom we our love disclose?. . . . . . . . . . . . . . . . 263 Other Poems  7    32
      Nor with Love to cloake Disdaine,. . . . . . . . . . . . . . 263 Other Poems  7    40
      In whose love I pleasure take, . . . . . . . . . . . . . . . 263 Other Poems  7    62
LOVED
      That thus preserves my loved life: . . . . . . . . . . . . .  13 Arcadia I    5     2
      Loved I am, and yet complaine of Love: . . . . . . . . . . .  41 Arcadia II  20     1
      Let me be lov'd, or els not loved be.. . . . . . . . . . . .  41 Arcadia II  20    14
```

		PAGE	TITLE		LINE
LOVED	(CONTINUED)				
And yet the prince (that lov'd him) not offend..		95	3rd Eclogues	64	54
"Long have I love'd, (alas thou worthy arte)		97	3rd Eclogues	64	97
Long have I lov'd, (alas love craveth love).		97	3rd Eclogues	64	98
Long have I lov'd thy selfe, alas my harte		97	3rd Eclogues	64	99
He still hop'd well, because I loved truth;.		99	3rd Eclogues	66	38
Love never had me opprest, but that I saw to be lov'd. . . .		123	4th Eclogues	74	44
So that thee like heaven I loved..		156	Cert Sonnets	27	4
I saw and liked, I liked but loved not,.		165	Astrophil	2	5
I loved, but straight did not what Love decreed:		165	Astrophil	2	6
Do they above love to be lov'd, and yet.		180	Astrophil	31	12
Only lov'd Tyrants, just in cruelty, ...		185	Astrophil	42	6
That love she did, but loved a Love not blind, ...		196	Astrophil	62	6
Which would not let me, whom she loved, decline.		196	Astrophil	62	7
That where before hart loved and eyes did see, ...		223	Astrophil	88	12
Lord I have loved well		306	Psalm XXVI		25
To play when that their loved dammes, are stoln or gone					
astray?.		343	Possibly	1	6
One love they lov'd, one life they liv'd..		241	Other Poems	3	4
Left Nous to coast the loved beauty ny..		249	Other Poems	4	284
To make thee nor thy better-loved rue:.		258	Other Poems	5	81
The Ewe another loved, ...		259	Other Poems	5	122
LOVE-INSTRUCTED					
Then did he slack his love-enstructed pace..		250	Other Poems	4	308
LOVELIEST					
Histor. Those woordes dyd once the Loveliest shepard use . .		24	1st Eclogues	9	62
LOVELY					
Though not so white as is thy lovely face, ...		4	Lady of May	2	20
No lovely praise was ever got with killing".		16	1st Eclogues	7	81
Whose faire bodily gifts are fram'd most lovely to each ey..		33	1st Eclogues	13	55
The lovely blowe with rare reward, my prayer is.		51	2nd Eclogues	28	112
Or while that shepheards love a lovely face.		56	2nd Eclogues	29	125
Of goodnes to receive lovely direction..		68	2nd Eclogues	34	4
The lovely clusters of her brests, ...		87	Arcadia III	62	53
In which most lovely traine, ...		92	3rd Eclogues	63	53
O lovelie starre, entitled of the morning, ...		111	4th Eclogues	71	9
If that love be a fault, more fault in you to be lovely: ..		123	4th Eclogues	74	43
Faire seeke not to be feard, most lovely beloved by thy					
servants,.		143	Cert Sonnets	14	1
No lovely Paris made thy Hellen his:		181	Astrophil	33	6
The ground of this fierce Love and lovely hate:.		195	Astrophil	60	11
Anger invests with such a lovely grace,.		203	Astrophil	73	13
To beautie's lovely light, ...		216	A&S 6th Song		32
His lovely face on them doth bide.		284	Psalm XI		22
As Venus' bird the white, swift, lovely Dove		251	Other Poems	4	353
Where we once our lovely sheepe, ...		262	Other Poems	7	21
LOVE-OPEN					
And surely taught by his love-open eye,.		251	Other Poems	4	378
LOVER					
And Love, which lover hurts is inhumanitie".		16	1st Eclogues	7	66
Lay all your feare upon your fearefull lover:.		17	1st Eclogues	7	91
Thus shall you both reward a lover true, ...		97	3rd Eclogues	64	107
From the image of thy lover?		225	A&S 10th Song		6
He envied such a death in sight of lover,.		259	Other Poems	5	124
LOVER'S					
Then take my shape, and play a lover's parte:.		79	Arcadia III	51	12
Your eyes may tread a Lover's maze..		86	Arcadia III	62	32
In life of lover's hart, ...		152	Cert Sonnets	23	10
Can judge of Love, thou feel'st a Lover's case;.		180	Astrophil	31	6
Of Lover's ruine some sad Tragedie:.		187	Astrophil	45	13
LOVERS					
What do lovers seeke for, long seeking for to enjoy? Joy.. .		63	2nd Eclogues	31	13
Are Poets then the onely lovers true, ...		146	Cert Sonnets	17	31
Some Lovers speake when they their Muses entertaine, ...		167	Astrophil	6	1
Those Lovers scorne whom that Love doth possesse?.		180	Astrophil	31	13
Of Lovers never knowne, a grievous case, ...		187	Astrophil	45	6
Dumbe Swannes, not chatring Pies, do Lovers prove..		192	Astrophil	54	13
The mansion seat of blisse, and just excuse of Lovers; . . .		213	A&S 5th Song		21
Of foes the spoile is evill, far worse of constant lovers. .		214	A&S 5th Song		48
Like Lovers do their Love, ...		261	Other Poems	6	43
LOVERS'					
Beautie his Booke, his play lovers' dissention:.		48	2nd Eclogues	28	42
LOVE'S					
That verie shame with Love's high title dignifie..		14	1st Eclogues	7	3
But if thou hast a Love, in that Love's passion, ...		15	1st Eclogues	7	16
Her length the earth in Love's chiefe clothing dressed.. . .		17	1st Eclogues	7	87
If shee still hate love's lawe,.		19	1st Eclogues	7	V150
But for that Love's desire most rules the eyes,.		22	1st Eclogues	8	41
Shall such morning deaws be an ease to the heate of a love's					
fire?		34	1st Eclogues	13	88
Then base and sower is Love's most high vocation..		48	2nd Eclogues	28	24
Quite from my selfe to love Love's contemplation;.		48	2nd Eclogues	28	32
Was vertue cladde in constant love's attire.		77	Arcadia III	48	2
Stay to true love's melody:.		140	Cert Sonnets	7	39
Behold Love's mightie hand		158	Cert Sonnets	28	38
Which ever hath Love's yoke despised:.		159	Cert Sonnets	29	15
At length to Love's decrees, I forc'd, agreed, ...		165	Astrophil	2	7
By my love judging what Love's paine might be.		173	Astrophil	16	8
By Love's owne selfe, but with so curious drought, ...		184	Astrophil	38	7
Each soule doth at Love's feet his weapons lay,.		186	Astrophil	43	7

LOVE'S	(CONTINUED)	PAGE	TITLE		LINE
Where blushing red, that Love's selfe them doth love,. . . .		186	Astrophil	43	10
According to my Lord Love's owne behest:		189	Astrophil	50	6
Be love's indeed, in Stella's selfe he may		191	Astrophil	52	10
Of them, who in their lips Love's standerd beare;.		191	Astrophil	54	6
And therefore by her Love's authority, ...		196	Astrophil	62	9
Griefe but Love's winter liverie is, the Boy		201	Astrophil	70	7
In Lillies' neast, where Love's selfe lies along..		208	Astrophil	83	8
The globe of weale, lips Love's indentures make:		210	Astrophil	85	13
(Spurd with love's spur, though gald and shortly raind . . .		230	Astrophil	98	7
To make a Lyzard dull to taste Love's daintie food:.		209	A&S 3rd Song		8
The poore-clad truth of love's wrong-ordred lot.		242	Other Poems	4	14
Can Love's duties best fulfill:.		263	Other Poems	7	38
LOVES					
We love, and have our loves rewarded..		14	1st Eclogues	6	1
Nor true love loves those loves with others mingled be.. . .		14	1st Eclogues	7	12
How much more we do love, so the lesse our loves be					
beleeved		32	1st Eclogues	13	20
The jealous eye, the more it lookes, it loves.		42	Arcadia II	22	7
For though life irkes, in life my loves protected be.. . . .		51	2nd Eclogues	28	125
He loves my hart, for once it was his owne:.		76	Arcadia III	45	7
Into my breste, and loves renewed swimme..		85	Arcadia III	61	12
Whose loves may ever bide, ...		91	3rd Eclogues	63	14
The golden meane who loves, lives safely free.		143	Cert Sonnets	12	4
And judgment loves,.		316	Psalm XXXIII		20
Who loves with good his servants good to blesse.		323	Psalm XXXV		70
With whose fine stepps all loves and joyes conspire.		250	Other Poems	4	302
LOVES'					
And others long to tell their loves' condition:.		19	1st Eclogues	7	171
And others long to tell their loves' condicion..		20	1st Eclogues	7	V971
"Only for my two loves' sake, Sir Ed. D. and M. F. G.. . . .		263	Other Poems	7	61
LOVETH					
I loving still a love that loveth none,.		148	Cert Sonnets	19	16
That she loveth me so dearely, ...		222	A&S 9th Song		32
Firm on his way, his way God loveth, ...		326	Psalm XXXVII		58
LOVE-THOUGHTS					
Twinckling starres Love-thoughts provoke:.		210	A&S 4th Song		8
LOVE-TOYS					
But these be your love-toyes, which still are spent.		106	3rd Eclogues	67	94
LOVING					
As loving not, accus'd, in Love I die.		41	Arcadia II	20	2
Make her as much more base by loving me.		72	Arcadia III	38	17
Sicke to the death, still loving my disease.		74	Arcadia III	41	8
Then is the quiet joy of loving wife;.		103	3rd Eclogues	67	8
More loving eyes she draws, more hate thou hast.		141	Cert Sonnets	8	14
I loving still a love that loveth none,.		148	Cert Sonnets	19	16
Loving in truth, and faine in verse my love to show, ...		165	Astrophil	1	1
To keepe the pace of their first loving state.		173	Astrophil	17	4
And knowing, love, and loving, lay apart		177	Astrophil	24	7
Like loving brothers' case		215	A&S 6th Song		15
Or loving, have so frothy thoughts, as easly thence to move:		217	A&S 7th Song		10
With loving homage kisse that only son he hath,.		272	Psalm II		27
For so Thy loving hand		305	Psalm XXVI		10
O then extend Thy loving heart		324	Psalm XXXVI		27
God, loving right, doth not forsake.		326	Psalm XXXVII		69
As much more loving, as lesse combersome..		255	Other Poems	4	504
Shunn lothed-loving bankes with conning crooke:.		257	Other Poems	5	29
Never striving, but in loving.		262	Other Poems	7	24
LOVINGLY					
Lovingly like friends did keepe, ...		262	Other Poems	7	22
LOVINGNESS					
Thy kindnes, lovingnes;.		303	Psalm XXV		22
LOW					
Rysing from lowe, are to the highest bente;.		78	Arcadia III	49	16
Transforme themselves to lowe dejected vallies:.		112	4th Eclogues	71	38
To so lowe ebbe that wonted were to flowe.		146	Cert Sonnets	17	15
And stately hilles disdaine to looke so low.		147	Cert Sonnets	18	8
And know those Bodies high raigne on the low..		178	Astrophil	26	11
Th'indifferent Judge betweene the high and low;.		184	Astrophil	39	4
For late with heart most high, with eyes most low, ...		196	Astrophil	63	5
O joy, too high for my low stile to show:.		200	Astrophil	69	1
And yet their high hearts look so low.		290	Psalm XVII		31
To raise in words what in effect is lowe:.		242	Other Poems	4	2
While thus they ran a low, but leaveld race, ...		243	Other Poems	4	57
To visite so low folkes did much disdaine, ...		243	Other Poems	4	63
A maid train'd up from high or low degree, ...		247	Other Poems	4	210
LOWER					
Doth lowre, nay, chide; nay, threat for only this:		203	Astrophil	73	7
LOWERING					
Lowring beautie chastens me:		203	A&S 2nd Song		26
LOWERS					
But even for that shall suffer mightie Lowers.		28	1st Eclogues	10	72
Must goe for that, if for her lowres he care:.		104	3rd Eclogues	67	42
My mistresse lowers and saith I do not love:		145	Cert Sonnets	17	1
LOWEST					
And lowest stops doo yeeld the hyest sounde.		81	Arcadia III	54	16
And lowest sinke not downe to jote of ill:		99	3rd Eclogues	66	32
LOWLY					
What be the sweet creatures wher lowly demaunds be not					
heard Hard.		65	2nd Eclogues	31	41

```
                                                          PAGE   TITLE          LINE
LUCK
    Youth, lucke, and praise, even fild my veines with pride.. .  191 Astrophil     53    4
LUCKLESS
    And each way luckles, yet in humble guise. . . . . . . . . .  249 Other Poems    4  277
LUCKLEST
    Or els; "Nay faith, mine is the lucklest lot,. . . . . . . .  104 3rd Eclogues 67   43
LUCKY
    Some luckie wits impute it but to chaunce; . . . . . . . . .  185 Astrophil     41    8
LULLED
    And o my Muse, though oft you luld her in your lap,. . . . .  213 A&S 5th Song        25
LULLS
    Of those fortune lulls, so small rest rests in a kingdome. .   34 1st Eclogues 13   90
LULLY
    Lully, lully, my babe, hope cradle bringeth. . . . . . . . .  139 Cert Sonnets  6    4
LURK
    The neck, in which strange graces lurke. . . . . . . . . . .   87 Arcadia III  62   48
LURKING
    Like lurking lion in his denn. . . . . . . . . . . . . . . .  282 Psalm X            37
    Now like his Whelp in den that lurking stayes. . . . . . . .  290 Psalm XVII         34
LUST
    But thou foule Cupid, syre to lawlesse lust, . . . . . . . .   92 3rd Eclogues 63   55
    Cupid's lust gone, and gone is bitter strife,. . . . . . . .   93 3rd Eclogues 63   94
    The Horse, good shape; the Sparrow, lust to playe; . . . . .  101 3rd Eclogues 66   81
    My ship, desire, with winde of lust long tost, . . . . . . .  151 Cert Sonnets 22   55
    When he his lust doth ease,. . . . . . . . . . . . . . . . .  281 Psalm X            10
    Least we should ever feare the lust. . . . . . . . . . . . .  283 Psalm X            79
    Let God save him, in whom was all his lust.. . . . . . . . .  299 Psalm XXII         20
    Unto whose ever hating lust. . . . . . . . . . . . . . . . .  308 Psalm XXVII        55
    A lustles song for sooth thinks hee that hath more lust to
        cry. . . . . . . . . . . . . . . . . . . . . . . . . . .  343 Possibly      1    8
LUSTER
    Whose gentle rayes suche Luster fynde, . . . . . . . . . . .   89 Arcadia III  62 V115
    Frame daintiest lustre, mixt of shades and light?. . . . . .  168 Astrophil     7    4
    Thy justice in most shining luster,. . . . . . . . . . . . .  325 Psalm XXXVII       14
    As rubies lustre, when they rubbed be. . . . . . . . . . . .  252 Other Poems    4  396
LUSTFUL
    He liked me, but pitied lustfull youth:. . . . . . . . . . .   99 3rd Eclogues 66   36
LUSTING
    The fulness of thy own heart's lusting;. . . . . . . . . . .  324 Psalm XXXVII       10
LUSTLESS
    A lustles song for sooth thinks hee that hath more lust to
        cry. . . . . . . . . . . . . . . . . . . . . . . . . . .  343 Possibly      1    8
LUSTS
    Our foolish lustes in honest rules to stay.. . . . . . . . .  103 3rd Eclogues 67    3
LUTE
    My Lute within thy selfe thy tunes enclose,. . . . . . . . .   81 Arcadia III  54    1
LUTE'S
    Yeldeth a lute's tune, . . . . . . . . . . . . . . . . . . .   30 1st Eclogues 12   16
*LYING
    Her whom I dread; so that with prostrate lying . . . . . . .   17 1st Eclogues  7   86
    And shalt root out the tongues to lying bent:. . . . . . . .  275 Psalm V            14
    To hearts that hate all lying. . . . . . . . . . . . . . . .  284 Psalm XI            8
    Those lying lipps from Cousening head remove,. . . . . . . .  284 Psalm XII           8
    Ev'n such I say, whose lying tongue. . . . . . . . . . . . .  308 Psalm XXVII        58
LYRE
    With voice more fit to wed Amphion's lyre, . . . . . . . . .  200 Astrophil     68    6
    To cadence of the tunes, which Amphyon's lyre did yeeld, . .  208 A&S 3rd Song        4
M
    "Only for my two loves' sake, Sir Ed. D. and M. F. G.. . . .  263 Other Poems    7   61
MAD
    And stoppe mine eares, lest I growe mad with Musicke.. . . .  112 4th Eclogues 71   60
    For since mad March great promise made of me,. . . . . . . .  175 Astrophil     21    9
    And gain'd by Mars, could yet mad Mars so tame,. . . . . . .  204 Astrophil     75    7
    And I, mad with delight, want wit to cease,. . . . . . . . .  207 Astrophil     81   13
    Pas mad with fall, and madder with the shame,. . . . . . . .  249 Other Poems    4  269
    Most mad with beames which he thought Cosma sent,. . . . . .  249 Other Poems    4  270
    With such mad haste he did to Cosma goe, . . . . . . . . . .  249 Other Poems    4  271
MADDED
    I am enclosed with young Bulls' madded route,. . . . . . . .  299 Psalm XXII         27
MADDER
    Pas mad with fall, and madder with the shame,. . . . . . . .  249 Other Poems    4  269
MADE
    Why thee a living man they had made dead.. . . . . . . . . .   11 Arcadia I     1    7
    Lalus. This mayde, thus made for joyes, o Pan bemone her,. .   17 1st Eclogues  7   97
    And pastimes make, as Nature things hath made. . . . . . . .   18 1st Eclogues  7  127
    Nature made all, but me of dolours made: . . . . . . . . . .   18 1st Eclogues  7  143
    Oh he is mard that is for others made. . . . . . . . . . . .   19 1st Eclogues  7  166
    Lalus. Oh he is mard that is for others made.. . . . . . . .   19 1st Eclogues  7  167
    Thy toong hath made of Cupid's deepe incision. . . . . . . .   20 1st Eclogues  7 V969
    Is made, forsooth, a Jurate of his woes, . . . . . . . . . .   23 1st Eclogues  9   39
    And statute made he never shoulde have voice,. . . . . . . .   29 1st Eclogues 10   86
    R. The joyes you have shall be made permanent. . . . . . . .   47 2nd Eclogues 27   35
    O tongues right ladders made to clime dishonour, . . . . . .   50 2nd Eclogues 28   90
    Of singing match we made, whence he with shame did trudge. .   52 2nd Eclogues 29   16
    My pipe and song made him both songe and pipe forsweare. . .   52 2nd Eclogues 29   20
    Which made a Bay, made Bay a holy tree:. . . . . . . . . . .   54 2nd Eclogues 29   61
    Made uniforme to any state reposed.. . . . . . . . . . . . .   57 2nd Eclogues 30   31
    Swelling with sighes, made pale with minde's disease,. . . .   58 2nd Eclogues 30   48
    What causes first made these torments on me to light? Light.   64 2nd Eclogues 31   23
    Eysight made me to yeelde, but what first pierst to myne
        eies? Eies.. . . . . . . . . . . . . . . . . . . . . . .   64 2nd Eclogues 31   26
```

```
MADE                    (CONTINUED)                          PAGE    TITLE          LINE
    Doth proclaime with a sound made all by men's mouths . . . .    68  2nd Eclogues 33    20
    (Of passions darke, made darke by beautie's light) . . . . .    72  Arcadia III  39     2
    And yet as hard, as brawne made hard by arte:. . . . . . . .    76  Arcadia III  46    16
    He made the simple wench his wrath abide.. . . . . . . . . .    95  3rd Eclogues 64    30
    In fine he made her gesse, there was some sweet. . . . . . .    95  3rd Eclogues 64    35
    Thus may you see, the jealous wretch was made. . . . . . . .    97  3rd Eclogues 64   121
    Rulers will thinke all things made them to please, . . . . .   100  3rd Eclogues 66    73
    Thus Man was made; thus Man their Lord became: . . . . . . .   101  3rd Eclogues 66   106
    But they or spent, or made of slender might, . . . . . . . .   102  3rd Eclogues 66   134
    To sheepe, whom love, not knowledge, made to heare, . . . . .  103  3rd Eclogues 66   156
    The house is made a very lothsome cage, . . . . . . . . . . .  105  3rd Eclogues 67    49
    We made for paine, our paines they made to cherish:. . . . .   106  3rd Eclogues 67   107
    Now Prince's losse hath made our damage publique, . . . . . .  109  Arcadia IV   70     4
    Breath made of flames, wits knowing nought but damage, . . .   109  Arcadia IV   70    28
    Hath made it selfe a crier of the morning, . . . . . . . . .   112  4th Eclogues 71    26
    My fire is more, then can be made with forrests; . . . . . .   112  4th Eclogues 71    56
    Klaius. These forrests eke, made wretched by our musique,. .   113  4th Eclogues 71    74
    (Which made of heav'nly stuffe no mortal chaunge doth bynde)   117  4th Eclogues 73    32
    Such proffer made, which she well showd with smiling cheere.   120  4th Eclogues 73   144
    To stand unto my will: their will they made me know. . . . .   121  4th Eclogues 73   157
    And thou o traytour Sleepe, made for to be our rest, . . . .   121  4th Eclogues 73   183
    Since Death on Vertue's fort hath made invasion. . . . . . .   128  4th Eclogues 75   102
    Bountifulnes hath made his last conclusion:. . . . . . . . .   128  4th Eclogues 75   119
    And farewell Prince, whom goodnesse hath made glorious.. . .   129  4th Eclogues 75   142
    In justice quit, of honour made no breach: . . . . . . . . .   135  Cert Sonnets  1    12
    A three foote stoole in Greece, made Trumpets sound, . . . .   146  Cert Sonnets 17    19
    Whilst that methought I justly made my bost. . . . . . . . .   147  Cert Sonnets 17    42
    Compar'd to me, made me in lightnesse found: . . . . . . . .   147  Cert Sonnets 17    47
    My Diane made me shew, . . . . . . . . . . . . . . . . . . .   158  Cert Sonnets 28    10
    Nor thinke the match unev'nly made, . . . . . . . . . . . . .  159  Cert Sonnets 29    10
    True, that on earth we are but pilgrims made, . . . . . . . .  167  Astrophil     5    12
    When Nature made her chiefe worke, Stella's eyes, . . . . . .  168  Astrophil     7     1
    But she most faire, most cold, made him thence take his
        flight . . . . . . . . . . . . . . . . . . . . . . . . .   169  Astrophil     8    12
    Of Stella's browes made him two better bowes, . . . . . . . .  173  Astrophil    17    10
    For since mad March great promise made of me, . . . . . . . .  175  Astrophil    21     9
    To warme with ill-made fire cold Moscovy; . . . . . . . . . .  180  Astrophil    30     4
    Wherewith my father once made it halfe tame; . . . . . . . .   180  Astrophil    30    10
    No lovely Paris made thy Hellen his: . . . . . . . . . . . .   181  Astrophil    33     6
    Made manifest by such a victorie, . . . . . . . . . . . . . .  185  Astrophil    40    10
    Sent forth the beames, which made so faire my race.. . . . .   185  Astrophil    41    14
    Where Vertue is made strong by Beautie's might, . . . . . . .  188  Astrophil    48     2
    And now hath made me to his hand so right, . . . . . . . . .   189  Astrophil    49    13
    Who hard by made a window send forth light.. . . . . . . . .   191  Astrophil    53     9
    Wo, having made with many fights his owne. . . . . . . . . .   193  Astrophil    57     1
    Nor that he made the Flouredeluce so fraid, . . . . . . . . .  204  Astrophil    75     9
    Be your words made (good Sir) of Indian ware, . . . . . . . .  225  Astrophil    92     1
    Griefe find the words, for thou hast made my braine. . . . .   228  Astrophil    94     1
    By love were made apt to consort with me.. . . . . . . . . .   229  Astrophil    95    11
    Have made, but forst by Nature still to flie, . . . . . . . .  233  Astrophil   103    10
    Where birds wanton musicke made, . . . . . . . . . . . . . .   217  A&S 8th Song        2
    Would have made tongue's language plaine; . . . . . . . . . .  219  A&S 8th Song       66
    Which fall he made to do his neighbor wrong. . . . . . . . .   278  Psalm VII          42
    Yet hast Thou made even him an owner . . . . . . . . . . . .   279  Psalm VIII         19
    He made my cumbrous way to me most plainly right.. . . . . .   292  Psalm XVIII        60
    To match with light foot staggs he made my foot so light . .   292  Psalm XVIII        61
    By them is made Thy servants' trade. . . . . . . . . . . . .   295  Psalm XIX          45
    Made worshipers before Almighty Thee.. . . . . . . . . . . .   300  Psalm XXII         68
    They that be made even fatt, with earth's fatt good, . . . .   300  Psalm XXII         71
    Now made, O Lord maintain, . . . . . . . . . . . . . . . . .   304  Psalm XXV          68
    For I have made my race. . . . . . . . . . . . . . . . . . .   305  Psalm XXVI          2
    Let those lips be made dumbe which love to ly, . . . . . . .   313  Psalm XXXI         49
    His Word made heavnly Coast, . . . . . . . . . . . . . . . .   316  Psalm XXXIII       22
    O Soul, rejoyce, we made this wretch our prey. . . . . . . .   323  Psalm XXXV         62
    Yea beasts made safe thy goodness try. . . . . . . . . . . .   323  Psalm XXXVI        18
    Thou knowst made declaration, . . . . . . . . . . . . . . . .  331  Psalm XL           36
    With sight made dymme with dayly teares another's sport to
        see. . . . . . . . . . . . . . . . . . . . . . . . . . .   343  Possibly      1     4
    W. What seale? D. My hart deepe graven. W. Who made the band
        so fast?. . . . . . . . . . . . . . . . . . . . . . . .    343  Possibly      1    27
    A garland made on temples for to weare, . . . . . . . . . . .  244  Other Poems   4    74
    For they seem'd made even of skie-mettall best, . . . . . . .  244  Other Poems   4   100
    Made them his owne before they had it wist.. . . . . . . . .   246  Other Poems   4   159
    Which made hir yeeld to deck this shepheards' band, . . . . .  247  Other Poems   4   215
    Thus on a hillock set, he made his mone. . . . . . . . . . .   253  Other Poems   4   440
    Made wolves (not inward wolves) my ewes to spare; . . . . . .  254  Other Poems   4   486
    Out shreaking pipe made of some witched tree. . . . . . . . .  255  Other Poems   4   516
    Which made his Strephon think himselfe in hell.. . . . . . .   256  Other Poems   4   540
    And thus, with eyes made dimme . . . . . . . . . . . . . . .   256  Other Poems   5    12
    Often Reedes me musicke made, . . . . . . . . . . . . . . . .  263  Other Poems   7    44
    Made to listen unto me, . . . . . . . . . . . . . . . . . . .  263  Other Poems   7    56
MADEST
    In vaine thou madest me to vaine things aspire, . . . . . . .  161  Cert Sonnets 31    10
    Thou gavest me their necks, on them Thou mad'est me passe. .   292  Psalm XVIII        73
    Like storehouse Thou of blessings mad'st, . . . . . . . . . .  297  Psalm XXI          21
    And madest me gladsom weeds enjoy, . . . . . . . . . . . . .   311  Psalm XXX          36
    Lo Thou a span's length madest my living line; . . . . . . .   330  Psalm XXXIX        15
MADNESS
    O madness of these folks, thus loosely led, . . . . . . . . .  286  Psalm XIV          13
```

```
MAGIC                                                    PAGE    TITLE          LINE
    "For though like waxe, this magique makes me waste,. . . . .  254 Other Poems    4   489
MAGNIFY
    Yea even my songs thy name shall magnify,. . . . . . . . .    279 Psalm IX           4
MAID
    Lalus. This mayde, thus made for joyes, o Pan bemone her,. .   17 1st Eclogues   7    97
    If Eagle fierce could so in Grecian Mayd delight,. . . . . .  209 A&S 3rd Song        9
    They saw a maid who thitherward did runne,. . . . . . . . .   244 Other Poems    4    83
    And saw this fairest maid of fairer minde, . . . . . . . . .  244 Other Poems    4    90
    That it was Love that shin'de in shining maid: . . . . . . .  246 Other Poems    4   164
    A maid train'd up from high or low degree, . . . . . . . . .  247 Other Poems    4   210
MAIDEN
    Yet ah, my Mayd'n Muse doth blush to tell the best.. . . . .  205 Astrophil     77    14
MAIDS
    But you faire maides, at length this true shall find,. . . .  192 Astrophil     54    11
    With mery maids a Maying they do go, . . . . . . . . . . . .  243 Other Poems    4    50
MAIMED
    That bad his friend, but then new maim'd, to be. . . . . . .  236 Astrophil    106    13
MAIN
    As his maine force, choise sport, and easefull stay. . . . .  186 Astrophil     43     4
    Nay sorrow comes with such maine rage, that he . . . . . . .  229 Astrophil     95     9
MAINTAIN
    Be none of us, or els maintaine our fashion: . . . . . . . .   15 1st Eclogues   7    14
    That onely light doth all my life maintaine; . . . . . . . .   39 Arcadia II    16     4
    This vowe receave, this vowe o Gods maintaine; . . . . . . .   40 Arcadia II    18     5
    Thus outward helps my inward griefes maintaine.. . . . . . .   42 Arcadia II    21    12
    Feede on my sheepe, your Native joyes mayntayne, . . . . . .   43 Arcadia II    23    13
    Leave off my sheep my mourninge to maintayne, . . . . . . .    44 Arcadia II    24    13
    Where all good haps a perfect state maintaine? . . . . . . .   58 2nd Eclogues  30    40
    Her lipps are the riches the warres to maintaine,. . . . . .   67 2nd Eclogues  33     9
    Whiche dazeling still, dothe still maynteine my sight; . . .   70 Arcadia III   35     6
    O Himen long their coupled joyes maintaine.. . . . . . . . .   91 3rd Eclogues  63     9
    Above line repeated at following locations . . . . . . . . .   91 3rd Eclogues  63    18
                 . . . . . . . . . . . . . . . . . . . . . . . .   91 3rd Eclogues  63    27
                 . . . . . . . . . . . . . . . . . . . . . . . .   92 3rd Eclogues  63    36
                 . . . . . . . . . . . . . . . . . . . . . . . .   92 3rd Eclogues  63    45
                 . . . . . . . . . . . . . . . . . . . . . . . .   92 3rd Eclogues  63    54
                 . . . . . . . . . . . . . . . . . . . . . . . .   93 3rd Eclogues  63    63
                 . . . . . . . . . . . . . . . . . . . . . . . .   93 3rd Eclogues  63    72
                 . . . . . . . . . . . . . . . . . . . . . . . .   93 3rd Eclogues  63    81
                 . . . . . . . . . . . . . . . . . . . . . . . .   93 3rd Eclogues  63    90
    For Himen will their coupled joyes maintaine.. . . . . . . .   94 3rd Eclogues  63    99
    That we our kind doo labour to maintaine;. . . . . . . . . .  105 3rd Eclogues  67    71
    Thought, reason, sense, time, you, and I, maintaine. . . . .  148 Cert Sonnets  19    18
    Eternall Love maintaine thy life in me.. . . . . . . . . . .  144 Cert Sonnets  32    14
    I am resolv'd thy errour to maintaine, . . . . . . . . . . .  199 Astrophil     67    13
    Who word to neighbour given doth faithfully maintain . . . .  287 Psalm XV            9
    He then shall maintayn his lott. . . . . . . . . . . . . . .  288 Psalm XVI          15
    Me in increasing still, Thy kindnes did maintaine;. . . . .   292 Psalm XVIII        65
    Now made, O Lord maintain, . . . . . . . . . . . . . . . . .  304 Psalm XXV          68
    Whose shield shall us maintaine. . . . . . . . . . . . . . .  318 Psalm XXXIII       78
MAINTAINED
    Let so our fruites grow up, that nature be maintainde: . . .   45 Arcadia II    26    13
    Then let my life long time on earth maintained be, . . . . .   61 2nd Eclogues  30   147
    Strephon. For she, whose parts maintaine a perfect musique,  113 4th Eclogues  71    61
    Our bodies be in living power maintained,. . . . . . . . . .  128 4th Eclogues  75   107
    For Thou my cause, my right Thou hast maintaind, . . . . . .  279 Psalm IX            8
MAINTAINETH
    Onely by you Cupid his crowne maintaineth. . . . . . . . . .  197 A&S 1st Song       12
MAINTAINING
    My life-maintaining heart, . . . . . . . . . . . . . . . . .  332 Psalm XL           49
MAINTAINS
    For ev'n in forge colde water fire maintaines. . . . . . . .  246 Other Poems    4   156
MAJESTY
    And if from Majestie of sacred lights, . . . . . . . . . . .  186 Astrophil     42    12
    And Humblenesse growes one with Majestie.. . . . . . . . . .  188 Astrophil     48     4
    Self-gard with mildnes, Sport with Majesty:. . . . . . . . .  247 Other Poems    4   214
*MAKE
    Since vertues all, to make her title, pleased be.. . . . . .   15 1st Eclogues   7    39
    How oft with raine of teares skies make confession,. . . . .   15 1st Eclogues   7    43
    Of fayrer death how can I make election? . . . . . . . . . .   16 1st Eclogues   7    72
    That she, whose looke alone might make me blessed, . . . . .   17 1st Eclogues   7    83
    And pastimes make, as Nature things hath made. . . . . . . .   18 1st Eclogues   7   127
    Or with desire to make such foe a frend, . . . . . . . . . .   22 1st Eclogues   9     9
    But this light choller that doth make you bolde, . . . . . .   25 1st Eclogues   9   105
    Till aige it self do make it self esteemde.. . . . . . . . .   26 1st Eclogues   9   141
    And thowe Laelaps let not pride make thee brim . . . . . . .   26 1st Eclogues  10    10
    (For age doth make him of a wolvish hew) . . . . . . . . . .   27 1st Eclogues  10    17
    And to the woods or brookes, who do make such dreery
        recitall . . . . . . . . . . . . . . . . . . . . . . . .   33 1st Eclogues  13    42
    Ewe doth make me be thinke what kind of bow the boy holdeth.   35 1st Eclogues  13   121
    But to my selfe what wish can I make for a salve to my
        sorrowes,. . . . . . . . . . . . . . . . . . . . . . . .   37 1st Eclogues  13   157
    Make me, o vertuous Shame, thy lawes neglect.. . . . . . . .   40 Arcadia II    18    12
    And make me heare the plaints I would refraine:. . . . . . .   42 Arcadia II    21    11
    And of their wounds make brave lame showes:.. . . . . . . .    44 Arcadia II    25     8
    To make these woods resounde thy lamentation?. . . . . . . .   47 2nd Eclogues  28     2
    Seekes to make ech thing badge of his sweet passion. . . . .   47 2nd Eclogues  28     6
    Dorus. But what doth make thee Dicus so suspicious . . . . .   47 2nd Eclogues  28     7
    If noble be thy bandes, make them notorious: . . . . . . . .   47 2nd Eclogues  28    14
```

293

*MAKE (CONTINUED)	PAGE	TITLE		LINE
Who glories in his love, doth make Love glorious:.	47	2nd Eclogues	28	16
And Venus seemes, to make up her, she spent herselfe.. . . .	49	2nd Eclogues	28	66
Nico. Couldst thou make Lalus flie? so nightingales avoide,.	52	2nd Eclogues	29	17
Nico. I thinke it well: such voice would make one musicke				
hate:.	52	2nd Eclogues	29	21
For Pas well knowes what layes can Nico make..	54	2nd Eclogues	29	74
I spied a thrush where she did make her nest,.	54	2nd Eclogues	29	82
She did the water wash, and make more fine..	55	2nd Eclogues	29	107
Their hopes on haps, and do not make despaire.	58	2nd Eclogues	30	42
In this strange violence, to make resistance..	67	2nd Eclogues	33	2
Wheare he was bounde, to make his marting place, ...	70	Arcadia III	36	4
Make present ease receave the better taste..	70	Arcadia III	36	6
Make great the losse, so grete the feare to misse.	71	Arcadia III	37	12
Make her as much more base by loving me.	72	Arcadia III	38	17
Do serve, to make my inward powers darke:.	73	Arcadia III	39	8
But cannot make resolved darkenes lighte:.	73	Arcadia III	39	12
The heavens conspir'd, to make my vitall sparke.	73	Arcadia III	40	3
What were it els, but to make each thing blinde?	79	Arcadia III	50	13
Let no strange dreme make her fayre body starte.	79	Arcadia III	51	8
What be her giftes, that make her equall thee, ...	80	Arcadia III	52	8
Make me still feare, thy faire appearing showe..	82	Arcadia III	56	14
Which skill dooth make in Princes' bowers.	87	Arcadia III	62	50
Sweete Ilands make in that sweete land..	90	Arcadia III	62	129
And make their issue showe	92	3rd Eclogues	63	41
Or with her beawtie fit to make a pray,.	94	3rd Eclogues	64	8
(For they have toongs to make a poore man blamed	94	3rd Eclogues	64	21
Thou art of blood; joy not to make things bleede:.	103	3rd Eclogues	66	150
Make home more paine then following of the cart.	104	3rd Eclogues	67	30
Who justly make our hearts the seates of sorow?.	109	Arcadia IV	70	8
O that we had, to make our woes more publique, ...	109	Arcadia IV	70	25
And make me wish my selfe layd under mountaines, ...	112	4th Eclogues	71	36
Enough to make a fertill minde lie waste..	114	4th Eclogues	72	30
Klaius. Enough to make a fertill minde lie waste	114	4th Eclogues	72	31
Favour to make my chiefe and onely hire.	115	4th Eclogues	72	55
So much more strong againe let fastest concorde make.. . . .	120	4th Eclogues	73	120
In ashes of despaire (though burnt) shall make thee live". .	121	4th Eclogues	73	174
So high, as should make such a paine notorious:.	129	4th Eclogues	75	140
And make his paine to keepe us safe his pleasure?.	129	4th Eclogues	76	24
Since force doth faint, and sight doth make me blind:. . . .	135	Cert Sonnets	1	4
Resolv'd to make me patterne of his might, ...	135	Cert Sonnets	2	2
Like those whom dreames make uglie monsters see, ...	136	Cert Sonnets	2	11
For why should I, whom free choise slave doth make,.	146	Cert Sonnets	17	9
She saith, because I make no wofull laies,.	146	Cert Sonnets	17	27
Who silence force to make their words more deare:..	147	Cert Sonnets	17	49
Their master is faire warn'd his will to make.	150	Cert Sonnets	22	20
Pleasure might cause her reade, reading might make her know,	165	Astrophil	1	3
Tc make my selfe beleeve, that all is well,.	166	Astrophil	2	13
Till that good God make Church and Churchman starve.	167	Astrophil	5	8
She even in blacke doth make all beauties flow?.	168	Astrophil	7	11
Which others said did make their soules to pine:	173	Astrophil	16	6
To them that would make speech of speech arise,.	178	Astrophil	27	4
Of other's children changelings use to make,.	178	Astrophil	28	2
Which makes the patents of true worldly blisse, ...	183	Astrophil	37	13
O make in me those civill warres to cease;	184	Astrophil	39	7
Thinke Nature me a man of armes did make..	185	Astrophil	41	11
Who while they make Love conquer, conquer Love,.	185	Astrophil	42	3
Till without fewell you can make hot fire.	188	Astrophil	46	14
Doth make my heart give to my tongue the lie..	188	Astrophil	47	14
No Patience, if thou wilt my good, then make	193	Astrophil	56	12
Deare, why make you more of a dog then me?	194	Astrophil	59	1
No kings be crown'd but they some covenants make.	200	Astrophil	69	14
Those lips, which make death's pay a meane price for a				
kisse	205	Astrophil	77	6
The globe of weale, lips Love's indentures make:	210	Astrophil	85	13
No doome should make one's heav'n become his hell.	212	Astrophil	86	14
Stella whose eyes make all my tempests cleere, ...	222	Astrophil	87	3
United powers make each the stronger prove..	223	Astrophil	88	14
Ne if I would, could I just title make,.	224	Astrophil	90	9
Whose pants do make unspilling creame to flow, ...	231	Astrophil	100	6
As thy lookes sturre, runs up and downe to make..	232	Astrophil	101	10
Which Nature' selfe did make, and selfe engraind the same? .	232	Astrophil	102	6
Doth make me most to wish thy comfort neere.	235	Astrophil	106	8
Make in my heavy mould new thoughts to grow:	236	Astrophil	106	11
Through pores of sencelesse trees, as it could make them				
move:.	208	A&S 3rd Song		2
To make a Lyzard dull to taste Love's daintie food:.	209	A&S 3rd Song		8
Lo you grow proud with this, for tyrans make folke bow:. . .	214	A&S 5th Song		61
"But the wrongs love beares, will make	234	A&S 11th Song		31
Which can make me thus to leave you, ...	235	A&S 11th Song		44
Fit oratours to make	215	A&S 6th Song		9
Nor withered leafe shall make yt faile to flourish..	270	Psalm I		10
Wher godly men do their assembly make.	270	Psalm I		18
Why do these earthly kings and lords such meetings make, . .	271	Psalm II		3
Such one I say, that when I make	273	Psalm IV		13
And make Thy wayes to me more plainly known, ...	275	Psalm V		23
Can of thy prayse the tongues entombed make.	276	Psalm VI		15
Thou the path wilt make me tread	288	Psalm XVI		37
Make us in mervailes of Thy mercy know	290	Psalm XVII		22
Now like a lion gaping to make preyes, ...	290	Psalm XVII		33

294

*MAKE	(CONTINUED)	PAGE	TITLE		LINE
Yea Thou dost make me serv'd by folks I never knew;.		293	Psalm XVIII		79
Let him notorious make		296	Psalm XX		11
Thou as in fiery Ov'en shalt make.		297	Psalm XXI		31
And ready make Thy vengefull bowe.		298	Psalm XXI		47
Of my poore weedes thy do partition make		299	Psalm XXII		43
They shall to children's children make notorious		300	Psalm XXII		77
My soul, which Thou didst make,.		304	Psalm XXV		67
Thy Face to shine upon Thy servant make, ...		313	Psalm XXXI		43
The lord with pardon doth make cleane, ...		314	Psalm XXXII		2
In fitt time make to Thee his moane, ...		315	Psalm XXXII		20
His heritage to make..		317	Psalm XXXIII		48
That seek my bane, O make me understand.		321	Psalm XXXV		5
Let Angel thine a scattring make them go..		321	Psalm XXXV		12
For causeles they did seek to make me dy..		321	Psalm XXXV		16
Who make a Cause to joy of my decay;		323	Psalm XXXV		64
But make such glad, and full of joyfulness,.		323	Psalm XXXV		67
Let not proud feet make me their thrall, ...		324	Psalm XXXVI		31
On him and he will make it speed..		324	Psalm XXXVII		12
And of Thy Judgement make a muster		325	Psalm XXXVII		15
Who to make warr with God praesumed;		326	Psalm XXXVII		50
And of the earth make Thee an owner, ...		327	Psalm XXXVII		87
Whom my fall doth make rejoyce..		328	Psalm XXXVIII		48
That fooles of me may make their game.		330	Psalm XXXIX		28
My God, O make no stay.		332	Psalm XL		70
W. If wages make you want, what food is that she gives?. . .		344	Possibly	1	33
Yeelde yeelde O yeelde, who first this Fort did make,. . . .		345	Possibly	4	9
One day (o day, that shin'de to make them darke!)		243	Other Poems	4	65
Should price of hir, as in a market, make.		245	Other Poems	4	123
There did he make hir laugh in spite of woe, ...		247	Other Poems	4	197
Do coupled towards either couple make, ...		248	Other Poems	4	234
With greater powr, then she did make them wend		251	Other Poems	4	375
Now make me thinke that there is not a fende,.		254	Other Poems	4	463
Tc make it selfe to my least creature slave:.		255	Other Poems	4	511
And make you faire with shadow of her hue:		257	Other Poems	5	32
Sc may your Make, this wholsome springtime aire, ...		257	Other Poems	5	42
Tc make thee nor thy better-loved rue:		258	Other Poems	5	81
These markes shall make thee wise:		259	Other Poems	5	111
Make but one Minde in Bodies three..		260	Other Poems	6	6
Above line repeated at following locations		260	Other Poems	6	12
. . . .		260	Other Poems	6	18
. . . .		260	Other Poems	6	24
. . . .		261	Other Poems	6	30
. . . .		261	Other Poems	6	36
. . . .		261	Other Poems	6	42
. . . .		261	Other Poems	6	48
. . . .		261	Other Poems	6	54
May make treaty to god Pan).		263	Other Poems	7	58

MAKER'S
| With outward maker's force, or like an inward father.. . . . | | 118 | 4th Eclogues | 73 | 48 |

MAKES
Your mind is wise, your wisedome makes you mild, ...		3	Lady of May	1	9
What coye account she makes of estimation?		15	1st Eclogues	7	34
Possesse she doth, and makes my soule her slave:		17	1st Eclogues	7	112
Whome wit makes vaine, or blinded with his eyes, ...		23	1st Eclogues	9	35
The ancient oke well makes a fired blocke:		25	1st Eclogues	9	87
Then who makes us such judges over all?.		29	1st Eclogues	10	96
Mirtle makes my request, my request is crown'd with a willowe.		35	1st Eclogues	13	118
Ashe makes speares which shieldes do resist, her force no repulse takes:		36	1st Eclogues	13	136
Which makes all eyes doo honour unto you..		38	Arcadia II	15	8
Which makes us most immortall shape to weare,.		40	Arcadia II	18	14
And makes our home good sport with dauncing bolt upright.. .		53	2nd Eclogues	29	46
Griefe onely makes his wretched state to see		58	2nd Eclogues	30	32
The labourer, whome tyred boddie makes		71	Arcadia III	37	7
Where too much sight, makes all the bodie blinde,.		73	Arcadia III	40	11
Where hers, whom worth makes highest over all, ...		78	Arcadia III	49	17
Whose motion makes all graces move..		89	Arcadia III	62	96
Whose eeven descent makes equall falle,.		89	Arcadia III	62	V104
And makes them fremb'd, who frendes by nature are,.		104	3rd Eclogues	67	38
When lo with hugest noise (such noise a tower makes. . . .		118	4th Eclogues	73	51
Though I be hers, she makes of me no treasure.		137	Cert Sonnets	3	24
Just accord all musike makes;.		140	Cert Sonnets	7	14
Her breath which makes a sower answer sweete,.		141	Cert Sonnets	9	6
Hath not such paine as it makes others have:		142	Cert Sonnets	11	10
It makes them flie that which they faine would have: . . .		145	Cert Sonnets	16	6
Red Porphir is, which locke of pearle makes sure:.		169	Astrophil	9	6
That her sweete breath makes oft thy flames to rise, . . .		170	Astrophil	12	4
That her Grace gracious makes thy wrongs, that she		170	Astrophil	12	6
Stella's faire haire, her face he makes his shield,. . . .		171	Astrophil	13	10
And if these rules did faile, proofe makes me sure,. . . .		178	Astrophil	26	12
That makes me oft my best friends overpasse, ...		178	Astrophil	27	12
That Noblenesse it selfe makes thus unkind?.		186	Astrophil	44	8
Of Hope, which makes it seeme faire to the eye..		189	Astrophil	49	8
Makes me fall from her sight, then sweetly she		195	Astrophil	60	6
But no scuse serves, she makes her wrath appeare		203	Astrophil	73	9
That voyce, which makes the soule plant himselfe in the eares:		205	Astrophil	77	9
Makes me in my best thoughts and quietst judgement see,. . .		205	Astrophil	77	12

MAKES   (CONTINUED)   PAGE   TITLE   LINE
      And love doth hold my hand, and makes me write.. . . . . . . 224 Astrophil   90   14
      But feeling proofe makes me say they mistake it furre: . . . 232 Astrophil   102   11
      It is but love, which makes his paper perfit white . . . . . 232 Astrophil   102   12
      With no worse curse then absence makes me tast.. . . . . . . 235 Astrophil   105   14
      And makes me then bow downe my head, and say,. . . . . 237 Astrophil   108   9
      Who makes a man live then glad when he dieth?. . . . . 197 A&S 1st Song   26
      And which is worse, makes me most guiltlesse torments have,. 214 A&S 5th Song   59
      Joying till joy makes us languish. . . . . 227 A&S 10th Song   42
      "Iove makes earth the water drink,. . . . . 219 A&S 8th Song   61
      Lcve to earth makes water sinke; . . . . 219 A&S 8th Song   62
      Ev'en Feare makes strangers shew much love though much
            untrue.. . . . . 293 Psalm XVIII   81
      The lord whose strength makes battails fight.. . . . . 302 Psalm XXIV   20
      For such he makes his secret kncw, ... 304 Psalm XXV   53
      He makes to be . . . . 307 Psalm XXVII   29
      His voice makes hindes their calves to cast, ... 310 Psalm XXIX   22
      His voice makes bald the forest wast;. . . . . 310 Psalm XXIX   23
      Thy Mercy is! which makes mankind. . . . . 324 Psalm XXXVI   20
      Whose wages makes me beg the more, who feeds me till I
            sterve,. . . . . 343 Possibly   1   20
      They catch, while he (foole!) to himself makes love: . . . . 243 Other Poems   4   46
      But fore-accounting oft makes builders misse.. . . . . 244 Other Poems   4   79
      "For though like waxe, this magique makes me waste,. . . . . 254 Other Poems   4   489
MAKEST
      Thus freed from mutin men, thou makest me to raign,. . . . . 293 Psalm XVIII   78
      Ev'n where Thou makest Thy honour's biding place.. . . . . . 306 Psalm XXXVI   27
      Since it is Thou that makest one such? . . . . 330 Psalm XXXIX   30
      Thou moth like mak'st his beauty fading be;. . . . . 330 Psalm XXXIX   35
MAKETH
      When by the winde it maketh a noyse, I do thinke she doth
            answer.. . . . .   36 1st Eclogues 13   145
      Let Pas now know, how Nico maketh layes. . . . .   54 2nd Eclogues 29   71
      My fall her glorie maketh, ... 136 Cert Sonnets 3   11
      And maketh weak. . . . . 317 Psalm XXXIII   35
MAKING
      Sings out her woes, a thorne her song-booke making:. . . . . 137 Cert Sonnets 4   4
      Sleepe then a litle, pap content is making:. . . . . 139 Cert Sonnets 6   8
      With that faire breast making woe's darknesse cleare:. . . . 193 Astrophil   57   11
      Making those Lillies and those Roses grow, ... 231 Astrophil   100   2
      In a ground of so firme making,. . . . . 234 A&S 11th Song   34
      On thy blessed making hand . . . . 289 Psalm XVI   43
      Making hir beames his bravery and might: . . . . 246 Other Poems   4   146
      Her happy-making hand, of whome one looke. . . . . 248 Other Poems   4   247
MALADIES
      Nurse inwarde maladyes, which have not scope to be breath'd
            out, ...   35 1st Eclogues 13   104
MALAPERT
      Thy words, though full of malapert offence,. . . . .   25 1st Eclogues 9   108
MALCONTENT
      There he wandring malecontent, ... 262 Other Poems   7   13
MALE
      Palmes do rejoyce to be joynd by the match of a male to a
            female,. . . . .   36 1st Eclogues 13   137
MALEDICTION
      To wretched me, the last worst malediction.. . . . .   61 2nd Eclogues 30   148
MALICE
      Who doth his soule to endlesse malice bend.. . . . .   22 1st Eclogues 9   10
      Envying shallow toyes with malice deepe. . . . . 104 3rd Eclogues 67   39
      Hast in their malice broken. . . . . 273 Psalm III   30
      When in hearts they malice meane.. . . . . 309 Psalm XXVIII   15
      But malice shall the wicked choake,. . . . . 320 Psalm XXXIV   75
MAN
      Why thee a living man they had made dead.. . . . .   11 Arcadia I   1   7
      Whose vertues strange, and beuties such, as no man them may
            know?. . . . .   12 Arcadia I   3   2
      Thanked be I that keepe a man, ...   13 Arcadia I   5   3
      So if my man must praises have,. . . . .   13 Arcadia I   5   5
      Above line repeated at following location. . . . .   13 Arcadia I   5   11
      O wretched state of man in selfe division! . . . .   20 1st Eclogues 7 V966
      Above line repeated at following location. . . . .   20 1st Eclogues 7 V967
      Thus halfe a man, with man he easly haunts,. . . . .   21 1st Eclogues 8   31
      An olde man heare, who would thy fancies raise.. . . . . . .   22 1st Eclogues 9   5
      Philisides. Who ever taught a skillesse man to teach, . . .   22 1st Eclogues 9   16
      Would scorne in man (their king) such feeble shows.. . . . .   23 1st Eclogues 9   43
      What man is he hath hath his freedome solde? . . . .   24 1st Eclogues 9   56
      Is he a manlike man, that doth not know man. . . . .   24 1st Eclogues 9   57
      A fickle Sex, and trew in trust to no man,.. . . . .   24 1st Eclogues 9   59
      No man doth wish his horse should aged bee.. . . . .   24 1st Eclogues 9   86
      I yet should know a young man speaketh now,. . . . .   25 1st Eclogues 9   97
      For proofe of man, who sprong of heav'nly fire . . . .   25 1st Eclogues 9   100
      Philisides. Hath any man heard what this old man said? . . .   26 1st Eclogues 9   135
      Thou heardst even now a yong man snebb me sore,.. . . . . .   27 1st Eclogues 10   22
      Geron. Fy man, fy man, what wordes hath thy tonge lent?. . .   28 1st Eclogues 10   61
      What can justice availe, to a man that tells not his owne
            case?. . . . .   32 1st Eclogues 13   22
      But yet well I doo finde each man most wise in his owne
            case . . . .   33 1st Eclogues 13   70
      Dorus. O glittring miseries of man, if this be the fortune.   34 1st Eclogues 13   89
      A man to feare a woman's moodie eye, ...   49 2nd Eclogues 28   75

296

MAN   (CONTINUED)   PAGE   TITLE   LINE
    The child feeles that; the man that feeling knowes,. . . . . 57 2nd Eclogues 30   23
    This man, this talking beast, this walking tree. . . . . . . 58 2nd Eclogues 30   34
    Bculon. O man, take heed, how thou the Gods do move. . . . . 59 2nd Eclogues 30   65
    Then man to yeeld to female lamentations?. . . . . 61 2nd Eclogues 30 141
    Woe to poore man: ech outward thing annoyes him. . . . . . . 62 2nd Eclogues 30 170
    Can then a cause be so light that forceth a man to go die?
        Aye. . . . . 64 2nd Eclogues 31   24
    What great name may I give to so heav'nly a woman? A
        woe-man . . . . 64 2nd Eclogues 31   37
    What man grafts in a tree dissimulation? . . . . 69 2nd Eclogues 34   28
    The marchante man, whome gayne dothe teache the Sea. . . . . 70 Arcadia III 36   1
    The marchante man, whome many seas have toughte. . . . . . . 71 Arcadia III 37   1
    A Banisht man, long bard from his desire . . . . 75 Arcadia III 44   1
    Seeke then and see, what man esteemeth best, ... 75 Arcadia III 44   5
    Happy man, happy wife. 94 3rd Eclogues 63   95
    As in a sommer day a man might see:. . . . . 94 3rd Eclogues 64   4
    (For they have toongs to make a poore man blamed . . . . . . 94 3rd Eclogues 64   21
    Glad was the man when he had heard her out,. . . . . 96 3rd Eclogues 64   63
    For feare he did, least he the young man might . . . . 96 3rd Eclogues 64   65
    For to the courte her man was calld by name, ... 96 3rd Eclogues 64   77
    And one man still, credit with her preserve. . . . . 98 3rd Eclogues 65   4
    Man was not man their dwellings in to hem. . . . . 100 3rd Eclogues 66   49
    Thus Man was made; thus Man their Lord became: . . . . 101 3rd Eclogues 66 106
    But yet o man, rage not beyond thy neede:. . . . . 103 3rd Eclogues 66 148
    Beleeve me man, there is no greater blisse,. . . . . 103 3rd Eclogues 67   7
    No wife but I hath such a man, God wot". . . . . 104 3rd Eclogues 67   45
    Nc mortall man the cuppe of suretie drinkes. . . . . 105 3rd Eclogues 67   60
    Man oft is plag'de with aire, is burnt with fire,. . . . . . 105 3rd Eclogues 67   67
    No man doth speake aright, who speakes in feare. . . . . . . 106 3rd Eclogues 67   84
    Unarmde (alas) unwarn'd to take a man asleepe? . . . . 122 4th Eclogues 73 186
    (Teares and teares of a man) had no returne to remorse;. . . 122 4th Eclogues 74   16
    But, but alas, like a man condemn'd doth crave to be heard
        speake,. . . . . 122 4th Eclogues 74   23
    Unto the man, whom now such miseries you awarde? . . . . . . 124 4th Eclogues 74   74
    If then a man in most ill case may give you a farewell;. . . 124 4th Eclogues 74   85
    But unto Man, age ever death doth sende. . . . . 127 4th Eclogues 75   84
    But Man which helpeth them, helplesse must perish. . . . . . 127 4th Eclogues 75   87
    The same man still in whom wysdome prevailes,. . . . . 143 Cert Sonnets 12   17
    No man doubts, whom beautie killeth, ... 156 Cert Sonnets 26   27
    But for that man with paine this truth descries, ... 177 Astrophil   25   5
    Thinke Nature me a man of armes did make. . . . . 185 Astrophil   41   11
    Where well he knowes, no man to him can come. . . . . 186 Astrophil   43   14
    Who makes a man live then glad when he dieth?. . . . . 197 A&S 1st Song   26
    And all I said so well, as no man it denied. . . . . 212 A&S 5th Song   12
    Time doth worke what no man knoweth.". . . . . 234 A&S 11th Song   17
    So all things whereto that man doth bend,. . . . . 270 Psalm I   11
    The murdrous man, and so the fraudulent. . . . . 275 Psalm V   16
    For this same man will not learn to repent,. . . . . 278 Psalm VII   33
    A pitt was digg'd, by this man vainly strong,. . . . . 278 Psalm VII   40
    Then think I, Ah, what is this Man,. . . . . 278 Psalm VIII   13
    And let not man have upper hand of Thee, ... 281 Psalm IX   62
    For lo with pride the wicked man . . . . 281 Psalm X   5
    Of earthly man, a lord of dust.. . . . . 283 Psalm X   80
    Even for the sighs, true sighs of man distrest . . . . 285 Psalm XII   15
    The foolish man by flesh and fancy led . . . . 286 Psalm XIV   1
    Then what man would so soon seek gold. . . . . 294 Psalm XIX   41
    Who is the man that ever can . . . . 295 Psalm XIX   49
    This man for everlasting;. . . . . 297 Psalm XXI   22
    Even he whose life no help of man can quicken. . . . . 300 Psalm XXII   74
    Ev'n like a dead man dreamed out of mind,. . . . . 313 Psalm XXXI   35
    Bless'ed is the man whose filthy stain . . . . 314 Psalm XXXII   1
    Another man be stonge. 320 Psalm XXXIV   52
    Thy grace with safety man fulfills,. . . . . 323 Psalm XXXVI   17
    The man whom God directs doth stand. . . . . 326 Psalm XXXVII   57
    Yet I the man that was betaken . . . . 326 Psalm XXXVII   62
    But I like a man become,. . . . . 328 Psalm XXXVIII   37
    Look but on this: man still doth riches heape. . . . . 330 Psalm XXXIX   21
    So what is man but vanity? . . . . 330 Psalm XXXIX   36
    What man Thy thoughts can count to Thee. . . . . 331 Psalm XL   22
    Judg of th' afflicted man; . . . . 332 Psalm XLI   2
    For never was there man more crossely crost then he. . . . . 241 Other Poems   1   4
    She mov'd hir lims, and drew the aged man,. . . . . 249 Other Poems   4   283
    But God gives them instinct the man to shun, ... 249 Other Poems   4   295
    He found man's vertue is but part of man,. . . . . 253 Other Poems   4   421
    And part must folowe where whole man doth goe. . . . . 253 Other Poems   4   422
    In this wood a man I met,. . . . . 262 Other Poems   7   7
    Grant, I say (if seely man . . . . 263 Other Poems   7   57
MANACIES
    Nor golden manacles, stand for a paradise, ... 69 2nd Eclogues 34   25
MANAGE
    That in the Manage myselfe takes delight. . . . . 189 Astrophil   49   14
MANGLED
    My mangled mind huge horrors still doe fright, ... 74 Arcadia III 42   5
    With price of mangled mind thy worthlesse ware,. . . . . . . 161 Cert Sonnets 31   6
MANIFEST
    Made manifest by such a victorie,. . . . . 185 Astrophil   40   10
MANIFOLD
    With passe-port of thy graces manifold:. . . . . 275 Psalm V   18
    My God Thy wondrous works how manifold,. . . . . 331 Psalm XL   21

		PAGE	TITLE		LINE
MANKIND					
But mankind is for aye to nought resolved.		127	4th Eclogues	75	81
But I a worm, not I of mankind am, ...		299	Psalm XXII		15
Unto due thoughts mankind his thoughts shall order, ...		300	Psalm XXII		66
Or shall Thy Truth on mankind layd		311	Psalm XXX		29
Thy Mercy is! which makes mankind.		324	Psalm XXXVI		20
MANLIKE					
Is he a manlike man, that doth not know man.		24	1st Eclogues	9	57
MANLY					
(Although simply atyrde) your manly affection utter.		32	1st Eclogues	13	16
MANNER					
And what manner a mind which had to that humor a vaine. Vaine.		63	2nd Eclogues	31	9
But fewe dayes past while she good maner us'de, ...		95	3rd Eclogues	64	26
Such maner time there was (what time I n'ot)		100	3rd Eclogues	66	43
By no pretence claime any maner place.		191	Astrophil	52	11
From carelesnesse did in no maner grow, ...		227	Astrophil	93	7
MANNERS					
If that be sinne which doth the maners frame, ...		172	Astrophil	14	9
I, cumbred with good maners, answer do, ...		180	Astrophil	30	13
If him new-learned manners had not stai'd.		246	Other Poems	4	166
MAN'S					
"Tush, tush", said nature, "this is all but a trifle, a man's selfe.		29	1st Eclogues	11	7
In silence, from a man's owne selfe with company robbed. . .		35	1st Eclogues	13	106
In sicke-man's franzie rather takes compassion, ...		50	2nd Eclogues	29	96
Where man's mind hath a freed consideration.		68	2nd Eclogues	34	3
In curled knots man's thought to hold:		85	Arcadia III	62	4
In shape, which by man's eye might be perceived;		127	4th Eclogues	75	71
Was this man's death the fruite of your dissention?		128	4th Eclogues	75	108
Farewell o pearl, the poore man's plenteous treasure:		129	4th Eclogues	76	2
Farewell o golden staffe, the weake man's might:		129	4th Eclogues	76	3
Wisdome farewell, the skillesse man's direction:		129	4th Eclogues	76	5
The child of curse, man's weaknesse foster-child, ...		141	Cert Sonnets	10	2
Thou blind man's marke, thou foole's self chosen snare, . . .		161	Cert Sonnets	31	1
Rich in all beauties which man's eye can see:		183	Astrophil	37	6
The poore man's wealth, the prisoner's release, ...		184	Astrophil	39	3
And now man's wrongs in me, poore beast, descrie.		189	Astrophil	49	4
No witchcraft is so evill, as which man's mind destroyeth. .		215	A&S 5th Song		78
The lord doth search the just man's reines, ...		284	Psalm XI		17
But hunt with craft the quiet man's annoy;		322	Psalm XXXV		52
Chafe not at some man's great good fortune		325	Psalm XXXVII		18
I know that man's foule sin doth cause Thy wrath..		330	Psalm XXXIX		33
He found man's vertue is but part of man, ...		253	Other Poems	4	421
MANSION					
Yet deare soile, if a soule closed in a mansion.		69	2nd Eclogues	34	31
The mansion seat of blisse, and just excuse of Lovers; . . .		213	A&S 5th Song		21
MANSIONS					
What needed so high sprites such mansions blind?		57	2nd Eclogues	30	14
MANTLE					
Each thing with mantle black the night doth soothe;		98	3rd Eclogues	66	5
MAN-WOOD					
Women man-wood, and men effeminate..		28	1st Eclogues	10	60
MANY					
Who is an heire of many hundred sheep.		18	1st Eclogues	7	117
That which we see in many time hath wrought, ...		22	1st Eclogues	9	14
Come from marble bowers, many times the gay harbor of anguish, ...		34	1st Eclogues	13	92
Nico. Thy monument is layd in many a tree, ...		56	2nd Eclogues	29	129
Those beames that set so many harts on fire?		59	2nd Eclogues	30	84
The marchante man, whome many seas have toughte.		71	Arcadia III	37	1
That streight was done with many a boistrous threat, ...		97	3rd Eclogues	64	115
Then gan in guiltlesse earth full many a wound, ...		102	3rd Eclogues	66	115
If many Kalaes our Arcadia gave, ...		104	3rd Eclogues	67	22
For true it is, that they feare many whom many feare.. . . .		143	Cert Sonnets	14	2
Ah haire, how many dayes, ...		158	Cert Sonnets	28	9
Beauties, which were of manie Carrets fine, ...		172	Astrophil	16	2
Wo, having made with many fights his owne.		193	Astrophil	57	1
So manie eyes ay seeking their owne woe, ...		206	Astrophil	78	12
I saw thy selfe with many a smiling line		232	Astrophil	103	2
How many Ones there be		272	Psalm III		4
Indeed full many folkes have said, ...		274	Psalm IV		24
And cruely in many peices teare.		277	Psalm VII		5
With many liberall blessing:		297	Psalm XXI		10
Many mighty wrongfull foes, ...		329	Psalm XXXVIII		57
Which many seeing hearts shall rayse		331	Psalm XL		13
Where bold and hurtles many plays he tries, ...		247	Other Poems	4	194
A-field they goe, where many lookers be, ...		247	Other Poems	4	217
"Where how many Creatures be, ...		263	Other Poems	7	49
So many pufft in minde I see, ...		263	Other Poems	7	50
MAP					
But thinke that all the Map of my state I display, ...		168	Astrophil	6	13
MAR					
Which thought doth marre my piping declaration, ...		19	1st Eclogues	7	168
To marre my minde, and with my hurt to please, ...		149	Cert Sonnets	21	2
MARBLE					
Come from marble bowers, many times the gay harbor of anguish, ...		34	1st Eclogues	13	92
This marble chose, as of like temper knowne:		40	Arcadia II	19	2
A woman's hand with constant marble stone.		40	Arcadia II	19	6

MARBLE   (CONTINUED)   PAGE   TITLE   LINE
    My words full weake, the marble full of might; . . . .   41 Arcadia II   19   7
    My words in store, the marble all alone; . . . .   41 Arcadia II   19   8
    My words blacke inke, the marble kindly white; . . . .   41 Arcadia II   19   9
    My words unseene, the marble still in sight, ...   41 Arcadia II   19   10
    A woman's hand, with constant marble stone.. . . . .   41 Arcadia II   19   12
    Like pomels round of Marble cleere:. . . . .   87 Arcadia III   62   55
    Hard like a rich marbell: hard, but a faire Diamond. . . . . 122 4th Eclogues   74   14
    My mistresse' Marble hart, ... 160 Cert Sonnets   30   24
    Marble mixt red and white do enterlace.. . . . . 169 Astrophil   9   8
    Such marble eares, no cunning wordes can charme, ... 346 Possibly   5   2
MARCH
    For since mad March great promise made of me, ... 175 Astrophil   21   9
MARCHED
    Stella alone with face unarmed marcht, ... 176 Astrophil   22   9
MARCHETH
    Because in brave array heere marcheth she, ... 223 Astrophil   88   3
MARCHFANE
    Like comfits round in marchpane set. . . . .   89 Arcadia III   62 112
MARGIN
    What blushing notes doest thou in margine see? . . . . 199 Astrophil   67   8
MARK
    But in a palme when I marke, how he doth rise under a
        burden . . . .   36 1st Eclogues   13 127
    Their ireful shotte against so weake a marke, ...   73 Arcadia III   40   6
    Thy running course cannot such beawties marke: . . . .   80 Arcadia III   52   11
    Must I be onely the marke, shall prove that Vertue is
        angrie . . . . 123 4th Eclogues   74   33
    And doo not onely marke the accents last, ... 126 4th Eclogues   75   32
    The Rockes which were of constant mind the marke . . . . . . 147 Cert Sonnets   18   5
    Thou blind man's marke, thou foole's selfe chosen snare, . . 161 Cert Sonnets   31   1
    Is no fit marke to pierce with his fine pointed dart:. . . . 168 Astrophil   8   3
    Who marke in thee what is in thee most faire.. . . . . 201 Astrophil   71   11
    To lay his then marke wanting shafts of sight, ... 230 Astrophil   99   3
    That with such poysonous care my lookes you marke, ... 233 Astrophil   104   2
    He leasure wants to mark all this. . . . . 282 Psalm X   48
    I plain sweet Lord, my plaint for pitty mark; . . . . 289 Psalm XVII   2
    For like a marke Thou shalt arow . . . . 298 Psalm XXI   45
    To me and mark what I do say, ... 319 Psalm XXXIV   42
    Mark the upright, the just attend, ... 327 Psalm XXXVII   93
    Thus did I think: I well will mark my way, ... 329 Psalm XXXIX   1
    But Dick my counsell marke: run from the place of wo:. . . . 344 Possibly   1   41
    Busy with oker did their shoulders marke, ... 243 Other Poems   4   69
    (His marke a Piller was devoid of stay, ... 243 Other Poems   4   70
    His eye, that ev'n did marke hir troden grasse, ... 251 Other Poems   4 379
MARKED
    If by the parties ment our meanings rightly be marked, . . .   37 1st Eclogues   13 174
    Strephon as yonge, yet markt with humble eies . . . . 243 Other Poems   4   36
MARKET
    Should price of hir, as in a market, make. . . . . 245 Other Poems   4 123
MARKING
    Which night and day he calls to marking mind.. . . . . 270 Psalm I   6
    More marking hir, then how himselfe did goe, ... 249 Other Poems   4 290
MARKS
    Least that some markes of jealousie you beare. . . . .   97 3rd Eclogues   64 124
    Can those blacke beames such burning markes engrave. . . . . 188 Astrophil   47   2
    That tedious leasure marks each wrinckled line:. . . . . . . 230 Astrophil   98   11
    These markes shall make thee wise: . . . . 259 Other Poems   5 111
MARRED
    Oh he is mard that is for others made. . . . .   19 1st Eclogues   7 166
    Lalus. Oh he is mard that is for others made.. . . . .   19 1st Eclogues   7 167
    Thinking how it hath mard my shepheard's trade.. . . . . . .   19 1st Eclogues   7 169
    My young mind marde, whom Love doth windlas so, ... 175 Astrophil   21   2
    Peace, foolish wit, with wit my wit is mard. . . . . 182 Astrophil   34   11
MARRIAGE
    From holy marriage, sweete and surest meane. . . . . 103 3rd Eclogues   67   2
    Marrie therefore; for marriage will destroy. . . . . 107 3rd Eclogues   67 115
MARRIED
    That married had a trick and bonny lasse . . . .   94 3rd Eclogues   64   3
    These fiftie winters maried have I beene; . . . . 106 3rd Eclogues   67   86
MARROW
    Sorowe suck up the marowe of my might, ...   74 Arcadia III   42   10
    Lord help, for ev'en my bones their marrow spend . . . . . . 276 Psalm VI   7
MARRY
    Marrie therefore; for marriage will destroy. . . . . 107 3rd Eclogues   67 115
    Who hath the eyes which marrie state with pleasure, ... 197 A&S 1st Song   5
MARS
    O Mars, for what doth serve thy armed axe? . . . .   60 2nd Eclogues   30 110
    In fine, since strife of thought but marres the mind, . . . 135 Cert Sonnets   1   8
    Phoebus was Judge betweene Jove, Mars, and Love, ... 171 Astrophil   13   1
    But in Vert field Mars bare a golden speare, ... 171 Astrophil   13   5
    Each had his creast, Mars caried Venus' glove, ... 171 Astrophil   13   7
    Because that Mars, growne slacker in her love, ... 173 Astrophil   17   2
    And gain'd by Mars, could yet mad Mars so tame, ... 204 Astrophil   75   7
    Leave to Mars the force of hands, ... 211 A&S 4th Song   45
MARS'S
    The boy refusde for feare of Marse's hate, ... 173 Astrophil   17   5
    In Marse's liverie, prauncing in the presse: . . . . 191 Astrophil   53   6
MARTIAL
    In Martiall sports I had my cunning tride, ... 191 Astrophil   53   1

	PAGE	TITLE		LINE
MARTING				
Wheare he was bounde, to make his marting place, ...	70	Arcadia III	36	4
MARVEI				
What marvaile then I take a woman's hew, ...	12	Arcadia I	2	13
Mastix. What marvaile if in youth such faults be done, . . .	27	1st Eclogues	10	25
What marvaile tho a Prince transforme himselfe to a Pastor?.	34	1st Eclogues	13	91
MARVELS				
My speeches all Thy marvailes shall descry:.	279	Psalm IX		2
Make us in mervailes of Thy mercy know	290	Psalm XVII		22
MASK				
Silence doth seeme the maske of base oppression.	47	2nd Eclogues	28	15
MASKED				
That bravely maskt, their fancies may be told:	166	Astrophil	3	2
MASKS				
My friend, that oft saw through all maskes my wo,.	200	Astrophil	69	5
MASS				
So mazde a masse, or if in me it growes, ...	149	Cert Sonnets	22	9
But streight his shining eyes this misty masse disclos'd.. .	291	Psalm XVIII		26
MAST				
Pine is a maste to a shippe, to my shippe shall hope for a				
maste serve?	36	1st Eclogues	13	129
Sore beaten doth her mast of Comforte spende:.	114	4th Eclogues	72	45
MASTER				
Reason. Thou Rebell vile, come, to thy master yelde.	46	2nd Eclogues	27	1
A hill most fitte for such a master, ...	88	Arcadia III	62	79
Their master is faire warn'd his will to make.	150	Cert Sonnets	22	20
Go you not from your master in his woe:.	254	Other Poems	4	487
If thou know not for whome thy Master dies,.	259	Other Poems	5	110
MASTER'S				
Come shepheard's weedes, become your master's minde:	13	Arcadia I	4	1
Wayle in my woes, taste of your master's payne,.	44	Arcadia II	24	11
All strife for toyes, and clayming master's right:	93	3rd Eclogues	63	67
On servants' shame oft Maister's blame doth sit;	236	Astrophil	107	12
Heare your wofull maister's story, ...	221	A&S 9th Song		12
MASTERING				
Her eyes so maistering me, that such objection	16	1st Eclogues	7	68
MASTIX				
Come narr good Mastix, tis now full tway score	27	1st Eclogues	10	20
Of yeeres (alas) since I good Mastix knewe..	27	1st Eclogues	10	21
Mastix. What marvaile if in youth such faults be done, . . .	27	1st Eclogues	10	25
MATCH				
Thy health too meane a match for my infection.	15	1st Eclogues	7	21
Let not thy tonge become a firy matche.	29	1st Eclogues	10	89
Palmes do rejoyce to be joynd by the match of a male to a				
female,.	36	1st Eclogues	13	137
Of singing match we made, whence he with shame did trudge. .	52	2nd Eclogues	29	16
Pas. Kisse her? now mayst thou kisse. I have a fitter match;	53	2nd Eclogues	29	39
Nor thinke the match unev'nly made,.	159	Cert Sonnets	29	10
To match with light foot staggs he made my foot so light . .	292	Psalm XVIII		61
Nor my life's cause match with bloodseeker's case, ...	306	Psalm XXVI		30
MATCHED				
Where proofes justly do teach, thus matcht, such worth to be				
nought worth.	34	1st Eclogues	13	83
Mock'st thou those Diamonds which only be matcht by the				
gods Ods.	65	2nd Eclogues	31	47
The first, thus matcht, were scarcely Gentlemen.	171	Astrophil	13	14
Pas Cosma matcht, yet angry with his fault,.	250	Other Poems	4	318
MATCHLESS				
The more his matchlesse giftes do deepely sinck.	85	Arcadia III	61	11
The matchlesse paire, even praise doth staine.	86	Arcadia III	62	16
MATE				
But if I had bene there, th'adst met another mate.	52	2nd Eclogues	29	22
This sowre-breath'd mate tast of those sugred lips..	194	Astrophil	59	11
Thou planted hast this earthly mate.	279	Psalm VIII		18
His well knowne friend, but yet his unknowne mate, ...	255	Other Poems	4	528
To mate with whom he liveth, ...	261	Other Poems	6	50
MATED				
Thus in my pilgrimaige of mated mynde, ...	71	Arcadia III	36	13
MATE-IN-ARMS				
Though oft himselfe my mate-in-armes he sware.	228	Astrophil	95	8
MATES				
Ne for bad mates in way of sinning waiteth	270	Psalm I		3
Of things vain, with vaine mates they bable all, ...	284	Psalm XII		4
And so thereafter He, and all his Mates.	286	Psalm XIV		4
These mates to be amated..	297	Psalm XXI		32
Yea neighbors, more, my mates were so agast.	313	Psalm XXXI		32
Joyne Mates in mirth to me,.	260	Other Poems	6	1
"My old mates I grieve to see, ...	262	Other Poems	7	19
Striving with my Mates in Song,.	263	Other Poems	7	45
MATTERETH				
Deadly wounds inward bleed, ech sleight sore mattereth.. . .	14	1st Eclogues	7	9
MATTERS				
"Nought can reason availe in heav'nly matters"..	68	2nd Eclogues	33	26
And use but you for matters to rehearse?	146	Cert Sonnets	17	35
MAUGRE				
O voice, o face, maugre my speeche's might,.	194	Astrophil	58	12
Maugre their force I will set him at rest.	285	Psalm XII		18
MAW				
Go bawling curre, thy hungry maw go fill,.	255	Other Poems	4	517

```
                                                        PAGE    TITLE           LINE
MAWS
    To crammed mawes a spratt new Stomake brings. . . . . . . . .  245 Other Poems      4   134
MAY
    If now the May of my yeares much decline,. . . . . . . . . .  175 Astrophil       21    10
    When mery May first early calls the morne, . . . . . . . . .  243 Other Poems      4    49
MAYING
    With merry maids a Maying they do go,. . . . . . . . . . . .  243 Other Poems      4    50
MAYPOLE
    While daunce about the may-pole is begun,. . . . . . . . . .  243 Other Poems      4    55
MAYST
    How thou from foolish love maist purge thy sense. . . . . . .   25 1st Eclogues     9   110
    If once thou maist that fancie glosse destroy. . . . . . . .   25 1st Eclogues     9   117
    I warne thee therefore (since thou maist have choice). . . .   29 1st Eclogues    10    88
    Thou mayest love her that I may see thy sightfulnesse. . . .   51 2nd Eclogues    28   113
    Pas. Kisse her? now mayst thou kisse. I have a fitter match;   53 2nd Eclogues    29    39
    For good thou mayst yet proove in sheepish sound. . . . . . .   56 2nd Eclogues    29   137
    To that where thou thy Cupid maist avowe,. . . . . . . . . .  106 3rd Eclogues    67   101
    Sweet swelling lip, well maist thou swell in pride,. . . . .  206 Astrophil       80     1
    There unseen thou maist be bold, . . . . . . . . . . . . . .  226 A&S 10th Song         16
    Will. Thou late of wages playn'dst: what wages mayst thou
        have?. . . . . . . . . . . . . . . . . . . . . . . . . .  344 Possibly         1    31
    So maist thou long abide . . . . . . . . . . . . . . . . . .  258 Other Poems      5    67
    That on his wings the leavell thou maist finde . . . . . . .  259 Other Poems      5   107
    "Therefore Pan, if thou mayst be . . . . . . . . . . . . . .  263 Other Poems      7    55
MAZE
    Your eyes may tread a Lover's maze. . . . . . . . . . . . . .   86 Arcadia III     62    32
MAZED
    Nor mas'de head thinke, nor faltring tonge recite. . . . . .   74 Arcadia III     42    14
    So mazde a masse, or if in me it growes, . . . . . . . . . .  149 Cert Sonnets    22     9
    Of his mazde powers keepes perfit harmony: . . . . . . . . .  230 Astrophil       99     8
    But they do faile, and in their mazed corners rew. . . . . .  293 Psalm XVIII           82
MAZEFUL
    In both a mazefull solitarinesse:. . . . . . . . . . . . . .  229 Astrophil       96     9
MEADS
    Like late mowne meades, late cut from joy I live. . . . . . .  147 Cert Sonnets    18    11
    Rockes, woods, hilles, caves, dales, meads, brookes, answere
        me, . . . . . . . . . . . . . . . . . . . . . . . . . . .  147 Cert Sonnets    18    13
MEAGER
    With meager lookes, as if they still did smart;. . . . . . .  104 3rd Eclogues    67    28
    But heavy was her pace, and such a meagre cheere,. . . . . .  118 4th Eclogues    73    69
MEAGERLY
    Approach of death, alas thou helpest meagerly, . . . . . . .  128 4th Eclogues    75   110
*MEAN
    By princely meane be stolne, and yet not lost. . . . . . . .   11 Arcadia I        1     2
    Thy health too meane a match for my infection. . . . . . . .   15 1st Eclogues     7    21
    "O" cried I, "of so meane worke be discharged: . . . . . . .   16 1st Eclogues     7    76
    What meane is there, alas, we can hope our losse to recover?   32 1st Eclogues    13    27
    In meane caves oft treasure abides, to an hostry a king
        comes. . . . . . . . . . . . . . . . . . . . . . . . . .   36 1st Eclogues    13   153
    And if a meane were found, fortune th' whole course of it
        hinders. . . . . . . . . . . . . . . . . . . . . . . . .   37 1st Eclogues    13   159
    Arte? what can be that art which thou dost meane by thy
        speche? Speche. . . . . . . . . . . . . . . . . . . . . .   64 2nd Eclogues    31    29
    But keeping holesome meane,. . . . . . . . . . . . . . . . .   93 3rd Eclogues    63    80
    From holy marriage, sweete and surest meane. . . . . . . . .  103 3rd Eclogues    67     2
    Desire's best meane, harvest of hartes affected, . . . . . .  108 Arcadia IV      69     2
    And so most ready am this meane of peace to trie. . . . . . .  121 4th Eclogues    73   152
    (Unto thy selfe I do meane those graces dwell so within
        thee . . . . . . . . . . . . . . . . . . . . . . . . . .  122 4th Eclogues    74     9
    The golden meane who loves, lives safely free. . . . . . . .  143 Cert Sonnets    12     4
    When I say "Stella", I do meane the same . . . . . . . . . .  179 Astrophil       28     5
    But now I meane no more your helpe to trie,. . . . . . . . .  192 Astrophil       55     9
    But (God wot) wot not what they meane by it: . . . . . . . .  204 Astrophil       74     6
    Those lips, which make death's pay a meane price for a
        kisse . . . . . . . . . . . . . . . . . . . . . . . . . .  205 Astrophil       77     6
    Teaching the meane, at once to take and give . . . . . . . .  206 Astrophil       79     9
    Or do you meane my tender eares to spare,. . . . . . . . . .  225 Astrophil       92     4
    What ayles this heathenish rage? What do theis people meane.  271 Psalm II              1
    When in hearts they malice meane,. . . . . . . . . . . . . .  309 Psalm XXVIII          15
    By fortune meane, in Nature borne a Queene,. . . . . . . . .  244 Other Poems      4    91
    That the meane estate is best, . . . . . . . . . . . . . . .  264 Other Poems      7    76
MEANER
    Then quickly did the meaner cattell finde, . . . . . . . . .  102 3rd Eclogues    66   135
    Yet were the hid and meaner beauties parcht, . . . . . . . .  176 Astrophil       22    12
    Although they be of meaner parents gott: . . . . . . . . . .  242 Other Poems      4    12
MEANEST
    Worst fell to smallest birds, and meanest heard, . . . . . .  102 3rd Eclogues    66   141
    Glutted with them now plaies with meanest things. . . . . . .  245 Other Poems      4   132
MEANING
    The seed Fast-meaning is, no truth to misse: . . . . . . . .  115 4th Eclogues    72    53
    Your morall notes straight my hid meaning teare. . . . . . .  233 Astrophil      104    12
    Sent from false heart, on double meaning stay'd. . . . . . .  284 Psalm XII             6
    From Ill word, and ill meaning sound. . . . . . . . . . . . .  289 Psalm XVII           12
    But God shall scorn their moody meaning, . . . . . . . . . .  325 Psalm XXXVII         35
    Gratefull meaning show thee, . . . . . . . . . . . . . . . .  337 Psalm XLIII          27
    Meaning with absence to refresh the thought. . . . . . . . .  246 Other Poems      4   175
MEANINGS
    If by the parties ment our meanings rightly be marked, . . .   37 1st Eclogues    13   174
MEANLY
    To set a pearle in steele so meanely varnished?. . . . . . .   16 1st Eclogues     7    63
```

MEANLY   (CONTINUED)   PAGE   TITLE   LINE
    Are then humane mindes priviledg'd so meanly,. . . . .   31 1st Eclogues 12   17
*MEANS
    Jcyn'd, by thy beauty adorn'd, be no meanes these greefes to
        abolish:.. . . . .   34 1st Eclogues 13   99
    Whom both nature seemes to debarr from meanes to be helped,.   37 1st Eclogues 13 158
    But who by meanes of wisdome hie . . . .   44 Arcadia II   25   5
    Turned anew by your meanes,. . . . .   154 Cert Sonnets 25   24
    How Poles' right king meanes, without leave of hoast,. . . . 180 Astrophil   30   3
MEANT
    If by the parties ment our meanings rightly be marked, . . .   37 1st Eclogues 13 174
    Of waiting thoughts all to her service ment? . . . .   78 Arcadia III 49   12
    As if he meant his lordship common be. . . . .   102 3rd Eclogues 66 112
    As stuffe meant for the sale set out to glaring showe) . . . 118 4th Eclogues 73   72
    As of a friend that meant not much amisse: . . . . 193 Astrophil   56   8
    For all love, all faith is meant thee, ... 220 A&S 8th Song   92
    For when great griefes to me be ment,. . . . . 307 Psalm XXVII   25
    While nought but game, the selfe-hurt wanton ment. . . . . . 247 Other Poems   4 192
MEANWHILE
    Meane while my heart confers with Stella's beames, ... 190 Astrophil   51   12
MEASURE
    Her father's corne (moving her faire limmes) measure.. . . .   16 1st Eclogues 7   75
    Measure my case, how by thy beautie's filling. . . . .   16 1st Eclogues 7   77
    Time, place, life, wit scarcely her rare gifts measure doth.   49 2nd Eclogues 29   60
    Of humane life to be the quiet measure,. . . . . 108 Arcadia IV   69   4
    And if that any counsell you to measure. . . . . 126 4th Eclogues 75   49
    What in your face mine eyes do measure.. . . . . 159 Cert Sonnets 29   9
    Only for you the heav'n forgate all measure. . . . . 197 A&S 1st Song   8
    If stones good measure daunc'd, the Theban walles to build,. 208 A&S 3rd Song   3
    Can abide to keepe no measure, ... 221 A&S 9th Song   7
    Become the measure.. . . . . 276 Psalm VI   4
    Lord unto me my time's just measure give,. . . . . 329 Psalm XXXIX   13
MEASURING
    Whose hearts are set on measuring a verse: . . . . 146 Cert Sonnets 17   32
MEAT
    With water drinke, herbes meate, and naked hide, ... 101 3rd Eclogues 66 109
    D. Teares drink, sorowes meat, wherewith, not I, but in me
        my death lives..   344 Possibly   1   34
MEDEA'S
    But never did Medea's golden weed. . . . . 252 Other Poems   4 409
MEDICINE
    What medecin may I finde for a paine that draw's me to
        death Death.. . . . .   63 2nd Eclogues 31   6
    O poisonous medecin! what worse to me can be then it? It...   63 2nd Eclogues 31   7
    What medicin then, can such desease remove . . . .   85 Arcadia III 61   13
MEDITATE
    Consider what I meditate in me:. . . . . 274 Psalm V   2
MEDITATION
    And my heart's meditation, ... 295 Psalm XIX   62
MEEK
    Nor meek abiding of the patient wight. . . . . 281 Psalm IX   58
    Meeke to the Meek Thou art, The good thy goodness taste; . . 292 Psalm XVIII   50
    The meek he doth in judgment lead, ... 303 Psalm XXV   35
    But meek men shall the earth possesse, ... 325 Psalm XXXVII   29
MEEKER
    Pray that my sunne go downe with meeker beames to bed. . . . 205 Astrophil   76   14
MEET
    But when in shade we meet of mirtle bowes, ...   18 1st Eclogues 7 128
    And when I meete these trees, in the earth's faire lyvery
        clothed, ...   35 1st Eclogues 13 113
    Pas. Alas, when I in spring meet roses rathe,. . . . .   54 2nd Eclogues 29   78
    When they though divers do together meete: . . . .   92 3rd Eclogues 63   34
    In that which he so fear'd that she should meet. . . . . . .   95 3rd Eclogues 64   36
    To her, where I my heart safeliest shall meet. . . . . 209 Astrophil   84   6
    But heere I do store of faire Ladies meete,. . . . . 236 Astrophil   106   9
    Did for mutuall comfort meete, ... 218 A&S 8th Song   6
    Heavenly Stella meete with you,. . . . . 222 A&S 9th Song   48
    And with these Words, when they meet, prayse Thy Name. . . . 300 Psalm XXII   52
    But did entend next bout with her to meete,. . . . . 248 Other Poems   4 250
    Though him to meete at all she sturred nought. . . . . 250 Other Poems   4 326
    While deare Uran, whose course was Pas to meet,. . . . . . . 250 Other Poems   4 330
    His fancies still did hir in half-way meet,. . . . . 251 Other Poems   4 371
MEETING
    Graunt pleasure to our meeting:. . . . . 260 Other Poems   6   2
MEETINGS
    Why do these earthly kings and lords such meetings make, . . 271 Psalm II   3
MELAMPUS
    Geron. Downe, downe Melampus; what? your fellow bite?. . . .   26 1st Eclogues 10   1
    For though Melampus like a wolfe doo looke,. . . . .   27 1st Eclogues 10   16
MELANCHOLY
    The Hare, her sleights; the Cat, his melancholie;. . . . . . 101 3rd Eclogues 66   92
    Whence those same fumes of melancholy rise,. . . . . 176 Astrophil   23   3
MELODIES
    With monefull melodies, for enough our greefes be revealed,.   37 1st Eclogues 13 173
MELODY
    Stay to true love's melody:. . . . . 140 Cert Sonnets 7   39
    More oft then to a chamber melodie;. . . . . 209 Astrophil   84   4
MELT
    My earthy moulde doth melte in watrie teares.. . . . .   19 1st Eclogues 7 151
    Dorus. My earthy moulde doth melte in watrie teares, ...   19 1st Eclogues 7 152

302

MELT   (CONTINUED)   PAGE TITLE   LINE
 Which nothing spares, to melt that Virgin-waxe . . . . 60 2nd Eclogues 30 108
 What kind of fires they be in which those spirits melt,. . . 153 Cert Sonnets 24 7
 Doth melt away though it be inmost seated. . . . . 299 Psalm XXII   34
MELTING
 Their snowy haire teare off in melting paine. . . . . 254 Other Poems 4 478
MELTS
 Melts downe his lead into my boyling brest,. . . . . 236 Astrophil 108 2
 My life melts with too much thinking;. . . . . 227 A&S 10th Song 45
 My heart melts remembring so,. . . . . 334 Psalm XLII   13
MEMORY
 But if my memory thus must be thralled . . . . 61 2nd Eclogues 30 164
 Elephant gave a perfect memorie: . . . . 101 3rd Eclogues 66 83
 Girt fast by memorie, and while I spurre . . . . 189 Astrophil 49 10
 Where memory sets foorth the beames of love. . . . . 223 Astrophil 88 11
 What? Doth their Memory no longer last?. . . . . 280 Psalm IX   18
MEN
 Old men themselves, doe love young wives to choose:. . . . . 25 1st Eclogues 9 88
 Oh when will men leave off to judge by haire,. . . . . 25 1st Eclogues 9 93
 Women man-wood, and men effeminate. . . . . 28 1st Eclogues 10 60
 Men tongd like lotches sucking others sorrowe. . . . . 50 2nd Eclogues 28 V885
 Away vayne Cares, by which fewe men do thinke . . . . 83 Arcadia III 59 3
 The dreadfull cries of murdred men in forrests.. . . . . . 112 4th Eclogues 71 48
 Aske, if in great men good men so do thronge,. . . . . . . 126 4th Eclogues 75 43
 They are but words therefore which men do buy, ... 128 4th Eclogues 75 115
 Why those that die, men say they do depart:. . . . . 148 Cert Sonnets 20 2
 End the way, where all men stay. No, no, no, no. . . . . . 155 Cert Sonnets 26 22
 From them that use men thus, ... 160 Cert Sonnets 30 9
 Above line repeated at following locations . . . . 160 Cert Sonnets 30 19
 . . . . 160 Cert Sonnets 30 29
 "Eut will not wise men thinke thy words fond ware?". . . . . 182 Astrophil 34 7
 O eyes, o eares of men, how are you charmed! . . . . 209 A&S 3rd Song 18
 For neither shall the men in sin delighted . . . . 270 Psalm I   15
 Wher godly men do their assembly make. . . . . 270 Psalm I   18
 These men like potshards weake.. . . . . 271 Psalm II   22
 O men, whose Fathers were but men, ... 273 Psalm IV   6
 Thy work it is such men safe in to hemm. . . . . 275 Psalm V   39
 So shall all men with laudes inviron thee. . . . . 277 Psalm VII   19
 But still be Thou to just men justest guide. . . . . 277 Psalm VII   27
 Who dost Thy saving health to true men bend. . . . . 277 Psalm VII   30
 When Godless men be snar'd in their own snares:. . . . . . 281 Psalm IX   52
 But men to be. . . . . 281 Psalm IX   65
 He waites to spoyle the simple men:. . . . . 282 Psalm X   38
 For what, alas, have just men done?. . . . . 284 Psalm XI   11
 No men are left, that charity do love, ... 284 Psalm XII   2
 Nay even the race of good men are decay'd. . . . . 284 Psalm XII   3
 Good and godly men I love. . . . . 288 Psalm XVI   8
 That Thou by Faithfull Men wilt stand. . . . . 290 Psalm XVII   23
 From men I say, and from men's worldly trade,. . . . . . . 290 Psalm XVII   38
 Thus freed from mutin men, thou makest me to raign,. . . . 293 Psalm XVIII 78
 Let trust of some men be . . . . 296 Psalm XX   26
 Nay shame of men, the people's scorning game.. . . . . . . 299 Psalm XXII   16
 To sinning men his path. . . . . 303 Psalm XXV   34
 Feare might of men?. 307 Psalm XXVII   6
 Ye men of Pow'er even by birth-right,. . . . . 309 Psalm XXIX   2
 I hated have those men whose thoughts do cleave. . . . . . 312 Psalm XXXI   16
 I understand what rayling great men spred; . . . . 313 Psalm XXXI   37
 Nor strong men have. 317 Psalm XXXIII 59
 For God's own eyes on good men sit . . . . 320 Psalm XXXIV 55
 That wicked men do seeme to flourish,. . . . . 324 Psalm XXXVII 2
 But meek men shall the earth possesse, ... 325 Psalm XXXVII 29
 Ev'ill men work ill to utmost right, ... 325 Psalm XXXVII 33
 Small goodes in good men better is . . . . 325 Psalm XXXVII 41
 If this in them be true, as true in men think I. . . . . . 343 Possibly 1 7
 While those restles desires in great men rife. . . . . . . 243 Other Poems 4 62
 When we doe but flatter men: . . . . 263 Other Poems 7 34
 Of all men to thee retaining,. . . . . 263 Other Poems 7 65
MENALCAS
 Pas. My voice the lambe did winne, Menalcas was our judge: . 52 2nd Eclogues 29 15
MENALCAS'
 Disuse your selves from sweete Menalcas' voice:. . . . . . . 13 Arcadia I 4 6
MEND
 Nothing can mend one point that in her lies. . . . . 17 1st Eclogues 7 108
 The filthy snake her aged coate can mende, ... 127 4th Eclogues 75 82
 You see what I can say; mend yet your froward mind,. . . . 215 A&S 5th Song 88
MENDED
 A Nimph thus turnde, but mended in translation.. . . . . . 15 1st Eclogues 7 36
 Eyes, let your Teares with gazing now be mended, ... 84 Arcadia III 59 14
MEN'S
 And yet they say he talkes in greate men's bowers? . . . . 28 1st Eclogues 10 68
 That men's harts be thy seate and endlesse fame be thy
  servant, ... 36 1st Eclogues 13 148
 Doth proclaime with a sound made all by men's mouths . . . 68 2nd Eclogues 33 20
 Men's lives, untill it be imbraste.. . . . . 87 Arcadia III 62 66
 The Oratour so farre men's harts doth bind,. . . . . 193 Astrophil 58 2
 How faine would I paint thee to all men's eyes,. . . . . . 207 Astrophil 81 7
 Thou those men's teeth which byte, ... 273 Psalm III   28
 From men I say, and from men's worldly trade,. . . . . . . 290 Psalm XVII   38
 This shall men's fancys frame. . . . . 319 Psalm XXXIV 17
 God keeps account of good men's dayes, ... 325 Psalm XXXVII 45

```
MEN'S               (CONTINUED)                         PAGE    TITLE          LINE
    To great men's peacock pride,. . . . . . . . . . . . .   331  Psalm XL          18
MERCHANT
    The marchante man, whome gayne dothe teache the Sea. . . . .   70  Arcadia III  36    1
    The marchante man, whome many seas have toughte. . . . . . .   71  Arcadia III  37    1
MERCIES
    All mercys shall be swarmed. . . . . . . . . . . . . . . .   315  Psalm XXXII       39
MERCIFUL
    Then me redeem Lord then be mercifull. . . . . . . . . . .   306  Psalm XXVI        36
MERCURY
    Mercury kill'd his false sire for this act,. . . . . . . . .    21  1st Eclogues  8   17
    Klaius. O Mercurie, foregoer to the evening, . . . . . . . .   111  4th Eclogues 71    7
MERCY
    Have mercy therfore still on me, . . . . . . . . . . . . .   273  Psalm IV           4
    But mercy, lord, let Mercy thyne descend . . . . . . . . .   276  Psalm VI           5
    Mercy, O Mercy lord, for Mercy's sake, . . . . . . . . . .   276  Psalm VI          13
    Have mercie, mercie lord I once did say, . . . . . . . . .   280  Psalm IX          36
    Make us in mervailes of Thy mercy know . . . . . . . . . .   290  Psalm XVII        22
    This mercy is so sure. . . . . . . . . . . . . . . . . . .   301  Psalm XXIII       23
    And mercy spredd abroad. . . . . . . . . . . . . . . . . .   304  Psalm XXV         40
    Of thee some mercy take, . . . . . . . . . . . . . . . . .   304  Psalm XXV         45
    O look, O help, let mercy fall,. . . . . . . . . . . . . .   304  Psalm XXV         59
    Heare to have mercy eke of me. . . . . . . . . . . . . . .   307  Psalm XXVII       38
    Lord heare, let mercy thine be stay'd. . . . . . . . . . .   311  Psalm XXX         31
    Thy mercy shall fill me with jollity,. . . . . . . . . . .   312  Psalm XXXI        19
    O Lord, of Thee let me still mercy winn, . . . . . . . . .   312  Psalm XXXI        25
    Upon his mercy beare.. . . . . . . . . . . . . . . . . . .   318  Psalm XXXIII      72
    O let thy mercy great. . . . . . . . . . . . . . . . . . .   318  Psalm XXXIII      82
    Lord, how the heav'ns thy mercy fills, . . . . . . . . . .   323  Psalm XXXVI       13
    Thy Mercy is! which makes mankind. . . . . . . . . . . . .   324  Psalm XXXVI       20
    Me still in truth and mercy save,. . . . . . . . . . . . .   332  Psalm XL          42
    Have mercy lord on me, . . . . . . . . . . . . . . . . . .   333  Psalm XLI         14
    On me let mercy fall,. . . . . . . . . . . . . . . . . . .   333  Psalm XLI         34
MERCY'S
    Mercy, O Mercy lord, for Mercy's sake, . . . . . . . . . .   276  Psalm VI          13
    Thy Mercy's tendernes;. . . . . . . . . . . . . . . . . .   303  Psalm XXV         20
    Ev'n for Thy mercy's sake, O Lord. . . . . . . . . . . . .   303  Psalm XXV         30
    And save me in, and for Thy mercie's sake. . . . . . . . .   313  Psalm XXXI        44
MERELY
    And yet leave me helplesse meerely?. . . . . . . . . . . .   222  A&S 9th Song      35
    At best is merely vanity.. . . . . . . . . . . . . . . . .   330  Psalm XXXIX       18
MERIT
    Ne yet for what I see, your beauties merite ought. . . . .   121  4th Eclogues 73  164
MERITS
    Cleofila. Hardy shephearde, such as thy meritts, such may be
        her insight . . . . . . . . . . . . . . . . . . . . .    37  1st Eclogues 13  155
    No vertue merits praise, once toucht with blot of Treason. .   214  A&S 5th Song      66
    Their merits to requite. . . . . . . . . . . . . . . . . .   333  Psalm XLI         36
MERRILY
    Sing lowd and merrily, . . . . . . . . . . . . . . . . . .   316  Psalm XXXIII      15
MERRY
    She thinks I leade and live too merrie daies.. . . . . . .   146  Cert Sonnets 17   30
    Mery with him, and not thinke of his woe.. . . . . . . . .   236  Astrophil   106   14
    Merry flocke, such one forgo,. . . . . . . . . . . . . . .   221  A&S 9th Song       8
    When mery May first early calls the morne, . . . . . . . .   243  Other Poems   4   49
    With mery maids a Maying they do go, . . . . . . . . . . .   243  Other Poems   4   50
MESEEMED
    Although their fame (me seemd) from truth. . . . . . . . .   119  4th Eclogues 73   80
MESEEMS
    Strephon. Me seemes I see the high and stately mountaines, .   112  4th Eclogues 71   37
    Me seemes I heare in these ill-changed forrests, . . . . .   112  4th Eclogues 71   39
    Me seemes I feele the comfort of the morning . . . . . . .   112  4th Eclogues 71   41
    Klaius. Me seemes I see a filthie clowdie evening, . . . .   112  4th Eclogues 71   43
    Me seemes I feele a noysome sent, the morning. . . . . . .   112  4th Eclogues 71   45
    Me seemes I heare, when I doo heare sweete musique,. . . .   112  4th Eclogues 71   47
    Part of my paine me seemes engraved lyes.. . . . . . . . .   147  Cert Sonnets 18    4
    Yet there, me seemes, I heare her singing loud.. . . . . .   255  Other Poems   4  508
MESSAGE
    So that eyes' message be of her received,. . . . . . . . .    30  1st Eclogues 12    3
    Above line repeated at following location. . . . . . . . .    31  1st Eclogues 12   27
    So that eyes' message doo returne rejected,. . . . . . . .    30  1st Eclogues 12    7
MESSENGER
    For messenger of inward good.. . . . . . . . . . . . . . .   156  Cert Sonnets 27    8
    Morne's messenger, with rose enameld skies . . . . . . . .   231  Astrophil    99   10
MET
    But if I had bene there, th'adst met another mate. . . . .    52  2nd Eclogues 29   22
    Oh! I do know what guest I have mett; it is Echo. 'T is
        Echo . . . . . . . . . . . . . . . . . . . . . . . . .    63  2nd Eclogues 31    3
    Well mett Echo, aproche: then tell me thy will too. I will
        too. . . . . . . . . . . . . . . . . . . . . . . . . .    63  2nd Eclogues 31    4
    Along whose ridge such bones are met,. . . . . . . . . . .    89  Arcadia III  62  111
    When with a fire he first met. . . . . . . . . . . . . . .   154  Cert Sonnets 25   17
    On horsebacke met him in his furious race, . . . . . . . .   176  Astrophil    22    6
    That Vertue, if it once met with our eyes, . . . . . . . .   177  Astrophil    25    3
    While Strephon might with preatie Nous have met, . . . . .   249  Other Poems   4  279
    Of all the games that here ere now I met:. . . . . . . . .   254  Other Poems   4  494
    My two and I be met, . . . . . . . . . . . . . . . . . . .   260  Other Poems   6   19
    In this wood a man I met,. . . . . . . . . . . . . . . . .   262  Other Poems   7    7
METAL
    Not so; although my mettall were most mutable, . . . . . .    47  2nd Eclogues 28   10
```

305

That with his fault he might her goodnes know. . . . .   97 3rd Eclogues 64   114
Might freely rome, or rest, as seemed them:. . . . .   100 3rd Eclogues 66   48
The Lion, harte; the Ounce gave active might;. . . . . 101 3rd Eclogues 66   80
Crocodile, teares, which might be falsely spilde:. . . . . . 101 3rd Eclogues 66   96
Gainst those of might, of whom in feare they stood,. . . . . 102 3rd Eclogues 66   130
But they or spent, or made of slender might, ... 102 3rd Eclogues 66   134
As for the gentle birds, like case might rewe. . . . . 102 3rd Eclogues 66   139
And in despite of that displeasure's might,. . . . . 113 4th Eclogues 72   6
Infected so with her sweet poyson's might, ... 115 4th Eclogues 72   78
Such vitall sparke, that her mine eyes might see.. . . . . . 115 4th Eclogues 72   84
As tender conscience might with furious panges assaulte. . . 117 4th Eclogues 73   20
Now bolder waxt, waxt prowde, that I such sway might beare: 121 4th Eclogues 73   159
Least it might thee allure home to thy selfe to returne, . . 122 4th Eclogues 74   8
As might learne Temp'rance voyde of a rage's events. . . . . 124 4th Eclogues 74   64
In shape, which by man's eye might be perceived; . . . . . . 127 4th Eclogues 75   71
Farewell o golden staffe, the weake man's might: . . . . . . 129 4th Eclogues 76   3
We Orphans lefte, void of all publique might?. . . . . 129 4th Eclogues 76   12
Orphans in deede, depriv'd of father's might, ... 129 4th Eclogues 76   13
When that we feare our hatefull neighbours' might, ... 129 4th Eclogues 76   20
For ever lamed of our suerest might; . . . . 130 4th Eclogues 76   28
Let us against our selves employ our might,. . . . . 130 4th Eclogues 76   35
Farewell our might, farewell our daunted pleasure: . . . . . 130 4th Eclogues 76   38
Disarming humane mindes of native might: . . . . 131 Arcadia V   77   6
Resolv'd to make me patterne of his might, ... 135 Cert Sonnets 2   2
More happie I, might I in bondage bide.. . . . . 144 Cert Sonnets 15   14
Even thus might I, for doubts which I conceave . . . . 145 Cert Sonnets 16   9
And thus might I for feare of may be, leave. . . . . 145 Cert Sonnets 16   11
If othes might serve, even by the Stygian lake,. . . . . . . 146 Cert Sonnets 17   6
Or thinking still my thoughts might have good end: . . . . . 147 Cert Sonnets 19   2
Then might I thinke what thoughts were best to thinke: . . . 148 Cert Sonnets 19   5
Then might I wisely swimme or gladly sinke.. . . . . 148 Cert Sonnets 19   6
Or for my love some love I might obtaine,. . . . . 148 Cert Sonnets 19   10
Then might I hope a change or ease of minde, ... 148 Cert Sonnets 19   11
If further place might further me to ease. . . . . 149 Cert Sonnets 21   4
Draw in thy beames, and humble all thy might,. . . . . 161 Cert Sonnets 32   5
That she (deare she) might take some pleasure of my paine: 165 Astrophil   1 V 2
That the deare She might take some pleasure of my paine: . . 165 Astrophil   1   2
Pleasure might cause her reade, reading might make her know, 165 Astrophil   1   3
Knowledge might pitie winne, and pitie grace obtaine,. . . . 165 Astrophil   1   4
Where with most ease and warmth he might employ his art: . . 168 Astrophil   8   7
By my love judging what Love's paine might be. . . . . 173 Astrophil   16   8
To mortall eyes might sweetly shine in her.. . . . . 177 Astrophil   25   11
I might, unhappie word, o me, I might, ... 181 Astrophil   33   1
Where Vertue is made strong by Beautie's might,. . . . . . . 188 Astrophil   48   2
Might winne some grace in your sweet skill arraid. . . . . . 192 Astrophil   55   4
Untill by your inspiring I might know, ... 192 Astrophil   55   7
How their blacke banner might be best displaid.. . . . . . . 192 Astrophil   55   8
When I might reade those letters faire of blisse,. . . . . . 193 Astrophil   56   5
Hoping that when they might find Stella alone, ... 193 Astrophil   57   5
O voice, o face, maugre my speeche's might,. . . . . 194 Astrophil   58   12
That hand, which without touch holds more then Atlas might;. 205 Astrophil   77   5
That in no more but these I might be fully blest:. . . . . . 205 Astrophil   77   13
Stella, while now by honour's cruell might,. . . . . 224 Astrophil   91   1
Yet truth (if Caitif's breath mighte call thee) this . . . . 227 Astrophil   93   5
Silence in both displaies his sullen might,. . . . . 229 Astrophil   96   5
When sorrow (using mine owne fier's might) . . . . 236 Astrophil   108   1
If Love might sweet'n so a boy of shepheard' brood,. . . . . 209 A&S 3rd Song   7
Of Musick's wondrous might:. . . . . 216 A&S 6th Song   34
The common sence, which might. . . . . 216 A&S 6th Song   43
Stella's selfe might not refuse thee.. . . . . 220 A&S 8th Song   96
How long shall I with foes' triumphant might . . . . 285 Psalm XIII   7
When silent night might seeme all faults to hide,. . . . . . 289 Psalm XVII   9
My God, and helping God, my might and trustfull might, . . . 290 Psalm XVIII   3
And so besides our God, who is indue'd with might? . . . . . 292 Psalm XVIII   58
My saving might, lord in Thy sight,. . . . . 295 Psalm XIX   63
Lord in Thy strength, lord in Thy might, ... 298 Psalm XXI   49
They look, they gaze, my boanes might be rehearsed;. . . . . 299 Psalm XXII   42
My desolated life from dogged might. . . . . 299 Psalm XXII   48
Who is this glorious King in might and power riding? . . . . 302 Psalm XXIV   19
Feare might of men?. . . . . 307 Psalm XXVII   6
Ascribe all glory and all might. . . . . 309 Psalm XXIX   3
For still I say Thou art my only might.. . . . . 312 Psalm XXXI   12
The might of people's hand. . . . . 317 Psalm XXXIII   36
To them that know Thee and Thy might,. . . . . 324 Psalm XXXVI   28
My heart pants, gon is my might; . . . . 328 Psalm XXXVIII   28
And rayse me up that I may once have might . . . . 333 Psalm XLI   35
Giveth me my might,. . . . . 336 Psalm XLIII   8
One said he brake acrosse; full well it so might be: . . . . 241 Other Poems   1   3
(Lest greedy eies to them might challenge lay) . . . . 243 Other Poems   4   68
Well might he others beare, but leane to none) . . . . 244 Other Poems   4   72
No grasse, no trees, nor yet hir sparrow might . . . . 245 Other Poems   4   111
Making hir beames his bravery and might: . . . . 246 Other Poems   4   146
But fearing lest all white might seeme too good,. . . . . . 246 Other Poems   4   151
He might on knees confesse his faulty part,. . . . . 247 Other Poems   4   190
While Strephon might with preatie Nous have met, ... 249 Other Poems   4   279
Happy, o happy! if they so might bide, ... 252 Other Poems   4   401
And thou my dogg, whose truth and valiant might. . . . . . . 254 Other Poems   4   485
MIGHTST
As where thou soone mightst helpe, most faith dost most
    oppresse,. . . . . 213 A&S 5th Song   41

```
MIGHTY                                                    PAGE    TITLE           LINE
   But even for that shall suffer mightie Lovers. . . . . . . .    28  1st Eclogues 10    72
   Seeing, Alas, so mightie powers bende. . . . . . . . . . . .    73  Arcadia III  40     5
   Behold Love's mightie hand . . . . . . . . . . . . . . . .    158  Cert Sonnets 28    38
   Like some weake Lords, neighbord by mighty kings,. . . . . .   179  Astrophil    29     1
   So did he save me from my mighty furious foe,. . . . . . . .   291  Psalm XVIII        36
   To runne their mighty races. . . . . . . . . . . . . . . .     294  Psalm XIX          24
   Nay Basan mighty Bulls close me about. . . . . . . . . . . .   299  Psalm XXII         28
   Their help from mighty hands.. . . . . . . . . . . . . . . .   317  Psalm XXXIII       60
   Many mighty wrongfull foes,. . . . . . . . . . . . . . . . .   329  Psalm XXXVIII      57
   With my reedes, sound mighty praise; . . . . . . . . . . . .   264  Other Poems   7    68
MILD
   Your mind is wise, your wisedome makes you mild, . . . . . .     3  Lady of May   1     9
   As smooth as Pan, as Juno milde, like goddesse Iris faste. .    12  Arcadia I     3     6
   Milde as a Lambe, more daintie then a Conie is:. . . . . . .    15  1st Eclogues  7    31
MILDNESS
   Self-gard with mildnes, Sport with Majesty:. . . . . . . . .   247  Other Poems   4   214
MILD-SEEMING
   The sheep, mild-seeming face; climing, the Beare;. . . . . .   101  3rd Eclogues 66    90
MILK
   Two thousand sheepe I have as white as milke,. . . . . . . .     4  Lady of May   2    19
   As white as milke, and comming to the call,. . . . . . . . .    54  2nd Eclogues 29    85
   Like wine and milke that mingled stood.. . . . . . . . . . .    86  Arcadia III  62    30
   Milke hands, rose cheeks, or lips more sweet, more red,. . .   225  Astrophil    91     7
   Who hath the breast, whose milke doth passions nourish,. . .   197  A&S 1st Song       17
   Yet but a babe, with milke of Sight he nurst:. . . . . . . .   247  Other Poems   4   202
   Strephon so chas'd did seme in milke to swimme.. . . . . . .   249  Other Poems   4   288
   Her chery lipps, milke hands, and golden haire . . . . . . .   254  Other Poems   4   461
MILKEN
   Then that which beares the mylken name.. . . . . . . . . . .    87  Arcadia III  62    60
   Her milken breasts the nurse of child-like love,. . . . . . .  141  Cert Sonnets  9     7
   I said, thine eyes were starres, thy breasts the milk'n way,  212  A&S 5th Song       10
MILK-WHITE
   To sett, for foile of his milk-white to serve. . . . . . . .   244  Other Poems   4    86
MILLICNS
   Millions of yeares this old drivell Cupid lives; . . . . . .    22  1st Eclogues  8    43
   Phoenix but one, of Crowes we milllions have:. . . . . . . .   104  3rd Eclogues 67    20
MIND
   Whose mind is such, as wisest minds appall,. . . . . . . . .     3  Lady of May   1     3
   Your mind is wise, your wisedome makes you mild, . . . . . .     3  Lady of May   1     9
   The highest note comes oft from basest mind, . . . . . . . .     4  Lady of May   2    13
   My foule mishap came yet from fairest mind.. . . . . . . . .     5  Lady of May   3    18
   Transformd in shew, but more transformd in minde,. . . . . .    11  Arcadia I     2     1
   Come shepheard's weedes, become your master's minde: . . . .    13  Arcadia I     4     1
   And if for want of use thy minde ashamed is,. . . . . . . . .    14  1st Eclogues  7     2
   Her minde, beames, state farre from thy weake wings
      banished . . . . . . . . . . . . . . . . . . . . . . . . .    16  1st Eclogues  7    65
   Her peereles height my minde to high erection. . . . . . . .    16  1st Eclogues  7    70
   Heare plaints come forth from dungeon of my minde. . . . . .    18  1st Eclogues  7   133
   My minde for weeds your vertue's liverie weares. . . . . . .    18  1st Eclogues  7   137
   If still her minde be such,. . . . . . . . . . . . . . . . .    19  1st Eclogues  7   150
   Philisides. Who minds to please the minde drownd in annoyes.    22  1st Eclogues  9     6
   Geron. Alas what falls are falne unto thy minde? . . . . . .    23  1st Eclogues  9    32
   What ayleth thee, and if they knew thy minde . . . . . . . .    23  1st Eclogues  9    42
   Uttring a serpent's minde with serpent's hisse.. . . . . . .    24  1st Eclogues  9    71
   And thinke them olde, that have the oldest minde,. . . . . .    25  1st Eclogues  9    94
   Then let thy minde with better bookes be tamed,. . . . . . .    25  1st Eclogues  9   120
   Such active minde but seldome passion sees.. . . . . . . . .    26  1st Eclogues  9   134
   But in a minde that would his flames should not be
      repressed  . . . . . . . . . . . . . . . . . . . . . . . .    33  1st Eclogues 13    60
   Whence may I show to my minde any light of a possible
      escape . . . . . . . . . . . . . . . . . . . . . . . . . .    37  1st Eclogues 13   161
   My purest minde; whose temper hard doth showe. . . . . . . .    40  Arcadia II   18     8
   My words, in hope to blaze my stedfast minde,. . . . . . . .    40  Arcadia II   19     1
   Now in this sande I would discharge my minde,. . . . . . . .    42  Arcadia II   21    13
   A quiet minde none but thy selfe can lend to thee,. . . . . .    51  2nd Eclogues 28   101
   Nought could impart such heates to friendly mind.. . . . . .    51  2nd Eclogues 28   105
   The quiet mind (whereof my selfe empairer is,. . . . . . . .    51  2nd Eclogues 28   114
   Without her love, then any mind who fairer is. . . . . . . .    51  2nd Eclogues 28   116
   To frame of Earth a vessell of the minde,. . . . . . . . . .    57  2nd Eclogues 30    12
   In thy high minde) get her thy husband's grace.. . . . . . .    60  2nd Eclogues 30   114
   Thus is our mind with too much minding spilled.. . . . . . .    62  2nd Eclogues 30   175
   And what manner a mind which had to that humor a vaine?
      Vaine. . . . . . . . . . . . . . . . . . . . . . . . . . .    63  2nd Eclogues 31     9
   Reason, tell me thy mind, if here be reason. . . . . . . . .    67  2nd Eclogues 33     1
   Where man's mind hath a freed consideration. . . . . . . . .    68  2nd Eclogues 34     3
   Be thow, sweete glove, the Anker of my mynde,. . . . . . . .    70  Arcadia III  35     7
   Thus in my pilgrimaige of mated mynde, . . . . . . . . . . .    71  Arcadia III  36    13
   Phaebus yeelde up thy title in my minde. . . . . . . . . . .    72  Arcadia III  38    11
   My minde ere now led foorth by reason's light: . . . . . . .    73  Arcadia III  39     4
   Since, as I say, both minde and sences darke . . . . . . . .    73  Arcadia III  39     9
   For what is life to dayly dyinge minde,. . . . . . . . . . .    73  Arcadia III  40     9
   So to my minde, while passions daylie growe, . . . . . . . .    74  Arcadia III  41     3
   My mangled mind huge horrors still doe fright, . . . . . . .    74  Arcadia III  42     5
   Is not my skill, nor reach of mortall minde. . . . . . . . .    79  Arcadia III  50    16
   Her minde amaz'de can neither's helpe applie.. . . . . . . .    81  Arcadia III  54     4
   Though (yoked so) my minde with sicknes fainte,. . . . . . .    83  Arcadia III  57     7
   Get hence foule Griefe, the canker of the minde: . . . . . .    83  Arcadia III  59     1
   My minde hath tasted.. . . . . . . . . . . . . . . . . . . .    83  Arcadia III  59     8
   But ah, alas! (In vayne) my minde, sight, thought, . . . . .    84  Arcadia III  60    11
```

307

MIND   (CONTINUED)   PAGE   TITLE   LINE
    I turne my minde to all formes of annoyes, ...   113   4th Eclogues 72   3
    Enough to make a fertill minde lie waste..   114   4th Eclogues 72   30
    Klaius. Enough to make a fertill minde lie waste   114   4th Eclogues 72   31
    So I in simple course, and unentangled minde   117   4th Eclogues 73   25
    A living coarse I lay: but ah, my wakefull minde   117   4th Eclogues 73   31
    Such thoughts, me thought, I thought, and straind my single
        mind   118   4th Eclogues 73   49
    As little hunting minde (God knowes) did there appeere.. . . 118   4th Eclogues 73   70
    "Sweet Mira mine" (quote she) "the pleasure of my minde, . . 119   4th Eclogues 73   93
    Diana deare; my minde to love and not to hate.   120   4th Eclogues 73   148
    Her beautie kindle shall within thy foolish minde, ...   121   4th Eclogues 73   171
    Then let us holde the blisse of peacefull minde, ...   131   Arcadia V   77   13
    In fine, since strife of thought but marres the mind,. . . . 135   Cert Sonnets 1   8
    Or doth she thinke all paine the minde forbeares?.   142   Cert Sonnets 11   5
    Right so my minde, caught by his guiding eye   144   Cert Sonnets 15   5
    In humble mind a constant faith to prove,.   145   Cert Sonnets 17   3
    The Rockes which were of constant mind the marke   147   Cert Sonnets 18   5
    Then might I hope a change or ease of minde, ...   148   Cert Sonnets 19   11
    Depart, a word so gentle to my minde,.   148   Cert Sonnets 20   3
    To marre my minde, and with my hurt to please, ...   149   Cert Sonnets 21   2
    Mine eyes the streight, the roomie cave, my minde, ...   150   Cert Sonnets 22   35
    An Angell's mind, but in a woman caste:.   151   Cert Sonnets 22   67
    Immortall is her minde:.   152   Cert Sonnets 23   22
    While to my minde the out side stood,.   156   Cert Sonnets 27   7
    In her unmatched mind: 160   Cert Sonnets 30   34
    With price of mangled mind thy worthlesse ware,.   161   Cert Sonnets 31   6
    Who should my mind to higher things prepare.   161   Cert Sonnets 31   8
    And thou my mind aspire to higher things:.   161   Cert Sonnets 32   2
    But never heeds the fruit of writer's mind:.   170   Astrophil   11   8
    O let me prop my mind, yet in his growth   174   Astrophil   19   12
    My young mind marde, whom Love doth windlas so,.   175   Astrophil   21   2
    Which inward sunne to Heroicke minde displaies,.   177   Astrophil   25   8
    Stella's great powrs, that so confuse my mind.   182   Astrophil   34   14
    Unto my mind, is Stella's image, wrought   183   Astrophil   38   6
    That hast my mind, none of the basest, brought   184   Astrophil   40   3
    My words I know do well set forth my mind, ...   186   Astrophil   44   1
    My mind bemones his sense of inward smart;   186   Astrophil   44   2
    So that I cannot chuse but write my mind,.   190   Astrophil   50   9
    And thinke so still, so Stella know my mind, ...   192   Astrophil   54   9
    Each sence of mine, each gift, each power of mind, ...   193   Astrophil   57   2
    Or else pronouncing grace, wherewith his mind.   194   Astrophil   58   7
    Now since her chast mind hates this love in me,.   195   Astrophil   61   9
    With chastned mind, I straight must shew that she.   195   Astrophil   61   10
    Frcm nobler course, fit for my birth and mind: 196   Astrophil   62   8
    With windowes ope then most my mind doth lie,.   230   Astrophil   99   5
    Such light in sense, with such a darkned mind.   231   Astrophil   99   14
    Of such heaven stuffe, to cloath so heavenly mynde.. 232   Astrophil   101   14
    No witchcraft is so evill, as which man's mind destroyeth.. . 215   A&S 5th Song   78
    You see what I can say; mend yet your froward mind,. 215   A&S 5th Song   88
    And in them thy mind discover, ...   225   A&S 10th Song   3
    Whose throne is in the mind, ...   217   A&S 6th Song   50
    Save thy mind which yet surpasseth..   219   A&S 8th Song   44
    Which night and day he calls to marking mind..   270   Psalm I   6
    Therfore (O Kings), be wise, O Rulers rule your mind,. . . . 271   Psalm II   23
    Thou first prepare'dst their mind.   283   Psalm X   75
    Indeed O you, you that be such of mind,.   300   Psalm XXII   63
    Vainly doth not puff up his mind;.   302   Psalm XXIV   10
    Ev'n like a dead man dreamed out of mind,.   313   Psalm XXXI   35
    The thinckinges of that mind   317   Psalm XXXIII   40
    Fix We our mind, ...   318   Psalm XXXIII   77
    I both in mind, and bones shall gladded be..   321   Psalm XXXV   20
    Of pleasurs past the reach of mind?.   324   Psalm XXXVI   24
    For my mind on my God bideth,.   335   Psalm XLII   25
    When thou hast mynd to weepe, seeke out som smoky room:. . . 343   Possibly   1   11
    That comfort in these sports you like, my mynde his comfort
        tryes.   343   Possibly   1   14
    Was once my mynde, my temper, and my lyfe, ...   344   Possibly   2   6
    A salve, freshe ayre, and hyghe contented mynde.   345   Possibly   2   14
    Such was his minde, if you another take: 345   Possibly   4   11
    Both free of minde, both did clear-dealing love, ...   243   Other Poems   4   39
    And saw this fairest maid of fairer minde, ...   244   Other Poems   4   90
    To long-perplexed minde breed long delight..   245   Other Poems   4   112
    Make but one Minde in Bodies three..   260   Other Poems   6   6
    Above line repeated at following locations   260   Other Poems   6   12
           260   Other Poems   6   18
           260   Other Poems   6   24
           261   Other Poems   6   30
           261   Other Poems   6   36
           261   Other Poems   6   42
           261   Other Poems   6   48
           261   Other Poems   6   54
    So many pufft in minde I see,.   263   Other Poems   7   50
MINDED
    A baite most fit, for hungrie minded guest..   75   Arcadia III 44   10
    Whether the Turkish new-moone minded be.   179   Astrophil   30   1
    Of those eyes, and blinder minded.   220   A&S 8th Song   84
    But who aright poore-minded be   283   Psalm X   61
MINDING
    Thus is our mind with too much minding spilled..   62   2nd Eclogues 30   175

```
MINDING              (CONTINUED)                        PAGE    TITLE           LINE
    Both so and thus, she minding Love should be . . . . . . .  168  Astrophil        7    12
MIND'S
    Swelling with sighes, made pale with minde's disease,. . . .   58  2nd Eclogues 30    48
    To stranger weights my minde's waste soile is bound, . . . .  149  Cert Sonnets 22     5
MINDS
    Whose mind is such, as wisest minds appall,. . . . . . . . .    3  Lady of May      1     3
    Philisides. Who minds to please the minde drownd in annoyes.   22  1st Eclogues  9     6
    Frcm former feare, they had of your good mindes, . . . . . .   26  1st Eclogues 10     5
    Into our mindes let us a little fall,. . . . . . . . . . . .   29  1st Eclogues 10    94
    Are then humane mindes priviledg'd so meanly,. . . . . . . .   31  1st Eclogues 12    17
    Give us foresightfull mindes: give us minds to obaye . . . .   45  Arcadia II   26    11
    How be the minds dispos'd that can not tast thy physick?
      Sick.. . . . . . . . . . . . . . . . . . . . . . . . . . .   63  2nd Eclogues 31    17
    Thou li'st false Echo, their minds as vertu be just. Just. .   65  2nd Eclogues 31    46
    Such mindes with sweet affections for to fill, . . . . . . .   92  3rd Eclogues 63    61
    Sweete supple mindes which soone to wisdome bowe . . . . . .  106  3rd Eclogues 67   103
    Far from my thoughts was ought, whereto their minds aspire,.  117  4th Eclogues 73    15
    In mortall mindes our mindes but planets' names preserve:. .  120  4th Eclogues 73   113
    Thus, thus the mindes, which over all doo clime, . . . . . .  127  4th Eclogues 75    88
    Which to our darkned mindes was best direction;. . . . . . .  129  4th Eclogues 76     9
    Disarming humane mindes of native might: . . . . . . . . . .  131  Arcadia V    77     6
    To starving minds such is God Cupid's dish.. . . . . . . . .  136  Cert Sonnets  2    14
    Since then truth to all minds telleth, . . . . . . . . . . .  140  Cert Sonnets  7    18
    Such causelesse feares when coward minds do take,. . . . . .  145  Cert Sonnets 16     5
    Infected mindes infect each thing they see.. . . . . . . . .  147  Cert Sonnets 18    14
    In weakened minds, quicke apprehending breed,. . . . . . . .  199  Astrophil    66     3
    Thy selfe, doest strive all minds that way to move,. . . . .  201  Astrophil    71    10
    Bids you leave such minds to nourish." . . . . . . . . . . .  234  A&S 11th Song      27
    Or knowing, have so muddy minds, as not to be in love; . . .  217  A&S 7th Song        9
    By them whose minds on hatefull thoughts do stay:. . . . . .  280  Psalm IX           38
    To humble broken minds . . . . . . . . . . . . . . . . . . .  320  Psalm XXXIV        65
    With cruel minds my very soul to teare.. . . . . . . . . . .  322  Psalm XXXV         28
    I say, I say the Righteous minds . . . . . . . . . . . . . .  326  Psalm XXXVII       73
    Their chearfull minds, till pois'ned was their cheare, . . .  243  Other Poems   4    41
*MINE
    And feede mine eares, mine eyes, my hart in you. . . . . . .    3  Lady of May      1    12
    That Goddesse mine, my blessed being sees". . . . . . . . . .    4  Lady of May      3     6
    Fcr from without came to mine eyes the blowe,. . . . . . . .   11  Arcadia I     2     5
    Whereto mine inward thoughts did faintly yeeld;. . . . . . .   11  Arcadia I     2     6
    And thus my eyes, are plaste still in one sight. . . . . . .   12  Arcadia I     2  V809
    Let crowes picke out mine eyes, which saw too much:. . . . .   19  1st Eclogues  7   149
    New friend of mine; I yeeld to thy habilitie:. . . . . . . .   19  1st Eclogues  7   174
    Let crowes picke out mine eyes which too much sawe.. . . . .   19  1st Eclogues  7  V149
    Good Lalus mine, I yeld to thy abilitie; . . . . . . . . . .   20  1st Eclogues  7  V974
    Be as thou art, but be with mine at one. . . . . . . . . . .   27  1st Eclogues 10    15
    If mine eyes can speake to doo harty errande,. . . . . . . .   30  1st Eclogues 12     1
    Or mine eyes' language she doo hap to judge of,. . . . . . .   30  1st Eclogues 12     2
    Above line repeated at following location. . . . . . . . . .   31  1st Eclogues 12    26
    Vertue, richesse, beawties of mine shall great be reputed. .   34  1st Eclogues 13    81
    Jaylor I am to my selfe, prison and prisoner to myne owne
      selfe. . . . . . . . . . . . . . . . . . . . . . . . . . .   37  1st Eclogues 13   163
    In vaine, mine Eyes, you labour to amende. . . . . . . . . .   38  Arcadia II   14     1
    Since sighes (into mine inward fornace turnd) . . . . . . . .   38  Arcadia II   14     7
    Since there mine eyes have played so false a parte,. . . . .   38  Arcadia II   14    11
    Since so mine eyes are subject to your sight,. . . . . . . .   39  Arcadia II   16     1
    No fancy mine, nor others' wronge suspect. . . . . . . . . .   40  Arcadia II   18    11
    Over these brookes trusting to ease mine eyes, . . . . . . .   41  Arcadia II   21     1
    (Mine eyes even great in labour with their teares) . . . . .   41  Arcadia II   21     2
    Since streame, aier, sand, mine eyes and eares conspire: . .   42  Arcadia II   21    17
    Passion. No, Tyrant; no: mine, mine shall be the fielde. . .   46  2nd Eclogues 27     2
    Pas. My gray-hood is mine owne, all be it be but gray, . . .   52  2nd Eclogues 29     7
    Nico. Mine was the scrippe: but thou, that seeming raged
      with love, . . . . . . . . . . . . . . . . . . . . . . . .   52  2nd Eclogues 29     9
    I leave mine eyes unwipte my cheekes to bathe. . . . . . . .   54  2nd Eclogues 29    80
    I said, my hands well paide her for mine eyes, . . . . . . .   55  2nd Eclogues 29   115
    What myne hath erst throwne downe so faire a tower?. . . . .   59  2nd Eclogues 30    96
    O eyes of mine, where once she saw her face, . . . . . . . .   60  2nd Eclogues 30   116
    And in thy case do glasse mine owne debilitie: . . . . . . .   60  2nd Eclogues 30   129
    Plangus. If through mine eares pearce any consolacyons . . .   61  2nd Eclogues 30   143
    Eysight made me to yeelde, but what first pierst to myne
      eies? Eies.. . . . . . . . . . . . . . . . . . . . . . . .   64  2nd Eclogues 31    26
    Her cannons be her eys, myne eys the walls be, . . . . . . .   68  2nd Eclogues 33    13
    Nowe that myne eyes their cheerefull sunn dothe misse. . . .   70  Arcadia III  35     5
    Since all the thinges which give mine eyes their light . . .   73  Arcadia III  39     5
    I plaine with cause, my woes are all myne owne.. . . . . . .   75  Arcadia III  43     6
    I holde his deare, and myne he cannot misse: . . . . . . . .   75  Arcadia III  45     3
    That she is myne, as I to her am true. . . . . . . . . . . .   76  Arcadia III  46     6
    That she be myne, as I to her am true. . . . . . . . . . . .   76  Arcadia III  46    12
    And in this growing barke growe verses myne. . . . . . . . .   77  Arcadia III  47    12
    My hopes which do but to mine owne aspire? . . . . . . . . .   80  Arcadia III  53     4
    Mine owne? o word on whose sweete sound doth pray. . . . . .   80  Arcadia III  53     5
    Mine owne, embraced, sought, knot, fire, desease.. . . . . .   84  Arcadia III  60    14
    A spotlesse mine of Alablaster.. . . . . . . . . . . . . . .   88  Arcadia III  62    80
    A neighbor mine not long agoe there was, . . . . . . . . . .   94  3rd Eclogues 64     1
    With old true tales he woont mine eares to fill, . . . . . .   99  3rd Eclogues 66    33
    Or els; "Nay faith, mine is the lucklest lot,. . . . . . . .  104  3rd Eclogues 67    43
    When without shame he saith, "these be mine owne". . . . . .  106  3rd Eclogues 67   114
    And stoppe mine eares, lest I growe mad with Musicke.. . . .  112  4th Eclogues 71    60
    Mine eyes did light upon her shining hewe, . . . . . . . . .  115  4th Eclogues 72    75
```

309

*MINE	(CONTINUED)	PAGE	TITLE		LINE
Such vitall sparke, that her mine eyes might see........		115	4th Eclogues	72	84
Did suffer drousie lids mine eyes then cleare to blinde: ..		117	4th Eclogues	73	26
When it blowne up with myne a fall of ruine takes)		118	4th Eclogues	73	52
"Sweet Mira mine" (quote she) "the pleasure of my minde, ..		119	4th Eclogues	73	93
First be mine eyes pulde out, first be my braine perished; .		124	4th Eclogues	74	60
O notes of mine your selves together tie:..........		127	4th Eclogues	75	76
Now that the mine is lost of all our treasure, ...		129	4th Eclogues	76	10
Thine earth now springs, mine fadeth,............		137	Cert Sonnets	4	11
Above line repeated at following location.		137	Cert Sonnets	4	23
Sleepe Babie mine, Desire, nurse Beautie singeth:......		139	Cert Sonnets	6	1
Thy cries, o Babie, set mine head on aking:........		139	Cert Sonnets	6	2
Since babie mine, from me thy watching springeth,......		139	Cert Sonnets	6	7
Of mine owne wordes, my owne good hap betray,........		145	Cert Sonnets	16	10
For in each thing wherto mine eye doth range,.......		147	Cert Sonnets	18	3
Myne eyes thence drawne, where lived all their light,....		149	Cert Sonnets	21	5
Mine eyes the streight, the roomie cave, my minde, ...		150	Cert Sonnets	22	35
Ladie mine eyes remained,....		154	Cert Sonnets	25	3
What in your face mine eyes do measure............		159	Cert Sonnets	29	9
To me mine eyes the true shape carie.............		159	Cert Sonnets	29	13
But knowne worth did in mine of time proceed,.......		165	Astrophil	2	3
Which Cupid's selfe from Beautie's myne did draw:......		169	Astrophil	9	13
Mine eyes (shall I say curst or blest) beheld........		173	Astrophil	16	10
That mine owne writings like bad servants show		175	Astrophil	21	3
Sure you say well, your wisdome's golden mine.		175	Astrophil	21	12
To hatch mine eyes, and that unpitted thought.		183	Astrophil	38	2
That once come there, the sobs of mine annoyes		187	Astrophil	44	13
Let not mine eyes be hel-driv'n from that light:		188	Astrophil	48	7
Pardon mine eares, both I and they do pray,.........		190	Astrophil	51	1
My heart then quak'd, then dazled were mine eyes,.....		191	Astrophil	53	10
So sweete sounds straight mine eare and heart do hit,....		192	Astrophil	55	13
Each sence of mine, each gift, each power of mind, ...		193	Astrophil	57	2
Let clouds bedimme my face, breake in mine eye,.....		198	Astrophil	64	5
By Nature borne, I gave to thee mine eyes.........		198	Astrophil	65	8
Mine eyes, my light, my heart, my life, alas,........		198	Astrophil	65	9
But when mine eyes backe to their heav'n did move, ...		199	Astrophil	66	13
I, I, o I may say, that she is mine.............		200	Astrophil	69	11
Care shining in mine eyes, faith in my sprite, ...		202	Astrophil	72	11
Of gentle force, so that mine eyes dare gladly play.....		205	Astrophil	76	6
My heart cries "ah", it burnes, mine eyes now dazled be: ..		205	Astrophil	76	11
Have chang'd desert, let mine owne conscience be		212	Astrophil	86	2
Let wo gripe on my heart, shame loade mine eye........		212	Astrophil	86	4
Graved in mine Epitaph a Poet's name:............		224	Astrophil	90	8
They please I do confesse, they please mine eyes,......		225	Astrophil	91	9
Can scarce discerne the shape of mine owne paine.......		228	Astrophil	94	4
Or if thy love of plaint yet mine forbeares,........		228	Astrophil	94	9
Mine eyes then only winke, for spite perchance,......		230	Astrophil	98	13
That wormes should have their Sun, and I want mine......		230	Astrophil	98	14
In tombe of lids then buried are mine eyes,.........		231	Astrophil	99	12
Envious wits what hath bene mine offence,..........		233	Astrophil	104	1
That to each word, nay sigh of mine you harke:.......		233	Astrophil	104	3
If I but stars upon mine armour beare, ...		233	Astrophil	104	10
But cease mine eyes, your teares do witnesse well.		235	Astrophil	105	9
Thou toldst mine eyes should helpe their famisht case? ...		235	Astrophil	106	6
When sorrow (using mine owne fier's might)		236	Astrophil	108	1
That mine eyes thine eyes may see?		225	A&S 10th Song		2
And showers from mine eyes proceeding.		221	A&S 9th Song		5
No sooner said, but (lo) myne Enemyes sink		280	Psalm IX		46
When waking of this sleep of mine.		290	Psalm XVII		47
Strengthning mine arms that they could break an Iron bow...		292	Psalm XVIII		63
So farr from seing myne unhealthfull eyes, ...		298	Psalm XXII		3
And open'd mine own wickedness,..............		315	Psalm XXXII		14
Of mine eyes abandons me..		328	Psalm XXXVIII		30
Telling mine iniquityes.		329	Psalm XXXVIII		54
Miso mine owne pigsnie, thou shalt heare news o' Damaetas. .		241	Other Poems	2	1
As pin'd a face as mine I saw againe..........		254	Other Poems	4	476
Do you remember still you once were mine,.........		254	Other Poems	4	495
Doth daily haunt: but so, that mine become		255	Other Poems	4	503
"Alas! a cloud hath overcast mine eies:..........		255	Other Poems	4	505
MINGLED					
Nor true love loves those loves with others mingled be....		14	1st Eclogues	7	12
Like wine and milke that mingled stood............		86	Arcadia III	62	30
MINSTRELSY					
But now to silence turn'd his minstralsie.		28	1st Eclogues	10	75
MIRA					
"Sweet Mira mine" (quote she) "the pleasure of my minde, ..		119	4th Eclogues	73	93
And Mira I admirde: her shape sank in my brest........		119	4th Eclogues	73	100
To yonder Nymphe therefore (to Mira I did point)		121	4th Eclogues	73	165
First having all their giftes upon faire Mira spred.		121	4th Eclogues	73	178
So Mira long may be.		256	Other Poems	5	17
Mira may looke her face, ...		257	Other Poems	5	31
That Mira may thee feede		258	Other Poems	5	83
MIRACIE					
What veiles then doo prevaile, but to a more miracle?....		123	4th Eclogues	74	50
MIRACLES					
Only with you not miracles are wonders..		197	A&S 1st Song		32
MIRACULOUS					
Or would she her miraculous power show,...........		168	Astrophil	7	9
MIRA'S					
Of Mira's beames eclipst by absence bad.		256	Other Poems	5	11

```
MIRA'S                  (CONTINUED)                      PAGE    TITLE           LINE
    But pulld by Mira's hande, . . . . . . . . . . . . . . . .   257 Other Poems     5    47
    Of Mira's lipps divide . . . . . . . . . . . . . . . . . .   258 Other Poems     5    57
    It may be part of Mira's peticoate, . . . . . . . . . . .    258 Other Poems     5    71
MIRE
    Doth plunge my wel-form'd soule even in the mire . . . . .   172 Astrophil      14     7
    Or like a broken pott in myer tredd. . . . . . . . . . . .   313 Psalm XXXI           36
MIRROR
    Now the ambitiouse Larke with mirror cleare. . . . . . . .   243 Other Poems     4    45
MIRTH
    As for my mirth, how could I but be glad, . . . . . . . .    147 Cert Sonnets   17    41
    Nectar of Mirth, since I Jove's cup do keepe. . . . . . .    201 Astrophil      70     4
    All mirth farewell, let me in sorrow live. . . . . . . . .   231 Astrophil     100    14
    Unto whom mirth is displeasure, . . . . . . . . . . . . .    221 A&S 9th Song          9
    Mirth with respect, few words with curtesy, . . . . . . .    247 Other Poems     4   212
    First killing mirth, then banishing all rest, . . . . . .    253 Other Poems     4   431
    Joyne Mates in mirth to me, . . . . . . . . . . . . . . .    260 Other Poems     6     1
    Cause all the mirth you can, . . . . . . . . . . . . . . .   261 Other Poems     6    37
    Mixing mirth our Songs among, . . . . . . . . . . . . . .    263 Other Poems     7    46
MISCHIEF
    That there where thou confest thy mischiefe lyes . . . . .    23 1st Eclogues    9    33
    No, no, our mischiefe growes in this vile fortune, . . . .   109 Arcadia IV     70    31
    Nor of my fortune ought, but mischieve crave. . . . . . .    114 4th Eclogues   72    20
    Strephon. Nor of my fortune ought but mischiefe crave, . .   114 4th Eclogues   72    21
    And great with child of mischeif travaild long, . . . . .   278 Psalm VII            38
    Both mischief and iniquity . . . . . . . . . . . . . . . .   282 Psalm X              30
    All wrong and mischeife lyes, . . . . . . . . . . . . . .    283 Psalm X              58
    And therfore soon would mischeife Thee . . . . . . . . . .   315 Psalm XXXII          35
    Abed on mischief museth he, . . . . . . . . . . . . . . .    323 Psalm XXXVI          11
    And deigne to deeme your neighbors' mischefe neare, . . .    242 Other Poems     4    11
MISCHIEF'S
    Only rich in mischiefe's treasure. . . . . . . . . . . . .   221 A&S 9th Song         10
MISCHIEFS
    Thus then (I say) my mischiefes have contributed . . . . .    49 2nd Eclogues   28    67
    For mischeefes greate, daye after day doth showe: . . . .     82 Arcadia III    56    13
MISCHIEVOUS
    But all their bad mischeivous skill. . . . . . . . . . . .   298 Psalm XXI            43
MISCONCEIVED
    If he to them his dutie misconceaved). . . . . . . . . . .    94 3rd Eclogues   64    22
MISER
    More gladde to me, then to a miser monie is. . . . . . . .    15 1st Eclogues    7    33
    And learn'd what ill a miser state doth breed, . . . . . .    21 1st Eclogues    8    22
MISERIES
    Which should most miseries, cast on a worme that I am. . .    29 1st Eclogues   11     2
    Dorus. O glittring miseries of man, if this be the fortune .  34 1st Eclogues   13    89
    That doost so well their miseries define? . . . . . . . .     59 2nd Eclogues   30    79
    Unto the man, whom now such miseries you awarde? . . . . .   124 4th Eclogues   74    74
    To know my miseries, but chaste and cruell: . . . . . . .    136 Cert Sonnets    3    10
MISER'S
    Farewell Complaint, the miser's only pleasure: . . . . . .    83 Arcadia III    59     2
    That bagged baggage of a miser's mudd, . . . . . . . . . .   245 Other Poems     4   122
MISERY
    Fortune thus gan say; "misery and misfortune is all one, . .  29 1st Eclogues   11     3
    That aptest is to figure miserie, . . . . . . . . . . . .    125 4th Eclogues   75    11
    Or want I sense to feele my miserie? . . . . . . . . . . .   188 Astrophil      47     5
    Gone is the winter of my miserie. . . . . . . . . . . . .    200 Astrophil      69     7
    A monster, other's harme, selfe-miserie, . . . . . . . . .   206 Astrophil      78     5
    Tast misery. . . . . . . . . . . . . . . . . . . . . . . .   301 Psalm XXIII           3
    Yea and from dreadfull misery. . . . . . . . . . . . . . .   319 Psalm XXXIV          15
MISFORTUNE
    Fortune thus gan say; "misery and misfortune is all one, . .  29 1st Eclogues   11     3
    And of misfortune, fortune hath only the gift. . . . . . .    29 1st Eclogues   11     4
    Hath no misfortune, but that Rich she is . . . . . . . . .   183 Astrophil      37    14
    Though all his plotts without misfortune . . . . . . . . .   325 Psalm XXXVII         19
MISHAP
    My foule mishap came yet from fairest mind . . . . . . . .     5 Lady of May     3    18
    Come learners then to me, the modell of mishappe, . . . .    153 Cert Sonnets   24    15
MISHAPS
    Gives happs or mishapps, ev'n as he ordreth his hearte . .    29 1st Eclogues   11     8
    Happy be those mishapps which, justly proportion holding, .   32 1st Eclogues   13    17
MISLED
    I am from you, light of my life, mis-led, . . . . . . . .    224 Astrophil      91     2
MISO
    Miso mine owne pigsnie, thou shalt heare news o' Damaetas. .  241 Other Poems     2     1
MISS
    But take this beast, if beasts you feare to misse, . . . .     4 Lady of May     2    29
    What time for her Juno her Jove did misse, . . . . . . . .    21 1st Eclogues    8    15
    P. Will hath his will, when Reason's will doth misse. . . .    46 2nd Eclogues   27     8
    P. How know we that, since present joyes we misse? . . . .    47 2nd Eclogues   27    38
    Which who doth misse his eyes are but delusions, . . . . .    51 2nd Eclogues   28   108
    But still our dazeled eyes their way do misse, . . . . . .    59 2nd Eclogues   30    74
    But Plangus, lest I may your sicknesse misse . . . . . . .    62 2nd Eclogues   30   182
    Nowe that myne eyes their cheerefull sunn dothe misse. . .    70 Arcadia III    35     5
    Make great the losse, so grete the feare to misse. . . . .    71 Arcadia III    37    12
    I holde his deare, and myne he cannot misse: . . . . . . .    75 Arcadia III    45     3
    But who those ruddie lippes can misse? . . . . . . . . . .    87 Arcadia III    62    37
    Though full of scorne, would not his duty misse, . . . . .    96 3rd Eclogues   64    69
    Which who so wants, halfe of himselfe doth misse . . . . .   103 3rd Eclogues   67     9
    The seed Fast-meaning is, no truth to misse: . . . . . . .   115 4th Eclogues   72    53
    Feeling my pulse, misse my disease . . . . . . . . . . . .   153 Cert Sonnets   24     9
```

```
MISS                    (CONTINUED)                        PAGE   TITLE          LINE
     I find how heav'nly day wretch I did misse.. . . . . . . . .  181 Astrophil    33     4
     Thou needs must misse, and so thou needs must smart. . . . .  188 Astrophil    46    11
     Leave following that, which it is gaine to misse. . . . . .   188 Astrophil    47    11
     And thinke I should not your large precepts misse? . . . . .  192 Astrophil    56     4
     What wonder then if he his lesson misse, . . . . . . . . . .  203 Astrophil    73     3
     That grace, which Venus weepes that she her selfe doth
       misse . . . . . . . . . . . . . . . . . . . . . . . . . .   205 Astrophil    77     4
     But wit confus'd with too much care did misse. . . . . . . .  227 Astrophil    93     8
     Niggard Time threats, if we misse. . . . . . . . . . . . . .  211 A&S 4th Song        31
     Naught his allseeing sight can miss, . . . . . . . . . . . .  284 Psalm XI            15
     For where he most would hit, he ever yet did misse.. . . . .  241 Other Poems   1     2
     But fore-accounting oft makes builders misse, . . . . . . .   244 Other Poems   4    79
MISSED
     The third his lesson mist, till all do smarte. . . . . . . .   27 1st Eclogues 10    45
     That you, guiltlesse thereof, your Nectar mist:. . . . . . .  235 Astrophil   105    10
     Me thought some staves he mist: if so, not much amisse:. . .  241 Other Poems   1     1
MISSING
     With idle paines, and missing ayme, do guesse. . . . . . . .  176 Astrophil    23     4
MIST
     Alas while we are wrapt in foggie mist . . . . . . . . . . .   59 2nd Eclogues 30    68
MISTAKE
     But feeling proofe makes me say they mistake it furre: . . .  232 Astrophil   102    11
MISTLETOE
     Like Oke and Mistletoe.. . . . . . . . . . . . . . . . . . .   92 3rd Eclogues 63    51
MISTRESS
     And to conclude thy mistresse is a woman. . . . . . . . . .    24 1st Eclogues  9    61
     Dorus. Blest be the name, wherewith my mistres named is: . .   49 2nd Eclogues 28    55
     For how would you the mistresse' thoughts bereave. . . . . .   78 Arcadia III  49    11
     My burning tongue hath bred my mistresse paine, . . . . . .   141 Cert Sonnets  9     2
     My mistresse lowers and saith I do not love: . . . . . . . .  145 Cert Sonnets 17     1
     Some good old dumpe, that Chaucer's mistresse knew, . . . .   146 Cert Sonnets 17    34
     That onely I the onely Mistresse had:. . . . . . . . . . . .  147 Cert Sonnets 17    43
     Dick. Here then and learn to sigh: a mistress I doo serve, .  343 Possibly      1    19
     Who seem'd orethrown was mistresse of the field: . . . . . .  251 Other Poems   4   347
MISTRESS'
     Thy mistresse' song is now a sorrow's crie,. . . . . . . . .   81 Arcadia III  54     2
     She waited mistresse' will: who thus disclosd her spright. .  119 4th Eclogues 73    92
     My mistresse' Marble hart, . . . . . . . . . . . . . . . . .  160 Cert Sonnets 30    24
MISTS
     Tush absence, while thy mistes eclipse that light, . . . . .  223 Astrophil    88     9
MISTY
     So darke with misty vapors, which arise. . . . . . . . . . .  228 Astrophil    94     2
     But streight his shining eyes this misty masse disclos'd.. .  291 Psalm XVIII         26
MISWENT
     Will. What? is thy Bagpipe broke, or are thy lambs miswent;.  343 Possibly      1    15
MIXED
     Where azurde veines well mixt appeere. . . . . . . . . . . .   87 Arcadia III  62    56
     A simple soule should breed so mixed woes. . . . . . . . . .  149 Cert Sonnets 22    10
     Though hope were mixt with feare, . . . . . . . . . . . . .   158 Cert Sonnets 28     6
     Frame daintiest lustre, mixt of shades and light?. . . . . .  168 Astrophil     7     4
     Marble mixt red and white do enterlace.. . . . . . . . . . .  169 Astrophil     9     8
     Sighs of woes were glad sighs mixt, . . . . . . . . . . . .   218 A&S 8th Song        18
MIXING
     Mixing mirth our Songs among, . . . . . . . . . . . . . . .   263 Other Poems   7    46
MIXTURE
     Which elements with mortall mixture breed: . . . . . . . . .  167 Astrophil     5    11
     With such bad mixture of my night and day, . . . . . . . . .  224 Astrophil    89    12
MIZZAR'S
     And from Mizzar's hilly head.. . . . . . . . . . . . . . . .  335 Psalm XLII          28
MOAN
     Sweet vertue's lawe barres not a causefull mone. . . . . . .   22 1st Eclogues  9    18
     Of lothsome dayes, whose losse how canst thou mone, . . . .    59 2nd Eclogues 30    78
     We mone that lost, which had we did bemone.. . . . . . . . .   59 2nd Eclogues 30    82
     My still kept course, while others sleepe, to mone.. . . . .  184 Astrophil    40     4
     The courtly Nymphs, acquainted with the mone . . . . . . . .  191 Astrophil    54     5
     Should scone be pierc'd with sharpnesse of the mone. . . . .  193 Astrophil    57     8
     He will give good eare to my moane.. . . . . . . . . . . . .  273 Psalm IV            15
     His eyes unto my Case, his eares unto my moane.. . . . . . .  291 Psalm XVIII         14
     My life with heavyness, my yeares with moane . . . . . . . .  312 Psalm XXXI          28
     But Thou didst heare, when I to Thee did moane.. . . . . . .  313 Psalm XXXI          63
     In fitt time make to Thee his moane, . . . . . . . . . . . .  315 Psalm XXXII         20
     As bragging that free of all passions' mone. . . . . . . . .  244 Other Poems   4    71
     Thus on a hillock set, he made his mone. . . . . . . . . . .  253 Other Poems   4   440
     And, but bewitch'd, who to his flock would mone? . . . . . .  254 Other Poems   4   460
MOANFUL
     With monefull melodies, for enough our greefes be revealed, .  37 1st Eclogues 13   173
     Boulon. How long wilt thou with monefull musicke staine. . .   58 2nd Eclogues 30    38
MOANING
     With glad moning passed anguish, . . . . . . . . . . . . . .  227 A&S 10th Song       39
MOANS
     And though my mones be not in musicke bound, . . . . . . . .   81 Arcadia III  54     7
MOCK
     Indeed the poore opprest by you, you mock, . . . . . . . . .  287 Psalm XIV           19
MOCKING
     The lookers now at me poore wretch be mocking, . . . . . . .  299 Psalm XXII          17
MOCKS
     One saith, He mockes; the other saith, he playes;. . . . . .   27 1st Eclogues 10    44
MOCKST
     Mock'st thou those Diamonds which only be matcht by the
       gods Ods. . . . . . . . . . . . . . . . . . . . . . . . .    65 2nd Eclogues 31    47
```

		PAGE	TITLE		LINE
MODEL					
Come learners then to me, the modell of mishappe,.		153	Cert Sonnets	24	15
MODELS					
But why? because of you they models be,.		225	Astrophil	91	10
Models such be wood-globes of glistring skies.		225	Astrophil	91	11
MOIST					
Warme snow, moyst pearle, softe ivorie..		90	Arcadia III	62	126
MOISTENED					
My moystned bed proofes of my sorrow showeth:.		276	Psalm VI		18
How rosy moist'ned lipps about his beake		244	Other Poems	4	95
MOISTENING					
My moystning strength is like a potsherd dride,.		299	Psalm XXII		35
MOISTNESS					
A clenly cloth thy moistnes for to wipe:		257	Other Poems	5	55
MOISTURE					
When rooted moisture failes, or groweth drie,.		128	4th Eclogues	75	113
Thy teares expresse night's native moisture right.		229	Astrophil	96	8
*MOLD					
My earthy moulde doth melte in watrie teares..		19	1st Eclogues	7	151
Dorus. My earthy moulde doth melte in watrie teares,.		19	1st Eclogues	7	152
But so his humor I frame, in a mould of choller adusted, . .		29	1st Eclogues	11	9
When all this Earth, this damme or mould of ours,.		100	3rd Eclogues	66	44
And doth she know what mould her beautie beares?		142	Cert Sonnets	11	2
A woman's mould, but like an Angell graste,.		151	Cert Sonnets	22	66
From out thy heavy mould, that inbent eyes		228	Astrophil	94	3
Make in my heavy mould new thoughts to grow:		236	Astrophil	106	11
MOLE					
Asse, pacience; the Mole, a working thought;		101	3rd Eclogues	66	86
Like to the Mowlle with want of guiding sight, ...		149	Cert Sonnets	21	7
A blinded Mowlle, or else a burned flye.		149	Cert Sonnets	21	14
MOLEHILLS					
Hart-broken so, that molehilles seeme high mountaines, . . .		111	4th Eclogues	71	23
MOMENT					
Each moment lost, part of my hap destroyes:.		80	Arcadia III	53	11
MOMUS'					
And for a tast of all these gifts, she borowes Momus' grace.		12	Arcadia I	3	8
MONARCHY					
Of her high heart giv'n me the monarchie:.		200	Astrophil	69	10
MONEY					
More gladde to me, then to a miser monie is.		15	1st Eclogues	7	33
Or glittering golden mony?		294	Psalm XIX		42
MONKEY					
Monkie, sweet breath; the Cow, her faire eyes brought; . . .		101	3rd Eclogues	66	88
MONSTER					
Pas. Tell this (and Phoebus be) what monster growes.		56	2nd Eclogues	29	144
Here wrong's name is unheard: slander a monster is..		69	2nd Eclogues	34	26
The smoke of hell, the monster called paine, ...		140	Cert Sonnets	8	2
A monster, other's harme, selfe-miserie, ...		206	Astrophil	78	5
MONSTER'S					
Nico. Tell me (and be my Pan) the monster's name,.		56	2nd Eclogues	29	141
MONSTERS					
Like those whom dreames make uglie monsters see, ...		136	Cert Sonnets	2	11
MONSTROUS					
Monstrous appeares, long trueth received late, ...		85	Arcadia III	61	6
Am banisht now among the monstrous mountaines.		111	4th Eclogues	71	16
Hailestones of teares, of sighes a monstrous blast,.		114	4th Eclogues	72	33
MONUMENT					
Nico. Thy monument is layd in many a tree, ...		56	2nd Eclogues	29	129
Yet let us leave a monument in publique.		109	Arcadia IV	70	15
Grant yet, grant yet a looke, to the last monument of his					
anguish, ...		122	4th Eclogues	74	3
Can death beautie become? must I be such a monument?		123	4th Eclogues	74	32
MONUMENTS					
So become our tombes monuments of her praise;.		30	1st Eclogues	12	10
MOOD					
Have you not seene her mood, ...		158	Cert Sonnets	28	21
MOODS					
As in their moodes to take a lingring pawse?		146	Cert Sonnets	17	24
MOODY					
A man to feare a woman's moodie eye, ...		49	2nd Eclogues	28	75
But God shall scorn their moody meaning, ...		325	Psalm XXXVII		35
MOON					
For as the Moone the eie doth please,.		13	Arcadia I	5	7
The sleepy kisse the moone stale:.		66	2nd Eclogues	32	28
"No" saies faire moone, "my lighte		82	Arcadia III	55	12
Like to the Moone when after chaunge		86	Arcadia III	62	11
The moone a sunder rent (O godes, o pardon me, ...		118	4th Eclogues	73	55
The Moone a sunder rent; whereat with sodaine fall		118	4th Eclogues	73	57
Whether the Turkish new-moone minded be.		179	Astrophil	30	1
With how sad steps, o Moone, thou climb'st the skies,. . . .		180	Astrophil	31	1
Then ev'n of fellowship, o Moone, tell me.		180	Astrophil	31	9
This small light the Moone bestowes, ...		210	A&S 4th Song		19
When Moone and starrs my thoughtes beholdeth		278	Psalm VIII		11
MOONY					
Your presence (sister deare) first to my Moony spheare,. . .		119	4th Eclogues	73	103
MOPSA'S					
What length of verse can serve brave Mopsa's good to show, .		12	Arcadia I	3	1
MORAL					
In morall rules let raging woes contained be?.		61	2nd Eclogues	30	151
Your morall notes straight my hid meaning teare.		233	Astrophil	104	12

313

	PAGE	TITLE		LINE
More high then stars, more firme then flintie field.	3	Lady of May	2	9
His wished weale, what more he could require:.	4	Lady of May	3	4
Transformd in shew, but more transformd in minde,.	11	Arcadia I	2	1
Milde as a Lambe, more daintie then a Conie is:.	15	1st Eclogues	7	31
More gladde to me, then to a miser monie is.	15	1st Eclogues	7	33
While still more wretch, more wicked he doth prove:.	22	1st Eclogues	8	44
Thy wit dost use still still more harmes to finde.	23	1st Eclogues	9	34
There is no hate that can thee more oppresse.	23	1st Eclogues	9	49
Knowing no more, then what poore tryall showes,.	28	1st Eclogues	10	53
And worse of other more, till by assent.	29	1st Eclogues	10	82
And we shall find more spottes then Leopard's skinne.. . . .	29	1st Eclogues	10	95
How much more we do love, so the lesse our loves be beleeved	32	1st Eclogues	13	20
Farre more happy be you, whose greatnes gets a free accesse,	33	1st Eclogues	13	54
Nor yet, fancy so drest, do receive more plausible hearing:.	35	1st Eclogues	13	101
Thus her giftes most sweet, thus more danger to be neere her, ...	36	1st Eclogues	13	126
For bellowes serve to kindle more the fire..	38	Arcadia II	14	8
What I call wrong, I doo the same, and more:	41	Arcadia II	20	6
The jealous eye, the more it lookes, it loves.	42	Arcadia II	22	7
Whose wounds are salves, whose yokes please more then pleasure doth:	49	2nd Eclogues	28	56
Her naked legge, more white then whitest snowe..	55	2nd Eclogues	29	101
She did the water wash, and make more fine..	55	2nd Eclogues	29	107
That (shining now) she then might shine more farre..	56	2nd Eclogues	29	122
I silent herd more wordes of witt.	57	2nd Eclogues	30	2
But more I plaine, I feele my woes the more.	57	2nd Eclogues	30	10
Her face which was more lively in my hart;	60	2nd Eclogues	30	117
For what can breed more peevish incongruities,.	61	2nd Eclogues	30	140
Let us some grammar learne of more congruities..	61	2nd Eclogues	30	142
O much more then words: those words serv'd more to me blesse Lesse.	64	2nd Eclogues	31	31
More in his owne he toyld he gladdes the more.	71	Arcadia III	36	12
My dreeades augment the more in passion's mighte,.	72	Arcadia III	37	17
And how much more her worth surmounteth thee,.	72	Arcadia III	38	16
Make her as much more base by loving me.	72	Arcadia III	38	17
O breath more sweete, then is the growing beane, ...	76	Arcadia III	46	2
Gay haire more gaie then straw when harvest lyes,.	76	Arcadia III	46	7
To over pressed brestes, more greevous waight.	82	Arcadia III	56	8
Thus thus the more I love, the wronge the more	85	Arcadia III	61	5
But ah the more I hate, the more I thinke.	85	Arcadia III	61	9
Whome I doe hate, the more I thinke on him,.	85	Arcadia III	61	10
The more his matchlesse giftes do deeply sinck.	85	Arcadia III	61	11
Whiter indeed; more white then snow,.	85	Arcadia III	62	7
A way more worthie beautie's fame, ...	87	Arcadia III	62	59
More white then Neptune's fomie face,.	88	Arcadia III	62	69
Those thighes, for Ovid's song more fitte;	88	Arcadia III	62	88
More white then whitest bone of whall.	89	Arcadia III	62	104
Have much more care of them that them do keepe,.	92	3rd Eclogues	63	39
This done, thou hast no more, but leave the rest	98	3rd Eclogues	65	13
For for my sheepe I dreaded mickle more.	99	3rd Eclogues	66	18
Beyond the heaven, far more beyond your witts.	99	3rd Eclogues	66	28
And aye more awe towards him for to plant, ...	101	3rd Eclogues	66	102
Make home more paine then following of the cart.	104	3rd Eclogues	67	30
O that we had, to make our woes more publique, ...	109	Arcadia IV	70	25
Long since my thoughts more desert be then forrests:. . . .	112	4th Eclogues	71	28
Long since I hate the night, more hate the morning:.	112	4th Eclogues	71	34
My fire is more, then can be made with forrests:.	112	4th Eclogues	71	56
My state more base, then are the basest vallies:	112	4th Eclogues	71	57
I wish no evenings more to see, each evening;.	112	4th Eclogues	71	58
Whose beawties shin'de more then the blushing morning, . . .	113	4th Eclogues	71	62
(More swift then falcon's stoope to feeding Falconer's call)	118	4th Eclogues	73	58
Straunge were the Ladies' weedes; yet more unfit then strange.	118	4th Eclogues	73	65
The other had with arte (more then our women knowe,.	118	4th Eclogues	73	71
So much more strong againe let fastest concorde make.. . . .	120	4th Eclogues	73	120
More then Nestor's yeares, more then a King's diademe. . . .	122	4th Eclogues	74	20
And with more, by the lawes that to Revenge doo belong.. . .	123	4th Eclogues	74	42
If that love be a fault, more fault in you to be lovely: . .	123	4th Eclogues	74	43
What veiles then doo prevaile, but to a more miracle?. . . .	123	4th Eclogues	74	50
Did not a rosed breath, from lips more rosie proceeding, . .	124	4th Eclogues	74	79
With much more: now what doo I finde, but Care to abhor me,.	124	4th Eclogues	74	81
Since so she will, whose will is to me more then a lawe. . .	124	4th Eclogues	74	84
Example more prevailing then direction,.	128	4th Eclogues	75	131
Feare is more paine, then is the paine it feares,.	131	Arcadia V	77	5
Would often kill to breed more feeling paine,.	135	Cert Sonnets	2	4
Aire let me draw no more thy breath in anguish:.	136	Cert Sonnets	3	14
Have more cause to lament me,.	137	Cert Sonnets	4	19
Since wanting is more woe then too much having..	137	Cert Sonnets	4	20
But no more wordes, thoughe such a worde bee spoken, ...	138	Cert Sonnets	5	17
Nor no more wording with a worde to spill mee.	138	Cert Sonnets	5	18
More loving eyes she draws, more hate thou hast.	141	Cert Sonnets	8	14
So stay her toung, that she no more say no..	142	Cert Sonnets	10	14
That sense feeles more then what doth sense containe?. . . .	142	Cert Sonnets	11	8
More happie I, might I in bondage bide..	144	Cert Sonnets	15	14
Who silence force to make their words more deare:.	147	Cert Sonnets	17	49
You fairer still, and still more cruell bent,.	148	Cert Sonnets	19	15
Of trueth, farre more then Alablaster pure,.	150	Cert Sonnets	22	39
A bird which gets more life then ship had lost..	151	Cert Sonnets	22	54

No more in thy sweetnesse glorie,. . . . .   156 Cert Sonnets 27   17
That no more thy beames availe thee. . . . .   156 Cert Sonnets 27   20
Lay not thy colours more to view,. . . . .   157 Cert Sonnets 27   23
Churches or schooles are for thy seate more fit: . . . . .   166 Astrophil   4   6
They sun-like should more dazle then delight?. . . . . . .   168 Astrophil   7   8
Stella; now she is nam'd, need more be said? . . . .   173 Astrophil   16   11
Then that I lose no more for Stella's sake.. . . . .   174 Astrophil   18   14
Wealth breeding want, more blist, more wretched grow.. . .   177 Astrophil   24   4
That I had bene more foolish or more wise. . . . .   181 Astrophil   33   14
But more I crie, lesse grace she doth impart. . . . . . .   186 Astrophil   44   6
Though false, yet with free scope more grace doth breed. .   187 Astrophil   45   10
And yet to breake more staves did me addresse: . . . . . .   191 Astrophil   53   2
But now I meane no more your helpe to trie,. . . . .   192 Astrophil   55   9
But as he then more short or slacke doth raine,. . . . . .   194 Astrophil   58   4
Deare, why make you more of a dog then me? . . . .   194 Astrophil   59   1
Deare, love me not, that you may love me more. . . . . . .   196 Astrophil   62   14
Nc more, my deare, no more these counsels trie,. . . . . .   198 Astrophil   64   1
My wealth no more, and no whit lesse my need,. . . . . . .   199 Astrophil   66   7
Rather then by more truth to get more paine. . . . .   199 Astrophil   67   14
With voice more fit to wed Amphion's lyre. . . . .   200 Astrophil   68   6
I must no more in thy sweet passions lie;. . . . .   202 Astrophil   72   7
That hand, which without touch holds more then Atlas might;. 205 Astrophil   77   5
That in no more but these I might be fully blest:. . . . .   205 Astrophil   77   13
Pardon that fault, once more graunt me the place,. . . . .   208 Astrophil   82   12
Nay, more foole I, oft suffered you to sleepe. . . . . . .   208 Astrophil   83   7
More oft then to a chamber melodie;. . . . .   209 Astrophil   84   4
And nothing then the cause more sweet could be,. . . . . .   223 Astrophil   87   13
While no night is more darke then is my day, ...   224 Astrophil   89   10
Milke hands, rose cheeks, or lips more sweet, more red,. .   225 Astrophil   91   7
Yet growest more wretched then thy nature beares. . . . .   228 Astrophil   94   13
Which ay most faire, now more then most faire show,. . . .   231 Astrophil   100   3
To write therein more fresh the story of delight,. . . . .   232 Astrophil   102   13
Foole, more foole, for no more taking. . . . .   203 A&S 2nd Song   28
More cause a like effect at leastwise bringeth:. . . . . .   208 A&S 3rd Song   5
So to raise my hap more hie; . . . .   211 A&S 4th Song   21
Threat'n what may be done, yet do more then you threat'n..   213 A&S 5th Song   33
Thinke now no more to heare of warme fine odourd snow, . .   213 A&S 5th Song   37
Thinke no more but die in me,. . . . .   227 A&S 10th Song   46
More then in my reason's sight.. . . . .   234 A&S 11th Song   30
No, the more fooles it do shake,. . . . .   234 A&S 11th Song   33
Ccme no more, least I get anger.". . . . .   234 A&S 11th Song   37
Musicke more loftly swels. . . . .   216 A&S 6th Song   25
Love more affected seemes. . . . .   216 A&S 6th Song   31
And wonder more esteemes. . . . .   216 A&S 6th Song   33
"Never season was more fit,. . . . .   219 A&S 8th Song   53
Never roome more apt for it; . . . .   219 A&S 8th Song   54
Thy griefe more then death would grieve me.. . . . .   220 A&S 8th Song   76
"If more may be sayd, I say, ...   220 A&S 8th Song   89
"Therefore, Deere, this no more move,. . . . .   220 A&S 8th Song   97
Stella who more love hath proved,. . . . .   221 A&S 9th Song   22
I say no more but this:. . . . .   272 Psalm III   22
Where I have found more heart's delight. . . . .   274 Psalm IV   28
And make Thy wayes to me more plainly known, ...   275 Psalm V   23
Of these bad folkes, more lifted up with pride . . . . . .   285 Psalm XII   26
More than they now do bragg, when He shall take. . . . . .   286 Psalm XIV   17
What would they more? And I would not their case.. . . . .   290 Psalm XVII   45
This much, yet more, when I by him this freedom gate,. . .   292 Psalm XVIII   40
Yea neighbors, more, my mates were so agast. . . . .   313 Psalm XXXI   32
Who was to me more than most gracious, ...   313 Psalm XXXI   59
Farr farr more sure, than walls most firmly fast.. . . . .   313 Psalm XXXI   60
For he spake not more soone.. . . . .   317 Psalm XXXIII   31
Ev'en gnashing teeth, to witness more their spight.. . . .   322 Psalm XXXV   42
He lends, he gives, more he doth spend . . . .   326 Psalm XXXVII   65
The more his seed in blessing flourish;. . . . .   326 Psalm XXXVII   66
And yet more,. . . . .   327 Psalm XXXVIII   5
But still the more that I did hold my peace, ...   329 Psalm XXXIX   7
The more my sorrow did encrease,. . . . .   329 Psalm XXXIX   8
The more me thought my heart was hott in me; . . . .   329 Psalm XXXIX   9
But they are more than can by me be told.. . . . .   331 Psalm XL   24
More than my head hath haires; . . . .   332 Psalm XL   47
A lustles song for sooth thinks hee that hath more lust to
    cry. . . . .   343 Possibly   1   8
Whose wages makes me beg the more, who feeds me till I
    sterve,. . . . .   343 Possibly   1   20
D. Her heavenly looks, which more and more do give me cause
    to crave.. . . . .   344 Possibly   1   32
For nothing can more tedious bee, then plaint, in time of
    joy.. . . . .   344 Possibly   1   46
More prayse to us we never looke to winne, ...   346 Possibly   5   11
For never was there man more crossely crost then he. . . .   241 Other Poems   1   4
Thinking it just more therein to delight . . . .   246 Other Poems   4   178
Desire the more he suckt, more sought the brest, ...   247 Other Poems   4   203
"Another time", quoth she, "become more wise". . . . . . .   249 Other Poems   4   275
Did hold hir fast for feare of more disgrace,. . . . . . .   249 Other Poems   4   278
More marking hir, then how himselfe did goe, ...   249 Other Poems   4   290
Much more his sight encrease his hote desire:. . . . . . .   249 Other Poems   4   298
Till that he spied old Geron could no more,. . . . .   250 Other Poems   4   307
But this straunge race more straunge conceits did yeeld: .   251 Other Poems   4   345
But, ah! hir darts did farre more depely goe . . . .   251 Other Poems   4   352

315

MORE	(CONTINUED)	PAGE	TITLE		LINE
Which more it mov'd, the more it sweeter was..........		252	Other Poems	4	400
More then, besides hir, all the earth could show.......		252	Other Poems	4	408
Help him, who can no more hir sight foregoe.		253	Other Poems	4	420
As much more loving, as lesse combersome............		255	Other Poems	4	504
Wilt thou have more? more have, if more I be.........		255	Other Poems	4	514
More envied Phoebus for his westerne flyinge		259	Other Poems	5	126

MORN
Sure shepherd's signe, that morne would soone fetch day. . .		103	3rd Eclogues	66	161
And yet could not by rising Morne foresee.		181	Astrophil	33	12
With such a rosie morne, whose beames most freshly gay . . .		205	Astrophil	76	7
When mery May first early calls the morne, ...		243	Other Poems	4	49
This morne alone to lonely walke did passe,.........		255	Other Poems	4	533

MORNING
Shall such morning deaws be an ease to the heate of a love's fire?		34	1st Eclogues	13	88
In her brave Calves, lyke morning skyes, ...		89	Arcadia III	62	V102
Which to my woes gives still an early morning:		111	4th Eclogues	71	5
O lovelie starre, entitled of the morning, ...		111	4th Eclogues	71	9
Am growne a shrich-owle to my selfe each morning......		111	4th Eclogues	71	18
Klaius. I that was once delighted every morning, ...		111	4th Eclogues	71	19
Hath made it selfe a crier of the morning, ...		112	4th Eclogues	71	26
Long since I hate the night, more hate the morning:.....		112	4th Eclogues	71	34
Me seemes I feele the comfort of the morning		112	4th Eclogues	71	41
Me seemes I feele a noysome sent, the morning.		112	4th Eclogues	71	45
I doo detest night, evening, day, and morning.		112	4th Eclogues	71	54
Klaius. Curse to my selfe my prayer is, the morning: ...		112	4th Eclogues	71	55
Whose beawties shin'de more then the blushing morning, ...		113	4th Eclogues	71	62
Who, where she went, bare in her forhead morning,......		113	4th Eclogues	71	70
Our morning hymne this is, and song at evening.......		113	4th Eclogues	71	75
Whose faire skin, beamy eyes, like morning sun on snow,...		169	Astrophil	8	9
Soule's joy, bend not those morning starres from me, ...		188	Astrophil	48	1
Who hath the crimson weeds stolne from my morning skies? ..		232	Astrophil	102	4
With earlyest entry of the Morning prime,..........		274	Psalm V		7

MORNING'S
| As on sweet flowrs when morning's drops we see........ | | 252 | Other Poems | 4 | 398 |

MORN'S
| Morne's messenger, with rose enameld skies .... | | 231 | Astrophil | 99 | 10 |

MORPHEUS
| Morpheus, the lively sonne of deadly sleepe, ... | | 180 | Astrophil | 32 | 1 |

MORROW
| One day layes up stuffe of griefe for the morrow:..... | | 62 | 2nd Eclogues | 30 | 176 |
| To see my night of evils, which hath no morow........ | | 136 | Cert Sonnets | 3 | 8 |

MORSEI
| What if Laelaps a better morsell fyndes........... | | 26 | 1st Eclogues | 10 | 7 |

MORTAI
As in it selfe to nourish mortall strife...........		57	2nd Eclogues	30	28
Is not my skill, nor reach of mortall minde.		79	Arcadia III	50	16
Nc mortall man the cuppe of suretie drinkes.........		105	3rd Eclogues	67	60
Turnde to the mortall serene of an evening..........		112	4th Eclogues	71	42
(Which made of heav'nly stuffe no mortal chaunge doth bynde)		117	4th Eclogues	73	32
Whence our immortall soules to mortall earth doo flowe:...		118	4th Eclogues	73	46
In mortall mindes our mindes but planets' names preserve:..		120	4th Eclogues	73	113
With mortall disdaine, bent to unendly revenge?.......		123	4th Eclogues	74	36
So that I live to pay a mortall fee, ...		136	Cert Sonnets	2	9
Small losse of mortall treasure, ...		152	Cert Sonnets	23	19
But to mortall		155	Cert Sonnets	26	17
Which elements with mortall mixture breed:		167	Astrophil	5	11
To mortall eyes might sweetly shine in her..........		177	Astrophil	25	11
Oppressing mortall sense, my death proceed,.........		186	Astrophil	42	13
From heavenly standing hits each mortall wight.......		229	Astrophil	97	4
When far spent night perswades each mortall eye, ...		230	Astrophil	99	1
Nc mortall gifts, no earthly fruites, now here descended be:		217	A&S 7th Song		14
O lord that rul'st Our mortall lyne.		278	Psalm VIII		1
Above line repeated at following location.		279	Psalm VIII		33
To give unawares a Mortall blow.		284	Psalm XI		7
But hast enlargd my feet from mortall ginn........		312	Psalm XXXI		24
Beholds our mortall race;...................		317	Psalm XXXIII		51
A creeping serpentlike of mortall woe.		252	Other Poems	4	412

MORTIFY
| Paine willes me die, yet will of death I mortifie: ..... | | 51 | 2nd Eclogues | 28 | 124 |

MOST
"Nothing", sayd he, "for most I joy in this,........		4	Lady of May	3	5
An uncouth love, which Nature hateth most...........		11	Arcadia I	1	4
We finde most sweete affection's snare,...........		14	1st Eclogues	6	3
The wood cries most, before it throughly kindled be, ...		14	1st Eclogues	7	8
Shallow brookes murmure most, deep silent slide away;....		14	1st Eclogues	7	11
Which of us two deserveth most compassion.		15	1st Eclogues	7	18
But for that Love's desire most rules the eyes,.......		22	1st Eclogues	8	41
Oft comes reliefe when most we seeme in trappe......		23	1st Eclogues	9	24
That erst I knewe, and with most plainefull muse;.....		24	1st Eclogues	9	63
And herein most their folly vaine appeares.........		24	1st Eclogues	9	78
Ath strongest soule, when most his raynes do bowe......		25	1st Eclogues	9	101
Which should most miseries, cast on a worme that I am. ...		29	1st Eclogues	11	2
But most wretched I am, now love awakes my desire......		30	1st Eclogues	11	20
But if eyes faile then, when I most doo need them, ...		30	1st Eclogues	12	5
Whose faire bodily gifts are fram'd most lovely to each ey..		33	1st Eclogues	13	55
But yet well I doo finde each man most wise in his owne case		33	1st Eclogues	13	70
Now by thy words I begin, most famous Lady, to gather. . . .		34	1st Eclogues	13	94

MOST   (CONTINUED)   PAGE   TITLE   LINE

Figge that yeeldes most pleasante frute, his shaddow is
    hurtefull, ...   35 1st Eclogues 13   125
Thus be her giftes most sweet, thus more danger to be neere
    her, ...   36 1st Eclogues 13   126
Which makes us most immortall shape to weare, ...   40 Arcadia II   18   14
When pittie most I crave, I cruell prove: . . . .   41 Arcadia II   20   3
R. But Reason will, that Reason governe most. . . . .   46 2nd Eclogues 27   5
Not so; although my mettall were most mutable, ...   47 2nd Eclogues 28   10
Her beames have wrought therin most suer impression: . . . .   47 2nd Eclogues 28   11
Thou then, that framste both words and voice most skilfully,   48 2nd Eclogues 28   19
Then base and sower is Love's most high vocation. . . . . .   48 2nd Eclogues 28   24
As thou doest thinke) should most of all disquiet me . . . .   51 2nd Eclogues 28 115
We thinke they hurt, when most they do assist. . . . . . .   59 2nd Eclogues 30   70
Will spoile the earth of his most rich attire. . . . . . .   59 2nd Eclogues 30   88
Selfe-guiltie folke most prone to feele compassion. . . . .   60 2nd Eclogues 30 V130
He heapes in inward griefe, that most destroyes him. . . . .   62 2nd Eclogues 30 172
But when I first did fal, what brought most fall to my hart?
    Arte. . . . .   64 2nd Eclogues 31   28
Oh when shall I be knowne, wher most to be knowne I do
    longe Long. . . . .   64 2nd Eclogues 31   32
Silly rewarde! yet among women hath she of vertu the most.
    Most. . . . .   64 2nd Eclogues 31   36
Horrible is this blasphemy unto the most holy. O lie. . . .   65 2nd Eclogues 31   45
Moste lothe to loose, the moste approching hope. . . . . .   71 Arcadia III 37   6
And highest thoughts, downeward most headlong throw? . . . .   73 Arcadia III 40   12
A baite most fit, for hungrie minded guest. . . . .   75 Arcadia III 44   10
Call me but yours, my title is most hye: . . . .   79 Arcadia III 50   17
Holde me most yours, then my longe suite is signde. . . . .   79 Arcadia III 50   18
A hill most fitte for such a master, ...   88 Arcadia III 62   79
And most bewitch the wretched eye, ...   90 Arcadia III 62   138
In which most lovely traine, ...   92 3rd Eclogues 63   53
Be fled as things most vaine, ...   93 3rd Eclogues 63   71
Subscription was, yours most, if you will prove. . . . . .   96 3rd Eclogues 64   90
The pandare of the thing, he most did feare, ...   97 3rd Eclogues 64 122
(For envie harbreth most in feeblest hartes) . . . . 100 3rd Eclogues 66   58
I studie that which moste may me displease, ...   113 4th Eclogues 72   5
Embrace that most, that most my soule destroyes. . . . . .   113 4th Eclogues 72   7
These foule, most foule, disastres to me fell; . . . . . .   116 4th Eclogues 72   97
Us to attend, in this most private time and place. . . . .   119 4th Eclogues 73   96
And so most ready am this meane of peace to trie. . . . . .   121 4th Eclogues 73 152
Despaire most tragicall clause to a deadly request). . . .   122 4th Eclogues 74   12
Can those eyes, that of eyes drownd in most harty flowing
    teares, ...   122 4th Eclogues 74   15
If then a man in most ill case may give you a farewell; . .   124 4th Eclogues 74   85
Who most the silly shepheard's pipe did pryse, ...   125 4th Eclogues 75   2
The wynde most oft the hugest Pine-tree greeves: . . . . .   143 Cert Sonnets 12   7
Faire seeke not to be feard, most lovely beloved by thy
    servants, ...   143 Cert Sonnets 14   1
For such a thought most highlie prized, ...   159 Cert Sonnets 29   14
It is most true, that eyes are form'd to serve . . . . . .   167 Astrophil   5   1
It is most true, what we call Cupid's dart, ...   167 Astrophil   5   5
Where with most ease and warmth he might employ his art: . . 168 Astrophil   8   7
But she most faire, most cold, made him thence take his
    flight . . . .   169 Astrophil   8   12
Thou doest proceed in thy most serious wayes: . . . .   170 Astrophil   11   2
Or at the most on some fine picture stayes, ...   170 Astrophil   11   7
But that my wealth I have most idly spent. . . . .   174 Astrophil   18   8
When most I glorie, then I feele most shame: . . . .   174 Astrophil   19   3
The wisest scholler of the wight most wise . . . .   177 Astrophil   25   1
It is most true, for since I her did see, ...   177 Astrophil   25   12
Seeme most alone in greatest companie, ...   178 Astrophil   27   2
Till now, wrapt in a most infernall night, ...   181 Astrophil   33   3
Who though most rich in these and everie part, ...   183 Astrophil   37   12
O eyes, where humble lookes most glorious prove, ...   185 Astrophil   42   5
Whose curelesse wounds even now most freshly bleed: . . . .   189 Astrophil   48   11
Of cunningst fishers most troubled streames, ...   190 Astrophil   51   10
Since they do weare his badge, most firmely prove. . . . .   190 Astrophil   52   4
But them (so sweete is she) most sweetly sing, ...   193 Astrophil   57   10
Which wooed wo, most ravishing delight . . . .   194 Astrophil   58   13
For late with heart most high, with eyes most low, ...   196 Astrophil   63   5
And all in vaine, for while thy breath most sweet, ...   200 Astrophil   68   9
Who marke in thee what is in thee most faire. . . . .   201 Astrophil   71   11
O heav'nly foole, thy most kisse-worthie face, ...   203 Astrophil   73   12
With such a rosie morne, whose beames most freshly gay . . . 205 Astrophil   76   7
Most rich, when most his riches it impart: . . . .   206 Astrophil   79   7
Most sweet-faire, most faire-sweet, do not alas, ...   208 Astrophil   82   7
Thus while th' effect most bitter was to me, ...   223 Astrophil   87   12
Now that of absence the most irksome night, ...   223 Astrophil   89   1
With windowes ope then most my mind doth lie, ...   230 Astrophil   99   5
Which ay most faire, now more then most faire show, ...   231 Astrophil   100   3
Doth make me most to wish thy comfort neere. . . . .   235 Astrophil   106   8
Most rude dispaire my daily unbidden guest, ...   236 Astrophil   108   7
Teaching sleepe most faire to be?. . . . .   202 A&S 2nd Song   2
I said, thou wert most faire, and so indeed thou art: . . .   212 A&S 5th Song   7
I said, thou wert most sweet, sweet poison to my heart: . .   212 A&S 5th Song   8
See now those feathers pluckt, wherewith thou flewst most
    high: . . . .   213 A&S 5th Song   22
As where thou soone mightst helpe, most faith dost most
    oppresse, ...   213 A&S 5th Song   41

```
MOST                    (CONTINUED)                         PAGE   TITLE           LINE
    And which is worse, makes me most guiltlesse torments have,.  214  A&S 5th Song      59
    Thinke of that most gratefull time,. . . . . . . . . . . .   226  A&S 10th Song     25
    Thinke of my most Princely power,. . . . . . . . . . . . .   226  A&S 10th Song     31
    That ravishing delight in them most sweete tunes do not
        raise;  . . . . . . . . . . . . . . . . . . . . . . .   217  A&S 7th Song       2
    In a grove most rich of shade, . . . . . . . . . . . . . .   217  A&S 8th Song       1
    Unto the lord most strong:  . . . . . . . . . . . . . . .    273  Psalm III         32
    These most ungratefull rebels unto Thee. . . . . . . . . .   275  Psalm V           32
    O Lord most high.. . . . . . . . . . . . . . . . . . . . .   279  Psalm IX           5
    Shew forth his Acts, and this as Act most high,. . . . . .   280  Psalm IX          32
    That I within the ports most beautyfull. . . . . . . . . .   280  Psalm IX          41
    Most surely caught.. . . . . . . . . . . . . . . . . . . .   280  Psalm IX          50
    In time most fitt for Thee . . . . . . . . . . . . . . . .   281  Psalm X            3
    Still plagues the poore the most he can:  . . . . . . . .    281  Psalm X            6
    Whose life doth seeme most greatly blest . . . . . . . . .   290  Psalm XVII        39
    My refuge, refuge then, when moste I am forlorn;  . . . . .  291  Psalm XVIII        5
    Whom then shall I invoke but Thee most worthy prayse,. . .   291  Psalm XVIII        6
    He made my cumbrous way to me most plainly right.. . . . .   292  Psalm XVIII       60
    Most circumspectly guarded,. . . . . . . . . . . . . . . .   295  Psalm XIX         46
    Most secret from all knowledg. . . . . . . . . . . . . . .   295  Psalm XIX         52
    Ev'n in the day when most Thy troubles be;  . . . . . . .    295  Psalm XX           2
    To thee, O Lord most just, . . . . . . . . . . . . . . . .   302  Psalm XXV          1
    Prove me O Lord most high, . . . . . . . . . . . . . . . .   305  Psalm XXVI         7
    The works perform'd by Thee most wondrous great. . . . . .   305  Psalm XXVI        24
    Most cruel words.. . . . . . . . . . . . . . . . . . . . .   308  Psalm XXVII       60
    Yea from the grave's most hungry jawes;. . . . . . . . . .   311  Psalm XXX          7
    To Vanitys, which most trust most deceave, . . . . . . . .   312  Psalm XXXI        17
    Let me not tast of shame, O lord most high,. . . . . . . .   313  Psalm XXXI        45
    Do throw their words against the most upright. . . . . . .   313  Psalm XXXI        51
    That trust in Thee, ev'n in most open sight! . . . . . . .   313  Psalm XXXI        54
    Who was to me more than most gracious, . . . . . . . . . .   313  Psalm XXXI        59
    Farr farr more sure, than walls most firmly fast.. . . . .   313  Psalm XXXI        60
    To him most strong,. . . . . . . . . . . . . . . . . . . .   316  Psalm XXXIII      14
    Most righteous is.. . . . . . . . . . . . . . . . . . . . .  316  Psalm XXXIII      17
    Then on that lord most kind. . . . . . . . . . . . . . . .   318  Psalm XXXIII      76
    Most great and grievous paines doth beare, . . . . . . . .   320  Psalm XXXIV       70
    When most he seemes opprest. . . . . . . . . . . . . . . .   320  Psalm XXXIV       72
    Even where I do most store of people find; . . . . . . . .   322  Psalm XXXV        47
    Most to Thy lawdes will I my speeches bind.. . . . . . . .   322  Psalm XXXV        48
    Let them be cloathd in most confounding shame, . . . . . .   323  Psalm XXXV        65
    Thy truth above the Clouds, most high, . . . . . . . . . .   323  Psalm XXXVI       14
    Thy justice in most shining luster,. . . . . . . . . . . .   325  Psalm XXXVII      14
    By God's most sure, and sweet salvation; . . . . . . . . .   327  Psalm XXXVII      98
    When most his troubles clime.. . . . . . . . . . . . . . .   332  Psalm XLI          4
    Therfore I said in most infirmity, . . . . . . . . . . . .   333  Psalm XLI         13
    By most cruel sprites, . . . . . . . . . . . . . . . . . .   336  Psalm XLIII        4
    In thy hill most holy. . . . . . . . . . . . . . . . . . .   336  Psalm XLIII       18
    Whose lyverie is such, as most I freeze apparelled most,. .  343  Possibly      1   21
    For where he most would hit, he ever yet did misse.. . . .   241  Other Poems   1    2
    But most cryed, "O well broke": O foole full gaily blest:.   241  Other Poems   1    5
    While most with hir he lesse did kepe with thee. . . . . .   247  Other Poems   4  221
    Most mad with beames which he thought Cosma sent,. . . . .   249  Other Poems   4  270
    Laid hold on him with most lay-holding grace.. . . . . . .   250  Other Poems   4  310
    Then so I faile, when most I would do well,. . . . . . . .   254  Other Poems   4  467
    This song she singes in most commaunding wise: . . . . . .   255  Other Poems   4  509
    As three most joyntly set, . . . . . . . . . . . . . . . .   260  Other Poems   6   21
MOTE
    Pas. And I am here the same, so mote I thrive and thee,. .    52  2nd Eclogues 29    3
    This mote from out his eye, this inward burre, . . . . . .   246  Other Poems   4  172
MOTH
    Woe, lyke a moth, my face's beauty eates . . . . . . . . .   276  Psalm VI          21
MOTHER
    Let me forget I am sonne to my mother, . . . . . . . . . .    61  2nd Eclogues 30  163
    Each sight draws on a thought, thought mother of science,.   69  2nd Eclogues 34   11
    Let mother earth now decke her selfe in flowers, . . . . .    91  3rd Eclogues 63    1
    With sinlesse sleepe, and silence, wisdome's mother, . . .   108  Arcadia IV  69    10
    And mother Earth, now clad in mourning weeds, did breath .   117  4th Eclogues 73    9
    That which their mother hight, or els their silly seed.. .   119  4th Eclogues 73   84
    His mother deare Cupid offended late,. . . . . . . . . . .   173  Astrophil  17      1
    Your faire mother is a bed,. . . . . . . . . . . . . . . .   211  A&S 4th Song      37
    Both Rebell to the Sonne, and Vagrant from the mother; . .   214  A&S 5th Song      69
    Will. A tyme there is for all, my Mother often sayes,. . .   343  Possibly      1    9
    To mother sea you come,. . . . . . . . . . . . . . . . . .   257  Other Poems   5   34
MOTHER'S
    With father's death, and mother's guiltie shame, . . . . .    21  1st Eclogues  8   19
    School'd onely by his mother's tender eye: . . . . . . . .   203  Astrophil  73      2
    At mother's breastes, thou didst good hope betake me.. . .   299  Psalm XXII        22
    Though Father's Care, and Mother's love, . . . . . . . . .   308  Psalm XXVII       49
    Like one that should his Mother's death lament.. . . . . .   322  Psalm XXXV        36
MOTHERS
    Mothers and Nurses of all vaine annoy. . . . . . . . . . .   107  3rd Eclogues 67  117
MOTH-LIKE
    Thou moth like mak'st his beauty fading be;. . . . . . . .   330  Psalm XXXIX       35
MOTION
    Dicus. Dorus, tell me, where is thy wonted motion. . . . .    47  2nd Eclogues 28    1
    Skowts each motion is, the hands the horsmen,. . . . . . .    67  2nd Eclogues 33    8
    Whose motion makes all graces move.. . . . . . . . . . . .    89  Arcadia III 62    96
    Those lampes of heav'nly fire to fixed motion bound, . . .   118  4th Eclogues 73   43
    Those lookes, whose beames be joy, whose motion is delight,. 205  Astrophil  77      1
```

```
MOTION                     (CONTINUED)                        PAGE    TITLE        LINE
    With motion of his rage did to the bottom shake. . . . . . . 291 Psalm XVIII        17
    Each motion seeming shott from beautie's bow,. . . . . . . . 244 Other Poems   4  106
MOTIONS
    No, no, thy motions bee. . . . . . . . . . . . . . . . . . .  80 Arcadia III  52   12
    But straight I saw motions of lightning grace, . . . . . . . 175 Astrophil    20   12
MOUGHT
    She troubled was (alas that it mought be!) . . . . . . . . . 245 Other Poems   4  113
MOUNT
    Their flames mount up, my powers prostrate lie:. . . . . . .  42 Arcadia II   22   11
    Who thus proceeds, for aye, in sacred Mount shall raign. . . 287 Psalm XV           13
MOUNTAINS
    The caves were full, the mountaines voide of goates: . . . .  98 3rd Eclogues 66   11
    Strephon. Yee Gote-heard Gods, that love the grassie
       mountaines,. . . . . . . . . . . . . . . . . . . . . . . 111 4th Eclogues 71    1
    O heavenlie huntresse of the savage mountaines,. . . . . . . 111 4th Eclogues 71    8
    Am banisht now among the monstrous mountaines. . . . . . . . 111 4th Eclogues 71   16
    Hart-broken so, that molehilles seeme high mountaines, . . . 111 4th Eclogues 71   23
    And hath with wailing strength clim'd highest mountaines:. . 112 4th Eclogues 71   27
    And make me wish my selfe layd under mountaines, . . . . . . 112 4th Eclogues 71   36
    Strephon. Me seemes I see the high and stately mountaines, . 112 4th Eclogues 71   37
    As soon as Sunne begins to clime the mountaines: . . . . . . 112 4th Eclogues 71   44
    With envie I doo hate the loftie mountaines; . . . . . . . . 112 4th Eclogues 71   52
    Shamed I hate my selfe in sight of mountaines, . . . . . . . 112 4th Eclogues 71   59
    Who much did passe in state the stately mountaines,. . . . . 113 4th Eclogues 71   63
    Turning to desarts our best pastur'de mountaines.. . . . . . 113 4th Eclogues 71   72
    Strephon. These mountaines witnesse shall, so shall these
       vallies, . . . . . . . . . . . . . . . . . . . . . . . . 113 4th Eclogues 71   73
    The mountaines great with childe I thought brought foorth a
       mouse. . . . . . . . . . . . . . . . . . . . . . . . . . 118 4th Eclogues 73   76
    The Mountains proudly high, and their ffoundations bent. . . 291 Psalm XVIII        16
    The courteous mountaines, griev'd at my disgrace,. . . . . . 254 Other Poems   4  477
    The stedfast mountaynes moved,. . . . . . . . . . . . . . . . 260 Other Poems   6   14
MOUNTING
    But hopes to gaine some helpe by mounting hie, . . . . . . . 144 Cert Sonnets 15    3
MOURN
    My bed, while I with black night mourn alone,. . . . . . . . 276 Psalm VI           19
    Lo I now to mourn begin. . . . . . . . . . . . . . . . . . . 329 Psalm XXXVIII      52
MOURNFUL
    Shall I, whose eares her mournefull words did seaze, . . . .  58 2nd Eclogues 30   50
MOURNFULLY
    And mournfully bewailing,. . . . . . . . . . . . . . . . . . 137 Cert Sonnets  4    5
MOURNING
    Leave off my sheep my mourninge to maintayne,. . . . . . . .  44 Arcadia II   24   13
    Can I forget, from how much mourning plainfulnes . . . . . .  61 2nd Eclogues 30  155
    Weare these my words as mourning weedes of woes, . . . . . .  81 Arcadia III  54    5
    This mourning inck, in which my hart doth bleede.. . . . . .  96 3rd Eclogues 64   96
    And mother Earth, now clad in mourning weeds, did breath . . 117 4th Eclogues 73    9
    Lilly in mourning blacke thy whitenes die: . . . . . . . . . 125 4th Eclogues 75   28
    For mourning night her blacke weedes may display.. . . . . . 126 4th Eclogues 75   54
    Or if thy mourning notes be fully spent, . . . . . . . . . . 127 4th Eclogues 75   64
    Ring out your belles, let mourning shewes be spread, . . . . 159 Cert Sonnets 30    1
    Placed ever there, gave him this mourning weed,. . . . . . . 168 Astrophil     7   13
    Silent and sad in mourning weedes doth dight:. . . . . . . . 229 Astrophil    97    8
    Still still for them I humbly mourning went. . . . . . . . . 322 Psalm XXXV         35
    Still in mourning chear arayd. . . . . . . . . . . . . . . . 328 Psalm XXXVIII      18
MOURNS
    Mournes she in truth, and thinks that others faine?. . . . . 142 Cert Sonnets 11    3
MOUSE
    A king upon a mouse, a strong foe to a rat,. . . . . . . . .  53 2nd Eclogues 29   32
    He eft would kill a mouse, but he disdaines the fight, . . .  53 2nd Eclogues 29   45
    The mountaines great with childe I thought brought foorth a
       mouse. . . . . . . . . . . . . . . . . . . . . . . . . . 118 4th Eclogues 73   76
    Ah, that, that do I not conceive; to the heaven when a mouse
       climes. . . . . . . . . . . . . . . . . . . . . . . . . 122 4th Eclogues 74   21
    That you heard was but a Mouse,. . . . . . . . . . . . . . . 211 A&S 4th Song       25
MOUTH
    Her haire pure Crapal-stone; her mouth O heavenly wyde;. . .  12 Arcadia I     3   11
    With wordes so vyld, from vilder mouth proceeding. . . . . .  50 2nd Eclogues 28 V 82
    For faithfull hart, cleane hands, and mouth as true: . . . .  99 3rd Eclogues 66   25
    My mouth too tender is for thy hard bit. . . . . . . . . . . 166 Astrophil     4    8
    My mouth doth water, and my breast doth swell, . . . . . . . 183 Astrophil    37    1
    Thus much my heart compeld my mouth to say,. . . . . . . . . 207 Astrophil    80    9
    But now spite of my heart my mouth will stay,. . . . . . . . 207 Astrophil    80   10
    Sweet lip, you teach my mouth with one sweet kisse.. . . . . 207 Astrophil    80   14
    Stop you my mouth with still still kissing me.. . . . . . . . 207 Astrophil    81   14
    For in their mouth not One cleere word is spent, . . . . . . 275 Psalm V            25
    Yet from his mouth doth spring . . . . . . . . . . . . . . . 282 Psalm X            27
    Flames issued from his mouth, and burning coales out went; . 291 Psalm XVIII        19
    From lion's mouth O help, and shew to heare me . . . . . . . 299 Psalm XXII         49
    By breath of his mouth stands. . . . . . . . . . . . . . . . 316 Psalm XXXIII       24
    And in my mouth continualy . . . . . . . . . . . . . . . . . 318 Psalm XXXIV         3
    The good mouth will in Wisdom bide,. . . . . . . . . . . . . 326 Psalm XXXVII       77
    I mussle will my mouth while in the sight. . . . . . . . . . 329 Psalm XXXIX         3
    So in my mouth he did a song afford, . . . . . . . . . . . . 331 Psalm XL           11
    With hand and mouth, with lapp and brest keepe warme,. . . . 258 Other Poems   5   84
MOUTHS
    Doth proclaime with a sound made all by men's mouths . . . .  68 2nd Eclogues 33   20
    Al filthy mouths that glory in their vice. . . . . . . . . .  98 3rd Eclogues 65   12
    But valiant Rebels oft in fooles' mouthes purchase fame: . . 214 A&S 5th Song       67
```

                                  319

```
MOUTHS            (CONTINUED)                        PAGE    TITLE        LINE
   With gaping mouthes, these folks on me have charged, . . . .   299 Psalm XXII       29
   Whose mouths Thy self dost bridle, . . . . . . . . . . . .   315 Psalm XXXII      33
MOVE
   As without breath, no pipe doth move,. . . . . . . . . . .    14 1st Eclogues   6      7
   And if enchantment can a harde hart move,. . . . . . . . .    17 1st Eclogues   7    100
   And thinck she is a she, that doth thee move.. . . . . . .    23 1st Eclogues   9     52
   Boulon. O man, take heed, how thou the Gods do move.     .    59 2nd Eclogues 30     65
   Boulon. Thy wailing words do much my spirits move, . . . .    60 2nd Eclogues 30    125
   Whose motion makes all graces move.. . . . . . . . . . . .    89 3rd Eclogues 62     96
   The goodman starting, askt what did her move?. . . . . . .    95 3rd Eclogues 64     47
   He will absent himselfe, least he should move. . . . . . .    95 3rd Eclogues 64     58
   Doth breake, now toong unto thy name doth move,. . . . . .    97 3rd Eclogues 64    100
   But cald, she came apace; a pace wherein did move. . . . .   119 4th Eclogues 73     89
   I praisde her eyes whom never chance doth move, . . . . .    141 Cert Sonnets   9      5
   Which seeming lesse, yet nobler life doth move.. . . . . .   151 Cert Sonnets 22     60
   And should in soule up to our countrey move: . . . . . . .   167 Astrophil      5     13
   His paper, pale dispaire, and paine his pen doth move. . .   168 Astrophil      6     11
   With pricking shot he did not throughly move,. . . . . . .   173 Astrophil     17      3
   Move not thy heavy grace, thou shalt in me,. . . . . . . .   184 Astrophil     39     13
   O eyes, which do the Spheares of beautie move, . . . . . .   185 Astrophil     42      1
   Are humbled thoughts, which bit of Reverence move, . . . .   189 Astrophil     49      6
   Not this faire outside, which our hearts doth move.. . . .   190 Astrophil     52      8
   If he waite well, I never thence would move: . . . . . . .   194 Astrophil     59      3
   But when mine eyes backe to their heav'n did move, . . . .   199 Astrophil     66     13
   Thy selfe, doest strive all minds that way to move,. . . .   201 Astrophil     71     10
   She comes, and streight therewith her shining twins do move.  204 Astrophil     76      1
   If you heare that they seeme my hart to move,. . . . . . .   225 Astrophil     91     13
   Through pores of sencelesse trees, as it could make them
       move:. . . . . . . . . . . . . . . . . . . . . . . . .   208 A&S 3rd Song          2
   Or loving, have so frothy thoughts, as easily thence to move:  217 A&S 7th Song         10
   Time and place for me may move you.. . . . . . . . . . . .   219 A&S 8th Song         52
   "Therefore, Deere, this no more move,. . . . . . . . . . .   220 A&S 8th Song         97
   Their abject lips no breath but flattery move. . . . . . .   284 Psalm XII             5
   Allarme allarme, let not their beauties move . . . . . . .   346 Possibly       5      5
   And both had skill in verse their voice to move. . . . . .   243 Other Poems    4     40
   Now bolt and cudgill squirrels' leape do move. . . . . . .   243 Other Poems    4     44
   Their sences rude plaine objects only move,. . . . . . . .   245 Other Poems    4    143
   Mov'd not himselfe, nor suffred hir to move. . . . . . . .   250 Other Poems    4    328
   So did Uran, the narr the swifter move,. . . . . . . . . .   251 Other Poems    4    357
MOVED
   Now whether mov'd with selfe unworthines,. . . . . . . . .    94 3rd Eclogues 64      7
   (Which life is cald) were mov'd their spirits to repose, .   116 4th Eclogues 73      5
   Diana did begin. "What mov'd me to invite. . . . . . . . .   119 4th Eclogues 73    102
   If Greekes themselves were mov'd with so small cause . . .   146 Cert Sonnets 17     21
   My poore reason thy words moved, . . . . . . . . . . . . .   156 Cert Sonnets 27      3
   Then can in good eawes be moved. . . . . . . . . . . . . .   221 A&S 9th Song         24
   Nay soon as he but moved . . . . . . . . . . . . . . . . .   297 Psalm XXI             6
   She mov'd hir lims, and drew the aged man, . . . . . . . .   249 Other Poems    4    283
   The aire hir swete race mov'd doth blow the fire.. . . . .   249 Other Poems    4    300
   Mov'd not himselfe, nor suffred hir to move. . . . . . . .   250 Other Poems    4    328
   Which more it mov'd, the more it sweeter was.. . . . . . .   252 Other Poems    4    400
   The stedfast mountaynes moved, . . . . . . . . . . . . . .   260 Other Poems    6     14
MOVES
   Love wakes the jealous eye least thence it moves:. . . . .    42 Arcadia II    22      6
   (Even like a toppe which nought but whipping moves). . . .    58 2nd Eclogues 30     33
   Love moves thy paine, and like a faithfull page, . . . . .   232 Astrophil    101      9
MOVING
   Her father's corne (moving her faire limmes) measure.. . .    16 1st Eclogues   7     75
   The ever-turning spheares, the never-moving ground;. . . .   118 4th Eclogues 73     44
   Moving, she seem'd at once to kisse, and speake. . . . . .   244 Other Poems    4     96
MOVINGS
   Where bee those movinges, the Delights, the graces?. . . .   138 Cert Sonnets   5     11
MOWING
   Ape great thing gave, though he did mowing stand,. . . . .   101 3rd Eclogues 66     97
   And said to me wide mowing as they could,. . . . . . . . .   322 Psalm XXXV           53
MOWN
   Like late mowne meades, late cut from joy I live.. . . . .   147 Cert Sonnets 18     11
MOWS
   With mowes and nodds they stand about me flocking. . . . .   299 Psalm XXII           18
MUCH
   Which so much reason beares, . . . . . . . . . . . . . . .    18 1st Eclogues   7    148
   Let crowes picke out mine eyes, which saw too much:. . . .    19 1st Eclogues   7    149
   Let crowes picke out mine eyes which too much sawe. . . . .    19 1st Eclogues   7  V149
   (At Juno's suite who much did Argus love). . . . . . . . .    22 1st Eclogues   8     46
   Thy too much zeale, I feare thy braine hath spent. . . . .    28 1st Eclogues 10     63
   How much more we do love, so the lesse our loves be
       beleeved . . . . . . . . . . . . . . . . . . . . . . .    32 1st Eclogues 13     20
   Still seeking Love, love found as much I flie. . . . . . .    41 Arcadia II    20      4
   With stroking hurt, and too much cramming kill.. . . . . .    41 Arcadia II    20     12
   Yet thus much Love, O Love, I crave of thee: . . . . . . .    41 Arcadia II    20     13
   Cosma's faire beames emblemish much his raies. . . . . . .    55 2nd Eclogues 29     98
   Boulon. Thy wailing words do much my spirits move, . . . .    60 2nd Eclogues 30    125
   Can I forget, from how much mourning plainfulnes . . . . .    61 2nd Eclogues 30    155
   Thus is our mind with too much minding spilled.. . . . . .    62 2nd Eclogues 30    175
   O much more then words: those words serv'd more to me
       blesse Lesse. . . . . . . . . . . . . . . . . . . . .     64 2nd Eclogues 31     31
   O how much I do like your solitarines! . . . . . . . . . .    68 2nd Eclogues 34      2
   Above line repeated at following location. . . . . . . . .    69 2nd Eclogues 34     16
   And how much more her worth surmounteth thee,. . . . . . .    72 Arcadia III   38     16
```

MUCH   (CONTINUED)   PAGE   TITLE   LINE
    Make her as much more base by loving me. . . . .   72 Arcadia III 38   17
    Where too much sight, makes all the bodie blinde,. . . . . .   73 Arcadia III 40   11
    Thus honour, liking, trust, much, farre, and deepe,. . . . .   84 Arcadia III 60   5
    Save one as much as other cleere:. . . . .   86 Arcadia III 62   20
    Have much more care of them that them do keepe,. . . . . . .   92 3rd Eclogues 63   39
    The courtlie shepheard much agast at this, ...   96 3rd Eclogues 64   67
    But let us pick our good from out much bad:. . . . .   105 3rd Eclogues 67   62
    But with much studie learne late to repent.. . . . .   106 3rd Eclogues 67   96
    Who hath our sight with too much sight infected, ...   108 Arcadia IV   69   6
    Who much did passe in state the stately mountaines,. . . . .   113 4th Eclogues 71   63
    Those names abasht me much, when those great names I hard: .   119 4th Eclogues 73   79
    Too much her peerles parts, nor yet could them despise.. . .   119 4th Eclogues 73   88
    Betwixt us two; how much that discord foule hath stain'd . .   119 4th Eclogues 73   106
    Proofe speakes too much to us that feeling triall have.. . .   119 4th Eclogues 73   108
    So much more strong againe let fastest concorde make.. . . .   120 4th Eclogues 73   120
    Should my too-much sight cause so true a Sunne to be lost? .   124 4th Eclogues 74   58
    What? was I then worthie such good, now worthie so muche
        evill? . . . .   124 4th Eclogues 74   77
    With much more: now what doo I finde, but Care to abhor me,.   124 4th Eclogues 74   81
    With too much griefe me thinkes you are dissolved. . . . . .   127 4th Eclogues 75   77
    Since wanting is more woe then too much having.. . . . . . .   137 Cert Sonnets 4   20
    Pressing too much upon ill harbourd shore. . . . .   142 Cert Sonnets 12   3
    We have a fish, by strangers much admirde, ...   150 Cert Sonnets 22   21
    Of which, how much may pierce to that sweete seate,. . . . .   151 Cert Sonnets 22   46
    I can speake what I feele, and feele as much as they,. . . .   168 Astrophil   6   12
    If now the May of my yeares much decline,. . . . .   175 Astrophil   21   10
    While too much wit (forsooth) so troubled me,. . . . .   181 Astrophil   33   10
    O Stella deare, how much thy power hath wrought, ...   184 Astrophil   40   2
    I much do guesse, yet find no truth save this, ...   187 Astrophil   44   9
    As of a friend that meant not much amisse: . . . .   193 Astrophil   56   8
    I cannot brag of word, much lesse of deed, ...   199 Astrophil   66   5
    "Or so?" Much lesse: "How then?" Sure thus it is:. . . . . .   204 Astrophil   74   13
    Thus much my heart compeld my mouth to say,. . . . .   207 Astrophil   80   9
    Of highest wish, I wish you so much blisse,. . . . .   209 Astrophil   84   13
    But wit confus'd with too much care did misse. . . . .   227 Astrophil   93   8
    Sure they prevaile as much with me, as he. . . . .   236 Astrophil   106   12
    My life melts with too much thinking;. . . . .   227 A&S 10th Song   45
    Him great harmes had taught much care, ...   218 A&S 8th Song   9
    But rather much he fancys this . . . .   281 Psalm X   15
    This much, yet more, when I by him this freedom gate,. . . .   292 Psalm XVIII   40
    Ev'en Peare makes strangers shew much love though much
        untrue. . . . .   293 Psalm XVIII   81
    From much abomination.   295 Psalm XIX   60
    Who never doth deceive, and much lesse his deceaving . . . .   302 Psalm XXIV   11
    Thus much I said, this being said. . . . .   311 Psalm XXX   33
    Bow down thine eare to heare how much I need,. . . . .   312 Psalm XXXI   4
    In him much joy, ...   318 Psalm XXXIII   80
    As Brothers, or as Friends beloved much; . . . .   322 Psalm XXXV   34
    The Wicked watch the righteous much. . . . .   326 Psalm XXXVII   81
    But I do hush, Why do I say thus much, ...   330 Psalm XXXIX   29
    Didst like, much lesse didst crave;. . . . .   331 Psalm XL   27
    And in me so much dismaid? . . . .   334 Psalm XLII   18
    Above line repeated at following location. . . . .   335 Psalm XLII   50
    Much may that was not yet, Allarme allarme.. . . . .   346 Possibly   5   12
    Me thought some staves he mist: if so, not much amisse:. . .   241 Other Poems   1   1
    Who share in woe, weygh others have as much. . . . .   242 Other Poems   4   16
    To visite so low folkes did much disdaine, ...   243 Other Poems   4   63
    A heardman rich of much account was he,. . . . .   245 Other Poems   4   117
    Much more his sight encreast his hote desire:. . . . .   249 Other Poems   4   298
    As much more loving, as lesse combersome.. . . . .   255 Other Poems   4   504
MUD
    That bagged baggage of a miser's mudd, ...   245 Other Poems   4   122
MUDDY
    As fishe sure tryall hath of muddy slyme.. . . . .   28 1st Eclogues 10   54
    Is chaunced to my life, that from such muddy abundance . . .   34 1st Eclogues 13   96
    Which heav'nly purest gifts defile in muddy cares. . . . . .   117 4th Eclogues 73   18
    Or knowing, have so muddy minds, as not to be in love; . . .   217 A&S 7th Song   9
MULE
    Oh be not like a horse or mule,. . . . .   315 Psalm XXXII   31
MULTITUDE
    The multitude to Jove a suite empartes,. . . . .   100 3rd Eclogues 66   61
MULTITUDES
    Even multitudes be they. . . . .   272 Psalm III   7
MURDER
    For murdre done, which never erst was seene, ...   102 3rd Eclogues 66   127
    If thus thou murther thy posteritie. . . . .   105 3rd Eclogues 67   78
    Who may and will not save, murder in truth committeth. . . .   214 A&S 5th Song   54
    But murder, private fault, seems but a toy to thee,. . . . .   214 A&S 5th Song   55
MURDERED
    The dreadfull cries of murdred men in forrests.. . . . . . .   112 4th Eclogues 71   48
MURDERER
    The name of murdrer now on thy faire forehead sitteth: . . .   214 A&S 5th Song   51
MURDERING
    Our sports murdering our selves, our musiques wailing, . . .   109 Arcadia IV   70   29
    See there that boy, that murthring boy I say,. . . . .   174 Astrophil   20   2
    Thou English murdring theefe, wilt have harts for thy pray:.   214 A&S 5th Song   50
    You then ungratefull thiefe, you murdring Tyran you, ...   215 A&S 5th Song   85
MURDEROUS
    The murdrous man, and so the fraudulent. . . . .   275 Psalm V   16

	PAGE	TITLE		LINE
MURMUR				
Shallow brookes murmure most, deep silent slide away;. . . .	14	1st Eclogues	7	11
MURMURINGS				
When with Dovelike murmurings, ...	226	A&S 10th Song		38
MURMURS				
To mutter murmures vaine?.	271	Psalm II		2
MURRAIN				
No woolves dare howle, no murrayne can prevaile, ...	43	Arcadia II	23	8
Away ragg'd rams, care I what murraine kill?	255	Other Poems	4	515
MUSCOVITE				
Is gone, and now like slave-borne Muscovite, ...	166	Astrophil	2	10
MUSCOVY				
To warme with ill-made fire cold Moscovy;.	180	Astrophil	30	4
*MUSE				
Thus shrewdly burdned then, how can my Muse escape?.	12	Arcadia I	3	3
Yet high is my attempt. O Muse historifie.	15	1st Eclogues	7	23
Lalus. Muse hold your peace: but thou, my God Pan, glorify .	15	1st Eclogues	7	25
Dorus. Farre other care, o Muse, my sorrow tries,.	17	1st Eclogues	7	106
But ah my Muse I would thou hadst facilitie,.	19	1st Eclogues	7	176
That erst I knewe, and with most plainefull muse;.	24	1st Eclogues	9	63
Joyning your sweete voice to the rurall muse of a deserte, .	31	1st Eclogues	13	2
That to the sacred Muse my anoyes somewhat be revealed,. . .	31	1st Eclogues	13	9
Sacred Muse, who in one contaynes what nine do in all them..	31	1st Eclogues	13	10
Give therefore to the Muse great praise in whose very				
likenes.	33	1st Eclogues	13	62
Burnt in my selfe, I muse at others' fire:	41	Arcadia II	20	5
My muse what ails this ardour.	65	2nd Eclogues	32	1
Above line repeated at following locations	66	2nd Eclogues	32	9
. . . .	66	2nd Eclogues	32	19
. . . .	66	2nd Eclogues	32	30
. . . .	67	2nd Eclogues	32	40
My muse I yeeld, my muse singe,.	67	2nd Eclogues	32	50
But back unto her back, my Muse, ...	89	Arcadia III	62	109
His death our death. But ah; my Muse hath swarved,.	129	4th Eclogues	75	136
Cease Muse therfore: thy dart o Death applie;.	129	4th Eclogues	75	141
They shall not last: with Citherne silent muse	143	Cert Sonnets	12	14
My Muse therefore, for onely thou canst tell,.	146	Cert Sonnets	17	11
"Foole," said my Muse to me, "looke in thy heart and write."	165	Astrophil	1	14
For me in sooth, no Muse but one I know:	166	Astrophil	3	9
Deeme that my Muse some fruit of knowledge plies:.	176	Astrophil	23	6
Sing then my Muse, now Io Pean sing, ...	196	Astrophil	63	9
My Muse may well grudge at my heav'nly joy,.	201	Astrophil	70	1
Come then my Muse, shew thou height of delight	201	Astrophil	70	9
Cease eager Muse, peace pen, for my sake stay,.	201	Astrophil	70	12
Yet ah, my Mayd'n Muse doth blush to tell the best..	205	Astrophil	77	14
And that my Muse to some eares not unsweet,.	209	Astrophil	84	2
My Muse and I must you of dutie greet.	209	Astrophil	84	7
Doubt you to whom my Muse these notes entendeth, ...	196	A&S 1st Song		1
Above line repeated at following location.	197	A&S 1st Song		33
And o my Muse, though oft you luld her in your lap,.	213	A&S 5th Song		25
Revenge, revenge, my Muse, Defiance' trumpet blow:	213	A&S 5th Song		32
And such skill in my Muse you reconcil'd shall find, ...	215	A&S 5th Song		89
MUSED				
Oft have I musde, but now at length I finde, ...	148	Cert Sonnets	20	1
And as I mus'd such World to see,.	329	Psalm XXXIX		10
MUSES				
Yee Muses all which chaste affects allow,.	91	3rd Eclogues	63	19
Muses graunt guiftes, Nymphes long and joyned life	93	3rd Eclogues	63	92
Your dolefull tunes sweete Muses now applie.	125	4th Eclogues	75	3
Above line repeated at following locations	125	4th Eclogues	75	15
. . . .	125	4th Eclogues	75	30
. . . .	126	4th Eclogues	75	48
. . . .	126	4th Eclogues	75	60
. . . .	127	4th Eclogues	75	78
. . . .	127	4th Eclogues	75	96
. . . .	128	4th Eclogues	75	117
Some Lovers speake when they their Muses entertaine, ...	167	Astrophil	6	1
Muses, I oft invoked your holy ayde, ...	192	Astrophil	55	1
And Muses scorne with vulgar braines to dwell, ...	203	Astrophil	74	3
The new Pernassus, where the Muses bide, ...	207	Astrophil	80	5
MUSES'				
I rather wisht thee clime the Muses' hill, ...	169	Astrophil	10	3
With words, wherein the Muses' treasures be, ...	195	Astrophil	60	7
Nede not the stately Muses' helpe invoke	242	Other Poems	4	7
MUSETH				
Abed on mischief museth he,.	323	Psalm XXXVI		11
MUSIC				
No musike kindly without love. . . , ...	14	1st Eclogues	6	8
Their wooll your weede, I will you Musique yeeld	18	1st Eclogues	7	124
If the sencelesse spheares doo yet hold a musique, ...	30	1st Eclogues	12	13
When trees daunce to the pype, and swift streames stay by				
the musicke, ...	33	1st Eclogues	13	47
When with the kawing crowes their musicke is annoide.. . . .	52	2nd Eclogues	29	18
Nico. I thinke it well: such voice would make one musicke				
hate:.	52	2nd Eclogues	29	21
But this is one that doth his musicke staine.	54	2nd Eclogues	29	62
Boulon. How long wilt thou with monefull musicke staine. . .	58	2nd Eclogues	30	38
And though my mones be not in musicke bound, ...	81	Arcadia III	54	7
Let voice of Sighes into cleare musike runne,.	84	Arcadia III	59	13
Since Lalus' musick oft doth yeeld you praise, ...	92	3rd Eclogues	63	29

```
MUSIC              (CONTINUED)                              PAGE    TITLE           LINE
  He said, the Musique best thilke powers pleasd . . . . . . .   99  3rd Eclogues 66    29
  Vouchsafe your silent eares to playning musique, . . . . . .  111  4th Eclogues 71     4
  Above line repeated at following location. . . . . . . . . .  111  4th Eclogues 71    11
  I that was once esteem'd for pleasant musique, . . . . . . .  111  4th Eclogues 71    15
  I that was once the musique of these vallies,. . . . . . . .  111  4th Eclogues 71    21
  And fill the vales with cries in steed of musique. . . . . .  111  4th Eclogues 71    24
  Strephon. Long since alas, my deadly Swannish musique. . . .  112  4th Eclogues 71    25
  Have praide me leave my strange exclaiming musique,. . . . .  112  4th Eclogues 71    32
  The Nightingales doo learne of Owles their musique:. . . . .  112  4th Eclogues 71    40
  Me seemes I heare, when I doo heare sweete musique,. . . . .  112  4th Eclogues 71    47
  I curse the fidling finders out of Musicke:. . . . . . . . .  112  4th Eclogues 71    51
  And stoppe mine eares, lest I growe mad with Musicke.. . . .  112  4th Eclogues 71    60
  Strephon. For she, whose parts maintaine a perfect musique,   113  4th Eclogues 71    61
  She, whose lest word brings from the sphaeres their musique,  113  4th Eclogues 71    68
  Klaius. These forrests eke, made wretched by our musique,. .  113  4th Eclogues 71    74
  For even the hearbes our hatefull musique stroyes, . . . . .  116  4th Eclogues 72   103
  (A musique sweet to one in carefull musing plaste) . . . . .  117  4th Eclogues 73     8
  Just accord all musike makes;. . . . . . . . . . . . . . . .  140  Cert Sonnets  7    14
  Wise silence is best musicke unto blisse.. . . . . . . . . .  201  Astrophil    70    14
  Sweetner of musicke, wisedome's beautifier:. . . . . . . . .  207  Astrophil    80     6
  While sobd out words a perfect Musike give.. . . . . . . . .  231  Astrophil   100    11
  Which now my breast orecharg'd to Musicke lendeth? . . . . .  196  A&S 1st Song        2
  Above line repeated at following location. . . . . . . . . .  197  A&S 1st Song       34
  Beauty, musicke, sweetnesse, love. . . . . . . . . . . . . .  226  A&S 10th Song      34
  For that doth Musike speake, . . . . . . . . . . . . . . . .  215  A&S 6th Song        8
  Musicke more loftly swels. . . . . . . . . . . . . . . . . .  216  A&S 6th Song       25
  Musicke doth witnesse call . . . . . . . . . . . . . . . . .  216  A&S 6th Song       37
  Which Musicke can in sky . . . . . . . . . . . . . . . . . .  217  A&S 6th Song       51
  Where birds wanton musicke made, . . . . . . . . . . . . . .  217  A&S 8th Song        2
  Her eares where Musique lives, . . . . . . . . . . . . . . .  258  Other Poems   5    60
  With sound of musicke living.. . . . . . . . . . . . . . . .  260  Other Poems   6    10
  Often Reedes me musicke made,. . . . . . . . . . . . . . . .  263  Other Poems   7    44
MUSIC'S
  If Orpheus' voyce had force to breathe such musicke's love .  208  A&S 3rd Song        1
  Of Musick's wondrous might:. . . . . . . . . . . . . . . . .  216  A&S 6th Song       34
  With sweet musick's skill. . . . . . . . . . . . . . . . . .  337  Psalm XLIII        26
MUSICS
  Our sports murdering our selves, our musiques wailing, . . .  109  Arcadia IV   70    29
MUSING
  Deepe musing to himselfe, which after-mewing showes, . . . .   53  2nd Eclogues 29    35
  He never musing standes, but with himselfe will play . . . .   53  2nd Eclogues 29    43
  (A musique sweet to one in carefull musing plaste) . . . . .  117  4th Eclogues 73     8
  As I thus musing stood, Diana cald to her. . . . . . . . . .  119  4th Eclogues 73    81
MUST
  Greater is she who must the judgement give.. . . . . . . . .    3  Lady of May   2     6
  To high conceipts the song must needes be high,. . . . . . .    3  Lady of May   2     8
  The gods must help, and pretious things must serve to shew
      her shape. . . . . . . . . . . . . . . . . . . . . . . .   12  Arcadia I     3     4
  So if my man must praises have,. . . . . . . . . . . . . . .   13  Arcadia I     5     5
  What then must I that keepe the knave? . . . . . . . . . . .   13  Arcadia I     5     6
  So if my man must praises have,. . . . . . . . . . . . . . .   13  Arcadia I     5    11
  What then must I that keepe the knave? . . . . . . . . . . .   13  Arcadia I     5    12
  Bent to such one, in whom, my selfe must say,. . . . . . . .   17  1st Eclogues  7   107
  Yet patient must abide.. . . . . . . . . . . . . . . . . . .   20  1st Eclogues  7  V960
  Though woes now live, at length thy woes must dye. . . . . .   22  1st Eclogues  9    12
  Though cradle witted, must not honnor loose. . . . . . . . .   25  1st Eclogues  9    92
  Loth to dye young, and then you must be olde,. . . . . . . .   25  1st Eclogues  9   103
  Youth will have will: Age must to age therefore. . . . . . .   27  1st Eclogues 10    24
  Which must frame contempt to the fittest purchase of
      honnour  . . . . . . . . . . . . . . . . . . . . . . . .   32  1st Eclogues 13    38
  Olive paintes me the peace that I must aspire to by
      conquest . . . . . . . . . . . . . . . . . . . . . . . .   35  1st Eclogues 13   117
  In you it is, you must the judgement give. . . . . . . . . .   39  Arcadia II   17     8
  Of my due faith, which needs must be immutable?. . . . . . .   47  2nd Eclogues 28     8
  That Nico must with Pas compared be? . . . . . . . . . . . .   54  2nd Eclogues 29    65
  Plangus must live to see Eronae's death. . . . . . . . . . .   58  2nd Eclogues 30    55
  Plangus must live some helpe for her to trie . . . . . . . .   58  2nd Eclogues 30    56
  If she must dye, then hath she past the line . . . . . . . .   59  2nd Eclogues 30    77
  In whose decay Vertue's faire shrine must fall.. . . . . . .   59  2nd Eclogues 30    91
  Burnt by the Sunne, she first must build her nest. . . . . .   60  2nd Eclogues 30   103
  Selfe-guiltie folke must prove to feele compassion.. . . . .   60  2nd Eclogues 30   130
  But if my memory thus must be thralled . . . . . . . . . . .   61  2nd Eclogues 30   164
  But hoarse and drye, my pipes I nowe must spare. . . . . . .   62  2nd Eclogues 30   190
  But you must pay, the gage of promist weale. . . . . . . . .   76  Arcadia III  46    18
  Loath, I must leave his chiefe resort. . . . . . . . . . . .   88  Arcadia III  62    84
  The best things still must be forgotten. . . . . . . . . . .   88  Arcadia III  62    86
  As I began, so must I ende.. . . . . . . . . . . . . . . . .   90  Arcadia III  62   144
  And as for me (sweete husband) I must beare". . . . . . . . .   96  3rd Eclogues 64    62
  Whether he needes must goe for feare of blame. . . . . . . .   96  3rd Eclogues 64    78
  Three dayes before that he must sure depart, . . . . . . . .   96  3rd Eclogues 64    79
  "The jealous wretch must now to Courte be gone:. . . . . . .   97  3rd Eclogues 64   103
  I will you lende; the rest your selves must give,. . . . . .  101  3rd Eclogues 66    76
  Must goe for that, if for her lowres he care:. . . . . . . .  104  3rd Eclogues 67    42
  Which must by this immortall be preserved, . . . . . . . . .  105  3rd Eclogues 67    77
  Whereby that being aye must be conserved.. . . . . . . . . .  106  3rd Eclogues 67    81
  Thy house by thee must live, or els be gone: . . . . . . . .  106  3rd Eclogues 67   110
  Then must I save, what in my chiefly raignes,. . . . . . . .  114  4th Eclogues 72    24
  Till by such hap, as I must ever rewe, . . . . . . . . . . .  115  4th Eclogues 72    74
  That thus I must, while in this death I dwell, . . . . . . .  116  4th Eclogues 72    89
```

323

MUST	(CONTINUED)	PAGE	TITLE		LINE
But now we muste needs yeelde, to what our otnes require". .		121	4th Eclogues	73	169
And that he thence must part where to live onely I lyved... .		123	4th Eclogues	74	30
Can death beautie become? must I be such a monument?		123	4th Eclogues	74	32
Must I be onely the marke, shall prove that Vertue is angrie		123	4th Eclogues	74	33
All my'offence was Love: with Love then must I be chastned,.		123	4th Eclogues	74	41
That he for want of elbowe roome must die?		126	4th Eclogues	75	44
But Man which helpeth them, helplesse must perish.		127	4th Eclogues	75	87
Must finish then by death's detested crime..		127	4th Eclogues	75	90
Peace Due alledgeance, Duty must bee broken, ...		138	Cert Sonnets	5	19
Releast from Court, where envie needes must be..		143	Cert Sonnets	12	6
Finding those beames, which I must ever love,.		149	Cert Sonnets	21	1
And wretched I must yeeld to this, ...		157	Cert Sonnets	27	31
True, and yet true that I must Stella love..		167	Astrophil	5	14
Effects of lively heat, must needs in nature grow.		169	Astrophil	8	11
But with your Rubarb words yow must contend.		171	Astrophil	14	5
That I respects for both our sakes must show:		181	Astrophil	33	11
Where truth it selfe must speake like flatterie?		182	Astrophil	35	2
For of my life I must a riddle tell.		183	Astrophil	37	4
That thou must want or food, or dwelling place..		187	Astrophil	46	4
Thou needs must misse, and so thou needs must smart.		188	Astrophil	46	11
I may, I must, I can, I will, I do		188	Astrophil	47	10
While each pretends that Stella must be his:		190	Astrophil	52	2
While with the people's shouts I must confesse,.		191	Astrophil	53	3
With chastned mind, I straight must shew that she.		195	Astrophil	61	10
Now from thy fellowship I needs must part, ...		202	Astrophil	72	5
I must no more in thy sweet passions lie:.		202	Astrophil	72	7
Vertue's gold now must head my Cupid's dart.		202	Astrophil	72	8
That Anger' selfe I needs must kisse againe.		203	Astrophil	73	14
But you must needs with those lips billing be?		208	Astrophil	83	12
My Muse and I must you of dutie greet.		209	Astrophil	84	7
Or if I needs (sweet Judge) must torments have,.		212	Astrophil	86	11
Or if such heavenly signes must prove annoy,.		231	Astrophil	100	13
Who will read must first learne spelling..		203	A&S 2nd Song		24
Princes in subjects wrongd, must deeme themselves abused.. .		213	A&S 5th Song		30
Sweet babes must babies have, but shrewd gyrles must be beat n..		213	A&S 5th Song		36
In this pleasant spring must see		222	A&S 9th Song		28
To that high doome, which I by Thee must get..		277	Psalm VII		18
Though battaile's brunt I needs must beare,.		307	Psalm XXVII		15
Who never more must rise..		333	Psalm XLI		28
And lookes so neere unto my cure that I must needes be lost.		343	Possibly	1	22
But hence, even hence, I must needes goe; such is my dogged fate..		344	Possibly	1	48
In shine or storme must sett the clowted shoe:		242	Other Poems	4	20
And so must see great cause before they love..		245	Other Poems	4	144
Must strive with waiting foot, and watching eye.		248	Other Poems	4	228
And he by law of Barly-brake must run.		249	Other Poems	4	296
To hell he goes, and Nous with him must dwell..		250	Other Poems	4	313
But so she must. And now the third assault		250	Other Poems	4	316
And part must folowe where whole man doth goe.		253	Other Poems	4	422
MUSTER					
And of Thy Judgement make a muster		325	Psalm XXXVII		15
MUSTERED					
Of fortune's Diademes, by beauty mustred..		67	2nd Eclogues	33	5
MUTABLE					
Not so; although my mettall were most mutable, ...		47	2nd Eclogues	28	10
MUTE					
If the mute timber when it hath the life lost, ...		30	1st Eclogues	12	15
But who doth feare, or bideth muet wilfully, ...		48	2nd Eclogues	28	17
And so I nothing said, I muet stood, ...		329	Psalm XXXIX		5
MUTINE					
Thus freed from mutin men, thou makest me to raign,.		293	Psalm XVIII		78
MUTTER					
To mutter murmures vaine?.		271	Psalm II		2
MUTUAL					
With mutuall embracements them to twyne:		91	3rd Eclogues	63	16
While we for mutuall spight a striving passion fed..		120	4th Eclogues	73	118
Did for mutuall comfort meete, ...		218	A&S 8th Song		6
But of a straunger mutuall help doth take:		248	Other Poems	4	238
MUZZLE					
I mussle will my mouth while in the sight.		329	Psalm XXXIX		3
MYRRH					
Lawrell shews what I seeke, by the Mirre is show'd how I seeke it,.		35	1st Eclogues	13	116
The weeping Myrrhe I thinke will not denie		125	4th Eclogues	75	13
MYRTLE					
But when in shade we meet of mirtle bowes, ...		18	1st Eclogues	7	128
Or pleasant mirtell, may teach th'unfortunate Echo		31	1st Eclogues	13	13
Mirtle makes my request, my request is crown'd with a willowe..		35	1st Eclogues	13	118
MYSELF					
False in my selfe, thus have I lost the field.		11	Arcadia I	2	8
My sight in her faire limmes, I then assure my selfe,. . . .		16	1st Eclogues	7	56
Can I be poore, that her golde haire procure my selfe? . . .		16	1st Eclogues	7	58
Till I get her, shall I to sheep enure my selfe?		16	1st Eclogues	7	60
Bent to such one, in whom, my selfe must say,.		17	1st Eclogues	7	107
Cleofila. Worthy shepeheard, by my song to my selfe all favor is happned,.		31	1st Eclogues	13	8

MYSELF	(CONTINUED)	PAGE	TITLE		LINE
Then do I shape to my selfe that forme which raigns so within me, ...		36	1st Eclogues	13	142
But to my selfe what wish can I make for a salve to my sorrowes, ...		37	1st Eclogues	13	157
Jaylor I am to my selfe, prison and prisoner to myne owne selfe.		37	1st Eclogues	13	163
That in my selfe your selfe true love doth plant;		39	Arcadia II	16	8
Blots to the stone, shame to my selfe I finde:		40	Arcadia II	19	4
Burnt in my selfe, I muse at others' fire:		41	Arcadia II	20	5
Quite from my selfe to love Love's contemplation;		48	2nd Eclogues	28	32
The quiet mind (whereof my selfe empairer is, ...		51	2nd Eclogues	28	114
Thus weakned by my selfe, no helpe remaineth.		68	2nd Eclogues	33	17
Wher who so wynns, I put my selfe to flight.		74	Arcadia III	42	8
Thus cruell to my selfe how canst thou crave		77	Arcadia III	47	7
Which barde desires, (barde by my selfe) imparte.		77	Arcadia III	47	11
As oh! my selfe, whose woes are never lighte		82	Arcadia III	56	9
Then ever for my selfe since I was bore:		99	3rd Eclogues	66	19
And thinke, I did my selfe from sorrow save.		104	3rd Eclogues	67	24
Am growne a shrich-owle to my selfe each morning.		111	4th Eclogues	71	18
And make me wish my selfe layd under mountaines, ...		112	4th Eclogues	71	36
Klaius. Curse to my selfe my prayer is, the morning:		112	4th Eclogues	71	55
Shamed I hate my selfe in sight of mountaines, ...		112	4th Eclogues	71	59
All what I am: if I my selfe will save, ...		114	4th Eclogues	72	23
But I cannot; who then my selfe should flie, ...		114	4th Eclogues	72	39
So close unto my selfe my wrackes doo lie.		114	4th Eclogues	72	40
Strephon. So close unto my selfe my wrackes doo lie;		114	4th Eclogues	72	41
My ship, my selfe, whose course to love doth bende, ...		114	4th Eclogues	72	44
I have my selfe, and all what life containeth, ...		128	4th Eclogues	75	101
Then to my selfe, not though Jove grew a suter of hers. . . .		143	Cert Sonnets	13	2
By your good helpe, or in my selfe to finde.		148	Cert Sonnets	19	12
A stranger fish, my selfe not yet expirde, ...		150	Cert Sonnets	22	25
My selfe unto th' Anatomy desirde, ...		150	Cert Sonnets	22	27
Now thus this wonder to my selfe I frame, ...		151	Cert Sonnets	22	69
But alwayes one my selfe with eagle eyde trueth to flie, . .		153	Cert Sonnets	24	24
Within my selfe to seeke my onelie hire:		161	Cert Sonnets	31	13
Biting my trewand pen, beating my selfe for spite, ...		165	Astrophil	1	13
To make my selfe beleeve, that all is well, ...		166	Astrophil	2	13
With what sharpe checkes I in my selfe am shent, ...		173	Astrophil	18	1
And by just counts my selfe a banckrout know		173	Astrophil	18	3
I see my course to lose my selfe doth bend:		174	Astrophil	18	12
Fawne on my self, and others to despise:		178	Astrophil	27	8
But to my selfe my selfe did give the blow, ...		181	Astrophil	33	9
For though I oft my selfe of them bemone, ...		189	Astrophil	48	9
That in the Manage myselfe takes delight.		189	Astrophil	49	14
And anchor fast my selfe on Vertue's shore.		196	Astrophil	62	11
Come, come, and let me powre my selfe on thee;		200	Astrophil	69	6
And do I then my selfe this vaine scuse give?.		227	Astrophil	93	9
Tho worlds quite me, shall I my selfe forgive?		227	Astrophil	93	11
Your Client poore my selfe, shall Stella handle so?.		213	A&S 5th Song		31
O if my self find not, ...		226	A&S 10th Song		7
Can learne, how my selfe to sunder		234	A&S 11th Song		14
In my selfe the smart I try, ...		220	A&S 8th Song		94
But I my self will to Thy house addresse		275	Psalm V		17
Now I, now I my self forgotten find, ...		313	Psalm XXXI		34
Till my self did my faults confess		315	Psalm XXXII		13
So I my self accus'd to God, ...		315	Psalm XXXII		16
I did pull down my self, fasting for such;		322	Psalm XXXV		31
Dick. Faith in my self and worth in her, which no proofe can undoo.		343	Possibly	1	26
So have I cause my selfe to plaine, but no cause to complayne.		344	Possibly	1	36
Sometimes to her newes of my selfe to tell		254	Other Poems	4	469
NAILS					
Or with a fair hand's nailes (o hand which nailes me to this death).		123	4th Eclogues	74	55
NAKED					
A naked god, young, blind, with arrowes two.		20	1st Eclogues	8	6
Or naked he, disguis'd in all untruth?		21	1st Eclogues	8	8
Her naked legge, more white then whitest snowe.		55	2nd Eclogues	29	101
Nico. She once starke nak'd did bathe a little tine;		55	2nd Eclogues	29	105
Full glad they were and tooke the naked sprite, ...		101	3rd Eclogues	66	78
With water drinke, herbes meate, and naked hide, ...		101	3rd Eclogues	66	109
Her right arme naked was, discovered was her breast.		118	4th Eclogues	73	68
Since naked sence can conquer reason armed:		135	Cert Sonnets	1	6
That it, despisde in true bud naked shew, ...		192	Astrophil	55	3
For when, nak'd boy, thou couldst no harbour find.		198	Astrophil	65	5
Or hers whom naked the Trojan boy did see.		207	Astrophil	82	4
But nake'd before thine eyes		283	Psalm X		57
NAME					
In one, whose name to name were high presumption, ...		15	1st Eclogues	7	38
Dorus. Lady your selfe, whom nether name I dare, ...		18	1st Eclogues	7	131
Therein his name, there his chiefe triumph lyes.		22	1st Eclogues	8	42
Let not a glittring name thy fancie dresse		23	1st Eclogues	9	47
In these woods to resounde the renowmed name of a goddesse: .		31	1st Eclogues	13	14
Pleasd to receave that name by rebounding answere of Echo, .		33	1st Eclogues	13	44
Dorus. Blest be the name, wherewith my mistres named is: . .		49	2nd Eclogues	28	55
A prettie curre it is; his name iwis is Catch, ...		53	2nd Eclogues	29	40
Pas. Thy name (O Cosma) shall with praise be spread, ...		56	2nd Eclogues	29	126
With name engrav'd: so though thy bodie die, ...		56	2nd Eclogues	29	130

NAME	(CONTINUED)	PAGE	TITLE		LINE
Nico. Tell me (and be my Pan) the monster's name,		56	2nd Eclogues	29	141
But glorious name of wretched humaine-kind?.		57	2nd Eclogues	30	16
What great name may I give to so heav'nly a woman? A woe-man		64	2nd Eclogues	31	37
Here wrong's name is unheard: slander a monster is.		69	2nd Eclogues	34	26
Then that which beares the mylken name.		87	Arcadia III	62	60
For to the courte her man was calld by name,		96	3rd Eclogues	64	77
Doth breake, now toong unto thy name doth move,		97	3rd Eclogues	64	100
And then who shall the name of Histor nourish?		106	3rd Eclogues	67	111
In Nature's name to suffer such a harme,		125	4th Eclogues	75	17
Whose porches rich (which name of cheekes endure)		169	Astrophil	9	7
Which dare claime from those lights the name of best,		169	Astrophil	9	11
But if (both for your love and skill) your name.		172	Astrophil	15	12
My verie inke turnes straight to Stella's name;		174	Astrophil	19	6
Doth even grow rich, naming my stella's name.		182	Astrophil	35	11
Because their forefront bare sweet Stella's name.		190	Astrophil	50	14
That Stella (o deare name) that Stella is.		190	Astrophil	52	6
But on her name incessantly to crie:		192	Astrophil	55	11
For let me but name her whom I do love,		192	Astrophil	55	12
Edward named fourth, as first in praise I name,		204	Astrophil	75	2
As consterd in true speech, the name of heav'n it beares,		205	Astrophil	77	11
Graved in mine Epitaph a Poet's name:		224	Astrophil	90	8
If her lips daignd to sweeten my poore name.		225	Astrophil	92	13
The name of murdrer now on thy faire forehead sitteth:		214	A&S 5th Song		51
Which beare his people's name,		273	Psalm III		35
And love the sweet sound of thy name, rejoyce.		275	Psalm V		34
And will to highest Name yeild prayses high.		278	Psalm VII		48
How through the World thy Name doth shine:		278	Psalm VIII		2
Above line repeated at following location.		279	Psalm VIII		34
Yea even my songs thy name shall magnify,		279	Psalm IX		4
That Name of God a fable is.		281	Psalm X		16
Nay to name their names disdain.		288	Psalm XVI		12
My name their eares, their eares their hearts to me enchaine		293	Psalm XVIII		80
I to Thy Name will sing, and this my song shall bee:		293	Psalm XVIII		89
Let name of Jacob's God,		295	Psalm XX		3
Upon God's holy name,		296	Psalm XX		29
And with these Words, when they meet, prayse Thy Name.		300	Psalm XXII		52
Ascribe due glory to his Name,		310	Psalm XXIX		4
Then since my tongue delights that name to blesse,		312	Psalm XXXI		8
Who hope on his Name just.		318	Psalm XXXIII		81
His Name may honourd be.		319	Psalm XXXIV		12
That wicked be, their very name.		320	Psalm XXXIV		59
And his name perish quite?		333	Psalm XLI		20
He quickly learn'd Urania was her name,		247	Other Poems	4	185
Like some which seeke to salve their blotted name.		248	Other Poems	4	231
Urania name, whose force he knew so well,		256	Other Poems	4	538
NAMED					
No stile is held for base, where Love well named is:		14	1st Eclogues	7	4
Dorus. Blest be the name, wherewith my mistres named is:		49	2nd Eclogues	28	55
Stella; now she is nam'd, need more be said?		173	Astrophil	16	11
Edward named fourth, as first in praise I name,		204	Astrophil	75	2
I should blush when thou art named."		220	A&S 8th Song		100
Who shall climb to the hill which God's own hill is named,		302	Psalm XXIV		5
NAMELESS					
(But namelesse he, for blamelesse he shall be)		94	3rd Eclogues	64	2
NAMELY					
Of all the birdes, but namely those were grieved,		29	1st Eclogues	10	83
NAME'S					
For his name's sake.		301	Psalm XXIII		9
O Lord for Thy name's sake		304	Psalm XXV		43
NAMES					
Tell yet againe me the names of these faire form'd to do ev'lls. Dev'lls.		65	2nd Eclogues	31	49
Those names abasht me much, when those great names I hard:		119	4th Eclogues	73	79
Our names are quite forgot, our temples are defac'd:		119	4th Eclogues	73	109
In mortall mindes our mindes but planets' names preserve:		120	4th Eclogues	73	113
Nay to name their names disdain.		288	Psalm XVI		12
NAMING					
And in our wailfull naming him our pleasure:		130	4th Eclogues	76	32
Doth even grow rich, naming my stella's name.		182	Astrophil	35	11
NAR					
Come narr good Mastix, tis now full tway score		27	1st Eclogues	10	20
So did Uran, the narr the swifter move,		251	Other Poems	4	357
NARROW					
To narrow brests he comes all wrapt in gaine:		21	1st Eclogues	8	37
Peake hath a Cave, whose narrow entries finde.		150	Cert Sonnets	22	31
NARROWLY					
Howe can they be unkind? speake for th'hast narroly pri'de. pride.		65	2nd Eclogues	31	43
NATIONS					
And joy therein, though Nations count it shame.		179	Astrophil	28	8
And turn to God, and all the Nations be.		300	Psalm XXII		67
NATIVE					
Feede on my sheepe, your Native joyes mayntayne,		43	Arcadia II	23	13
But Lillies such whose native smell		87	Arcadia III	62	63
Disarming humane mindes of native might:		131	Arcadia V	77	6
Love borne in Greece, of late fled from his native place,		168	Astrophil	8	1
Thy teares expresse night's native moisture right.		229	Astrophil	96	8

		PAGE	TITLE		LINE
NATIVE	(CONTINUED)				
The Fish of Sea the Native heire,.		279	Psalm VIII		30
NATURE					
An uncouth love, which Nature hateth most.		11	Arcadia I	1	4
And pastimes make, as Nature things hath made.		18	1st Eclogues	7	127
Nature made all, but me of dolours made:		18	1st Eclogues	7	143
Fortune, Nature, Love, long have contended about me, ...		29	1st Eclogues	11	1
"Tush, tush", said nature, "this is all but a trifle, a man's selfe.		29	1st Eclogues	11	7
Where thou poore nature left'st all thy due glory, to fortune.		30	1st Eclogues	11	15
Nature abasht went back: fortune blusht: yet she replide thus:.		30	1st Eclogues	11	17
Thus, thus, alas! wofull in nature, unhappy by fortune,. . .		30	1st Eclogues	11	19
Nature against we do seeme to rebell, seeme fooles in a vaine sute..		32	1st Eclogues	13	24
Nature worketh enough with a small help for the revealing. .		33	1st Eclogues	13	61
Whom both nature seemes to debarr from meanes to be helped,.		37	1st Eclogues	13	158
Let so our fruites grow up, that nature be maintainde: . . .		45	Arcadia II	26	13
R. By nature you to Reason faith have sworne.		46	2nd Eclogues	27	11
Fortune store, Nature health, Love grant perswasion.		51	2nd Eclogues	28	100
His nature? nay, himselfe? for so it is.		59	2nd Eclogues	30	72
That nature, soverayne of earthly dwellers,.		68	2nd Eclogues	33	21
Clymes even unto the starres, Nature is under it..		68	2nd Eclogues	34	9
For nature hathe that never fayling scoope,.		71	Arcadia III	37	5
Nature her selfe enameld it.		90	Arcadia III	62	124
And makes them fremb'd, who frendes by nature are,.		104	3rd Eclogues	67	38
While that we doo what nature doth require,.		105	3rd Eclogues	67	65
Nature above all things requireth this,.		105	3rd Eclogues	67	70
Sorow pay we unto the rights of Nature,.		109	Arcadia IV	70	5
In such a case where it appeares that nature		109	Arcadia IV	70	9
Arcadia's gemme the noblest childe of nature.		109	Arcadia IV	70	18
O nature doting olde, o blinded nature,.		109	Arcadia IV	70	19
Seas in our eyes, and brasen tongues by nature,.		109	Arcadia IV	70	26
But forced are to burthen feeble nature.		110	Arcadia IV	70	34
His nature feares to die who lives still wailing..		110	Arcadia IV	70	39
Nature to me for torment did emparte;.		113	4th Eclogues	72	13
And thinking this, thinke Nature, Life, and Death.		114	4th Eclogues	72	16
Ah let us all against foule Nature crie:		127	4th Eclogues	75	92
For how can Nature unto this reply?.		127	4th Eclogues	75	94
Late harbors in her face whom nature wrought,.		141	Cert Sonnets	8	7
A Ladie in despite of nature chaste,.		151	Cert Sonnets	22	62
But Copying is, what in her Nature writes.		166	Astrophil	3	14
Rebels to Nature, strive for their owne smart.		167	Astrophil	5	4
When Nature made her chiefe worke, Stella's eyes,.		168	Astrophil	7	1
Effects of lively heat, must needs in nature grow.		169	Astrophil	8	11
In nature apt to like when I did see		172	Astrophil	16	1
Till that his grandame Nature pittying it, ...		173	Astrophil	17	9
And not in Nature for best fruits unfit:		174	Astrophil	19	13
For me, I do Nature unidle know, ...		178	Astrophil	26	9
Where Nature doth with infinite agree?		182	Astrophil	35	4
With so sweete voice, and by sweete Nature so, ...		183	Astrophil	36	9
Thinke Nature me a man of armes did make..		185	Astrophil	41	11
The heav'nly nature of that place is such, ...		187	Astrophil	44	12
By Nature borne, I gave to thee mine eyes.		198	Astrophil	65	8
Who will in fairest booke of Nature know,.		201	Astrophil	71	1
Least joy, by Nature apt sprites to enlarge, ...		210	Astrophil	85	3
Yet growest more wretched then thy nature beares,.		228	Astrophil	94	13
To whom nor art nor nature graunteth light,.		230	Astrophil	99	2
Nature with care sweates for her darling's sake, ...		232	Astrophil	101	12
Have made, but forst by Nature still to flie,.		233	Astrophil	103	10
Whose senses in so evill consort, their stepdame Nature laies,.		217	A&S 7th Song		1
With nature pleas'd, content with present case,.		243	Other Poems	4	59
By fortune meane, in Nature borne a Queene,.		244	Other Poems	4	91
So is in her the best of Nature spent,.		249	Other Poems	4	299
NATURE'S					
Thy yonger shall with Nature's blisse embrace.		11	Arcadia I	1	3
Such force hath Love above poore Nature's power.		19	1st Eclogues	7	161
Dorus. Such force hath Love above poore Nature's power,. . .		19	1st Eclogues	7	162
Thus nature's Diamond, receave thy conquest, ...		68	2nd Eclogues	33	27
In nature's pride your heads to heav'nwarde heave, ...		77	Arcadia III	49	2
While thy known course, observing nature's right,.		82	Arcadia III	56	11
The cattell wild, or tame, in nature's bowers.		100	3rd Eclogues	66	47
Turning all nature's course to selfe displeasure..		108	Arcadia IV	69	8
With nature's praise are wont in safest home to take.. . . .		117	4th Eclogues	73	14
And laying downe my head, did nature's rule observe, ...		117	4th Eclogues	73	27
On Nature's sweet repast, as healthfull senses ledd.		117	4th Eclogues	73	40
In Nature's name to suffer such a harme,.		125	4th Eclogues	75	17
We Nature's workes doo helpe, she us defaces.		127	4th Eclogues	75	93
Since nature's workes be good, and death doth serve.		131	Arcadia V	77	1
As nature's worke: why should we feare to dye?		131	Arcadia V	77	2
On nature's sweetest light..		151	Cert Sonnets	23	4
Above line repeated at following location.		152	Cert Sonnets	23	36
Having before me Nature's treasure,.		159	Cert Sonnets	29	6
Invention, Nature's child, fled step-dame Studie's blowes, .		165	Astrophil	1	10
Prepar'd by Nature's chiefest furniture, ...		169	Astrophil	9	2
Or reach the fruite of Nature's choisest tree, ...		169	Astrophil	10	4
So when thou saw'st in Nature's cabinet, ...		170	Astrophil	11	9
Unable quite to pay even Nature's rent,.		174	Astrophil	18	5

327

NATURE'S   (CONTINUED)   PAGE   TITLE   LINE
    Who since he hath, by Nature's speciall grace, ...   206 Astrophil   78   9
    Nature's praise, Vertue's stall, Cupid's cold fire,. . . . .   206 Astrophil   80   3
    By linkes of Love, and only Nature's art:. . . . .   207 Astrophil   81   6
    Which Nature' selfe did make, and selfe engraind the same? .   232 Astrophil   102   6
    Who keepes the key of Nature's chiefest treasure?. . . . . .   197 A&S 1st Song   6
    Rebell by Nature's law, Rebell by law of reason, ...   214 A&S 5th Song   63
    And Liban' self with Nature's skorn, ...   310 Psalm XXIX   17
    To Nature's heir, the faire Urania, pay, ...   251 Other Poems   4   364
    Is by nature's giftes procured.. . . . .   263 Other Poems   7   36
NATURES
    Whom troubles tosse, whose natures need doth quell,. . . . .   285 Psalm XII   14
NAUGHT
    Which being nought seems somewhat to the eyen, ...   19 1st Eclogues   7   164
    Which breeds nought else but gloses of deceits.. . . . . . .   20 1st Eclogues   8   4
    Naught in himselfe ech other to abuse. . . . .   21 1st Eclogues   8   24
    And belly nought is left, such sure is he, ...   24 1st Eclogues   9   82
    Either a sleepe be all if nought assaile,. . . . .   27 1st Eclogues 10   29
    And doth not feele, that life is nought but time . . . . . .   28 1st Eclogues 10   50
    But if he nought do desire, what can Heraclitus aile?. . . .   30 1st Eclogues 11   12
    Where proofes justly do teach, thus matcht, such worth to be
        nought worth. . . . .   34 1st Eclogues 13   83
    But nought els do behold (else is nought worth the
        beholding . . . .   36 1st Eclogues 13   150
    Nought could impart such heates to friendly mind.. . . . . .   51 2nd Eclogues 28   105
    Her cleared lookes, nought els, in stormes can quiet me. . .   51 2nd Eclogues 28   119
    Among us all we should find out some thing of nought.. . . .   51 2nd Eclogues 29   2
    (Even like a toppe which nought but whipping moves). . . . .   58 2nd Eclogues 30   33
    "Nought can reason availe in heav'nly matters".. . . . . . .   68 2nd Eclogues 33   26
    Nought disturbs thy quiet, all to thy service yeeld, ...   69 2nd Eclogues 34   10
    Ye helplesse Sighes, blowe out your breath to nought,. . . .   83 Arcadia III   59   5
    Amid my sheepe, though I sawe nought to feare, ...   99 3rd Eclogues 66   15
    For clerkly reed, and hating what is naught, ...   99 3rd Eclogues 66   24
    The Ermion, whitest skinne, spotted with nougat; . . . . . .   101 3rd Eclogues 66   89
    Breath made of flames, wits knowing nought but damage, . . .   109 Arcadia IV   70   28
    The darkened heav'n my soule which nought can see; . . . . .   114 4th Eclogues 72   35
    But mankind is for aye to nought resolved. . . . .   127 4th Eclogues 75   81
    And can crie helpe with nought but grones and starts:. . . .   136 Cert Sonnets   2   12
    Worth as nought worth rejected,. . . . .   159 Cert Sonnets 30   5
    Desiring nought but how to kill desire.. . . . .   161 Cert Sonnets 31   14
    Readie of wit and fearing nought but shame:. . . . .   172 Astrophil   14   11
    That Plato I read for nought, but if he tame . . . .   175 Astrophil   21   5
    Leaving me nought but wailing eloquence: . . . .   184 Astrophil   38   11
    Now brought abed, hath brought nought foorth, but nought.. .   278 Psalm VII   39
    Naught his allseing sight can miss,. . . . .   284 Psalm XI   15
    And bring to naught those watching pawes.. . . . .   290 Psalm XVII   36
    Whose hands do handle nought,. . . . .   306 Psalm XXVI   31
    Shall need nought that is good.. . . . .   319 Psalm XXXIV   40
    Whom he doth curse to naught shall rott. . . . .   326 Psalm XXXVII   56
    Which to avoyde, quenche, loose noughte booted stryfe. . . .   344 Possibly   2   8
    That naught withstandes Desire, Allarme allarme. . . . . . .   346 Possibly   5   4
    With triumph's shews would shew he nought did feare. . . . .   244 Other Poems   4   78
    While nought but game, the selfe-hurt wanton ment. . . . . .   247 Other Poems   4   192
    Though him to meete at all she sturred nought. . . . .   250 Other Poems   4   326
NAUGHTY
    No, nor with Thee the naughty Ones shall dwel, ...   274 Psalm V   11
    Yea worse than doggs, a naughty wicked rout. . . . .   299 Psalm XXII   40
    The Naughty borrowes paying not, ...   326 Psalm XXXVII   53
    Those vile scoffes of naughty ones . . . .   335 Psalm XLII   45
NAVEL
    But that her navel doth unite, ...   88 Arcadia III   62   73
NAY
    Whose force had such force so to transforme, nay to reforme
        me,. . . . .   37 1st Eclogues 13   166
    Nay rather then my ease discontentation. . . . .   51 2nd Eclogues 28   120
    Pas. Nay like to nightingales the other birds give eare: . .   52 2nd Eclogues 29   19
    His nature? nay, himselfe? for so it is. . . . .   59 2nd Eclogues 30   72
    Nay even cold Death enflamde with hot desire . . . .   59 2nd Eclogues 30   86
    Nay higher thoughtes (though thralled thoughtes) I call. . .   78 Arcadia III   49   13
    Or els; "Nay faith, mine is the lucklest lot,. . . . .   104 3rd Eclogues 67   43
    And loth this time, could life, nay thinke, that life. . . .   113 4th Eclogues 72   12
    Me thought, nay sure I was, I was in fairest wood. . . . . .   117 4th Eclogues 73   35
    "Nay then (Diana said) the chastnesse I will give. . . . . .   121 4th Eclogues 73   173
    "Nay thou (said both) shalt see such beames shine in her
        face . . . .   121 4th Eclogues 73   175
    Nay to the heav'ns your just complayninges sende,. . . . . .   126 4th Eclogues 75   37
    Absented? nay I say for ever banished. . . . .   128 4th Eclogues 75   125
    The babe cries "nay, for that abide I waking". . . . .   139 Cert Sonnets   6   9
    Nay former blisse addes to present paine,. . . . .   153 Cert Sonnets 24   13
    Nay, that may breed my fame, it is so rare:. . . . .   182 Astrophil   34   6
    That lap doth lap, nay lets, in spite of spite,. . . . . . .   194 Astrophil   59   10
    For Grammer sayes (to Grammer who sayes nay) . . . .   196 Astrophil   63   13
    Stolne to my heart, since last faire night, nay day, ...   199 Astrophil   66   10
    Doth lowre, nay, chide; nay, threat for only this: . . . . .   203 Astrophil   73   7
    Nay, more foole I, oft suffered you to sleepe. . . . .   208 Astrophil   83   7
    Nay sorrow comes with such maine rage, that he . . . .   229 Astrophil   95   9
    That to each word, nay sigh of mine you harke, ...   233 Astrophil   104   3
    What, is not this enough? nay farre worse commeth here;. . .   214 A&S 5th Song   73
    See, do you see this face? a face? nay image of the skies, .   217 A&S 7th Song   15
    Nay ev'n my soul fell troubles do appall;. . . . .   276 Psalm VI   9

NAY   (CONTINUED)   PAGE   TITLE   LINE

	PAGE	TITLE		LINE
Nay if I wrought not for his Freedome's sake	277	Psalm VII		11
And they are faln, nay perisht at Thy sight:	279	Psalm IX		7
Nay so proud is his puffed thought	281	Psalm X		13
Nay even the race of good men are decay'd.	284	Psalm XII		3
Nay give me eyes, and light, least that I sleep.	285	Psalm XIII		11
Nay to name their names disdain.	288	Psalm XVI		12
Nay unto Thee they cry'd, but thou heardst not their cryes..	293	Psalm XVIII		75
Nay soon as he but moved	297	Psalm XXI		6
Nay shame of men, the people's scorning game..	299	Psalm XXII		16
Nay Basan mighty Bulls close me about.	299	Psalm XXII		28
Nay I did even detest.	305	Psalm XXVI		16
Nay like young Calves in leapes are born,	310	Psalm XXIX		16
A span? nay nothing in Thyn eyne..	330	Psalm XXXIX		16
Nay ev'n unto hir home he oft would go,	247	Other Poems	4	193
"Nay each thing is bewitcht to know my case:	254	Other Poems	4	473
"Nay, what neede the Arte to those,	263	Other Poems	7	31

NE

	PAGE	TITLE		LINE
Ne let white haires, which on my face doo grow,	38	Arcadia II	15	5
Ne pleasure here, ne fame gott..	66	2nd Eclogues	32	39
Ne dare once shew thy face,	93	3rd Eclogues	63	87
Ne can he faile, for prince hath for him sent:	97	3rd Eclogues	64	104
I sate me downe: for see to goe ne could,	99	3rd Eclogues	66	20
Ne could my soule it selfe accuse of such a faulte,	117	4th Eclogues	73	19
Ne yet for what I see, your beauties merite ought.	121	4th Eclogues	73	164
Which inke onely relates, but ne laments, ne replies?	122	4th Eclogues	74	18
Ne doo I care how rude be my invention,	128	4th Eclogues	75	104
Ne if I would, could I just title make,	224	Astrophil	90	9
Ne for bad mates in way of sinning waiteth	270	Psalm I		3
Ne yet shall suffred be a place to take,	270	Psalm I		17
Ne let thy rage, of my due punishment.	276	Psalm VI		3

NEAR

	PAGE	TITLE		LINE
Seeke skill of hearbes in hills, haunt brookes neere night,	26	1st Eclogues	9	127
Thus be her giftes most sweet, thus more danger to be neere her,	36	1st Eclogues	13	126
Nico. As I of late, neer bushes usde my sive,	54	2nd Eclogues	29	81
But when I did come neere with heate and hope,	54	2nd Eclogues	29	88
As neere his home, when storme or shelf he feares;	71	Arcadia III	37	4
As thou drawest on, so let my blisse draw neere.	80	Arcadia III	53	10
Some say it doth betoken wonders neare	81	Arcadia III	55	2
Did goe his way, but sojourn'd neere thereby,	96	3rd Eclogues	64	71
For neere acquaintance dooth diminish reverent feare..	121	4th Eclogues	73	160
Neere Wilton sweete, huge heapes of stones are found,	149	Cert Sonnets	22	1
Neare therabout, into your Poesie wring;	172	Astrophil	15	4
How faire a day was neare, o punisht eyes,	181	Astrophil	33	13
In Beautie's throne, see now who dares come neare.	203	Astrophil	73	10
Frcm comming neare those Cherries banish me:	208	Astrophil	82	8
So neere, in so good time, so free a place?.	235	Astrophil	105	2
Doth make me most to wish thy comfort neere.	235	Astrophil	106	8
By aiding when fierce unicorns come neare me..	299	Psalm XXII		50
Shall never dare come neare him.	315	Psalm XXXII		24
This lord is ever ever neare,	320	Psalm XXXIV		66
Who helpest those, whose ruin was so neere,	321	Psalm XXXV		23
And lookes so neere unto my cure that I must needes be lost.	343	Possibly	1	22
And deigne to deeme your neighbors' mischefe neare,.	242	Other Poems	4	11
To wedd Antaxius their neighbour neare.	245	Other Poems	4	116
So on the downs we see, neere Wilton faire,	251	Other Poems	4	342
Did beate their hands, which durst so neere to presse.	252	Other Poems	4	406
Late neere a crosse I met an ougly Cat.	253	Other Poems	4	448
A widow turtle neere on bared root	256	Other Poems	5	6

NEARER

	PAGE	TITLE		LINE
Then void of neerer cares, the depth of things to find..	118	4th Eclogues	73	50
Till Strephon's plaining voice him nearer drew,	256	Other Poems	4	535

NEARLY

	PAGE	TITLE		LINE
O be not farr, since pain so nearly presseth,	299	Psalm XXII		25

NEARNESS

	PAGE	TITLE		LINE
But (like a point in midst of a circle) is still of a neernesse,	31	1st Eclogues	13	6

NECK

	PAGE	TITLE		LINE
To weare upon her neck, that open lies..	55	2nd Eclogues	29	119
The neck, in which strange graces lurke.	87	Arcadia III	62	48
Whose necke becomes such yoke of tyranny?.	188	Astrophil	47	4
When in her necke you did Love ditties peepe;	208	Astrophil	83	6
Leave that sir Phip, least off your necke be wroong.	208	Astrophil	83	14
Her faire necke a foule yoke bare,	218	A&S 8th Song		10
Then let his foot uppon my neck be set:	277	Psalm VII		14

NECKS

	PAGE	TITLE		LINE
Thou gavest me their necks, on them Thou mad'est me passe..	292	Psalm XVIII		73

NECTAR

	PAGE	TITLE		LINE
Nectar of Mirth, since I Jove's cup do keepe..	201	Astrophil	70	4
And through those lips drinke Nectar from that toong;	208	Astrophil	83	13
That you, guiltlesse thereof, your Nectar mist:.	235	Astrophil	105	10
At her lips my Nectar drinking..	227	A&S 10th Song		48

NEED

	PAGE	TITLE		LINE
Save when great need of them perforce apeare..	27	1st Eclogues	10	36
But if eyes faile then, when I most doo need them,	30	1st Eclogues	12	5
P. We now have peace, your peace we doo not neede.	46	2nd Eclogues	27	28
And vertue do in greatest need neglect.	58	2nd Eclogues	30	64
But yet o man, rage not beyond thy needs:	103	3rd Eclogues	66	148
Stella; now she is nam'd, need more be said?	173	Astrophil	16	11

NEED	(CONTINUED)	PAGE	TITLE		LINE
To them that do such entertainment need, ...		190	Astrophil	51	3
My wealth no more, and no whit lesse my need,.		199	Astrophil	66	7
Theeves steal for need, and steale but goods, which paine					
recovers,.		214	A&S 5th Song		45
For all I neede, that with such foes do byde.		275	Psalm V		24
Whom troubles tosse, whose natures need doth quell,.		285	Psalm XII		14
Bow down thine eare to heare how much I need,.		312	Psalm XXXI		4
And when neede were, from pride in privy plight, ...		313	Psalm XXXI		55
Shall need nought that is good.		319	Psalm XXXIV		40
Nede not the stately Muses' helpe invoke		242	Other Poems	4	7
When, if nede were, they could at quintain run:.		243	Other Poems	4	56
"Nay, what neede the Arte to those,.		263	Other Poems	7	31
NEEDED					
What needed so high sprites such mansions blind?		57	2nd Eclogues	30	14
NEEDFUL					
Ready to store their campes of needfull things:.		179	Astrophil	29	4
NEEDING					
Not needing charming skill,.		92	3rd Eclogues	63	60
NEEDS					
To high conceipts the song must needes be high,.		3	Lady of May	2	8
Of my due faith, which needs must be immutable?.		47	2nd Eclogues	28	8
Nico would needes with Pas his bagpipe blowe.		54	2nd Eclogues	29	68
The tippe no jewell needes to weare:		87	Arcadia III	62	35
Whether he needes must goe for feare of blame.		96	3rd Eclogues	64	78
But now we muste needs yeelde, to what our othes require". .		121	4th Eclogues	73	169
Releast from Court, where envie needes must be.		143	Cert Sonnets	12	6
But if that needs thou wilt usurping be, ...		167	Astrophil	4	9
Effects of lively heat, must needs in nature grow.		169	Astrophil	8	11
But thou wouldst needs fight both with love and sence, . . .		170	Astrophil	10	9
Thou needs must smart, and so thou needs must smart.		188	Astrophil	46	11
Now from thy fellowship I needs must part, ...		202	Astrophil	72	5
That Anger' selfe I needs must kisse againe.		203	Astrophil	73	14
But you must needs with those lips billing be?		208	Astrophil	83	12
Or if I needs (sweet Judge) must torments have,.		212	Astrophil	86	11
To this great cause, which needs both use and art, ...		236	Astrophil	107	8
Though battaile's brunt I needs must beare, ...		307	Psalm XXVII		15
My tongue would needs and thus I spake:.		329	Psalm XXXIX		12
And lookes so neere unto my cure that I must needes be lost.		343	Possibly	1	22
But hence, even hence, I must needes goe; such is my dogged					
fate.		344	Possibly	1	48
NEEDY					
Him as thy slave, and now long needy Fame.		182	Astrophil	35	10
NEER					
Let them be ne'r a sunder, ...		261	Other Poems	6	56
NEGATIVES					
That in one speech two Negatives affirme.		196	Astrophil	63	14
NEGLECT					
Make me, o vertuous Shame, thy lawes neglect.		40	Arcadia II	18	12
And vertue do in greatest need neglect.		58	2nd Eclogues	30	64
NEGLECTED					
Whose light is cause we have our lives neglected		108	Arcadia IV	69	7
NEIGHBOR					
A neighbor mine not long agoe there was, ...		94	3rd Eclogues	64	1
Which fall he made to do his neighbor wrong.		278	Psalm VII		42
Nor neighbour hurts by deed, nor doth with slaunder stain. .		287	Psalm XV		6
Who word to neighbour given doth faithfully maintain		287	Psalm XV		9
From my plague, kynn, neighbour, Friend, ...		328	Psalm XXXVIII		31
Still my orethwart neighbour is.		329	Psalm XXXVIII		51
To wedd Antaxius their neighbour neare.		245	Other Poems	4	116
NEIGHBORED					
Like some weake Lords, neighbord by mighty kings,.		179	Astrophil	29	1
NEIGHBORS					
The neighbours all did crie, "alas what asse doth bray?" . .		52	2nd Eclogues	29	26
Gainst neighbors good for womanish debate.		93	3rd Eclogues	63	70
Weepe neighbours, weepe, do you not heare it said, ...		160	Cert Sonnets	30	11
To which sweet springs of waters neighbours be,.		270	Psalm I		8
Neighbors friendly entertain		309	Psalm XXVIII		14
Yea neighbors, more, my mates were so agast.		313	Psalm XXXI		32
By neighbors prai'd she went abroad therby,.		247	Other Poems	4	207
NEIGHBORS'					
When that we feare our hatefull neighbours' might, ...		129	4th Eclogues	76	20
And deigne to deeme your neighbors' mischefe neare, ...		242	Other Poems	4	11
NEIGHING					
With neighing, blaying, braying, and barking,.		100	3rd Eclogues	66	62
NEITHER					
Then cries to sencelesse things, which neither knowes. . . .		23	1st Eclogues	9	41
Neither he beares reverence to a Prince nor pittie to					
begger		31	1st Eclogues	13	5
Neither doubt you a whit, time will your passion utter. . . .		33	1st Eclogues	13	58
And yet neither of us great or blest deemeth his owne selfe.		33	1st Eclogues	13	73
If neither by that helpe, thou canst clime up to thy fancie,		34	1st Eclogues	13	100
Both still do worke, in neither finde I rest:.		42	Arcadia II	22	3
That since the having them to neither's due, ...		56	2nd Eclogues	29	148
Is neither freed, nor yet to service bound, ...		144	Cert Sonnets	15	2
Hath neither leave to live, nor doome to dye,.		144	Cert Sonnets	15	7
But so confusde, that neither any eye.		149	Cert Sonnets	22	2
Of all my thoughts hath neither stop nor start,.		176	Astrophil	23	13
He blessed is, who neither loosely treads.		270	Psalm I		1
For neither shall the men in sin delighted		270	Psalm I		15

330

```
NEITHER              (CONTINUED)                      PAGE   TITLE            LINE
   Dick. Bound as I neither power have, nor would have power to
     stir. . . . . . . . . . . . . . . . . . . . . . . . .  343  Possibly       1    24
NEITHER'S
   Her minde amaz'de can neither's helpe applie. . . . . . .  81  Arcadia III  54     4
NEPTUNE'S
   Fire no liquor can coole: Neptune's seate would be dryd up
     there. . . . . . . . . . . . . . . . . . . . . . . . .  32  1st Eclogues 13   32
   More white then Neptune's fomie face, . . . . . . . . . .  88  Arcadia III  62   69
   (Who Neptune's webb on daunger's distaff spun) . . . . . 251  Other Poems   4  374
NEST
   I spied a thrush where she did make her nest, . . . . . .  54  2nd Eclogues 29   82
   Burnt by the Sunne, she first must build her nest. . . .  60  2nd Eclogues 30  103
   Or as the silly birde in well acquainted nest. . . . . . 117  4th Eclogues 73   23
   To honor turnd, doth dwell in honor's nest, . . . . . . . 151  Cert Sonnets 22   47
   Neast of young joyes, schoolmaster of delight, . . . . . 206  Astrophil    79    8
   In Lillies' neast, where Love's selfe lies along. . . . . 208  Astrophil    83    8
   A nest for my yong praise in Lawrell tree: . . . . . . . 224  Astrophil    90    6
   And my yong soule flutters to thee his nest, . . . . . . 236  Astrophil   108    6
   I dwell, layd up in safest neast. . . . . . . . . . . . . 274  Psalm IV          35
   Of wicked wights the nest, . . . . . . . . . . . . . . . 305  Psalm XXVI        17
   Epeirus high, was honest Klaius' nest, . . . . . . . . . 242  Other Poems   4   25
   Betwixt them two the peeper tooke his nest, . . . . . . . 244  Other Poems   4  102
NESTOR'S
   More then Nestor's yeares, more then a King's diademe. . . 122  4th Eclogues 74   20
   What Nestor's counsell can my flames alay, . . . . . . . 182  Astrophil    35    5
NESTS
   Of Venus' babe the wanton nests: . . . . . . . . . . . .  87  Arcadia III  62   54
   Sometimes we see small birds from nests do pull. . . . . 245  Other Poems   4  136
NET
   And hopes the flickring winde with net to holde, . . . .  24  1st Eclogues  9   54
   Adonis' end, Venus' nett, . . . . . . . . . . . . . . . .  66  2nd Eclogues 32   27
   And in that nett, which they well hidden think, . . . . . 280  Psalm IX          48
   When hee once drau'th his wily nett. . . . . . . . . . . 282  Psalm X           40
   My feet from tangling net. . . . . . . . . . . . . . . . 304  Psalm XXV         58
   Preserve me from the wyly wrappinge nett . . . . . . . . 312  Psalm XXXI        10
   For causeless they both pitt and net did sett, . . . . . 321  Psalm XXXV        15
   Fall in self pitt, be caught in their own nett.. . . . . 321  Psalm XXXV        18
NETHER
   Dorus. Lady your selfe, whom nether name I dare, . . . .  18  1st Eclogues  7  131
NETS
   That from her lockes, thy day-nets, none scapes free, . . . 170  Astrophil  12    2
NEVER
   For water cold did never promise fire: . . . . . . . . .   3  Lady of May   2    4
   Happie be they which well beleeve, and never seeke the rest.  12  Arcadia I   3   14
   I never found long love such wealth hath paide to me". . . .  16  1st Eclogues  7   54
   Doth beauties keep, which never Sunne can burne, . . . .  18  1st Eclogues  7  118
   With long large eares where never rumour dyes. . . . . .  21  1st Eclogues  8   28
   His cloven foote doth never treade aright. . . . . . . .  21  1st Eclogues  8   30
   Or stop a breach, that never Cannon sawe?. . . . . . . .  22  1st Eclogues  9   17
   And never hathe therof arightelye deemde . . . . . . . .  26  1st Eclogues  9  139
   Of my good sheepe, thou never trews time tooke: . . . . .  27  1st Eclogues 10   14
   And statute made he never shoulde have voice, . . . . . .  29  1st Eclogues 10   86
   Oh no, no, hardye shepeheard, worth can never enter a title,  34  1st Eclogues 13   82
   Dicus. The harte well set doth never shunne confession: . .  47  2nd Eclogues 28   13
   Largesse his hands could never skill of sparefulnesse. . . .  48  2nd Eclogues 28   45
   He never musing standes, but with himselfe will play . . . .  53  2nd Eclogues 29   43
   Nico. If never I did faile your holy-dayes, . . . . . . .  54  2nd Eclogues 29   69
   In this weake worke, that it can never be. . . . . . . .  57  2nd Eclogues 30   30
   Upon thy spoiles, which never should lye waste?. . . . .  59  2nd Eclogues 30   93
   End? but I can never end, love will not give me the leave.
     Leave. . . . . . . . . . . . . . . . . . . . . . . . .  63  2nd Eclogues 31   16
   Yet never rock, nor race, suche terror brought, . . . . .  71  Arcadia III  37    3
   For nature hathe that never fayling scoope, . . . . . . .  71  Arcadia III  37    5
   My thoughts forget: my thoughts, which never swerve. . .  72  Arcadia III  38    3
   This cave is darke, but it had never light.. . . . . . .  75  Arcadia III  43    1
   There never was a better bargaine driv'ne. . . . . . . .  75  Arcadia III  45    4
   The giver giv'n from gifte shall never parte.. . . . . .  77  Arcadia III  47   14
   As oh! my selfe, whose woes are never lighte . . . . . .  82  Arcadia III  56    9
   And never ended. . . . . . . . . . . . . . . . . . . . .  84  Arcadia III  59   16
   Which never part but that they showe . . . . . . . . . .  87  Arcadia III  62   41
   Whence never word in vaine did flowe.. . . . . . . . . .  87  Arcadia III  62   45
   Yet never shall my song omitte . . . . . . . . . . . . .  88  Arcadia III  62   87
   Which never may decrease . . . . . . . . . . . . . . . .  91  3rd Eclogues 63    5
   He forst her thinke that which she never thought.. . . .  95  3rd Eclogues 64   34
   Then gave he him the blow which never smarted. . . . . .  97  3rd Eclogues 64  120
   Never hard hand, nor ever raines too light.. . . . . . .  98  3rd Eclogues 65    8
   Because (though hurt) they never heard her grone.. . . . 102  3rd Eclogues 66  119
   For murdre done, which never erst was seene, . . . . . . 102  3rd Eclogues 66  127
   Wherein the birde doth never sing but cry; . . . . . . . 105  3rd Eclogues 67   50
   And for th'event we never ought be sad.. . . . . . . . . 105  3rd Eclogues 67   66
   There never past foule word, I dare well say.. . . . . . 106  3rd Eclogues 67   93
   (Which may be know'n, but never help't with wailing) . . . 109  Arcadia IV   70   14
   And smirkly thus gan say. "I never sought debate . . . . 120  4th Eclogues 73  147
   I never spited you, but thought you overwise.. . . . . . 121  4th Eclogues 73  150
   That thou shalt never dare seeke helpe of wretched case".. . 121  4th Eclogues 73  176
   Love never had me opprest, but that I saw to be lov'd. . . . 123  4th Eclogues 74   44
   Thy selfe henceforth the light doo never see.. . . . . . 125  4th Eclogues 75   24
   Sounde of my griefes, and let it never ende, . . . . . . 126  4th Eclogues 75   35
   Within it selfe, and never taketh ende: . . . . . . . . . 127  4th Eclogues 75   80
```

                                331

NEVER   (CONTINUED)   PAGE   TITLE   LINE
    The stile of heavie hart can never flie. . . . .   129 4th Eclogues 75   139
    Since shunning paine, I ease can never find: . . . .   135 Cert Sonnets 1   1
    Where bee now those wordes never Idelly wasted,. . . . . .   138 Cert Sonnets 5   7
    But betweene those armes, never else do leave mee; . . . .   138 Cert Sonnets 5   23
    I praisde her eyes whom never chance doth move,. . . . . .   141 Cert Sonnets 9   5
    I never did my vowed word forsake: . . . .   146 Cert Sonnets 17   8
    My lake is sense, whose dulling streames never runne,. . .   150 Cert Sonnets 22   15
    A light which dying never, ...   152 Cert Sonnets 23   7
    She never dies but lasteth . . . .   152 Cert Sonnets 23   9
    In never dying faith:. . . . .   152 Cert Sonnets 23   14
    Thou web of will, whose end is never wrought;. . . . . . .   161 Cert Sonnets 31   4
    Grow rich in that which never taketh rust: . . . .   161 Cert Sonnets 32   3
    But never heeds the fruit of writer's mind:. . . . .   170 Astrophil   11   8
    The raines of Love I love, though never slake, ...   179 Astrophil   28   7
    That never I with clos'd-up sense do lie,. . . . .   181 Astrophil   32   6
    For though I never see them, but straight wayes. . . . . .   186 Astrophil   42   9
    Of Lovers never knowne, a grievous case, ...   187 Astrophil   45   6
    If he waite well, I never thence would move: . . . .   194 Astrophil   59   3
    I never dranke of Aganippe well, ...   203 Astrophil   74   1
    So ample eares as never good newes know: . . . .   206 Astrophil   78   13
    Only of you the flatterer never lieth. . . . .   197 A&S 1st Song   28
    For I protest, my sight never thy face enjoyeth, ...   215 A&S 5th Song   75
    Never doth thy beauty florish. . . . .   234 A&S 11th Song   29
    "Never season was more fit, ...   219 A&S 8th Song   53
    Never roome more apt for it; . . . .   219 A&S 8th Song   54
    Tho I blisse enherit never.. . . . .   221 A&S 9th Song   20
    That hatefull never cease. . . . .   272 Psalm III   2
    And that forgetfull sort, which never cares. . . . .   281 Psalm IX   54
    That after God he never sought,. . . . .   281 Psalm X   14
    This gotten blisse shall never part, ...   282 Psalm X   24
    Who with deceitfull tongue hath never usd to faine,. . . .   287 Psalm XV   5
    My never peirced shield, my ever saving horn,. . . . . . .   290 Psalm XVIII   4
    Yea Thou dost make me serv'd by folks I never knew;. . . .   293 Psalm XVIII   79
    They are unrighteous never.. . . . .   294 Psalm XIX   40
    And flames of never quenched fire. . . . .   297 Psalm XXI   35
    But God Thy eare my crying never heareth.. . . . .   298 Psalm XXIII   6
    And so can never I . . . .   301 Psalm XXIII   2
    Who never doth deceive, and much lesse his deceaving . . .   302 Psalm XXIV   11
    Who search of God's face never leave.. . . . .   302 Psalm XXIV   16
    Shall never suffer shame;. . . . .   303 Psalm XXV   8
    For never day such changing wrought. . . . .   303 Psalm XXV   17
    I held for sure that I should never slyde. . . . .   305 Psalm XXVI   6
    That I should never be undone, ...   311 Psalm XXX   21
    Therfore my tongue shall never lack. . . . .   311 Psalm XXX   37
    Never therfore let me confounded be, ...   312 Psalm XXXI   2
    Shall never dare come neare him. . . . .   315 Psalm XXXII   24
    Shall never blush for shame. . . . .   319 Psalm XXXIV   20
    Laying such things, as never in mee weare; . . . .   322 Psalm XXXV   26
    Who never word of peace yet utter would, ...   322 Psalm XXXV   51
    They are cast down, and never shal . . . .   324 Psalm XXXVI   35
    And never found again shal be. . . . .   325 Psalm XXXVII   28
    In perill they shall perish never, ...   325 Psalm XXXVII   47
    To justice never saw forsaken, ...   326 Psalm XXXVII   63
    And Thy good state shall never end.. . . . .   326 Psalm XXXVII   68
    Though I did seek, I never found.. . . . .   327 Psalm XXXVII   92
    About these never conquered walles to swarme,. . . . . . .   346 Possibly   5   10
    More prayse to us we never looke to winne, ...   346 Possibly   5   11
    For never was there man more crossely crost then he. . . .   241 Other Poems   1   4
    Never the earth on his round shoulders bare. . . . .   247 Other Poems   4   209
    In sum, proud Boreas never ruled fleet . . . .   251 Other Poems   4   373
    But never did Medea's golden weed. . . . .   252 Other Poems   4   409
    So may you never dy, ...   257 Other Poems   5   46
    Who never joy, but when. . . . .   261 Other Poems   6   39
    Never striving, but in loving. . . . .   262 Other Poems   7   24
NEVERMORE
    I will but kisse, I never more will bite.. . . . .   208 Astrophil   82   14
    Who never more must rise.. . . . .   333 Psalm XLI   28
NEVER-MOVING
    The ever-turning spheares, the never-moving ground;. . . .   118 4th Eclogues 73   44
NEW
    My day newe cares; my ginnes my daily sight, ...   18 1st Eclogues 7   140
    New plucked from the place where it did breed, ...   19 1st Eclogues 7   159
    New friend of mine; I yeeld to thy habilitie:. . . . . . .   19 1st Eclogues 7   174
    He proules ech place stil in new colours deckt,. . . . . .   21 1st Eclogues 8   35
    Olde houses are throne downe for new we see: . . . .   24 1st Eclogues 9   84
    Lyke to my noble thoughtes, still new, well plac'd, to me
      fruteles.. . . . .   35 1st Eclogues 13   124
    Olde aged oke cutt downe, of newe works serves to the
      building:. . . . .   36 1st Eclogues 13   134
    Alas, if you a Phoenix new will have . . . .   60 2nd Eclogues 30   102
    I waste my harte, which still newe torment tryes,. . . . .   75 Arcadia III 43   5
    And thou deare flesh, as soft as wooll new drest,. . . . .   76 Arcadia III 46   15
    Aurora like new out of bed,. . . . .   86 Arcadia III 62   24
    Rubies, Cherries, and Roses new, ...   87 Arcadia III 62   39
    And in himselfe new doubting causes nurst. . . . .   94 3rd Eclogues 64   12
    And that it had enflam'd a new desire. . . . .   95 3rd Eclogues 64   38
    And if forsooth there come some new found ware,. . . . . .   104 3rd Eclogues 67   40
    Hate fully growne, Absence new sprongen out. . . . .   115 4th Eclogues 72   58
    While late bare earth, proud of new clothing springeth,. .   137 Cert Sonnets 4   3

NEW   (CONTINUED)   PAGE   TITLE   LINE

	PAGE	TITLE		LINE
Yet lives untill his life be new requirde.	150	Cert Sonnets	22	24
Ennobling new found Tropes with problemes old:	166	Astrophil	3	6
In her sight I a lesson new have speld,.	173	Astrophil	16	12
And straight therewith, like wags new got to play, ...	173	Astrophil	17	13
Stella, whence doth this new assault arise,.	182	Astrophil	36	1
But wilt new warre upon thine owne begin?.	183	Astrophil	36	8
Then servant's wracke, where new doubts honor brings;. . . .	187	Astrophil	45	11
To such a schoole-mistresse, whose lessons new	188	Astrophil	46	10
So may you still have somewhat new to say.	190	Astrophil	51	4
The new Pernassus, where the Muses bide, ...	207	Astrophil	80	5
Make in my heavy mould new thoughts to grow:	236	Astrophil	106	11
That bad his friend, but then new maim'd, to be.	236	Astrophil	106	13
Now child, a lesson new you shall begin to spell:.	213	A&S 5th Song		35
"What if you new beauties see, ...	234	A&S 11th Song		21
Will not they stir new affection?"	234	A&S 11th Song		22
New perfumed with flowers fresh growing, ...	217	A&S 8th Song		4
New joy, new joy unto Our King,.	296	Psalm XXI		1
Doth rise againe, new joyes shall rise.	311	Psalm XXX		18
A new, sing a new song	316	Psalm XXXIII		13
New song unto our God of prayse, ...	331	Psalm XL		12
Thy wallet or thy Tarbox lost, or thy new rayment rent?. . .	343	Possibly	1	16
To crammed mawes a spratt new Stomake brings..	245	Other Poems	4	134
So in you ever new	257	Other Poems	5	30
NEWBORN				
With new-borne sighes and denisend wit do sing;.	172	Astrophil	15	8
NEW-CCINED				
Of Love, new-coind to helpe my beggery,.	196	Astrophil	62	13
NEW-FCUND				
Or gemmes, or frutes of new-found Paradise,.	207	Astrophil	81	2
NEW-LEARNED				
If him new-learned manners had not stai'd.	246	Other Poems	4	166
NEWLY				
Where greene leaves did newly bud.	262	Other Poems	7	4
NEW-MCON				
Whether the Turkish new-moone minded be.	179	Astrophil	30	1
NEWS				
Pas. O Nymphes, I tell you newes, for Pas you knowe:	54	2nd Eclogues	29	66
Long be thy woes for such newes, but how recks she my				
thoughts? Oughts..	64	2nd Eclogues	31	33
Is it to carry newes	80	Arcadia III	52	3
So ample eares as never good newes know:	206	Astrophil	78	13
Miso mine owne pigsnie, thou shalt heare news o' Damaetas. .	241	Other Poems	2	1
Sometimes to her newes of my selfe to tell	254	Other Poems	4	469
NEXT				
First fower but say, next fowr their saying seale, ...	76	Arcadia III	46	17
But did entend next bout with her to meete,.	248	Other Poems	4	250
NICE				
How nice to touch? how all her speeches peized be?	15	1st Eclogues	7	35
NICO				
Nico. And are you there old Pas? in troth I ever thought,. .	51	2nd Eclogues	29	1
Nico. Ah now I see, why thou art in thy selfe so blind:. . .	52	2nd Eclogues	29	5
Nico. Mine was the scrippe: but thou, that seeming raged				
with love, ...	52	2nd Eclogues	29	9
Nico. In deed the witch thy dam her crouch from shoulder				
spred, ...	52	2nd Eclogues	29	13
Nico. Couldst thou make Lalus flie? so nightingales avoide,.	52	2nd Eclogues	29	17
Nico. I thinke it well: such voice would make one musicke				
hate:.	52	2nd Eclogues	29	21
Nico. Well aimed by my hat: for as thou sangst last day; . .	52	2nd Eclogues	29	25
Nico. Content: but I will lay a wager hereunto,.	53	2nd Eclogues	29	29
Nico. Who doubts but Pas' fine pipe againe will bring. . . .	53	2nd Eclogues	29	51
Since Nico doth to sing so widely gape?.	53	2nd Eclogues	29	55
Nico his place farre better furnish will..	53	2nd Eclogues	29	56
Nico. Was this not he, who for Siringa's scape	53	2nd Eclogues	29	57
Nico. O Faunes, O Fairies all, and do you see, ...	54	2nd Eclogues	29	63
That Nico must with Pas compared be?	54	2nd Eclogues	29	65
Nico would needes with Pas his bagpipe blowe..	54	2nd Eclogues	29	68
Nico. If never I did faile your holy-dayes,.	54	2nd Eclogues	29	69
Let Pas now know, how Nico maketh layes.	54	2nd Eclogues	29	71
For Pas well knowes what layes can Nico make..	54	2nd Eclogues	29	74
Nico. Alas how oft I looke on cherries ripe, ...	54	2nd Eclogues	29	75
Nico. As I of late, neer bushes usde my sive,.	54	2nd Eclogues	29	81
Nico. I oft doo sue, and Leuca saith, I shall, ...	54	2nd Eclogues	29	87
Nico. When Leuca dooth appeare, the Sunne for shame.	55	2nd Eclogues	29	93
Nico. Leuca to me did yester-morning showe	55	2nd Eclogues	29	99
Nico. She once starke nak'd did bathe a little tine;	55	2nd Eclogues	29	105
Nico. To river's banke, being a walking brought, ...	55	2nd Eclogues	29	111
Nico. O if I had a ladder for the skies, ...	55	2nd Eclogues	29	117
Nico. Nothing (O Leuca) shall thy fame deface, ...	56	2nd Eclogues	29	123
Nico. Thy monument is layd in many a tree, ...	56	2nd Eclogues	29	129
Nico. Peace, peace good Pas, thou weeriest even the ground .	56	2nd Eclogues	29	135
Nico. Tell me (and be my Pan) the monster's name,.	56	2nd Eclogues	29	141
NIGGARD				
Giving frankly niggard No:	202	A&S 2nd Song		10
Niggard Time threats, if we misse.	211	A&S 4th Song		31
Then do they pull from sharpe and niggard thorne	243	Other Poems	4	51
NIGGARDLY				
The welkin had full niggardly enclosed	98	3rd Eclogues	66	8

Peace? what barrs me my tongue? who is it that comes me so
    ny? I. . . . .   62 2nd Eclogues 31   2
Now fled, then cherished? then so nie, now so remote?. . . . 124 4th Eclogues 74   78
Left Nous to coast the loved beauty ny. . . . . 249 Other Poems   4 284
Till spying well she welnigh weary was,. . . . . 251 Other Poems   4 377

NIGHT
My charme should be, she haunt me day and night. . . . . . .   17 1st Eclogues 7 105
Seeke skill of hearbes in hills, haunt brookes neere night,.   26 1st Eclogues 9 127
Yet for that night, my Caban dyd them kepe . . . .   62 2nd Eclogues 30 188
Be thow my starre in this my darkest night,. . . . .   70 Arcadia III 35   4
Become the cause of my darke ouglie night? . . . .   74 Arcadia III 42   2
Till her eyes shine, I live in darkest night. . . . .   79 Arcadia III 51   14
With ouglie cloke the darke envious night: . . . .   82 Arcadia III 55   8
Each thing with mantle black the night doth soothe;. . . . .   98 3rd Eclogues 66   5
The night growne old, her blacke head waxen gray,. . . . . . 103 3rd Eclogues 66 160
O Night, the ease of care, the pledge of pleasure, ... 108 Arcadia IV   69   1
Long since I hate the night, more hate the morning:. . . . . 112 4th Eclogues 71   34
I doo detest night, evening, day, and morning. . . . . 112 4th Eclogues 71   54
With Sunne's depart: and now the darkenes of the night . . . 116 4th Eclogues 73   2
For mourning night her blacke weedes may display. . . . . . . 126 4th Eclogues 75   54
To see my night of evils, which hath no morow. . . . . 136 Cert Sonnets 3   8
But for to spangle the blacke weeds of night:. . . . . 178 Astrophil   26   6
Till now, wrapt in a most infernall night, ... 181 Astrophil   33   3
This night while sleepe begins with heavy wings. . . . . . . 183 Astrophil   38   1
Stolne to my heart, since last faire night, nay day, ... 199 Astrophil   66   10
Now that of absence the most irksome night,. . . . . 223 Astrophil   89   1
Leaving my Hemisphere, leave me in night,. . . . . 223 Astrophil   89   4
Each day seemes long, and longs for long-staid night,. . . . 224 Astrophil   89   5
The night as tedious, wooes th'approch of day; . . . . 224 Astrophil   89   6
Languish with horrors of the silent night,. . . . . 224 Astrophil   89   8
Suffering the evils both of the day and night, ... 224 Astrophil   89   9
While no night is more darke then is my day, ... 224 Astrophil   89   10
Nor no day hath lesse quiet then my night: . . . . 224 Astrophil   89   11
With such bad mixture of my night and day, ... 224 Astrophil   89   12
That living thus in blackest winter night, ... 224 Astrophil   89   13
With absence' Vaile, I live in Sorowe's night. . . . . 224 Astrophil   91   4
Thought with good cause thou likest so well the night, . . . 229 Astrophil   96   1
Night bard from Sun, thou from thy owne sunne's light; . . . 229 Astrophil   96   4
In night of sprites the gastly powers stur,. . . . . 229 Astrophil   96   10
Dian that faine would cheare her friend the Night, ... 229 Astrophil   97   1
But ah poore Night, in love with Phoebus' light, ... 229 Astrophil   97   5
While the blacke horrors of the silent night,. . . . . 230 Astrophil   98   9
When far spent night perswades each mortall eye, ... 230 Astrophil   99   1
Takes in that sad hue, which with th'inward night. . . . . . 230 Astrophil   99   7
Curst be the night which did your strife resist, ... 235 Astrophil   105   12
Clips streight my wings, streight wraps me in his night, . . 236 Astrophil   108   8
As his light was her eyes, her death his endlesse night: . . 209 A&S 3rd Song   10
Night hath closd all in her cloke, ... 210 A&S 4th Song   7
"Who is it that this darke night,. . . . . 233 A&S 11th Song   1
Which night and day he calls to marking mind. . . . . 270 Psalm I   1   6
My bed, while I with black night mourn alone,. . . . . 276 Psalm VI   19
Ev'n when night with his black wing. . . . . 288 Psalm XVI   21
When silent night might seeme all faults to hide,. . . . . . 289 Psalm XVII   9
And night to night succeding right . . . . 293 Psalm XIX   7
O God the night is privy to my plaint, ... 298 Psalm XXII   7
For so both day and night did stand. . . . . 315 Psalm XXXII   10
Day and night my teares out flowing. . . . . 334 Psalm XLII   9
I by night shall singing last, ... 335 Psalm XLII   38
The day seemes long, but night is odious . . . . 253 Other Poems   4 435
The day well fed, the night in faithfull folde:. . . . . . . 258 Other Poems   5   68

NIGHT-BIRDS
Of reason, from whose light those night-birds flie;. . . . . 201 Astrophil   71   7

NIGHTINGALE
As for the Nightingale, woodmusique's King,. . . . .   99 3rd Eclogues 66   13
Nightingale, voice, entising songes to saye. . . . . 101 3rd Eclogues 66   82
The Nightingale, as soone as aprill bringeth . . . . 137 Cert Sonnets 4   1

NIGHTINGALES
Dorus. Nightingales seldome sing, the Pie still chattereth:.   14 1st Eclogues 7   7
Nico. Couldst thou make Lalus flie? so nightingales avoide,.   52 2nd Eclogues 29   17
Pas. Nay like to nightingales the other birds give eare: . .   52 2nd Eclogues 29   19
The Nightingales doo learne of Owles their musique:. . . . . 112 4th Eclogues 71   40
The Nightingales for woe their songs refraine: . . . . 254 Other Poems   4 474

NIGHT'S
Which now in night's deepe shade sheep heard of me. . . . . .   99 3rd Eclogues 66   42
Thy teares expresse night's native moisture right. . . . . . 229 Astrophil   96   8
But, but (alas) night's side the ods hath fur, ... 229 Astrophil   96   12

NIMBLE
I have (and long shall have) a white great nimble cat, . . .   53 2nd Eclogues 29   31
So nimble feet as stirre still, though on thornes: . . . . . 206 Astrophil   78   11
They lay snares they nimble be. . . . . 328 Psalm XXXVIII   34

NINE
Sacred Muse, who in one contaynes what nine do in all them..   31 1st Eclogues 13   10
Let daintie wits crie on the Sisters nine, ... 166 Astrophil   3   1

NIPS
With chumpish lookes, hard words, and secret nips, ...   95 3rd Eclogues 64   31

NIS
For nothing can endure where order n'is. . . . . 100 3rd Eclogues 66   51

NO
To one that hath no wealth, and wants his wit. . . . .   4 Lady of May   2   24

	PAGE	TITLE		LINE
Bound but to you, no wealth but you I would:	4	Lady of May	2	28
It is no shame, since Hercules was he"..	5	Lady of May	3	12
Whose vertues strange, and beuties such, as no man them may know?.	12	Arcadia I	3	2
We love, and are no whit regarded.	14	1st Eclogues	6	2
As without breath, no pipe doth move,.	14	1st Eclogues	6	7
No musike kindly without love.	14	1st Eclogues	6	8
No stile is held for base, where Love well named is:	14	1st Eclogues	7	4
No, though the heav'ns for high attempts have blamed me, . .	15	1st Eclogues	7	22
Who though she be no Bee, yet full of honie is:.	15	1st Eclogues	7	29
"Thou art no souldier fitte for Cupid's garrison..	16	1st Eclogues	7	51
No lovely praise was ever got with killing".	16	1st Eclogues	7	81
No charme holdes her, but well possesse she may;	17	1st Eclogues	7	111
No thralles like them that inward bondage have..	17	1st Eclogues	7	114
I have no shewes of wealth: my wealth is you,.	18	1st Eclogues	7	135
I finde no shade, but where my Sunne doth burne:	18	1st Eclogues	7	144
No place to turne; without, within it fryes:	18	1st Eclogues	7	145
No, nothing so; an old false knave he is,.	21	1st Eclogues	8	13
The witts abusde with will no counsayle take.	23	1st Eclogues	9	22
There is no hate that can thee more oppresse..	23	1st Eclogues	9	49
A fickle Sex, and trew in trust to no man,.	24	1st Eclogues	9	59
No man doth wish his horse should aged bee..	24	1st Eclogues	9	86
Knowing no more, then what poore tryall showes,.	28	1st Eclogues	10	53
No sword soe bytes as that evill toole annoyes..	29	1st Eclogues	10	90
But farewell nowe, thy fault is no great sinne,.	29	1st Eclogues	10	97
Fire no liquor can coole: Neptune's seate would be dryd up there.	32	1st Eclogues	13	32
(Since no estates be so base, but love vouchsafeth his arrow	33	1st Eclogues	13	50
Since no refuge doth serve from woundes we do carry about us	33	1st Eclogues	13	51
Oh no, no, hardye shepeheard, worth can never enter a title,	34	1st Eclogues	13	82
Joyn'd, by thy beauty adorn'd, be no meanes these greefes to abolish:.	34	1st Eclogues	13	99
Cyprus promiseth helpe, but a helpe where comes no recomforte..	35	1st Eclogues	13	119
Ashe makes speares which shieldes do resist, her force no repulse takes:	36	1st Eclogues	13	136
That where you are no wished good can want;.	39	Arcadia II	16	6
My virgin life no spotted thought shall staine..	40	Arcadia II	18	6
No fancy mine, nor others' wronge suspect.	40	Arcadia II	18	11
Clusters of clowdes, which no Sunne ever cleares..	41	Arcadia II	21	4
The sound to this strange aier no sooner goes,.	42	Arcadia II	21	9
No woolves dare howle, no murrayne can prevaile, ...	43	Arcadia II	23	8
While our sonne shynes no clowdie greeves assaile.	43	Arcadia II	23	12
Your woll is riche: no tonge can tell my gayne..	43	Arcadia II	23	14
Leave of my sheepe: it is no tyme to feede,.	43	Arcadia II	24	1
Your sweetest flowers, your herbes, no service yeeld,. . . .	43	Arcadia II	24	5
You beare no woll, and losse is all my gayne..	44	Arcadia II	24	14
Passion. No, Tyrant: no: mine, mine shall be the fielde. . .	46	2nd Eclogues	27	2
P. No Reason yet had ever skill to show it..	47	2nd Eclogues	27	40
No, no: no wordes ennoble selfe-nobilitie.	48	2nd Eclogues	28	28
No eare nor taile he hath, least they should him disgrace, .	53	2nd Eclogues	29	41
Since cause of griefe no cause from life removes..	58	2nd Eclogues	30	37
No, no: Despaire my dayly lesson saith,.	58	2nd Eclogues	30	53
O Venus (if her praise no envy frames,.	60	2nd Eclogues	30	113
Doth th'infected wretch, of his ev'll th'extremity know? No.	63	2nd Eclogues	31	19
Alas it is no glory.	65	2nd Eclogues	32	3
Alas it is no comfort, ...	65	2nd Eclogues	32	5
Alas it is no wisdome.	65	2nd Eclogues	32	7
Wherin no eare can have joy, ...	66	2nd Eclogues	32	37
Thus weakned by my selfe, no helpe remaineth..	68	2nd Eclogues	33	17
Bownded with no limitts, borne with a wing of hope	68	2nd Eclogues	34	8
Here no treason is hidd, vailed in innocence,.	69	2nd Eclogues	34	17
Keepe thy sprite from abuse, here no abuse doth haunte.. . .	69	2nd Eclogues	34	27
Beaten with waves, no sooner kennes the baye	70	Arcadia III	36	3
But at no change, so pinching care he takes, ...	71	Arcadia III	37	9
Can taste no sweetes, the sower onely please:.	74	Arcadia III	41	2
No cave, no wasting waxe, no wordes of griefe, ...	75	Arcadia III	43	7
Who hold this fast no greater wealth require..	75	Arcadia III	44	8
No smaller wound, alas! farr deeper have..	77	Arcadia III	47	4
Such pearcing wordes as no thoughts els conceave:.	78	Arcadia III	49	8
No no, such force with my small force to trye.	79	Arcadia III	50	15
Let no strange dreme make her fayre body starte.	79	Arcadia III	51	8
No, no, thy motions bee.	80	Arcadia III	52	12
With circkled course, which no wise stay can trye, ...	81	Arcadia III	54	10
"No" saies faire moone, "my lighte	82	Arcadia III	55	12
No wondre then, though sighte my sighte did tainte,.	83	Arcadia III	57	5
For no thing, time, nor place, can loose, quench, ease,. . .	84	Arcadia III	60	13
No lampe, whose light by Art is got, ...	86	Arcadia III	62	17
No Sunne, which shines, and seeth not, ...	86	Arcadia III	62	18
No purer then the pretie eares..	86	Arcadia III	62	28
No talke untaught can finde the way.	86	Arcadia III	62	34
The tippe no jewell needes to weare:	87	Arcadia III	62	35
No tongue can her perfections tell,.	90	Arcadia III	62	145
Which that no chaunce may staine,.	91	3rd Eclogues	63	8
No pride shall them oppresse,.	94	3rd Eclogues	63	96
Desiring, that no griefe in him he bread	97	3rd Eclogues	64	111
For sure, no jealousie can that prevent, ...	97	3rd Eclogues	64	125

NO	(CONTINUED)	PAGE	TITLE		LINE
	This done, thou hast no more, but leave the rest	98	3rd Eclogues	65	13
	No beast should freely speake, but onely he.	101	3rd Eclogues	66	105
	Deeme me no gloire to swell in tyrannie.	103	3rd Eclogues	66	149
	Beleeve me man, there is no greater blisse,.	103	3rd Eclogues	67	7
	Histor. No doubt to whom so good chance did betide,. . . .	104	3rd Eclogues	67	13
	No wife but I hath such a man, God wot".	104	3rd Eclogues	67	45
	Shall in this life embrace no worthy thing:.	105	3rd Eclogues	67	59
	No mortall man the cuppe of suretie drinkes.	105	3rd Eclogues	67	60
	No man doth speake aright, who speakes in feare.	106	3rd Eclogues	67	84
	And yet finde no such faults in womankind.	106	3rd Eclogues	67	87
	The sure refuge, by thee and by no other	108	Arcadia IV	69	13
	Since no evill fortune equalls publique damage:.	108	Arcadia IV	70	3
	No, no, our mischiefe growes in this vile fortune, ...	109	Arcadia IV	70	31
	I wish no evenings more to see, each evening;.	112	4th Eclogues	71	58
	Whereto I yeeld, and seeke no other breath,.	114	4th Eclogues	72	18
	No being now, but sorowe I can have:	114	4th Eclogues	72	27
	The seed Fast-meaning is, no truth to misse:	115	4th Eclogues	72	53
	(Which made of heav'nly stuffe no mortal chaunge doth bynde)	117	4th Eclogues	73	32
	What essence dest'nie hath; if fortune be or no;	118	4th Eclogues	73	45
	No knee once bowed, forsooth, for them they say we serve.. .	120	4th Eclogues	73	114
	Are we their servants growne? no doubt a noble staye:. . .	120	4th Eclogues	73	115
	(Teares and teares of a man) had no returne to remorse;. .	122	4th Eclogues	74	16
	That they, which have no lives, should live so long, . . .	126	4th Eclogues	75	41
	O well thou doost that thou no longer bidest;.	126	4th Eclogues	75	53
	Of what was good, where now no good doth lie;.	127	4th Eclogues	75	74
	Me thinkes, my sound no place with sorrow filleth.	127	4th Eclogues	75	99
	No, no, for ever gone is all our pleasure;	130	4th Eclogues	76	25
	In justice quit, of honour made no breach:	135	Cert Sonnets	1	12
	Longing to have, having no wit to wish,.	136	Cert Sonnets	2	13
	To see my night of evils, which hath no morow.	136	Cert Sonnets	3	8
	Alas, all onely she no pitie taketh.	136	Cert Sonnets	3	9
	Aire let me draw no more thy breath in anguish:.	136	Cert Sonnets	3	14
	Though I be hers, she makes of me no treasure.	137	Cert Sonnets	3	24
	Alas she hath no other cause of anguish.	137	Cert Sonnets	4	13
	Where bee those wellcomes by no worthe deserved?	138	Cert Sonnets	5	10
	But no more wordes, thoughe such a worde bee spoken. . . .	138	Cert Sonnets	5	17
	Nor no more wording with a worde to spill mee.	138	Cert Sonnets	5	18
	No, though tongue to roofe be cleaved, ...	139	Cert Sonnets	7	8
	For no dumbnesse nor death bringeth.	140	Cert Sonnets	7	38
	And so no helpe gainst envy of those powers?	142	Cert Sonnets	10	12
	So stay her toung, that she no more say no:.	142	Cert Sonnets	10	14
	No, no, she is too wise, she knowes her face	142	Cert Sonnets	11	9
	O happie Dove if she no bondage tried:.	144	Cert Sonnets	15	13
	She saith, because I make no worull laies,.	146	Cert Sonnets	17	27
	On whome all love, in whom no love is plaste,.	151	Cert Sonnets	22	63
	O no, O no, tryall onely shewse.	153	Cert Sonnets	24	10
	No, no, no, no, I cannot hate my foe,.	155	Cert Sonnets	26	1
	Above line repeated at following locations	155	Cert Sonnets	26	12
	. . . .	156	Cert Sonnets	26	23
	Burneth bright in fairest light. No, no, no, no.	155	Cert Sonnets	26	11
	They have no cause to be sorie,.	155	Cert Sonnets	26	20
	End the way, where all men stay. No, no, no, no.	155	Cert Sonnets	26	22
	No man doubts, whom beautie killeth, ...	156	Cert Sonnets	26	27
	Though in paine, cannot complaine. No, no, no, no.	156	Cert Sonnets	26	33
	For no faire signe can credit winne,.	156	Cert Sonnets	27	15
	No more in thy sweetnesse glorie,.	156	Cert Sonnets	27	17
	That no more thy beames availe thee.	156	Cert Sonnets	27	20
	No other shepheard should have scope,.	158	Cert Sonnets	28	7
	If I ware you or no, ...	158	Cert Sonnets	28	12
	No further debt on me is laid, ...	159	Cert Sonnets	29	2
	For me in sooth, no Muse but one I know:	166	Astrophil	3	9
	Least if no vaile those brave gleames did disguise,. . . .	168	Astrophil	7	7
	Is no fit marke to pierce with his fine pointed dart:. . .	168	Astrophil	8	3
	O no, her heart is such a Cittadell, ...	171	Astrophil	12	12
	And which is worse, no good excuse can show,.	174	Astrophil	18	7
	I see and yet no greater sorow take,.	174	Astrophil	18	13
	Then that I lose no more for Stella's sake..	174	Astrophil	18	14
	So Tyran he no fitter place could spie.	175	Astrophil	20	5
	Having no scarfe of clowds before his face,.	176	Astrophil	22	3
	To have for no cause birthright in the skie, ...	178	Astrophil	26	5
	I beg no subject to use eloquence,.	179	Astrophil	28	9
	Looke at my hands for no such quintessence;.	179	Astrophil	28	11
	If in the Scotch court be no weltring yet;	180	Astrophil	30 V	11
	"Foole," answers he, "no Indes such treasures hold,. . . .	181	Astrophil	32	12
	No lovely Paris made thy Hellen his:	181	Astrophil	33	6
	No force, no fraud, robd thee of thy delight,.	181	Astrophil	33	7
	Hath no misfortune, but that Rich she is..	183	Astrophil	37	14
	Where well he knowes, no man to him can come..	186	Astrophil	43	14
	Her heart, sweete heart, is of no Tygre's kind:.	186	Astrophil	44	4
	And yet she heares, yet I no pitty find;	186	Astrophil	44	5
	I much do guesse, yet find no truth save this, ...	187	Astrophil	44	9
	May get no almes but scorne of beggerie.	188	Astrophil	47	8
	By no pretence claime any maner place.	191	Astrophil	52	11
	"What now sir foole," said he, "I would no lesse,.	191	Astrophil	53	7
	He cannot love: no, no, let him alone.".	191	Astrophil	54	8
	But now I meane no more your helpe to trie,.	192	Astrophil	55	9
	That I well find no eloquence like it.	192	Astrophil	55	14
	No Patience, if thou wilt my good, then make	193	Astrophil	56	12
	That no pace else their guided steps can find, ...	194	Astrophil	58	3

NO   (CONTINUED)   PAGE   TITLE   LINE

Line	Page	Title	No.	Line
Least once should not be heard, twise said, No, No..	196	Astrophil	63	8
No more, my deare, no more these counsels trie,	198	Astrophil	64	1
Let me no steps but of lost labour trace,	198	Astrophil	64	6
That giv'st no better eare to my just cries:	198	Astrophil	65	2
For when, nak'd boy, thou couldst no harbour find.	198	Astrophil	65	5
My wealth no more, and no whit lesse my need,	199	Astrophil	66	7
No kings be crown'd but they some covenants make..	200	Astrophil	69	14
I must no more in thy sweet passions lie;	202	Astrophil	72	7
But no scuse serves, she makes her wrath appeare	203	Astrophil	73	9
I am no pick-purse of another's wit.	204	Astrophil	74	8
Guesse we the cause: "What, is it thus?" Fie no:	204	Astrophil	74	12
No wind, no shade can coole, what helpe then in my case, ..	205	Astrophil	76	12
That in no more but these I might be fully blest:..	205	Astrophil	77	13
And no spurre can his resty race renew,..	207	Astrophil	80	12
By no encrochment wrongd, nor time forgot:	209	Astrophil	84	10
And that you know, I envy you no lot	209	Astrophil	84	12
No doome should make one's heav'n become his hell.	212	Astrophil	86	14
While no night is more darke then is my day,	224	Astrophil	89	10
Nor no day hath lesse quiet then my night:	224	Astrophil	89	11
Not them, o no, but you in them I love.	225	Astrophil	91	14
From carelesnesse did in no maner grow,	227	Astrophil	93	7
Faint coward joy no longer tarry dare,	228	Astrophil	95	5
Her selfe (to shew no other joy hath place).	229	Astrophil	97	7
O teares, no teares, but raine from beautie's skies,	231	Astrophil	100	1
Such teares, sighs, plaints, no sorrow is, but joy:	231	Astrophil	100	12
With no worse curse then absence makes me tast..	235	Astrophil	105	14
Giving frankly niggard No:	202	A&S 2nd Song		10
What No her tongue sleeping useth.	202	A&S 2nd Song		12
Foole, more foole, for no more taking.	203	A&S 2nd Song		28
"No, no, no, no, my Deare, let be.".	210	A&S 4th Song		6
Above line repeated at following locations	210	A&S 4th Song		12
"	210	A&S 4th Song		18
"	211	A&S 4th Song		24
"	211	A&S 4th Song		30
"	211	A&S 4th Song		36
"	211	A&S 4th Song		42
"	211	A&S 4th Song		48
"	211	A&S 4th Song		54
Better place no wit can find,	210	A&S 4th Song		13
And all I said so well, as no man it denied.	212	A&S 5th Song		12
Thinke now no more to heare of warme fine odourd snow, ...	213	A&S 5th Song		37
No vertue merits praise, once toucht with blot of Treason..	214	A&S 5th Song		66
No witchcraft is so evill, as which man's mind destroyeth..	215	A&S 5th Song		78
Let no tongue aspire to tell,	226	A&S 10th Song		10
Thought see thou no place forbeare,	226	A&S 10th Song		19
Thinke no more but die in me,	227	A&S 10th Song		46
Time doth worke what no man knoweth."	234	A&S 11th Song		17
Deere, do reason no such spite,	234	A&S 11th Song		28
No, the more fooles it do shake,	234	A&S 11th Song		33
Come no more, least I get anger."	234	A&S 11th Song		37
As no exceptions tutch..	216	A&S 6th Song		42
No mortall gifts, no earthly fruites, now here descended be:	217	A&S 7th Song		14
But no fault there is in praying.	219	A&S 8th Song		48
"Therefore, Deere, this no more move,	220	A&S 8th Song		97
Can abide to keepe no measure,	221	A&S 9th Song		7
No, she hates me, wellaway,	222	A&S 9th Song		41
No help for you remaineth.	272	Psalm III		9
I say no more but this:.	272	Psalm III		22
No, nor with Thee the naughty Ones shall dwel,	274	Psalm V		11
O let their wickedness no longer bide.	277	Psalm VII		25
Whose life no life but of Thee holdeth,	278	Psalm VIII		12
What? Doth their Memory no longer last?.	280	Psalm IX		18
No sooner said, but (lo) myne Enemyes sink	280	Psalm IX		46
In them no cause is growing.	284	Psalm XI		12
No men are left, that charity do love,	284	Psalm XII		2
Their abject lips no breath but flattery move.	284	Psalm XII		5
Yea in no age thy blisse from them departs..	285	Psalm XII		24
No, No I trust on thee, and joy in Thy	286	Psalm XIII		17
There is no God that raigneth.	286	Psalm XIV		3
On my soul no power shall have:	288	Psalm XVI		32
There is no speech, no language which.	293	Psalm XIX		9
There be no eyn but reade the line	294	Psalm XIX		13
There be no Rea'ms hidd from his beames,	294	Psalm XIX		27
No sooner my child eyes could look abroad,	299	Psalm XXII		23
Even he whose life no help of man can quicken.	300	Psalm XXII		74
No whit feare ill.	301	Psalm XXIII		12
To Thy Works they give no ey..	309	Psalm XXVIII		21
No end shall find.	317	Psalm XXXIII		41
We have no plea but trust.	318	Psalm XXXIII		84
Noe feare of God doth once appeare	323	Psalm XXXVI		5
Though he do fall no wracke he proveth,	326	Psalm XXXVII		59
No time within his limites binds..	326	Psalm XXXVII		76
No sound part (causd by Thy wrath)	327	Psalm XXXVIII		7
My God, O make no stay..	332	Psalm XL		70
Dick. Faith in my self and worth in her, which no proofe can undoo..	343	Possibly	1	26
So have I cause my selfe to plaine, but no cause to complayne.	344	Possibly	1	36
Desire's great force, no forces can withhold:.	345	Possibly	4	3

NO   (CONTINUED)   PAGE   TITLE   LINE
    Allarme allarme, here will no yeelding be, ...   346 Possibly   5   1
    Such marble eares, no cunning wordes can charme, ...   346 Possibly   5   2
    No force, though force be used, Allarme allarme. . . . . .   346 Possibly   5   8
    A Shepheard's tale no height of stile desires. . . . . . .   242 Other Poems   4   1
    They found, they felt, they had no lease of blisse. . . . . 244 Other Poems   4   80
    No grasse, no trees, nor yet hir sparrow might . . . . . .   245 Other Poems   4 111
    In whome no evill did raigne, nor good appeare, ... 245 Other Poems   4 118
    No, no, it was in spite of wisdome's song, ...   247 Other Poems   4 222
    Nous cri'de, and chafd, but he no other can. . . . .   249 Other Poems   4 285
    Till that he spied old Geron could no more, ... 250 Other Poems   4 307
    Nous sware it was no right; for his default. . . . .   250 Other Poems   4 314
    For then wise Klaius found no absence can. . . . .   253 Other Poems   4 419
    Help him, who can no more hir sight foregoe. . . . .   253 Other Poems   4 420
    Strephon, poor youth, because he saw no smoke, ...   253 Other Poems   4 427
    No sleeps, but dreams, no dreams, but visions straunge, . . 253 Other Poems   4 436
    Leave sheepe, leave all, I will no piecing have. . . . . .   255 Other Poems   4 512
    So may no fortune breed. . . . .   258 Other Poems   5   80
    And gives her kidds no food, but willow's barke." . . . . . 259 Other Poems   5 113
NOBILITY
    On me to cast those eyes, where shine nobilitie. . . . . .   19 1st Eclogues 7 178
    No, no: no wordes ennoble selre-nobilitie. . . . .   48 2nd Eclogues 28   28
NOBLE
    O noble age who place their only blisse. . . . .   24 1st Eclogues 9   69
    Lyke to my noble thoughtes, still new, well plac'd, to me
        fruteles. . . . .   35 1st Eclogues 13 124
    When that noble toppe doth nodd, I beleeve she salutes me; . 36 1st Eclogues 13 144
    Bownd and bownd by so noble bandes, as loth to be unbownd, . 37 1st Eclogues 13 162
    If noble be thy bandes, make them notorious: . . . .   47 2nd Eclogues 28   14
    Thus noble golde, downe to the bottome goes, ...   81 Arcadia III 54   13
    Well grounded, noble, due, spite, rage, disdaine, ...   84 Arcadia III 60   10
    This noble Cedar's pretious roote: . . . .   89 Arcadia III 62 106
    Are we their servants growne? no doubt a noble staye: . . . 120 4th Eclogues 73 115
    Seeking to quench in me the noble fire, ... 200 Astrophil   68   7
    He lifted me unto a largly noble place. . . . . 292 Psalm XVIII   42
    Yea noble hight of Rocky Hill. . . . .   307 Psalm XXVII   28
    To yeeld she found hir noble heart did ake: . . . . 245 Other Poems   4 125
NOBLENESS
    That Noblenesse it selfe makes thus unkind?. . . . .   186 Astrophil   44   8
NOBLER
    Where helping weaker sort, the nobler beastes, ...   102 3rd Eclogues 66 121
    Which seeming lesse, yet nobler life doth move. . . . . . . 151 Cert Sonnets 22   60
    Nobler desires, least else that friendly foe, ... 175 Astrophil   21   7
    From nobler course, fit for my birth and mind: . . . . . .   196 Astrophil   62   8
    O blisse, fit for a nobler state then me: . . . . 200 Astrophil   69   2
    Teaching dumbe lips a nobler exercise. . . . .   207 Astrophil   81   4
NOBLEST
    The noblest kinde rejects not others' woes. . . . .   18 1st Eclogues 7 134
    Thus be our noblest parts dryed up with sorrow: . . . . . .   62 2nd Eclogues 30 174
    Arcadia's gemme the noblest childe of nature. . . . . 109 Arcadia IV   70   18
    Yet noblest Conquerours do wreckes avoid. . . . . 185 Astrophil   40   11
NOBLY
    In speeches nobly placed: . . . . 216 A&S 6th Song   26
    He nobly saves his King, and kindness keeps in store, . . . 293 Psalm XVIII   90
NOBODY
    Unto no body my woman saith she had rather a wife be, . . . 143 Cert Sonnets 13   1
NOD
    When that noble toppe doth nodd, I beleeve she salutes me; . 36 1st Eclogues 13 144
NODS
    With mowes and nodds they stand about me flocking. . . . .   299 Psalm XXII   18
NOISE
    Which shootes strongly with out any noyse and deadly without
        smarte. . . . .   35 1st Eclogues 13 122
    When by the winde it maketh a noyse, I do thinke she doth
        answer. . . . .   36 1st Eclogues 13 145
    When lo with hugest noise (such noise a tower makes. . . .   118 4th Eclogues 73   51
    (Or such a noise it was, as highest thunders sende, ... 118 4th Eclogues 73   53
    A chamber deafe to noise, and blind to light: . . . . 184 Astrophil   39   10
    One deep with noyse of his fall. . . . .   335 Psalm XLII   29
NOISOME
    Me seemes I feele a noysome sent, the morning. . . . . . .   112 4th Eclogues 71   45
    From out that noysome gulfe, which gaping lies . . . . . .   205 Astrophil   78   3
    That to hir breast he gave a noysome blowe. . . . . 249 Other Poems   4 272
NONE
    Be none of us, or els maintaine our fashion: . . . .   15 1st Eclogues 7   14
    My pastimes none: time passeth on my fall: . . . .   18 1st Eclogues 7 142
    None but I, workes by desire: by desire have I kindled in
        his soule. . . . .   30 1st Eclogues 11   13
    Aire, we do still with sighes encrease; to the fire? we do
        want none. . . . .   32 1st Eclogues 13   30
    None can speake of a wound with skill, if he have not a
        wound felt. . . . .   33 1st Eclogues 13   71
    A quiet mind none but thy selfe can lend to thee, ...   51 2nd Eclogues 28 101
    These wordes are full of woes, yet feele they none. . . . .   75 Arcadia III 43   3
    You none can clayme but you your selfe by right, ...   79 Arcadia III 50   19
    Who yet was good, because she knewe none ill, ...   94 3rd Eclogues 64   14
    But yet the common Damme none did bemone: . . . . 102 3rd Eclogues 66 118
    Revil'd for ech small fault, sometimes for none: . . . . .   105 3rd Eclogues 67   53
    Now kindnesse profred is, none kinder is that I: . . . . .   121 4th Eclogues 73 151
    I loving still a love that loveth none, ... 148 Cert Sonnets 19   16

NONE   (CONTINUED)   PAGE   TITLE   LINE

	PAGE	TITLE		LINE
That from her lockes, thy day-nets, none scapes free,. . . .	170	Astrophil	12	2
Then be they close, and so none shall displease.	182	Astrophil	34	8
That hast my mind, none of the basest, brought	184	Astrophil	40	3
As I may well recount, but none can prize:	198	Astrophil	65	4
Feare not else, none can us spie:.	211	A&S 4th Song		22
And all my help from none but Thee is sent,.	277	Psalm VII		29
None, I say still, shall ruind be.	321	Psalm XXXIV		79
And he not being, she was none..	241	Other Poems	3	2
Well might he others beare, but leane to none)	244	Other Poems	4	72
While into none doubt of his love did sinke,.	247	Other Poems	4	199
And none invisible, but Spirites, can goe.	253	Other Poems	4	456
And yet, deare soule, I know she hurteth none:	254	Other Poems	4	458
He treble beas for helpe, but none can get:.	254	Other Poems	4	492

NOON

But lo, while I do speake, it groweth noone with me, ...	205	Astrophil	76	9

NOONDAY

Like to the glory of noone day..	325	Psalm XXXVII		16

NORTH

But finding these North clymes do coldly him embrace,. . . .	168	Astrophil	8	5
By north or south still rich adorned live:	256	Other Poems	5	16

NOSE

Her nose, her chinne pure ivorie weares:	86	Arcadia III	62	27

NOSTRILS

He came, but came with smoake from out his nostrills sent, .	291	Psalm XVIII		18

NOTE

Tune up my voice, a higher note I yeeld, ...	3	Lady of May	2	7
The highest note comes oft from basest mind, ...	4	Lady of May	2	13
Not limited to a whispringe note, the Lament of a Courtier,.	35	1st Eclogues	13	110
So grow thy wooll of note, ...	258	Other Poems	5	69

NOTES

From those cleere notes which freely may rejoyce..	13	Arcadia I	4	8
The cheerefull notes these pleasant places yeeld,.	58	2nd Eclogues	30	39
The birds' eyes closde, closed their chirping notes. . . .	98	3rd Eclogues	66	12
Where highest notes to godlines are raisd,.	99	3rd Eclogues	66	31
Or if thy mourning notes be fully spent, ...	127	4th Eclogues	75	64
O notes of mine your selves together tie:.	127	4th Eclogues	75	76
What blushing notes doest thou in margine see?	199	Astrophil	67	8
In well raisde notes, my pen the best it may	201	Astrophil	70	10
Your morall notes straight my hid meaning teare.	233	Astrophil	104	12
Doubt you to whom my Muse these notes entendeth, ...	196	A&S 1st Song		1
Above line repeated at following location.	197	A&S 1st Song		33
For warbling notes from inward chearing flow.	242	Other Poems	4	4

NOTHING

"Nothing", sayd he, "for most I joy in this, ...	4	Lady of May	3	5
A heape of sweetes she is, where nothing spilled is; . . .	15	1st Eclogues	7	28
Nothing can mend one point that in her lies.	17	1st Eclogues	7	108
No, nothing so; an old false knave he is,.	21	1st Eclogues	8	13
Were in his dayes: which heard, one nothing heares,. . . .	24	1st Eclogues	9	76
That nothing winnes the heaven, but what doth earth forsake.	45	Arcadia II	26	16
To such a force soone chaunge were nothing sutable.. . . .	47	2nd Eclogues	28	12
But in the place found nothing but a rope.	55	2nd Eclogues	29	92
Nico. Nothing (O Leuca) shall thy fame deface, ...	56	2nd Eclogues	29	123
Which nothing spares, to melt that Virgin-waxe	60	2nd Eclogues	30	108
Hurte not the face, which nothing can amende".	82	Arcadia III	55	15
Where nothing but impression lackes.	88	Arcadia III	62	76
All waywardnes, which nothing kindly brookes,.	93	3rd Eclogues	63	66
Yet (for I nothing sawe) I feared sore;.	99	3rd Eclogues	66	16
For nothing can endure where order n'is.	100	3rd Eclogues	66	51
With such a will that nothing can asswage.	105	3rd Eclogues	67	51
Looks over the world, and can find nothing such, ...	169	Astrophil	9	10
With doing all, leave nothing done but paine.	210	Astrophil	85	8
And nothing then the cause more sweet could be,.	223	Astrophil	87	13
For nothing from my wit or will doth flow, ...	224	Astrophil	90	12
Love feares nothing else but anger..	203	A&S 2nd Song		20
Will streight-way nothing bee..	283	Psalm X		68
For nothing they can ever want	319	Psalm XXXIV		34
Nothing in my body sound;.	328	Psalm XXXVIII		21
And so I nothing said, I muet stood, ...	329	Psalm XXXIX		5
A span? nay nothing in Thyn eyne..	330	Psalm XXXIX		16
For nothing can more tedious bee, then plaint, in time of joy. . .	344	Possibly	1	46
Who nothing earthly, but of fire and aire, ...	250	Other Poems	4	338
Those eies, which nothing themselves can see, ...	253	Other Poems	4	451
Till straunge delight, delight to nothing ware;.	254	Other Poems	4	482
Let nothing mee remove	261	Other Poems	6	45

NOTORIOUS

If noble be thy bandes, make them notorious:	47	2nd Eclogues	28	14
So high, as should make such a paine notorious:.	129	4th Eclogues	75	140
Let him notorious make	296	Psalm XX		11
They shall to children's children make notorious	300	Psalm XXII		77

NOURISH

As in it selfe to nourish mortall strife..	57	2nd Eclogues	30	28
And then who shall the name of Histor nourish?	106	3rd Eclogues	67	111
And seeke to nourish that, which now contaynes	114	4th Eclogues	72	22
My life forgets to nourish languisht sprites;.	186	Astrophil	42	10
Nor nourish speciall lockes of vowed haire,.	191	Astrophil	54	3
Who hath the breast, whose milke doth passions nourish,. . .	197	A&S 1st Song		17
Bids you leave such minds to nourish."	234	A&S 11th Song		27
Whose braunches faile not timely fruite to nourish,.	270	Psalm I		9

```
NOURISH              (CONTINUED)                    PAGE    TITLE           LINE
      Nor envy in thy bosome nourish . . . . . . . . . . . . . . . .  324  Psalm XXXVII       3
      Then fly all ev'ill and goodness nourish,. . . . . . . . . .    326  Psalm XXXVII      67
NOUS
      Faire Nous with Pas the lott to hell did sende:. . . . . . . .  248  Other Poems   4   244
      From Nous and Cosma all their beauty tooke.. . . . . . . . .    248  Other Poems   4   248
      So he with Nous to Geron turn'd their race,. . . . . . . . .    248  Other Poems   4   251
      But Nous that slipt from Pas, did catch the clowne.. . . . .    248  Other Poems   4   262
      While Strephon might with preatie Nous have met,. . . . . .     249  Other Poems   4   279
      Left Nous to coast the loved beauty ny. . . . . . . . . . . .   249  Other Poems   4   284
      Nous cri'de, and chafd, but he no other can. . . . . . . . .    249  Other Poems   4   285
      Still shunning Nous to lengthen pleasing race, . . . . . . .    250  Other Poems   4   306
      To hell he goes, and Nous with him must dwell. . . . . . . .    250  Other Poems   4   313
      Nous sware it was no right; for his default. . . . . . . . .    250  Other Poems   4   314
      Nous counseld Strephon Geron to pursue,. . . . . . . . . . .    250  Other Poems   4   321
      Drew dainty Nous, that she not able so . . . . . . . . . . .    250  Other Poems   4   335
NOW
      Come Espilus, come now declare thy skill,. . . . . . . . . .      3  Lady of May   2     1
      When being askt, now that he did obtaine . . . . . . . . . .      4  Lady of May   3     3
      Now thanked be the great God Pan,. . . . . . . . . . . . . .     13  Arcadia I     5     1
      Sing then, and see (for now thou hast inflamed me) . . . . .     15  1st Eclogues  7    20
      Now my hoarse voice doth faile this occupation,. . . . . . .     19  1st Eclogues  7   170
      But now hoarse voyce, doth faile this occupation. . . . . .      20  1st Eclogues  7  V970
      Till now at length that Jove him office gives, . . . . . . .     22  1st Eclogues  8    45
      Though woes now live, at length thy woes must dye. . . . . .     22  1st Eclogues  9    12
      I yet should know a young man speaketh now,. . . . . . . . .     25  1st Eclogues  9    97
      Come narr good Mastix, tis now full tway score . . . . . . .     27  1st Eclogues 10    20
      Thou heardst even now a yong man snebb me sore,. . . . . . .     27  1st Eclogues 10    22
      But now to silence turn'd his minstralsie. . . . . . . . . .     28  1st Eclogues 10    75
      But farewell nowe, thy fault is no great sinne,. . . . . . .     29  1st Eclogues 10    97
      But most wretched I am, now love awakes my desire. . . . . .     30  1st Eclogues 11    20
      Now by thy words I begin, most famous Lady, to gather. . . .     34  1st Eclogues 13    94
      But ceasse worthy shepheard, nowe ceasse we to weery the
          hearers. . . . . . . . . . . . . . . . . . . . . . . . .     37  1st Eclogues 13   172
      In vaine, my Hart, now you with sight are burnd, . . . . . .     38  Arcadia II   14     5
      Reason, I vaine (now you have lost my hart). . . . . . . . .     38  Arcadia II   14     9
      Now in this sande I would discharge my minde,. . . . . . . .     42  Arcadia II   21    13
      My sun is gon, Nowe clowdie greeves assayle. . . . . . . . .     44  Arcadia II   24    12
      P. We now have peace, your peace we doo not neede. . . . . .     46  2nd Eclogues 27    28
      By telling how she was, how now she framed is. . . . . . . .     49  2nd Eclogues 28    53
      Nico. Ah now I see, why thou art in thy selfe so blind:. . .     52  2nd Eclogues 29     5
      Pas. Kisse her? now mayst thou kisse. I have a fitter match;     53  2nd Eclogues 29    39
      Let Pas now know, how Nico maketh layes. . . . . . . . . . .     54  2nd Eclogues 29    71
      Unto my pipe, O Nimphes, nowe helpe my pipe, . . . . . . . .     54  2nd Eclogues 29    73
      That (shining now) she then might shine more farre.. . . . .     56  2nd Eclogues 29   122
      What greater ills have now the heavens in store, . . . . . .     57  2nd Eclogues 30     6
      But hoarse and drye, my pipes I nowe must spare. . . . . . .     62  2nd Eclogues 30   190
      And now fame the herald of her true honour,. . . . . . . . .     68  2nd Eclogues 33    19
      Nowe that myne eyes their cheerefull sunn dothe misse. . . .     70  Arcadia III  35     5
      But nowe successe hathe gott above annoyes,. . . . . . . . .     71  Arcadia III  36    17
      Nowe that I spye the haven my thoughtes requyre, . . . . . .     72  Arcadia III  37    15
      Nowe that some flower of fruict, my paynes do prove, . . . .     72  Arcadia III  37    16
      My minde ere now led foorth by reason's light: . . . . . . .     73  Arcadia III  39     4
      Thy mistresse' song is now a sorrow's crie,. . . . . . . . .     81  Arcadia III  54     2
      But nowe each where doth range . . . . . . . . . . . . . . .     82  Arcadia III  55     7
      Aurora now thou shewst thy blushing light. . . . . . . . . .     82  Arcadia III  56     1
      But now the fitt is past: and time hath giv'ne . . . . . . .     83  Arcadia III  57     9
      Eyes, let your Teares with gazing now be mended, . . . . . .     84  Arcadia III  59    14
      Of huge complaintes, that now it is despis'de. . . . . . . .     85  Arcadia III  61     4
      But bow all knees, now of her knees. . . . . . . . . . . . .     89  Arcadia III  62    93
      Now course doth leade me to her hand,. . . . . . . . . . . .     90  Arcadia III  62   121
      Let mother earth now decke her selfe in flowers, . . . . . .     91  3rd Eclogues 63     1
      Now whether mov'd with selfe unworthines,. . . . . . . . . .     94  3rd Eclogues 64     7
      Doth breake, now toong unto thy name doth move,. . . . . . .     97  3rd Eclogues 64   100
      "The jealous wretch must now to Courte be gone:. . . . . . .     97  3rd Eclogues 64   103
      Now is the time we may be here alone,. . . . . . . . . . . .     97  3rd Eclogues 64   105
      Now that he had her words so truely tried: . . . . . . . . .     97  3rd Eclogues 64   112
      But now the courtier gan to smell the feate, . . . . . . . .     97  3rd Eclogues 64   117
      How sheepheards did of yore, how now they thrive,. . . . . .     99  3rd Eclogues 66    34
      Which now in night's deepe shade sheep heard of me.. . . . .     99  3rd Eclogues 66    42
      That they now skilld not, how from him to wend;. . . . . . .    102  3rd Eclogues 66   114
      Who now his owne, full like his owne he used.. . . . . . . .    102  3rd Eclogues 66   142
      Now fancie's fits, now fortune's balefull stowers: . . . . .    103  3rd Eclogues 66   157
      Thou seest, how friske, and jolly now he is, . . . . . . . .    103  3rd Eclogues 67     5
      Yet now the roote of him abase you would.. . . . . . . . . .    106  3rd Eclogues 67    99
      Goe to, goe to, and Cupid now applie . . . . . . . . . . . .    106  3rd Eclogues 67   100
      Histor. Perchaunce I will, but nowe me thinkes it tyme . . .    107  3rd Eclogues 67   118
      These stately starrs in their now shining faces, . . . . . .    108  Arcadia IV   69     9
      Now Prince's losse hath made our damage publique,. . . . . .    109  Arcadia IV   70     4
      Am banisht now among the monstrous mountaines. . . . . . . .    111  4th Eclogues 71    16
      And seeke to nourish that, which now contaynes . . . . . . .    114  4th Eclogues 72    22
      No being now, but sorowe I can have: . . . . . . . . . . . .    114  4th Eclogues 72    27
      And now I faine would reape, I reape but this, . . . . . . .    115  4th Eclogues 72    57
      And this hath got; the catcher now is caught,. . . . . . . .    115  4th Eclogues 72    66
      But now those living lights absented be, . . . . . . . . . .    116  4th Eclogues 72    85
      Full dead before, I now to dust should fall, . . . . . . . .    116  4th Eclogues 72    86
      But now an ende, (o Klaius) now an ende, . . . . . . . . . .    116  4th Eclogues 72   102
      Now was our heav'nly vaulte deprived of the light. . . . . .    116  4th Eclogues 73     1
      With Sunne's depart: and now the darkenes of the night . . .    116  4th Eclogues 73     2
      Now each thing which enjoy'd that firie quickning sparke . .    116  4th Eclogues 73     4
```

NOW	(CONTINUED)	PAGE	TITLE		LINE
And mother Earth, now clad in mourning weeds, did breath . .		117	4th Eclogues	73	9
Be silent therefore now, and so be silent still.		119	4th Eclogues	73	97
And hither now, vouchsafe to take with willing eare.		119	4th Eclogues	73	104
Those thousand altars faire now in the dust to lie?.		119	4th Eclogues	73	112
And now before we seeke by wise Apollo's skill		120	4th Eclogues	73	125
Now resteth onely this, which of us two is she, ...		120	4th Eclogues	73	135
Now kindnesse profred is, none kinder is that I:		121	4th Eclogues	73	151
Now bolder waxt, waxt prowde, that I such sway might beare:.		121	4th Eclogues	73	159
But now we muste needs yeelde, to what our othes require". .		121	4th Eclogues	73	169
And now fully beleeves helpe to be quite perished;		122	4th Eclogues	74	2
Can those eyes now yeeld to the kind conceit of a sorow, . .		122	4th Eclogues	74	17
Now that he finds to what end his life and love be reserved,		123	4th Eclogues	74	29
Unto the man, whom now such miseries you awarde?		124	4th Eclogues	74	74
Think what a world is now, think who hath altred her hart. .		124	4th Eclogues	74	76
What? was I then worthie such good, now worthie so muche evill?		124	4th Eclogues	74	77
Now fled, then cherished? then so nie, now so remote?. . . .		124	4th Eclogues	74	78
With much more: now what doo I finde, but Care to abhor me,.		124	4th Eclogues	74	81
And banished doo I live, nor now will seeke a recov'rie, . .		124	4th Eclogues	74	83
Your dolefull tunes sweete Muses now applie.		125	4th Eclogues	75	3
Above line repeated at following locations		125	4th Eclogues	75	15
. . . .		125	4th Eclogues	75	30
. . . .		126	4th Eclogues	75	48
. . . .		126	4th Eclogues	75	60
. . . .		127	4th Eclogues	75	78
. . . .		127	4th Eclogues	75	96
. . . .		128	4th Eclogues	75	117
In trees) now through your porous barkes receave		125	4th Eclogues	75	5
Let golde now rust, let Diamonds waste in thee:.		125	4th Eclogues	75	22
Vertue is dead, now set thy triumph here..		127	4th Eclogues	75	72
Now set thy triumph in this world, bereaved.		127	4th Eclogues	75	73
Of what was good, where now no good doth lie;.		127	4th Eclogues	75	74
Justice, justice is now (alas) oppressed:.		128	4th Eclogues	75	118
For what place now is lefte for our affection.		129	4th Eclogues	76	7
Now that of purest lampe is queint the light, ...		129	4th Eclogues	76	8
Now that the mine is lost of all our treasure, ...		129	4th Eclogues	76	10
Now death hath swallow'd up our worldly pleasure, ...		129	4th Eclogues	76	11
Shall we now finde a guide of such affection, ...		129	4th Eclogues	76	22
Let them be clearde, and now begin to see, ...		131	Arcadia V	77	11
Thine earth now springs, mine fadeth, ...		137	Cert Sonnets	4	11
Above line repeated at following location.		137	Cert Sonnets	4	23
Where bee nowe those Joyes, that I lately tasted?.		138	Cert Sonnets	5	5
Where bee nowe those eyes ever Inly persers?		138	Cert Sonnets	5	6
Where bee now those wordes never Idelly wasted, ...		138	Cert Sonnets	5	7
O paine I now recant the praise I gave, ...		141	Cert Sonnets	9	13
An Asse's shade ere now hath bred debate..		146	Cert Sonnets	17	20
And see you not that I fall now to ryme?		146	Cert Sonnets	17	40
But now, if ere my face with joy be clad:.		147	Cert Sonnets	17	44
In clyming steepe, now hard refusall show:		147	Cert Sonnets	18	6
The shading woods seeme now my Sunne to darke, ...		147	Cert Sonnets	18	7
The restfull Caves now restlesse visions give, ...		147	Cert Sonnets	18	9
Oft have I musde, but now at length I finde, ...		148	Cert Sonnets	20	1
But now the starres with their strange course do binde . . .		148	Cert Sonnets	20	5
Now dead, doth shew departure is a death..		148	Cert Sonnets	20	12
Now thus this wonder to my selfe I frame, ...		151	Cert Sonnets	22	69
Now thy sweetnesse sowre is deemed, ...		156	Cert Sonnets	27	9
Now even that footstep of lost libertie.		166	Astrophil	2	9
Is gone, and now like slave-borne Muscovite, ...		166	Astrophil	2	10
And now employ the remnant of my wit, ...		166	Astrophil	2	12
Vertue alas, now let me take some rest, ...		166	Astrophil	4	1
The windowes now through which this heav'nly guest		169	Astrophil	9	9
Stella: now she is nam'd, need more be said?		173	Astrophil	16	11
I now have learn'd Love right, and learn'd even so, ...		173	Astrophil	16	13
Poore passenger, passe now thereby I did, ...		175	Astrophil	20	9
If now the May of my yeares much decline, ...		175	Astrophil	21	10
Dig deepe with learning's spade, now tell me this, ...		175	Astrophil	21	13
What now the Dutch in their full diets boast;		180	Astrophil	30	6
How Holland hearts, now so good townes be lost, ...		180	Astrophil	30	7
Till now, wrapt in a most infernall night, ...		181	Astrophil	33	3
Him as thy slave, and now long needy Fame.		182	Astrophil	35	10
I curst thee oft, I pitie now thy case, ...		187	Astrophil	46	1
Alas poore wag, that now a scholler art.		188	Astrophil	46	9
Whose curelesse wounds even now most freshly bleed:.		189	Astrophil	48	11
And now man's wrongs in me, poore beast, descrie..		189	Astrophil	49	4
And now hath made me to his hand so right, ...		189	Astrophil	49	13
And now my pen these lines had dashed quite, ...		190	Astrophil	50	12
"What now sir foole," said he, "I would no lesse, ...		191	Astrophil	53	7
"What?" say they of me, "now I dare sweare, ...		191	Astrophil	54	7
But now I meane no more your helpe to trie, ...		192	Astrophil	55	9
But now that I, alas, do want her sight, ...		193	Astrophil	56	9
Growne now his slaves, he forst them out to find		193	Astrophil	57	3
Now judge by this: in piercing phrases late, ...		194	Astrophil	58	9
Now I, wit-beaten long by hardest Fate, ...		195	Astrophil	60	9
Now with slow words, now with dumbe eloquence.		195	Astrophil	61	2
Now since her chast mind hates this love in me, ...		195	Astrophil	61	9
O Grammer rules, o now your vertues show;.		196	Astrophil	63	1
Sing then my Muse, now Io Pean sing, ...		196	Astrophil	63	9
In this old world, growne now so too too wise:		198	Astrophil	65	6
Doth Stella now begin with piteous eye, ...		199	Astrophil	67	2

	PAGE	TITLE		LINE
She oft hath drunke my teares, now hopes to enjoy.	201	Astrophil	70	3
Now from thy fellowship I needs must part,	202	Astrophil	72	5
Vertue's gold now must head my Cupid's dart.	202	Astrophil	72	8
Now banisht art, but yet alas how shall?	202	Astrophil	72	14
In Beautie's throne, see now who dares come neare.	203	Astrophil	73	10
Benighted in cold wo, but now appeares my day,	204	Astrophil	76	3
My heart cries "ah", it burnes, mine eyes now dazled be:	205	Astrophil	76	11
Cease we to praise, now pray we for a kisse.	206	Astrophil	79	14
But now spite of my heart my mouth will stay,	207	Astrophil	80	10
Now blessed you, beare onward blessed me	209	Astrophil	84	5
In hart both sight and love now coupled be;	223	Astrophil	88	13
Now that of absence the most irksome night,	223	Astrophil	89	1
Stella, while now by honour's cruell might,	224	Astrophil	91	1
For my poore soule, which now that sicknesse tries,	228	Astrophil	94	6
So gratefull now you waite upon my care.	228	Astrophil	95	4
Which ay most faire, now more then most faire show,	231	Astrophil	100	3
Stella now learnes (strange case) to weepe in thee.	231	Astrophil	101	8
What saist thou now, where is that dainty cheere	235	Astrophil	106	5
But thou art gone, now that selfe felt disgrace.	235	Astrophil	106	7
Which now my breast orecharg'd to Musicke lendeth?	196	A&S 1st Song		2
Above line repeated at following location.	197	A&S 1st Song		34
Now will I teach her that she,	202	A&S 2nd Song		3
Now will I with that boy prove	202	A&S 2nd Song		7
Now will I attempt to know,	202	A&S 2nd Song		11
Now will I invade the fort;	202	A&S 2nd Song		15
Now will I alas refraine,	203	A&S 2nd Song		19
Now will I but venture this,	203	A&S 2nd Song		23
Now will I away hence flee:	203	A&S 2nd Song		27
Onely joy, now here you are,	210	A&S 4th Song		1
But now that hope is lost, unkindnesse kils delight,	212	A&S 5th Song		13
For rage now rules the reynes, which guided were by Pleasure	213	A&S 5th Song		15
I thinke now of thy faults, who late thought of thy praise,	213	A&S 5th Song		16
That speech falles now to blame, which did thy honour raise,	213	A&S 5th Song		17
See now those feathers pluckt, wherewith thou flewst most high:	213	A&S 5th Song		22
Now child, a lesson new you shall begin to spell:	213	A&S 5th Song		35
Thinke now no more to heare of warme fine odourd snow,	213	A&S 5th Song		37
Now God forbid. A theefe, and of worst theeves the cheefe:	213	A&S 5th Song		44
The name of murderer now on thy faire forehead sitteth:	214	A&S 5th Song		51
Of foule rebellion then I do appeach thee now;	214	A&S 5th Song		62
I now then staine thy white with vagabunding shame,	214	A&S 5th Song		68
No mortall gifts, no earthly fruites, now here descended be:	217	A&S 7th Song		14
But now teares themselves did smile,	218	A&S 8th Song		14
Sigh they did, but now betwixt	218	A&S 8th Song		17
These birds sing: "Now use the season.".	219	A&S 8th Song		56
Now be still, yet still beleeve me,	220	A&S 8th Song		75
Up lord now time it is:	272	Psalm III		23
Who causeless now, yeelds me a hatefull heart,	277	Psalm VII		12
Now brought abed, hath brought nought foorth, but nought...	278	Psalm VII		39
Because my Foes to fly are now constraind.	279	Psalm IX		6
His farr off sight now hoodwinkt is,	282	Psalm X		47
I now should Fall aflying?	283	Psalm XI		4
Ah, now even for their sakes, that taste of Woe,	285	Psalm XII		13
More than they now do bragg, when He shall take.	286	Psalm XIV		17
Now like a lion gaping to make preyes,	290	Psalm XVII		33
Now like his Whelp in den that lurking stayes.	290	Psalm XVII		34
Now in mee knowledg sayes.	296	Psalm XX		21
The lookers now at me poore wretch be mocking,	299	Psalm XXII		17
And now am brought, alas, brought by Thy power	299	Psalm XXII		37
New made, O Lord maintain,	304	Psalm XXV		68
Now, Now shall He lift up my head.	307	Psalm XXVII		31
Lo I thus waild, now daunce for joy.	311	Psalm XXX		34
Now I, now I my self forgotten find,	313	Psalm XXXI		34
O now accord	316	Psalm XXXIII		8
O now be bent.	316	Psalm XXXIII		11
Aha! Sir, now we see you where we should..	322	Psalm XXXV		54
Lo there I now foresee their fall.	324	Psalm XXXVI		33
I have been younge now old I am,	326	Psalm XXXVII		61
Lo I now to mourn begin.	329	Psalm XXXVIII		52
As now to say to me,	332	Psalm XL		59
Now is hee wrackt say they, lo, there he lyes.	333	Psalm XLI		27
So then be blest now then, at home, abroad,	334	Psalm XLI		45
Where is now Thy God so good?.	334	Psalm XLII		12
Where hath now your God his biding?.	335	Psalm XLII		48
Now let those lightsome sights we see thy darknes overcome.	343	Possibly	1	12
Yeelde yeelde O yeelde, now is it time to yeelde,	345	Possibly	4	13
Allarme allarme, companions nowe beginne,	346	Possibly	5	9
As all the rest, so now the stone.	241	Other Poems	3	7
Now for a clod-like hare in fourm they peere,	243	Other Poems	4	43
Now bolt and cudgill squirrels' leape do move.	243	Other Poems	4	44
Now the ambitiouse Larke with mirror cleare.	243	Other Poems	4	45
And now at keels they trie a harmles chaunce,	243	Other Poems	4	47
And now their curr they teach to fetch and daunce.	243	Other Poems	4	48
Glutted with them now plaies with meanest things...	245	Other Poems	4	132
So now for pray these shepheards two he tooke,	245	Other Poems	4	137
Therefore Love arm'd in hir now takes the fielde,	245	Other Poems	4	145
Were now his darts leaving his wonted fight.	246	Other Poems	4	148
And cal'd, now wounded, purpose to his aide:	246	Other Poems	4	162

NOW	(CONTINUED)	PAGE	TITLE		LINE
And now, proud Rebell gan for to gainsay		246	Other Poems	4	173
And therfore finding force now faint to be,.		248	Other Poems	4	255
But so she must. And now the third assault		250	Other Poems	4	316
Now runnes, and takes hir in his clipping armes.		252	Other Poems	4	384
He found that Reason's self now reasons found.		253	Other Poems	4	423
Now make me thinke that there is not a fende,.		254	Other Poems	4	463
And now the dropping trees do wepe for me, ...		254	Other Poems	4	479
And now faire evenings blush my shame to see..		254	Other Poems	4	480
Though thus, and worse, though now I am at last, ...		254	Other Poems	4	493
Of all the games that here ere now I met:.		254	Other Poems	4	494
Come shepheard's boy, let now thy heart be bowd.		255	Other Poems	4	510
I aske, now answere me..		256	Other Poems	5	20
What fitts me now but teares, and sighings sadd?		259	Other Poems	5	97
Which Holland sweet now gently sendeth in, ...		259	Other Poems	5	106
Since I am now come hether,.		261	Other Poems	6	38
Now joyned be our hands, ...		261	Other Poems	6	55
Now in servile Court remayning...		262	Other Poems	7	12
NUMBER					
All numbring artes her endlesse graces number not:		49	2nd Eclogues	28	59
Whose care is cause that they in number growe, ...		92	3rd Eclogues	63	38
In number like the hearde.		92	3rd Eclogues	63	42
The number best beloved, ...		261	Other Poems	6	26
NUMBERING					
All numbring artes her endlesse graces number not:		49	2nd Eclogues	28	59
NUMBERS					
Whose numbers, wayes, greatnesse, eternitie, ...		178	Astrophil	26	3
NUMBERS'					
From fancie's earth passing all numbers' bound,.		149	Cert Sonnets	22	7
NUMBROUS					
Their numbrous strength redouble..		272	Psalm III		6
NUMID					
Like Numid Lions by the hunters chas'd,.		249	Other Poems	4	291
NURSE					
Nurse inwarde maladyes, which have not scope to be breath'd					
out, ...		35	1st Eclogues	13	104
Alas (said I) this babe dooth nurce my thought..		55	2nd Eclogues	29	113
Sleepe Babie mine, Desire, nurse Beautie singeth:.		139	Cert Sonnets	6	1
Her milken breasts the nurse of child-like love, ...		141	Cert Sonnets	9	7
You seeke to nurse at fullest breasts of Fame, ...		172	Astrophil	15	13
NURSED					
And in himselfe new doubting causes nurst.		94	3rd Eclogues	64	12
But as you with my breast I oft have nurst,.		228	Astrophil	95	3
Yet but a babe, with milke of Sight he nurst:.		247	Other Poems	4	202
NURSES					
Mothers and Nurses of all vaine annoy.		107	3rd Eclogues	67	117
NURSETH					
Thus be my thoughts disperst, thus thinking nurseth a					
thinking,.		36	1st Eclogues	13	139
NYMPH					
A Nimph thus turnde, but mended in translation..		15	1st Eclogues	7	36
Her waiting Nymphe, a Nymphe that did excell as farr		119	4th Eclogues	73	82
To yonder Nymphe therefore (to Mira I did point)		121	4th Eclogues	73	165
O the fayre Nymphe torne to doo woemen honor,.		138	Cert Sonnets	5	3
Above line repeated at following location.		138	Cert Sonnets	5	27
Towardes Aurora's Court a Nymph doth dwell,.		183	Astrophil	37	5
Nymph of the gard'n, where all beauties be:		207	Astrophil	82	1
Sweet gard'n Nymph, which keepes the Cherrie tree, ...		208	Astrophil	82	5
NYMPHS					
To whether with best cause the Nymphes faire flowers					
affoord		52	2nd Eclogues	29	28
Pas. O Nymphes, I tell you newes, for Pas you knowe:		54	2nd Eclogues	29	66
Unto my pipe, O Nimphes, nowe helpe my pipe, ...		54	2nd Eclogues	29	73
Yee Nymphes which in the waters empire have, ...		92	3rd Eclogues	63	28
Muses graunt guiftes, Nymphes long and joyned life		93	3rd Eclogues	63	92
Yee Nimphes which haunt the springs in pleasant vallies, . .		111	4th Eclogues	71	2
The first with cloth's tuckt up as Nymphes in woods do					
range ,.		118	4th Eclogues	73	66
The courtly Nymphs, acquainted with the mone		191	Astrophil	54	5
Bringing with her those starry Nimphs, whose chace		229	Astrophil	97	3
O					
Her haire pure Crapal-stone; her mouth O heavenly wyde;. . .		12	Arcadia I	3	11
Yet high is my attempt. O Muse historifie.		15	1st Eclogues	7	23
Thy pipe, o Pan, shall helpe, though I sing sorilie.		15	1st Eclogues	7	27
O happie Gods, which by inward assumption.		15	1st Eclogues	7	40
With armour of my hart, he cried "O vanitie, ...		16	1st Eclogues	7	62
"O" cried I, "of so meane worke be discharged:		16	1st Eclogues	7	76
Dorus. Once, o sweete once, I saw with dread oppressed . . .		17	1st Eclogues	7	85
Lalus. This mayde, thus made for joyes, o Pan bemone her,. .		17	1st Eclogues	7	97
Dorus. Farre other care, o Muse, my sorrow tries,.		17	1st Eclogues	7	106
Which if you will (o doo) bestow on me,.		18	1st Eclogues	7	121
Oh he is mard that is for others made.		19	1st Eclogues	7	166
Lalus. Oh he is mard that is for others made..		19	1st Eclogues	7	167
O wretched state of man in selfe division!		20	1st Eclogues	7	V966
Above line repeated at following location.		20	1st Eclogues	7	V967
O well thou saiest! a feeling declaration.		20	1st Eclogues	7	V968
Philisides. O gods, how long this old foole hath annoi'd . .		24	1st Eclogues	9	66
My wearied ears! O gods yet graunt me this,.		24	1st Eclogues	9	67
O noble age who place their only blisse.		24	1st Eclogues	9	69
Oh when will men leave off to judge by haire, ...		25	1st Eclogues	9	93

343

O   (CONTINUED)   PAGE   TITLE   LINE

But o happy be you, which safe from fyry reflection. . . . .   31 1st Eclogues 13   11
But yet, alas! O but yet alas! our happs be but hard happs,.   32 1st Eclogues 13   37
Oh no, no, hardye shepeheard, worth can never enter a title,   34 1st Eclogues 13   82
Dorus. O glittring miseries of man, if this be the fortune .   34 1st Eclogues 13   89
"Onley Juell, O only Juell, which only deservest . . . . . .   36 1st Eclogues 13   147
O descende for a while, from this greate height to behold
    me . . . .   36 1st Eclogues 13   149
O be it so, graunte such an event, O Gods, that event give..   37 1st Eclogues 13   169
O heavenly soule, in humaine shape conteind: . . . .   38 Arcadia II   15   2
This vowe receave, this vowe o Gods maintaine; . . . .   40 Arcadia II   18   5
Make me, o vertuous Shame, thy lawes neglect.. . . . .   40 Arcadia II   18   12
O Chastitie, the chiefe of heavenly lightes, ...   40 Arcadia II   18   13
Yet thus much Love, O Love, I crave of thee: . . . .   41 Arcadia II   20   13
O only sonne that suche a fruite can breede. . . . .   43 Arcadia II   23   3
O blessed sonne whence all this blessing goes. . . . .   43 Arcadia II   23   6
O cruell sonne thy hate this harme dothe breede. . . . . . .   43 Arcadia II   24   3
R. O foolish thing, which glory doeste destroye. . . . . . .   46 2nd Eclogues 27   19
P. O glorious title of a foolish toye. . . . .   46 2nd Eclogues 27   20
R. O sacred Reason, helpe our vertuous toiles. . . . .   46 2nd Eclogues 27   23
P. O Passion, passe on feeble Reason's spoiles.. . . . . . .   46 2nd Eclogues 27   24
O then it shines; then are the heav'ns distributed,. . . . .   49 2nd Eclogues 28   65
O heards take heed; for I a woolfe have found; . . . .   50 2nd Eclogues 28   83
O sheepheards' boyes, eschue these tongues of venome,. . . .   50 2nd Eclogues 28   87
O tongues right ladders made to clime dishonour, ...   50 2nd Eclogues 28   90
Nico. O Faunes, O Fairies all, and do you see, ...   54 2nd Eclogues 29   63
Pas. O Nymphes, I tell you newes, for Pas you knowe: . . . .   54 2nd Eclogues 29   66
Unto my pipe, O Nimphes, nowe helpe my pipe, ...   54 2nd Eclogues 29   73
Nico. O if I had a ladder for the skies, ...   55 2nd Eclogues 29   117
Pas. O if I had Apollo's golden carre, ...   56 2nd Eclogues 29   120
Nico. Nothing (O Leuca) shall thy fame deface, ...   56 2nd Eclogues 29   123
Pas. Thy name (O Cosma) shall with praise be spread, ...   56 2nd Eclogues 29   126
Erona dye? O heaven (if heaven there be) . . . .   58 2nd Eclogues 30   59
Boulon. O man, take heed, how thou the Gods do move. . . . .   59 2nd Eclogues 30   65
O Vertue weake, shall death his triumph set. . . . .   59 2nd Eclogues 30   92
And shall (o me) all this in ashes rest? . . . .   60 2nd Eclogues 30   101
O Mars, for what doth serve thy armed axe? . . . .   60 2nd Eclogues 30   110
O Venus (if her praise no envy frames, ...   60 2nd Eclogues 30   113
O eyes of mine, where once she saw her face, ...   60 2nd Eclogues 30   116
O braine, where thought of her hath onely place; . . . . . .   60 2nd Eclogues 30   118
O hand, which toucht her hand when we did part;. . . . . . .   60 2nd Eclogues 30   119
O lippes, that kist that hand with my teares sprent; . . . .   60 2nd Eclogues 30   120
O toonge, then dumbe, not daring tell my smart;. . . . . . .   60 2nd Eclogues 30   121
O soule, whose love in her is onely spent, ...   60 2nd Eclogues 30   122
Oh! I do know what guest I have mett; it is Echo. 'T is
    Echo . . . .   63 2nd Eclogues 31   3
O poisonous medecin! what worse to me can be then it? It...   63 2nd Eclogues 31   7
Oh! what is it? what is it that may be a salve to my Love?
    Love.. . . . .   63 2nd Eclogues 31   12
O much more then words: those words serv'd more to me
    blesse Lesse. . . . .   64 2nd Eclogues 31   31
Oh when shall I be knowne, wher most to be knowne I do
    longe Long. . . . .   64 2nd Eclogues 31   32
Horrible is this blasphemy unto the most holy. O lie.. . . .   65 2nd Eclogues 31   45
O sweet woods the delight of solitarines!. . . . .   68 2nd Eclogues 34   1
Above line repeated at following locations . . . .   69 2nd Eclogues 34   15
                                           . . . .   69 2nd Eclogues 34   29
O how much I do like your solitarines! . . . .   68 2nd Eclogues 34   2
Above line repeated at following location. . . . .   69 2nd Eclogues 34   16
O how well I do like your solitarines! . . . .   69 2nd Eclogues 34   30
Oh! if such a one have bent to a lonely life . . . .   69 2nd Eclogues 34   39
O Words which fall like sommer deaw on me, ...   76 Arcadia III 46   1
O breath more sweete, then is the growing beane, ...   76 Arcadia III 46   2
O toong in which, all honyed likoures bee, ...   76 Arcadia III 46   3
O voice that doth, the Thrush in shrilnes staine,. . . . . .   76 Arcadia III 46   4
O brest in which two white sheepe swell in pride:. . . . . .   76 Arcadia III 46   10
Do not disdaine, o streight up raised Pine,. . . . .   77 Arcadia III 47   1
By her who was (O blessed you) content,. . . . .   78 Arcadia III 49   5
And so by you (O blessed you) hath sent, ...   78 Arcadia III 49   7
And while o sleepe thou closest up her sight,. . . . .   79 Arcadia III 51   5
O harbour all her partes in easefull plighte:. . . . .   79 Arcadia III 51   7
But yet o dreame, if thou wilt not departe . . . .   79 Arcadia III 51   9
O Titan faire the giver of the daie? . . . .   80 Arcadia III 52   2
O Stealing time the subject of delaie, ...   80 Arcadia III 53   1
Mine owne? o word on whose sweete sound doth pray. . . . . .   80 Arcadia III 53   5
O time, become the chariot of my joyes:. . . . .   80 Arcadia III 53   9
As oh! my selfe, whose woes are never lighte . . . .   82 Arcadia III 56   9
O heav'n awake shewe forth thy stately face, ...   91 3rd Eclogues 63   10
O Himen long their coupled joyes maintaine.. . . . .   91 3rd Eclogues 63   9
Above line repeated at following locations . . . .   91 3rd Eclogues 63   18
                                           . . . .   91 3rd Eclogues 63   27
                                           . . . .   92 3rd Eclogues 63   36
                                           . . . .   92 3rd Eclogues 63   45
                                           . . . .   92 3rd Eclogues 63   54
                                           . . . .   93 3rd Eclogues 63   63
                                           . . . .   93 3rd Eclogues 63   72
                                           . . . .   93 3rd Eclogues 63   81
                                           . . . .   93 3rd Eclogues 63   90
"O beasts, take heed what you of me desire.. . . . . 100 3rd Eclogues 66   72
But yet o man, rage not beyond thy neede:. . . . . 103 3rd Eclogues 66   148

O

(CONTINUED)	PAGE	TITLE	LINE
O Histor, seeke within thy selfe to flourish:.	106	3rd Eclogues 67	109
O Night, the ease of care, the pledge of pleasure, ...	108	Arcadia IV 69	1
O nature doting olde, o blinded nature,.	109	Arcadia IV 70	19
O that we had, to make our woes more publique, ...	109	Arcadia IV 70	25
Klaius. O Mercurie, foregoer to the evening, ...	111	4th Eclogues 71	7
O heavenlie huntresse of the savage mountaines,.	111	4th Eclogues 71	8
O lovelie starre, entitled of the morning, ...	111	4th Eclogues 71	9
O faire, o onely faire, from thee, alas, ...	116	4th Eclogues 72	96
Since thou from me (o me) o Sunne didst passe.	116	4th Eclogues 72	98
But now an ende, (o Klaius) now an ende, ...	116	4th Eclogues 72	102
The moone a sunder rent (O godes, o pardon me, ...	118	4th Eclogues 73	55
And bending humbled eyes (o eyes the Sunne of sight)	119	4th Eclogues 73	91
Is this thy fruite O strife? those thousand churches hie,. .	119	4th Eclogues 73	111
Was it a dreame? O dreame, how hast thou wrought in me,. . .	121	4th Eclogues 73	181
And thou o traytour Sleepe, made for to be our rest, ...	121	4th Eclogues 73	183
O cowarde Cupid thus doost thou my honour keepe, ...	122	4th Eclogues 73	185
O you (alas so I rind) cause of his onely ruine.	122	4th Eclogues 74	4
Dread not a whit (O goodly cruell) that pittie may enter . .	122	4th Eclogues 74	5
O faire, O fairest, are such the triumphs to thy fairnesse?.	123	4th Eclogues 74	31
Unto revenge? O sweete, on a wretch wilt thou be revenged? .	123	4th Eclogues 74	37
Or with a fair hand's nailes (o hand which nailes me to this death).	123	4th Eclogues 74	55
O wretch, what do I say? should that faire face be defaced?.	124	4th Eclogues 74	57
O not but such love you say you could have afoorded, ...	124	4th Eclogues 74	63
O sweet simplicitie: from whence should Love be so learned?.	124	4th Eclogues 74	65
Shall I not? o may I not thus yet refresh the remembrance, .	124	4th Eclogues 74	71
And you o trees (if any life there lies.	125	4th Eclogues 75	4
And you, o flowers, which sometimes Princes were,.	125	4th Eclogues 75	25
O Hiacinthe let Ai be on thee still.	125	4th Eclogues 75	29
O Echo, all these woods with roaring fill, ...	126	4th Eclogues 75	31
O light of Sunne, which is entit'led day,.	126	4th Eclogues 75	52
O well thou doost that thou no longer bidest;.	126	4th Eclogues 75	53
O Phoebus with good cause thy face thou hidest,.	126	4th Eclogues 75	55
O Philomela with thy brest oppressed	126	4th Eclogues 75	61
And if, o Sunne, thou ever didst appeare,.	127	4th Eclogues 75	70
O notes of mine your selves together tie:.	127	4th Eclogues 75	76
O Elements, by whose (they say) contention,.	128	4th Eclogues 75	106
O Phisicke's power, which (some say) hath refrayned.	128	4th Eclogues 75	109
Cease Muse therfore: thy dart o Death applie;.	129	4th Eclogues 75	141
Farewell o Sunn, Arcadia's clearest light:.	129	4th Eclogues 76	1
Farewell o pearl, the poore man's plenteous treasure:. . . .	129	4th Eclogues 76	2
Farewell o golden staffe, the weake man's might:.	129	4th Eclogues 76	3
Farewell o Joy, the wofull's onely pleasure.	129	4th Eclogues 76	4
I yeeld, o Love, unto thy loathed yoke,.	135	Cert Sonnets 1	9
O Philomela faire, o take some gladnesse,.	137	Cert Sonnets 4	9
Above line repeated at following location.	137	Cert Sonnets 4	21
O My thoughtes' sweete foode, my my onely owner, ...	138	Cert Sonnets 5	1
O my heavens for taste by thie heavenly pleasure,.	138	Cert Sonnets 5	2
O the fayre Nymphe borne to doo woemen honor,.	138	Cert Sonnets 5	3
O hideous absence, by thee am I thralled.	138	Cert Sonnets 5	13
O my vayne worde gon, Ruyn of my glory...	138	Cert Sonnets 5	14
O deue allegiance, by thee am I called	138	Cert Sonnets 5	15
Then come, O come, then do I come, receyve (mee),.	138	Cert Sonnets 5	21
O my Thoughtes' sweete foode, my (my) onely Owner, ...	138	Cert Sonnets 5	25
O my heavens for Taste, by thy heavenly pleasure,.	138	Cert Sonnets 5	26
O the fayre Nymphe borne to doo woemen honor,.	138	Cert Sonnets 5	27
Thy cries, o Babie, set mine head on aking:.	139	Cert Sonnets 6	2
O Faire, o sweet, when I do looke on thee, ...	139	Cert Sonnets 7	1
Above line repeated at following locations	139	Cert Sonnets 7	11
. . . .	140	Cert Sonnets 7	21
. . . .	140	Cert Sonnets 7	31
Her legges (O legges) her ay well stepping feete..	141	Cert Sonnets 9	8
O paine I now recant the praise I gave,.	141	Cert Sonnets 9	13
And have I heard her say, "o cruell paine!".	142	Cert Sonnets 11	1
O happie Dove if she no bondage tried:	144	Cert Sonnets 15	13
O this it is, the knotted straw is found	146	Cert Sonnets 17	16
O no, O no, tryall onely shewse.	153	Cert Sonnets 24	10
Words, o words of heavenlie knowledge, ...	157	Cert Sonnets 27	35
What changes here, o haire,.	157	Cert Sonnets 28	1
O teares of guilefull breast,.	158	Cert Sonnets 28	14
Tell me o haire of gold, ...	158	Cert Sonnets 28	17
Leave me o Love, which reachest but to dust, ...	161	Cert Sonnets 32	1
O take fast hold, let that light be thy guide, ...	162	Cert Sonnets 32	9
In truth, o Love, with what a boyish kind.	170	Astrophil 11	1
O no, her heart is such a Cittadell, ...	171	Astrophil 12	12
O how for joy he leapes, o how he crowes,.	173	Astrophil 17	12
O let me prop my mind, yet in his growth	174	Astrophil 19	12
O fooles, or over-wise, alas the race.	176	Astrophil 23	12
With how sad steps, o Moone, thou climb'st the skies,. . . .	180	Astrophil 31	1
Then ev'n of fellowship, o Moone, tell me.	180	Astrophil 31	9
I might, unhappie word, o me, I might, ...	181	Astrophil 33	1
How faire a day was neare, o punisht eyes, ...	181	Astrophil 33	13
Come sleepe, o sleepe, the certaine knot of peace, ...	184	Astrophil 39	1
O make in me those civill warres to cease;	184	Astrophil 39	7
O Stella deare, how much thy power hath wrought, ...	184	Astrophil 40	2
O do not let thy Temple be destroyd.	185	Astrophil 40	14
O eyes, which do the Spheares of beautie move, ...	185	Astrophil 42	1
O eyes, where humble lookes most glorious prove, ...	185	Astrophil 42	5
Do not, o do not from poore me remove, ...	186	Astrophil 42	7

345

O

	(CONTINUED)	PAGE	TITLE		LINE
Yet still on me, o eyes, dart downe your rayes:.	186	Astrophil	42	11
Her face? O Love, a Rogue thou then shouldst be, ...	187	Astrophil	46	6
Unkind, I love you not: O me, that eye	188	Astrophil	47	13
What ever may ensue, o let me be	188	Astrophil	48	5
O looke, o shine, o let me die and see.	188	Astrophil	48	8
That Stella (o deare name) that Stella is.	190	Astrophil	52	6
O voice, o face, maugre my speeche's might,.	194	Astrophil	58	12
O Doctor Cupid, thou for me reply, ...	195	Astrophil	61	12
O Grammer rules, o now your vertues show;.	196	Astrophil	63	1
For Grammer sayes (o this deare Stella weighe,).	196	Astrophil	63	12
O give my passions leave to run their race:.	198	Astrophil	64	2
O thinke I then, what paradise of joy.	200	Astrophil	68	13
O joy, too high for my low stile to show:.	200	Astrophil	69	1
O blisse, fit for a nobler state then me:.	200	Astrophil	69	2
My spring appeares, o see what here doth grow.	200	Astrophil	69	8
I, I, o I may say, that she is mine.	200	Astrophil	69	11
O heav'nly foole, thy most kisse-worthie face, ...	203	Astrophil	73	12
O how the pleasant aires of true love be	205	Astrophil	78	1
O kisse, which doest those ruddie gemmes impart, ...	207	Astrophil	81	1
O kisse, which soules, even soules together ties, ...	207	Astrophil	81	5
O ease your hand, treate not so hard your slave:	212	Astrophil	86	9
Not them, o no, but you in them I love.	225	Astrophil	91	14
O God, thinke you that satisfies my care?.	225	Astrophil	92	8
O fate, o fault, o curse, child of my blisse,.	227	Astrophil	93	1
O teares, no teares, but raine from beautie's skies, . . .	231	Astrophil	100	1
O honied sighs, which from that breast do rise,.	231	Astrophil	100	5
O plaints conserv'd in such a sugred phraise,.	231	Astrophil	100	9
O happie Tems, that didst my Stella beare, ...	232	Astrophil	103	1
They did themselves (o sweetest prison) twine.	232	Astrophil	103	8
With sight thereof cride out; o faire disgrace,.	233	Astrophil	103	13
O absent presence Stella is not here;.	235	Astrophil	106	1
O let not fooles in me thy workes reprove, ...	236	Astrophil	107	13
But o foole, thinke of the danger, ...	203	A&S 2nd Song		17
Oh sweet kisse, but ah she is waking,.	203	A&S 2nd Song		25
O stones, o trees, learne hearing, Stella singeth.	208	A&S 3rd Song		6
O birds, o beasts, looke Love, lo, Stella shineth.	209	A&S 3rd Song		12
O eyes, o eares of men, how are you charmed!	209	A&S 3rd Song		18
I said, my soule was thine (o that I then had lyed). . . .	212	A&S 5th Song		9
And o my Muse, though oft you luld her in your lap,. . . .	213	A&S 5th Song		25
O deare life, when shall it be,.	225	A&S 10th Song		1
O if my self find not, ...	226	A&S 10th Song		7
O my thought my thoughts surcease, ...	227	A&S 10th Song		43
O unjustest fortune's sway,.	235	A&S 11th Song		43
O You that heare this voice, ...	215	A&S 6th Song		1
O you that see this face,.	215	A&S 6th Song		2
O let them heare these sacred tunes, and learne in wonder's schooles,.	217	A&S 7th Song		5
O let them see these heavenly beames, and in faire letters reede.	217	A&S 7th Song		11
"Graunt, o graunt, but speech alas,.	219	A&S 8th Song		45
Graunt, o me, what am I saying?.	219	A&S 8th Song		47
"Graunt, o deere, on knees I pray, ...	219	A&S 8th Song		49
Stella whom o heavens do blesse, ...	221	A&S 9th Song		18
And say (O kings) yet have I set my King upon.	271	Psalm II		13
Therfore (O Kings), be wise, O Rulers rule your mind,. . .	271	Psalm II		23
O they be rightly blest.	272	Psalm II		32
Heare me, O heare me when I call	273	Psalm IV		1
O God, God of my Equity, ...	273	Psalm IV		2
O men, whose Fathers were but men, ...	273	Psalm IV		6
O tremble then with awfull will:	273	Psalm IV		16
Ponder the words, O lord, that I do say, ...	274	Psalm V		1
O, hearken to my voice, which calls on Thee, ...	274	Psalm V		3
Guide me, O in thy justice be my guide:.	275	Psalm V		22
Mercy, O Mercy lord, for Mercy's sake, ...	276	Psalm VI		13
O Lord my God, Thou art my trustfull stay.	277	Psalm VII		1
O save me from this Persecution's showre:.	277	Psalm VII		2
O lord, my God, if I did not forbeare.	277	Psalm VII		7
Arise, O lord, in wrath thy self upsett.	277	Psalm VII		16
Therfore, O lord, lift up Thy throne on high	277	Psalm VII		20
O let their wickednesse no longer bide.	277	Psalm VII		25
O lord that rul'st Our mortall lyne.	278	Psalm VIII		1
Above line repeated at following location.	279	Psalm VIII		33
With all my heart O lord I will prayse Thee, ...	279	Psalm IX		1
O Lord most high.	279	Psalm IX		5
O bragging Foe, where is the endlesse wast.	280	Psalm IX		16
O prayse the lord, this Syon dweller good, ...	280	Psalm IX		31
With terrors great, O Lord, do thou them fright:	281	Psalm IX		63
O God our only starr,.	281	Psalm X		2
O let proud him be throughly caught.	281	Psalm X		7
O with how simple look	282	Psalm X		41
O lord Our only God, ...	282	Psalm X		50
O be thou still the Orphan's aide.	283	Psalm X		77
But Thou (O lord) give them a thorough fall, ...	284	Psalm XII		7
Then Thou (O lord) shalt keep the Good stil sure.	285	Psalm XII		22
How long, O lord, shall I forgotten be?.	285	Psalm XIII		1
O madness of these folks, thus loosely led,.	286	Psalm XIV		13
In Tabernacle Thyne, O lord, who shall remayne?.	287	Psalm XV		1
O let my sentence passe from Thyne own face;	289	Psalm XVII		5
Shew then O Lord Thy wondrous kindnesse show, ...	290	Psalm XVII		21

O   (CONTINUED)   PAGE   TITLE   LINE

Thee will I love, O Lord, with all my heart's delight, . . .   290 Psalm XVIII   1
With blasting breath O Lord, that in thy chiding went. . . .   291 Psalm XVIII   33
O law of his How perfect 'tis. . . . .   294 Psalm XIX   29
O lord cleanse me from faults that be. . . . .   295 Psalm XIX   51
O God my God I cry while day appeareth; . . . .   298 Psalm XXII   5
O God the night is privy to my plaint, ...   298 Psalm XXII   7
O be not farr, since pain so nearly presseth,. . . . . . .   299 Psalm XXII   25
But be not farr O Lord, my strength, my comfort; . . . . .   299 Psalm XXII   45
From lion's mouth O help, and shew to heare me . . . . . .   299 Psalm XXII   49
Indeed O you, you that be such of mind,. . . . .   300 Psalm XXII   63
To thee, O Lord most just, ...   302 Psalm XXV   1
Ev'n for Thy mercy's sake, O Lord. . . . .   303 Psalm XXV   30
O Lord for Thy name's sake . . . .   304 Psalm XXV   43
Oh, is there one with his Feare fraught? . . . .   304 Psalm XXV   47
O look, O help, let mercy fall,. . . . .   304 Psalm XXV   59
Now made, O Lord maintain, ...   304 Psalm XXV   68
O Lord from all his troubles fell. . . . .   305 Psalm XXV   78
Prove me O Lord most high, ...   305 Psalm XXVI   7
O Lord I will. . . . .   308 Psalm XXVII   41
Forsake not me, O leave me not,. . . . .   308 Psalm XXVII   46
O God of my. . . . .   308 Psalm XXVII   47
Oh, give me not, for there are sproong . . . .   308 Psalm XXVII   56
O my strength stop not Thine eare, ...   308 Psalm XXVIII   2
O lord Thou hast exalted me. . . . .   310 Psalm XXX   1
Thy endless prayse: O God my King. . . . .   311 Psalm XXX   38
O lord that art the God of verity. . . . .   312 Psalm XXXI   15
O Lord, of Thee let me still mercy winn, ...   312 Psalm XXXI   25
Let me not tast of shame, O lord most high,. . . . .   313 Psalm XXXI   45
Oh! of thy grace what endlesse pleasure flowes . . . . . .   313 Psalm XXXI   52
Oh be not like a horse or mule,. . . . .   315 Psalm XXXII   31
Rejoice in God, O ye . . . .   316 Psalm XXXIII   1
O prayse with harp the lord, ...   316 Psalm XXXIII   7
O now accord . . . .   316 Psalm XXXIII   8
O now be bent. . . . .   316 Psalm XXXIII   11
O let thy mercy great. . . . .   318 Psalm XXXIII   82
Thy force O Lord against their force oppose, ...   321 Psalm XXXV   2
That seek my bane, O make me understand. . . . .   321 Psalm XXXV   5
Ev'en bones shall say O God, who is Thy peere, ...   321 Psalm XXXV   21
Oh! on my soul let not these tumults hitt. . . . .   322 Psalm XXXV   44
O lord, do not absent Thy self from me!. . . . .   322 Psalm XXXV   56
O Soul, rejoyce, we made this wretch our prey. . . . . . .   323 Psalm XXXV   62
O Lord how excellent a thing . . . .   324 Psalm XXXVI   19
O then extend Thy loving heart . . . .   324 Psalm XXXVI   27
O then Thy righteousness impart. . . . .   324 Psalm XXXVI   29
Hast O Lord, that I be stayd . . . .   329 Psalm XXXVIII   64
This being thus, For what O Lord wait I? . . . .   330 Psalm XXXIX   23
O helpe o help me, this farr yet I crave,. . . . .   330 Psalm XXXIX   25
O he indeed is blessed,. . . . .   331 Psalm XL   15
Vouchsafe me help O Lord, and help with hast;. . . . . . .   332 Psalm XL   51
My God, O make no stay.. . . . .   332 Psalm XL   70
O heale my soul, let there Thy cure begin. . . . .   333 Psalm XLI   15
O yea, my Friend to whom I did impart. . . . .   333 Psalm XLI   29
Therfore, O Lord, abandond thus of all,. . . . .   333 Psalm XLI   33
Whome Thou, O place of places all, dost place. . . . . . .   334 Psalm XLI   43
Oh so! O be it so! . . . .   334 Psalm XLI   48
I will say: O lord my tower, ...   335 Psalm XLII   41
Dick. Oh hence! o cruell word! which even doggs do hate: .   344 Possibly   1   47
Yeelde yeelde, O yeelde, you that this Forte do holde, . .   345 Possibly   4   1
Then to Desier's desire, O yeelde O yeelde.. . . . .   345 Possibly   4   4
Yeelde yeelde O yeelde, trust not on beautie's pride,. . .   345 Possibly   4   5
Claymes but to gaine his due, O yeelde O yeelde. . . . . .   345 Possibly   4   8
Yeelde yeelde O yeelde, who first this Fort did make,. . .   345 Possibly   4   9
Defence herein doth wrong, O yeelde O yeelde,. . . . . . .   345 Possibly   4   12
Yeelde yeelde O yeelde, now is it time to yeelde,. . . . .   345 Possibly   4   13
Before thassault beginne, O yeelde O yeelde. . . . .   345 Possibly   4   14
But most cryed, "O well broke": O foole full gaily blest:.   241 Other Poems   1   5
Miso mine owne pigsnie, thou shalt heare news o' Damaetas.   241 Other Poems.   2   1
But you, o you, that thinke not teares too deare . . . . .   242 Other Poems   4   9
Ther was (o seldome blessed word of was!). . . . .   242 Other Poems   4   17
One day (o day, that shin'de to make them darke!). . . . .   243 Other Poems   4   65
(O happy Dove that art compar'd to hir!) . . . .   251 Other Poems   4   354
Happy, o happy! if they so might bide, ...   252 Other Poems   4   401
"O earth, once answere give, ...   256 Other Poems   5   14
"Tell me o Turtle true, ...   258 Other Poems   5   79
O fortune too too badd,. . . . .   259 Other Poems   5   98
Oh! what doth wailing winne? . . . .   259 Other Poems   5   103

OAK

The ancient oke well makes a fired blocke: 25   1st Eclogues   9   87
Olde aged oke cutt downe, of newe works serves to the
     building:.   36   1st Eclogues 13   134
Like Oke and Mistletoe..   92   3rd Eclogues 63   51

OAK'S

But thus in oke's true shade recounted he.   99   3rd Eclogues 66   41

OATH

That they by solemne oth their Deities would binde . . . .   121 4th Eclogues 73   156

OATHS

But now we muste needs yeelde, to what our othes require". .   121 4th Eclogues 73   169
If othes might serve, even by the Stygian lake,. . . . . .   146 Cert Sonnets 17   6

```
OBEISANCE                                                    PAGE    TITLE        LINE
    Commands all creatures, to yeeld obeysance . . . . . . . .  68  2nd Eclogues 33   22
OBEY
    Give us foresightfull mindes: give us minds to obaye . . . .  45  Arcadia II   26   11
    So well she can command, and yet obay, . . . . . . . . . .  106  3rd Eclogues 67   89
    And having bound them fast by Styx, they should obaye. . .  121  4th Eclogues 73  161
OBEYED
    "Venus come on": said she, "Diane you are obaide". . . . . .  119  4th Eclogues 73   78
OBJECT
    Barr'd from their chiefest object of delightfulnesse,. . . .  51  2nd Eclogues 28  109
    Nor ey receaves due object,. . . . . . . . . . . . . . . .   66  2nd Eclogues 32   38
    Shall I not once object, that you, you graunted a favour . .  124  4th Eclogues 74   73
    In object best to knit and strength our sight, . . . . . .  168  Astrophil     7    6
    (As his sole object of felicitie). . . . . . . . . . . . .  212  Astrophil    86    7
    Dead glasse, doost thou thy object so imbrace, . . . . . .  235  Astrophil   105    3
OBJECTION
    Her eyes so maistering me, that such objection . . . . . .   16  1st Eclogues  7   68
OBJECTS
    Leave sense, and those which sense's objects be. . . . . .  169  Astrophil    10    7
    Both in their objects such,. . . . . . . . . . . . . . . .  216  A&S 6th Song       41
    Their sences rude plaine objects only move,. . . . . . . .  245  Other Poems   4  143
OBLATION
    And for a sure sacrifice I do dayly oblation offer . . . .   37  1st Eclogues 13  170
OBSCURED
    This cheerefull aire with your obscured cheere,. . . . . .  127  4th Eclogues 75   68
OBSERVE
    And laying downe my head, did nature's rule observe, . . . .  117  4th Eclogues 73   27
OBSERVING
    While thy known course, observing nature's right,. . . . .   82  Arcadia III  56   11
OBTAIN
    When being askt, now that he did obtaine . . . . . . . . .    4  Lady of May   3    3
    Or wrapt in flesh what do they here obtaine, . . . . . . .   57  2nd Eclogues 30   15
    Or for my love some love I might obtaine, . . . . . . . . .  148  Cert Sonnets 19   10
    Knowledge might pitie winne, and pitie grace obtaine,. . . .  165  Astrophil     1    4
    That Ballance weigh'd what sword did late obtaine, . . . .  204  Astrophil    75    8
    Let my whispering voyce obtaine, . . . . . . . . . . . . .  210  A&S 4th Song        3
    Lord, of Thy Holy Hill who shall the rest obtayne? . . . .  287  Psalm XV            2
OBTAINED
    At length obtain the point of his desire, . . . . . . . . .    4  Lady of May   3    2
    Guided so well, that I obtain'd the prize, . . . . . . . .  185  Astrophil    41    2
OBTAINETH
    That who so that grace obtaineth,. . . . . . . . . . . . .  140  Cert Sonnets  7   25
OCCASION
    From any joy, which might her griefe occasion. . . . . . .   51  2nd Eclogues 28  122
    Thou art the father of occasion deare: . . . . . . . . . .   81  Arcadia III  53   12
OCCUPATION
    Now my hoarse voice doth faile this occupation,. . . . . .   19  1st Eclogues  7  170
    But now hoarse voyce, doth faile this occupation,. . . . .   20  1st Eclogues  7 V970
OCEAN
    First the rivers shall ceasse to repay their fludds to the
        Ocean:. . . . . . . . . . . . . . . . . . . . . . . .   33  1st Eclogues 13   65
    For by his power the land upon the Ocean raigneth, . . . .  302  Psalm XXIV          3
OCEANS
    What Oceans of delight in me do flow. . . . . . . . . . . .  200  Astrophil    69    4
ODDS
    Such oddes I willing lay; for him and you I know. . . . . .   53  2nd Eclogues 29   48
    Mock'st thou those Diamonds which only be matcht by the
        gods Ods . . . . . . . . . . . . . . . . . . . . . . .   65  2nd Eclogues 31   47
    Ods? what an ods is there since them to the heav'ns I
        prefer Erre. . . . . . . . . . . . . . . . . . . . . .   65  2nd Eclogues 31   48
    But, but (alas) night's side the ods hath fur, . . . . . .  229  Astrophil    96   12
ODIOUS
    The day seemes long, but night is odious . . . . . . . . .  253  Other Poems   4  435
ODORED
    Thinke now no more to heare of warme fine odourd snow, . . .  213  A&S 5th Song       37
ODORS
    The Indian odours doth excell. . . . . . . . . . . . . . .   87  Arcadia III  62   64
O'ER
    I set you ore the flock I dearly love, . . . . . . . . . .   26  1st Eclogues 10    2
    To worthy Coredens he gave me o'er. . . . . . . . . . . . .   99  3rd Eclogues 66   40
    I hosts by thee orecome, by Thee ore walls I fly;. . . . .  292  Psalm XVIII        54
    He ran, but ran with eye ore shoulder cast,. . . . . . . .  249  Other Poems   4  289
O'ERCAST
    Sleepy darkness doth o're cast,. . . . . . . . . . . . . .  288  Psalm XVI          22
O'ERCASTING
    These doubting clouds ore-casting heav'nly braine, . . . .  245  Other Poems   4  127
O'ERCHARGED
    Let folke orecharg'd with braine against me crie,. . . . .  198  Astrophil    64    4
    Which now my breast orecharg'd to Musicke lendeth? . . . .  196  A&S 1st Song        2
    Above line repeated at following location. . . . . . . . .  197  A&S 1st Song       34
O'ERCOME
    Old age orecome, the greater honour gives. . . . . . . . .   39  Arcadia II   15   12
    R. though we cannot orecome, our cause is just. . . . . . .   47  2nd Eclogues 27   31
    P. let us orecome, and let us be unjust. . . . . . . . . .   47  2nd Eclogues 27   32
    I hosts by thee orecome, by Thee ore walls I fly;. . . . .  292  Psalm XVIII        54
O'ERFLOWS
    Leave of my sheepe: it is no tyme to feede,. . . . . . . .   43  Arcadia II   24    4
O'ERHEATED
    Whose heart with these huge flames, like wax o're heated,. .  299  Psalm XXII         33
```

```
O'ERTAKE                                                        PAGE    TITLE            LINE
  When, when will death o'retake this wretched wight . . . . .  333 Psalm XLI             19
O'ERTHROWN
  In which do light small birds of thoughts orethrowne:. . . .   18 1st Eclogues    7   141
  Who seemed orethrown was mistresse of the field. . . . . . .  251 Other Poems     4   347
O'ERTHWART
  Still my orethwart neighbour is. . . . . . . . . . . . . . .  329 Psalm XXXVIII        51
OFF
  Oh when will men leave off to judge by haire,. . . . . . . .   25 1st Eclogues    9    93
  Who of his tongue the lickowr gladly powrs,. . . . . . . . .   28 1st Eclogues   10    71
  Leave of my sheepe: it is no tyme to feede,. . . . . . . . .   43 Arcadia II     24     1
  Leave of my sheepe, my shower of teeres oreflowes, . . . . .   43 Arcadia II     24     4
  Leave of my sheepe, my sighes burne up your filde, . . . . .   43 Arcadia II     24     7
  Leave of my sheepe, sorrowe hathe hoysed sayle,. . . . . . .   44 Arcadia II     24    10
  Leave off my sheep my mourninge to maintayne,. . . . . . . .   44 Arcadia II     24    13
  Thou art farre off, thy kingdome is above: . . . . . . . . .   72 Arcadia III    38     7
  Yet first but wooll, or fethers off he teard:. . . . . . . .  102 3rd Eclogues   66   143
  They leave off al, and say, death comes too eagerlie.. . . .  128 4th Eclogues   75   114
  And thence cast off, where his sweete hurt he found, . . . .  144 Cert Sonnets   15     6
  Leave that sir Phip, least off your necke be wroong. . . . .  208 Astrophil      83    14
  His farr off sight now hoodwinkt is, . . . . . . . . . . . .  282 Psalm X              47
  And quite cutt off, with helpless end. . . . . . . . . . . .  327 Psalm XXXVII         96
  Farr off wend; . . . . . . . . . . . . . . . . . . . . . . .  328 Psalm XXXVIII        32
  Shaking off all sadnes,. . . . . . . . . . . . . . . . . . .  336 Psalm XLIII          21
  Their snowy haire teare off in melting paine.. . . . . . . .  254 Other Poems     4   478
OFFENCE
  Thy words, though full of malapert offence,. . . . . . . . .   25 1st Eclogues    9   108
  As th'offence was done, and goe beyond if he can.. . . . . .  123 4th Eclogues   74    40
  All my'offence was Love: with Love then must I be chastned,.  123 4th Eclogues   74    41
  Envious wits what hath bene mine offence,. . . . . . . . . .  233 Astrophil     104     1
OFFENCES
  Boulon. Who still doth seeke against himselfe offences,. . .   62 2nd Eclogues   30   167
  Praesumptuous sins' offences, . . . . . . . . . . . . . . .  295 Psalm XIX            54
OFFEND
  And yet the prince (that lov'd him) not offend.. . . . . . .   95 3rd Eclogues   64    54
  Feare to offend, will worthie to appeare,. . . . . . . . . .  202 Astrophil      72    10
OFFENDED
  His mother deare Cupid offended late,. . . . . . . . . . . .  173 Astrophil      17     1
OFFER
  And for a sure sacrifice I do dayly oblation offer . . . . .   37 1st Eclogues   13   170
  That in my heart I offer still to thee,. . . . . . . . . . .  185 Astrophil      40    13
  This large offer of our blisse,. . . . . . . . . . . . . . .  211 A&S 4th Song         32
OFFEREDST
  Reason thou kneel'dst, and offeredst straight to prove . . .  170 Astrophil      10    13
OFFERING
  Thou sacrifice nor offring,. . . . . . . . . . . . . . . . .  331 Psalm XL             25
  Burnt offring nor sin offring, . . . . . . . . . . . . . . .  331 Psalm XL             26
OFFERINGS
  Our offrings spoil'd, our priests from priesthood are
    displac'd. . . . . . . . . . . . . . . . . . . . . . . . .  119 4th Eclogues   73   110
  Their blood offrings I do shun,. . . . . . . . . . . . . . .  288 Psalm XVI            11
  That in good part he did Thy Offrings take;. . . . . . . . .  296 Psalm XX             12
  Thy offrings so that they to ashes turn. . . . . . . . . . .  296 Psalm XX             15
  Offrings of joy in Temple His, . . . . . . . . . . . . . . .  307 Psalm XXVII          34
OFFICE
  Till now at length that Jove him office gives, . . . . . . .   22 1st Eclogues    8    45
  If you, on you I lay what in my office be. . . . . . . . . .  120 4th Eclogues   73   134
  While everie office themselves will discharge, . . . . . . .  210 Astrophil      85     7
OFFSPRING
  When that we see our ofspring gaily bent,. . . . . . . . . .   28 1st Eclogues   10    59
  To see her ofspring seeke a good increase, . . . . . . . . .   91 3rd Eclogues   63     2
  As they so theirs, Him shall their ofspring serve, . . . . .  300 Psalm XXII           75
OFT
  Whose face doth oft the bravest sort enchaunt, . . . . . . .    3 Lady of May     1     2
  Your face hurts oft, but still it doth delight,. . . . . . .    3 Lady of May     1     8
  The highest note comes oft from basest mind, . . . . . . . .    4 Lady of May     2    13
  And plaine speach oft then quaint phrase better framed is. .   14 1st Eclogues    7     6
  How oft with raine of teares skies make confession,. . . . .   15 1st Eclogues    7    43
  Lalus. How oft my dolefull Sire cried to me, "tarrie sonne".   16 1st Eclogues    7    49
  When first he spied my love? how oft he said to me,. . . . .   16 1st Eclogues    7    50
  Dorus. How oft, when reason saw love of her harnished. . . .   16 1st Eclogues    7    61
  Nor stormes doo turne: fairenes serves oft to wealth.. . . .   18 1st Eclogues    7   119
  Poore Painters oft with silly Poets joyne, . . . . . . . . .   20 1st Eclogues    8     1
  Oft comes reliefe when most we seeme in trappe.. . . . . . .   23 1st Eclogues    9    24
  We oft are angrier, with the feeble flie . . . . . . . . . .   28 1st Eclogues   10    64
  And preciouse couches full oft are shak't with a feaver. . .   34 1st Eclogues   13    86
  Then kneling to the ground, oft thus do I speake to that
    Image: . . . . . . . . . . . . . . . . . . . . . . . . . .   36 1st Eclogues   13   146
  In meane caves oft treasure abides, to an hostry a king
    comes. . . . . . . . . . . . . . . . . . . . . . . . . . .   36 1st Eclogues   13   153
  And so behinde foule clowdes full oft faire starres do ly
    hidden". . . . . . . . . . . . . . . . . . . . . . . . . .   36 1st Eclogues   13   154
  With flamie breathe doo issue oft in sound:. . . . . . . . .   42 Arcadia II     21     8
  His wings desire oft clipt with desperation: . . . . . . . .   48 2nd Eclogues   28    44
  She oft her lookes, the starres her favour bend to thee: . .   51 2nd Eclogues   28    99
  Dorus. Well do I prove, errour lies oft in zeale,. . . . . .   51 2nd Eclogues   28   103
  Which oft he lifteth up, and stayes his lifted pawe, . . . .   53 2nd Eclogues   29    34
  Nico. Alas how oft I looke on cherries ripe, . . . . . . . .   54 2nd Eclogues   29    75
  Nico. I oft doo sue, and Leuca saith, I shall, . . . . . . .   54 2nd Eclogues   29    87
  Pas. So oft these woods have heard me "Cosma" crie,. . . . .   56 2nd Eclogues   29   132

                                  349
```

OFT	(CONTINUED)	PAGE	TITLE		LINE
Sweete speaking oft a currish hart reclaimes..........		60	2nd Eclogues	30	115
Oft prove I: but what salve, when Reason seeks to be gone?					
One................................		63	2nd Eclogues	31	11
Can fancies want eies, or he fall that steppeth aloft? Oft..		64	2nd Eclogues	31	22
Ofte scorching sonne, ofte clowdie darkenes feares,......		71	Arcadia III	36	9
(Which oft to hope laies out a guilefull baite,........		82	Arcadia III	56	2
Passion rebelde, oft reason's strength hath shaked......		82	Arcadia III	57	4
There ofte steales out that round cleane foote........		89	Arcadia III	62	105
Since Lalus' musick oft doth yeeld you praise,........		92	3rd Eclogues	63	29
Bussing her oft, and in his hart full faine,.........		95	3rd Eclogues	64	51
Of that small light oft watching shepheards see.......		98	3rd Eclogues	66	7
And (but they drad their Prince they ofte should want) ...		101	3rd Eclogues	66	100
Man oft is plag'de with aire, is burnt with fire,......		105	3rd Eclogues	67	67
Which oft hath Echo tir'd in secrete forrests.........		111	4th Eclogues	71	12
Whose footsteps I with kisses oft did trace,.........		115	4th Eclogues	72	73
That thou full oft shalt wish thy judging eyes were blinde".		121	4th Eclogues	73	172
For oft in paine to paine my painefull heart		141	Cert Sonnets	9	3
Fear'st not a face that oft whole harts devowres,......		142	Cert Sonnets	10	10
The wynde most oft the hugest Pine-tree greeves:......		143	Cert Sonnets	12	7
To hie conceits whose fruits are oft but small,.......		144	Cert Sonnets	15	10
Oft have I musde, but now at length I finde,.........		148	Cert Sonnets	20	1
Alas how oft with teares,...................		158	Cert Sonnets	28	13
Oft turning others' leaves, to see if thence would flow...		165	Astrophil	1	7
Yet hiding royall bloud full oft in rurall vaine.......		167	Astrophil	6	8
That her sweete breath makes oft thy flames to rise,....		170	Astrophil	12	4
Who oft fore-judge my after-following race,.........		178	Astrophil	26	13
Because I oft in darke abstracted guise,...........		178	Astrophil	27	1
Which lookes too oft in his unflattring glasse:.......		178	Astrophil	27	10
That makes me oft my best friends overpasse,........		178	Astrophil	27	12
A Prophet oft, and oft an historie,.............		181	Astrophil	32	3
Oft cruell fights well pictured forth do please......		181	Astrophil	34	4
Stella oft sees the verie face of wo		187	Astrophil	45	1
I curst thee oft, I pitie now thy case,...........		187	Astrophil	46	1
For though I oft my selfe of them bemone,..........		189	Astrophil	48	9
Muses, I oft invoked your holy ayde, ...		192	Astrophil	55	1
And oft whole troupes of saddest words I staid,......		192	Astrophil	55	5
He barks, my songs thine owne voyce oft doth prove:....		194	Astrophil	59	6
Oft with true sighes, oft with uncalled teares,......		195	Astrophil	61	1
My friend, that oft saw through all maskes my wo,.....		200	Astrophil	69	5
She oft hath drunke my teares, now hopes to enjoy.....		201	Astrophil	70	3
And oft so clings to my pure Love, that I..........		202	Astrophil	72	2
Love still a boy, and oft a wanton is,...........		203	Astrophil	73	1
Although lesse gifts impe feathers oft on Fame,......		204	Astrophil	75	4
Nay, more foole I, oft suffered you to sleepe.		208	Astrophil	83	7
More oft then to a chamber melodie;.............		209	Astrophil	84	4
That to win me, oft shewes a present pay?.........		223	Astrophil	88	4
But as you with my breast I oft have nurst,........		228	Astrophil	95	3
Though oft himselfe my mate-in-armes he sware.		228	Astrophil	95	8
Shewes her oft at the full her fairest face,.......		229	Astrophil	97	2
With sweete soft shades thou oft invitest me		230	Astrophil	98	5
Sweetnesse, that breathes and pants as oft as she:....		231	Astrophil	101	2
Where those red cheeks, which oft with faire encrease did					
frame..............................		232	Astrophil	102	2
On servants' shame oft Maister's blame doth sit;.....		236	Astrophil	107	12
And o my Muse, though oft you luld her in your lap,....		213	A&S 5th Song		25
But valiant Rebels oft in fooles' mouthes purchase fame: ..		214	A&S 5th Song		67
For proof, oft lain in wait he is.............		282	Psalm X		31
He oft layeth out his hook,................		282	Psalm X		42
The lions oft lack food,.................		319	Psalm XXXIV		37
Those raveners' whelps oft starved be,..........		319	Psalm XXXIV		38
But fore-accounting oft makes builders misse,......		244	Other Poems	4	79
So oft in feasts with costly chaunges cladd........		245	Other Poems	4	133
Nay ev'n unto hir home he oft would go,..........		247	Other Poems	4	193
For hearing him so oft with wordes of woe.........		256	Other Poems	4	537
His oft sigh-broken dittie,................		259	Other Poems	5	115
Oft each other's friendship proving,...........		262	Other Poems	7	23
OFTEN					
Would often kill to breed more feeling paine,......		135	Cert Sonnets	2	4
Whereof, with whom, how often did she talke,......		225	Astrophil	92	11
Will. A tyme there is for all, my Mother often sayes,...		343	Possibly	1	9
For creeping rimes, which often sighings choke......		242	Other Poems	4	8
Often Reedes me musicke made,..............		263	Other Poems	7	44
OIL					
As well may thincke with oyle to coole the fire:		22	1st Eclogues	9	8
With oyle Thou dost anoynt my head,...........		301	Psalm XXIII		19
OKER					
Busy with oker did their shoulders marke,.........		243	Other Poems	4	69
OLD					
How is he young, that tam'de old Phoebus' youth?		21	1st Eclogues	8	10
No, nothing so; an old false knave he is,.........		21	1st Eclogues	8	13
Millions of yeares this old drivell Cupid lives;.....		22	1st Eclogues	8	43
An olde man heare, who would thy fancies raise.....		22	1st Eclogues	9	5
Philisides. O gods, how long this old foole hath annoi'd ..		24	1st Eclogues	9	66
This life-deadman in this old dungeon flong........		24	1st Eclogues	9	83
Olde houses are throne downe for new we see:.......		24	1st Eclogues	9	84
Old men themselves, doe love young wives to choose:....		25	1st Eclogues	9	88
And thinke them olde, that have the oldest minde,....		25	1st Eclogues	9	94
Loth to dye young, and then you must be olde,.......		25	1st Eclogues	9	103
Philisides. Hath any man heard what this old man said? ...		26	1st Eclogues	9	135

350

OLD	(CONTINUED)	PAGE	TITLE		LINE
Olde aged oke cutt downe, of newe works serves to the building:.		36	1st Eclogues	13	134
Let not old age disgrace my high desire, ...		38	Arcadia II	15	1
Old wood inflam'de, doth yeeld the bravest fire, ...		38	Arcadia II	15	3
Old age is wise and full of constant truth;.		39	Arcadia II	15	9
Old age well stayed from raunging humor lives:		39	Arcadia II	15	10
Old age hath knowne what ever was in youth:.		39	Arcadia II	15	11
Old age orecome, the greater honour gives.		39	Arcadia II	15	12
And to old age since you your selfe aspire,.		39	Arcadia II	15	13
Let not old age disgrace my high desire.		39	Arcadia II	15	14
Though thousands old, a Boy entit'led still.		41	Arcadia II	20	10
Nico. And are you there old Pas? in troth I ever thought,. .		51	2nd Eclogues	29	1
Pas. But here is Dicus old; let him then speake the woord, .		52	2nd Eclogues	29	27
To let that witolde beast consume in flames.		60	2nd Eclogues	30	111
Go sing the fall of old Thebes,.		66	2nd Eclogues	32	21
The songe I sange old Languet had me taught, ...		99	3rd Eclogues	66	22
With old true tales he woont mine eares to fill,.		99	3rd Eclogues	66	33
The night growne old, her blacke head waxen gray,.		103	3rd Eclogues	66	160
O nature doting olde, O blinded nature,.		109	Arcadia IV	70	19
Time ever old, and yonge is still revolved		127	4th Eclogues	75	79
Some good old dumpe, that Chaucer's mistresse knew,.		146	Cert Sonnets	17	34
Ennobling new found Tropes with problemes old:		166	Astrophil	3	6
Thy scepter use in some old Catoe's brest;		166	Astrophil	4	5
Which from the ribs of old Parnassus flowes,.		172	Astrophil	15	2
In this old world, growne now so too too wise:		198	Astrophil	65	6
Desire, though thou my old companion art,.		202	Astrophil	72	1
I have been younge now old I am, ...		326	Psalm XXXVII		61
Geron, though olde yet gamesome, kept one ende		248	Other Poems	4	242
Till that he spied old Geron could no more,.		250	Other Poems	4	307
So that Uran, whose arme old Geron bore,.		250	Other Poems	4	309
For he was olde, and easly would be cought:.		250	Other Poems	4	322
While Geron olde came safe to Cosma true,.		250	Other Poems	4	325
"My old mates I grieve to see, ...		262	Other Poems	7	19
OLDEST					
The oldest Rammes are culled from the flocke:.		24	1st Eclogues	9	85
And thinke them olde, that have the oldest minde,.		25	1st Eclogues	9	94
OLIVE					
Olive paintes me the peace that I must aspire to by conquest		35	1st Eclogues	13	117
OLYMPUS					
What judge you doth a hillocke shew, by the lofty Olympus? .		34	1st Eclogues	13	75
OMIT					
Yet never shall my song omitte		88	Arcadia III	62	87
ONCE					
Lalus. Once my well-waiting eyes espied my treasure, ...		16	1st Eclogues	7	73
Dorus. Once, o sweete once, I saw with dread oppressed . . .		17	1st Eclogues	7	85
Such weight it hath which once is full possest.		20	1st Eclogues	7	V961
Above line repeated at following location.		20	1st Eclogues	7	V962
Histor. Those woordes dyd once the Loveliest shepard use . .		24	1st Eclogues	9	62
Who once a white long beard, well handle does, ...		25	1st Eclogues	9	90
If once thou maist that fancie glosse destroy.		25	1st Eclogues	9	117
Who once all birdes, in sweetly-singing past, ...		28	1st Eclogues	10	74
Pas. Cosma once said, she left the wicket ope, ...		55	2nd Eclogues	29	90
Nico. She once starke nak'd did bathe a little time;		55	2nd Eclogues	29	105
Pas. She once, to coole her selfe, stood in a well,.		55	2nd Eclogues	29	108
Pas. As in a glasse I held she once did looke,.		55	2nd Eclogues	29	114
O eyes of mine, where once she saw her face,.		60	2nd Eclogues	30	116
I darkned am, who once had clearest sight.		75	Arcadia III	43	4
He loves my hart, for once it was his owne:.		76	Arcadia III	45	7
Ne dare once shew thy face,.		93	3rd Eclogues	63	87
When once this entred was, in woman's hart,.		95	3rd Eclogues	64	37
Whereto two parties once be full content.		97	3rd Eclogues	64	126
For once the Lion by the Lambe did lie;.		100	3rd Eclogues	66	52
Strephon. I that was once free-burges of the forrests, . . .		111	4th Eclogues	71	13
I that was once esteem'd for pleasant musique, ...		111	4th Eclogues	71	15
Klaius. I that was once delighted every morning, ...		111	4th Eclogues	71	19
I that was once the musique of these vallies,.		111	4th Eclogues	71	21
No knee once bowed, forsooth, for them they say we serve... .		120	4th Eclogues	73	114
With age's force decay'd, yet once the heaven was his.. . .		120	4th Eclogues	73	124
What sweete joyes I had once, and what a place I did hold? .		124	4th Eclogues	74	72
Shall I not once object, that you, you graunted a favour . .		124	4th Eclogues	74	73
I know not I, but once in detestation.		128	4th Eclogues	75	100
When once one is for Atropos distrained.		128	4th Eclogues	75	111
Which once said what I conceaved,.		139	Cert Sonnets	7	5
A Satyre once did runne away for dread,.		145	Cert Sonnets	16	1
If from my soule this love would once depart,.		148	Cert Sonnets	19	9
Once to approch this hayer..		158	Cert Sonnets	28	8
Seeing how once you saw I liv'd,.		158	Cert Sonnets	28	31
"Her eyes were once his dart".		160	Cert Sonnets	30	26
That Vertue, if it once met with our eyes, ...		177	Astrophil	25	3
Wherewith my father once made it halfe tame;		180	Astrophil	30	10
And ah what hope, that hope should once see day, ...		182	Astrophil	35	7
That once come there, the sobs of mine annoyes		187	Astrophil	44	13
Least once should not be heard, twise said, No, No..		196	Astrophil	63	8
But that which once may win thy cruell hart:		198	Astrophil	64	13
Teaching the meane, at once to take and give		206	Astrophil	79	9
Pardon that fault, once more graunt me the place,.		208	Astrophil	82	12
Cannot heavn's food, once felt, keepe stomakes free.		223	Astrophil	88	7
Who womankind at once both deckes and stayneth?.		197	A&S 1st Song		10

ONCE   (CONTINUED)   PAGE TITLE   LINE

Nc vertue merits praise, once toucht with blot of Treason. . 214 A&S 5th Song 66
Whose beames, where they once are darted,. . . . . 218 A&S 8th Song 35
Wherof if but a sparke once kindled be, you all. . . . . . 272 Psalm II   29
Have mercie, mercie lord I once did say, ... 280 Psalm IX   36
When hee once drau'th his wily nett. . . . . 282 Psalm X   40
Noe feare of God doth once appeare . . . . 323 Psalm XXXVI   5
And rayse me up that I may once have might . . . . 333 Psalm XLI   35
Was once my mynde, my temper, and my lyfe, ... 344 Possibly 2   6
Allarme allarme, when once the fight is warme, ... 346 Possibly 5 13
Moving, she seem'd at once to kisse, and speake. . . . . . . 244 Other Poems 4 96
Do you remember still you once were mine,. . . . . 254 Other Poems 4 495
"C earth, once answere give, ... 256 Other Poems 5 14
Once to Shepheard's God retayning, ... 262 Other Poems 7 11
Where we once our lovely sheepe, ... 262 Other Poems 7 21

ONE

To one whose state is raised over all, ... 3 Lady of May 1   1
Who in one selfe these diverse gifts can plant;. . . . . . . 3 Lady of May 1   4
To one that hath no wealth, and wants his wit. . . . . 4 Lady of May 2 24
That such a one is witnesse of my hart,. . . . . 5 Lady of May 3 14
All this one the this fatall yere shall hitte. . . . . 11 Arcadia I 1 V807
Thus are my eyes still Captive to one sight: . . . . 12 Arcadia I 2   9
Thus all my thoughts are slaves to one thought still:. . . . 12 Arcadia I 2 10
And thus my eyes, are plaste still in one sight. . . . . . . 12 Arcadia I 2 V809
And thus my thoughtes, can thinke but one thing still. . . . 12 Arcadia I 2 V810
Then power out plaint, and in one word say this: . . . . . . 13 Arcadia I 4   9
In one, whose name to name were high presumption,. . . . . . 15 1st Eclogues 7 38
Bent to such one, in whom, my selfe must say,. . . . . 17 1st Eclogues 7 107
Nothing can mend one point that in her lies. . . . . 17 1st Eclogues 7 108
While that one body shine. . . . . 19 1st Eclogues 7 165
One brings the stuffe, the other stamps the coine, ... 20 1st Eclogues 8   3
Time shall in one my life and sorrowes end,. . . . . 23 1st Eclogues 9 19
Still were I one, this still should be my case,. . . . . . . 23 1st Eclogues 9 28
Were in his dayes: which heard, one nothing heares,. . . . . 24 1st Eclogues 9 76
Where all my paines one looke of hers hath paid. . . . . . . 26 1st Eclogues 9 137
Be as thou art, but be with mine at one. . . . . 27 1st Eclogues 10 15
One saith, He mockes; the other saith, he playes;. . . . . . 27 1st Eclogues 10 44
Fortune thus gan say; "misery and misfortune is all one, . . 29 1st Eclogues 11   3
Sacred Muse, who in one contaynes what nine do in all them.. 31 1st Eclogues 13 10
Ease I do feele (such ease as falls to one wholy diseased) . 35 1st Eclogues 13 114
And witnesse am, how ill agree in one,. . . . . 40 Arcadia II 19   5
May witnesse beare, how ill agree in one,. . . . . 41 Arcadia II 19 11
The one of Love, the other Jealousie,. . . . . 42 Arcadia II 22   2
The one aloft doth holde the other hie.. . . . . 42 Arcadia II 22   5
One wonder yet farre passeth my conceate:. . . . . 42 Arcadia II 22 13
Nico. I thinke it well: such voice would make one musicke
 hate:. . . . . 52 2nd Eclogues 29 21
But this is one that doth his musicke staine.. . . . . 54 2nd Eclogues 29 62
The one, which tother would refrayne.. . . . . 57 2nd Eclogues 30   4
Where chaunge of thoughts one foole to other shewes, ... 57 2nd Eclogues 30 21
Then let me eke forget one hand from other:. . . . . 61 2nd Eclogues 30 161
One day layes up stuffe of griefe for the morrow:. . . . . . 62 2nd Eclogues 30 176
Oft prove I: but what salve, when Reason seeks to be gone?
 One. . . . . 63 2nd Eclogues 31 11
Oh! if such a one have bent to a lonely life . . . . 69 2nd Eclogues 34 39
Unite in one, my state thus still to save; . . . . 70 Arcadia III 35 15
By just exchange, one for the other giv'ne.. . . . . 75 Arcadia III 45   2
His hart in me, keepes me and him in one,. . . . . 76 Arcadia III 45   5
Yet joyning formes one sight of beautie breede.. . . . . . . 78 Arcadia III 50   4
Yet all well knit to one faire end do passe: . . . . 78 Arcadia III 50   8
All what I am, still one, his owne, doe finde. . . . . 78 Arcadia III 50 10
All what you are still one, his owne to finde, ... 79 Arcadia III 50 11
Save one as much as other cleere:. . . . . 86 Arcadia III 62 20
There may one see, and yet not see . . . . 88 Arcadia III 62 67
Live one in two, a well united paire,. . . . . 91 3rd Eclogues 63   7
Let one time (but long first) close up their daies,. . . . . 92 3rd Eclogues 63 31
One grave their bodies seaze:. . . . . 92 3rd Eclogues 63 32
One streame both streames containe,. . . . . 92 3rd Eclogues 63 35
And thus she did. One day to him she came, ... 95 3rd Eclogues 64 43
And one man still, credit with her preserve. . . . . 98 3rd Eclogues 65   4
(The one doth force, the latter doth entise) . . . . 98 3rd Eclogues 65 10
Phoenix but one, of Crowes we milllions have:. . . . . 104 3rd Eclogues 67 20
A silence sweet each where with one consent embraste . . . . 117 4th Eclogues 73   7
(A musique sweet to one in carefull musing plaste) . . . . . 117 4th Eclogues 73   8
And so she was attirde, as one that did not prize. . . . . . 119 4th Eclogues 73 87
Let one the Princesse be, to her the other yeeld:. . . . . . 120 4th Eclogues 73 129
But if among yourselves some one tree growe, ... 125 4th Eclogues 75 10
One Echo to another Echo cast. . . . . 126 4th Eclogues 75 34
In one true chest to rob all Vertue's treasure?. . . . . . . 126 4th Eclogues 75 47
One word of woe another after traineth:. . . . . 128 4th Eclogues 75 103
When once one is for Atropos distrained. . . . . 128 4th Eclogues 75 111
One of other beautie takes.. . . . . 140 Cert Sonnets 7 17
And so for one that felt god Cupid's dart, ... 146 Cert Sonnets 17 29
Me to leave, with whome I leave my hart. . . . . 148 Cert Sonnets 20   6
But alwayes one my selfe with eagle eyde trueth to flie, . . 153 Cert Sonnets 24 24
In one that changeth so, ... 158 Cert Sonnets 28 26
Better then one captiv'd perceiveth, ... 159 Cert Sonnets 29 16
For me in sooth, no Muse but one I know: . . . . 166 Astrophil 3   9
I sweare, my heart such one shall shew to thee,. . . . . . . 167 Astrophil 4 12
But one worse fault, Ambition, I confesse, ... 178 Astrophil 27 11

```
ONE                          (CONTINUED)                    PAGE    TITLE              LINE
      If French can yet three parts in one agree; . . . . . . . .  180 Astrophil   30    5
      Within what bounds can one his liking stay, . . . . . . . .  182 Astrophil   35    3
      And Humblenesse growes one with Majestie. . . . . . . . . .  188 Astrophil   48    4
      One hand forgott to rule, th'other to fight. . . . . . . .   191 Astrophil   53   11
      What, a whole weeke without one peece of looke, . . . . . .  192 Astrophil   56    3
      That in one speech two Negatives affirme.. . . . . . . . .   196 Astrophil   63   14
      Fortune wheeles still with me in one sort slow, . . . . . .  199 Astrophil   66    6
      One from the other scarcely can descrie. . . . . . . . . .   202 Astrophil   72    3
      Sweet lip, you teach my mouth with one sweet kisse.. . . . . 207 Astrophil   80   14
      I caught at one of them a hungrie bit; . . . . . . . . . . . 208 Astrophil   82   11
      Since kind or chance gives both one liverie, . . . . . . .   229 Astrophil   96    2
      Slow heavinesse in both holds one degree, . . . . . . . . .  229 Astrophil   96    6
      Thou then whom partiall heavens conspir'd in one to frame, . 213 A&S 5th Song      19
      Who faileth one, is false, though trusty to another. . . . . 214 A&S 5th Song      72
      It is one who from thy sight, . . . . . . . . . . . . . . .   233 A&S 11th Song      3
      Merry flocke, such one forgo, . . . . . . . . . . . . . . .  221 A&S 9th Song       8
      When He chose me, a godly One: . . . . . . . . . . . . . .   273 Psalm IV          12
      Such one I say, that when I make . . . . . . . . . . . . . . 273 Psalm IV          13
      For in their mouth not One cleere word is spent, . . . . .   275 Psalm V           25
      To slay the hurtless One, . . . . . . . . . . . . . . . . .  282 Psalm X           34
      Not One that good remaineth. . . . . . . . . . . . . . . .   286 Psalm XIV          6
      One that his Wisdome learneth.. . . . . . . . . . . . . . .  286 Psalm XIV          9
      All plung'd in stinking filth, not One well bent, . . . . .  286 Psalm XIV         11
      Not One, that God discerneth.. . . . . . . . . . . . . . .   286 Psalm XIV         12
      Deare beloved Holy One, . . . . . . . . . . . . . . . . . .  288 Psalm XVI         35
      And since there is not One, who it redresseth. . . . . . .   299 Psalm XXII        26
      Oh, is there one with his Feare fraught? . . . . . . . . .   304 Psalm XXV         47
      One thing in deed I did and will . . . . . . . . . . . . . . 307 Psalm XXVII       19
      Therfore shall evry godly One. . . . . . . . . . . . . . .   315 Psalm XXXII       19
      So that not one of them is broke; . . . . . . . . . . . . .  320 Psalm XXXIV       74
      Like one that should his Mother's death lament.. . . . . .   322 Psalm XXXV        36
      Since it is Thou that makest one such? . . . . . . . . . .   330 Psalm XXXIX       30
      When but with one look of his. . . . . . . . . . . . . . .   334 Psalm XLII        21
      One deep with noyse of his fall. . . . . . . . . . . . . .   335 Psalm XLII        29
      One said he brake acrosse; full well it so might be: . . . . 241 Other Poems  1     3
      They joi'd one joy, one griefe they griev'd, . . . . . . .   241 Other Poems  3     3
      One love they lov'd, one life they liv'd.. . . . . . . . . . 241 Other Poems  3     4
      The hand was one, one was the sword. . . . . . . . . . . .   241 Other Poems  3     5
      That tombes the two, is justly one. . . . . . . . . . . . .  241 Other Poems  3     8
      A paire of frends, or rather one cal'd two, . . . . . . . .  242 Other Poems  4    18
      One day (o day, that shin'de to make them darke!). . . . .   243 Other Poems  4    65
      In some such one she lik'd not his desire, . . . . . . . .   245 Other Poems  4   119
      With one good dawnce, or letter finely pend, . . . . . . .   245 Other Poems  4   140
      Till one faire eav'n an howr ere Sun did rest, . . . . . .   247 Other Poems  4   205
      Geron, though olde yet gamesome, kept one ende . . . . . .   248 Other Poems  4   242
      Her happy-making hand, of whome one looke. . . . . . . . .   248 Other Poems  4   247
      One day he with his flock abroad did raunge: . . . . . . .   253 Other Poems  4   438
      With traitor lime the one, . . . . . . . . . . . . . . . .   258 Other Poems  5    87
      Then want one hower those eyes which my joyes keepe. . . . . 259 Other Poems  5   102
      Make but one Minde in Bodies three. . . . . . . . . . . . .  260 Other Poems  6     6
      Above line repeated at following locations . . . . . . . .   260 Other Poems  6    12
          . . . . . . . . . . . . . . . . . . . . . . . . . . . .  260 Other Poems  6    18
          . . . . . . . . . . . . . . . . . . . . . . . . . . . .  260 Other Poems  6    24
          . . . . . . . . . . . . . . . . . . . . . . . . . . . .  261 Other Poems  6    30
          . . . . . . . . . . . . . . . . . . . . . . . . . . . .  261 Other Poems  6    36
          . . . . . . . . . . . . . . . . . . . . . . . . . . . .  261 Other Poems  6    42
          . . . . . . . . . . . . . . . . . . . . . . . . . . . .  261 Other Poems  6    48
          . . . . . . . . . . . . . . . . . . . . . . . . . . . .  261 Other Poems  6    54
      As one for ever joyned bee.. . . . . . . . . . . . . . . .   261 Other Poems  6    60
      One among the rest electing. . . . . . . . . . . . . . . .   262 Other Poems  7    17
ONE'S
      Sucking one's ill, another to infect.. . . . . . . . . . .    21 1st Eclogues  8   36
      Or where one's love so constant bene, . . . . . . . . . . .  158 Cert Sonnets 28   27
      No doome should make one's heav'n become his hell. . . . .   212 Astrophil   86   14
ONES
      How many Ones there be . . . . . . . . . . . . . . . . . .   272 Psalm III          4
      No, nor with Thee the naughty Ones shall dwel, . . . . . .   274 Psalm V           11
      His Holy ones; they are preserved. . . . . . . . . . . . .   326 Psalm XXXVII      70
      Those vile scoffes of naughty ones . . . . . . . . . . . .   335 Psalm XLII        45
ONLY
      Which hath in others' head his only being. . . . . . . . .    20 1st Eclogues  7 V964
      O noble age who place their only blisse. . . . . . . . . .    24 1st Eclogues  9   69
      Only fond youth admires a rotten stocke. . . . . . . . . .    25 1st Eclogues  9   89
      And of misfortune, fortune hath only the gift. . . . . . .    29 1st Eclogues 11    4
      Happy be you that may to the saint, your onely Idea, . . .    32 1st Eclogues 13   15
      You doo approch to the fruite your onely desirs be to
          gather . . . . . . . . . . . . . . . . . . . . . . . .    33 1st Eclogues 13   63
      Her praise, whence to the world all praise had his only
          beginning: . . . . . . . . . . . . . . . . . . . . . .    33 1st Eclogues 13   69
      Then by my high Cedar, rich Ruby, and only shining Sunne,..   34 1st Eclogues 13   80
      "Onley Juell, O only Juell, which only deservest . . . . .    36 1st Eclogues 13  147
      That onely light doth all my life maintaine; . . . . . . .    39 Arcadia II   16    4
      To onely thee my constant course I beare.. . . . . . . . .    40 Arcadia II   18   16
      O only sonne that suche a fruite can breede. . . . . . . .    43 Arcadia II   23    3
      The hart, eye, eare here onely find his treasure doth: . . .  49 2nd Eclogues 28   58
      Whose onely face the little heaven is, . . . . . . . . . .    51 2nd Eclogues 28  107
      Her onely cure from surfet-woes can diet me: . . . . . . .    51 2nd Eclogues 28  117
      That hath foure legs, and with two onely goes, . . . . . .    56 2nd Eclogues 29  142
      That hath foure eyes, and onely two can frame. . . . . . .    56 2nd Eclogues 29  143
```

ONLY	(CONTINUED)	PAGE	TITLE		LINE
And all but jests, save onely sorrowe's rage.		57	2nd Eclogues	30	22
Griefe onely makes his wretched state to see		58	2nd Eclogues	30	32
O braine, where thought of her hath onely place;		60	2nd Eclogues	30	118
O soule, whose love in her is onely spent, ...		60	2nd Eclogues	30	122
As if by death she onely might be saved?		61	2nd Eclogues	30	160
Think so, for of my desired blisse it is only the course.					
Curse.		64	2nd Eclogues	31	39
Mock'st thou those Diamonds which only be matcht by the					
gods Ods.		65	2nd Eclogues	31	47
To blase my onely secretts?.		65	2nd Eclogues	32	2
Above line repeated at following location.		66	2nd Eclogues	32	31
Wherein do only flowrish		66	2nd Eclogues	32	32
That only can redresse thee, ...		67	2nd Eclogues	32	48
But onely that my goddesse		67	2nd Eclogues	32	56
Under this, this her owne, her only dearling.		68	2nd Eclogues	33	23
Contemplation here holdeth his only seate:		68	2nd Eclogues	34	7
Can taste no sweetes, the sower onely please:.		74	Arcadia III	41	2
You onely yours, too farr beyond desarte..		79	Arcadia III	50	22
Preserve those beames, this age's onely lighte:		79	Arcadia III	51	2
Farewell Complaint, the miser's only pleasure:		83	Arcadia III	59	2
Which onely thus unhappie be,.		86	Arcadia III	62	21
Which onely still doth Lillies yeeld:.		87	Arcadia III	62	62
It title had, unto my only love, ...		96	3rd Eclogues	64	89
Was onely won'd with such as beastes begot:.		100	3rd Eclogues	66	45
Onely the owle still warnde them not to seech		100	3rd Eclogues	66	68
No beast should freely speake, but onely he.		101	3rd Eclogues	66	105
Who onely sees the ill is worse then blind..		106	3rd Eclogues	67	85
Favour to make my chiefe and onely hire.		115	4th Eclogues	72	55
O faire, o onely faire, from thee, alas, ...		116	4th Eclogues	72	96
Doth hide his head with cares but onely how to rest:		117	4th Eclogues	73	24
To onely thee thou seest we graunt this speciall grace . . .		119	4th Eclogues	73	95
Now resteth onely this, which of us two is she,.		120	4th Eclogues	73	135
O you (alas so I find) cause of his onely ruine.		122	4th Eclogues	74	4
Which inke onely relates, but ne laments, ne replies?. . . .		122	4th Eclogues	74	18
Gives an adieu to the world, as to his onely delight:. . . .		123	4th Eclogues	74	26
And that he thence must part where to live onely I lyved.. .		123	4th Eclogues	74	30
Must I be onely the marke, shall prove that Vertue is					
angrie		123	4th Eclogues	74	33
First let Cimmerian darknes be my onel'habitaco'n:		124	4th Eclogues	74	59
And doo not onely marke the accents last,.		126	4th Eclogues	75	32
To well felte griefe, plainte is the onely pleasure.		126	4th Eclogues	75	51
Farewell o Joy, the wofull's onely pleasure.		129	4th Eclogues	76	4
He would not arm'd with beautie, only raigne		135	Cert Sonnets	2	5
For all his strife can onlie bondage gaine..		135	Cert Sonnets	2	8
Alas, all onely she no pitie taketh, ...		136	Cert Sonnets	3	9
O My thoughtes' sweete foode, my my onely owner, ...		138	Cert Sonnets	5	1
Above line repeated at following location.		138	Cert Sonnets	5	25
Thou paine the onely guest of loath'd constraint,.		141	Cert Sonnets	10	1
My Muse therefore, for onely thou canst tell,.		146	Cert Sonnets	17	11
Are Poets then the onely lovers true,.		146	Cert Sonnets	17	31
That onely I the onely Mistresse had:.		147	Cert Sonnets	17	43
O no, O no, tryall onely shewse.		153	Cert Sonnets	24	10
Within my selfe to seeke my onelie hire:		161	Cert Sonnets	31	13
But only Stella's eyes and Stella's hart..		176	Astrophil	23	14
He knowes not) grow in only follie rich.		177	Astrophil	24	14
By only those two starres in Stella's face..		178	Astrophil	26	14
So in my swelling breast that only I		178	Astrophil	27	7
Princesse of Beautie, for whose only sake.		179	Astrophil	28	6
Love onely reading unto me this art.		179	Astrophil	28	14
That she, me thinks, not onely shines but sings.		184	Astrophil	38	8
Only lov'd Tyrants, just in cruelty, ...		185	Astrophil	42	6
She heard my plaints, and did not only heare,.		193	Astrophil	57	9
Alas, if you graunt only such delight.		194	Astrophil	59	12
That heav'n of joyes throwes onely downe on me		195	Astrophil	60	3
Alas, if this the only mettall be.		196	Astrophil	62	12
Stella, the onely Planet of my light, ...		200	Astrophil	68	1
Chiefe good, whereto my hope doth only aspire, ...		200	Astrophil	68	3
These things are left me by my only Deare;		202	Astrophil	72	12
School'd onely by his mother's tender eye:		203	Astrophil	73	2
Doth lowre, nay, chide; nay, threat for only this:		203	Astrophil	73	7
But only for this worthy knight durst prove.		204	Astrophil	75	13
The onely light of joy, the onely warmth of Love..		204	Astrophil	76	4
Scortch not, but onely do darke chilling sprites remove. . .		205	Astrophil	76	8
And onely cherish doth with injurie.		206	Astrophil	78	8
By linkes of Love, and only Nature's art:.		207	Astrophil	81	6
Safe in my soule, which only doth to thee.		212	Astrophil	86	6
Only with paines my paines thus eased be,.		227	Astrophil	93	12
Only true sighs, you do not go away, ...		229	Astrophil	95	12
Mine eyes then only winke, for spite perchance,.		230	Astrophil	98	13
Onely unto the heav'n of Stella's face..		235	Astrophil	105	7
There shines a joy from thee my only light;.		236	Astrophil	108	4
And in my joyes for thee my only annoy..		237	Astrophil	108	14
Only in you my song begins and endeth.		196	A&S 1st Song		4
Only for you the heav'n forgate all measure.		197	A&S 1st Song		8
Onely by you Cupid his crowne maintaineth.		197	A&S 1st Song		12
Onely to you her Scepter Venus granteth.		197	A&S 1st Song		16
Onelie through you the tree of life doth flourish.		197	A&S 1st Song		20
Onely at you all envie hopelesse rueth..		197	A&S 1st Song		24
Only of you the flatterer never lieth.		197	A&S 1st Song		28

```
ONLY                    (CONTINUED)                        PAGE     TITLE          LINE
    Only with you not miracles are wonders.. . . . . . . . . .   197 A&S 1st Song      32
    Only in you my song begins and endeth. . . . . . . . . .    197 A&S 1st Song      36
    The two only darts of Love:. . . . . . . . . . . . . .      202 A&S 2nd Song       6
    Onely joy, now here you are, . . . . . . . . . . . . . .    210 A&S 4th Song       1
    Which (I protest) proceed from only Cruell thee, . . . . .  214 A&S 5th Song      53
    Only thought aymes at the pleasure.. . . . . . . . . . .    226 A&S 10th Song     12
    Is only true delight.. . . . . . . . . . . . . . . . . .    215 A&S 6th Song      12
    Only rich in mischiefe's treasure. . . . . . . . . . . .    221 A&S 9th Song      10
    Sorrow onely then hath glory,. . . . . . . . . . . . . .    221 A&S 9th Song      14
    Himselfe onely winter-sterved. . . . . . . . . . . . . .    222 A&S 9th Song      30
    With loving homage kisse that only son he hath,. . . . . .  272 Psalm II          27
    And then they that in him their only trust do rest,. . . .  272 Psalm II          31
    And only hunt, where lyes do ly? . . . . . . . . . . . .    273 Psalm IV          10
    By power of whose only brest,. . . . . . . . . . . . . .    274 Psalm IV          34
    May only joy in all Thy saving wayes . . . . . . . . . .    280 Psalm IX          44
    O God our only starr,. . . . . . . . . . . . . . . . . .    281 Psalm X            2
    O lord Our only God, . . . . . . . . . . . . . . . . . .    282 Psalm X           50
    The throne of Heav'n is only His:. . . . . . . . . . . .    284 Psalm XI          14
    God my only portion is . . . . . . . . . . . . . . . . .    288 Psalm XVI         13
    On whom against my Foes my only safty stayes?. . . . . . .  291 Psalm XVIII        7
    Of him that only thunders; . . . . . . . . . . . . . . .    293 Psalm XIX          2
    He only leanes on highest Thing, . . . . . . . . . . . .    297 Psalm XXI         27
    Remember, only King, . . . . . . . . . . . . . . . . . .    303 Psalm XXV         19
    For Thou the Lord, Thou only art,. . . . . . . . . . . .    304 Psalm XXV         71
    For still I say Thou art my only might.. . . . . . . . .    312 Psalm XXXI        12
    He me, he only brought.. . . . . . . . . . . . . . . . .    319 Psalm XXXIV       16
    Thou only, Thou, art hee . . . . . . . . . . . . . . . .    332 Psalm XL          68
    Their sences rude plaine objects only move,. . . . . . . .  245 Other Poems   4  143
    "Only for my two loves' sake, Sir Ed. D. and M. F. G.. . .  263 Other Poems   7   61
    Only two do me delight . . . . . . . . . . . . . . . . .    263 Other Poems   7   63
ONWARD
    Now blessed you, beare onward blessed me . . . . . . . . .  209 Astrophil     84    5
OPAL
    Her forhead jacinth like, her cheekes of opall hue,. . . .   12 Arcadia I     3    9
OPE
    Pas. Cosma once said, she left the wicket ope, . . . . . .   55 2nd Eclogues 29   90
    With windowes ope then most my mind doth lie,. . . . . . .  230 Astrophil     99    5
OPEN
    I cried, and was with open rayes rewarded: . . . . . . . .   17 1st Eclogues  7   94
    To open eyes all beauties he doth raine; . . . . . . . . .   22 1st Eclogues  8   39
    To weare upon her neck, that open lies.. . . . . . . . . .   55 2nd Eclogues 29  119
    Which at firste voly gave too open entry,. . . . . . . . .   68 2nd Eclogues 33   14
    Be thou the knot of this their open vowe,. . . . . . . . .   92 3rd Eclogues 63   47
    Where open hartes do holde so constant place,. . . . . . .   93 3rd Eclogues 63   88
    Either to do like him, which open shone, . . . . . . . . .  176 Astrophil     22   10
    The same key op'n can, which can locke up a treasure.. . .  213 A&S 5th Song      18
    Their throat, it is an Open swallowing grave,. . . . . . .  275 Psalm V           27
    That trust in Thee, ev'n in most open sight! . . . . . . .  313 Psalm XXXI        54
    And surely taught by his love-open eye,. . . . . . . . . .  251 Other Poems   4  378
    Come she, and sweet the aire with open brest,. . . . . . .  254 Other Poems   4  466
OPENED
    That opened furthe my seale of comforte is) . . . . . . .    70 Arcadia III  35    3
    Was held, in opend sense it flies away,. . . . . . . . . .  184 Astrophil     38   10
    And open'd mine own wickednes,. . . . . . . . . . . . . .   315 Psalm XXXII       14
OPENEST
    Thou openest heavnly Doore . . . . . . . . . . . . . . .    283 Psalm X           73
OPENING
    Opening rubies, pearles deviding.. . . . . . . . . . . . .  226 A&S 10th Song     30
OPENS
    Which breakes the clowdes and opens forth the light, . . .  161 Cert Sonnets 32    7
    A double key, which opens to the heart,. . . . . . . . . .  206 Astrophil     79    6
OPERATION
    Here you fully do finde this strange operation of love,. . . 31 1st Eclogues 13    3
OPINIONS
    Nor conning humorists' puddled opinions, . . . . . . . . .   69 2nd Eclogues 34   20
OPPOSE
    That dare themselves to him oppose,. . . . . . . . . . . .  282 Psalm X           22
    Thy force O Lord against their force oppose, . . . . . . .  321 Psalm XXXV         2
OPPRESS
    There is no hate that can thee more oppresse.. . . . . . .   23 1st Eclogues  9   49
    No pride shall them oppresse,. . . . . . . . . . . . . . .   94 3rd Eclogues 63   96
    Fell jealousie did so his braine oppresse, . . . . . . . .   94 3rd Eclogues 64    9
    As where thou soone mightst helpe, most faith dost most
        oppresse,. . . . . . . . . . . . . . . . . . . . . .   213 A&S 5th Song      41
    With heaped weights of their own sins oppresse . . . . . .  275 Psalm V           31
OPPRESSED
    Where eares be burnt, eyes dazled, harts opprest?. . . . .    3 Lady of May   1    6
    Dorus. Once, o sweete once, I saw with dread oppressed . . .  17 1st Eclogues  7   85
    When Cedars to the ground be opprest by the weight of an
        emmott,. . . . . . . . . . . . . . . . . . . . . . .    34 1st Eclogues 13   77
    (Opprest with ruinouse conceites) by the helpe of an
        outcrye . . . . . . . . . . . . . . . . . . . . . .    35 1st Eclogues 13  109
    How hast thou framde the paine wherewith I am opprest? . . .  121 4th Eclogues 73  184
    Love never had me opprest, but that I saw to be lov'd. . . .  123 4th Eclogues 74   44
    O Philomela with thy brest oppressed . . . . . . . . . . .  126 4th Eclogues 75   61
    Justice, justice is now (alas) oppressed:. . . . . . . . .  128 4th Eclogues 75  118
    If vaine love have my simple soule opprest,. . . . . . . .  166 Astrophil      4    3
    Through that darke fornace to my hart opprest, . . . . . .  236 Astrophil    108    3
    Both within themselves oppressed,. . . . . . . . . . . . .  218 A&S 8th Song       7
```

OPPRESSED	(CONTINUED)	PAGE	TITLE		LINE
Thou lord also th' Oppressed wilt defend		280	Psalm IX		26
Indeed the pocre opprest by you, you mock, ...		287	Psalm XIV		19
So can I not be opprest, ...		288	Psalm XVI		27
See how I am opprest		304	Psalm XXV		63
When most he seemes opprest.		320	Psalm XXXIV		72
Whose foule weights have me opprest.		327	Psalm XXXVIII		12
Of my Cause oppressed.		336	Psalm XLIII		3
Where with heate oppreste I was, ...		262	Other Poems	7	2
OPPRESSETH					
What griefe her breast oppresseth, ...		137	Cert Sonnets	4	7
While the Foe oppresseth me?		335	Psalm XLII		44
OPPRESSING					
Oppressing mortall sense, my death proceed, ...		186	Astrophil	42	13
OPPRESSION					
Silence doth seeme the maske of base oppression.		47	2nd Eclogues	28	15
His youth delight, his age the soule's oppression:		48	2nd Eclogues	28	39
OPPROBRIOUS					
Showes, guilty harte doth deeme his state opprobrious. . . .		48	2nd Eclogues	28	18
ORANGE					
Trust in the shade of pleasing Orange tree;		180	Astrophil	30	8
ORATOR					
The Oratour so farre men's harts doth bind, ...		193	Astrophil	58	2
ORATORS					
Fit oratours to make		215	A&S 6th Song		9
ORDAINED					
And so thou hast all things ordained		279	Psalm VIII		23
ORDAINETH					
Sir wrong his tombe ordaineth, ...		160	Cert Sonnets 30		23
ORDER					
Where senses do behold th'order of heav'nly hoste, ...		68	2nd Eclogues 34		5
For nothing can endure where order n'is.		100	3rd Eclogues 66		51
Cranes, order; Storkes, to be appearing holie;		101	3rd Eclogues 66		94
Shepherd of shepherds, whose well setled order		128	4th Eclogues 75		128
And hast Thy deadly armes in order brought		278	Psalm VII		35
Unto due thoughts mankind his thoughts shall order, ...		300	Psalm XXII		66
ORDERED					
The poore-clad truth of love's wrong-ordred lot.		242	Other Poems	4	14
ORDERETH					
Gives happs or mishapps, ev'n as he ordreth his hearte.. . .		29	1st Eclogues 11		8
ORIENT					
All things that earst I sawe, as orient pearles exceed, . . .		119	4th Eclogues 73		83
ORPHAN					
My Orphan sence flies to the inward sight, ...		223	Astrophil	88	10
Bare me in hand, that in this Orphane place, ...		235	Astrophil	106	3
ORPHAN'S					
O be thou still the Orphan's aide.		283	Psalm X		77
ORPHANS					
We Orphans lefte, void of all publique might?.		129	4th Eclogues 76		12
Orphans in deede, depriv'd of father's might:.		129	4th Eclogues 76		13
ORPHEUS'					
If Orpheus' voyce had force to breathe such musicke's love .		208	A&S 3rd Song		1
Sweete Orpheus' Harpe, whose sound		260	Other Poems	6	13
OTHER					
Seeke other thoughts thy life or death to find;		4	Lady of May	2	15
For other be those tunes which sorrow tyes, ...		13	Arcadia I	4	7
Dorus. Farre other care, o Muse, my sorrow tries, ...		17	1st Eclogues	7	106
One brings the stuffe, the other stamps the coine, ...		20	1st Eclogues	8	3
Naught in himselfe ech other to abuse.		21	1st Eclogues	8	24
And let thine eyes to other sports be framed..		25	1st Eclogues	9	122
One saith, He mockes; the other saith, he playes;.		27	1st Eclogues 10		44
And worse of other more, till by assent.		29	1st Eclogues 10		82
I waile their lotte, but will not other prove.		39	Arcadia II	17	4
The one of Love, the other Jealousie, ...		42	Arcadia II	22	2
The one aloft doth holde the other hie..		42	Arcadia II	22	5
Pas. Nay like to nightingales the other birds give eare: . .		52	2nd Eclogues 29		19
Where chaunge of thoughts one foole to other shewes, ...		57	2nd Eclogues 30		21
Then let me eke forget one hand from other:		61	2nd Eclogues 30		161
By just exchange, one for the other giv'ne..		75	Arcadia III	45	2
Save one as much as other cleere:		86	Arcadia III	62	20
Each other still allow:		92	3rd Eclogues 63		50
Ech other beast likewise his present brings:		101	3rd Eclogues 66		99
Let other fowler spots away be blowne;		105	3rd Eclogues 67		55
The sure refuge, by thee and by no other		108	Arcadia IV	69	13
Whereto I yeeld, and seeke no other breath, ...		114	4th Eclogues 72		18
The other had with arte (more then our women knowe, ...		118	4th Eclogues 73		71
Both our estates, while each the other did deprave, ...		119	4th Eclogues 73		107
Let one the Princesse be, to her the other yeeld:.		120	4th Eclogues 73		129
Alas she hath no other cause of anguish.		137	Cert Sonnets	4	13
One of other beautie takes..		140	Cert Sonnets	7	17
No other shepheard should have scope, ...		158	Cert Sonnets 28		7
The other sees it but disguised.		159	Cert Sonnets 29		18
Use all to helpe his other conquerings:		179	Astrophil	29	8
With either lip he doth the other kisse:		186	Astrophil	43	11
One hand forgott to rule, th'other to fight.		191	Astrophil	53	11
Nor other sugring of my speech to prove, ...		192	Astrophil	55	10
Looking on me, while I lookt other way:		199	Astrophil	66	12

	PAGE	TITLE		LINE
OTHER (CONTINUED)				
One from the other scarcely can descrie, ...	202	Astrophil	72	3
The prettie death, while each in other live.	206	Astrophil	79	11
If thou praise not, all other praise is shame.	224	Astrophil	90	4
Her selfe (to shew no other joy hath place).	229	Astrophil	97	7
Each to other do imparte,.	227	A&S 10th Song		41
Every other vulgar light.	233	A&S 11th Song		5
It selfe to the other lends.	216	A&S 6th Song		18
But each in the other blessed.	218	A&S 8th Song		8
But of the Other side, the poore in sprite	281	Psalm IX		56
But so of happy other side	284	Psalm XI		21
Who to other Gods do run,.	288	Psalm XVI		10
Other deeps of Woes doth call, ...	335	Psalm XLII		30
He, that the other in some yeares did passe, ...	242	Other Poems	4	21
At other end Uran did Strephon lend.	248	Other Poems	4	246
Nous cri'de, and chafd, but he no other can.	249	Other Poems	4	285
The other end Geron with Uran garde.	250	Other Poems	4	319
The other left alone,.	258	Other Poems	5	88
Scarce each other can abide, ...	263	Other Poems	7	52
OTHER'S				
Burnt in my selfe, I muse at others' fire:	41	Arcadia II	20	5
Disdainst we see thee staind with other's light.	80	Arcadia III	52	15
His ugly evill in other's good to hide,.	141	Cert Sonnets	8	6
Of other's children changelings use to make, ...	178	Astrophil	28	2
A monster, other's harme, selfe-miserie, ...	206	Astrophil	78	5
For other's ease, their frutte, or free estate,.	345	Possibly	2	10
Oft each other's friendship proving, ...	262	Other Poems	7	23
OTHERS				
Nor true love loves those loves with others mingled be.. . .	14	1st Eclogues	7	12
Oh he is mard that is for others made.	19	1st Eclogues	7	166
Lalus. Oh he is mard that is for others made..	19	1st Eclogues	7	167
And others long to tell their loves' condition:.	19	1st Eclogues	7	171
And others long to tell their loves' condicion..	20	1st Eclogues	7	V971
For he woulde sing, but others were defaste;	28	1st Eclogues	10	76
Let others deck their pride with skarres,.	44	Arcadia II	25	7
Men tongd like lotches sucking others sorrowe.	50	2nd Eclogues	28	V885
At which, whether the others did repine, ...	100	3rd Eclogues	66	57
Mournes she in truth, and thinks that others faine?. . . .	142	Cert Sonnets	11	3
Hath not such paine as it makes others have:	142	Cert Sonnets	11	10
Which others said did make their soules to pine:	173	Astrophil	16	6
The Sunne which others burn'd, did her but kisse..	176	Astrophil	22	14
Others, because the Prince my service tries, ...	176	Astrophil	23	7
Fawne on my self, and others to despise:	178	Astrophil	27	8
My still kept course, while others sleepe, to mone.. . . .	184	Astrophil	40	4
Others, because of both sides I do take.	185	Astrophil	41	9
In chariots arm'd, Others in chivalry;	296	Psalm XX		27
Shew that we do not grudge at all when others do rejoyce.. .	343	Possibly	1	2
Who share in woe, weygh others have as much.	242	Other Poems	4	16
Well might he others beare, but leane to none)	244	Other Poems	4	72
OTHERS'				
Who frownes at others' feastes, dooth better bide away.. . .	15	1st Eclogues	7	15
The noblest kinde rejects not others' woes..	18	1st Eclogues	7	134
Which hath in others' head his only being.	20	1st Eclogues	7	V964
No fancy mine, nor others' wronge suspect.	40	Arcadia II	18	11
Who others' vertue doubt, themselves are vicious..	47	2nd Eclogues	28	9
His breast doth fill with earth of others' woe,.	50	2nd Eclogues	28	85
Since from these good the others' good doth flowe, ...	92	3rd Eclogues	63	40
Who others' woes and plaints can chastly beare:.	142	Cert Sonnets	10	7
Feares she to feele, and feeles not others' feares?. . . .	142	Cert Sonnets	11	4
Oft turning others' leaves, to see if thence would flow. .	165	Astrophil	1	7
And others' feete still seem'd but strangers in my way.. .	165	Astrophil	1	11
Without my plumes from others' wings I take.	224	Astrophil	90	11
With others' blott, till all do tast of shame.	248	Other Poems	4	232
It ended, but the others' woe began, ...	252	Other Poems	4	417
OUGHT				
And for th'event we never ought be sad..	105	3rd Eclogues	67	66
Ought to be king, from whose rules who do swerve,.	167	Astrophil	5	3
OUNCE				
The Lion, harte; the Ounce gave active might;.	101	3rd Eclogues	66	80
OURS				
When all this Earth, this damme or mould of ours,.	100	3rd Eclogues	66	44
Crie, "Victorie, this faire day all is ours.".	171	Astrophil	12	11
For who is God, besides this Great Jehova Ours?.	292	Psalm XVIII		57
OURSELVES				
That huntinge faultes, our selves we did not catch.. . . .	29	1st Eclogues	10	93
R. We with ourselves abide a daily strife.	46	2nd Eclogues	27	25
Our sports murdering our selves, our musiques wailing, . .	109	Arcadia IV	70	29
Let hating of our selves be our affection, ...	130	4th Eclogues	76	33
Let us against our selves employ our might,.	130	4th Eclogues	76	35
An image is, which for our selves we carve;.	167	Astrophil	5	6
OUT				
Then power out plaint, and in one word say this:	13	Arcadia I	4	9
Let crowes picke out mine eyes, which saw too much:. . . .	19	1st Eclogues	7	149
Let crowes picke out mine eyes which too much sawe.. . . .	19	1st Eclogues	7	V149
Who well can set a passion out to show:.	25	1st Eclogues	9	112
Since that we see our saddest Shepheards out	27	1st Eclogues	10	26
Or all abroade if but a Cubb start out.	27	1st Eclogues	10	30
Nurse inwarde maladyes, which have not scope to be breath'd				
out, ...	35	1st Eclogues	13	104
My weedes, Desire, cut out in endlesse foldes.	39	Arcadia II	17	6

OUT   (CONTINUED)   PAGE   TITLE   LINE
      Among us all we should find out some thing of nought.. . . . .   51 2nd Eclogues 29   2
      While I was warbling out your wonted praise,. . . . .   54 2nd Eclogues 29   67
      Due sighes blowe out all sparkes of joyfull light, ...   74 Arcadia III 42   11
      (Which oft to hope laies out a guilefull baite,. . . . . . .   82 Arcadia III 56   2
      Ye helplesse Sighes, blowe out your breath to nought,. . . .   83 Arcadia III 59   5
      Aurora like new out of bed,. . . . .   86 Arcadia III 62   24
      There ofte steales out that round cleane foote . . . .   89 Arcadia III 62   105
      And out gan cry, "ah well away for shame,. . . . .   95 3rd Eclogues 64   45
      Glad was the man when he had heard her out,. . . . .   96 3rd Eclogues 64   63
      But let us pick our good from out much bad:. . . . .   105 3rd Eclogues 67   62
      Which drawne-out line doth hold all humane blisse. . . . . .   105 3rd Eclogues 67   72
      That private panges can not breath out in publique . . . . .   109 Arcadia IV 70   32
      I curse the fidling finders out of Musicke:. . . . .   112 4th Eclogues 71   51
      Hate fully growne, Absence new sprongen out. . . . .   115 4th Eclogues 72   58
      As stuffe meant for the sale set out to glaring showe) . . .   118 4th Eclogues 73   72
      When I such guests did see come out of such a house, ...   118 4th Eclogues 73   75
      I would have spoken out: but out they both did crie;. . . .   121 4th Eclogues 73   167
      Bubling out doth breathe signes of his hugie dolours:. . . .   123 4th Eclogues 74   28
      First be mine eyes pulde out, first be my braine perished; .   124 4th Eclogues 74   60
      Out of our sight in turne of hand is vanished. . . . .   128 4th Eclogues 75   127
      And putting out our eyes seeke we our light. . . . .   130 4th Eclogues 76   36
      Sings out her woes, a thorne her song-booke making:. . . . .   137 Cert Sonnets 4   4
      (With gall cut out) closde up againe by art, ...   150 Cert Sonnets 22   23
      Ring out your belles, let mourning shewes be spread, ...   159 Cert Sonnets 30   1
      In this small course which birth drawes out to death,. . . .   144 Cert Sonnets 32   10
      While teares powre out his inke, and sighs breathe out his
          words: . . . .   168 Astrophil   6   10
      Breathe out the flames which burne within my heart,. . . . .   179 Astrophil   28   13
      With shield of proofe shield me from out the prease. . . . .   184 Astrophil   39   5
      And cannot chuse but put out what I write, ...   190 Astrophil   50   10
      Growne now his slaves, he forst them out to find . . . . . .   193 Astrophil   57   3
      What sighes stolne out, or kild before full borne? . . . . .   199 Astrophil   67   9
      Envie, put out thine eyes, least thou do see . . . .   200 Astrophil   69   3
      Shall paint out joy, though but in blacke and white. . . . .   201 Astrophil   70   11
      From out that noysome gulfe, which gaping lies . . . .   205 Astrophil   78   3
      Or of thy gifts at least shade out some part. . . . .   207 Astrophil   81   8
      Out traytour absence, darest thou counsell me,. . . . . . .   223 Astrophil   88   1
      From out thy heavy mould, that inbent eyes . . . .   228 Astrophil   94   3
      Would faine drive cloudes from out my heavy cheere. . . . .   230 Astrophil   97   11
      But when Aurora leades out Phoebus' daunce,. . . . .   230 Astrophil   98   12
      While sobd out words a perfect Musike give. . . . .   231 Astrophil   100   11
      With sight thereof cride out; o faire disgrace,. . . . . . .   233 Astrophil   103   13
      From out my ribs, and puffing prove that I . . . .   233 Astrophil   104   13
      Candles out, and curtaines spread: . . . .   211 A&S 4th Song   38
      And all eares worse then deafe, that heard not out thy
          storie. . . . .   212 A&S 5th Song   6
      And shalt root out the tongues to lying bent:. . . . .   275 Psalm V   14
      Thou dost put out, and quite consuming send. . . . .   280 Psalm IX   14
      Shall not be scrap'd from out of heavnly scoar:. . . . . . .   281 Psalm IX   57
      He oft layeth out his hook,. . . . .   282 Psalm X   42
      From out Thy land by them anoy'd. . . . .   283 Psalm X   72
      He came, but came with smoake from out his nostrills sent, .   291 Psalm XVIII 18
      Flames issued from his mouth, and burning coales out went: .   291 Psalm XVIII 19
      Then out his arrowes fly, and streight they scatterd been, .   291 Psalm XVIII 29
      From out his veiling places, ...   294 Psalm XIX   22
      Root out their generation. . . . .   297 Psalm XXI   40
      Whose loosed bones quite out of joint be wryde;. . . . . . .   299 Psalm XXII   32
      And tongue is prest to publish out thy prayse. . . . .   306 Psalm XXVI   39
      Ev'n like a dead man dreamed out of mind,. . . . .   313 Psalm XXXI   35
      I said that I from out Thy sight was cast; . . . .   313 Psalm XXXI   62
      From out his troubles all. . . . .   319 Psalm XXXIV 24
      And drink from out Thy pleasures' spring,. . . . .   324 Psalm XXXVI 23
      Like laurell fresh himself out spreading.. . . . .   327 Psalm XXXVII 90
      The fire took fire and forcibly out brake, ...   329 Psalm XXXIX 11
      As soon as out they go.. . . . .   333 Psalm XLI   24
      Day and night my teares out flowing. . . . .   334 Psalm XLII   9
      When thou hast mynd to weepe, seeke out som smoky room:. . .   343 Possibly   1   11
      The trees spred out their armes to shade hir face, ...   245 Other Poems   4   109
      This mote from out his eye, this inward burre, ...   246 Other Poems   4   172
      With shafts shott out from their back-turned bow.. . . . . .   251 Other Poems   4   351
      Out shreaking pipe made of some witched tree.. . . . .   255 Other Poems   4   516
      Which thus breath'd out with earthquake of his hart. . . . .   256 Other Poems   4   544
OUTCRY
      (Cpprest with ruinouse conceites) by the helpe of an
          outcrye . . . .   35 1st Eclogues 13   109
OUTSIDE
      While to my minde the out side stood,. . . . .   156 Cert Sonnets 27   7
      Not this faire outside, which our hearts doth move. . . . .   190 Astrophil   52   8
      Not for his faire outside, nor well lined braine,. . . . . .   204 Astrophil   75   3
OUTWARD
      With outward force and inward treason spoild.. . . . .   11 Arcadia I   2   4
      Yeld outward shew, what inward change he tryes:. . . . . . .   13 Arcadia I   4   2
      With cutward joyes, which inly cannot sincke,. . . . .   22 1st Eclogues 9   7
      And yet his outward heate our teares would quench, but an
          inward . . . .   32 1st Eclogues 13   31
      Since outward pleasures be but halting helpes to decayd
          soules). . . . .   33 1st Eclogues 13   52
      Thus outward helps my inward griefes maintaine.. . . . . . .   42 Arcadia II   21   12
      Woe to poore man: ech outward thing annoyes him. . . . . . .   62 2nd Eclogues 30   170

OUTWARD   (CONTINUED)   PAGE   TITLE   LINE
    My inward hurte should spare thy outward rine? . . . .   77 Arcadia III   47   8
    Right so my inwarde partes, and outward glasse, ... 78 Arcadia III   50   6
    And inward griefe seale up with outward wailing. . . . . . . 109 Arcadia IV   70   6
    With outward maker's force, or like an inward father. . . . . 118 4th Eclogues   73   48
    They are the outward seale: . . . .   152 Cert Sonnets   23   30
    Playing and shining in each outward part: . . . .   170 Astrophil   11   13
    Outward, all outward goods . . . .   304 Psalm XXV   51
    With inward wo, an outward sack cloth ware. . . . .   322 Psalm XXXV   30
OVEN
    Thou as in fiery Ov'en shalt make. . . . .   297 Psalm XXI   31
OVER
    To one whose state is raised over all, ...   3 Lady of May   1   1
    Then who makes us such judges over all?. . . . .   29 1st Eclogues   10   96
    Over these brookes trusting to ease mine eyes, ...   41 Arcadia II   21   1
    Where hers, whom worth makes highest over all, ...   78 Arcadia III   49   17
    Thus, thus the mindes, which over all doo clime, ...   127 4th Eclogues   75   88
    Lcoks over the world, and can find nothing such, ...   169 Astrophil   9   10
    Deere, therefore be not jealous over me, ...   225 Astrophil   91   12
    Triumphing over me.   333 Psalm XLI   40
    Over me all thy waves went; . . . .   335 Psalm XLII   34
    Pas could not stay, but over him did rake, ...   248 Other Poems   4 259
    They looked down to triumph over pride: . . . .   252 Other Poems   4 403
OVERCAME
    I would know by what right this palenesse overcame . . . . . 232 Astrophil   102   7
OVERCAST
    "Alas! a cloud hath overcast mine eies: . . . .   255 Other Poems   4 505
OVERCCME
    She had chiefe Goddesses in beautie overcome. . . . .   120 4th Eclogues   73 146
    With darkest shade doth overccme my day; . . . .   223 Astrophil   89   2
    Now let those lightsome sights we see thy darknes overcome.   343 Possibly   1   12
OVERGCNE
    Because thou hast thy fellow overgone, ...   27 1st Eclogues   10   11
OVERLCADEN
    Tir'de as a jade in overloden carte, ...   253 Other Poems   4 443
OVERPASS
    That makes me oft my best friends overpasse, ...   178 Astrophil   27   12
OVERPASSED
    But feare forgott, and paynes all overpaste, ...   70 Arcadia III   36   5
OVER-PRESSED
    To over pressed brestes, more greevous waight. . . . . . .   82 Arcadia III   56   8
OVERSPREAD
    And that faire you my Sunne, thus overspred. . . . .   224 Astrophil   91   3
OVERTAKE
    Thy hand thy foes shall overtake, ...   297 Psalm XXI   29
OVERTHROW
    Both these conspird poore Reason's overthrowe; . . . .   11 Arcadia I   2   7
    There shall he find all vices' overthrow, ...   201 Astrophil   71   5
    As how to watch our overthrow, ...   290 Psalm XVII   32
    For they to overthrow Thy Will . . . .   298 Psalm XXI   41
OVERTHROWN
    With reason's strife, by senses overthrowne, ...   148 Cert Sonnets   19   14
    Weigh then how I by thee am overthrowne: . . . .   185 Astrophil   40   8
OVERTHWART
    Alas, what cause is there so overthwart, ...   186 Astrophil   44   7
OVERTRODDEN
    And state throwen downe to over-troden vallies. . . . . . .   112 4th Eclogues   71   30
OVER-WISE
    I never spited you, but thought you overwise. . . . .   121 4th Eclogues   73 150
    O fooles, or over-wise, alas the race. . . . .   176 Astrophil   23   12
OVID'S
    Those thighes, for Ovid's song more fitte; . . . .   88 Arcadia III   62   88
OWE
    Which unto it by birthright I do ow: . . . .   174 Astrophil   18   6
    Such coltish gyres, that to my birth I owe . . . .   175 Astrophil   21   6
    I owe Thee prayse, I will prayse Thee. . . . .   310 Psalm XXX   3
    What great thanks I ow thee. . . . .   337 Psalm XLIII   30
OWL
    Onely the owle still warnde them not to seech. . . . . . .   100 3rd Eclogues   66   68
    Am growne a shrich-owle to my selfe each morning. . . . . .   111 4th Eclogues   71   18
OWLS
    The Nightingales doo learne of Owles their musique: . . . .   112 4th Eclogues   71   40
OWLY
    Our owly eyes, which dimm'd with passions bee, ...   131 Arcadia V   77   9
OWN
    In thy owne seate a forraine state shall sit. . . . .   11 Arcadia I   1   8
    Love well thine owne: me thinkes, woolle's whitenes passeth
        all: . . . .   16 1st Eclogues   7   53
    But fondlings fonde, know not your owne desire . . . . . .   25 1st Eclogues   9 102
    To be a player of thine owne annoy. . . . .   25 1st Eclogues   9 119
    By justice' worke they their owne faultes disclose: . . . .   27 1st Eclogues   10   42
    Our owne demeane, and soone we wondre shall. . . . .   29 1st Eclogues   10   92
    What can justice availe, to a man that tells not his owne
        case?. . . . .   32 1st Eclogues   13   22
    But yet well I doo finde each man most wise in his owne
        case . . . .   33 1st Eclogues   13   70
    And neither of us great or blest deemeth his owne selfe.   33 1st Eclogues   13   73
    In silence, from a man's owne selfe with company robbed. . .   35 1st Eclogues   13 106
    Jaylor I am to my selfe, priscn and prisoner to myne owne
        selfe. . . . .   37 1st Eclogues   13 163

OWN   (CONTINUED)   PAGE   TITLE   LINE
Of my owne harte, where thoughts be the temple, sighte is an
  aultar. . . . .   37 1st Eclogues 13   171
P. Reason hath eyes to see his owne ill case. . . . .   46 2nd Eclogues 27   16
Or if sheepe's cries can helpe the Sunne's owne braverie,. .   48 2nd Eclogues 28   25
In thy owne proofe he gets so straunge possession, ...   48 2nd Eclogues 28   35
To helpe, or hurt in thee her owne infection. . . . .   49 2nd Eclogues 28   54
For that construction thy owne wordes do beare. . . . . . .   49 2nd Eclogues 28   74
Pas. My gray-hood is mine owne, all be it be but gray, . . .   52 2nd Eclogues 29   7
Such beames so like his owne, which might have might . . . .   60 2nd Eclogues 30   105
And in thy case do glasse mine owne debilitie: . . . . . .   60 2nd Eclogues 30   129
To sing my owne decaid state. . . . .   65 2nd Eclogues 32   4
Under this, this her owne, her only dearling. . . . .   68 2nd Eclogues 33   23
More in his owne he toyld he gladdes the more. . . . .   71 Arcadia III 36   12
I plaine with cause, my woes are all myne owne. . . . . . .   75 Arcadia III 43   6
He loves my hart, for once it was his owne: . . . .   76 Arcadia III 45   7
All what I am, still one, his owne, doe finde. . . . .   78 Arcadia III 50   10
All what you are still one, his owne to finde, ...   79 Arcadia III 50   11
My hopes which do but to mine owne aspire? . . . .   80 Arcadia III 53   4
Mine owne? o word on whose sweete sound doth pray. . . . . .   80 Arcadia III 53   5
Mine owne, embraced, sought, knot, fire, desease. . . . . .   84 Arcadia III 60   14
To their owne worke this priviledge they graunt, ... 101 3rd Eclogues 66   103
Who now his owne, full like his owne he used. . . . . 102 3rd Eclogues 66   142
When without shame he saith, "these be mine owne". . . . . . 106 3rd Eclogues 67   114
How hast thou torne thy selfe! sought thine owne damage! . . 109 Arcadia IV   70   20
Then decke me as thine owne; thy helpe I borowe, ... 114 4th Eclogues 72   28
Of mine owne wordes, my owne good hap betray,. . . . . 145 Cert Sonnets 16   10
Rebels to Nature, strive for their owne smart. . . . . 167 Astrophil   5   4
My best wits still their owne disgrace invent: . . . . 174 Astrophil   19   5
That mine owne writings like bad servants show . . . . 175 Astrophil   21   3
Or carelesse of the wealth because her owne: . . . . 176 Astrophil   22   11
And damning their owne selves to Tantal's smart, ... 177 Astrophil   24   3
But wilt new warre upon thine owne begin?. . . . . 183 Astrophil   36   8
By Love's owne selfe, but with so curious drought, ... 184 Astrophil   38   7
According to my Lord Love's owne behest: . . . . 189 Astrophil   50   6
Wo, having made with many fights his owne. . . . . 193 Astrophil   57   1
Prints his owne lively forme in rudest braine. . . . . 194 Astrophil   58   8
He barks, my songs thine owne voyce oft doth prove:. . . . . 194 Astrophil   59   6
Her graunt to me, by her owne vertue know. . . . . 196 Astrophil   63   4
Who his owne joy to his owne hurt applies, ... 206 Astrophil   78   7
So manie eyes ay seeking their owne woe, ... 206 Astrophil   78   12
Have chang'd desert, let mine owne conscience be . . . . . . 212 Astrophil   86   2
Can scarce discerne the shape of mine owne paine. . . . . . 228 Astrophil   94   4
Kils his owne children, teares, finding tha they. . . . . . 229 Astrophil   95   10
Night bard from Sun, thou from thy owne sur e's light; . . . 229 Astrophil   96   4
Till it have wrought what thy owne will at ends. . . . . . . 236 Astrophil   107   11
When sorrow (using mine owne fier's might) . . . . 236 Astrophil   108   1
Whose owne fault casts him downe, hardly high seat recovers. 213 A&S 5th Song   24
Thou lord, Thou lord, the saver of Thyne Owne. . . . . 275 Psalm V   21
With heaped weights of their own sins oppresse . . . . 275 Psalm V   31
And his own evill his own head shall appall. . . . . 278 Psalm VII   45
To rule the Works of Thyne own hands . . . . 279 Psalm VIII   22
Is their own foot, ledd by their own ill thought,. . . . . . 280 Psalm IX   49
When Godless men be snar'd in their own snares:. . . . . . . 281 Psalm IX   52
In craft of his own crafty thought!. . . . . 281 Psalm X   8
Say, Thou dost not Thyn Own regard?. . . . . 283 Psalm X   56
Ev'en the body of Thyne Own, ... 288 Psalm XVI   34
O let my sentence passe from Thyne own face; . . . . 289 Psalm XVII   5
That God from fall his own Anoynted stayes.. . . . . 296 Psalm XX   22
And God shall them in his own court reserve. . . . . 300 Psalm XXII   76
Who shall climb to the hill which God's own hill is named, . 302 Psalm XXIV   5
And to the proud in deeds pays home their own. . . . . 314 Psalm XXXI   66
And open'd mine own wickednes,. . . . . 315 Psalm XXXII   14
For God's own eyes on good men sit . . . . 320 Psalm XXXIV   55
Fall in self pitt, be caught in their own nett.. . . . . . . 321 Psalm XXXV   18
The fulness of thy own heart's lusting;. . . . . 324 Psalm XXXVII   10
The wicked by his own pride bannish;. . . . . 325 Psalm XXXVII   26
Their swords shall their own hearts embrew. . . . . 325 Psalm XXXVII   40
Miso mine owne pigsnie, thou shalt heare news o' Damaetas. . 241 Other Poems   2   1
Made them his owne before they had it wist.. . . . . 246 Other Poems   4   159
When Strephon, cursing his owne backwardnes, ... 252 Other Poems   4   388
To his owne witt, thought upon thought did swell,. . . . . . 256 Other Poems   4   542
With thoughts which thoughts their owne tormentors tried,. . 259 Other Poems   5   119
OWNER
So faire a fielde would well become an owner. . . . .   17 1st Eclogues 7   99
O My thoughtes' sweete foode, my my onely owner, ... 138 Cert Sonnets 5   1
Above line repeated at following location. . . . . 138 Cert Sonnets 5   25
Yet hast Thou made even him an owner . . . . 279 Psalm VIII   19
And of the earth make Thee an owner, ... 327 Psalm XXXVII   87
OWNERS'
As if they would of owners' humour be, ... 242 Other Poems   4   31
OXEN
Both sheep and Oxen wholy hast,. . . . . 279 Psalm VIII   26
OX'S
Eyes faire and great, like faire great oxe's eyes, ...   76 Arcadia III 46   9
P
P. If Reason will, that Passions be not free.. . . . .   46 2nd Eclogues 27   4
P. And Passion will, that Passion rule the rost. . . . . . .   46 2nd Eclogues 27   6
P. Will hath his will, when Reason's will doth misse.. . . .   46 2nd Eclogues 27   8
P. And let him die, so that he die content.. . . . .   46 2nd Eclogues 27   10

P	(CONTINUED)	PAGE	TITLE		LINE
P. Not so, but fellowlike together borne..		46	2nd Eclogues	27	12
P. Who Passion doth forsake, lives void of joy..		46	2nd Eclogues	27	14
P. Reason hath eyes to see his owne ill case..		46	2nd Eclogues	27	16
P. And is not Reason dimde with Passion's might?		46	2nd Eclogues	27	18
P. O glorious title of a foolish toye.		46	2nd Eclogues	27	20
P. Because our weaknes weakeneth all your might.		46	2nd Eclogues	27	22
P. O Passion, passe on feeble Reason's spoiles..		46	2nd Eclogues	27	24
P. We gladly use the sweetnes of our life.		46	2nd Eclogues	27	26
P. We now have peace, your peace we doo not neede.		46	2nd Eclogues	27	28
P. Who be too weake, do feigne they be too good.		47	2nd Eclogues	27	30
P. Let us orecome, and let us be unjust.		47	2nd Eclogues	27	32
P. What shall we winne by taking Reason's yoke?.		47	2nd Eclogues	27	34
P. But so we shall with griefe learne to repent.		47	2nd Eclogues	27	36
P. How know we that, since present joyes we misse?		47	2nd Eclogues	27	38
P. No Reason yet had ever skill to show it..		47	2nd Eclogues	27	40
Welcome my two to me, E.D. F.G. P.S..		261	Other Poems	6	25
PACE					
With Cupid she fore-sees, and goes god Vulcan's pace:. . . .		12	Arcadia I	3	7
But heavy was her pace, and such a meagre cheere,.		118	4th Eclogues	73	69
But cald, she came apace; a pace wherein did move.		119	4th Eclogues	73	89
To keepe the pace of their first loving state.		173	Astrophil	17	4
That no pace else their guided steps can find, ...		194	Astrophil	58	3
Then did he slack his love-enstructed pace..		250	Other Poems	4	308
With love drawne on, so fast with pace unmeet.		250	Other Poems	4	334
PACIFIED					
With chafe enough, till she him pacified:.		97	3rd Eclogues	64	110
PAGE					
Where Cupid is sworne page to Chastity?.		182	Astrophil	35	8
Love moves thy paine, and like a faithfull page, ...		232	Astrophil	101	9
Curst be the page from whome the bad torch fell, ...		235	Astrophil	105	11
PAID					
I never found long love such wealth hath paide to me". . . .		16	1st Eclogues	7	54
Where all my paines one looke of hers hath paid.		26	1st Eclogues	9	137
I said, my hands well paide her for mine eyes, ...		55	2nd Eclogues	29	115
Sweet Ladie you remaine well paid.		159	Cert Sonnets	29	4
That wittie Lewis to him a tribute paid.		204	Astrophil	75	11
PAIN					
A good foole call'd with paine, perhapps may be, ...		28	1st Eclogues	10	71
Enjoye my joyes, as you dyd taste my payne,.		43	Arcadia II	23	11
Wayle in my woes, taste of your master's payne,.		44	Arcadia II	24	11
Latona's sonne, whose birth in paine and travaile long . . .		45	Arcadia II	26	7
Paine willes me die, yet will of death I mortifie:		51	2nd Eclogues	28	124
Where death is feard, and life is held with paine.		57	2nd Eclogues	30	19
Thus is our thought with paine for thistles tilled:.		62	2nd Eclogues	30	173
What medecin may I finde for a paine that draw's me to					
death Death..		63	2nd Eclogues	31	6
Thus sweete paine, I do yeeld, what ere I can yeelde.. . . .		68	2nd Eclogues	33	29
Bitter griefe tastes me best, paine is my ease,.		74	Arcadia III	41	7
In which delightfull paine,.		91	3rd Eclogues	63	17
Make home more paine then following of the cart.		104	3rd Eclogues	67	30
We made for paine, our paines they made to cherish:.		106	3rd Eclogues	67	107
Vaine is their paine, who labour in Despaire.		115	4th Eclogues	72	60
Strephon. Vaine is their paine, who labour in Despaire.. . .		115	4th Eclogues	72	61
How hast thou framde the paine wherewith I am opprest? . . .		121	4th Eclogues	73	184
So high, as should make such a paine notorious:.		129	4th Eclogues	75	140
And make his paine to keepe us safe his pleasure?.		129	4th Eclogues	76	24
Feare is more paine, then is the paine it feares,.		131	Arcadia V	77	5
Since shunning paine, I ease can never find:		135	Cert Sonnets	1	1
Would often kill to breed more feeling paine,.		135	Cert Sonnets	2	4
The smoke of hell, the monster called paine, ...		140	Cert Sonnets	8	2
Ah saucy paine let not thy errour last,.		141	Cert Sonnets	8	13
My burning tongue hath bred my mistresse paine,.		141	Cert Sonnets	9	2
For oft in paine to paine my painefull heart		141	Cert Sonnets	9	3
Paine heard her praise, and full of inward fire, ...		141	Cert Sonnets	9	9
O paine I now recant the praise I gave,.		141	Cert Sonnets	9	13
Thou paine the onely guest of loath'd constraint,.		141	Cert Sonnets	10	1
Thou paine, thou hated paine, from heav'n exilde,.		141	Cert Sonnets	10	4
And have I heard her say, "o cruell paine!".		142	Cert Sonnets	11	1
Or doth she thinke all paine the minde forbeares?		142	Cert Sonnets	11	5
Hath not such paine as it makes others have:		142	Cert Sonnets	11	10
But this she thinks, our paine hye cause excuseth,.		142	Cert Sonnets	11	13
Where her who should rule paine, false paine abuseth.. . . .		142	Cert Sonnets	11	14
Part of my paine me seemes engravell lyes..		147	Cert Sonnets	18	4
I yeeld and strive, I kisse and curse the paine:		148	Cert Sonnets	19	17
Doth answere well the paine:		152	Cert Sonnets	23	18
Nay former blisse addes to present paine,.		153	Cert Sonnets	24	13
Though in paine, cannot complaine. No, no, no, no.		156	Cert Sonnets	26	33
That the deare She might take some pleasure of my paine: . .		165	Astrophil	1	2
That she (deare she) might take some pleasure of my paine: .		165	Astrophil	1 V	2
Of force of heav'nly beames, infusing hellish paine:		167	Astrophil	6	3
His paper, pale dispaire, and paine his pen doth move. . . .		168	Astrophil	6	11
That to win it, is all the skill and paine.		171	Astrophil	12	14
Alas have I not paine enough my friend,.		171	Astrophil	14	1
By my love judging what Love's paine might be.		173	Astrophil	16	8
But for that man with paine this truth descries, ...		177	Astrophil	25	5
Where Love is chastnesse, Paine doth learne delight, ...		188	Astrophil	48	3
Rather then by more truth to get more paine.		199	Astrophil	67	14
Those scarlet judges, threatning bloudy paine?		203	Astrophil	73	11
With doing all, leave nothing done but paine..		210	Astrophil	85	8

361

PAIN	(CONTINUED)	PAGE	TITLE		LINE
Can scarce discerne the shape of mine owne paine		228	Astrophil	94	4
Love moves thy paine, and like a faithfull page,		232	Astrophil	101	9
All folkes prest at thy will thy paine to 'swage,		232	Astrophil	101	11
Sweete reward for sharpest paine:		210	A&S 4th Song		4
Suffer not her to laugh, while both we suffer paine:		213	A&S 5th Song		29
Theeves steal for need, and steale but goods, which paine recovers,		214	A&S 5th Song		45
Upon his pate, his pain employed thus.		278	Psalm VII		44
When wycked soules be turn'd to hellish paine,		281	Psalm IX		53
Yet perish shall (although his paine be sore)		281	Psalm IX		59
And forsee their wretched paine.		288	Psalm XVI		9
O be not farr, since pain so nearly presseth,		299	Psalm XXII		25
Do pine, my strength with pain is wholy gon,		312	Psalm XXXI		29
Thus I prest down with weight of pain,		315	Psalm XXXII		7
And did due pain forgive me.		315	Psalm XXXII		18
And keep from Famin's paine.		318	Psalm XXXIII		75
Leaving in paine their wel-fed hungry eies..		246	Other Poems	4	168
Their snowy haire teare off in melting paine.		254	Other Poems	4	478
To thinke, and thinke with paine		256	Other Poems	5	10
PAINFULL					
Cherish the hives of wisely painfull Bees:		26	1st Eclogues	9	132
For oft in paine to paine my painefull heart		141	Cert Sonnets	9	3
PAINFULNESS					
"Erona dye, and end this ougly painefulnes"?		61	2nd Eclogues	30	157
PAINLESS					
This waxe doth waste it selfe, yet painelesse dyes..		75	Arcadia III	43	2
PAINS					
Where all my paines one looke of hers hath paid.		26	1st Eclogues	9	137
But in the sandes my paynes foretolde I finde,		42	Arcadia II	21	15
What be the joyes for which to enjoy they went to the paines Paines..		63	2nd Eclogues	31	14
So are thy pains my pains too.		67	2nd Eclogues	32	42
But feare forgott, and paynes all overpaste,		70	Arcadia III	36	5
Nowe that some flower of fruict, my paynes do prove,		72	Arcadia III	37	16
Can holde, shew, tell, my paines without reliefe..		75	Arcadia III	43	8
To ease those paines, which on desire do waite).		82	Arcadia III	56	4
We made for paine, our paines they made to cherish:		106	3rd Eclogues	67	107
Which is the hatefull web of Sorowe's paines..		114	4th Eclogues	72	25
But that eternall paines my soule have hent,		116	4th Eclogues	72	87
But vaine it is to thinke those paines should cease,		116	4th Eclogues	72	94
With idle paines, and missing ayme, do guesse.		176	Astrophil	23	4
With me those paines for God's sake do not take:		179	Astrophil	28	3
So sweets my paines, that my paines me rejoyce..		193	Astrophil	57	14
In justice paines come not till faults do call;		212	Astrophil	86	10
Only with paines my paines thus eased be,		227	Astrophil	93	12
And age pull'd on with paines all freshness fretteth:		276	Psalm VI		22
Ponder the paines, which on me loaden be		280	Psalm IX		37
On me the paines of death already gan to prey,		291	Psalm XVIII		8
Most great and grievous paines doth beare,		320	Psalm XXXIV		70
Foul faults sore pains do reach me,		332	Psalm XL		46
Then sports grew paines, all talking tediouse,		253	Other Poems	4	433
PAINT					
Thus Painters Cupid paint, thus Poets do,		20	1st Eclogues	8	5
As you paint them: but well in you I finde,		106	3rd Eclogues	67	83
To paint my living death, and endlesse smart:		146	Cert Sonnets	17	28
Weakely did seeme to paint death's ougly dart.		148	Cert Sonnets	20	4
May paint my face without seeing mee,		153	Cert Sonnets	24	3
I sought fit words to paint the blackest face of woe,		165	Astrophil	1	5
While with a feeling skill I paint my hell..		166	Astrophil	2	14
Shall paint out joy, though but in blacke and white.		201	Astrophil	70	11
How faine would I paint thee to all men's eyes,		207	Astrophil	81	7
What inke is blacke inough to paint my wo?		227	Astrophil	93	3
Paint woe's blacke face so lively to my sight,		230	Astrophil	98	10
PAINTED					
In painted clothes, because they call it love.		23	1st Eclogues	9	48
Sorrowes ill easde, where sorrowes painted be.		41	Arcadia II	21	6
Painted in my beclowded stormie face:		187	Astrophil	45	2
With golden leaves, and painted babery,		246	Other Poems	4	181
PAINTER					
Like cunning Painter shadowing white..		89	Arcadia III	62	98
Would she in beamie blacke, like painter wise,		168	Astrophil	7	3
PAINTER'S					
Her haire, which by the helpe of painter's cunning, shinde..		118	4th Eclogues	73	74
PAINTERS					
Poore Painters oft with silly Poets joyne,		20	1st Eclogues	8	1
Thus Painters Cupid paint, thus Poets do,		20	1st Eclogues	8	5
PAINTS					
Olive paintes me the peace that I must aspire to by conquest		35	1st Eclogues	13	117
PAIR					
The matchlesse paire, even praise doth staine.		86	Arcadia III	62	16
Live one in two, a well united paire,		91	3rd Eclogues	63	7
A paire of frends, or rather one cal'd two,		242	Other Poems	4	18
PALACE					
How to the woods love runnes as well as rydes to the Pallace		31	1st Eclogues	13	4
In sorrows torments, then, tyed to the pompes of a pallace,		35	1st Eclogues	13	103
PALATE					
Which both the pallate, and the eyes delight..		26	1st Eclogues	9	131

```
                                                              PAGE    TITLE           LINE
PALE
    Swelling with sighes, made pale with minde's disease,. . . .   58 2nd Eclogues 30    48
    In shewe and sent pale violets,. . . . . . . . . . . . . . .   89 Arcadia III  62   107
    His paper, pale dispaire, and paine his pen doth move. . . .  168 Astrophil     6    11
PALENESS
    That in that palenesse beautie's white we see; . . . . . . .  231 Astrophil   101     6
    I would know by what right this palenesse overcame . . . . .  232 Astrophil   102     7
PALM
    But in a palme when I marke, how he doth rise under a
        burden . . . . . . . . . . . . . . . . . . . . . . . . .   36 1st Eclogues 13   127
PALMS
    Palmes do rejoyce to be joynd by the match of a male to a
        female,. . . . . . . . . . . . . . . . . . . . . . . . .   36 1st Eclogues 13   137
PALSY
    Dead palsie sicke of all my chiefest parts:. . . . . . . . .  136 Cert Sonnets  2    10
PAN
    (Therion) When wanton Pan, deceiv'd with Lion's skin,. . . .    5 Lady of May   3     7
    "Poore Pan" (he sayd) "although thou beaten be,. . . . . . .    5 Lady of May   3    11
    As smooth as Pan, as Juno milde, like goddesse Iris faste. .   12 Arcadia I     3     6
    Now thanked be the great God Pan,. . . . . . . . . . . . . .   13 Arcadia I     5     1
    Lalus. Muse hold your peace: but thou, my God Pan, glorify .   15 1st Eclogues  7    25
    Thy pipe, o Pan, shall helpe, though I sing sorilie. . . . .   15 1st Eclogues  7    27
    Lalus. This mayde, thus made for joyes, o Pan bemone her,. .   17 1st Eclogues  7    97
    Pan is not dead, since Pas beginnes to sing. . . . . . . . .   53 2nd Eclogues 29    53
    Nico. Tell me (and be my Pan) the monster's name,. . . . . .   56 2nd Eclogues 29   141
    Pan, father Pan, the god of silly sheepe,. . . . . . . . . .   92 3rd Eclogues 63    37
    Pan store of babes, vertue their thoughts well staid,. . . .   93 3rd Eclogues 63    93
    Let Pan our good God see,. . . . . . . . . . . . . . . . . .  260 Other Poems   6     3
    "Therefore Pan, if thou mayst be . . . . . . . . . . . . . .  263 Other Poems   7    55
    May make treaty to god Pan). . . . . . . . . . . . . . . . .  263 Other Poems   7    58
PANDAR
    The pandare of the thing, he most did feare, . . . . . . . .   97 3rd Eclogues 64   122
PANGS
    What be the pangs they beare, and whence those pangs be
        derived, . . . . . . . . . . . . . . . . . . . . . . . .   33 1st Eclogues 13    43
    That private panges can not breath out in publique . . . . .  109 Arcadia IV   70    32
    As tender conscience might with furious panges assaulte. . .  117 4th Eclogues 73    20
    And knowne those pangs that the losers prove,. . . . . . . .  153 Cert Sonnets 24     2
PANTING
    While brickle houreglas runnes, guide thou our panting race:   45 Arcadia II   26    10
    Cannot be staid within my panting breast,. . . . . . . . . .  189 Astrophil    50     2
    So my soul in panting playeth, . . . . . . . . . . . . . . .  334 Psalm XLII          3
    To feele the panting heart, which through hir syde . . . . .  252 Other Poems   4   405
PANTS
    Whose pants do make unspilling creame to flow, . . . . . . .  231 Astrophil   100     6
    Sweetnesse, that breathes and pants as oft as she: . . . . .  231 Astrophil   101     2
    Which pants as though it still should leape to thee: . . . .  236 Astrophil   107     6
    My heart pants, gon is my might; . . . . . . . . . . . . . .  328 Psalm XXXVIII      28
PAP
    Sleepe then a litle, pap content is making:. . . . . . . . .  139 Cert Sonnets  6     8
    That in her breast thy pap well sugred lies, . . . . . . . .  170 Astrophil    12     5
    And then, a heav'nly child, gave her Ambrosian pap:. . . . .  213 A&S 5th Song       26
PAPER
    Goodnes the penne, heaven paper is,. . . . . . . . . . . . .   90 Arcadia III  62   142
    His paper, pale dispaire, and paine his pen doth move. . . .  168 Astrophil     6    11
    It is but love, which makes his paper perfit white . . . . .  232 Astrophil   102    12
PARADISE
    Nor golden manacles, stand for a paradise, . . . . . . . . .   69 2nd Eclogues 34    25
    O thinke I then, what paradise of joy. . . . . . . . . . . .  200 Astrophil    68    13
    Or gemmes, or frutes of new-found Paradise, . . . . . . . . .  207 Astrophil    81     2
PARCH
    Whiche my chefe partte, doth passe throughe, parche, and
        tye . . . . . . . . . . . . . . . . . . . . . . . . . .  344 Possibly      2     2
PARCHED
    Yet were the hid and meaner beauties parcht, . . . . . . . .  176 Astrophil    22    12
PARDON
    What pardon can availe? or who employes him. . . . . . . . .   62 2nd Eclogues 30   168
    The moone a sunder rent (O godes, o pardon me, . . . . . . .  118 4th Eclogues 73    55
    Sweetnesse sweetly pardon folly, . . . . . . . . . . . . . .  157 Cert Sonnets 27    33
    I do confesse, pardon a fault confest, . . . . . . . . . . .  166 Astrophil     4     7
    Yet Deare, let me this pardon get of you,. . . . . . . . . .  188 Astrophil    46    12
    Pardon mine eares, both I and they do pray,. . . . . . . . .  190 Astrophil    51     1
    Pardon that fault, once more graunt me the place,. . . . . .  208 Astrophil    82    12
    And pardon all my faults.. . . . . . . . . . . . . . . . . .  304 Psalm XXV          64
    The lord with pardon doth make cleane, . . . . . . . . . . .  314 Psalm XXXII         2
PARDONED
    His damme a beast was pardon'd beastly fact. . . . . . . . .   21 1st Eclogues  8    18
PARENTS
    For what they see their parents love or hate . . . . . . . .   28 1st Eclogues 10    56
    Although they be of meaner parents gott: . . . . . . . . . .  242 Other Poems   4    12
    With tedious brawlings of her parents deare, . . . . . . . .  245 Other Poems   4   114
    Her parents liking well it should be so, . . . . . . . . . .  247 Other Poems   4   195
    By Parents train'd the Tartars wilde are tought, . . . . . .  251 Other Poems   4   350
PARENTS'
    Yet beares he still his parents' stately gifts,. . . . . . .   21 1st Eclogues  8    25
    Faine would be free, but dreadeth parents' ire.. . . . . . .  245 Other Poems   4   120
PARIS
    No lovely Paris made thy Hellen his: . . . . . . . . . . . .  181 Astrophil    33     6
PARIS'
    As though she were the same, as when by Paris' doome . . . .  120 4th Eclogues 73   145
```

363

PARLIAMENT
    Of fowles there called was a parliament. . . . .   29 1st Eclogues 10   84
PARNASSUS
    Which from the ribs of old Parnassus flowes,. . . . . 172 Astrophil   15   2
    The new Pernassus, where the Muses bide, ... 207 Astrophil   80   5
    Highway since you my chiefe Pernassus be,. . . . . 209 Astrophil   84   1
PARROT
    I pray thee what hath ere the Parret gott, ...   28 1st Eclogues 10   67
    And Parot, ready tongue, that to applie. . . . . 101 3rd Eclogues 66   84
PART
    Then thow earst knew? rather take part with him. . . . . . .   26 1st Eclogues 10   8
    For that I finde in them parte of my estate represented. . .   35 1st Eclogues 13 115
    Since there mine eyes have played so false a parte,. . . . .   38 Arcadia II   14   11
    In whose chiefe parte your worthes implanted be? . . . . . .   39 Arcadia II   16   10
    And cast from me part of my burdnous cares:. . . . .   42 Arcadia II   21   14
    O hand, which toucht her hand when we did part;. . . . . . .   60 2nd Eclogues 30 119
    Chief band I saye, which tyes my chiefest parte, ...   70 Arcadia III   35   12
    My cheefest parte, wherin do chieflye stand. . . . .   70 Arcadia III   35   13
    So smooth as sleekestone-like, it smoothes each parte, . . .   76 Arcadia III   46   14
    The giver giv'n from gifte shall never parte.. . . . .   77 Arcadia III   47   14
    Then take my shape, and play a lover's parte:. . . . .   79 Arcadia III   51   12
    Each moment lost, part of my hap destroyes:. . . . .   80 Arcadia III   53   11
    Fore-felt Desire, begin to savour parte. . . . .   83 Arcadia III   59   11
    In whose each part all pens may dwell? . . . .   85 Arcadia III   62   2
    Which never part but that they showe . . . .   87 Arcadia III   62   41
    Thus hath each part his beautie's part,. . . . .   90 Arcadia III   62 133
    In whose each part all pens may dwell. . . . .   90 Arcadia III   62 146
    Vertue (if not a God) yet God's chiefe parte,. . . . .   92 3rd Eclogues 63   46
    There rested then, to play a woman's part, ...   95 3rd Eclogues 64   39
    A letter such which might from either part . . . .   96 3rd Eclogues 64   81
    Till forste to parte, with harte and eyes even sore, ...   99 3rd Eclogues 66   39
    But since you will, part of my heav'nly fire . . . . 100 3rd Eclogues 66   75
    I thinke from me, not from my woes to parte. . . . . 113 4th Eclogues 72   10
    Klaius. I think from me, not from my woes to parte,. . . . . 113 4th Eclogues 72   11
    And that he thence must part where to live onely I lyved.. . 123 4th Eclogues 74   30
    Where each part in such peace dwelleth,. . . . . 140 Cert Sonnets   7   16
    For because my cheefe part singeth,. . . . . 140 Cert Sonnets   7   35
    Or art thou free from above bid play this part, ... 142 Cert Sonnets 10   11
    Part of my paine me seemes engraved lyes.. . . . . 147 Cert Sonnets 18   4
    That parting thus my chiefest part I part. . . . . 148 Cert Sonnets 20   8
    Part of my life, the loathed part to me, ... 148 Cert Sonnets 20   9
    But that good part, wherein all comforts be, ... 148 Cert Sonnets 20   11
    From joy I part still living in annoy. . . . . 148 Cert Sonnets 20   14
    Which caught, to cruell search yeelds his chiefe part: . . . 150 Cert Sonnets 22   22
    In love, his chiefest part.. . . . . 152 Cert Sonnets 23   12
    The inward light: and that the heavenly part . . . . 167 Astrophil   5   2
    Not usde to frozen clips, he strave to find some part, . . . 168 Astrophil   8   6
    Playing and shining in each outward part:. . . . . 170 Astrophil   11   13
    Who though most rich in these and everie part, ... 183 Astrophil   37   12
    Now from thy fellowship I needs must part, ... 202 Astrophil   72   5
    Pleasingst consort, where each sence holds a part, ... 206 Astrophil   79   3
    Or of thy gifts at least shade out some part.. . . . . 207 Astrophil   81   8
    I saw that sighes her sweetest lips did part,. . . . . 223 Astrophil   87   7
    Thanke may you have for such a thankfull part, ... 229 Astrophil   95   13
    They first resort unto that soveraigne part; . . . . 236 Astrophil   107   4
    For wearing Venus' badge, in every part of thee, ... 214 A&S 5th Song   70
    If I have beene unkynd for friendly part: . . . . 277 Psalm VII   10
    This gotten blisse shall never part, ... 282 Psalm X   24
    And of my Child's part the blisse, ... 288 Psalm XVI   14
    That in good part he did Thy Offrings take;. . . . . 296 Psalm XX   12
    It is a comely part. . . . . 316 Psalm XXXIII   4
    No sound part (causd by Thy wrath) . . . . 327 Psalm XXXVIII   7
    So that my surest part,. . . . . 332 Psalm XL   48
    Whiche my chefe partte, doth passe throughe, parche, and
       tye . . . . 344 Possibly   2   2
    But when the rod began to play his part, ... 246 Other Poems   4 183
    He might on knees confesse his faulty part,. . . . . 247 Other Poems   4 190
    Which absence wisht: love plai'd a victor's part:. . . . . . 248 Other Poems   4 223
    He found man's vertue is but part of man,. . . . . 253 Other Poems   4 421
    And part must folowe where whole man doth goe. . . . . 253 Other Poems   4 422
    Breeding huge stormes with in his inward parte,. . . . . . . 256 Other Poems   4 543
    It may be part of Mira's peticoate,. . . . . 258 Other Poems   5   71
PARTAGE
    Have not I fair partage gott?. . . . . 288 Psalm XVI   18
PARTAKER
    Me-thinkes I am partaker of thy passion, ...   60 2nd Eclogues 30 128
PARTED
    Tell me poore wretch, parted from wretched prey, ... 258 Other Poems   5   89
PARTHENIA
    Argalus and Parthenia. 241 Other Poems   3   9
PARTIAL
    Yet with repining at so partiall lot.. . . . . 165 Astrophil   2   8
    Thou then whom partiall heavens conspir'd in one to frame, . 213 A&S 5th Song   19
    To both sides partiall is: . . . . 216 A&S 6th Song   46
PARTIES
    If by the parties ment our meanings rightly be marked, . . .   37 1st Eclogues 13 174
    Whereto two parties once be full content.. . . . .   97 3rd Eclogues 64 126
PARTING
    That parting thus my chiefest part I part. . . . . 148 Cert Sonnets 20   8
    After parting ought forgot,. . . . . 226 A&S 10th Song   8

```
PARTITION                                                         PAGE    TITLE           LINE
     Of my poore weedes thy do partition make . . . . . . . . .   299  Psalm XXII          43
PARTS
     As for those parts unknowne, which hidden sure are best: . .  12  Arcadia I      3     13
     Can I, that know her sacred parts, restrained be . . . . . .  61  2nd Eclogues  30    149
     Thus be our noblest parts dryed up with sorrow:. . . . . . .  62  2nd Eclogues  30    174
     Right so my inwarde partes, and outward glasse,. . . . . . .  78  Arcadia III   50      6
     O harbour all her partes in easefull plighte:. . . . . . . .  79  Arcadia III   51      7
     (As even in beasts their dammes leave chaunging parts) . . . 100  3rd Eclogues  66     60
     Strephon. For she, whose parts maintainde a perfect musique, 113  4th Eclogues  71     61
     Too much her peerles parts, nor yet could them despise.. . . 119  4th Eclogues  73     88
     Dead palsie sicke of all my chiefest parts:. . . . . . . . . 136  Cert Sonnets   2     10
     If thus, alas: yet while those partes have wo, . . . . . . . 142  Cert Sonnets  10     13
     Yea worse then death, death parts both woe and joy,. . . . . 148  Cert Sonnets  20     13
     If French can yet three parts in one agree;. . . . . . . . . 180  Astrophil     30      5
     When fire seven times hath spent his earthly parts.. . . . . 285  Psalm XII            21
     Strephon, whose eies on hir back-parts did play, . . . . . . 250  Other Poems    4    333
PARTY
     A friend each party drawes,. . . . . . . . . . . . . . . . . 216  A&S 6th Song         29
PAS
     Nico. And are you there old Pas? in troth I ever thought,. .  51  2nd Eclogues  29      1
     Pas. And I am here the same, so mote I thrive and then,. . .  52  2nd Eclogues  29      3
     Pas. My gray-hood is mine owne, all be it be but gray, . . .  52  2nd Eclogues  29      7
     Pas. Ah foole; so Courtiers do. But who did lively skippe, .  52  2nd Eclogues  29     11
     Pas. My voice the lambe did winne, Menalcas was our judge: .  52  2nd Eclogues  29     15
     Pas. Nay like to nightingales the other birds give eare: . .  52  2nd Eclogues  29     19
     Pas. Another sure as is a gander from a goose: . . . . . . .  52  2nd Eclogues  29     23
     Pas. But here is Dicus old; let him then speake the woord, .  52  2nd Eclogues  29     27
     Pas. Kisse her? now mayst thou kisse. I have a fitter match;  53  2nd Eclogues  29     39
     Pan is not dead, since Pas beginnes to sing. . . . . . . . .  53  2nd Eclogues  29     53
     Pas. Who evermore will love Apollo's quill,. . . . . . . . .  53  2nd Eclogues  29     54
     Pas. This is not he that failed her to gaine,. . . . . . . .  54  2nd Eclogues  29     60
     That Nico must with Pas compared be? . . . . . . . . . . . .  54  2nd Eclogues  29     65
     Pas. O Nymphes, I tell you newes, for Pas you knowe: . . . .  54  2nd Eclogues  29     66
     Nico would needes with Pas his bagpipe blowe. . . . . . . . . 54  2nd Eclogues  29     68
     Let Pas now know, how Nico maketh layes. . . . . . . . . . .  54  2nd Eclogues  29     71
     Pas. If each day hath bene holy for your sake, . . . . . . .  54  2nd Eclogues  29     72
     For Pas well knowes what layes can Nico make.. . . . . . . .  54  2nd Eclogues  29     74
     Pas. Alas, when I in spring meet roses rathe,. . . . . . . .  54  2nd Eclogues  29     78
     Pas. But long have I a sparrow gailie drest,. . . . . . . . . 54  2nd Eclogues  29     84
     Pas. Cosma once said, she left the wicket ope, . . . . . . .  55  2nd Eclogues  29     90
     Pas. When Cosma doth come forth, the Sun displaies . . . . .  55  2nd Eclogues  29     96
     Pas. But yesternight by light I did receave. . . . . . . . .  55  2nd Eclogues  29    102
     Pas. She once, to coole her selfe, stood in a well,. . . . .  55  2nd Eclogues  29    108
     Pas. As in a glasse I held she once did looke, . . . . . . .  55  2nd Eclogues  29    114
     Pas. O if I had Apollo's golden carre, . . . . . . . . . . .  56  2nd Eclogues  29    120
     Pas. Thy name (O Cosma) shall with praise be spread, . . . .  56  2nd Eclogues  29    126
     Pas. So oft these woods have heard me "Cosma" crie, . . . .   56  2nd Eclogues  29    132
     Nico. Peace, peace good Pas, thou weeriest even the ground .  56  2nd Eclogues  29    135
     Pas. My father hath at home a prettie Jay, . . . . . . . . .  56  2nd Eclogues  29    138
     Pas. Tell this (and Phoebus be) what monster growes. . . . .  56  2nd Eclogues  29    144
     With Cosma, for whose love Pas past in woe.. . . . . . . . . 248  Other Poems    4    243
     Faire Nous with Pas the lott to hell did sende:. . . . . . . 248  Other Poems    4    244
     Pas thought it hell, while he was Cosma fro. . . . . . . . . 248  Other Poems    4    245
     The play began: Pas durst not Cosma chace, . . . . . . . . . 248  Other Poems    4    249
     But light-legd Pas had gott the middle space.. . . . . . . . 248  Other Poems    4    253
     And so when Pas hand-reached him to take,. . . . . . . . . . 248  Other Poems    4    257
     Pas could not stay, but over him did rake, . . . . . . . . . 248  Other Poems    4    259
     But Nous that slipt from Pas, did catch the clowne.. . . . . 248  Other Poems    4    262
     So laughing all, yet Pas to ease some dell,. . . . . . . . . 249  Other Poems    4    263
     Who should to Pas, but they would her prevent. . . . . . . . 249  Other Poems    4    268
     Pas mad with fall, and madder with the shame,. . . . . . . . 249  Other Poems    4    269
     She quick, and proud, and who did Pas despise, . . . . . . . 249  Other Poems    4    273
     Thus Pas did kisse hir hand with little grace, . . . . . . . 249  Other Poems    4    276
     Till Uran seing Pas to Cosma fly,. . . . . . . . . . . . . . 249  Other Poems    4    286
     Pas Cosma matcht, yet angry with his fault,. . . . . . . . . 250  Other Poems    4    318
     For Pas, whether it were for feare, or love, . . . . . . . . 250  Other Poems    4    327
     While deare Uran, whose course was Pas to meet,. . . . . . . 250  Other Poems    4    330
     Her breath, then short, seem'd loth from home to pas, . . .  252  Other Poems    4    399
PAS'
     Nico. Who doubts but Pas' fine pipe againe will bring. . . .  53  2nd Eclogues  29     51
PASS
     The thought of which doth passe all worldly pelfe. . . . . .  18  1st Eclogues   7    130
     While, "Let us passe our time" each shepeheard saies.. . . .  28  1st Eclogues  10     48
     First let them die, then passe the starres,. . . . . . . . .  44  Arcadia II    25      9
     P. O Passion, passe on feeble Reason's spoiles.. . . . . . .  46  2nd Eclogues  27     24
     Yet all well knit to one faire end do passe: . . . . . . . .  78  Arcadia III   50      8
     For you do passe your selfe, in vertue's might.. . . . . . .  79  Arcadia III   50     20
     That Albion clives in whitenes passe:. . . . . . . . . . . .  88  Arcadia III   62     91
     He farre did passe the rest of Shepheards all. . . . . . . .  94  3rd Eclogues  64     18
     Which little time did fitlie bring to passe. . . . . . . . .  96  3rd Eclogues  64     76
     Riches of children passe a Prince's throne;. . . . . . . . . 106  3rd Eclogues  67    112
     Who much did passe in state the stately mountaines,. . . . . 113  4th Eclogues  71     63
     Since thou from me (o me) o Sunne didst passe. . . . . . . . 116  4th Eclogues  72     98
     For though she passe all things, yet what is all . . . . . . 174  Astrophil     19      9
     Poore passenger, passe now thereby I did,. . . . . . . . . . 175  Astrophil     20      9
     Yet let this thought thy Tygrish courage passe:. . . . . . . 198  Astrophil     65     11
     Beauties which do in excellencie passe . . . . . . . . . . . 207  Astrophil     82      2
     Knowing worlds passe, ere she enough can find. . . . . . . . 232  Astrophil    101     13
     But if I by a happy window passe,. . . . . . . . . . . . . . 233  Astrophil    104      9
```

PASS   (CONTINUED)   PAGE   TITLE   LINE
    Failes me fearing on to passe, ... 219 A&S 8th Song   46
    O let my sentence passe from Thyne own face; . . . . . . 289 Psalm XVII   5
    Thou gavest me their necks, on them Thou mad'est me passe. . 292 Psalm XVIII   73
    Since youth and they do passe; . . . . 303 Psalm XXV   28
    Confounded be, and passe away like smoake, ... 313 Psalm XXXI   47
    Whiche my chefe partte, doth passe throughe, parche, and
      tye . . . . 344 Possibly   2   2
    He, that the other in some yeares did passe, ... 242 Other Poems 4   21
    Giving his reason pasport for to passe,. . . . . 252 Other Poems 4   381
    This morne alone to lonely walke did passe,. . . . . . . 255 Other Poems 4   533
PASSED
    Is past with me, my bloud is waxen colde.. . . . .   25 1st Eclogues 9   107
    And when that time is paste, death holdes his heeles.. . .   28 1st Eclogues 10   51
    Who once all birdes, in sweetly-singing past,. . . . . .   28 1st Eclogues 10   74
    If she must dye, then hath she past the line . . . . . .   59 2nd Eclogues 30   77
    But now the fitt is past: and time hath giv'ne . . . . .   83 Arcadia III 57   9
    But fewe dayes past while she good maner us'de,. . . . .   95 3rd Eclogues 64   26
    There never past foule word, I dare well say,. . . . . . 106 3rd Eclogues 67   93
    In straightnes past the Cedars of the forrests,. . . . . 113 4th Eclogues 71   64
    Till that it hath all woods and waters past. . . . . . . 126 4th Eclogues 75   36
    With glad moning passed anguish, ... 227 A&S 10th Song   39
    By them is past in sweetest taste. . . . . 294 Psalm XIX   43
    When time's time shall be past.. . . . . 317 Psalm XXXIII   42
    With Cosma, for whose love Pas past in woe.. . . . . . . 248 Other Poems 4   243
    D. Wonder that by two so black eyes the glittering stars be
      past.. . . . . 343 Possibly   1   28
PASSENGER
    Yet to a passenger will bonnet vaile.. . . . .   27 1st Eclogues 10   33
    Poore passenger, passe now thereby I did,. . . . . 175 Astrophil   20   9
PASSETH
    Love well thine owne: me thinkes, woolle's whitenes passeth
      all: . . . .   16 1st Eclogues 7   53
    My pastimes none: time passeth on my fall: . . . .   18 1st Eclogues 7   142
    One wonder yet farre passeth my conceate:. . . . .   42 Arcadia II   22   13
    Whose face all, all beauty passeth,. . . . . 219 A&S 8th Song   43
PASSING
    Passing the hate-spott Ermelin.. . . . .   89 Arcadia III 62   116
    From fancie's earth passing all numbers' bound,. . . . . 149 Cert Sonnets 22   7
    Passing all ghesse, whence into me should fly. . . . . . 149 Cert Sonnets 22   8
PASSION
    But if thou hast a Love, in that Love's passion, ...   15 1st Eclogues 7   16
    Who well can set a passion out to show:. . . . .   25 1st Eclogues 9   112
    Passion beares halfe when puffing wit doth blowe, ...   25 1st Eclogues 9   114
    Such active minde but seldome passion sees.. . . . . . .   26 1st Eclogues 9   134
    Into the faire looker on, pastime, not passion, enters.. . .   32 1st Eclogues 13   41
    Neither doubt you a whit, time will your passion utter. . .   33 1st Eclogues 13   58
    Into my live's bondage, yet may disburden a passion. . . .   35 1st Eclogues 13   108
    Passion. No, Tyrant; no: mine, mine shall be the fielde.. .   46 2nd Eclogues 27   2
    P. And Passion will, that Passion rule the rost. . . . .   46 2nd Eclogues 27   6
    R. Whom Passion leades unto his death is bent. . . . . .   46 2nd Eclogues 27   9
    R. Who Passion doth ensue, lives in annoy. . . . .   46 2nd Eclogues 27   13
    P. Who Passion doth forsake, lives void of joy.. . . . .   46 2nd Eclogues 27   14
    R. Passion is blinde, and treades an unknowne trace. . . .   46 2nd Eclogues 27   15
    P. O Passion, passe on feeble Reason's spoiles.. . . . .   46 2nd Eclogues 27   24
    R. Yet Passion, yeeld at length to Reason's stroke.. . . .   47 2nd Eclogues 27   33
    Seekes to make ech thing badge of his sweet passion. . . .   47 2nd Eclogues 28   6
    Thou soone may have some helpe, or change of passion.. . .   50 2nd Eclogues 28   98
    Me-thinkes I am partaker of thy passion, ...   60 2nd Eclogues 30   128
    So greate a passion all feele, ...   66 2nd Eclogues 32   16
    Passion rebelde, oft reason's strength hath shaked.. . . .   82 Arcadia III 57   4
    While we for mutuall spight a striving passion fed.. . . . 120 4th Eclogues 73   118
    Well: but faultie I was: Reason to my Passion yeelded, . . . 124 4th Eclogues 74   67
    Passion unto my rage, Rage to a hasty revenge. . . . . . 124 4th Eclogues 74   68
    Leaving him so passion rent, ... 221 A&S 8th Song   102
    Leaving him to passion rent, ... 221 A&S 8th Song   V102
PASSION'S
    P. And is not Reason dimde with Passion's might? . . . .   46 2nd Eclogues 27   18
    My dreeades augment the more in passion's mighte,. . . .   72 Arcadia III 37   17
    Fancie we feele, encludes all passion's mighte,. . . . .   82 Arcadia III 57   3
    Had reason's weight for passion's ease rejected. . . . .   83 Arcadia III 57   8
    Of passyon's hilles reaching to reason's skie. . . . . . 149 Cert Sonnets 22   6
PASSIONS
    But let us sing, sweet tunes do passions ease, ...   22 1st Eclogues 9   4
    P. If Reason will, that Passions be not free.. . . . . .   46 2nd Eclogues 27   4
    R. Dare Passions then abide in Reason's light? . . . . .   46 2nd Eclogues 27   17
    Which Passions kill, and Reason do deface. . . . .   47 2nd Eclogues 27   42
    Of our selfe-love (so passions do deceave) . . . .   59 2nd Eclogues 30   69
    Since that the stormy rage of passions darcke. . . . . .   72 Arcadia III 39   1
    (Of passions darke, made darke by beautie's light) . . .   72 Arcadia III 39   2
    So to my minde, while passions daylie growe, ...   74 Arcadia III 41   3
    (Tide to the stake of doubt) strange passions baite, . . .   82 Arcadia III 56   10
    Those passions which to youthfull head doo clime,. . . . 107 3rd Eclogues 67   116
    Our owly eyes, which dimm'd with passions bee, ... 131 Arcadia V   77   9
    My wit doth strive those passions to defend, ... 174 Astrophil   18   10
    O give my passions leave to run their race:. . . . . . . 198 Astrophil   64   2
    I must no more in thy sweet passions lie;. . . . . 202 Astrophil   72   7
    Who hath the breast, whose milke doth passions nourish,. . . 197 A&S 1st Song   17
PASSIONS'
    As bragging that free of all passions' mone. . . . . . . 244 Other Poems 4   71

366

		PAGE	TITLE		LINE
PASSPORT					
With passe-port of thy graces manifold:.		275	Psalm V		18
Giving his reason pasport for to passe,.		252	Other Poems	4	381
PASS-PRAISE					
That skin, whose passe-praise hue scorns this poore terme of white:.		205	Astrophil	77	7
PAST					
To couple comming harmes with sorrowes past?		57	2nd Eclogues 30		7
Though present times and past with evils be snarde,.		143	Cert Sonnets 12		13
To be (in things past bounds of wit) fooles, if they be not fooles.		217	A&S 7th Song		6
Of pleasurs past the reach of mind?.		324	Psalm XXXVI		24
To seek Thy beauty past conceit;		332	Psalm XL		62
And past all hope his chapps to frustrate so.		251	Other Poems	4	344
PASTIME					
Into the faire looker on, pastime, not passion, enters. . . .		32	1st Eclogues 13		41
With what pastime, time's journey she beguilde,.		225	Astrophil	92	12
PASTIMES					
And pastimes make, as Nature things hath made.		18	1st Eclogues	7	127
My pastimes none: time passeth on my fall:		18	1st Eclogues	7	142
Was ever apt: but you my pastimes did despise.		121	4th Eclogues 73		149
PASTOR					
Well may a Pastor plaine, but alas his plaints be not esteem de.		32	1st Eclogues 13		39
Say then what vantage do we get, by the trade of a Pastor? .		33	1st Eclogues 13		49
What marvaile tho a Prince transforme himselfe to a Pastor?.		34	1st Eclogues 13		91
PASTORAL					
Because in wrestling and in pastorall.		94	3rd Eclogues 64		17
PASTORS					
Raging in woes first pastors tought to plaine?		53	2nd Eclogues 29		58
PASTORS'					
Dorus. Lady, reservd by the heav'ns to do pastors' company honnor,.		31	1st Eclogues 13		1
PASTURE					
The pasture rich, the wooll as soft as silke,.		4	Lady of May	2	21
Their pasture is faire hilles of fruitlesse Love:.		39	Arcadia II	17	2
With sonne's approche your pasture fertill growes,.		43	Arcadia II	23	2
My sonne is gon, your pasture barrein growes,.		43	Arcadia II	24	2
As for to finde a pasture strowed with golde,.		104	3rd Eclogues 67		14
He rests me in green pasture his..		301	Psalm XXIII		4
PASTURED					
Turning to desarts our best pastur'de mountaines..		113	4th Eclogues 71		72
PATE					
Upon his pate, his pain employed thus.		278	Psalm VII		44
PATENTS					
Which make the patents of true worldly blisse,.		183	Astrophil	37	13
PATH					
Thou the path wilt make me tread		288	Psalm XVI		37
Teach me, thus vext, what path to go..		303	Psalm XXV		12
To sinning men his path.		303	Psalm XXV		34
PATHS					
The unworn paths, his rule embraceth..		279	Psalm VIII		32
The Paths of my great God?		304	Psalm XXV		38
From the paths of folly, ...		336	Psalm XLIII		15
PATIENCE					
(And pacience hath) let him goe learne of him.		24	1st Eclogues	9	73
Asse, pacience; the Mole, a working thought;		101	3rd Eclogues 66		86
And you poore beastes, in patience bide your hell,.		103	3rd Eclogues 66		153
Fy, schoole of Patience, Fy, your lesson is.		192	Astrophil	56	1
No Patience, if thou wilt my good, then make		193	Astrophil	56	12
Her come, and heare with patience my desire.		193	Astrophil	56	13
And then with patience bid me beare my fire.		193	Astrophil	56	14
PATIENT					
Yet patient must abide..		20	1st Eclogues	7	V960
Thou righteous art, Thou strong, thou patient,.		277	Psalm VII		31
Nor meek abiding of the patient wight..		281	Psalm IX		58
Wait on the lord with patient hope,.		325	Psalm XXXVII		17
While long I did with patient constancy.		330	Psalm XL		1
PATTERN					
This paterne good, unto our children goes, ...		28	1st Eclogues 10		55
Resolv'd to make me patterne of his might, ...		135	Cert Sonnets	2	2
PAUSE					
As in their moodes to take a lingring pawse?		146	Cert Sonnets 17		24
PAVILION					
About which hee dimme clouds like a Pavilion brings, ...		291	Psalm XVIII		24
PAVILIONS					
From strife of tongues in Thy Pavilions plac't..		313	Psalm XXXI		57
PAW					
Which oft he lifteth up, and stayes his lifted pawe, ...		53	2nd Eclogues 29		34
Hurtles was Tyger's pawe and Serpent's hisse..		100	3rd Eclogues 66		54
PAWN					
This is my pawne; the price let Dicus' judgement show: . . .		53	2nd Eclogues 29		47
PAWS					
Though strongly hedg'd of bloudy Lyon's pawes, ...		204	Astrophil	75	10
So piercing pawes, as spoyle when they embrace,.		206	Astrophil	78	10
And bring to naught those watching pawes..		290	Psalm XVII		36
PAY					
But you must pay, the gage of promist weale.		76	Arcadia III	46	18
Sorow pay we unto the rights of Nature,.		109	Arcadia IV	70	5
So that I live to pay a mortall fee, ...		136	Cert Sonnets	2	9

PAY   (CONTINUED)   PAGE   TITLE   LINE
      Unable quite to pay even Nature's rent,. . . . . 174 Astrophil   18   5
      I will good tribute pay if thou do so. . . . . 184 Astrophil   39   8
      Those lips, which make death's pay a meane price for a
            kisse . . . . 205 Astrophil   77   6
      That to win me, oft shewes a present pay?. . . . . 223 Astrophil   88   4
      So my good deeds they pay with this ev'ill share,. . . . . . 322 Psalm XXXV   27
      To Nature's heir, the faire Urania, pay, ... 251 Other Poems   4 364
      So when to pay your due. . . . . 257 Other Poems   5   33
PAYING
      The Naughty borrowes paying not, ... 326 Psalm XXXVII   53
PAYS
      And to the proud in deeds pays home their own. . . . . 314 Psalm XXXI   66
PEACE
      Lalus. Muse hold your peace: but thou, my God Pan, glorify .   15 1st Eclogues 7   25
      Olive paintes me the peace that I must aspire to by
            conquest . . . .   35 1st Eclogues 13 117
      R. But yet our strife sure peace in end doth breede. . . . .   46 2nd Eclogues 27   27
      P. We now have peace, your peace we doo not neede. . . . . .   46 2nd Eclogues 27   28
      Nico. Peace, peace good Pas, thou weeriest even the ground .   56 2nd Eclogues 29 135
      Faire Rocks, goodly rivers, sweet woods, when shall I see
            peace? Peace.. . . . .   62 2nd Eclogues 31   1
      Peace? what barrs me my tongue? who is it that comes me so
            ny? I. . . . .   62 2nd Eclogues 31   2
      And warr of thoughts is swallow'd up in peace. . . . .   91 3rd Eclogues 63   4
      The seate of peace, the throne which is erected. . . . . . . 108 Arcadia IV   69   3
      Where life is death, and death cannot breed peace. . . . . . 116 4th Eclogues 72   95
      Let us a perfect peace betwixt us two resolve: . . . . 120 4th Eclogues 73 127
      And so most ready am this meane of peace to trie.. . . . . . 121 4th Eclogues 73 152
      As well he was in peace a safest treasure: . . . . 129 4th Eclogues 76   17
      Peace Due alledgeance, Duty must bee broken, ... 138 Cert Sonnets 5   19
      Where each part in such peace dwelleth,. . . . . 140 Cert Sonnets 7   16
      And pleasd with our soft peace, staid here his flying race.. 168 Astrophil   8   4
      Peace, foolish wit, with wit my wit is mard. . . . . 182 Astrophil   34   11
      Come sleepe, o sleepe, the certaine knot of peace, ... 184 Astrophil   39   1
      Cease eager Muse, peace pen, for my sake stay, ... 201 Astrophil   70   12
      Then since (deare life) you faine would have me peace, . . . 207 Astrophil   81   12
      Ah bed, the field where joye's peace some do see,. . . . . . 230 Astrophil   98   1
      "Peace, I thinke that some give eare:. . . . . 234 A&S 11th Song   36
      So I in peace, and peacefull blisse. . . . . 274 Psalm IV   31
      That they in peace shall blessed live. . . . . 310 Psalm XXIX   29
      Seek peace and follow after it,. . . . . 320 Psalm XXXIV   54
      Who never word of peace yet utter would, ... 322 Psalm XXXV   51
      They shall have peace in plenteousness.. . . . . 325 Psalm XXXVII   32
      His end shall be in peace enjoyed:. . . . . 327 Psalm XXXVII   94
      But still the more that I did hold my peace, ... 329 Psalm XXXIX   7
PEACEFUL
      Then let us holde the blisse of peacefull minde, ... 131 Arcadia V   77   13
      So I in peace, and peacefull blisse. . . . . 274 Psalm IV   31
PEACOCK
      All peacock pride, and fruites of peacock's pride. . . . . .   93 3rd Eclogues 63   73
      To great men's peacock pride,. . . . . 331 Psalm XL   18
PEACOCK'S
      The peacocke's pride, the pye's pild flatterye,. . . . . . .   28 1st Eclogues 10   77
      All peacock pride, and fruites of peacock's pride. . . . . .   93 3rd Eclogues 63   73
      His death-bed peacock's follie,. . . . . 160 Cert Sonnets 30   13
PEAK
      Peake hath a Cave, whose narrow entries finde. . . . . 150 Cert Sonnets 22   31
PAEAN
      Sing then my Muse, now Io Pean sing, ... 196 Astrophil   63   9
PEARL
      Her twinkling eies bedeckt with pearle, her lips of Saphir
            blew:. . . . .   12 Arcadia I   3   10
      To set a pearle in steele so meanely varnished?. . . . . . .   16 1st Eclogues 7   63
      Where well couched abides a coffer of pearle,. . . . .   67 2nd Eclogues 33   10
      Thus pure pearle, I do yeeld, my senses and soule. . . . . .   68 2nd Eclogues 33   28
      Of pretious pearle the double rowe,. . . . .   87 Arcadia III 62   42
      Warme snow, moyst pearle, softe ivorie. . . . .   90 Arcadia III 62 126
      Farewell o pearl, the poore man's plenteous treasure:. . . . 129 4th Eclogues 76   2
      Red Porphir is, which locke of pearle makes sure:. . . . . . 169 Astrophil   9   6
      Whence hast thou Ivorie, Rubies, pearle and gold,. . . . . . 181 Astrophil   32   10
PEARLS
      All things that earst I sawe, as orient pearles exceed,. . . 119 4th Eclogues 73   83
      Let pearls be wan with woe their damme doth beare: . . . . . 125 4th Eclogues 75   23
      For me, I wept to see pearles scattered so,. . . . . 223 Astrophil   87   9
      Opening rubies, pearles deviding. . . . . 226 A&S 10th Song   30
PEARLS'
      Nor blushing Lillies, nor pearles' ruby-hidden row,. . . . . 213 A&S 5th Song   38
PEDANT
      Unto Cupid that boy shall a Pedante be found?. . . . . 124 4th Eclogues 74   66
PEEP
      When in her necke you did Love ditties peepe;. . . . . 208 Astrophil   83   6
PEEPER
      Betwixt them two the peeper tooke his nest,. . . . . 244 Other Poems   4 102
PEEPING
      She chirping ran, he peeping flew away,. . . . . 244 Other Poems   4   87
*PEER
      Can liken them without all peere,. . . . .   86 Arcadia III 62   19
      Even so (alas) a Lady Dian's peere,. . . . . 230 Astrophil   97   9
      Ev'en bones shall say O God, who is Thy peere, ... 321 Psalm XXXV   21

*PEER   (CONTINUED)   PAGE   TITLE   LINE

	PAGE	TITLE		LINE
Now for a clod-like hare in fourm they peere, ...	243	Other Poems	4	43
PEERLESS				
Her peereles height my minde to high erection.	16	1st Eclogues	7	70
Too much her peerles parts, nor yet could them despise.. . .	119	4th Eclogues	73	88
PEEVISH				
For what can breed more peevish incongruities, ...	61	2nd Eclogues	30	140
PEISE				
His eyelidds peyse our going..	284	Psalm XI		16
PEISED				
How nice to touch? how all her speeches peized be?	15	1st Eclogues	7	35
PELF				
The thought of which doth passe all worldly pelfe.	18	1st Eclogues	7	130
PEN				
An ende, an ende, my dulde penn cannot write, ...	74	Arcadia III	42	13
Goodnes the penne, heaven paper is, ...	90	Arcadia III	62	142
Biting my trewand pen, beating my selfe for spite, ...	165	Astrophil	1	13
His paper, pale dispaire, and paine his pen doth move. . . .	168	Astrophil	6	11
And yet my words, as them my pen doth frame, ...	174	Astrophil	19	7
And now my pen these lines had dashed quite, ...	190	Astrophil	50	12
In well raisde notes, my pen the best it may	201	Astrophil	70	10
Cease eager Muse, peace pen, for my sake stay, ...	201	Astrophil	70	12
Then grew my tongue and pen records unto thy glory:.	212	A&S 5th Song		3
PENNED				
While I there speache in my rude ryminge pende..	62	2nd Eclogues	30	187
With one good dawnce, or letter finely pend, ...	245	Other Poems	4	140
PENS				
In whose each part all pens may dwell?	85	Arcadia III	62	2
Above line repeated at following location.	90	Arcadia III	62	146
PENSIVE				
On pensive soules (in steede of restfull baite).	82	Arcadia III	56	6
PENSIVENESS				
The curious wits, seeing dull pensivenesse	176	Astrophil	23	1
PEOPLE				
What ayles this heathenish rage? What do theis people meane.	271	Psalm II		1
Thou, lord, the people shalt in judgment try:.	277	Psalm VII		22
God's people do devower, ...	286	Psalm XIV		15
Lord then still Thy people save, ...	309	Psalm XXVIII		33
God to his people strength shall give, ...	310	Psalm XXIX		28
Ev'en people that, ev'en those	317	Psalm XXXIII		46
Even where I do most store of people find;	322	Psalm XXXV		47
PEOPLE'S				
While with the people's shouts I must confesse, ...	191	Astrophil	53	3
Which beare his people's name, ...	273	Psalm III		35
Nay shame of men, the people's scorning game...	299	Psalm XXII		16
The might of people's hand..	317	Psalm XXXIII		36
PERCEIVE				
Will at length perceave these flames by her beames to be				
kindled, ...	37	1st Eclogues	13	167
Lest that Argus eyes perceive you.".	235	A&S 11th Song		42
PERCEIVED				
In shape, which by man's eye might be perceived;	127	4th Eclogues	75	71
PERCEIVETH				
Better then one captiv'd perceiveth, ...	159	Cert Sonnets	29	16
PERCHANCE				
And me perchaunce your constant temper lend.	23	1st Eclogues	9	20
A Cage (guilded perchaunce) is all his lott.	28	1st Eclogues	10	69
Histor. Perchaunce I will, but nowe me thinkes it tyme . . .	107	3rd Eclogues	67	118
Mine eyes then only winke, for spite perchance, ...	230	Astrophil	98	13
PERCHED				
At length he perch'd himself in Stella's joyfull face, . . .	168	Astrophil	8	8
PERCHING				
Pearching within square royall rooves, ...	89	Arcadia III	62	114
PERFECT				
In perfect light, which could not me deceave, ...	55	2nd Eclogues	29	100
Where all good haps a perfect state maintaine?	58	2nd Eclogues	30	40
But still, although we faile of perfect rightfulnes, ...	61	2nd Eclogues	30	137
No Elephant so perfect beares.	86	Arcadia III	62	V 28
In worth, in taste, in perfitte hewe:	87	Arcadia III	62	40
(For then their language was a perfect speech)	100	3rd Eclogues	66	65
Elephant gave a perfect memorie:	101	3rd Eclogues	66	83
Strephon. For she, whose parts maintainde a perfect musique,	113	4th Eclogues	71	61
Indeed a perfect hewe, indeed a sweet consent.	119	4th Eclogues	73	85
In whom of all my rules the perfect proofe I finde, ...	119	4th Eclogues	73	94
Let us a perfect peace betwixt us two resolve:	120	4th Eclogues	73	127
Unto her rested sense a perfect waking, ...	137	Cert Sonnets	4	2
She knows the sicknesse of that perfect place.	142	Cert Sonnets	11	11
That face, whose lecture shewes what perfect beautie is: . .	205	Astrophil	77	2
While sobd out words a perfect Musike give..	231	Astrophil	100	11
It is but love, which makes paper perfit white	232	Astrophil	102	12
The perfect beauties be..	216	A&S 6th Song		23
A perfect harmony.	216	A&S 6th Song		24
Of his mazde powers keepes perfit harmony:	230	Astrophil	99	8
O law of his How perfect 'tis.	294	Psalm XIX		29
To grant Thy Will and perfect Thy entent, ...	296	Psalm XX		17
Which when he did in perfect image show, ...	256	Other Poems	4	541
PERFECTION				
I challenge thee by shew of her perfection, ...	15	1st Eclogues	7	17
Their dwellers rapt with sight of her perfection	15	1st Eclogues	7	44
With large encrease, and wooll of fine perfection, ...	49	2nd Eclogues	28	50

369

PERFECTION   (CONTINUED)   PAGE   TITLE   LINE

    Wit learnes in thee perfection to expresse,. . . . . 182 Astrophil   35   12
    (Image like of Saints' perfection) . . . . 234 A&S 11th Song   24
PERFECTION'S
    And not content to be Perfection's heire . . . . 201 Astrophil   71   9
PERFECTIONS
    What toong can her perfections tell. . . . .   85 Arcadia III 62   1
    No tongue can her perfections tell,. . . . .   90 Arcadia III 62 145
PERFORCE
    Save when great need of them perforce apeare. . . . .   27 1st Eclogues 10   36
    But perforce disgest, all bitter juices of horror. . . . . .   35 1st Eclogues 13 105
    Yet Fancie would perforce employ his skill,. . . . . 115 4th Eclogues 72   65
PERFORMED
    She answer'd was with looke, and well performed behest:. . . 119 4th Eclogues 73   99
    Who feare Thee shall my vowes performed see. . . . . 300 Psalm XXII   60
    The works perform'd by Thee most wondrous great. . . . . . . 305 Psalm XXVI   24
PERFUMED
    New perfumed with flowers fresh growing, ... 217 A&S 8th Song   4
PERHAPS
    A good foole call'd with paine, perhapps may be, ...   28 1st Eclogues 10   71
    And everie floure, not sweet perhaps, which growes . . . . . 172 Astrophil   15   3
    My harmes on Ink's poore losse, perhaps some find. . . . . . 182 Astrophil   34   13
    Bid'n, perhaps he fetcheth thee a glove, ... 194 Astrophil   59   7
    That I perhaps am somewhat kinne to thee;. . . . . 198 Astrophil   65   12
PERIL
    In perill they shall perish never, ... 325 Psalm XXXVII   47
PERISH
    But Man which helpeth them, helplesse must perish. . . . . . 127 4th Eclogues 75   87
    The way they go shal be their way to perish. . . . . 271 Psalm I   22
    From your way perish shall . . . . 272 Psalm II   30
    Yet perish shall (although his paine be sore). . . . . 281 Psalm IX   59
    For those badd folks at last shall perish, ... 325 Psalm XXXVII   23
    In perill they shall perish never, ... 325 Psalm XXXVII   47
    And his name perish quite? . . . . 333 Psalm XLI   20
PERISHED
    And now fully beleeves helpe to be quite perished; . . . . . 122 4th Eclogues 74   2
    First be mine eyes pulde out, first be my braine perished; . 124 4th Eclogues 74   60
    And they are faln, nay perisht at Thy sight: . . . . 279 Psalm IX   7
PERJURED
    As perjur'd cowards in adversity . . . . 248 Other Poems 4 239
PERJURY
    With perjury doth falsly bind. . . . . 302 Psalm XXIV   12
PERMANENT
    R. The joyes you have shall be made permanent. . . . .   47 2nd Eclogues 27   35
PERPETUALLY
    Perpetualy.. . . . . 280 Psalm IX   25
PERPLEXED
    To long-perplexed minde breed long delight.. . . . . 245 Other Poems 4 112
    Up and downe perplexed went, ... 262 Other Poems 7   14
PERPLEXITY
    That full of doubts, thou of perplexity; . . . . 229 Astrophil   96   7
PERSECUTION'S
    O save me from this Persecution's showre:. . . . . 277 Psalm VII   2
PERSERS
    Where bee nowe those eyes ever Inly persers? . . . . 138 Cert Sonnets 5   6
PERSEVER
    Tho against me shee persever,. . . . . 221 A&S 9th Song   19
PERSON
    Whose eyes a person vile do hold in vile disdain . . . . . 287 Psalm XV   7
PERSUADES
    What words so ere she speakes perswades for thee,. . . . . . 171 Astrophil   12   7
    When far spent night perswades each mortall eye, ... 230 Astrophil   99   1
PERSUASION
    But how he doth by might, or by persuasion . . . .   49 2nd Eclogues 28   46
    Fortune store, Nature health, Love grant perswasion. . . . .   51 2nd Eclogues 28 100
PERSUASIONS
    And still th'effect of thy perswasions prove:. . . . . 167 Astrophil   4   11
PERTAINETH
    And reason, since the Croune to God pertaineth,. . . . . . . 300 Psalm XXII   69
PERTAINS
    For busines, where it pertaines him not, ...   28 1st Eclogues 10   65
PERUSE
    Yet stay and well peruse,. . . . .   80 Arcadia III 52   7
PETRARCH'S
    You that poore Petrarch's long deceased woes,. . . . . 172 Astrophil   15   7
PETTICOAT
    It may be part of Mira's peticoate,. . . . . 258 Other Poems 5   71
PHAETON'S
    In him, the thoughts of Phaeton's damme to grave.. . . . . .   60 2nd Eclogues 30 106
PHILIP
    Good brother Philip, I have borne you long,. . . . . 208 Astrophil   83   1
PHILISIDES
    Geron. Up, up Philisides, let sorrowes goe,. . . . .   22 1st Eclogues 9   1
    Philisides. Who minds to please the minde drownd in annoyes.   22 1st Eclogues 9   6
    Philisides. Who ever taught a skillesse man to teach,. . . .   22 1st Eclogues 9   16
    Philisides. If fortune's lappe became my dwelling place, . .   23 1st Eclogues 9   26
    Philisides. O gods, how long this old foole hath annoi'd . .   24 1st Eclogues 9   66
    Philisides. Hath any man heard what this old man said? . . .   26 1st Eclogues 9 135
    The ladd Philisides. . . . . 256 Other Poems 5   1

PHILOMELA
  O Philomela with thy brest oppressed . . . . 126 4th Eclogues 75 61
  O Philomela faire, o take some gladnesse, ... 137 Cert Sonnets 4 9
  Above line repeated at following location. . . . . 137 Cert Sonnets 4 21
PHILOSOPHY
  Nor in hid wayes to guide Philosophie: . . . . 179 Astrophil 28 10
PHIP
  Leave that sir Phip, least off your necke be wroong. . . . . 208 Astrophil 83 14
PHLEGMATIC
  In thy cold stuffe a flegmatike delight? . . . . 193 Astrophil 56 11
PHOEBUS
  Pas. Tell this (and Phoebus be) what monster growes. . . . . 56 2nd Eclogues 29 144
  Phaebus farewell, a sweeter Saint I serve, ... 72 Arcadia III 38 1
  Above line repeated at following location. . . . . 72 Arcadia III 38 6
  Phaebus yeelde up thy title in my minde. . . . . 72 Arcadia III 38 11
  O Phoebus with good cause thy face thou hidest, ... 126 4th Eclogues 75 55
  Phoebus was Judge betweene Jove, Mars, and Love, ... 171 Astrophil 13 1
  Phoebus drew wide the curtaines of the skies . . . . 171 Astrophil 13 12
  Phoebus, that shepheard high, ... 257 Other Poems 5 22
  More envied Phoebus for his westerne flyinge . . . . 259 Other Poems 5 126
PHOEBUS'
  How is he young, that tam'de old Phoebus youth? . . . . . . 21 1st Eclogues 8 10
  Of Phoebus' violence in shade of stately Ciprus tree, ... 31 1st Eclogues 13 12
  Blushing at sight of Phoebus' pride. . . . . 86 Arcadia III 62 26
  Be victor still of Phoebus' golden treasure: . . . . 108 Arcadia IV 69 5
  By Phoebus' doome, with sugred sentence sayes, ... 177 Astrophil 25 2
  But ah poore Night, in love with Phoebus' light, ... 229 Astrophil 97 5
  But when Aurora leades out Phoebus' daunce, ... 230 Astrophil 98 12
  Ah what doth Phoebus' gold that wretch availe, ... 237 Astrophil 108 10
  Walking in bright Phoebus' blaze . . . . 262 Other Poems 7 1
PHOENIX
  Alas, if you a Phoenix new will have . . . . 60 2nd Eclogues 30 102
  The Phoenix wings be not so rare . . . . 89 Arcadia III 62 118
  Who would not have a Phoenix if he could? . . . . 104 3rd Eclogues 67 16
  Phoenix but one, of Crowes we milllions have: . . . . 104 3rd Eclogues 67 20
  Yet I shall die in Phoenix fire. . . . . 153 Cert Sonnets 24 27
  When I demaund of Phenix Stella's state, ... 225 Astrophil 92 6
  And then the Phoenix feared to be cought. . . . . 251 Other Poems 4 360
PHRASE
  And plaine speach oft then quaint phrase better framed is. . 14 1st Eclogues 7 6
  Can I forget in how straunge phrase she craved . . . . 61 2nd Eclogues 30 158
  Since in such phrase his faith he did attire. . . . . 80 Arcadia III 53 8
  But failst thou not in phrase so heav'nly hie? . . . . 199 Astrophil 67 6
  O plaints conserv'd in such a sugred phraise, ... 231 Astrophil 100 9
  Strive we that in some worthy phrase . . . . 319 Psalm XXXIV 11
PHRASES
  Or Pindare's Apes, flaunt they in phrases fine, ... 166 Astrophil 3 3
  Phrases and Problemes from my reach do grow, ... 166 Astrophil 3 10
  Now judge by this: in piercing phrases late, ... 194 Astrophil 58 9
PHYSIC
  Geron. What can amend where physick is refusde? . . . . 23 1st Eclogues 9 21
  How be the minds dispos'd that can not tast thy physick?
    Sick. . . . . 63 2nd Eclogues 31 17
  Beleeve them not, for Phisicke true doth finde, ... 147 Cert Sonnets 17 51
PHYSICIANS'
  Great be Physitions' brags, but aid is beggerly, ... 128 4th Eclogues 75 112
PHYSIC'S
  O Phisicke's power, which (some say) hath refrayned. . . . . 128 4th Eclogues 75 109
PICK
  Let crowes picke out mine eyes, which saw too much: . . . . . 19 1st Eclogues 7 149
  Let crowes picke out mine eyes which too much sawe. . . . . . 19 1st Eclogues 7 V149
  But let us pick our good from out much bad: . . . . 105 3rd Eclogues 67 62
PICKPURSE
  I am no pick-purse of another's wit. . . . . 204 Astrophil 74 8
PICTURE
  And see by this picture to you presented, ... 128 4th Eclogues 75 122
  Without the picture be found true. . . . . 157 Cert Sonnets 27 24
  Or at the most on some fine picture stayes, ... 170 Astrophil 11 7
PICTURED
  Oft cruell fights well pictured forth do please. . . . . . . 181 Astrophil 34 4
PICTURES
  I will thinke theye pictures be, ... 234 A&S 11th Song 23
  With hear-say, pictures, or a window looke, ... 245 Other Poems 4 139
PIE
  Dorus. Nightingales seldome sing, the Pie still chattereth: . 14 1st Eclogues 7 7
PIE'S
  The peacocke's pride, the pye's pild flatterye, ... 28 1st Eclogues 10 77
PIECE
  What, a whole weeke without one peece of looke, ... 192 Astrophil 56 3
  Some beautie's peece, as amber colourd hed, ... 225 Astrophil 91 6
  But golde can guild a rotten piece of wood, ... 245 Other Poems 4 124
PIECEMEAL
  With Iron scepter bruse thou shalt, and peece meale breake . 271 Psalm II 21
PIECES
  And cruely in many peices teare. . . . . 277 Psalm VII 5
PIECING
  Leave sheepe, leave all, I will no piecing have. . . . . . . 255 Other Poems 4 512
PIED
  Enam'ling with pied flowers their thoughts of gold: . . . . . 166 Astrophil 3 4
  May then yong his pide weedes showing, ... 217 A&S 8th Song 3

PIED   (CONTINUED)   PAGE   TITLE   LINE
    Deckt with pyde flowers sweetely smelling. . . . . 262 Other Poems   7   6
PIERCE
    Plangus. If through mine eares pearce any consolacyons . . . 61 2nd Eclogues 30 143
    A plaint of guiltlesse hurt doth pierce the skie. . . . . . 103 3rd Eclogues 66 152
    Of which, how much may pierce to that sweete seate, ... 151 Cert Sonnets 22   46
    Is no fit marke to pierce with his fine pointed dart:. . . . 168 Astrophil   8   3
    But thou didst peirce my eare, ... 331 Psalm XL   28
    Did me pearce, burne, and bynde, long since and late, ... 345 Possibly   2 12
    So have I heard to pierce pursuing shield. . . . . 251 Other Poems   4 349
PIERCED
    Eysight made me to yeelde, but what first pierst to myne
        eies? Eies. . . . .   64 2nd Eclogues 31   26
    Held, pearst, possest, my judgement, sence, and will, ...   84 Arcadia III 60   6
    But ere I could flie thence, it pierc'd my heart. . . . . . 175 Astrophil   20 14
    Should soone be pierc'd with sharpnesse of the mone. . . . . 193 Astrophil   57   8
    My never peirced shield, my ever saving horn, ... 290 Psalm XVIII   4
    My humble hands, my fainting feet they peirced; . . . . . . 299 Psalm XXII   41
    For thy shafts have pierc't me sore, ... 327 Psalm XXXVIII   3
    Hir hands which pierc'd the soule's seav'n-double shield, . . 246 Other Poems   4 147
PIERCER
    Undermin'd with a speech the pearcer of thoughts. . . . . .   68 2nd Eclogues 33   16
PIERCING
    Are hurt, not helpt, with piercing of the light: . . . . . .   73 Arcadia III 39 10
    Such pearcing wordes as no thoughts els conceave: . . . . .   78 Arcadia III 49   8
    Now judge by this: in piercing phrases late, ... 194 Astrophil   58   9
    So piercing pawes, as spoyle when they embrace, ... 206 Astrophil   78 10
    Even god himself sent down his peircing ey . . . . 286 Psalm XIV   7
    Where piercing witts do quickly apprehend, ... 245 Other Poems   4 142
PIES
    Dumbe Swannes, not chatring Pies, do Lovers prove, ... 192 Astrophil   54 13
PIGSNEY
    Miso mine owne pigsnie, thou shalt heare news o' Damaetas. . 241 Other Poems   2   1
PIKES
    Her loose haire be the shott, the brestes the pykes be, . . .   67 2nd Eclogues 33   7
PILED
    The peacocke's pride, the pye's pild flatterye, ...   28 1st Eclogues 10   77
PILFERING
    For pilfring Lalus' lambe, with crouch to blesse thy head. .   52 2nd Eclogues 29   14
PILGRIMAGE
    Plangus. Alas how long this pilgrimage doth last? . . . . .   57 2nd Eclogues 30   5
    Thus in my pilgrimaige of mated mynde, ...   71 Arcadia III 36 13
PILGRIMS
    True, that on earth we are but pilgrims made, ... 167 Astrophil   5 12
PILIAR
    (His marke a Piller was devoid of stay, ... 243 Other Poems   4 70
PILLOWS
    Take thou of me smooth pillowes, sweetest bed, ... 184 Astrophil   39   9
PINCHING
    But at no change, so pinching care he takes, ...   71 Arcadia III 37   9
PINDARE'S
    Or Pindare's Apes, flaunt they in phrases fine, ... 166 Astrophil   3   3
*PINE
    Pine is a maste to a shippe, to my shippe shall hope for a
        maste serve? . . . .   36 1st Eclogues 13 129
    Pine is hye, hope is as hie, sharpe leav'd, sharpe yet be my
        hope's budds. . . . .   36 1st Eclogues 13 130
    Do not disdaine, o streight up raised Pine, ...   77 Arcadia III 47   1
    Which others said did make their soules to pine: . . . . . . 173 Astrophil   16   6
    Late tyr'd with wo, even ready for to pine . . . . 195 Astrophil   62   1
    Do pine, my strength with pain is wholy gon, ... 312 Psalm XXXI   29
    And pine away with daily wasting woe? . . . . 257 Other Poems   5 26
PINED
    As pin'd a face as mine I saw againe. . . . . 254 Other Poems   4 476
PINES
    You goodly pines, which still with brave assent. . . . . . .   77 Arcadia III 49   1
PINE-TREE
    The wynde most oft the hugest Pine-tree greeves: . . . . . . 143 Cert Sonnets 12   7
PINING
    In river as I look'd my pining face, ... 254 Other Poems   4 475
PIN'S
    I thought those babes of some pinne's hurt did whine, ... 173 Astrophil   16   7
PIPE
    As without breath, no pipe doth move, ...   14 1st Eclogues 6   7
    Thy pipe, o Pan, shall helpe, though I sing sorilie. . . . .   15 1st Eclogues 7 27
    Silly shepheard's poore pype, when his harsh sound testifis
        our woes, ...   32 1st Eclogues 13   40
    When trees daunce to the pype, and swift streames stay by
        the musicke, ...   33 1st Eclogues 13   47
    Then may I hope, my pipe may have abilitie, ...   48 2nd Eclogues 28   26
    My pipe and song made him both songe and pipe forsweare. . .   52 2nd Eclogues 29   20
    Nico. Who doubts but Pas' fine pipe againe will bring. . . .   53 2nd Eclogues 29   51
    Unto my pipe, O Nimphes, nowe helpe my pipe, ...   54 2nd Eclogues 29   73
    (A little flocke; but well my pipe they couthe) . . . . . .   98 3rd Eclogues 66   2
    Thus did I sing, and pipe eight sullen houres. . . . . 103 3rd Eclogues 66 155
    Who most the silly shepheard's pipe did pryse, ... 125 4th Eclogues 75   2
    Another humbler wit to shepheard's pipe retires, ... 167 Astrophil   6   7
    "But you my pipe, whilome my chief delight, ... 254 Other Poems   4 481
    Out shreaking pipe made of some witched tree. . . . . 255 Other Poems   4 516
    With that (yet kissed first) his pipe he burst. . . . . . . 255 Other Poems   4 520

PIPE   (CONTINUED)   PAGE   TITLE   LINE
    His pipe was at his foote, ... 256 Other Poems   5   4
    "Tell me my seely pipe, ...   257 Other Poems   5   53
    "Earth, brooke, flowrs, pipe, lambe, Dove. . . . . 259 Other Poems   5   92
PIPES
    But hoarse and drye, my pipes I nowe must spare. . . . . .   62 2nd Eclogues 30 190
    And eke their pipes did well, as frends, agree. . . . . . . 242 Other Poems   4   32
PIPING
    Which thought doth marre my piping declaration, ...   19 1st Eclogues 7 168
    As farre as any shepheards piping be: . . . .   56 2nd Eclogues 29 127
    Did piping leade, the Sunne already sanke. . . . .   98 3rd Eclogues 66   3
    Absent alone canst thou then piping be? . . . .   258 Other Poems   5   65
PISTLE
    The pistle selfe, such kinde of wordes it had, ...   96 3rd Eclogues 64   91
PIT
    In her cheekes pit thou didst thy pitfould set, ... 170 Astrophil   11   11
    A pitt was digg'd, by this man vainly strong, ... 278 Psalm VII   40
    But in the pitt he ruind first did fall, ...   278 Psalm VII   41
    Down in the pitt, which they themselves had wrought: . . .   280 Psalm IX   47
    To the pitt where flesh doth end. . . . . 308 Psalm XXVIII   5
    When I within the pitt do bide; . . . .   311 Psalm XXX   27
    For causeless they both pitt and net did sett, ...   321 Psalm XXXV   15
    Fall in self pitt, be caught in their own nett. . . . . . . 321 Psalm XXXV   18
    And me from pitt bemyred, ... 331 Psalm XL   5
*PITCH
    From wooden bones, and bloud of pitch doth flie. . . . . .   151 Cert Sonnets 22   53
    About them pitch who him do feare, ...   319 Psalm XXXIV   26
PITEOUS
    Doth Stella now begin with piteous eye, ... 199 Astrophil   67   2
    Tell her in your piteous blaying, ... 222 A&S 9th Song   49
PITFALLS
    Or catch the birds with pitfalls, or with lyme, ...   26 1st Eclogues 9 124
PITFOLD
    In her cheekes pit thou didst thy pitfould set, ... 170 Astrophil   11   11
PITIED
    He liked me, but pitied lustfull youth: . . . .   99 3rd Eclogues 66   36
PITY
    Neither he beares reverence to a Prince nor pittie to
        begger . . . .   31 1st Eclogues 13   5
    And will pitty the wound festred so strangely within me. . . 37 1st Eclogues 13 168
    When pittie most I crave, I cruell prove: . . . .   41 Arcadia II   20   3
    We pittie deeme that which but weakenes is: . . . .   62 2nd Eclogues 30 180
    Dread not a whit (O goodly cruell) that pittie may enter . . 122 4th Eclogues 74   5
    The earth with pitie dull the center keepeth: . . . . 136 Cert Sonnets 3   4
    Alas, all onely she no pitie taketh, ...   136 Cert Sonnets 3   9
    Knowledge might pitie winne, and pitie grace obtaine, . . . 165 Astrophil   1   4
    Such smart may pitie claime of any hart, ...   186 Astrophil   44   3
    And yet she heares, yet I no pitty find; . . . .   186 Astrophil   44   5
    And yet she heares, and yet no pitie I find; . . . .   186 Astrophil   44 V 5
    But cannot skill to pitie my disgrace, ...   187 Astrophil   45   3
    Pitie thereof gate in her breast such place. . . . .   187 Astrophil   45   7
    I am not I, pitie the tale of me. . . . . 187 Astrophil   45   14
    I curst thee oft, I pitie now thy case, ... 187 Astrophil   46   1
    Shewes love and pitie to my absent case. . . . . 195 Astrophil   60   8
    While gracefull pitty beauty beautifies. . . . . 231 Astrophil   100   4
    Shall a heavenly grace want pitty?" . . . . 219 A&S 8th Song   64
    Great Pity. . . . . 286 Psalm XIII   18
    I plain sweet Lord, my plaint for pitty mark; . . . . 289 Psalm XVII   2
    With face the plot of pittie, ... 259 Other Poems   5 118
    Taking pitty on his case, ... 264 Other Poems   7   74
PITYING
    Till that his grandame Nature pittying it, ...   173 Astrophil   17   9
PLACE
    Yet all my health I place in your good-will. . . . .   18 1st Eclogues 7 120
    No place to turne; without, within it fryes: . . . .   18 1st Eclogues 7 145
    New plucked from the place where it did breed, ...   19 1st Eclogues 7 159
    He proules ech place stil in new colours deckt, ...   21 1st Eclogues 8   35
    Philisides. If fortune's lappe became my dwelling place, . .   23 1st Eclogues 9   26
    O noble age who place their only blisse. . . . .   24 1st Eclogues 9   69
    Selfe-lost and wandring, banished that place we doe come
        from, ...   32 1st Eclogues 13   26
    What place is there left, we may hope our woes to recomfort?   32 1st Eclogues 13   28
    R.p. Then let us both to heavenly rules give place, ...   47 2nd Eclogues 27   41
    Time, place, life, wit scarcely her rare gifts measure doth.   49 2nd Eclogues 28   60
    Nico his place farre better furnish will. . . . .   53 2nd Eclogues 29   56
    But in the place found nothing but a rope. . . . .   55 2nd Eclogues 29   92
    I would come downe, and yeeld to her my place, ...   56 2nd Eclogues 29 121
    That sweetens all the place; she is the guest. . . . . . .   59 2nd Eclogues 30   99
    O braine, where thought of her hath onely place; . . . . .   60 2nd Eclogues 30 118
    Where but a baiting place is all our portion. . . . .   61 2nd Eclogues 30 136
    Wheare he was bounde, to make his marting place, ...   70 Arcadia III 36   4
    I like this place, wheare at the least the darke . . . . .   73 Arcadia III 39   13
    Is left a Sunne, whose beames thy place may use? . . . . .   80 Arcadia III 52   6
    Comfort, step thou in place of wonted sadnes. . . . .   83 Arcadia III 59   10
    For no thing, time, nor place, can loose, quench, ease, . .   84 Arcadia III 60   13
    The gartring place with child-like signe, ...   89 Arcadia III 62   99
    Becomming every time and place, ...   90 Arcadia III 62 136
    Where open hartes do holde so constant place, ...   93 3rd Eclogues 63   88
    Place Sorrowe's triumph on my conquered harte: . . . . . .   114 4th Eclogues 72   17
    Since then my harte did loose his wonted place, ... 115 4th Eclogues 72   77

```
PLACE                    (CONTINUED)                              PAGE      TITLE        LINE
       Of heaven, of earth, of hell, of time and place was come...  118  4th Eclogues 73    62
       Us to attend, in this most private time and place. . . . .  119  4th Eclogues 73    96
       What sweete joyes I had once, and what a place I did hold? . 124  4th Eclogues 74    72
       And vertuous soules so soone should lose their place?. . . . 126  4th Eclogues 75    42
       Me thinkes, my sound no place with sorrow filleth. . . . .  127  4th Eclogues 75    99
       For what place now is lefte for our affection. . . . . . .  129  4th Eclogues 76     7
       Place standeth still amazed. . . . . . . . . . . . . . . .  136  Cert Sonnets  3     7
       Place see my grave uptorne: . . . . . . . . . . . . . . .   136  Cert Sonnets  3    19
       Fire, aire, sea, earth, fame, time, place, shew your power.. 136  Cert Sonnets  3    20
       Long sham'd to be accurst in every place, . . . . . . . .   141  Cert Sonnets  8     3
       She knows the sicknesse of that perfect place. . . . . . .  142  Cert Sonnets 11    11
       If further place might further me to ease. . . . . . . . .  149  Cert Sonnets 21     4
       Decke that poore place with Alablaster linde... . . . . . . 150  Cert Sonnets 22    34
       For if my place give me great pleasure, . . . . . . . . . . 159  Cert Sonnets 29     5
       Love borne in Greece, of late fled from his native place,.  168  Astrophil     8     1
       Gold is the covering of that stately place.. . . . . . . .  169  Astrophil     9     4
       So Tyran he no fitter place could spie,. . . . . . . . . .  175  Astrophil    20     5
       And staid pleasd with the prospect of the place, . . . . .  175  Astrophil    20    10
       Progressing then from faire twinnes' gold'n place: . . . .  175  Astrophil    22     4
       Scourge of it selfe, still climing slipprie place, . . . .  176  Astrophil    23    10
       Unseene, unheard, while thought to highest place . . . . .  178  Astrophil    27    13
       What, may it be that even in heav'nly place. . . . . . . .  180  Astrophil    31     3
       The baiting place of wit, the balme of woe, . . . . . . . . 184  Astrophil    39     2
       The heav'nly nature of that place is such, . . . . . . . .  187  Astrophil    44    12
       Pitie thereof gate in her breast such place. . . . . . . .  187  Astrophil    45     7
       That thou must want or food, or dwelling place.. . . . . .  187  Astrophil    46     4
       By no pretence claime any maner place. . . . . . . . . . .  191  Astrophil    52    11
       When my good Angell guides me to the place,. . . . . . . .  194  Astrophil    60     1
       Her flamie glistring lights increase with time and place;.. 205  Astrophil    76    10
       Pardon that fault, once more graunt me the place, . . . . . 208  Astrophil    82    12
       What, doth high place ambitious thoughts augment?. . . . .  208  Astrophil    83     9
       But give apt servants their due place, let eyes. . . . . .  210  Astrophil    85     9
       If this darke place yet shew like candle light,. . . . . .  225  Astrophil    91     5
       Her selfe (to shew no other joy hath place). . . . . . . .  229  Astrophil    97     7
       Let honor selfe to thee graunt highest place.. . . . . . .  233  Astrophil   103    14
       So neere, in so good time, so free a place?. . . . . . . .  235  Astrophil   105     2
       Bare me in hand, that in this Orphane place, . . . . . . .  235  Astrophil   106     3
       Better place no wit can find, . . . . . . . . . . . . . . . 210  A&S 4th Song      13
       I thought each place was darke but where thy lights would
          be . . . . . . . . . . . . . . . . . . . . . . . . . .   212  A&S 5th Song       5
       To take up the place for me; . . . . . . . . . . . . . . .  226  A&S 10th Song     14
       Thought see thou no place forbeare,. . . . . . . . . . . .  226  A&S 10th Song     19
       Deserves the former place: . . . . . . . . . . . . . . . .  215  A&S 6th Song       4
       Time and place for me may move you.. . . . . . . . . . . .  219  A&S 8th Song      52
       Seeke a better place of feeding, . . . . . . . . . . . . .  221  A&S 9th Song       2
       Ne yet shall suffred be a place to take, . . . . . . . . .  270  Psalm I           17
       Of grain and wine fills stoaring place.. . . . . . . . . .  274  Psalm IV          30
       In such a place Unknown. . . . . . . . . . . . . . . . . .  282  Psalm X           33
       To beare his sacred flight, in secret place then clos'd, .  291  Psalm XVIII       23
       He lifted me unto a largly noble place.. . . . . . . . . .  292  Psalm XVIII       42
       Who shall stand in his Holy place? . . . . . . . . . . . .  302  Psalm XXIV         6
       Ev'n where Thou makest Thy honour's biding place.. . . . .  306  Psalm XXVI        27
       Thou art my safe and secret place. . . . . . . . . . . . .  315  Psalm XXXII       25
       Who dwell in dusty place.. . . . . . . . . . . . . . . . .  317  Psalm XXXIII      54
       Thou shalt have both good food and place.. . . . . . . . .  324  Psalm XXXVII       8
       Whome Thou, O place of places all, dost place. . . . . . .  334  Psalm XLI         43
       But Dick my counsell marke: run from the place of wo:. . .  344  Possibly      1   41
       Of clime-fall Court, the envy-hatching place:. . . . . . .  243  Other Poems   4   61
       With length laid downe she deckt the lonely place. . . . .  244  Other Poems   4  107
       The two that in mid place, Hell called were, . . . . . . .  248  Other Poems   4  227
       Vertue's proofe, fortune's victor, beautie's place.. . . .  252  Other Poems   4  392
       So I left him in that place, . . . . . . . . . . . . . . .  264  Other Poems   7   73
PLACED
       And thus my eyes, are plaste still in one sight. . . . . .   12  Arcadia I     2 V809
       Lyke to my noble thoughtes, still new, well plac'd, to me
          fruteles. . . . . . . . . . . . . . . . . . . . . . . .   35  1st Eclogues 13  124
       Yet be my hopes thus plast, here fixed lives my recomforte,. 37  1st Eclogues 13  164
       Like players plast to fill a filthy stage, . . . . . . . .   57  2nd Eclogues 30   20
       Who hath his hire, hath well his labour plast: . . . . . .  108  Arcadia IV   68    1
       (A musique sweet to one in carefull musing plaste) . . . .  117  4th Eclogues 73    8
       And having plaste my thoughts, my thoughts thus placed me.. 117  4th Eclogues 73   34
       For ever banish'd from well plac'd affection;. . . . . . .  130  4th Eclogues 76   29
       On whome all love, in whom no love is plaste, . . . . . . . 151  Cert Sonnets 22   63
       Placed ever there, gave him this mourning weed, . . . . . . 168  Astrophil     7   13
       By being placed in such a wretch as I. . . . . . . . . . .  228  Astrophil    94   14
       In speeches nobly placed: . . . . . . . . . . . . . . . . . 216  A&S 6th Song      26
       Where thou art not formost placed, . . . . . . . . . . . .  220  A&S 8th Song      87
       Thou hatest all whose works in evill are plac't. . . . . .  275  Psalm V           13
       Thou under his Dominion plac't . . . . . . . . . . . . . .  279  Psalm VIII        25
       And whose bodys placed be. . . . . . . . . . . . . . . . .  289  Psalm XVI         42
       But in his church his Fame is plac't.. . . . . . . . . . .  310  Psalm XXIX        24
       And ev'en my bones consume where they be plac't. . . . . .  312  Psalm XXXI        30
       From strife of tongues in Thy Pavilions plac't.. . . . . .  313  Psalm XXXI        57
PLACES
       The cheerefull notes these pleasant places yeeld, . . . . .  58  2nd Eclogues 30   39
       Thou arte therefore of these our desart places . . . . . .  108  Arcadia IV   69   12
       We last short while, and build long lasting places:. . . .  127  4th Eclogues 75   91
       They fit for heavenly places, . . . . . . . . . . . . . . . 152  Cert Sonnets 23   23
       All the places, . . . . . . . . . . . . . . . . . . . . . . 155  Cert Sonnets 26    6
```

PLACES	(CONTINUED)	PAGE	TITLE	LINE
From out his veiling places, ...		294	Psalm XIX	22
Set them in pointed places, ...		298	Psalm XXI	46
Whome Thou, O place of places all, dost place.		334	Psalm XLI	43
PLACEST				
Thou placest him upon all lands.		279	Psalm VIII	21
PLACING				
Can I forget, when they in prison placing her, ...		61	2nd Eclogues 30	152
In our well-doing placing all his pleasure, ...		129	4th Eclogues 76	15
PLAGUE				
With plague of deepe disdaine:		159	Cert Sonnets 30	4
Beautie's plague, Vertue's scourge, succour of lies:		206	Astrophil 78	6
A still felt plague, to selfe condemning me:		212	Astrophil 86	3
Who tempt, and tempted plague, are Devils in true defining..		215	A&S 5th Song	84
From my plague, kynn, neighbour, Friend, ...		328	Psalm XXXVIII	31
PLAGUED				
Thus plag'de how can I frame to my soare any hope of				
amendemente?		37	1st Eclogues 13	160
Man oft is plag'de with aire, is burnt with fire, ...		105	3rd Eclogues 67	67
Where plagu'd for rash attempt, gives up his ghost, ...		151	Cert Sonnets 22	57
PLAGUES				
My plaintes call wolves, my plagues in you prevaile, ...		43	Arcadia II 24	8
With so sweete plagues my happie harmes infected be:		51	2nd Eclogues 28	123
Still plagues the poore the most he can:		281	Psalm X	6
Ah! yet from me let Thy plagues be displac't, ...		330	Psalm XXXIX	31
***PLAIN**				
And plaine speach oft then quaint phrase better framed is. .		14	1st Eclogues 7	6
Well may a Pastor plaine, but alas his plaints be not				
esteem de.		32	1st Eclogues 13	39
Raging in woes first pastors tought to plaine?		53	2nd Eclogues 29	58
Then earste I knewe: But first dyd playne.		57	2nd Eclogues 30	3
But more I plaine, I feele my woes the more.		57	2nd Eclogues 30	10
I plaine with cause, my woes are all myne owne..		75	Arcadia III 43	6
Which being pure and plaine, ...		93	3rd Eclogues 63	62
Not spying faults, nor in plaine errors blinde, ...		98	3rd Eclogues 65	7
That heavie earth, not fierie sprites may plaine?.		142	Cert Sonnets 11	6
Would have made tongue's language plaine;		219	A&S 8th Song	66
Whose deeds of Righteous heart, whose hearty words be plain,		287	Psalm XV	4
I plain sweet Lord, my plaint for pitty mark;		289	Psalm XVII	2
So have I cause my selfe to plaine, but no cause to				
complayne.		344	Possibly 1	36
Their sences rude plaine objects only move, ...		245	Other Poems 4	143
PLAINEDST				
Will. Thou late of wages playn'dst: what wages mayst thou				
have?.		344	Possibly 1	31
PLAINETH				
Underneath my window playneth?".		233	A&S 11th Song	2
PLAINFUL				
That erst I knewe, and with most plainefull muse;		24	1st Eclogues 9	63
PLAINFULNESS				
Can I forget, from how much mourning plainfulnes		61	2nd Eclogues 30	155
PLAINING				
Vouchsafe your silent eares to playning musique, ...		111	4th Eclogues 71	4
Above line repeated at following location.		111	4th Eclogues 71	11
Your dolefull tunes, to them still playning say, ...		126	4th Eclogues 75	50
Then give a quiet eare unto my playning:		127	4th Eclogues 75	65
A plaining songe plaine-singing voice requires, ...		242	Other Poems 4	3
Till Strephon's plaining voice him nearer drew, ...		256	Other Poems 4	535
PLAINLY				
In thy face I plainly see, ...		140	Cert Sonnets 7	29
And make Thy wayes to me more plainly known, ...		275	Psalm V	23
He made my cumbrous way to me most plainly right..		292	Psalm XVIII	60
PLAIN-SINGING				
A plaining songe plaine-singing voice requires, ...		242	Other Poems 4	3
PLAINT				
Then power out plaint, and in one word say this:		13	Arcadia I 4	9
Helples his plaint, who spoyles himselfe of blisse..		13	Arcadia I 4	10
A plaint of guiltlesse hurt doth pierce the skie..		103	3rd Eclogues 66	152
Her helpe to this, this justest cause of plaint.		125	4th Eclogues 75	14
To well felte griefe, plainte is the onely pleasure.		126	4th Eclogues 75	51
From such deepe plaint as should such woes descrie, ...		129	4th Eclogues 75	137
To some a sweetest plaint, a sweetest stile affords, ...		168	Astrophil 6	9
Or if thy love of plaint yet mine forbeares, ...		228	Astrophil 94	9
I plain sweet Lord, my plaint for pitty mark;		289	Psalm XVII	2
O God the night is privy to my plaint, ...		298	Psalm XXII	7
Yet to my plaint Thou hast not audience lent..		298	Psalm XXII	8
For nothing can more tedious bee, then plaint, in time of				
joy.		344	Possibly 1	46
PLAINTFUL				
Do not thy hart, to plaintfull custome bring, ...		22	1st Eclogues 9	3
Harke plaintfull ghostes, infernall furies harke		73	Arcadia III 40	1
That here is juster cause of plaintfull sadnesse:.		137	Cert Sonnets 4	10
Above line repeated at following location.		137	Cert Sonnets 4	22
PLAINTS				
Heare plaints come forth from dungeon of my minde.		18	1st Eclogues 7	133
Well may a Pastor plaine, but alas his plaints be not				
esteem de.		32	1st Eclogues 13	39
And thinke ther she do dwell and heare what plaintes I do				
utter:		36	1st Eclogues 13	143
And make me heare the plaints I would refraine:.		42	Arcadia II 21	11

PLAINTS	(CONTINUED)	PAGE	TITLE		LINE
My plaintes call wolves, my plagues in you prevaile, ...		43	Arcadia II	24	8
The tunes be cryes, the words plaints, ...		66	2nd Eclogues 32		35
Who others' woes and plaints can chastly beare:.		142	Cert Sonnets 10		7
She heard my plaints, and did not only heare,.		193	Astrophil	57	9
O plaints conserv'd in such a sugred phraise,.		231	Astrophil	100	9
Such teares, sighs, plaints, no sorrow is, but joy:.		231	Astrophil	100	12
My crying plaints to him alone,.		273	Psalm IV		14
PLANET					
Stella, the onely Planet of my light,.		200	Astrophil	68	1
PLANETS					
Shall such high Plannets tend to the losse of a worme? . . .		123	4th Eclogues 74		38
While those faire planets on thy streames did shine.		232	Astrophil	103	4
PLANETS'					
In mortall mindes our mindes but planets' names preserve:. .		120	4th Eclogues 73		113
PLANGUS					
Plangus. Alas how long this pilgrimage doth last?.		57	2nd Eclogues 30		5
Plangus. Curst be good haps, and curst be they that build. .		58	2nd Eclogues 30		41
Plangus must live to see Eronae's death.		58	2nd Eclogues 30		55
Plangus must live some helpe for her to trie		58	2nd Eclogues 30		56
Plangus doth live, and shall Erona dye?.		58	2nd Eclogues 30		58
Plangus. And shall shee dye? shall cruell fier spill		59	2nd Eclogues 30		83
Plangus. If through mine eares pearce any consolacyons . . .		61	2nd Eclogues 30		143
Let me forget that Plangus I am called:.		61	2nd Eclogues 30		162
But Plangus, lest I may your sicknesse misse		62	2nd Eclogues 30		182
While Plangus dyd a storie strainge declare.		62	2nd Eclogues 30		189
PLANT					
Who in one selfe these diverse gifts can plant;.		3	Lady of May	1	4
That in my selfe your selfe true love doth plant;.		39	Arcadia II	16	8
And aye more awe towards him for to plant, ...		101	3rd Eclogues 66		102
That voyce, which makes the soule plant himselfe in the					
eares:		205	Astrophil	77	9
And on his Testimonys plant.		304	Psalm XXV		42
Who faithfull feares in him do plant;.		319	Psalm XXXIV		35
PLANTED					
Such planted gifts enrich even beggers' sight:		3	Lady of May	1	10
He shall be lyke a freshly planted tree, ...		270	Psalm I		7
Thou planted hast this earthly mate.		279	Psalm VIII		18
In quiet home they shall be planted,.		325	Psalm XXXVII		30
PLANTETH					
Who hath the feet, whose step all sweetnesse planteth, . . .		197	A&S 1st Song		13
PLANTS					
Thus halfe a beast, ech beastly vice he plants,.		21	1st Eclogues 8		33
Those pleasant plants, those sweete and frutefull trees, . .		26	1st Eclogues 9		130
My heeles and plants thou didst from stumbling slip					
sustaine , ...		292	Psalm XVIII		67
PLATO					
That Plato I read for nought, but if he tame		175	Astrophil	21	5
PLAUSIBLE					
Nor yet, fancy so drest, do receive more plausible hearing:.		35	1st Eclogues 13		101
PLAY					
Beautie his Booke, his play lovers' dissention:.		48	2nd Eclogues 28		42
He never musing standes, but with himselfe will play		53	2nd Eclogues 29		43
Then take my shape, and play a lover's parte:.		79	Arcadia III 51		12
There rested then, to play a woman's part, ...		95	3rd Eclogues 64		39
The Horse, good shape; the Sparrow, lust to playe;		101	3rd Eclogues 66		81
Or art thou from above bid play this part, ...		142	Cert Sonnets 10		11
And straight therewith, like wags new got to play, ...		173	Astrophil	17	13
When he will play, then in her lips he is, ...		186	Astrophil	43	9
When for so soft a ro●d deare play he trie?		203	Astrophil	73	4
Of gentle force, so that mine eyes dare gladly play.		205	Astrophil	76	6
Some play, while he is disarmed.		202	A&S 2nd Song		8
Who ever Lambkins saw (yet lambkins love to play).		343	Possibly	1	5
To play when that their loved dammes, are stoln or gone					
astray?.		343	Possibly	1	6
But when the rod began to play his part, ...		246	Other Poems	4	183
The play began: Pas durst not Cosma chace, ...		248	Other Poems	4	249
Strephon, whose eies on hir back-parts did play, ...		250	Other Poems	4	333
Who earnest found what they accounted play..		251	Other Poems	4	366
Nor beat you for your play,.		257	Other Poems	5	36
PLAYED					
Since there mine eyes have played so false a parte,.		38	Arcadia II	14	11
But while I thus with this yong Lyon plaid;.		173	Astrophil	16	9
Which absence wisht: love plai'd a victor's part:.		248	Other Poems	4	223
PLAYER					
To be a player of thine owne annoy..		25	1st Eclogues 9		119
PLAYERS					
Like players plast to fill a filthy stage, ...		57	2nd Eclogues 30		20
PLAYETH					
So my soul in panting playeth, ...		334	Psalm XLII		3
PLAYFELLOW					
Friend without change, playfellow without strife,.		103	3rd Eclogues 67		10
PLAYING					
Playing and shining in each outward part:.		170	Astrophil	11	13
Let us the while be playing, ...		261	Other Poems	6	32
PLAYS					
One saith, He mockes; the other saith, he playes;.		27	1st Eclogues 10		44
Austere she is, when he would honest playes;		104	3rd Eclogues 67		34
With thousand pretty childish plaies, ...		158	Cert Sonnets 28		11
With guilded leaves or colourd Velume playes,.		170	Astrophil	11	6

PLAYS	(CONTINUED)	PAGE	TITLE		LINE
When she with skirts tuckt very hy, with girles at stoolball playes.		343	Possibly	1	10
In chastest plaies, till home they walke a rowe,		243	Other Poems	4	54
Glutted with them now plaies with meanest things.		245	Other Poems	4	132
Where bold and hurtles many plays he tries,		247	Other Poems	4	194

PLEA
| We have no plea but trust. | | 318 | Psalm XXXIII | | 84 |

PLEAD
| Who at thy beer, as at a barre, shall plead. | | 11 | Arcadia I | 1 | 6 |
| The barre to plead their right, | | 215 | A&S 6th Song | | 11 |

PLEASANT
Those pleasant plants, those sweete and frutefull trees,		26	1st Eclogues	9	130
Or pleasant mirtell, may teach th'unfortunate Echo		31	1st Eclogues	13	13
Figge that yeeldes most pleasante frute, his shaddow is hurtefull,		35	1st Eclogues	13	125
The cheerefull notes these pleasant places yeeld,		58	2nd Eclogues	30	39
So may thy song be pleasant.		66	2nd Eclogues	32	29
The handle of this plesant worke,		87	Arcadia III	62	47
Yee Nimphes which haunt the springs in pleasant vallies,		111	4th Eclogues	71	2
I that was once esteem'd for pleasant musique,		111	4th Eclogues	71	15
O how the pleasant aires of true love be		205	Astrophil	78	1
In this pleasant spring must see		222	A&S 9th Song		28
In a goodly pleasant ground?		288	Psalm XVI		17

PLEASE
For as the Moone the eie doth please,		13	Arcadia I	5	7
Philisides. Who minds to please the minde drownd in annoyes.		22	1st Eclogues	9	6
Whose wounds are salves, whose yokes please more then pleasure doth:		49	2nd Eclogues	28	56
Can taste no sweetes, the sower onely please:		74	Arcadia III	2	
Do please all eyes, and spotlesse do endure.		91	3rd Eclogues	63	25
Rulers will thinke all things made them to please,		100	3rd Eclogues	66	73
And with the chaunge of them my fancie please.		113	4th Eclogues	72	4
And let him be our judge: the lad doth please me well".		121	4th Eclogues	73	153
To marre my minde, and with my hurt to please,		149	Cert Sonnets	21	2
They should still daunce to please a gazer's sight.		178	Astrophil	26	8
Oft cruell fights well pictured forth do please.		181	Astrophil	34	4
In verse, and that my verse best wits doth please?		204	Astrophil	74	11
They please I do confesse, they please mine eyes,		225	Astrophil	91	9
Soone with my death I will please thee.		211	A&S 4th Song		53
Faining love, somewhat to please me:		222	A&S 9th Song		42
Of seely boies please unacquainted sight:		246	Other Poems	4	182
In flowry fielde a gladder eye to please:		256	Other Poems	5	3
If it please thee be reflected,		264	Other Poems	7	71

PLEASED
Since vertues all, to make her title, pleased be.		15	1st Eclogues	7	39
Pleasd to receave that name by rebounding answere of Echo,		33	1st Eclogues	13	44
He said, the Musique best thilke powers pleasd		99	3rd Eclogues	66	29
Pleased with the light, that his small corse doth burne:		149	Cert Sonnets	21	12
Who hath his fancie pleased,		151	Cert Sonnets	23	1
But who hath fancies pleased,		152	Cert Sonnets	23	33
And pleasd with our soft peace, staid here his flying race.		168	Astrophil	8	4
And staid pleasd with the prospect of the place,		175	Astrophil	20	10
The' afflicted then shall eat, and be well pleased,		300	Psalm XXII		61
With nature pleas'd, content with present case,		243	Other Poems	4	59

PLEASING
Trust in the shade of pleasing Orange tree;		180	Astrophil	30	8
Wing'd with whose breath, so pleasing Zephires blow,		231	Astrophil	100	7
Still shunning Nous to lengthen pleasing race,		250	Other Poems	4	306
With their ever-pleasing sight,		263	Other Poems	7	64

PLEASINGEST
| Pleasingst consort, where each sence holds a part, | | 206 | Astrophil | 79 | 3 |

PLEASURE
Drawes up; and if, hope fayling, ende live's pleasure,		16	1st Eclogues	7	71
Whose wounds are salves, whose yokes please more then pleasure doth:		49	2nd Eclogues	28	56
Ne pleasure here, ne fame gott.		66	2nd Eclogues	32	39
Farewell Complaint, the miser's only pleasure:		83	Arcadia III	59	2
In stede of Thought, true pleasure be begunne,		84	Arcadia III	59	15
O Night, the ease of care, the pledge of pleasure,		108	Arcadia IV	69	1
"Sweet Mira mine" (quote she) "the pleasure of my minde,		119	4th Eclogues	73	93
To well felte griefe, plainte is the onely pleasure.		126	4th Eclogues	75	51
Farewell o Joy, the wofull's onely pleasure.		129	4th Eclogues	76	4
Now death hath swallow'd up our worldly pleasure,		129	4th Eclogues	76	11
In our well-doing placing all his pleasure,		129	4th Eclogues	76	15
And make his paine to keepe us safe his pleasure?		129	4th Eclogues	76	24
No, no, for ever gone is all our pleasure;		130	4th Eclogues	76	25
And in our wailfull naming him our pleasure:		130	4th Eclogues	76	32
Farewell our might, farewell our daunted pleasure:		130	4th Eclogues	76	38
O my heavens for taste by thie heavenly pleasure,		138	Cert Sonnets	5	2
Above line repeated at following location.		138	Cert Sonnets	5	26
Looke then and dye, the pleasure		152	Cert Sonnets	23	17
When to my deadlie pleasure,		154	Cert Sonnets	25	1
To my dying heart some pleasure,		155	Cert Sonnets	26	9
For if my place give me great pleasure,		159	Cert Sonnets	29	5
What ever fades, but fading pleasure brings.		161	Cert Sonnets	32	4
That the deare She might take some pleasure of my paine:		165	Astrophil	1	2
That she (deare she) might take some pleasure of my paine:		165	Astrophil	1 V	2
Pleasure might cause her reade, reading might make her know,		165	Astrophil	1	3
Who hath the eyes which marrie state with pleasure,		197	A&S 1st Song		5

377

PLEASURE   (CONTINUED)   PAGE   TITLE   LINE

For rage now rules the reynes, which guided were by
    Pleasure . . . . 213 A&S 5th Song   15
Only thought aymes at the pleasure.. . . . . 226 A&S 10th Song   12
Such pleasure take in Vanity,. . . . . 273 Psalm IV   9
Oh! of thy grace what endlesse pleasure flowes . . . . 313 Psalm XXXI   52
The pleasure of my God attend, ... 330 Psalm XL   2
Graunt pleasure to our meeting:. . . . . 260 Other Poems   6   2
Then this false, fine, Courtly pleasure. . . . . 263 Other Poems   7   48
In whose love I pleasure take, ... 263 Other Poems   7   62
PLEASURES
Then Love allowes, our pleasures to enrich,. . . . . 18 1st Eclogues 7 129
Since outward pleasures be but halting helpes to decayd
    soules). . . . . 33 1st Eclogues 13   52
Shall in endlesse pleasures stand! . . . . 289 Psalm XVI   44
Of pleasurs past the reach of mind?. . . . . 324 Psalm XXXVI   24
PLEASURES'
And drink from out Thy pleasures' spring,. . . . . 324 Psalm XXXVI   23
PLEDGE
Fayre hand, the fayrest pledge of fayrer harte,. . . . . 70 Arcadia III 35   10
O Night, the ease of care, the pledge of pleasure, ... 108 Arcadia IV 69   1
PLENTEOUS
Farewell o pearl, the poore man's plenteous treasure:. . . . . 129 4th Eclogues 76   2
The plenteous sweets, (can sweets so sharply grow?). . . . . . 243 Other Poems   4   52
PLENTEOUSNESS
They shall have peace in plenteousness.. . . . . 325 Psalm XXXVII   32
PLENTY
The lord such plenty hath, ... 303 Psalm XXV   32
And of grasse was plenty dwelling, ... 262 Other Poems   7   5
PLIES
Deeme that my Muse some fruit of knowledge plies:. . . . . . . 176 Astrophil   23   6
PLIGHT
Or howe do I, captiv'd in this darke plight, ... 74 Arcadia III 42   3
O harbour all her partes in easefull plighte:. . . . . 79 Arcadia III 51   7
And when neede were, from pride in privy plight, ... 313 Psalm XXXI   55
PLOT
Both ruines, ruiners, and ruin'd plott . . . . 280 Psalm IX   19
With face the plot of pittie,. . . . . 259 Other Poems   5 118
PLOT'S
With ground plot's fall shall be undone: . . . . 284 Psalm XI   10
PLOTS
Though all his plotts without misfortune . . . . 325 Psalm XXXVII   19
PLOW
A Lillie field, with plowe of Rose which tilled is.. . . . . . 15 1st Eclogues 7   30
I long doo plowe with plough of deepe Desire:. . . . . 115 4th Eclogues 72   52
PLOWED
Thy stars be fal'n, plowed is thy flintie ground:. . . . . . .   4 Lady of May   2   16
PLOWS
He water plowes, and soweth in the sand, ... 24 1st Eclogues 9   53
PLUCKED
New plucked from the place where it did breed, ... 19 1st Eclogues 7 159
See now those feathers pluckt, wherewith thou flewst most
    high:. . . . . 213 A&S 5th Song   22
PLUM
Lips red and plum, as cherrie's ruddy side,. . . . . 76 Arcadia III 46   8
PLUMES
Without my plumes from others' wings I take. . . . . 224 Astrophil   90   11
PLUNGE
Doth plunge my wel-form'd soule even in the mire . . . . 172 Astrophil   14   7
Thou well hast known what plung my soul was in . . . . 312 Psalm XXXI   21
PLUNGED
Better yet do I live, that though by my thoughts I be
    plunged. . . . . 35 1st Eclogues 13 107
Deepe plunged in earth, deprived of the skie.. . . . . 149 Cert Sonnets 21   8
All plung'd in stinking filth, not One well bent,. . . . . . . 286 Psalm XIV   11
POESY
Neare therabout, into your Poesie wring; . . . . 172 Astrophil   15   4
POET
A Poet eke, as humours fly or creepe,. . . . . 181 Astrophil   32   4
POET'S
By wise discourse, sweete tunes, or Poet's fiction;. . . . . . 61 2nd Eclogues 30 144
Graved in mine Epitaph a Poet's name:. . . . . 224 Astrophil   90   8
POETS
Poore Painters oft with silly Poets joyne, ... 20 1st Eclogues 8   1
Thus Painters Cupid paint, thus Poets do,. . . . . 20 1st Eclogues 8   5
Which Poets say, the gods them selves do feare,. . . . . 146 Cert Sonnets 17   7
Are Poets then the onely lovers true,. . . . . 146 Cert Sonnets 17   31
POETS'
Some do I heare of Poets' furie tell,. . . . . 204 Astrophil   74   5
POINT
At length obtain the point of his desire, ...   4 Lady of May   3   2
Nothing can mend one point that in her lies. . . . . 17 1st Eclogues 7 108
At blowe point, hotcocles, or els at keeles. . . . . 28 1st Eclogues 10   47
But (like a point in midst of a circle) is still of a
    neernesse, ... 31 1st Eclogues 13   6
Watched when she a furder point might gaine, ... 96 3rd Eclogues 64   75
To yonder Nymphe therefore (to Mira I did point) . . . . 121 4th Eclogues 73 165
Which through a bleeding heart his point did shove:. . . . . . 171 Astrophil   13   6
Nor give each speech a full point of a grone,. . . . . 191 Astrophil   54   4
All to this point, how my poore life to take.. . . . . 313 Psalm XXXI   39

```
                                                         PAGE    TITLE           LINE
POINTED
     Is no fit marke to pierce with his fine pointed dart:. . . .  168 Astrophil      8    3
     Set them in pointed places,. . . . . . . . . . . . . . . .   298 Psalm XXI          46
POINTING
     Not pointing to fit folkes each undercharge, . . . . . . .   210 Astrophil     85    6
POINTS
     That I Climb'd highest hill, he me warr points did show, . . 292 Psalm XVIII        62
POISON
     As who by being poisond doth poison know.. . . . . . . . .   173 Astrophil     16   14
     That poison foule of bubling pride doth lie. . . . . . . .   178 Astrophil     27    6
     I said, thou wert most sweet, sweet poison to my heart:. . . 212 A&S 5th Song        8
     On Creon's child his poison sooner throw,. . . . . . . . .   252 Other Poems    4  410
POISON'S
     Infected so with her sweet poyson's might, . . . . . . . .   115 4th Eclogues 72   78
POISONED
     As who by being poisond doth poison know.. . . . . . . . .   173 Astrophil     16   14
     Their chearfull minds, till pois'ned was their cheare, . . . 243 Other Poems    4   41
     But lickrous, Poison'd, faine to her would goe,. . . . . .   246 Other Poems    4  165
POISONOUS
     Then with the poisnous todes that quiet lie. . . . . . . .    28 1st Eclogues 10   66
     O poisonous medecin! what worse to me can be then it? It..    63 2nd Eclogues 31    7
     That with such poysonous care my lookes you marke, . . . .   233 Astrophil    104    2
POLES'
     How Poles' right king meanes, without leave of hoast,. . . . 180 Astrophil     30    3
POLICY
     The beastes had sure some beastly pollicie:. . . . . . . .   100 3rd Eclogues 66   50
POMMELS
     Like pomels round of Marble cleere:. . . . . . . . . . . .    87 Arcadia III   62   55
POMP
     And by thy pompe our losse will be conceaved.. . . . . . .   127 4th Eclogues 75   75
POMPS
     In sorrows torments, then, tyed to the pompes of a pallace,.  35 1st Eclogues 13  103
     Who under courtly pompes doo hatch a base desire.. . . . .   117 4th Eclogues 73   16
PONDER
     They seldome ponder what to them is due. . . . . . . . . .   104 3rd Eclogues 67   27
     Ponder the words, O lord, that I do say, . . . . . . . . .   274 Psalm V            1
     Ponder the paines, which on me loaden be . . . . . . . . .   280 Psalm IX          37
POOR
     He is not poore who can his freedome save, . . . . . . . .     4 Lady of May    2   27
     "Poore Pan" (he sayd) "although thou beaten be,. . . . . .     5 Lady of May    3   11
     Both these conspird poore Reason's overthrowe; . . . . . .    11 Arcadia I      2    7
     Can I be poore, that her golde haire procure my selfe? . . .  16 1st Eclogues  7   58
     Such force hath Love above poore Nature's power. . . . . .    19 1st Eclogues  7  161
     Dorus. Such force hath Love above poore Nature's power,. . .  19 1st Eclogues  7  162
     Poore Painters oft with silly Poets joyne, . . . . . . . .    20 1st Eclogues  8    1
     Knowing no more, then what poore tryall showes, . . . . .     28 1st Eclogues 10   53
     Where thou poore nature left'st all thy due glory, to
         fortune. . . . . . . . . . . . . . . . . . . . . . . .    30 1st Eclogues 11   15
     Silly shepheard's poore pype, when his harsh sound testifis
         our woes,. . . . . . . . . . . . . . . . . . . . . . .    32 1st Eclogues 13   40
     If thou (alas poore if) do winne, then winne thou this,. . .  53 2nd Eclogues 29   37
     Woe to poore man: ech outward folly annoyes him. . . . . .    62 2nd Eclogues 30  170
     (For they have toongs to make a poore man blamed . . . . .    94 3rd Eclogues 64   21
     And you poore beastes, in patience bide your hell, . . . .   103 3rd Eclogues 66  153
     And thou poore Earth, whom fortune doth attaint. . . . . .   125 4th Eclogues 75   16
     Farewell o pearl, the poore man's plenteous treasure:. . .   129 4th Eclogues 76    2
     As this poore beast who did his rest forsake,. . . . . . .   145 Cert Sonnets 16    7
     Decke that poore place with Alablaster linde.. . . . . . .   150 Cert Sonnets 22   34
     My poore reason thy words moved, . . . . . . . . . . . . .   156 Cert Sonnets 27    3
     And strange things cost too deare for my poore sprites.. . . 166 Astrophil      3   11
     Of touch they are, and poore I am their straw. . . .· . . .  169 Astrophil      9   14
     You that poore Petrarch's long deceased woes, . . . . . .    172 Astrophil     15    7
     Poore passenger, passe now thereby I did,. . . . . . . . .   175 Astrophil     20    9
     My harmes on Ink's poore losse, perhaps some find. . . . .   182 Astrophil     34   13
     The poore man's wealth, the prisoner's release,. . . . . .   184 Astrophil     39    3
     Do not, o do not from poore me remove, . . . . . . . . . .   186 Astrophil     42    7
     Alas poore wag, that now a scholler art. . . . . . . . . .   188 Astrophil     46    9
     And now man's wrongs in me, poore beast, descrie.. . . . .   189 Astrophil     49    4
     While those poore babes their death in birth do find:. . . . 190 Astrophil     50   11
     Poore Layman I, for sacred rites unfit.. . . . . . . . . .   203 Astrophil     74    4
     That skin, whose passe-praise hue scorns this poore terme of
         white:. . . . . . . . . . . . . . . . . . . . . . . .   205 Astrophil     77    7
     Poore hope's first wealth, ostage of promist weale,. . . .   206 Astrophil     79   12
     If her lips daignd to sweeten my poore name. . . . . . . .   225 Astrophil     92   13
     For my poore soule, which now that sicknesse tries,. . . .   228 Astrophil     94    6
     But ah poore Night, in love with Phoebus' light,. . . . .    229 Astrophil     97    5
     Your Client poore my selfe, shall Stella handle so?. . . .   213 A&S 5th Song       31
     Her poore slave's unjust decaying. . . . . . . . . . . . .   222 A&S 9th Song       50
     That all against poore me. . . . . . . . . . . . . . . . .   272 Psalm III           5
     But of the Other side, the poore in sprite . . . . . . . .   281 Psalm IX          56
     Still plagues the poore the most he can: . . . . . . . . .   281 Psalm X            6
     To trap poor soules he goes! . . . . . . . . . . . . . . .   282 Psalm X           44
     To prayers of the poore: . . . . . . . . . . . . . . . . .   283 Psalm X           74
     That poore from ruine may be stayd:. . . . . . . . . . . .   283 Psalm X           78
     Indeed the poore opprest by you, you mock, . . . . . . . .   287 Psalm XIV         19
     Up then thou liftst the poore, and down the proud wilt cast; 292 Psalm XVIII       52
     The lookers now at me poore wretch be mocking, . . . . . .   299 Psalm XXII        17
     Of my poore weedes thy do partition make . . . . . . . . .   299 Psalm XXII        43
     For I am poore, and left of all. . . . . . . . . . . . . .   304 Psalm XXV         60
     All to this point, how my poore life to take.. . . . . . .   313 Psalm XXXI        39
```

POOR (CONTINUED) PAGE TITLE LINE

That hunt so poore a prey as is my soule.. . . . . 321 Psalm XXXV 8
Who poore and weake from rich and strong dost free,. . . . . 321 Psalm XXXV 22
This while, though poore, they in themselves did raigne. . . 243 Other Poems 4 64
And full, poore foole, of boyish bravery,. . . . . 244 Other Poems 4 77
Of them, poore soules: and cutting Reason's raines,. . . . . 246 Other Poems 4 158
Strephon, poor youth, because he saw no smoke, ... 253 Other Poems 4 427
Canst thou, poore lamme, become another's lamme? . . . . . . 258 Other Poems 5 76
Tell me poore wretch, parted from wretched prey, ... 258 Other Poems 5 89
In poore shepheard's base degree?. . . . . 262 Other Poems 7 26

POOR-CLAD
The poore-clad truth of love's wrong-ordred lot. . . . . . . 242 Other Poems 4 14

POORLY
Poorely counterfeiting thee.. . . . . 234 A&S 11th Song 25

POOR-MINDED
But who aright poore-minded be . . . . 283 Psalm X 61

POPLAR
Popler changeth his hew from a rising sunne to a setting:. . 36 1st Eclogues 13 132

PORCHES
Whose porches rich (which name of cheekes endure). . . . . . 169 Astrophil 9 7

PORES
Through pores of sencelesse trees, as it could make them
move:. . . . . 208 A&S 3rd Song 2

POROUS
In trees) now through your porous barkes receave . . . . . 125 4th Eclogues 75 5

PORPHYR
Red Porphir is, which locke of pearle makes sure:. . . . . . 169 Astrophil 9 6

PORPHYRY
With dearest tops of porphyrie.. . . . . 87 Arcadia III 62 57

PORTION
Where but a baiting place is all our portion.. . . . . 61 2nd Eclogues 30 136
God my only portion is . . . . 288 Psalm XVI 13
And count this life their Portion best . . . . 290 Psalm XVII 40

PORTRAIT
To portrait that which in this world is best.. . . . . 189 Astrophil 50 8

PORTS
That I within the ports most beautifull. . . . . 280 Psalm IX 41

POSSESSE
All this I give, let me possesse thy grace,. . . . . 4 Lady of May 2 22
No charme holdes her, but well possesse she may;. . . . . . . 17 1st Eclogues 7 111
Possesse she doth, and makes my soule her slave: . . . . . . 17 1st Eclogues 7 112
Feede on my sheepe, possesse your fruitefull fyeld,. . . . . 43 Arcadia II 23 7
She doth possesse, thy Image is defaste, ... 72 Arcadia III 38 12
Though each possesse a divers working kinde, ... 78 Arcadia III 50 7
Yet pride I thinke doth not my soule possesse, ... 178 Astrophil 27 9
Those Lovers scorne whom that Love doth possesse?. . . . . . 180 Astrophil 31 13
Honour is honour'd, that thou doest possesse . . . . 182 Astrophil 35 9
But meek men shall the earth possesse, ... 325 Psalm XXXVII 29
Emprison hir, who both them did possesse . . . . 252 Other Poems 4 390

POSSESSED
Such weight it hath which once is full possest.. . . . . . . 20 1st Eclogues 7 V961
Above line repeated at following location. . . . . 20 1st Eclogues 7 V962
Wyth two strange fires of equall heate possest,. . . . . . . 42 Arcadia II 22 1
And how possest he strengthens his invasion? . . . . 48 2nd Eclogues 28 36
With sense possest, and claim'd by reason's right: . . . . . 74 Arcadia III 42 6
By inward letts, of them his state possest, ... 75 Arcadia III 44 2
Held, pearst, possest, my judgement, sence, and will,. . . . 84 Arcadia III 60 6
Till deadly sleepe at length possest my living coarse. . . . 117 4th Eclogues 73 30
By his seed eke possest. . . . . 304 Psalm XXV 52

POSSESSETH
As farre as Love possesseth any head.. . . . . 56 2nd Eclogues 29 128

POSSESSING
Shall have the land in their possessing, ... 326 Psalm XXXVII 74

POSSESSION
Enjoy her soule, in bodie's faire possession,. . . . . 15 1st Eclogues 7 41
In thy owne proofe he gets so straunge possession, ... 48 2nd Eclogues 28 35

POSSIBILITY
Her eyes the force beyond my possibilitie. . . . . 48 2nd Eclogues 28 30

POSSIBLE
You, though feares do abash, in you still possible hopes be: 32 1st Eclogues 13 23
Whence may I show to my minde any light of a possible
escape . . . . 37 1st Eclogues 13 161

POSTERITY
If thus thou murther thy posteritie. . . . . 105 3rd Eclogues 67 78

POT
Or like a broken pott in myer tredd. . . . . 313 Psalm XXXI 36

POTSHERD
My moystning strength is like a potsherd dride,. . . . . . . 299 Psalm XXII 35

POTSHERDS
These men like potshards weake.. . . . . 271 Psalm II 22

POUR
Then power out plaint, and in one word say this: . . . . . . 13 Arcadia I 4 9
While teares powre out his inke, and sighs breathe out his
words: . . . . 168 Astrophil 6 10
Come, come, and let me powre my selfe on thee; . . . . 200 Astrophil 69 6
And thy words of refuse, do powre even hell on mee:. . . . . 215 A&S 5th Song 83

POURS
Is that huge storme, which powres it selfe on me:. . . . . . 114 4th Eclogues 72 32

POWDERED
Broadred with buls and swans, powdred with golden raine: . . 167 Astrophil 6 6

POWER   PAGE   TITLE   LINE

	PAGE	TITLE		LINE
Thus is my power transformed to your will.	12	Arcadia I	2	12
The power I will invoke dwelles in her eyes:	17	1st Eclogues	7	104
Such force hath Love above poore Nature's power.	19	1st Eclogues	7	161
Dorus. Such force hath Love above poore Nature's power,.	19	1st Eclogues	7	162
Hath power that Sex with bridle to withhold?	24	1st Eclogues	9	58
As that hatefull death can abridge them of powre,.	31	1st Eclogues	12	18
Thou doest desire, and with free power to holde.	83	Arcadia III	58	2
Our bodies be in living power maintained,.	128	4th Eclogues	75	107
O Phisicke's power, which (some say) hath refrayned.	128	4th Eclogues	75	109
Fire, aire, sea, earth, fame, time, place, shew your power..	136	Cert Sonnets	3	20
Of deathe's power,	155	Cert Sonnets	26	19
Or would she her miraculous power show,.	168	Astrophil	7	9
So Stella's heart, finding what power Love brings,	179	Astrophil	29	5
Since thou in me so sure a power doest keepe,.	181	Astrophil	32	5
O Stella deare, how much thy power hath wrought,	184	Astrophil	40	2
Each sence of mine, each gift, each power of mind,	193	Astrophil	57	2
Your power in your beautie stands:	211	A&S 4th Song		46
Thinke of my most Princely power,.	226	A&S 10th Song		31
By power of whose only brest,.	274	Psalm IV		34
While I am voyd of any helping pow'r.	277	Psalm VII		6
The power of Thy through-seing eyes?	283	Psalm X		54
Wee both have power, and will our tales to tell,	285	Psalm XII		11
The just into his power.	286	Psalm XIV		18
On my soul no power shall have:.	288	Psalm XVI		32
Shall use destroying power,.	297	Psalm XXI		34
Thy power still be praised..	298	Psalm XXI		52
And now am brought, alas, brought by Thy power	299	Psalm XXII		37
For by his power the land upon the Ocean raigneth,	302	Psalm XXIV		3
Who is this glorious King in might and power riding?	302	Psalm XXIV		19
My foes, to utmost of their pow'r.	307	Psalm XXVII		8
Ye men of Pow'er even by birth-right,.	309	Psalm XXIX		2
Have power again to raised be.	324	Psalm XXXVI		36
Do well and trust on heavnly power,.	324	Psalm XXXVII		7
Dick. Bound as I neither power have, nor would have power to stir.	343	Possibly	1	24
With greater powr, then she did make them wend	251	Other Poems	4	375
POWERS				
For (woe is me) my powers all I finde.	11	Arcadia I	2	3
Who of his tongue the lickowr gladly powrs,.	28	1st Eclogues	10	70
Yee living powres enclosed in stately shrine	40	Arcadia II	18	1
Their flames mount up, my powers prostrate lie:.	42	Arcadia II	22	11
To those high powers, which idly sit above,.	58	2nd Eclogues	30	63
Do serve, to make my inward powers darke:.	73	Arcadia III	39	8
Seeing, Alas, so mightie powers bende.	73	Arcadia III	40	5
Where justest love doth vanquish Cupid's powers.	91	3rd Eclogues	63	3
He said, the Musique best thilke powers pleasd	99	3rd Eclogues	66	29
Then since such pow'rs conspire unto our damage.	109	Arcadia IV	70	13
Free all my powers were from those captiving snares,	117	4th Eclogues	73	17
Celestiall powers to wormes, Jove's children serve to claye.	120	4th Eclogues	73	116
And so no helpe gainst envy of those powers?	142	Cert Sonnets	10	12
Deale thou with powers of thoughts, leave love to will..	169	Astrophil	10	8
Thou countest Stella thine, like those whose powers.	171	Astrophil	12	9
Bends all his powers, even unto Stella's grace..	178	Astrophil	27	14
Stella's great powrs, that so confuse my mind.	182	Astrophil	34	14
Doth fall to stray, and my chiefe powres are brought	183	Astrophil	38	3
United powers make each the stronger prove..	223	Astrophil	88	14
In night of sprites the gastly powers stur.	229	Astrophil	96	10
Of his mazde powers keepes perfit harmony:	230	Astrophil	99	8
Of all the powers which life bestowes on me,	236	Astrophil	107	2
This God then girded me in his Almighty pow'rs,.	292	Psalm XVIII		59
Yea heares with powers and helps cf helpfull hand.	296	Psalm XX		25
PRAISE				
Yet hath sir Sunne the greatest praise,.	13	Arcadia I	5	9
Her praise, whose praise to learne your skill hath framed me.	15	1st Eclogues	7	24
No lovely praise was ever got with killing".	16	1st Eclogues	7	81
Seeke to espie her faultes as well as praise,.	25	1st Eclogues	9	121
So become our tombes monuments of her praise;.	30	1st Eclogues	12	10
Thus not ending, endes the due praise of her praise;	31	1st Eclogues	12	21
Give therefore to the Muse great praise in whose very likenes.	33	1st Eclogues	13	62
Ere that I leave with song of praise her praise to solemnize	33	1st Eclogues	13	68
Her praise, whence to the world all praise had his only beginning:	33	1st Eclogues	13	69
To helpe her praise, who decks me in her slaverie.	48	2nd Eclogues	28	27
The auncient prayse to Arcad shepheards' skill?.	53	2nd Eclogues	29	52
While I was warbling out your wconted praise,.	54	2nd Eclogues	29	67
Pas. Thy name (O Cosma) shall with praise be spread,	56	2nd Eclogues	29	126
Goe winne of him (for chattering) praise or shame:	56	2nd Eclogues	29	139
O Venus (if her praise no envy frames,	60	2nd Eclogues	30	113
The matchlesse paire, even praise doth staine.	86	Arcadia III	62	16
Of whose high praise, and praisefull blisse,	90	Arcadia III	62	141
Since Lalus' musick oft doth yeeld you praise,	92	3rd Eclogues	63	29
Her strength from him, his praise from her do growe.	92	3rd Eclogues	63	52
If he do praise the dog, she likes the cat..	104	3rd Eclogues	67	54
With nature's praise are wont in safest home to take..	117	4th Eclogues	73	14
But such they say we be: this praise our discord bred,	120	4th Eclogues	73	117
He hopes for some small praise since she hath great,	141	Cert Sonnets	8	11

381

PRAISE	(CONTINUED)	PAGE	TITLE		LINE
With her due praise did of my state complaine, ...		141	Cert Sonnets	9	4
Paine heard her praise, and full of inward fire, ...		141	Cert Sonnets	9	9
Her face (this age's praise) the thiefe doth kisse..		141	Cert Sonnets	9	12
O paine I now recant the praise I gave,.		141	Cert Sonnets	9	13
I call it praise to suffer Tyrannie;		166	Astrophil	2	11
Not thou by praise, but praise in thee is raisde:.		182	Astrophil	35	13
It is a praise to praise, when thou art praisde.		182	Astrophil	35	14
Abase her praise, saying she doth excell:.		183	Astrophil	37	8
His praise to sleight, which from good use doth rise;. . . .		185	Astrophil	41	7
Youth, lucke, and praise, even fild my veines with pride...		191	Astrophil	53	4
Edward named fourth, as first in praise I name,.		204	Astrophil	75	2
That skin, whose passe-praise hue scorns this poore terme of					
white:.		205	Astrophil	77	7
Cease we to praise, now pray we for a kisse.		206	Astrophil	79	14
Nature's praise, Vertue's stall, Cupid's cold fire,.		206	Astrophil	80	3
Without how farre this praise is short of you, ...		207	Astrophil	80	13
She builds her fame on higher seated praise:		207	Astrophil	81	10
If thou praise not, all other praise is shame.		224	Astrophil	90	4
A nest for my yong praise in Lawrell tree:		224	Astrophil	90	6
That eloquence it selfe envies your praise,.		231	Astrophil	100	10
To you, to you, all song of praise is due, ...		196	A&S 1st Song		3
Above line repeated at following locations		197	A&S 1st Song		7
. . . .		197	A&S 1st Song		11
. . . .		197	A&S 1st Song		15
. . . .		197	A&S 1st Song		19
. . . .		197	A&S 1st Song		23
. . . .		197	A&S 1st Song		27
. . . .		197	A&S 1st Song		31
. . . .		197	A&S 1st Song		35
I thinke now of thy faults, who late thought of thy praise,..		213	A&S 5th Song		16
No vertue merits praise, once toucht with blot of Treason. .		214	A&S 5th Song		66
He layes on this chiefe praise, ...		216	A&S 6th Song		47
Chiefe praise on that he laies..		216	A&S 6th Song		48
Can of thy prayse the tongues entombed make.		276	Psalm VI		15
With all my heart O lord I will prayse Thee, ...		279	Psalm IX		1
O prayse the lord, this Syon dweller good, ...		280	Psalm IX		31
Of syon's Daughter may sing forth Thy prayse:.		280	Psalm IX		42
For he himself doth prayse,.		281	Psalm X		9
Whom then shall I invoke but Thee most worthy prayse,. . . .		291	Psalm XVIII		6
And with these Words, when they meet, prayse Thy Name. . . .		300	Psalm XXII		52
Who feare the lord all prayse and glory beare him;		300	Psalm XXII		53
In congregation great I will prayse Thee,.		300	Psalm XXII		59
And tongue is prest to publish out thy prayse.		306	Psalm XXVI		39
To prayse the lord..		307	Psalm XXVII		36
I owe Thee prayse, I will prayse Thee.		310	Psalm XXX		3
Prayse, Prayse this lord then evermore		311	Psalm XXX		10
Thy endless prayse: O God my King.		311	Psalm XXX		38
Then prayse, then prayse I do the lord of us,.		313	Psalm XXXI		58
O prayse with harp the lord, ...		316	Psalm XXXIII		7
Inhabit shall his prayse..		318	Psalm XXXIV		4
Somewhat to speake of his due praise,.		319	Psalm XXXIV		10
Thy justice witness shall and speake Thy prayse.		323	Psalm XXXV		72
New song unto our God of prayse, ...		331	Psalm XL		12
Still gladly say, Unto our God bee prayse.		332	Psalm XL		64
More prayse to us we never looke to winne, ...		346	Possibly	5	11
Each way, as she, that age's praise, did bend.		251	Other Poems	4	376
With my reedes, sound mighty praise;		264	Other Poems	7	68
PRAISED					
I praisde her eyes whom never chance doth move,.		141	Cert Sonnets	9	5
It is a praise to praise, when thou art praisde.		182	Astrophil	35	14
"If those eyes you praised, be		220	A&S 8th Song		81
Thy power still be praised..		298	Psalm XXI		52
And God shall be by those his seekers praysed.		300	Psalm XXII		62
God is my God, by me praysed..		335	Psalm XLII		56
PRAISEFUL					
Of whose high praise, and praisefull blisse, ...		90	Arcadia III	62	141
PRAISES					
So if my man must praises have,.		13	Arcadia I	5	5
Above line repeated at following location.		13	Arcadia I	5	11
That all these cruell words your praises shall be proved...		215	A&S 5th Song		90
And will to highest Name yeild prayses high.		278	Psalm VII		48
But let me give prayses high		309	Psalm XXVIII		24
Leading them his prayses singing,.		334	Psalm XLII		15
PRAISING					
They ever shall send thee their praysing voyce,.		275	Psalm V		35
PRANCING					
In Marse's liverie, prauncing in the presse:		191	Astrophil	53	6
PRATING					
Whereby Thou stop'st Thyne Enemy's prating		278	Psalm VIII		7
PRATTLED					
Nor time pratled away, cradle of ignorance,.		69	2nd Eclogues	34	22
PRAY					
I pray thee what hath ere the Parret gott, ...		28	1st Eclogues	10	67
With sluttish song: I pray thee learne to blea,.		56	2nd Eclogues	29	136
And therefore pray him that of courtesie		95	3rd Eclogues	64	57
I pray thee doo to Lalus' sample leane:		103	3rd Eclogues	67	4
Pardon mine eares, both I and they do pray,.		190	Astrophil	51	1
Pray that my sunne go downe with meeker beames to bed. . . .		205	Astrophil	76	14
Cease we to praise, now pray we for a kisse.		206	Astrophil	79	14

PRAY   (CONTINUED)   PAGE   TITLE   LINE
     Thou English murdring theefe, wilt have harts for thy pray:.   214 A&S 5th Song   50
     "Graunt, o deere, on knees I pray, ...   219 A&S 8th Song   49
     And hearken how I pray to Thee. . . . .   273 Psalm IV   5
     My King, my God for I to thee will pray. . . . .   274 Psalm V   4
     And pray that still Thou guide my way. . . . .   289 Psalm XVII   15
     What I pray; . . . .   328 Psalm XXXVIII   26
PRAYED
     Have praide me leave my strange exclaiming musique, ... 112 4th Eclogues 71   32
     I prayd with prayers which my breast did touch: . . . . 322 Psalm XXXV   32
     By neighbors prai'd she went abroad therby, ... 247 Other Poems   4   207
PRAYER
     The lovely blowe with rare reward, my prayer is. . . . . . .   51 2nd Eclogues 28   112
     Klaius. Curse to my selfe my prayer is, the morning: . . . . 112 4th Eclogues 71   55
     For unto Thee I will my prayer send, ... 274 Psalm V   6
PRAYERS
     To prayers of the poore: . . . . 283 Psalm X   74
     When as to him Our Prayers do appeare. . . . . 296 Psalm XX   35
     I prayd with prayers which my breast did touch; . . . . 322 Psalm XXXV   32
     Praying, prayers still bequeathing . . . . 335 Psalm XLII   39
PRAYING
     But no fault there is in praying. . . . . 219 A&S 8th Song   48
     Then thus to Thee I praying cry'd: . . . . 311 Psalm XXX   25
     Praying, prayers still bequeathing . . . . 335 Psalm XLII   39
PREASE
     With shield of proofe shield me from out the prease. . . . . 184 Astrophil   39   5
PRECEDENCE
     To whom precedence shall of both accorded be. . . . .   120 4th Eclogues 73   136
PRECEPTS
     And thinke I should not your large precepts misse? . . . . . 192 Astrophil   56   4
     As my young Dove may in your precepts wise . . . . 196 Astrophil   63   3
PRECIOUS
     The gods must help, and pretious things must serve to shew
          her shape. . . . .   12 Arcadia I   3   4
     And preciouse couches full oft are shak't with a feaver. . .   34 1st Eclogues 13   86
     Of pretious pearle the double rowe, ...   87 Arcadia III   62   42
     This noble Cedar's pretious roote: . . . .   89 Arcadia III   62   106
PREFER
     Ods? what an ods is there since them to the heav'ns I
          prefer Erre. . . . .   65 2nd Eclogues 31   48
PREFERS
     Their first caught sence prefers to teacher's blowes. . . . . 28 1st Eclogues 10   57
PRENTICE
     Sonets be not bound prentise to annoy: . . . . 201 Astrophil   70   5
PRENTICESHIP
     His childhood woonder, prenticeship attention, ...   48 2nd Eclogues 28   38
PREPARE
     Who should my mind to higher things prepare. . . . . 161 Cert Sonnets 31   8
     Before she could prepare to be unkind, ... 193 Astrophil   57   6
PREPARED
     With feare of change, the courage well preparde: . . . . . . 143 Cert Sonnets 12   11
     Prepar'd by Nature's chiefest furniture, ... 169 Astrophil   9   2
     Yet each prepar'd, with fanne's wel-shading grace, ... 176 Astrophil   22   7
     Which He prepar'd, to give his judgments high: . . . . 280 Psalm IX   22
     With inbow'd bosome well for hir prepar'd, ... 252 Other Poems   4   387
PREPAREDST
     Thou first prepare'dst their mind. . . . . 283 Psalm X   75
PREPARES
     What God prepares. . . . . 281 Psalm IX   55
PRESAGE
     With cries first borne, the pressage of his life, ... 57 2nd Eclogues 30   24
PRESENCE
     But with thy cheerefull presence helpe to grace. . . . . . .   91 3rd Eclogues 63   12
     Your presence (sister deare) first to my Moony spheare, . . . 119 4th Eclogues 73   103
     To greater woes by presence I returne, ... 149 Cert Sonnets 21   10
     Whose presence, absence, absence presence is; . . . . 195 Astrophil   60   13
     That presence, which doth give darke hearts a living light: . 205 Astrophil   77   3
     O absent presence Stella is not here; . . . . 235 Astrophil   106   1
     And as a Queene, who from her presence sends . . . . 236 Astrophil   107   9
     Woe me, from me why is Thy presence taken? . . . . 298 Psalm XXII   2
     Thy deare presence farr from me; . . . . 329 Psalm XXXVIII   63
     To which hir presence such a feaver brought. . . . . 246 Other Poems   4   176
*PRESENT
     Since whitenesse doth present the sweetest show, ...   38 Arcadia II   15   7
     Thou purest stone, whose purenesse doth present. . . . . . .   40 Arcadia II   18   7
     P. How know we that, since present joyes we misse? . . . . .   47 2nd Eclogues 27   38
     Make present ease receave the better taste. . . . .   70 Arcadia III   36   6
     That doth present those even browes, ...   86 Arcadia III   62   9
     Ech other beast likewise his present brings: . . . . 101 3rd Eclogues 66   99
     Though present times and past with evils be snarde, ... 143 Cert Sonnets 12   13
     Where former blisse present evils do staine, ... 153 Cert Sonnets 24   12
     Nay former blisse addes to present paine, ... 153 Cert Sonnets 24   13
     That to win me, oft shewes a present pay? . . . . 223 Astrophil   88   4
     Who is still my present aid; . . . . 335 Psalm XLII   54
     Sure aid present comfort. . . . .   337 Psalm XLIII   36
     With nature pleas'd, content with present case, ... 243 Other Poems   4   59
PRESENTED
     And see by this picture to you presented, ... 128 4th Eclogues 75   122
PRESERVE
     (Whiche hyding didest preserve that beawtie's light, ...   70 Arcadia III   35   2

                                  383

PRESERVE	(CONTINUED)	PAGE	TITLE		LINE
She heav'n on earth with beauties doth preserve.	. . . . . .	72	Arcadia III	38	8
Though each of them, his private forme preserve,	. . . . . .	78	Arcadia III	50	3
Preserve those beames, this age's onely lighte:	. . . . . .	79	Arcadia III	51	2
And one man still, credit with her preserve.	. . . .	98	3rd Eclogues	65	4
Which senses up doth shut the senses to preserve.	. . . . .	117	4th Eclogues	73	28
In mortall mindes our mindes but planets' names preserve:	. .	120	4th Eclogues	73	113
Since feare is vaine, but when it may preserve,	. . . .	131	Arcadia V	77	3
Preserve me from the wyly wrapping nett	. . . .	312	Psalm XXXI		10
PRESERVED					
Which must by this immortall be preserved,	. . . .	105	3rd Eclogues	67	77
As in his health we healthfull were preserved,	. . . . . .	128	4th Eclogues	75	134
While in pride flowers be preserved,	. . . .	222	A&S 9th Song		29
By Thee preserv'd, in Thee they shall abide,	. . . .	285	Psalm XII		23
Ev'n from the Waters' depth my God preserved me so.	. . . . .	291	Psalm XVIII		35
Let him be lifted up, that hath preserved me!	. . . .	293	Psalm XVIII		84
His Holy ones; they are preserved.	. . . .	326	Psalm XXXVII		70
PRESERVES					
That thus preserves my loved life:	. . . .	13	Arcadia I	5	2
For this Our lord preserves the faith full race.	. . . . .	314	Psalm XXXI		65
PRESS					
In Marse's liverie, prauncing in the presse:	. . . .	191	Astrophil	53	6
Did beate their hands, which durst so neere to presse.	. . .	252	Other Poems	4	406
PRESSED					
But thou white skinne, as white as cruddes well prest,	. . .	76	Arcadia III	46	13
To over pressed brestes, more greevous waight.	. . . .	82	Arcadia III	56	8
Tuckt up even with the knees, with bowe and arrowes prest:	.	118	4th Eclogues	73	67
A field there is where, if a stake be prest.	. . . .	150	Cert Sonnets	22	41
All folkes prest at thy will thy paine to 'swage,	. . . . .	232	Astrophil	101	11
And tongue is prest to publish out thy prayse.	. . . . . .	306	Psalm XXVI		39
Thus I prest down with weight of pain,	. . . .	315	Psalm XXXII		7
So prest with sins I cannot see my case.	. . . .	332	Psalm XL		44
Be prest our reedes to fill,	. . . .	260	Other Poems	6	9
PRESSETH					
O be not farr, since pain so nearly presseth,	. . . .	299	Psalm XXII		25
PRESSING					
Pressing too much upon ill harbourd shore.	. . . .	142	Cert Sonnets	12	3
PRESUMED					
Who to make warr with God praesumed;	. . . .	326	Psalm XXXVII		50
PRESUMPTION					
In one, whose name to name were high presumption,	. . . . .	15	1st Eclogues	7	38
PRESUMPTUOUS					
Praesumptuous sins' offences,	. . . .	295	Psalm XIX		54
PRETENCE					
By no pretence claime any maner place.	. . . .	191	Astrophil	52	11
For with pretence from Strephon hir to garde,	. . . .	252	Other Poems	4	385
PRETENDS					
While each pretends that Stella must be his:	. . . .	190	Astrophil	52	2
PRETEXT					
Slander wants a pretext, flattery gone beyond:	. . . . . .	69	2nd Eclogues	34	38
PRETTY					
A prettie curre it is; his name iwis is Catch,	. . . . . .	53	2nd Eclogues	29	40
I would climbe up, and bring a prettie starre,	. . . . . .	55	2nd Eclogues	29	118
Pas. My father hath at home a prettie Jay,	. . . .	56	2nd Eclogues	29	138
No purer then the pretie eares.	. . . .	86	Arcadia III	62	28
That dothe present those prety Browes,	. . . .	86	Arcadia III	62 V	9
With thousand prety childish plaies,	. . . .	158	Cert Sonnets	28	11
A prety case! I hoped her to bring	. . . .	193	Astrophil	57	12
The prettie death, while each in other live.	. . . .	206	Astrophil	79	11
While Strephon might with preatie Nous have met,	. . . . .	249	Other Poems	4	279
PREVAIL					
What counsell can prevaile, or light give light?	. . . . .	23	1st Eclogues	9	36
No woolves dare howle, no murrayne can prevaile,	. . . . .	43	Arcadia II	23	8
My plaintes call wolves, my plagues in you prevaile,	. . .	43	Arcadia II	24	8
Shall barr that wrong, and though it not prevaile.	. . . .	82	Arcadia III	55	13
So as if I prevaile, you give your giftes to me:	. . . . .	120	4th Eclogues	73	133
What veiles then doo prevaile, but to a more miracle?.	. . .	123	4th Eclogues	74	50
Sure they prevaile as much with me, as he.	. . . .	236	Astrophil	106	12
So strangely (alas) thy works in me prevaile,	. . . . . .	237	Astrophil	108	12
PREVAILED					
Prevailed,	. . . .	286	Psalm XIII		14
PREVAILING					
Example more prevailing then direction,	. . . .	128	4th Eclogues	75	131
For Thereus' force on her chaste will prevailing,	. . . .	137	Cert Sonnets	4	37
So did he save me from their then prevailing hate,	. . . .	291	Psalm XVIII		37
While prevayling foes.	. . . .	336	Psalm XLIII		11
PREVAILS					
The same man still in whom wysdome prevailes,	. . . .	143	Cert Sonnets	12	17
PREVENT					
For sure, no jealousie can that prevent,	. . . .	97	3rd Eclogues	64	125
Up lord prevent those gaping jawes	. . . .	290	Psalm XVII		35
Will. What care takes shee for thee? D. Hir care is to					
prevent.	. . . .	344	Possibly	1	37
Who should to Pas, but they would her prevent.	. . . . . .	249	Other Poems	4	268
PREVENTST					
Yea thou prevent'st e're ask he could,	. . . .	297	Psalm XXI		9
PREY					
Mine owne? o word on whose sweete sound doth pray.	. . . . .	80	Arcadia III	53	5
Or with her beawtie fit to make a pray,	. . . .	94	3rd Eclogues	64	8
(First sealing up my heart as pray of his)	. . . .	141	Cert Sonnets	9	10

PREY	(CONTINUED)	PAGE	TITLE		LINE
The sweete pursute of my desired pray.		145	Cert Sonnets	16	12
Till bloudie bullet get him wrongfull pray..		175	Astrophil	20	4
Could hope by Cupid's helpe on you to pray;.		186	Astrophil	43	2
From base desire on earthly cates to pray?		223	Astrophil	88	8
On me the paines of death already gan to prey, ...		291	Psalm XVIII		8
That hunt so poore a prey as is my soule.		321	Psalm XXXV		8
O Soul, rejoyce, we made this wretch our prey.		323	Psalm XXXV		62
So now for pray these shepheards two he tooke, ...		245	Other Poems	4	137
Tell me poore wretch, parted from wretched prey, ...		258	Other Poems	5	89

PREYS
| Now like a lion gaping to make preyes, ... | | 290 | Psalm XVII | | 33 |

PRICE
Or when a rich rubie's just price be the worth of a walnut,.		34	1st Eclogues	13	78
This is my pawne; the price let Dicus' judgement show: . . .		53	2nd Eclogues	29	47
Of rarest price, both heav'n and earth her bower..		59	2nd Eclogues	30	100
With price of mangled mind thy worthlesse ware,.		161	Cert Sonnets	31	6
Those lips, which make death's pay a meane price for a					
kisse		205	Astrophil	77	6
Should price of hir, as in a market, make.		245	Other Poems	4	123

PRICKING
| With pricking shot he did not throughly move, ... | | 173 | Astrophil | 17 | 3 |

PRIDE
And thowe Laelaps let not pride make thee brim		26	1st Eclogues	10	10
The peacocke's pride, the pye's pild flatterye,.		28	1st Eclogues	10	77
Let others deck their pride with skarres,.		44	Arcadia II	25	7
Howe can they be unkind? speake for th'hast narroly pri'de.					
pride.		65	2nd Eclogues	31	43
Whence can pride come there, since springs of beawty be					
thence? Thence..		65	2nd Eclogues	31	44
O brest in which two white sheepe swell in pride:.		76	Arcadia III	46	10
In nature's pride your heads to heav'nwarde heave, ...		77	Arcadia III	49	2
Blushing at sight of Phoebus' pride.		86	Arcadia III	62	26
All peacock pride, and fruites of peacock's pride.		93	3rd Eclogues	63	73
No pride shall them oppresse,.		94	3rd Eclogues	63	96
Yet like a coward fearing stranger's pride,.		95	3rd Eclogues	64	29
Who at the first, wanting, or hiding pride,.		101	3rd Eclogues	66	107
Foode without fulnes, counsaile without pride, ...		103	3rd Eclogues	67	11
Shrewdnes so stirres, pride so puffes up their hart, ...		104	3rd Eclogues	67	26
An humble pride, a skorne that favour staines:		151	Cert Sonnets	22	65
But shining forth of heate in his chiefe pride;.		176	Astrophil	22	4
That poison foule of bubling pride doth lie.		178	Astrophil	27	6
Yet pride I thinke doth not my soule possesse, ...		178	Astrophil	27	9
Youth, lucke, and praise, even fild my veines with pride...		191	Astrophil	53	4
Sweet swelling lip, well maist thou swell in pride,.		206	Astrophil	80	1
Thine eyes my pride, thy lips my history:.		224	Astrophil	90	3
While in pride flowers be preserved, ...		222	A&S 9th Song		29
For lo with pride the wicked man		281	Psalm X		5
In falsehood wrapt, but in their pride display'd..		284	Psalm XII		9
Of these bad folkes, more lifted up with pride		285	Psalm XII		26
Which full of spight, of Pride and cruelty,.		313	Psalm XXXI		50
And when neede were, from pride in privy plight, ...		313	Psalm XXXI		55
The wicked by his own pride bannisht;.		325	Psalm XXXVII		26
To great men's peacock pride,.		331	Psalm XL		18
Yeelde yeelde O yeelde, trust not on beautie's pride,. . . .		345	Possibly	4	5
They looked down to triumph over pride:.		252	Other Poems	4	403
Like to Junoe's birdes of pride, ...		263	Other Poems	7	51

PRIED
| Howe can they be unkind? speake for th'hast narroly pri'de" | | | | | |
| pride.. . . . . | | 65 | 2nd Eclogues | 31 | 43 |

PRIESTHOOD
| Our offrings spoil'd, our priests from priesthood are | | | | | |
| displac'd. . . . . | | 119 | 4th Eclogues | 73 | 110 |

PRIESTS
| Our offrings spoil'd, our priests from priesthood are | | | | | |
| displac'd. . . . . | | 119 | 4th Eclogues | 73 | 110 |

PRIME
Ly but to sleepe, and in the earely prime.		26	1st Eclogues	9	126
To age thus doe they draw there youthfull pryme, ...		28	1st Eclogues	10	52
With earliest entry of the Morning prime,.		274	Psalm V		7

PRINCE
Neither he beares reverence to a Prince nor pittie to					
begger		31	1st Eclogues	13	5
What marvaile tho a Prince transforme himselfe to a Pastor?.		34	1st Eclogues	13	91
To whome our prince did beare a great good will, ...		94	3rd Eclogues	64	16
And yet the prince (that lov'd him) not offend..		95	3rd Eclogues	64	54
Ne can he faile, for prince hath for him sent:.		97	3rd Eclogues	64	104
And (but they drad their Prince they ofte should want) . . .		101	3rd Eclogues	66	100
How well last day before our Prince you could..		106	3rd Eclogues	67	97
And farewell Prince, whom goodnesse hath made glorious.. . .		129	4th Eclogues	75	142
Others, because the Prince my service tries, ...		176	Astrophil	23	7
A rightfull Prince by unright deeds a Tyran groweth.		214	A&S 5th Song		60
And yet against thy Prince thy force dost dayly prove: . . .		214	A&S 5th Song		65

PRINCELY
| By princely meane be stolne, and yet not lost. . . . . | | 11 | Arcadia I | 1 | 2 |
| Thinke of my most Princely power,. . . . . | | 226 | A&S 10th Song | | 31 |

PRINCE'S
As Prince's losse or change:		81	Arcadia III	55	3
Of Prince's harte quite lost the ruine strange..		81	Arcadia III	55	6
Riches of children passe a Prince's throne;.		106	3rd Eclogues	67	112

PRINCE'S   (CONTINUED)   PAGE   TITLE   LINE
    Now Prince's losse hath made our damage publique,. . . . . .   109 Arcadia IV   70   4
    Of Prince's losse your selves for tokens reare.. . . . . . .   125 4th Eclogues   75   27
PRINCES
    And you, o flowers, which sometimes Princes were,. . . . . .   125 4th Eclogues   75   25
    Princes in subjects wrongd, must deeme themselves abused.. .   213 A&S 5th Song   30
PRINCES'
    Which skill dooth make in Princes' bowers. . . . .   87 Arcadia III   62   50
PRINCESS
    Let one the Princesse be, to her the other yeeld:. . . . . .   120 4th Eclogues   73 129
    Princesse of Beautie, for whose only sake. . . . .   179 Astrophil   28   6
    Stella since thou so right a Princesse art . . . .   236 Astrophil   107   1
    Then reason, Princesse hy, ...   217 A&S 6th Song   49
PRINT
    Shewes easie print in mettall fine.. . . . .   89 Arcadia III   62 100
    Lo, he was gon, print of his treading, ...   327 Psalm XXXVII   91
PRINTS
    Prints his owne lively forme in rudest braine. . . . .   194 Astrophil   58   8
PRISON
    Jaylor I am to my selfe, prison and prisoner to myne owne
        selfe. . . . .   37 1st Eclogues   13 163
    Can I forget, when they in prison placing her, ...   61 2nd Eclogues   30 152
    That hardly usde, who ever prison broke, ...   135 Cert Sonnets   1   11
    They did themselves (o sweetest prison) twine. . . . .   232 Astrophil   103   8
PRISONER
    Jaylor I am to my selfe, prison and prisoner to myne owne
        selfe. . . . .   37 1st Eclogues   13 163
PRISONER'S
    The poore man's wealth, the prisoner's release,. . . . . . .   184 Astrophil   39   3
PRISONERS
    A fire, to burne the prisoners he gaines,. . . . .   246 Other Poems   4 154
PRIVATE
    Then do I thinke in deed, that better it is to be private. .   35 1st Eclogues   13 102
    Though each of them, his private forme preserve, ...   78 Arcadia III   50   3
    That private panges can not breath out in publique . . . . .   109 Arcadia IV   70   32
    Us to attend, in this most private time and place. . . . . .   119 4th Eclogues   73   96
    Private with welth, publike with quiet garnished.. . . . . .   128 4th Eclogues   75 129
    But murder, private fault, seems but a toy to thee,. . . . .   214 A&S 5th Song   55
PRIVATENESS
    All privatenes, selfe-seeking, inward spite, ...   93 3rd Eclogues   63   65
PRIVILEGE
    To their owne worke this priviledge they graunt, ...   101 3rd Eclogues   66 103
    And so by priviledge of sacred seate,. . . . .   141 Cert Sonnets   8   9
    By sence's priviledge, can scape from thee.. . . . .   183 Astrophil   36   14
PRIVILEGED
    Are then humane mindes priviledg'd so meanly,. . . . .   31 1st Eclogues   12   17
PRIVY
    O God the night is privy to my plaint, ...   298 Psalm XXII   7
    Which they for me with privy craft have set, ...   312 Psalm XXXI   11
    And when neede were, from pride in privy plight, ...   313 Psalm XXXI   55
PRIZE
    And so she was attirde, as one that did not prize. . . . . .   119 4th Eclogues   73   87
    Who most the silly shepheard's pipe did pryse, ...   125 4th Eclogues   75   2
    Guided so well, that I obtain'd the prize, ...   185 Astrophil   41   2
    As I may well recount, but none can prize: . . . .   198 Astrophil   65   4
PRIZED
    Thinges rightelie prizde, love is the bande of love. . . . .   83 Arcadia III   57   14
    For such a thought most highlie prized,. . . . .   159 Cert Sonnets   29   14
PROBLEMS
    Ennobling new found Tropes with problemes old: . . . .   166 Astrophil   3   6
    Phrases and Problemes from my reach do grow, ...   166 Astrophil   3   10
PROCEED
    Seeme to proceede, so well it was devisde. . . . .   96 3rd Eclogues   64   82
    But knowne worth did in mine of time proceed,. . . . .   165 Astrophil   2   3
    Thou doest proceed in thy most serious wayes:. . . . .   170 Astrophil   11   2
    Oppressing mortall sense, my death proceed,. . . . .   186 Astrophil   42   13
    So may your tongue still fluently proceed, ...   190 Astrophil   51   2
    Which (i protest) proceed from only Cruell thee, ...   214 A&S 5th Song   53
PROCEEDETH
    And in whome faire death proceedeth, ...   156 Cert Sonnets   26   29
PROCEEDING
    With wordes so vyld, from vilder mouth proceeding. . . . . .   50 2nd Eclogues   28 V 82
    Did not a rosed breath, from lips more rosie proceeding, . .   124 4th Eclogues   74   79
    And showers from mine eyes proceeding. . . . .   221 A&S 9th Song   5
    The trade of them, that just proceeding love;. . . . .   271 Psalm I   20
    From so fair book proceeding,. . . . .   294 Psalm XIX   14
PROCEEDS
    Who thus proceeds, for aye, in sacred Mount shall raign. . .   287 Psalm XV   13
PROCLAIM
    Doth proclaime with a sound made all by men's mouths . . . .   68 2nd Eclogues   33   20
PROCURE
    Can I be poore, that her golde haire procure my selfe? . . .   16 1st Eclogues   7   58
    And know great causes, great effects procure:. . . . .   178 Astrophil   26   10
PROCURED
    Is by nature's giftes procured.. . . . .   263 Other Poems   7   36
PRODUCE
    So that we can long time produce their time: . . . .   127 4th Eclogues   75   86
PROFESS
    Professe in deed I do not Cupid's art; . . . .   192 Astrophil   54   10

```
PROFFER                                                     PAGE    TITLE              LINE
    Such proffer made, which she well showd with smiling cheere.  120 4th Eclogues 73  144
PROFFERED
    Nor courteous ruin of proffered usury, . . . . . . . . . . .   69 2nd Eclogues 34    21
    Now kindnesse profred is, none kinder is that I: . . . . . .  121 4th Eclogues 73   151
PROFIT
    That profit may ensue to him that best can do. . . . . . . .   53 2nd Eclogues 29    30
PROGRESSING
    Progressing then from faire twinnes' gold'n place: . . . . .  175 Astrophil      22     2
PROGRESSION
    Dorus. Sight is his roote, in thought is his progression,. .   48 2nd Eclogues 28    37
PROMISE
    For water cold did never promise fire: . . . . . . . . . . .    3 Lady of May     2     4
    My tempred hart; by thee my promise sent . . . . . . . . . .   40 Arcadia II     18     9
    Do you say still, this is her promise due, . . . . . . . . .   76 Arcadia III    46     5
    Joyne you with me, to seale this promise due,. . . . . . . .   76 Arcadia III    46    11
    For since mad March great promise made of me,. . . . . . . .  175 Astrophil      21     9
    When some faire Ladies, by hard promise tied,. . . . . . . .  176 Astrophil      22     5
PROMISED
    But you must pay, the gage of promist weale. . . . . . . . .   76 Arcadia III    46    18
    Poore hope's first wealth, ostage of promist weale,. . . . .  206 Astrophil      79    12
PROMISETH
    Cyprus promiseth helpe, but a helpe where comes no
        recomforte.. . . . . . . . . . . . . . . . . . . . . . .   35 1st Eclogues 13   119
PROMISING
    Promising wonders, wonder to invite, . . . . . . . . . . . .  178 Astrophil      26     4
PRONE
    Selfe-guiltie folke most prone to feele compassion.. . . . .   60 2nd Eclogues 30 V130
PRONOUNCING
    Or else pronouncing grace, wherewith his mind. . . . . . . .  194 Astrophil      58     7
PROOF
    For proofe of man, who sprong of heav'nly fire . . . . . . .   25 1st Eclogues  9   100
    In thy owne proofe he gets so straunge possession, . . . . .   48 2nd Eclogues 28    35
    Then greefe, unkindnes, proofe, tooke, kindled, tought,. . .   84 Arcadia III    60     9
    In whom of all my rules the perfect proofe I finde,. . . . .  119 4th Eclogues 73    94
    Proofe speakes too much to us that feeling triall have.. . .  119 4th Eclogues 73   108
    Forc'd by a tedious proofe, that Turkish hardned hart, . . .  168 Astrophil       8     2
    And if these rules did faile, proofe makes me sure,. . . . .  178 Astrophil      26    12
    With shield of proofe shield me from out the prease. . . . .  184 Astrophil      39     5
    Love by sure proofe I may call thee unkind,. . . . . . . . .  198 Astrophil      65     1
    But feeling proofe makes me say they mistake it furre: . . .  232 Astrophil     102    11
    The proofe of Beautie's worth, th'enheritrix of fame,. . . .  213 A&S 5th Song          20
    For proof, oft lain in wait he is.. . . . . . . . . . . . .   282 Psalm X               31
    Thou that by proofe acquainted art . . . . . . . . . . . . .  289 Psalm XVII             7
    For proof, while I my race did run . . . . . . . . . . . . .  311 Psalm XXX             19
    Dick. Faith in my self and worth in her, which no proofe can
        undoo.. . . . . . . . . . . . . . . . . . . . . . . . .  343 Possibly        1    26
    Vertue's proofe, fortune's victor, beautie's place.. . . . .  252 Other Poems     4   392
PROOFS
    Vertue you have, of vertue you have left proufes to the
        whole world, . . . . . . . . . . . . . . . . . . . . . .   33 1st Eclogues 13    56
    Where proofes justly do teach, thus matcht, such worth to be
        nought worth. . . . . . . . . . . . . . . . . . . . . .    34 1st Eclogues 13    83
    My moystned bed proofes of my sorrow showeth:. . . . . . . .  276 Psalm VI              18
    Thou righteous proofes to hearts, and reines dost send,. . .  277 Psalm VII             28
    That by sharp proofes, the heathen themselves may see. . . .  281 Psalm IX              64
PROP
    O let me prop my mind, yet in his growth . . . . . . . . . .  174 Astrophil      19    12
    With heavnly strength Thy earthly strength to prop.. . . . .  295 Psalm XX              10
PROPHET
    A Prophet oft, and oft an historie,. . . . . . . . . . . . .  181 Astrophil      32     3
PROPORTION
    Happy be those mishapps which, justly proportion holding,. .   32 1st Eclogues 13    17
    To hold these worldly things in such proportion, . . . . . .   60 2nd Eclogues 30   132
    With sad eyes I their weake proportion see,. . . . . . . . .  189 Astrophil      50     7
PROPORTIONED
    That were in Court a well proportion'd hooke,. . . . . . . .  245 Other Poems     4   141
PROSPECT
    And staid pleasd with the prospect of the place, . . . . . .  175 Astrophil      20    10
    And I, but for because my prospect lies. . . . . . . . . . .  179 Astrophil      29    13
PROSPER
    Shall prosper still, with well succeeding end. . . . . . . .  270 Psalm I               12
PROSTRATE
    Her whom I dread; so that with prostrate lying . . . . . . .   17 1st Eclogues  7    86
    Their flames mount up, my powers prostrate lie:. . . . . . .   42 Arcadia II     22    11
PROTECTED
    For though life irkes, in life my loves protected be.. . . .   51 2nd Eclogues 28   125
PROTECTION
    Dorus. Thy challenge great, but greater my protection: . . .   15 1st Eclogues  7    19
    Lastly what so she be, that's my protection. . . . . . . . .   49 2nd Eclogues 28    72
PROTECTOR
    And Protector bee. . . . . . . . . . . . . . . . . . . . . .  336 Psalm XLIII            2
PROTEST
    I do protest and seeke with service due, . . . . . . . . . .  145 Cert Sonnets 17     2
    Which (I protest) proceed from only Cruell thee, . . . . . .  214 A&S 5th Song          53
    For I protest, my sight never thy face enjoyeth, . . . . . .  215 A&S 5th Song          75
PROTESTS
    For she protests to banish thee her face,. . . . . . . . . .  187 Astrophil      46     5
    Delight protests he is not for the accurst,. . . . . . . . .  228 Astrophil      95     7
```

PROUD | PAGE | TITLE | LINE
A servant Sex, soone prowde if they be coi'de, ... | 24 | 1st Eclogues | 9 | 60
Now bolder waxt, waxt prowde, that I such sway might beare:. | 121 | 4th Eclogues | 73 | 159
While late bare earth, proud of new clothing springeth,. . . | 137 | Cert Sonnets | 4 | 3
Are Beauties there as proud as here they be? . . . . | 180 | Astrophil | 31 | 11
Lo you grow proud with this, for tyrans make folke bow:. . . | 214 | A&S 5th Song | | 61
O let proud him be throughly caught. . . . . | 281 | Psalm X | | 7
Nay so proud is his puffed thought . . . . | 281 | Psalm X | | 13
Up then thou liftst the poore, and down the proud wilt cast; | 292 | Psalm XVIII | | 52
And to the proud in deeds pays home their own. . . . . | 314 | Psalm XXXI | | 66
Let not proud feet make me their thrall, ... | 324 | Psalm XXXVI | | 31
Free of proud feares, brave begg'ry, smiling strife. . . . . | 243 | Other Poems | 4 | 60
Proud grew the grasse that under hir did growe,. . . . . . . | 244 | Other Poems | 4 | 108
Thus proud and fierce unto the hearts he stept . . . . | 246 | Other Poems | 4 | 157
And now, proud Rebell gan for to gainsay . . . . | 246 | Other Poems | 4 | 173
His heels grow'n proud did seme at heav'n to shake.. . . . . | 248 | Other Poems | 4 | 261
She quick, and proud, and who did Pas despise, ... | 249 | Other Poems | 4 | 273
With proud aspect, disdaining greater hast.. . . . . | 249 | Other Poems | 4 | 293
To downe proud hearts that would not willing dye.. . . . . . | 250 | Other Poems | 4 | 304
In sum, proud Boreas never ruled fleet . . . . | 251 | Other Poems | 4 | 373
With him proud battell proved. . . . . | 259 | Other Poems | 5 | 123
PROUDLY
The Mountains proudly high, and their ffoundations bent. . . | 291 | Psalm XVIII | | 16
Proudly bedeckt in Aprill's livory,. . . . . | 253 | Other Poems | 4 | 453
PROVE
Affection's charmes in my behalfe to prove.. . . . . | 17 | 1st Eclogues | 7 | 102
While still more wretch, more wicked he doth prove:. . . . . | 22 | 1st Eclogues | 8 | 44
Begin (and halfe the worke is dcne) to prove . . . . | 23 | 1st Eclogues | 9 | 50
When they shall such devided weakenesse prove? . . . . | 26 | 1st Eclogues | 10 | 6
I waile their lotte, but will not other prove. . . . . | 39 | Arcadia II | 17 | 4
When pittie most I crave, I cruell prove:. . . . . | 41 | Arcadia II | 20 | 3
Dorus. Well do I prove, errour lies oft in zeale,. . . . . . | 51 | 2nd Eclogues | 28 | 103
For good thou mayst yet proove in sheepish sound.. . . . . . | 56 | 2nd Eclogues | 29 | 137
Blasphemous words the speaker vaine do prove.. . . . . | 59 | 2nd Eclogues | 30 | 67
That sorrowe's worke against my will I prove.. . . . . | 60 | 2nd Eclogues | 30 | 127
Selfe-guiltie folke must prove to feele compassion.. . . . . | 60 | 2nd Eclogues | 30 | 130
Hath not Reason enough vehemence the desire to reprove?
Prove. . . . . | 63 | 2nd Eclogues | 31 | 10
Oft prove I: but what salve, when Reason seeks to be gone?
One. . . . . | 63 | 2nd Eclogues | 31 | 11
Nowe that some flower of fruict, my paynes do prove, ... | 72 | Arcadia III | 37 | 16
Thy force I feare, her force I still do prove. . . . . | 72 | Arcadia III | 38 | 10
Crying in me: eye hopes deceitefull prove. . . . . | 83 | Arcadia III | 57 | 13
Subscription was, yours most, if you will prove. . . . . . . | 96 | 3rd Eclogues | 64 | 90
Must I be onely the marke, shall prove that Vertue is
angrie . . . . | 123 | 4th Eclogues | 74 | 33
Shall prove that fiercenes can with a white dove abide?. . . | 123 | 4th Eclogues | 74 | 34
In humble mind a constant faith to prove,. . . . . | 145 | Cert Sonnets | 17 | 3
I deemd it best some absence for to prove, ... | 149 | Cert Sonnets | 21 | 3
And knowne those pangs that the losers prove,. . . . . | 153 | Cert Sonnets | 24 | 2
And still th'effect of thy perswasions prove:. . . . . | 167 | Astrophil | 4 | 11
Reason thou kneel'dst, and offeredst straight to prove . . . | 170 | Astrophil | 10 | 13
Who threatned stripes, if he his wrath did prove:. . . . . . | 173 | Astrophil | 17 | 6
Vertue's great beautie in that face I prove, ... | 177 | Astrophil | 25 | 13
O eyes, where humble lookes most glorious prove, ... | 185 | Astrophil | 42 | 5
Our horsmanships, while by strange worke I prove . . . . . . | 189 | Astrophil | 49 | 2
Since they do weare his badge, most firmely prove. . . . . . | 190 | Astrophil | 52 | 4
Dumbe Swannes, not chatring Pies, do Lovers prove, ... | 192 | Astrophil | 54 | 13
Nor other sugring of my speech to prove, ... | 192 | Astrophil | 55 | 10
He barks, my songs thine owne voyce oft doth prove:. . . . . | 194 | Astrophil | 59 | 6
But only for this worthy knight durst prove. . . . . | 204 | Astrophil | 75 | 13
She comes with light and warmth, which like Aurora prove . . | 205 | Astrophil | 76 | 5
United powers make each the stronger prove.. . . . . | 223 | Astrophil | 88 | 14
Or if such heavenly signes must prove annoy, ... | 231 | Astrophil | 100 | 13
From out my ribs, and puffing prove that I . . . . | 233 | Astrophil | 104 | 13
Now will I with that boy prove . . . . | 202 | A&S 2nd Song | | 7
And if the trees, nor stones stirre not the same to prove, . | 209 | A&S 3rd Song | | 14
And yet against thy Prince thy force dost dayly prove: . . . | 214 | A&S 5th Song | | 65
While she doth against me prove. . . . . | 226 | A&S 10th Song | | 35
Time doth as the subject prove. . . . . | 234 | A&S 11th Song | | 18
Cease in these effects to prove: . . . . | 220 | A&S 8th Song | | 74
For while his wayes do prove,. . . . . | 282 | Psalm X | | 17
This is all the best I prove,. . . . . | 288 | Psalm XVI | | 7
Prove me O Lord most high, ... | 305 | Psalm XXVI | | 7
The darte, the beames, the stringe so stronge I prove; . . . | 344 | Possibly | 2 | 1
The honest sports of earthy lcdging prove; . . . . | 243 | Other Poems | 4 | 42
Dcth on hir wings hir utmost swiftnes prove, ... | 251 | Other Poems | 4 | 355
PROVED
Finding that but wordes they proved. . . . . | 156 | Cert Sonnets | 27 | 12
That all these cruell words your praises shall be proved... | 215 | A&S 5th Song | | 90
Stella who more love hath proved,. . . . . | 221 | A&S 9th Song | | 22
With him proud battell proved. . . . . | 259 | Other Poems | 5 | 123
PROVES
Griefe is the stone which finest judgement proves: . . . . . | 58 | 2nd Eclogues | 30 | 35
PROVETH
Though he do fall no wracke he proveth,. . . . . | 326 | Psalm XXXVII | | 59
PROVING
Oft each other's friendship proving, ... | 262 | Other Poems | 7 | 23
PROVOKE
Twinckling starres Love-thoughts provoke:. . . . . | 210 | A&S 4th Song | | 8

```
                                                          PAGE   TITLE           LINE
PROVOKED
     Yet each day art provoakt, thyne Ire to show,. . . . . . . .  277  Psalm VII          32
PROWLS
     He proules ech place stil in new colours deckt,. . . . . . .   21  1st Eclogues  8    35
PRY
     To lye, faine, gloze, to steale, pry, and accuse,. . . . . .   21  1st Eclogues  8    23
     To lye, to steale, to pry, and to accuse,. . . . . . . . . .   21  1st Eclogues  8  V 23
PUBLIC
     Since no evill fortune equalls publique damage:. . . . . . .  108  Arcadia IV   70     3
     Now Prince's losse hath made our damage publique,. . . . . .  109  Arcadia IV   70     4
     Choosing alas! this our theatre publique,. . . . . . . . . .  109  Arcadia IV   70    11
     Yet let us leave a monument in publique. . . . . . . . . . .  109  Arcadia IV   70    15
     Publique our losse: so, see, thy shame is publique.. . . . .  109  Arcadia IV   70    24
     O that we had, to make our woes more publique, . . . . . . .  109  Arcadia IV   70    25
     That private panges can not breath out in publique . . . . .  109  Arcadia IV   70    32
     With all our deathes shew we this damage publique. . . . . .  110  Arcadia IV   70    38
     Private with welth, publike with quiet garnished.. . . . . .  128  4th Eclogues 75   129
     We Orphans lefte, void of all publique might?. . . . . . . .  129  4th Eclogues 76    12
     Be you still faire, honourd by publike heed, . . . . . . . .  209  Astrophil    84     9
PUBLISH
     "Art not asham'd to publish thy disease?". . . . . . . . . .  182  Astrophil    34     5
     And tongue is prest to publish out thy prayse. . . . . . . .  306  Psalm XXVI         39
PUDDLED
     Nor conning humorists' puddled opinions, . . . . . . . . . .   69  2nd Eclogues 34    20
PUFF
     Vainly doth not puff up his mind;. . . . . . . . . . . . . .  302  Psalm XXIV         10
PUFFED
     When Love puft up with rage of hy disdaine,. . . . . . . . .  135  Cert Sonnets  2     1
     Nay so proud is his puffed thought . . . . . . . . . . . . .  281  Psalm X            13
     So many pufft in minde I see,. . . . . . . . . . . . . . . .  263  Other Poems   7    50
PUFFING
     Passion beares high when puffing wit doth blowe, . . . . . .   25  1st Eclogues  9   114
     First did with puffing kisse those lockes display: . . . . .  233  Astrophil   103    11
     From out my ribs, and puffing prove that I . . . . . . . . .  233  Astrophil   104    13
PUFFS
     Shrewdnes so stirres, pride so puffes up their hart, . . . .  104  3rd Eclogues 67    26
PUING
     The birdes likewise with chirpes, and puing could, . . . . .  100  3rd Eclogues 66    66
PUISSANT
     Wise Counsellors, stout Captaines, puissant Kings, . . . . .  245  Other Poems   4   130
PULING
     Puiling, and whimpring, or else scolding flat, . . . . . . .  104  3rd Eclogues 67    29
PULL
     I did pull down my self, fasting for such; . . . . . . . . .  322  Psalm XXXV         31
     Then do they pull from sharpe and niggard thorne . . . . . .  243  Other Poems   4    51
     Sometimes we see small birds from nests do pull. . . . . . .  245  Other Poems   4   136
PULLED
     And loden so puls downe, puld downe destroyes. . . . . . . .   50  2nd Eclogues 28    86
     First be mine eyes pulde out, first be my braine pulde; .  .  124  4th Eclogues 74    60
     And age pull'd on with paines all freshness fretteth:. . . .  276  Psalm VI           22
     Klaius in deede would faine have puld a way. . . . . . . . .  246  Other Poems   4   171
     But pulld by Mira's hande, . . . . . . . . . . . . . . . . .  257  Other Poems   5    47
PULLS
     And loden so puls downe, puld downe destroyes. . . . . . . .   50  2nd Eclogues 28    86
PULSE
     Feeling my pulse, misse my disease.. . . . . . . . . . . . .  153  Cert Sonnets 24     9
PUNISHED
     How faire a day was neare, o punisht eyes, . . . . . . . . .  181  Astrophil    33    13
PUNISHMENT
     Ne let thy rage, of my due punishment. . . . . . . . . . . .  276  Psalm VI            3
     And yeeld himselfe unto hir punishment,. . . . . . . . . . .  247  Other Poems   4   191
PUPPET
     Let not a puppet abuse thy sprite, Kings' Crownes do not
          helpe them . . . . . . . . . . . . . . . . . . . . . .   34  1st Eclogues 13    84
PURCHASE
     Which must frame contempt to the fittest purchase of
          honnour . . . . . . . . . . . . . . . . . . . . . . .   32  1st Eclogues 13    38
     But valiant Rebels oft in fooles' mouthes purchase fame: . .  214  A&S 5th Song       67
PURCHASED
     As their deeds have purchas'd it,. . . . . . . . . . . . . .  309  Psalm XXVIII       17
PURE
     Her haire pure Crapal-stone; her mouth O heavenly wyde;. . .   12  Arcadia I     3    11
     Thus pure pearle, I do yeeld, my senses and soule. . . . . .   68  2nd Eclogues 33    28
     Her nose, her chinne pure ivorie weares: . . . . . . . . . .   86  Arcadia III  62    27
     And like to lillies pure . . . . . . . . . . . . . . . . . .   91  3rd Eclogues 63    24
     Which being pure and plaine, . . . . . . . . . . . . . . . .   93  3rd Eclogues 63    62
     They seemd to me) on whom did waite a Virgin pure: . . . . .  118  4th Eclogues 73    64
     Of trueth, farre more then Alablaster pure,. . . . . . . . .  150  Cert Sonnets 22    39
     Deceiv'd the quaking boy, who thought from so pure light,. .  169  Astrophil     8    10
     Hath his front built of Alabaster pure;. . . . . . . . . . .  169  Astrophil     9     3
     But know that I in pure simplicitie, . . . . . . . . . . . .  179  Astrophil    28    12
     And oft so clings to my pure Love, that I. . . . . . . . . .  202  Astrophil    72     2
     These are God's words, God's words are ever pure,. . . . . .  285  Psalm XII          19
     Pure, Purer than the silver throughly try'd. . . . . . . . .  285  Psalm XII          20
     My joy shall be pure to enjoy thy face,. . . . . . . . . . .  290  Psalm XVII         46
     Pure to the pure, Thou dealst with crooked crookedly;. . . .  292  Psalm XVIII        51
PURELY
     Thy way is soundly sure, Thy word is purely tryd;. . . . . .  292  Psalm XVIII        55
     So purely wise it gives the eyes . . . . . . . . . . . . . .  294  Psalm XIX          35
```

		PAGE	TITLE		LINE
PURENESS					
Thou purest stone, whose purenesse doth present.		40	Arcadia II	18	7
According as he saw the pureness of my hand.		292	Psalm XVIII		49
All pureness ever to embrace;.		302	Psalm XXIV		8
PURER					
No purer then the pretie eares..		86	Arcadia III	62	28
Pure, Purer than the silver throughly try'd.		285	Psalm XII		20
PUREST					
Thou purest stone, whose purenesse doth present.		40	Arcadia II	18	7
My purest minde; whose temper hard doth showe.		40	Arcadia II	18	8
I sawe her arme, where purest Lillies cleave..		55	2nd Eclogues	29	104
With losse of purest blood themselves to teare,.		58	2nd Eclogues	30	46
Let us not winke though void of purest sightfulnes..		61	2nd Eclogues	30	139
Which heav'nly purest gifts defile in muddy cares.		117	4th Eclogues	73	18
Now that of purest lampe is queint the light,.		129	4th Eclogues	76	8
But of his death flies up a purest love, ...		151	Cert Sonnets	22	59
And fooles can thinke those Lampes of purest light,.		177	Astrophil	26	2
"But your reason's purest light, ...		234	A&S 11th Song		26
Of purest Metal dressing..		297	Psalm XXI		12
His compleat harneis was hir purest white.		246	Other Poems	4	150
PURGE					
How thou from foolish love maist purge thy sense..		25	1st Eclogues	9	110
PURIFIED					
So shall I bide well purify'd.		295	Psalm XIX		59
PURLING					
You that do search for everie purling spring,.		172	Astrophil	15	1
PURPOSE					
For ere that either had his purpose done,.		244	Other Poems	4	81
And cal'd, now wounded, purpose to his aide:		246	Other Poems	4	162
PURSUE					
What Foes I did persue my force did them attaine,.		292	Psalm XVIII		68
Let Angel thine persue them as they fly, ...		321	Psalm XXXV		13
Nous counseld Strephon Geron to pursue,.		250	Other Poems	4	321
PURSUING					
So have I heard to pierce pursuing shield.		251	Other Poems	4	349
PURSUIT					
The sweete pursute of my desired pray.		145	Cert Sonnets	16	12
PURSUIVANTS					
Hir feet be Pursevants from Cupid sent,.		249	Other Poems	4	301
PUT					
To put it with my hand in Cosma's brest.		54	2nd Eclogues	29	86
Wher who so wynns, I put my selfe to flight.		74	Arcadia III	42	8
Be hence aye put to flight,.		93	3rd Eclogues	63	68
In choller put, with whom he would not fight..		96	3rd Eclogues	64	66
And cannot chuse but put out what I write, ...		190	Astrophil	50	10
Envie, put out thine eyes, least thou do see		200	Astrophil	69	3
Thou dost put out, and quite consuming send.		280	Psalm IX		14
All, all my trust lord I have put in Thee, ...		312	Psalm XXXI		1
However they putt in their claimes,.		315	Psalm XXXII		23
But throw them down, put them to endlesse blame, ...		323	Psalm XXXV		63
The happy wretch she putt into hir breast, ...		244	Other Poems	4	98
PUTRIFY					
My wounds putrify and stink, ...		328	Psalm XXXVIII		13
PUTS					
With inward cries putts up a bitter role		85	Arcadia III	61	3
PUTTING					
And putting out our eyes seeke we our light.		130	4th Eclogues	76	36
PYTHON'S					
Thou God, whose youth was deckt with spoyle of Python's skin		44	Arcadia II	26	5
QUAINT					
And plaine speach oft then quaint phrase better framed is. .		14	1st Eclogues	7	6
QUAKE					
They love indeed, who quake to say they love..		192	Astrophil	54	14
Nor ever call on god, but they shall quake		286	Psalm XIV		16
And so the Earth did fall to tremble, and to quake		291	Psalm XVIII		15
QUAKED					
My heart then quak'd, then dazled were mine eyes,.		191	Astrophil	53	10
QUAKING					
Deceiv'd the quaking boy, who thought from so pure light,. .		169	Astrophil	8	10
QUEEN					
But to the Cedar, Queene of woods, when I lifte my beteard eyes,.		36	1st Eclogues	13	141
I have a wife worthie to be a Queene,.		106	3rd Eclogues	67	88
Queene Vertue's court, which some call Stella's face,. . . .		169	Astrophil	9	1
And as a Queene, who from her presence sends		236	Astrophil	107	9
By fortune meane, in Nature borne a Queene,.		244	Other Poems	4	91
QUEEN-APPLE'S					
Or like the fresh Queene-apple's side, ...		86	Arcadia III	62	25
QUEINT					
Now that of purest lampe is queint the light,.		129	4th Eclogues	76	8
QUELL					
Whom troubles tosse, whose natures need doth quell,.		285	Psalm XII		14
QUENCH					
And yet his outward heate our teares would quench, but an inward		32	1st Eclogues	13	31
What hope to quench, where each thing blowes the fire? . . .		42	Arcadia II	21	18
For no thing, time, nor place, can loose, quench, ease,. . .		84	Arcadia II	60	13
Fuell to seeke and not to quench the fire:		95	3rd Eclogues	64	40
Seeking to quench in me the noble fire, ...		200	Astrophil	68	7

QUENCH   (CONTINUED)   PAGE   TITLE   LINE
  Which to avoyde, quenche, loose noughte booted stryfe. . . . 344 Possibly   2   8
QUENCHED
  And flames of never quenched fire. . . . . 297 Psalm XXI   35
QUESTION
  Which soone as it did batefull question frame, ... 247 Other Poems   4   189
QUESTIONS
  These questions busie wits to me do frame; . . . . 180 Astrophil   30   12
  That to my questions you so totall are?. . . . . 225 Astrophil   92   5
  With their dayly questions throwing: . . . . 334 Psalm XLII   11
QUICK
  My wits, quicke in vaine thoughts, in vertue lame: . . . . . 175 Astrophil   21   4
  In weakened minds, quicke apprehending breed,. . . . . 199 Astrophil   66   3
  Know, that small Love is quicke, and great Love doth amaze:. 209 A&S 3rd Song   16
  Of quick strength is an horse,. . . . .   317 Psalm XXXIII   61
  She quick, and proud, and who did Pas despise, ... 249 Other Poems   4   273
QUICKEN
  Even he whose life no help of man can quicken. . . . . 300 Psalm XXII   74
QUICKENING
  Now each thing which enjoy'd that firie quickning sparke . . 116 4th Eclogues 73   4
QUICKLY
  Quickly secure, and easilie in doubt,. . . . .   27 1st Eclogues 10   28
  That quickly they would her burne, drowne, or smother, . . .   61 2nd Eclogues 30   159
  Then quickly did the meaner cattell finde, ... 102 3rd Eclogues 66   135
  Shall quickly me from what she hates remove. . . . . 195 Astrophil   61   11
  For quickly ends his wrathfull Will, ... 311 Psalm XXX   13
  Where piercing witts do quickly apprehend, ... 245 Other Poems   4   142
  He quickly learn'd Urania was her name,. . . . . 247 Other Poems   4   185
  He quickly knew what witchcraft gave the blow. . . . . 256 Other Poems   4   539
QUIET
  Then with the poisnous todes that quiet lie. . . . .   28 1st Eclogues 10   66
  A quiet mind none but thy selfe can lend to thee,. . . . . .   51 2nd Eclogues 28   101
  The quiet mind (whereof my selfe empairer is,. . . . .   51 2nd Eclogues 28   114
  Her cleared lookes, nought els, in stormes can quiet me. . .   51 2nd Eclogues 28   119
  Nought disturbs thy quiet, all to thy service yeeld, ...   69 2nd Eclogues 34   10
  Then is the quiet joy of loving wife;. . . . . 103 3rd Eclogues 67   8
  Of humane life to be the quiet measure,. . . . . 108 Arcadia IV   69   4
  Ye Satyrs joyde with free and quiet forrests,. . . . . 111 4th Eclogues 71   3
  My senses such release, as they which quiet live,. . . . . . 117 4th Eclogues 73   12
  Then give a quiet eare unto my playning: . . . . 127 4th Eclogues 75   65
  Private with welth, publike with quiet garnished.. . . . . . 128 4th Eclogues 75   129
  From filth of foreworne house, and quiet lives,. . . . . . . 143 Cert Sonnets 12   5
  Nor no day hath lesse quiet then my night: . . . . 224 Astrophil   89   11
  But hunt with craft the quiet man's annoy; . . . . 322 Psalm XXXV   52
  In quiet home they shall be planted. . . . . 325 Psalm XXXVII   30
QUIETEST
  Makes me in my best thoughts and quietst judgement see,. . . 205 Astrophil   77   12
QUIET'S
  But when he will for quiet's sake remove . . . . 186 Astrophil   43   12
QUILL
  Pas. Who evermore will love Apollo's quill,. . . . .   53 2nd Eclogues 29   54
QUINTAIN
  When, if nede were, they could at quintain run:. . . . . . . 243 Other Poems   4   56
QUINTESSENCE
  Looke at my hands for no such quintessence;. . . . . 179 Astrophil   28   11
  Those words, which do sublime the quintessence of blisse:. . 205 Astrophil   77   8
QUIT
  In justice quit, of honour made no breach: . . . . 135 Cert Sonnets 1   12
  Tho worlds quite me, shall I my selfe forgive? . . . . 227 Astrophil   93   11
QUITE
  They live in force, I quite consumed die.. . . . .   42 Arcadia II   22   12
  Quite from my selfe to love Love's contemplation;. . . . . .   48 2nd Eclogues 28   32
  Of windes quite contrarie in waves of will:. . . . .   59 2nd Eclogues 30   81
  Of Prince's harte quite lost the ruine strange.. . . . . . .   81 Arcadia III   55   6
  Be those despaires, which have my hopes quite wast.. . . . . 114 4th Eclogues 72   37
  And unto death, quite drownde in Dolours, brought.. . . . .   115 4th Eclogues 72   68
  Our names are quite forgot, our temples are defac'd: . . . . 119 4th Eclogues 73   109
  And now fully beleeves helpe to be quite perished; . . . . . 122 4th Eclogues 74   2
  Fire burne me quite, till sense of burning leave me: . . . . 136 Cert Sonnets 3   13
  Unable quite to pay even Nature's rent,. . . . . 174 Astrophil   18   5
  With dearth of words, or answers quite awrie,. . . . . 178 Astrophil   27   3
  And now my pen these lines had dashed quite, ... 190 Astrophil   50   12
  Yet thought and speech do live, though metamorphosd quite: . 212 A&S 5th Song   14
  Thou dost put out, and quite consuming send. . . . . 280 Psalm IX   14
  Be quite forgott.. . . . . 280 Psalm IX   20
  God sleeps, or hath forgotten quite, ... 282 Psalm X   46
  Whose loosed bones quite out of joint be wryde;. . . . . . . 299 Psalm XXII   32
  Let me not ruin quite; . . . . 302 Psalm XXV   4
  From earth quite to displace.. . . . . 320 Psalm XXXIV   60
  Then abjects, while I was unwitting quite, ... 322 Psalm XXXV   39
  And quite cutt off, with helpless end. . . . . 327 Psalm XXXVII   96
  Senseles quite,. . . . . 328 Psalm XXXVIII   41
  And his name perish quite? . . . . 333 Psalm XLI   20
  Absented quite from you, ... 257 Other Poems   5   38
QUIVER
  While Love on me doth all his quiver spend,. . . . . 171 Astrophil   14   4
QUIVERS
  Clos'd with their quivers in sleep's armory; . . . . 230 Astrophil   99   4
QUOTH
  "Husband", quoth she, "go to him by and by,. . . . .   95 3rd Eclogues 64   55

391

	QUOTH	(CONTINUED)	PAGE	TITLE		LINE
	"Alas", quoth she, "thus women's shame doth creepe".		96	3rd Eclogues	64	87
	"Sweet Mira mine" (quote she) "the pleasure of my minde, . .		119	4th Eclogues	73	93
	"Yet thou shalt not go free (quoth Venus) such a fire. . . .		121	4th Eclogues	73	170
	"Another time", quoth she, "become more wise".		249	Other Poems	4	275
R						
	R. Can Reason then a Tyraunt counted be?		46	2nd Eclogues	27	3
	R. But Reason will, that Reason governe most.		46	2nd Eclogues	27	5
	R. Your will is will; but Reason reason is.		46	2nd Eclogues	27	7
	R. Whom Passion leades unto his death is bent.		46	2nd Eclogues	27	9
	R. By nature you to Reason faith have sworne.		46	2nd Eclogues	27	11
	R. Who Passion doth ensue, lives in annoy.		46	2nd Eclogues	27	13
	R. Passion is blinde, and treades an unknowne trace.		46	2nd Eclogues	27	15
	R. Dare Passions then abide in Reason's light?		46	2nd Eclogues	27	17
	R. O foolish thing, which glory doeste destroye.		46	2nd Eclogues	27	19
	R. Weakenes you are, dare you with our strength fight? . . .		46	2nd Eclogues	27	21
	R. O sacred Reason, helpe our vertuous toiles.		46	2nd Eclogues	27	23
	R. We with ourselves abide a daily strife.		46	2nd Eclogues	27	25
	R. But yet our strife sure peace in end doth breede.		46	2nd Eclogues	27	27
	R. We are too strong: but Reason seekes not blood.		47	2nd Eclogues	27	29
	R. Though we cannot orecome, our cause is just.		47	2nd Eclogues	27	31
	R. Yet Passion, yeeld at length to Reason's stroke.		47	2nd Eclogues	27	33
	R. The joyes you have shall be made permanent.		47	2nd Eclogues	27	35
	R. Repent indeed, but that shall be your blisse.		47	2nd Eclogues	27	37
	R. You know it not: of Reason therefore know it.		47	2nd Eclogues	27	39
*RACE						
	While brickle houreglas runnes, guide thou our panting race:		45	Arcadia II	26	10
	Yet never rock, nor race, suche terror brought, ...		71	Arcadia III	37	3
	And stay the starrs' inconstant constant race, ...		126	4th Eclogues	75	38
	And pleasd with our soft peace, staid here his flying race. .		168	Astrophil	8	4
	On horsebacke met him in his furious race, ...		176	Astrophil	22	6
	O fooles, or over-wise, alas the race.		176	Astrophil	23	12
	Who oft fore-judge my after-following race, ...		178	Astrophil	26	13
	Sent forth the beames, which made so faire my race.		185	Astrophil	41	14
	But when the ruggedst step of Fortune's race		195	Astrophil	60	5
	O give my passions leave to run their race:		198	Astrophil	64	2
	And no spurre can his resty race renew, ...		207	Astrophil	80	12
	Was not in fault, who bent thy dazling race.		235	Astrophil	105	6
	And what the race of him descended		279	Psalm VIII		15
	In race of life their Feet to guide.		284	Psalm XI		23
	Nay even the race of good men are decay'd.		284	Psalm XII		3
	If of this Clayey race he could espy		286	Psalm XIV		8
	His race is even from ends of heaven		294	Psalm XIX		25
	And from among the humane race		297	Psalm XXI		39
	For I have made my race.		305	Psalm XXVI		2
	For proof, while I my race did run		311	Psalm XXX		19
	For this Our lord preserves the faith full race.		314	Psalm XXXI		65
	Beholds our mortall race;		317	Psalm XXXIII		51
	While thus they ran a low, but leaveld race, ...		243	Other Poems	4	57
	So he with Nous to Geron turn'd their race, ...		248	Other Poems	4	251
	The aire hir swete race mov'd doth blow the fire.		249	Other Poems	4	300
	Still shunning Nous to lengthen pleasing race, ...		250	Other Poems	4	306
	But this straunge race more straunge conceits did yeeld: . .		251	Other Poems	4	345
	Till with long race deare she was breathles brought, ...		251	Other Poems	4	359
	Hir race did not hir beautie's beames augment, ...		252	Other Poems	4	393
	And giving to his sight a wandring race, ...		255	Other Poems	4	526
	So may your sliding race		257	Other Poems	5	28
RACES						
	To runne their mighty races.		294	Psalm XIX		24
RACK						
	(Delay, the racke of unrefrain'd desire)		80	Arcadia III	53	2
RAGE						
	But forste with raige, his raige on theym upbrayde.		24	1st Eclogues	9	65
	Whyle hote desyres do Raigne in fancie's rage, ...		26	1st Eclogues	9	140
	Is she in rage? so is the Sunne in sommer hot, ...		49	2nd Eclogues	28	61
	Then rage for rage: rather my wish I send to thee, ...		50	2nd Eclogues	28	97
	And all but jests, save onely sorrowe's rage.		57	2nd Eclogues	30	22
	But if thy rage some brave revenge will finde, ...		72	Arcadia III	38	13
	Since that the stormy rage of passions darcke		72	Arcadia III	39	1
	Well grounded, noble, due, spite, rage, disdaine, ...		84	Arcadia III	60	10
	But yet o man, rage not beyond thy neede:		103	3rd Eclogues	66	148
	But who doo let their tongues shew well their rage, ...		105	3rd Eclogues	67	47
	Passion unto my rage, Rage to a hasty revenge.		124	4th Eclogues	74	68
	When Love puft up with rage of hy disdaine, ...		135	Cert Sonnets	2	1
	Trying high seas, nor while Sea rage you flee, ...		142	Cert Sonnets	12	2
	Alas, I lie: rage hath this errour bred, ...		160	Cert Sonnets	30	31
	But harder Judges judge ambition's rage, ...		176	Astrophil	23	9
	With rage of Love, I cald my Love unkind;		195	Astrophil	62	2
	Nay sorrow comes with such maine rage, that he		229	Astrophil	95	9
	For rage now rules the reynes, which guided were by					
	Pleasure		213	A&S 5th Song		15
	Strength of liking, rage of longing.		226	A&S 10th Song		24
	What ayles this heathenish rage? What do theis people meane.		271	Psalm II		1
	Ne let thy rage, of my due punishment.		276	Psalm VI		3
	Against such rage of foes: Awake for me.		277	Psalm VII		17
	With motion of his rage did to the bottom shake.		291	Psalm XVIII		17
	In rage Thy servant do not chase.		308	Psalm XXVII		45
	Fume not, rage not, frett not I say, ...		325	Psalm XXXVII		21
	Lord while that thy rage doth bide, ...		327	Psalm XXXVIII		1
	What rage in them, that love in him did show.		249	Other Poems	4	294

RAGE   (CONTINUED)   PAGE   TITLE   LINE
    But after this to greater rage it broke, ... 253 Other Poems   4 429
RAGED
    Nico. Mine was the scrippe: but thou, that seeming raged
        with love, ...   52 2nd Eclogues 29   9
RAGE'S
    As might learne Temp'rance voyde of a rage's events. . . . . 124 4th Eclogues 74   64
RAGGED
    Away ragg'd rams, care I what murraine kill? . . . . 255 Other Poems   4 515
    Like Rogue, all ragged goe, ...   257 Other Poems   5   25
RAGING
    Raging in woes first pastors tought to plaine? . . . .   53 2nd Eclogues 29   58
    In morall rules let raging woes contained be?. . . . .   61 2nd Eclogues 30   151
    Thus toyled in my work of raging love, ...   71 Arcadia III 37   14
    With rageing jaws environ me . . . . 307 Psalm XXVII   9
RAIL
    Against me swarm, ceaseless to raile at me.. . . . . 322 Psalm XXXV   40
RAILING
    I understand what rayling great men spred; . . . . 313 Psalm XXXI   37
RAIMENT
    Thy wallet or thy Tarbox lost, or thy new rayment rent?. . . 343 Possibly   1   16
RAIN
    How oft with raine of teares skies make confession,. . . . .   15 1st Eclogues 7   43
    To open eyes all beauties he doth raine; . . . .   22 1st Eclogues 8   39
    Or like the drops of raine.. . . . .   92 3rd Eclogues 63   44
    The aire in raine for my afflicticn weepeth: . . . . 136 Cert Sonnets 3   2
    Whose clowdie thoughts let fall an inward raine. . . . . . . 150 Cert Sonnets 22   36
    Broadred with buls and swans, powdred with golden raine: . . 167 Astrophil   6   6
    O teares, no teares, but raine from beautie's skies, ... 231 Astrophil   100   1
    At length in rowes of Kisse-cheeke teares they raine.. . . . 245 Other Poems   4 128
RAINING
    Witnesse your wofull teares with daily rayning.. . . . . . . 127 4th Eclogues 75   69
RAINS
    Ath strongest soule, when most his raynes do bowe. . . . . .   25 1st Eclogues 9   101
    The raines of Love I love, though never slake, ... 179 Astrophil   28   7
    On them storms, brimstone, coales he raines, ... 284 Psalm XI   19
RAISE
    Whose sprite all sprites can spoile, raise, damne, or save:.   17 1st Eclogues 7   110
    An olde man heare, who would thy fancies raise.. . . . . . .   22 1st Eclogues 9   5
    At whose approach the Sunne rase in the evening, ... 113 4th Eclogues 71   69
    Strange flames of Love it in our soules would raise; . . . . 177 Astrophil   25   4
    So to raise my hap more hie; . . . . 211 A&S 4th Song   21
    That speech falles now to blame, which did thy honour raise, 213 A&S 5th Song   17
    That ravishing delight in them most sweete tunes do not
        raise; . . . .   217 A&S 7th Song   2
    I bett those folks as small as dust, which wind doth rayse;. 293 Psalm XVIII   76
    May joy and banners raise. . . . . 296 Psalm XX   19
    Which many seeing hearts shall rayse . . . . 331 Psalm XL   13
    And rayse me up that I may once have might . . . . 333 Psalm XLI   35
    To raise in words what in effect is lowe:. . . . . 242 Other Poems   4   2
RAISED
    To one whose state is raised over all, ...   3 Lady of May   1   1
    Dorus. Such Kala is: but ah, my fancies raysed be. . . . . .   15 1st Eclogues 7   37
    Where highest notes to godlines are raisd, ...   99 3rd Eclogues 66   31
    My soule is bliste, secure joyde, and fortune raysed. . . .   108 Arcadia IV   69   14
    Let here his eyes be raised. . . . . 151 Cert Sonnets 23   3
    Above line repeated at following locations . . . .   0 Other Poems   0   0
    . . . . 152 Cert Sonnets 23   35
    Not thou by praise, but praise in thee is raisde:. . . . . . 182 Astrophil   35   13
    My forces razde, thy banners raisd within: . . . . 183 Astrophil   36   6
    In well raisde notes, my pen the best it may . . . . 201 Astrophil   70   10
    Thy Honour high be raised. . . . . 298 Psalm XXI   50
    Have power again to raised be. . . . . 324 Psalm XXXVI   36
    And in fine my soul be raysed, ... 335 Psalm XLII   55
RAISING
    By raysing up, upon thy selfe to stand.. . . . .   23 1st Eclogues 9   51
RAKE
    Then in the Dust let him my hcnour rake. . . . . 277 Psalm VII   15
    Pas could not stay, but over him did rake, ... 248 Other Poems   4 259
RAM
    His Ramme, who to recover.. . . . .   259 Other Poems   5 121
RAMPIRE
    Nor ramper did abide; my braine was up blowne, ...   68 2nd Eclogues 33   15
RAMS
    The oldest Rammes are culled from the flocke:. . . . .   24 1st Eclogues 9   85
    Away ragg'd rams, care I what murraine kill? . . . . 255 Other Poems   4 515
RAN
    She ranne away, and threw at me a ball.. . . . .   54 2nd Eclogues 29   89
    While thus they ran a low, but leaveld race, ... 243 Other Poems   4   57
    She chirping ran, he peeping flew away, ...   244 Other Poems   4   87
    With whome to joyne fast ran Urania sweet: . . . . 248 Other Poems   4 252
    For as Urania after Cosma ran, ... 249 Other Poems   4 281
    He ran, but ran with eye ore shoulder cast, ...   249 Other Poems   4 289
RANGE
    But nowe each where doth range . . . .   82 Arcadia III 55   7
    Her horned head abroad doth raunge:. . . . .   86 Arcadia III 62   12
    The first with cloth's tuckt up as Nymphes in woods do
        range , ... 118 4th Eclogues 73   66
    For in each thing wherto mine eye doth range, ...   147 Cert Sonnets 18   3
    One day he with his flock abroad did raunge: . . . . 253 Other Poems   4 438

RANGE	(CONTINUED)	PAGE	TITLE		LINE
Give leave your flockes to range,.		261	Other Poems	6	31

RANGING
| Old age well stayed from raunging humor lives: . . . . | | 39 | Arcadia II | 15 | 10 |

RANSACKED
| A conquerd, yelden, ransackt heart to winne? . . . . | | 182 | Astrophil | 36 | 2 |

RAPE
| Recount the rape of Europe,. . . . . | | 66 | 2nd Eclogues | 32 | 26 |

RAPT
| Their dwellers rapt with sight of her perfection . . . . . . | | 15 | 1st Eclogues | 7 | 44 |
| Though rapt with beautie's hooke, I did impart . . . . | | 150 | Cert Sonnets | 22 | 26 |

RARE
What circle then in so rare force beares swaye?.		17	1st Eclogues	7	109
Time, place, life, wit scarcely her rare gifts measure doth.		49	2nd Eclogues	28	60
The lovely blowe with rare reward, my prayer is.		51	2nd Eclogues	28	112
In this rare subject from thy common right:.		79	Arcadia III	51	10
The Phoenix wings be not so rare		89	Arcadia III	62	118
Nay, that may breed my fame, it is so rare:.		182	Astrophil	34	6
With choisest words, thy words with reasons rare,.		200	Astrophil	68	10

RARELY
| Drowsy am I, and yet can rarely slepe. . . . . | | 253 | Other Poems | 4 | 446 |

RAREST
And for Rose-water sould of rarest smell..		55	2nd Eclogues	29	110
Of rarest price, both heav'n and earth her bower..		59	2nd Eclogues	30	100
With choise delights and rarest company,.		230	Astrophil	97	10

RASE
This said, this done, he rase even tir'd with rest,.		255	Other Poems	4	521
Then rase, but rase on leggs with faintnes bended, ...		259	Other Poems	5	116
He rase, and streight espied		259	Other Poems	5	120

RASH
| Where plagu'd for rash attempt, gives up his ghost,. . . . . | | 151 | Cert Sonnets | 22 | 57 |

RASHLY
| I should so rashly ripp up.. . . . . | | 66 | 2nd Eclogues | 32 | 18 |

RAT
| A king upon a mouse, a strong foe to a rat,. . . . . | | 53 | 2nd Eclogues | 29 | 32 |

RATE
| That you allow me them by so small rate? . . . . | | 225 | Astrophil | 92 | 2 |

RATHE
| Pas. Alas, when I in spring meet roses rathe,. . . . . | | 54 | 2nd Eclogues | 29 | 78 |

RATHER
This tyran Love; or rather do suppresse.		23	1st Eclogues	9	45
Rather to wrong then unto just defence,.		25	1st Eclogues	9	106
Then thow earst knew? rather take part with him.		26	1st Eclogues	10	8
In sicke-man's franzie rather takes compassion,.		50	2nd Eclogues	28	96
Then rage for rage: rather my wish I send to thee, ...		50	2nd Eclogues	28	97
Nay rather then my ease discontentation.		51	2nd Eclogues	28	120
Rather then have thy all-beholding eye		126	4th Eclogues	75	56
Unto no body my woman saith she had rather a wife be,. . . .		143	Cert Sonnets	13	1
I rather wisht thee clime the Muses' hill, ...		169	Astrophil	10	3
Rather then by more truth to get more paine.		199	Astrophil	67	14
To lose his Crowne, rather then faile his Love..		204	Astrophil	75	14
But rather much he fancys this		281	Psalm X		15
A paire of frends, or rather one cal'd two,.		242	Other Poems	4	18
Or rather, till thou die,.		258	Other Poems	5	77
I rather would my sheepe		259	Other Poems	5	99

RATIFY
| To conquere, and his conquest how to ratifie,. . . . . | | 49 | 2nd Eclogues | 28 | 47 |

RATLING
| Into your rimes, running in ratling rowes: . . . . | | 172 | Astrophil | 15 | 6 |

RAVEN
| Where famine ravine taught their hungrie chestes,. . . . . . | | 102 | 3rd Eclogues | 66 | 124 |

RAVENER'S
| Led by Thy Word the Rav'ner's stepps I shun, ... | | 289 | Psalm XVII | | 14 |

RAVENERS'
| Those raveners' whelps oft starved be, ... | | 319 | Psalm XXXIV | | 38 |

RAVENOUS
| Extolling ravenous gain: . . . . | | 281 | Psalm X | | 11 |

RAVENS
| Upon thy face let coaly Ravens swarme: . . . . | | 125 | 4th Eclogues | 75 | 19 |

RAVISHED
| Ravisht, staid not, till in her golden haire . . . . | | 232 | Astrophil | 103 | 7 |
| He ravished with sight how gracefully. . . . . | | 249 | Other Poems | 4 | 282 |

RAVISHING
| Which wooed wo, most ravishing delight . . . . | | 194 | Astrophil | 58 | 13 |
| That ravishing delight in them most sweete tunes do not raise; . . . . | | 217 | A&S 7th Song | | 2 |

RAYED
| Mine was the scrippe: but thou, that seeming rayed with love . . . . | | 52 | 2nd Eclogues | 29 V | 9 |

RAYS
I cried, and was with open rayes rewarded:		17	1st Eclogues	7	94
Cosma's faire beames emblemish much his raies.		55	2nd Eclogues	29	98
Thy beames I like, but her cleare rayes I love:.		72	Arcadia III	38	9
Like to my brother's raies, yet those I sende.		82	Arcadia III	55	14
Whose gentle rayes suche Luster fynde, ...		89	Arcadia III	62	V115
For soone as they strake thee with Stella's rayes, ...		170	Astrophil	10	12
Yet still on me, o eyes, dart downe your rayes:.		186	Astrophil	42	11
Their rayes to me, who in her tedious absence lay.		204	Astrophil	76	2

RAZED
| On her, who hath in me thy temple raste, ... | | 72 | Arcadia III | 38 | 14 |

394

RAZED	(CONTINUED)	PAGE	TITLE		LINE
My forces razde, thy banners raisd within:		183	Astrophil	36	6
REACH					
Looke to thy selfe; reach not beyond humanitie:.		16	1st Eclogues	7	64
Is not my skill, nor reach of mortall minde.		79	Arcadia III	50	16
But all, for all reach not my wailefull will:.		126	4th Eclogues	75	33
Phrases and Problemes from my reach do grow, ...		166	Astrophil	3	10
Or reach the fruite of Nature's choisest tree, ...		169	Astrophil	10	4
Beauties so farre from reach of words, that we		183	Astrophil	37	7
Though my Works reach not to Thee.		287	Psalm XVI		6
Of pleasurs past the reach of mind?.		324	Psalm XXXVI		24
Foul faults sore pains do reach me,.		332	Psalm XL		46
REACHED					
And so when Pas hand-reached him to take,.		248	Other Poems	4	257
He thrise reacht, thrise deceiv'd when hir to beare.		250	Other Poems	4	340
REACHEST					
Leave me o Love, which reachest but to dust, ...		161	Cert Sonnets	32	1
REACHING					
Of passyon's hilles reaching to reason's skie, ...		149	Cert Sonnets	22	6
READ					
While shepheards' tunes be heard, or rimes be read, ...		56	2nd Eclogues	29	124
And in whose eyes my dayly doome I reede..		72	Arcadia III	38	5
The goodman read on both sides the content,.		96	3rd Eclogues	64	88
As thou wilt deigne to reade, and gentlie reede, ...		96	3rd Eclogues	64	95
And this was all, and this the husband read.		97	3rd Eclogues	64	109
Let Dirge be sung, and Trentals rightly read, ...		160	Cert Sonnets	30	21
Pleasure might cause her reade, reading might make her know,		165	Astrophil	1	3
How then? even thus: in Stella's face I reed,.		166	Astrophil	3	12
That Plato I read for nought, but if he tame		175	Astrophil	21	5
I reade it in thy lookes, thy languisht grace, ...		180	Astrophil	31	7
Then thinke my deare, that you in me do reed		187	Astrophil	45	12
When I might reade those letters faire of blisse,.		193	Astrophil	56	5
Stella's sweete breath the same to me did reed..		194	Astrophil	58	11
So children still reade you with awfull eyes,.		196	Astrophil	63	2
Let him but learne of Love to reade in thee, ...		201	Astrophil	71	3
That all thy hurts in my hart's wracke I reede;.		227	Astrophil	93	13
Who will read must first learne spelling..		203	A&S 2nd Song		24
O let them see these heavenly beames, and in faire letters					
reede.		217	A&S 7th Song		11
There be no eyn but reade the line		294	Psalm XIX		13
READING					
Pleasure might cause her reade, reading might make her know,		165	Astrophil	1	3
Love onely reading unto me this art..		179	Astrophil	28	14
For evry body's reading.		294	Psalm XIX		16
READY					
And Parot, ready tongue, that to applie.		101	3rd Eclogues	66	84
And so most ready am this meane of peace to trie..		121	4th Eclogues	73	152
Readie of wit and fearing nought but shame:.		172	Astrophil	14	11
Ready to store their campes of needfull things:.		179	Astrophil	29	4
Late tyr'd with wo, even ready for to pine		195	Astrophil	62	1
And ready art to let Thyne arrowes go.		278	Psalm VII		36
All ready, ready to my snaring grave to go..		291	Psalm XVIII		11
And ready make Thy vengefull bowe.		298	Psalm XXI		47
REALM					
This realme of blisse, while vertuous course I take, ...		200	Astrophil	69	13
Thou, sweetest subject, werte borne in the realme of Love, .		214	A&S 5th Song		64
The Heathen for thy Child's right, and will thy realme					
extend		271	Psalm II		19
That Realm in deed hath blisse		317	Psalm XXXIII		43
REALMS					
He that is my revenge, in whom I realmes subdue, ...		293	Psalm XVIII		85
And that by right upon all Realmes he raigneth..		300	Psalm XXII		70
REAMS					
There be no Rea'ms hidd from his beames, ...		294	Psalm XIX		27
REAP					
And now I faine would reape, I reape but this, ...		115	4th Eclogues	72	57
And knowes not who the fruit shall reap.		330	Psalm XXXIX		22
REAPED					
These bolde words she did heare, this fruite I reaped, . . .		17	1st Eclogues	7	82
REAR					
Of Prince's losse your selves for tokens reare..		125	4th Eclogues	75	27
Jove on his helme the thunderbolt did reare..		171	Astrophil	13	8
But God shall him to safety reare.		320	Psalm XXXIV		71
REARED					
Of yonglings, which thy selfe with love hast rearde, ...		92	3rd Eclogues	63	43
And safe again He rear'd mee		272	Psalm III		18
REASON					
Thus Reason to his servants yeelds his right;.		12	Arcadia I	2	11
Thus reason to his Servantes gyves his right		12	Arcadia I	2	V811
Dorus. How oft, when reason saw love of her harnished. . . .		16	1st Eclogues	7	61
Thus Reason said: but she came, Reason vanished;		16	1st Eclogues	7	67
Which so much reason beares, ...		18	1st Eclogues	7	148
Reason, I vaine (now you have lost my hart).		38	Arcadia II	14	9
Reason. Thou Rebell vile, come, to thy master yelde.		46	2nd Eclogues	27	1
R. Can Reason then a Tyraunt counted be?		46	2nd Eclogues	27	3
P. If Reason will, that Passions be not free..		46	2nd Eclogues	27	4
R. But Reason will, that Reason governe most..		46	2nd Eclogues	27	5
R. Your will is will; but Reason reason is..		46	2nd Eclogues	27	7
R. By nature you to Reason faith have sworne..		46	2nd Eclogues	27	11
P. Reason hath eyes to see his owne ill case..		46	2nd Eclogues	27	16

REASON   (CONTINUED)   PAGE   TITLE   LINE
  P. And is not Reason dimde with Passion's might? . . . . . .   46 2nd Eclogues 27   18
  R. O sacred Reason, helpe our vertuous toiles. . . . .   46 2nd Eclogues 27   23
  R. We are too strong: but Reason seekes not blood. . . . . .   47 2nd Eclogues 27   29
  R. You know it not: of Reason therefore know it. . . . . . .   47 2nd Eclogues 27   39
  P. No Reason yet had ever skill to show it.. . . . .   47 2nd Eclogues 27   40
  Which Passions kill, and Reason do deface. . . . .   47 2nd Eclogues 27   42
  Or Reason lie a slave to servile Sense,. . . . .   49 2nd Eclogues 28   76
  So love encroches on your charmed reason,. . . . .   50 2nd Eclogues 28   93
  Yet Reason saith, Reason should have abilitie, ...   60 2nd Eclogues 30   131
  Hath not Reason enough vehemence the desire to reprove?
      Prove. . . . .   63 2nd Eclogues 31   10
  Oft prove I: but what salve, when Reason seeks to be gone?
      One. . . . .   63 2nd Eclogues 31   11
  Reason, tell me thy mind, if here be reason. . . . .   67 2nd Eclogues 33   1
  Say then Reason, I say what is thy counsell? . . . .   67 2nd Eclogues 33   6
  Above line repeated at following locations . . . .   67 2nd Eclogues 33   12
         . . . .   68 2nd Eclogues 33   18
         . . . .   68 2nd Eclogues 33   24
  Reason sighes but in end he thus doth answere. . . . .   68 2nd Eclogues 33   25
  "Nought can reason availe in heav'nly matters".. . . . . . .   68 2nd Eclogues 33   26
  Reason looke to thy selfe, I serve a goddesse. . . . .   68 2nd Eclogues 33   30
  For reason will, great sight of hoped blisse,. . . . .   71 Arcadia III 37   11
  Her cable, Reason, breakes from anchor, Hope:. . . . . 114 4th Eclogues 72   46
  You be the cause that I love: what Reason blameth a shadowe, 123 4th Eclogues 74   45
  Well: but faultie I was: Reason to my Passion yeelded, . . . 124 4th Eclogues 74   67
  And aske the reason of that speciall grace,. . . . . 126 4th Eclogues 75   40
  Since naked sence can conquer reason armed:. . . . . 135 Cert Sonnets 1   6
  Or reason foyld would not in vaine contend:. . . . . 147 Cert Sonnets 19   4
  Thought, reason, sense, time, you, and I, maintaine. . . . . 148 Cert Sonnets 19   18
  Can count them just, nor reason reason trye, ... 149 Cert Sonnets 22   3
  Of sorrowe's droppes, till colder reason binde . . . . 150 Cert Sonnets 22   37
  Reason abasht retyred, ... 154 Cert Sonnets 25   7
  My poore reason thy words moved, ... 156 Cert Sonnets 27   3
  Reason hath thy words removed, ... 156 Cert Sonnets 27   11
  The litle reason that is left in me, ... 167 Astrophil   4   10
  Reason, in faith thou art well serv'd, that still. . . . . . 169 Astrophil   10   1
  Reason thou kneel'dst, and offeredst straight to prove . . . 170 Astrophil   10   13
  By reason good, good reason her to love. . . . . 170 Astrophil   10   14
  Of reason, from whose light those night-birds flie;. . . . . 201 Astrophil   71   17
  They are amaz'd, but you with reason armed,. . . . . 209 A&S 3rd Song   17
  Rebell by Nature's law, Rebell by law of reason, ... 214 A&S 5th Song   63
  Deere, do reason no such spite,. . . . . 234 A&S 11th Song   28
  Then reason, Princesse hy, ... 217 A&S 6th Song   49
  Smiling ayre allowes my reason,. . . . . 219 A&S 8th Song   55
  And reason, since the Croune to God pertaineth,. . . . . . . 300 Psalm XXII   69
  Giving his reason pasport for to passe,. . . . . 252 Other Poems   4   381
  While guilty thoughts accus'd his Reason weake). . . . . . . 255 Other Poems   4   532
REASON'S
  Both these conspird poore Reason's overthrowe; . . . .   11 Arcadia I   2   7
  P. Will hath his will, when Reason's will doth misse.. . . .   46 2nd Eclogues 27   8
  R. Dare Passions then abide in Reason's light? . . . .   46 2nd Eclogues 27   17
  P. O Passion, passe on feeble Reason's spoiles.. . . . . . .   46 2nd Eclogues 27   24
  R. Yet Passion, yeeld at length to Reason's stroke.. . . . .   47 2nd Eclogues 27   33
  P. What shall we winne by taking Reason's yoke?. . . . . . .   47 2nd Eclogues 27   34
  My minde ere now led foorth by reason's light: . . . .   73 Arcadia III 39   4
  With sense possest, and claim'd by reason's right: . . . . .   74 Arcadia III 42   6
  Passion rebelde, oft reason's strength hath shaked.. . . . .   82 Arcadia III 57   4
  Had reason's weight for passion's ease rejected. . . . . . .   83 Arcadia III 57   8
  Which were not evill, well vew'd in reason's light.. . . . . 131 Arcadia V   77   8
  But vertue sets so high, that reason's light,. . . . . 135 Cert Sonnets 2   7
  If rebell sence would reason's law receyve;. . . . . 147 Cert Sonnets 19   3
  With reason's strife, by senses overthrowne,. . . . . 148 Cert Sonnets 19   14
  Of passyon's hilles reaching to reason's skie, ... 149 Cert Sonnets 22   6
  When into Reason's audite I do go: . . . . 173 Astrophil   18   2
  Since Reason's selfe doth blow the cole in me? . . . . 182 Astrophil   35   6
  "But your reason's purest light, ... 234 A&S 11th Song   26
  More then in my reason's sight.. . . . . 234 A&S 11th Song   30
  Wholy devoy'd of Reason's rule,. . . . . 315 Psalm XXXII   32
  Of them, poore soules: and cutting Reason's raines,. . . . . 246 Other Poems   4   158
  He found that Reason's self now reasons found. . . . . 253 Other Poems   4   423
REASONS
  Such wandring reasons in thy speech I finde. . . . .   25 1st Eclogues 9   98
  Cloth'd with fine tropes, with strongest reasons lin'd,. . . 194 Astrophil   58   6
  With choisest words, thy words with reasons rare,. . . . . . 200 Astrophil   68   10
  Thy reasons firmly set on Vertue's feet; . . . . 200 Astrophil   68   11
  He found that Reason's self now reasons found. . . . . 253 Other Poems   4   423
REBEL
  Rebell, Rebell, in golden fetters binde. . . . .   23 1st Eclogues 9   44
  Those rebell thoughts which are thy slaves by kinde. . . . .   23 1st Eclogues 9   46
  Nature against we do seeme to rebell, seeme fooles in a
      vaine sute.. . . . .   32 1st Eclogues 13   24
  Reason. Thou Rebell vile, come, to thy master yelde. . . . .   46 2nd Eclogues 27   1
  With rebell force, hath closde in dungeon darke. . . . . . .   73 Arcadia III 39   3
  "Fie, fie, what have we done? ungodly rebell fie.. . . . . . 121 4th Eclogues 73   168
  If rebell sence would reason's law receyve;. . . . . 147 Cert Sonnets 19   3
  Rebell by Nature's law, Rebell by law of reason, ... 214 A&S 5th Song   63
  Both Rebell to the Sonne, and Vagrant from the mother; . . . 214 A&S 5th Song   69
  You Rebell run away, to Lord and Lady untrue,. . . . . 215 A&S 5th Song   86
  And now, proud Rebell gan for to gainsay . . . . 246 Other Poems   4   173

```
                                                       PAGE    TITLE           LINE
REBELIED
    Passion rebelde, oft reason's strength hath shaked.. . . . .   82 Arcadia III  57    4
REBELLION
    Of foule rebellion then I do appeach thee now; . . . . . . .  214 A&S 5th Song      62
REBELLIOUS
    And save them from rebellious hand.. . . . . . . . . . . . .  290 Psalm XVII        24
    Nor my Rebellious blott, . . . . . . . . . . . . . . . . . .  303 Psalm XXV         27
REBELS
    Rebels to Nature, strive for their owne smart. . . . . . . .  167 Astrophil      5   4
    But valiant Rebels oft in fooles' mouthes purchase fame: . .  214 A&S 5th Song      67
    These most ungratefull rebels unto Thee. . . . . . . . . . .  275 Psalm V           32
    Who freed me from my foes, from rebells guarded me,. . . . .  293 Psalm XVIII       86
REBOUND
    But that it dooth with Echoe's force rebound . . . . . . . .   42 Arcadia II   21   10
REBOUNDING
    Pleasd to receave that name by rebounding answere of Echo, .   33 1st Eclogues 13   44
REBUKE
    Least I rebuke sustain;. . . . . . . . . . . . . . . . . . .  304 Psalm XXV         70
    Rebuke and wracke on those wrong doers throw,. . . . . . . .  321 Psalm XXXV         9
REBUKED
    The Gentiles Thou rebuked sorely hast, . . . . . . . . . . .  279 Psalm IX          11
RECANT
    O paine I now recant the praise I gave,. . . . . . . . . . .  141 Cert Sonnets 9    13
RECEIPT
    Receipt to me, within thy bosome darke.. . . . . . . . . . .   73 Arcadia III  40    8
    Deepe in the earth, what hath in earth receipt . . . . . . .  150 Cert Sonnets 22   42
RECEIVE
    In those weake harts that his advice receave.. . . . . . . .   21 1st Eclogues 8    34
    Pleasd to receave that name by rebounding answere of Echo, .   33 1st Eclogues 13   44
    Nor yet, fancy so drest, do receive more plausible hearing:.   35 1st Eclogues 13  101
    This vowe receave, this vowe o Gods maintaine; . . . . . . .   40 Arcadia II   18    5
    Pas. But yesternight by light I did receave. . . . . . . . .   55 2nd Eclogues 29  102
    What glorie from our losse can he receave? . . . . . . . . .   59 2nd Eclogues 30   73
    Thus nature's Diamond, receave thy conquest, . . . . . . . .   68 2nd Eclogues 33   27
    Of goodnes to receive lovely direction.. . . . . . . . . . .   68 2nd Eclogues 34    4
    Her stepps, gladd we receave, gladd we receave her eys.. . .   69 2nd Eclogues 34   40
    Make present ease receave the better taste.. . . . . . . . .   70 Arcadia III  36    6
    Of some late grace a greater grace receave,. . . . . . . . .   77 Arcadia III  49    4
    In trees) now through your porous barkes receave . . . . . .  125 4th Eclogues 75    5
    Then come, O come, then do I come, receyve (mee),. . . . . .  138 Cert Sonnets 5    21
    If rebell sence would reason's law receave;. . . . . . . . .  147 Cert Sonnets 19    3
    Receive good acceptation!. . . . . . . . . . . . . . . . . .  295 Psalm XIX         64
    Sweet Righteousness shall he receive,. . . . . . . . . . . .  302 Psalm XXIV        14
    Stay then Thy wrath, that I may strength receive . . . . . .  330 Psalm XXXIX       41
RECEIVED
    So that eyes' message be of her receaved,. . . . . . . . . .   30 1st Eclogues 12    3
    Above line repeated at following location. . . . . . . . . .   31 1st Eclogues 12   27
    His hart his wound receaved from my sight: . . . . . . . . .   76 Arcadia III  45    9
    Monstrous appeares, long trueth receaved late, . . . . . . .   85 Arcadia III  61    6
    And as a courtier was with cheere receaved,. . . . . . . . .   94 3rd Eclogues 64   20
RECEIVES
    Nor ey receaves due object,. . . . . . . . . . . . . . . . .   66 2nd Eclogues 32   38
RECEIVETH
    Though he the lively forme receiveth:. . . . . . . . . . . .  159 Cert Sonnets 29   17
RECITAL
    And to the woods or brookes, who do make such dreery
        recitall . . . . . . . . . . . . . . . . . . . . . . . .   33 1st Eclogues 13   42
    And so refuse to behold of these strange wounds the
        recitall . . . . . . . . . . . . . . . . . . . . . . . .  122 4th Eclogues 74    7
RECITE
    Nor mas'de head thinke, nor faltring tonge recite. . . . . .   74 Arcadia III  42   14
RECKLESSNESS
    With recklesness what may thy house betide,. . . . . . . . .   93 3rd Eclogues 63   75
RECKS
    Long be thy woes for such newes, but how recks she my
        thoughts? Oughts.. . . . . . . . . . . . . . . . . . . .   64 2nd Eclogues 31   33
RECLAIMS
    Sweete speaking oft a currish hart reclaimes.. . . . . . . .   60 2nd Eclogues 30  115
RECOMFORT
    What place is there left, we may hope our woes to recomfort?   32 1st Eclogues 13   28
    Cyprus promiseth helpe, but a helpe where comes no
        recomforte.. . . . . . . . . . . . . . . . . . . . . . .   35 1st Eclogues 13  119
    Yet be my hopes thus plast, here fixed lives my recomforte,.   37 1st Eclogues 13  164
    But God is Their recomfort.. . . . . . . . . . . . . . . . .  287 Psalm XIV         21
RECONCILED
    And such skill in my Muse you reconcil'd shall find, . . . .  215 A&S 5th Song      89
RECORD
    With the voyce of truth to recorde to all worldes, . . . . .   31 1st Eclogues 12   19
    But in Thy kindness me record, . . . . . . . . . . . . . . .  303 Psalm XXV         29
RECORDS
    Then grew my tongue and pen records unto thy glory:. . . . .  212 A&S 5th Song       3
RECOUNT
    Recount the rape of Europe,. . . . . . . . . . . . . . . . .   66 2nd Eclogues 32   26
    Let all the earth with scorne recount my case, . . . . . . .  198 Astrophil     64   7
    As I may well recount, but none can prize: . . . . . . . . .  198 Astrophil     65   4
RECOUNTED
    But thus in oke's true shade recounted he. . . . . . . . . .   99 3rd Eclogues 66   41
RECOVER
    So I your sight, you shall your selves recover". . . . . . .   17 1st Eclogues 7    93
    What meane is there, alas, we can hope our losse to recover?   32 1st Eclogues 13   27
```

```
RECOVER                    (CONTINUED)                     PAGE    TITLE          LINE
     His Ramme, who to recover. . . . . . . . . . . . . . . .  259 Other Poems    5   121
RECCVERED
     To well recoverd state. . . . . . . . . . . . . . . . . .  333 Psalm XLI          12
RECOVERS
     Whose owne fault casts him downe, hardly high seat recovers.  213 A&S 5th Song    24
     Theeves steal for need, and steale but goods, which paine
          recovers, . . . . . . . . . . . . . . . . . . . . .   214 A&S 5th Song    45
RECOVERY
     And banished doo I live, nor now will seeke a recov'rie, . .  124 4th Eclogues 74  83
RED
     And thinke from Cosma's sweet red lips I live, . . . . . .   54 2nd Eclogues 29  79
     Lips red and plum, as cherrie's ruddy side, . . . . . . . .   76 Arcadia III  46   8
     Like Christall, underlayde with Redd, . . . . . . . . . .    86 Arcadia III  62 V 24
     Red Porphir is, which locke of pearle makes sure: . . . . .  169 Astrophil     9   6
     Marble mixt red and white do enterlace. . . . . . . . . . .  169 Astrophil     9   8
     Where blushing red, that Love's selfe them doth love, . . .  186 Astrophil    43  10
     Milke hands, rose cheeks, or lips more sweet, more red, . .  225 Astrophil    91   7
     Where those red cheeks, which oft with faire encrease did
          frame. . . . . . . . . . . . . . . . . . . . . . . .  232 Astrophil   102   2
     Sc may the cheries redd. . . . . . . . . . . . . . . . . .  258 Other Poems    5  56
REDDEST
     While beautie's reddest inke Venus for him doth sturre. . .  232 Astrophil   102  14
REDE
     Because I red him, as I would my son. . . . . . . . . . . .   27 1st Eclogues 10  23
     For clerkly reed, and hating what is naught, . . . . . . .    99 3rd Eclogues 66  24
REDEEM
     Then me redeem Lord then be mercifull. . . . . . . . . . .   306 Psalm XXXVI       36
     God doth all soules redeeme. . . . . . . . . . . . . . . .   321 Psalm XXXIV       77
REDOUELE
     Their numbrous strength redouble. . . . . . . . . . . . . .  272 Psalm III          6
REDRESS
     That only can redresse thee, . . . . . . . . . . . . . . .    67 2nd Eclogues 32  48
     Thinke that I thinke state errours to redresse. . . . . . .  176 Astrophil    23   8
REDRESSED
     To have his harmes with wisdome's helpe redrest. . . . . .    75 Arcadia III  44   4
     Such cursed harmes as cannot be redressed. . . . . . . . .   126 4th Eclogues 75  63
REDRESSETH
     And since there is not One, who it redresseth. . . . . . .   299 Psalm XXII        26
REEDS
     Be prest our reedes to fill, . . . . . . . . . . . . . . .   260 Other Poems    6   9
     Often Reedes me musicke made, . . . . . . . . . . . . . . .  263 Other Poems    7  44
     With my reedes, sound mighty praise; . . . . . . . . . . .   264 Other Poems    7  68
REFECTION
     As thou wilt give our soules a deare refection, . . . . . .   49 2nd Eclogues 28  52
REFINETH
     Earth gave that Love, heav'n I trcw Love refineth: . . . .   209 A&S 3rd Song      11
REFLECTED
     Enterchangeably reflected. . . . . . . . . . . . . . . . .   218 A&S 8th Song      16
     If it please thee be reflected, . . . . . . . . . . . . . .  264 Other Poems    7  71
REFLECTION
     But o happy be you, which safe from fyry reflection. . . .    31 1st Eclogues 13  11
     A greater good by her divine reflection; . . . . . . . . .    49 2nd Eclogues 28  68
REFORM
     Whose force had such force so to transforme, nay to reforme
          me, . . . . . . . . . . . . . . . . . . . . . . . . .   37 1st Eclogues 13 166
REFRAIN
     And make me heare the plaints I would refraine: . . . . . .   42 Arcadia II   21  11
     The one, which tother would refrayne. . . . . . . . . . . .   57 2nd Eclogues 30   4
     Doth him, his face, his words, leave, shunne, refraine, . .   84 Arcadia III  60  12
     Now will I alas refraine, . . . . . . . . . . . . . . . . .  203 A&S 2nd Song      19
     Frome bitinge Usury who ever doth refrain, . . . . . . . .   287 Psalm XV          11
     The Nightingales for woe their songs refraine: . . . . . .   254 Other Poems    4 474
REFRAINED
     O Phisicke's power, which (some say) hath refrayned. . . .   128 4th Eclogues 75 109
REFRESH
     Shall I not? o may I not thus yet refresh the remembrance, .  124 4th Eclogues 74  71
     As can refresh the hell where my soule fries. . . . . . . .  231 Astrophil   100   8
     Meaning with absence to refresh the thought. . . . . . . .   246 Other Poems    4 175
REFRESHING
     Seeking some refreshing brook, . . . . . . . . . . . . . .   334 Psalm XLII         2
REFUGE
     Since no refuge doth serve from woundes we do carry about
          us . . . . . . . . . . . . . . . . . . . . . . . . .    33 1st Eclogues 13  51
     The sure refuge, by thee and by no other . . . . . . . . .   108 Arcadia IV   69  13
     My refuge, refuge then, when moste I am forlorn; . . . . .   291 Psalm XVIII        5
REFUSAL
     In clyming steepe, now hard refusall show: . . . . . . . .   147 Cert Sonnets 18   6
REFUSE
     And so refuse to behold of these strange wounds the
          recitall . . . . . . . . . . . . . . . . . . . . . .  122 4th Eclogues 74   7
     And thy words of refuse, do powre even hell on mee: . . . .  215 A&S 5th Song    83
     Stella's selfe might not refuse them. . . . . . . . . . . .  220 A&S 8th Song    96
REFUSED
     Geron. What can amend where physick is refusde?. . . . . .    23 1st Eclogues  9  21
     The boy refusde for feare of Marse's hate, . . . . . . . .   173 Astrophil    17   5
     Stella hath refused me, . . . . . . . . . . . . . . . . . .  221 A&S 9th Song    21
     Above line repeated at following location. . . . . . . . .   222 A&S 9th Song    26
REFUSETH
     Her tongue waking still refuseth, . . . . . . . . . . . . .  202 A&S 2nd Song       9
```

		PAGE	TITLE	LINE
REGARD				
	Gratefulnes, sweetnes, holy love, hartie regard)	122	4th Eclogues 74	10
	Say, Thou dost not Thyn Own regard?.	283	Psalm X	56
	My eyes still my God regard.	288	Psalm XVI	25
REGARDED				
	We love, and are no whit regarded.	14	1st Eclogues 6	2
	Honor, the cause, desart is not regarded..	17	1st Eclogues 7	96
REGIMENT				
	Of vertue's regiment, shining in harnesse.	67	2nd Eclogues 33	4
REHEARSE				
	And use but you for matters to rehearse?	146	Cert Sonnets 17	35
REHEARSED				
	They look, they gaze, my boanes might be rehearsed;.	299	Psalm XXII	42
REHEARSERS				
	Wcundes to Rehersers?.	138	Cert Sonnets 5	8
REIGN				
	Whyle hote desyres do Raigne in fancie's rage.	26	1st Eclogues 9	140
	Since in sweete you all goods so richly raigne,.	39	Arcadia II 16	5
	Balles to the starres, and thralles to Fortune's raigne; . .	57	2nd Eclogues 30	17
	Where that all blisse may raigne,.	91	3rd Eclogues 63	26
	In her let beautie both, and chastnesse fully raigne.. . . .	120	4th Eclogues 73	132
	He would not arm'd with beautie, only raigne	135	Cert Sonnets 2	5
	And know those Bodies high raigne on the low..	178	Astrophil 26	11
	Of all the kings that ever here did raigne,.	204	Astrophil 75	1
	For then the lord in judgment shewes to raigne	281	Psalm IX	51
	Who thus proceeds, for aye, in sacred Mount shall raign. . .	287	Psalm XV	13
	Thus freed from mutin men, thou makest me to raign,.	293	Psalm XVIII	78
	Nor reign upon my senses..	295	Psalm XIX	56
	This while, though poore, they in themselves did raigne. . .	243	Other Poems 4	64
	In whome no evill did raigne, nor good appeare,.	245	Other Poems 4	118
REIGNED				
	I know full well you know, what discord long hath raign'd. .	119	4th Eclogues 73	105
	That even his feet have on them raigned.	279	Psalm VIII	24
REIGNETH				
	So it be seene what sorrow in me raigneth.	128	4th Eclogues 75	105
	To see what faire sight there raigneth,.	140	Cert Sonnets 7	26
	Who hath the lips, where wit in fairnesse raigneth,.	197	A&S 1st Song	9
	In thee my glory raigneth.	272	Psalm III	12
	There is no God that raigneth.	286	Psalm XIV	3
	And that by right upon all Realmes he raigneth..	300	Psalm XXII	70
	For by his power the land upon the Ocean raigneth, ...	302	Psalm XXIV	3
REIGNING				
	In all whose workes vainess is ever raigning:.	276	Psalm VI	26
REIGNS				
	Then do I shape to my selfe that forme which raigns so with			
	in me,.	36	1st Eclogues 13	142
	Then must I save, what in my chiefly raignes,..	114	4th Eclogues 72	24
	A seate where beauty shines and vertue raignes,.	141	Cert Sonnets 8	10
	In my reines hot torment raignes,.	328	Psalm XXXVIII	19
REIN				
	The raine wherewith my Rider doth me tie,..	189	Astrophil 49 V	5
	But as he them more short or slacke doth raine,.	194	Astrophil 58	4
REINED				
	(Spurd with love's spur, though gald and shortly raind . . .	230	Astrophil 98	7
REINS				
	Never hard hand, nor ever raines too light..	98	3rd Eclogues 65	8
	Where fairnesse yeelds to wisdome's shortest raines.	151	Cert Sonnets 22	64
	The raines wherewith my Rider doth me tie, ...	189	Astrophil 49	5
	For rage now rules the reynes, which guided were by			
	Pleasure	213	A&S 5th Song	15
	Thou righteous proofes to hearts, and reines dost send,. . .	277	Psalm VII	28
	The lord doth search the just man's reines,.	284	Psalm XI	17
	In my inward reynes I taste.	288	Psalm XVI	23
	Yea sound my reines, and inmost of my heart;	305	Psalm XXVI	9
	Of furious floods he holds the reines, ...	310	Psalm XXIX	26
	In my reines hot torment raignes,.	328	Psalm XXXVIII	19
	Of them, poore soules: and cutting Reason's raines,.	246	Other Poems 4	158
REJECTED				
	So that eyes' message doo returne rejected,.	30	1st Eclogues 12	7
	Had reason's weight for passion's ease rejected.	83	Arcadia III 57	8
	Worth as nought worth rejected,.	159	Cert Sonnets 30	5
	And I from thee not rejected."	264	Other Poems 7	72
REJECTS				
	The noblest kinde rejects not others' woes..	18	1st Eclogues 7	134
REJOICE				
	(Espilus) Thus joyfully in chosen tunes rejoyce, ...	5	Lady of May 3	13
	From those cleere notes which freely may rejoyce..	13	Arcadia I 4	8
	Palmes do rejoyce to be joynd by the match of a male to a			
	female,.	36	1st Eclogues 13	137
	So sweets my paines, that my paines me rejoyce..	193	Astrophil 57	14
	The very essence of their tunes, when Angels do rejoyce. . .	217	A&S 7th Song	18
	Serve God, serve him with feare: Rejoyce in him but so,. . .	271	Psalm II	25
	And love the sweet sound of thy name, rejoyce.	275	Psalm V	34
	Get hence you ev'ill, who in my ev'ill rejoyce,.	276	Psalm VI	25
	Rejoice in God, O ye	316	Psalm XXXIII	1
	To witness thus rejoice..	316	Psalm XXXIII	12
	O Soul, rejoyce, we made this wretch our prey.	323	Psalm XXXV	62
	Whom my fall doth make rejoyce..	328	Psalm XXXVIII	48
	Shew that we do not grudge at all when others do rejoyce.. .	343	Possibly 1	2

	PAGE	TITLE	LINE
RELATES			
Which inke onely relates, but ne laments, ne replies? . . .	122	4th Eclogues 74	18
RELATION			
Yeeld to our eares a sweet and sound relation, ...	48	2nd Eclogues 28	20
RELEASE			
Alas I doo; from which to finde release, ...	116	4th Eclogues 72	92
My senses such release, as they which quiet live,.	117	4th Eclogues 73	12
The poore man's wealth, the prisoner's release,.	184	Astrophil 39	3
RELEASED			
Releast from Court, where envie needes must be..	143	Cert Sonnets 12	6
RELENT			
Relent those thoughts, which then did so displease?	58	2nd Eclogues 30	52
RELENTING			
But finding th'approch of death with an inly relenting,. . .	123	4th Eclogues 74	25
RELIC			
Ruine's relique, care's web, and sorrowe's foode:.	23	1st Eclogues 9	29
RELICS			
But ah her flight hath my dead reliques spent.	115	4th Eclogues 72	80
Strephon. But ah her flight hath my dead reliques spent, . .	115	4th Eclogues 72	81
RELIEF			
Oft comes reliefe when most we seeme in trappe..	23	1st Eclogues 9	24
Can holde, shew, tell, my paines without reliefe..	75	Arcadia III 43	8
RELIEVED			
But he were by me releeved..	222	A&S 9th Song	40
RELYING			
May be still to thee relying..	263	Other Poems 7	60
REMAIN			
And let her have the giftes that should in both remaine: . .	120	4th Eclogues 73	131
Till knit with cold, though there unknowne remaine,.	150	Cert Sonnets 22	33
Sweet Ladie you remaine well paid.	159	Cert Sonnets 29	4
In Tabernacle Thyne, O lord, who shall remayne?.	287	Psalm XV	1
Whether I silent did remain, ...	315	Psalm XXXII	8
REMAINED			
Ladie mine eyes remained,.	154	Cert Sonnets 25	3
REMAINEDST			
If Thou remainedst Idle.	315	Psalm XXXII	36
REMAINETH			
Thus weakned by my selfe, no helpe remaineth..	68	2nd Eclogues 33	17
So then since that heaven remaineth, ...	140	Cert Sonnets 7	28
No help fcr you remaineth.	272	Psalm III	9
Not One that good remaineth.	286	Psalm XIV	6
REMAINING			
Now in servile Court remayning..	262	Other Poems 7	12
Grant me with those two remaining.	263	Other Poems 7	66
REMAINS			
Hardly remains fyer hid, where skill is bent to the hiding,.	33	1st Eclogues 13	59
These wonders England breedes, the last remaines,.	151	Cert Sonnets 22	61
And this his rule for aye remains.	310	Psalm XXIX	27
There remains.	328	Psalm XXXVIII	20
REMEDY			
He did demaunde what remedy to finde;.	95	3rd Eclogues 64	52
REMEMBER			
Whom that Great God remember can?.	278	Psalm VIII	14
Remember, only King, ...	303	Psalm XXV	19
But Lord remember not.	303	Psalm XXV	25
Do you remember still you once were mine,.	254	Other Poems 4	495
REMEMBERING			
Ye saints of his, remembring still	311	Psalm XXX	11
My heart melts remembring so,.	334	Psalm XLII	13
REMEMBRANCE			
Shall I not? o may I not thus yet refresh the remembrance, .	124	4th Eclogues 74	71
While remembrance doth both states containe.	153	Cert Sonnets 24	14
Thy remembrance to divorce,.	225	A&S 10th Song	5
Who is our Lord, with due remembrance wayte.	296	Psalm XX	30
To Thy remembrance bring	303	Psalm XXV	21
Let those things Thy remembrance grave,.	303	Psalm XXV	23
Will. What keepeth safe thy band? D. Remembrance is the Chest.	344	Possibly 1	29
REMNANT			
And now employ the remnant of my wit,.	166	Astrophil 2	12
REMORSE			
Is Late remorse in follie dearely bought..	49	2nd Eclogues 28	78
(Teares and teares of a man) had no returne to remorse;. . .	122	4th Eclogues 74	16
Remorse in you to doe this Fortresse harme,.	346	Possibly 5	6
REMORSED			
Wrong sturres remorsed greefe, griefe's deadly sore.	85	Arcadia III 61	7
REMOTE			
Now fled, then cherished? then so nie, now so remote?. . . .	124	4th Eclogues 74	78
REMOTEST			
But what? I say from earth's remotest border	300	Psalm XXII	65
REMOVE			
Do you not thincke this will the wolves remove	26	1st Eclogues 10	4
What medicin then, can such desease remove	85	Arcadia III 61	13
But for all this I can not her remove.	145	Cert Sonnets 17	4
Dc not, o do not from poore me remove,.	186	Astrophil 42	7
But when he will for quiet's sake remove	186	Astrophil 43	12
Shall quickly me from what she hates remove.	195	Astrophil 61	11
Scortch not, but onely do darke chilling sprites remove. . .	205	Astrophil 76	8
"But time will these thoughts remove:.	234	A&S 11th Song	16
Those lying lipps from Cousening head remove,.	284	Psalm XII	8

REMOVE   (CONTINUED)   PAGE   TITLE   LINE
    Let nothing mee remove . . . .   261 Other Poems   6   45
REMOVED
    Reason hath thy words removed, ...   156 Cert Sonnets 27   11
    Nor he removed be. . . . .   282 Psalm X   25
REMOVES
    Since cause of griefe no cause from life removes.. . . . . .   58 2nd Eclogues 30   37
RENDER
    Dorus. Unto the Gods with a thanckfull heart all thankes I
        do render, ...   32 1st Eclogues 13   35
RENDERED
    She sackes my rendred sprite.. . . . .   155 Cert Sonnets 26   4
    Above line repeated at following locations . . . .   155 Cert Sonnets 26   15
    . . . .   156 Cert Sonnets 26   26
RENEW
    Ah woe is me, my woes renewe;. . . . .   90 Arcadia III 62   120
    Our yoong yeares to renew (for so he saith he will). . . . .   120 4th Eclogues 73   126
    Who thinke themselves well blest, if they renew. . . . . . .   146 Cert Sonnets 17   33
    And no spurre can his resty race renew,. . . . .   207 Astrophil   80   12
    And he shall your establishment renew. . . . .   314 Psalm XXXI   69
    Are you not dried? Can you your self renew?. . . . .   257 Other Poems   5   39
RENEWED
    Into my breste, and loves renewed swimme.. . . . .   85 Arcadia III 61   12
RENEWETH
    Who long dead beautie with increase reneweth?. . . . .   197 A&S 1st Song   22
RENOWN
    Rich in the treasure of deserv'd renowne,. . . . .   183 Astrophil   37   9
    With limitlesse renowne. . . . .   217 A&S 6th Song   54
    And their Renoune, which seemed so lyke to last, ...   280 Psalm IX   13
RENOWNED
    In these woods to resounde the renowmed name of a goddesse..   31 1st Eclogues 13   14
*RENT
    My thoughtes then hers, who first your ryne did rente, . . .   78 Arcadia III 49   14
    The moone a sunder rent (O godes, o pardon me, ...   118 4th Eclogues 73   55
    The Moone a sunder rent; whereat with sodaine fall . . . . .   118 4th Eclogues 73   57
    Unable quite to pay even Nature's rent,. . . . .   174 Astrophil   18   5
    Hart rent thy selfe, thou doest thy selfe but right, ...   181 Astrophil   33   5
    Leaving him so passion rent, ...   221 A&S 8th Song   102
    Leaving him to passion rent, ...   221 A&S 8th Song   V102
    Wound and rent me to the bones,. . . . .   335 Psalm XLII   46
    Thy wallet or thy Tarbox lost, or thy new rayment rent?. . .   343 Possibly   1   16
REPAIR
    Thither the World for justice shall repaire, ...   280 Psalm IX   23
REPAST
    On Nature's sweet repast, as healthfull senses ledd. . . . .   117 4th Eclogues 73   40
REPAY
    First the rivers shall ceasse to repay their fludds to the
        Occean:. . . . .   33 1st Eclogues 13   65
    If thou doo not repay his deeds for thee,. . . . .   105 3rd Eclogues 67   74
REPELLING
    But her hands his hands repelling, ...   219 A&S 8th Song   67
REPENT
    P. But so we shall with griefe learne to repent. . . . . . .   47 2nd Eclogues 27   36
    R. Repent indeed, but that shall be your blisse. . . . . . .   47 2nd Eclogues 27   37
    So hastily that which they would repent: . . . .   100 3rd Eclogues 66   69
    But with much studie learne late to repent.. . . . .   106 3rd Eclogues 67   96
    I willing run, yet while I run, repent.. . . . .   174 Astrophil   19   4
    Yet witches may repent, thou art far worse then they,. . . .   215 A&S 5th Song   79
    For this same man will not learn to repent, ...   278 Psalm VII   33
REPENTING
    Voyde of wishing and repenting.. . . . .   264 Other Poems   7   78
REPINE
    While that we do at his sweete scourge repine, ...   59 2nd Eclogues 30   75
    At which, whether the others did repine, ...   100 3rd Eclogues 66   57
REPINING
    Yet with repining at so partiall lot.. . . . .   165 Astrophil   2   8
REPLIED
    Nature abasht went back: fortune blusht: yet she replide
        thus:. . . . .   30 1st Eclogues 11   17
REPLIES
    Which inke onely relates, but ne laments, ne replies?. . . .   122 4th Eclogues 74   18
REPLY
    For how can Nature unto this reply?. . . . .   127 4th Eclogues 75   94
    O Doctor Cupid, thou for me reply, ...   195 Astrophil   61   12
REPOSE
    (Which life is cald) were mov'd their spirits to repose, . .   116 4th Eclogues 73   5
REPOSED
    Made uniforme to any state reposed.. . . . .   57 2nd Eclogues 30   31
REPRESENTED
    For that I finde in them parte of my estate represented. . .   35 1st Eclogues 13   115
REPRESS
    Word with word do not represse.. . . . .   328 Psalm XXXVIII   42
REPRESSED
    But in a minde that would his flames should not be
        repressed . . . .   33 1st Eclogues 13   60
REPROACH
    See what clouds of reproch small darke thy honour's skie,..   213 A&S 5th Song   23
    All my fierce Foes reproach on mee did cast; . . . .   313 Psalm XXXI   31
    All trouble, all reproche. . . . .   320 Psalm XXXIV   64

401

```
                                                                 PAGE    TITLE        LINE
REPROACHES
     Dicus. Dorus you wander farre in great reproches; . . . . .  50  2nd Eclogues 28    92
REPROVE
     Hath not Reason enough vehemence the desire to reprove?
          Prove. . . . . . . . . . . . . . . . . . . . . . . . .  63  2nd Eclogues 31    10
     O let not fooles in me thy workes reprove, . . . . . . . . . 236  Astrophil   107    13
REPULSE
     Ashe makes speares which shieldes do resist, her force no
          repulse takes: . . . . . . . . . . . . . . . . . . . .  36  1st Eclogues 13   136
     Gave repulse all grace excelling.. . . . . . . . . . . . . . 219  A&S 8th Song       68
REPUTATION
     Of singing take to thee the reputation.. . . . . . . . . . .  19  1st Eclogues  7   172
     Dorus. Of singing take to thee the reputation. . . . . . . .  19  1st Eclogues  7   173
     Of singing thou hast got the reputation. . . . . . . . . . .  20  1st Eclogues  7  V972
     Above line repeated at following location. . . . . . . . . .  20  1st Eclogues  7  V973
REPUTED
     Vertue, richesse, beawties of mine shall great be reputed. .  34  1st Eclogues 13    81
REQUEST
     Mirtle makes my request, my request is crown'd with a
          willowe. . . . . . . . . . . . . . . . . . . . . . . .  35  1st Eclogues 13   118
     Despaire most tragicall clause to a deadly request). . . . . 122  4th Eclogues 74    12
     The earth, her eares: the stake is my request: . . . . . . . 151  Cert Sonnets 22    45
REQUIRE
     His wished weale, what more he could require:. . . . . . . .   4  Lady of May   3     4
     And sorrows do require some respitt unto the sences. . . . .  37  1st Eclogues 13   175
     Nowe that I spye the haven my thoughtes requyre, . . . . . .  72  Arcadia III  37    15
     Who hold this fast no greater wealth require.. . . . . . . .  75  Arcadia III  44     8
     While that we doo what nature doth require,. . . . . . . . . 105  3rd Eclogues 67    65
     Our yeares doo it require: you see we both doo feele . . . . 120  4th Eclogues 73   121
     But now we muste needs yeelde, to what our othes require". . 121  4th Eclogues 73   169
     In wind or water streame do require to be writ.. . . . . . . 143  Cert Sonnets 13     4
     That He enquiringe, doth require just blood, . . . . . . . . 280  Psalm IX           33
REQUIRED
     Yet lives untill his life be new requirde. . . . . . . . . . 150  Cert Sonnets 22    24
REQUIRES
     That life and length of life requires, . . . . . . . . . . . 320  Psalm XXXIV        46
     A plaining songe plaine-singing vcice requires,. . . . . . . 242  Other Poems   4     3
REQUIRETH
     Leasure to weigh what due deserte requireth. . . . . . . . .  83  Arcadia III  57    10
     Nature above all things requireth this,. . . . . . . . . . . 105  3rd Eclogues 67    70
REQUITE
     Their merits to requite. . . . . . . . . . . . . . . . . . . 333  Psalm XLI          36
RESERVE
     "And ev'n in that love, shall I reserve him a spite".. . . .  30  1st Eclogues 11    18
     And God shall them in his own court reserve. . . . . . . . . 300  Psalm XXII         76
RESERVED
     Dorus. Lady, reservd by the heav'ns to do pastors' company
          honnor,. . . . . . . . . . . . . . . . . . . . . . . .  31  1st Eclogues 13     1
     Now that he finds to what end his life and love be reserved, 123  4th Eclogues 74    29
     Lady have you reserved,. . . . . . . . . . . . . . . . . . . 154  Cert Sonnets 25    19
RESIST
     Ashe makes speares which shieldes do resist, her force no
          repulse takes: . . . . . . . . . . . . . . . . . . . .  36  1st Eclogues 13   136
     And shall sensive things be sc sencelesse as to resist
          sence  . . . . . . . . . . . . . . . . . . . . . . . .  36  1st Eclogues 13   138
     To causefull wrath, which thou canst not resist. . . . . . .  59  2nd Eclogues 30    66
     Curst be the night which did your strife resist, . . . . . . 235  Astrophil   105    12
     But if they had, could shephockes this resist? . . . . . . . 246  Other Poems   4   160
RESISIANCE
     In this strange violence, to make resistance.. . . . . . . .  67  2nd Eclogues 33     2
RESOLVE
     And they againe resolve. . . . . . . . . . . . . . . . . . .  19  1st Eclogues  7   153
     Let us a perfect peace betwixt us two resolve: . . . . . . . 120  4th Eclogues 73   127
RESOLVED
     But cannot make resolved darkenes lighte:. . . . . . . . . .  73  Arcadia III  39    12
     But mankind is for aye to nought resolved. . . . . . . . . . 127  4th Eclogues 75    81
     Resolv'd to make me patterne of his might, . . . . . . . . . 135  Cert Sonnets  2     2
     For me alas I am full resolv'd . . . . . . . . . . . . . . . 153  Cert Sonnets 24    19
     I am resolv'd thy errour to maintaine, . . . . . . . . . . . 199  Astrophil    67    13
RESORT
     That to your strength your foes have sure resorte. . . . . .  38  Arcadia II   14    12
     Loath, I must leave his chiefe resort. . . . . . . . . . . .  88  Arcadia III  62    84
     My worke her workes to know, her dwelling my resorte.. . . . 117  4th Eclogues 73    42
     By them who of his rude resort complaine,. . . . . . . . . . 141  Cert Sonnets  8     4
     They first resort unto that soveraigne part; . . . . . . . . 236  Astrophil   107     4
     Sleeping, grants a free resort:. . . . . . . . . . . . . . . 202  A&S 2nd Song       14
RESCUND
     In these woods to resounde the renowmed name of a goddesse..  31  1st Eclogues 13    14
     To make these woods resounde thy lamentation?. . . . . . . .  47  2nd Eclogues 28     2
     That after death, to heav'n in woods' resound, . . . . . . .  56  2nd Eclogues 29   133
     The straunge resounde of these my causefull cries: . . . . . 125  4th Eclogues 75     6
     Yea through the Waters doth resound. . . . . . . . . . . . . 310  Psalm XXIX          9
RESPECT
     Show that Thy eyes respect a faithfull case; . . . . . . . . 289  Psalm XVII          6
     Mirth with respect, few words with curtesy,. . . . . . . . . 247  Other Poems   4   212
RESPECTS
     That I respects for both our sakes must show:. . . . . . . . 181  Astrophil    33    11
RESPITE
     And sorrows do require some respitt unto the sences. . . . .  37  1st Eclogues 13   175
     Sweete, for a while give respite to my hart, . . . . . . . . 236  Astrophil   107     5
```

*REST

	PAGE	TITLE		LINE
How dare I, wretch, seeke there my woes to rest, ...	3	Lady of May	1	5
Happie be they which well beleeve, and never seeke the rest.	12	Arcadia I	3	14
As for the rest, howe shepeheardes spend their daies, ...	28	1st Eclogues	10	46
Of those fortune lulls, so small rest rests in a kingdome. .	34	1st Eclogues	13	90
Bcth still do worke, in neither finde I rest:.	42	Arcadia II	22	3
With so strong lives, that bodie cannot rest	56	2nd Eclogues	29	145
And shall (o me) all this in ashes rest?	60	2nd Eclogues	30	101
Can thoughts still thinking so rest unappalled?.	61	2nd Eclogues	30	166
Of this we live, in this wee finde our rest, ...	75	Arcadia III	44	7
He farre did passe the rest of Shepheards all.	94	3rd Eclogues	64	18
This done, thou hast no more, but leave the rest	98	3rd Eclogues	65	13
Icleped starres; each thing to rest disposed:.	98	3rd Eclogues	66	10
Might freely rome, or rest, as seemed them:.	100	3rd Eclogues	66	48
I will you lende; the rest your selves must give, ...	101	3rd Eclogues	66	76
Doth hide his head with cares but onely how to rest:	117	4th Eclogues	73	24
The rest I cannot tell, for therewithall I wak'd	121	4th Eclogues	73	179
And thou o traytour Sleepe, made for to be our rest, ...	121	4th Eclogues	73	183
Unto my children alway good rest taking:.	139	Cert Sonnets	6	5
As this poore beast who did his rest forsake, ...	145	Cert Sonnets	16	7
The wood, above doth soone consuming rest.	150	Cert Sonnets	22	44
But all the rest, which feare durst not applie, ...	151	Cert Sonnets	22	49
She is the cause that all the rest I am.	151	Cert Sonnets	22	70
Vertue alas, now let me take some rest, ...	166	Astrophil	4	1
For that at length yet doth invite some rest, ...	229	Astrophil	96	13
To steale some rest, but wretch I am constraind, ...	230	Astrophil	98	6
Restlesse rest, and living dying.	218	A&S 8th Song		20
And then they that in him their only trust do rest, ...	272	Psalm II		31
Will lay me down, and take my rest:.	274	Psalm IV		32
Maugre their fcrce I will set him at rest.	285	Psalm XII		18
Lord, of Thy Holy Hill who shall the rest obtayne?	287	Psalm XV		2
Yea my flesh in hope shall rest.	288	Psalm XVI		30
Inward, an inward rest, ...	304	Psalm XXV		50
Nor my sins let my bones rest;	327	Psalm XXXVIII		9
When bedd from rest becomes his seat of woe, ...	333	Psalm XLI		9
As all the rest, so now the stone.	241	Other Poems	3	7
So Klaius' soule did in his Strephon rest.	242	Other Poems	4	29
Till one faire eav'n an howr ere Sun did rest, ...	247	Other Poems	4	205
Among the rest that there did take delight	251	Other Poems	4	361
First killing mirth, then banishing all rest, ...	253	Other Poems	4	431
This said, this done, he rase even tir'd with rest, ...	255	Other Poems	4	521
One among the rest electing.	262	Other Poems	7	17
Learning this among the rest, ...	264	Other Poems	7	75

RESTED

There rested then, to play a woman's part, ...	95	3rd Eclogues	64	39
Unto her rested sense a perfect waking, ...	137	Cert Sonnets	4	2

RESTETH

Now resteth onely this, which of us two is she, ...	120	4th Eclogues	73	135

RESTFUL

On pensive soules (in steede of restfull baite).	82	Arcadia III	56	6
The restfull Caves now restlesse visions give, ...	147	Cert Sonnets	18	9

RESTLESS

The restfull Caves now restlesse visions give, ...	147	Cert Sonnets	18	9
But finding not those restlesse flames in me, ...	173	Astrophil	16	5
Restlesse rest, and living dying.	218	A&S 8th Song		20
While those restles desires in great men rife.	243	Other Poems	4	62

RESTORE

He shall me restore to blisse, ...	334	Psalm XLII		22

RESTORED

Which cannot be restor'd by time nor industrie:.	214	A&S 5th Song		47
Should be restor'd by him above.	308	Psalm XXVII		51
Let them not restored be;	309	Psalm XXVIII		23
For it is Thou, that hast restord my light, ...	312	Psalm XXXI		14

RESTRAIN

That they thy sting restraine, ...	93	3rd Eclogues	63	89

RESTRAINED

Can I, that know her sacred parts, restrained be	61	2nd Eclogues	30	149
But their tongues restraind from walking, ...	218	A&S 8th Song		23

RESTS

Of those fortune lulls, so small rest rests in a kingdome. .	34	1st Eclogues	13	90
Disdaind with this, in deserts sought their restes;	102	3rd Eclogues	66	123
He rests me in green pasture his.	301	Psalm XXIII		4

RESTY

And no spurre can his resty race renew, ...	207	Astrophil	80	12

RETAINING

Once to Shepheard's God retayning, ...	262	Other Poems	7	11
Of all men to thee retaining, ...	263	Other Poems	7	65

RETIRED

Reason abasht retyred, ...	154	Cert Sonnets	25	7
From dungeon he retired, ...	331	Psalm XL		6

RETIRES

Another humbler wit to shepheard's pipe retires, ...	167	Astrophil	6	7

RETRAIT

Best charge, and bravest retrait in Cupid's fight, ...	206	Astrophil	79	5

RETURN

So that eyes' message doo returne rejected, ...	30	1st Eclogues	12	7
Least it might thee allure home to thy selfe to returne, . .	122	4th Eclogues	74	8
(Teares and teares of a man) had no returne to remorse; . . .	122	4th Eclogues	74	16
Wo, wo to me, on me returne the smart:	141	Cert Sonnets	9	1
To greater woes by presence I returne, ...	149	Cert Sonnets	21	10

```
RETURN                       (CONTINUED)                   PAGE    TITLE            LINE
    Let me home returne, stark blinded . . . . . . . . . . . .  220 A&S 8th Song       83
RETURNED
    That I e're I return'd destroyd them utterly . . . . . . . .  292 Psalm XVIII       69
REVEAL
    My lipps shall still reveale,. . . . . . . . . . . . . . . .  331 Psalm XL          38
REVEALED
    That to the sacred Muse my anoyes somewhat be revealed,. . .   31 1st Eclogues 13    9
    With monefull melodies, for enough our greefes be revealed,.   37 1st Eclogues 13  173
REVEALING
    Nature worketh enough with a small help for the revealing. .   33 1st Eclogues 13   61
REVEALS
    That forced with grief reveales what greeved eyes dyd see) .  118 4th Eclogues 73   56
REVENGE
    But if thy rage some brave revenge will finde, . . . . . . .   72 Arcadia III  38   13
    And eke revenge his wrong suspecting you". . . . . . . . . .   97 3rd Eclogues 64  108
    With mortall disdaine, bent to unendly revenge?. . . . . . .  123 4th Eclogues 74   36
    Unto revenge? O sweete, on a wretch wilt thou be revenged? .  123 4th Eclogues 74   37
    And to revenge who doo bend, would in that kind be revenged,  123 4th Eclogues 74   39
    And with more, by the lawes that to Revenge doo belong.. . .  123 4th Eclogues 74   42
    Passion unto my rage, Rage to a hasty revenge. . . . . . . .  124 4th Eclogues 74   68
    His Sire's revenge, joyn'd with a kingdome's gaine:. . . . .  204 Astrophil    75    6
    Revenge, revenge, my Muse, Defiance' trumpet blow: . . . . .  213 A&S 5th Song      32
    Bent to revenge and ever hating. . . . . . . . . . . . . . .  278 Psalm VIII         8
    He that is my revenge, in whom I realmes subdue, . . . . . .  293 Psalm XVIII       85
REVENGED
    Unto revenge? O sweete, on a wretch wilt thou be revenged? .  123 4th Eclogues 74   37
    And to revenge who doo bend, would in that kind be revenged,  123 4th Eclogues 74   39
REVERENCE
    Neither he beares reverence to a Prince nor pittie to
        begger . . . . . . . . . . . . . . . . . . . . . . . . .   31 1st Eclogues 13    5
    Are humbled thoughts, which bit of Reverence move, . . . . .  189 Astrophil    49    6
REVERENT
    For neere acquaintance dooth diminish reverent feare.. . . .  121 4th Eclogues 73  160
REVILED
    Revil'd for ech small fault, sometimes for none: . . . . . .  105 3rd Eclogues 67   53
REVIVED
    Till thou shalt revived be,. . . . . . . . . . . . . . . . .  227 A&S 10th Song     47
REVIVES
    He me revives, leads me the way. . . . . . . . . . . . . . .  301 Psalm XXIII        7
REVIVETH
    Elme embraste by a vine, embracing fancy reviveth. . . . . .   36 1st Eclogues 13  131
REVOLVED
    Time ever old, and yonge is still revolved . . . . . . . . .  127 4th Eclogues 75   79
REWARD
    Justely to graunt thy rewarde, such envie I beare to thy
        fortune. . . . . . . . . . . . . . . . . . . . . . . . .   37 1st Eclogues 13  156
    The lovely blowe with rare reward, my prayer is. . . . . . .   51 2nd Eclogues 28  112
    Silly rewarde! yet among women hath she of vertu the most.
        Most. . . . . . . . . . . . . . . . . . . . . . . . . .    64 2nd Eclogues 31   36
    Thus shall you both reward a lover true, . . . . . . . . . .   97 3rd Eclogues 64  107
    Nor breake my word though reward come late,. . . . . . . . .  153 Cert Sonnets 24   21
    Which for reward spoile it with vaine annoyes. . . . . . . .  174 Astrophil    18   11
    Is sawcinesse reward of curtesise?. . . . . . . . . . . . .   208 Astrophil    83   10
    Sweete reward for sharpest paine:. . . . . . . . . . . . . .  210 A&S 4th Song       4
    My justice, my just hands thus did the lord reward,. . . . .  292 Psalm XVIII       43
    Spare not them, give them reward . . . . . . . . . . . . . .  309 Psalm XXVIII      16
REWARDED
    We love, and have our loves rewarded.. . . . . . . . . . . .   14 1st Eclogues  6    1
    I cried, and was with open rayes rewarded: . . . . . . . . .   17 1st Eclogues  7   94
    Shall to the world appeare that faith and love be rewarded .  123 4th Eclogues 74   35
    Thus is his death rewarded,. . . . . . . . . . . . . . . . .  152 Cert Sonnets 23   15
    Shall fully be rewarded. . . . . . . . . . . . . . . . . . .  295 Psalm XIX         48
REWARDETH
    Cowards Love with losse rewardeth. . . . . . . . . . . . . .  202 A&S 2nd Song      16
RHUBARB
    But with your Rubarb words yow must contend. . . . . . . . .  171 Astrophil    14    5
RHYME
    And see you not that I fall now to ryme? . . . . . . . . . .  146 Cert Sonnets 17   40
RHYMES
    While shepheards' tunes be heard, or rimes be read,. . . . .   56 2nd Eclogues 29  124
    Into your rimes, running in ratling rowes: . . . . . . . . .  172 Astrophil    15    6
    If still I force her in sad rimes to creepe: . . . . . . . .  201 Astrophil    70    2
    For creeping rimes, which often sighings choke.. . . . . . .  242 Other Poems   4    8
RHYMING
    While I there speache in my rude ryminge pende.. . . . . . .   62 2nd Eclogues 30  187
RIBS
    Her ribbes in white well armed be. . . . . . . . . . . . . .   88 Arcadia III  62   68
    Which from the ribs of old  Parnassus flowes,. . . . . . . .  172 Astrophil    15    2
    From out my ribs, and puffing prove that I . . . . . . . . .  233 Astrophil   104   13
RICH
    The pasture rich, the wooll as soft as silke,. . . . . . . .    4 Lady of May   2   21
    Or when a rich rubie's just price be the worth of a walnut,.   34 1st Eclogues 13   78
    Then by my high Cedar, rich Ruby, and only shining Sunne,. .   34 1st Eclogues 13   80
    Your woll is riche: no tonge can tell my gayne.. . . . . . .   43 Arcadia II   23   14
    Will spoile the earth of his most rich attire. . . . . . . .   59 2nd Eclogues 30   88
    Hard like a rich marbell: hard, but a faire Diamond. . . . .  122 4th Eclogues 74   14
    Grow rich in that which never taketh rust: . . . . . . . . .  161 Cert Sonnets 32    3
    Whose porches rich (which name of cheekes endure) . . . . .  169 Astrophil     9    7
    Rich fooles there be, whose base and filthy hart . . . . . .  176 Astrophil    24    1
```

```
RICH                         (CONTINUED)            PAGE   TITLE           LINE
    But that rich foole, who by blind Fortune's lot. . . . . . .   177 Astrophil     24    9
    He knowes not) grow in only follie rich. . . . . . . . . .     177 Astrophil     24   14
    Doth even grow rich, naming my stella's name. . . . . . . . .  182 Astrophil     35   11
    Rich in all beauties which man's eye can see:. . . . . . . .   183 Astrophil     37    6
    Rich in the treasure of deserv'd renowne. . . . . . . . . .    183 Astrophil     37    9
    Rich in the riches of a royall hart, . . . . . . . . . . . .   183 Astrophil     37   10
    Rich in those gifts which give th'eternall crowne; . . . . .   183 Astrophil     37   11
    Who though most rich in these and everie part, . . . . . .     183 Astrophil     37   12
    Hath no misfortune, but that Rich she is. . . . . . . . . .    183 Astrophil     37   14
    Most rich, when most his riches it impart: . . . . . . . . .   206 Astrophil     79    7
    But thou rich in all joyes, doest rob my joyes from me, . . .  214 A&S 5th Song        46
    In a grove most rich of shade, . . . . . . . . . . . . . . .   217 A&S 8th Song         1
    Only rich in mischiefe's treasure. . . . . . . . . . . . .     221 A&S 9th Song        10
    Who poore and weake from rich and strong dost free, . . . . .  321 Psalm XXXV          22
    A heardman rich of much account was he, . . . . . . . . . .    245 Other Poems    4  117
    By north or south still rich adorned live: . . . . . . . . .   256 Other Poems    5   16
RICHES
    I saw that riches fall, and fell a crying; . . . . . . . .      17 1st Eclogues   7   88
    Her lipps are the riches the warres to maintaine, . . . . . .   67 2nd Eclogues  33    9
    Riches of children passe a Prince's throne; . . . . . . . .    106 3rd Eclogues  67  112
    Since thou my riches arte, and that thou haste . . . . . . .   114 4th Eclogues  72   29
    Rich in the riches of a royall hart, . . . . . . . . . . . .   183 Astrophil     37   10
    Copartner of the riches of that sight: . . . . . . . . . .     188 Astrophil     48    6
    Most rich, when most his riches it impart: . . . . . . . . .   206 Astrophil     79    7
    That they in riches flourish do. . . . . . . . . . . . . .     290 Psalm XVII          43
    Look but on this: man still doth riches heape. . . . . . . .   330 Psalm XXXIX         21
RICHESSE
    And vertue is gratefull with bewty and riches adorned, . . .    33 1st Eclogues  13 V 57
    Vertue, richesse, beawties of mine shall great be reputed. .    34 1st Eclogues  13   81
RICHEST
    The richest gemme of Love and life enjoyes, . . . . . . . . .  177 Astrophil     24   10
RICHLY
    Since in sweete you all goods so richly raigne, . . . . . . .   39 Arcadia II    16    5
    In time that, richly di'de, . . . . . . . . . . . . . . . .    258 Other Poems    5   70
RICHNESS
    And vertue is gratefull with bewty and richnes adorned, . . .   33 1st Eclogues  13   57
RID
    And rid me from the wrongs which cruel Witts did brew; . . .   293 Psalm XVIII         87
RIDDLE
    For of my life I must a riddle tell. . . . . . . . . . . . .   183 Astrophil     37    4
RIDDLES
    Will. What? these are riddles sure, art thou then bound to
        her? . . . . . . . . . . . . . . . . . . . . . . . . . .   343 Possibly       1   23
RIDE
    In highest way of heav'n the Sunne did ride, . . . . . . .     175 Astrophil     22    1
RIDER
    The raines wherewith my Rider doth me tie, . . . . . . . . .   189 Astrophil     49    5
RIDES
    How to the woods love runnes as well as rydes to the
        Pallace . . . . . . . . . . . . . . . . . . . . . . . .     31 1st Eclogues  13    4
RIDGE
    Along whose ridge such bones are met, . . . . . . . . . . . .   89 Arcadia III   62  111
RIDING
    Who is this glorious King in might and power riding? . . . .   302 Psalm XXIV          19
RIFE
    A Shop of shame, a Booke where blots be rife . . . . . . . .    57 2nd Eclogues  30   26
    Not sparing me, in whom his workes be rife: . . . . . . . .    114 4th Eclogues  72   15
    While those restles desires in great men rife. . . . . . .     243 Other Poems    4   62
*RIGHT
    Thus Reason to his servants yeelds his right; . . . . . . .     12 Arcadia I      2   11
    Thus reason to his Servantes gyves his right . . . . . . .      12 Arcadia I      2 V811
    If he be blind, how hitteth he so right? . . . . . . . . .      21 1st Eclogues   8    9
    Goe graft againe, and seeke to graft them right, . . . . .      26 1st Eclogues   9  129
    Give right sound to the eares, and enter aright to the
        judgement; . . . . . . . . . . . . . . . . . . . . . . .    32 1st Eclogues  13   18
    O tongues right ladders made to clime dishonour, . . . . .      50 2nd Eclogues  28   90
    With sense possest, and claim'd by reason's right: . . . . .    74 Arcadia III   42    6
    Right so my thoughts, whereon my hart I feede . . . . . . .     78 Arcadia III   50    5
    Right so my inwarde partes, and outward glasse, . . . . . .     78 Arcadia III   50    6
    You none can clayme but you your selfe by right, . . . . .      79 Arcadia III   50   19
    In this rare subject from thy common right: . . . . . . . .     79 Arcadia III   51   10
    Care upon care (in steede of doing right). . . . . . . . .      82 Arcadia III   56    7
    While thy known course, observing nature's right, . . . . .     82 Arcadia III   56   11
    All strife for toyes, and clayming master's right: . . . .      93 3rd Eclogues  63   67
    Not sturring thoughts, nor yet denying right, . . . . . . .     98 3rd Eclogues  65    6
    Her right arme naked was, discovered was her breast. . . . .   118 4th Eclogues  73   68
    Right so my boiling hart, enflam'de with fire of a faire
        eye . . . . . . . . . . . . . . . . . . . . . . . . . .    123 4th Eclogues  74   27
    Right so my minde, caught by his guiding eye . . . . . . .     144 Cert Sonnets  15    5
    By conquest's right in steade of searching kill. . . . . .     150 Cert Sonnets  22   30
    I now have learn'd Love right, and learn'd even so, . . . .    173 Astrophil     16   13
    Your words my friend (right healthfull caustiks) blame . . .   175 Astrophil     21    1
    How Poles' right king meanes, without leave of hoast, . . .    180 Astrophil     30    3
    Hart rent thy selfe, thou doest thy selfe but right, . . . .   181 Astrophil     33    5
    And if these things, as being thine by right, . . . . . . .    184 Astrophil     39   12
    And now hath made me to his hand so right, . . . . . . . .     189 Astrophil     49   13
    That his right badge is but worne in the hart: . . . . . .     192 Astrophil     54   12
    Which, coupling Doves, guides Venus' chariot right. . . . .    206 Astrophil     79    4
    Thy teares expresse night's native moisture right. . . . .     229 Astrophil     96    8
```

```
*RIGHT              (CONTINUED)                           PAGE    TITLE          LINE
    I would know by what right this palenesse overcame . . . . .  232 Astrophil  102    7
    Stella since thou so right a Princesse art . . . . . . . . .  236 Astrophil  107    1
    The barre to plead their right,. . . . . . . . . . . . . . .  215 A&S 6th Song     11
    The Heathen for thy Child's right, and will thy realme
        extend . . . . . . . . . . . . . . . . . . . . . . . .  271 Psalm II          19
    For Thou my cause, my right Thou hast maintaind, . . . . . .  279 Psalm IX           8
    Of judging right.. . . . . . . . . . . . . . . . . . . . . .  279 Psalm IX          10
    Up lord, and judg the Gentyls in Thy right . . . . . . . . .  281 Psalm IX          61
    And he my right hand doth guard, . . . . . . . . . . . . . .  288 Psalm XVI         26
    He made my cumbrous way to me most plainly right.. . . . . .  292 Psalm XVIII       60
    Thou gavest me saving shield, Thy right hand was my stay;. .  292 Psalm XVIII       64
    And night to night succeding right . . . . . . . . . . . . .  293 Psalm XIX          7
    Gcd's doomes be right, and cheer the sprite, . . . . . . . .  294 Psalm XIX         33
    And that by right upon all Realmes he raigneth.. . . . . . .  300 Psalm XXII        70
    Teach lord, lord lead me Thy right way,. . . . . . . . . . .  308 Psalm XXVII       52
    Direct me how to go, and guide me right, . . . . . . . . . .  312 Psalm XXXI         9
    Ev'ill men work ill to utmost right, . . . . . . . . . . . .  325 Psalm XXXVII      33
    God, loving right, doth not forsake. . . . . . . . . . . . .  326 Psalm XXXVII      69
    Let them guide me right. . . . . . . . . . . . . . . . . . .  336 Psalm XLIII       14
    Nous sware it was no right; for his default. . . . . . . . .  250 Other Poems   4  314
RIGHTEOUS
    Thou righteous proofes to hearts, and reines dost send,. . .  277 Psalm VII         28
    Thou righteous art, Thou strong, thou patient,. . . . . . .  277 Psalm VII         31
    Whose deeds of Righteous heart, whose hearty words be plain,  287 Psalm XV           4
    That righteous be; . . . . . . . . . . . . . . . . . . . . .  316 Psalm XXXIII       2
    Mcst righteous is. . . . . . . . . . . . . . . . . . . . . .  316 Psalm XXXIII      17
    I say, I say the Righteous minds . . . . . . . . . . . . . .  326 Psalm XXXVII      73
    The Wicked watch the righteous much. . . . . . . . . . . . .  326 Psalm XXXVII      81
RIGHTEOUSNESS
    His righteousness, and this his doing glorious.. . . . . . .  300 Psalm XXII        78
    Which righteousness doth take, . . . . . . . . . . . . . . .  301 Psalm XXIII        8
    Sweet Righteousness shall he receive,. . . . . . . . . . . .  302 Psalm XXIV        14
    Of grace and righteousness . . . . . . . . . . . . . . . . .  303 Psalm XXV         31
    But save me, save me in Thy righteousness, . . . . . . . . .  312 Psalm XXXI         3
    He righteousness approves. . . . . . . . . . . . . . . . . .  316 Psalm XXXIII      19
    That yet beare love unto my righteousness; . . . . . . . . .  323 Psalm XXXV        68
    Thy Righteousness like hugest hills, . . . . . . . . . . . .  323 Psalm XXXVI       15
    O then Thy righteousness impart. . . . . . . . . . . . . . .  324 Psalm XXXVI       29
    Of This sweet righteousness. . . . . . . . . . . . . . . . .  331 Psalm XL          37
RIGHTFUL
    A rightfull Prince by unright deeds a Tyran groweth. . . . .  214 A&S 5th Song      60
    In my sound rightfull way, . . . . . . . . . . . . . . . . .  334 Psalm XLI         42
RIGHTFULNESS
    But still, although we faile of perfect rightfulnes, . . . .   61 2nd Eclogues 30 137
    Doth cherish rightfulness. . . . . . . . . . . . . . . . . .  316 Psalm XXXIII       6
RIGHTLY
    If by the parties ment our meanings rightly be marked, . . .   37 1st Eclogues 13 174
    Thinges rightelie prizde, love is the bande of love. . . . .   83 Arcadia III  57  14
    Thy common-wealth may rightly grieved be,. . . . . . . . . .  105 3rd Eclogues 67  76
    Let Dirge be sung, and Trentals rightly read,. . . . . . . .  160 Cert Sonnets 30  21
    O they be rightly blest. . . . . . . . . . . . . . . . . . .  272 Psalm II          32
    She went, they staid; or rightly for to say, . . . . . . . .  246 Other Poems   4  169
RIGHTS
    Sorow pay we unto the rights of Nature,. . . . . . . . . . .  109 Arcadia IV   70    5
RIGORCUS
    Where rigrows exile lockes up all my sense?. . . . . . . . .  233 Astrophil   104    8
RIND
    Her soule, arm'd but with such a dainty rind,. . . . . . . .  193 Astrophil    57    7
RINE
    My inward hurte should spare thy outward rine? . . . . . . .   77 Arcadia III  47    8
    My thoughtes then hers, who first your ryne did rente, . . .   78 Arcadia III  49  14
RING
    Ring out your belles, let mourning shewes be spread, . . . .  159 Cert Sonnets 30   1
RIP
    I should so rashly ripp up.. . . . . . . . . . . . . . . . .   66 2nd Eclogues 32  18
RIPE
    Nico. Alas how oft I looke on cherries ripe, . . . . . . . .   54 2nd Eclogues 29  75
RISE
    But in a palme when I marke, how he doth rise under a
        burden . . . . . . . . . . . . . . . . . . . . . . . .   36 1st Eclogues 13 127
    But there againe the flesh doth rise . . . . . . . . . . . .   89 Arcadia III  62 101
    Some cause there is, which of strange cause doth rise: . . .  147 Cert Sonnets 18   2
    Thus do I fall to rise thus, . . . . . . . . . . . . . . . .  154 Cert Sonnets 25  27
    That her sweete breath makes oft thy flames to rise, . . . .  170 Astrophil    12    4
    Whence those same fumes of melancholy rise,. . . . . . . . .  176 Astrophil    23    3
    His praise to sleight, which from good use doth rise; . . .  185 Astrophil    41    7
    O honied sighs, which from that breast do rise,. . . . . . .  231 Astrophil   100    5
    Then rise and come abroad, . . . . . . . . . . . . . . . . .  282 Psalm X           49
    Not I but thou throw'st down those, who 'gainst me do rise;.  292 Psalm XVIII       72
    Doth rise again, new joyes shall rise. . . . . . . . . . . .  311 Psalm XXX         18
    But rise, but wake that I may judgment gett. . . . . . . . .  322 Psalm XXXV        57
    Who never more must rise.. . . . . . . . . . . . . . . . . .  333 Psalm XLI         28
RISING
    Pcpler changeth his hew from a rising sunne to a setting:. .   36 1st Eclogues 13 132
    Rysing from lowe, are to the highest bente;. . . . . . . . .   78 Arcadia III  49  16
    And yet could not by rising Morne foresee. . . . . . . . . .  181 Astrophil    33  12
RITES
    Poore Layman I, for sacred rites unfit.. . . . . . . . . . .  203 Astrophil    74    4
```

	PAGE	TITLE		LINE
RIVAL				
Thus Death becomes a rivall to us all, ...	59	2nd Eclogues	30	89
RIVAL'S				
With Jove's disdaine at such a rival's seed, ...	21	1st Eclogues	8	20
RIVER				
In river as I look'd my pining face, ...	254	Other Poems	4	475
RIVER'S				
Nico. To river's banke, being a walking brought, ...	55	2nd Eclogues	29	111
Lay by a river's side, ...	256	Other Poems	5	2
RIVERS				
First the rivers shall ceasse to repay their fludds to the Ocean:	33	1st Eclogues	13	65
Faire Rocks, goodly rivers, sweet woods, when shall I see peace? Peace.	62	2nd Eclogues	31	1
And like two rivers sweete, ...	92	3rd Eclogues	63	33
ROAM				
Might freely rome, or rest, as seemed them:	100	3rd Eclogues	66	48
ROAR				
Yea I roare, ...	328	Psalm XXXVIII		23
ROARED				
Or roar'd, my bones still wasted;	315	Psalm XXXII		9
ROARING				
Roring, and howling for to have a King.	100	3rd Eclogues	66	63
O Echo, all these woods with roaring fill, ...	126	4th Eclogues	75	31
So farr from hearing to my roaring cryes.	298	Psalm XXII		4
Like lions fierce, with roaring jawes enlarged.	299	Psalm XXII		30
ROB				
In one true chest to rob all Vertue's treasure?	126	4th Eclogues	75	47
But thou rich in all joyes, doest rob my joyes from me, . . .	214	A&S 5th Song		46
Yet gentle English theeves do rob, but will not slay;	214	A&S 5th Song		49
ROBBED				
In silence, from a man's owne selfe with company robbed. . .	35	1st Eclogues	13	106
For ever robbed of our royall treasure.	130	4th Eclogues	76	30
No force, no fraud, robd thee of thy delight, ...	181	Astrophil	33	7
ROCK				
Yet never rock, nor race, suche terror brought, ...	71	Arcadia III	37	3
On rocke, Despaire, the buriall of my blisse.	114	4th Eclogues	72	50
Klaius. On rocke, Despaire, the buriall of my blisse	115	4th Eclogues	72	51
My strength my strongest rock, which my defence hast borne, .	290	Psalm XVIII		2
Then live Jehova still, my rock still blessed be;	293	Psalm XVIII		83
Be my strong rock, be Thou my forteress.	312	Psalm XXXI		6
Indeed Thou art my rock, my Forteress;	312	Psalm XXXI		7
ROCKS				
Faire Rocks, goodly rivers, sweet woods, when shall I see peace? Peace.	62	2nd Eclogues	31	1
Where rockes do wayte, for theym the wyndes do chase, ...	70	Arcadia III	36	2
When strugling rocks he would imbrace.	88	Arcadia III	62	70
The Rockes which were of constant mind the marke	147	Cert Sonnets	18	5
Rockes, woods, hilles, caves, dales, meads, brookes, answere me, ...	147	Cert Sonnets	18	13
Which rotting on the rockes, their death do dye:	151	Cert Sonnets	22	52
ROCKY				
Yea noble hight of Rocky Hill.	307	Psalm XXVII		28
A steadfast rocky stone, ...	331	Psalm XL		9
ROD				
When for so soft a rod deare play he trie?	203	Astrophil	73	4
Thy rodd and Thy staffe be	301	Psalm XXIII		14
And his sweet grace streight easd the rod.	315	Psalm XXXII		17
But when the rod began to play his part, ...	246	Other Poems	4	183
ROGUE				
Her face? O Love, a Rogue thou then shouldst be, ...	187	Astrophil	46	6
Like Rogue, all ragged goe, ...	257	Other Poems	5	25
ROLL				
With inward cries putts up a bitter role	85	Arcadia III	61	3
Within the sinners' roll, ...	306	Psalm XXVI		29
Who for my hurt each way their thoughts did roll.	321	Psalm XXXV		10
For in Thy book's roll I am writt, ...	331	Psalm XL		32
ROME				
From all the world, her heart is then his rome, ...	186	Astrophil	43	13
ROOF				
My tong to this my roofe cleaves, ...	66	2nd Eclogues	32	12
No, though tongue to roofe be cleaved, ...	139	Cert Sonnets	7	8
My cleaving tongue close to my roofe doth bide.	299	Psalm XXII		36
ROOFS				
Pearching within square royall rooves, ...	89	Arcadia III	62	114
ROOM				
And farre unfit to hold so good a roome.	94	3rd Eclogues	64	6
That he for want of elbowe roome must die?	126	4th Eclogues	75	44
Never roome more apt for it;	219	A&S 8th Song		54
When thou hast mynd to weepe, seeke out som smoky room: . . .	343	Possibly	1	11
ROOMS				
Large roomes within, where droppes distill amaine:	150	Cert Sonnets	22	32
ROOMY				
Mine eyes the streight, the roomie cave, my minde, ...	150	Cert Sonnets	22	35
ROOST				
P. And Passion will, that Passion rule the rost.	46	2nd Eclogues	27	6
ROOT				
Dorus. Sight is his roote, in thought is his progression, . .	48	2nd Eclogues	28	37
Sweete roote say thou, the roote of my desire.	77	Arcadia III	48	1
This noble Cedar's pretious roote:	89	Arcadia III	62	106

ROOT	(CONTINUED)	PAGE	TITLE		LINE
Yet now the roote of him abase you would.		106	3rd Eclogues	67	99
And shalt root out the tongues to lying bent:.		275	Psalm V		14
Root out their generation.		297	Psalm XXI		40
A widow turtle neere on bared root		256	Other Poems	5	6

ROOTED

| But when his seate so rooted he had found, ... | | 102 | 3rd Eclogues | 66 | 113 |
| When rooted moisture failes, or groweth drie,. . . . . | | 128 | 4th Eclogues | 75 | 113 |

ROOTS

| The flying sprites which trees by rootes up teare. . . . . . | | 114 | 4th Eclogues | 72 | 36 |
| My feete are turn'd to rootes, my hart becommeth lead, . . . | | 215 | A&S 5th Song | | 77 |

ROPE

| But in the place found nothing but a rope. . . . . | | 55 | 2nd Eclogues | 29 | 92 |

*ROSE

A Lillie field, with plowe of Rose which tilled is..		15	1st Eclogues	7	30
Milke hands, rose cheeks, or lips more sweet, more red,. . .		225	Astrophil	91	7
Morne's messenger, with rose enameld skies		231	Astrophil	99	10

ROSED

| Did not a rosed breath, from lips more rosie proceeding, . . | | 124 | 4th Eclogues | 74 | 79 |

ROSES

Pas. Alas, when I in spring meet roses rathe,.		54	2nd Eclogues	29	78
Rubies, Cherries, and Roses new, ...		87	Arcadia III	62	39
Where roses gueuls are borne in silver field..		171	Astrophil	13	11
Making those Lillies and those Roses grow, ...		231	Astrophil	100	2
Where be those Roses gone, which sweetned so our eyes? . . .		232	Astrophil	102	1
There those roses for to kisse,.		226	A&S 10th Song		28

ROSE-WATER

| And for Rose-water sould of rarest smell.. . . . . | | 55 | 2nd Eclogues | 29 | 110 |

ROSY

Did not a rosed breath, from lips more rosie proceeding, . .		124	4th Eclogues	74	79
A rosie garland, and a wearie hed:		184	Astrophil	39	11
With such a rosie morne, whose beames most freshly gay . . .		205	Astrophil	76	7
How rosy moist'ned lipps about his beake		244	Other Poems	4	95

ROT

| Whom he doth curse to naught shall rott. . . . . | | 326 | Psalm XXXVII | | 56 |

ROTTEN

Not rotten sheepe, but high crownes she surpasseth all.. . .		16	1st Eclogues	7	57
Only fond youth admires a rotten stocke.		25	1st Eclogues	9	89
When rotten Fame will tell their blowes.		44	Arcadia II	25	10
But rotten bleeding argues evill complection		50	2nd Eclogues	28	V883
But golde can guild a rotten piece of wood,.		245	Other Poems	4	124

ROTTING

| Which rotting on the rockes, their death do dye: . . . . . . | | 151 | Cert Sonnets | 22 | 52 |

ROUND

The circle is my (round about her) sight:.		17	1st Eclogues	7	103
Who hunting round the strongest for to kill, ...		50	2nd Eclogues	28	84
Like pomels round of Marble cleere:.		87	Arcadia III	62	55
There ofte steales out that round cleane foote		89	Arcadia III	62	105
Like comfits round in marchpane set.		89	Arcadia III	62	112
Though legions round be layd,.		272	Psalm III		20
His Angels Armys round		319	Psalm XXXIV		25
Never the earth on his round shoulders bare.		247	Other Poems	4	209
With larger round, to shun the folowing feet..		250	Other Poems	4	332

ROUT

| I am enclosed with young Bulls' madded route,. . . . . | | 299 | Psalm XXII | | 27 |
| Yea worse than doggs, a naughty wicked rout. . . . . | | 299 | Psalm XXII | | 40 |

ROW

Of pretious pearle the double rowe,.		87	Arcadia III	62	42
Nor blushing Lillies, nor pearles' ruby-hidden row,.		213	A&S 5th Song		38
And set their arrows in a rowe		284	Psalm XI		6
In chastest plaies, till home they walke a rowe, ...		243	Other Poems	4	54

ROWS

| Into your rimes, running in ratling rowes: . . . . | | 172 | Astrophil | 15 | 6 |
| At length in rowes of Kisse-cheeke teares they raine.. . . . | | 245 | Other Poems | 4 | 128 |

ROYAL

Pearching within square royall rooves, ...		89	Arcadia III	62	114
For ever robbed of our royall treasure..		130	4th Eclogues	76	30
Yet hiding royall bloud full oft in rurall vaine..		167	Astrophil	6	8
Rich in the riches of a royall hart, ...		183	Astrophil	37	10

RP

| R.P. Then let us both to heavenly rules give place,. . . . . | | 47 | 2nd Eclogues | 27 | 41 |

RUBBED

| As rubies lustre, when they rubbed be. . . . . | | 252 | Other Poems | 4 | 396 |

RUBBING

| Or rubbing hurt the sore, I here doo end.. . . . . | | 62 | 2nd Eclogues | 30 | 183 |

RUBIES

Rubies, Cherries, and Roses new, ...		87	Arcadia III	62	39
Whence hast thou Ivorie, Rubies, pearle and gold,.		181	Astrophil	32	10
Opening rubies, pearles deviding..		226	A&S 10th Song		30
As rubies lustre, when they rubbed be.		252	Other Poems	4	396

RUBY

| Then by my high Cedar, rich Ruby, and only shining Sunne,. . | | 34 | 1st Eclogues | 13 | 80 |

RUBY-HIDDEN

| Nor blushing Lillies, nor pearles' ruby-hidden row,. . . . . | | 213 | A&S 5th Song | | 38 |

RUBY'S

| Or when a rich rubie's just price be the worth of a walnut,. | | 34 | 1st Eclogues | 13 | 78 |

RUDDY

A ruddie haire his cote, with fine long specled face:. . . .		53	2nd Eclogues	29	42
Lips red and plum, as cherrie's ruddy side,.		76	Arcadia III	46	8
But who those ruddie lippes can misse?		87	Arcadia III	62	37

```
RUDDY                         (CONTINUED)                    PAGE   TITLE              LINE
    O kisse, which doest those ruddie gemmes impart, . . . . . .  207  Astrophil      81      1
RUDE
    While I there speache in my rude ryminge pende.. . . . . . .   62  2nd Eclogues 30    187
    Ne doo I care how rude be my invention, . . . . . . . . . .   128  4th Eclogues 75    104
    By them who of his rude resort complaine,. . . . . . . . . .  141  Cert Sonnets  8      4
    Not by rude force, but sweetest soveraigntie . . . . . . . .  201  Astrophil     71      6
    Most rude dispaire my daily unbidden guest, . . . . . . . .   236  Astrophil    108      7
    Their sences rude plaine objects only move, . . . . . . . .   245  Other Poems   4    143
RUDEST
    Prints his owne lively forme in rudest braine. . . . . . . .  194  Astrophil     58      8
RUE
    As for the gentle birds, like case might rewe. . . . . . . .  102  3rd Eclogues 66    139
    Till by such hap, as I must ever rewe, . . . . . . . . . . .  115  4th Eclogues 72     74
    But they do faile, and in their mazed corners rew. . . . . .  293  Psalm XVIII         82
    To make thee nor thy better-loved rue: . . . . . . . . . . .  258  Other Poems   5     81
RUETH
    Onely at you all envie hopelesse rueth.. . . . . . . . . . .  197  A&S 1st Song        24
RUGGEDST
    But when the ruggedst step of Fortune's race . . . . . . . .  195  Astrophil     60      5
RUIN
    Nor courteous ruin of proffered usury, . . . . . . . . . . .   69  2nd Eclogues 34     21
    Of Prince's harte quite lost the ruine strange.. . . . . . .   81  Arcadia III  55      6
    Ruine, the winde, hath blowne her from her scope:. . . . . .  114  4th Eclogues 72     48
    When it blowne up with myne a fall of ruine takes) . . . . .  118  4th Eclogues 73     52
    O you (alas so I find) cause of his onely ruine. . . . . . .  122  4th Eclogues 74      4
    O my vayne worde gon, Ruyn of my glory.. . . . . . . . . . .  138  Cert Sonnets  5     14
    But yet in vaine thou hast my ruine sought, . . . . . . . .   161  Cert Sonnets 31      9
    Of sinfull thoughts, which do in ruine end?. . . . . . . . .  172  Astrophil     14      8
    Of Lover's ruine some sad Tragedie:. . . . . . . . . . . . .  187  Astrophil     45     13
    Let my chaunge to ruine be.. . . . . . . . . . . . . . . . .  234  A&S 11th Song       10
    Let their vile thoughts the thinkers' ruin be. . . . . . . .  275  Psalm V             30
    That poore from ruine may be stayd:. . . . . . . . . . . . .  283  Psalm X             78
    Least my Foe bragg, that in my ruin hee. . . . . . . . . . .  286  Psalm XIII          13
    Let me not ruin quite; . . . . . . . . . . . . . . . . . . .  302  Psalm XXV            4
    Who helpest those, whose ruin was so neere, . . . . . . . .   321  Psalm XXXV          23
    That lift themselves my ruin for to frame. . . . . . . . . .  323  Psalm XXXV          66
    Who victor seem'd, was to his ruine brought: . . . . . . . .  251  Other Poems   4    346
RUINED
    But in the pitt he ruind first did fall, . . . . . . . . . .  278  Psalm VII           41
    Both ruines, ruiners, and ruin'd plott . . . . . . . . . . .  280  Psalm IX            19
    None, I say still, shall ruind be.. . . . . . . . . . . . . .  321  Psalm XXXIV         79
RUINERS
    Both ruines, ruiners, and ruin'd plott . . . . . . . . . . .  280  Psalm IX            19
RUING
    Rewing change of wonted state, . . . . . . . . . . . . . . .  262  Other Poems   7      9
RUINOUS
    (Opprest with ruinouse conceites) by the helpe of an
        outcrye . . . . . . . . . . . . . . . . . . . . . . . .    35  1st Eclogues 13    109
    Which lest the ruinous want of government dissolve;. . . . .  120  4th Eclogues 73    128
RUIN'S
    Ruine's relique, care's web, and sorrowe's foode: . . . . .    23  1st Eclogues  9     29
    A wreched wracke, a glasse of Ruine's ende.. . . . . . . . .   73  Arcadia III  40      4
RUINS
    Dwell in my ruines, feede with sucking smarte, . . . . . . .  113  4th Eclogues 72      9
    The ruines of her conquest to espie: . . . . . . . . . . . .  199  Astrophil     67      3
    Both ruines, ruiners, and ruin'd plott . . . . . . . . . . .  280  Psalm IX            19
RULE
    P. And Passion will, that Passion rule the rost. . . . . . .   46  2nd Eclogues 27      6
    And laying downe my head, did nature's rule observe, . . . .  117  4th Eclogues 73     27
    "How ill both you can rule, well hath your discord taught: .  121  4th Eclogues 73    163
    Yet craving law of armes, whose rule doth teach, . . . . . .  135  Cert Sonnets  1     10
    Where her who should rule paine, false paine abuseth.. . . .  142  Cert Sonnets 11     14
    One hand forgott to rule, th'other to fight. . . . . . . . .  191  Astrophil     53     11
    If Rule by force without all claime a Tyran showeth, . . . .  214  A&S 5th Song        57
    Therfore (O Kings), be wise, O Rulers rule your mind, . . .   271  Psalm II            23
    Sinne from all rule in you depose, . . . . . . . . . . . . .  273  Psalm IV            17
    To rule the Works of Thyne own hands . . . . . . . . . . . .  279  Psalm VIII          22
    The unworn paths, his rule embraceth.. . . . . . . . . . . .  279  Psalm VIII          32
    And this his rule for aye remains. . . . . . . . . . . . . .  310  Psalm XXIX          27
    Wholy devoy'd of Reason's rule, . . . . . . . . . . . . . .   315  Psalm XXXII         32
RULED
    How elder rul'd their flocks, and cur'd their smart, . . . .  243  Other Poems   4     37
    In sum, proud Boreas never ruled fleet . . . . . . . . . . .  251  Other Poems   4    373
RULERS
    Rulers will thinke all things made them to please, . . . . .  100  3rd Eclogues 66     73
    Therfore (O Kings), be wise, O Rulers rule your mind, . . .   271  Psalm II            23
RULES
    But for that Love's desire most rules the eyes, . . . . . .    22  1st Eclogues  8     41
    R.p. Then let us both to heavenly rules give place, . . . .    47  2nd Eclogues 27     41
    In morall rules let raging woes contained be?. . . . . . . .   61  2nd Eclogues 30    151
    Our foolish lustes in honest rules to stay.. . . . . . . . .  103  3rd Eclogues 67      3
    Where they by wisdome's Rules directed are, . . . . . . . .   106  3rd Eclogues 67    104
    In whom of all my rules the perfect proofe I finde, . . . .   119  4th Eclogues 73     94
    Ought to be king, from whose rules who do swerve, . . . . .   167  Astrophil      5      3
    And if these rules did faile, proofe makes me sure, . . . .   178  Astrophil     26     12
    Rules with a becke, so tyrannizeth thee, . . . . . . . . . .  187  Astrophil     46      3
    O Grammer rules, o now your vertues show;. . . . . . . . . .  196  Astrophil     63      1
    For rage now rules the reynes, which guided were by
        Pleasure . . . . . . . . . . . . . . . . . . . . . . . .  213  A&S 5th Song        15
```

		PAGE	TITLE	LINE

RULES   (CONTINUED)
    For what lord rules our bold emboldned breast. . . . . 285 Psalm XII   12
RULEST
    O lord that rul'st Our mortall lyne. . . . . 278 Psalm VIII   1
    Above line repeated at following location. . . . . 279 Psalm VIII   33
RULING
    In ruling of a house so well shee's seene. . . . . 106 3rd Eclogues 67   90
    The Voice of that lord ruling us . . . . 310 Psalm XXIX   10
RUMOR
    With long large eares where never rumour dyes. . . . . 21 1st Eclogues 8   28
    They deeme, and of their doome the rumour flies, ... 178 Astrophil 27   5
RUN
    Let voice of Sighes into cleare musike runne, ... 84 Arcadia III 59   13
    A Satyre once did runne away for dread, ... 145 Cert Sonnets 16   1
    My lake is sense, whose still streames never runne, ... 150 Cert Sonnets 22   15
    I willing run, yet while I run, repent. . . . . 174 Astrophil 19   4
    O give my passions leave to run their race: . . . . 198 Astrophil 64   2
    From my deare Captainnesse to run away?. . . . . 223 Astrophil 88   2
    And from lowts to run away.. . . . . 235 A&S 11th Song   45
    Who to other Gods do run, ... 288 Psalm XVI   10
    Not weighing ought how fleshly fancys run, ... 289 Psalm XVII   13
    To runne their mighty races. . . . . 294 Psalm XIX   24
    For proof, while I my race did run . . . . 311 Psalm XXX   19
    To looke and run to him for aid, ... 319 Psalm XXXIV   18
    But Dick my counsell marke: run from the place of wo: . . . . 344 Possibly 1   41
    When, if nede were, they could at quintain run: . . . . 243 Other Poems 4   56
    They saw a maid who thitherward did runne, ... 244 Other Poems 4   83
    And he by law of Barly-brake must run. . . . . 249 Other Poems 4   296
    To runne, brake from his hands, and let him goe. . . . . . . 250 Other Poems 4   336
    Though with soft leggs, did run as fast as he. . . . . 250 Other Poems 4   339
    His soule did fly as she was seen to run. . . . . 251 Other Poems 4   372
RUNAGATE
    The wretch compell'd a runnagate became, ... 21 1st Eclogues 8   21
RUNAWAY
    Unto Dianae's train thou runaway didst flee: . . . . 214 A&S 5th Song   71
    You Rebell run away, to Lord and Lady untrue, ... 215 A&S 5th Song   86
RUNNING
    Thy running course cannot such beawties marke: . . . . 80 Arcadia III 52   11
    Their running fall into a constant vaine . . . . 150 Cert Sonnets 22   38
    Into your rimes, running in ratling rowes: . . . . 172 Astrophil 15   6
    Unto the dust of my death's running hower; . . . . 299 Psalm XXII   38
    But as his heate with running did augment, ... 249 Other Poems 4   297
RUNS
    How to the woods love runnes as well as rydes to the
        Pallace . . . . 31 1st Eclogues 13   4
    While brickle houreglas runnes, guide thou our panting race: 45 Arcadia II 26   10
    Time runnes away for sorow: . . . . 136 Cert Sonnets 3   6
    As thy lookes sturre, runs up and downe to make. . . . . . . 232 Astrophil 101   10
    Now runnes, and takes hir in his clipping armes. . . . . . . 252 Other Poems 4   384
RURAL
    Joyning your sweete voice to the rurall muse of a deserte, . 31 1st Eclogues 13   2
    Of growing trees, yee rurall Gods that wield . . . . 40 Arcadia II 18   2
    Yet hiding royall bloud full oft in rurall vaine. . . . . . . 167 Astrophil 6   8
RUST
    Which though of glittring golde, shall heere take rust . . . 92 3rd Eclogues 63   57
    Let golde now rust, let Diamonds waste in thee: . . . . 125 4th Eclogues 75   22
    Grow rich in that which never taketh rust: . . . . 161 Cert Sonnets 32   3
S
    Welcome my two to me, E.D. F.G. P.S. . . . . 261 Other Poems 6   25
SABLES
    Joves golden shield did Eagle sables beare, ... 171 Astrophil 13   3
SACK
    Thou didst ungird my dolefull sack . . . . 311 Psalm XXX   35
SACKCLOTH
    With inward wo, an outward sack cloth ware.. . . . . 322 Psalm XXXV   30
SACKS
    She sackes my rendred sprite.. . . . . 155 Cert Sonnets 26   4
    Above line repeated at following locations . . . . 155 Cert Sonnets 26   15
    . . . . 156 Cert Sonnets 26   26
SACRED
    That to the sacred Muse my anoyes somewhat be revealed, . . 31 1st Eclogues 13   9
    Sacred Muse, who in one contaynes what nine do in all them.. 31 1st Eclogues 13   10
    R. O sacred Reason, helpe our vertuous toiles. . . . . 46 2nd Eclogues 27   23
    Can I, that know her sacred parts, restrained be . . . . . . 61 2nd Eclogues 30   149
    To this chaste love your sacred favours bow, ... 91 3rd Eclogues 63   21
    And so by priviledge of sacred seate, ... 141 Cert Sonnets 8   9
    And in my braine some sacred humour flowe: . . . . 146 Cert Sonnets 17   38
    As sacred things, far from all daunger's show. . . . . 177 Astrophil 24   8
    And if from Majestie of sacred lights, ... 186 Astrophil 42   12
    Poore Layman I, for sacred rites unfit.. . . . . 203 Astrophil 74   4
    O let them heare these sacred tunes, and learne in wonder's
        schooles, ... 217 A&S 7th Song   5
    Who thus proceeds, for aye, in sacred Mount shall raign. . . 287 Psalm XV   13
    My cryes clim'd up and he bent down from sacred throne, . . 291 Psalm XVIII   13
    To beare his sacred flight, in secret place then clos'd, . . 291 Psalm XVIII   23
SACRIFICE
    Like beast for sacrifice, where save the tong. . . . . 24 1st Eclogues 9   81
    And for a sure sacrifice I do dayly oblation offer . . . . . 37 1st Eclogues 13   170
    Thou sacrifice nor offring, ... 331 Psalm XL   25
    But on his eies his heart did sacrifise. . . . . 251 Other Poems 4   368

SACRIFICES   PAGE   TITLE   LINE
  The sacrifices sacrify . . . . 274 Psalm IV   21
  So shall I sacrifices spred, ... 307 Psalm XXVII   33
SACRIFY
  The sacrifices sacrify . . . . 274 Psalm IV   21
SACRILEGE
  What sacriledge hath such a saint disgrast?. . . . . 59 2nd Eclogues 30   97
SAD
  And for th'event we never ought be sad.. . . . . 105 3rd Eclogues 67   66
  With how sad steps, o Moone, thou climb'st the skies,. . . . 180 Astrophil   31   1
  Of Lover's ruine some sad Tragedie:. . . . . 187 Astrophil   45   13
  With sad eyes I their weake proportion see,. . . . . 189 Astrophil   50   7
  Even those sad words even in sad me did breed. . . . . . . 194 Astrophil   58   14
  If still I force her in sad rimes to creepe: . . . . 201 Astrophil   70   2
  And her sad words my sadded sence did heare. . . . . 223 Astrophil   87   8
  Silent and sad in mourning weedes doth dight:. . . . . . . 229 Astrophil   97   8
  Takes in that sad hue, which with th'inward night. . . . . 230 Astrophil   99   7
  Each thing both sweet and sadd . . . . 256 Other Poems   5   8
  What fitts me now but teares, and sighings sadd? . . . . . 259 Other Poems   5   97
SADDED
  And her sad words my sadded sence did heare. . . . . 223 Astrophil   87   8
SADDEST
  Since that we see our saddest Shepheards out . . . . 27 1st Eclogues 10   26
  And oft whole troupes of saddest words I staid,. . . . . . 192 Astrophil   55   5
SADDLE
  The Wand is Will, thou Fancie Saddle art,. . . . . 189 Astrophil   49   9
SADLY
  Both sadly blacke, both blackly darkned be,. . . . . 229 Astrophil   96   3
SADNESS
  Comfort, step thou in place of wonted sadnes.. . . . . . . 83 Arcadia III 59   10
  That here is juster cause of plaintfull sadnesse:. . . . . 137 Cert Sonnets   4   10
  Above line repeated at following location. . . . . 137 Cert Sonnets   4   22
  Shaking off all sadnes,. . . . . 336 Psalm XLIII   21
SAFE
  But o happy be you, which safe from fyry reflection. . . . 31 1st Eclogues 13   11
  And make his paine to keepe us safe his pleasure?. . . . . 129 4th Eclogues 76   24
  Safe in my soule, which only doth to thee. . . . . 212 Astrophil   86   6
  And safe again He rear'd mee . . . . 272 Psalm III   18
  Thy work it is such men safe in to hemm. . . . . 275 Psalm V   39
  Thou art my safe and secret place. . . . . 315 Psalm XXXII   25
  To keep them safe and sound. . . . . 319 Psalm XXXIV   28
  Yea beasts made safe thy goodness try. . . . . 323 Psalm XXXVI   18
  The Lord will keep his life yet safe and sound . . . . . . 333 Psalm XLI   5
  Will. What keepeth safe thy band? D. Remembrance is the
    Chest. . . . . 344 Possibly   1   29
  While Geron olde came safe to Cosma true,. . . . . 250 Other Poems   4   325
SAFELIEST
  To her, where I my heart safeliest shall meet. . . . . . . 209 Astrophil   84   6
SAFELY
  The golden meane who loves, lives safely free. . . . . . . 143 Cert Sonnets 12   4
  For he me safely kept. . . . . 272 Psalm III   17
  Cosma this while to Strephon safely came,. . . . . 249 Other Poems   4   265
SAFEST
  With nature's praise are wont in safest home to take.. . . 117 4th Eclogues 73   14
  As well he was in peace a safest treasure: . . . . 129 4th Eclogues 76   17
  I dwell, layd up in safest neast.. . . . . 274 Psalm IV   35
SAFETY
  Dicus. Thy safetie sure is wrapped in destruction: . . . . 49 2nd Eclogues 28   73
  Whose shade safety doth hold, danger avoideth her: . . . . 69 2nd Eclogues 34   34
  On whom against my Foes my only safty stayes?. . . . . . . 291 Psalm XVIII   7
  His safety from Thee flowing!. . . . . 296 Psalm XXI   4
  Some safty unto me;. 305 Psalm XXV   74
  And, so I did safety gett, ... 309 Psalm XXVIII   28
  But God shall him to safety reare. . . . . 320 Psalm XXXIV   71
  Thy grace with safety man fulfills,. . . . . 323 Psalm XXXVI   17
SAID
  "Nothing", sayd he, "for most I joy in this, ... 4 Lady of May   3   5
  "Poore Pan" (he sayd) "although thou beaten be,. . . . . . 5 Lady of May   3   11
  When first he spied my love? how oft he said to me,. . . . 16 1st Eclogues   7   50
  Thus Reason said: but she came, Reason vanished;. . . . . . 16 1st Eclogues   7   67
  Yet not of wemen Judging as he said, ... 24 1st Eclogues   9   64
  Philisides. Hath any man heard what this old man said? . . . 26 1st Eclogues   9   135
  "Tush, tush", said nature, "this is all but a trifle, a
    man's selfe. . . . . 29 1st Eclogues 11   7
  Love smiled, and thus said; "Want joynd to desire is
    unhappy . . . . 30 1st Eclogues 11   11
  Pas. Cosma once said, she left the wicket ope, ... 55 2nd Eclogues 29   90
  Alas (said I) this babe dooth nurce my thought.. . . . . . 55 2nd Eclogues 29   113
  I said, my hands well paide her for mine eyes, ... 55 2nd Eclogues 29   115
  She sigh'd and sayd, the bad guest sought her love.. . . . 95 3rd Eclogues 64   48
  He said, the Musique best thilke powers pleasd . . . . . . 99 3rd Eclogues 66   29
  A King, in language theirs they said they would: . . . . . 100 3rd Eclogues 66   64
  Jove wisely said (for wisedome wisely sayes) . . . . 100 3rd Eclogues 66   71
  But walking forth, the first thus to the second saide, . . . 118 4th Eclogues 73   77
  "Venus come on": said she, "Diane you are obaide". . . . . 119 4th Eclogues 73   78
  "Nay then (Diana said) the chastnesse I will give. . . . . 121 4th Eclogues 73   173
  "Nay thou (said both) shalt see such beames shine in her
    face . . . . 121 4th Eclogues 73   175
  Which once said what I conceaved,. . . . . 139 Cert Sonnets   7   5
  On things, were by a woman said, ... 158 Cert Sonnets 28   39

SAID	(CONTINUED)	PAGE	TITLE		LINE
Weepe neighbours, weepe, do you not heare it said, ...		160	Cert Sonnets	30	11
"Foole," said my Muse to me, "looke in thy heart and write."		165	Astrophil	1	14
Which others said did make their soules to pine:		173	Astrophil	16	6
Stella; now she is nam'd, need more be said?		173	Astrophil	16	11
"What now sir foole," said he, "I would no lesse,.		191	Astrophil	53	7
Sweet said that I true love in her should find..		196	Astrophil	62	4
Least once should not be heard, twise said, No, No..		196	Astrophil	63	8
Say all, and all well sayd, still say the same..		225	Astrophil	92	14
I said, thou wert most faire, and so indeed thou art:. . . .		212	A&S 5th Song		7
I said, thou wert most sweet, sweet poison to my heart:. . .		212	A&S 5th Song		8
I said, my soule was thine (o that I then had lyed).		212	A&S 5th Song		9
I said, thine eyes were starres, thy breasts the milk'n way,		212	A&S 5th Song		10
And all I said so well, as no man it denied.		212	A&S 5th Song		12
"Astrophil" sayd she, "my love		220	A&S 8th Song		73
"If more may be sayd, I say, ...		220	A&S 8th Song		89
Indeed full many folkes have said, ...		274	Psalm IV		24
No sooner said, but (lo) myne Enemyes sink		280	Psalm IX		46
Thus much I said, this being said.		311	Psalm XXX		33
I said that I from out Thy sight was cast;		313	Psalm XXXI		62
And said to me wide mowing as they could,.		322	Psalm XXXV		53
For I sayd, heare, least they be		328	Psalm XXXVIII		46
And so I nothing said, I muet stood, ...		329	Psalm XXXIX		5
Thus bound I said, lo, lord I am at hand,.		331	Psalm XL		31
Therfore I said in most infirmity, ...		333	Psalm XLI		13
To him my thanks shall be said		335	Psalm XLII		53
One said he brake acrosse; full well it so might be:		241	Other Poems	1	3
This said, this done, he rase even tir'd with rest,.		255	Other Poems	4	521
With teares, he saide, or sorrow said for him.		256	Other Poems	5	13
This said, at length he ended.		259	Other Poems	5	114

SAIDST

| In dede thou said'st it was thy frend to see,. . . . . | | 247 | Other Poems | 4 | 219 |

SAIL

We shepeheards are like them that under saile.		27	1st Eclogues	10	31
Feede on my sheepe, sorrow hathe stricken sayle, ...		43	Arcadia II	23	10
Leave of my sheepe, sorrowe hathe hoysed sayle,.		44	Arcadia II	24	10

SAILS

| In too full winde draw in thy swelling sailes. . . . . | | 143 | Cert Sonnets | 12 | 18 |
| Beware full sailes drowne not thy tottring barge:. . . . . . | | 209 | Astrophil | 85 | 2 |

SAINT

Happy be you that may to the saint, your onely Idea, ...		32	1st Eclogues	13	15
Thy sainte is dead, or dead is thy devotion.		47	2nd Eclogues	28	3
What sacriledge hath such a saint disgrast?.		59	2nd Eclogues	30	97
Seeking the Sainct in whome all graces dwell,.		71	Arcadia III	36	14
Phaebus farewell, a sweeter Saint I serve,.		72	Arcadia III	38	1
Above line repeated at following location.		72	Arcadia III	38	6
As for to lose thy gemme, our earthly Sainct,.		125	4th Eclogues	75	18
So captives to his Saint both soule and sence, ...		195	Astrophil	61	6

SAINTS

| Ye saints of his, remembring still . . . . | | 311 | Psalm XXX | | 11 |
| Feare God ye saints of his,. . . . . | | 319 | Psalm XXXIV | | 33 |

SAINTS'

| (Image like of Saints' perfection) . . . . | | 234 | A&S 11th Song | | 24 |

SAKE

But deck therewith my soule for your sake dying.		17	1st Eclogues	7	90
Yet for my sake discover us thy griefe..		23	1st Eclogues	9	23
Pas. If each day hath bene holy for your sake, ...		54	2nd Eclogues	29	72
Then that I lose no more for Stella's sake..		174	Astrophil	18	14
With me those paines for God's sake do not take:		179	Astrophil	28	3
Princesse of Beautie, for whose only sake.		179	Astrophil	28	6
But when he will for quiet's sake remove		186	Astrophil	43	12
Cease eager Muse, peace pen, for my sake stay, ...		201	Astrophil	70	12
Nature with care sweates for her darling's sake, ...		232	Astrophil	101	12
Mercy, O Mercy lord, for Mercy's sake, ...		276	Psalm VI		13
Nay if I wrought not for his Freedome's sake		277	Psalm VII		11
For his name's sake.		301	Psalm XXIII		9
Ev'n for Thy mercy's sake, O Lord.		303	Psalm XXV		30
O Lord for Thy name's sake		304	Psalm XXV		43
And save me in, and for Thy mercie's sake.		313	Psalm XXXI		44
"Only for my two loves' sake, Sir Ed. D. and M. F. G.. . . .		263	Other Poems	7	61

SAKES

Who for our sakes will thinke all travaile light,.		129	4th Eclogues	76	23
That I respects for both our sakes must show:.		181	Astrophil	33	11
Ah, now even for their sakes, that taste of Woe, ...		285	Psalm XII		13

SALE

| As stuffe meant for the sale set out to glaring showe) . . . | | 118 | 4th Eclogues | 73 | 72 |

SALUTE

| Cals each wight to salute the floure of blisse;. . . . . . . | | 231 | Astrophil | 99 | 11 |

SALUTES

| When that noble toppe doth nodd, I beleeve she salutes me; . | | 36 | 1st Eclogues | 13 | 144 |

SALVATION

Salvation doth belong.		273	Psalm III		31
That springs from Thy salvation;		297	Psalm XXI		18
A blessing from the lord, from God of his salvation.		302	Psalm XXIV		13
The strong God my salvation is..		306	Psalm XXVII		2
Salvation high..		308	Psalm XXVII		48
By God's most sure, and sweet salvation;		327	Psalm XXXVII		98
My salvation is in thee.		329	Psalm XXXVIII		66

SALVE

| (Therion) Thus wofully I in wo this salve do find, ... | | 5 | Lady of May | 3 | 17 |

412

SALVE   (CONTINUED)   PAGE   TITLE   LINE
    But to my selfe what wish can I make for a salve to my
        sorrowes, ...   37 1st Eclogues 13   157
    Oft prove I: but what salve, when Reason seeks to be gone?
        One. . . . .   63 2nd Eclogues 31   11
    Oh! what is it? what is it that may be a salve to my Love?
        Love. . . . .   63 2nd Eclogues 31   12
    Deeper engrav'd, which salve nor time can save, ... 77 Arcadia III 47   5
    A salve, freshe ayre, and hyghe contented mynde. . . . . 345 Possibly   2   14
    Like some which seeke to salve their blotted name. . . . 248 Other Poems   4   231
SALVES
    Whose wounds are salves, whose yokes please more then
        pleasure doth: . . . .   49 2nd Eclogues 28   56
SAME
    What I call wrong, I doo the same, and more: . . . . . .   41 Arcadia II   20   6
    Pas. And I am here the same, so mote I thrive and thee, . . 52 2nd Eclogues 29   3
    Torne with her hands, and those same hands of snow . . .   58 2nd Eclogues 30   45
    She studied cunning how the same to blinde. . . . . 95 3rd Eclogues 64   42
    And did the same, although with mickle feare. . . . . . . 96 3rd Eclogues 64   64
    As though she were the same, as when by Paris' doome . . . 120 4th Eclogues 73   145
    The same man still in whom wysdome prevailes, ... 143 Cert Sonnets 12   17
    Since that in selfe same metall coin'd, ... 159 Cert Sonnets 29   3
    You have the same in my hands, seeing. . . . . 159 Cert Sonnets 29   8
    That see my wracke, and yet embrace the same? . . . . . . 174 Astrophil   19   2
    Whence those same fumes of melancholy rise, ... 176 Astrophil   23   3
    When I say "Stella", I do meane the same . . . . 179 Astrophil   28   5
    How Ulster likes of that same golden bit, ... 180 Astrophil   30   9
    But that they stopt his furie from the same, ... 190 Astrophil   50   13
    Stella's sweete breath the same to me did reed. . . . . . 194 Astrophil   58   11
    And I do sweare even by the same delight, ... 208 Astrophil   82   13
    Say all, and all well sayd, still say the same. . . . . . 225 Astrophil   92   14
    Which Nature' selfe did make, and selfe engraind the same? . 232 Astrophil   102   6
    And if the trees, nor stones stirre not the same to prove, . 209 A&S 3rd Song   14
    Long stay ere he graunt the same: . . . . 211 A&S 4th Song   33
    The same key op'n can, which can locke up a treasure. . . . 213 A&S 5th Song   18
    And on those blessed same, ... 273 Psalm III   34
    For Thou art that same God, far from delight . . . . . . 274 Psalm V   9
    For this same man will not learn to repent, ... 278 Psalm VII   33
    And who doth frame to keep the same. . . . . 295 Psalm XIX   47
    Link not me in self same chain . . . . 309 Psalm XXVIII   11
    Of sanctuary do the same. . . . . 310 Psalm XXIX   6
    He knowes the same, ... 317 Psalm XXXIII   56
    Is bent, but bent against those same . . . . 320 Psalm XXXIV   58
    For those same eyes his flatterers be. . . . . 323 Psalm XXXVI   7
    He knew hir haunt, and haunted in the same, ... 247 Other Poems   4   187
    As this same sprite about my fancies blinde, ... 255 Other Poems   4   502
    These same words, or this effecting: . . . . 262 Other Poems   7   18
SAMOTHEA
    Of samothea lande; a lande, which whilom stood . . . . . 117 4th Eclogues 73   36
SAMPLE
    I pray thee doo to Lalus' sample leane: . . . . 103 3rd Eclogues 67   4
SANCTUARY
    From sanctuary high. . . . . 295 Psalm XX   6
    Where Thy sanctuary stands, ... 309 Psalm XXVIII   8
    Of sanctuary do the same. . . . . 310 Psalm XXIX   6
SAND
    He water plowes, and soweth in the sand, ... 24 1st Eclogues 9   53
    Now in this sande I would discharge my minde, ... 42 Arcadia II   21   13
    Since streame, aier, sand, mine eyes and eares conspire: . . 42 Arcadia II   21   17
    And written in the sand. . . . . 158 Cert Sonnets 28   40
SANDS
    But in the sandes my paynes foretolde I finde, ... 42 Arcadia II   21   15
SANDY
    On sandie banke of late, ... 158 Cert Sonnets 28   33
SANG
    And sange unto my sheepe lest stray they should. . . . . 99 3rd Eclogues 66   21
    The songe I sange old Languet had me taught, ... 99 3rd Eclogues 66   22
SANGST
    Nico. Well aimed by my hat: for as thou sangst last day; . . 52 2nd Eclogues 29   25
SANK
    Did piping leade, the Sunne already sanke. . . . . 98 3rd Eclogues 66   3
    And Mira I admirde: her shape sank in my brest. . . . . . 119 4th Eclogues 73   100
SAPPHIRE
    Her twinkling eies bedeckt with pearle, her lips of Saphir
        blew: . . . . 12 Arcadia I   3   10
SAPPHIRE-COLORED
    There fall those Saphir-coloured brookes, ... 90 Arcadia III 62   127
SATE
    I sate me downe: for see to goe ne could, ... 99 3rd Eclogues 66   20
    Brake bow, brake shafts, while Cupid weeping sate: . . . 173 Astrophil   17   8
    My Friend I say, who at my table sate, ... 333 Psalm XLI   31
    He saw behind a bush where Klaius sate: . . . . 255 Other Poems   4   527
    Sate wailing without boot. . . . . 256 Other Poems   5   7
SATIN
    But soft and supple satten like. . . . . 88 Arcadia III 62   82
SATISFIES
    O God, thinke you that satisfies my care? . . . . 225 Astrophil   92   8
SATISFY
    Dicus. But so thy sheepe may thy good wishes satisfie. . . . 49 2nd Eclogues 28   49

```
                                                              PAGE    TITLE       LINE
SATURN
    Like great god Saturn faire, and like faire Venus chaste:. .   12 Arcadia I      3    5
    Although we be divine, our grandsire Saturne is. . . . . .    120 4th Eclogues 73  123
SATYR
    A Satyre once did runne away for dread,. . . . . . . . . .    145 Cert Sonnets 16    1
    Better like I thy Satyre deerest Dyer, . . . . . . . . . .    145 Cert Sonnets 16   13
SATYRS
    Ye Satyrs joyde with free and quiet forrests, . . . . . . .   111 4th Eclogues 71    3
SAUCINESS
    Is sawcinesse reward of curtesie?. . . . . . . . . . . . .    208 Astrophil    83   10
    With how sweet sawes she blam'd their sawcines:. . . . . .    252 Other Poems   4  404
SAUCY
    Ah saucy paine let not thy errour last,. . . . . . . . . .    141 Cert Sonnets  8   13
    Sweet, it was saucie Love, not humble I. . . . . . . . . .    203 Astrophil    73    8
SAVAGE
    O heavenlie huntresse of the savage mountaines,. . . . . .    111 4th Eclogues 71    8
SAVE
    He is not poore who can his freedome save, . . . . . . . .      4 Lady of May   2   27
    Thy father bids thee save, and chides for spilling.. . . .     16 1st Eclogues  7   79
    Save then my soule, spill not my thoughts well heaped, . .     16 1st Eclogues  7   80
    Whose sprite all sprites can spoile, raise, damne, or save:.   17 1st Eclogues  7  110
    Like beast for sacrifice, where save the tong. . . . . . .     24 1st Eclogues  9   81
    Save when great need of them perforce apeare.. . . . . . .     27 1st Eclogues 10   36
    Save that dayly we may discerne what fire we do burne in.. .   33 1st Eclogues 13   53
    Save what a worke, by thy selfe is wrought: and since I am
        altred . . . . . . . . . . . . . . . . . . . . . . .       36 1st Eclogues 13  151
    A blooddy helpe with blood to save:. . . . . . . . . . . .     44 Arcadia II   25    2
    And all but jests, save onely sorrowe's rage.. . . . . . .     57 2nd Eclogues 30   22
    But well you know, the gentle Sunne would save . . . . . .     60 2nd Eclogues 30  104
    Unite in one, my state thus still to save; . . . . . . . .     70 Arcadia III  35   15
    Deeper engrav'd, which salve nor time can save,. . . . . .     77 Arcadia III  47    5
    Save one as much as other cleere:. . . . . . . . . . . . .     86 Arcadia III  62   20
    And thinke, I did my selfe from sorrow save. . . . . . . .    104 3rd Eclogues 67   24
    All what I am: if I my selfe will save,. . . . . . . . . .    114 4th Eclogues 72   23
    Then must I save, what in my chiefly raignes,. . . . . . .    114 4th Eclogues 72   24
    Hath yet such health, as it my life can save.. . . . . . .    142 Cert Sonnets 11   12
    Thinking not why, but how himselfe to save.. . . . . . . .    145 Cert Sonnets 16    8
    I much do guesse, yet find no truth save this, . . . . . .    187 Astrophil    44    9
    Who may and will not save, murder in truth committeth. . .    214 A&S 5th Song      54
    Save thy mind which yet surpasseth.. . . . . . . . . . . .    219 A&S 8th Song      44
    O save me from this Persecution's showre:. . . . . . . . .    277 Psalm VII          2
    Save me lord, for why Thou art . . . . . . . . . . . . . .    287 Psalm XVI          1
    And save them from rebellious hand.. . . . . . . . . . . .    290 Psalm XVII        24
    Save me from them Thou usest as thy blade, . . . . . . . .    290 Psalm XVII        37
    So did he save me from my mighty furious foe,. . . . . . .    291 Psalm XVIII       36
    So did he save me from their then prevailing hate, . . . .    291 Psalm XVIII       37
    Let God save him, in whom was all his lust.. . . . . . . .    299 Psalm XXII        20
    Ah! from the sword yet save my vital sprite, . . . . . . .    299 Psalm XXII        47
    Lord then still Thy people save, . . . . . . . . . . . . .    309 Psalm XXVIII      33
    But save me, save in Thy righteousness,. . . . . . . . . .    312 Psalm XXXI         3
    Save me from foes who seek my bane to bake.. . . . . . . .    313 Psalm XXXI        42
    And save me in, and for Thy mercie's sake. . . . . . . . .    313 Psalm XXXI        44
    Hosts do the King not save,. . . . . . . . . . . . . . . .    317 Psalm XXXIII      58
    His sight is them to save. . . . . . . . . . . . . . . . .    318 Psalm XXXIII      73
    And will save whom his sight cleere. . . . . . . . . . . .    320 Psalm XXXIV       67
    Save me distrest from lion's cruel kind. . . . . . . . . .    322 Psalm XXXV        45
    He shall save them from all the fetches. . . . . . . . . .    327 Psalm XXXVII     102
    From my transgressions me to save. . . . . . . . . . . . .    330 Psalm XXXIX       26
    Me still in truth and mercy save,. . . . . . . . . . . . .    332 Psalm XL          42
    Save me from bad wights. . . . . . . . . . . . . . . . . .    336 Psalm XLIII        5
SAVED
    Hath sav'd his charge? it is even I. . . . . . . . . . . .     44 Arcadia II   25    6
    Who hath sav'd all? it is even I.. . . . . . . . . . . . .     44 Arcadia II   25   12
    As if by death she onely might be saved? . . . . . . . . .     61 2nd Eclogues 30  160
    And sav'd me from foes' laughing scorn;. . . . . . . . . .    310 Psalm XXX          2
    Then shall I joy in thee, then sav'd by Thee . . . . . . .    321 Psalm XXXV        19
SAVER
    Thou lord, Thou lord, the saver of Thyne Owne. . . . . . .    275 Psalm V           21
    Ah, when from syon shall the saver come, . . . . . . . . .    287 Psalm XIV         22
SAVES
    He nobly saves his King, and kindness keeps in store,. . .    293 Psalm XVIII       90
SAVEST
    The life of him Thou savest. . . . . . . . . . . . . . . .    297 Psalm XXI         16
    Who savest me from troblous case,. . . . . . . . . . . . .    315 Psalm XXXII       26
SAVING
    Saving the glowe worme, which would curteous be. . . . . .     98 3rd Eclogues 66    6
    Who dost Thy saving health to true men bend. . . . . . . .    277 Psalm VII         30
    May only joy in all Thy saving wayes . . . . . . . . . . .    280 Psalm IX          44
    My never peirced shield, my ever saving horn,. . . . . . .    290 Psalm XVIII        4
    Thou gavest me saving shield, Thy right hand was my stay;. .   292 Psalm XVIII       64
    My saving might, lord in Thy sight,. . . . . . . . . . . .    295 Psalm XIX         63
    That in thy saving We.. . . . . . . . . . . . . . . . . . .    296 Psalm XX          18
    The saving me from smart,. . . . . . . . . . . . . . . . .    303 Psalm XXV         16
    Let them that love Thy saving seat . . . . . . . . . . . .    332 Psalm XL          63
SAVIOR
    Assist us Saviour deare; . . . . . . . . . . . . . . . . .    296 Psalm XX          33
SAVOR
    Fore-felt Desire, begin to savour parte. . . . . . . . . .     83 Arcadia III  59   11
SAW
    Dorus. How oft, when reason saw love of her harnished. . .     16 1st Eclogues  7   61
```

SAW   (CONTINUED)   PAGE   TITLE   LINE

	PAGE	TITLE		LINE
Dorus. Once, o sweete once, I saw with dread oppressed . . .	17	1st Eclogues	7	85
I saw that riches fall, and fell a crying;	17	1st Eclogues	7	88
Let crowes picke out mine eyes, which saw too much:.	19	1st Eclogues	7	149
Let crowes picke out mine eyes which too much sawe.	19	1st Eclogues	7	V149
Or stop a breach, that never Cannon sawe?.	22	1st Eclogues	9	17
I sawe her arme, where purest Lillies cleave.	55	2nd Eclogues	29	104
Shall I that saw Eronae's shining haire.	58	2nd Eclogues	30	44
Shall I that saw those brests, where beauties flow,.	58	2nd Eclogues	30	47
And saw those eyes (those Sonnes) such shoures to shew,. . .	58	2nd Eclogues	30	49
O eyes of mine, where once she saw her face, ...	60	2nd Eclogues	30	116
Amid my sheepe, though I sawe nought to feare, ...	99	3rd Eclogues	66	15
Yet (for I nothing sawe) I feared sore;.	99	3rd Eclogues	66	16
But sawe they would, and he to deserts went.	100	3rd Eclogues	66	70
Tho when they saw their foen of greatnes kilde.	102	3rd Eclogues	66	133
When falcon they, and gossehauke saw in mewe.	102	3rd Eclogues	66	140
All things that earst I sawe, as orient pearles exceed,. . .	119	4th Eclogues	73	83
I that was first agast, when first I saw their showe:. . . .	121	4th Eclogues	73	158
Love never had me opprest, but that I saw to be lov'd. . .	123	4th Eclogues	74	44
I see since I saw you:	157	Cert Sonnets	28	2
Who ever saw such woe?	158	Cert Sonnets	28	28
Seeing how once you saw I liv'd, ...	158	Cert Sonnets	28	31
I saw this woman sit,.	158	Cert Sonnets	28	34
I saw and liked, I liked but loved not,.	165	Astrophil	2	5
But straight I saw motions of lightning grace,.	175	Astrophil	20	12
My friend, that oft saw through all maskes my wo,.	200	Astrophil	69	5
I saw that teares did in her eyes appeare;	223	Astrophil	87	6
I saw that sighes her sweetest lips did part,.	223	Astrophil	87	7
I saw thy selfe with many a smiling line	232	Astrophil	103	2
If I saw my good dog grieved,.	222	A&S 9th Song		37
According as he saw the pureness of my hand.	292	Psalm XVIII		49
To justice never saw forsaken, ...	326	Psalm XXXVII		63
Who ever Lambkins saw (yet lambkins love to play).	343	Possibly	1	5
They saw a maid who thitherward did runne, ...	244	Other Poems	4	83
And saw this fairest maid of fairer minde, ...	244	Other Poems	4	90
Strephon, poor youth, because he saw no smoke, ...	253	Other Poems	4	427
As pin'd a face as mine I saw againe:.	254	Other Poems	4	476
He saw behind a bush where Klaius sate:.	255	Other Poems	4	527

SAWS

	PAGE	TITLE		LINE
With how sweet sawes she blam'd their sawcines:.	252	Other Poems	4	404

SAWST

	PAGE	TITLE		LINE
So when thou saw'st in Nature's cabinet.	170	Astrophil	11	9

SAY

	PAGE	TITLE		LINE
Then power out plaint, and in one word say this:	13	Arcadia I	4	9
Bent to such one, in whom, my selfe must say,.	17	1st Eclogues	7	107
And yet they say he talkes in great men's bowers?.	28	1st Eclogues	10	68
Fortune thus gan say; "misery and misfortune is all one,. .	29	1st Eclogues	11	3
Say then what vantage do we get, by the trade of a Pastor?.	33	1st Eclogues	13	49
And may I not (say I then) gett up though griefs be so weightie?.	36	1st Eclogues	13	128
Thus then (I say) my mischiefes have contributed	49	2nd Eclogues	28	67
Histor. Thus dyd they saye and then awaye dyd wende; . . .	62	2nd Eclogues	30	185
Yet say againe thy advise for th' ev'lls that I told thee. I told thee.	63	2nd Eclogues	31	18
Say then Reason, I say what is thy counsell?	67	2nd Eclogues	33	6
Above line repeated at following locations	67	2nd Eclogues	33	12
. . . .	67	2nd Eclogues	33	18
. . . .	68	2nd Eclogues	33	18
. . . .	68	2nd Eclogues	33	24
Chief band I saye, which tyes my chiefest parte, ...	70	Arcadia III	35	12
Since, as I say, both minde and sences darke, ...	73	Arcadia III	39	9
Do you say still, this is her promise due, ...	76	Arcadia III	46	5
First fower but say, next fowr their saying seale, ...	76	Arcadia III	46	17
Sweete roote say thou, the roote of my desire.	77	Arcadia III	48	1
Kisse her from me, and say unto her spirite, ...	79	Arcadia III	51	13
Some say it doth betoken wonders neare	81	Arcadia III	55	2
So good a say invites the eye, ...	87	Arcadia III	62	51
Nightingale, voice, entising songes to saye.	101	3rd Eclogues	66	82
There never past foule word, I dare well say.	106	3rd Eclogues	67	93
No knee once bowed, forsooth, for them they say we serve. .	120	4th Eclogues	73	114
But such they say we be: this praise our discord bred, . .	120	4th Eclogues	73	117
And smirkly thus gan say. "I never sought debate	120	4th Eclogues	73	147
To all what I decreed, did thus my verdict saye.	121	4th Eclogues	73	162
O wretch, what do I say? should that faire face be defaced?.	124	4th Eclogues	74	57
O not but such love you say you could have afoorded, . . .	124	4th Eclogues	74	63
Say, that I well shuld finde in what a care I was had? . .	124	4th Eclogues	74	80
Your dolefull tunes, to them still playning say, ...	126	4th Eclogues	75	50
That she her child, I say, her best child killeth?	127	4th Eclogues	75	95
O Elements, by whose (they say) contention,.	128	4th Eclogues	75	106
O Phisicke's power, which (some say) hath refrayned. . . .	128	4th Eclogues	75	109
They leave off al, and say, death comes too eagerlie. . . .	128	4th Eclogues	75	114
Absented? nay I say for ever banished.	128	4th Eclogues	75	125
Fame say I was not borne:.	136	Cert Sonnets	3	17
They that heav'n have knowne, do say	140	Cert Sonnets	7	24
So stay her toung, that she no more say no..	142	Cert Sonnets	10	14
And have I heard her say, "o cruell paine!".	142	Cert Sonnets	11	1
Which Poets say, the gods them selves do feare, ...	146	Cert Sonnets	17	7
Why those that die, men say they do depart:.	148	Cert Sonnets	20	2
Mine eyes (shall I say curst or blest) beheld.	173	Astrophil	16	10
See there that boy, that murthring boy I say,.	174	Astrophil	20	2
Sure you say well, your wisdome's golden mine.	175	Astrophil	21	12

```
SAY                  (CONTINUED)                    PAGE   TITLE          LINE
    When I say "Stella", I do meane the same . . . . . . . . .  179 Astrophil     28    5
    What may words say, or what may words not say, . . . . . .  182 Astrophil     35    1
    So may you still have somewhat new to say. . . . . . . . .  190 Astrophil     51    4
    Looke here, I say." I look'd, and Stella spide, . . . . . . 191 Astrophil     53    8
    "What he?" say they of me, "now I dare sweare, . . . . . .  191 Astrophil     54    7
    They love indeed, who quake to say they love . . . . . . .  192 Astrophil     54   14
    I, I, o I may say, that she is mine. . . . . . . . . . . .  200 Astrophil     69   11
    Thus much my heart compeld my mouth to say, . . . . . . . . 207 Astrophil     80    9
    You say forsooth, you left her well of late. . . . . . . .  225 Astrophil     92    7
    Say all, and all well sayd, still say the same. . . . . . . 225 Astrophil     92   14
    But feeling proofe makes me say they mistake it furre: . .  232 Astrophil    102   11
    Stella, I say my Stella, should appeare. . . . . . . . . .  235 Astrophil    106    4
    And scorning say, "See what it is to love.". . . . . . . .  236 Astrophil    107   14
    And makes me then bow downe my head, and say, . . . . . . . 237 Astrophil    108    9
    Yet a sleepe, me thinkes they say, . . . . . . . . . . . .  211 A&S 4th Song       27
    Yet worse then worst, I say thou art a theefe, a theefe? .  213 A&S 5th Song       43
    A witch I say thou art, though thou so faire appeare; . . . 214 A&S 5th Song       74
    Alas, that I am forst such evill of thee to say, . . . . .  215 A&S 5th Song       80
    I say thou art a Devill, though clothd in Angel's shining:  215 A&S 5th Song       81
    You see what I can say; mend yet your froward mind, . . . . 215 A&S 5th Song       88
    "Well, be gone, be gone I say, . . . . . . . . . . . . . .  235 A&S 11th Song      41
    Say whether of the choice. . . . . . . . . . . . . . . . .  215 A&S 6th Song        3
    Say whether thou wilt crowne, . . . . . . . . . . . . . . . 217 A&S 6th Song       53
    "If more may be sayd, I say, . . . . . . . . . . . . . . .  220 A&S 8th Song       89
    Come let us break their bonds, say they, and fondly say: .  271 Psalm II            7
    And say (O kings) yet have I set my King upon. . . . . . .  271 Psalm II           13
    And say that he did say: . . . . . . . . . . . . . . . . .  271 Psalm II           16
    That to my soul do say, . . . . . . . . . . . . . . . . . . 272 Psalm III           8
    I say no more but this: . . . . . . . . . . . . . . . . . . 272 Psalm III          22
    Such one I say, that when I make . . . . . . . . . . . . .  273 Psalm V            13
    Ponder the words, O lord, that I do say, . . . . . . . . .  274 Psalm V             1
    Have mercie, mercie lord I once did say, . . . . . . . . .  280 Psalm IX           36
    Say, Thou dost not Thyn Own regard?. . . . . . . . . . . .  283 Psalm X            56
    Our tongues, say they, beyond them all shall go, . . . . .  285 Psalm XII          10
    That to God my God I say . . . . . . . . . . . . . . . . .  287 Psalm XVI           4
    Say then, Is not my life not found. . . . . . . . . . . . . 288 Psalm XVI          16
    I say again that I have calld on Thee. . . . . . . . . . .  289 Psalm XVII         17
    And boldly say Thou wilt give eare to me, . . . . . . . . . 289 Psalm XVII         18
    From men I say, and from men's worldly trade, . . . . . . . 290 Psalm XVII         38
    Therfore I say again this goodness he me sent. . . . . . .  292 Psalm XVIII        47
    Let God help him (say they) whom he did trust; . . . . . .  299 Psalm XXII         19
    But what? I say from earth's remotest border, . . . . . . . 300 Psalm XXII         65
    I say, and say again, . . . . . . . . . . . . . . . . . . . 305 Psalm XXV          75
    Seek ye my Face, when Thou didst say, . . . . . . . . . . . 307 Psalm XXVII        39
    Ev'n such I say, whose lying tongue. . . . . . . . . . . .  308 Psalm XXVII        58
    Blesse Thyne heritage I say, . . . . . . . . . . . . . . .  309 Psalm XXVIII       34
    Full of successe, fond I did say . . . . . . . . . . . . .  311 Psalm XXX          20
    For still I say Thou art my only might.. . . . . . . . . .  312 Psalm XXXI         12
    But I did trust in Thee, lord, I did say . . . . . . . . .  313 Psalm XXXI         40
    Bee strong I say his strength confirm in you, . . . . . . . 314 Psalm XXXI         67
    I say but tast and see . . . . . . . . . . . . . . . . . .  319 Psalm XXXIV        29
    To me and mark what I do say, . . . . . . . . . . . . . . . 319 Psalm XXXIV        42
    None, I say still, shall ruind be. . . . . . . . . . . . .  321 Psalm XXXIV        79
    Ev'en bones shall say O God, who is Thy peere, . . . . . .  321 Psalm XXXV         21
    Let them not, Lord, within their hearts thus say: . . . . . 323 Psalm XXXV         61
    Yet let them say, laud be to God alwayes . . . . . . . . .  323 Psalm XXXV         69
    What guilty wickedness doth say, . . . . . . . . . . . . .  323 Psalm XXXVI         2
    Fume not, rage not, frett not I say, . . . . . . . . . . .  325 Psalm XXXVII       21
    I say, I say the Righteous minds . . . . . . . . . . . . .  326 Psalm XXXVII       73
    But I do hush, Why do I say thus much, . . . . . . . . . .  330 Psalm XXXIX        29
    As now to say to me, . . . . . . . . . . . . . . . . . . .  332 Psalm XL           59
    Still gladly say, Unto our God bee prayse. . . . . . . . .  332 Psalm XL           64
    While thus, alas, they say: . . . . . . . . . . . . . . . . 333 Psalm XLI          18
    Now is hee wrackt say they, lo, there he lyes. . . . . . .  333 Psalm XLI          27
    My Friend I say, who at my table sate, . . . . . . . . . .  333 Psalm XLI          31
    I will say: O lord my tower, . . . . . . . . . . . . . . .  335 Psalm XLII         41
    She went, they staid; or rightly for to say, . . . . . . .  246 Other Poems    4  169
    Say then, can this but of enchantment come?. . . . . . . .  254 Other Poems    4  472
    Say all, and I with them, . . . . . . . . . . . . . . . . . 259 Other Poems    5   93
    Grant, I say (if seely man . . . . . . . . . . . . . . . .  263 Other Poems    7   57
SAYEST
    O well thou saiest! a feeling declaration. . . . . . . . .   20 1st Eclogues   7 V968
    What saist thou now, where is that dainty cheere . . . . .  235 Astrophil    106    5
SAYETH
    One saith, He mockes; the other saith, he playes; . . . . .  27 1st Eclogues  10   44
    Sweete Juniper saith this, thoh I burne, yet I burne in a
        sweete fire. . . . . . . . . . . . . . . . . . . . . .   35 1st Eclogues  13  120
    Nico. I oft doo sue, and Leuca saith, I shall, . . . . . .   54 2nd Eclogues  29   87
    No, no: Despaire my dayly lesson saith, . . . . . . . . . .  58 2nd Eclogues  30   53
    And saith, although I seeke my life to flie, . . . . . . .   58 2nd Eclogues  30   54
    Yet Reason saith, Reason should have abilitie, . . . . . .   60 2nd Eclogues  30  131
    "Alas" she saith "I am thine, . . . . . . . . . . . . . . .  67 2nd Eclogues  32   41
    When without shame he saith, "these be mine owne". . . . .  106 3rd Eclogues  67  114
    Our young yeares to renew (for so he saith he will). . . .  120 4th Eclogues  73  126
    And be it as he saith". Venus was glad to heare. . . . . .  120 4th Eclogues  73  143
    Unto no body my woman saith she had rather a wife be, . . . 143 Cert Sonnets  13    1
    My mistresse lowers and saith I do not love: . . . . . . .  145 Cert Sonnets  17    1
    She saith, because I make no wofull laies, . . . . . . . .  146 Cert Sonnets  17   27
    "Scholler," saith Love, "bend hitherward your wit.". . . .  174 Astrophil     19   14
```

SAYETH	(CONTINUED)	PAGE	TITLE		LINE
Her eyes, her lips, her all, saith Love do this, ...		190	Astrophil	52	3
And I will (sayeth His King) the lord's decree display,. . .		271	Psalm II		15
And sayeth in his bragging heart,.		282	Psalm X		23
Thus freely saith he in his sprite:.		282	Psalm X		45
I will get up saith God, and my help show.		285	Psalm XII		16

SAYING
First fower but say, next fowr their saying seale, ...		76	Arcadia III	46	17
Not in his sayings saying I, but we:		102	3rd Eclogues	66	111
To grieve me worse, in saying that Desire.		171	Astrophil		6
Abase her praise, saying she doth excell:.		183	Astrophil	37	8
Graunt, o me, what am I saying?.		219	A&S 8th Song		47

SAYINGS
| Not in his sayings saying I, but we: . . . . | | 102 | 3rd Eclogues | 66 | 111 |

SAYS
While, "Let us passe our time" each shepeheard saies.. . . .		28	1st Eclogues	10	48
Dooth hide himselfe: for to himselfe he sayes, ...		55	2nd Eclogues	29	94
"No" saies faire moone, "my lighte		82	Arcadia III	55	12
But that her fore-head sayes in me		85	Arcadia III	62	5
Jove wisely said (for wisedome wisely sayes)		100	3rd Eclogues	66	71
Still contrarie to what her husband sayes;		104	3rd Eclogues	67	32
By Phoebus' doome, with sugred sentence sayes, ...		177	Astrophil	25	2
For Grammer sayes (o this deare Stella weighe,)		196	Astrophil	63	12
For Grammer sayes (to Grammer who sayes nay)		196	Astrophil	63	13
But she forbids, with blushing words, she sayes, ...		207	Astrophil	81	9
Now in mee knowledg sayes.		296	Psalm XX		21
Even truth that for me sayes		306	Psalm XXVI		37
Will. A tyme there is for all, my Mother often sayes,. . . .		343	Possibly	1	9

SCANT
| Or if that they be skante, if this be wronge?. . . . . | | 126 | 4th Eclogues | 75 | 45 |

SCAPE
| Nico. Was this not he, who for Siringa's scape . . . . | | 53 | 2nd Eclogues | 29 | 57 |
| By sence's priviledge, can scape from thee.. . . . . | | 183 | Astrophil | 36 | 14 |

SCAPES
| That from her lockes, thy day-nets, none scapes free,. . . . | | 170 | Astrophil | 12 | 2 |

SCARCE
And scarce discerne the dawne of comming day,.		131	Arcadia V	77	10
Can scarce discerne the shape of mine owne paine..		228	Astrophil	94	4
Scarce each other can abide, ...		263	Other Poems	7	52

SCARCELY
Time, place, life, wit scarcely her rare gifts measure doth.		49	2nd Eclogues	28	60
The first, thus matcht, were scarcely Gentlemen.		171	Astrophil	13	14
One from the other scarcely can descrie, ...		202	Astrophil	72	3
Thence, so farre thence, that scarcely any sparke.		233	Astrophil	104	6
Yet thoughts do flie, though I can scarcely creep.		253	Other Poems	4	444

SCARF
| Having no scarfe of clowds before his face,. . . . . | | 176 | Astrophil | 22 | 3 |

SCARLET
| Those scarlet judges, threatning bloudy paine? . . . . | | 203 | Astrophil | 73 | 11 |

SCARS
| Let others deck their pride with skarres,. . . . . | | 44 | Arcadia II | 25 | 7 |

SCATTER
| Or scatter on her bedd,. . . . . | | 257 | Other Poems | 5 | 49 |

SCATTERED
Hye tyme for me, for scattered were my sheepe.		62	2nd Eclogues	30	186
Fond fancie's scum, and dregs of scattred thought, ...		161	Cert Sonnets	31	2
For me, I wept to see pearles scattered so,.		223	Astrophil	87	9
But lyke vyle chaffe with wind shal scattred be.		270	Psalm I		14
Then out his arrowes fly, and streight they scatterd been, .		291	Psalm XVIII		29

SCATTERETH
| Ech eare suckes up the words a true love scattereth, ... | | 14 | 1st Eclogues | 7 | 5 |

SCATTERING
| Let Angel thine a scattring make them go.. . . . . | | 321 | Psalm XXXV | | 12 |

SCENT
In shewe and sent pale violets,.		89	Arcadia III	62	107
Me seemes I feele a noysome sent, the morning..		112	4th Eclogues	71	45
But from the sent of some infectious grave:.		114	4th Eclogues	72	19

SCEPTER
Thy scepter use in some old Catoe's brest;		166	Astrophil	4	5
To leave the scepter of all subject things,.		183	Astrophil	38	4
Onely to you her Scepter Venus granteth.		197	A&S 1st Song		16
With Iron scepter bruse thou shalt, and peece méale breake .		271	Psalm II		21

SCEPTERS
| Your scepters here, if to your eares divine. . . . . | | 40 | Arcadia II | 18 | 3 |

SCHOLAR
"Scholler," saith Love, "bend hitherward your wit.".		174	Astrophil	19	14
The wisest scholler of the wight most wise		177	Astrophil	25	1
Alas poore wag, that now a scholler art.		188	Astrophil	46	9

SCHOOL
| Fy, schoole of Patience, Fy, your lesson is. . . . . | | 192 | Astrophil | 56 | 1 |

SCHOOLED
| School'd onely by his mother's tender eye: . . . . | | 203 | Astrophil | 73 | 2 |

SCHOOLMASTER
| Neast of young joyes, schoolmaster of delight, ... | | 206 | Astrophil | 79 | 8 |

SCHOOLMISTRESS
| To such a schoole-mistresse, whose lessons new . . . . | | 188 | Astrophil | 46 | 10 |

SCHOOLS
Experience doubts, and schooles holde disputation.		49	2nd Eclogues	28	48
Churches or schooles are for thy seate more fit:		166	Astrophil	4	6
The schooles where Venus hath learn'd Chastitie.		185	Astrophil	42	4

		PAGE	TITLE	LINE
SCHOOLS	**(CONTINUED)**			
O let them heare these sacred tunes, and learne in wonder's schooles,.		217	A&S 7th Song	5
SCIENCE				
Each sight draws on a thought, thought mother of science,. .		69	2nd Eclogues 34	11
SCOFFERS				
With scoffers false I was their feast's delight, ...		322	Psalm XXXV	41
SCOFFS				
Those vile scoffes of naughty ones		335	Psalm XLII	45
SCOLDING				
Puiling, and whimpring, or else scolding flat, ...		104	3rd Eclogues 67	29
SCOOP				
For nature hathe that never fayling scoope,.		71	Arcadia III 37	5
SCOPE				
Nurse inwarde maladyes, which have not scope to be breath'd out,.		35	1st Eclogues 13	104
Who judge that honour, which hath scope to slander..		50	2nd Eclogues 28	91
In graunting such a scope to filthy fortune,.		109	Arcadia IV 70	21
Ruine, the winde, hath blowne her from her scope:.		114	4th Eclogues 72	48
No other shepheard should have scope,.		158	Cert Sonnets 28	7
Though false, yet with free scope more grace doth breed. . .		187	Astrophil 45	10
And setting Thee for scope		305	Psalm XXVI	4
And them who do the scope.		318	Psalm XXXIII	70
Attain unto their wished scope..		325	Psalm XXXVII	20
SCORCH				
Scortch not, but onely do darke chilling sprites remove. . .		205	Astrophil 76	8
SCORCHED				
My voice is hoarse, my throte scorcht, ...		66	2nd Eclogues 32	11
SCORCHING				
Ofte scorching sonne, ofte clowdie darkenes feares,.		71	Arcadia III 36	9
SCORE				
Come narr good Mastix, tis now full tway score		27	1st Eclogues 10	20
Shall not be scrap'd from out of heavnly scoar:.		281	Psalm IX	57
Thou wouldst not set me on their score		311	Psalm XXX	8
While I do score my losses on the winde, ...		255	Other Poems 4	498
SCORN				
Would scorne in man (their king) such feeble shows..		23	1st Eclogues 9	43
Though full of scorne, would not his duty misse, ...		96	3rd Eclogues 64	69
An humble pride, a skorne that favour staines:		151	Cert Sonnets 22	65
And Faith faire scorne doth gaine.		159	Cert Sonnets 30	6
Though dustie wits dare scorne Astrologie, ...		177	Astrophil 26	1
Those Lovers scorne whom that Love doth possesse?.		180	Astrophil 31	13
May get no almes but scorne of beggerie.		188	Astrophil 47	8
Let all the earth with scorne recount my case, ...		198	Astrophil 64	7
And Muses scorne with vulgar braines to dwell, ...		203	Astrophil 74	3
He shall laugh them to scorn,.		271	Psalm II	10
And Liban' self with Nature's skorn, ...		310	Psalm XXIX	17
And sav'd me from foes' laughing scorn;.		310	Psalm XXX	2
But God shall scorn their moody meaning, ...		325	Psalm XXXVII	35
SCORNED				
If so great services may scorned be:		198	Astrophil 65	10
SCORNERS				
Nor yet himself with idle scorners seateth:.		270	Psalm I	4
SCORN-GOLD				
Brave crest to him hir scorn-gold haire did yeeld, ...		246	Other Poems 4	149
SCORNING				
And scorning say, "See what it is to love.".		236	Astrophil 107	14
Nay shame of men, the people's scorning game..		299	Psalm XXII	16
SCORNS				
That skin, whose passe-praise hue scorns this poore terme of white:.		205	Astrophil 77	7
SCOTCH				
If in the Scotch court be no weltring yet;		180	Astrophil 30 V	11
SCOTTISH				
If in the Scottishe Court be weltring yet;		180	Astrophil 30	11
SCOURGE				
While that we do at his sweete scourge repine, ...		59	2nd Eclogues 30	75
The scourge of life, and death's extreame disgrace,.		140	Cert Sonnets 8	1
Scourge of it selfe, still climing slipprie place, ...		176	Astrophil 23	10
Beautie's plague, Vertue's scourge, succour of lies:		206	Astrophil 78	6
SCOURGING				
For when his sin Thy scourging hath, ...		330	Psalm XXXIX	34
SCOUTS				
Skowts each motion is, the hands the horsmen,.		67	2nd Eclogues 33	8
SCRAPED				
Shall not be scrap'd from out of heavnly scoar:.		281	Psalm IX	57
SCRIP				
Not as the scrippe thou stalest, while Dorcas sleeping lay..		52	2nd Eclogues 29	8
Nico. Mine was the scrippe: but thou, that seeming raged with love,.		52	2nd Eclogues 29	9
SCUM				
Fond fancie's scum, and dregs of scattred thought, ...		161	Cert Sonnets 31	2
SCUSE				
But no scuse serves, she makes her wrath appeare		203	Astrophil 73	9
And do I then my selfe this vaine scuse give?.		227	Astrophil 93	9
SEA				
Earth, sea, ayre, fire, heav'n, hell, and gastly sprite. . .		23	1st Eclogues 9	40
The marchante man, whome gayne dothe teache the Sea.		70	Arcadia III 36	1
Let all the Sea thy teares accounted be:		125	4th Eclogues 75	20
The sea to ebbe for griefe his flowing turneth:.		136	Cert Sonnets 3	3

SEA   (CONTINUED)   PAGE   TITLE   LINE
    Sea drownd in thee, of tedious life bereave me:. . . . . . .   136 Cert Sonnets 3   15
    Fire, aire, sea, earth, fame, time, place, shew your power..   136 Cert Sonnets 3   20
    Trying high seas, nor while Sea rage you flee, ...   142 Cert Sonnets 12   2
    That, from that sea deriv'd, teares' spring did flow.. . . .   187 Astrophil   45   8
    Nor of that golden sea, whose waves in curles are brok'n:. .   213 A&S 5th Song   39
    The Fish of Sea the Native heire,. . . . .   279 Psalm VIII   30
    To mother sea you come,. . . . .   257 Other Poems   5   34
SEAL
    Yet is it seale, though errour, of true hart.. . . . .   51 2nd Eclogues 28   104
    That opened furthe my seale of comforte is) . . . .   70 Arcadia III 35   3
    Joyne you with me, to seale this promise due,. . . . .   76 Arcadia III 46   11
    First fower but say, next fowr their saying seale, ...   76 Arcadia III 46   17
    With beautie's seale, and vertue faire disguis'de, ...   85 Arcadia III 61   2
    A daintie seale of virgin-waxe,. . . . .   88 Arcadia III 62   75
    And inward griefe seale up with outward wailing. . . . . . .   109 Arcadia IV   70   6
    They are the outward seale:. . . . .   152 Cert Sonnets 23   30
    W. What seale? D. My hart deepe graven. W. Who made the band
        so fast?. . . . .   343 Possibly   1   27
SEALED
    She seald it first, then she the sealing brake,. . . . . . .   96 3rd Eclogues 64   83
    Like as the Dove which seeled up doth flie,. . . . .   144 Cert Sonnets 15   1
SEALING
    She seald it first, then she the sealing brake,. . . . . . .   96 3rd Eclogues 64   83
    (First sealing up my heart as pray of his) . . . .   141 Cert Sonnets 9   10
SEARCH
    His eyes are curious search, but vailde with warefulnesse:.   48 2nd Eclogues 28   43
    Which caught, to cruell search yeelds his chiefe part: . . .   150 Cert Sonnets 22   22
    You that do search for everie purling spring,. . . . .   172 Astrophil   15   1
    Search them, and wyked he. . . . .   283 Psalm X   67
    The lord doth search the just man's reines,. . . . .   284 Psalm XI   17
    Who search of God's face never leave.. . . . .   302 Psalm XXIV   16
SEARCHING
    By conquest's right in steade of searching kill. . . . . . .   150 Cert Sonnets 22   30
    Then was I by thy searching insight try'd, ...   289 Psalm XVII   10
SEAS
    With strong foes on land, on seas with contrary tempests . .   29 1st Eclogues 11   5
    The marchante man, whome many seas have toughte. . . . . . .   71 Arcadia III 37   1
    Seas in our eyes, and brasen tongues by nature,. . . . . . .   109 Arcadia IV   70   26
    Trying high seas, nor while Sea rage you flee, ...   142 Cert Sonnets 12   2
    So deepe in seas of vertue beauties ly.. . . . .   151 Cert Sonnets 22   58
    The waters of the seas . . . .   316 Psalm XXXIII   25
SEASON
    But it is season for to end our singing, ...   50 2nd Eclogues 28   94
    "Never season was more fit, ...   219 A&S 8th Song   53
    These birds sing: "Now use the season.". . . . .   219 A&S 8th Song   56
SEAT
    In thy owne seate a forraine state shall sit.. . . . .   11 Arcadia I   1   8
    Fire no liquor can coole: Neptune's seate would be dryd up
        there. . . . .   32 1st Eclogues 13   32
    That men's harts be thy seate and endlesse fame be thy
        servant, ...   36 1st Eclogues 13   148
    That that deare Dyamond, where wisdome holdeth a sure seate,   37 1st Eclogues 13   165
    Thy heated harte my seat is. . . . .   67 2nd Eclogues 32   43
    Contemplation here holdeth his only seate: . . . .   68 2nd Eclogues 34   7
    But wilt thy selfe in such a seate delighte, ...   79 Arcadia III 51   11
    Such living beames should her black seate assaile, ...   82 Arcadia III 55   10
    And wisdome to his wonted seate aspireth.. . . . .   83 Arcadia III 57   12
    In that sweete seate the Boy doth sport: . . . .   88 Arcadia III 62   83
    But when his seate so rooted he had found, ...   102 3rd Eclogues 66   113
    The seate of peace, the throne which is erected. . . . . . .   108 Arcadia IV   69   3
    And so by priviledge of sacred seate,. . . . .   141 Cert Sonnets 8   9
    A seate where beauty shines and vertue raignes,. . . . . . .   141 Cert Sonnets 8   10
    Of which, how much may pierce to that sweete seate,. . . . .   151 Cert Sonnets 22   46
    Churches or schooles are for thy seate more fit: . . . . . .   166 Astrophil   4   6
    The mansion seat of blisse, and just excuse of Lovers; . . .   213 A&S 5th Song   21
    Whose owne fault casts him downe, hardly high seat recovers.   213 A&S 5th Song   24
    A seat for me. . . . .   307 Psalm XXVII   30
    His justice seat the World sustains, ...   310 Psalm XXIX   25
    Let them that love Thy saving seat . . . .   332 Psalm XL   63
    When bedd from rest becomes his seat of woe, ...   333 Psalm XLI   9
SEATED
    She builds her fame on higher seated praise: . . . .   207 Astrophil   81   10
    Doth melt away though it be inmost seated.. . . . .   299 Psalm XXII   34
    Which seated is, in spotlesse honor's fielde,. . . . .   345 Possibly   4   2
SEATETH
    Nor yet himself with idle scorners seateth:. . . . .   270 Psalm I   4
SEAT'S
    And keep it joynde, fearing your seate's consumption.. . . .   15 1st Eclogues 7   42
SEATS
    Who justly make our hearts the seates of sorow?. . . . . . .   109 Arcadia IV   70   8
SECOND
    First, second, last, did binde, enforce, and arme, ...   84 Arcadia III 60   3
    The second sweetly-fenced warde, ...   87 Arcadia III 62   43
    But walking forth, the first thus to the second saide, . . .   118 4th Eclogues 73   77
    And all to second barly-brake are bent:. . . . .   249 Other Poems   4   266
SECRET
    My thoughts imprisonde in my secreat woes, ...   42 Arcadia II   21   7
    Sweete glove the wittnes of my secrett blisse. . . . .   70 Arcadia III 35   1
    Those secret joyes, which heaven to me emparte, ...   70 Arcadia III 35   14

419

SECRET   (CONTINUED)   PAGE   TITLE   LINE
      And have to Lalus shewd your secret skill, ...   91 3rd Eclogues 63   20
      With chumpish lookes, hard words, and secret nips, ...   95 3rd Eclogues 64   31
      Eagle, high looke; Wolfe secrete crueltie: . . . .   101 3rd Eclogues 66   87
      Which touch the father's hart with secret joy, ...   106 3rd Eclogues 67 113
      With secret sense of our eternall damage, ...   110 Arcadia IV   70   35
      Which oft hath Echo tir'd in secrete forrests. . . . .   111 4th Eclogues 71   12
      Of what thou seest: close up in secrete knot thy will". . . .   119 4th Eclogues 73   98
      Nor so faire levell in so secret stay, ...   175 Astrophil   20   6
      "If to secret of my hart, ...   220 A&S 8th Song   85
      In secret by-way villages. . . . .   282 Psalm X   32
      To beare his sacred flight, in secret place then clos'd, . .   291 Psalm XVIII   23
      Most secret from all knowledg. . . . .   295 Psalm XIX   52
      For such he makes his secret know, ...   304 Psalm XXV   53
      Thou art my safe and secret place. . . . .   315 Psalm XXXII   25
SECRETS
      To blase my onely secretts?. . . . .   65 2nd Eclogues 32   2
      Above line repeated at following location. . . . .   66 2nd Eclogues 32   31
      With Inward secrets of my heart. . . . .   289 Psalm XVII   8
      The secrets of my heart, ...   333 Psalm XLI   30
SECURE
      Quickly secure, and easilie in doubt, ...   27 1st Eclogues 10   28
SEE
      That see my good, and judgeth my desert: . . . .   5 Lady of May   3   16
      Since what I see, thinke, know is all but you? . . . .   12 Arcadia I   2   14
      Sing then, and see (for now thou hast inflamed me) . . . . .   15 1st Eclogues 7   20
      Such as you see, such still you shall me finde.. . . . . . .   18 1st Eclogues 7 122
      Of all those fooles that will have all they see. . . . . . .   22 1st Eclogues 8   48
      That which we see in many time hath wrought, ...   22 1st Eclogues 9   14
      Olde houses are throne downe for new we see: . . . .   24 1st Eclogues 9   84
      Such sight have they that see with goggling eyes.. . . . . .   25 1st Eclogues 9 113
      Histor. Thus may you see, howe youthe estemeth aige. . . . .   26 1st Eclogues 9 138
      Since that we see our saddest Shepheards out . . . .   27 1st Eclogues 10   26
      That sport it is to see with howe great art . . . .   27 1st Eclogues 10   41
      For what they see their parents love or hate . . . .   28 1st Eclogues 10   56
      When that we see our ofspring gaily bent, ...   28 1st Eclogues 10   59
      That her I see, though you did lose your light.. . . . . . .   38 Arcadia II   14   4
      In watry glasse my watrie eyes I see:. . . . .   41 Arcadia II   21   5
      And see therein how well the writer fares. . . . .   42 Arcadia II   21   16
      P. Reason hath eyes to see his owne ill case.. . . . .   46 2nd Eclogues 27   16
      Thou mayest love her that I may see thy sightfulnesse. . . .   51 2nd Eclogues 28 113
      Nico. Ah now I see, why thou art in thy selfe so blind:.. . .   52 2nd Eclogues 29   5
      Do you not heare his voice, and see his shape? . . . .   53 2nd Eclogues 29   59
      Nico. O Faunes, O Fairies all, and do you see, ...   54 2nd Eclogues 29   63
      Me thinkes I see the lippes my Leuca hath, ...   54 2nd Eclogues 29   76
      Griefe onely makes his wretched state to see . . . .   58 2nd Eclogues 30   32
      Plangus must live to see Eronae's death. . . . .   58 2nd Eclogues 30   55
      Serve all thy starrie eyes this shame to see?. . . . .   58 2nd Eclogues 30   61
      What ere you see, thinke, touch, kisse, speake, or love, . .   60 2nd Eclogues 30 123
      Faire Rocks, goodly rivers, sweet woods, when shall I see
            peace? Peace.. . . . .   62 2nd Eclogues 31   1
      Seeke then and see, what man esteemeth best, ...   75 Arcadia III   44   5
      Bend all thy light to see. . . . .   80 Arcadia III   52   9
      Disdainst we see thee staind with other's light. . . . . . .   80 Arcadia III   52   15
      Two gleaming Sunnes of splendour like I see, ...   81 Arcadia III   55   4
      A whiter beautie you may see.. . . . .   85 Arcadia III   62   6
      Because themselves cannot see.. . . . .   86 Arcadia III   62   22
      There may one see, and yet not see . . . .   88 Arcadia III   62   67
      To see her ofspring seeke a good increase, ...   91 3rd Eclogues 63   2
      As in a sommer day a man might see:. . . . .   94 3rd Eclogues 64   4
      Thus may you see, the jealous wretch was made. . . . .   97 3rd Eclogues 64 121
      Then such be he, as she his worth may see, ...   98 3rd Eclogues 65   3
      Of that small light oft watching shepheards see. . . . . . .   98 3rd Eclogues 66   7
      I sate me downe: for see to goe ne could,. . . . .   99 3rd Eclogues 66   20
      Publique our losse: so, see, thy shame is publique.. . . . .   109 Arcadia IV   70   24
      Long since I see my joyes come to their evening, ...   112 4th Eclogues 71   29
      Strephon. Me seemes I see the high and stately mountaines, .   112 4th Eclogues 71   37
      Klaius. Me seemes I see a filthie clowdie evening, ...   112 4th Eclogues 71   43
      I wish no evenings more to see, each evening;. . . . .   112 4th Eclogues 71   58
      The darkened heav'n my soule which nought can see; . . . . .   114 4th Eclogues 72   35
      So that I see, although my sight empaire, ...   115 4th Eclogues 72   59
      Such vitall sparke, that her mine eyes might see. . . . . . .   115 4th Eclogues 72   84
      That forced with grief reveales what greeved eyes dyd see) .   118 4th Eclogues 73   56
      When I such guests did see come out of such a house, ...   118 4th Eclogues 73   75
      Our yeares doo it require: you see we both doo feele . . . .   120 4th Eclogues 73 121
      Ne yet for what I see, your beauties merite ought. . . . . .   121 4th Eclogues 73 164
      "Nay thou (said both) shalt see such beames shine in her
            face . . . .   121 4th Eclogues 73 175
      That I things erst unseene should first in dreaming see? . .   121 4th Eclogues 73 182
      Thy selfe henceforth the light doo never see. . . . .   125 4th Eclogues 75   24
      And see by this picture to you presented, ...   128 4th Eclogues 75 122
      For see alas, who is from you absented.. . . . .   128 4th Eclogues 75 124
      Let them be clearde, and now begin to see, ...   131 Arcadia V   77   11
      Like those whom dreames make uglie monsters see, ...   136 Cert Sonnets   2   11
      The fire to see my wrongs for anger burneth: . . . .   136 Cert Sonnets   3   1
      To see my night of evils, which hath no morow. . . . .   136 Cert Sonnets   3   8
      Place see my grave uptorne:. . . . .   136 Cert Sonnets   3   19
      To see what faire sight there raigneth, ...   140 Cert Sonnets   7   26
      In thy face I plainly see, ...   140 Cert Sonnets   7   29
      And see you not that I fall now to ryme? . . . .   146 Cert Sonnets 17   40

420

SEE   (CONTINUED)   PAGE   TITLE   LINE

In Dales I see each way a hard assent: 147   Cert Sonnets 18   10
Infected mindes infect each thing they see.   147   Cert Sonnets 18   14
But eyes these beauties see not, ...   152   Cert Sonnets 23   25
I see since I saw you: 157   Cert Sonnets 28   2
To see me as you see?.   158   Cert Sonnets 28   32
That doth both shine and give us sight to see.   161   Cert Sonnets 32   8
Then farewell world, thy uttermost I see, ...   144   Cert Sonnets 32   13
Oft turning others' leaves, to see if thence would flow. . . .   165   Astrophil   1   7
Or seeke heavn's course, or heavn's inside to see: 169   Astrophil   10   5
In nature apt to like when I did see   172   Astrophil   16   1
I see my course to lose my selfe doth bend:.   174   Astrophil   18   12
I see and yet no greater sorow take, ...   174   Astrophil   18   13
That see my wracke, and yet embrace the same?.   174   Astrophil   19   2
See there that boy, that murthring boy I say, ...   174   Astrophil   20   2
It is most true, for since I her did see, ...   177   Astrophil   25   12
And then would not, or could not see my blisse:.   181   Astrophil   33   2
And ah what hope, that hope should once see day, ...   182   Astrophil   35   7
Rich in all beauties which man's eye can see:.   183   Astrophil   37   6
Livelier then else-where, Stella's image see.   184   Astrophil   39   14
For though I never see them, but straight wayes.   186   Astrophil   42   9
For when he will see who dare him gainesay, ...   186   Astrophil   43   5
If Love learne not alone to love and see, ...   187   Astrophil   46   7
O looke, o shine, o let me die and see.   188   Astrophil   48   8
With sad eyes I their weake proportion see, ...   189   Astrophil   50   7
Till that her blush taught me my shame to see.   191   Astrophil   53   14
Where all my good I do in Stella see, ...   194   Astrophil   60   2
And do I see some cause a hope to feede, ...   199   Astrophil   66   1
What blushing notes doest thou in margine see?   199   Astrophil   67   8
Envie, put out thine eyes, least thou do see   200   Astrophil   69   3
My spring appeares, o see what here doth grow.   200   Astrophil   69   8
In Beautie's throne, see now who dares come neare.   203   Astrophil   73   10
Makes me in my best thoughts and quietst judgement see, . . .   205   Astrophil   77   12
Or hers whom naked the Trojan boy did see.   207   Astrophil   82   4
I see the house, my heart thy selfe containe.   209   Astrophil   85   1
See Beautie's totall summe summ'd in her face: 210   Astrophil   85   10
For me, I wept to see pearles scattered so, ...   223   Astrophil   87   9
That where before hart loved and eyes did see, ...   223   Astrophil   88   12
Ah bed, the field where joye's peace some do see, ...   230   Astrophil   98   1
That in that palenesse beautie's white we see;   231   Astrophil   101   6
And scorning say, "See what it is to love.".   236   Astrophil   107   14
See the hand which waking gardeth, ...   202   A&S 2nd Song   13
See now those feathers pluckt, wherewith thou flewst most
    high:.   213   A&S 5th Song   22
See what clouds of reproch small darke thy honour's skie, . .   213   A&S 5th Song   23
You see what I can say; mend yet your froward mind, ...   215   A&S 5th Song   88
That mine eyes thine eyes may see?   225   A&S 10th Song   2
Thought see thou no place forbeare, ...   226   A&S 10th Song   19
Leave to see, and leave to wonder.".   234   A&S 11th Song   12
"What if you new beauties see, ...   234   A&S 11th Song   21
O you that see this face, ...   215   A&S 6th Song   2
Who have so leaden eyes, as not to see sweet beautie's show,   217   A&S 7th Song   7
O let them see these heavenly beames, and in faire letters
    reede.   217   A&S 7th Song   11
Heare then, but then with wonder heare; see but adoring see,   217   A&S 7th Song   13
See, do you see this face? a face? nay image of the skies, .   217   A&S 7th Song   15
See how it the leaves doth kisse.   219   A&S 8th Song   58
In this pleasant spring must see   222   A&S 9th Song   28
Such blessings shall not wycked wretches see   270   Psalm I   13
That evry folk Thy wondrous Acts may see.   277   Psalm VII   21
That by sharp proofes, the heathen themselves may see. . . .   281   Psalm IX   64
Nor danger ever see: 282   Psalm X   26
I shall see Thee in likeness Thine.   290   Psalm XVII   48
As he before his eyes did see my justice stand, ...   292   Psalm XVIII   48
Who feare Thee shall my vowes performed see.   300   Psalm XXII   60
See how I am opprest   304   Psalm XXV   63
Beleiv'd God's goodness for to see, ...   308   Psalm XXVII   62
The highest Cedars broken see, ...   310   Psalm XXIX   14
Throughout doth see.   317   Psalm XXXIII   53
I say but tast and see   319   Psalm XXXIV   29
But lo, soon as they did me staggering see, ...   322   Psalm XXXV   37
Lord wilt thou see, and wilt Thou suffer it?   322   Psalm XXXV   43
Aha! Sir, now we see you where we should.   322   Psalm XXXV   54
And in thy light shall We see light.   324   Psalm XXXVI   26
Who do ev'ill works: lo I doe see.   324   Psalm XXXVI   34
Frett not Thy self, if thou do see   324   Psalm XXXVII   1
Watch but a while, and Thou shalt see.   325   Psalm XXXVII   25
Yea thou shalt see the ev'ill decay.   327   Psalm XXXVII   88
And as I mus'd such World to see, ...   329   Psalm XXXIX   10
What do we seeke? the greatest state I see   330   Psalm XXXIX   17
So prest with sins I cannot see my case.   332   Psalm XL   44
With sight made dymme with dayly teares another's sport to
    see.   343   Possibly   1   4
Now let those lightsome sights we see thy darknes overcome.   343   Possibly   1   12
Courage therefore, and let the stately see   346   Possibly   5   3
Then shall you see them yelde, Allarme allarme.   346   Possibly   5   14
Well for to see they kept themselves unsene, ...   244   Other Poems   4   89
Sometimes we see small birds from nests do pull.   245   Other Poems   4   136
And so must see great cause before they love.   245   Other Poems   4   144
In dede thou said'st it was thy frend to see, ...   247   Other Poems   4   219

SEE   (CONTINUED)   PAGE TITLE   LINE

```
SEE               (CONTINUED)                        PAGE   TITLE        LINE
    There may you see, soone as the middle two . . . . . . . . 248 Other Poems  4  233
    So on the downs we see, neere Wilton faire,. . . . . . . . 251 Other Poems  4  342
    To see the sportes of double-shining day,. . . . . . . . . 251 Other Poems  4  362
    As on sweet flowrs when morning's drops we see.. . . . . . 252 Other Poems  4  398
    To see hir eies, with how true humblenes . . . . . . . . . 252 Other Poems  4  402
    To see, to feele, to heare, to tast, to know . . . . . . . 252 Other Poems  4  407
    Those eies, which nothing like themselves can see, . . . . 253 Other Poems  4  451
    "When I see her, my sinewes shake for feare, . . . . . . . 253 Other Poems  4  457
    I still do see, though I be still alone. . . . . . . . . . 254 Other Poems  4  462
    And now faire evenings blush my shame to see.. . . . . . . 254 Other Poems  4  480
    And yet I see her shine amid the cloud.. . . . . . . . . . 255 Other Poems  4  506
    Let Pan our good God see,. . . . . . . . . . . . . . . . . 260 Other Poems  6    3
    "My old mates I grieve to see, . . . . . . . . . . . . . . 262 Other Poems  7   19
    So many pufft in minde I see,. . . . . . . . . . . . . . . 263 Other Poems  7   50
SEECH
    Onely the owle still warnde them not to seech. . . . . . . 100 3rd Eclogues 66  68
SEED
    With seede of woes my hart brimme-full is charged. . . . .  16 1st Eclogues  7  78
    With Jove's disdaine at such a rival's seed, . . . . . . .  21 1st Eclogues  8  20
    Cleofila. First shall fertill grounds not yeeld increase of
      a good seed: . . . . . . . . . . . . . . . . . . . . . .  33 1st Eclogues 13  64
    From her, in whome is sowne their freedome's seede,. . . .  72 Arcadia III  38   4
    (As Tygers, leopards, beares, and Lions' seed) . . . . . . 102 3rd Eclogues 66 122
    The seed Fast-meaning is, no truth to misse: . . . . . . . 115 4th Eclogues 72  53
    That which their mother hight, or els their silly seed.. . 119 4th Eclogues 73  84
    For David his Anoynt, and his seed ever more.. . . . . . . 293 Psalm XVIII  91
    You Isra'el's seed, you come of Jacob, feare him.. . . . . 300 Psalm XXII   54
    Jacob this is Thy seed, God seeking generation,. . . . . . 302 Psalm XXIV   15
    By his seed eke possest. . . . . . . . . . . . . . . . . . 304 Psalm XXV    52
    Nor that his seed to begging came. . . . . . . . . . . . . 326 Psalm XXXVII 64
    The more his seed in blessing flourish;. . . . . . . . . . 326 Psalm XXXVII 66
SEEING
    And lives in fancye's seing. . . . . . . . . . . . . . . .  20 1st Eclogues  7 V965
    Seeing, Alas, so mightie powers bende. . . . . . . . . . .  73 Arcadia III  40   5
    And seeing feele in me . . . . . . . . . . . . . . . . . .  81 Arcadia III  55   5
    Not seeing earst such token in the wife, . . . . . . . . .  96 3rd Eclogues 64  68
    May paint my face without seeing mee,. . . . . . . . . . . 153 Cert Sonnets 24   3
    Seeing how once you saw I liv'd, . . . . . . . . . . . . . 158 Cert Sonnets 28  31
    You have the same in my hands, seeing. . . . . . . . . . . 159 Cert Sonnets 29   8
    The curious wits, seeing dull pensivenesse . . . . . . . . 176 Astrophil    23   1
    I, seeing better sights in sight's decay,. . . . . . . . . 184 Astrophil    38  12
    Or seeing jets, blacke, but in blacknesse bright.. . . . . 225 Astrophil    91   8
    Seeing hope yeeld when this wo strake him furst: . . . . . 228 Astrophil    95   6
    Or seeing, have so wodden wits, as not that worth to know; 217 A&S 7th Song      8
    Seing me so long to beare. . . . . . . . . . . . . . . . . 222 A&S 9th Song     33
    The power of Thy through-seing eyes? . . . . . . . . . . . 283 Psalm X      54
    Both light and force of seing. . . . . . . . . . . . . . . 294 Psalm XIX    36
    So farr from seing myne unhealthfull eyes, . . . . . . . . 298 Psalm XXII    3
    Which many seeing hearts shall rayse . . . . . . . . . . . 331 Psalm XL     13
    Of Thy face to have a seing? . . . . . . . . . . . . . . . 334 Psalm XLII    8
    Till Uran seing Pas to Cosma fly,. . . . . . . . . . . . . 249 Other Poems   4 286
    So joy I, in you seeing; . . . . . . . . . . . . . . . . . 261 Other Poems   6  44
SEEK
    How dare I, wretch, seeke there my woes to rest, . . . . .   3 Lady of May   1   5
    Seeke other thoughts thy life or death to find;. . . . . .   4 Lady of May   2  15
    Happie be they which well beleeve, and never seeke the rest. 12 Arcadia I    3  14
    My hart doth seeke another estimation. . . . . . . . . . .  19 1st Eclogues  7 175
    Seeke to espie her faultes as well as praise,. . . . . . .  25 1st Eclogues  9 121
    Seeke skill of hearbes in hills, haunt brookes neere night, 26 1st Eclogues  9 127
    Goe graft againe, and seeke to graft them right, . . . . .  26 1st Eclogues  9 129
    But so unheard, condemn'd, kept thence we do seeke to abide
      in,. . . . . . . . . . . . . . . . . . . . . . . . . . .  32 1st Eclogues 13  25
    With bolde clamor unheard, unmarckt, what I seeke what I
      suffer:. . . . . . . . . . . . . . . . . . . . . . . . .  35 1st Eclogues 13 112
    Lawrell shews what I seeke, by the Mirre is show'd how I
      seeke it,. . . . . . . . . . . . . . . . . . . . . . . .  35 1st Eclogues 13 116
    With sighes you seeke to coole your hotte desire:. . . . .  38 Arcadia II   14   6
    My head you seeke, as to your strongest forte. . . . . . .  38 Arcadia II   14  10
    Theere seeke defence where weakenesse is the force:. . . .  49 2nd Eclogues 28  77
    And saith, although I seeke my life to flie, . . . . . . .  58 2nd Eclogues 30  54
    Seeke we to tame these childish superfluities: . . . . . .  61 2nd Eclogues 30 138
    Boulon. Who still doth seeke against himselfe offences,. .  62 2nd Eclogues 30 167
    What do lovers seeke for, long seeking for to enjoy? Joy..  63 2nd Eclogues 31  13
    Nor ought I seeke to shun death, . . . . . . . . . . . . .  67 2nd Eclogues 32  55
    Seeke then and see, what man esteemeth best, . . . . . . .  75 Arcadia III  44   5
    To see her ofspring seeke a good increase, . . . . . . . .  91 3rd Eclogues 63   2
    Fuell to seeke and not to quench the fire: . . . . . . . .  95 3rd Eclogues 64  40
    Iron to seeke, which gainst it selfe should bend,. . . . . 102 3rd Eclogues 66 116
    For I seeke not their shame, but still me thinkes, . . . . 105 3rd Eclogues 67  56
    O Histor, seeke within thy selfe to flourish:. . . . . . . 106 3rd Eclogues 67 109
    Earth thou didst seeke, and store of earth thou hast.. . . 108 Arcadia IV   68   2
    Whereto I yeeld, and seeke no other breath,. . . . . . . . 114 4th Eclogues 72  18
    And seeke to nourish that, which now contaynes . . . . . . 114 4th Eclogues 72  22
    And now before we seeke by wise Apollo's skill . . . . . . 120 4th Eclogues 73 125
    That thou shalt never dare seeke helpe of wretched case".. 121 4th Eclogues 73 176
    Such thing cannot I seeke (Despaire hath giv'n me my answer. 122 4th Eclogues 74 11
    And banished doo I live, nor now will seeke a recov'rie, . 124 4th Eclogues 74  83
    Whence, whence alas, shall we seeke our direction! . . . . 129 4th Eclogues 76  19
    And putting out our eyes seeke we our light. . . . . . . . 130 4th Eclogues 76  36
```

SEEK   (CONTINUED)   PAGE   TITLE   LINE

Faire seeke not to be feard, most lovely beloved by thy
    servants,. 143 Cert Sonnets 14   1
I do protest and seeke with service due, ... 145 Cert Sonnets 17   2
Thus what I seeke is in you: . . . . 155 Cert Sonnets 25 33
Within my selfe to seeke my onelie hire: . . . . 161 Cert Sonnets 31 13
Or seeke heavn's course, or heavn's inside to see: . . . . . 169 Astrophil   10   5
You seeke to nurse at fullest breasts of Fame, ... 172 Astrophil   15 13
Stella thinke not that I by verse seeke fame,. . . . . 224 Astrophil   90   1
Who seeke, who hope, who love, who live but thee;. . . . . . 224 Astrophil   90   2
Seeke a better place of feeding, ... 221 A&S 9th Song   2
That seek to Thee. 280 Psalm IX   30
Then what man would so soon seek gold. . . . . 294 Psalm XIX   41
Seek ye my Face, when Thou didst say,. . . . . 307 Psalm XXVII   39
Seek Thy face still. . . . . 308 Psalm XXVII   42
Save me from foes who seek my bane to bake.. . . . . 313 Psalm XXXI   42
But who seek God with constancy. . . . . 319 Psalm XXXIV   39
Seek peace and follow after it,. . . . . 320 Psalm XXXIV   54
That seek my bane, O make me understand. . . . . 321 Psalm XXXV   5
For causeles they did seek to make me dy. . . . . 321 Psalm XXXV   16
And seek of life for to bereave him; . . . . 326 Psalm XXXVII 82
Though I did seek, I never found. . . . . 327 Psalm XXXVII 92
What do we seeke? the greatest state I see . . . . 330 Psalm XXXIX 17
To seek Thy beauty past conceit; . . . . 332 Psalm XL   62
When thou hast mynd to weepe, seeke out som smoky room:. . . 343 Possibly   1 11
Like some which seeke to salve their blotted name. . . . . . 248 Other Poems 4 231
SEEKERS
And God shall be by those his seekers praysed. . . . . 300 Psalm XXII   62
SEEKETH
Who seeketh heav'n and comes of heav'nly breath. . . . . . . 144 Cert Sonnets 32 12
SEEKING
Still seeking Love, love found as much I flie. . . . . 41 Arcadia II   20   4
What do lovers seeke for, long seeking for to enjoy? Joy... 63 2nd Eclogues 31 13
Seeking the Sainct in whome all graces dwell,. . . . . 71 Arcadia III 36 14
All privatenes, selfe-seeking, inward spite, ... 93 3rd Eclogues 63 65
Seeking to quench in me the noble fire,. . . . . 200 Astrophil   68   7
So manie eyes ay seeking their owne woe, ... 206 Astrophil   78 12
Jacob this is Thy seed, God seeking generation,. . . . . . . 302 Psalm XXIV   15
Seeking some refreshing brook, ... 334 Psalm XLII   2
SEEKS
R. We are too strong: but Reason seekes not blood. . . . . . 47 2nd Eclogues 27 29
Seekes to make ech thing badge of his sweet passion. . . . . 47 2nd Eclogues 28   6
Oft prove I: but what salve, when Reason seeks to be gone?
    One. . . . . 63 2nd Eclogues 31 11
Who seekes to knowe, acquaintes hym self with hell;. . . . . 71 Arcadia III 36 16
Since bashfull dread seekes where he knowes me harmed: . . . 135 Cert Sonnets 1   2
SEEK-SORROW
And thou, seke-sorow Klaius, them among: . . . . 247 Other Poems 4 218
SEEKST
But, foole, seekst not to get into her hart. . . . . 170 Astrophil   11 14
SEELY
The seely wretch with foule affliction staind, ... 300 Psalm XXII   56
Of shepheards two the seely case to show,. . . . . 242 Other Poems 4   6
Of seely boies please unacquainted sight:. . . . . 246 Other Poems 4 182
"Tell me my seely pipe,. . . . . 257 Other Poems 5 53
Seely shepheards are not witting . . . . 262 Other Poems 7 29
Grant, I say (if seely man . . . . 263 Other Poems 7 57
SEEM
His horned head doth seeme the heaven to spight: . . . . . . 21 1st Eclogues 8 29
Oft comes reliefe when most we seeme in trappe.. . . . . . . 23 1st Eclogues 9 24
Nature against we do seeme to rebell, seeme fooles in a
    vaine sute... 32 1st Eclogues 13 24
Such this smale greatnes, doth seeme compar'd to the
    greatest.. . . . . 34 1st Eclogues 13 76
Or to the Sun for wonders seeme small sparks of a candle:. . 34 1st Eclogues 13 79
Seeme to your eyes of a disgracefull hewe: . . . . 38 Arcadia II   15   6
Silence doth seeme the maske of base oppression. . . . . . . 47 2nd Eclogues 28 15
If three-leav'd grasse seeme to the sheepe unsavorie,. . . . 48 2nd Eclogues 28 23
Joie's strangers seeme, I cannot bide their showe, ... 74 Arcadia III 41   5
Seeme to proceede, so well it was devisde. . . . . 96 3rd Eclogues 64 82
Hart-broken so, that molehilles seeme high mountaines, . . . 111 4th Eclogues 71 23
Whose eyes seeme chaste, because they looke on ground: . . . 147 Cert Sonnets 17 50
The shading woods seeme now my Sunne to darke, ... 147 Cert Sonnets 18   7
Weakely did seeme to paint death's ougly dart. . . . . 148 Cert Sonnets 20   4
Seeme most alone in greatest companie. . . . . 178 Astrophil   27   2
Of Hope, which makes it seeme faire to the eye.. . . . . . . 189 Astrophil   49   8
If you heare that they seeme my hart to move,. . . . . 225 Astrophil   91 13
When silent night might seeme all faults to hide,. . . . . . 289 Psalm XVII   9
Whose life doth seeme most greatly blest . . . . 290 Psalm XVII   39
That wicked men do seeme to flourish,. . . . . 324 Psalm XXXVII   2
But fearing lest all white might seeme too good, ... 246 Other Poems 4 151
His heels grow'n proud did seme at heav'n to shake. . . . . . 248 Other Poems 4 261
Strephon so chas'd did seme in milke to swimme.. . . . . . . 249 Other Poems 4 288
All visions seeme, at every bush I start:. . . . . 253 Other Poems 4 445
SEEMED
Seemde but to spoyle the foode of thoughts long famished... 16 1st Eclogues 7 69
Might freely rome, or rest, as seemed them:. . . . . 100 3rd Eclogues 66 48
That last day seem'd, he could not chew a beane. . . . . . . 103 3rd Eclogues 67   6
They seemd to me) on whom did waite a Virgin pure: . . . . . 118 4th Eclogues 73 64
She seemed full of jealous feares, ... 158 Cert Sonnets 28 15

		PAGE	TITLE		LINE
SEEMED	(CONTINUED)				
And others' feete still seem'd but strangers in my way....		165	Astrophil	1	11
They fled with blush, which guiltie seem'd of love......		199	Astrophil	66	14
While craftily you seem'd your cut to keepe, ...		208	Astrophil	83	3
And their Renoune, which seemed so lyke to last, ...		280	Psalm IX		13
Moving, she seem'd at once to kisse, and speake.		244	Other Poems	4	96
For they seem'd made even of skie-mettall best,.......		244	Other Poems	4	100
Strephon, whose absence seem'd unto thee long,.......		247	Other Poems	4	220
The hidden beauties seem'd in waite to lye,.........		250	Other Poems	4	303
So caught, him seem'd he caught of joyes the bell, ...		250	Other Poems	4	311
Who victor seem'd, was to his ruine brought:		251	Other Poems	4	346
Who seem'd orethrown was mistresse of the field:		251	Other Poems	4	347
Her breath, then short, seem'd loth from home to pas,....		252	Other Poems	4	399
SEEMING					
Nico. Mine was the scrippe: but thou, that seeming raged with love, ...		52	2nd Eclogues	29	9
The sheep, mild-seeming face; climing, the Beare;......		101	3rd Eclogues	66	90
Which seeming lesse, yet nobler life doth move.......		151	Cert Sonnets	22	60
His will false-seeming holie		160	Cert Sonnets	30	15
Each motion seeming shott from beautie's bow,.......		244	Other Poems	4	106
SEEMS					
Which being nought seems somewhat to the eyen,.......		19	1st Eclogues	7	164
Great to thee my estate seemes, thy estate is blest by my judgement:		33	1st Eclogues	13	72
Whom both nature seemes to debarr from meanes to be helped,.		37	1st Eclogues	13	158
And Venus seemes, to make up her, she spent herselfe.. ...		49	2nd Eclogues	28	66
Wce, but seems to me joy, that agrees to my thought so. I thought so...		64	2nd Eclogues	31	38
The Waspe seemes gay, but is a combrous thing.		104	3rd Eclogues	67	21
That whereas blacke seemes Beautie's contrary, ...		168	Astrophil	7	10
Each day seemes long, and longs for long-staid night,....		224	Astrophil	89	5
But murder, private fault, seems but a toy to thee,.....		214	A&S 5th Song		55
Love more affected seemes.		216	A&S 6th Song		31
When most he seemes opprest.		320	Psalm XXXIV		72
The day seemes long, but night is odious		253	Other Poems	4	435
SEEN					
Lalus. If thou wilt not be seene, thy face goe hide away,..		15	1st Eclogues	7	13
Seen, and unknowne; heard, but without attention.......		19	1st Eclogues	7	179
Yet have I seene when well a wolfe he shooke........		27	1st Eclogues	10	18
That it both seene and felte may with you live".		101	3rd Eclogues	66	77
For murdre done, which never erst was seene, ...		102	3rd Eclogues	66	127
In ruling of a house so well shee's seene.		106	3rd Eclogues	67	90
So it be seene what sorrow in me raigneth.		128	4th Eclogues	75	105
Have you not seene her mood, ...		158	Cert Sonnets	28	21
Who hath such beautie seene.		158	Cert Sonnets	28	25
Yet swam in joy, such love in her was seene.		223	Astrophil	87	11
The gulfs of waters then were through their Chanels seen,..		291	Psalm XVIII		31
This thou hast seen, and wilt thou silent be?........		322	Psalm XXXV		55
I have the Wicked seen full sound, ...		327	Psalm XXXVII		89
So have I sene trim bookes in velvet dight		246	Other Poems	4	180
His soule did fly as she was seen to run..........		251	Other Poems	4	372
Wayling till death, shun you not to be seene?........		258	Other Poems	5	91
SEES					
That Goddesse mine, my blessed being sees"..........		4	Lady of May	3	6
Such active minde but seldome passion sees..........		26	1st Eclogues	9	134
My tongue doth tell what fancie sees............		89	Arcadia III	62	94
Who onely sees the ill is worse then blind..........		106	3rd Eclogues	67	85
The other sees it but disguised.		159	Cert Sonnets	29	18
Stella oft sees the verie face of wo		187	Astrophil	45	1
As what my hart still sees thou canst not spie?.......		235	Astrophil	105	4
SEEST					
But thanke the cause, thou seest, when he is dim........		27	1st Eclogues	10	12
Thou seest, how friske, and jolly now he is, ...		103	3rd Eclogues	67	5
To onely thee thou seest we graunt this speciall grace ...		119	4th Eclogues	73	95
Of what thou seest: close up in secrete knot thy will"....		119	4th Eclogues	73	98
Thou seest each side the walking doth endure		285	Psalm XII		25
Will. Thou seest my eares do itch at it: good Dick thy sorow tell.		343	Possibly	1	18
SEETH					
No Sunne, which shines, and seeth not, ...		86	Arcadia III	62	18
SEIZE					
Shall I, whose eares her mournefull words did seaze, ...		58	2nd Eclogues	30	50
Whose fyrie chaines, uppon his freedome seaze, ...		74	Arcadia III	41	4
One grave their bodies seaze:		92	3rd Eclogues	63	32
Seaze on all to her belonging;		226	A&S 10th Song		21
All her hate, death soone would seaze me,..........		222	A&S 9th Song		44
SELDOM					
Dorus. Nightingales seldome sing, the Pie still chattereth:.		14	1st Eclogues	7	7
Such active minde but seldome passion sees..........		26	1st Eclogues	9	134
They seldome ponder what to them is due.		104	3rd Eclogues	67	27
Ther was (o seldome blessed word of was!).		242	Other Poems	4	17
SELF					
Who in one selfe these diverse gifts can plant;.......		3	Lady of May	1	4
"Tush, tush", said nature, "this is all but a trifle, a man's selfe.		29	1st Eclogues	11	7
And yet neither of us great or blest deemeth his owne selfe.		33	1st Eclogues	13	73
In silence, from a man's owne selfe with company robbed. ..		35	1st Eclogues	13	106
Jaylor I am to my selfe, prison and prisoner to myne owne selfe.		37	1st Eclogues	13	163
Unto my selfe let after-livers know.		40	Arcadia II	18	10

SELF	(CONTINUED)	PAGE	TITLE		LINE
Since in my hands selfe goodly sight she tooke..		55	2nd Eclogues	29	116
Now whether mov'd with selfe unworthines,.		94	3rd Eclogues	64	7
The pistle selfe, such kinde of wordes it had, ...		96	3rd Eclogues	64	91
Turning all nature's course to selfe displeasure..		108	Arcadia IV	69	8
Since that in selfe same metall coin'd,.		159	Cert Sonnets	29	3
Thou blind man's marke, thou foole's selfe chosen snare, . .		161	Cert Sonnets	31	1
Which Cupid's selfe from Beautie's myne did draw:.		169	Astrophil	9	13
Since Reason's selfe doth blow the cole in me?		182	Astrophil	35	6
By Love's owne selfe, but with so curious drought, ...		184	Astrophil	38	7
Where blushing red, that Love's selfe them doth love,. . . .		186	Astrophil	43	10
Be Love's indeed, in Stella's selfe he may		191	Astrophil	52	10
Let Vertue have that Stella's selfe; yet thus, ...		191	Astrophil	52	13
The thorowest words, fit for woe's selfe to grone, ...		193	Astrophil	57	4
That Anger' selfe I needs must kisse againe.		203	Astrophil	73	14
In Lillies' neast, where Love's selfe lies along..		208	Astrophil	83	8
Cannot such grace your silly selfe content,.		208	Astrophil	83	11
A still felt plague, to selfe condemning me:		212	Astrophil	86	3
Which Nature' selfe did make, and selfe engraind the same? .		232	Astrophil	102	6
Let honor selfe to thee graunt highest place..		233	Astrophil	103	14
But thou art gone, now that selfe felt disgrace.		235	Astrophil	106	7
Stella's selfe might not refuse thee.		220	A&S 8th Song		96
But doth God' self disdain..		281	Psalm X		12
His judgments be self verity,.		294	Psalm XIX		39
Link not me in self same chain		309	Psalm XXVIII		11
And Liban' self with Nature's skorn, ...		310	Psalm XXIX		17
Fall in self pitt, be caught in their own nett..		321	Psalm XXXV		18
He found that Reason's self now reasons found.		253	Other Poems	4	423
With in himselfe of hir deare selfe to speake, ...		255	Other Poems	4	534
SELF-CONCEIT					
Who for a selfe-conceipt will that forbeare, ...		105	3rd Eclogues	67	80
SELF-DESTRUCTION					
Where it should be to selfe-destruction bound?		57	2nd Eclogues	30	13
SELF-DIVISION					
O wretched state of man in selfe division!		20	1st Eclogues	7	V966
Above line repeated at following location.		20	1st Eclogues	7	V967
SELF-GUARD					
Self-gard with mildnes, Sport with Majesty:.		247	Other Poems	4	214
SELF-GUILTY					
Selfe-guiltie folke must prove to feele compassion..		60	2nd Eclogues	30	130
SELF-HURT					
While nought but game, the selfe-hurt wanton ment.		247	Other Poems	4	192
SELF-LIKE					
Where by his words his self-like cause he knew..		256	Other Poems	4	536
SELF-LOST					
Selfe-lost and wandring, banished that place we doe come					
from,.		32	1st Eclogues	13	26
SELF-LOVE					
Of our selfe-love (so passions do deceave)		59	2nd Eclogues	30	69
SELF-MISERY					
A monster, other's harme, selfe-miserie, ...		206	Astrophil	78	5
SELFNESS					
That wholly hers, all selfnesse he forbeares,.		195	Astrophil	61	7
SELF-NOBILITY					
No, no: no wordes ennoble selfe-nobilitie.		48	2nd Eclogues	28	28
SELF-SEEKING					
All privatenes, selfe-seeking, inward spite, ...		93	3rd Eclogues	63	65
SELL					
I would the earth, I would the heavens sell.		116	4th Eclogues	72	93
SELLS					
Who sells not guiltlesse cause, for filthy love of gain: . .		287	Psalm XV		12
SELVES					
And damning their owne selves to Tantal's smart, ...		177	Astrophil	24	3
Their sugred selves to kisse thy happy hedd:		258	Other Poems	5	58
SENATORS					
Like Senators a harmeles empire had.		100	3rd Eclogues	66	56
SEND					
Since to my hart her shape you so did sende;		38	Arcadia II	14	3
Then rage for rage: rather my wish I send to thee, ...		50	2nd Eclogues	28	97
Unto my woes the hatefull heavens do sende,.		73	Arcadia III	40	2
Like to my brother's raies, yet those I sende.		82	Arcadia III	55	14
To teare the bowels, that good corne should send..		102	3rd Eclogues	66	117
(Or such a noise it was, as highest thunders sende,.		118	4th Eclogues	73	53
Into thy hart by the sight of this Epistle I send:		122	4th Eclogues	74	6
Nay to the heav'ns your just complayninges sende,.		126	4th Eclogues	75	37
But unto Man, age ever death doth sende.		127	4th Eclogues	75	84
Who hard by made a window send forth light..		191	Astrophil	53	9
Thought therefore I will send thee,.		226	A&S 10th Song		13
For unto Thee I will my prayer send, ...		274	Psalm V		6
They ever shall send thee their praysing voyce,.		275	Psalm V		35
Since ever thou to them wilt succour send.		275	Psalm V		36
Thou righteous proofes to hearts, and reines dost send,. . .		277	Psalm VII		28
Thou dost put out, and quite consuming send.		280	Psalm IX		14
Which to Thy self my soul will send.		290	Psalm XVII		20
Send unto desolation		297	Psalm XXI		38
To thee Lord my cry I send..		308	Psalm XXVIII		1
Send Thy truth and light,.		336	Psalm XLIII		13
Faire Nous with Pas the lott to hell did sende:.		248	Other Poems	4	244
SENDETH					
Which Holland sweet now gently sendeth in, ...		259	Other Poems	5	106

		PAGE	TITLE	LINE
SENDS				
As happie shewes of corne when harvest sendes;		71	Arcadia III 37	10
Approching warmes (not else) dead logges up sends, ...		150	Cert Sonnets 22	12
And as a Queene, who from her presence sends		236	Astrophil 107	9
SENSE				
How thou from foolish love maist purge thy sense.		25	1st Eclogues 9	110
Their first caught sence prefers to teacher's blowes.		28	1st Eclogues 10	57
And shall sensive things be so sencelesse as to resist sence		36	1st Eclogues 13	138
Or Reason lie a slave to servile Sense, ...		49	2nd Eclogues 28	76
With sense possest, and claim'd by reason's right:		74	Arcadia III 42	6
Tc her sweete sence, sweete sleepe, some ease imparte, . . .		79	Arcadia III 51	3
Her sence too weake to beare her spirit's mighte.		79	Arcadia III 51	4
Held, pearst, possest, my judgement, sence, and will, ...		84	Arcadia III 60	6
My soule is bliste, sence joyde, and fortune raysed.		108	Arcadia IV 69	14
With secret sense of our eternall damage, ...		110	Arcadia IV 70	35
Since naked sence can conquer reason armed:		135	Cert Sonnets 1	6
Fire burne me quite, till sense of burning leave me:		136	Cert Sonnets 3	13
Unto her rested sense a perfect waking, ...		137	Cert Sonnets 4	2
That sense feeles more then what doth sense containe?		142	Cert Sonnets 11	8
If rebell sence would reason's law receyve;		147	Cert Sonnets 19	3
Thought, reason, sense, time, you, and I, maintaine.		148	Cert Sonnets 19	18
My lake is sense, whose still streames never runne, ...		150	Cert Sonnets 22	5
Nor sence that grace descryes:		152	Cert Sonnets 23	26
For though my sense be from me, ...		154	Cert Sonnets 25	21
And I be dead who want sense, ...		154	Cert Sonnets 25	22
Al my sense thy sweetnesse gained, ...		156	Cert Sonnets 27	1
Wouldst brabling be with sence and love in me:		169	Astrophil 10	2
Leave sense, and those which sense's objects be.		169	Astrophil 10	7
But thou wouldst needs fight both with love and sence, . . .		170	Astrophil 10	9
That never I with clos'd-up sense do lie, ...		181	Astrophil 32	6
I start, looke, hearke, but what in closde up sence.		184	Astrophil 38	9
Was held, in opend sense it flies away, ...		184	Astrophil 38	10
Oppressing mortall sense, my death proceed, ...		186	Astrophil 42	13
My mind bemones his sense of inward smart;		186	Astrophil 44	2
Or want I sense to feele my miserie?		188	Astrophil 47	5
Each sence of mine, each gift, each power of mind, ...		193	Astrophil 57	2
So captives to his Saint both soule and sence, ...		195	Astrophil 61	6
Pleasingst consort, where each sence holds a part, ...		206	Astrophil 79	3
And her sad words my sadded sence did heare.		223	Astrophil 87	8
My Orphan sence flies to the inward sight, ...		223	Astrophil 88	10
Which even to sence, sence of it selfe denies, ...		228	Astrophil 94	7
Such light in sense, with such a darkned mind.		231	Astrophil 99	14
Where rigrows exile lockes up all my sense?.		233	Astrophil 104	8
The common sence, which might.		216	A&S 6th Song	43
Sense of love to love inspiring.		219	A&S 8th Song	60
SENSELESS				
Then cries to sencelesse things, which neither knowes. . . .		23	1st Eclogues 9	41
If the sencelesse spheares doo yet hold a musique, ...		30	1st Eclogues 12	13
And shall sensive things be so sencelesse as to resist sence		36	1st Eclogues 13	138
Through pores of sencelesse trees, as it could make them move:		208	A&S 3rd Song	2
Senseles quite, ...		328	Psalm XXXVIII	41
Spake unto a sencelesse tree, ...		262	Other Poems 7	16
SENSE'S				
Leave sense, and those which sense's objects be.		169	Astrophil 10	7
While he each thing in sense's ballance wayes, ...		177	Astrophil 25	6
By Sence's priviledge, can scape from thee.		183	Astrophil 36	14
SENSES				
And sorrows do require some respitt unto the sences.		37	1st Eclogues 13	175
Which do envenome both the soule and senses.		50	2nd Eclogues 28	88
To that strange stroke which conquer'd all my senses, ...		61	2nd Eclogues 30	165
Thus pure pearle, I do yeeld, my senses and soule.		68	2nd Eclogues 33	28
Where senses do behold th'order of heav'nly hoste, ...		68	2nd Eclogues 34	5
Since, as I say, both minde and sences darke		73	Arcadia III 39	9
My hart in him, his thoughtes and senses guides:		76	Arcadia III 45	6
My senses such release, as they which quiet live, ...		117	4th Eclogues 73	12
Which senses up doth shut the senses to preserve.		117	4th Eclogues 73	28
On Nature's sweet repast, as healthfull senses ledd.		117	4th Eclogues 73	40
With reason's strife, by senses overthrowne, ...		148	Cert Sonnets 19	14
Gladly my senses yeelded.		154	Cert Sonnets 25	8
Gladly my senses yeelding, ...		154	Cert Sonnets 25	9
Thus be my senses on you:		155	Cert Sonnets 25	31
Who hath the voyce, which soule from sences sunders, ...		197	A&S 1st Song	29
With my greedy licorous sences, ...		226	A&S 10th Song	33
Whose senses in so evill consort, their stepdame Nature laies, ...		217	A&S 7th Song	1
Senses all asunder breakes;		219	A&S 8th Song	38
Ncr reign upon my senses.		295	Psalm XIX	56
Their sences rude plaine objects only move, ...		245	Other Poems 4	143
SENSIVE				
And shall sensive things be so sencelesse as to resist sence		36	1st Eclogues 13	138
SENT				
My tempred hart; by thee my promise sent		40	Arcadia II 18	9
And so by you (O blessed you) hath sent, ...		78	Arcadia III 49	7
She told him that the courtier had it sent:		96	3rd Eclogues 64	86
Ne can he faile, for prince hath for him sent:		97	3rd Eclogues 64	104
And of some sent from that sweet enemie Fraunce;		185	Astrophil 41	4

SENT	(CONTINUED)	PAGE	TITLE		LINE

SENT
    Sent forth the beames, which made so faire my race. . . . . . 185 Astrophil 41 14
    Stella's eyes sent to me the beames of blisse, ... 199 Astrophil 66 11
    And all my help from none but Thee is sent, ... 277 Psalm VII 29
    Sent from false heart, on double meaning stay'd. . . . . . . 284 Psalm XII 6
    Even god himself sent down his peircing ey . . . . 286 Psalm XIV 7
    He came, but came with smoake from out his nostrills sent, . 291 Psalm XVIII 18
    Then sent he from above, and took me from below, ... 291 Psalm XVIII 34
    Therfore I say again this goodness he me sent. . . . . 292 Psalm XVIII 47
    Yea fire from himself sent, ... 296 Psalm XX 14
    Most mad with beames which he thought Cosma sent, ... 249 Other Poems 4 270
    Hir feet be Pursevants from Cupid sent, ... 249 Other Poems 4 301
    When he from you is sent, ... 257 Other Poems 5 51
SENTENCE
    By Phoebus' doome, with sugred sentence sayes, ... 177 Astrophil 25 2
    Then lord, my lord, give sentence on my side . . . . 277 Psalm VII 23
    O let my sentence passe from Thyne own face; . . . . 289 Psalm XVII 5
SENTENTIOUS
    As with sententious lips to set a title vaine on it: . . . . 217 A&S 7th Song 4
SERENE
    Turnde to the mortall serene of an evening. . . . . 112 4th Eclogues 71 42
SERIOUS
    Thou doest proceed in thy most serious wayes: . . . . 170 Astrophil 11 2
SERPENT-LIKE
    A creeping serpentlike of mortall woe. . . . . 252 Other Poems 4 412
SERPENT'S
    Uttring a serpent's minde with serpent's hisse. . . . . . . 24 1st Eclogues 9 71
    Hurtles was Tyger's pawe and Serpent's hisse. . . . . 100 3rd Eclogues 66 54
SERVANT
    A servant Sex, soone prowde if they be coi'de, ... 24 1st Eclogues 9 60
    That men's harts be thy seate and endlesse fame be thy
      servant, ... 36 1st Eclogues 13 148
    Thy servant keep, least in him creep . . . . 295 Psalm XIX 53
    In rage Thy servant do not chase. . . . . 308 Psalm XXVII 45
    Thy Face to shine upon Thy servant make, ... 313 Psalm XXXI 43
SERVANT'S
    Then servant's wracke, where new doubts honor brings; . . . 187 Astrophil 45 11
SERVANTS
    Thus Reason to his servants yeelds his right; . . . . 12 Arcadia I 2 11
    Thus reason to his Servantes gyves his right . . . . 12 Arcadia I 2 V811
    Dearely the servants doo their wages buy, ... 105 3rd Eclogues 67 52
    Are we their servants growne? no doubt a noble staye: . . . 120 4th Eclogues 73 115
    Faire seeke not to be feard, most lovely beloved by thy
      servants, ... 143 Cert Sonnets 14 1
    That mine owne writings like bad servants show . . . . . . 175 Astrophil 21 3
    But give apt servants their due place, let eyes. . . . . . 210 Astrophil 85 9
    Who loves with good his servants good to blesse. . . . . . 323 Psalm XXXV 70
SERVANTS'
    On servants' shame oft Maister's blame doth sit; . . . . . 236 Astrophil 107 12
    By them is made Thy servants' trade. . . . . 295 Psalm XIX 45
SERVE
    What length of verse can serve brave Mopsa's good to show, . 12 Arcadia I 3 1
    The gods must help, and pretious things must serve to shew
      her shape. . . . . 12 Arcadia I 3 4
    Let swanne's example siker serve for thee, ... 28 1st Eclogues 10 73
    Since no refuge doth serve from woundes we do carry about
      us . . . . 33 1st Eclogues 13 51
    Pine is a maste to a shippe, to my shippe shall hope for a
      maste serve? . . . . 36 1st Eclogues 13 129
    For fellowes serve to kindle more the fire. . . . . 38 Arcadia II 14 8
    My sheepe are thoughts, which I both guide and serve: . . . 39 Arcadia II 17 1
    Serve all thy starrie eyes this shame to see? . . . . 58 2nd Eclogues 30 61
    O Mars, for what doth serve thy armed axe? . . . . 60 2nd Eclogues 30 110
    Reason looke to thy selfe, I serve a goddesse. . . . . . . 68 2nd Eclogues 33 30
    Phaebus farewell, a sweeter Saint I serve, ... 72 Arcadia III 38 1
    Above line repeated at following location. . . . . 72 Arcadia III 38 6
    Do serve, to make my inward powers darke: . . . . 73 Arcadia III 39 8
    Like divers flowers, whose divers beauties serve . . . . . 78 Arcadia III 50 1
    No knee once bowed, forsooth, for them they say we serve. . 120 4th Eclogues 73 114
    Celestiall powers to wormes, Jove's children serve to claye. 120 4th Eclogues 73 116
    Since nature's workes be good, and death doth serve. . . . 131 Arcadia V 77 1
    If othes might serve, even by the Stygian lake, ... 146 Cert Sonnets 17 6
    It is most true, that eyes are form'd to serve . . . . . . 167 Astrophil 5 1
    Serve him with shot, her lips his heralds arre: . . . . . . 179 Astrophil 29 10
    Serve God, serve him with feare: Rejoyce in him but so, . . 271 Psalm II 25
    As they so theirs, Him shall their ofspring serve, ... 300 Psalm XXII 75
    Dick. Here then and learn to sigh: a mistress I doo serve, . 343 Possibly 1 19
    To sett, for foile of his milke-white to serve. . . . . . . 244 Other Poems 4 86
SERVED
    O much more then words: those words serv'd more to me
      blesse Lesse. . . . . 64 2nd Eclogues 31 31
    Reason, in faith thou art well serv'd, that still. . . . . 169 Astrophil 10 1
    Astrophil that so wel served, ... 222 A&S 9th Song 27
    Yea Thou dost make me serv'd by folks I never knew; . . . . 293 Psalm XVIII 79
SERVES
    Nor stormes doo turne: fairenes serves oft to wealth. . . . 18 1st Eclogues 7 119
    Olde aged oke cutt downe, of newe works serves to the
      building: . . . . 36 1st Eclogues 13 134
    Where witt but serves, to have true tast of woes. . . . . . 57 2nd Eclogues 30 25
    But no scuse serves, she makes her wrath appeare . . . . . 203 Astrophil 73 9

427

```
SERVES                    (CONTINUED)                    PAGE    TITLE          LINE
    Serves thy beames but to disclose, . . . . . . . . . . . . .  210  A&S 4th Song     20
    What serves alas the blood of me . . . . . . . . . . . . .  311  Psalm XXX        26
SERVETH
    Sweete soule let not a wretch that serveth sheepe, . . . . .    4  Lady of May   2  17
    What skill servethe a soare of a wrong infirmity judged? . .   32  1st Eclogues 13  21
SERVICE
    Eache flower eache herbe dothe to your service yeeld, . . . .   43  Arcadia II   23   5
    Your sweetest flowers, your herbes, no service yeeld, . . . .   43  Arcadia II   24   5
    Nought disturbs thy quiet, all to thy service yeeld, . . . .   69  2nd Eclogues 34  10
    Of waiting thoughts all to her service ment? . . . . . . . .   78  Arcadia III  49  12
    But that her husband thought her service bent. . . . . . . .   95  3rd Eclogues 64  27
    Is neither freed, nor yet to service bound, . . . . . . . .   144  Cert Sonnets 15   2
    I do protest and seeke with service due, . . . . . . . . . .  145  Cert Sonnets 17   2
    Others, because the Prince my service tries, . . . . . . . .  176  Astrophil    23   7
    Service and Honor, wonder with delight, . . . . . . . . . .   202  Astrophil    72   9
SERVICEABLE
    The goodman bad his wife be serviceable. . . . . . . . . . .   94  3rd Eclogues 64  24
SERVICES
    If so great services may scorned be: . . . . . . . . . . . .  198  Astrophil    65  10
SERVILE
    Or Reason lie a slave to servile Sense, . . . . . . . . . . .   49  2nd Eclogues 28  76
    Now in servile Court remayning. . . . . . . . . . . . . . .   262  Other Poems   7  12
SET
    To set a pearle in steele so meanely varnished? . . . . . .    16  1st Eclogues  7  63
    Who well can set a passion out to show: . . . . . . . . . .    25  1st Eclogues  9 112
    I set you ore the flock I dearly love, . . . . . . . . . . .   26  1st Eclogues 10   2
    Dicus. The harte well set doth never shunne confession: . .    47  2nd Eclogues 28  13
    Those beames that set so many harts on fire? . . . . . . . .   59  2nd Eclogues 30  84
    O Vertue weake, shall death his triumph set. . . . . . . . .   59  2nd Eclogues 30  92
    Doth force us there to set our chiefe delightfulnes, . . . .   61  2nd Eclogues 30 135
    Like comfits round in marchpane set. . . . . . . . . . . . .   89  Arcadia III  62 112
    As stuffe meant for the sale set out to glaring showe) . . .  118  4th Eclogues 73  72
    Vertue is dead, now set thy triumph here.. . . . . . . . . .  127  4th Eclogues 75  72
    Now set thy triumph in this world, bereaved. . . . . . . . .  127  4th Eclogues 75  73
    Thy cries, o Babie, set mine head on aking: . . . . . . . .   139  Cert Sonnets  6   2
    Whose hearts are set on measuring a verse: . . . . . . . . .  146  Cert Sonnets 17  32
    In her cheekes pit thou didst thy pitfould set, . . . . . .   170  Astrophil    11  11
    Wrackes Triumphs be, which Love (high set) doth breed. . . .  186  Astrophil    42  14
    My words I know do well set forth my mind, . . . . . . . . .  186  Astrophil    44   1
    Nor do not use set colours for to weare, . . . . . . . . . .  191  Astrophil    54   2
    Thy reasons firmly set on Vertue's feet, . . . . . . . . . .  200  Astrophil    68  11
    As with sententious lips to set a title vaine on it: . . . .  217  A&S 7th Song      4
    Love did set his lips asunder, . . . . . . . . . . . . . . .  218  A&S 8th Song     27
    And say (O kings) yet have I set my King upon. . . . . . . .  271  Psalm II         13
    Then let his foot uppon my neck be set: . . . . . . . . . .   277  Psalm VII        14
    And set their arrows in a rowe . . . . . . . . . . . . . . .  284  Psalm XI          6
    Maugre their force I will set him at rest. . . . . . . . . .  285  Psalm XII        18
    Their Words be set in letters great. . . . . . . . . . . . .  294  Psalm XIX        15
    Thou, Thou it is that hast him set . . . . . . . . . . . . .  297  Psalm XXI        19
    Set them in pointed places, . . . . . . . . . . . . . . . .   298  Psalm XXI        46
    They were set free when they upon Thee called, . . . . . . .  298  Psalm XXII       13
    But still on this Lord set?. . . . . . . . . . . . . . . . .  304  Psalm XXV        56
    Who doth, and will set free. . . . . . . . . . . . . . . . .  304  Psalm XXV        57
    All my trust on him was sett; . . . . . . . . . . . . . . .   309  Psalm XXVIII     27
    Thou wouldst not set me on their score . . . . . . . . . . .  311  Psalm XXX         8
    Which they for me with privy craft have set, . . . . . . . .  312  Psalm XXXI       11
    On us be set, . . . . . . . . . . . . . . . . . . . . . . .   318  Psalm XXXIII     83
    For causeless they both pitt and net did sett, . . . . . . .  321  Psalm XXXV       15
    Let not their joy upon my woes be sett. . . . . . . . . . .   322  Psalm XXXV       60
    Abroad his stepps be wrongly sett. . . . . . . . . . . . . .  323  Psalm XXXVI      12
    In shine or storme must sett the clowted shoe: . . . . . . .  242  Other Poems   4  20
    To sett, for foile of his milke-white to serve.. . . . . . .  244  Other Poems   4  86
    Thus on a hillock set, he made his mone. . . . . . . . . . .  253  Other Poems   4 440
    Whose foote doth set a heav'n on cursed thee, . . . . . . .   256  Other Poems   5  19
    As three most joyntly set, . . . . . . . . . . . . . . . . .  260  Other Poems   6  21
    On lamenting wholy set: . . . . . . . . . . . . . . . . . .   262  Other Poems   7   8
SETS
    Whose steppe on earth all beautie sets.. . . . . . . . . . .   89  Arcadia III  62 108
    But vertue sets so high, that reason's light, . . . . . . .   135  Cert Sonnets  2   7
    Where memory sets foorth the beames of love. . . . . . . . .  223  Astrophil    88  11
    On them he sets his love: . . . . . . . . . . . . . . . . .   282  Psalm X          18
    The heavnly Frame sets forth the Fame. . . . . . . . . . . .  293  Psalm XIX         1
SETST
    Thou setst a bate betweene my will and wit, . . . . . . . .   166  Astrophil     4   2
    Thou sett'st me free, when I was thrall, . . . . . . . . . .  273  Psalm IV          3
    Before me Thou a table setst, . . . . . . . . . . . . . . .   301  Psalm XXIII      16
SETTING
    Popler changeth his hew from a rising sunne to a setting: . .   36  1st Eclogues 13 132
    Setting Thy self in Throne, which shined bright. . . . . . .  279  Psalm IX          9
    And setting Thee for scope . . . . . . . . . . . . . . . . .  305  Psalm XXVI        4
    Setting my feet upon . . . . . . . . . . . . . . . . . . . .  331  Psalm XL          8
    But yet a setting foorth it some way lent: . . . . . . . . .  252  Other Poems   4 395
SETTLED
    The wife thus having settled husband's braine, . . . . . . .   96  3rd Eclogues 64  73
    Shepherd of shepherds, whose well setled order . . . . . . .  128  4th Eclogues 75 128
    Bewray it selfe in my long setled eyes, . . . . . . . . . .   176  Astrophil    23   2
SEVEN
    When fire seven times hath spent his earthly parts.. . . . .  285  Psalm XII        21
```

	PAGE	TITLE		LINE
SEVEN-DOUBLE				
Hir hands which pierc'd the soule's seav'n-double shield,. .	246	Other Poems	4	147
SEVERED				
So should our sever'd bodies three	261	Other Poems	6	59
SEX				
Hath power that Sex with bridle to withhold?	24	1st Eclogues	9	58
A fickle Sex, and trew in trust tc no man, ...	24	1st Eclogues	9	59
A servant Sex, soone prowde if they be coi'de, ...	24	1st Eclogues	9	60
SHADE				
But when in shade we meet of mirtle bowes, ...	18	1st Eclogues	7	128
I finde no shade, but where my Sunne doth burne:	18	1st Eclogues	7	144
That I growe like a shade, ...	19	1st Eclogues	7	163
Of Phoebus' violence in shade of stately Ciprus tree,. . . .	31	1st Eclogues	13	12
Which ever shines, though hid from earth by earthly shade, .	44	Arcadia II	26	3
Betwixt the good and shade of good divided,.	62	2nd Eclogues	30	179
Faire trees' shade is enough fortification,.	69	2nd Eclogues	34	13
Whose shade safety doth hold, danger avoideth her:	69	2nd Eclogues	34	34
But thus in oke's true shade recounted he.	99	3rd Eclogues	66	41
Which now in night's deepe shade sheep heard of me..	99	3rd Eclogues	66	42
Where shade from Sunne, and sporte I sought in evening,.. . .	111	4th Eclogues	71	14
An Asse's shade ere now hath bred debate...	146	Cert Sonnets	17	20
The glasse to you but gives a shade, ...	159	Cert Sonnets	29	12
Whereof this Beautie can be but a shade, ...	167	Astrophil	5	10
Trust in the shade of pleasing Orange tree;	180	Astrophil	30	8
Nor ever did in shade of Tempe sit:.	203	Astrophil	74	2
No wind, no shade can coole, what helpe then in my case, . .	205	Astrophil	76	12
Or of thy gifts at least shade out some part..	207	Astrophil	81	8
With darkest shade doth overccme my day;	223	Astrophil	89	2
In a grove most rich of shade, ...	217	A&S 8th Song		1
In Thy wings' shade then let me hidden ly.	290	Psalm XVII		26
Of death's dark shade I will	301	Psalm XXIII		11
The trees spred out their armes to shade hir face, ...	245	Other Poems	4	109
"Well was I, while under shade	263	Other Poems	7	43
SHADES				
Frame daintiest lustre, mixt of shades and light?.	168	Astrophil	7	4
With sweete soft shades thou oft invitest me	230	Astrophil	98	5
They are but shades not true things where we live, ...	330	Psalm XXXIX		19
Vain shades and vain, in vain to grieve.	330	Psalm XXXIX		20
SHADING				
The shading woods seeme now my Sunne to darke, ...	147	Cert Sonnets	18	7
Yet each prepar'd, with fanne's wel-shading grace, ...	176	Astrophil	22	7
Then in good Dog, faire field, or shading tree..	246	Other Poems	4	179
SHADOW				
Figge that yeeldes most pleasante frute, his shaddow is				
hurtefull,.	35	1st Eclogues	13	125
The Sunne is hid; his kindly shadowe combers not..	49	2nd Eclogues	28	63
Hastened from us with barre of shadow darke, ...	80	Arcadia III	52	13
You be the cause that I love: what Reason blameth a shadowe,	123	4th Eclogues	74	45
Trust in the shadow of thy wing.	324	Psalm XXXVI		21
And make you faire with shadow of her hue:	257	Other Poems	5	32
SHADOWING				
Like cunning Painter shadowing white..	89	Arcadia III	62	98
SHADOWS				
The Sunne is hid; his kindly shadows cumber not.	49	2nd Eclogues	28	V 63
SHADY				
While they did ward sun-beames with shady bay, ...	243	Other Poems	4	66
I got to a shady wood, ...	262	Other Poems	7	3
SHAFTS				
The bloudy shaftes of Cupid's warre, ...	90	Arcadia III	62	131
Brake bow, brake shafts, while Cupid weeping sate:	173	Astrophil	17	8
To lay his then marke wanting shafts of sight, ...	230	Astrophil	99	3
Thy fingers Cupid's shafts, thy voyce the Angel's lay: . . .	212	A&S 5th Song		11
For thy shafts have pierc't me sore, ...	327	Psalm XXXVIII		4
With shafts shott out from their back-turned bow..	251	Other Poems	4	351
SHAKE				
My eys be dym, my lyms shake,.	66	2nd Eclogues	32	10
No, the more fooles it do shake, ...	234	A&S 11th Song		33
With motion of his rage did to the bottom shake.	291	Psalm XVIII		17
His heels grow'n proud did seme at heav'n to shake..	248	Other Poems	4	261
"When I see her, my sinewes shake for feare, ...	253	Other Poems	4	457
SHAKED				
And precious couches full oft are shak't with a feaver. . .	34	1st Eclogues	13	86
Passion rebelde, for reason's strength hath shaked..	82	Arcadia III	57	4
And found with deadly feare that all my sinewes shak'd.. . .	121	4th Eclogues	73	180
SHAKING				
Shaking off all sadnes,.	336	Psalm XLIII		21
SHALLCW				
As shallow brookes do yeeld the greatest sound,.	4	Lady of May	2	14
Shallow brookes murmure most, deep silent slide away;. . . .	14	1st Eclogues	7	11
Envying shallow toyes with malice deepe.	104	3rd Eclogues	67	39
SHALT				
Thou, with thy wife, adultry shalt commit.	11	Arcadia I	1	10
Looke further then, so shalt thou finde at least,.	75	Arcadia III	44	9
And thou shalt finde, in women vertues lie..	106	3rd Eclogues	67	102
"Yet thou shalt not go free (quoth Venus) such a fire. . . .	121	4th Eclogues	73	170
That thou full oft shalt wish thy judging eyes were blinde".	121	4th Eclogues	73	172
"Nay thou (said both) shalt see such beames shine in her				
face	121	4th Eclogues	73	175
That thou shalt never dare seeke helpe of wretched case".. .	121	4th Eclogues	73	176
That Vertue, thou thy selfe shalt be in love..	167	Astrophil	4	14

		PAGE	TITLE		LINE

SHALT (CONTINUED)
Move not thy heavy grace, thou shalt in me,.		184	Astrophil	39	13
Till thou shalt revived be,.		227	A&S 10th Song		47
With Iron scepter bruse thou shalt, and peece meale breake .		271	Psalm II		21
And shalt root out the tongues to lying bent:.		275	Psalm V		14
Thou, lord, the people shalt in judgment try:.		277	Psalm VII		22
Then Thou (O lord) shalt keep the Good stil sure.		285	Psalm XII		22
Thou as in fiery Ov'en shalt make.		297	Psalm XXI		31
Their fruit shalt Thou from earthly face		297	Psalm XXI		37
For like a marke Thou shalt arow		298	Psalm XXI		45
Thou shalt have both good food and place.		324	Psalm XXXVII		8
Watch but a while, and Thou shalt see.		325	Psalm XXXVII		25
Yea thou shalt see the ev'ill decay.		327	Psalm XXXVII		88
Miso mine owne pigsnie, thou shalt heare news o' Damaetas. .		241	Other Poems	2	1

SHAME
To wo and shame the wretch did enter in, ...		5	Lady of May	3	9
It is no shame, since Hercules was he".		5	Lady of May	3	12
That verie shame with Love's high title dignifie.		14	1st Eclogues	7	3
With father's death, and mother's guiltie shame, ...		21	1st Eclogues	8	19
The Cockow's shame, the Goose's good intent, ...		28	1st Eclogues	10	80
Make me, o vertuous Shame, thy lawes neglect.		40	Arcadia II	18	12
Blots to the stone, shame to my selfe I finde:		40	Arcadia II	19	4
Dorus. If Sunnie beames shame heav'nly habitation;		48	2nd Eclogues	28	22
Of singing match we made, whence he with shame did trudge. .		52	2nd Eclogues	29	16
Nico. When Leuca dooth appeare, the Sunne for shame. . . .		55	2nd Eclogues	29	93
Goe winne of him (for chattering) praise or shame:		56	2nd Eclogues	29	139
A Shop of shame, a Booke where blots be rife		57	2nd Eclogues	30	26
Serve all thy starrie eyes this shame to see?.		58	2nd Eclogues	30	61
Blush on for shame: that still with thee do light.		82	Arcadia III	56	5
And out gan cry, "ah well away for shame,.		95	3rd Eclogues	64	45
A young girle's hart, to that were shame for both, ...		95	3rd Eclogues	64	59
"Alas", quoth she, "thus women's shame doth creepe". . . .		96	3rd Eclogues	64	87
For I seeke not their shame, but still me thinkes, ...		105	3rd Eclogues	67	56
When without shame he saith, "these be mine owne".		106	3rd Eclogues	67	114
Publique our losse: so, see, thy shame is publique.		109	Arcadia IV	70	24
By shame and griefe, helpe, helpe me to lament		126	4th Eclogues	75	62
His winding sheete is shame, ...		160	Cert Sonnets	30	14
Readie of wit and fearing nought but shame:.		172	Astrophil	14	11
When most I glorie, then I feele most shame:		174	Astrophil	19	3
Great expectation, weare a traine of shame..		175	Astrophil	21	8
And joy therein, though Nations count it shame.		179	Astrophil	28	8
Till that her blush taught me my shame to see.		191	Astrophil	53	14
Let wo gripe on my heart, shame loade mine eye..		212	Astrophil	86	4
If thou praise not, all other praise is shame.		224	Astrophil	90	4
The height of honor in the kindly badge of shame?.		232	Astrophil	102	3
On servants' shame oft Maister's blame doth sit;		236	Astrophil	107	12
I now then staine thy white with vagabunding shame, ...		214	A&S 5th Song		68
Behold their broken shame!		296	Psalm XX		31
Nay shame of men, the people's scorning game.		299	Psalm XXII		16
Shall never suffer shame;.		303	Psalm XXV		8
Let me not tast of shame, O lord most high,.		313	Psalm XXXI		45
Shall never blush for shame.		319	Psalm XXXIV		20
Let them be cloathd in most confounding shame, ...		323	Psalm XXXV		65
Let me not be thrown down to so base shame		330	Psalm XXXIX		27
Let them have shame, yea blush for shame,.		332	Psalm XL		52
Let them with shame be cloyed;		332	Psalm XL		55
For guerdon of their shame,.		332	Psalm XL		57
Where failing is a shame, and breaking is his best.. . . .		241	Other Poems	1	6
With others' blott, till all do tast of shame.		248	Other Poems	4	232
Pas mad with fall, and madder with the shame,.		249	Other Poems	4	269
And now faire evenings blush my shame to see.		254	Other Poems	4	480

SHAMED
Shamed I hate my selfe in sight of mountaines, ...		112	4th Eclogues	71	59
Long sham'd to be accurst in every place,.		141	Cert Sonnets	8	3
Nor blam'd for bloud, nor sham'd for sinfull deed.		209	Astrophil	84	11
They shall be sham'd and vext, that breed my crying, . . .		276	Psalm VI		30

SHAMEFUL
| Their shamefull flying. . . . . | | 276 | Psalm VI | | 32 |
| Confound those folks, thrust them in shamefull hole. . . . | | 321 | Psalm XXXV | | 7 |

SHAPE
The gods must help, and pretious things must serve to shew					
her shape.		12	Arcadia I	3	4
Cloth'd in the shape which soonest may deceave:.		21	1st Eclogues	8	32
Then do I shape to my selfe that forme which raigns so with					
in me, ...		36	1st Eclogues	13	142
Since to my hart her shape you so did sende;		38	Arcadia II	14	3
O heavenly soule, in humaine shape conteind:		38	Arcadia II	15	2
Which makes us most immortall shape to weare,.		40	Arcadia II	18	14
Do you not heare his voice, and see his shape?		53	2nd Eclogues	29	59
Then take my shape, and play a lover's parte:.		79	Arcadia III	51	12
The Horse, good shape; the Sparrow, lust to playe;		101	3rd Eclogues	66	81
And Mira I admirde: her shape sank in my brest..		119	4th Eclogues	73	100
In shape, which by man's eye might be perceived;		127	4th Eclogues	75	71
To me mine eyes the true shape carie.		159	Cert Sonnets	29	13
Love of her selfe, takes Stella's shape, that she.		177	Astrophil	25	10
Can scarce discerne the shape of mine owne paine.		228	Astrophil	94	4
Viewing the shape of darknesse and delight,.		230	Astrophil	99	6
Who hid in Angel's shape my life would ende.		254	Other Poems	4	464

SHARE
| That is their share assigned.. . . . . | | 284 | Psalm XI | | 20 |

SHARE	(CONTINUED)	PAGE	TITLE		LINE
So my good deeds they pay with this ev'ill share,.		322	Psalm XXXV		27
Who share in woe, weygh others have as much.		242	Other Poems	4	16

SHARED
| Ev'en so be their guerdon shar'd. . . . . | | 309 | Psalm XXVIII | | 20 |

SHARP
Pine is hye, hope is as hie, sharpe leav'd, sharpe yet be my					
hope's budds.		36	1st Eclogues	13	130
Thinke, my harde haps have blunted death's sharpe knife, . .		113	4th Eclogues	72	14
With what sharpe checkes I in my selfe am shent, ...		173	Astrophil	18	1
That busie archer his sharpe arrowes tries?.		180	Astrophil	31	4
My horse, he spurres with sharpe desire my hart:		189	Astrophil	49	11
That by sharp proofes, the heathen themselves may see. . . .		281	Psalm IX		64
Then do they pull from sharpe and niggard thorne		243	Other Poems	4	51

SHARPEST
| Sweete reward for sharpest paine:. . . . . | | 210 | A&S 4th Song | | 4 |

SHARPLY
| The plenteous sweets, (can sweets so sharply grow?). . . . . | | 243 | Other Poems | 4 | 52 |

SHARPNESS
| Should soone be pierc'd with sharpnesse of the mone. . . . . | | 193 | Astrophil | 57 | 8 |

SHEEP
Sweete soule let not a wretch that serveth sheepe, ...		4	Lady of May	2	17
Two thousand sheepe I have as white as milke,.		4	Lady of May	2	19
Not rotten sheepe, but high crownes she surpasseth all. . .		16	1st Eclogues	7	57
Till I get her, shall I to sheep enure my selfe?		16	1st Eclogues	7	60
Who is an heire of many hundred sheep.		18	1st Eclogues	7	117
Constant and kind: my sheep your foode shall breed,.		18	1st Eclogues	7	123
Of my good sheepe, thou never trews time tooke:.		27	1st Eclogues	10	14
My sheepe are thoughts, which I both guide and serve:. . . .		39	Arcadia II	17	1
What wooll my sheepe shall beare, whyle thus they live,. . .		39	Arcadia II	17	7
Feede on my sheepe, my chardge my comforte feede,.		43	Arcadia II	23	1
Feede on my sheepe, your fayer sweete feeding flowes,. . . .		43	Arcadia II	23	4
Feede on my sheepe, possesse your fruitefull fyeld,.		43	Arcadia II	23	7
Feede on my sheepe, sorrow hathe stricken sayle, ...		43	Arcadia II	23	10
Feede on my sheepe, your Native joyes mayntayne, ...		43	Arcadia II	23	13
Leave of my sheepe: it is no tyme to feede,.		43	Arcadia II	24	1
Leave of my sheepe, my shower of teeres oreflowes, ...		43	Arcadia II	24	4
Leave of my sheepe, my sighes burne up your filde, ...		43	Arcadia II	24	7
Leave of my sheepe, sorrowe hathe hoysed sayle,.		44	Arcadia II	24	10
Leave off my sheep my mourninge to maintayne,.		44	Arcadia II	24	13
If three-leav'd grasse seeme to the sheepe unsavorie,. . . .		48	2nd Eclogues	28	23
Dicus. But so thy sheepe may thy good wishes satisfie. . . .		49	2nd Eclogues	28	49
Hye tyme for me, for scattered were my sheepe.		62	2nd Eclogues	30	186
O brest in which two white sheepe swell in pride:.		76	Arcadia III	46	10
Pan, father Pan, the god of silly sheepe,.		92	3rd Eclogues	63	37
Amid my sheepe, though I sawe nought to feare,.		99	3rd Eclogues	66	15
For for my sheepe I dreaded mickle more.		99	3rd Eclogues	66	18
And sange unto my sheepe lest stray they should.		99	3rd Eclogues	66	21
Which now in night's deepe shade sheep heard of me..		99	3rd Eclogues	66	42
The sheep, mild-seeming face; climing, the Beare;.		101	3rd Eclogues	66	90
To sheepe, whom love, not knowledge, made to heare,.		103	3rd Eclogues	66	156
And gamesome then, when he thinkes on his sheepe;.		104	3rd Eclogues	67	35
Both sheep and Oxen wholy hast,.		279	Psalm VIII		26
The shepheards will grow leane I trow, their sheep will ill					
be fed.		344	Possibly	1	40
And taught his shepe hir shepe in food to thwart..		247	Other Poems	4	188
I am as dull as winter-sterved sheep,.		253	Other Poems	4	442
Leave sheepe, leave all, I will no piecing have.		255	Other Poems	4	512
I rather would my sheepe		259	Other Poems	5	99
Where we once our lovely sheepe, ...		262	Other Poems	7	21

SHEEPHOOK
| My sheepehooke is wanne hope, which all upholdes:. . . . . . | | 39 | Arcadia II | 17 | 5 |

SHEEPHOOKS
| But if they had, could shephookes this resist? . . . . | | 246 | Other Poems | 4 | 160 |

SHEEPISH
| For good thou mayst yet proove in sheepish sound.. . . . . . | | 56 | 2nd Eclogues | 29 | 137 |

SHEEP'S
| Or if sheepe's cries can helpe the Sunne's owne braverie,. . | | 48 | 2nd Eclogues | 28 | 25 |

SHEET
| His winding sheete is shame, ... | | 160 | Cert Sonnets | 30 | 14 |
| Like in a winding sheet, wretch I already lay, ... | | 291 | Psalm XVIII | | 10 |

SHELF
| As neere his home, when storme or shelf he feares; . . . . . | | 71 | Arcadia III | 37 | 4 |

SHENT
With what sharpe checkes I in my selfe am shent, ...		173	Astrophil	18	1
Lord, let not me a worme by thee be shent, ...		276	Psalm VI		1
The World's foundations then lay bare because he shent . . .		291	Psalm XVIII		32
So to have done amisse, so to be shent..		244	Other Poems	4	104

SHEPHERD
Histor. Those woordes dyd once the Loveliest shepard use . .		24	1st Eclogues	9	62
While, "Let us passe our time" each shepeheard saies.. . . .		28	1st Eclogues	10	48
So small accompt of time the shepeheard feeles		28	1st Eclogues	10	49
Cleofila. Worthy shepeheard, by my song to my selfe all					
favor is happned,.		31	1st Eclogues	13	8
Happy shepheard, with thanks to the Gods, still thinke to be					
thankfull,.		32	1st Eclogues	13	33
Oh no, no, hardye shepeheard, worth can never enter a title,		34	1st Eclogues	13	82
Cleofila. Hardy shephearde, such as thy meritts, such may be					
her insight		37	1st Eclogues	13	155
But ceasse worthy shepheard, nowe ceasse we to weery the					
hearers.		37	1st Eclogues	13	172

SHEPHERD   (CONTINUED)   PAGE   TITLE   LINE
    Unto his house a jollie shepeheard went, ...   94 3rd Eclogues 64   15
    The courtlie shepheard much agast at this, ...   96 3rd Eclogues 64   67
    Languet, the shepheard best swift Ister knewe, ...   99 3rd Eclogues 66   23
    Since that to death is gone the shepheard hie, ... 125 4th Eclogues 75   1
    Shepherd of shepherds, whose well setled order . . . . . . 128 4th Eclogues 75   128
    No other shepheard should have scope, ... 158 Cert Sonnets 28   7
    If Love might sweet'n so a boy of shepheard' brood, ... 209 A&S 3rd Song   7
    The lord the lord my shepheard is, ... 301 Psalm XXIII   1
    Phoebus, that shepheard high, ... 257 Other Poems   5   22
SHEPHERDESS
    Stella fiercest shepherdesse, ... 221 A&S 9th Song   16
SHEPHERD'S
    Come shepheard's weedes, become your master's minde: . . . .   13 Arcadia I   4   1
    Come shepheard's weedes, attend my woefull cryes: . . . . .   13 Arcadia I   4   5
    Thinking how it hath mard my shepheard's trade. . . . . . .   19 1st Eclogues   7 169
    Silly shepheard's poore pype, when his harsh sound testifis
        our woes, ...   32 1st Eclogues 13   40
    As farre as any shepheards piping be: . . . .   56 2nd Eclogues 29 127
    Sure shepherd's signe, that morne would soone fetch day. . . 103 3rd Eclogues 66 161
    Who most the silly shepheard's pipe did pryse, ... 125 4th Eclogues 75   2
    Another humbler wit to shepheard's pipe retires, ... 167 Astrophil   6   7
    A Shepheard's tale no height of stile desires. . . . . 242 Other Poems   4   1
    Klaius for skill of herbs and shepheard's art. . . . . 243 Other Poems   4   33
    Which made hir yeeld to deck this shepheards' band, ... 247 Other Poems   4 215
    Come shepheard's boy, let now thy heart be bowd. . . . . . . 255 Other Poems   4 510
    Once to Shepheard's God retayning, ... 262 Other Poems   7   11
    In poore shepheard's base degree? . . . . 262 Other Poems   7   26
    Greater was that shepheard's treasure, ... 263 Other Poems   7   47
SHEPHERDS
    Since that we see our saddest Shepheards out . . . .   27 1st Eclogues 10   26
    We shepeheards are like them that under saile . . . .   27 1st Eclogues 10   31
    And such discord twixt greatest shepheards flowes, ...   27 1st Eclogues 10   40
    As for the rest, howe shepeheardes spend their daies, . . .   28 1st Eclogues 10   46
    Or while that shepheards love a lovely face. . . . .   56 2nd Eclogues 29 125
    He farre did passe the rest of Shepheards all. . . . .   94 3rd Eclogues 64   18
    Of that small light oft watching shepheards see. . . . . . .   98 3rd Eclogues 66   7
    How sheepheards did of yore, how now they thrive, ...   99 3rd Eclogues 66   34
    Shepheards bewaile your uttermost confusion; . . . . 128 4th Eclogues 75 121
    Shepherd of shepherds, whose well setled order . . . . . . 128 4th Eclogues 75 128
    The shepheards will grow leane I trow, their sheep will ill
        be fed. . . . . 344 Possibly   1   40
    Of shepheards two the seely case to show, ... 242 Other Poems   4   6
    So now for pray these shepheards two he tooke, ... 245 Other Poems   4 137
    These sports shepheards deviz'd such faults to show. . . . . 248 Other Poems   4 241
    Seely shepheards are not witting . . . . 262 Other Poems   7   29
    "Therefore shepheardes wanting skill, ... 263 Other Poems   7   37
SHEPHERDS'
    O sheepheards' boyes, eschue these tongues of venome, . . .   50 2nd Eclogues 28   87
    The auncient prayse to Arcad shepheards' skill? . . . . . .   53 2nd Eclogues 29   52
    While shepheards' tunes be heard, or rimes be read, ...   56 2nd Eclogues 29 124
SHIELD
    Your state is great, your greatnesse is our shield, ...   3 Lady of May   1   7
    And from the stormes our sweeteste sonne will shield. . . .   43 Arcadia II   23   9
    My sun is gon, from stormes what shall us sheelde? . . . . .   43 Arcadia II   24   9
    For all these certaine blowes the surest shield. . . . . . .   58 2nd Eclogues 30   43
    Joves golden shield did Eagle sables beare. . . . . 171 Astrophil   13   3
    Stella's faire haire, her face he makes his shield, ... 171 Astrophil   13   10
    With shield of proofe shield me from out the prease. . . . . 184 Astrophil   39   5
    Yet lord thou art my shield, ... 272 Psalm III   11
    With kindest care, as with a certain shield. . . . . 275 Psalm V   40
    My never peirced shield, my ever saving horn, ... 290 Psalm XVIII   4
    To them that trust in Thee a shield thou dost abide. . . . . 292 Psalm XVIII   56
    Thou gavest me saving shield, Thy right hand was my stay; . . 292 Psalm XVIII   64
    Shield me from these assaults; . . . . 304 Psalm XXV   62
    That God is my strength my shield; . . . . 309 Psalm XXVIII   26
    Whose shield shall us maintaine. . . . . 318 Psalm XXXIII   78
    Take up Thy shield and for my succour stand, ... 321 Psalm XXXV   3
    Will. God shield us from such Dames. If so our Downes be
        sped, ... 344 Possibly   1   39
    Fayrenesse though fayer, is but a feeble shielde, ... 345 Possibly   4   6
    Hir hands which pierc'd the soule's seav'n-double shield, . . 246 Other Poems   4 147
    So have I heard to pierce pursuing shield. . . . . 251 Other Poems   4 349
SHIELDS
    Ashe makes speares which shieldes do resist, her force no
        repulse takes: . . . .   36 1st Eclogues 13 136
    To hurt himselfe, what shields can be defenses? . . . . . .   62 2nd Eclogues 30 169
SHIFTS
    Some gazing still, some winking wilye shiftes, ...   21 1st Eclogues   8   27
SHINE
    Shine eyes on me, that both our lives be guarded; . . . . .   17 1st Eclogues   7   92
    While that one body shine. . . . .   19 1st Eclogues   7 165
    On me to cast those eyes, where shine nobilitie. . . . . . .   19 1st Eclogues   7 178
    From Cosma's eyes, which full in darkenes shine, ...   55 2nd Eclogues 29 103
    That (shining now) she then might shine more farre. . . . . .   56 2nd Eclogues 29 122
    Till her eyes shine, I live in darkest night. . . . .   79 Arcadia III   51   14
    "Nay thou (said both) shalt see such beames shine in her
        face . . . . 121 4th Eclogues 73 175
    But foole, foole that I am, those eyes would shine from a
        dark cave. . . . . 123 4th Eclogues 74   49

SHINE   (CONTINUED)   PAGE   TITLE   LINE

That doth both shine and give us sight to see. . . . . 161 Cert Sonnets 32   8
Or else let them in statelier glorie shine,. . . . . 166 Astrophil   3   5
To mortall eyes might sweetly shine in her.. . . . . 177 Astrophil   25   11
Keepe still my Zenith, ever shine on me. . . . . 186 Astrophil   42   8
O looke, o shine, o let me die and see.. . . . . 188 Astrophil   48   8
She in whose eyes Love, though unfelt, doth shine, ... 196 Astrophil   62   3
For Stella hath with words where faith doth shine, ... 200 Astrophil   69   9
While those faire planets on thy streames did shine. . . . . 232 Astrophil 103 4
How through the World thy Name doth shine: . . . . 278 Psalm VIII   2
Above line repeated at following location. . . . . 279 Psalm VIII   34
Their eyes do swim, their face doth shine in fatt, ... 290 Psalm XVII   29
Thy Face to shine upon Thy servant make, ... 313 Psalm XXXI   43
In shine or storme must sett the clowted shoe: . . . . 242 Other Poems   4 20
And yet I see her shine amid the cloud.. . . . . 255 Other Poems   4 506
SHINED
Whose beawties shin'de more then the blushing morning, . . . 113 4th Eclogues 71 62
Her haire, which by the helpe of painter's cunning, shinde.. 118 4th Eclogues 73 74
Setting Thy self in Throne, which shined bright. . . . . . . 279 Psalm IX   9
One day (o day, that shin'de to make them darke!) . . . . . 243 Other Poems   4 65
That it was Love that shin'de in shining maid: . . . . 246 Other Poems   4 164
For simple goodnes shined in his eyes. . . . . 247 Other Poems   4 196
SHINES
To swelling harts he shines in honour's fire:. . . . . 21 1st Eclogues 8 38
While our sonne shynes no clowdie greeves assaile. . . . . . 43 Arcadia II 23 12
Which ever shines, though hid from earth by earthly shade, . 44 Arcadia II 26   3
O then it shines: then are the heav'ns distributed,. . . . . 49 2nd Eclogues 28 65
No Sunne, which shines, and seeth not, ... 86 Arcadia III 62 18
A seate where beauty shines and vertue raignes,. . . . . . . 141 Cert Sonnets 8 10
That she, me thinks, not onely shines but sings. . . . . . . 184 Astrophil   38   8
There shines a joy from thee my only light;. . . . . 236 Astrophil 108 4
She is the heardesse faire that shines in darke. . . . . . . 259 Other Poems   5 112
SHINEST
Cupid, because thou shin'st in Stella's eyes,. . . . . 170 Astrophil   12   1
SHINETH
That inward sunne in thine eyes shineth so.. . . . . 201 Astrophil   71   8
O birds, o beasts, looke Love, lo, Stella shineth. . . . . . 209 A&S 3rd Song   12
SHINING
Then by my high Cedar, rich Ruby, and only shining Sunne,. . 34 1st Eclogues 13 80
That (shining now) she then might shine more farre. . . . . 56 2nd Eclogues 29 122
Shall I that saw Eronae's shining haire. . . . . 58 2nd Eclogues 30 44
Of vertue's regiment, shining in harnesse. . . . . 67 2nd Eclogues 33   4
Howe is my Sunn, whose beames are shining bright,. . . . . . 74 Arcadia III 42   1
These stately starrs in their now shining faces, ... 108 Arcadia IV 69   9
Mine eyes did light upon her shining hewe, ... 115 4th Eclogues 72 75
Who burnt his lips to kisse faire shining fire.. . . . . . . 145 Cert Sonnets 16 14
But when my Sunne her shining twinnes there bends, ... 150 Cert Sonnets 22 16
Playing and shining in each outward part:. . . . . 170 Astrophil   11 13
But shining forth of heate in his chiefe pride;. . . . . . . 176 Astrophil   22   4
Care shining in mine eyes, faith in my sprite, ... 202 Astrophil   72 11
She comes, and streight therewith her shining twins do move. 204 Astrophil   76   1
I say thou art a Devill, though clothd in Angel's shining: . 215 A&S 5th Song 81
"Steila, in whose shining eyes,. . . . . 218 A&S 8th Song 33
The shining clearness of thy face: . . . . 274 Psalm IV   27
But streight his shining eyes this misty masse disclos'd.. . 291 Psalm XVIII 26
The shining Lord he is my light, ... 306 Psalm XXVII   1
Thy justice in most shining luster,. . . . . 325 Psalm XXXVII 14
That it was Love that shin'de in shining maid: . . . . 246 Other Poems   4 164
To see the sportes of double-shining day,. . . . . 251 Other Poems   4 362
SHIP
Pine is a maste to a shippe, to my shippe shall hope for a
    maste serve?. . . . . 36 1st Eclogues 13 129
Thus tossed in my shipp of huge desyre,. . . . . 71 Arcadia III 37 13
My ship, my selfe, whose course to love doth bende,. . . . . 114 4th Eclogues 72 44
A bird which gets more life then ship had lost.. . . . . . . 151 Cert Sonnets 22 54
My ship, desire, with winde of lust long tost, ... 151 Cert Sonnets 22 55
SHIPS
Of ships, by shipwrack cast on Albion coast, ... 151 Cert Sonnets 22 51
SHIPWRACK
Of ships, by shipwrack cast on Albion coast, ... 151 Cert Sonnets 22 51
SHIRION
And shirion like young Unicorn.. . . . . 310 Psalm XXIX   18
SHOE
In shine or storme must sett the clowted shoe: . . . . 242 Other Poems   4 20
SHOES
From the cruell headache, nor shooes of golde doo the gowt
    heale,. . . . . 34 1st Eclogues 13 85
SHONE
Either to do like him, which open shone, ... 176 Astrophil   22 10
SHOOK
Yet have I seene when well a wolfe he shooke.. . . . . 27 1st Eclogues 10 18
But thus with irefull eyes, and face that shooke with spite. 119 4th Eclogues 73 101
SHOOT
How farre they shoote awrie! the true cause is,. . . . . . . 185 Astrophil   41 12
SHOOTS
Which shootes strongly with out any noyse and deadly without
    smarte. . . . . 35 1st Eclogues 13 122
SHOP
A Shop of shame, a Booke where blots be rife . . . . 57 2nd Eclogues 30 26

		PAGE	TITLE		LINE
SHORE					
Pressing too much upon ill harbourd shore.		142	Cert Sonnets	12	3
And anchor fast my selfe on Vertue's shore..		196	Astrophil	62	11
SHORES					
How thy lee shores by my sighes stormed be!.		230	Astrophil	98	4
SHORT					
Unto the heav'ns? our wings be too short; th' earth thinks us a burden;		32	1st Eclogues	13	29
In travaile of our life (a short but tedious space).		45	Arcadia II	26	9
We last short while, and build long lasting places:.		127	4th Eclogues	75	91
But as he them more short or slacke doth raine, ...		194	Astrophil	58	4
But with short breath, long lookes, staid feet and walking hed, ...		205	Astrophil	76	13
Without how farre this praise is short of you, ...		207	Astrophil	80	13
For their short time is in his sight.		325	Psalm XXXVII		36
With gazing looks, short sighs, unsettled feet, ...		251	Other Poems	4	369
Her breath, then short, seem'd loth from home to pas, . . .		252	Other Poems	4	399
SHORT-BITTEN					
Train'd in the life which on short-bitten grasse		242	Other Poems	4	19
SHORTEST					
Where fairnesse yeelds to wisdome's shortest raines.		151	Cert Sonnets	22	64
SHORTLY					
(Spurd with love's spur, though gald and shortly raind . . .		230	Astrophil	98	7
SHOT					
Her loose haire be the shott, the brestes the pykes be, . .		67	2nd Eclogues	33	7
Their ireful shotte against so weake a marke, ...		73	Arcadia III	40	6
Or canons thunder-like, all shot togither, lende)		118	4th Eclogues	73	54
Not at first sight, nor with a dribbed shot.		165	Astrophil	2	1
With pricking shot he did not throughly move, ...		173	Astrophil	17	3
There himselfe with his shot he close doth lay..		175	Astrophil	20	8
Serve him with shot, her lips his heralds arre:.		179	Astrophil	29	10
How farre they shot awrie! the true cause is, ...		185	Astrophil	41 V	12
Deare Killer, spare not thy sweet cruell shot:		189	Astrophil	48	13
The Arrow being shot from far, doth give the smaller blowe..		344	Possibly	1	42
So brave a shott, deere fyre and bewtye strange.		345	Possibly	2	11
Each motion seeming shott from beautie's bow, ...		244	Other Poems	4	106
With shafts shott out from their back-turned bow..		251	Other Poems	4	351
A shot unheard gave me a wound unseene?.		253	Other Poems	4	454
SHOULDER					
Nico. In deed the witch thy dam her crouch from shoulder spred, ...		52	2nd Eclogues	29	13
He ran, but ran with eye ore shoulder cast, ...		249	Other Poems	4	289
SHOULDERS					
Her shoulders be like two white Doves, ...		89	Arcadia III	62	113
The great beames gone, the house on shoulders light: . . .		102	3rd Eclogues	66	136
Busy with oker did their shoulders marke..		243	Other Poems	4	69
Never on the earth on his round shoulders bare.		247	Other Poems	4	209
SHOULDST					
Why shouldst thou toyle our thornie soile to till?		169	Astrophil	10	6
Her face? O Love, a Rogue thou then shouldst be, ...		187	Astrophil	46	6
SHOUTS					
While with the people's shouts I must confesse, ...		191	Astrophil	53	3
SHOVE					
Which through a bleeding heart his point did shove:		171	Astrophil	13	6
But she in chafe him from her lap did shove, ...		173	Astrophil	17	7
SHOW					
Shew how thou canst deserve so brave desire, ...		3	Lady of May	2	2
Transform'd in shew, but more transform'd in minde, ...		11	Arcadia I	2	1
What length of verse can serve brave Mopsa's good to show, .		12	Arcadia I	3	1
The gods must help, and pretious things must serve to shew her shape.		12	Arcadia I	3	4
Yeld outward shew, what inward change he tryes:.		13	Arcadia I	4	2
I challenge thee by shew of her perfection, ...		15	1st Eclogues	7	17
Who well can set a passion out to show:.		25	1st Eclogues	9	112
What judge you doth a hillocke shew, by the lofty Olympus? .		34	1st Eclogues	13	75
Whence may I show to my minde any light of a possible escape		37	1st Eclogues	13	161
Since whitenesse doth present the sweetest show, ...		38	Arcadia II	15	7
My purest minde; whose temper hard doth showe.		40	Arcadia II	18	8
P. No Reason yet had ever skill to show it..		47	2nd Eclogues	27	40
This is my pawne; the price let Dicus' judgement show:. . .		53	2nd Eclogues	29	47
Nico. Leuca to me did yester-morning showe		55	2nd Eclogues	29	99
And saw those eyes (those Sonnes) such shoures to shew, . .		58	2nd Eclogues	30	49
To shew the wound without cure.		65	2nd Eclogues	32	4
While that the light may shewe the horrors darke		73	Arcadia III	39	11
Joie's strangers seeme, I cannot bide their showe, ...		74	Arcadia III	41	5
Can holde, shew, tell, my paines without reliefe..		75	Arcadia III	43	8
For mischeefes greate, daye after day doth showe:.		82	Arcadia III	56	13
Make me still feare, thy faire appearing showe..		82	Arcadia III	56	14
Which never part but that they showe		87	Arcadia III	62	41
In shewe and sent pale violets, ...		89	Arcadia III	62	107
O heav'n awake shewe forth thy stately face, ...		91	3rd Eclogues	63	10
And make their issue showe		92	3rd Eclogues	63	41
Ne dare once shew thy face, ...		93	3rd Eclogues	63	87
"Thus shall you show that him you do not doubt, ...		96	3rd Eclogues	64	61
But that he would, to him the letter show.		97	3rd Eclogues	64	113
But who doo let their tongues shew well their rage, ...		105	3rd Eclogues	67	47
With all our deathes shew we this damage publique.		110	Arcadia IV	70	38
As stuffe meant for the sale set out to glaring showe) . . .		118	4th Eclogues	73	72
I that was first agast, when first I saw their showe:. . . .		121	4th Eclogues	73	158

SHOW (CONTINUED)
PAGE   TITLE   LINE

Let it embassage beare your grieves to showe.. . . . .   125 4th Eclogues 75   12
Fire, aire, sea, earth, fame, time, place, shew your power.. 136 Cert Sonnets 3   20
In hard estate with stowt shew valor use,. . . . . 143 Cert Sonnets 12   16
In clyming steepe, now hard refusall show: . . . . 147 Cert Sonnets 18   6
Now dead, doth shew departure is a death.. . . . . 148 Cert Sonnets 20   12
My Diane made me shew, ... 158 Cert Sonnets 28   10
Loving in truth, and faine in verse my love to show, ... 165 Astrophil   1   1
I sweare, my heart such one shall shew to thee,. . . . . . . 167 Astrophil   4   12
Or would she her miraculous power show,. . . . . 168 Astrophil   7   9
And which is worse, no good excuse can show, ... 174 Astrophil   18   7
That mine owne writings like bad servants show . . . . 175 Astrophil   21   3
As sacred things, far from all daunger's show. . . . . 177 Astrophil   24   8
To shew her skin, lips, teeth and head so well?. . . . . . . 181 Astrophil   32   11
That I respects for both our sakes must shew:. . . . . 181 Astrophil   33   11
In all sweete stratagems sweete Arte can show, ... 183 Astrophil   36   11
Yet hearing late a fable, which did show . . . . 187 Astrophil   45   5
That it, despisde in true but naked shew,. . . . . 192 Astrophil   55   3
With chastned mind, I straight must shew that she. . . . . . 195 Astrophil   61   10
O Grammer rules, o now your vertues show; . . . . 196 Astrophil   63   1
Of everie image, which may comfort show? . . . . 199 Astrophil   66   4
O joy, too high for my low stile to show:. . . . . 200 Astrophil   69   1
Come then my Muse, shew thou height of delight . . . . 201 Astrophil   70   9
Stella, those faire lines, which true goodnesse show.. . . . 201 Astrophil   71   4
If this darke place yet shew like candle light,. . . . . . . 225 Astrophil   91   5
What sobs can give words grace my griefe to show?. . . . . . 227 Astrophil   93   2
Her selfe (to shew no other joy hath place). . . . . 229 Astrophil   97   7
She could not shew my blind braine waies of joy, ... 230 Astrophil   97   13
Which ay most faire, now more then most faire show,. . . . . 231 Astrophil   100   3
Who have so leaden eyes, as not to see sweet beautie's show, 217 A&S 7th Song   7
Which to stones I els would show:. . . . . 221 A&S 9th Song   13
Yet each day art provoakt, thyne Ire to show,. . . . . 277 Psalm VII   32
Shew forth his Acts, and this as Act most high,. . . . . . . 280 Psalm IX   32
I will get up saith God, and my help show. . . . . 285 Psalm XII   16
Show that Thy eyes respect a faithfull case; . . . . 289 Psalm XVII   6
Shew then O Lord Thy wondrous kindness show, ... 290 Psalm XVII   21
This my Distresse to God with wailfull cryes I show, ... 291 Psalm XVIII   12
That I Climb'd highest hill, he me warr points did show, . . 292 Psalm XVIII   62
Ev'en Feare makes strangers shew much love though much
   untrue.. . . . . 293 Psalm XVIII   81
From lion's mouth O help, and shew to heare me . . . . 299 Psalm XXII   49
Yea Lord to me Thy wayes do show;. . . . . 303 Psalm XXV   11
To such he doth his Cov'nant show. . . . . 304 Psalm XXV   54
In great show, ... 329 Psalm XXXVIII   56
Shew me how long I have to live. . . . . 329 Psalm XXXIX   14
Ev'en heapes of wicked thoughts which streight they show . . 333 Psalm XLI   23
Gratefull meaning show thee, ... 337 Psalm XLIII   27
Shew that we do not grudge at all when others do rejoyce.. . 343 Possibly   1   2
My freedom, with show of hir beames, with virtue my content. 344 Possibly   1   38
Of shepheards two the seely case to show,. . . . . 242 Other Poems   4   6
With triumph's shews would shew he nought did feare. . . . . 244 Other Poems   4   78
But she on elbow lean'd, with sighs did show . . . . 245 Other Poems   4   110
These sports shepheards deviz'd such faults to show. . . . . 248 Other Poems   4   241
What rage in them, that love in him did show.. . . . . 249 Other Poems   4   294
More then, besides hir, all the earth could show.. . . . . . 252 Other Poems   4   408
Which when he did in perfect image show, ... 256 Other Poems   4   541
SHOWED
Lawrell shews what I seeke, by the Mirre is show'd how I
   seeke it,. . . . .   35 1st Eclogues 13   116
And have to Lalus shewd your secret skill, ... 91 3rd Eclogues 63   20
And with some words which shewed little care,. . . . . 97 3rd Eclogues 64   118
Such proffer made, which she well showd with smiling cheere. 120 4th Eclogues 73   144
In Cryes to Thee I shewd my Cause. . . . . 311 Psalm XXX   5
In summe, I shew'd, that I to them was bent. . . . . 322 Psalm XXXV   33
SHOWER
Leave of my sheepe, my shower of teeres oreflowes, ... 43 Arcadia II   24   4
O save me from this Persecution's showre:. . . . . 277 Psalm VII   2
SHOWERS
And saw those eyes (those Sonnes) such shoures to shew,. . . 58 2nd Eclogues 30   49
Some fresh and fruitfull showers upon my sunne-burn'd
   braine . . . . 165 Astrophil   1   8
And showers from mine eyes proceeding. . . . . 221 A&S 9th Song   5
SHOWETH
If Rule by force without all claime a Tyran showeth, ... 214 A&S 5th Song   57
My moystned bed proofes of my sorrow showeth:. . . . . 276 Psalm VI   18
SHOWING
Life showing, dead indeed: . . . . 19 1st Eclogues 7   160
May then yong his pide weedes showing, ... 217 A&S 8th Song   3
SHOWS
I have no shewes of wealth: my wealth is you,. . . . . 18 1st Eclogues 7   135
Would scorne in man (their king) such feeble shows.. . . . . 23 1st Eclogues 9   43
It shews they fetch their wit from youthfull yeares. . . . . 24 1st Eclogues 9   80
Knowing no more, then what poore tryall showes,. . . . . . . 28 1st Eclogues 10   53
Lawrell shews what I seeke, by the Mirre is show'd how I
   seeke it,. . . . .   35 1st Eclogues 13   116
And of their wounds make brave lame showes:. . . . . 44 Arcadia II   25   8
Showes, guilty harte doth deeme his state opprobrious. . . . 48 2nd Eclogues 28   18
Deepe musing to himselfe, which after-mewing showes, ... 53 2nd Eclogues 29   35
Where chaunge of thoughts one foole to other shewes, ... 57 2nd Eclogues 30   21
As happie shewes of corne when harvest sendes; . . . . 71 Arcadia III 37   10

435

SHOWS   (CONTINUED)   PAGE   TITLE   LINE
    The world doth yeeld such ill consorted shows, ...   81 Arcadia III   54   9
    His workes, showes, suites, with wit, grace, and vow's
        might . . . .   84 Arcadia III   60   4
    Shewes easie print in mettall fine.. . . . .   89 Arcadia III   62   100
    O no, O no, tryall onely shewse. . . . . 153 Cert Sonnets 24   10
    Ring out your belles, let mourning shewes be spread, ... 159 Cert Sonnets 30   1
    Shewes love and pitie to my absent case. . . . . 195 Astrophil   60   8
    That face, whose lecture shewes what perfect beautie is: . . 205 Astrophil   77   2
    That to win me, oft shewes a present pay?. . . . . 223 Astrophil   88   4
    Shewes her oft at the full her fairest face, ... 229 Astrophil   97   2
    For then the lord in judgment shewes to raigne . . . . 281 Psalm IX   51
    And with how humble showes . . . . 282 Psalm X   43
    Shewes his handworking wonders.. . . . . 293 Psalm XIX   4
    With triumph's shews would shew he nought did feare. . . . . 244 Other Poems   4   78
SHOWST
    Aurora now thou shewst thy blushing light. . . . .   82 Arcadia III   56   1
SHREWD
    All churlish wordes, shrewd answeres, crabbed lookes,. . . .   93 3rd Eclogues 63   64
    Fals to shrewd turnes, and I was in his way. . . . . 173 Astrophil   17   14
    Sweet babes must babies have, but shrewd gyrles must be
        beat n. . . . . 213 A&S 5th Song   36
SHREWDLY
    Thus shrewdly burdned then, how can my Muse escape?. . . . .   12 Arcadia I   3   3
SHREWDNESS
    Shrewdnes so stirres, pride so puffes up their hart, ... 104 3rd Eclogues 67   26
SHRICH-OWL
    Am growne a shrich-owle to my selfe each morning.. . . . . . 111 4th Eclogues 71   18
SHRIEKING
    Out shreaking pipe made of some witched tree.. . . . . . . 255 Other Poems   4   516
SHRILINESS
    O voice that doth, the Thrush in shrilnes staine,. . . . . .   76 Arcadia III   46   4
SHRINE
    Yee living powres enclosed in stately shrine . . . .   40 Arcadia II   18   1
    In whose decay Vertue's faire shrine must fall.. . . . . .   59 2nd Eclogues 30   91
SHRINES
    That shrines in flesh so true a Deitie,. . . . . 167 Astrophil   4   13
SHRINKING
    Tho I in want be shrinking,. . . . . 332 Psalm XL   65
    With shrinking legges, but with a swelling brest,. . . . . . 255 Other Poems   4   523
SHRINKS
    Geron. Who for ech fickle feare from vertue shrinkes,. . . . 105 3rd Eclogues 67   58
SHUN
    Dicus. The harte well set doth never shunne confession:. . .   47 2nd Eclogues 28   13
    Nor ought I seeke to shun death, ...   67 2nd Eclogues 32   55
    Doth him, his face, his words, leave, shunne, refraine,. . .   84 Arcadia III   60   12
    Their blood offrings I do shun,. . . . . 288 Psalm XVI   11
    Led by Thy Word the Rav'ner's stepps I shun, ... 289 Psalm XVII   14
    But God gives them instinct the man to shun, ... 249 Other Poems   4   295
    With larger round, to shun the folowing feet.. . . . . . . 250 Other Poems   4   332
    He that before shund hir to shun such harmes,. . . . . . . 252 Other Poems   4   383
    Shunn lothed-loving bankes with conning crooke:. . . . . . 257 Other Poems   5   29
    Wayling till death, shun you not to be seene?. . . . . . . 258 Other Poems   5   91
SHUNNED
    He that before shund hir to shun such harmes,. . . . . . . 252 Other Poems   4   383
SHUNNING
    Since shunning paine, I ease can never find: . . . . 135 Cert Sonnets   1   1
    Who shunning vanity and works of vaineness leaving,. . . . . 302 Psalm XXIV   9
    Still shunning Nous to lengthen pleasing race, ... 250 Other Poems   4   306
SHUT
    Which senses up doth shut the senses to preserve.. . . . . 117 4th Eclogues 73   28
SICK
    How be the minds dispos'd that can not tast thy physick?
        Sick.. . . . .   63 2nd Eclogues 31   17
    Like those sicke folkes, in whome strange humors flowe,. . .   74 Arcadia III   41   1
    Sicke to the death, still loving my disease. . . . .   74 Arcadia III   41   8
    Dead palsie sicke of all my chiefest parts:. . . . . 136 Cert Sonnets   2   10
    Stella is sicke, and in that sicke bed lies. . . . . 231 Astrophil   101   1
    And grace, sicke too, such fine conclusions tries, ... 231 Astrophil   101   3
    Beauty is sicke, but sicke in so faire guise,. . . . . 231 Astrophil   101   5
    Sicke, thirsty, glad (though but of empty glasse:) . . . . . 233 Astrophil   104   11
    And turn his couch, where sick he couched late,. . . . . . 333 Psalm XLI   11
SICK-BED
    Stella is sicke, and in that sicke bed lies. . . . . 231 Astrophil   101   1
SICKER
    Let swanne's example siker serve for thee, ...   28 1st Eclogues 10   73
SICK-MAN'S
    In sicke-man's franzie rather takes compassion,. . . . . .   50 2nd Eclogues 28   96
SICKNESS
    But Plangus, lest I may your sicknesse misse . . . .   62 2nd Eclogues 30   182
    Though (yoked so) my minde with sicknes fainte,. . . . . .   83 Arcadia III   57   7
    So in his sicknesse grew our sure infection. . . . . 128 4th Eclogues 75   135
    She knows the sicknesse of that perfect place. . . . . . . 142 Cert Sonnets 11   11
    For my poore soule, which now that sickenesse tries,. . . . . 228 Astrophil   94   6
    That sickenesse brags it selfe best graced to be.. . . . . 231 Astrophil   101   4
    Their judgements hackney on, the fault on sicknesse lay, . . 232 Astrophil   102   10
    And whose? ev'n who when they sickness bare. . . . . 322 Psalm XXXV   29
SIDE
    Lips red and plum, as cherrie's ruddy side,. . . . .   76 Arcadia III   46   8
    Or like the fresh Queene-apple's side, ...   86 Arcadia III   62   25

SIDE   (CONTINUED)   PAGE TITLE   LINE

	PAGE	TITLE		LINE
Might of each side astray be brought,.	88	Arcadia III	62	72
In my free side? or am I borne a slave,.	188	Astrophil	47	3
But, but (alas) night's side the ods hath fur,.	229	Astrophil	96	12
This side doth beauty take,.	215	A&S 6th Song		7
Then lord, my lord, give sentence on my side	277	Psalm VII		23
But of the Other side, the poore in sprite	281	Psalm IX		56
But so of happy other side	284	Psalm XI		21
Thou seest each side the walking doth endure	285	Psalm XII		25
To feele the panting heart, which through hir syde	252	Other Poems	4	405
Lay by a river's side, ...	256	Other Poems	5	2

SIDES

	PAGE	TITLE		LINE
The goodman read on both sides the content,.	96	3rd Eclogues	64	88
Others, because of both sides I do take.	185	Astrophil	41	9
To both sides partiall is:	216	A&S 6th Song		46
For troubles of all sides have me within..	312	Psalm XXXI		26

SIEVE

	PAGE	TITLE		LINE
Nico. As I of late, neer bushes usde my sive,.	54	2nd Eclogues	29	81

SIGH

	PAGE	TITLE		LINE
That to each word, nay sigh of mine you harke,.	233	Astrophil	104	3
Sigh they did, but now betwixt	218	A&S 8th Song		17
Lo, I am tir'd, while still I sigh and groane:	276	Psalm VI		17
Dick. Here then and learn to sigh: a mistress I doo serve, .	343	Possibly	1	19

SIGH-BROKEN

	PAGE	TITLE		LINE
His oft sigh-broken dittie,.	259	Other Poems	5	115

SIGHED

	PAGE	TITLE		LINE
She sigh'd and sayd, the bad guest sought her love..	95	3rd Eclogues	64	48
I sighd her sighes, and wailed for her wo, ...	223	Astrophil	87	10
How cloth'd, how waited on, sighd she or smilde, ...	225	Astrophil	92	10

SIGHINGS

	PAGE	TITLE		LINE
For creeping rimes, which often sighings choke..	242	Other Poems	4	8
What fitts me now but teares, and sighings sadd?	259	Other Poems	5	97

SIGHS

	PAGE	TITLE		LINE
To aire of sighes, sighes to the harte's fire turne, ...	19	1st Eclogues	7	154
Aire, we do still with sighes encrease; to the fire? we do want none.	32	1st Eclogues	13	30
With sighes you seeke to coole your hotte desire:.	38	Arcadia II	14	6
Since sighes (into mine inward fornace turnd).	38	Arcadia II	14	7
Leave of my sheepe, my sighes burne up your filde, ...	43	Arcadia II	24	7
Swelling with sighes, made pale with minde's disease,. . . .	58	2nd Eclogues	30	48
Reason sighes but in end he thus doth answere.	68	2nd Eclogues	33	25
Hold deere his work, with sighes eache change attendes,. . .	71	Arcadia III	37	8
Due sighes blowe out all sparkes of joyfull light, ...	74	Arcadia III	42	11
Ye helplesse Sighes, blowe out your breath to nought,. . .	83	Arcadia III	59	5
Let voice of Sighes into cleare musike runne,.	84	Arcadia III	59	13
Hailestones of teares, of sighes a monstrous blast,.	114	4th Eclogues	72	33
That all the earth my woes, sighes, teares may know,. . . .	146	Cert Sonnets	17	39
While teares powre out his inke, and sighs breathe out his words:.	168	Astrophil	6	10
With new-borne sighes and denisend wit do sing;.	172	Astrophil	15	8
Oft with true sighes, oft with uncalled teares,.	195	Astrophil	61	1
What sighes stolne out, or kild before full borne?	199	Astrophil	67	9
I saw that sighes her sweetest lips did part,.	223	Astrophil	87	7
I sighd her sighes, and wailed for her wo, ...	223	Astrophil	87	10
I cry thy sighs; my deere, thy teares I bleede..	227	Astrophil	93	14
Yet sighs, deere sighs, indeede true friends you are,. . . .	228	Astrophil	95	1
Only true sighs, you do not go away, ...	229	Astrophil	95	12
How thy lee shores by my sighes stormed be!.	230	Astrophil	98	4
O honied sighs, which from that breast do rise,.	231	Astrophil	100	5
Such teares, sighs, plaints, no sorrow is, but joy:.	231	Astrophil	100	12
Sighs of woes were glad sighs mixt,.	218	A&S 8th Song		18
Even for the sighs, true sighs of man distrest	285	Psalm XII		15
My sighs are not hid from thee;.	328	Psalm XXXVIII		27
But she on elbow lean'd, with sighs did show	245	Other Poems	4	110
With gazing looks, short sighs, unsettled feet,.	251	Other Poems	4	369
Filling his eies with teares, with sighs his brest..	253	Other Poems	4	432

SIGHT

	PAGE	TITLE		LINE
Such planted gifts enrich even beggers' sight:	3	Lady of May	1	10
Thus are my eyes still Captive to one sight:	12	Arcadia I	2	9
And thus my eyes, are plaste still in one sight.	12	Arcadia I	2	V809
With gentle beames not hurting sight:.	13	Arcadia I	5	8
Their dwellers rapt with sight of her perfection	15	1st Eclogues	7	44
My sight in her faire limmes, I then assure my selfe,. . . .	16	1st Eclogues	7	56
So I your sight, you shall your selves recover".	17	1st Eclogues	7	93
The circle is my (round about her) sight:	17	1st Eclogues	7	103
My day newe cares; my ginnes my daily sight, ...	18	1st Eclogues	7	140
Then each conceit that enters in by sight, ...	23	1st Eclogues	9	38
Such sight have they that see with goggling eyes..	25	1st Eclogues	9	113
Of my owne harte, where thoughts be the temple, sighte is an aultar.	37	1st Eclogues	13	171
With flowing teares your fault of hasty sight:	38	Arcadia II	14	2
In vaine, my Hart, now you with sight are burnd, ...	38	Arcadia II	14	5
Since so mine eyes are subject to your sight,.	39	Arcadia II	16	1
That in your sight they fixed have my braine;.	39	Arcadia II	16	2
My words unseene, the marble still in sight, ...	41	Arcadia II	19	10
And in our little world dost crave our inward sight,. . . .	44	Arcadia II	26	2
Dorus. Sight is his roote, in thought is his progression,..	48	2nd Eclogues	28	37
Since in my hands selfe goodly sight she tooke..	55	2nd Eclogues	29	116
Each sight draws on a thought, thought mother of science,..	69	2nd Eclogues	34	11
Whiche dazeling still, dothe still maynteine my sight; . . .	70	Arcadia III	35	6

SIGHT	(CONTINUED)	PAGE	TITLE		LINE
For reason will, great sight of hoped blisse, ...		71	Arcadia III	37	11
Where too much sight, makes all the bodie blinde, ...		73	Arcadia III	40	11
Come clowdie feares, close up my daseled sight, ...		74	Arcadia III	42	9
I darkned am, who once had clearest sight.		75	Arcadia III	43	4
His hart his wound receaved from my sight:		76	Arcadia III	45	9
Yet joyning formes one sight of beautie breede.		78	Arcadia III	50	4
And while o sleepe thou closest up her sight, ...		79	Arcadia III	51	5
(Her sight where love did forge his fayrest darte)		79	Arcadia III	51	6
Because that thou, the author of our sight, ...		80	Arcadia III	52	14
Too weake for them our weaker sighte doth vaile.		82	Arcadia III	55	11
Beautie hath force to catche the humane sight.		82	Arcadia III	57	1
Sight doth bewitch, the fancie evill awaked.		82	Arcadia III	57	2
No wondre then, though sighte my sighte did tainte, ...		83	Arcadia III	57	5
But ah, alas! (In vayne) sight, thought, ...		84	Arcadia III	60	11
Blushing at sight of Phoebus' pride.		86	Arcadia III	62	26
In curious circle, busie sight:		88	Arcadia III	62	74
The bellie there gladde sight doth fill, ...		88	Arcadia III	62	77
Whose bought incav'd doth yeeld such sight, ...		89	Arcadia III	62	97
Who hath our sight with too much sight infected, ...		108	Arcadia IV	69	6
Shamed I hate my selfe in sight of mountaines, ...		112	4th Eclogues	71	59
Blinded with beames, fell darkenes is my sight:		113	4th Eclogues	72	8
So that I see, although my sight empaire, ...		115	4th Eclogues	72	59
And hers on me, astonisht with that sight.		115	4th Eclogues	72	76
And bending humbled eyes (o eyes the Sunne of sight)		119	4th Eclogues	73	91
Into thy hart by the sight of this Epistle I send:		122	4th Eclogues	74	6
Should my too-much sight cause so true a Sunne to be lost? .		124	4th Eclogues	74	58
Fould with this sight, while thou thy chariot guidest. . . .		126	4th Eclogues	75	57
Out of our sight in turne of hand is vanished.		128	4th Eclogues	75	127
Since force doth faint, and sight doth make me blind:		135	Cert Sonnets	1	4
On those affectes which easily yeeld to sight, ...		135	Cert Sonnets	2	6
To see what faire sight there raigneth, ...		140	Cert Sonnets	7	26
Like to the Mowlle with want of guiding sight, ...		149	Cert Sonnets	21	7
With fruits of happie sight, ...		151	Cert Sonnets	23	2
From sight of her faire eyes:		152	Cert Sonnets	23	28
With fruits of happie sight, ...		152	Cert Sonnets	23	34
That doth both shine and give us sight to see.		161	Cert Sonnets	32	8
Not at first sight, nor with a dribbed shot.		165	Astrophil	2	1
In object best to knit and strength our sight, ...		168	Astrophil	7	6
In her sight I a lesson new have speld, ...		173	Astrophil	16	12
They should still daunce to please a gazer's sight.		178	Astrophil	26	8
Copartner of the riches of that sight:		188	Astrophil	48	6
But now that I, alas, do want her sight, ...		193	Astrophil	56	9
Makes me fall from her sight, then sweetly she		195	Astrophil	60	6
Fed by thy worth, and kindled by thy sight?		200	Astrophil	68	8
My Orphan sence flies to the inward sight, ...		223	Astrophil	88	10
In hart both sight and love now coupled be;		223	Astrophil	88	13
While I dispaire by Sunne's sight to enjoy.		230	Astrophil	97	14
Paint woe's blacke face so lively to my sight, ...		230	Astrophil	98	10
To lay his then marke wanting shafts of sight, ...		230	Astrophil	99	3
With sight thereof cride out; o faire disgrace, ...		233	Astrophil	103	13
Unhappie sight, and hath thee vanisht by.		235	Astrophil	105	1
For I protest, my sight never thy face enjoyeth, ...		215	A&S 5th Song		75
It is one who from thy sight, ...		233	A&S 11th Song		3
More then in my reason's sight.		234	A&S 11th Song		30
A lesson fit, both sight and skill, love and firme love to					
breede, ...		217	A&S 7th Song		12
But her sight his cares did banish, ...		218	A&S 8th Song		11
In his sight her yoke did vanish		218	A&S 8th Song		12
But, lord, lift Thou upon our sight.		274	Psalm IV		26
Nor glorious Fooles stand in Thy awfull sight.		274	Psalm V		12
And they are faln, nay perisht at Thy sight:		279	Psalm IX		7
His farr off sight now hoodwinkt is, ...		282	Psalm X		47
Naught his allseing sight can miss, ...		284	Psalm XI		15
Shall feel in Thy face's sight		289	Psalm XVI		40
By him because I did find in his eyes' sight grace, ...		292	Psalm XVIII		41
My saving might, lord in Thy sight, ...		295	Psalm XIX		63
I lift my in ward sight;		302	Psalm XXV		2
That in the streets from sight of me they fled.		313	Psalm XXXI		33
That trust in Thee, ev'n in most open sight!		313	Psalm XXXI		54
I said that I from out Thy sight was cast;		313	Psalm XXXI		62
But lo Jehova's sight.		318	Psalm XXXIII		67
His sight is them to save.		318	Psalm XXXIII		73
And will save whom his sight cleere.		320	Psalm XXXIV		67
For their short time is in his sight.		325	Psalm XXXVII		36
I mussle will my mouth while in the sight.		329	Psalm XXXIX		3
For my God Thy sight		336	Psalm XLIII		7
With sight made dymme with dayly teares another's sport to					
see.		343	Possibly	1	4
Whille I that syghte, desyre, and vowe forbare, ...		344	Possibly	2	7
Of seely boies please unacquainted sight:		246	Other Poems	4	182
Yet but a babe, with milke of Sight he nurst:		247	Other Poems	4	202
With sight of feare from frends to fremb'd do flie.		248	Other Poems	4	240
He ravished with sight how gracefully.		249	Other Poems	4	282
Much more his sight encreast his hote desire:		249	Other Poems	4	298
And did the tribute of their wondring sight.		251	Other Poems	4	363
Help him, who can no more hir sight foregoe.		253	Other Poems	4	420
And you my flock, care of my carefull sight, ...		254	Other Poems	4	483
And giving to his sight a wandring race, ...		255	Other Poems	4	526
(With blushing soule at sight of judgement's glasse, ...		255	Other Poems	4	531

438

SIGHT	(CONTINUED)	PAGE	TITLE		LINE
He envied such a death in sight of lover,.		259	Other Poems	5	124
With their ever-pleasing sight,.		263	Other Poems	7	64
SIGHTFULNESS					
Thou mayest love her that I may see thy sightfulnesse. . . .		51	2nd Eclogues 28		113
Let us not winke though void of purest sightfulnes..		61	2nd Eclogues 30		139
SIGHT'S					
I, seeing better sights in sight's decay,.		184	Astrophil	38	12
SIGHTS					
I, seeing better sights in sight's decay,.		184	Astrophil	38	12
Now let those lightsomme sights we see thy darknes overcome.		343	Possibly	1	12
SIGN					
The gartring place with child-like signe,.		89	Arcadia III	62	99
Sure shepherd's signe, that morne would soone fetch day. . .		103	3rd Eclogues 66		161
Sore signe it is, the Lord's last thred is spun.		150	Cert Sonnets 22		14
For no faire signe can credit winne, ...		156	Cert Sonnets 27		15
SIGNED					
Holde me most yours, then my longe suite is signde.		79	Arcadia III	50	18
SIGNIFIED					
As yet love she signified.		220	A&S 8th Song		72
SIGNIFY					
Lalus. Come Dorus, come, let songs thy sorowes signifie: . .		14	1st Eclogues 7		1
SIGNS					
Bubling out doth breathe signes of his hugie dolours:. . . .		123	4th Eclogues 74		28
That so I may signes of my sorrowe leave.		125	4th Eclogues 75		9
Or if such heavenly signes must prove annoy, ...		231	Astrophil	100	13
SILENCE					
But now to silence turn'd his minstralsie.		28	1st Eclogues 10		75
Since when I thinke he hath in silence lived..		29	1st Eclogues 10		87
In silence, from a man's owne selfe with company robbed. . .		35	1st Eclogues 13		106
Silence doth seeme the maske of base oppression.		47	2nd Eclogues 28		15
Either dull silence, or eternall chat;		104	3rd Eclogues 67		31
With sinlesse sleepe, and silence, wisdome's mother, ...		108	Arcadia IV	69	10
A silence sweet each where with one consent embraste		117	4th Eclogues 73		7
Who silence force to make their words more deare:.		147	Cert Sonnets 17		49
Wise silence is best musicke unto blisse..		201	Astrophil	70	14
Silence in both displaies his sullen might,.		229	Astrophil	96	5
Love it selfe did silence breake;.		218	A&S 8th Song		26
Let them in bedd of endless silence dy..		313	Psalm XXXI		48
I silence kept ev'n in the good.		329	Psalm XXXIX		6
SILENT					
Shallow brookes murmure most, deep silent slide away;. . . .		14	1st Eclogues 7		11
I silent herd more wordes of witt.		57	2nd Eclogues 30		2
Of written greefes, yet be the silent ground..		81	Arcadia III	54	8
Vouchsafe your silent eares to playning musique, ...		111	4th Eclogues 71		4
Above line repeated at following location.		111	4th Eclogues 71		11
Be silent therefore now, and so be silent still.		119	4th Eclogues 73		97
They shall not last: with Citherne silent muse		143	Cert Sonnets 12		14
But my heart burnes, I cannot silent be..		207	Astrophil	81	11
Languisht with horrors of the silent night, ...		224	Astrophil	89	8
Silent and sad in mourning weedes doth dight:.		229	Astrophil	97	8
While the blacke horrors of the silent night,.		230	Astrophil	98	9
When silent night might seeme all faults to hide,.		289	Psalm XVII		9
Whether I silent did remain, ...		315	Psalm XXXII		8
This thou hast seen, and wilt thou silent be?.		322	Psalm XXXV		55
SILENTLY					
How silently, and with how wanne a face, ...		180	Astrophil	31	2
SILK					
The pasture rich, the wooll as soft as silke,.		4	Lady of May	2	21
As she a black-silke cap on him begunne.		244	Other Poems	4	85
SILLY					
Poore Painters oft with silly Poets joyne, ...		20	1st Eclogues 8		1
Silly shepheard's poore pype, when his harsh sound testifis our woes,.		32	1st Eclogues 13		40
Unto a silly caban, though weake, yet stronger against woes.		34	1st Eclogues 13		93
Thus children doo the silly birds they finde,.		41	Arcadia II	20	11
Silly rewarde! yet among women hath she of vertu the most. Most..		64	2nd Eclogues 31		36
Pan, father Pan, the god of silly sheepe,.		92	3rd Eclogues 63		37
While thus he fear'd the silly innocent, ...		94	3rd Eclogues 64		13
At last for sport their sillie lives did spill..		103	3rd Eclogues 66		147
Or as the silly birde in well acquainted nest.		117	4th Eclogues 73		23
That which their mother hight, or els their silly seed.. . .		119	4th Eclogues 73		84
Who most the silly shepheard's pipe did pryse, ...		125	4th Eclogues 75		2
Like to the silly Sylvan,.		154	Cert Sonnets 25		15
On silly me do not the burthen lay,.		190	Astrophil	51	5
Cannot such grace your silly selfe content,.		208	Astrophil	83	11
And by the syly stand.		282	Psalm X		52
SILVANUS					
(Espilus) Silvanus long in love, and long in vaine,.		4	Lady of May	3	1
SILVER					
Her skin like burnisht gold, her hands like silver ure untryde.		12	Arcadia I	3	12
Which leaded are with silver skinne, ...		89	Arcadia III	62	115
Like Whitest Snowe, in silver Brooke,.		88	Arcadia III	62 V	69
In cofer of dimme clowdes his silver groates,.		98	3rd Eclogues 66		9
Where roses gueuls are borne in silver field..		171	Astrophil	13	11
Pure, Purer than the silver throughly try'd.		285	Psalm XII		20
SIMILES					
Or with strange similies enrich each line, ...		166	Astrophil	3	7

	PAGE	TITLE	LINE
SIMPLE			
Where simple love, which chastnesse doth imparte,.	92	3rd Eclogues 63	58
He made the simple wench his wrath abide..	95	3rd Eclogues 64	30
So I in simple course, and unentangled minde	117	4th Eclogues 73	25
A simple soule should breed so mixed woes.	149	Cert Sonnets 22	10
If vaine love have my simple soule opprest,.	166	Astrophil 4	3
He waites to spoyle the simple men:.	282	Psalm X	38
O with how simple look	282	Psalm X	41
Which if it last, Woe to all simple Hearts..	285	Psalm XII	27
For simple goodnes shined in his eyes.	247	Other Poems 4	196
SIMPLEST			
To simplest Wisdom lending.	294	Psalm XIX	32
SIMPLICITY			
Such goodnes that in her simplicitie triumphs:	69	2nd Eclogues 34	36
O sweet simplicitie: from whence should Love be so learned?.	124	4th Eclogues 74	65
But know that I in pure simplicitie, ...	179	Astrophil 28	12
SIMPLY			
(Although simply atyrde) your manly affection utter.	32	1st Eclogues 13	16
SIN			
But farewell nowe, thy fault is no great sinne,.	29	1st Eclogues 10	97
(So humble knowledge can throw downe the snakish sinne). . .	44	Arcadia II 26	6
That to the duke, he would his sinne declare,.	97	3rd Eclogues 64	116
If that be sinne which doth the maners frame,.	172	Astrophil 14	9
If that be sinne which in fixt hearts doth breed	172	Astrophil 14	12
Then Love is sinne, and let me sinfull be.	172	Astrophil 14	14
For neither shall the men in sin delighted	270	Psalm I	15
But they that sinne, in sinfull breast do cherish;	271	Psalm I	21
Sinne from all rule in you depose, ...	273	Psalm IV	17
Least such things sin in Thy self cherish, ...	325	Psalm XXXVII	22
For my sin,.	329	Psalm XXXVIII	53
I know that man's foule sin doth cause Thy wrath..	330	Psalm XXXIX	33
For when his sin Thy scourging hath, ...	330	Psalm XXXIX	34
Burnt offring nor sin offring, ...	331	Psalm XL	26
Where 'gainst Thee lay my sin.	333	Psalm XLI	16
SINCE			
It is no shame, since Hercules was he"..	5	Lady of May 3	12
Since what I see, thinke, know is all but you?	12	Arcadia I 2	14
Nor be abasht, since such a guest you finde,.	13	Arcadia I 4	3
Since vertues all, to make her title, pleased be..	15	1st Eclogues 7	39
Since she faire fierce to such a state me calls, ...	23	1st Eclogues 9	30
Since all his force against himselfe he tries..	23	1st Eclogues 9	37
That since they still alledge, When they were yong:.	24	1st Eclogues 9	79
Of yeeres (alas) since I good Mastix knewe..	27	1st Eclogues 10	21
Since that we see our saddest Shepheards out	27	1st Eclogues 10	26
Since when I thinke he hath in silence lived..	29	1st Eclogues 10	87
I warne thee therefore (since thou maist have choice). . . .	29	1st Eclogues 10	88
(Since no estates be so base, but love vouchsafeth his arrow	33	1st Eclogues 13	50
Since no refuge doth serve from woundes we do carry about us	33	1st Eclogues 13	51
Since outward pleasures be but halting helpes to decayd soules).	33	1st Eclogues 13	52
Save what a worke, by thy selfe is wrought: and since I am altred	36	1st Eclogues 13	151
Since to my hart her shape you so did sende;	38	Arcadia II 14	3
Since sighes (into mine inward fornace turnd)	38	Arcadia II 14	7
Since there mine eyes have played so false a parte,.	38	Arcadia II 14	11
And since in vaine I find were all my strife,.	38	Arcadia II 14	13
Since whitenesse doth present the sweetest show, ...	38	Arcadia II 15	7
And to old age since you your selfe aspire, ...	39	Arcadia II 15	13
Since so mine eyes are subject to your sight,.	39	Arcadia II 16	1
Since so my harte is filled with that light, ...	39	Arcadia II 16	3
Since in sweete you all goods so richly raigne,.	39	Arcadia II 16	5
Since so your living image lives in me,.	39	Arcadia II 16	7
Since streame, aier, sand, mine eyes and eares conspire: . .	42	Arcadia II 21	17
P. How know we that, since present joyes we misse?	47	2nd Eclogues 27	38
Pan is not dead, since Pas beginnes to sing.	53	2nd Eclogues 29	53
Since Nico doth to sing so widely gape?.	53	2nd Eclogues 29	55
But ever since that well is well besought, ...	55	2nd Eclogues 29	109
Since in my hands selfe goodly sight she tooke..	55	2nd Eclogues 29	116
That since the having them to neither's due, ...	56	2nd Eclogues 29	148
Long since my voice is hoarce, and throte is sore, ...	57	2nd Eclogues 30	8
Since cause of griefe no cause from life removes..	58	2nd Eclogues 30	37
Then then what do I gaine, since unto hir will I do winde? Winde.	64	2nd Eclogues 31	34
Whence can pride come there, since springs of beawty be thence? Thence.	65	2nd Eclogues 31	44
Ods? what an ods is there since them to the heav'ns I prefer Erre..	65	2nd Eclogues 31	48
Synce love with care, and hope with feare do fight..	72	Arcadia III 37	18
Since that the stormy rage of passions darcke.	72	Arcadia III 39	1
Since all the thinges which give mine eyes their light . . .	73	Arcadia III 39	5
Since, as I say, both minde and sences darke	73	Arcadia III 39	9
Since that my thoughtes, as streight as streightnes thine, .	77	Arcadia III 47	3
Since in such phrase his faith he did attire..	80	Arcadia III 53	8
Since Lalus' musick oft doth yeeld you praise, ...	92	3rd Eclogues 63	29
Since from these good the others' good doth flowe, ...	92	3rd Eclogues 63	40
Then ever for my selfe since I was bore:	99	3rd Eclogues 66	19
But since you will, part of my heav'nly fire	100	3rd Eclogues 66	75
Since wayling is a bud of causefull sorowe,.	108	Arcadia IV 70	1

	PAGE	TITLE		LINE
Since sorow is the follower of evill fortune,	108	Arcadia IV	70	2
Since no evill fortune equalls publique damage:	108	Arcadia IV	70	3
Then since such pow'rs conspire unto our damage.	109	Arcadia IV	70	13
Since sorow then concludeth all our fortune,	110	Arcadia IV	70	37
Strephon. Long since alas, my deadly Swannish musique.	112	4th Eclogues	71	25
Long since my thoughts more desert be then forrests:	112	4th Eclogues	71	28
Long since I see my joyes come to their evening,	112	4th Eclogues	71	29
Klaius. Long since the happie dwellers of these vallies,	112	4th Eclogues	71	31
Long since I hate the night, more hate the morning:	112	4th Eclogues	71	34
Long since my thoughts chase me like beasts in forrests,	112	4th Eclogues	71	35
Since thou my riches arte, and that thou haste	114	4th Eclogues	72	29
Since then my harte did loose his wonted place,	115	4th Eclogues	72	77
Since thou from me (o me) o Sunne didst passe.	116	4th Eclogues	72	98
That with a body't goes? since by a body it is.	123	4th Eclogues	74	46
You should have your face (since Love is ill) blemished.	123	4th Eclogues	74	56
Since so she will, whose will is to me more then a lawe.	124	4th Eclogues	74	84
Since that to death is gone the shepheard hie,	125	4th Eclogues	75	1
Since Death on Vertue's fort hath made invasion.	128	4th Eclogues	75	102
Of any since God AEsculapius ceased.	128	4th Eclogues	75	116
Since nature's workes be good, and death doth serve.	131	Arcadia V	77	1
Since feare is vaine, but when it may preserve,	131	Arcadia V	77	3
Since this we feele, greate losse we cannot finde.	131	Arcadia V	77	14
Since shunning paine, I ease can never find:	135	Cert Sonnets	1	1
Since bashfull dread seekes where he knowes me harmed:	135	Cert Sonnets	1	2
Since will is won, and stopped eares are charmed:	135	Cert Sonnets	1	3
Since force doth faint, and sight doth make me blind:	135	Cert Sonnets	1	4
Since loosing long, the faster still I bind:	135	Cert Sonnets	1	5
Since naked sence can conquer reason armed:	135	Cert Sonnets	1	6
Since heart in chilling feare with yce is warmed:	135	Cert Sonnets	1	7
In fine, since strife of thought but marres the mind,	135	Cert Sonnets	1	8
Since wanting is more woe then too much having..	137	Cert Sonnets	4	20
Since babie mine, from me thy watching springeth,	139	Cert Sonnets	6	7
Since then truth to all minds telleth,	140	Cert Sonnets	7	18
So then since that heaven remaineth,	140	Cert Sonnets	7	28
He hopes for some small praise since she hath great,	141	Cert Sonnets	8	11
In wonted walkes, since wonted fancies change,	147	Cert Sonnets	18	1
But since my thoughts in thinking still are spent,	148	Cert Sonnets	19	13
Since she lives in his death..	152	Cert Sonnets	23	16
Since his treasure	155	Cert Sonnets	26	10
Since our lives be not immortall,	155	Cert Sonnets	26	16
I see since I saw you:	157	Cert Sonnets	28	2
Since they did warrant me.	158	Cert Sonnets	28	20
Since that in selfe same metall coin'd,	159	Cert Sonnets	29	3
For since mad March great promise made of me,	175	Astrophil	21	9
It is most true, for since I her did see,	177	Astrophil	25	12
Since thou in me so sure a power doest keepe,	181	Astrophil	32	5
Since Reason's selfe doth blow the cole in me?	182	Astrophil	35	6
Whereto long since, through my long battred eyes,	182	Astrophil	36	3
And there long since, Love thy Lieutenant lies,	183	Astrophil	36	5
Long since forc'd by thy beames, but stone nor tree.	183	Astrophil	36	13
Since then thou hast so farre subdued me,	185	Astrophil	40	12
Since to himselfe he doth your gifts apply,	186	Astrophil	43	3
Blind-hitting boy, since that thee and me.	187	Astrophil	46	2
Yet since my death-wound is already got,	189	Astrophil	48	12
Since they do weare his badge, most firmely prove.	190	Astrophil	52	4
Well Love, since this demurre our sute doth stay,	191	Astrophil	52	12
To witlesse things, then Love I hope (since wit.	194	Astrophil	59	13
Now since her chast mind hates this love in me,	195	Astrophil	61	9
Since in thine armes, if learnd fame truth hath spread,	198	Astrophil	65	13
Stolne to my heart, since last faire night, nay day,	199	Astrophil	66	10
Nectar of Mirth, since I Jove's cup do keepe..	201	Astrophil	70	4
Who since he hath, by Nature's speciall grace,	206	Astrophil	78	9
Since best wits thinke it wit thee to admire:	206	Astrophil	80	2
Then since (deare life) you faine would have me peace,	207	Astrophil	81	12
Highway since you my chiefe Pernassus be,	209	Astrophil	84	1
Since Stella's eyes, wont to give me my day,	223	Astrophil	89	3
Since all my words thy beauty doth endite,	224	Astrophil	90	13
Since kind or chance gives both one liverie,	229	Astrophil	96	2
Stella since thou so right a Princesse art	236	Astrophil	107	1
Since sweet sleep her eyes hath charmed,	202	A&S 2nd Song		5
Since she disdaining me, doth you in me disdaine:	213	A&S 5th Song		28
That not I, but since I love you,	219	A&S 8th Song		51
Since ever thou to them wilt succour send.	275	Psalm V		36
Since I do trust Jehova still,	283	Psalm XI		1
And since my lipps feign not with Thee,	289	Psalm XVII		3
O be not farr, since pain so nearly presseth,	299	Psalm XXII		25
And since there is not One, who it redresseth.	299	Psalm XXII		26
And reason, since the Croune to God pertaineth,	300	Psalm XXII		69
Since they Eternal Essence have.	303	Psalm XXV		24
Since youth and they do passe;	303	Psalm XXV		28
Since all my ayd in Thee I got;	308	Psalm XXVII		44
Then since my tongue delights that name to blesse,	312	Psalm XXXI		8
Since he their hearts doth frame,	317	Psalm XXXIII		55
Since it is Thou that makest one such?	330	Psalm XXXIX		30
Since foes nor have, nor shall have cause to be.	333	Psalm XLI		39
Will. Dick, since we cannot dance, come let a chearefull voyce.	343	Possibly	1	1
Did me pearce, burne, and bynde, long since and late,	345	Possibly	2	12
For since warre is the ground of vertue's love,	346	Possibly	5	7

SINCE   (CONTINUED)   PAGE   TITLE   LINE

	PAGE	TITLE		LINE
Since I am now come hether,.	261	Other Poems	6	38
Since they know not how to faine,.	263	Other Poems	7	39

SINEWS

And found with deadly feare that all my sinewes shak'd. . . .	121	4th Eclogues	73	180
Then those delights through all their sinewes breed	252	Other Poems	4	411
"When I see her, my sinewes shake for feare, ...	253	Other Poems	4	457

SINFUL

Of sinfull thoughts, which do in ruine end?	172	Astrophil	14	8
Then Love is sinne, and let me sinfull be.	172	Astrophil	14	14
Nor blam'd for bloud, nor sham'd for sinfull deed.	209	Astrophil	84	11
But they that sinne, in sinfull breast do cherish;	271	Psalm I		21

SING

Dorus. Nightingales seldome sing, the Pie still chattereth:.	14	1st Eclogues	7	7
Sing then, and see (for now thou hast inflamed me)	15	1st Eclogues	7	20
Thy pipe, o Pan, shall helpe, though I sing sorilie.	15	1st Eclogues	7	27
But let us sing, sweet tunes do passions ease, ...	22	1st Eclogues	9	4
For he woulde sing, but others were defaste;	28	1st Eclogues	10	76
Yet dying, and dead, doo we sing her honour;	30	1st Eclogues	12	9
Or when an Echo begins unmov'd to sing them a love song. . .	33	1st Eclogues	13	48
But still when thou dost sing, me thinkes a colt is loose. .	52	2nd Eclogues	29	24
And if I better sing, let me thy Cosma kisse.	53	2nd Eclogues	29	38
Dicus. Sing then my lads, but sing with better vaine then				
yet, ...	53	2nd Eclogues	29	49
Pan is not dead, since Pas beginnes to sing.	53	2nd Eclogues	29	53
Since Nico doth to sing so widely gape?.	53	2nd Eclogues	29	55
To sing my owne decaid state.	65	2nd Eclogues	32	4
If that to sing thou arte bent	66	2nd Eclogues	32	20
Go sing the fall of old Thebes, ...	66	2nd Eclogues	32	21
My muse I yeeld, my muse singe, ...	67	2nd Eclogues	32	50
It August was, he daynde not then to sing.	99	3rd Eclogues	66	14
Thus did I sing, and pipe eight sullen houres.	103	3rd Eclogues	66	155
Wherein the birde doth never sing but cry;	105	3rd Eclogues	67	50
Heart and soule do sing in me.	139	Cert Sonnets	7	3
Above line repeated at following locations	139	Cert Sonnets	7	10
. . . .	139	Cert Sonnets	7	13
. . . .	140	Cert Sonnets	7	20
. . . .	140	Cert Sonnets	7	23
. . . .	140	Cert Sonnets	7	30
. . . .	140	Cert Sonnets	7	33
. . . .	140	Cert Sonnets	7	40
. . . .	140	Cert Sonnets	7	27
Forced are to sing alway;	146	Cert Sonnets	17	37
Take harp and sing in this our versing time:	172	Astrophil	15	8
With new-borne sighes and denisend wit do sing;	193	Astrophil	57	10
But them (so sweete is she) most sweetly sing, ...	196	Astrophil	63	9
Sing then my Muse, now Io Pean sing, ...	201	Astrophil	70	6
Trebles sing high, as well as bases deepe:	219	A&S 8th Song		56
These birds sing: "Now use the season.".	280	Psalm IX		42
Of syon's Daughter may sing forth Thy prayse:	283	Psalm X		69
So lord we shall Thy Title sing.	293	Psalm XVIII		89
I to Thy Name will sing, and this my song shall bee:	311	Psalm XXX		39
I will thee thanks for ever sing.	316	Psalm XXXIII		13
A new, sing a new song	316	Psalm XXXIII		15
Sing lowd and merrily, ...	337	Psalm XLIII		29
I will sing abroad				

SINGER

The singer is the song's theame.	66	2nd Eclogues	32	36

SINGETH

Or else who singeth worse, my skill will hardly hit.	53	2nd Eclogues	29	50
Sleepe Babie mine, Desire, nurse Beautie singeth:	139	Cert Sonnets	6	1
For because my cheefe part singeth, ...	140	Cert Sonnets	7	35
O stones, o trees, learne hearing, Stella singeth.	208	A&S 3rd Song		6
Stella, whose voice when it singeth, ...	219	A&S 8th Song		39

SINGING

Of singing take to thee the reputation.	19	1st Eclogues	7	172
Dorus. Of singing take to thee the reputation.	19	1st Eclogues	7	173
Of singing thou hast got the reputation.	20	1st Eclogues	7	V972
Above line repeated at following location.	20	1st Eclogues	7	V973
Who once all birdes, in sweetly-singing past, ...	28	1st Eclogues	10	74
But it is season for to end our singing, ...	50	2nd Eclogues	28	94
Of singing match we made, whence he with shame did trudge. .	52	2nd Eclogues	29	16
Viols with singing Voice, ...	316	Psalm XXXIII		9
Leading them his prayses singing, ...	334	Psalm XLII		15
I by night shall singing last, ...	335	Psalm XLII		38
A plaining songe plaine-singing voice requires, ...	242	Other Poems	4	3
Yet there, me seemes, I heare her singing loud.	255	Other Poems	4	508
Ye Hymnes and singing skill.	260	Other Poems	6	7

SINGLE

Is this sweet doubling of our single life.	103	3rd Eclogues	67	12
Such thoughts, me thought, I thought, and straind my single				
mind	118	4th Eclogues	73	49
And Strephon single, turned after him.	249	Other Poems	4	287
He single thus, hop'd soone with hir to be, ...	250	Other Poems	4	337

SINGLED

Hardly they heard, which by good hunters singled be.	14	1st Eclogues	7	10

SINGS

Sings out her woes, a thorne her song-booke making:	137	Cert Sonnets	4	4
That she, me thinks, not onely shines but sings.	184	Astrophil	38	8
This song she singes in most commaunding wise:	255	Other Poems	4	509

		PAGE	TITLE		LINE
SINK					
	With outward joyes, which inly cannot sincke, ...	22	1st Eclogues	9	7
	The more his matchlesse giftes do deepely sinck.	85	Arcadia III	61	11
	The sinke of filth, be counted huswifery:	93	3rd Eclogues	63	79
	And lowest sinke not downe to jote of ill:	99	3rd Eclogues	66	32
	Care that I sinke in griefe, Care that I live banished? . . .	124	4th Eclogues	74	82
	Then might I wisely swimme or gladly sinke.	148	Cert Sonnets	19	6
	Love to earth makes water sinke;	219	A&S 8th Song		62
	No sooner said, but (lo) myne Enemyes sink	280	Psalm IX		46
	In the sinck	328	Psalm XXXVIII		14
	While into none doubt of his love did sinke, ...	247	Other Poems	4	199
SINLESS					
	With sinlesse sleepe, and silence, wisdome's mother, ...	108	Arcadia IV	69	10
SINNERS'					
	Within the sinners' roll, ...	306	Psalm XXVI		29
SINNING					
	Ne for bad mates in way of sinning waiteth	270	Psalm I		3
	To sinning men his path.	303	Psalm XXV		34
SINS					
	Their soules fowl sinns for inmost lyning have:	275	Psalm V		26
	With heaped weights of their own sins oppresse	275	Psalm V		31
	Sins brew'd in youthfull glass, ...	303	Psalm XXV		26
	Imputes not sins to be abhord, ...	314	Psalm XXXII		5
	Nor my sins let my bones rest;	327	Psalm XXXVIII		9
	So prest with sins I cannot see my case.	332	Psalm XL		44
SINS'					
	Praesumptuous sins' offences, ...	295	Psalm XIX		54
SION					
	My Holy Hill Syon.	271	Psalm II		14
	O prayse the lord, this Syon dweller good, ...	280	Psalm IX		31
	Ah, when from syon shall the saver come, ...	287	Psalm XIV		22
SION'S					
	Of syon's Daughter may sing forth Thy prayse:	280	Psalm IX		42
	From Syon's holy top;	295	Psalm XX		8
SIR					
	Yet hath sir Sunne the greatest praise, ...	13	Arcadia I	5	9
	Sir wrong his tombe ordaineth, ...	160	Cert Sonnets	30	23
	"What now sir foole," said he, "I would no lesse, ...	191	Astrophil	53	7
	Leave that sir Phip, least off your necke be wroong. . . .	208	Astrophil	83	14
	Be your words made (good Sir) of Indian ware, ...	225	Astrophil	92	1
	Aha! Sir, now we see you where we should.	322	Psalm XXXV		54
	"Only for my two loves' sake, Sir Ed. D. and M. F. G. . .	263	Other Poems	7	61
SIRE					
	Lalus. How oft my dolefull Sire cried to me, "tarrie sonne".	16	1st Eclogues	7	49
	Mercury kill'd his false sire for this act, ...	21	1st Eclogues	8	17
	But thou foule Cupid, syre to lawlesse lust, ...	92	3rd Eclogues	63	55
	But from thy heart, while my sire charmeth thee, ...	181	Astrophil	32	13
	Then hayle, then firie coales, then thundred heavnly sire, .	291	Psalm XVIII		27
SIRE'S					
	His Sire's revenge, joynd with a kingdome's gaine:	204	Astrophil	75	6
SIRINGA'S					
	Nico. Was this not he, who for Siringa's scape	53	2nd Eclogues	29	57
SISTER					
	Your presence (sister deare) first to my Moony spheare, . .	119	4th Eclogues	73	103
SISTERS					
	Let daintie wits crie on the Sisters nine, ...	166	Astrophil	3	1
SIT					
	In thy owne seate a forraine state shall sit.	11	Arcadia I	1	8
	And in thy throne, a forayne state shall sitte	11	Arcadia I	1	V806
	As I behynde a Busshe dyd sitt	57	2nd Eclogues	30	1
	To those high powers, which idly sit above, ...	58	2nd Eclogues	30	63
	Where whitenes dooth for ever sitte:	90	Arcadia III	62	123
	I saw this woman sit, ...	158	Cert Sonnets	28	34
	Nor ought do care, though some above me sit, ...	198	Astrophil	64	11
	Nor ever did in shade of Tempe sit:	203	Astrophil	74	2
	I would know whether she did sit or walke, ...	225	Astrophil	92	9
	On servants' shame oft Maister's blame doth sit;	236	Astrophil	107	12
	But God shall sit in his Eternal chaire.	280	Psalm IX		21
	For God's own eyes on good men sit	320	Psalm XXXV		55
	I will thank Thee, where congregations sitt, ...	322	Psalm XXXV		46
SITS					
	To have a feeling tast of him that sitts	99	3rd Eclogues	66	27
	He sits me fast, how ever I do sturre:	189	Astrophil	49	12
SITTETH					
	The name of murdrer now on thy faire forehead sitteth: . . .	214	A&S 5th Song		51
SIX					
	Of Barly-brake among the six befell.	250	Other Poems	4	317
SKIES					
	How oft with raine of teares skies make confession, ...	15	1st Eclogues	7	43
	Nico. O if I had a ladder for the skies, ...	55	2nd Eclogues	29	117
	With cries to skies, and curses to the ground, ...	57	2nd Eclogues	30	9
	In her brave calves, like christall skies.	89	Arcadia III	62	102
	That her cleare voyce lifts thy fame to the skies.	171	Astrophil	12	8
	Phoebus drew wide the curtaines of the skies	171	Astrophil	13	12
	Lookes to the skies, and in a ditch doth fall?	174	Astrophil	19	11
	And so nor will, nor can, behold those skies	177	Astrophil	25	7
	With how sad steps, o Moone, thou climb'st the skies, . .	180	Astrophil	31	1
	She lightning Love, displaying Venus' skies, ...	196	Astrophil	63	7
	Models such be wood-globes of glistring skies.	225	Astrophil	91	11
	Morne's messenger, with rose enameld skies	231	Astrophil	99	10

```
SKIES                    (CONTINUED)                              PAGE   TITLE        LINE
      O teares, no teares, but raine from beautie's skies, . . . .  231 Astrophil  100    1
      Who hath the crimson weeds stolne from my morning skies? . .  232 Astrophil  102    4
      See, do you see this face? a face? nay image of the skies, .  217 A&S 7th Song       15
      Are the lights of Cupid's skies, . . . . . . . . . . . . . .  218 A&S 8th Song       34
      But of the skyes the teaching cryes. . . . . . . . . . . . .  293 Psalm XIX          11
      And lo, his Call the skyes did clime;. . . . . . . . . . . .  319 Psalm XXXIV        22
SKILL
      Come Espilus, come now declare thy skill,. . . . . . . . . .    3 Lady of May   2    1
      Her praise, whose praise to learne your skill hath framed
          me . . . . . . . . . . . . . . . . . . . . . . . . . . .   15 1st Eclogues  7   24
      Seeke skill of hearbes in hills, haunt brookes neere night,.   26 1st Eclogues  9  127
      What skill servethe a soare of a wrong infirmity judged? . .   32 1st Eclogues 13   21
      Hardly remains fyer hid, where skill is bent to the hiding,.   33 1st Eclogues 13   59
      None can speake of a wound with skill, if he have not a
          wound felt. . . . . . . . . . . . . . . . . . . . . . .    33 1st Eclogues 13   71
      P. No Reason yet had ever skill to show it.. . . . . . . . .   47 2nd Eclogues 27   40
      Largesse his hands could never skill of sparefulnesse. . . .   48 2nd Eclogues 28   45
      Or else who singeth worse, my skill will hardly hit. . . . .   53 2nd Eclogues 29   50
      The auncient prayse to Arcad shepheards' skill?. . . . . . .   53 2nd Eclogues 29   52
      Is not my skill, nor reach of mortall minde. . . . . . . . .   79 Arcadia III  50   16
      Which skill dooth make in Princes' bowers. . . . . . . . . .   87 Arcadia III  62   50
      And have to Lalus shewd your secret skill, . . . . . . . . .   91 3rd Eclogues 63   20
      Not needing charming skill,. . . . . . . . . . . . . . . . .   92 3rd Eclogues 63   60
      With his sweet skill my skillesse youth he drewe,. . . . . .   99 3rd Eclogues 66   26
      Ante, industrie; and Connie, skill to builde;. . . . . . . .  101 3rd Eclogues 66   93
      Yet Fancie would perforce employ his skill,. . . . . . . . .  115 4th Eclogues 72   65
      And now before we seeke by wise Apollo's skill . . . . . . .  120 4th Eclogues 73  125
      While with a feeling skill I paint my hell.. . . . . . . . .  166 Astrophil     2   14
      That to win it, is all the skill and paine.. . . . . . . . .  171 Astrophil    12   14
      But if (both for your love and skill) your name. . . . . . .  172 Astrophil    15   12
      Horsemen my skill in horsmanship advaunce; . . . . . . . . .  185 Astrophil    41    5
      But cannot skill to pitie my disgrace, . . . . . . . . . . .  187 Astrophil    45    3
      Might winne some grace in your sweet skill arraid. . . . . .  192 Astrophil    55    4
      And such skill in my Muse you reconcil'd shall find, . . . .  215 A&S 5th Song       89
      A lesson fit, both sight and skill, love and firme love to
          breede,. . . . . . . . . . . . . . . . . . . . . . . . .  217 A&S 7th Song       12
      Is so of skill bereaved, . . . . . . . . . . . . . . . . . .  293 Psalm XIX          10
      But all their bad mischeivous skill. . . . . . . . . . . . .  298 Psalm XXI          43
      With sweet musick's skill. . . . . . . . . . . . . . . . . .  337 Psalm XLIII        26
      Klaius for skill of herbs and shepheard's art. . . . . . . .  243 Other Poems   4   33
      And both had skill in verse their voice to move. . . . . . .  243 Other Poems   4   40
      Ye Hymnes and singing skill. . . . . . . . . . . . . . . . .  260 Other Poems   6    7
      Let heere thy skill abound,. . . . . . . . . . . . . . . . .  260 Other Poems   6   15
      "Therefore shepheardes wanting skill,. . . . . . . . . . . .  263 Other Poems   7   37
SKILLED
      That they now skilld not, how from him to wend;. . . . . . .  102 3rd Eclogues 66  114
      In sweetest strength, so sweetly skild withall,. . . . . . .  183 Astrophil    36   10
SKILLESS
      Philisides. Who ever taught a skillesse man to teach,. . . .   22 1st Eclogues  9   16
      With his sweet skill my skillesse youth he drewe,. . . . . .   99 3rd Eclogues 66   26
      Wisdome farewell, the skillesse man's direction: . . . . . .  129 4th Eclogues 76    5
SKILFULLY
      Thou then, that framste both words and voice most skilfully,   48 2nd Eclogues 28   19
SKIM
      If from his words the falshood he do skim. . . . . . . . . .   24 1st Eclogues  9   77
SKIN
      (Therion) When wanton Pan, deceiv'd with Lion's skin,. . . .    5 Lady of May   3    7
      Her skin like burnisht gold, her hands like silver ure
          untryde. . . . . . . . . . . . . . . . . . . . . . . . .   12 Arcadia I     3   12
      Want I white wooll, whose eyes her white skinne garnished? .   16 1st Eclogues  7   59
      And we shall find more spottes then Leopard's skinne. . . . .   29 1st Eclogues 10   95
      Thou God, whose youth was deckt with spoyle of Python's
          skin . . . . . . . . . . . . . . . . . . . . . . . . . .   44 Arcadia II   26    5
      But thou white skinne, as white as cruddes well prest, . . .   76 Arcadia III  46   13
      Which leaded are with silver skinne, . . . . . . . . . . . .   89 Arcadia III  62  115
      The Ermion, whitest skinne, spotted with nought;. . . . . . .  101 3rd Eclogues 66   89
      Whose faire skin, beamy eyes, like morning sun on snow,. . .  169 Astrophil     8    9
      Her flesh his food, her skin his armour brave, . . . . . . .  179 Astrophil    29   12
      To shew her skin, lips, teeth and head so well?. . . . . . .  181 Astrophil    32   11
      That skin, whose passe-praise hue scorns this poore terme of
          white:. . . . . . . . . . . . . . . . . . . . . . . . . .  205 Astrophil    77    7
      With skinne in sorrow died,. . . . . . . . . . . . . . . . .  259 Other Poems   5  117
SKINS
      From that foe's wounds their tender skinnes to hide. . . . .  176 Astrophil    22    8
SKIP
      Pas. Ah foole; so Courtiers do. But who did lively skippe, .   52 2nd Eclogues 29   11
SKIRTS
      When she with skirts tuckt very hy, with girles at stoolball
          playes. . . . . . . . . . . . . . . . . . . . . . . . . .  343 Possibly      1   10
SKY
      A plaint of guiltlesse hurt doth pierce the skie.. . . . . .  103 3rd Eclogues 66  152
      And well (me thinks) becomes this vaultie skie . . . . . . .  126 4th Eclogues 75   58
      Deepe plunged in earth, deprived of the skie.. . . . . . . .  149 Cert Sonnets 21    8
      Of passyon's hilles reaching to reason's skie, . . . . . . .  149 Cert Sonnets 22    6
      To have for no cause birthright in the skie, . . . . . . . .  178 Astrophil    26    5
      See what clouds of reproch small darke thy honour's skie,. .  213 A&S 5th Song       23
      Which Musicke can in sky . . . . . . . . . . . . . . . . . .  217 A&S 6th Song       51
      The lord looks from the sky, . . . . . . . . . . . . . . . .  317 Psalm XXXIII       49
```

```
SKY-METAL                                                   PAGE    TITLE          LINE
    For they seem'd made even of skie-mettall best,. . . . . . .  244 Other Poems    4   100
SLACK
    But as he them more short or slacke doth raine,. . . . . . .  194 Astrophil     58    4
    Then did he slack his love-enstructed pace. . . . . . . . . . 250 Other Poems    4   308
SLACKER
    Because that Mars, growne slacker in her love, . . . . . . .  173 Astrophil     17    2
SLAIN
    And jealousie is slaine: . . . . . . . . . . . . . . . . . .   94 3rd Eclogues 63   98
    But him her host that unkind guest had slaine. . . . . . . .  184 Astrophil     38   14
SLAKE
    The raines of Love I love, though never slake, . . . . . . .  179 Astrophil     28    7
SLANDER
    Who judge that honour, which hath scope to slander. . . . . .  50 2nd Eclogues 28   91
    Here wrong's name is unheard: slander a monster is. . . . . .  69 2nd Eclogues 34   26
    Slander wants a pretext, flattery gone beyond: . . . . . . .   69 2nd Eclogues 34   38
    Nor neighbour hurts by deed, nor doth with slaunder stain. .  287 Psalm XV            6
SLAVE
    Sweete soule, to whom I vowed am a slave,. . . . . . . . . .    3 Lady of May    2   11
    Possesse she doth, and makes my soule her slave: . . . . . .   17 1st Eclogues   7  112
    Or Reason lie a slave to servile Sense, . . . . . . . . . . .   49 2nd Eclogues 28   76
    Thou art my Lord, and I thy vowed slave. . . . . . . . . . .  135 Cert Sonnets   1   14
    For why should I, whom free choise slave doth make,. . . . .  146 Cert Sonnets  17    9
    Upon that coast, am giv'n up for a slave. . . . . . . . . . .  179 Astrophil     29   14
    Him as thy slave, and now needy Fame. . . . . . . . . . . .   182 Astrophil     35   10
    In my free side? or am I borne a slave,. . . . . . . . . . .  188 Astrophil     47    3
    When Cupid, having me his slave describe . . . . . . . . . .  191 Astrophil     53    5
    O ease your hand, treate not so hard your slave: . . . . . .  212 Astrophil     86    9
    For thou doest lord my heart, who am not borne thy slave,. .  214 A&S 5th Song       58
    Let them not have me for their slave . . . . . . . . . . . .  295 Psalm XIX          55
    And witness me Thy slave. . . . . . . . . . . . . . . . . .   331 Psalm XL           30
    To make it selfe to my least looke a slave:. . . . . . . . .  255 Other Poems    4  511
SLAVE-BORN
    Is gone, and now like slave-borne Muscovite, . . . . . . . .  166 Astrophil      2   10
SLAVERY
    To helpe her praise, who decks me in her slaverie. . . . . .   48 2nd Eclogues 28   27
SLAVE'S
    Her poore slave's unjust decaying. . . . . . . . . . . . . .  222 A&S 9th Song       50
SLAVES
    Thus all my thoughts are slaves to one thought still:. . . .   12 Arcadia I      2   10
    Those rebell thoughts which are thy slaves by kinde. . . . .   23 1st Eclogues   9   46
    Growne now his slaves, he forst them out to find . . . . . .  193 Astrophil     57    3
    As heart-bound slaves: and happy then embrace. . . . . . . .  252 Other Poems    4  391
SLAY
    Slay mee not, for stay doo not hyde thy blisses, . . . . . .  138 Cert Sonnets   5   22
    A kind of grace it is to slay with speed. . . . . . . . . . :  189 Astrophil     48   14
    Yet gentle English theeves do rob, but will not slay;. . . .  214 A&S 5th Song       49
    To slay the hurtless One,. . . . . . . . . . . . . . . . . .  282 Psalm X            34
SLEEK
    Like Alablaster faire and sleeke,. . . . . . . . . . . . . .   88 Arcadia III   62   81
SLEEKSTONE-LIKE
    So smooth as sleekestone-like, it smoothes each parte, . . .   76 Arcadia III   46   14
SLEEP
    Ly but to sleepe, and in the earely prime. . . . . . . . . .   26 1st Eclogues   9  126
    Doubte is his sleepe, he waketh in invention;. . . . . . . .   48 2nd Eclogues 28   40
    To her sweete sence, sweete sleepe, some ease imparte, . . .   79 Arcadia III   51    3
    And while o sleepe thou closest up her sight,. . . . . . . .   79 Arcadia III   51    5
    With sinlesse sleepe, and silence, wisdome's mother, . . . .  108 Arcadia IV    69   10
    Till deadly sleepe at length possest my living coarse. . . .  117 4th Eclogues 73   30
    And thou o traytour Sleepe, made for to be our rest, . . . .  121 4th Eclogues 73  183
    Sleepe Babie mine, Desire, nurse Beautie singeth:. . . . . .  139 Cert Sonnets   6    1
    Sleepe then a litle, pap content is making:. . . . . . . . .  139 Cert Sonnets   6    8
    Morpheus, the lively sonne of deadly sleepe, . . . . . . . .  180 Astrophil     32    1
    This night while sleepe begins with heavy wings. . . . . . .  183 Astrophil     38    1
    Cald it anew, and wooed sleepe againe: . . . . . . . . . . .  184 Astrophil     38   13
    Come sleepe, o sleepe, the certaine knot of peace, . . . . .  184 Astrophil     39    1
    My still kept course, while others sleepe, to mone. . . . .   184 Astrophil     40    4
    Nay, more foole I, oft suffered you to sleepe. . . . . . . .  208 Astrophil     83    7
    Teaching sleepe most faire to be?. . . . . . . . . . . . . .  202 A&S 2nd Song        2
    Since sweet sleep her eyes hath charmed, . . . . . . . . . .  202 A&S 2nd Song        5
    Jealousie it selfe doth sleepe:. . . . . . . . . . . . . . .  210 A&S 4th Song       10
    Dumbe sleepe holdeth all the house:. . . . . . . . . . . . .  211 A&S 4th Song       26
    Nay give me eyes, and light, least that I sleep. . . . . . .  285 Psalm XIII         11
    When waking of this sleep of mine. . . . . . . . . . . . . .  290 Psalm XVII         47
    "But your reason's purest light, . . . . . . . . . . . . . .  234 A&S 11th Song      26
SLEEPETH
    Love is not dead, but sleepeth . . . . . . . . . . . . . . .  160 Cert Sonnets  30   33
SLEEPING
    Not as the scrippe thou stalest, while Dorcas sleeping lay. .   52 2nd Eclogues 29    8
    What No her tongue sleeping useth. . . . . . . . . . . . . .  202 A&S 2nd Song       12
    Sleeping, grants a free resort:. . . . . . . . . . . . . . .  202 A&S 2nd Song       14
SLEEP'S
    Clos'd with their quivers in sleep's armory; . . . . . . . .  230 Astrophil     99    4
SLEEPS
    God sleeps, or hath forgotten quite, . . . . . . . . . . . .  282 Psalm X            46
    No sleeps, but dreams, no dreams, but visions straunge,. . .  253 Other Poems    4  436
SLEEPY
    The sleepy kisse the moone stale:. . . . . . . . . . . . . .   66 2nd Eclogues 32   28
    Sleepy darkness doth o're cast,. . . . . . . . . . . . . . .  288 Psalm XVI          22

                                    445
```

	PAGE	TITLE		LINE
SLEEVES				
With sleeves turnde up, loose haire, and brestes enlarged, .	16	1st Eclogues	7	74
SLEIGHT				
Deadly wounds inward bleed, ech sleight sore mattereth....	14	1st Eclogues	7	9
His praise to sleight, which from good use doth rise;....	185	Astrophil	41	7
SLEIGHTS				
The Hare, her sleights; the Cat, his melancholie;......	101	3rd Eclogues	66	92
SLENDER				
But they or spent, or made of slender might, ...	102	3rd Eclogues	66	134
But of such wives we finde a slender crew;	104	3rd Eclogues	67	25
SLEPT				
I layd me down and slept,..................	272	Psalm III		16
SLID				
Engulfed in despaire, slid downe from fortune's lappe: ...	153	Cert Sonnets	24	16
SLIDE				
Shallow brookes murmure most, deep silent slide away;....	14	1st Eclogues	7	11
And fellow-like let his dominion slide;...........	101	3rd Eclogues	66	110
And thinke how evill becommeth him to slide, ...	144	Cert Sonnets	32	11
Whence words, not words, but heav'nly graces slide......	206	Astrophil	80	4
On me all this, who do like water slide;	299	Psalm XXII		31
I held for sure that I should never slyde........	305	Psalm XXVI		6
What comes therof? he shall not slide............	326	Psalm XXXVII		80
SLIDED				
So are we from our high creation slided...........	62	2nd Eclogues	30	181
SLIDETH				
From the grounds where Jordan slideth............	335	Psalm XLII		27
SLIDING				
So may your sliding race	257	Other Poems	5	28
SLIME				
As fishe sure tryall hath of muddy slyme...........	28	1st Eclogues	10	54
SLIP				
Least yet I slip or go astray.	289	Psalm XVII		16
My heeles and plants thou didst from stumbling slip				
sustaine ,....................	292	Psalm XVIII		67
So from base slip is stayed..................	297	Psalm XXI		28
SLIPPED				
But Nous that slipt from Pas, did catch the clowne......	248	Other Poems	4	262
SLIPPERS				
So that you may on hyer slippers stay............	93	3rd Eclogues	63	76
SLIPPERY				
His good strong staffe my slippry yeares ubore:	99	3rd Eclogues	66	37
Scourge of it selfe, still climing slipprie place, ...	176	Astrophil	23	10
But let their flight be dark and slippery;	321	Psalm XXXV		14
SLOW				
Now with slow words, now with dumbe eloquence.......	195	Astrophil	61	2
Fortune wheeles still with me in one sort slow,.......	199	Astrophil	66	6
Slow heavinesse in both holds one degree,..........	229	Astrophil	96	6
SLUMBERING				
Let not these slumbring clowds thy beawties hide,......	91	3rd Eclogues	63	11
SLUTTERY				
Yet let not sluttery,....................	93	3rd Eclogues	63	78
SLUTTISH				
With sluttish song: I pray thee learne to blea,.......	56	2nd Eclogues	29	136
SLUTTISHNESS				
Nor yet shall yeeld to loathsome sluttishnes,.......	94	3rd Eclogues	63	97
SLY				
Let their sly witts unwares destruction get, ...	321	Psalm XXXV		17
SMALL				
With twenty ginnes we will the small birds take,....	18	1st Eclogues	7	126
In which do light small birds of thoughts orethrowne:....	18	1st Eclogues	7	141
So small accompt of time the shepeheard feeles	28	1st Eclogues	10	49
Nature worketh enough with a small help for the revealing. .	33	1st Eclogues	13	61
Such this smale greatnes, doth seeme compar'd to the				
greatest......................	34	1st Eclogues	13	76
Or to the Sun for wonders seeme small sparks of a candle:..	34	1st Eclogues	13	79
Of those fortune lulls, so small rest rests in a kingdome. .	34	1st Eclogues	13	90
The fuell small: how be the fires so great?.	42	Arcadia II	22	14
Hath all thy whirling course so small effect?.......	58	2nd Eclogues	30	60
No no, such force with my small force to trye.	79	Arcadia III	50	15
Whose Atlas is a smallest small, ...	89	Arcadia III	62	103
Of that small light oft watching shepheards see.	98	3rd Eclogues	66	7
Revil'd for ech small fault, sometimes for none:	105	3rd Eclogues	67	53
He hopes for some small praise since she hath great, ...	141	Cert Sonnets	8	11
To hie conceits whose fruits are oft but small,......	144	Cert Sonnets	15	10
In tender harts, small things engender hate:	146	Cert Sonnets	17	17
If Greekes themselves were mov'd with so small cause	146	Cert Sonnets	17	21
Pleased with the light, that his small corse doth burne: ..	149	Cert Sonnets	21	12
Small losse of mortall treasure, ...	152	Cert Sonnets	23	19
In this small course which birth drawes out to death,....	144	Cert Sonnets	32	10
Nor this, nor that, nor any such small cause,.......	204	Astrophil	75	12
That you allow me them by so small rate?	225	Astrophil	92	2
Know, that small Love is quicke, and great Love doth amaze:.	209	A&S 3rd Song		16
This small light the Moone bestowes, ...	210	A&S 4th Song		19
See what clouds of reproch small darke thy honour's skie,..	213	A&S 5th Song		23
"This small wind which so sweete is, ...	219	A&S 8th Song		57
I bett those folks as small as dust, which wind doth rayse;.	293	Psalm XVIII		76
Small goodes in good men better is	325	Psalm XXXVII		41
Sometimes we see small birds from nests do pull.	245	Other Poems	4	136
SMALLER				
No smaller wound, alas! farr deeper have..	77	Arcadia III	47	4

446

		PAGE	TITLE		LINE
SMALLER	(CONTINUED)				
The Arrow being shot from far, doth give the smaller blowe..		344	Possibly	1	42
SMALLEST					
Whose Atlas is a smallest small, ...		89	Arcadia III	62	103
Worst fell to smallest birds, and meanest heard, ...		102	3rd Eclogues	66	141
SMART					
Who yelds to woe, doth encrease his smart.		22	1st Eclogues	9	2
The third his lesson mist, till all do smarte.		27	1st Eclogues	10	45
Which shootes strongly with out any noyse and deadly without					
smarte.		35	1st Eclogues	13	122
O toonge, then dumbe, not daring tell my smart;		60	2nd Eclogues	30	121
So still me thought in me his hurt did smart:		76	Arcadia III	45	12
Live long, and long witnesse my chosen smarte, ...		77	Arcadia III	47	10
With meager lookes, as if they still did smart;		104	3rd Eclogues	67	28
Dwell in my ruines, feede with sucking smarte, ...		113	4th Eclogues	72	9
Wo, wo to me, on me returne the smart:		141	Cert Sonnets	9	1
To paint my living death, and endlesse smart:		146	Cert Sonnets	17	28
Rebels to Nature, strive for their owne smart.		167	Astrophil	5	4
And damning their owne selves to Tantal's smart, ...		177	Astrophil	24	3
What harder thing then smart, and not to speake?		182	Astrophil	34	10
My mind bemones his sense of inward smart;		186	Astrophil	44	2
Such smart may pitie claime of any hart, ...		186	Astrophil	44	3
Thou needs must misse, and so thou needs must smart.		188	Astrophil	46	11
Alas I found, that she with me did smart, ...		223	Astrophil	87	5
In my selfe the smart I try, ...		220	A&S 8th Song		94
The saving me from smart, ...		303	Psalm XXV		16
How elder rul'd their flocks, and cur'd their smart, ...		243	Other Poems	4	37
Faine would, but could not fly from golden smart.		246	Other Poems	4	184
SMARTED					
Then gave he him the blow which never smarted.		97	3rd Eclogues	64	120
SMELL					
And for Rose-water sould of rarest smell..		55	2nd Eclogues	29	110
But Lillies such whose native smell.		87	Arcadia III	62	63
But now the courtier gan to smell the feate, ...		97	3rd Eclogues	64	117
When I doo smell the flowers of these vallies:		112	4th Eclogues	71	46
In that, which of fowle wickedness doth smel:		274	Psalm V		10
SMELLING					
Deckt with pyde flowers sweetely smelling.		262	Other Poems	7	6
SMILE					
Did smile on me, and then away she leaped.		17	1st Eclogues	7	84
Teaching blind eyes both how to smile and weepe, ...		181	Astrophil	32	8
Hath cheekes to smile, as well as eyes to weepe.		201	Astrophil	70	8
But now teares themselves did smile, ...		218	A&S 8th Song		14
SMILED					
Love smiled, and thus said; "Want joynd to desire is					
unhappy		30	1st Eclogues	11	11
How cloth'd, how waited on, sighd she or smilde, ...		225	Astrophil	92	10
SMILES					
Cupid then smiles, for on his crest there lies		171	Astrophil	13	9
SMILING					
Such proffer made, which she well showd with smiling cheere.		120	4th Eclogues	73	144
I saw thy selfe with many a smiling line		232	Astrophil	103	2
Smiling ayre allowes my reason, ...		219	A&S 8th Song		55
Free of proud feares, brave begg'ry, smiling strife.		243	Other Poems	4	60
SMIRKLY					
And smirkly thus gan say. "I never sought debate		120	4th Eclogues	73	147
SMOKE					
When yonger dooth in smoke his vertue spend.		38	Arcadia II	15	4
The smoke of hell, the monster called paine, ...		140	Cert Sonnets	8	2
He came, but came with smoake from out his nostrills sent, .		291	Psalm XVIII		18
Confounded be, and passe away like smoake, ...		313	Psalm XXXI		47
Ev'en with the smoake shall wast away.		326	Psalm XXXVII		52
Strephon, poor youth, because he saw no smoke, ...		253	Other Poems	4	427
SMOKY					
In vaine thou kindlest all thy smokie fire;		161	Cert Sonnets	31	11
When thou hast mynd to weepe, seeke out som smoky room: . . .		343	Possibly	1	11
SMOOTH					
As smooth as Pan, as Juno milde, like goddesse Iris faste. .		12	Arcadia I	3	6
So smooth as sleekestone-like, it smoothes each parte, . . .		76	Arcadia III	46	14
With hanches smooth as looking glasse.		88	Arcadia III	62	92
Take thou of me smooth pillowes, sweetest bed, ...		184	Astrophil	39	9
How falles it then, that with so smooth an ease.		204	Astrophil	74	9
SMOOTHES					
So smooth as sleekestone-like, it smoothes each parte, . . .		76	Arcadia III	46	14
SMOTHER					
That quickly they would her burne, drowne, or smother, . . .		61	2nd Eclogues	30	159
SNAKE					
Goe snake hide thee in dust, ...		93	3rd Eclogues	63	86
The filthy snake her aged coate can mende, ...		127	4th Eclogues	75	82
SNAKISH					
(So humble knowledge can throw downe the snakish sinne). . .		44	Arcadia II	26	6
SNAKY					
Nor envie's snaky ey, finds any harbor here, ...		69	2nd Eclogues	34	18
Where envie's snaky ey, winketh or els dyeth, ...		69	2nd Eclogues	34	37
SNARE					
We finde most sweete affection's snare, ...		14	1st Eclogues	6	3
Thou blind man's marke, thou foole's selfe chosen snare, . .		161	Cert Sonnets	31	1
Hardned, and coulde, farr from affectione's snare.		344	Possibly	2	5
SNARED					
Though present times and past with evils be snarde, ...		143	Cert Sonnets	12	13

		PAGE	TITLE		LINE
SNARED	(CONTINUED)				
When Godless men be snar'd in their own snares:.		281	Psalm IX		52
SNARES					
Free all my powers were from those captiving snares, ...		117	4th Eclogues 73		17
When Godless men be snar'd in their own snares:.		281	Psalm IX		52
They lay snares they nimble be..		328	Psalm XXXVIII		34
SNARING					
All ready, ready to my snaring grave to go..		291	Psalm XVIII		11
SNATCH					
Didst snatch from Cosma's hand her greene ywroughten glove..		52	2nd Eclogues 29		10
SNEB					
Thou heardst even now a yong man snebb me sore,.		27	1st Eclogues 10		22
SNOW					
Her naked legge, more white then whitest snowe..		55	2nd Eclogues 29		101
Torne with her hands, and those same hands of snow		58	2nd Eclogues 30		45
Whiter indeed; more white then snow, ...		85	Arcadia III 62		7
Warme snow, moyst pearle, softe ivorie..		90	Arcadia III 62		126
Like Whitest Snowe, in silver Brooke,.		88	Arcadia III 62 V		69
Whose faire skin, beamy eyes, like morning sun on snow,. . .		169	Astrophil 8		9
Thinke now no more to heare of warme fine odourd snow, . . .		213	A&S 5th Song		37
SNOWY					
Their snowy haire teare off in melting paine..		254	Other Poems 4		478
SNUGGING					
Where snugging well he well appear'd content		244	Other Poems 4		103
*SO					
So dare I, wretch, my bashfull feare subdue, ...		3	Lady of May 1		11
Shew how thou canst deserve so brave desire, ...		3	Lady of May 2		2
Let not wild woods so great a treasure have.		3	Lady of May 2		12
Among his flocke so sweete a treasure keepe.		4	Lady of May 2		18
Though not so white as is thy lovely face, ...		4	Lady of May 2		20
So if my man must praises have,.		13	Arcadia I 5		5
Above line repeated at following location.		13	Arcadia I 5		11
To set a pearle in steele so meanely varnished?.		16	1st Eclogues 7		63
Her eyes so maistering me, that such objection		16	1st Eclogues 7		68
"O" cried I, "of so meane worke be discharged:		16	1st Eclogues 7		76
Her whom I dread; so that with prostrate lying		17	1st Eclogues 7		86
"Let not dead earth enjoy so deare a cover,.		17	1st Eclogues 7		89
So I your sight, you shall your selves recover".		17	1st Eclogues 7		93
So faire a fielde would well become an owner..		17	1st Eclogues 7		99
What circle then in so rare force beares swaye?.		17	1st Eclogues 7		109
Which so much reason beares, ...		18	1st Eclogues 7		148
So doth my life within it selfe dissolve.		19	1st Eclogues 7		156
Lalus. So doth my life within it selfe dissolve, ...		19	1st Eclogues 7		157
To worke my Goddesse so by thy invention,.		19	1st Eclogues 7		177
If he be blind, how hitteth he so right?		21	1st Eclogues 8		9
No, nothing so; an old false knave he is,.		21	1st Eclogues 8		13
Or trayne the fox that traines so crafty laies..		26	1st Eclogues 9		125
Who have their lesson so long time begonne?.		27	1st Eclogues 10		27
So small accompt of time the shepeheard feeles		28	1st Eclogues 10		49
No sword soe bytes as that evill toole annoyes..		29	1st Eclogues 10		90
Still doo I crosse this wretch, what so he taketh in hand"..		29	1st Eclogues 11		6
But so his humor I frame, in a mould of choller adusted, . .		29	1st Eclogues 11		9
So that eyes' message be of her received, ...		30	1st Eclogues 12		3
So that eyes' message doo returne rejected,.		30	1st Eclogues 12		7
So become our tombes monuments of her praise;.		30	1st Eclogues 12		10
So becomes our losse the triumph of her gayne;		30	1st Eclogues 12		11
Are then humane mindes priviledg'd so meanly,.		31	1st Eclogues 12		17
So that eyes' message be of her received, ...		31	1st Eclogues 12		27
How much more we do love, so the lesse our loves be beleeved		32	1st Eclogues 13		20
But so unheard, condemn'd, kept thence we do seeke to abide in,.		32	1st Eclogues 13		25
(Since no estates be so base, but love vouchsafeth his arrow		33	1st Eclogues 13		50
Of those fortune lulls, so small rest rests in a kingdome. .		34	1st Eclogues 13		90
Ncr yet, fancy so drest, do receive more plausible hearing:.		35	1st Eclogues 13		101
And may I not (say I then) gett up though griefs be so weightie?.		36	1st Eclogues 13		128
So my desires by my feare, cutt downe, be the frames of her honour...		36	1st Eclogues 13		135
And shall sensive things be sc sencelesse as to resist sence		36	1st Eclogues 13		138
Then do I shape to my selfe that forme which raigns so with in me, ...		36	1st Eclogues 13		142
And so behinde foule clowdes full oft faire starres do ly hidden"..		36	1st Eclogues 13		154
Bownd and bownd by so noble bandes, as loth to be unbownd, .		37	1st Eclogues 13		162
Whose force had such force so to transforme, nay to reforme me,.		37	1st Eclogues 13		166
And will pitty the wound festred sc strangely within me. . .		37	1st Eclogues 13		168
O be it so, graunte such an event, O Gods, that event give..		37	1st Eclogues 13		169
Since to my hart her shape you so did sende;		38	Arcadia II 14		3
Since there mine eyes have played so false a parte,.		38	Arcadia II 14		11
Since so mine eyes are subject to your sight,.		39	Arcadia II 16		1
Since so my harte is filled with that light, ...		39	Arcadia II 16		3
Since in sweete you all goods so richly raigne,.		39	Arcadia II 16		5
Since so your living image lives in me,.		39	Arcadia II 16		7
The fuell small: how be the fires so great?.		42	Arcadia II 22		14
(So humble knowledge can throw downe the snakish sinne) . . .		44	Arcadia II 26		6
Let so our fruites grow up, that nature be maintainde: . . .		45	Arcadia II 26		13

			PAGE	TITLE		LINE
*SO	(CONTINUED)					
But so our hartes keepe downe, with vice they be not stainde			45	Arcadia II	26	14
P. And let him die, so that he die content..			46	2nd Eclogues	27	10
P. Not so, but fellowlike together borne..			46	2nd Eclogues	27	12
P. But so we shall with griefe learne to repent.			47	2nd Eclogues	27	36
Dorus. But what doth make thee Dicus so suspicious			47	2nd Eclogues	28	7
Not so; although my mettall were most mutable,			47	2nd Eclogues	28	10
In thy owne proofe he gets so straunge possession, ...			48	2nd Eclogues	28	35
Dicus. But so thy sheepe may thy good wishes satisfie. . . .			49	2nd Eclogues	28	49
So she thy love, her eyes thy eyes may gratifie,			49	2nd Eclogues	28	51
Is she in rage? so is the Sunne in sommer hot, ...			49	2nd Eclogues	28	61
Lastly what so she be, that's my protection.			49	2nd Eclogues	28	72
With words so vile, which viler breath doth breed.			50	2nd Eclogues	28	82
And loden so puls downe, puld downe destroyes.			50	2nd Eclogues	28	86
So love encroches on your charmed reason,.			50	2nd Eclogues	28	93
With so sweete plagues my happie harmes infected be:			51	2nd Eclogues	28	123
Pas. And I am here the same, so mote I thrive and thee,. . .			52	2nd Eclogues	29	3
Nico. Ah now I see, why thou art in thy selfe so blind:. . .			52	2nd Eclogues	29	5
Pas. Ah foole; so Courtiers do. But who did lively skippe . .			52	2nd Eclogues	29	11
Nico. Couldst thou make Lalus flie? so nightingales avoide,.			52	2nd Eclogues	29	17
Since Nico doth to sing so widely gape?.			53	2nd Eclogues	29	55
For me to come, and so she did: I came,.			55	2nd Eclogues	29	91
With name engrav'd: so though thy bodie die, ...			56	2nd Eclogues	29	130
Pas. So oft these woods have heard me "Cosma" crie,.			56	2nd Eclogues	29	132
For so yet of a conquest speake thou may..			56	2nd Eclogues	29	140
With so strong lives, that bodie cannot rest			56	2nd Eclogues	29	145
Dicus. Enough, enough: so ill hath done the best,.			56	2nd Eclogues	29	147
What needed so high sprites such mansions blind?			57	2nd Eclogues	30	14
This bodie is: this bodie so composed, ...			57	2nd Eclogues	30	27
So divers be the Elements disposed			57	2nd Eclogues	30	29
Relent those thoughts, which then did so displease?.			58	2nd Eclogues	30	52
Though in despaire, for love so forcethe me;			58	2nd Eclogues	30	57
Hath all thy whirling course so small effect?.			58	2nd Eclogues	30	60
Of our selfe-love (so passions do deceave)			59	2nd Eclogues	30	69
His nature? nay, himselfe? for so it is.			59	2nd Eclogues	30	72
That doost so well their miseries define?.			59	2nd Eclogues	30	79
Those beames that set so many harts on fire?			59	2nd Eclogues	30	84
What myne hath erst throwne downe so faire a tower?.			59	2nd Eclogues	30	96
Such beames so like his owne, which might have might			60	2nd Eclogues	30	105
Can thoughts still thinking so rest unappalled?.			61	2nd Eclogues	30	166
So are we from our high creation slided.			62	2nd Eclogues	30	181
Peace? what barrs me my tongue? who is it that comes me so ny? I.			62	2nd Eclogues	31	2
Can then a cause be so light that forceth a man to go die? Aye.			64	2nd Eclogues	31	24
What great name may I give to so heav'nly a woman? A woe-man			64	2nd Eclogues	31	37
Woe, but seems to me joy, that agrees to my thought so. I thought so..			64	2nd Eclogues	31	38
Think so, for of my desired blisse it is only the course. Curse.			64	2nd Eclogues	31	39
So greate a passion all feele, ...			66	2nd Eclogues	32	16
To think a soare so deadly			66	2nd Eclogues	32	17
I should so rashly ripp up..			66	2nd Eclogues	32	18
So may thy songe be famous;.			66	2nd Eclogues	32	24
So may thy song be pleasant.			66	2nd Eclogues	32	29
So are thy pains my pains too.			67	2nd Eclogues	32	42
But at no change, so pinching care he takes,.			71	Arcadia III	37	9
Make great the losse, so grete the feare to misse.			71	Arcadia III	37	12
So that the windowes of my inward light.			73	Arcadia III	39	7
Seeing, Alas, so mightie powers bende.			73	Arcadia III	40	5
Their ireful shotte against so weake a marke,.			73	Arcadia III	40	6
So to my minde, while passions daylie growe, ...			74	Arcadia III	41	3
Looke further then, so shalt thou finde at least,.			75	Arcadia III	44	9
So still he thought in me his hurt did smart:.			76	Arcadia III	45	12
So smooth as sleekestone-like, it smoothes each parte, . . .			76	Arcadia III	46	14
And so by you (O blessed you) hath sent, ...			78	Arcadia III	49	7
His thoughtes in you, where so sweete thoughtes were spent,.			78	Arcadia III	49	10
Right so my thoughts, whereon my hart I feede:			78	Arcadia III	50	5
Right so my inwarde partes, and outward glasse,.			78	Arcadia III	50	6
So both are yours: I, bound with gaged harte:.			79	Arcadia III	50	21
As thou drawest on, so let my blisse draw neere.			80	Arcadia III	53	10
Though (yoked so) my minde with sicknes fainte,.			83	Arcadia III	57	7
All thoughts so spronge, are from their dwelling driv'n, . .			83	Arcadia III	57	11
So that therein appeares some blood, ...			86	Arcadia III	62	29
So good a say invites the eye, ...			87	Arcadia III	62	51
The Phoenix wings be not so rare			89	Arcadia III	62	118
As I began, so must I ende..			90	Arcadia III	62	144
No Elephant so perfect beares.			86	Arcadia III	62	V 28
And so to him and her your giftes distill, ...			91	3rd Eclogues	63	22
So that you may on hyer slippers stay.			93	3rd Eclogues	63	76
Where open hartes do holde so constant place,.			93	3rd Eclogues	63	88
And farre unfit to hold so good a roome.			94	3rd Eclogues	64	6
Fell jealousie did so his braine oppresse, ...			94	3rd Eclogues	64	9
And so she was, and all with good intent,.			95	3rd Eclogues	64	25
In that which he so fear'd that she should meet.			95	3rd Eclogues	64	36
Seeme to proceede, so well it was devisde.			96	3rd Eclogues	64	82
So may thy flockes encrease, thy deere hart glad,.			96	3rd Eclogues	64	93
So may each thing, even as thou wishest lighte,.			96	3rd Eclogues	64	94

*SO	(CONTINUED)	PAGE	TITLE		LINE
Now that he had her words so truely tried:		97	3rd Eclogues	64	112
So hastily that which they would repent:		100	3rd Eclogues	66	69
But when his seate so rooted he had found,		102	3rd Eclogues	66	113
Which who so wants, halfe of himselfe doth misse.		103	3rd Eclogues	67	9
Histor. No doubt to whom so good chance did betide,		104	3rd Eclogues	67	13
Shrewdnes so stirres, pride so puffes up their hart,		104	3rd Eclogues	67	26
But certainly so long we may be glad,		105	3rd Eclogues	67	64
So well she can command, and yet obay,		106	3rd Eclogues	67	89
In ruling of a house so well shee's seene.		106	3rd Eclogues	67	90
As we to get are fram'd, so they to spare:		106	3rd Eclogues	67	106
Publique our losse: so, see, thy shame is publique..		109	Arcadia IV	70	24
Sc darkened am, that all my day is evening,		111	4th Eclogues	71	22
Hart-broken so, that molehilles seeme high mountaines,		111	4th Eclogues	71	23
Strephon. These mountaines witnesse shall, so shall these vallies,		113	4th Eclogues	71	73
So close unto my selfe my wrackes doo lie.		114	4th Eclogues	72	40
Strephon. So close unto my selfe my wrackes doo lie;		114	4th Eclogues	72	41
So that I see, although my sight empaire,		115	4th Eclogues	72	59
For so did I, when with my angle, Will,		115	4th Eclogues	72	62
Infected so with her sweet poyson's might,		115	4th Eclogues	72	78
So I in simple course, and unentangled minde		117	4th Eclogues	73	25
And so she was attirde, as one that did not prize.		119	4th Eclogues	73	87
Be silent therefore now, and so be silent still.		119	4th Eclogues	73	97
So much more strong againe let fastest concorde make..		120	4th Eclogues	73	120
Our young yeares to renew (for so he saith he will).		120	4th Eclogues	73	126
So as if I prevaile, you give your giftes to me:		120	4th Eclogues	73	133
For that (so that you like) hereby doth lie a youth.		120	4th Eclogues	73	137
Ard so most ready am this meane of peace to trie..		121	4th Eclogues	73	152
O you (alas so I find) cause of his onely ruine.		122	4th Eclogues	74	4
And so refuse to behold of these strange wounds the recitall		122	4th Eclogues	74	7
(Unto thy selfe I do meane those graces dwell so within thee		122	4th Eclogues	74	9
Right so my boiling hart, enflam'de with fire of a faire eye		123	4th Eclogues	74	27
Ev'n as I am, so I should unto that haire be a thrall.		123	4th Eclogues	74	54
Should my too-much sight cause so true a Sunne to be lost?		124	4th Eclogues	74	58
O sweet simplicitie: from whence should Love be so learned?.		124	4th Eclogues	74	65
Such faith, so staineles, inviolate, violent?.		124	4th Eclogues	74	70
What? was I then worthie such good, now worthie so muche evill?		124	4th Eclogues	74	77
Now fled, then cherished? then so nie, now so remote?.		124	4th Eclogues	74	78
Since so she will, whose will is to me more then a lawe.		124	4th Eclogues	74	84
That so I may signes of my sorrowe leave..		125	4th Eclogues	75	9
That they, which have no lives, should live so long,		126	4th Eclogues	75	41
And vertuous soules so soone should lose their place?.		126	4th Eclogues	75	42
Aske, if in great men good men so do thronge,		126	4th Eclogues	75	43
So that we can long time produce their time:		127	4th Eclogues	75	86
So it be seene what sorrow in me raigneth.		128	4th Eclogues	75	105
Sc in his sicknesse grew our sure infection.		128	4th Eclogues	75	135
So high, as should make such a paine notorious:..		129	4th Eclogues	75	140
But vertue sets so high, that reason's light,		135	Cert Sonnets	2	7
So that I live to pay a mortall fee,		136	Cert Sonnets	2	9
In whom all joyes so well agree,		139	Cert Sonnets	7	2
Above line repeated at following locations		139	Cert Sonnets	7	12
		140	Cert Sonnets	7	22
		140	Cert Sonnets	7	32
So then since that heaven remaineth,		140	Cert Sonnets	7	28
And so by priviledge of sacred seate,		141	Cert Sonnets	8	9
And so no helpe gainst envy of those powers?		142	Cert Sonnets	10	12
So stay her toung, that she no more say no..		142	Cert Sonnets	10	14
Right so my minde, caught by his guiding eye		144	Cert Sonnets	15	5
To so lowe ebbe that wonted were to flowe.		146	Cert Sonnets	17	15
If Greekes themselves were mov'd with so small cause		146	Cert Sonnets	17	21
And so for one that felt god Cupid's dart,		146	Cert Sonnets	17	29
And stately hilles disdaine to looke so low.		147	Cert Sonnets	18	8
Depart, a word so gentle to my minde,		148	Cert Sonnets	20	3
But so confusde, that neither any eye.		149	Cert Sonnets	22	2
What force brought them to so unlikely ground.		149	Cert Sonnets	22	4
Sc mazde a masse, or if in me it growes,		149	Cert Sonnets	22	9
A simple soule should breed so mixed woes.		149	Cert Sonnets	22	10
So deepe in seas of vertue beauties ly..		151	Cert Sonnets	22	58
So may they live still sorie		152	Cert Sonnets	23	31
For so faire a flame embraces,		155	Cert Sonnets	26	5
Sc that I in her beames dying,		156	Cert Sonnets	26	31
So that thee like heaven I loved..		156	Cert Sonnets	27	4
Till that I sware my faith so stood,		158	Cert Sonnets	28	23
In one that changeth so,		158	Cert Sonnets	28	26
Or where one's love so constant bene,		158	Cert Sonnets	28	27
From so ungratefull fancie,		160	Cert Sonnets	30	7
Above line repeated at following locations		160	Cert Sonnets	30	17
		160	Cert Sonnets	30	27
Therefore from so vile fancie,		161	Cert Sonnets	30	37
Yet with repining at so partiall lot..		165	Astrophil	2	8
That shrines in flesh so true a Deitie,		167	Astrophil	4	13
In colour blacke, why wrapt she beames so bright?.		168	Astrophil	7	2
Both so and thus, she minding Love should be		168	Astrophil	7	12
Deceiv'd the quaking boy, who thought from so pure light,		169	Astrophil	8	10
So when thou saw'st in Nature's cabinet.		170	Astrophil	11	9

*SO   (CONTINUED)   PAGE   TITLE   LINE

Line text	PAGE	TITLE		LINE
That those lips swell, so full of thee they bee,	170	Astrophil	12	3
What words so ere she speakes perswades for thee,	171	Astrophil	12	7
Sc fortified with wit, stor'd with disdaine,	171	Astrophil	12	13
I now have learn'd Love right, and learn'd even so,	173	Astrophil	16	13
So Tyran he no fitter place could spie,	175	Astrophil	20	5
Nor so faire levell in so secret stay,	175	Astrophil	20	6
My young mind marde, whom Love doth windlas so,	175	Astrophil	21	2
Hath this world ought so faire as Stella is?	175	Astrophil	21	14
And so nor will, nor can, behold those skies	177	Astrophil	25	7
So in my swelling breast that only I	178	Astrophil	27	7
I list not dig so deepe for brasen fame.	179	Astrophil	28	4
So Stella's heart, finding what power Love brings,	179	Astrophil	29	5
How Holland hearts, now so good townes be lost,	180	Astrophil	30	7
Since thou in me so sure a power doest keepe,	181	Astrophil	32	5
To shew her skin, lips, teeth and head so well?.	181	Astrophil	32	11
While too much wit (forsooth) so troubled me,	181	Astrophil	33	10
Nay, that may breed my fame, it is so rare:	182	Astrophil	34	6
Then be they close, and so none shall displease.	182	Astrophil	34	8
Stella's great powrs, that so confuse my mind.	182	Astrophil	34	14
With so sweete voice, and by sweete Nature so,	183	Astrophil	36	9
In sweetest strength, so sweetly skild withall,	183	Astrophil	36	10
Beauties so farre from reach of words, that we	183	Astrophil	37	7
By Love's owne selfe, but with so curious drought,	184	Astrophil	38	7
I will good tribute pay if thou do so.	184	Astrophil	39	8
Since then thou hast so farre subdued me,	185	Astrophil	40	12
Guided so well, that I obtain'd the prize,	185	Astrophil	41	2
Sent forth the beames, which made so faire my race..	185	Astrophil	41	14
Alas, what cause is there so overthwart,	186	Astrophil	44	7
Rules with a becke, so tyrannizeth thee,	187	Astrophil	46	3
Thou needs must misse, and so thou needs must smart.	188	Astrophil	46	11
So long (though he from booke myche to desire)	188	Astrophil	46	13
And now hath made me to his hand so right,	189	Astrophil	49	13
And yet as soone as they so formed be,	189	Astrophil	50	5
Sc that I cannot chuse but write my mind,	190	Astrophil	50	9
Sc may your tongue still fluently proceed,	190	Astrophil	51	2
So may you still have somewhat new to say.	190	Astrophil	51	4
And is even irkt that so sweet Comedie,	190	Astrophil	51	13
And thinke so still, so Stella know my mind,	192	Astrophil	54	9
With choisest flowers my speech to engarland so;	192	Astrophil	55	2
So sweete sounds straight mine eare and heart do hit,	192	Astrophil	55	13
But them (so sweete is she) most sweetly sing,	193	Astrophil	57	10
So sweets my paines, that my paines me rejoyce..	193	Astrophil	57	14
The Oratour so farre men's harts doth bind,	193	Astrophil	58	2
Litle he is, so litle worth is he;	194	Astrophil	59	5
So dull am, that I cannot looke into	195	Astrophil	60	10
So captives to his Saint both soule and sence,	195	Astrophil	61	6
So children still reade you with awfull eyes,	196	Astrophil	63	2
In this old world, growne now so too too wise:	198	Astrophil	65	6
If so great services may scorned be:	198	Astrophil	65	10
But failst thou not in phrase so heav'nly hie?	199	Astrophil	67	6
It is, so faire a Vertue to enjoy.	200	Astrophil	68	14
That inward sunne in thine eyes shineth so..	201	Astrophil	71	8
So while thy beautie drawes the heart to love,	201	Astrophil	71	12
And oft so clings to my pure Love, that I.	202	Astrophil	72	2
When for so soft a rod deare play he trie?	203	Astrophil	73	4
How falles it then, that with so smooth an ease,	204	Astrophil	74	9
"Or so?" Much lesse: "How then?" Sure thus it is:	204	Astrophil	74	13
And gain'd by Mars, could yet mad Mars so tame,	204	Astrophil	75	7
Nor that he made the Flouredeluce so fraid,	204	Astrophil	75	9
Of gentle force, so that mine eyes dare gladly play.	205	Astrophil	76	6
So piercing pawes, as spoyle when they embrace,	206	Astrophil	78	10
So nimble feet as stirre still, though on thornes:	206	Astrophil	78	11
So manie eyes ay seeking their owne woe,	206	Astrophil	78	12
So ample eares as never good newes know:	206	Astrophil	78	13
Of highest wish, I wish you so much blisse,	209	Astrophil	84	13
O ease your hand, treate not so hard your slave:	212	Astrophil	86	9
For me, I wept to see pearles scattered so,	223	Astrophil	87	9
Is faith so weake? Or is such force in thee?	223	Astrophil	88	5
Nor so ambitious am I, as to frame	224	Astrophil	90	5
That you allow me them by so small rate?	225	Astrophil	92	2
That to my questions you so totall are?.	225	Astrophil	92	5
Witnesse with me, that my foule stumbling so,	227	Astrophil	93	6
Sc darke with misty vapors, which arise.	228	Astrophil	94	2
As of a caitife worthy so to die,	228	Astrophil	94	10
So gratefull now you waite upon my care.	228	Astrophil	95	4
Thought with good cause thou likest so well the night,	229	Astrophil	96	1
Even so (alas) a Lady Dian's peere,	230	Astrophil	97	9
Paint woe's blacke face so lively to my sight,	230	Astrophil	98	10
Wing'd with whose breath, so pleasing Zephires blow,	231	Astrophil	100	7
Beauty is sicke, but sicke in so faire guise,	231	Astrophil	101	5
Of such heaven stuffe, to cloath so heavenly mynde..	232	Astrophil	101	14
Where be those Roses gone, which sweetned so our eyes?	232	Astrophil	102	1
While wanton winds with beauties so devine	232	Astrophil	103	6
She so discheveld, blusht; from window I	233	Astrophil	103	12
Thence, so faire thence, that scarcely any sparke.	233	Astrophil	104	6
So neere, in so good time, so free a place?.	235	Astrophil	105	2
Dead glasse, doost thou thy object so imbrace,	235	Astrophil	105	3
Curst be the Cochman which did drive so fast,	235	Astrophil	105	13
False flattering hope, that with so faire a face,	235	Astrophil	106	2

451

Stella since thou so right a Princesse art . . . .   236 Astrophil   107   1
So strangely (alas) thy works in me prevaile,. . . . .   237 Astrophil   108   12
Yet those lips so sweetly swelling,. . . . .   203 A&S 2nd Song   21
If Love might sweet'n so a boy of shepheard' brood,. . . . .   209 A&S 3rd Song   7
If Eagle fierce could so in Grecian Mayd delight,. . . . . .   209 A&S 3rd Song   9
So to raise my hap more hie; . . . .   211 A&S 4th Song   21
That brought me so high to fall: . . . .   211 A&S 4th Song   52
I said, thou wert most faire, and so indeed thou art:. . . .   212 A&S 5th Song   7
And all I said so well, as no man it denied. . . . .   212 A&S 5th Song   12
Your Client poore my selfe, shall Stella handle so?. . . . .   213 A&S 5th Song   31
But of thy soule, so fraught with such ungratefulnesse,. . .   213 A&S 5th Song   40
A witch I say thou art, though thou so faire appeare;. . . .   214 A&S 5th Song   74
No witchcraft is so evill, as which man's mind destroyeth. .   215 A&S 5th Song   78
In a ground of so firme making,. . . . .   234 A&S 11th Song   34
But both to both so bent,. . . . .   216 A&S 6th Song   35
Whose senses in so evill consort, their stepdame Nature
    laies, ...   217 A&S 7th Song   1
Or if they do delight therein, yet are so cloyed with wit, .   217 A&S 7th Song   3
Who have so leaden eyes, as not to see sweet beautie's show,   217 A&S 7th Song   7
Or seeing, have so wodden wits, as not that worth to know; .   217 A&S 7th Song   8
Or knowing, have so muddy minds, as not to be in love; . . .   217 A&S 7th Song   9
Or loving, have so frothy thoughts, as easily thence to move: 217 A&S 7th Song   10
"This small wind which so sweete is, ...   219 A&S 8th Song   57
And if dumbe things be so witty, ...   219 A&S 8th Song   63
Half as deere as you to me,. . . . .   220 A&S 8th Song   82
Leaving him so passion rent, ...   221 A&S 8th Song   102
Astrophil that so wel served,. . . . .   222 A&S 9th Song   27
That she loveth me so dearely, ...   222 A&S 9th Song   32
Seing me so long to beare. . . . .   222 A&S 9th Song   33
Coles of love that burne so clearely;. . . . .   222 A&S 9th Song   34
So all things whereto that man doth bend,. . . . .   270 Psalm I   11
Serve God, serve him with feare: Rejoyce in him but so,. . .   271 Psalm II   25
So I in peace, and peacefull blisse. . . . .   274 Psalm IV   31
So shall my voice clime to thyne eares betime: . . . .   274 Psalm V   5
The murdrous man, and so the fraudulent. . . . .   275 Psalm V   16
So shall all they that trust in thee do bend,. . . . .   275 Psalm V   33
So shall all men with laudes inviron thee. . . . .   277 Psalm VII   19
And so thou hast all things ordained . . . .   279 Psalm VIII   23
And their Renoune, which seemed so lyke to last,. . . . . .   280 Psalm IX   13
Why standest Thou so farr, ...   281 Psalm X   1
Nay so proud is his puffed thought . . . .   281 Psalm X   13
Why should the evill, sc evill despise . . . .   283 Psalm X   53
And why should he in heart so hard . . . .   283 Psalm X   55
So lord we shall Thy Title sing. . . . .   283 Psalm X   69
But so of happy other side . . . .   284 Psalm XI   21
And so thereafter He, and all his Mates. . . . .   286 Psalm XIV   4
So can I not be opprest,. . . . .   288 Psalm XVI   27
So my heart is fully glad, ...   288 Psalm XVI   28
So in joy my glory clad, ...   288 Psalm XVI   29
And yet their high hearts look so low. . . . .   290 Psalm XVII   31
Whose bellyes so with daintys Thou dost fill . . . .   290 Psalm XVII   41
And so with hidden treasures grant their Will, ...   290 Psálm XVII   42
And so the Earth did fall to tremble, and to quake . . . . .   291 Psalm XVIII   15
Ev'n from the Waters' depth my God preserved me so.. . . . .   291 Psalm XVIII   35
So did he save me from my mighty furious foe,. . . . .   291 Psalm XVIII   36
Sc did he save me from their then prevailing hate, ...   291 Psalm XVIII   37
And so besides our God, who is indue'd with might? . . . . .   292 Psalm XVIII   58
To match with light foot staggs he made my foot so light . .   292 Psalm XVIII   61
The firmament, so strangely bent,. . . . .   293 Psalm XIX   3
Is so of skill bereaved, ...   293 Psalm XIX   10
From so fair book proceeding,. . . . .   294 Psalm XIX   14
Sc purely wise it gives the eyes . . . .   294 Psalm XIX   35
And so endures for ever, ...   294 Psalm XIX   38
Then what man would so soon seek gold. . . . .   294 Psalm XIX   41
So shall my spryte be still upright. . . . .   295 Psalm XIX   57
So shall I bide well purify'd . . . .   295 Psalm XIX   59
Sc let words sprung from my weake tongue,. . . . .   295 Psalm XIX   61
Thy offrings so that they to ashes turn. . . . .   296 Psalm XX   15
And so let him consent . . . .   296 Psalm XX   16
In so high estimation.   297 Psalm XXI   20
Sc from base slip is stayed. . . . .   297 Psalm XXI   28
That Thee so ev'ill have hated;. . . . .   297 Psalm XXI   30
And so shall in Our songs' delight,. . . . .   298 Psalm XXI   51
So farr from seing myne unhealthfull eyes, ...   298 Psalm XXII   3
Sc farr from hearing to my roaring cryes.. . . . .   298 Psalm XXII   4
O be not farr, since pain so nearly presseth,. . . . .   299 Psalm XXII   25
As they so theirs, Him shall their ofspring serve, ...   300 Psalm XXII   75
And so can never I . . . .   301 Psalm XXIII   2
And so my cup dost fill. . . . .   301 Psalm XXIII   20
This mercy is so sure.   301 Psalm XXIII   23
For so Thy loving hand . . . .   305 Psalm XXVI   10
They stumble so. . . . .   307 Psalm XXVII   11
So shall I sacrifices spred, ...   307 Psalm XXVII   33
Ev'en so be their guerdon shar'd.. . . . .   309 Psalm XXVIII   20
And, so I did safety gett, ...   309 Psalm XXVIII   28
So shall I with joy be filld,. . . . .   309 Psalm XXVIII   29
So my songs his lauds shall yeeld. . . . .   309 Psalm XXVIII   30
Yea neighbors, more, my mates were so agast. . . . .   313 Psalm XXXI   32
For so both day and night did stand. . . . .   315 Psalm XXXII   10

So I my self accus'd to God, ...   315 Psalm XXXII   16
So his high heavnly face . . . .   320 Psalm XXXIV   57
So that not one of them is broke;. . . . .   320 Psalm XXXIV   74
That hunt so poore a prey as is my soule.. . . . .   321 Psalm XXXV   8
Who helpest those, whose ruin was so neere,. . . . .   321 Psalm XXXV   23
So my good deeds they pay with this ev'ill share,. . . . .   322 Psalm XXXV   27
Which wicked folks do hold so deare;. . . . .   323 Psalm XXXVI   3
Before his eyes that so doth stray.. . . . .   323 Psalm XXXVI   6
And so I nothing said, I muet stood, ...   329 Psalm XXXIX   5
Let me not be thrown down to so base shame . . . .   330 Psalm XXXIX   27
So what is man but vanity? . . . .   330 Psalm XXXIX   36
So in my mouth he did a song afford, ...   331 Psalm XL   11
Whose trust is so addressed, ...   331 Psalm XL   16
So prest with sins I cannot see my case. . . . .   332 Psalm XL   44
So that my surest part,. . . . .   332 Psalm XL   48
Who so unpitteous be . . . .   332 Psalm XL   58
So then be blest now, then, at home, abroad, ...   334 Psalm XLI   45
Oh so! O be it so! . . . .   334 Psalm XLI   48
So my soul in panting playeth, ...   334 Psalm XLII   3
Where is now Thy God so good?. . . . .   334 Psalm XLII   12
My heart melts remembring so,. . . . .   334 Psalm XLII   13
Why art Thou my soul so sorry. . . . .   334 Psalm XLII   17
And in me so much dismaid? . . . .   334 Psalm XLII   18
Why art Thou my soul so sorry. . . . .   335 Psalm XLII   49
And in me so much dismaid? . . . .   335 Psalm XLII   50
And lookes so neere unto my cure that I must needes be lost.   343 Possibly   1   22
W. What seale? D. My hart deepe graven. W. Who made the band
    so fast?. . . . .   343 Possibly   1   27
D. Wonder that by two so black eyes the glittering stars be
    past.. . . . .   343 Possibly   1   28
So have I cause my selfe to plaine, but no cause to
    complayne. . . . .   344 Possibly   1   36
Will. God shield us from such Dames. If so our Downes be
    sped,. . . . .   344 Possibly   1   39
The darte, the beames, the stringe so stronge I prove; . . .   344 Possibly   2   1
So brave a shott, deere fyre and bewtye strange. . . . . .   345 Possibly   2   11
Me thought some staves he mist: if so, not much amisse:. . .   241 Other Poems   1   1
One said he brake acrosse; full well it so might be: . . . .   241 Other Poems   1   3
As all the rest, so now the stone. . . . .   241 Other Poems   3   7
So Klaius' soule did in his Strephon rest. . . . .   242 Other Poems   4   29
Yet not so wise, as of unstained harte:. . . . .   243 Other Poems   4   35
So that the grave did not his words despise. . . . .   243 Other Poems   4   38
The plenteous sweets, (can sweets so sharply grow?). . . . .   243 Other Poems   4   52
To visite so low folkes did much disdaine. . . . .   243 Other Poems   4   63
So to have done amisse, so to be shent.. . . . .   244 Other Poems   4 104
So oft in feasts with costly chaunges cladd. . . . .   245 Other Poems   4 133
So Lords with sport of Stagg and Hearon full . . . .   245 Other Poems   4 135
So now for pray these shepheards two he tooke, ...   245 Other Poems   4 137
And so must see great cause before they love.. . . . . . .   245 Other Poems   4 144
So have I sene trim bookes in velvet dight . . . .   246 Other Poems   4 180
Her parents liking well it should be so, ...   247 Other Poems   4 195
So as good thoughts of him in all arise, ...   247 Other Poems   4 198
So he with Nous to Geron turn'd their race,. . . . .   248 Other Poems   4 251
And so when Pas hand-reached him to take,. . . . .   248 Other Poems   4 257
So laughing all, yet Pas to ease some dell,. . . . .   249 Other Poems   4 263
Strephon so chas'd did seme in milke to swimme.. . . . . .   249 Other Poems   4 288
So is in her the best of Nature spent, ...   249 Other Poems   4 299
So that Uran, whose arme old Geron bore, ...   250 Other Poems   4 309
So caught, him seem'd he caught of joyes the bell, ...   250 Other Poems   4 311
And thought it heav'n so to be drawn to hell.. . . . . . .   250 Other Poems   4 312
But so she must. And now the third assault . . . .   250 Other Poems   4 316
And so to take the gemme Urania sought.. . . . .   250 Other Poems   4 324
So they three did togither idly stay,. . . . .   250 Other Poems   4 329
With love drawne on, so fast with pace unmeet. . . . . . .   250 Other Poems   4 334
Drew dainty Nous, that she not able so . . . .   250 Other Poems   4 335
So on the downs we see, neere Wilton faire,. . . . .   251 Other Poems   4 342
And past all hope his chapps to frustrate so.. . . . . . .   251 Other Poems   4 344
So have I heard to pierce pursuing shield. . . . .   251 Other Poems   4 349
So did Uran, the narr the swifter move,. . . . .   251 Other Poems   4 357
Whither it would, so it would let him dy,. . . . .   252 Other Poems   4 382
Came to hir back, and so with double warde . . . .   252 Other Poems   4 389
Happy, o happy! if they so might bide, ...   252 Other Poems   4 401
Did beate their hands, which durst so neere to presse. . . .   252 Other Poems   4 406
And so that even the barly-brake did end.. . . . .   252 Other Poems   4 416
So doth he yeeld, so takes he on his yoke, ...   253 Other Poems   4 425
He was invisible that hurt me so,. . . . .   253 Other Poems   4 455
Then most I faile, when most I would do well,. . . . . . .   254 Other Poems   4 467
That at me so amaz'd my fellowes jest: . . . .   254 Other Poems   4 468
While I was I, and so had cause to care; . . . .   254 Other Poems   4 484
Doth daily haunt: but so, that mine become . . . .   255 Other Poems   4 503
For hearing him so oft with wordes of woe. . . . .   256 Other Poems   4 537
Urania name, whose force he knew so well,. . . . .   256 Other Poems   4 538
So may thy stately grace . . . .   256 Other Poems   5   15
So Mira long may be.. . . . .   256 Other Poems   5   17
So may your sliding race . . . .   257 Other Poems   5   28
So in you ever new . . . .   257 Other Poems   5   30
So when to pay your due.. . . . .   257 Other Poems   5   33
So may your Make, this wholsome springtime aire, ...   257 Other Poems   5   42
So may you never dy, ...   257 Other Poems   5   46

*SO	(CONTINUED)	PAGE	TITLE		LINE
So may thee still betide		257	Other Poems	5	54
So may the cheries redd.		258	Other Poems	5	56
So may her eares be ledd,.		258	Other Poems	5	59
So maist thou long abide		258	Other Poems	5	67
So grow thy wooll of note, ...		258	Other Poems	5	69
So may no fortune breed.		258	Other Poems	5	80
So may thy blessings swarme.		258	Other Poems	5	82
So I unlucky lad		259	Other Poems	5	95
Joyne hearts and hands, so let it be,.		260	Other Poems	6	5
Above line repeated at following locations		260	Other Poems	6	11
. . . .		260	Other Poems	6	17
. . . .		260	Other Poems	6	23
. . . .		261	Other Poems	6	29
. . . .		261	Other Poems	6	35
. . . .		261	Other Poems	6	41
. . . .		261	Other Poems	6	47
. . . .		261	Other Poems	6	53
So joy I, in you seeing;		261	Other Poems	6	44
So should our sever'd bodies three		261	Other Poems	6	59
So many pufft in minde I see, ...		263	Other Poems	7	50
"So shall I to thee alwayes, ...		264	Other Poems	7	67
So I left him in that place, ...		264	Other Poems	7	73
SOBBED					
While sobd out words a perfect Musike give..		231	Astrophil	100	11
SOBBING					
For god hath heard the weeping sobbing voice		276	Psalm VI		27
SOBER					
Such is their speech, who be of sober wit;		104	3rd Eclogues	67	46
Or did she else that sober hue devise, ...		168	Astrophil	7	5
SOBS					
That once come there, the sobs of mine annoyes		187	Astrophil	44	13
What sobs can give words grace my griefe to show?.		227	Astrophil	93	2
SOFT					
The pasture rich, the wooll as soft as silke,.		4	Lady of May	2	21
And thou deare flesh, as soft as wooll new drest,.		76	Arcadia III	46	15
But soft and supple satten like.		88	Arcadia III	62	82
Warme snow, moyst pearle, softe ivorie..		90	Arcadia III	62	126
And pleasd with our soft peace, staid here his flying race..		168	Astrophil	8	4
Let her go. Soft, but here she comes. Go to, ...		188	Astrophil	47	12
When for so soft a rod deare play he trie?		203	Astrophil	73	4
As though that faire soft hand did you great wrong.. . . .		208	Astrophil	83	4
With sweete soft shades thou oft invitest me		230	Astrophil	98	5
Though with soft leggs, did run as fast as he.		250	Other Poems	4	339
SOIL					
Yet deare soile, if a soule closed in a mansion.		69	2nd Eclogues	34	31
To stranger weights my minde's waste soile is bound, . . .		149	Cert Sonnets	22	5
Why shouldst thou toyle our thornie soile to till?		169	Astrophil	10	6
SOJOURNED					
Did goe his way, but sojourn'd neere thereby, ...		96	3rd Eclogues	64	71
SOLD					
What man is he that hath his freedome solde?		24	1st Eclogues	9	56
My brest to swords, my soule to hell have solde.		50	2nd Eclogues	28	80
And for Rose-water sould of rarest smell..		55	2nd Eclogues	29	110
SOLDIER					
"Thou art no souldier fitte for Cupid's garrison..		16	1st Eclogues	7	51
SOLE					
His sole exec'tour blâme..		160	Cert Sonnets	30	16
(As his sole object of felicitie).		212	Astrophil	86	7
SOLEMN					
That they by solemne oth their Deities would binde		121	4th Eclogues	73	156
SOLEMNIZE					
Ere that I leave with song of praise her praise to solemnize		33	1st Eclogues	13	68
SOLITARINESS					
O sweet woods the delight of solitarines!.		68	2nd Eclogues	34	1
Above line repeated at following locations		69	2nd Eclogues	34	15
. . . .		69	2nd Eclogues	34	29
O how much I do like your solitarines!		68	2nd Eclogues	34	2
Above line repeated at following location.		69	2nd Eclogues	34	16
O how well I do like your solitarines!		69	2nd Eclogues	34	30
And thinke not she doth hurt our solitarines, ...		69	2nd Eclogues	34	41
For such company decks such solitarines.		69	2nd Eclogues	34	42
In both a mazefull solitarinesse:		229	Astrophil	96	9
SOME					
Some hurt accuse a third with horny head..		21	1st Eclogues	8	12
Some gazing still, some winking wilye shiftes, ...		21	1st Eclogues	8	27
In hunting fearefull beastes, do spend some dayes, ...		25	1st Eclogues	9	123
And sorrows do require some respitt unto the sences. . . .		37	1st Eclogues	13	175
But when to give some grace she doth content herselfe, . .		49	2nd Eclogues	28	64
Thou soone may have some helpe, or change of passion.. . .		50	2nd Eclogues	28	98
Among us all we should find out some thing of nought.. . .		51	2nd Eclogues	29	2
Plangus must live some helpe for her to trie		58	2nd Eclogues	30	56
Let doltes in haste some altars faire erect.		58	2nd Eclogues	30	62
Let us some grammar learne of more congruities..		61	2nd Eclogues	30	142
Nowe that some flower of fruict, my paynes do prove, . . .		72	Arcadia III	37	16
But if thy rage some brave revenge will finde, ...		72	Arcadia III	38	13
Of some late grace a greater grace receave, ...		77	Arcadia III	49	4
To her sweete sence, sweete sleepe, some ease imparte, . .		79	Arcadia III	51	3
Some say it doth betoken wonders neare		81	Arcadia III	55	2

454

SOME (CONTINUED)   PAGE   TITLE   LINE

So that therein appeares some blood, ... 86 Arcadia III 62   29
In fine he made her gesse, there was some sweet. . . . . . 95 3rd Eclogues 64   35
And with some words which shewed little care,. . . . . . . 97 3rd Eclogues 64 118
Least that some markes of jealousie you beare. . . . . . . 97 3rd Eclogues 64 124
The beastes had sure some beastly pollicie:. . . . . 100 3rd Eclogues 66   50
And if forsooth there come some new found ware,. . . . . . 104 3rd Eclogues 67   40
But from the sent of some infectious grave:. . . . . 114 4th Eclogues 72   19
But if among yourselves some one tree growe, ... 125 4th Eclogues 75   10
O Phisicke's power, which (some say) hath refrayned. . . . 128 4th Eclogues 75 109
O Philomela faire, o take some gladnesse,. . . . . 137 Cert Sonnets 4   9
Above line repeated at following location. . . . . 137 Cert Sonnets 4   21
He hopes for some small praise since she hath great, . . . 141 Cert Sonnets 8   11
But hopes to gaine some helpe by mounting hie, ... 144 Cert Sonnets 15   3
Some good old dumpe, that Chaucer's mistresse knew,. . . . 146 Cert Sonnets 17   34
And in my braine some sacred humour flowe: . . . . 146 Cert Sonnets 17   38
Some cause there is, which of strange cause doth rise: . . 147 Cert Sonnets 18   2
Or for my love some love I might obtaine, ... 148 Cert Sonnets 19   10
Lives to impart my wearie clay some breath.. . . . . 148 Cert Sonnets 20   10
I deemd it best some absence for to prove, ... 149 Cert Sonnets 21   3
To my dying heart some pleasure, ... 155 Cert Sonnets 26   9
That the deare She might take some pleasure of my paine: . 165 Astrophil   1   2
That she (deare she) might take some pleasure of my paine: . 165 Astrophil   1 V 2
Some fresh and fruitfull showers upon my sunne-burn'd
  braine . . . . 165 Astrophil   1   8
Vertue alas, now let me take some rest,. . . . . 166 Astrophil   4   1
Thy scepter use in some old Catoe's brest; . . . . 166 Astrophil   4   5
Some Lovers speake when they their Muses entertaine, . . . 167 Astrophil   6   1
To some a sweetest plaint, a sweetest stile affords, . . . 168 Astrophil   6   9
Not usde to frozen clips, he strave to find some part, . . 168 Astrophil   8   6
To my close heart, where while some firebrands he did lay, . 169 Astrophil   8   13
Queene Vertue's court, which some call Stella's face,. . . 169 Astrophil   9   1
For like a child that some faire booke doth find, ... 170 Astrophil   11   5
Or at the most on some fine picture stayes,. . . . . 170 Astrophil   11   7
I thought those babes of some pinne's hurt did whine,. . . 173 Astrophil   16   7
When some faire Ladies, by hard promise tied, ... 176 Astrophil   22   5
Some that know how my spring I did addresse, ... 176 Astrophil   23   5
Deeme that my Muse some fruit of knowledge plies:. . . . . 176 Astrophil   23   6
Or for some brawle, which in that chamber hie, ... 178 Astrophil   26   7
Like some weake Lords, neighbord by mighty kings,. . . . . 179 Astrophil   29   1
My harmes on Ink's poore losse, perhaps some find. . . . . 182 Astrophil   34   13
And of some sent from that sweet enemie Fraunce; . . . . . 185 Astrophil   41   4
Some luckie wits impute it but to chaunce: . . . . 185 Astrophil   41   8
Of Lover's ruine some sad Tragedie:. . . . . 187 Astrophil   45   13
But find some Hercules to beare, in steed. . . . . 190 Astrophil   51   7
Might winne some grace in your sweet skill arraid. . . . . 192 Astrophil   55   4
Then some good body tell me how I do,. . . . . 195 Astrophil   60   12
Nor ought do care, though some above me sit, ... 198 Astrophil   64   11
And do I see some cause a hope to feede, ... 199 Astrophil   66   1
No kings be crown'd but they some covenants make.. . . . . 200 Astrophil   69   14
"But ah," Desire still cries, "give me some food." . . . . 201 Astrophil   71   14
Some do I heare of Poets' furie tell,. . . . . 204 Astrophil   74   5
Or of thy gifts at least shade out some part.. . . . . . . 207 Astrophil   81   8
And that my Muse to some eares not unsweet,. . . . . 209 Astrophil   84   2
Some beautie's peece, as amber colourd hed,. . . . . 225 Astrophil   91   6
For that at length yet doth invite some rest,. . . . . . . 229 Astrophil   96   13
Ah bed, the field where joye's peace some do see,. . . . . 230 Astrophil   98   1
To steale some rest, but wretch I am constraind, ... 230 Astrophil   98   6
Some play, while he is disarmed.. . . . . 202 A&S 2nd Song   8
"Peace, I thinke that some give eare:. . . . . 234 A&S 11th Song   36
Where you may nave some defence. . . . . 221 A&S 9th Song   3
That like a byrd to some strong hill . . . . 283 Psalm XI   3
Although some Worldly losse therby he may sustaine,. . . . 287 Psalm XV   10
Let trust of some men be . . . . 296 Psalm XX   26
Of thee some mercy take, ... 304 Psalm XXV   45
Some safty unto me;. 305 Psalm XXV   74
Strive we that in some worthy phrase . . . . 319 Psalm XXXIV   11
Chafe not at some man's great good fortune . . . . 325 Psalm XXXVII   18
Seeking some refreshing brook, ... 334 Psalm XLII   2
When thou hast mynd to weepe, seeke out som smoky room:. . 343 Possibly   1   11
Me thought some staves he mist: if so, not much amisse:. . 241 Other Poems   1   1
He, that the other in some yeares did passe, ... 242 Other Poems   4   21
Then some grene gowns are by the lasses worne. . . . . . . 243 Other Poems   4   53
In some such one she lik'd not his desire, ... 245 Other Poems   4 119
Like some which seeke to salve their blotted name. . . . . 248 Other Poems   4 231
So laughing all, yet Pas to ease some dell,. . . . . 249 Other Poems   4 263
But yet a setting foorth it some way lent: . . . . 252 Other Poems   4 395
Out shreaking pipe made of some witched tree.. . . . . . . 255 Other Poems   4 516
SOMEONE
Some one his song in Jove, and Jove's strange tales attires, 167 Astrophil   6   5
SOMETHING
Use something else to chast'n me withall,. . . . . 212 Astrophil   86   12
SOMETIME
And try with bayt how fish will bite sometime. . . . . . . 26 1st Eclogues 9 128
With sweatie browes, sometyme with watrie eyes,. . . . . . 71 Arcadia III 36   8
Apollo wakes, and bow hath sometime sparde.. . . . . 143 Cert Sonnets 12   15
SOMETIMES
But sometimes to the woods, sometimes to the heavens do
  decyphire, ... 35 1st Eclogues 13 111
Revil'd for ech small fault, sometimes for none: . . . . . 105 3rd Eclogues 67   53

455

SOMETIMES   (CONTINUED)   PAGE   TITLE   LINE
    And you, o flowers, which sometimes Princes were,. . . . . .   125 4th Eclogues 75   25
    The doore by which sometimes comes forth her Grace,. . . . .   169 Astrophil   9   5
    Sometimes we see small birds from nests do pull. . . . . . .   245 Other Poems   4   136
    Sometimes to her newes of my selfe to tell . . . .   254 Other Poems   4   469
SOMEWHAT
    Which being nought seems somewhat to the eyen, ...   19 1st Eclogues 7   164
    That to the sacred Muse my anoyes somewhat be revealed,. . .   31 1st Eclogues 13   9
    So may you still have somewhat new to say. . . . .   190 Astrophil   51   4
    Somewhat thy lead'n counsels, which I tooke. . . . .   193 Astrophil   56   7
    That I perhaps am somewhat kinne to thee;. . . . .   198 Astrophil   65   12
    Faining love, somewhat to please me: . . . .   222 A&S 9th Song   42
    Somewhat to speake of his due praise,. . . . .   319 Psalm XXXIV   10
SON
    Lalus. How oft my dolefull Sire cried to me, "tarrie sonne".   16 1st Eclogues 7   49
    My sonne, keepe this, that my long toyle hath laide to me: .   16 1st Eclogues 7   52
    Because I red him, as I would my son.. . . . .   27 1st Eclogues 10   23
    Latona's sonne, whose birth in paine and travaile long . . .   45 Arcadia II   26   7
    Let me forget I am sonne to my mother, ...   61 2nd Eclogues 30   163
    Joyne with thy sonne, to ease my long annoys.. . . . .   81 Arcadia III 53   13
    Morpheus, the lively sonne of deadly sleepe,. . . . .   180 Astrophil   32   1
    Both Rebell to the Sonne, and Vagrant from the mother; . . .   214 A&S 5th Song   69
    Thou art my son in deed, this day begott by me:. . . . . . .   271 Psalm II   17
    With loving homage kisse that only son he hath,. . . . . . .   272 Psalm II   27
SONG
    To high conceipts the song must needes be high,. . . . . . .   3 Lady of May   2   8
    Cleofila. Worthy shepeheard, by my song to my selfe all
        favor is happned,.   31 1st Eclogues 13   8
    Or when an Echo begins unmov'd to sing them a love song. . .   33 1st Eclogues 13   48
    Ere that I leave with song of praise her praise to
        solemnize . . . .   33 1st Eclogues 13   68
    My pipe and song made him both songe and pipe forsweare. . .   52 2nd Eclogues 29   20
    With sluttish song: I pray thee learne to blea,. . . . . . .   56 2nd Eclogues 29   136
    So may thy songe be famous;. . . . .   66 2nd Eclogues 32   24
    So may thy song be pleasant. . . . .   66 2nd Eclogues 32   29
    The song thereof a last will,. . . . .   66 2nd Eclogues 32   34
    But all thy songe herein knitt:. . . . .   67 2nd Eclogues 32   51
    Thy mistresse' song is now a sorrow's crie,. . . . .   81 Arcadia III 54   2
    Yet never shall my song omitte . . . .   88 Arcadia III 62   87
    Those thighes, for Ovid's song more fitte; . . . .   88 Arcadia III 62   88
    The songe I sange old Languet had me taught, ...   99 3rd Eclogues 66   22
    Our morning hymne this is, and song at evening.. . . . . . .   113 4th Eclogues 71   75
    This song from deathe's sorrow springeth:. . . . .   140 Cert Sonnets 7   36
    Some one his song in Jove, and Jove's strange tales attires,   167 Astrophil   6   5
    I bare (with Envie) yet I bare your song,. . . . .   208 Astrophil   83   5
    To you, to you, all song of praise is due, ...   196 A&S 1st Song   3
    Above line repeated at following locations . . . .   197 A&S 1st Song   7
        . . . .   197 A&S 1st Song   11
        . . . .   197 A&S 1st Song   15
        . . . .   197 A&S 1st Song   19
        . . . .   197 A&S 1st Song   23
        . . . .   197 A&S 1st Song   27
        . . . .   197 A&S 1st Song   31
        . . . .   197 A&S 1st Song   35
    Only in you my song begins and endeth. . . . .   196 A&S 1st Song   4
    Above line repeated at following location. . . . .   197 A&S 1st Song   36
    That therewith my song is broken.. . . . .   221 A&S 8th Song   104
    I to Thy Name will sing, and this my song shall bee: . . . .   293 Psalm XVIII   89
    And song accord. . . . .   307 Psalm XXVII   35
    A new, sing a new song . . . .   316 Psalm XXXIII   13
    So in my mouth he did a song afford, ...   331 Psalm XL   11
    New song unto our God of prayse, ...   331 Psalm XL   12
    In my song shall be display'd. . . . .   334 Psalm XLII   20
    Above line repeated at following location. . . . .   335 Psalm XLII   52
    A lustles song for sooth thinks hee that hath more lust to
        cry. . . . .   343 Possibly   1   8
    A plaining songe plaine-singing voice requires,. . . . . . .   242 Other Poems   4   3
    No, no, it was in spite of wisdome's song, ...   247 Other Poems   4   222
    This song she singes in most commaunding wise: . . . .   255 Other Poems   4   509
    "My song clime thou the winde. . . . .   259 Other Poems   5   105
    Striving with my Mates in Song,. . . . .   263 Other Poems   7   45
SONG-BOOK
    Sings out her woes, a thorne her song-booke making:. . . . .   137 Cert Sonnets 4   4
SONG'S
    The singer is the song's theame. . . . .   66 2nd Eclogues 32   36
    Song's Ditty.. . . . .   286 Psalm XIII   20
SONGS
    Lalus. Come Dorus, come, let songs thy sorowes signifie: . .   14 1st Eclogues 7   1
    Nightingale, voice, entising songes to saye. . . . .   101 3rd Eclogues 66   82
    He barks, my songs thine owne voyce oft doth prove:. . . . .   194 Astrophil   59   6
    Yea even my songs thy name shall magnify,. . . . .   279 Psalm IX   4
    So my songs his lauds shall yeeld. . . . .   309 Psalm XXVIII   30
    To songs and joyfull byding. . . . .   315 Psalm XXXII   27
    The Nightingales for woe their songs refraine: . . . .   254 Other Poems   4   474
    Mixing mirth our Songs among,. . . . .   263 Other Poems   7   46
SONGS'
    And so shall in Our songs' delight,. . . . .   298 Psalm XXI   51
SONNETS
    Sonets be not bound prentise to annoy: . . . .   201 Astrophil   70   5

```
SONS                                                             PAGE     TITLE          LINE
    Gallein's adoptive sonnes, who by a beaten way . . . . . .   232  Astrophil   102     9
SOON
    A servant Sex, soone prowde if they be coi'de, . . . . . .    24  1st Eclogues   9    60
    That soone the world of his false tong be void.. . . . . .    24  1st Eclogues   9    68
    Within thy selfe, thou soone wilt be ashamed. . . . . . .     25  1st Eclogues   9   118
    Our owne demeane, and soone we wondre shall. . . . . . . .    29  1st Eclogues  10    92
    To such a force soone chaunge were nothing sutable. . . .     47  2nd Eclogues  28    12
    Thou soone may have some helpe, or change of passion. . . .   50  2nd Eclogues  28    98
    And soone forget the swincke due to their hire. . . . . .    100  3rd Eclogues  66    74
    Sure shepherd's signe, that morne would soone fetch day. . . 103  3rd Eclogues  66   161
    Lalus' example I would soone ensue,. . . . . . . . . . . .   104  3rd Eclogues  67    23
    Sweete supple mindes which soone to wisdome bowe . . . . .   106  3rd Eclogues  67   103
    As soon as Sunne begins to clime the mountaines: . . . . .   112  4th Eclogues  71    44
    And vertuous soules so soone should lose their place?. . .   126  4th Eclogues  75    42
    The Nightingale, as soone as aprill bringeth . . . . . . .   137  Cert Sonnets   4     1
    The wood, above doth soone consuming rest. . . . . . . . .   150  Cert Sonnets  22    44
    For soone as they strake thee with Stella's rayes, . . . .   170  Astrophil     10    12
    My boiling sprites did thither soone incline,. . . . . . .   172  Astrophil     16     3
    And yet as soone as they so formed be, . . . . . . . . . .   189  Astrophil     50     5
    Should soone be pierc'd with sharpnesse of the mone. . . .   193  Astrophil     57     8
    Becomes a clog) will soone ease me of it. . . . . . . . .    194  Astrophil     59    14
    But soone as thought of thee breeds my delight, . . . . .    236  Astrophil    108     5
    Soone with my death I will please thee. . . . . . . . . . .  211  A&S 4th Song         53
    As where thou soone mightst helpe, most faith dost most
        oppresse, . . . . . . . . . . . . . . . . . . . . . .    213  A&S 5th Song         41
    All her hate, death soone would seaze me,. . . . . . . . .   222  A&S 9th Song         44
    Then what man would so soon seek gold. . . . . . . . . . .   294  Psalm XIX            41
    Nay soon as he but moved . . . . . . . . . . . . . . . . .   297  Psalm XXI             6
    In clouds of teares, but soon as sun . . . . . . . . . . .   311  Psalm XXXII          17
    And therfore soon would mischeife Thee . . . . . . . . . .   315  Psalm XXXII          35
    For he spake not more soone. . . . . . . . . . . . . . . .   317  Psalm XXXIII         31
    But lo, soon as they did me staggering see,. . . . . . . .   322  Psalm XXXV           37
    They soone shall be cutt down like grasse. . . . . . . . .   324  Psalm XXXVII          5
    As soon as out they go.. . . . . . . . . . . . . . . . . .   333  Psalm XLI            24
    The later borne, yet too soone, Strephon hight.. . . . . .   242  Other Poems    4    24
    Which soone as it did batefull question frame, . . . . . .   247  Other Poems    4   189
    There may you see, soone as the middle two . . . . . . . .   248  Other Poems    4   233
    He single thus, hop'd soone with hir to be,. . . . . . . .   250  Other Poems    4   337
SOONER
    The sound to this strange aier no sooner goes, . . . . . .    42  Arcadia II    21     9
    I sooner would, then thus my eares defile. . . . . . . . .    50  2nd Eclogues  28    81
    Beaten with waves, no sooner kennes the baye . . . . . . .    70  Arcadia III   36     3
    Where, "sooner die then change my state",. . . . . . . . .   158  Cert Sonnets  28    35
    No sooner said, but (lo) myne Enemyes sink . . . . . . . .   280  Psalm IX             46
    No sooner my child eyes could look abroad, . . . . . . . .   299  Psalm XXII           23
    Who trusts him sooner shall. . . . . . . . . . . . . . . .   318  Psalm XXXIII         64
    On Creon's child his poison sooner throw,. . . . . . . . .   252  Other Poems    4   410
    Sconer these than those in hearing.. . . . . . . . . . . .   263  Other Poems    7    54
SOONEST
    Cloth'd in the shape which soonest may deceave:. . . . . .    21  1st Eclogues   8    32
SOOTH
    For me in sooth, no Muse but one I know: . . . . . . . . .   166  Astrophil      3     9
SOOTHE
    Each thing with mantle black the night doth soothe;. . . .    98  3rd Eclogues  66     5
SOPHISTRY
    Driv'n else to graunt by Angel's sophistrie, . . . . . . .   195  Astrophil     61    13
SORE
    Deadly wounds inward bleed, ech sleight sore mattereth.. .    14  1st Eclogues   7     9
    Thou heardst even now a yong man snebb me sore,. . . . . .    27  1st Eclogues  10    22
    What skill servethe a soare of a wrong infirmity judged? . .  32  1st Eclogues  13    21
    Thus plag'de how can I frame to my soare any hope of
        amendemente? . . . . . . . . . . . . . . . . . . . . .    37  1st Eclogues  13   160
    Long since my voice is hoarce, and throte is sore, . . . .    57  2nd Eclogues  30     8
    Or rubbing hurt the sore, I here doo end.. . . . . . . . .    62  2nd Eclogues  30   183
    To think a soare so deadly . . . . . . . . . . . . . . . .    66  2nd Eclogues  32    17
    Wrong sturres remorsed greefe, griefe's deadly sore. . . .    85  Arcadia III   61     7
    Yet (for I nothing sawe) I feared sore;. . . . . . . . . .    99  3rd Eclogues  66    16
    Till forste to parte, with harte and eyes even sore, . . .    99  3rd Eclogues  66    39
    Sore beaten doth her mast of Comforte spende:. . . . . . .   114  4th Eclogues  72    45
    Sore signe it is, the Lord's last thred is spun. . . . . .   150  Cert Sonnets  22    14
    Yet perish shall (although his paine be sore). . . . . . .   281  Psalm IX             59
    For thy shafts have pierc't me sore, . . . . . . . . . . .   327  Psalm XXXVIII         4
    I am weake and broken sore,. . . . . . . . . . . . . . . .   328  Psalm XXXVIII        22
    Foul faults sore pains do reach me,. . . . . . . . . . . .   332  Psalm XL             46
    Thus, fast he fled from her he follow'd sore,. . . . . . .   250  Other Poems    4   305
SORELY
    The Gentiles Thou rebuked sorely hast, . . . . . . . . . .   279  Psalm IX             11
SORRILY
    Thy pipe, o Pan, shall helpe, though I sing sorilie. . . .    15  1st Eclogues   7    27
SORROW
    For other be those tunes which sorrow tyes,. . . . . . . .    13  Arcadia I      4     7
    Dorus. Farre other care, o Muse, my sorrow tries,. . . . .    17  1st Eclogues   7   106
    Feede on my sheepe, sorrow hathe stricken sayle, . . . . .    43  Arcadia II    23    10
    Leave of my sheepe, sorrowe hathe hoysed sayle,. . . . . .    44  Arcadia II    24    10
    Men tongd like lotches sucking others sorrowe. . . . . . .    50  2nd Eclogues  28  V885
    Thus be our noblest parts dryed up with sorrow:. . . . . .    62  2nd Eclogues  30   174
    Sorowe suck up the marowe of my might, . . . . . . . . . .    74  Arcadia III   42    10
    And thinke, I did my selfe from sorrow save. . . . . . . .   104  3rd Eclogues  67    24
    Since wayling is a bud of causefull sorowe,. . . . . . . .   108  Arcadia IV    70     1
```

```
SORROW                          (CONTINUED)              PAGE    TITLE            LINE
     Since sorow is the follower of evill fortune,. . . . . . .   108  Arcadia IV    70     2
     Sorow pay we unto the rights of Nature,. . . . . . . . . .   109  Arcadia IV    70     5
     Who justly make our hearts the seates of sorow?. . . . . .   109  Arcadia IV    70     8
     Of willing teares, torne heare, and cries of sorrow. . . .   109  Arcadia IV    70    16
     Cast thy stepmother eyes upon our sorowe,. . . . . . . . .   109  Arcadia IV    70    23
     A yelling voice, and heartes compos'd of sorow,. . . . . .   109  Arcadia IV    70    27
     And sorow feede, feeding our soules with sorow.. . . . . .   110  Arcadia IV    70    36
     Since sorow then concludeth all our fortune, . . . . . . .   110  Arcadia IV    70    37
     Sorow then cherish me, for I am sorowe:. . . . . . . . . .   114  4th Eclogues  72    26
     No being now, but sorowe I can have: . . . . . . . . . . .   114  4th Eclogues  72    27
     Can those eyes now yeeld to the kind conceit of a sorow, . .  122  4th Eclogues  74    17
     That so I may signes of my sorrowe leave.. . . . . . . . .   125  4th Eclogues  75     9
     Me thinkes, my sound no place with sorrow filleth. . . . .   127  4th Eclogues  75    99
     So it be seene what sorrow in me raigneth. . . . . . . . .   128  4th Eclogues  75   105
     Time runnes away for sorow:. . . . . . . . . . . . . . . .   136  Cert Sonnets   3     6
     This song from deathe's sorrow springeth:. . . . . . . . .   140  Cert Sonnets   7    36
     I see and yet no greater sorow take, . . . . . . . . . . .   174  Astrophil     18    13
     Nay sorrow comes with such maine rage, that he . . . . . .   229  Astrophil     95     9
     Such teares, sighs, plaints, no sorrow is, but joy:. . . .   231  Astrophil    100    12
     All mirth farewell, let me in sorrow live. . . . . . . . .   231  Astrophil    100    14
     When sorrow (using mine owne fier's might) . . . . . . . .   236  Astrophil    108     1
     Sorrow onely then hath glory,. . . . . . . . . . . . . . .   221  A&S 9th Song        14
     My moystned bed proofes of my sorrow showeth:. . . . . . .   276  Psalm VI            18
     The more my sorrow did encrease, . . . . . . . . . . . . .   329  Psalm XXXIX          8
     Will. Thou seest my eares do itch at it: good Dick thy sorow
          tell. . . . . . . . . . . . . . . . . . . . . . . . .   343  Possibly       1    18
     And thou, seke-sorow Klaius, them among: . . . . . . . . .   247  Other Poems    4   218
     With teares, he saide, or sorrow said for him. . . . . . .   256  Other Poems    5    13
     With skinne in sorrow died,. . . . . . . . . . . . . . . .   259  Other Poems    5   117
SORROW'S
     Ruine's relique, care's web, and sorrowe's foode:. . . . .    23  1st Eclogues   9    29
     And all but jests, save onely sorrowe's rage. . . . . . . .    57  2nd Eclogues  30    22
     That sorrowe's worke against my will I prove.. . . . . . .    60  2nd Eclogues  30   127
     That sorrowe's weight dothe balance up thies joyes.. . . .    71  Arcadia III   36    18
     Thy mistresse' song is now a sorrow's crie,. . . . . . . .    81  Arcadia III   54     2
     Place Sorrowe's triumph on my conquered harte: . . . . . .   114  4th Eclogues  72    17
     Which is the hatefull web of Sorowe's paines.. . . . . . .   114  4th Eclogues  72    25
     Of sorrowe's droppes, till colder reason binde . . . . . .   150  Cert Sonnets  22    37
     The lothsome buds growne on sorrowe's tree.. . . . . . . .   153  Cert Sonnets  24     5
     With absence' Vaile, I live in Sorowe's night. . . . . . .   224  Astrophil     91     4
     As grudging me my sorrowe's eloquence? . . . . . . . . . .   233  Astrophil    104     4
     D. Teares drink, sorowes meat, wherewith, not I, but in me
          my death lives. . . . . . . . . . . . . . . . . . . .   344  Possibly       1    34
SORROWS
     Lalus. Come Dorus, come, let songs thy sorowes signifie: . .   14  1st Eclogues   7     1
     Geron. Up, up Philisides, let sorrowes goe,. . . . . . . .    22  1st Eclogues   9     1
     Time shall in one my life and sorrowes end,. . . . . . . .    23  1st Eclogues   9    19
     In sorrows torments, then, tyed to the pompes of a pallace,. .  35  1st Eclogues  13   103
     But to my selfe what wish can I make for a salve to my
          sorrowes,. . . . . . . . . . . . . . . . . . . . . .    37  1st Eclogues  13   157
     And sorrows do require some respitt unto the sences. . . .    37  1st Eclogues  13   175
     Sorrowes ill easde, where sorrowes painted be. . . . . . .    41  Arcadia II    21     6
     To couple comming harmes with sorrowes past? . . . . . . .    57  2nd Eclogues  30     7
SORRY
     The sorry fruites of anguish,. . . . . . . . . . . . . . .    66  2nd Eclogues  32    33
     Still to be sory.. . . . . . . . . . . . . . . . . . . . .   138  Cert Sonnets   5    16
     So may they live still sorie . . . . . . . . . . . . . . .   152  Cert Sonnets  23    31
     They have no cause to be sorie,. . . . . . . . . . . . . .   155  Cert Sonnets  26    20
     For thy knitting haire be sorie: . . . . . . . . . . . . .   156  Cert Sonnets  27    18
     When tis excellently sory. . . . . . . . . . . . . . . . .   221  A&S 9th Song        15
     Why art Thou my soul so sorry. . . . . . . . . . . . . . .   334  Psalm XLII          17
     Above line repeated at following location. . . . . . . . .   335  Psalm XLII          49
SORT
     Whose face doth oft the bravest sort enchaunt, . . . . . .     3  Lady of May    1     2
     Where helping weaker sort, the nobler beastes, . . . . . .   102  3rd Eclogues  66   121
     Fortune wheeles still with me in one sort slow,. . . . . .   199  Astrophil     66     6
     And that forgetfull sort, which never cares. . . . . . . .   281  Psalm IX            54
     Like the wiser sorte, whose learning,. . . . . . . . . . .   263  Other Poems    7    41
SOUGHT
     Both equall hurt, in this change sought our blisse:. . . .    76  Arcadia III   45    13
     Mine owne, embraced, sought, knot, fire, desease.. . . . .    84  Arcadia III   60    14
     Grumbling at her when she his kindnes sought,. . . . . . .    95  3rd Eclogues  64    32
     She sigh'd and sayd, the bad guest sought her love.. . . .    95  3rd Eclogues  64    48
     Disdaind with this, in deserts sought their restes;. . . .   102  3rd Eclogues  66   123
     How hast thou torne thy selfe! sought thine owne damage! . .  109  Arcadia IV    70    20
     Where shade from Sunne, and sporte I sought in evening,. . .  111  4th Eclogues  71    14
     I sought to catch the fish Torpedo faire.. . . . . . . . .   115  4th Eclogues  72    63
     And smirkly thus gan say. "I never sought debate . . . . .   120  4th Eclogues  73   147
     But yet in vaine thou hast my ruine sought,. . . . . . . .   161  Cert Sonnets  31     9
     I sought fit words to paint the blackest face of woe,. . .   165  Astrophil      1     5
     Upon a wretch, that long thy grace hath sought;. . . . . .   185  Astrophil     40     7
     That after God he never sought,. . . . . . . . . . . . . .   281  Psalm X             14
     Thus I begin. I sought . . . . . . . . . . . . . . . . . .   319  Psalm XXXIV         13
     And sought with deeds Thy will to hitt;. . . . . . . . . .   331  Psalm XL            33
     Who jointly sought my bale to frame; . . . . . . . . . . .   332  Psalm XL            53
     Desire the more he suckt, more sought the brest, . . . . .   247  Other Poems    4   203
     And so to take the gemme Urania sought.. . . . . . . . . .   250  Other Poems    4   324
SOUGHT-FOR
     Their sought-for treasure. . . . . . . . . . . . . . . . .    83  Arcadia III   59     4
```

SOUL

		PAGE	TITLE		LINE
Sweete soule, to whom I vowed am a slave,.		3	Lady of May	2	11
Sweete soule let not a wretch that serveth sheepe, ...		4	Lady of May	2	17
Enjoy her soule, in bodie's faire possession,.		15	1st Eclogues	7	41
Save then my soule, spill not my thoughts well heaped, . . .		16	1st Eclogues	7	80
But deck therewith my soule for your sake dying.		17	1st Eclogues	7	90
Possesse she doth, and makes my soule her slave:		17	1st Eclogues	7	112
Who doth his soule to endlesse malice bend..		22	1st Eclogues	9	10
Ath strongest soule, when most his raynes do bowe.		25	1st Eclogues	9	101
None but I, workes by desire: by desire have I kindled in his soule.		30	1st Eclogues	11	13
Fleshly vaile consumes; but a soule hath his life, ...		31	1st Eclogues	12	22
Life to this our soule..		31	1st Eclogues	12	24
Comfort into my soule. I do finde, I do find what a blessing		34	1st Eclogues	13	95
O heavenly soule, in humaine shape conteind:		38	Arcadia II	15	2
A voice may come, which troubled soule doth yeld:.		40	Arcadia II	18	4
Till spotlesse soule unto thy bosome flye, ...		40	Arcadia II	18	17
My brest to swords, my soule to hell have solde.		50	2nd Eclogues	28	80
Which do envenome both the soule and senses.		50	2nd Eclogues	28	88
O soule, whose love in her is onely spent, ...		60	2nd Eclogues	30	122
While that my soule, she, she lives in affliction;		61	2nd Eclogues	30	146
My sowle beginnes to take leave.		66	2nd Eclogues	32	15
Thus pure pearle, I do yeeld, my senses and soule.		68	2nd Eclogues	33	28
Yet deare soile, if a soule closed in a mansion.		69	2nd Eclogues	34	31
My greedy soule, with gripe of inward fire:.		80	Arcadia III	53	6
The love which is imprinted in my soule.		85	Arcadia III	61	1
My soule is bliste, sence joyde, and fortune raysed.		108	Arcadia IV	69	14
Embrace that most, that most my soule destroyes.		113	4th Eclogues	72	7
The darkened heav'n my soule which nought can see;		114	4th Eclogues	72	35
But that eternall paines my soule have hent, ...		116	4th Eclogues	72	87
Ne could my soule it selfe accuse of such a faulte,.		117	4th Eclogues	73	19
Heart and soule do sing in me.		139	Cert Sonnets	7	3
Above line repeated at following locations		139	Cert Sonnets	7	10
. . . .		139	Cert Sonnets	7	13
. . . .		140	Cert Sonnets	7	20
. . . .		140	Cert Sonnets	7	23
. . . .		140	Cert Sonnets	7	30
. . . .		140	Cert Sonnets	7	33
. . . .		140	Cert Sonnets	7	40
If from my soule this love would once depart,.		148	Cert Sonnets	19	9
A simple soule should breed so mixed woes.		149	Cert Sonnets	22	10
Where my soule I have engaged?		157	Cert Sonnets	27	28
If vaine love have my simple scule opprest,.		166	Astrophil	4	3
And should in soule up to our countrey move:		167	Astrophil	5	13
Doth plunge my wel-form'd soule even in the mire		172	Astrophil	14	7
By my soule judging what Love's paine might be..		173	Astrophil	16 V	8
Yet pride I thinke doth not my soule possesse,.		178	Astrophil	27	9
That not my soule, which at thy foot did fall, ...		183	Astrophil	36	12
Each soule doth at Love's feet his weapons lay, ...		186	Astrophil	43	7
That vertuous soule, sure heire of heav'nly blisse:.		190	Astrophil	52	7
Her soule, arm'd but with such a dainty rind,.		193	Astrophil	57	7
But I unbid, fetch even my soule to thee..		194	Astrophil	59	8
So captives to his Saint both soule and sence, ...		195	Astrophil	61	6
That voyce, which makes the soule plant himselfe in the eares:		205	Astrophil	77	9
Safe in my soule, which only doth to thee.		212	Astrophil	86	6
For my poore soule, which now that sicknesse tries,.		228	Astrophil	94	6
As can refresh the hell where my soule fries.		231	Astrophil	100	8
And my yong soule flutters to thee his nest, ...		236	Astrophil	108	6
Who hath the voyce, which soule from sences sunders, ...		197	A&S 1st Song		29
I said, my soule was thine (o that I then had lyed).		212	A&S 5th Song		9
But of thy soule, so fraught with such ungratefulnesse,. . .		213	A&S 5th Song		40
For thy face tempts my soule to leave the heav'n for thee, .		215	A&S 5th Song		82
But my soule shall harbour there..		234	A&S 11th Song		40
That to my soul do say,.		272	Psalm III		8
Nay ev'n my soul fell troubles do appall;.		276	Psalm VI		9
Least lion like He do my soule devoure, ...		277	Psalm VII		4
Witness Thou my soule with me.		287	Psalm XVI		3
On my soul no power shall have:.		288	Psalm XVI		32
Which to Thy self my soul will send.		290	Psalm XVII		20
The very soul amending,.		294	Psalm XIX		30
My soul, which Thou didst make,.		304	Psalm XXV		67
Sweet lord, write not my soul.		306	Psalm XXVI		28
Thou well hast known what plung my soul was in		312	Psalm XXXI		21
My eye, my Gutts, yea my soul grief doth wast, ...		312	Psalm XXXI		27
My soul shall glory still.		318	Psalm XXXIV		5
That hunt so poore a prey as is my soule..		321	Psalm XXXV		8
With cruel minds my very soul to teare..		322	Psalm XXXV		28
Oh! on my soul let not these tumults hitt.		322	Psalm XXXV		44
O Soul, rejoyce, we made this wretch our prey.		323	Psalm XXXV		62
O heale my soul, let there Thy cure begin.		333	Psalm XLI		15
So my soul in panting playeth, ...		334	Psalm XLII		3
My soul thirsts indeed in me		334	Psalm XLII		5
Why art Thou my soul so sorry.		334	Psalm XLII		17
Ah my soul it self appaleth, ...		334	Psalm XLII		23
Why art Thou my soul so sorry.		335	Psalm XLII		49
And in fine my soul be raysed, ...		335	Psalm XLII		55
Why art Thou my soul		337	Psalm XLIII		31
So Klaius' soule did in his Strephon rest.		242	Other Poems	4	29
Kindly, sweete soule, she did unkindnes take,.		245	Other Poems	4	121

SOUL   (CONTINUED)   PAGE   TITLE   LINE
    His soule did fly as she was seen to run.. . . . .   251 Other Poems   4   372
    And yet, deare soule, I know she hurteth none: . . . .   254 Other Poems   4   458
    (With blushing soule at sight of judgement's glasse, ...   255 Other Poems   4   531
SOUL-INVADING
    Heare you this soule-invading voice, and count it but a
        voice? . . . .   217 A&S 7th Song   17
SOUL'S
    His youth delight, his age the soule's oppression: . . . . .   48 2nd Eclogues 28   39
    Soule's joy, bend not those morning starres from me, ...   188 Astrophil   48   1
    Their soules fowl sinns for inmost lyning have:. . . . . . .   275 Psalm V   26
    Hir hands which pierc'd the soule's seav'n-double shield,. .   246 Other Poems   4   147
SOULS
    But wretched be the soules which, vaild in a contrary
        subject, ...   32 1st Eclogues 13   19
    Since outward pleasures be but halting helpes to decayd
        soules). . . . .   33 1st Eclogues 13   52
    As thou wilt give our soules a deare refection,. . . . . . .   49 2nd Eclogues 28   52
    On pensive soules (in steede of restfull baite). . . . . . .   82 Arcadia III 56   6
    And sorow feede, feeding our soules with sorow.. . . . . . .   110 Arcadia IV   70   36
    Whence our immortall soules to mortall earth doo flowe:. . .   118 4th Eclogues 73   46
    And vertuous soules so soone should lose their place?. . . .   126 4th Eclogues 75   42
    Which others said did make their soules to pine: . . . . . .   173 Astrophil   16   6
    Strange flames of Love it in our soules would raise; . . . .   177 Astrophil   25   4
    O kisse, which soules, even soules together ties . . . . . .   207 Astrophil   81   5
    When Wycked soules be turn'd to hellish paine, ...   281 Psalm IX   53
    To trap poor soules he goes! . . . .   282 Psalm X   44
    God doth all soules redeeme. . . . .   321 Psalm XXXIV   77
    To them that be in soules upright. . . . .   324 Psalm XXXVI   30
    To have their hate on good soules wroken;. . . . .   325 Psalm XXXVII   38
    Of them, poore soules: and cutting Reason's raines,. . . . .   246 Other Poems   4   158
SOUND
    As shallow brookes do yeeld the greatest sound,. . . . . . .   4 Lady of May   2   14
    Give right sound to the eares, and enter aright to the
        judgement; . . . .   32 1st Eclogues 13   18
    Silly shepheard's poore pype, when his harsh sound testifis
        our woes,. . . . .   32 1st Eclogues 13   40
    With flamie breathe doo issue oft in sound:. . . . .   42 Arcadia II   21   8
    The sound to this strange aier no sooner goes, ...   42 Arcadia II   21   9
    Yeeld to our eares a sweet and sound relation,.. . . . . . .   48 2nd Eclogues 28   20
    For good thou mayst yet proove in sheepish sound.. . . . . .   56 2nd Eclogues 29   137
    Doth proclaime with a round made all by men's mouths . . . .   68 2nd Eclogues 33   20
    Mine owne? o word on whose sweete sound doth pray. . . . . .   80 Arcadia III 53   5
    And lowest stops doo yeeld the hyest sounde. . . . .   81 Arcadia III 54   16
    Scunde of my griefes, and let it never ende, ...   126 4th Eclogues 75   35
    Me thinkes, my sound no place with sorrow filleth. . . . . .   127 4th Eclogues 75   99
    Nor held in evill, nor suffered to be sound, ...   144 Cert Sonnets 15   8
    With sound of horne, which he him selfe did blow,. . . . . .   145 Cert Sonnets 16   2
    A three foote stoole in Greece, made Trumpets sound, ...   146 Cert Sonnets 17   19
    Ncr trumpets sound I heard, nor friendly cries;. . . . . . .   191 Astrophil   53   12
    And love the sweet sound of thy name, rejoyce. . . . .   275 Psalm V   34
    From Ill word, and ill meaning sound.. . . . .   289 Psalm XVII   12
    Scund and upright with him, to wickednes not bent. . . . . .   292 Psalm XVIII   46
    Yea sound my reines, and inmost of my heart; . . . .   305 Psalm XXVI   9
    His voyce doth threatning thunders sound,. . . . .   310 Psalm XXIX   8
    To keep them safe and sound. . . . .   319 Psalm XXXIV   28
    I have the Wicked seen full sound, ...   327 Psalm XXXVII   89
    Nc sound part (causd by Thy wrath) . . . .   327 Psalm XXXVIII   7
    Nothing in my body sound;. . . . .   328 Psalm XXXVIII   21
    The Lord will keep his life yet safe and sound . . . .   333 Psalm XLI   5
    In my sound rightfull way, ...   334 Psalm XLI   42
    With sound of musicke living.. . . . .   260 Other Poems   6   10
    Sweete Orpheus' Harpe, whose sound . . . .   260 Other Poems   6   13
    With my reedes, sound mighty praise; . . . .   264 Other Poems   7   68
SOUNDING
    Tell, if that breath, which thee thy sounding gives, ...   258 Other Poems   5   63
SOUNDLY
    Thy way is soundly sure, Thy word is purely tryd;. . . . . .   292 Psalm XVIII   55
SOUNDS
    So sweete sounds straight mine eare and heart do hit,. . . .   192 Astrophil   55   13
SOUR
    That sweete, but sower despairefull care.. . . . .   14 1st Eclogues 6   4
    Then base and sower is Love's most high vocation.. . . . . .   48 2nd Eclogues 28   24
    Can taste no sweetes, the sower onely please:. . . . .   74 Arcadia III 41   2
    Her breath which makes a sower answer sweete,. . . . .   141 Cert Sonnets 9   6
    Now thy sweetnesse sowre is deemed,. . . . .   156 Cert Sonnets 27   9
SOUR-BREATHED
    This sowre-breath'd mate tast of those sugred lips.. . . . .   194 Astrophil   59   11
SOUTH
    By north or south still rich adorned live: . . . .   256 Other Poems   5   16
SOVEREIGN
    Her vertue is soveraine, fortune a vassal of hers".. . . . .   30 1st Eclogues 11   16
    That nature, soverayne of earthly dwellers,. . . . .   68 2nd Eclogues 33   21
    They first resort unto that soveraigne part; . . . .   236 Astrophil   107   4
    "Stella soveraigne of my joy,. . . . .   218 A&S 8th Song   29
SOVEREIGNTY
    Whether with words this soveraignty he gaine,. . . . .   194 Astrophil   58   5
    Not by rude force, but sweetest soveraigntie . . . .   201 Astrophil   71   6
SOWETH
    He water plowes, and soweth in the sand, ...   24 1st Eclogues 9   53

```
SOWN                                                           PAGE    TITLE            LINE
   From her, in whome is sowne their freedome's seede,. . . . .  72  Arcadia III   38     4
SPACE
   In travaile of our life (a short but tedious space). . . . .  45  Arcadia II    26     9
   Than they whose stoare in harvest space. . . . . . . . . . .  274  Psalm IV            29
   But light-legd Pas had gott the middle space. . . . . . . .  248  Other Poems    4   253
SPADE
   Dig deepe with learning's spade, now tell me this, . . . . .  175  Astrophil     21    13
SPAKE
   (For both togither spake, each loth to be behinde) . . . . .  121  4th Eclogues 73   155
   Then she spake; her speech was such, . . . . . . . . . . . .  220  A&S 8th Song        69
   Then spake he his lowd voyce, then hailestones coales and
      fire. . . . . . . . . . . . . . . . . . . . . . . . . . .  291  Psalm XVIII         28
   For he spake not more soone. . . . . . . . . . . . . . . . .  317  Psalm XXXIII        31
   My tongue would needs and thus I spake:. . . . . . . . . . .  329  Psalm XXXIX         12
   Spake unto a sencelesse tree,. . . . . . . . . . . . . . . .  262  Other Poems    7    16
SPAN
   A span? nay nothing in Thyn eyne. . . . . . . . . . . . . .  330  Psalm XXXIX         16
SPANGLE
   But for to spangle the blacke weeds of night:. . . . . . .  178  Astrophil     26     6
SPAN'S
   Lo Thou a span's length madest my living line; . . . . . .  330  Psalm XXXIX         15
SPARE
   But hoarse and drye, my pipes I nowe must spare. . . . . .   62  2nd Eclogues 30   190
   My inward hurte should spare thy outward rine? . . . . . .   77  Arcadia III   47     8
   As we to get are fram'd, so they to spare: . . . . . . . .  106  3rd Eclogues 67   106
   Why should we spare our voice from endlesse wailing, . . .  109  Arcadia IV    70     7
   Deare Killer, spare not thy sweet cruell shot: . . . . . .  189  Astrophil     48    13
   Or do you meane my tender eares to spare,. . . . . . . . .  225  Astrophil     92     4
   Spare not them, give them reward . . . . . . . . . . . . .  309  Psalm XXVIII        16
   Made wolves (not inward wolves) my ewes to spare;. . . . .  254  Other Poems    4   486
SPARED
   Apollo wakes, and bow hath sometime sparde.. . . . . . . .  143  Cert Sonnets 12    15
SPAREFULNESS
   Largesse his hands could never skill of sparefulnesse. . .   48  2nd Eclogues 28    45
SPARES
   Which nothing spares, to melt that Virgin-waxe . . . . . .   60  2nd Eclogues 30   108
SPARING
   Not sparing me, in whom his workes be rife:. . . . . . . .  114  4th Eclogues 72    15
SPARK
   The heavens conspir'd, to make my vitall sparke. . . . . .   73  Arcadia III   40     3
   In earthly clothes enclosde a heavenly sparke. . . . . . .   80  Arcadia III   52    10
   Such vitall sparke, that her mine eyes might see.. . . . .  115  4th Eclogues 72    84
   Now each thing which enjoy'd that firie quickning sparke .  116  4th Eclogues 73     4
   Thence, so farre thence, that scarcely any sparke. . . . .  233  Astrophil    104     6
   Wherof if but a sparke once kindled be, you all. . . . . .  272  Psalm II            29
SPARKS
   Or to the Sun for wonders seeme small sparks of a candle:. .   34  1st Eclogues 13    79
   Due sighes blowe out all sparkes of joyfull light, . . . .   74  Arcadia III   42    11
SPARROW
   Pas. But long have I a sparrow gailie drest, . . . . . . .   54  2nd Eclogues 29    84
   The Horse, good shape; the Sparrow, lust to playe; . . . .  101  3rd Eclogues 66    81
   To catch hir sparrow which from hir did swerve,. . . . . .  244  Other Poems    4    84
   No grasse, no trees, nor yet hir sparrow might . . . . . .  245  Other Poems    4   111
SPARROW'S
   The Falcon's fercenes, Sparrow's letchery, . . . . . . . .   28  1st Eclogues 10    79
SPARROWS
   There came a chariot faire by doves and sparrowes guided:. .  118  4th Eclogues 73    59
SPARTANS
   Or do you cutted Spartanes imitate?. . . . . . . . . . . .  225  Astrophil     92     3
SPEAK
   Foole that I am that with my dogges speake grewe.. . . . .   27  1st Eclogues 10    19
   Doe speake high wordes, when all the coaste is cleare, . .   27  1st Eclogues 10    32
   If mine eyes can speake to doo harty errande,. . . . . . .   30  1st Eclogues 12     1
   But if eyes can speake to doo harty errande, . . . . . . .   31  1st Eclogues 12    25
   None can speake of a wound with skill, if he have not a
      wound felt.. . . . . . . . . . . . . . . . . . . . . . .   33  1st Eclogues 13    71
   Then kneling to the ground, oft thus do I speake to that
      Image: . . . . . . . . . . . . . . . . . . . . . . . . .   36  1st Eclogues 13   146
   Pas. But here is Dicus old; let him then speake the woord, .   52  2nd Eclogues 29    27
   For so yet of a conquest speake thou may.. . . . . . . . .   56  2nd Eclogues 29   140
   What ere you see, thinke, touch, kisse, speake, or love, . .   60  2nd Eclogues 30   123
   Howe can they be unkind? speake for th'hast narroly pri'de.
      pride.. . . . . . . . . . . . . . . . . . . . . . . . .   65  2nd Eclogues 31    43
   To speake without an answere.. . . . . . . . . . . . . . .   65  2nd Eclogues 32     6
   No beast should freely speake, but onely he. . . . . . . .  101  3rd Eclogues 66   105
   Lord, what bywords they speake, what spite they spit?. . . .  105  3rd Eclogues 67    48
   No man doth speake aright, who speakes in feare. . . . . .  106  3rd Eclogues 67    84
   To speak with her, while freely speak we maye. . . . . . .  107  3rd Eclogues 67   120
   But, but alas, like a man condemn'd doth crave to be heard
      speake, . . . . . . . . . . . . . . . . . . . . . . . .  122  4th Eclogues 74    23
   Thus great with child to speake, and helplesse in my
      throwes . . . . . . . . . . . . . . . . . . . . . . . .  165  Astrophil      1    12
   Some Lovers speake when they their Muses entertaine, . . . .  167  Astrophil      6     1
   I can speake what I feele, and feele as much as they,. . . .  168  Astrophil      6    12
   What words so ere she speake perswades for thee, . . . . .  171  Astrophil     12 V  7
   "What idler thing, then speake and not be hard?" . . . . .  182  Astrophil     34     9
   What harder thing then smart, and not to speake? . . . . .  182  Astrophil     34    10
   Where truth it selfe must speake like flatterie? . . . . .  182  Astrophil     35     2
   My thoughts I speake, and what I speake doth flow. . . . .  204  Astrophil     74    10
```

SPEAK   (CONTINUED)   PAGE   TITLE   LINE
     But lo, while I do speake, it groweth noone with me, ...   205 Astrophil   76   9
     And even while I do speake, my death wounds bleeding be: . .   214 A&S 5th Song   52
     For that doth Musike speake, ...   215 A&S 6th Song   8
     But when their tongues could not speake, ...   218 A&S 8th Song   25
     Thus to speake in love and wonder: . . . .   218 A&S 8th Song   28
     And bravely speake to them, with breath of wrathful fire,. .   271 Psalm II   11
     Somewhat to speake of his due praise,. . . . .   319 Psalm XXXIV   10
     Speake thou for me against wrong speaking foes,. . . . . . .   321 Psalm XXXV   1
     Thy justice witness shall and speake Thy prayse. . . . . . .   323 Psalm XXXV   72
     Moving, she seem'd at once to kisse, and speake. . . . . . .   244 Other Poems   4   96
     With in himselfe of hir deare selfe to speake, ...   255 Other Poems   4   534
SPEAKER
     Blasphemous words the speaker vaine do prove. . . . .   59 2nd Eclogues 30   67
SPEAKETH
     I yet should know a young man speaketh now,. . . . .   25 1st Eclogues 9   97
SPEAKING
     Sweete speaking oft a currish hart reclaimes. . . . .   60 2nd Eclogues 30   115
     What be the fruites of speaking arte? what growes by the
        words? Words. . . . .   64 2nd Eclogues 31   30
     Speake thou for me against wrong speaking foes,. . . . . . .   321 Psalm XXXV   1
     Speaking ev'ill, thinking deceit. . . . .   328 Psalm XXXVIII 36
     Little hearing, speaking lesse;. . . . .   328 Psalm XXXVIII 39
     I fain of them would speaking be;. . . . .   331 Psalm XL   23
SPEAKS
     No man doth speake aright, who speakes in feare. . . . . . .   106 3rd Eclogues 67   84
     Proofe speakes too much to us that feeling triall have. . . . 119 4th Eclogues 73   108
     But who by hearesay speakes, and hath not fully felt . . . .   153 Cert Sonnets 24   6
     What words so ere she speakes perswades for thee,. . . . . .   171 Astrophil   12   7
     "Stella, whose voice when it speakes,. . . . .   219 A&S 8th Song   37
SPEAR
     But in Vert field Mars bare a golden speare, ...   171 Astrophil   13   5
SPEARS
     Ashe makes speares which shieldes do resist, her force no
        repulse takes: . . . .   36 1st Eclogues 13   136
SPECIAL
     Let speciall care upon thy flock be staid, ...   26 1st Eclogues 9   133
     To all her limmes a spetiall grace,. . . . .   90 Arcadia III 62   135
     To onely thee thou seest we graunt this speciall grace . . .   119 4th Eclogues 73   95
     And aske the reason of that speciall grace,. . . . .   126 4th Eclogues 75   40
     Nor nourish speciall lockes of vowed haire,. . . . .   191 Astrophil   54   3
     Who since he hath, by Nature's speciall grace, ...   206 Astrophil   78   9
SPECKLED
     A ruddie haire his cote, with fine long specled face:. . . .   53 2nd Eclogues 29   42
SPECULATION
     Such wisedome, that in her lives speculation:. . . . .   69 2nd Eclogues 34   35
SPED
     Will. God shield us from such Dames. If so our Downes be
        sped,. . . . .   344 Possibly   1   39
SPEECH
     And plaine speech oft then quaint phrase better framed is. .   14 1st Eclogues 7   6
     Such wandring reasons in thy speech I finde. . . . .   25 1st Eclogues 9   98
     While I there speache in my rude ryminge pende. . . . . . .   62 2nd Eclogues 30   187
     Arte? what can be that art which thou dost meane by thy
        speche? Speche. . . . .   64 2nd Eclogues 31   29
     Undermin'd with a speech the pearcer of thoughts. . . . . .   68 2nd Eclogues 33   16
     Vertue, beawtie, and speach, did strike, wound, charme,. . .   84 Arcadia III 60   1
     (For then their language was a perfect speech) . . . .   100 3rd Eclogues 66   65
     Such is their speech, who be of sober wit; . . . .   104 3rd Eclogues 67   46
     To them that would make speech of speech arise,. . . . . . .   178 Astrophil   27   4
     By such unsuted speech should hindred be. . . . .   190 Astrophil   51   14
     Nor give each speech a full point of a grone,. . . . .   191 Astrophil   54   4
     With choisest flowers my speech to engarland so; . . . . . .   192 Astrophil   55   2
     Nor other sugring of my speech to prove, ...   192 Astrophil   55   10
     That in one speech two Negatives affirme. . . . .   196 Astrophil   63   14
     Her eye's-speech is translated thus by thee: . . . .   199 Astrophil   67   5
     As consterd in true speech, the name of heav'n it beares,. .   205 Astrophil   77   11
     Let eares heare speech, which wit to wonder ties,. . . . . .   210 Astrophil   85   11
     Thought waited on delight, and speech did follow thought:. .   212 A&S 5th Song   2
     Yet thought and speech do live, though metamorphosd quite:. . 212 A&S 5th Song   14
     That speech falles now to blame, which did thy honour raise,   213 A&S 5th Song   17
     "Graunt, o graunt, but speech alas,. . . . .   219 A&S 8th Song   45
     There his hands in their speech, faine . . . .   219 A&S 8th Song   65
     Then she spake; her speech was such, ...   220 A&S 8th Song   69
     There is no speech, no language which. . . . .   293 Psalm XIX   9
     Speeche without ende were better not begin. . . . .   259 Other Poems   5   104
SPEECHES
     How nice to touch? how all her speeches peized be? . . . . .   15 1st Eclogues 7   35
     In speeches nobly placed:. . . . .   216 A&S 6th Song   26
     My speeches all Thy marvailes shall descry:. . . . .   279 Psalm IX   2
     Most to Thy lawdes will I my speeches bind. . . . .   322 Psalm XXXV   48
SPEECH'S
     O voice, o face, maugre my speeche's might,. . . . .   194 Astrophil   58   12
SPEED
     A kind of grace it is to slay with speed. . . . .   189 Astrophil   48   14
     Deliver me, Deliver me in speed, ...   312 Psalm XXXI   5
     On him and he will make it speed. . . . .   324 Psalm XXXVII   12
SPEEDY
     In speedie helpe, thanke worthie frends appeare. . . . . . .   81 Arcadia III 53   14

```
                                                      PAGE    TITLE            LINE
SPELL
    Now child, a lesson new you shall begin to spell:. . . . . .  213 A&S 5th Song      35
SPELLED
    In her sight I a lesson new have speld,. . . . . . . . . . .  173 Astrophil    16   12
SPELLING
    Who will read must first learne spelling.. . . . . . . . . .  203 A&S 2nd Song      24
SPEND
    In hunting fearefull beastes, do spend some dayes, . . . . .   25 1st Eclogues  9  123
    As for the rest, howe shepeheardes spend their daies,. . . .   28 1st Eclogues 10   46
    When yonger dooth in smoke his vertue spend. . . . . . . . .   38 Arcadia II   15    4
    Sore beaten doth her mast of Comforte spende:. . . . . . . .  114 4th Eclogues 72   45
    And while their line of yeares they did in vertue spende.. .  117 4th Eclogues 73   38
    While Love on me doth all his quiver spend, . . . . . . . . .  171 Astrophil    14    4
    Why doest thou spend the treasures of thy sprite,. . . . . .  200 Astrophil    68    5
    Lord help, for ev'en my bones their marrow spend . . . . . .  276 Psalm VI           7
    He lends, he gives, more he doth spend . . . . . . . . . . .  326 Psalm XXXVII      65
    To spend for harms, although they touch you not: . . . . . .  242 Other Poems   4   10
SPENDS
    That without love she spends her yeares of love: . . . . . .   17 1st Eclogues  7   98
SPENT
    This winde he spent: but when my Kala glasseth all . . . . .   16 1st Eclogues  7   55
    Thy too much zeale, I feare thy braine hath spent. . . . . .   28 1st Eclogues 10   63
    And Venus seemes, to make up her, she spent herselfe.. . . .   49 2nd Eclogues 28   66
    O soule, whose love in her is onely spent, . . . . . . . . .   60 2nd Eclogues 30  122
    His thoughtes in you, where so sweete thoughtes were spent,.   78 Arcadia III  49   10
    But they or spent, or made of slender might, . . . . . . . .  102 3rd Eclogues 66  134
    But these be your love-toyes, which still are spent. . . . .  106 3rd Eclogues 67   94
    But ah her flight hath my dead reliques spent. . . . . . . .  115 4th Eclogues 72   80
    Strephon. But ah her flight hath my dead reliques spent, . .  115 4th Eclogues 72   81
    Or if thy mourning notes be fully spent, . . . . . . . . . .  127 4th Eclogues 75   64
    But since my thoughts in thinking still are spent, . . . . .  148 Cert Sonnets 19   13
    What streames of teares she spent, . . . . . . . . . . . . .  158 Cert Sonnets 28   22
    But that my wealth I have most idly spent. . . . . . . . . .  174 Astrophil    18    8
    Avise themselves that they are vainely spent.. . . . . . . .  174 Astrophil    19    8
    When far spent night perswades each mortall eye, . . . . . .  230 Astrophil    99    1
    I thought all words were lost, that were not spent of thee:.  212 A&S 5th Song       4
    As both in both are spent. . . . . . . . . . . . . . . . . .  216 A&S 6th Song      36
    For in their mouth not One cleere word is spent, . . . . . .  275 Psalm V           25
    When fire seven times hath spent his earthly parts.. . . . .  285 Psalm XII         21
    That Thy anger being spent, . . . . . . . . . . . . . . . . .  335 Psalm XLII        36
    So is in her the best of Nature spent, . . . . . . . . . . .  249 Other Poems   4  299
SPHERE
    Your presence (sister deare) first to my Moony spheare,. . .  119 4th Eclogues 73  103
SPHERES
    If the sencelesse spheares doo yet hold a musique, . . . . .   30 1st Eclogues 12   13
    For the blacke starres those Spheares containe,. . . . . . .   86 Arcadia III  62   15
    She, whose lest word brings from the spheares their musique,  113 4th Eclogues 71   68
    The ever-turning spheares, the never-moving ground;. . . . .  118 4th Eclogues 73   44
    O eyes, which do the Spheares of beautie move, . . . . . . .  185 Astrophil    42    1
SPIED
    When first he spied my love? how oft he said to me,. . . . .   16 1st Eclogues  7   50
    I spied a thrush where she did make her nest,. . . . . . . .   54 2nd Eclogues 29   82
    Looke here, I say." I look'd, and Stella spide,. . . . . . .  191 Astrophil    53    8
    Till that he spied old Geron could no more,. . . . . . . . .  250 Other Poems   4  307
SPILL
    Save then my soule, spill not my thoughts well heaped, . . .   16 1st Eclogues  7   80
    Plangus. And shall shee dye? shall cruell fier spill . . . .   59 2nd Eclogues 30   83
    At last for sport their sillie lives did spill.. . . . . . .  103 3rd Eclogues 66  147
    Ncr no more wording with a worde to spill mee. . . . . . . .  138 Cert Sonnets  5   18
    Your fearfull words why do you spill . . . . . . . . . . . .  283 Psalm XI           2
    That it doth spill. . . . . . . . . . . . . . . . . . . . . .  301 Psalm XXIII       21
SPILLED
    A heape of sweetes she is, where nothing spilled is; . . . .   15 1st Eclogues  7   28
    Thus is our mind with too much minding spilled.. . . . . . .   62 2nd Eclogues 30  175
    Crocodile, teares, which might be falsely spilde:. . . . . .  101 3rd Eclogues 66   96
SPILLETH
    Alas, me thinkes, my weakned voice but spilleth, . . . . . .  127 4th Eclogues 75   97
SPILLING
    Thy father bids thee save, and chides for spilling.. . . . .   16 1st Eclogues  7   79
SPIRIT
    Kisse her from me, and say unto her spirite, . . . . . . . .   79 Arcadia III  51   13
    Whose spirit falshood flyeth.. . . . . . . . . . . . . . . .  314 Psalm XXXII        6
SPIRITED
    In thee or sprites or spirited gastlinesse:. . . . . . . . .  229 Astrophil    96   11
SPIRIT'S
    Her sence too weake to beare her spirit's mighte.. . . . . .   79 Arcadia III  51    4
SPIRITS
    Boulon. Thy wailing words do much my spirits move, . . . . .   60 2nd Eclogues 30  125
    (Which life is cald) were mov'd their spirits to repose, . .  116 4th Eclogues 73    5
    Earth take this earth, wherein my spirits languish.. . . . .  136 Cert Sonnets  3   16
    Till wounded, blind, and wearied Spirites, lose. . . . . . .  144 Cert Sonnets 15   11
    I heare a crye of spirits faint and blinde,. . . . . . . . .  148 Cert Sonnets 20    7
    What kind of fires they be in which those spirits melt,. . .  153 Cert Sonnets 24    7
    And none invisible, but Spirites, can goe. . . . . . . . . .  253 Other Poems   4  456
SPIRITS'
    Despaire my fielde; the flowers spirits' warrs:. . . . . . .   18 1st Eclogues  7  139
    Wherein she suffring all her spirits' languish,. . . . . . .  137 Cert Sonnets  4   15
SPIT
    Talking time borrowe for to spitt their vennim . . . . . . .   50 2nd Eclogues 28 V886
    Lord, what bywords they speake, what spite they spit?. . . .  105 3rd Eclogues 67   48
```

SPITE

		PAGE	TITLE		LINE
His horned head doth seeme the heaven to spignt:		21	1st Eclogues	8	29
"And ev'n in that love, shall I reserve him a spite".		30	1st Eclogues	11	18
Therefore, alas, you use vile Vulcan's spight, ...		60	2nd Eclogues	30	107
With swelling hart in spite and due disdainfulnes.		61	2nd Eclogues	30	153
Who full of guiltie spite, ...		82	Arcadia III	55	9
Well grounded, noble, due, spite, rage, disdaine,.		84	Arcadia III	60	10
All privatenes, selfe-seeking, inward spite, ...		93	3rd Eclogues	63	65
Lord, what bywords they speake, what spite they spit?. . . .		105	3rd Eclogues	67	48
But thus with irefull eyes, and face that shooke with spite.		119	4th Eclogues	73	101
While we for mutuall spight a striving passion fed.		120	4th Eclogues	73	118
Like foe, whose wits inclin'd to deadly spite, ...		135	Cert Sonnets	2	3
Biting my trewand pen, beating my selfe for spite, ...		165	Astrophil	1	13
That lap doth lap, nay lets, in spite of spite,.		194	Astrophil	59	10
But now spite of my heart my mouth will stay,.		207	Astrophil	80	10
Mine eyes then only winke, for spite perchance,.		230	Astrophil	98	13
Deere, do reason no such spite, ...		234	A&S 11th Song		28
Venom'd with godless spight, ...		273	Psalm III		29
Which full of spight, of Pride and cruelty,.		313	Psalm XXXI		50
Ev'en gnashing teeth, to witness more their spight.		322	Psalm XXXV		42
There did he make hir laugh in spite of woe, ...		247	Other Poems	4	197
No, no, it was in spite of wisdome's song, ...		247	Other Poems	4	222

SPITED

| I never spited you, but thought you overwise. . . . . | | 121 | 4th Eclogues | 73 | 150 |

SPITEFULNESS

| As for thy wish to my enraged spitefulnesse, ... | | 51 | 2nd Eclogues | 28 | 111 |

SPLENDOR

| Two gleaming Sunnes of splendour like I see, ... | | 81 | Arcadia III | 55 | 4 |

SPOIL

Seemde but to spoyle the foode of thoughts long famished.. .		16	1st Eclogues	7	69
Whose sprite all sprites can spoile, raise, damne, or save:.		17	1st Eclogues	7	110
Cormoraunt's glutt, Kite's spoile, king fisher's waste,. . .		28	1st Eclogues	10	78
Thou God, whose youth was deckt with spoyle of Python's					
skin		44	Arcadia II	26	5
Will spoile the earth of his most rich attire.		59	2nd Eclogues	30	88
Which for reward spoile it with vaine annoyes.		174	Astrophil	18	11
So piercing pawes, as spoyle when they embrace,.		206	Astrophil	78	10
Of foes the spoile is evill, far worse of constant lovers. .		214	A&S 5th Song		48
He waites to spoyle the simple men:.		282	Psalm X		38

SPOILED

With outward force and inward treason spoild.		11	Arcadia I	2	4
Is gone, is gone from these our spoyled forrests,.		113	4th Eclogues	71	71
Our offrings spoil'd, our priests from priesthood are					
displac'd.		119	4th Eclogues	73	110
Farewell our light, farewell our spoiled treasure:		130	4th Eclogues	76	37

SPOILING

| Spoiling their flock, or while twixt them they strive. . . . | | 99 | 3rd Eclogues | 66 | 35 |

SPOILS

Helples his plaint, who spoyles himselfe of blisse..		13	Arcadia I	4	10
That we be her spoiles?.		31	1st Eclogues	12	20
P. O Passion, passe on feeble Reason's spoiles..		46	2nd Eclogues	27	24
Upon thy spoiles, which never should lye waste?.		59	2nd Eclogues	30	93
From him whose force did in their spoiles appeare.		321	Psalm XXXV		24

SPOKEN

I would have spoken out: but out they both did crie; . . .		121	4th Eclogues	73	167
But no more wordes, thoughe such a worde bee spoken, ...		138	Cert Sonnets	5	17
Ungratefull who is cald, the worst of evils is spok'n. . . .		213	A&S 5th Song		42
With what she had done and spoken, ...		221	A&S 8th Song		103

SPORT

That sport it is to see with howe greate art		27	1st Eclogues	10	41
And makes our home good sport with dauncing bolt upright.. .		53	2nd Eclogues	29	46
In that sweete seate the Boy doth sport:		88	Arcadia III	62	83
At last for sport their sillie lives did spill..		103	3rd Eclogues	66	147
Where shade from Sunne, and sporte I sought in evening,. . .		111	4th Eclogues	71	14
Her giftes my study was, her beauties were my sporte:. . . .		117	4th Eclogues	73	41
As his maine force, choise sport, and easefull stay.		186	Astrophil	43	4
In sport I suckt, while she asleepe did lie, ...		203	Astrophil	73	6
With sight made dymme with dayly teares another's sport to					
see.		343	Possibly	1	4
So Lords with sport of Stagg and Hearon full		245	Other Poems	4	135
Self-gard with mildnes, Sport with Majesty:.		247	Other Poems	4	214

SPORTS

And let thine eyes to other sports be framed..		25	1st Eclogues	9	122
Our sports murdering our selves, our musiques wailing, . . .		109	Arcadia IV	70	29
In Martiall sports I had my cunning tride, ...		191	Astrophil	53	1
That comfort in these sports you like, my mynde his comfort					
tryes.		343	Possibly	1	14
The honest sports of earthy lodging prove.		243	Other Poems	4	42
These sports shepheards deviz'd such faults to show.		248	Other Poems	4	241
To see the sportes of double-shining day,.		251	Other Poems	4	362
Then sports grew paines, all talking tediouse, ...		253	Other Poems	4	433
"The sportes wherin I wonted to do well, ...		254	Other Poems	4	465

SPOT

| Passing the hate-spott Ermelin. . . . . | | 89 | Arcadia III | 62 | 116 |

SPOTLESS

Till spotlesse soule unto thy bosome flye, '.		40	Arcadia II	18	17
A spotlesse mine of Alablaster..		88	Arcadia III	62	80
Do please all eyes, and spotlesse do endure.		91	3rd Eclogues	63	25
(She beckned unto me) as yet of spotlesse truth, ...		120	4th Eclogues	73	138
But if all faith, like spotlesse Ermine ly		212	Astrophil	86	5

SPOTLESS   (CONTINUED)   PAGE   TITLE   LINE
  Ev'en spotless verity. . . . . 304 Psalm XXV   39
  Which seated is, in spotlesse honor's fielde, ... 345 Possibly   4   2
SPOTS
  And titles are but spots to such a worthe, ... 18 1st Eclogues   7   132
  And we shall find more spottes then Leopard's skinne. . . . . 29 1st Eclogues   10   95
  Let other fowler spots away be blowne; . . . . 105 3rd Eclogues   67   55
SPOTTED
  My virgin life no spotted thought shall staine. . . . . 40 Arcadia II   18   6
  The Ermion, whitest skinne, spotted with nought; . . . . . . 101 3rd Eclogues   66   89
  Who, their spotted thoughts to cloak, ... 309 Psalm XXVIII   13
SPOUSE
  Who would have sworne his spowse diana was, ... 96 3rd Eclogues   64   74
SPRAT
  To crammed mawes a spratt new Stomake brings. . . . . 245 Other Poems   4   134
SPREAD
  Nico. In deed the witch thy dam her crouch from shoulder
    spred, ... 52 2nd Eclogues   29   13
  Pas. Thy name (O Cosma) shall with praise be spread, ... 56 2nd Eclogues   29   126
  Her cheekes with kindly claret spred. . . . . 86 Arcadia III   62   23
  First having all their giftes upon faire Mira spred. . . . . 121 4th Eclogues   73   178
  Ring out your belles, let mourning shewes be spread, ... 159 Cert Sonnets   30   1
  Since in thine armes, if learnd fame truth hath spread, . . . 198 Astrophil   65   13
  Candles out, and curtaines spread: . . . . 211 A&S 4th Song   38
  To him my voyce I spread, ... 272 Psalm III   14
  And mercy spredd abroad. . . . . 304 Psalm XXV   40
  So shall I sacrifices spred, ... 307 Psalm XXVII   33
  I understand what rayling great men spred; . . . . 313 Psalm XXXI   37
  For my faults are highly spred . . . . 327 Psalm XXXVIII   10
  The trees spred out their armes to shade hir face, ... 245 Other Poems   4   109
SPREADING
  Like laurell fresh himself out spreading. . . . . 327 Psalm XXXVII   90
SPRENT
  O lippes, that kist that hand with my teares sprent; . . . . 60 2nd Eclogues   30   120
*SPRING
  Pas. Alas, when I in spring meet roses rathe, ... 54 2nd Eclogues   29   78
  You that do search for everie purling spring, ... 172 Astrophil   15   1
  Some that know how my spring I did addresse, ... 176 Astrophil   23   5
  That, from that sea deriv'd, teares' spring did flow. . . . . 187 Astrophil   45   8
  My spring appeares, o see what here doth grow. . . . . 200 Astrophil   69   8
  In this pleasant spring must see . . . . 222 A&S 9th Song   28
  Yet from his mouth doth spring . . . . 282 Psalm X   27
  And drink from out Thy pleasures' spring, ... 324 Psalm XXXVI   23
SPRINGETH
  While late bare earth, proud of new clothing springeth, . . . 137 Cert Sonnets   4   3
  Since babie mine, from me thy watching springeth, ... 139 Cert Sonnets   6   7
  This song from deathe's sorrow springeth: . . . . 140 Cert Sonnets   7   36
  Where that heat of all heates springeth, ... 155 Cert Sonnets   26   7
*SPRINGS
  Whence can pride come there, since springs of beawty be
    thence? Thence. . . . . 65 2nd Eclogues   31   44
  Yee Nimphes which haunt the springs in pleasant vallies, . . 111 4th Eclogues   71   2
  Thine earth now springs, mine fadeth, ... 137 Cert Sonnets   4   11
  Above line repeated at following location. . . . . 137 Cert Sonnets   4   23
  To which sweet springs of waters neighbours be, ... 270 Psalm I   8
  That springs from Thy salvation; . . . . 297 Psalm XXI   18
  Tell me, if your diverted springs become . . . . 257 Other Poems   5   37
SPRINGTIME
  So may your Make, this wholsome springtime aire, ... 257 Other Poems   5   42
  Tell me, if husband springtime leave your lande, ... 257 Other Poems   5   50
SPRITE
  Teach me what circle may acquaint her sprite, ... 17 1st Eclogues   7   101
  Whose sprite all sprites can spoile, raise, damne, or save:. 17 1st Eclogues   7   110
  Earth, sea, ayre, fire, heav'n, hell, and gastly sprite. . . 23 1st Eclogues   9   40
  Let not a puppet abuse thy sprite, Kings' Crownes do not
    helpe them . . . . 34 1st Eclogues   13   84
  Echo, what do I gett yelding my sprite to my grieves?
    Grieves. . . . . 63 2nd Eclogues   31   5
  Keepe thy sprite from abuse, here no abuse doth haunte. . . . 69 2nd Eclogues   34   27
  Tyre on, despaier, uppon my tyred sprite. . . . . 74 Arcadia III   42   12
  "My sweetest joy, the comfort of my sprite, ... 96 3rd Eclogues   64   92
  Full glad they were and tooke the naked sprite, ... 101 3rd Eclogues   66   78
  She waited mistresse' will: who thus disclosd her spright. . 119 4th Eclogues   73   92
  She sackes my rendred sprite. . . . . 155 Cert Sonnets   26   4
  Above line repeated at following locations . . . . 155 Cert Sonnets   26   15
  . . . . 156 Cert Sonnets   26   26
  Or sprite, disdaine of such disdaine to have? . . . . 188 Astrophil   47   6
  Why doest thou spend the treasures of thy sprite, ... 200 Astrophil   68   5
  Care shining in mine eyes, faith in my sprite, ... 202 Astrophil   72   11
  But of the Other side, the poore in sprite . . . . 281 Psalm IX   56
  Thus freely saith he in his sprite: . . . . 282 Psalm X   45
  How long shall I consult with carefull sprite . . . . 285 Psalm XIII   5
  God's doomes be right, and cheer the sprite, ... 294 Psalm XIX   33
  So shall my spryte be still upright. . . . . 295 Psalm XIX   57
  Ah! from the sword yet save my vital sprite, ... 299 Psalm XXII   47
  Into Thy hands I do commend my sprite, ... 312 Psalm XXXI   13
  In sprite afflicted finds. . . . . 320 Psalm XXXIV   68
  In sprite that I shall have Thy helping hand. . . . . 321 Psalm XXXV   6
  As this same sprite about my fancies blinde, ... 255 Other Poems   4   502

	PAGE	TITLE		LINE
SPRITES				
Whose sprite all sprites can spoile, raise, damne, or save:.	17	1st Eclogues	7	110
Holde thou my hart, establish thou my sprights:.	40	Arcadia II	18	15
What needed so high sprites such mansions blind?	57	2nd Eclogues	30	14
The flying sprites which trees by rootes up teare.	114	4th Eclogues	72	36
That heavie earth, not fierie sprites may plaine?.	142	Cert Sonnets	11	6
And strange things cost too deare for my poore sprites.. . .	166	Astrophil	3	11
My boiling sprites did thither soone incline,.	172	Astrophil	16	3
My life forgets to nourish languisht sprites;.	186	Astrophil	42	10
Scortch not, but onely do darke chilling sprites remove. . .	205	Astrophil	76	8
Least joy, by Nature apt sprites to enlarge, ...	210	Astrophil	85	3
In night of sprites the gastly powers stur,.	229	Astrophil	96	10
In thee or sprites or spirited gastlinesse:.	229	Astrophil	96	11
By most cruel sprites, ...	336	Psalm XLIII		4
SPRUNG				
For proofe of man, who sprong of heav'nly fire	25	1st Eclogues	9	100
All thoughts so spronge, are from their dwelling driv'n, . .	83	Arcadia III	57	11
From sucklings hath Thy honour sproong,.	278	Psalm VIII		5
So let words sprung from my weake tongue,.	295	Psalm XIX		61
Oh, give me not, for there are sproong	308	Psalm XXVII		56
SPRUNGEN				
Hate fully growne, Absence new sprongen out.	115	4th Eclogues	72	58
SPUN				
Sore signe it is, the Lord's last thred is spun.	150	Cert Sonnets	22	14
(Who Neptune's webb on daunger's distaff spun)	251	Other Poems	4	374
SPUR				
Girt fast by memorie, and while I spurre	189	Astrophil	49	10
And no spurre can his resty race renew,.	207	Astrophil	80	12
(Spurd with love's spur, though gald and shortly raind . . .	230	Astrophil	98	7
SPURRED				
(Spurd with love's spur, though gald and shortly raind . . .	230	Astrophil	98	7
SPURS				
My horse, he spurres with sharpe desire my hart:	189	Astrophil	49	11
SPY				
She byd me spie her babie in the brooke, ...	55	2nd Eclogues	29	112
Nowe that I spye the haven my thoughtes requyre, ...	72	Arcadia III	37	15
So Tyran he no fitter place could spie,.	175	Astrophil	20	5
As what my hart still sees thou canst not spie?.	235	Astrophil	105	4
Feare not else, none can us spie:.	211	A&S 4th Song		22
SPYING				
Nct spying faults, nor in plaine errors blinde,.	98	3rd Eclogues	65	7
Till spying well she welnigh weary was,.	251	Other Poems	4	377
SQUARE				
Pearching within square royall rooves, ...	89	Arcadia III	62	114
SQUIRRELS'				
Now bolt and cudgill squirrels' leape do move.	243	Other Poems	4	44
STAFF				
His good strong staffe my slippry yeares upbore:	99	3rd Eclogues	66	37
Farewell o golden staffe, the weake man's might:.	129	4th Eclogues	76	3
But He, staffe of my age, He staid my stumbling state. . . .	291	Psalm XVIII		39
Thy rodd and Thy staffe be	301	Psalm XXIII		14
STAG				
The Stagge did give the harme eschewing feare.	101	3rd Eclogues	66	91
So Lords with sport of Stagg and Hearon full	245	Other Poems	4	135
STAGE				
Like players plast to fill a filthy stage, ...	57	2nd Eclogues	30	20
STAGGERING				
But lo, soon as they did me staggering see,.	322	Psalm XXXV		37
STAGS				
To match with light foot staggs he made my foot so light . .	292	Psalm XVIII		61
STAIN				
My virgin life no spotted thought shall staine..	40	Arcadia II	18	6
But this is one that doth his musicke staine..	54	2nd Eclogues	29	62
Boulon. How long wilt thou with monefull musicke staine. . .	58	2nd Eclogues	30	38
O voice that doth, the Thrush in shrilnes staine,.	76	Arcadia III	46	4
The matchlesse paire, even praise doth staine.	86	Arcadia III	62	16
Which that no chaunce may staine,.	91	3rd Eclogues	63	8
Or cruell (still) time did your beautie staine:.	148	Cert Sonnets	19	8
Where former blisse present evils do staine, ...	153	Cert Sonnets	24	12
I now then staine thy white with vagabunding shame,.	214	A&S 5th Song		68
Staine with your blasphemys? till when	273	Psalm IV		8
Nor neighbour hurts by deed, nor doth with slaunder stain. .	287	Psalm XV		6
Bless'ed is the man whose filthy stain	314	Psalm XXXII		1
STAINED				
But so our hartes keepe downe, with vice they be not stainde	45	Arcadia II	26	14
Disdainst we see thee staind with other's light.	80	Arcadia III	52	15
If you helpe not our wedlocke will be staind".	95	3rd Eclogues	64	46
Betwixt us two; how much that discord foule hath stain'd . .	119	4th Eclogues	73	106
How is thy grace by my strange fortune staind!	230	Astrophil	98	3
The seely wretch with foule affliction staind, ...	300	Psalm XXII		56
STAINETH				
Who womankind at once both deckes and stayneth?.	197	A&S 1st Song		10
STAINING				
Yee dimmy clowdes, which well employ your staynyng	127	4th Eclogues	75	67
STAINLESS				
For faultlesse length, and stainelesse hewe, ...	90	Arcadia III	62	119
Such faith, so staineles, inviolate, violent?.	124	4th Eclogues	74	70
STAINS				
Her staines are beames; vertue the fault she blamed is.. . .	49	2nd Eclogues	28	57

STAINS   (CONTINUED)   PAGE   TITLE   LINE
  Streight as Cedar, a voice staines the Cannary birds,. . . .   69 2nd Eclogues 34   33
  Within her beames wrapping his cruell staines. . . . . . .   141 Cert Sonnets 8   12
  An humble pride, a skorne that favour staines: . . . . . .   151 Cert Sonnets 22   65
STAKE
  (Tide to the stake of doubt) strange passions baite, ...   82 Arcadia III 56   10
  A field there is where, if a stake be prest. . . . .   150 Cert Sonnets 22   41
  The earth, her eares: the stake is my request: . . . . . .   151 Cert Sonnets 22   45
  Deeper still they drive the stake. . . . .   234 A&S 11th Song   35
STALE
  The sleepy kisse the moone stale:. . . . .   66 2nd Eclogues 32   28
  Then did on him who first stale downe the fire, ...   171 Astrophil   14   3
STALEST
  Not as the scrippe thou stalest, while Dorcas sleeping lay..   52 2nd Eclogues 29   8
STALK
  But like the feeble flower (whose stalke cannot sustaine . .   117 4th Eclogues 73   21
STALKS
  With Lycoras stalkes of Porphiry,. . . . .   87 Arcadia III 62 V 57
STALL
  Nature's praise, Vertue's stall, Cupid's cold fire,. . . . .   206 Astrophil   80   3
STAMMERING
  Wry words, and stam'ring, or els doltish dombe,. . . . . .   254 Other Poems   4   471
STAMPS
  One brings the stuffe, the other stamps the coine, ...   20 1st Eclogues 8   3
STAND
  By raysing up, upon thy selfe to stand.. . . . .   23 1st Eclogues 9   51
  Nor golden manacles, stand for a paradise, ...   69 2nd Eclogues 34   25
  My cheefest parte, wherin do chieflye stand. . . . .   70 Arcadia III 35   13
  Ape great thing gave, though he did mowing stand,. . . . .   101 3rd Eclogues 66   97
  To stand unto my will: their will they made me know. . . .   121 4th Eclogues 73   157
  Nor glorious Fooles stand in Thy awfull sight. . . . . . .   274 Psalm V   12
  And by the syly stand. . . . .   282 Psalm X   52
  Shall in endlesse pleasures stand! . . . .   289 Psalm XVI   44
  That Thou by Faithfull Men wilt stand. . . . .   290 Psalm XVII   23
  As he before his eyes did see my justice stand,. . . . . .   292 Psalm XVIII   48
  Wee stand upright, while they their fall did frame.. . . .   296 Psalm XX   32
  With mowes and nodds they stand about me flocking. . . . .   299 Psalm XXII   18
  Who shall stand in his Holy place? . . . .   302 Psalm XXIV   6
  Before my eyes did stand . . . .   305 Psalm XXVI   11
  For so both day and night did stand. . . . .   315 Psalm XXXII   10
  He badd it and it did stand.. . . . .   317 Psalm XXXIII   33
  Take up Thy shield and for my succour stand, ...   321 Psalm XXXV   3
  The man whom God directs doth stand. . . . .   326 Psalm XXXVII   57
  Yea lord Thy law within my heart doth stand: . . . .   331 Psalm XL   34
STANDARD
  Of them, who in their lips Love's standerd beare;. . . . . .   191 Astrophil   54   6
STANDEST
  Why standest Thou so farr, ...   281 Psalm X   1
STANDETH
  Place standeth still amazed. . . . .   136 Cert Sonnets 3   7
STANDING
  From heavenly standing hits each mortall wight.. . . . . .   229 Astrophil   97   4
STANDS
  He never musing standes, but with himselfe will play . . . .   53 2nd Eclogues 29   43
  Your power in your beautie stands: . . . .   211 A&S 4th Song   46
  The ballance evnly stands; . . . .   283 Psalm X   60
  Where Thy sanctuary stands,. . . . .   309 Psalm XXVIII   8
  By breath of his mouth stands. . . . .   316 Psalm XXXIII   24
STAR
  I would climbe up, and bring a prettie starre, ...   55 2nd Eclogues 29   118
  Be thow my starre in this my darkest night,. . . . .   70 Arcadia III 35   4
  O lovelie starre, entitled of the morning,. . . . .   111 4th Eclogues 71   9
  And yet my Starre, because a sugred kisse. . . . .   203 Astrophil   73   5
  Stella starre of heavenly fier,. . . . .   218 A&S 8th Song   31
  O God our only starr,. . . . .   281 Psalm X   2
STARK
  Nico. She once starke nak'd did bathe a little tine; . . . .   55 2nd Eclogues 29   105
  Let me home returne, stark blinded . . . .   220 A&S 8th Song   83
STARRY
  Serve all thy starrie eyes this shame to see?. . . . .   58 2nd Eclogues 30   61
  Bringing with her those starry Nimphs, whose chace . . . . .   229 Astrophil   97   3
STARS
  More high then stars, more firme then flintie field. . . . .   3 Lady of May   2   9
  Thy stars be fal'n, plowed is thy flintie ground:. . . . . .   4 Lady of May   2   16
  The starres thy state, fortune may change thy happe. . . . .   23 1st Eclogues 9   25
  And all the starres conspired to my good,. . . . .   23 1st Eclogues 9   27
  Whose wit the starres, whose fortune fortune thralls.. . . .   23 1st Eclogues 9   31
  And so behinde foule clowdes full oft faire starres do ly
    hidden". . . . .   36 1st Eclogues 13   154
  First let them die, then passe the starres,. . . . .   44 Arcadia II   25   9
  She oft her lookes, the starres her favour bend to thee: . .   51 2nd Eclogues 28   99
  Balles to the starres, and thralles to Fortune's raigne; . .   57 2nd Eclogues 30   17
  Clymes even unto the starres, Nature is under it.. . . . . .   68 2nd Eclogues 34   9
  To Westerne wightes, what starres in East appeare? . . . . .   80 Arcadia III 52   4
  For the blacke starres those Spheares containe,. . . . . . .   86 Arcadia III 62   15
  Icleped starres; each thing to rest disposed:. . . . . . .   98 3rd Eclogues 66   10
  These stately starrs in their now shining faces, ...   108 Arcadia IV   69   9
  Did light those beamye stars which greater light did darke:.   116 4th Eclogues 73   3
  But now the starres with their strange course do binde . . .   148 Cert Sonnets 20   5
  By only those two starres in Stella's face.. . . . .   178 Astrophil   26   14

467

		PAGE	TITLE		LINE
STARS	(CONTINUED)				
Soule's joy, bend not those morning starres from me, ...		188	Astrophil	48	1
When Sun is hid, can starres such beames display?.		223	Astrophil	88	6
If I but stars upon mine armour beare, ...		233	Astrophil	104	10
Twinckling starres Love-thoughts provoke:.		210	A&S 4th Song		8
I said, thine eyes were starres, thy breasts the milk'n way,		212	A&S 5th Song		10
When Moone and starrs my thoughtes beholdeth		278	Psalm VIII		11
D. Wonder that by two so black eyes the glittering stars be past.		343	Possibly	1	28
STARS'					
And stay the starrs' inconstant constant race, ...		126	4th Eclogues	75	38
START					
Or all abroade if but a Cubb start out..		27	1st Eclogues	10	30
Let no strange dreme make her fayre body starte.		79	Arcadia III	51	8
Of all my thoughts hath neither stop nor start, ...		176	Astrophil	23	13
I start, looke, hearke, but what in closde up sence.		184	Astrophil	38	9
All visions seeme, at every bush I start:.		253	Other Poems	4	445
STARTING					
The goodman starting, askt what did her move?.		95	3rd Eclogues	64	47
STARTS					
And can crie helpe with nought but grones and starts:. . . .		136	Cert Sonnets	2	12
STARVE					
On barren sweetes they feede, and feeding sterve:.		39	Arcadia II	17	3
Till that good God make Church and Churchman starve.		167	Astrophil	5	8
Whose wages makes me beg the more, who feeds me till I sterve,.		343	Possibly	1	20
STARVED					
Himselfe onely winter-sterved.		222	A&S 9th Song		30
Those raveners' whelps oft starved be, ...		319	Psalm XXXIV		38
I am as dull as winter-sterved sheep, ...		253	Other Poems	4	442
STARVING					
To starving minds such is God Cupid's dish..		136	Cert Sonnets	2	14
STATE					
To one whose state is raised over all, ...		3	Lady of May	1	1
Your state is great, your greatnesse is our shield, ...		3	Lady of May	1	7
In thy owne seate a forraine state shall sit..		11	Arcadia I	1	8
And in thy throne, a forayne state shall sitte		11	Arcadia I	1	V806
Her minde, beames, state farre from thy weake wings banished		16	1st Eclogues	7	65
O wretched state of man in selfe division!		20	1st Eclogues	7	V966
Above line repeated at following location.		20	1st Eclogues	7	V967
And learn'd what ill a miser state doth breed, ...		21	1st Eclogues	8	22
The starres thy state, fortune may change thy happe.		23	1st Eclogues	9	25
Since she faire fierce to such a state me calls, ...		23	1st Eclogues	9	30
Showes, guilty harte doth deeme his state opprobrious. . . .		48	2nd Eclogues	28	18
Made uniforme to any state reposed..		57	2nd Eclogues	30	31
Griefe onely makes his wretched state to see		58	2nd Eclogues	30	32
Where all good haps a perfect state maintaine?		58	2nd Eclogues	30	40
In what state was I then, when I tooke this deadly disease? ease.		63	2nd Eclogues	31	8
To sing my owne decaid state..		65	2nd Eclogues	32	4
Unite in one, my state thus still to save;		70	Arcadia III	35	15
Thus then my forme, and thus my state I finde, ...		73	Arcadia III	40	13
By inward letts, of them his state possest, ...		75	Arcadia III	44	2
Blacke incke becommes the state wherein I dye.		81	Arcadia III	54	6
And state throwen downe to over-troden vallies..		112	4th Eclogues	71	30
My state more base, then are the basest vallies:		112	4th Eclogues	71	57
Who much did passe in state the stately mountaines, ...		113	4th Eclogues	71	63
With her due praise did of my state complaine, ...		141	Cert Sonnets	9	4
And write the state how my fancies bee, ...		153	Cert Sonnets	24	4
Nor change in change, though change change my state.		153	Cert Sonnets	24	23
Where, "sooner die then change my state", ...		158	Cert Sonnets	28	35
But thinke that all the Map of my state I display, ...		168	Astrophil	6	13
To keepe the pace of their first loving state.		173	Astrophil	17	4
Thinke that I thinke state errours to redresse..		176	Astrophil	23	8
To me that feele the like, thy state descries.		180	Astrophil	31	8
O blisse, fit for a nobler state then me:.		200	Astrophil	69	2
When I demaund of Phenix Stella's state, ...		225	Astrophil	92	6
Who hath the eyes which marrie state with pleasure, ...		197	A&S 1st Song		5
For though in lesse than Angel's state		279	Psalm VIII		17
But He, staffe of my age, He staid my stumbling state. . . .		291	Psalm XVIII		39
And Thy good state shall never end..		326	Psalm XXXVII		68
What do we seeke? the greatest state I see		330	Psalm XXXIX		17
To well recoverd state.		333	Psalm XLI		12
Did kick against my state.		333	Psalm XLI		32
Rewing change of wonted state, ...		262	Other Poems	7	9
STATELIER					
Or else let them in statelier glorie shine, ...		166	Astrophil	3	5
STATELY					
Yet beares he still his parents' stately gifts, ...		21	1st Eclogues	8	25
Of Phoebus' violence in shade of stately Ciprus tree, ...		31	1st Eclogues	13	12
Yee living powres enclosed in stately shrine.		40	Arcadia II	18	1
Where sweet graces erect the stately banner.		67	2nd Eclogues	33	3
Yet still, faire tree, lifte up thy stately line, ...		77	Arcadia III	47	9
Faire under these doth stately growe, ...		87	Arcadia III	62	46
Lift up their stately swelling bankes;		88	Arcadia III	62	90
O heav'n awake shewe forth thy stately face, ...		91	3rd Eclogues	63	10
These stately starrs in their now shining faces, ...		108	Arcadia IV	69	9
Strephon. Me seemes I see the high and stately mountaines, .		112	4th Eclogues	71	37
Who much did passe in state the stately mountaines, ...		113	4th Eclogues	71	63

```
STATELY           (CONTINUED)                          PAGE    TITLE          LINE
  A stately tombe to cover him deceased. . . . . . . . . . . . 126  4th Eclogues 75   59
  The stately towers come downe with greater fall: . . . . . . 143  Cert Sonnets 12    8
  And stately hilles disdaine to looke so low. . . . . . . . . 147  Cert Sonnets 18    8
  Gold is the covering of that stately place.. . . . . . . . . 169  Astrophil     9    4
  Courage therefore, and let the stately see . . . . . . . . . 346  Possibly      5    3
  Nede not the stately Muses' helpe invoke . . . . . . . . . . 242  Other Poems   4    4
  So may thy stately grace . . . . . . . . . . . . . . . . . . 256  Other Poems   5   15
STATES
  While remembrance doth both states containe. . . . . . . . . 153  Cert Sonnets 24   14
  Of Conquerd states, wherby such fame you gott? . . . . . . . 280  Psalm IX          17
STATUIE
  And statute made he never shoulde have voice,. . . . . . . .  29  1st Eclogues 10   86
STATUTES
  Still to his judgments lookt, still for his statutes car'd,. 292  Psalm XVIII       45
STAVES
  And yet to breake more staves did me addresse: . . . . . . . 191  Astrophil    53    2
  Me thought some staves he mist: if so, not much amisse:. . . 241  Other Poems   1    1
*STAY
  When trees daunce to the pype, and swift streames stay by
       the musicke, . . . . . . . . . . . . . . . . . . . . . .  33  1st Eclogues 13   47
  What foresight tels; our thoughts upon thy knowledge staye.. 45  Arcadia II   26   12
  Yet stay and well peruse,. . . . . . . . . . . . . . . . . .  80  Arcadia III  52    7
  What strange dessein hast thou my hopes to staie,. . . . . .  80  Arcadia III  53    3
  With circkled course, which no wise stay can trye, . . . . .  81  Arcadia III  54   10
  So that you may on hyer slippers stay. . . . . . . . . . . .  93  3rd Eclogues 63   76
  Our foolish lustes in honest rules to stay.. . . . . . . . . 103  3rd Eclogues 67    3
  Are we their servants growne? no doubt a noble staye:. . . . 120  4th Eclogues 73  115
  And stay the starrs' inconstant constant race, . . . . . . . 126  4th Eclogues 75   38
  Slay mee not, for stay doo not hyde thy blisses, . . . . . . 138  Cert Sonnets  5   22
  Stay to true love's melody:. . . . . . . . . . . . . . . . . 140  Cert Sonnets  7   39
  So stay her toung, that she no more say no.. . . . . . . . . 142  Cert Sonnets 10   14
  End the way, where all men stay. No, no, no, no. . . . . . . 155  Cert Sonnets 26   22
  But words came halting forth, wanting Invention's stay,. . . 165  Astrophil     1    9
  Nor so faire levell in so secret stay, . . . . . . . . . . . 175  Astrophil    20    6
  Within what bounds can one his liking stay,. . . . . . . . . 182  Astrophil    35    3
  As his maine force, choise sport, and easefull stay. . . . . 186  Astrophil    43    4
  Well Love, since this demurre our sute doth stay,. . . . . . 191  Astrophil    52   12
  Cease eager Muse, peace pen, for my sake stay, . . . . . . . 201  Astrophil    70   12
  But now spite of my heart my mouth will stay,. . . . . . . . 207  Astrophil    80   10
  And faine those Aeols' youthes there would their stay. . . . 233  Astrophil   103    9
  Long stay ere he graunt the same:. . . . . . . . . . . . . . 211  A&S 4th Song      33
  (Knees on ground he then did stay) . . . . . . . . . . . . . 219  A&S 8th Song      50
  My Deare God stay me.. . . . . . . . . . . . . . . . . . . . 276  Psalm VI          12
  O Lord my God, Thou art my trustfull stay. . . . . . . . . . 277  Psalm VII          1
  By them whose minds on hatefull thoughts do stay:. . . . . . 280  Psalm IX          38
  Thou my lord, Thou art my stay,. . . . . . . . . . . . . . . 287  Psalm XVI          5
  Thou gavest me saving shield, Thy right hand was my stay;. . 292  Psalm XVIII       64
  On beauty His my eyes to stay. . . . . . . . . . . . . . . . 307  Psalm XXVII       22
  For then my Hill Good God did stay;. . . . . . . . . . . . . 311  Psalm XXX         22
  Thou art my God, my time on thee doth stay;. . . . . . . . . 313  Psalm XXXI        41
  Who stay for God, in blisse shall stay.. . . . . . . . . . . 325  Psalm XXXVII      24
  Stay then Thy wrath, that I may strength receive . . . . . . 330  Psalm XXXIX       41
  And my weake steps did stay. . . . . . . . . . . . . . . . . 331  Psalm XL          10
  My God, O make no stay.. . . . . . . . . . . . . . . . . . . 332  Psalm XL          70
  But triumph well may I, whom Thou dost stay. . . . . . . . . 334  Psalm XLI         41
  (His marke a Piller was devoid of stay,. . . . . . . . . . . 243  Other Poems   4   70
  Till hard by them both he and she did stay.. . . . . . . . . 244  Other Poems   4   88
  Pas could not stay, but over him did rake, . . . . . . . . . 248  Other Poems   4  259
  So they three did togither idly stay,. . . . . . . . . . . . 250  Other Poems   4  329
  She chide you not for stay,. . . . . . . . . . . . . . . . . 257  Other Poems   5   35
*STAYED
  Let speciall care upon thy flock be staid, . . . . . . . . .  26  1st Eclogues  9  133
  Old age well stayed from raunging humor lives: . . . . . . .  39  Arcadia II   15   10
  Pan store of babes, vertue their thoughts well staid,. . . .  93  3rd Eclogues 63   93
  He stayd untill the goodman was departed,. . . . . . . . . .  97  3rd Eclogues 64  119
  Whose stormelike course staid not till hard by me it bided.. 118  4th Eclogues 73   60
  Thus my beleefe was staid, . . . . . . . . . . . . . . . . . 158  Cert Sonnets 28   37
  And pleasd with our soft peace, staid here his flying race.. 168  Astrophil     8    4
  Well staid with truth in word and faith of deed, . . . . . . 172  Astrophil    14   10
  And staid pleasd with the prospect of the place, . . . . . . 175  Astrophil    20   10
  Cannot be staid within my panting breast,. . . . . . . . . . 189  Astrophil    50    2
  And oft whole troupes of saddest words I staid,. . . . . . . 192  Astrophil    55    5
  But with short breath, long lookes, staid feet and walking
       hed, . . . . . . . . . . . . . . . . . . . . . . . . . . 205  Astrophil    76   13
  Each day seemes long, and longs for long-staid night,. . . . 224  Astrophil    89    5
  Ravisht, staid not, till in her golden haire . . . . . . . . 232  Astrophil   103    7
  Of just desires, on justice stayd, . . . . . . . . . . . . . 274  Psalm IV          22
  That poore from ruine may be stayd:. . . . . . . . . . . . . 283  Psalm X           78
  Sent from false heart, on double meaning stay'd. . . . . . . 284  Psalm XII          6
  But He, staffe of my age, He staid my stumbling state. . . . 291  Psalm XVIII       39
  So from base slip is stayed. . . . . . . . . . . . . . . . . 297  Psalm XXI         28
  Lord heare, let mercy thine be stay'd. . . . . . . . . . . . 311  Psalm XXX         31
  Whose faces on his comfort staid . . . . . . . . . . . . . . 319  Psalm XXXIV       19
  Still, still the godly shall be stay'd . . . . . . . . . . . 327  Psalm XXXVII      97
  Hast O Lord, that I be stayd . . . . . . . . . . . . . . . . 329  Psalm XXXVIII     64
  If him new-learned manners had not stai'd. . . . . . . . . . 246  Other Poems   4  166
  She went, they staid; or rightly for to say, . . . . . . . . 246  Other Poems   4  169
  She staid in them, they went in thought with hyr:. . . . . . 246  Other Poems   4  170
  Or she from thee be staide,. . . . . . . . . . . . . . . . . 258  Other Poems   5   74
```

```
STAYING                                                           PAGE     TITLE          LINE
    (He staying thus) was faine abroad to stray. . . . . . . .    250 Other Poems    4   331
*STAYS
    Which oft he lifteth up, and stayes his lifted pawe, . . . .   53 2nd Eclogues 29    34
    She bids him goe, and yet from jorney stayes. . . . . . . .   104 3rd Eclogues 67    36
    Or at the most on some fine picture stayes,. . . . . . . . .  170 Astrophil    11     7
    Now like his Whelp in den that lurking stayes. . . . . . . .  290 Psalm XVII          34
    On whom against my Foes my only safty stayes?. . . . . . . .  291 Psalm XVIII          7
    That God from fall his own Anoynted stayes.. . . . . . . . .  296 Psalm XX            22
    My foot on justice stayes, . . . . . . . . . . . . . . . . .  306 Psalm XXVI          38
STEADFAST
    My words, in hope to blaze my stedfast minde,. . . . . . . .   40 Arcadia II   19     1
    A steadfast rocky stone, . . . . . . . . . . . . . . . . . .  331 Psalm XL             9
    The stedfast mountaynes moved, . . . . . . . . . . . . . . .  260 Other Poems    6    14
STEAL
    To lye, faine, gloze, to steale, pry, and accuse,. . . . . .   21 1st Eclogues  8    23
    To lye, to steale, to pry, and to accuse,. . . . . . . . . .   21 1st Eclogues  8 V 23
    Till wrong, contempt, deceipt, did growe, steale, creepe,. .   84 Arcadia III  60     7
    Sweet Stella's image I do steale to mee". . . . . . . . . . .  181 Astrophil    32    14
    To steale some rest, but wretch I am constraind, . . . . . .  230 Astrophil    98     6
    Theeves steal for need, and steale but goods, which paine
        recovers, . . . . . . . . . . . . . . . . . . . . . . .  214 A&S 5th Song        45
    That Foxes leave to steale, because they finde they dy
        therefore. . . . . . . . . . . . . . . . . . . . . . . .  344 Possibly      1    44
STEALING
    O Stealing time the subject of delaie, . . . . . . . . . . .   80 Arcadia III  53     1
    Do invite a stealing kisse:. . . . . . . . . . . . . . . . .  203 A&S 2nd Song        22
STEALS
    There ofte steales out that round cleane foote . . . . . . .   89 Arcadia III  62   105
STEEL
    To set a pearle in steele so meanely varnished?. . . . . . .   16 1st Eclogues  7    63
STEELS
    Harde to be gott, but got constant, to be helde like
        steeles  Eeles.. . . . . . . . . . . . . . . . . . . . .   65 2nd Eclogues 31    42
STEEP
    In clyming steepe, now hard refusall show: . . . . . . . . .  147 Cert Sonnets 18     6
STELLA
    True, and yet true that I must Stella love.. . . . . . . . .  167 Astrophil     5    14
    When trembling voice brings forth that I do Stella love. . .  168 Astrophil     6    14
    Stella, thou straight lookst babies in her eyes, . . . . . .  170 Astrophil    11    10
    Thou countest Stella thine, like those whose powers. . . . .  171 Astrophil    12     9
    Stella behold, and then begin to endite. . . . . . . . . . .  172 Astrophil    15    14
    Stella: now she is nam'd, need more be said? . . . . . . . .  173 Astrophil    16    11
    Hath this world ought so faire as Stella is? . . . . . . . .  175 Astrophil    21    14
    Stella alone with face unarmed marcht, . . . . . . . . . . .  176 Astrophil    22     9
    When I say "Stella", I do meane the same . . . . . . . . . .  179 Astrophil    28     5
    But by thy worke my Stella I descrie, . . . . . . . . . . . .  181 Astrophil    32     7
    Stella, whence doth this new assault arise,. . . . . . . . .  182 Astrophil    36     1
    O Stella deare, how much thy power hath wrought, . . . . . .  184 Astrophil    40     2
    Stella lookt on, and from her heavenly face. . . . . . . . .  185 Astrophil    41    13
    Stella oft sees the verie face of wo . . . . . . . . . . . .  187 Astrophil    45     1
    Stella, the fulnesse of my thoughts of thee. . . . . . . . .  189 Astrophil    50     1
    While each pretends that Stella must be his: . . . . . . . .  190 Astrophil    52     2
    That Stella (o deare name) that Stella is. . . . . . . . . .  190 Astrophil    52     6
    Looke here, I say." I look'd, and Stella spide, . . . . . . .  191 Astrophil    53     8
    And thinke so still, so Stella know my mind, . . . . . . . .  192 Astrophil    54     9
    Hoping that when they might find Stella alone, . . . . . . .  193 Astrophil    57     5
    Where all my good I do in Stella see, . . . . . . . . . . . .  194 Astrophil    60     2
    For Grammer sayes (o this deare Stella weighe,) . . . . . . .  196 Astrophil    63    12
    Doth Stella now begin with piteous eye, . . . . . . . . . . .  199 Astrophil    67     2
    Stella, the onely Planet of my light, . . . . . . . . . . . .  200 Astrophil    68     1
    For Stella hath with words where faith doth shine, . . . . .  200 Astrophil    69     9
    Stella, those faire lines, which true goodnesse show.. . . .  201 Astrophil    71     4
    When I was forst from Stella ever deere, . . . . . . . . . .  222 Astrophil    87     1
    Stella food of my thoughts, hart of my hart, . . . . . . . .  222 Astrophil    87     2
    Stella whose eyes make all my tempests cleere, . . . . . . .  222 Astrophil    87     3
    Stella thinke not that I by verse seeke fame,. . . . . . . .  224 Astrophil    90     1
    Stella, while now by honour's cruell might, . . . . . . . . .  224 Astrophil    91     1
    Through me, wretch me, even Stella vexed is. . . . . . . . .  227 Astrophil    93     4
    Stella is sicke, and in that sicke bed lies. . . . . . . . .  231 Astrophil   101     1
    Stella now learnes (strange case) to weepe in thee.. . . . .  231 Astrophil   101     8
    O happie Tems, that didst my Stella beare, . . . . . . . . .  232 Astrophil   103     1
    Do Stella love. Fooles, who doth it deny?. . . . . . . . . .  233 Astrophil   104    14
    O absent presence Stella is not here;. . . . . . . . . . . .  235 Astrophil   106     1
    Stella, I say my Stella, should appeare. . . . . . . . . . .  235 Astrophil   106     4
    Stella since thou so right a Princesse art . . . . . . . . .  236 Astrophil   107     1
    O stones, o trees, learne hearing, Stella singeth. . . . . .  208 A&S 3rd Song         6
    O birds, o beasts, looke Love, lo, Stella shineth. . . . . .  209 A&S 3rd Song        12
    Your Client poore my selfe, shall Stella handle so?. . . . .  213 A&S 5th Song        31
    Astrophil with Stella sweete, . . . . . . . . . . . . . . . .  218 A&S 8th Song         5
    "Stella soveraigne of my joy,. . . . . . . . . . . . . . . .  218 A&S 8th Song        29
    Stella starre of heavenly fier, . . . . . . . . . . . . . . .  218 A&S 8th Song        31
    Stella loadstar of desier. . . . . . . . . . . . . . . . . .  218 A&S 8th Song        32
    "Stella, in whose shining eyes, . . . . . . . . . . . . . . .  218 A&S 8th Song        33
    "Stella, whose voice when it speakes,. . . . . . . . . . . .  219 A&S 8th Song        37
    Stella, whose voice when it singeth, . . . . . . . . . . . .  219 A&S 8th Song        39
    "Stella, in whose body is. . . . . . . . . . . . . . . . . .  219 A&S 8th Song        41
    Stella fiercest shepherdesse,. . . . . . . . . . . . . . . .  221 A&S 9th Song        16
    Stella whom o heavens do blesse, . . . . . . . . . . . . . .  221 A&S 9th Song        18
    Stella hath refused me,. . . . . . . . . . . . . . . . . . .  221 A&S 9th Song        21
```

STELLA	(CONTINUED)	PAGE	TITLE		LINE
Stella who more love hath proved,.		221	A&S 9th Song		22
Stella hath refused me,.		222	A&S 9th Song		26
Heavenly Stella meete with you,.		222	A&S 9th Song		48

STELLA'S

How then? even thus: in Stella's face I reed,.		166	Astrophil	3	12
When Nature made her chiefe worke, Stella's eyes,.		168	Astrophil	7	1
At length he perch'd himself in Stella's joyfull face, . . .		168	Astrophil	8	8
Queene Vertue's court, which some call Stella's face,. . . .		169	Astrophil	9	1
For soone as they strake thee with Stella's rayes, ...		170	Astrophil	10	12
Cupid, because thou shin'st in Stella's eyes,.		170	Astrophil	12	1
Stella's faire haire, her face he makes his shield,.		171	Astrophil	13	10
Of Stella's browes made him two better bowes,.		173	Astrophil	17	10
Then that I lose no more for Stella's sake..		174	Astrophil	18	14
My verie inke turnes straight to Stella's name;.		174	Astrophil	19	6
But only Stella's eyes and Stella's hart..		176	Astrophil	23	14
Love of her selfe, takes Stella's shape, that she.		177	Astrophil	25	10
By only those two starres in Stella's face.		178	Astrophil	26	14
Bends all his powers, even unto Stella's grace..		178	Astrophil	27	14
So Stella's heart, finding what power Love brings, ...		179	Astrophil	29	5
Sweet Stella's image I do steale to mee"..		181	Astrophil	32	14
Stella's great powrs, that so confuse my mind.		182	Astrophil	34	14
Doth even grow rich, naming my stella's name..		182	Astrophil	35	11
Unto my mind, is Stella's image, wrought		183	Astrophil	38	6
Livelier then else-where, Stella's image see..		184	Astrophil	39	14
Because their forefront bare sweet Stella's name..		190	Astrophil	50	14
Meane while my heart confers with Stella's beames, ...		190	Astrophil	51	12
Be Love's indeed, in Stella's selfe he may		191	Astrophil	52	10
Let Vertue have that Stella's selfe; yet thus, ...		191	Astrophil	52	13
Stella's sweete breath the same to me did reed..		194	Astrophil	58	11
I Stella's eyes assayll, invade her eares;		195	Astrophil	61	3
Stella's eyes sent to me the beames of blisse,.		199	Astrophil	66	11
My lips are sweet, inspired with Stella's kisse.		204	Astrophil	74	14
Hundreds of yeares you Stella's feet may kisse..		209	Astrophil	84	14
Since Stella's eyes, wont to give me my day,.		223	Astrophil	89	3
When I demaund of Phenix Stella's state, ...		225	Astrophil	92	6
Onely unto the heav'n of Stella's face,.		235	Astrophil	105	7
Stella's selfe might not refuse thee..		220	A&S 8th Song		96

STEP

Comfort, step thou in place of wonted sadnes..		83	Arcadia III	59	10
Whose steppe on earth all beautie sets..		89	Arcadia III	62	108
Our life is but a step in dustie way..		131	Arcadia V	77	12
But when the ruggedst step of Fortune's race		195	Astrophil	60	5
Who hath the feet, whose step all sweetnesse planteth, . . .		197	A&S 1st Song		13
Who hath the feet, whose step of sweetnesse planteth,. . . .		197	A&S 1st Song		V 13

STEPDAME

Invention, Nature's child, fled step-dame Studie's blowes, .		165	Astrophil	1	10
Whose senses in so evill consort, their stepdame Nature laies, ...		217	A&S 7th Song		1

STEFMOTHER

Cast thy stepmother eyes upon our sorowe,.		109	Arcadia IV	70	23

STEPPED

Thus proud and fierce unto the hearts he stept		246	Other Poems	4	157

STEPPETH

Can fancies want eies, or he fall that steppeth aloft? Oft..		64	2nd Eclogues	31	22

STEPPING

Her legges (O legges) her ay well stepping feete..		141	Cert Sonnets	9	8

STEPS

Her stepps, gladd we receave, gladd we receave her eys.. . .		69	2nd Eclogues	34	40
Tread in my steppes, or follow not..		153	Cert Sonnets	24	18
With how sad steps, o Moone, thou climb'st the skies,. . . .		180	Astrophil	31	1
That no pace else their guided steps can find, ...		194	Astrophil	58	3
Let me no steps but of lost labour trace,.		198	Astrophil	64	6
The straying stepps as wicked Counsel leads;		270	Psalm I		2
Led by Thy Word the Rav'ner's stepps I shun, ...		289	Psalm XVII		14
Unto my strengthned stepps Thou didst enlarge the way, . . .		292	Psalm XVIII		66
My stepps shall guided be, ...		306	Psalm XXVI		35
Abroad his stepps be wrongly sett.		323	Psalm XXXVI		12
And my weake steps did stay.		331	Psalm XL		10
With whose fine stepps all loves and joyes conspire.		250	Other Poems	4	302

STIFF

Whose mettall stiff he knew he could not bende		245	Other Poems	4	138

*STILL

Your face hurts oft, but still it doth delight,.		3	Lady of May	1	8
But still take heede least thou thy selfe submit		4	Lady of May	2	23
Thus are my eyes still Captive to one sight:		12	Arcadia I	2	9
Thus all my thoughts are slaves to one thought still:. . . .		12	Arcadia I	2	10
And thus my eyes, are plaste still in one sight.		12	Arcadia I	2	V809
And thus my thoughtes, can thinke but one thing still. . . .		12	Arcadia I	2	V810
Dorus. Nightingales seldome sing, the Pie still chattereth:.		14	1st Eclogues	7	7
Such as you see, such still you shall me finde..		18	1st Eclogues	7	122
If still her minde be such,.		19	1st Eclogues	7	150
If shee still hate love's lawe,.		19	1st Eclogues	7	V150
Yet beares he still his parents' stately gifts,.		21	1st Eclogues	8	25
Some gazing still, some winking wilye shiftes, ...		21	1st Eclogues	8	27
He proules ech place stil in new colours deckt,.		21	1st Eclogues	8	35
While still more wretch, more wicked he doth prove:.		22	1st Eclogues	8	44
Still were I one, this still should be my case,.		23	1st Eclogues	9	28
Thy wit dost use still still more harmes to finde.		23	1st Eclogues	9	34
That since they still alledge, When they were yong:.		24	1st Eclogues	9	79

```
*STILL                   (CONTINUED)                    PAGE   TITLE        LINE
  I way them not, but still will thee advize . . . . . . . . .   25  1st Eclogues  9  109
  Still doo I crosse this wretch, what so he taketh in hand"..   29  1st Eclogues 11    6
  But (like a point in midst of a circle) is still of a
    neernesse, . . . . . . . . . . . . . . . . . . . . . . .     31  1st Eclogues 13    6
  You, though feares do abash, in you still possible hopes be:   32  1st Eclogues 13   23
  Aire, we do still with sighes encrease; to the fire? we do
    want none. . . . . . . . . . . . . . . . . . . . . . . .     32  1st Eclogues 13   30
  Happy shepheard, with thanks to the Gods, still thinke to be
    thankfull, . . . . . . . . . . . . . . . . . . . . . . .     32  1st Eclogues 13   33
  Of carking agonies (to estates which still be adherent). . .   34  1st Eclogues 13   97
  Lyke to my noble thoughts, still new, well plac'd, to me
    fruteles. . . . . . . . . . . . . . . . . . . . . . . . .    35  1st Eclogues 13  124
  My words unseene, the marble still in sight, . . . . . . . .   41  Arcadia II   19   10
  Still seeking Love, love found as much I flie. . . . . . . .   41  Arcadia II   20    4
  Though thousands old, a Boy entit'led still. . . . . . . . .   41  Arcadia II   20   10
  Both still do worke, in neither finde I rest:. . . . . . . .   42  Arcadia II   22    3
  But still when thou dost sing, me thinkes a colt is loose. .   52  2nd Eclogues 29   24
  But still (me thought) with beauties from her fell, . . . .   55  2nd Eclogues 29  106
  The after-folkes shall wonder still at thee. . . . . . . . .   56  2nd Eclogues 29  131
  But still our dazeled eyes their way do misse, . . . . . . .   59  2nd Eclogues 30   74
  But still, although we faile of perfect rightfulnes, . . . .   61  2nd Eclogues 30  137
  Can thoughts still thinking so rest unappalled?. . . . . . .   61  2nd Eclogues 30  166
  Boulon. Who still doth seeke against himselfe offences, . . .  62  2nd Eclogues 30  167
  Whiche dazeling still, dothe still maynteine my sight; . . .   70  Arcadia III  35    6
  Unite in one, my state thus still to save; . . . . . . . . .   70  Arcadia III  35   15
  Thy force I feare, her force I still do prove. . . . . . . .   72  Arcadia III  38   10
  Do foster still, the fruite of fancies darke:. . . . . . . .   73  Arcadia III  39    6
  Sicke to the death, still loving my disease. . . . . . . . .   74  Arcadia III  41    8
  My mangled mind huge horrors still doe fright, . . . . . . .   74  Arcadia III  42    5
  I waste my harte, which still newe torment tryes.. . . . . .   75  Arcadia III  43    5
  So still me thought in me his hurt did smart:. . . . . . . .   76  Arcadia III  45   12
  Do you say still, this is her promise due, . . . . . . . . .   76  Arcadia III  46    5
  Yet still, faire tree, lifte up thy stately line, . . . . .   77  Arcadia III  47    9
  You goodly pines, which still with brave assent. . . . . . .   77  Arcadia III  49    1
  All what I am, still one, his owne, doe finde. . . . . . . .   78  Arcadia III  50   10
  All what you are still one, his owne to finde, . . . . . . .   79  Arcadia III  50   11
  Blush on for shame: that still with thee do light. . . . . .   82  Arcadia III  56    5
  Make me still feare, thy faire appearing showe.. . . . . . .   82  Arcadia III  56   14
  Which blessed still themselves doo kisse.. . . . . . . . . .   87  Arcadia III  62   38
  Which onely still doth Lillies yeeld:. . . . . . . . . . . .   87  Arcadia III  62   62
  The best things still must be forgotten. . . . . . . . . . .   88  Arcadia III  62   86
  That still he be her head, she be his harte, . . . . . . . .   92  3rd Eclogues 63   48
  Each other still allow:. . . . . . . . . . . . . . . . . . .   92  3rd Eclogues 63   50
  And one man still, credit with her preserve. . . . . . . . .   98  3rd Eclogues 65    4
  He still hop'd well, because I loved truth;. . . . . . . . .   99  3rd Eclogues 66   38
  Onely the owle still warnde them not to seech. . . . . . . .  100  3rd Eclogues 66   68
  With meager lookes, as if they still did smart;. . . . . . .  104  3rd Eclogues 67   28
  Still contrarie to what her husband sayes; . . . . . . . . .  104  3rd Eclogues 67   32
  For I seeke not their shame, but still me thinkes, . . . . .  105  3rd Eclogues 67   56
  That still our little world may know his king. . . . . . . .  105  3rd Eclogues 67   63
  But these be your toyes, which still are spent. . . . . . .  106  3rd Eclogues 67   94
  Be victor still of Phoebus' golden treasure: . . . . . . . .  108  Arcadia IV   69    5
  His nature feares to die who lives still wailing.. . . . . .  110  Arcadia IV   70   39
  Which to my woes gives still an early morning: . . . . . . .  111  4th Eclogues 71    5
  Yet living still in her, while her beames lent . . . . . . .  115  4th Eclogues 72   83
  And keepe it still within this body thrall:. . . . . . . . .  116  4th Eclogues 72   88
  Be silent therefore now, and so be silent still. . . . . . .  119  4th Eclogues 73   97
  O Hiacinthe let Ai be on thee still. . . . . . . . . . . . .  125  4th Eclogues 75   29
  Your dolefull tunes, to them still playning say, . . . . . .  126  4th Eclogues 75   50
  Time ever old, and yonge is still revolved . . . . . . . . .  127  4th Eclogues 75   79
  Still studying how to us to be a light.. . . . . . . . . . .  129  4th Eclogues 76   16
  And unto death bend still our thoughts' direction. . . . . .  130  4th Eclogues 76   34
  Since loosing long, the faster still I bind: . . . . . . . .  135  Cert Sonnets  1    5
  Place standeth still amazed. . . . . . . . . . . . . . . . .  136  Cert Sonnets  3    7
  Yet still her eyes give to my flames their fuell.. . . . . .  136  Cert Sonnets  3   12
  Still to be sory.. . . . . . . . . . . . . . . . . . . . . .  138  Cert Sonnets  5   16
  The same man still in whom wysdome prevailes, . . . . . . .  143  Cert Sonnets 12   17
  Or thinking still my thoughts might have good end: . . . . .  147  Cert Sonnets 19    2
  Or cruell (still) time did your beautie staine:. . . . . . .  148  Cert Sonnets 19    8
  But since my thoughts in thinking still are spent, . . . . .  148  Cert Sonnets 19   13
  You fairer still, and still more cruell bent,. . . . . . . .  148  Cert Sonnets 19   15
  I loving still a love that loveth none, . . . . . . . . . .  148  Cert Sonnets 19   16
  From joy I part still living in annoy. . . . . . . . . . . .  148  Cert Sonnets 20   14
  My lake is sense, whose still streames never runne, . . . .  150  Cert Sonnets 22   15
  Which though despisde, yet still doth truth endure.. . . . .  150  Cert Sonnets 22   40
  Thus is her life still guarded, . . . . . . . . . . . . . .  152  Cert Sonnets 23   13
  So may they live still sorie . . . . . . . . . . . . . . . .  152  Cert Sonnets 23   31
  And others' feete still seem'd but strangers in my way.. . .  165  Astrophil     1   11
  And still th'effect of thy perswasions prove:. . . . . . . .  167  Astrophil     4   11
  Reason, in faith thou art well serv'd, that still. . . . . .  169  Astrophil    10    1
  My best wits still their owne disgrace invent: . . . . . . .  174  Astrophil    19    5
  Scourge of it selfe, still climing slipprie place, . . . . .  176  Astrophil    23   10
  Lies hatching still the goods wherein they flow: . . . . . .  176  Astrophil    24    2
  They should still daunce to please a gazer's sight.. . . . .  178  Astrophil    26    8
  But know not how, for still I thinke of you. . . . . . . . .  180  Astrophil    30   14
  My still kept course, while others sleepe, to mone.. . . . .  184  Astrophil    40    4
  That in my heart I offer still to thee, . . . . . . . . . .  185  Astrophil    40   13
  Keepe still my Zenith, ever shine on me. . . . . . . . . . .  186  Astrophil    42    8
  Yet still on me, o eyes, dart downe your rayes:. . . . . . .  186  Astrophil    42   11
```

*STILL   (CONTINUED)   PAGE TITLE   LINE

```
So may your tongue still fluently proceed, . . . . . . . . .   190 Astrophil   51    2
So may you still have somewhat new to say. . . . . . . . . .   190 Astrophil   51    4
And thinke so still, so Stella know my mind, . . . . . . . .   192 Astrophil   54    9
So children still reade you with awfull eyes,. . . . . . . .   196 Astrophil   63    2
Fortune wheeles still with me in one sort slow,. . . . . . .   199 Astrophil   66    6
Desire still on the stilts of feare doth go. . . . . . . . .   199 Astrophil   66    8
If still I force her in sad rimes to creepe: . . . . . . . .   201 Astrophil   70    2
"But ah," Desire still cries, "give me some food." . . . . .   201 Astrophil   71   14
Love still a boy, and oft a wanton is, . . . . . . . . . . .   203 Astrophil   73    1
So nimble feet as stirre still, though on thornes: . . . . .   206 Astrophil   78   11
Stop you my mouth with still still kissing me. . . . . . . .   207 Astrophil   81   14
Be you still faire, honourd by publike heed, . . . . . . . .   209 Astrophil   84    9
A still felt plague, to selfe condemning me: . . . . . . . .   212 Astrophil   86    3
Say all, and all well sayd, still say the same.. . . . . . .   225 Astrophil   92   14
Thou though still tired, yet still doost it detest.. . . . .   229 Astrophil   96   14
That hue, whose force my hart still unto thraldome ties? . .   232 Astrophil  102    8
Have made, but forst by Nature still to flie,. . . . . . . .   233 Astrophil  103   10
As what my hart still sees thou canst not spie?. . . . . . .   235 Astrophil  105    4
Which pants as though it still should leape to thee: . . . .   236 Astrophil  107    6
Her tongue waking still refuseth,. . . . . . . . . . . . . .   202 A&S 2nd Song      9
You witch, you Divill, (alas) you still of me beloved, . . .   215 A&S 5th Song     87
With time still th' affection groweth. . . . . . . . . . . .   234 A&S 11th Song    19
Deeper still they drive the stake. . . . . . . . . . . . . .   234 A&S 11th Song    35
Now be still, yet still beleeve me,. . . . . . . . . . . . .   220 A&S 8th Song     75
Shall prosper still, with well succeeding end. . . . . . . .   270 Psalm I          12
Have mercy therfore still on me, . . . . . . . . . . . . . .   273 Psalm IV          4
Talk with your hearts, and yet be still. . . . . . . . . . .   273 Psalm IV         18
Lo, I am tir'd, while still I sigh and groane: . . . . . . .   276 Psalm VI         17
But still be Thou to just men justest guide. . . . . . . . .   277 Psalm VII        27
Still plagues the poore the most he can: . . . . . . . . . .   281 Psalm X           6
Whom to their losse he still doth get. . . . . . . . . . . .   282 Psalm X          39
O be thou still the Orphan's aide. . . . . . . . . . . . . .   283 Psalm X          77
Since I do trust Jehova still, . . . . . . . . . . . . . . .   283 Psalm XI          1
Then Thou (O lord) shalt keep the Good stil sure.. . . . . .   285 Psalm XII        22
Still therfore of Thy Graces shall be my . . . . . . . . . .   286 Psalm XIII       19
My eyes still my God regard. . . . . . . . . . . . . . . . .   288 Psalm XVI        25
And pray that still Thou guide my way. . . . . . . . . . . .   289 Psalm XVII       15
Who for my Death still me enclose. . . . . . . . . . . . . .   290 Psalm XVII       28
Still to his judgments lookt, still for his statutes car'd,.   292 Psalm XVIII      45
Me in encreasing still, Thy kindness did maintaine;. . . . .   292 Psalm XVIII      65
Then live Jehova still, my rock still blessed be;. . . . . .   293 Psalm XVIII      83
So shall my spryte be still upright. . . . . . . . . . . . .   295 Psalm XIX        57
Defend Thee still from all Thy foes abroad.. . . . . . . . .   295 Psalm XX          5
Thy power still be praised. . . . . . . . . . . . . . . . . .  298 Psalm XXI        52
Our Fathers still in thee their trust did beare, . . . . . .   298 Psalm XXII       11
By waters still and sweet. . . . . . . . . . . . . . . . . .   301 Psalm XXIII       5
But still on this Lord set?. . . . . . . . . . . . . . . . .   304 Psalm XXV        56
My woes are still encreast;. . . . . . . . . . . . . . . . .   304 Psalm XXV        61
That I may still expresse. . . . . . . . . . . . . . . . . .   305 Psalm XXVI       22
My trust still hold. . . . . . . . . . . . . . . . . . . . .   307 Psalm XXVII      18
In house of High Jehova still, . . . . . . . . . . . . . . .   307 Psalm XXVII      21
Seek Thy face still. . . . . . . . . . . . . . . . . . . . .   308 Psalm XXVII      42
Lord then still Thy people save, . . . . . . . . . . . . . .   309 Psalm XXVIII     33
Ye saints of his, remembring still . . . . . . . . . . . . .   311 Psalm XXX        11
For still I say Thou art my only might.. . . . . . . . . . .   312 Psalm XXXI       12
O Lord, of Thee let me still mercy winn, . . . . . . . . . .   312 Psalm XXXI       25
You that do trust in him who still is true,. . . . . . . . .   314 Psalm XXXI       68
Or roar'd, my bones still wasted;. . . . . . . . . . . . . .   315 Psalm XXXII       9
My soul shall glory still. . . . . . . . . . . . . . . . . .   318 Psalm XXXIV       5
None, I say still, shall ruind be. . . . . . . . . . . . . .   321 Psalm XXXIV      79
Still still for them I humbly mourning went. . . . . . . . .   322 Psalm XXXV       35
Still, still the godly shall be stay'd . . . . . . . . . . .   327 Psalm XXXVII     97
Still Thy hands upon me be.. . . . . . . . . . . . . . . . .   327 Psalm XXXVIII     6
Still in mourning chear arayd. . . . . . . . . . . . . . . .   328 Psalm XXXVIII    18
Still my orethwart neighbour is. . . . . . . . . . . . . . .   329 Psalm XXXVIII    51
But still the more that I did hold my peace, . . . . . . . .   329 Psalm XXXIX       7
Look but on this: man still doth riches heape. . . . . . . .   330 Psalm XXXIX      21
My lipps shall still reveale, . . . . . . . . . . . . . . . .  331 Psalm XL         38
Me still in truth and mercy save,. . . . . . . . . . . . . .   332 Psalm XL         42
Still gladly say, Unto our God bee prayse. . . . . . . . . .   332 Psalm XL         64
World without end, let still his blessing flow;. . . . . . .   334 Psalm XLI        47
Yet thus still my hope is grounded,. . . . . . . . . . . . .   335 Psalm XLII       35
Praying, prayers still bequeathing . . . . . . . . . . . . .   335 Psalm XLII       39
Who is still my present aid; . . . . . . . . . . . . . . . .   335 Psalm XLII       54
Wait on God, for still . . . . . . . . . . . . . . . . . . .   337 Psalm XLIII      34
Still both their flocks flocking togither went,. . . . . . .   242 Other Poems   4   30
Like dropsy folke still drinke to be a thyrst. . . . . . . .   247 Other Poems   4  204
And still, beleve me, Strephon was at hand.. . . . . . . . .   247 Other Poems   4  216
Still shunning Nous to lengthen pleasing race, . . . . . . .   250 Other Poems   4  306
(Yet beauty still as fast as she did sturre) . . . . . . . .   251 Other Poems   4  358
His fancies still did hir in half-way meet,. . . . . . . . .   251 Other Poems   4  371
Till finding still his evill encreasing thus,. . . . . . . .   253 Other Poems   4  437
I still do see, though I be still alone. . . . . . . . . . .   254 Other Poems   4  462
Do you remember still you once were mine,. . . . . . . . . .   254 Other Poems   4  495
Still to be hers, about her aye to flie, . . . . . . . . . .   255 Other Poems   4  501
By north or south still rich adorned live: . . . . . . . . .   256 Other Poems   5   16
So may thee still betide . . . . . . . . . . . . . . . . . .   257 Other Poems   5   54
Still for thy Dam with bea-waymenting crie?. . . . . . . . .   258 Other Poems   5   78
May be still to thee relying.. . . . . . . . . . . . . . . .   263 Other Poems   7   60
```

	PAGE	TITLE		LINE
STILTS				
Desire still on the stilts of feare doth go.	199	Astrophil	66	8
STING				
That they thy sting restraine, ...	93	3rd Eclogues 63		89
The humming Waspe, if it had not a stinge, ...	104	3rd Eclogues 67		17
Doth add her force unto the sting of fortune:.	109	Arcadia IV	70	10
STINK				
My wounds putrify and stink, ...	328	Psalm XXXVIII		13
STINKING				
All plung'd in stinking filth, not One well bent,.	286	Psalm XIV		11
STIR				
Vertue of late, with vertuous care to ster	177	Astrophil	25	9
He sits me fast, how ever I do sturre:	189	Astrophil	49	12
So nimble feet as stirre still, though on thornes:	206	Astrophil	78	11
In night of sprites the gastly powers stur,.	229	Astrophil	96	10
As thy lookes sturre, runs up and downe to make.	232	Astrophil	101	10
While beautie's reddest inke Venus for him doth sturre.. . .	232	Astrophil	102	14
And if the trees, nor stones stirre not the same to prove, .	209	A&S 3rd Song		14
Will not they stir new affection?"	234	A&S 11th Song		22
Dick. Bound as I neither power have, nor would have power to				
stir.	343	Possibly	1	24
(Yet beauty still as fast as she did sturre)	251	Other Poems	4	358
STIRRED				
Though him to meete at all she sturred nought.	250	Other Poems	4	326
STIRRING				
All sturring husband's hate.	93	3rd Eclogues 63		69
Not sturring thoughts, nor yet denying right,.	98	3rd Eclogues 65		6
STIRS				
Sturres me to thinke what dangers lye in waite..	82	Arcadia III	56	12
Wrong sturres remorsed greefe, griefe's deadly sore. . . .	85	Arcadia III	61	7
Shrewdnes so stirres, pride so puffes up their hart, . . .	104	3rd Eclogues 67		26
STOCK				
Only fond youth admires a rotten stocke.	25	1st Eclogues	9	89
Their Counsills are your Common jesting stock, ...	287	Psalm XIV		20
STOIC-LIKE				
Who Stoick-like in clowdie hew appeare:.	147	Cert Sonnets 17		48
STOLE				
Then did on him who first stole downe the fire,.	171	Astrophil	14 V	3
STOLEN				
By princely meane be stolne, and yet not lost.	11	Arcadia I	1	2
When for a treene-dish stolne, thy father did thee whippe! .	52	2nd Eclogues 29		12
And sure at length stolne goods do come to light	172	Astrophil	15	11
Stolne to my heart, since last faire night, nay day, . . .	199	Astrophil	66	10
What sighes stolne out, or kild before full borne?	199	Astrophil	67	9
Who hath the crimson weeds stolne from my morning skies? . .	232	Astrophil	102	4
To play when that their loved dammes, are stoln or gone				
astray?.	343	Possibly	1	6
(Stolne from her yoong by theeves' unchoosing hast). . . .	254	Other Poems	4	491
STOMACH				
To crammed mawes a spratt new Stomake brings.	245	Other Poems	4	134
STOMACHS				
Cannot heavn's food, once felt, keepe stomakes free. . . .	223	Astrophil	88	7
STONE				
Her haire pure Crapal-stone; her mouth O heavenly wyde;. . .	12	Arcadia I	3	11
Thou purest stone, whose purenesse doth present.	40	Arcadia II	18	7
Blots to the stone, shame to my selfe I finde:	40	Arcadia II	19	5
A woman's hand with constant marble stone.	40	Arcadia II	19	6
Above line repeated at following location.	41	Arcadia II	19	12
Griefe is the stone which finest judgement proves:	58	2nd Eclogues 30		35
Is chang'd to stone, in hardnesse, cold, and weight, . . .	150	Cert Sonnets 22		43
Long since forc'd by thy beames, but stone nor tree. . . .	183	Astrophil	36	13
A steadfast rocky stone.	331	Psalm XL		9
As all the rest, so now the stone.	241	Other Poems	3	7
STONES				
Neere Wilton sweete, huge heapes of stones are found,. . . .	149	Cert Sonnets 22		1
If stones good measure daunc'd, the Theban walles to build,.	208	A&S 3rd Song		3
O stones, o trees, learne hearing, Stella singeth.	208	A&S 3rd Song		6
The birds, beasts, stones and trees feele this, and feeling				
love:	209	A&S 3rd Song		13
And if the trees, nor stones stirre not the same to prove, .	209	A&S 3rd Song		14
Which to stones I els would show:.	221	A&S 9th Song		13
STOOD				
Pas. She once, to coole her selfe, stood in a well,. . . .	55	2nd Eclogues 29		108
Like wine and milke that mingled stood..	86	Arcadia III	62	30
Gainst those of might, of whom in feare they stood,. . . .	102	3rd Eclogues 66		130
Of samothea lande; a lande, which whilom stood	117	4th Eclogues 73		36
As I thus musing stood, Diana cald to her.	119	4th Eclogues 73		81
While to my minde the out side stood,.	156	Cert Sonnets 27		7
Till that I sware my faith so stood, ...	158	Cert Sonnets 28		23
And so I nothing said, I muet stood, ...	329	Psalm XXXIX		5
To strive she fear'd how it with vertue stoode..	245	Other Poems	4	126
He stood, but turn'd, as Girosol, to Sun:.	251	Other Poems	4	370
STOOL				
A three foote stoole in Greece, made Trumpets sound, . . .	146	Cert Sonnets 17		19
STOOLBALL				
When she with skirts tuckt very hy, with girles at stoolball				
playes.	343	Possibly	1	10
STOOP				
(More swift then falcon's stoope to feeding Falconer's call)	118	4th Eclogues 73		58

STOP

	PAGE	TITLE		LINE
Or stop a breach, that never Cannon sawe?.	22	1st Eclogues	9	17
And stoppe mine eares, lest I growe mad with Musicke.	112	4th Eclogues	71	60
Of all my thoughts hath neither stop nor start,.	176	Astrophil	23	13
Stop you my mouth with still still kissing me.	207	Astrophil	81	14
O my strength stop not Thine eare, ...	308	Psalm XXVIII		2
Yea take Thy lance and stop the way of those	321	Psalm XXXV		4
Heare lord my suits and cryes, stop not thyn eares	330	Psalm XXXIX		37

STOPPED

Since will is won, and stopped eares are charmed:.	135	Cert Sonnets	1	3
But that they stopt his furie from the same, ...	190	Astrophil	50	13

STOPS

And lowest stops doo yeeld the hyest sounde.	81	Arcadia III	54	16

STOPST

Whereby Thou stop'st Thyne Enemy's prating	278	Psalm VIII		7

STORE

My words in store, the marble all alone;	41	Arcadia II	19	8
I waile for want, and yet am chckte with store..	41	Arcadia II	20	8
Fortune store, Nature health, Love grant perswasion.	51	2nd Eclogues	28	100
What greater ills have now the heavens in store, ...	57	2nd Eclogues	30	6
But harveste come, and corne in fertill store, ...	71	Arcadia III	36	11
Pan store of babes, vertue their thoughts well staid,. . . .	93	3rd Eclogues	63	93
Earth thou didst seeke, and store of earth thou hast.	108	Arcadia IV	68	2
Ready to store their campes of needfull things:.	179	Astrophil	29	4
But heere I do store of faire Ladies meete.	236	Astrophil	106	9
Than they whose stoare in harvest space.	274	Psalm IV		29
He nobly saves his King, and kindness keeps in store,. . . .	293	Psalm XVIII		90
Behold my Foes, what store they be,.	304	Psalm XXV		65
Even where I do most store of people find;	322	Psalm XXXV		47

STORED

So fortified with wit, stor'd with disdaine, ...	171	Astrophil	12	13

STOREHOUSE

Like storehouse Thou of blessings mad'st,.	297	Psalm XXI		21

STORING

Of grain and wine fills stoaring place..	274	Psalm IV		30

STORKS

Cranes, order; Storkes, to be appearing holie;	101	3rd Eclogues	66	94

STORM

As neere his home, when storme or shelf he feares;	71	Arcadia III	37	4
Is that huge storme, which powres it selfe on me:.	114	4th Eclogues	72	32
In shine or storme must sett the clowted shoe:	242	Other Poems	4	20

STORMED

How thy lee shores by my sighes stormed be!.	230	Astrophil	98	4

STORMLIKE

Whose stormelike course staid not till hard by me it bided..	118	4th Eclogues	73	60

STORMS

Nor stormes doo turne: fairenes serves oft to wealth.. . . .	18	1st Eclogues	7	119
And from the stormes our sweeteste sonne will shield.. . . .	43	Arcadia II	23	9
My sun is gon, from stormes what shall us sheelde?	43	Arcadia II	24	9
Her cleared lookes, nought els, in stormes can quiet me. . .	51	2nd Eclogues	28	119
Winde, tempests, and stormes, yet in ende what gives she desire? Ire.	64	2nd Eclogues	31	35
What stormes founde me, what tormentes I dyd fynde,.	71	Arcadia III	36	15
The diffrence is; all folkes those stormes forbeare:	114	4th Eclogues	72	38
Of living deaths, deare wounds, faire stormes and freesing fires:	167	Astrophil	6	4
From the stormes in my breast breeding,.	221	A&S 9th Song		4
On them storms, brimstone, coales he raines, ...	284	Psalm XI		19
Breeding huge stormes with in his inward parte,.	256	Other Poems	4	543

STORMY

Since that the stormy rage of passions darcke.	72	Arcadia III	39	1
Painted in my beclowded stormie face:.	187	Astrophil	45	2

STORY

While Plangus dyd a storie strainge declare.	62	2nd Eclogues	30	189
To write therein more fresh the story of delight,.	232	Astrophil	102	13
And all eares worse then deafe, that heard not out thy storie..	212	A&S 5th Song		6
Heare your wofull maister's story, ...	221	A&S 9th Song		12
A heavn'ly story?.	276	Psalm VI		16
Upon the heavns engrav'n the story..	278	Psalm VIII		4

STOURS

Now fancie's fits, now fortune's balefull stowers.	103	3rd Eclogues	66	157

STOUT

In hard estate with stowt shew valor use,.	143	Cert Sonnets	12	16
Wise Counseliors, stout Captaines, puissant Kings, ...	245	Other Poems	4	130

STRAIGHT

But straight they fledde, summond by cruell honor, ...	17	1st Eclogues	7	95
Streight as Cedar, a voice staines the Cannary birds,. . . .	69	2nd Eclogues	34	33
Do not disdaine, o streight up raised Pine,.	77	Arcadia III	47	1
Since that my thoughtes, as streight as streightnes thine, .	77	Arcadia III	47	3
That streight was done with many a boistrous threat, ...	97	3rd Eclogues	64	115
Which streight the Earth yclothed in his claye:.	101	3rd Eclogues	66	79
But streight there issued forth two Ladies (Ladies sure. . .	118	4th Eclogues	73	63
I loved, but straight did not what Love decreed:	165	Astrophil	2	6
Reason thou kneel'dst, and offeredst straight to prove . . .	170	Astrophil	10	13
Stella, thou straight lookst babies in her eyes, ...	170	Astrophil	11	10
And straight therewith, like wags new got to play, ...	173	Astrophil	17	13
My verie inke turnes straight to Stella's name;.	174	Astrophil	19	6
But straight I saw motions of lightning grace, ...	175	Astrophil	20	12
The first that straight my fancie's error brings	183	Astrophil	38	5

475

STRAIGHT (CONTINUED)   PAGE   TITLE   LINE

	PAGE	TITLE		LINE
Are metamorphosd straight to tunes of joyes.	187	Astrophil	44	14
So sweete sounds straight mine eare and heart do hit,. . . .	192	Astrophil	55	13
With chastned mind, I straight must shew that she..	195	Astrophil	61	10
I joyed, but straight thus watred was my wine, ...	196	Astrophil	62	5
She comes, and streight therewith her shining twins do move.	204	Astrophil	76	1
Your morall notes straight my hid meaning teare.	233	Astrophil	104	12
Clips streight my wings, streight wraps me in his night, . .	236	Astrophil	108	8
Love therewith is streight imparted.	218	A&S 8th Song		36
And turn their backs, and strait on backs appeare.	276	Psalm VI		31
But streight his shining eyes this misty masse disclos'd.. .	291	Psalm XVIII		26
Then out his arrowes fly, and streight they scatterd been,. .	291	Psalm XVIII		29
But, ah he strait his face did hide, ...	311	Psalm XXX		23
And his sweet grace streight easd the rod.	315	Psalm XXXII		17
Ev'en heapes of wicked thoughts which streight they show . .	333	Psalm XLI		23
Klaius streight felt, and groned at the blowe, ...	246	Other Poems	4	161
And streight for failing, grav'd it in his heart:.	247	Other Poems	4	186
Then couples three be streight allotted there, ...	248	Other Poems	4	225
He rase, and streight espied	259	Other Poems	5	120

STRAIGHTNESS

Since that my thoughtes, as streight as streightnes thine, .	77	Arcadia III	47	3
In straightnes past the Cedars of the forrests,.	113	4th Eclogues	71	64

STRAIGHTWAY

Will streight-way nothing be..	283	Psalm X		68

STRAIGHTWAYS

For though I never see them, but straight wayes.	186	Astrophil	42	9

STRAIN

Thee to thy wracke beyond thy limits straine..	210	Astrophil	85	4

STRAINED

Such thoughts, me thought, I thought, and straind my single mind	118	4th Eclogues	73	49

STRAIT

Mine eyes the streight, the roomie cave, my minde, ...	150	Cert Sonnets	22	35

STRAKE

For soone as they strake thee with Stella's rayes, ...	170	Astrophil	10	12
Seeing hope yeeld when this wo strake him furst:	228	Astrophil	95	6

STRANGE

Whose vertues strange, and beuties such, as no man them may know?.	12	Arcadia I	3	2
To fill the world with strange but vaine conceits:	20	1st Eclogues	8	2
Here you fully do finde this strange operation of love,. . .	31	1st Eclogues	13	3
To this strange death I vainely yeeld my life.	38	Arcadia II	14	14
The sound to this strange aier no sooner goes,.	42	Arcadia II	21	9
Wyth two strange fires of equall heate possest,.	42	Arcadia II	22	1
In thy owne proofe he gets so straunge possession,.	48	2nd Eclogues	28	35
Can I forget in how straunge phrase she craved	61	2nd Eclogues	30	158
To that strange stroke which conquer'd all my senses,. . . .	61	2nd Eclogues	30	165
While Plangus dyd a storie strainge declare.	62	2nd Eclogues	30	189
In this strange violence, to make resistance..	67	2nd Eclogues	33	2
Like those sicke folkes, in whome strange humors flowe,. . .	74	Arcadia III	41	1
Let no strange dreme make her fayre body starte.	79	Arcadia III	51	8
What strange dessein hast thou my hopes to staie,.	80	Arcadia III	53	3
Of Prince's harte quite lost the ruine strange..	81	Arcadia III	55	6
(Tide to the stake of doubt) strange passions baite, . . .	82	Arcadia III	56	10
The neck, in which strange graces lurke.	87	Arcadia III	62	48
For there with strange compact dooth lie	90	Arcadia III	62	125
Have praide me leave my strange exclaiming musique,.	112	4th Eclogues	71	32
Straunge were the Ladies' weedes; yet more unfit then strange.	118	4th Eclogues	73	65
And so refuse to behold of these strange wounds the recitall	122	4th Eclogues	74	7
The straunge resounde of these my causefull cries:	125	4th Eclogues	75	6
Till these straunge altrings you did hap to trie;.	125	4th Eclogues	75	26
What courage strange hath caught thy caitife hart, ...	142	Cert Sonnets	10	9
Deeming strange evill in that he did not know..	145	Cert Sonnets	16	4
Some cause there is, which of strange cause doth rise: . . .	147	Cert Sonnets	18	2
But now the starres with their strange course do binde . . .	148	Cert Sonnets	20	5
Or with strange similies enrich each line, ...	166	Astrophil	3	7
And strange things cost too deare for my poore sprites.. . .	166	Astrophil	3	11
Some one his song in Jove, and Jove's strange tales attires,	167	Astrophil	6	5
Strange flames of Love it in our soules would raise;	177	Astrophil	25	4
Our horsmanships, while by strange worke I prove	189	Astrophil	49	2
How is thy grace by my strange fortune staind!	230	Astrophil	98	3
Stella now learnes (strange case) to weepe in thee..	231	Astrophil	101	8
So brave a shott, deere fyre and bewtye strange..	345	Possibly	2	11
But this straunge race more straunge conceits did yeeld: . .	251	Other Poems	4	345
No sleeps, but dreams, no dreams, but visions straunge,. . .	253	Other Poems	4	436
Till straunge delight, delight to nothing ware;	254	Other Poems	4	482

STRANGELY

And will pitty the wound festred so strangely within me. . .	37	1st Eclogues	13	168
So strangely (alas) thy works in me prevaile,.	237	Astrophil	108	12
The firmament, so strangely bent,.	293	Psalm XIX		3

STRANGER

To stranger weights my minde's waste soile is bound, ...	149	Cert Sonnets	22	5
A stranger fish, my selfe not yet expirde, ...	150	Cert Sonnets	22	25
For I with Thee on earth a stranger am	330	Psalm XXXIX		39
But of a straunger mutuall help doth take:	248	Other Poems	4	238

STRANGER'S

Yet like a coward fearing stranger's pride,.	95	3rd Eclogues	64	29

STRANGERS

	PAGE	TITLE		LINE
Joie's strangers seeme, I cannot bide their showe, ...	74	Arcadia III	41	5
We have a fish, by strangers much admirde, ...	150	Cert Sonnets	22	21
And others' feete still seem'd but strangers in my way.. . .	165	Astrophil	1	11
Ev'en Feare makes strangers shew much love though much untrue.	293	Psalm XVIII		81

STRATAGEMS

| In all sweete stratagems sweete Arte can show, ... | 183 | Astrophil | 36 | 11 |

STRAVE

| Not usde to frozen clips, he strave to find some part, . . . | 168 | Astrophil | 8 | 6 |
| Geron strave hard, but aged were his feet, ... | 248 | Other Poems | 4 | 254 |

STRAW

Gay haire more gaie then straw when harvest lyes,.	76	Arcadia III	46	7
O this it is, the knotted straw is found	146	Cert Sonnets	17	16
Of touch they are, and poore I am their straw.	169	Astrophil	9	14

STRAY

But with such turnes the voice to stray, ...	86	Arcadia III	62	33
And sange unto my sheepe lest stray they should.	99	3rd Eclogues	66	21
Doth fall to stray, and my chiefe powres are brought	183	Astrophil	38	3
Yea tho I should thro vallys stray	301	Psalm XXIII		10
Before his eyes that so doth stray..	323	Psalm XXXVI		6
Least by my tongue I hap to stray;	329	Psalm XXXIX		2
(He staying thus) was faine abroad to stray.	250	Other Poems	4	331

STRAYED

| Or thou from her be straide, ... | 258 | Other Poems | 5 | 75 |

STRAYERS

| But strayers vile shall be destroyed . . . . | 327 | Psalm XXXVII | | 95 |

STRAYING

Of straying wayes, when valiant errour guides:	190	Astrophil	51	11
But alas, if in your straying.	222	A&S 9th Song		47
The straying stepps as wicked Counsel leads;	270	Psalm I		2
Sure, sure the Floods of straying streames	315	Psalm XXXII		22
Your flockes will not be straying.	261	Other Poems	6	34

STREAM

Since streame, aier, sand, mine eyes and eares conspire: . .	42	Arcadia II	21	17
One streame both streames containe,.	92	3rd Eclogues	63	35
In wind or water streame do require to be writ..	143	Cert Sonnets	13	4

STREAMS

When trees daunce to the pype, and swift streames stay by the musicke.	33	1st Eclogues	13	47
One streame both streames containe,.	92	3rd Eclogues	63	35
My lake is sense, whose still streames never runne,.	150	Cert Sonnets	22	15
What streames of teares she spent, ...	158	Cert Sonnets	28	22
Of cunningst fishers in most troubled streames,.	190	Astrophil	51	10
While those faire planets on thy streames did shine.	232	Astrophil	103	4
Sure, sure the Floods of straying streames	315	Psalm XXXII		22

STREETS

| That in the streets from sight of me they fled.. . . . . . . | 313 | Psalm XXXI | | 33 |

STRENGTH

That to your strength your foes have sure resorte.	38	Arcadia II	14	12
R. Weakenes you are, dare you with our strength fight? . . .	46	2nd Eclogues	27	21
Passion rebelde, oft reason's strength hath shaked..	82	Arcadia III	57	4
Her strength from him, his praise from her do growe.	92	3rd Eclogues	63	52
And hath with wailing strength clim'd highest mountaines:..	112	4th Eclogues	71	27
In object best to knit and strength our sight, ...	168	Astrophil	7	6
In sweetest strength, so sweetly skild withall,.	183	Astrophil	36	10
Towne-folkes my strength; a daintier judge applies	185	Astrophil	41	6
Strength of liking, rage of longing.	226	A&S 10th Song		24
Their numbrous strength redouble..	272	Psalm III		6
My strength my strongest rock, which my defence hast borne,.	290	Psalm XVIII		2
For why, my fighting strength by Thy strength strengthned was.	292	Psalm XVIII		71
With heavnly strength Thy earthly strength to prop..	295	Psalm XX		10
Lord from Thy strength is growing;	296	Psalm XXI		2
Lord in Thy strength, lord in Thy might, ...	298	Psalm XXI		49
My moystning strength is like a potsherd dride,.	299	Psalm XXII		35
But be not farr O Lord, my strength, my comfort;	299	Psalm XXII		45
The lord whose strength makes battails fight..	302	Psalm XXIV		20
That hand whose strength should help of bribes is full.. . .	306	Psalm XXVI		33
This lord with strength my life doth blisse;	306	Psalm XXVII		4
O my strength stop not Thine eare, ...	308	Psalm XXVIII		2
That God is my strength my shield;	309	Psalm XXVIII		26
God on them his strength doth lay.	309	Psalm XXVIII		31
God to his people strength shall give, ...	310	Psalm XXIX		28
Do pine, my strength with pain is wholy gon, ...	312	Psalm XXXI		29
Bee strong I say his strength confirm in you,.	314	Psalm XXXI		67
Of quick strength is an horse, ...	317	Psalm XXXIII		61
He shall be their true strength and aid.	327	Psalm XXXVII		100
Above line repeated at following location.	327	Psalm XXXVII		101
Stay then Thy wrath, that I may strength receive	330	Psalm XXXIX		41
In God his strength shall grow,.	333	Psalm XLI		10

STRENGTHENED

| Unto my strengthned stepps Thou didst enlarge the way, . . . | 292 | Psalm XVIII | | 66 |
| For why, my fighting strength by Thy strength strengthned was. . . . . | 292 | Psalm XVIII | | 71 |

STRENGTHENING

| Strengthning mine arms that they could break an Iron bow... | 292 | Psalm XVIII | | 63 |

STRENGTHENS

| And how possest he strengthens his invasion? . . . . | 48 | 2nd Eclogues | 28 | 36 |

STRENGTHS

	PAGE	TITLE		LINE
For both, alas, their strengthes together tie:	42	Arcadia II	22	4
Or know your strengths, and then you shall do well..	103	3rd Eclogues 66		154

STREPHON

Strephon. Yee Gote-heard Gods, that love the grassie mountaines,.	111	4th Eclogues 71		1
Strephon. I that was once free-burges of the forrests,. . .	111	4th Eclogues 71		13
Strephon. Long since alas, my deadly Swannish musique. . . .	112	4th Eclogues 71		25
Strephon. Me seemes I see the high and stately mountaines, .	112	4th Eclogues 71		37
Strephon. I wish to fire the trees of all these forrests;. .	112	4th Eclogues 71		49
Strephon. For she, whose parts maintainde a perfect musique,	113	4th Eclogues 71		61
Strephon. These mountaines witnesse shall, so shall these vallies, ...	113	4th Eclogues 71		73
Strephon. I Joye in griefe, and doo detest all joyes:. . . .	113	4th Eclogues 72		1
Strephon. Nor of my fortune ought but mischiefe crave, . . .	114	4th Eclogues 72		21
Strephon. So close unto my selfe my wrackes doo lie;	114	4th Eclogues 72		41
Strephon. Vaine is their paine, who labour in Despaire.. . .	115	4th Eclogues 72		61
Strephon. But ah her flight hath my dead reliques spent, . .	115	4th Eclogues 72		81
Strephon. I joye in griefe, and doo detest all joyes.. . . .	116	4th Eclogues 72		101
The later borne, yet too soone, Strephon hight..	242	Other Poems	4	24
To Strephon Aeole's land first breathing lent:	242	Other Poems	4	26
So Klaius' soule did in his Strephon rest.	242	Other Poems	4	34
Strephon was yonge, yet markt with humble eies	243	Other Poems	4	36
Strephon with leavy twiggs of Laurell tree	244	Other Poems	4	73
Strephon, fond boy, delighted did not knowe, ...	246	Other Poems	4	163
Strephon did leape with joy and jolitie, ...	246	Other Poems	4	177
And still, beleve me, Strephon was at hand..	247	Other Poems	4	216
Strephon, whose absence seem'd unto thee long, ...	247	Other Poems	4	220
At other end Uran did Strephon lend.	248	Other Poems	4	246
Cosma this while to Strephon safely came,.	249	Other Poems	4	265
While Strephon might with preatie Nous have met, ...	249	Other Poems	4	279
And Strephon single, turned after him.	249	Other Poems	4	287
Strephon so chas'd did seme in milke to swimme..	249	Other Poems	4	288
I thinke you thinke Strephon bent thitherward.	250	Other Poems	4	320
Nous counseld Strephon Geron to pursue,.	250	Other Poems	4	321
Strephon, whose eies on hir back-parts did play, ...	250	Other Poems	4	333
That she would faine the catch of Strephon flie, ...	252	Other Poems	4	380
For with pretence from Strephon hir to garde,.	252	Other Poems	4	385
When Strephon, cursing his owne backwardnes, ...	252	Other Poems	4	388
Strephon, poor youth, because he saw no smoke, ...	253	Other Poems	4	427
Which made his Strephon think himselfe in hell..	256	Other Poems	4	540

STREPHON'S

As Strephon's eare and heart to Klaius bent:	242	Other Poems	4	28
Till Strephon's plaining voice him nearer drew,.	256	Other Poems	4	535

STRICKEN

Feede on my sheepe, sorrow hathe stricken sayle, ...	43	Arcadia II	23	10
To him shall kneel who to the dust be stricken,.	300	Psalm XXII		73

STRIFE

Who ended hath this fearefull strife:.	13	Arcadia I	5	4
And since in vaine I find were all my strife,.	38	Arcadia II	14	13
R. We with ourselves abide a daily strife.	46	2nd Eclogues 27		25
R. But yet our strife sure peace in end doth breede.	46	2nd Eclogues 27		27
As in it selfe to nourish mortall strife.	57	2nd Eclogues 30		28
All strife for toyes, and clayming master's right:	93	3rd Eclogues 63		67
Cupid's lust gone, and gone is bitter strife, ...	93	3rd Eclogues 63		94
Knowing that evill becomes a houshold strife, ...	96	3rd Eclogues 64		70
Friend without change, playfellow without strife,.	103	3rd Eclogues 67		10
Is this thy fruite O strife? those thousand churches hie,. .	119	4th Eclogues 73		111
In fine, since strife of thought but marres the mind,. . . .	135	Cert Sonnets	1	8
For all his strife can onlie bondage gaine..	135	Cert Sonnets	2	8
With reason's strife, by senses overthrowne, ...	148	Cert Sonnets	19	14
A strife is growne betweene Vertue and Love, ...	190	Astrophil	52	1
Curst be the night which did your strife resist, ...	235	Astrophil	105	12
From strife of tongues in Thy Pavilions plac't..	313	Psalm XXXI		57
Which to avoyde, quenche, loose noughte booted stryfe. . . .	344	Possibly	2	8
Free of proud feares, brave begg'ry, smiling strife.	243	Other Poems	4	60

STRIKE

Vertue, beawtie, and speach, did strike, wound, charme,. . .	84	Arcadia III	60	1

STRIKES

Ffayre, thorow fayre strykes of heedefull Looke.	88	Arcadia III	62 V	70

STRING

The darte, the beames, the stringe so stronge I prove; . . .	344	Possibly	2	1

STRINGED

Let ten-stringd instrument	316	Psalm XXXIII		10

STRINGS

Thus in thy selfe, least strings are loudest founde, ...	81	Arcadia III	54	15
On Cupid's bow how are my heart-strings bent,.	174	Astrophil	19	1

STRIPES

Who threatned stripes, if he his wrath did prove:.	173	Astrophil	17	6

STRIVE

I cease to strive, with double conquest foild:	11	Arcadia I	2	2
Spoiling their flock, or while twixt them they strive. . . .	99	3rd Eclogues 66		35
I yeeld and strive, I kisse and curse the paine:	148	Cert Sonnets	19	17
Rebels to Nature, strive for their owne smart.	167	Astrophil	5	4
My wit doth strive those passions to defend, ...	174	Astrophil	18	10
Thy selfe, doest strive all minds that way to move,.	201	Astrophil	71	10
Sweet alas, why strive you thus?	211	A&S 4th Song		43
Strive we that in some worthy phrase	319	Psalm XXXIV		11
To strive she fear'd how it with vertue stoode..	245	Other Poems	4	126
Must strive with waiting foot, and watching eye.	248	Other Poems	4	228

	PAGE	TITLE	LINE

STRIVING
While we for mutuall spight a striving passion fed.. . . . . . 120 4th Eclogues 73 118
Striving abroad a foraging to go,. . . . . 192 Astrophil 55 6
Never striving, but in loving. . . . . 262 Other Poems 7 24
Striving with my Mates in Song,. . . . . 263 Other Poems 7 45

STROKE
R. Yet Passion, yeeld at length to Reason's stroke.. . . . . 47 2nd Eclogues 27 33
To that strange stroke which conquer'd all my senses,. . . . 61 2nd Eclogues 30 165
Who hath the hand which without stroke subdueth, ... 197 A&S 1st Song 21
That of the stroke, the heat, and knott of love, ... 344 Possibly 2 3
Thad'st killed with a stroke,. . . . . 259 Other Poems 5 100

STROKES
For with thy handy stroakes I wast.. . . . . 330 Psalm XXXIX 32

STROKING
With stroking hurt, and too much cramming kill.. . . . . . . 41 Arcadia II 20 12

STRONG
With strong foes on land, on seas with contrary tempests . . 29 1st Eclogues 11 5
R. We are too strong: but Reason seekes not blood. . . . . . 47 2nd Eclogues 27 29
A king upon a mouse, a strong foe to a rat,. . . . . 53 2nd Eclogues 29 32
With so strong lives, that bodie cannot rest . . . . 56 2nd Eclogues 29 145
His good strong staffe my slippry yeares upbore: . . . . . . 99 3rd Eclogues 66 37
So much more strong againe let fastest concorde make.. . . . 120 4th Eclogues 73 120
But Thereus' love, on her by strong hand wrokne, ... 137 Cert Sonnets 4 14
Where Vertue is made strong by Beautie's might,. . . . . . . 188 Astrophil 48 2
Her strong darts, but weake defences.. . . . . 226 A&S 10th Song 36
Unto the lord most strong: . . . . 273 Psalm III 32
Thou righteous art, Thou strong, thou patient, ... 277 Psalm VII 31
A pitt was digg'd, by this man vainly strong,. . . . . 278 Psalm VII 40
That like a byrd to some strong hill . . . . 283 Psalm XI 3
The strong God my salvation is:. . . . . 306 Psalm XXVII 2
Hope, Trust in God, bee strong, and he . . . . 308 Psalm XXVII 64
Is strong though he be gracious, ... 310 Psalm XXIX 11
Be my strong rock, be Thou my forteress. . . . . 312 Psalm XXXI 6
Bee strong I say his strength confirm in you,. . . . . 314 Psalm XXXI 67
To him most strong,. . . . . 316 Psalm XXXIII 14
Nor strong men have. . . . . 317 Psalm XXXIII 59
Who poore and weake from rich and strong dost free,. . . . . 321 Psalm XXXV 22
The darte, the beames, the stringe so stronge I prove; . . . 344 Possibly 2 1
When strong Desire, which vertue's love doth guide,. . . . . 345 Possibly 4 7

STRONGER
Unto a silly caban, though weake, yet stronger against woes. 34 1st Eclogues 13 93
United powers make each the stronger prove.. . . . . 223 Astrophil 88 14

STRONGEST
Whose strongest hope in your weake comfort lyes. . . . . . . 13 Arcadia I 4 4
Ath strongest soule, when most his raynes do bowe. . . . . . 25 1st Eclogues 9 101
My head you seeke, as to your strongest forte: . . . . 38 Arcadia II 14 10
Who hunting round the strongest for to kill, ... 50 2nd Eclogues 28 84
Cloth'd with fine tropes, with strongest reasons lin'd,. . . 194 Astrophil 58 6
The strongest judgements weake:. . . . . 215 A&S 6th Song 10
My strength my strongest rock, which my defence hast borne,. 290 Psalm XVIII 2

STRONGLY
Which shootes strongly with out any noyse and deadly without
  smarte. . . . . 35 1st Eclogues 13 122
Though strongly hedg'd of bloudy Lyon's pawes, ... 204 Astrophil 75 10

STROWED
As for to finde a pasture strowed with golde,. . . . . 104 3rd Eclogues 67 14

STROY
Let them not fleere, who me would causless stroy,. . . . . . 322 Psalm XXXV 50

STROYS
For even the hearbes our hatefull musique stroyes, ... 116 4th Eclogues 72 103

STRUGGLE
But they do swell and struggle forth of me,. . . . . 189 Astrophil 50 3

STRUGGLING
When strugling rocks he would imbrace. . . . . 88 Arcadia III 62 70

STUDIED
She studied cunning how the same to blinde.. . . . . 95 3rd Eclogues 64 42

STUDIES
Our studies fixt upon the falles of fortune. . . . . 109 Arcadia IV 70 30

STUDY
But with much studie learne late to repent.. . . . . 106 3rd Eclogues 67 96
I studie that which moste may me displease,. . . . . 113 4th Eclogues 72 5
Her giftes my study was, her beauties were my sporte:. . . . 117 4th Eclogues 73 41

STUDYING
Still studying how to us to be a light.. . . . . 129 4th Eclogues 76 16
Studying inventions fine, her wits to entertaine:. . . . . . 165 Astrophil 1 6

STUDY'S
Invention, Nature's child, fled step-dame Studie's blowes, . 165 Astrophil 1 10

STUFF
One brings the stuffe, the other stamps the coine, ... 20 1st Eclogues 8 3
One day layes up stuffe of griefe for the morrow:. . . . . . 62 2nd Eclogues 30 176
That childish stuffe which knowes not frendes from foes, . . 81 Arcadia III 54 11
(Which made of heav'nly stuffe no mortal chaunge doth bynde) 117 4th Eclogues 73 32
As stuffe meant for the sale set out to glaring showe) . . . 118 4th Eclogues 73 72
In thy cold stuffe a flegmatike delight? . . . . 193 Astrophil 56 11
Of such heaven stuffe, to cloath so heavenly mynde.. . . . . 232 Astrophil 101 14

STUMBLE
They stumble so. . . . . 307 Psalm XXVII 11

STUMBLING
Witnesse with me, that my foule stumbling so,. . . . . 227 Astrophil 93 6
But He, staffe of my age, He staid my stumbling state. . . . 291 Psalm XVIII 39

	PAGE	TITLE		LINE
STUMBLING (CONTINUED)				
My heeles and plants thou didst from stumbling slip				
sustaine , ...	292	Psalm XVIII		67
STUNG				
With a cruell answer stong..	139	Cert Sonnets	7	7
Another man be stonge.	320	Psalm XXXIV		52
STYGIAN				
If othes might serve, even by the Stygian lake,.	146	Cert Sonnets 17		6
STYLE				
No stile is held for base, where Love well named is:	14	1st Eclogues	7	4
The stile of heavie hart can never flie.	129	4th Eclogues 75		139
To some a sweetest plaint, a sweetest stile affords, ...	168	Astrophil	6	9
O joy, too high for my low stile to show:.	200	Astrophil	69	1
A Shepheard's tale no height of stile desires.	242	Other Poems	4	1
STYX				
And having bound them fast by Styx, they should obaye. . . .	121	4th Eclogues 73		161
SUAGE				
All folkes prest at thy will thy paine to 'swage,.	232	Astrophil	101	11
SUBDUE				
So dare I, wretch, my bashfull feare subdue, ...	3	Lady of May	1	11
He that is my revenge, in whom I realmes subdue, ...	293	Psalm XVIII		85
SUBDUED				
Since then thou hast so farre subdued me,.	185	Astrophil	40	12
SUBDUETH				
Who hath the hand which without stroke subdueth, ...	197	A&S 1st Song		21
SUBJECT				
But wretched be the soules which, vaild in a contrary				
subject, ...	32	1st Eclogues 13		19
Since so mine eyes are subject to your sight,.	39	Arcadia II	16	1
In this rare subject from thy ccmmon right:.	79	Arcadia III	51	10
O Stealing time the subject of delaie, ...	80	Arcadia III	53	1
I beg no subject to use eloquence, ...	179	Astrophil	28	9
To leave the scepter of all subject things, ...	183	Astrophil	38	4
Thou, sweetest subject, werte borne in the realme of Love, .	214	A&S 5th Song		64
Time doth as the subject prove,.	234	A&S 11th Song		18
SUBJECTS				
Princes in subjects wrongd, must deeme themselves abused.. .	213	A&S 5th Song		30
SUBLIME				
Those words, which do sublime the quintessence of blisse:. .	205	Astrophil	77	8
SUBMIT				
But still take heede least thou thy selfe submit	4	Lady of May	2	23
SUBSCRIPTION				
Subscription was, yours most, if you will prove.	96	3rd Eclogues 64		90
SUBSTANCE				
Longing to be with losse of substance gay.	93	3rd Eclogues 63		74
If that the substance faile within..	156	Cert Sonnets 27		16
SUBTLETY				
He thought gray haires afforded subtletie.	248	Other Poems	4	256
SUCCEEDING				
Shall prosper still, with well succeeding end.	270	Psalm I		12
And night to night succeding right	293	Psalm XIX		7
Though ill deeds well succeeding be.	324	Psalm XXXVII		4
SUCCESS				
But nowe successe hathe gott above annoyes,.	71	Arcadia III	36	17
But Grammer's force with sweet successe confirme,.	196	Astrophil	63	11
Full of successe, fond I did say	311	Psalm XXX		20
SUCCOR				
Beautie's plague, Vertue's scourge, succour of lies:	206	Astrophil	78	6
Since ever thou to them wilt succour send.	275	Psalm V		36
The succour of the succourless	283	Psalm X		63
Is but a succour vaine,.	318	Psalm XXXIII		63
Take up Thy shield and for my succour stand, ...	321	Psalm XXXV		3
SUCCORLESS				
The succour of the succourless	283	Psalm X		63
SUCH				
Whose mind is such, as wisest minds appall,.	3	Lady of May	1	3
Such planted gifts enrich even beggers' sight:	3	Lady of May	1	10
That such a one is witnesse of my hart,.	5	Lady of May	3	14
Both they themselves unto such two shall wed,.	11	Arcadia I	1	5
Whose vertues strange, and beuties such, as no man them may				
know?.	12	Arcadia I	3	2
Nor be abasht, since such a guest you finde, ...	13	Arcadia I	4	3
Dorus. Such Kala is: but ah, my fancies raysed be.	15	1st Eclogues	7	37
I never found long love such wealth hath paide to me". . . .	16	1st Eclogues	7	54
Her eyes so maistering me, that such objection	16	1st Eclogues	7	68
Bent to such one, in whom, my selfe must say,.	17	1st Eclogues	7	107
Such as you see, such still you shall me finde..	18	1st Eclogues	7	122
And titles are but spots to such a worthe, ...	18	1st Eclogues	7	132
If still her minde be such,.	19	1st Eclogues	7	150
Such force hath Love above poore Nature's power.	19	1st Eclogues	7	161
Dorus. Such force hath Love above poore Nature's power,. . .	19	1st Eclogues	7	162
Such weight it hath which once is full possest.	20	1st Eclogues	7	V961
Above line repeated at following location.	20	1st Eclogues	7	V962
With Jove's disdaine at such a rival's seed, ...	21	1st Eclogues	8	20
Or with desire to make such foe a frend, . , ...	22	1st Eclogues	9	9
Since she faire fierce to such a state me calls, ...	23	1st Eclogues	9	30
Would scorne in man (their king) such feeble shows.. . . .	23	1st Eclogues	9	43
Such hartes of brasse, wise heads, and garments trim	24	1st Eclogues	9	75
And belly nought is left, such sure is he, ...	24	1st Eclogues	9	82
Such wandring reasons in thy speech I finde.	25	1st Eclogues	9	98

SUCH   (CONTINUED)   PAGE   TITLE   LINE
     Such sight have they that see with goggling eyes.. . . . . . .   25 1st Eclogues 9 113
     Such active minde but seldome passion sees.. . . . .   26 1st Eclogues 9 134
     When they shall such devided weakenesse prove? . . . .   26 1st Eclogues 10   6
     Mastix. What marvaile if in youth such faults be done, . . .   27 1st Eclogues 10   25
     With such intemperance, that each way grows. . . . .   27 1st Eclogues 10   38
     And such discord twixt greatest shepheards flowes, ...   27 1st Eclogues 10   40
     Then who makes us such judges over all?. . . . .   29 1st Eclogues 10   96
     And to the woods or brookes, who do make such dreery
         recitall . . . .   33 1st Eclogues 13   42
     Such this smale greatnes, doth seeme compar'd to the
         greatest... . . . .   34 1st Eclogues 13   76
     Where proofes justly do teach, thus matcht, such worth to be
         nought worth. . . . .   34 1st Eclogues 13   83
     Shall such morning deaws be an ease to the heate of a love's
         fire? . . . .   34 1st Eclogues 13   88
     Is chaunced to my life, that from such muddy abundance . . .   34 1st Eclogues 13   96
     Ease I do feele (such ease as falls to one wholy diseased) .   35 1st Eclogues 13 114
     Thus to my sonne do I yeeld, such lookes her beames do
         aforde me. . . . .   36 1st Eclogues 13 133
     Cleofila. Hardy shephearde, such as thy meritts, such may be
         her insight . . . .   37 1st Eclogues 13 155
     Justely to graunt thy rewarde, such envie I beare to thy
         fortune. . . . .   37 1st Eclogues 13 156
     Whose force had such force so to transforme, nay to reforme
         me,. . . . .   37 1st Eclogues 13 166
     O be it so, graunte such an event, O Gods, that event give..   37 1st Eclogues 13 169
     Such life to leade, such death I vow to dye. . . . .   40 Arcadia II   18   18
     O only sonne that suche a fruite can breede. . . . .   43 Arcadia II   23   3
     To such a force soone chaunge were nothing sutable.. . . . .   47 2nd Eclogues 28   12
     Such anger bringing: as for me, my fancie. . . . .   50 2nd Eclogues 28   95
     Nought could impart such heates to friendly mind.. . . . . .   51 2nd Eclogues 28 105
     Nico. I thinke it well: such voice would make one musicke
         hate:. . . . .   52 2nd Eclogues 29   21
     Such oddes I willing lay; for him and you I know.. . . . . .   53 2nd Eclogues 29   48
     And suffer such a wrong? a wrong I trowe,. . . . .   54 2nd Eclogues 29   64
     What needed so high sprites such mansions blind? . . . . . .   57 2nd Eclogues 30   14
     And saw those eyes (those Sonnes) such shoures to shew,. . .   58 2nd Eclogues 30   49
     But such we are with inward tempest blowne . . . .   59 2nd Eclogues 30   80
     What sacriledge hath such a saint disgrast?. . . . .   59 2nd Eclogues 30   97
     Such beames so like his owne, which might have might . . . .   60 2nd Eclogues 30 105
     They uttred are in such a feeling fashion, ...   60 2nd Eclogues 30 126
     To hold these worldly things in such proportion, ...   60 2nd Eclogues 30 132
     Long be thy woes for such newes, but how recks she my
         thoughts? Oughts... . . . .   64 2nd Eclogues 31   33
     Dev'lls? if in hell such dev'lls do abide, to the hells I do
         go. Go. . . . .   65 2nd Eclogues 31   50
     Such wisedome, that in her lives speculation:. . . . .   69 2nd Eclogues 34   35
     Such goodnes that in her simplicitie triumphs: . . . .   69 2nd Eclogues 34   36
     Oh! if such a one have bent to a lonely life . . . .   69 2nd Eclogues 34   39
     For such company decks such solitarines. . . . .   69 2nd Eclogues 34   42
     Yet never rock, nor race, suche terror brought,. . . . . . .   71 Arcadia III 37   3
     Though you besides such graces earth hath lent,. . . . . . .   77 Arcadia III 49   3
     Such pearcing wordes as no thoughts els conceave:. . . . . .   78 Arcadia III 49   8
     No no, such force with my small force to trye. . . . .   79 Arcadia III 50   15
     But wilt thy selfe in such a seate delighte, ...   79 Arcadia III 51   11
     Thy running course cannot such beawties marke: . . . .   80 Arcadia III 52   11
     Since in such phrase his faith he did attire... . . . . . .   80 Arcadia III 53   8
     The world doth yeeld such ill consorted shows, ...   81 Arcadia III 54   9
     Such living beames should her black seate assaile, ...   82 Arcadia III 55   10
     What medicin then, can such desease remove . . . .   85 Arcadia III 61   13
     But with such turnes the voice to stray, ...   86 Arcadia III 62   33
     Such be I thinke the sumptuous towers. . . . .   87 Arcadia III 62   49
     But Lillies such whose native smell. . . . .   87 Arcadia III 62   63
     A hill most fitte for such a master, ...   88 Arcadia III 62   79
     For such an use the world hath gotten, ...   88 Arcadia III 62   85
     Whose bought incav'd doth yeeld such sight,. . . . .   89 Arcadia III 62   97
     Along whose ridge such bones are met,. . . . .   89 Arcadia III 62 111
     Whose gentle rayes suche Luster fynde, ...   89 Arcadia III 62 V115
     Her Nose and Chynn suche Ivory weares, ...   86 Arcadia III 62 V 27
     Such mindes with sweet affections for to fill, ...   92 3rd Eclogues 63   61
     To such an end as he might be abus'de. . . . .   95 3rd Eclogues 64   28
     Not seeing earst such token in the wife, ...   96 3rd Eclogues 64   68
     A letter such which might from either part . . . .   96 3rd Eclogues 64   81
     The pistle selfe, such kinde of wordes it had, ...   96 3rd Eclogues 64   91
     Then such be he, as she his worth may see, ...   98 3rd Eclogues 65   3
     Such maner time there was (what time I n'ot) . . . .   100 3rd Eclogues 66   43
     Was onely won'd with such as beastes begot:. . . . .   100 3rd Eclogues 66   45
     But of such wives we finde a slender crew; . . . .   104 3rd Eclogues 67   25
     No wife but I hath such a man, God wot". . . . .   104 3rd Eclogues 67   45
     Such is their speech, who be of sober wit; . . . .   104 3rd Eclogues 67   46
     With such a will that nothing can asswage. . . . .   105 3rd Eclogues 67   51
     And God forbid, women such cattell were, ...   106 3rd Eclogues 67   82
     And yet finde no such faults in womankind. . . . .   106 3rd Eclogues 67   87
     We beare our double yoke with such consent,. . . . .   106 3rd Eclogues 67   92
     In such a case where it appeares that nature . . . .   109 Arcadia IV   70   9
     Then since such pow'rs conspire unto our damage. . . . . . .   109 Arcadia IV   70   13
     In graunting such a scope to filthy fortune, ...   109 Arcadia IV   70   21
     Till by such hap, as I must ever rewe, ...   115 4th Eclogues 72   74
     Such vitall sparke, that her mine eyes might see.. . . . . .   115 4th Eclogues 72   84

SUCH (CONTINUED)   PAGE TITLE LINE

My senses such release, as they which quiet live,. . . . . . 117 4th Eclogues 73 12
Ne could my soule it selfe accuse of such a faulte,. . . . . 117 4th Eclogues 73 19
Such thoughts, me thought, I thought, and straind my single
 mind . . . . 118 4th Eclogues 73 49
When lo with hugest noise (such noise a tower makes. . . . . 118 4th Eclogues 73 51
(Or such a noise it was, as highest thunders sende,. . . . . 118 4th Eclogues 73 53
But heavy was her pace, and such a meagre cheere,. . . . . . 118 4th Eclogues 73 69
When I such guests did see come out of such a house, ... 118 4th Eclogues 73 75
But such they say we be: this praise our discord bred, . . . 120 4th Eclogues 73 117
Such proffer made, which she well showd with smiling cheere. 120 4th Eclogues 73 144
Now bolder waxt, waxt prowde, that I such sway might beare:. 121 4th Eclogues 73 159
"Yet thou shalt not go free (quoth Venus) such a fire. . . . 121 4th Eclogues 73 170
"Nay thou (said both) shalt see such beames shine in her
 face . . . . 121 4th Eclogues 73 175
Such thing cannot I seeke (Despaire hath giv'n me my answer. 122 4th Eclogues 74 11
Such thing cannot he hope, that knowes thy determinat
 hardnes; . . . . 122 4th Eclogues 74 13
O faire, O fairest, are such the triumphs to thy fairnesse?. 123 4th Eclogues 74 31
Can death beautie become? must I be such a monument? . . . . 123 4th Eclogues 74 32
Shall such high Plannets tend to the losse of a worme? . . . 123 4th Eclogues 74 38
Ere that I should consent to doo such excessive a dammage. . 124 4th Eclogues 74 61
O not but such love you say you could have afoorded, ... 124 4th Eclogues 74 63
But what's this for a fault, for which such faieth be
 abolisht,. . . . . 124 4th Eclogues 74 69
Such faith, so staineles, inviolate, violent?. . . . . 124 4th Eclogues 74 70
Unto the man, whom now such miseries you awarde? . . . . . . 124 4th Eclogues 74 74
What? was I then worthie such good, now worthie so muche
 evill? . . . . 124 4th Eclogues 74 77
In Nature's name to suffer such a harme, ... 125 4th Eclogues 75 17
Such cursed harmes as cannot be redressed. . . . . 126 4th Eclogues 75 63
From such as were to dye for him contented.. . . . . 128 4th Eclogues 75 126
From such deepe plaint as should such woes descrie,. . . . . 129 4th Eclogues 75 137
So high, as should make such a paine notorious:. . . . . . . 129 4th Eclogues 75 140
Shall we now finde a guide of such affection,. . . . . 129 4th Eclogues 76 22
To starving minds such is God Cupid's dish.. . . . . 136 Cert Sonnets 2 14
But no more wordes, thoughe such a worde bee spoken, ... 138 Cert Sonnets 5 17
Where each part in such peace dwelleth,. . . . . 140 Cert Sonnets 7 16
Hath not such paine as it makes others have: . . . . 142 Cert Sonnets 11 10
Hath yet such health, as it my life can save.. . . . . 142 Cert Sonnets 11 12
Such causelesse feares when coward minds do take,. . . . . . 145 Cert Sonnets 16 5
Should Ladies faire be tyed to such hard lawes,. . . . . . . 146 Cert Sonnets 17 23
Who hath such beautie seene. . . . . 158 Cert Sonnets 28 25
Who ever saw such woe? . . . . 158 Cert Sonnets 28 28
For such a thought most highlie prized,. . . . . 159 Cert Sonnets 29 14
From such a femall franzie . . . . 160 Cert Sonnets 30 8
Above line repeated at following location. . . . . 160 Cert Sonnets 30 18
From such femall franzie,. . . . . 160 Cert Sonnets 30 28
To call such wit a franzie,. . . . . 161 Cert Sonnets 30 38
I sweare, my heart such one shall shew to thee,. . . . . . . 167 Astrophil 4 12
Looks over the world, and can find nothing such, ... 169 Astrophil 9 10
O no, her heart is such a Cittadell,. . . . . 171 Astrophil 12 12
You take wrong waies, those far-fet helpes be such,. . . . . 172 Astrophil 15 9
Such coltish gyres, that to my birth I owe . . . . 175 Astrophil 21 6
Yet to those fooles heav'n such wit doth impart, ... 177 Astrophil 24 5
And can with foule abuse such beauties blot; . . . . 177 Astrophil 24 11
Looke at my hands for no such quintessence;. . . . . 179 Astrophil 28 11
"Foole," answers he, "no Indes such treasures hold,. . . . . 181 Astrophil 32 12
Made manifest by such a victorie,. . . . . 185 Astrophil 40 10
Such smart may pitie claime of any hart, ... 186 Astrophil 44 3
The heav'nly nature of that place is such, ... 187 Astrophil 44 12
Pitie thereof gate in her breast such place. . . . . 187 Astrophil 45 7
To such a schoole-mistresse, whose lessons new . . . . 188 Astrophil 46 10
Can those blacke beames such burning markes engrave. . . . . 188 Astrophil 47 2
Whose necke becomes such yoke of tyranny?. . . . . 188 Astrophil 47 4
Or sprite, disdaine of such disdaine to have?. . . . . 188 Astrophil 47 6
To them that do such entertainment need, ... 190 Astrophil 51 3
By such unsuted speech should hindred be.. . . . . 190 Astrophil 51 14
Her soule, arm'd but with such a dainty rind,. . . . . 193 Astrophil 57 7
Alas, if you graunt only such delight. . . . . 194 Astrophil 59 12
Thou whom to me such my good turnes should bind, ... 198 Astrophil 65 3
Hast thou found such and such like arguments?. . . . . 199 Astrophil 67 10
Anger invests with such a lovely grace,. . . . . 203 Astrophil 73 13
Nor this, nor that, nor any such small cause,. . . . . 204 Astrophil 75 12
With such a rosie morne, whose beames most freshly gay . . . 205 Astrophil 76 7
That conversation sweet, where such high comforts be,. . . . 205 Astrophil 77 10
Is it not evill that such a Devill wants hornes? . . . . . . 206 Astrophil 78 14
Cannot such grace your silly selfe content,. . . . . 208 Astrophil 83 11
Yet swam in joy, such love in her was seene. . . . . 223 Astrophil 87 11
Is faith so weake? Or is such force in thee? . . . . 223 Astrophil 88 5
When Sun is hid, can starres such beames display?. . . . . . 223 Astrophil 88 6
With such bad mixture of my night and day, ... 224 Astrophil 89 12
Models such be wood-globes of glistring skies. . . . . 225 Astrophil 91 11
By being placed in such a wretch as I. . . . . 228 Astrophil 94 14
Nay sorrow comes with such maine rage, that he . . . . 229 Astrophil 95 9
Thanke may you have for such a thankfull part, ... 229 Astrophil 95 13
Such light in sense, with such a darkned mind. . . . . 231 Astrophil 99 14
O plaints conserv'd in such a sugred phraise,. . . . . 231 Astrophil 100 9
Such teares, sighs, plaints, no sorrow is, but joy:. . . . . 231 Astrophil 100 12
Or if such heavenly signes must prove annoy, ... 231 Astrophil 100 13

SUCH   (CONTINUED)   PAGE   TITLE   LINE

And grace, sicke too, such fine conclusions tries, ...   231 Astrophil 101   3
Of such heaven stuffe, to cloath so heavenly mynde.. . . . .   232 Astrophil 101   14
That with such poysonous care my lookes you marke, ...   233 Astrophil 104   2
Whose grace is such, that when it chides doth cherish? . . .   197 A&S 1st Song   18
If Orpheus' voyce had force to breathe such musicke's love .   208 A&S 3rd Song   1
But of thy soule, so fraught with such ungratefulnesse,. . .   213 A&S 5th Song   40
Alas, that I am forst such evill of thee to say, ...   215 A&S 5th Song   80
And such skill in my Muse you reconcil'd shall find, ...   215 A&S 5th Song   89
Bids you leave such minds to nourish." . . . .   234 A&S 11th Song   27
Deere, do reason no such spite,. . . . .   234 A&S 11th Song   28
Both in their objects such,. . . . .   216 A&S 6th Song   41
Then she spake; her speech was such,. . . . .   220 A&S 8th Song   69
While such wise she love denied, ...   220 A&S 8th Song   71
Merry flocke, such one forgo,. . . . .   221 A&S 9th Song   8
Such blessings shall not wycked wretches see . . . .   270 Psalm I   13
Why do these earthly kings and lords such meetings make, . .   271 Psalm II   3
Such pleasure take in Vanity,. . . . .   273 Psalm IV   9
Such one I say, that when I make . . . .   273 Psalm IV   13
From whence shall come to us such ayd? . . . .   274 Psalm IV   25
For all I neede, that with such foes do byde.. . . . .   275 Psalm V   24
Thy work it is such men safe in to hemm. . . . .   275 Psalm V   39
Ever from deed of any such desart: . . . .   277 Psalm VII   8
Against such rage of foes: Awake for me. . . . .   277 Psalm VII   17
Of Conquerd states, wherby such fame you gott? . . . .   280 Psalm IX   17
In such a place Unknown. . . . .   282 Psalm X   33
With such brave wounds, that they under my feet did ly.. . .   292 Psalm XVIII   70
Indeed O you, you that be such of mind,. . . . .   300 Psalm XXII   63
For never day such changing wrought. . . . .   303 Psalm XXV   17
The lord such plenty hath, ...   303 Psalm XXV   32
To such as keep his Covenant . . . .   304 Psalm XXV   41
For such he makes his secret know, ...   304 Psalm XXV   53
To such he doth his Cov'nant show. . . . .   304 Psalm XXV   54
And from the haunts of such bad folks did fly. . . . .   305 Psalm XXVI   18
Ev'n such I say, whose lying tongue. . . . .   308 Psalm XXVII   58
And watch and ward for such do beare . . . .   319 Psalm XXXIV   27
And blessing such with length desires, ...   320 Psalm XXXIV   47
Laying such things, as never in mee weare; . . . .   322 Psalm XXXV   26
I did pull down my self, fasting for such; . . . .   322 Psalm XXXV   31
But make such glad, and full of joyfulness,. . . . .   323 Psalm XXXV   67
Least such things sin in Thy self cherish, ...   325 Psalm XXXVII   22
Nor let him be condemn'd by such.. . . . .   327 Psalm XXXVII   84
In my heart such grief is found. . . . .   328 Psalm XXXVIII   24
I ev'en as such kind of wight, ...   328 Psalm XXXVIII   40
And as I mus'd such World to see,. . . . .   329 Psalm XXXIX   10
Since it is Thou that makest one such? . . . .   330 Psalm XXXIX   30
In such longing thoughts it falleth. . . . .   334 Psalm XLII   24
Cast down in such dole,. . . . .   337 Psalm XLIII   32
Whose lyverie is such, as most I freeze apparelled most, . .   343 Possibly   1   21
Will. God shield us from such Dames. If so our Downes be
    sped,. . . . .   344 Possibly   1   39
But hence, even hence, I must needes goe; such is my dogged
    fate.. . . . .   344 Possibly   1   48
Such was his minde, if you another take: . . . .   345 Possibly   4   11
Such marble eares, no cunning wordes can charme, ...   346 Possibly   5   2
Who may be glad, be glad you be not such:. . . . .   242 Other Poems   4   15
In some such one she lik'd not his desire, ...   245 Other Poems   4 119
To which hir presence such a feaver brought. . . . .   246 Other Poems   4 176
These sports shepheards deviz'd such faults to show. . . . .   248 Other Poems   4 241
With such mad haste he did to Cosma goe, ...   249 Other Poems   4 271
He that before shund hir to shun such harmes,. . . . .   252 Other Poems   4 383
He envied such a death in sight of lover,. . . . .   259 Other Poems   5 124
Such comfort, fervent love . . . .   261 Other Poems   6   51
It belongs to such alone . . . .   262 Other Poems   7   27
SUCK
Where drawing breath, I sucke the aire of woe: . . . .   73 Arcadia III 40   10
Sorowe suck up the marowe of my might, ...   74 Arcadia III 42   10
Let breath sucke up those sweetes, let armes embrace . . . .   210 Astrophil   85   12
SUCKED
In sport I suckt, while she asleepe did lie, ...   203 Astrophil   73   6
Desire the more he suckt, more sought the brest, ...   247 Other Poems   4 203
SUCKING
Sucking one's ill, another to infect.. . . . .   21 1st Eclogues 8   36
Men tongd like lotches sucking others sorrowe. . . . .   50 2nd Eclogues 28 V885
Dwell in my ruines, feede with sucking smarte, ...   113 4th Eclogues 72   9
SUCKLINGS
From sucklings hath Thy honour sproong,. . . . .   278 Psalm VIII   5
SUCKS
Ech eare suckes up the words a true love scattereth, ...   14 1st Eclogues 7   5
SUDDEN
Till of these thoughts thy sodaine ende bereaved me. . . . .   48 2nd Eclogues 28   33
The Moone a sunder rent; whereat with sodaine fall . . . . .   118 4th Eclogues 73   57
SUE
Nico. I oft doo sue, and Leuca saith, I shall, ...   54 2nd Eclogues 29   87
SUFFER
But even for that shall suffer mightie Lovers. . . . .   28 1st Eclogues 10   72
With bolde clamor unheard, unmarckt, what I seeke what I
    suffer:. . . . .   35 1st Eclogues 13 112
And suffer such a wrong? a wrong I trowe,. . . . .   54 2nd Eclogues 29   64
Did suffer drousie lids mine eyes then cleare to blinde; . .   117 4th Eclogues 73   26

SUFFER   (CONTINUED)   PAGE   TITLE   LINE
    In Nature's name to suffer such a harme, ... 125 4th Eclogues 75   17
    I call it praise to suffer Tyrannie; . . . . 166 Astrophil   2   11
    Suffer not her to laugh, while both we suffer paine: . . . . 213 A&S 5th Song   29
    Shall never suffer shame;. . . . . 303 Psalm XXV   8
    Lord wilt thou see, and wilt Thou suffer it? . . . . 322 Psalm XXXV   43
SUFFERED
    Nor held in evill, nor suffered to be sound, ... 144 Cert Sonnets 15   8
    Nay, more foole I, oft suffered you to sleepe. . . . . 208 Astrophil   83   7
    Ne yet shall suffred be a place to take, ... 270 Psalm I   17
    Mcv'd not himselfe, nor suffred hir to move. . . . . 250 Other Poems   4   328
SUFFERING
    Wherein she suffring all her spirits' languish,. . . . . . . 137 Cert Sonnets 4   15
    Suffering the evils both of the day and night, ... 224 Astrophil   89   9
SUFFICE
    Of conquest, do not these effects suffice, ... 183 Astrophil   36   7
    Let it suffise that he himselfe forgoe.. . . . . 254 Other Poems   4   488
SUGARED
    Which flanked with two sugred flankes, ... 88   Arcadia III 62   89
    That in her breast thy pap well sugred lies, ... 170 Astrophil   12   5
    By Phoebus' doome, with sugred sentence sayes, ... 177 Astrophil   25   2
    This sowre-breath'd mate tast of those sugred lips.. . . . . 194 Astrophil   59   11
    And yet my Starre, because a sugred kisse. . . . . 203 Astrophil   73   5
    O plaints conserv'd in such a sugred phraise,. . . . . 231 Astrophil   100   9
    Which do breath a sugred blisse, ... 226 A&S 10th Song   29
    Their sugred selves to kisse thy happy hedd: . . . . 258 Other Poems   5   58
SUGARING
    Nor other sugring of my speech to prove, ... 192 Astrophil   55   10
SUING
    Which from suing voice do fly. . . . . 309 Psalm XXVIII   10
SUIT
    Lalus. But if my Kala this my suite denies,. 18   1st Eclogues 7   147
    (At Juno's suite who much did Argus love). 22   1st Eclogues 8   46
    Nature against we do seeme to rebell, seeme fooles in a
        vaine sute.. 32   1st Eclogues 13   24
    Holde me most yours, then my longe suite is signde.. 79   Arcadia III 50   18
    The multitude to Jove a suite empartes,. . . . . 100 3rd Eclogues 66   61
    Well Love, since this demurre our sute doth stay,. . . . . . 191 Astrophil   52   12
    Ah, my sute granted is, I feele my breast doth swell:. . . . 213 A&S 5th Song   34
    The lord my suite did heare, and gently heare, ... 276 Psalm VI   29
    My suite is just, just lord to my suite hark;. . . . . 289 Psalm XVII   1
SUITABLE
    To such a force soone chaunge were nothing sutable.. 47   2nd Eclogues 28   12
SUITOR
    Then to my selfe, not though Jove grew a suter of hers.. . . 143 Cert Sonnets 13   2
SUITS
    His workes, showes, suites, with wit, grace, and vow's
        might 84   Arcadia III 60   4
    Up to Our God, when Thy suites granted be. . . . . 296 Psalm XX   20
    Heare lord my suits and cryes, stop not thyn eares . . . . . 330 Psalm XXXIX   37
SULLEN
    Thus did I sing, and pipe eight sullen houres. . . . . 103 3rd Eclogues 66   155
    Sweet Ladie, as for those whose sullen cheare, ... 147 Cert Sonnets 17   46
    Silence in both displaies his sullen might,. . . . . 229 Astrophil   96   5
SUM
    See Beautie's totall summe summ'd in her face: . . . . 210 Astrophil   85   10
    In summe, I shew'd, that I to them was bent. . . . . 322 Psalm XXXV   33
    In sum, proud Boreas never ruled fleet . . . . 251 Other Poems   4   373
SUMMED
    See Beautie's totall summe summ'd in her face: . . . . 210 Astrophil   85   10
SUMMER
    Is she in rage? so is the Sunne in sommer hot, ... 49   2nd Eclogues 28   61
    O Words which fall like sommer deaw on me, ... 76   Arcadia III 46   1
    As in a sommer day a man might see:. 94   3rd Eclogues 64   4
    I feele the flames of hottest sommer day.. . . . . 224 Astrophil   89   14
SUMMONED
    But straight they fledde, summond by cruell honor, ... 17   1st Eclogues 7   95
SUMPTUOUS
    Such be I thinke the sumptuous towers. 87   Arcadia III 62   49
SUN
    Yet hath sir Sunne the greatest praise,. 13   Arcadia I   5   9
    Doth beauties keep, which never Sunne can burne, ... 18   1st Eclogues 7   118
    I finde no shade, but where my Sunne doth burne: 18   1st Eclogues 7   144
    Or to the Sun for wonders seeme small sparks of a candle:. . 34   1st Eclogues 13   79
    Then by my high Cedar, rich Ruby, and only shining Sunne,. . 34   1st Eclogues 13   80
    Pcpler changeth his hew from a rising sunne to a setting:. . 36   1st Eclogues 13   132
    Thus to my sonne do I yeeld, such lookes her beames do
        aforde me.. 36   1st Eclogues 13   133
    Clusters of clowdes, which no Sunne ever cleares.. 41   Arcadia II   21   4
    O only sonne that suche a fruite can breede. 43   Arcadia II   23   3
    O blessed sonne whence all this blessing goes. 43   Arcadia II   23   6
    And from the stormes our sweeteste sonne will shield.. . . . 43   Arcadia II   23   9
    While our sonne shynes no clowdie greeves assaile. 43   Arcadia II   23   12
    My sonne is gon, your pasture barrein growes,. 43   Arcadia II   24   2
    O cruell sonne thy hate this harme dothe breede. 43   Arcadia II   24   3
    My sonne alas from me for ever goes. 43   Arcadia II   24   6
    My sun is gon, from stormes what shall us sheelde? 43   Arcadia II   24   9
    My sun is gon, Nowe clowdie greeves assayle. 44   Arcadia II   24   12
    Is she in rage? so is the Sunne in sommer hot, ... 49   2nd Eclogues 28   61
    The Sunne is hid; his kindly shadowe combers not.. 49   2nd Eclogues 28   63

```
SUN                         (CONTINUED)                    PAGE    TITLE          LINE
    Nico. When Leuca dooth appeare, the Sunne for shame. . . . .   55  2nd Eclogues 29    93
    Pas. When Cosma doth come forth, the Sun displaies . . . . .   55  2nd Eclogues 29    96
    By what eclipse shall that Sonne be defaste? . . . . . . . .   59  2nd Eclogues 30    95
    Burnt by the Sunne, she first must build her nest. . . . . .   60  2nd Eclogues 30   103
    But well you know, the gentle Sunne would save . . . . . .    60  2nd Eclogues 30   104
    Nowe that myne eyes their cheerefull sunn dothe misse. . . .   70  Arcadia III  35     5
    Ofte scorching sonne, ofte clowdie darkenes feares,. . . . .   71  Arcadia III  36     9
    Howe is my Sunn, whose beames are shining bright,. . . . .    74  Arcadia III  42     1
    And to the sunne with waxen winges to flie?. . . . . . . .    79  Arcadia III  50    14
    Is left a Sunne, whose beames thy place may use? . . . . .    80  Arcadia III  52     6
    No Sunne, which shines, and seeth not, . . . . . . . . . .    86  Arcadia III  62    18
    Did piping leade, the Sunne already sanke. . . . . . . . .    98  3rd Eclogues 66     3
    Where shade from Sunne, and sporte I sought in evening,. . .  111  4th Eclogues 71    14
    As soon as Sunne begins to clime the mountaines: . . . . .   112  4th Eclogues 71    44
    I give the Sunne a last farewell each evening; . . . . . .   112  4th Eclogues 71    50
    At whose approach the Sunne rase in the evening, . . . . .   113  4th Eclogues 71    69
    Since thou from me (o me) o Sunne didst passe. . . . . . .   116  4th Eclogues 72    98
    And bending humbled eyes (o eyes the Sunne of sight) . . . .  119  4th Eclogues 73    91
    Should my too-much sight cause so true a Sunne to be lost?    124  4th Eclogues 74    58
    O light of Sunne, which is entit'led day, . . . . . . . . .  126  4th Eclogues 75    52
    And if, o Sunne, thou ever didst appeare,. . . . . . . . .   127  4th Eclogues 75    70
    Farewell o Sunn, Arcadia's clearest light: . . . . . . . .   129  4th Eclogues 76     1
    Where ys Ah that face, that a Sunne defaces? . . . . . . .   138  Cert Sonnets  5     9
    The shading woods seeme now my Sunne to darke, . . . . . .   147  Cert Sonnets 18     7
    The Bruertons have a Lake, which when the Sunne. . . . . .   150  Cert Sonnets 22    11
    But when my Sunne her shining twinnes there bends, . . . .   150  Cert Sonnets 22    16
    Up to the sunne, although the sunne my wings do frie:. . . .  153  Cert Sonnets 24    25
    As you, alas, my Sunne bends;. . . . . . . . . . . . . . .   154  Cert Sonnets 25    26
    Whose faire skin, beamy eyes, like morning sun on snow,. . .  169  Astrophil     8     9
    In highest way of heav'n the Sunne did ride, . . . . . . .   175  Astrophil    22     1
    The Sunne which others burn'd, did her but kisse. . . . . .  176  Astrophil    22    14
    Which inward sunne to Heroicke minde displaies,. . . . . .   177  Astrophil    25     8
    That inward sunne in thine eyes shineth so.. . . . . . . .   201  Astrophil    71     8
    Pray that my sunne go downe with meeker beames to bed. . . .  205  Astrophil    76    14
    When Sun is hid, can starres such beames display?. . . . .   223  Astrophil    88     6
    And that faire you my Sunne, thus overspred.. . . . . . .    224  Astrophil    91     3
    Night bard from Sun, thou from thy owne sunne's light; . . .  229  Astrophil    96     4
    That wormes should have their Sun, and I want mine.. . . .    230  Astrophil    98    14
    In clouds of teares, but soon as sun . . . . . . . . . . .   311  Psalm XXX          17
    Dick. What joy the joyfull sunne gives unto bleared eyes:.    343  Possibly      1    13
    Till one faire eav'n an howr ere Sun did rest, . . . . . .   247  Other Poems   4   205
    He stood, but turn'd, as Girosol, to Sun:. . . . . . . . .   251  Other Poems   4   370
SUNBEAMS
    While they did ward sun-beames with shady bay, . . . . . .   243  Other Poems   4    66
SUNBURNED
    Some fresh and fruitfull showers upon my sunne-burn'd
        braine . . . . . . . . . . . . . . . . . . . . . . . .   165  Astrophil     1     8
SUNDER
    Can learne, how my selfe to sunder . . . . . . . . . . . .   234  A&S 11th Song      14
SUNDERS
    Who hath the voyce, which soule from sences sunders, . . . .  197  A&S 1st Song       29
SUNDRY
    That he, to whome these sondrie giftes I binde,. . . . . .    78  Arcadia III  50     9
SUNG
    Let Dirge be sung, and Trentals rightly read,. . . . . . .   160  Cert Sonnets 30    21
SUN-LIKE
    They sun-like should more dazle then delight?. . . . . . .   168  Astrophil     7     8
SUNNY
    Dorus. If Sunnie beames shame heav'nly habitation; . . . .    48  2nd Eclogues 28    22
SUN'S
    With sonne's approche your pasture fertill growes, . . . .    43  Arcadia II   23     2
    Or if sheepe's cries can helpe the Sunne's owne braverie,.    48  2nd Eclogues 28    25
    With Sunne's depart: and now the darkenes of the night . .   116  4th Eclogues 73     2
    Night bard from Sun, thou from thy owne sunne's light; . . .  229  Astrophil    96     4
    While I dispaire by Sunne's sight to enjoy.. . . . . . . .   230  Astrophil    97    14
    There by his Grace for sun's fair face . . . . . . . . . .   294  Psalm XIX          19
SUNS
    And saw those eyes (those Sonnes) such shoures to shew,. .    58  2nd Eclogues 30    49
    When two Sunnes do appeare . . . . . . . . . . . . . . . .    81  Arcadia III  55     1
    Two gleaming Sunnes of splendour like I see, . . . . . . .    81  Arcadia III  55     4
    By taking her two Sunnes from these darke vallies. . . . .   113  4th Eclogues 71    66
    They to the beamie Sunnes went,. . . . . . . . . . . . . .   154  Cert Sonnets 25    12
SUPERFLUITIES
    Seeke we to tame these childish superfluities: . . . . . .    61  2nd Eclogues 30   138
SUPPLE
    But soft and supple satten like. . . . . . . . . . . . . .    88  Arcadia III  62    82
    Sweete supple mindes which soone to wisdome bowe . . . . .   106  3rd Eclogues 67   103
SUPPLY
    That they, aswell as they, Hell may supplie: . . . . . . .   248  Other Poems   4   230
SUPPRESS
    This tyran Love; or rather do suppresse. . . . . . . . . .    23  1st Eclogues  9    45
SURCEASE
    O my thought my thoughts surcease, . . . . . . . . . . . .   227  A&S 10th Song      43
SURE
    Great sure is she, on whom our hopes do live,. . . . . . .     3  Lady of May   2     5
    As for those parts unknowne, which hidden sure are best: .    12  Arcadia I     3    13
    Geron. Yet sure an end, to each thing time doth give,. . .    22  1st Eclogues  9    11
    And belly nought is left, such sure is he, . . . . . . . .    24  1st Eclogues  9    82
    As fishe sure tryall hath of muddy slyme.. . . . . . . . .    28  1st Eclogues 10    54
```

SURE   (CONTINUED)   PAGE   TITLE   LINE

      That that deare Dyamond, where wisdome holdeth a sure seate,   37 1st Eclogues 13   165
      And for a sure sacrifice I do dayly oblation offer . . . . .   37 1st Eclogues 13   170
      That to your strength your foes have sure resorte. . . . . .   38 Arcadia II   14   12
      R. But yet our strife sure peace in end doth breede. . . . .   46 2nd Eclogues 27   27
      Her beames have wrought therin most suer impression: . . . .   47 2nd Eclogues 28   11
      Dicus. Thy safetie sure is wrapped in destruction: . . . . .   49 2nd Eclogues 28   73
      Pas. Another sure as is a gander from a goose: . . . .   52 2nd Eclogues 29   23
      But thou, sure Hope, tickle my leaping heart.. . . . .   83 Arcadia III   59   9
      Three dayes before that he must sure depart, ...   96 3rd Eclogues 64   79
      For sure, no jealousie can that prevent, ...   97 3rd Eclogues 64 125
      The beastes had sure some beastly pollicie:. . . . . 100 3rd Eclogues 66   50
      Sure shepherd's signe, that morne would soone fetch day. . . 103 3rd Eclogues 66 161
      The sure refuge, by thee and by no other . . . . 108 Arcadia IV   69   13
      Me thought, nay sure I was, I was in fairest wood. . . . . . 117 4th Eclogues 73   35
      But streight there issued forth two Ladies (Ladies sure. . . 118 4th Eclogues 73   63
      So in his sickness grew our sure infection. . . . . 128 4th Eclogues 75 135
      You better sure shall live, not evermore . . . . 142 Cert Sonnets 12   1
      Red Porphir is, which locke of pearle makes sure:. . . . . . 169 Astrophil   9   6
      And sure at length stolne goods do come to light . . . . . . 172 Astrophil   15   11
      Sure you say well, your wisdome's golden mine. . . . . 175 Astrophil   21   12
      And if these rules did faile, proofe makes me sure,. . . . . 178 Astrophil   26   12
      Sure, if that long with Love acquainted eyes . . . . 180 Astrophil   31   5
      Since thou in me so sure a power doest keepe,. . . . . 181 Astrophil   32   5
      That vertuous soule, sure heire of heav'nly blisse:. . . . . 190 Astrophil   52   7
      Love by sure proofe I may call thee unkind,. . . . . 198 Astrophil   65   1
      "Or so?" Much lesse: "How then?" Sure thus it is:. . . . . . 204 Astrophil   74   13
      Sure they prevaile as much with me, as he. . . . . 236 Astrophil   106   12
      Absence sure will helpe, if I. . . . . 234 A&S 11th Song   13
      Then Thou (O lord) shalt keep the Good stil sure.. . . . . . 285 Psalm XII   22
      Thy way is soundly sure, Thy word is purely tryd;. . . . . . 292 Psalm XVIII   55
      God's witness sure for aye doth dure . . . . 294 Psalm XIX   31
      This mercy is so sure. 301 Psalm XXIII   23
      Sure, sure who hope in Thee. . . . . 303 Psalm XXV   7
      I held for sure that I should never slyde. . . . . 305 Psalm XXVI   6
      Farr farr more sure, than walls most firmly fast.. . . . . . 313 Psalm XXXI   60
      Sure, sure the Floods of straying streames . . . . 315 Psalm XXXII   22
      Our hearts sure shall enjoy. . . . . 318 Psalm XXXIII   79
      By God's most sure, and sweet salvation; . . . . 327 Psalm XXXVII   98
      Sure I do but halting go,. . . . . 329 Psalm XXXVIII   49
      Sure aid present comfort.. . . . . 337 Psalm XLIII   36
      Will. What? these are riddles sure, art thou then bound to
          her? . . . . 343 Possibly   1   23
      Sure I bewitched am, it is even that:.. . . . . 253 Other Poems   4   447
SURELY
      Most surely caught.. . . . . 280 Psalm IX   50
      And surely taught by his love-open eye,. . . . . 251 Other Poems   4   378
SUREST
      For all these certaine blowes the surest shield. . . . . . .   58 2nd Eclogues 30   43
      From holy marriage, sweete and surest meane. . . . . 103 3rd Eclogues 67   2
      For ever lamed of our suerest might; . . . . 130 4th Eclogues 76   28
      So that my surest part,. . . . . 332 Psalm XL   48
SURETY
      No mortall man the cuppe of suretie drinkes. . . . . 105 3rd Eclogues 67   60
SURFEIT-WOES
      Her onely cure from surfet-woes can diet me: . . . .   51 2nd Eclogues 28 117
SURMOUNTETH
      And how much more her worth surmounteth thee,. . . . .   72 Arcadia III   38   16
SURPASS
      Whose fruit doth farre th' Esperian tast surpasse: . . . . . 208 Astrophil   82   6
SURPASSETH
      Not rotten sheepe, but high crownes she surpasseth all.. . .   16 1st Eclogues 7   57
      Save thy mind which yet surpasseth.. . . . . 219 A&S 8th Song   44
SUSPECT
      No fancy mine, nor others' wronge suspect. . . . .   40 Arcadia II   18   11
SUSPECTING
      (How can he love suspecting treacherie?. . . . .   93 3rd Eclogues 63   84
      And eke revenge his wrong suspecting you". . . . .   97 3rd Eclogues 64 108
SUSPICIOUS
      Dorus. But what doth make thee Dicus so suspicious . . . . .   47 2nd Eclogues 28   7
SUSTAIN
      But like the feeble flower (whose stalke cannot sustaine . . 117 4th Eclogues 73   21
      Although some Worldly losse therby he may sustaine,. . . . . 287 Psalm XV   10
      My heeles and plants thou didst from stumbling slip
          sustaine , ... 292 Psalm XVIII   67
      Least I rebuke sustain;. . . . . 304 Psalm XXV   70
SUSTAINS
      His justice seat the World sustains, ... 310 Psalm XXIX   25
SWALLOWED
      And warr of thoughts is swallow'd up in peace. . . . .   91 3rd Eclogues 63   4
      Now death hath swallow'd up our worldly pleasure,. . . . . . 129 4th Eclogues 76   11
SWALLOWING
      Their throat, it is an Open swallowing grave,. . . . . 275 Psalm V   27
SWAM
      Yet swam in joy, such love in her was seene. . . . . 223 Astrophil   87   11
SWAN
      There was the swan of dignitie deprived, ...   29 1st Eclogues 10   85
      Where Leda's swanne his feathers mewes,. . . . .   89 Arcadia III   62   110
      As to Swanne in last disease:. . . . . 140 Cert Sonnets 7   37

```
SWANNISH                                                    PAGE    TITLE          LINE
    Strephon. Long since alas, my deadly Swannish musique. . . .  112 4th Eclogues 71   25
SWAN'S
    Let swanne's example siker serve for thee, . . . . . . . . .   28 1st Eclogues 10   73
    If the Swanne's sweet voice be not heard, but at death,. . .   30 1st Eclogues 12   14
SWANS
    Broadred with buls and swans, powdred with golden raine: . .  167 Astrophil     6    6
    Dumbe Swannes, not chatring Pies, do Lovers prove, . . . . .  192 Astrophil    54   13
    Friends like to blacke Swannes appearing,. . . . . . . . . .  263 Other Poems   7   53
SWARE
    Till that I sware my faith so stood, . . . . . . . . . . . .  158 Cert Sonnets 28   23
    To blaze these last, and sware devoutly then,. . . . . . . .  171 Astrophil    13   13
    Though oft himselfe my mate-in-armes he sware. . . . . . . .  228 Astrophil    95    8
    Nous sware it was no right; for his default. . . . . . . . .  250 Other Poems   4  314
SWARM
    Upon thy face let coaly Ravens swarme: . . . . . . . . . . .  125 4th Eclogues 75   19
    In whose sweete heav'n Angels of high thoughts swarme? . . .  142 Cert Sonnets 10    8
    The while a swarm of foes with vexing feates . . . . . . . .  276 Psalm VI          23
    Against me swarm, ceaseless to raile at me.. . . . . . . . .  322 Psalm XXXV        40
    About these never conquered walles to swarme,. . . . . . . .  346 Possibly      5   10
    So may thy blessings swarme. . . . . . . . . . . . . . . . .  258 Other Poems   5   82
SWARMED
    All mercys shall be swarmed. . . . . . . . . . . . . . . . .  315 Psalm XXXII       39
SWARMS
    What swarmes of vertues did in his youth flye. . . . . . . .   24 1st Eclogues  9   74
SWAY
    What circle then in so rare force beares swaye?. . . . . . .   17 1st Eclogues  7  109
    Now bolder waxt, waxt prowde, that I such sway might beare:.  121 4th Eclogues 73  159
    Of Atlas tyr'd, your wisedome's heav'nly sway. . . . . . . .  190 Astrophil    51    8
    O unjustest fortune's sway,. . . . . . . . . . . . . . . . .  235 A&S 11th Song     43
SWEAR
    And sweare she is not worthy thee to have. . . . . . . . . .  141 Cert Sonnets  9   14
    I sweare, my heart such one shall shew to thee,. . . . . . .  167 Astrophil     4   12
    "What he?" say they of me, "now I dare sweare, . . . . . . .  191 Astrophil    54    7
    And this I sweare by blackest brooke of hell,. . . . . . . .  204 Astrophil    74    7
    And I do sweare even by the same delight,. . . . . . . . . .  208 Astrophil    82   13
    In truth I sweare, I wish not there should be. . . . . . . .  224 Astrophil    90    7
    I sweare by her I love and lacke, that I . . . . . . . . . .  235 Astrophil   105    5
    Wo to me, and do you sweare. . . . . . . . . . . . . . . . .  211 A&S 4th Song      49
    Why alas doth she then sweare, . . . . . . . . . . . . . . .  222 A&S 9th Song      31
SWEATING
    The little coine his sweating browes have got, . . . . . . .  104 3rd Eclogues 67   41
SWEATS
    Nature with care sweates for her darling's sake, . . . . . .  232 Astrophil   101   12
SWEATY
    With sweatie browes, sometyme with watrie eyes,. . . . . . .   71 Arcadia III  36    8
SWEET
    Sweete soule, to whom I vowed am a slave,. . . . . . . . . .    3 Lady of May   2   11
    Sweete soule let not a wretch that serveth sheepe, . . . . .    4 Lady of May   2   17
    Among his flocke so sweete a treasure keepe. . . . . . . . .    4 Lady of May   2   18
    Disuse your selves from sweete Menalcas' voice:. . . . . . .   13 Arcadia I     4    6
    We finde most sweete affection's snare,. . . . . . . . . . .   14 1st Eclogues  6    3
    That sweete, but sower despairefull care.. . . . . . . . . .   14 1st Eclogues  6    4
    Dorus. Once, o sweete once, I saw with dread oppressed . . .   17 1st Eclogues  7   85
    But let us sing, sweet tunes do passions ease, . . . . . . .   22 1st Eclogues  9    4
    Sweet vertue's lawe barres not a causefull mone. . . . . . .   22 1st Eclogues  9   18
    Those pleasant plants, those sweete and frutefull trees, . .   26 1st Eclogues  9  130
    If the Swanne's sweet voice be not heard, but at death,. . .   30 1st Eclogues 12   14
    Joyning your sweete voice to the rurall muse of a deserte, .   31 1st Eclogues 13    2
    Sweete Juniper saith this, thoh I burne, yet I burne in a
        sweete fire. . . . . . . . . . . . . . . . . . . . . . .   35 1st Eclogues 13  120
    Thus is her giftes most sweet, thus more danger to be neere
        her, . . . . . . . . . . . . . . . . . . . . . . . . . .   36 1st Eclogues 13  126
    Since in sweete you all goods so richly raigne,. . . . . . .   39 Arcadia II   16    5
    Feede on my sheepe, your fayer sweete feeding flowes,. . . .   43 Arcadia II   23    4
    Seekes to make ech thing badge of his sweet passion. . . . .   47 2nd Eclogues 28    6
    Yeeld to our eares a sweet and sound relation, . . . . . . .   48 2nd Eclogues 28   20
    With so sweete plagues my happie harmes infected be: . . . .   51 2nd Eclogues 28  123
    And thinke from Cosma's sweet red lips I live, . . . . . . .   54 2nd Eclogues 29   79
    While that we do at his sweete scourge repine, . . . . . . .   59 2nd Eclogues 30   75
    Sweete speaking oft a currish hart reclaimes.. . . . . . . .   60 2nd Eclogues 30  115
    By wise discourse, sweete tunes, or Poet's fiction;. . . . .   61 2nd Eclogues 30  144
    Faire Rocks, goodly rivers, sweet woods, when shall I see
        peace? Peace... . . . . . . . . . . . . . . . . . . . .   62 2nd Eclogues 31    1
    What be the sweet creatures wher lowly demaunds be not
        heard Hard. . . . . . . . . . . . . . . . . . . . . . .   65 2nd Eclogues 31   41
    Where sweet graces erect the stately banner. . . . . . . . .   67 2nd Eclogues 33    3
    Her legges carriage is of all the sweet campe: . . . . . . .   67 2nd Eclogues 33   11
    Thus sweete paine, I do yeeld, what ere I can yeelde.. . . .   68 2nd Eclogues 33   29
    O sweet woods the delight of solitarines!. . . . . . . . . .   68 2nd Eclogues 34    1
    Above line repeated at following locations . . . . . . . . .   69 2nd Eclogues 34   15
        . . . . . . . . . . . . . . . . . . . . . . . . . . . .   69 2nd Eclogues 34   29
    Sweet birds kindly do graunt harmony unto thee,. . . . . . .   69 2nd Eclogues 34   12
    As sweete as violetts, faire as a lilly is,. . . . . . . . .   69 2nd Eclogues 34   32
    Sweete glove the wittnes of my secrett blisse. . . . . . . .   70 Arcadia III  35    1
    Be thow, sweete glove, the Anker of my mynde,. . . . . . . .   70 Arcadia III  35    7
    Sweete glove, the sweete despoyles of sweetest hand, . . . .   70 Arcadia III  35    9
    O breath more sweete, then is the growing beane, . . . . . .   76 Arcadia III  46    2
    Sweete roote say thou, the roote of my desire. . . . . . . .   77 Arcadia III  48    1
    His thoughtes in you, where so sweete thoughtes were spent,.   78 Arcadia III  49   10
```

SWEET	(CONTINUED)	PAGE	TITLE		LINE
To her sweete sence, sweete sleepe, some ease imparte, . . .		79	Arcadia III	51	3
Mine owne? o word on whose sweete sound doth pray.		80	Arcadia III	53	5
In that sweete seate the Boy doth sport:		88	Arcadia III	62	83
Sweete Ilands make in that sweete land.		90	Arcadia III	62	129
And like two rivers sweete, ...		92	3rd Eclogues	63	33
Such mindes with sweet affections for to fill, ...		92	3rd Eclogues	63	61
In fine he made her gesse, there was some sweet.		95	3rd Eclogues	64	35
And as for me (sweete husband) I must beare".		96	3rd Eclogues	64	62
And geve a long desire a sweet content..		97	3rd Eclogues	64	106
With his sweet skill my skillesse youth he drewe,.		99	3rd Eclogues	66	26
Monkie, sweet breath; the Cow, her faire eyes brought; . . .		101	3rd Eclogues	66	88
From holy marriage, sweete and surest meane.		103	3rd Eclogues	67	2
Is this sweet doubling of our single life.		103	3rd Eclogues	67	12
Sweete supple mindes which soone to wisdome bowe		106	3rd Eclogues	67	103
Me seemes I heare, when I doo heare sweete musique,.		112	4th Eclogues	71	47
Infected so with her sweet poyson's might, ...		115	4th Eclogues	72	78
A silence sweet each where with one consent embraste		117	4th Eclogues	73	7
(A musique sweet to one in carefull musing plaste)		117	4th Eclogues	73	8
On Nature's sweet repast, as healthfull senses ledd.		117	4th Eclogues	73	40
Indeed a perfect hewe, indeed a sweet consent.		119	4th Eclogues	73	85
"Sweet Mira mine" (quote she) "the pleasure of my minde, . .		119	4th Eclogues	73	93
Unto revenge? O sweete, on a wretch wilt thou be revenged? .		123	4th Eclogues	74	37
O sweet simplicitie: from whence should Love be so learned?.		124	4th Eclogues	74	65
What sweete joyes I had once, and what a place I did hold? .		124	4th Eclogues	74	72
Bend your thoghts to the dear sweet words which then to me					
giv'n were:.		124	4th Eclogues	74	75
Your dolefull tunes sweete Muses now applie.		125	4th Eclogues	75	3
Above line repeated at following locations		125	4th Eclogues	75	15
. . . .		125	4th Eclogues	75	30
. . . .		126	4th Eclogues	75	48
. . . .		126	4th Eclogues	75	60
. . . .		127	4th Eclogues	75	78
. . . .		127	4th Eclogues	75	96
. . . .		128	4th Eclogues	75	117
O My thoughtes' sweete foode, my my onely owner, ...		138	Cert Sonnets	5	1
Above line repeated at following location.		138	Cert Sonnets	5	25
O Faire, o sweet, when I do looke on thee, ...		139	Cert Sonnets	7	1
Above line repeated at following locations		139	Cert Sonnets	7	11
. . . .		140	Cert Sonnets	7	21
. . . .		140	Cert Sonnets	7	31
Sweete thinke not I am at ease,.		140	Cert Sonnets	7	34
Her breath which makes a sower answer sweete,.		141	Cert Sonnets	9	6
In whose sweete heav'n Angels of high thoughts swarme? . . .		142	Cert Sonnets	10	8
And thence cast off, where his sweete hurt he found, ...		144	Cert Sonnets	15	6
The sweete pursute of my desired pray.		145	Cert Sonnets	16	12
Sweet Ladie, as for those whose sullen cheare, ...		147	Cert Sonnets	17	46
Alas sweet Brookes do in my teares augment:.		147	Cert Sonnets	18	12
Neere Wilton sweete, huge heapes of stones are found,. . . .		149	Cert Sonnets	22	1
Of which, how much may pierce to that sweete seate,.		151	Cert Sonnets	22	46
Sweet Ladie you remaine well paid.		159	Cert Sonnets	29	4
To that sweet yoke, where lasting freedomes be:.		161	Cert Sonnets	32	6
That her sweete breath makes oft thy flames to rise, ...		170	Astrophil	12	4
And everie floure, not sweet perhaps, which growes		172	Astrophil	15	3
As that sweete blacke which vailes the heav'nly eye:		175	Astrophil	20	7
Let him, deprived of sweet but unfelt joyes, ...		177	Astrophil	24	12
Sweet Stella's image I do steale to mee".		181	Astrophil	32	14
With so sweete voice, and by sweete Nature so, ...		183	Astrophil	36	9
In all sweete stratagems sweete Arte can show, ...		183	Astrophil	36	11
And of some sent from that sweet enemie Fraunce;		185	Astrophil	41	4
Faire eyes, sweet lips, deare heart, that foolish I.		186	Astrophil	43	1
Her heart, sweete heart, is of no Tygre's kind:.		186	Astrophil	44	4
Deare Killer, spare not thy sweet cruell shot:		189	Astrophil	48	13
Because their forefront bare sweet Stella's name..		190	Astrophil	50	14
And is even irkt that so sweet Comedie,.		190	Astrophil	51	13
Might winne some grace in your sweet skill arraid.		192	Astrophil	55	4
So sweete sounds straight mine eare and heart do hit,. . . .		192	Astrophil	55	13
But them (so sweete is she) most sweetly sing, ...		193	Astrophil	57	10
Stella's sweete breath the same to me did reed..		194	Astrophil	58	11
But this at last is her sweet breath'd defence:.		195	Astrophil	61	4
Sweet said that I true love in her should find..		196	Astrophil	62	4
But Grammer's force with sweet successe confirme,.		196	Astrophil	63	11
And all in vaine, for while thy breath most sweet, ...		200	Astrophil	68	9
I must no more in thy sweet passions lie;.		202	Astrophil	72	7
Sweet, it was saucie Love, not humble I.		203	Astrophil	73	8
My lips are sweet, inspired with Stella's kisse.		204	Astrophil	74	14
That conversation sweet, where such high comforts be,. . . .		205	Astrophil	77	10
Sweet kisse, thy sweets I faine would sweetly endite,. . . .		206	Astrophil	79	1
Sweet swelling lip, well maist thou swell in pride,.		206	Astrophil	80	1
Sweet lip, you teach my mouth with one sweet kisse..		207	Astrophil	80	14
Sweet gard'n Nymph, which keepes the Cherrie tree, ...		208	Astrophil	82	5
Most sweet-faire, most faire-sweet, do not alas, ...		208	Astrophil	82	7
Or if I needs (sweet Judge) must torments have,.		212	Astrophil	86	11
And nothing then the cause more sweet could be,.		223	Astrophil	87	13
Milke hands, rose cheeks, or lips more sweet, more red,. . .		225	Astrophil	91	7
With sweete soft shades thou oft invitest me		230	Astrophil	98	5
But when birds charme, and that sweete aire, which is. . . .		231	Astrophil	99	9
Who may with charme of conversation sweete,.		236	Astrophil	106	10
Sweete, for a while give respite to my hart, ...		236	Astrophil	107	5
Since sweet sleep her eyes hath charmed, ...		202	A&S 2nd Song		5

```
SWEET                        (CONTINUED)                    PAGE    TITLE         LINE
     Oh sweet kisse, but ah she is waking,. . . . . . . . . . .  203 A&S 2nd Song     25
     Sweete reward for sharpest paine:. . . . . . . . . . . . .  210 A&S 4th Song      4
     These sweet flowers on fine bed too, . . . . . . . . . . .  210 A&S 4th Song     15
     Sweet then, while each thing doth frame: . . . . . . . . .  211 A&S 4th Song     34
     Sweet alas, why strive you thus? . . . . . . . . . . . . .  211 A&S 4th Song     43
     I said, thou wert most sweet, sweet poison to my heart:. . .  212 A&S 5th Song     8
     Sweet babes must babies have, but shrewd gyrles must be
        beat n.. . . . . . . . . . . . . . . . . . . . . . . .  213 A&S 5th Song     36
     Fearing (sweete) you to endanger,. . . . . . . . . . . . .  234 A&S 11th Song    39
     That ravishing delight in them most sweete tunes do not
        raise; . . . . . . . . . . . . . . . . . . . . . . . .  217 A&S 7th Song      2
     Who have so leaden eyes, as not to see sweet beautie's show,  217 A&S 7th Song      7
     Astrophil with Stella sweete,. . . . . . . . . . . . . . .  218 A&S 8th Song      5
     "This small wind which so sweete is, . . . . . . . . . . .  219 A&S 8th Song     57
     To which sweet springs of waters neighbours be,. . . . . .  270 Psalm I           8
     And love the sweet sound of thy name, rejoyce. . . . . . .  275 Psalm V          34
     Turne Thee, sweet lord, and from this Ougly fall . . . . .  276 Psalm VI         11
     I plain sweet Lord, my plaint for pitty mark;. . . . . . .  289 Psalm XVII        2
     By waters still and sweet. . . . . . . . . . . . . . . . .  301 Psalm XXIII       5
     Sweet Righteousness shall he receive,. . . . . . . . . . .  302 Psalm XXIV       14
     Sweet lord, write not my soul. . . . . . . . . . . . . . .  306 Psalm XXVI       28
     And his sweet grace streight easd the rod. . . . . . . . .  315 Psalm XXXII      17
     How sweet how gracious is his grace. . . . . . . . . . . .  319 Psalm XXXIV      30
     By God's most sure, and sweet salvation; . . . . . . . . .  327 Psalm XXXVII     98
     Of This sweet righteousness. . . . . . . . . . . . . . . .  331 Psalm XL         37
     With sweet musick's skill. . . . . . . . . . . . . . . . .  337 Psalm XLIII      26
     Kindly, sweete soule, she did unkindnes take,. . . . . . .  245 Other Poems  4  121
     At Barly brake hir swete swift foot to trie. . . . . . . .  247 Other Poems  4  208
     With whome to joyne fast ran Urania sweet: . . . . . . . .  248 Other Poems  4  252
     The aire hir swete race mov'd doth blow the fire.. . . . .  249 Other Poems  4  300
     As on sweet flowrs when morning's drops we see. . . . . . .  252 Other Poems  4  398
     With how sweet sawes she blam'd their sawcines:. . . . . .  252 Other Poems  4  404
     Come she, and sweet the aire with open brest,. . . . . . .  254 Other Poems  4  466
     Each thing both sweet and sadd . . . . . . . . . . . . . .  256 Other Poems  5    8
     Which Holland sweet now gently sendeth in, . . . . . . . .  259 Other Poems  5  106
     Sweete Orpheus' Harpe, whose sound . . . . . . . . . . . .  260 Other Poems  6   13
     To joyne sweet friends beloved. . . . . . . . . . . . . . .  260 Other Poems  6   16
SWEETEN
     If her lips daignd to sweeten my poore name. . . . . . . .  225 Astrophil    92   13
     If Love might sweet'n so a boy of shepheard' brood,. . . .  209 A&S 3rd Song      7
SWEETENED
     Where be those Roses gone, which sweetned so our eyes? . . .  232 Astrophil   102    1
SWEETENER
     Which even of sweetnesse sweetest sweetner art:. . . . . .  206 Astrophil    79    2
     Sweetner of musicke, wisedome's beautifier:. . . . . . . .  207 Astrophil    80    6
SWEETENING
     Breathing all blisse and sweetning to the heart, . . . . .  207 Astrophil    81    3
SWEETENS
     That sweetens all the place; she is the guest. . . . . . .   59 2nd Eclogues 30   99
SWEETER
     Phaebus farewell, a sweeter Saint I serve,. . . . . . . . .   72 Arcadia III  38    1
     Above line repeated at following location. . . . . . . . .   72 Arcadia III  38    6
     Which more it mov'd, the more it sweeter was.. . . . . . .  252 Other Poems   4  400
SWEETEST
     Whose cleerest eyes I blisse, and sweetest voyce,. . . . .    5 Lady of May   3   15
     Since whitenesse doth present the sweetest show, . . . . .   38 Arcadia II   15    7
     And from the stormes our sweeteste sonne will shield.. . .   43 Arcadia II   23    9
     Your sweetest flowers, your herbes, no service yeeld,. . .   43 Arcadia II   24    5
     Her words in syrup laid of sweetest breath,. . . . . . . .   58 2nd Eclogues 30   51
     Sweete glove, the sweete despoyles of sweetest hand, . . .   70 Arcadia III  35    9
     "My sweetest joy, the comfort of my sprite,. . . . . . . .   96 3rd Eclogues 64   92
     On nature's sweetest light.. . . . . . . . . . . . . . . .  151 Cert Sonnets 23    4
     Above line repeated at following location. . . . . . . . .  152 Cert Sonnets 23   36
     To some a sweetest plaint, a sweetest stile affords, . . .  168 Astrophil     6    9
     In sweetest strength, so sweetly skild withall,. . . . . .  183 Astrophil    36    9
     Take thou of me smooth pillowes, sweetest bed, . . . . . .  184 Astrophil    39    9
     Not by rude force, but sweetest soveraigntie . . . . . . .  201 Astrophil    71    6
     Which even of sweetnesse sweetest sweetner art:. . . . . .  206 Astrophil    79    2
     I saw that sighes her sweetest lips did part,. . . . . . .  223 Astrophil    87    7
     They did themselves (o sweetest prison) twine.. . . . . . .  232 Astrophil   103    8
     Thou, sweetest subject, werte borne in the realme of Love,  214 A&S 5th Song     64
     By them is past in sweetest taste. . . . . . . . . . . . .  294 Psalm XIX        43
SWEET-FAIR
     Most sweet-faire, most faire-sweet, do not alas, . . . . .  208 Astrophil    82    7
SWEETLY
     Sweetnesse sweetly pardon folly, . . . . . . . . . . . . .  157 Cert Sonnets 27   33
     To mortall eyes might sweetly shine in her.. . . . . . . .  177 Astrophil    25   11
     In sweetest strength, so sweetly skild withall,. . . . . .  183 Astrophil    36   10
     But them (so sweete is she) most sweetly sing, . . . . . .  193 Astrophil    57   10
     Makes me fall from her sight, then sweetly she . . . . . .  195 Astrophil    60    6
     Sweet kisse, thy sweets I faine would sweetly endite,. . .  206 Astrophil    79    1
     Yet those lips so sweetly swelling,. . . . . . . . . . . .  203 A&S 2nd Song     21
     Deckt with pyde flowers sweetely smelling. . . . . . . . .  262 Other Poems   7    6
SWEETLY-FENCED
     The second sweetly-fenced warde, . . . . . . . . . . . . .   87 Arcadia III  62   43
SWEETLY-SINGING
     Who once all birdes, in sweetly-singing past,. . . . . . .   28 1st Eclogues 10   74
SWEETNESS
     P. We gladly use the sweetnes of our life. . . . . . . . .   46 2nd Eclogues 27   26
```

SWEETNESS   (CONTINUED)   PAGE TITLE   LINE
    Gratefulnes, sweetnes, holy love, hartie regard) . . . . . .   122 4th Eclogues 74   10
    Al my sense thy sweetnesse gained, ...   156 Cert Sonnets 27   1
    Now thy sweetnesse sowre is deemed, ...   156 Cert Sonnets 27   9
    Nc more in thy sweetnesse glorie, ...   156 Cert Sonnets 27   17
    Sweetnesse sweetly pardon folly, ...   157 Cert Sonnets 27   33
    Which even of sweetnesse sweetest sweetner art: . . . . . .   206 Astrophil   79   2
    Sweetnesse, that breathes and pants as oft as she: . . . . .   231 Astrophil   101   2
    Who hath the feet, whose step all sweetnesse planteth, . . .   197 A&S 1st Song   13
    Who hath the feet, whose step of sweetnesse planteth, ... 197 A&S 1st Song   V 13
    Beauty, musicke, sweetnesse, love. . . . .   226 A&S 10th Song   34
SWEETS
    A heape of sweetes she is, where nothing spilled is; . . . .   15 1st Eclogues 7   28
    On barren sweetes they feede, and feeding sterve: . . . . . .   39 Arcadia II   17   3
    Can taste no sweetes, the sower onely please: . . . .   74 Arcadia III 41   2
    So sweets my paines, that my paines me rejoyce. . . . . 193 Astrophil   57   14
    Sweet kisse, thy sweets I faine would sweetly endite, ... 206 Astrophil   79   1
    Let breath sucke up those sweetes, let armes embrace . . . .   210 Astrophil   85   12
    The plenteous sweets, (can sweets so sharply grow?). . . . .   243 Other Poems   4   52
SWELL
    O brest in which two white sheepe swell in pride: . . . . . .   76 Arcadia III 46   10
    Deeme it no gloire to swell in tyrannie. . . . .   103 3rd Eclogues 66   149
    That those lips swell, so full of thee they bee, ...   170 Astrophil   12   3
    My mouth doth water, and my breast doth swell, ...   183 Astrophil   37   1
    But they do swell and struggle forth of me, ...   189 Astrophil   50   3
    Sweet swelling lip, well maist thou swell in pride, ... 206 Astrophil   80   1
    Ah, my sute granted is, I feele my breast doth swell: . . . . 213 A&S 5th Song   34
    Against all them, that against him do swell, ...   285 Psalm XII   17
    To his owne witt, thought upon thought did swell, ... 256 Other Poems   4   542
SWELLED
    That those lips sweld, so full of thee they bee, ...   170 Astrophil   12 V 3
SWELLING
    To swelling harts he shines in honour's fire: . . . .   21 1st Eclogues 8   38
    Swelling with sighes, made pale with minde's disease, ...   58 2nd Eclogues 30   48
    With swelling hart in spite and due disdainfulnes. . . . . .   61 2nd Eclogues 30   153
    Lift up their stately swelling bankes; . . . .   88 Arcadia III 62   90
    In too full winde draw in thy swelling sailes. . . . .   143 Cert Sonnets 12   18
    So in my swelling breast that only I . . . .   178 Astrophil   27   7
    Sweet swelling lip, well maist thou swell in pride, ... 206 Astrophil   80   1
    Yet those lips so sweetly swelling, ...   203 A&S 2nd Song   21
    And cruel words their swelling tongues do chatt, ...   290 Psalm XVII   30
    With shrinking legges, but with a swelling brest, ... 255 Other Poems   4   523
SWELLS
    Musicke more loftly swels. . . . .   216 A&S 6th Song   25
SWERVE
    My thoughts forget: my thoughts, which never swerve. . . . .   72 Arcadia III 38   3
    Ought to be king, from whose rules who do swerve, ... 167 Astrophil   5   3
    To catch hir sparrow which from hir did swerve, ...   244 Other Poems   4   84
SWERVED
    His death our death. But ah; my Muse hath swarved, ...   129 4th Eclogues 75   136
    Howe bee wee swerved? . . . .   138 Cert Sonnets 5   12
    From time to time, but who be swerved. . . . .   326 Psalm XXXVII   71
SWIFT
    When trees daunce to the pype, and swift streames stay by
          the musicke, ...   33 1st Eclogues 13   47
    Languet, the shepheard best swift Ister knewe, ...   99 3rd Eclogues 66   23
    (More swift then falcon's stoope to feeding Falconer's call)   118 4th Eclogues 73   58
    At Barly brake hir swete swift foot to trie. . . . .   247 Other Poems   4   208
    As Venus' bird the white, swift, lovely Dove . . . .   251 Other Poems   4   353
SWIFTER
    So did Uran, the narr the swifter move, ...   251 Other Poems   4   357
SWIFTNESS
    Doth on hir wings hir utmost swiftnes prove, ...   251 Other Poems   4   355
SWIM
    Into my breste, and loves renewed swimme. . . . .   85 Arcadia III 61   12
    Then might I wisely swimme or gladly sinke. . . . .   148 Cert Sonnets 19   6
    Their eyes do swim, their face doth shine in fatt, ...   290 Psalm XVII   29
    Strephon so chas'd did seme in milke to swimme. . . . . . .   249 Other Poems   4   288
SWINK
    And soone forget the swincke due to their hire. . . . . . .   100 3rd Eclogues 66   74
SWORD
    No sword soe bytes as that evill toole annoyes. . . . . . .   29 1st Eclogues 10   90
    With sword of wit, giving wounds of dispraise, ...   170 Astrophil   10   10
    That Ballance weigh'd what sword did late obtaine, ...   204 Astrophil   75   8
    Therfore thou whetst Thy sword, and bend'st Thy bow, ...   278 Psalm VII   34
    Ah! from the sword yet save my vital sprite, ...   299 Psalm XXII   47
    The hand was one, one was the sword. . . . .   241 Other Poems   3   5
SWORDS
    My brest to swords, my soule to hell have solde. . . . . . .   50 2nd Eclogues 28   80
    The ev'ill bent bowes, and swords they drew, ...   325 Psalm XXXVII   37
    Their swords shall their own hearts embrew. . . . .   325 Psalm XXXVII   40
SWORN
    R. By nature you to Reason faith have sworne. . . . .   46 2nd Eclogues 27   11
    Who would have sworne his spowse diana was, ...   96 3rd Eclogues 64   74
    Where Cupid is sworne page to Chastity?. . . . .   182 Astrophil   35   8
SYLVAN
    Like to the silly Sylvan, ...   154 Cert Sonnets 25   15
SYRUP
    Her words in syrup laid of sweetest breath, ...   58 2nd Eclogues 30   51

'T   PAGE   TITLE   LINE

  Oh! I do know what guest I have mett; it is Echo. 'T is
    Echo . . . .   63 2nd Eclogues 31   3
  For to my dimmed eyes beganne t'appeare. . . . . 103 3rd Eclogues 66   159
  Then may I hope t'atchieve grace of a heavenly tiger.. . . . 122 4th Eclogues 74   22
  That with a body't goes? since by a body it is.. . . . . . . 123 4th Eclogues 74   46
TABERNACLE
  In Tabernacle Thyne, O lord, who shall remayne?. . . . . .   287 Psalm XV   1
  The tabernacle builded,. . . . .   294 Psalm XIX   18
  In Tabernacle His hee will . . . .   307 Psalm XXVII   26
  Tabernacle high. . . . .   336 Psalm XLIII   17
TABLE
  And for this Courtier should well like his table,. . . . . . 94 3rd Eclogues 64   23
  Before me Thou a table setst,. . . . .   301 Psalm XXIII   16
  My Friend I say, who at my table sate, ...   333 Psalm XLI   31
TACKLING
  Fancie, her tackling, torne away doth flie:. . . . .   114 4th Eclogues 72   47
TAIL
  Fine eares, long taile he hath, with Lion's curbed clawe,. . 53 2nd Eclogues 29   33
  No eare nor taile he hath, least they should him disgrace, . 53 2nd Eclogues 29   41
TAINT
  No wondre then, though sighte my sighte did tainte,. . . . . 83 Arcadia III 57   5
TAKE
  But still take heede least thou thy selfe submit . . . . . .   4 Lady of May   2   23
  Them can I take, but you I cannot hold:. . . . .   4 Lady of May   2   26
  But take this beast, if beasts you feare to misse, ...   4 Lady of May   2   29
  What marvaile then I take a woman's hew, ... 12 Arcadia I   2   13
  With twenty ginnes we will the small birds take, ... 18 1st Eclogues 7   126
  Of singing take to thee the reputation.. . . . . 19 1st Eclogues 7   172
  Dorus. Of singing take to thee the reputation. . . . . 19 1st Eclogues 7   173
  The witts abusde with will no counsayle take.. . . . . 23 1st Eclogues 9   22
  Then thow earst knew? rather take part with him. . . . . . . 26 1st Eclogues 10   8
  Let this assured holde our judgements ever take, ... 45 Arcadia II   26   15
  O heards take heed; for I a woolfe have found; . . . . 50 2nd Eclogues 28   83
  That will I take, and to my Leuca give. . . . .   54 2nd Eclogues 29   83
  Boulon. O man, take heed, how thou the Gods do move. . . . . 59 2nd Eclogues 30   65
  My sowle beginnes to take leave. . . . . 66 2nd Eclogues 32   15
  Then take my shape, and play a lover's parte:. . . . . 79 Arcadia III 51   12
  Which though of glittring golde, shall heere take rust . . . 92 3rd Eclogues 63   57
  And to her jealous husband did it take.. . . . . 96 3rd Eclogues 64   84
  Take heed therefore, how you ensue that trade, ... 97 3rd Eclogues 64   123
  "O beasts, take heed what you of me desire.. . . . . 100 3rd Eclogues 66   72
  With nature's praise are wont in safest home to take.. . . . 117 4th Eclogues 73   14
  And hither now, vouchsafe to take with willing eare. . . . . 119 4th Eclogues 73   104
  Unarmde (alas) unwarn'd to take a man asleepe? . . . . 122 4th Eclogues 73   186
  Earth take this earth, wherein my spirits languish.. . . . . 136 Cert Sonnets 3   16
  O Philomela faire, o take some gladnesse,. . . . . 137 Cert Sonnets 4   9
  Above line repeated at following location. . . . . 137 Cert Sonnets 4   21
  Such causelesse feares when coward minds do take,. . . . . . 145 Cert Sonnets 16   5
  As in their moodes to take a lingring pawse? . . . . 146 Cert Sonnets 17   24
  Take harp and sing in this our versing time: . . . . 146 Cert Sonnets 17   37
  But when that failes, my dead hopes up to take,. . . . . . . 150 Cert Sonnets 22   19
  O take fast hold, let that light be thy guide, ... 162 Cert Sonnets 32   9
  That the deare She might take some pleasure of my paine: . . 165 Astrophil   1   2
  That she (deare she) might take some pleasure of my paine: . 165 Astrophil   1 V 2
  Vertue alas, now let me take some rest,. . . . . 166 Astrophil   4   1
  But she most faire, most cold, made him thence take his
    flight . . . . 169 Astrophil   8   12
  You take wrong waies, those far-fet helpes be such,. . . . . 172 Astrophil   15   9
  I see and yet no greater sorow take, ... 174 Astrophil   18   13
  With me those paines for God's sake do not take: . . . . . . 179 Astrophil   28   3
  Take thou of me smooth pillowes, sweetest bed, ... 184 Astrophil   39   9
  Others, because of both sides I do take. . . . . 185 Astrophil   41   9
  What, dost thou thinke that I can ever take. . . . . 193 Astrophil   56   10
  Will she take time, before all wracked be? . . . . 199 Astrophil   67   4
  This realme of blisse, while vertuous course I take, ... 200 Astrophil   69   13
  Teaching the meane, at once to take and give . . . . 206 Astrophil   79   9
  Thou but of all the kingly Tribute take. . . . . 210 Astrophil   85   14
  Without my plumes from others' wings I take. . . . . 224 Astrophil   90   11
  Take me to thee, and thee to me. . . . . 210 A&S 4th Song   5
  Above line repeated at following locations . . . . 210 A&S 4th Song   11
     . . . . 210 A&S 4th Song   17
     . . . . 211 A&S 4th Song   23
     . . . . 211 A&S 4th Song   29
     . . . . 211 A&S 4th Song   35
     . . . . 211 A&S 4th Song   41
     . . . . 211 A&S 4th Song   47
  Yong folkes, take time while you may:. . . . . 211 A&S 4th Song   28
  To take up the place for me; . . . . 226 A&S 10th Song   14
  Fearing her beames, take with thee . . . . 226 A&S 10th Song   23
  This side doth beauty take,. . . . . 215 A&S 6th Song   7
  Ne yet shall suffred be a place to take, ... 270 Psalm I   17
  And counsel jointly take,. . . . . 271 Psalm II   4
  Such pleasure take in Vanity,. . . . . 273 Psalm IV   9
  Yet know this too, that God did take . . . . 273 Psalm IV   11
  Will lay me down, and take my rest:. . . . . 274 Psalm IV   32
  Then let my Foe chase me, and chasing take:. . . . . 277 Psalm VII   13
  More than they now do bragg, when He shall take. . . . . . . 286 Psalm XIV   17
  That in good part he did Thy Offrings take;. . . . . 296 Psalm XX   12
  And yet ev'en from the womb thy self did'st take me; . . . . 299 Psalm XXII   21

TAKE   (CONTINUED)   PAGE   TITLE   LINE
    And do cast lots, who should my vesture take.. . . . .   299 Psalm XXII   44
    Which righteousness doth take, ...   301 Psalm XXIII   8
    Of thee some mercy take, ...   304 Psalm XXV   45
    And me from these ills take. . . . .   304 Psalm XXV   69
    All to this point, how my poore life to take.. . . . .   313 Psalm XXXI   39
    Who him for their lord take; . . . .   317 Psalm XXXIII   45
    Take up Thy shield and for my succour stand, ...   321 Psalm XXXV   3
    Yea take Thy lance and stop the way of those . . . .   321 Psalm XXXV   4
    Dc not take. . . . .   329 Psalm XXXVIII   62
    Dick. Good Will, I cannot take thy good advice, before . . .   344 Possibly   1   43
    Such was his minde, if you another take: . . . .   345 Possibly   4   11
    Kindly, sweete soule, she did unkindnes take,. . . . . .   245 Other Poems 4 121
    But of a straunger mutuall help doth take: . . . .   248 Other Poems 4 238
    And so when Pas hand-reached him to take,. . . . .   248 Other Poems 4 257
    And so to take the gemme Urania sought.. . . . .   250 Other Poems 4 324
    Among the rest that there did take delight . . . .   251 Other Poems 4 361
    Do fondly take away. . . . .   258 Other Poems 5   86
    In whose love I pleasure take, ...   263 Other Poems 7   62
TAKEN
    Woe me, from me why is Thy presence taken? . . . .   298 Psalm XXII   2
TAKES
    Ashe makes speares which shieldes do resist, her force no
        repulse takes: . . . .   36 1st Eclogues 13 136
    In sicke-man's franzie rather takes compassion,. . . . . .   50 2nd Eclogues 28   96
    But at no change, so pinching care he takes, ...   71 Arcadia III 37   9
    When it blowne up with myne a fall of ruine takes) . . . .   118 4th Eclogues 73   52
    One of other beautie takes.. . . . .   140 Cert Sonnets 7   17
    Love of her selfe, takes Stella's shape, that she.. . . .   177 Astrophil   25   10
    That in the Manage myselfe takes delight.. . . . .   189 Astrophil   49   14
    Takes in that sad hue, which with th'inward night. . . . .   230 Astrophil   99   7
    Will. What care takes shee for thee? D. Hir care is to
        prevent. . . . .   344 Possibly   1   37
    Therefore Love arm'd in hir now takes the fielde,. . . . .   245 Other Poems 4 145
    Now runnes, and takes hir in his clipping armes. . . . . .   252 Other Poems 4 384
    So doth he yeeld, so takes he on his yoke, ...   253 Other Poems 4 425
TAKETH
    Still doo I crosse this wretch, what so he taketh in hand".. . 29 1st Eclogues 11   6
    Within it selfe, and never taketh ende:. . . . .   127 4th Eclogues 75   80
    Alas, all onely she no pitie taketh, ...   136 Cert Sonnets 3   9
    Grow rich in that which never taketh rust: . . . .   161 Cert Sonnets 32   3
TAKING
    P. What shall we winne by taking Reason's yoke?. . . . . .   47 2nd Eclogues 27   34
    By taking her two Sunnes from these darke vallies. . . . .   113 4th Eclogues 71   66
    Unto my children alway good rest taking: . . . .   139 Cert Sonnets 6   5
    Foole, more foole, for no more taking. . . . .   203 A&S 2nd Song   28
    And Klaius taking for his yonglings carke, ...   243 Other Poems 4   67
    Taking pitty on his case, ...   264 Other Poems 7   74
TALE
    I am not I, pitie the tale of me.. . . . .   187 Astrophil   45   14
    A Shepheard's tale no height of stile desires. . . . . . .   242 Other Poems 4   1
TALENTS
    Whose talents held young Ganimed above:. . . . .   171 Astrophil   13   4
TALES
    With old true tales he woont mine eares to fill, ...   99 3rd Eclogues 66   33
    Scme one his song in Jove, and Jove's strange tales attires, 167 Astrophil   6   5
    Wee both have power, and will our tales to tell, ...   285 Psalm XII   11
TALK
    No talke untaught can finde the way. . . . .   86 Arcadia III 62   34
    Whereof, with whom, how often did she talke, ...   225 Astrophil   92   11
    Talk with your hearts, and yet be still. . . . .   273 Psalm IV   18
TALKING
    Talking time borrowe for to spitt their vennim . . . . . .   50 2nd Eclogues 28 V886
    This man, this talking beast, this walking tree. . . . . .   58 2nd Eclogues 30   34
    Till their harts had ended talking.. . . . .   218 A&S 8th Song   24
    Then sports grew paines, all talking tediouse, ...   253 Other Poems 4 433
TALKS
    And yet they say he talkes in greate men's bowers? . . . .   28 1st Eclogues 10   68
TAME
    Seeke we to tame these childish superfluities: . . . . . .   61 2nd Eclogues 30 138
    The cattell wild, or tame, in nature's bowers. . . . . . .   100 3rd Eclogues 66   47
    That Plato I read for nought, but if he tame . . . .   175 Astrophil   21   5
    Wherewith my father once made it halfe tame; . . . .   180 Astrophil   30   10
    And gain'd by Mars, could yet mad Mars so tame,. . . . . .   204 Astrophil   75   7
TAMED
    How is he young, that tam'de old Phoebus' youth? . . . . .   21 1st Eclogues 8   10
    Then let thy minde with better bookes be tamed,. . . . . .   25 1st Eclogues 9 120
TANGLING
    My feet from tangling net. . . . .   304 Psalm XXV   58
TANTAL'S
    And damning their owne selves to Tantal's smart, ...   177 Astrophil   24   3
TARBOX
    Thy wallet or thy Tarbox lost, or thy new rayment rent?. . . 343 Possibly   1   16
TARRY
    Lalus. How oft my dolefull Sire cried to me, "tarrie sonne". 16 1st Eclogues 7   49
    That of those beames in you do tarie:. . . . .   159 Cert Sonnets 29   11
    Faint coward joy no longer tarry dare, ...   228 Astrophil   95   5
    Long I will not after tary,. . . . .   226 A&S 10th Song   15
TARTARS
    By Parents train'd the Tartars wilde are tought, ...   251 Other Poems 4 350

TASTE
```
                                                       PAGE    TITLE        LINE
And for a tast of all these gifts, she borowes Momus' grace.   12  Arcadia I      3     8
Enjoye my joyes, as you dyd taste my payne,. . . . . . .       43  Arcadia II    23    11
Wayle in my woes, taste of your master's payne,. . . . . .     44  Arcadia II    24    11
Where witt but serves, to have true tast of woes.. . . . .     57  2nd Eclogues 30    25
How be the minds dispos'd that can not tast thy physick?
    Sick. . . . . . . . . . . . . . . . . . . . . . . . . .    63  2nd Eclogues 31    17
Make present ease receave the better taste.. . . . . . . .     70  Arcadia III  36     6
Employ thy might, that she my fires may taste. . . . . . .     72  Arcadia III  38    15
Can taste no sweetes, the sower onely please:. . . . . . .     74  Arcadia III  41     2
In worth, in taste, in perfitte hewe:. . . . . . . . . . .     87  Arcadia III  62    40
So true a Taste invites the Eye, . . . . . . . . . . . . .     87  Arcadia III  62 V 51
To have a feeling tast of him that sitts . . . . . . . . .     99  3rd Eclogues 66    27
At length for glutton taste he did them kill:. . . . . . .    103  3rd Eclogues 66   146
O my heavens for taste by thie heavenly pleasure,. . . . .    138  Cert Sonnets  5     2
O my heavens for Taste, by thy heavenly pleasure,. . . . .    138  Cert Sonnets  5    26
This sowre-breath'd mate tast of those sugred lips.. . . .    194  Astrophil    59    11
Whose fruit doth farre th' Esperian tast surpasse: . . . .    208  Astrophil    82     6
With no worse curse then absence makes me tast.. . . . . .    235  Astrophil   105    14
To make a Lyzard dull to taste Love's daintie food:. . . .    209  A&S 3rd Song        8
Can tast comfort but of thee,. . . . . . . . . . . . . . .    220  A&S 8th Song       78
Ah, now even for their sakes, that taste of Woe, . . . . .    285  Psalm XII          13
In my inward reynes I taste. . . . . . . . . . . . . . . .    288  Psalm XVI          23
Meeke to the Meek Thou art, The good thy goodness taste; . .  292  Psalm XVIII        50
By them is past in sweetest taste. . . . . . . . . . . . .    294  Psalm XIX          43
Tast misery. . . . . . . . . . . . . . . . . . . . . . . .    301  Psalm XXIII         3
Let me not tast of shame, O lord most high,. . . . . . . .    313  Psalm XXXI         45
I say but tast and see . . . . . . . . . . . . . . . . . .    319  Psalm XXXIV        29
I by day thy love shall tast,. . . . . . . . . . . . . . .    335  Psalm XLII         37
With others' blott, till all do tast of shame. . . . . . .    248  Other Poems   4   232
To see, to feele, to heare, to tast, to know . . . . . . .    252  Other Poems   4   407
```
TASTED
```
My minde hath tasted. . . . . . . . . . . . . . . . . . .      83  Arcadia III  59     8
Asking her how she tasted Courtier's lips, . . . . . . . .     95  3rd Eclogues 64    33
Where bee nowe those Joyes, that I lately tasted?. . . . .    138  Cert Sonnets  5     5
My life hott torments tasted.. . . . . . . . . . . . . . .    315  Psalm XXXII        12
```
TASTES
```
Bitter griefe tastes me best, paine is my ease,. . . . . .     74  Arcadia III  41     7
```
TAUGHT
```
Philisides. Who ever taught a skillesse man to teach,. . . .   22  1st Eclogues  9    16
Raging in woes first pastors tought to plaine? . . . . . .     53  2nd Eclogues 29    58
The marchante man, whome many seas have toughte. . . . . .     71  Arcadia III  37     9
Then greefe, unkindnes, proofe, tooke, kindled, tought,. . .   84  Arcadia III  60     9
With weeping eyes (her eyes she taught to weepe) . . . . .     96  3rd Eclogues 66    85
The songe I sange old Languet had me taught, . . . . . . .     99  3rd Eclogues 66    22
Where famine ravine taught their hungrie chestes,. . . . .    102  3rd Eclogues 66   124
The dogge was in a coller taught his kinde.. . . . . . . .    102  3rd Eclogues 66   138
"How ill both you can rule, well hath your discord taught: .  121  4th Eclogues 73   163
Lyke crafty wretch by time and travell tought, . . . . . .    141  Cert Sonnets  8     5
For vertue hath this better lesson taught, . . . . . . . .    161  Cert Sonnets 31    12
Till that her blush taught me my shame to see. . . . . . .    191  Astrophil    53    14
Venus is taught with Dian's wings to flie: . . . . . . . .    202  Astrophil    72     6
Him great harmes had taught much care, . . . . . . . . . .    218  A&S 8th Song        9
He shall be by best teacher taught.. . . . . . . . . . . .    304  Psalm XXV          48
Chastned but thus, and thus his lesson tought, . . . . . .    244  Other Poems   4    97
And taught his shepe hir shepe in food to thwart.. . . . .    247  Other Poems   4   188
By Parents train'd the Tartars wilde are tought, . . . . .    251  Other Poems   4   350
And surely taught by his love-open eye,. . . . . . . . . .    251  Other Poems   4   378
```
TEACH
```
Teach me what circle may acquaint her sprite,. . . . . . .     17  1st Eclogues  7   101
Philisides. Who ever taught a skillesse man to teach,. . . .   22  1st Eclogues  9    16
Or pleasant mirtell, may teach th'unfortunate Echo . . . .     31  1st Eclogues 13    13
Where proofes justly do teach, thus matcht, such worth to be
    nought worth. . . . . . . . . . . . . . . . . . . . . .     34  1st Eclogues 13    83
Doth teach, to learne the good what travailes do belong: . .   45  Arcadia II   26     8
The marchante man, whome gayne dothe teache the Sea. . . .     70  Arcadia III  36     1
For I to teach the world complainte am bent. . . . . . . .    127  4th Eclogues 75    66
Yet craving law of armes, whose rule doth teach, . . . . .    135  Cert Sonnets  1    10
Which in her face teach vertue, I could brooke . . . . . .    193  Astrophil    56     6
Sweet lip, you teach my mouth with one sweet kisse.. . . .    207  Astrophil    80    14
Now will I teach her that she, . . . . . . . . . . . . . .    202  A&S 2nd Song        3
In darkness teach cleere knowledg. . . . . . . . . . . . .    293  Psalm XIX           8
Teach me, thus vext, what path to go.. . . . . . . . . . .    303  Psalm XXV          12
Teach me for why Thou art. . . . . . . . . . . . . . . . .    303  Psalm XXV          14
And teach the humble how to tread. . . . . . . . . . . . .    303  Psalm XXV          36
Teach lord, lord lead me Thy right way,. . . . . . . . . .    308  Psalm XXVII        52
Come, Come, the way I will teach Thee, . . . . . . . . . .    315  Psalm XXXII        29
For I will teach to you the way. . . . . . . . . . . . . .    320  Psalm XXXIV        43
But tryall well doth teach me, . . . . . . . . . . . . . .    332  Psalm XL           45
And now their curr they teach to fetch and daunce. . . . .    243  Other Poems   4    48
```
TEACHER
```
He shall be by best teacher taught.. . . . . . . . . . . .    304  Psalm XXV          48
```
TEACHER'S
```
Their first caught sence prefers to teacher's blowes.. . . .   28  1st Eclogues 10    57
```
TEACHING
```
Teaching blind eyes both how to smile and weepe, . . . . .    181  Astrophil    32     8
Teaching the meane, at once to take and give . . . . . . .    206  Astrophil    79     9
Teaching dumbe lips a nobler exercise. . . . . . . . . . .    207  Astrophil    81     4
Teaching sleepe most faire to be?. . . . . . . . . . . . .    202  A&S 2nd Song        2
But of the skyes the teaching cryes. . . . . . . . . . . .    293  Psalm XIX          11
```

```
                                                         PAGE    TITLE          LINE
TEAR
    With losse of purest blood themselves to teare,. . . . . . .    58  2nd Eclogues 30    46
    To teare the bowels, that good corne should send.. . . . . .   102  3rd Eclogues 66   117
    The flying sprites which trees by rootes up teare. . . . . .   114  4th Eclogues 72    36
    Your morall notes straight my hid meaning teare. . . . . . .   233  Astrophil   104    12
    And cruely in many peices teare. . . . . . . . . . . . . . .   277  Psalm VII           5
    With cruel minds my very soul to teare.. . . . . . . . . . .   322  Psalm XXXV         28
    Amid my flock with woe my voice I teare, . . . . . . . . . .   254  Other Poems   4   459
    Their snowy haire teare off in melting paine.. . . . . . . .   254  Other Poems   4   478
TEARED
    Yet first but wooll, or fethers off he teard:. . . . . . . .   102  3rd Eclogues 66   143
TEAR'S
    D. Teares drink, sorowes meat, wherewith, not I, but in me
       my death lives.. . . . . . . . . . . . . . . . . . . . .    344  Possibly      1    34
*TEARS
    How oft with raine of teares skies make confession,. . . . .    15  1st Eclogues  7    43
    My foode is teares; my tunes waymenting yeeld: . . . . . . .    18  1st Eclogues  7   138
    My earthy moulde doth melte in watrie teares.. . . . . . . .    19  1st Eclogues  7   151
    Dorus. My earthy moulde doth melte in watrie teares, . . . .    19  1st Eclogues  7   152
    And yet his outward heate our teares would quench, but an
       inward. . . . . . . . . . . . . . . . . . . . . . . . . .    32  1st Eclogues 13    31
    With flowing teares your fault of hasty sight: . . . . . . .    38  Arcadia II   14     2
    (Mine eyes even great in labour with their teares) . . . . .    41  Arcadia II   21     2
    Leave of my sheepe, my shower of teeres oreflowes, . . . . .    43  Arcadia II   24     4
    O lippes, that kist that hand with my teares sprent; . . . .    60  2nd Eclogues 30   120
    The laborer, which cursed earthe up teares . . . . . . . . .    71  Arcadia III  36     7
    Teares, drowne your selves, for woe (your cause) is wasted,.    83  Arcadia III  59     6
    Eyes, let your Teares with gazing now be mended, . . . . . .    84  Arcadia III  59    14
    Crocodile, teares, which might be falsely spilde:. . . . . .   101  3rd Eclogues 66    96
    Of willing teares, torne heare, and cries of sorrow. . . . .   109  Arcadia IV   70    16
    Hailestones of teares, of sighes a monstrous blast,. . . . .   114  4th Eclogues 72    33
    Can those eyes, that of eyes drownd in most harty flowing
       teares,. . . . . . . . . . . . . . . . . . . . . . . . .    122  4th Eclogues 74    15
    (Teares and teares of a man) had no returne to remorse;. . .   122  4th Eclogues 74    16
    Let all the Sea thy teares accounted be: . . . . . . . . . .   125  4th Eclogues 75    20
    Witnesse your wofull teares with daily rayning.. . . . . . .   127  4th Eclogues 75    69
    Let teares for him therefore be all our treasure,. . . . . .   130  4th Eclogues 76    31
    That eyes weepe worse then hart in bloodie teares? . . . . .   142  Cert Sonnets 11     7
    That all the earth my woes, sighes, teares may know, . . . .   146  Cert Sonnets 17    39
    Alas sweet Brookes do in my teares augment:. . . . . . . . .   147  Cert Sonnets 18    12
    Alas how oft with teares,. . . . . . . . . . . . . . . . . .   158  Cert Sonnets 28    13
    O teares of guilefull breast,. . . . . . . . . . . . . . . .   158  Cert Sonnets 28    14
    What streames of teares she spent, . . . . . . . . . . . . .   158  Cert Sonnets 28    22
    While teares powre out his inke, and sighs breathe out his
       words: . . . . . . . . . . . . . . . . . . . . . . . . .    168  Astrophil     6    10
    Oft with true sighes, oft with uncalled teares,. . . . . . .   195  Astrophil    61     1
    She oft hath drunke my teares, now hopes to enjoy. . . . . .   201  Astrophil    70     3
    I saw that teares did in her eyes appeare; . . . . . . . . .   223  Astrophil    87     6
    I cry thy sighs; my deere, thy teares I bleede.. . . . . . .   227  Astrophil    93    14
    Yet waile thy selfe, and waile with causefull teares, . . .   228  Astrophil    94    11
    Kils his owne children, teares, finding that they. . . . . .   229  Astrophil    95    10
    Thy teares expresse night's native moisture right. . . . . .   229  Astrophil    96     8
    O teares, no teares, but raine from beautie's skies, . . . .   231  Astrophil   100     1
    Such teares, sighs, plaints, no sorrow is, but joy:. . . . .   231  Astrophil   100    12
    But cease mine eyes, your teares do witnesse well. . . . . .   235  Astrophil   105     9
    But now teares themselves did smile, . . . . . . . . . . . .   218  A&S 8th Song       14
    With my teares floweth.. . . . . . . . . . . . . . . . . . .   276  Psalm VI           20
    In clouds of teares, but soon as sun . . . . . . . . . . . .   311  Psalm XXX          17
    At these my words all cloath'd in teares:. . . . . . . . . .   330  Psalm XXXIX        38
    Day and night my teares out flowing. . . . . . . . . . . . .   334  Psalm XLII          9
    With sight made dymme with dayly teares another's sport to
       see. . . . . . . . . . . . . . . . . . . . . . . . . . .    343  Possibly      1     4
    But you, o you, that thinke not teares too deare . . . . . .   242  Other Poems   4     9
    At length in rowes of Kisse-cheeke teares they raine.. . . .   245  Other Poems   4   128
    Filling his eies with teares, with sighs his brest.. . . . .   253  Other Poems   4   432
    With teares, he saide, or sorrow said for him. . . . . . . .   256  Other Poems   5    13
    What fitts me now but teares, and sighings sadd? . . . . . .   259  Other Poems   5    97
TEARS'
    That, from that sea deriv'd, teares' spring did flow.. . . .   187  Astrophil    45     8
TEDIOUS
    In travaile of our life (a short but tedious space). . . . .    45  Arcadia II   26     9
    Sea drownd in thee, of tedious life bereave me:. . . . . . .   136  Cert Sonnets  3    15
    Forc'd by a tedious proofe, that Turkish hardned hart, . . .   168  Astrophil     8     2
    Or doth the tedious burd'n of long wo. . . . . . . . . . . .   199  Astrophil    66     2
    Their rayes to me, who in her tedious absence lay. . . . . .   204  Astrophil    76     2
    The night as tedious, wooes th'approch of day; . . . . . . .   224  Astrophil    89     6
    That tedious leasure marks each wrinckled line:. . . . . . .   230  Astrophil    98    11
    For nothing can more tedious bee, then plaint, in time of
       joy. . . . . . . . . . . . . . . . . . . . . . . . . . .    344  Possibly      1    46
    With tedious brawlings of her parents deare, . . . . . . . .   245  Other Poems   4   114
    Then sports grew paines, all talking tediouse, . . . . . . .   253  Other Poems   4   433
TEETH
    For hungrie throte their flesh with teeth he brused: . . . .   102  3rd Eclogues 66   145
    To shew her skin, lips, teeth and head so well?. . . . . . .   181  Astrophil    32    11
    Thou those men's teeth which byte, . . . . . . . . . . . . .   273  Psalm III          28
    Ev'en gnashing teeth, to witness more their spight.. . . . .   322  Psalm XXXV         42
    Gnashing their teeth full of disdeigning;. . . . . . . . . .   325  Psalm XXXVII       34
TELL
    And others long to tell their loves' condition:. . . . . . .    19  1st Eclogues  7   171
    And others long to tell their loves' condicion.. . . . . . .    20  1st Eclogues  7  V971
```

TELL	(CONTINUED)	PAGE	TITLE		LINE
Your woll is riche: no tonge can tell my gayne..		43	Arcadia II	23	14
When rotten Fame will tell their blowes.		44	Arcadia II	25	10
Dicus. Dorus, tell me, where is thy wonted motion.		47	2nd Eclogues 28		1
Goe on therefore, and tell us, by what fashion		48	2nd Eclogues 28		34
Pas. O Nymphes, I tell you newes, for Pas you knowe:		54	2nd Eclogues 29		66
Nico. Tell me (and be my Pan) the monster's name,.		56	2nd Eclogues 29		141
Pas. Tell this (and Phoebus be) what monster growes.		56	2nd Eclogues 29		144
O toonge, then dumbe, not daring tell my smart;.		60	2nd Eclogues 30		121
Well mett Echo, aproche: then tell me thy will too. I will too.		63	2nd Eclogues 31		4
Yet tell what light thinge I had in me to draw me to die? Eye.		64	2nd Eclogues 31		25
Tell yet againe me the names of these faire form'd to do ev'lls. Dev'lls.		65	2nd Eclogues 31		49
Reason, tell me thy mind, if here be reason.		67	2nd Eclogues 33		1
Can holde, shew, tell, my paines without reliefe..		75	Arcadia III	43	8
What toong can her perfections tell.		85	Arcadia III	62	1
My tongue doth tell what fancie sees..		89	Arcadia III	62	94
No tongue can her perfections tell,.		90	Arcadia III	62	145
And tell him that you finde I doo him tell,.		95	3rd Eclogues 64		56
Thus both did come to me, and both began to tell		121	4th Eclogues 73		154
The rest I cannot tell, for therewithall I wak'd		121	4th Eclogues 73		179
My Muse therefore, for onely thou canst tell,.		146	Cert Sonnets 17		11
Tell me the cause of this my causelesse woe, ...		146	Cert Sonnets 17		12
Tell how ill thought disgrac'd my doing well:.		146	Cert Sonnets 17		13
Tell how my joyes and hopes thus fowly fell.		146	Cert Sonnets 17		14
Tell me o haire of gold, ...		158	Cert Sonnets 28		17
Dig deepe with learning's spade, now tell me this, ...		175	Astrophil	21	13
Then ev'n of fellowship, o Moone, tell me.		180	Astrophil	31	9
Vouchsafe of all acquaintance this to tell,.		181	Astrophil	32	9
For of my life I must a riddle tell.		183	Astrophil	37	4
Then some good body tell me how I do,.		195	Astrophil	60	12
Some do I heare of Poets' furie tell,.		204	Astrophil	74	5
Yet ah, my Mayd'n Muse doth blush to tell the best.. . . .		205	Astrophil	77	14
Let no tongue aspire to tell,.		226	A&S 10th Song		10
Tell her in your piteous blaying,.		222	A&S 9th Song		49
Wee both have power, and will our tales to tell, ...		285	Psalm XII		11
Will. Thou seest my eares do itch at it: good Dick thy sorow tell.		343	Possibly	1	18
Sometimes to her newes of my selfe to tell		254	Other Poems	4	469
"Tell me you wanton brooke,.		257	Other Poems	5	27
Tell me, if your diverted springs become		257	Other Poems	5	37
"Tell me you flowers faire,.		257	Other Poems	5	40
Tell me, if husband springtime leave your lande, ...		257	Other Poems	5	50
"Tell me my seely pipe,.		257	Other Poems	5	53
Tell, if that breath, which thee thy sounding gives, . . .		258	Other Poems	5	63
"Tell me my lamb of gold,.		258	Other Poems	5	66
Tell me, if wolves the throte.		258	Other Poems	5	72
"Tell me o Turtle true,.		258	Other Poems	5	79
Tell me if greedy arme,.		258	Other Poems	5	85
Tell me poore wretch, parted from wretched prey, ...		258	Other Poems	5	89
Daring not to tell to mee, ...		262	Other Poems	7	15
TELLETH					
Since then truth to all minds telleth, ...		140	Cert Sonnets	7	18
His tongue of heavnly judgments telleth, ...		326	Psalm XXXVII		78
TELLING					
By telling how she was, how now she framed is.		49	2nd Eclogues 28		53
Where Israel Thy lawdes is ever telling;		298	Psalm XXII		10
Telling mine iniquityes.		329	Psalm XXXVIII		54
TELLS					
What can justice availe, to a man that tells not his owne case?.		32	1st Eclogues 13		22
What foresight tels; our thoughts upon thy knowledge staye..		45	Arcadia II	26	12
TEMPE					
Nor ever did in shade of Tempe sit:.		203	Astrophil	74	2
TEMPER					
And weakest harts to constant temper brought..		22	1st Eclogues	9	15
And me perchaunce your constant temper lend.		23	1st Eclogues	9	20
My purest minde; whose temper hard doth showe..		40	Arcadia II	18	8
This marble chose, as of like temper knowne:		40	Arcadia II	19	2
Who love can temper thus,.		161	Cert Sonnets 30		39
He blessed is, who with wise temper can.		332	Psalm XLI		1
Was once my mynde, my temper, and my lyfe, ...		344	Possibly	2	6
TEMPERANCE					
As might learne Temp'rance voyde of a rage's events.		124	4th Eclogues 74		64
TEMPERED					
My tempred hart; by thee my promise sent		40	Arcadia II	18	9
TEMPERS					
Tempers her words to trampling horses feet,.		209	Astrophil	84	3
TEMPEST					
But such we are with inward tempest blowne		59	2nd Eclogues 30		80
Or me wretch his tempest thunders.		335	Psalm XLII		32
TEMPESTS					
With strong foes on land, on seas with contrary tempests . .		29	1st Eclogues 11		5
Winde, tempests, and stormes, yet in ende what gives she desire? Ire.		64	2nd Eclogues 31		35
Willd me these tempests of vaine love to flie, ...		196	Astrophil	62	10
Stella whose eyes make all my tempests cleere, ...		222	Astrophil	87	3

495

TEMPESTUOUS
    Yet I confess in that tempestuous haste. . . . .   313 Psalm XXXI   61
TEMPLE
    Of my owne harte, where thoughts be the temple, sighte is an
        aultar. . . . .   37 1st Eclogues 13   171
    On her, who hath in me thy temple raste, ...   72 Arcadia III 38   14
    And, fooles, adore in temple of our hart, ... 167 Astrophil   5   7
    O do not let thy Temple be destroyd. . . . . 185 Astrophil   40   14
    Towards the Temple of Thy Holyness.. . . . . 275 Psalm V   20
    God in his Holy Temple is, ... 284 Psalm XI   13
    His Temple too.. . . . . 307 Psalm XXVII   24
    Offrings of joy in Temple His, ... 307 Psalm XXVII   34
*TEMPLES
    Our names are quite forgot, our temples are defac'd: . . . . 119 4th Eclogues 73   109
    A garland made on temples for to weare, ... 244 Other Poems   4   74
TEMPT
    Who tempt, and tempted plague, are Devils in true defining.. 215 A&S 5th Song   84
TEMPTED
    Who tempt, and tempted plague, are Devils in true defining.. 215 A&S 5th Song   84
TEMPTS
    For thy face tempts my soule to leave the heav'n for thee, . 215 A&S 5th Song   82
TEND
    Shall such high Plannets tend to the losse of a worme? . . . 123 4th Eclogues 74   38
TENDER
    With her faire hande, your tender barkes to cleave, ...   78 Arcadia III 49   6
    Her tender Ribbes well armed bee, ...   88 Arcadia III 62 V 68
    As tender conscience might with furious panges assaulte. . . 117 4th Eclogues 73   20
    In tender harts, small things engender hate: . . . . 146 Cert Sonnets 17   17
    My mouth too tender is for thy hard bit. . . . . 166 Astrophil   4   8
    From that foe's wounds their tender skinnes to hide. . . . . 176 Astrophil   22   8
    School'd onely by his mother's tender eye: . . . . 203 Astrophil   73   2
    Or do you meane my tender eares to spare, ... 225 Astrophil   92   4
    Then lord from me draw not Thy tender grace, ... 332 Psalm XL   41
    How tenderly hir tender hands betweene . . . . 244 Other Poems   4   93
TENDERLY
    How tenderly hir tender hands betweene . . . . 244 Other Poems   4   93
TENDERNESS
    Thy Mercy's tenderness;. . . . . 303 Psalm XXV   20
TEN-STRINGED
    Let ten-stringd instrument . . . . 316 Psalm XXXIII   10
TENT
    Hide me, ev'n closely in his Tent; . . . . 307 Psalm XXVII   27
TENTS
    Her breasts his tents, legs his triumphall carre: . . . . . . 179 Astrophil   29   11
TERM
    That skin, whose passe-praise hue scorns this poore terme of
        white: . . . . 205 Astrophil   77   7
TERROR
    Yet never rock, nor race, suche terror brought, ...   71 Arcadia III 37   3
TERRORS
    With terrors great, O Lord, do thou them fright: . . . . . . 281 Psalm IX   63
TESTIFIES
    Silly shepheard's poore pype, when his harsh sound testifis
        our woes, ...   32 1st Eclogues 13   40
TESTIFY
    Blinde Cupid's workes with wonder testifie?. . . . . 106 3rd Eclogues 67   98
TESTIFYING
    With armes crost, yet testifying . . . . 218 A&S 8th Song   19
TESTIMONIES
    And on his Testimonys plant. . . . . 304 Psalm XXV   42
TEXT
    Looke on againe, the faire text better trie: . . . . 199 Astrophil   67   7
*TH
    Or pleasant mirtell, may teach th'unfortunate Echo . . . . .   31 1st Eclogues 13   13
    Unto the heav'ns? our wings be too short; th' earth thinks
        us a burden; . . . .   32 1st Eclogues 13   29
    And if a meane were found, fortune th' whole course of it
        hinders. . . . .   37 1st Eclogues 13   159
    But if I had bene there, th'adst met another mate. . . . . .   52 2nd Eclogues 29   22
    Yet say againe thy advise for th' ev'lls that I told thee. I
        told thee. . . . .   63 2nd Eclogues 31   18
    Doth th'infected wretch, of his ev'll th'extremity know? No.   63 2nd Eclogues 31   19
    Howe can they be unkind? speake for th'hast narroly pri'de.
        pride. . . . .   65 2nd Eclogues 31   43
    Where senses do behold th'order of heav'nly hoste, ...   68 2nd Eclogues 34   5
    And for th'event we never ought be sad. . . . . 105 3rd Eclogues 67   66
    But finding th'approch of death with an inly relenting, . . . 123 4th Eclogues 74   25
    As th'offence was done, and goe beyond if he can. . . . . . 123 4th Eclogues 74   40
    My selfe unto th' Anatomy desirde, ... 150 Cert Sonnets 22   27
    And still th'effect of thy perswasions prove: . . . . 167 Astrophil   4   11
    And find th'effect, for I do burne in love.. . . . . 177 Astrophil   25   14
    Rich in those gifts which give th'eternall crowne; . . . . . 183 Astrophil   37   11
    Th'indifferent Judge betweene the high and low; . . . . 184 Astrophil   39   4
    One hand forgott to rule, th'other to fight. . . . . 191 Astrophil   53   11
    Th' anatomy of all my woes I wrate, ... 194 Astrophil   58   10
    Whose fruit doth farre th' Esperian tast surpasse: . . . . . 208 Astrophil   82   6
    Thus while th' effect most bitter was to me, ... 223 Astrophil   87   12
    The night as tedious, wooes th'approch of day; . . . . 224 Astrophil   89   6
    Takes in that sad hue, which with th'inward night. . . . . . 230 Astrophil   99   7
    The proofe of Beautie's worth, th'enheritrix of fame, ... 213 A&S 5th Song   20

	PAGE	TITLE		LINE
With time still th' affection groweth.	234	A&S 11th Song		19
Thou lord also th' Oppressed wilt defend	280	Psalm IX		26
Th' afflicted cry.	280	Psalm IX		35
In th' Innocence of Me	305	Psalm XXVI		19
Judg of th' afflicted man;	332	Psalm XLI		2
Before thassault beginne, O yeelde O yeelde.	345	Possibly	4	14
If th' author of thy blisse.	257	Other Poems	5	21
Thad'st killed with a stroke,	259	Other Poems	5	100

THAMES

	PAGE	TITLE		LINE
O happie Tems, that didst my Stella beare,	232	Astrophil	103	1

THAN

	PAGE	TITLE		LINE
More high then stars, more firme then flintie field.	3	Lady of May	2	9
And plaine speach oft then quaint phrase better framed is.	14	1st Eclogues	7	6
Milde as a Lambe, more daintie then a Conie is:	15	1st Eclogues	7	31
More gladde to me, then to a miser monie is.	15	1st Eclogues	7	33
Rather to wrong then unto just defence,	25	1st Eclogues	9	106
Then thow earst knew? rather take part with him.	26	1st Eclogues	10	8
Then jarle: lo, lo, even these how envie blindes.	26	1st Eclogues	10	9
Knowing no more, then what poore tryall showes,	28	1st Eclogues	10	53
Yet thou art mickle warse then ere was I,	28	1st Eclogues	10	62
Then with the poisnous todes that quiet lie.	28	1st Eclogues	10	66
And we shall find more spottes then Leopard's skinne.	29	1st Eclogues	10	95
In sorrows torments, then, tyed to the pompes of a pallace,	35	1st Eclogues	13	103
Whose wounds are salves, whose yokes please more then pleasure doth:	49	2nd Eclogues	28	56
I sooner would, then thus my eares defile.	50	2nd Eclogues	28	81
Then rage for rage: rather my wish I send to thee,	50	2nd Eclogues	28	97
Without her love, then any mind who fairer is.	51	2nd Eclogues	28	116
Nay rather then my ease discontentation.	51	2nd Eclogues	28	120
Dicus. Sing then my lads, but sing with better vaine then yet,	53	2nd Eclogues	29	49
Her naked legge, more white then whitest snow.	55	2nd Eclogues	29	101
Then earste I knew: But first dyd playne	57	2nd Eclogues	30	3
Then man to yeeld to female lamentations?	61	2nd Eclogues	30	141
O poisonous medecin! what worse to me can be then it? It..	63	2nd Eclogues	31	7
O much more then words: those words serv'd more to me blesse Lesse.	64	2nd Eclogues	31	31
O breath more sweete, then is the growing beane,	76	Arcadia III	46	2
Gay haire more gaie then straw when harvest lyes,	76	Arcadia III	46	7
My thoughtes then hers, who first your ryne did rente,	78	Arcadia III	49	14
Then hers, to whom my thoughts alonely thrall.	78	Arcadia III	49	15
Whiter indeed; more white then snow,	85	Arcadia III	62	7
No purer then the pretie eares.	86	Arcadia III	62	28
Then that which beares the mylken name.	87	Arcadia III	62	60
More white then Neptune's fomie face,	88	Arcadia III	62	69
More white then whitest bone of whall.	89	Arcadia III	62	104
Then ever for my selfe since I was bore:	99	3rd Eclogues	66	19
Then is the quiet joy of loving wife;	103	3rd Eclogues	67	8
Make home more paine then following of the cart.	104	3rd Eclogues	67	30
Who onely sees the ill is worse then blind.	106	3rd Eclogues	67	85
Long since my thoughts more desert be then forrests:	112	4th Eclogues	71	28
My fire is more, then can be made with forrests;	112	4th Eclogues	71	56
My state more base, then are the basest vallies:	112	4th Eclogues	71	57
Whose beawties shin'de more then the blushing morning,	113	4th Eclogues	71	62
(More swift then falcon's stoope to feeding Falconer's call)	118	4th Eclogues	73	58
Straunge were the Ladies' weedes; yet more unfit then strange.	118	4th Eclogues	73	65
The other had with arte (more then our women knowe,	118	4th Eclogues	73	71
Who may this doubt discerne: for better, witt, then lot.	120	4th Eclogues	73	139
Now kindnesse profred is, none kinder is then I:	121	4th Eclogues	73	151
More then Nestor's yeares, more then a King's diademe.	122	4th Eclogues	74	20
Since so she will, whose will is to me more then a lawe.	124	4th Eclogues	74	84
Rather then have thy all-beholding eye	126	4th Eclogues	75	56
Example more prevailing then direction,	128	4th Eclogues	75	131
Feare is more paine, then is the paine it feares,	131	Arcadia V	77	5
Since wanting is more woe then too much having..	137	Cert Sonnets	4	20
That eyes weepe worse then hart in bloodie teares?	142	Cert Sonnets	11	7
That sense feeles more then what doth sense containe?.	142	Cert Sonnets	11	8
Then to my selfe, not though Jove grew a suter of hers..	143	Cert Sonnets	13	2
Yea worse then death, death parts both woe and joy,	148	Cert Sonnets	20	13
Of trueth, farre more then Alablaster pure,	150	Cert Sonnets	22	39
A bird which gets more life then ship had lost.	151	Cert Sonnets	22	54
Where, 'sooner die then change my state',	158	Cert Sonnets	28	35
Better then one captiv'd perceiveth,	159	Cert Sonnets	29	16
They sun-like should more dazle then delight?.	168	Astrophil	7	8
Then did on him who first stale downe the fire,	171	Astrophil	14	3
Then that I lose no more for Stella's sake..	174	Astrophil	18	14
"What idler thing, then speake and not be hard?"	182	Astrophil	34	9
What harder thing then smart, and not to speake?	182	Astrophil	34	10
Livelier then else-where, Stella's image see.	184	Astrophil	39	14
Then servant's wracke, where new doubts honor brings;	187	Astrophil	45	11
Deare, why make you more of a dog then me?	194	Astrophil	59	1
Rather then by more truth to get more paine.	199	Astrophil	67	14
O blisse, fit for a nobler state then me:	200	Astrophil	69	2
To lose his Crowne, rather then faile his Love..	204	Astrophil	75	14
That hand, which without touch holds more then Atlas might;	205	Astrophil	77	5
More oft then to a chamber melodie;	209	Astrophil	84	4
Then those blest eyes, where all my hopes do dwell,	212	Astrophil	86	13
And nothing then the cause more sweet could be,	223	Astrophil	87	13

```
THAN                              (CONTINUED)                    PAGE    TITLE         LINE
      While no night is more darke then is my day, . . . . . . . .   224 Astrophil   89   10
      Nor no day hath lesse quiet then my night: . . . . . . . . .   224 Astrophil   89   11
      Yet growest more wretched then thy nature beares,. . . . . .   228 Astrophil   94   13
      Which ay most faire, now more then most faire show,. . . . .  231 Astrophil  100    3
      With no worse curse then absence makes me tast.. . . . . . .   235 Astrophil  105   14
      And all eares worse then deafe, that heard not out thy
          storie. . . . . . . . . . . . . . . . . . . . . . . . . .  212 A&S 5th Song      6
      Threat'n what may be done, yet do more then you threat'n.. .   213 A&S 5th Song     33
      Yet worse then worst, I say thou art a theefe, a theefe? . .   213 A&S 5th Song     43
      Yet witches may repent, thou art far worse then they,. . . .  215 A&S 5th Song     79
      More then in my reason's sight.. . . . . . . . . . . . . . .   234 A&S 11th Song    30
      Thy griefe more then death would grieve me.. . . . . . . . .   220 A&S 8th Song     76
      Then can in good eawes be moved. . . . . . . . . . . . . . .   221 A&S 9th Song     24
      Than they whose stoare in harvest space. . . . . . . . . . .   274 Psalm IV         29
      For though in lesse than Angel's state . . . . . . . . . . .   279 Psalm VIII       17
      Pure, Purer than the silver throughly try'd. . . . . . . . .   285 Psalm XII        20
      More than they now do bragg, when He shall take. . . . . . .   286 Psalm XIV        17
      Yea worse than doggs, a naughty wicked rout.. . . . . . . .    299 Psalm XXII       40
      Who was to me more than most gracious, . . . . . . . . . . .   313 Psalm XXXI       59
      Farr farr more sure, than walls most firmly fast.. . . . . .   313 Psalm XXXI       60
      Than it was done;. . . . . . . . . . . . . . . . . . . . . .   317 Psalm XXXIII     32
      Than true deliverance gain.. . . . . . . . . . . . . . . . .   318 Psalm XXXIII     66
      Than of bad folks the wealthy wonder,. . . . . . . . . . . .   325 Psalm XXXVII     42
      But they are more than can by me be told.. . . . . . . . . .   331 Psalm XL         24
      More than my head hath haires; . . . . . . . . . . . . . . .   332 Psalm XL         47
      For nothing can more tedious bee, then plaint in time of
          joy . . . . . . . . . . . . . . . . . . . . . . . . . . .  344 Possibly     1   46
      For never was there man more crossely crost then he. . . . .   241 Other Poems  1    4
      Then in good Dog, faire field, or shading tree.. . . . . . .   246 Other Poems  4  179
      More marking hir, then how himselfe did goe,. . . . . . . .    249 Other Poems  4  290
      More then, besides hir, all the earth could show.. . . . . .   252 Other Poems  4  408
      Then those delights through all their sinews breed . . . . .   252 Other Poems  4  411
      Of faire Urania, fairer then a greene, . . . . . . . . . . .   253 Other Poems  4  452
      Then want one hower those eyes which my joyes keepe. . . . .   259 Other Poems  5  102
      Then this false, fine, Courtly pleasure. . . . . . . . . . .   263 Other Poems  7   48
      Sooner these than those in hearing.. . . . . . . . . . . . .   263 Other Poems  7   54
THANK
      But thanke the cause, thou seest, when he is dim.. . . . . .    27 1st Eclogues 10   12
      "I con thee thanke" to whom thy dogges be deare, . . . . . .    27 1st Eclogues 10   34
      Thanke may you have for such a thankfull part, . . . . . . .   229 Astrophil   95   13
      I will thank Thee, where congregations sitt, . . . . . . . .   322 Psalm XXXV       46
      Thank my God I will, . . . . . . . . . . . . . . . . . . . .   337 Psalm XLIII      35
THANKED
      Now thanked be the great God Pan,. . . . . . . . . . . . . .    13 Arcadia I     5    1
      Thanked be I that keepe a man, . . . . . . . . . . . . . . .    13 Arcadia I     5    3
THANKFUL
      Happy shepheard, with thanks to the Gods, still thinke to be
          thankfull,. . . . . . . . . . . . . . . . . . . . . . . .   32 1st Eclogues 13   33
      Dorus. Unto the Gods with a thanckfull heart all thankes I
          do render, . . . . . . . . . . . . . . . . . . . . . . .    32 1st Eclogues 13   35
      Thanke may you have for such a thankfull part, . . . . . . .   229 Astrophil   95   13
THANKFULLY
      With thankes and wishes, wishing thankfully. . . . . . . . .   209 Astrophil   84    8
THANKFULNESS
      With voyce of thankfulness . . . . . . . . . . . . . . . . .   305 Psalm XXVI       23
      For cherfull thankfulness, . . . . . . . . . . . . . . . . .   316 Psalm XXXIII      3
THANKS
      Happy shepheard, with thanks to the Gods, still thinke to be
          thankfull,. . . . . . . . . . . . . . . . . . . . . . . .   32 1st Eclogues 13   33
      Dorus. Unto the Gods with a thanckfull heart all thankes I
          do render, . . . . . . . . . . . . . . . . . . . . . . .    32 1st Eclogues 13   35
      You have my thankes, Let me your comforte have.. . . . . . .    70 Arcadia III  35   16
      With thankes and wishes, wishing thankfully. . . . . . . . .   209 Astrophil   84    8
      I will give thanks unto the lord of Us . . . . . . . . . . .   278 Psalm VII        46
      Among the Gentiles then I, Lord, yeild thanks to Thee, . . .   293 Psalm XVIII      88
      With thanks his Holyness therfore; . . . . . . . . . . . . .   311 Psalm XXX        12
      Shall ever dust give thanks to Thee, . . . . . . . . . . . .   311 Psalm XXX        28
      I will thee thanks for ever sing.. . . . . . . . . . . . . .   311 Psalm XXX        39
      Give hearty thanks to him on high, . . . . . . . . . . . . .   318 Psalm XXXIV       2
      To him my thanks shall be said . . . . . . . . . . . . . . .   335 Psalm XLII       53
      What great thanks I ow thee. . . . . . . . . . . . . . . . .   337 Psalm XLIII      30
THANKWORTHIEST
      Thanke-worthiest yet when you shall breake my hart.. . . . .   229 Astrophil   95   14
THANKWORTHY
      In speedie helpe, thanke worthie frends appeare. . . . . . .    81 Arcadia III  53   14
THEATER
      Choosing alas! this our theatre publique,. . . . . . . . . .   109 Arcadia IV   70   11
THEBAN
      If stones good measure daunc'd, the Theban walles to build,.   208 A&S 3rd Song      3
THEBES
      Go sing the fall of old Thebes,. . . . . . . . . . . . . . .    66 2nd Eclogues 32   21
THEIRS
      A King, in language theirs they said they would: . . . . . .   100 3rd Eclogues 66   64
      As they so theirs, Him shall their ofspring serve, . . . . .   300 Psalm XXII       75
      To ev'ill, both they and theirs shall wrack. . . . . . . . .   326 Psalm XXXVII     72
THEME
      The singer is the song's theame. . . . . . . . . . . . . . .    66 2nd Eclogues 32   36
THEMSELVES
      Both they themselves unto such two shall wed,. . . . . . . .    11 Arcadia I     1    5
```

THEMSELVES	(CONTINUED)	PAGE	TITLE		LINE
Old men themselves, doe love young wives to choose:		25	1st Eclogues	9	88
Who others' vertue doubt, themselves are vicious.		47	2nd Eclogues	28	9
Turnd from themselves, infected with their cage,		57	2nd Eclogues	30	18
With losse of purest blood themselves to teare,		58	2nd Eclogues	30	46
Because themselves they cannot see..		86	Arcadia III	62	22
Which blessed still themselves doo kisse..		87	Arcadia III	62	38
He chose themselves his guarders for to bene,		102	3rd Eclogues	66	129
Transforme themselves to lowe dejected vallies:		112	4th Eclogues	71	38
Which Poets say, the gods them selves do feare,		146	Cert Sonnets	17	7
If Greekes themselves were mov'd with so small cause		146	Cert Sonnets	17	21
Who thinke themselves well blest, if they renew.		146	Cert Sonnets	17	33
Failing themselves, with withered conscience dye.		151	Cert Sonnets	22	50
Avise themselves that they are vainely spent..		174	Astrophil	19	8
To keepe themselves and their chief cities free,		179	Astrophil		2
While everie office themselves will discharge,		210	Astrophil	85	7
They did themselves (o sweetest prison) twine.		232	Astrophil	103	8
Princes in subjects wrongd, must deeme themselves abused..		213	A&S 5th Song		30
Both within themselves oppressed,		218	A&S 8th Song		7
But now teares themselves did smile,		218	A&S 8th Song		14
Dcwn in the pitt, which they themselves had wrought:		280	Psalm IX		47
That by sharp proofes, the heathen themselves may see.		281	Psalm IX		64
That dare themselves to him oppose,		282	Psalm X		22
Commit their Cause, themselves, to Thee,		283	Psalm X		62
That lift themselves my ruin for to frame.		323	Psalm XXXV		66
This while, though poore, they in themselves did raigne.		243	Other Poems	4	64
Well for to see they kept themselves unsene,		244	Other Poems	4	89
Those eies, which nothing like themselves can see,		253	Other Poems	4	451

THEN

What marvaile then I take a woman's hew,		12	Arcadia I	2	13
Thus shrewdly burdned then, how can my Muse escape?.		12	Arcadia I	3	3
Then power out plaint, and in one word say this:		13	Arcadia I	4	9
What then must I that keepe the knave?		13	Arcadia I	5	6
Above line repeated at following location.		13	Arcadia I	5	12
Sing then, and see (for now thou hast inflamed me)		15	1st Eclogues	7	20
Of best things then what world can yeeld confection.		15	1st Eclogues	7	46
My sight in her faire limmes, I then assure my selfe,		16	1st Eclogues	7	56
Save then my soule, spill not my thoughts well heaped,		16	1st Eclogues	7	80
Did smile on me, and then away she leaped.		17	1st Eclogues	7	84
What circle then in so rare force beares swaye?.		17	1st Eclogues	7	109
Then Love allowes, our pleasures to enrich,		18	1st Eclogues	7	129
By Argus got on Io, then a cow:		21	1st Eclogues	8	14
Then vertue try, if she can worke in thee.		22	1st Eclogues	9	13
Then each conceit that enters in by sight,		23	1st Eclogues	9	38
Then cries to sencelesse things, which neither knowes.		23	1st Eclogues	9	41
Then who will heare a well autoris'd lye,		24	1st Eclogues	9	72
Loth to dye young, and then you must be olde,		25	1st Eclogues	9	103
Then let thy minde with better bookes be tamed,		25	1st Eclogues	9	120
Then him we kisse, whom late before we beatt		27	1st Eclogues	10	37
Then who makes us such judges over all?.		29	1st Eclogues	10	96
But if eyes faile then, when I most doo need them,		30	1st Eclogues	12	5
Are then humane mindes priviledg'd so meanly,		31	1st Eclogues	12	17
Then shall those thinges ease their inward horrible angwish.		33	1st Eclogues	13	46
Say then what vantage do we get, by the trade of a Pastor? .		33	1st Eclogues	13	49
Then by my high Cedar, rich Ruby, and only shining Sunne,		34	1st Eclogues	13	80
If then a boddily evill in a boddily gloze be not hidden,		34	1st Eclogues	13	87
Then do I thinke in deed, that better it is to be private.		35	1st Eclogues	13	102
And may I not (say I then) gett up though griefs be so weightie?		36	1st Eclogues	13	128
Then do I shape to my selfe that forme which raigns so with in me,		36	1st Eclogues	13	142
Then kneling to the ground, oft thus do I speake to that Image:		36	1st Eclogues	13	146
How can you him unworthy then decree,		39	Arcadia II	16	9
First let them die, then passe the starres,		44	Arcadia II	25	9
R. Can Reason then a Tyraunt counted be?		46	2nd Eclogues	27	3
R. Dare Passions then abide in Reason's light?		46	2nd Eclogues	27	17
R.p. Then let us both to heavenly rules give place,		47	2nd Eclogues	27	41
Thou then, that framste both words and voice most skilfully,		48	2nd Eclogues	28	19
Then base and sower is Love's most high vocation..		48	2nd Eclogues	28	24
Then may I hope, my pipe may have abilitie,		48	2nd Eclogues	28	26
O then it shines; then are the heav'ns distributed,		49	2nd Eclogues	28	65
Thus then (I say) my mischiefes have contributed		49	2nd Eclogues	28	67
Pas. But here is Dicus old; let him then speake the woord,		52	2nd Eclogues	29	27
If thou (alas poore if) do winne, then winne thou this,		53	2nd Eclogues	29	37
Dicus. Sing then my lads, but sing with better vaine then yet,		53	2nd Eclogues	29	49
That (shining now) she then might shine more farre.		56	2nd Eclogues	29	122
Relent those thoughts, which then did so displease?.		58	2nd Eclogues	30	52
If she must dye, then hath she past the line		59	2nd Eclogues	30	77
O toonge, then dumbe, not daring tell my smart;		60	2nd Eclogues	30	121
Then let my life long time on earth maintained be,		61	2nd Eclogues	30	147
Then let me eke forget one hand from other:		61	2nd Eclogues	30	161
Histor. Thus dyd they saye and then awaye dyd wende;		62	2nd Eclogues	30	185
Well mett Echo, aproche: then tell me thy will too. I will too.		63	2nd Eclogues	31	4
In what state was I then, when I tooke this deadly disease? ease.		63	2nd Eclogues	31	8
Then to an earnest Love what doth best victorie lend? Ende..		63	2nd Eclogues	31	15
Can then a cause be so light that forceth a man to go die? Aye.		64	2nd Eclogues	31	24

```
THEN                           (CONTINUED)                    PAGE    TITLE       LINE
    Then then what do I gaine, since unto hir will I do winde?
       Winde . . . . . . . . . . . . . . . . . . . . . . . .  64  2nd Eclogues 31    34
    Say then Reason, I say what is thy counsell? . . . . . .  67  2nd Eclogues 33     6
    Above line repeated at following locations . . . . . . .  67  2nd Eclogues 33    12
                  . . . . . . . . . . . . . . . . . . . . .   68  2nd Eclogues 33    18
                  . . . . . . . . . . . . . . . . . . . . .   68  2nd Eclogues 33    24

    Thus then my forme, and thus my state I finde, . . . . .  73  Arcadia III  40    13
    Seeke then and see, what man esteemeth best, . . . . . .  75  Arcadia III  44     5
    Looke further then, so shalt thou finde at least, . . .  75  Arcadia III  44     9
    Holde me most yours, then my longe suite is signde. . .  79  Arcadia III  50    18
    Then take my shape, and play a lover's parte: . . . . .  79  Arcadia III  51    12
    No wondre then, though sighte my sighte did tainte, . .  83  Arcadia III  57     5
    Then greefe, unkindnes, proofe, tooke, kindled, tought, . .  84  Arcadia III  60     9
    What medicin then, can such desease remove . . . . . . .  85  Arcadia III  61    13
    Her bellie then gladde sight doth fill, . . . . . . . .  88  Arcadia III  62 V 77
    There rested then, to play a woman's part, . . . . . . .  95  3rd Eclogues 64    39
    She seald it first, then she the sealing brake, . . . .  96  3rd Eclogues 64    83
    Then gave he him the blow which never smarted. . . . . .  97  3rd Eclogues 64   120
    Then such be he, as she his worth may see, . . . . . . .  98  3rd Eclogues 65     3
    It August was, he daynde not then to sing. . . . . . . .  99  3rd Eclogues 66    14
    Then founde I which thing is a charge to beare . . . . .  99  3rd Eclogues 66    17
    Unknowne as then were they that buylden towers: . . . . 100  3rd Eclogues 66    46
    (For then their language was a perfect speech) . . . . . 100  3rd Eclogues 66    65
    Then gan in guiltlesse earth full many a wound, . . . . 102  3rd Eclogues 66   115
    Then gan he factions in the beastes to breed; . . . . . 102  3rd Eclogues 66   120
    Then quickly did the meaner cattell finde, . . . . . . . 102  3rd Eclogues 66   135
    Or know your strengths, and then you shall do well. . . 103  3rd Eclogues 66   154
    But then I homeward call'd my lambkins deare: . . . . . 103  3rd Eclogues 66   158
    And gamesome then, when he thinkes on his sheepe; . . . 104  3rd Eclogues 67    35
    And then who shall the name of Histor nourish? . . . . . 106  3rd Eclogues 67   111
    Then since such pow'rs conspire unto our damage. . . . . 109  Arcadia IV   70    13
    Since sorow then concludeth all our fortune, . . . . . . 110  Arcadia IV   70    37
    Then must I save, what in my chiefly raignes, . . . . . 114  4th Eclogues 72    24
    Scrow then cherish me, for I am scrowe: . . . . . . . . 114  4th Eclogues 72    26
    Then decke me as thine owne; thy helpe I borowe, . . . . 114  4th Eclogues 72    28
    But I cannot; who then my selfe should flie, . . . . . . 114  4th Eclogues 72    39
    Are all in me: what helpe then can I trie? . . . . . . . 114  4th Eclogues 72    43
    Ev'n then Despaire did Hope already kill: . . . . . . . 115  4th Eclogues 72    64
    To death, as then disguisde in her faire face, . . . . . 115  4th Eclogues 72    69
    Since then my harte did loose his wonted place, . . . . 115  4th Eclogues 72    77
    When I, disgraced wretch, not wretched then, did give. . 117  4th Eclogues 73    11
    Did suffer drousie lids mine eyes then cleare to blinde; . . 117  4th Eclogues 73    26
    They first their use forgot, then fancies lost their force; . 117  4th Eclogues 73    29
    Then void of neerer cares, the depth of things to find. . . 118  4th Eclogues 73    50
    "Nay then (Diana said) the chastnesse I will give. . . . 121  4th Eclogues 73   173
    Then may I hope t'atchieve grace of a heavenly tiger. . . 122  4th Eclogues 74    22
    All my'offence was Love: with Love then must I be chastned, . 123  4th Eclogues 74    41
    What veiles then doo prevaile, but to a more miracle? . . 123  4th Eclogues 74    50
    Bend your thoghts to the dear sweet words which then to me
       giv'n were: . . . . . . . . . . . . . . . . . . . . . 124  4th Eclogues 74    75
    What? was I then worthie such good, now worthie so muche
       evill? . . . . . . . . . . . . . . . . . . . . . . . 124  4th Eclogues 74    77
    Now fled, then cherished? then so nie, now so remote? . . 124  4th Eclogues 74    78
    If then a man in most ill case may give you a farewell; . . 124  4th Eclogues 74    85
    Then give a quiet eare unto my playning: . . . . . . . . 127  4th Eclogues 75    65
    Must finish then by death's detested crime. . . . . . . 127  4th Eclogues 75    90
    Then let us holde the blisse of peacefull minde, . . . . 131  Arcadia V    77    13
    Then come, O come, then do I come, receyve (mee), . . . 138  Cert Sonnets  5    21
    Sleepe then a litle, pap content is making: . . . . . . 139  Cert Sonnets  6     8
    Since then truth to all minds telleth, . . . . . . . . . 140  Cert Sonnets  7    18
    So then since that heaven remaineth, . . . . . . . . . . 140  Cert Sonnets  7    28
    Else what in face, then in my fancie beare? . . . . . . 146  Cert Sonnets 17    10
    Are Poets then the onely lovers true, . . . . . . . . . 146  Cert Sonnets 17    31
    Then good Apollo do away thy bowe: . . . . . . . . . . . 146  Cert Sonnets 17    36
    Then might I thinke what thoughts were best to thinke: . . 148  Cert Sonnets 19     5
    Then might I wisely swimme or gladly sinke. . . . . . . 148  Cert Sonnets 19     6
    Then might I hope a change or ease of minde, . . . . . . 148  Cert Sonnets 19    11
    Then from his depth with force in her begunne, . . . . . 150  Cert Sonnets 22    17
    Looke then and dye, the pleasure . . . . . . . . . . . . 152  Cert Sonnets 23    17
    Come learners then to me, the modell of mishappe, . . . 153  Cert Sonnets 24    15
    If I then faultie be, . . . . . . . . . . . . . . . . . 158  Cert Sonnets 28    18
    Then farewell world, thy uttermost I see, . . . . . . . 144  Cert Sonnets 32     1
    How then? even thus: in Stella's face I reed, . . . . . 166  Astrophil     3    12
    What Love and Beautie be, then all my deed . . . . . . . 166  Astrophil     3    13
    Cupid then smiles, for on his crest there lies . . . . . 171  Astrophil    13     9
    To blaze these last, and sware devoutly then, . . . . . 171  Astrophil    13    13
    Then Love is sinne, and let me sinfull be. . . . . . . . 172  Astrophil    14    14
    Stella behold, and then begin to endite. . . . . . . . . 172  Astrophil    15    14
    When most I glorie, then I feele most shame: . . . . . . 174  Astrophil    19     3
    And then descried the glistring of his dart: . . . . . . 175  Astrophil    20    13
    Progressing then from faire twinnes' gold'n place: . . . 175  Astrophil    22     2
    Then ev'n of fellowship, o Moone, tell me. . . . . . . . 180  Astrophil    31     9
    And then would not, or could not see my blisse: . . . . 181  Astrophil    33     2
    Then be they close, and so none shall displease. . . . . 182  Astrophil    34     8
    Listen then Lordings with good eare to me, . . . . . . . 183  Astrophil    37     3
    Weigh then how I by thee am overthrowne: . . . . . . . . 185  Astrophil    40     8
    And then, thinke thus, although thy beautie be . . . . . 185  Astrophil    40     9
    Since then thou hast so farre subdued me, . . . . . . . 185  Astrophil    40    12
    Then with those eyes he lookes, lo by and by . . . . . . 186  Astrophil    43     6
```

THEN	(CONTINUED)	PAGE	TITLE		LINE
When he will play, then in her lips he is, ...		186	Astrophil	43	9
From all the world, her heart is then his rome,.		186	Astrophil	43	13
Then thinke my deare, that you in me do reed		187	Astrophil	45	12
Her face? O Love, a Rogue thou then shouldst be, ...		187	Astrophil	46	6
My heart then quak'd, then dazled were mine eyes,.		191	Astrophil	53	10
No Patience, if thou wilt my good, then make		193	Astrophil	56	12
And then with patience bid me beare my fire.		193	Astrophil	56	14
To witlesse things, then Love I hope (since wit.		194	Astrophil	59	13
Makes me fall from her sight, then sweetly she		195	Astrophil	60	6
Then some good body tell me how I do,.		195	Astrophil	60	12
Then his desires he learnes, his live's course thence. . . .		195	Astrophil	61 V	8
Sing then my Muse, now Io Pean sing, ...		196	Astrophil	63	9
O thinke I then, what paradise of joy.		200	Astrophil	68	13
Come then my Muse, shew thou height of delight		201	Astrophil	70	9
What wonder then if he his lesson misse, ...		203	Astrophil	73	3
How falles it then, that with so smooth an ease.		204	Astrophil	74	9
"Or so?" Much lesse: "How then?" Sure thus it is:.		204	Astrophil	74	13
No wind, no shade can coole, what helpe then in my case, . .		205	Astrophil	76	12
Then since (deare life) you faine would have me peace, . . .		207	Astrophil	81	12
And do I then my selfe this vaine scuse give?.		227	Astrophil	93	9
Do thou then (for thou canst) do thou complaine,.		228	Astrophil	94	5
Mine eyes then only winke, for spite perchance,.		230	Astrophil	98	13
To lay his then marke wanting shafts of sight,.		230	Astrophil	99	3
With windowes ope then most my mind doth lie,.		230	Astrophil	99	5
In tombe of lids then buried are mine eyes,.		231	Astrophil	99	12
That bad his friend, but then new maim'd, to be.		236	Astrophil	106	13
And makes me then bow downe my head, and say,.		237	Astrophil	108	9
Who makes a man live then glad when he dieth?.		197	A&S 1st Song		26
Sweet then, while each thing doth frame:		211	A&S 4th Song		34
Then grew my tongue and pen records unto thy glory:.		212	A&S 5th Song		3
I said, my soule was thine (o that I then had lyed).		212	A&S 5th Song		9
Thou then whom partiall heavens conspir'd in one to frame, .		213	A&S 5th Song		19
And then, a heav'nly child, gave her Ambrosian pap:.		213	A&S 5th Song		26
I lay then to thy charge unjustest Tyrannie, ...		214	A&S 5th Song		56
Of foule rebellion then I do appeach thee now;		214	A&S 5th Song		62
I now then staine thy white with vagabunding shame,.		214	A&S 5th Song		68
You then ungratefull thiefe, you murdring Tyran you, ...		215	A&S 5th Song		85
Then reason, Princesse hy, ...		217	A&S 6th Song		49
Heare then, but then with wonder heare; see but adoring see,		217	A&S 7th Song		13
May then yong his pide weedes showing, ...		217	A&S 8th Song		3
(Knees on ground he then did stay)		219	A&S 8th Song		50
Then she spake; her speech was such, ...		220	A&S 8th Song		69
Sorrow onely then hath glory,.		221	A&S 9th Song		14
Why alas doth she then sweare, ...		222	A&S 9th Song		31
Then adieu, deere flocke adieu:.		222	A&S 9th Song		46
And then they that in him their only trust do rest,.		272	Psalm II		31
O tremble then with awfull will:		273	Psalm IV		16
Then let my Foe chase me, and chasing take:.		277	Psalm VII		13
Then let his foot uppon my neck be set:.		277	Psalm VII		14
Then in the Dust let him my honour rake.		277	Psalm VII		15
Then lord, my lord, give sentence on my side		277	Psalm VII		23
Then think I, Ah, what is this Man,.		278	Psalm VIII		13
For then the lord in judgment shewes to raigne		281	Psalm IX		51
Then rise and come abroad, ...		282	Psalm X		49
Then eare to them enclin'd.		283	Psalm X		76
Then Thou (O lord) shalt keep the Good stil sure..		285	Psalm XII		22
He then shall maintayn my lott..		288	Psalm XVI		15
Say then, Is not my lot found.		288	Psalm XVI		16
Then was I by thy searching insight try'd, ...		289	Psalm XVII		10
And then by Thee was guiltless found		289	Psalm XVII		11
Then let my Words, my Crys ascend, ...		290	Psalm XVII		19
Shew then O Lord Thy wondrous kindness show, ...		290	Psalm XVII		21
Then keep me as the Apple of an Eye, ...		290	Psalm XVII		25
In Thy wings' shade then let me hidden ly.		290	Psalm XVII		26
My refuge, refuge then, when moste I am forlorn;		291	Psalm XVIII		5
Whom then shall I invoke but Thee most worthy prayse,. . . .		291	Psalm XVIII		6
To beare his sacred flight, in secret place then clos'd, . .		291	Psalm XVIII		23
Then hayle, then firie coales, then thundred heavnly sire, .		291	Psalm XVIII		27
Then spake he his lowd voyce, then hailestones coales and					
fire.		291	Psalm XVIII		28
Then out his arrowes fly, and streight they scatterd been, .		291	Psalm XVIII		29
The gulfs of waters then were through their Chanels seen,. .		291	Psalm XVIII		31
The World's foundations then lay bare because he shent . . .		291	Psalm XVIII		32
Then sent he from above, and took me from below, ...		291	Psalm XVIII		34
So did he save me from their then prevailing hate, ...		291	Psalm XVIII		37
Up then thou liftst the poore, and down the proud wilt cast;		292	Psalm XVIII		52
This God then girded me in his Almighty pow'rs,.		292	Psalm XVIII		59
Then live Jehova still, my rock still blessed be;.		293	Psalm XVIII		83
Among the Gentiles then I, Lord, yeild thanks to Thee, . . .		293	Psalm XVIII		88
Then what man would so soon seek gold.		294	Psalm XIX		41
Than I was giv'en to Thee, Thou wert my God.		299	Psalm XXII		24
To Brethren then I will declare Thy Fame,.		299	Psalm XXII		51
The' afflicted then shall eat, and be well pleased,.		300	Psalm XXII		61
Where then should my eyes be		304	Psalm XXV		55
Then me redeem Lord then be mercifull.		306	Psalm XXVI		36
And shall I then		307	Psalm XXVII		5
Then though against me armys were, ...		307	Psalm XXVII		13
Lord then still Thy people save, ...		309	Psalm XXVIII		33
Prayse, Prayse this lord then evermore		311	Psalm XXX		10

501

THEN	(CONTINUED)	PAGE	TITLE		LINE
For then my Hill Good God did stay;.		311	Psalm XXX		22
Then thus to Thee I praying cry'd:		311	Psalm XXX		25
Then since my tongue delights that name to blesse, ...		312	Psalm XXXI		8
Then prayse, then prayse I do the lord of us,.		313	Psalm XXXI		58
Then love him ye all ye that feel his grace, ...		314	Psalm XXXI		64
Then on that lord most kind.		318	Psalm XXXIII		76
Come then and join with me,.		319	Psalm XXXIV		9
Then shall I joy in thee, then sav'd by Thee		321	Psalm XXXV		19
Then abjects, while I was unwitting quite, ...		322	Psalm XXXV		39
Then, then let not my foes unjustly joy;		322	Psalm XXXV		49
O then extend Thy loving heart		324	Psalm XXXVI		27
O then Thy righteousness impart.		324	Psalm XXXVI		29
Then fly all ev'ill and goodness nourish,.		326	Psalm XXXVII		67
Do not, Lord, then me forsake, ...		329	Psalm XXXVIII		61
Stay then Thy wrath, that I may strength receive		330	Psalm XXXIX		41
Then lord from me draw not Thy tender grace, ...		332	Psalm XL		41
For then their hatefull heads close whispring be		333	Psalm XLI		25
So then be blest now, then, at home, abroad, ...		334	Psalm XLI		45
Why then hast thou left me?.		336	Psalm XLIII		9
Then lo, then I will		337	Psalm XLIII		25
Then God, yea my God,.		337	Psalm XLIII		28
Dick. Here then and learn to sigh: a mistress I doo serve, .		343	Possibly	1	19
Will. What? these are riddles sure, art thou then bound to					
her?		343	Possibly	1	23
Will. What living get you then? D. Disdayne; but just					
disdayne.		344	Possibly	1	35
Will. Then Dick let us go hence lest wee great folkes annoy.		344	Possibly	1	45
Then to Desier's desire, O yeelde O yeelde..		345	Possibly	4	4
Then shall you see them yelde, Allarme allarme..		346	Possibly	5	14
I then, whose burd'ned brest but thus aspires.		242	Other Poems	4	5
Then do they pull from sharpe and niggard thorne		243	Other Poems	4	51
Then some grene gowns are by the lasses worne.		243	Other Poems	4	53
For he then chosen was the dignitie.		244	Other Poems	4	75
For then Urania homeward did arise,.		246	Other Poems	4	167
Who then in Lion's cave did enter fyrst, ...		247	Other Poems	4	206
Then couples three be streight allotted there, ...		248	Other Poems	4	225
Then did he slack his love-enstructed pace..		250	Other Poems	4	308
And then the Phoenix feared to be cought..		251	Other Poems	4	360
With greater powr, then she did make them wend		251	Other Poems	4	375
As heart-bound slaves: and happy then embrace.		252	Other Poems	4	391
Her breath, then short, seem'd loth from home to pas,. . . .		252	Other Poems	4	399
For then wise Klaius found no absence can.		253	Other Poems	4	419
First killing mirth, then banishing all rest,.		253	Other Poems	4	431
Then sports grew paines, all talking tediouse, ...		253	Other Poems	4	433
Then so I faile, when most I would do well,.		254	Other Poems	4	467
I go about, but then is all my best.		254	Other Poems	4	470
Say then, can this but of enchantment come?.		254	Other Poems	4	472
On thy then blessed face,.		256	Other Poems	5	18
Absent alone canst thou then piping be?.		258	Other Poems	5	65
Then rase, but rase on leggs with faintnes bended, ...		259	Other Poems	5	116
It is to be used then, ...		263	Other Poems	7	33
THENCE					
But so unheard, condemn'd, kept thence we do seeke to abide					
in,.		32	1st Eclogues	13	25
Love wakes the jealous eye least thence it moves:.		42	Arcadia II	22	6
Whence can pride come there, since springs of beawty be					
thence? Thence.		65	2nd Eclogues	31	44
And thence those armes derived are;.		89	Arcadia III	62	117
Allow good company, but kepe from thence		98	3rd Eclogues	65	11
And that he thence must part where to live onely I lyved.. .		123	4th Eclogues	74	30
And thence cast off, where his sweete hurt he found, ...		144	Cert Sonnets	15	6
Myne eyes thence drawne, where lived all their light,. . . .		149	Cert Sonnets	21	5
Oft turning others' leaves, to see if thence would flow. . .		165	Astrophil	1	7
But she most faire, most cold, made him thence take his					
flight		169	Astrophil	8	12
But ere I could flie thence, it pierc'd my heart.		175	Astrophil	20	14
If he waite well, I never thence would move:		194	Astrophil	59	3
Thence his desires he learnes, his live's course thence. . .		195	Astrophil	61	8
Ah, is it not enough, that I am thence,.		233	Astrophil	104	5
Thence, so farre thence, that scarcely any sparke.		233	Astrophil	104	6
Or loving, have so frothy thoughts, as easly thence to move:		217	A&S 7th Song		10
Thence he to all his judgments shall apply		280	Psalm IX		24
Thence let him undertake		295	Psalm XX		9
And lately thence untwine:		257	Other Poems	5	44
THENCEFORTH					
That from thenceforth to all eternitie,.		101	3rd Eclogues	66	104
THERE					
How dare I, wretch, seeke there my woes to rest, ...		3	Lady of May	1	5
Therein his name, there his chiefe triumph lyes.		22	1st Eclogues	8	42
That there where thou confest thy mischiefe lyes		23	1st Eclogues	9	33
There is no hate that can thee more oppresse..		23	1st Eclogues	9	49
Of fowles there called was a parliament.		29	1st Eclogues	10	84
There was the swan of dignitie deprived, ...		29	1st Eclogues	10	85
What meane is there, alas, we can hope our losse to recover?		32	1st Eclogues	13	27
What place is there left, we may hope our woes to recomfort?		32	1st Eclogues	13	28
Fire no liquor can coole: Neptune's seate would be dryd up					
there.		32	1st Eclogues	13	32
And thinke ther she do dwell and heare what plaintes I do					
utter:		36	1st Eclogues	13	143

```
THERE              (CONTINUED)                              PAGE    TITLE        LINE
    Since there mine eyes have played so false a parte,. . . . .   38  Arcadia II    14    11
    I layde my face; my face wherein there lyes. . . . . . . . .   41  Arcadia II    21     3
    Theere seeke defence where weakenesse is the force:. . . . .   49  2nd Eclogues 28    77
    Nico. And are you there old Pas? in troth I ever thought,. .   51  2nd Eclogues 29     1
    But if I had bene there, th'adst met another mate. . . . . .   52  2nd Eclogues 29    22
    Erona dye? O heaven (if heaven there be) . . . . . . . . . .   58  2nd Eclogues 30    59
    Doth force us there to set our chiefe delightfulnes, . . . .   61  2nd Eclogues 30   135
    Whence can pride come there, since springs of beawty be
        thence? Thence. . . . . . . . . . . . . . . . . . . . .   65  2nd Eclogues 31    44
    Ods? what an ods is there since them to the heav'ns I
        prefer Erre. . . . . . . . . . . . . . . . . . . . . . .   65  2nd Eclogues 31    48
    There never was a better bargaine driv'ne. . . . . . . . . .   75  Arcadia III   45     4
    There may one see, and yet not see . . . . . . . . . . . . .   88  Arcadia III   62    67
    The bellie there gladde sight doth fill, . . . . . . . . . .   88  Arcadia III   62    77
    But there againe the flesh doth rise . . . . . . . . . . . .   89  Arcadia III   62   101
    There ofte steales out that round cleane foote . . . . . . .   89  Arcadia III   62   105
    For there with strange compact dooth lie . . . . . . . . . .   90  Arcadia III   62   125
    There fall those Saphir-coloured brookes,. . . . . . . . . .   90  Arcadia III   62   127
    A neighbor mine not long agoe there was, . . . . . . . . . .   94  3rd Eclogues 64     1
    In fine he made her gesse, there was some sweet. . . . . . .   95  3rd Eclogues 64    35
    There rested then, to play a woman's part, . . . . . . . . .   95  3rd Eclogues 64    39
    Such maner time there was (what time I n'ot) . . . . . . . .  100  3rd Eclogues 66    43
    Beleeve me man, there is no greater blisse,. . . . . . . . .  103  3rd Eclogues 67     7
    He were a foole, if there he did not bide. . . . . . . . . .  104  3rd Eclogues 67    15
    And if forsooth there come some new found ware,. . . . . . .  104  3rd Eclogues 67    40
    There never past foule word, I dare well say. . . . . . . .   106  3rd Eclogues 67    93
    But there I was, and there my calmie thoughts I fedd . . . .  117  4th Eclogues 73    39
    There came a chariot faire by doves and sparrowes guided:. .  118  4th Eclogues 73    59
    But streight there issued forth two Ladies (Ladies sure. . .  118  4th Eclogues 73    63
    As little hunting minde (God knowes) did there appeere.. . .  118  4th Eclogues 73    70
    And you o trees (if any life there lies. . . . . . . . . . .  125  4th Eclogues 75     4
    To see what faire sight there raigneth,. . . . . . . . . . .  140  Cert Sonnets  7    26
    Some cause there is, which of strange cause doth rise: . . .  147  Cert Sonnets 18     2
    But when my Sunne her shining twinnes there bends, . . . . .  150  Cert Sonnets 22    16
    Till knit with cold, though there unknowne remaine,. . . . .  150  Cert Sonnets 22    33
    A field there is where, if a stake be prest. . . . . . . . .  150  Cert Sonnets 22    41
    Placed ever there, gave him this mourning weed,. . . . . . .  168  Astrophil     7    13
    Cupid then smiles, for on his crest there lies . . . . . . .  171  Astrophil    13     9
    See there that boy, that murthring boy I say,. . . . . . . .  174  Astrophil    20     2
    There himselfe with his shot he close doth lay.. . . . . . .  175  Astrophil    20     8
    Rich fooles there be, whose base and filthy hart . . . . . .  176  Astrophil    24     1
    Is constant Love deem'd there but want of wit? . . . . . . .  180  Astrophil    31    10
    Are Beauties there as proud as here they be? . . . . . . . .  180  Astrophil    31    11
    Do they call Vertue there ungratefulnesse? . . . . . . . . .  180  Astrophil    31    14
    And there long since, Love thy Lieutenant lies,. . . . . . .  183  Astrophil    36     5
    Alas, what cause is there so overthwart, . . . . . . . . . .  186  Astrophil    44     7
    That once come there, the sobs of mine annoyes . . . . . . .  187  Astrophil    44    13
    Doubt there hath bene, when with his golden chaine . . . . .  193  Astrophil    58     1
    And yet amid all feares a hope there is. . . . . . . . . . .  199  Astrophil    66     9
    There shall he find all vices' overthrow,. . . . . . . . . .  201  Astrophil    71     5
    In truth I sweare, I wish not there should be. . . . . . . .  224  Astrophil    90     7
    Though harbengers of death lodge there his traine. . . . . .  228  Astrophil    94     8
    And faine those Aeols' youthes there would their stay. . . .  233  Astrophil   103     9
    There shines a joy from thee my only light;. . . . . . . . .  236  Astrophil   108     4
    There unseen thou maist be bold, . . . . . . . . . . . . . .  226  A&S 10th Song      16
    There those roses for to kisse,. . . . . . . . . . . . . . .  226  A&S 10th Song      28
    But my soule shall harbour there.. . . . . . . . . . . . . .  234  A&S 11th Song      40
    But no fault there is in praying.. . . . . . . . . . . . . .  219  A&S 8th Song       48
    There his hands in their speech, faine . . . . . . . . . . .  219  A&S 8th Song       65
    How many Ones there be . . . . . . . . . . . . . . . . . . .  272  Psalm III          4
    There is no God that raigneth. . . . . . . . . . . . . . . .  286  Psalm XIV          3
    There is no speech, no language which. . . . . . . . . . . .  293  Psalm XIX          9
    There be no eyn but reade the line . . . . . . . . . . . . .  294  Psalm XIX         13
    There by his Grace for sun's fair face . . . . . . . . . . .  294  Psalm XIX         19
    There be no Rea'ms hidd from his beames, . . . . . . . . . .  294  Psalm XIX         27
    And since there is not One, who it redresseth. . . . . . . .  299  Psalm XXII        26
    There where the Lord of all. . . . . . . . . . . . . . . . .  301  Psalm XXIII       26
    Oh, is there one with his Feare fraught? . . . . . . . . . .  304  Psalm XXV         47
    Oh, give me not, for there are sproong . . . . . . . . . . .  308  Psalm XXVII       56
    Lo there I now foresee their fall. . . . . . . . . . . . . .  324  Psalm XXXVI       33
    There remains. . . . . . . . . . . . . . . . . . . . . . . .  328  Psalm XXXVIII     20
    O heale my soul, let there Thy cure begin. . . . . . . . . .  333  Psalm XLI         15
    Now is hee wrackt say they, lc, there he lyes. . . . . . . .  333  Psalm XLI         27
    Will. A tyme there is for all, my Mother often sayes,. . . .  343  Possibly      1     9
    For never was there man more crossely crost then he. . . . .  241  Other Poems   1     4
    Ther was (o seldome blessed word of was!). . . . . . . . . .  242  Other Poems   4    17
    There did he make hir laugh in spite of woe, . . . . . . . .  247  Other Poems   4   197
    Then couples three be streight allotted there, . . . . . . .  248  Other Poems   4   225
    There may you see, soone as the middle two . . . . . . . . .  248  Other Poems   4   233
    Among the rest that there did take delight . . . . . . . . .  251  Other Poems   4   361
    He did not there doe homage of his eies, . . . . . . . . . .  251  Other Poems   4   367
    Now make me thinke that there is not a fende,. . . . . . . .  254  Other Poems   4   463
    Yet there, me seemes, I heare her singing loud.. . . . . . .  255  Other Poems   4   508
    There he wandring malecontent, . . . . . . . . . . . . . . .  262  Other Poems   7    13
THEREABOUT
    Neare therabout, into your Poesie wring; . . . . . . . . . .  172  Astrophil    15     4
THEREABOUTS
    Neare thereabouts, into your Poesie wring: . . . . . . . . .  172  Astrophil    15  V  4
```

```
THEREAFTER                                                PAGE    TITLE            LINE
    And so thereafter He, and all his Mates. . . . . . . . . .  286 Psalm XIV            4
THEREBY
    And hope therby to ease their inward horrible anguish, . . .  33 1st Eclogues 13     45
    And though thereby my fancie was infected, . . . . . . . .   83 Arcadia III  57      6
    Did goe his way, but sojourn'd neere thereby, . . . . . . .  96 3rd Eclogues 64     71
    Poore passenger, passe now thereby I did, . . . . . . . . . 175 Astrophil    20      9
    Although some Worldly losse therby he may sustaine, . . . . 287 Psalm XV            10
    By neighbors prai'd she went abroad therby, . . . . . . . . 247 Other Poems   4    207
THEREFORE
    Youth will have will: Age must to age therefore. . . . . .   27 1st Eclogues 10     24
    I warne thee therefore (since thou maist have choice). . .   29 1st Eclogues 10     88
    Give therefore to the Muse great praise in whose very
        likenes. . . . . . . . . . . . . . . . . . . . . . . .   33 1st Eclogues 13     62
    R. You know it not: of Reason therefore know it. . . . . .   47 2nd Eclogues 27     39
    Goe on therefore, and tell us, by what fashion . . . . . .   48 2nd Eclogues 28     34
    Therefore, alas, you use vile Vulcan's spight, . . . . . .   60 2nd Eclogues 30    107
    And therefore he a courtier was benamed, . . . . . . . . .   94 3rd Eclogues 64     19
    And therefore pray him that of courtesie . . . . . . . . .   95 3rd Eclogues 64     57
    Take heed therefore, how you ensue that trade, . . . . . .   97 3rd Eclogues 64    123
    And shall we not therefore their use desire? . . . . . . .  105 3rd Eclogues 67     69
    Marrie therefore; for marriage will destroy. . . . . . . .  107 3rd Eclogues 67    115
    Thou arte therefore of these our desart places . . . . . .  108 Arcadia IV   69     12
    Therefore esteeming all good blessings toyes, . . . . . . . 116 4th Eclogues 72     99
    Be silent therefore now, and so be silent still. . . . . .  119 4th Eclogues 73     97
    To yonder Nymphe therefore (to Mira I did point) . . . . .  121 4th Eclogues 73    165
    They are but words therefore which men do buy, . . . . . .  128 4th Eclogues 75    115
    Cease Muse therfore: thy dart o Death applie; . . . . . . . 129 4th Eclogues 75    141
    Let teares for him therefore be all our treasure, . . . . . 130 4th Eclogues 76     31
    My Muse therefore, for onely thou canst tell, . . . . . . . 146 Cert Sonnets 17     11
    Therefore from so vile fancie, . . . . . . . . . . . . . .  161 Cert Sonnets 30     37
    And therefore, though her beautie and her grace. . . . . .  191 Astrophil    52      9
    And therefore by her Love's authority, . . . . . . . . . .  196 Astrophil    62      9
    Deere, therefore be not jealous over me, . . . . . . . . .  225 Astrophil    91     12
    Thought therefore I will send thee, . . . . . . . . . . . . 226 A&S 10th Song       13
    "Therefore, Deere, this no more move, . . . . . . . . . . . 220 A&S 8th Song        97
    Therfore (O Kings), be wise, O Rulers rule your mind, . . . 271 Psalm II            23
    Have mercy therfore still on me, . . . . . . . . . . . . .  273 Psalm IV             4
    Therfore, O lord, lift up Thy throne on high . . . . . . .  277 Psalm VII           20
    Therfore thou whetst Thy sword, and bend'st Thy bow, . . .  278 Psalm VII           34
    Therfore he doth defy all those. . . . . . . . . . . . . .  282 Psalm X             21
    Still therfore of Thy Graces shall be my . . . . . . . . .  286 Psalm XIII          19
    Therfore I say again this goodness he me sent. . . . . . .  292 Psalm XVIII         47
    Hide not therfore from me that face, . . . . . . . . . . .  308 Psalm XXVII         43
    Therfore while that I may cry, . . . . . . . . . . . . . .  309 Psalm XXVIII         6
    With thanks his Holyness therfore; . . . . . . . . . . . .  311 Psalm XXX           12
    Therfore my tongue shall never lack. . . . . . . . . . . .  311 Psalm XXX           37
    Never therfore let me confounded be, . . . . . . . . . . .  312 Psalm XXXI           2
    Therfore shall evry godly One. . . . . . . . . . . . . . .  315 Psalm XXXII         19
    And therfore soon would mischeife Thee . . . . . . . . . .  315 Psalm XXXII         35
    Therfore I said in most infirmity, . . . . . . . . . . . .  333 Psalm XLI           13
    Therfore, O Lord, abandond thus of all, . . . . . . . . . . 333 Psalm XLI           33
    That Foxes leave to steale, because they finde they dy
        therefore. . . . . . . . . . . . . . . . . . . . . . .  344 Possibly      1     44
    Courage therefore, and let the stately see . . . . . . . .  346 Possibly      5      3
    Therefore Love arm'd in hir now takes the fielde, . . . . . 245 Other Poems   4    145
    And therfore finding force now faint to be, . . . . . . . . 248 Other Poems   4    255
    "Therefore shepheardes wanting skill, . . . . . . . . . . . 263 Other Poems   7     37
    "Therefore Pan, if thou mayst be . . . . . . . . . . . . .  263 Other Poems   7     55
THEREIN
    Therein his name, there his chiefe triumph lyes. . . . . .   22 1st Eclogues  8     42
    And see therein how well the writer fares. . . . . . . . .   42 Arcadia II   21     16
    Her beames have wrought therin most suer impression: . . .   47 2nd Eclogues 28     11
    So that therein appeares some blood, . . . . . . . . . . .   86 Arcadia III  62     29
    And joy therein, though Nations count it shame. . . . . . . 179 Astrophil    28      8
    To write therein more fresh the story of delight, . . . . . 232 Astrophil   102     13
    Or if they do delight therein, yet are so cloyed with wit, . 217 A&S 7th Song        3
    Thinking it just more therein to delight . . . . . . . . .  246 Other Poems   4    178
    Not knowing who did draw with him therin; . . . . . . . . . 253 Other Poems   4    426
THEREOF
    And never hathe therof arightelye deemde . . . . . . . . .   26 1st Eclogues  9    139
    The song thereof a last will, . . . . . . . . . . . . . . .  66 2nd Eclogues 32     34
    Not though thereof the cause her selfe she know: . . . . .  187 Astrophil    45      4
    Pitie thereof gate in her breast such place. . . . . . . .  187 Astrophil    45      7
    That any laud to me thereof should grow, . . . . . . . . .  224 Astrophil    90     10
    With sight thereof cride out; o faire disgrace, . . . . . . 233 Astrophil   103     13
    That you, guiltlesse thereof, your Nectar mist: . . . . . . 235 Astrophil   105     10
    What comes therof? he shall not slide. . . . . . . . . . .  326 Psalm XXXVII        80
THEREON
    Thereon his name, there his chiefe triumph lyes. . . . . .   22 1st Eclogues  8 V  42
    Shall dwell thereon, and this their blessing . . . . . . .  326 Psalm XXXVII        75
THERETO
    W. Who bound thee? D. Love my Lord. W. What witnesses
        therto . . . . . . . . . . . . . . . . . . . . . . . .  343 Possibly      1     25
THEREUS'
    For Thereus' force on her chaste will prevailing. . . . . . 137 Cert Sonnets  4      8
    But Thereus' love, on her by strong hand wrokne, . . . . .  137 Cert Sonnets  4     14
THEREWITH
    But deck therewith my soule for your sake dying. . . . . .   17 1st Eclogues  7     90
    And straight therewith, like wags new got to play, . . . .  173 Astrophil    17     13
```

THEREWITH   (CONTINUED)   PAGE   TITLE   LINE

	PAGE	TITLE		LINE
She comes, and streight therewith her shining twins do move.	204	Astrophil	76	1
Love therewith is streight imparted.	218	A&S 8th Song		36
That therewith my song is broken..	221	A&S 8th Song		104
THEREWITHAL				
The rest I cannot tell, for therewithall I wak'd	121	4th Eclogues	73	179
Therewithall away she went,.	221	A&S 8th Song		101
THERICN				
(Therion) When wanton Pan, deceiv'd with Lion's skin,.	5	Lady of May	3	7
(Therion) Thus wofully I in wo this salve do find,	5	Lady of May	3	17
THESE				
Who in one selfe these diverse gifts can plant;.	3	Lady of May	1	4
And ere that all these blowes thy head doo hit,.	11	Arcadia I	1	9
Both these conspird poore Reason's overthrowe;	11	Arcadia I	2	7
And for a tast of all these gifts, she borowes Momus' grace.	12	Arcadia I	3	8
These bolde words she did heare, this fruite I reaped,	17	1st Eclogues	7	82
Then jarle: lo, lo, even these how envie blindes..	26	1st Eclogues	10	9
These cocklinges cockred we bewaile to late,	28	1st Eclogues	10	58
In these woods to resounde the renowmed name of a goddesse..	31	1st Eclogues	13	14
Jcyn'd, by thy beauty adorn'd, be no meanes these greefes to abolish:	34	1st Eclogues	13	99
And when I meete these trees, in the earth's faire lyvery clothed,	35	1st Eclogues	13	113
Will at length perceave these flames by her beames to be kindled,	37	1st Eclogues	13	167
Over these brookes trusting to ease mine eyes,	41	Arcadia II	21	1
These fires increase: in these I dayly burne:.	42	Arcadia II	22	8
To make these woods resounde thy lamentation?.	47	2nd Eclogues	28	2
Till of these thoughts thy sodaine ende bereaved me.	48	2nd Eclogues	28	33
O sheepheards' boyes, eschue these tongues of venome,.	50	2nd Eclogues	28	87
Our best defenses are to flie these adders..	50	2nd Eclogues	28	89
Pas. So oft these woods have heard me "Cosma" crie,.	56	2nd Eclogues	29	132
The cheerefull notes these pleasant places yeeld,.	58	2nd Eclogues	30	39
For all these certaine blowes the surest shield.	58	2nd Eclogues	30	43
To hold these worldly things in such proportion,	60	2nd Eclogues	30	132
Seeke we to tame these childish superfluities:	61	2nd Eclogues	30	138
If ought I cease these hideous exclamations,	61	2nd Eclogues	30	145
What causes first made these torments on me to light? Light.	64	2nd Eclogues	31	23
Tell yet againe me the names of these faire form'd to do ev'lls. Dev'lls.	65	2nd Eclogues	31	49
That sorrowe's weight dothe balance up thies joyes..	71	Arcadia III	36	18
These wordes are full of woes, yet feele they none..	75	Arcadia III	43	3
That he, to whome these sondrie giftes I binde,	78	Arcadia III	50	9
Weare these my words as mourning weedes of woes,	81	Arcadia III	54	5
Faire under these doth stately growe,.	87	Arcadia III	62	46
Betwixt these two a way doth lie,.	87	Arcadia III	62	58
In thies delights the wandring thought	88	Arcadia III	62	71
Let not these slumbring clowds thy beawties hide,.	91	3rd Eclogues	63	11
Since from these good the others' good doth flowe,	92	3rd Eclogues	63	40
These fiftie winters maried have I beene;.	106	3rd Eclogues	67	86
But these be your love-toyes, which still are spent.	106	3rd Eclogues	67	94
When without shame he saith, "these be mine owne".	106	3rd Eclogues	67	114
These stately starrs in their now shining faces,	108	Arcadia IV	69	9
Thou arte therefore of these our desart places	108	Arcadia IV	69	12
While that my voice doth fill these wofull vallies,.	111	4th Eclogues	71	10
I that was once the musique of these vallies,	111	4th Eclogues	71	21
Klaius. Long since the happie dwellers of these vallies, .	112	4th Eclogues	71	31
Me seemes I heare in these ill-changed forrests,	112	4th Eclogues	71	39
When I doo smell the flowers of these vallies:	112	4th Eclogues	71	46
Strephon. I wish to fire the trees of all these forrests:.	112	4th Eclogues	71	49
By taking her two Sunnes from these darke vallies.	113	4th Eclogues	71	66
Is gone, is gone from these our spoyled forrests,.	113	4th Eclogues	71	71
Strephon. These mountaines witnesse shall, so shall these vallies,	113	4th Eclogues	71	73
Klaius. These forrests eke, made wretched by our musique,.	113	4th Eclogues	71	74
These foule, most foule, disastres to me fell;	116	4th Eclogues	72	97
What life it is, and how that all these lives doo gather,.	118	4th Eclogues	73	47
And so refuse to behold of these strange wounds the recitall	122	4th Eclogues	74	7
The straunge resounde of these my causefull cries:	125	4th Eclogues	75	6
Till these straunge altrings you did hap to trie,.	125	4th Eclogues	75	26
O Echo, all these woods with roaring fill,.	126	4th Eclogues	75	31
These be her words, but a woman's words to a love that is eager,	143	Cert Sonnets	13	3
If I could thinke how these my thoughts to leave,.	147	Cert Sonnets	19	1
These wonders England breedes, the last remaines,.	151	Cert Sonnets	22	61
But eyes these beauties see not,	152	Cert Sonnets	23	25
But finding these North clymes do coldly him embrace,.	168	Astrophil	8	5
To blaze these last, and sware devoutly then,.	171	Astrophil	13	13
And if these rules did faile, proofe makes me sure,.	178	Astrophil	26	12
These questions busie wits to me do frame;	180	Astrophil	30	12
Of conquest, do not these effects suffice,	183	Astrophil	36	7
Who though most rich in these and everie part,	183	Astrophil	37	12
And if these things, as being thine by right,.	184	Astrophil	39	12
While these poore babes their death in birth do find:.	190	Astrophil	50 V	11
And now my pen these lines had dashed quite,	190	Astrophil	50	12
Willd me these tempests of vaine love to flie,	196	Astrophil	62	10
Nc more, my deare, no more these counsels trie,.	198	Astrophil	64	1
These things are left me by my only Deare;	202	Astrophil	72	12
That in no more but these I might be fully blest:.	205	Astrophil	77	13

THESE	(CONTINUED)	PAGE	TITLE		LINE
Doubt you to whom my Muse these notes entendeth, ...		196	A&S 1st Song		1
Above line repeated at following location.		197	A&S 1st Song		33
These sweet flowers on fine bed too, ...		210	A&S 4th Song		15
That all these cruell words your praises shall be proved.. .		215	A&S 5th Song		90
"Eut time will these thoughts remove:.		234	A&S 11th Song		16
These gentle Lawyers wage, ...		215	A&S 6th Song		14
O let them heare these sacred tunes, and learne in wonder's schooles,.		217	A&S 7th Song		5
O let them see these heavenly beames, and in faire letters reede.		217	A&S 7th Song		11
These birds sing: "Now use the season.".		219	A&S 8th Song		56
Cease in these effects to prove:		220	A&S 8th Song		74
What ayles this heathenish rage? What do theis people meane.		271	Psalm II		1
Why do these earthly kings and lords such meetings make, . .		271	Psalm II		3
These men like potshards weake.		271	Psalm II		22
These most ungratefull rebels unto Thee.		275	Psalm V		32
These are God's words, God's words are ever pure, ...		285	Psalm XII		19
Of these bad folkes, more lifted up with pride		285	Psalm XII		26
O madness of these folks, thus loosely led,.		286	Psalm XIV		13
These Canibals, who as if they were bread.		286	Psalm XIV		14
These mates to be amated..		297	Psalm XXI		32
Shall these bad wights devouer...		297	Psalm XXI		36
With gaping mouthes, these folks on me have charged, ...		299	Psalm XXII		29
Whose heart with these huge flames, like wax o're heated,. .		299	Psalm XXII		33
And with these Words, when they meet, prayse Thy Name. . . .		300	Psalm XXII		52
Shield me from these assaults;		304	Psalm XXV		62
And me from these ills take.		304	Psalm XXV		69
Oh! on my soul let not these tumults hitt.		322	Psalm XXXV		44
At these my words all cloath'd in teares;.		330	Psalm XXXIX		38
That comfort in these sports you like, my mynde his comfort tryes.		343	Possibly	1	14
Will. What? these are riddles sure, art thou then bound to her?		343	Possibly	1	23
About these never conquered walles to swarme,.		346	Possibly	5	10
These doubting clouds ore-casting heav'nly braine, ...		245	Other Poems	4	127
So now for pray these shepheards two he tooke, ...		245	Other Poems	4	137
These sports shepheards deviz'd such faults to show.		248	Other Poems	4	241
"Alas! what weights are these that lode my heart!.		253	Other Poems	4	441
"For, but by charms, how fall these things on me,.		253	Other Poems	4	449
These markes shall make thee wise:		259	Other Poems	5	111
These same words, or this effecting:		262	Other Poems	7	18
Sconer these than those in hearing..		263	Other Poems	7	54
THICKEST					
Cloudes even of Waters dark, and thickest ayre compos'd; . .		291	Psalm XVIII		25
THIEF					
Her face (this age's praise) the thiefe doth kisse..		141	Cert Sonnets	9	12
Who like a theefe, hid in darke bush doth ly,.		175	Astrophil	20	3
Yet worse then worst, I say thou art a theefe, a theefe? . .		213	A&S 5th Song		43
Now God forbid. A theefe, and of worst theeves the cheefe: .		213	A&S 5th Song		44
Thou English murdring theefe, wilt have harts for thy pray:.		214	A&S 5th Song		50
You then ungratefull thiefe, you murdring Tyran you, ...		215	A&S 5th Song		85
THIEVES					
Now God forbid. A theefe, and of worst theeves the cheefe: .		213	A&S 5th Song		44
Theeves steal for need, and steale but goods, which paine recovers,.		214	A&S 5th Song		45
Yet gentle English theeves do rob, but will not slay;. . . .		214	A&S 5th Song		49
THIEVES'					
(Stolne from her yoong by theeves' unchoosing hast).		254	Other Poems	4	491
THIGHS					
Those thighes, for Ovid's song more fitte;		88	Arcadia III	62	88
THILKE					
He said, the Musique best thilke powers pleasd		99	3rd Eclogues	66	29
THINE					
Love well thine owne: me thinkes, woolle's whitenes passeth all:		16	1st Eclogues	7	53
To be a player of thine owne annoy..		25	1st Eclogues	9	91
And let thine eyes to other sports be framed..		25	1st Eclogues	9	122
"Alas" she saith "I am thine,.		67	2nd Eclogues	32	41
Since that my thoughtes, as streight as streightnes thine, .		77	Arcadia III	47	3
How hast thou torne thy selfe! sought thine owne damage! . .		109	Arcadia IV	70	20
Then decke me as thine owne; thy helpe I borowe, ...		114	4th Eclogues	72	28
Thine earth now springs, mine fadeth, ...		137	Cert Sonnets	4	11
Above line repeated at following location.		137	Cert Sonnets	4	23
Thou countest Stella thine, like those whose powers.		171	Astrophil	12	9
But wilt new warre upon thine owne begin?.		183	Astrophil	36	8
And if these things, as being thine by right,.		184	Astrophil	39	12
He barks, my songs thine owne voyce oft doth prove:.		194	Astrophil	59	6
Since in thine armes, if learnd fame truth hath spread,. . .		198	Astrophil	65	13
Envie, put out thine eyes, least thou do see		200	Astrophil	69	3
That inward sunne in thine eyes shineth so..		201	Astrophil	71	8
Thine eyes my pride, thy lips my history:.		224	Astrophil	90	3
I said, my soule was thine (o that I then had lyed).		212	A&S 5th Song		9
I said, thine eyes were starres, thy breasts the milk'n way,		212	A&S 5th Song		10
That mine eyes thine eyes may see?		225	A&S 10th Song		2
So shall my voice clime to thyne eares betime:		274	Psalm V		5
Thou lord, Thou lord, the saver of Thyne Owne.		275	Psalm V		21
But mercy, lord, let Mercy thyne descend		276	Psalm VI		5
Yet each day art provoakt, thyne Ire to show,.		277	Psalm VII		32
And ready art to let Thyne arrowes go.		278	Psalm VII		36

THINE (CONTINUED)
	PAGE	TITLE		LINE
That hast of thine unmatched glory	278	Psalm VIII		3
Whereby Thou stop'st Thyne Enemy's prating	278	Psalm VIII		7
To rule the Works of Thyne own hands	279	Psalm VIII		22
Say, Thou dost not Thyn Own regard?.	283	Psalm X		56
But nake'd before thine eyes	283	Psalm X		57
In Tabernacle Thyne, O lord, who shall remayne?.	287	Psalm XV		1
Ev'en the body of Thyne Own, ...	288	Psalm XVI		34
Thyne Ears voutchsafe to bend to me.	289	Psalm XVII		4
O let my sentence passe from Thyne own face;	289	Psalm XVII		5
I shall see Thee in likeness Thine.	290	Psalm XVII		48
O my strength stop not Thine eare, ...	308	Psalm XXVIII		2
Blesse Thyne heritage I say, ...	309	Psalm XXVIII		34
Lord heare, let mercy thine be stay'd.	311	Psalm XXX		31
Bow down thine eare to heare how much I need,.	312	Psalm XXXI		4
For my annoyes have come before thyne eye, ...	312	Psalm XXXI		20
Let Angel thine a scattring make thee go.	321	Psalm XXXV		12
Let Angel thine persue them as they fly, ...	321	Psalm XXXV		13
A span? nay nothing in Thyn eyne.	330	Psalm XXXIX		16
Heare lord my suits and cryes, stop not thyn eares	330	Psalm XXXIX		37
Yearely decke thine Altar shall:	264	Other Poems	7	70

THING
	PAGE	TITLE		LINE
And thus my thoughtes, can thinke but one thing still. . . .	12	Arcadia I	2	V810
Geron. Yet sure an end, to each thing time doth give, ...	22	1st Eclogues	9	11
Thus both trees and each thing ells, be the bookes of a fancy.	36	1st Eclogues	13	140
What hope to quench, where each thing blowes the fire? . . .	42	Arcadia II	21	18
A foolish thing with fooles to deale:	44	Arcadia II	25	3
R. O foolish thing, which glory doeste destroye.	46	2nd Eclogues	27	19
Seekes to make ech thing badge of his sweet passion.	47	2nd Eclogues	28	6
Among us all we should find out some thing of nought.. . . .	51	2nd Eclogues	29	2
Thy gray-hood hides the thing, that thou despairst to find..	52	2nd Eclogues	29	6
Woe to poore man: ech outward thing annoyes him.	62	2nd Eclogues	30	170
Yet tell what light thinge I had in me to draw me to die? Eye.	64	2nd Eclogues	31	25
What were it els, but to make each thing blinde?	79	Arcadia III	50	13
For no thing, time, nor place, can loose, quench, ease,. . .	84	Arcadia III	60	13
Graunt to the thing which we for Lalus crave.	92	3rd Eclogues	63	30
So may each thing, even as thou wishest lighte,.	96	3rd Eclogues	64	94
The pandare of the thing, he most did feare, ...	97	3rd Eclogues	64	122
Each thing with mantle black the night doth soothe;.	98	3rd Eclogues	66	5
Icleped starres; each thing to rest disposed:.	98	3rd Eclogues	66	10
Then founde I which thing is a charge to beare	99	3rd Eclogues	66	17
Ape great thing gave, though he did mowing stand,.	101	3rd Eclogues	66	97
The Waspe seemes gay, but is a combrous thing.	104	3rd Eclogues	67	21
Shall in this life embrace no worthy thing:	105	3rd Eclogues	67	59
Now each thing which enjoy'd that firie quickning sparke . .	116	4th Eclogues	73	4
Such thing cannot I seeke (Despaire hath giv'n me my answer.	122	4th Eclogues	74	11
Such thing cannot he hope, that knowes thy determinat hardnes;	122	4th Eclogues	74	13
For in each thing wherto mine eye doth range,.	147	Cert Sonnets	18	3
Infected mindes infect each thing they see..	147	Cert Sonnets	18	14
While he each thing in sense's ballance wayes, ...	177	Astrophil	25	6
"What idler thing, then speake and not be hard?"	182	Astrophil	34	9
What harder thing then smart, and not to speake?	182	Astrophil	34	10
I crav'd the thing which ever she denies:.	196	Astrophil	63	6
Sweet then, while each thing doth frame:	211	A&S 4th Song		34
He only leanes on highest Thing, ...	297	Psalm XXI		27
One thing in deed I did and will	307	Psalm XXVII		19
O Lord how excellent a thing	324	Psalm XXXVI		19
"Nay each thing is bewitcht to know my case:	254	Other Poems	4	473
Each thing both sweet and sadd	256	Other Poems	5	8

THINGS
	PAGE	TITLE		LINE
The gods must help, and pretious things must serve to shew her shape.	12	Arcadia I	3	4
Of best things then what world can yeeld confection.	15	1st Eclogues	7	46
She is her selfe, of best things the collection.	15	1st Eclogues	7	48
And pastimes make, as Nature things hath made.	18	1st Eclogues	7	127
Then cries to sencelesse things, which neither knowes. . . .	23	1st Eclogues	9	41
Then shall those thinges ease their inward horrible angwish.	33	1st Eclogues	13	46
And shall sensive things be so sencelesse as to resist sence	36	1st Eclogues	13	138
To hold these worldly things in such proportion, ...	60	2nd Eclogues	30	132
Since all the thinges which give mine eyes their light . . .	73	Arcadia III	39	5
Thinges rightelie prizde, love is the bande of love.	83	Arcadia III	57	14
The best things still must be forgotten.	88	Arcadia III	62	86
Be fled as things most vaine, ...	93	3rd Eclogues	63	71
Rulers will thinke all things made them to please, ...	100	3rd Eclogues	66	73
Thou art of blood; joy not to make things bleede:.	103	3rd Eclogues	66	150
Nature above all things requireth this,.	105	3rd Eclogues	67	70
Then void of neerer cares, the depth of things to find.. . .	118	4th Eclogues	73	50
All things that earst I sawe, as orient pearles exceed,. . .	119	4th Eclogues	73	83
That I things erst unseene should first in dreaming see? . .	121	4th Eclogues	73	182
In tender harts, small things engender hate:	146	Cert Sonnets	17	17
On things, were by a woman said, ...	158	Cert Sonnets	28	39
Who should my mind to higher things prepare.	161	Cert Sonnets	31	8
In vaine thou madest me to vaine things aspire,.	161	Cert Sonnets	31	10
And thou my mind aspire to higher things:.	161	Cert Sonnets	32	2
And strange things cost too deare for my poore sprites.. . .	166	Astrophil	3	11
For though she passe all things, yet what is all	174	Astrophil	19	9

THINGS	(CONTINUED)	PAGE	TITLE		LINE
As sacred things, far from all daunger's show.		177	Astrophil	24	8
Ready to store their campes of needfull things:.		179	Astrophil	29	4
To leave the scepter of all subject things,.		183	Astrophil	38	4
And if these things, as being thine by right,.		184	Astrophil	39	12
Alas, if Fancy drawne by imag'd things,.		187	Astrophil	45	9
To witlesse things, then Love I hope (since wit.		194	Astrophil	59	13
These things are left me by my only Deare;		202	Astrophil	72	12
To be (in things past bounds of wit) fooles, if they be not fooles..		217	A&S 7th Song		6
And if dumbe things be so witty,.		219	A&S 8th Song		63
So all things whereto that man doth bend,.		270	Psalm I		11
And so thou hast all things ordained		279	Psalm VIII		23
And what thinges els of waters traceth		279	Psalm VIII		31
Of things vain, with vaine mates they bable all, ...		284	Psalm XII		4
Let those things Thy remembrance grave, ...		303	Psalm XXV		23
Laying such things, as never in mee weare;		322	Psalm XXXV		26
Least such things sin in Thy self cherish, ...		325	Psalm XXXVII		22
They are but shades not true things where we live, ...		330	Psalm XXXIX		19
Lockt fast with knowing that she is, of worldly things the best..		344	Possibly	1	30
Glutted with them now plaies with meanest things..		245	Other Poems	4	132
"For, but by charms, how fall these things on me,.		253	Other Poems	4	449
THINK					
Since what I see, thinke, know is all but you?		12	Arcadia I	2	14
And thus my thoughtes, can thinke but one thing still. . . .		12	Arcadia I	2	V810
As well may thincke with oyle to coole the fire:		22	1st Eclogues	9	8
And thinck she is a she, that doth thee move..		23	1st Eclogues	9	52
And thinke them olde, that have the oldest minde,.		25	1st Eclogues	9	94
First thinke they erre, that thinke them gayly wise, ...		25	1st Eclogues	9	111
Do you not thincke this will the wolves remove		26	1st Eclogues	10	4
Since when I thinke he hath in silence lived..		29	1st Eclogues	10	87
Happy shepheard, with thanks to the Gods, still thinke to be thankfull,.		32	1st Eclogues	13	33
Then do I thinke in deed, that better it is to be private. .		35	1st Eclogues	13	102
And thinke ther she do dwell and heare what plaintes I do utter:		36	1st Eclogues	13	143
When by the winde it maketh a noyse, I do thinke she doth answer..		36	1st Eclogues	13	145
As thou doest thinke) should most of all disquiet me		51	2nd Eclogues	28	115
Nico. I thinke it well: such voice would make one musicke hate:.		52	2nd Eclogues	29	21
And thinke from Cosma's sweet red lips I live, ...		54	2nd Eclogues	29	79
We thinke they hurt, when most they do assist.		59	2nd Eclogues	30	70
What ere you see, thinke, touch, kisse, speake, or love, . .		60	2nd Eclogues	30	123
The asse did hurt when he did thinke to kisse.		62	2nd Eclogues	30	184
Think so, for of my desired blisse it is only the course. Curse.		64	2nd Eclogues	31	39
To think a soare so deadly		66	2nd Eclogues	32	17
And thinke not she doth hurt our solitarines,.		69	2nd Eclogues	34	41
Nor mas'de head thinke, nor faltring tonge recite.		74	Arcadia III	42	14
Or doost thou thinke that heare.		80	Arcadia III	52	5
Sturres me to thinke what dangers lye in waite..		82	Arcadia III	56	12
Thought, thinke to ende, too long the frute of thought . . .		83	Arcadia III	59	7
But ah the more I hate, the more I thinke.		85	Arcadia III	61	9
Whome I doe hate, the more I thinke on him,.		85	Arcadia III	61	10
Such be I thinke the sumptuous towers.		87	Arcadia III	62	49
He forst her thinke that which she never thought..		95	3rd Eclogues	64	34
And thinke not that thy answere answere is,.		97	3rd Eclogues	64	101
This thinke I well, the beasts with courage clad		100	3rd Eclogues	66	55
Rulers will thinke all things made them to please, ...		100	3rd Eclogues	66	73
Thou fearest death; thinke they are loth to die.		103	3rd Eclogues	66	151
And thinke, I did my selfe from sorrow save.		104	3rd Eclogues	67	24
I thinke from me, not from my woes to parte.		113	4th Eclogues	72	10
Klaius. I think from me, not from my woes to parte,.		113	4th Eclogues	72	11
And loth this time, calld life, nay thinke, that life. . . .		113	4th Eclogues	72	12
Thinke, my harde haps have blunted death's sharpe knife, . .		113	4th Eclogues	72	14
And thinking this, thinke Nature, Life, and Death.		114	4th Eclogues	72	16
But vaine it is to thinke those paines should cease, ...		116	4th Eclogues	72	94
Think what a world is now, think who hath altred her hart. .		124	4th Eclogues	74	76
The weeping Myrrhe I thinke will not denie		125	4th Eclogues	75	13
Who for our sakes will thinke all travaile light,.		129	4th Eclogues	76	23
Sweete thinke not I am at ease,.		140	Cert Sonnets	7	34
Or doth she thinke all paine the minde forbeares?.		142	Cert Sonnets	11	5
Who thinke themselves will blest, if they renew.		146	Cert Sonnets	17	33
Thinke Hanniball did laugh when Carthage lost.		147	Cert Sonnets	17	45
If I could thinke how these my thoughts to leave,.		147	Cert Sonnets	19	1
Then might I thinke what thoughts were best to thinke: . . .		148	Cert Sonnets	19	5
Thus what I thinke is of you:.		155	Cert Sonnets	25	32
Nor thinke the match unev'nly made,.		159	Cert Sonnets	29	10
And thinke how evill becommeth him to slide, ...		144	Cert Sonnets	32	11
But thinke that all the Map of my state I display, ...		168	Astrophil	6	13
Thinke that I thinke state errours to redresse..		176	Astrophil	23	8
And fooles can thinke those Lampes of purest light,.		177	Astrophil	26	2
Yet pride I thinke doth not my soule possesse,.		178	Astrophil	27	9
But know not how, for still I thinke of you.		180	Astrophil	30	14
"But will not wise men thinke thy words fond ware?".		182	Astrophil	34	7
And then, thinke thus, although thy beautie be		185	Astrophil	40	9
Thinke Nature me a man of armes did make..		185	Astrophil	41	11
Then thinke my deare, that you in me do reed		187	Astrophil	45	12

THINK   (CONTINUED)   PAGE   TITLE   LINE

And thinke so still, so Stella know my mind, ... 192 Astrophil   54   9
And thinke I should not your large precepts misse? . . . . 192 Astrophil   56   4
What, dost thou thinke that I can ever take. . . . . 193 Astrophil   56   10
O thinke I then, what paradise of joy. . . . . 200 Astrophil   68   13
Since best wits thinke it wit thee to admire;. . . . . . . 206 Astrophil   80   2
Stella thinke not that I by verse seeke fame, ... 224 Astrophil   90   1
O God, thinke you that satisfies my care?. . . . . 225 Astrophil   92   8
Mery with him, and not thinke of his woe.. . . . . 236 Astrophil   106   14
But o foole, thinke of the danger, ... 203 A&S 2nd Song   17
I thinke now of thy faults, who late thought of thy praise,. 213 A&S 5th Song   16
Thinke now no more to heare of warme fine odourd snow, . . 213 A&S 5th Song   37
Thinke of that most gratefull time,. . . . . 226 A&S 10th Song   25
Thinke of my most Princely power,. . . . . 226 A&S 10th Song   31
Thinke, thinke of those dalyings,. . . . . 226 A&S 10th Song   37
Thinke no more but die in me,. . . . . 227 A&S 10th Song   46
I will thinke theye pictures be, ... 234 A&S 11th Song   23
"Peace, I thinke that some give eare:. . . . . 234 A&S 11th Song   36
Then think I, Ah, what is this Man,. . . . . 278 Psalm VIII   13
And in that nett, which they well hidden think, ... 280 Psalm IX   48
And what think you may be. . . . . 304 Psalm XXV   37
Thus did I think: I well will mark my way, ... 329 Psalm XXXIX   1
If this in them be true, as true in men think I. . . . . . 343 Possibly   1   7
But you, o you, that thinke not teares too deare . . . . . 242 Other Poems   4   9
For not himselfe to be in love did thinke. . . . . 247 Other Poems   4 200
I thinke you thinke Strephon bent thitherward. . . . . . . 250 Other Poems   4 320
Now make me thinke that there is not a fende,. . . . . . . 254 Other Poems   4 463
Which made his Strephon think himselfe in hell.. . . . . . 256 Other Poems   4 540
To thinke, and thinke with paine . . . . 256 Other Poems   5   10
THINKERS'
Let their vile thoughts the thinkers' ruin be. . . . . . . 275 Psalm V   30
THINKING
Thinking how it hath mard my shepheard's trade.. . . . . .   19 1st Eclogues 7 169
Thus be my thoughts disperst, thus thinking nurseth a
   thinking,. . . . .   36 1st Eclogues 13 139
Can thoughts still thinking so rest unappalled?. . . . . .   61 2nd Eclogues 30 166
And thinking this, thinke Nature, Life, and Death. . . . . 114 4th Eclogues 72 16
Thinking not why, but how himselfe to save.. . . . . 145 Cert Sonnets 16   8
Or thinking still my thoughts might have good end: . . . . 147 Cert Sonnets 19   2
But since my thoughts in thinking still are spent, ... 148 Cert Sonnets 19 13
My life melts with too much thinking;. . . . . 227 A&S 10th Song   45
Speaking ev'ill, thinking deceit.. . . . . 328 Psalm XXXVIII   36
Yet God on me is thinking, ... 332 Psalm XL   66
Thinking it just more therein to delight . . . . 246 Other Poems   4 178
THINKINGS
The thinckinges of that mind . . . . 317 Psalm XXXIII   40
THINKS
Unto the heav'ns? our wings be too short; th' earth thinks
   us a burden; . . . .   32 1st Eclogues 13 29
To witnes, that he thinkes his thoughts delicious, ...   47 2nd Eclogues 28   5
Me thinkes I see the lippes my Leuca hath, ...   54 2nd Eclogues 29 76
And gamesome then, when he thinkes on his sheepe;. . . . . 104 3rd Eclogues 67 35
Mournes she in truth, and thinks that others faine?. . . . 142 Cert Sonnets 11   3
But this she thinks, our paine hye cause excuseth, ... 142 Cert Sonnets 11 13
She thinks I leade and live too merrie daies.. . . . . . . 146 Cert Sonnets 17 30
She thinkes you do letters write:. . . . . 211 A&S 4th Song   39
A lustles song for sooth thinks hee that hath more lust to
   cry. . . . . 343 Possibly   1   8
THINNEST
Lyke thynnest Lawne with Tynsell lynde,. . . . .   89 Arcadia III 62 V116
THIRD
Some hurt accuse a third with horny head.. . . . .   21 1st Eclogues 8   12
The third his lesson mist, till all do smarte. . . . . . .   27 1st Eclogues 10 45
But so she must. And now the third assault . . . . 250 Other Poems   4 316
THIRSTING
Thirsting on my God to look. . . . . 334 Psalm XLII   4
THIRSTS
My soul thirsts indeed in me . . . . 334 Psalm XLII   5
THIRSTY
Sicke, thirsty, glad (though but of empty glasse:) . . . . 233 Astrophil   104   11
THIS
All this I give, let me possesse thy grace,. . . . .   4 Lady of May   2   22
But take this beast, if beasts you feare to misse, ...   4 Lady of May   2   29
"Nothing", sayd he, "for most I joy in this, ...   4 Lady of May   3   5
Till this he tooke for comfort of his lot: . . . .   5 Lady of May   3   10
(Therion) Thus wofully I in wo this salve do find, ...   5 Lady of May   3   19
All this one the this fatall yere shall hitte. . . . . . .   11 Arcadia I   1 V807
Then power out plaint, and in one word say this: . . . . .   13 Arcadia I   4   9
Who ended hath this fearefull strife:. . . . .   13 Arcadia I   5   4
My sonne, keepe this, that my long toyle hath laide to me: 16 1st Eclogues 7   52
This winde he spent: but when my Kala glasseth all . . . .   16 1st Eclogues 7   55
These bolde words she did heare, this fruite I reaped, . .   17 1st Eclogues 7   82
Lalus. This mayde, thus made for joyes, o Pan bemone her,.   17 1st Eclogues 7   97
Lalus. But if my Kala this my suite denies,. . . . .   18 1st Eclogues 7 147
Now my hoarse voice doth faile this occupation,. . . . . .   19 1st Eclogues 7 170
But now hoarse voyce, doth faile this occupation,. . . . .   20 1st Eclogues 7 V970
Mercury kill'd his false sire for this act,. . . . .   21 1st Eclogues 8   17
Millions of yeares this old drivell Cupid lives; . . . . .   22 1st Eclogues 8   43
In this our world a hang-man for to be, ...   22 1st Eclogues 8   47
Still were I one, this still should be my case, ...   23 1st Eclogues 9   28

509

THIS	(CONTINUED)	PAGE	TITLE		LINE
This tyran Love; or rather do suppresse.		23	1st Eclogues	9	45
Philisides. O gods, how long this old foole hath annoi'd		24	1st Eclogues	9	66
My wearied ears! O gods yet graunt me this,		24	1st Eclogues	9	67
This life-deadman in this old dungeon flong.		24	1st Eclogues	9	83
But this light choller that doth make you bolde,		25	1st Eclogues	9	105
Philisides. Hath any man heard what this old man said?		26	1st Eclogues	9	135
Do you not thincke this will the wolves remove		26	1st Eclogues	10	4
This paterne good, unto our children goes,		28	1st Eclogues	10	55
Still doo I crosse this wretch, what so he taketh in hand".		29	1st Eclogues	11	6
"Tush, tush", said nature, "this is all but a trifle, a man's selfe.		29	1st Eclogues	11	7
Life to this our soule.		31	1st Eclogues	12	24
Here you fully do finde this strange operation of love,		31	1st Eclogues	13	3
For yet (weigh this alas!) great is not great to a greater.		34	1st Eclogues	13	74
Such this smale greatnes, doth seeme compar'd to the greatest.		34	1st Eclogues	13	76
Dorus. O glittring miseries of man, if this be the fortune.		34	1st Eclogues	13	89
Sweete Juniper saith this, thoh I burne, yet I burne in a sweete fire.		35	1st Eclogues	13	120
O descende for a while, from this greate height to behold me.		36	1st Eclogues	13	149
To this strange death I vainely yeeld my life.		38	Arcadia II	14	14
This vowe receave, this vowe o Gods maintaine;		40	Arcadia II	18	5
This marble chose, as of like temper knowne:		40	Arcadia II	19	2
This is thy worke, thou God for ever blinde:		41	Arcadia II	20	9
The sound to this strange aier no sooner goes,		42	Arcadia II	21	9
Now in this sande I would discharge my minde,		42	Arcadia II	21	13
O blessed sonne whence all this blessing goes.		43	Arcadia II	23	6
O cruell sonne thy hate this harme dothe breede.		43	Arcadia II	24	3
Let this assured holde our judgements ever take,		45	Arcadia II	26	15
Throwne on this earth the Chaos of confusions.		51	2nd Eclogues	28	110
Despairde in all this flocke to find a knave, but thee.		52	2nd Eclogues	29	4
If thou (alas poore if) do winne, then winne thou this,		53	2nd Eclogues	29	37
This is my pawne; the price let Dicus' judgement show:		53	2nd Eclogues	29	47
Nico. Was this not he, who for Siringa's scape		53	2nd Eclogues	29	57
Pas. This is not he that failed her to gaine,		54	2nd Eclogues	29	60
But this is one that doth his musicke staine.		54	2nd Eclogues	29	62
Alas (said I) this babe dooth nurce my thought.		55	2nd Eclogues	29	113
Pas. Tell this (and Phoebus be) what monster growes.		56	2nd Eclogues	29	144
Plangus. Alas how long this pilgrimage doth last?		57	2nd Eclogues	30	5
This bodie is: this bodie so composed,		57	2nd Eclogues	30	27
In this weake worke, that it can never be.		57	2nd Eclogues	30	30
This man, this talking beast, this walking tree.		58	2nd Eclogues	30	34
Serve all thy starrie eyes this shame to see?		58	2nd Eclogues	30	61
And shall (o me) all this in ashes rest?		60	2nd Eclogues	30	101
"Erona dye, and end this ougly painefulnes"?		61	2nd Eclogues	30	157
In what state was I then, when I tooke this deadly disease? ease.		63	2nd Eclogues	31	8
Horrible is this blasphemy unto the most holy. O lie.		65	2nd Eclogues	31	45
My muse what ails this ardour.		65	2nd Eclogues	32	1
Above line repeated at following locations		66	2nd Eclogues	32	9
. . .		66	2nd Eclogues	32	19
. . .		66	2nd Eclogues	32	30
. . .		67	2nd Eclogues	32	40
My tong to this my roofe cleaves,		66	2nd Eclogues	32	12
In this strange violence, to make resistance.		67	2nd Eclogues	33	2
Under this, this her owne, her only dearling.		68	2nd Eclogues	33	23
Be thow my starre in this this my darkest night,		70	Arcadia III	35	4
I like this place, wheare at the least the darke		73	Arcadia III	39	13
Or howe do I, captiv'd in this darke plight,		74	Arcadia III	42	3
Betwixt which two in me I have this fight,		74	Arcadia III	42	7
This cave is darke, but it had never light.		75	Arcadia III	43	1
This waxe doth waste it selfe, yet painelesse dyes.		75	Arcadia III	43	2
All is but this, this is our labour's hire,		75	Arcadia III	44	6
Of this we live, in this wee finde our rest,		75	Arcadia III	44	7
Who hold this fast no greater wealth require.		75	Arcadia III	44	8
Both equall hurt, in this change sought our blisse:		76	Arcadia III	45	13
Do you say still, this is her promise due,		76	Arcadia III	46	5
Joyne you with me, to seale this promise due,		76	Arcadia III	46	11
And in this growing barke growe verses myne.		77	Arcadia III	47	12
Preserve those beames, this age's onely lighte:		79	Arcadia III	51	2
In this rare subject from thy common right:		79	Arcadia III	51	10
Let him drinke this, whome long in armes to folde.		83	Arcadia III	58	1
The handle of this plesant worke,		87	Arcadia III	62	47
This leades unto the joyous field,		87	Arcadia III	62	61
This noble Cedar's pretious roote:		89	Arcadia III	62	106
How all this is but a faire Inne		90	Arcadia III	62	139
To this chaste love your sacred favours bow,		91	3rd Eclogues	63	21
Be thou the knot of this their open vowe,		92	3rd Eclogues	63	47
And for this Courtier should well like his table,		94	3rd Eclogues	64	23
When once this entred was, in woman's hart,		95	3rd Eclogues	64	37
The courtlie shepheard much agast at this,		96	3rd Eclogues	64	67
This mourning inck, in which my hart doth bleede.		96	3rd Eclogues	64	96
And this was all, and this the husband read.		97	3rd Eclogues	64	109
This done, thou hast no more, but leave the rest		98	3rd Eclogues	65	13
When all this Earth, this damme or mould of ours,		100	3rd Eclogues	66	44
This thinke I well, the beasts with courage clad		100	3rd Eclogues	66	55
To their owne worke this priviledge they graunt,		101	3rd Eclogues	66	103
Disdaind with this, in deserts sought their restes;		102	3rd Eclogues	66	123

THIS   (CONTINUED)   PAGE   TITLE   LINE

	PAGE	TITLE		LINE
Is this sweet doubling of our single life.	103	3rd Eclogues	67	12
But this bad world, few golden fieldes doth bring,	104	3rd Eclogues	67	19
Shall in this life embrace no worthy thing:.	105	3rd Eclogues	67	59
Nature above all things requireth this,	105	3rd Eclogues	67	70
Which must by this immortall be preserved,	105	3rd Eclogues	67	77
And yet in all this time, betwixt us tway,	106	3rd Eclogues	67	91
We go unto the Bryde, and use this daye.	107	3rd Eclogues	67	119
Choosing alas! this our theatre publique,	109	Arcadia IV	70	11
No, no, our mischiefe growes in this vile fortune,	109	Arcadia IV	70	31
With all our deathes shew we this damage publique.	110	Arcadia IV	70	38
Our morning hymne this is, and song at evening..	113	4th Eclogues	71	75
And loth this time, calld love, nay thinke, that life.	113	4th Eclogues	72	12
And thinking this, thinke Nature, Life, and Death.	114	4th Eclogues	72	16
And now I faine would reape, I reape but this,	115	4th Eclogues	72	57
And this hath got; the catcher now is caught,	115	4th Eclogues	72	66
And keepe it still within this body thrall:.	116	4th Eclogues	72	88
That thus I must, while in this death I dwell,	116	4th Eclogues	72	89
To onely thee thou seest we graunt this speciall grace	119	4th Eclogues	73	95
Us to attend, in this most private time and place.	119	4th Eclogues	73	96
Is this thy fruite O strife? those thousand churches hie,	119	4th Eclogues	73	111
But such they say we be: this praise our discord bred,	120	4th Eclogues	73	117
Now resteth onely this, which of us two is she,	120	4th Eclogues	73	135
Who may this doubt discerne: for better, witt, then lot.	120	4th Eclogues	73	139
This crowne of amber faire (an amber crowne she held).	120	4th Eclogues	73	141
And so most ready am this meane of peace to trie.	121	4th Eclogues	73	152
Into thy hart by the sight of this Epistle I send:	122	4th Eclogues	74	6
Or with a fair hand's nailes (o hand which nailes me to this death).	123	4th Eclogues	74	55
Unto the earth, by the hurt of this her heavenly jewell.	124	4th Eclogues	74	62
But what's this for a fault, for which such faieth be abolisht,	124	4th Eclogues	74	69
Her helpe to this, this justest cause of plaint.	125	4th Eclogues	75	14
Or if that they be skante, if this be wronge?.	126	4th Eclogues	75	45
Did Wisedome this our wretched time espie.	126	4th Eclogues	75	46
Fould with this sight, while thou thy chariot guidest.	126	4th Eclogues	75	57
And well (me thinks) becomes this vaultie skie	126	4th Eclogues	75	58
This cheerefull aire with your obscured cheere,	127	4th Eclogues	75	68
Now set thy triumph in this world, bereaved.	127	4th Eclogues	75	73
For how can Nature unto this reply?.	127	4th Eclogues	75	94
The vehement course of this just lamentation:	127	4th Eclogues	75	98
Was this man's death the fruite of your dissention?.	128	4th Eclogues	75	108
And see by this picture to you presented.	128	4th Eclogues	75	122
Since this we feele, greate losse we cannot finde.	131	Arcadia V	77	14
Earth take this earth, wherein my spirits languish..	136	Cert Sonnets	3	16
This you heare is not my tongue,	139	Cert Sonnets	7	4
This song from deathe's sorrow springeth:	140	Cert Sonnets	7	36
Her face (this age's praise) the thiefe doth kisse..	141	Cert Sonnets	9	12
Or art thou from above bid play this part,	142	Cert Sonnets	10	11
But this she thinks, our paine hye cause excuseth,	142	Cert Sonnets	11	13
As this poore beast who did his rest forsake,	145	Cert Sonnets	16	7
But for all this I can not her remove.	145	Cert Sonnets	17	4
Tell me the cause of this my causelesse woe,	146	Cert Sonnets	17	12
O this it is, the knotted straw is found	146	Cert Sonnets	17	16
Take harp and sing in this our versing time:	146	Cert Sonnets	17	37
If from my soule this love would once depart,	148	Cert Sonnets	19	9
Now thus this wonder to my selfe I frame,	151	Cert Sonnets	22	69
This heaven in it doth binde..	152	Cert Sonnets	23	24
And wretched I must yeeld to this,	157	Cert Sonnets	27	31
How ill fits you this greene to weare,	157	Cert Sonnets	28	3
Once to approch this hayer..	158	Cert Sonnets	28	8
I saw this woman sit,	158	Cert Sonnets	28	34
Of this high grace with blisse conjoyn'd	159	Cert Sonnets	29	1
Alas, I lie: rage hath this errour bred,	160	Cert Sonnets	30	31
For vertue hath this better lesson taught,	161	Cert Sonnets	31	12
In this small course which birth drawes out to death,	144	Cert Sonnets	32	10
Whereof this Beautie can be but a shade,	167	Astrophil	5	10
Placed ever there, gave him this mourning weed,	168	Astrophil	7	13
The windowes now through which this heav'nly guest.	169	Astrophil	9	9
Crie, "Victorie, this faire day all is ours.".	171	Astrophil	12	11
But while I thus with this yong Lyon plaid;	173	Astrophil	16	9
Dig deepe with learning's spade, now tell me this,	175	Astrophil	21	13
Hath this world ought so faire as Stella is?	175	Astrophil	21	14
Her daintiest bare went free; the cause was this,	176	Astrophil	22	13
But for that man with paine this truth descries,	177	Astrophil	25	5
Love onely reading unto me this art.	179	Astrophil	28	14
To fill his hornes this yeare on Christian coast;	179	Astrophil	30	2
Vouchsafe of all acquaintance this to tell,	181	Astrophil	32	9
Stella, whence doth this new assault arise,	182	Astrophil	36	1
This night while sleepe begins with heavy wings.	183	Astrophil	38	1
Having this day my horse, my hand, my launce	185	Astrophil	41	1
My bloud from them, who did excell in this,	185	Astrophil	41	10
I much do guesse, yet find no truth save this,	187	Astrophil	44	9
Yet Deare, let me this pardon get of you,	188	Astrophil	46	12
To portrait that which in this world is best..	189	Astrophil	50	8
Her eyes, her lips, her all, saith Love do this,	190	Astrophil	52	3
Not this faire outside, which our hearts doth move.	190	Astrophil	52	8
Well Love, since this demurre our sute doth stay,	191	Astrophil	52	12
But you faire maides, at length this true shall find,	192	Astrophil	54	11
Whether with words this soveraignty he gaine,	194	Astrophil	58	5

511

THIS   (CONTINUED)   PAGE   TITLE   LINE

Phrase	PAGE	TITLE		LINE
Now judge by this: in piercing phrases late,	194	Astrophil	58	9
This sowre-breath'd mate tast of those sugred lips..	194	Astrophil	59	11
The ground of this fierce Love and lovely hate:.	195	Astrophil	60	11
But this at last is her sweet breath'd defence:.	195	Astrophil	61	4
Now since her chast mind hates this love in me,.	195	Astrophil	61	9
Alas, if this the only mettall be.	196	Astrophil	62	12
For Grammer sayes (o this deare Stella weighe,).	196	Astrophil	63	12
In this old world, growne now so too too wise:	198	Astrophil	65	6
Yet let this thought thy Tygrish courage passe:.	198	Astrophil	65	11
Labour to kill in me this killing care:.	200	Astrophil	68	12
This realme of blisse, while vertuous course I take,	200	Astrophil	69	13
I give you here my hand for truth of this,	201	Astrophil	70	13
Doth lowre, nay, chide; nay, threat for only this:	203	Astrophil	73	7
And this I sweare by blackest brooke of hell,.	204	Astrophil	74	7
Nor this, nor that, nor any such small cause,.	204	Astrophil	75	12
But only for this worthy knight durst prove.	204	Astrophil	75	13
That skin, whose passe-praise hue scorns this poore terme of white:.	205	Astrophil	77	7
Loathing all lies, doubting this Flatterie is:	207	Astrophil	80	11
Without how farre this praise is short of you,	207	Astrophil	80	13
Alas, whence came this change of lookes? If I.	212	Astrophil	86	1
If this darke place yet shew like candle light,.	225	Astrophil	91	5
Yet truth (if Caitif's breath mighte call thee) this	227	Astrophil	93	5
And do I then my selfe this vaine scuse give?.	227	Astrophil	93	9
I have (live I and know this) harmed thee,	227	Astrophil	93	10
Seeing hope yeeld when this wo strake him furst:	228	Astrophil	95	6
I would know by what right this palenesse overcame	232	Astrophil	102	7
Of comfort dare come to this dungeon darke,.	233	Astrophil	104	7
Bare me in hand, that in this Orphane place,	235	Astrophil	106	3
To this great cause, which needs both use and art,	236	Astrophil	107	8
Now will I but venture this,	203	A&S 2nd Song		23
The birds, beasts, stones and trees feele this, and feeling love:	209	A&S 3rd Song		13
Nor beasts, nor birds do come unto this blessed gaze,.	209	A&S 3rd Song		15
This small light the Moone bestowes,	210	A&S 4th Song		19
This large offer of our blisse,	211	A&S 4th Song		32
Lo you grow proud with this, for tyrans make folke bow:.	214	A&S 5th Song		61
What, is not this enough? nay farre worse commeth here;.	214	A&S 5th Song		73
"Who is it that this darke night,	233	A&S 11th Song		1
"Well in absence this will dy,	234	A&S 11th Song		11
O You that heare this voice,	215	A&S 6th Song		1
O you that see this face,.	215	A&S 6th Song		2
Feare not to judge this bate,	215	A&S 6th Song		5
This side doth beauty take,	215	A&S 6th Song		7
And in this faultlesse face,	216	A&S 6th Song		22
Be Arbiter of this,	216	A&S 6th Song		44
He layes on this chiefe praise,	216	A&S 6th Song		47
See, do you see this face? a face? nay image of the skies,	217	A&S 7th Song		15
Heare you this soule-invading voice, and count it but a voice?	217	A&S 7th Song		17
"This small wind which so sweete is,	219	A&S 8th Song		57
"Therefore, Deere, this no more move,	220	A&S 8th Song		97
In this caitife hart to be,	221	A&S 9th Song		23
In this pleasant spring must see	222	A&S 9th Song		28
What ayles this heathenish rage? What do theis people meane.	271	Psalm II		1
Thou art my son in deed, this day begott by me:.	271	Psalm II		17
I say no more but this:.	272	Psalm III		22
Yet know this too, that God did take	273	Psalm IV		11
Turne Thee, sweet lord, and from this Ougly fall	276	Psalm VI		11
O save me from this Persecution's showre:.	277	Psalm VII		2
For this same man will not learn to repent,.	278	Psalm VII		33
A pitt was digg'd, by this man vainly strong,.	278	Psalm VII		40
Then think I, Ah, what is this Man,.	278	Psalm VIII		13
Thou planted hast this earthly mate.	279	Psalm VIII		18
O prayse the lord, this Syon dweller good,	280	Psalm IX		31
Shew forth his Acts, and this as Act most high,.	280	Psalm IX		32
But rather much he fancys this	281	Psalm X		15
This gotten blisse shall never part,	282	Psalm X		24
He leasure wants to mark all this.	282	Psalm X		48
His guiltie heart with this fond thought hath fed,	286	Psalm XIV		2
If of this Clayey race he could espy	286	Psalm XIV		8
This is all the best I prove,	288	Psalm XVI		7
And count this life their Portion best	290	Psalm XVII		40
When waking of this sleep of mine.	290	Psalm XVII		47
This my Distresse to God with wailfull cryes I show,	291	Psalm XVIII		12
But streight his shining eyes unto this misty masse disclos'd..	291	Psalm XVIII		26
This much, yet more, when I by him this freedom gate,	292	Psalm XVIII		40
Therfore I say again this goodnesse he me sent.	292	Psalm XVIII		47
For who is God, besides this Great Jehova Ours?.	292	Psalm XVIII		57
This God then girded me in his Almighty pow'rs,	292	Psalm XVIII		59
I to Thy Name will sing, and this my song shall bee:	293	Psalm XVIII		89
This man for everlasting;.	297	Psalm XXI		22
And why all this? Because Our King	297	Psalm XXI		25
On me all this, who do like water slide;	299	Psalm XXII		31
Hasten to help me, in this deep discomfort.	299	Psalm XXII		46
But when he calld this lord did give him hearing..	300	Psalm XXII		58
His righteousness, and this his doing glorious..	300	Psalm XXII		78
This mercy is so sure.	301	Psalm XXIII		23
Jacob this is Thy seed, God seeking generation,	302	Psalm XXIV		15

THIS	(CONTINUED)	PAGE	TITLE		LINE
Who is this glorious King in might and power riding?		302	Psalm XXIV		19
Who is This Glorious King? The lord of armyes guiding,		302	Psalm XXIV		23
But still on this Lord set?.		304	Psalm XXV		56
This lord with strength my life doth blisse;		306	Psalm XXVII		4
In this I would.		307	Psalm XXVII		17
And this his rule for aye remains.		310	Psalm XXIX		27
Prayse, Prayse this lord then evermore		311	Psalm XXX		10
On me, from me help this annoy...		311	Psalm XXX		32
Thus much I said, this being said.		311	Psalm XXX		33
All to this point, how my poore life to take...		313	Psalm XXXI		39
For this Our lord preserves the faith full race.		314	Psalm XXXI		65
Whom this lord chose,.		317	Psalm XXXIII		47
This lord and he did heare my cry,		319	Psalm XXXIV		14
This shall men's fancys frame.		319	Psalm XXXIV		17
For lo, this Wretch did call,.		319	Psalm XXXIV		21
How this Our lord to feare..		320	Psalm XXXIV		44
This lord is ever ever neare,.		320	Psalm XXXIV		66
So my good deeds they pay with this ev'ill share,.		322	Psalm XXXV		27
This thou hast seen, and wilt thou silent be?.		322	Psalm XXXV		55
O Soul, rejoyce, we made this wretch our prey.		323	Psalm XXXV		62
And this delight to them is granted,		325	Psalm XXXVII		31
Shall dwell thereon, and this their blessing		326	Psalm XXXVII		75
Look but on this: man still doth riches heape.		330	Psalm XXXIX		21
This being thus, For what O Lord wait I?		330	Psalm XXXIX		23
O helpe o help me, this farr yet I crave,.		330	Psalm XXXIX		25
Of This sweet righteousness.		331	Psalm XL		37
Aha! This is good game..		332	Psalm XL		60
When, when will death o'retake this wretched wight		333	Psalm XLI		19
But what? This doth already well appeare		333	Psalm XLI		37
If this in them be true, as true in men think I.		343	Possibly	1	7
Yeelde yeelde, O yeelde, you that this Forte do holde,		345	Possibly	4	1
Yeelde yeelde O yeelde, who first this Fort did make,.		345	Possibly	4	9
Remorse in you to doe this Fortresse harme,		346	Possibly	5	6
While thus they liv'd, (this was indede a life).		243	Other Poems	4	58
This while, though poore, they in themselves did raigne.		243	Other Poems	4	64
And saw this fairest maid of fairer minde,		244	Other Poems	4	90
This done, but done with captive-killing grace,		244	Other Poems	4	105
Besides this force, within hir eies he kept.		246	Other Poems	4	153
But if they had, could shephockes this resist?		246	Other Poems	4	160
This mote from out his eye, this inward burre,		246	Other Poems	4	172
Which made hir yeeld to deck this shepheards' band,		247	Other Poems	4	215
Cosma this while to Strephon safely came,		249	Other Poems	4	265
But all this while another course he fet...		249	Other Poems	4	280
But this straunge race more straunge conceits did yeeld:		251	Other Poems	4	345
But after this to greater rage it broke,		253	Other Poems	4	429
Say then, can this but of enchantment come?.		254	Other Poems	4	472
"For though like waxe, this magique makes me waste,.		254	Other Poems	4	489
As this same sprite about my fancies blinde,		255	Other Poems	4	502
This song she singes in most commaunding wise:		255	Other Poems	4	509
This said, this done, he rase even tir'd with rest,.		255	Other Poems	4	521
This morne alone to lonely walke did passe,.		255	Other Poems	4	533
So may your Make, this wholsome springtime aire,		257	Other Poems	5	42
This said, at length he ended.		259	Other Poems	5	114
In this wood a man I met.		262	Other Poems	7	7
These same words, or this effecting:		262	Other Poems	7	18
Then this false, fine, Courtly pleasure.		263	Other Poems	7	48
Learning this among the rest,.		264	Other Poems	7	75
THISTLES					
Thus is our thought with paine for thistles tilled:.		62	2nd Eclogues	30	173
THITHER					
My boiling sprites did thither soone incline,		172	Astrophil	16	3
Thither the World for justice shall repaire,		280	Psalm IX		23
THITHERWARD					
They saw a maid who thitherward did runne,		244	Other Poems	4	83
I thinke you thinke Strephon bent thitherward.		250	Other Poems	4	320
THORN					
Sings out her woes, a thorne her song-booke making:.		137	Cert Sonnets	4	4
Thy thorne without, my thorne my heart invadeth.		137	Cert Sonnets	4	12
Above line repeated at following location.		137	Cert Sonnets	4	24
Then do they pull from sharpe and niggard thorne		243	Other Poems	4	51
THORNS					
So nimble feet as stirre still, though on thornes:		206	Astrophil	78	11
THORNY					
Why shouldst thou toyle our thornie soile to till?		169	Astrophil	10	6
THOROUGH					
Ffayre, thorow fayre strykes of heedefull Looke.		88	Arcadia III	62 V	70
But Thou (O lord) give them a thorough fall,		284	Psalm XII		7
THOROUGHEST					
The thorowest words, fit for woe's selfe to grone,		193	Astrophil	57	4
THOSE					
As for those parts unknowne, which hidden sure are best:		12	Arcadia I	3	13
For other be those tunes which sorrow tyes,.		13	Arcadia I	4	7
From those cleere notes which freely may rejoyce...		13	Arcadia I	4	8
Nor true love loves those loves with others mingled be...		14	1st Eclogues	7	12
On me to cast those eyes, where shine nobilitie.		19	1st Eclogues	7	178
In those weake harts that his advice receave...		21	1st Eclogues	8	34
Of all those fooles that will have all they see.		22	1st Eclogues	8	48
Those rebell thoughts which are thy slaves by kinde.		23	1st Eclogues	9	46
Histor. Those woordes dyd once the Loveliest shepard use		24	1st Eclogues	9	62

THOSE   (CONTINUED)   PAGE   TITLE   LINE

Those pleasant plants, those sweete and frutefull trees, . .   26 1st Eclogues 9   130
Of all the birdes, but namely those were grieved,. . . . . .   29 1st Eclogues 10   83
Happy be those mishapps which, justly proportion holding,. .   32 1st Eclogues 13   17
What be the pangs they beare, and whence those pangs be
   derived, ...   33 1st Eclogues 13   43
Then shall those thinges ease their inward horrible angwish.   33 1st Eclogues 13   46
Of those fortune lulls, so small rest rests in a kingdome. .   34 1st Eclogues 13   90
Torne with her hands, and those same hands of snow . . . . .   58 2nd Eclogues 30   45
Shall I that saw those brests, where beauties flow,. . . . .   58 2nd Eclogues 30   47
And saw those eyes (those Sonnes) such shoures to shew,. . .   58 2nd Eclogues 30   49
Relent those thoughts, which then did so displease?. . . . .   58 2nd Eclogues 30   52
To those high powers, which idly sit above,. . . . .   58 2nd Eclogues 30   63
Those beames that set so many harts on fire? . . . .   59 2nd Eclogues 30   84
O much more then words: those words serv'd more to me
   blesse Lesse. . . . .   64 2nd Eclogues 31   31
Mock'st thou those Diamonds which only be matcht by the
   gods Ods. . . . .   65 2nd Eclogues 31   47
Those secrett joyes, which heaven to me emparte, ...   70 Arcadia III   35   14
Like those sicke folkes, in whome strange humors flowe,. . .   74 Arcadia III   41   1
Preserve those beames, this age's onely lighte:. . . . . . .   79 Arcadia III   51   2
Like to my brother's raies, yet those I sende. . . . .   82 Arcadia III   55   14
To ease those paines, which on desire do waite). . . . . . .   82 Arcadia III   56   4
That doth present those even browes, ...   86 Arcadia III   62   9
For the blacke starres those Spheares containe,. . . . . . .   86 Arcadia III   62   15
But who those ruddie lippes can misse? . . . .   87 Arcadia III   62   37
Those thighes, for Ovid's song more fitte; . . . .   88 Arcadia III   62   88
And thence those armes derived are;. . . . .   89 Arcadia III   62   117
There fall those Saphir-coloured brookes,. . . . .   90 Arcadia III   62   127
And Arches bee to those fayre Lyddes . . . .   86 Arcadia III   62 V 13
By those great beastes, as for the weaker's good,. . . . . . 102 3rd Eclogues 66   128
Gainst those of might, of whom in feare they stood,. . . . . 102 3rd Eclogues 66   130
Those passions which to youthfull head doo clime, ... 107 3rd Eclogues 67   116
Be those despaires, which have my hopes quite wast.. . . . . 114 4th Eclogues 72   37
The diffrence is; all folkes those stormes forbeare: . . . . 114 4th Eclogues 72   38
But now those living lights absented be, ... 116 4th Eclogues 72   85
But vaine it is to thinke those paines should cease, ... 116 4th Eclogues 72   94
Did light those beamye stars which greater light did darke:. 116 4th Eclogues 73   3
Free all my powers were from those captiving snares, ... 117 4th Eclogues 73   17
Those lampes of heav'nly fire to fixed motion bound, ... 118 4th Eclogues 73   43
Those names abasht me much, when those great names I hard: . 119 4th Eclogues 73   79
Of all those Graces' giftes the heavens have ever lent.. . . 119 4th Eclogues 73   86
Is this thy fruite O strife? those thousand churches hie,. . 119 4th Eclogues 73   111
Those thousand altars faire now in the dust to lie?. . . . . 119 4th Eclogues 73   112
(Unto thy selfe I do meane those graces dwell so within
   thee . . . . 122 4th Eclogues 74   9
Can those eyes, that of eyes drownd in most harty flowing
   teares,. . . . . 122 4th Eclogues 74   15
Can those eyes now yeeld to the kind conceit of a sorow, . . 122 4th Eclogues 74   17
You should those faire eyes have with a veile covered. . . . 123 4th Eclogues 74   48
But foole, foole that I am, those eyes would shine from a
   dark cave. . . . . 123 4th Eclogues 74   49
Or those golden lockes, those lockes which lock me to
   bondage, ... 123 4th Eclogues 74   51
On those affectes which easily yeeld to sight, ... 135 Cert Sonnets 2   6
Like those whom dreames make uglie monsters see, ... 136 Cert Sonnets 2   11
Where bee nowe those Joyes, that I lately tasted?. . . . . . 138 Cert Sonnets 5   5
Where bee nowe those eyes ever Inly persers? . . . . 138 Cert Sonnets 5   6
Where bee now those wordes never Idelly wasted,. . . . . . . 138 Cert Sonnets 5   7
Where bee those wellcomes by no worthe deserved? . . . . . . 138 Cert Sonnets 5   10
Where bee those movinges, the Delights, the graces?. . . . . 138 Cert Sonnets 5   11
But betweene those armes, never else do leave mee; . . . . . 138 Cert Sonnets 5   23
And so no helpe gainst envy of those powers? . . . . 142 Cert Sonnets 10   12
If thus, alas: yet while those partes have wo, ... 142 Cert Sonnets 10   13
To twist those broyles, which hardly would untwine:. . . . . 146 Cert Sonnets 17   22
Sweet Ladie, as for those whose sullen cheare, ... 147 Cert Sonnets 17   46
Why those that die, men say they do depart:. . . . . 148 Cert Sonnets 20   2
Finding those beames, which I must ever love,. . . . . 149 Cert Sonnets 21   1
And knowne those pangs that the losers prove,. . . . . 153 Cert Sonnets 24   2
What kind of fires they be in which those spirits melt,. . . 153 Cert Sonnets 24   7
Those bands alas shall not be dissolv'd. . . . . 153 Cert Sonnets 24   20
For if those flames burne my desire, ... 153 Cert Sonnets 24   26
That trust those killing eyes, I would,. . . . . 158 Cert Sonnets 28   19
That of those beames in you do tarie:. . . . . 159 Cert Sonnets 29   11
Least if no vaile those brave gleames did disguise,. . . . . 168 Astrophil   7   7
Which dare claime from those lights the name of best,. . . . 169 Astrophil   9   11
Leave sense, and those which sense's objects be. . . . . . . 169 Astrophil   10   7
That those lips swell, so full of thee they bee, ... 170 Astrophil   12   3
Thou countest Stella thine, like those whose powers. . . . . 171 Astrophil   12   9
Of those three gods, whose armes the fairest were: . . . . . 171 Astrophil   13   2
You take wrong waies, those far-fet helpes be such,. . . . . 172 Astrophil   15   9
But finding not those restlesse flames in me,. . . . . 173 Astrophil   16   5
I thought those babes of some pinne's hurt did whine,. . . . 173 Astrophil   16   7
Of all those goods, which heav'n to me hath lent:. . . . . . 173 Astrophil   18   4
My wit doth strive those passions to defend. . . . . 174 Astrophil   18   10
Whence those same fumes of melancholy rise,. . . . . 176 Astrophil   23   3
Yet to those fooles heav'n such wit doth impart, ... 177 Astrophil   24   5
(Exil'd for ay from those high treasures, which. . . . . . . 177 Astrophil   24   13
And so nor will, nor can, behold those skies . . . . 177 Astrophil   25   7
And fooles can thinke those Lampes of purest light,. . . . . 177 Astrophil   26   2

514

THOSE   (CONTINUED)   PAGE   TITLE   LINE

And know those Bodies high raigne on the low.. . . . .   178 Astrophil   26   11
By only those two starres in Stella's face.. . . . .   178 Astrophil   26   14
With me those paines for God's sake do not take: . . . . . .   179 Astrophil   28   3
Those Lovers scorne whom that Love doth possesse?. . . . . .   180 Astrophil   31   13
Rich in those gifts which give th'eternall crowne; . . . . .   183 Astrophil   37   11
Of those fierce darts, dispaire at me doth throw:. . . . . .   184 Astrophil   39   6
O make in me those civill warres to cease; . . . .   184 Astrophil   39   7
Then with those eyes he lookes, lo by and by . . . .   186 Astrophil   43   6
Those daintie dores unto the Court of blisse,. . . . .   187 Astrophil   44   11
Can those blacke beames such burning markes engrave. . . . .   188 Astrophil   47   2
Soule's joy, bend not those morning starres from me, ...   188 Astrophil   48   1
While those poore babes their death in birth do find:. . . .   190 Astrophil   50   11
When I might reade those letters faire of blisse,. . . . . .   193 Astrophil   56   5
Even those sad words even in sad me did breed. . . . .   194 Astrophil   58   14
This sowre-breath'd mate tast of those sugred lips.. . . . .   194 Astrophil   59   11
Stella, those faire lines, which true goodnesse show.. . . .   201 Astrophil   71   4
Of reason, from whose light those night-birds flie;. . . . .   201 Astrophil   71   7
Those scarlet judges, threatning bloudy paine? . . . .   203 Astrophil   73   11
Those lookes, whose beames be joy, whose motion is delight,.   205 Astrophil   77   1
Those lips, which make death's pay a meane price for a
  kisse . . . .   205 Astrophil   77   6
Those words, which do sublime the quintessence of blisse:. .   205 Astrophil   77   8
Infected by those vapours, which arise . . . .   205 Astrophil   78   2
O kisse, which doest those ruddie gemmes impart, ...   207 Astrophil   81   1
From comming neare those Cherries banish me: . . . .   208 Astrophil   82   8
But you must needs with those lips billing be? . . . .   208 Astrophil   83   12
And through those lips drinke Nectar from that toong;. . . .   208 Astrophil   83   13
Let breath sucke up those sweetes, let armes embrace . . . .   210 Astrophil   85   12
Then those blest eyes, where all my hopes do dwell,. . . . .   212 Astrophil   86   13
Bringing with her those starry Nimphs, whose chace . . . . .   229 Astrophil   97   3
Making those Lillies and those Roses grow, ...   231 Astrophil   100   2
And joy, which is inseperate from those eyes,. . . . .   231 Astrophil   101   7
Where be those Roses gone, which sweetned so our eyes? . . .   232 Astrophil   102   1
Where those red cheeks, which oft with faire encrease did
  frame. . . . .   232 Astrophil   102   2
How doth the colour vade of those vermillion dies, ...   232 Astrophil   102   5
While those faire planets on thy streames did shine. . . . .   232 Astrophil   103   4
And faine those Aeols' youthes there would their stay. . . .   233 Astrophil   103   9
First did with puffing kisse those lockes display: . . . . .   233 Astrophil   103   11
Yet those lips so sweetly swelling,. . . . .   203 A&S 2nd Song   21
See now those feathers pluckt, wherewith thou flewst most
  high:. . . . .   213 A&S 5th Song   22
Those faire wonders to behold, ...   226 A&S 10th Song   17
There those roses for to kisse,. . . . .   226 A&S 10th Song   28
Thinke, thinke of those dalyings,. . . . .   226 A&S 10th Song   37
Be not yet those fancies changed?" . . . .   234 A&S 11th Song   7
"If those eyes you praised, be . . . .   220 A&S 8th Song   81
Of those eyes, and blinder minded. . . . .   220 A&S 8th Song   84
Thou those men's teeth which byte, ...   273 Psalm III   28
And on those blessed same, ...   273 Psalm III   34
Therfore he doth defy all those. . . . .   282 Psalm X   21
Those lying lipps from Cousening head remove,. . . . .   284 Psalm XII   8
Up lord prevent those gaping jawes . . . .   290 Psalm XVII   35
And bring to naught those watching pawes.. . . . .   290 Psalm XVII   36
Not I but thou throw'st down those, who 'gainst me do rise;.   292 Psalm XVIII   72
I bett those folks as small as dust, which wind doth rayse;.   293 Psalm XVIII   76
And God shall be by those his seekers praysed. . . . .   300 Psalm XXII   62
Let not those foes that me annoy . . . .   303 Psalm XXV   5
Let those things Thy remembrance grave,. . . . .   303 Psalm XXV   23
And with those hands about Thy Altar waite,. . . . .   305 Psalm XXVI   21
Because of those . . . .   308 Psalm XXVII   53
To thy self those words apply. . . . .   309 Psalm XXVIII   9
I hated have those men whose thoughts do cleave. . . . . . .   312 Psalm XXXI   16
Let those lipps be made dumbe which love to ly, ...   313 Psalm XXXI   49
To whom feare Thee? what thou hast done for those. . . . . .   313 Psalm XXXI   53
Ev'en people that, ev'en those . . . .   317 Psalm XXXIII   46
Those raveners' whelps oft starved be, ...   319 Psalm XXXIV   38
Is bent, but bent against those same . . . .   320 Psalm XXXIV   58
Yea take Thy lance and stop the way of those . . . .   321 Psalm XXXV   4
Confound those folks, thrust them in shamefull hole. . . . .   321 Psalm XXXV   7
Rebuke and wracke on those wrong doers throw,. . . . .   321 Psalm XXXV   9
Who helpest those, whose ruin was so neere,. . . . .   321 Psalm XXXV   23
For those same eyes his flatterers be. . . . .   323 Psalm XXXVI   7
For those badd folks at last shall perish, ...   325 Psalm XXXVII   23
Those vile scoffes of naughty ones . . . .   335 Psalm XLII   45
Now let those lightsomme sights we see thy darknes overcome.   343 Possibly   1   12
And in those gifts that years distribute doe,. . . . .   242 Other Poems   4   22
While those restles desires in great men rife. . . . .   243 Other Poems   4   62
Then those delights through all their sinews breed . . . . .   252 Other Poems   4   411
That from those eies where heav'nly apples bene, ...   253 Other Poems   4   450
Those eies, which nothing like themselves can see, ...   253 Other Poems   4   451
Then want one hower those eyes which my joyes keepe. . . . .   259 Other Poems   5   102
"Nay, what neede the Arte to those,. . . . .   263 Other Poems   7   31
Sooner these than those in hearing.. . . . .   263 Other Poems   7   54
Grant me with those two remaining. . . . .   263 Other Poems   7   66
THOUGH
Though not so white as is thy lovely face, ...   4 Lady of May   2   20
No, though the heav'ns for high attempts have blamed me, . .   15 1st Eclogues   7   22
Thy pipe, o Pan, shall helpe, though I sing sorilie. . . . .   15 1st Eclogues   7   27

THOUGH	(CONTINUED)	PAGE	TITLE		LINE
Who though she be no Bee, yet full of honie is:.		15	1st Eclogues	7	29
Though woes now live, at length thy woes must dye.		22	1st Eclogues	9	12
Though cradle witted, must not honnor loose.		25	1st Eclogues	9	92
Thy words, though full of malapert offence,.		25	1st Eclogues	9	108
For though Melampus like a wolfe doo looke,.		27	1st Eclogues	10	16
You, though feares do abash, in you still possible hopes be:		32	1st Eclogues	13	23
What marvaile tho a Prince transforme himselfe to a Pastor?.		34	1st Eclogues	13	91
Unto a silly caban, though weake, yet stronger against woes.		34	1st Eclogues	13	93
Better yet do I live, that though by my thoughts I be plunged.		35	1st Eclogues	13	107
Sweete Juniper saith this, thoh I burne, yet I burne in a sweete fire.		35	1st Eclogues	13	120
And may I not (say I then) gett up though griefs be so weightie?.		36	1st Eclogues	13	128
That her I see, though you did lose your light..		38	Arcadia II	14	4
Though thousands old, a Boy entit'led still.		41	Arcadia II	20	10
Which ever shines, though hid from earth by earthly shade, .		44	Arcadia II	26	3
R. Though we cannot orecome, our cause is just..		47	2nd Eclogues	27	31
Yet is it seale, though errour, of true hart..		51	2nd Eclogues	28	104
For though life irkes, in life my loves protected be.. . . .		51	2nd Eclogues	28	125
With name engrav'd: so though thy bodie die, ...		56	2nd Eclogues	29	130
Though in despaire, for love so forcethe me;		58	2nd Eclogues	30	57
Let us not winke though void of purest sightfulnes..		61	2nd Eclogues	30	139
Though you besides such graces earth hath lent,.		77	Arcadia III	49	3
Nay higher thoughtes (though thralled thoughtes) I call. . .		78	Arcadia III	49	13
Though each of them, his private forme preserve, ...		78	Arcadia III	50	3
Though each possesse a divers working kinde, ...		78	Arcadia III	50	7
And though my mones be not in musicke bound, ...		81	Arcadia III	54	7
Shall barr that wrong, and though it not prevaile.		82	Arcadia III	55	13
No wondre then, though sighte my sighte did tainte,.		83	Arcadia III	57	5
And though thereby my fancie was infected, ...		83	Arcadia III	57	6
Though (yoked so) my minde with sicknes fainte,.		83	Arcadia III	57	7
When they though divers do together meete:		92	3rd Eclogues	63	34
Which though of glittring golde, shall heere take rust . . .		92	3rd Eclogues	63	57
And (though against his will) on him she leand,.		95	3rd Eclogues	64	44
Though full of scorne, would not his duty misse.		96	3rd Eclogues	64	69
Amid my sheepe, though I saw nought to feare, ...		99	3rd Eclogues	66	15
Ape should thing gave, though he did mowing stand,.		101	3rd Eclogues	66	97
Because (though hurt) they never heard her grone..		102	3rd Eclogues	66	119
Tho when they saw their foen of greatnes kilde..		102	3rd Eclogues	66	133
Her flight from me, from me, though dead to me,.		115	4th Eclogues	72	82
As though she were the same, as when by Paris' doome		120	4th Eclogues	73	145
In ashes of despaire (though burnt) shall make thee live". .		121	4th Eclogues	73	174
Ah, that, that do I not conceive, though that to me leefe were		122	4th Eclogues	74	19
But foole, foole that I am, tho I had but a hair of her head found,.		123	4th Eclogues	74	53
Though I be hers, she makes of me no treasure.		137	Cert Sonnets	3	24
But no more wordes, thoughe such a worde bee spoken, ...		138	Cert Sonnets	5	17
No, though tongue to roofe be cleaved, ...		139	Cert Sonnets	7	8
Though present times and past with evils be snarde,.		143	Cert Sonnets	12	13
Then to my selfe, not though Jove grew a suter of hers.. . .		143	Cert Sonnets	13	2
Though rapt with beautie's hooke, I did impart		150	Cert Sonnets	22	26
Till knit with cold, though there unknowne remaine,.		150	Cert Sonnets	22	33
Which though despisde, yet still doth truth endure..		150	Cert Sonnets	22	40
Keeping that forme, though void of wonted heate:.		151	Cert Sonnets	22	48
Nor breake my word though reward come late,.		153	Cert Sonnets	24	21
Nor change in change, though change change my state.		153	Cert Sonnets	24	23
For though my sense be from me,.		154	Cert Sonnets	25	21
Though in paine, cannot complaine. No, no, no, no..		156	Cert Sonnets	26	33
Though hope were mixt with feare, ...		158	Cert Sonnets	28	6
Though he the lively forme receiveth:.		159	Cert Sonnets	29	17
For though she passe all things, yet what is all		174	Astrophil	19	9
Though dustie wits dare scorne Astrologie, ...		177	Astrophil	26	1
The raines of Love I love, though never slake, ...		179	Astrophil	28	7
And joy therein, though Nations count it shame..		179	Astrophil	28	8
Who though most rich in these and everie part, ...		183	Astrophil	37	12
For though I never see them, but straight wayes.		186	Astrophil	42	9
Not though thereof the cause her selfe she know:		187	Astrophil	45	4
Though false, yet with free scope more grace doth breed. . .		187	Astrophil	45	10
So long (though he from booke myche to desire)		188	Astrophil	46	13
Who for long faith, tho dayly helpe I crave, ...		188	Astrophil	47	7
For though I oft my selfe of them bemone, ...		189	Astrophil	48	9
And therefore, though her beautie and her grace.		191	Astrophil	52	9
She in whose eyes Love, though unfelt, doth shine, ...		196	Astrophil	62	3
Nor ought do care, though some above me sit, ...		198	Astrophil	64	11
And though she give but thus conditionly		200	Astrophil	69	12
Shall paint out joy, though but in blacke and white.		201	Astrophil	70	11
Desire, though thou my old companion art,.		202	Astrophil	72	1
Though strongly hedg'd of bloudy Lyon's pawes, ...		204	Astrophil	75	10
So nimble feet as stirre still, though on thornes:		206	Astrophil	78	11
For though full of desire, emptie of wit,.		208	Astrophil	82	9
As though that faire soft hand did you great wrong..		208	Astrophil	83	4
Tho worlds quite me, shall I my selfe forgive?		227	Astrophil	93	11
Though harbengers of death lodge there his traine.		228	Astrophil	94	8
That though in wretchednesse thy life doth lie,.		228	Astrophil	94	12
Though oft himselfe my mate-in-armes he sware.		228	Astrophil	95	8
Thou though still tired, yet still doost it detest..		229	Astrophil	96	14
But wo is me, though joy it selfe were she,.		230	Astrophil	97	12

516

```
THOUGH                     (CONTINUED)                    PAGE  TITLE           LINE
   (Spurd with love's spur, though gald and shortly raind . . .   230 Astrophil   98    7
   Sicke, thirsty, glad (though but of empty glasse:) . . . . .   233 Astrophil  104   11
   Which pants as though it still should leape to thee: . . . .   236 Astrophil  107    6
   Yet thought and speech do live, though metamorphosd quite: .   212 A&S 5th Song     14
   And o my Muse, though oft you luld her in your lap,. . . . .   213 A&S 5th Song     25
   Who faileth one, is false, though trusty to another. . . . .   214 A&S 5th Song     72
   A witch I say thou art, though thou so faire appeare;. . . .   214 A&S 5th Song     74
   I say thou art a Devill, though clothd in Angel's shining: .   215 A&S 5th Song     81
   Though from me you be estranged, . . . . . . . . . . . . . .   234 A&S 11th Song     9
   Least, though I leave not thy love,. . . . . . . . . . . . .   220 A&S 8th Song     98
   Tho against me shee persever,. . . . . . . . . . . . . . . .   221 A&S 9th Song     19
   Tho I blisse enherit never.. . . . . . . . . . . . . . . . .   221 A&S 9th Song     20
   Though legions round be layd,. . . . . . . . . . . . . . . .   272 Psalm III        20
   For though in lesse than Angel's state . . . . . . . . . . .   279 Psalm VIII       17
   Though my Works reach not to Thee. . . . . . . . . . . . . .   287 Psalm XVI         6
   Ev'en Feare makes strangers shew much love though much
      untrue. . . . . . . . . . . . . . . . . . . . . . . . . .   293 Psalm XVIII      81
   Doth melt away though it be inmost seated. . . . . . . . . .   299 Psalm XXII       34
   Yea tho I should thro vallys stray . . . . . . . . . . . . .   301 Psalm XXIII      10
   Though it be great in me.. . . . . . . . . . . . . . . . . .   304 Psalm XXV        46
   Then though against me armys were,. . . . . . . . . . . . .    307 Psalm XXVII      13
   Though battaile's brunt I needs must beare,. . . . . . . . .   307 Psalm XXVII      15
   Though Father's Care, and Mother's love. . . . . . . . . . .   308 Psalm XXVII      49
   Is strong though he be gracious, . . . . . . . . . . . . . .   310 Psalm XXIX       11
   Though ill deeds well succeeding be. . . . . . . . . . . . .   324 Psalm XXXVII      4
   Though all his plotts without misfortune . . . . . . . . . .   325 Psalm XXXVII     19
   Though he do fall no wracke he proveth,. . . . . . . . . . .   326 Psalm XXXVII     59
   Though I did seek, I never found.. . . . . . . . . . . . . .   327 Psalm XXXVII     92
   Tho I in want be shrinking,. . . . . . . . . . . . . . . . .   332 Psalm XL         65
   To God's Altars tho. . . . . . . . . . . . . . . . . . . . .   336 Psalm XLIII      19
   Dick. Ah Will, though I grudge not, I count it feeble glee .   343 Possibly    1     3
   Fayrenesse though fayer, is but a feeble shielde,. . . . . .   345 Possibly    4     6
   No force, though force be used, Allarme allarme. . . . . . .   346 Possibly    5     8
   This while, though poore, they in themselves did raigne. . .   243 Other Poems 4    64
   Geron, though olde yet gamesome, kept one ende . . . . . . .   248 Other Poems 4   242
   Though they do fly, yet backwardly do glowe. . . . . . . . .   249 Other Poems 4   292
   Though him to meete at all she sturred nought. . . . . . . .   250 Other Poems 4   326
   Though with soft leggs, did run as fast as he. . . . . . . .   250 Other Poems 4   339
   Yet thoughts do flie, though I can scarcely creep. . . . . .   253 Other Poems 4   444
   I still do see, though I be still alone. . . . . . . . . . .   254 Other Poems 4   462
   "For though like waxe, this magique makes me waste,. . . . .   254 Other Poems 4   489
   Though thus, and worse, though now I am at last, . . . . . .   254 Other Poems 4   493
THOUGHT
   Thus all my thoughts are slaves to one thought still:. . . .    12 Arcadia I   2    10
   The thought of which doth passe all worldly pelfe. . . . . .    18 1st Eclogues 7  130
   Which thought doth marre my piping declaration,. . . . . . .    19 1st Eclogues 7  168
   My virgin life no spotted thought shall staine.. . . . . . .    40 Arcadia II  18    6
   Dorus. Sight is his roote, in thought is his progression,. .    48 2nd Eclogues 28  37
   Dorus. If I had thought to heare blasphemous wordes, . . . .    50 2nd Eclogues 28  79
   Nico. And are you there old Pas? in troth I ever thought,. .    51 2nd Eclogues 29   1
   But still (me thought) with beauties from her fell,. . . . .    55 2nd Eclogues 29 106
   Alas (said I) this babe dooth nurce my thought. . . . . . .     55 2nd Eclogues 29 113
   O braine, where thought of her hath onely place; . . . . . .    60 2nd Eclogues 30 118
   Thus is our thought with paine for thistles tilled:. . . . .    62 2nd Eclogues 30 173
   Woe, but seems to me joy, that agrees to my thought so. I
      thought so.. . . . . . . . . . . . . . . . . . . . . . .     64 2nd Eclogues 31  38
   Each sight draws on a thought, thought mother of science,. .    69 2nd Eclogues 34  11
   May keepe my thoughtes, from thought of wonted light.. . . .    73 Arcadia III 39   14
   So still me thought in me his hurt did smart:. . . . . . . .    76 Arcadia III 45   12
   Thought, thinke to ende, too long the frute of thought . . .    83 Arcadia III 59    7
   In stede of Thought, true pleasure be begunne,. . . . . . .     84 Arcadia III 59   15
   But ah, alas! (In vayne) my minde, sight, thought, . . . . .    84 Arcadia III 60   11
   In curled knots man's thought to hold: . . . . . . . . . . .    85 Arcadia III 62    4
   In thies delights the wandring thought . . . . . . . . . . .    88 Arcadia III 62   71
   But that her husband thought her service bent. . . . . . . .    95 3rd Eclogues 64  27
   He forst her thinke that which she never thought.. . . . . .    95 3rd Eclogues 64  34
   Asse, pacience; the Mole, a working thought; . . . . . . . .   101 3rd Eclogues 66  86
   Despise delight, am tyrde with thought of ease;. . . . . . .   113 4th Eclogues 72   2
   Such thoughts, me thought, I thought, and straind my single
      mind . . . . . . . . . . . . . . . . . . . . . . . . . .    118 4th Eclogues 73  49
   I, wretch, astonisht was, and thought the deathfull doome. .   118 4th Eclogues 73  61
   The mountaines great with childe I thought brought foorth a
      mouse. . . . . . . . . . . . . . . . . . . . . . . . . .    118 4th Eclogues 73  76
   I never spited you, but thought you overwise.. . . . . . . .   121 4th Eclogues 73 150
   In fine, since strife of thought that marres the mind,. . .    135 Cert Sonnets 1    8
   From deepe vaine thought that I may not be true. . . . . . .   145 Cert Sonnets 17   5
   Tell how ill thought disgrac'd my doing well:. . . . . . . .   146 Cert Sonnets 17  13
   Thought, reason, sense, time, you, and I, maintaine. . . . .   148 Cert Sonnets 19  18
   For such a thought most highlie prized,. . . . . . . . . . .   159 Cert Sonnets 29  14
   Fond fancie's scum, and dregs of scattred thought,. . . . .    161 Cert Sonnets 31   2
   Deceiv'd the quaking boy, who thought from so pure light,. .   169 Astrophil   8    10
   And, Love, I thought that I was full of thee:. . . . . . . .   172 Astrophil  16     4
   I thought those babes of some pinne's hurt did whine,. . . .   173 Astrophil  16     7
   Unseene, unheard, while thought to highest place . . . . . .   178 Astrophil  27    13
   To hatch mine eyes, and that unbitted thought. . . . . . . .   183 Astrophil  38     2
   Thou canst vouchsafe the influence of a thought. . . . . . .   184 Astrophil  40     6
   Yet let this thought thy Tygrish courage passe:. . . . . . .   198 Astrophil  65    11
   Thought with good cause thou likest so well the night, . . .   229 Astrophil  96     1
   But soone as thought of thee breeds my delight,. . . . . . .   236 Astrophil 108     5
```

THOUGHT	(CONTINUED)	PAGE	TITLE		LINE
Thought waited on delight, and speech did follow thought:. .		212	A&S 5th Song		2
I thought all words were lost, that were not spent of thee:.		212	A&S 5th Song		4
I thought each place was darke but where thy lights would be		212	A&S 5th Song		5
Yet thought and speech do live, though metamorphosd quite: .		212	A&S 5th Song		14
I thinke now of thy faults, who late thought of thy praise,.		213	A&S 5th Song		16
Only thought aymes at the pleasure.		226	A&S 10th Song		12
Thought therefore I will send thee,.		226	A&S 10th Song		13
Thought see thou no place forbeare,.		226	A&S 10th Song		19
O my thought my thoughts surcease, ...		227	A&S 10th Song		43
"If that any thought in me,.		220	A&S 8th Song		77
Lo he that first conceiv'd a wretched thought, ...		278	Psalm VII		37
Is their own foot, ledd by their own ill thought,.		280	Psalm IX		49
In craft of his own crafty thought!.		281	Psalm X		8
Nay so proud is his puffed thought		281	Psalm X		13
His guiltie heart with this fond thought hath fed, ...		286	Psalm XIV		2
In thought and conversation.		295	Psalm XIX		58
But led by wicked thought.		306	Psalm XXVI		32
She staid in them, they went in thought with hyr:.		246	Other Poems	4	170
Meaning with absence to refresh the thought.		246	Other Poems	4	175
Pas thought it hell, while he was Cosma fro.		248	Other Poems	4	245
He thought gray haires afforded subtletie.		248	Other Poems	4	256
Most mad with beames which he thought Cosma sent,.		249	Other Poems	4	270
And thought it heav'n so to be drawn to hell.		250	Other Poems	4	312
To his owne witt, thought upon thought did swell, ...		256	Other Poems	4	542
THOUGHTS					
Are all my thoughts, in which I live or die:		3	Lady of May	2	10
Seeke other thoughts thy life or death to find;.		4	Lady of May	2	15
Whereto mine inward thoughts did faintly yeeld;.		11	Arcadia I	2	6
Thus all my thoughts are slaves to one thought still:. . .		12	Arcadia I	2	10
And thus my thoughtes, can thinke but one thing still. . .		12	Arcadia I	2	V810
Seemde but to spoyle the foode of thoughts long famished...		16	1st Eclogues	7	69
Save then my soule, spill not my thoughts well heaped, . .		16	1st Eclogues	7	80
My eyes the sparkes, my thoughts the fatall knot.		17	1st Eclogues	7	113
In which do light small birds of thoughts orethrowne:. . .		18	1st Eclogues	7	141
Those rebell thoughts which are thy slaves by kinde. . . .		23	1st Eclogues	9	46
Truly not I, who did my thoughts engage, ...		26	1st Eclogues	9	136
Better yet do I live, that though by my thoughts I be plunged.		35	1st Eclogues	13	107
Lyke to my noble thoughtes, still new, well plac'd, to me fruteles..		35	1st Eclogues	13	124
Thus be my thoughts disperst, thus thinking nurseth a thinking,.		36	1st Eclogues	13	139
Of my owne harte, where thoughts be the temple, sighte is an aultar.		37	1st Eclogues	13	171
My sheepe are thoughts, which I both guide and serve:. . .		39	Arcadia II	17	1
My thoughts imprisonde in my secreat woes, ...		42	Arcadia II	21	7
What foresight tels; our thoughts upon thy knowledge staye..		45	Arcadia II	26	12
To witnes, that he thinkes his thoughts delicious, ...		47	2nd Eclogues	28	5
Till of these thoughts thy sodaine ende bereaved me. . . .		48	2nd Eclogues	28	33
Where chaunge of thoughts one foole to other shewes, . . .		57	2nd Eclogues	30	21
Relent those thoughts, which then did so displease?. . . .		58	2nd Eclogues	30	52
In him, the thoughts of Phaeton's damme to grave:.		60	2nd Eclogues	30	106
Can thoughts still thinking so rest unappalled?.		61	2nd Eclogues	30	166
Long be thy woes for such newes, but how recks she my thoughts? Oughts..		64	2nd Eclogues	31	33
My fancy amazde, my thoughtes dull'd,.		66	2nd Eclogues	32	13
Undermin'd with a speech the pearcer of thoughts..		68	2nd Eclogues	33	16
And wise thoughts do behold what the creator is:		68	2nd Eclogues	34	6
Nowe that I spye the haven my thoughtes requyre, ...		72	Arcadia III	37	15
My thoughts forget: my thoughts, which never swerve. . . .		72	Arcadia III	38	3
May keepe my thoughtes, from thought of wonted light.. . .		73	Arcadia III	39	14
And highest thoughts, downeward most headlong throw? . . .		73	Arcadia III	40	12
My hart in him, his thoughtes and senses guides:		76	Arcadia III	45	6
That wounding thee, my thoughtes in thee I grave:.		77	Arcadia III	47	2
Since that my thoughtes, as streight as streightnes thine, .		77	Arcadia III	47	3
Such pearcing wordes as no thoughts els conceave:.		78	Arcadia III	49	8
His thoughtes in you, where so sweete thoughtes were spent,.		78	Arcadia III	49	10
For how would you the mistresse' thoughts bereave.		78	Arcadia III	49	11
Of waiting thoughts all to her service ment?		78	Arcadia III	49	12
Nay higher thoughtes (though thralled thoughtes) I call. .		78	Arcadia III	49	13
My thoughtes then hers, who first your ryne did rente, . .		78	Arcadia III	49	14
Then hers, to whom my thoughts alonely thrall.		78	Arcadia III	49	15
Right so my thoughts, whereon my hart I feede:		78	Arcadia III	50	5
All thoughts so spronge, are from their dwelling driv'n, .		83	Arcadia III	57	11
And warr of thoughts is swallow'd up in peace.		91	3rd Eclogues	63	4
Pan store of babes, vertue their thoughts well staid,. . .		93	3rd Eclogues	63	93
Not sturring thoughts, nor yet denying right,.		98	3rd Eclogues	65	6
Long since my thoughts more desert be then forrests: . . .		112	4th Eclogues	71	28
Long since my thoughts chase me like beasts in forrests, .		112	4th Eclogues	71	35
I harowe it with Thoughts, which all conspire.		115	4th Eclogues	72	54
Far from my thoughts was ought, whereto their minds aspire,.		117	4th Eclogues	73	15
And having plaste my thoughts, my thoughts thus placed me..		117	4th Eclogues	73	34
But there I was, and there my calmie thoughts I fedd . . .		117	4th Eclogues	73	39
Such thoughts, me thought, I thought, and straind my single mind		118	4th Eclogues	73	49
Bend your thoghts to the dear sweet words which then to me giv'n were:.		124	4th Eclogues	74	75
In whose sweete heav'n Angels of high thoughts swarme? . .		142	Cert Sonnets 10		8

THOUGHTS   (CONTINUED)   PAGE   TITLE   LINE
    If I could thinke how these my thoughts to leave,. . . . . . 147 Cert Sonnets 19   1
    Or thinking still my thoughts might have good end:. . . . . 147 Cert Sonnets 19   2
    Then might I thinke what thoughts were best to thinke: . . . 148 Cert Sonnets 19   5
    But since my thoughts in thinking still are spent, ... 148 Cert Sonnets 19   13
    Yet live with thoughts closde up, till that she will . . . . 150 Cert Sonnets 22   29
    Whose clowdie thoughts let fall an inward raine. . . . . . . 150 Cert Sonnets 22   36
    Enam'ling with pied flowers their thoughts of gold:. . . . . 166 Astrophil   3   4
    Deale thou with powers of thoughts, leave love to will.. . . 169 Astrophil   10   8
    Of sinfull thoughts, which do in ruine end?. . . . . 172 Astrophil   14   8
    My wits, quicke in vaine thoughts, in vertue lame: . . . . . 175 Astrophil   21   4
    Of all my thoughts hath neither stop nor start,. . . . . . . 176 Astrophil   23   13
    My tongue doth itch, my thoughts in labour be: . . . . 183 Astrophil   37   2
    Are humbled thoughts, which bit of Reverence move, ... 189 Astrophil   49   6
    Stella, the fulnesse of my thoughts of thee. . . . . 189 Astrophil   50   1
    My thoughts I speake, and what I speake doth flow. . . . . . 204 Astrophil   74   10
    Makes me in my best thoughts and quietst judgement see,. . . 205 Astrophil   77   12
    What, doth high place ambitious thoughts augment?. . . . . . 208 Astrophil   83   9
    Stella food of my thoughts, hart of my hart, ... 222 Astrophil   87   2
    The field where all my thoughts to warre be traind,. . . . . 230 Astrophil   98   2
    Make in my heavy mould new thoughts to grow: . . . . 236 Astrophil   106   11
    And on my thoughts give thy Lieftenancy. . . . . 236 Astrophil   107   7
    Twinckling starres Love-thoughts provoke:. . . . . 210 A&S 4th Song   8
    O my thought my thoughts surcease, ... 227 A&S 10th Song   43
    "But time will these thoughts remove:. . . . . 234 A&S 11th Song   16
    Or loving, have so frothy thoughts, as easly thence to move: 217 A&S 7th Song   10
    Let their vile thoughts the thinkers' ruin be. . . . . 275 Psalm V   30
    When Moone and starrs my thoughtes beholdeth . . . . 278 Psalm VIII   11
    By them whose minds on hatefull thoughts do stay:. . . . . . 280 Psalm IX   38
    Unto due thoughts mankind his thoughts shall order,. . . . . 300 Psalm XXII   66
    Who, their spotted thoughts to cloak,. . . . . 309 Psalm XXVIII   13
    I hated have those men whose thoughts do cleave. . . . . . . 312 Psalm XXXI   16
    Who for my hurt each way their thoughts did roll.. . . . . . 321 Psalm XXXV   10
    His deeds, yea thoughtes all good forgett; . . . . 323 Psalm XXXVI   10
    What man Thy thoughts can count to Thee. . . . . 331 Psalm XL   22
    Ev'en heapes of wicked thoughts which streight they show . . 333 Psalm XLI   23
    With hurtfull thoughts to me.. . . . . 333 Psalm XLI   26
    In such longing thoughts it falleth. . . . . 334 Psalm XLII   24
    So as good thoughts of him in all arise, ... 247 Other Poems   4   198
    On thoughts he feeds, his lookes their figure chaunge, . . . 253 Other Poems   4   434
    Yet thoughts do flie, though I can scarcely creep. . . . . . 253 Other Poems   4   444
    While guilty thoughts accus'd his Reason weake). . . . . . . 255 Other Poems   4   532
    With thoughts which thoughts their owne tormentors tried,. . 259 Other Poems   5   119
THOUGHTS'
    And unto death bend still our thoughts' direction. . . . . . 130 4th Eclogues 76   34
    O My thoughtes' sweete foode, my my onely owner, ... 138 Cert Sonnets 5   1
    Above line repeated at following location. . . . . 138 Cert Sonnets 5   25
THOUSAND
    Two thousand sheepe I have as white as milke,. . . . .   4 Lady of May   2   19
    Two thousand deere in wildest woods I have,. . . . .   4 Lady of May   2   25
    A horned head, cloven foote, and thousand eyes,. . . . . . .   21 1st Eclogues 8   26
    Is this thy fruite O strife? those thousand churches hie,. . 119 4th Eclogues 73   111
    Those thousand altars faire now in the dust to lie?. . . . . 119 4th Eclogues 73   112
    With thousand prety childish plaies, ... 158 Cert Sonnets 28   11
THOUSANDS
    Though thousands old, a Boy entit'led still. . . . .   41 Arcadia II   20   10
THRALL
    Her to enjoy, where joy it selfe is thrall,. . . . .   59 2nd Eclogues 30   87
    Then hers, to whom my thoughts alonely thrall. . . . .   78 Arcadia III 49   15
    And keepe it still within this body thrall:. . . . . 116 4th Eclogues 72   88
    Ev'n as I am, so I should unto that haire be a thrall. . . . 123 4th Eclogues 74   54
    Thou sett'st me free, when I was thrall, ... 273 Psalm IV   3
    Let not proud feet make me their thrall, ... 324 Psalm XXXVI   31
THRALLDOM
    And are not forst fonde thraldome to allow.. . . . . 106 3rd Eclogues 67   105
    That hue, whose force my hart still unto thraldome ties? . . 232 Astrophil   102   8
    Yet will not I greife, ashes, thralldom change . . . . 345 Possibly   2   9
THRALLED
    But if my memory thus must be thralled . . . .   61 2nd Eclogues 30   164
    Nay higher thoughtes (though thralled thoughtes) I call. . .   78 Arcadia III 49   13
    O hideous absence, by thee am I thralled.. . . . . 138 Cert Sonnets 5   13
THRALLS
    No thralles like them that inward bondage have.. . . . . . .   17 1st Eclogues 7   114
    Whose wit the starres, whose fortune fortune thralls.. . . .   23 1st Eclogues 9   31
    Balles to the starres, and thralles to Fortune's raigne; . .   57 2nd Eclogues 30   17
THREAD
    Sore signe it is, the Lord's last thred is spun. . . . . . . 150 Cert Sonnets 22   14
THREADS
    Her haire fine threeds of finest gould . . . .   85 Arcadia III 62   3
THREAT
    That streight was done with many a boistrous threat, ...   97 3rd Eclogues 64   115
    Doth lowre, nay, chide; nay, threat for only this: . . . . . 203 Astrophil   73   7
THREATEN
    Threat'n what may be done, yet do more then you threat'n.. . 213 A&S 5th Song   33
THREATENED
    Who threatned stripes, if he his wrath did prove:. . . . . . 173 Astrophil   17   6
    With eyes which threatned they would drowne his face,. . . . 255 Other Poems   4   524
THREATENING
    Those scarlet judges, threatning bloudy paine? . . . . 203 Astrophil   73   11
    His voyce doth threatning thunders sound,. . . . . 310 Psalm XXIX   8

519

```
                                                                PAGE    TITLE           LINE
THREATENS
    In cheeks and lipps the Tyran threatens bloud. . . . . . .  246 Other Poems     4   152
THREATS
    Niggard Time threats, if we misse. . . . . . . . . . . . .  211 A&S 4th Song        31
THREE
    Three dayes before that he must sure depart, . . . . . . .   96 3rd Eclogues 64    79
    A three foote stoole in Greece, made Trumpets sound, . . .  146 Cert Sonnets 17    19
    Of those three gods, whose armes the fairest were: . . . .  171 Astrophil    13     2
    If French can yet three parts in one agree;. . . . . . . .  180 Astrophil    30     5
    Then couples three be streight allotted there, . . . . . .  248 Other Poems     4   225
    So they three did togither idly stay,. . . . . . . . . . .  250 Other Poems     4   329
    Make but one Minde in Bodies three.. . . . . . . . . . . .  260 Other Poems     6     6
    Above line repeated at following locations . . . . . . . .  260 Other Poems     6    12
                    . . . . . . . . . . . . . . . . . . . . .  260 Other Poems     6    18
                    . . . . . . . . . . . . . . . . . . . . .  260 Other Poems     6    24
                    . . . . . . . . . . . . . . . . . . . . .  261 Other Poems     6    30
                    . . . . . . . . . . . . . . . . . . . . .  261 Other Poems     6    36
                    . . . . . . . . . . . . . . . . . . . . .  261 Other Poems     6    42
                    . . . . . . . . . . . . . . . . . . . . .  261 Other Poems     6    48
                    . . . . . . . . . . . . . . . . . . . . .  261 Other Poems     6    54
    As three most joyntly set, . . . . . . . . . . . . . . . .  260 Other Poems     6    21
    So should our sever'd bodies three . . . . . . . . . . . .  261 Other Poems     6    59
THREE-LEAVED
    If three-leav'd grasse seeme to the sheepe unsavorie,. . .   48 2nd Eclogues 28    23
THREW
    She ranne away, and threw at me a ball.. . . . . . . . . .   54 2nd Eclogues 29    89
THRICE
    Lord he is in thrice blessed case. . . . . . . . . . . . .  319 Psalm XXXIV        31
    He thrise reacht, thrise deceiv'd when hir to beare. . . .  250 Other Poems     4   340
THRIVE
    Pas. And I am here the same, so mote I thrive and thee,. .   52 2nd Eclogues 29     3
    How sheepheards did of yore, how now they thrive,. . . . .   99 3rd Eclogues 66    34
THROAT
    Long since my voice is hoarce, and throte is sore, . . . .   57 2nd Eclogues 30     8
    My voice is hoarse, my throte scorcht, . . . . . . . . . .   66 2nd Eclogues 32    11
    For hungrie throte their flesh with teeth he brused: . . .  102 3rd Eclogues 66   145
    Her throate in tunes expresseth. . . . . . . . . . . . . .  137 Cert Sonnets  4     6
    Their throat, it is an Open swallowing grave,. . . . . . .  275 Psalm V            27
    Tell me, if wolves the throte. . . . . . . . . . . . . . .  258 Other Poems     5    72
THROES
    Thus great with child to speake, and helplesse in my
            throwes . . . . . . . . . . . . . . . . . . . . .  165 Astrophil     1    12
THRONE
    And in thy throne, a forayne state shall sitte . . . . . .   11 Arcadia I      1 V806
    From heav'nly throne to her heav'n use digression? . . . .   15 1st Eclogues  7    45
    Riches of children passe a Prince's throne;. . . . . . . .  106 3rd Eclogues 67   112
    The seate of peace, the throne which is erected. . . . . .  108 Arcadia IV    69     3
    Alas, if from the height of Vertue's throne, . . . . . . .  184 Astrophil    40     5
    In Beautie's throne, see now who dares come neare. . . . .  203 Astrophil    73    10
    Whose throne is in the mind, . . . . . . . . . . . . . . .  217 A&S 6th Song       50
    Therfore, O lord, lift up Thy throne on high . . . . . . .  277 Psalm VII          20
    Setting Thy self in Throne, which shined bright. . . . . .  279 Psalm IX            9
    The throne of Heav'n is only His:. . . . . . . . . . . . .  284 Psalm XI           14
    My cryes clim'd up and he bent down from sacred throne,. .  291 Psalm XVIII        13
THRONG
    Aske, if in great men good men so do thronge,. . . . . . .  126 4th Eclogues 75    43
THROUGH
    Plangus. If through mine eares pearce any consolacyons . .   61 2nd Eclogues 30   143
    In trees) now through your porous barkes receave . . . . .  125 4th Eclogues 75     5
    The windowes now through which this heav'nly guest . . . .  169 Astrophil     9     9
    Which through a bleeding heart his point did shove:. . . .  171 Astrophil    13     6
    Whereto long since, through my long battred eyes,. . . . .  182 Astrophil    36     3
    That through my heart their beamie darts be gone,. . . . .  189 Astrophil    48    10
    My friend, that oft saw through all maskes my wo,. . . . .  200 Astrophil    69     5
    And through those lips drinke Nectar from that toong;. . .  208 Astrophil    83    13
    Through me, wretch me, even Stella vexed is. . . . . . . .  227 Astrophil    93     4
    Through that darke fornace to my hart opprest, . . . . . .  236 Astrophil   108     3
    Onelie through you the tree of life doth flourish. . . . .  197 A&S 1st Song       20
    Through pores of sencelesse trees, as it could make them
            move:. . . . . . . . . . . . . . . . . . . . . .  208 A&S 3rd Song        2
    How through the World thy Name doth shine: . . . . . . . .  278 Psalm VIII          2
    Above line repeated at following location. . . . . . . . .  279 Psalm VIII         34
    The gulfs of waters then were through their Chanels seen,.  291 Psalm XVIII        31
    Yea tho I should thro vallys stray . . . . . . . . . . . .  301 Psalm XXIII        10
    Through him the floods to their beds fell. . . . . . . . .  302 Psalm XXIV          4
    Yea through the Waters doth resound. . . . . . . . . . . .  310 Psalm XXIX          9
    Whiche my chefe partte, doth passe throughe, parche, and
            tye . . . . . . . . . . . . . . . . . . . . . . .  344 Possibly      2     2
    To feele the panting heart, which through hir syde . . . .  252 Other Poems     4   405
    Then those delights through all their sinews breed . . . .  252 Other Poems     4   411
THROUGHLY
    The wood cries most, before it throughly kindled be, . . .   14 1st Eclogues  7     8
    With pricking shot he did not throughly move,. . . . . . .  173 Astrophil    17     3
    O let proud him be throughly caught. . . . . . . . . . . .  281 Psalm X             7
    Pure, Purer than the silver throughly try'd. . . . . . . .  285 Psalm XII          20
THROUGHOUT
    Throughout my days.. . . . . . . . . . . . . . . . . . . .  280 Psalm IX           45
    Throughout all ages last.. . . . . . . . . . . . . . . . .  317 Psalm XXXIII       39
    Throughout doth see. . . . . . . . . . . . . . . . . . . .  317 Psalm XXXIII       53
```

THROUGH-SEEING   PAGE   TITLE   LINE

The power of Thy through-seing eyes? . . . .   283 Psalm X   54

THROW

(So humble knowledge can throw downe the snakish sinne). . .   44 Arcadia II   26   6
And highest thoughts, downeward most headlong throw? . . . .   73 Arcadia III 40   12
Of those fierce darts, dispaire at me doth throw:. . . . . .   184 Astrophil   39   6
He against me doth throw, but down it shall. . . . .   278 Psalm VII   43
The floods of wickednesse on me did horrors throw, ...   291 Psalm XVIII   9
Do throw their words against the most upright. . . . .   313 Psalm XXXI   51
Rebuke and wracke on those wrong doers throw,. . . . .   321 Psalm XXXV   9
But throw them down, put them to endlesse blame, ...   323 Psalm XXXV   63
On Creon's child his poison sooner throw,. . . . .   252 Other Poems   4 410

THROWETH

His heat to all he throweth. . . . .   294 Psalm XIX   28

THROWING

With their dayly questions throwing: . . . .   334 Psalm XLII   11

THROWN

Olde houses are throne downe for new we see: . . . .   24 1st Eclogues 9   84
Throwne on this earth the Chaos of confusions. . . . .   51 2nd Eclogues 28 110
What myne hath erst throwne downe so faire a tower?. . . . .   59 2nd Eclogues 30   96
And state throwen downe to over-troden vallies.. . . . . . .   112 4th Eclogues 71   30
First throwne on my desire,. . . . .   155 Cert Sonnets 26   3
Above line repeated at following locations . . . .   155 Cert Sonnets 26 14
    . . . .   156 Cert Sonnets 26 25
Let them be thrown down by Thee: . . . .   309 Psalm XXVIII   22
Let me not be thrown down to so base shame . . . .   330 Psalm XXXIX   27

THROWS

That heav'n of joyes throwes onely downe on me . . . .   195 Astrophil   60   3

THROWST

Not I but thou throw'st down those, who 'gainst me do rise;.   292 Psalm XVIII   72

THRUSH

I spied a thrush where she did make her nest,. . . . .   54 2nd Eclogues 29 82
O voice that doth, the Thrush in shrilnes staine,. . . . . .   76 Arcadia III 46   4

THRUST

Confound those folks, thrust them in shamefull hole. . . . .   321 Psalm XXXV   7

THUNDER

The highest hills the bolt of thunder cleeves: . . . .   143 Cert Sonnets 12   9

THUNDERBOLT

Jove on his helme the thunderbolt did reare. . . . .   171 Astrophil   13   8

THUNDERED

Thundred disdaines and lightnings of disgrace: . . . .   195 Astrophil   60   4
Then hayle, then firie coales, then thundred heavnly sire, .   291 Psalm XVIII   27

THUNDER-LIKE

Or canons thunder-like, all shot togither, lende). . . . . .   118 4th Eclogues 73 54

THUNDERS

Thunders of cries; lightnings my wilde lookes be,. . . . . .   114 4th Eclogues 72 34
(Or such a noise it was, as highest thunders sende,. . . . .   118 4th Eclogues 73 53
Whose force but yours the bolts of beautie thunders? . . . .   197 A&S 1st Song   30
Of him that only thunders; . . . .   293 Psalm XIX   2
His voyce doth threatning thunders sound,. . . . .   310 Psalm XXIX   8
On me wretch his tempest thunders. . . . .   335 Psalm XLII   32

THUS

(Espilus) Thus joyfully in chosen tunes rejoyce, ...   5 Lady of May   3   13
(Therion) Thus wofully I in wo this salve do find, ...   5 Lady of May   3   17
False in my selfe, thus have I lost the field. . . . .   11 Arcadia I   2   8
Thus are my eyes still Captive to one sight: . . . .   12 Arcadia I   2   9
Thus all my thoughts are slaves to one thought still:. . . .   12 Arcadia I   2   10
Thus Reason to his servants yeelds his right; . . . .   12 Arcadia I   2   11
Thus is my power transformed to your will. . . . .   12 Arcadia I   2   12
And thus my eyes, are plaste still in one sight. . . . . . .   12 Arcadia I   2 V809
And thus my thoughtes, can thinke but one thing still. . . .   12 Arcadia I   2 V810
Thus reason to his Servantes gyves his right . . . .   12 Arcadia I   2 V811
Thus shrewdly burdned then, how can my Muse escape?. . . . .   12 Arcadia I   3   3
That thus preserves my loved life: . . . .   13 Arcadia I   5   2
A Nimph thus turnde, but mended in translation. . . . .   15 1st Eclogues 7   36
Thus Reason said: but she came, Reason vanished; . . . . . .   16 1st Eclogues 7   67
Lalus. This mayde, thus made for joyes, o Pan bemone her,. .   17 1st Eclogues 7   97
Thus doth my life within it selfe dissolve. . . . .   19 1st Eclogues 7 V156
Above line repeated at following location. . . . .   19 1st Eclogues 7 V157
Thus Painters Cupid paint, thus Poets do, ...   20 1st Eclogues 8   5
Thus halfe a man, with man he easly haunts, ...   21 1st Eclogues 8   31
Thus halfe a beast, ech beastly vice he plants,. . . . . . .   21 1st Eclogues 8   33
Histor. Thus may you see, howe youthe estemeth aige. . . . .   26 1st Eclogues 9 138
To age thus doe they draw there youthfull pryme, ...   28 1st Eclogues 10   52
Fortune thus gan say; "misery and misfortune is all one, . .   29 1st Eclogues 11   3
Love smiled, and thus said; "Want joynd to desire is
   unhappy . . . .   30 1st Eclogues 11 11
Nature abasht went back: fortune blusht: yet she replide
   thus:. . . . .   30 1st Eclogues 11 17
Thus, thus, alas! wofull in nature, unhappy by fortune,. . .   30 1st Eclogues 11 19
Thus not ending, endes the due praise of her praise; . . . .   31 1st Eclogues 12 21
Where proofes justly do teach, thus matcht, such worth to be
   nought worth. . . . .   34 1st Eclogues 13 83
Thus be her giftes most sweet, thus more danger to be neere
   her, ...   36 1st Eclogues 13 126
Thus to my sonne do I yeeld, such lookes her beames do
   aforde me. . . . .   36 1st Eclogues 13 133
Thus be my thoughts disperst, thus thinking nurseth a
   thinking, ...   36 1st Eclogues 13 139
Thus both trees and each thing ells, be the bookes of a
   fancy. . . . .   36 1st Eclogues 13 140

	PAGE	TITLE		LINE
Then kneling to the ground, oft thus do I speake to that Image:	36	1st Eclogues	13	146
Thus by thy worke, disdaine not that which is by thy selfe done	36	1st Eclogues	13	152
Thus plag'de how can I frame to my soare any hope of amendemente?	37	1st Eclogues	13	160
Yet be my hopes thus plast, here fixed lives my recomforte,	37	1st Eclogues	13	164
What wooll my sheepe shall beare, whyle thus they live,	39	Arcadia II	17	7
Thus children doo the silly birds they finde,	41	Arcadia II	20	11
Yet thus much Love, O Love, I crave of thee:	41	Arcadia II	20	13
Thus outward helps my inward griefes maintaine	42	Arcadia II	21	12
Thus then (I say) my mischiefes have contributed	49	2nd Eclogues	28	67
Thus she is framde: her eyes are my direction;	49	2nd Eclogues	28	70
I sooner would, then thus my eares defile.	50	2nd Eclogues	28	81
Thus I commend to thee all our former love	51	2nd Eclogues	28	102
Thus for ech change my changelesse hart I fortifie	51	2nd Eclogues	28	126
Thus Death becomes a rivall to us all,	59	2nd Eclogues	30	89
But if my memory thus must be thralled	61	2nd Eclogues	30	164
Thus is our thought with paine for thistles tilled:	62	2nd Eclogues	30	173
Thus be our noblest parts dryed up with sorrow:	62	2nd Eclogues	30	174
Thus is our mind with too much minding spilled.	62	2nd Eclogues	30	175
Histor. Thus dyd they saye and then awaye dyd wende;	62	2nd Eclogues	30	185
Thus weakned by my selfe, no helpe remaineth	68	2nd Eclogues	33	17
Reason sighes but in end he thus doth answere.	68	2nd Eclogues	33	25
Thus nature's Diamond, receave thy conquest,	68	2nd Eclogues	33	27
Thus pure pearle, I do yeeld, my senses and soule.	68	2nd Eclogues	33	28
Thus sweete paine, I do yeeld, what ere I can yeelde	68	2nd Eclogues	33	29
Unite in one, my state thus still to save;	70	Arcadia III	35	15
Thus in my pilgrimaige of mated mynde,	71	Arcadia III	36	13
Thus tossed in my shipp of huge desyre,	71	Arcadia III	37	13
Thus toyled in my work of raging love,	71	Arcadia III	37	14
Thus then my forme, and thus my state I finde,	73	Arcadia III	40	13
Thus cruell to my selfe how canst thou crave	77	Arcadia III	47	7
Thus noble golde, downe to the bottome goes,	81	Arcadia III	54	13
Thus in thy selfe, least strings are loudest founde,	81	Arcadia III	54	15
Thus honour, liking, trust, much, farre, and deepe,	84	Arcadia III	60	5
Thus thus the more I love, the wronge the more	85	Arcadia III	61	5
Which onely thus unhappie be,	86	Arcadia III	62	21
Thus hath each part his beautie's part,	90	Arcadia III	62	133
While thus he fear'd the silly innocent,	94	3rd Eclogues	64	13
And thus she did. One day to him she came,	95	3rd Eclogues	64	43
"Thus shall you show that him you do not doubt,	96	3rd Eclogues	64	61
The wife thus having settled husband's braine,	96	3rd Eclogues	64	73
"Alas", quoth she, "thus women's shame doth creepe".	96	3rd Eclogues	64	87
Thus shall you both reward a lover true,	97	3rd Eclogues	64	107
Thus may you see, the jealous wretch was made.	97	3rd Eclogues	64	121
But thus in oke's true shade recounted he.	99	3rd Eclogues	66	41
Thus Man was made; thus Man their Lord became:	101	3rd Eclogues	66	106
Thus did I sing, and pipe eight sullen houres.	103	3rd Eclogues	66	155
If thus thou murther thy posteritie.	105	3rd Eclogues	67	78
Thus, thus alas, I had my losse in chase.	115	4th Eclogues	72	70
Klaius. Thus, thus alas, I had my losse in chase,	115	4th Eclogues	72	71
That thus I must, while in this death I dwell,	116	4th Eclogues	72	89
And having plaste my thoughts, my thoughts thus placed me.	117	4th Eclogues	73	34
But walking forth, the first thus to the second saide,	118	4th Eclogues	73	77
As I thus musing stood, Diana cald to her.	119	4th Eclogues	73	81
She waited mistresse' will: who thus disclosd her spright.	119	4th Eclogues	73	92
But thus with irefull eyes, and face that shooke with spite.	119	4th Eclogues	73	101
And smirkly thus gan say. "I never sought debate	120	4th Eclogues	73	147
Thus both did come to me, and both began to tell	121	4th Eclogues	73	154
To all what I decreed, did thus my verdict saye.	121	4th Eclogues	73	162
O cowarde Cupid thus doost thou my honour keepe,	122	4th Eclogues	73	185
Shall I not? o may I not thus yet refresh the remembrance,	124	4th Eclogues	74	71
Thus, thus the mindes, which over all doo clime,	127	4th Eclogues	75	88
If thus, alas: yet while those partes have wo,	142	Cert Sonnets	10	13
Fearing and feared thus from himselfe he fled,	145	Cert Sonnets	16	3
Even thus might I, for doubts which I conceave	145	Cert Sonnets	16	9
And thus might I for feare of may be, leave.	145	Cert Sonnets	16	11
Tell how my joyes and hopes thus fowly fell.	146	Cert Sonnets	17	14
That parting thus my chiefest part I part.	148	Cert Sonnets	20	8
Now thus this wonder to my selfe I frame,	151	Cert Sonnets	22	69
Thus is her life still guarded,	152	Cert Sonnets	23	13
Thus is his death rewarded,	152	Cert Sonnets	23	15
Thus to betray my hart's fort,	154	Cert Sonnets	25	10
Thus do I fall to rise thus,	154	Cert Sonnets	25	27
Thus do I dye to live thus,	154	Cert Sonnets	25	28
Thus may I not be from you:	155	Cert Sonnets	25	30
Thus be my senses on you:	155	Cert Sonnets	25	31
Thus what I thinke is of you:	155	Cert Sonnets	25	32
Thus what I seeke is in you:	155	Cert Sonnets	25	33
Thus my beleefe was stayde.	158	Cert Sonnets	28	37
From them that use men thus,	160	Cert Sonnets	30	9
Above line repeated at following locations	160	Cert Sonnets	30	19
. . . .	160	Cert Sonnets	30	29
. . . .	161	Cert Sonnets	30	39
Who love can temper thus,	161	Cert Sonnets	30	39
Thus great with child to speake, and helplesse in my throwes	165	Astrophil	1	12
How then? even thus: in Stella's face I reed,	166	Astrophil	3	12
Both so and thus, she minding Love should be	168	Astrophil	7	12

THUS   (CONTINUED)   PAGE   TITLE   LINE
    The first, thus matcht, were scarcely Gentlemen. . . . . . .   171 Astrophil   13   14
    But while I thus with this yong Lyon plaid;. . . . .   173 Astrophil   16   9
    And thus her heart escapes, but thus her eyes. . . . .   179 Astrophil   29   9
    Thus write I while I doubt to write, and wreake. . . . . . .   182 Astrophil   34   12
    And then, thinke thus, although thy beautie be . . . .   185 Astrophil   40   9
    That Noblenesse it selfe makes thus unkind?. . . . .   186 Astrophil   44   8
    What, have I thus betrayed my libertie?. . . . .   188 Astrophil   47   1
    But Vertue thus that title doth disprove,. . . . .   190 Astrophil   52   5
    Let Vertue have that Stella's selfe; yet thus, ...   191 Astrophil   52   13
    I joyed, but straight thus watred was my wine, ...   196 Astrophil   62   5
    Her eye's-speech is translated thus by thee: . . . .   199 Astrophil   67   5
    And though she give but thus conditionly . . . .   200 Astrophil   69   12
    Guesse we the cause: "What, is it thus?" Fie no: . . . . . .   204 Astrophil   74   12
    "Or so?" Much lesse? "How then?" Sure thus it is:. . . . . .   204 Astrophil   74   13
    Thus much my heart compeld my mouth to say,. . . . .   207 Astrophil   80   9
    Thus while th' effect most bitter was to me, ...   223 Astrophil   87   12
    That living thus in blackest winter night, ...   224 Astrophil   89   13
    And that faire you my Sunne, thus overspred. . . . .   224 Astrophil   91   3
    Only with paines my paines thus eased be,. . . . .   227 Astrophil   93   12
    Sweet alas, why strive you thus? . . . .   211 A&S 4th Song   43
    Which can make me thus to leave you, ...   235 A&S 11th Song   44
    Thus doth the voice and face,. . . . .   215 A&S 6th Song   13
    Thus to speake in love and wonder: . . . .   218 A&S 8th Song   28
    Tyran honour doth thus use thee, ...   220 A&S 8th Song   95
    Upon his pate, his pain employed thus. . . . .   278 Psalm VII   44
    Thus freely saith he in his sprite:. . . . .   282 Psalm X   45
    Thus languish? . . . .   285 Psalm XIII   8
    O madness of these folks, thus loosely led,. . . . .   286 Psalm XIV   13
    Who thus proceeds, for aye, in sacred Mount shall raign. . .   287 Psalm XV   13
    My justice, my just hands thus did the lord reward,. . . . .   292 Psalm XVIII   43
    Thus freed from mutin men, thou makest me to raign,. . . . .   293 Psalm XVIII   78
    Thus thus shall all my days be fede, ...   301 Psalm XXIII   22
    Teach me, thus vext, what path to go.. . . . .   303 Psalm XXV   12
    Then thus to Thee I praying cry'd: . . . .   311 Psalm XXX   25
    Thus much I said, this being said. . . . .   311 Psalm XXX   33
    Thus I prest down with weight of pain, ...   315 Psalm XXXII   7
    Thus I begin. I sought . . . .   319 Psalm XXXIV   13
    Let them not, Lord, within their hearts thus say:. . . . . .   323 Psalm XXXV   61
    Ev'n thus it self it doth display, ...   323 Psalm XXXVI   4
    Thus did I think: I well will mark my way, ...   329 Psalm XXXIX   1
    My tongue would needs and thus I spake:. . . . .   329 Psalm XXXIX   12
    This being thus, For what O Lord wait I? . . . .   330 Psalm XXXIX   23
    But I do hush, Why do I say thus much, ...   330 Psalm XXXIX   29
    Thus bound I said, lo, lord I am at hand,. . . . .   331 Psalm XL   31
    While thus, alas, they say:. . . . .   333 Psalm XLI   18
    Therfore, O Lord, abandond thought of all,. . . . .   333 Psalm XLI   33
    Yet thus still my hope is grounded,. . . . .   335 Psalm XLII   35
    Dick. I would it were but thus, for thus it were too well. .   343 Possibly   1   17
    I then, whose burd'ned brest but thus aspires. . . . .   242 Other Poems 4   5
    While thus they ran a low, but leaveld race, ...   243 Other Poems 4   57
    While thus they liv'd, (this was indede a life). . . . . . .   243 Other Poems 4   58
    Chastned but thus, and thus his lesson tought, ...   244 Other Poems 4   97
    Thus proud and fierce unto the hearts he stept . . . .   246 Other Poems 4 157
    Thus Pas did kisse hir hand with little grace. . . . .   249 Other Poems 4 276
    Thus, fast he fled from her he follow'd sore,. . . . .   250 Other Poems 4 305
    (He staying thus) was faine abroad to stray. . . . .   250 Other Poems 4 331
    He single thus, hop'd soone with hir to be,. . . . .   250 Other Poems 4 337
    Till finding still his evill encreasing thus,. . . . .   253 Other Poems 4 437
    Thus on a hillock set, he made his mone. . . . .   253 Other Poems 4 440
    Though thus, and worse, though now I am at last, ...   254 Other Poems 4 493
    Which thus breath'd out with earthquake of his hart. . . . .   256 Other Poems 4 544
    And thus, with eyes made dimme . . . .   256 Other Poems 5   12
THWART
    And taught his shepe hir shepe in food to thwart. . . . . . . 247 Other Poems 4 188
THYSELF
    But still take heede least thou thy selfe submit . . . . . .   4 Lady of May 2   23
    Looke to thy selfe; reach not beyond humanitie:. . . . . . .   16 1st Eclogues 7   64
    By raysing up, upon thy selfe to stand . . . .   23 1st Eclogues 9   51
    Within thy selfe, thou soone wilt be ashamed . . . .   25 1st Eclogues 9 118
    Save what a worke, by thy selfe is wrought: and since I am
        altred. . . . .   36 1st Eclogues 13 151
    Thus by thy worke, disdaine not that which is by thy selfe
        done.. . . . . 36 1st Eclogues 13 152
    A quiet mind none but thy selfe can lend to thee,. . . . . .   51 2nd Eclogues 28 101
    Nico. Ah now I see, why thou art in thy selfe so blind:. . .   52 2nd Eclogues 29   5
    Curs'd be thy selfe for cursing that which leades me to
        joies. Toies.. . . . . 65 2nd Eclogues 31 40
    Reason looke to thy selfe, I serve a goddesse. . . . .   68 2nd Eclogues 33 30
    Nor danger to thy selfe if be not in thy selfe.. . . . . . .   69 2nd Eclogues 34 14
    But wilt thy selfe in such a seate delighte, ...   79 Arcadia III 51 11
    My Lute within thy selfe thy tunes enclose,. . . . .   81 Arcadia III 54   1
    Thus in thy selfe, least strings are loudest founde, ...   81 Arcadia III 54 15
    Of yonglings, which thy selfe with love hast rearde, ...   92 3rd Eclogues 63 43
    Long have I lov'd thy selfe, alas my harte . . . .   97 3rd Eclogues 64 99
    O Histor, seeke within thy selfe to flourish:. . . . .   106 3rd Eclogues 67 109
    How hast thou torne thy selfe! sought thine owne damage! . .   109 Arcadia IV   70 20
    Least it might thee allure home to thy selfe to returne, . .   122 4th Eclogues 74   8
    (Unto thy selfe I do meane those graces dwell so within
        thee . . . . 122 4th Eclogues 74   9

THYSELF	(CONTINUED)	PAGE	TITLE		LINE
Thy selfe henceforth the light doo never see.........		125	4th Eclogues	75	24
That Vertue, thou thy selfe shalt be in love.........		167	Astrophil	4	14
Hart rent thy selfe, thou doest thy selfe but right, ...		181	Astrophil	33	5
Thy selfe, doest strive all minds that way to move,.....		201	Astrophil	71	10
I see the house, my heart thy selfe containe,........		209	Astrophil	85	1
Yet waile thy selfe, and waile with causefull teares,....		228	Astrophil	94	11
I saw thy selfe with many a smiling line		232	Astrophil	103	2
Arise, O lord, in wrath thy self upsett.		277	Psalm VII		16
Setting Thy self in Throne, which shined bright.		279	Psalm IX		9
Which to Thy self my soul will send.		290	Psalm XVII		20
And yet ev'en from the womb thy self did'st take me;....		299	Psalm XXII		21
To thy self those words apply.		309	Psalm XXVIII		9
Whose mouths Thy self dost bridle, ...		315	Psalm XXXII		33
O lord, do not absent Thy self from me!...........		322	Psalm XXXV		56
Frett not Thy self, if thou do see		324	Psalm XXXVII		1
Least such things sin in Thy self cherish, ...		325	Psalm XXXVII		22
Doth not thy selfe, when he long absent is,........		257	Other Poems	5	24
TICKLE					
But thou, sure Hope, tickle my leaping heart.........		83	Arcadia III	59	9
TIDES					
For me, while you discourse of courtly tides,........		190	Astrophil	51	9
TIE					
For both, alas, their strengthes together tie:		42	Arcadia II	22	4
O notes of mine your selves together tie:..........		127	4th Eclogues	75	76
Ty me haire your captive wholly, ...		157	Cert Sonnets	27	34
The raines wherewith my Rider doth me tie,.........		189	Astrophil	49	5
Whiche my chefe partte, doth passe throughe, parche, and tye		344	Possibly	2	2
TIED					
In sorrows torments, then, tyed to the pompes of a pallace,.		35	1st Eclogues	13	103
(Tide to the stake of doubt) strange passions baite, ...		82	Arcadia III	56	10
Should Ladies faire be tyed to such hard lawes,.......		146	Cert Sonnets	17	23
Beautie tied to vertue,.................		154	Cert Sonnets	25	6
Fetters tyed, do waite the hower		155	Cert Sonnets	26	18
When some faire Ladies, by hard promise tied,........		176	Astrophil	22	5
And ti'de them fast to leade his triumph badd, ...		245	Other Poems	4	131
TIES					
For other be those tunes which sorrow tyes,.........		13	Arcadia I	4	7
Chief band I saye, which tyes my chiefest parte, ...		70	Arcadia III	35	12
O kisse, which soules, even soules together ties		207	Astrophil	81	5
Let eares heare speech, which wit to wonder ties,......		210	Astrophil	85	11
That hue, whose force my hart still unto thraldome ties? ..		232	Astrophil	102	8
TIETH					
Who hath the haire which, loosest, fastest, tieth,.....		197	A&S 1st Song		25
TIGER					
First may a trusty Greyhounde transforme himselfe to a Tigre		33	1st Eclogues	13	66
Then may I hope t'atchieve grace of a heavenly tiger.....		122	4th Eclogues	74	22
TIGERISH					
Yet let this thought thy Tygrish courage passe:.......		198	Astrophil	65	11
TIGER'S					
Hurtles was Tyger's pawe and Serpent's hisse.........		100	3rd Eclogues	66	54
Her heart, sweete heart, is of no Tygre's kind:......		186	Astrophil	44	4
TIGERS					
(As Tygers, leopards, beares, and Lions' seed)		102	3rd Eclogues	66	122
*TILL					
Till this he tooke for comfort of his lot:		5	Lady of May	3	10
Till I get her, shall I to sheep enure my selfe?		16	1st Eclogues	7	60
Till now at length that Jove him office gives,.......		22	1st Eclogues	8	45
Till aige it self do make it self esteemde..........		26	1st Eclogues	9	141
The third his lesson mist, till all do smarte........		27	1st Eclogues	10	45
And worse of other more, till by assent.		29	1st Eclogues	10	82
Till spotlesse soule unto thy bosome flye,.........		40	Arcadia II	18	17
Till of these thoughts thy sodaine ende bereaved me.		48	2nd Eclogues	28	33
Till with lickt beard, his eye of fire espie his foes. ...		53	2nd Eclogues	29	36
She lay for dead, till I helpt with unlasing her?......		61	2nd Eclogues	30	154
Till my frayle barke his haven agayn do fynde.		70	Arcadia III	35	8
Till her eyes shine, I live in darkest night.........		79	Arcadia III	51	14
Till wrong, contempt, deceit, did growe, steale, creepe,..		84	Arcadia III	60	7
With chafe enough, till she him pacified:..........		97	3rd Eclogues	64	110
Till forste to parte, with harte and eyes even sore, ...		99	3rd Eclogues	66	39
And drawes the dolor on till wery evening.		111	4th Eclogues	71	6
Till by such hap, as I must ever rewe,...........		115	4th Eclogues	72	74
Till deadly sleepe at length possest my living coarse. ...		117	4th Eclogues	73	30
Whose stormelike course staid not till hard by me it bided..		118	4th Eclogues	73	60
Till these straunge altrings you did hap to trie,.....		125	4th Eclogues	75	26
Till that it hath all woods and waters past.		126	4th Eclogues	75	36
Till that they doo unto our dolours bende:		126	4th Eclogues	75	39
Fire burne me quite, till sense of burning leave me:		136	Cert Sonnets	3	13
Till want of force do force her fall to ground;.......		144	Cert Sonnets	15	4
Till wounded, blind, and wearied Spirites, lose.		144	Cert Sonnets	15	11
Yet live with thoughts closde up, till that she will		150	Cert Sonnets	22	29
Till knit with cold, though there unknowne remaine,.....		150	Cert Sonnets	22	33
Of sorrowe's droppes, till colder reason binde		150	Cert Sonnets	22	37
Till that I sware my faith so stood, ...		158	Cert Sonnets	28	23
Till due desert she find..		160	Cert Sonnets	30	36
Till by degrees it had full conquest got...........		165	Astrophil	2	4
Till that good God make Church and Churchman starve.		167	Astrophil	5	8
Why shouldst thou toyle our thornie soile to till?		169	Astrophil	10	6

*TILL	(CONTINUED)	PAGE	TITLE		LINE
Till downe-right blowes did foyle thy cunning fence:		170	Astrophil	10	11
Till that his grandame Nature pittying it,		173	Astrophil	17	9
Till bloudie bullet get him wrongfull pray..		175	Astrophil	20	4
Till now, wrapt in a most infernall night,		181	Astrophil	33	3
Till without fewell you can make hot fire.		188	Astrophil	46	14
Till that in words thy figure be exprest..		189	Astrophil	50	4
Till that her blush taught me my shame to see.		191	Astrophil	53	14
His who till death lookt in a watrie glasse,		207	Astrophil	82	3
In justice paines come not till faults do call;		212	Astrophil	86	10
Ravisht, staid not, till in her golden haire		232	Astrophil	103	7
Till it have wrought what thy owne will attends.		236	Astrophil	107	11
Joying till joy makes us languish.		227	A&S 10th Song		42
Till thou shalt revived be,		227	A&S 10th Song		47
Till their harts had ended talking..		218	A&S 8th Song		24
Till when will ye my honour high		273	Psalm IV		7
Staine with your blasphemys? till when		273	Psalm IV		7
Till my self did my faults confess		315	Psalm XXXII		13
Till his known ev'ill do hatred get.		323	Psalm XXXVI		8
Whose wages makes me beg the more, who feeds me till I sterve,		343	Possibly	1	20
Their chearfull minds, till pois'ned was their cheare,		243	Other Poems	4	41
In chastest plaies, till home they walke a rowe,		243	Other Poems	4	54
Till hard by them both he and she did stay..		244	Other Poems	4	88
Till one faire eav'n an howr ere Sun did rest,		247	Other Poems	4	205
With others' blott, till all do tast of shame.		248	Other Poems	4	232
Till Uran seing Pas to Cosma fly,		249	Other Poems	4	286
Till that he spied old Geron could no more,		250	Other Poems	4	307
Till with long race deare she was breathles brought,		251	Other Poems	4	359
Till spying well she welnigh weary was,		251	Other Poems	4	377
Till she brake from their armes (although in deed.		252	Other Poems	4	413
Till of his life it did full conquest win,		253	Other Poems	4	430
Till finding still his evill encreasing thus,		253	Other Poems	4	437
Till straunge delight, delight to nothing ware;		254	Other Poems	4	482
Till my eies had their curse from blessed eine.		254	Other Poems	4	496
Till Strephon's plaining voice him nearer drew,		256	Other Poems	4	535
Or rather, till thou die,		258	Other Poems	5	77
Wayling till death, shun you not to be seene?.		258	Other Poems	5	91
TILLED					
A Lillie field, with plowe of Rose which tilled is..		15	1st Eclogues	7	30
Thus is our thought with paine for thistles tilled:.		62	2nd Eclogues	30	173
TIMBER					
If the mute timber when it hath the life lost,		30	1st Eclogues	12	15
TIME					
My pastimes none: time passeth on my fall:		18	1st Eclogues	7	142
What time for her Juno her Jove did misse,		21	1st Eclogues	8	15
Geron. Yet sure an end, to each thing time doth give,		22	1st Eclogues	9	11
That which we see in many time hath wrought,		22	1st Eclogues	9	14
Time shall in one my life and sorrowes end,		23	1st Eclogues	9	19
Of my good sheepe, thou never trews time tooke:		27	1st Eclogues	10	14
Who have their lesson so long time begonne?.		27	1st Eclogues	10	27
While, "Let us passe our time" each shepeheard saies..		28	1st Eclogues	10	48
So small accompt of time the shepeheard feeles		28	1st Eclogues	10	49
And doth not feele, that life is nought but time		28	1st Eclogues	10	50
And when that time is paste, death holdes his heeles..		28	1st Eclogues	10	51
Neither doubt you a whit, time will your passion utter..		33	1st Eclogues	13	58
Leave of my sheepe: it is no tyme to feede,		43	Arcadia II	24	1
Time, place, life, wit scarcely her rare gifts measure doth.		49	2nd Eclogues	28	60
Talking time borrowe for to spitt their vennim		50	2nd Eclogues	28	V886
Then let my life long time on earth maintained be,		61	2nd Eclogues	30	147
Hye tyme for me, for scattered were my sheepe.		62	2nd Eclogues	30	186
Nor time pratled away, cradle of ignorance,		69	2nd Eclogues	34	22
Deeper engrav'd, which salve nor time can save,		77	Arcadia III	47	5
O Stealing time the subject of delaie,		80	Arcadia III	53	1
O time, become the chariot of my joyes:		80	Arcadia III	53	9
That trusts in time, to finde the way aright		82	Arcadia III	56	3
But now the fitt is past: and time hath giv'ne		83	Arcadia III	57	9
For no thing, time, nor place, can loose, quench, ease,		84	Arcadia III	60	13
Becomming every time and place,		90	Arcadia III	62	136
Let one time (but long first) close up their daies,		92	3rd Eclogues	63	31
Which little time did fitlie bring to passe.		96	3rd Eclogues	64	76
Now is the time we may be here alone,		97	3rd Eclogues	64	105
To vertue, fortune, time and woman's brest..		98	3rd Eclogues	65	14
Such maner time there was (what time I n'ot)		100	3rd Eclogues	66	43
And yet in all this time, betwixt us tway,		106	3rd Eclogues	67	91
Histor. Perchaunce I will, but nowe me thinkes it tyme		107	3rd Eclogues	67	118
And loth this time, calld life, nay thinke, that life.		113	4th Eclogues	72	12
Of heaven, of earth, of hell, of time and place was come..		118	4th Eclogues	73	62
Us to attend, in this most private time and place.		119	4th Eclogues	73	96
Did Wisedome this our wretched time espie.		126	4th Eclogues	75	46
Time ever old, and yonge is still revolved		127	4th Eclogues	75	79
So that we can long time produce their time:		127	4th Eclogues	75	86
Time runnes away for sorow:		136	Cert Sonnets	3	6
Time haste my dying hower:		136	Cert Sonnets	3	18
Fire, aire, sea, earth, fame, time, place, shew your power..		136	Cert Sonnets	3	20
Lyke crafty wretch by time and travell tought,		141	Cert Sonnets	8	5
Take harp and sing in this our versing time:		146	Cert Sonnets	17	37
Or cruell (still) time did your beautie staine:		148	Cert Sonnets	19	8
Thought, reason, sense, time, you, and I, maintaine.		148	Cert Sonnets	19	18
But knowne worth did in mine of time proceed,		165	Astrophil	2	3

TIME	(CONTINUED)	PAGE	TITLE		LINE
What can be hoped my harvest time will be?		175	Astrophil	21	11
Will she take time, before all wracked be?		199	Astrophil	67	4
Her flamie glistring lights increase with time and place;.		205	Astrophil	76	10
By no encrochment wrongd, nor time forgot:		209	Astrophil	84	10
Sc neere, in so good time, so free a place?		235	Astrophil	105	2
Yong folkes, take time while you may:.		211	A&S 4th Song		28
Niggard Time threats, if we misse.		211	A&S 4th Song		31
Which cannot be restor'd by time nor industrie:		214	A&S 5th Song		47
Thinke of that most gratefull time,.		226	A&S 10th Song		25
"But time will these thoughts remove:.		234	A&S 11th Song		16
Time doth worke what no man knoweth.".		234	A&S 11th Song		17
Time doth as the subject prove,.		234	A&S 11th Song		18
With time still th' affection groweth.		234	A&S 11th Song		19
Time and place for me may move you..		219	A&S 8th Song		52
Up lord now time it is:.		272	Psalm III		23
That they to Thee in troublous tyme may flee:		280	Psalm IX		27
In time most fitt for Thee.		281	Psalm X		3
Lord help, it is high time for me to call,		284	Psalm XII		1
Thou art my God, my time on thee doth stay;.		313	Psalm XXXI		41
In fitt time make to Thee his mcane,		315	Psalm XXXII		20
And God freed him, in his worst time		319	Psalm XXXIV		23
For their short time is in his sight.		325	Psalm XXXVII		36
From time to time, but who be swerved.		326	Psalm XXXVII		71
Nc time within his limites binds.		326	Psalm XXXVII		76
In time of greatest tribulation.		327	Psalm XXXVII		99
For God shall him deliver in the time.		332	Psalm XLI		3
Will. A tyme there is for all, my Mother often sayes,.		343	Possibly	1	9
Fcr nothing can more tedious bee, then plaint, in time of joy.		344	Possibly	1	46
Yeelde yeelde O yeelde, now is it time to yeelde,		345	Possibly	4	13
"Another time", quoth she, "become more wise".		249	Other Poems	4	275
To beare the bondes which Time nor wit could breake,		255	Other Poems	4	530
In time that, richly di'de,		258	Other Poems	5	70
TIMELY					
Whose braunches faile not timely fruite to nourish,		270	Psalm I		9
TIME'S					
The weakning worke of Time's for ever-whirling wheele.		120	4th Eclogues	73	122
With what pastime, time's journey she beguilde,		225	Astrophil	92	12
When time's times shall be past.		317	Psalm XXXIII		42
Lord unto me my time's just measure give,		329	Psalm XXXIX		13
TIMES					
Come from marble bowers, many times the gay harbor of anguish,		34	1st Eclogues	13	92
Though present times and past with evils be snarde,		143	Cert Sonnets	12	13
When fire seven times hath spent his earthly parts.		285	Psalm XII		21
When time's times shall be past.		317	Psalm XXXIII		42
TINE					
Nico. She once starke nak'd did bathe a little tine;		55	2nd Eclogues	29	105
TINSEL					
Lyke thynnest Lawne with Tynsell lynde,		89	Arcadia III	62	V116
TIP					
The tippe no jewell needes to weare:		87	Arcadia III	62	35
The tippe is jewell of the eare.		87	Arcadia III	62	36
TIPPED					
But arrowes two, and tipt with gold or leade:		21	1st Eclogues	8	11
TIRE					
Tyre on, despaier, upon my tyred sprite..		74	Arcadia III	42	12
Upon whose breast a fiercer Gripe doth tire.		171	Astrophil	14	2
TIRED					
The labourer, whome tyred boddie makes		71	Arcadia III	37	7
Tyre on, despaier, upon my tyred sprite..		74	Arcadia III	42	12
Which oft hath Echo tir'd in secrete forrests.		111	4th Eclogues	71	12
Despise delight, am tyrde with thought of ease;.		113	4th Eclogues	72	2
Of Atlas tyr'd, your wisedome's heav'nly sway.		190	Astrophil	51	8
Late tyr'd with wo, even ready for to pine		195	Astrophil	62	1
Tired with the dusty toiles of busie day,.		224	Astrophil	89	7
Thou though still tired, yet still doost it detest..		229	Astrophil	96	14
Lo, I am tir'd, my little I sigh and groane:		276	Psalm VI		17
Tir'de as a jade in overloden carte,		253	Other Poems	4	443
This said, this done, he rase even tir'd with rest,		255	Other Poems	4	521
TIS					
Come narr good Mastix, tis now full tway score		27	1st Eclogues	10	20
Ccme, come my currs, tis late I will goe in.		29	1st Eclogues	10	98
When tis excellently sory.		221	A&S 9th Song		15
O law of his How perfect 'tis.		294	Psalm XIX		29
TITAN					
O Titan faire the giver of the daie?		80	Arcadia III	52	2
TITLE					
That verie shame with Love's high title dignifie..		14	1st Eclogues	7	3
Since vertues all, to make her title, pleased be..		15	1st Eclogues	7	39
Oh no, no, hardye shepeheard, worth can never enter a title,		34	1st Eclogues	13	82
P. O glorious title of a foolish toye.		46	2nd Eclogues	27	20
Ncr trifling title of vanity dazleth us,		69	2nd Eclogues	34	24
Phaebus yeelde up thy title in my minde.		72	Arcadia III	38	11
Call me but yours, my title is most hye:		79	Arcadia III	50	17
Thy title great, I justlie chalenge may,		80	Arcadia III	53	7
It title had, unto my only love,		96	3rd Eclogues	64	89
But Vertue thus that title doth disprove,		190	Astrophil	52	5
Ne if I would, could I just title make,		224	Astrophil	90	9

TITLE	(CONTINUED)	PAGE	TITLE	LINE
As with sententious lips to set a title vaine on it:		217	A&S 7th Song	4
So lord we shall Thy Title sing.		283	Psalm X	69
TITLES				
And titles are but spots to such a worthe, ...		18	1st Eclogues 7	132
TOADS				
Then with the poisnous todes that quiet lie.		28	1st Eclogues 10	66
TOGETHER				
For both, alas, their strengthes together tie:		42	Arcadia II 22	4
P. Not so, but fellowlike together borne..		46	2nd Eclogues 27	12
When they though divers do together meete:		92	3rd Eclogues 63	34
Or canons thunder-like, all shot togither, lende).		118	4th Eclogues 73	54
(For both togither spake, each loth to be behinde)		121	4th Eclogues 73	155
O notes of mine your selves together tie:.		127	4th Eclogues 75	76
O kisse, which soules, even soules together ties		207	Astrophil 81	5
Still both their flocks flocking togither went,.		242	Other Poems 4	30
So they three did togither idly stay,.		250	Other Poems 4	329
I am with you together..		261	Other Poems 6	40
TOIL				
My sonne, keepe this, that my long toyle hath laide to me: .		16	1st Eclogues 7	52
Why shouldst thou toyle our thornie soile to till?		169	Astrophil 10	6
TOILED				
More in his owne he toyld he gladdes the more.		71	Arcadia III 36	12
Thus toyled in my work of raging love, ...		71	Arcadia III 37	14
TOILS				
R. O sacred Reason, helpe our vertuous toiles.		46	2nd Eclogues 27	23
Tired with the dusty toiles of busie day,.		224	Astrophil 89	7
TOKEN				
Not seeing earst such token in the wife, ...		96	3rd Eclogues 64	68
TOKENS				
Of Prince's losse your selves for tokens reare..		125	4th Eclogues 75	27
TOLD				
Yet say againe thy advise for th' ev'lls that I told thee. I				
told thee..		63	2nd Eclogues 31	18
She told him that the courtier had it sent:.		96	3rd Eclogues 64	86
That bravely maskt, their fancies may be told:		166	Astrophil 3	2
But they are more than can by me be told..		331	Psalm XL	24
I tolde you Klaius was the haples wight.		251	Other Poems 4	365
TOLDST				
Thou toldst mine eyes should helpe their famisht case? . . .		235	Astrophil 106	6
TOMB				
A stately tombe to cover him deceased.		126	4th Eclogues 75	59
Sir wrong his tombe ordaineth, ...		160	Cert Sonnets 30	23
In tombe of lids then buried are mine eyes,.		231	Astrophil 99	12
TOMBS				
So become our tombes monuments of her praise;.		30	1st Eclogues 12	10
That tombes the two, is justly one..		241	Other Poems 3	8
TONGUE				
Thy toong hath made of Cupid's deepe incision.		20	1st Eclogues 7	V969
That soone the world of his false tong be void..		24	1st Eclogues 9	68
Like beast for sacrifice, where save the tong..		24	1st Eclogues 9	81
Geron. Fy man, fy man, what wordes hath thy tonge lent?. . .		28	1st Eclogues 10	61
Who of his tongue the lickowr gladly powrs,.		28	1st Eclogues 10	70
Let not thy tonge become a firy matche,.		29	1st Eclogues 10	89
Your woll is riche: no tonge can tell my gayne..		43	Arcadia II 23	14
O toonge, then dumbe, not daring tell my smart;.		60	2nd Eclogues 30	121
Peace? what barrs me my tongue? who is it that comes me so				
ny? I..		62	2nd Eclogues 31	2
My tong to this my roofe cleaves,.		66	2nd Eclogues 32	12
Nor mas'de head thinke, nor faltring tonge recite.		74	Arcadia III 42	14
O toong in which, all honyed likoures bee, ...		76	Arcadia III 46	3
What toong can her perfections tell.		85	Arcadia III 62	1
Her heav'nly-dewed tongue to garde..		87	Arcadia III 62	44
My tongue doth tell what fancie sees..		89	Arcadia III 62	94
No tongue can her perfections tell,.		90	Arcadia III 62	145
Doth breake, now toong unto thy name doth move,.		97	3rd Eclogues 64	100
And Parot, ready tongue, that to applie.		101	3rd Eclogues 66	84
This you heare is not my tongue, ...		139	Cert Sonnets 7	4
No, though tongue to roofe be cleaved, ...		139	Cert Sonnets 7	8
My burning tongue hath bred my mistresse paine,.		141	Cert Sonnets 9	2
So stay her toung, that she no more say no..		142	Cert Sonnets 10	14
My tongue doth itch, my thoughts in labour be:		183	Astrophil 37	2
Doth make my heart give to my tongue the lie..		188	Astrophil 47	14
So may your tongue still fluently proceed, ...		190	Astrophil 51	2
And through those lips drinke Nectar from that toong;. . . .		208	Astrophil 83	13
Her tongue waking still refuseth,.		202	A&S 2nd Song	9
What No her tongue sleeping useth.		202	A&S 2nd Song	12
Then grew my tongue and pen records unto thy glory:. . . .		212	A&S 5th Song	3
Let no tongue aspire to tell,.		226	A&S 10th Song	10
Which the deere tongue would afford, ...		218	A&S 8th Song	22
Wherto their tongue is flattring Instrument.		275	Psalm V	28
Thy force hath flow'd from Babie's tongue.		278	Psalm VIII	6
Under his tongue do harbour'd ly		282	Psalm X	29
Who with deceitfull tongue hath never usd to faine,.		287	Psalm XV	5
So let words sprung from my weake tongue,.		295	Psalm XIX	61
My cleaving tongue close to my roofe doth bide..		299	Psalm XXII	36
And tongue is prest to publish out thy prayse.		306	Psalm XXVI	39
Ev'n such I say, whose lying tongue.		308	Psalm XXVII	58
Therfore my tongue shall never lack.		311	Psalm XXX	37
Then since my tongue delights that name to blesse, ...		312	Psalm XXXI	8

527

TONGUE   (CONTINUED)   PAGE   TITLE   LINE
    Keep well thy lipps and tongue . . . . 320 Psalm XXXIV   49
    As for my tongue, while I have any dayes,. . . . . 323 Psalm XXXV   71
    His tongue of heavnly judgments telleth, ... 326 Psalm XXXVII   78
    Least by my tongue I hap to stray; . . . . 329 Psalm XXXIX   2
    My tongue would needs and thus I spake:. . . . . 329 Psalm XXXIX   12
TONGUED
    Men tongd like lotches sucking others sorrowe. . . . . . .   50 2nd Eclogues 28 V885
TONGUE'S
    Would have made tongue's language plaine;. . . . . 219 A&S 8th Song   66
TONGUES
    O sheepheards' boyes, eschue these tongues of venome,. . . .   50 2nd Eclogues 28   87
    O tongues right ladders made to clime dishonour, ...   50 2nd Eclogues 28   90
    (For they have toongs to make a poore man blamed . . . . .   94 3rd Eclogues 64   21
    But who doo let their tongues shew well their rage,. . . . . 105 3rd Eclogues 67   47
    Seas in our eyes, and brasen tongues by nature,. . . . . . 109 Arcadia IV   70   26
    But their tongues restraind from walking,. . . . . 218 A&S 8th Song   23
    But when their tongues could not speake, ... 218 A&S 8th Song   25
    And shalt root out the tongues to lying bent:. . . . . 275 Psalm V   14
    Can of thy prayse the tongues entombed make. . . . . 276 Psalm VI   15
    Our tongues, say they, beyond them all shall go, ... 285 Psalm XII   10
    And cruel Words their swelling tongues do chatt, ... 290 Psalm XVII   30
    From strife of tongues in Thy Pavilions plac't.. . . . . . . 313 Psalm XXXI   57
TOO
    Thy health too meane a match for my infection. . . . .   15 1st Eclogues 7   21
    Let crowes picke out mine eyes, which saw too much:. . . .   19 1st Eclogues 7 149
    Let crowes picke out mine eyes which too much sawe.. . . . .   19 1st Eclogues 7 V149
    These cocklinges cockred we bewaile to late, ...   28 1st Eclogues 10   58
    Thy too much zeale, I feare thy braine hath spent. . . . . .   28 1st Eclogues 10   63
    Unto the heav'ns? our wings be too short; th' earth thinks
        us a burden; . . . .   32 1st Eclogues 13   29
    With stroking hurt, and too much cramming kill.. . . . . . .   41 Arcadia II   20   12
    R. We are too strong: but Reason seekes not blood. . . . . .   47 2nd Eclogues 27   29
    P. Who be too weake, do feigne they be too good. . . . . . .   47 2nd Eclogues 27   30
    In him, the thoughts of Phaeton's damme to grave.. . . . . .   60 2nd Eclogues 30 106
    Thus is our mind with too much minding spilled.. . . . . . .   62 2nd Eclogues 30 175
    Well mett Echo, aproche: then tell me thy will too. I will
        too. . . . .   63 2nd Eclogues 31   4
    So are thy pains my pains too. . . . .   67 2nd Eclogues 32   42
    My voice, too hott to keepe in.. . . . .   67 2nd Eclogues 32   45
    Which at firste voly gave too open entry,. . . . .   68 2nd Eclogues 33   14
    Where too much sight, makes all the bodie blinde,. . . . . .   73 Arcadia III 40   11
    You onely yours, too farr beyond desarte.. . . . .   79 Arcadia III 50   22
    Her sence too weake to beare her spirit's mighte.. . . . . .   79 Arcadia III 51   4
    Too weake for them our weaker sighte doth vaile. . . . . . .   82 Arcadia III 55   11
    Thought, thinke to ende, too long the frute of thought . . .   83 Arcadia III 59   7
    Never hard hand, nor ever raines too light.. . . . .   98 3rd Eclogues 65   8
    Who hath our sight with too much sight infected, ... 108 Arcadia IV   69   6
    Too much her peerles parts, nor yet could them despise.. . . 119 4th Eclogues 73   88
    Proofe speakes too much to us that feeling triall have.. . . 119 4th Eclogues 73 108
    With too much griefe me thinkes you are dissolved. . . . . . 127 4th Eclogues 75   77
    They leave off al, and say, death comes too eagerlie.. . . . 128 4th Eclogues 75 114
    Since wanting is more woe then too much having.. . . . . . . 137 Cert Sonnets 4   20
    No, no, she is too wise, she knowes her face . . . . 142 Cert Sonnets 11   9
    Pressing too much upon ill harbourd shore. . . . . 142 Cert Sonnets 12   3
    In too full winde draw in thy swelling sailes. . . . . 143 Cert Sonnets 12   18
    I would it not, their mettall is too fine, ... 146 Cert Sonnets 17   25
    She thinks I leade and live too merrie daies.. . . . . 146 Cert Sonnets 17   30
    Desire, desire I have too dearely bought,. . . . . 161 Cert Sonnets 31   5
    Too long, too long asleepe thou hast me brought, ... 161 Cert Sonnets 31   7
    And strange things cost too deare for my poore sprites.. . . 166 Astrophil   3   11
    My mouth too tender is for thy hard bit. . . . . 166 Astrophil   4   8
    But finding these North clymes too coldly him embrace, . . . 168 Astrophil   8 V 5
    Which lookes too oft in his unflattring glasse:. . . . . . . 178 Astrophil   27   10
    While too much wit (forsooth) so troubled me,. . . . . 181 Astrophil   33   10
    Far far too long to learne it without booke: . . . . 192 Astrophil   56   2
    In this old world, growne now so too too wise: . . . . 198 Astrophil   65   6
    O joy, too high for my low stile to show:. . . . . 200 Astrophil   69   1
    But wit confus'd with too much care did misse. . . . . 227 Astrophil   93   8
    And grace, sicke too, such fine conclusions tries, ... 231 Astrophil 101   3
    When she wakes, is too too cruell. . . . . 202 A&S 2nd Song
    These sweet flowers on fine bed too, ... 210 A&S 4th Song   15
    My life melts with too much thinking;. . . . . 227 A&S 10th Song   45
    Which too deep in me is framed,. . . . . 220 A&S 8th Song   99
    Yet know this too, that God did take . . . . 273 Psalm IV   11
    Thy judgments are too high . . . . 282 Psalm X   19
    His Temple too.. . . . . 307 Psalm XXVII   24
    Dick. I would it were but thus, for thus it were too well. . 343 Possibly   1   17
    But you, o you, that thinke not teares too deare . . . . . . 242 Other Poems   4   9
    The later borne, yet too soone, Strephon hight.. . . . . . . 242 Other Poems   4   24
    But fearing lest all white might seeme too good, ... 246 Other Poems   4 151
    The lesson which but late he learn'd too furre:. . . . . . . 246 Other Poems   4 174
    O fortune too too badd,. . . . . 259 Other Poems   5   98
TOOK
    Till this he tooke for comfort of his lot: . . . .   5 Lady of May   3   10
    Of my good sheepe, thou never trews time tooke:. . . . . . .   27 1st Eclogues 10   14
    If Love tooke thee by force, or caught thee guilefully.. . .   48 2nd Eclogues 28   21
    Since in my hands selfe goodly sight she tooke.. . . . . . .   55 2nd Eclogues 29 116
    In what state was I then, when I tooke this deadly disease?
        ease.. . . . .   63 2nd Eclogues 31   8

TOOK   (CONTINUED)   PAGE   TITLE   LINE

    Then greefe, unkindnes, proofe, tooke, kindled, tought,. . .   84 Arcadia III   60   9
    Full glad they were and tooke the naked sprite,. . . . . . . 101 3rd Eclogues 66   78
    Love of her selfe, tooke Stella's shape, that she. . . . . . 177 Astrophil   25 V 10
    Somewhat thy lead'n counsels, which I tooke. . . . . 193 Astrophil   56   7
    Which all from Thee their Essence took . . . . 278 Psalm VIII   10
    Then sent he from above, and took me from below,. . . . . .   291 Psalm XVIII   34
    The fire took fire and forcibly out brake,. . . . .   329 Psalm XXXIX   11
    Betwixt them two the peeper tooke his nest,. . . . . 244 Other Poems   4 102
    So now for pray these shepheards two he tooke, ... 245 Other Poems   4 137
    From Nous and Cosma all their beauty tooke.. . . . . 248 Other Poems   4 248
    Up with hir fist, and tooke him on the face, ... 249 Other Poems   4 274
    She fled, and tooke: he folow'd, and was cought. . . . . . . 251 Other Poems   4 348
TOOL
    No sword soe bytes as that evill toole annoyes.. . . . . . .   29 1st Eclogues 10   90
TOO-MUCH
    Should my too-much sight cause so true a Sunne to be lost? . 124 4th Eclogues 74   58
*TOP
    When that noble toppe doth nodd, I beleeve she salutes me; .   36 1st Eclogues 13 144
    (Even like a toppe which nought but whipping moves). . . . .   58 2nd Eclogues 30   33
    His weighty top) his top doth downeward drooping leane:. . . 117 4th Eclogues 73   22
    From Syon's holy top;. 295 Psalm XX   8
TOPS
    With dearest tops of porphyrie.. . . . .   87 Arcadia III   62   57
TORCH
    Curst be the page from whome the bad torch fell, ... 235 Astrophil   105   11
TORMENT
    I waste my harte, which still newe torment tryes.. . . . . .   75 Arcadia III   43   5
    Nature to me for torment did emparte;. . . . . 113 4th Eclogues 72   13
    When to my livelie torment,. . . . . 154 Cert Sonnets 25   2
    In my reines hot torment raignes,. . . . . 328 Psalm XXXVIII   19
TORMENTORS
    With thoughts which thoughts their owne tormentors tried,. . 259 Other Poems   5 119
TORMENTS
    In sorrows torments, then, tyed to the pompes of a pallace,.   35 1st Eclogues 13 103
    What causes first made these torments on me to light? Light.   64 2nd Eclogues 31   23
    What stormes founde me, what tormentes I dyd fynde,. . . . .   71 Arcadia III   36   15
    Or if I needs (sweet Judge) must torments have,. . . . . . . 212 Astrophil   86   11
    And which is worse, makes me most guiltlesse torments have,. 214 A&S 5th Song   59
    And of hideous torments ease me. . . . . 222 A&S 9th Song   45
    My life hott torments tasted.. . . . . 315 Psalm XXXII   12
TORN
    Torne with her hands, and those same hands of snow . . . . .   58 2nd Eclogues 30   45
    Of willing teares, torne heare, and cries of sorrow. . . . . 109 Arcadia IV   70   16
    How hast thou torne thy selfe! sought thine owne damage! . . 109 Arcadia IV   70   20
    Fancie, her tackling, torne away doth flie:. . . . . 114 4th Eclogues 72   47
    Torne you should disperse unto the blasts of a winde.. . . . 123 4th Eclogues 74   52
    For when my heart with woes was torn,. . . . . 311 Psalm XXX   4
TORPEDO
    I sought to catch the fish Torpedo faire.. . . . . 115 4th Eclogues 72   63
TOSS
    With care's hard hand) to turne and tosse in thee. . . . . . 230 Astrophil   98   8
    Whom troubles tosse, whose natures need doth quell,. . . . . 285 Psalm XII   14
TOSSED
    Thus tossed in my shipp of huge desyre,. . . . .   71 Arcadia III   37   13
    My ship, desire, with winde of lust long tost, ... 151 Cert Sonnets 22   55
TOTAL
    See Beautie's totall summe summ'd in her face: . . . . 210 Astrophil   85   10
    That to my questions you so totall are?. . . . . 225 Astrophil   92   5
TOTHER
    The one, which tother would refrayne.. . . . .   57 2nd Eclogues 30   4
TOTTERING
    Beware full sailes drowne not thy tottring barge:. . . . . . 209 Astrophil   85   2
TOUCH
    How nice to touch? how all her speeches peized be? . . . . .   15 1st Eclogues   7   35
    What ere you see, thinke, touch, kisse, speake, or love, . .   60 2nd Eclogues 30 123
    Which touch the father's hart with secret joy, ... 106 3rd Eclogues 67 113
    Of touch they are that without touch doth touch, ... 169 Astrophil   9   12
    Of touch they are, and poore I am their straw. . . . . 169 Astrophil   9   14
    As do bewray a want of inward tuch:. . . . . 172 Astrophil   15   10
    That when the breath of my complaints doth tuch. . . . . . . 187 Astrophil   44   10
    That hand, which without touch holds more then Atlas might;. 205 Astrophil   77   5
    As no exceptions tutch.. . . . . 216 A&S 6th Song   42
    As but eares but hart did tuch:. . . . . 220 A&S 8th Song   70
    I prayd with prayers which my breast did touch;. . . . . . . 322 Psalm XXXV   32
    To spend for harms, although they touch you not: . . . . . . 242 Other Poems   4   10
TOUCHED
    Even turtle toutcht he with hypocrisie.. . . . .   28 1st Eclogues 10   81
    O hand, which toucht her hand when we did part;. . . . . . .   60 2nd Eclogues 30 119
    No vertue merits praise, once toucht with blot of Treason. . 214 A&S 5th Song   66
TOUCHING
    And crown'd the earth with his first touching crowne:. . . . 248 Other Poems   4 260
TOUCHSTONE
    Me with Thy touch-stone try, ... 305 Psalm XXVI   8
TOWARD
    Toward Aurora's Court a Nymph doth dwell,. . . . . 183 Astrophil   37 V 5
    Toward Lamkins best beloved. . . . . 221 A&S 9th Song   25
    The two in hell did toward Cosma frame,. . . . . 249 Other Poems   4 267
TOWARDS
    And aye more awe towards him for to plant, ... 101 3rd Eclogues 66 102

TOWARDS   (CONTINUED)   PAGE   TITLE   LINE
   Towardes Aurora's Court a Nymph doth dwell,. . . . .   183 Astrophil   37   5
   Towards the Temple of Thy Holyness. . . . .   275 Psalm V   20
   Do coupled towards either couple make, ...   248 Other Poems   4   234
TOWER
   What myne hath erst throwne downe so faire a tower?. . . . .   59 2nd Eclogues 30   96
   When lo with hugest noise (such noise a tower makes. . . . .   118 4th Eclogues 73   51
   I will say: O lord my tower, ...   335 Psalm XLII   41
TOWERS
   Such be I thinke the sumptuous towers. . . . .   87 Arcadia III 62   49
   Unknowne as then were they that buylden towers:. . . . . . .   100 3rd Eclogues 66   46
   The stately towers come downe with greater fall: . . . . . .   143 Cert Sonnets 12   8
TOWNFOLKS
   Towne-folkes my strength; a daintier judge applies . . . . .   185 Astrophil   41   6
TOWNS
   How Holland hearts, now so good townes be lost, ...   180 Astrophil   30   7
TOY
   But is indeed a toy, if not a toy, ...   25 1st Eclogues 9   115
   P. O glorious title of a foolish toye. . . . .   46 2nd Eclogues 27   20
   But murder, private fault, seems but a toy to thee, ...   214 A&S 5th Song   55
TOYING
   Not toying kinde, nor causlesly unkinde, ...   98 3rd Eclogues 65   5
TOYS
   Curs'd be thy selfe for cursing that which leades me to
     joies. . . . .   65 2nd Eclogues 31   40
   All strife for toyes, and clayming master's right: . . . . .   93 3rd Eclogues 63   67
   Envying shallow toyes with malice deepe. . . . .   104 3rd Eclogues 67   39
   But these be your love-toyes, which still are spent. . . . .   106 3rd Eclogues 67   94
   Therefore esteeming all good blessings toyes, ...   116 4th Eclogues 72   99
   My youth doth waste, my knowledge brings forth toyes, . . .   174 Astrophil   18   9
TRACE
   R. Passion is blinde, and treades an unknowne trace. . . . .   46 2nd Eclogues 27   15
   Whose footsteps I with kisses oft did trace, ...   115 4th Eclogues 72   73
   Let me no steps but of lost labour trace, ...   198 Astrophil   64   6
TRACETH
   And what thinges els of waters traceth . . . .   279 Psalm VIII   31
TRADE
   Thinking how it hath mard my shepheard's trade. . . . . . .   19 1st Eclogues 7   169
   Say then what vantage do we get, by the trade of a Pastor? .   33 1st Eclogues 13   49
   Take heed therefore, how you ensue that trade, ...   97 3rd Eclogues 64   123
   The trade of them, that just proceeding love; . . . .   271 Psalm I   20
   From men I say, and from men's worldly trade, ...   290 Psalm XVII   38
   By them is made Thy servants' trade. . . . .   295 Psalm XIX   45
TRAGEDY
   Of Lover's ruine some sad Tragedie: . . . .   187 Astrophil   45   13
TRAGICAL
   Despaire most tragicall clause to a deadly request) . . . .   122 4th Eclogues 74   12
*TRAIN
   Or trayne the fox that traines so crafty laies. . . . . . .   26 1st Eclogues 9   125
   In which most lovely traine, ...   92 3rd Eclogues 63   53
   Great expectation, weare a traine of shame. . . . .   175 Astrophil   21   8
   Though harbengers of death lodge there his traine. . . . . .   228 Astrophil   94   8
   Unto Dianae's train thou runaway didst flee: . . . .   214 A&S 5th Song   71
   Even he, that leads of life an uncorrupted traine, ...   287 Psalm XV   3
TRAINED
   The field where all my thoughts to warre be traind, ...   230 Astrophil   98   2
   Train'd in the life which on short-bitten grasse . . . . . .   242 Other Poems   4   19
   A maid train'd up from high or low degree, ...   247 Other Poems   4   210
   By Parents train'd the Tartars wilde are tought, ...   251 Other Poems   4   350
TRAINETH
   One word of woe another after traineth: . . . .   128 4th Eclogues 75   103
TRAINS
   Or trayne the fox that traines so crafty laies. . . . . . .   26 1st Eclogues 9   125
TRAITOR
   And thou o traytour Sleepe, made for to be our rest, ...   121 4th Eclogues 73   183
   Out traytour absence, darest thou counsell me, ...   223 Astrophil   88   1
   With traitor lime the one, ...   258 Other Poems   5   87
TRAMPLING
   Tempers her words to trampling horses feet, ...   209 Astrophil   84   3
TRANSFORM
   First may a trusty Greyhounde transforme himselfe to a
     Tigre . . . .   33 1st Eclogues 13   66
   What marvaile tho a Prince transforme himselfe to a Pastor?.   34 1st Eclogues 13   91
   Whose force had such force so to transforme, nay to reforme
     me, ...   37 1st Eclogues 13   166
   Transforme themselves to lowe dejected vallies: . . . . . .   112 4th Eclogues 71   38
TRANSFORMED
   Transformd in shew, but more transformd in minde, ...   11 Arcadia I   2   1
   Thus is my power transformed to your will. . . . .   12 Arcadia I   2   12
   Whence he was transformed late, ...   262 Other Poems   7   10
TRANSGRESSIONS
   From my transgressions me to save. . . . .   330 Psalm XXXIX   26
TRANSLATED
   Her eye's-speech is translated thus by thee: . . . .   199 Astrophil   67   5
TRANSLATION
   A Nimph thus turnde, but mended in translation. . . . . . .   15 1st Eclogues 7   36
TRAP
   Oft comes reliefe when most we seeme in trappe. . . . . . .   23 1st Eclogues 9   24
   To trap poor soules he goes! . . . .   282 Psalm X   44

```
TRAVAIL                                                      PAGE    TITLE           LINE
     Latona's sonne, whose birth in paine and travaile long . . .   45 Arcadia II    26    7
     In travaile of our life (a short but tedious space). . . . .   45 Arcadia II    26    9
     Who for our sakes will thinke all travaile light,. . . . . .  129 4th Eclogues  76   23
TRAVAILED
     And great with child of mischeif travaild long,. . . . . . .  278 Psalm VII          38
TRAVAILS
     Doth teach, to learne the good what travailes do belong: . .   45 Arcadia II    26    8
TRAVEL
     Lyke crafty wretch by time and travell tought, . . . . . . .  141 Cert Sonnets   8    5
TREACHERY
     (How can he love suspecting treacherie?. . . . . . . . . .    93 3rd Eclogues  63   84
TREAD
     His cloven foote doth never treade aright. . . . . . . . . .   21 1st Eclogues   8   30
     Your eyes may tread a Lover's maze.. . . . . . . . . . . . .   86 Arcadia II    26   32
     Tread in my steppes, or follow not.. . . . . . . . . . . . .  153 Cert Sonnets  24   18
     Thou the path wilt make me tread . . . . . . . . . . . . . .  288 Psalm XVI          37
     And teach the humble how to tread. . . . . . . . . . . . . .  303 Psalm XXV          36
     Or like a broken pott in myer tredd. . . . . . . . . . . . .  313 Psalm XXXI         36
TREADING
     Lo, he was gon, print of his treading, . . . . . . . . . . .  327 Psalm XXXVII       91
TREADS
     R. Passion is blinde, and treades an unknowne trace. . . . .   46 2nd Eclogues  27   15
     He blessed is, who neither loosely treads. . . . . . . . . .  270 Psalm I             1
TREASON
     With outward force and inward treason spoild.. . . . . . . .   11 Arcadia I      2    4
     Here no treason is hidd, vailed in innocence,. . . . . . . .   69 2nd Eclogues  34   17
     No vertue merits praise, once toucht with blot of Treason. .  214 A&S 5th Song       66
TREASURE
     Let not wild woods so great a treasure have. . . . . . . . .    3 Lady of May    2   12
     Among his flocke so sweete a treasure keepe. . . . . . . . .    4 Lady of May    2   18
     Lalus. Once my well-waiting eyes espied my treasure, . . . .   16 1st Eclogues   7   73
     In meane caves oft treasure abides, to an hostry a king
       comes. . . . . . . . . . . . . . . . . . . . . . . . . . .   36 1st Eclogues  13  153
     The hart, eye, eare here onely find his treasure doth: . . .   49 2nd Eclogues  28   58
     Their sought-for treasure. . . . . . . . . . . . . . . . . .   83 Arcadia III   59    4
     Be victor still of Phoebus' golden treasure: . . . . . . . .  108 Arcadia IV    69    5
     In one true chest to rob all Vertue's treasure?. . . . . . .  126 4th Eclogues  75   47
     Farewell o pearl, the poore man's plenteous treasure:. . . .  129 4th Eclogues  76    2
     Now that the mine is lost of all our treasure, . . . . . . .  129 4th Eclogues  76   10
     As well he was in peace a safest treasure: . . . . . . . . .  129 4th Eclogues  76   17
     Who long have gap't to get Arcadians' treasure.. . . . . . .  129 4th Eclogues  76   21
     For ever robbed of our royall treasure.. . . . . . . . . . .  130 4th Eclogues  76   30
     Let teares for him therefore be all our treasure,. . . . . .  130 4th Eclogues  76   31
     Farewell our light, farewell our spoiled treasure: . . . . .  130 4th Eclogues  76   37
     Though I be hers, she makes of me no treasure. . . . . . . .  137 Cert Sonnets   3   24
     Lady my Treasure.. . . . . . . . . . . . . . . . . . . . . .  138 Cert Sonnets   5    4
     Above line repeated at following location. . . . . . . . . .  138 Cert Sonnets   5   28
     As treasure house where her best gifts abyde.. . . . . . . .  141 Cert Sonnets   8    8
     Small losse of mortall treasure, . . . . . . . . . . . . . .  152 Cert Sonnets  23   19
     Since his treasure . . . . . . . . . . . . . . . . . . . . .  155 Cert Sonnets  26   10
     Having before me Nature's treasure,. . . . . . . . . . . . .  159 Cert Sonnets  29    6
     Rich in the treasure of deserv'd renowne,. . . . . . . . . .  183 Astrophil     37    9
     Who keepes the key of Nature's chiefest treasure?. . . . . .  197 A&S 1st Song        6
     The same key op'n can, which can locke up a treasure.. . . .  213 A&S 5th Song       18
     Nor debard from beautie's treasure,. . . . . . . . . . . . .  226 A&S 10th Song       9
     Only rich in mischiefe's treasure. . . . . . . . . . . . . .  221 A&S 9th Song       10
     And depths in treasure his.. . . . . . . . . . . . . . . . .  316 Psalm XXXIII       27
     Greater was that shepheard's treasure, . . . . . . . . . . .  263 Other Poems    7   47
TREASURES
     Locke up, faire liddes, the treasures of my harte: . . . . .   79 Arcadia III   51    1
     (Exil'd for ay from those high treasures, which. . . . . . .  177 Astrophil     24   13
     "Foole," answers he, "no Indes such treasures hold,. . . . .  181 Astrophil     32   12
     With words, wherein the Muses' treasures be, . . . . . . . .  195 Astrophil     60    7
     Why doest thou spend the treasures of thy sprite,. . . . . .  200 Astrophil     68    5
     And so with hidden treasures grant their Will, . . . . . . .  290 Psalm XVII         42
TREAT
     O ease your hand, treate not so hard your slave: . . . . . .  212 Astrophil     86    9
TREATY
     May make treaty to god Pan). . . . . . . . . . . . . . . . .  263 Other Poems    7   58
TREBLE
     He treble beas for helpe, but none can get:. . . . . . . . .  254 Other Poems    4  492
TREBLES
     Trebles sing high, as well as bases deepe: . . . . . . . . .  201 Astrophil     70    6
TREE
     Of Phoebus' violence in shade of stately Ciprus tree,. . . .   31 1st Eclogues  13   12
     Which made a Bay, made Bay a holy tree:. . . . . . . . . . .   54 2nd Eclogues  29   61
     Nico. Thy monument is layd in many a tree, . . . . . . . . .   56 2nd Eclogues  29  129
     This man, this talking beast, this walking tree. . . . . . .   58 2nd Eclogues  30   34
     What man grafts in a tree dissimulation? . . . . . . . . . .   69 2nd Eclogues  34   28
     Yet still, faire tree, lifte up thy stately line,. . . . . .   77 Arcadia III   47    9
     But if among yourselves some one tree growe, . . . . . . . .  125 4th Eclogues  75   10
     The wynde most oft the hugest Pine-tree greeves: . . . . . .  143 Cert Sonnets  12    7
     The lothsome buds growne on sorrowe's tree.. . . . . . . . .  153 Cert Sonnets  24    5
     Or reach the fruite of Nature's choisest tree, . . . . . . .  169 Astrophil     10    4
     Trust in the shade of pleasing Orange tree;. . . . . . . . .  180 Astrophil     30    8
     Long since forc'd by thy beames, but stone nor tree. . . . .  183 Astrophil     36   13
     Sweet gard'n Nymph, which keepes the Cherrie tree,. . . . . .  208 Astrophil     82    5
     A nest for my yong praise in Lawrell tree: . . . . . . . . .  224 Astrophil     90    6
     Onelie through you the tree of life doth flourish. . . . . .  197 A&S 1st Song       20
```

TREE	(CONTINUED)	PAGE	TITLE		LINE
Ech tree in his best attiring,		219	A&S 8th Song		59
He shall be lyke a freshly planted tree,		270	Psalm I		7
Strephon with leavy twiggs of Laurell tree		244	Other Poems	4	73
Then in good Dog, faire field, or shading tree		246	Other Poems	4	179
Out shreaking pipe made of some witched tree		255	Other Poems	4	516
Spake unto a sencelesse tree,		262	Other Poems	7	16
TREENE-DISH					
When for a treene-dish stolne, thy father did thee whippe!		52	2nd Eclogues 29		12
TREES					
Those pleasant plants, those sweete and frutefull trees,		26	1st Eclogues 9		130
When trees daunce to the pype, and swift streames stay by the musicke,		33	1st Eclogues 13		47
And when I meete these trees, in the earth's faire lyvery clothed,		35	1st Eclogues 13		113
Firr trees great and greene, fixt on a hye hill but a barrein,		35	1st Eclogues 13		123
Thus both trees and each thing ells, be the bookes of a fancy.		36	1st Eclogues 13		140
Of growing trees, yee rurall Gods that wield		40	Arcadia II 18		2
Strephon. I wish to fire the trees of all these forrests;		112	4th Eclogues 71		49
The flying sprites which trees by rootes up teare.		114	4th Eclogues 72		36
And from our burning breath the trees doo bende.		116	4th Eclogues 72		104
And you o trees (if any life there lies.		125	4th Eclogues 75		4
In trees) now through your porous barkes receave		125	4th Eclogues 75		5
The very trees with grafting we can cherish,		127	4th Eclogues 75		85
Through pores of sencelesse trees, as it could make them move:		208	A&S 3rd Song		2
O stones, o trees, learne hearing, Stella singeth.		208	A&S 3rd Song		6
The birds, beasts, stones and trees feele this, and feeling love:		209	A&S 3rd Song		13
And if the trees, nor stones stirre not the same to prove,		209	A&S 3rd Song		14
The trees spred out their armes to shade hir face,		245	Other Poems	4	109
No grasse, no trees, nor yet hir sparrow might		245	Other Poems	4	111
And now the dropping trees doo wepe for me,		254	Other Poems	4	479
TREES'					
Faire trees' shade is enough fortification,		69	2nd Eclogues 34		13
TREMBLE					
O tremble then with awfull will:		273	Psalm IV		16
And so the Earth did fall to tremble, and to quake		291	Psalm XVIII		15
TREMBLING					
When trembling voice brings forth that I do Stella love.		168	Astrophil 6		14
That joy with trembling go		271	Psalm II		26
His voice have trembling deserts try'd,		310	Psalm XXIX		20
TRENTALS					
Let Dirge be sung, and Trentals rightly read,		160	Cert Sonnets 30		21
TRIAL					
Knowing no more, then what poore tryall showes,		28	1st Eclogues 10		53
As fishe sure tryall hath of muddy slyme.		28	1st Eclogues 10		54
Proofe speakes too much to us that feeling triall have.		119	4th Eclogues 73		108
O no, O no, tryall onely shewse.		153	Cert Sonnets 24		10
Let fyre for tryall burn,		296	Psalm XX		13
But tryall well doth teach me,		332	Psalm XL		45
TRIBULATION					
In time of greatest tribulation.		327	Psalm XXXVII		99
TRIBUTE					
From hidnest depth, which tribute when it ends,		150	Cert Sonnets 22		13
I will good tribute pay if thou do so.		184	Astrophil 39		8
That wittie Lewis to him a tribute paid.		204	Astrophil 75		11
Thou but of all the kingly Tribute take.		210	Astrophil 85		14
And did the tribute of their wondring sight.		251	Other Poems	4	363
TRICK					
That married had a trick and bonny lasse		94	3rd Eclogues 64		3
TRIED					
Now that he had her words so truely tried:		97	3rd Eclogues 64		112
O happie Dove if she no bondage tried:		144	Cert Sonnets 15		13
In Martiall sports I had my cunning tride,		191	Astrophil 53		1
Pure, Purer than the silver throughly try'd.		285	Psalm XII		20
Then was I by thy searching insight try'd,		289	Psalm XVII		10
Thy way is soundly sure, Thy word is purely tryd;		292	Psalm XVIII		55
His voice have trembling deserts try'd,		310	Psalm XXIX		20
With thoughts which thoughts their owne tormentors tried,		259	Other Poems	5	119
TRIES					
Yeld outward shew, what inward change he tryes:		13	Arcadia I 4		2
Dorus. Farre other care, o Muse, my sorrow tries,		17	1st Eclogues 7		106
Since all his force against himselfe he tries.		23	1st Eclogues 9		37
I waste my harte, which still newe torment tryes		75	Arcadia III 43		5
Others, because the Prince my service tries,		176	Astrophil 23		7
That busie archer his sharpe arrowes tries?		180	Astrophil 31		4
For my poore soule, which now that sicknesse tries,		228	Astrophil 94		6
And grace, sicke too, such fine conclusions tries,		231	Astrophil 101		3
That comfort in these sports you like, my mynde his comfort tryes.		343	Possibly 1		14
Where bold and hurtles many plays he tries,		247	Other Poems	4	194
TRIFLE					
"Tush, tush", said nature, "this is all but a trifle, a man's selfe.		29	1st Eclogues 11		7
TRIFLING					
Nor trifling title of vanity dazleth us,		69	2nd Eclogues 34		24

TRIM
    Such hartes of brasse, wise heads, and garments trim . . . .   24 1st Eclogues 9   75
    So have I sene trim bookes in velvet dight . . . . 246 Other Poems 4 180
TRINITY
    A happy blessed Trinitie;. . . . . 260 Other Poems 6   20
TRIUMPH
    Therein his name, there his chiefe triumph lyes. . . . . . .   22 1st Eclogues 8   42
    So becomes our losse the triumph of her gayne; . . . .   30 1st Eclogues 12   11
    O Vertue weake, shall death his triumph set. . . . .   59 2nd Eclogues 30   92
    Place Sorrowe's triumph on my conquered harte: . . . . 114 4th Eclogues 72   17
    Vertue is dead, now set thy triumph here. . . . . 127 4th Eclogues 75   72
    Now set thy triumph in this world, bereaved. . . . . 127 4th Eclogues 75   73
    But triumph well may I, whom Thou dost stay. . . . . 334 Psalm XLI   41
    And ti'de them fast to leade his triumph badd, ... 245 Other Poems 4 131
    They looked down to triumph over pride:. . . . . 252 Other Poems 4 403
TRIUMPHAL
    Her breasts his tents, legs his triumphall carre:. . . . . . 179 Astrophil   29   11
TRIUMPHANT
    How long shall I with foes' triumphant might . . . . 285 Psalm XIII   7
TRIUMPHER
    Faire triumpher of annoy,. . . . . 218 A&S 8th Song   30
TRIUMPHING
    Heav'ns envy not at my high triumphing:. . . . . 196 Astrophil   63   10
    Triumphing over me. . . . . 333 Psalm XLI   40
TRIUMPH'S
    With triumph's shews would shew he nought did feare. . . . . 244 Other Poems 4   78
TRIUMPHS
    Such goodnes that in her simplicitie triumphs: . . . .   69 2nd Eclogues 34   36
    O faire, O fairest, are such the triumphs to thy fairnesse?. 123 4th Eclogues 74   31
    Wrackes Triumphs be, which Love (high set) doth breed. . . . 186 Astrophil   42   14
TRODDEN
    His eye, that ev'n did marke hir troden grasse, ... 251 Other Poems 4 379
TROJAN
    A horse's worth laid wast the Troyan ground: . . . . 146 Cert Sonnets 17   18
    Or hers whom naked the Trojan boy did see. . . . . 207 Astrophil   82   4
TROOPS
    And oft whole troupes of saddest words I staid, ... 192 Astrophil   55   5
    How in troops I wont to go, ... 334 Psalm XLII   14
TROPES
    Ennobling new found Tropes with problemes old: . . . . 166 Astrophil   3   6
    Cloth'd with fine tropes, with strongest reasons lin'd, . . . 194 Astrophil   58   6
TROPHIES
    Where they would leave trophees of cruell damage, ... 109 Arcadia IV   70   12
TROTH
    Nico. And are you there old Pas? in troth I ever thought, . .   51 2nd Eclogues 29   1
TROUBLE
    To breed my grievous trouble, ... 272 Psalm III   3
    All trouble, all reproche. . . . . 320 Psalm XXXIV   64
TROUBLED
    A voice may come, which troubled soule doth yeld: . . . . . .   40 Arcadia II   18   4
    While too much wit (forsooth) so troubled me, ... 181 Astrophil   33   10
    Of cunningst fishers in most troubled streames, ... 190 Astrophil   51   10
    She troubled was (alas that it mought be!) . . . . 245 Other Poems 4 113
TROUBLES
    Which troubles their daye's worke, and joyes of evening: . . 112 4th Eclogues 71   33
    Nay ev'n my soul fell troubles do appall; . . . . 276 Psalm VI   9
    Whom troubles tosse, whose natures need doth quell, ... 285 Psalm XIII   14
    Ev'n in the day when most Thy troubles be; . . . . 295 Psalm XX   2
    O Lord from all his troubles fell. . . . . 305 Psalm XXV   78
    For troubles of all sides have me within. . . . . 312 Psalm XXXI   26
    From out his troubles all. . . . . 319 Psalm XXXIV   24
    When most his troubles clime. . . . . 332 Psalm XLI   4
TROUBLOUS
    That they to Thee in troublous tyme may flee: . . . . 280 Psalm IX   27
    And at my fall they joy that, troublous, me. . . . . 286 Psalm XIII   15
    Who savest me from troblous case, ... 315 Psalm XXXII   26
TROW
    And suffer such a wrong? a wrong I trowe, ...   54 2nd Eclogues 29   64
    Earth gave that Love, heav'n I trow Love refineth: . . . . . 209 A&S 3rd Song   11
    Is that love? forsooth I trow, ... 222 A&S 9th Song   36
    The shepheards will grow leane I trow, their sheep will ill
      be fed. . . . . 344 Possibly   1   40
TRUANT
    Biting my trewand pen, beating my selfe for spite, ... 165 Astrophil   1   13
TRUCE
    Of my good sheepe, thou never trews time tooke:. . . . . . .   27 1st Eclogues 10   14
TRUDGE
    Of singing match we made, whence he with shame did trudge. .   52 2nd Eclogues 29   16
TRUE
    Ech eare suckes up the words a true love scattereth, ...   14 1st Eclogues 7   5
    Nor true love loves those loves with others mingled be. . . .   14 1st Eclogues 7   12
    A fickle Sex, and trew in trust to no man, ...   24 1st Eclogues 9   59
    True cause of evils, and cause of causelesse woe. . . . . . .   25 1st Eclogues 9 116
    That in my selfe your selfe true love doth plant; . . . . . .   39 Arcadia II   16   8
    Yet is it seale, though errour, of true hart. . . . .   51 2nd Eclogues 28 104
    Where witt but serves, to have true tast of woes. . . . . . .   57 2nd Eclogues 30   25
    And now fame the herald of her true honour, ...   68 2nd Eclogues 33   19
    Trew harte, whose trewthe dothe yeeld to trewest bande, . . .   70 Arcadia III 35   11
    My true love hath my hart, and I have his, ...   75 Arcadia III 45   1
    Above line repeated at following location. . . . .   76 Arcadia III 45   14

533

TRUE	(CONTINUED)	PAGE	TITLE		LINE
That she is myne, as I to her am true.		76	Arcadia III	46	6
That she be myne, as I to her am true.		76	Arcadia III	46	12
In stede of Thought, true pleasure be begunne, ...		84	Arcadia III	59	15
So true a Taste invites the Eye, ...		87	Arcadia III	62 V	51
Thus shall you both reward a lover true, ...		97	3rd Eclogues	64	107
First be he true, fcr truth doth truth deserve:		98	3rd Eclogues	65	2
For faithfull hart, cleane hands, and mouth as true:		99	3rd Eclogues	66	25
With old true tales he woont mine eares to fill, ...		99	3rd Eclogues	66	33
But thus in oke's true shade recounted he.		99	3rd Eclogues	66	41
Should my too-much sight cause so true a Sunne to be lost? .		124	4th Eclogues	74	58
In one true chest to rob all Vertue's treasure?		126	4th Eclogues	75	47
Stay to true love's melody:		140	Cert Sonnets	7	39
Fcr true it is, that they feare many whom many feare.. . . .		143	Cert Sonnets	14	2
From deepe vaine thought that I may not be true.		145	Cert Sonnets	17	5
Are Poets then the onely lovers true, ...		146	Cert Sonnets	17	31
Beleeve them not, for Phisicke true doth finde, ...		147	Cert Sonnets	17	51
Without the picture be found true.		157	Cert Sonnets	27	24
To me mine eyes the true shape carie..		159	Cert Sonnets	29	13
That shrines in flesh so true a Deitie, ...		167	Astrophil	4	13
It is most true, that eyes are form'd to serve		167	Astrophil	5	1
It is most true, what we call Cupid's dart, ...		167	Astrophil	5	5
True, that true Beautie Vertue is indeed, ...		167	Astrophil	5	9
True, that on earth we are but pilgrims made, ...		167	Astrophil	5	12
True, and yet true that I must Stella love..		167	Astrophil	5	14
It is most true, for since I her did see, ...		177	Astrophil	25	12
Which make the patents of true worldly blisse, ...		183	Astrophil	37	13
How farre they shoote awrie! the true cause is, ...		185	Astrophil	41	12
But you faire maides, at length this true shall find, . . .		192	Astrophil	54	11
That it, despisde in true but naked shew, ...		192	Astrophil	55	3
Oft with true sighes, oft with uncalled teares, ...		195	Astrophil	61	1
Sweet said that I true love in her should find..		196	Astrophil	62	4
Hcpe, art thou true, or doest thou flatter me?		199	Astrophil	67	1
Stella, those faire lines, which true goodnesse show.. . . .		201	Astrophil	71	4
As consterd in true speech, the name of heav'n it beares,..		205	Astrophil	77	11
O how the pleasant aires of true love be		205	Astrophil	78	1
Yet sighs, deere sighs, indeede true friends you are, . . .		228	Astrophil	95	1
Only true sighs, you do not go away, ...		229	Astrophil	95	12
Who tempt, and tempted plague, are Devils in true defining..		215	A&S 5th Song		84
Is only true delight..		215	A&S 6th Song		12
Who dost Thy saving health to true men bend.		277	Psalm VII		30
Even for the sighs, true sighs of man distrest		285	Psalm XII		15
Which to life true life doth lead:		288	Psalm XVI		38
You that do trust in him who still is true, ...		314	Psalm XXXI		68
Than true deliverance gain..		318	Psalm XXXIII		66
In that deare lord with true delight, ...		318	Psalm XXXIV		6
He shall be their true strength and aid.		327	Psalm XXXVII		100
Above line repeated at following location.		327	Psalm XXXVII		101
They are but shades not true things where we live, ...		330	Psalm XXXIX		19
If this in them be true, as true in men think I.		343	Possibly	1	7
Did it for just Desire's true children builde, ...		345	Possibly	4	10
While Geron olde came safe to Cosma true, ...		250	Other Poems	4	325
To see hir eies, with how true humblenes		252	Other Poems	4	402
"Tell me o Turtle true, ...		258	Other Poems	5	79
Friendship true in hart assured, ...		263	Other Poems	7	35
TRUEST					
Trew harte, whose trewthe dothe yeeld to trewest bande,. . .		70	Arcadia III	35	11
TRULY					
Truly not I, who did my thoughts engage, ...		26	1st Eclogues	9	136
Now that he had her words so truely tried:		97	3rd Eclogues	64	112
Who him do truly feare, ...		318	Psalm XXXIII		69
TRUMPET					
Revenge, revenge, my Muse, Defiance' trumpet blow:		213	A&S 5th Song		32
TRUMPETS					
A three foote stoole in Greece, made Trumpets sound, ...		146	Cert Sonnets	17	19
Ncr trumpets sound I heard, nor friendly cries;.		191	Astrophil	53	12
Who else for whom Fame worthy trumpets wanteth?.		197	A&S 1st Song		14
TRUST					
A fickle Sex, and trew in trust to no man, ...		24	1st Eclogues	9	59
Thus honour, liking, trust, much, farre, and deepe, ...		84	Arcadia III	60	5
How can she love where love cannot win trust?)		93	3rd Eclogues	63	85
That trust those killing eyes, I would, ...		158	Cert Sonnets	28	19
Trust in the shade of pleasing Orange tree;		180	Astrophil	30	8
"Trust me while I thee deny, ...		220	A&S 8th Song		93
And then they they that in him their only trust do rest, . .		272	Psalm II		31
Trust in that lord, that cannot ly, ...		274	Psalm IV		23
So shall all they that trust in thee do bend, ...		275	Psalm V		33
They that know Thee, on Thee their trust will bend, ...		280	Psalm IX		28
Since I do trust Jehova still, ...		283	Psalm XI		1
No, No I trust on thee, and joy in Thy		286	Psalm XIII		17
To them that trust in Thee a shield thou dost abide. . . .		292	Psalm XVIII		56
Let trust of some men be		296	Psalm XX		26
In heaven his trust hath layed;.		297	Psalm XXI		26
Our Fathers still in thee their trust did beare, ...		298	Psalm XXII		11
Let God help him (say they) whom he did trust;		299	Psalm XXII		19
My God in Thee I trust, ...		302	Psalm XXV		3
That I from trust in Thee was brought.		303	Psalm XXV		18
Of whom the trust lives in my heart.		304	Psalm XXV		72
My trust still hold.		307	Psalm XXVII		18
Hope, Trust in God, bee strong, and he		308	Psalm XXVII		64

534

```
TRUST                      (CONTINUED)                      PAGE   TITLE            LINE
     All my trust on him was sett;. . . . . . . . . . . . . .  309  Psalm XXVIII        27
     All, all my trust lord I have put in Thee, . . . . . . .  312  Psalm XXXI           1
     To Vanitys, which most trust most deceave, . . . . . . .  312  Psalm XXXI          17
     But I did trust in Thee, lord, I did say . . . . . . . .  313  Psalm XXXI          40
     That trust in Thee, ev'n in most open sight! . . . . . .  313  Psalm XXXI          54
     You that do trust in him who still is true, . . . . . . . 314  Psalm XXXI          68
     But who on God his trust invokes,. . . . . . . . . . . .  315  Psalm XXXII         38
     We have no plea but trust. . . . . . . . . . . . . . . .  318  Psalm XXXIII        84
     Whose trust is all on thee.. . . . . . . . . . . . . . .  319  Psalm XXXIV         32
     Who him their trust esteeme. . . . . . . . . . . . . . .  321  Psalm XXXIV         80
     Trust in the shadow of thy wing. . . . . . . . . . . . .  324  Psalm XXXVI         21
     Do well and trust on heavnly power, . . . . . . . . . . . 324  Psalm XXXVII         7
     Because on him their trust is laid.. . . . . . . . . . .  327  Psalm XXXVII       104
     To feare with trust, and trust with feare the Lord.. . .  331  Psalm XL            14
     Whose trust is so addressed, . . . . . . . . . . . . . .  331  Psalm XL            16
     Yeelde yeelde O yeelde, trust not on beautie's pride,. . . 345  Possibly       4     5
TRUSTED
     They trusted and by Thee deliverd were.. . . . . . . . .  298  Psalm XXII          12
TRUSTFUL
     O Lord my God, Thou art my trustfull stay. . . . . . . .  277  Psalm VII            1
     My God, and helping God, my might and trustfull might, . . 290  Psalm XVIII         3
     Of all my trustfull hope,. . . . . . . . . . . . . . . .  305  Psalm XXVI           5
TRUSTING
     Over these brookes trusting to ease mine eyes, . . . . . .  41  Arcadia II   21    1
     Guide Thee by him, lay all thy trusting. . . . . . . . .  324  Psalm XXXVII        11
TRUSTS
     That trusts in time, to finde the way aright . . . . . . .  82  Arcadia III  56    3
     Who trusts him sooner shall. . . . . . . . . . . . . . .  318  Psalm XXXIII        64
TRUSTY
     First may a trusty Greyhounde transforme himselfe to a
       Tigre . . . . . . . . . . . . . . . . . . . . . . . . .   33  1st Eclogues 13   66
     Who faileth one, is false, though trusty to another. . . . 214  A&S 5th Song        72
TRUTH
     With the voyce of truth to recorde to all worldes, . . . .  31  1st Eclogues 12   19
     Old age is wise and full of constant truth;. . . . . . .   39  Arcadia II   15    9
     Trew harte, whose trewthe dothe yeeld to trewest bande,. . .  70  Arcadia III  35   11
     Monstrous appeares, long trueth received late, . . . . .   85  Arcadia III  61    6
     First be he true, for truth doth truth deserve:. . . . .   98  3rd Eclogues 65    2
     He still hop'd well, because I loved truth;. . . . . . .   99  3rd Eclogues 66   38
     The seed Fast-meaning is, no truth to misse: . . . . . .  115  4th Eclogues 72   53
     Although their fame (me seemd) from truth had greatly jard.. 119  4th Eclogues 73   80
     (She beckned unto me) as yet of spotlesse truth, . . . .  120  4th Eclogues 73  138
     Since then truth to all minds telleth, . . . . . . . . .  140  Cert Sonnets  7   18
     Mournes she in truth, and thinks that others faine?. . . . 142  Cert Sonnets 11    3
     Of trueth, farre more then Alablaster pure,. . . . . . .  150  Cert Sonnets 22   39
     Which though despisde, yet still doth truth endure.. . .  150  Cert Sonnets 22   40
     But alwayes one my selfe with eagle eyde trueth to flie, . . 153  Cert Sonnets 24   24
     Loving in truth, and faine in verse my love to show, . . . 165  Astrophil     1    1
     In truth, o Love, with what a boyish kind. . . . . . . .  170  Astrophil    11    1
     Well staid with truth in word and faith of deed, . . . .  172  Astrophil    14   10
     But for that man with paine this truth descries, . . . .  177  Astrophil    25    5
     Where truth it selfe must speake like flatterie? . . . .  182  Astrophil    35    2
     I much do guesse, yet find no truth save this, . . . . .  187  Astrophil    44    9
     Since in thine armes, if learnd fame truth hath spread,. . . 198  Astrophil    65   13
     Rather then by more truth to get more paine. . . . . . .  199  Astrophil    67   14
     I give you here my hand for truth of this, . . . . . . .  201  Astrophil    70   13
     In truth I sweare, I wish not there should be. . . . . .  224  Astrophil    90    7
     Yet truth (if Caitif's breath mighte call thee) this . .  227  Astrophil    93    5
     Who may and will not save, murder in truth committeth. . . 214  A&S 5th Song        54
     The eare, his truth to trie: . . . . . . . . . . . . . .  216  A&S 6th Song        38
     Guide me as Thy Truth guides;. . . . . . . . . . . . . .  303  Psalm XXV           13
     That from Thy truth will not depart. . . . . . . . . . .  305  Psalm XXVI          12
     Even truth that for me sayes . . . . . . . . . . . . . .  306  Psalm XXVI          37
     In Truth of heart I answerd Thee,. . . . . . . . . . . .  307  Psalm XXVII         40
     Or shall Thy Truth on mankind layd . . . . . . . . . . .  311  Psalm XXX           29
     Thy truth above the Clouds, most high, . . . . . . . . .  323  Psalm XXXVI         14
     Thy Truth, health, gratiousness. . . . . . . . . . . . .  331  Psalm XL            40
     Me still in truth and mercy save,. . . . . . . . . . . .  332  Psalm XL            42
     Send Thy truth and light,. . . . . . . . . . . . . . . .  336  Psalm XLIII         13
     The poore-clad truth of love's wrong-ordred lot. . . . .  242  Other Poems   4   14
     And thou my dogg, whose truth and valiant might. . . . .  254  Other Poems   4  485
TRY
     Then vertue try, if she can worke in thee. . . . . . . .   22  1st Eclogues  9   13
     And try with bayt how fish will bite sometime. . . . . .   26  1st Eclogues  9  128
     Plangus must live some helpe for her to trie . . . . . .   58  2nd Eclogues 30   56
     No no, such force with my small force to trye. . . . . .   79  Arcadia III  50   15
     With circkled course, which no wise stay can trye, . . .   81  Arcadia III  54   10
     Are all in me: what helpe then can I trie? . . . . . . .  114  4th Eclogues 72   43
     And so most ready am this meane of peace to trie.. . . .  121  4th Eclogues 73  152
     Till these straunge altrings you did hap to trie,. . . .  125  4th Eclogues 75   26
     Can count them just, nor reason reason trye, . . . . . .  149  Cert Sonnets 22    3
     I on my horse, and Love on me doth trie. . . . . . . . .  189  Astrophil    49    1
     But now I meane no more your helpe to trie,. . . . . . .  192  Astrophil    55    9
     No more, my deare, no more these counsels trie,. . . . .  198  Astrophil    64    1
     Looke on againe, the faire text better trie: . . . . . .  199  Astrophil    67    7
     When for so soft a rod deare play he trie? . . . . . . .  203  Astrophil    73    4
     The eare, his truth to trie: . . . . . . . . . . . . . .  216  A&S 6th Song        38
     In my selfe the smart I try, . . . . . . . . . . . . . .  220  A&S 8th Song        94
     Thou, lord, the people shalt in judgment try:. . . . . .  277  Psalm VII           22
```

```
TRY                    (CONTINUED)                      PAGE    TITLE        LINE
  Me with Thy touch-stone try, . . . . . . . . . . . . . . . .   305 Psalm XXVI           8
  Yea beasts made safe thy goodness try . . . . . . . . . . .    323 Psalm XXXVI          18
  And now at keels they trie a harmles chaunce,. . . . . . .     243 Other Poems    4     47
  At Barly brake hir swete swift foot to trie. . . . . . . .     247 Other Poems    4    208
TRYING
  Trying high seas, nor while Sea rage you flee, . . . . . . .   142 Cert Sonnets 12      2
  Glory trying,. . . . . . . . . . . . . . . . . . . . . . . .   156 Cert Sonnets 26     32
TUCKED
  The first with cloth's tuckt up as Nymphes in woods do
    range ,. . . . . . . . . . . . . . . . . . . . . . . . . .   118 4th Eclogues 73     66
  Tuckt up even with the knees, with bowe and arrowes prest: .   118 4th Eclogues 73     67
  When she with skirts tuckt very hy, with girles at stoolball
    playes. . . . . . . . . . . . . . . . . . . . . . . . . .    343 Possibly       1     10
TUMBLED
  The fox on knees and elbowes tombled downe:. . . . . . . .     248 Other Poems    4    258
TUMULTS
  Oh! on my soul let not these tumults hitt. . . . . . . . .     322 Psalm XXXV          44
TUNE
  Tune up my voice, a higher note I yeeld, . . . . . . . . .       3 Lady of May    2      7
  Yeldeth a lute's tune, . . . . . . . . . . . . . . . . . . .    30 1st Eclogues 12     16
TUNES
  (Espilus) Thus joyfully in chosen tunes rejoyce, . . . . .       5 Lady of May    3     13
  For other be those tunes which sorrow tyes,. . . . . . . .      13 Arcadia I      4      7
  My foode is teares; my tunes waymenting yeeld: . . . . . .      18 1st Eclogues 7     138
  But let us sing, sweet tunes do passions ease, . . . . . .      22 1st Eclogues 9      4
  While shepheards' tunes be heard, or rimes be read,. . . .      56 2nd Eclogues 29    124
  By wise discourse, sweete tunes, or Poet's fiction;. . . .      61 2nd Eclogues 30    144
  The tunes be cryes, the words plaints, . . . . . . . . . .      66 2nd Eclogues 32     35
  My Lute within thy selfe thy tunes enclose,. . . . . . . .      81 Arcadia III  54      1
  Your dolefull tunes sweete Muses now applie. . . . . . . .     125 4th Eclogues 75      3
  Above line repeated at following locations . . . . . . . .     125 4th Eclogues 75     15
                                                                 125 4th Eclogues 75     30
  . . . . . . . . . . . . . . . . . . . . . . . . . . . . . .    126 4th Eclogues 75     48
  . . . . . . . . . . . . . . . . . . . . . . . . . . . . . .    126 4th Eclogues 75     60
  . . . . . . . . . . . . . . . . . . . . . . . . . . . . . .    127 4th Eclogues 75     78
  . . . . . . . . . . . . . . . . . . . . . . . . . . . . . .    127 4th Eclogues 75     96
  . . . . . . . . . . . . . . . . . . . . . . . . . . . . . .    128 4th Eclogues 75    117
  Your dolefull tunes, to them still playning say, . . . . .     126 4th Eclogues 75     50
  Her throate in tunes expresseth. . . . . . . . . . . . . .     137 Cert Sonnets  4      6
  Are metamorphosd straight to tunes of joyes. . . . . . . .     187 Astrophil     44     14
  To cadence of the tunes, which Amphion's lyre did yeeld, . .   208 A&S 3rd Song         4
  That ravishing delight in them most sweete tunes do not
    raise; . . . . . . . . . . . . . . . . . . . . . . . . . .   217 A&S 7th Song         2
  O let them heare these sacred tunes, and learne in wonder's
    schooles,. . . . . . . . . . . . . . . . . . . . . . . . .   217 A&S 7th Song         5
  The very essence of their tunes, when Angels do rejoyce. . .   217 A&S 7th Song        18
TURKISH
  Forc'd by a tedious proofe, that Turkish hardned hart, . . .   168 Astrophil      8      2
  Whether the Turkish new-moone minded be. . . . . . . . . .     179 Astrophil     30      1
TURN
  Nor stormes doo turne: fairenes serves oft to wealth.. . . .    18 1st Eclogues  7    119
  No place to turne; without, within it fryes: . . . . . . .      18 1st Eclogues  7    145
  To aire of sighes, sighes to the harte's fire turne, . . . .    19 1st Eclogues  7    154
  My Lyvelye joyes to dolefull ashes turne:. . . . . . . . .      42 Arcadia II    22     10
  I turne my minde to all formes of annoyes, . . . . . . . .     113 4th Eclogues 72      3
  Out of our sight in turne of hand is vanished. . . . . . .     128 4th Eclogues 75    127
  With care's hard hand) to turne and tosse in thee. . . . .     230 Astrophil     98      8
  Turne Thee, sweet lord, and from this Ougly fall . . . . .     276 Psalm VI            11
  And turn their backs, and strait on backs appeare. . . . .     276 Psalm VI            31
  Thy offrings so that they to ashes turn. . . . . . . . . .     296 Psalm XX            15
  And turn to God, and all the Nations be. . . . . . . . . .     300 Psalm XXII          67
  And turn his couch, where sick he couched late,. . . . . .     333 Psalm XLI           11
  Do turne from thee his eye,. . . . . . . . . . . . . . . . .   257 Other Poems    5     23
TURNED
  A Nimph thus turnde, but mended in translation.. . . . . . .    15 1st Eclogues  7     36
  With sleeves turnde up, loose haire, and brestes enlarged, .    16 1st Eclogues  7     74
  But now to silence turn'd his minstralsie. . . . . . . . .      28 1st Eclogues 10     75
  Since sighes (into mine inward fornace turnd). . . . . . .      38 Arcadia II    14      7
  Turnd from themselves, infected with their cage, . . . . .      57 2nd Eclogues 30     18
  Turnde to the mortall serene of an evening.. . . . . . . .     112 4th Eclogues 71     42
  To honor turnd, doth dwell in honor's nest,. . . . . . . .     151 Cert Sonnets 22     47
  Turned anew by your meanes,. . . . . . . . . . . . . . . .     154 Cert Sonnets 25     24
  My feete are turn'd to rootes, my hart becommeth lead, . . .   215 A&S 5th Song        77
  When Wycked soules be turn'd to hellish paine, . . . . . .     281 Psalm IX            53
  So he with Nous to Geron turn'd their race,. . . . . . . .     248 Other Poems    4    251
  And Strephon single, turned after him. . . . . . . . . . .     249 Other Poems    4    287
  With shafts shott out from their back-turned bow.. . . . .     251 Other Poems    4    351
  He stood, but turn'd, as Girosol, to Sun:. . . . . . . . .     251 Other Poems    4    370
TURNETH
  The sea to ebbe for griefe his flowing turneth:. . . . . .     136 Cert Sonnets  3      3
TURNING
  Turning all nature's course to selfe displeasure.. . . . . .   108 Arcadia IV    69      8
  Turning to desarts our best pastur'de mountaines.. . . . .     113 4th Eclogues 71     72
  The ever-turning spheares, the never-moving ground;. . . .     118 4th Eclogues 73     44
  Oft turning others' leaves, to see if thence would flow. . .   165 Astrophil      1      7
TURNS
  But with such turnes the voice to stray, . . . . . . . . .      86 Arcadia III   62     33
  Unto the flowre that ay turnes,. . . . . . . . . . . . . .     154 Cert Sonnets 25     25
  Fals to shrewd turnes, and I was in his way. . . . . . . .     173 Astrophil     17     14
```

TURNS	(CONTINUED)	PAGE	TITLE		LINE
My verie inke turnes straight to Stella's name;.		174	Astrophil	19	6
Thou whom to me such my good turnes should bind, ...		198	Astrophil	65	3
Nor ever turns aside		331	Psalm XL		19
He hopes, with dainty turns she doth him flee.		251	Other Poems	4	341

TURTLE
Even turtle toutcht he with hypocrisie..		28	1st Eclogues 10		81
In the faithfull Turtle dove..		234	A&S 11th Song		20
A widow turtle neere on bared root		256	Other Poems	5	6
"Tell me o Turtle true,.		258	Other Poems	5	79

TURTLE-DOVE
| And as the Turtle-Dove . . . . | | 261 | Other Poems | 6 | 49 |

TURTLES
| But like the turtells faire. . . . . | | 91 | 3rd Eclogues 63 | | 6 |

TUSH
| "Tush, tush", said nature, "this is all but a trifle, a man's selfe. . . . . | | 29 | 1st Eclogues 11 | | 7 |
| Tush absence, while thy mistes eclipse that light, ... | | 223 | Astrophil | 88 | 9 |

TUTOR'S
| Like busie boyes, to winne their tutor's harte,. . . . . . . | | 27 | 1st Eclogues 10 | | 43 |

TWAY
| Come narr good Mastix, tis now full tway score . . . . . . | | 27 | 1st Eclogues 10 | | 20 |
| And yet in all this time, betwixt us tway, ... | | 106 | 3rd Eclogues 67 | | 91 |

TWENTY
| With twenty ginnes we will the small birds take, ... | | 18 | 1st Eclogues 7 | | 126 |

TWICE
| Least once should not be heard, twise said, No, No.. . . . . | | 196 | Astrophil | 63 | 8 |

TWIGS
| Strephon with leavy twiggs of Laurell tree . . . . | | 244 | Other Poems | 4 | 73 |

TWINE
| With mutuall embracements them to twyne: . . . . | | 91 | 3rd Eclogues 63 | | 16 |
| They did themselves (o sweetest prison) twine. . . . . | | 232 | Astrophil | 103 | 8 |

TWINED
| A wanton woman's face, and with curld knots had twinde . . . | | 118 | 4th Eclogues 73 | | 73 |

TWINKLING
| Her twinkling eies bedeckt with pearle, her lips of Saphir blew:. . . . . | | 12 | Arcadia I | 3 | 10 |
| Twinckling starres Love-thoughts provoke:. . . . . | | 210 | A&S 4th Song | | 8 |

TWINS
| But when my Sunne her shining twinnes there bends, ... | | 150 | Cert Sonnets 22 | | 16 |
| She comes, and streight therewith her shining twins do move. | | 204 | Astrophil | 76 | 1 |

TWINS'
| Progressing then from faire twinnes' gold'n place: . . . . . | | 175 | Astrophil | 22 | 2 |

TWIST
| To twist those broyles, wnich hardly would untwine:. . . . . | | 146 | Cert Sonnets 17 | | 22 |

TWIXT
| And such discord twixt greatest shepheards flowes, ... | | 27 | 1st Eclogues 10 | | 40 |
| Spoiling their flock, or while twixt them they strive. . . . | | 99 | 3rd Eclogues 66 | | 35 |

TWO
Two thousand sheepe I have as white as milke,.		4	Lady of May	2	19
Two thousand deere in wildest woods I have,.		4	Lady of May	2	25
Both they themselves unto such two shall wed,.		11	Arcadia I	1	5
Which of us two deserveth most compassion.		15	1st Eclogues 7		18
A naked god, young, blind, with arrowes two.		20	1st Eclogues 8		6
But arrowes two, and tipt with gold or leade:		21	1st Eclogues 8		11
Wyth two strange fires of equall heate possest,.		42	Arcadia II	22	1
That hath foure legs, and with two onely goes, ...		56	2nd Eclogues 29		142
That hath foure eyes, and onely two can frame.		56	2nd Eclogues 29		143
Betwixt which two in me I have this fight, ...		74	Arcadia III	42	7
O brest in which two white sheepe swell in pride:.		76	Arcadia III	46	10
When two Sunnes do appeare		81	Arcadia III	55	1
Two gleaming Sunnes of splendour like I see, ...		81	Arcadia III	55	4
Betwixt these two a way doth lie,.		87	Arcadia III	62	58
Which flanked with two sugred flankes, ...		88	Arcadia III	62	89
Her shoulders be like two white Doves		89	Arcadia III	62	113
Live one in two, a well united paire,.		91	3rd Eclogues 63		7
And like two rivers sweete,.		92	3rd Eclogues 63		33
Whereto two parties once be full content..		97	3rd Eclogues 64		126
By taking her two Sunnes from these darke vallies.		113	4th Eclogues 71		66
But streight there issued forth two Ladies (Ladies sure. . .		118	4th Eclogues 73		63
Betwixt us two; how much that discord foule hath stain'd . .		119	4th Eclogues 73		106
Let us a perfect peace betwixt us two resolve:		120	4th Eclogues 73		127
Now resteth onely this, which of us two is she, ...		120	4th Eclogues 73		135
Of Stella's browes made him two better bowes,.		173	Astrophil	17	10
By only those two starres in Stella's face..		178	Astrophil	26	14
That in one speech two Negatives affirme...		196	Astrophil	63	14
The two only darts of Love:.		202	A&S 2nd Song		6
Of which the two life-giving lights are figured in her eyes:		217	A&S 7th Song		16
D. Wonder that by two so black eyes the glittering stars be past..		343	Possibly	1	28
That tombes the two, is justly one..		241	Other Poems	3	8
Of shepheards two the seely case to show,.		242	Other Poems	4	6
A paire of frends, or rather one cal'd two,.		242	Other Poems	4	18
Betwixt them two the peeper tooke his nest,.		244	Other Poems	4	102
So now for pray these shepheards two he tooke, ...		245	Other Poems	4	137
They of both ends the middle two doe flie, ...		248	Other Poems	4	226
The two that in mid place, Hell called were, ...		248	Other Poems	4	227
There may you see, soone as the middle two		248	Other Poems	4	233
The two in hell did toward Cosma frame,.		249	Other Poems	4	267
My two and I be met, ...		260	Other Poems	6	19

```
TWO                      (CONTINUED)                       PAGE   TITLE           LINE
     Welcome my two to me, E.D. F.G. P.S. . . . . . . . . . . . .   261 Other Poems      6    25
     "Only for my two loves' sake, Sir Ed. D. and M. F. G. . . . .  263 Other Poems      7    61
     Only two do me delight . . . . . . . . . . . . . . . . . . .   263 Other Poems      7    63
     Grant me with those two remaining. . . . . . . . . . . . . .   263 Other Poems      7    66
TYRAN
     This tyran Love; or rather do suppresse. . . . . . . . . . .    23 1st Eclogues    9    45
     So Tyran he no fitter place could spie,. . . . . . . . . . .   175 Astrophil       20     5
     If Rule by force without all claime a Tyran showeth, . . . .   214 A&S 5th Song          57
     A rightfull Prince by unright deeds a Tyran groweth. . . . .   214 A&S 5th Song          60
     You then ungratefull thiefe, you murdring Tyran you, . . . .   215 A&S 5th Song          85
     Tyran honour doth thus use thee, . . . . . . . . . . . . . .   220 A&S 8th Song          95
     In cheeks and lipps the Tyran threatens bloud. . . . . . . .   246 Other Poems      4   152
TYRANNICAL
     But our Desire's tyrannicall extortion . . . . . . . . . . .    60 2nd Eclogues   30   134
TYRANNIZETH
     Rules with a becke, so tyrannizeth thee, . . . . . . . . . .   187 Astrophil       46     3
TYRANNY
     Deeme it no gloire to swell in tyrannie. . . . . . . . . . .   103 3rd Eclogues   66   149
     I call it praise to suffer Tyrannie; . . . . . . . . . . . .   166 Astrophil        2    11
     Whose necke becomes such yoke of tyranny?. . . . . . . . . .   188 Astrophil       47     4
     I lay then to thy charge unjustest Tyrannie, . . . . . . . .   214 A&S 5th Song          56
TYRANS
     Lo you grow proud with this, for tyrans make folke bow:. . .   214 A&S 5th Song          61
TYRANT
     Passion. No, Tyrant; no: mine, mine shall be the fielde. . .    46 2nd Eclogues   27     2
     R. Can Reason then a Tyraunt counted be? . . . . . . . . . .    46 2nd Eclogues   27     3
TYRANTS
     Only lov'd Tyrants, just in cruelty, . . . . . . . . . . . .   185 Astrophil       42     6
UGLY
     "Erona dye, and end this ougly painefulnes"? . . . . . . . .    61 2nd Eclogues   30   157
     The warres of ougly Centaurs,. . . . . . . . . . . . . . . .    66 2nd Eclogues   32    22
     Become the cause of my darke ouglie night? . . . . . . . . .    74 Arcadia III    42     2
     With ouglie cloke the darke envious night: . . . . . . . . .    82 Arcadia III    55     8
     While each conceate an ouglie figure beares, . . . . . . . .   131 Arcadia V      77     7
     Like those whom dreames make uglie monsters see, . . . . . .   136 Cert Sonnets    2    11
     His ugly evill in other's good to hide,. . . . . . . . . . .   141 Cert Sonnets    8     6
     Weakely did seeme to paint death's ougly dart. . . . . . . .   148 Cert Sonnets   20     4
     Turne Thee, sweet lord, and from this Ougly fall . . . . . .   276 Psalm VI             11
     Failes me, with ugly feares. . . . . . . . . . . . . . . . .   332 Psalm XL             50
     Late neere a crosse I met an ougly Cat.. . . . . . . . . . .   253 Other Poems      4   448
ULSTER
     How Ulster likes of that same golden bit,. . . . . . . . . .   180 Astrophil       30     9
UNABLE
     Unable quite to pay even Nature's rent,. . . . . . . . . . .   174 Astrophil       18     5
UNACQUAINTED
     Of seely boies please unacquainted sight:. . . . . . . . . .   246 Other Poems      4   182
UNAPPALLED
     Can thoughts still thinking so rest unappalled?. . . . . . .    61 2nd Eclogues   30   166
UNARMED
     Unarmde (alas) unwarn'd to take a man asleepe? . . . . . . .   122 4th Eclogues   73   186
     Stella alone with face unarmed marcht, . . . . . . . . . . .   176 Astrophil       22     9
UNAWARES
     To give unawares a Mortall blow. . . . . . . . . . . . . . .   284 Psalm XI              7
UNBID
     But I unbid, fetch even my soule to thee.. . . . . . . . . .   194 Astrophil       59     8
UNBIDDEN
     Most rude dispaire my daily unbidden guest,. . . . . . . . .   236 Astrophil      108     7
UNBITTED
     To hatch mine eyes, and that unbitted thought. . . . . . . .   183 Astrophil       38     2
UNBOUND
     Bownd and bownd by so noble bandes, as loth to be unbownd, .    37 1st Eclogues   13   162
UNCALLED
     Oft with true sighes, oft with uncalled teares,. . . . . . .   195 Astrophil       61     1
UNCHASTITY
     A loathing of all loose unchastitie, . . . . . . . . . . . .   172 Astrophil       14    13
UNCHOOSING
     (Stolne from her yoong by theeves' unchoosing hast). . . . .   254 Other Poems      4   491
UNCORRUPTED
     Even he, that leads of life an uncorrupted traine, . . . . .   287 Psalm XV              3
UNCOUTH
     An uncouth love, which Nature hateth most. . . . . . . . . .    11 Arcadia I       1     4
UNDER
     We shepeheards are like them that under saile. . . . . . . .    27 1st Eclogues   10    31
     But in a palme when I marke, how he doth rise under a
        burden . . . . . . . . . . . . . . . . . . . . . . . . . .    36 1st Eclogues   13   127
     Under this, this her owne, her only dearling,. . . . . . . .    68 2nd Eclogues   33    23
     Clymes even unto the starres, Nature is under it.. . . . . .    68 2nd Eclogues   34     9
     Faire under these doth stately growe,. . . . . . . . . . . .    87 Arcadia III    62    46
     And make me wish my selfe layd under mountaines, . . . . . .   112 4th Eclogues   71    36
     Who under courtly pompes doo hatch a base desire.. . . . . .   117 4th Eclogues   73    16
     Thou under his Dominion plac't . . . . . . . . . . . . . . .   279 Psalm VIII           25
     Under his tongue do harbour'd ly . . . . . . . . . . . . . .   282 Psalm X              29
     With such brave wounds, that they under my feet did ly.. . .   292 Psalm XVIII          70
     Proud grew the grasse that under hir did growe,. . . . . . .   244 Other Poems      4   108
     "Well was I, while under shade . . . . . . . . . . . . . . .   263 Other Poems      7    43
UNDERCHARGE
     Not pointing to fit folkes each undercharge, . . . . . . . .   210 Astrophil       85     6
UNDERLAYED
     Like Christall, underlayde with Redd,. . . . . . . . . . . .    86 Arcadia III    62 V 24
```

		PAGE	TITLE	LINE

UNDERMINED
    Undermin'd with a speech the pearcer of thoughts........ 68 2nd Eclogues 33 16
UNDERNEATH
    Underneath my window playneth?"................. 233 A&S 11th Song   2
UNDERSTAND
    I understand what rayling great men spred; .... 313 Psalm XXXI   37
    That seek my bane, O make me understand. .... 321 Psalm XXXV   5
UNDERSTANDS
    Their works he understands.. .... 317 Psalm XXXIII   57
UNDERTAKE
    Thence let him undertake .... 295 Psalm XX   9
UNDERTAKEN
    That ere by them ought undertaken be,............ 236 Astrophil   107   3
UNDERTAKING
    Love at length leave undertaking." .... 234 A&S 11th Song 32
UNDO
    Dick. Faith in my self and worth in her, which no proofe can
        undoo... .... 343 Possibly   1   26
    They false and fearfull do their hands undoe,........ 248 Other Poems   4 235
UNDONE
    With ground plot's fall shall be undone: .... 284 Psalm XI   10
    That I should never be undone, ... 311 Psalm XXX   21
UNENDLY
    With mortall disdaine, bent to unendly revenge? .... 123 4th Eclogues 74 36
UNENTANGLED
    So I in simple course, and unentangled minde .... 117 4th Eclogues 73 25
UNEVENLY
    Nor thinke the match unev'nly made,............. 159 Cert Sonnets 29 10
UNFELT
    Let him, deprived of sweet but unfelt joyes, ... 177 Astrophil   24   12
    She in whose eyes Love, though unfelt, doth shine, ... 196 Astrophil   62   3
UNFIT
    And farre unfit to hold so good a roome. .... 94 3rd Eclogues 64   6
    Straunge were the Ladies' weedes; yet more unfit then
        strange. .... 118 4th Eclogues 73 65
    And not in Nature for best fruits unfit: .... 174 Astrophil   19   13
    Poore Layman I, for sacred rites unfit.. .... 203 Astrophil   74   4
UNFLATTERING
    Which lookes too oft in his unflattring glasse:....... 178 Astrophil   27   10
UNFORTUNATE
    Or pleasant mirtell, may teach th'unfortunate Echo ..... 31 1st Eclogues 13 13
UNGIRD
    Thou didst ungird my dolefull sack .... 311 Psalm XXX   35
UNGODLY
    "Fie, fie, what have we done? ungodly rebell fie....... 121 4th Eclogues 73 168
UNGRATEFUL
    From so ungratefull fancie,.................. 160 Cert Sonnets 30   7
    Above line repeated at following locations .... 160 Cert Sonnets 30 17
    . . . . 160 Cert Sonnets 30 27
    Ungratefull who is cald, the worst of evils is spok'n. ... 213 A&S 5th Song 42
    You then ungratefull thiefe, you murdring Tyran you, ... 215 A&S 5th Song 85
    These most ungratefull rebels unto Thee. .... 275 Psalm V   32
UNGRATEFULNESS
    Do they call Vertue there ungratefulnesse? .... 180 Astrophil   31   14
    But of thy soule, so fraught with such ungratefulnesse,.. 213 A&S 5th Song 40
UNHANDSOME
    But he himselfe a foule unhansome groome,.......... 94 3rd Eclogues 64   5
UNHAPPY
    Love smiled, and thus said; "Want joynd to desire is
        unhappy .... 30 1st Eclogues 11 11
    Thus, thus, alas! wofull in nature, unhappy by fortune,.. 30 1st Eclogues 11 19
    Which onely thus unhappie be,................. 86 Arcadia III 62 21
    I might, unhappie word, o me, I might,............ 181 Astrophil   33   1
    Unhappie sight, and hath she vanisht by. .... 235 Astrophil 105   1
UNHEALTHFUL
    So farr from seing myne unhealthfull eyes, ... 298 Psalm XXII   3
UNHEARD
    But so unheard, condemn'd, kept thence we do seeke to abide
        in,........................... 32 1st Eclogues 13 25
    With bolde clamor unheard, unmarckt, what I seeke what I
        suffer:.......................... 35 1st Eclogues 13 112
    Here wrong's name is unheard: slander a monster is....... 69 2nd Eclogues 34 26
    Unseene, unheard, while thought to highest place ...... 178 Astrophil   27   13
    A shot unheard gave me a wound unseene?. .... 253 Other Poems   4 454
    "Be you with me while I unheard do cry,........... 255 Other Poems   4 497
UNICORN
    And shirion like young Unicorn.. .... 310 Psalm XXIX   18
UNICORNS
    By aiding when fierce unicorns come neare me........ 299 Psalm XXII   50
UNIDLE
    For me, I do Nature unidle know, ... 178 Astrophil   26   9
UNIFORM
    Made uniforme to any state reposed.. .... 57 2nd Eclogues 30 31
UNITE
    Unite in one, my state thus still to save; .... 70 Arcadia III 35 15
    But that her navel doth unite, ... 88 Arcadia III 62 73
    And yet unite the eyes,.................... 152 Cert Sonnets 23   6
UNITED
    Live one in two, a well united paire,............ 91 3rd Eclogues 63   7
    United powers make each the stronger prove.. .... 223 Astrophil   88   14

```
                                                         PAGE    TITLE          LINE
UNITY
    In firmest band of Unitie. . . . . . . . . . . . . . .   260 Other Poems     6    22
UNJUST
    P. Let us orecome, and let us be unjust. . . . . . . .    47 2nd Eclogues 27    32
    The evill of evils, just cause to be unjust, . . . . . . .   93 3rd Eclogues 63    83
    Her poore slave's unjust decaying. . . . . . . . . . . .  222 A&S 9th Song        50
    Against me witnesses unjust, . . . . . . . . . . . . .   308 Psalm XXVII         57
UNJUSTEST
    I lay then to thy charge unjustest Tyrannie, . . . . . .  214 A&S 5th Song        56
    O unjustest fortune's sway,. . . . . . . . . . . . . . .  235 A&S 11th Song       43
UNJUSTLY
    Then, then let not my foes unjustly joy; . . . . . . . .  322 Psalm XXXV          49
UNKIND
    Howe can they be unkind? speake for th'hast narroly pri'de.
        pride. . . . . . . . . . . . . . . . . . . . . . . .   65 2nd Eclogues 31    43
    Not toying kinde, nor causlesly unkinde, . . . . . . . .   98 3rd Eclogues 65     5
    But him her host that unkind guest had slaine. . . . . .  184 Astrophil    38    14
    That Noblenesse it selfe makes thus unkind?. . . . . . .  186 Astrophil    44     8
    Unkind, I love you not: O me, that eye . . . . . . . . .  188 Astrophil    47    13
    Before she could prepare to be unkind, . . . . . . . . .  193 Astrophil    57     6
    With rage of Love, I cald my Love unkind:. . . . . . . .  195 Astrophil    62     2
    Love by sure proofe I may call thee unkind, . . . . . . .  198 Astrophil    65     1
    If I have been unkynd for friendly part: . . . . . . . .  277 Psalm VII          10
UNKINDNESS
    Then greefe, unkindnes, proofe, tooke, kindled, tought,. . .   84 Arcadia III  60     9
    Unkindnes breedes, unkindnes fostreth hate.. . . . . . . .   85 Arcadia III  61     8
    But now that hope is lost, unkindnesse kils delight, . . . .  212 A&S 5th Song       13
    Kindly, sweete soule, she did unkindnes take,. . . . . . .  245 Other Poems    4   121
UNKNOWN
    As for those parts unknowne, which hidden sure are best: . .   12 Arcadia I    3    13
    Seen, and unknowne; heard, but without attention.. . . . .   19 1st Eclogues  7   179
    R. Passion is blinde, and treades an unknowne trace. . . . .   46 2nd Eclogues 27    15
    Unknowe as then were they that buylden towers:. . . . . . .  100 3rd Eclogues 66    46
    Till knit with cold, though there unknowne remaine,. . . . .  150 Cert Sonnets 22    33
    In such a place Unknown. . . . . . . . . . . . . . . . .  282 Psalm X            33
    His well knowne friend, but yet his unknowne mate, . . . . .  255 Other Poems    4   528
UNLASING
    She lay for dead, till I helpt with unlasing her?. . . . .   61 2nd Eclogues 30   154
UNLIKELY
    What force brought them to so unlikely ground. . . . . . .  149 Cert Sonnets 22     4
UNLUCKY
    So I unlucky lad . . . . . . . . . . . . . . . . . . . .  259 Other Poems    5    95
UNMARKED
    With bolde clamor unheard, unmarckt, what I seeke what I
        suffer:. . . . . . . . . . . . . . . . . . . . . . .   35 1st Eclogues 13   112
UNMATCHED
    In face and eyes unmatched being,. . . . . . . . . . . .  159 Cert Sonnets 29     7
    In her unmatched mind: . . . . . . . . . . . . . . . . .  160 Cert Sonnets 30    34
    That hast of thine unmatched glory . . . . . . . . . . .  278 Psalm VIII          3
UNMEET
    With love drawne on, so fast with pace unmeet. . . . . .  250 Other Poems    4   334
UNMOVED
    Or when an Echo begins unmov'd to sing them a love song. . .   33 1st Eclogues 13    48
UNPARTIAL
    Lett our unpartiall eyes a litle watche. . . . . . . . .   29 1st Eclogues 10    91
UNPITEOUS
    Who so unpitteous be . . . . . . . . . . . . . . . . . .  332 Psalm XL           58
UNPROVIDED
    And whose good happ, doth leave him unprovided,. . . . . .   62 2nd Eclogues 30   177
UNREFRAINED
    (Delay, the racke of unrefrain'd desire) . . . . . . . .   80 Arcadia III  53     2
UNREMOVED
    In friendship unremoved. . . . . . . . . . . . . . . . .  261 Other Poems    6    28
UNRIGHT
    A rightfull Prince by unright deeds a Tyran groweth. . . .  214 A&S 5th Song        60
UNRIGHTEOUS
    They are unrighteous never.. . . . . . . . . . . . . . .  294 Psalm XIX          40
UNSAVORY
    If three-leav'd grasse seeme to the sheepe unsavorie,. . . .   48 2nd Eclogues 28    23
UNSEEN
    My words unseene, the marble still in sight, . . . . . . .   41 Arcadia II   19    10
    That I things erst unseene should first in dreaming see? . .  121 4th Eclogues 73   182
    Unseene, unheard, while thought to highest place . . . . .  178 Astrophil    27    13
    There unseen thou maist be bold, . . . . . . . . . . . .  226 A&S 10th Song       16
    Well for to see they kept themselves unsene, . . . . . . .  244 Other Poems    4    89
    A shot unheard gave me a wound unseene?. . . . . . . . .  253 Other Poems    4   454
UNSETTLED
    With gazing looks, short sighs, unsettled feet,. . . . . .  251 Other Poems    4   369
UNSPEAKABLY
    Unspeakably his heart Thou glad'st,. . . . . . . . . . .  297 Psalm XXI          23
UNSPILLING
    Whose pants do make unspilling creame to flow, . . . . . .  231 Astrophil   100     6
UNSTAINED
    Yet not so wise, as of unstained harte:. . . . . . . . .  243 Other Poems    4    35
UNSUITED
    By such unsuted speech should hindred be.. . . . . . . .  190 Astrophil    51    14
UNSWEET
    And that my Muse to some eares not unsweet,. . . . . . .  209 Astrophil    84     2
UNTAUGHT
    No talke untaught can finde the way. . . . . . . . . . .   86 Arcadia III  62    34
```

UNTIL		PAGE	TITLE		LINE
In being heard untill the hearer dye		24	1st Eclogues	9	70
In ease, untill that bodie life forgoes.		56	2nd Eclogues	29	146
Men's lives, untill it be imbraste..		87	Arcadia III	62	66
He stayd untill the goodman was departed,.		97	3rd Eclogues	64	119
Yet lives untill his life be new requirde.		150	Cert Sonnets	22	24
Untill by your inspiring I might know, ...		192	Astrophil	55	7
UNTO					
Both they themselves unto such two shall wed,.		11	Arcadia I	1	5
Geron. Alas what falls are falne unto thy minde?		23	1st Eclogues	9	32
Rather to wrong then unto just defence,.		25	1st Eclogues	9	106
This paterne good, unto our children goes, ...		28	1st Eclogues	10	55
Infernall agonies unto a bewtye divine,.		30	1st Eclogues	11	14
Or if eyes' language be not unto her knowne, ...		30	1st Eclogues	12	6
Unto the heav'ns? our wings be too short; th' earth thinks us a burden;		32	1st Eclogues	13	29
Dorus. Unto the Gods with a thanckfull heart all thankes I do render, ...		32	1st Eclogues	13	35
Unto a silly caban, though weake, yet stronger against woes.		34	1st Eclogues	13	93
And sorrows do require some respitt unto the sences.		37	1st Eclogues	13	175
Which makes all eyes doo honour unto you..		38	Arcadia II	15	8
Unto my selfe let after-livers know.		40	Arcadia II	18	10
Till spotlesse soule unto thy bosome flye, ...		40	Arcadia II	18	17
R. Whom Passion leades unto his death is bent.		46	2nd Eclogues	27	9
Unto my pipe, O Nimphes, nowe helpe my pipe, ...		54	2nd Eclogues	29	73
Let all for her, and unto her be bent.		60	2nd Eclogues	30	124
Then then what do I gaine, since unto hir will I do winde? Winde.		64	2nd Eclogues	31	34
Horrible is this blasphemy unto the most holy. O lie.. . . .		65	2nd Eclogues	31	45
Clymes even unto the starres, Nature is under it..		68	2nd Eclogues	34	9
Sweet birds kindly do graunt harmony unto thee,.		69	2nd Eclogues	34	12
Unto my woes the hatefull heavens do sende,.		73	Arcadia III	40	2
Kisse her from me, and say unto her spirite, ...		79	Arcadia III	51	13
This leades unto the joyous field, ...		87	Arcadia III	62	61
But back unto her back, my Muse, ...		89	Arcadia III	62	109
He leane to her, she unto him do bow:.		92	3rd Eclogues	63	49
Unto his house a jollie shepeheard went, ...		94	3rd Eclogues	64	15
It title had, unto my only love, ...		96	3rd Eclogues	64	89
Doth breake, now toong unto thy name doth move,.		97	3rd Eclogues	64	100
And sange unto my sheepe lest stray they should.		99	3rd Eclogues	66	21
In granting unto him a grandsire's gaine.		105	3rd Eclogues	67	75
We go unto the Bryde, and use this daye..		107	3rd Eclogues	67	119
Sorow pay we unto the rights of Nature,.		109	Arcadia IV	70	5
Doth add her force unto the sting of fortune:.		109	Arcadia IV	70	10
Then since such pow'rs conspire unto our damage.		109	Arcadia IV	70	13
So close unto my selfe my wrackes doo lie.		114	4th Eclogues	72	40
Strephon. So close unto my selfe my wrackes doo lie;		114	4th Eclogues	72	41
And unto death, quite drownde in Dolours, brought.		115	4th Eclogues	72	68
(She beckned unto me) as yet of spotlesse truth, ...		120	4th Eclogues	73	138
To stand unto my will: their will they made me know.		121	4th Eclogues	73	157
Unto the caitife wretch, whom long affliction holdeth, . . .		122	4th Eclogues	74	1
(Unto thy selfe I do meane those graces dwell so within thee		122	4th Eclogues	74	9
Unto revenge? O sweete, on a wretch wilt thou be revenged? .		123	4th Eclogues	74	37
Torne you should disperse unto the blasts of a winde.. . . .		123	4th Eclogues	74	52
Ev'n as I am, so I should unto that haire be a thrall. . . .		123	4th Eclogues	74	54
Unto the earth, by the hurt of this her heavenly jewell. . .		124	4th Eclogues	74	62
Unto Cupid that boy shall a Pedante be found?.		124	4th Eclogues	74	66
Passion unto my rage, Rage to a hasty revenge.		124	4th Eclogues	74	68
Unto the man, whom now such miseries you awarde?		124	4th Eclogues	74	74
Till that they doo unto our dolours bende:		126	4th Eclogues	75	39
Then give a quiet eare unto my playning:		127	4th Eclogues	75	65
But unto Man, age ever death doth sende.		127	4th Eclogues	75	84
For how can Nature unto this reply?.		127	4th Eclogues	75	94
And unto death bend still our thoughts' direction.		130	4th Eclogues	76	34
I yeeld, o Love, unto thy loathed yoke.		135	Cert Sonnets	1	9
Unto her rested sense a perfect waking,.		137	Cert Sonnets	4	2
Unto my children alway good rest taking:		139	Cert Sonnets	6	5
Unto no body my woman saith she had rather a wife be,. . . .		143	Cert Sonnets	13	1
My selfe unto th' Anatomy desirde, ...		150	Cert Sonnets	22	27
Unto the flowre that ay turnes, ...		154	Cert Sonnets	25	25
Which unto it by birthright I do ow:		174	Astrophil	18	6
That unto me, who fare like him that both.		174	Astrophil	19	10
Bends all his powers, even unto Stella's grace..		178	Astrophil	27	14
Love onely reading unto me this art.		179	Astrophil	28	14
Unto my mind, is Stella's image, wrought		183	Astrophil	38	6
Those daintie dores unto the Court of blisse,.		187	Astrophil	44	11
Wise silence is best musicke unto blisse..		201	Astrophil	70	14
That hue, whose force my hart still unto thraldome ties? . .		232	Astrophil	102	8
Onely unto the heav'n of Stella's face,.		235	Astrophil	105	7
They first resort unto that soveraigne part;		236	Astrophil	107	4
Nor beasts, nor birds do come unto this blessed gaze,. . . .		209	A&S 3rd Song		15
Then grew my tongue and pen records unto thy glory:.		212	A&S 5th Song		3
Unto Dianae's train thou runaway didst flee:		214	A&S 5th Song		71
Unto whom mirth is displeasure,.		221	A&S 9th Song		9
Unto the lord most strong:		273	Psalm III		32
For unto Thee I will my prayer send, ...		274	Psalm V.		6
Give them their due unto their guiltiness, ...		275	Psalm V		29
These most ungratefull rebels unto Thee.		275	Psalm V		32
I will give thanks unto the lord of Us		278	Psalm VII		46

541

```
UNTO                    (CONTINUED)                              PAGE    TITLE           LINE
     His eyes unto my Case, his eares unto my moane..  . . . . . .  291  Psalm XVIII        14
     He lifted me unto a largly noble place.. . . . . . . . . . . . 292  Psalm XVIII        42
     Unto my strengthned stepps Thou didst enlarge the way,  . . .  292  Psalm XVIII        66
     Nay unto Thee they cry'd, but thou heardst not their cryes..   293  Psalm XVIII        75
     Day unto day doth it display, . . . . . . . . . . . . . . . .  293  Psalm XIX           5
     New joy, new joy unto Our King,. . . . . . . . . . . . . . . . 296  Psalm XXI           1
     Lo! ev'en unto Eternity. . . . . . . . . . . . . . . . . . . . 297  Psalm XXI          15
     Send unto desolation . . . . . . . . . . . . . . . . . . . . . 297  Psalm XXI          38
     Unto the dust of my death's running hower; . . . . . . . . . . 299  Psalm XXII         38
     Unto due thoughts mankind his thoughts shall order,. . . . . . 300  Psalm XXII         66
     Some safty unto me;. . . . . . . . . . . . . . . . . . . . . . 305  Psalm XXV          74
     Unto whose ever hating lust. . . . . . . . . . . . . . . . . . 308  Psalm XXVII        55
     Unto Thy heart . . . . . . . . . . . . . . . . . . . . . . . . 308  Psalm XXVII        65
     Ascribe unto the lord of light,. . . . . . . . . . . . . . . . 309  Psalm XXIX          1
     That yet beare love unto my righteousness; . . . . . . . . . . 323  Psalm XXXV         68
     Attain unto their wished scope.. . . . . . . . . . . . . . . . 325  Psalm XXXVII       20
     He will exalt thee unto honour . . . . . . . . . . . . . . . . 327  Psalm XXXVII       86
     Lord unto me my time's just measure give,. . . . . . . . . . . 329  Psalm XXXIX        13
     New song unto our God of prayse, . . . . . . . . . . . . . . . 331  Psalm XL           12
     Still gladly say, Unto our God bee prayse. . . . . . . . . . . 332  Psalm XL           64
     And will not him unto the will expose. . . . . . . . . . . . . 333  Psalm XLI           7
     Dick. What joy the joyfull sunne gives unto bleared eyes:. .   343  Possibly        1  13
     And lookes so neere unto my cure that I must needes be lost.   343  Possibly        1  22
     Thus proud and fierce unto the hearts he stept . . . . . . .   246  Other Poems     4 157
     And yeeld himselfe unto hir punishment,. . . . . . . . . . .   247  Other Poems     4 191
     Nay ev'n unto hir home he oft would go,. . . . . . . . . . .   247  Other Poems     4 193
     Strephon, whose absence seem'd unto thee long, . . . . . . .   247  Other Poems     4 220
     Spake unto a sencelesse tree,. . . . . . . . . . . . . . . .   262  Other Poems     7  16
     Made to listen unto me,. . . . . . . . . . . . . . . . . . .   263  Other Poems     7  56
UNTRIED
     Her skin like burnisht gold, her hands like silver ure
       untryde. . . . . . . . . . . . . . . . . . . . . . . . . .    12  Arcadia I       3  12
UNTRUE
     You Rebell run away, to Lord and Lady untrue,. . . . . . . .   215  A&S 5th Song       86
     Ev'en Feare makes strangers shew much love though much
       untrue.. . . . . . . . . . . . . . . . . . . . . . . . . .   293  Psalm XVIII        81
UNTRUTH
     Or naked he, disguis'd in all untruth? . . . . . . . . . . .    21  1st Eclogues    8   8
UNTWINE
     To twist those broyles, which hardly would untwine:. . . . .   146  Cert Sonnets 17    22
     And lately thence untwine: . . . . . . . . . . . . . . . . .   257  Other Poems     5  44
UNWARES
     He burnt unwares his wings, and cannot fly away. . . . . . .   169  Astrophil       8  14
     Let their sly witts unwares destruction get, . . . . . . . .   321  Psalm XXXV         17
UNWARNED
     Unarmde (alas) unwarn'd to take a man asleepe? . . . . . . .   122  4th Eclogues 73   186
UNWIPED
     I leave mine eyes unwipte my cheekes to bathe. . . . . . . .    54  2nd Eclogues 29    80
UNWITTING
     Then abjects, while I was unwitting quite, . . . . . . . . .   322  Psalm XXXV         39
UNWORN
     The unworn paths, his rule embraceth.. . . . . . . . . . . .   279  Psalm VIII         32
UNWORTHINESS
     Now whether mov'd with selfe unworthines,. . . . . . . . . .    94  3rd Eclogues 64     7
UNWORTHY
     How can you him unworthy then decree,. . . . . . . . . . . .    39  Arcadia II      16   9
UP
     Tune up my voice, a higher note I yeeld, . . . . . . . . . .     3  Lady of May     2   7
     Ech eare suckes up the words a true love scattereth, . . . .    14  1st Eclogues    7   5
     Drawes up; and if, hope fayling, ende live's pleasure, . . .    16  1st Eclogues    7  71
     With sleeves turnde up, loose haire, and brestes enlarged, .    16  1st Eclogues    7  74
     Geron. Up, up Philisides, let sorrowes goe,. . . . . . . . .    22  1st Eclogues    9   1
     By raysing up, upon thy selfe to stand.. . . . . . . . . . .    23  1st Eclogues    9  51
     Who hath his hopes laid up in woman's hand.. . . . . . . . .    24  1st Eclogues    9  55
     Fire no liquor can coole: Neptune's seate would be dryd up
       there. . . . . . . . . . . . . . . . . . . . . . . . . . .    32  1st Eclogues 13   32
     If neither by that helpe, thou canst clime up to thy fancie,    34  1st Eclogues 13  100
     And may I not (say I then) gett up though griefs be so
       weightie?. . . . . . . . . . . . . . . . . . . . . . . . .    36  1st Eclogues 13  128
     Their flames mount up, my powers prostrate lie:. . . . . . .    42  Arcadia II      22  11
     Leave of my sheepe, my sighes burne up your filde, . . . . .    43  Arcadia II      24   7
     Let so our fruites grow up, that nature be maintainde: . . .    45  Arcadia II      26  13
     And Venus seemes, to make up her, she spent herselfe.. . . .    49  2nd Eclogues 28   66
     Which oft he lifteth up, and stayes his lifted pawe, . . . .    53  2nd Eclogues 29   34
     I would climbe up, and bring a prettie starre, . . . . . . .    55  2nd Eclogues 29  118
     Thus be our noblest parts dryed up with sorrow:. . . . . . .    62  2nd Eclogues 30  174
     One day layes up stuffe of griefe for the morrow:. . . . . .    62  2nd Eclogues 30  176
     I should so rashly ripp up.. . . . . . . . . . . . . . . . .    66  2nd Eclogues 32   18
     Nor ramper did abide; my braine was up blowne, . . . . . . .    68  2nd Eclogues 33   15
     The laborer, which cursed earthe up teares . . . . . . . . .    71  Arcadia III     36   7
     That sorrowe's weight dothe balance up thies joyes.. . . . .    71  Arcadia III     36  18
     Phaebus yeelde up thy title in my minde. . . . . . . . . . .    72  Arcadia III     38  11
     Come clowdie feares, close up my daseled sight,. . . . . . .    74  Arcadia III     42   9
     Sorowe suck up the marowe of my might, . . . . . . . . . . .    74  Arcadia III     42  10
     Yet still, faire tree, lifte up thy stately line,. . . . . .    77  Arcadia III     47   9
     Locke up, faire liddes, the treasures of my harte: . . . . .    79  Arcadia III     51   1
     And while o sleepe thou closest up her sight, . . . . . . . .   79  Arcadia III     51   5
     With inward cries putts up a bitter role . . . . . . . . . .    85  Arcadia III     61   3
     Lift up their stately swelling bankes; . . . . . . . . . . .    88  Arcadia III     62  90
```

UP   (CONTINUED)   PAGE TITLE   LINE

And warr of thoughts is swallow'd up in peace. . . . . . . 91 3rd Eclogues 63 4
Let one time (but long first) close up their daies,. . . . . 92 3rd Eclogues 63 31
Shrewdnes so stirres, pride so puffes up their hart, ... 104 3rd Eclogues 67 26
And inward griefe seale up with outward wailing. . . . . . 109 Arcadia IV 70 6
The flying sprites which trees by rootes up teare. . . . . . 114 4th Eclogues 72 36
Which senses up doth shut the senses to preserve,. . . . . 117 4th Eclogues 73 28
Flew up with freer wings of fleshly bondage free;. . . . . 117 4th Eclogues 73 33
When it blowne up with myne a fall of ruine takes) . . . . . 118 4th Eclogues 73 52
The first with cloth's tuckt up as Nymphes in woods do
 range ,. . . . . 118 4th Eclogues 73 66
Tuckt up even with the knees, with bowe and arrowes prest: . 118 4th Eclogues 73 67
Of what thou seest: close up in secrete knot thy will". . . . 119 4th Eclogues 73 98
Now death hath swallow'd up our worldly pleasure,. . . . . 129 4th Eclogues 76 11
When Love puft up with rage of hy disdaine,. . . . . 135 Cert Sonnets 2 1
(First sealing up my heart as pray of his) . . . . 141 Cert Sonnets 9 10
Like as the Dove which seeled up doth flie,. . . . . 144 Cert Sonnets 15 1
But with his wings of fancies up he goes,. . . . . 144 Cert Sonnets 15 9
Approching warmes (not else) dead logges up sends,. . . . . 150 Cert Sonnets 22 12
But when that failes, my dead hopes up to take,. . . . . . . 150 Cert Sonnets 22 19
(With gall cut out) closde up againe by art,. . . . . 150 Cert Sonnets 22 23
Yet live with thoughts closde up, till that she will . . . . 150 Cert Sonnets 22 29
Where plagu'd for rash attempt, gives up his ghost,. . . . . 151 Cert Sonnets 22 57
But of his death flies up a purest love, ... 151 Cert Sonnets 22 59
Up to the sunne, although the sunne my wings do frie:. . . . 153 Cert Sonnets 24 25
And should in soule up to our cuntrey move: . . . . 167 Astrophil 5 13
Having got up a breach by fighting well,. . . . . 171 Astrophil 12 10
Upon that coast, am giv'n up for a slave. . . . . 179 Astrophil 29 14
That never I with clos'd-up sense do lie,. . . . . 181 Astrophil 32 6
I start, looke, hearke, but what in closde up sence. . . . . 184 Astrophil 38 9
Let breath sucke up those sweetes, let armes embrace . . . . 210 Astrophil 85 12
As thy lookes sturre, runs up and downe to make. . . . . . . 232 Astrophil 101 10
Where rigrows exile lockes up all my sense?. . . . . 233 Astrophil 104 8
The same key op'n can, which can locke up a treasure.. . . . 213 A&S 5th Song 18
To take up the place for me; . . . . 226 A&S 10th Song 14
The lord lifts up my head, ... 272 Psalm III 13
Up lord now time it is:. . . . . 272 Psalm III 23
I dwell, layd up in safest neast.. . . . . 274 Psalm IV 35
Therfore, O lord, lift up Thy throne on high . . . . 277 Psalm VII 20
Up lord, and judg the Gentyls in Thy right . . . . 281 Psalm IX 61
Lift up Thy heavnly hand . . . . 282 Psalm X 51
I will get up saith God, and my help show. . . . . 285 Psalm XII 16
Of these bad folkes, more lifted up with pride . . . . 285 Psalm XII 26
Up lord prevent those gaping jawes . . . . 290 Psalm XVII 35
My cryes clim'd up and he bent down from sacred throne, . . . 291 Psalm XVIII 13
For they had caught me up, when I was weake in Woe;. . . . . 291 Psalm XVIII 38
Up then thou liftst the poore, and down the proud wilt cast; 292 Psalm XVIII 52
Up Thou dost light my light, and cleare my darkned eye. . . . 292 Psalm XVIII 53
Let him be lifted up, that hath preserved me!. . . . . 293 Psalm XVIII 84
Up to Our God, when Thy suites granted be. . . . . 296 Psalm XX 20
Vainly doth not puff up his mind;. . . . . 302 Psalm XXIV 10
Lift up your heads you Gates, and you doores ever biding,. . 302 Psalm XXIV 17
Above line repeated at following location. . . . . 302 Psalm XXIV 21
On my complaint build up their joy.. . . . . 303 Psalm XXV 6
Now, Now shall He lift up my head. . . . . 307 Psalm XXVII 31
Feed and lift them up for aye. . . . . 309 Psalm XXVIII 35
Take up Thy shield and for my succour stand, ... 321 Psalm XXXV 3
And rayse me up that I may once have might . . . . 333 Psalm XLI 35
A maid train'd up from high or low degree, ... 247 Other Poems 4 210
Up with hir fist, and tooke him on the face, ... 249 Other Poems 4 274
Up and downe perplexed went,. . . . . 262 Other Poems 7 14
UPBORE
His good strong staffe my slippry yeares upbore: . . . . . . 99 3rd Eclogues 66 37
UPBORN
And was from evill by Thee upborn, ... 311 Psalm XXX 6
UPBRAID
But forste with raige, his raige on theym upbrayde.. . . . . 24 1st Eclogues 9 65
UPHELD
He is upheld by heavnly hand.. . . . . 326 Psalm XXXVII 60
UPHOLDS
My sheepehooke is wanne hope, which all upholdes:. . . . . . 39 Arcadia II 17 5
But God upholds the just in blisse.. . . . . 325 Psalm XXXVII 44
UPON
Lay all your feare upon your fearefull lover:. . . . . 17 1st Eclogues 7 91
By raysing up, upon thy selfe to stand.. . . . . 23 1st Eclogues 9 51
Let speciall care upon thy flock be staid,. . . . . 26 1st Eclogues 9 133
What foresight tels; our thoughts upon thy knowledge staye.. 45 Arcadia II 26 12
A king upon a mouse, a strong foe to a rat,. . . . . 53 2nd Eclogues 29 32
To weare upon her neck, that open lies.. . . . . 55 2nd Eclogues 29 119
Upon thy spoiles, which never should lye waste?. . . . . . . 59 2nd Eclogues 30 93
Whyle upon chaunce, his fruite of labour lyes; . . . . 71 Arcadia III 36 10
Whose fyrie chaines, uppon his freedome seaze, ... 74 Arcadia III 41 4
Tyre on, despaier, uppon my tyred sprite.. . . . . 74 Arcadia III 42 12
Care upon care (in steede of doing right). . . . . 82 Arcadia III 56 7
Pearching uppon square Royall Rooves,. . . . . 89 Arcadia III 62 V114
Cast thy stepmother eyes upon our sorowe,. . . . . 109 Arcadia IV 70 23
Our studies fixt upon the falles of fortune. . . . . 109 Arcadia IV 70 30
Mine eyes did light upon her shining hewe, ... 115 4th Eclogues 72 75
First having all their giftes upon faire Mira spred. . . . . 121 4th Eclogues 73 178
And let my breath upon your braunches cleave,. . . . . 125 4th Eclogues 75 7

UPON   (CONTINUED)   PAGE   TITLE   LINE
    Upon thy face let coaly Ravens swarme: . . . .   125 4th Eclogues 75   19
    Pressing too much upon ill harbourd shore. . . . .   142 Cert Sonnets 12   3
    Some fresh and fruitfull showers upon my sunne-burn'd
        braine . . . .   165 Astrophil   1   8
    Upon whose breast a fiercer Gripe doth tire. . . . .   171 Astrophil   14   2
    Upon that coast, am giv'n up for a slave.. . . . .   179 Astrophil   29   14
    But wilt new warre upon thine owne begin?. . . . .   183 Astrophil   36   8
    Upon a wretch, that long thy grace hath sought;. . . . . .   185 Astrophil   40   7
    So gratefull now you waite upon my care. . . . .   228 Astrophil   95   4
    Upon thy cheerefull face, joye's livery weare: . . . . . .   232 Astrophil   103   3
    If I but stars upon mine armour beare, ...   233 Astrophil   104   10
    And say (O kings) yet have I set my King upon. . . . . . .   271 Psalm II   13
    But, lord, lift Thou upon our sight. . . . .   274 Psalm IV   26
    Then let his foot uppon my neck be set:. . . . .   277 Psalm VII   14
    Upon his pate, his pain employed thus. . . . .   278 Psalm VII   44
    Upon the heavns engrav'n the story.. . . . .   278 Psalm VIII   4
    When I upon the Heav'ns do look. . . . .   278 Psalm VIII   9
    Thou placest him upon all lands. . . . .   279 Psalm VIII   21
    Nor reign upon my senses.. . . . .   295 Psalm XIX   56
    Upon God's holy name,. . . . .   296 Psalm XX   29
    They were set free when they upon Thee called, ...   298 Psalm XXII   13
    And that by right upon all Realmes he raigneth.. . . . . .   300 Psalm XXII   70
    For by his power the land upon the Ocean raigneth, ...   302 Psalm XXIV   3
    For all my hope fixt upon God doth ly. . . . .   312 Psalm XXXI   18
    Thy Face to shine upon Thy servant make, ...   313 Psalm XXXI   43
    Upon his mercy beare.. . . . .   318 Psalm XXXIII   72
    Let not their joy upon my woes be sett.. . . . .   322 Psalm XXXV   60
    Still Thy hands upon me be.. . . . .   327 Psalm XXXVIII   6
    Setting my feet upon . . . .   331 Psalm XL   8
    To his owne witt, thought upon thought did swell,. . . . .   256 Other Poems   4   542
UPPER
    And let not man have upper hand of Thee, ...   281 Psalm IX   62
UPRAISED
    Do not disdaine, o streight up raised Pine,. . . . .   77 Arcadia III 47   1
UPRIGHT
    And makes our home good sport with dauncing bolt upright..   53 2nd Eclogues 29   46
    To be forsooth upright,. . . . .   216 A&S 6th Song   45
    Scund and upright with him, to wickednes not bent. . . . .   292 Psalm XVIII   46
    So shall my spryte be still upright. . . . .   295 Psalm XIX   57
    Wee stand upright, while they their fall did frame.. . . .   296 Psalm XX   32
    Do throw their words against the most upright. . . . . . .   313 Psalm XXXI   51
    To them that be in soules upright. . . . .   324 Psalm XXXVI   30
    Mark the upright, the just attend, ...   327 Psalm XXXVII   93
UPRIGHTNESS
    Let my uprightness gaine . . . .   305 Psalm XXV   73
UPSET
    Arise, O lord, in wrath thy self upsett. . . . .   277 Psalm VII   16
UPTORN
    Place see my grave uptorne:. . . . .   136 Cert Sonnets 3   19
URAN
    At other end Uran did Strephon lend. . . . .   248 Other Poems   4   246
    Geron with Uran were condemn'd to hell.. . . . .   249 Other Poems   4   264
    Till Uran seing Pas to Cosma fly,. . . . .   249 Other Poems   4   286
    So that Uran, whose arme old Geron bore, ...   250 Other Poems   4   309
    The other end Geron with Uran garde. . . . .   250 Other Poems   4   319
    While deare Uran, whose course was Pas to meet,. . . . . .   250 Other Poems   4   330
    So did Uran, the narr the swifter move,. . . . .   251 Other Poems   4   357
URANIA
    For then Urania homeward did arise,. . . . .   246 Other Poems   4   167
    He quickly learn'd Urania was her name,. . . . .   247 Other Poems   4   185
    With whome to joyne fast ran Urania sweet: . . . .   248 Other Poems   4   252
    For as Urania after Cosma ran, ...   249 Other Poems   4   281
    And so to take the gemme Urania sought.. . . . .   250 Other Poems   4   324
    To Nature's heir, the faire Urania, pay, ...   251 Other Poems   4   364
    Of faire Urania, fairer then a greene, ...   253 Other Poems   4   452
    Urania name, whose force he knew so well,. . . . .   256 Other Poems   4   538
URE
    Her skin like burnisht gold, her hands like silver ure
        untryde. . . . .   12 Arcadia I   3   12
US
    Be none of us, or els maintaine our fashion: . . . .   15 1st Eclogues 7   14
    Which of us two deserveth most compassion. . . . .   15 1st Eclogues 7   18
    But let us sing, sweet tunes do passions ease, ...   22 1st Eclogues 9   4
    Yet for my sake discover us thy griefe.. . . . .   23 1st Eclogues 9   23
    While, "Let us passe our time" each shepheard saies.. . .   28 1st Eclogues 10   48
    Into our mindes let us a little fall,. . . . .   29 1st Eclogues 10   94
    Then who makes us such judges over all?. . . . .   29 1st Eclogues 10   96
    Unto the heav'ns? our wings be too short; th' earth thinks
        us a burden; . . . .   32 1st Eclogues 13   29
    Since no refuge doth serve from woundes we do carry about
        us . . . .   33 1st Eclogues 13   51
    And yet neither of us great or blest deemeth his owne selfe.   33 1st Eclogues 13   73
    Which makes us most immortall shape to weare,. . . . . . .   40 Arcadia II   18   14
    My sun is gon, from stormes what shall us sheelde? . . . .   43 Arcadia II   24   9
    Give us foresightfull mindes: give us minds to obaye . . .   45 Arcadia II   26   11
    P. Let us orecome, and let us be unjust. . . . .   47 2nd Eclogues 27   32
    R.p. Then let us both to heavenly rules give place,. . . .   47 2nd Eclogues 27   41
    Goe on therefore, and tell us, by what fashion . . . . . .   48 2nd Eclogues 28   34
    Among us all we should find out some thing of nought.. . .   51 2nd Eclogues 29   2

	(CONTINUED)	PAGE	TITLE	LINE
To harme us wormes should that high Justice leave.		59	2nd Eclogues 30	71
The kindly way to beate us on to blisse.		59	2nd Eclogues 30	76
Thus Death becomes a rivall to us all,		59	2nd Eclogues 30	89
Doth force us there to set our chiefe delightfulnes,		61	2nd Eclogues 30	135
Let us not winke though void of purest sightfulnes..		61	2nd Eclogues 30	139
Let us some grammar learne of more congruities...		61	2nd Eclogues 30	142
Nor trifling title of vanity dazleth us,		69	2nd Eclogues 34	24
Hastened from us with barre of shadow darke,		80	Arcadia III 52	13
But let us pick our good from out much bad:		105	3rd Eclogues 67	62
And yet in all this time, betwixt us tway,		106	3rd Eclogues 67	91
Yet let us leave a monument in publique.		109	Arcadia IV 70	15
Us to attend, in this most private time and place.		119	4th Eclogues 73	96
Betwixt us two; how much that discord foule hath stain'd		119	4th Eclogues 73	106
Proofe speakes too much to us that feeling triall have...		119	4th Eclogues 73	108
But let us wiser be; and what foule discorde brake,		120	4th Eclogues 73	119
Let us a perfect peace betwixt us two resolve:		120	4th Eclogues 73	127
Now resteth onely this, which of us two is she,		120	4th Eclogues 73	135
Becommeth us: in us fortune determines not..		120	4th Eclogues 73	140
Ah let us all against foule Nature crie:		127	4th Eclogues 75	92
We Nature's workes doo helpe, she us defaces..		127	4th Eclogues 75	93
Which he of us for ever hath deserved.		129	4th Eclogues 75	138
Still studying how to us to be a light..		129	4th Eclogues 76	16
And make his paine to keepe us safe his pleasure?.		129	4th Eclogues 76	24
Let us against our selves employ our might,.		130	4th Eclogues 76	35
Then let us holde the blisse of peacefull minde,		131	Arcadia V 77	13
Good Lord deliver us..		160	Cert Sonnets 30	10
Above line repeated at following locations		160	Cert Sonnets 30	20
. . . .		160	Cert Sonnets 30	30
. . . .		160	Cert Sonnets 30	40
That doth both shine and give us sight to see.		161	Cert Sonnets 32	8
That Vertue but that body graunt to us..		191	Astrophil 52	14
Us in their best language woo:		210	A&S 4th Song	16
Feare not else, none can us spie:.		211	A&S 4th Song	22
Concord better fitteth us:		211	A&S 4th Song	44
Joying till joy makes us languish.		227	A&S 10th Song	42
Come let us break their bonds, say they, and fondly say:		271	Psalm II	7
From whence shall come to us such ayd?		274	Psalm IV	25
I will give thanks unto the lord of Us		278	Psalm VII	46
Make us in mervailes of Thy mercy know		290	Psalm XVII	22
Assist us Saviour deare;		296	Psalm XX	33
The Voice of that lord ruling us		310	Psalm XXIX	10
Then prayse, then prayse I do the lord of us,		313	Psalm XXXI	58
Whose shield shall us maintaine.		318	Psalm XXXIII	78
On us be set,.		318	Psalm XXXIII	83
Will. God shield us from such Dames. If so our Downes be sped,		344	Possibly 1	39
Will. Then Dick let us go hence lest wee great folkes annoy.		344	Possibly 1	45
More prayse to us we never looke to winne,		346	Possibly 5	11
Let us the while be playing,		261	Other Poems 6	32

And if for want of use thy minde ashamed is,		14	1st Eclogues 7	2
From heav'nly throne to her heav'n use digression?		15	1st Eclogues 7	45
Thy wit dost use still still more harmes to finde.		23	1st Eclogues 9	34
Histor. Those woordes dyd once the Loveliest shepard use		24	1st Eclogues 9	62
He is a beast, that beaste's use will allowe		25	1st Eclogues 9	99
P. We gladly use the sweetnes of our life.		46	2nd Eclogues 27	26
Therefore, alas, you use vile Vulcan's spight,		60	2nd Eclogues 30	107
Is left a Sunne, whose beames thy place may use?		80	Arcadia III 52	6
For such an use the world hath gotten,		88	Arcadia III 62	85
He did to beastes' best use his cunning frame;		101	3rd Eclogues 66	108
And shall we not therefore their use desire?		105	3rd Eclogues 67	69
We go unto the Bryde, and use this daye.		107	3rd Eclogues 67	119
And wanting use of eyes their eyes began to close:		116	4th Eclogues 73	6
They first their use forgot, then fancies lost their force;.		117	4th Eclogues 73	29
For it was of use bereaved,		139	Cert Sonnets 7	6
In hard estate with stowt shew valor use,		143	Cert Sonnets 12	16
And use but you for matters to rehearse?		146	Cert Sonnets 17	35
Use thy words but to bewaile thee,		156	Cert Sonnets 27	19
From them that use men thus,		160	Cert Sonnets 30	9
Above line repeated at following locations		160	Cert Sonnets 30	19
. . . .		160	Cert Sonnets 30	29
Thy scepter use in some old Catoe's brest;		166	Astrophil 4	5
Of other's children changelings use to make,		178	Astrophil 28	2
I beg no subject to use eloquence,		179	Astrophil 28	9
Use all to helpe his other conquerings:.		179	Astrophil 29	8
His praise to sleight, which from good use doth rise;.		185	Astrophil 41	7
Nor do not use set colours for to weare,		191	Astrophil 54	2
Use something else to chast'n me withall,		212	Astrophil 86	12
To this great cause, which needs both use and art,		236	Astrophil 107	8
Whom iron doores do keepe from use of day?		237	Astrophil 108	11
These birds sing: "Now use the season."		219	A&S 8th Song	56
Tyran honour doth thus use thee,		220	A&S 8th Song	95
Shall use destroying power,		297	Psalm XXI	34

Nico. As I of late, neer bushes usde my sive,		54	2nd Eclogues 29	81
But fewe dayes past while she good maner us'de,		95	3rd Eclogues 64	26
Who now his owne, full like his owne he used..		102	3rd Eclogues 66	142
And when they were well us'de to be abused,		102	3rd Eclogues 66	144
That hardly usde, who ever prison broke,		135	Cert Sonnets 1	11

		PAGE	TITLE		LINE
USED	(CONTINUED)				
	Not usde to frozen clips, he strave to find some part, . . .	168	Astrophil	8	6
	Who with deceitfull tongue hath never usd to faine,.	287	Psalm XV		5
	Against them usd by wicked wretches, ...	327	Psalm XXXVII		103
	No force, though force be used, Allarme allarme.	346	Possibly	5	8
	It is to be used then, ...	263	Other Poems	7	33
USEST					
	Save me from them Thou usest as thy blade, ...	290	Psalm XVII		37
USETH					
	What No her tongue sleeping useth.	202	A&S 2nd Song		12
USING					
	When sorrow (using mine owne fier's might)	236	Astrophil	108	1
USURPING					
	But if that needs thou wilt usurping be, ...	167	Astrophil	4	9
USURY					
	Nor courteous ruin of proffered usury, ...	69	2nd Eclogues 34		21
	Frome bitinge Usury who ever doth refrain, ...	287	Psalm XV		11
UTMOST					
	His utmost light: for well his witte doth know,.	55	2nd Eclogues 29		97
	My foes, to utmost of their pow'r.	307	Psalm XXVII		8
	Ev'ill men work ill to utmost right, ...	325	Psalm XXXVII		33
	Doth on hir wings hir utmost swiftnes prove, ...	251	Other Poems	4	355
UTTER					
	(Although simply atyrde) your manly affection utter.	32	1st Eclogues 13		16
	Neither doubt you a whit, time will your passion utter. . .	33	1st Eclogues 13		58
	And thinke ther she do dwell and heare what plaintes I do				
	utter:	36	1st Eclogues 13		143
	Who never word of peace yet utter would, ...	322	Psalm XXXV		51
UTTERED					
	They uttred are in such a feeling fashion, ...	60	2nd Eclogues 30		126
UTTERING					
	Uttring a serpent's minde with serpent's hisse..	24	1st Eclogues 9		71
UTTERLY					
	That I e're I return'd destroyd them utterly	292	Psalm XVIII		69
UTTERMOST					
	Shepheards bewaile your uttermost confusion;	128	4th Eclogues 75		121
	Then farewell world, thy uttermost I see,.	144	Cert Sonnets 32		13
VADE					
	How doth the colour vade of those vermillion dies, ...	232	Astrophil	102	5
VAGABONDING					
	I now then staine thy white with vagabunding shame,.	214	A&S 5th Song		68
VAGRANT					
	Both Rebell to the Sonne, and Vagrant from the mother; . . .	214	A&S 5th Song		69
VAIN					
	(Espilus) Silvanus long in love, and long in vaine,.	4	Lady of May	3	1
	To fill the world with strange but vaine conceits:	20	1st Eclogues 8		2
	Whome wit makes vaine, or blinded with his eyes, ...	23	1st Eclogues 9		35
	And herein most their folly vaine appeares	24	1st Eclogues 9		78
	Nature against we do seeme to rebell, seeme fooles in a				
	vaine sute.	32	1st Eclogues 13		24
	In vaine, mine Eyes, you labour to amende.	38	Arcadia II	14	1
	In vaine, my Hart, now you with sight are burnd, ...	38	Arcadia II	14	5
	Reason, I vaine (now you have lost my hart).	38	Arcadia II	14	9
	And since in vaine I find were all my strife,.	38	Arcadia II	14	13
	Blasphemous words the speaker vaine do prove,.	59	2nd Eclogues 30		67
	And what manner a mind which had to that humor a vaine?				
	Vaine.	63	2nd Eclogues 31		9
	Away vayne Cares, by which fewe men do finde	83	Arcadia III 59		3
	But ah, alas! (In vayne) my minde, sight, thought, ...	84	Arcadia III 60		11
	Whence never word in vaine did flowe..	87	Arcadia III 62		45
	Be fled as things most vaine,.	93	3rd Eclogues 65		71
	As farre from want, as farre from vaine expence, ...	98	3rd Eclogues 65		9
	Mothers and Nurses of all vaine annoy.	107	3rd Eclogues 67		117
	Vaine is their paine, who labour in Despaire.	115	4th Eclogues 72		60
	Strephon. Vaine is their paine, who labour in Despaire.. . .	115	4th Eclogues 72		61
	But vaine it is to thinke those paines should cease, ...	116	4th Eclogues 72		94
	For vaine equalitie is but contention's field.	120	4th Eclogues 73		130
	Since feare is vaine, but when it may preserve,.	131	Arcadia V	77	3
	O my vayne worde gon, Ruyn of my glory.	138	Cert Sonnets 5		14
	From deepe vaine thought that I may not be true.	145	Cert Sonnets 17		5
	Or reason foyld would not in vaine contend:.	147	Cert Sonnets 19		4
	But yet in vaine thou hast my ruine sought,.	161	Cert Sonnets 31		9
	In vaine thou madest me to vaine things aspire,.	161	Cert Sonnets 31		10
	In vaine thou kindlest all thy smokie fire;.	161	Cert Sonnets 31		11
	If vaine love have my simple soule opprest,.	166	Astrophil	4	3
	Which for reward spoile it with vaine annoyes.	174	Astrophil	18	11
	My wits, quicke in vaine thoughts, in vertue lame:	175	Astrophil	21	4
	Willd me these tempests of vaine love to flie, ...	196	Astrophil	62	10
	And all in vaine, for while thy breath most sweet, ...	200	Astrophil	68	9
	And do I then my selfe this vaine scuse give?.	227	Astrophil	93	9
	As with sententious lips to set a title vaine on it:	217	A&S 7th Song		4
	To mutter murmures vaine?.	271	Psalm II		2
	Of things vain, with vaine mates they bable all, ...	284	Psalm XII		4
	Is but a succour vaine,.	318	Psalm XXXIII		63
	Vain shades and vain, in vain to grieve.	330	Psalm XXXIX		20
VAINLY					
	To this strange death I vainely yeeld my life.	38	Arcadia II	14	14
	Avise themselves that they are vainely spent..	174	Astrophil	19	8
	A pitt was digg'd, by this man vainly strong,.	278	Psalm VII		40
	Vainly doth not puff up his mind;.	302	Psalm XXIV		10

VAINNESS	PAGE	TITLE	LINE
In all whose workes vainess is ever raigning:.	276	Psalm VI	26
Who shunning vanity and works of vaineness leaving,.	302	Psalm XXIV	9
Who be to vaineness bent:.	305	Psalm XXVI	14

VALES
| And fill the vales with cries in steed of musique. . . . . | 111 | 4th Eclogues 71 | 24 |

VALIANT
Of straying wayes, when valiant errour guides:	190	Astrophil 51	11
Nor that he could young-wise, wise-valiant frame	204	Astrophil 75	5
But valiant Rebels oft in fooles' mouthes purchase fame: . .	214	A&S 5th Song	67
And thou my dogg, whose truth and valiant might.	254	Other Poems 4	485

VALLEYS
Yee Nimphes which haunt the springs in pleasant vallies,. . .	111	4th Eclogues 71	2
While that my voice doth fill these wofull vallies,.	111	4th Eclogues 71	10
Of huge despaire, and foule affliction's vallies,.	111	4th Eclogues 71	17
I that was once the musique of these vallies,.	111	4th Eclogues 71	21
And state throwen downe to over-troden vallies..	112	4th Eclogues 71	30
Klaius. Long since the happie dwellers of these vallies, . .	112	4th Eclogues 71	31
Transforme themselves to lowe dejected vallies:.	112	4th Eclogues 71	38
When I doo smell the flowers of these vallies:	112	4th Eclogues 71	46
And with despite despise the humble vallies:	112	4th Eclogues 71	53
My state more base, then are the basest vallies:	112	4th Eclogues 71	57
By taking her two Sunnes from these darke vallies,.	113	4th Eclogues 71	66
Klaius. For she, with whom compar'd, the Alpes are vallies,.	113	4th Eclogues 71	67
Strephon. These mountaines witnesse shall, so shall these vallies, ...	113	4th Eclogues 71	73
Yea tho I should thro vallys stray	301	Psalm XXIII	10

VALOR
| In hard estate with stowt shew valor use,. . . . . | 143 | Cert Sonnets 12 | 16 |

VANISH
| In his sight her yoke did vanish . . . . | 218 | A&S 8th Song | 12 |

VANISHED
Thus Reason said: but she came, Reason vanished;	16	1st Eclogues 7	67
Out of our sight in turne of hand is vanished.	128	4th Eclogues 75	127
Unhappie sight, and hath she vanisht by.	235	Astrophil 105	1
Look after him, he shall be vannisht	325	Psalm XXXVII	27

VANITIES
| To Vanitys, which most trust most deceave, ... | 312 | Psalm XXXI | 17 |

VANITY
With armour of my hart, he cried "O vanitie, ...	16	1st Eclogues 7	62
Nor trifling title of vanity dazleth us, ...	69	2nd Eclogues 34	24
Such pleasure take in Vanity,.	273	Psalm IV	9
Who shunning vanity and works of vaineness leaving,.	302	Psalm XXIV	9
At best is merely vanity..	330	Psalm XXXIX	18
So what is man but vanity?	330	Psalm XXXIX	36

VANQUISH
| Where justest love doth vanquish Cupid's powers. . . . . . . | 91 | 3rd Eclogues 63 | 3 |

VANTAGE
| Say then what vantage do we get, by the trade of a Pastor? . | 33 | 1st Eclogues 13 | 49 |

VAPORS
| Infected by those vapours, which arise . . . . | 205 | Astrophil 78 | 2 |
| So darke with misty vapors, which arise. . . . . | 228 | Astrophil 94 | 2 |

VARNISHED
| To set a pearle in steele so meanely varnished?. . . . . . . | 16 | 1st Eclogues 7 | 63 |

VASSAL
| Her vertue is soveraine, fortune a vassal of hers". . . . . . | 30 | 1st Eclogues 11 | 16 |

VAULT
| Now was our heav'nly vaulte deprived of the light. . . . . . | 116 | 4th Eclogues 73 | 1 |
| About that Vault he goeth, ... | 294 | Psalm XIX | 26 |

VAULTY
| And well (me thinks) becomes this vaultie skie . . . . | 126 | 4th Eclogues 75 | 58 |

VEHEMENCE
| Hath not Reason enough vehemence the desire to reprove? Prove. . . . . | 63 | 2nd Eclogues 31 | 10 |

VEHEMENT
| The vehement course of this just lamentation:. . . . . | 127 | 4th Eclogues 75 | 98 |

VEIL
Yet to a passenger will bonnet vaile..	27	1st Eclogues 10	33
Fleshly vaile consumes; but a soule hath his life, ...	31	1st Eclogues 12	22
Too weake for them our weaker sighte doth vaile.	82	Arcadia III 55	11
You should those faire eyes have with a veile covered. . . .	123	4th Eclogues 74	48
Least if no vaile those brave gleames did disguise,.	168	Astrophil 7	7
With absence' Vaile, I live in Sorowe's night.	224	Astrophil 91	4

VEILED
But wretched be the soules which, vaild in a contrary subject, ...	32	1st Eclogues 13	19
His eyes are curious search, but vailde with warefulnesse: .	48	2nd Eclogues 28	43
Here no treason is hidd, vailed in innocence,.	69	2nd Eclogues 34	17

VEILING
| From out his veiling places, ... | 294 | Psalm XIX | 22 |

VEILS
| What veiles then doo prevaile, but to a more miracle?. . . . | 123 | 4th Eclogues 74 | 50 |
| As that sweete blacke which vailes the heav'nly eye: . . . . | 175 | Astrophil 20 | 7 |

VEIN
Dicus. Sing then my lads, but sing with better vaine then yet, ...	53	2nd Eclogues 29	49
And what manner a mind which had to that humor a vaine? Vaine.	63	2nd Eclogues 31	9
Their running fall into a constant vaine	150	Cert Sonnets 22	38
Yet hiding royall bloud full oft in rurall vaine..	167	Astrophil 6	8

```
                                                            PAGE    TITLE          LINE
VEINS
     Where azurde veines well mixt appeere. . . . . . . . . .  87  Arcadia III   62    56
     Youth, lucke, and praise, even fild my veines with pride.. . 191  Astrophil   53    4
VELUM
     With guilded leaves or coloured Velume playes,. . . . . . . 170  Astrophil   11    6
VELVET
     So have I sene trim bookes in velvet dight . . . . . . . . 246  Other Poems   4  180
VENGEFUL
     And ready make Thy vengefull bowe. . . . . . . . . . . . . 298  Psalm XXI         47
VENGM
     O sheepheards' boyes, eschue these tongues of venome,. . . .  50  2nd Eclogues 28   87
     Talking time borrowe for to spitt their vennim . . . . . .  50  2nd Eclogues 28 V886
VENGMED
     Venom'd with godless spight, . . . . . . . . . . . . . . . 273  Psalm III         29
VENOMOUS
     Nor flatterers' venomous insinuations, . . . . . . . . . .  69  2nd Eclogues 34   19
VENTURE
     Now will I but venture this, . . . . . . . . . . . . . . . 203  A&S 2nd Song      23
VENUS
     Like great god Saturn faire, and like faire Venus chaste:. .  12  Arcadia I     3    5
     And Venus seemes, to make up her, she spent herselfe.. . . .  49  2nd Eclogues 28   66
     Thy Venus' child, whose beautie Venus lackes?. . . . . . .  60  2nd Eclogues 30  112
     O Venus (if her praise no envy frames, . . . . . . . . . .  60  2nd Eclogues 30  113
     "Venus come on": said she, "Diane you are obaide". . . . . 119  4th Eclogues 73   78
     And be it as he saith". Venus was glad to heare. . . . . . 120  4th Eclogues 73  143
     "Yet thou shalt not go free (quoth Venus) such a fire. . . 121  4th Eclogues 73  170
     The schooles where Venus hath learn'd Chastitie. . . . . . 185  Astrophil   42    4
     Venus is taught with Dian's wings to flie: . . . . . . . . 202  Astrophil   72    6
     That grace, which Venus weepes that she her selfe doth
        misse .. . . . . . . . . . . . . . . . . . . . . . . . 205  Astrophil   77    4
     While beautie's reddest inke Venus for him doth sturre.. . 232  Astrophil  102   14
     Onely to you her Scepter Venus granteth. . . . . . . . . . 197  A&S 1st Song      16
     Which to their eies the bowles of Venus brought, . . . . . 244  Other Poems   4   99
VENUS'
     Thy Venus' child, whose beautie Venus lackes?. . . . . . .  60  2nd Eclogues 30  112
     Adonis' end, Venus' nett,. . . . . . . . . . . . . . . . .  66  2nd Eclogues 32   27
     Of Venus' babe the wanton nests: . . . . . . . . . . . . .  87  Arcadia III   62   54
     Each had his creast, Mars caried Venus' glove, . . . . . . 171  Astrophil   13    7
     She lightning Love, displaying Venus' skies, . . . . . . . 196  Astrophil   63    7
     Which, coupling Doves, guides Venus' chariot right.. . . . 206  Astrophil   79    4
     For wearing Venus' badge, in every part of thee, . . . . . 214  A&S 5th Song      70
     As Venus' bird the white, swift, lovely Dove . . . . . . . 251  Other Poems   4  353
VERDICT
     To all what I decreed, did thus my verdict saye. . . . . . 121  4th Eclogues 73  162
VERITY
     His judgments be self verity,. . . . . . . . . . . . . . . 294  Psalm XIX         39
     Ev'en spotless verity. . . . . . . . . . . . . . . . . . . 304  Psalm XXV         39
     O lord that art the God of verity.. . . . . . . . . . . . . 312  Psalm XXXI        15
VERMILION
     How doth the colour vade of those vermillion dies, . . . . 232  Astrophil  102    5
VERSE
     What length of verse can serve brave Mopsa's good to show, .  12  Arcadia I     3    1
     Whose hearts are set on measuring a verse: . . . . . . . . 146  Cert Sonnets 17   32
     Loving in truth, and faine in verse my love to show, . . . 165  Astrophil    1    1
     In verse, and that my verse best wits doth please? . . . . 204  Astrophil   74   11
     Stella thinke not that I by verse seeke fame,. . . . . . . 224  Astrophil   90    1
     And both had skill in verse their voice to move. . . . . . 243  Other Poems   4   40
VERSES
     And in this growing barke growe verses myne. . . . . . . .  77  Arcadia III   47   12
VERSING
     Take harp and sing in this our versing time: . . . . . . . 146  Cert Sonnets 17   37
VERT
     But in Vert field Mars bare a golden speare, . . . . . . . 171  Astrophil   13    5
VERY
     That verie shame with Love's high title dignifie.. . . . .  14  1st Eclogues  7    3
     Give therefore to the Muse great praise in whose very
        likenes. . . . . . . . . . . . . . . . . . . . . . . .  33  1st Eclogues 13   62
     The house is made a very lothsome cage,. . . . . . . . . . 105  3rd Eclogues 67   49
     His very being he hath not deserved, . . . . . . . . . . . 105  3rd Eclogues 67   79
     The very trees with grafting we can cherish, . . . . . . . 127  4th Eclogues 75   85
     My verie inke turnes straight to Stella's name;. . . . . . 174  Astrophil   19    6
     Stella oft sees the verie face of wo . . . . . . . . . . . 187  Astrophil   45    1
     The very essence of their tunes, when Angels do rejoyce. . . 217  A&S 7th Song      18
     The very soul amending,. . . . . . . . . . . . . . . . . . 294  Psalm XIX         30
     My very flesh for to devoure,. . . . . . . . . . . . . . . 307  Psalm XXVII       10
     That wicked be, their very name. . . . . . . . . . . . . . 320  Psalm XXXIV       59
     Indeed the very best . . . . . . . . . . . . . . . . . . . 320  Psalm XXXIV       69
     With cruel minds my very soul to teare.. . . . . . . . . . 322  Psalm XXXV        28
     When she with skirts tuckt very hy, with girles at stoolball
        playes. . . . . . . . . . . . . . . . . . . . . . . . 343  Possibly     1   10
VESSEI
     To frame of Earth a vessell of the minde,. . . . . . . . .  57  2nd Eclogues 30   12
VESTURE
     And do cast lots, who should my vesture take.. . . . . . . 299  Psalm XXII        44
VEX
     And vex them in his ire. . . . . . . . . . . . . . . . . . 271  Psalm II          12
VEXED
     I had bene vext, if vext I had not beene.. . . . . . . . . 223  Astrophil   87   14
     Through me, wretch me, even Stella vexed is. . . . . . . . 227  Astrophil   93    4
     They shall be sham'd and vext, that breed my crying, . . . 276  Psalm VI          30
```

548

VEXED	(CONTINUED)	PAGE	TITLE		LINE
To help who vexed be!.		281	Psalm X		4
Teach me, thus vext, what path to go..		303	Psalm XXV		12
VEXING					
The glasses of thy dayly vexing care?"		181	Astrophil	34	3
The while a swarm of foes with vexing feates		276	Psalm VI		23
VICE					
Thus halfe a beast, ech beastly vice he plants,.		21	1st Eclogues	8	33
First shall vertue be vice, and bewty be counted a blemishe,		33	1st Eclogues	13	67
But so our hartes keepe downe, with vice they be not					
stainde		45	Arcadia II	26	14
That they all vice may kill:		91	3rd Eclogues	63	23
Al filthy mouths that glory in their vice.		98	3rd Eclogues	65	12
VICES'					
There shall he find all vices' overthrow,.		201	Astrophil	71	5
VICIOUS					
Who others' vertue doubt, themselves are vicious..		47	2nd Eclogues	28	9
VICTOR					
Be victor still of Phoebus' golden treasure:		108	Arcadia IV	69	5
Who victor seem'd, was to his ruine brought:		251	Other Poems	4	346
Vertue's proofe, fortune's victor, beautie's place.. . . .		252	Other Poems	4	392
VICTOR'S					
Which absence wisht: love plai'd a victor's part:.		248	Other Poems	4	223
VICTORY					
Then to an earnest Love what doth best victorie lend? Ende..		63	2nd Eclogues	31	15
Crie, "Victorie, this faire day all is ours.".		171	Astrophil	12	11
Made manifest by such a victorie,.		185	Astrophil	40	10
VIEW					
Lay not thy colours more to view,.		157	Cert Sonnets	27	23
VIEWED					
Which were not evill, well vew'd in reason's light.. . . .		131	Arcadia V	77	8
VIEWING					
Viewing the shape of darknesse and delight,.		230	Astrophil	99	6
VILD					
With wordes so vyld, from vilder mouth proceeding.		50	2nd Eclogues	28 V	82
VILDER					
With wordes so vyld, from vilder mouth proceeding.		50	2nd Eclogues	28 V	82
VILE					
Reason. Thou Rebell vile, come, to thy master yelde. . . .		46	2nd Eclogues	27	1
With words so vile, which viler breath doth breed.		50	2nd Eclogues	28	82
Therefore, alas, you use vile Vulcan's spight, ...		60	2nd Eclogues	30	107
From any joy, know fortune's vile displacing her,.		61	2nd Eclogues	30	150
But above all away vile jealousie, ...		93	3rd Eclogues	63	82
No, no, our mischiefe growes in this vile fortune, ...		109	Arcadia IV	70	31
Therefore from so vile fancie, ...		161	Cert Sonnets	30	37
But lyke vyle chaffe with wind shal scattred be.		270	Psalm I		14
Let their vile thoughts the thinkers' ruin be..		275	Psalm V		30
Whose eyes a person vile do hold in vile disdain		287	Psalm XV		7
And as vile chaff away the wind doth blow,.		321	Psalm XXXV		11
But strayers vile shall be destroyed		327	Psalm XXXVII		95
Those vile scoffes of naughty ones		335	Psalm XLII		45
VILER					
With words so vile, which viler breath doth breed.		50	2nd Eclogues	28	82
VILLAGE-LORD					
Of village-Lord that whitsontide to beare:		244	Other Poems	4	76
VILLAGES					
In secret by-way villages.		282	Psalm X		32
VINE					
Elme embraste by a vine, embracing fancy reviveth.		36	1st Eclogues	13	131
Like to the Elme and Vyne, ...		91	3rd Eclogues	63	15
VIOLENCE					
Of Phoebus' violence in shade of stately Ciprus tree,. . .		31	1st Eclogues	13	12
In this strange violence, to make resistance..		67	2nd Eclogues	33	2
With violence of heav'nly.		154	Cert Sonnets	25	5
VIOLENT					
Such faith, so staineles, inviolate, violent?.		124	4th Eclogues	74	70
VIOLETS					
As sweete as violetts, faire as a lilly is,.		69	2nd Eclogues	34	32
In shewe and sent pale violets,.		89	Arcadia III	62	107
VIOLS					
Viols with singing Voice,.		316	Psalm XXXIII		9
VIRGIN					
My virgin life no spotted thought shall staine..		40	Arcadia II	18	6
They seemd to me) on whom did waite a Virgin pure:		118	4th Eclogues	73	64
VIRGIN-WAX					
Which nothing spares, to melt that Virgin-waxe		60	2nd Eclogues	30	108
A daintie seale of virgin-waxe,.		88	Arcadia III	62	75
VIRTUE					
Then vertue try, if she can worke in thee.		22	1st Eclogues	9	13
With vertue fraught and full of holy feare!.		25	1st Eclogues	9	95
Her vertue is soveraine, fortune a vassal of hers".. . . .		30	1st Eclogues	11	16
Vertue you have, of vertue you have left proufes to the					
whole world, ...		33	1st Eclogues	13	56
And vertue is gratefull with bewty and richnes adorned,. . .		33	1st Eclogues	13	57
First shall vertue be vice, and bewty be counted a blemishe,		33	1st Eclogues	13	67
Vertue, richesse, beawties of mine shall great be reputed. .		34	1st Eclogues	13	81
Desteny keepes me aloofe. For if all thy estate to thy					
verture.		34	1st Eclogues	13	98
When yonger dooth in smoke his vertue spend.		38	Arcadia II	15	4
Who others' vertue doubt, themselves are vicious..		47	2nd Eclogues	28	9

VIRTUE	(CONTINUED)	PAGE	TITLE		LINE
Her staines are beames; vertue the fault she blamed is.. . . .		49	2nd Eclogues	28	57
And vertue do in greatest need neglect..		58	2nd Eclogues	30	64
O Vertue weake, shall death his triumph set.		59	2nd Eclogues	30	92
Silly rewarde! yet among women hath she of vertu the most. Most..		64	2nd Eclogues	31	36
Thou li'st false Echo, their minds as vertu be just. Just. .		65	2nd Eclogues	31	46
Was vertue cladde in constant love's attire.		77	Arcadia III	48	2
Vertue, beawtie, and speach, did strike, wound, charme,. . .		84	Arcadia III	60	1
With beautie's seale, and vertue faire disguis'de, ...		85	Arcadia III	61	2
Vertue (if not a God) yet God's chiefe parte,.		92	3rd Eclogues	63	46
Pan store of babes, vertue their thoughts well staid,. . . .		93	3rd Eclogues	63	93
To vertue, fortune, time and woman's brest..		98	3rd Eclogues	65	14
Geron. Who for ech fickle feare from vertue shrinkes,. . . .		105	3rd Eclogues	67	58
And while their line of yeares they did in vertue spende...		117	4th Eclogues	73	38
Must I be onely the marke, shall prove that Vertue is angrie		123	4th Eclogues	74	33
Vertue is dead, now set thy triumph here..		127	4th Eclogues	75	72
But vertue sets so high, that reason's light,.		135	Cert Sonnets	2	7
A seate where beauty shines and vertue raignes,.		141	Cert Sonnets	8	10
So deepe in seas of vertue beauties ly..		151	Cert Sonnets	22	58
Beautie tied to vertue, ...		154	Cert Sonnets	25	6
For vertue hath this better lesson taught, ...		161	Cert Sonnets	31	12
Vertue alas, now let me take some rest,.		166	Astrophil	4	1
That Vertue, thou thy selfe shalt be in love..		167	Astrophil	4	14
True, that true Beautie Vertue is indeed,.		167	Astrophil	5	9
My wits, quicke in vaine thoughts, in vertue lame:		175	Astrophil	21	4
That Vertue, if it once met with our eyes,.		177	Astrophil	25	3
Vertue of late, with vertuous care to ster		177	Astrophil	25	9
Do they call Vertue there ungratefulnesse?		180	Astrophil	31	14
Vertue awake, Beautie but beautie is,.		188	Astrophil	47	9
Where Vertue is made strong by Beautie's might,.		188	Astrophil	48	2
A strife is growne betweene Vertue and Love,.		190	Astrophil	52	1
But Vertue thus that title doth disprove,.		190	Astrophil	52	5
Let Vertue have that Stella's selfe; yet thus,.		191	Astrophil	52	13
That Vertue but that body graunt to us..		191	Astrophil	52	14
Which in her face teach vertue, I could brooke		193	Astrophil	56	6
Her graunt to me, by her owne vertue know.		196	Astrophil	63	4
Thou art my Wit, and thou my Vertue art.		198	Astrophil	64	14
It is, so faire a Vertue to enjoy.		200	Astrophil	68	14
How Vertue may best lodg'd in beautie be,.		201	Astrophil	71	2
As fast thy Vertue bends that love to good:.		201	Astrophil	71	13
No vertue merits praise, once toucht with blot of Treason. .		214	A&S 5th Song		66
Why? because I vertue chose.		329	Psalm XXXVIII		60
My freedom, with show of hir beames, with virtue my content.		344	Possibly	1	38
To strive she fear'd how it with vertue stoode..		245	Other Poems	4	126
He found man's vertue is but part of man,.		253	Other Poems	4	421
VIRTUE'S					
My minde for weeds your vertue's liverie weares.		18	1st Eclogues	7	137
Sweet vertue's lawe barres not a causefull mone.		22	1st Eclogues	9	18
In whose decay Vertue's faire shrine must fall...		59	2nd Eclogues	30	91
Of vertue's regiment, shining in harnesse.		67	2nd Eclogues	33	4
For you do passe your selfe, in vertue's might..		79	Arcadia III	50	20
In one true chest to rob all Vertue's treasure?.		126	4th Eclogues	75	47
Since Death on Vertue's fort hath made invasion.		128	4th Eclogues	75	102
Queene Vertue's court, which some call Stella's face,. . . .		169	Astrophil	9	1
Vertue's great beautie in that face I prove,.		177	Astrophil	25	13
Alas, if from the height of Vertue's throne, ...		184	Astrophil	40	5
And anchor fast my selfe on Vertue's shore..		196	Astrophil	62	11
Thy reasons firmly set on Vertue's feet, ...		200	Astrophil	68	11
Vertue's gold now must head my Cupid's dart.		202	Astrophil	72	8
Beautie's plague, Vertue's scourge, succour of lies:		206	Astrophil	78	6
Nature's praise, Vertue's stall, Cupid's cold fire,.		206	Astrophil	80	3
When strong Desire, which vertue's love doth guide,.		345	Possibly	4	7
For since warre is the ground of vertue's love,.		346	Possibly	5	7
Vertue's proofe, fortune's victor, beautie's place..		252	Other Poems	4	392
VIRTUES					
Whose vertues strange, and beuties such, as no man them may know?.		12	Arcadia I	3	2
Since vertues all, to make her title, pleased be..		15	1st Eclogues	7	39
What swarmes of vertues did in his youth flye.		24	1st Eclogues	9	74
And thou shalt finde, in women vertues lie..		106	3rd Eclogues	67	102
Whom curst do blesse, whose weakenesse vertues arme, ...		142	Cert Sonnets	10	6
Whose beames be joyes, whose joyes all vertues be, ...		185	Astrophil	42	2
O Grammer rules, o now your vertues show;.		196	Astrophil	63	1
VIRTUOUS					
Make me, o vertuous Shame, thy lawes neglect..		40	Arcadia II	18	12
R. O sacred Reason, helpe our vertuous toiles.		46	2nd Eclogues	27	23
And vertuous soules so soone should lose their place?. . . .		126	4th Eclogues	75	42
Vertue of late, with vertuous care to ster		177	Astrophil	25	9
That vertuous soule, sure heire of heav'nly blisse:.		190	Astrophil	52	7
This realme of blisse, while vertuous course I take, ...		200	Astrophil	69	13
VISION					
That I become a vision		20	1st Eclogues	7	V963
VISIONS					
The restfull Caves now restlesse visions give, ...		147	Cert Sonnets	18	9
No sleeps, but dreams, no dreams, but visions straunge,. . .		253	Other Poems	4	436
All visions seeme, at every bush I start:.		253	Other Poems	4	445
VISIT					
To visite so low folkes did much disdaine, ...		243	Other Poems	4	63

```
                                                           PAGE    TITLE         LINE
VISITINGS
   Their courteous visitings are courting lyes, . . . . . . . .   333 Psalm XLI          21
VITAL
   The heavens conspir'd, to make my vitall sparke. . . . . . .    73 Arcadia III   40    3
   Such vitall sparke, that her mine eyes might see. . . . . .    115 4th Eclogues 72   84
   Ah! from the sword yet save my vital sprite, . . . . . . . .   299 Psalm XXII         47
VOCATION
   Then base and sower is Love's most high vocation. . . . . .     48 2nd Eclogues 28   24
VOICE
   Tune up my voice, a higher note I yeeld, . . . . . . . . . .     3 Lady of May    2    7
   Whose cleerest eyes I blisse, and sweetest voyce, . . . . . .     5 Lady of May    3   15
   Disuse your selves from sweete Menalcas' voice:. . . . . . .    13 Arcadia I      4    6
   Now my hoarse voice doth faile this occupation, . . . . . .     19 1st Eclogues   7  170
   But now hoarse voyce, doth faile this occupation, . . . . .     20 1st Eclogues   7 V970
   And statute made he never shoulde have voice, . . . . . . .     29 1st Eclogues  10   86
   If the Swanne's sweet voice be not heard, but at death, . . .    30 1st Eclogues  12   14
   With the voyce of truth to recorde to all worldes, . . . . .    31 1st Eclogues  12   19
   Joyning your sweete voice to the rurall muse of a deserte, .    31 1st Eclogues  13    2
   A voice may come, which troubled soule doth yeld:. . . . . .    40 Arcadia II    18    4
   Thou then, that framste both words and voice most skilfully,    48 2nd Eclogues 28   19
   As for your doubts: her voice was it deceaved me, . . . . .     48 2nd Eclogues 28   29
   Pas. My voice the lambe did winne, Menalcas was our judge: .    52 2nd Eclogues 29   15
   Nico. I thinke it well: such voice would make one musicke
         hate:. . . . . . . . . . . . . . . . . . . . . . . . .    52 2nd Eclogues 29   21
   Do you not heare his voice, and see his shape? . . . . . . .    53 2nd Eclogues 29   59
   Long since my voice is hoarce, and throte is sore, . . . . .    57 2nd Eclogues 30    8
   My voice is hoarse, my throte scorcht, . . . . . . . . . . .    66 2nd Eclogues 32   11
   My voice, too hott to keepe in. . . . . . . . . . . . . . .     67 2nd Eclogues 32   45
   Streight as Cedar, a voice staines the Cannary birds, . . .     69 2nd Eclogues 34   33
   O voice that doth, the Thrush in shrilnes staine, . . . . .     76 Arcadia III   46    4
   Let voice of Sighes into cleare musike runne, . . . . . . .     84 Arcadia III   59   13
   But with such turnes the voice to stray, . . . . . . . . . .    86 Arcadia III   62   33
   Nightingale, voice, entising songes to saye. . . . . . . . .   101 3rd Eclogues 66   82
   Why should we spare our voice from endlesse wailing, . . . .   109 Arcadia IV    70    7
   A yelling voice, and heartes compos'd of sorow, . . . . . .    109 Arcadia IV    70   27
   While that my voice doth fill these wofull vallies, . . . . .   111 4th Eclogues 71   10
   Alas, me thinkes, my weakned voice but spilleth, . . . . . .   127 4th Eclogues 75   97
   When trembling voice brings forth that I do Stella love. . .   168 Astrophil      6   14
   That her cleare voyce lifts thy fame to the skies. . . . . .   171 Astrophil     12    8
   With so sweete voice, and by sweete Nature so, . . . . . . .   183 Astrophil     36    9
   To feele my griefes, and she with face and voice . . . . . .   193 Astrophil     57   13
   O voice, o face, maugre my speeche's might, . . . . . . . .    194 Astrophil     58   12
   He barks, my songs thine owne voyce oft doth prove: . . . .    194 Astrophil     59    6
   With voice more fit to wed Amphion's lyre, . . . . . . . . .   200 Astrophil     68    6
   That voyce, which makes the soule plant himselfe in the
         eares: . . . . . . . . . . . . . . . . . . . . . . . .   205 Astrophil     77    9
   Who hath the voyce, which soule from sences sunders, . . . .   197 A&S 1st Song       29
   If Orpheus' voyce had force to breathe such musicke's love .   208 A&S 3rd Song        1
   Let my whispering voyce obtaine, . . . . . . . . . . . . . .   210 A&S 4th Song        3
   Thy fingers Cupid's shafts, thy voyce the Angel's lay: . . .   212 A&S 5th Song       11
   O You that heare this voice, . . . . . . . . . . . . . . . .   215 A&S 6th Song        1
   Thus doth the voice and face, . . . . . . . . . . . . . . .    215 A&S 6th Song       13
   Heare you this soule-invading voice, and count it but a
         voice? . . . . . . . . . . . . . . . . . . . . . . . .   217 A&S 7th Song       17
   "Stella, whose voice when it speakes, . . . . . . . . . . .    219 A&S 8th Song       37
   Stella, whose voice when it singeth, . . . . . . . . . . . .   219 A&S 8th Song       39
   To him my voyce I spread, . . . . . . . . . . . . . . . . .    272 Psalm III          14
   O, hearken to my voice, which calls on Thee, . . . . . . . .   274 Psalm V             3
   So shall my voice clime to thyne eares betime: . . . . . . .   274 Psalm V             5
   They ever shall send thee their praysing voyce, . . . . . .    275 Psalm V            35
   For god hath heard the weeping sobbing voice . . . . . . . .   276 Psalm VI           27
   Then spake he his lowd voyce, then hailestones coales and
         fire. . . . . . . . . . . . . . . . . . . . . . . . .    291 Psalm XVIII        28
   With voyce of thankfulnes . . . . . . . . . . . . . . . . .    305 Psalm XXVI         23
   Heare lord when I my voice display, . . . . . . . . . . . .     307 Psalm XXVII        37
   Which from suing voice do fly. . . . . . . . . . . . . . . .   309 Psalm XXVIII       10
   His voice is on the Waters found, . . . . . . . . . . . . .     310 Psalm XXIX          7
   His voyce doth threatning thunders sound, . . . . . . . . .    310 Psalm XXIX          8
   The Voice of that lord ruling us . . . . . . . . . . . . . .   310 Psalm XXIX         10
   By voice of high Jehova we . . . . . . . . . . . . . . . . .   310 Psalm XXIX         13
   His voice doth flashing flames divide, . . . . . . . . . . .   310 Psalm XXIX         19
   His voice have trembling deserts try'd, . . . . . . . . . .    310 Psalm XXIX         20
   His voice makes hindes their calves to cast, . . . . . . . .   310 Psalm XXIX         22
   His voice makes bald the forest wast; . . . . . . . . . . .    310 Psalm XXIX         23
   Viols with singing Voice, . . . . . . . . . . . . . . . . .    316 Psalm XXXIII        9
   My God Thou wilt heare my voice; . . . . . . . . . . . . . .   328 Psalm XXXVIII      45
   Will. Dick, since we cannot dance, come let a chearefull
         voyce. . . . . . . . . . . . . . . . . . . . . . . . .   343 Possibly       1    1
   A plaining songe plaine-singing voice requires, . . . . . .    242 Other Poems    4    3
   And both had skill in verse their voice to move. . . . . . .   243 Other Poems    4   40
   Amid my flock with woe my voice I teare, . . . . . . . . . .   254 Other Poems    4  459
   Till Strephon's plaining voice him nearer drew, . . . . . .    256 Other Poems    4  535
VOICED
   Dicus. Thy words well voic'd, well gra'ste had almost heaved
         me. . . . . . . . . . . . . . . . . . . . . . . . . .     48 2nd Eclogues 28   31
VOID
   That soone the world of his false tong be void. . . . . . .     24 1st Eclogues   9   68
   P. Who Passion doth forsake, lives void of joy. . . . . . .     46 2nd Eclogues 27   14
   Let us not winke though void of purest sightfulnes. . . . .     61 2nd Eclogues 30  139
   The caves were full, the mountaines voide of goates: . . . .    98 3rd Eclogues 66   11
```

VOID   (CONTINUED)   PAGE   TITLE   LINE
  Then void of neerer cares, the depth of things to find.. . . . 118 4th Eclogues 73   50
  As might learne Temp'rance voyde of a rage's events. . . . . 124 4th Eclogues 74   64
  We Orphans lefte, void of all publique might?. . . . . . . 129 4th Eclogues 76   12
  Keeping that forme, though void of wonted heate: . . . . . . 151 Cert Sonnets 22   48
  For it is void of hate.. . . . . 215 A&S 6th Song   6
  While I am voyd of any helping pow'r.. . . . . 277 Psalm VII   6
  Voyde of me in field to bee, ... 262 Other Poems   7 20
  Voyde of wishing and repenting.. . . . . 264 Other Poems   7 78
VOLLEY
  Which at firste voly gave too open entry,. . . . .   68 2nd Eclogues 33   14
VOUCHSAFE
  Vouchsafe your silent eares to playning musique, ... 111 4th Eclogues 71   4
  Above line repeated at following location. . . . . 111 4th Eclogues 71   11
  And hither now, vouchsafe to take with willing eare. . . . 119 4th Eclogues 73   104
  Vouchsafe of all acquaintance this to tell,. . . . . 181 Astrophil   32   9
  Thou canst vouchsafe the influence of a thought. . . . . . 184 Astrophil   40   6
  Thyne Ears voutchsafe to bend to me. . . . . 289 Psalm XVII   4
  Vouchsafe me help O Lord, and help with hast;. . . . . . . 332 Psalm XL   51
VOUCHSAFETH
  (Since no estates be so base, but love vouchsafeth his
    arrow . . . .   33 1st Eclogues 13   50
VOW
  This vowe receave, this vowe o Gods maintaine; . . . . . .   40 Arcadia II   18   5
  Such life to leade, such death I vow to dye. . . . .   40 Arcadia II   18 18
  Be thou the knot of this their open vowe,. . . . .   92 3rd Eclogues 63   47
  Whille I that syghte, desyre, and vowe forbare,. . . . . . 344 Possibly   2   7
VOWED
  Sweete soule, to whom I vowed am a slave,. . . . .   3 Lady of May   2 11
  Thou art my Lord, and I thy vowed slave. . . . . 135 Cert Sonnets   1 14
  I never did my vowed word forsake: . . . . 146 Cert Sonnets 17   8
  Nor nourish speciall lockes of vowed haire,. . . . . 191 Astrophil   54   3
VOW'S
  His workes, showes, suites, with wit, grace, and vow's
    might . . . .   84 Arcadia III   60   4
VOWS
  Who feare Thee shall my vowes performed see. . . . . 300 Psalm XXII   60
VULCAN'S
  With Cupid she fore-sees, and goes god Vulcan's pace:. . . .   12 Arcadia I   3   7
  Therefore, alas, you use vile Vulcan's spight, ...   60 2nd Eclogues 30   107
VULGAR
  And Muses scorne with vulgar braines to dwell, ... 203 Astrophil   74   3
  Every other vulgar light.. . . . . 233 A&S 11th Song   5
W
  W. Who bound thee? D. Love my Lord. W. What witnesses
    therto . . . . 343 Possibly   1 25
  W. What seale? D. My hart deepe graven. W. Who made the band
    so fast?. . . . . 343 Possibly   1 27
  W. If wages make you want, what food is that she gives?. . . 344 Possibly   1 33
WAG
  Alas poore wag, that now a scholler art. . . . . 188 Astrophil   46   9
  Cupid the wagg, that lately conquer'd had. . . . . 245 Other Poems   4 129
WAGE
  These gentle Lawyers wage, ... 215 A&S 6th Song   14
WAGER
  Nico. Content: but I will lay a wager hereunto,. . . . . .   53 2nd Eclogues 29   29
WAGES
  Dearely the servants doo their wages buy,. . . . . 105 3rd Eclogues 67   52
  Whose wages makes me beg the more, who feeds me till I
    sterve,. . . . . 343 Possibly   1 20
  Will. Thou late of wages playn'dst: what wages mayst thou
    have?. . . . . 344 Possibly   1 31
  W. If wages make you want, what food is that she gives?. . . 344 Possibly   1 33
WAGS
  And straight therewith, like wags new got to play, ... 173 Astrophil   17 13
WAIL
  I waile their lotte, but will not other prove. . . . . . .   39 Arcadia II   17   4
  I waile for want, and yet am chokte with store.. . . . . .   41 Arcadia II   20   8
  Wayle in my woes, taste of your master's payne,. . . . . .   44 Arcadia II   24 11
  Yet waile thy selfe, and waile with causefull teares,. . . . 228 Astrophil   94 11
WAILED
  I sighd her sighes, and wailed for her wo, ... 223 Astrophil   87 10
  Lo I that waild, now daunce for joy. . . . . 311 Psalm XXX   34
WAILFUL
  But all, for all reach not my wailefull will:. . . . . . . 126 4th Eclogues 75   33
  And in our wailfull naming him our pleasure: . . . . 130 4th Eclogues 76   32
  This my Distresse to God with wailfull cryes I show, ... 291 Psalm XVIII   12
WAILING
  Boulon. Thy wailing words do much my spirits move, ...   60 2nd Eclogues 30   125
  Since wayling is a bud of causefull sorowe,. . . . . 108 Arcadia IV   70   1
  And inward griefe seale up with outward wailing. . . . . . 109 Arcadia IV   70   6
  Why should we spare our voice from endlesse wailing, ... 109 Arcadia IV   70   7
  (Which may be know'n, but never help't with wailing) . . . . 109 Arcadia IV   70 14
  By thy impe's losse to fill the world with wailing.. . . . . 109 Arcadia IV   70 22
  Our sports murdering our selves, our musiques wailing, . . . 109 Arcadia IV   70 29
  The furious inward griefes with hellish wailing: . . . . . 109 Arcadia IV   70 33
  His nature feares to die who lives still wailing.. . . . . . 110 Arcadia IV   70 39
  And hath with wailing strength clim'd highest mountaines:.. . 112 4th Eclogues 71   27
  Leaving me nought but wailing eloquence: . . . . 184 Astrophil   38 11
  Sate wailing without boot. . . . . 256 Other Poems   5   7

WAILING   (CONTINUED)   PAGE   TITLE   LINE
    Wayling till death, shun you not to be seene?. . . . . 258 Other Poems   5   91
    Oh! what doth wailing winne? . . . .   259 Other Poems   5   103
WAIT
    Where rockes do wayte, for theym the wyndes do chase,. . . .   70 Arcadia III   36   2
    To ease those paines, which on desire do waite). . . . . .   82 Arcadia III   56   4
    Sturres me to thinke what dangers lye in waite.. . . . . .   82 Arcadia III   56   12
    They seemd to me) on whom did waite a Virgin pure: . . . . . 118 4th Eclogues 73   64
    Fetters tyed, do waite the hower . . . .   155 Cert Sonnets 26   18
    If he waite well, I never thence would move: . . . .   194 Astrophil   59   3
    So gratefull now you waite upon my care. . . . .   228 Astrophil   95   4
    For proof, oft lain in wait he is. . . . .   282 Psalm X   31
    Who is our Lord, with due remembrance wayte. . . . .   296 Psalm XX   30
    And with those hands about Thy Altar waite,. . . . .   305 Psalm XXVI   21
    Wait on the lord with patient hope,. . . . .   325 Psalm XXXVII   17
    Wait thou on God and keep his way, ...   327 Psalm XXXVII   85
    But who for my life do waite,. . . . .   328 Psalm XXXVIII   33
    This being thus, For what O Lord wait I? . . . .   330 Psalm XXXIX   23
    I wait on Thee with hopefull ey. . . . .   330 Psalm XXXIX   24
    Wait on God, for yet his glory . . . .   334 Psalm XLII   19
    Above line repeated at following location. . . . .   335 Psalm XLII   51
    Wait on God, for still . . . .   337 Psalm XLIII   34
    The hidden beauties seem'd in waite to lye,. . . . .   250 Other Poems   4   303
WAITED
    She waited mistresse' will: who thus disclosd her spright. . 119 4th Eclogues 73   92
    How cloth'd, how waited on, sighd she or smilde, ...   225 Astrophil   92   10
    Thought waited on delight, and speech did follow thought:. . 212 A&S 5th Song   2
WAITETH
    Ne for bad mates in way of sinning waiteth . . . .   270 Psalm I   3
WAITING
    Lalus. Once my well-waiting eyes espied my treasure, ...   16 1st Eclogues 7   73
    Of waiting thoughts all to her service ment? . . . .   78 Arcadia III   49   12
    Her waiting Nymphe, a Nymphe that did excell as farr . . . . 119 4th Eclogues 73   82
    And will my waiting eyes to thee ward bend.. . . . .   274 Psalm V   8
    Must strive with waiting foot, and watching eye. . . . . .   248 Other Poems   4   228
WAITS
    He waites to spoyle the simple men:. . . . .   282 Psalm X   38
WAKE
    But rise, but wake that I may judgment gett. . . . .   322 Psalm XXXV   57
WAKED
    The rest I cannot tell, for therewithall I wak'd . . . . .   121 4th Eclogues 73 179
WAKEFUL
    A living coarse I lay: but ah, my wakefull minde . . . . .   117 4th Eclogues 73   31
WAKES
    Love wakes the jealous eye least thence it moves:. . . . .   42 Arcadia II   22   6
    Apollo wakes, and bow hath sometime sparde.. . . . .   143 Cert Sonnets 12   15
    When she wakes, is too too cruell. . . . .   202 A&S 2nd Song   4
WAKETH
    Doubte is his sleepe, he waketh in invention;. . . . . . .   48 2nd Eclogues 28   40
WAKING
    Unto her rested sense a perfect waking,. . . . .   137 Cert Sonnets 4   2
    The Babe cries "way, thy love doth keepe me waking". . . . . 139 Cert Sonnets 6   3
    Above line repeated at following location. . . . .   139 Cert Sonnets 6   6
    The babe cries "nay, for that abide I waking". . . . . . .   139 Cert Sonnets 6   9
    Her tongue waking still refuseth,. . . . .   202 A&S 2nd Song   9
    See the hand which waking gardeth, ...   202 A&S 2nd Song   13
    Oh sweet kisse, but ah she is waking,. . . . .   203 A&S 2nd Song   25
    When waking of this sleep of mine. . . . .   290 Psalm XVII   47
WALK
    I would know whether she did sit or walke, ...   225 Astrophil   92   9
    Why walk I in woes . . . .   336 Psalm XLIII   10
    In chastest plaies, till home they walke a rowe, ...   243 Other Poems   4   54
    This morne alone to lonely walke did passe,. . . . .   255 Other Poems   4 533
WALKED
    Because I walk'd his wayes, nor gainst him ev'ly went, . . . 292 Psalm XVIII   44
WALKING
    Nico. To river's banke, being a walking brought, ...   55 2nd Eclogues 29 111
    This man, this talking beast, this walking tree. . . . . .   58 2nd Eclogues 30   34
    But walking forth, the first thus to the second saide, . . . 118 4th Eclogues 73   77
    But with short breath, long lookes, staid feet and walking
        hed, ...   205 Astrophil   76   13
    But their tongues restraint from walking,. . . . .   218 A&S 8th Song   23
    Thou seest each side the walking doth endure . . . .   285 Psalm XII   25
    Walking in bright Phoebus' blaze . . . .   262 Other Poems   7   1
WALKS
    In wonted walkes, since wonted fancies change, ...   147 Cert Sonnets 18   1
WALLET
    Thy wallet or thy Tarbox lost, or thy new rayment rent?. . . 343 Possibly   1   16
WALLS
    Her cannons be her eys, myne eys the walls be, ...   68 2nd Eclogues 33   13
    If stones good measure daunc'd, the Theban walles to build,. 208 A&S 3rd Song   3
    I hosts by thee orecome, by Thee ore walls I fly;. . . . . . 292 Psalm XVIII   54
    Farr farr more sure, than walls most firmly fast.. . . . .   313 Psalm XXXI   60
    About these never conquered walles to swarme,. . . . . . .   346 Possibly   5   10
WALNUT
    Or when a rich rubie's just price be the worth of a walnut,.   34 1st Eclogues 13   78
WAN
    My sheepehooke is wanne hope, which all upholdes:. . . . .   39 Arcadia II   17   5
    Let pearls be wan with woe their damme doth beare: . . . . . 125 4th Eclogues 75   23
    How silently, and with how wanne a face, ...   180 Astrophil   31   2

```
                                                          PAGE    TITLE          LINE
WAND
     The Wand is Will, thou Fancie Saddle art,. . . . . . . . . .  189 Astrophil    49     9
WANDER
     Dicus. Dorus you wander farre in great reproches;. . . . . .   50 2nd Eclogues 28    92
WANDERING
     Such wandring reasons in thy speech I finde. . . . . . . . .   25 1st Eclogues  9    98
     Selfe-lost and wandring, banished that place we doe come
        from,. . . . . . . . . . . . . . . . . . . . . . . . . .   32 1st Eclogues 13    26
     In thies delights the wandring thought . . . . . . . . . . .   88 Arcadia III  62    71
     For ever wandring from all good direction; . . . . . . . . .  130 4th Eclogues 76    26
     Who bends not wandring eyes. . . . . . . . . . . . . . . . .  331 Psalm XL            17
     And giving to his sight a wandring race, . . . . . . . . . .  255 Other Poems   4   526
     There he wandring malecontent, . . . . . . . . . . . . . . .  262 Other Poems   7    13
WANT
     And if for want of use thy minde ashamed is, . . . . . . . .   14 1st Eclogues  7     2
     Want I white wooll, whose eyes her white skinne garnished? .   16 1st Eclogues  7    59
     Love smiled, and thus said; "Want joynd to desire is
        unhappy . . . . . . . . . . . . . . . . . . . . . . . .    30 1st Eclogues 11    11
     Aire, we do still with sighes encrease; to the fire? we do
        want none. . . . . . . . . . . . . . . . . . . . . . . .   32 1st Eclogues 13    30
     That where you are no wished good can want;. . . . . . . . .   39 Arcadia II   16     6
     I waile for want, and yet am chokte with store.. . . . . . .   41 Arcadia II   20     8
     Can fancies want eies, or he fall that steppeth aloft? Oft..   64 2nd Eclogues 31    22
     As farre from want, as farre from vaine expence, . . . . . .   98 3rd Eclogues 65     9
     And (but they drad their Prince they ofte should want) . . .  101 3rd Eclogues 66   100
     Which lest the ruinous want of government dissolve;. . . . .  120 4th Eclogues 73   128
     That he for want of elbowe roome must die? . . . . . . . . .  126 4th Eclogues 75    44
     Till want of force do force her fall to ground;. . . . . . .  144 Cert Sonnets 15     4
     Like to the Mowlle with want of guiding sight, . . . . . . .  149 Cert Sonnets 21     7
     And I be dead who want sense,. . . . . . . . . . . . . . . .  154 Cert Sonnets 25    22
     As do bewray a want of inward tuch:. . . . . . . . . . . . .  172 Astrophil    15    10
     Wealth breeding want, more blist, more wretched grow.. . . .  177 Astrophil    24     4
     Is constant Love deem'd there but want of wit? . . . . . . .  180 Astrophil    31    10
     That thou must want or food, or dwelling place.. . . . . . .  187 Astrophil    46     4
     Or want I sense to feele my miserie? . . . . . . . . . . . .  188 Astrophil    47     5
     But now that I, alas, do want her sight, . . . . . . . . . .  193 Astrophil    56     9
     And I, mad with delight, want wit to cease,. . . . . . . . .  207 Astrophil    81    13
     That wormes should have their Sun, and I want mine.. . . . .  230 Astrophil    98    14
     Shall a heavenly grace want pitty?". . . . . . . . . . . . .  219 A&S 8th Song        64
     For nothing they can ever want . . . . . . . . . . . . . . .  319 Psalm XXXIV         34
     Nor want in dearth their want to ease. . . . . . . . . . . .  325 Psalm XXXVII        48
     Tho I in want be shrinking,. . . . . . . . . . . . . . . . .  332 Psalm XL            65
     W. If wages make you want, what food is that she gives?. . .  344 Possibly      1    33
     Then want one hower those eyes which my joyes keepe. . . . .  259 Other Poems   5   102
WANTETH
     Who else for whom Fame worthy trumpets wanteth?. . . . . . .  197 A&S 1st Song        14
WANTING
     And wanting her, my weeping eyes I wipe. . . . . . . . . . .   54 2nd Eclogues 29    77
     Who at the first, wanting, or hiding pride,. . . . . . . . .  101 3rd Eclogues 66   107
     And wanting use of eyes their eyes began to close: . . . . .  116 4th Eclogues 73     6
     Since wanting is more woe then too much having.. . . . . . .  137 Cert Sonnets  4    20
     But words came halting forth, wanting Invention's stay,. . .  165 Astrophil     1     9
     To lay his then marke wanting shafts of sight, . . . . . . .  230 Astrophil    99     3
     "Therefore shepheardes wanting skill,. . . . . . . . . . . .  263 Other Poems   7    37
WANTON
     (Therion) When wanton Pan, deceiv'd with Lion's skin,. . . .    5 Lady of May   3     7
     Of Venus' babe the wanton nests:. . . . . . . . . . . . . .    87 Arcadia III  62    54
     A wanton woman's face, and with curld knots had twinde . . .  118 4th Eclogues 73    73
     Love still a boy, and oft a wanton is, . . . . . . . . . . .  203 Astrophil    73     1
     While wanton winds with beauties so devine . . . . . . . . .  232 Astrophil   103     6
     Where birds wanton musicke made, . . . . . . . . . . . . . .  217 A&S 8th Song         2
     While nought but game, the selfe-hurt wanton ment. . . . . .  247 Other Poems   4   192
     "Tell me you wanton brooke,. . . . . . . . . . . . . . . . .  257 Other Poems   5    27
WANTS
     To one that hath no wealth, and wants his wit. . . . . . . .    4 Lady of May   2    24
     Slander wants a pretext, flattery gone beyond: . . . . . . .   69 2nd Eclogues 34    38
     Which who so wants, halfe of himselfe doth misse.. . . . . .  103 3rd Eclogues 67     9
     Is it not evill that such a Devill wants hornes? . . . . . .  206 Astrophil    78    14
     He leasure wants to mark all this. . . . . . . . . . . . . .  282 Psalm X             48
WAR
     The bloudy shaftes of Cupid's warre, . . . . . . . . . . . .   90 Arcadia III  62   131
     And warr of thoughts is swallow'd up in peace. . . . . . . .   91 3rd Eclogues 63     4
     She warre doth ever with his kinsfolke keepe,. . . . . . . .  104 3rd Eclogues 67    37
     In warr his wit and word was our direction.. . . . . . . . .  129 4th Eclogues 76    18
     But wilt new warre upon thine owne begin?. . . . . . . . . .  183 Astrophil    36     8
     The field where all my thoughts to warre be traind,. . . . .  230 Astrophil    98     2
     That I Climb'd highest hill, he me warr points did show, . .  292 Psalm XVIII         62
     Who to make warr with God praesumed; . . . . . . . . . . . .  326 Psalm XXXVII        50
     For since warre is the ground of vertue's love,. . . . . . .  346 Possibly      5     7
WARBLING
     While I was warbling out your woonted praise,. . . . . . . .   54 2nd Eclogues 29    67
     For warbling notes from inward chearing flow.. . . . . . . .  242 Other Poems   4     4
*WARD
     The second sweetly-fenced warde, . . . . . . . . . . . . . .   87 Arcadia III  62    43
     And will my waiting eyes to thee ward bend.. . . . . . . . .  274 Psalm V              8
     And watch and ward for such do beare . . . . . . . . . . . .  319 Psalm XXXIV         27
     He did himself to me ward bend,. . . . . . . . . . . . . . .  330 Psalm XL             3
     While they did ward sun-beames with shady bay, . . . . . . .  243 Other Poems   4    66
     Came to hir back, and so with double warde . . . . . . . . .  252 Other Poems   4   389
```

```
*WARE                                                          PAGE    TITLE        LINE
      And if forsooth there come some new found ware,. . . . . . .  104  3rd Eclogues 67   40
      If I ware you or no,. . . . . . . . . . . . . . . . . . .     158  Cert Sonnets 28   12
      With price of mangled mind thy worthlesse ware,. . . . . . .  161  Cert Sonnets 31    6
      "But will not wise men thinke thy words fond ware?". . . . .  182  Astrophil    34    7
      Be your words made (good Sir) of Indian ware,. . . . . . .   225  Astrophil    92    1
WAREFULNESS
      His eyes are curious search, but vailde with warefulnesse: .   48  2nd Eclogues 28   43
      He met hir full, but full of warefulnes, . . . . . . . . .   252  Other Poems   4  386
WARM
      Warme well thy wits, if thou wilt win her will,. . . . . . .    3  Lady of May   2    3
      Warme snow, moyst pearle, softe ivorie.. . . . . . . . . . .   90  Arcadia III  62  126
      To warme with ill-made fire cold Moscovy;. . . . . . . . .   180  Astrophil    30    4
      Thinke now no more to heare of warme fine odourd snow, . . .  213  A&S 5th Song      37
      Allarme allarme, when once the fight is warme, . . . . . . .  346  Possibly      5   13
      With hand and mouth, with lapp and brest keepe warme,. . . .  258  Other Poems   5   84
WARMED
      Since heart in chilling feare with yce is warmed:. . . . . .  135  Cert Sonnets  1    7
WARMS
      Approching warmes (not else) dead logges up sends, . . . . .  150  Cert Sonnets 22   12
WARMTH
      Where with most ease and warmth he might employ his art: . .  168  Astrophil     8    7
      The onely light of joy, the onely warmth of Love.. . . . . .  204  Astrophil    76    4
      She comes with light and warmth, which like Aurora prove . .  205  Astrophil    76    5
WARN
      I warne thee therefore (since thou maist have choice). . . .   29  1st Eclogues 10   88
WARNED
      Onely the owle still warnde them not to seech. . . . . . . .  100  3rd Eclogues 66   68
      Their master is faire warn'd his will to make. . . . . . . .  150  Cert Sonnets 22   20
WARRANT
      Since they did warrant me. . . . . . . . . . . . . . . . . .  158  Cert Sonnets 28   20
WARS
      Despaire my fielde; the flowers spirits' warrs:. . . . . . .   18  1st Eclogues  7  139
      The warres of ougly Centaurs,. . . . . . . . . . . . . . . .   66  2nd Eclogues 32   22
      Her lipps are the riches the warres to maintaine,. . . . . .   67  2nd Eclogues 33    9
      O make in me those civill warres to cease; . . . . . . . . .  184  Astrophil    39    7
WASH
      She did the water wash, and make more fine.. . . . . . . . .   55  2nd Eclogues 29  107
WASHED
      My hands shall washed be,. . . . . . . . . . . . . . . . . .  305  Psalm XXVI        20
WASP
      The humming Waspe, if it had not a stinge, . . . . . . . . .  104  3rd Eclogues 67   17
      Before all flies the Waspe accept I would. . . . . . . . . .  104  3rd Eclogues 67   18
      The Waspe seemes gay, but is a combrous thing. . . . . . . .  104  3rd Eclogues 67   21
WASTE
      Cormoraunt's glutt, Kite's spoile, king fisher's waste,. . .   28  1st Eclogues 10   78
      Upon thy spoiles, which never should lye waste?. . . . . . .   59  2nd Eclogues 30   93
      This waxe doth waste it selfe, yet painelesse dyes.. . . . .   75  Arcadia III  43    2
      I waste my harte, which still newe torment tryes.. . . . . .   75  Arcadia III  43    5
      Waste it is calde, for it doth waste . . . . . . . . . . . .   87  Arcadia III  62   65
      Enough to make a fertill minde lie waste.. . . . . . . . . .  114  4th Eclogues 72   30
      Klaius. Enough to make a fertill minde lie waste . . . . . .  114  4th Eclogues 72   31
      Be those despaires, which have my hopes quite wast.. . . . .  114  4th Eclogues 72   37
      Let golde now rust, let Diamonds waste in thee:. . . . . . .  125  4th Eclogues 75   22
      A horse's worth laid wast the Troyan ground: . . . . . . . .  146  Cert Sonnets 17   18
      To stranger weights my minde's waste soile is bound, . . . .  149  Cert Sonnets 22    5
      My youth doth waste, my knowledge brings forth toyes,. . . .  174  Astrophil    18    9
      O bragging Foe, where is the endless wast. . . . . . . . . .  280  Psalm IX          16
      His voice makes bald the forest wast;. . . . . . . . . . . .  310  Psalm XXIX        23
      My eye, my Gutts, yea my soul grief doth wast, . . . . . . .  312  Psalm XXXI        27
      Ev'en with the smoake shall wast away. . . . . . . . . . . .  326  Psalm XXXVII      52
      For with thy handy stroakes I wast.. . . . . . . . . . . . .  330  Psalm XXXIX       32
      Let them be curst away that would me wast; . . . . . . . . .  332  Psalm XL          54
      "For though like waxe, this magique makes me waste,. . . . .  254  Other Poems   4  489
WASTED
      Teares, drowne your selves, for woe (your cause) is wasted,.   83  Arcadia III  59    6
      Where bee now those wordes never Idelly wasted,. . . . . . .  138  Cert Sonnets  5    7
      Or roar'd, my bones still wasted;. . . . . . . . . . . . . .  315  Psalm XXXII        9
WASTETH
      He ever dies that wasteth. . . . . . . . . . . . . . . . . .  152  Cert Sonnets 23   11
WASTING
      No cave, no wasting waxe, no wordes of griefe, . . . . . . .   75  Arcadia III  43    7
      While my God with wasting wonders. . . . . . . . . . . . . .  335  Psalm XLII        31
      And pine away with daily wasting woe?. . . . . . . . . . . .  257  Other Poems   5   26
WATCH
      Lett our unpartiall eyes a litle watche. . . . . . . . . . .   29  1st Eclogues 10   91
      As how to watch our overthrow, . . . . . . . . . . . . . . .  290  Psalm XVII        32
      And watch and ward for such do beare . . . . . . . . . . . .  319  Psalm XXXIV       27
      Watch but a while, and Thou shalt see. . . . . . . . . . . .  325  Psalm XXXVII      25
      The Wicked watch the righteous much. . . . . . . . . . . . .  326  Psalm XXXVII      81
WATCHED
      Watched when she a furder point might gaine, . . . . . . . .   96  3rd Eclogues 64   75
WATCHING
      Of that small light oft watching shepheards see. . . . . . .   98  3rd Eclogues 66    7
      Since babie mine, from me thy watching springeth,. . . . . .  139  Cert Sonnets  6    7
      And bring to naught those watching pawes.. . . . . . . . . .  290  Psalm XVII        36
      Must strive with waiting foot, and watching eye. . . . . . .  248  Other Poems   4  228
WATER
      For water cold did never promise fire: . . . . . . . . . . .    3  Lady of May   2    4
      He water plowes, and soweth in the sand, . . . . . . . . . .   24  1st Eclogues  9   53
```

```
WATER                    (CONTINUED)                        PAGE   TITLE          LINE
    She did the water wash, and make more fine.. . . . . . . . . .   55  2nd Eclogues 29   107
    And for Rose-water sould of rarest smell.. . . . . . . . . .    55  2nd Eclogues 29   110
    With water drinke, herbes meate, and naked hide, . . . . . .   101  3rd Eclogues 66   109
    In water dround, in earth his buriall is;. . . . . . . . . .   105  3rd Eclogues 67    68
    In wind or water streame do require to be writ.. . . . . . .   143  Cert Sonnets 13     4
    My mouth doth water, and my breast doth swell, . . . . . . .   183  Astrophil    37     1
    "love makes earth the water drink, . . . . . . . . . . . . .   219  A&S 8th Song        61
    Love to earth makes water sinke; . . . . . . . . . . . . . .   219  A&S 8th Song        62
    On me all this, who do like water slide; . . . . . . . . . .   299  Psalm XXII         31
    For ev'n in forge colde water fire maintaines. . . . . . . .   246  Other Poems   4   156
WATERED
    In watry glasse my watred eyes I see:. . . . . . . . . . . .    41  Arcadia II   21 V   5
    With sweatie browes, sometyme with watered eyes, . . . . . .    71  Arcadia III  36 V   8
    I joyed, but straight thus watred was my wine, . . . . . . .   196  Astrophil    62     5
WATERS
    Yee Nymphes which in the waters empire have, . . . . . . . .    92  3rd Eclogues 63    28
    Till that it hath all woods and waters past. . . . . . . . .   126  4th Eclogues 75    36
    To which sweet springs of waters neighbours be,. . . . . . .   270  Psalm I             8
    And what thinges els of waters traceth . . . . . . . . . . .   279  Psalm VIII         31
    Cloudes even of Waters dark, and thickest ayre compos'd; . .   291  Psalm XVIII        25
    The gulfs of waters then were through their Chanels seen,. .   291  Psalm XVIII        31
    By waters still and sweet. . . . . . . . . . . . . . . . . .   301  Psalm XXIII         5
    His voice is on the Waters found,. . . . . . . . . . . . . .   310  Psalm XXIX          7
    Yea through the Waters doth resound. . . . . . . . . . . . .   310  Psalm XXIX          9
    The waters of the seas . . . . . . . . . . . . . . . . . . .   316  Psalm XXXIII       25
WATERS'
    Ev'n from the Waters' depth my God preserved me so.. . . . .   291  Psalm XVIII        35
WATERY
    My earthy moulde doth melte in watrie teares.. . . . . . . .    19  1st Eclogues  7   151
    Dorus. My earthy moulde doth melte in watrie teares, . . . .    19  1st Eclogues  7   152
    In watry glasse my watrie eyes I see:. . . . . . . . . . . .    41  Arcadia II   21     5
    With sweatie browes, sometyme with watrie eyes,. . . . . . .    71  Arcadia III  36     8
    Long drowned hopes to watrie eyes it lends:. . . . . . . . .   150  Cert Sonnets 22    18
    His who till death lookt in a watrie glasse, . . . . . . . .   207  Astrophil    82     3
WAVES
    Of windes quite contrarie in waves of will:. . . . . . . . .    59  2nd Eclogues 30    81
    Beaten with waves, no sooner kennes the baye . . . . . . . .    70  Arcadia III  36     3
    Brused with waves of Care, but broken is . . . . . . . . . .   114  4th Eclogues 72    49
    Nor of that golden sea, whose waves in curles are brok'n:. .   213  A&S 5th Song       39
    Over me all thy waves went;. . . . . . . . . . . . . . . . .   335  Psalm XLII         34
WAX
    Which nothing spares, to melt that Virgin-waxe . . . . . . .    60  2nd Eclogues 30   108
    This waxe doth waste it selfe, yet painelesse dyes.. . . . .    75  Arcadia III  43     2
    No cave, no wasting waxe, no wordes of griefe, . . . . . . .    75  Arcadia III  43     7
    A daintie seale of virgin-waxe, . . . . . . . . . . . . . . .   88  Arcadia III  62    75
    Whose heart with these huge flames, like wax o're heated,. .   299  Psalm XXII         33
    "For though like waxe, this magique makes me waste,. . . . .   254  Other Poems   4   489
WAXED
    Now bolder waxt, waxt prowde, that I such sway might beare:.   121  4th Eclogues 73   159
*WAXEN
    Is past with me, my bloud is waxen colde.. . . . . . . . . .    25  1st Eclogues  9   107
    And to the sunne with waxen winges to flie?. . . . . . . . .    79  Arcadia III  50    14
    The night growne old, her blacke head waxen gray,. . . . . .   103  3rd Eclogues 66   160
*WAY
    With such intemperance, that each way grows. . . . . . . . .    27  1st Eclogues 10    38
    But still our dazeled eyes their way do misse, . . . . . . .    59  2nd Eclogues 30    74
    The kindly way to beate us on to blisse. . . . . . . . . . .    59  2nd Eclogues 30    76
    That trusts in time, to finde the way aright . . . . . . . .    82  Arcadia III  56     3
    No talke untaught can finde the way. . . . . . . . . . . . .    86  Arcadia III  62    34
    Betwixt these two a way doth lie,. . . . . . . . . . . . . .    87  Arcadia III  62    58
    A way more worthie beautie's fame, . . . . . . . . . . . . .    87  Arcadia III  62    59
    Did goe his way, but sojourn'd neere thereby,. . . . . . . .    96  3rd Eclogues 64    71
    Our life is but a step in dustie way. . . . . . . . . . . . .  131  Arcadia V    77    12
    The Babe cries "way, thy love doth keepe me waking". . . . .   139  Cert Sonnets  6     3
    Above line repeated at following locations . . . . . . . . .   139  Cert Sonnets  6     6
    In Dales I see each way a hard assent: . . . . . . . . . . .   147  Cert Sonnets 18    10
    End the way, where all men stay. No, no, no, no. . . . . . .   155  Cert Sonnets 26    22
    And others' feete still seem'd but strangers in my way.. . .   165  Astrophil     1    11
    Fals to shrewd turnes, and I was in his way. . . . . . . . .   173  Astrophil    17    14
    In highest way of heav'n the Sunne did ride, . . . . . . . .   175  Astrophil    22     1
    Looking on me, while I lookt other way:. . . . . . . . . . .   199  Astrophil    66    12
    Thy selfe, doest strive all minds that way to move,. . . . .   201  Astrophil    71    10
    Gallein's adoptive sonnes, who by a beaten way . . . . . . .   232  Astrophil   102     9
    Counting but dust what in the way did lie. . . . . . . . . .   235  Astrophil   105     8
    I said, thine eyes were starres, thy breasts the milk'n way,  212  A&S 5th Song       10
    Ne for bad mates in way of sinning waiteth . . . . . . . . .   270  Psalm I             3
    The way they go shal be their way to perish. . . . . . . . .   271  Psalm I            22
    From your way perish shall . . . . . . . . . . . . . . . . .   272  Psalm II           30
    Deliver me in my endangerd way . . . . . . . . . . . . . . .   277  Psalm VII           3
    And pray that still Thou guide my way. . . . . . . . . . . .   289  Psalm XVII         15
    Thy way is soundly sure, Thy word is purely tryd;. . . . . .   292  Psalm XVIII        55
    He made my cumbrous way to me most plainly right.. . . . . .   292  Psalm XVIII        60
    Unto my strengthned stepps Thou didst enlarge the way, . . .   292  Psalm XVIII        66
    He me revives, leads me the way. . . . . . . . . . . . . . .   301  Psalm XXIII         7
    Teach lord, lord lead me Thy right way,. . . . . . . . . . .   308  Psalm XXVII        52
    While I that way hold my hands . . . . . . . . . . . . . . .   309  Psalm XXVIII        7
    Come, Come, the way I will teach Thee, . . . . . . . . . . .   315  Psalm XXXII        29
    For I will teach to you the way. . . . . . . . . . . . . . .   320  Psalm XXXIV        43
    Yea take Thy lance and stop the way of those . . . . . . . .   321  Psalm XXXV          4
```

*WAY	(CONTINUED)	PAGE	TITLE		LINE
Who for my hurt each way their thoughts did roll..		321	Psalm XXXV		10
Firm on his way, his way God loveth, ...		326	Psalm XXXVII		58
Wait thou on God and keep his way, ...		327	Psalm XXXVII		85
Thus did I think: I well will mark my way, ...		329	Psalm XXXIX		1
In my sound rightfull way, ...		334	Psalm XLI		42
And each way luckles, yet in humble guise.		249	Other Poems	4	277
Each way, as she, that age's praise, did bend.		251	Other Poems	4	376
But yet a setting foorth it some way lent:		252	Other Poems	4	395
WAYMENTING					
My foode is teares; my tunes waymenting yeeld:		18	1st Eclogues	7	138
Still for thy Dam with bea-waymenting crie?.		258	Other Poems	5	78
WAYS					
Thou doest proceed in thy most serious wayes:.		170	Astrophil	11	2
You take wrong waies, those far-fet helpes be such,.		172	Astrophil	15	9
Whose numbers, wayes, greatnesse, eternitie, ...		178	Astrophil	26	3
Nor in hid wayes to guide Philosophie:		179	Astrophil	28	10
Of straying wayes, when valiant errour guides:		190	Astrophil	51	11
She could not shew my blind braine waies of joy, ...		230	Astrophil	97	13
And make Thy wayes to me more plainly known, ...		275	Psalm V		23
May only joy in all Thy saving wayes		280	Psalm IX		44
For while in wayes do prove,.		282	Psalm X		17
Because I walk'd his wayes, nor gainst him ev'ly went, . . .		292	Psalm XVIII		44
I bett them as the clay is bett in beaten wayes.		293	Psalm XVIII		77
Yea Lord to me Thy wayes do show;.		303	Psalm XXV		11
But fill their hearts with joy, who bend their wayes		332	Psalm XL		61
WAYWARDNESS					
All waywardnes, which nothing kindly brookes,.		93	3rd Eclogues	63	66
WEAK					
Whose strongest hope in your weake comfort lyes.		13	Arcadia I	4	4
Her minde, beames, state farre from thy weake wings					
banished		16	1st Eclogues	7	65
In those weake harts that his advice receave..		21	1st Eclogues	8	34
Unto a silly caban, though weake, yet stronger against woes.		34	1st Eclogues	13	93
My words full weake, the marble full of might;		41	Arcadia II	19	7
P. Who be too weake, do feigne they be too good.		47	2nd Eclogues	27	30
In this weake worke, that it can never be.		57	2nd Eclogues	30	30
O Vertue weake, shall death his triumph set.		59	2nd Eclogues	30	92
Their ireful shotte against so weake a marke,.		73	Arcadia III	40	6
Her sence too weake to beare her spirit's mighte..		79	Arcadia III	51	4
Too weake for them our weaker sighte doth vaile.		82	Arcadia III	55	11
Farewell o golden staffe, the weake man's might:		129	4th Eclogues	76	3
Like some weake Lords, neighbord by mighty kings,.		179	Astrophil	29	1
With sad eyes I their weake proportion see,.		189	Astrophil	50	7
Nor do like Lords, whose weake confused braine,.		210	Astrophil	85	5
Is faith so weake? Or is such force in thee?		223	Astrophil	88	5
Her strong darts, but weake defences..		226	A&S 10th Song		36
The strongest judgements weake:.		215	A&S 6th Song		10
These men like potshards weake..		271	Psalm II		22
For I am weake, and in my weakness languish;		276	Psalm VI		6
For they had caught me up, when I was weake in Woe;.		291	Psalm XVIII		38
So let words sprung from my weake tongue, ...		295	Psalm XIX		61
And maketh weak.		317	Psalm XXXIII		35
Who poore and weake from rich and strong dost free,.		321	Psalm XXXV		22
I am weake and broken sore,.		328	Psalm XXXVIII		22
And my weake steps did stay.		331	Psalm XL		10
While guilty thoughts accus'd his Reason weake).		255	Other Poems	4	532
WEAKENED					
Thus weakned by my selfe, no helpe remaineth..		68	2nd Eclogues	33	17
Alas, me thinkes, my weakned voice but spilleth, ...		127	4th Eclogues	75	97
In weakened minds, quicke apprehending breed,.		199	Astrophil	66	3
WEAKENETH					
P. Because our weaknes weakeneth all your might.		46	2nd Eclogues	27	22
WEAKENING					
The weakning worke of Time's for ever-whirling wheele. . . .		120	4th Eclogues	73	122
WEAKER					
Whiche beares the bytt a weaker force doth guide,.		20	1st Eclogues	7	V959
Too weake for them our weaker sighte doth vaile.		82	Arcadia III	55	11
Where helping weaker sort, the nobler beastes, ...		102	3rd Eclogues	66	121
WEAKER'S					
By those great beastes, as for the weaker's good,.		102	3rd Eclogues	66	128
WEAKEST					
And weakest harts to constant temper brought..		22	1st Eclogues	9	15
WEAKLY					
Weakely did seeme to paint death's ougly dart.		148	Cert Sonnets 20		4
WEAKNESS					
When they shall such devided weakenesse prove?		26	1st Eclogues	10	6
R. Weakenes you are, dare you with our strength fight? . . .		46	2nd Eclogues	27	21
P. Because our weaknes weakeneth all your might.		46	2nd Eclogues	27	22
Theere seeke defence where weakenesse is the force:.		49	2nd Eclogues	28	77
We pittie deeme that which but weakenes is:.		62	2nd Eclogues	30	180
The child of curse, man's weakenesse foster-child,.		141	Cert Sonnets 10		2
Whom curst do blesse, whose weakenesse vertues arme, ...		142	Cert Sonnets 10		6
For I am weake, and in my weakness languish;		276	Psalm VI		6
WEAL					
His wished weale, what more he could require:.		4	Lady of May	3	4
But you must pay, the gage of promist weale.		76	Arcadia III	46	18
Which die not in that weale.		152	Cert Sonnets 23		32
Poore hope's first wealth, ostage of promist weale,.		206	Astrophil	79	12
The globe of weale, lips Love's indentures make:		210	Astrophil	85	13

```
WEALTH                                                          PAGE    TITLE            LINE
    To one that hath no wealth, and wants his wit. . . . . . . .   4  Lady of May    2    24
    Bound but to you, no wealth but you I would: . . . . . . . .   4  Lady of May    2    28
    I never found long love such wealth hath paide to me". . . .  16  1st Eclogues   7    54
    Nor stormes doo turne: fairenes serves oft to wealth. . . .   18  1st Eclogues   7   119
    I have no shewes of wealth: my wealth is you,. . . . . . . .  18  1st Eclogues   7   135
    Who hold this fast no greater wealth require. . . . . . . .   75  Arcadia III   44     8
    Private with welth, publike with quiet garnished. . . . . . 128  4th Eclogues  75   129
    But that my wealth I have most idly spent. . . . . . . . . . 174  Astrophil     18     8
    Or carelesse of the wealth because her owne: . . . . . . . . 176  Astrophil     22    11
    Wealth breeding want, more blist, more wretched grow. . . . . 177  Astrophil     24     4
    The poore man's wealth, the prisoner's release,. . . . . . . 184  Astrophil     39     3
    My wealth no more, and no whit lesse my need,. . . . . . . . 199  Astrophil     66     7
    World of my wealth, and heav'n of my delight. . . . . . . . 200  Astrophil     68     4
    Poore hope's first wealth, ostage of promist weale,. . . . . 206  Astrophil     79    12
WEALTHY
    Than of bad folks the wealthy wonder,. . . . . . . . . . . . 325  Psalm XXXVII          42
WEAPONS
    Each soule doth at Love's feet his weapons lay,. . . . . . . 186  Astrophil     43     7
WEAR
    Which makes us most immortall shape to weare,. . . . . . . .  40  Arcadia II    18    14
    To weare upon her neck, that open lies. . . . . . . . . . .   55  2nd Eclogues  29   119
    Weare these my words as mourning weedes of woes, . . . . . .  81  Arcadia III   54     5
    The tippe no jewell needes to weare: . . . . . . . . . . . .  87  Arcadia III   62    35
    How ill fits you this greene to weare, . . . . . . . . . . . 157  Cert Sonnets  28     3
    Great expectation, weare a traine of shame. . . . . . . . . 175  Astrophil     21     8
    Since they do weare his badge, most firmely prove. . . . . . 190  Astrophil     52     4
    Nor do not use set colours for to weare, . . . . . . . . . . 191  Astrophil     54     2
    Upon thy cheerefull face, joye's livery weare: . . . . . . . 232  Astrophil    103     3
    Who weare his blessed livery;. . . . . . . . . . . . . . . . 321  Psalm XXXIV          78
    With inward wo, an outward sack cloth ware. . . . . . . . . 322  Psalm XXXV           30
    A garland made on temples for to weare,. . . . . . . . . . . 244  Other Poems    4    74
    Till straunge delight, delight to nothing ware;. . . . . . . 254  Other Poems    4   482
WEARIED
    My wearied ears! O gods yet graunt me this,. . . . . . . . .  24  1st Eclogues   9    67
    Till wounded, blind, and wearied Spirites, lose. . . . . . . 144  Cert Sonnets  15    11
    In absence blind, and wearied with that woe, . . . . . . . . 149  Cert Sonnets  21     9
WEARIEST
    Nico. Peace, peace good Pas, thou weeriest even the ground . 56  2nd Eclogues  29   135
WEARING
    For wearing Venus' badge, in every part of thee, . . . . . . 214  A&S 5th Song         70
WEARS
    My minde for weeds your vertue's liverie weares. . . . . . .  18  1st Eclogues   7   137
    Her nose, her chinne pure ivorie weares: . . . . . . . . . .  86  Arcadia III   62    27
WEARY
    But ceasse worthy shepheard, nowe ceasse we to weery the
        hearers. . . . . . . . . . . . . . . . . . . . . . . . .  37  1st Eclogues  13   172
    And drawes the dolor on till very evening. . . . . . . . . . 111  4th Eclogues  71     6
    Lives to impart my wearie clay some breath. . . . . . . . . 148  Cert Sonnets  20    10
    A rosie garland, and a wearie hed: . . . . . . . . . . . . . 184  Astrophil     39    11
    Till spying well she welnigh weary was,. . . . . . . . . . . 251  Other Poems    4   377
WEB
    Ruine's relique, care's web, and sorrowe's foode:. . . . . .  23  1st Eclogues   9    29
    Which is the hatefull web of Sorowe's paines. . . . . . . . 114  4th Eclogues  72    25
    Thou web of will, whose end is never wrought;. . . . . . . . 161  Cert Sonnets  31     4
    (Who Neptune's webb on daunger's distaff spun) . . . . . . . 251  Other Poems    4   374
WED
    Both they themselves unto such two shall wed,. . . . . . . .  11  Arcadia I      1     5
    With voice more fit to wed Amphion's lyre, . . . . . . . . . 200  Astrophil     68     6
    To wedd Antaxius their neighbour neare. . . . . . . . . . . 245  Other Poems    4   116
WEDLOCK
    If you helpe not our wedlocke will be staind". . . . . . . .  95  3rd Eclogues  64    46
WEED
    Their wooll your weede, I will you Musique yeeld . . . . . .  18  1st Eclogues   7   124
    To decke the earth with his well-colourde weede, . . . . . .  78  Arcadia III   50     2
    Placed ever there, gave him this mourning weed,. . . . . . . 168  Astrophil      7    13
    But never did Medea's golden weed. . . . . . . . . . . . . . 252  Other Poems    4   409
WEEDS
    Come shepheard's weedes, become your master's minde: . . . .  13  Arcadia I      4     1
    Come shepheard's weedes, attend my woefull cryes:. . . . . .  13  Arcadia I      4     5
    My minde for weeds your vertue's liverie weares. . . . . . .  18  1st Eclogues   7   137
    My weedes, Desire, cut out in endlesse foldes. . . . . . . .  39  Arcadia II    17     6
    Weare these my words as mourning weedes of woes, . . . . . .  81  Arcadia III   54     5
    And mother Earth, now clad in mourning weeds, did breath . . 117  4th Eclogues  73     9
    Straunge were the Ladies' weedes; yet more unfit then
        strange. . . . . . . . . . . . . . . . . . . . . . . . . 118  4th Eclogues  73    65
    For mourning night her blacke weedes may display. . . . . . 126  4th Eclogues  75    54
    But for to spangle the blacke weeds of night:. . . . . . . . 178  Astrophil     26     6
    Silent and sad in mourning weedes doth dight:. . . . . . . . 229  Astrophil     97     8
    Who hath the crimson weeds stolne from my morning skies? . . 232  Astrophil    102     4
    May then yong his pide weedes showing, . . . . . . . . . . . 217  A&S 8th Song          3
    Of my poore weedes thy do partition make . . . . . . . . . . 299  Psalm XXII           43
    And madest me gladsom weeds enjoy, . . . . . . . . . . . . . 311  Psalm XXX            36
WEEK
    What, a whole weeke without one peece of looke,. . . . . . . 192  Astrophil     56     3
WEEP
    With weeping eyes (her eyes she taught to weepe) . . . . . .  96  3rd Eclogues  64    85
    That eyes weepe worse then hart in bloodie teares? . . . . . 142  Cert Sonnets  11     7
    Weepe neighbours, weepe, do you not heare it said, . . . . . 160  Cert Sonnets  30    11
    Teaching blind eyes both how to smile and weepe, . . . . . . 181  Astrophil     32     8
```

WEEP   (CONTINUED)   PAGE   TITLE   LINE
  Hath cheekes to smile, as well as eyes to weepe. . . . . . .   201 Astrophil   70   8
  Stella now learnes (strange case) to weepe in thee.. . . . .   231 Astrophil   101   8
  When thou hast mynd to weepe, seeke out som smoky room:. . .   343 Possibly   1   11
  And now the dropping trees do wepe for me, ...   254 Other Poems   4 479
WEEPETH
  The aire in raine for my affliction weepeth: . . . .   136 Cert Sonnets 3   2
  Wo to me, alas she weepeth!. . . . .   157 Cert Sonnets 27   25
WEEPING
  And wanting her, my weeping eyes I wipe. . . . .   54 2nd Eclogues 29   77
  With weeping eyes (her eyes she taught to weepe) . . . . . .   96 3rd Eclogues 64   85
  The weeping Myrrhe I thinke will not denie . . . .   125 4th Eclogues 75   13
  Brake bow, brake shafts, while Cupid weeping sate: . . . . .   173 Astrophil   17   8
  For god hath heard the weeping sobbing voice . . . .   276 Psalm VI   27
WEEPS
  That grace, which Venus weepes that she her selfe doth
    misse . . . .   205 Astrophil   77   4
WEIGH
  I way them not, but still will thee advize . . . .   25 1st Eclogues 9 109
  For yet (weigh this alas!) great is not great to a greater..   34 1st Eclogues 13   74
  Leasure to weigh what due deserte requireth. . . . .   83 Arcadia III 57   10
  Weigh then how I by thee am overthrowne: . . . .   185 Astrophil   40   8
  For Grammer sayes (o this deare Stella weighe,). . . . . . .   196 Astrophil   63   12
  Who share in woe, weygh others have as much. . . . .   242 Other Poems   4   16
WEIGHED
  That Ballance weigh'd what sword did late obtaine, ...   204 Astrophil   75   8
WEIGHING
  Not weighing ought how fleshly fancys run, ...   289 Psalm XVII   13
WEIGHS
  While he each thing in sense's ballance wayes, ...   177 Astrophil   25   6
WEIGHT
  Such weight it hath which once is full possest.. . . . . . .   20 1st Eclogues 7 V961
  Above line repeated at following location. . . . .   20 1st Eclogues 7 V962
  When Cedars to the ground be opprest by the weight of an
    emmott,. . . . .   34 1st Eclogues 13   77
  That sorrowe's weight dothe balance up thies joyes.. . . . .   71 Arcadia III 36   18
  To over pressed brestes, more greevous waight. . . . .   82 Arcadia III 56   8
  Had reason's weight for passion's ease rejected. . . . . . .   83 Arcadia III 57   8
  Is chang'd to stone, in hardnesse, cold, and weight, ...   150 Cert Sonnets 22   43
  Thus I prest down with weight of pain, ...   315 Psalm XXXII   7
WEIGHTS
  To stranger weights my minde's waste soile is bound, ...   149 Cert Sonnets 22   5
  With heaped weights of their own sins oppresse . . . .   275 Psalm V   31
  Whose foule weights have me opprest. . . . .   327 Psalm XXXVIII   12
  "Alas! what weights are these that lode my heart!. . . . . .   253 Other Poems   4 441
  Her ears the weights of wit. . . . .   259 Other Poems   5 109
WEIGHTY
  And may I not (say I then) gett up though griefs be so
    weightie?. . . . .   36 1st Eclogues 13 128
  His weighty top) his top doth downeward drooping leane:. . .   117 4th Eclogues 73   22
WELCOME
  Welcome my two to me, E.D. F.G. P.S. . . . .   261 Other Poems   6   25
WELCOMES
  Where bee those wellcomes by no worthe deserved? . . . . . .   138 Cert Sonnets 5   10
WELKIN
  The welkin had full niggardly enclosed . . . .   98 3rd Eclogues 66   8
*WELL
  Warme well thy wits, if thou wilt win her will,. . . . . . .   3 Lady of May   2   3
  Happie be they which well beleeve, and never seeke the rest.   12 Arcadia I   3   14
  No stile is held for base, where Love well named is: . . . .   14 1st Eclogues 7   4
  Love well thine owne: me thinkes, woolle's whitenes passeth
    all: . . . .   16 1st Eclogues 7   53
  Save then my soule, spill not my thoughts well heaped, . . .   16 1st Eclogues 7   80
  So faire a fielde would well become an owner. . . . .   17 1st Eclogues 7   99
  No charme holdes her, but well possesse she may; . . . . . .   17 1st Eclogues 7 111
  O well thou saiest! a feeling declaration. . . . .   20 1st Eclogues 7 V968
  As well may thincke with oyle to coole the fire: . . . . . .   22 1st Eclogues 9   8
  Then who will heare a well autoris'd lye,. . . . .   24 1st Eclogues 9   72
  The ancient oke well makes a fired blocke: . . . .   25 1st Eclogues 9   87
  Who once a white long beard, well handle does, ...   25 1st Eclogues 9   90
  Who well can set a passion out to show:. . . . .   25 1st Eclogues 9 112
  Seeke to espie her faultes as well as praise,. . . . .   25 1st Eclogues 9 121
  Yet have I seene when havl a wolfe he shooke.. . . . .   27 1st Eclogues 10   18
  How to the woods love runnes as well as rydes to the
    Pallace . . . .   31 1st Eclogues 13   4
  Well may a Pastor plaine, but alas his plaints be not
    esteem de. . . . .   32 1st Eclogues 13   39
  But yet well I doo finde each man most wise in his owne
    case . . . .   33 1st Eclogues 13   70
  Lyke to my noble thoughtes, still new, well plac'd, to me
    fruteles... . . . .   35 1st Eclogues 13 124
  Old age well stayed from raunging humor lives: . . . .   39 Arcadia II   15   10
  And see therein how well the writer fares. . . . .   42 Arcadia II   21   16
  Dicus. The harte well set doth never shunne confession:. . .   47 2nd Eclogues 28   13
  Dicus. Thy words well voic'd, well gra'ste had almost heaved
    me. . . . .   48 2nd Eclogues 28   31
  Dorus. Well do I prove, errour lies oft in zeale,. . . . . .   51 2nd Eclogues 28 103
  Nico. I thinke it well: such voice would make one musicke
    hate:. . . . .   52 2nd Eclogues 29   21
  Nico. Well aimed by my hat: for as thou sangst last day; . .   52 2nd Eclogues 29   25

For Pas well knowes what layes can Nico make.. . . . .   54 2nd Eclogues 29   74
His utmost light: for well his witte doth know,. . . . . . .   55 2nd Eclogues 29   97
Pas. She once, to coole her selfe, stood in a well,. . . . .   55 2nd Eclogues 29   108
But ever since that well is well besought, ...   55 2nd Eclogues 29   109
I said, my hands well paide her for mine eyes, ...   55 2nd Eclogues 29   115
That doost so well their miseries define?. . . . .   59 2nd Eclogues 30   79
But well you know, the gentle Sunne would save . . . .   60 2nd Eclogues 30   104
Well mett Echo, aproche: then tell me thy will too. I will
    too. . . . .   63 2nd Eclogues 31   4
Where well couched abides a coffer of pearle,. . . . .   67 2nd Eclogues 33   10
O how well I do like your solitarines! . . . .   69 2nd Eclogues 34   30
Nor brooke oughte els but well acquainted woe. . . . .   74 Arcadia III 41   6
But thou white skinne, as white as cruddes well prest, . . .   76 Arcadia III 46   13
Yet all well knit to one faire end do passe: . . . .   78 Arcadia III 50   8
Yet stay and well peruse,. . . . .   80 Arcadia III 52   7
Well grounded, noble, due, spite, rage, disdaine,. . . . . .   84 Arcadia III 60   10
Where azurde veines well mixt appeere. . . . .   87 Arcadia III 62   56
Her ribbes in white well armed be. . . . .   88 Arcadia III 62   68
Live one in two, a well united paire,. . . . .   91 3rd Eclogues 63   7
Pan store of babes, vertue their thoughts well staid,. . . .   93 3rd Eclogues 63   93
And for this Courtier should well like his table,. . . . . .   94 3rd Eclogues 64   23
But (for his jealous eye she well did finde) . . . .   95 3rd Eclogues 64   41
Seeme to proceede, so well it was devisde. . . . .   96 3rd Eclogues 64   82
(A little flocke; but well my pipe they couthe). . . . . . .   98 3rd Eclogues 66   2
He still hop'd well, because I loved truth;. . . . .   99 3rd Eclogues 66   38
This thinke I well, the beasts with courage clad . . . . . .   100 3rd Eclogues 66   55
And when they were well us'de to be abused,. . . . .   102 3rd Eclogues 66   144
Or know your strengths, and then you shall do well.. . . . .   103 3rd Eclogues 66   154
But who doo let their tongues shew well their rage,. . . . .   105 3rd Eclogues 67   47
As you paint them: but well in you I finde,. . . . .   106 3rd Eclogues 67   83
So well she can command, and yet obay,. . . . .   106 3rd Eclogues 67   89
In ruling of a house so well shee's seene. . . . .   106 3rd Eclogues 67   90
There never past foule word, I dare well say. . . . .   106 3rd Eclogues 67   93
How well last day before our Prince you could. . . . .   106 3rd Eclogues 67   97
Who hath his hire, hath well his labour plast: . . . .   108 Arcadia IV 68   1
Or as the silly birde in well acquainted nest. . . . .   117 4th Eclogues 73   23
She answer'd was with looke, and well performed behest:. . .   119 4th Eclogues 73   99
I know full well you know, what discord long hath raign'd.   119 4th Eclogues 73   105
Such proffer made, which she well showd with smiling cheere.   120 4th Eclogues 73   144
And let him be our judge: the lad doth please me well".. . .   121 4th Eclogues 73   153
"How ill both you can rule, well hath your discord taught: 121 4th Eclogues 73   163
Well: but faultie I was: Reason to my Passion yeelded, . . .   124 4th Eclogues 74   67
Say, that I well shuld finde in what a care I was had? . . .   124 4th Eclogues 74   80
To well felte griefe, plainte is the onely pleasure. . . . .   126 4th Eclogues 75   51
O well thou doost that thou no longer bidest;. . . . .   126 4th Eclogues 75   53
And well (me thinks) becomes this vaultie skie . . . .   126 4th Eclogues 75   58
Yee dimmy clowdes, which well employ your stayning . . . . .   127 4th Eclogues 75   67
Shepherd of shepherds, whose well setled order . . . .   128 4th Eclogues 75   128
As well he was in peace a safest treasure: . . . .   129 4th Eclogues 76   17
For ever banish'd from well plac'd affection;. . . . .   130 4th Eclogues 76   29
Which were not evill, well vew'd in reason's light.. . . . .   131 Arcadia V   77   8
In whom all joyes so well agree, ...   139 Cert Sonnets 7   2
Above line repeated at following locations . . . .   139 Cert Sonnets 7   12
     . . . .   140 Cert Sonnets 7   22
     . . . .   140 Cert Sonnets 7   32
Her legges (O legges) her ay well stepping feete.. . . . . .   141 Cert Sonnets 9   8
With feare of change, the courage well preparde: . . . . . .   143 Cert Sonnets 12   11
Tell how ill thought disgrac'd my doing well:. . . . .   146 Cert Sonnets 17   13
Who thinke themselves well blest, if they renew. . . . . . .   146 Cert Sonnets 17   33
Doth answere well the paine: . . . .   152 Cert Sonnets 23   18
Indeed I well did hope. . . . .   158 Cert Sonnets 28   5
Sweet Ladie you remaine well paid. . . . .   159 Cert Sonnets 29   4
To make my selfe beleeve, that all is well,. . . . .   166 Astrophil   2   13
Reason, in faith thou art well serv'd, that still. . . . . .   169 Astrophil   10   1
That in her breast thy pap well sugred lies, ...   170 Astrophil   12   5
Having got up a breach by fighting well, ...   171 Astrophil   12   10
Well staid with truth in word and faith of deed, ...   172 Astrophil   14   10
Sure you say well, your wisdome's golden mine. . . . .   175 Astrophil   21   12
To shew her skin, lips, teeth and head so well?. . . . . . .   181 Astrophil   32   11
Oft cruell fights well pictured forth do please. . . . . . .   181 Astrophil   34   4
Guided so well, that I obtain'd the prize, ...   185 Astrophil   41   2
Where well he knowes, no man to him can come.. . . . .   186 Astrophil   43   14
My words I know do well set forth my mind, ...   186 Astrophil   44   1
Well Love, since this demurre our sute doth stay,. . . . . .   191 Astrophil   52   12
That I well find no eloquence like it. . . . .   192 Astrophil   55   14
If he waite well, I never thence would move: . . . .   194 Astrophil   59   3
As I may well recount, but none can prize: . . . .   198 Astrophil   65   4
Well, how so thou interpret the contents,. . . . .   199 Astrophil   67   12
My Muse may well grudge at my heav'nly joy,. . . . .   201 Astrophil   70   1
Trebles sing high, as well as bases deepe. . . . .   201 Astrophil   70   6
Hath cheekes to smile, as well as eyes to weepe. . . . . . .   201 Astrophil   70   8
In well raisde notes, my pen the best it may . . . .   201 Astrophil   70   10
I never dranke of Aganippe well, ...   203 Astrophil   74   1
Not for his faire outside, nor well lined braine,. . . . . .   204 Astrophil   75   3
Sweet swelling lip, well maist thou swell in pride,. . . . .   206 Astrophil   80   1
You say forsooth, you left her well of late. . . . .   225 Astrophil   92   7
Say all, and all well sayd, still say the same.. . . . . . .   225 Astrophil   92   14
Thought with good cause thou likest so well the night, . . .   229 Astrophil   96   1
But cease mine eyes, your teares do witnesse well. . . . . .   235 Astrophil   105   9

*WELL	(CONTINUED)	PAGE	TITLE	LINE
And all I said so well, as no man it denied.		212	A&S 5th Song	12
"Well in absence this will dy,		234	A&S 11th Song	11
"Well, be gone, be gone I say,		235	A&S 11th Song	41
Astrophil that so wel served,		222	A&S 9th Song	27
Shall prosper still, with well succeeding end.		270	Psalm I	12
And in that nett, which they well hidden think,		280	Psalm IX	48
All plung'd in stinking filth, not One well bent,		286	Psalm XIV	11
So shall I bide well purify'd.		295	Psalm XIX	59
Wee may well call thy glory great.		297	Psalm XXI	17
The" afflicted then shall eat, and be well pleased,		300	Psalm XXII	61
Lord I have loved well		306	Psalm XXVI	25
Well may the Evening cloath the eyes		311	Psalm XXX	16
Thou well hast known what plung my soul was in		312	Psalm XXXI	21
Whose fault well hidden lyeth.		314	Psalm XXXII	3
Knowing full well that beasts they be.		315	Psalm XXXII	34
Full well his ey		317	Psalm XXXIII	50
Keep well thy lipps and tongue		320	Psalm XXXIV	49
For why the Well of life Thou art.		324	Psalm XXXVI	25
Though ill deeds well succeeding be.		324	Psalm XXXVII	4
Do well and trust on heavnly power,		324	Psalm XXXVII	7
Thus did I think: I well will mark my way,		329	Psalm XXXIX	1
But tryall well doth teach me,		332	Psalm XL	45
To well recoverd state..		333	Psalm XLI	12
But what? This doth already well appeare		333	Psalm XLI	37
But triumph well may I, whom Thou dost stay.		334	Psalm XLI	41
Dick. I would it were but thus, for thus it were too bad.		343	Possibly 1	17
One said he brake acrosse; full well it so might be:		241	Other Poems 1	3
But most cryed, "O well broke": O foole full gaily blest:		241	Other Poems 1	5
And eke their pipes did well, as frends, agree..		242	Other Poems 4	32
Well might he others beare, but leane to none)		244	Other Poems 4	72
Behold (beholding well it doth deserve).		244	Other Poems 4	82
Well for to see they kept themselves unsene,		244	Other Poems 4	89
How well apaid she was hir birde to finde:		244	Other Poems 4	92
Where snugging well he well appear'd content		244	Other Poems 4	103
That were in Court a well proportion'd hooke,		245	Other Poems 4	141
Her parents liking well it should be so,		247	Other Poems 4	195
That they, aswell as they, Hell may supplie:		248	Other Poems 4	230
Till spying well she welnigh weary was,		251	Other Poems 4	377
With inbow'd bosome well for hir prepar'd,		252	Other Poems 4	387
"The sportes wherin I wonted to do well,		254	Other Poems 4	465
Then so I faile, when most I would do well,		254	Other Poems 4	467
His well knowne friend, but yet his unknowne mate,		255	Other Poems 4	528
Urania name, whose force he knew so well,		256	Other Poems 4	538
The day well fed, the night in faithfull folde:		258	Other Poems 5	68
"Well was I, while under shade		263	Other Poems 7	43
WELLAWAY				
And out gan cry, "ah well away for shame,		95	3rd Eclogues 64	45
No, she hates me, wellaway,		222	A&S 9th Song	41
WELL-COLORED				
To decke the earth with his well-colourde weede,		78	Arcadia III 50	2
WELL-DESERVED				
From coming to the well deserved end,		277	Psalm VII	26
WELL-DOING				
In our well-doing placing all his pleasure,		129	4th Eclogues 76	15
WELL-FED				
Leaving in paine their wel-fed hungry eies..		246	Other Poems 4	168
WELL-FORMED				
Doth plunge my wel-form'd soule even in the mire		172	Astrophil 14	7
WELLING				
And fare-welling the flocke did homeward wend,		252	Other Poems 4	415
WELL-NIGH				
Till spying well she welnigh weary was,		251	Other Poems 4	377
WELL-SHADING				
Yet each prepar'd, with fanne's wel-shading grace,		176	Astrophil 22	7
WELL-WAITING				
Lalus. Once my well-waiting eyes espied my treasure,		16	1st Eclogues 7	73
WELTERING				
If in the Scottishe Court be weltring yet;		180	Astrophil 30	11
WENCH				
He made the simple wench his wrath abide..		95	3rd Eclogues 64	30
WEND				
Histor. Thus dyd they saye and then awaye dyd wende;		62	2nd Eclogues 30	185
How they might get that guest, from them to wend,		95	3rd Eclogues 64	53
That they now skilld not, how from him to wend:		102	3rd Eclogues 66	114
And wyked folkes from thee to wrack do wend.		279	Psalm IX	12
With hugy darknes, which about his feet did wend,		291	Psalm XVIII	21
Farr off wend;		328	Psalm XXXVIII	32
With greater powr, then she did make them wend		251	Other Poems 4	375
And fare-welling the flocke did homeward wend,		252	Other Poems 4	415
WENT				
Nature abasht went back: fortune blusht: yet she replide thus:		30	1st Eclogues 11	17
What be the joyes for which to enjoy they went to the paines Paines..		63	2nd Eclogues 31	14
Unto his house a jollie shepeheard went,		94	3rd Eclogues 64	15
But sawe they would, and he to deserts went.		100	3rd Eclogues 66	70
Who, where she went, bare in her forhead morning,		113	4th Eclogues 71	70
That, leaving me for dead, to her it went:		115	4th Eclogues 72	79
They to the beamie Sunnes went,		154	Cert Sonnets 25	12

561

WENT   (CONTINUED)   PAGE   TITLE   LINE

	PAGE	TITLE		LINE
Her daintiest bare went free; the cause was this,.	176	Astrophil	22	13
Therewithall away she went,.	221	A&S 8th Song		101
And, lo, he finds that all astraying went, ...	286	Psalm XIV		10
Flames issued from his mouth, and burning coales out went; .	291	Psalm XVIII		19
With blasting breath O Lord, that in thy chiding went. . . .	291	Psalm XVIII		33
Because I walk'd his wayes, nor gainst him ev'ly went, . . .	292	Psalm XVIII		44
Still still for them I humbly mourning went.	322	Psalm XXXV		35
Over me all thy waves went;.	335	Psalm XLII		34
Still both their flocks flocking togither went,.	242	Other Poems	4	30
She went, they staid; or rightly for to say, ...	246	Other Poems	4	169
She staid in them, they went in thought with hyr:.	246	Other Poems	4	170
By neighbors prai'd she went abroad therby,.	247	Other Poems	4	207
The dainty dew on face and body went	252	Other Poems	4	397
Up and downe perplexed went,.	262	Other Poems	7	14

WEPT

	PAGE	TITLE		LINE
For me, I wept to see pearles scattered so,.	223	Astrophil	87	9
Wept they had, alas the while, ...	218	A&S 8th Song		13
Whose boiling heat encreased as she wept:.	246	Other Poems	4	155

WERE

	PAGE	TITLE		LINE
In one, whose name to name were high presumption,.	15	1st Eclogues	7	38
Still were I one, this still should be my case,.	23	1st Eclogues	9	28
Were in his dayes: which heard, one nothing heares,.	24	1st Eclogues	9	76
That since they still alledge, When they were yong:.	24	1st Eclogues	9	79
Geron. If that thy face were hid, or I were blinde,.	25	1st Eclogues	9	96
For he woulde sing, but others were defaste;	28	1st Eclogues	10	76
Of all the birdes, but namely those were grieved,.	29	1st Eclogues	10	83
And if a meane were found, fortune th' whole course of it				
hinders.	37	1st Eclogues	13	159
And since in vaine I find were all my strife,.	38	Arcadia II	14	13
Not so; although my mettall were most mutable,.	47	2nd Eclogues	28	10
To such a force soone chaunge were nothing sutable.. . . .	47	2nd Eclogues	28	12
In divers kinds; yet as he were not filled,.	62	2nd Eclogues	30	171
Hye tyme for me, for scattered were my sheepe.	62	2nd Eclogues	30	186
His thoughtes in you, where so sweete thoughtes were spent,.	78	Arcadia III	49	10
What were it els, but to make each thing blinde?	79	Arcadia III	50	13
That if he absent were but halfe a daye, ...	94	3rd Eclogues	64	10
A young girle's hart, to that were shame for both, ...	95	3rd Eclogues	64	59
Whereto you knowe, his honest harte were loath..	95	3rd Eclogues	64	60
The caves were full, the mountaines voide of goates: . . .	98	3rd Eclogues	66	11
Unknowne as then were they that buylden towers:.	100	3rd Eclogues	66	46
Full glad they were and tooke the naked sprite,.	101	3rd Eclogues	66	78
They all consented were to give him wings:	101	3rd Eclogues	66	101
Blith were the commons, cattell of the fielde, ...	102	3rd Eclogues	66	132
And when they were well us'de to be abused,.	102	3rd Eclogues	66	144
He were a foole, if there he did not bide.	104	3rd Eclogues	67	15
And God forbid, women such cattell were,.	106	3rd Eclogues	67	82
(Which life is cald) were mov'd their spirits to repose, .	116	4th Eclogues	73	5
Free all my powers were from those captiving snares, . . .	117	4th Eclogues	73	17
Her giftes my study was, her beauties were my sporte:. . .	117	4th Eclogues	73	41
Straunge were the Ladies' weedes; yet more unfit then				
strange.	118	4th Eclogues	73	65
As though she were the same, as when by Paris' doome . . .	120	4th Eclogues	73	145
That thou full oft shalt wish thy judging eyes were blinde".	121	4th Eclogues	73	172
Ah, that, that do I not conceive, though that to me leefe				
were	122	4th Eclogues	74	19
Bend your thoghts to the dear sweet words which then to me				
giv'n were:.	124	4th Eclogues	74	75
And you, o flowers, which sometimes Princes were,.	125	4th Eclogues	75	25
From such as were to dye for him contented..	128	4th Eclogues	75	126
As in his health we healthfull were preserved, ...	128	4th Eclogues	75	134
Which were not evill, well vew'd in reason's light.. . . .	131	Arcadia V	77	8
To so lowe ebbe that wonted were to flowe.	146	Cert Sonnets	17	15
If Greekes themselves were mov'd with so small cause . . .	146	Cert Sonnets	17	21
The Rockes which were of constant mind the marke	147	Cert Sonnets	18	5
Then might I thinke what thoughts were best to thinke: . .	148	Cert Sonnets	19	5
Though hope were mixt with feare,.	158	Cert Sonnets	28	6
On things, were by a woman said, ...	158	Cert Sonnets	28	39
"Her eyes were once his dart".	160	Cert Sonnets	30	26
Of those three gods, whose armes the fairest were:	171	Astrophil	13	2
The first, thus matcht, were scarcely Gentlemen.	171	Astrophil	13	14
Beauties, which were of manie Carrets fine,.	172	Astrophil	16	2
Yet were the hid and meaner beauties parcht, ...	176	Astrophil	22	12
My heart then quak'd, then dazled were mine eyes,.	191	Astrophil	53	10
By love were made apt to consort with me..	229	Astrophil	95	11
But wo is me, though joy it selfe were she,.	230	Astrophil	97	12
I thought all words were lost, that were not spent of thee:.	212	A&S 5th Song		4
I said, thine eyes were starres, thy breasts the milk'n way,	212	A&S 5th Song		10
For rage now rules the reynes, which guided were by				
Pleasure	213	A&S 5th Song		15
Sighs of woes were glad sighs mixt,.	218	A&S 8th Song		18
But he were by me releeved..	222	A&S 9th Song		40
O men, whose Fathers were but men, ...	273	Psalm IV		6
These Canibals, who as if they were bread.	286	Psalm XIV		14
The gulfs of waters then were through their Chanels seen,. .	291	Psalm XVIII		31
They trusted and by Thee deliverd were..	298	Psalm XXII		12
They were set free when they upon Thee called, ...	298	Psalm XXII		13
They hop'd on Thee, and they were not appalled..	298	Psalm XXII		14
Then though against me armys were, ...	307	Psalm XXVII		13
While battaile's brunt on me were laid	307	Psalm XXVII		16

WERE	(CONTINUED)	PAGE	TITLE		LINE
Yea neighbors, more, my mates were so agast.		313	Psalm XXXI		32
And when neede were, from pride in privy plight, ...		313	Psalm XXXI		55
Laying such things, as never in mee weare;		322	Psalm XXXV		26
Dick. I would it were but thus, for thus it were too well. .		343	Possibly	1	17
But East and West were join'd by frendship's hest.		242	Other Poems	4	27
When, if nede were, they could at quintain run:.		243	Other Poems	4	56
That were in Court a well proportion'd hooke, ...		245	Other Poems	4	141
Were now his darts leaving his wonted fight.		246	Other Poems	4	148
The two that in mid place, Hell called were, ...		248	Other Poems	4	227
Geron strave hard, but aged were his feet, ...		248	Other Poems	4	254
Geron with Uran were condemn'd to hell.		249	Other Poems	4	264
For Pas, whether it were for feare, or love, ...		250	Other Poems	4	327
For they were ever in the best degree, ...		252	Other Poems	4	394
Do you remember still you once were mine, ...		254	Other Poems	4	495
Fearing the worst, not knowing what were best, ...		255	Other Poems	4	525
His lambs were him beside, ...		256	Other Poems	5	5
Speeche without ende were better not begin..		259	Other Poems	5	104
WERT					
I said, thou wert most faire, and so indeed thou art:. . . .		212	A&S 5th Song		7
I said, thou wert most sweet, sweet poison to my heart:. . .		212	A&S 5th Song		8
Thou, sweetest subject, werte borne in the realme of Love, .		214	A&S 5th Song		64
Than I was giv'en to Thee, Thou wert my God.		299	Psalm XXII		24
WEST					
But East and West were join'd by frendship's hest.		242	Other Poems	4	27
WESTERN					
To Westerne wightes, what starres in East appeare?		80	Arcadia III	52	4
More envied Phoebus for his westerne flyinge		259	Other Poems	5	126
WESTWARD					
And alwaies westward eying, ...		259	Other Poems	5	125
WHALE					
More white then whitest bone of whall.		89	Arcadia III	62	104
WHAT					
His wished weale, what more he could require:.		4	Lady of May	3	4
What marvaile then I take a woman's hew, ...		12	Arcadia I	2	13
Since what I see, thinke, know is all but you?		12	Arcadia I	2	14
What length of verse can serve brave Mopsa's good to show, .		12	Arcadia I	3	1
Yeld outward shew, what inward change he tryes:.		13	Arcadia I	4	2
What then must I that keepe the knave?		13	Arcadia I	5	6
Above line repeated at following location.		13	Arcadia I	5	12
What coye account she makes of estimation?		15	1st Eclogues	7	34
Of best things then what world can yeeld confection. . . .		15	1st Eclogues	7	46
Teach me what circle may acquaint her sprite,.		17	1st Eclogues	7	101
What circle then in so rare force beares swaye?.		17	1st Eclogues	7	109
What time for her Juno her Jove did misse.		21	1st Eclogues	8	15
And learn'd what ill a miser state doth breed, ...		21	1st Eclogues	8	22
Geron. What can amend where physick is refusde?.		23	1st Eclogues	9	21
Geron. Alas what falls are falne unto thy minde?		23	1st Eclogues	9	32
What counsell can prevaile, or light give light?		23	1st Eclogues	9	36
What ayleth thee, and if they knew thy minde		23	1st Eclogues	9	42
What man is he that hath his freedome solde?		24	1st Eclogues	9	56
What swarmes of vertues did in his youth flye.		24	1st Eclogues	9	74
Philisides. Hath any man heard what this old man said? . .		26	1st Eclogues	9	135
Geron. Downe, downe Melampus; what? your fellow bite?. . .		26	1st Eclogues	10	1
What if Laelaps a better morsell fyndes.		26	1st Eclogues	10	7
Mastix. What marvaile if in youth such faults be done, . .		27	1st Eclogues	10	25
Knowing no more, then what poore tryall showes,.		28	1st Eclogues	10	53
For what they see their parents love or hate		28	1st Eclogues	10	56
Geron. Fy man, fy man, what wordes hath thy tonge lent?. .		28	1st Eclogues	10	61
I pray thee what hath ere the Parret gott, ...		28	1st Eclogues	10	67
Still doo I crosse this wretch, what so he taketh in hand"..		29	1st Eclogues	11	6
But if he nought do desire, what can Heraclitus aile?. . .		30	1st Eclogues	11	12
Sacred Muse, who in one contaynes what nine do in all them..		31	1st Eclogues	13	10
What skill servethe a soare of a wrong infirmity judged? . .		32	1st Eclogues	13	21
What can justice availe, to a man that tells not his owne case:.		32	1st Eclogues	13	22
What meane is there, alas, we can hope our losse to recover?		32	1st Eclogues	13	27
What place is there left, we may hope our woes to recomfort?		32	1st Eclogues	13	28
What be the pangs they beare, and whence those pangs be derived, ...		33	1st Eclogues	13	43
Say then what vantage do we get, by the trade of a Pastor? .		33	1st Eclogues	13	49
Save that dayly we may discerne what fire we do burne in.. .		33	1st Eclogues	13	53
What judge you doth a hillocke shew, by the lofty Olympus? .		34	1st Eclogues	13	75
What marvaile tho a Prince transforme himselfe into a Pastor?.		34	1st Eclogues	13	91
Comfort into my soule. I do finde, I do find what a blessing		34	1st Eclogues	13	95
With bolde clamor unheard, unmarckt, what I seeke what I suffer:.		35	1st Eclogues	13	112
Lawrell shews what I seeke, by the Mirre is show'd how I seeke it,.		35	1st Eclogues	13	116
Ewe doth make me be thinke what kind of bow the boy holdeth.		35	1st Eclogues	13	121
And thinke ther she do dwell and heare what plaintes I do utter:.		36	1st Eclogues	13	143
Save what a worke, by thy selfe is wrought: and since I am altred		36	1st Eclogues	13	151
But to my selfe what wish can I make for a salve to my sorrowes,.		37	1st Eclogues	13	157
What wooll my sheepe shall beare, whyle thus they live,.. .		39	Arcadia II	17	7
What I call wrong, I doo the same, and more:		41	Arcadia II	20	6
What hope to quench, where each thing blowes the fire? . . .		42	Arcadia II	21	18
My sun is gon, from stormes what shall us sheelde?		43	Arcadia II	24	9

Doth teach, to learne the good what travailes do belong: . .   45 Arcadia II   26   8
What foresight tels; our thoughts upon thy knowledge staye..   45 Arcadia II   26   12
That nothing winnes the heaven, but what doth earth forsake.   45 Arcadia II   26   16
P. What shall we winne by taking Reason's yoke?. . . . . . .   47 2nd Eclogues 27   34
Dorus. But what doth make thee Dicus so suspicious . . . . .   47 2nd Eclogues 28   7
Goe on therefore, and tell us, by what fashion . . . .   48 2nd Eclogues 28   34
Lastly what so she be, that's my protection. . . . .   49 2nd Eclogues 28   72
The neighbours all did crie, "alas what asse doth bray?" . .   52 2nd Eclogues 29   26
For Pas well knowes what layes can Nico make.. . . . .   54 2nd Eclogues 29   74
Pas. Tell this (and Phoebus be) what monster growes. . . . .   56 2nd Eclogues 29   144
What greater ills have now the heavens in store, ...   57 2nd Eclogues 30   6
What needed so high sprites such mansions blind? . . . . . .   57 2nd Eclogues 30   14
Or wrapt in flesh what do they here obtaine, ...   57 2nd Eclogues 30   15
What glorie from our losse can he receave? . . . .   59 2nd Eclogues 30   73
By what eclipse shall that Sonne be defaste? . . . .   59 2nd Eclogues 30   95
What myne hath erst throwne downe so faire a tower?. . . . .   59 2nd Eclogues 30   96
What sacriledge hath such a saint disgrast?. . . . .   59 2nd Eclogues 30   97
O Mars, for what doth serve thy armed axe? . . . .   60 2nd Eclogues 30   110
What ere you see, thinke, touch, kisse, speake, or love, . .   60 2nd Eclogues 30   123
For what can breed more peevish incongruities, ...   61 2nd Eclogues 30   140
What pardon can availe? or who employes him. . . . .   62 2nd Eclogues 30   168
To hurt himselfe, what shields can be defenses?. . . . . . .   62 2nd Eclogues 30   169
Peace? what barrs me my tongue? who is it that comes me so
    ny? I. . . . .   62 2nd Eclogues 31   2
Oh! I do know what guest I have mett; it is Echo. @T is
    Echo . . . .   63 2nd Eclogues 31   3
Echo, what do I gett yelding my sprite to my grieves?
    Grieves. . . . .   63 2nd Eclogues 31   5
What medecin may I finde for a paine that draw's me to
    death Death.. . . . .   63 2nd Eclogues 31   6
O poisonous medecin! what worse he can be then it? It.. .   63 2nd Eclogues 31   7
In what state was I then, when I tooke this deadly disease?
    ease. . . . .   63 2nd Eclogues 31   8
And what manner a mind which had to that humor a vaine?
    Vaine. . . . .   63 2nd Eclogues 31   9
Oft prove I: but what salve, when Reason seeks to be gone?
    One. . . . .   63 2nd Eclogues 31   11
Oh! what is it? what is it that may be a salve to my Love?
    Love. . . . .   63 2nd Eclogues 31   12
What do lovers seeke for, long seeking for to enjoy? Joy.. .   63 2nd Eclogues 31   13
What be the joyes for which to enjoy they went to the
    paines Paines.. . . . .   63 2nd Eclogues 31   14
Then to an earnest Love what doth best victorie lend? Ende..   63 2nd Eclogues 31   15
But if he know not his harms what guides hath he whil'st he
    be blind? Blind. . . . .   63 2nd Eclogues 31   20
What blinde guides can he have that leanes to a fancy? A
    fancy. . . . .   63 2nd Eclogues 31   21
What causes first made these torments on me to light? Light.   64 2nd Eclogues 31   23
Yet tell what light thinge I had in me to draw me to die?
    Eye. . . . .   64 2nd Eclogues 31   25
Eysight made me to yeelde, but what first pierst to myne
    eies? Eies.. . . . .   64 2nd Eclogues 31   26
Eies' hurters, eies hurt, but what from them to me fall's?
    Fall's.. . . . .   64 2nd Eclogues 31   27
But when I first did fal, what brought most fall to my hart?
    Arte. . . . .   64 2nd Eclogues 31   28
Arte? what can be that art which thou dost meane by thy
    speche? Speche.. . . . .   64 2nd Eclogues 31   29
What be the fruites of speaking arte? what growes by the
    words? Words.. . . . .   64 2nd Eclogues 31   30
Then then what do I gaine, since unto hir will I do winde?
    Winde. . . . .   64 2nd Eclogues 31   34
Winde, tempests, and stormes, yet in ende what gives she
    desire? Ire. . . . .   64 2nd Eclogues 31   35
What great name may I give to so heav'nly a woman? A
    woe-man . . . .   64 2nd Eclogues 31   37
What be the sweet creatures wher lowly demaunds be not
    heard Hard. . . . .   65 2nd Eclogues 31   41
Ods? what an ods is there since them to the heav'ns I
    prefer Erre. . . . .   65 2nd Eclogues 31   48
My muse what ails this ardour. . . . .   65 2nd Eclogues 32   1
Above line repeated at following locations . . . .   66 2nd Eclogues 32   9
                                                                     66 2nd Eclogues 32   19
    . . . .   66 2nd Eclogues 32   30
                                                                     67 2nd Eclogues 32   40
Say then Reason, I say what is thy counsell? . . . .   67 2nd Eclogues 33   6
Above line repeated at following locations . . . .   67 2nd Eclogues 33   12
                                                                     68 2nd Eclogues 33   18
    . . . .   68 2nd Eclogues 33   24
Thus sweete paine, I do yeeld, what ere I can yeelde.. . . .   68 2nd Eclogues 33   29
And wise thoughts do behold what the creator is: . . . . . .   68 2nd Eclogues 34   6
What man grafts in a tree dissimulation? . . . .   69 2nd Eclogues 34   28
What stormes founde me, what tormentes I dyd fynde,. . . . .   71 Arcadia III   36   15
What horrors breede, wheare wynd dominion beares,. . . . . .   71 Arcadia III   37   2
For what is life to dayly dyinge minde,. . . . .   73 Arcadia III   40   9
Seeke then and see, what man esteemeth best, ...   75 Arcadia III   44   5
All what I am, still one, his owne, doe finde. . . . .   78 Arcadia III   50   10
All what you are still one, his owne to finde, ...   79 Arcadia III   50   11
What were it els, but to make each thing blinde? . . . . . .   79 Arcadia III   50   13

To Westerne wightes, what starres in East appeare? . . . . .   80 Arcadia III   52   4
What be her giftes, that make her equall thee, ...   80 Arcadia III   52   8
What strange dessein hast thou my hopes to staie, ...   80 Arcadia III   53   3
Sturres me to thinke what dangers lye in waite.. . . . . . .   82 Arcadia III   56   12
Leasure to weigh what due deserte requireth. . . . .   83 Arcadia III   57   10
What medicin then, can such desease remove . . . .   85 Arcadia III   61   13
What toong can her perfections tell. . . . .   85 Arcadia III   62   1
My tongue doth tell what fancie sees.. . . . .   89 Arcadia III   62   94
With recklesness what may thy house betide, ...   93 3rd Eclogues 63   75
He gest the worst (you wot what is the worst). . . . .   94 3rd Eclogues 64   11
The goodman starting, askt what did her move?. . . . .   95 3rd Eclogues 64   47
He did demaunde what remedy to finde:. . . . .   95 3rd Eclogues 64   52
For clerkly reed, and hating what is naught, ...   99 3rd Eclogues 66   24
Such maner time there was (what time I n'ot) . . . . 100 3rd Eclogues 66   43
"O beasts, take heed what you of me desire.. . . . . 100 3rd Eclogues 66   72
They seldome ponder what to them is due. . . . . 104 3rd Eclogues 67   27
Still contrarie to what her husband sayes; . . . . 104 3rd Eclogues 67   32
Lord, what bywords they speake, what spite they spit?. . . . 105 3rd Eclogues 67   48
While that we doo what nature doth require, ... 105 3rd Eclogues 67   65
All what I am: if I my selfe will save, ... 114 4th Eclogues 72   23
Then must I save, what in my chiefly raignes, ... 114 4th Eclogues 72   24
Are all in me: what helpe then can I trie? . . . . 114 4th Eclogues 72   43
What essence dest'nie hath; if fortune be or no; . . . . . 118 4th Eclogues 73   45
What life it is, and how that all these lives doo gather, . 118 4th Eclogues 73   47
That forced with grief reveales what greeved eyes dyd see) 118 4th Eclogues 73   56
Of what thou seest: close up in secrete knot thy will". . . 119 4th Eclogues 73   98
Diana did begin. "What mov'd me to invite. . . . . 119 4th Eclogues 73 102
I know full well you know, what discord long hath raign'd.. 119 4th Eclogues 73 105
But let us wiser be; and what foule discorde brake, ... 120 4th Eclogues 73 119
If you, on you I lay what in my office be. . . . . 120 4th Eclogues 73 134
To all what I decreed, did thus my verdict saye. . . . . . 121 4th Eclogues 73 162
Ne yet for what I see, your beauties merite ought. . . . . 121 4th Eclogues 73 164
"Fie, fie, what have we done? ungodly rebell fie. . . . . . 121 4th Eclogues 73 168
But now we muste needs yeelde, to what our othes require". . 121 4th Eclogues 73 169
Now that he finds to what end his life and love be reserved, 123 4th Eclogues 74   29
You be the cause that I love: what Reason blameth a shadowe, 123 4th Eclogues 74   45
What veiles then doo prevaile, but to a more miracle?. . . . 123 4th Eclogues 74   50
O wretch, what do I say? should that faire face be defaced?. 124 4th Eclogues 74   57
But what's this for a fault, for which such faieth be
    abolisht, ... 124 4th Eclogues 74   69
What sweete joyes I had once, and what a place I did hold?   124 4th Eclogues 74   72
Think what a world is now, think who hath altred her hart. . 124 4th Eclogues 74   76
What? was I then worthie such good, now worthie so muche
    evill? . . . . 124 4th Eclogues 74   77
Say, that I well shuld finde in what a care I was had? . . . 124 4th Eclogues 74   80
With much more: now what doo I finde, but Care to abhor me, 124 4th Eclogues 74   81
Of what was good, where now no good doth lie; . . . . 127 4th Eclogues 75   74
I have my selfe, and all what life containeth, ... 128 4th Eclogues 75 101
So it be seene what sorrow in me raigneth. . . . . 128 4th Eclogues 75 105
For what place now is lefte for our affection. . . . . 129 4th Eclogues 76   7
What griefe her breast oppresseth, ... 137 Cert Sonnets   4   7
Which once said what I conceaved, ... 139 Cert Sonnets   7   5
To see what faire sight there raigneth, ... 140 Cert Sonnets   7   26
What courage strange hath caught thy caitife hart. . . . . . 142 Cert Sonnets 10   9
And doth she know what mould her beautie beares? . . . . . . 142 Cert Sonnets 11   2
That sense feeles more then what doth sense containe?. . . . 142 Cert Sonnets 11   8
Else what in face, then in my fancie beare?. . . . . 146 Cert Sonnets 17   10
Then what I thinke what thoughts were best to thinke: . . . 148 Cert Sonnets 19   5
What force brought them to so unlikely ground. . . . . 149 Cert Sonnets 22   4
Deepe in the earth, what hath in earth receipt . . . . 150 Cert Sonnets 22   42
What kind of fires they be in which those spirits melt, . . 153 Cert Sonnets 24   7
Shall gesse, and faile, what doth displease, ... 153 Cert Sonnets 24   8
Finde to what harme they hastned, ... 154 Cert Sonnets 25   14
Thus what I thinke is of you: . . . . 155 Cert Sonnets 25   32
Thus what I seeke is in you: . . . . 155 Cert Sonnets 25   33
All what I am, it is you. . . . . 155 Cert Sonnets 25   34
Foole in me, what follie creepeth, ... 157 Cert Sonnets 27   26
What changes here, o haire, ... 157 Cert Sonnets 28   1
What streames of teares she spent, ... 158 Cert Sonnets 28   22
What in your face mine eyes do measure. . . . . 159 Cert Sonnets 29   9
I loved, but straight did not what Love decreed: . . . . . . 165 Astrophil   2   6
What Love and Beautie be, then all my deed . . . . 166 Astrophil   3   13
But Copying is, what in her Nature writes. . . . . 166 Astrophil   3   14
Leave what thou likest not, deale not thou with it.. . . . . 166 Astrophil   4   4
It is most true, what we call Cupid's dart, ... 167 Astrophil   5   5
Of hopes begot by feare, of wot not what desires: . . . . . 167 Astrophil   6   6
I can speake what I feele, and feele as much as they, . . . 168 Astrophil   6   12
In truth, o Love, with what a boyish kind. . . . . 170 Astrophil   11   1
What words so ere she speakes perswades for thee, ... 171 Astrophil   12   7
By my love judging what Love's paine might be. . . . . 173 Astrophil   16   8
With what sharpe checkes I in my selfe am shent, ... 173 Astrophil   18   1
For though she passe all things, yet what is all . . . . . . 174 Astrophil   19   9
What can be hoped my harvest time will be? . . . . 175 Astrophil   21   11
As what their hands do hold, their heads do know, ... 177 Astrophil   24   6
So Stella's heart, finding what power Love brings, ... 179 Astrophil   29   5
What now the Dutch in their full diets boast; . . . . 180 Astrophil   30   6
What, may it be that even in heav'nly place. . . . . 180 Astrophil   31   3
Come let me write, "And to what end?" To ease. . . . . 181 Astrophil   34   1
"What idler thing, then speake and not be hard?" . . . . . . 182 Astrophil   34   9

What harder thing then smart, and not to speake? . . . . . .   182 Astrophil   34   10
What may words say, or what may words not say, ...   182 Astrophil   35   1
Within what bounds can one his liking stay,. . . . .   182 Astrophil   35   3
What Nestor's counsell can my flames alay, ...   182 Astrophil   35   5
And ah what hope, that hope should once see day, ...   182 Astrophil   35   7
I start, looke, hearke, but what in closde up sence. . . . .   184 Astrophil   38   9
Alas, what cause is there so overthwart, ...   186 Astrophil   44   7
What, have I thus betrayed my libertie?. . . . .   188 Astrophil   47   1
And cannot chuse but put out what I write, ...   190 Astrophil   50   10
"What now sir foole," said he, "I would no lesse,. . . . . .   191 Astrophil   53   7
"What he?" say they of me, "now I dare sweare, ...   191 Astrophil   54   7
What, a whole weeke without one peece of looke,. . . . . . .   192 Astrophil   56   3
What, dost thou thinke that I can ever take. . . . .   193 Astrophil   56   10
Shall quickly me from what she hates remove. . . . .   195 Astrophil   61   11
What blushing notes doest thou in margine see? . . . .   199 Astrophil   67   8
What sighes stolne out, or kild before full borne? . . . . .   199 Astrophil   67   9
O thinke I then, what paradise of joy. . . . .   200 Astrophil   68   13
What Oceans of delight in me do flow.. . . . .   200 Astrophil   69   4
My spring appeares, o see what here doth grow. . . . .   200 Astrophil   69   8
Who marke in thee what is in thee most faire.. . . . .   201 Astrophil   71   11
What wonder then if he his lesson misse, ...   203 Astrophil   73   3
But (God wot) wot not what they meane by it: . . . .   204 Astrophil   74   6
My thoughts I speake, and what I speake doth flow. . . . . .   204 Astrophil   74   10
Guesse we the cause: "What, is it thus?" Pie no: . . . . . .   204 Astrophil   74   12
That Ballance weigh'd what sword did late obtaine, ...   204 Astrophil   75   8
No wind, no shade can coole, what helpe then in my case, . .   205 Astrophil   76   12
That face, whose lecture shewes what perfect beautie is: . .   205 Astrophil   77   2
What, doth high place ambitious thoughts augment?. . . . . .   208 Astrophil   83   9
With what pastime, time's journey she beguilde,. . . . . . .   225 Astrophil   92   12
What sobs can give words grace my griefe tc show?. . . . . .   227 Astrophil   93   2
What inke is blacke inough to paint my wo? . . . .   227 Astrophil   93   3
I would know by what right this palenesse overcame . . . . .   232 Astrophil   102   7
Envious wits what hath bene mine offence,. . . . .   233 Astrophil   104   1
As what my hart still sees thou canst not spie?. . . . . . .   235 Astrophil   105   4
Counting but dust what in the way did lie. . . . .   235 Astrophil   105   8
What saist thou now, where is that dainty cheere . . . . . .   235 Astrophil   106   5
Till it have wrought what thy owne will attends. . . . . . .   236 Astrophil   107   11
And scorning say, "See what it is to love.". . . . .   236 Astrophil   107   14
Ah what doth Phoebus' gold that wretch availe, ...   237 Astrophil   108   10
What No her tongue sleeping useth. . . . .   202 A&S 2nd Song   12
See what clouds of reproch small darke thy honour's skie,. .   213 A&S 5th Song   23
Threat'n what may be done, yet do more then you threat'n.. .   213 A&S 5th Song   33
What, is not this enough? nay farre worse commeth here;. . .   214 A&S 5th Song   73
You see what I can say; mend yet your froward mind,. . . . .   215 A&S 5th Song   88
In what high joyes I shall dwell,. . . . .   226 A&S 10th Song   11
From what in my hart doth ly. . . . .   234 A&S 11th Song   15
Time doth worke what no man knoweth.". . . . .   234 A&S 11th Song   17
"What if you new beauties see, ...   234 A&S 11th Song   21
Graunt, o me, what am I saying?. . . . .   219 A&S 8th Song   47
With what she had done and spoken, ...   221 A&S 8th Song   103
What ayles this heathenish rage? What do theis people meane. 271 Psalm II   1
Consider what I meditate in me:. . . . .   274 Psalm V   2
Then think I, Ah, what is this Man,. . . . .   278 Psalm VIII   13
And what the race of him descended . . . .   279 Psalm VIII   15
And what thinges els of waters traceth . . . .   279 Psalm VIII   31
What? Doth their Memory no longer last?. . . . .   280 Psalm IX   18
What God prepares. . . . .   281 Psalm IX   55
For what, alas, have just men done?. . . . .   284 Psalm XI   11
For what lord rules our bold emboldned breast. . . . .   285 Psalm XII   12
What? ever?. . . . .   285 Psalm XIII   2
What would they more? And I would not their case.. . . . . .   290 Psalm XVII   45
What Foes I did persue my force did them attaine,. . . . . .   292 Psalm XVIII   68
Then what man would so soon seek gold. . . . .   294 Psalm XIX   41
Lord what delight to him doth bring. . . . .   296 Psalm XXI   3
Thou hast given what his heart would have, ...   297 Psalm XXI   5
His lips to crave, what he would crave . . . .   297 Psalm XXI   7
But what? I say from earth's remotest border . . . .   300 Psalm XXII   65
The earth is God's, and what the Globe of earth containeth,.   302 Psalm XXIV   1
Teach me, thus vext, what path to go.. . . . .   303 Psalm XXV   12
And what think you may be. . . . .   304 Psalm XXV   37
Behold my Foes, what store they be,. . . . .   304 Psalm XXV   65
What had I been, except I had. . . . .   308 Psalm XXVII   61
And what was I but wretched clay?. . . . .   311 Psalm XXX   24
What serves alas the blood of me . . . .   311 Psalm XXX   26
Thou well hast known what plung my soul was in . . . .   312 Psalm XXXI   21
I understand what rayling great men spred; . . . .   313 Psalm XXXI   37
Oh! of thy grace what endlesse pleasure flowes . . . .   313 Psalm XXXI   52
To whom feare Thee? what thou hast done for those. . . . . .   313 Psalm XXXI   53
To me and mark what I do say,. . . . .   319 Psalm XXXIV   42
What guilty wickedness doth say, ...   323 Psalm XXXVI   2
What comes therof? he shall not slide. . . . .   326 Psalm XXXVII   80
What I pray; . . . .   328 Psalm XXXVIII   26
What do we seeke? the greatest state I see . . . .   330 Psalm XXXIX   17
This being thus, For what O Lord wait I?. . . . . 330 Psalm XXXIX   23
So what is man but vanity? . . . .   330 Psalm XXXIX   36
What man Thy thoughts can count to Thee. . . . .   331 Psalm XL   22
But what? This doth already well appeare . . . .   333 Psalm XLI   37
What great thanks I ow thee. . . . .   337 Psalm XLIII   30
What ayles Thy discomfort? . . . .   337 Psalm XLIII   33

WHAT   (CONTINUED)   PAGE   TITLE   LINE

Dick. What joy the joyfull sunne gives unto bleared eyes:. .   343 Possibly   1   13
Will. What? is thy Bagpipe broke, or are thy lambs miswent;.   343 Possibly   1   15
Will. What? these are riddles sure, art thou then bound to
     her? . . . .   343 Possibly   1   23
W. Who bound thee? D. Love my Lord. W. What witnesses
     therto . . . .   343 Possibly   1   25
W. What seale? D. My hart deepe graven. W. Who made the band
     so fast?. . . . .   343 Possibly   1   27
Will. What keepeth safe thy band? D. Remembrance is the
     Chest. . . . .   344 Possibly   1   29
Will. Thou late of wages playn'dst: what wages mayst thou
     have?. . . . .   344 Possibly   1   31
Will. What living get you then? D. Disdayne; but just
     disdayne. . . . .   344 Possibly   1   35
Will. What care takes shee for thee? D. Hir care is to
     prevent. . . . .   344 Possibly   1   37
To raise in words what in effect is lowe:. . . . .   242 Other Poems   4   2
What rage in them, that love in him did show. . . . .   249 Other Poems   4   294
Who earnest found what they accounted play. . . . .   251 Other Poems   4   366
Did not conceive what fire he had within. . . . .   253 Other Poems   4   428
"Alas! what weights are these that lode my heart!. . . . . .   253 Other Poems   4   441
Away ragg'd rams, care I what murraine kill? . . . .   255 Other Poems   4   515
Fearing the worst, not knowing what were best, ...   255 Other Poems   4   525
He quickly knew what witchcraft gave the blow. . . . .   256 Other Poems   4   539
What fitts me now but teares, and sighings sadd? . . . . . .   259 Other Poems   5   97
Oh! what doth wailing winne? . . . .   259 Other Poems   5   103
What in art of Love is fitting. . . . .   262 Other Poems   7   30
"Nay, what neede the Arte to those,. . . . .   263 Other Poems   7   31
WHATE'ER
Thus sweete paine, I do yeeld, what ere I can yeelde.. . . .   68 2nd Eclogues 33   29
WHATEVER
Old age hath knowne what ever was in youth:. . . . .   39 Arcadia II   15   11
What ever fades, but fading pleasure brings. . . . .   161 Cert Sonnets 32   4
What ever may ensue, o let me be . . . .   188 Astrophil   48   5
WHEEL
The weaking worke of Time's for ever-whirling wheele. . . .   120 4th Eclogues 73   122
WHEELS
Fortune wheeles still with me in one sort slow,. . . . . . .   199 Astrophil   66   6
WHELP
Now like his whelp in den that lurking stayes. . . . .   290 Psalm XVII   34
WHELPS
Those raveners' whelps oft starved be, ...   319 Psalm XXXIV   38
WHEN

When being askt, now that he did obtaine . . . .   4 Lady of May   3   3
(Therion) When wanton Pan, deceiv'd with Lion's skin,. . . .   5 Lady of May   3   7
When first he spied my love? how oft he said to me,. . . . .   16 1st Eclogues 7   50
This winde he spent: but when my Kala glasseth all . . . . .   16 1st Eclogues 7   55
Dorus. How oft, when reason saw love of her harnished. . . .   16 1st Eclogues 7   61
But when in shade we meet of mirtle bowes, ...   18 1st Eclogues 7   128
Oft comes reliefe when most we seeme in trappe.. . . . . . .   23 1st Eclogues 9   24
That since they still alledge, When they were yong:. . . . .   24 1st Eclogues 9   79
Oh when will men leave off to judge by haire,. . . . .   25 1st Eclogues 9   93
Ath strongest soule, when most his raynes do bowe. . . . . .   25 1st Eclogues 9   101
Passion beares high when puffing wit doth blowe,. . . . . . .   25 1st Eclogues 9   114
When they shall such devided weakenesse prove? . . . .   26 1st Eclogues 10   6
But thanke the cause, thou seest, when he is dim. . . . . . .   27 1st Eclogues 10   12
Yet have I seene when well a wolfe he shooke.. . . . .   27 1st Eclogues 10   18
Doe speake high wordes, when all the coaste is cleare, . . .   27 1st Eclogues 10   32
Save when great need of them perforce apeare.. . . . .   27 1st Eclogues 10   36
And when that time is paste, death holdes his heeles.. . . .   28 1st Eclogues 10   51
When that we see our ofspring gaily bent,. . . . .   28 1st Eclogues 10   59
Since when I thinke he hath in silence lived.. . . . .   29 1st Eclogues 10   87
But if eyes faile then, when I most doo need them, ...   30 1st Eclogues 12   5
If the mute timber when it hath the life lost, ...   30 1st Eclogues 12   15
Silly shepheard's poore pype, when his harsh sound testifis
     our woes,. . . . .   32 1st Eclogues 13   40
When trees daunce to the pype, and swift streames stay by
     the musicke, ...   33 1st Eclogues 13   47
Or when an Echo begins unmov'd to sing them a love song. . .   33 1st Eclogues 13   48
When Cedars to the ground be opprest by the weight of an
     emmott,. . . . .   34 1st Eclogues 13   77
Or when a rich rubie's just price be the worth of a walnut,.   34 1st Eclogues 13   78
And when I meete these trees, in the earth's faire lyvery
     clothed,. . . . .   35 1st Eclogues 13   113
But in a palme when I marke, how he doth rise under a
     burden . . . .   36 1st Eclogues 13   127
But to the Cedar, Queene of woods, when I lifte my beteard
     eyes,. . . . .   36 1st Eclogues 13   141
When that noble toppe doth nodd, I beleeve she salutes me; .   36 1st Eclogues 13   144
When by the winde it maketh a noyse, I do thinke she doth
     answer.. . . . .   36 1st Eclogues 13   145
When yonger dooth in smoke his vertue spend. . . . .   38 Arcadia II   15   4
When pittie most I crave, I cruell prove:. . . . .   41 Arcadia II   20   3
When rotten Fame will tell their blowes. . . . .   44 Arcadia II   25   10
P. Will hath his will, when Reason's will doth misse.. . . .   46 2nd Eclogues 27   8
But when to give some grace she doth content herselfe, . . .   49 2nd Eclogues 28   64
When for a treene-dish stolne, thy father did thee whippe! .   52 2nd Eclogues 29   12
When with the kawing crowes their musicke is annoide.. . . .   52 2nd Eclogues 29   18
But still when thou dost sing, me thinkes a colt is loose. .   52 2nd Eclogues 29   24

WHEN	(CONTINUED)	PAGE	TITLE	LINE
Pas. Alas, when I in spring meet roses rathe,.		54	2nd Eclogues 29	78
But when I did come neere with heate and hope,.		54	2nd Eclogues 29	88
Nico. When Leuca dooth appeare, the Sunne for shame.		55	2nd Eclogues 29	93
Pas. When Cosma doth come forth, the Sun displaies		55	2nd Eclogues 29	96
We thinke they hurt, when most they do assist.		59	2nd Eclogues 30	70
O hand, which toucht her hand when we did part;.		60	2nd Eclogues 30	119
Can I forget, when they in prison placing her, ...		61	2nd Eclogues 30	152
The asse did hurt when he did thinke to kisse.		62	2nd Eclogues 30	184
Faire Rocks, goodly rivers, sweet woods, when shall I see peace? Peace...		62	2nd Eclogues 31	1
In what state was I then, when I tooke this deadly disease? ease.		63	2nd Eclogues 31	8
Oft prove I: but what salve, when Reason seeks to be gone? One.		63	2nd Eclogues 31	11
But when I first did fal, what brought most fall to my hart? Arte.		64	2nd Eclogues 31	28
Oh when shall I be knowne, wher most to be knowne I do longe Long.		64	2nd Eclogues 31	32
As neere his home, when storme or shelf he feares;		71	Arcadia III 37	4
As happie shewes of corne when harvest sendes;		71	Arcadia III 37	10
Gay haire more gaie then straw when harvest lyes,.		76	Arcadia III 46	7
When worthlesse corke, aloft doth floting lye.		81	Arcadia III 54	14
When two Sunnes do appeare		81	Arcadia III 55	1
Like to the Moone when after chaunge		86	Arcadia III 62	11
When strugling rocks he would imbrace.		88	Arcadia III 62	70
When they though divers do together meete:		92	3rd Eclogues 63	34
Grumbling at her when she his kindnes sought,.		95	3rd Eclogues 64	32
When once this entred was, in woman's hart,.		95	3rd Eclogues 64	37
Glad was the man when he had heard her out,.		96	3rd Eclogues 64	63
Watched when she a furder point might gaine, ...		96	3rd Eclogues 64	75
When all this Earth, this damme or mould of ours,.		100	3rd Eclogues 66	44
But when his seate so rooted he had found, ...		102	3rd Eclogues 66	113
Tho when they saw their foen of greatnes kilde..		102	3rd Eclogues 66	133
When falcon they, and gossehauke saw in mewe..		102	3rd Eclogues 66	140
And when they were well us'de to be abused,.		102	3rd Eclogues 66	144
Austere she is, when he would honest playes;		104	3rd Eclogues 67	34
And gamesome then, when he thinkes on his sheepe;.		104	3rd Eclogues 67	35
When without shame he saith, "these be mine owne".		106	3rd Eclogues 67	114
When I doo smell the flowers of these vallies:		112	4th Eclogues 71	46
Me seemes I heare, when I doo heare sweete musique,.		112	4th Eclogues 71	47
For so did I, when with my angle, Will,.		115	4th Eclogues 72	62
When first that crowned Basiliske I knewe,.		115	4th Eclogues 72	72
When I, disgraced wretch, not wretched then, did give. . . .		117	4th Eclogues 73	11
When lo with hugest noise (such noise a tower makes.		118	4th Eclogues 73	51
When it blowne up with myne a fall of ruine takes)		118	4th Eclogues 73	52
When I such guests did see come out of such a house, ...		118	4th Eclogues 73	75
Those names abasht me much, when those great names I hard: .		119	4th Eclogues 73	79
Tc worthiest let him give, when both he hath beheld:		120	4th Eclogues 73	142
As though she were the same, as when by Paris' doome		120	4th Eclogues 73	145
I that was first agast, when first I saw their showe:. . . .		121	4th Eclogues 73	158
Ah, that, that do I not conceive; to the heaven when a mouse climes.		122	4th Eclogues 74	21
When they by yeares' experience get best graces, ...		127	4th Eclogues 75	89
When once one is for Atropos distrained.		128	4th Eclogues 75	111
When rooted moisture failes, or groweth drie,.		128	4th Eclogues 75	113
When that we feare our hatefull neighbours' might,.		129	4th Eclogues 76	20
Since feare is vaine, but when it may preserve,.		131	Arcadia V 77	3
When Love puft up with rage of hy disdaine,.		135	Cert Sonnets 2	1
O Faire, when I do looke on thee, ...		139	Cert Sonnets 7	1
Above line repeated at following locations		139	Cert Sonnets 7	11
. . . .		140	Cert Sonnets 7	21
. . . .		140	Cert Sonnets 7	31
Such causelesse feares when coward minds do take,.		145	Cert Sonnets 16	5
Thinke Hanniball did laugh when Carthage lost.		147	Cert Sonnets 17	45
The Bruertons have a Lake, which when the Sunne.		150	Cert Sonnets 22	11
From hidnest depth, which tribute when it ends,.		150	Cert Sonnets 22	13
But when my Sunne her shining twinnes there bends, ...		150	Cert Sonnets 22	16
But when that failes, my dead hopes up to take,.		150	Cert Sonnets 22	19
When to my deadlie pleasure, ...		154	Cert Sonnets 25	1
When to my livelie torment,.		154	Cert Sonnets 25	2
When with a fire he first met		154	Cert Sonnets 25	17
Scme Lovers speake when they their Muses entertaine, ...		167	Astrophil 6	1
When trembling voice brings forth that I do Stella love. . .		168	Astrophil 6	14
When Nature made her chiefe worke, Stella's eyes,.		168	Astrophil 7	1
That when the heav'n to thee his best displayes, ...		170	Astrophil 11	3
So when thou saw'st in Nature's cabinet.		170	Astrophil 11	9
In nature apt to like when I did see		172	Astrophil 16	1
When into Reason's audite I do go:		173	Astrophil 18	2
When most I glorie, then I feele most shame:		174	Astrophil 19	3
When some faire Ladies, by hard promise tied,.		176	Astrophil 22	5
When I say "Stella", I do meane the same		179	Astrophil 28	5
It is a praise to praise, when thou art praisde.		182	Astrophil 35	14
Fcr when he will see who dare him gainesay,.		186	Astrophil 43	5
When he will play, then in her lips he is,.		186	Astrophil 43	9
But when he will for quiet's sake remove		186	Astrophil 43	12
That when the breath of my complaints doth tuch.		187	Astrophil 44	10
Of straying wayes, when valiant errour guides:		190	Astrophil 51	11
When Cupid, having me his slave describe		191	Astrophil 53	5
When I might reade those letters faire of blisse,.		193	Astrophil 56	5

568

WHEN	(CONTINUED)	PAGE	TITLE		LINE
Hoping that when they might find Stella alone, ...		193	Astrophil	57	5
Doubt there hath bene, when with his golden chaine		193	Astrophil	58	1
When my good Angell guides me to the place, ...		194	Astrophil	60	1
But when the ruggedst step of Fortune's race		195	Astrophil	60	5
For when, nak'd boy, thou couldst no harbour find.		198	Astrophil	65	5
But when mine eyes backe to their heav'n did move, ...		199	Astrophil	66	13
When for so soft a rod deare play he trie?		203	Astrophil	73	4
So piercing pawes, as spoyle when they embrace, ...		206	Astrophil	78	10
Most rich, when most his riches it impart:		206	Astrophil	79	7
When in her necke you did Love ditties peepe;		208	Astrophil	83	6
When I was forst from Stella ever deere, ...		222	Astrophil	87	1
When Sun is hid, can starres send beames display?		223	Astrophil	88	6
When I demaund of Phenix Stella's state, ...		225	Astrophil	92	6
Seeing hope yeeld when this wo strake him furst:		228	Astrophil	95	6
Thanke-worthiest yet when you shall breake my hart.		229	Astrophil	95	14
But when Aurora leades out Phoebus' daunce, ...		230	Astrophil	98	12
When far spent night perswades each mortall eye, ...		230	Astrophil	99	1
But when birds charme, and that sweete aire, which is. . . .		231	Astrophil	99	9
When sorrow (using mine owne fier's might)		236	Astrophil	108	1
Whose grace is such, that when it chides doth cherish? . . .		197	A&S 1st Song		18
Who makes a man live then glad when he dieth?		197	A&S 1st Song		26
When she wakes, is too too cruell.		202	A&S 10th Song		4
O deare life, when shall it be, ...		225	A&S 10th Song		1
When my leaping hart will clime, ...		226	A&S 10th Song		26
When I blessed shall devower, ...		226	A&S 10th Song		32
When with Dovelike murmurings, ...		226	A&S 10th Song		38
Deere when you find change in me, ...		234	A&S 11th Song		8
The very essence of their tunes, when Angels do rejoyce. . .		217	A&S 7th Song		18
But when their tongues could not speake, ...		218	A&S 8th Song		25
"Stella, whose voice when it speakes, ...		219	A&S 8th Song		37
Stella, whose voice when it singeth, ...		219	A&S 8th Song		39
I should blush when thou art named."		220	A&S 8th Song		100
When tis excellently sory.		221	A&S 9th Song		15
Consist, when they to highest doome are cited, ...		270	Psalm I		16
Heare me, O heare me when I call		273	Psalm IV		1
Thou sett'st me free, when I was thrall, ...		273	Psalm IV		3
Till when will ye my honour high		273	Psalm IV		7
Staine with your blasphemys? till when		273	Psalm IV		8
When He chose me, a godly One:		273	Psalm IV		12
Such one I say, that when I make		273	Psalm IV		13
And when your chamber you do close, ...		273	Psalm IV		19
When I upon the Heav'ns do look.		278	Psalm VIII		9
When Moone and starrs my thoughtes beholdeth		278	Psalm VIII		11
When Godless men be snar'd in their own snares:		281	Psalm IX		52
When Wycked soules be turn'd to hellish paine, ...		281	Psalm IX		53
When he his lust doth ease, ...		281	Psalm X		10
When hee once drau'th his wily nett.		282	Psalm X		40
When fire seven times hath spent his earthly parts.		285	Psalm XII		21
More than they now do bragg, when He shall take.		286	Psalm XIV		17
Ah, when from syon shall the saver come, ...		287	Psalm XIV		22
Ev'n when night with his black wing.		288	Psalm XVI		21
When silent night might seeme all faults to hide, ...		289	Psalm XVII		9
When waking of this sleep of mine.		290	Psalm XVII		47
My refuge, refuge then, when moste I am forlorn;		291	Psalm XVIII		5
For they had caught me up, when I was weake in Woe;		291	Psalm XVIII		38
This much, yet more, when I by him this freedom gate, . . .		292	Psalm XVIII		40
Ev'n in the day when most Thy troubles be;		295	Psalm XX		2
When Thou on it dost cry, ...		295	Psalm XX		4
Up to Our God, when Thy suites granted be.		296	Psalm XX		20
They were set free when they upon Thee called, ...		298	Psalm XXII		13
By aiding when fierce unicorns come neare me		299	Psalm XXII		50
And with these Words, when they meet, prayse Thy Name. . . .		300	Psalm XXII		52
But when he calld this lord did give him hearing.		300	Psalm XXII		58
Ev'n when foe's envious cry.		301	Psalm XXIII		17
When wicked folk, even they that be.		307	Psalm XXVII		7
For when great griefes to me be ment, ...		307	Psalm XXVII		25
Heare lord when I my voice display, ...		307	Psalm XXVII		37
Seek ye my Face, when Thou didst say, ...		307	Psalm XXVII		39
When in hearts they malice meane.		309	Psalm XXVIII		15
For when my heart with woes was torn, ...		311	Psalm XXX		4
When I within the pitt do bide;		311	Psalm XXX		27
And when neede were, from pride in privy plight, ...		313	Psalm XXXI		55
But Thou didst heare, when I to Thee did moane.		313	Psalm XXXI		63
When Thou wilt deign to heare him.		315	Psalm XXXII		21
When time's times shall be past.		317	Psalm XXXIII		42
The just when harms approach		320	Psalm XXXIV		61
When most he seemes opprest.		320	Psalm XXXIV		72
And whose? ev'n his who when they sickness bare.		322	Psalm XXXV		29
Who joy but they, when they assembled bee?		322	Psalm XXXV		38
For when his sin Thy scourging hath, ...		330	Psalm XXXIX		34
When most his troubles clime.		332	Psalm XLI		4
When bedd from rest becomes his seat of woe, ...		333	Psalm XLI		9
When, when will death o'retake this wretched wight		333	Psalm XLI		19
Ah, when comes my blessed being, ...		334	Psalm XLII		7
When but with one look of his.		334	Psalm XLII		21
When foes ask with foule deriding, ...		335	Psalm XLII		47
Shew that we do not grudge at all when others do rejoyce. . .		343	Possibly	1	2
To play when that their loved dammes, are stoln or gone astray?		343	Possibly	1	6

WHEN   (CONTINUED)   PAGE   TITLE   LINE

When she with skirts tuckt very hy, with girles at stoolball
    playes. . . . .   343 Possibly   1   10
When thou hast mynd to weepe, seeke out som smoky room:. . .   343 Possibly   1   11
When strong Desire, which vertue's love doth guide, ...   345 Possibly   4   7
Allarme allarme, when once the fight is warme, ...   346 Possibly   5   13
When mery May first early calls the morne, ...   243 Other Poems   4   49
When, if nede were, they could at quintain run: . . . . . .   243 Other Poems   4   56
But when the rod began to play his part, ...   246 Other Poems   4 183
And so when Pas hand-reached him to take, ...   248 Other Poems   4 257
He thrise reacht, thrise deceiv'd when hir to beare. . . . .   250 Other Poems   4 340
When Strephon, cursing his owne backwardnes, ...   252 Other Poems   4 388
As rubies lustre, when they rubbed be. . . . .   252 Other Poems   4 396
As on sweet flowrs when morning's drops we see. . . . .   252 Other Poems   4 398
"When I see her, my sinewes shake for feare, ...   253 Other Poems   4 457
Then so I faile, when most I would do well, ...   254 Other Poems   4 467
Which when he did in perfect image show, ...   256 Other Poems   4 541
Doth not thy selfe, when he long absent is, ...   257 Other Poems   5   24
So when to pay your due. . . . .   257 Other Poems   5   33
When he from you is sent, ...   257 Other Poems   5   51
Who never joy, but when. . . . .   261 Other Poems   6   39
When we doe but flatter men: . . . .   263 Other Poems   7   34
WHENAS
When as to him Our Prayers do appeare. . . . .   296 Psalm XX   35
WHENCE
What be the pangs they beare, and whence those pangs be
    derived, ...   33 1st Eclogues 13   43
Her praise, whence to the world all praise had his only
    beginning: . . . .   33 1st Eclogues 13   69
Whence may I show to my minde any light of a possible
    escape . . . .   37 1st Eclogues 13 161
O blessed sonne whence all this blessing goes. . . . .   43 Arcadia II   23   6
Of singing match we made, whence he with shame did trudge. .   52 2nd Eclogues 29   16
Whence can pride come there, since springs of beawty be
    thence? Thence. . . . .   65 2nd Eclogues 31   44
Whence never word in vaine did flowe. . . . .   87 Arcadia III 62   45
Whence our immortall soules to mortall earth doo flowe: . .   118 4th Eclogues 73   46
O sweet simplicitie: from whence should Love be so learned?.   124 4th Eclogues 74   65
Whence, whence alas, shall we seeke our direction! . . . . .   129 4th Eclogues 76   19
Passing all ghesse, whence into me should fly. . . . .   149 Cert Sonnets 22   8
To come from whence you be, ...   158 Cert Sonnets 28   30
Whence those same fumes of melancholy rise, ...   176 Astrophil   23   3
Whence hast thou Ivorie, Rubies, pearle and gold, ...   181 Astrophil   32   10
Stella, whence doth this new assault arise, ...   182 Astrophil   36   1
Whence words, not words, but heav'nly graces slide. . . . . .   206 Astrophil   80   4
Alas, whence came this change of lookes? If I . . . .   212 Astrophil   86   1
From whence shall come to us such ayd? . . . .   274 Psalm IV   25
Whence he was transformed late, ...   262 Other Poems   7   10
WHERE
Where eares be burnt, eyes dazled, harts opprest?. . . . . .   3 Lady of May   1   6
Came to the bed, where wound for kisse he got, ...   5 Lady of May   3   8
No stile is held for base, where Love well named is: . . . .   14 1st Eclogues 7   4
A heape of sweetes she is, where nothing spilled is; . . . .   15 1st Eclogues 7   28
I finde no shade, but where my Sunne doth burne: . . . . . .   18 1st Eclogues 7 144
New plucked from the place where it did breed, ...   19 1st Eclogues 7 159
On me to cast those eyes, where shine nobilitie. . . . . . .   19 1st Eclogues 7 178
With long large eares where never rumour dyes. . . . .   21 1st Eclogues 8   28
Geron. What can amend where physick is refusde?. . . . . . .   23 1st Eclogues 9   21
That there where thou confest thy mischiefe lyes . . . . . .   23 1st Eclogues 9   33
Like beast for sacrifice, where save the tong. . . . .   24 1st Eclogues 9   81
Where all my paines one looke of hers hath paid. . . . . . .   26 1st Eclogues 9 137
For busines, where it pertaines him not, ...   28 1st Eclogues 10   65
Where thou poore nature left'st all thy due glory, to
    fortune. . . . .   30 1st Eclogues 11   15
Hardly remains fyer hid, where skill is bent to the hiding, .   33 1st Eclogues 13   59
Where proofes justly do teach, thus matcht, such worth to be
    nought worth. . . . .   34 1st Eclogues 13   83
Cyprus promiseth helpe, but a helpe where comes no
    recomforte. . . . .   35 1st Eclogues 13 119
That that deare Dyamond, where wisdome holdeth a sure seate,   37 1st Eclogues 13 165
Of my owne harte, where thoughts be the temple, sighte is an
    aultar. . . . .   37 1st Eclogues 13 171
That where you are no wished good can want; . . . .   39 Arcadia II   16   6
Sorrowes ill easde, where sorrowes painted be. . . . .   41 Arcadia II   21   6
What hope to quench, where each thing blowes the fire? . . .   42 Arcadia II   21   18
Dicus. Dorus, tell me, where is thy wonted motion. . . . . .   47 2nd Eclogues 28   1
Theere seeke defence where weakenesse is the force: . . . . .   49 2nd Eclogues 28   77
I spied a thrush where she did make her nest, ...   54 2nd Eclogues 29   82
I sawe her arme, where purest Lillies cleave. . . . .   55 2nd Eclogues 29 104
Ah where was first that cruell cunning found, ...   57 2nd Eclogues 30   11
Where it should be to selfe-destruction bound? . . . .   57 2nd Eclogues 30   13
Where death is feard, and life is held with paine. . . . . .   57 2nd Eclogues 30   19
Where chaunge of thoughts one foole to other shewes, ...   57 2nd Eclogues 30   21
Where witt but serves, to have true tast of woes. . . . . . .   57 2nd Eclogues 30   25
A Shop of shame, a Booke where blots be rife . . . .   57 2nd Eclogues 30   26
Where all good haps a perfect state maintaine? . . . .   58 2nd Eclogues 30   40
Shall I that saw those brests, where beauties flow, ...   58 2nd Eclogues 30   47
Her to enjoy, where joy it selfe is thrall, ...   59 2nd Eclogues 30   87
O eyes of mine, where once she saw her face, ...   60 2nd Eclogues 30 116
O braine, where thought of her hath onely place; . . . . . .   60 2nd Eclogues 30 118

```
WHERE                      (CONTINUED)                      PAGE    TITLE          LINE
     Where but a baiting place is all our portion. . . . . . . .   61  2nd Eclogues 30  136
     Oh when shall I be knowne, wher most to be knowne I do
          longe  Long. . . . . . . . . . . . . . . . . . . . . .   64  2nd Eclogues 31   32
     what be the sweet creatures wher lowly demaunds be not
          heard  Hard. . . . . . . . . . . . . . . . . . . . . .   65  2nd Eclogues 31   41
     Where sweet graces erect the stately banner. . . . . . . .   67  2nd Eclogues 33    3
     Where well couched abides a coffer of pearle, . . . . . . .   67  2nd Eclogues 33   10
     Where man's mind hath a freed consideration. . . . . . . .   68  2nd Eclogues 34    3
     Where senses do behold th'order of heav'nly hoste, . . . .   68  2nd Eclogues 34    5
     Where envie's snaky ey, winketh or els dyeth, . . . . . . .   69  2nd Eclogues 34   37
     Where rockes do wayte, for theym the wyndes do chase, . . .   70  Arcadia III  36    2
     Wheare he was bounde, to make his marting place, . . . . .   70  Arcadia III  36    4
     What horrors breede, wheare wynd dominion beares, . . . . .   71  Arcadia III  37    2
     I like this place, wheare at the least the darke . . . . .   73  Arcadia III  39   13
     Where drawing breath, I sucke the aire of woe: . . . . . .   73  Arcadia III  40   10
     Where too much sight, makes all the bodie blinde, . . . . .   73  Arcadia III  40   11
     Wher who so wynns, I put my selfe to flight. . . . . . . .   74  Arcadia III  42    8
     His thoughtes in you, where so sweete thoughtes were spent,   78  Arcadia III  49   10
     Where hers, whom worth makes highest over all, . . . . . .   78  Arcadia III  49   17
     (Her sight where love did forge his fayrest darte) . . . .   79  Arcadia III  51    6
     But nowe each where doth range . . . . . . . . . . . . . .   82  Arcadia III  55    7
     Where love draws hate, and hate engendreth love? . . . . .   85  Arcadia III  61   14
     Where azurde veines well mixt appeere. . . . . . . . . . .   87  Arcadia III  62   56
     Where nothing but impression lackes. . . . . . . . . . . .   88  Arcadia III  62   76
     Where Leda's swanne his feathers mewes, . . . . . . . . . .   89  Arcadia III  62  110
     Where whitenes dooth for ever sitte: . . . . . . . . . . .   90  Arcadia III  62  123
     Where justest love doth vanquish Cupid's powers. . . . . .   91  3rd Eclogues 63    3
     Where that all blisse may raigne, . . . . . . . . . . . . .   91  3rd Eclogues 63   26
     Where simple love, which chastnesse doth imparte, . . . . .   92  3rd Eclogues 63   58
     How can she love where love cannot win trust?) . . . . . .   93  3rd Eclogues 63   85
     Where open hartes do holde so constant place, . . . . . . .   93  3rd Eclogues 63   88
     Where highest notes to godlines are raisd, . . . . . . . .   99  3rd Eclogues 66   31
     For nothing can endure where order n'is. . . . . . . . . .  100  3rd Eclogues 66   51
     Where helping weaker sort, the nobler beastes, . . . . . .  102  3rd Eclogues 66  121
     Where famine ravine taught their hungrie chestes, . . . . .  102  3rd Eclogues 66  124
     To that where thou thy Cupid maist avowe, . . . . . . . . .  106  3rd Eclogues 67  101
     Where they by wisdome's Rules directed are, . . . . . . . .  106  3rd Eclogues 67  104
     In such a case where it appeares that nature . . . . . . .  109  Arcadia IV   70    9
     Where they would leave trophees of cruell damage, . . . . .  109  Arcadia IV   70   12
     Where shade from Sunne, and sporte I sought in evening, . .  111  4th Eclogues 71   14
     Who, where she went, bare in her forhead morning, . . . . .  113  4th Eclogues 71   70
     Where life is death, and death cannot breed peace. . . . .  116  4th Eclogues 72   95
     A silence sweet each where with one consent embraste . . .  117  4th Eclogues 73    7
     And that he thence must part where to live onely I lyved..   123  4th Eclogues 74   30
     Of what was good, where now no good doth lie; . . . . . . .  127  4th Eclogues 75   74
     Since bashfull dread seekes where he knowes me harmed: . .  135  Cert Sonnets  1    2
     Where bee nowe those Joyes, that I lately tasted? . . . . .  138  Cert Sonnets  5    5
     Where bee nowe those eyes ever Inly persers? . . . . . . .  138  Cert Sonnets  5    6
     Where bee now those wordes never Idelly wasted, . . . . . .  138  Cert Sonnets  5    7
     Where ys Ah that face, that a Sunne defaces? . . . . . . .  138  Cert Sonnets  5    9
     Where bee those wellcomes by no worthe deserved? . . . . .  138  Cert Sonnets  5   10
     Where bee those movinges, the Delights, the graces?. . . .  138  Cert Sonnets  5   11
     Where each part in such peace dwelleth, . . . . . . . . . .  140  Cert Sonnets  7   16
     As treasure house where her best gifts abyde.. . . . . . .  141  Cert Sonnets  8    8
     A seate where beauty shines and vertue raignes, . . . . . .  141  Cert Sonnets  8   10
     Where her who should rule paine, false paine abuseth.. . .  142  Cert Sonnets 11   14
     Releast from Court, where envie needes must be.. . . . . .  143  Cert Sonnets 12    6
     And thence cast off, where his sweete hurt he found, . . .  144  Cert Sonnets 15    6
     Both force to flie and knowledge where to fall.. . . . . .  144  Cert Sonnets 15   12
     Myne eyes thence drawne, where lived all their light, . . .  149  Cert Sonnets 21    5
     Large roomes within, where droppes distill amaine: . . . .  150  Cert Sonnets 22   32
     A field there is where, if a stake be prest. . . . . . . .  150  Cert Sonnets 22   41
     Where plagu'd for rash attempt, gives up his ghost, . . . .  151  Cert Sonnets 22   57
     Where fairnesse yeelds to wisdome's shortest raines. . . .  151  Cert Sonnets 22   64
     Where former blisse present evils do staine, . . . . . . .  153  Cert Sonnets 24   12
     Where by the death of all deaths, . . . . . . . . . . . . .  154  Cert Sonnets 25   13
     Where that heat of all heates springeth, . . . . . . . . .  155  Cert Sonnets 26    7
     End the way, where all men stay. No, no, no, no. . . . . .  155  Cert Sonnets 26   22
     Where my soule I have engaged? . . . . . . . . . . . . . .  157  Cert Sonnets 27   28
     Or where one's love so constant bene, . . . . . . . . . . .  158  Cert Sonnets 28   27
     Where, "sooner die then change my state", . . . . . . . . .  158  Cert Sonnets 28   35
     Where she his counsell keepeth, . . . . . . . . . . . . . .  160  Cert Sonnets 30   35
     To that sweet yoke, where lasting freedomes be: . . . . . .  161  Cert Sonnets 32    6
     Where with most ease and warmth he might employ his art: .  168  Astrophil     8    7
     To my close heart, where while some firebrands he did lay, .  169  Astrophil     8   13
     Where roses gueuls are borne in silver field.. . . . . . .  171  Astrophil    13   11
     Where truth it selfe must speake like flatterie? . . . . .  182  Astrophil    35    2
     Where Nature doth with infinite agree? . . . . . . . . . .  182  Astrophil    35    4
     Where Cupid is sworne page to Chastity?. . . . . . . . . .  182  Astrophil    35    8
     The schooles where Venus hath learn'd Chastitie. . . . . .  185  Astrophil    42    4
     O eyes, where humble lookes most glorious prove, . . . . .  185  Astrophil    42    5
     Where blushing red, that Love's selfe them doth love, . . .  186  Astrophil    43   10
     Where well he knowes, no man to him can come.. . . . . . .  186  Astrophil    43   14
     Then servant's wracke, where new doubts honor brings;. . .  187  Astrophil    45   11
     Where Vertue is made strong by Beautie's might, . . . . . .  188  Astrophil    48    2
     Where Love is chastnesse, Paine doth learne delight, . . .  188  Astrophil    48    3
     Where all my good I do in Stella see, . . . . . . . . . . .  194  Astrophil    60    2
     For Stella hath with words where faith doth shine, . . . .  200  Astrophil    69    9
     That conversation sweet, where such high comforts be, . . .  205  Astrophil    77   10
```

WHERE	(CONTINUED)	PAGE	TITLE		LINE
Pleasingst consort, where each sence holds a part,		206	Astrophil	79	3
The friendly fray, where blowes both wound and heale,		206	Astrophil	79	10
Breakefast of Love, but lo, lo, where she is,		206	Astrophil	79	13
The new Pernassus, where the Muses bide,		207	Astrophil	80	5
Where Beautie's blush in Honour's graine is dide..		207	Astrophil	80	8
Nymph of the gard'n, where all beauties be:.		207	Astrophil	82	1
In Lillies' neast, where Love's selfe lies along..		208	Astrophil	83	8
Tc her, where I my heart safeliest shall meet.		209	Astrophil	84	6
Then those blest eyes, where all my hopes do dwell,		212	Astrophil	86	13
Where memory sets foorth the beames of love.		223	Astrophil	88	11
That where before hart loved and eyes did see,		223	Astrophil	88	12
Ah bed, the field where joye's peace some do see,		230	Astrophil	98	1
The field where all my thoughts to warre be traind,		230	Astrophil	98	2
As can refresh the hell where my soule fries..		231	Astrophil	100	8
Where be those Roses gone, which sweetned so our eyes?		232	Astrophil	102	1
Where those red cheeks, which oft with faire encrease did frame.		232	Astrophil	102	2
Where rigrows exile lockes up all my sense?.		233	Astrophil	104	8
What saist thou now, where is that dainty cheere		235	Astrophil	106	5
Who hath the lips, where wit in fairnesse raigneth,		197	A&S 1st Song		9
I thought each place was darke but where thy lights would be		212	A&S 5th Song		5
As where thou soone mightst helpe, most faith dost most oppresse,		213	A&S 5th Song		41
Where birds wanton musicke made,		217	A&S 8th Song		2
Whose beames, where they once are darted,		218	A&S 8th Song		35
Where thou art not formost placed,		220	A&S 8th Song		87
Where you may have some defence.		221	A&S 9th Song		3
Wher godly men do their assembly make.		270	Psalm I		18
And only hunt, where lyes do ly?		273	Psalm IV		10
Where I have found more heart's delight.		274	Psalm IV		28
O bragging Foe, where is the endless wast.		280	Psalm IX		16
Where who may contemplate Thee		289	Psalm XVI		39
Where Israel Thy lawdes is ever telling;		298	Psalm XXII		10
There where the Lord of all.		301	Psalm XXIII		26
Where then should my eyes be		304	Psalm XXV		55
The House where Thou dost dwell,		306	Psalm XXVI		26
Ev'n where Thou makest Thy honour's biding place..		306	Psalm XXVI		27
To the pitt where flesh doth end..		308	Psalm XXVIII		5
Where Thy sanctuary stands,		309	Psalm XXVIII		8
Ev'en Deserts where the Arabs byde..		310	Psalm XXIX		21
But his deare favour where it lyes .		311	Psalm XXX		14
And ev'en my bones consume where they be plac't.		312	Psalm XXXI		30
Feare was each where, while they their counsells led		313	Psalm XXXI		38
Ev'en where he dwelleth hee.		317	Psalm XXXIII		52
I will thank Thee, where congregations sitt,		322	Psalm XXXV		46
Even where I do most store of people find;		322	Psalm XXXV		47
Aha! Sir, now we see you where we should..		322	Psalm XXXV		54
They are but shades not true things where we live,		330	Psalm XXXIX		19
Where I in horrors lay,		331	Psalm XL		7
And turn his couch, where sick he couched late,		333	Psalm XLI		11
Where 'gainst Thee lay my sin.		333	Psalm XLI		16
Where is now Thy God so good?.		334	Psalm XLII		12
From the grounds where Jordan slideth.		335	Psalm XLII		27
Where hath now your God his biding?.		335	Psalm XLII		48
For where he most would hit, he ever yet did misse..		241	Other Poems	1	2
Where failing is a shame, and breaking is his best..		241	Other Poems	1	6
Where snugging well he well appear'd content		244	Other Poems	4	103
Where piercing witts do quickly apprehend,		245	Other Poems	4	142
Where bold and hurtles many plays he tries,		247	Other Poems	4	194
A-field they goe, where many lookers be,		247	Other Poems	4	217
And part must folowe where whole man doth goe.		253	Other Poems	4	422
And comming where he hop'd to be alone,		253	Other Poems	4	439
That from those eies where heav'nly apples bene,		253	Other Poems	4	450
He saw behind a bush where Klaius sate:.		255	Other Poems	4	527
Where by his words his self-like cause he knew..		256	Other Poems	4	536
Her eares where Musique lives,		258	Other Poems	5	60
Where with heate oppreste I was,		262	Other Poems	7	2
Where greene leaves did newly bud.		262	Other Poems	7	4
Where we once our lovely sheepe.		262	Other Poems	7	21
"Where how many Creatures be,		263	Other Poems	7	49
WHEREAS					
Whereas if I a gratefull gardien have,		135	Cert Sonnets	1	13
That whereas blacke seemes Beautie's contrary,		168	Astrophil	7	10
WHEREAT					
The Moone a sunder rent; whereat with sodaine fall		118	4th Eclogues	73	57
Whereat I did but jeast.		158	Cert Sonnets	28	16
WHEREBY					
Whereby that being aye must be conserved..		106	3rd Eclogues	67	81
Whereby Thou stop'st Thyne Enemy's prating		278	Psalm VIII		7
Of Conquerd states, wherby such fame you gott?		280	Psalm IX		17
WHEREIN					
I layde my face; my face wherein there lyes.		41	Arcadia II	21	3
Wherein do only flowrish		66	2nd Eclogues	32	32
Wherin no eare can have joy,		66	2nd Eclogues	32	37
Wherin I burne, thy breath is		67	2nd Eclogues	32	44
My cheefest parte, wherin do chieflye stand.		70	Arcadia III	35	13
Blacke incke becommes the state wherein I dye.		81	Arcadia III	54	6
Wherein the birde doth never sing but cry;		105	3rd Eclogues	67	50

WHEREIN	(CONTINUED)	PAGE	TITLE		LINE
But cald, she came apace; a pace wherein did move.		119	4th Eclogues	73	89
Earth take this earth, wherein my spirits languish..		136	Cert Sonnets	3	16
Wherein she suffring all her spirits' languish,		137	Cert Sonnets	4	15
But that good part, wherein all comforts be,		148	Cert Sonnets	20	11
Lies hatching still the goods wherein they flow:		176	Astrophil	24	2
With words, wherein the Muses' treasures be,		195	Astrophil	60	7
"The sportes wherin I wonted to do well,		254	Other Poems	4	465

WHERECF

The quiet mind (whereof my selfe empairer is,		51	2nd Eclogues	28	114
Whereof this Beautie can be but a shade,		167	Astrophil	5	10
Whereof, with whom, how often did she talke,		225	Astrophil	92	11
Wherof if but a sparke once kindled be, you all.		272	Psalm II		29

WHERECN

Right so my thoughts, whereon my hart I feede:		78	Arcadia III	50	5

WHERETO

Whereto mine inward thoughts did faintly yeeld;		11	Arcadia I	2	6
Of that, whereto he feard she was enclinde,		95	3rd Eclogues	64	50
Whereto you knowe, his honest harte were loath.		95	3rd Eclogues	64	60
Whereto two parties once be full content..		97	3rd Eclogues	64	126
Whereto I yeeld, and seeke no other breath,		114	4th Eclogues	72	18
Far from my thoughts was ought, whereto their minds aspire,		117	4th Eclogues	73	15
For in each thing wherto mine eye doth range,		147	Cert Sonnets	18	3
Whereto long since, through my long battred eyes,		182	Astrophil	36	3
Chiefe good, whereto my hope dcth only aspire,		200	Astrophil	68	3
So all things whereto that man doth bend,		270	Psalm I		11
Wherto their tongue is flattring Instrument.		275	Psalm V		28
Wherto my heart did give me;		315	Psalm XXXII		15

WHEREWITH

Dorus. Blest be the name, wherewith my mistres named is:		49	2nd Eclogues	28	55
How hast thou framde the paine wherewith I am opprest?		121	4th Eclogues	73	184
Wherewith my father once made it halfe tame;		180	Astrophil	30	10
The raines wherewith my Rider doth me tie,		189	Astrophil	49	5
Or else pronouncing grace, wherewith his mind.		194	Astrophil	58	7
See now those feathers pluckt, wherewith thou flewst most high:		213	A&S 5th Song		22
D. Teares drink, sorowes meat, wherewith, not I, but in me my death lives..		344	Possibly	1	34

WHETHER

To whether with best cause the Nymphes faire flowers affoord		52	2nd Eclogues	29	28
Now whether mov'd with selfe unworthines,		94	3rd Eclogues	64	7
Whether he needes must goe for feare of blame.		96	3rd Eclogues	64	78
At which, whether the others did repine,		100	3rd Eclogues	66	57
Whether the Turkish new-moone minded be.		179	Astrophil	30	1
Whether with words this soveraignty he gaine,		194	Astrophil	58	5
I would know whether she did sit or walke,		225	Astrophil	92	9
Whether absence have had force		225	A&S 10th Song		4
Say whether of the choice.		215	A&S 6th Song		3
Say whether thou wilt crowne,		217	A&S 6th Song		53
Whether I silent did remain,		315	Psalm XXXII		8
Fcr Pas, whether it were for feare, or love,		250	Other Poems	4	327

WHETST

Therfore thou whetst Thy sword, and bend'st Thy bow,		278	Psalm VII		34

WHICH

Are all my thoughts, in which I live or die:		3	Lady of May	2	10
An uncouth love, which Nature hateth most.		11	Arcadia I	1	4
As for those parts unknowne, which hidden sure are best:		12	Arcadia I	3	13
Happie be they which well beleeve, and never seeke the rest.		12	Arcadia I	3	14
For other be those tunes which sorrow tyes,		13	Arcadia I	4	7
From those cleere notes which freely may rejoyce..		13	Arcadia I	4	8
Hardly they heard, which by good hunters singled be.		14	1st Eclogues	7	10
Which of us two deserveth most compassion.		15	1st Eclogues	7	18
A Lillie field, with plowe of Rose which tilled is..		15	1st Eclogues	7	30
O happie Gods, which by inward assumption.		15	1st Eclogues	7	40
And Love, which lover hurts is inhumanitie".		16	1st Eclogues	7	66
Doth beauties keep, which never Sunne can burne,		18	1st Eclogues	7	118
Which if you will (o doo) bestow on me,		18	1st Eclogues	7	121
The thought of which doth passe all worldly pelfe.		18	1st Eclogues	7	130
In which do light small birds of thoughts orethrowne:		18	1st Eclogues	7	141
Which so much reason beares,		18	1st Eclogues	7	148
Let crowes picke out mine eyes, which saw too much:		19	1st Eclogues	7	149
Let crowes picke out mine eyes which too much sawe..		19	1st Eclogues	7	V149
Which doth to ashes burne:		19	1st Eclogues	7	155
Which being nought seems somewhat to the eyen,		19	1st Eclogues	7	164
Which thought doth marre my piping declaration,		19	1st Eclogues	7	168
Whiche beares the bytt a weaker force doth guide,		20	1st Eclogues	7	V959
Such weight it hath which once is full possest..		20	1st Eclogues	7	V961
Above line repeated at following location.		20	1st Eclogues	7	V962
Which hath in others' head his only being.		20	1st Eclogues	7	V964
Which breeds nought else but gloses of deceits..		20	1st Eclogues	8	4
Cloth'd in the shape which soonest may deceave:		21	1st Eclogues	8	32
But for that Love is worst, which rules the eyes,		22	1st Eclogues	8	V 41
With outward joyes, which inly cannot sincke,		22	1st Eclogues	9	7
That which we see in many time hath wrought,		22	1st Eclogues	9	14
Then cries to sencelesse things, which neither knowes.		23	1st Eclogues	9	41
Those rebell thoughts which are thy slaves by kinde.		23	1st Eclogues	9	46
Were in his dayes: which heard, one nothing heares,		24	1st Eclogues	9	76
Fondly blame that to which your selves aspire.		25	1st Eclogues	9	104
Which both the pallate, and the eyes delight..		26	1st Eclogues	9	131

Which should most miseries, cast on a worme that I am. . . .   29 1st Eclogues 11   2
Which is helde in love, love it is, that hath joynde . . . .   31 1st Eclogues 12   23
But o happy be you, which safe from fyry reflection. . . . .   31 1st Eclogues 13   11
Happy be those mishapps which, justly proportion holding,. .   32 1st Eclogues 13   17
But wretched be the soules which, vaild in a contrary
     subject, ... 32 1st Eclogues 13   19
Which must frame contempt to the fittest purchase of
     honnour . . . .   32 1st Eclogues 13   38
Of carking agonies (to estates which still be adherent). . .   34 1st Eclogues 13   97
Nurse inwarde maladyes, which have not scope to be breath'd
     out, ... 35 1st Eclogues 13 104
Which shootes strongly with out any noyse and deadly without
     smarte. . . . .   35 1st Eclogues 13 122
Ashe makes speares which shieldes do resist, her force no
     repulse takes: . . . .   36 1st Eclogues 13 136
Then do I shape to my selfe that forme which raigns so with
     in me, ...   36 1st Eclogues 13 142
"Cnley Juell, O only Juell, which cnly deservest . . . . . .   36 1st Eclogues 13 147
Thus by thy worke, disdaine not that which is by thy selfe
     done.. . . . .   36 1st Eclogues 13 152
Ne let white haires, which on my face doo grow,. . . . . . .   38 Arcadia II   15   5
Which makes all eyes doo honour unto you.. . . . .   38 Arcadia II   15   8
My sheepe are thoughts, which I both guide and serve:. . . .   39 Arcadia II   17   1
My sheepehooke is wanne hope, which all upholdes:. . . . . .   39 Arcadia II   17   5
A voice may come, which troubled soule doth yeld:. . . . . .   40 Arcadia II   18   4
Which makes us most immortall shape to weare,. . . . .   40 Arcadia II   18   14
Clusters of clowdes, which no Sunne ever cleares.. . . . . .   41 Arcadia II   21   4
Which ever shines, though hid from earth by earthly shade, .   44 Arcadia II   26   3
R. O foolish thing, which glory doeste destroye. . . . . . .   46 2nd Eclogues 27   19
Which Passions kill, and Reason do deface. . . . .   47 2nd Eclogues 27   42
Of my due faith, which needs must be immutable?. . . . . . .   47 2nd Eclogues 28   8
With words so vile, which viler breath doth breed. . . . . .   50 2nd Eclogues 28   82
Which do envenome both the soule and senses. . . . .   50 2nd Eclogues 28   88
Who judge that honour, which hath scope to slander.. . . . .   50 2nd Eclogues 28   91
Which who doth misse his eyes are but delusions, ...   51 2nd Eclogues 28 108
From any joy, which might her griefe occasion. . . . .   51 2nd Eclogues 28 122
Which oft he lifteth up, and stayes his lifted pawe, ...   53 2nd Eclogues 29   34
Deepe musing to himselfe, which after-mewing showes, ...   53 2nd Eclogues 29   35
Which made a Bay, made Bay a holy tree:. . . . .   54 2nd Eclogues 29   61
In perfect light, which could not me deceave,. . . . .   55 2nd Eclogues 29 100
From Cosma's eyes, which full in darkenes shine, ...   55 2nd Eclogues 29 103
Let cat and dog fight which shall have both you. . . . . . .   56 2nd Eclogues 29 149
The one, which tother would refrayne. . . . .   57 2nd Eclogues 30   4
(Even like a toppe which nought but whipping moves). . . . .   58 2nd Eclogues 30   33
Griefe is the stone which finest judgement proves: . . . . .   58 2nd Eclogues 30   35
Relent those thoughts, which then did so displease?. . . . .   58 2nd Eclogues 30   52
To those high powers, which idly sit above,. . . . .   58 2nd Eclogues 30   63
Tc causefull wrath, which thou canst not resist. . . . . . .   59 2nd Eclogues 30   66
We mone that lost, which had we did bemone. . . . .   59 2nd Eclogues 30   82
Upon thy spoiles, which never should lye waste?. . . . . . .   59 2nd Eclogues 30   93
Such beames so like his owne, which might have might . . . .   60 2nd Eclogues 30 105
Which nothing spares, to melt that Virgin-waxe . . . .   60 2nd Eclogues 30 108
Which while it is, it is all Asia's light. . . . .   60 2nd Eclogues 30 109
Her face which was more lively in my hart; . . . .   60 2nd Eclogues 30 117
O hand, which toucht her hand when we did part;. . . . . . .   60 2nd Eclogues 30 119
Tc that strange stroke which conquer'd all my senses,. . . .   61 2nd Eclogues 30 165
We pittie deeme that which but weakenes is:. . . . .   62 2nd Eclogues 30 180
And what manner a mind which had to that humor a vaine?
     Vaine.. . . . .   63 2nd Eclogues 31   9
What be the joyes for which to enjoy they went to the
     paines Paines..   63 2nd Eclogues 31   14
Arte? what can be that art which thou dost meane by thy
     speche? Speche..   64 2nd Eclogues 31   29
Curs'd be thy selfe for cursing that which leades me to
     joies. Toies.. . . . .   65 2nd Eclogues 31   40
Mock'st thou those Diamonds which only be matcht by the
     gods Ods.. . . . .   65 2nd Eclogues 31   47
Which at firste voly gave too open entry,. . . . .   68 2nd Eclogues 33   14
(Whiche hyding didest preserve that beawtie's light, ...   70 Arcadia III 35   2
Whiche dazeling still, dothe still maynteine my sight; . . .   70 Arcadia III 35   6
Chief band I saye, which tyes my chiefest parte, ...   70 Arcadia III 35   12
Those secrett joyes, which heaven to me emparte, ...   70 Arcadia III 35   14
The laborer, which cursed earthe up teares . . . .   71 Arcadia III 36   7
My thoughts forget: my thoughts, which never swerve. . . . .   72 Arcadia III 38   3
Since all the thinges which give mine eyes their light . . .   73 Arcadia III 39   5
Betwixt which two in me I have this fight, ...   74 Arcadia III 42   7
I waste my harte, which still newe torment tryes.. . . . . .   75 Arcadia III 43   5
Hid heere his hopes, by which he might aspire. . . . .   75 Arcadia III 44   7
O Words which fall like sommer deaw on me, ...   76 Arcadia III 46   1
O toong in which, all honyed likoures bee, ...   76 Arcadia III 46   3
O brest in which two white sheepe swell in pride:. . . . . .   76 Arcadia III 46   10
Deeper engrav'd, which salve nor time can save,. . . . . . .   77 Arcadia III 47   5
Which barde desires, (barde by my selfe) imparte.. . . . . .   77 Arcadia III 47   11
You goodly pines, which still with brave assent. . . . . . .   77 Arcadia III 49   1
My hopes which do but to mine owne aspire? . . . .   80 Arcadia III 53   4
With circkled course, which no wise stay can trye, ...   81 Arcadia III 54   10
That childish stuffe which knowes not frendes from foes, . .   81 Arcadia III 54   11
Hurte not the face, which nothing can amende". . . . .   82 Arcadia III 55   15
(Which oft to hope laies out a guilefull baite,. . . . . . .   82 Arcadia III 56   2

To ease those paines, which on desire do waite). . . . . . .   82 Arcadia III 56   4
Away vayne Cares, by which fewe men do finde . . . .   83 Arcadia III 59   3
The love which is imprinted in my soule. . . . .   85 Arcadia III 61   1
Which on cold winter's face doth grow. . . . .   85 Arcadia III 62   8
No Sunne, which shines, and seeth not, ...   86 Arcadia III 62   18
Which onely thus unhappie be, ...   86 Arcadia III 62   21
Which blessed still themselves doo kisse. . . . .   87 Arcadia III 62   38
Which never part but that they showe . . . .   87 Arcadia III 62   41
The neck, in which strange graces lurke. . . . .   87 Arcadia III 62   48
Which skill dooth make in Princes' bowers. . . . .   87 Arcadia III 62   50
Then that which beares the mylken name.. . . . .   87 Arcadia III 62   60
Which onely still doth Lillies yeeld:. . . . .   87 Arcadia III 62   62
Which flanked with two sugred flankes, ...   88 Arcadia III 62   89
Which leaded are with silver skinne, ...   89 Arcadia III 62 115
Which conduit-like with curious crookes, ...   90 Arcadia III 62 128
Which doth even beautie beautifie, ...   90 Arcadia III 62 137
Of fairer guest, which dwells within, ...   90 Arcadia III 62 140
Which never may decrease . . . .   91 3rd Eclogues 63   5
Which that no chaunce may staine, ...   91 3rd Eclogues 63   8
In which delightfull paine, ...   91 3rd Eclogues 63   17
Yee Muses all which chaste affects allow, ...   91 3rd Eclogues 63   19
Yee Nymphes which in the waters empire have, ...   92 3rd Eclogues 63   28
Graunt to the thing which we for Lalus crave.. . . . .   92 3rd Eclogues 63   30
Of yonglings, which thy selfe with love hast rearde, ...   92 3rd Eclogues 63   43
In which most lovely traine, ...   92 3rd Eclogues 63   53
Which though of glittring golde, shall heere take rust . . .   92 3rd Eclogues 63   57
Where simple love, which chastnesse doth imparte, ...   92 3rd Eclogues 63   58
Which being pure and plaine, ...   93 3rd Eclogues 63   62
All waywardnes, which nothing kindly brookes, ...   93 3rd Eclogues 63   66
He forst her thinke that which she never thought.. . . . . .   95 3rd Eclogues 64   34
In that which he so fear'd that she should meet. . . . . . .   95 3rd Eclogues 64   36
Which little time did fitlie bring to passe. . . . .   96 3rd Eclogues 64   76
A letter such which might from either part . . . .   96 3rd Eclogues 64   81
This mourning inck, in which my hart doth bleede.. . . . . .   96 3rd Eclogues 64   96
And with some words which shewed little care, ...   97 3rd Eclogues 64 118
Then gave he him the blow which never smarted. . . . .   97 3rd Eclogues 64 120
Saving the glowe worme, which would curteous be. . . . . . .   98 3rd Eclogues 66   6
Then founde I which thing is a charge to beare . . . .   99 3rd Eclogues 66   17
Which now in night's deepe shade sheep heard of me.. . . . .   99 3rd Eclogues 66   42
At which, whether the others did repine, ... 100 3rd Eclogues 66   57
So hastily that which they would repent: . . . . 100 3rd Eclogues 66   69
Which streight the Earth yclothed in his claye:. . . . . . . 101 3rd Eclogues 66   79
Crocodile, teares, which might be falsely spilde:. . . . . . 101 3rd Eclogues 66   96
Iron to seeke, which gainst it selfe should bend, ...   102 3rd Eclogues 66 116
Which being done he afterwards would kill. . . . . 102 3rd Eclogues 66 126
For murdre done, which never erst was seene, ... 102 3rd Eclogues 66 127
Which who so wants, halfe of himselfe doth misse.. . . . . . 103 3rd Eclogues 67   9
Which drawne-out line doth hold all humane blisse. . . . . . 105 3rd Eclogues 67   72
Which must by this immortall be preserved, ... 105 3rd Eclogues 67   77
But these be your love-toyes, which still are spent. . . . . 106 3rd Eclogues 67   94
Sweete supple mindes which soone to wisdome bowe . . . . . . 106 3rd Eclogues 67 103
Which touch the father's hart with secret joy, ... 106 3rd Eclogues 67 113
Those passions which to youthfull head doo clime, ...   107 3rd Eclogues 67 116
The seate of peace, the throne which is erected. . . . . . . 108 Arcadia IV   69   3
Witnesse his wrong which by thy helpe is eased:. . . . . . . 108 Arcadia IV   69   11
(Which may be know'n, but never help't with wailing) . . . . 109 Arcadia IV   70   14
Yee Nimphes which haunt the springs in pleasant vallies, . . 111 4th Eclogues 71   2
Which to my woes gives still an early morning: . . . . 111 4th Eclogues 71   5
Which oft hath Echo tir'd in secrete forrests. . . . . 111 4th Eclogues 71   12
Which troubles their daye's worke, and joyes of evening: . . 112 4th Eclogues 71   33
I studie that which moste may me displease, ...   113 4th Eclogues 72   5
And seeke to nourish that, which now contaynes . . . . 114 4th Eclogues 72   22
Which is the hatefull web of Sorowe's paines.. . . . . 114 4th Eclogues 72   25
Is that huge storme, which powres it selfe on me:. . . . . . 114 4th Eclogues 72   32
The darkened heav'n my soule which nought can see; . . . . . 114 4th Eclogues 72   35
The flying sprites which trees by rootes up teare. . . . . . 114 4th Eclogues 72   36
Be those despaires, which have my hopes quite wast.. . . . . 114 4th Eclogues 72   37
I harowe it with Thoughts, which all conspire. . . . . 115 4th Eclogues 72   54
Lamde with the angle, which it selfe did beare, ...   115 4th Eclogues 72   67
Alas I doo; from which to finde release, ... 116 4th Eclogues 72   92
Did light those beamye stars which greater light did darke:. 116 4th Eclogues 73   3
Now each thing which enjoy'd that firie quickning sparke .   116 4th Eclogues 73   4
(Which life is cald) were mov'd their spirits to repose, . . 116 4th Eclogues 73   5
My senses such release, as they which quiet live, ...   117 4th Eclogues 73   12
Which heav'nly purest gifts defile in muddy cares. . . . . . 117 4th Eclogues 73   18
Which senses up doth shut the senses to preserve. . . . . .   117 4th Eclogues 73   28
(Which made of heav'nly stuffe no mortal chaunge doth bynde) 117 4th Eclogues 73   32
Of samothea lande; a lande, which whilom stood . . . . 117 4th Eclogues 73   36
Her haire, which by the helpe of painter's cunning, shinde.. 118 4th Eclogues 73   74
That which their mother hight, or els their silly seed.. . . 119 4th Eclogues 73   84
Which lest the ruinous want of government dissolve; . . . .   120 4th Eclogues 73 128
Now resteth onely this, which of us two is she, ...   120 4th Eclogues 73 135
Such proffer made, which she well showd with smiling cheere. 120 4th Eclogues 73 144
Which inke onely relates, but ne laments, ne replies?. . . . 122 4th Eclogues 74   18
Or those golden lockes, those lockes which lock me to
    bondage, ... 123 4th Eclogues 74   51
Or with a fair hand's nailes (o hand which nailes me to this
    death). . . . . 123 4th Eclogues 74   55
But what's this for a fault, for which such faieth be
    abolisht, ... 124 4th Eclogues 74   69

Bend your thoghts to the dear sweet words which then to me
    giv'n were:. . . . .   124 4th Eclogues 74   75
And you, o flowers, which sometimes Princes were,. . . . . .   125 4th Eclogues 75   25
That they, which have no lives, should live so long, ...   126 4th Eclogues 75   41
O light of Sunne, which is entit'led day,. . . . .   126 4th Eclogues 75   52
Yee dimmy clowdes, which well employ your stayning . . . . .   127 4th Eclogues 75   67
In shape, which by man's eye might be perceived;. . . . . .   127 4th Eclogues 75   71
But Man which helpeth them, helplesse must perish. . . . . .   127 4th Eclogues 75   87
Thus, thus the mindes, which over all doo clime,. . . . . .   127 4th Eclogues 75   88
O Phisicke's power, which (some say) hath refrayned. . . . .   128 4th Eclogues 75   109
They are but words therefore which men do buy,. . . . . . .   128 4th Eclogues 75   115
Which he of us for ever hath deserved. . . . .   129 4th Eclogues 75   138
Which to our darkned mindes was best direction;. . . . . . .   129 4th Eclogues 76   9
Why should we feare that which we cannot flye? . . . .   131 Arcadia V   77   4
Which were not evill, well vew'd in reason's light. . . . .   131 Arcadia V   77   8
Our owly eyes, which dimm'd with passions bee, ...   131 Arcadia V   77   9
On those affectes which easily yeeld to sight, ...   135 Cert Sonnets 2   6
To see my night of evils, which hath no morow. . . . .   136 Cert Sonnets 3   8
Which once said what I conceaved,. . . . .   139 Cert Sonnets 7   5
Her breath which makes a sower answer sweete,. . . . .   141 Cert Sonnets 9   6
Like as the Dove which seeled up doth flie,. . . . .   144 Cert Sonnets 15   1
With sound of horne, which he him selfe did blow,. . . . . .   145 Cert Sonnets 16   2
It makes them flie that which they faine would have: . . . .   145 Cert Sonnets 16   6
Even thus might I, for doubts which I conceave . . . .   145 Cert Sonnets 16   9
Which Poets say, the gods them selves do feare,. . . . . . .   146 Cert Sonnets 17   7
To twist those broyles, which hardly would untwine:. . . . .   146 Cert Sonnets 17   22
Scme cause there is, which of strange cause doth rise: . . .   147 Cert Sonnets 18   2
The Rockes which were of constant mind the marke . . . . . .   147 Cert Sonnets 18   5
Finding those beames, which I must ever love,. . . . .   149 Cert Sonnets 21   1
Even as the flye, which to the flame doth goe,. . . . . . .   149 Cert Sonnets 21   11
The Bruertons have a Lake, which when the Sunne. . . . . . .   150 Cert Sonnets 22   11
From hidnest depth, which tribute when it ends,. . . . . . .   150 Cert Sonnets 22   13
Which caught, to cruell search yeelds his chiefe part: . . .   150 Cert Sonnets 22   22
Which though despisde, yet still doth truth endure. . . . .   150 Cert Sonnets 22   40
Of which, how much may pierce to that sweete seate,. . . . .   151 Cert Sonnets 22   46
But all the rest, which feare durst not applie,. . . . . . .   151 Cert Sonnets 22   49
Which rotting on the rockes, their death do dye: . . . . . .   151 Cert Sonnets 22   52
A bird which gets more life then ship had lost.. . . . . . .   151 Cert Sonnets 22   54
Which seeming lesse, yet nobler life doth move.. . . . . . .   151 Cert Sonnets 22   60
A light which doth dissever, ...   152 Cert Sonnets 23   5
A light which dying never, ...   152 Cert Sonnets 23   7
Which as of inward glorie. . . . .   152 Cert Sonnets 23   29
Which die not in that weale. . . . .   152 Cert Sonnets 23   32
What kind of fires they be in which those spirits melt,. . .   153 Cert Sonnets 24   7
Which Epitaph containeth,. . . . .   160 Cert Sonnets 30   25
Leave me o Love, which reachest but to dust, ...   161 Cert Sonnets 32   1
Grow rich in that which never taketh rust: . . . .   161 Cert Sonnets 32   3
Which breakes the clowdes and opens forth the light,. . . .   161 Cert Sonnets 32   7
In this small course which birth drawes out to death,. . . .   144 Cert Sonnets 32   10
Love gave the wound, which while I breathe will bleed: . . .   165 Astrophil   2   2
Of herbes or beastes, which Inde or Afrike hold. . . . . . .   166 Astrophil   3   8
An image is, which for our selves we carve;. . . . .   167 Astrophil   5   6
Which elements with mortall mixture breed: . . . .   167 Astrophil   5   11
Queene Vertue's court, which some call Stella's face,. . . .   169 Astrophil   9   1
The doore by which sometimes comes forth her Grace,. . . . .   169 Astrophil   9   5
Red Porphir is, which locke of pearle makes sure:. . . . . .   169 Astrophil   9   6
Whose porches rich (which name of cheekes endure). . . . . .   169 Astrophil   9   7
The windowes now through which this heav'nly guest . . . . .   169 Astrophil   9   9
Which dare claime from those lights the name of best,. . . .   169 Astrophil   9   11
Which Cupid's selfe from Beautie's myne did draw:. . . . . .   169 Astrophil   9   13
Leave sense, and those which sense's objects be. . . . . . .   169 Astrophil   10   7
Which through a bleeding heart his point did shove:. . . . .   171 Astrophil   13   6
Of sinfull thoughts, which do in ruine end?. . . . .   172 Astrophil   14   8
If that be sinne which doth the maners frame,. . . . .   172 Astrophil   14   9
If that be sinne which in fixt hearts doth breed . . . . . .   172 Astrophil   14   12
Which from the ribs of old Parnassus flowes,. . . . .   172 Astrophil   15   2
And everie floure, not sweet perhaps, which growes . . . . .   172 Astrophil   15   3
Beauties, which were of manie Carrets fine,. . . . .   172 Astrophil   16   2
Which others said did make their soules to pine: . . . . . .   173 Astrophil   16   6
Of all those goods, which heav'n to me hath lent:. . . . . .   173 Astrophil   18   4
Which unto it by birthright I do cw:. . . . .   174 Astrophil   18   6
And which is worse, no good excuse can show, ...   174 Astrophil   18   7
Which for reward spoile it with vaine annoyes. . . . .   174 Astrophil   18   11
As that sweete blacke which vailes the heav'nly eye: . . . .   175 Astrophil   20   7
Either to do like him, which open shone, ...   176 Astrophil   22   10
The Sunne which others burn'd, did her but kisse.. . . . . .   176 Astrophil   22   14
(Exil'd for ay from those high treasures, which. . . . . . .   177 Astrophil   24   13
Which inward sunne to Heroicke minde displaies,. . . . . . .   177 Astrophil   25   8
Or for some brawle, which in that chamber hie, ...   178 Astrophil   26   7
Which lookes too oft in his unflattring glasse:. . . . . . .   178 Astrophil   27   10
Breathe out the flames which burne within my heart,. . . . .   179 Astrophil   28   13
A burthned hart. "How can words ease, which are. . . . . . .   181 Astrophil   34   2
That not my soule, which at thy foot did fall, ...   183 Astrophil   36   12
Rich in all beauties which man's eye can see:. . . . .   183 Astrophil   37   6
Rich in those gifts which give th'eternall crowne; . . . . .   183 Astrophil   37   11
Which make the patents of true worldly blisse, ...   183 Astrophil   37   13
His praise to sleight, which from good use doth rise;. . . .   185 Astrophil   41   7
Sent forth the beames, which made so faire my race.. . . . .   185 Astrophil   41   14
O eyes, which do the Spheares of beautie move, ...   185 Astrophil   42   1

Wrackes Triumphs be, which Love (high set) doth breed. . . .   186 Astrophil   42   14
Yet hearing late a fable, which did show . . . .   187 Astrophil   45   5
Leave following that, which it is gaine to misse.. . . . . .   188 Astrophil   47   11
Are humbled thoughts, which bit of Reverence move, ...   189 Astrophil   49   6
Of Hope, which makes it seeme faire to the eye.. . . . . . .   189 Astrophil   49   8
To portrait that which in this world is best.. . . . .   189 Astrophil   50   8
Not this faire outside, which our hearts doth move.. . . . .   190 Astrophil   52   8
Which in her face teach vertue, I could brooke . . . .   193 Astrophil   56   6
Somewhat thy lead'n counsels, which I tooke. . . . .   193 Astrophil   56   7
Which wooed wo, most ravishing delight . . . .   194 Astrophil   58   13
Which would not let me, whom she loved, decline. . . . . . .   196 Astrophil   62   7
I crav'd the thing which ever she denies:. . . . .   196 Astrophil   63   6
But that which once may win thy cruell hart: . . . .   198 Astrophil   64   13
Of everie image, which may comfort show? . . . .   199 Astrophil   66   4
They fled with blush, which guiltie seem'd of love.. . . . .   199 Astrophil   66   14
Stella, those faire lines, which true goodnesse show.. . . .   201 Astrophil   71   4
She comes with light and warmth, which like Aurora prove . .   205 Astrophil   76   5
That presence, which doth give darke hearts a living light:.   205 Astrophil   77   3
That grace, which Venus weepes that she her selfe doth
  misse .. . .   205 Astrophil   77   4
That hand, which without touch holds more then Atlas might;.   205 Astrophil   77   5
Those lips, which make death's pay a meane price for a
  kisse .. . .   205 Astrophil   77   6
Those words, which do sublime the quintessence of blisse:. .   205 Astrophil   77   8
That voyce, which makes the soule plant himselfe in the
  eares: . . . .   205 Astrophil   77   9
Infected by those vapours, which arise . . . .   205 Astrophil   78   2
From out that noysome gulfe, which gaping lies . . . .   205 Astrophil   78   3
Which even of sweetnesse sweetest sweetner art:. . . . . . .   206 Astrophil   79   2
Which, coupling Doves, guides Venus' chariot right.. . . . .   206 Astrophil   79   4
A double key, which opens to the heart,. . . . .   206 Astrophil   79   6
O kisse, which doest those ruddie gemmes impart, ...   207 Astrophil   81   1
O kisse, which soules, even soules together ties . . . . . .   207 Astrophil   81   5
Beauties which do in excellencie passe . . . .   207 Astrophil   82   2
Sweet gard'n Nymph, which keepes the Cherrie tree, ...   208 Astrophil   82   5
Let eares heare speech, which wit to wonder ties,. . . . . .   210 Astrophil   85   11
Safe in my soule, which only doth to thee. . . . .   212 Astrophil   86   6
So darke with misty vapors, which arise. . . . .   228 Astrophil   94   2
For my poore soule, which now that sicknesse tries,. . . . .   228 Astrophil   94   6
Which even to sence, sence of it selfe denies, ...   228 Astrophil   94   7
Takes in that sad hue, which with th'inward night. . . . . .   230 Astrophil   99   7
But when birds charme, and that sweete aire, which is. . . .   231 Astrophil   99   9
Which ay most faire, now more then most faire show,. . . . .   231 Astrophil   100   3
O honied sighs, which from that breast do rise,. . . . . . .   231 Astrophil   100   5
And joy, which is inseperate from those eyes,. . . . .   231 Astrophil   101   7
Where be those Roses gone, which sweetned so our eyes? . . .   232 Astrophil   102   1
Where those red cheeks, which oft with faire encrease did
  frame. . . . .   232 Astrophil   102   2
Which Nature' selfe did make, and selfe engraind the same? .   232 Astrophil   102   6
It is but love, which makes his paper perfit white . . . . .   232 Astrophil   102   12
Curst be the night which did your strife resist, ...   235 Astrophil   105   12
Curst be the Cochman which did drive so fast,. . . . .   235 Astrophil   105   13
Of all the powers which life bestowes on me, ...   236 Astrophil   107   2
Which pants as though it still should leape to thee: . . . .   236 Astrophil   107   6
To this great cause, which needs both use and art, ...   236 Astrophil   107   8
Which now my breast orecharg'd to Musicke lendeth? . . . . .   196 A&S 1st Song   2
Who hath the eyes which marrie state with pleasure,. . . . .   197 A&S 1st Song   5
Who hath the hand which without stroke subdueth,. . . . . .   197 A&S 1st Song   21
Who hath the haire which, loosest, fastest tieth,. . . . . .   197 A&S 1st Song   25
Who hath the voyce, which soule from sences sunders,. . . . . 197 A&S 1st Song   29
Which now my breast orecharg'd to Musicke lendeth? . . . . .   197 A&S 1st Song   34
See the hand which waking gardeth, ...   202 A&S 2nd Song   13
To cadence of the tunes, which Amphyon's lyre did yeeld, . .   208 A&S 3rd Song   4
For rage now rules the reynes, which guided were by
  Pleasure . . . .   213 A&S 5th Song   15
That speech falles now to blame, which did thy honour raise, 213 A&S 5th Song   17
The same key op'n can, which can locke up a treasure.. . . .   213 A&S 5th Song   18
Theeves steal for need, and steale but goods, which paine
  recovers,. . . . .   214 A&S 5th Song   45
Which cannot be restor'd by time nor industrie:. . . . . . .   214 A&S 5th Song   47
Which (I protest) proceed from only Cruell thee, ...   214 A&S 5th Song   53
And which is worse, makes me most guiltlesse torments have,. 214 A&S 5th Song   59
No witchcraft is so evill, as which man's mind destroyeth. . 215 A&S 5th Song   78
Which in them my hopes do cary.. . . . .   226 A&S 10th Song   18
Which do breath a sugred blisse, ...   226 A&S 10th Song   29
Which can make me thus to leave you, ...   235 A&S 11th Song   44
The common sence, which might. . . . .   216 A&S 6th Song   43
Which Musicke can in sky . . . .   217 A&S 6th Song   51
Of which the two life-giving lights are figured in her eyes: 217 A&S 7th Song   16
Which the deere tongue would afford, ...   218 A&S 8th Song   22
Save thy mind which yet surpasseth.. . . . .   219 A&S 8th Song   44
"This small wind which so sweete is, ...   219 A&S 8th Song   57
Which too deep in me is framed, ... 220 A&S 8th Song   99
Which to stones I els would show:. . . . .   221 A&S 9th Song   13
Which night and day he calls to marking mind.. . . . .   270 Psalm I   6
To which sweet springs of waters neighbours be,. . . . . . .   270 Psalm I   8
Which all against me gather,. . . . . 272 Psalm III   21
Thou those men's teeth which byte, ...   273 Psalm III   28
Which beare his people's name, ...   273 Psalm III   35

WHICH	(CONTINUED)	PAGE	TITLE	LINE
O, hearken to my voice, which calls on Thee, ...		274	Psalm V	3
In that, which of fowle wickedness doth smel:.		274	Psalm V	10
To that high doome, which I by Thee must get.		277	Psalm VII	18
Which fall he made to do his neighbor wrong.		278	Psalm VII	42
Which all from Thee their Essence took		278	Psalm VIII	10
Which in the fertile fields be feeding,.		279	Psalm VIII	28
Setting Thy self in Throne, which shined bright.		279	Psalm IX	9
And their Renoune, which seemed so lyke to last, ...		280	Psalm IX	13
Which He prepar'd, to give his judgments high:		280	Psalm IX	22
Which he forgetteth not, nor letteth dy.		280	Psalm IX	34
Ponder the paines, which on me loaden be		280	Psalm IX	37
Down in the pitt, which they themselves had wrought: . . .		280	Psalm IX	47
And in that nett, which they well hidden think,.		280	Psalm IX	48
And that forgetfull sort, which never cares.		281	Psalm IX	54
Which if it last, Woe to all simple Hearts..		285	Psalm XII	27
Do works which earth corrupt and Heaven hates, ...		286	Psalm XIV	5
Which to life true life doth lead:		288	Psalm XVI	38
Which to Thy self my soul will send.		290	Psalm XVII	20
My strength my strongest rock, which my defence hast borne,.		290	Psalm XVIII	2
With hugy darknes, which about his feet did wend.		291	Psalm XVIII	21
About which hee dimme clouds like a Pavilion brings, . . .		291	Psalm XVIII	24
I bett those folks as small as dust, which wind doth rayse;.		293	Psalm XVIII	76
And rid me from the wrongs which cruel Witts did brew; . .		293	Psalm XVIII	87
There is no speech, no language which.		293	Psalm XIX	9
Which righteousness doth take, ...		301	Psalm XXIII	8
Who shall climb to the hill which God's own hill is named, .		302	Psalm XXIV	5
My soul, which Thou didst make,.		304	Psalm XXV	67
Which from suing voice do fly.		309	Psalm XXVIII	10
Ev'en Cedars, which on liban be, ...		310	Psalm XXIX	15
Which they for me with privy craft have set, ...		312	Psalm XXXI	11
To Vanitys, which most trust most deceave, ...		312	Psalm XXXI	17
Let those lips be made dumbe which love to ly, ...		313	Psalm XXXI	49
Which full of spight, of Pride and cruelty,.		313	Psalm XXXI	50
I prayd with prayers which my breast did touch;.		322	Psalm XXXV	32
Which wicked folks do hold so deare;		323	Psalm XXXVI	3
Thy Mercy is! which makes mankind.		324	Psalm XXXVI	20
Which many seeing hearts shall rayse		331	Psalm XL	13
Which should Thy lessons beare		331	Psalm XL	29
Ev'en heapes of wicked thoughts which streight they show . .		333	Psalm XLI	23
As the chafed hart which brayeth		334	Psalm XLII	1
Dick. Faith in my self and worth in her, which no proofe can undoo.		343	Possibly 1	26
D. Her heavenly looks, which more and more do give me cause to crave.		344	Possibly 1	32
Dick. Oh hence! o cruell word! which even doggs do hate: . .		344	Possibly 1	47
Whiche my chefe partte, doth passe throughe, parche, and tye		344	Possibly 2	2
Which to avoyde, quenche, loose noughte booted stryfe. . . .		344	Possibly 2	8
Which seated is, in spotlesse honor's fielde,.		345	Possibly 4	2
When strong Desire, which vertue's love doth guide,.		345	Possibly 4	7
For creeping rimes, which often sighings choke.		242	Other Poems 4	8
Train'd in the life which on short-bitten grasse		242	Other Poems 4	19
To catch hir sparrow which from hir did swerve,.		244	Other Poems 4	84
Which to their eies the bowles of Venus brought, ...		244	Other Poems 4	99
Hir hands which pierc'd the soule's seav'n-double shield,. .		246	Other Poems 4	147
The lesson which but late he learn'd too furre:.		246	Other Poems 4	174
To which hir presence such a feaver brought.		246	Other Poems 4	176
Which soone as it did batefull question frame, ...		247	Other Poems 4	189
Which made hir yeeld to deck this shepheards' band,.		247	Other Poems 4	215
Which absence wisht: love plai'd a victor's part:.		248	Other Poems 4	223
Like some which seeke to salve their blotted name.		248	Other Poems 4	231
Most mad with beames which he thought Cosma sent,.		249	Other Poems 4	270
Which more it mov'd, the more it sweeter was..		252	Other Poems 4	400
To feele the panting heart, which through hir syde		252	Other Poems 4	405
Did beate their hands, which durst so neere to presse. . .		252	Other Poems 4	406
To fasten knotts, which fancy first had bound.		253	Other Poems 4	424
Those eies, which nothing like themselves can see, ...		253	Other Poems 4	451
In which by will, my will and wits I binde:.		255	Other Poems 4	500
With eyes which threatned they would drowne his face,. . . .		255	Other Poems 4	524
To beare the bondes which Time nor wit could breake, . . .		255	Other Poems 4	530
Which made his Strephon think himselfe in hell..		256	Other Poems 4	540
Which when he did in perfect image show, ...		256	Other Poems 4	541
Which thus breath'd out with earthquake of his hart. . . .		256	Other Poems 4	544
Tell, if that breath, which thee thy sounding gives, . . .		258	Other Poems 5	63
Then want one hower those eyes which my joyes keepe.		259	Other Poems 5	102
Which Holland sweet now gently sendeth in, ...		259	Other Poems 5	106
With thoughts which thoughts their owne tormentors tried,. .		259	Other Poems 5	119
WHICHEVER				
Which ever hath Love's yoke despised:.		159	Cert Sonnets 29	15
WHILE				
While that one body shine.		19	1st Eclogues 7	165
While still more wretch, more wicked he doth prove:. . . .		22	1st Eclogues 8	44
Whyle hote desyres do Raigne in fancie's rage.		26	1st Eclogues 9	140
While, "Let us passe our time" each shepheard saies.. . . .		28	1st Eclogues 10	48
O descende for a while, from this greate height to behold me		36	1st Eclogues 13	149
What wooll my sheepe shall beare, whyle thus they live,. . .		39	Arcadia II 17	7
While our sonne shynes no clowdie greeves assaile.		43	Arcadia II 23	12
While brickle houreglas runnes, guide thou our panting race:		45	Arcadia II 26	10

WHILE	(CONTINUED)	PAGE	TITLE		LINE
Not as the scrippe thou stalest, while Dorcas sleeping lay..		52	2nd Eclogues	29	8
While I was warbling out your wconted praise,........		54	2nd Eclogues	29	67
While shepheards' tunes be heard, or rimes be read,.....		56	2nd Eclogues	29	124
Or while that shepheards love a lovely face.........		56	2nd Eclogues	29	125
Alas while we are wrapt in foggie mist		59	2nd Eclogues	30	68
While that we do at his sweete scourge repine, ...		59	2nd Eclogues	30	75
Which while it is, it is all Asia's light.		60	2nd Eclogues	30	109
While that my soule, she, she lives in affliction;		61	2nd Eclogues	30	146
While I there speache in my rude ryminge pende........		62	2nd Eclogues	30	187
While Plangus dyd a storie strainge declare.		62	2nd Eclogues	30	189
Whyle upon chaunce, his fruite of labour lyes;.......		71	Arcadia III	36	10
While that the light may shewe the horrors darke		73	Arcadia III	39	11
So to my minde, while passions daylie growe, ...		74	Arcadia III	41	3
And while o sleepe thou closest up her sight,.......		79	Arcadia III	51	5
While thy known course, observing nature's right,.....		82	Arcadia III	56	11
While thus he fear'd the silly innocent, ...		94	3rd Eclogues	64	13
But fewe dayes past while she good maner us'de,..		95	3rd Eclogues	64	26
Spoiling their flock, or while twixt them they strive. ...		99	3rd Eclogues	66	35
While that we doo what nature doth require,........		105	3rd Eclogues	67	65
To speak with her, while freely speak we maye........		107	3rd Eclogues	67	120
While that my voice doth fill these wofull vallies,.....		111	4th Eclogues	71	10
Yet living still in her, while her beames lent		115	4th Eclogues	72	83
That thus I must, while in this death I dwell, ...		116	4th Eclogues	72	89
An honour to the world, while Honour was their ende, ...		117	4th Eclogues	73	37
And while their line of yeares they did in vertue spende...		117	4th Eclogues	73	38
Both our estates, while each the other did deprave,....		119	4th Eclogues	73	107
While we for mutuall spight a striving passion fed..		120	4th Eclogues	73	118
Fould with this sight, while thou thy chariot guidest. ..		126	4th Eclogues	75	57
We last short while, and build long lasting places:....		127	4th Eclogues	75	91
While he did live, farre, farre was all disorder;.....		128	4th Eclogues	75	130
While each conceate an ouglie figure beares, ...		131	Arcadia V	77	7
While late bare earth, proud of new clothing springeth,...		137	Cert Sonnets	4	3
If thus, alas: yet while those partes have wo, ...		142	Cert Sonnets	10	13
Trying high seas, nor while Sea rage you flee, ...		142	Cert Sonnets	12	2
While remembrance doth both states containe.		153	Cert Sonnets	24	14
While to my minde the out side stood,..........		156	Cert Sonnets	27	7
Love gave the wound, which while I breathe will bleed: ...		165	Astrophil	2	2
While with a feeling skill I paint my hell........		166	Astrophil	2	14
While teares powre out his inke, and sighs breathe out his words:		168	Astrophil	6	10
To my close heart, where while some firebrands he did lay, .		169	Astrophil	8	13
While Love on me doth all his quiver spend,........		171	Astrophil	14	4
But while I thus with this yong Lyon plaid;.......		173	Astrophil	16	9
Brake bow, brake shafts, while Cupid weeping sate:		173	Astrophil	17	8
I willing run, yet while I run, repent..		174	Astrophil	19	4
While that blacke hue from me the bad guest hid:		175	Astrophil	20	11
While he each thing in sense's ballance wayes, ...		177	Astrophil	25	6
Unseene, unheard, while thought to highest place		178	Astrophil	27	13
But from thy heart, while my sire charmeth thee, ...		181	Astrophil	32	13
While too much wit (forsooth) so troubled me,........		181	Astrophil	33	10
Thus write I while I doubt to write, and wreake.......		182	Astrophil	34	12
This night while sleepe begins with heavy wings.......		183	Astrophil	38	1
My still kept course, while others sleepe, to mone.....		184	Astrophil	40	4
Who while they make Love conquer, conquer Love,......		185	Astrophil	42	3
Our horsmanships, while by strange worke I prove		189	Astrophil	49	2
Girt fast by memorie, and while I spurre		189	Astrophil	49	10
While those poore babes their death in birth do find:....		190	Astrophil	50	11
For me, while you discourse of courtly tides,.......		190	Astrophil	51	9
While each pretends that Stella must be his:		190	Astrophil	52	2
While with the people's shouts I must confesse,......		191	Astrophil	53	3
Yet while I languish, him that bosome clips........		194	Astrophil	59	9
Looking on me, while I lookt other way:..........		199	Astrophil	66	12
And all in vaine, for while thy breath most sweet, ...		200	Astrophil	68	9
This realme of blisse, while vertuous course I take, ...		200	Astrophil	69	13
So while thy beautie drawes the heart to love, ...		201	Astrophil	71	12
While each doth blow the fier of my hart;........		202	Astrophil	72	4
In sport I suckt, while she asleepe did lie, ...		203	Astrophil	73	6
But lo, while I do speake, it groweth noone with me, ...		205	Astrophil	76	9
The prettie death, while each in other live.		206	Astrophil	79	11
While craftily you seem'd your cut to keepe, ...		208	Astrophil	83	3
While everie office themselves will discharge, ...		210	Astrophil	85	7
Thus while th' effect most bitter was to me, ...		223	Astrophil	87	12
Tush absence, while thy mistes eclipse that light, ...		223	Astrophil	88	9
While no night is more darke then is my day, ...		224	Astrophil	89	10
Stella, while now by honour's cruell might,........		224	Astrophil	91	1
While I dispaire by Sunne's sight to enjoy..		230	Astrophil	97	14
While the blacke horrors of the silent night,.......		230	Astrophil	98	9
While gracefull pitty beauty beautifies.		231	Astrophil	100	4
While sobd out words a perfect Musike give..		231	Astrophil	100	11
While beautie's reddest inke Venus for him doth sturre....		232	Astrophil	102	14
While those faire planets on thy streames did shine. ...		232	Astrophil	103	4
While wanton winds with beauties so devine		232	Astrophil	103	6
Sweete, for a while give respite to my hart, ...		236	Astrophil	107	5
Some play, while he is disarmed.		202	A&S 2nd Song		8
Yong folkes, take time while you may:...........		211	A&S 4th Song		28
Sweet then, while each thing doth frame:		211	A&S 4th Song		34
While favour fed my hope, delight with hope was brought, ..		212	A&S 5th Song		1
Suffer not her to laugh, while both we suffer paine:		213	A&S 5th Song		29
And even while I do speake, my death wounds bleeding be: ..		214	A&S 5th Song		52

	PAGE	TITLE		LINE
While she doth against me prove.	226	A&S 10th Song		35
That each, while each contends,	216	A&S 6th Song		17
Wept they had, alas the while,	218	A&S 8th Song		13
While their eyes by love directed,	218	A&S 8th Song		15
While such wise she love denied,	220	A&S 8th Song		71
"Trust me while I thee deny,	220	A&S 8th Song		93
While in pride flowers be preserved,	222	A&S 9th Song		29
While Thou art in the heat of thy displeasure:	276	Psalm VI		2
Lo, I am tir'd, while still I sigh and groane:	276	Psalm VI		17
My bed, while I with black night mourn alone,	276	Psalm VI		19
The while a swarm of foes with vexing feates	276	Psalm VI		23
While I am voyd of any helping pow'r	277	Psalm VII		6
For while his wayes do prove,	282	Psalm X		17
Wee stand upright, while they their fall did frame.	296	Psalm XX		32
O God my God I cry while day appeareth;	298	Psalm XXII		5
While battaile's brunt on me were laid	307	Psalm XXVII		16
Therfore while that I may cry,	309	Psalm XXVIII		6
While I that way hold my hands	309	Psalm XXVIII		7
For proof, while I my race did run	311	Psalm XXX		19
Feare was each where, while they their counsells led	313	Psalm XXXI		38
Then abjects, while I was unwitting quite,	322	Psalm XXXV		39
As for my tongue, while I have any dayes,	323	Psalm XXXV		71
Watch but a while, and Thou shalt see.	325	Psalm XXXVII		25
Lord while that thy rage doth bide,	327	Psalm XXXVIII		1
But the while they live and grow	329	Psalm XXXVIII		55
I mussle will my mouth while in the sight.	329	Psalm XXXIX		3
While long I did with patient constancy.	330	Psalm XL		1
While thus, alas, they say:	333	Psalm XLI		18
While my God with wasting wonders.	335	Psalm XLII		31
While the Foe oppresseth me?	335	Psalm XLII		44
While prevayling foes.	336	Psalm XLIII		11
Whille I that syghte, desyre, and vowe forbare,	344	Possibly	2	7
They catch, while he (foole!) to himself makes love:	243	Other Poems	4	46
While daunce about the may-pole is begun,	243	Other Poems	4	55
While thus they ran a low, but leaveld race,	243	Other Poems	4	57
While thus they liv'd, (this was indede a life)	243	Other Poems	4	58
While those restles desires in great men rife.	243	Other Poems	4	62
This while, though poore, they in themselves did raigne.	243	Other Poems	4	64
While they did ward sun-beames with shady bay,	243	Other Poems	4	66
While nought but game, the selfe-hurt wanton ment.	247	Other Poems	4	192
While into none doubt of his love did sinke,	247	Other Poems	4	199
While most with hir he lesse did kepe with thee.	247	Other Poems	4	221
Pas thought it hell, while he was Cosma fro.	248	Other Poems	4	245
Cosma this while to Strephon safely came,	249	Other Poems	4	265
While Strephon might with preatie Nous have met,	249	Other Poems	4	279
But all this while another course he fet.	249	Other Poems	4	280
While Geron olde came safe to Cosma true,	250	Other Poems	4	325
While deare Uran, whose course was Pas to meet,	250	Other Poems	4	330
While I was I, and so had cause to care;	254	Other Poems	4	484
"Be you with me while I unheard do cry,	255	Other Poems	4	497
While I do score my losses on the winde,	255	Other Poems	4	498
While I in heart my will write ere I die.	255	Other Poems	4	499
While guilty thoughts accus'd his Reason weake)	255	Other Poems	4	532
Let us the while be playing,	261	Other Poems	6	32
"Well was I, while under shade	263	Other Poems	7	43
WHILES				
Whiles he each thing in sense's ballance wayes,	177	Astrophil	25 V	6
WHILOM				
Of samothea lande; a lande, which whilom stood	117	4th Eclogues 73		36
"But you my pipe, whilome my chief delight,	254	Other Poems	4	481
WHILST				
But if he know not his harms what guides hath he whil'st he be blind?	63	2nd Eclogues 31		20
Whilst that methought I justly made my bost.	147	Cert Sonnets 17		42
WHIMPERING				
Puiling, and whimpring, or else scolding flat,	104	3rd Eclogues 67		29
WHINE				
I thought those babes of some pinne's hurt did whine,	173	Astrophil	16	7
WHIP				
When for a treene-dish stolne, thy father did thee whippe!	52	2nd Eclogues 29		12
WHIPPING				
(Even like a toppe which nought but whipping moves).	58	2nd Eclogues 30		33
WHIRLING				
Hath all thy whirling course so small effect?	58	2nd Eclogues 30		60
The weakning worke of Time's for ever-whirling wheele.	120	4th Eclogues 73		122
WHISPERING				
Not limited to a whispringe note, the Lament of a Courtier,	35	1st Eclogues 13		110
Let my whispering voyce obtaine,	210	A&S 4th Song		3
For then their hatefull heads close whispring be	333	Psalm XLI		25
WHIT				
We love, and are no whit regarded.	14	1st Eclogues 6		2
Neither doubt you a whit, time will your passion utter.	33	1st Eclogues 13		58
Dread not a whit (O goodly cruell) that pittie may enter	122	4th Eclogues 74		5
My wealth no more, and no whit lesse my need,	199	Astrophil	66	7
No whit feare ill.	301	Psalm XXIII		12
WHITE				
Two thousand sheepe I have as white as milke,	4	Lady of May	2	19
Though not so white as is thy lovely face,	4	Lady of May	2	20
Want I white wooll, whose eyes her white skinne garnished?	16	1st Eclogues	7	59

WHITE	(CONTINUED)	PAGE	TITLE		LINE
Who once a white long beard, well handle does, ...		25	1st Eclogues	9	90
Ne let white haires, which on my face doo grow,.		38	Arcadia II	15	5
My words blacke inke, the marble kindly white;		41	Arcadia II	19	9
I have (and long shall have) a white great nimble cat, . . .		53	2nd Eclogues	29	31
As white as milke, and comming to the call,.		54	2nd Eclogues	29	85
Her naked legge, more white then whitest snowe..		55	2nd Eclogues	29	101
O brest in which two white sheepe swell in pride:.		76	Arcadia III	46	10
But thou white skinne, as white as cruddes well prest, . . .		76	Arcadia III	46	13
Whiter indeed; more white then snow, ...		85	Arcadia III	62	7
Her ribbes in white well armed be.		88	Arcadia III	62	68
More white then Neptune's fomie face,.		88	Arcadia III	62	69
Like cunning Painter shadowing white.		89	Arcadia III	62	98
More white then whitest bone of whall.		89	Arcadia III	62	104
Her shoulders be like two white Doves, ...		89	Arcadia III	62	113
Shall prove that fiercenes can with a white dove abide?. . .		123	4th Eclogues	74	34
Marble mixt red and white do enterlace.		169	Astrophil	9	8
Shall paint out joy, though but in blacke and white.		201	Astrophil	70	11
That skin, whose passe-praise hue scorns this poore terme of white:.		205	Astrophil	77	7
That in that palenesse beautie's white we see;		231	Astrophil	101	6
It is but love, which makes his paper perfit white		232	Astrophil	102	12
I now then staine thy white with vagabunding shame,.		214	A&S 5th Song		68
To sett, for foile of his milke-white to serve.		244	Other Poems	4	86
His compleat harneis was hir purest white.		246	Other Poems	4	150
But fearing lest all white might seeme too good, ...		246	Other Poems	4	151
As Venus' bird the white, swift, lovely Dove		251	Other Poems	4	353
WHITENESS					
Love well thine owne: me thinkes, woolle's whitenes passeth all:.		16	1st Eclogues	7	53
Since whitenesse doth present the sweetest show, ...		38	Arcadia II	15	7
That Albion clives in whitenes passe:.		88	Arcadia III	62	91
Where whitenes dooth for ever sitte:		90	Arcadia III	62	123
Lilly in mourning blacke thy whitenes die:		125	4th Eclogues	75	28
WHITER					
A whiter beautie you may see..		85	Arcadia III	62	6
Whiter indeed; more white then snow, ...		85	Arcadia III	62	7
WHITEST					
Her naked legge, more white then whitest snowe..		55	2nd Eclogues	29	101
More white then whitest bone of whall.		89	Arcadia III	62	104
Like Whitest Snowe, in silver Brooke,.		88	Arcadia III	62 V	69
The Ermion, whitest skinne, spotted with nought;		101	3rd Eclogues	66	89
WHITHER					
Whither it would, so it would let him dy,.		252	Other Poems	4	382
WHITSUNTIDE					
Of village-Lord that whitsontide to beare:		244	Other Poems	4	76
WHO					
Who in one selfe these diverse gifts can plant;.		3	Lady of May	1	4
Greater is she who must the judgement give..		3	Lady of May	2	6
He is not poore who can his freedome save, ...		4	Lady of May	2	27
Who at thy beer, as at a barre, shall plead.		11	Arcadia I	1	6
Helples his plaint, who spoyles himselfe of blisse..		13	Arcadia I	4	10
Who ended hath this fearefull strife:.		13	Arcadia I	5	4
Who can despaire, whom hope doth beare?.		14	1st Eclogues	6	5
And who can hope, who feeles despaire?		14	1st Eclogues	6	6
Who frownes at others' feastes, dooth better bide away.. . .		15	1st Eclogues	7	15
My Kala's giftes: who with all good gifts filled is.		15	1st Eclogues	7	26
Who though she be no Bee, yet full of honie is:.		15	1st Eclogues	7	29
Who is an heire of many hundred sheep.		18	1st Eclogues	7	117
Nor helpe by life or death who living dyes..		18	1st Eclogues	7	146
(At Juno's suite who much did Argus love).		22	1st Eclogues	8	46
Who yelds to woe, doth but encrease his smart..		22	1st Eclogues	9	2
An olde man heare, who would thy fancies raise..		22	1st Eclogues	9	5
Philisides. Who minds to please the minde drownd in annoyes.		22	1st Eclogues	9	6
Who doth his soule to endlesse malice bend..		22	1st Eclogues	9	10
Philisides. Who ever taught a skillesse man to teach,. . . .		22	1st Eclogues	9	16
Who hath his hopes laid up in woman's hand..		24	1st Eclogues	9	55
O noble age who place their only blisse.		24	1st Eclogues	9	69
Then who will heare a well autoris'd lye,.		24	1st Eclogues	9	72
Who once a white long beard, well handle does, ...		25	1st Eclogues	9	90
For proofe of man, who sprong of heav'nly fire		25	1st Eclogues	9	100
Who well can set a passion out to show:.		25	1st Eclogues	9	112
Truly not I, who did my thoughts engage, ...		26	1st Eclogues	9	136
Who have their lesson so long time begonne?.		27	1st Eclogues	10	27
Who of his tongue the lickowr gladly powrs,.		28	1st Eclogues	10	70
Who once all birdes, in sweetly-singing past,.		28	1st Eclogues	10	74
Then who makes us such judges over all?.		29	1st Eclogues	10	96
Sacred Muse, who in one contaynes what nine do in all them..		31	1st Eclogues	13	10
And to the woods or brookes, who do make such dreery recitall		33	1st Eclogues	13	42
But who by meanes of wisdome hie		44	Arcadia II	25	5
Who hath sav'd all? it is even I..		44	Arcadia II	25	12
R. Who Passion doth ensue, lives in annoy.		46	2nd Eclogues	27	13
P. Who Passion doth forsake, lives void of joy..		46	2nd Eclogues	27	14
P. Who be too weake, do feigne they be too good.		47	2nd Eclogues	27	30
For who doth holde his love in estimation, ...		47	2nd Eclogues	28	4
Who others' vertue doubt, themselves are vicious:.		47	2nd Eclogues	28	9
Who glories in his love, doth make Love glorious:.		47	2nd Eclogues	28	16
But who doth feare, or bideth muet wilfully, ...		48	2nd Eclogues	28	17
To helpe her praise, who decks me in her slaverie.		48	2nd Eclogues	28	27

	PAGE	TITLE	LINE
Who hunting round the strongest for to kill, ...	50	2nd Eclogues 28	84
Who judge that honour, which hath scope to slander..	50	2nd Eclogues 28	91
Which who doth misse his eyes are but delusions, ...	51	2nd Eclogues 28	108
Without her love, then any mind who fairer is.	51	2nd Eclogues 28	116
Pas. Ah foole; so Courtiers do. But who did lively skippe, .	52	2nd Eclogues 29	11
Or else who singeth worse, my skill will hardly hit.	53	2nd Eclogues 29	50
Nico. Who doubts but Pas' fine pipe againe will bring. . . .	53	2nd Eclogues 29	51
Pas. Who evermore will love Apollo's quill, ...	53	2nd Eclogues 29	54
Nico. Was this he, why not, for Siringa's scape	53	2nd Eclogues 29	57
For who grieves not hath but a blockish braine, ...	58	2nd Eclogues 30	36
Boulon. Who still doth seeke against himselfe offences, . . .	62	2nd Eclogues 30	167
What pardon can availe? or who employes him.	62	2nd Eclogues 30	168
Peace? what barrs me my tongue? who is it that comes me so ny? I.	62	2nd Eclogues 31	2
Who seekes to knowe, acquaintes hym self with hell;	71	Arcadia III 36	16
On her, who hath in me thy temple raste, ...	72	Arcadia III 38	14
I darkned am, who once had clearest sight.	75	Arcadia III 43	4
Who hold this fast no greater wealth require..	75	Arcadia III 44	8
By her who was (O blessed you) content, ...	78	Arcadia III 49	5
My thoughtes then hers, who first your ryne did rente, . . .	78	Arcadia III 49	14
Who full of guiltie spite, ...	82	Arcadia III 55	9
But who those ruddie lippes can misse?	87	Arcadia III 62	37
Who yet was good, because she knewe none ill, ...	94	3rd Eclogues 64	14
Who would have sworne his spowse diana was, ...	96	3rd Eclogues 64	74
Who doth desire that chaste his wife should be, ...	98	3rd Eclogues 65	1
Who at the first, wanting, or hiding pride, ...	101	3rd Eclogues 66	107
Who now his owne, full like his owne he used..	102	3rd Eclogues 66	142
Which who so wants, halfe of himselfe doth misse.	103	3rd Eclogues 67	9
Who would not have a Phoenix if he could?.	104	3rd Eclogues 67	16
And makes them fremb'd, who frendes by nature are, ...	104	3rd Eclogues 67	38
Such is their speech, who be of sober wit;	104	3rd Eclogues 67	46
But who doo let their tongues shew well their rage, ...	105	3rd Eclogues 67	47
Geron. Who for ech fickle feare from vertue shrinkes, . . .	105	3rd Eclogues 67	58
Who for a selfe-conceipt will that forbeare, ...	105	3rd Eclogues 67	80
No man doth speake aright, who speakes in feare.	106	3rd Eclogues 67	84
Who onely sees the ill is worse then blind..	106	3rd Eclogues 67	85
And then who shall the name of Histor nourish?	106	3rd Eclogues 67	111
Who hath his hire, will hath his labour plast:	108	Arcadia IV 68	1
Who hath our sight with too much sight infected, ...	108	Arcadia IV 69	6
Who justly make our hearts the seates of sorow?.	109	Arcadia IV 70	8
His nature feares to die who lives still wailing..	110	Arcadia IV 70	39
Who much did passe in state the stately mountaines, ...	113	4th Eclogues 71	63
Who, where she went, bare in her forhead morning, ...	113	4th Eclogues 71	70
But I cannot; who then my selfe should flie, ...	114	4th Eclogues 72	39
Vaine is their paine, who labour in Despaire..	115	4th Eclogues 72	60
Strephon. Vaine is their paine, who labour in Despaire.. . .	115	4th Eclogues 72	61
Who under courtly pompes doo hatch a base desire..	117	4th Eclogues 73	16
She waited mistresse' will: who thus disclosd her spright. .	119	4th Eclogues 73	92
Who may this doubt discerne: for better, witt, then lot. . .	120	4th Eclogues 73	139
And to revenge who doo bend, would in that kind be revenged,	123	4th Eclogues 74	39
Think what a world is now, think who hath altred her hart..	124	4th Eclogues 74	76
Who most the silly shepheard's pipe did pryse, ...	125	4th Eclogues 75	2
For see alas, who is from you absented..	128	4th Eclogues 75	124
Who long have gap't to get Arcadians' treasure..	129	4th Eclogues 76	21
Who for our sakes will thinke all travaile light, ...	129	4th Eclogues 76	23
That hardly usde, who ever prison broke, ...	135	Cert Sonnets 1	11
But I who dayly craving, ...	137	Cert Sonnets 4	17
By them who of his rude resort complaine, ...	141	Cert Sonnets 8	4
Who others' woes and plaints can chastly beare:	142	Cert Sonnets 10	7
Where her who should rule paine, false paine abuseth.. . . .	142	Cert Sonnets 11	14
The golden meane who loves, lives safely free.	143	Cert Sonnets 12	4
As this poore beast who did his rest forsake, ...	145	Cert Sonnets 16	7
Who burnt his lips to kisse faire shining fire..	145	Cert Sonnets 16	14
Who thinke themselves well blest, if they renew.	146	Cert Sonnets 17	33
Who Stoick-like in clowdie hew appeare:	147	Cert Sonnets 17	48
Who silence force to make their words more deare:	147	Cert Sonnets 17	49
Who hath his fancie pleased, ...	151	Cert Sonnets 23	1
Who may immortall gaine.	152	Cert Sonnets 23	20
But who hath fancies pleased, ...	152	Cert Sonnets 23	33
Who hath ever felt the change of love, ...	153	Cert Sonnets 24	1
But who by hearesay speakes, and hath not fully felt	153	Cert Sonnets 24	6
And I be dead who want sense, ...	154	Cert Sonnets 25	22
Who with glorie.	155	Cert Sonnets 26	21
Who hath such beautie seene.	158	Cert Sonnets 28	25
Who love can temper thus, ...	161	Cert Sonnets 30	39
Who should my mind to higher things prepare.	161	Cert Sonnets 31	8
Who seeketh heav'n and comes of heav'nly breath.	144	Cert Sonnets 32	12
Ought to be king, from whose rules who do swerve, ...	167	Astrophil 5	3
To honor all their deaths, who for her bleed..	168	Astrophil 7	14
Deceiv'd the quaking boy, who thought from so pure light, . .	169	Astrophil 8	10
Then did on him who first stale downe the fire, ...	171	Astrophil 14	3
As who by being poisond doth poison know..	173	Astrophil 16	14
Who threatned stripes, if he his wrath did prove:	173	Astrophil 17	6
That unto me, who fare like him that both..	174	Astrophil 19	10
Who like a theefe, hid in darke bush doth ly, ...	175	Astrophil 20	3
But that rich foole, who by blind Fortune's lot.	177	Astrophil 24	9
Who oft fore-judge my after-following race, ...	178	Astrophil 26	13
Who though most rich in these and everie part, ...	183	Astrophil 37	12
My bloud from them, who did excell in this, ...	185	Astrophil 41	10

WHO	(CONTINUED)	PAGE	TITLE		LINE
Who while they make Love conquer, conquer Love,.		185	Astrophil	42	3
For when he will see who dare him gainesay,.		186	Astrophil	43	5
Who for long faith, tho dayly helpe I crave,.		188	Astrophil	47	7
Who hard by made a window send forth light...		191	Astrophil	53	9
Of them, who in their lips Love's standerd beare;.		191	Astrophil	54	6
They love indeed, who quake to say they love.		192	Astrophil	54	14
That who indeed infelt affection beares, .		195	Astrophil	61	5
For Grammer sayes (to Grammer who sayes nay)		196	Astrophil	63	13
Who will in fairest booke of Nature know,.		201	Astrophil	71	1
Who marke in thee what is in thee most faire.		201	Astrophil	71	11
In Beautie's throne, see now who dares come neare.		203	Astrophil	73	10
Their rayes to me, who in her tedious absence lay.		204	Astrophil	76	2
Who his owne joy to his owne hurt applies, .		206	Astrophil	78	7
Who since he hath, by Nature's speciall grace, .		206	Astrophil	78	9
His who till death lookt in a watrie glasse, .		207	Astrophil	82	3
Who seeke, who hope, who love, who live but thee;.		224	Astrophil	90	2
Forst by their Lord, who is asham'd to find. .		231	Astrophil	99	13
Who hath the crimson weeds stolne from my morning skies? .		232	Astrophil	102	4
Gallein's adoptive sonnes, who by a beaten way .		232	Astrophil	102	9
Do Stella love. Fooles, who doth it deny?.		233	Astrophil	104	14
Was not in fault, who bent thy dazling race. .		235	Astrophil	105	6
Who may with charme of conversation sweete,.		236	Astrophil	106	10
And as a Queene, who from her presence sends .		236	Astrophil	107	9
Who hath the eyes which marrie state with pleasure,.		197	A&S 1st Song		5
Who keepes the key of Nature's chiefest treasure?.		197	A&S 1st Song		6
Who hath the lips, where wit in fairnesse raigneth,.		197	A&S 1st Song		9
Who womankind at once both deckes and stayneth?.		197	A&S 1st Song		10
Who hath the feet, whose step all sweetnesse planteth, .		197	A&S 1st Song		13
Who else for whom Fame worthy trumpets wanteth?.		197	A&S 1st Song		14
Who hath the breast, whose milke doth passions nourish,.		197	A&S 1st Song		17
Who hath the hand which without stroke subdueth, .		197	A&S 1st Song		21
Who long dead beautie with increase reneweth?.		197	A&S 1st Song		22
Who hath the haire which, loosest, fastest tieth,.		197	A&S 1st Song		25
Who makes a man live then glad when he dieth?.		197	A&S 1st Song		26
Who hath the voyce, which soule from sences sunders, .		197	A&S 1st Song		29
Who will read must first learne spelling..		203	A&S 2nd Song		24
I thinke now of thy faults, who late thought of thy praise,		213	A&S 5th Song		16
Ungratefull who is cald, the worst of evils is spok'n. .		213	A&S 5th Song		42
Who may and will not save, murder in truth committeth. .		214	A&S 5th Song		54
For thou doest lord my heart, who am not borne thy slave,.		214	A&S 5th Song		58
Who faileth one, is false, though trusty to another. .		214	A&S 5th Song		72
Who tempt, and tempted plague, are Devils in true defining..		215	A&S 5th Song		84
"Who is it that this darke night,.		233	A&S 11th Song		1
It is one who from thy sight,.		233	A&S 11th Song		3
Who have so leaden eyes, as not to see sweet beautie's show,		217	A&S 7th Song		7
Stella who more love hath proved,.		221	A&S 9th Song		22
He blessed is, who neither loosely treads.		270	Psalm I		1
But He shall them deride who by the heavns is borne, .		271	Psalm II		9
Get hence you ev'ill, who in my ev'ill rejoyce,.		276	Psalm VI		25
Who causeless now, yeelds me a hatefull heart, .		277	Psalm VII		12
Who dost Thy saving health to true men bend. .		277	Psalm VII		30
To help who vexed be!.		281	Psalm X		4
But who aright poore-minded be .		283	Psalm X		61
Who hast the heath'ny folk destroyd. .		283	Psalm X		71
Who be to God enclined..		284	Psalm XI		24
These Canibals, who as if they were bread. .		286	Psalm XIV		14
In Tabernacle Thyne, O lord, who shall remayne?.		287	Psalm XV		1
Lord, of Thy Holy Hill who shall the rest obtayne? .		287	Psalm XV		2
Who with deceitfull tongue hath never usd to faine,.		287	Psalm XV		5
Who word to neighbour given doth faithfully maintain .		287	Psalm XV		9
Who sells not guiltlesse cause, for filthy love of gain:.		287	Psalm XV		12
Who thus proceeds, for aye, in sacred Mount shall raign. .		287	Psalm XV		13
Who to other Gods do run,.		288	Psalm XVI		10
Who dost ever counsell mee,.		288	Psalm XVI		20
Where who may contemplate Thee .		289	Psalm XVI		39
Who for my Death still me enclose.		290	Psalm XVII		28
For who is God, besides this Great Jehova Ours?.		292	Psalm XVIII		57
And so besides our God, who is indue'd with might? .		292	Psalm XVIII		58
Not I but thou throw'st down those, who 'gainst me do rise;.		292	Psalm XVIII		72
Behold they cry, but who to them his help applys?.		292	Psalm XVIII		74
Who freed me from my foes, from rebells guarded me,.		293	Psalm XVIII		86
Who forth doth come like a bridegrome.		294	Psalm XIX		21
And who doth frame to keep the same. .		295	Psalm XIX		47
Who is the man that ever can .		295	Psalm XIX		49
Who is our Lord, with due remembrance wayte. .		296	Psalm XX		30
And since there is not One, who it redresseth. .		299	Psalm XXII		26
On me all this, who do like water slide; .		299	Psalm XXII		31
And do cast lots, who should my vesture take..		299	Psalm XXII		44
Who feare the lord all prayse and glory beare him;.		300	Psalm XXII		53
Who feare Thee shall my vowes performed see. .		300	Psalm XXII		60
To him shall kneel who to the dust be stricken,.		300	Psalm XXII		73
And all who in that Globe do dwell;.		302	Psalm XXIV		2
Who shall climb to the hill which God's own hill is named, .		302	Psalm XXIV		5
Who shall stand in his Holy place? .		302	Psalm XXIV		6
Who shunning vanity and works of vaineness leaving,.		302	Psalm XXIV		9
Who never doth deceive, and much lesse his deceaving .		302	Psalm XXIV		11
Who search of God's face never leave..		302	Psalm XXIV		16
Who is this glorious King in might and power riding? .		302	Psalm XXIV		19
Who is This Glorious King? The lord of armyes guiding, .		302	Psalm XXIV		23

Sure, sure who hope in Thee. . . . .   303 Psalm XXV   7
Who doth, and will set free. . . . .   304 Psalm XXV   57
Who hate, yea hate me cruely.. . . . .   304 Psalm XXV   66
Who be to vaineness bent,. . . . .   305 Psalm XXVI   14
Who shall be able me to fright?. . . . .   306 Psalm XXVII   3
Who, their spotted thoughts to cloak,. . . . .   309 Psalm XXVIII   13
Who his Anoynted helped have.. . . . .   309 Psalm XXVIII   32
Save me from foes who seek my bane to bake.. . . . .   313 Psalm XXXI   42
Who was to me more than most gracious, ...   313 Psalm XXXI   59
You that do trust in him who still is true,. . . . .   314 Psalm XXXI   68
Who savest me from troblous case,. . . . .   315 Psalm XXXII   26
But who cn God his trust invokes,. . . . .   315 Psalm XXXII   38
Joy be to you, who do enjoy. . . . .   316 Psalm XXXII   41
And who abroad . . . .   317 Psalm XXXIII   29
Who him for their lord take; . . . .   317 Psalm XXXIII   45
Who dwell in dusty place.. . . . .   317 Psalm XXXIII   54
Who trusts him sooner shall. . . . .   318 Psalm XXXIII   64
Who him do truly feare,. . . . .   318 Psalm XXXIII   69
And them who do the scope. . . . .   318 Psalm XXXIII   70
Who hope on his Name just. . . . .   318 Psalm XXXIII   81
About them pitch who him do feare, ...   319 Psalm XXXIV   26
Who faithfull feares in him do plant; . . . .   319 Psalm XXXIV   35
But who seek God with constancy. . . . .   319 Psalm XXXIV   39
Among you, who is here . . . .   320 Psalm XXXIV   45
Who hate the good shall fall.. . . . .   320 Psalm XXXIV   76
Who weare his blessed livery;. . . . .   321 Psalm XXXIV   78
Who him their trust esteeme. . . . .   321 Psalm XXXIV   80
Who for my hurt each way their thoughts did roll.. . . . . .   321 Psalm XXXV   10
Ev'en bones shall say O God, who is Thy peere, ...   321 Psalm XXXV   21
Who poore and weake from rich and strong dost free,. . . . .   321 Psalm XXXV   22
Who helpest those, whose ruin was so neere,. . . . .   321 Psalm XXXV   23
Who did me wrong, against me witness beare . . . .   322 Psalm XXXV   25
And whose? ev'n his who when they sickness bare. . . . . . .   322 Psalm XXXV   29
Who joy but they, when they assembled bee? . . . .   322 Psalm XXXV   38
Let them not fleere, who me would causless stroy,. . . . . .   322 Psalm XXXV   50
Who never word of peace yet utter would, ...   322 Psalm XXXV   51
Who make a Cause to joy of my decay; . . . .   323 Psalm XXXV   64
Who loves with good his servants good to blesse. . . . . . .   323 Psalm XXXV   70
Who shall in Thy house fatness find. . . . .   324 Psalm XXXVI   22
Who do ev'ill works: lo I doe see. . . . .   324 Psalm XXXVI   34
Who stay for God, in blisse shall stay.. . . . .   325 Psalm XXXVII   24
Who to make warr with God praesumed; . . . .   326 Psalm XXXVII   50
From time to time, but who be swerved. . . . .   326 Psalm XXXVII   71
But who for my life do waite,. . . . .   328 Psalm XXXVIII   33
Who hunt me, ...   328 Psalm XXXVIII   35
Who do ev'ill for good, to me. . . . .   329 Psalm XXXVIII   58
And knowes not who the fruit shall reap. . . . .   330 Psalm XXXIX   22
Who bends not wandring eyes. . . . .   331 Psalm XL   17
Who jointly sought my bale to frame; . . . .   332 Psalm XL   53
Who so unpitteous be . . . .   332 Psalm XL   58
But fill their hearts with joy, who bend their wayes . . . .   332 Psalm XL   61
He blessed is, who with wise temper can. . . . .   332 Psalm XLI   1
Who never more must rise.. . . . .   333 Psalm XLI   28
My Friend I say, who at my table sate, ...   333 Psalm XLI   31
Who is still my present aid; . . . .   335 Psalm XLII   54
Who ever Lambkins saw (yet lambkins love to play). . . . . .   343 Possibly   1   5
Whose wages makes me beg the more, who feeds me till I
    sterve,. . . . .   343 Possibly   1   20
W. Who bound thee? D. Love my Lord. W. What witnesses
    therto . . . .   343 Possibly   1   25
W. What seale? D. My hart deepe graven. W. Who made the band
    so fast?. . . . .   343 Possibly   1   27
Yeelde yeelde O yeelde, who first this Fort did make,. . . .   345 Possibly   4   9
Who may be glad, be glad you be not such:. . . . .   242 Other Poems   4   15
Who share in woe, weygh others have as much. . . . .   242 Other Poems   4   16
They saw a maid who thitherward did runne, ...   244 Other Poems   4   83
Who would have hir in will and worde agree . . . .   245 Other Poems   4   115
Who then in Lion's cave did enter fyrst, ...   247 Other Poems   4   206
Who should to Pas, but they would her prevent. . . . .   249 Other Poems   4   268
She quick, and proud, and who did Pas despise, ...   249 Other Poems   4   273
Who would be caught, that she should go to hell: . . . . . .   250 Other Poems   4   315
Who nothing earthly, but of fire and aire, ...   250 Other Poems   4   338
Who victor seem'd, was to his ruine brought: . . . .   251 Other Poems   4   346
Who seem'd orethrown was mistresse of the field: . . . . . .   251 Other Poems   4   347
Who earnest found what they accounted play.. . . . .   251 Other Poems   4   366
(Who Neptune's webb on daunger's distaff spun) . . . .   251 Other Poems   4   374
Emprison hir, who both them did possesse . . . .   252 Other Poems   4   390
Help him, who can no more hir sight foregoe. . . . .   253 Other Poems   4   420
Not knowing who did draw with him therin;. . . . .   253 Other Poems   4   426
And, but bewitch'd, who to his flock would mone? . . . . . .   254 Other Poems   4   460
Who hid in Angel's shape my life would ende. . . . .   254 Other Poems   4   464
Klaius the wretch, who lately yelden was . . . .   255 Other Poems   4   529
His Ramme, who to recover. . . . .   259 Other Poems   5   121
Who never joy, but when. . . . .   261 Other Poems ˙6   39
WHOEVER
Who ever saw such woe? . . . .   158 Cert Sonnets 28   28
Frome bitinge Usury who ever doth refrain, ...   287 Psalm XV   11
WHOIE
Vertue you have, of vertue you have left proufes to the
    whole world, ...   33 1st Eclogues 13   56

WHOLE	(CONTINUED)	PAGE	TITLE		LINE
And if a meane were found, fortune th' whole course of it					
hinders.		37	1st Eclogues	13	159
Fear'st not a face that oft whole harts devowres,.		142	Cert Sonnets	10	10
Whole armies of thy beauties entred in..		182	Astrophil	36	4
And oft whole troupes of saddest words I staid,.		192	Astrophil	55	5
What, a whole weeke without one peece of looke,.		192	Astrophil	56	3
And part must folowe where whole man doth goe.		253	Other Poems	4	422
WHOLESOME					
But keeping holesome meane,.		93	3rd Eclogues	63	80
So may your Make, this wholsome springtime aire, ...		257	Other Poems	5	42
WHOLLY					
Ease I do feele (such ease as falls to one wholy diseased) .		35	1st Eclogues	13	114
Ty me haire your captive wholly, ...		157	Cert Sonnets	27	34
That wholly hers, all selfnesse he forbeares,.		195	Astrophil	61	7
Both sheep and Oxen wholy hast,.		279	Psalm VIII		26
Do pine, my strength with pain is wholy gon, ...		312	Psalm XXXI		29
Wholy devoy'd of Reason's rule,.		315	Psalm XXXII		32
On lamenting wholy set:.		262	Other Poems	7	8
WHOM					
Great sure is she, on whom our hopes do live,.		3	Lady of May	2	5
Sweete soule, to whom I vowed am a slave,.		3	Lady of May	2	11
Judge you to whom all beautie's force is lent.		4	Lady of May	2	31
Judge you of Love, to whom all Love is bent.		4	Lady of May	2	32
Who can despaire, whom hope doth beare?.		14	1st Eclogues	6	5
Her whom I dread; so that with prostrate lying		17	1st Eclogues	7	86
Bent to such one, in whom, my selfe must say,.		17	1st Eclogues	7	107
Dorus. Lady your selfe, whom nether name I dare		18	1st Eclogues	7	131
Whome wit makes vaine, or blinded with his eyes, ...		23	1st Eclogues	9	35
"I con thee thanke" to whom thy dogges be deare, ...		27	1st Eclogues	10	34
Then him we kisse, whom late before we beatt		27	1st Eclogues	10	37
Whom both nature seemes to debarr from meanes to be helped,.		37	1st Eclogues	13	158
R. Whom Passion leades unto his death is bent.		46	2nd Eclogues	27	9
The marchante man, whome gayne dothe teache the Sea.		70	Arcadia III	36	1
Seeking the Sainct in whome all graces dwell,.		71	Arcadia III	36	14
The marchante man, whome many seas have toughte.		71	Arcadia III	37	1
The labourer, whome tyred boddie makes		71	Arcadia III	37	7
From her, in whome is sowne their freedome's seede,.		72	Arcadia III	38	4
Like those sicke folkes, in whome strange humors flowe,. . .		74	Arcadia III	41	1
Then hers, to whom my thoughts alonely thrall.		78	Arcadia III	49	15
Where hers, whom worth makes highest over all, ...		78	Arcadia III	49	17
That he, to whome these sondrie giftes I binde,.		78	Arcadia III	50	9
Let him drinke this, whome long in armes to folde.		83	Arcadia III	58	1
Whome I doe hate, the more I thinke on him,.		85	Arcadia III	61	10
To whome our prince did beare a great good will, ...		94	3rd Eclogues	64	16
In choller put, with whom he would not fight..		96	3rd Eclogues	64	66
Gainst those of might, of whom in feare they stood,.		102	3rd Eclogues	66	130
To sheepe, whom love, not knowledge, made to heare,.		103	3rd Eclogues	66	156
Histor. No doubt to whom so good chance did betide,.		104	3rd Eclogues	67	13
Klaius. For she, with whom compar'd, the Alpes are vallies,.		113	4th Eclogues	71	67
Not sparing me, in whom his workes be rife:.		114	4th Eclogues	72	15
They seemd to me) on whom did waite a Virgin pure:		118	4th Eclogues	73	64
In whom of all my rules the perfect proofe I finde,.		119	4th Eclogues	73	94
To whom precedence shall of both accorded be..		120	4th Eclogues	73	136
Unto the caitife wretch, whom long affliction holdeth, . . .		122	4th Eclogues	74	1
Unto the man, whom now such miseries you awarde?		124	4th Eclogues	74	74
And thou poore Earth, whom fortune doth attaint.		125	4th Eclogues	75	16
And farewell Prince, whom goodnesse hath made glorious.. . .		129	4th Eclogues	75	142
Like those whom dreames make uglie monsters see,.		136	Cert Sonnets	2	11
In whom all joyes so well agree, ...		139	Cert Sonnets	7	2
Above line repeated at following locations		139	Cert Sonnets	7	12
. . . .		140	Cert Sonnets	7	22
. . . .		140	Cert Sonnets	7	32
Late harbors in her face whom nature wrought, ...		141	Cert Sonnets	8	7
I praisde her eyes whom never chance doth move,.		141	Cert Sonnets	9	5
Whom curst do blesse, whose weakenesse vertues arme, ...		142	Cert Sonnets	10	6
The same man still in whom wysdome prevailes,.		143	Cert Sonnets	12	17
For true it is, that they feare many whom many feare.. . . .		143	Cert Sonnets	14	2
For why should I, whom free choise slave doth make,.		146	Cert Sonnets	17	9
Me one to leave, with whome I leave my hart.		148	Cert Sonnets	20	6
On whome all love, in whom no love is plaste,.		151	Cert Sonnets	22	63
No man doubts, whom beautie killeth, ...		156	Cert Sonnets	26	27
And in whome faire death proceedeth, ...		156	Cert Sonnets	26	29
My young mind marde, whom Love doth windlas so,.		175	Astrophil	21	2
Those Lovers scorne whom that Love doth possesse?.		180	Astrophil	31	13
For let me but name her whom I do love,.		192	Astrophil	55	12
Which would not let me, whom she loved, decline.		196	Astrophil	62	7
Thou whom to me such my good turnes should bind, ...		198	Astrophil	65	3
Or hers whom naked the Trojan boy did see.		207	Astrophil	82	4
Whereof, with whom, how often did she talke, ...		225	Astrophil	92	11
To whom nor art nor nature graunteth light,.		230	Astrophil	99	2
Curst be the page from whome the bad torch fell, ...		235	Astrophil	105	11
Whom she imployes, dismisse from thee my wit,.		236	Astrophil	107	10
Whom iron doores do keepe from use of day?		237	Astrophil	108	11
Doubt you to whom my Muse these notes entendeth, ...		196	A&S 1st Song		1
Who else for whom Fame worthy trumpets wanteth?.		197	A&S 1st Song		14
Doubt you to whom my Muse these notes intendeth, ...		197	A&S 1st Song		33
Thou then whom partiall heavens conspir'd in one to frame, .		213	A&S 5th Song		19
Leave a wretch, in whom all wo		221	A&S 9th Song		6
Unto whom mirth is displeasure,.		221	A&S 9th Song		9

585

```
WHOM          (CONTINUED)                                    PAGE    TITLE        LINE
    Stella whom o heavens do blesse, . . . . . . . . . . . . .  221  A&S 9th Song     18
    In God on whom you build . . . . . . . . . . . . . . . .    272  Psalm III        10
    Whom that Great God remember can?. . . . . . . . . . . .    278  Psalm VIII       14
    Whom to their losse he still doth get. . . . . . . . . .    282  Psalm X          39
    Whom troubles tosse, whose natures need doth quell,. . . .  285  Psalm XII        14
    Whom then shall I invoke but Thee most worthy prayse,. . .  291  Psalm XVIII       6
    On whom against my Foes my only safty stayes?. . . . . .    291  Psalm XVIII       7
    He that is my revenge, in whom I realmes subdue, . . . . .  293  Psalm XVIII      85
    Let God help him (say they) whom he did trust; . . . . . .  299  Psalm XXII       19
    Let God save him, in whom was all his lust.. . . . . . .    299  Psalm XXII       20
    The God in whom abides . . . . . . . . . . . . . . . . .    303  Psalm XXV        15
    Of whom the trust lives in my heart. . . . . . . . . . .    304  Psalm XXV        72
    Whom Death to his cold bosom drawes. . . . . . . . . . .    311  Psalm XXX         9
    To whom feare Thee? what thou hast done for those. . . . .  313  Psalm XXXI       53
    Blessed in deed to whom the lord . . . . . . . . . . . .    314  Psalm XXXII       4
    Whom this lord chose,. . . . . . . . . . . . . . . . . .    317  Psalm XXXIII     47
    And will save whom his signt cleere. . . . . . . . . . .    320  Psalm XXXIV      67
    Lo whom God blest he blessed liveth, . . . . . . . . . .    326  Psalm XXXVII     55
    Whom he doth curse to naught shall rott. . . . . . . . .    326  Psalm XXXVII     56
    The man whom God directs doth stand. . . . . . . . . . .    326  Psalm XXXVII     57
    Whom my fall doth make rejoyce.. . . . . . . . . . . . .    328  Psalm XXXVIII    48
    O yea, my Friend to whom I did impart. . . . . . . . . .    333  Psalm XLI        29
    But triumph well may I, whom Thou dost stay. . . . . . .    334  Psalm XLI        41
    Whome Thou, O place of places all, dost place. . . . . .    334  Psalm XLI        43
    In whome no evill did raigne, nor good appeare,. . . . . .  245  Other Poems   4  118
    Her happy-making hand, of whome one looke. . . . . . . .    248  Other Poems   4  247
    With whome to joyne fast ran Urania sweet: . . . . . . .    248  Other Poems   4  252
    Whome hills from her do hemme, . . . . . . . . . . . . .    259  Other Poems   5   96
    If thou know not for whome thy Master dies,. . . . . . .    259  Other Poems   5  110
    To mate with whom he liveth, . . . . . . . . . . . . . .    261  Other Poems   6   50
    To whome arte of Love is knowne: . . . . . . . . . . . .    262  Other Poems   7   28
    To whom we our love disclose?. . . . . . . . . . . . . .    263  Other Poems   7   32
WHOSE
    To one whose state is raised over all, . . . . . . . . .      3  Lady of May   1    1
    Whose face doth oft the bravest sort enchaunt, . . . . .      3  Lady of May   1    2
    Whose mind is such, as wisest minds appall,. . . . . . .      3  Lady of May   1    3
    Whose cleerest eyes I blisse, and sweetest voyce,. . . .      5  Lady of May   3   15
    Whose vertues strange, and beuties such, as no man them may
        know?. . . . . . . . . . . . . . . . . . . . . . . .     12  Arcadia I     3    2
    Whose strongest hope in your weake comfort lyes. . . . .     13  Arcadia I     4    4
    Her praise, whose praise to learne your skill hath framed
        me . . . . . . . . . . . . . . . . . . . . . . . . .     15  1st Eclogues  7   24
    In one, whose name to name were high presumption,. . . .     15  1st Eclogues  7   38
    Want I white wooll, whose eyes her white skinne garnished?.  16  1st Eclogues  7   59
    That she, whose looke alone might make me blessed, . . . .   17  1st Eclogues  7   83
    Whose sprite all sprites can spoile, raise, damne, or save:. 17  1st Eclogues  7  110
    Whose wit the starres, whose fortune fortune thralls.. . .   23  1st Eclogues  9   31
    Farre more happy be you, whose greatnes gets a free accesse, 33  1st Eclogues 13   54
    Whose faire bodily gifts are fram'd most lovely to each ey.. 33  1st Eclogues 13   55
    Give therefore to the Muse great praise in whose very
        likenes. . . . . . . . . . . . . . . . . . . . . . .     33  1st Eclogues 13   62
    Whose force had such force so to transforme, nay to reforme
        me,. . . . . . . . . . . . . . . . . . . . . . . . .     37  1st Eclogues 13  166
    In whose chiefe parte your worthes implanted be? . . . .     39  Arcadia II   16   10
    Thou purest stone, whose purenesse doth present. . . . .     40  Arcadia II   18    7
    My purest minde; whose temper hard doth showe. . . . . .     40  Arcadia II   18    8
    Apollo great, whose beames the greater world do light, . .   44  Arcadia II   26    1
    Whose lights do ever live, but in our darkenesse fade; . .   44  Arcadia II   26    4
    Thou God, whose youth was deckt with spoyle of Python's
        skin . . . . . . . . . . . . . . . . . . . . . . . .     44  Arcadia II   26    5
    Latona's sonne, whose birth in paine and travaile long . .   45  Arcadia II   26    7
    Whose wounds are salves, whose yokes please more then
        pleasure doth: . . . . . . . . . . . . . . . . . . .     49  2nd Eclogues 28   56
    Whose onely face the little heaven is, . . . . . . . . .     51  2nd Eclogues 28  107
    Whose cries are ladders made to climb dishonor . . . . .     50  2nd Eclogues 28 V 34
    Shall I, whose eares her mournefull words did seaze, . .     58  2nd Eclogues 30   50
    Of lothsome dayes, whose losse how canst thou mone,. . . .   59  2nd Eclogues 30   78
    In whose decay Vertue's faire shrine must fall.. . . . .     59  2nd Eclogues 30   91
    Thy Venus' child, whose beautie Venus lackes?. . . . . .     60  2nd Eclogues 30  112
    O soule, whose love in her is onely spent, . . . . . . .     60  2nd Eclogues 30  122
    And whose good happ, doth leave him unprovided,. . . . . .   62  2nd Eclogues 30  177
    Whose shade safety doth hold, danger avoideth her: . . . .   69  2nd Eclogues 34   34
    Trew harte, whose trewthe dothe yeeld to trewest bande,. . . 70  Arcadia III  35   11
    And in whose eyes my dayly doome I reede.. . . . . . . .     72  Arcadia III  38    5
    Whose fyrie chaines, uppon his freedome seaze, . . . . .     74  Arcadia III  41    4
    Howe is my Sunn, whose beames are shining bright,. . . . .   74  Arcadia III  42    1
    Like divers flowers, whose divers beauties serve . . . .     78  Arcadia III  50    1
    Is left a Sunne, whose beames thy place may use? . . . .     80  Arcadia III  52    6
    Mine owne? o word on whose sweete sound doth pray. . . .     80  Arcadia III  53    5
    As oh! my selfe, whose woes are never lighte . . . . . .     82  Arcadia III  56    9
    In whose each part all pens may dwell? . . . . . . . . .     85  Arcadia III  62    2
    Whose equall lynes their angles bowes, . . . . . . . . .     86  Arcadia III  62   10
    Whose winke ech bold attempt forbids,. . . . . . . . . .     86  Arcadia III  62   14
    Nc lampe, whose light by Art is got,. . . . . . . . . . .    86  Arcadia III  62   17
    In whose Incirclets if you gaze, . . . . . . . . . . . .     86  Arcadia III  62   31
    But Lillies such whose native smell. . . . . . . . . . .     87  Arcadia III  62   63
    Whose motion makes all graces move.. . . . . . . . . . .     89  Arcadia III  62   96
    Whose bought incav'd doth yeeld such sight,. . . . . . .     89  Arcadia III  62   97
    Whose Atlas is a smallest small, . . . . . . . . . . . .     89  Arcadia III  62  103
```

586

WHOSE	(CONTINUED)	PAGE	TITLE		LINE
Whose steppe on earth all beautie sets..		89	Arcadia III	62	108
Along whose ridge such bones are met,.		89	Arcadia III	62	111
Of whose high praise, and praisefull blisse, ...		90	Arcadia III	62	141
In whose each part all pens may dwell.		90	Arcadia III	62	146
Whose eeven descent makes equall falle,.		89	Arcadia III	62	V104
Whose gentle rayes suche Luster fynde, ...		89	Arcadia III	62	V115
Whose loves may ever bide, ...		91	3rd Eclogues	63	14
Whose care is cause that they in number growe, ...		92	3rd Eclogues	63	38
Whose light is cause we have our lives neglected		108	Arcadia IV	69	7
Strephon. For she, whose parts maintainde a perfect musique,		113	4th Eclogues	71	61
Whose beawties shin'de more then the blushing morning, . . .		113	4th Eclogues	71	62
She, whose lest word brings from the spheares their musique,		113	4th Eclogues	71	68
At whose approach the Sunne rase in the evening, ...		113	4th Eclogues	71	69
My ship, my selfe, whose course to love doth bende,.		114	4th Eclogues	72	44
Whose footsteps I with kisses oft did trace, ...		115	4th Eclogues	72	73
Whose braines boile not in woes, nor brests with beatings ake, ...		117	4th Eclogues	73	13
But like the feeble flower (whose stalke cannot sustaine . .		117	4th Eclogues	73	21
Whose stormelike course staid not till hard by me it bided..		118	4th Eclogues	73	60
Since so she will, whose will is to me more then a lawe. . .		124	4th Eclogues	74	84
O Elements, by whose (they say) contention,.		128	4th Eclogues	75	106
Shepherd of shepherds, whose well setled order		128	4th Eclogues	75	128
Yet craving law of armes, whose rule doth teach, ...		135	Cert Sonnets	1	10
Like foe, whose wits inclin'd to deadly spite,.		135	Cert Sonnets	2	3
How holdst thou her, whose eyes constraint doth feare, . . .		142	Cert Sonnets	10	5
Whom curst do blesse, whose weakenesse vertues arme, ...		142	Cert Sonnets	10	6
In whose sweete heav'n Angels of high thoughts swarme? . . .		142	Cert Sonnets	10	8
To hie conceits whose fruits are oft but small,.		144	Cert Sonnets	15	10
Whose hearts are set on measuring a verse:		146	Cert Sonnets	17	32
Sweet Ladie, as for those whose sullen cheare, ...		147	Cert Sonnets	17	46
Whose eyes seeme chaste, because they looke on ground: . . .		147	Cert Sonnets	17	50
My lake is sense, whose still streames never runne,.		150	Cert Sonnets	22	15
Peake hath a Cave, whose narrow entries finde.		150	Cert Sonnets	22	31
Whose clowdie thoughts let fall an inward raine.		150	Cert Sonnets	22	36
Thou web of will, whose end is never wrought;.		161	Cert Sonnets	31	4
Ought to be king, from whose rules who do swerve,.		167	Astrophil	5	3
Whose faire skin, beamy eyes, like morning sun on snow,. . .		169	Astrophil	8	9
Whose porches rich (which name of cheekes endure).		169	Astrophil	9	7
Thou countest Stella thine, like those whose powers.		171	Astrophil	12	9
Of those three gods, whose armes the fairest were:		171	Astrophil	13	2
Whose talents held young Ganimed above:.		171	Astrophil	13	4
Upon whose breast a fiercer Gripe doth tire.		171	Astrophil	14	2
Rich fooles there be, whose base and filthy hart		176	Astrophil	24	1
Whose numbers, wayes, greatnesse, eternitie, ...		178	Astrophil	26	3
Princesse of Beautie, for whose only sake.		179	Astrophil	28	6
Whose beames be joyes, whose joyes all vertues be, ...		185	Astrophil	42	2
To such a schoole-mistresse, whose lessons new		188	Astrophil	46	10
Whose necke becomes such yoke of tyranny?.		188	Astrophil	47	4
Whose curelesse wounds even now most freshly bleed:.		189	Astrophil	48	11
Whose presence, absence, absence presence is;.		195	Astrophil	60	13
She in whose eyes Love, though unfelt, doth shine, ...		196	Astrophil	62	3
Of reason, from whose light those night-birds flie;.		201	Astrophil	71	7
With such a rosie morne, whose beames most freshly gay . . .		205	Astrophil	76	7
Those lookes, whose beames be joy, whose motion is delight,		205	Astrophil	77	1
That face, whose lecture shewes what perfect beautie is: . .		205	Astrophil	77	2
That skin, whose passe-praise hue scorns this poore terme of white:.		205	Astrophil	77	7
Whose fruit doth farre th' Esperian tast surpasse:		208	Astrophil	82	6
Nor do like Lords, whose weake confused braine.		210	Astrophil	85	5
Stella whose eyes make all my tempests cleere,.		222	Astrophil	87	3
Bringing with her those starry Nimphs, whose chace		229	Astrophil	97	3
Whose pants do make unspilling creame to flow, ...		231	Astrophil	100	6
Wing'd with whose breath, so pleasing Zephires blow, ...		231	Astrophil	100	7
That hue, whose force my hart still·unto thraldome ties? . .		232	Astrophil	102	8
Who hath the feet, whose step all sweetnesse planteth, . . .		197	A&S 1st Song		13
Who hath the breast, whose milke doth passions nourish,. . .		197	A&S 1st Song		17
Whose grace is such, that when it chides doth cherish? . . .		197	A&S 1st Song		18
Whose force but yours the bolts of beautie thunders?		197	A&S 1st Song		30
Whose owne fault casts him downe, hardly high seat recovers.		213	A&S 5th Song		24
Nor of that golden sea, whose waves in curles are brok'n:. .		213	A&S 5th Song		39
Whose throne is in the mind, ...		217	A&S 6th Song		50
Whose senses in so evill consort, their stepdame Nature laies, ...		217	A&S 7th Song		1
"Stella, in whose shining eyes,.		218	A&S 8th Song		33
Whose beames, where they once are darted,.		218	A&S 8th Song		35
"Stella, whose voice when it speakes,.		219	A&S 8th Song		37
Stella, whose voice when it singeth, ...		219	A&S 8th Song		39
"Stella, in whose body is.		219	A&S 8th Song		41
Whose face all, all beauty passeth,.		219	A&S 8th Song		43
Whose braunches faile not timely fruite to nourish,.		270	Psalm I		9
O men, whose Fathers were but men, ...		273	Psalm IV		6
Than they whose stoare in harvest space.		274	Psalm IV		29
By power of whose only brest, ...		274	Psalm IV		34
Thou hatest all whose works in evill are plac't.		275	Psalm V		13
In all whose workes vainess is ever raigning:.		276	Psalm VI		26
Whose life no life but of Thee holdeth,.		278	Psalm VIII		12
By them whose minds on hatefull thoughts do stay:.		280	Psalm IX		38
Whose fury bends to harme:		283	Psalm X		66
Whom troubles tosse, whose natures need doth quell,.		285	Psalm XII		14

WHOSE	(CONTINUED)	PAGE	TITLE		LINE
Whose deeds of Righteous heart, whose hearty words be plain,		287	Psalm XV		4
Whose eyes a person vile do hold in vile disdain		287	Psalm XV		7
And whose bodys placed be.		289	Psalm XVI		42
Whose life doth seeme most greatly blest		290	Psalm XVII		39
Whose bellyes so with daintys Thou dost fill		290	Psalm XVII		41
Whose loosed bones quite out of joint be wryde;		299	Psalm XXII		32
Whose heart with these huge flames, like wax o're heated,.		299	Psalm XXII		33
Even he whose life no help of man can quicken.		300	Psalm XXII		74
He that hath hurtless hands, whose inward heart is framed.		302	Psalm XXIV		7
The lord whose strength makes battails fight..		302	Psalm XXIV		20
Whose hands do handle nought,.		306	Psalm XXVI		31
That hand whose strength should help of bribes is full..		306	Psalm XXVI		33
Unto whose ever hating lust.		308	Psalm XXVII		55
Ev'n such I say, whose lying tongue.		308	Psalm XXVII		58
I hated have those men whose thoughts do cleave.		312	Psalm XXXI		16
Bless'ed is the man whose filthy stain		314	Psalm XXXII		1
Whose fault well hidden lyeth.		314	Psalm XXXII		3
Whose spirit falshood flyeth..		314	Psalm XXXII		6
Whose mouths Thy self dost bridle,		315	Psalm XXXII		33
In them whose heart.		316	Psalm XXXIII		5
Whose God he is,		317	Psalm XXXIII		44
Whose shield shall us maintaine.		318	Psalm XXXIII		78
Whose faces on his comfort staid		319	Psalm XXXIV		19
Whose trust is all on thee..		319	Psalm XXXIV		32
Who helpest those, whose ruin was so neere,.		321	Psalm XXXV		23
From him whose force did in their spoiles appeare.		321	Psalm XXXV		24
And whose? ev'n his who when they sickness bare.		322	Psalm XXXV		29
Whose foule weights have me opprest.		327	Psalm XXXVIII		12
Whose trust is so addressed,		331	Psalm XL		16
Whose wages makes me beg the more, who feeds me till I sterve,.		343	Possibly	1	20
Whose lyverie is such, as most I freeze apparelled most,		343	Possibly	1	21
I then, whose burd'ned brest but thus aspires.		242	Other Poems	4	9
Whose mettall stiff he knew he could not bende		245	Other Poems	4	138
Whose boiling heat encreased as she wept:.		246	Other Poems	4	155
Strephon, whose absence seem'd unto thee long,		247	Other Poems	4	220
With Cosma, for whose love Pas past in woe..		248	Other Poems	4	243
With whose fine stepps all lookes and joyes conspire.		250	Other Poems	4	302
So that Uran, whose arme old Geron bore,		250	Other Poems	4	309
While deare Uran, whose course was Pas to meet,.		250	Other Poems	4	330
Strephon, whose eies on hir back-parts did play,		250	Other Poems	4	333
And thou my dogg, whose truth and valiant might.		254	Other Poems	4	485
Or like a lambe whose dam away is fet,		254	Other Poems	4	490
Urania name, whose force he knew so well,.		256	Other Poems	4	538
Whose foote doth set a heav'n on cursed thee,.		256	Other Poems	5	19
Sweete Orpheus' Harpe, whose sound		260	Other Poems	6	13
Like the wiser sorte, whose learning,.		263	Other Poems	7	41
In whose love I pleasure take,		263	Other Poems	7	62
WHOSO					
Wher who so wynns, I put my selfe to flight.		74	Arcadia III	42	8
That who so that grace obtaineth,.		140	Cert Sonnets	7	25
But who so will instructed be.		315	Psalm XXXII		28
WHY					
Why thee a living man they had made dead..		11	Arcadia I	1	7
Nico. Ah now I see, why thou art in thy selfe so blind:.		52	2nd Eclogues	29	5
Why doost thou haste away.		80	Arcadia III	52	1
Why should we spare our voice from endlesse wailing,		109	Arcadia IV	70	7
As nature's worke: why should we feare to dye?		131	Arcadia V	77	2
Why should we feare that which we cannot flye?		131	Arcadia V	77	4
Thinking not why, but how himselfe to save..		145	Cert Sonnets	16	8
For why should I, whom free choise slave doth make,.		146	Cert Sonnets	17	9
Why those that die, men say they do depart:.		148	Cert Sonnets	20	2
In colour blacke, why wrapt she beames so bright?.		168	Astrophil	7	2
Why shouldst thou toyle our thornie soile to till?		169	Astrophil	10	6
Deare, why make you more of a dog then me?		194	Astrophil	59	1
Why doest thou spend the treasures of thy sprite,.		200	Astrophil	68	5
But why? because of you they models be,.		225	Astrophil	91	10
Sweet alas, why strive you thus?		211	A&S 4th Song		43
"Why alas, and are you he?		234	A&S 11th Song		6
Why alas doth she then sweare,		222	A&S 9th Song		31
Why do these earthly kings and lords such meetings make,		271	Psalm II		3
Why standest Thou so farr,		281	Psalm X		1
Why should the evill, so evill despise		283	Psalm X		53
And why should he in heart so hard		283	Psalm X		55
Your fearfull words why do you spill		283	Psalm XI		2
Save me lord, for why Thou art		287	Psalm XVI		1
For why, my fighting strength by Thy strength strengthned was.		292	Psalm XVIII		71
And why all this? Because Our King		297	Psalm XXI		25
My God my God why hast Thou me forsaken?		298	Psalm XXII		1
Woe me, from me why is Thy presence taken?		298	Psalm XXII		2
Teach me for why Thou art.		303	Psalm XXV		14
For why the Well of life Thou art.		324	Psalm XXXVI		25
Why? because I virtue chose.		329	Psalm XXXVIII		60
But I do hush, Why do I say thus much,		330	Psalm XXXIX		29
And hearkned how, and why that I did cry,.		331	Psalm XL		4
Why art Thou my soul so sorry.		334	Psalm XLII		17
Above line repeated at following location.		335	Psalm XLII		49
Why am I forgott by Thee?.		335	Psalm XLII		42

WHY	(CONTINUED)	PAGE	TITLE	LINE
Why should grief my heart devower, ...		335	Psalm XLII	43
Why then hast thou left me?.		336	Psalm XLIII	9
Why walk I in woes		336	Psalm XLIII	10
Why art Thou my soul		337	Psalm XLIII	31

WICKED

While still more wretch, more wicked he doth prove:.		22	1st Eclogues 8	44
The straying stepps as wicked Counsel leads;		270	Psalm I	2
Such blessings shall not wycked wretches see		270	Psalm I	13
And wyked folkes from thee to wrack do wend.		279	Psalm IX	12
When Wycked soules be turn'd to hellish paine, ...		281	Psalm IX	53
For lo with pride the wicked man		281	Psalm X	5
Breake Thou the wyked arm.		283	Psalm X	65
Search them, and wyked he.		283	Psalm X	67
But hates, abhorrs the wycked braines, ...		284	Psalm XI	18
From my destroying Wicked Foes		290	Psalm XVII	27
Yea worse than doggs, a naughty wicked rout.		299	Psalm XXII	40
Of wicked wights the nest, ...		305	Psalm XXVI	17
But led by wicked thought.		306	Psalm XXVI	32
When wicked folk, even they that be.		307	Psalm XXVII	7
With the wicked working folk		309	Psalm XXVIII	12
As deserves their wicked witt;		309	Psalm XXVIII	18
For I have call'd on Thee, let wicked folk		313	Psalm XXXI	46
Woes, woes shall come to wicked folks;		315	Psalm XXXII	37
That wicked be, their very name.		320	Psalm XXXIV	59
But malice shall the wicked choake, ...		320	Psalm XXXIV	75
Which wicked folks do hold so deare;		323	Psalm XXXVI	3
That wicked men do seeme to flourish, ...		324	Psalm XXXVII	2
The wicked by his own pride bannisht;		325	Psalm XXXVII	26
For wycked arms shall breake asunder, ...		325	Psalm XXXVII	43
The Wicked watch the righteous much.		326	Psalm XXXVII	81
I have the Wicked seen full sound, ...		327	Psalm XXXVII	89
Against them usd by wicked wretches, ...		327	Psalm XXXVII	103
I do abide of wicked wight.		329	Psalm XXXIX	4
Ev'en heapes of wicked thoughts which streight they show . .		333	Psalm XLI	23

WICKEDNESS

In that, which of fowle wickedness doth smel:.		274	Psalm V	10
If ought my hands of wyckednes do bear:.		277	Psalm VII	9
O let their wickedness no longer bide.		277	Psalm VII	25
The floods of wickedness on me did horrors throw, ...		291	Psalm XVIII	9
Scund and upright with him, to wickedness not bent.		292	Psalm XVIII	46
And open'd mine own wickedness, ...		315	Psalm XXXII	14
What guilty wickedness doth say, ...		323	Psalm XXXVI	2

WICKET

Pas. Cosma once said, she left the wicket ope, ...		55	2nd Eclogues 29	90

WIDE

Her haire pure Crapal-stone; her mouth O heavenly wyde; . . .		12	Arcadia I 3	11
Phoebus drew wide the curtaines of the skies		171	Astrophil 13	12
And said to me wide mowing as they could, ...		322	Psalm XXXV	53

WIDELY

Since Nico doth to sing so widely gape?.		53	2nd Eclogues 29	55

WIDOW

A widow turtle neere on bared root		256	Other Poems 5	6

WIELD

Of growing trees, yee rurall Gods that wield		40	Arcadia II 18	2

WIFE

Thou, with thy wife, adultry shalt commit.		11	Arcadia I 1	10
Happy man, happy wife.		94	3rd Eclogues 63	95
The goodman bad his wife be serviceable.		94	3rd Eclogues 64	24
Nct seeing earst such token in the wife, ...		96	3rd Eclogues 64	68
The wife thus having settled husband's braine, ...		96	3rd Eclogues 64	73
Who doth desire that chaste his wife should be, ...		98	3rd Eclogues 65	1
Then is the quiet joy of loving wife;		103	3rd Eclogues 67	8
No wife but I hath such a man, God wot".		104	3rd Eclogues 67	45
I have a wife worthie to be a Queene, ...		106	3rd Eclogues 67	88
Unto no body my woman saith she had rather a wife be, . . .		143	Cert Sonnets 13	1

WIGHT

The wisest scholler of the wight most wise		177	Astrophil 25	1
From heavenly standing hits each mortall wight.		229	Astrophil 97	4
Cals each wight to salute the floure of blisse;		231	Astrophil 99	11
Nor meek abiding of the patient wight.		281	Psalm IX	58
I ev'en as such kind of wight, ...		328	Psalm XXXVIII	40
I do abide of wicked wight.		329	Psalm XXXIX	4
When, when will death o'retake this wretched wight		333	Psalm XLI	19
Was Klaius cald, (ah Klaius, wofull wight!).		242	Other Poems 4	23
I tolde you Klaius was the haples wight.		251	Other Poems 4	365

WIGHTS

To Westerne wightes, what starres in East appeare?		80	Arcadia III 52	4
Shall these bad wights devouer.		297	Psalm XXI	36
Of wicked wights the nest, ...		305	Psalm XXVI	17
Save me from bad wights.		336	Psalm XLIII	5

WILD

Let not wild woods so great a treasure have.		3	Lady of May 2	12
The cattell wild, or tame, in nature's bowers.		100	3rd Eclogues 66	47
Hunting the wilde inhabiters of forrests, ...		111	4th Eclogues 71	20
Thunders of cries; lightnings my wilde lookes be, ...		114	4th Eclogues 72	34
By Parents train'd the Tartars wilde are tought, ...		251	Other Poems 4	350

WILDEST

Two thousand deere in wildest woods I have, ...		4	Lady of May 2	25

589

WILILY
    Full Wylily intended;. . . . . 298 Psalm XXI   42
*WILL
    Warme well thy wits, if thou wilt win her will,. . . . . . . 3 Lady of May   2   3
    Thus is my power transformed to your will. . . . . 12 Arcadia I   2 12
    Yet all my health I place in your good-will. . . . . 18 1st Eclogues 7 120
    The witts abuse with will no counsayle take. . . . . 23 1st Eclogues 9   22
    He is a beast, that beaste's use will allowe . . . . 25 1st Eclogues 9   99
    Youth will have will: Age must to age therefore. . . . . . . 27 1st Eclogues 10 24
    Bard of my will, I have beyond desire: . . . . 41 Arcadia II   20   7
    P. If Reason will, that Passions be not free. . . . . 46 2nd Eclogues 27   4
    R. But Reason will, that Reason governe most. . . . . 46 2nd Eclogues 27   5
    P. And Passion will, that Passion rule the rost. . . . . . . 46 2nd Eclogues 27   6
    R. Your will is will; but Reason reason is. . . . . 46 2nd Eclogues 27   7
    P. Will hath his will, when Reason's will doth misse. . . . 46 2nd Eclogues 27   8
    Paine willes me die, yet will of death I mortifie: . . . . . 51 2nd Eclogues 28 124
    Of windes quite contrarie in waves of will:. . . . . 59 2nd Eclogues 30 81
    That sorrowe's worke against my will I prove. . . . . 60 2nd Eclogues 30 127
    Well mett Echo, aproche: then tell me thy will too. I will
       too. . . . . 63 2nd Eclogues 31   4
    Then then what do I gaine, since unto hir will I do winde?
       Winde. . . . . 64 2nd Eclogues 31 34
    The song thereof a last will,. . . . . 66 2nd Eclogues 32 34
    Held, pearst, possest, my judgement, sence, and will,. . . . 84 Arcadia III 60   6
    To whome our prince did beare a great good will, ... 94 3rd Eclogues 64 16
    And (though against his will) on him she leand,. . . . . . . 95 3rd Eclogues 64 44
    Was jumpe concorde betweene our wit and will: . . . . 99 3rd Eclogues 66 30
    But since you will, part of my heav'nly fire . . . . 100 3rd Eclogues 66 75
    With such a will that nothing can asswage. . . . . 105 3rd Eclogues 67 51
    For so did I, when with my angle, Will,. . . . . 115 4th Eclogues 72 62
    She waited mistresse' will: who thus disclosd her spright. . 119 4th Eclogues 73 92
    Of what thou seest: close up in secrete knot thy will". . . 119 4th Eclogues 73 98
    To stand unto my will: their will they made me know. . . . . 121 4th Eclogues 73 157
    Since so she will, whose will is to me more then a lawe. . . 124 4th Eclogues 74 84
    But all, for all reach not my wailefull will:. . . . . 126 4th Eclogues 75 33
    Since will is won, and stopped eares are charmed:. . . . . . 135 Cert Sonnets 1   3
    For Thereus' force on her chaste will prevailing. . . . . . 137 Cert Sonnets 4   8
    Full womanlike complaines her will was brokne. . . . . 137 Cert Sonnets 4 16
    Their master is faire warn'd his will to make. . . . . 150 Cert Sonnets 22 20
    His will false-seeming holie . . . . 160 Cert Sonnets 30 15
    Thou web of will, whose end is never wrought;. . . . . 161 Cert Sonnets 31   4
    Thou setst a bate betweene my will and wit,. . . . . 166 Astrophil   4   2
    Deale thou with powers of thoughts, leave love to will. . . 169 Astrophil 10   8
    The Wand is Will, thou Fancie Saddle art,. . . . . 189 Astrophil 49   9
    But do not will me from my Love to flie. . . . . 198 Astrophil 64   8
    Feare to offend, will worthie to appeare,. . . . . 202 Astrophil 72 10
    For nothing from my wit or will doth flow, ... 224 Astrophil 90 12
    All folkes prest at thy will thy paine to 'swage,. . . . . . 232 Astrophil 101 11
    Till it have wrought what thy owne will attends. . . . . . . 236 Astrophil 107 11
    O tremble then with awfull will: . . . . 273 Psalm IV   16
    Wee both have power, and will our tales to tell, ... 285 Psalm XII   11
    And so with hidden treasures grant their Will, ... 290 Psalm XVII   42
    To grant Thy Will and perfect Thy entent,. . . . . 296 Psalm XX   17
    For they to overthrow Thy Will . . . . 298 Psalm XXI   41
    For quickly ends his wrathfull Will, ... 311 Psalm XXX   13
    And sought with deeds Thy will to hitt;. . . . . 331 Psalm XL   33
    And will not him unto the will expose. . . . . 333 Psalm XLI   7
    Will. Dick, since we cannot dance, come let a chearefull
       voyce. . . . . 343 Possibly   1   1
    Dick. Ah Will, though I grudge not, I count it feeble glee . 343 Possibly   1   3
    Will. A tyme there is for all, my Mother often sayes,. . . . 343 Possibly   1   9
    Will. What? is thy Bagpipe broke, or are thy lambs miswent;. 343 Possibly   1 15
    Will. Thou seest my eares do itch at it: good Dick thy sorow
       tell. . . . . 343 Possibly   1 18
    Will. What? these are riddles sure, art thou then bound to
       her? . . . . 343 Possibly   1 23
    Will. What keepeth safe thy band? D. Remembrance is the
       Chest. . . . . 344 Possibly   1 29
    Will. Thou late of wages playn'dst: what wages mayst thou
       have?. . . . . 344 Possibly   1 31
    Will. What living get you then? D. Disdayne; but just
       disdayne. . . . . 344 Possibly   1 35
    Will. What care takes shee for thee? D. Hir care is to
       prevent. . . . . 344 Possibly   1 37
    Will. God shield us from such Dames. If so our Downes be
       sped,. . . . . 344 Possibly   1 39
    Dick. Good Will, I cannot take thy good advice, before . . . 344 Possibly   1 43
    Will. Then Dick let us go hence lest wee great folkes annoy. 344 Possibly   1 45
    Who would have hir in will and worde agree . . . . 245 Other Poems 4 115
    While I in heart my will write ere I die. . . . . 255 Other Poems 4 499
    In which by will, my will and wits I binde:. . . . . 255 Other Poems 4 500
    Hides their inward will of harming. . . . . 263 Other Poems 7 42
WILLED
    Willd me these tempests of vaine love to flie, ... 196 Astrophil 62 10
WILLFULLY
    But who doth feare, or bideth muet wilfully, ... 48 2nd Eclogues 28 17
WILLING
    Such oddes I willing lay; for him and you I know. . . . . . 53 2nd Eclogues 29 48
    Of willing teares, torne heare, and cries of sorrow. . . . . 109 Arcadia IV 70 16
    And hither now, vouchsafe to take with willing eare. . . . . 119 4th Eclogues 73 104

```
WILLING                    (CONTINUED)              PAGE   TITLE            LINE
    I willing run, yet while I run, repent.. . . . . . . . . .  174 Astrophil      19    4
    Doth willing graunt, that in the frontiers he. . . . . . . .  179 Astrophil      29    7
    To downe proud hearts that would not willing dye.. . . . . .  250 Other Poems     4  304
WILLOW
    Mirtle makes my request, my request is crown'd with a
        willowe. . . . . . . . . . . . . . . . . . . . . . . . .   35 1st Eclogues 13  118
WILLOW'S
    And gives her kidds no food, but willow's barke.". . . . .  259 Other Poems     5  113
WILLS
    Paine willes me die, yet will of death I mortifie: . . . .   51 2nd Eclogues 28  124
WILT
    Warme well thy wits, if thou wilt win her will,. . . . . . .    3 Lady of May   2    3
    Lalus. If thou wilt not be seene, thy face goe hide away,. .   15 1st Eclogues  7   13
    Within thy selfe, thou soone wilt be ashamed . . . . . . . .   25 1st Eclogues  9  118
    As thou wilt give our soules a deare refection,. . . . . . .   49 2nd Eclogues 28   52
    Boulon. How long wilt thou with monefull musicke staine. . .   58 2nd Eclogues 30   38
    But yet o dreame, if thou wilt not departe . . . . . . . . .   79 Arcadia III  51    9
    But wilt thy selfe in such a seate delighte, . . . . . . . .   79 Arcadia III  51   11
    As thou wilt deigne to reade, and gentlie reede, . . . . . .   96 3rd Eclogues 64   95
    Unto revenge? O sweete, on a wretch wilt thou be revenged? .  123 4th Eclogues 74   37
    But if that needs thou wilt usurping be, . . . . . . . . . .  167 Astrophil      4    9
    But wilt new warre upon thine owne begin?. . . . . . . . . .  183 Astrophil     36    8
    No Patience, if thou wilt my good, then make . . . . . . . .  193 Astrophil     56   12
    Thou English murdring theefe, wilt have harts for thy pray:.  214 A&S 5th Song        50
    Say whether thou wilt crowne, . . . . . . . . . . . . . . .  217 A&S 6th Song        53
    Since ever thou to them wilt succour send. . . . . . . . . .  275 Psalm V             36
    Alas, how long, my God, wilt Thou delay me?. . . . . . . . .  276 Psalm VI            10
    Thou lord also th' Oppressed wilt defend . . . . . . . . . .  280 Psalm IX            26
    For Thou lord found by them wilt ever be . . . . . . . . . .  280 Psalm IX            29
    How long wilt Thou Thy hidden face from me . . . . . . . . .  285 Psalm XIII           3
    For I know thou wilt defend. . . . . . . . . . . . . . . . .  288 Psalm XVI           33
    Thou the path wilt make me tread . . . . . . . . . . . . . .  288 Psalm XVI           37
    And boldly say Thou wilt give eare to me,. . . . . . . . . .  289 Psalm XVII          18
    That Thou by Faithfull Men wilt stand. . . . . . . . . . . .  290 Psalm XVII          23
    Up then thou liftst the poore, and down the proud wilt cast;  292 Psalm XVIII         52
    When Thou wilt deign to heare him. . . . . . . . . . . . . .  315 Psalm XXXII         21
    Lord wilt thou see, and wilt Thou suffer it? . . . . . . . .  322 Psalm XXXV          43
    This thou hast seen, and wilt thou silent be?. . . . . . . .  322 Psalm XXXV          55
    My God Thou wilt heare my voice; . . . . . . . . . . . . . .  328 Psalm XXXVIII       45
    Wilt thou have more? more have, if more I be. . . . . . . .  255 Other Poems     4  514
WILTON
    Neere Wilton sweete, huge heapes of stones are found,. . . .  149 Cert Sonnets 22    1
    So on the downs we see, neere Wilton faire,. . . . . . . . .  251 Other Poems     4  342
WILY
    Some gazing still, some winking wilye shiftes, . . . . . . .   21 1st Eclogues  8   27
    When hee once drau'th his wily nett. . . . . . . . . . . . .  282 Psalm X             40
    Preserve me from the wyly wrappinge nett . . . . . . . . . .  312 Psalm XXXI          10
WIN
    Warme well thy wits, if thou wilt win her will,. . . . . . .    3 Lady of May   2    3
    Like busie boyes, to winne their tutor's harte,. . . . . . .   27 1st Eclogues 10   43
    P. What shall we winne by taking Reason's yoke?. . . . . . .   47 2nd Eclogues 27   34
    Pas. My voice the lambe did winne, Menalcas was our judge:.   52 2nd Eclogues 29   15
    If thou (alas poore if) do winne, then winne thou this,. . .   53 2nd Eclogues 29   37
    Goe winne of him (for chattering) praise or shame: . . . . .   56 2nd Eclogues 29  139
    How can she love where love cannot win trust?) . . . . . . .   93 3rd Eclogues 63   85
    For no faire signe can credit winne, . . . . . . . . . . . .  156 Cert Sonnets 27   15
    Knowledge might pitie winne, and pitie grace obtaine,. . . .  165 Astrophil      1    4
    That to win it, is all the skill and paine. . . . . . . . .  171 Astrophil     12   14
    A conquerd, yelden, ransackt heart to winne? . . . . . . . .  182 Astrophil     36    2
    Might winne some grace in your sweet skill arraid. . . . . .  192 Astrophil     55    4
    But that which once may win thy cruell hart: . . . . . . . .  198 Astrophil     64   13
    That to win me, oft shewes a present pay?. . . . . . . . . .  223 Astrophil     88    4
    O Lord, of Thee let me still mercy winn, . . . . . . . . . .  312 Psalm XXXI          25
    More prayse to us we never looke to winne, . . . . . . . . .  346 Possibly        5   11
    Till of his life it did full conquest win, . . . . . . . . .  253 Other Poems     4  430
    Oh! what doth wailing winne? . . . . . . . . . . . . . . . .  259 Other Poems     5  103
*WIND
    This winde he spent: but when my Kala glasseth all . . . . .   16 1st Eclogues  7   55
    And hopes the flickring winde with net to holde, . . . . . .   24 1st Eclogues  9   54
    When by the winde it maketh a noyse, I do thinke she doth
        answer. . . . . . . . . . . . . . . . . . . . . . . . .   36 1st Eclogues 13  145
    Then what do I gaine, since unto hir will I do winde?
        Winde. . . . . . . . . . . . . . . . . . . . . . . . . .   64 2nd Eclogues 31   34
    Winde, tempests, and stormes, yet in ende what gives she
        desire? Ire. . . . . . . . . . . . . . . . . . . . . . .   64 2nd Eclogues 31   35
    What horrors breede, wheare wynd dominion beares,. . . . . .   71 Arcadia III  37    2
    Ruine, the winde, hath blowne her from her scope:. . . . . .  114 4th Eclogues 72   48
    Torne you should disperse unto the blasts of a winde.. . . .  123 4th Eclogues 74   52
    The wynde most oft the hugest Pine-tree greeves: . . . . . .  143 Cert Sonnets 12    7
    In too full winde draw in thy swelling sailes. . . . . . . .  143 Cert Sonnets 12   18
    In wind or water streame do require to be writ.. . . . . . .  143 Cert Sonnets 13    4
    My ship, desire, with winde of lust long tost, . . . . . . .  151 Cert Sonnets 22   55
    No wind, no shade can coole, what helpe then in my case, . .  205 Astrophil     76   12
    "This small wind which so sweete is, . . . . . . . . . . . .  219 A&S 8th Song        57
    But lyke vyle chaffe with wind shal scattred be. . . . . . .  270 Psalm I             14
    I bett those folks as small as dust, which wind doth rayse;.  293 Psalm XVIII         76
    And as vile chaff away the wind doth blow, . . . . . . . . .  321 Psalm XXXV          11
    While I do score my losses on the winde, . . . . . . . . . .  255 Other Poems     4  498
    'My song clime thou the winde. . . . . . . . . . . . . . . .  259 Other Poems     5  105
```

                                   591

```
WINDING                                                  PAGE    TITLE          LINE
    His winding sheete is shame, . . . . . . . . . . . . .  160 Cert Sonnets 30   14
    Like in a winding sheet, wretch I already lay, . . . . . . .  291 Psalm XVIII       10
WINDLASS
    My young mind marde, whom Love doth windlas so, . . . . . . .  175 Astrophil   21    2
WINDOW
    Who hard by made a window send forth light.. . . . . . . . .  191 Astrophil   53    9
    She so discheveld, blusht; from window I . . . . . . . . . .  233 Astrophil  103   12
    But if I by a happy window passe, . . . . . . . . . . . . . .  233 Astrophil  104    9
    Underneath my window playneth?". . . . . . . . . . . . . . .  233 A&S 11th Song      2
    With hear-say, pictures, or a window looke, . . . . . . . . .  245 Other Poems  4  139
WINDOW-GLASS
    With Diamond in window-glasse she graved, . . . . . . . . . .   61 2nd Eclogues 30  156
WINDOWS
    So that the windowes of my inward light. . . . . . . . . . .   73 Arcadia III  39    7
    The windowes now through which this heav'nly guest . . . . .  169 Astrophil    9    9
    With windowes ope then most my mind doth lie, . . . . . . . .  230 Astrophil   99    5
WINDS
    Of windes quite contrarie in waves of will: . . . . . . . . .   59 2nd Eclogues 30   81
    Where rockes do wayte, for theym the wyndes do chase, . . . .   70 Arcadia III  36    2
    While wanton winds with beauties so devine . . . . . . . . .  232 Astrophil  103    6
    The Cherubins their backs, the winds did yeild their wings, .  291 Psalm XVIII       22
WINE
    Like wine and milke that mingled stood.. . . . . . . . . . .   86 Arcadia III  62   30
    I joyed, but straight thus watred was my wine, . . . . . . .  196 Astrophil   62    5
    Of grain and wine fills stoaring place.. . . . . . . . . . .  274 Psalm IV          30
WING
    Bownded with no limitts, borne with a wing of hope . . . . .   68 2nd Eclogues 34    8
    Ev'n when night with his black wing. . . . . . . . . . . . .  288 Psalm XVI         21
    Trust in the shadow of thy wing. . . . . . . . . . . . . . .  324 Psalm XXXVI       21
WINGED
    Wing'd with whose breath, so pleasing Zephires blow, . . . .  231 Astrophil  100    7
WINGS
    Her minde, beames, state farre from thy weake wings
        banished . . . . . . . . . . . . . . . . . . . . . . . .   16 1st Eclogues  7   65
    Unto the heav'ns? our wings be too short; th' earth thinks
        us a burden; . . . . . . . . . . . . . . . . . . . . . .   32 1st Eclogues 13   29
    They feede on me, and with my wings do flie: . . . . . . . .   42 Arcadia II   22    9
    His wings desire oft clipt with desperation: . . . . . . . .   48 2nd Eclogues 28   44
    And to the sunne with waxen winges to flie?. . . . . . . . .   79 Arcadia III  50   14
    The Phoenix wings be not so rare . . . . . . . . . . . . . .   89 Arcadia III  62  118
    They all consented were to give him wings: . . . . . . . . .  101 3rd Eclogues 66  101
    Flew up with freer wings of fleshly bondage free; . . . . . .  117 4th Eclogues 73   33
    But with his wings of fancies up he goes, . . . . . . . . . .  144 Cert Sonnets 15    9
    Up to the sunne, although the sunne my wings do frie: . . . .  153 Cert Sonnets 24   25
    He burnt unwares his wings, and cannot fly away. . . . . . .  169 Astrophil    8   14
    This night while sleepe begins with heavy wings. . . . . . .  183 Astrophil   38    1
    Venus is taught with Dian's wings to flie: . . . . . . . . .  202 Astrophil   72    6
    With wings of Love in aire of wonder flie, . . . . . . . . .  212 Astrophil   86    8
    Without my plumes from others' wings I take. . . . . . . . .  224 Astrophil   90   11
    Clips streight my wings, streight wraps me in his night, . .  236 Astrophil  108    8
    The Cherubins their backs, the winds did yeild their wings, .  291 Psalm XVIII       22
    Doth on wings hir utmost swiftnes prove, . . . . . . . . . .  251 Other Poems  4  355
    That on his wings the leavell thou maist finde . . . . . . .  259 Other Poems  5  107
WINGS'
    In Thy wings' shade then let me hidden ly. . . . . . . . . .  290 Psalm XVII        26
WINK
    Let us not winke though void of purest sightfulnes.. . . . .   61 2nd Eclogues 30  139
    Whose winke ech bold attempt forbids.. . . . . . . . . . . .   86 Arcadia III  62   14
    Mine eyes then only winke, for spite perchance, . . . . . . .  230 Astrophil   98   13
WINKETH
    Where envie's snaky ey, winketh or els dyeth, . . . . . . . .   69 2nd Eclogues 34   37
WINKING
    Some gazing still, some winking wilye shiftes, . . . . . . .   21 1st Eclogues  8   27
    With winking eyes aye bent . . . . . . . . . . . . . . . . .  282 Psalm X           35
WINS
    That nothing winnes the heaven, but what doth earth forsake.   45 Arcadia II   26   16
    Wher who so wynns, I put my selfe to flight. . . . . . . . .   74 Arcadia III  42    8
WINTER
    Gone is the winter of my miserie, . . . . . . . . . . . . . .  200 Astrophil   69    7
    Griefe but Love's winter liverie is, the Boy . . . . . . . .  201 Astrophil   70    7
    That living thus in blackest winter night, . . . . . . . . .  224 Astrophil   89   13
WINTER'S
    Which on cold winter's face doth grow. . . . . . . . . . . .   85 Arcadia III  62    8
WINTERS
    These fiftie winters maried have I beene; . . . . . . . . . .  106 3rd Eclogues 67   86
    Fowle Winters as they come, away they shall. . . . . . . . .  143 Cert Sonnets 12   12
WINTER-STARVED
    Himselfe onely winter-sterved. . . . . . . . . . . . . . . .  222 A&S 9th Song      30
    I am as dull as winter-sterved sheep, . . . . . . . . . . . .  253 Other Poems  4  442
WIPE
    And wanting her, my weeping eyes I wipe. . . . . . . . . . .   54 2nd Eclogues 29   77
    A clenly cloth thy moistnes for to wipe: . . . . . . . . . .  257 Other Poems  5   55
WISDOM
    Your mind is wise, your wisedome makes you mild, . . . . . .    3 Lady of May   1    9
    That that deare Dyamond, where wisdome holdeth a sure seate,   37 1st Eclogues 13  165
    But who by meanes of wisdome hie . . . . . . . . . . . . . .   44 Arcadia II   25    5
    Alas it is no wisdome. . . . . . . . . . . . . . . . . . . .   65 2nd Eclogues 32    7
    Such wisedome, that in her lives speculation: . . . . . . . .   69 2nd Eclogues 34   35
    And wisdome to his wonted seate aspireth.. . . . . . . . . .   83 Arcadia III  57   12
```

592

WISDOM   (CONTINUED)   PAGE   TITLE   LINE
     Jove wisely said (for wisedome wisely sayes) . . . .   100 3rd Eclogues 66   71
     Sweete supple mindes which soone to wisdome bowe . . . . . .   106 3rd Eclogues 67   103
     Did Wisedome this our wretched time espie. . . . .   126 4th Eclogues 75   46
     Wisdome farewell, the skillesse man's direction: . . . . . .   129 4th Eclogues 76   5
     The same man still in whom wysdome prevailes,. . . . .   143 Cert Sonnets 12   17
     One that his Wisdom learneth. . . . .   286 Psalm XIV   9
     To simplest Wisdom lending.. . . . .   294 Psalm XIX   32
     The good mouth will in Wisdom bide,. . . . .   326 Psalm XXXVII   77
WISDOM'S
     To have his harmes with wisdome's helpe redrest. . . . . . .   75 Arcadia III 44   4
     Where they by wisdome's Rules directed are,. . . . .   106 3rd Eclogues 67   104
     With sinlesse sleepe, and silence, wisdome's mother, ...   108 Arcadia IV   69   10
     Where fairnesse yeelds to wisdome's shortest raines. . . . .   151 Cert Sonnets 22   64
     Sure you say well, your wisdome's director. . . . .   175 Astrophil   21   12
     Of Atlas tyr'd, your wisdome's heav'nly sway. . . . .   190 Astrophil   51   8
     Sweetner of musicke, wisdome's beautifier:. . . . .   207 Astrophil   80   6
     No, no, it was in spite of wisdome's song, ...   247 Other Poems   4   222
WISDOMS
     That to thy advauncement their wisdomes have thee abased... .   32 1st Eclogues 13   34
     That to my advauncement their wisdomes have me abased. . . .   32 1st Eclogues 13   36
     The high conceits thy heav'nly wisedomes breed . . . .   72 Arcadia III 38   2
*WISE
     Your mind is wise, your wisedome makes you mild, ...   3 Lady of May   1   9
     Such hartes of brasse, wise heads, and garments trim . . . .   24 1st Eclogues 9   75
     First thinke they erre, that thinke them gayly wise, ...   25 1st Eclogues 9   111
     But yet well I doo finde each man most wise in his owne
       case . . . .   33 1st Eclogues 13   70
     Old age is wise and full of constant truth;. . . . .   39 Arcadia II   15   9
     By wise discourse, sweete tunes, or Poet's fiction;. . . . .   61 2nd Eclogues 30   144
     And wise thoughts do behold what the creator is: . . . . . .   68 2nd Eclogues 34   6
     With circkled course, which no wise stay can trye, ...   81 Arcadia III 54   10
     And now before we seeke by wise Apollo's skill . . . .   120 4th Eclogues 73   125
     I never spited you, but thought you overwise.. . . . .   121 4th Eclogues 73   150
     No, no, she is too wise, she knowes her face . . . .   142 Cert Sonnets 11   9
     Would she in beamie blacke, like painter wise, ...   168 Astrophil   7   3
     O fooles, or over-wise, alas the race. . . . .   176 Astrophil   23   12
     The wisest scholler of the wight most wise . . . .   177 Astrophil   25   1
     That I had bene more foolish or more wise. . . . .   181 Astrophil   33   14
     "But will not wise men thinke thy words fond ware?". . . . .   182 Astrophil   34   7
     As my young Dove may in your precepts wise . . . .   196 Astrophil   63   3
     In this old world, growne now so too too wise: . . . .   198 Astrophil   65   6
     Wise silence is best musicke unto blisse.. . . . .   201 Astrophil   70   14
     Nor that he could young-wise, wise-valiant frame . . . . . .   204 Astrophil   75   5
     While such wise she love denied, ...   220 A&S 8th Song   71
     Therfore (O Kings), be wise, O Rulers rule your mind,. . . .   271 Psalm II   23
     So purely wise it gives the eyes . . . .   294 Psalm XIX   35
     He blessed is, who with wise temper can. . . . .   332 Psalm XLI   1
     Among the wisest was accounted wise, ...   243 Other Poems   4   34
     Yet not so wise, as of unstained harte:. . . . .   243 Other Poems   4   35
     Wise Counsellors, stout Captaines, puissant Kings, ...   245 Other Poems   4   130
     "Another time", quoth she, "become more wise". . . . .   249 Other Poems   4   275
     For then wise Klaius found no absence can. . . . .   253 Other Poems   4   419
     This song she singes in most commaunding wise: . . . .   255 Other Poems   4   509
     These markes shall make thee wise: . . . .   259 Other Poems   5   111
WISELY
     Cherish the hives of wisely painfull Bees: . . . .   26 1st Eclogues 9   132
     Jove wisely said (for wisedome wisely sayes) . . . .   100 3rd Eclogues 66   71
     Then might I wisely swimme or gladly sinke.. . . . .   148 Cert Sonnets 19   6
WISER
     But let us wiser be; and what foule discorde brake,. . . . .   120 4th Eclogues 73   119
     Like the wiser sorte, whose learning,. . . . .   263 Other Poems   7   41
WISEST
     Whose mind is such, as wisest minds appall,. . . . .   3 Lady of May   1   3
     The wisest scholler of the wight most wise . . . .   177 Astrophil   25   1
     Among the wisest was accounted wise, ...   243 Other Poems   4   34
WISE-VALIANT
     Nor that he could young-wise, wise-valiant frame . . . . . .   204 Astrophil   75   5
WISH
     No man doth wish his horse should aged bee.. . . . .   24 1st Eclogues 9   86
     But to my selfe what wish can I make for a salve to my
       sorrowes,. . . . .   37 1st Eclogues 13   157
     Then rage for rage: rather my wish I send to thee, ...   50 2nd Eclogues 28   97
     As for thy wish to my enraged spitefulnesse, ...   51 2nd Eclogues 28   111
     And make me wish my selfe layd under mountaines, ...   112 4th Eclogues 71   36
     Strephon. I wish to fire the trees of all these forrests;. .   112 4th Eclogues 71   49
     I wish no evenings more to see, each evening;. . . . .   112 4th Eclogues 71   58
     That thou full oft shalt wish thy judging eyes were blinde".   121 4th Eclogues 73   172
     Longing to have, having no wit to wish,. . . . .   136 Cert Sonnets 2   13
     Nor hope, nor wishe another course to frame, ...   198 Astrophil   64   12
     Of highest wish, I wish you so much blisse,. . . . .   209 Astrophil   84   13
     In truth I sweare, I wish not there should be. . . . .   224 Astrophil   90   7
     Doth make me most to wish thy comfort neere. . . . .   235 Astrophil   106   8
     I do any wish impart,.   220 A&S 8th Song   86
     Be both wish and I defaced.. . . . .   220 A&S 8th Song   88
WISHED
     His wished weale, what more he could require:. . . . .   4 Lady of May   3   4
     That where you are no wished good can want;. . . . .   39 Arcadia II   16   6
     I rather wisht thee clime the Muses' hill, ...   169 Astrophil   10   3
     Attain unto their wished scope.. . . . .   325 Psalm XXXVII   20

		PAGE	TITLE		LINE
WISHED	(CONTINUED)				
Which absence wisht: love plai'd a victor's part:.		248	Other Poems	4	223
WISHES					
Dicus. But so thy sheepe may thy good wishes satisfie. . . .		49	2nd Eclogues	28	49
With thankes and wishes, wishing thankfully.		209	Astrophil	84	8
WISHEST					
So may each thing, even as thou wishest lighte,.		96	3rd Eclogues	64	94
WISHING					
With thankes and wishes, wishing thankfully.		209	Astrophil	84	8
Voyde of wishing and repenting..		264	Other Poems	7	78
WIST					
Made them his owne before they had it wist..		246	Other Poems	4	159
WIT					
To one that hath no wealth, and wants his wit.		4	Lady of May	2	24
Whose wit the starres, whose fortune fortune thralls.. . . .		23	1st Eclogues	9	31
Thy wit dost use still still more harmes to finde.		23	1st Eclogues	9	34
Whome wit makes vaine, or blinded with his eyes, ...		23	1st Eclogues	9	35
It shews they fetch their wit from youthfull yeares.		24	1st Eclogues	9	80
Passion beares high when puffing wit doth blowe, ...		25	1st Eclogues	9	114
Time, place, life, wit scarcely her rare gifts measure doth.		49	2nd Eclogues	28	60
His utmost light: for well his witte doth know,.		55	2nd Eclogues	29	97
I silent herd more wordes of witt.		57	2nd Eclogues	30	1
Where witt but serves, to have true tast of woes..		57	2nd Eclogues	30	25
His workes, showes, suites, with wit, grace, and vow's					
might		84	Arcadia III	60	4
Was jumpe concorde betweene our wit and will:.		99	3rd Eclogues	66	30
Such is their speech, who be of sober wit;		104	3rd Eclogues	67	46
Who may this doubt discerne: for better, witt, then lot. . .		120	4th Eclogues	73	139
In warr his wit and word was our direction..		129	4th Eclogues	76	18
Longing to have, having no wit to wish,.		136	Cert Sonnets	2	13
To call such wit a franzie,.		161	Cert Sonnets	30	38
And now employ the remnant of my wit,.		166	Astrophil	2	12
Thou setst a bate betweene my will and wit,.		166	Astrophil	4	2
Another humbler wit to shepheard's pipe retires, ...		167	Astrophil	6	7
With sword of wit, giving wounds of dispraise, ...		170	Astrophil	10	10
Sc fortified with wit, stor'd with disdaine, ...		171	Astrophil	12	13
Readie of wit and fearing nought but shame:.		172	Astrophil	14	11
With new-borne sighes and denisend wit do sing;.		172	Astrophil	15	8
My wit doth strive those passions to defend, ...		174	Astrophil	18	10
"Scholler," saith Love, "bend hitherward your wit.".		174	Astrophil	19	14
Yet to those fooles heav'n such wit doth impart, ...		177	Astrophil	24	5
Is constant Love deem'd there but want of wit?		180	Astrophil	31	10
While too much wit (forsooth) so troubled me,.		181	Astrophil	33	10
Peace, foolish wit, with wit my wit is mard.		182	Astrophil	34	11
Wit learnes in thee perfection to expresse,.		182	Astrophil	35	12
The baiting place of wit, the balme of woe,.		184	Astrophil	39	2
To witlesse things, then Love I hope (since wit..		194	Astrophil	59	13
I do not envie Aristotle's wit,.		198	Astrophil	64	9
Thou art my Wit, and thou my Vertue art.		198	Astrophil	64	14
I am no pick-purse of another's wit.		204	Astrophil	74	8
Since best wits thinke it wit thee to admire;.		206	Astrophil	80	2
And I, mad with delight, want wit to cease,.		207	Astrophil	81	13
For though full of desire, emptie of wit,.		208	Astrophil	82	9
Let eares heare speech, which wit to wonder ties,.		210	Astrophil	85	11
For nothing from my wit or will doth flow,.		224	Astrophil	90	12
But wit confus'd with too much care did misse.		227	Astrophil	93	8
Whom she imployes, dismisse from thee my wit,.		236	Astrophil	107	10
Who hath the lips, where wit in fairnesse raigneth,.		197	A&S 1st Song		9
Better place no wit can find,.		210	A&S 4th Song		13
Or if they do delight therein, yet are so cloyed with wit, .		217	A&S 7th Song		3
To be (in things past bounds of wit) fooles, if they be not					
fooles..		217	A&S 7th Song		6
As deserves their wicked witt;		309	Psalm XXVIII		18
To beare the bondes which Time nor wit could breake, ...		255	Other Poems	4	530
Tc his owne witt, thought upon thought did swell,.		256	Other Poems	4	542
Her ears the weights of wit.		259	Other Poems	5	109
WIT-BEATEN					
Now I, wit-beaten long by hardest Fate,.		195	Astrophil	60	9
WITCH					
Nico. In deed the witch thy dam her crouch from shoulder					
spred,.		52	2nd Eclogues	29	13
A witch I say thou art, though thou so faire appeare;. . . .		214	A&S 5th Song		74
You witch, you Divill, (alas) you still of me beloved, . . .		215	A&S 5th Song		87
WITCHCRAFT					
No witchcraft is so evill, as which man's mind destroyeth. .		215	A&S 5th Song		78
He quickly knew what witchcraft gave the blow.		256	Other Poems	4	539
WITCHED					
Out shreaking pipe made of some witched tree..		255	Other Poems	4	516
WITCHES					
Yet witches may repent, thou art far worse then they,. . . .		215	A&S 5th Song		79
WITHAL					
In sweetest strength, so sweetly skild withall,.		183	Astrophil	36	10
Use someting else to chast'n me withall,.		212	Astrophil	86	12
WITHER					
And wither like green herb or flower;.		324	Psalm XXXVII		6
Wither not you, languisht with discontent?		257	Other Poems	5	52
WITHERED					
Failing themselves, with withered conscience dye..		151	Cert Sonnets	22	50
Nor withered leafe shall make yt faile to flourish..		270	Psalm I		10

WITHHOLD	PAGE	TITLE		LINE
Hath power that Sex with bridle to withhold?	24	1st Eclogues	9	58
Desire's great force, no forces can withhold:.	345	Possibly	4	3
WITHIN				
No place to turne; without, within it fryes:	18	1st Eclogues	7	145
So doth my life within it selfe dissolve, ...	19	1st Eclogues	7	156
Lalus. So doth my life within it selfe dissolve, ...	19	1st Eclogues	7	157
Within thy selfe, thou soone wilt be ashamed	25	1st Eclogues	9	118
Then do I shape to my selfe that forme which raigns so with				
in me, ...	36	1st Eclogues	13	142
And will pitty the wound festred so strangely within me. . .	37	1st Eclogues	13	168
Receipt to me, within thy bosome darke..	73	Arcadia III	40	8
My Lute within thy selfe thy tunes enclose,.	81	Arcadia III	54	1
Pearching within square royall rooves, ...	89	Arcadia III	62	114
Of fairer guest, which dwells within,.	90	Arcadia III	62	140
O Histor, seeke within thy selfe to flourish:.	106	3rd Eclogues	67	109
And keepe it still within this body thrall:.	116	4th Eclogues	72	88
Her beautie kindle shall within thy foolish minde, ...	121	4th Eclogues	73	171
(Unto thy selfe I do meane those graces dwell so within				
thee	122	4th Eclogues	74	9
Within it selfe, and never taketh ende:.	127	4th Eclogues	75	80
Within her beames wrapping his cruell staines.	141	Cert Sonnets	8	12
Large roomes within, where droppes distill amaine:	150	Cert Sonnets	22	32
If that the substance faile within..	156	Cert Sonnets	27	16
Within my selfe to seeke my onelie hire:	161	Cert Sonnets	31	13
Breathe out the flames which burne within my heart,.	179	Astrophil	28	13
Within what bounds can one his liking stay,.	182	Astrophil	35	3
My forces razde, thy banners raisd within:	183	Astrophil	36	6
Cannot be staid within my panting breast,.	189	Astrophil	50	2
Both within themselves oppressed,.	218	A&S 8th Song		7
That I within the ports most beautyfull.	280	Psalm IX		41
Within the bounds of Innocence to byde,.	305	Psalm XXVI		3
Within the sinners' roll,.	306	Psalm XXVI		29
When I within the pitt do bide;.	311	Psalm XXX		27
Within the hand of hatefull enmitie, ...	312	Psalm XXXI		23
For troubles of all sides have me within..	312	Psalm XXXI		26
Let them not, Lord, within their hearts thus say:.	323	Psalm XXXV		61
No time within his limites binds.	326	Psalm XXXVII		76
Yea lord Thy law within my heart doth stand;	331	Psalm XL		34
Besides this force, within his eies he kept.	246	Other Poems	4	153
Did not conceive what fire he had within..	253	Other Poems	4	428
With in himselfe of hir deare selfe to speake, ...	255	Other Poems	4	534
Breeding huge stormes with in his inward parte,.	256	Other Poems	4	543
Within my heart you be	261	Other Poems	6	27
Within the Elmy grange,.	261	Other Poems	6	33
*WITHOUT				
For from without came to mine eyes the blowe,.	11	Arcadia I	2	5
As without breath, no pipe doth move,.	14	1st Eclogues	6	7
No musike kindly without love.	14	1st Eclogues	6	8
That without love she spends her yeares of love:	17	1st Eclogues	7	98
No place to turne; without, within it fryes:	18	1st Eclogues	7	145
Seen, and unknowne; heard, but without attention.	19	1st Eclogues	7	179
Which shootes strongly with out any noyse and deadly without				
smarte.	35	1st Eclogues	13	122
Without her love, then any mind who fairer is.	51	2nd Eclogues	28	116
To speake without an answere..	65	2nd Eclogues	32	6
To shew the wound without cure..	65	2nd Eclogues	32	8
Can holde, shew, tell, my paines without reliefe..	75	Arcadia III	43	8
Can liken them without all peere,.	86	Arcadia III	62	19
Friend without change, playfellow without strife,.	103	3rd Eclogues	67	10
Foode without fulnes, counsaile without pride, ...	103	3rd Eclogues	67	11
When without shame he saith, "these be mine owne".	106	3rd Eclogues	67	114
Thy thorne without, my thorne my heart invadeth.	137	Cert Sonnets	4	12
Above line repeated at following location.	137	Cert Sonnets	4	24
May paint my face without seeing mee,.	153	Cert Sonnets	24	3
Without the picture be found true.	157	Cert Sonnets	27	24
Of touch they are that without touch doth touch, ...	169	Astrophil	9	12
How Poles' right king meanes, without leave of hoast,. . .	180	Astrophil	30	3
Without desire to feed of further grace.	187	Astrophil	46	8
Till without fewell you can make hot fire.	188	Astrophil	46	14
Far far too long to learne it without booke:	192	Astrophil	56	2
What, a whole weeke without one peece of looke,.	192	Astrophil	56	3
That I love not, without I leave to love..	195	Astrophil	61	14
That hand, which without touch holds more then Atlas might:.	205	Astrophil	77	5
Without how farre this praise is short of you, ...	207	Astrophil	80	13
Without my plumes from others' wings I take.	224	Astrophil	90	11
Who hath the hand which without stroke subdueth,.	197	A&S 1st Song		21
If Rule by force without all claime a Tyran showeth, . . .	214	A&S 5th Song		57
Though all his plotts without misfortune	325	Psalm XXXVII		19
For on Thee, lord, without end	328	Psalm XXXVIII		43
World without end, let still his blessing flow;.	334	Psalm XLI		47
Sate wailing without boot.	256	Other Poems	5	7
Speeche without ende were better not begin..	259	Other Poems	5	104
That I, without thy denying, ...	263	Other Poems	7	59
WITHSTANDS				
That naught withstandes Desire, Allarme allarme.	346	Possibly	5	4
WITLESS				
To witlesse things, then Love I hope (since wit.	194	Astrophil	59	13
WITNESS				
That such a one is witnesse of my hart,.	5	Lady of May	3	14

WITNESS   (CONTINUED)   PAGE TITLE   LINE

	PAGE	TITLE		LINE
And witnesse am, how ill agree in one, ...	40	Arcadia II	19	5
May witnesse beare, how ill agree in one,.	41	Arcadia II	19	11
To witnes, that he thinkes his thoughts delicious, ...	47	2nd Eclogues	28	5
Sweete glove the wittnes of my secrett blisse.	70	Arcadia III	35	1
Live long, and long witnesse my chosen smarte, ...	77	Arcadia III	47	10
Witnesse his wrong which by thy helpe is eased:.	108	Arcadia IV	69	11
Strephon. These mountaines witnesse shall, so shall these				
vallies, ...	113	4th Eclogues	71	73
Witnesse your wofull teares with daily rayning..	127	4th Eclogues	75	69
My hand doth not beare witnesse with my hart,.	146	Cert Sonnets	17	26
Witnesse of life to them that living die:.	180	Astrophil	32	2
Witnesse with me, that my foule stumbling so,.	227	Astrophil	93	6
But cease mine eyes, your teares do witnesse well.	235	Astrophil	105	9
Musicke doth witnesse call	216	A&S 6th Song		37
For death doth kill the Witness of thy glory;.	276	Psalm VI		14
Witness Thou my soule with me.	287	Psalm XVI		3
God's witness sure for aye doth dure	294	Psalm XIX		31
To witness you rejoice.	316	Psalm XXXIII		12
Who did me wrong, against me witness beare	322	Psalm XXXV		25
Ev'en gnashing teeth, to witness more their spight..	322	Psalm XXXV		42
Thy justice witness shall and speake Thy prayse.	323	Psalm XXXV		72
And witness me Thy slave..	331	Psalm XL		30

WITNESSES

	PAGE	TITLE		LINE
Against me witnesses unjust, ...	308	Psalm XXVII		57
W. Who bound thee? D. Love my Lord. W. What witnesses				
therto	343	Possibly	1	25

WIT-OLD

	PAGE	TITLE		LINE
To let that witolde beast consume in flames.	60	2nd Eclogues	30	111

WITS

	PAGE	TITLE		LINE
Warme well thy wits, if thou wilt win her will,.	3	Lady of May	2	3
The witts abusde with will no counsayle take..	23	1st Eclogues	9	22
Beyond the heaven, far more beyond your witts.	99	3rd Eclogues	66	28
Breath made of flames, wits knowing nought but damage, . . .	109	Arcadia IV	70	28
Like foe, whose wits inclin'd to deadly spite, ...	135	Cert Sonnets	2	3
Studying inventions fine, her wits to entertaine:.	165	Astrophil	1	6
Let daintie wits crie on the Sisters nine, ...	166	Astrophil	3	1
My best wits still their owne disgrace invent:	174	Astrophil	19	5
My wits, quicke in vaine thoughts, in vertue lame:	175	Astrophil	21	4
The curious wits, seeing dull pensivenesse	176	Astrophil	23	1
Though dustie wits dare scorne Astrologie, ...	177	Astrophil	26	1
These questions busie wits to me do frame;	180	Astrophil	30	12
Some luckie wits impute it but to chaunce;	185	Astrophil	41	8
In verse, and that my verse best wits doth please?	204	Astrophil	74	11
Since best wits thinke it wit thee to admire:.	206	Astrophil	80	2
Envious wits what hath bene mine offence,.	233	Astrophil	104	1
Or seeing, have so wodden wits, as not that worth to know; .	217	A&S 7th Song		8
And rid me from the wrongs which cruel Witts did brew; . . .	293	Psalm XVIII		87
Let their sly witts unwares destruction get, ...	321	Psalm XXXV		17
Where piercing witts do quickly apprehend, ...	245	Other Poems	4	142
In which by will, my will and wits I binde:.	255	Other Poems	4	500

WITTED

	PAGE	TITLE		LINE
Though cradle witted, must not honnor loose.	25	1st Eclogues	9	92

WITTING

	PAGE	TITLE		LINE
Seely shepheards are not witting	262	Other Poems	7	29

WITTY

	PAGE	TITLE		LINE
That wittie Lewis to him a tribute paid.	204	Astrophil	75	11
And if dumbe things be so witty, ...	219	A&S 8th Song		63

WIVES

	PAGE	TITLE		LINE
Old men themselves, doe love young wives to choose:.	25	1st Eclogues	9	88
But of such wives we finde a slender crew;	104	3rd Eclogues	67	25

WOE

	PAGE	TITLE		LINE
To wo and shame the wretch did enter in, ...	5	Lady of May	3	9
(Therion) Thus wofully I in wo this salve do find, ...	5	Lady of May	3	17
For (woe is me) my powers all I finde.	11	Arcadia I	2	3
Who yelds to woe, doth but encrease his smart.	22	1st Eclogues	9	2
True cause of evils, and cause of causelesse woe..	25	1st Eclogues	9	116
His breast doth fill with earth of others' woe,.	50	2nd Eclogues	28	85
Woe to poore man: ech outward thing annoyes him.	62	2nd Eclogues	30	170
Woe, but seems to me joy, that agrees to my thought so. I				
thought so..	64	2nd Eclogues	31	38
Where drawing breath, I sucke the aire of woe:	73	Arcadia III	40	10
Nor brooke oughte els but well acquainted woe.	74	Arcadia III	41	6
Teares, drowne your selves, for woe (your cause) is wasted,.	83	Arcadia III	59	6
Ah woe is me, my woes renewe;.	90	Arcadia III	62	120
But, woe is me, the yeare is gone about, ...	115	4th Eclogues	72	56
Farewell, long farewell, all my woe, all my delight.	124	4th Eclogues	74	86
My breath distinguish'd into wordes of woe, ...	125	4th Eclogues	75	8
Let pearls be wan with woe their damme doth beare:	125	4th Eclogues	75	23
One word of woe another after traineth:.	128	4th Eclogues	75	103
Since wanting is more woe then too much having..	137	Cert Sonnets	4	20
Wo, wo to me, on me returne the smart:	141	Cert Sonnets	9	1
Brother to woe, and father of complaint:	141	Cert Sonnets	10	3
If thus, alas: yet while those partes have wo, ...	142	Cert Sonnets	10	13
Tell me the cause of this my causelesse woe, ...	146	Cert Sonnets	17	12
Yea worse then death, death parts both woe and joy,.	148	Cert Sonnets	20	13
In absence blind, and wearied with that woe, ...	149	Cert Sonnets	21	9
Wo to me, alas she weepeth!.	157	Cert Sonnets	27	25
Who ever saw such woe?	158	Cert Sonnets	28	28
I sought fit words to paint the blackest face of woe,. . . .	165	Astrophil	1	5

WOE   (CONTINUED)   PAGE   TITLE   LINE
    The baiting place of wit, the balme of woe,. . . . .   184 Astrophil   39   2
    Stella oft sees the verie face of wo . . . .   187 Astrophil   45   1
    wo, having made with many fights his owne. . . . . 193 Astrophil   57   1
    Which wooed wo, most ravishing delight . . . .   194 Astrophil   58   13
    Late tyr'd with wo, even ready for to pine . . . . 195 Astrophil   62   1
    Or doth the tedious burd'n of long wo. . . . .   199 Astrophil   66   2
    My friend, that oft saw through all maskes my wo,. . . . . . 200 Astrophil   69   5
    Benighted in cold wo, but now appeares my day, ... 204 Astrophil   76   3
    So manie eyes ay seeking their owne woe, ... 206 Astrophil   78   12
    Let wo gripe on my heart, shame loade mine eye... . . . . .   212 Astrophil   86   4
    I sighd her sighes, and wailed for her wo, ...   223 Astrophil   87   10
    What inke is blacke inough to paint my wo? . . . . 227 Astrophil   93   3
    Seeing hope yeeld when this wo strake him furst: . . . . . . 228 Astrophil   95   6
    But wo is me, though joy it selfe were she,. . . . . 230 Astrophil   97   12
    Mery with him, and not thinke of his woe... . . . .   236 Astrophil   106   14
    Wo to me, and do you sweare. . . . . 211 A&S 4th Song   49
    Leave a wretch, in whom all wo . . . . 221 A&S 9th Song   6
    Woe, lyke a moth, my face's beauty eates . . . . 276 Psalm VI   21
    Ah, now even for their sakes, that taste of Woe, ... 285 Psalm XII   13
    Which if it last, Woe to all simple Hearts.. . . . . 285 Psalm XII   27
    For they had caught me up, when I was weake in Woe;. . . . . 291 Psalm XVIII   38
    Woe me, from me why is Thy presence taken? . . . . 298 Psalm XXII   2
    With inward wo, an outward sack cloth ware.. . . . . 322 Psalm XXXV   30
    And my woe . . . . 329 Psalm XXXVIII   50
    When bedd from rest becomes his seat of woe, ... 333 Psalm XLI   9
    But Dick my counsell marke: run from the place of wo:. . . . 344 Possibly   1   41
    Who share in woe, weygh others have as much. . . . . 242 Other Poems   4   16
    There did he make hir laugh in spite of woe, ... 247 Other Poems   4   197
    With Cosma, for whose love Pas past in woe.. . . . . 248 Other Poems   4   243
    A creeping serpentlike of mortall woe. . . . . 252 Other Poems   4   412
    It ended, but the others' woe began, ... 252 Other Poems   4   417
    Began at least to be conceiv'd as woe, ... 252 Other Poems   4   418
    Amid my flock with woe my voice I teare, ... 254 Other Poems   4   459
    The Nightingales for woe their songs refraine: . . . . 254 Other Poems   4   474
    Go you not from your master in his woe: . . . .   254 Other Poems   4   487
    For hearing him so oft with wordes of woe. . . . . 256 Other Poems   4   537
    And pine away with daily wasting woe?. . . . . 257 Other Poems   5   26
WOEFUL
    Come shepheard's weedes, attend my woefull cryes:. . . . . .   13 Arcadia I   4   5
    Thus, thus, alas! wofull in nature, unhappy by fortune,. . .   30 1st Eclogues 11   19
    While that my voice doth fill these wofull vallies,. . . . . 111 4th Eclogues 71   10
    Witnesse your wofull teares with daily rayning.. . . . . . . 127 4th Eclogues 75   69
    She saith, because I make no wofull laies, ... 146 Cert Sonnets 17   27
    Heare your wofull maister's story, ... 221 A&S 9th Song   12
    was Klaius cald, (ah Klaius, wofull wight!). . . . . 242 Other Poems   4   23
WOEFUL'S
    Farewell o Joy, the wofull's onely pleasure. . . . . 129 4th Eclogues 76   4
WOEFULLY
    (Therion) Thus wofully I in wo this salve do find, ...   5 Lady of May   3   17
WOE-MAN
    What great name may I give to so heav'nly a woman? A
      woe-man . . . .   64 2nd Eclogues 31   37
WOE'S
    The thorowest words, fit for woe's selfe to grone, ... 193 Astrophil   57   4
    With that faire breast making woe's darknesse cleare:. . . . 193 Astrophil   57   11
    Paint woe's blacke face so lively to my sight, ... 230 Astrophil   98   10
WOES
    How dare I, wretch, seeke there my woes to rest, ...   3 Lady of May   1   5
    With seede of woes my hart brimme-full is charged. . . . . .   16 1st Eclogues 7   78
    The noblest kinde rejects not others' woes.. . . . .   18 1st Eclogues 7   134
    Though woes now live, at length thy woes must dye. . . . . .   22 1st Eclogues 9   12
    Is made, forsooth, a Jurate of his woes, ...   23 1st Eclogues 9   39
    What place is there left, we may hope our woes to recomfort?   32 1st Eclogues 13   28
    Silly shepheard's poore pype, when his harsh sound testifis
      our woes, ...   32 1st Eclogues 13   40
    Unto a silly caban, though weake, yet stronger against woes.   34 1st Eclogues 13   93
    My thoughts imprisonde in my secreat woes, ...   42 Arcadia II   21   7
    Wayle in my woes, taste of your master's payne,. . . . . . .   44 Arcadia II   24   11
    Her onely cure from surfet-woes can diet me: . . . .   51 2nd Eclogues 28   117
    Raging in woes first pastors tought to plaine? . . . .   53 2nd Eclogues 29   58
    But more I plaine, I feele my woes the more.. . . . .   57 2nd Eclogues 30   10
    Where witt but serves, to have true tast of woes:. . . . . .   57 2nd Eclogues 30   25
    In morall rules let raging woes contained be?. . . . .   61 2nd Eclogues 30   151
    Long be thy woes for such newes, but how recks she my
      thoughts? Oughts. . . . .   64 2nd Eclogues 31   33
    Unto my woes the hatefull heavens do sende,. . . . .   73 Arcadia III 40   2
    These wordes are full of woes, yet feele they none.. . . . .   75 Arcadia III 43   3
    I plaine with cause, my woes are all myne owne.. . . . . . .   75 Arcadia III 43   6
    Weare these my words as mourning weedes of woes, ...   81 Arcadia III 54   5
    As oh! my selfe, whose woes are never lighte . . . .   82 Arcadia III 56   9
    Ah woe is me, my woes renewe;. . . . .   90 Arcadia III 62   120
    O that we had, to make our woes more publique, ... 109 Arcadia IV   70   25
    Which to my woes gives still an early morning: . . . . 111 4th Eclogues 71   5
    I thinke from me, not from my woes to parte. . . . . 113 4th Eclogues 72   10
    Klaius. I think from me, not from my woes to parte,. . . . . 113 4th Eclogues 72   11
    Whose braines boile not in woes, nor brests with beatings
      ake, ...   117 4th Eclogues 73   13
    From such deepe plaint as should such woes descrie,. . . . . 129 4th Eclogues 75   137
    Sings out her woes, a thorne her song-booke making:. . . . . 137 Cert Sonnets 4   4

WOES	(CONTINUED)	PAGE	TITLE	LINE
Who others' woes and plaints can chastly beare:		142	Cert Sonnets 10	7
That all the earth my woes, sighes, teares may know,		146	Cert Sonnets 17	39
To greater woes by presence I returne,		149	Cert Sonnets 21	10
A simple soule should breed so mixed woes.		149	Cert Sonnets 22	10
The bitter juice of forsaken woes,		153	Cert Sonnets 24	11
You that poore Petrarch's long deceased woes,		172	Astrophil 15	7
Th' anatomy of all my woes I wrate,		194	Astrophil 58	10
That in my woes for thee thou art my joy,		237	Astrophil 108	13
Thy delights my woes increase,		227	A&S 10th Song	44
Sighs of woes were glad sighs mixt,		218	A&S 8th Song	18
My woes are still encreast:		304	Psalm XXV	61
For when my heart with woes was torn,		311	Psalm XXX	4
Woes, woes shall come to wicked folks:		315	Psalm XXXII	37
Let not their joy upon my woes be sett...		322	Psalm XXXV	60
For endless woes me compast have,		332	Psalm XL	43
Other deeps of Woes doth call,		335	Psalm XLII	30
Why walk I in woes		336	Psalm XLIII	10
WOLF				
For though Melampus like a wolfe doo looke,		27	1st Eclogues 10	16
Yet have I seene when well a wolfe he shooke...		27	1st Eclogues 10	18
O heards take heed; for I a woolfe have found;		50	2nd Eclogues 28	83
Eagle, high looke; Wolfe secrete crueltie:		101	3rd Eclogues 66	87
WOLVES				
Do you not thincke this will the wolves remove		26	1st Eclogues 10	4
No woolves dare howle, no murrayne can prevaile,		43	Arcadia II 23	8
My plaintes call wolves, my plagues in you prevaile,		43	Arcadia II 24	8
Made wolves (not inward wolves) my ewes to spare;		254	Other Poems 4	486
Tell me, if wolves the throte.		258	Other Poems 5	72
WOLVISH				
(For age doth make him of a wolvish hew)		27	1st Eclogues 10	17
WOMAN				
And to conclude thy mistresse is a woman..		24	1st Eclogues 9	61
What great name may I give to so heav'nly a woman? A woe-man		64	2nd Eclogues 31	37
That ever fell to honest woman yet:		104	3rd Eclogues 67	44
Unto no body my woman saith she had rather a wife be,		143	Cert Sonnets 13	1
An Angell's mind, but in a woman caste:		151	Cert Sonnets 22	67
I saw this woman sit,		158	Cert Sonnets 28	34
On things, were by a woman said,		158	Cert Sonnets 28	39
WOMANISH				
Gainst neighbors good for womanish debate.		93	3rd Eclogues 63	70
WOMANKIND				
And yet finde no such faults in womankind.		106	3rd Eclogues 67	87
Choler adust is joyed in woman-kinde,		147	Cert Sonnets 17	52
Who womankind at once both deckes and stayneth?		197	A&S 1st Song	10
WOMANLIKE				
Full womanlike complaines her will was brokne.		137	Cert Sonnets 4	16
WOMAN'S				
What marvaile then I take a woman's hew,		12	Arcadia I 2	13
Who hath his hopes laid up in woman's hand..		24	1st Eclogues 9	55
A woman's hand with constant marble stone.		40	Arcadia II 19	6
Above line repeated at following location.		41	Arcadia II 19	12
A man to feare a woman's moodie eye,		49	2nd Eclogues 28	75
When once this entred was, in woman's hart,		95	3rd Eclogues 64	37
There rested then, to play a woman's part,		95	3rd Eclogues 64	39
To vertue, fortune, time and woman's brest.		98	3rd Eclogues 65	14
A wanton woman's face, and with curld knots had twinde		118	4th Eclogues 73	73
These be her words, but a woman's words to a love that is eager,		143	Cert Sonnets 13	3
A woman's mould, but like an Angell graste,		151	Cert Sonnets 22	66
WOMB				
And yet ev'en from the womb thy self did'st take me;		299	Psalm XXII	21
WOMEN				
Yet not of wemen Judging as he said,		24	1st Eclogues 9	64
Women man-wood, and men effeminate..		28	1st Eclogues 10	60
Silly rewarde! yet among women hath she of vertu the most. Most.		64	2nd Eclogues 31	36
And God forbid, women such cattell were,		106	3rd Eclogues 67	82
And thou shalt finde, in women vertues lie.		106	3rd Eclogues 67	102
The other had with arte (more then our women knowe,		118	4th Eclogues 73	71
O the fayre Nymphe borne to doo woemen honor,		138	Cert Sonnets 5	3
Above line repeated at following location.		138	Cert Sonnets 5	27
WOMEN'S				
"Alas", quoth she, "thus women's shame doth creepe".		96	3rd Eclogues 64	87
WON				
Since will is won, and stopped eares are charmed:		135	Cert Sonnets 1	3
WONDER				
Our owne demeane, and soone we wondre shall.		29	1st Eclogues 10	92
One wonder yet farre passeth my conceate:		42	Arcadia II 22	13
His childhood woonder, prenticeship attention,		48	2nd Eclogues 28	38
The after-folkes shall wonder still at thee.		56	2nd Eclogues 29	131
No wondre then, though sighte my sighte did tainte,		83	Arcadia III 57	5
My harte, eyes, eares, with wonder, love, delight:		84	Arcadia III 60	2
Blinde Cupid's workes with wonder testifie?		106	3rd Eclogues 67	98
Fame is with wonder blazed:		136	Cert Sonnets 3	5
Now thus this wonder to my selfe I frame,		151	Cert Sonnets 22	69
Promising wonders, wonder to invite,		178	Astrophil 26	4
Service and Honor, wonder with delight,		202	Astrophil 72	9
What wonder then if he his lesson misse,		203	Astrophil 73	3

WONDER   (CONTINUED)   PAGE   TITLE   LINE
      Let eares heare speech, which wit to wonder ties,. . . . . . 210 Astrophil   85   11
      With wings of Love in aire of wonder flie,. . . . . 212 Astrophil   86   8
      Leave to see, and leave to wonder.". . . . . 234 A&S 11th Song   12
      And wonder more esteemes . . . . 216 A&S 6th Song   33
      Heare then, but then with wonder heare; see but adoring see, 217 A&S 7th Song   13
      Thus to speake in love and wonder: . . . . 218 A&S 8th Song   28
      Than of bad folks the wealthy wonder,. . . . . 325 Psalm XXXVII   42
      D. Wonder that by two so black eyes the glittering stars be
      past. . . . . 343 Possibly   1   28
      By metamorphoz'd wonder. . . . . 261 Other Poems   6   58
WONDERING
      And did the tribute of their wondring sight. . . . . 251 Other Poems   4   363
WONDER'S
      O let them heare these sacred tunes, and learne in wonder's
      schooles,. . . . . 217 A&S 7th Song   5
WONDERS
      Or to the Sun for wonders seeme small sparks of a candle:. .   34 1st Eclogues 13   79
      Some say it doth betoken wonders neare . . . .   81 Arcadia III 55   2
      These wonders England breedes, the last remaines,. . . . . . 151 Cert Sonnets 22   61
      Promising wonders, wonder to invite, ... 178 Astrophil   26   4
      Only with you not miracles are wonders.. . . . . 197 A&S 1st Song   32
      Those faire wonders to behold, ... 226 A&S 10th Song   17
      Shewes his handworking wonders.. . . . . 293 Psalm XIX   4
      while my God with wasting wonders. . . . . 335 Psalm XLII   31
WONDROUS
      Of Musick's wondrous might:. . . . . 216 A&S 6th Song   34
      That evry folk Thy wondrous Acts may see.. . . . . 277 Psalm VII   21
      Shew then O Lord Thy wondrous kindness show, ... 290 Psalm XVII   21
      The works perform'd by Thee most wondrous great. . . . . . . 305 Psalm XXVI   24
      My God Thy wondrous works how manifold,. . . . . 331 Psalm XL   21
WONED
      Was onely won'd with such as beastes begot:. . . . . 100 3rd Eclogues 66   45
WONT
      With old true tales he woont mine eares to fill, ...   99 3rd Eclogues 66   33
      With nature's praise are wont in safest home to take.. . . . 117 4th Eclogues 73   14
      Since Stella's eyes, wont to give me my day, ... 223 Astrophil   89   3
      How in troops I wont to go,. . . . . 334 Psalm XLII   14
WONTED
      Dicus. Dorus, tell me, where is thy wonted motion. . . . . .   47 2nd Eclogues 28   1
      While I was warbling out your woonted praise,. . . . .   54 2nd Eclogues 29   67
      May keepe my thoughtes, from thought of wonted light.. . . .   73 Arcadia III 39   14
      And wisdome to his wonted seate aspireth.. . . . .   83 Arcadia III 57   12
      Comfort, step thou in place of wonted sadnes.. . . . .   83 Arcadia III 59   10
      Since then my harte did loose his wonted place,. . . . . . . 115 4th Eclogues 72   77
      To so lowe ebbe that wonted were to flowe. . . . . 146 Cert Sonnets 17   15
      In wonted walkes, since wonted fancies change, ... 147 Cert Sonnets 18   1
      Keeping that forme, though void of wonted heate: . . . . . . 151 Cert Sonnets 22   48
      Were now his darts leaving his wonted fight. . . . . 246 Other Poems   4   148
      "The sportes wherin I wonted to do well, ... 254 Other Poems   4   465
      Rewing change of wonted state, ... 262 Other Poems   7   9
WOO
      Us in their best language woo: . . . . 210 A&S 4th Song   16
*WOOD
      The wood cries most, before it throughly kindled be, ...   14 1st Eclogues 7   8
      Women man-wood, and men effeminate.. . . . .   28 1st Eclogues 10   60
      Old wood inflam'de, doth yeeld the bravest fire, ...   38 Arcadia II   15   3
      Me thought, nay sure I was, I was in fairest wood. . . . . . 117 4th Eclogues 73   35
      The wood, above doth soone consuming rest. . . . . 150 Cert Sonnets 22   44
      But golde can guild a rotten piece of wood,. . . . . 245 Other Poems   4   124
      I got to a shady wood, ... 262 Other Poems   7   3
      In this wood a man I met,. . . . . 262 Other Poems   7   7
WOODEN
      From wooden bones, and bloud of pitch doth flie. . . . . . . 151 Cert Sonnets 22   53
      Or seeing, have so wodden wits, as not that worth to know; . 217 A&S 7th Song   8
WOOD-GLOBES
      Models such be wood-globes of glistring skies. . . . . 225 Astrophil   91   11
WOODMUSIC'S
      As for the Nightingale, woodmusique's King,. . . . .   99 3rd Eclogues 66   13
WOODS
      Let not wild woods so great a treasure have. . . . .   3 Lady of May   2   12
      Two thousand deere in wildest woods I have,. . . . .   4 Lady of May   2   25
      How to the woods love runnes as well as rydes to the
      Pallace . . . .   31 1st Eclogues 13   4
      In these woods to resounde the renowmed name of a goddesse..   31 1st Eclogues 13   14
      And to the woods or brookes, who do make such dreery
      recitall . . . .   33 1st Eclogues 13   42
      But sometimes to the woods, sometimes to the heavens do
      decyphire, ...   35 1st Eclogues 13   111
      But to the Cedar, Queene of woods, when I lifte my beteard
      eyes,. . . . .   36 1st Eclogues 13   141
      To make these woods resounde thy lamentation?. . . . .   47 2nd Eclogues 28   2
      Pas. So oft these woods have heard me "Cosma" crie,. . . . .   56 2nd Eclogues 29   132
      Faire Rocks, goodly rivers, sweet woods, when shall I see
      peace? Peace.. . . . .   62 2nd Eclogues 31   1
      O sweet woods the delight of solitarines!. . . . .   68 2nd Eclogues 34   1
      Above line repeated at following locations . . . .   69 2nd Eclogues 34   15
      . . . .   69 2nd Eclogues 34   29
      The first with cloth's tuckt up as Nymphes in woods do
      range ,. . . . . 118 4th Eclogues 73   66

WOODS	(CONTINUED)	PAGE	TITLE		LINE
O Echo, all these woods with roaring fill, ...		126	4th Eclogues	75	31
Till that it hath all woods and waters past.		126	4th Eclogues	75	36
The shading woods seeme now my Sunne to darke, ...		147	Cert Sonnets	18	7
Rockes, woods, hilles, caves, dales, meads, brookes, answere me, ...		147	Cert Sonnets	18	13
WOODS'					
That after death, to heav'n in woods' resound, ...		56	2nd Eclogues	29	133
WOOED					
Cald it anew, and wooed sleepe againe:		184	Astrophil	38	13
Which wooed wo, most ravishing delight		194	Astrophil	58	13
WOOL					
The pasture rich, the wooll as soft as silke, ...		4	Lady of May	2	21
Want I white wooll, whose eyes her white skinne garnished? .		16	1st Eclogues	7	59
Their wooll your weede, I will you Musique yeeld		18	1st Eclogues	7	124
What wooll my sheepe shall beare, whyle thus they live, . . .		39	Arcadia II	17	7
Your woll is riche: no tonge can tell my gayne.		43	Arcadia II	23	14
You beare no woll, and losse is all my gayne.		44	Arcadia II	24	14
With large encrease, and wooll of fine perfection, ...		49	2nd Eclogues	28	50
And thou deare flesh, as soft as wooll new drest, ...		76	Arcadia III	46	15
Yet first but wooll, or fethers off he teard:		102	3rd Eclogues	66	143
So grow thy wooll of note, ...		258	Other Poems	5	69
WOOL'S					
Love well thine owne: me thinkes, woolle's whitenes passeth all:		16	1st Eclogues	7	53
WOOS					
The night as tedious, wooes th'approch of day;		224	Astrophil	89	6
WORD					
Then power out plaint, and in one word say this:		13	Arcadia I	4	9
Pas. But here is Dicus old; let him then speake the woord, .		52	2nd Eclogues	29	27
My harte my worde, my worde hath giv'ne my harte.		77	Arcadia III	47	13
Mine owne? o word on whose sweete sound doth pray.		80	Arcadia III	53	5
Whence never word in vaine did flowe.		87	Arcadia III	62	45
There never past foule word, I dare well say.		106	3rd Eclogues	67	93
She, whose lest word brings from the spheares their musique,		113	4th Eclogues	71	68
One word of woe another after traineth:		128	4th Eclogues	75	103
In warr his wit and word was our direction.		129	4th Eclogues	76	18
O my vayne worde gon, Ruyn of my glory.		138	Cert Sonnets	5	14
But no more wordes, thoughe such a worde bee spoken, ...		138	Cert Sonnets	5	17
Ncr no more wording with a worde to spill mee.		138	Cert Sonnets	5	18
I never did my vowed word forsake:		146	Cert Sonnets	17	8
Depart, a word so gentle to my minde, ...		148	Cert Sonnets	20	3
Ncr breake my word though reward come late, ...		153	Cert Sonnets	24	21
Well staid with truth in word and faith of deed, ...		172	Astrophil	14	10
I might, unhappie word, o me, I might, ...		181	Astrophil	33	1
I cannot brag of word, much lesse of deed, ...		199	Astrophil	66	5
That to each word, nay sigh of mine you harke, ...		233	Astrophil	104	3
Their eares hungry of each word.		218	A&S 8th Song		21
For in their mouth not One cleere word is spent, ...		275	Psalm V		25
Who word to neighbour given doth faithfully maintain		287	Psalm XV		9
From Ill word, and ill meaning sound.		289	Psalm XVII		12
Led by Thy Word the Rav'ner's stepps I shun, ...		289	Psalm XVII		14
Thy way is soundly sure, Thy word is purely tryd;		292	Psalm XVIII		55
Because that word of his		316	Psalm XXXIII		16
His Word made heavnly Coast, ...		316	Psalm XXXIII		22
Who never word of peace yet utter would, ...		322	Psalm XXXV		51
Word with my soule do not represse.		328	Psalm XXXVIII		42
Dick. Oh hence! o cruell word! which even doggs do hate: . .		344	Possibly	1	47
Ther was (o seldome blessed word of was!).		242	Other Poems	4	17
Who would have hir in will and worde agree		245	Other Poems	4	115
WORDING					
Ncr no more wording with a worde to spill mee.		138	Cert Sonnets	5	18
WORDS					
Ech eare suckes up the words a true love scattereth, ...		14	1st Eclogues	7	5
These bolde words she did heare, this fruite I reaped, . . .		17	1st Eclogues	7	82
Histor. Those woordes dyd once the Loveliest shepard use . .		24	1st Eclogues	9	62
If from his words the falshood he do skim.		24	1st Eclogues	9	77
Thy words, though full of malapert offence, ...		25	1st Eclogues	9	108
Doe speake high wordes, when all the coaste is cleare, . . .		27	1st Eclogues	10	32
Geron. Fy man, fy man, what wordes hath thy tonge lent?. . .		28	1st Eclogues	10	61
Now by thy words I begin, most famous Lady, to gather. . . .		34	1st Eclogues	13	94
My words, in hope to blaze my stedfast minde, ...		40	Arcadia II	19	1
But loe, my words defaste, my fancies blinde, ...		40	Arcadia II	19	3
My words full weake, the marble full of might;		41	Arcadia II	19	7
My words in store, the marble all alone;		41	Arcadia II	19	8
My words blacke inke, the marble kindly white;		41	Arcadia II	19	9
My words unseene, the marble still in sight, ...		41	Arcadia II	19	10
Thou then, that framste both words and voice most skilfully,		48	2nd Eclogues	28	19
Nc, no: no wordes ennoble selfe-nobilitie.		48	2nd Eclogues	28	28
Dicus. Thy words well voic'd, well gra'ste had almost heaved me.		48	2nd Eclogues	28	31
For that construction thy owne wordes do beare.		49	2nd Eclogues	28	74
Dorus. If I had thought to heare blasphemous wordes, ...		50	2nd Eclogues	28	79
With words so vile, which viler breath doth breed.		50	2nd Eclogues	28	82
But for to find thy words did her disgrace, ...		51	2nd Eclogues	28	106
I silent herd more wordes of witt.		57	2nd Eclogues	30	2
Shall I, whose eares her mournefull words did seaze, ...		58	2nd Eclogues	30	50
Her words in syrup laid of sweetest breath, ...		58	2nd Eclogues	30	51
Blasphemous words the speaker vaine do prove.		59	2nd Eclogues	30	67
Boulon. Thy wailing words do much my spirits move, ...		60	2nd Eclogues	30	125

600

	PAGE	TITLE		LINE
What be the fruites of speaking arte? what growes by the words? Words..	64	2nd Eclogues	31	30
O much more then words: those words serv'd more to me blesse Lesse.	64	2nd Eclogues	31	31
The tunes be cryes, the words plaints,	66	2nd Eclogues	32	35
These wordes are full of woes, yet feele they none...	75	Arcadia III	43	3
No cave, no wasting waxe, no wordes of griefe,	75	Arcadia III	43	7
O Words which fall like sommer deaw on me,	76	Arcadia III	46	1
Such pearcing wordes as no thoughts els conceave:	78	Arcadia III	49	8
Weare these my words as mourning weedes of woes,	81	Arcadia III	54	5
Doth him, his face, his words, leave, shunne, refraine,..	84	Arcadia III	60	12
All churlish wordes, shrewd answeres, crabbed lookes,....	93	3rd Eclogues	63	64
With chumpish lookes, hard words, and secret nips,	95	3rd Eclogues	64	31
The pistle selfe, such kinde of wordes it had,	96	3rd Eclogues	64	91
Now that he had her words so truely tried:	97	3rd Eclogues	64	112
And with some words which shewed little care,.......	97	3rd Eclogues	64	118
Bend your thoghts to the dear sweet words which then to me giv'n were:.	124	4th Eclogues	74	75
My breath distinguish'd into wordes of woe,.......	125	4th Eclogues	75	8
They are but words therefore which men do buy,.....	128	4th Eclogues	75	115
Where bee now those wordes never Idelly wasted,....	138	Cert Sonnets	5	7
But no more wordes, thoughe such a worde bee spoken, ...	138	Cert Sonnets	5	17
These be her words, but a woman's words to a love that is eager,	143	Cert Sonnets	13	3
Of mine owne wordes, my owne good hap betray,......	145	Cert Sonnets	16	10
Who silence force to make their words more deare:.....	147	Cert Sonnets	17	49
My poore reason thy words moved,...........	156	Cert Sonnets	27	3
Reason hath thy words removed,...........	156	Cert Sonnets	27	11
Finding that but wordes they proved...........	156	Cert Sonnets	27	12
Use thy words but to bewaile thee,..........	156	Cert Sonnets	27	19
Words, o words of heavenlie knowledge,..........	157	Cert Sonnets	27	35
Know my words their faults acknowledge..........	157	Cert Sonnets	27	36
As her words had it bent?.............	158	Cert Sonnets	28	24
I sought fit words to paint the blackest face of woe,....	165	Astrophil	1	5
But words came halting forth, wanting Invention's stay,..	165	Astrophil	1	9
While teares powre out his inke, and sighs breathe out his words:	168	Astrophil	6	10
What words so ere she speakes perswades for thee,......	171	Astrophil	12	7
But with your Rubarb words yow must contend.........	171	Astrophil	14	5
And yet my words, as them my pen doth frame,........	174	Astrophil	19	7
Your words my friend (right healthfull caustiks) blame ...	175	Astrophil	21	1
With dearth of words, or answers quite awrie,........	178	Astrophil	27	3
A burthned hart. "How can words ease, which are......	181	Astrophil	34	2
"But will not wise men thinke thy words fond ware?"....	182	Astrophil	34	7
What may words say, or what may words not say,	182	Astrophil	35	1
Beauties so farre from reach of words, that we	183	Astrophil	37	7
My words I know do well set forth my mind,........	186	Astrophil	44	1
Till that in words thy figure be exprest..	189	Astrophil	50	4
And oft whole troupes of saddest words I staid,.....	192	Astrophil	55	5
The thorowest words, fit for woe's selfe to grone,.....	193	Astrophil	57	4
Whether with words this soveraignty he gaine,.......	194	Astrophil	58	5
Even those sad words even in sad me did breed.......	194	Astrophil	58	14
With words, wherein the Muses' treasures be,.......	195	Astrophil	60	7
Now with slow words, now with dumbe eloquence.......	195	Astrophil	61	2
With choisest words, thy words with reasons rare,.....	200	Astrophil	68	10
For Stella hath with words where faith doth shine,	200	Astrophil	69	9
Those words, which do sublime the quintessence of blisse:..	205	Astrophil	77	8
Whence words, not words, but heav'nly graces slide......	206	Astrophil	80	4
But she forbids, with blushing words, she sayes,......	207	Astrophil	81	9
Tempers her words to trampling horses feet,.........	209	Astrophil	84	3
And her sad words my sadded sence did heare.........	223	Astrophil	87	8
Since all my words thy beauty doth endite,.........	224	Astrophil	90	13
Be your words made (good Sir) of Indian ware,.....	225	Astrophil	92	1
What sobs can give words grace my griefe to show?.....	227	Astrophil	93	2
Griefe find the words, for thou hast made my braine.....	228	Astrophil	94	1
While sobd out words a perfect Musike give........	231	Astrophil	100	11
I thought all words were lost, that were not spent of thee:.	212	A&S 5th Song		4
And thy words of refuse, do powre even hell on mee:.....	215	A&S 5th Song		83
That all these cruell words your praises shall be proved...	215	A&S 5th Song		90
Ponder the words, O lord, that I do say,..........	274	Psalm V		1
Your fearfull words why do you spill	283	Psalm XI		2
These are God's words, God's words are ever pure,......	285	Psalm XII		19
Whose deeds of Righteous heart, whose hearty words be plain,	287	Psalm XV		4
Then let my Words, my Crys ascend, ...	290	Psalm XVII		19
And cruel Words their swelling tongues do chatt,......	290	Psalm XVII		30
Their Words be set in letters great...........	294	Psalm XIX		15
So let words sprung from my weake tongue,..........	295	Psalm XIX		61
And with these Words, when they meet, prayse Thy Name. ...	300	Psalm XXII		52
Most cruel words..................	308	Psalm XXVII		60
To thy self those words apply................	309	Psalm XXVIII		9
Do throw their words against the most upright.........	313	Psalm XXXI		51
Or that by words enwrapt in guile.............	320	Psalm XXXIV		51
His words deceit, iniquity	323	Psalm XXXVI		9
At these my words all cloath'd in teares;.........	330	Psalm XXXIX		38
My Foes' ev'ill words their hate of me display	333	Psalm XLI		17
Such marble eares, no cunning wordes can charme,......	346	Possibly	5	2
To raise in words what in effect is lowe:..........	242	Other Poems	4	2
So that the grave did not his words despise.........	243	Other Poems	4	38
Mirth with respect, few words with curtesy,........	247	Other Poems	4	212

WORDS	(CONTINUED)	PAGE	TITLE		LINE
Wry words, and stam'ring, or els doltish dombe,.		254	Other Poems	4	471
Where by his words his self-like cause he knew..		256	Other Poems	4	536
For hearing him so oft with wordes of woe.		256	Other Poems	4	537
These same words, or this effecting:		262	Other Poems	7	18

WORK
"O" cried I, "of so meane worke be discharged:	16	1st Eclogues	7	76
To worke my Goddesse so by thy invention,.	19	1st Eclogues	7	177
Then vertue try, if she can worke in thee.	22	1st Eclogues	9	13
Begin (and halfe the worke is done) to prove	23	1st Eclogues	9	50
By justice' worke they their owne faultes disclose:.	27	1st Eclogues	10	42
Save what a worke, by thy selfe is wrought: and since I am altred	36	1st Eclogues	13	151
Thus by thy worke, disdaine not that which is by thy selfe done.	36	1st Eclogues	13	152
This is thy worke, thou God for ever blinde:	41	Arcadia II	20	9
Both still do worke, in neither finde I rest:.	42	Arcadia II	22	3
In this weake worke, that it can never be.	57	2nd Eclogues	30	30
That sorrowe's worke against my will I prove.	60	2nd Eclogues	30	127
Hold deere his work, with sighes eache change attendes,. . .	71	Arcadia III	37	8
Thus toyled in my work of raging love, ...	71	Arcadia III	37	14
The handle of this plesant worke,.	87	Arcadia III	62	47
To their owne worke this priviledge they graunt, ...	101	3rd Eclogues	66	103
Which troubles their daye's worke, and joyes of evening: . .	112	4th Eclogues	71	33
My worke her workes to know, her dwelling my resorte.. . . .	117	4th Eclogues	73	42
The weakning worke of Time's for ever-whirling wheele. . . .	120	4th Eclogues	73	122
As nature's worke: why should we feare to dye?	131	Arcadia V	77	2
When Nature made her chiefe worke, Stella's eyes,.	168	Astrophil	7	1
But by thy worke my Stella I descrie,.	181	Astrophil	32	7
Our horsmanships, while by strange worke I prove	189	Astrophil	49	2
Time doth worke what no man knoweth.".	234	A&S 11th Song		17
Thy work it is to blesse, thou blessest them;.	275	Psalm V		37
Thy work it is such men safe in to hemm.	275	Psalm V		39
Ev'ill men work ill to utmost right, ...	325	Psalm XXXVII		33

WORKETH
| Nature worketh enough with a small help for the revealing. . | 33 | 1st Eclogues | 13 | 61 |

WORKING
Though each possesse a divers working kinde, ...	78	Arcadia III	50	7
Asse, pacience; the Mole, a working thought;	101	3rd Eclogues	66	86
With the wicked working folk	309	Psalm XXVIII		12

WORKS
None but I, workes by desire: by desire have I kindled in his soule.	30	1st Eclogues	11	13
Olde aged oke cutt downe, of newe works serves to the building:.	36	1st Eclogues	13	134
His workes, showes, suites, with wit, grace, and vow's might	84	Arcadia III	60	4
Blinde Cupid's workes with wonder testifie?.	106	3rd Eclogues	67	98
Not sparing me, in whom his workes be rife:.	114	4th Eclogues	72	15
My worke her workes to know, her dwelling my resorte.. . . .	117	4th Eclogues	73	42
We Nature's workes doo helpe, she us defaces..	127	4th Eclogues	75	93
Since nature's workes be good, and death doth serve.	131	Arcadia V	77	1
O let not fooles in me thy workes reprove, ...	236	Astrophil	107	13
So strangely (alas) thy works in me prevaile,.	237	Astrophil	108	12
Thou hatest all whose works in evill are plac't.	275	Psalm V		13
In all whose workes vainess is ever raigning:.	276	Psalm VI		26
To rule the Works of Thyne own hands	279	Psalm VIII		22
Do works which earth corrupt and Heaven hates, ...	286	Psalm XIV		5
Though my Works reach not to Thee.	287	Psalm XVI		6
Who shunning vanity and works of vaineness leaving,.	302	Psalm XXIV		9
The works perform'd by Thee most wondrous great.	305	Psalm XXVI		24
To Thy Works they give no ey..	309	Psalm XXVIII		21
Their works he understands.	317	Psalm XXXIII		57
Who do ev'ill works: lo I doe see.	324	Psalm XXXVI		34
My God Thy wondrous works how manifold,.	331	Psalm XL		21

WORLD
Of best things then what world can yeeld confection.	15	1st Eclogues	7	46
To fill the world with strange but vaine conceits:	20	1st Eclogues	8	2
In this our world a hang-man for to be,.	22	1st Eclogues	8	47
That soone the world of his false tong be void..	24	1st Eclogues	9	68
Vertue you have, of vertue you have left proufes to the whole world, ...	33	1st Eclogues	13	56
Her praise, whence to the world all praise had his only beginning:	33	1st Eclogues	13	69
Apollo great, whose beames the greater world do light, . . .	44	Arcadia II	26	1
And in our little world dost cleare our inward sight,. . . .	44	Arcadia II	26	2
The world the garden is, she is the flower	59	2nd Eclogues	30	98
The world doth yeeld such ill consorted shows, ...	81	Arcadia III	54	9
For such an use the world hath gotten, ...	88	Arcadia III	62	85
Beyond our worlde, and ere I gatt my boothe.	98	3rd Eclogues	66	4
But this bad world, few golden fieldes doth bring, ...	104	3rd Eclogues	67	19
That still our little world may know his king.	105	3rd Eclogues	67	63
By thy impe's losse to fill the world with wailing..	109	Arcadia IV	70	22
An honour to the world, while Honour was their ende, ...	117	4th Eclogues	73	37
The bande of beauties all, the little world of Love.	119	4th Eclogues	73	90
Gives an adieu to the world, as to his onely delight:. . . .	123	4th Eclogues	74	26
Shall to the world appeare that faith and love be rewarded. .	123	4th Eclogues	74	35
Think what a world is now, think who hath altred her hart. .	124	4th Eclogues	74	76
For I to teach the world complainte am bent.	127	4th Eclogues	75	66
Now set thy triumph in this world, bereaved.	127	4th Eclogues	75	73

WORLD	(CONTINUED)	PAGE	TITLE		LINE
Then farewell world, thy uttermost I see,.		144	Cert Sonnets	32	13
Lcoks over the world, and can find nothing such, ...		169	Astrophil	9	10
Hath this world ought so faire as Stella is?		175	Astrophil	21	14
From all the world, her heart is then his rome,.		186	Astrophil	43	13
Tc portrait that which in this world is best..		189	Astrophil	50	8
In this old world, growne now so too too wise:		198	Astrophil	65	6
Wcrld of my wealth, and heav'n of my delight.		200	Astrophil	68	4
Hcw through the World thy Name doth shine:		278	Psalm VIII		2
Atove line repeated at following location.		279	Psalm VIII		34
Thither the World for justice shall repaire, ...		280	Psalm IX		23
His justice seat the World sustains, ...		310	Psalm XXIX		25
Of world a dweller is.		317	Psalm XXXIII		30
And as I mus'd such World to see,.		329	Psalm XXXIX		10
Wcrld without end, let still his blessing flow;.		334	Psalm XLI		47
WORLDIY					
The thought of which doth passe all worldly pelfe.		18	1st Eclogues	7	130
To hold these worldly things in such proportion, ...		60	2nd Eclogues	30	132
Now death hath swallow'd up our worldly pleasure,.		129	4th Eclogues	76	11
Which make the patents of true worldly blisse, ...		183	Astrophil	37	13
Although some Worldly losse therby he may sustaine,.		287	Psalm XV		10
From men I say, and from men's worldly trade,.		290	Psalm XVII		38
Lcckt fast with knowing that she is, of worldly things the best..		344	Possibly	1	30
WORLD'S					
Ycu that are borne to be the worlde's eye, ...		79	Arcadia III	50	12
Farr as World's farthest end.		271	Psalm II		20
The World's foundations then lay bare because he shent . . .		291	Psalm XVIII		32
WORLDS					
With the voyce of truth to recorde to all worldes, ...		31	1st Eclogues	12	19
Tho worlds quite me, shall I my selfe forgive?		227	Astrophil	93	11
Knowing worlds passe, ere she enough can find.		232	Astrophil	101	13
WORM					
Which should most miseries, cast on a worme that I am. . . .		29	1st Eclogues	11	2
Shall such high Plannets tend to the losse of a worme? . . .		123	4th Eclogues	74	38
Lcrd, let not me a worme by thee be shent, ...		276	Psalm VI		1
But I a worm, not I of mankind am, ...		299	Psalm XXII		15
WORMS					
Tc harme us wormes should that high Justice leave.		59	2nd Eclogues	30	71
Celestiall powers to wormes, Jove's children serve to claye.		120	4th Eclogues	73	116
That wormes should have their Sun, and I want mine..		230	Astrophil	98	14
WORN					
That his right badge is but worne in the hart:		192	Astrophil	54	12
Then some grene gowns are by the lasses worne.		243	Other Poems	4	53
WORSE					
Yet thou art mickle warse then ere was I,.		28	1st Eclogues	10	62
And worse of other more, till by assent.		29	1st Eclogues	10	82
Or else who singeth worse, my skill will hardly hit.		53	2nd Eclogues	29	50
O poisonous medecin! what worse to me can be then it? It...		63	2nd Eclogues	31	7
Who onely sees the ill is worse then blind..		106	3rd Eclogues	67	85
That eyes weepe worse then hart in bloodie teares?		142	Cert Sonnets	11	7
Yea worse then death, death parts both woe and joy,.		148	Cert Sonnets	20	13
Tc grieve me worse, in saying that Desire.		171	Astrophil	14	6
And which is worse, no good excuse can show, ...		174	Astrophil	18	7
But one worse fault, Ambition, I confesse, ...		178	Astrophil	27	11
With no worse curse then absence makes me tast..		235	Astrophil	105	14
And all eares worse then deafe, that heard not out thy storie..		212	A&S 5th Song		6
Yet worse then worst, I say thou art a theefe, a theefe? . .		213	A&S 5th Song		43
Of foes the spoile is evill, far worse of constant lovers..		214	A&S 5th Song		48
And which is worse, makes me most guiltlesse torments have,.		214	A&S 5th Song		59
What, is not this enough? nay farre worse commeth here;. . .		214	A&S 5th Song		73
Yet witches may repent, thou art far worse then they,. . . .		215	A&S 5th Song		79
Yea worse than doggs, a naughty wicked rout.		299	Psalm XXII		40
Though thus, and worse, though now I am at last, ...		254	Other Poems	4	493
"Absence is death, or worse, to them that love."		259	Other Poems	5	94
WORSHIPERS					
Made worshipers before Almighty Thee..		300	Psalm XXII		68
WORST					
But for that Love is worst, which rules the eyes,.		22	1st Eclogues	8 V	41
To wretched me, the last worst malediction..		61	2nd Eclogues	30	148
He gest the worst (you wot what is the worst).		94	3rd Eclogues	64	11
Wcrst fell to smallest birds, and meanest heard, ...		102	3rd Eclogues	66	141
Let Fortune lay on me her worst disgrace,.		198	Astrophil	64	3
That do not leave your least friend at the wurst,.		228	Astrophil	95	2
Ungratefull who is cald, the worst of evils is spok'n. . . .		213	A&S 5th Song		42
Yet worse then worst, I say thou art a theefe, a theefe? . .		213	A&S 5th Song		43
Now God forbid. A theefe, and of worst theeves the cheefe: .		213	A&S 5th Song		44
And God freed him, in his worst time		319	Psalm XXXIV		23
Fearing the worst, not knowing what were best, ...		255	Other Poems	4	525
WORTH					
And titles are but spots to such a worthe, ...		18	1st Eclogues	7	132
Or when a rich rubie's just price the worth of a walnut,. .		34	1st Eclogues	13	78
Oh no, no, hardye shepeheard, worth can never enter a title,		34	1st Eclogues	13	82
Where proofes justly do teach, thus matcht, such worth to be nought worth..		34	1st Eclogues	13	83
But nought els do behold (else is nought worth the beholding		36	1st Eclogues	13	150
And how much more her worth surmounteth thee,.		72	Arcadia III	38	16
Where hers, whom worth makes highest over all, ...		78	Arcadia III	49	17

```
WORTH                      (CONTINUED)                        PAGE   TITLE             LINE
    In worth, in taste, in perfitte hewe:. . . . . . . . . . .  87   Arcadia III  62     40
    Then such be he, as she his worth may see, . . . . . . . .  98   3rd Eclogues 65      3
    Where bee those wellcomes by no worthe deserved? . . . . . 138   Cert Sonnets  5     10
    A horse's worth laid wast the Troyan ground: . . . . . . . 146   Cert Sonnets 17     18
    Thy haire not worth a haire esteemed:. . . . . . . . . . . 156   Cert Sonnets 27     10
    Worth as nought worth rejected,. . . . . . . . . . . . . . 159   Cert Sonnets 30      5
    But knowne worth did in mine of time proceed,. . . . . . . 165   Astrophil     2      3
    Litle he is, so litle worth is he; . . . . . . . . . . . . 194   Astrophil    59      5
    Fed by thy worth, and kindled by thy sight?. . . . . . . . 200   Astrophil    68      8
    The proofe of Beautie's worth, th'enneritrix of fame,. . . 213   A&S 5th Song        20
    Or seeing, have so wodden wits, as not that worth to know; . 217  A&S 7th Song         8
    Dick. Faith in my self and worth in her, which no proofe can
        undoo.. . . . . . . . . . . . . . . . . . . . . . . . . 343  Possibly      1     26
WORTHIEST
    To worthiest let him give, when both he hath beheld: . . . . 120  4th Eclogues 73    142
WORTHLESS
    When worthlesse corke, aloft doth floting lye. . . . . . . .  81  Arcadia III  54     14
    With price of mangled mind thy worthlesse ware,. . . . . . . 161  Cert Sonnets 31      6
WORTHS
    In whose chiefe parte your worthes implanted be? . . . . . .  39  Arcadia II   16     10
WORTHY
    Cleofila. Worthy shepheard, by my song to my selfe all
        favor is happned,. . . . . . . . . . . . . . . . . . . .  31  1st Eclogues 13      8
    But ceasse worthy shepheard, nowe ceasse we to weery the
        hearers. . . . . . . . . . . . . . . . . . . . . . . . .  37  1st Eclogues 13    172
    Let Death first dye; be thou his worthy let. . . . . . . . .  59  2nd Eclogues 30     94
    A way more worthie beautie's fame, . . . . . . . . . . . . .  87  Arcadia III  62     59
    "Long have I love'd, (alas thou worthy arte) . . . . . . . .  97  3rd Eclogues 64     97
    To worthy Coredens he gave me ore. . . . . . . . . . . . . .  99  3rd Eclogues 66     40
    Shall in this life embrace no worthy thing:. . . . . . . . . 105  3rd Eclogues 67     59
    I have a wife worthie to be a Queene,. . . . . . . . . . . . 106  3rd Eclogues 67     88
    What? was I then worthie such good, now worthie so muche
        evill? . . . . . . . . . . . . . . . . . . . . . . . . . 124  4th Eclogues 74     77
    And sweare she is not worthy thee to have. . . . . . . . . . 141  Cert Sonnets  9     14
    Feare to offend, will worthie to appeare,. . . . . . . . . . 202  Astrophil    72     10
    O heav'nly foole, thy most kisse-worthie face, . . . . . . . 203  Astrophil    73     12
    But only for this worthy knight durst prove. . . . . . . . . 204  Astrophil    75     13
    As of a caitife worthy so to die,. . . . . . . . . . . . . . 228  Astrophil    94     10
    Who else for whom Fame worthy trumpets wanteth?. . . . . . . 197  A&S 1st Song        14
    Whom then shall I invoke but Thee most worthy prayse,. . . . 291  Psalm XVIII          6
    Strive we that in some worthy phrase . . . . . . . . . . . . 319  Psalm XXXIV         11
WOT
    He gest the worst (you wot what is the worst). . . . . . . .  94  3rd Eclogues 64     11
    No wife but I hath such a man, God wot". . . . . . . . . . . 104  3rd Eclogues 67     45
    Of hopes begot by feare, of wot not what desires:. . . . . . 167  Astrophil     6      2
    But (God wot) wot not what they meane by it: . . . . . . . . 204  Astrophil    74      6
WOULDST
    Wouldst brabling be with sence and love in me: . . . . . . . 169  Astrophil    10      2
    But thou wouldst needs fight both with love and sence, . . . 170  Astrophil    10      9
    But thou Desire, because thou wouldst have all,. . . . . . . 202  Astrophil    72     13
    But if thou wouldst garded be, . . . . . . . . . . . . . . . 226  A&S 10th Song       22
    Thou wouldst not set me on their score . . . . . . . . . . . 311  Psalm XXX            8
WOUND
    Came to the bed, where wound for kisse he got, . . . . . . .   5  Lady of May   3      8
    None can speake of a wound with skill, if he have not a
        wound felt.. . . . . . . . . . . . . . . . . . . . . . .  33  1st Eclogues 13     71
    And will pitty the wound festred so strangely within me. . .  37  1st Eclogues 13    168
    To shew the wound without cure.. . . . . . . . . . . . . . .  65  2nd Eclogues 32      8
    His hart his wound receaved from my sight: . . . . . . . . .  76  Arcadia III  45      9
    No smaller wound, alas! farr deeper have.. . . . . . . . . .  77  Arcadia III  47      4
    Vertue, beawtie, and speach, did strike, wound, charme,. . .  84  Arcadia III  60      1
    Then gan in guiltlesse earth full many a wound,. . . . . . . 102  3rd Eclogues 66    115
    Love gave the wound, which while I breathe will bleed: . . . 165  Astrophil     2      2
    Flie, fly, my friends, I have my death wound; fly, . . . . . 174  Astrophil    20      1
    Yet since my death-wound is already got, . . . . . . . . . . 189  Astrophil    48     12
    The friendly fray, where blowes both wound and heale,. . . . 206  Astrophil    79     10
    Wound and rent me to the bones,. . . . . . . . . . . . . . . 335  Psalm XLII          46
    A shot unheard gave me a wound unseene?. . . . . . . . . . . 253  Other Poems   4    454
WOUNDED
    My hart was wounded, with his wounded hart.. . . . . . . . .  76  Arcadia III  45     10
    Giv'ne to my harte, by my fore wounded eyne: . . . . . . . .  77  Arcadia III  47      6
    Till wounded, blind, and wearied Spirites, lose. . . . . . . 144  Cert Sonnets 15     11
    Wounded, inflam'de, knitt to the deathe I dye. . . . . . . . 344  Possibly      2      4
    And cal'd, now wounded, purpose to his aide: . . . . . . . . 246  Other Poems   4    162
WOUNDING
    That wounding thee, my thoughtes in thee I grave:. . . . . .  77  Arcadia III  47      2
WOUNDS
    Deadly wounds inward bleed, ech sleight sore mattereth.. . .  14  1st Eclogues  7      9
    Since no refuge doth serve from woundes we do carry about
        us . . . . . . . . . . . . . . . . . . . . . . . . . . .  33  1st Eclogues 13     51
    And of their wounds make brave lame showes:. . . . . . . . .  44  Arcadia II   25      8
    Whose wounds are salves, whose yokes please more then
        pleasure doth: . . . . . . . . . . . . . . . . . . . . .  49  2nd Eclogues 28     56
    And so refuse to behold of these strange wounds the
        recitall . . . . . . . . . . . . . . . . . . . . . . . . 122  4th Eclogues 74      7
    Woundes to Rehersers?. . . . . . . . . . . . . . . . . . . . 138  Cert Sonnets  5      8
    Of living deaths, deare wounds, faire stormes and freesing
        fires: . . . . . . . . . . . . . . . . . . . . . . . . . 167  Astrophil     6      4
    With sword of wit, giving wounds of dispraise, . . . . . . . 170  Astrophil    10     10
```

```
WOUNDS         (CONTINUED)                              PAGE    TITLE            LINE
   From that foe's wounds their tender skinnes to hide. . . . .   176  Astrophil    22     8
   Whose curelesse wounds even now most freshly bleed:. . . . .   189  Astrophil    48    11
   And even while I do speake, my death wounds bleeding be: . .   214  A&S 5th Song         52
   With such brave wounds, that they under my feet did ly. . . .  292  Psalm XVIII          70
   My wounds putrify and stink, . . . . . . . . . . . . . . . .   328  Psalm XXXVIII        13
   And in my woundes, my flames and bondes I fynde. . . . . . .   345  Possibly      2    13
WRACK
   A wreched wracke, a glasse of Ruine's ende.. . . . . . . . .    73  Arcadia III   40     4
   That see my wracke, and yet embrace the same?. . . . . . . .   174  Astrophil    19     2
   Then servant's wracke, where new doubts honor brings;. . . .   187  Astrophil    45    11
   Thee to thy wracke beyond thy limits straine.. . . . . . . .   210  Astrophil    85     4
   That all thy hurts in my hart's wracke I reede;. . . . . . .   227  Astrophil    93    13
   And wyked folkes from thee to wrack do wend. . . . . . . . .   279  Psalm IX             12
   Lightning on lightning he did for their wrack augment; . . .   291  Psalm XVIII          30
   Rebuke and wracke on those wrong doers throw, . . . . . . .    321  Psalm XXXV            9
   Though he do fall no wracke he proveth, . . . . . . . . . .    326  Psalm XXXVII         59
   To ev'ill, both they and theirs shall wrack. . . . . . . . .   326  Psalm XXXVII         72
WRACKED
   Will she take time, before all wracked be? . . . . . . . .    199  Astrophil    67     4
   Now is hee wrackt say they, lo, there he lyes. . . . . . . .   333  Psalm XLI            27
WRACKS
   So close unto my selfe my wrackes doo lie. . . . . . . . . .   114  4th Eclogues 72    40
   Strephon. So close unto my selfe my wrackes doo lie; . . . .   114  4th Eclogues 72    41
   Wrackes Triumphs be, which Love (high set) doth breed. . . .   186  Astrophil    42    14
WRAPPED
   To narrow brests he comes all wrapt in gaine:. . . . . . . .    21  1st Eclogues  8    37
   Dicus. Thy safetie sure is wrapped in destruction: . . . . .    49  2nd Eclogues 28    73
   Or wrapt in flesh what do they here obtaine, . . . . . . . .    57  2nd Eclogues 30    15
   Alas while we are wrapt in foggie mist . . . . . . . . . .     59  2nd Eclogues 30    68
   Death wrapt in flesh, to living grave assign'd.. . . . . . .    73  Arcadia III   40    14
   In colour blacke, why wrapt she beames so bright?. . . . . .   168  Astrophil     7     2
   Till now, wrapt in a most infernall night, . . . . . . . . .   181  Astrophil    33     3
   In falsehood wrapt, but in their pride display'd.. . . . . .   284  Psalm XII             9
WRAPPING
   Within her beames wrapping his cruell staines. . . . . . . .   141  Cert Sonnets  8    12
   Preserve me from the wyly wrappinge nett . . . . . . . . . .   312  Psalm XXXI           10
WRAPS
   Clips streight my wings, streight wraps me in his night, . .   236  Astrophil   108     8
WRATE
   Th' anatomy of all my woes I wrate,. . . . . . . . . . . . .   194  Astrophil    58    10
WRATH
   To causefull wrath, which thou canst not resist. . . . . . .    59  2nd Eclogues 30    66
   He made the simple wench his wrath abide. . . . . . . . . .     95  3rd Eclogues 64    30
   Who threatned stripes, if he his wrath did prove:. . . . . .   173  Astrophil    17     6
   But no scuse serves, she makes her wrath appeare . . . . . .   203  Astrophil    73     9
   Least you enflame his wrath. . . . . . . . . . . . . . . . .   272  Psalm II             28
   Arise, O lord, in wrath thy self upsett. . . . . . . . . . .   277  Psalm VII            16
   No sound part (causd by Thy wrath) . . . . . . . . . . . . .   327  Psalm XXXVIII         7
   I know that man's foule sin doth cause Thy wrath.. . . . . .   330  Psalm XXXIX          33
   Stay then Thy wrath, that I may strength receive . . . . . .   330  Psalm XXXIX          41
WRATHFUL
   And bravely speake to them, with breath of wrathful fire,. .   271  Psalm II             11
   For quickly ends his wrathfull Will, . . . . . . . . . . . .   311  Psalm XXX            13
WREAK
   Thus write I while I doubt to write, and wreake. . . . . . .   182  Astrophil    34    12
WRECKS
   Yet noblest Conquerours do wreckes avoid.. . . . . . . . . .   185  Astrophil    40    11
WRESTLING
   Because in wrestling and in pastorall. . . . . . . . . . . .    94  3rd Eclogues 64    17
WRETCH
   How dare I, wretch, seeke there my woes to rest, . . . . . .     3  Lady of May   1     5
   So dare I, wretch, my bashfull feare subdue, . . . . . . . .     3  Lady of May   1    11
   Sweete soule let not a wretch that serveth sheepe, . . . . .     4  Lady of May   2    17
   To wo and shame the wretch did enter in, . . . . . . . . . .     5  Lady of May   3     9
   The wretch compell'd a runnagate became, . . . . . . . . . .    21  1st Eclogues  8    21
   While still more wretch, more wicked he doth prove:. . . . .    22  1st Eclogues  8    44
   Still doo I crosse this wretch, what so he taketh in hand".. .   29  1st Eclogues 11     6
   Doth th'infected wretch, of his ev'll th'extremity know? No.    63  2nd Eclogues 31    19
   "The jealous wretch must now to Courte be gone:. . . . . . .    97  3rd Eclogues 64   103
   Thus may you see, the jealous wretch was made. . . . . . . .    97  3rd Eclogues 64   121
   Hath cast me, wretch, into eternall evening, . . . . . . . .   113  4th Eclogues 71    65
   When I, disgraced wretch, not wretched then, did give. . . .   117  4th Eclogues 73    11
   I, wretch, astonisht was, and thought the deathfull doome. .   118  4th Eclogues 73    61
   Unto the caitife wretch, whom long affliction holdeth, . . .   122  4th Eclogues 74     1
   Unto revenge? O sweete, on a wretch wilt thou be revenged?.    123  4th Eclogues 74    37
   O wretch, what do I say? should that faire face be defaced?.   124  4th Eclogues 74    57
   Lyke crafty wretch by time and travell tought, . . . . . . .   141  Cert Sonnets  8     5
   I find how heav'nly day wretch I did misse.. . . . . . . . .   181  Astrophil    33     4
   Upon a wretch, that long thy grace hath sought;. . . . . . .   185  Astrophil    40     7
   Through me, wretch me, even Stella vexed is.. . . . . . . .    227  Astrophil    93     4
   By being placed in such a wretch as I. . . . . . . . . . . .   228  Astrophil    94    14
   To steale some rest, but wretch I am constraind, . . . . . .   230  Astrophil    98     6
   Ah what doth Phoebus' gold that wretch availe, . . . . . . .   237  Astrophil   108    10
   Leave a wretch, in whom all wo . . . . . . . . . . . . . . .   221  A&S 9th Song          6
   Like in a winding sheet, wretch I already lay, . . . . . . .   291  Psalm XVIII          10
   The lookers now at me poore wretch be mocking, . . . . . . .   299  Psalm XXII           17
   The seely wretch with foule affliction staind, . . . . . . .   300  Psalm XXII           56
   For lo, this Wretch did call,. . . . . . . . . . . . . . . .   319  Psalm XXXIV          21
   O Soul, rejoyce, we made this wretch our prey. . . . . . . .   323  Psalm XXXV           62
```

                                     605

WRETCH   (CONTINUED)   PAGE   TITLE   LINE

	PAGE	TITLE		LINE
Or me wretch his tempest thunders.	335	Psalm XLII		32
The happy wretch she putt into hir breast,	244	Other Poems	4	98
Klaius the wretch, who lately yelden was	255	Other Poems	4	529
Tell me poore wretch, parted from wretched prey,	258	Other Poems	5	89

WRETCHED

	PAGE	TITLE		LINE
O wretched state of man in selfe division!	20	1st Eclogues	7	V966
Above line repeated at following location.	20	1st Eclogues	7	V967
But most wretched I am, now love awakes my desire.	30	1st Eclogues	11	20
But wretched be the soules which, vaild in a contrary subject,	32	1st Eclogues	13	19
But glorious name of wretched humaine-kind?.	57	2nd Eclogues	30	16
Griefe onely makes his wretched state to see	58	2nd Eclogues	30	32
To wretched me, the last worst malediction..	61	2nd Eclogues	30	148
A wreched wracke, a glasse of Ruine's ende..	73	Arcadia III	40	4
And most bewitch the wretched eye,	90	Arcadia III	62	138
Klaius. These forrests eke, made wretched by our musique,.	113	4th Eclogues	71	74
When I, disgraced wretch, not wretched then, did give.	117	4th Eclogues	73	11
That thou shalt never dare seeke helpe of wretched case".	121	4th Eclogues	73	176
Did Wisedome this our wretched time espie.	126	4th Eclogues	75	46
And wretched I must yeeld to this,	157	Cert Sonnets	27	31
Wealth breeding want, more blist, more wretched grow..	177	Astrophil	24	4
Yet growest more wretched then thy nature beares,	228	Astrophil	94	13
Lo he that first conceiv'd a wretched thought,	278	Psalm VII		37
And forsee their wretched paine.	288	Psalm XVI		9
And what was I but wretched clay?.	311	Psalm XXX		24
On wretched mee thy heavy hand,	315	Psalm XXXII		11
When, when will death o'retake this wretched wight.	333	Psalm XLI		19
Tell me poore wretch, parted from wretched prey,	258	Other Poems	5	89

WRETCHEDNESS

	PAGE	TITLE		LINE
That though in wretchednesse thy life doth lie,	228	Astrophil	94	12

WRETCHES

	PAGE	TITLE		LINE
Such blessings shall not wycked wretches see	270	Psalm I		13
Against them usd by wicked wretches,	327	Psalm XXXVII		103

WRIED

	PAGE	TITLE		LINE
Whose loosed bones quite out of joint be wryde;	299	Psalm XXII		32

WRING

	PAGE	TITLE		LINE
Neare therabout, into your Poesie wring;	172	Astrophil	15	4

WRINKLED

	PAGE	TITLE		LINE
That tedious leasure marks each wrinckled line:	230	Astrophil	98	11

WRIT

	PAGE	TITLE		LINE
In wind or water streame do require to be writ..	143	Cert Sonnets	13	4
She with her finger writ:.	158	Cert Sonnets	28	36
Writ each character of blisse,	219	A&S 8th Song		42
For in Thy book's roll I am writt,	331	Psalm XL		32

WRITE

	PAGE	TITLE		LINE
An ende, an ende, my dulde penn cannot write,	74	Arcadia III	42	13
And write the state how my fancies bee,	153	Cert Sonnets	24	4
"Foole," said my Muse to me, "looke in thy heart and write."	165	Astrophil	1	14
Come let me write, "And to what end?" To ease.	181	Astrophil	34	1
Thus write I while I doubt to write, and wreake.	182	Astrophil	34	12
As good to write as for to lie and grone..	184	Astrophil	40	1
So that I cannot chuse but write my mind,	190	Astrophil	50	9
And cannot chuse but put out what I write,	190	Astrophil	50	10
And love doth hold my hand, and makes me write..	224	Astrophil	90	14
To write therein more fresh the story of delight,	232	Astrophil	102	13
She thinkes you do letters write:	211	A&S 4th Song		39
Write, but first let me endite:	211	A&S 4th Song		40
Sweet lord, write not my soul.	306	Psalm XXVI		28
While I in heart my will write ere I die..	255	Other Poems	4	499

WRITER

	PAGE	TITLE		LINE
And see therein how well the writer fares.	42	Arcadia II	21	16

WRITER'S

	PAGE	TITLE		LINE
But never heeds the fruit of writer's mind:	170	Astrophil	11	8

WRITES

	PAGE	TITLE		LINE
But Copying is, what in her Nature writes.	166	Astrophil	3	14

WRITINGS

	PAGE	TITLE		LINE
That mine owne writings like bad servants show	175	Astrophil	21	3

WRITTEN

	PAGE	TITLE		LINE
Of written greefes, yet be the silent ground..	81	Arcadia III	54	8
She written had (but in a hand disguisde).	96	3rd Eclogues	64	80
And written in the sand.	158	Cert Sonnets	28	40

WROKEN

	PAGE	TITLE		LINE
But Thereus' love, on her by strong hand wrokne,	137	Cert Sonnets	4	14
My causeless wrongs hast wroken.	273	Psalm III		27
To have their hate on good soules wroken;	325	Psalm XXXVII		38

WRONG

	PAGE	TITLE		LINE
Rather to wrong then unto just defence,	25	1st Eclogues	9	106
What skill servethe a soare of a wrong infirmity judged?	32	1st Eclogues	13	21
No fancy mine, nor others' wronge suspect.	40	Arcadia II	18	11
What I call wrong, I doo the same, and more:	41	Arcadia II	20	6
And suffer such a wrong? a wrong I trowe,	54	2nd Eclogues	29	64
Shall barr that wrong, and though it not prevaile.	82	Arcadia III	55	13
Till wrong, contempt, deceipt, did growe, steale, creepe,	84	Arcadia III	60	7
Thus thus the more I love, the wronge the more	85	Arcadia III	61	5
Wrong sturres remorsed greefe, griefe's deadly sore.	85	Arcadia III	61	7
And eke revenge his wrong suspecting you".	97	3rd Eclogues	64	108
Witnesse his wrong which by thy helpe is eased:	108	Arcadia IV	69	11
Or if that they be skante, if this be wronge?.	126	4th Eclogues	75	45
Sir wrong his tombe ordaineth,	160	Cert Sonnets	30	23

WRONG	(CONTINUED)	PAGE	TITLE		LINE
You take wrong waies, those far-fet helpes be such,.		172	Astrophil	15	9
As though that faire soft hand did you great wrong..		208	Astrophil	83	4
Which fall he made to do his neighbor wrong.		278	Psalm VII		42
All wrong and mischeife lyes,.		283	Psalm X		58
Speake thou for me against wrong speaking foes,.		321	Psalm XXXV		1
Who did me wrong, against me witness beare		322	Psalm XXXV		25
Defence herein doth wrong, O yeelde O yeelde,.		345	Possibly	4	12
WRONGDOERS					
Rebuke and wracke on those wrong doers throw,.		321	Psalm XXXV		9
WRONGED					
By no encrochment wrongd, nor time forgot:		209	Astrophil	84	10
Princes in subjects wrongd, must deeme themselves abused...		213	A&S 5th Song		30
WRONGFUL					
Till bloudie bullet get him wrongfull pray..		175	Astrophil	20	4
Many mighty wrongfull foes,.		329	Psalm XXXVIII		57
WRONGLY					
Abroad his stepps be wrongly sett.		323	Psalm XXXVI		12
WRONG-ORDERED					
The poore-clad truth of love's wrong-ordred lot.		242	Other Poems	4	14
WRONG'S					
Here wrong's name is unheard: slander a monster is.. . . .		69	2nd Eclogues 34		26
WRONGS					
The fire to see my wrongs for anger burneth:		136	Cert Sonnets	3	1
That her Grace gracious makes thy wrongs, that she		170	Astrophil	12	6
And now man's wrongs in me, poore beast, descrie..		189	Astrophil	49	4
"But the wrongs love beares, will make		234	A&S 11th Song		31
My causeless wrongs hast wroken.		273	Psalm III		27
And rid me from the wrongs which cruel Witts did brew; . .		293	Psalm XVIII		87
That causeless wrongs do frame..		303	Psalm XXV		10
WROUGHT					
That which we see in many time hath wrought, ...		22	1st Eclogues	9	14
Save what a worke, by thy selfe is wrought: and since I am					
altred		36	1st Eclogues 13		151
Her beames have wrought therin most suer impression: . . .		47	2nd Eclogues 28		11
Was it a dreame? O dreame, how hast thou wrought in me,. .		121	4th Eclogues 73		181
Late harbors in her face whom nature wrought,.		141	Cert Sonnets	8	7
Thou web of will, whose end is never wrought;.		161	Cert Sonnets 31		4
Unto my mind, is Stella's image, wrought		183	Astrophil	38	6
O Stella deare, how much thy power hath wrought, ...		184	Astrophil	40	2
Till it have wrought what thy owne will attends.		236	Astrophil	107	11
Nay if I wrought not for his Freedome's sake		277	Psalm VII		11
Down in the pitt, which they themselves had wrought: . . .		280	Psalm IX		47
For never day such changing wrought.		303	Psalm XXV		17
And that the bias of hir bloud was wrought..		244	Other Poems	4	101
WRUNG					
Leave that sir Phip, least off your necke be wroong. . . .		208	Astrophil	83	14
WRY					
Wry words, and stam'ring, or els doltish dombe,.		254	Other Poems	4	471
YCLEPED					
Icleped starres; each thing to rest disposed:.		98	3rd Eclogues 66		10
YCLOTHED					
Which streight the Earth yclothed in his claye:.		101	3rd Eclogues 66		79
YE					
Yee living powres enclosed in stately shrine		40	Arcadia II	18	1
Of growing trees, yee rurall Gods that wield		40	Arcadia II	18	2
Ye helplesse Sighes, blowe out your breath to nought,. . .		83	Arcadia III	59	5
Yee Muses all which chaste affects allow,.		91	3rd Eclogues 63		19
Yee Nymphes which in the waters empire have,.		92	3rd Eclogues 63		28
Strephon. Yee Gote-heard Gods, that love the grassie					
mountaines,.		111	4th Eclogues 71		1
Yee Nimphes which haunt the springs in pleasant vallies, . .		111	4th Eclogues 71		2
Ye Satyrs joyde with free and quiet forrests,.		111	4th Eclogues 71		3
Yee dimmy clowdes, which well employ your staying		127	4th Eclogues 75		67
But with your Rubarb words ye must contend		171	Astrophil	14 V	5
Till when will ye my honour high		273	Psalm IV		7
Seek ye my Face, when Thou didst say,.		307	Psalm XXVII		39
Ye men of Pow'er even by birth-right,.		309	Psalm XXIX		2
Ye saints of his, remembring still		311	Psalm XXX		11
Then love him ye all ye that feel his grace, ...		314	Psalm XXXI		64
Rejoice in God, O ye		316	Psalm XXXIII		1
Feare God ye saints of his,.		319	Psalm XXXIV		33
Ye Hymnes and singing skill.		260	Other Poems	6	7
YEA					
Yea worse then death, death parts both woe and joy,. . . .		148	Cert Sonnets 20		13
Yea even my songs thy name shall magnify,.		279	Psalm IX		4
Yea in no age thy blisse from them departs..		285	Psalm XII		24
Yea my flesh in hope shall rest.		288	Psalm XVI		30
Yea Thou dost make me serv'd by folks I never knew;. . . .		293	Psalm XVIII		79
Yea fire from himself sent,.		296	Psalm XX		14
Yea heares with powers and helps of helpfull hand.		296	Psalm XX		25
Yea thou prevent'st e're ask he could, ...		297	Psalm XXI		9
Yea worse than doggs, a naughty wicked rout.		299	Psalm XXII		40
Yea tho I should thro vallys stray		301	Psalm XXIII		10
And long yea long abide I shall, ...		301	Psalm XXIII		25
Yea Lord to me Thy wayes do show;.		303	Psalm XXV		11
Who hate, yea hate me cruely..		304	Psalm XXV		66
Yea sound my reines, and inmost of my heart;		305	Psalm XXVI		9
Yea noble hight of Rocky Hill.		307	Psalm XXVII		28
Yea through the Waters doth resound.		310	Psalm XXIX		9

YEA   (CONTINUED)   PAGE   TITLE   LINE

Entry	PAGE	TITLE	LINE
Yea from the grave's most hungry jawes;.	311	Psalm XXX	7
My eye, my Gutts, yea my soul grief doth wast,	312	Psalm XXXI	27
Yea neighbors, more, my mates were so agast.	313	Psalm XXXI	32
Yea and from dreadfull misery.	319	Psalm XXXIV	15
Yea take Thy lance and stop the way of those	321	Psalm XXXV	4
His deeds, yea thoughtes all good forgett;	323	Psalm XXXVI	10
Yea beasts made safe thy goodness try.	323	Psalm XXXVI	18
Yea thou shalt see the ev'ill decay.	327	Psalm XXXVII	88
Yea I roare,	328	Psalm XXXVIII	23
Yea lord Thy law within my heart doth stand;	331	Psalm XL	34
Let them have shame, yea blush for shame,	332	Psalm XL	52
Yea let them be destroyed.	332	Psalm XL	56
O yea, my Friend to whom I did impart.	333	Psalm XLI	29
Then God, yea my God,	337	Psalm XLIII	28

YEAR

Entry	PAGE	TITLE	LINE
All this one the this fatall yere shall hitte.	11	Arcadia I	1 V807
But, woe is me, the yeare is gone about,	115	4th Eclogues 72	56
To fill his hornes this yeare on Christian coast;	179	Astrophil 30	2

YEARLY

Entry	PAGE	TITLE	LINE
Yearely decke thine Altar shall:	264	Other Poems 7	70

YEARS

Entry	PAGE	TITLE	LINE
That without love she spends her yeares of love:	17	1st Eclogues 7	98
Millions of yeares this old drivell Cupid lives;	22	1st Eclogues 8	43
It shews they fetch their wit from youthfull yeares.	24	1st Eclogues 9	80
Of yeeres (alas) since I good Mastix knewe..	27	1st Eclogues 10	21
His good strong staffe my slippry yeares upbore:	99	3rd Eclogues 66	37
And while their line of yeares they did in vertue spende...	117	4th Eclogues 73	38
Our yeares doo it require: you see we both doo feele	120	4th Eclogues 73	121
Our young yeares to renew (for so he saith he will).	120	4th Eclogues 73	126
More then Nestor's yeares, more then a King's diademe.	122	4th Eclogues 74	20
If now the May of my yeares much decline,	175	Astrophil 21	10
Hundreds of yeares you Stella's feet may kisse..	209	Astrophil 84	14
My life with heavyness, my yeares with moane	312	Psalm XXXI	28
He, that the other in some yeares did passe,	242	Other Poems 4	21
And in those gifts that years distribute doe,	242	Other Poems 4	22

YEARS'

Entry	PAGE	TITLE	LINE
When they by yeares' experience get best graces,	127	4th Eclogues 75	89

YELLING

Entry	PAGE	TITLE	LINE
A yelling voice, and heartes compos'd of sorow,	109	Arcadia IV 70	27

YESTERMORNING

Entry	PAGE	TITLE	LINE
Nico. Leuca to me did yester-morning showe	55	2nd Eclogues 29	99

YESTERNIGHT

Entry	PAGE	TITLE	LINE
Pas. But yesternight by light I did receave.	55	2nd Eclogues 29	102

YET

Entry	PAGE	TITLE	LINE
My foule mishap came yet from fairest mind..	5	Lady of May 3	18
By princely meane be stolne, and yet not lost.	11	Arcadia I 1	2
Yet hath sir Sunne the greatest praise,	13	Arcadia I 5	9
Yet high is my attempt. O Muse historifie.	15	1st Eclogues 7	23
Who though she be no Bee, yet full of honie is:	15	1st Eclogues 7	29
Yet all my health I place in your good-will.	18	1st Eclogues 7	120
Yet patient must abide.	20	1st Eclogues 7	V960
Yet beares he still his parents' stately gifts,	21	1st Eclogues 8	25
Geron. Yet sure an end, to each thing time doth give,	22	1st Eclogues 9	11
Yet for my sake discover us thy griefe.	23	1st Eclogues 9	23
Yet not of wemen Judging as he said,	24	1st Eclogues 9	64
My wearied ears! O gods yet graunt me this,	24	1st Eclogues 9	67
I yet should know a young man speaketh now,	25	1st Eclogues 9	97
Yet have I seene when well a wolfe he shooke..	27	1st Eclogues 10	18
Yet to a passenger will bonnet vaile.	27	1st Eclogues 10	33
Yet thou art mickle warse then ere was I,	28	1st Eclogues 10	62
And yet they say he takes in greate men's bowers?	28	1st Eclogues 10	68
Nature abasht went back: fortune blusht: yet she replide thus:	30	1st Eclogues 11	17
Hope we do live yet.	30	1st Eclogues 12	4
Yet dying, and dead, doo we sing her honour;	30	1st Eclogues 12	9
If the sencelesse spheares doo yet hold a musique,	30	1st Eclogues 12	13
Hope we doo live yet..	31	1st Eclogues 12	28
And yet his outward heate our teares would quench, but an inward	32	1st Eclogues 13	31
But yet, alas! O but yet alas! our happs be but hard happs,	32	1st Eclogues 13	37
But yet well I doo finde each man most wise in his owne case	33	1st Eclogues 13	70
And yet neither of us great or blest deemeth his owne selfe.	33	1st Eclogues 13	73
For yet (weigh this alas!) great is not great to a greater..	34	1st Eclogues 13	74
Unto a silly caban, though weake, yet stronger against woes.	34	1st Eclogues 13	93
Nor yet, fancy so drest, do receive more plausible hearing:	35	1st Eclogues 13	101
Better yet do I live, that though by my thoughts I be plunged.	35	1st Eclogues 13	107
Into my live's bondage, yet may disburden a passion.	35	1st Eclogues 13	108
Sweete Juniper saith this, thoh I burne, yet I burne in a sweete fire.	35	1st Eclogues 13	120
Pine is hye, hope is as hie, sharpe leav'd, sharpe yet be my hope's budds.	36	1st Eclogues 13	130
Yet be my hopes thus plast, here fixed lives my recomforte,	37	1st Eclogues 13	164
Loved I am, and yet complaine of Love:	41	Arcadia II 20	1
I waile for want, and yet am chokte with store.	41	Arcadia II 20	8
Yet thus much Love, O Love, I crave of thee:	41	Arcadia II 20	13
One wonder yet farre passeth my conceate:	42	Arcadia II 22	13
R. But yet our strife sure peace in end doth breede.	46	2nd Eclogues 27	27

608

	(CONTINUED)	PAGE	TITLE		LINE
R. Yet Passion, yeeld at length to Reason's stroke......		47	2nd Eclogues	27	33
P. No Reason yet had ever skill to shew it..........		47	2nd Eclogues	27	40
Yet harvest brings. Doth she alas absent herselfe?.....		49	2nd Eclogues	28	62
Yet is it seale, though errour, of true hart........		51	2nd Eclogues	28	104
Paine willes me die, yet will of death I mortifie:.....		51	2nd Eclogues	28	124
Dicus. Sing then my lads, but sing with better vaine then yet...........................		53	2nd Eclogues	29	49
For good thou mayst yet proove in sheepish sound.......		56	2nd Eclogues	29	137
For so yet of a conquest speake thou may...........		56	2nd Eclogues	29	140
Yet Reason saith, Reason should have abilitie,.......		60	2nd Eclogues	30	131
In divers kinds; yet as he were not filled,........		62	2nd Eclogues	30	171
Yet for that night, my Caban dyd them kepe.........		62	2nd Eclogues	30	188
Yet say againe thy advise for th' ev'lls that I told thee. I told thee....................		63	2nd Eclogues	31	18
Yet tell what light thinge I had in me to draw me to die? Eye...........................		64	2nd Eclogues	31	25
Winde, tempests, and stormes, yet in ende what gives she desire? Ire.......................		64	2nd Eclogues	31	35
Silly rewarde! yet among women hath she of vertu the most. Most...........................		64	2nd Eclogues	31	36
Tell yet againe me the names cf these faire form'd to do ev'lls. Dev'lls.....................		65	2nd Eclogues	31	49
Yet deare soile, if a soule closed in a mansion.......		69	2nd Eclogues	34	31
Yet never rock, nor race, suche terror brought,......		71	Arcadia III	37	3
This waxe doth waste it selfe, yet painelesse dyes.....		75	Arcadia III	43	2
These wordes are full of woes, yet feele they none.....		75	Arcadia III	43	3
And yet as hard, as brawne made hard by arte:.......		76	Arcadia III	46	16
Yet still, faire tree, lifte up thy stately line,.....		77	Arcadia III	47	9
Yet yeeld your graunt, a baser hand may leave.......		78	Arcadia III	49	9
Yet joyning formes one sight of beautie breede.......		78	Arcadia III	50	4
Yet all well knit to one faire end do passe:.......		78	Arcadia III	50	8
But yet o dreame, if thou wilt not departe........		79	Arcadia III	51	9
Yet stay and well peruse,.................		80	Arcadia III	52	7
Of written greefes, yet be the silent ground.......		81	Arcadia III	54	8
Like to my brother's raies, yet those I sende.......		82	Arcadia III	55	14
There may one see, and yet not see............		88	Arcadia III	62	67
Yet never shall my song omitte.............		88	Arcadia III	62	87
Vertue (if not a God) yet God's chiefe parte,......		92	3rd Eclogues	63	46
Yet let not sluttery,...................		93	3rd Eclogues	63	78
Nor yet shall yeeld to loathsome sluttishnes,......		94	3rd Eclogues	63	97
Who yet was good, because she knewe none ill,......		94	3rd Eclogues	64	14
Yet like a coward fearing stranger's pride,.......		95	3rd Eclogues	64	29
And yet the prince (that lov'd him) not offend.....		95	3rd Eclogues	64	54
That yet the ground hereof he might espie........		96	3rd Eclogues	64	72
Not sturring thoughts, nor yet denying right,......		98	3rd Eclogues	65	6
Yet (for I nothing sawe) I feared sore;.........		99	3rd Eclogues	66	16
But yet the common Damme none did bemone;........		102	3rd Eclogues	66	118
Yet first but wooll, or fethers off he teard:......		102	3rd Eclogues	66	143
But yet o man, rage not beyond thy neede:........		103	3rd Eclogues	66	148
She bids him goe, and yet from jorney stayes......		104	3rd Eclogues	67	36
That ever fell to honest woman yet:...........		104	3rd Eclogues	67	44
And yet finde no such faults in womankind........		106	3rd Eclogues	67	87
So well she can command, and yet obay,.........		106	3rd Eclogues	67	89
And yet in all this time, betwixt us tway,.......		106	3rd Eclogues	67	91
Yet now the roote of him abase you would........		106	3rd Eclogues	67	99
Yet let us leave a monument in publique........		109	Arcadia IV	70	15
Yet Fancie would perforce employ his skill,......		115	4th Eclogues	72	65
Yet living still in her, while her beames lent		115	4th Eclogues	72	83
Straunge were the Ladies' weedes; yet more unfit then strange........................		118	4th Eclogues	73	65
Too much her peerles parts, nor yet could them despise....		119	4th Eclogues	73	88
With age's force decay'd, yet once the heaven was his. ...		120	4th Eclogues	73	124
(She beckned unto me) as yet of spotlesse truth, ...		120	4th Eclogues	73	138
Ne yet for what I see, your beauties merite ought......		121	4th Eclogues	73	164
"Yet thou shalt not go free (quoth Venus) such a fire....		121	4th Eclogues	73	170
Grant yet, grant yet a looke, to the last monument of his anguish,......................		122	4th Eclogues	74	3
Shall I not? o may I not thus yet refresh the remembrance, .		124	4th Eclogues	74	71
Yet craving law of armes, whose rule doth teach,.....		135	Cert Sonnets	1	10
Yet still her eyes give to my flames their fuell.....		136	Cert Sonnets	3	12
If thus, alas: yet while those partes have wo,.....		142	Cert Sonnets	10	13
Hath yet such health, as it my life can save.......		142	Cert Sonnets	11	12
Is neither freed, nor yet to service bound,.......		144	Cert Sonnets	15	2
Yet lives untill his life be new requirde.........		150	Cert Sonnets	22	24
A stranger fish, my selfe not yet expirde,.......		150	Cert Sonnets	22	25
Yet live with thoughts closde up, till that she will . ..		150	Cert Sonnets	22	29
Which though despisde, yet still doth truth endure....		150	Cert Sonnets	22	40
Which seeming lesse, yet nobler life doth move......		151	Cert Sonnets	22	60
And yet unite the eyes,................		152	Cert Sonnets	23	6
Yet eyes deprived be not,...............		152	Cert Sonnets	23	27
Yet I shall die in Phoenix fire.............		153	Cert Sonnets	24	27
Yet, yet, a life to their death,............		154	Cert Sonnets	25	18
Yet do we both live in you...............		154	Cert Sonnets	25	23
But yet in vaine thou hast my ruine sought,......		161	Cert Sonnets	31	9
Yet with repining at so partiall lot..........		165	Astrophil	2	8
True, and yet true that I must Stella love........		167	Astrophil	5	14
Yet hiding royall bloud full oft in rurall vaine.....		167	Astrophil	6	8
Yet of that best thou leav'st the best behind.......		170	Astrophil	11	4
I see and yet no greater sorow take,..........		174	Astrophil	18	13

YET   (CONTINUED)   PAGE TITLE   LINE

	PAGE	TITLE		LINE
That see my wracke, and yet embrace the same?	174	Astrophil	19	2
I willing run, yet while I run, repent..	174	Astrophil	19	4
And yet my words, as them my pen doth frame, ...	174	Astrophil	19	7
For though she passe all things, yet what is all	174	Astrophil	19	9
O let me prop my mind, yet in his growth	174	Astrophil	19	12
Yet each prepar'd, with fanne's wel-shading grace, ...	176	Astrophil	22	7
Yet were the hid and meaner beauties parcht, ...	176	Astrophil	22	12
Yet to those fooles heav'n such wit doth impart, ...	177	Astrophil	24	5
Yet pride I thinke doth not my soule possesse, ...	178	Astrophil	27	9
If French can yet three parts in one agree;.	180	Astrophil	30	5
If in the Scottishe Court be weltring yet;	180	Astrophil	30	11
Do they above love to be lov'd, and yet.	180	Astrophil	31	12
And yet could not by rising Morne foresee.	181	Astrophil	33	12
Yet noblest Conquerours do wreckes avoid.	185	Astrophil	40	11
Yet still on me, o eyes, dart downe your rayes:.	186	Astrophil	42	11
And yet she heares, yet I no pitty find;	186	Astrophil	44	5
I much do guesse, yet find no truth save this, ...	187	Astrophil	44	9
And yet she heares, and yet no pitie I find;	186	Astrophil	44 V	5
Yet hearing late a fable, which did show	187	Astrophil	45	5
Though false, yet with free scope more grace doth breed. . .	187	Astrophil	45	10
Yet Deare, let me this pardon get of you,.	188	Astrophil	46	12
Yet since my death-wound is already got, ...	189	Astrophil	48	12
And yet as soone as they so formed be, ...	189	Astrophil	50	5
Let Vertue have that Stella's selfe; yet thus, ...	191	Astrophil	52	13
And yet to breake more staves did me addresse:	191	Astrophil	53	2
If he be faire, yet but a dog can be..	194	Astrophil	59	4
Yet while I languish, him that bosome clips, ...	194	Astrophil	59	9
Yet let this thought thy Tygrish courage passe:.	198	Astrophil	65	11
And yet amid all feares a hope there is.	199	Astrophil	66	9
Now banisht art, but yet alas how shall?	202	Astrophil	72	14
And yet my Starre, because a sugred kisse.	203	Astrophil	73	5
And gain'd by Mars, could yet mad Mars so tame,.	204	Astrophil	75	7
Yet ah, my Mayd'n Muse doth blush to tell the best..	205	Astrophil	77	14
I bare (with Envie) yet I bare your song,.	208	Astrophil	83	5
Yet swam in joy, such love in her was seene.	223	Astrophil	87	11
If this darke place yet shew like candle light,.	225	Astrophil	91	5
Yet truth (if Caitif's breath mighte call thee) this	227	Astrophil	93	5
Or if thy love of plaint yet mine forbeares, ...	228	Astrophil	94	9
Yet waile thy selfe, and waile with causefull teares,. . . .	228	Astrophil	94	11
Yet growest more wretched then thy nature beares,.	228	Astrophil	94	13
Yet sighs, deere sighs, indeede true friends you are,. . . .	228	Astrophil	95	1
Thanke-worthiest yet when you shall breake my hart..	229	Astrophil	95	14
For that at length yet doth invite some rest,.	229	Astrophil	96	13
Thou though still tired, yet still doost it detest..	229	Astrophil	96	14
Yet those lips so sweetly swelling,.	203	A&S 2nd Song		21
Yet a sleepe, me thinkes they say, ...	211	A&S 4th Song		27
Yet thought and speech do live, though metamorphosd quite: .	212	A&S 5th Song		14
Threat'n what may be done, yet do more then you threat'n.. .	213	A&S 5th Song		33
Yet worse then worst, I say thou art a theefe, a theefe? . .	213	A&S 5th Song		43
Yet gentle English theeves do rob, but will not slay;. . . .	214	A&S 5th Song		49
And yet against thy Prince thy force dost dayly prove: . . .	214	A&S 5th Song		65
Yet witches may repent, thou art far worse then they,. . . .	215	A&S 5th Song		79
You see what I can say; mend yet your froward mind,.	215	A&S 5th Song		88
Be not yet those fancies changed?"	234	A&S 11th Song		7
Or if they do delight therein, yet are so cloyed with wit, .	217	A&S 7th Song		3
With armes crost, yet testifying	218	A&S 8th Song		19
Save thy mind which yet surpasseth..	219	A&S 8th Song		44
As yet love she signified.	220	A&S 8th Song		72
Now be still, yet still beleeve me,.	220	A&S 8th Song		75
Yet alas before you go,.	221	A&S 9th Song		11
Fiercest but yet fairest ever;	221	A&S 9th Song		17
And yet leave me helplesse meerely?.	222	A&S 9th Song		35
Nor yet himself with idle scorners seateth:.	270	Psalm I		4
Ne yet shall suffred be a place to take, ...	270	Psalm I		17
And say (O kings) yet have I set my King upon.	271	Psalm II		13
Yet lord thou art my shield, ...	272	Psalm III		11
Yet know this too, that God did take	273	Psalm IV		11
Talk with your hearts, and yet be still.	273	Psalm IV		18
Yourselves yet to yourselves disclose.	273	Psalm IV		20
Yet each day art provoakt, thyne Ire to show,.	277	Psalm VII		32
Yet hast Thou made even him an owner	279	Psalm VIII		19
Yet perish shall (although his paine be sore).	281	Psalm IX		59
Yet from his mouth doth spring	282	Psalm X		27
Least yet I slip or go astray.	289	Psalm XVII		16
And yet their high hearts look so low.	290	Psalm XVII		31
This much, yet more, when I by him this freedom gate,. . . .	292	Psalm XVIII		40
Yet to my plaint Thou hast not audience lent..	298	Psalm XXII		8
And yet ev'en from the womb thy self did'st take me;	299	Psalm XXII		21
Ah! from the sword yet save my vital sprite, ...	299	Psalm XXII		47
For he hath not abhorrd nor yet disdain'd..	300	Psalm XXII		55
Abandon me, yet my decay..	308	Psalm XXVII		50
Thou hast hid them: yet leaving them thy light,.	313	Psalm XXXI		56
Yet I confess in that tempestuous haste.	313	Psalm XXXI		61
And yet his force.	317	Psalm XXXIII		62
Who never word of peace yet utter would,.	322	Psalm XXXV		51
That yet beare love unto my righteousness;	323	Psalm XXXV		68
Yet let them say, laud be to God alwayes	323	Psalm XXXV		69
Yet I the man that was betaken	326	Psalm XXXVII		62
And yet more,.	327	Psalm XXXVIII		5

YET (CONTINUED)   PAGE   TITLE   LINE

	PAGE	TITLE		LINE
O helpe o help me, this farr yet I crave,.	330	Psalm XXXIX		25
Ah! yet from me let Thy plagues be displac't,.	330	Psalm XXXIX		31
Yet God on me is thinking, ...	332	Psalm XL		66
The Lord will keep his life yet safe and sound	333	Psalm XLI		5
Wait on God, for yet his glory	334	Psalm XLII		19
Yet thus still my hope is grounded,.	335	Psalm XLII		35
Wait on God, for yet his glory	335	Psalm XLII		51
Who ever Lambkins saw (yet lambkins love to play).	343	Possibly	1	5
Yet will not I greife, ashes, thralldom change	345	Possibly	2	9
Much may that was not yet, Allarme allarme..	346	Possibly	5	12
For where he most would hit, he ever yet did misse..	241	Other Poems	1	2
The later borne, yet too soone, Strephon hight..	242	Other Poems	4	24
Yet not so wise, as of unstained harte:.	243	Other Poems	4	35
Strephon was yonge, yet markt with humble eies	243	Other Poems	4	36
No grasse, no trees, nor yet hir sparrow might	245	Other Poems	4	111
Yet but a babe, with milke of Sight he nurst:.	247	Other Poems	4	202
Geron, though olde yet gamesome, kept one ende	248	Other Poems	4	242
So laughing all, yet Pas to ease some dell,.	249	Other Poems	4	263
And each way luckles, yet in humble guise.	249	Other Poems	4	277
Though they do fly, yet backwardly do glowe.	249	Other Poems	4	292
Pas Cosma matcht, yet angry with his fault,.	250	Other Poems	4	318
(Yet beauty still as fast as she did sturre)	251	Other Poems	4	358
But yet a setting foorth it some way lent:	252	Other Poems	4	395
Yet thoughts do flie, though I can scarcely creep.	253	Other Poems	4	444
Drowsy am I, and yet can rarely slepe.	253	Other Poems	4	446
And yet, deare soule, I know she hurteth none:	254	Other Poems	4	458
And yet I see her shine amid the cloud..	255	Other Poems	4	506
Yet there, me seemes, I heare her singing loud..	255	Other Poems	4	508
With that (yet kissed first) his pipe he burst,.	255	Other Poems	4	520
His well knowne friend, but yet his unknowne mate, ...	255	Other Poems	4	528

YEW

	PAGE	TITLE		LINE
Ewe doth make me be thinke what kind of bow the boy holdeth.	35	1st Eclogues	13	121

YIELD

	PAGE	TITLE		LINE
Tune up my voice, a higher note I yeeld, ...	3	Lady of May	2	7
As shallow brookes do yeeld the greatest sound, ...	4	Lady of May	2	14
Whereto mine inward thoughts did faintly yeeld;.	11	Arcadia I	2	6
Yeld outward shew, what inward change he tryes:.	13	Arcadia I	4	2
Of best things then what world can yeeld confection. . . .	15	1st Eclogues	7	46
Their wooll your weede, I will you Musique yeeld	18	1st Eclogues	7	124
My foode is teares; my tunes waymenting yeeld:	18	1st Eclogues	7	138
New friend of mine; I yeeld to thy habilitie:.	19	1st Eclogues	7	174
Good Lalus mine, I yeld to thy abilitie;	20	1st Eclogues	7	V974
Cleofila. First shall fertill grounds not yeeld increase of a good seed:	33	1st Eclogues	13	64
Thus to my sonne do I yeeld, such lookes her beames do aforde me.	36	1st Eclogues	13	133
To this strange death I vainely yeeld my life.	38	Arcadia II	14	14
Old wood inflam'de, doth yeeld the bravest fire, ...	38	Arcadia II	15	3
A voice may come, which troubled soule doth yeld:.	40	Arcadia II	18	4
Eache flower eache herbe dothe to your service yeeld,. . .	43	Arcadia II	23	5
Your sweetest flowers, your herbes, no service yeeld,. . .	43	Arcadia II	24	5
Reason. Thou Rebell vile, come, to thy master yelde. . . .	46	2nd Eclogues	27	1
R. Yet Passion, yeeld at length to Reason's stroke.. . . .	47	2nd Eclogues	27	33
Yeeld to our eares a sweet and sound relation, ...	48	2nd Eclogues	28	20
I would come downe, and yeeld to her my place,.	56	2nd Eclogues	29	121
The cheerefull notes these pleasant places yeeld,.	58	2nd Eclogues	30	39
Then man to yeeld to female lamentations?.	61	2nd Eclogues	30	141
Eysight made me to yeelde, but what first pierst to myne eies? Eies..	64	2nd Eclogues	31	26
My muse I yeeld, my muse singe,.	67	2nd Eclogues	32	50
Commands all creatures, to yeeld obeysance	68	2nd Eclogues	33	22
Thus pure pearle, I do yeeld, my senses and soule.	68	2nd Eclogues	33	28
Thus sweete paine, I do yeeld, what ere I can yeelde.. . .	68	2nd Eclogues	33	29
Nought disturbs thy quiet, all to thy service yeeld, . . .	69	2nd Eclogues	34	10
Trew harte, whose trewthe dothe trewthe yeeld to trewest bande,. . .	70	Arcadia III	35	11
Phaebus yeelde up thy title in my minde.	72	Arcadia III	38	11
Yet yeeld your graunt, a baser hand may leave.	78	Arcadia III	49	9
The world doth yeeld such ill consorted shows, ...	81	Arcadia III	54	9
And lowest stops doo yeeld the hyest sounde.	81	Arcadia III	54	16
Which onely still doth Lillies yeeld:.	87	Arcadia III	62	62
Whose bought incav'd doth yeeld such sight,.	89	Arcadia III	62	97
Since Lalus' musick oft doth yeeld you praise, ...	92	3rd Eclogues	63	29
Nor yet shall yeeld to loathsome sluttishnes,.	94	3rd Eclogues	63	97
Camaeleon, ease to chaunge; Ducke, ease to yelde;.	101	3rd Eclogues	66	95
Whereto I yeeld, and seeke no other breath,.	114	4th Eclogues	72	18
Let one the Princesse be, to her the other yeeld:.	120	4th Eclogues	73	129
But now we muste needs yeelde, to what our othes require". .	121	4th Eclogues	73	169
Can those eyes now yeeld to the kind conceit of a sorow,. .	122	4th Eclogues	74	17
I yeeld, o Love, unto thy loathed yoke,.	135	Cert Sonnets	1	9
On those affectes which easily yeeld to sight, ...	135	Cert Sonnets	2	6
I yeeld and strive, I kisse and curse the paine:	148	Cert Sonnets	19	17
And wretched I must yeeld to this, ...	157	Cert Sonnets	27	31
Do easly yeeld, that all their coasts may be	179	Astrophil	29	3
Seeing hope yeeld when this wo strake him furst:	228	Astrophil	95	6
To cadence of the tunes, which Amphyon's lyre did yeeld, . .	208	A&S 3rd Song		4
And will to highest Name yeild prayses high.	278	Psalm VII		48
The Cherubins their backs, the winds did yeild their wings,.	291	Psalm XVIII		22
Among the Gentiles then I, Lord, yeild thanks to Thee, . . .	293	Psalm XVIII		88
So my songs his lauds shall yeeld.	309	Psalm XXVIII		30

YIELD   (CONTINUED)   PAGE   TITLE   LINE
    Yeelde yeelde, O yeelde, you that this Forte do holde, . . .   345 Possibly   4   1
    Then to Desier's desire, O yeelde O yeelde.. . . . .   345 Possibly   4   4
    Yeelde yeelde O yeelde, trust not on beautie's pride,. . . .   345 Possibly   4   5
    Claymes but to gaine his due, O yeelde O yeelde. . . . . . .   345 Possibly   4   8
    Yeelde yeelde O yeelde, who first this Fort did make,. . . .   345 Possibly   4   9
    Defence herein doth wrong, O yeelde O yeelde,. . . . .   345 Possibly   4   12
    Yeelde yeelde O yeelde, now is it time to yeelde,. . . . . .   345 Possibly   4   13
    Before thassault beginne, O yeelde O yeelde. . . . .   345 Possibly   4   14
    Then shall you see them yelde, Allarme allarme. . . . . . .   346 Possibly   5   14
    Tc yeeld she found hir noble heart did ake:. . . . .   245 Other Poems   4   125
    Brave crest to him hir scorn-gold haire did yeeld,. . . . .   246 Other Poems   4   149
    And yeeld himselfe unto hir punishment,. . . . .   247 Other Poems   4   191
    Which made hir yeeld to deck this shepheards' band,. . . . .   247 Other Poems   4   215
    But this straunge race more straunge conceits did yeeld: . .   251 Other Poems   4   345
    So doth he yeeld, so takes he on his yoke, ...   253 Other Poems   4   425
YIELDED
    Well: but faultie I was: Reason to my Passion yeelded, . . .   124 4th Eclogues 74   67
    Gladly my senses yeelded.. . . . .   154 Cert Sonnets 25   8
YIELDEN
    A conquerd, yelden, ransackt heart to winne? . . . .   182 Astrophil   36   2
    Klaius the wretch, who lately yelden was . . . .   255 Other Poems   4   529
YIELDETH
    Yeldeth a lute's tune, ...   30 1st Eclogues 12   16
YIELDING
    Echo, what do I gett yelding my sprite to my grieves?
        Grieves. . . . .   63 2nd Eclogues 31   5
    Gladly my senses yeelding, ...   154 Cert Sonnets 25   9
    Allarme allarme, here will no yeelding be, ...   346 Possibly   5   1
YIELDS
    Thus Reason to his servants yeelds his right;. . . . .   12 Arcadia I   2   11
    Who yelds to woe, doth but encrease his smart. . . . .   22 1st Eclogues 9   2
    Figge that yeeldes most pleasante frute, his shaddow is
        hurtefull,. . . . .   35 1st Eclogues 13   125
    Which caught, to cruell search yeelds his chiefe part: . . .   150 Cert Sonnets 22   22
    Where fairnesse yeelds to wisdome's shortest raines. . . . .   151 Cert Sonnets 22   64
    Who causeless now, yeelds me a hatefull heart, ...   277 Psalm VII   12
YOKE
    P. What shall we winne by taking Reason's yoke?. . . . . . .   47 2nd Eclogues 27   34
    We beare our double yoke with such consent,. . . . .   106 3rd Eclogues 67   92
    I yeeld, o Love, unto thy loathed yoke,. . . . .   135 Cert Sonnets 1   9
    Which ever hath Love's yoke despised:. . . . .   159 Cert Sonnets 29   15
    To that sweet yoke, where lasting freedomes be:. . . . . . .   161 Cert Sonnets 32   6
    Whose necke becomes such yoke of tyranny?. . . . .   188 Astrophil   47   4
    Cupid's yoke to loose or bind: . . . .   210 A&S 4th Song   14
    Her faire necke a foule yoke bare, ...   218 A&S 8th Song   10
    In his sight her yoke did vanish . . . .   218 A&S 8th Song   12
    So doth he yeeld, so takes he on his yoke, ...   253 Other Poems   4   425
YOKED
    Though (yoked so) my minde with sicknes fainte,. . . . . . .   83 Arcadia III   57   7
YOKES
    Whose wounds are salves, whose yokes please more then
        pleasure doth: . . . .   49 2nd Eclogues 28   56
    And cast their yoakes away.. . . . .   271 Psalm II   8
YOND
    On yond foule flocke belonging not to me." . . . .   255 Other Poems   4   518
YONDER
    To yonder Nymphe therefore (to Mira I did point) . . . . . .   121 4th Eclogues 73   165
YORE
    How sheepheards did of yore, how now they thrive,. . . . . .   99 3rd Eclogues 66   34
YOUNG
    A naked god, young, blind, with arrowes two. . . . .   20 1st Eclogues 8   6
    A naked god, blinde young, with arrowes two. . . . .   20 1st Eclogues 8   V 6
    How is he young, that tam'de old Phoebus' youth? . . . . . .   21 1st Eclogues 8   10
    That since they still alledge, When they were yong:. . . . .   24 1st Eclogues 9   79
    Old men themselves, doe love young wives to choose:. . . . .   25 1st Eclogues 9   88
    I yet should know a young man speaketh now,. . . . .   25 1st Eclogues 9   97
    Loth to dye young, and then you must be olde,. . . . .   25 1st Eclogues 9   103
    Thou heardst even now a yong man snebb me sore,. . . . . . .   27 1st Eclogues 10   22
    A young girle's hart, to that were shame for both, ...   95 3rd Eclogues 64   59
    For feare he did, least he the young man might . . . .   96 3rd Eclogues 64   65
    Our young yeares to renew (for so he saith he will). . . . .   120 4th Eclogues 73   126
    Time ever old, and yonge is still revolved . . . .   127 4th Eclogues 75   79
    Whose talents held young Ganimed above:. . . . .   171 Astrophil   13   4
    But while I thus with this yong Lyon plaid;. . . . .   173 Astrophil   16   9
    My young mind marde, whom Love doth Winlas so,. . . . . . .   175 Astrophil   21   2
    Holds my young braine captiv'd in golden cage. . . . .   176 Astrophil   23   11
    As my young Dove may in your precepts wise . . . .   196 Astrophil   63   3
    Neast of young joyes, schoolmaster of delight, ...   206 Astrophil   79   8
    A nest for my yong praise in Lawrell tree: . . . .   224 Astrophil   90   6
    And my yong soule flutters to thee his nest, ...   236 Astrophil   108   6
    Ycng folkes, take time while you may:. . . . .   211 A&S 4th Song   28
    May then yong his pide weedes showing, ...   217 A&S 8th Song   3
    I am enclosed with young Bulls' madded route,. . . . .   299 Psalm XXII   27
    Nay like young Calves in leapes are born,. . . . .   310 Psalm XXIX   16
    And shirion like young Unicorn. . . . . 310 Psalm XXIX   18
    I have been younge now old I am, ...   326 Psalm XXXVII   61
    Strephon was yonge, yet markt with humble eies . . . .   243 Other Poems   4   36
    (Stolne from her yoong by theeves' unchoosing hast). . . . .   254 Other Poems   4   491

	PAGE	TITLE		LINE

YOUNGER
Thy yonger shall with Nature's blisse embrace. . . . . 11 Arcadia I 1 3
When yonger dooth in smoke his vertue spend. . . . . 38 Arcadia II 15 4

YOUNGLINGS
Of yonglings, which thy selfe with love hast rearde, ... 92 3rd Eclogues 63 43
And Klaius taking for his yonglings carke, ... 243 Other Poems 4 67

YOUNG-WISE
Nor that he could young-wise, wise-valiant frame . . . . . . 204 Astrophil 75 5

YOURS
To liken her? Decke yours with your comparison:. . . . . . 15 1st Eclogues 7 47
Call me but yours, my title is most hye: . . . . 79 Arcadia III 50 17
Holde me most yours, then my longe suite is signde.. . . . . 79 Arcadia III 50 18
Sc both are yours: I, bound with gaged harte:. . . . . . . 79 Arcadia III 50 21
You onely yours, too farr beyond desarte.. . . . . 79 Arcadia III 50 22
Subscription was, yours most, if you will prove. . . . . . 96 3rd Eclogues 64 90
Whose force but yours the bolts of beautie thunders? . . . . 197 A&S 1st Song 30

YOURSELF
Dorus. Lady your selfe, whom nether name I dare, ... 18 1st Eclogues 7 131
And to old age since you your selfe aspire,. . . . . 39 Arcadia II 15 13
That in my selfe your selfe true love doth plant;. . . . . . 39 Arcadia II 16 8
Ycu none can clayme but you your selfe by right, ... 79 Arcadia III 50 19
For you do passe your selfe, in vertue's might.. . . . . . . 79 Arcadia III 50 20
Are you not dried? Can you your self renew?. . . . . 257 Other Poems 5 39

YOURSELVES
Disuse your selves from sweete Menalcas' voice:. . . . . . . 13 Arcadia I 4 6
So I your sight, you shall your selves recover". . . . . . . 17 1st Eclogues 7 93
Fondly blame that to which your selves aspire. . . . . 25 1st Eclogues 9 104
Them to defend, not with your selves to fight. . . . . 26 1st Eclogues 10 3
Teares, drowne your selves, for woe (your cause) is wasted,. 83 Arcadia III 59 6
I will you lende; the rest your selves must give,. . . . . . 101 3rd Eclogues 66 76
But if among yourselves some one tree growe, ... 125 4th Eclogues 75 10
Of Prince's losse your selves for tokens reare.. . . . . . . 125 4th Eclogues 75 27
O notes of mine your selves together tie:. . . . . 127 4th Eclogues 75 76
Yourselves yet to yourselves disclose. . . . . 273 Psalm IV 20

YOUTH
How is he young, that tam'de old Phoebus' youth? . . . . . . 21 1st Eclogues 8 10
What swarmes of vertues did in his youth flye. . . . . 24 1st Eclogues 9 74
Only fond youth admires a rotten stocke. . . . . 25 1st Eclogues 9 89
Histor. Tnus may you see, howe youthe estemeth aige. . . . . 26 1st Eclogues 9 138
Youth will have will: Age must to age therefore. . . . . . . 27 1st Eclogues 10 24
Mastix. What marvaile if in youth such faults be done, . . . 27 1st Eclogues 10 25
Old age hath knowne what ever was in youth:. . . . . 39 Arcadia II 15 11
Thou God, whose youth was deckt with spoyle of Python's
skin . . . . 44 Arcadia II 26 5
His youth delight, his age the soule's oppression: . . . . . 48 2nd Eclogues 28 39
With his sweet skill my skillesse youth he drewe,. . . . . . 99 3rd Eclogues 66 26
He liked me, but pitied lustfull youth:. . . . . 99 3rd Eclogues 66 36
For that (so that you like) hereby doth lie a youth. . . . . 120 4th Eclogues 73 137
And getting youth againe, in youth doth flourish:. . . . . . 127 4th Eclogues 75 83
My youth doth waste, my knowledge brings forth toyes,. . . . 174 Astrophil 18 9
Youth, lucke, and praise, even fild my veines with pride.. . 191 Astrophil 53 4
Since youth and they do passe; . . . . 303 Psalm XXV 28
Strephon, poor youth, because he saw no smoke, ... 253 Other Poems 4 427

YOUTHFUL
It shews they fetch their wit from youthfull yeares. . . . . 24 1st Eclogues 9 80
To age thus doe they draw there youthfull pryme, ... 28 1st Eclogues 10 52
Those passions which to youthfull head doo clime,. . . . . . 107 3rd Eclogues 67 116
Sins brew'd in youthfull glass,. . . . . 303 Psalm XXV 26

YOUTHS
And faine those Aeols' youthes there would their stay. . . . 233 Astrophil 103 9

YWROUGHTEN
Didst snatch from Cosma's hand her greene ywroughten glove.. 52 2nd Eclogues 29 10

ZEAL
Thy too much zeale, I feare thy braine hath spent. . . . . . 28 1st Eclogues 10 63
Dorus. Well do I prove, errour lies oft in zeale,. . . . . . 51 2nd Eclogues 28 103

ZENITH
Keepe still my Zenith, ever shine on me. . . . . 186 Astrophil 42 8

ZEPHYRS
Wing'd with whose breath, so pleasing Zephires blow, ... 231 Astrophil 100 7

APPENDIX

*Index Words
in Order of Frequency*

1740
To
1629
The
1415
And
1409
My
1339
Of
1257
In
1255
I
1001
That
861
With
787
A
754
But
738
Be
691
Me
665
Is
655
His
608
For
585
Thy
527
Her
523
So
509
He
498
Do
466
Not
443
Which
433
All
424
Doth
409
Thou
392
From
389
O
385
You
370
Did
350
This
348
No
343
Their
342
Love
337
As
326
By
322
They
What
308
Who
299
Then
290
She
Thee
286
Shall
272
On
271
Now
266
It

253
Such
252
Let
242
Yet
239
Eyes
232
Have
231
Will
229
When
If
214
Our
208
Heart
205
Still
197
More
Or
195
Thus
194
Them
193
Was
Where
190
Your
Can
186
Him
Whose
182
Hath
177
Those
176
How
171
Lord
169
See
Sweet
166
May
163
Most
161
God
Well
155
We
153
Make
152
While
149
Like
144
Are
139
Good
Since
137
Fair
Only
136
One
135
Nor
129
Though
128
Mind
126
Say
124
Myself
122
Even
Words
120
Mine
118
Would

116
Life
115
Might
113
Light
Sight
112
Long
111
Never
These
109
Unto
105
Than
104
Should
103
Thoughts
101
Face
100
Find
Man
99
At
98
Made
96
Alas
Each
Think
95
High
94
Both
Death
Must
93
There
91
Oft
Praise
Some
90
Up
89
Soul
88
Place
Show
87
Own
86
Art
85
Were
83
Take
Yield
82
Great
81
Time
80
Am
79
Give
78
Had
Know
Out
75
Ever
Help
Joy
74
Come
Much
Thyself
72
Fear
Pain
71
Dear
70
Go
Heavenly

Thought
69
First
Till
True
Us
Voice
67
Desire
66
Cause
Earth
Force
65
Beauty
Reason
Woe
64
Leave
Part
63
Hand
Hope
62
Fire
61
Best
Full
Sun
Too
60
Grace
Once
59
Bliss
Nature
Stella
58
Day
Far
Poor
Seek
56
Delight
Makes
Name
Night
55
Virtue
54
Bear
Die
Hear
Itself
53
Beams
Joys
Said
Wit
52
Inward
Live
Men
51
An
End
Fly
Other
Tell
50
Down
Fall
Hast
Pas
Prove
Tears
49
Eye
Hands
Hearts
Heaven
Lie
Sure
48
Right
Therefore
47
Cannot
Dost
Here

Shame
Tongue
Way
Woes
46
Look
45
Could
Keep
Lips
Thine
Things
Upon
44
Care
Ears
Evil
Nay
Set
Song
Two
43
Himself
Music
Save
Sense
Sing
Stay
Vain
42
Ah
Indeed
Old
Rest
Within
41
Naught
New
State
Trust
Without
40
Breast
Strange
Truth
39
Because
Fortune
Hold
Just
Sheep
Why
38
Due
Kiss
Muse
Sorrow
37
Away
Cruel
Dark
Ease
Found
Hate
Lest
Power
Saw
Self
Strength
Thing
36
Bent
Forever
Speak
World
35
Else
Head
Move
Sighs
Soon
Strephon
34
Against
Change
Grief
Honor
Lo
Skill
Stella's

Word
33
Breath
Case
Glory
Peace
Pleasure
Pride
Same
Straight
Use
Wretch
32
Beauties
Blind
Grow
Late
Nature's
Race
Th
31
Better
Breed
Cries
Fancy
Lay
Nothing
Rage
Wicked
30
Cry
Dan
Gifts
Hair
Minds
Nico
Sound
Want
Wilt
Yea
29
Dead
Fame
Feel
Foes
Foul
Frame
Grant
Last
Maintain
Small
Themselves
Treasure
White
28
Beauty's
Before
Blessed
Get
Lies
Taste
Wise
27
Being
Black
Free
Gone
Heard
Ill
Lives
Love's
Near
None
Pains
Pass
Weak
Young
26
Any
Comfort
Course
Forth
Happy
Hard
King
Many
Miss
Speech
Sprite
Stayed

26
Work
25
Brought
Heavens
Hell
Into
Klaius
Passion
Rich
Seem
Serve
24
Bend
Call
Dorus
Faith
Farewell
Feet
Fool
Glad
Hurt
Judge
Length
Looks
Methinks
Powers
Quite
Shade
Shalt
Stars
Strong
23
Appear
Called
Chief
Ear
Field
Fine
Golden
Got
Hopes
Loss
Loved
Mean
Mercy
Mortal
Shows
Sleep
Tunes
Wretched
22
Age
Air
Bad
Blow
Despair
Disdain
Ere
Food
Holy
Living
Lost
Pity
Reason's
Seat
Send
Shine
Spite
Thence
Try
Witness
Works
21
Absence
Again
Although
Aye
Bow
Brain
Burn
Done
Fault
Fit
Folks
Gain
Justice
Little
Mark
Needs

Others
Placed
Proud
Senses
Shield
Smart
Spent
Stand
Through
Went
Wits
Wonder
Worth
Wrong
20
Beasts
Birds
Cupid's
Daily
Deep
Dwell
Feed
Fill
Ground
Kind
Learn
Man's
P
Pipe
Read
Run
Sayeth
Shining
Teach
Tree
Waste
Whence
Wind
Worse
19
Alone
Bind
Caught
Cosma
Didst
Endless
Fast
Faults
Gave
God's
Gold
Oppressed
Please
R
Seeing
Sought
Sweetest
Taught
Trees
Wait
Win
Wings
Yourselves
18
About
Bide
Body
Bound
Came
Child
Constant
Cupid
Dare
Fain
Flames
Flock
Friend
Fruit
Geron
Greater
Highest
Hue
Impart
Laid
Less
Lovely
Morning
Mountains
Mouth
Perfect

Play
Receive
Seemed
Skies
Souls
Stately
Strife
Virtue's
Woods
Ye
Youth
17
Abide
Above
Apply
Become
Been
Boy
Cast
Comes
Cursed
Earthly
Fancies
Flow
Flowers
Gives
Guide
Herself
Hid
Judgment
Kill
Known
Left
Loving
Need
Ruin
Secret
Sent
Shepherd
Sore
Three
Worthy
16
Alarm
Blood
Born
Clear
Content
Counsel
Crave
Fears
Forced
Gods
Hers
House
Join
Meseems
Off
Outward
Proof
Pure
Rather
Sake
Seen
Shape
Shepherds
Took
Ways
Wish
15
Abroad
After
Among
Another
Answer
Arms
Bears
Begin
Behold
Clouds
Deadly
Deridan
Evening
Fail
False
Fools
Foot
Home
Knew
Lalus

Meet
Ne
Neither
Others'
Pan
Passions
Past
Plain
Quiet
Shepherd's
Silent
Silly
Sin
Wealth
Write
14
Blest
Bodies
Break
Cease
Cold
Doubt
Enough
Envy
Every
Foe
Goodness
Graces
Grave
Griefs
Heat
Hide
Hill
Instead
Knows
Lot
Moan
Muses
Reign
Rise
Sacred
Says
Slave
Spread
Touch
Turn
Turned
Valleys
Very
Vile
Wailing
Wear
Weeds
Wherein
Wisdom
Wound
Wounds
Years
13
Aught
Base
Beast
Brave
Brings
Children
Climb
Close
Coupled
Darkness
Days
Disgrace
Dust
Enjoy
Fight
Forests
Friends
Glass
Guest
Harms
Having
Humble
Image
Increase
Lady
Loves
Low
Marble
Mayst
Met
Methought

Mourning
Noble
Parts
Pray
Present
Public
Rebel
Rejoice
Rule
Scorn
Seed
Shot
Silence
Sit
Skin
Sprites
Store
Takes
Title
Venus
Wonted
Wrought
12
Aid
Annoy
Bed
Beyond
Bones
Breasts
Broken
Crown
Dart
Dick
Display
Doleful
Echo
Evils
Faithful
Father
Fell
Flesh
Given
Glorious
Hence
Knowledge
Law
Lead
Lesson
Lift
Men's
Moved
Naked
Nest
Notes
Nous
Plaint
Prey
Purest
Raise
Raised
Revenge
Rules
Sad
Seems
Side
Sorrow's
Stain
Steps
Stood
Thanks
Thinking
Tongues
Under
Void
Whereto
Whether
Yourself
11
Affection
Anguish
Aspire
Bring
Canst
Catch
Causeless
Cheer
Court
Curse
Deeds
Dog

Draws
Embrace
Fairest
Felt
Fled
Fortune's
Goes
Hateful
Held
Hidden
Horse
Hymen
Joined
Knowing
Land
Line
Measure
Mother
Open
Ourselves
Over
Paint
Plaints
Pleasant
Possess
Presence
Prince
Put
Reins
Righteousness
Safe
Sea
Singing
Son
Sport
Storms
Swear
Throne
Tired
Ugly
Water
Wife
Woman's
Worst
10
Agree
Annoys
Band
Banished
Blessing
Blows
Cherish
Closed
D
Dainty
Dance
Deliver
Desert
Desires
Dicus
Direction
Doom
Draw
Dying
Fearing
Feeling
Fie
Finding
Foolish
Framed
Fruits
Grown
Hap
Haps
Hearing
Heavy
Hot
Judgments
La
Labor
Lamb
Lays
Led
Lose
Mighty
Mischief
Moon
Nourish
Pay
Plangus

10	Phoebus'	Meant	Duty	Unknown	Guiltless
Pleased	Pit	Milk	Dwelling	Uran	Hardly
Remove	Point	Mold	Effect	Verse	Haunt
Reward	Possessed	Neighbors	Eke	Virtues	Heads
Service	Preserve	Net	Error	Vouchsafe	Hearty
Shun	Reach	Pierced	Estate	Walking	Heed
Sick	Ready	Places	Failing	Wandering	Helpless
Sink	Require	Plays	Fairer	Wanting	Herbs
Soft	Riches	Pressed	Feeble	Watery	Higher
Spend	Round	Pretty	Feeding	Wherewith	Holdeth
Stir	Saving	Prevail	Fiery	Whole	Inflamed
Strive	Scope	Quickly	Fixed	Wholly	Iron
Suffer	Seal	Rain	Flies	Wickedness	Jehova
Suit	Shines	Red	Forbear	Woeful	Jewel
Sweetness	Short	Rent	Form	Woman	Kindled
Swelling	Simple	Root	Gainst	Wood	Knot
Tedious	Solitariness	Safety	Gladly	Worldly	Lilies
Together	Sooner	Saint	Goods	Wrongs	Lion's
Tries	Sorrows	Servants	Grass	Yours	Lived
Used	Spoil	Sharp	Grieved	6	Locks
Waters	Sports	Sickness	Half	Always	Maid
Wool	Stone	Sky	Harvest	Angel's	Meaning
Wrack	Swell	Songs	Height	Appears	Misery
Yoke	Temple	Sorry	Honest	Apt	Mixed
9	Tender	Spare	Honor's	Ashes	Named
Absent	Therein	Spring	Hoped	Augment	Names
Anger	Throw	Stolen	Horrors	Bands	Native
Approach	Thrown	Stray	Human	Beaten	News
Armed	Triumph	Subject	Husband	Begun	Nobler
Asunder	Unkind	Sugared	Keeps	Bends	Object
Bless	War	Sweetly	Kindness	Besides	Offerings
Blush	Weep	Sweets	Kings	Biding	Order
Brake	Wight	Tear	Languish	Bitter	Pasture
Breathe	Wrath	Thereof	Lap	Bloody	Phrase
Brooks	8	Thinks	Leads	Bringeth	Piercing
Build	Arm	Tried	Leuca	Busy	Plaining
Burnt	Arrows	Troubles	Looked	Causeful	Plant
Cares	Becomes	Turns	Loose	Charge	Praised
Chaste	Began	Upright	Mad	Charm	Praises
Cheeks	Begins	Urania	Making	Choice	Price
Conquest	Between	Venus'	Metal	Coast	Private
Cried	Betwixt	Waking	Mira	Conceit	Proceed
Dam	Blame	Wanton	Motion	Conquered	Promise
Damage	Blushing	Weakness	Neck	Courage	Quench
Death's	Bright	Weight	Neighbor	Courtier	Range
Deck	Chase	Wend	Noise	Crying	Refrain
Despise	Cheerful	Wisdom's	Obtain	Curious	Renew
Drew	Chiefest	Women	Other's	Danger	Resort
Dumb	Coming	Wonders	Pace	Darts	Return
Either	Complain	Wrapped	Patience	Defend	Rightly
Espy	Confess	7	People	Defense	Rocks
Eyes'	Creep	Ails	Perish	Desire's	Roses
Favor	Cunning	Allow	Philisides	Detest	Rude
Feared	Cut	Already	Phoenix	Devour	Scattered
Fierce	Delights	Arise	Pierce	Dim	Search
Filthy	Depart	Ask	Pine	Discord	Seely
Flourish	Disease	Asleep	Preserved	Dread	Seest
Flower	Dove	Babe	Ran	Dressed	Senseless
Folk	Erst	Bare	Rare	Drowned	Serves
Forget	Eternal	Barley-brake	Rays	Easily	Shadow
Forsooth	Falls	Barred	Reigneth	Effects	Shafts
Fully	Fed	Believe	Remembrance	Eloquence	Shined
Greatest	Flight	Beloved	Repent	Employ	Ship
Green	Folly	Bird	Righteous	Ended	Showed
Grows	Fond	Bleed	Rock	Endure	Sins
Haste	Forgot	Blinded	S	Enter	Smoke
Hills	Forsake	Bold	Salvation	Fancy's	Snow
Hit	Gan	Bondage	Salve	Father's	Spake
Infected	Gentle	Book	Seas	Fearful	Spark
Ink	Guides	Bosom	Seeking	Feels	Speaking
Jove	Guilty	Brook	Sees	Feign	Special
Justly	Harm	Cave	Sir	Fertile	Spill
Kindly	Health	Chance	Slide	Filled	Star
Leaving	Heart's	Clad	Sometimes	Fires	Stones
Lend	Histor	Clothed	Somewhat	Fish	Story
Lent	Holds	Cloudy	Spirits	Flattery	Sun's
Lights	Huge	Company	Spotless	Floods	Swarm
Lively	Hungry	Conceits	Springs	Fort	Sword
Livery	Immortal	Count	Stained	Freed	Taking
Lovers	Jealous	Darkened	Stays	Freely	Thereby
Lust	Jealousy	Deed	Steal	Fresh	Thorn
Mars	Kept	Deem	Stop	Friendly	Thousand
Mirth	Knees	Defaced	Streams	Gay	Thrall
Mistress	Language	Deprived	Strongest	Glove	Throat
Nymph	Learned	Dies	Stuff	Goddess	Thunders
Nymphs	Least	Divers	Temper	Godly	Told
Pardon	Legs	Double	Thief	Grateful	Torn
Pearl	Loath	Doubts	Tied	Grew	Trade
Pen	Match	Drink	Torments	Growing	Train
Phoebus	Mates	Dull	Tyran	Guess	Tread

6
Treasures
Trial
Ungrateful
Unheard
Unseen
Until
Vanity
Veil
Vexed
Virtucus
Ward
Warm
Weigh
Whatever
Whoso
Willing
Wolves
Wondrous
Wounded
Yields
5
Abuse
Acquainted
Afford
Aged
Amazed
Amid
Ardor
Aright
Arrow
Assail
Attend
Avail
Back
Badge
Bait
Balance
Beamy
Beat
Behind
Birth
Bit
Blamed
Blaze
Blessings
Blown
Boiling
Bred
Broke
Burden
Burning
Cage
Calls
Careful
Cat
Caves
Changed
Chasteness
Chose
Circle
Claim
Clay
Cloak
Coals
Common
Compared
Conceive
Conceived
Consent
Contain
Contrary
Cool
Cosma's
Counsels
Courtly
Cure
Dazzled
Dearly
Decay
Deceive
Decked
Dei
Descend
Descry
Deserts
Despised
Destroyed
Diana
Disguised

Displayed
Divine
Dogs
Dungeon
Embraced
Enclosed
Ends
Ensue
Evermore
Eyen
Fa
Faint
Fairness
Female
Finds
Firm
Flee
Flocks
Flowing
Follow
Former
Freedom
Frenzy
Furious
Further
Giving
Goodly
Graced
Gracious
Grammar
Greatness
Greedy
Groan
Guarded
Guided
Harbor
Hark
Hates
Hears
Heir
Hellish
Helped
Helps
Hire
Hoarse
Hour
Humor
Hunting
Invite
Ire
Jaws
Jove's
Joyed
Killing
Knit
Ladies
Large
Lean
Leaves
Leridan
Lifted
Liked
Limbs
Lion
Lords
Lover
Lover's
Lying
Madest
Maintained
Malice
Mankind
Manner
Marred
Master
Master's
Mate
Means
Meek
Melt
Memory
Merry
Miseries
Morn
Mother's
Mouse
Mouths
Nightingales
Nurse
Odds

Often
Oppress
Owner
Paid
Pangs
Parents
Passed
Passion's
Patient
People's
Perfection
Perhaps
Plague
Prepared
Prince's
Proofs
Pulled
Queen
Quick
Quoth
Reasons
Received
Reigns
Remain
Remains
Resist
Resolved
Resound
Rewarded
Rotten
Running
Runs
Sacrifice
Sate
Saved
Saying
Scarcely
Seeks
Seize
Servant
Sets
Setting
Shake
Silver
Singeth
Sire
Smell
Smooth
Sort
Sour
Speaks
Spheres
Spoils
Sprung
Spy
Stands
Start
Step
Straying
Stroke
Style
Succor
Sustain
Swift
Tame
Teaching
Teeth
Thank
Therewith
Tie
Ties
Top
Toys
Tribute
Unhappy
Unkindness
Vice
Vow
W
Wages
Wail
Walk
Walls
Wants
Watch
Waves
Weal
Weary
Weeping
Weights

Whit
Whiteness
Wild
Window
Winds
Wished
Wot
Wouldst
4
Abashed
Absented
Abused
Accord
Afflicted
Affliction
Age's
Alablaster
Anew
Angel
Angels
Apollo's
Appall
Appearing
Argus
Armies
Ashamed
Assault
Attempt
Attire
Aurora
Author
Avoid
Babes
Baby
Bar
Bay
Beard
Bemoan
Bereaved
Bewail
Bite
Bleeding
Blot
Borne
Boulon
Bowed
Bowers
Bows
Breeding
Breeds
Bringing
Brother
Brows
Burned
Bush
Caitiff
Carry
Cattle
Cedars
Challenge
Chamber
Chariot
Charmed
Chastity
Cherries
Choler
Chosen
Clearest
Cleave
Colors
Compassion
Complaint
Condemned
Conquer
Conspire
Conspired
Conversation
Corn
Courteous
Coward
Cradle
Craft
Creatures
Crowned
Crows
Deaths
Decayed
Deceived
Declare
Deemed

Defile
Degree
Deign
Delay
Depth
Deserved
Destroys
Devils
Diamond
Discern
Disclose
Displays
Displease
Displeasure
Doing
Dolors
Doors
Downward
Drawn
Dream
Dried
Drops
Drown
Durst
Dusty
Eagle
Eased
Entertain
Entitled
Equal
Equity
Essence
Esteemed
Estimation
Excel
Exiled
Express
Fails
Fat
Fate
Feathers
Fetch
Fetters
Few
Figure
Flows
Flying
Forehead
Forgotten
Four
Friendship
Fuel
Fullness
Fur
Gaily
Game
Gaping
Gather
Gazing
Gem
Gladness
Glittering
Goodman
Granted
Grieve
Grievous
Grip
Groweth
Guard
Guiding
Handle
Harmony
Hating
Heal
Heaps
Helping
Heritage
Hiding
Host
Hunt
Hurtless
Hurts
Idly
Inclined
Indite
Infection
Invention
Israel
Ivory
Joyful

Judging
Kala
Keepeth
Killed
Knave
Knots
Lalus'
Lambkins
Lament
Languished
Lasting
Lately
Lauds
Laugh
Laurel
Laws
Letters
Lids
Lightning
Liking
Loathsome
Lock
Longer
Longing
Makest
Maketh
Marks
Matched
Mazed
Merchantman
Mercy's
Mira's
Misfortune
Monster
Monument
Muddy
Murder
Murdering
Musing
Mutual
Naughty
Nectar
Noblest
Note
Notorious
Number
Offence
Ones
Ore
Orecome
Ought
Overthrow
Owe
Painted
Panting
Pants
Passeth
Pearls
Peer
Perchance
Piping
Plagues
Plaintful
Planted
Pleasures
Poets
Poison
Prayers
Precious
Prevailing
Prevent
Princess
Prison
Prize
Proceeding
Proved
Raging
Rase
Realm
Rebels
Recomfort
Refuge
Refused
Rejected
Remaineth
Remember
Reputation
Request
Restless
Restored

Thereus'	Tossed	Twixt	Venom	Whereas	Withered
Therewithal	Total	Tyrant	Vexing	Whereat	Withhold
Therion	Toward	Unarmed	View	Whichever	Witnesses
Thither	Trap	Understand	Village-lord	Whilom	Witty
Thitherward	Treads	Undo	Vine	Whilst	Wives
Threat	Tremble	Undone	Violets	Whiter	Wooden
Threaten	Trim	Unfelt	Virgin	Wholesome	Wooed
Threatened	Triumphing	Ungratefulne-	Virgin-wax	Willow's	Worn
Threatening	Trojan	ss	Vulcan's	Wilton	Worthless
Thrive	Troops	United	Vulgar	Winding	Wracked
Thrush	Tropes	Unjustest	Wag	Winking	Wrapping
Thundered	Trouble	Untrue	Wailed	Wins	Wretches
Tiger	Trusting	Untwine	Warbling	Winter-starv-	Wrongdoers
Tiger's	Trusts	Unwares	Warefulness	ed	Wronged
Tilled	Trusty	Upholds	Warned	Winters	Wrongful
Tip	Trying	Upraised	Waxed	Wipe	Yielded
Tire	Tune	Usury	Wears	Wiser	Yielden
Toil	Turkish	Uttermost	Weepeth	Wishes	Yokes
Toiled	Turtle-dove	Vapors	Weighty	Wishing	Younger
Toils	Tway	Vault	Well-deserved	Witchcraft	Younglings
Tombs	Twine	Veils	Western	Withal	Zeal
Toss	Twinkling	Veins	Whenas	Wither	
	Twins				